The Polish American
Encyclopedia

The Polish American Encyclopedia

GENERAL EDITOR

James S. Pula
Purdue University

ASSOCIATE EDITORS

M. B. B. Biskupski
Central Connecticut State University

William E. Galush
Loyola University, Chicago

Anna D. Jaroszyńska-Kirchmann
Eastern Connecticut State University

Thomas J. Napierkowski
University of Colorado–Colorado Springs

Neal Pease
University of Wisconsin–Milwaukee

Donald E. Pienkos
University of Wisconsin–Milwaukee

Cheryl A. Pula
Dunham Public Library

John Radzilowski
University of Alaska–Southeast

McFarland & Company, Inc., Publishers
Jefferson, North Carolina, and London

LIBRARY OF CONGRESS CATALOGUING-IN-PUBLICATION DATA

The Polish American encyclopedia / general editor, James S. Pula ;
associate editors, M.B.B. Biskupski ... [et al.].
p.   cm.
Includes bibliographical references and index.

ISBN 978-0-7864-3308-7
illustrated case binding : 50# alkaline paper ∞

1. Polish Americans — Encyclopedias.   2. Polish Americans — Biography —
Encyclopedias.   I. Pula, James S., 1946–   II. Biskupski, Mieczyslaw B.
E184.P7P6836   2011   973'.049185 — dc22   2010038616

British Library cataloguing data are available

Front cover imagery © 2011 Shutterstock

Manufactured in the United States of America

*McFarland & Company, Inc., Publishers
Box 611, Jefferson, North Carolina 28640
www.mcfarlandpub.com*

To the memory of Stanislaus A. Blejwas

Authors of Individual Entries

Kathleen Alaimo
St. Xavier University

Frederick J. Augustyn
Library of Congress

Anthony J. Bajdek
Northeastern University

T. Lindsay Baker
Tarleton State University

Don Binkowski
Independent Scholar

M. B. B. Biskupski
Central Connecticut State University

Brian Bonkosky
Independent Author

Jason C. Booza
Wayne State University

Carl L. Bucki
Independent Researcher

John J. Bukowczyk
Wayne State University

Romuald K. Byczkiewicz
Central Connecticut State University

Krystyna Cap
Johns Hopkins University

Jude Carroll
Sisters of the Holy Family of Nazareth

Krysta Close
University of Southern California

Geraldine Coleman
Loyola Academy

Stanley L. Cuba
Kirkland Museum of Fine and Decorative Arts

Silvia G. Dapía
John Jay College, City University of New York

Anamika Dasgupta
York College, City University of New York

Piotr Derengowski
University of Gdańsk

Mary Krane Derr
Freelance Writer and Poet

John Drobnicki
York College, City University of New York

Thomas Duszak
State Library of Pennsylvania

Ewa Dzurak
College of Staten Island

Mary Patrice Erdmans
Central Connecticut State University

Halina Filipowicz
University of Wisconsin–Madison

Patricia Finnegan
Syracuse, New York

Halina Florkowska Frančić
Jagiellonian University

Jacek Galazka
Independent Editor

William J. Galush
Loyola University Chicago

Mary Edward Gira
Congregation of the Sisters of the Resurrection of Our Lord Jesus Christ

Luis J. Gonzalez
Hunter College, City University of New York

Joseph E. Gore
The Kościuszko Foundation

Guillermo Gregorio
Purdue University North Central

Regina Grol
University of North Carolina–Chapel Hill

Thaddeus V. Gromada
Polish Institute of Arts & Sciences

John Grondelski
Independent Scholar

Ludwik Grzebień
Society of Jesus, Poland

Anne Gurnack
University of Wisconsin–Parkside

Joseph T. Hapak
Moraine Valley Community College

Daryl Ann Hiller
Independent Scholar

Thomas L. Hollowak
Langsdale Library

Beth Holmgren
Duke University

Richard J. Hunter, Jr.
Seton Hall University

Anna D. Jaroszyńska-Kirchmann
Eastern Connecticut State University

Francis Casimir Kajencki
Southwest Polonia Press

Madge Karecki
Sisters of St. Joseph of the Third Order of St. Francis

Gabriela Pawlus Kasprzak
University of Toronto

Sophie Hodorowicz Knab
Niagara Community College

David Koenigstein
Bronx Community College, City University of New York

Mark A. Kohan
Polish American Journal

Frank B. Koper
SS. Cyril & Methodius Seminary

Alexander R. Koproski
Stamford, Connecticut

Iwona Korga
Józef Piłsudski Institute

Grażyna J. Kozaczka
Cazenovia College

Jerome Krase
Brooklyn College

Charles S. Kraszewski
King's College

Karl Krueger
Lutheran Theological Seminary

Jerzy Krzyżanowski
Ohio State University

Timothy Kulbicki
St. Mary's Seminary and University

Piotr Kuhiwczak
University of Warwick

Leonard Kurdek
Polish Museum of America

Anthony J. Kuzniewski
College of the Holy Cross

Steven M. Leahy
American University in Bosnia and Herzegovina

Włodek Łopaczyński
National Institutes of Health

Sławomir Lotysz
University of Zielona Góra

Héctor R. Lozada
Seton Hall University

Matthew Lyons
Balch Institute for Ethnic Studies

Karen Majewski
Orchard Lake Schools

Anna Mazurkiewicz
University of Gdańsk

Lucyna Migala
Lira Ensemble

Christina Miller
York College, City University of New York

Myron Momryk
Library and Archives Canada

Harriet Napierkowski
University of Colorado–Colorado Springs

Thomas Napierkowski
University of Colorado–Colorado Springs

Eugene P. Nassar
Utica College

Martin S. Nowak
Polish American Journal

Peter J. Obst
Poles in America Foundation, Inc.

Eric Opiela
Opiela Booth PLLC

Richard J. Orli
Arlington, Virginia

Emil Orzechowski
Jagiellonian University

Halina Osysko
Commission on Education, Polish American Congress

Dominic A. Pacyga
Columbia College/Chicago

Robert D. Parmet
York College, City University of New York

John Pawlikowski
Catholic Theological Union

Neal Pease
University of Wisconsin–Milwaukee

Angela T. Pienkos
Polish American Historical Association

Donald E. Pienkos
University of Wisconsin–Milwaukee

Thomas Pniewski
The Kościuszko Foundation

Joseph L. Pudlo, Jr.
Polish Legion of American Veterans

Cheryl A. Pula
Dunham Public Library

James S. Pula
Purdue University

John Radzilowski
University of Alaska Southeast

Biff Rocha
Benedictine College

Janusz W. Romanski
Widener University

Edward L. Rowny
U.S. Army, Retired

Susan Sanchez-Barnett
Baltimore County Public Schools

Scott Scheidlower
York College, City University of New York

Frederic Skalny
Polish Heritage Society of Rochester, New York

Wanda Slawinska
Buffalo State College–State University of New York

Bartosz H. Stanisławski
Syracuse University

David Stefancic
St. Mary's College (Indiana)

Ben S. Stefanski II
Polish American Cultural Center, Cleveland, Ohio

Dorothy Pula Strohecker
Baltimore, Maryland

Jonathan Swarts
Purdue University North Central

Maria Swiecicka-Ziemianek
Temple University

Edward R. Szemraj
Canisius College

Anna Szpindor
Polish Medical Society

Robert Szymczak
Pennsylvania State University–Beaver Campus

Thomas Tarapacki
Polish American Journal

Ewa Thompson
Rice University

Maja Trochimczyk
Moonrise Press

Kathleen Urbanic
Polish Community Archives, St. Stanislaus Parish, Rochester, New York

Michael T. Urbanski
Central Connecticut State University

Pien Versteegh
University of Tilburg, Netherlands

Estelle P. Wachtel-Torres
Polish-American Arts Society of Washington

Adam Walaszek
Jagiellonian University

Isaac A. Weiner
Georgia State University

Joseph W. Wieczerzak
Bronx Community College

Geraldine Wodarczyk
Sisters of the Holy Family of Nazareth

Joanna Wojdon
University of Wrocław

Ewa Wołyńska
Central Connecticut State University

Bozena U. Zaremba
Freelance Journalist and Translator

Theodore L. Zawistowski
Polish National Catholic Church Commission on History and Archives

Marek Zebrowski
University of Southern California

M. Janice Ziolkowski
Felician Sisters of North America

Joseph W. Zurawski
Polish Roman Catholic Union of America

Adam A. Zych
Lower Silesia University

Table of Contents

Acknowledgments

Creation of a work of this nature requires the collaboration of many people. Aside from those actively involved in authoring the entries, the Polish American Historical Association would like to extend its gratitude to Mark Kohan for providing back files of the *Polish American Journal*; Leonard Kurdek for his assistance in locating demographic and other information; Julita Siegel for her assistance in scanning illustrations; John Bukowczyk for providing lists of potential entries; Karen Majewski for facilitating access to the wealth of resources at the Polish Mission of the Orchard Lake Schools; Edith Pula, Paul Obrobina, and Robert Jadach who provided information to complete entries; and the staff of the Polish Museum of America that was exceptionally helpful during the entire duration of this project.

PAHA would like to thank the following individuals and institutions for their assistance in locating and permission to reprint illustrations from their collections: Maria Cieśla, Jan Lorys, Julita Siegel, Leonard Kurdek, Małgorzata Kot, and Krystyna Grell of The Polish Museum of America in Chicago; Marcin Chumiecki and Karen Majewski of the Polish Mission at the Orchard Lake Schools in Michigan; Ewa Wołyńska and Renata Vickery of the Connecticut Polish American Archives at Central Connecticut State University; Iwona Korga and Agnieszka Petka of the Józef Piłsudski Institute in New York; Michael Doylen, Ellen Engseth, and Ewa Barczyk at the University of Wisconsin–Milwaukee Libraries; Paul Obrobina, and Robert Jadach at the Polish National Alliance; Brenda L. Galloway-Wright of the Urban Archives at Temple University; the Kościuszko Foundation, the Library of Congress; the National Archives and Records Administration; and the United States Military History Institute. The abbreviations that follow correspond to identifying abbreviations that appear at the end of the captions accompanying the illustrations and indicate the source of each.

CCSU   Connecticut Polish American Archives, Central Connecticut State University (-EL = Edmund Liszka Collection; -ES = Rev. Eugene A. Solega Collection; -HG = Henry Gwiazda Papers; -LP = Lottie Pozniak Collection; -JW = Monsignor John P. Wodarski Collection; -RG = Roman Galinski Papers; -RM = Raymond Marciniec Collection; -SB = Stanislaus A. Blejwas Collection; -SM = Monsignor Stanislaus Musiel Collection)
JPI   Józef Piłsudski Institute of America (New York)
KF   Kościuszko Foundation
LC   Library of Congress
OLS   Orchard Lake Schools, Polish Mission
NARA   National Archives and Records Administration
PAHA   Polish American Historical Association
PMA   Polish Museum of America (Chicago)
PNA   Polish National Alliance
TU   Temple University, Urban Archives
USMHI   United States Military History Institute
UWM   University of Wisconsin–Milwaukee

Very special thanks go to the following for their generous financial support: the embassy of the Republic of Poland, the Józef Piłsudski Institute, the Kościuszko Foundation, the Polish American Historical Association, the Polish Institute of Arts and Sciences, the Polish Studies Program, Central Connecticut State University, and the Rosenstiel Foundation. Also Melvyn J. Andrews, Alfred Bialobrzeski, Don Binkowski, George S. Bobinski, Brian Bonkosky, Edward P. Czapor, Jadwiga Daniec, John A. Drobnicki, Walter Drzewieniecki, Thomas Duszak, Eugene E. Dziedzic, William J. Galush, Joseph E. Gore, Henry J. Gwiazda II, Thomas L. Hollowak, Anna D. Jaroszyńska-Kirchmann, Francis Casimir Kajencki, Alexander R. Koproski, Steven L. Kreseski, A. J. Krowinski, Alan B. Kubarek, Paul T. Kulas, Philip S. Majka, Stanley E. Milewski, Anthony J. Monczewski, Jr., Robert V. Ogrodnik, Matthew L. Panczyk, Donald E. Pienkos, the Polish Cultural Club of Greater Hartford, Polski Uniwersytet Ludowy, Richard P. Poremski, James S. Pula, Walter J. Rakoczy, the Raritan Valley Slavic Cultural and

Heritage Society, Chester S. Rog, Janusz Romanski, the Ben S. Stefanski II family, the Syracuse Polish Community, Inc., Anna Szpindor, Susan F. Tyszka, Mary Jane Urbanowicz, John B. Wlodkowski, Joanna Wojdon, Walter Zachariasiewicz, George and Jessie Zak Foundation, Maria Swiecicka Ziemianek, and Robert W. Zogorski.

Also, special thanks go to Frederick J. Augustyn, Jr., Thomas J. Czerwinski, Robert F. Dobek, John A. Garstka, Nellie Gomsi, Ann Gurnack, S. M. Kay, Anne Marie Knawa, Mark Kohan, Stephen Leahy, Danuta S. Lloyd, Monica S. Maciasz, Gerald M. Matcho, James L. Miara, Garrett S. Mierzejewski, Eugene P. Nassar, Adela Nowak, Gerald Ortell, Louis L. Patalita, Dennis Piotrowski, Donald F. Samull, Leonard Skowronski, Daniel Stone, Irena A. Szewiola, Ewa Thompson, Allan R. Treppa, Richard F. Warmowski, Cecilia Welna.

Preface

As the United States continues to mature as a pluralistic society, and to become more sensitive to the cultural past of its people and their contributions to the development of American life, an understanding of long-neglected groups becomes all the more important. *The Polish American Encyclopedia* is the first comprehensive reference work and research tool published on the Polish experience in the United States and its influence on the development of American history and culture. Poles constituted the second largest group of European immigrants arriving in the United States between 1870 and 1920, surpassed only by Italians. Further waves of migration after World War II and during the rise of Solidarność in Poland contributed to the maintenance of a strong Polish ethnic presence that has influenced materially the development of American social, economic, political and cultural history. According to the United States national census in 2000, nearly 9,000,000 Americans traced their roots to Poland, a figure many historians believe is understated due to the intermarriage of the post-immigrant generations and the initial confusion over nationality resulting from the partition of traditional Polish lands by Austria, Prussia and Russia in the 1790s. Because Poland no longer existed as an independent nation during the period of mass migration, Poles were routinely listed as arriving from one of the three partitioning powers.

This encyclopedia is designed to be a basic research tool for students, researchers and the general public. To enhance its value as a research tool, nearly all of the entries include references to other sources for those seeking additional information. The list of entries was derived from existing directories developed by various institutions and individual scholars and the further suggestions of experts in a wide variety of disciplines. Authors of the various entries are responsible for the content and accuracy of their submissions. Among the associate editors, general responsibilities were divided as follows: M. B. B. Biskupski, pre–1940 entries, scholars, and miscellaneous topics; William E. Galush, education and religious affairs; Anna D. Jaroszyńska-Kirchmann, immigration and post–1940 topics; Thomas J. Napierkowski, literature, journalism, and the fine arts; Neal Pease, sports, science, and business; Donald E. Pienkos, organizational life, politics, and organized labor; Cheryl A. Pula, performing arts, demographics and proofreading; John Radzilowski, military and miscellaneous topics.

The encyclopedia contains three types of entries: thematic, topical, and biographical.

1. *Thematic*: Thematic entries synthesize existing work to provide interpretations of and insight into important aspects of the Polish American experience. They serve as a framework for understanding the chronological progression of major themes such as organizational life, religious affairs, holiday celebrations, and participation in the labor movement.
2. *Topical*: Topical entries are intended to identify specific places, events, organizations, or cultural elements such as the Polish National Alliance, Hamtramck, the Latimer Massacre, *wigilia*, or the Polish Army in France.
3. *Biographical*: The purpose of the biographical entries is *not* to provide a *potpourri* of famous Polish Americans. Any such attempt would be necessarily incomplete. The purpose is to identify those who have made *significant* contributions at the regional or national level either to the history and culture of the United States, or to the development of American Polonia. Perhaps no other task was as difficult for the editors as identifying individuals to be included in the biographical entries. First, with only a very few exceptions, the editors limited inclusion to people who were Polish Americans. Poles who had not become U.S. citizens or had not resided and worked in the U.S. for a significant amount of time were not included because the intention of the encyclopedia was to develop a resource on American Polonia. The only exceptions to this rule were entries for people like Agaton Giller who had a fundamental influence on the organization of Poles in the U.S., or Henryk Sienkiewicz whose brief residence in the U.S. led to significant writings based on his experience there.

Second, because of the exceptionally large pool of potential candidates for inclusion, the editors determined to limit inclusion to people who made significant contributions as evidenced by membership in established halls of fame, the awarding of significant civilian or military awards, or noteworthy recognition within the Polish ethnic community. To do this, the editors consulted organizational directories, lists of award recipients, previously compiled registers of prominent individuals, and specialists in a wide variety of fields, both in the United States and abroad. Each person included in the encyclopedia was suggested by at least two of these sources and approved by the editors.

One problem the editors encountered was in defining the term "Polish American." Historically, Poland contained a multi-ethnic, multi-religious population within borders that changed frequently and often with great impact on the population. Would someone who migrated to the U.S. from the area of the Polish-Lithuanian Commonwealth be "Polish" even though the individual might be descended from some other ethnic group? Would someone of Polish ancestry born in an area which, at the time, was part of Russia or Ukraine nevertheless be considered Polish? Examples that come immediately to mind are Tadeusz Kościuszko (of Lithuanian-Ruthenian heritage) or John Shalikashvili (of Georgian ancestry). Surely both would be considered Poles because they spoke and wrote in Polish, supported Poland, and considered themselves to be Polish.

This scenario becomes even more problematical with the increasingly frequent intermarriage between groups in the United States. Who, exactly, was to be considered a Polish American? The editors decided that for the purposes of the encyclopedia, the same methodology applied to determining whether an immigrant was "Polish" would be used to define a "Polish American." To be included, an individual had to have at least one parent of Polish ancestry and, for those who were not ethnic Poles, had to in some way self-identify as Polish. For example, if the subject wrote in Polish or about Polish topics, or belonged to a Polish or Polish American organization, the person was considered "Polish" for the purpose of this work. Nevertheless, given the imprecision of human ethnicity, especially in more contemporary times, whatever system of identification is used will be open to criticism. The editors have also attempted to include individuals from a breadth of fields of endeavor, and to include those who made relatively unique contributions who may not have otherwise achieved the specific criteria for inclusion.

The editors encourage anyone identifying an error in this work to contact them so that future editions may be corrected.

How to Use This Encyclopedia

Alphabetization: Since this work is intended for English-speaking audiences, the Polish letters ą, ć, ę, ł, ń, ó, ś, ż, and ź are alphabetized as if they were English letters without the Polish diacriticals.

Authors: The author of each entry is identified at the end of the entry in italics. The institutional affiliation of each author, if any, is noted in the list of authors on page vi. Authors are responsible for the content and accuracy of their entries.

Bold Type: Within the entries, terms in bold type are cross references to entries in their own right.

See: Occasionally, organizations, people, or other entries may be known by alternate names. In these cases, the text indicates where a particular topic may be found by a "see—Xxxxx" notation.

Sources: Nearly all of the entries contain, after the end of the text, references to one or more sources of additional information on the topic of the entry.

Polish Pronunciation Guide

This pronunciation table for Polish letters and letter combinations
is presented courtesy of Ohio University Press.

a   as in *father*

ą   as the French *on*

c   as the *ts* in *cats*

ć   as a soft *ch*

ch   a gutteral h

cz   as the *ch* in *church*

ę   as the French *en*

g   a hard *g* as in *get*

i   as *ee*

j   as *y* in *yellow*

ł   as *w*

ń   combination *in* becomes *ine, en* becomes *ene,* and *on* becomes *oyne.*

ó   as *oo* in *boot*

rz   as the French *j* in *jardin*

ś   as *sh*

sz   as *sh* in *ship*

szcz   enunciating both sounds as the *sh* and *ch* in *fresh cheese*

u   as *oo* in *boot*

w   as *v*

ż   as a high pitched *zh*

ź   as a low pitched *zh*

The Encyclopedia

Abakanowicz, Magdalena (b. Falenty, Poland, June 20, 1930; d.—). Sculptor. Magdalena Abakanowicz was born to aristocratic parents. Her father, Konstanty, was of Polonized Tatar ancestry and a descendant of Abaka-Khan, great grandson of Genghis Khan. With the outbreak of World War II, Abakanowicz and her family fled their estate; among the many casualties of both Nazi and Soviet occupation were her uncle, Piotr Abakanowicz, a commander of the Polish resistance, and his wife, who were arrested and sentenced to death by the Polish Communist secret police. In the immediate postwar period, Abakanowicz's family moved to Gdańsk where, between 1945 and 1947, she finished her high school education in nearby Tczew and completed two years of art school in Gdynia. In 1949, she briefly attended the Gdańsk Academy of Fine Arts in Sopot, an institution known for its emphasis on ceramics and textile design, before transferring to the Warsaw Academy of Fine Arts in 1950. Beginning in the 1960s, she received critical acclaim for her work. Her early experimentation with textiles gave way to the mammoth, freestanding, three-dimensional woven fiber works called "Abakans" that would come to define her early career. First exhibited at the International 1964 Biennial of Tapestry in Lausanne, Switzerland, her Abakans would go on to win the Grand Prix at the São Paulo Biennial the following year. In 1965, Abakanowicz also received honors from the Polish Ministry of Art and Culture and was awarded a faculty position at the Academy of Fine Arts

Magdelena Abakanowicz, artist, at the unveiling of "Agora" in Chicago, 2006 (*PMA*).

in Poznań. By the 1970s, her installations and exhibits reached the United States, meeting with particular acclaim in Los Angeles and Pasadena. From 1973 to 1982, Abakanowicz produced four sets of figurative and non-figurative sculptures respectively titled *Heads* (1973–75), *Seated Figures* (1974–79), *Backs* (1976–82), and *Embryology* (1978–81). These works drew heavily on historic Polish themes, symbols, and images, including the spirit of Polish Romanticism, Slavic legends, Polish folklore, and Christian symbolism. By the 1980s, increasing political repression by the Communist regime in the face of the growing Solidarity Trade Union movement led Abakanowicz to remain abroad, teaching and traveling throughout the United States and Canada. Although she insisted on political neutrality, her sculpture cycles of standing crowds are said to have reflected the prevailing sociopolitical climate in Poland between 1986 and 1990. While in the United States in 1983–84, Abakanowicz taught sculpture at UCLA and California State University–Fullerton. Although she is most well known for her work with textiles, she has also exhibited drawings and paintings. Her installations span the globe; some of her permanent outdoor sculptures can be found in Dallas, New York City, Paris, Jerusalem, Lisbon, and Seoul. Between 2004 and 2006, she added Chicago's Grant Park to this list, with a project called *Agora*. Abakanowicz holds several honorary doctorates including those from the Royal College of Art in London, the Rhode Island School of Design, the Massachusetts College of Art in Boston, and the Pratt Institute in New York.—*Krystyna Cap*

Sources: Michael Brenson, "Magdalena Abakanowicz's 'Abakans,'" *Art Journal*, Vol. 54, no. 1 (1995), 56–61; Joanna Inglot, *The Figurative Sculpture of Magdalena Abakanowicz: Bodies, Environments, and Myths* (Berkeley and Los Angeles: University of California Press, 1989).

Abramowicz, Alfred Leo (b. Chicago, Illinois, January 27, 1919; d. Chicago, Illinois, September 12, 1999). Catholic bishop. The son of Polish immigrants, Abramowicz attended Quigley Preparatory Seminary and later earned his masters degree from St. Mary of the Lake Seminary in Mundelein, Illinois. Shortly thereafter he was ordained on May 1, 1943, and assigned as assistant pastor at the parish of the Immaculate Conception. From 1949 until 1952 he studied in Rome to earn a licentiate in Canon Law from the Gregorian University. Returning to the United States,

Abramowicz became a resident of Holy Name Cathedral, also holding a post on the Archdiocese of Chicago's Marriage Tribunal. In 1966 Pope Pius XII named him a papal chamberlain with the title of "Monsignor." On May 8, 1968, at the age of forty-nine, Abramowicz was appointed as Auxiliary Bishop of Chicago and Titular Bishop of Pesto, one of very few Poles to achieve this position at that time. As a bishop, Abramowicz was a successful advocate for **Polonia**. In 1966 he helped organize Chicago's celebration of the Millennium of Christianity in Poland. He was the national director of the **Catholic League for Religious Assistance to Poland** for over thirty years, as well as being a member of the **Polish Roman Catholic Union** in America, Knights of Columbus, Polish American Association, Chaplain of War Veterans, and many other organizations designed to help immigrants. As part of the Catholic Church's interreligious effort he directed the theological work of the Commission for Dialogue with Jews in the United States. Abramowicz served as a judge during the beatification processes of several Polish candidates for sainthood. His friend Karol Wojtyła visited the parish of the Five Holy Martyrs, where Abramowicz was pastor, in 1969 and 1976. It was Wojtyła's three day visit in October of 1979 as Pope John Paul II that brought the parish international attention. A collector of Pope John Paul II memorabilia, after retiring on January 24, 1995, Abramowicz donated many of his personal mementos to the **Polish Museum of America**. Some of these artifacts became part of the museum's permanent exhibit devoted to the Pope. Under the direction of Cardinal George, the Archdiocese of Chicago began to invite seminarians and priests to come from Poland to Chicago. The Bishop Abramowicz Seminary, named in his honor, serves as the first stop for newly arriving recruits from Poland who, after one year of intensive study of the English language and American culture, complete their education and are assigned to the wide variety of Catholic parishes in the Archdiocese.—*Biff Rocha*

Sources: obituaries in *Chicago Sun Times*, September 13, 1999; *Milwaukee Journal Sentinel*, September 15, 1999.

Abramowicz, Danny (b. Bellingham, Washington, September 6, 1945; d.—). Football player. Despite success playing college football at Xavier University, Abramowicz was not regarded highly as a professional prospect and was among the last selections made in the 1967 National Football League draft. Nevertheless, he turned in a productive career as a wide receiver for two NFL teams from 1967 to 1974. Abramowicz had his best seasons with his original squad, the New Orleans Saints, and in 1969 he was named first team All-Pro while leading the league in receptions. Following retirement, at various times he served stints as an assistant coach with two NFL teams, worked as an analyst on New Orleans Saints radio broadcasts, and hosted his own television program on the EWTN Catholic network. Abramowicz was inducted into the National Polish-American Sports Hall of Fame in 1992.—*Neal Pease*

SOURCE: "Danny Abramowicz," National Polish-American Sports Hall of Fame website, www.polish sportshof.com.

Adamowski, Benjamin S. (b. Chicago, Illinois, November 20, 1906; d. Chicago, Illinois, March 1982). Politician. The son of a Chicago alderman, Adamowski earned his law degree from DePaul University in 1928. Elected to the Illinois State Assembly in 1930 at age 23, he was chosen majority leader of the Assembly in 1935. Initially a loyal member of the Chicago Democratic Party organization built by Mayor Anton Cermak and led after his death by Mayor Edward Kelly, Adamowski broke with the organization after it refused to re-slate the independent-minded, well-respected Judge Edmund Jarecki in the 1938 election. From then on, Adamowski was an independent force in the Democratic Party and an increasingly bitter opponent of Richard J. Daley, his one time friend and state assembly colleague. After military service in

Benjamin S. Adamowski, politician. Photograph ca. 1940–42 (*PMA*).

World War II, Adamowski reentered political life and in 1955 campaigned for the Democratic Party mayoral nomination won by Daley, by then the chairman of Cook County (mainly Chicago) Democratic Party organization. Adamowski then left the Democrats for the Republicans and in 1956 was elected to the office of State's Attorney of Cook County. For the next four years he aggressively sought to expose corruption in Daley's Chicago organization. His efforts were enough to make his defeat in the 1960 election one of Daley's top priorities. While national attention focused on the presidential election and John Kennedy's paper-thin 8,800 victory margin in Illinois over Richard Nixon (out of 4.76 million votes cast), Adamowski was also defeated by 15,000 votes. Adamowski declared the results fraudulent, but Nixon eventually chose not to lodge a challenge, enabling Kennedy to win the presidency and at the same time ending Adamowski's own recount bid.

In 1963 Adamowski mounted another campaign against Daley, who was seeking his third term as mayor. In the election he won over 590,000 votes (45 percent) and carried 18 of the city's 50 wards, all of them in the heavily Polish northwest, southwest and southeast sides of the city. His effort was the strongest mayoral campaign Daley ever confronted and the last great demonstration of the power of Polish ethnic voting in Chicago. However, Adamowski was swamped in those wards populated by African Americans and in the white wards having the largest numbers of city and county patronage employees. He also garnered practically no financial backing from his party or from wealthy conservative businessmen. Columnist **Mike Royko** labeled the Daley campaign against Adamowski "vindictive" and dominated by real fear that a taxpayer revolt coupled with anger over city hall corruption might end his rule. Historian Edward Kantowicz, in his excellent book on Polish Americans in Chicago politics, states that Adamowski's hot temper and resulting inability to remain a loyal party man were his flaws as a politician, thus preventing him from rising higher in Illinois politics. But it is unclear whether any Chicago Polish American politician—including **John Smulski** in the early 1900s, Matt Szymczak in the 1920s, or Congressmen **Roman Pucinski** or **Daniel Rostenkowski** in the 1970s—could have done much better than Adamowski in political environments dominated by ambitious party bosses who distrusted every serious possible Polish American mayoral aspirant. Smulski and Szymczak got out of politics, the former for a career in banking and national Polonia affairs, the latter for a governorship in the Fed-

eral Reserve System. Pucinski's effort against a colorless Democratic organization nominee failed in 1977; Rostenkowski never challenged the party leadership. Leon Walkowicz, in his 1953 history of Chicago **Polonia**, described Adamowski, on the eve of his first mayoral campaign, as "the youngest, most popular, most energetic, most competent, hardest working representative of the younger generation and without question our political leader."—*Donald E. Pienkos*

SOURCES: Edward Kantowicz, *Polish American Politics in Chicago, 1880–1940* (Chicago: University of Chicago Press, 1975); Mike Royko, *Boss: Mayor Richard J. Daley of Chicago* (New York: Dutton, 1971); Tomasz Inglot and John Pelissero, "Ethnic Political Power in a Machine City: Chicago's Poles at Rainbow's End," *Urban Affairs Quarterly*, Vol. 28 (June 1993).

Adamski, George (b. Poland, April 17, 1891; d. Washington, D.C., April 23, 1965). Ufologist. Moving to the United States with his family at the age of two, he settled in Dunkirk, NY. He later joined the U.S. Army, serving in the 13th Cavalry and participating in the punitive expedition against Pancho Villa in Mexico (1915–16). After working at Yellowstone National Park, a flour mill in Oregon, and a stint as a bootlegger, he moved to Laguna Beach, California, where he founded the Royal Order of Tibet dedicated to the study of scientific philosophy. He organized a farming and research community near Palomar Mountain in 1940, where he also worked as a handyman at a hamburger stand. In 1946 he claimed to have seen a cigar-shaped space ship during a meteor shower, and the following year circulated a photograph he said showed a spaceship near his property. In 1950 he took a photograph, supposedly of a formation of six alien spacecraft flying in formation. Two years later he asserted he was present when a spaceship landed in the Colorado Desert where he met beings from Venus. He also stated he traveled more than 50,000 miles in spaceships with beings from Mars and Saturn, and had classified photographs of the far side of the moon showing mountains, lakes, trees, and cities. Though most UFO researchers write him off as a charlatan, Adamski was a popular international lecturer on the subject of UFOs, even having an audience with Queen Juliana of the Netherlands. He wrote several books, including *Flying Saucers Have Landed* (1953), *Inside the Spaceships* (1955), and *Flying Saucers Farewell* (1961). After his death, some of his followers established the George Adamski Foundation to carry on his work with UFOs and cosmic philosophy.—*Cheryl A. Pula*

SOURCES: Colin Bennett, *Looking for Orthon: The Story of George Adamski, the First Flying Saucer Contactee, and How He Changed the World* (New York:

Paraview Press, 2001); Lou Zinsstag and Timothy Good, *George Adamski: The Untold Story* (Beckenham, UK: Ceit Publications, 1983).

Agriculture. Although never amounting to more than ten to fifteen percent of American Polonia, Polish Americans engaged in agriculture have always been an integral part of Polish American history, and in fact the first Polish American communities were rural communities. The majority of Polish immigrants to the United States came from rural backgrounds, yet few sought to return to the life they had known in the old country. The reasons for this stem from the economics of farming in east-central Europe and the United States. Most Polish immigrants from **Galicia** and the Congress Kingdom came to the New World in response to the need for wage labor. Immigrant wages helped to support the rural family economy in east-central Europe and were not meant to recreate a different rural experience but to sustain what already existed. Wage labor immigrants often migrated as individuals and even when they stayed in the U.S. they often did not possess sufficient family labor or money to begin farming. Moreover, in many regions of partitioned Poland, as in other impoverished areas of Europe, there was a clear association between farming and poverty. Immigrants went to America to escape poverty, not become paupers yet again.

It is significant that the majority of Polish farming communities in the U.S. drew their population from the German partition of occupied Poland. In these regions, peasant emancipation had begun earlier and agriculture was more modernized and profitable. Immigrants from western Poland were more likely than their neighbors in the Austrian and Russian zones to arrive in America as settler immigrants; that is, they came as a family unit with the intent of permanent settlement rather than as individuals seeking wage labor. In addition, these immigrants came to America earlier and thus often had better access to farmland and since many spoke German they could learn about opportunities from their German neighbors who heavily settled many rural areas of the Midwest and Great Plains.

The first Polish communities in the United States were rural settlements beginning with **Panna Maria**, Texas, settled in 1854 by a shipload of Silesian immigrants, followed soon by rural settlements in Wisconsin, Minnesota, Michigan, and Illinois. These early immigrants tended to be Silesians, Kashubs, or Poznanians and their settlements were often drawn from a few villages in Europe. Early Polonia farming settlements frequently spawned daughter colonies. The **Kashub** community of Winona, Minnesota, for example, created daughter communities in Holloway, Minnesota, Day County, South Dakota, and St. Philip, Montana. In some instances there was specific point to point migration. For example, settlers from the **Silesian** village of Syców settled in Wells, Minnesota, and some of their children pioneered the small community of Windsor, North Dakota. Direct migration from Poland to the rural U.S. was not unknown, especially before the 1880s, but this was not the experience of most rural Polish Americans. Instead, most Polonia farming communities were formed from immigrants drawn from urban or mining areas (such as the Pennsylvania coal country). Polish immigrants spent anywhere from a year to a decade in such settings earning money that would later be used to buy land, tools, animals, and seed. In some cases, Poles purchased farm land in a promising rural community and then returned to the city for a few more years of wage labor before finally taking up their farm. After settling on the farm, it was quite common to continue working elsewhere for wages. In the Midwest, Polish farmers spent the winters in logging camps in northern Michigan, Minnesota or Wisconsin. In New England and on Long Island, local factories remained an important economic option. Older sons or daughters could be sent to the city to live with friends or relatives to work for the winter or for a year or more. Some Polish farming communities developed a kind of mixed economy. In Winona, for example, Polish farmers spent part of the year on their farms and part working in the city's saw mills.

Polish rural communities were formed by two distinct processes. The first was settlement by chain migration. This was a common process which resulted in a slow but steady increase in the size of the community until it reached a point of critical mass that allowed it to develop and support institutions such as a parish church. Chain migration communities were among the first Polonia rural settlements but chain migration also created the later Polish farming communities in New England and on Long Island. In some instances, Polish settlers from Poznania followed their former German neighbors and took up land near German American settlements. At Tabor, in southeast South Dakota, Polish settlers followed Czech immigrants. A second process was colonization or the creation of planned rural communities. The first efforts to create rural Polish communities occurred in the 1870s. The **Polish Roman Catholic Union of America** (PRCUA) and later its rival the **Polish National Alliance** (PNA) took the lead in promoting colonies as a way to create (or re-create) Polish rural life in America and remove immigrants from the allegedly baneful influences of city life. In most cases, Polish organizations joined forces with railroad companies eager to settle state and federal land grants with farmers who would provide traffic for their rail lines. In some instances, local Catholic dioceses were also involved. In Minnesota, Archbishop John Ireland originally promoted farming settlements for Irish immigrants but when the effort stalled for lack of interest he turned to other Catholic immigrant groups including Poles. The railroads provided various incentives, such as free excursions to the proposed colony for potential colonists, relatively easy terms of purchase, and land to be set aside for a Polish parish and cemetery. In return, Polish organizations promoted the venture via their newspapers and in some cases by using agents who toured Polonia communities to talk up the virtues of the new colonies.

The height of colonization occurred between the mid 1870s and the 1890s, though

A typical Polish farm couple in Michigan, ca. 1920s (*OLS*).

colonization schemes continued to be promoted as late as the 1920s. A significant number of successful colonies were created. For example, the Polish farming communities of central Nebraska were the result of a PRCUA–sponsored effort in the 1870s led by one of the Union's founders, **Jan Barzyński**. Secular promoters associated with the PNA sponsored colonies in Arkansas and Minnesota. PNA Censor **Franciszek Gryglaszewski** was especially active in promoting Minnesota colonies in the 1880s. The tiny town of Grygla in northwestern Minnesota stands in tribute to his efforts. In several instances, railroads themselves used Polish speaking agents and took out ads in Polonia newspapers to promote settlement. The Great Northern Railroad and its subsidiaries promoted enduring Polish colonies in Sturgeon Lake, Minnesota, and Pe Ell, Washington. After the 1890s, Polish immigrants were also drawn to colonies in the Canadian provinces of Manitoba and Saskatchewan. Most colonies drew settlers from established Polonia concentrations, especially Chicago, Milwaukee, Minneapolis or the mining regions of Pennsylvania. In some cases, colonists came from other rural communities and rarely directly from Europe. Most colonists seemed to have roots in western Poland, but some colonies did attract adherents with origins in Galicia and the Congress Kingdom.

Although most colonization efforts were legitimate, there were quite a few that were of dubious value. This was especially true of later colonization ventures that focused on promoting land of poor quality. After the turn of the century, ventures aimed at creating Polish colonies in Mississippi, Florida, or the Upper Peninsula of Michigan were commonly promoted in the Polonia press. Some ventures were fraudulent. In the 1880s and 1890s, **Feliks Pietrowicz** (one of the founders of the Polish Falcons) and a business partner promoted a series of colonies in Minnesota and Wisconsin. Pietrowicz and his partner were arrested for fraud after a Wisconsin venture in which Polish immigrants bought forest land in the northern part of the state but were denied the right to cut any of the timber on their own land, making it virtually worthless. The depression of the early 1890s, the basic hardships of rural life, the lack of good farmland, and bad publicity created by dubious or fraudulent business practices of some promoters served to severely reduce interest in colonization ventures. By 1900, they had become a curiosity as the majority of Polish immigrants opted for life in urban centers and mining communities where wage labor was widely available.

From a cultural standpoint, Polish-American rural communities were not uniform. Some smaller communities never developed the critical mass needed to sustain any institution other than a parish church (and in some cases not even that). Others developed a wide range of institutions to rival their urban counterpart. The Polish Franciscan center at Pulaski, Wisconsin, featured one of the largest Catholic churches in rural America, a monastery, a minor seminary, and a publishing house. Even small communities could support major endeavors. The Polish community of Silver Lake, Minnesota, once had three military companies with full dress to commemorate Polish historical events, including one unit garbed as the famed "Reapers of Death" from **Tadeusz Kościuszko**'s 1794 rebellion in Poland. In 1894, Silver Lake sent its own delegation to the international exposition in Lwów bearing examples of the produce of the community's farmers to display. Some communities remained relatively separate from the larger trends of Polonia life, but thanks to

newspapers, railroads, and family ties to urban centers, true isolation was rare. The Polish farmers of Wilno, in southwest Minnesota, often made yearly visits during the winter to their relatives in Chicago and Minneapolis and in turn hosted their city kin during the summer months. By contrast, some of the Polish communities settled at a very early stage by chain migration directly from Poland remained apart from the urban centers. In these areas, Polish farmers often more closely reproduced the social relations and landscape of their homeland. One example is the phenomenon of roadside crosses found in Polish farming communities of central Wisconsin.

From an economic standpoint, Polish American farmers faced the same problems as their neighbors and there was little room for innovation. Exceptions to this were the Polish immigrants who took over old Yankee farms in New England and turned the exhausted soil of the region into productive truck farms. In the Midwest and Great Plains, Polish farmers tended to be cash-grain farmers, although like their German and Czech neighbors successful Polish farm families were highly diversified which provided a degree of protection from falling commodity prices. Observers noted that Polish American farmers placed a higher reliance on family labor than their native-born counterparts and delayed the purchase of machinery for longer. It was rare for any American farmer in the late nineteenth or twentieth centuries to grow wealthy from farming and this was certainly the case with Polish immigrants who often arrived in America with little ready capital. Yet, extant case studies of Polish farming communities indicate that most Polish farmers were able to hold their own and even modestly increase the size of their holdings. Some were able to parlay success on the land into opening small-town businesses, including creameries, general stores, or implement dealerships. To be sure, there were also some who struggled mightily to keep hold of their land or eked out a living as renters or even sharecroppers.

In general, the state of the American farm economy has worked against the perpetuation of the type of family farms Polish immigrants sought to establish. Yet, many Polish farm families in the Midwest and Great Plains have achieved the designation of "century farms," having been operated by the same family for at least one hundred years. Communities such as Pulaski, Wilno, or Silver Lake continue to maintain a strong local Polish identity. In 2010, Loup County, Nebraska, had the highest concentration of people of Polish ancestry of any county in the nation. This persistence is a measure of proof in the success of Polish im-

This farmers' market was located in the heavily Polish community of Stevens Point, Wisconsin (*OLS*).

migrant farmers and their descendants in American agriculture.—*John Radzilowski*

SOURCES: John Radzilowski, "A New Poland in the Old Northwest: Polish Farming Colonies on the Northern Great Plains," *Polish American Studies*, Vol. 59, no. 2 (Autumn 2002), 79–96; Lucjan Kocik, *Polski Farmer w Ameryce: Studium na Przykładzie stanu Wisconsin w USA* (Wrocław: Ossolineum, 1990); John Radzilowski, "Hidden Cosmos: The Life Worlds of Polish Immigrants in Two Minnesota Communities, 1875–1925," Ph.D. diss., Arizona State University, 1999.

Alfred Jurzykowski Foundation, Inc. As an expression of his desire to assist the peoples of Poland and Brazil both charitably and in the educational fields, Alfred Jurzykowski, using his personal funds, established the Alfred Jurzykowski Foundation, Inc. It was incorporated July 11, 1960, as a Membership Corporation of the State of New York and subsequently became a not-for-profit corporation receiving Federal tax-exempt status November 22, 1965. The choice of Poland was because it was his paternal birthplace and Brazil as the country where he successfully industrialized the automobile industry and was the fifty percent owner of Mercedes-Benz do Brasil. His interest was sold after his death and the proceeds transferred to the Foundation. In 1963 the Foundation's Board of Trustees adopted a four-point program in anticipation of the forthcoming celebration in 1966 of the one-thousandth anniversary of the Polish state. The first point was to provide scholarships for studies in the United States for persons of creative ability from Poland. Rather than grant the stipends and scholarships directly, the Foundation trustees decided to use established Polish cultural institutions having the proper experience. This program was implemented by the **Kosciuszko Foundation** which received annual grants for the purpose of financing scholarships and incidental expenses for gifted Polish students, artists, and musicians to study or perform in the United States. In this way the Jurzykowski Foundation was able to fill a critical vacuum in the area of international exchanges. For a period of time, the **Polish Institute of Arts and Sciences of America** was selected as the institution to provide grants in the area of arts and sciences.

The second point was to provide financial support to Polish cultural institutions outside of Poland. This was implemented by grants to many well-known institutions in **Polonia** including the Polish Institute of Arts and Sciences of America, the **Piłsudski Institute** of America for Research in the Modern History of Poland, the Polish Institute and Sikorski Museum in London, and the Societe Historique et Litteraire Polonaise in Paris. An im-

portant step in this regard was the purchase of a building at 55 East 66th Street, New York City, and leased for an initial three-year term to the Polish Institute of Arts and Sciences of America at an annual rent of $1.00 and renewed for successive three-year terms until the building was sold in 1986. Grants also were made to a number of universities to finance Polish studies, foremost being a major grant in 1971 to Harvard University to establish a Chair in Polish Language and Literature. The Chair was first held by Professor Wiktor Weintraub.

The third point was the annual awards for Polish artists and scholars wherever they resided. The fourth point was providing financial aid to particularly deserving institutions within the scope of the Foundation's charitable activities including support in medical research and other organizations active in other charitable and educational fields including the American Research Hospital in Poland, the Polish Assistance, Inc., the New York Public Library, and the Committee for the Blind of Poland. In February 2000 the Foundation approved a major grant of $1,000,000 for the establishment of a Department of Environmental Studies at the University of Mining and Metallurgy, Akademia Gorniczo-Hutnicza in Kraków, payable in ten annual grants to the Kosciuszko Foundation which was contractually responsible to oversee the project and to disperse the funds to the University against project benchmarks.

Grants usually ranged from $5,000 to $50,000. In 2002 the Foundation awarded 38 grants in the amount of $2,102,050. Alfred Jurzykowski served as the Foundation's first president until his death in July 1966. His wife, Milena Jurzykowski, succeeded her husband as president on November 22, 1966, to be succeeded by Alexis Coudert upon her death who, in turn, was succeeded by Morris Cohen who served as both president and executive director until his death in October 1984. Thereupon, Bluma Cohen, who was a trustee, became the Foundation's manager, executive director and vice president and served as such until the Foundation's dissolution in October 2007 when its assets were equally divided between two private foundations established by the Jurzykowski daughters: Pleroma, Inc., organized by Christine Jurzykowski and Almi Foundation, Inc. (formerly The Mach Foundation) organized by Yolande Jurzykowski.—*Joseph E. Gore*

SOURCE: *The Kosciuszko Foundation Monthly News Letter*, Vol. XXXII, No. 1 (1977–78), 310.

Alliance College. In 1912, the **Polish National Alliance** of America (PNA), embarked

on an ambitious project to create the first, and thus far only, secular Polish American college in North America. The purpose of the institution was to provide immigrants and their children with an opportunity for an education beyond the parochial school that would provide upward mobility in American society while maintaining the cultural values and traditions which defined the ethnic group. The idea of a Polish American institution of higher learning was formally initiated in 1903 at the annual PNA convention. There, delegates approved a special education and school committee charged with the task of raising money and determining the feasibility of a school to be owned and operated by the Alliance. Several years later, in 1911, the committee won formal approval from the Board of Directors to establish s school, named Alliance College (Kolegium Związkowy), "that would be conducted in a genuinely civic and patriotic spirit ... identifying the best in American and Polish culture." To house the school, PNA leaders quickly chose a defunct hotel in the small town of Cambridge Springs in northwestern Pennsylvania. The Rider Hotel, as it was known, formerly served as a health resort and mineral spa for the nation's wealthy at the beginning of the twentieth century. Consequently, the building included many luxurious amenities, fine architecture, and lay on 160 acres of picturesque land that, at the time, made its $175,000 price tag seem a bargain.

On October 26, 1912, President William Howard Taft, assuming the role of honored speaker, formally dedicated Alliance College to much fanfare. The PNA initially organized Alliance as a four year secondary school along with a finishing program for young boys in the primary grades. In its first year, Alliance attracted 326 students, but its failure to receive accreditation from the Commonwealth of Pennsylvania created doubts about its future. The following year, enrollment dropped to 135 boys. Upon achieving accreditation in 1914, however, and the opening of a new, successful technical training program, enrollments steadily increased. In that same year, the PNA established an officer training program at Alliance College in anticipation of America's involvement in the First World War that could potentially bring about Poland's independence. Approximately 500 Polish American men, along with 220 non–Poles, traveled to Cambridge Springs to participate in the program that would eventually prove instrumental in preparing men for battle in the **Polish Army in France**.

During the 1920s, school leaders expanded Alliance College with a new gymnasium in addition to introducing a new two-year junior college beginning in the 1924-25 academic year. The program added college level courses to Alliance's already extensive educational offerings, allowing the school to become more competitive with American institutions while responding to young Polish Americans who, though still small in number, increasingly desired to attend American universities. With the addition of the new junior college, Alliance attracted a record number of 390 students in 1925 surpassing expectations.

In early 1931, disaster struck. During an evening snow squall on January 20 a small fire broke out on the fourth floor of the school which quickly engulfed the building. The raging fire that ensued took only two hours to level the school to its stone foundation. Fortunately, everyone escaped safely with but few suffering minor injuries. The residents of Cambridge Springs graciously opened their homes, hotels, schools, and churches to aid displaced students and prevent any interruption in studies. The source of the fire was a short circuit caused by the building's primitive and faulty wiring. The biggest tragedy of the fire was not so much the loss of the school but the loss of the library and museum which housed invaluable Polish treasures including letters and artifacts from Polish monarchs, the priceless works of Adam Mickiewicz, and rare pieces of Polish art. Although a new dormitory neared completion at the time of the fire, rebuilding the rest of the school proved challenging because of the difficult economic depression of the 1930s coupled with the school's lack of funds and the PNA's own financial difficulties. Worse still, enrollments in the school declined steadily throughout the 1930s and 1940s, from approximately 240 in 1930 to 32 in 1944. This resulted in a painfully slow reconstruction of the school, with Alliance Hall completed in 1934 and Washington Hall in 1942.

Despite its problems, the leadership of the PNA and the school remained committed to Alliance. Thanks to a campaign spearheaded by PNA President **Charles Rozmarek**, Alliance began the 1948 academic year as a liberal arts college with the right to confer degrees in the arts and sciences. This transformation of the school into a four-year collegiate institution was achieved in an effort to make Alliance College more competitive in postwar America. The move proved worthwhile for the school as enrollments grew during the 1950s and 1960s, reaching a peak of 630 in 1969. Meanwhile, the campus experienced its own improvements with the addition of new dormitories and modern academic facilities in an effort to bring Alliance on par with other leading academic institutions. The

An aerial view of Alliance College in Cambridge Springs, Pennsylvania (*PMA*).

1960s also saw the birth of the school's most renowned student activities. Growing student interest in the music and dance heritage of Poland led to creation of the Kujawiaki dance group in 1964. Unlike other dance groups, the Kujawiaki were quickly recognized around the country for their commitment to authentic Polish dances, music, and costumes from various regions of Poland.

The 1970s, however, brought a reversal of fortunes for the small liberal arts school. Economic stagnation coupled with changing attitudes toward higher education in America caused colleges and universities across the nation to experience significant declines in student populations. The resulting loss of funds from tuition and rising inflation forced many small, private colleges to close while larger institutions cut costs significantly in order to stay afloat. This unanticipated change in the higher education environment brought hardships and spiraling decline to Alliance College. In 1977, only 177 students were actively enrolled at the school compared to over 600 less than a decade earlier. The lack of tuition income and reduced subsidies from the PNA, which suffered its own financial troubles, created serious budget deficits. For the next two decades, school officials and the PNA did what they could to cut costs, increase recognition of the school, and explore more creative methods of fundraising. Despite their efforts, Alliance suffered deteriorating facilities, high faculty turn-over, weak programs, and a detached administration, all of which damaged morale among students and faculty while tarnishing the school's reputation. A modest

rise in enrollment, improved fundraising efforts, and increased PNA subsidies in the 1980s did little to reverse Alliance's distressing situation. On February 20, 1987, the PNA School Commission voted 36 to 6 in favor of a resolution to suspend operation of Alliance College effective June 30 of that year. The Commission cited soaring operational costs, long-term liabilities, massive debt to the PNA, and lack of interest and support from the college's primary constituencies as the reasons behind their decision. An additional worry of the School Commission came from the Middle States Association of Colleges and Schools which never gave formal confirmation concerning Alliance's accreditation for the following 1987-88 academic year. According to the Middle States Commission, it could no longer accredit the school for more than one year at a time due to the continued low enrollment and unstable financial situation. In order to earn accreditation for the future, the PNA would have to commit at least one million dollars annually for a minimum of ten years, in addition to other funds needed to operate the college. Considering that the school was already indebted to the PNA for approximately three million dollars, contributing another ten million dollars over the next ten years was deemed too large a burden for the PNA.

Shortly after Alliance's seventy-third and final commencement in May 1987, the campus was closed and offered for sale. It took three years to find a buyer; however, in late December 1990, the 188 acres and 13 buildings which formerly made up Alliance College were purchased by the Commonwealth of Pennsylvania for a sum of three million dollars. Due to the outstanding debt of the college to the PNA, the organization actually walked away with a loss of approximately $425,000. Today, the property, a shadow of its former self, serves as a minimum security prison for women. Yet, the spirit of Alliance College remains strong among those who had personal contact with America's only secular Polish American college.—*Michael T. Urbanski*

SOURCES: Arthur Coleman, "Alliance College, American Cradle of Polish Heritage," *Zgoda*, June 1 and 15, July 1 and 15, August 1 and 15, 1957; "Report of the Committee on Alliance College," *Zgoda*, December 1, 1991, 8; Walery Fronczak, ed., *Pamiętnik Jubileuszowy Kolegium ZNP, 1912–1937* (Cambridge Springs, PA: Alliance College Alumni Association, 1937); Michael T. Urbanski, "Polite Avoidance: The Story Behind the Closing of Alliance College," *Polish American Studies*, Vol. 66, no. 1 (2009), 25–42.

Alliance of Poles in America. A fraternal insurance and cultural organization, the Alliance of Poles in America originated in 1895 when members of Group 143 of the **Polish National Alliance** (PNA) in Cleveland protested against admission of socialists and non–Catholics, a decision taken during the eleventh convention of the PNA. On September 22, 1895, a group of 65 people led by the grocer Tomasz Żółnowski formed the Alliance of Poles of Ohio. A week later four other groups joined. The Alliance's first convention took place in January 1897 with Żółnowski elected its first president. The goal of the organization was to unite Catholic Poles, Americans of Polish descent, Lithuanians, Ruthenians, Slovaks, and other immigrants from the pre-partitioned Polish-Lithuanian Commonwealth. By the beginning of the twentieth century, the Alliance included some Lithuanian and mixed lodges. The weekly *Polonia w Ameryce* (Polonia in America) became the semi-official organ of the group. The organization eventually expanded to other cities in Ohio, Michigan, and Pennsylvania, resulting in July 1917 in a change in its name to the Alliance of Poles in America. The Alliance began publishing its official organ, *Związkowiec* (The Alliancer) in 1926 when it numbered 133 groups with a total of 18,429 members. By 1973 it had shrunk to 60 lodges including 15,000 members. In 1983 it reported some 20,000 and assets $7 million. The organization offered insurance policies, mortgage loans, a welfare fund for sick and disabled persons, and college scholarships for youth. In 1925 it constructed a headquarters, a hall, and library in the Polish district in Cleveland. On January 1, 2005, it merged with the Polish National Alliance.—*Adam Walaszek*

SOURCE: D. Van Tassel and J. J. Grabowski, eds., *The Encyclopedia of Cleveland, History* (Bloomington-Indianapolis: Indiana University Press, 1987).

Alliance of Polish Socialists in America *see* **Polish Socialist Alliance in America.**

American Center of Polish Culture, Inc. *see* **National Polish Center.**

American Committee for the Investigation of the Katyn Massacre. The formation of the American Committee for the Investigation of the Katyn Massacre was announced during a press conference in New York's Waldorf Astoria Hotel on November 21, 1949. Its purpose was to identify those guilty of the massacre of thousands of Polish officers in a forest near Katyń during World War II. The formation of the Committee was preceded by the activities of the **Polish American Congress** and American journalists, especially Julius Epstein of the New York *Herald Tribune*, who tried to arouse the interest of the U.S. administration and of the United Nations over the Katyń case. Support came from Arthur Bliss Lane, former U.S. ambassador to Poland, who agreed to chair the Committee. Other founding members included Epstein as executive secretary, Arthur Max Eastman as executive vice-president, George Creel (Chief of the Office of Information during World War I), William Donovan and Allen Dulles (former officers of the Office of Strategic Services), James Farley (former Postmaster General), **Blair Gunther** (Pittsburgh Judge and a Polish American activist), **Charles Rozmarek** (president of the Polish American Congress and the **Polish National Alliance**), prominent anti–Communist Clare Booth Luce, and journalists George Sokolsky and Dorothy Thompson. The organization received initial funding from the Polish American Congress and the National Committee for a Free Europe despite the refusal of a tax exempt status from the U.S. Bureau of Internal Revenue.

The activities of the Committee were threefold. First, it sought to obtain and preserve evidence on the Katyń massacre. It interviewed Polish ex-prisoners of the Soviets, Soviet defectors, and the leaders of the Polish emigration. It also collected written documents from the Polish government-in-exile and from German sources. Second, it attempted to publicize the case among the American public. The committee members made speeches, wrote pamphlets, and circulated memoranda. The third goal was to interest the United States Congress in the matter. Letters were sent to members of Congress asking for official action. The first results

came on June 26, 1951, when a resolution was introduced by Congressman Timothy Sheehan, Republican of Chicago, to create a "select committee to [...] conduct a full and complete investigation of all aspects of the massacre of 4,000 Polish officers in the Katyń Forest, near Smolensk." The motion was shelved, but the Committee kept mobilizing the American public to exert pressure on Congress and on September 18, 1951, the bill was reintroduced by John Madden, Democrat of Indiana. This time it was unanimously accepted. A seven-member select Congressional committee was formed to "conduct a full and complete investigation [...] of the massacre of thousands of Polish officers buried in a mass grave in the Katyń Forest." The American Committee for the Investigation of the Katyń Massacre thus accomplished its goal of initiating an official investigation of the Katyń atrocity. Subsequently it disbanded, turning its files over to the Congressional investigators who completed their work in December, 1952, when they concluded that the Soviets were guilty of the crime and recommended that their final report be delivered to the United Nations.—*Joanna Wojdon*

SOURCE: Robert Szymczak, "A Matter of Honor: Polonia and the Congressional Investigation of the Katyn Forest Massacre," *Polish American Studies*, Vol. XLI, no. 1 (Spring 1984), 25–65.

American Committee for the Resettlement of Polish Displaced Persons (ACRPDP). Formed in Chicago by the **Polish American Congress** in response to the passage of the Displaced Persons Act of 1948, the organization's purpose was to "help select eligible displaced persons of Polish nationality in the designated D.P. Camps in Europe ... [and] provide them with necessaries, secure their transportation from the port of entry to the place of resettlement in the United States, provide them with jobs and housing facilities and to work with the Federal D.P. Commission and all related governmental, civic, and private agencies in this regard." It was also "to raise funds in order to successfully carry out the resettlement program of the DPs." The ACRPDP was the only Polish American resettlement agency directly accredited by the U.S. Displaced Persons Commission, and recognized by the International Refugee Organization and other agencies, as an independent agency, which could issue its own "assurances" for sponsoring entry of displaced persons into the U.S. without the necessity of securing individual affidavits. Following the passage of the 1950 Amendments to the Displaced Persons Act, which established a quota of 18,000 for the admittance of Polish veterans in Great Britain, the ACRPDP obtained recognition from the State Department to administer this resettlement program. As a result, about 11,000 Polish veterans, together with their families, were resettled in the U.S. By the time the law expired on December 31, 1951, the ACRPDP had obtained assurances for about 35,000 Polish displaced persons.

The first authorities of the ACRPDP included: Chairman Judge **Blair F. Gunther**, Secretary-Treasurer Edward E. Plusdrak, and Directors **Adela Lagodzińska**, the Rev. Walerian Karcz, Jan A. Stanek, Józef Pawlowski, Franciszka Dymek, and Tadeusz Adesko. The ACRPDP organized 27 state divisions, and cooperated with both national and local Polonia organizations, relying especially on the structures of the **Polish National Alliance**. It also had its representatives in Germany (Col. Bolesław Wichrowski and **Frances Dymek**) and Great Britain. The ACRPDP representatives secured assurances, which included guarantees for jobs and housing, processed the paperwork, and met incoming displaced persons at the ports of entry, where they often organized official welcomes and provided the arriving refugees with food and medical attention. Next, they directed the displaced persons to their destinations, giving them loans to cover costs of inland transportation. The ACRPDP also secured temporary lodging for the displaced persons who either had to travel farther or whose sponsors had not shown up. The committee struggled to cover the costs of the resettlement. In 1949, it organized a well-publicized fund drive, which, however, fell short of the expected goals. It forced the committee to accept sizeable loans from the Polish National Alliance and the Displaced Persons Commission. For the next few years after the expiration of the Displaced Persons Act, the ACRPDP focused on repaying those loans by collecting outstanding accounts from individual displaced persons.

In 1954, the State Department again accredited the ACRPDP to administer resettlement of Polish refugees coming under the new Refugee Relief Act of 1953. In 1955–57, the ACRPDP assisted Polish refugees brought over to the U.S., while the officers of the National Catholic Welfare Conference represented the committee in the work abroad. During this time more than a thousand persons arrived in the U.S. due to the ACRPDP's efforts. Although the committee continued to exist till 1968, the level of its activities in the 1960s had been very low, except for the lobbying effort by the PAC Washington Office, which theoretically represented also the ACRPDP. The ACRPDP cooperated (as well as competed) with two other major Polonia agencies in the area of the resettlement: The

Polish Immigration Committee (New York), and the Rada Polonii Amerykańskiej (after 1946 as **Polish American Council**)—both affiliated with the National Catholic Welfare Conference.—*Anna D. Jaroszyńska-Kirchmann*

SOURCES: Anna D. Jaroszyńska-Kirchmann, *The Exile Mission: The Polish Political Diaspora and Polish Americans, 1939–1956* (Athens, OH: Ohio University Press, 2004); Anna D. Jaroszyńska, "The American Committee for the Resettlement of Polish Displaced Persons (1948–1968) in the Manuscript Collection of the Immigration History Research Center," *Polish American Studies*, Vol. 46, no. 1 (Spring 1987), 67–74; Joanna Wojdon, *W imieniu sześciu milionów ... Kongres Polonii Amerykańskiej w latach 1944–1968* (Toruń: Wydawnictwo Adam Marszałek, 2005).

American Council for Polish Culture, Inc.

Founded in Detroit in July 1948, the ACPC is a national non-profit, charitable, cultural, and educational organization that serves as a network and provides national leadership among affiliated Polish American cultural organizations throughout the United States. In 2009, the Council represented the interests of some 25 affiliated organizations in fifteen states and the District of Columbia, published a quarterly publication titled *Polish Heritage*, and offered several scholarship programs. The Council meets in annual convention at sites around the country, usually sponsored by its affiliate organizations. In 1991, after the fall of communism in Poland, the Council sponsored its first convention in Poland, and in 2002 convened in Kraków. The ACPC Board is comprised of five elected officers and twelve elected national directors, as well as representatives from each of the Council's affiliates, past ACPC presidents, and appointed and standing committee members. Among the ACPC's activities was a major fundraising effort to found the American Center of Polish Culture (now the **Polish National Center**) which opened in Washington, D.C., in 1992; raising funds for the restoration of the monument to Gen. **Kazimierz Pułaski** in Savannah, Georgia; raising some $50,000 to open the first community computer center in Eastern Europe in Siedlce, Poland, in 1992; presenting an original sculptured plaque to the Harper's Ferry National Park in honor of Cyprian Norwid; contributing the "Polish Perspectives" exhibition at the annual National Conference of the Social Studies; sponsoring a scholarship of a student to engage in summer study in Poland; supports an annual operatic award in honor of **Marcella Sembrich**; provides scholarships to Polish Americans for advanced college study; and sponsors an annual Youth Leadership Conference in Washington, D.C.—*Włodek Lopaczynski*

SOURCES: Anna Chrypinska, *Our Second Quarter Century 1973–1998. The History of the American Council for Polish Culture* (n.p.: American Council for

Polish Culture, 1998); Charles A. Baretski, *Our Quarter-Century: The History of the American Council of Polish Cultural Clubs, 1948–1973* (Newark: American Council of Polish Cultural Clubs, 1973).

American Council of Polish Cultural Clubs *see* American Council for Polish Culture.

American Institute of Polish Culture, Inc.

Founded by **Blanka A. Rosenstiel** in 1972, the American Institute of Polish Culture (AIPC) is a non-profit corporation located in Miami, Florida, dedicated to increasing awareness of Polish history and culture and encouraging the scientific and aesthetic activities of Polish Americans. The AIPC sponsors lectures, book publications and signings, conferences, seminars, poetry readings, radio and television programs, art exhibits, Polish film series, and other cultural and educational events. The Institute has also translated into English and published more than twenty books and published the annual *Good News* journal which includes articles on Polish history and culture and biographical information on prominent Poles and Polish Americans. The AIPC awards scholarships, sponsors an annual International Polonaise Ball, and in 1977 founded the Chopin Foundation of the United States to support the education of young American musicians and promote appreciation of the music of Fryderyk Chopin. In 1998 it established the Kościuszko Chair in Polish Studies at the University of Virginia that was later moved in 2008 to the Institute of World Politics in Washington, D.C. The AIPC publishes the annual *Good News* magazine to promote awareness of its mission.—*Donald E. Pienkos*

SOURCE: Annual *Good News* magazines.

American Polish Labor Council.

The American Polish Labor Council (APLC) was an *ad hoc* political adjunct of the Congress of Industrial Organizations (CIO) Political Action Committee established in January 1944 to aid in the re-election of President Franklin Delano Roosevelt for a fourth term. At this time, there was no national political action umbrella group for Polish Americans, the establishment of the **Polish American Congress** being five months in the future. Sidney Hillman, president of the powerful Amalgamated Clothing Workers of America (ACWA), labor's closest advisor to FDR, and chairman of the CIO's Political Action Committee, spearheaded the Polish Labor Council with the help of **Bolesław K. Gebert**. The ACWA, the CIO, and its political action committee, all headed by Hillman, combined with the **American Slav Congress** to promote the Democratic Party and the election of FDR.

With the Republican candidate, Governor Thomas E. Dewey, making overtures to **Polonia**, it was especially important that the CIO, which claimed to represent the vast majority of blue collar Polish workers, take an active part in maintaining their loyalty to FDR. Key to these efforts was the support of **Leo Krzycki**, president of the American Slav Congress, who assumed leadership of the Labor Council. A noted one-time socialist leader, Krzycki and the pro–Soviet American Slav Congress supported FDR because of his pro-labor orientation and his policy of recognizing the Soviet Union and his subsequent wartime alliance with the USSR. An important step in the political process was a meeting between Hillman and Krzycki in Cleveland, OH, on January 16, 1944. "The purpose of these committees," Krzycki proclaimed, "is to combat insidious propaganda of fifth columnists and reactionary elements in the Polish communities and to mobilize Americans of Polish descent in support of our commander-in-chief, Franklin D. Roosevelt, and his foreign and domestic policies." Officers of the APLC included many of Polonia's prominent labor activists: Albert A. Krzywonos served as recording secretary; John A. Zaremba as secretary-treasurer; and the vice presidents included Chester Kosmalski (United Auto Workers), Stanley Strobeck (steel workers), Joseph Cetnar (electrical workers), John Sobczak (ACWA), Conrad Komorowski (farm equipment workers), Joseph Poskonka (packing house workers), Adolph Prywara (shipbuilders), Dolores Pinta (mine and mill workers), **Stanley Nowak** (public employees), Frank Mierkiewicz (fur and leather workers), Joseph Pyzik (American-Polish Trades Council), Wacław Andrzejewski (office workers), and Joseph Janusz (cooks). "Not surprisingly," political scientist Donald E. Pienkos concluded, "both organizations [the American Slav Congress and American Polish Labor Council] were accorded substantial recognition in Washington as better representing Polish American opinion than the 'anti–Soviet' KNAPP" (**National Committee of Americans of Polish Descent**). The APLC published two pamphlets for general distribution, *We've Come a Long Way with Roosevelt* (1944), a political campaign piece, and Ignace Złotowski's *What Is Happening in Poland?* (1945), which was designed to promote a pro–Soviet policy. The APLC's second national conference, held in Washington, D.C., in April 1945, was more involved with pro–Soviet interests than American labor issues. The APLC's activities generally ceased with the presidency of Harry S Truman, who pursued an anti–Soviet policy, particularly as enunci-

ated in his "Truman Doctrine" address to Congress in March 1947.

The Polish American Labor Council in Detroit, an anti–Communist group with a name similar to the APLC, registered as a corporation two weeks after the CIO group and opposed its action in the area of foreign affairs. It continued as an arm of the Polish American Congress long after the demise of the CIO labor council. Throughout their existence, both Labor Councils were closely monitored by the Foreign Nationalities Bureau of the Office of Strategic Services.—*Don Binkowski*

SOURCES: Bolesław Gebert, "Progressive Traditions Among Polish-Americans During World War II," in Grzegorz Babiński and Mirosław Frančić, eds., *Poles in History and Culture of the United States of America* (Wrocław: Zakład Narodowy Im. Ossolińskich, 1979), 99–115; Donald E. Pienkos, *For Your Freedom Through Ours: Polish American Efforts on Poland's Behalf, 1863–1991* (Boulder CO: East European Monographs, 1991); Don Binkowski, *Leo Krzycki and the Detroit Left* (Philadelphia: Xlibris, 2001).

American Relief for Poland *see* **Polish American Council.**

American Slav Congress. When Germany invaded Poland in 1939, various Polish American organizations formed support groups for the Polish government-in-exile in London. The groups spread across the country from Chicago to New York, but one group stood out from the rest, the American Slav Congress. The American Slav Congress was a late comer on the scene, having been formed only after the invasion of the Soviet Union in 1941. Moscow acted first to unite all Slavs against a common German enemy when it called its own All Slav Congress in late 1941. The call for Slavic unity harkened back to World War I and before, when imperial Russia portrayed itself as the great protector of the Slavs. The new call for Slavic unity against the fascist menace was first answered by **Joseph Yablonski**, a labor leader in the United Mine Workers Union in the United States in November of 1941. The call was then picked up by **Bolesław Gebert** who became the founder and directing force behind the American Slav Congress. It was later revealed that he was an NKVD agent with the code name Ataman. The first meeting of the Congress was held April 25–26, 1942, in Detroit. **Leo Krzycki**, a founder of the Congress of Industrial Organizations (CIO), was chosen as the chair. He became the front man for Gebert, with Moscow referring to Krzycki as a "progressive" thinking individual.

Initially the Congress gave and received support from the London exile government. Even Jan Stanczyk, the Exile Minister of Labor, offered his personal support. But the honeymoon lasted for only about a year.

When news of the Katyń Massacre came out and Moscow severed diplomatic relations with the exile government in 1943, Krzycki and the American Slav Congress broke with London and remained loyal to Moscow, supporting the Moscow-backed Committee of Polish Patriots. When Moscow proposed a shift in Polish borders to the Oder-Niese River line, Krzycki and the Slav Congress lent the action its full support. It was also arranged for Krzycki and two other representatives from the Congress to travel to Moscow to visit Stalin in 1944. Krzycki was later dropped from the list so as not to compromise his standing in Washington, D.C., but his two closest allies, the Rev. **Stanisław Orlemański** and **Oskar Lange**, did make the trip. Lange was to become a leading member of the Soviet-backed Polish government; however, Orlemański was severely reprimanded by his superiors who did not approve of his trip and dropped out of political life. Krzycki and the Congress continued to support the Moscow-backed regimes established in Eastern Europe after the war by hosting their representatives when they visited the U.S. or by visiting in the late 1940s various East European states from Poland to Bulgaria. There, Krzycki was hailed as a Hero of Labor.

The American Slav Congress was under constant surveillance by the FBI and the OSS during the war, and by the CIA after the war. In 1950 it was put on the list of communist supported organizations by the U.S. Attorney General. The Congress officially ended its activities on November 6, 1951, but continued to remain on government lists until 1955 when it was officially dropped as a subversive organization. **Polonia** gave little support to the American Slav Congress, and it would remain a fringe group from after World War II until its demise in 1951.—*David Stefancic*

SOURCES: Donald Binkowski, *Leo Krzycki and the Detroit Left* (Philadelphia: Xlibris Books, 2002); Earl Hayes and Harvey Klehr, *Venona* (New Haven: Yale University Press, 1999).

Ameryka-Echo (*America-Echo*). **Antoni A. Paryski** began publishing a weekly *Ameryka* on September 21, 1889. In 1902, he bought Buffalo's *Echo*, which superseded the earlier *Głos Wolny* (Voice of Freedom), brought it to Toledo, and combined it with *Ameryka*, establishing *Ameryka-Echo* on December 6, 1902. The weekly was a part of Paryski's larger publishing enterprise, Paryski Publishing Company, which also printed other newspapers, books, manuals, and other publications. Circulation of *Ameryka-Echo* grew steadily, placing it in the forefront of the Polish press in the United States. According to *Ayer's Directory*, *Ameryka-Echo*'s circulation was 8,500 in 1895; 12,640 in 1899; and 14,000 in 1905. Since its inception, *Ameryka*, and then *Ameryka-Echo* supported the national-liberal camp, with Paryski himself a member of the **Polish National Alliance**. Throughout his career as *Ameryka-Echo*'s editor and publisher, Paryski built a reputation for independence and repeatedly claimed that his newspaper remained free from any party and political influences and did not represent any particular interests. Instead, anti-clericalism, vicious at times, became the newspaper's most characteristic feature. *Ameryka-Echo* openly criticized the Roman Catholic Church and attacked individual priests, accusing them of greed, corruption, immorality, and exploitation of parishioners. In response, the Roman Catholic clergy insisted that people who subscribed to, or even read, Paryski's paper were expected to confess it as a sin, were often refused absolution, and were encouraged to boycott businesses that advertised in *Ameryka-Echo*. In 1912, several bishops of Midwestern states officially condemned Polish newspapers, among them *Ameryka-Echo*, which generated persistent claims by local priests that the publishers of the weekly had been excommunicated.

In 1904, *Ameryka-Echo* added four pages, the so-called "Dodatek" (Addition), which included serialized novels, and articles on artistic, literary, and educational topics. The masthead of the "Dodatek" carried a motto "Precz z obłudą, naprzód z wolą ludu," or "away with hypocrisy, [and] ahead with the will of the people." Paryski's self-proclaimed mission became self-education for the people (oświata), which carried real freedom and empowerment, and protected the people against exploitation. Paryski used thousands of so-called "education agents" (agenci oświatowi), as sales agents, sending them from home to home collecting newspaper subscriptions and book orders. In 1915, a daily edition of *Ameryka-Echo* appeared for a year, and was again briefly revived in 1917. By 1922 the circulation jumped to 40,000. A year later, *Ameryka-Echo* reached a circulation of 105,000 copies, which was at that time the highest among the entire Polish American press. Riding the wave of prosperity and popularity, Paryski decided to again add a daily edition of *Ameryka-Echo*, while keeping a weekly weekend edition in an unchanged format. In 1924, Paryski printed almost 40,000 copies of the daily and 112,000 copies of the weekly. During the next five years, *Ameryka-Echo* gained record circulation; the daily fluctuated between 40,000 and 43,000 copies (except in 1928, when the daily dropped to 28,000), while the weekly reached an unprecedented 120,000 copies.

During the Great Depression, in 1934, Paryski decided to discontinue the daily to focus solely on the weekly. The circulation remained high. *Ayer's Directory* lists the circulation of the daily for the years 1931–34 as close to 25,000, with the weekly reaching 95,000. Beginning in 1935, however, circulation numbers began a steady downward trend. In 1935, *Ameryka-Echo* printed 80,400 copies, 74,900 copies in 1936, and 68,900 copies in each of the years from 1937 to 1940. Paryski probably served as the editor-in-chief from the inception of *Ameryka-Echo* until 1921, when he hired Mieczysław Stanisław Dunin (1922–28) as editor. After Dunin's death, Frank T. Friedel (1933–43) served as editor. Many prominent Polonia journalists were associated with *Ameryka-Echo*. In the late 1920s its editorial staff included, among others, Józef Lubicz, Jan Swojski, and Janina Dunin (who designed and headed a section for women). Among regular contributors and correspondents were **Tadeusz Siemiradzki**, Tomasz Kozak, Józef Sawicki, Julian Korski-Grove, **Stanisław Osada**, **Melania Nesterowicz**, Stefan Nesterowicz, Seweryn Skulski, Józef Bronowicz, S. B. Sandusky, F. Jagiełło, Mieczysław Friedel, and **Czesław Łukaszkiewicz**. A sizable group of regular contributors represented the **Polish National Catholic Church**, including Bishop **Franciszek Bończak**, Bishop **Leon Grochowski**, Bishop Józef Zielonka, the Rev. B. Krupski, the Rev. M.S. Lesik, the Rev. W. K. Strzelec, the Rev. A Ziarko, and the Rev. **Józef L. Zawistowski**.

After Paryski's death in 1935, *Ameryka-Echo* continued its general direction and profile. During the 1940s, circulation of *Ameryka-Echo* remained between 20,000 and 22,000. However, by 1956 it dropped to 16,263, beginning a steady downward trend for the rest of the decade. In 1942–45, Paryski's Sorbonne-educated daughter, Marie Paryski-Rosiński, became the editor-in-chief; and following her tragic death in a car accident, her husband, Dr. Victor Rosiński took over as an editor-in-chief. After Rosiński's death, J. Szczęsny Leśniewicz became editor-in-chief in 1955. Due to the decreasing subscription base and rising costs of production, in 1956 a private corporation, with Marian Wojciechowski as administrative manager and Leśniewicz as primary share holders, purchased *Ameryka-Echo*, while the Paryski Publishing Company, headed by founder's son, Thaddeus Paryski, continued to provide facilities and printing services.

With Rosiński's death, the character of *Ameryka-Echo* began a gradual transformation. Wojciechowski insisted that the vehemently anti-clerical sections of the newspaper be suspended, and Thaddeus Paryski agreed to the change. *Ameryka-Echo* was now to avoid discussing and criticizing any religion or denomination. Both Leśniewicz and Wojciechowski belonged to the new wave of postwar Polish exiles and sought to improve the intellectual level of the weekly, as well as its Polish language standards, in an effort to appeal to the more educated and less anti-clerical postwar arrivals. In 1959–60, *Ameryka-Echo* expanded to include a Buffalo edition, trying to fill the void left by the 1957 closing of **Dziennik dla Wszystkich**. The rising costs of printing and postal services, however, became a real strain on *Ameryka-Echo*'s finances. It was finally sold to a Chicago group where it merged with **Dziennik Chicagoski** under the editorship of Józef F. Białasiewicz. *Ameryka-Echo* continued its Buffalo edition, but the majority of materials in the newspaper were now shared with *Dziennik Chicagoski*, and the number of pages decreased from sixteen to twelve. Circulation, which hovered around 15,000, shot up to 22,687 in 1961 and 1962, for a while reflecting positively on the change. Circulation numbers, however, began another downward spiral from 19,357 in 1963 to 14,660 in 1970 and 12,700 in 1971. Both *Dziennik Chicagoski* and *Ameryka-Echo* closed in 1971. *Ameryka-Echo*'s last issue appeared on May 9, 1971. The Paryski Publishing Company did not last much longer; the 84-year-old company, one of the largest printing firms in the Toledo area, went out of business in November of 1972.—*Anna Jaroszyńska-Kirchmann*

Masthead of *Ameryka-Echo* published in Buffalo, New York (*PMA*).

SOURCES: Anna D. Jaroszyńska-Kirchmann, "As if

at a Public Meeting: Polish American Readers, Writers, and Editors of *Ameryka-Echo*, 1922–1969," in Bruce S. Elliott, David A. Gerber, and Suzanne M. Sinke, eds., *Letters Across Borders: The Epistolary Practices of International Migrants* (New York: Palgrave, 2006), 200–22; Theodore L. Zawistowski, "*Ameryka-Echo* as a Source for Polish National Catholic Church History: First Impressions," *PNCC Studies*, Vol. 16 (1995), 61–72; Anna D. Jaroszyńska-Kirchmann, "Between Polish Positivism and American Capitalism: The Educational Agents' Experiment in the Polish-American Community, 1889–1914," *History of Education Quarterly*, Vol. 48, no. 4 (2008), 485–507.

Am-Pol Eagle. The *Am-Pol Eagle* is a weekly newspaper that primarily serves the Polish communities of Buffalo and Western New York. Pilot issues of the newspaper were published on July 28 and in August of 1960. Regular weekly publication then began on September 15, 1960, and has continued without interruption since that date. The *Am-Pol Eagle* was established by Matthew W. Pelczyński, who served as editor and publisher until his death in 1993. He was succeeded by Renee Harzewski, who continued as publisher until 2006. The newspaper's managing editor, Roger L. Puchalski, was then named publisher in January of 2007. The *Am-Pol Eagle* began as a four page newspaper, but quickly expanded its coverage to an average of between sixteen and twenty pages. Although the newspaper contains some segments in the Polish language, it is written primarily in English. Initially, the newspaper filled a void created by the closing of Buffalo's Polish daily, the **Dziennik dla Wszystkich**, in 1957. Recognized for the reporting of cultural news affecting the Polonia of Western New York, the *Am-Pol Eagle* has also provided leadership on issues of concern to that community. For example, its editorials have opposed defamation, and have given support to historic preservation, to educational programs, and to the maintenance of Polish churches and institutions. The newspaper has also promoted the election of qualified Polish American candidates for public office. In 2006, the Buffalo and Erie County Historical Society presented its Niederlander Award to the *Am-Pol Eagle* in recognition of the newspaper's ongoing contributions to preservation of the history of Western New York.—*Carl L. Bucki*

Masthead of Western New York's *Am-Pol Eagle* (*OLS*).

SOURCES: Jan Wepsiec, *Polish American Serial Publications: 1842–1966, An Annotated Bibliography* (Chicago: by the author, 1968); *Am-Pol Eagle*, August 13, 2009.

Anarchism, Polish American *see* **Radicalism, Polish American.**

Andrews, Stanley (Stanisław Andrzejewski; b. Chicago, Illinois, August 28, 1891; d. Los Angeles, California, June 23, 1969). Actor. An early interest in stage and radio productions led Andrews to his first significant role as the voice of Daddy Warbucks on the popular *Little Orphan Annie* radio show (1931–36). During his career he appeared as a character actor in more than 250 movies including *All the King's Horses* (1934), *Mr. Deeds Goes to Town* (1936), *The Lone Ranger* (1938), *Blondie* (1938), *Andy Hardy Gets Spring Fever* (1939), *Beau Geste* (1939), *Mr. Smith Goes to Washington* (1939), *The Ox-Bow Incident* (1943), *It's a Wonderful Life* (1946), *Road to Rio* (1947), *The Lemon Drop Kid* (1951). His final role was in *Cry Terror!* (1958). From 1952 to 1965 he starred as The Old Ranger in the very popular television series *Death Valley Days* until the sponsors opted for a younger man, Ronald Reagan. His television career also included guest appearances on *The Adventures of Superman*, *Range Rider*, *The Lone Ranger*, *The Cisco Kid*, *Annie Oakley*, *The Adventures of Rin Tin Tin*, *The Adventures of Wild Bill Hickok* and *Maverick.—James S. Pula*

SOURCES: *Current Biography*, Vol. 13 (June 1952); obituary, *New York Times*, June 26, 1969.

Andrzejkowicz, Juliusz (b. Wilno district, Lithuania, September 1821; d. Philadelphia, Pennsylvania, April 3, 1898). Polonia activist, businessman. Because of his involvement in revolutionary activities against the occupying powers, his property was confiscated in 1848 and he fled first to France and then to the United States in 1854. Settling in Philadelphia where he engaged in business, he eventually opened a paint and chemical store under the name of Andrzejkowicz and Dunk. He maintained close ties with Polish émigré circles in France, and also presided over the Polish com-

Juliusz Andrzejkowicz, first president of the Polish National Alliance (*OLS*).

mittee formed in the U.S. to rally support for the January Insurrection in 1863. In May of 1879, he was among the first individuals to respond to a letter of **Agaton Giller** advocating the organization of Poles in the United States. On February 15, 1880, in consequence of his efforts to establish a new organization along the lines Giller proposed, Andrzejkowicz was elected president of the newly-formed group which was named the **Polish National Alliance** (PNA) and registered as the first member of Group No. 1. The national convention (or sejm) of the Alliance elected him **censor**, an office he held for the next three years. The Fourth Sejm in 1883 named him honorary president for life. Andrzejkowicz was a strong supporter of the creation of a Polish National Treasury in Rapperswil, Switzerland, serving on its National Commission. In 1886–87 he traveled in Europe to advocate the unification of émigré organizations into a general national alliance which he called a National Polish League. He also used his presence in Europe to strongly protest against Germanization policies in the German-occupied zones of partitioned Poland. Andrzejkowicz helped to organize assistance for veterans of the Polish national uprisings living in the West.—*Adam Walaszek*

SOURCES: "Juliusz Andrzejkowicz," *Zgoda*, April 14, 1898, 1; Donald E. Pienkos, *PNA: A Centennial History of the Polish National Alliance of the United States of North America* (Boulder, CO: East European Monographs, 1984).

Anthony, Michael (Michael Anthony Sobolewski; b. Chicago, Illinois, June 20, 1954; d.—). Musician. One of five children born to Polish immigrant parents, he moved with his family as a child to California where he graduated from Arcadia High School in 1972. Acquiring an interest in music while growing up, he played trumpet in the junior high school marching band, he then learned to play the guitar and bass. Following graduation from high school, he formed the band Poverty's Children, as well as playing in several other bands. Enrolling in Pasadena City College, he met Alex Van Halen who soon asked him to join his group as bassist. In 1974 he joined Eddie Van Halen, Alex Van Halen, and David Lee Roth to form the hit hard rock band Van Halen. After signing a contract with Warner Brothers in 1978, the band released ten albums between 1979 and 1995. During this period Anthony acquired a popular reputation not only for his bass play, but for his concert solos replete with stage theatrics. In 2004 he was replaced as bassist by Wolfgang Van Halen, the son of the band's founder Eddie Van Halen. Anthony also appeared with Sammy Hagar's band The Waboritas and briefly joined the groups Planet Us and The Other Half. In 2007 he formed Mad Anthony Xpress. In addition to his music, Anthony also markets hot sauce, hot mustard and barbeque sauce through his on-line Mad Anthony Café.—*James S. Pula*

SOURCE: "Michael Anthony," *Almanac of Famous People* (Detroit: Thomson Gale, 2007).

Anti-Defamation Commission *see* Polish American Congress Anti-Defamation Commission.

Antolak, Sylvester (b. St. Clairsville, Ohio, September 10, 1916; d. Cisterna di Littoria, Italy, May 24, 1944). Soldier, Medal of Honor recipient. Growing up in St. Clairsville, Ohio, Antolak enlisted in Company B, 15th Infantry Regiment, 3rd Infantry Division

Sylvester Antolak, Medal of Honor recipient (*NARA*).

where he rose to the rank of sergeant. During the Allied breakout from the Anzio beachhead in Italy, near Cisterna di Littoria on May 24, 1944, Sgt. Antolak led his unit in an assault on German machine gun positions. Although wounded three times, he continued his advance into intense German fire killing two Germans and forcing ten to surrender. Refusing medical attention, he continued to lead the advance on the German positions until killed. For bravery and sacrifice he was awarded the Medal of Honor, the citation of which read in part: "[H]e charged 200 yards over flat, coverless terrain to destroy an enemy machinegun nest during the second day of the offensive which broke through the German cordon of steel around the Anzio beachhead. Fully 30 yards in advance of his squad, he ran into withering enemy machinegun, machine-pistol and rifle fire. Three times he was struck by bullets and knocked to the ground, but each time he struggled to his feet to continue his relentless advance. With one shoulder deeply gashed and his right arm shattered, he continued to rush directly into the enemy fire concentration with his submachine gun wedged under his uninjured arm until within 15 yards of the enemy strong point, where he opened fire at deadly close range, killing 2 Germans and forcing the remaining 10 to surrender. He reorganized his men and, refusing to seek medical attention so badly needed, chose to lead the way toward another strong point 100 yards distant. Utterly disregarding the hail of bullets concentrated upon him, he had stormed ahead nearly three-fourths of the space between strong points when he was instantly killed by hostile enemy fire. Inspired by his example, his squad went on to overwhelm the enemy troops. By his supreme sacrifice, superb fighting courage, and heroic devotion to the attack, Sgt. Antolak was directly responsible for eliminating 20 Germans, capturing an enemy machinegun, and clearing the path for his company to advance." The *USS Sgt. Sylvester Antolak*, AP-192, was named in his honor.—*James S. Pula*

SOURCES: R. J. Proft, *United States of America's Congressional Medal of Honor Recipients and Their Official Citations* (Columbia Heights, MN: Highland House II, 2002); *The Medal of Honor of the United States Army* (Washington, D.C.: U.S. Government Printing Office, 1948), 53.

Anuszkiewicz, Richard (b. Erie, Pennsylvania, May 23, 1930; d.—). Artist. Educated at the Cleveland Institute of Art (BFA, 1953), he earned a Pulitzer Traveling Fellowship to study at the National Academy of Design in New York (1953), after which he studied with color theorist Josef Albers at Yale University, receiving a MFA degree in 1955

Richard Anuszkiewicz, a leader in the Op Art Movement (*Stanley L. Cuba*).

and a B.S. degree in education from Kent State University (1956). In 1957 he moved to New York where he soon established himself as a leader in the Op Art Movement along with Julian Stanczak, with whom he roomed at Yale. Noted especially for his mathematical precision and his focus on the psychology and physiology of visual perception, his use of color also brought critical acclaim. His teaching career encompassed Artist-in-Residence appointments at Dartmouth College, the University of Wisconsin, Cornell University, Kent State University, and the School of Visual Arts. His solo exhibitions appeared in Colombia, Germany, Italy, Japan, Switzerland, and various locations in the U.S. His work has been recognized with the Charles of the Ritz Painting Award, Philosopher's Stone Prize (1963), Silvermine Guild (1964), Cleveland Arts Prize (1977), Hassam Fund Purchase Prize (1980, 1988), New York State Art Teachers' Association Award (1994), Emil and Dines Carlson Award (1995), New Jersey Pride Award (1996), Richard Florsheim Fund Grant (1997), Lee Krasner Award (2000), and Lorenzo di Medici Medal-Florence Biennale (2005).—*Stanley L. Cuba*

SOURCES: *Richard Anuszkiewicz: A Survey* (New York: David Findlay, Jr., Fine Art, 2005); Floyd Ratliff, Sanford Wurmfeld, *Color Function Painting: The Art of Josef Albers, Julian Stanczak and Richard Anuszkiewicz. Selections from the Collection of Neil K. Rector* (Winston-Salem: Wake Forest University Fine Arts Gallery, 1996); Martin H. Bush, *Richard Anuszkiewicz. Constructions and Paintings: 1986–1991* (New York: ACA Galleries, 1991); Karl Lunde, *Anuszkiewicz* (New York: Harry N. Abrams, Inc., 1977); Paul Cummings, *A Dictionary of Contemporary American Artists* (London: St. James Press, 1971).

Archacki, Henryk (b. Pieczyska, Poland, August 21, 1907; d. New Rochelle, New York, August 13, 1998). Artist, journalist. Migrating to Chicago in 1908, Archacki graduated from Carl Schurz High School and in 1928 began writing for the youth and sports pages of Chicago's *Dziennik Związkowy* (Alliance Daily News). He was then hired as a graphic artist by Republic Engraving and Design Company, which then sent him to run its Brooklyn, New York, studio in November 1930. When Republic went out of business, Archacki formed his own graphic design firm, Pioneer Rubber and Engraving Company, creating everything from rubber stamps to advertising. He also began to draw cartoons about Polish oddities and historical figures, which he called "Do you know that," which he based on Ripley's popular *Believe it or Not!* His cartoons appeared in many Polish publications over the years, including the *American Polonia Reporter* and the *Polish American Journal*. During his career he drew about 3,000 cartoons, earning him the title of "the Polish Ripley." In 1931 he also became sports editor for *Poland* magazine and *Czas*, the organ of the **Polish National Alliance of Brooklyn**. In 1967, he began writing an English-language page for *Straż*, the official publication of the **Polish National Union**, by invitation of Bishop **Leon Grochowski**, Primate of the **Polish National Catholic Church**. In 1937, Archacki was initiated into the Kosciuszko Lodge, Free Order of Masons, in the Bronx, New York, becoming its Worshipful Master in 1943. His article, "A Brief History of Polish Freemasonry," appeared in the lodge's fifteenth anniversary historical brochure, published in 1943. In 1978, he was made Right Worshipful and appointed by New York's Grand Master to be the Representative to the Grand Lodge of Montana. He

Henry Archacki, artist, journalist, and Polonia activist (*PMA*).

continued to be active in Masonic affairs into the 1990s.

Archacki was one of the founders of the Commission for Research on Polish Immigration within the **Polish Institute of Arts and Sciences** in America in 1942, which later became the **Polish American Historical Association**. Aside from preserving the memory of various Poles by illustrating and writing about them, he was also involved in honoring and preserving the mortal remains of some of them. Under his leadership, the Kosciuszko Lodge was instrumental in having the graves of Union Civil War General **Włodzimierz Krzyżanowski** and his wife moved from Greenwood Cemetery in Brooklyn to Arlington National Cemetery in 1937. In 1961, he helped form the American Polish Civil War Centennial Committee, whose purpose was to commemorate and investigate the contributions of Polish Americans in the Civil War. He was appointed the New York State Chairman of the **Kosciuszko Garden** Fund at West Point Military Academy in 1967. A great admirer of pianist and statesman **Ignacy Jan Paderewski**, Archacki wore a goatee in honor of his idol, and was present in 1958 when his brother-in-law, Conrad Wycki, accidentally discovered the resting place of Paderewski's heart in a mausoleum in Cypress Hills Cemetery in Brooklyn. Paderewski's wish was that his body would be returned to a free Poland after his death, but that his heart would remain in the United States. Archacki formed the Paderewski Heart Memorial Committee and arranged to have the heart moved to the **Shrine of Our Lady of Częstochowa in Doylestown**, Pennsylvania, where it was interred in 1986 in a commemorative urn with a bronze bas-relief designed by sculptor **Andrzej Pityński**. After this was accomplished, the Committee dropped the word "heart" from its name, and the goal of the Paderewski Memorial Committee became returning Paderewski's body to a free Poland, and also trying to decide when Poland was "free enough" to do so. The body was moved from Arlington National Cemetery in June 1992 and interred at St. John's Cathedral in Warsaw.

Among Archacki's honors were a medal from the Polish government-in-exile (1965); the Centennial Award from *Zgoda*, the official publication of the **Polish National Alliance** (1981); and the Distinguished Service Award from the Polish American Historical Association (1988). The cremated remains of Archacki and his wife are interred at the Shrine of Our Lady of Częstochowa in Doylestown, Pennsylvania, with a bas-relief of their likenesses designed by Andrzej Pityński.—*John Drobnicki*

SOURCES: Francis Bolek, ed., *Who's Who in Polish America* (3rd ed., Harbinger House, 1943); Edward Pinkowski, "Death of Henry Archacki," *Bulletin of the Polish Genealogical Society of California*, Vol. 11 (April 1999).

Architecture, Polish Cathedral Style. Typical of the older Polish-American urban communities of New England, the Middle Atlantic states and the Midwest where the larger settlements of the Great Migration (1880–1914) occurred, these churches were constructed from the donations of the working poor on a grand style as works of not only religious devotion, but group identity and community pride. Characterized by extensive internal and external ornamentation that has been compared to Spanish Baroque style, the decorations usually reflected the regional culture of the areas in Poland where the immigrants originated. Many of these edifices are modeled on churches in Poland, with a strong preference for Renaissance and Baroque styles. According to Peter Williams, "the ambitious prelates in the Great Lakes Polonias often chose to make monumental statements in the Renaissance style of their mother country. The scale of these structures was often enormous, both in the great size of these parishes and the episcopal ambitions of their clerical leaders." Prominent examples of this style include churches such as St. Stanislaus Kostka in Chicago, St. Hedwig in Chicago, St. Adalbert in Buffalo, St. Florian in Hamtramck (MI), Our Lady of Mt. Carmel in Wyandotte (MI), St. Stanislaus in Slavic Village (Cleveland, OH), St. John Cantius in Tremont (OH), St. Stanislaus in Milwaukee, St. Josaphat Basilica in Milwaukee, St. Stanislaus Kostka in Pittsburgh, and Immaculate Heart of Mary in Pittsburgh.—*James S. Pula*

SOURCES: Edward R. Kantowicz, *The Archdiocese of Chicago: A Journey of Faith*: (Ireland: Booklink, 2006); Peter W. Williams, *Houses of God: Region, Religion, and Architecture in the United States* (Urbana: University of Illinois Press, 1997), 179.

Archives, Polish American. "Polish American Archives" in this entry refers to archives either founded by American Polonia or preserving the archival materials that were produced by Polish Americans that can be found in the United States and Poland.

The **Polish Museum of America**, located in Chicago, Illinois, is a Polish American institution founded in 1935 by the **Polish Roman Catholic Union**. **Mieczysław Haiman** was its first director. The archival holdings form an important part of the entire collection and include the institutional files of Rada Polonii Amerykańskiej (Polish War Relief, **American Relief for Poland**; 1938–70), Polish **National Department** (Wydział Narodowy; 1916–22), the Relief Committee for Poland in America (Polski Centralny Komitet Ratunkowy; 1914–18), and the Polish Museum itself, as well as of the local branches of the Polish American fraternals from the Chicago area. Among the personal files that should be mentioned are those of the volunteers of the **Polish Army in France** (1917) and famous Poles who lived in America — including **Helena Modjeska**, **Ignacy Jan Paderewski**, Władysław Orkan, **Henryk Sienkiewicz**, Wacław Gawroński — and of Polish American figures — Mieczysław Haiman, **Marcelina Sembrich-Kochańska**, Donald Bilinski, **Francis Bolek**, Bishop Jan Cieplak. Information about many other Polish Americans can be found in the biographical collection of the Museum, as can printed documents of Polish American parishes, archival maps, photographs and postcards, as well as a large collection of Polish American newspapers.

The **Central Archives of American Polonia** in Orchard Lake, Michigan, were organized by the Rev. **Joseph Swastek**. Many materials were donated by Polish American priests including **Francis Bolek**, Kazimierz Bobrowski (pertaining to the Polish Catholic Mission in Bombay), Walerian Jasiński, **Mieczysław Madaj**, **Antoni Małłek** (including the minutes of **Alliance College** in Cambridge Springs, PA), Jacek Przygoda, and Wojciech Rojek. A collection of Bishop **Stephen Woźnicki** concentrates on the American Catholic Church's aid to the Church in Poland. Donations from **Edward Różański** highlight different aspects of Polish American life, while Różański also transferred to Orchard Lake a portion of the papers and memorabilia of **Aloysius Mazewski**, president of the **Polish American Congress** and **Polish National Alliance** (1967–88). Other collections are devoted to various organizations including the Polish Army Second Corps of Gen. Władysław Anders, the First Polish Armored Division of General Stanisław Maczek, the Polish Home Army, the Polish Air Force, the Association of Former Political Prisoners of World War II, the **Polish Army Veterans' Association**, Polish **Scouting**, and the **Polish Singers' Alliance in America**. Thematic collections include the Archive, Library and Museum of Emigrant Writers (with archival materials and scripts of such writers as **Aleksander Janta**, **Melchior Wańkowicz**, Wacław Iwaniuk, Józef Cat-Mackiewicz, Jarosław Iwaszkiewicz, and Julian Ejsmont), Polonia Radio and TV (based on the donations of Msgr. W. Rojek, Robert Lewandowski and Dr. Walter Sikora) and of Polonia Education (materials from the Polish American schools, the Society of Polish

Youth of Passaic, NJ, and from the Commission of Education of the Polish American Congress). The collections are partly catalogued with the finding aids either printed or placed on the library computers.

The **Polish Institute of Arts and Sciences of America** was formed in 1942 by the Polish scholars in exile. As of 2000, its archive consisted of 65 collections, but with much of the material devoted to Polish, not Polish American history. Included are the papers of leaders of Polish political parties who settled in the United States after World War II including Karol Popiel (Polish Christian Democratic Party), Jerzy Ptakowski (Polish National Party), Zygmunt Zaremba and Feliks Mantel (Polish Socialist Party), and Tadeusz Cieplak (Polish Peasant Union-in-Exile). The papers of Zygmunt Tebinka, Consul General of Poland in Montreal, and of the Polish Embassy in the United States (1919–45) are also available. Polish writers who lived in the United States are represented by **Jan Lechoń**, **Kazimierz Wierzyński**, Andrzej Bobkowski, Wacław Solski, and Bohdan Pawłowicz. The collections also include the papers of the founders and prominent members of PIASA — **Oskar Halecki**, **Wacław Lednicki**, **Feliks Gross**, **Ludwik Krzyżanowski**, **Edmund Urbański**, Jan Wyskota-Zakrzewski, **Frank Renkiewicz**, Frank B. Roman, the Gutowski family, Paul Supiński, Paul Super, Włodzimierz Drzewieniecki, and Ludomira Markiewicz. Organizational records include those of the Polish Federalist Association Division in Chicago, Polish Freedom Movement "Independence and Democracy" (NiD), and Polish American organizations from the New York City area, among them the Polish Association of Former Political Prisoners in New York (1952–82), Democratic Opposition Movement (1963–88), Polish American Relief Committee in New York (1914–17), Polish American and Austrian Friendship Committee in New York (1979–84), Polish American Academic Association (1960–63), Roman Dmowski Institute in New York (since 1954), Assembly of Representatives of Polish American Organizations in New York (1995–2000), **Polish American Congress** Commission of Education (since 1986), and PIASA itself. The Charles Burke Memorial Collection of photographs presenting different aspects of the Polish and Polish American life from 1914 onward is also worth mentioning. An on-line inventory of the PIASA archives is available at www.piasa.org.

The **Józef Piłsudski Institute of America** was founded in New York in 1943 by Piłsudskiites-in-exile headed by Wacław Jędrzejewicz, the first executive director. The core of

the collection was initially the Belweder Archive of the Piłsudski Institute for Research in the Modern History of Poland, evacuated from Warsaw in September 1939. Institutional collections include those of the **National Committee of Americans of Polish Descent** (KNAPP; 1942–65), **National Defense Committee** (1912–40), Consulate General in New York (1930–45), Independent Intelligence Unit "Estezet" (1941–45), and the Institute itself. Among about a hundred individual collections are those of ambassadors Józef Lipski, Michał Sokolnicki, and Juliusz Łukasiewicz, Generals Kazimierz Sosnkowski and Władysław Bortnowski, and also Jan Weinstein, Władysław Pobóg-Malinowski, Tadeusz Katelbach, Stanisław Gierat, Antoni Koper, and **Marian Kamil Dziewanowski**. A research guide is available at www.pilsudski.org.

The Connecticut **Polish American Archives at Central Connecticut State University** was established in 1986 with a grant from the National Historical Publications and Record Commission. As of 2003 they comprised 682 linear feet of material in 68 personal and 45 institutional collections. Special emphasis is placed on the Polish American life in New England and to the post–World War II period. Files national in scope are those of the **American Council for Polish Culture**, North American Study Center for Polish Affairs (**STUDIUM**), and Solidarity International. Materials of the **National Polish American-Jewish American Council** can be found in the papers of **Stanislaus A. Blejwas**. A partial inventory is available online at library.ccsu.edu/about/departments/cppa/.

The **Polish National Catholic Church** has its own archives in Scranton, Pennsylvania. It is divided into two parts. The Bishop **Hodur** Archives of the Central Diocese of the Polish National Catholic Church consist of the records of the Bishop Hodur Biography Commission of 1970s and records of the cathedral rectory of the PNCC's Central Diocese. The Archives of the Polish National Catholic Church document the history of the PNCC. There are minutes of synods, administrative bodies, official Church documents, and personal papers of its prime bishops, as well as other materials relating to the PNCC.

The Immigration History Research Center at the University of Minnesota in St. Paul, founded in 1965, is the American institution that holds the largest amount of Polish American archival materials. Its Polish collection was initiated by **Frank Renkiewicz**. Records of over 100 individuals and organizations cover the period from the nineteenth through the twenty-first century. Represented are priests, political and cultural activists, poets and writers, the Polish American press, and local chapters of fraternal and other organizations. Documents pertaining to Polish Americans may also be found in collections of other ethnic groups, including the papers of Michael Novak and the **Assembly of Captive European Nations**. Printed inventories by **Anna D. Jaroszyńska-Kirchmann** are available for five collections: Paryski Publishing Company (publisher of *Ameryka-Echo*; 1930–60, 210 linear feet), Polish American Congress (1944–72, 47 feet), **Aloysius A. Mazewski** (1944–88, 79 feet), Edward and Loda **Różański** (1940–91, 43 feet), and the **American Committee for Resettlement of Polish Displaced Persons** (1949–68). Research guides can be found online at www.ihrc.umn.edu.

The **Balch Institute of Ethnic Studies** in Philadelphia, which opened in 1976 and merged into the Historical Society of Pennsylvania in 2002, is another offspring of the ethnic revival. Its Polish American collection documents the history of the Polish American press including the papers of **Henry Dende** and his *Polish-American Journal*, the Polish Star Publishing Company and Gwiazda, and Bronisław Pluta. There are also records of the **Polish Union of the United States of North America** in Wilkes-Barre (1906–84, 192 feet), the Polish Beneficial Association, and other local organizations and the Pennsylvania branches of national Polish American organizations. A detailed inventory is available online at www.hsp.org.

The Hoover Institution in Stanford, California, was founded in 1919. Its first archival holdings pertaining to Poland came from the Paris Peace conference and the California sojourn of **Ignacy Jan Paderewski**. The Polish collection expanded after World War II when the archive of the Ministry of Foreign Affairs of the Polish government in-exile was moved to Stanford. The files of the Polish diplomatic and consular posts in the U.S. include those for the Washington embassy and the Consulates in New York, Chicago, Pittsburgh, Detroit, and San Francisco, as well as the honorary consulates in Houston and New Orleans. The collection of the Polish Information Center in New York documents Polish propaganda efforts in America during World War II, while the papers of Stanisław Mikołajczyk and Stefan Korboński, as well as the records of Radio Free Europe, represent the political emigration after World War II. Polonia leaders of the San Francisco area have donated their personal papers and documents of the organizations in which they were active. The description of the collections is available at www.hoover.org.

Documents pertaining to the Polish American past can be found in other American archives, especially in the cities with the larger Polonian population at the Milwaukee Urban Archives (a part of the University of Wisconsin–Milwaukee) and the Western Reserve Historical Society in Cleveland.

In Poland the main repository of the documents relating to the Polish American history for a long time has been the Archiwum Akt Nowych (Central Archive for Modern Records) in Warsaw. In the Paderewski Archive there are documents pertaining to the activities of Polonia before 1945 performed by the Polish **National Department**, Polish Central Relief Agency, **National Defense Committee**, The **Kosciuszko Foundation**, Polish American fraternals, parishes, and schools. There are separate collections of the Polish National Committee, **Światpol** (World Alliance of Poles Abroad), and the Organizational Council of the Poles Abroad. Records pertaining to the Polish American life can be found in the collection of the Ministry of Foreign Affairs (1918–39), the Polish Embassy in Washington, and the Consulate General in New York. As for the post–World War II period, only a few documents pertaining to Polonia have been identified in the collections of the Committee for Cultural Cooperation Abroad (1950–56), National Subscription Committee for School Building (1959–65), Ministry of Information and Propaganda, and other ministries and offices. There is a small portion of the records of the "Polonia" Society in Warsaw.

In 1992 "Wspólnota Polska" established the Center for the Documentation of Polish Emigration at the "Dom Polonii" in Pułtusk. Two anchors of its archival holdings are the "Gift of Stanley Naj" of Chicago and the papers of the "Polonia" Society for Cooperation with Polonia Abroad (Towarzystwo Łączności z Polonią Zagraniczną "Polonia"; 1955–89). The archival part of the "Gift of Stanley Naj" was organized into the following collections pertaining to Polish American history: Father Dr. Józef Orłowski Collection (1903–63), Leon Walkowicz Collection and the Felicja Walkowicz Archive (1910–79), Eugeniusz Walkiewicz Collection of Musical Scores (1901–55), Fr. **Lucjan Bójnowski** Collection (1889–1931), The Records of the Newspaper *Ameryka-Echo* (1958–66), The Records of the Holy Family Library in Chicago (1923–87), Józefina Rzewska Collection (1933–85), The Polish Combatant Organizations (1920–81), Polish American parishes, Polish American Congress (1927–84), The Polish National Department (Wydział Narodowy) 1914–25; Recruiting Centers for the Haller Army (1917–18), the **Polish Museum of America** (1960–

83), the Polish National Alliance (1903–88), the **Polonia** Press-Clippings (1912–80), and Collection of Recordings of the Polish Section of the BBC broadcasts. Detailed description has been put at www.odwp.pl.—*Joanna Wojdon*

SOURCE: *Polish American Studies*, Vol. LX, no. 1 (Spring 2003) is an issue dedicated to Polish American archives.

Arctowski, Henryk (b. Warsaw, Poland, July 15, 1871; d. Washington, D.C., February 21, 1958, Washington, D.C.). Explorer, scientist. Born in Russian-occupied Poland, Arctowski left to attend the university first in Liège, Belgium, then the Sorbonne in Paris where he studied geology and chemistry. In 1895 he contacted Adrien de Gerlache de Gomery who was organizing a Belgian scientific expedition to Antarctica. He was hired as a director for scientific studies on board the *Belgica*, which sailed for Antarctica in 1897. In early 1898 the ship became trapped in sea ice for a year, forcing the crew to become the first people to spend an entire winter below the Antarctic Circle. Arctowski carried out research in geology, oceanography, and meteorology during the expedition, discovering the halo and arcs that form around the sun as light passes through ice crystals in the air. Returning to Uccle, Belgium, he worked on data collected during the voyage, which led him to the conclusion that the South Andes and the Antarctic Peninsula were geologically similar. In 1909 Arctowski moved to New York where he took a position as director of the natural sciences division of the New York Public Library. During this time he continued his scientific work, becoming one of the world's leading experts on climate change. In 1919 he was named chief scientist of an expedition to the Spitsbergen Islands north of the Arctic Circle. That same year he prepared the "Report on Poland" for the U.S. delegation to the Paris Peace Conference, a work containing 2,500 pages of informative text, maps, and charts.

Henryk Arctowski, explorer, scientist, and expert on climate change (*OLS*).

Returning to Poland in 1920, Arctowski turned down an offer to become the government's Minister of Education in favor of a position as chairman of Geophysics and Meteorology at Jan Kazimierz University in Lwów, where he received an honorary doctorate. When World War II began in September 1939, he was in Washington attending a conference as president of the International Commission on Climate Changes. He therefore remained in the U.S., began working as a researcher at the Smithsonian Institution in 1940, and was granted U.S. citizenship. Ill health forced him to retire in 1950. During his career he published more than 400 scientific works and was a strong advocate of international cooperation in scientific research. His name has been given to the Polish research station in Antarctica and to Arctowski Peninsula, Arctowski Peak, and Arctowski Nunataks on that continent, and to Mt. Arctowski and Arctowski Glacier in Spitzbergen. In 1969, his widow established the triennial Arctowski Medal to honor outstanding contributions to the study of solar physics and solar-terrestrial relationships.—*Martin S. Nowak*

SOURCES: Frederick A. Cook, *Through the First Arctic Night* (LaVergne, TN: Lightning Source, 2007); Marilyn J. Landis, *Antarctica: Exploring the Extreme* (Chicago: Chicago Review Press, 2003).

Art *see* Fine Arts.

Assembly of Captive European Nations (ACEN).

ACEN was an international organization of nine Eastern European national émigré groups and five international organizations formally established in New York on September 20, 1954, to advance the restoration of independence to the countries of East and Central Europe. Founded under the aegis of the National Committee for a Free Europe (later the Free Europe Committee), from its inception ACEN included representation from the councils (or committees) in exile from Albania, Bulgaria, Czechoslovakia, Estonia, Hungary, Latvia, Lithuania, Poland and Romania. The associated international organizations which sent their delegates to ACEN were the Christian Democratic Union of Central Europe (CDUCE), the International Center of Free Trade Unionists in Exile (ICFTUE), the International Peasant Union (IPU), the Liberal Democratic Union of Central Eastern Europe (LDUCEE), and the Socialist Union of Central Eastern Europe (SUCEE).

The ACEN charter listed the goals of the Assembly as follows: To sustain the morale of the peoples behind the Iron Curtain, strengthen their will to resist, preserve democratic ideals, promote research on Eastern Europe, provide assistance to refugees, but also supply information on Soviet methods to the free world, seek international support for liberation of Central and Eastern Europe and co-operate with the Council of Europe and European Movement with the aim of assuring an adequate representation of the captive European nations in those bodies, and of preparing the way for the integration of these nations into a United Europe, following their liberation. Their aim of a "peaceful liberation" was to be achieved by providing for free elections and immediate withdrawal of Soviet troops.

In its formal structure, ACEN purposely bore resemblance to the United Nations; that is, it was comprised of the Plenary Assembly, General Committee, Secretariat and working committees. The Assembly's one year sessions began in September and they usually convened in New York, parallel to the sessions of the U.N. Five special sessions were also organized by the Council of Europe in Strasbourg. The Assembly's plenary sessions were presided over in rotation by the chairmen of national delegations or by members of the General Committee. Each national delegation had one seat in the General Committee, and its meetings were presided over by ACEN's chairman, who was elected for a one-year term. The chairman was assisted by the permanent Secretariat. The Secretary General could serve for more than one term, as was the case with Romanian diplomat Brutus Coste who was in that position from 1954 to 1965.

Each of the Eastern European nations had one delegation to ACEN, except for the Poles. Since the Assembly's inception there were two Polish delegations with eight people in each. One represented the Polish National Democratic Committee headed by the former Polish vice-premier Stanisław Mikołajczyk, a delegation presided over by Karol Popiel, and another that spoke on behalf of the London-based Political Council headed by Stefan Korboński. This duality reflected the divisions among the Poles gathered around the London-based Polish government in exile. In an attempt to unite the divided Polish exiles, a new body—the Provisional Council of National Unity—was established on July 31, 1954. Its chapter in New York City was formed on December 11, 1955. In response, ACEN acknowledged only one delegation of London-based exiles headed by Stefan Korboński in 1956. This delegation consisted of eleven members. The remaining five seats were reserved for representatives of Stanisław Mikołajczyk should he ever wish to fill them. Then, due to both American and internal pressures, on March 18, 1958 the link with London was terminated. On December 6, 1959 the Polish Council of Unity, an organization independent of London, was formed and thus the Polish delegation to ACEN changed again. Despite the internal divisions, the Polish contribution to ACEN's activities was significant.

Firstly, due to the numbers of Polish Americans, the activities and initiatives undertaken by the Polish delegation to ACEN had the potential of garnering noteworthy support, and hence exercise influence on the American government. As ACEN members found it hard, or often impossible to assimilate, rejecting naturalization on principle in the belief that they were the genuine spokesmen for their compatriots behind the Iron Curtain (that is, "the voice of the captive people"), they claimed not to be involved in matters which pertained to domestic affairs in the U.S.

Secondly, while the majority of the exiled parliamentarians, diplomats, party leaders, journalists and lawyers from Eastern Europe, representing an array of political outlooks, posed an excellent source for enhancing both the popular knowledge of communism and providing valuable intelligence to the U.S. government. The arriving Poles, who experienced fighting both Nazi and Soviet totalitarianisms, helped to raise awareness among ACEN members that attention should be directed not to their ideological views but to the sole fact of brutal, foreign domination and exploitation of their homelands.

Thirdly, the worldwide network of Polish diasporas helped to create an extensive web of ACEN offices and delegations. Particularly noteworthy were the activities of **Jerzy Lerski** in Tokyo and Zygmunt Zawadowski in Beirut. Naturally, all of ACEN's national delegations used their contacts with compatriots. In 1956 the ACEN offices opened in London, Paris and Bonn, remaining in operation until 1973. All in all, ACEN's delegations were present on all continents except for Africa and Antarctica.

Finally, Polish authors extensively contributed to various ACEN publications, of which the most successful was the *ACEN News*. From 1957 to 1967, **Feliks Gadomski** edited the *Survey of Recent Developments in the Nine Captive Countries*. Those materials, published with the help of the Free Europe Committee, were distributed free of charge to libraries, schools, and institutions throughout the United States and abroad (and also translated into many languages including Swedish or Arabic). Furthermore, ACEN's representatives were publishing in major American daily newspapers and magazines, their articles often being inserted into the *Congressional Record*. They were present at many academic conferences, authored their own publications and reports, and were in high demand among the American political and academic elites.

One of ACEN's most prominent and influential members was Korboński, the organization's chairman in 1958–59, 1966–67 and 1971–85. Along with men like George M. Dimitrov (Bulgaria), Vilis Masens (Latvia), Vaclovas Sidzikauskas (Lithuania), Ferenc Nagy (Hungary), Petr Zenkl and Józef Lettrich (Czechoslovakia), Alexander Kutt (Estonia) and Vasil Germenji (Albania), Korboński's personal contacts helped open many of Washington's doors to ACEN delegations. His books were promoted by ACEN, translated and distributed in many countries of the world with the assistance of the Free Europe Committee. The other prominent Polish exiles that were involved in ACEN over different periods of time were, among others, Stanisław Bańczyk, Bolesław Biega, Michał Mościcki, Zygmunt Nagórski, Adam Niebieszczański, Otto Pehr, **Bolesław Wierzbiański**, and Stanisław Wójcik. Their activities contributed to bringing the Eastern European question before Western audiences.

As ACEN's activities were funded by the CIA (1954–71), private donations generating just a fraction of this organization's resources, it is understandable that its activities were influenced and restricted by the U.S. government by the means of approving its budget. However, once the concealed sponsorship became public in 1971, ACEN was deprived of financial support. Nevertheless, the Assembly's members decided not to give up and on May 22, 1972, changed its formal structure by creating ACEN, Inc., which was registered by the Supreme Court of the state of New York with all nine Eastern European nations represented. Despite significant financial burdens, ACEN, Inc. continued its limited operations until 1989.

Over the 35 years of its continued existence, ACEN became a cohesive information headquarters and research center on Eastern Europe, as well as a lobbying group. Its importance and major achievements rested with its ability to maintain Eastern Europe on the agenda of American foreign policy and in the eye of public opinion. Through its presence and use of the U.S. and international mass media, with the support of the U.S. Congress, personal contacts with foreign policy makers, the use of both private and public organizations, ACEN's own publications, exhibits and lecture series its members managed to keep the hope for freedom in Eastern Europe alive long enough to see it come about. The archives of the Assembly of Captive European Nations are located in the Immigration History Research Center, University of Minnesota, while the Feliks Gadomski Papers are in the Zakład Narodowy im Ossolińskich, Wrocław, Poland.—*Anna Mazurkiewicz*

SOURCE: Anna Mazurkiewicz, "Assembly of the Captive European Nations: 'The Voice of the Silenced Peoples,'" in Ieva Zake, ed., *Anti-Communist Minorities: The Political Activism of Ethnic Refugees in the United States* (New York: Palgrave MacMillan, 2009).

Assimilation *see* **Ethnic Identity and Assimilation.**

Athletics *see* **Sports, Polish Americans in.**

Ax, Emanuel (b. Lwów, Poland [present-day Ukraine]; June 8, 1949; d.—). Pianist. Ax's parents were Jewish survivors of the Nazi concentration camps. His father, a speech coach at the Lwów Theater of Opera and Ballet, began bringing Emanuel to work when he was four years old. At six, Emanuel started to play the violin, but by seven switched to piano under his father's tutelage. In 1957, the family relocated to Warsaw and later secured exit visas to Canada. Initially they joined relatives already living in Winnipeg, Manitoba. By 1961, Emanuel Ax and his parents settled in New York City, which became his permanent base. Between the ages of thirteen and fifteen, Ax's desire to become a classical pianist solidified. He attended every piano concert by his heroes **Artur Rubinstein** and Vladimir Horowitz that he could. For fourteen years, he studied piano at the Juilliard School of Music with Kraków native Mieczysław Munz (1900–76), a once-acclaimed performer who turned to teaching in the 1940s because of a hand disability. The Boys Clubs of America Epstein Scholarship Program funded Ax's studies at Juilliard. In 1970, the same year he became a naturalized U.S. citizen, Ax achieved a bachelor's degree in French from Columbia University. In 1969, he gave a piano concert tour of South and Central America. During the early 1970s, he placed in the Chopin,

Emanuel Ax, internationally recognized pianist (**OLS**).

Vianna da Motta, and Queen Elizabeth of Belgium international piano performance competitions. His debut in New York City came on March 12, 1973, at Alice Tully Hall. In 1974, he won first place in the first Artur Rubinstein Competition in Tel Aviv, Israel, and then embarked on a long tour of the United States. In 1975, Ax won the Michaels Award for Young Concert Artists. Two years later, he made his debut in London. He received the Avery Fisher Prize in 1979.

Ax established himself as an especially lyrical, contemplative interpreter of the Classical and Romantic piano repertoires, particularly the compositions of Mozart, Hadyn, Chopin, Tchiakovsky, Rachmaninoff, Brahms, and Debussy. He appeared at the Tanglewood and Ravinia Festivals and soloed with many of the world's most prestigious symphony orchestras, including those in New York, Chicago, Boston, Los Angeles, London, and Israel. In 2004 he was featured in a BBC documentary on the Holocaust. This Emmy Award–winning program was first broadcast to mark sixty years since the liberation of Auschwitz. For the 2005-06 concert season Ax was Pianist-in-Residence with the Berlin (Germany) Philharmonic. Even as he excelled in solo performance with orchestras, Ax was acclaimed for his other musical collaborations, particularly with such noted chamber musicians as violinist Isaac Stern and cellist Yo-Yo Ma. Ax and his wife Yuko Nozaki also performed together many times: as duo piano soloists at New York's Carnegie Hall; with symphony orchestras around the U.S.; in the Distinguished Artist Series co-sponsored by New York City's Metropolitan Museum of Art and 92nd Street Y; and in a Mark Morris Dance Company effort that started with the 2006 Mostly Mozart Festival.

Ax differed from some of his classical music peers in his active encouragement of contemporary music composers and his interest in performing their work. He premiered at least three compositions dedicated to him personally: *Century Rolls* by John Adams (with the Cleveland Orchestra, 1997); *Seeing* by Christopher Rouse (with the New York Philharmonic, 1999); and *Extremity of Sky* by Melinda Wagner (with Daniel Barenboim and the Chicago Symphony, 2003). Ax also introduced Bright Sheng's *Red Silk Dance* (2000, with the Boston Symphony) and *Song and Dance of Tears* (2003, with Yo-Yo Ma, David Zinman, and the New York Philharmonic). In 2002 he premiered Polish composer Krzysztof Penderecki's piano concerto *Resurrection* with the Philadelphia Orchestra. In 1987 he signed an exclusive recording contract with Sony. As of 2008, he had won a total of seven classical music Grammy Awards: two for Best Instrumental Soloist Performance Without Orchestra, and five for Best Chamber Music Performance with Ma, Stern, and other well-known collaborators.

Ax developed an enduring reputation for his humility as much as for his versatile musical achievements. When an interviewer asked him if he ever "felt captive to the piano," he responded, "No, but that's probably because I don't work hard enough." However, he did grant that "[t]he basic form of my life is music."—*Mary Krane Derr*

SOURCES: "Emanuel Ax," in Laura Kuhn, ed., *Baker's Biographical Dictionary of Musicians, Ninth Edition* (New York: Schirmer Books, 2001); "Emanuel Ax," *Who's Who In America* (Chicago: A. N. Marquis, 2005); David Dubal, *Reflections From the Keyboard: The World of the Concert Pianist* (New York: Schirmer Books and London: Prentice Hall International, 1997.

Babiarz, John E., Sr. (b. Wilmington, Delaware, June 6, 1915; d. Wilmington, Delaware, June 5, 2004). Politician. He grew up on Wilmington's East Side where he was a life member of St. Stanislaus Kostka Church. Graduating from Wilmington High School and the University of Delaware (1937), he served with the U.S. Army in the Middle East during World War II. A charter member of V.F.W. White Eagle Post No. 7006 in Wilmington, he was elected Delaware V.F.W. state commander in 1950. His memberships included **Polish Falcons** Nest 20, the **Polish National Alliance**, and the Polish Library Association. He served as president and director of the Kosciuszko Savings and Loan Association in Wilmington. Elected Register in Chancery in 1948, he became chief clerk of the Delaware State House of Representatives in 1954 before being elected city council president in 1956 and mayor of Wilmington in 1960. During his two terms as mayor he modernized city government with the passage of the home rule charter that strengthened the office of mayor as city executive in charge of municipal departments and instituted a merit system for employees. Following the assassination of Martin Luther King, Jr., on April 4, 1968, armed National Guard troops were summoned on April 9 to quell the riots in the African American section of Wilmington. After one week Mayor Babiarz requested their withdrawal, but Governor Charles L. Terry, Jr., overruled him. The troops remained until the end of Terry's term when Governor Russell W. Peterson ordered their withdrawal on his first day in office on January 21, 1969. The construction of I-95 through the city occurred during Babiarz's term as mayor, with hundreds of homes—including many in Hedgeville, the Polish neighborhood—being demolished. The mayor had supported the routing of I-95 on the outskirts of Wilmington rather than directly through it. Babiarz was defeated in his bid for a third term in 1968. Later he served as president of the Better Business Bureau (1969–73) and was appointed state secretary of the Department of Administrative Services in 1973. During a term as director of commerce (1977–81) he concentrated on the development of the Port of Wilmington. The Delaware Division of the **Polish American Congress** formally honored him for his accomplishments in 1986. Mayor John E. Babiarz Park at the foot of East Seventh St. on the Christina River was dedicated on May 27, 1997. He is buried at Cathedral Cemetery in Wilmington.—*Thomas Duszak*

SOURCES: "Interview with Mary Babiarz, Polish Immigrant" in the Special Collections, University of Delaware Library, June 14, 1969; Harris B. McDowell, "Polish Millenium [sic]," *Congressional Record*, Cong. 89–2, Vol. 112, pt. 7 (May 2, 1966), 9495–97; Jim Parks, "Former Wilmington Mayor at the Hub of 1960s Change," *News Journal* (Wilmington), May 27, 1993, Crossroads sect., 1–2; "The Wilmington Riots: A City Divided," *News Journal*, April 5, 1998, F1-8; Adam Taylor, "Babiarz Was City's First Modern Mayor," *News Journal*, June 8, 2004, B1, 6.

Bajdek, Anthony J. (b. Lynn, Massachusetts, October 7, 1938; d.—). Polonia activist, historian. Bajdek earned baccalaureate (1964) and masters' (1966) degrees in history from Northeastern University where, as an undergraduate, he was president of the Phi Alpha Theta National Honor Society in History and vice president of Pi Sigma Alpha National Honor Society in Political Science. In 1964 he was awarded both a teaching fellowship by Northeastern and a doctoral assistantship by Boston College. As a faculty member at Northeastern, he also served as assistant dean, associate dean, and interim dean before retiring in July 2004 after 39 years of administrative service. He completed 42 consecutive years of teaching in 2008 as a Senior Lecturer in History. Bajdek served as National Vice President for American Affairs of the **Polish American Congress**, president of the Polish American Congress of Eastern Massachusetts, and president of the American Association of the Friends of Kościuszko at West Point. In 2003, he founded the latter organization which sponsors the Annual **Kościuszko** Conference and Observance at West Point. The observance is held at the Kościuszko Monument of 1828, the world's second oldest monument to Kościuszko after the Kościuszko Mound (Kopiec Kościuszki) of 1823 in Kraków, Poland. In May 2004 he introduced into the Massachusetts legislature the first Visa Waiver for Poland Joint Resolution in the nation and worked for successful passage of similar resolutions in New Jersey (October 2004), Vermont (January 2005), Pennsylvania (April 2005), Connecticut and Maine (May 2005), Nebraska, New York, and Ohio (June 2005), Michigan (June 2006), Arizona (April 2007), and Illinois (October 2007). In 2009, he proposed, the Massachusetts legislature enacted, and the governor approved H. 3035, whereby under Massachusetts General Laws, Chapter 6, a statutory annual commemoration of "Polish American Congress Day" is observed statewide on October 30. Among his recognitions are the Knight's Cross of the Order of Merit of the Republic of Poland (2002), the Distinguished Polish American Award (2004) by the New England Chapter of the Kościuszko Foundation, and National Citizen of the Year (2009) by the **Am-Pol Eagle** of Buffalo, NY. In 2008 in Kraków, the Kosciuszko Mound Committee (Komitet Kopca Kościuszki) awarded him its special Kościuszko Medal in recognition of his efforts to connect the mutual work of "kindred spirit and purpose" of the Association and that of the Committee, established in 1823 to care for the Mound in perpetuity.—*Anthony J. Bajdek*

SOURCE: "Bajdek is *Am-Pol Eagle* National Citizen of the Year," *Am-Pol Eagle*, February 26, 2009, 1, 3.

Bakanowski, Adolf Sixtus (b. Mohylówka, Poland, March 28, 1840; d. Kraków, Poland, May 22, 1916). Priest. Bakanowski completed his secondary education in Niemirów and in 1856 entered the seminary in Kamieniec Podolski where he studied for two years before being sent to the Ecclesiastical Academy in St. Petersburg. Following his ordination on May 28, 1863, he enlisted in an infantry regiment to fight the Russians during the January Insurrection in the same year. With the failure of the revolt, he made his way to Austrian Galicia and then to Rome. After joining the **Resurrectionists**, in the fall of 1866 he went to their missions in Texas as Vicar General, serving in **Panna Maria** until

The Rev. Adolf Bakanowski, pioneer priest in Texas and Chicago (*OLS*).

July of 1870. While there he was responsible for constructing a school and rectory. In 1870, following a visit to the Vatican, he was assigned as pastor at St. Stanislaus Kostka Parish in Chicago. In 1873 he returned to Europe as a delegate to the election of the General of the Resurrectionist Order and later served as Superior of the Order in Vienna for eight years. His memoirs form an important source for the study of the early Polish settlements in Texas.—*James S. Pula*

SOURCES: Adolf Bakanowski, "My Memoirs — Texas Sojourn (1866–70)," *Polish American Studies*, Vol. 25, no. 2 (1968), 106–24; Adolf Bakanowski, *Polish Circuit Rider, the Texas Memoirs of Adolf Bakanowski, O.R. (1866–1870)* (Cheshire, CT: Cherry Hill Books, 1971).

Baker, Carroll (Karolina Piekarski; b. Johnstown, Pennsylvania, May 28, 1931; d.—). Actress. Beginning her career in show business, Baker worked for a year as a magician's assistant before landing a small part in the film *Easy to Love* (1953). After studying at the New York Actor's Studio, she appeared in the Broadway production *All Summer Long* which brought her to the attention of director Elia Kazan who cast her in the title role in *Baby Doll* (1956). The movie brought her an Academy Award nomination and instant stardom. She appeared in a steady stream of films thereafter, including *The Big Country* (1958), *The Miracle* (1959), *But Not for Me* (1959), *Something Wild* (1961), *How the West Was Won* (1962), *Station Six-Sahara* (1962), *The Carpetbaggers* (1964), *Sylvia* (1965), *Harlow* (1965), and *Mister Moses* (1965). She also appeared in the Broadway production of *Come on Strong* (1962). After a prolonged legal battle with Paramount Pictures, Baker moved to Italy for several years where she starred in hard-edged Italian thrillers including *The Sweet Body of Deborah* (1968), *Paranoia* (1970), and *Baba Yaga* (1973). A lead role in *Andy Warhol's Bad* (1977) brought her back to the United States, and the decade also saw her return to the stage in productions of *Lucy Crown* and *Motive*. During the 1980s, Baker moved into character work, playing the mother of murdered Playboy Playmate Dorothy Stratten in *Star 80* (1983) and Jack Nicholson's wife in *Ironweed* (1987). In 1990, she played a villainess in the Arnold Schwarzenegger film *Kindergarten Cop*. Her film and television work continued sporadically through the 1990s, and the 2006 DVD release of *Baby Doll* features a documentary with Baker reflecting on the impact the film had on her career. Baker has a star on the Hollywood Walk of Fame at 1725 Vine Street.—*Patricia Finnegan*

SOURCES: Carroll Baker, *Baby Doll, An Autobiography* (New York: Arbor House, 1983); Cobbett Steinberg, *Film Facts* (New York: Facts on File, Inc., 1980), 23.

Bakos, Józef (b. Buffalo, New York, September 23, 1891; d. Santa Fe, New Mexico, April 25, 1977). Artist. Educated at the Albright Art School, Buffalo (1912–16), he later studied privately with artist John E. Thompson in Buffalo (1917-18), and later Denver, Colorado (1918-19). Relocating to Santa Fe, NM, in 1920, he spent the rest of his life there acquiring notoriety as a painter and wood carver. Together with Walter Mruk, Fremont Ellis, Will Shuster, and Willard Nash, he was a founding member in 1921 of *Los Cinco Pintores* (The Five Painters), Santa Fe's first modernist art group. He also taught at the University of Colorado at Boulder (1919-20), the Santa Fe Art School (1930s), and the Chappell School of Art, an affiliate of the University of Denver (1932–34). His works appeared in solo exhibitions in Buffalo and throughout the American Southwest. Among his honors were prizes at the Colorado State Fair, Pueblo (1919); Purchase, First Biennial, Whitney Museum of American Art (1932); New Mexico State Fair, Albuquerque (Purchase Award, 1954, 1962; Second Prize, Watercolor, 1962).—*Stanley L. Cuba*

SOURCES: Stanley L. Cuba, "The Art of Jozef Bakos," in *Jozef Bakos: An Early Modernist (1891–1977)* (Santa Fe: Museum of Fine Arts, Museum of New Mexico, 1988); Sharyn Rohlfson Udall, *Santa Fe Art Colony, 1900–1942* (Santa Fe: Gerald Peters Art Gallery, 1987); Charles C. Eldredge, Julie Schimmel, William H. Truettner, *Art in New Mexico, 1900–1945: Paths to Taos and Santa Fe* (Washington, D.C.: National Museum of American Art, Smithsonian Institution, and New York: Abbeville Press, 1986); Sharyn Rohlfson Udall, *Modernist Painting in New Mexico 1913–1935* (Albuquerque: University of New Mexico Press, 1984).

Balch Institute for Ethnic Studies. The Balch Institute for Ethnic Studies was founded in 1971 in Philadelphia, Pennsylvania, to document and interpret the broad range of ethnic and immigrant experiences in the United States. Since then, the institute has collected approximately four million manuscripts, 60,000 printed works, 12,000 graphics, and 4,500 three-dimensional artifacts, representing over sixty ethnic groups. In 2002, the Balch Institute merged with the Historical Society of Pennsylvania (HSP), which maintains the institute's archival and library collections and continues its educational work in ethnic history. Among HSP's holdings from the Balch Institute, Polish American–related materials include some sixty-six manuscript collections (with 290 linear feet of material) and an estimated 1,200 printed works. The manuscript collections primarily document Polish Americans in the Philadelphia and Scranton-Wilkes-Barre areas. The records of the **Polish Union of the United States of North America**, a fraternal benefit society founded in 1890, form over two-thirds of the manuscript

material by volume and primarily include death claims and other policyholder files. Other fraternal benefit collections include records of the Polish Beneficial Association based in Philadelphia and the **Polish National Alliance** of the United States of North America, whose origins are in that city.

Polish American newspaper publishing is represented in the records of the Polish Star Publishing Company (which published *Gwiazda* newspaper) and the *Polish American Journal*, as well as the papers of newspapermen Stefan Sokolowski, Bronisław Pluta, and **Henry Dende** (an editor of the *Polish-American Journal* who also served as president of the Polish Union of the United States of North America).

Documenting Polish American involvement in local politics are the papers of Leon Kolankiewicz and Joseph Zazyczny, both of whom served on the Philadelphia City Council in the mid–twentieth century. The Kolankiewicz papers also document Polish war relief work during both world wars, complementing the records of the Philadelphia Chapter of **American Relief for Poland** (Rada Polonii Amerykańskiej). The papers of Zygmunt Nagorski, Sr., and Eugene Kleban document the careers of two Polish intellectuals who settled in the United States following World War II. Nagorski served in the Polish government-in-exile during the war; in the United States he practiced law and wrote about the postwar situation in Poland and Europe. Kleban was a member of the Polish Army General Staff and a prisoner of war in Germany, who after the war worked with displaced persons in Britain and then became a professor of sociology and industrial relations in the U.S. Both men were leaders in the **Polish Institute of Arts and Sciences of America**.

Notable among the printed collections are over thirty Polish-American newspapers, some available in paper format, others on microfilm. Titles include *Czas* (Brooklyn), *Dziennik Zjednoczenia* (Chicago), *Dziennik Związkowy* (Chicago), *Sokół Polski* (New York City, Pittsburgh), and *Zgoda* (Chicago), among many others. Finding aids for many of the manuscript collections listed above can be found on the Historical Society of Pennsylvania's website, www.hsp.org. For more information about HSP collections from the Balch Institute, one may also contact the Director of Archives, Historical Society of Pennsylvania, 1300 Locust Street, Philadelphia, PA 19107.—*Matthew Lyons*

SOURCES: Monique Bourque and R. Joseph Anderson, *A Guide to Manuscript and Microfilm Collections of the Research Library of the Balch Institute for Ethnic Studies* (Philadelphia: The Balch Institute for Ethnic Studies, 1992); Matthew Lyons and Gwendolyn

Kaminski, "Furthering the Balch Institute Legacy: Eastern European–Related Collections at the Historical Library of Pennsylvania," *Slavic & East European Information Resources*, Vol. 7, nos. 2/3 (2006), 121–37.

Baldyga, Leonard J. (b. Cicero, Illinois, March 19, 1932; d.—). Diplomat, Polonia activist. Baldyga earned a B.S. degree in communications from Southern Illinois University (1959) and an master's degree in international affairs from Columbia University (1962). Following an early career as a journalist and editor, he joined the U.S. Foreign Service in 1962, serving in Senegal, Poland, and Austria. From 1970 to 1972, he was Country Affairs Officer for Romania and Czechoslovakia. He was assigned as public affairs officer in Warsaw (1972–75) and Mexico City (1976–78), after which he attended the State Department's Senior Seminar in International Affairs (1978-79). In 1979 he was promoted to Deputy Director of European Affairs for the Soviet Union and Eastern Europe (1979–81) and then to Director of European Affairs (1981–83). From 1979 to 1983 he also served as the U.S. Information Agency's principal negotiator for bilateral cultural and scientific agreements with the Soviet Bloc. In 1983 he was assigned as Minister-Counselor for Public Affairs in Rome (1983–88) and New Delhi (1988–91), but in 1992 returned to his former position as Director of European Affairs. He retired two years later with the rank of Career Minister. As a result of his foreign service work, he was honored with the Presidential Distinguished Service Award (1984), the Presidential Merit Service Award (1988), the USIA Distinguished Service Award (twice), and the Edward R. Murrow Award for Excellence in Public Diplomacy (1988). He was decorated with the Officer's Cross Order of Merit in 1994 and the Commander's Cross in 2002, both from the Republic of Poland. Baldyga was also honored with the Edward R. Murrow Fellowship at the Fletcher School of Law and Diplomacy at Tufts University, where he served as Acting Director of the Murrow Center and taught seminars in international political communication and public diplomacy. Following his retirement from the foreign service, he was Senior Consultant for Central and East European Programs at the International Research & Exchange Board and was an active member of the boards of directors of the Sabre Foundation and of the **Polish Institute of Arts and Sciences** and was a member of the editorial board of the Polish Edition of *Encyclopedia Britannica*. In May 2009 he was the commencement speaker at the graduation ceremony of Southern Illinois University's College of Mass Communication and Media Arts and honored as its Alumni of the Year.—*James S. Pula*

Banachowski, Andy (b. San Mateo, California, August 16, 1945; b.—). Volleyball player, coach. As a collegiate volleyball player at UCLA, Banachowski was twice an All-American and a member of national championship squads in 1965 and 1967. In 1965, he became women's volleyball coach at UCLA, a post he retains to date. During his lengthy tenure, he became the most successful coach in the history of amateur women's volleyball. He has coached six national championship teams at UCLA, and won numerous national, regional, and conference coach of the year honors. Banachowski is a member of the American Volleyball Coaches Association Hall of Fame, and was the first women's coach named to the National Volleyball Hall of Fame. In 2000, he won the USA Volleyball All Time Great Coach Award. He was inducted into the National Polish-American Sports Hall of Fame in 2009.—*Neal Pease*

SOURCE: "Andy Banachowski," Volleyball Hall of Fame website, www.volleyhall.org/banachowski.html.

Banaszak, Peter Andrew "Pete" (b. Crivitz, Wisconsin, May 21, 1944; d.—). Football player. In high school, Banaszak starred in football, basketball, and track. As a running back in college he excelled playing for the University of Miami, becoming a fifth round pick of the American Football League Oakland Raiders in 1966. He played for the Raiders from 1966 through 1978, finishing his career with 3,772 rushing yards, 121 receptions for 1,022 yards, and 51 touchdowns. He played in two Super Bowls as a member of the Raiders, scoring two touchdowns in the Raiders' 32–14 win over the Minnesota Vikings in Super Bowl XI. During his twelve years with the Raiders they won at least ten games each year on a fourteen game schedule. He played in some of the most memorable games and plays of the famous Oakland Raiders franchise like the Heidi Game, Franco Harris' Immaculate Reception, Super Bowls II and XI, the Sea-of-Hands, Ghost-to-the-Post, and the Holy Roller in which he "fumbled" the ball to Dave Casper for the winning touchdown against the San Diego Chargers in 1979. He led the team in rushing and scoring in 1975 with 187 carries for 672 yards and 16 rushing touchdowns, which stands as the second highest touchdown total in one season in Raider history. That year he was selected as the Oakland Raiders' Most Valuable Player. Banaszak holds the Raiders team career record for rushing touchdowns with 52 and played in 121 consecutive games which stands as the fourth longest on the squad. Following his playing career he co-hosted a post-game radio program after Jacksonville Jaguar games. He

was inducted into the National Polish-American Sports Hall of Fame in 1990.—*Luis J. Gonzalez*

SOURCE: Robert Boyles and Paul Guido, *Fifty Years of College Football: A Modern History of America's Most Colorful Sport* (Wilmington, DE: Sideline Communications, 2005), 147.

Bańczakiewicz, Ludwik (b. Poland, ca 1800; d. United States, ca. 1840). Educator. After serving as a cadet captain in the 10th Regiment, Grenadiers of the Guard, he joined the November Uprising (1830-31) and was forced into exile with its failure. Bańczakiewicz was chosen chairman of the committee elected by the exiles to represent them in America. Although the details are sketchy, he went to Washington, D.C., to present a request to Congress for a land grant to the exiles, then journeyed to Boston, but apparently became disillusioned when the Polish committee dissolved and, announcing that he wanted to avoid unpleasantness, he enlisted in the U.S. Navy in Boston and in 1834 shipped out aboard the *USS Potomac* for a cruise to France, Portugal, Spain, Italy, and the Papal States, eventually transferring to the *USS John Adams* in February 1835. Although listed as a seaman, naval records indicate that he taught languages. He apparently died of yellow fever, but the sources are not specific on the date which is believed to have been in 1839 or 1840. Nevertheless, he is recognized as the head of the first Polish organization established on U.S. soil.—*James S. Pula*

SOURCE: Ladislas John Siekaniec, *The Polish Contribution to Early American Education, 1608–1865* (San Francisco: R & E Research Associates, 1976).

Baptists, Polish American. During the nineteenth and early twentieth centuries, Baptist missionaries worked to spread their faith to immigrants in the United States under the auspices of the American Baptist Home Mission Society. They enjoyed considerable success among Protestant German and Scandinavian immigrants in the mid- to late 1800s. Evangelization among Roman Catholic immigrants from Eastern Europe, for whom religious faith and ethnic identity were deeply intertwined, proved a greater challenge. The first Polish Baptist missions opened in Detroit (1888) and Buffalo (1891), each led initially by the Rev. Józef Antoszewski, a minister born in Poland who was able to preach in the immigrants' own language. Similarly, a Baptist mission in the Polish settlement of Rochester, NY, was established by a Polish-born minister in 1911, the Rev. Ludwik Adamus who was a native of Galicia and had completed his training at the Rochester Theological Seminary. Aware of the independent church movement spreading through Polish settlements in the northeastern states, the Home Mission Society was hopeful that its work among Poles would prove fruitful, that large numbers of those dissatisfied with American Catholicism would embrace the teachings of Baptism. However, only fourteen Polish Baptist churches with a total of 1,400 members had taken root in the United States in 1921. Similarly disappointing numbers of converts were realized among other immigrant groups from Eastern Europe. In 2008, the Polish Baptist Association in the U.S. and Canada included approximately 700 baptized members organized in ten churches and missions, including churches in Chicago, Minneapolis, New York, Philadelphia, and Toronto.—*Kathleen Urbanic*

SOURCES: Lawrence B. Davis, *Immigrants, Baptists, and the Protestant Mind in America* (Urbana: University of Illinois Press, 1973); Joel Hayden, *Religious Work Among the Poles* (Cleveland: Board of Home Missions of the Presbyterian Church, U.S.A., 1916).

Baran, Paul (b. Grodno, Poland, April 29, 1926; d.—). Engineer. Born in Poland, Baran and his family migrated to the United States in 1928. Baran received his undergraduate degree in electrical engineering from the Drexel Institute of Technology in Philadelphia, Pennsylvania, in 1949. After graduation, Baran briefly worked as a technician for the Eckert-Mauchly Computer Corporation from 1949-50 and for Raymond Rosen Engineering Products Company in 1950. He married and moved to Los Angeles shortly thereafter where he worked for the Hughes Aircraft Company in Redondo Beach, California. At the same time, Baran took night classes at UCLA, eventually completing a master's degree in engineering in 1959. In the same year he assumed a position in the Computer Sciences Department of the Mathematics Division of the Rand Corporation, a not-for-profit organization closely tied to the U.S. Air Force, then involved in communication and technology research and development at the height of the Cold War. A major concern among U.S. scientists and defense strategists in this period was the development of survivable command and control communication networks that could withstand a first-strike nuclear attack. In the early 1960s, weaknesses were thought to be inherent in the "centralized networks" of telecommunications. In contrast to preexisting centralized networks in which information was carried by single nodes or centers, Baran alternatively proposed "distributed networks," or "packet switching," in which data would travel along multiple nodes simultaneously and would be reassembled upon arrival at its destination. This, it was argued, offered increased security in the event that one or more information-carrying nodes

Paul Baran, pioneer of digital networks (*OLS*).

were destroyed as a result of nuclear attack. Baran's conceptualization of "distributed networks" also hinged on digital technology in a period where telecommunications was still analog. In 1965, the U.S. Air Force approved Baran's research, but the implementation of the project was delayed when the Department of Defense could not find a company willing to adopt his digital networks. Impressed by Baran's work, the Pentagon's Advanced Research Projects Agency (ARPA) began implementing Baran's project in conjunction with the research of Dr. Donald Davies of the British National Physics Laboratory (NPL), who had also been developing the concept of packet switching. The project, known as ARPNET, took Baran and Davies' nodes and established an online network of four sites for the purpose of resource sharing. In subsequent years an additional twelve sites connected. Many credit Baran as being the "grandfather of the internet," as packet switching technology formed its basis, growing out of the foundations of ARPNET. Baran left Rand in 1968 to co-found the Institute for the Future, a nonprofit organization engaged in forecast research in the field of communications. Several years later, he also developed Cabledata Associates, Equatorial Communications, Telebit, and Packet/Stratacom. Additionally, Baran cofounded Metricom and Ricochet Wireless (1986), InterFax (1989), Com21 (1995), and GoBackTV (2003). In 1989 he was awarded UCLA's Advanced Computing Technologies Pioneer Award for his work on packet switching and in 2001 the Franklin Institute's Bower Award and Prize for Achievement in Science.—*Krystyna Cap*

SOURCES: "Oral History Interview with Paul Baran," interview by Judy O'Neill, transcript, March 5, 1990, Charles Babbage Institute Collections, Uni-

versity of Minnesota, Minneapolis; Kristina Fiore, "Cold War Comm Work Lays Grounds for 'Net Shopping,'" *Electronic Design*, Vol. 55, no. 23 (2007), 72; Rich Karlgaard, "Chip + Net = Ah!" *National Review*, Vol. 52, no. 11 (2000), 42–44.

Barańczak, Stanisław (pseudonym Barbara Stawiczak; b. Poznań, Poland, November 13, 1946; d.—). Poet, scholar. Barańczak studied Polish philology at the Adam Mickiewicz University in his home city, receiving his doctorate in 1973. He began his teaching career at his alma mater, but was punitively terminated in 1977 for his anti–Communist activities in the Komitet Obrony Robotników (Committee for Workers' Defense), a precursor of Solidarność (Solidarity). With the rise of Solidarity in 1980, he returned to his position at Adam Mickiewicz University. On being awarded the Jurzykowski Prize that same year, he left Poland for the United States where, since 1980, he has been associated with Harvard University. Barańczak is one of the leading contemporary poets of Poland and a member of the first group of Polish poets born either during the Second World War, or after its conclusion, thus having no direct experience of Poland before the Soviet imposition of communist government. His generation is usually described as the Nowa Fala (New Wave). It is also spoken of as the "Generation of '68," since many of them came into maturity during the student riots of that year. Also, some of them, Barańczak included, are referenced as "linguistic poets," as their poetry often turns on puns, wordplay, and a sarcastic mimicry of the debased language of official propaganda. As a poet, Barańczak debuted in 1965 in the journal *Odra*; his first volume of verse was *Korekta twrazy* (A Proof of the Face), published three years later. Since that time, he has published some ten volumes of verse. Arguably the most important of his poetic works is the anti-heroic verse cycle *Sztuczne oddychanie* (Artificial Respiration, 1974), which recounts one day in the life of a nameless "gray man," the citizen of the Communist Polish People's Republic, and serves as a kind of coda to the romantic traditions of Polish poetry. In it, the poet expresses the despairing hopelessness of life in a totalitarian society, in which no effective individual act is possible, whether heroic or banal. Even suicide is meaningless—no salvific act is possible, on behalf of others, or even on behalf of one's self. Because Barańczak's poetry is so dependent upon clever rhymes, wordplay, and a necessary field of reference in the reality of propaganda and the daily life of Poland under communism, it is extremely difficult to translate. Some idea of Barańczak's poetic gifts can be obtained from the one volume of his selected poetry in English, *The Weight of the Body* (1989). He is also one of the preeminent modern Polish verse translators. He has translated Shakespeare for the stage, and brought out numerous volumes of the English poets in his translation. Many of the poets he has chosen to translate are such as appeal to his love of clever, difficult, "dense" poetry, such as the Metaphysicals of the seventeenth century: Henry Vaughan, John Donne, George Herbert, and the demanding nineteenth-century Jesuit poet Gerard Manley Hopkins. His co-translation (with Nobel laureate Seamus Heaney) of Renaissance poet Jan Kochanowski's *Laments* (1995) is one of the most noteworthy modern English translations of Polish poetry. Barańczak's critical output is wide-ranging and consists of interpretations of Adam Ważyk, **Czesław Miłosz**, Miron Białoszewski, and many other poets, translation theory and literary history. His book on the poetry of Zbigniew Herbert, *Uciekinier z Utopii* (1984) is available in English under the title *A Fugitive from Utopia* (1987); and the English-language *Breathing Under Water and Other East European Essays* (1990) and *Polish Poetry of the Last Two Decades of Communist Rule: Spoiling Cannibals' Fun* (1990) collect some of his critical insights on the literature of Poland and East-Central Europe. He has served on the editorial boards of many important Polish journals, both in Poland and abroad. In the United States, he was editor-in-chief of *The Polish Review* (New York City) from 1986–1990.—*Charles S. Kraszewski*

SOURCES: *Zaufać nieufności* (To Trust Distrust, 1993), a wide-ranging interview on themes both autobiographical and literary, which offers the reader a wealth of information and insight on Barańczak himself, his Poland, and literature in general. Charles S. Kraszewski, "The Harmonic Bell-Jar: Wierzyński, Barańczak and the Poetics of Anti-Heroic Dissent," *The Polish Review*, Vol. 52, no. 2 (2007), 193–214; "Barancczak, Stanislaw," *Contemporary Authors* (Detroit: Gale Research Company, New Revision Series), Vol. 77, 43–48.

Baranski, Christine Jane (b. Buffalo, New York, May 2, 1952; d.—). Actress. After attending Villa Maria Academy in Buffalo, Baranski studied at Juilliard, debuted in the Off-Broadway show *Coming Attractions* in 1980, and made her Broadway debut in the same year in *Hide & Seek*. She received a Tony Award as Best Featured Actress in a Play for *The Real Thing* (1984), and went on to star in other Broadway hits and at the Kennedy Center in Washington, D.C., where she starred in productions of *Sweeney Todd* (2002) and *Mame* (2006). She won two Tony Awards, two Drama Desk Awards, and gained critical acclaim for her performances in the films *The Birdcage* where she won a Screen Actors Guild Award (1996) and *Chicago* where she garnered

a Broadcast Film Critics Association Award. She won a Screen Actors Guild Award and an Emmy Award for Best Supporting Actress in a Comedy Series for her role on the CBS sitcom *Cybill* (1995) and another Emmy nomination for her guest appearance on the NBC series *Frasier*.—*James S. Pula*

SOURCE: Miranda Spencer, "Christine Baranski," *Biography*, Vol. 3, no. 8 (August 1999), 22.

Bardziłowska, Stefania (Stefania Walczewska; b. Zagórz, Poland, May 8, 1895; d.—). Polonia activist. Walczewska migrated to the U.S. before the outbreak of World War I. In 1917 she married Walerian Bardziłowski, the owner of a tailoring business in Boston. During World War II she became famous for her extensive correspondence with Polish soldiers in Africa, the Middle East, and Western Europe. It is estimated that she accumulated about one thousand addresses, sending letters and packages containing various goods to lonely Polish soldiers who called her "Wojenna Mamusia" (Military Mother). She also provided financial support for Polish soldiers and civilians alike. Following the war she helped displaced persons find missing family members, provided assistance to those seeking a visa to enter the U.S., and also helped immigrants to find jobs once they arrived. In 1946, during his visit to the United States, General Tadeusz Bór-Komorowski of the Polish army decorated Bardziłowska with the Cross of Merit for her social and charitable work during the war.—*Iwona Korga*

SOURCES: Piłsudski Institute of America Archives, Bardzilowska Stefania Collection no 33, 25 archival units of letters of S. Bardziłowska to Polish soldiers; Bronisław Rejnowski, *Listy do Panii Bardziłowskiej* (Warsaw: Filatelista, 2006).

Stefania Bardziłowska, known as "Wojenna Mamusia" (OLS).

Barszczewski, Stefan (b. Warsaw, Poland, June 21, 1862; d. Poland, 1937). Journalist. Barszczewski came to the United States in 1887 and found work at the *Dziennik Chicagoski* (Polish Chicago Daily). At age nineteen, he became associated with the **Polish National Alliance** and in 1894 wrote its first official history, *Związek Narodowy Polski w Stanach Zjednoczonych Ameryki Północnej: Jego Rozwoj, Działalność i Stan Obecny*, on the occasion of the one hundredth anniversary of the Kościuszko (see **Tadeusz Kościuszko**) uprising of 1794. This book, long believed lost, was rediscovered in the 1970s and reissued by the PNA at the time of its centennial in 1980. In 1896 Barszczewski was elected editor of the newly established newspaper of the **Polish Falcons Alliance**, *Sokół* (The Falcon). The following year he was elected editor-in-chief of the weekly official PNA publication, *Zgoda* (Harmony). He held both positions until 1901 when he resigned from both posts due to poor health and returned to live permanently in Poland. There he worked on several newspapers, including the *Kuryer Warszawski* (Warsaw Courier). He also authored a number of plays that were staged in Polonia and wrote many short stories.—*Donald E. Pienkos*

SOURCES: Arthur L. Waldo, *Sokólstwo: przednia straż narodu, dzieje idei i organizacji w Ameryce* (Pittsburgh: Nakł. Sokólstwa Polskiego w Ameryce, 1953), Vol. 1; Donald E. Pienkos, *PNA: A Centennial History of the Polish National Alliance* (Boulder, CO: East European Monographs, 1984).

Bartkowiak, Andrzej Wojciech (b. Łódź, Poland, March 6, 1950; d.—). Cinematographer, actor, director. Trained at the Polish Film School in Łódź, he migrated to the United States in 1972. The first work he did in America was filming commercials for television. He began his film career as the cinematographer for *Deadly Hero* in 1976, but had his first big break when he worked as the director of photography for Sidney Lumet's crime classic, *Prince of the City* (1981). The two men became good friends, and over the next dozen years worked together on no less than eleven films. Bartkowiak earned a reputation as a cinematographer who specialized in setting and shooting realistic, sometimes gritty urban scenes, setting a standard in the art. He is also renowned for his work using light and shadow to create atmosphere, often resulting in a color film that looks like black and white, or using soft tones to impart an "old" look to a film. He became much in demand after the film *Speed* (1994), when his photography contributed greatly to the tension of the film, most of which took place on a speeding bus. As a director, he has also been responsible for such films as *Exit Wounds*

(2001) and *Doom* (2005). His work as a cinematographer includes *Thirteen* Days (2000) about the Cuban Missile Crisis, *Dante's Peak* (1997), *Falling Down* (1993), *Twins* (1988), and many more. Among his honors are Academy award nominations for three of his films—*The Verdict* (1982), *Terms of Endearment* (1983), and *Prizzi's Honor* (1986).—*Cheryl A. Pula*

SOURCE: Sidney Lumet, *Making Movies* (New York: Vintage, 1996).

Bartkowski, Steven Joseph (b. Des Moines, Iowa, November 12, 1952; d.—). Football player. This native Iowan went west and attended the University of California where he played both baseball and football, though he would become famous as a quarterback for the Golden Bears. Assistant coach Paul Hackett stated Bartkowski was the only quarterback he had ever seen who could throw a football 100 yards. Though his first two years were anything but sterling as a backup quarterback to Vince Ferragamo, once he became the starter he was selected as an All-American in his senior year 1974, leading the nation with 2,580 yards passing. He was a first round pick in the National Football League draft in 1975, the first California graduate so named. As a pro, he set an Atlanta Falcons record for passing touchdowns with 31 in 1980, and became Atlanta's all-time passing leader with 23,470 yards. He also led the League in passer rating with a 97.6 accuracy percentage. He was wearing number 10 on his jersey. Bartkowski played for Atlanta for ten years, from 1975 to 1985, then one year each with the Washington Redskins (1985) and the Los Angeles Rams (1986). Bartkowski is among elite quarterbacks, in that he is one of only seven who achieved two consecutive seasons with 30 touchdowns (1980-81), sharing the honor with the likes of legendary New York Giants quarterback Y.A. Tittle, among others. After his football career, he worked for DPR Construction, Inc., a general contracting firm, and was a member of the Board of Directors of the Atlanta Falcons, as well as several charities. He was named All-American (1974), NFL Rookie of the Year (1975), *Sporting News* Rookie of the Year (1975), a two time selection for the Pro Bowl (1980, 1981), and an All-Pro Selection (1980).—*Cheryl A. Pula*

SOURCE: Dan DeHaan, *Intercepted by Christ: Biography of Steve Bartkowski* (Lilburn, GA: Cross Roads Books, 1980).

Barzyński, Jan (b. Tomaszów Lubelski, in Russian Poland, 1848; d. Chicago, Illinois, April 27, 1886). Journalist, politician. While Barzyński was studying law in Warsaw, the Russian police placed him under surveillance

Jan Barzyński, prominent journalist and politician (*PMA*).

in 1870, causing him to migrate to Texas where he worked with his brother **Wincenty Barzyński** in San Antonio and also served as a representative of the Polish newspaper *Orzeł Polski* (Polish Eagle) published in Washington, Missouri. In 1872 he began publishing his own newspaper, *Pielgrzym* (Pilgrim), in Union, Missouri. On its pages he argued for the unification of all Catholic Poles in America to help them retain their "faith, learn the language and history of Poland," but at the same time he supported the policy of assimilation contending that a Pole in America ought to "be given a chance to become a good Yankee." *Pielgrzym* sharply criticized Chicago's organization **Gmina Polska** (Polish Commune), its main ideological opponent. In an attempt to fulfill his plan to unify Catholic Polonia, he tried to form a national organization in 1874, but it proved unsuccessful. Then, jointly with **Teodor Gieryk** and **Peter Kiołbassa**, Barzyński organized a convention of Poles in Chicago (October 14–16, 1874), during which delegates established the **Polish Roman Catholic Union**, a Catholic fraternal, which would also strengthen the Catholic faith among immigrants, a factor Barzyński considered to be a cornerstone of **Polskość** (Polishness). In 1874 he established the newspaper *Gazeta Polska Katolicka* (Polish Catholic Gazette), moving it to Chicago in 1875 where he edited it until 1880 when it passed into the hands of **Władysław Smulski**. Barzyński then moved to St. Paul, Nebraska, where he organized Polish rural settlements. He also wrote *Elementarz* (primers) for the first and second grade in parochial schools (1878) and edited *kalendarz* (calendars, much like almanacs), a very popular form of publication

among Polish immigrants in the U.S.—*Adam Walaszek*

SOURCES: Andrzej Brożek, *Polish Americans 1854–1939* (Warsaw: Interpress, 1985); T. Lindsay Baker, "The Early Years of Rev. Wincenty Barzyński," *Polish American Studies*, Vol. 32, no. 1 (1975), 29–52; Meroe J. Owens, "Jan Barzynski, Land Agent," *Nebraska History*, Vol. 36 (June 1955).

Barzyński, Wincenty Michał (b. Sulisławice, near Sandomierz in Galicia, Poland, September 20, 1838; d. Chicago, Illinois, May 2, 1899). Priest, Polonia activist. A controversial figure who was both admired and hated, it would be difficult to overestimate Barzyński's impact on the developments in Chicago's Polish community. Ordained on October 28, 1861, in Lublin, he participated in the January Uprising of 1863 by organizing local underground support for Polish troops, but with the failure of the revolt had to escape to Kraków. Arrested, he spent ten months in prison. Deported to Paris in 1865, he was attracted to the Congregation of the Resurrection, an order founded in Paris in 1836 by Polish émigré priests to unite Catholicism and the cause of Polish national independence. Moving to Rome, he joined the **Congregation of the Resurrection**, making his vows on September 18, 1866. On the following day he left for the United States along with **Adolf Bakanowski** and Feliks Zwiardowski. The Resurrectionists sent him to Texas where he served as organizer and pastor of St. Michael's parish in San Antonio (1868). After moving to St. Hedwig in 1873, the following year he became pastor of St. Stanislaus Kostka in Chicago, serving there from September 6, 1874, until his death in 1899, heading a parish of some 40,000 to 50,000 parishioners, the

The Rev. Wincenty Barzyński, initiator of the Polish Roman Catholic Union (*PMA*).

largest Polish parish in the city, in the country, and—some say—one of the largest in the world. A strong personality buttressed by exceptional determination made Barzyński one of the most important figures in the lengthy ideological struggles between the clerical faction, led by the Resurrectionists, and the nationalists in the city and the country. This was reflected in the long rivalry between Holy Trinity parish, supported by independentists from the **Gmina Polska** and the St. Joseph Society, and St. Stanislaus Kostka parish. Barzyński's goal was to create cultural and spiritual unity among Poles in the city. He also attempted to unify all of Chicago's Polish Catholics under the jurisdiction of the Resurrectionists, a policy that led to various conflicts within the community, as well as with church authorities. Additionally, his leadership was the subject of complaints about trusteeship problems, including the administration of parish funds, ownership of church property, and ideological and political struggles between Poles of different orientations. Barzyński called the first meeting of the **Polish Roman Catholic Union** (PRCU) in Chicago on October 10, 1874. His initiative led to the formation in 1875 of the Association of Polish Roman Catholic Priests in the United States (Towarzystwo Księży Rzymsko-Katolickich Polskich w Stanach Zjednoczonych), associated with the PRCU, one of two rival Polish priests' associations to promote clerical unity, assist bishops, and provide guidance to the laity. In 1887 he also organized the Polish Publishing Company which printed the weekly *Wiara i Ojczyzna* (Faith and Fatherland) that, in 1899, became *Naród Polski* (The Polish Nation). In December 1890 his company began printing *Dziennik Chicagoski* (Chicago Daily News), the official organ of PRCU, and also *Kropidło* (The Aspergillum), the highly polemical, anti–**Polish National Alliance** weekly. Barzyński engaged in constant, and often acrimonious, struggles with the Polish National Alliance. In 1891 he founded St. Stanislaus Kostka College in Chicago, the oldest Polish high school in America. In 1894, Barzyński was among the initiators of the **Polish League in America**, an organization he planned to unite Poles of different political and ideological camps to support the interests of Polish Americans. Although the organization initially included activists from different ideological camps, the organization was short-lived. He organized various societies, confraternities, sodalities, Polish Catholic parishes in Chicago, schools, charity institutions and played a crucial role in the formation of institutional Polonia. His brothers were **Jan Barzyński**, a journalist, and

Józef Barzyński, a priest, who served in Chicago as well.—*Adam Walaszek*

Sources: Andrzej Brożek, *Polish Americans 1854–1939* (Warsaw: Interpress, 1985); Wacław Kruszka, *Historia polska w Ameryce* (Milwaukee: Drukiem Spółki Wydawniczej Kuryera, 1905, 1907, Vols. 5, 10); T. Lindsay Baker, "The Early Years of Rev. Wincenty Barzyński," *Polish American Studies*, Vol. 31, no. 1 (1975), 29–52; Joseph J. Parot, *Polish Catholics in Chicago 1850–1920. A Religious History* (DeKalb: Northern Illinois University Press, 1981).

Bekker, Mieczysław Grzegorz (b. Strzyżów, Poland, May 25, 1905; d. Santa Barbara, California, January 8, 1989). Engineer. Bekker played an important role in the exploration of the moon by designing the Lunar Rover Vehicle (LRV), and was a leading expert in vehicle design for off-road movement. Born in Austrian-occupied southern Poland, he graduated form Warsaw Technical University in 1929. After serving for two years in the Polish army, he went to work for the Ministry of Military Affairs where he worked on designing tanks and other off-road vehicles. He is credited with originating the engineering discipline called terramechanics. At the outbreak of World War II in September 1939, Bekker was with an army unit that evacuated to Romania after the fall of Warsaw. Six months later he made his way to France where he found employment with the French Ministry of Defense working on tanks. In 1942 he accepted an offer from the Canadian government to work on armored vehicle research. The following year he joined the Canadian army in which he rose to the rank of lieutenant colonel.

In 1956, Bekker accepted a professorship at the University of Michigan where he also

Mieczysław Bekker holding a model of the Moon Rover that he designed for NASA (*OLS*).

worked at the Army Vehicle Laboratory in Detroit. Five years later he was hired by General Motors as a specialist in vehicle design in Santa Barbara, California, where his main task was development of an extraterrestrial vehicle for use in exploring the moon, but he was also a military adviser to the U.S. and Canada. Bekker took the lead role for General Motors in engineering the LRV which was chosen by NASA for the moon mission. His vehicle was first used on Apollo 15, the fourth U.S. mission to the moon, on July 30, 1971, with other versions used during the Apollo 16 and Apollo 17 missions. Altogether, the three rovers logged more than 75 miles, reached a top speed of twelve miles per hour, and performed flawlessly.

Bekker authored many books and articles pertaining to his work on off-road vehicles, received several patents for inventions connected to his designs, and received several honorary doctorates.—*Martin S. Nowak*

Sources: Gordon Davis, ed., *Who's Who in Engineering* (New York: American Association of Engineering Societies, 1988); Carl W. Hall, ed., *A Biographical Dictionary of People in Engineering* (West Lafayette, IN: Purdue University Press, 2008).

Benatar, Pat (Patricia Mae Andrzejewski; b. Brooklyn, New York, January 10, 1953; d.—). Singer. After high school, Benatar enrolled in the Juilliard School of Music, but dropped out to pursue a career in health. After a year of study she again dropped out at age nineteen, married, and took a job as a bank teller in Richmond, Virginia. She quit in 1973 to work as a singer in a nightclub featuring music of the 1920s. Two years later her singing impressed Rick Newman, owner of the popular club Catch a Rising Star, who signed her to appear as a regular. At Halloween in 1977 she went on stage dressed in a vampire outfit and received standing ovations even though she performed her normal repertoire of songs. The following year she signed with Chrysalis Records with her first album appearing in August 1979. She was an instant hit, being nominated for eight Grammy Awards in the next ten years and winning four consecutive Grammy Awards for Best Female Rock Performance (1980–83). She also took home American Music Awards for Favorite Female Pop/Rock Vocalist in 1981 and 1983, along with Favorite Female Pop/Rock Video Artist in 1985. She was named *Rolling Stone*'s Favorite Female Vocalist twice and she is ranked as one of the most successful female vocalists in history by *Billboard* magazine. She was one of the top selling artists of the 1980s, including two multi-platinum albums, five platinum albums, three gold albums, and nineteen "Top 40" singles.—*James S. Pula*

SOURCE: Jancee Dunn, "Pat Benatar," *Rolling Stone*, no. 908 (October 31, 2002), 132; "Pat Benatar," *People Magazine*, Vol. 54, no. 5 (July 31, 2000), 86.

Benda, Władysław Teodor (W.T.) (b. Poznań, Poland, January 15, 1873; d. Newark, New Jersey, November 30, 1948). Artist. Educated at the Fine Arts School in Kraków where he studied under Władysław Łuszczkiewicz, Florian Cynk, and Izydor Jabloński (1882–93), he later continued his studies in Vienna. Invited in 1898 by his aunt, the famous actress **Helena Modjeska** (Modrzejewska), to move to California, he did so in 1900, continuing his studies at the Hopkins Institute in San Francisco. In 1902 he relocated to New York where he studied at the Art Students League with Robert Henri and the Chase School of Art. He became a U.S. citizen in 1911. A painter, graphic artist, illustrator, mask maker, set and costume designer, lecturer, and author, he was recognized as a foremost authority on masks, and known for his "Benda Girl" during the "Golden Age of American Illustration." During both World Wars he produced posters for Polish War Relief. As an illustrator, his work appeared in the following magazines: *American, Associated Sunday Magazine, Century, Collier's, Cosmopolitan, Hearst's International, Liberty, Life, McClure's, Saturday Evening Post, Scribner's, Vanity Fair,* and *Women's Home Companion*. His illustrations also appeared in Jacob A. Riis, *The Old Town* (1909); Gene Stratton-Porter, *A Girl of the Limberlost* (1909); Jacob A. Riis, *Neighbors: Life Stories of the Other Half* (1914); H.G. Dwight, *Stamboul Nights* (1916); Willa Cather, *My Antonia* (1918); and Gilda Varesi Archibald & Dorothea Donn-Byrne, *Enter Madame: A Play in Three Acts* (1921). During his career, Benda lectured widely before audiences at art institutes, educational institutions, and public settings. His

W. T. Benda, artist, illustrator, and developer of the "Benda Girl" (*PMA*).

publications include *Masks* (1944), and among his awards were the Silver Medal at the Panama Pacific International Exhibition in San Francisco (1915) and the Order of Polonia Restituta awarded by the Polish Government after World War I. Collections of his work can be found at the Brandywine River Museum, Chadds Ford, PA; **Kosciuszko Foundation**, New York; Library of Congress, Washington, D.C.; Museum of the City of New York; **Polish Museum of America**, Chicago; and Washington County Museum of Fine Arts, Hagerstown, MD.—*Stanley L. Cuba*

SOURCES: *W. T. Benda Memorial Exhibition: Masks, Paintings, Drawings* (New York: The Kosciuszko Foundation House, 1949); Judy L. Larson, *American Illustration 1890–1925: Romance, Adventure & Suspense* (Calgary, Canada: Glenbow-Alberta Institute, 1986); Jadwiga I. Daniec, "In the Footsteps of W. T. Benda, 1873–1948," *The Polish Review*, Vol. 39, no. 1 (1994), 21–43.

Benet, Sula (Sula Benetowa; b. Warsaw, Poland, October 6, 1903; d. New York, New York, November 12, 1982). Anthropologist. Because of her family's business, Benet spent her childhood in Russia and Ukraine where she attended school. She later enrolled in the humanities program at the Free Polish University (Wolna Wszechnica Polska), majored in cultural anthropology, and graduated in 1936. That fall, she arrived to New York City and soon thereafter enrolled in graduate studies in the Columbia University Anthropology Department where she worked closely with Ruth Benedict, especially interviewing European war refugees for the purpose of creating a profile of their cultures and their national character. After the war she led a Polish group at the university in the Research in Contemporary Cultures (RCC) project. She defended her dissertation in 1944 and it was published in *American Anthropologists* in two parts: "The Paleolithic Period in Poland," and "The Magdalenian Culture in Poland." As part of her responsibilities in the RCC project, she prepared reports about Polish culture including "Polish Festivals and Folklore," "Courage: Cumulative Effects of Sacrifice" (published by the University of Chicago Press in *The Study of Culture at a Distance*; 1953), and "Patterns of Thought and Behavior in the Culture of Poland: A Study of National Culture." In 1951 she published her first book, *Song, Dance and Customs of Peasant Poland*, with an introduction by Margaret Mead. It is a sweeping monograph of Polish folk culture that reached far back into history. Materials for the book were gathered from literature, fieldwork in Poland conducted in 1947-48, and interviews conducted in New York.

Benet joined the anthropology department at Hunter College of the City University of New York in 1944, and also taught at Fairleigh Dickinson University in New Jersey and Pratt Institute in New York. She published the popular folklore books *Riddles of Many Lands* (1956) and *Festival Menus Round the World* (1957). She was also interested in other Slavic cultures, especially Russian, and translated the work *The Village of Viriatino: An Ethnographic Study of a Russian Village from Before the Revolution to the Present* (1970). While working on this project she made contact with many Soviet anthropologists which allowed her to organize fieldwork in Abkhasia financed by CUNY and The Wenner-Gren Foundation. This resulted in publication of *Abkhasians: The Long Living People of the Caucasus* (1974). Her interest in longevity led to publication of "Why They Live to be 100, or Even Older in Abkhasia," an article in the *New York Times* on December, 26, 1971. She retired from Hunter College in 1973 with the title of Professor Emerita and joined the Research Institute for the Study of Man in New York where she worked on the Longevity Project. In 1976 she published *How to Live to Be 100: The Lifestyle of the People of the Caucasus.*—*Ewa Dzurak*

SOURCE: Walter H. Waggoner, "Dr. Sula Benet 76, a Specialist in Longevity and East Europe," *New York Times*, November 13, 1982.

Bernard, Carlos (Carlos Bernard Papierski; b. Evanston, Illinois, October 12, 1962; d.—). Actor. The son of a Polish father and a Spanish mother, Bernard was raised in Chicago. He began his education at Illinois State University before earning an MFA degree from the American Conservatory Theater in San Francisco. He began his acting career in the Mark Taper Forum production of *Scenes from an Execution* and in A.C.T. productions of *Good, As You Like It, Hamlet, The Diary of Anne Frank,* and *The Cherry Orchard*. He made guest appearances on several television shows including *Walker, Texas Ranger, Silk Stalkings* and *Babylon 5*, and in the films *Mars and Beyond, The Colonel's Last Flight,* and *Vegas, City of Dreams*. He was a regular on the daytime soap opera *The Young and the Restless*, but is best known for his role as Tony Almeida in Fox Television's drama *24*, which began in 2001.—*James S. Pula*

SOURCES: *People*, Vol. 59, no. 18 (May 12, 2003), Vol. 64, no. 16 (October 17, 2005), and Vol. 65, no. 12 (March 27, 2006).

Bernardine Sisters of the Third Order of St. Francis *see* **Franciscan Sisters.**

Bialasiewicz, Józef (b. Russian occupied Poland, December 6, 1912; d. Chicago, Illinois, October 28, 1986). Journalist. Bialasiewicz completed his studies in law at the University of Warsaw and began work as a newspaper reporter for the *Gazeta Warszawska* (Warsaw Gazette) in 1930, involving himself at the same time in the Szczerbiec Society (Jagged Sword), a Polish patriotic group. After the outbreak of World War II, he worked in the underground press and wrote for the newspaper *Państwo Polskie* (Polish State). Arrested by the Gestapo, he was sent to Auschwitz. At war's end, he was able to reach Bavaria where he became the head of the Polish Committee there, serving as editor of the *Wiadomości Polskie* (Polish News) and organizing the Union of Polish Journalists in the West. In this period he was also active in working with such Polish émigré publications as *Kultura* (Culture) in Paris and *Orzel Biały* (The White Eagle). In 1949 Bialasiewicz arrived in the United States, where he organized the Mutual Aid Society of the New Emigration (Stowarzyszenie Samopomocy Nowej Emigracji). He began work as a newsman at the ***Dziennik Chicagoski*** (Chicago Daily News) and served as its editor from 1958 until the paper's demise in 1971. During these years he established the Polish American Book Store in Chicago. After 1968 Bialasiewicz was president of the reorganized Union of Polish Journalists in America and headed the Polish language weekly *Polonia*. From 1977 until his death he worked for the ***Dziennik Związkowy*** (Alliance Daily) in Chicago. His son, Dr. Wojciech Bialasiewicz, later served as editor-in-chief of the *Dziennik Związkowy*. He is himself the author of a valuable book in the Polish language that details American Polonia's responses to the invasion of Poland in 1939.—*Donald E. Pienkos*

SOURCE: Wojciech Wierzewski, "Sto Trzydzieska Slynnych Polaków w Ameryce" (Unpublished manuscript in the archives of the University of Wisconsin–Milwaukee, 2000).

Bialkowska, Mother Mary Clara (Anna Bialkowska; b. Wiecborka, Prussian occupied Poland, June 1, 1872; d. Garfield Heights, Ohio, December 12, 1955). Catholic nun. After migrating to the U.S. with her parents at age six, Bialkowska settled in the Polish neighborhood that developed around St. Stanislaus Parish in Milwaukee, Wisconsin. Despite being educated by the German School Sisters of Notre Dame, Bialkowska gravitated to the **Felician Sisters** in Detroit, but she left the group in October 1888, only a year after she entered. Nevertheless, this experience had long-lasting effects on her life, especially her appreciation for the Polish language. Even years later as a Sister of St. Joseph of the Third Order of St. Francis, she insisted that younger members of the congregation use the sound patterns of the Polish upper class

she learned from the Felician Sisters. Sometime before May of 1890 she entered the School Sisters of St. Francis. On July 15, 1891, she received the habit and the name Sister Mary Kleta. She was immediately sent out to teach in Wisconsin and after making her first vows she went to Pennsylvania and Illinois. In 1897, at the age of twenty-five, she was transferred to Sweetest Heart of Mary School in Detroit where she served as superior and principal, becoming recognized for her administrative ability. The next year she was sent to St. Mary of Perpetual Help School that had an enrollment of over 1,000 Polish students. While at St. Mary's, Sr. Kleta became disturbed by the fact that Polish sisters were being sent to serve the wealthy in a sanitarium in Milwaukee while there was a critical shortage of Polish teachers in parish schools. At the urging of the pastor of St. Mary's, the Rev. Stanley Nawrocki, Sr. Kleta agreed to organize and lead a movement of separation from the School Sisters of St. Francis to form a new congregation with the purpose of ministering to youth. Her companion in this project was Sister **Felicia Jaskulska**. They were supported in their efforts by Bishop Sebastian Messmer of the Diocese of Green Bay, Wisconsin, the Rev. Łukasz Peściński in Stevens Point, and the Rev. Stanley Nawrocki in Chicago. The bishop promised them his guidance and protection; the priests provided on-the-spot advice and encouragement.

By 1902, Sr. Kleta pronounced her perpetual vows in the new congregation and changed her name to Sister Clara. At the congregation's first General Chapter she was elected as the assistant to the superior general, Mother Felicia, and was named to supervise the building of the motherhouse. Mother Clara shared Mother Felicia's vision of educating sisters so they could better serve the Polish immigrant community. Together, they enlarged the congregation's commitment to parish schools in rural Wisconsin, as well as in the urban centers of Chicago and Detroit. Mother Clara Bialkowska taught the sisters Polish so they could better serve the children in the schools. Saturdays and weekday evenings were devoted to English classes and a variety of subjects necessary for a well-rounded elementary school curriculum.—*Madge Karecki*

SOURCE: Josephine Marie Peplinski, *A Fitting Response: The History of the Sisters of St. Joseph of the Third Order of St. Francis Part II The Growth, 1902–1962* (South Bend: Sisters of St. Joseph of the Third Order of St. Francis, 1992).

Bielaski, Alexander (Aleksander Bielawski; born in Lithuania, August 1, 1811; d. Belmont, Missouri, November 7, 1861). Engineer, soldier. After studying at the Russian Military

Aleksander Bielaski, engineer and American Civil War officer (*PMA*).

School in St. Petersburg, he joined the Russian Engineer Corps. With the outbreak of the November Uprising in Poland in 1830, Bielaski immediately joined Polish troops under Gen. Dembinski's command as a non-commissioned officer. At the Battle of Grochów (February 25, 1831) he was severely wounded by a shot in a face that cost him all of his teeth on the right side. When the insurrection collapsed, Bielaski migrated to Bourges, France, from which he continued his travel to the United States in 1832. His qualifications gained him an appointment as an engineer building railroads. From 1835 to 1837 he conducted a topographical survey in Florida. In 1837 he settled in Illinois, taking work as an engineer with the Illinois Central Railroad. In 1841 he became a naturalized citizen, marrying in the following year. From 1843 to 1844 he worked as an engineer in Mexico. Despite the fact that the Mexican government offered him naturalization and high military rank, he returned to his home in Springfield. In 1844 he was appointed as a primary draftsman in the Patent Office, holding this position until the outbreak of the Civil War. In 1861 he enlisted in the Union army. Assigned to Gen. John A. McClernand's staff with the rank of captain, he fell in his first battle with Confederates at Belmont, Missouri, where he was shot down while leading an attack of the 27th Illinois Infantry with its colors in his hands. Bielaski's superiors saluted him for his heroic death. His body was never found.—*Piotr Derengowski*

SOURCE: Joseph A. Wytrwal, "Lincoln's Friend—Captain A. Bielaski," *Polish American Studies*, Vol. XIV, no. 3–4 (1957), 65–67.

Bielaski, Alexander Bruce (b. Montgomery County, Maryland, April 2, 1883; d. New York, February 19, 1964). Attorney, FBI Director. After receiving his law degree from George Washington University in 1904,

Bielaski joined the Department of Justice where he assisted in the reorganization of the court system in Oklahoma before its entry into the Union. Following this assignment he joined the Bureau of Investigation (now the Federal Bureau of Investigation), rising quickly to head that agency by 1912. During his tenure as chief, the scope of Bureau responsibilities grew considerably. After leaving government service for private practice in 1919, he returned to serve in undercover operations against violations of the prohibition laws in New York City. Between 1929 and 1959 he led the National Board of Fire Underwriters' arson investigation unit, and in 1938 served as president of the Society of Former Special Agents. —*James S. Pula*

SOURCES: G. T. A. O'Toole, *The Encyclopedia of American Intelligence and Espionage: From the Revolutionary War to the Present* (New York: Facts on File, 1988); "Bruce Bielaski, Justice Aide, Dies," *New York Times,* February 20, 1964.

Bielaski, Oscar (b. Washington, D.C., March 21, 1847; d. Washington, D.C., November 8, 1911). Baseball player. Oscar Bielaski holds the double distinction of being the first athlete of Polish extraction to play major league baseball, and to earn a livelihood in professional sports. The son of Polish immigrants, Bielaski learned baseball while serving in the Union army during the Civil War, when the game soon to emerge as the recognized American national pastime was a favorite leisure activity of soldiers. The dawn of professional baseball gave him the opportunity to profit from this newly acquired skill. In 1872 he joined his hometown Washington Nationals of the National Association, the pioneer "major league," then in its second year of operation. Over the course of a modest career, the right handed hitting Bielaski played five seasons for three different teams, primarily as a right fielder, compiling a lifetime batting average of .241. In 1876, his final season, his Chicago White Stockings won the inaugural championship of the National League. Following his retirement from sport, Bielaski worked and coached baseball at the Washington Navy Yard. He is buried in Arlington National Cemetery. In 2005 he was inducted into the National Polish-American Sports Hall of Fame. —*Neal Pease*

SOURCES: "Oscar Bielaski," National Polish-American Sports Hall of Fame website, www.polishsportshof.com; "Oscar Bielaski: First Pol-Am Major Leaguer," *Polish American Journal,* June 16, 1962.

Bigos. Also known as "Hunter's Stew," *bigos* is a traditional food reflecting its peasant origins through its typical ingredients of mushrooms, cabbage, onions, carrots, potatoes, and other vegetables grown on peasant farms, along with fruits, wild berries and meat from pigs, sheep and cattle interspersed with wild game and venison. If there is a Polish national dish it is *bigos*, which comes in as many varieties as the mind may conceive and the available foodstuffs provide. Though a typical peasant dish, versions of *bigos* also graced the tables of the burghers and gentry, often including exotic mixtures of rare and expensive meats and spices. —*James S. Pula*

SOURCE: Marie Sokolowski, et al., eds., *Treasured Polish Recipes for Americans* (Minneapolis: Polanie Publishing Company, 1988), 66–67.

Birds of Passage. Sometimes also known as "sojourners," this is a term used by historians of migration movements to refer to immigrants who have no intention of residing permanently in the area to which they move. This was especially true of immigrants from the southern and eastern regions of Europe arriving in the U.S. between 1880 and World War I, many of whom arrived with the intention of earning some money so they could return to their home country and purchase land or otherwise pursue a better life for themselves and their families. It has been estimated that between 1907 and 1911, for every one hundred immigrants who arrived from Southern and Eastern Europe, 44 left to return to those areas. For Italians, it has been estimated that 73 left for every 100 who arrived; for Poles, the figure was lower. An exception to this general trend was the Jews, the vast majority arriving from the eastern portions of Europe, who included very few "birds of passage." Polish historians have estimated that about 33 percent of the Poles who migrated to America eventually returned to Poland. —*James S. Pula*

SOURCES: Ewa Morawska, "Labor Migrations of Poles in the Atlantic World Economy, 1880–1914," *Comparative Studies in Society and History,* Vol. 31, no. 2 (1989); Adam Walaszek, "Return Migration from the USA to Poland," in Daniel Kubat, ed., *The Politics of Return. International Return Migration in Europe* (New York: Center for Migration Studies, 1984).

Biskupski, M. B. B. (Mieczysław Bolesław Bieńkowski Biskupski; b. Chicago, Illinois, September 24, 1948; d.—). Historian. The son of Polish émigrés who arrived in America from Mazowsze and the northeast *kresy* in the early years of the twentieth century, Biskupski earned his B.A. (1971) and M.A. (1972) in history from the University of California, Los Angeles. He completed his graduate work at Yale, earning a prestigious fellowship from the university in 1972 and dissertation research grants from Yale's Russian and Eastern European Studies Center. In 1975 he earned his M.Phil. from Yale and his Ph.D. in 1981. His dissertation, titled "The United States and the Rebirth of Poland, 1914–1918," examined the Polish Question in America and the reasons behind Woodrow Wilson's eventual support for an independent Poland. During his time at Yale, Biskupski served as a lecturer in the history department and held dissertation fellowships from the Fulbright-Hays Foundation and the International Studies Association/Ford Foundation. After receiving his doctorate, he taught at Millersville University of Pennsylvania, the University of Rochester, and St. John Fisher College, where he was an Associate Professor of history and international studies and Director of the Institute for Polish Studies. In 1995 he held a prestigious Fulbright Research Professorship at the Institute of History, University of Warsaw, and was named a Fellow of the Central European University in Budapest, Hungary, in 1997. Biskupski served as managing editor of the academic journal *East Central Europe* (1982–91) and as president of the **Polish American Historical Association** (1988–90). He was a member of the boards of directors of both the **Polish Institute of Arts and Sciences of America** and the Polish American Historical Association. In 2002 he was appointed to the **Stanislaus A. Blejwas** Endowed Chair in Polish and Polish American Studies established in 1997 at Central Connecticut State University in New Britain, CT. He is the recipient of several honors and awards for scholarly distinction, including the Officer's Cross of the Order of Merit of the Republic of Poland (2000) and the Honor Roll for Polish Science from the Ministry of Education in Poland (2001). Biskupski received PAHA's **Mieczysław Haiman** Award (2004), given annually to scholars for continuous advancement of the study of Polish American history and culture. His publications include *Ideology, Politics and Diplomacy* (2005), *The History of Poland* (2000), and such edited volumes as *Pastor of the Poles: Polish-American Essays* (with Stanislaus A. Blejwas; 1982), *Polish Democratic Thought from the Renaissance to the Great Migration* (with **James S. Pula**; 1991), and *The Origins of Modern Polish Democracy* (with James S. Pula and Piotr Wróbel; 2010), as well as many refereed articles appearing in *Polin: Studies in Polish Jewry,* **Polish Review,** *War and Society, Slavic Review, Slavonic and East European Review,* and **Polish American Studies.** —*Krystyna Cap*

SOURCE: Bolesław Wierzbiański, *Who's Who in Polish America* (New York: Bicentennial Publishing Corp., 1996), 33.

Black-Polish Coalition. The Black-Polish Coalition of Buffalo, New York, was a relatively short-lived but instructive effort during the 1980s at dialogue and cooperation between two of the largest ethnic communities in the city. During the decade, tensions between the two communities were increasing. In Buffalo, as in other historically industrial Great Lakes cities, union-protected, well-paying manufacturing jobs were becoming less available and competition for them fiercer. "White ethnics," including Polish Americans, were leaving their longtime urban enclaves for the suburbs, at the same time that substantial numbers of African Americans were moving in. On Buffalo's East Side, this was happening in *Sercii Polonia* (The Heart of **Polonia**), in the Broadway Fillmore neighborhood. Hindered by stereotypes of working-class "white ethnics" as bigots, the black newcomers did not always understand that Buffalo's now dwindling Polonia had long offered its historic residents a safe haven against the rampant discrimination in "mainstream" U.S. culture. The Polish residents sometimes translated their sense of loss into hostility and blame towards blacks, forgetting what it was like to be a people who also knew the sting of oppression, and buying into stereotypes of their new neighbors as criminals and welfare cheats.

The 1980s also marked a resurgence in the sort of anti-racist, culturally pluralistic progressive politics that had, for example, drawn both blacks and Poles into the labor movement during the early twentieth century. This revival helped create an opening for the formation of a Black-Polish organization in Buffalo. The immediate stimulus was a particularly heated dispute between the two communities over a Buffalo Common Council proposal to completely eliminate the Broadway Fillmore district. This plan would have increased black political representation in city politics, while decreasing Polish. When the scheme failed, Bill Falkowski asked in the January 1984 issue of the Buffalo-based *Polish American Voice* whether a coalition between the groups was now feasible and desirable. Falkowski thought that indeed it was, but Poles needed to first "respect the humanity of their Black neighbors" and blacks to "understand how Poles feel about their neighborhoods." As **John Bukowczyk** notes, the Coalition was made possible by a reciprocal recognition "that both groups shared common ground around the issues of identity and powerlessness and that neither had caused the other's problems." Soon afterwards, the Black-Polish Coalition of Buffalo formally launched with hopes of educating the two communities about one another's cultures and confronting the shared problems of crime and urban decay.

The Coalition conducted several events in the Broadway Fillmore neighborhood that promoted interethnic dialogue. One was a well-attended screening of the film drama *The Killing Floor* (1985) at the Polish Community Center. Directed by Bill Duke and starring Damien Leake, Moses Gunn, and Dennis Farina, this award-winning film, set in 1917 to 1919, originally aired on PBS-TV's *American Playhouse* series. Based on a true story, it is about an African American man, Frank Custer, who migrates north to Chicago in search of a decent living. He finds work in the brutal meatpacking industry, where many Polish immigrants as well as blacks have ended up. Cooperating with Poles, Custer becomes involved in a labor union and tries to recruit other blacks, despite their deep mistrust of anything initiated by whites.

The Coalition also inspired a joint Martin Luther King Jr./**Tadeusz Kościuszko** parade in the neighborhood. Although King's human rights service was by then well-known beyond the African American community, non–Poles were still not generally aware of Kościuszko's. Consistent with his support for the American independence struggle against the English, Kościuszko emancipated the serfs on his estate and transferred ownership of the land to them. Traveling through the American South, he noted the parallels between serfdom and the enslavement of Africans. In his American will, he allocated his Revolutionary War income to the purchase then liberation and education of African American slaves (see **Kościuszko's Will**).

The Black-Polish Coalition met every two weeks for almost two years. According to member David Franczyk, then editor of ***Polish American Journal*** and later Buffalo Common Council president, the organization came to an end because it "focused on ephemeral events" and thus "did not create the groundwork for a more enduring future." He also cited "some political leaders who felt threatened by the Coalition, and some in both communities who preferred to perpetuate negative stereotypes about each group; for example, Pol-Ams who thought blacks destroyed the neighborhood, and blacks who thought all Poles were racist." In addition, he mentioned demographic trends in the Broadway-Fillmore area. From the 1980s into the 1990s, much housing was demolished there and not replaced. Along with the continued departures of Polish Americans, blacks also left. Asked what the Coalition meant to him personally, Franczyk replied: "I was gratified that interaction between Pol-Ams and African Americans was not wholly negative, as the Coalition focused on those things which promoted cultural tolerance, understanding, and the desire to mitigate the rebuilding of a distressed ethnic community." —*Mary Krane Derr*

SOURCES: John J. Bukowczyk, *A History of the Polish Americans* (New Brunswick, NJ: Transaction Publishers, 2008); Bill Falkowski, "Is a Black/Polish Coalition Now Possible?" *Polish American Voice*, January 1984.

Black-Polish Conference. The Black-Polish Conference (BPC) arose in the aftermath of the riots —"the Great Rebellion," in the words of some — that devastated Detroit, Michigan, for five days in late July, 1967. Forty-three people were killed, most of them black. Possibly 1,189 were injured. Over 2,000 buildings were burned down, including small businesses that African Americans and white ethnics owned and depended on for their livelihoods. The riots only intensified national and local attention to the disrespected civil rights of racial and ethnic minorities and to urban difficulties like poverty, poor labor conditions, inadequate health care, and substandard housing. In 1968, the noted Roman Catholic sociologist Rev. Andrew Greeley charged Polish Americans with anti-black racism: a charge that many Polish Americans deemed an unfair, inaccurate, and pernicious stereotype. A challenge arose from the Detroit Archdiocesan Priests Conference for Polish Affairs, the local group for Polish American clergy. On April 10, 1968, the group's 100 members met for a seminar at **Saints Cyril and Methodius Seminary** in Orchard Lake, Michigan. They passed a resolution asserting every person's right, whatever his or her "color, race, or national origin," to "freedom of opportunity ... in housing, education, employment, use of public facilities ... and [to] a decent standard of living." They connected this resolution to the Polish people's own long struggle against discrimination. The resolution inspired John Conyers, a Detroit-area Congressman and an African American, to meet with Revs. Daniel Bogus and Fabian Slominski, the chairs of the Polish priests' association. The three men discussed the possibility of Polish-Black action on local social justice matters. By December 1968, they convened a series of exploratory meetings between civic and religious leaders from both communities. As Conyers' aide Leon Atchison observed, "The fur flew at the first meeting. All the fears and animosity, the latent and overt hostility were very apparent." Yet the participants' mutual candor allowed them to "get things out of their system" and cultivate "a healthy respect" for one another. An anonymous and practically minded politician noted that "respect for each others' political power," not "love," was the necessary force to start a Black-Polish coalition: "Love can come later." The Rev. Bogus agreed that the coalition required "hard organizing and a realistic approach.... You don't accomplish this goal through idealistic pronouncements about brotherhood or the value of good race relations."

A series of events in late March 1969 severely tested the BPC's charter members. On Detroit's west side, a black militant organization called the Republic of New Afrika (RNA) held its first anniversary convention under the legal protection of armed security guards at the New Bethel Baptist Church. The pastor of the church was Reverend C. L. Franklin, noted civil rights leader (and father of legendary soul singer Aretha Franklin). As the convention dispersed, two young Polish police officers on patrol, Michael Czapski and Richard Worobec, had an altercation with the security guards. Czapski was killed and Worobec severely injured. Four civilians were also hurt. Severely damaging the church in the process, police arrested over 150 people from the meeting, including children, and imprisoned them incommunicado without charging them. Judge George Crockett, an African American, conducted an impromptu court in the police station and released almost all the prisoners on the grounds that there was no evidence against them. His actions evoked further rage among Polish Detroiters, as did the Black community's widespread support for him. Through these difficult incidents, the BPC meetings persisted and allowed members of both the Black and Polish communities to air critical grievances in a fashion that defused interethnic tensions, rather than escalating them. Later in the year, the BPC performed a similar task when Roman Stanley Gribbs, a Polish American, was elected Detroit mayor by a narrow margin over Richard H. Austin, later Michigan's first black Secretary of State.

The Black-Polish Conference officially launched itself in June 1969. While more moderate than the many black militant groups then quite active in the city, the BPC did not adopt a conservative "colorblind" approach to racial strife and racial justice. Indeed, it spoke of cooperating on solutions to shared problems "without losing our ethnic identities." Many Detroit residents expressed skepticism and surprise about the new group and its agenda. They repeated the entrenched stereotype of Poles as "too socially conservative and hostile to black demands." The BPC was undeterred, noting in its statement of purpose that "two out of every three Detroiters is either Black or Polish" and that the two communities had a high degree of daily contact with each other. Indeed, at the time, the city's population was 44 percent African American and twenty percent Polish. The BPC's declared expressed aims were "to promote increased knowledge of the history and culture of each community

by the other through public meetings and cultural and educational programs; to develop and expand the channels of communication between the two groups, particularly on matters of current community concern, not only between the leadership, but also between the individuals in each community; and, to sponsor specific programs of mutual benefit to the Black and Polish communities."

Early on, the BPC claimed over 4,000 members and the backing of leaders from both communities. **Frank Renkiewicz** named these leaders as "Polish priests and black ministers, the president of the Polish-American Chamber of Commerce, the head of the local [Booker T. Washington] black businessmen's association, university professors and administrators, political figures such as Conyers and ... Polish Congressman **Lucien Nedzi**, civil rights workers, neighborhood organizers, journalists such as [editor Stanley] Krajewski of the *Polish Daily News* and Mitchell Lewandowski of the *Hamtramck Citizen*, leaders of the traditionally conservative Polish-American Congress, and Frank Ditto, head of a militant black organization called the East Side Voice for an Independent Detroit." Ditto was the same community organizer whom *Time Magazine* (June 13, 1969) portrayed according to the menacing stereotype of the "angry Black man": "burly, brooding ... prowl[ing] the streets in a dashiki, arous[ing] fear or hatred in many whites."

The BPC actively encouraged Black and Polish clubs, associations, and churches to have joint meetings and explore cooperative plans of action. By 1971 the BPC had formed an executive committee. The Rev. Bogus and Rep. Conyers headed it and took turns chairing BPC meetings. Partly because of public concerns about religious and political ambition and bias, the executive committee was changed into a board of directors. The BPC also had a steering committee with 45 members who met regularly. The Conference had achieved official nonprofit status. It was receiving foundation grants, starting with $50,000 from the New Detroit Corporation and the Priests' Conference for Polish Affairs. It had a small paid staff and much volunteer support, as well as the aid of clerical workers and consultants from the Human Relations Division of the Detroit Archdiocese. The BPC regularly published a newsletter with a diverse readership. By 1972, grants from the National Center for Urban Ethnic Affairs allowed the BPC to expand its staff, conduct more community meetings, and launch hoped-for initiatives. The BPC sought improvements in public housing and city services delivery and challenged environmental racism in the form of

public dumps. It fed lunches to needy children and started programs for elderly people and youths. It cosponsored an African American cultural festival as well as a trip to Poland. The BPC's greatest attempt to recruit more grassroots members was its proposed community-based health plan for uninsured patients.

By the mid–1970s, the BPC apparently suffered a decline. Understanding the organization's decline as well as its enduring effects requires more research into archival materials. BPC documents can be found in the Walter P. Reuther Library of Labor and Urban Affairs, Wayne State University, especially in the Chris & Marti Alston, Kenneth V. and Sheila M. Cockrel, Detroit Commission on Community Relations — Human Rights Department, New Detroit, and Rosa Parks Collections. Although it did not continue, the BPC remains an intriguing model of cooperation between two racial/ethnic groups that are still often considered one another's natural antagonists. This model merits further study.

Although others likely existed at least one clear legacy of the BPC remained as of 2009. This was the Metro Health Foundation (MHF) of Detroit. During the early 1970s, the BPC identified the lack of community-based health programs and access to primary health care as among the most urgent unmet needs of Detroit and Hamtramck residents. Although the MHF did not begin until 1986, it traced itself directly back to the BPC's community needs assessment. By 2005, the MHF had assets of $8.1 million. Its community outreach programs advocated for better primary care access. The Foundation made grants to fund primary health services such as prenatal care and education for pregnant teens, senior prescription assistance, medical transportation, and medical care for homeless persons. Both Polish and African Americans benefited from MHF activities.—*Mary Krane Derr*

SOURCES: John Bukowczyk, *And My Children Did Not Know Me: A History of the Polish Americans* (Bloomington: Indiana University Press, 1987); Dennis Deslippe, "'We Must Bring Together a New Coalition': The Challenge of Working-Class White Ethnics to Color-Blind Conservatism in the 1970s," *International Labor and Working-Class History*, Vol. 74 (2008), 148–70; Dan Georgakas and Marvin Surkin, *Detroit, I Do Mind Dying: A Study in Urban Revolution* (Cambridge, MA: South End Press, 1998); Glenn F. Kossick, "Metro Health Foundation," *Grantmakers in Health Bulletin*, May 15, 2006; Frank Renkiewicz, ed., *The Poles in America, 1608–1972: A Chronology and Fact Book* (Dobbs Ferry, NY: Oceana Publications, 1973); Heather Ann Thompson, *Whose Detroit? Politics, Labor, and Race in a Modern American City* (Ithaca, NY: Cornell University Press, 2004); Perry L. Weed, *The White Ethnic Movement and Ethnic Politics* (New York: Praeger Publishers, 1973).

Blazejowski, Carol (b. Elizabeth, New Jersey, September 29, 1956; d. —). Basketball player. Blazejowski earned All-America honors in basketball at Montclair State College three straight seasons (1976–78), and won the inaugural award as the top college women's player in the country in 1978. She left Montclair State as holder of collegiate records as the top career scorer in women's basketball (both total points and per game average) and for most points scored in a game at Madison Square Garden by a player of either sex. "The Blaze" played a single season in the Women's Pro Basketball League in 1980-81, winning its most valuable player award, before the collapse of the WPBL brought an end to her playing days. Afterward, she worked in the front offices of the National Basketball Association. She became vice president and general manager of the New York Liberty of the Women's National Basketball Association in 1997, and president/general manager of the team in 2008. Blazejowski is a member of the Naismith Memorial Basketball Hall of Fame, the Women's Basketball Hall of Fame, and was elected to the National Polish-American Sports Hall of Fame in 1994.—*Neal Pease*

SOURCE: "Carol Blazejowski," National Polish-American Sports Hall of Fame website, www.polishsportshof.com.

Blazonczyk, Edward "Eddie" (b. Chicago, Illinois, July 12, 1941; d.—). Musician. Blazonczyk began his career in the early 1950s when he formed a four-piece group named "Happy Eddie and His Polka Jesters" to play at Polish weddings and other events. In 1958 he signed with Mercury Records as "Eddie Bell and the Bel-Aires," writing and recording Pop music and appearing on early television shows including Dick Clark's *American Bandstand* and *The Jim Loundsbury Show*. In 1962 he returned to the Polka genre with a new group he called "Versatones," recording his first album, "Polka Parade," in 1963 on the Bel-Aire label. Since then they have recorded more than sixty albums. Popularity brought tours of the U.S., Canada, France, Italy, and Poland. Among their more than 125 honors and awards, the Versatones have been nominated eighteen times for Grammy Awards, winning for their album "Another Polka Celebration" in 1986. His recording of "Angeline Be Mine Polka" was voted the best single in 1969, and the group was named "The Nation's Number One Polka Band" in 1967. The U.S. Polka Association presented him with its Lifetime Achievement Award (2002). He was inducted into the International Polka Hall of Fame in 1970. See also **Polka**.—*James S. Pula*

SOURCE: Charles Keil, Angeliki V. Keil, and Dick Blau, *Polka Happiness* (Philadelphia, Temple University Press, 1992).

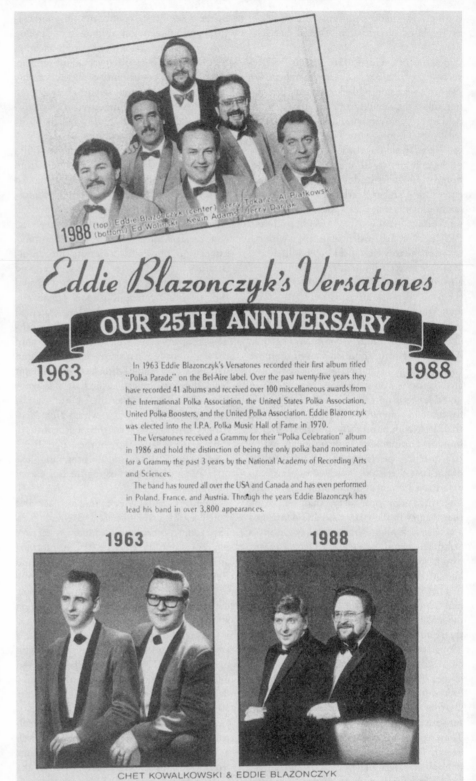

Twenty-fifth anniversary poster for Eddie Blazonczyk and his "Versatones" (*PMA*).

Blejwas, Stanislaus A. (b. Brooklyn, New York, October 5, 1941; d. New Britain, Connecticut, September 21, 2001). Historian. Raised in Clark, New Jersey, Blejwas earned his baccalaureate *summa cum laude* at Providence College (1963) before receiving his Ph.D. in Modern European and Polish History at Columbia University (1973). After accepting a position in the history department at Central Connecticut State University, he

Stan Blejwas, historian and founder of the Chair in Polish and Polish American Studies at Central Connecticut State University (*CCSU-BC*).

rose to the rank of professor and was named to the prestigious honorary position of Connecticut State University Professor. At Central Connecticut, Blejwas vigorously pursued for more than two decades his dream of developing an endowed program in Polish studies at the institution. His work was rewarded in 1997 with the creation of the Endowed Chair of Polish and Polish American Studies, the name of which was changed following his death to the Stanislaus A. Blejwas Chair of Polish and Polish American Studies. This was only the second fully endowed position in Polish studies in the U.S. A noted historian of Poland and the Poles in the U.S., Blejwas's publications included *Pastor of the Poles: Polish American Essays Presented to Right Reverend Monsignor John P. Wodarski in Honor of the Fiftieth Anniversary of His Ordination* (1982, with M. B. Biskupski), *Realism in Polish Politics: Survival and National Revival in Nineteenth Century Poland* (1984), *St. Stanislaus B. & M. Parish, Meriden, Connecticut: A Century of Connecticut Polonia: 1891–1991* (1991), and *The Polish Singers Alliance of America, 1888–1998: Choral Patriotism* (2005). Among his many recognitions were a fellowship at the Institute on East Central Europe (1963), an Honorary Fellowship at Columbia University (1966), a Fulbright-Hays Fellowship to Poland (1967), a **Kosciuszko Foundation** Doctoral Dissertation Award (1974), a grant from the Connecticut Humanities Council (1982), the Mieczysław Haiman Award of the **Polish American Historical Association** for contributions to the field, a grant from the Kosciuszko Foundation and the Polish Ministry of Education for research at the Polish State Archives and the Polish Foreign Ministry Archives, and a distinguished service award from the Polish American Historical Association of which he was elected president. In 1994, President Bill Clinton appointed Blejwas to the United States Holocaust Memorial Council, a position he was re-appointed to in 1999. In 1996 President Aleksander Kwasniewski of the Republic of Poland awarded him the Officer of Swords of the Order of Merit of the Republic of Poland, the highest state decoration in Poland. In 2000 the Polish government presented him with the Foreign Minister's Diploma of Recognition for his promotion of Polish culture abroad.—*James S. Pula*

SOURCES: *Polish American Studies*, Vol. LIX, no. 1 (2002) is dedicated to Blejwas and contains six articles on him and his work; obituary, *Hartford Courant*, September 25, 2001.

Blenski, Michael (b. Boboda, Poland, September 27, 1862; d. Milwaukee, Wisconsin, March 23, 1932). Politician, Polonia activist. Proud of his **Kaszubian** heritage, Blenski only "became" a Pole in the U.S. Coming to Milwaukee in 1880, he worked first as a pattern maker and later as a bookkeeper. Active in local politics, he was elected to the Wisconsin legislature in 1892. In 1893, he was appointed by President Grover Cleveland as the executive secretary of the newly created U.S. Weather Bureau in Washington, D.C. Earning his law degree from Georgetown University, Blenski returned to Milwaukee where he won election to a civil court judgeship in 1909, holding this office until his death and gaining a reputation for his good humor both on and off the bench. In 1916, as a member of the **Kosciuszko Guard**, a unit of the Wisconsin National Guard comprised almost entirely of Poles from Milwaukee, he took part in Gen. John Pershing's expedition to Mexico to capture the one-time revolutionary turned outlaw Pancho Villa. Blenski became a member of the **Polish National Alliance** and won election as a vice **censor** of the PNA in 1903. From 1915 to 1924 he served as censor of the Alliance.—*Donald E. Pienkos*

SOURCE: Donald E. Pienkos, *PNA: A Centennial History of the Polish National Alliance* (Boulder, CO: East European Monographs, 1984).

Michael Blenski, politician and Polonia activist (*OLS*).

Boarding. Although generally frowned upon in Poland, the practice of taking in boarders became commonplace in early Polish American working-class families. With the low wages paid to unskilled industrial workers during the period of the mass migration between 1870 and 1920, families had to adapt to meet the financial needs of supporting themselves. Women began working outside the household in factory or other jobs, a practice rarely seen in Poland, and children went to work early to increase family income. For those who owned homes, financial strategies included renting out rooms. This usually began by taking in relatives or friends, but it soon spread to include non-relatives as families found it a lucrative source of additional income. In fact, Poles had a higher percentage of households with boarders or lodgers than any other European ethnic group with 48.4 percent of homes including boarders as compared to an average of 32.9 percent for other European groups. In cases where enough boarders were present to make it financially worthwhile, the woman of the house did not seek employment outside the home, but instead acted as a housekeeper, purchasing food, cooking meals, washing and mending clothes, and otherwise operating what amounted to a small hotel. For these services, boarders paid additional fees beyond their basic rent, enabling families to meet expenses and improve their collective lives.—*James S. Pula*

SOURCE: James S. Pula, *Polish Americans: An Ethnic Community* (New York: Twayne Publishers, 1995), 26.

Bobko, Karol Joseph "Bo" (b. New York, New York, December 23, 1937; d.—). Astronaut. A member of the first graduating class at the U.S. Air Force Academy in 1959, he received his pilot's wings in 1960 before completing his M.S. degree in Aerospace Engineering at the University of Southern California in 1970. On active duty as a fighter pilot between 1961 and 1965, he then attended the Aerospace Research Pilots School at Edwards Air Force Base, California, before joining the astronaut program in 1966. Qualifying as an astronaut in 1969, he participated in the Skylab Medical Experiments Altitude Test (SMEAT), was a member of the support group for the Apollo-Soyuz Test Project (ASTP), and a member of the support crew for the Space Shuttle Approach and Landing Tests at Edwards Air Force Base where he served as the prime chase pilot during Approach and Landing Test (ALT) flights. He participated in three space flights, totaling 386 hours in space, including serving as pilot on the maiden voyage of the spacecraft *Challenger* (April 4–9, 1983) and mission commander on the *Discovery* (April 12–19, 1985) and the maiden voyage of the *Atlantis* (October 3–7, 1985). Rising to the rank of colonel, he was honored with three NASA Flight Medals, two NASA Exceptional Service Medals, six Group Achievement Awards, the Defense Superior Service Medal, Legion of Merit, Defense Meritorious Service Medal, the Air Force Distinguished Flying Cross, two Meritorious Service Medals, and the Air Force Academy Jabara Award. Following retirement from the Air Force and the astronaut program in 1988, he served as principal in the firm of Booz Allen & Hamilton, Inc., specializing in high performance training simulation, hardware and software systems engineering, spacecraft checkout and testing, space station development and program integration. In 2000 he moved to SPACEHAB as Vice President for Strategic Programs, then took a position as program manager for support of the NASA Ames Simulation Laboratories with SAIC in 2005.—*James S. Pula*

SOURCE: National Aeronautics and Space Administration, Lyndon B. Johnson Space Center, http://www.jsc.nasa.gov/Bios/htmlbios/bobko-kj.ktml.

Bobrowicz, Edmund V. (b. Milwaukee, Wisconsin, May 1, 1919; d. Green Bay, Wisconsin, March 16, 2003). Union leader, Congressman. After serving in the U.S. Army in the South Pacific during World War II, he became active as an organizer for the Congress of Industrial Organization's left-wing Fur and Leather Workers' Union, defeating the conservative Democratic three-term incumbent congressman, **Thaddeus Wasilewski**, in the August 13, 1946 primary for nomination as U.S. Representative in Milwaukee's heavily Polish American fourth district. He accomplished that with the assistance of the CIO's Political Action Committee. A month later, in September, the *Milwaukee Journal* claimed that he was a Communist. Although Bobrowicz denied the accusation, it was a cause for both national and state Democratic Party concern in the Cold War climate of the time and led State Democratic National Committeeman Robert E. Tehan to attempt to purge Bobrowicz from the party. According to the *Time* magazine issue of October 14, 1946, Tehan stated that he was "convinced that Bobrowicz [was] a Communist Party member." Daniel Webster Hoan, long-time Socialist and anti–Communist mayor of Milwaukee (1916–40), who had become a Democrat during World War II, encouraged Democrats to repudiate Bobrowicz's candidacy, but his name could not be removed from the ballot. Bobrowicz competed in the general election in November 1946 and lost to the Republican challenger. Bobrowicz's defeat as the Democratic Party candidate was undoubtedly due to Wasilewski's decision to campaign as an independent candidate. In 1948, Bobrowicz sought the same congressional seat, this time as the candidate of the newly organized Progressive Party which supported the presidential campaign of Henry A. Wallace, Franklin D. Roosevelt's vice president during his third term. However, in 1948 the state CIO removed Bobrowicz, together with six others, from its leadership roster for "misinforming CIO members" about the pro-Soviet stance of Wallace's party. But the more radical Fur and Leather Workers' union, unlike most other labor unions, opposed Truman and supported Wallace and Bobrowicz. Subsequently, Bobrowicz was badly defeated in the general election. He continued to serve as an official in his union and later moved to Green Bay.—*Frederick J. Augustyn*

SOURCES: John Earl Haynes, *Red Scare or Red Menace? American Communism and Anticommunism in the Cold War Era* (Chicago: Ivan R. Dee, 1996), 128; Chicago *Daily Tribune*, September 28, 1946, 8; *New York Times*, August 3, 1946, 13 and August 14, 1946, 1; *Time*, September 30, 1946, October 14, 1946, October 21, 1946, and November 18, 1946; Angela T. Pienkos, ed., *Ethnic Politics in Urban America: The Polish Experience in Four Cities* (Chicago: Polish American Historical Association, 1978).

Boeck, Leopold Julian (b. Chełm, Poland, November 14, 1823; d. Philadelphia, Pennsylvania, May 18, 1896). Educator. After completing his early education in Chełm, he continued his studies at the Universities of Breslau and Berlin. Although he earned a doctorate of philosophy degree, sources differ on whether this was awarded by the University of Bonn or the University of Berlin. Becoming involved in Polish revolutionary activities, he fled with General Józef Bem to Hungary where he served in the unsuccessful revolt led by Lajos Kossuth. Imprisoned for a time in Constantinople where he fled, he eventually arrived in Paris in 1849 or 1850, obtaining a professorship in mathematics at the Sorbonne. From Paris, Boeck migrated to the U.S. via England, settling in New York where he was employed as a teacher. Prior to the Civil War, he founded in New York City what is considered to be the first polytechnic institute in U.S., but it closed when most of his students volunteered for military service on the outbreak of the war in 1861. Following the war he reestablished the school, advertising it as a "School of Engineers and Chemists" that also taught modern languages, but closed its doors for good when he accepted a position as professor of applied mathematics and engineering at the University of Virginia in 1867. In 1873, President Ulysses S. Grant named him "Scientific Commissioner" to the Universal Exposition in Vienna, and in 1877 President Rutherford B. Hayes appointed him in the same capacity to the exposition in Philadelphia. He completed his career with an appointment as professor of modern languages at the University of Pennsylvania.—*James S. Pula*

SOURCES: Ladislas John Siekaniec, *The Polish Contribution to Early American Education, 1608–1865* (San Francisco: R&E Research Associates, 1976); obituary in the Philadelphia *Public Ledger*, May 19, 1896.

Bójnowski, Lucyan (b. Swierzbutów, Poland, February 5, 1868; d. New Britain, Connecticut, July 28, 1960). Priest, Polonia activist. Bójnowski grew up in a family of *szlachta* (petty landowning nobility) from which he inherited a strong sense of service to the less fortunate. After receiving a classical education at the lyceum in Suwałki, fearing conscription into the tsarist army he determined to go to America over his father's objections. Arriving in the U.S. in 1888, Bójnowski entered the **Saints Cyril and Methodius Seminary** in Orchard Lake, Michigan, in the following year. He pursued further studies at St. John's Seminary in Brighton, Massachusetts, and was ordained on January 30, 1895. He was assigned to New Britain, Connecticut, where he was responsible for the construction of the original wooden church of Sacred Heart of Jesus Parish. As the long-term pastor of Sacred Heart, he grew to wield potent political influence in the community. Over the years he built the parish into one of the largest in the diocese, replaced the wooden structure with a magnificent stone edifice and added a convent, two parochial schools, an orphanage, a home for the aged, a printing operation, a Polish bank, a host of parish organizations, and a newspaper that boasted some 30,000 subscribers. To these enterprises he founded the Sisters of the Immaculate Conception. In the battles that tore **Polonia** asunder at the end of the nineteenth century, Bójnowski opposed the **independent** religious movement but at the same time strongly championed the Polish cause both within the Roman Catholic Church where he advocated Polish bishops and the patriotic cause of Poland's independence. He attended the first Polish Catholic Congress in Buffalo in 1896, launched a spirited defense of the educational level at Saints Cyril and Methodius Seminary, and successfully defended his parish against the influence of independents and their one-time allies in the New Britain socialist movement and the **Polish National Alliance**. A strong advocate of organization within Polonia, he encouraged the establish-

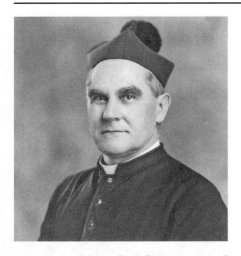

Msgr. Lucjan Bójnowski, Polonia activist and leader of Connecticut Polish Catholics (*PMA*).

ment of political, cultural, and self-help societies within the parish and the Polish community. During World War I he served as a recruiting officer for the **Polish Army in France** and was active in supporting fundraising activities on behalf of Poland, with his parish contributing close to $183,000 for Polish causes. During the postwar years, Bójnowski was a strong advocate of preserving Polish language and culture in the face of increasing pressure for "americanization," both within and outside the church, which was then defined to require that immigrants shed all vestiges of their ethnic heritage. Conversely, he continued to be a staunch opponent of the **Polish National Catholic Church**. What he advocated quite passionately was that Polish Americans become citizens, learn about American culture and politics, to take advantage of educational opportunities, but to also preserve their own religious and cultural traditions. However, his authoritarian rule also led to serious conflict within his parish and the surrounding community, eventually leading to the creation of Holy Cross Parish as a second Polish Catholic church in New Britain. During World War II, Bójnowski was once again active in Polish relief efforts and promoting the Polish cause, yet he also engaged in contentious polemics with other Polonia leaders with whom he disagreed. His often unbecoming rhetoric helped to drive further wedges in Polonia at the expense of unity in support of Poland. He supported the establishment of the **Polish American Congress** and led New Britain's contingent to its initial meeting, but even there he attempted to exclude those whose beliefs he did not share. In the postwar years he engaged in further controversies, including his criticism of newly arrived displaced persons who he characterized as divisive and lazy. In 1946 he was given the title

of monsignor in recognition of his past accomplishments in building his parish. Bójnowski's papers are located at the Connecticut Polish American Archives at Central Connecticut State University.—*James S. Pula*

SOURCES: Daniel S. Buczek, *Immigrant Pastor: The Life of the Right Reverend Monsignor Lucyan Bójnowski of New Britain, Connecticut* (Waterbury, CT: Heminway Corporation, 1974); Bronislas A. Jezierski, "Father Lucian Bójnowski 1868–1960," *Polish American Studies*, Vol. 16, no. 3–4 (1959), 99–108.

Bolek, Francis (b. Zależe, Galicia, September 11, 1886; d. Buffalo, New York, July 7, 1958). Priest, journalist. Upon completion of a master degree in theological studies in Przemyśl, Bolek was ordained a priest in 1910. He served as curate at parishes in Komarno (1910–12) and Biecz (1912–14) before becoming military chaplain in the Austro-Hungarian Army (1914–18) and later in the Polish Army (1918–22). Taken as a prisoner of war during the Polish-Bolshevik conflict, he was imprisoned in Moscow for eighteen months until his release in 1922 through the efforts of Prime Minister Wincenty Witos. When Bolek returned to Poland in 1922, he established the Adam Mickiewicz Gimnazjum in Pruzany where he taught Polish literature until 1924. He visited the United States for the first time in 1924, staying in Chicago until he returned to Poland later that year.

In 1925, he returned to America to become curate at St. Stanislaus Parish in Detroit. From February 5 to December 10, 1927, he was a curate at SS. Cyril and Methodius Parish, Milwaukee, Wisconsin, after which he served as professor of Polish literature from 1927 to 1931 at **Alliance College**, Cambridge Springs, Pennsylvania. On June 15, 1931, Bolek organized St. Stanislaus Kostka Parish in Sharon, Pennsylvania, where he served until July, 1941. For the first time in the history of Polish parishes, St. Stanislaus Kostka Parish was incorporated as a "Polish Roman Catholic Congregation, Inc." Bolek continued his education at Columbia University (1941–43) in New York, where he earned three master's degrees in philosophy, sociology, and education, as well as a doctorate in philosophy in 1948. Simultaneously, he taught Polish literature during the years 1941–46 at St. Francis College in Athol Springs, New York, and additionally, in 1944-45 served as professor of Polish at Canisius College in Buffalo.

During his priestly ministry in America, Bolek organized eighteen Polish schools and 27 youth clubs involving several thousand Poles. He collected statistical material related to the life of Polonia, published about thirty books, more than twenty pamphlets, and hundreds of articles. His publications include the following books: *Naród i lud w dzielach*

Stanisława Wyspiańskiego (1912); *Parafie polskie w Ameryce. Opisy hisoryczno-statystyczne* (Vol. I, published in 1930 in *Kuryer Polski* in Milwaukee under the pen name the Rev. Józef Janicki); *Towns and Places Founded by Polish Immigrants in the United States* (1931); *Who's Who in Polish America* (1939, 1940, 1943, and 1970 reprint); *Arcybiskup Cieplak i nasza młodziez* (1926); *The Polish American School System* (New York, 1948).

Bolek participated extensively in the life of **Polonia**. He held professional memberships in Polonian and American educational organizations, participated in founding the Congress of American Polonia and the League of Religious Assistance to Poland, was actively involved in developing the **Kosciuszko Foundation**, and was a frequent speaker at the Polish Museum in Chicago. In 1942, Bolek became a co-founder of the Commission for Polish Immigration Research at the **Polish Institute of Arts and Sciences** in New York. At the first congress, his paper, "A Plan for the Polish-American Encyclopedia: The American Pole," was to become a lifetime pursuit. In 1954, Volume I of *The Polish American Encyclopedia* appeared in print. Later, the Commission for Polish Immigration Research was transformed into a professional organization, the **Polish American Historical Association**. He participated annually in PAHA proceedings, presenting interesting and original papers on the history of Polonia and expressing concern about its integration and population in America.

As an educator, Bolek was also closely associated with Columbia University, especially its American Association of Teachers of Slavonic and East European Languages. In

The Rev. Francis Bolek, author and editor of an important early work, *Who's Who* in Polish America (*PMA*).

1945, Dean Arthur E. Christy appointed Bolek editor of the Polish section of the prominent *Index of Comparative Literature*, which was published jointly by The American Library Association, The Association of American Colleges, and The National Council of Teachers of English. When Bolek died in 1958 at the age of 72 he left behind an impressive scholarly legacy. However, his greatness lies in the fact that he was the first to recognize the need to produce a biographical dictionary of Polonia and a Polish American encyclopedia.—*Frank B. Koper*

SOURCES: Francis Bolek, ed., *Who's Who in Polish America* (New York: Harbinger House, 1943); the Rev. Roman Nir, *Catalog of the Archives of Reverend Professor Francis Bolek* (Orchard Lake, MI: The Central Archives of American Polonia in Orchard Lake, 1998), Vol. II.

Bolesławski, Richard (Bolesław Ryszard Srednicki; b. Dębowa Góra, Russian occupied Poland, February 4, 1889; d. Hollywood, California, January 17, 1937). Motion picture director. Bolesławski graduated from the cavalry officer school in Tver and later studied acting at the Moscow Art Theater. During the First World War he saw action in the imperial cavalry, but left Russia for Poland following the Bolshevik Revolution of November 1917. There he took the name Ryszard Bolesławski and directed the semi-documentary motion picture *Cud nad Wisła* (The Miracle on the Vistula) that told the story of General Józef Piłsudski's decisive victory over General Mikhail Tukhachevsky's Bolshevik Red Army in August 1920. After a short stay in Germany as an actor, Bolesławski sailed for the U.S. where he and actress Maria Ouspenskaya organized the American Laboratory Theater in New York. The training program was based on the theories of "method acting" originated in Russia by Konstantin Stanislavsky; one of their students was Lee Strasberg, who with Stella Adler organized the Group Theater in 1931. One of their later students was Marlon Brando. Offered the opportunity to direct motion pictures in Hollywood, Bolesławski enjoyed an impressive, exhausting career as a director that ended with his death a week short of his 48th birthday. Among his twenty films, in which he used many of Hollywood's top stars of the era, were *Rasputin and the Empress* which featured the famed Barrymore trio, Ethel, John and Lionel, in their only film together (1932); *Clive of India* starring Ronald Coleman and Loretta Young); *Les Miserables* with Frederick March and Charles Laughton; and *O'Shaughnessy's Boy* featuring Wallace Beery and Jackie Cooper. All three movies came out in 1935.—*Donald E. Pienkos*

SOURCE: Wojciech Wierzewski, "Sto Trzydzieska Slynnych Polaków w Ameryce" (Unpublished manuscript in the archives of the University of Wisconsin-Milwaukee, 2000).

Bończak, Franciszek (b. Podgórze, Poland, December 1, 1881; d. Elk Grove, Illinois, September 21, 1967). Bishop. Growing up under Austrian rule in partitioned Poland, Bończak received his early education in local schools where he joined the secret nationalist student organization Jedność (Unity). After completing his education he worked on the newspapers *Wieniec* (The Wreath) and *Pszczółka* (The Little Bee), both of which supported the cause of the peasantry. After moving to Vienna to study medicine, he was conscripted into the Austrian army and passed the examination for the rank of second lieutenant. Wishing to avoid active duty, he migrated to the U.S., settling in Chicago in 1902. There he was employed by Bishop **Antoni Kozłowski**, a leader in the **independent** movement, on his weekly newspaper *Reforma* (Reform), soon becoming editor of the publication which changed it name to *Lud* (The People). Bończak soon entered the seminary and was ordained on December 29, 1903. After brief service in Chicago and nearby Hegewisch, Bończak was sent east by Kozłowski to organize unaffiliated independent parishes and presumably encourage the formation of new schismatic parishes. His first stop was at Sts. Peter and Paul Parish in Passaic, NJ. He attended the first synod of the **Polish National Catholic Church** held in 1904 and the subsequent Special Synod in 1906. By 1910, PNCC Bishop **Franciszek Hodur** appointed Bończak as pastor of St. Adalbert's PNCC parish in Priceburg (modern Dickson City), PA. He was elevated quickly to Vicar General of the Central Territory comprising nine parishes in Pennsylvania and Maryland. He supported PNCC affiliation with the International Old Catholic Congress and strongly supported transplanting the PNCC movement to Poland. In addition to his normal duties, Bończak organized and directed choirs and served as vice rector of the **Savonarola Theological Seminary**. In 1914 he moved to Milwaukee with instructions to found a PNCC parish to serve independents in that city and its environs. He was successful in establishing Sts. Peter and Paul Parish and Holy Name of Jesus Parish in South Milwaukee. Remaining active in PNCC administrative matters, Bończak was elected bishop and in 1922 Hodur sent him to spread the church to Poland, an assignment he held for the next five years. Upon his return he served briefly in Detroit, then moved back to Milwaukee and began authoring a series of theological

tracts written in clear language aimed at the broader general audience of laymen. Although he retired in 1954, in 1959 he became embroiled in a controversy when he chose to consecrate the Rev. Bernard Goławski as a bishop against the wishes of Prime Bishop **Leon Grochowski**.—*James S. Pula*

SOURCES: Joseph W. Wieczerzak, "Bishop Francis Bończak: A Biographical Introduction," *PNCC Studies*, Vol. 14 (1993), 21–45; Theodore L. Zawistowski, "Bishop Francis Bończak: At the Point of Return," *PNCC Studies*, Vol. 14 (1993), 47–57.

Bootkoski, Paul Gregory (b. Newark, New Jersey, July 4, 1940; d.—). Bishop. Bootkoski attended Queen of Peace Grammar School in North Arlington (NJ), St. Benedict's Prep in Newark, and Seton Hall University. He studied for the priesthood at Immaculate Conception Seminary, Darlington, NJ, and was ordained by Archbishop Thomas A. Boland on May 28, 1966. After serving at Sacred Heart Church in Bloomfield, Holy Spirit Church in Orange, and St. Michael's in Cranford, all in New Jersey, in 1972 he joined the staff at Seton Hall University where he was named Director of Campus Ministry (1974) and Assistant Vice-President for Student Affairs (1980). In 1983 he became pastor of St. Mary of the Assumption Church in Elizabeth, NJ, moving to St. Gabriel in Saddle River in 1990. The following year Pope John Paul II named him Monsignor, and five years later he became Vicar for Priests in the Archdiocese. In 1991 he was promoted to auxiliary bishop of the Archdiocese of Newark on July 8, 1997, the first Polish American to be elevated to this position. He was consecrated bishop on September 5 of the same year. He was elevated to Bishop of the Metuchen Diocese in March 2002. Bootkoski has been a leader in the movement to address the serious problem of sexual abuse by priests within the Diocese of Metuchen, and within the Catholic Church in the U.S. in general. Among his other reforms, he appointed a lay person to a major leadership position in the diocese, expanded the diocesan review board to include three abuse victims, reviewed the diocesan files to identify possible cases of abuse, and invited local prosecutors to speak to priests about sexual abuse. In June 2003 the Survivors Network of those Abused by Priests (SNAP), the leading national support and advocacy group for victims, named Bootkoski its "model bishop" for his efforts to identify, prosecute, and eliminate clergy who engage in sexual abuse, as well as provide support for their victims.—*James S. Pula*

SOURCE: David O'Reilly, "N.J. Bishop Is a Hero to Survivors of Abuse: Activists Praise Metuchen's Shepherd for Response to Crisis," Philadelphia *Inquirer*, June 29, 2003.

Boryla, Vincent Joseph "Moose" (b. East Chicago, Indiana, March 11, 1927; d.—). Basketball player. Following graduation from East Chicago Washington High School in 1944, Boryla played college basketball for Notre Dame where he earned All-American honors as a freshman, and the University of Denver, earning distinction as an AAU All-American (1946-47 and 1947-48) and was part of the U.S. team that won the gold medal at the 1948 Summer Olympics in London. In 1948-49 he was named outstanding collegian to play in Madison Square Garden by a vote of the Metropolitan Sports Writers Association. Following college, Boryla played for the New York Knicks in the early 1950s, and later became the Knicks' coach, from 1956 to 1958. Later in his career he became general manager of the American Basketball Association's Denver Nuggets early in their history when they were first the Kansas City ABA team and then the Denver Larks. He was also the general manager of the ABA's Utah Stars. Boryla later rejoined the Nuggets when the franchise joined the NBA, winning the NBA Executive of the Year Award in 1984. He was inducted into the Indiana Basketball Hall of Fame (1986) and the National Polish-American Sports Hall of Fame (1984).—*Luis J. Gonzalez*

SOURCES: Karen C. Heisler, *Fighting Irish Legends, Lists and Lore* (Champaign, IL: Sports Publishing, 2006); Indiana Basketball Hall of Fame.

Bratkowski, Zeke (Edmund Raymond Bratkowski; b. Danville, Illinois, October 20, 1931; d.—). Football player. Bratkowski picked up the nickname "Zeke" as a child when he wore a baseball jersey with the name of the Chicago White Sox slugger Zeke Bonura. An All-American quarterback at the University of Georgia in 1952 and 1953, he was twice named the Southeast Conference "Passer of the Year." As a junior in 1952 he led the nation in passing yardage, and as a senior he led the nation in punting average at 42.6 yards per punt. Drafted seventeenth in the NFL draft by the Chicago Bears in 1953, he spent nine seasons with them (1954–60) before being traded to the Los Angeles Rams (1961–63) and then the Green Bay Packers (1963–71) where he became a backup to Bart Starr. He played for the Packers until 1973 when he was traded back to the Chicago Bears. Bratkowski played a total of thirteen years in the NFL passing for more than 10,000 yards. After his playing career, he became an offensive coordinator and quarterback coach for 26 seasons with Chicago, Baltimore, Indianapolis, Philadelphia, and the New York Jets. He was also quarterback coach with the Cleveland Browns, the Jets, the Packers, and the Baltimore Ravens.

Bratkowski was elected to the State of Georgia Sports Hall of Fame in 1980, the Green Bay Packers Hall of Fame in 1989, and the National Polish-American Sports Hall of Fame in 1995.—*Patricia Finnegan*

SOURCE: National Polish American Sports Hall of Fame web site.

Brief, Bunny (Anthony John Grzeszkowski?; b. Remus, Michigan, July 3, 1892; d. Milwaukee, Wisconsin, February 11, 1963). Baseball player. While sources differ regarding his original name, this Michigan native became known as Bunny Brief once he began a professional baseball career. He played for a short time in the major leagues for three different teams between 1912 and 1917, but without notable success. However, he became the first star home run hitter of the minor leagues, duplicating on that level the power game being introduced by Babe Ruth in the majors. A right handed hitting first baseman-outfielder, Brief won eight minor league home run championships, a feat still unsurpassed, and also led his league in runs, runs batted in, hits, and triples in multiple seasons. He enjoyed his greatest fame and accomplishment as a standout in the American Association from 1918 to 1928, playing first with Kansas City, then closing his career in Milwaukee, where he became a favorite of the sizable Polish-American community. Brief retired as the holder of the record for most lifetime minor league home runs with 342, a mark since eclipsed, and still tops the American Association lists for career round trippers with 256. After his playing days ended, he remained in Milwaukee and served as the longtime supervisor of that city's municipal youth baseball program.—*Neal Pease*

SOURCES: "Bunny Brief, Hitting Hero," *American Association Almanac*, Vol. 1, no. 2 (2001); Neal Pease, "Diamonds Out of the Coal Mines: Slavic Americans in Baseball," in L. Baldassaro and R. A. Johnson, eds., *The American Game: Baseball and Ethnicity* (Carbondale: Southern Illinois University, 2002).

Broda, Walter Edward "Turk" (b. Brandon, Manitoba, May 15, 1914; d. Canada, October 17, 1972). Hockey player. Broda began his professional career as a hockey goalie in the International Hockey League with the champion Detroit Olympics in 1934. He was an immediate hit, leading the league in both wins and goals against average, both in the regular season and in the playoffs. He became one of the most sought after goalies and was ultimately sold to the Maple Leafs in 1936 for the then steep price of $7,500. In 1941 he won the Vezina Trophy awarded annually to the National Hockey League's goaltender judged to be the best at this position by the General Managers of each team of the league. In 1942

he led Toronto to a Stanley Cup while being selected as a goaltender to the league All-Star team. From 1943 to 1945, Broda served in the Canadian Army. After returning from the war he rejoined the NHL, later leading Toronto to three more Stanley Cups (1947–49) while winning a second Vezina Trophy and being selected to the NHL All-Star team in 1948. In 1951, he won his last Stanley Cup with Toronto, retiring in 1952. His career statistics included more than 300 wins in an era when seasons were only 48–60 games long, 62 shutouts, and a lifetime goals against average of 2.53. With five Stanley Cup rings, he is regarded as perhaps the best clutch goaltender of all time. His 13 playoff shutouts in 102 games and goals against average 1.98, attest to Turk Broda's indispensable role with the Toronto Maple Leafs dynasty of the 1940s. He was inducted into the Hockey Hall of Fame in 1967 and the National Polish-American Sports Hall of Fame in 2005. In 1998, he was ranked number 60 on *The Hockey News'* list of the 100 Greatest Hockey Players.—*Luis J. Gonzalez*

SOURCES: M. R. Carroll, Andrew Podnieks and Michael Harling, eds., *Concise Encyclopedia of Hockey* (Vancouver, BC: Greystone Books, 2001), 19; Brian McFarlane, *Brian McFarlane's History of Hockey* (Champaign, IL: Sports Pub., 1997); Chris McDonell, *Hockey's Greatest Stars: Legends & Young Lions* (Buffalo, NY: Firefly Books, 2005).

Brodowski, Zbigniew Edmund (b. Poznań, Poland, November 16, 1852; d. Eberswalde, Germany, August 11, 1901). Journalist, diplomat. Born in the Prussian-ruled zone of partitioned Poland, Brodowski was the son of a judge in Poznań. He studied at the Universities of Breslau (Wrocław) and Leipzig (Lipsk) and came to America in 1876 after completing his education. Originally employed as an editor of the *Kuryer Nowoyorski* (New York Courier), he won some notoriety by writing an article condemning what he saw as a shabby history of Poland printed in the *Gazeta Polska* (Polish Gazette) of Chicago. Traveling to California, he worked on the construction of the San Francisco cable car line and there became acquainted with such Polish personalities of the time as the actress **Helena Modjeska** (Modrzejewska), General **Włodzimierz Krzyżanowski** (a civil war veteran, Polish patriot, and member of the **Polish National Alliance**), and the novelist **Henryk Sienkiewicz**. His writing out west won him praise with his stories appearing in both Polish and American newspapers. In 1884 he traveled to Chicago where he first edited the *Gazeta Chicagoska* (The Chicago Gazette), then *Zgoda* (Harmony; 1885–89), the official publication of the Polish National Alliance. As editor of *Zgoda* he gained a rep-

Edmund Zbigniew Brodowski, journalist, editor and diplomat (*PMA*).

utation for energetic polemics aimed at the rival **Polish Roman Catholic Union** and **Resurrectionist Order**, in which he defended the PNA's nationalist ideology. At this time he also wrote a memorandum calling for Poland's independence that was sent to Berlin and Vienna.

As a commissioner of the Chicago Park District in 1890, Brodowski found employment for hundreds of Polish immigrants. In 1895 he was elected president of the PNA. His brief two year tenure in office witnessed construction of the PNA building with its offices, library, and printing house. He resigned in August 1897 to accept the post of U.S. Consul in Breslau, Germany. However, because of his previous writings and speeches on behalf of Polish reunification and independence, the German government refused to accept his appointment. Eventually, Brodowski was reassigned as American consul in Fuerth, Bavaria, and later Solingen in the Rhineland. Brodowski became widely known for his articles in the German press defending American policy during the Spanish-American War. He published his recollections in the Kraków periodical *Czas* and in the Warsaw *Tygodnik Ilustrowany.—Donald E. Pienkos*

SOURCES: Stanisław Osada, *Historia Związku Narodowego Polskiego i rozwój ruchu narodowego Polskiego w Ameryce Północnej* (Chicago: Nakładem i drukiem Związku Narodowego Polskiego, 1905); Donald E. Pienkos, *PNA: A Centennial History of the Polish National Alliance of the United States of North America* (Boulder, CO: East European Monographs, 1984); J. Olbiński, "Edmund Zbigniew Brodowski," *Zgoda*, August 22, 1901, 1; Stanisław Osada, *Historia Związku Narodowego Polskiego* (Chicago: Polish National Alliance, 1957), Vol. 1.

Bronson, Charles (Karolis Bucinskis, Charles Dennis Buchinsky, Charles Buchinski; b. Ehrenfeld, Pennsylvania, November 3, 1921;

d. Los Angeles, California, August 30, 2003). Actor. The eleventh of fifteen children born to a Lithuanian-Polish coal-miner father who died when he was eleven, and mother who died when he was thirteen, he faced a life in the coal mines until 1943 when he was drafted into the United States Army Air Corps. While serving as a tail gunner on a B-29 Superfortress in the Pacific Theater he was wounded, but completed 25 missions over Japan. After the war he went to art school in Philadelphia on the G.I. Bill, then moved to Atlantic City, New Jersey, where he supported himself with menial jobs. He moved to New York to play stock theater along with his roommate, Jack Klugman. In 1949 he moved to California, enrolled at the Pasadena Playhouse, and was "discovered" by director Henry Hathaway, who offered him his first film role in 1951's *You're in the Navy Now.* Three years later, the infamous McCarthy hearings were in full swing, and he decided to change his last name to "Bronson," so his Slavic name would not arouse suspicions. He chose his new name from the Bronson Gate at Paramount Studios on the corner of Bronson Street and Melrose Avenue. Due to his rough hewn features, he was typically typecast as a tough or criminal. Once asked about his appearance, Bronson said, "I guess I look like a rock quarry that someone has dynamited." A critic said he was "a Clark Gable who had been left out in the sun too long." Even so, he received plaudits almost every time he appeared, giving memorable and often gritty performances in such classics as *Machine Gun Kelly, The Dirty Dozen, The Great Escape, The Battle of the Bulge, The Magnificent Seven* and others. He appeared in a television series, *Man with a Camera*, with parts in others such as *The Twi-

Charles Bronson, award-winning actor (*OLS*).

light Zone* and *Have Gun Will Travel.* Amazingly popular in Europe, Bronson did not become a major star in the United States until 1974 when his most popular film *Death Wish* was released. Bronson's last film was *Death Wish V* in 1994. During his career he appeared in over 60 films. Bronson was active in raising funds for the John Wayne Cancer Institute. His honors include a Golden Globe in 1972; a Gold Star Award as the industry's number one international star (1979); and a Star on the Hollywood Walk of Fame.—*Cheryl A. Pula*

SOURCES: Charles Bronson, *Bronson* (London, UK: Blake, 2000); Charles Bronson, *Insanity: My Mad Life* (London, UK: John Blake, 2003); David Downing, *Charles Bronson* (New York: St. Martin's Press, 1983); W. A. Harbinson, *Bronson!* (London, UK: H. W. Allen, 1976); Jerry Vermilye, *The Films of Charles Bronson* (Secaucus, NJ: Citadel Press, 1980).

Brotherhood of Dispersed Solidarity Members (Wspólnota Rozproszonych Członków NSZZ Solidarność). Organized in the fall of 1984 by Solidarity activists Jarosław Chołodecki, Hubert Romanowski, and Wojciech Sukiennik, the main goals of the organization were to help the opposition in Poland and to unite Solidarity refugees living abroad. This organization was affiliated with the international Conference of Solidarity Support Organizations. This loosely-knit group of two dozen people, operating mostly in Chicago, represent the type of political activity undertaken during the 1980s by refugees on behalf of Poland. Brotherhood members were educated professionals — all of them had advanced degrees and worked in professional occupations. All Brotherhood activists were former members of Solidarność or they had been actively involved with the opposition in Poland before relocating to the United States. Several once held prominent positions in Solidarność and had been jailed by the Jaruzelski regime for their political activities. Two Brotherhood members had been on the National Coordinating Commission of Solidarność, and nine members had been chairmen or vice chairmen of regional Solidarność committees. Brotherhood dues were considered union dues and they were assessed by the same standard used for union dues in Poland, one percent of annual income. The money raised was sent to Poland to support regional and local underground opposition publications and centers of activity. Other Brotherhood activities included organizing lectures, demonstrating, and circulating petitions. Brotherhood members also operated through a second group, the Club of Catholic Intellectuals, known as KIK from its Polish name *Klub Inteligentcji Katolickiej.* KIK in Chicago was modeled after KIK in Poland, an organization created in the late 1950s for the purpose of discussing social, economic, and religious issues. In Chicago, Brotherhood leaders and other recent immigrants founded KIK in 1986, to serve as a discussion group and to bring together educated members in Polonia interested in Polish affairs. KIK was composed of roughly 40 recent Polish immigrants. In addition, World War II émigrés regularly attended meetings, and younger Polish Americans were occasionally present. All Brotherhood members were KIK members, but not all KIK members were Brotherhood members. Neither organization was incorporated. Both organizations disbanded shortly after the elections in 1989 ushered in a new economic and political system in Poland. Several members of the Brotherhood moved into consulate positions in the United States including Krzysztof Kasprzyk who later was Consul General of the Polish Consulate in California and then New York, as well as Hubert Romanowski, who in 1990, became the first non communist Consul General of the Chicago consulate since 1939.—*Mary Patrice Erdmans*

SOURCES: Mary Patrice Erdmans, "Recent Political Action on Behalf of Poland: The Interrelationships Among Polonia's Cohorts, 1978–1990," in Helena Znaniecka Lopata, *Polish Americans* (New Brunswick, NJ: Transaction Publishers, 1994), chapter 8; Mary Patrice Erdmans, *Opposite Poles: Immigrants and Ethnics in Polish Chicago, 1976–1990* (University Park, PA: Pennsylvania State Press, 1998).

Browalski, Edmund S. (b. Detroit, Michigan, March 6, 1918; d. Garden City, Michigan, January 3, 1985). Sports journalist. After playing sandlot and professional baseball in his youth, Browalski pursued a lengthy career as a sportswriter and booster of Polish-American athletics in the Detroit area. In 1941, he joined the staff of the *Polish Daily News* of Hamtramck, and eventually became the longtime sports editor of that paper. "Big Ed" Browalski spent many years as official scorer for the Detroit Tigers major league baseball team, and the Detroit chapter of the Baseball Writers Association of America gives an annual award in his name. He also served as president of the Bowling Writers' Association of America. In 1973, Browalski took the lead in the creation of the **National Polish-American Sports Hall of Fame** in **Hamtramck**, and is regarded as the founder of the organization. He was himself inducted into the Hall of Fame in 1983.—*Neal Pease*

SOURCE: "Ed Browalski," National Polish-American Sports Hall of Fame website, www.polish sportshof.com.

Brudzinski, Bob (b. Fremont, Ohio, January 1, 1955; d.—). Football player. Brudzinski played college football at Ohio State University (1973–76) where he starred at defensive end. He was named All-Big Ten in 1975 and 1976, and won All-America honors in the latter year. After being chosen in the first round of the 1977 professional draft, he played for thirteen seasons as a linebacker in the National Football League. He played in three Super Bowls: in 1979, with the Los Angeles Rams, his original team, and in 1982 and 1984 with the Miami Dolphins. Following his retirement from football, Brudzinski became a restaurateur in Florida. He was inducted into the National Polish-American Sports Hall of Fame in 2005.—*Neal Pease*

SOURCE: "Bob Brudzinski," National Polish-American Sports Hall of Fame website, www.polish sportshof.com.

Bruskewitz, Fabian Wendelin (b. Milwaukee, Wisconsin, September 6, 1935; d.—). Catholic bishop. Tracing Polish ancestry through his paternal grandmother, he was educated at St. Lawrence Seminary at Mount Calvary, Wisconsin, and at the Pontifical North American College in Rome. He was ordained a priest in 1960. After brief assignments as assistant pastor in one of Wisconsin's parishes and teaching at St. Francis Seminary, he was transferred to Rome where he worked in the Congregation for Catholic Education for 11 years, obtaining his doctorate in dogmatic theology at the Gregorian University in 1969. In 1980 he was appointed pastor of St. Bernard's Parish in Milwaukee, and in 1992 Pope John Paul II named him bishop of the Diocese of Lincoln, Nebraska, where he has served since.

An activist bishop known for his orthodoxy and fidelity to the Catholic Magisterium, he has taken many initiatives meant to strengthen and deepen the Faith in his diocese. He was responsible for opening two new Catholic schools, two new seminaries, and two new parishes in the diocese situated in a demographically shrinking part of the United States. He was instrumental in keeping the Madonna Rehabilitation Hospital in Lincoln under Catholic sponsorship and in building low-income housing in that city. Under his leadership the Diocese of Lincoln exhibited a marked increase in vocations to the priesthood. He also began a public campaign against organizations such as "Catholics for a Free Choice" or "A Call to Action" whose activities he viewed as contradictory to Catholic teaching. As part of this campaign, he declared that membership in Planned Parenthood, the Hemlock Society, all Masonic organizations, and the Society of St. Pius X (an arch-conservative group of former Catholics) was incompatible with membership in the Catholic Church. He was also a vocal critic of abortion and homosexuality. During the 2004 presidential campaign he declared that he would deny the Eucharist to presidential candidate John Kerry, a Catholic who supported legislation permitting abortion.

Bruskewitz's leadership ability made him a powerful advocate of orthodoxy in the National Conference of Catholic Bishops. In his response to the document "Always Our Children: A Pastoral Message to Parents of Homosexual Children," issued under the auspices of the U.S. Bishops' Conference in 1997, he wrote a paper arguing that the text contradicted the *Catechism of the Catholic Church*. The response was published in the Catholic bimonthly *Inside the Vatican* in 1998 and was widely discussed. Bruskewitz was also the author of *A Shepherd Speaks* (1997), a compendium of Catholic beliefs. In 1999 he was named one of the "Top 100 Catholics of the Twentieth Century" by the *Daily Catholic*. He wrote columns for the *Southern Nebraska Register,* the *Evangelization Station,* and other Catholic periodicals, and was a frequent speaker at Catholic conferences. In 2006 Bishop Bruskewitz's diocese was the only Roman Catholic diocese in the country that declined to participate in the audit of compliance with the non–Catholic Charter for the Protection of Children and Young People. In his refusal to comply Bishop Bruskewitz argued that some members of the Charter were advocates of partial birth abortion, other types of abortion, the cloning of human embryos, and other forms of behavior incompatible with Catholic morality. Under Bishop Bruskewitz, the Diocese of Lincoln recorded no cases of sexual abuse of minors or other types of sexual misconduct by members of the clergy or lay Catholic educational staff.—*Ewa Thompson*

SOURCE: Fabian Bruskewitz, *Bishop Fabian Bruskewitz: A Shepherd Speaks* (Fort Collins, CO: Igantius Press, 1997).

Brzezinski, Emilie Leonia "Mika" (b. New York, New York, May 2, 1967; d.—). Journalist. The daughter of Dr. **Zbigniew Brzeziński**, Mika Brzezinski attended the Madeira High School, a private school for girls in McLean, Virginia. After graduation she attended Georgetown University for two years and graduated from Williams College, a private, residential, top rated liberal arts college in Williamstown, MA, with a degree in English (1989). She served as an intern at Washington's WUSA and WRC and began her career as a journalist at ABC's "World News This Morning" in 1990. In 1991 she moved to Fox affiliate WTIC-TV/WTIC-DT in Hartford Connecticut and in 1992 to CBS affiliate WFSB-TV/WFSB-DT in Hartford where, in 1995, she became a weekday morning anchor. Two years later, in 1997, she became an anchor and correspondent for CBS "Up to the Minute News Page." In 2000 she worked for MSNBC on the "Home Page" show and returned to CBS as a correspondent in 2001. This made her a principal "Ground Zero" reporter for the events of September 11, 2001. At CBS she served as correspondent, substitute, and segment anchor, and contributed frequently to the CBS Sunday Morning news. In 2007 she returned to MSNBC reporting the "Up to the Minute" news Update, then moved to a position as co-host of the MSNBC's "Morning Joe" with Joe Scarborough, a former congressman and onetime Republican lawmaker from Pensacola, as well as anchor of MSNBC Live, and a co-host of a radio program. In 2009 she was under contract with P. Weinstein Book Publishers for a book entitled "Sometimes You Have to Take a Step Back," to be published in the spring, 2010.—*Maria Swiecicka-Ziemianek*

SOURCE: "Mika Brzezinski," *Biography Resource Center Online* (Detroit: Gale, 2009).

Brzeziński, Zbigniew Kazimierz (b. Warsaw, Poland, March 28, 1928; d.—). Political scientist, statesman. The son of a Polish diplomat, Brzeziński spent his early years in Germany during the rise of the Nazis (1931–35), and the Soviet Union during the Stalinist purges (1936–38). The family then moved to Canada where he attended McGill University before moving to the United States to earn his doctorate at Harvard University in 1953. A professor at Harvard, in 1958 he became an American citizen, and a year later left to teach at Columbia University. An advisor to the presidential campaign of John F. Kennedy in

1960, he urged policies of non-aggression in Europe. Throughout his career, Brzeziński supported anti-communist policies from the Cuban Missile Crisis in 1962 to involvement in the Vietnam conflict. Serving presidential administrations from Kennedy through Bill Clinton, he co-founded the Trilateral Commission to strengthen industrial ties between nations of the free world. During Jimmy Carter's presidential bid, Brzeziński served as his primary foreign policy advisor and, after Carter's election, was named National Security Advisor where he came into conflict with Secretary of State Cyrus Vance over Eastern European policy. His many books include *The Permanent Purge: Politics in Soviet Totalitarianism* (1956), *Soviet Bloc: Unity and Conflict* (1967), *Power and Principle: Memoirs of the National Security Advisor, 1977–1981* (1983), *Grand Failure: The Birth and Death of Communism in the Twentieth Century* (1993), *Out of Control: Global Turmoil on the Eve of the 21st Century* (1993), and *America and the World: Conversations on the Future of American Foreign Policy* (2008). Brzeziński is a trustee for the Center for Strategic and International Studies, and has honorary degrees from many colleges and universities. Among his many awards are the Presidential Medal of Freedom, Poland's Order of the White Eagle, the Hubert Humphrey Award for Public Service, the U Thant Award, and the David Rockefeller International Leadership Award.—*Cheryl A. Pula*

SOURCES: Zbigniew Brzezinski, *Power and Principle: Memoirs of the National Security Advisor, 1977–1981* (New York: Farrar, Strauss and Giroux, 1983); Patrick Vaughan, *Brzezinski: A Life on the Grand Chessboard of Power* (New York: Times, 2008).

Budney, Michael Paul (b. Ulatowo-Adamy, Poland, October 3, 1911; d.—). Businessman. Born while his parents were visiting Poland, Budney returned with them to the U.S. when he was six months old. Educated in the public schools in New Britain, CT, he went to work as a machinist at age fifteen. In 1940, together with his siblings, he rented a garage and began manufacturing tool holders under the name Atlantic Machine Tool Works. After three years the business proved successful enough for them to construct their own building in Newington, with their major customer being Pratt and Whitney Aircraft. When it became difficult for the company to fill orders due to the scarcity of fine precision equipment in the 1950s, Budney, as president of the company, purchased a metal casting foundry in Southington to create their own machine tools. Known as the Atlantic Series Jig Bores and the Atlantic Series Grinding and Milling Machines, these inventions were so

Michael Budney produced precision equipment for Pratt & Whitney and other major corporations (*OLS*).

successful that by the early 1960s the U.S. government was sponsoring their worldwide distribution at machine trade shows in Europe and Africa. By the 1960s, Atlantic Machine, as it was commonly known, employed 2,600 skilled engineers, machinists, toolmakers, and inspectors. Over the years, Budney's company provided employment, housing, and transportation for thousands of Polish immigrants. It was, in itself, a microcosmic "Polish community" with in-house Polish-speaking medical staff, housing, and transportation assistance. Atlantic Machine had a "personnel recruiter" working in conjunction with the Polish Immigration Committee of New York who traveled several times each week to New York City to assist Polish immigrants arriving in search of employment, a home, and a future. In addition, Budney personally signed "Affidavits of Support" to guarantee employment and housing to hundreds Poles, permitting them to migrate from Poland and Western Europe to the United States. Between the 1940s and the late 1960s, Budney ventured into other projects ranging from dairy farming to motel construction and management. Draftsmen and engineers from Atlantic Machine assisted in the design and construction of motels in the central Connecticut area and along its shoreline. The first was aptly named Atlantic, which was followed by the Siesta, White Swan, Towne House, and Niantic Motor Lodge. Temporary lodging accommodations for many of Atlantic's workforce were provided at these motels with bus transportation supplied to and from work. The workforce was an integral part of Atlantic's success. Atlantic Machine was sold in 1969 to Ex-Cell-

Dr. Zbigniew Brzeziński, national security advisor to President Carter (*PMA*).

O Corporation, an international manufacturer based in Detroit, Michigan. Budney continued as president for one year and, in 1971, departed the business he founded 28 years earlier. From the original small garage, it had grown to a 350,000-square-foot "small city" that employed thousands. At that time, most of the founding family members chose to retire, but Budney, at age 59, went on to create several other manufacturing businesses. With his son, Hank, and his brother Henry, Budney founded "Berlin Manufacturing," employing a predominantly Polish workforce of about eighty people through the mid–1970s. In 1983, Michael, his daughter and two sons formed "The Budney Company" which grew to employ about 100 Polish-speaking, skilled personnel. In 2008, at age 97, Budney was president and CEO of Budney Industries in Berlin, CT.—*Iwona Korga*

Bukoski, Anthony (b. Superior, Wisconsin, October 18, 1945; d.—). Author, critic, professor. A third generation Polish American, Bukoski was born and raised in a Polish enclave centered on St. Adalbert Roman Catholic Church where he attended the parish grade school. This centering of family life around church, school, and neighborhood is particularly important in Bukoski's case since most of his creative works focus on recovering and preserving the ethnic identity of the time and place of his youth and young adulthood. He graduated from Cathedral High School in Superior and began undergraduate work at Wisconsin State College-Superior. After his freshman year he enlisted in the United States Marine Corps. Upon his discharge in 1967, he returned to his studies, receiving his bachelor's degree at Wisconsin State (1970), his A.M. from Brown University (1973) and his M.F.A. (1976) and Ph.D. (1984) degrees from the University of Iowa. Bukoski taught for one year at Northwestern State University of Louisiana (1985-86), but in 1987 accepted a position on the faculty of the University of Wisconsin-Superior. He has published five short story collections: *Twelve Below Zero* (1986; reprinted 2008), *Children of Strangers* (1993), *Polonaise* (1999), *Time Between Trains* (2003), and *North of the Port* (2008). Virtually all of his short stories study the people of the Polish East End of Superior, and his achievement has been compared to that of Sherwood Anderson and Flannery O'-Connor. His books have been favorably reviewed in numerous publications, including *Booklist* which made *Time Between Trains* an "Editors' Choice" and selected it as one of the best books of 2003. In addition to his books, Bukoski's short stories and essays have ap-

Anthony Bukoski, novelist, critic and professor of English (*Anthony Bukoski*).

peared in various prestigious journals and anthologies from the University of Iowa Press and Columbia University Press in its Eastern European Monograph Series.

Among his many awards, Bukoski has won four Outstanding Achievement Awards from the Wisconsin Library Association and three Anne Powers Book-length Fiction Awards from the Council of Wisconsin Writers. The Robert E. Gard Wisconsin Idea Foundation presented him with its 2005 award "For the excellence with which [the author's] stories celebrate his grass roots, the Polish East End of Superior, Wisconsin, thus bringing that community to life in literature." The **Polish American Historical Association** has twice given him its Creative Arts Award and once awarded him its **Oskar Halecki** Prize. In 2002, he was awarded the first Literary Prize presented by the Polish Institute of Houston "For excellence in presenting the life of American Polish communities in the Midwest." The same year he was named R. V. Cassill Fellow in Fiction by the Christopher Isherwood Foundation. In 1997, Diane Glancy, Paul Gruchow, and Bukoski were featured in the PBS video "A Sense of Place: A Portrait of Three Midwestern Writers." In December 2003, a week of stories from *The Time Between Trains* was broadcast on Wisconsin Public Radio's "Chapter a Day" program. In February 2004, the Actor Liev Schreiber read the title story from *The Time Between Trains* in live performance at Symphony Space in Manhattan as part of the "Selected Shorts: A Celebration of the Short Story" series. Mr. Schreiber's reading was subsequently broadcast on National Public Radio. In 2008 *Booklist* concluded "Bukoski's heart-piercing,

poetic fiction of place and ethnicity makes one wish to be Polish, too, despite the heartbreak."—*Thomas J. Napierkowski*

SOURCES: David Bowen, "The Land of Graves and Crosses: An Interview with Anthony Bukoski," *Main Street Rag*, Vol. 8, No. 3 (Fall 2003), 9–16; Michael Longrie, "Replaying the Past: An Interview with Anthony Bukoski," *Wisconsin Academy Review*, Vol. 42, No. 1 (Winter 1995-96), 29–33; Joel Friederich, "Rooted to Place," *Wisconsin People & Ideas*, Vol. 54, No. 3 (Summer 2008), 14–18.

Bukowczyk, John J. (b. Perth Amboy, New Jersey, June 16, 1950; d.—). Historian. Raised in Perth Amboy, Bukowczyk received his B.A. degree in history and political science from Northwestern University (1972) before earning his M.A. in history from Harvard University (1973) and his doctorate from the same institution (1980). Following graduation, he accepted a position in the history department at Wayne State University in Detroit, Michigan, specializing in American immigration/ethnic history and urban history. His research focuses on the construction, maintenance, and transformation of personal, civic, and ethnic identities; urban and regional economic development; urban ethnic, race, and class relations; and the relationship between group rights and social justice. His work on American Polonia, *And My Children Did Not Know Me: A History of the Polish-Americans* (1987; reprinted in 2008) was recognized with the Oscar Halecki Prize for the best publication on Polish American history and culture from the **Polish American Historical Association**, an organization he later served as president. His later work, *Permeable Border: The Great Lakes Basin as Transnational Region* (2005) was awarded the 2006 Albert B. Corey Prize by the American Historical Association and the Canadian Historical Association for "the best book on Canadian-American relations or on the history of both countries." Bukowczyk's research has also been recognized with the Gold Cross (1st Class) of the Order of Merit of the Republic of Poland (2000), the Detroit 300 Polish Heritage Award from the Detroit 300 Polish American Heritage Committee (2001), and the Polish American Historical Association's Distinguished Service Award (2002).—*Anamika Dasgupta*

SOURCES: "John Bukowczyk," *Dictionary of International Biography* (Cambridge: International Biographical Centre, 1998); *Marquis Who's Who in the Midwest* (New Providence, NJ: Marquis Who's Who, 1997); *The International Authors and Writers Who's Who* (Cambridge: International Biographical Centre, 1993).

Burke, William "Billy" (William Ignatius Burkowski; b. Union City, Connecticut, December 14, 1902; d. Clearwater, Florida, April 19, 1972). Golfer. Burkowski first became involved in golf as a caddie at the Naugatuck Golf Club in Connecticut. For many years,

American golf was largely considered the domain of the wealthy, and it was unusual for the son of a working class Polish immigrant to take up the sport, much less excel at it. The story goes that Burkowski became a caddie to earn some money when he was fifteen. He eventually started playing the game himself, but could not afford clubs or a bag, so some members gave him clubs and he carried them in his hands. He kept playing despite losing the ring finger and severely injuring the little finger on his left hand while working in a steel mill. At age sixteen, "The Boy Marvel" won the Naugatuck club championship in a driving rainstorm. Supporters bought him a golf bag so he could play in the state amateur, which he lost on the final hole. The following year, 1923, he went on to win the state amateur. That victory led to Burkowski, who anglicized his name to Burke, getting a job as a golf pro at the Mattatuck Golf Course in Waterbury CT.

In 1931 Burke went to the U.S. Open at the Inverness Club in Toledo. He trailed the leader, George Von Elm of California, by two strokes at the start of the 36-hole final round on Sunday, July 4. At the end of regular play, Burke and Von Elm were tied. On the following day they played a 36-hole playoff to decide the title, and ended the day still tied. On Tuesday they launched another 36-hole playoff, but this time Burke ended up winning by a single stroke. After 144 holes and 589 stokes, Billy Burke was the U.S. Open champion. Burke's victory was particularly significant not only because he used steel-shafted clubs, but also because the lengthy playoff caused a change in all future playoff formats. Although the Open win was the high point, Burke enjoyed a fine career. He won ten career tournaments, and finished third at the Masters twice. Burke played in 159 career PGA Tour tournaments, finishing in the top ten an amazing eighty times. He was also considered one of the finest Ryder Cup team members of his era, going undefeated in the 1931 and 1933 Ryder Cups. Burke was inducted into the PGA Hall of Fame in 1966. — *Thomas Tarapacki*

SOURCE: *Time*, July 13, 1931.

Burton, Sala Galante (Sala Galante; b. Białystok, Poland, April 1, 1925; d. Washington, D.C., February 1, 1987). Congresswoman. The wife and widow of Phillip Burton, a liberal Democratic Representative from California whom she had met in 1950 at a California Young Democrats convention and subsequently married in 1953, Sala Burton was born into a Jewish family, left Poland in 1939, and attended public schools in San Francisco and San Francisco University. She was multilingual, speaking English, Polish, German, Yiddish, French, and Russian. Burton served as associate director of the California Public Affairs Institute (1948–50), vice president of the California Democratic Council (1951–54), which she had helped organize, president of the San Francisco Democratic Women's Forum (1957–59), and delegate to the Democratic National Conventions in 1956, 1976, 1980, and 1984. She was president of the Democratic Wives of the House and Senate from 1972 through 1974 and legislative chair of the Women's National Democratic Club and its liaison to the House. Burton was also a member of the Advisory Board of the National Council on Soviet Jewry and a lobbyist for the Equal Rights Amendment. She was initially her husband's "silent partner," counseling him on political issues such as opposition to the Reagan administration's foreign and environmental policies. Burton was subsequently elected as a Democrat to the Ninety-eighth Congress representing the Fifth District. This was through a special election to fill the vacancy caused by the death of her husband on April 10, 1983. She garnered 55 percent of the vote, thereby avoiding a runoff by winning an outright majority of votes cast. Burton was the host House member for the 1984 Democratic National Convention in San Francisco and was reelected to the two succeeding Congresses, serving on the Education and Labor and the Rules Committees. Because of her cancer treatments, Burton had already announced that she would not run for re-election in 1988 and instead endorsed former California Democratic Party chair Nancy Pelosi in her first run for public office. The special election to replace Sala Burton ushered in Pelosi who in January 2007 became the first female Speaker of the House. — *Frederick J. Augustyn*

SOURCE: "Sala Galante Burton," *Women in Congress, 1917–2006* (Washington: Government Printing Office, 2006).

Burzyński, Stanisław Rajmund (b. Lublin, Poland, January 23, 1943; d.—). Physician, scientist. After receiving his medical degree with distinction in 1967 and doctorate in biochemistry in 1968 from the Medical Academy (Akademia Medyczna) in Lublin, he completed his internship and residency in internal medicine at the Lublin Medical Academy and emigrated to the United States to work as a research associate at Baylor College of Medicine, Houston, Texas (1970–72), and as assistant professor (1972–77). At Baylor, he pursued research initiated in Poland, discovering that cancer patients have fewer peptides in their blood and hypothesizing that certain peptides play a role in reprogramming cancer cells, a finding that may have therapeutic value. Several purified peptides, which Burzyński termed antineoplastons, appeared to have antineoplastic (anti-cancer) potential. In 1977 he left Baylor to open a private practice in nearby Stafford, Texas, where he began manufacturing and administering antineoplastons to cancer patients, ultimately establishing the Burzynski Clinic and Burzynski Research Institute. In 1983, the Federal Food and Drug Administration filed a civil suit in Federal Court against Burzyński for violations of the Food, Drug and Cosmetics Act. After years of state and federal legal proceedings, he was acquitted of all charges in 1997. Based on encouraging preliminary data, in 1993 the National Cancer Institute initiated clinical trials to assess antineoplaston therapy. The studies were conducted by the Mayo Clinic, Memorial Sloan Kettering Cancer Center, and the Warren G. Magnuson Clinical Center at the National Institutes of Health, but in 1995 the studies were closed amidst controversy with no definitive results. With "treatment IND" (Investigational New Drug) permits from the Federal Food and Drug Administration, Burzyński offers antineoplaston treatments to patients who previously received conventional treatment, or who have conditions that are unlikely to respond to existing treatment or for which no treatment exists. Thousands of such patients have been treated, with reports of tumor regression and cure. While Burzyński has published numerous articles in peer-reviewed scientific journals, he is widely criticized for failure to perform a well-designed, appropriately monitored and controlled clinical trial to convincingly establish the efficacy and toxicity of antineoplastons. He also has published hypotheses regarding genetic control of aging and markets a number of products purported to possess anti-aging effects. He holds several patents related to treatments for autoimmune diseases, neuro-fibromatosis, AIDS, and cancer. Burzyński received national attention when, periodically, individuals with cancer took legal action to be treated with antineoplastons rather than conventional therapy, or fought insurance companies to pay for the treatments (participation in clinical trials is generally not covered by insurance). Media coverage of these cases, protests, lobbying efforts, hearings and bills in Congress, and the establishment of the National Center for Complementary and Alternative Medicine, reflect heightened public interest in patients' rights to choose treatment, the government's role in approving treatment, and alternatives to conventional medical care. Burzyński has many supporters, has received awards for his work (including the Polish Cross of Merit), and participates in national and international medical and scientific conferences. He is a member of the American Medical Association (AMA), American Association for the Advancement of Science (AAAS), American Association for Cancer Research (AACR), Society for Neuroscience, Society for Neuro-Oncology, Texas Medical Society, Harris County Medical Society (HCMS), the Polish National Alliance, and Sigma Xi.—*Christina Miller*

SOURCE: Bolesław Wierzbiański, *Who's Who in Polish America* (New York: Bicentennial Publishing Corp., 1996), 54.

Call Northside 777. Had it not been for a phone that did not ring, the first major Hollywood film to focus on Polish America might never have happened. While awaiting that phone call, *Chicago Times* reporter Terry Colangelo passed the time by reading the next day's October 10, 1944, issue of the *Times*. A notice in the classified section caught her eye: "$5,000 Reward for Killers of Officer Lundy on December 9, 1932. Call GRO 1758, 12–7 PM." Sensing a story behind that ad, Colangelo circled it and placed it on editor Karin Walsh's desk (called Brian Kelly in the film). Walsh then sent reporter James P. McGuire, a former private-eye, to find out who placed the ad and why. What emerged from that inquiry is a poignant story of a Polish immigrant mother's sacrifice, founded on her faith that justice would eventually prevail. "Every Biting Word.... Every Sensational Scene Is True!" proclaimed *Call Northside 777*'s print ad upon its release in February 1948, but that was not entirely so. Several scenes — including the film's title — were fictionalized, and some key events in the actual story were overlooked.

Patrolman William D. Lundy was slain on December 9, 1932, in the rear of a delicatessen, located in south-side Chicago's Back-of-the-Yards neighborhood. Prohibition was still the law of the land, but both Lundy and coal-driver John Zagata (renamed Bundy and Jan Gruska respectively in *CN777*) knew that deli-owner Vera Walush (the film's Wanda Skutnik) conducted that era's typical backroom sideline. After filling Vera's shed, the Polish American coal-man bought a drink for himself and Lundy. Zagata then saw two men enter, announcing a hold-up. Seven bullets entered Lundy's body as he grappled with them. The gunmen fled. Joe Majczek (*CN777*'s Frank Wiecek, played by Richard Conte) and Ted Marcinkiewicz (the movie's Tomek Zaleska) were convicted of that murder on November 10, 1933, based solely on Walush's testimony. Their punishment was 99 years in

prison, instead of the death sentence normally imposed on cop-killers.

Times man McGuire (played by Jimmy Stewart) traveled to the neat-as-a-pin, Back-of-the-Yards home of Tillie Majczek. Short and wiry, she explained in heavily-accented English why she had placed that ad. "Sit," she told Mcguire. "Joe don't kill nobody." To prove that, Tillie saved $5,000 over the course of eleven years by scrubbing floors in a downtown Chicago office building. She presented McGuire with a thirty-page history of her son's case, which Joe had compiled in prison. The major revelation in Joe's typewritten account was that Judge Charles P. Molthrop, who presided over the case, had promised him a retrial. Verifying that claim was impossible since Molthrop had died in 1935. However, McGuire was easily able to track down John Zagata, the only eyewitness to the murder besides Walush. Zagata had testified at the trial that he could not identify Lundy's slayers, who were much taller than Joe and Ted.

Zagata surprised the reporter by assailing Walush's testimony. He was adamant about Walush's inability to get a clear look at the killers. He also recalled that the judge assured Joe a new trial. William Fitzgerald, the judge's bailiff, would further tell the *Times* that Molthrop had accused Walush of perjury in his chambers. McGuire interviewed Majczek's ex-wife, Helen, who divorced Joe with his consent about 1939. Legally unable to testify at the trial, Helen insisted Joe was at home with her at the time of the murder. In his review of the trial transcript, McGuire found that six witnesses testified Ted was elsewhere at the time of the Lundy shooting. Stewart's character, Jim McNeal, was a composite of the two *Times* reporters who actually covered the case: McGuire, who did the digging, and veteran journalist John McPhaul, who digested McGuire's findings. Little did the pair realize they would wind up writing a multiple-award-winning series of thirty articles over the course of ten months. The series began October 11, 1944.

Combing through old police files unearthed long-hidden facts. McGuire found Walush's initial statement to the police, never presented at the trial, in which she was asked if she could describe the killers: "No, I was so scared that I ran away before I could look at them." Joe's original arrest record also indicated that he was held 34 hours before being booked. That unusually long time supported Majczek's contention that Walush had difficulty identifying him. Affidavits which the *Times* obtained from Walush's friend, Bessie Barron, and Judge Molthrop's son, David, corroborated

Majczek's claim of innocence. Persistent sleuthing on McGuire's part revealed that the state's attorney had threatened Molthrop with the end of his career had he pursued a second trial.

It was the prevailing political climate in late 1932 that tipped the scales of justice against Joe: Chicago was about to sponsor the Century of Progress World's Fair in 1933. There were six unsolved murders in the week of Lundy's murder alone. Calling crime an obstacle to the fair's success, businessmen demanded action from city hall. Further dooming Majczek was the inept manner in which his often inebriated trial attorney, William W. O'Brien, represented him. O'Brien, who was later disbarred, refused to let Joe testify. He also failed to thoroughly question prosecution witnesses. O'Brien's appeal of the verdict to the Illinois Supreme Court was equally slipshod. That court upheld the verdicts on April 17, 1935.

Tillie Majczek uncannily knew her son had passed "with flying colors" a polygraph test McGuire/McPhaul had arranged in early December 1944. In late March 1945, a pardon board hearing was arranged. Attorney Walker Butler represented Joe. Despite knowing the Chicago police and state's attorney would vigorously oppose a pardon, and that, moreover, she was gambling with Joe's chances for parole, Tillie was unmoved, maintaining: "Joe did not kill the policeman. The board will find that out." The undaunted mother's lonely struggle for justice ended when officials of major Polish American organizations rallied to Joe's defense — a chain of events that *CN777* ignores. Passing resolutions asking the governor to grant Joe a fair hearing were the Polish Welfare Association (now known as the Polish American Association), the **Polish Roman Catholic Union**, Polish Alma Mater (later merged with the **Polish National Alliance**), and various Polish American organizations on the city's southeast side. The pardon board convened on April 10, 1945.

Normal procedure dictated that a decision would be reached within six weeks after the hearing. Yet more than four months passed by in silence — contrary to how the hearing played out in the movie. Then, suddenly, on August 15, 1945, Joe Majczek walked out of Joliet's Stateville Prison a free man. In his hands was a certificate of a full pardon signed by then Gov. Dwight Green. McGuire had every hope of a headline upon Joe's release, but the end of World War II that same day understandably thwarted his wish. Absent from *CN777* was the backdrop of that war, during which both Tillie and the *Times* had received scores of letters of support from members of the armed services. Shortly after his release, Joe Majczek said he harbored no grudge against society for his unjust confinement. While incarcerated, he took a college correspondence course and became a model clerk in the prison infirmary.

Old-fashioned gumshoe work, not the film's fictitious blow-up of a date on a newspaper is what freed Joe Majczek (Marcinkiewicz would be exonerated in 1950). *CN777* neither won, nor was nominated for, any Academy Awards, though noted movie critic James Agee felt its soundtrack deserved a special Oscar. Seasoned stage-actress Kasia Orzazewska, who played the role of Tillie Wiecek, had previously appeared on Broadway four times. She began her stage career at age fifteen, playing in Polish-language stock companies across various American cities. Both her performance and the movie were uniformly praised by film critics, except for the film's weak ending.

For rectifying a miscarriage of justice, the *Chicago Times* and its reporters were honored with journalism's top awards from the Sigma Delta Chi Fraternity, National Headliners Club and the American Newspaper Guild. The *Times* refused Tillie's reward, and Lundy's murder remains unsolved. The precedent set by the Majczek-Marckinkiewicz conviction is reflected in the entire first chapter of Judge Jerome Frank and Barbara Frank's *Not Guilty* (1957), a critique of the U.S. criminal justice system. The case has also been cited in legal journals up to the fairly recent present: the *Stanford Law Review* (November 1987) and *Tennessee Law Review* (Summer 1989). It also appears on Northwestern University's Center on Wrongful Convictions website.—*Leonard Kurdek*

SOURCES: Jerome Frank and Barbara Frank, *Not Guilty* (Garden City, NY: Doubleday and Company, Inc., 1957); The People of the State of Illinois, Defendant in Error, *vs.* Joseph Majczek *et al.* Plaintiffs in Error, in 360 *Ill.* 261 (1935), 261–268 (Illinois Supreme Court Ruling in the Majczek Case); series on Tillie and Joe Majczek in the *Chicago Daily Times*, October 11-December 8, 1944, March 26-April 11, 1945, and August 15-August 19, 1945 (articles from 1944 generally begin on page 3 or 4; articles from 1945 in general begin page 5 or 6).

Canada, Poles in. One would wonder whether the historical development of Polonia north of the 49th parallel would be significantly different from their ethnic compatriots south of the Canadian border, especially since they inhabit one continent with predominantly Protestant attitudes and values, similar migration patterns, and even more importantly, a Polish migration that tended to be drawn from the same regions, levels of education and socio-economic backgrounds.

Nevertheless, the differences between the two groups outweigh the similarities. In the 1930s, the Polish Vice-Consul to Canada, Roman Mazurkiewicz wrote *Polskie Wychodztwo i Osadnictwo w kanadzie* (Polish Emigration and Settlement in Canada), commenting on the differences between Poles in Canada and America, with the latter lending themselves to a faster assimilation. According to his assessment, by the mid–1930s, Poles in America were referring to themselves as "Americans of Polish heritage." This form of self-identification was not used by Poles in Canada, who still referred to themselves as "Poles in Canada." Such a statement does not indicate that Polish Americans lacked a sense of Polishness, but it does denote a different evolution of the Poles living to the north, in particular, when it came to the establishment of Polish organizations (both secular and religious), financial institutions, class mobility, founding of Polish neighborhoods, attitudes towards their homeland and their self-identity.

Chronologically, Polish chain migration to Canada can be divided into five distinct phases: (a) late nineteenth century (1850s-1880s); (b) pre–World War I (1890s-1914); (c) interwar (1919–1939); (d) post–World War II (1940s-1970s); and (e) post–Solidarity (1980s-1993). Four critical issues informed their journey to Canada: reasons for migration (economic vs. political); length of migration (temporary vs. permanent); socio-economic standing of incoming group; and place of settlement (rural vs. urban). Determining the number of Polish migrants prior to the establishment of the Polish state is a difficult and complex process. In the late nineteenth and early twentieth centuries, Canadian immigration officials were not concerned with recording the ethnic identity of incoming migrants, attributing national identity to place of originating residence or birth. Hence, Poles were recorded as Prussians, Austrians or Russians. At times, even the name of a region was listed as a national identity, such as in the case of "Galicians" (see **Galicia**). Oftentimes, communication between immigrant and host country was problematic, with the entrant unable to express his or her nationality in English. This problem was further compounded by a lack of national awareness amongst the earlier migrants, and a non-existent Polish bureaucracy to record those leaving its borders and advocate on behalf of its citizens.

The arrival of Polish immigrants to Canada can be traced to the mid–eighteenth century. Though deserving mention, the migration before the mid–nineteenth century consisted of only a few individuals who left Poland amidst

the partitioning process and in its aftermath (especially following the uprisings in the early 1830s and later 1840s). These individuals tended to be highly educated and from the upper classes (gentry). They quickly assimilated into Canadian society participating in the development of the colony. Individuals such as Capitan Karol Blaszkowicz (Blaskowitz), for example, who came in 1759, joined General Wolfe's army during the last phases of the Franco-English battle at Québec City and Montréal. Dominik Barcz from Gdańsk settled in Lower Canada in the mid–1700s, published two newspapers, and sat on the Legislative Council. Physician and surgeon August Glabiński (Globenski) and his sons became high-ranking officers in the Canadian militia involved in the War of 1812 and the Rebellion of 1837-38. One of the best known pioneers, **Kazimierz Gzowski**, arrived in 1841. A professional engineer by trade, he was responsible for building seven bridges (in particular, the bridge linking Fort Erie with Buffalo), ports, railways, Yonge Street in Toronto, and several other civil engineering projects. Not only was he a colonel in the militia, he also became Deputy Lieutenant Governor of Ontario and was Knighted by Queen Victoria.

The first significant group of migrants — though small in numbers — came from the Prussian partition and settled in the Renfrew area of Eastern Ontario during the mid–1850s. The Kaszubs (see **Kashub**), who eventually numbered approximately 500 families, were drawn to this region for its free land and visual similarity to the terrain they had left behind in Poland. Thereafter, other clusters of Poles spread throughout Ontario and Québec (Berlin, Montréal, Toronto, Hamilton, Sudbury); Winnipeg, Manitoba; Vancouver, British Columbia; and Sydney, Nova Scotia. During this period — and given the obscurity of accurate statistics — the Polish group comprised approximately 2,500 and 3,500. Prior to the First World War, one has to examine the Census information provided for 1901, 1911, and 1921 to reach an estimate of Poles in Canada. Accordingly, 6,255, 33,652, and 53,403 Poles respectively were self-identified as living in Canada. However, between 1896 and 1919, another estimate indicates that roughly 115,000 migrants of Polish origin settled in Canada, with a peak reached in 1907.

The interwar period faces its own challenges as ethnic Ukrainians, Byelorussians and Jews were included with Poles when recorded by Canadian authorities. Furthermore, upon entering the country as Poles, some of these minorities went on to re-identify themselves with their appropriate ethnicity. According to Canadian figures, "Polish" migration during the period from 1918 to 1939 was estimated as ranging from 147,348 to 153,291. Fortunately, these figures can be compared with those of the Polish government and a more accurate picture arises. Based on Polish sources, between 1920 and 1939, approximately 136,558 to 143,543 (150,196 for 1918 to 1939) Polish immigrants made their way to Canada, the second largest overseas group following that of the United States and ahead of Argentina. By 1928, over forty percent of the trans-Atlantic Polish migration was directed toward Canada. Within this group, an estimated 40.4 percent were Ukrainians, fourteen percent were Jews and 7.4 percent were Byelorussians. Most interwar migrants originated from the poorest areas of reconstituted Poland, mainly Galicia and the Eastern Borderlands.

The post–World War II period saw 113,310 people of Polish origin arriving between 1946 and 1959, with most coming during the first decade after war's end. The 1951 Canadian Census indicates the Polish population to be 219,845. The following two decades saw a decrease in the number of migrating Poles, falling to 34,854. These numbers rose slightly during the 1980s to 48,950 emigrants. Census statistics point to 323,517 Poles in 1961 and 316,430 in 1971. During the post–Communist period (1989–93), migration to Canada rose to its third highest level since the pre–World War I period to 67,157. In the 2001 census, 260,415 Canadians identified themselves as ethnically Polish, while 556,665 claimed some degree of Polish heritage (multiple identities). The fluctuating figures of migrating Poles speak to two central influences behind these movements — push and pull factors: the types of conditions found in Poland along with the economic and political factors, such as immigration policy, that drew Poles to Canada. Prior to the Second World War, migration was fueled by poor economic conditions in Poland. In some instances, ethnic or political persecution also played a role. In the case of the Kaszubs, for example, economic conditions were exacerbated by Otto von Bismarck's **Kulturkampf** policy, which encouraged the Germanization of the Polish population. Consequently, Kaszubs migrated with entire families for the intended purpose of permanent settlement.

The second phase of migration tended to come from the Russian and Austrian sectors of Poland. A booming population in Russian Poland, along with a lack of access to land — centered in the hands of large landowners — resulted in mass poverty. The situation was similar in Austrian Poland, the most industrially under-developed partitioned region, where small family plots of land, continuously subdivided amongst progeny, led to meager subsistence living. Both groups of Polish immigrants tended to be peasants or farmers; they were illiterate, uneducated and had little or no sense of national identity. In these cases, a sense of Polish national identity was developed post migration, with the latter group composed of single men drawn to Canada by its opportunities and following a pattern of chain migration with no particular interest in permanent settlement. This male dominated group engaged in physically intensive labor such as mining, lumbering, railroad construction and/or commercial agriculture, and was inclined to "settle" in the western parts of Canada: Manitoba, Saskatchewan and Alberta.

The interwar migrants were somewhat different than their predecessors. By 1918, Poland reappeared as an independent republic. Yet, delayed agrarian reforms along with slow industrialization, created a situation whereby even in the 1930s, three quarters of Poland's population still lived in villages and 64 percent of its population was employed in agriculture. These factors led to a post-war population boom which was exacerbated by repatriation and decreasing land holdings, resulting in a surplus labor force that could not be absorbed. Polish emigration and repatriation policies underwent a change in response to this economic situation: closing the doors to those trying to return to Poland and easing the bureaucracy for those wanting to leave. Moreover, it was hoped that this migrating workforce would help to jump-start the economy with an influx of remittances being sent back to family. Most migrants from this period were men, who had a developed sense of national identity, a basic (elementary) level of education, and experience in organizing and/or participating in organization life. Yet they were not interested in permanent settlement. Their primary goal was to earn enough income to pay off debts and/or to purchase (larger) tracts of land back home. They came to western Canada to work primarily on farms and supplemented their income in the off-season by taking up employment in mining, lumbering and railway building. Nevertheless, a shift from rural to urban migration took place during this period, which was further stimulated by the Great Depression. From this point onward, Polish migrants would head to cities and not farms when coming to Canada. The economic downturn also transformed temporary migrants into permanent settlers, with women (and children) traveling across the ocean to meet their husbands in Canada.

The migration following the Second World War consisted of exiled individuals who were well-educated in professional and technical fields, such as engineering. Many were former military serving in the Polish Armed forces and were now considered displaced persons with no desire to return to a Communist country. Their migration was political in nature with many perceiving themselves as political exiles. The largest number of Polish immigrants had come by 1952. Throughout the late 1950s and 1960s, an increasing number of migrating women resulted in a more balanced sex ratio. A similar pattern characterized the post–Solidarity migratory phase. During the 1960s and 1970s, most came as either "landed immigrants" sponsored by families or charitable organizations or by claiming refugee status. Some were able to continue employment in their fields of training, but others had to take on menial, low-paying jobs. The post–Solidarity period commenced with the enactment of Martial Law in Poland in December of 1981. Primarily emigrating from cities and towns, these migrating families came to Canada mostly as (sponsored) refugees intent on permanent settlement and searching for economic betterment. Highly qualified and educated, the majority settled in urban centers of Ontario.

The spike of Polish immigrants experienced during the second migratory phase (1890s to 1914) coincided with changes to Canada's immigration policy, which was driven by economics and a desire to increase the population in the western provinces. In 1896, Clifford Sifton became the Minister of the Interior in charge of immigration. Under his tenure, and with decreasing migration from Britain, Canada opened its doors to "stalwart peasant[s] in ... sheep-skin coat[s]" from Central and Eastern Europe, who were expected to settle new land in western Canada and strengthen the new nation against America's Manifest Destiny. The Canadian government enticed newcomers with loans and grants of large tracts of land for settlement. This boom in immigration came also with a thriving economy that required workers. A similar economic situation occurred in the 1920s, resulting in more Central and Eastern European emigrants making their way to Canada. The increasing numbers of Polish migrants during the interwar period resulted from a shift in American immigration policy that effectively closed its borders to Poles. This time around, the Canadian government turned to the Canadian National Railway and the Canadian Pacific Railway to promote immigration to Canada. Under the Railway Agreement, nearly 200,000 Central and Eastern Europeans were brought to Manitoba, Saskatchewan and Alberta.

The Great Depression of the 1930s and the war years effectively closed the door to immigrants who could no longer meet the (rising) financial requirement, which had now risen to $1,000 per Polish family (and was much higher for other "non-desirables," such as Jews). During these years, Canada had not developed a real refugee policy that would respond to broad international principles. This would change in the post-war period when under the International Refugee Organization, Canada would accept displaced persons. Additionally, family reunification under the sponsorship system greatly benefited European immigrants. Only in the 1950s were changes made to Canada's immigration policy whereby greater emphasis was placed on occupation and education of immigrants as opposed to their ethnic backgrounds or family connections. Restrictions placed on an immigrant, such as working in a specific field and living in a certain region, were now lifted. The focus on economic growth aligned with immigration policy, producing a shift from unskilled labor to skilled (post-industrial model) labor. There was also a successful push for greater openness to immigrants and refugees, differing from the movement that emphasized occupational selectiveness, resulting in a stronger commitment to cultural pluralism (multiculturalism) by the Canadian government in the 1970s and 1980s. These changes to Canadian immigration policy affected the type of immigrant arriving in Canada, from one toiling on land to a highly-educated generation of professionals who saw Canada as their adopted homeland.

The development of the Polish community also reflected these broad transformations. The evolution of the Polish community can be relegated to two main external factors: the type of migration—permanent or temporary, and Canadian attitudes towards migrants. Throughout the nineteenth and early twentieth centuries and in spite of the Canadian government's weariness towards the assimilatory capabilities of "foreigners"—fearing a decline in the country's social and moral order, and a dilution of cultural values—the government did not officiate over a program of assimilation. Instead, migrating ethnic groups were chosen for their "assimilatory abilities," which would quickly permit them to become successful and productive Canadian citizens. Nevertheless, the expansive nature of the country, its few urban centers (especially in the West) and coping with a significant French minority (driven to preserve and maintain its own language and culture) made rapid assimilation challenging. The French-Canadian model of cultural preservation served as a prototype to be emulated by immigrants. Moreover, a migration predominantly temporary in nature gave way to slower establishment of secular and financial organizations and newspapers.

Initially, the formation of Polish community commenced with and evolved around a church, considered the center of religious and community life. This was followed by the establishment of church-based organizations that served the cultural and financial needs of the community. Once enough organizational experience had been gained, and as with each new migratory wave, community life expanded to include lay organizations. Some of these retained remnants of religious ideals while others rejected them altogether. In the interwar period, a movement attempting to consolidate smaller organizations into larger federations became the answer to strengthening the various Polish settlements and organizations. Importance was still placed on maintaining ties with the homeland, with a slight exception of the Związek Polaków w Kanadzie (Polish Friendly Alliance of Canada), which became more interested in Polish-Canadian interests as opposed to Polish state interests. In the post–World War II period, secular organizations that responded to different class needs multiplied. The establishment of professional organizations was the most noticeable reflection of that trend. The 1940s and 1950s also witnessed the first large scale organizational efforts that were directed at "Polish-Canadian" interests, emphasizing a shift away from ties with the motherland to the importance and permanence of the Polish community within mainstream Canadian society. This trend would continue into the 1980s and 1990s.

The formation of Polish institutions was primarily driven by a need to preserve Polish language, culture and history. Originally, as migrations were to be temporary, the onus fell on maintaining one's religious faith with less worry being placed on loss of language and culture. After all, it was thought that language and culture could not be lost within a year or two. With an increase in the permanence of migratory groups, especially in the interwar years, Polish institutions became a means against losing Polish identity, which now became identified with knowledge of language, culture and history. The Catholic Church became the first step in preserving a sense of Polishness.

Since the church had played a central role within the Polish village, during the first three waves of migration, this was the first type of institution to be established by Poles, especially in rural areas. Under some circumstances, urban areas tended to first experience small lay organizations of a self-improvement variety, which made the establishment of a church a part of their constitutional goals. In most cases, the lack of English or French made it difficult for Poles to engage in existing church services. This, coupled with a desire to recreate community life left behind in the old country, led Poles to petition their respective Archdioceses for Polish-speaking clergy. This was followed by the establishment of church-building committees, which began the process of developing ethnic parishes. Generally speaking, bishops responded positively to such requests by obtaining the services of Polish-speaking missionaries or visiting clergy, and by aiding with financial and moral support for such emerging parishes.

While other forms of organized associations were created at a slow pace, churches were always a primary concern. In Ontario, the Poles of Berlin (Kitchener) established a mission church in 1862, the year of their arrival, and by the 1870s were served by the Resurrectionists. They shared the church with Germans and only in 1912 formed a separate Polish parish. Similarly, the Kaszubs made use of a local Irish parish until they received regular visitations from Polish clergy. In 1870 they established their first chapel (St. Stanislaus Kostka) in Wilno under the initiative of the Rev. Józef Specht; this was followed by a church in 1895 — Mary Queen of Poland. Another St. Stanislaus Kostka church was built in Copper Cliff (near Sudbury) in 1898 under the direction of two Polish Jesuits, but by 1901 there were no Polish priests serving this church until the Rev. D.P. Biernacki visited from Barry's Bay starting in 1911. Even though Poles referred to it as a Polish church, the parish served Italians, French Canadians, Irish, and Ukrainian Greek Catholics. Toronto saw a growth of two parishes within a span of a decade: St. Stanislaus Kostka parish was established in 1911 with the help of philanthropist Eugene O'Keefe and served by the Rev. Joseph Hinzmann. Four years later, another Polish parish, St. Mary's, was founded under the initiative of the Rev. Marian Wachowiak, who formed the building fund for the construction of the church that served the needs of approximately 250 Polish families.

The Polish community in Québec was concentrated in Montréal. Two parishes were founded: Our Lady Queen of Poland (1907) and Holy Trinity (1933), which had begun as a mission in 1916. Before the 1920s, the hub of Polish migration centered in Western Canada (with the largest centre in Winnipeg) was in need of Polish priests. Archbishop of St. Boniface, Adelard Langevin, attempted to obtain a Polish priest to serve the community under the urging of a Polish church building committee formed in Winnipeg in 1897. Two Oblates of Mary Immaculate and brothers, Jan and Wojciech Kulawy, were invited; the former becoming a missionary to Slavs and Germans in the West, and the latter directing the building of the Winnipeg parish of Holy Ghost (1899). In early twentieth century, Polish parishes were also founded in Saskatchewan: Candiac (1908), Regina (1912); and in Alberta: Coleman (1904), Roundhill (1905), Edmonton (1913). The rise of Polish communities and their demand for clergy always outweighed the supply of available priests. In 1929, there were only 42 priests (of whom twenty served in cities) for 33 parishes and 157 missions; in 1938 the number of priests rose to 75, while the number of parishes nearly doubled to 62 (and 120 missions). It was only with the arrival of the Oblates of Mary Immaculate and in particular, their expansion into Eastern Canada in the 1930s that a stable flow of priests was reached.

In the old land, clergy were held in high esteem, and this respect was transplanted to Canadian soil. During the first three migratory phases, the priest was inclined to have a higher level of education than his flock and was better versed in English (or French). Besides, the Canadian context enhanced his role. Priests were no longer responsible merely with fulfilling a religious function; they began to serve as mediators between the Polish community and Canadian society. When new immigrants would arrive in a Canadian city, it was either family or a priest who would help them to acclimatize to their surroundings. Well into the 1930s, priests also served as the first teachers of the Polish language and history, and functioned as organizers of mutual aid associations and libraries, social directors, and legal representatives. They provided the organizational expertise that lay members lacked.

The parish also became a place where religious and national sentiments — such as the celebration of national festivals — were realized by the Polish community. The activities of St. Stanislaus Kostka in Toronto, for instance, ranged from the religious to those cultivating the national aspirations of the community and those aiding the poor. Religious societies such as the Holy Rosary Confraternity and the Holy Name Society were established complementing a Polish language school, parish or-

chestra and even a mutual aid society — the Mutual Association of St. Stanislaus. Other such organizations focused on drama, sports and youth clubs, as well as immigrant aid. Winnipeg's Holy Ghost parish had a Youth Club (1907), Society of Polish Immigrants (1908), Polish Association of Bart Glowacki (1909), White Eagle Club (1931), and Women's Association (1933). The parish became one of the means of protecting against the loss of identity — a source of social-cultural existence, reaching beyond the spiritual and religious. In most cases throughout all migratory periods, national churches emerged within an already existing Polish neighborhood, consolidating its ethnic character.

The relationship between laity and clergy, however, was not one without certain tensions. The laity were the prime initiators behind the establishment of Polish parishes, raising the necessary funds to pay for the priest and for the erection of the church building. Such financial responsibilities were new to the Polish immigrants and resulted in increased participation in the running of the parish, at times, conflicting with the pastor's role. Another source of antagonism was rooted in factional regionalism, whereby some priests were not accepted as the community did not recognize their "Polishness," accusing them, for instance, of being Teutonic Knights (Krzyżacy), as in the case of the Kulawy brothers. The novelty of the Canadian environment convinced some Poles to explore other religious denominations.

Since the Canadian Catholic hierarchy was quite accommodating in promoting ethnic parishes, with little emphasis on overt assimilation, the American-based **Polish National Catholic Church** (PNCC) made little headway in Canada. An independent congregation breaking with the Holy Ghost parish in 1904 joined the PNCC three years later. In the following years, eleven parishes were formed mostly in Ontario and in Montréal, with the height of popularity reaching a peak in the 1960s with a membership of approximately 5,000. By 1991, this number dropped to a little more than a thousand. Instead, greater worry for the Catholic hierarchy came from conversion to Protestantism and the fear of socialist influence. During the 1940s and 1950s the proportion of Catholics among Poles steadily decreased, though increasing within all major Protestant denominations (especially in the Evangelical and Fundamentalist congregations). This changed in the early 1960s, when the numbers began to reverse with Catholic numbers once again rising and Protestantism declining. Until the 1970s, two Polish **Lutheran** congregations were active in Manitoba and

Ontario, and eight Baptist congregations in Ontario. Only the Jehovah's Witnesses and Pentecostal Assemblies saw slight increases. Overall, during the post–World War II period and into the 1980s and 1990s, churches (especially of the Catholic variety) continued to be built as Polish communities proliferated. The parish formed the basis of the Polish community providing immigrants with a sense of security and basis for (learning) organizational skills, which would assist Poles in establishing more diverse and secular organizations. In the early stages of migration before World War II, Poles established a number of secular organizations, which, while espousing ideals of Catholicism, were not administered by clergy. In most cases, secular organizations tended to be numerically small and too poor to purchase their own building facilities. Toronto's Sons of Poland under the Protection of the Mother of God, Queen of the Polish Kingdom, for instance, merged in 1921 with the St. Stanislaus Mutual Aid Association for the purpose of combining resources for the building of a hall. Secular organizations also had a shorter longevity as compared to their parish-based counterparts — out of 15 secular organizations formed in Winnipeg between 1902 and 1920, only two survived into the 1970s — and most were founded in urban centers. Many of them were of a fraternal or social nature, such as Berlin's Mutual Aid Society (1872), or Toronto's Association of Polish Citizens (1890s), which was superseded in 1908 by the Synowie Polscy (Sons of Poland). The latter stipulated in its constitution that its members were to be good Catholics, leading a moral life and not belong to any secret organizations condemned by the Church. The organization's purpose was to help individuals during times of illness, disability, and aid with funeral costs. Such objectives were typical of most fraternal organizations, tending to stress both moral and economic betterment along with the prerequisite of maintaining ties with the homeland.

Socialist organizations were also founded in this period, such as Montréal's Polish Socialists' Association (1906) or Toronto's Polish Socialist Party Association (1909–17). They were inclined to advocate for the social rights of workers and peasants along with Poland's independence. Coming into conflict with Canada's foreign policy toward Russia — especially during the First World War — some organizations were disbanded and socialists interned as enemy aliens. Socialist organizations would crop up once again during the Depression, when organizations such as the Polskie Towarzystwo Robotniczo-Farmerskie (Polish Workers' and Farmers' Association), active in Winnipeg since 1928, moved eastward to Toronto in 1936, becoming the Polish People's Association in Canada. Throughout the 1930s, this organization had significant popularity, reaching a membership of 4,000. Since it focused on class rather than ethnicity, its membership extended into the Ukrainian community; by 1938 they had fifteen branches in Ontario, four in Montréal, one in Nova Scotia and twenty throughout the Western provinces. As previously mentioned, these organizations were short-lived as the Canadian government found their ideological radicalism alarming.

Prior to the 1920s, Polish secular associations suffered from organizational difficulties, lacking planning and executive experience. This was compounded by poor communication arising from a weak common identity that typified the Polish immigrants before the Great War. Moreover, frequent mobility and large distances between urban and rural areas made collaboration between organizations difficult. The 1920s and 1930s ushered in a new age of organizational activity that began to reflect initial stages of permanent settlement and the necessity of adjustment to Canadian society, all while attempting to preserve the cultural heritage among the youth. With rising relative economic prosperity, concerns began to move beyond insurance and religious matters, extending to educational and cultural matters. Organizations became the nuclei of socio-cultural activities such as lectures, amateur theatre productions, celebrations of not only religious, but also historical and national anniversaries. Mutual aid associations were transformed into social clubs, and auxiliaries were formed to serve member interests in sports, theatre, adult education and/or political issues in Poland. These types of initiatives were of great consequence as most members tended to be single men with few alternatives to taverns, billiard halls and places of recreation and fellowship. The evolution within the organizational structure of the Polish associations also came as a result of the acquisition of administrative experience, and the involvement of the Polish government in the early 1920s, which began to take an active interest in Polish immigrant activity through advice, literature and funding.

The 1930s witnessed a shift away from a variety of isolated and independent Polish organizations to their amalgamation into larger institutions. Recognition was given to the weaknesses of multiple and disassociated groups — they were small, under funded and dispersed throughout Canada. In order to consolidate their strengths and to ensure their continued presence serving the cultural interests of Poles, four large federations were created: Stowarzyszenie Polaków w Kanadzie (Association of Poles in Canada; SPwK) established in 1933 with headquarters in Winnipeg; Związek Polaków w Kanadzie (The Polish Friendly Alliance in Canada; ZPwK) established in 1924 in Toronto; Zjednoczenie Zrzeszen Polskich w Kanadzie (Federation of Polish Societies in Canada; ZZPwK) founded in 1931 by the Polish consuls in Winnipeg; and Polskie Towarzystwo Robotniczo-Farmerskie (Polish Workers' and Farmers' Association; PTRF) which emerged in 1931.

Each of the federations had its own constitution to which the smaller organizations would defer, without necessarily infringing on the goals and interests of each of the comprising groups. All were concerned with maintaining Polish identity among the immigrants, but each of the four groups had a different approach. SPwK was a parish-based organization strongly popular in Western Canada. Led by clergy and laity, it worried about the rising popularity of socialism and anticlericalism. It was also created as an alternative to ZPwK and ZZPwK. Its paper, *Gazeta Katolicka* (Catholic Gazette) underscored religion and Polish national identity, promoting the notion of Polak-Katolik (Pole-Catholic). The ZZPwK was created under the guidance and influence of the Polish government, encompassing both secular and religious organizations in all parts of Canada. Its focus was on maintaining cultural distinctiveness through the establishment of Polish schools and libraries. While promoting closer ties between immigrants and their homeland, it hoped that Poles living abroad would retain their affiliation to the Republic, would strive to prevent the loss of youth through assimilation, and would recognize and support the Polish (Piłsudski) government. This, of course, was not to officially detract from the loyalty of Poles to Canada; nonetheless, the ZZPwK's aim was to identify the Polish community as an extension (i.e., province) of the old country. To compete with the other organizations, it published its own paper, *Czas* (Time), and by 1939, it had 80 affiliate members. The Polish government and its diplomatic envoys recognized the importance of maintaining ties with clergy (and religious organizations), which they acknowledged as a capable vehicle for maintaining Polish identity.

Based in Ontario, ZPwK was in many ways responding to the overly religious nature of the SPwK and the overt nationalism of the ZZPwK. It perceived the former as not doing enough to promote national activity, arguing that clergy placed the Church ahead of nationalism. The pro-Polish sentiments of the latter, according to ZPwK, placed too much stress on Polish domestic policies and state interests. Instead, the ZPwK called for Poles to affirm Canada as their chosen fatherland. By 1939, ZPwK had seventeen branches in Ontario, its own weekly newspaper, *Związkowiec* (Alliancer), auxiliary bodies, and schools. A fifth federation, Związek Narodowy Polski w Kanadzie (Polish National Union in Canada; ZNPwK; 1937), arose out of a dissident branch of the ZPwK (Group 9), rejecting ZPwK's growing anti-clericalism and radicalism, and of Polish Veterans Association Branch 114. They wanted to promote the Polish identity, retaining culture and ties with Poland without rejecting religion. The Second World War brought to an end the ZZPwK and the SPwK which lost membership due to migrating populations and a loss of western rural parishes. These losses came to benefit the ZPwK and the ZNPwK. The post-war period also prompted the establishment of new types of Polish organizations: Kongres Polonii Kanadyjskiej (Canadian Polish Congress; KPK; 1944), and veteran associations such as the Stowarzyszenie Polskich Kombatantów (Polish Combatants Association; SPK; 1947). The KPK broke with tradition and shifted its orientation to the Canadian context, with Poland retaining a symbolic position. Canada was now the source of immigrant loyalty, and Poles were to fulfill their duties and responsibilities to their new country. Veteran associations, on the other hand, maintained concern for the liberation of Poland (from Communism), and saw themselves as guardians of Polishness and Polish interests. Given that both organizations extended across Canada, each having a different vision — KPK experienced greater attachment to Canada than SPK (which perceived their migration as temporary) — tension emerged. Attempts at rapprochement produced a statement of common interests, including the continued struggle for Polish independence and against Communism, aiding the settlement of new immigrants in Canada and raising the position and participation of Polonia in mainstream society.

Another indication of the permanence of the Polish community in the post–World War II years was the establishment of credit unions. Normally, the popularity of credit unions — which grew out as a Catholic response to the effects of industrialization — was achieved among immigrants to Canada in the 1920s and 1930s, with the purpose of aiding the skilled and unskilled laborers obtain access to banking that was normally unreachable as a result of their economic status. The establishment of credit unions within an ethnic community was indicative of the growing economic stability within the community, while meeting the expanding economic needs of Poles, such as providing them with mortgages and a place to secure their savings. In the past, the temporary nature of migration encouraged the practice of sending most earnings back to the homeland as opposed to, for instance, investing it in the purchase of housing. The first Polish credit union was founded by Oblate Father Stanislaus Puchniak in August 1945 at St. Stanislaus Parish, Toronto; a second office was established in 1958 at St. Casimir's Parish.

Other than religious, fraternal and social organizations, professional associations and women's organizations were two further developments within the Polish community. During the post–World War II period, the arrival of many educated professionals resulted in the establishment of clubs with the purpose of aiding its members in upgrading their professional skills and advancing in their field(s). Women's organizations began as auxiliaries to male organizations, concerned primarily with catering services, charitable works, cultural activities and teaching in Polish language schools. During the 1950s the previous failed attempts at federating women's organizations finally succeeded with the creation of Federacja Kobiet Polskich w Kanadzie (The Federation of Polish Women in Canada), which quickly became affiliated with the KPK. They rejected an auxiliary status and stereotypical female roles, becoming strongly involved in politics, supporting the Polish government in exile. Another organization aimed at assisting Polish girls to obtain university education, the Koło Pan im. Marii Curie Skłodowskiej (Marie Curie Skłodowska Association of Toronto) was established in 1957, by Canadian-born graduates of the University of Toronto. The association, however, restricted its membership to university-educated women or wives of Polish professionals.

Polish organizations of all types functioned on the basis of preserving Polish language, culture and history, essentially acting as a guardian of Polish identity, and as a buffer against assimilation into Canadian society. Even KPK, which concentrated on the Canadian context, revoked assimilation. Polish organizational activity, whether secular or religious, began at the grassroots level, with a desire not to forget their heritage. Nevertheless, even attempts at preserving Polishness among the youth through organizations such as Harcerstwo/**Scouts** or through the estab-

lishment of the Stowarzyszenie Nauczycieli Polskich (Association of Polish Teachers), fissures between intergenerational groups began to grow. For those Canadian-born, Polishness became a form of heritage and was not met with the same vigor for preservation found among their parents. Moreover, organizations that held great popularity during the interwar and post-war years began to see a decline of membership in the 1980s when the incoming wave of migrants with different values and goals came into conflict with the ideals of their predecessors.

In trying to build and maintain self-sustaining Polish communities, education and print media (newspapers) became important bulwarks against identity loss, while simultaneously and indirectly facilitating adjustment to new conditions. As previously mentioned, the first newspaper to reach a dispersed community was the *Gazeta Katolicka* (Catholic Gazette, 1908–40), which underwent a number of transformations becoming *Gazeta Polska* (The Polish Gazette, 1940–50) and finally merging with *Głos Polski* (The Polish Voice), the mouthpiece of the ZNPwK. *Czas* (Time), *Związkowiec* (Alliancer), and the Communist *Budzik* (Alarm) and *Głos Pracy* (The Voice of Labor) all vied for popularity among the Polish readers. The Polish American press served as a model for its northern neighbors. Polish papers were deemed to be an extension of ethnic cultural life. Print media was the means through which Polish communities were able to stay connected, keeping abreast of events back home and within the international community. Newspapers also provided advice and information about immigrant life within Canada (and within given regional communities), while underscoring national consciousness and the uniqueness of the national identity of Poles. Their aim was to improve the educational and cultural levels of immigrants. However, since most press organs were associated with specific organizations, they became vehicles of propaganda, supporting the ideals of their sponsors. On a few occasions, Poles turned to the Polish American press to vocalize their criticisms. In comparison to other ethnic groups in Canada, the Canadian Polish press was not well developed, having a smaller number of periodicals. In part, this may have been the result of access to the Polish press coming from the United States and Poland. In the interwar years, special periodicals for Poles abroad were sponsored by the Polish government and organizations working for emigrants in foreign lands. The evolution of Polish Canadian press paralleled the development of the Polish community where concerns

with matters of the Polish state shifted to interests of Polish-Canadians.

Since the Solidarity period, the Polish community has continued to grow and expand moving from parish life to lay associations that attempted to maintain Polish language and culture among the older generation while encouraging Polish youth to rediscover their roots. Language maintenance in the latter case was benefited by the government-funded heritage language program, which provides language instruction outside of school hours. Courses on Polish language and history were also created at various Canadian universities. Polish retailers, retirement homes, and communities that encourage the retention of Polish identity have complemented Polish press, credit unions and parishes. The growth of the Polish community is evident in Mississauga, Ontario, for example, where Poles are the second largest ethnic minority. The largest Catholic parish in Canada, St. Maximilian Kolbe Polish Parish, is also found here. Given that over a decade has passed since the most recent group of immigrants, identity preservation is still strong within the community. The Rev. John Bednarz, OMI in discussing the nature of the Poles in the 1950s stated, "The Polish people ... kept their language and tradition much longer than other European immigrants, as evidenced by the 90-year old Polish colony in Pembroke diocese, where people still used the Polish language and kept many of the old traditions."—*Gabriela Pawlus Kasprzak*

SOURCES: Edward Hubicz, *Polish Churches in Manitoba* (London: Veritas Foundation Publication Centre, 1960); Martha McCarthy, *The Missionary Oblates of Mary Immaculate: St. Mary's Province* (Saskatoon: Missionary Oblates St. Mary's Province, 2004); Donald Avery and J. K. Fedorowicz, *The Poles in Canada* (Ottawa: Canadian Historical Association, 1982); Maria Cetnar, *Adaption of Polish Ethnic Group in Canada* (M.A. Thesis, University of Toronto, 1987); Benedykt Heydenkorn, *From Prairies to Cities: Papers on the Poles in Canada at the VIII World Congress of Sociology* (Toronto: Canadian-Polish Research Institute, 1975); Benedykt Heydenkorn, *A Community in Transition: the Polish Group in Canada* (Toronto: Canadian Polish Research Institute, 1985); Benedykt Heydenkorn, *Heritage and the Future: Essays on Poles in Canada* (Toronto: Canadian Polish Research Institute, 1988); Benedykt Heydenkorn, *Organizational Structure of the Polish-Canadian Community: The Federation of Polish Societies in Canada* (Toronto: Canadian Polish Research Institute, 1979); Benedykt Heydenkorn, *Past and Present: Selected Topics on the Polish group in Canada* (Toronto: Polish Alliance Press, 1974); Benedykt Heydenkorn, *Topics on Poles in Canada* (Toronto: Canadian Polish Congress, Canadian-Polish Research Institute, 1976); Rudolf Kogler, *The Polish Community in Canada* (Toronto: Canadian Polish Research Institute, 1976); Ludwik Kos-Rabcewicz-Zubkowski, *The Poles in Canada* (Toronto: Polish Alliance Press, 1968); William Makowski, *History and Integration of Poles in Canada* (Toronto: Canadian Polish Congress, 1967); Joanna Matejko, *Polish Settlers in Alberta: Reminiscences and Biographies* (Toronto: n.p., 1979); Henry Radecki, *A*

Member of a Distinguished Family: the Polish Group in Canada (Toronto: McClelland and Stewart, 1976); Henry Radecki, *Ethnic Organizational Dynamics: The Polish Group in Canada* (Waterloo, Ontario: Wilfrid Laurier University Press, 1979); Henry Radecki, *The History of the Polish Community in St. Catharines* (St. Catharines: Project History, 2002); Anna Reczynska, *For Bread and a Better Future: Emigration from Poland to Canada 1918–1939* (North York, Ontario: Multicultural History Society of Ontario, 1996); Frank Renkiewicz, ed, *The Polish Presence in Canada and America* (Toronto: Multicultural History Society of Ontario, 1982); Zofia Shahrodi, "From Sojourners to Settlers: The Formation of Polonia in Toronto and Hamilton, 1886–1929" (PhD diss., University of Toronto, 1989); Victor Turek and Benedykt Heydenkorn, *Poles in Manitoba* (Toronto: Polish Research Institute in Canada, 1967); Victor Turek, *The Polish-Language Press in Canada: its History and a Bibliographical List* (Toronto: Polish Alliance Press, 1962).

Catholic League for Religious Assistance to Poland. Shortly after the German invasion of Poland in September 1939, Pope Pius XII issued his Encyclical *Summi Pontificatus* on October 20 calling on Catholics to extend their "generous and brotherly sympathy" to the suffering Polish nation. In response, the Rev. Thomas Bona began to organize diocesan relief efforts for Poland in Chicago. His efforts were soon mirrored by Auxiliary Bishop **Stefan Woźnicki** in Detroit and other religious leaders in Polish American communities throughout the U.S. On April 28, 1943, thirteen leaders from various communities met in Detroit at the invitation of Auxiliary Bishop Woźnicki where they established a national organization to coordinate the various local efforts. The group planned a national meeting for Buffalo on May 18–19 which attracted 76 representatives from fifteen dioceses. The meeting established a national headquarters in Detroit, approved the name Liga Pomocy Religijnej Polsce (League for Religious Assistance to Poland), and agreed to begin publishing the journal *Liga* (The League) to promote its efforts. Those elected as officers of the organization were Nicholas Gronkowski, president; **Clara Świeczkowska**, vice president; Bishop Stefan Woźnicki, treasurer; and the Rev. E. Szumal, secretary. When Szumal resigned to assume a post at **Sts. Cyril and Methodius Seminary**, he was succeeded by the Rev. Stanislaus Piwowar. At a meeting in Cleveland in 1944, the organization's name was changed to the Liga Katolicka (Catholic League) and the headquarters moved to Chicago. The League was active in providing relief to Polish displaced persons and the rebuilding of Poland's churches in the postwar period. Between 1943 and 1959 the League provided $4,547,564.40.—*James S. Pula*

SOURCE: Alfred L. Abramowicz, "The Catholic League for Religious Assistance to Poland," *Polish American Studies*, Vol. 20, no. 1 (1963), 28–33.

Catholicism, Polish American. The history of the Roman Catholic faith among Polish Americans is an inseparable part of Polish American history. Catholicism helped to create and define the nature of what it meant to be Polish American — culturally, socially, and religiously. The vast majority of Polish immigrants came to America as Roman Catholics. Jews and Orthodox Christians who migrated from the Polish lands in the nineteenth and twentieth centuries almost always identified as something other than Polish once in America: Jewish American, Carpatho-Rusin, Ukrainian, and so on. There were small groups of Polish **Baptists**, Missouri-Synod **Lutherans**, Mariavites, and other denominations, as well as members of the dissident American-based **Polish National Catholic Church** (PNCC) and scattered individual atheists. Nevertheless, these groups, even taken together, never represented more than a small fraction of the overall Polish American community.

By the nineteenth century Catholicism became closely associated with nationalism in Poland. Aspects of Polish Catholicism took on a particularly messianic cast during the nineteenth century as Romantic writers and revolutionaries imagined Poland to be the "Christ among nations," put to death for the sins of Europe, and destined to rise once more, heralding liberation for all enslaved peoples. These trends were largely confined to intellectuals and political activists and in the mid–nineteenth century had only barely begun to touch the lives of ordinary Poles, most of whom lived in peasant villages in varying degrees of poverty. Primary loyalties of most Poles were to family, parish, and village. National identity in the modern sense developed slowly in the countryside and being Polish as such was so closely associated with Latin-rite Catholicism that Roman Catholicism was referred to colloquially as "the Polish faith." Thus, in the villages from which most of the mass emigration to the U.S. originated, people understood themselves to be Polish because they were Catholic but lacked any strong connection to a national political or cultural tradition.

Although parishes were important to many immigrant groups, scholars and contemporary observers alike agreed on the absolute centrality of Catholic parishes and parish life for Polish Americans. Local parishes were virtually synonymous with local **Polonia** communities. They were the home to most people and the majority of important organizations in the life of ordinary Polish immigrants. They provided the cultural and spiritual alpha and omega for generations of Polish Americans. As such, they served as the focus for the community's most profound beliefs, its most cherished hopes, and its bitterest conflicts and rivalries. Until Vatican II, Polish American clergy were the single most important element of the community's leadership, provided most of its teachers and nurses, and were among its most articulate writers and scholars.

Parishes were crucial to Polonia communities for a variety of reasons. Strong religious faith was at the core of the identity of most peasant immigrants. Moreover because the process of immigration disrupted or severely stretched family networks and peasant communities, the American parish represented a kind of substitute or replacement for things the immigrants were unable to bring to the New World. They provided a kind of social and cultural anchor for a people whose lives where often quite turbulent.

Despite its importance, Polish American religious life — perhaps due to its very ubiquity — has often been ignored or stereotyped by many secular scholars as a kind of embarrassing left-over from the Old Country. However, even a cursory comparison between the religious culture of Polish immigrants and their contemporaries in rural Poland indicates significant differences that reinforce the fact that Polish American Catholicism was as much affected by the process of immigration as every other aspect of Polish immigrant life. For example, Polish immigrants adopted new devotional forms instituted after Vatican I more readily than did their counterparts in Poland. Polish immigrants adapted to their faith new forms of lay piety that were becoming common in the American church long before they were common in the Old Country. Practices such as Forty-Hour Devotions that were "traditional" in the mid–twentieth century were very new in the 1880s and 1890s. Equally important was the massive development of lay societies, sodalities, and rosary groups, which were also encouraged by the reforms of Vatican I. The creation of new rituals almost wholly unknown in either the U.S. or Poland was also important. Broadly speaking, there were two types of celebrations or rituals: patriotic and religious. These events were elaborate and time-consuming spectacles that fulfilled a complex range of needs. Devotions, rituals, and celebrations bound together communities made up of diverse and often divisive elements. They temporarily held in abeyance the seemingly chaotic world of the immigrants and mitigated the pain of loss caused in no small part by their own life choices.

Polish American Catholicism also developed in response to the conditions of urban industrial life in which most immigrants found themselves. Polonia developed a wide range of self-help organizations, including fraternal societies, cultural and educational institutions, sports leagues, and a wide range of social groups. Many were directly based within parishes and many more were closely associated with them directly or indirectly.

A crucial feature of the parish community was the development of formal organizations, most of them led by the laity. The one major exception was the parish school which became ubiquitous in Polish immigrant parishes. Early schools were staffed by lay teachers (often the church organist) which proved less than optimal. The solution was to turn the schools over to women religious. After the turn of the century, teaching sisters staffed Polish parish schools almost exclusively. The development of parochial schools, along with the creation of orphanages, hospitals, old age homes, homes for unwed mothers, and other social institutions staffed primarily by women religious represented a tremendous mobilization of talent and resources by and for Polish immigrant communities that were economically and socially marginal in American society. Prior to World War I, two thirds of all Poles in professional occupations in Detroit were teaching sisters. Orders founded in Poland, such as the Sisters of St. Felix, found their greatest growth in the United States. For example, by 1955, 82 percent of **Felicians** were in the New World and only eighteen percent in Poland. Nuns not only taught school but developed curricula and wrote and published textbooks that emphasized Catholicism, dual Polish and American patriotism, and bilingualism. In addition to the development of women's orders, there was a corresponding growth in priestly vocations among Polish immigrants. The development of a Polish Seminary in Detroit was a particularly important development (see **Sts. Cyril and Methodius Seminary**). There was also a minor seminary founded in Chicago and a Polish Franciscan province and seminary established in Pulaski, Wisconsin.

The creation of lay societies in parishes represented an equally rich organizational development. The most common were mutual aid societies, rosary societies, and sodalities, but there were also a vast range of other organizations whose focus ranged from paramilitary drill to agricultural improvement to theater and literature. Parish organizations were run on a democratic basis and taught democratic political behavior. Such societies enforced moral standards and taught a code of conduct that emphasized fidelity and personal responsibility.

The importance of the parish to Polish American life was emphasized by the immense amount of resources devoted to the building of churches. The building and control of Polish parishes was a vital project that, like the development of a hybrid devotional culture and the founding of organizations, helped to bind together and order immigrant communities. Impoverished, working-class Polonia poured tremendous resources into building parish churches, schools, and related institutions. Although the energy and ability of pastors had much to do with the creation of the environment of the Polish Catholic parish, it was the active support and determination of the parishioners themselves that made possible the building of churches that rivaled the great cathedrals of Europe. Parishioners not only provided the material resources at great sacrifice to themselves and their families, and in some cases "sweat equity," they also helped to hire architects, approved and modified designs, commissioned statuary, and endowed bells and stained glass windows. This is all the more remarkable when we consider that nearly every one of these immigrant parishioners had grown up in remote villages in the "backwaters" of the modern world in thatched roof huts with dirt floors.

Such painful sacrifices bred a tremendous sense of ownership and pride, for in the old country only the nobility could endow

churches. This brought with it expectations of having a say in the running of the parish which they, not the bishop, had built, fueling conflicts over parish control. Indeed, nearly all conflicts within Polish parishes were over administrative, leadership, and financial issues rather than theology or doctrine. At the same time, the building of these parishes bound the Poles to America in a way no civics lesson could equal. As one scholar put it, Polish churches "stood as visible reminders that God had come with the immigrants on their long journey and that perhaps the voyage had been worth it. They were the stone and mortar roots that bound them to the soul of the new world."

Catholicism was particularly important in shaping Polish American identity. Strong ties to the parish were combined with dual national loyalties—American patriotism and loyalty to an abstract concept of Poland. This was accomplished through the medium of the parish, both by osmosis via the cultural and devotional life of the community and consciously through the clergy who encouraged all three attachments at various levels. Particularly in the second and third generations, priests and nuns were often the ones who promoted maintenance of Polish language and culture.

The post–World War II era in Polish American Catholic history was one of important

St. Mary's Church in Middletown, Connecticut, in the early 1940s. Polish Americans spent liberally on their churches as reflections of community pride (*CCSU-SC*).

transitions that remain poorly studied. Barriers of ethnic class prejudice eroded and the demographics of the immigrant community ensured that many second-generation Poles had formative life experiences during World War II. The hope that their children could succeed outside the ethnic ghetto led many parents to the painful decision to deliberately de-emphasize the use of the Polish language among their children, though it remained the language of everyday life in most parishes. Politically, the results of World War II and the loss of Polish independence led to an intensification of anti-communism that was further spurred by the arrival of a wave of educated Polish émigrés.

Polish American anti-communism dovetailed with the position of the American Church until the post–Vatican II era and the *Ostpolitik* of Popes John XXIII and Paul VI. Vatican II's American version hastened the decomposition of the immigrant parish community by de-emphasizing the importance of devotional life, decimating women's religious orders, and reducing support for parochial schools. Demographic and economic changes were also crucial as ethnic enclaves broke down due to out-migration, urban decay, and the changing political and racial composition of American cities. Each disruption of parish life had a negative impact on Polish American culture and language retention since the parish had always been the main incubator of both. Secular organizations and even the so-called ethnic revival of the 1970s could not replace the old parish community to the same extent.

During the pontificate of Pope John Paul II, there were some signs of renewal but by that time Polonia's institutional weakness made it difficult to take advantage of the cultural or spiritual potential of this dynamic new era in the life of the Church. Community leaders were either unwilling or unable to engage large parts of the Pope's sophisticated philosophical and theological message. There was been no major move to develop new initiatives, find inspiration in the voluminous writings of John Paul II, or to undertake some serious self-assessment. For ordinary Polish Americans, the picture is harder to frame and certainly more complex. The deep connection between being Polish-American and being Catholic was clearly strengthened by the witness of John Paul II and there is some evidence, both in old Polonia parishes and in those founded by newer immigrants, of a more serious devotional life. John Paul II played *the* major role in ending communism in Poland and east central Europe. Thus, his greatest impact on American Polonia was indirect. The fall of communism has created a very new situation for Polonia, one to which it has yet to fully adjust.

Successive waves of immigrants since the nineteenth century created a distinctive Polish American Catholic culture in the New World that while made up of American and Polish elements cannot have arisen or been sustained anywhere else. This was a culture poised on one hand somewhere between an imagined community that seamlessly blended Polish and American patriotism and on the other the intense localism of a community focused on its own internal affairs, problems, and politics. This fusion was fueled by a deep Catholicism and found its fullest expression in ritual and church architecture. Excluded for two generations from the political and economic mainstream, Polonia found in Catholicism values that eschewed political and economic success. Polish American culture and identity is not merely a hybrid of Polish and American elements, but a hybrid of ethnicity and faith. Polish American social history is characterized by this mingling of faith and ethnicity, and in later generations where ethnicity has faded into the background, faith has remained stronger and where ethnicity has revived it has done so in a Catholic context. Secular Polish Americanness has proved ephemeral and unsustainable over the generations so that the future history of Polonia may be determined by the extent and depth of secularization in the broader society.—*John Radziłowski*

SOURCES: Anthony J. Kuzniewski, "The Catholic Church in the Life of the Polish-Americans," in Frank Mocha, ed., *Poles in America: Bicentennial Essays* (Stevens Point, WI: Worzalla Publishing Company, 1978), 399–422; Daniel S. Buczek, *Immigrant Pastor: The Life of the Right Reverend Monsignor Lucyan Bójnowski of New Britain, Connecticut* (Waterbury, CT: Association of Polish Priests in Connecticut, 1974); John Iwicki, *Resurrectionist Charism: A History of the Congregation of the Resurrection* (Rome: n.p., 1986, 3 vols.); Edward R. Kantowicz, *Corporation Sole: Cardinal Mundelein and Chicago Catholicism* (Notre Dame: Notre Dame University Press, 1983); Wacław Kruszka, *A History of Poles in America to 1908*, James S. Pula et al., eds. (Washington, D.C.: Catholic University of America Press, 1993–2001, 4 vols.); William J. Galush, "Both Polish and Catholic: Immigrant Clergy in the American Church," *Catholic Historical Review*, Vol. 70, no. 3 (1984), 407–27; William J. Galush, "Faith and Fatherland: Dimensions of Polish-American Ethno-religion, 1875–1975," in Randall M. Miller and Thomas D. Marzik, eds., *Immigrants and Religion in Urban America* (Philadelphia: Temple University Press, 1977), 84–102; William J. Galush, "The Polish National Catholic Church: A Survey of Its Origins, Development and Missions," *Records of the American Catholic Historical Society of Philadelphia*, Vol. 83, no. 3–4 (1973), 131–49; Joseph John Parot, *Polish Catholics in Chicago, 1850–1920: A Religious History* (DeKalb: Northern Illinois University Press, 1981); Thaddeus C. Radzialowski, "Reflections on the History of the Felicians in America," *Polish American Studies*, Vol. 32, no. 1 (Spring 1975), 19–28; Thaddeus C. Radzilowski, "View from a Polish Ghetto: Reflections on the First 100 Years in Detroit," *Ethnicity*, Vol. 1 (1974), 125–50; John Radziłowski, *The Eagle and the Cross: A History of the Polish Roman Catholic Union of America, 1873–2000* (Boulder, CO: East European Monographs, 2003); John Radziłowski, "Miracle: American Polonia, Karol Wojtyła, and the Election of John Paul II," *Polish American Studies*, Vol. 63, no. 1 (Spring 2006), 79–87; John Radziłowski, "Rev. Wincenty Barzyński and a Polish Catholic Response to Industrial Capitalism," *Polish American Studies*, Vol. 58, no. 2 (Autumn 2001), 23–32; John Radziłowski, "A Social History of Polish-American Catholicism," *U.S. Catholic Historian*, Vol. 27, no. 3 (Summer 2009), 21–43; James S. Pula, "Polish-American Catholicism: A Case Study in Cultural Determinism," *U.S. Catholic Historian*, Vol. 27, no. 3 (Summer 2009), 1–19.

Cawetzka, Charles (b. Detroit, Michigan, March 1, 1877; d. Romulus, Michigan, October 23, 1951). Soldier, Medal of Honor recipient. A private in Company F, 30th U.S. Infantry, during the Spanish American War and the Philippine Insurrection, Cawetzka was engaged in action near Sariava on Luzon Island in the Philippines on August 23, 1900, when a fellow soldier was wounded and disabled. Disregarding his own safety, Cawetzka defended his fallen comrade until help arrived. Awarded the Medal of Honor for his actions, the citation noted that "Singlehanded, he defended a disabled comrade against a greatly superior force of the enemy."—*James S. Pula*

SOURCE: R. J. Proft, *United States of America's Congressional Medal of Honor Recipients and Their Official Citations* (Columbia Heights, MN: Highland House II, 2002).

Cebrowski, Arthur K. (b. Passaic, New Jersey, August 13, 1942; d. Bethesda, Maryland, November 12, 2005). Naval officer. A 1964 graduate of Villanova University, he earned a master's degree in Computer Systems Management from the Naval Postgraduate School and attended the Naval War College. Cebrowski entered the navy through the Reserve Officers Training Corps in 1964, serving as a naval aviator and commander of Fighter Squadron 41 and Carrier Air Wing Eight. His fleet commands included the assault ship USS *Guam*, the aircraft carrier USS *Midway*, and the USS *America* Battle Group. He had combat experience in Vietnam and Desert Storm. His Joint Chiefs of Staff (JCS) assignments included serving as the Director, Command, Control, Communications and Computers (J-6), Joint Staff. In 2001 he was appointed by Secretary of Defense Donald Rumsfeld to serve as Director of the Office of Force Transformation (OFT) in the U.S. Department of Defense where he remained until January 2005. In this position, he was responsible for serving as an advocate, focal point, and catalyst for the transformation of the United

States armed forces. As Director of Force Transformation, Vice Admiral Cebrowski worked to link transformation to strategic functions, evaluated the transformation efforts of the military departments, and promoted synergy by recommending steps to integrate on-going transformation activities among branches of the Department of Defense. Among his primary responsibilities, he monitored Service and Joint experimentation programs and made policy recommendations to the Secretary and Deputy Secretary of Defense. Known in the Department of Defense (DOD) as the father of network-centric warfare, he spent the last six years of his service in the department fighting an existing cultural climate of resistance to change. His true legacy may be his dogged effort to change DOD's culture. In April 2002, during a hearing before the Senate Armed Forces Committee Cebrowski stated, "Transformation is not just about technology and things. Rather, it is more about culture, behavior and the creation and exploitation of promising concepts to provide new sources of military power." He advocated, "The centralized control of information itself is a folly which will subvert the great advantage that America has in information technology and processes. The power of information is derived from access and speed, not from control and management." From his position in the DOD, he tried to push the service away from operating mega-billion-dollar carriers and their support ships. He favored a new age of warfare based on hundreds of mini-carriers and lightweight combat ships he called "Street fighters." Cebrowski was famous for his intellect and ability to cram a wide range of concepts and ideas into a short conversation. He believed fervently in his ideas and the importance of sharing them, taking the time to discuss his thoughts with anyone he encountered. Admiral Cebrowski retired on October 1, 2001, with over 37 years of service, after serving as the President of the Naval War College in Newport, Rhode Island.—*Luis J. Gonzalez*

SOURCE: Adam Bernstein, "Adm. Arthur Cebrowski Dies; Led Pentagon Think Tank," *Washington Post*, November 15, 2005, B6.

Ceglarski, Lenard Stanley "Len" (b. East Walpole, MA, June 27, 1926; d.—). Hockey player. An All-American hockey player, he was a high-scoring left wing on Boston College's 1949 NCAA Championship team and captain of the 1950-51 squad. He was also a member of the U.S. Olympic hockey team that won the silver medal at the 1952 Winter Olympic Games in Oslo, Norway. Ceglarski taught and coached at Walpole High for four years before beginning his collegiate coaching career by taking the reins of the Golden Knights program at Clarkson College of Technology (NY) in 1958. He was the fourth head coach in Clarkson's storied tradition. It took him only four seasons to guide the Golden Knights to their first NCAA championship tournament appearance in 1962 when Clarkson finished the season with a 22-3-1 record, losing in the final game of the playoffs to finish second. During the 1965-66 season, Ceglarski's team won the ECAC Tournament, and once again made it to the deciding game in the NCAA championships, finishing the season with a 24-3 record for which he was honored with his first Spencer Penrose Trophy, which annually goes to the national coach of the year. He also earned the prestigious honor in 1978 and 1985.

In 1972 he left Clarkson to coach his alma mater, Boston College. There he guided the "Eagles" to over 400 victories through two decades, retiring in 1992 with 689 career wins. At the time, it was the most in Division I history. In 2009, he ranked sixth behind leader Ron Mason's 924 wins. In 34 seasons (1958–1992), he became the winningest coach in history of college hockey with a record of 673-339-38 (254-97-11 in 14 seasons at Clarkson; 419-242-27 in 20 seasons at Boston College). He is the only man in this sport ever to coach 1,000 games.

Ceglarski was honored with the Bob Kullen Award (1984-85) for significant achievement as a head coach, the Lester Patrick Trophy for outstanding service to hockey (1990), and the Legend of College Hockey Award (1996). He was inducted into the Boston College Varsity Club Athletic Hall of Fame (1974), the National Polish American Sports Hall of Fame (1993), and the United States Hockey Hall of Fame (1992). The Len Ceglarski Award for Individual Sportsmanship is offered by the directors of Hockey East in his honor.—*Luis J. Gonzalez*

SOURCE: Brian McFarlane, *Brian McFarlane's History of Hockey* (Champaign, IL: Sports Publications, 1997).

Censor. The office of Censor is unique to the **Polish National Alliance**, and is best defined as the "Office of the Chief Judge of the PNA." It dates back to the creation of the Alliance in 1880, and has several connections. The founders were well aware of the office of censor, the defender of the public good, from their reading of the history of the ancient Roman republic. In addition, the founding leader of the Polish National Alliance, **Julius Andrzejkowicz**, was an aging man who resided in Philadelphia, far from Chicago where the organization voted to establish its headquarters. The office was thus established, in a sense, for him, with its chief power that of serving as a judicial authority in reviewing, and even vetoing, decisions of the Alliance's executive board, headed by the president. This power was considerably reduced in later years. The censor's authority over the editor of the PNA's official publication, *Zgoda* (Harmony), has also, for all practical purposes, ended.

From the outset a certain tension existed between the president and the censor of the Alliance. Both had wide ranging duties and both were elected by a vote of the delegates taking part in the PNA national convention (or Sejm). But the censor, without exception, has resided outside of Chicago, and thus was not expected to play any real role in the day to day administration of the Alliance. Nevertheless he had the right to attend Board meetings and express his views on matters pertaining to the fraternal's governance. In certain instances, most notably in the relations between Censor **Casimir Sypniewski** and President **Casimir Żychliński** in the 1920s and those between Censor **Blair Gunther** and President **Charles Rozmarek** in the 1950s, the tension between the two offices led to questions of primacy. Who was the final authority? These and other less public disputes (for example, between Censor **Francis Świętlik** and President Rozmarek in the late 1940s and between Censor Walter Dworakowski and President **Aloysius Mazewski** in the late 1960s) were invariably decided in favor of the president. The decline in the office of censor since 1968-69 has led to calls in the PNA for abolishing the office, since the censor is no longer responsible for reviewing the financial records of the fraternal and there is no **Alliance College** (since 1987) to direct—another duty once performed by the censor. Indeed, at the forty-first PNA convention in 1991, a vote to abolish the office narrowly failed, but only thanks to the intervention of President **Edward J. Moskal**.

One function of the censor, not exercised in years, is that of a spokesperson for the organization in defining the PNA mission, in cooperation with the president and Board of Directors, for the enlightenment of its members. The last censor to take on this role was Francis Świętlik. Most of those who have served as censor have been respected figures in their chosen professions. Thus, Andrzejkowicz (censor from 1880–82) and **Anthony Schreiber** (1905–13) were successful businessmen; **Franciszek Gryglaszewski** (1882–91), **Theodore Heliński** (1893–99), and Walter Dworakowski (1965–71) were public officials; **Michael Blenski** (1915–24) and Blair Gunther

(1947–59) were judges; Francis Swiętlik (1931–47) was a university law school dean; **Leon Sadowski** (1899–1905) was a physician; Casimir Sypniewski (1924–31) was an attorney; and **Casimir Lotarski** (1971–75) was a banker.—*Donald E. Pienkos*

SOURCE: Donald E. Pienkos, *PNA: A Centennial History of the Polish National Alliance of the United States of North America* (Boulder, CO: East European Monographs, 1984).

Census, 2000 United States. In the year 2000, the United States Census estimated there were some 55 million ethnic Poles living in the world with approximately seventy percent of those in Poland. It estimated the number of people of Polish descent living in the United States at about nine million. The following data provide a demographic, economic and occupational portrait of American Polonia based on data available from the U.S. Census Bureau's 2000 Summary File 4 and 2000 Public Use Microdata (PUMS) five percent file. Both these files provide detailed population characteristics for persons who self-identified as being of Polish ancestry. The vast majority of American Polonia are second and third generation descendants of Poles who arrived between 1900 and 1930. As a result, the geographic distribution of the population largely represents the original settlement patterns of their ancestors in the East and Midwest.

PLACE OF BIRTH OF PERSONS OF POLISH ANCESTRY

Place of Birth	Total
United States	8,460,301
Poland	418,532
Other Countries	64,403
Germany	35,713
Canada	17,506

PERSONS OF POLISH ANCESTRY BY METROPOLITAN AREA

Metropolitan Area	Total
Chicago, IL	831,774
Detroit, MI	479,659
Philadelphia, PA	288,440
New York, NY	268,228
Buffalo–Niagara Falls, NY	209,303
Pittsburgh, PA	209,032
Milwaukee–Waukesha, WI	190,076
Cleveland–Lorain–Elyria, OH	186,570
Minneapolis-St. Paul, MN	148,876
Los Angeles–Long Beach, CA	122,680
Boston, MA	120,245
Newark, NJ	120,193
Bergen–Passaic, NJ	95,403
St. Louis, MO	67,084
Houston, TX	59,254
Omaha, NE–IA	32,132
Jersey City, NJ	27,673

While the largest immigration of Poles to the United States occurred prior to World War I, the period between 1991 and 2003 saw 210,195 people emigrate directly from Poland. Although this pales in comparison to the influx of immigrants from Canada, India, and Mexico, it does demonstrate a continuing flow of Poles into the United States. Of this number, 37 percent arrived between 1989 and 1991, most of them settling in the metropolitan areas of Chicago and New York. Older gateway cities like Detroit, Cleveland, and Philadelphia only represented a small portion of the overall immigration during this period. By 2000, females of Polish ancestry comprised 51.4 percent of the Polish population, similar to the percentage overall in the United States. Similarly, 24.4 percent of the population is under the age of eighteen and 12.3 percent over the age of 65, which is within a percentage point of overall rates. Thus, much of Polonia is between the ages of 25 and 54 which represents the current American workforce.

PLACE OF RESIDENCE OF POLISH IMMIGRANTS ARRIVING BETWEEN 1989 AND 1998

Metropolitan Area	Total
Chicago, IL	68,349
New York, NY	30,689
Bergen–Passaic, NJ	9,795
Newark, NJ	6,828
Detroit, MI	4,728
Hartford, CT	4,441
Nassau–Suffolk, NY	3,807
Middlesex–Somerset–Hunterdon, NJ	2,667
Washington, D.C.–Maryland–Virginia	2,285
Jersey City, NJ	2,123
Philadelphia, PA–NJ	2,063

Persons of Polish ancestry have a slightly smaller percentage of family households where two or more persons are living together that are related by birth, marriage or adoption. Some 65.8 percent of Polish households, as compared to 68.5 percent for the nation as a whole, are family households. In terms of non-family households, the Polish population is slightly higher, but this represents the elderly portion of the population living alone. According to the 2000 Census, 9.5 percent of Polish households are occupied by a single person over the age of 65, most of which are female. Poles are higher than the national percentages for married couples at 54.2 percent of all families compared to 52.5 percent for the entire population. More significantly is the low percentage of female single parent families which is only 8.4 percent of all Polish families, while the average for the United States as a whole is 11.8 percent. The family structure of Poles living in America is related to the Catholic tradition of the population.

When compared to the national population, Poles 25 years of age and over are much better educated with 30.9 percent having a baccalaureate degree or higher, while less than 25 percent of the total population has the same educational attainment. In terms of graduate and advanced degrees, Poles are at 11.8 percent and the U.S. population is at 8.9 percent. At the opposite end of the spectrum, Poles without a high school diploma rank at half the 11.5 percent of the total population. Nearly half of the Polish immigrants 25 years of age and older that immigrated since 1989 have at least some college education and fifteen percent arrived with graduate degrees, the latter being higher than the average of 11.9 percent for all immigrants during this period.

Related to the education of American Polonia is the fact that the median Polish household earns nearly $10,000 more per year than the median U.S. household. Households of Polish ancestry earned $50,887 in 2000 compared to $41,994 for the national population. For full time employed persons, Polish males earned on average $43,079 and females $30,995 which was substantially higher than the national averages of $37,057 and $27,194 respectively. Furthermore, the poverty rate amongst Polish families is only 3.8 percent while the national average is much higher at 9.2 percent. Nearly one in ten families in the United States lives below the poverty threshold; the rate is less than half of that for Poles. Not only are fewer Polish families in poverty, but over 20 percent earned more than $100,000 in 2000. When compared to the educational and economic situation that they faced nearly a century ago, Polish Americans have made major advancements toward improving the quality of their lives, families and communities.

The data indicate that Poles fare better than the total population in terms of education, income and have fewer families in poverty. In addition, sixty percent of the population older than sixteen was in the labor force and only 2.6 percent were unemployed during 2000. In terms of occupation, 39 percent of Poles are employed as managers, professionals or other professions closely related to higher incomes. In terms of industrial jobs, many Poles are employed in manufacturing, retail, professional or human service fields. While the Polish population differed significantly from the overall population in other demographic characteristics, there is not much difference in the industrial diversity of the population.

DEMOGRAPHIC PROFILE OF THE UNITED STATES AND THE POLISH-AMERICAN POPULATION, 2000

	Polish Population Number	Polish Population Percent	Total Population Number	Total Population Percent
Total Population	8,977,235	100	281,421,906	100
SEX				
Male	4,364,644	48.6	137,916,186	49.0
Female	4,612,591	51.4	143,505,720	51.0
AGE				
Under 5 Years	548,870	6.1	19,046,754	6.8
5 to 9 Years	612,389	6.8	20,608,282	7.3
10 to 14 Years	645,835	7.2	20,618,199	7.3
15 to 19 Years	632,412	7.0	19,911,052	7.1
20 to 24 Years	566,225	6.3	19,025,980	6.8
25 to 34 Years	1,227,681	13.7	39,577,357	14.1
35 to 44 years	1,505,660	16.8	45,905,471	16.3
45 to 54 Years	1,353,664	15.1	37,578,609	13.4
55 to 59 Years	457,291	5.1	13,383,251	4.8
60 to 64 Years	327,181	3.6	10,787,979	3.8
65 to 74 Years	542,659	6.0	18,501,149	6.6
75 to 84 Years	439,726	4.9	12,317,262	4.4
85 Years and Over	117,642	1.3	4,160,561	1.5
HOUSEHOLDS BY TYPE				
Households (total)	3,558,022	100.0	105,539,122	100.0
Family Households	2,339,748	65.8	72,261,780	68.5
Married Couples	1,927,858	54.2	55,458,451	52.5
Female (no male)	297,149	8.4	12,500,761	11.8
Non-Family Households	1,218,274	34.2	33,277,342	31.5
Living Alone	981,790	27.6	27,203,724	25.8
5 Years and Over	339,772	9.5	9,849,325	9.3
EDUCATIONAL ATTAINMENT				
Pop. 25 Yrs & Over	5,971,504	100.0	182,211,639	100.0
Less than 9th Grade	205,639	3.4	13,755,477	7.5
9th-12th (no diploma)	485,242	8.1	21,960,148	12.1
High School Graduate	1,710,005	28.6	52,168,981	28.6
College, No Degree	1,270,335	21.3	38,351,595	21.0
Associate Degree	452,300	7.6	11,512,833	6.3
Bachelor's Degree	1,143,116	19.1	28,317,792	15.5
Grad./Profess. Degree	704,867	11.8	16,144,813	8.9
MARITAL STATUS				
Pop. 15 yrs & Over	7,170,141	100.0	221,148,671	100.0
Never Married	2,005,186	28.0	59,913,370	27.1
Married (not separated)	3,975,573	55.4	120,231,273	54.4
Separated	89,607	1.2	4,769,220	2.2
Widowed	469,974	6.6	14,674,500	6.6
Female	381,049	5.3	11,975,325	5.4
Divorced	629,801	8.8	21,560,308	9.7
Female	362,784	5.1	12,305,294	5.6
OCCUPATION				
Employed Civilian Population 16 Years and Over	4,646,470	100.0	129,721,512	100.0
Management, Profess., and Related Occupa.	1,819,078	39.1	43,646,731	33.6
Service Occupations	579,053	12.5	19,276,947	14.9
Sales & Office Occupa.	1,288,287	27.7	34,621,390	26.7
Farm., Fish. & Forestry	12,657	0.3	951,810	0.7
Constr., Extraction & Maintenance	392,147	8.4	12,256,138	9.4

	Polish Population Number	Polish Population Percent	Total Population Number	Total Population Percent
Production, Transportation & Material Moving	555,248	11.9	18,968,496	14.6
INDUSTRY				
Agriculture, Forestry, Fishing Hunting & Mining	40,088	0.9	2,426,053	1.9
Construction	278,304	6.0	8,801,507	6.8
Manufacturing	684,002	14.7	18,286,005	14.1
Wholesale Trade	174,213	3.7	4,666,757	3.6
Retail Trade	545,810	11.7	15,221,716	11.7
Transportation, Warehousing & Utilities	223,727	4.8	6,740,102	5.2
Information	160,555	3.5	3,996,564	3.1
Finance, Insurance, Real Estate, Rent & Lease	353,537	7.6	8,934,972	6.9
Professional, Science, Management & Admin.	487,524	10.5	12,061,865	9.3
Education, Health & Social Services	962,470	20.7	25,843,029	19.9
Arts, Entertainment, Recreation, Accommodation & Food Service	326,313	7.0	10,210,295	7.9
Other Services (except Public Administration)	198,300	4.3	6,320,632	4.9
Public Administration	211,627	4.6	6,212,015	4.8
INCOME IN 1999				
Households	3,558,022	100.0	105,539,122	100.0
Less than $10,000	213,631	6.0	10,067,027	9.5
$10,000 to $14,999	178,080	5.0	6,657,228	6.3
$15,000 to $24,999	373,237	10.5	13,536,965	12.8
$25,000 to $34,999	402,307	11.3	13,519,242	12.8
$35,000 to $49,999	572,851	16.1	17,446,272	16.5
$50,000 to $74,999	776,407	21.8	20,540,604	19.5
$75,000 to $99,999	457,363	12.9	10,799,245	10.2
$100,000 to $149,999	365,632	10.3	8,147,826	7.7
$150,000 to $199,999	106,802	3.0	2,322,038	2.2
$200,000 or More	111,712	3.1	2,502,675	2.4
Median Household Income in Dollars	50,887		41,994	
Families	2,339,748	100.0	72,261,780	100.0
Less than $10,000	58,972	2.5	4,155,386	5.8
$10,000 to $14,999	53,613	2.3	3,115,586	4.3
$15,000 to $24,999	169,533	7.2	7,757,397	10.7
$25,000 to $34,999	224,241	9.6	8,684,429	12.0
$35,000 to $49,999	368,460	15.7	12,377,108	17.1
$50,000 to $74,999	585,888	25.0	16,130,100	22.3
$75,000 to $99,999	378,133	16.2	9,009,327	12.5
$100,000 to $149,999	312,680	13.4	6,936,210	9.6
$150,000 to $199,999	92,259	3.9	1,983,673	2.7
$200,000 or More	95,969	4.1	2,112,564	2.9
Median Household Income in Dollars	61,635		50,046	
POVERTY STATUS in 1999 (Below Poverty Level)				
Families & Percent Below Poverty Level	89,542	3.8	6,620,945	9.2

STATE OF BIRTH OF PERSONS OF
POLISH ANCESTRY BORN IN
THE UNITED STATES
(TOTAL = 8,460,301), 2000

State of Birth	Total
Alabama	13,746
Alaska	8,180
Arizona	40,954
Arkansas	11,608
California	307,124
Colorado	48,106
Connecticut	282,027
Delaware	33,107
District of Columbia	26,438
Florida	124,734
Georgia	33,412
Hawaii	8,611
Idaho	8,498
Illinois	987,248
Indiana	187,569
Iowa	31,854
Kansas	29,138
Kentucky	21,706
Louisiana	16,042
Maine	17,731
Maryland	150,735
Massachusetts	323,310
Michigan	928,204
Minnesota	242,862
Mississippi	8,458
Missouri	84,251
Montana	15,778
Nebraska	73,559
Nevada	12,730
New Hampshire	32,164
New Jersey	549,515
New Mexico	11,230
New York	1,217,066
North Carolina	33,062
North Dakota	26,676
Ohio	462,533
Oklahoma	20,817
Oregon	30,747
Pennsylvania	993,409
Rhode Island	46,707
South Carolina	15,619
South Dakota	13,079
Tennessee	21,357
Texas	158,943
Utah	12,152
Vermont	14,152
Virginia	63,289
Washington	62,289
West Virginia	39,076
Wisconsin	520,873
Wyoming	9,899

See also **Immigration Patterns.**—*Jason C. Booza*

Central Archives of American Polonia. Located in Orchard Lake, Michigan, and affiliated with **Saints Cyril and Methodius Seminary**, the library and archival collections on Polish and Polish American subjects began to take shape under the seminary's first archivist, the Rev. **Józef Swastek** who actively sought to build the collections. By 2010, the archives contained materials on: Poland; **Saints Cyril and Methodius Seminary, St.**

Mary's College, St. Mary's Preparatory School, and various centers; the history of Polish immigrants in the U.S. and other countries and of Polish Americans; Polish American parishes; Polish organizations in America; biographies of Poles and Polish Americans; rare prints and books, some of which date to the sixteenth century; newspapers, magazines, and almanacs; genealogy; and special collections of stamps, coins, maps, photographs, posters and other items.—*James S. Pula*

SOURCES: Karen Majewski, "The Rare Book Collection, Alumni Memorial Library, St. Mary's College," *Polish American Studies*, Vol. 60, no. 1 (2003), 45–50; Roman Nir, "The Archives, Libraries, and Museums of Polonia at Orchard Lake," *Polish American Studies*, Vol. 60, no. 1 (2003), 51–80.

Central Polish Committee in America. A political organization of Poles in the U.S., the Committee was formed by Poles in New York on March 14, 1863, in support of the January Insurrection of 1863 against tsarist rule in Poland. Its initial officers included W. Mackiewicz as president and Romuald I. Jaworowski as vice president. The goal of the Committee was to "raise the sympathy of all nations" in favor of the Insurrection, influence American public opinion, collect funds to provide the insurgents with weapons and other necessary supplies, and to help volunteers travel to Europe to join the fight. Local branches of the organization existed in Albany (NY), Chicago, Leavenworth (KS), Philadelphia, San Francisco, St. Louis, and Washington (D.C.). In July 1863 the Polish Committee in Paris nominated **Henryk Kałussowski** as its delegate in the U.S. with the task of collecting funds for the struggle against Russia. In the same year the Committee initiated publication of *Echo z Polski* (Echo from Poland), the first Polish-language newspaper published in America. Edited by Jaworowski, the decidedly political newspaper supported the struggle against Russia, providing its readers with information from Europe. The publication lasted until December 1864. The organization enjoyed mixed success. The funds it collected did not meet expectations, while some two-thirds of the supplies it sent to the insurrectionists were confiscated by Austrian authorities. The Committee ceased activity around the middle of 1864 with the failure of the January Insurrection. The Committee's operations were greatly hampered by America's involvement in its Civil War (1861–65). Ironically, Russia's support for the Union, in contrast to Britain and France which leaned toward the Confederacy, led the North to side with the Tsar and not the Poles. A number of activists on the Central Polish Committee remained involved in the cause of Polish inde-

pendence, most notably Kałussowski and **Juliusz Andrzejkowicz**, the initiator of the **Polish National Alliance** in 1880.—*Adam Walaszek*

SOURCE: Florian Stasik, *Polish Political Emigres in the United States of America, 1831–1864* (Boulder & New York: East European Monographs, 2002).

Cetera, Peter Paul (b. Chicago, Illinois, September 13, 1944; d.—). Singer, songwriter, musician. The second of six children born into a Polish American family on the south side of Chicago, from an early age he was taught to harmonize with his siblings and learned to play the accordion. As a teenager he briefly attended seminary school, but left, learned to play guitar, and joined local rock and roll bands including the Exceptions. In 1967 he joined a group called Chicago, which needed a tenor voice. He became the band's bass player and shared lead singing duties. The group featured an innovative sound in the world of rock music, the heavy use of a horn section. The band moved to Los Angeles in 1968. Cetera began writing songs, though it took years before his writing abilities were accepted by the other band members. By the late 1970s it was Cetera who was writing and singing most of Chicago's hit songs, such as "If You Leave Me Now" and "Baby What a Big Surprise." In 1981, Cetera produced his first solo record album. In 1985 he left Chicago. He has enjoyed several best selling hit records including duets with Chaka Kahn and Cher.—*Martin S. Nowak*

SOURCE: Chris Jisi, "The Inspiration," *Bass Player*, Vol. 18, no. 12 (December 2007), 36–43.

Chain Migration. In recent decades the field of migration studies has become increasingly sophisticated in scope, refining contemporary understandings of human movement and revising long-standing analytical models. Efforts to bridge theoretical and conceptual chasms between the humanities and the social sciences have led scholars to produce more nuanced studies of human movement. The work of Charles Tilly, a pioneer in the field of migration studies, has been especially influential. Tilly's work has focused on the study of networks and of migration systems—the latter referring not only to a conceptually bounded geographic area in which human movement takes place, but also to the mechanisms that connect movement to various economic, political, and social processes. Tilly's migration systems depend on the permanency of a migrant's stay at the point of destination, as well as the distance between sending and receiving regions. In a seminal article, Tilly outlined his migration systems, which include four main types: local migration, circular migration, chain migration, and career migration. Tilly defined chain migration as movement "from one place to another via a set of social arrangements in which people at the destination provide aid, information, and encouragement to new immigrants. Such arrangements tend to produce a considerable proportion of experimental moves and a large backflow to the place of origin. At the destination, they also tend to produce durable clusters of people linked by common origin."

In the Polish-American case, chain migration generally applies to economic emigration that began in the mid- to late nineteenth century. Although political emigration from the partitioned lands began in the eighteenth century, becoming widespread among Polish intellectuals and political elites after the various insurrections, the mass transatlantic movement of Polish laborers and peasants settling in North and South America occurred later and was motivated more by economic than by political considerations, earning successive cohorts of migrants the label "for bread" (*za chlebem*) immigrants. In the late nineteenth century in particular, numerous factors combined to force Polish peasants from the land, including rural and urban overcrowding, post-emancipation landlessness, destruction of cottage industries and rural handicrafts, and widespread poverty. Among the earliest economic migrants were those from the Prussian Polish lands. Beginning in 1854, an estimated 1.4 million Poles moved to Western Germany, Western Europe, and the Western Hemisphere. At first emigration was largely cyclical, with seasonal migrants moving between the various partitioning empires and their home towns or provinces; however, by the 1860s and 1870s, the mass migration of Polish peasants from the Austrian, Prussian, and Russian partitions became more permanent than it was temporary and occurred in ever increasing numbers resulting as much from adverse socioeconomic and political conditions in the partitioning empires as from the relaxation of previously stringent anti-emigration laws. Scholars of Polish emigration generally point to the Rev. **Leopold Moczygęba**, a Polish priest and member of the Franciscan order, as one of the earliest examples of chain migration to America. Moczygęba and a group of Poles left Opole, Silesia, in 1854, for Texas, where they settled and eventually founded the first Polish settlement at **Panna Maria**. Moczygęba sent letters home to relatives in Płużnica, urging them to join him in America. Moczygęba and his first group of Polish immigrants were followed by successive cohorts of Poles, expanding the original Polish settlement in Panna Maria. After 1855, new groups of migrants established

another community around Bandera, Texas, where Moczygęba served the local parish in addition to Panna Maria. The 1850s saw additional Polish rural communities established at St. Hedwig, Texas (1857), Parisville, Michigan (1857), and Poland's Corner/Polonia, Wisconsin (1858). After the U.S. Civil War, Poles gravitated to burgeoning urban and industrial centers in Buffalo, Chicago, Cleveland, Detroit, Milwaukee, and Pittsburgh, where they worked as low-skilled laborers in coal, steel, metal, slaughtering, and meat-packing factories. Like Father Moczygęba and his letters home, other Polish immigrants — often temporary economic **sojourners** — encouraged further migration through the information and aid they provided, sending letters, money, or prepaid tickets back to their villages for family members to emigrate as well. As a result, increasingly sophisticated networks of Polish relief and work organizations, church groups, and other associations developed, easing some of the difficulties faced by migrants in the absence of preexisting assistance mechanisms.— *Krystyna Cap*

SOURCES: Charles Tilly, "Migration in Modern European History," in William H. McNeill and Ruth S. Adams, eds., *Human Migration: Patterns and Policies* (Bloomington and London: Indiana University Press, 1978), 48–72; Dorota Praszałowicz, "Overseas Migration from Partitioned Poland: Poznania and Eastern Galicia as Case Studies," *Polish American Studies*, Vol. 60, No. 2 (2003), 61–81.

Chesney, Chester Anton (b. Chicago, Illinois, March 9, 1916; d. Marco Island, Florida, September 20, 1986). Congressman. Chesney attended St. Hyacinth and Lane Technical High School and graduated from De Paul University in 1938. After playing professional football with the Chicago Bears in 1939 and 1940, he entered the United States Air Force in June 1941 as a private and was discharged as a major in 1946 after service in the Pacific and European Theaters. He was assistant chief of special service at the Veterans Administration in Hines, Illinois, in 1946 and 1947, did graduate work at the Northwestern University Graduate Commerce School in 1947, and served as an executive with Montgomery Ward & Co. in 1948 and 1949. Chesney was elected as a Democrat to the Eighty-first Congress (January 3, 1949-January 3, 1951). He was an unsuccessful candidate for reelection in 1950, a delegate to the 1968 Democratic National Convention, a twelve-year Democratic Party committeeman of Elk Grove Township, Illinois, and vice-president and director of Avondale Savings & Loan Association.— *Frederick J. Augustyn*

SOURCE: obituary, *Chicago Tribune*, September 23, 1986, sect. 2, 10.

Chmielińska, Stefania (b. Warsaw, Poland, March 16, 1866; d. Chicago, Illinois, February 24, 1939). Polonia activist. Chmielińska arrived in the U.S. in 1891 where she settled in Chicago as a seamstress and florist. In May 1898 she organized the first meeting of a group of women who agreed to form themselves into the **Polish Women's Alliance** Society. In November 1899 this group, and several others like it, met twice resulting in the establishment of the Polish Women's Alliance of America on a national basis with Chmielińska elected its provisional president. On June 12, 1900, the PWA held its founding convention in Chicago with 24 delegates representing eight women's groups and 264 members in all. Chmielińska was elected vice president at this meeting, but soon after took over as president from the absent chief executive. She went on to hold the presidency in 1900–02 and from 1906 to 1910. In the succeeding years she remained active in the Alliance, was a candidate for office on several occasions, and was elected vice president from 1916 to 1921. During her presidency, she won approval of a charter from the state of Illinois, initiated regular contacts with the poet Maria Konopnicka and other women leaders in Poland, made the first attempt to create the PWA of A's own newspaper, *Głos Polek* (The Voice of Polish Women; 1902), and established the fraternal's Educational Committee (Komitet Oświaty). In 1931 the PWA of A named her its first honorary president and proclaimed the organization's annual observance of May 22 as Founders' Day. Chmielińska was posthumously awarded the Gold Cross by the Polish government for her work on behalf of its independence and the betterment of immigrants in America. She

Stefania Chmielińska, initiator of the Polish Women's Alliance of America (*PMA*).

is remembered in the PWA of A as the "Mother of the Polish Women's Alliance of America." —*Donald E. Pienkos*

SOURCES: Jadwiga Karlowiczowa, *Historia Związku Polek w Ameryce przyczynki do poznania duszy wychodźtwa polskiego w Stanach Zjednoczonych Ameryki Pólnocnej* (Chicago: Wydana przez Związek Polek w Ameryce, 1938); Angela Pienkos and Donald E. Pienkos, "*In the Ideals of Women is the Strength of a Nation*": *A History of the Polish Women's Alliance of America* (Boulder, CO: East European Monographs, 2003); "Stefania Chmielińska — założycielka Związku Polek w Ameryce," *Polacy Zagranicą* (Warsaw), Vol. 10, no. 4 (1939), 17.

Chopin Theatre. The Chopin Theatre was designed in 1918 by M. F. Strunch Architects as a 987 seat theater at 1541–43 W. Division Street in the heart of the first Polish settlement in Chicago. The building changed names several times over the course of the twentieth century — from Chopin Theatre to Harding Theatre, back to Chopin and then to Pix Theatre from 1940 to 1980 — as the Polish community migrated north and west out of the original immigrant community. The Chopin Theatre was renovated as a bank for a brief period in the 1980s and then a nightclub. In 1990, the vacant building was purchased by Zygmunt Dyrkacz and gradually restored. A biologist by profession in Poland, Dyrkacz moved into the area in 1986. Called The Gallery Theatre when John Cusack and Jeremy Piven performed, the theatre changed back to its old name Chopin Theatre in 1993. Since its rebirth in 1990, Chopin Theatre's purpose has been to support, present and produce multi-cultural avant garde theater, literary, film, visual and performance art. It contains two stages, gallery space for art exhibits and a seating capacity of 220 for the largest stage. Programs have included national poetry, invited speakers, and dialogues on local, national and international issues, film festivals, Tony award-winning plays, and summer programs for children. While mostly a venue for American theater and art, it is also a cultural center for Polish art and theater. Chopin Theatre has produced over 110 of its own productions, mostly in Poland and Eastern Europe, and hosted performers from almost every state in U.S. and from over forty countries, including Pulitzer winners, writers, poets, actors, musicians and filmmakers. From 1990 to 2007, it had approximately 7,000 presentations (5,000 theatrical, 1,000 films, 800 poetry evenings, and over 100 music events). Its main presenters have included Chicago Filmmakers, Guild Complex, Young Chicago Authors, Collaboration Theater, Roadworks Productions as well as the Hypocrites, Signal Ensemble Theatre, Teatro Vista and Uma Productions. In 2002, Zygmunt Dyrkacz married African American Lela Headd, and they became co-owners and Artistic Directors of the theater. It was listed on the *Chicago Tribune*'s Best of Theaters in 2003, 2004 and 2005. —*Mary Patrice Erdmans*

SOURCE: Mary Patrice Erdmans, "New Polonia: Urban and Suburban," in John Koval, Larry Bennet, Michael Bennet, Roberta Garner, Fassil Demissie, and Kiljoong Kim, eds., *The New Chicago* (Philadelphia: Temple University Press, 2006), 115–27.

Cichowski, Seweryn *see* **Severin, Charles.**

Ciszek, Walter J. (b. Shenandoah, Pennsylvania, November 4, 1904; d. Bronx, New York, December 8, 1984). Priest, author. Born the seventh of thirteen children to Polish immigrants, he began study for the priesthood at the **SS. Cyril and Methodius Seminary** in Orchard Lake, Michigan, but then entered the Society of Jesus on September 7, 1928. After studies in the **Jesuit** novitiate at St. Andrew-on-Hudson in Poughkeepsie (NY), he professed his first vows on September 8, 1930, then continued his studies at St. Isaac Jogues in Wernersville, Pennsylvania, at Woodstock College in Maryland, and in Rome. While still a seminarian, Ciszek volunteered for service to the people of Russia, leading to his ordination in the Byzantine Rite of the Roman Catholic Church on June 24, 1937. In 1938 he was assigned to a parish in the eastern part of Poland, and was serving at that location when Germany attacked Poland on September 1, 1939. Ciszek used this invasion as an opportunity to enter the Soviet Union. In 1940, however, he was arrested by Soviet authorities who sentenced him to a term of 25 years in prison. Ultimately, he served five years in prison and ten years at forced labor in the mines of Siberia before being assigned to work as a garage mechanic near the Mongolian border. Believing him dead, his sister was surprised to receive a letter from him in 1955. The family then contacted the State Department, which eventually negotiated a prisoner exchange resulting in his release on October 11, 1963. Throughout his time in Russia, Ciszek continued to perform his priestly ministries on behalf of fellow prisoners and other co-workers. These experiences became the subject of a highly acclaimed book about his experience entitled *With God in Russia* that he co-authored with a fellow Jesuit, Daniel L. Flaherty, in 1964. Until his death, Ciszek worked at the John XXIII Ecumenical Center on the Bronx Campus of Fordham University. —*Carl L. Bucki*

SOURCES: "Liberated Priest was Ruled Dead," *New York Times*, October 12, 1963, 7; Walter J. Ciszek, S.J., and Daniel L. Flaherty, S.J., *With God in Russia* (New York: McGraw-Hill, 1964); "Walter M. Ciszek, 80; Jesuit Held by Soviet," *New York Times*, December 10, 1984, B14.

Club of Catholic Intellectuals *see* **Brotherhood of Dispersed Solidarity Members.**

Commission on Education. A segment of the American Agenda of the **Polish American Congress**, the Commission on Education was established in Washington, D.C., in 1984 partly in response to the political situation in Poland, but mainly to provide a sense of direction for the increasing number of Saturday schools and other supplementary schools throughout the United States. Chaired since its inception by Dr. Edmund Osysko, it provides a curriculum covering pre-school through twelfth grade instruction that correlates with the organization of the American

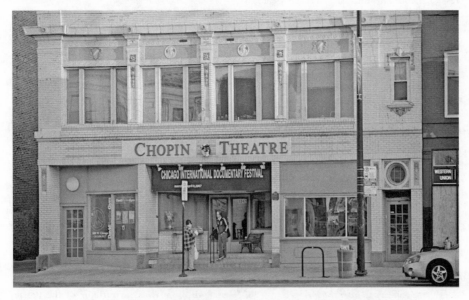

Chopin Theater, one of Chicago's great cultural landmarks (*PMA*).

educational system. As an ethnic group, Polish Americans have exhibited persistence in cultivating their heritage through the practice of religion, preservation of history, and development of literature. According to data from 2008, there were 165 supplementary schools registered in 27 states, some with enrollments in excess of 1,000 students. The Commission cooperates with the faculty of Columbia University in administering Polish Regents Examinations which offer academic credits to successful students. The Commission also organizes bi-annual Teachers' Conventions designed to strengthen the national teachers' network and promote greater professionalism. The tenth convention, held in Boston, MA, in 2008, attracted more than 450 participants.—*Halina Osysko*

SOURCE: Donald E. Pienkos, *PNA: A Centennial History of the Polish National Alliance of the United States of North America* (Boulder, CO: East European Monographs, 1984).

Committee of National Defense *see* **National Defense Committee.**

Congregation of the Resurrection *see* **Resurrection, Congregation of the.**

Congress of the Emigration (Sejm Wychództwa). The Congress of the Emigration was an extraordinary gathering held in Detroit, Michigan, in August 1918 under the auspices of the Polish **National Department** (Wydział Narodowy) led by **John Smulski** of Chicago. Its purpose was to unite **Polonia** in support of the cause of Poland's postwar independence and to raise funds in support of the future Polish state. The event brought together 946 delegates representing the Polish Catholic parishes and every significant secular organization of the Polish community, except for the **Polish Socialist Alliance** and the **Polish National Catholic Church**, the main backers of the rival Polish **National Defense Committee** (Komitet Obrony Narodowej; KON). In accord with its aim of representing the entire Polonia, delegates were elected in a strict proportional manner on the basis of the memberships of their sponsoring organizations. Roman Dmowski, leader of the National Democratic Party in Poland and chairman of the Polish National Committee in Paris, an erstwhile future Polish provisional governing authority spoke to the delegates at the Congress. So did **Ignacy Jan Paderewski**, the renowned pianist and patriot. In response to Paderewski's appeal, the delegates resolved to raise $10 million in support of the future independent Poland.

A key decision winning unanimous approval at the Congress was to make the Polish National Department the "central and chief organization of the entire emigration in America for Poland's independence." Smulski was chosen to be its president, with **Polish National Alliance** President **Casimir Żychliński** elected vice president, **Polish Roman Catholic Union** of America Treasurer Nicodemus Piotrowski treasurer, and Stanisław Szwajkart of the PRCUA its national secretary. Leaders of the PNA, PRCUA, **Polish Women's Alliance**, and **Polish Falcons** were elected to its Board of Directors. The end of World War I on November 11, 1918, only weeks after the Congress, took the wind out of the sails of its $10 million drive. Eventually $5.5 million was collected. When Józef Piłsudski proclaimed Poland's independence, his ascendency to the leadership of the new Polish state ended Roman Dmowski's immediate hopes of heading the country.

The National Department held a second Congress of the Emigration in November 1919 and a third in 1921. By then many in Polonia were calling for its dissolution. At the 1921 PNA convention a resolution to withdraw from the National Department was approved by a 321–106 vote. Clearly, the idea embodied in the slogan, "Wychodźtwo dla Wychodźtwa" (Emigrants for the Emigrants; meaning Polonia for Polonia) was in the air. In 1923, at its fourth congress in Cleveland the National Department was dissolved. Poland's independence was seen as completing its mission, thereby justifying the formation of a new Polonia-oriented federation, the Polish Welfare Council in America (Polska Rada Opieki Społecznej w Ameryce, PROSA) headed by Żychliński.—*Donald E. Pienkos*

SOURCES: Donald E. Pienkos, *For Your Freedom Through Ours: Polish American Efforts on Poland's Behalf, 1863–1991* (Boulder, CO: East European Monographs, 1991); William Galush, "American Poles and the New Poland," *Ethnicity*, Vol. 1, no. 3 (1974).

Connecticut Polish American Archive. The Polish Studies Program at Central Connecticut State University was initiated by local Polonia activists in 1974 with the donation of books on Poland. Community donations continued, leading to the creation of the Polish Heritage Collection. The gifts also included a substantial number of archival materials, and in 1986 the Program received a grant from the National Historical Publications and Records Commission to establish the Connecticut Polish American Archive (CPAA) with the mission to collect, preserve, and make accessible these materials. Finding aids to selected CPAA collections can be found on its web page at: http://library.ccsu.edu/about/depart ments/cpaa and on Connecticut Online Archive at http://library.wcsu.edu/cao and inventories to remaining CPAA collections are available on demand. The CPAA is a repository of documents related to the history of the Polish American community in the United States, with a special emphasis on the history of Polish Americans in Connecticut and New England. It is located in the Elihu Burritt Library at Central Connecticut University in New Britain, CT, and is an integral part of the **Stanislaus A. Blejwas** Endowed Chair in Polish & Polish American Studies. The core of the collection consists of records of Polish American organizations, societies, and institutions. The majority of the records pertain to local chapters of national institutions— **Polish American Congress**, Polish **Falcons**, all three Polish veteran organizations (**Polish Army Veterans Association** of America, **Polish Veterans of World War II, Inc.** and **Polish Legion of American Veterans**), fraternals (**Polish National Alliance**, **Polish Women's Alliance**, **Polish Roman Catholic Union**), cultural societies (**American Council for Polish Culture**, **Polish Singers Alliance** in America), Roman Catholic and the **Polish National Catholic Church** parishes, charitable organizations, the Polish Junior League, and Polish **scouting**. Some represent community organizing at the regional, state or town level including political clubs, societies, choirs, Sunday schools, and others. Two major collections contain complete archives of national entities: the **American Council of Polish Cultural Clubs** and the **North American Study Center for Polish Affairs**. Among CPAA's other holdings are several collections of grass-root Solidarity support organizations that cover their local, national, and international activities. The second largest group of archival materials consists of collections of personal papers. Among these are the papers of prominent Polish American figures with local links such as **Stanislaw A. Blejwas**, Ewa Gieratowa, Elizabeth Wasiutynski, Andrzej Blaszczynski, Thaddeus Maliszewski, Msgr. John P. Wodarski, Msgr. Alphonse J. Fiedorczyk, and many smaller collections with papers of local activists and ordinary Polish Americans of different generations. Three collections at CPAA record the publishing activities of the Polish American community all over the United States. These are the Polish American periodical collection, Polish American publications (non-serial) collection, and a Polish American anniversary and ephemeral imprints collection. The periodical collection holds titles produced from the 1870s to the present in different locations throughout the U.S. with a predominance of titles published on the east coast. Included are all formats of periodical publications—newspapers, magazines, scholarly publications, bulletins, newsletters, and yearbooks. The Polish American publications collection preserves all kind of monographic imprints (books, pamphlets, musical scores) published by large companies such as the Polish American Publishing Co., **Antoni Paryski**, **Władysław Dyniewicz**, the Worzalla Brothers, and W. H. Sajewski, as well as smaller publishing houses. The CPAA anniversary booklet collection consists of occasional booklets, programs, and other smaller ephemeral publications issued by Polish American parishes and local organizations, most of them based in New England, although there are many examples from other parts of the United States and Canada. In 2009 the CPAA started digitizing this collection and the pamphlets can be viewed at: http://content.library.ccsu.edu. The Archive also collects examples of music recordings made by Polish American bands and choirs.—*Ewa Wolyńska*

SOURCE: Ewa Wolyńska, "The Connecticut Polish American Archives, Central Connecticut State University," *Polish American Studies*, Vol. 60, no. 1 (2003), 13–17.

Constitution Day *see* Polish Constitution Day.

Constitution of the Third of May.

The first modern national constitution in Europe, and the second in the world after the American Constitution, it was passed on May 3, 1791 by the Four-Year Sejm of the Polish-Lithuanian Commonwealth. Authored primarily by King Stanisław August Poniatowski, Ignacy Potocki, and Hugo Kołłątaj, its purpose was to reform the political system of the Polish-Lithuanian Commonwealth in line with the key political ideas of the Enlightenment. It is historically important because it was aimed at alleviating political problems of the declining Polish-Lithuanian Commonwealth, which over preceding decades started becoming increasingly dysfunctional as a political entity due to serious systemic inefficiencies. To that effect, the Constitution of the Third of May weakened the position of the nobility, decreased the role played by the Senate, eliminated the principle of *liberum veto* (which had been used to deadlock deliberations of the Sejm), eliminated the so-called free election of kings (who had been elected by the nobility), prohibited the organization of confederations (semi-legal opposition groups that could be created against a specific policy of authorities' ruling), strengthened the executive, introduced the principle of government accountability to the Sejm, increased the rights of the townspeople, and gave peasants the promise of government and legal protection. The Constitution of the Third of May was abolished as a result of Russian military

intervention in 1792. Its historical significance cannot be overstated. From the national (Polish) perspective, the Constitution represented an enlightened, modern, and patriotic attempt to repair the failing political system and save the collapsing Polish-Lithuanian Commonwealth. Unfortunately, those efforts came too late. In 1795, the Third Partition took Poland off of the map of Europe for 123 years (until 1918). Regionally, the Constitution represented a major, albeit belated, voice of freedom and equality in a Europe in which absolutist regimes were becoming dominant powers. Lastly, from the global perspective, the Constitution ranks among the list of the most enlightened political achievements along with the American Declaration of Independence, American Constitution, and the French Revolution. Polish Americans recall and celebrate the Constitution of the Third of May as a significant contribution to democratic thought and process.—*Bartosz H. Stanislawski*

SOURCE: Adam Zamoyski, *The Polish Way: A Thousand-Year History of the Poles and Their Culture* (New York: Hippocrene Books, 1993).

Contoski, Victor J. (b. St. Paul, Minnesota, May 4, 1936; d.—). Poet, educator. Born to Polish American parents in 1936, Contoski was educated in Wisconsin and Minnesota, attending St. Benedict's Academy in Altoona, Wisconsin, Holy Cross grade school in northeast Minneapolis, and high school at St. Thomas Military Academy in St. Paul. After graduation, he majored in Latin and Greek at the University of Minnesota, receiving a Master's Degree in English in 1961. Upon graduation he traveled to Poland where he attended the Polish language school at the University of Łódź. While there, he was asked by faculty members to offer a course on American literature and soon after applied for and received a Fulbright Professorship at Łódź from 1963-64. While in Poland, Contoski met his wife, Wiesława Babula, whom he married in July 1962. In addition, Contoski also completed work on *Four Contemporary Polish Poets*, a bilingual volume concerning the works of Tadeusz Rożewicz, Stanisław Grochowiak, Jerzy Harasymowicz, and Roman Sliwonik, which was published upon his return to the United States. After leaving Poland, Contoski initially entered a doctorate program at Ohio State University, but transferred to the University of Wisconsin where he received his doctorate in English in 1969. He taught English at the University of Kansas until his retirement in 2007. Over the course of his lifetime Contoski has published some 200 poems, translated fifty works of contemporary Polish poetry, and written over 150 reviews in a variety of literary periodicals. His

published books of poetry include *Astronomers, Madonnas, and Prophecies* (1972), *Broken Treatises* (1973), *Names* (1979), and *Homecoming* (2000). Contoski's work has been translated into five languages, including Polish, Rumanian, and Japanese; and his *A Kansas Sequence* and *Quantrill's Raid on Lawrence* were set to music in 1983 and 1984 respectively. He is also a tournament chess player who won the U.S. Correspondence Chess Championship in 1976.—*Krystyna Cap*

SOURCE: "Kontoski, Victor," *Contemporary Authors* (Detroit: Gale Research Company, New Revision Series), Vol. 17, 71.

Coordinating Council of Free World Polonia. Following the Second World War, the Polish Ex-Combatants Association (Stowarzyszenie Polskich Kombatantów; SPK) promoted the idea of close cooperation within the Polish political diaspora. The idea gained momentum in the 1970s when the Canadian Polish Congress assumed organizational responsibilities, but the participation of the **Polish American Congress** in the preliminary work and in the Council itself was crucial to the success of the venture. The Conference "Polonia '75" in November, 1975, brought 56 representatives from eleven countries to Washington, D.C., where they made a decision to organize a permanent coordinating body. To establish what would become the Coordinating Council of Free World Polonia, the groups announced another conference, "Polonia of Tomorrow," to be held in Toronto in May, 1978. Membership was restricted to major **Polonia** organizations in the participating nations (Argentina, Australia, Belgium, Canada, Denmark, France, Germany, Great Britain, Italy, Netherlands, New Zealand, South Africa, Sweden, Switzerland, United States, and Uruguay), and to world federations (Polish Veterans in Exile Association, Polish Scouting Association, Polish Air Force Association, World Union of Veterans of Home Army, Polish Army Veterans' Association, Polish Women's Federation, and the Conference on Polish Museums, Archives and Libraries in the West). A permanent office opened in Toronto. Presidents of the Polish American Congress, the Canadian Polish Congress and the Federation of Poles in Great Britain comprised the organization's Board, with the president of the Canadian Polish Congress serving as president. In 1984, presidents of the French Polish Congress and of the Federation of Polish Organizations in Australia joined the Board, which meets annually. The Council's administrative decisions were regarded as recommendations that were not binding. The Council published a journal, with funds coming from the voluntary contributions of the member organizations. The purposes of the Council were twofold: (1) To help the Polish nation in its struggle for full freedom and sovereignty; and (2) to preserve and promote Polish culture and to exchange information between the people of Polish descent living around the globe. One of its first activities was to bring the plight of the Poles in Russia to the attention of world public opinion. A special American-Canadian-British commission pursued this question, with **Jan Nowak-Jeziorański**, the Polish American Congress representative on the commission, preparing a questionnaire and a series of publications about the fate of the Poles in the Soviet Union. In 1983, the St. Andrew Bobola Foundation was incorporated in Canada under the Council's auspices to gather funds for the Poles in Russia.

Other Council commissions addressed youth issues, education, information and mass media, books and the press, and collaboration with other captive nations. The Council adopted declarations in support of the democratic opposition in Poland, condemning the Communist regime and expressing solidarity with the Polish nation. Anniversaries of the battle of Monte Cassino were commemorated in 1984 and 1994, while 1980 was proclaimed the Katyń Year and 1981 and 1988 the Years of the Polish Youth. The Council encouraged its member organizations to help the Polish nation during the economic crisis of the 1980s. It promoted the "Medicine Bank," organized at the request of Lech Wałęsa in 1980, through which member organizations were directly involved in collecting and delivering shipments to Poland. Another of its accomplishments was successful fundraising for construction of the Polish Home of John Paul II in Rome. Officially opened on November 8, 1981, it serves Polish pilgrims to the Vatican. In August 1983, the Council sponsored the Summer University of World Polonia in Rome. In the 1990s it supported the democratic changes in Poland, reestablishing contacts with Polish authorities following the ascendancy of Solidarity. In 1990, the Council co-sponsored, together with **Wspólnota Polska**, the conference "Homeland—Emigration" ("Kraj—Emigracja") in Rome. The conference of Polonia in Kraków in 1992 also co-sponsored by the Council, brought together people of Polish descent from East and West. Organizational changes implemented at that time resulted in the replacement of the Council with the Council of World Polonia in 1994.—*Joanna Wojdon*

SOURCES: Artur Rynkiewicz, "Rada Koordynacyjna Polonii Wolnego Świata 1975–1994," in A. Szkuta, ed., *Kierownictwo obozu niepodległościowego na obczyźnie 1945–1990* (London 1996); Joanna Wojdon, "Polonia światowa z amerykańskiej perspektywy. Kulisy powstania Rady Koordynacyjnej Polonii Wolnego Świata w archiwach Kongresu Polonii Amerykańskiej," *Przegląd Polonijny*, no. 2 (2006).

Coveleski, Stanley (Stanisław Kowalewski; b. Shamokin, Pennsylvania, July 13, 1889; d. South Bend, Indiana, March 20, 1984). Baseball player. A native of the Pennsylvania coal country, the young Coveleski honed his baseball skills by throwing stones at targets between working shifts in the mines, according to his own account. Following in the footsteps of his brother Harry, he made his debut as a major league pitcher in 1912. He won 215 games over the course of a fourteen-year career as a pitcher in the American League, primarily for Cleveland and Washington. A right hander, Coveleski was noted for excellent control. He was one of a handful of hurlers permitted to continue to throw his most effective delivery, the spitball, after it was banned from the game. During the prime of his career, roughly the years 1917–1925, Coveleski was one of the outstanding pitchers in baseball, in various campaigns leading his league in such categories as earned run average, win-loss percentage, strikeouts, and shutouts. A plausible case can be made that he was the best pitcher in the American League in any of the three seasons 1920, 1923, or 1925. His teams won three American League pennants, and in 1920 he led the Cleveland Indians to victory in the World Series by winning three complete games, a feat unsurpassed in the annals of the sport. Following his retirement from baseball in 1928, Coveleski took up residence in South Bend, Indiana, for the rest of his life, and the minor league stadium in that city is named in his honor. In 1969 he was elected to the National

Stanley Coveleski, the first Slavic American elected to the National Baseball Hall of Fame (*LC*).

Baseball Hall of Fame, the Slavic-American player of earliest vintage so honored. He was inducted into the **National Polish-American Sports Hall of Fame** in 1976.—*Neal Pease*

SOURCES: "Stanley Coveleski" in Lawrence S. Ritter, ed., *The Glory of Their Times* (New York: Harper, 1992); Stanley Malinowski, "Throwing Stones Gave Coveleski Control, *Polish American Journal*, April 4, 1959.

Creekmur, Lou (b. Hopelawn, New Jersey, January 22, 1927; d. Tamarac, Florida, July 5, 2009). Football player. Creekmur was a standout lineman for the Detroit Lions of the National Football League from 1950 through 1959. As a collegian, he played at William and Mary from 1944 to 1949, with an interruption for military service in World War II. During his professional career with the Lions, he played primarily offensive guard and tackle. Creekmur won All-Pro honors seven times, played in eight Pro Bowls, and his Lions teams won three NFL championships. He is a member of the Pro Football Hall of Fame, and was inducted into the National Polish-American Sports Hall of Fame in 2001.—*Neal Pease*

SOURCE: "Lou Creekmur," National Polish-American Sports Hall of Fame website, www.polishsportshof.com.

Crime, Polish American. All ethnic groups have a criminal element and Polish Americans have been no exception. In the five decades prior to World War II, Poles were, along with Italians and Jews, considered a "problem group." Many upper-middle class native-born Anglos saw them as criminals, foreign radicals, or shiftless chiselers. Scholars saw them as especially prone to crime, family break-up, and what was termed "social disorganization." The University of Chicago School of Sociology, perhaps the most famous American contribution to the development of urban sociology, based much of its work on the problems of Poles in Chicago. The most important examples were William I. Thomas and **Florian Znanecki**'s classic work *The Polish Peasant in Europe and America* and Clifford Shaw's *The Jack-Roller*. Polish American newspapers were filled with stories of Polish misdeeds, drunkenness, and crime. Many Polish organizations spent a great deal of effort on the community's social problems—especially the problems of second-generation young people. Even Hollywood occasionally took notice, as the 1948 film *Call Northside 777* shows. This image was not without foundation. Polish immigrants and their children suffered from a host of serious social problems. Immigration put tremendous strains on families and the large pool of single male laborers under age 35 with access to disposable income resulted in widespread family break ups, alcoholism, and violence. Yet the most serious problems affected the young people of the second generation. Beginning around World War I, Polish communities across the country began to experience a baby boom. As early as 1910, the number of children of Polish immigrants exceeded the number of actual immigrants. These "baby boomers" entered the years of their lives in which crime peaks statistically during the 1910s and 1920s. The difficult social environment of industrial America and the problems of acculturation all contributed to a rapid increase in crime among Polish Americans. Between 1900 and 1925, arrests of Poles in Chicago grew by 252 percent, or two and a half times, faster than the growth of Poles in Chicago's population, especially in the first decade of the twentieth century. Disorderly conduct was the most common crime for which Poles were arrested. By the 1920s, juvenile delinquency rates were out of control.

In 1925, one quarter of all delinquent boys in Cook County were Polish, higher than any other group. A study of gangs in Chicago during the late 1920s showed that of all gangs that could be identified by ethnic group, the largest number were Polish. There were nearly 150 Polish street gangs in the city, compared to 48 Italian, 75 Irish, and 63 African American. In Detroit, Poles made up eleven percent of the population in 1930, but accounted for 27 percent of inmates in the city's juvenile detention facility. Polish street gangs were based in neighborhoods and made up of boys between the ages of eight and perhaps twenty. In addition to petty crime, and sometimes serious crime, gangs provided a sense of peer-group identity. One of the major functions of the Polish American gang, like its counterparts from other ethnic groups, was to defend "turf"—areas each ethnic group considered its own, be they streets, alleys, playgrounds, or fields. Thus, fights between rival gangs took on the character of miniature ethnic wars. In the summer of 1919 when Polish gangs clashed with Jewish gangs in south Chicago, it garnered a great deal of attention due to the political situation in Poland but was in fact quite common. In addition to fights with Jews, Polish gangs also clashed with many other groups. One account notes, "The residents of a Polish colony ... led by such gangs as the 'Hillers,' [i.e., **Górale**] who dug themselves in along canals, would wage pitched battles with many Greeks and Italians from the southwest. A boy was shot through the heart in one of these fights."

Although street gangs were the most organized criminal activity in Polonia, there were a number of more prominent gangsters of Polish ancestry. Joseph Saltis, although probably of Slovak ancestry, was identified as a Pole, employed many Polish gangsters, and went by the nickname "Polack Joe." He controlled bootlegging in most of South Chicago throughout the 1920s and used violence to enforce that control. Saltis became very wealthy from his illegal operations. He bought a mansion in Chicago and a resort near Hayward, Wisconsin, where he is credited with building the first golf course in northern Wisconsin for his private enjoyment. His gang was the first to use submachine guns and his operative Pete "Three Finger" Kunski (or Kozinski) specialized in the use of bombs to destroy rivals' speakeasies. Saltis and **Jake "Greasy Thumb" Guzik** allied themselves with Al Capone's South Side Gang in Chicago, with Guzik becoming Capone's chief financial advisor. Another major Polish gangster was **Hymie Weiss**, who was born Earl Wojciechowski to Polish Catholic parents but took a new Jewish-sounding name when he entered the world of crime. Weiss, a leader in Chicago's North Side Gang, was killed by South Side rivals in 1925. Saltis lost his fortune after the end of Prohibition and died from cirrhosis of the liver in 1947, a homeless alcoholic.

In Philadelphia, **Mickey Duffy** (born William Cusick), led the chief bootlegging ring, while in Cleveland a similar position was held by Joseph Filkowski and Joseph Starek. Why Polonia did not spawn more high-level gangsters is unknown. Likewise the reasons for the decline in crime rates among Polish Americans in the 1940s and 1950s remains poorly understood. One possible explanation is demographic in that the "baby boom" of Polish immigrants of the 1920s began to "age out" of the years in which crime is at its statistical peak in the period following World War II. Another factor is that many community leaders, especially those based in the tradition of Catholic Positivism, made a major effort to combat crime and deviant behavior. Among more recent Polish immigrants in the 1980s and 1990s, the same trends have not been in evidence although in the first decade of the twenty-first century a number of modest-sized Polish organized crime groups operated primarily in Chicago; New York, where the **Greenpoint Crew** engaged in a wide variety of criminal activities and **Richard "The Iceman" Kuklinski** was a trusted hit-man for the Gambino crime family; and Philadelphia where the **Kielbasa Posse** operated loansharking, bookmaking, and drug-running activities out of Port Richmond.—*John Radzilowski*

SOURCES: John Radzilowski, "Conflict Between Poles and Jews in Chicago, 1900–1930," *Polin: Studies in Polish Jewry*, Vol. 19 (2007), 117–33; John Radzilowski, "Crime, Delinquency, Deviance, and Reform in Polish Chicago, 1890s to 1940s," (New Britain, CT: Central Connecticut State University, 2002); John Radzilowski, "Fecund Newcomers or Dying Ethnics? Demographic Approaches to the History of Polish and Italian Immigrants and Their Children in the United States, 1880 to 1980," *Journal of American Ethnic History*, Vol. 27, no. 1 (Fall 2007).

Crimmins, Johnny (b. Detroit, Michigan, May 2, 1895; d. Wayne, Michigan, January 30, 1992). Bowler. One of the best bowlers in U.S. history, Crimmins owed much of his success to a very tight hook he developed that meant he was bothered less by varying lane conditions than other bowlers. From 1936 through 1940, he averaged 215 for 45 games to win the Elks National Tournament. In a two month stretch during the 1941 season he won four major tournaments: the Buddy Bomar Classic in Dallas, the Skang Mercurio Singles Tournament in Cleveland, the first National All-Star Tournament in Chicago, and the Rose Bowl Singles Classic in California. Crimmins was voted "Bowler of the Year 1942" by the nation's bowling writers. In four decades of competition, he won nearly 100 titles in major tournaments, averaging 195 in forty American Bowling Congress sanctioned tournaments. Considered the "Best cross-alley bowler in the country," he was inducted into the National Polish American Sports Hall of Fame in 1976.—*Luis J. Gonzalez*

SOURCE: "Crimmins, Johnny," http://www.polishsportshof.com/bios/Crimmins_j.html, May 2008.

Cultural Centers, Polish American. Beginning with the settlement of large numbers of Polish immigrants in the U.S. in the last quarter of the nineteenth century, there was interest among their leaders in preserving what they believed to be the best elements of Poland's cultural heritage among the immigrants and their offspring. Given this interest, it is not at all surprising that even the earliest immigrant voluntary institutions, most notably the churches and the fraternals, went far beyond their explicit reasons for existing and from the start also operated as true cultural centers. A visit to practically any of the existing churches funded by Polish Roman Catholics (as many as 900 were built), the scores of **Polish National Catholic** and Protestant churches as well, the many edifices of the fraternals, national and local, and the meeting places of the Polish American veterans organizations will provide an insight into the thinking of their organizers in sharing their appreciation of the Polish cultural experience.

After World War I, Polish Americans in various communities began the work of establishing a kind of culture center that was different in certain respects from what already existed in **Polonia**. Their aim was broader, and involved the effort to reach out to enlighten non–Poles, as well as Polish Americans, about the Polish cultural experience. Over the past eighty and more years, scores of Polish homes and centers have been created in communities throughout the United States. All have sought to meet one or more of a variety of perceived community needs. These have included (a) enabling Polish American groups to have meeting places where they could hold their functions; (b) serving as repositories of art, published materials, and other memorabilia donated for preservation by ethnically-minded individuals; (c) organizing artistic exhibits and film screenings that celebrate the Polish and Polish American experience; (d) sponsoring lectures on Polish themes; and (e) providing hospitable locations for social events in the community. Some centers have gone so far as to set up restaurant and banquet facilities for weddings and other family events. Most operate shops where Polish artwork, handicraft items, and books can be purchased.

In their excellent book, *The Polish Heritage Travel Guide to the U.S.A. and Canada* (1992), **Jacek Gałązka** and Albert Juszczak provide a fairly comprehensive list and description of the cultural centers in existence up to the time they gathered their data. This author identified more than 45 such centers from their book. Ten of these centers are listed below, by their date of origin, along with their general functions. All maintain impressive edifices, promote their aims to the general public, and have substantial numbers of supporters whose involvement in promoting the Polish heritage is likely to continue long into the future.

1. The **Kosciuszko Foundation**, located in the Borough of Manhattan in New York City. In existence since 1925, the Foundation is housed in a building containing a wealth of Polish art.

2. The **Polish Museum of America**, established in 1935 in Chicago and supported by the **Polish Roman Catholic Union** of America fraternal. It contains an impressive collection of Polish art, and includes many artifacts about the **Polish Army in France** created in World War I and the life of pianist-patriot **Ignacy Jan Paderewski**. It also maintains an extensive library and archive.

3. The Polish Seminary in Orchard Lake, Michigan (see **SS. Cyril and Methodius Seminary**), is the repository of an impressive gallery of Polish art brought to the U.S. for showing at the New York World's Fair in 1939, and houses a significant archive of Polish and Polish American materials. On the seminary grounds is the Chapel dedicated to the Virgin Mother of Częstochowa and the **National Polish-American Sports Hall of Fame**.

4. The **National Shrine of Our Lady of Częstochowa** in Doylestown, Pennsylvania (1966). The stained glass windows of this extraordinary Church tell the story of the history of Poland and of Polonia.

5. The **Thaddeus Kosciuszko National Memorial** in Philadelphia, created in 1972. **Tadeusz Kościuszko** resided in this modest building during his last visit to the U.S. in 1797. It contains historical interpretation exhibits about Kościuszko's life.

6. The **American Institute of Polish Culture** in Miami, Florida (1972). This organization promotes the Polish cultural heritage through its artistic exhibits and the displays it sends around the country for use elsewhere, by its publications, and in numerous other ways.

7. The **American Center for Polish Culture** in Washington, D.C. (1989). Lectures, musical programs, and art exhibits are regularly featured in this building.

8. The **Polish American Cultural Center** of Philadelphia, located in the heart of the city's historic district and established in 1988. This Center's museum is viewed by thousands of visitors each year.

9. The **Polish Center of Wisconsin**, established in 2000, and located in the city of Franklin, a suburb of Milwaukee. It functions, along with St. Josaphat Basilica Church and its John Paul II Cultural Center in Milwaukee, as a major center of Polish and Polish American cultural life. The Polish Center is connected with an annual outdoor festival of Polish and **Polonia** culture and music, a popular outdoor event held annually since 1982.

10. The **Pope John Paul II Cultural Center** in Washington, D.C. A Polish day is celebrated in October each year. There is a Polish room, and programs on Polish history and thought are held there.

A number of this country's institutions of higher education, and their libraries are repositories of Polish art, archival collections, photographs, and other valuable memorabilia. Among these are the State University of New York in Buffalo, Le Moyne College in Syracuse, New York, the University of Wisconsin-Milwaukee, the Hoover Institution of Stanford University, the Immigration History Research Center of the University of Minnesota, Central Connecticut State University in New Britain, Connecticut, and the University of Pittsburgh. The **Polish Institute of Arts and Sciences** of America and the **Piłsudski Institute**, both located in New York City, are important cultural centers. Other true centers of Polish culture are to be found in the Embassy and Consulates of the Republic of Poland, all of which display impressive collections of Polish art and sculpture, and sponsor lectures and other events for the public.

Gałązka and Juszczak listed cultural centers operating in the states of Arizona, California, Colorado, Connecticut, Florida, Illinois, Indiana, Maryland, Michigan, Minnesota, Mississippi, Missouri, New Jersey, New York, Pennsylvania, South Carolina, Washington, Wisconsin, and the District of Columbia. Undoubtedly, cultural centers are to be found elsewhere too, but apparently the authors did not find volunteers to provide such information for every state in the country. New centers have also come into existence since their book appeared.—*Donald E. Pienkos*

SOURCE: Jacek Galazka and Albert Juszczak, *The Polish Heritage Travel Guide to the U.S.A. and Canada* (Cornwall Bridge, CT: Polish Heritage Publications, 1992).

Curtius, Alexander (Aleksander Karol Kurcjusz or Kurczewicz; b. Poland, date unknown; d. unknown). Educator, physician. Although little is known of Curtius's early life, and in fact there has been no definite confirmation of the Polish form of his surname, he was apparently a professor in Lithuania before he arrived in New Amsterdam (later New York) in the early summer of 1659. There he accepted a position as schoolmaster for a new Latin school and is believed to be the first such teacher in New Amsterdam. It appears from the scanty records that he also tutored students individually and practiced medicine. Disagreements over his salary apparently led to his leaving New Amsterdam. By the end of 1661 he was back in the Netherlands, enrolled in the University of Leiden studying medicine.—*James S. Pula*

SOURCES: Ladislas John Siekaniec, *The Polish Contribution to Early American Education, 1608–1865* (San Francisco: R & E Research Associates, 1976); Edmund L. Kowalczyk, "Dr. Alexander Curtius," *Polish American Journal*, October 10, 1959), 2.

Customs, Polish American. Most customs and traditions associated with Polish Americans are associated with the liturgical calendar of the Roman Catholic faith. They are also closely tied to the cycles of the seasons, harvest time, and to family life, customs brought to America by the predominantly rural and agricultural society of Poland where most of the Polish immigrants originated during the late nineteenth and early twentieth centuries. Seeking a better life in America, the Poles settled in major industrial cities throughout the United States, but predominantly in cities along the Great Lakes such as Buffalo, Cleveland, Detroit, and Chicago. The communities they formed came to be called "Polonia." Over the years many customs have been lost to families through the death of the elderly, very often the culture bearers and keepers who knew and remembered the customs themselves or learned them from their parents and grandparents who migrated to this country. As each succeeding generation moves farther way from those initial immigrants, intermarries, or moves outside established Polish American communities, the ways of living and celebrating holidays and holy days as their ancestors once did becomes fainter and fainter. There is however, a core of customs and traditions that remain and are acknowledged as Polish American.

CHRISTMAS CUSTOMS

In many Polish American homes the most important part of the Christmas celebration is Christmas Eve, with the centerpiece being the Christmas Eve supper. The traditional Christmas Eve dinner is called **Wigilia** (the Vigil) and traditionally begins in the evening when the first star appears in the sky. Tradition dictates that there be an uneven number of people attending and that there always be an empty seat for any stranger who may appear, this being symbolic of the Christ Child. The meal begins with everyone gathering around the table covered with a crisp white tablecloth. The families who have access to it, place hay under the tablecloth or sprinkle the tablecloth with straw in memory of the hay in the manger where the Christ Child was born. Everyone joins together in saying a short prayer and expressing thankfulness for blessings received throughout the year. This is followed by the most important ceremony of the night, the breaking and sharing of the **opłatek** (wafer). The opłatek is an unconsecrated bread wafer of the type used during Holy Communion in many religious services. It is white in color and rectangular in shape, about three inches by six inches, and available either from the clergy in many Polish American parishes or from shops specializing in Polish food or gifts. It has pride of place on the Wigilia table. Many families place the opłatek on a special plate covered with bits of hay or straw as a reminder that Jesus Christ was born in a stable.

The sharing of the *opłatek* is led by the head of the household or the oldest member present. Choosing one of the other older individuals present, they offer each other good wishes for health and happiness, the fulfillment of hopes and dreams, sometimes asking for forgiveness if there has been discord or estrangement. Whoever is being offered the wishes breaks off a piece of the opłatek being offered

to them and eats it. They, in turn, offer good wishes in return to the person who has just wished them well. Everyone present has their own piece of wafer and must extend and exchange good wishes with everyone else, down to the smallest infant present. This is what family members fly across the world for — to be present among family and friends and the opportunity to openly express their love for one another or sometimes to seek reconciliation. Family members who cannot be present, send one another a piece of *opłatek* in the mail to say "I am with you in spirit and send you opłatek and wishes for health and peace and love in your life."

After everyone has an opportunity to exchange well wishes and share the wafer, the meal can begin. Tradition dictates that this meal is meatless and some cooks still strive to have an uneven number of dishes. The food eaten varies among the different regions in Poland, but all of them reflected the mainly agrarian nature of Poland. The meal can begin with soup made from mushrooms, peas or beets. There are fish dishes including *sledzie* (pickled herring), carp, or any type of preferred fish. Traditional side dishes include plain boiled potatoes, *kasza* (buckwheat groats), **pierogi** (dumplings filled with a potato and cheese mixture, plain farmer's cheese, sauerkraut, or fruit); **kapusta z grochem** (sauerkraut cooked with dried peas), or *kluski*

Polish American Christmas postcard from the 1930s (*OLS*).

z makiem (noodles with honey and poppy seeds). The meal concludes with *kompot* (stewed fruits), *makowiec* (poppy seed roll), or cookies made from honey. Still traditional in many homes is the conclusion of the meal with a very ancient dish called *kucya*, sometimes spelled kutia, made of cooked wheat berries, poppy seeds, honey, and nuts. It is one of Poland's most ancient Christmas Eve dishes. Typically everyone who is able attends the Shepard's Mass or Midnight Mass called the Pasterka.

NEW YEAR CUSTOMS

On New Year's Eve it is customary to eat herring and hold money in the palm of your hand at the stroke of midnight to assure plenty of it for the coming year. The Feast of Three Kings on January 6 officially closes the twelve days of Christmas. It honors the Three Wise Men who sought the Christ Child. The faithful attend Mass where the priest blesses chalk and distributes it to be brought home. The head of household writes the letters K+M+B over the door leading into the house for the initials of the Three Wise Men (Kasper, Melchior, and Baltazar) followed by the year.

EASTER CUSTOMS

On Shrove Tuesday, the Tuesday before Ash Wednesday, the Polish American community celebrates **Pączki** Day. According to tradition, the house prepares for the strict fasting season of Lent by ridding the house of all fats such as lard, butter, and eggs which were forbidden during Lent. In Poland, all types of rich foods were prepared including fried, fruit filled doughnuts called *pączki*. This round, yeast doughnut, deep fat fried and filled with a fruit jelly, is sold in bakeries throughout the Polish American community. For Polish American Catholics, Ash Wednesday ushers in the holy season of Lent. It begins with the anointing of foreheads with ashes. The ashes are obtained from the burning of palms from the previous year. The strict fast associated with the Lenten season has lessened considerably to the fasting from meat on Wednesdays and Fridays. Popular during this time is the eating of a fish fry offered at various local taverns and restaurants. Throughout the Lenten season there are regularly held services celebrating the Way of the Cross accompanied by the singing of the Bitter Laments, known as **Gorzkie Żale**, recalling the Lord's passion.

Palm Sunday begins the most important religious celebration of the Roman Catholic Church. The church service celebrates the triumphant entrance of Christ into Jerusalem with the faithful attending Mass receiving palms to commemorate the event. These blessed palms are taken home and tucked behind holy pictures. It is believed that the palms protect the house and its inhabitants against evil. A popular Holy Week tradition occurs on Holy Thursday. After the Mass of the Lord's Supper, the Eucharist is processed to a side altar called the altar of repose. At the conclusion of the church service, the faithful stay to pray and adore the Holy Eucharist. In many Polish American communities, particularly in big cities with many parishes, the faithful visit seven nearby churches to kneel in front of the altars of repose to pray and adore the Holy Eucharist (Eucharistic adoration). It is an ancient practice, probably originating in Rome, where early pilgrims visited the seven major basilicas as penance during the Lenten season. The seven areas may also be related to the historical seven deacons of Rome, whose responsibility was to minister to the poor in their region of the city.

The next day, on Good Friday, the afternoon church service focuses on the events of the death and Crucifixion of Jesus Christ. The churches are filled with the scent of incense and potted lilies, hyacinths, and daffodils. A figure of the crucified Christ is laid to rest in a specially constructed tomb at one of the side altars. It is surrounded by vigil lights, flowers, and greenery. The faithful come to pray and ask forgiveness of their sins.

On Holy Saturday the custom is to bring to the priest a basket of specially prepared food to be blessed. This is called *święconka* from the word *święcone*, which means "blessed." According to the Roman Catholic faith, each food placed in the basket has a particular significance. Included in the basket are a lamb made out of butter (*baranek*) which is a representation of the Lamb of God, and hard boiled eggs (*jajka*) symbolizing rebirth and new life. Sometimes the eggs are colored by the children; but sometimes they are simply died in onion skin. The basket also contains pork sausage called *kiełbasa* and ham in celebration of the New Testament which came into effect with Christ's resurrection; bread, with or without the symbol of a cross on top, recalling the bread of the Last Supper; horseradish (*chrzan*) that reminds the faithful of the bitterness and suffering of Christ culminating in the Resurrection; a sweet round yeast cake called a *baba* or *babka*, or in the shape of a loaf called a *placek*, rich with egg yolks and studded with raisins; a cake in the shape of a lamb; and other sweet rolls or cakes made with poppy seeds or almonds. After these basic foodstuffs, Polish Americans include whatever was traditional for their families, sometimes including water to be blessed,

Polish American Easter postcard from the 1930s (*OLS*).

salt and pepper, wine, and chocolate. The basket is decorated with greenery such as boxwood or pussy willows and covered with a cloth. The cloth is often something that came with an ancestor from the old country, or was embroidered or crocheted just for this purpose. Those who keep the tradition strive to make the basket as beautiful as they can. At the same time, the children bring their own baskets filled with chocolate bunnies, yellow chicks, and jelly beans and place their baskets next to those of their parents. The church is filled with the scent of flowers, incense, and sausage. The pastor prays over the food baskets and sprinkles them with holy water. The faithful then take their baskets home in eager anticipation of eating the food the following day.

Easter Sunday is the most important holy day of the year. The Mass of the Resurrection (the Rezurekcja) takes place at early light, usually 7:00 am. At the beginning of the service the priest attends the tomb of Christ to pray, takes the monstrance with the Holy Eucharist out of the tabernacle, and announces the resurrection by singing the words "Wesoły nam dzień dzis nastał (Joyful is the coming of this day)." The parishioners and organist join in with this centuries-old song of celebration of the risen Christ. Together with the other concelebrating priests, nuns, altar boys, parish leaders, and school children, the pastor leads a procession three times around the interior or exterior of the church, depending on the weather or parish preferences. At the conclu-

sion of the Mass, Polish Americans head home for a special early morning breakfast, also called *święconka*, the name taken from the basket of food blessed on Holy Saturday. The basket of food, along with a vast array of other foods prepared for the morning repast, is then consumed. The breakfast begins with the head of the household taking a blessed egg, dividing it into quarters or eighth's, depending on the number of individuals present, and offering a piece of the egg to all the assembled individuals along with well wishes and the joy of the day. Everyone then partakes and enjoys the food that was blessed the previous day.

Many communities with large Polish American populations celebrate the ancient Easter Monday custom of dyngus also called *śmigus-dyngus* (see **Dyngus Day**). The custom takes two different forms. One occurs with a ritual dousing of water. The other is the striking of someone with a green branch, generally pussy willows. Both originate from ancient "water" rites in Poland where splashing water or striking a girl with greenery assumed a magic role in producing fertility and new life. Currently, the day is still celebrated with males and females squirting each other with squirt guns and lightly hitting each other with pussy willow branches. Many communities host parades with individuals dressed in regional Polish costumes and numerous **polka** parties.

Autumn Customs

During the month of August there are two types of customs and traditions. The First is the celebration of Our Lady of the Herbs. In Poland the religious Feast of the Assumption on August 15 is also called Matka Boska Zielna (Blessed Mother of the Herbs), or Our Lady of the Herbs. The Blessed Mother is seen as the patron and keeper of the earth and all of its abundance. On this special feast day, every village housewife brought a bouquet of herbs, flowers, and grain that was collected from her garden, the fields, and orchards. She gathered dill, mint, rosemary, southernwood, parsley, hyssop, lovage, and comfrey, or whatever she had growing in her garden. To this she added her favorite flower such as sweet pea, tansy, or sunflower. A branch of a favorite fruit tree, such as apple or pear, is also tucked into the arrangement. Since August coincided with the time of the harvest, it was also the custom to take a few spikes of various grains including wheat, rye, and oats. After the blessing, the flowers were taken home and tucked behind holy pictures to protect the home against fire and lightning. This custom, at risk of dying out in the last decades, has had a significant revival in recent years in Polish American churches and communities.

The second major tradition is the hosting of harvest festivals called Dożynki. This is a remnant of the real harvest festivals that concluded the bringing in of the grains and bounty of the land in preparation for winter. In memory of their ancestors, many Polish American parishes still host a modified version of the event by bring in farmers to sell fruits, vegetables, and flowers, share traditional foods, and provide the opportunity to dance and celebrate.

FAMILY CUSTOMS

Weddings continue to be an important celebratory event in Polish American families. One of the very important old Polish rituals associated with the arrival of the guests at the wedding hall is greeting them with bread and salt. It is the role of the parents to meet guests at the door with a plate covered with one's best linen cloth containing small pieces of bread sprinkled with a tiny amount of salt. Each guest is greeted with the words "We greet you and invite you to this joyous occasion with this bread and salt." When the bride and groom enter, they are also greeted with the bread and salt. Symbolically, these items represent both the bitterness of life (salt) and the goodness (bread).

Another custom associated with Polish American weddings is the unveiling (*oczepiny*). This was one of the oldest and most important wedding customs in old Poland. The custom of the unveiling and capping ceremony was so essential, and played such a vital role in wedding activities, that where other wedding customs have completely disappeared, it has survived to this day and is part of the wedding tradition for any girl who wishes to celebrate her Polish heritage. At its heart, *oczepiny* is a rite of passage for the bride from that of a young maiden to that of married woman. This event usually takes place late in the evening after the guests have partaken of food, drink, and plenty of dancing and celebration. The bride is brought to the center of the dance floor and placed in a chair. She is surrounded by her bridesmaids and the other single women present, and her bridal veil or flowers are removed from her head, usually by the maid or matron of honor. Accompanied by the traditional Unveiling Song (Rośnie Trawka, sometimes called Dwanaście Aniołów), the veil or flowers are replaced with the cap of the married woman, called a *czepek*. In old Poland the placing of the cap on her head was an irrevocable moment for the bride, one from which there was no turning back. At this moment, and this moment only, she was officially a married lady. In America, the groom, not to be ignored, is also given a wide brimmed hat decorated lavishly with fruit and vegetables symbolizing fertility.—*Sophie Hodorowicz Knab*

SOURCES: Sophie Hodorowicz Knab, *Polish Customs, Traditions, & Folklore* (New York: Hippocrene Books, 1993); Deborah Anders Silverman, *Polish-American Folklore* (Urbana: University of Illinois Press, 2000).

Cwojdziński, Antoni (b. Brezezany na Ukranie, Russian Empire, October 9, 1896; d. London, England, August 7, 1972). Playwright, director. A playwright of comedies and satires that often spoofed popular misconceptions of science and psychology, Cwojdziński referred to his work as "scientific comedies" (*komedie naukowe*). He studied mathematics, physics, and chemistry at the universities of Lwów, Kraków, and Warsaw respectively. Briefly, he worked as an assistant of Theoretical Physics at the University of Warsaw. In the mid–1920s, his interests turned toward the arts and theater where he worked as an actor in several theatrical productions in Łódź, Katowice, Lwów, and Warsaw, among other places, for nearly a decade. He studied theatrical direction under Leon Schiller, began to direct productions as well as act, and then turned his talents to writing. He wrote and produced *Teoria Einstein* (Einstein's Theories) in 1934, which became a popular hit with audiences. The work spoofed popular misconceptions of science and the absurd conclusions drawn from a hasty reading of Einstein's theory of relativity. It won the Reynal Prize and enjoyed a run of 525 performances in 1934–36. Subsequent scientific comedies along a similar vein included *Epoka tempa* (The Pace of the this Epoch; 1935), *Freuda teoria snow* (Freud's Theory of Dreams; 1937), and *Temperamenty* (Temperament; 1938). Cwojdziński also dabbled in Poland's nascent film industry as an actor under the pseudonym Antoni Wojdan in several films before the war.

With the onset of war in September 1939, he remained in Warsaw for several months until the Germans took an interest in "an author who writes about Jewish scientists," as Cwojdziński put it. He fled to France and made his way to England and then the United States where, by 1941, he settled in New York. There he became a member of The Polish Artists' Theatre led by Leonidas Dudarew-Ossetyński. Based in New York, this theatre group was subsidized by the Polish government-in-exile in London. Operating 1942–45, it toured Boston, Buffalo, Chicago, Detroit, New York, and other cities. Its repertoire included the works of **Julian Tuwim**, **Jan Lechoń**, and other traditional Polish patriotic works and holiday performances such as the *Pastoralka*, a Christmas play based on Polish folk traditions. It also performed comedies and original works as well. These included Cwojdziński's *Piata kolumna w Warszawie* (Fifth Column in Warsaw; 1942), *Polska podziemna* (Polish Underground), and *Nimiec* (German). He also directed numerous productions.

With his wife, he briefly ran a radio station in Detroit. In 1944-45 he put together a series of one-act plays entitled *Warsawa w ogniu* (Warsaw in Flames) that ran in Boston and he tried to break into scores of towns and cities across the country. In the post-war years he settled in Chicago and collaborated in the theatrical group *Nasza Reduta* (Our Masked Ball) where he served primarily as a director. He also contributed to the local Polish radio hour and the Polish language press in the United States. After living in the U.S. for nearly 22 years, Cwojdziński relocated with his wife to England where he continued to work as a stage director and returned to writing his remaining science-themed comedies. He wrote and produced two comedies in London *Hipnoze* (Hypnosis) and *Obrona genów* (Struggle of the Genes), the latter dealing with popular misconceptions of hypnosis and parapsychology, genetics and nuclear war respectively. *Hypnosis* was set in the U.S. and featured Polish American characters. He returned to Poland in 1964 and staged a popular production of *Hypnosis*.

Cwojdziński's work was generally more well-received in Poland than it was abroad. His popular comedies *Freud's Theory of Dreams* and *Hypnosis* have been staged and made into films on a number of occasions.—*Romuald K. Byczkiewicz*

SOURCES: Kazimierz Braun, *A History of Polish Theater, 1939–1989: Spheres of Captivity and Freedom* (Westport, CT: Greenwood Press; 1996); Anna D. Jaroszyńska-Kirchmann, *The Exile Mission: The Polish Political Diaspora and Polish Americans, 1939–1956* (Athens, OH: Ohio University Press; 2004).

Cybis, Bolesław (b. Wilno, Poland, July 23, 1895; d. Trenton, New Jersey, May 31, 1958). Artist. Cybis was educated at the Academy of Fine Arts in St. Petersburg, Russia (1915), and at the Academy of Fine Arts in Warsaw where he studied with Tadeusz Pruszkowski (1923–25). Following the Russian Civil War in 1921 he sought refuge in Constantinople where he worked with artists Constantin Alajalov and Pavel Tchelitchev. After saving enough money to return to Warsaw, he entered the Fine Arts Academy, then went on to study Renaissance painters in Rome and Florence (1928). He lived and painted in Tripoli, Lybia (1932), and during the interwar period in Poland became a founding member of the painting group Bractwo św. Łukasza (Brotherhood of St.

Luke) and taught at the Academy of Fine Arts in Warsaw (1937). Traveling to the United States to spend time in the southwest sketching and painting American Indians (1939), he was stranded in New York by the outbreak of World War II. Cybis and his wife remained in the United States, becoming American citizens. Establishing himself as a painter, muralist, and sculptor, he founded Cybis Art Productions at the Steinway Mansion in Astoria, NY (1940), later relocating it to Trenton, NJ (1942), where he was one of the founders of the Cordey China Company. Around 1950 the couple started their own company, Cybis Porcelain, in Trenton. His honors include the Grand Prix for his ceiling mural at the Polish Pavilion of the International Art and Technique Exhibition, Paris (1937), and First Prize in the Christmas "Window Art" with fresco sculptures, Fifth Avenue, New York (1941).—*Stanley L. Cuba*

SOURCES: Irena Piotrowska, "American Painters and Illustrators of Polish Descent," in Revs. Francis Bolek and Ladislaus J. Siekaniec, eds., *Polish American Encyclopedia* (Buffalo, NY: Polish American Encyclopedia, 1954); Kenneth W. Prescott and James R. Mitchell, *Cybis in Retrospect* (Trenton: New Jersey State Museum, 1970).

Czarobski, Zygmont Pierre "Ziggy" (b. Chicago, Illinois, September 13, 1922; d. Aurora, Illinois, July 1, 1984). Football player. Czarobski entered the University of Notre Dame (1942-43), but his studies were interrupted for service in World War II. When he returned to school in 1946 he became the starting right tackle, leading Notre Dame to back-to-back national championships in 1946 and 1947. During this stretch, Notre Dame went 17-0-1 and outscored its opponents 562–76. Czarobski made both the International News Service and the Newspaper Enterprise Association All-America teams in 1947, then played professional football with the Chicago Rockets of the All-America Conference. After his pro football career ended, Czarboski became the administrative assistant to the Illinois Secretary of State. He also devoted much time and energy to charity, and once raised $202,000 in a single day for the Maryville Academy, a children's home. He was elected to the College Football Hall of Fame in 1977.—*Patricia Finnegan*

SOURCE: College Football National Hall of Fame Web Site.

Czas (Time). Established in Brooklyn, NY, in 1905, by the Czas Publishing Company, *Czas* was the official organ of the **Polish National Alliance of Brooklyn**. Its first editor was Józef Sawicki and it contained mostly organizational, local, and regional news.—*James S. Pula*

SOURCE: Jan Wepsiec, *Polish American Serial Publications: 1842–1966, An Annotated Bibliography* (Chicago: Jan Wepsiec, 1968), 37.

Czermański, Zdzisław (b. Kraków, Poland, April 30, 1896; d. New York, New York, January 27, 1970). Artist. Initially trained as a barber, optician, and photographer in Lwów, Poland, he later studied at the Free Academy of Fine Arts and with Kazimierz Sichulski in Lwów, then with Fernand Leger in Paris in the 1920s. During World War I, at age fourteen, he enlisted in Józef Piłsudski's legions, advancing to the rank of captain. In the 1920s and 1930s his work was published in *Szczutka* (Fillip) in Lwów, and in *Cyrulki Warszawski* (Barber of Warsaw) and *Wiadomości Literackie* (Literary News) in Warsaw. Known for his depictions of Marshal Piłsudski, he relocated to Paris in 1929 where his illustrations of Parisian street scenes appeared in *L'Illustration*, bringing him to the attention of the *Graphic* in London for whom he did work in 1931. Invited to the United States by the newly-founded *Fortune* magazine in October 1931, he traveled the country depicting political, financial, and cultural leaders, as well as scenes from urban and rural American life. Returning to Poland in 1934, with the German invasion in 1939 he escaped war-torn Poland with his wife via Wilno, Scandinavia, France, Portugal, and Brazil, arriving in New York where he spent the rest of his life. His drawings and caricatures were published in Europe in *Crapouillot, L'Art vivant, La Revue de l'art ancien et moderne, L'Illustration*, and the London *Graphic*; and in the United States in *American Mercury, Collier's, Cosmopolitan, Fortune, Esquire, Liberty, Life, Look, New York Times Book Review, Saturday Evening Post, The*

Zdzisław Czermański, a self-portrait (*Stanley L. Cuba*).

New Yorker, Time, and *Vogue*. Solo exhibitions of Czermański's work appeared in Detroit, Paris, New York, Warsaw, and Youngstown (OH), while his works appeared in many group exhibitions. Czermański's illustrations appeared in a number of books in Poland and France, as well the following published in the U.S.: *The Europeans* (1941), *Tale of a City* (1943), *The Forgotten Battlefield* (1944), *The Blue Flower: Best Stories of the Romanticists* (1946), and *American Transformations* (1959). Among his honors are the Gold Service Cross of the Polish government-in-exile in London and the **Alfred Jurzykowski Foundation** Prize.—*Stanley L. Cuba*

SOURCES: Frank E. Siudzinski, "The New American Offers Czermanski: Artists Draws Mickiewicz," *The New American* (New York), Vol. I, no. 2 (1932); "Czermanski Turns Art Against Artists: Polish-Born Portraits Goes to Work on Creative World's Wizards," *Look*, July 29, 1952; *Zdzisław Czermański 1900–1970: Rysunki* (Warsaw: Galeria Kordegarda, 1991).

Czestochowa, American (National Shrine of Our Lady of Czestochowa). Located in Doylestown, PA, the American Czestochowa was founded in 1955 by the Rev. Michael Zembrzuski as a home in the United States for the Pauline Fathers and Brothers (the Roman Catholic Religious Order of St. Paul the First Hermit) based at the Jasna Góra Monastery in Częstochowa, Poland. Through the generosity of a donation from the Rev. Stanisław K. Zdebel, a parcel of land was purchased at 654 Ferry Road (a place called Beacon Hill) near Doylestown and a barn on the property was adapted for use as the chapel of Our Lady of Częstochowa to house a copy of the religious icon of the Black Madonna, a representation of the Virgin Mary and Christ Child also known as Our Lady of Częstochowa. In the mid–1960s, construction began on a church designed by Polish architect Jerzy Szeptycki. This was a modern design, in a style then popular, made of poured concrete and a flat roof with the McCloskey Construction firm of Philadelphia engaged as prime contractor. The still unfinished building was dedicated on August 21, 1966, on a day when President Lyndon Baines Johnson made a brief visit to the Shrine. Also present on that occasion were Philadelphia Archbishop **John Cardinal Krol**, Pennsylvania Governor William Scranton, Philadelphia Mayor James Tate, and Senator Hugh Scott. Expenses resulting from the ambitious expansion program grew faster than donations, leaving the American Czestochowa deeply in debt. In addition, a series of unfavorable articles by Gannett News Service reporters Carlton J. Sherwood, William F. Schmick, and John M. Hanchette shed a negative light on the situation. Eventually, the debt was repaid through a fund raising cam-

National Shrine of Our Lady of Częstochowa in Doylestown, Pennsylvania (*Peter Obst*).

paign orchestrated by John Cardinal Krol and a loan obtained from the Knights of Columbus organization by the Prior of the Paulines, the Rev. Lucius Tyrasiński. The debt was fully repaid on August 30, 1981. On September 9, 1984, President Ronald Reagan, accompanied by Pennsylvania Governor Richard Thornburgh, visited the shrine. Eventually, this visit was memorialized with a sculpture portraying the president and his host, Polish Festival chair Jane Gowaty, sitting together at a picnic table.

By 2009 the Shrine included the main church with Chapels of St. Anne and of the Black Madonna, Our Lady of Częstochowa. Small chapels were dedicated to St. Paul the First Hermit, Our Lady of Nazareth, Divine Mercy, and Our Lady of Guadalupe. Outdoors there was a grotto honoring Our Lady of Lourdes, and a chapel for Our Lady of Fatima. A separate visitor center houses a cafeteria, museum, religious shop, and meeting rooms. The Ave Maria Retreat House has accommodations for groups and individuals. An impressive granite statue of Pope John Paul II by Stanisław Lutostański is located between the buildings. There is also a cemetery which is the final resting place of many Polonia notables. The Polish Army veterans' section is graced by "The Avenger," a large sculpture designed by **Andrzej Pityński**. A Polish American folk festival is held every Labor Day and on the weekend following. Two prominent Poles, **Jan Lechoń** and **Ignacy Jan Paderewski** are remembered with memorials

built into the walls of the vestibule in the main church, both executed by sculptor Andrzej Pityński. The Paderewski Memorial actually contains Paderewski's heart, separated from his body after death in 1941, later forgotten but eventually located in a Long Island mausoleum by historian **Henryk Archacki**.

The National Shrine of Our Lady of Czestochowa is not only the spiritual heart of Philadelphia **Polonia**, but attracts visitors and pilgrims from many states and abroad. A summer foot pilgrimage, that now includes groups from Trenton and Philadelphia, was initiated by the Rev. Ignacy Kuziemski of Great Meadows, NJ, in 1988 and has since become an annual event. Buses bring visitors for Sunday Mass, and for special religious events. This includes members of the New York Haitian community who consider the Black Madonna representation of the Virgin Mary to be their spiritual Mother. Because of this, the Pauline Fathers have added Holy Masses in French to the Sunday schedule.

In the future the Shrine will continue to play an important role in the spiritual life not only of Polonia, but other ethnic groups in the United States, not only as a place of worship but as a repository of various art works and memorabilia, for example, the paintings of Jan Styka and items relating to visits in 1969 and 1976 of Cardinal Karol Wojtyła before he became Pope John Paul II. The Pauline Fathers and Brothers use modern means of communication to send out the Gospel message through the Polish language broadcast,

the "Voice of Czestochowa" and an internet website.—*Peter J. Obst*

SOURCE: *50 Year Anniversary Journal* (Doylestown, PA: National Shrine of Our Lady of Czestochowa, 2005).

Czołgosz, Leon Franciszek (alias Fred C. Nieman; b. Detroit, Michigan, January 1[?], 1873; d. Auburn, New York, October, 29, 1901). Assassin. In 1891 Czołgosz's family settled in Cleveland, Ohio, later moving to Warrensville in the same state. Czołgosz made a living working in wire plants. By 1893 he had become highly critical of religion and capitalism. When he became unemployed in 1898 he displayed an increasing interest in the anarchist movement. Although he tried to become a member of the leftist Liberty Club (Klub Wolności) in Cleveland, there is no evidence that he was accepted to membership in this or any other socialist organization. He purportedly made a decision to assassinate the president of the United States upon learning of the murder of Italian King Humbert I in 1900, but he later confessed to being impressed by a flamboyant speech of Emma Goldman whom he listened to in Cleveland. On September 6, 1901, during the Pan-American Exposition in Buffalo, Czołgosz shot President William McKinley who died eight days later. Immediately apprehended at the scene, he was sentenced to death by hanging. Polish Americans strongly condemned the assassination, many even rejecting claims that he held Polish ancestry. Psychiatric observations of Czołgosz following his arrest were published by Walter Channing, and an account of the assassination is given in a highly anti-leftist novel by **Stanisław Osada**, *W dni-*

Leon Czołgosz, assassin of President William McKinley (*OLS*).

ach nędzy i zbrodni (In Days of Memory and Crime), published in 1908.—*Adam Walaszek*

SOURCES: "Czolgosz, Leon," in David D. Van Tassel and John J. Grabowski, eds., *The Encyclopedia of Cleveland History* (Bloomington, IN: Indiana University Press, 1987); A. Wesley Johns, *The Man Who Shot McKinley* (South Brunswick, NJ: A. S. Barnes and Co., Inc., 1970); Walter Channing, *The Mental Status of Czolgosz, the Assassin of President McKinley* (Baltimore: n.p., 1902).

Czyz, Bobby (b. Orange, New Jersey, February 10, 1962; d.—). Prize fighter. Czyz was a member of the U.S. Amateur Boxing Team in 1980, and injury prevented him from joining his teammates for a journey to Poland that ended in a fatal airplane crash. As a professional fighter from 1980–98, he compiled a record of 44-8-0. He held the world light heavyweight championship in 1986-87, and the world cruiserweight championship in 1991-92. In addition, Czyz was recognized in some quarters as the super cruiserweight titleholder in 1995-96. He also appeared as a broadcast boxing analyst. Czyz is a member of the New Jersey Boxing Hall of Fame, and in 2009 he was inducted into the **National Polish-American Sports Hall of Fame**.—*Neal Pease*

SOURCE: "Bobby Czyz," New Jersey Boxing Hall of Fame website, www.njboxinghof.org.

Czyzewski, Francis Kalist (b. South Bend, Indiana, June 30, 1904; d. South Bend, Indiana, December 6, 1976). Radio pioneer. An early inclination toward the priesthood drew Czyzewski to the seminary of the Holy Cross Fathers at the University of Notre Dame, but he later switched to journalism, earning his baccalaureate degree in 1920. After accepting a position as editor of the newspaper *Goniec Polski* (Polish Messenger), he organized a theater company in which he directed, acted, and authored plays. He later accepted a position on the editorial staff of the *South Bend Tribune*, which also owned radio station WSBT. This drew Czyzewski into radio as originator of *The Polish Hour*, which debuted in August 1929. It was the first Polish radio program broadcast in Indiana and only the third station to broadcast an original Polish language program in the United States. The program was the first to broadcast American and international news in Polish, and to mix Polish and English in its broadcasts to appeal to non–Polish listeners who enjoyed Polish music. In 1936 he was honored with the Silver Cross of Merit from the Republic of Poland for his work in promoting Polish culture. Czyzewski retired in 1974.—*James S. Pula*

SOURCE: Joseph Migala, *Polish Radio Broadcasting in the United States* (Boulder, CO: East European Monographs, 1987), 212–13.

Dąbrowski, Adam (b. Warsaw, Poland, September 10, 1880; d. Los Angeles, California, August 12, 1972). Sculptor. After studying at the Warsaw Fine Arts School with sculptor Xawery Dunikowski and painters Ferdynand Ruszczyć and Kazimierz Stabrowski (pre–1905), and at the Zakład Arystyczny Rzezbiarsko-Sztukatorski in Warsaw (1905), he migrated to New York in 1906. There, he opened his own shop on the Lower East Side (1912–23) and later a woodcarving school at 241 Fulton Street, Brooklyn (1929–34). He worked briefly in Cincinnati and subsequently Los Angeles (1937–72). Among his commissioned works were the Frick Mansion interiors and some of the trappings in Riverside Church (New York), St. Casimir's Church (Brooklyn, NY, and Shenandoah, PA), Church of the Blessed Sacrament (New York), altars, crucifixes and Stations of the Cross for ten Catholic and Protestant churches in southern California; **Polish Roman Catholic Union**, Chicago (1936); Essex Club, Newark, NJ; Philadelphia Public Ledger Building and Land Title Building, Philadelphia, PA; L.C. Phipps Mansion, Denver, CO; London Shop, Hollywood, CA. He also completed bas-reliefs of President Woodrow Wilson, **Kazimierz Pułaski**, **Tadeusz Kościuszko**, and Władysław Reymont. His works appeared in exhibitions in Chicago (IL), Larchmont (NY), New York, and Newark (NJ). Collections of his works are housed at Newark Museum, Princeton University, the **Polish Museum of America** (Chicago), and the **Polish Women's Alliance** (Chicago).—*Stanley L. Cuba*

SOURCES: Eugene Clute and Adam Dabrowski, *A Monograph of the Work of Adam Dabrowski, Sculptor in Wood* (Chicago: n.p., ca. 1920); "Adam Dabrowski," *Poland*, December 1928.

Dąbrowski, Józef Henryk (b. Żółtańce, partitioned Poland, January 27, 1842; d. Detroit, Michigan, February 15, 1903). Priest, educator. Born into a family of the lesser landed nobility, he was the eldest of five children. Privately tutored at an early age, he completed his primary and secondary education in nearby Lublin. In 1862 he entered Szkoła Główna or "Main School," as the restored University of Warsaw was then known, where he pursued studies in engineering. Forced to leave Poland because of his participation in the January Insurrection of 1863, Dąbrowski went first to Dresden, then to Switzerland for two years, and finally to Rome where he entered the charter class of the Polish Papal College founded by Pius IX in 1866. He completed philosophical and theological studies at the Gregorian University and was ordained in Rome on August 8, 1869. Advised by the Rev. **Leopold Moczygemba**, OFM Conv., founder of **Panna Maria**, Texas in 1854, and at the invitation of Bishop Joseph Melcher of Green Bay, Wisconsin, he arrived in the United States on December 31, 1869 to work among Polish Catholic immigrants in rural Wisconsin. During twelve years as a parish priest he built two churches, a mission chapel, a parochial school, a convent, and a rectory. In 1874 he brought the Sisters of the Congregation of St. Felix of Cantilice (the **Felicians**) to staff the parochial school in Polonia, Wisconsin. Both he and the sisters realized the paramount importance of education for the preservation of immigrant faith and the national spirit. In collaboration with the Felician Sisters, he drafted a course of study for an eight-grade elementary school and a four-year high school. Instruction was

Adam Dąbrowski, sculptor (*Stanley L. Cuba*).

Joseph Dąbrowski, founder of Saints Cyril and Methodius Seminary (*OLS*).

conducted in both Polish and English in all grades except the first. He assisted the sisters in establishing a novitiate and setting up a print shop, which published Polish textbooks for elementary grades. His efforts eventually won him the reputation as the founder of the Polish American school system.

In the Wisconsin wilderness Dąbrowski preached to the Chippewa, Winnebago, and Menominee Indians, baptized several hundred, and taught his new flock the ways of Euro-American agriculture. His Polish-Chippewa dictionary was designed to facilitate the mission; and, for a brief period, until they returned to their former ways, Native Americans also joined the Felician community. By 1879 the Felicians were teaching at St. Albertus Parish in Detroit. They were granted permission to move their motherhouse from rural Wisconsin to a centrally located city where they would enjoy greater support from priests and other religious. In 1882, for reasons of health and with the approval of Bishop Caspar Borgess, Dąbrowski also transferred his activities to Detroit, where he became pastor of St. Albertus and continued to guide the expansion of the Felician community and its network of schools and publications. He simultaneously collaborated in establishing **SS. Cyril and Methodius Seminary** and St. Mary's High School in 1885 for the training of bi-lingual Polish American priests. As rector of the Polish seminary (1885–1903) and director of the Felicians (1874–1903), he was instrumental in providing Polish parishes with priests and parochial schools with teachers, contributing more than any other single individual to their development.—*Frank B. Koper*

SOURCES: Joseph V. Swastek, "The Formative Years of the Polish Seminary in the United States," in F. Domanski, et al., eds., *The Contributions of the Poles to the Growth of Catholicism in the United States* (Rome: Typis Pontificiae Universitatis Gregorianae, 1959), 29–150; Frank Renkiewicz, *For God, Country, and Polonia: One Hundred Years of the Orchard Lake Schools* (Orchard Lake, MI: Center for Polish Studies and Culture, 1985), 13–47; Mary Edwina, "The Founder of the Polish Seminary," *Polish American Studies*, Vol. 8, no. 1–2 (1951), 21–28; Mary Benedicta, "Father Joseph Dąbrowski — Educator," *Polish American Studies*, Vol. 9, no. 1–2 (1952), 11–16; Mary Jeremiah, "Father Dąbrowski and the Felicians," *Polish American Studies*, Vol. 16, no. 1–2 (1959), 12–23; Joseph Swastek, "Father Dąbrowski Reconsidered," *Polish American Studies*, Vol. 26, no. 1 (1969), 30–40; Mary Benedicta Kolat, "Father Joseph Dabrowski, the Pioneer Priest and His Significant Contribution Toward Catholic American School System" (Detroit: Unpublished M.A. thesis, Wayne State University, 1950); Thaddeus C. Radzilowski, "Father Jozef Dąbrowski, the Orchard Lake Schools and the Shaping of Polish American Catholicism," *U.S. Catholic Historian*, Vol. 27, no. 3 (2009), 83–107.

Dake, Arthur (Arthur William Darkowski; b. Portland, Oregon, April 8, 1910; d. Reno, Nevada, April 28, 2000). Chess player.

Dake was the last living member of the great U.S. Chess Olympiad teams that won the title consecutively in Prague 1931, Folkestone 1933, and Warsaw 1935 where he had the best score in the entire Olympiad. At the age of sixteen he joined the merchant marine where he made voyages to China and Russia. He was an energetic man who was described by many as a friendly and positive individual. Dake did not learn chess until 1927 when he received instruction in the game at the Portland YMCA. He quickly established his reputation first in Portland and then in New York where he arrived in 1929 just in time for the Wall Street Crash. By the following year he became champion of the Marshall Chess Club. Becoming a professional chess player during a time of poverty, he hustled for a quarter a game on Coney Island, played rapid play and blitz chess events for money and coached, but like most of the depression era players he made hardly any money. Dake's career is unusual in that he did not enter a tournament until he was already a strong player and, as a result, virtually all of his tournament results, even from his very first tournament, were reported in publications such as the American Chess Bulletin. His first tournament was the 1930 New York State Championship, in which he finished third. In addition, his career as a tournament player was exceptionally short. Virtually all of his chess was played during the period 1930 to 1938. He then stayed virtually out of chess for 37 years until he made a comeback in 1975.

After marrying in 1935, he crossed the United States on simultaneous tours and the following year taught chess in Milwaukee schools. In 1937 he needed a steady income so he stayed away from competitive chess in

order to earn a stable income. His last major appearance was in the 1938 U.S. Chess Championships where he tied for sixth place. He did play some chess after this, including two draws in 1946 in the Russia versus the United States match in Moscow. In 1952 he placed fourth in the Hollywood tournament won by Svetosar Gligoric. He filled in during one round of the USA–USSR match in New York 1954, losing to David Bronstein. He returned more regularly to chess after his retirement as supervisor at Oregon's Department of Motor Vehicles. In 1973 he entered the Lone Pine tournament and had reasonable results in this event in 1974 and 1976. At age ninety, he spent his last night playing blackjack in the Sands Regency Casino in Reno, Nevada. He is a member of the U.S. Chess Hall of Fame.—*Luis J. Gonzalez*

SOURCES: Casey Bush, *Grandmaster from Oregon: The Life and Games of Arthur Dake* (Portland, OR: Portland Chess Press, 1991); Larry Parr, "Arthur Dake: An American Original," *Chess Life*, December 1984, 28; obituary, *New York Times*, May 11, 2000.

D'Alfonce, Joseph Emile (Józef Emil D'Alfons; b. Warsaw, Poland, 1813; d. Ripon, Yorkshire, England, December 1871). Educator. A descendant of a noble family from the Grand Duchy of Poznań, D'Alfonce attended the Imperial Military Academy in St. Petersburg, then studied military engineering in Warsaw. Siding with the Polish cause in the November Uprising (1830-31), he was reduced in rank to private and sent to the Caucasus, but escaped to France and then to the U.S. where he tutored for individual families. In 1851, he accepted a position as a gymnastics instructor at the University of Virginia. In the same year he published *Instructions in Gymnastics Containing a Full Description of More Than Eight Hundred Exercises, and Illustrated by Five Hundred Engravings*. In 1856 he was licensed to tutor students in French at the university. With the outbreak of the Civil War he was commissioned and sent to Richmond, but when he objected to the harsh treatment of Union prisoners an order was issued for his arrest and he barely escaped to the North, making his way penniless to New York. Joining the Union army, he served in the cavalry forces under Gen. Philip Sheridan. Following the war he returned to the University of Virginia, but left after a year, no doubt rejected by the faculty and students because of his service in the Union army. Moving north, he took a position as chair of modern languages at the Alexander Institute in White Plains, NY. Attempts by scholars to locate confirming evidence of D'Alfonse's service in the Confederate and Union forces has thus far not been successful.—*James S. Pula*

Arthur Dake, champion chess player (*OLS*).

SOURCES: Ladislas John Siekaniec, *The Polish Contribution to Early American Education, 1608–1865* (San Francisco: R & E Research Associates, 1976); "Biographical Sketch of Prof. J. E. D'Alfonce, *The Eastern State Journal* (White Plains, NY), November 27, 1886.

Dana, Walter (Władysław Danilowski; b. Warsaw, Poland, April 26, 1902; d. Miami Beach, Florida, March 4, 2000). Composer, pianist. After studying music in the Warsaw Conservatory and in Paris, he earned a degree in law from Warsaw University. While working with the Polish Foreign Office he also worked with the Quid Pro Quo Theater and founded the Chór Dana (Dana Choir) which performed throughout Europe and made two concert tours in the U.S. The creator of numerous film scores, he also served as director of music for the Polish Radio Network and director of the Tip Top Theatre, being honored for his efforts with Poland's Gold Cross of Merit and Italy's Royal Diamond Pin with Crown. When the Germans invaded Poland in 1939 he managed to escape, eventually migrating to the U.S. where he founded an American version of the Chór Dana, appearing on Polish radio stations in New York and Detroit. In 1946 he formed Dana Records which quickly became the leading label for Polka music. In 1952 *Billboard Magazine* ranked his label third behind only Victor and Columbia. Dana was able to introduce to audiences a host of new talent, many of whom went on to become household names in the Polka music field. His label eventually released 120 albums featuring about 1,300 songs. Among his awards were the Gold Cross of Merit from Poland and the Royal Diamond Pin with Crown from Italy. He was inducted into the Polka Hall of Fame in 1971. — *James S. Pula*

SOURCES: Bolesław Wierzbiański, ed., *Who's Who in Polish America* (New York: Bicentennial Publishing Corporation, 1996); Douglas Martin, "Walter Dana, Polka Promoter, Dies at 96," *New York Times*, March 13, 2000.

Danielewski, Ann "Poe" (b. New York, New York, March 23, 1968; d. —). Musician, songwriter. Born to avant-garde Polish film director **Tad Danielewski** and American actress Priscilla Machold, Ann Danielewski received the nickname "Poe" at the age of nine owing to an affinity for the writing of American poet, literary critic, and short-story writer Edgar Allan Poe, and, in particular, for his short story, "The Mask of the Red Death." As a child, Danielewski moved with her parents to Africa, India, and Europe, before returning to the United States and settling in Utah, where her father taught theater and film at Brigham Young University. After her parents' divorce, Danielewski spent the remainder of her adolescence living as a squatter in Manhattan's Lower East Side. While pursuing her

undergraduate degree in English on a full scholarship at Princeton University, she established her first band, continuing her music career in New York City upon graduation. In 1994, Atlantic Records signed Danielewski as a recording artist, and one year later she released her debut album, *Hello*. The successful singles "Angry Johnny" and "Trigger Happy Jack" pushed *Hello* to the top of music charts, earning the album gold-record status. In 2000, Danielewski released her second album, *Haunted*, which was inspired by her brother, **Mark Z. Danielewski**'s novel *House of Leaves*. The album's tracks also incorporated segments of her late father's tape recorded lectures, monologues, and voice recordings. *Haunted* was released in conjunction with *House of Leaves*, and together the Danielewskis embarked on a tour of Borders Books and Music stores across the United States to promote both the CD and the book. One of *Haunted*'s tracks, "Hey Pretty," was remixed after the album's release, adding the voice of Mark Danielewski as he read passages from his novel. Ann Danielewski's musical style has been described as a blend of electronica, folk, and rock music. Her 2000 cover of the Go-Gos' song "My Lips Are Sealed" appeared in the film *Gossip* (2000). — *Krystyna Cap*

SOURCE: Steve Baltin, "The Haunting Return of Poe," *Rolling Stone*, November 2, 2000.

Danielewski, Mark Z. (b. New York, New York, March 5, 1966; d. —). Author. The son of Polish émigré avant-garde film director **Tad Danielewski** and brother of singer-songwriter **Ann "Poe" Danielewski**, Mark Danielewski is author of two critically acclaimed novels, *House of Leaves* (Pantheon, 2000) and *Only Revolutions* (Pantheon, 2006), as well as *The Whalestoe Letters* (2000) and *The Fifty Year Sword* (2005). He holds degrees in English literature from Yale University (1988) and the University of Southern California School of Cinema-Television (1993). His first novel, *House of Leaves*, received the attention of critics for its daring visual and verbal experimentation. Touted as a sprawling post-postmodern work for its groundbreaking aesthetics — myriad footnotes, essays, inverted and backwards text, fragmented prose, overlapping textboxes, intersecting storylines, and other literary and verbal devices — the novel was also profoundly influenced by film techniques and graphic art, drawing inspiration from myriad sources, including *The Blair Witch Project*. Written in close collaboration with his sister, "Poe," *House of Leaves* inspired her 2000 album *Haunted*. His second novel, *Only Revolutions*, departs from the horror story-like quality of *House of Leaves*, telling a

time-traveling tale of two teenagers on a road trip across America. *Only Revolutions* was short-listed for the National Book Award, and reviewers have compared Danielewski's prose to James Joyce's *Ulysses*, Herman Melville's *Moby-Dick*, and Vladimir Nabokov's *Pale Fire* in depth and complexity. — *Krystyna Cap*

SOURCES: Larry McCaffery and Sinda Gregory, "Haunted House — An Interview with Mark Z. Danielewski," *Critique*, Vol. 44, no. 2 (2003), 99–135; Troy Patterson, "Complete 360," *New York Times Book Review* (November 5, 2006), 24.

Danielewski, Tad (b. Poland, March 29, 1921; d. Los Angeles, California, January 6, 1993). Teacher, director. An influential acting teacher who trained a generation of remarkable actors and a noted film and stage director, Danielewski served in the Polish Underground and was also confined in a German forced labor camp during World War II. After liberation, he directed a series of plays in the Polish and British army theatres and pursued his dramatic studies at the Royal Academy of Dramatic Art in London. He migrated to the United States in 1948, attended Ohio State University, and launched his career as a television and stage director. He directed twenty features for the CBS "Omnibus" series by the mid–1950s. He was active in New York theatre, directing a series of plays and organizing his own acting workshop which only took in professional actors on a one-on-one basis after they had successfully auditioned for him. Over the years, actors who praised his teaching style and technique include James Earl Jones, Martin Sheen, Sigourney Weaver, and Mercedes Ruehl. Ruehl singled out Danielewski for special thanks in her Oscar and Tony Awards acceptance speeches. Jones, in his memoir, credited Danielewski with preparing him for his stage roles in *Othello* and *Of Mice and Men*, and with teaching him "something else that precedes language," the "something that rages in every human being [and] rages in the best of dramatic characters.... Drama should always take us to the edge, where we don't know what is going to happen, or how far it is going to go." In 1957 Danielewski founded Stratton Productions, collaborating with Pearl S. Buck on several theatrical and film productions. He expanded into film direction with *The Big Wave* (1961), *No Exit* (1962), *The Guide* (1965; a collaboration with Pearl S. Buck), and *España puerta abierta* (1972). He was also part of a production team with the ABC network that won an Emmy award for the documentary series *Africa* in 1967. Danielewski continued to work with actors in his workshop and was a professor of theater and film at Brigham Young University (1977–88) and professor emeritus

at the University of Southern California.—
Romuald K. Byczkiewicz

SOURCE: "Tad Danielewski, An Acting Teacher and
a Director," *New York Times*, January 13, 1993, 19.

Data, Marisha (b. Chicago, Illinois, May
26, 1911; d. Chicago, Illinois, October 12,
1972). Musician. Data was attracted to music
early in her life and developed an impressively
varied vocal repertoire. She performed in concerts in Chicago's Grant Park and in *Gentlemen
Prefer Blondes* in summer stock at Music in
the Round in Skokie, Illinois. She was a
soloist with the Midwest and San Carlo Opera
Company where she starred in *Il Travatore*,
Hansel and Gretel, the *Barber of Seville*, and
other operatic productions. In addition to her
vocal talents, she was an accomplished actress
and comedienne, appearing in major cities
from New York through Chicago and in
Canada. As a singer, she recorded on the
Rondo, Capitol, Dana, Ridgemoor, and
Chicago Polka labels, but is best known for
her polka hits "Wishing Well Waltz" and "Vi-
olins Play For Me." She was inducted into the
Polka Music Hall of Fame in 1974. Data was
also generous in her support for charitable
causes. Her Marisha Data radio program
raised more than $10,000 to assist in restoring
the Salvatorian Fathers Seminary in Trzebina,
Poland; her efforts were responsible for the
sale of over $1 million in U.S. War Bonds; she
raised thousands of dollars for the Red Cross
and to fight infantile paralysis; for more than
ten years she made appearances in support of
crippled children in Poland and orphans in
Japan; she collected stamps for more than fifteen years to purchase medical supplies for
missionaries in Africa; she collected funds to
aid a facility for blind children in Laski,

**Marisha Data, singer, comedienne, and noted
philanthropist, 1949 (*PMA*).**

Poland; she appeared on behalf of veterans
homes and homes for the aged; and she
worked on behalf of many church and patriotic causes. In all of these efforts, she refused
any compensation and would not accept
payment for advertising them during her
shows.—*James S. Pula*

SOURCE: www.internationalpolka.com/data.htm.

Dębski, Aleksander (b. Mogielnica,
Poland, November 17, 1857; d. Warsaw, Poland,
March 6, 1935). Politician, socialist. Dębski
became involved in secret organizations in his
secondary school years. As a student of mathematics and physics at St. Petersburg's University, he joined a group of Polish socialists.
After a colleague's arrest, Dębski gave up studies and in 1883 came to Warsaw under a false
name and joined the "Great Proletariat," the
first Polish socialist party. He set up socialist
groups throughout the Kingdom of Poland
and was instrumental in making contacts with
Russian revolutionists. During tsarist repres-
sions against socialists in 1884, he fled to
Geneva, later moving between Zurich, Paris
and London while earning his living as a typesetter and printer. Dębski took an active part
in the Polish and European socialist movement. In 1892 he was elected to the executive
committee of the newly created Związek Za-
graniczny Socjalistów Polskich (Overseas Alliance of Polish Socialists). In May 1899 he
went to America to aid the Polish American
socialist movement, particularly in New York
and Chicago. He was active in the **Alliance
of Polish Socialists** and in the **Polish National Alliance**, where he was elected vice
censor in 1903. In 1904 Dębski obtained
American citizenship while continuing his appeals to the Polish American community to
aid Poland and organizing assistance for Polish
political émigrés in the revolutionary years of
1904–05. At the same time, he kept in contact
with Polish socialists in Europe, in whose disputes he supported the independence movement associated with Józef Piłsudski. In 1910
he took part in the Polish National Congress
held in Washington, D.C. (see **Polish National Congress of 1910**), that placed renewed
emphasis on **Polonia**'s commitment to Polish
independence. In 1912 Dębski was among the
co-founders of the **National Defense Committee** (KON) and entered its Central Committee. After the outbreak of World War I he
secretly assisted in sending Polish American
volunteers to Piłsudski's Legions. In 1914-15
and 1915–17 he visited his homeland as a
KON delegate, delivering $11,000 collected
by Polish Americans and a standard from the
Polish women of Chicago. He observed the
Legions in action and cooperated with Pił-

**Aleksander Dębski, socialist politician and co-
founder of the National Defense Committee
(*JPI*).**

sudski. As an American citizen he had to leave
Warsaw (which was occupied by the Germans)
when the U.S. declared war on Germany in
1917. After returning to America, Dębski submitted to Pres. Woodrow Wilson memoranda
on the independence of Poland and on humanitarian and economic aid. In 1917–22 he
was a publisher of *Telegram Codzienny* (Daily
Telegram), a KON-oriented New York daily.
On January 1, 1920 Dębski returned to Poland
where he supported Piłsudski until 1926 when
he came to regard the right-centrist government as incapable of dealing with social problems. After 1926 he was strongly opposed to the
dictatorial methods of the Piłsudski regime. He
remained a democrat, a socialist, and an active
member of the Polish Socialist Party (PPS). As
its representative in the Senate in 1930–35,
Dębski criticized governmental abuses and anti–
Semitic outbreaks.—*Joanna Wojdon*

SOURCES: Marian Marek Drozdowski, *Aleksander
Dębski* (Warsaw: Iskry, 1986); Norbert Barlicki, *Aleksander Dębski. Życie i działalność 1857–1935* (Warszawa:
Wydawnictwo Stowarzyszenia B. Wiezniów Polity-
cznych, 1937).

Dembinski, Louis (Ludwik Dębiński;
b. Tarnów, Poland, 1828; d. Philadelphia,
Pennsylvania, March 9, 1886). Educator. Arriving in the U.S. in 1849, he apparently studied and taught in New England before entering Yale University in 1855. While at Yale, he
is believed to have been the first Pole to be-

come a member of the Phi Beta Kappa honorary. Graduating in 1858, he moved to Clinton, LA, where he opened a school for boys and was elected to the examining committee of Centenary College. In October, 1860, he was elected principal of the public school in Clinton. When the Civil War broke out he was conscripted by Confederate authorities into the 16th Louisiana Infantry. By the spring of 1862 he returned to Clinton on sick leave, but following the Union seizure of New Orleans he worked as a clerk with the U.S. Provost Marshal's Office in that city. While he was there, neighbors burned his property, probably because of his cooperation with the Northern army. Dembinski soon became principal of the Claiborne Boys School in New Orleans. However, when the Union occupation ended following the war Dembinski was discharged because of his Northern sympathies. He moved to Westport, CT, in October, 1866, enrolled again in Yale University, and earned an M.A. degree from Yale the following year. Following graduation he moved to Sherburne, NY, where he again assumed a position as principal of the local public high school. He retired in July, 1875, and moved to Philadelphia where he began work in his father-in-law's pharmacy. After receiving the degree "Graduate in Pharmacy" from the Philadelphia College of Pharmacy and Science (1877), he pursued the profession of a pharmacist for the rest of his life.—*James S. Pula*

SOURCES: Ladislas John Siekaniec, *The Polish Contribution to Early American Education, 1608–1865* (San Francisco: R & E Research Associates, 1976); James William Mobley, "The Academy Movement in Louisiana," *Louisiana Historical Quarterly*, Vol. 30, no. 3 (July 1947).

Democratic Society of Polish Exiles in America (Towarzystwo Demokratyczne Wygnańców Polskich w Ameryce).

Formed in New York City in August 1852 under the leadership of Ludwik Szpaczek, the Democratic Society of Polish Exiles in America was an outgrowth of the Polish Democratic Society (Towarzystwo Demokratyczne Polski) formed by exiles in Paris and maintained close ties to it throughout the existence of the Society in America. It was formed in an attempt to provide an organizational umbrella for the greatly dispersed Polish political emigration in the U.S., to keep them informed about European events, organize attempts to support their countrymen in Europe, and also provide for needy members. Membership was open to "Every person born on Polish soil, regardless of his political or religious beliefs." The first committee included Szpaczek as president, someone with the surname Wróblewski as secretary, J. A. Szretter as treasurer, and committee members Aleksander Małuski, Ksawery Karczewski, Józef Kiczman, and J. Kępiński. The society remained active for about eight years, with varying membership that included at one time or another 157 names. In New York, where weekly meetings were held, attendance varied from about 20 to 35 people per meeting. Outside of New York, the most active centers were in Charleston, Cleveland, Philadelphia, St. Louis, and Troy (NY). A separate society in New Orleans declined regular cooperation with the New York group because of differing political philosophies. Though with limited funds that it raised from sympathetic supporters in New York City, the Society attempted to find employment for new arrivals, provided funds for the purchase of necessities, and also helped members to pay for transportation if they secured employment in other cities. In this, it was a precursor of the self-help organizations established on a much wider scale during the period of the mass migration between 1870 and 1920. The Society maintained ongoing relationships with other European exile groups, frequently attending meetings of French, German, Italian, Hungarian, and other groups of similar political exiles. The Society was a permanent member of the Union of Liberal Societies, formed in New York to coordinate activities of the various émigré groups. One of the Society's activities that drew participation from the other exile groups was the annual commemoration of the outbreak of the November Uprising in 1830. When called upon by Poles in Europe to participate in the Russo-Turkish War on the side of Turkey in an effort to weaken Russia's grip on Polish territory, the Society refused, arguing that Polish exiles ought to return to Europe only to participate directly in attempts to redeem the fatherland, not to join forces with a despotic government. Following 1855, contacts with European exiles lessened, and the political activities of the Society became fewer, its only notable success being the establishment of an active group in San Francisco. The death of Szpaczek in 1859 led to further decline in the organization's activity.—*James S. Pula*

SOURCE: Florian Stasik, *Polish Political Émigrés in the United States of America, 1831–1864* (Boulder, CO: East European Monographs, 2002).

Dende, Cornelian (Edmund Dende; b. Scranton, Pennsylvania, August 8, 1915; d. New York State, August 31, 1996).

Priest, journalist. Dende entered the Polish American St. Anthony of Padua Province of the Conventual **Franciscan** Friars (OFM Conv. or Black Franciscans) in 1934. After priesthood studies in Montréal (Canada), Lwów (Poland), Rome (Italy), and Granby (MA), Dende min-

The Rev. Cornelian Dende, journalist (*OLS*).

istered at Corpus Christi Church, Buffalo, NY, for a short time prior to being named co-director of the Catholic Press Agency, a news bureau accredited to the Polish government-in-exile during World War II. After serving at St. Joseph Church, Camden, NJ, Dende was named Novice Master first at St. Lawrence Novitiate in Becket, MA, in 1948. He then served at St. Joseph Cupertino Novitiate in Ellicott City, MD, and in 1958 was named Master of Students at St. Hyacinth Seminary in Granby, MA. The next year, upon the death of **Justin Figas** OFM Conv., the founding director of *The Rosary Hour*, a Polish-language weekly Sunday evening devotional radio program heard on some seventy-five stations, Dende was named director. He made significant organizational changes to the show, and in 1960 he moved from live to taped broadcasts, allowing greater flexibility and dissemination of taped materials. In addition to the tapes, the well-researched Polish language segments were printed and disseminated as well. Dende and the friars maintained a massive correspondence, offering spiritual direction, counsel, and moral guidance to Polish-language listeners and correspondents by the thousands each year. A regular devotional mail order campaign was also begun. In 1979 the format switched from a full hour broadcast November to April, to a half-hour broadcast weekly throughout the year. Guest presenters both from Poland and the United States addressed weekly themes in basic Christian doctrine, ethics, important figures in Polish culture, and prayer and spirituality to recent Polish immigrants and older immigrants retaining facility in the Polish language throughout the United States and Canada. Special appeals launched through the program financed ventures in both the United States and Poland, including St. Francis High School, Athol Springs, NY; St. Joseph Inter-community Hospital, Cheektowaga, NY; the Catholic University of Lublin, Poland; and the Metropolitan Seminary of the Archdiocese of Warsaw. Dende served as director until 1995. Among his numerous honors and recognition, he was twice awarded the Officer's Cross of the Order of *Polonia Restituta* by the government of Poland; twice National Citizen of the Year by the national weekly *Am-Pol Eagle*; the Gold Medal of Merit from the Catholic University of Lublin; the Papal award *Pro Ecclesia et Pontifice*; the Medal of Merit of the Cardinal Primate of Poland; and honorary doctorates from Alliance College and the Catholic University of Lublin.—*Timothy Kulbicki*

SOURCES: Alex Cymerman, "A Tribute to Fr. Cornelian Dende, OFM Conv.," in *The Franciscan Friars St. Anthony of Padua Province, USA, Pay Grateful Tribute* (Buffalo: Father Justin Rosary Hour, 1984); Jan Książek, *Radiowa Godzina Różańcowa Ojca Justyna 1931–1981* (Buffalo: Father Justin Rosary Hour, 1981); Tadeusz Zasępa, *Emigracyjni Katecheci Radiowej Godziny Różańcowej* (Buffalo: Father Justin Rosary Hour, 1984).

Dende, Henry J. (b, Scranton, Pennsylvania, October 21, 1918; d. Scranton, Pennsylvania, January 29, 2001). Editor, journalist. Dende earned his B.A. in journalism from the University of Scranton and also studied at **Alliance College**, Washington and Jefferson College, and the University of Warsaw. After serving in the U.S. Army (1942–45), from 1945 through 1969 he was editor of the *Polish-American Journal*, then published in Scranton, PA, turning it into a widely-read newspaper of national importance. He served as a member of the Scranton School Board (1951–69), president of the Lackawanna County Vocational-Technical School Board, and national president of the **Polish Union of the United States** of North America. Among his honors were Printing Man of the Year (1961), a special citation from the State Senate of Pennsylvania (1969), the **Kościuszko Foundation** Medal of Recognition, and invitations to the White House by every president from John F. Kennedy through Ronald Reagan.—*James S. Pula*

SOURCE: Bolesław Wierzbiański, *Who's Who in Polish America* (New York: Bicentennial Publishing Corp., 1996), 85.

Derdowski, Hieronim Jarosz (b. Wiele, Prussian-occupied Poland, March 9, 1852; d. Winona, Minnesota, August 13, 1902). Journalist, editor. Born in the Kashub region to a locally prominent family with gentry roots, Derdowski attended school in Chojnice and Braniewo, later enrolling in the minor seminaries in Chełmno and Pelpin. He was a precocious student, intensely Catholic and patriotic, as both a Pole and a **Kashub**. It was later claimed that he could speak eight languages fluently. Family accounts suggest he ran into trouble with some of his teachers and classmates due to a pronounced anti–Prussian attitude. When he was seventeen, he was sent to Rome to continue his studies with the goal of joining the priesthood. While there, he was caught up in the political struggles of the Papacy which was attempting to maintain an independent Papal territory in the face of Italian pressure. Derdowski joined a volunteer Papal guard under French leadership. In the wake of the Franco-Prussian War, the unit disbanded, and he wandered Europe finding occasional work as a tutor. About 1877 he returned to Poland, working as newspaper editor in Toruń. During this period he began publishing humorous and patriotic pieces on the Kashub region, including "Marszu Kaszubskiego" (Kashubian March), a kind of regional anthem based on the "Mazurka Dąbrowskiego" (Dąbrowski **Mazurka**), *O Panu Czorlińscim co do Pucka po sece jachoł* (1880), a humorous verse evoking rural Kashub life, and *Kaszube pod Widnem* (1883). The latter work was intensely patriotic, which drew the attention of the German authorities. Derdowski's poems and editorials earned him a number of brief stints in jail.

In 1885, Derdowski left Europe to come to America, settling briefly in New York, Chicago, and Detroit where he worked for a number of newspapers including *Pielgrzym Polski* (Polish Pilgrim). In 1886 he was invited to Winona, Minnesota, by the local pastor who had started a newspaper to serve the growing community of Kashub immigrants. The paper was christened *Wiarus* (Veteran), which translates as "the faithful soldier" or sometimes "The Veteran." *Wiarus* achieved wide circulation across the Midwest and Great Plains, serving many small farming communities as well as urban centers such as Detroit, Milwaukee, and Chicago. The paper's subscriber base was especially strong in communities with a large Kashub presence. Through this vehicle, he became one of the most influential and controversial editors in American **Polonia** during the late 1880s and 1890s. During the intense political struggles that rocked American Polonia in the 1880s and 1890s, Derdowski played the role of community gadfly. He criticized advocates of both the "nationalist" and "Catholic" camps, developing a particularly fierce conflict with **Michał Kruszka**, editor of *Kuryer Polski* (Polish Courier).

In 1892, Derdowski suffered a stroke that left him partially paralyzed. A large man, said by some to have weighed 400 pounds, Derdowski never fully recovered his health. He continued an active schedule as editor while writing several smaller poems and working on a comparative Polish-Kashub grammar, probably meant for New World immigrant communities. Following his death in Winona in 1902, his newspaper continued under the editorship of his wife until 1919.—*John Radzilowski*

SOURCES: Stanisław Janke, *Derdowski* (Gdańsk: Oficyna Czec, 2002); Paul Libera, "Polish Settlers in Winona, Minnesota," *Polish American Studies*, Vol. 15, no. 1–2 (January-June 1958), 18–29; obituary, *Wiarus*, September 21, 1902, 1; John Radzilowski, *Poles in Minnesota* (St. Paul: Minnesota Historical Society Press, 2006); Helene Derdowska Zimniewicz and Norah O'Leary Sorem, "Polish Troublemaker: Pioneer Trouble Shooter," *Gopher Historian*, Vol. 4, no. 3 (November 1949), 2–4, 13; Andrzej Bukowski, "Działalność literacka i społeczna Hieronima Derdowskiego w Ameryce," *Rocznik Gdański*, Vol. 19–20 (1960–61), 83–161; Andrzej Bukowski, *Działalność literacka i społeczna Hieronima Derdowskiego w Ameryce (1885–1902)* (Gdańsk: Gdańskie Towarzysrwo Naukowe, 1961).

de Reszke, Edouard (Edward; b. Warsaw, Poland, December 22, 1853; d. Garnek, Poland, May 25, 1917). Opera singer. Edward was the third of five children born to highly musical parents who owned and operated Warsaw's Hotel Saski. De Reszke's father was exiled for five years in Siberia after participating in the 1863 uprising, an experience which surely contributed to the boy's lifelong patriotism. In the pragmatic spirit of the Positivist era, Edward was schooled to become an agriculturalist. But when he returned to Warsaw after two years of study, his older brother Jan (see **Jean de Reszke**) discovered that Edward had developed a magnificent bass voice and took charge of his career. Thereafter Edward and Jan traveled to Italy for vocal studies. Always happiest when they were together, the two brothers became each other's best critics and most fervent supporters. Large men with considerable athletic abilities and enormous appetites, they loved to entertain their friends with joking and musical impersonations. At work on their music, Jan always assumed the role of taskmaster due to Edward's lesser intellectual drive and tendency towards indolence.

Following in his brother's impressive footsteps, Edward (who adopted the French "Edouard" for his international tours) won more immediate success onstage and proved a much more reliable performer in terms of his good health and affable temperament. His tremendously powerful, flexible voice served him very well because great basses earned much less than great tenors such as Jan (Jean) and Edouard had a wife and four daughters to support. Jean's ambition pushed Edouard to master an extraordinary spectrum of leading bass roles, ranging from French and Italian parts (Mephistopheles in Gounod's *Faust*, Don Basilio in *Il Barbiere di Siviglia*, Leporello in *Don Giovanni*) to Wagnerian characters (Heinrich in *Lohengrin*, Hans Sachs in *Die Meistersinger*, King Marke in *Tristan und Isolde*). Indeed, Verdi himself selected the very young Edouard to play the King of Egypt in the Paris debut of *Aida* on April 22, 1876. Like Jean, Edouard learned to sing all these roles in their original languages and performed consistently with his brother in Milan, Paris, London, St. Petersburg, Warsaw, and assorted American cities.

The famed de Reszke brothers helped usher "The Golden Age of Music" into 1890s American opera houses, attracting huge audiences who were awed by their astonishing voices and painstaking phrasing, diction, and acting. In both Chicago (1891) and New York (1892), Edouard first won American hearts as a surprisingly talented bass. Much like the Polish-become-American actress **Helena Modjeska**, these Polish brothers elevated Americans' estimations of Polish artistic achievement and, in the process, inspired the Polish immigrants who enthusiastically attended their performances. Edouard especially returned their admiration, singing to the gallery in American houses, where his transplanted compatriots could afford to sit. He was proud to see the peasant immigrants from his country transformed into respectable American citizens and art lovers.

While the de Reszkes enhanced the high culture reputation of Poland and the Poles in America, Edouard was also drawn to American popular culture — to African-American spirituals, popular songs, and even the cakewalk. Much as he relished the English music hall, so he thoroughly enjoyed American vaudeville, and the American press often printed rumors about his plans to appear on its stage. Such a move would have put paid to his operatic career, yet Edouard's interest reflected his broader appreciation of culture, his affinities for new types of entertainment as well as what was then deemed serious art.

After Edouard's final operatic performance as Mephistopheles on March 31, 1903, in New York, he attempted teaching, with and without his brother, in Paris, London, and Warsaw. World War I caught him in Poland, where he and his family suffered invasions, counter-invasions, deprivation, and illness on the estate he had built in Garnek in 1895. Cut off from his beloved brother Jean, who remained in France, Edouard never regained his health and died at home, surrounded by his wife and children.—*Beth Holmgren*

SOURCES: Henry T. Finck, *Success in Music and How It is Won* (New York: Charles Scribner's Sons, 1909); Clara Leiser, *Jean de Reszke and the Great Days of Opera* (New York: Minton, Balch & Company, 1934); Wojciech Matuszyński, *Władcy amerykańskiej sceny operowej. Jan i Edward Reszke (Złoty okres, 1891–1903)* (Częstochowa: Stowarzyszenie Przyjaciół "Gaude Mater," 2007).

De Reszke, Jean (Jan Mieczysław; b. Warsaw, Poland, January 14, 1850; d. Nice, France, April 3, 1925). Opera singer, voice teacher. The second of five children born to the musical de Reszke family in Warsaw, Jan pioneered an operatic career for himself and his two talented siblings, Edward (see **Edouard de Reszke**) and Józefina. Although he shared his family's fierce patriotism, deepened by his father's five years in Siberian exile after the 1863 uprising, Jan was dedicated first and foremost to the art of operatic singing. As youngsters, he and Edward would sneak into the cheap gallery seats at the opera while their parents enjoyed the music below, unaware that their boys were not asleep at home. In lieu of finishing a law degree, as his parents had wished, Jan went off to Italy for vocal training and made his 1874 debut in Venice as Alfonso in Donizetti's *La Favorita*. Ironically, Jan persisted unremarkably as a baritone while Edward and Józefina earned kudos as a powerful bass and a heroic soprano. Edward and his father ultimately persuaded Jan that his was a rich tenor voice, and he consequently spent several years traveling with his performing siblings, developing his upper register and studying new roles. Jan debuted as a tenor in an 1879 *Robert le Diable* produced in Madrid.

But he first conquered his audience as a great tenor when the composer Jules Massenet cast him as John the Baptist in the 1884 Paris performance of *Herodiade*.

Although Jan, who adopted the name "Jean" for the purpose of international touring, acquired four Polish estates over the course of his very successful career, he was far less preoccupied than Edward with his properties and the race horses he raised on them. His life completely revolved around opera. Jean's primary home in France did not signal a shift in his national allegiance, but his choice of the best vantage for perfecting his art and conducting an international career. Unlike Italian singers, he could not exercise the option of singing tenor leads in his native tongue while the rest of the cast performed in the opera's original language. Jean not only learned to sing in Italian, French, and German, but also meticulously rehearsed the proper vocal and emotional rendering of all his foreign language parts. A harsh self-critic, he constantly strived for the most beautiful performance of his role. Jean was also highly protective of his voice because he suffered chronic bouts of bronchitis. Less healthy and more exacting than Edward, he preferred to cancel an engagement rather than deliver a flawed performance.

Given his excellent *tenore robusto*, consummate musicianship, and keen intellectual and emotional grasp of each operatic composition, it is little wonder that many music critics pronounced him the best tenor of his day and the period of his stardom (roughly 1884–1902) the "age of Jean de Reszke." He was certainly the highest paid tenor, earning, for example, $2,450 plus a percentage of the box office re-

Edouard de Reszke, internationally acclaimed opera singer (*OLS*).

Jean de Reszke, internationally acclaimed opera singer (*OLS*).

ceipts for each performance during a New York tour. Jean's achievements as a tenor and a Pole were astounding, for he excelled in the major roles of Italian and French operas (Radames in *Aida*, Otello, Romeo in *Romeo et Juliette*, Faust, Don Jose in *Carmen*) as well as the much more physically demanding Wagnerian parts of Lohengrin, Walther in *Die Meistersinger*, Tristan, and Siegfried. Although critics opined that the latter parts injured his voice and hastened his retirement, Jean and Edward (under Jean's tutelage) proved to audiences in Europe and America that Wagnerian operas could be sung beautifully. Like other touring Polish artists, Jean advertised Poland's world-class and standard setting talent while his nation remained partitioned and oppressed by three imperial powers.

After his retirement from the stage in 1902, Jean continued to serve his art as an influential teacher, tutoring hundreds of students in the special theater he had constructed behind his Parisian home in Paris. News of the deaths of his son and brother Edward during World War I drove him into temporary seclusion. He and his wife eventually moved to Nice in 1919, where he resumed teaching until his death.—*Beth Holmgren*

SOURCES: Henry T. Finck, *Success in Music and How It is Won* (New York: Charles Scribner's Sons, 1909); Peter Geoffrey Hurst, *The Age of Jean de Reszke: Forty Years of Opera, 1874–1914* (London: Christopher Johnson, 1958); Clara Leiser, *Jean de Reszke and the Great Days of Opera* (New York: Minton, Balch & Company, 1934).

De Rosen, John Henry (Jan Henryk de Rosen; b. Warsaw, Poland, February 25, 1891; d. Arlington, Virginia, September 22, 1982). Artist, diplomat. Educated by his father, Jan Rosen, a court painter to Russian Tsars Alexander III and Nicholas II, de Rosen studied at the Lycée Carnot and the University of Lausanne, Switzerland. During World War I he volunteered for service in the French Army, later joining the **Polish Army in France** under General Józef Haller, attaining the rank of captain. He accompanied **Ignacy Jan Paderewski** to the Versailles Peace Conference (1919) and to Geneva, Switzerland, for the League of Nations before serving in the Polish Ministry of Foreign Affairs (1921–24). During the 1930s he taught at Lwów Polytechnic in Poland. Invited by the Polish Ambassador, Count Jerzy Potocki, to visit Washington, D.C., he was stranded there by the outbreak of World War II. During the war he served as a military aide at the Polish Embassy while also teaching at The Catholic University of America in Washington, D.C. (1939–45). As an artist, he is especially known for his murals, frescos, and mosaics on both religious and secular subjects.

His mosaics can be found in the National Shrine of the Immaculate Conception, Washington, D.C.; St. Matthew Cathedral, Washington, D.C.; and in various locations in Toledo (OH), Miami (FL), St. Louis (MO), and Oxford (MI). His stained glass windows are in the Armenian Catholic Cathedral in Lwów, and his murals and frescoes are located in Lwów, Stanisławów, Przemyśl, Podkowa Lesna, and Miejsce Piastowe in Poland as well as Vienna (Austria), Castel Gandolfo and Varese (Italy), and various locations in Arizona, California, Connecticut, the District of Columbia, Illinois, Maryland, New Jersey, New York, Ohio, and Pennsylvania. Collections of his works are located in the National Museum in Warsaw, Poland, and the St. Vincent Gallery at St. Vincent College, Latrobe, PA. His artistic and government work has been recognized with the Virtuti Militari Cross, Cross of Valor, Cross of Independence, Golden Laurel, and Polonia Restituta from Poland; the Legion of Honor, Croix de Guerre, and Cross of the Combatant from France; the Military Medal for Bravery in the Field from Great Britain; and the Papal Order of St. Gregory the Great.—*Stanley L. Cuba*

SOURCES: the Rev. Zdzisław Peszkowski, "Arystokracie Ducha-Mistrzowi Janowi de Rosen," *Sodalis Polonia* (Orchard Lake, MI: The Orchard Lake Schools), Vol. 56, no. 2 (February, 1976); the Rev. Walerian Jasinski, "Złoty Jubileusz Arystycznej Twórczołci Jana Henryka de Rosena," *Sodalis Polonia* (Orchard Lake, MI: The Orchard Lake Schools), Vol. 56, no. 2 (February, 1976); Olga Klug Iwanowska, "Genius with Blue Eyes," *The Quarterly Review* (American Council of Polish Cultural Clubs), October–December, 1975; "Artist Paints New Murals for Sacred Heart Church," *Pittsburgh Press*, December 16, 1953; "Murals Rich in Color Show Crucifixion Events," *Los Angeles Times*, September 7, 1953.

Derwinski, Edward Joseph (b. Chicago, Illinois, September 15, 1926; d.—). Congressman, banker. After graduating from Mount Carmel High School in 1944, Derwinski served as an infantryman in the U.S. Army in the Pacific and with the Occupation Forces in Japan in 1945-46. After his discharge, he earned a B.S. degree from Loyola University in Chicago (1951) and served as president of the West Pullman Savings & Loan Association (1950–75). He was elected to one term in the Illinois House of Representatives (1957-58) after which he gained election as a Republican to the Eighty-sixth and to the eleven succeeding Congresses (January 3, 1959-January 3, 1983). He was an unsuccessful candidate for re-nomination in 1982 when redistricting after the 1980 census carved up the 4th Congressional District, south and west of Chicago, with only fifteen percent of the original area remaining. This placed Derwinski in a party primary with fellow Republican Congressman

Edward Derwinski, congressman (*NARA*).

George O'Brien, a contest that Derwinski lost. During his political career he served as a delegate to the United Nations General Assembly (1971-72), chair of the U.S. delegation to the Interparliamentary Union (1970-72, 1978–80), and thereafter was appointed by President Ronald Reagan to be Counselor at the Department of State from March 18, 1983, to March 23, 1987 and Under Secretary of State for Security Assistance, Science and Technology, March 23, 1987, to January 21, 1989. Thus, he served in the State Department during the time leading up to the democratic revolutions in Eastern Europe. Derwinski became the first person to hold the upgraded Cabinet-level position of Secretary of the Department of Veterans Affairs (1989–92). A Polish American, Derwinski has worked on behalf of Eastern Europe more generally, and in 1996 he headed "Ethic Americans for Dole/Kemp." His personal and congressional papers and correspondence are located at the Illinois State Historical Library in Springfield, Illinois.—*Frederick J. Augustyn*

SOURCE: *Biographical Directory of the United States Congress, 1774-Present* (http://bioguide.congress.gov/).

Didur, Adam (b. Wola Sękowa, Austrian Poland, February 24, 1874; d. Katowice, Poland, January 7, 1946). Opera singer. Perhaps the greatest operatic bass of the early twentieth century, Didur began his training in Lwów but quickly moved to Milan where he studied under Franz Emmerich. He made his debut as Guardiano in Verdi's *La Forza del destino* in 1894 and soon began a peripatetic career which took him to many lands. He performed with the Warsaw Opera in the 1899–1903 seasons where he played a number of Italian roles but also appeared in Moniuszko's *Halka* and *Straszny Dwór*. He spent the 1903–

Adam Didur, considered the greatest bass opera singer of his era (*PMA*).

06 season at Milan's famous La Scala. In 1909 he performed in Russia including at the Bolshoi. Significantly, the Russians billed him variously as an "American" and an "Italian" bass; whereas, later, at New York's Metropolitan Opera, he was often listed as a "Russian." He was at Covent Garden in London in 1905–13 before settling for years in New York. In 1914, while at home in Austrian Poland, he was briefly incarcerated for refusing to join the Austrian army in service against the Russians. However, this episode remains obscure. From 1914 to 1929 Didur was the lead bass at New York's Metropolitan Opera. His most famous role at the Met was the lead in Mussorgsky's *Boris Gudonov*. His "signature" roles also included Mephisto in Gounod's *Faust* and Don Basilio in Rossini's *Il barbiere di Siviglia*. During Didur's long career at the Met he made an astonishing 729 appearances in many roles, as well as 182 additional performances with the touring company.

One of the major figures in a group of operatic giants to emerge at the turn of the century, a group which included the Poles **Marcella Sembrich-Kochanska** and the **de Reszke** brothers, his huge voice and exceptional versatility allowed him to sing scores of roles in six languages. He even occasionally sang baritone parts including the well-known Scarpio in *Tosca* and Tonio in *I Pagliacci*. In 1932 he retired and returned to Poland. The war found him in Warsaw where he spent the occupation engaged in teaching. With the end of hostilities he moved to Silesia where he founded the Państwowa Oprera Śląska in Bytom and served as its first Director. It was here, at the age of seventy, that he appeared once again in *Halka* in the Dziemba role, his last performance. A major figure at the Met

for many years, Didur was perhaps the greatest bass of his era and almost certainly the greatest opera talent ever produced by Poland. In 1992 a collection of his performances was released on CD.—*M. B. B. Biskupski*

SOURCES: Henryk Woznica, *Adam Didur* (Katowice: Katowickie Tow. Spoleczno-Kulturalne, 1988); W. Moore McLean, *Notable Personages of Polish Ancestry* (Detroit: The Unique Press, Inc., 1938); Adam Neuer, Józef Kanski, et al., *Adam Didur* (Kraków: Polskie Wydawnictwo Muzyczne, 2005).

Dillingham Commission *see* **Immigration Restriction, Affect on Polish Americans.**

Dingell, John David, Jr. (b. Colorado Springs, Colorado, July 8, 1926; d.—). Congressman, attorney. Dingell attended Capitol Page School, Washington, D.C., and Georgetown Preparatory School in Garrett Park, MD. He was a Congressional Page in the United States House of Representatives (1938–43), served in the U.S. Army (1944–46), and then earned his B.S. degree from Georgetown University (1949) and a J.D. from Georgetown University Law School (1952). After graduation he was a research assistant to U.S. Circuit Judge Theodore Levin (1952-53) before accepting a position as assistant prosecuting attorney of Wayne County, MI (1954-55). Elected as a Democrat to the Eighty-fourth Congress by a special election held to fill the vacancy caused by the death of his father, Representative **John D. Dingell, Sr.** (who had served from 1933–55), Dingell Jr. was reelected to twenty-seven succeeding Congresses. While in office he was a delegate to the Democratic National Conventions in 1956, 1960, 1968, 1980, and 1984, and served as chair of the Committee on Energy and Commerce (Ninety-seventh through One Hundred Third Congresses and One Hundred Tenth Congress). Dingell, who was of Polish and Scots-Irish descent (his grandfather having changed the family name from Dzieglewicz), was in 2010 the longest serving Representative and consequently the dean of the House, and the only House member with service since the 1950s. As senior House member, in 1995 he swore in Republican Newt Gingrich as House Speaker. Democratic Representative John Conyers of Michigan, the second most senior House member, once served on Dingell's staff. Together, both Dingells have represented southeastern Michigan for over 75 years. Dingell credited President Harry Truman's decision to drop the atomic bombs on Japan in August 1945 for saving his life and those of many others. He was known as a chairman to hold to a vigorous approach to oversight. Revealing the changing nature of Capitol Hill, however, after the November

John Dingell, congressman (*LC*).

election of 2008 Rep. Henry Waxman of California ousted the more senior Dingell, who was backed by the centrist Blue Dog Democrats, as chair of the Energy and Commerce Committee. Dingell was a strong supporter of organized labor and social welfare and, like his father, a champion of a national health insurance system. At least partially in his father's memory, Dingell Jr. introduced HR 15 (the same number as his district) the national health insurance bill that Dingell, Sr., cosponsored in 1943. Dingell helped to write the Medicare Bill in the 1960s, but he vociferously opposed the Republicans' 2003 Medicare prescription drug bill as inadequate. He largely opposed gun control (although he voted for the 1994 crime bill) and won support from the National Rifle Association (he was once on its board.) Yet, he was an environmentalist as well. A sportsman and hunter, Dingell's support of environmental measures related to his appreciation for the outdoors as evidenced by the fact that he helped to produce the 1990 Clean Air Act. He said that "living wild species are like a library of books still unread. Our heedless destruction of them is akin to burning the library without ever having read its books." He claims to be the automobile industry's chief Congressional supporter, because of the autoworkers whom he represents, and he has worked to block or delay automobile safety, fuel economy, and antipollution requirements, with mixed results. He backed labor's opposition to the 1993 North American Free Trade Agreement (NAFTA). Asked whether he might someday step down from his seat in Congress to allow his son Christopher, a lawyer and state senator, to run for it, Dingell said someday, but not soon. "There's an old Polish saying: Before you sell the bear's hide, you first have to shoot the bear."—*Frederick J. Augustyn*

SOURCES: *Biographical Directory of the United States Congress, 1774–Present* (http://bioguide.congress.gov/); Harreld S. Adams, "The Dingell-Lesinski 1964 Primary Race," *Western Political Quarterly*, Vol. 19 (December 1966), 688–96; David Rosenbaum, "Washington at Work: Michigan Democrat Presides as Capital's Inquisitor," *New York Times*, September 30, 1991, A1; John Fortier, "Dingell's Ouster Reveals Democrats' New Order," *Politico*, November 11, 2008; Wade Roush, "John Dingell: Dark Knight of Science," *Technology Review*, Vol. 95 (January 1992), 58–62; Rochelle Stanfield, "Plotting Every Move," *National Journal*, Vol. 20 (March 26, 1988), 792–97; *Wall Street Journal*, "A Glorious Mess," April 12, 2008, A8.

Dingell, John David, Sr. (the original family name was Dzieglewicz; b. Detroit, Michigan, February 2, 1894; d. Washington, D.C., September 19, 1955). Congressman. Dingell attended St. Casimir Parochial School in Detroit. After graduating he took correspondence courses while working as a newsboy, printer, journalist, and finally an engineer on a natural gas pipeline. He helped organize and served as a trustee of the Colorado Springs Labor College, which taught vocational skills to workers, especially Mexican immigrants. Elected to the Fifteenth Michigan District of the House of Representatives in 1932, Dingell was known as a New Dealer. In addition to supporting key New Deal programs, he also supported the St. Lawrence Seaway Project. In his first term, he served on the Insular Affairs Committee, Civil Service Committee, and the Committee on Patents. Consistent with his membership on the Committee on Insular Affairs, Dingell supported causes favoring the Philippine Islands during his entire career. In his second term, he won election to the powerful Ways and Means Committee, and played an important role in the passage of the original Social Security bill in 1935. The media recognized Dingell as one of the more influential House Democrats. At the time of his death, he was the second ranking member on the Ways and Means Committee. Although the legislation was not enacted, Dingell was best known for the 1943 Wagner-Murray-Dingell bill, which proposed a national health insurance program. This bill would have also created a national system responsible for all federal welfare programs. Dingell repeatedly reintroduced this bill for the rest of his life. While doctors derided this bill as socialized medicine, Dingell responded in 1946 by accusing the American Medical Association of maintaining an outmoded system that only benefited them. During World War II, Dingell called for the relief of Poland while denouncing Nazi Germany and the Soviet Union. He was a member of a 1944 Polish American delegation that met with President Franklin D. Roosevelt to plea for Poland. Dingell supported Zionist causes, including arming Jews in Palestine to fight the Axis, and in 1948 he criticized the State Department for not doing enough to help establish Israel as a nation. In 1952, the Roman Catholic Dingell went so far as to describe himself as a "Christian Zionist." While against Communism, Dingell opposed the establishment and continuation of the House Un-American Activities Committee and the red baiting activities of Senator Joseph R. McCarthy. John David Dingell, Sr., was succeeded in the House of Representatives by his son, **John David Dingell, Jr.**—*Steven M. Leahy*

SOURCES: Gerald R. Banister, "The Longest-Tenured Polish-American Congressman," *Polish American Studies*, Vol. 21, No. 1 (January-June 1964), 38–40; *New York Times* obituary, September 20, 1955.

Ditka, Michael "Mike" (Michael Keller Dyczko; b. Carnegie, Pennsylvania, October 18, 1939; d.—). Athlete, journalist. A graduate of Aliquippa High School, Ditka played football, basketball, and baseball. Recruited by Notre Dame and Penn State, he chose to attend the University of Pittsburgh (1958–60) where he played linebacker, defensive end, and tight end, earning All-American honors. Many sportswriters consider him one of the best college tight ends in history. In 1961 he was a first round draft pick of the Chicago Bears (1961–66), where he redefined the position of tight end when he became a premier pass receiver. As Rookie of the Year, he scored 12 touchdowns, amassed 1,076 yards of offense, and 56 catches. Three years later he caught 75 passes, a record for tight ends that stood until 1980. He was All-NFL four years in a row, and chosen for the Pro Bowl five years running. After the Bears, he played for the Philadelphia Eagles (1967–68) and Dallas Cowboys (1968–72), including the Cowboys' Super Bowl championship team of 1971. He played professionally for 12 years, then became assistant coach for the Cowboys (1969–72), and head coach for the Chicago Bears (1982–92). The Bears won the Super Bowl in 1985. He became a sportscaster with NBC (1992–97), then head coach of the New Orleans Saints (1997–2000). Ditka is only the second person to win the Super Bowl as both a player and coach. After retiring from football he returned to broadcasting, both on television and radio. He owns a chain of restaurants that bear his name and is part owner of the Chicago Rush Arena Football Team. Among his honors are Consensus All-American (1960), Pro Football Rookie of the Year (1961), five-time Pro Bowl player (1961–65), NFL 75th Anniversary All-Time Team Member, UPI NFL Coach of the Year (1985, 1988), College Football Hall of Fame (1986), AP NFL Coach of The Year (1985, 1988), *Sporting News* NFL Coach of the Year (1985), *Pro Football Weekly* NFL Coach of the Year (1988), Pro Football Hall of Fame (1988).—*Cheryl A. Pula*

SOURCES: Mike Ditka, *Ditka: An Autobiography* (Chicago: Bonus Books, 1986); Mike Ditka, *In Life, First You Kick Ass: Reflections on the 1985 Bears and Wisdom From Da Coach* (Champaign, IL: Sports Publishing, 1995); Armen Keteyian, *Ditka: Monster of the Midway* (New York: Pocket Books, 1992); Rich Wolfe, *Da Coach* (Chicago: Triumph Books, 1999).

Dlugosz, Louis (b. Lackawanna, New York, November 21, 1915; d. Mińsk, Mazowiecki, Poland, January 17, 2002). Sculptor. Dlugosz demonstrated an affinity for clay sculpture at an early age. By 1936, he had exhibited his first works at the Albright Art Gallery in Buffalo, New York. A Bethlehem Steel worker from the age of nineteen and later an employee of the Electro Refractories & Abrasive Corporation of Lackawanna, Dlugosz's art is well known for its "pretzel-bending" technique, which eared him critical acclaim within the art community. He received honors for his work with first prize at the Albright Art Gallery's Annual Exhibition by Artists of Western New York in 1940. Not long after, he exhibited his work at New York's Nierendorf Gallery where the Museum of Modern Art purchased two of his sculptures. In the same year, he entered the U.S. Army and was deployed to Europe where he remained for two years after his discharge in 1945. Under the GI Bill, he attended the Académie La Grand Chaumière in Paris. While in France, Dlugosz exhibited his *Head of Christ* sculpture at the Louvre. After returning to the United States, he studied at the Buffalo Art Institute for three years before assuming his old job at Bethlehem Steel. Among Dlugosz's most famous works are busts of Sioux leader Sitting Bull, Polish Solidarity leader Lech Wałęsa and former hostage Terry Anderson; the latter two reside in the permanent collection of the Museum of Modern Art in New York and the bust of Wałęsa was blessed by Pope John Paul II. Throughout his lifetime, Dlugosz's work was exhibited across North America, including the Riverside Museum in New York, the Nelson Gallery in Kansas City, The Garret Club in Buffalo and the Royal Ontario Museum in Toronto, Ontario. While visiting Poland in 2002, Dlugosz died and was buried in Mińsk, Mazowiecki.—*Krystyna Cap*

SOURCE: "He Labors for Art," *Mechanix Illustrated*, Vol. 53, no. 3 (March 1957), 103–05.

Dmochowski-Sanders, Henryk (Henryk Dmochowski; b. Zablocie, Lithuania, October 14, 1810; d. Józefowo, Lithuania, May 14, 1863). Artist, Polonia activist. Educated at the University of Wilno where he studied law

Henryk Dmochowski-Sanders, sculptor (*Stanley L. Cuba*).

(1825–28) and drawing (1826-27), Dmochowski later continued his studies at the Ecole des Beaux-Arts, Paris (1840s), and the atelier of François Rude whom he assisted with the sculptures for Napoleon's sarcophagus in Paris. During the November Uprising (1830-31) in Poland he was a member of Józef Zaliwski's partisan detachment. Following the failure of the revolt, he migrated to France in 1832 where he lived in Mattroy, Paris, and Tours. In 1833 he participated in the unsuccessful Zaliwski armed expedition in **Galicia** (the Austrian-occupied portion of partitioned Poland). Apprehended in 1834, he was turned over to the Austrian authorities who imprisoned him in the Kufstein fortress in the Tyrol (1837–41) where he did bread sculptures. Following his release he lived in France (1841–48), Lwów (1848), Milosław (1849), and London (1851). He migrated to the United States in 1852, settling in Philadelphia where he became a member of the patriotic Towarzystwo Demokratyczne Polskie (**Democratic Society of Poles in America**). His sculpture of his deceased wife and infant twins in the Laurel Hill Cemetery, Philadelphia, gained widespread acclaim. He later relocated to Washington, D.C., in 1857. Among his finest works as a sculptor are the marble bust of **Kazimierz Pułaski** for his monument in Savannah, Georgia, and his busts of Pułaski and **Tadeusz Kościuszko** executed on the request of Congress for the U.S. Capitol. In addition to his sculptures, which included busts of LaFayette,

Garibaldi, and many other political figures, he is also known for creating scores of medals, bas-reliefs, and miniature statuettes of prominent people of the pre-civil war era. He also wrote political articles that appeared in the American press. In 1861 he returned to Wilno where he completed a bust of Tytus Działyński, a statue of Barbara Radziwiłł, and a number of other works. During the January Insurrection in 1863 he served as a county commissioner of the Rząd Narodowy (National Government). Active in recruiting for the revolutionaries, he was later killed in a skirmish with Russian troops.—*Stanley L. Cuba*

SOURCES: Virgil E. McMahan, comp., *Washington, D.C. Artists Born Before 1900* (Washington, D.C.: Privately Printed, 1976); Zuzanna Proszyńska, "Henryk Dmochowski," *Słownik Artystów Polskich* (Wrocław: Zakład Narodowy im. Ossolińskich, 1975, Vol. II); Sister Mary Liguori, "Henry Dmochowski Saunders: Soldier-Sculptor," *Polish American Studies*, Vol. VI, no. 1–2 (1949), 18–25; Tadeusz Walendowski, "A Story Found on Laurel Hill," *Polish American Studies*, Vol. 58, no. 2 (2001), 95–105; Ryszard Mienicki, "Henryk Dmochowski," *Polski Słownik Biograficzny* (Kraków: Polska Akademia Umiejętności, 1939, Vol. V), 206-07.

Domanski, Vincent, Jr. (b. Philadelphia, Pennsylvania, February 1, 1894; d. Philadelphia, Pennsylvania, February 26, 1968). Philatelist. A world-renown expert on Polish stamps, Domanski was elected president of the Society of Philatelic Americans and the National Philatelic Museum in Philadelphia. He was a member of the organizing committee for the Centenary International Philatelic Exhibition in New York in 1947, prominent in organizing various other philatelic events, and was active in a variety of philatelic organizations. He was the co-author of *Postal History of the Kingdom of Poland, 1815–1870*, a CD that included two treatises on early Polish mail systems. In 1956 he was honored with the Award of Merit from the South Jersey Philatelic Exhibition, and was inducted into the American Philatelic Society Hall of Fame in 1968.—*James S. Pula*

SOURCE: www.stamps.org.

Drabowsky, Moe (Miron Drabowski; b. Ozanna, Poland, July 21, 1935; d. Little Rock, Arkansas, June 10, 2006). Baseball player. One of the few American ballplayers to have been born in Poland, Miron Drabowski migrated to the United States with his parents shortly before the start of the Second World War. At the age of 21, Moe Drabowsky — as he had become known — made his debut as a major league pitcher. A righthander, he turned in a journeyman career, compiling a record of 88–105 for eight teams over the course of seventeen seasons. Drabowsky is remembered best

for two incidents. In 1958, he surrendered the 3,000th lifetime hit collected by Stan Musial, by coincidence the greatest player of Polish extraction. Eight years later, he won the first game of the 1966 World Series with a stellar extended appearance in relief, propelling his Baltimore Orioles toward the championship. He also pitched for the Baltimore world champions of 1970. After retiring as a player, Drabowsky coached for three major league teams, and briefly managed in the minor leagues. In 1987, he returned to Poland to assist in organizing the first Polish Olympic baseball squad. He was inducted into the **National Polish-American Sports Hall of Fame** in 1999.—*Neal Pease*

SOURCE: Neal Pease, "Diamonds Out of the Coal Mines: Slavic Americans in Baseball," in Lawrence Baldassaro and Richard A. Johnson, eds., *The American Game: Baseball and Ethnicity* (Carbondale: Southern Illinois University, 2002).

Drama *see* **Literature, Polish American.**

Drzewieniecki, Włodzimierz Marian "Walter" (b. Piotrków Trybunalski, Poland, December 14, 1914; d. Kenmore, New York, February 13, 2010). Historian. Drzewieniecki graduated from the military college in Ostrow Mazowiecka (1937). After the outbreak of World War II, he served in the Polish army during the September Campaign in 1939, then participated in the Polish underground army before making his way to the Middle East where he joined the Carpathian Infantry Brigade. He attended the British Army Staff College in Haifa, Palestine (1943) and was then assigned to the General Staff of the Polish 2nd Corps attached to the British army during the Italian Campaign. Following the war he migrated to the U.S. in 1950 where he continued his education with a B.S. degree from the University of Wisconsin-Stevens Point (1957), and a M.A. degree (1958) and Ph. D. (1963) from the University of Chicago. During his career he held positions at the State University of New York at Oswego (SUNY; 1959–63) and SUNY-Buffalo (1963–73), the latter including appointment as director of the East European Institute (1967–72) and chair of the History Department (1969–71). He was the author of a number of publications on Polish history including *The German Polish Frontier* (1959), *Wrześniowe wspomnienia podporucznika* (1978), and *Przez Balkany do Brygady Karpackiej* (1990). He also organized various public exhibits, lectures, and cultural events in Buffalo where he served as vice president of the Polish Cultural Foundation from 1971 to 1975, and president 1965–71 and 1975–91. Among his many awards were the Order of Virtuti Militari, Order of Polonia

Restituta, and Cross of Valor, all from the Polish government-in-exile in London, and a first prize for his wartime memoirs from the Polish Academy of Sciences (1976).—*James S. Pula*

SOURCES: Bolesław Wierzbiański, ed., *Who's Who in Polish America* (New York: Bicentennial Publishing Corporation, 1996); "Drzewieniecki, Pol-Am scholar & Polish veteran, dies," *Am-Pol Eagle*, March 10, 2010.

Dubaniewicz, Peter Paul (b. Cleveland, Ohio, November 17, 1913; d. Cuyahoga, Ohio, August 16, 2003). Artist. Educated at the Cleveland Art Institute where he graduated in 1935 and the Boston Museum School of Fine Arts, during World War II he designed camouflage and training aids for the U.S. Army Engineer Board at Fort Belvoir, VA, later joining the U.S. Maritime Service. He traveled to Mexico in 1940, 1958, and 1965, and to Europe in 1974 for further art studies. As an educator, he taught at the Boston Museum School of Fine Arts (1938–41), the Cleveland Institute of Art (1945–81), Oberlin College, Oberlin, OH (1972); the Skowhegan School of Paintings and Sculpture, Skowhegan, ME; Case Western Reserve University, Cleveland (1978); and Cuyahoga Community College, Cleveland (1987-88). As an artist, he executed murals at the Carnival for Freedom, Boston Gardens, MA (1940), the Alliance of Poles Building in Cleveland (1950), the St. Alexis Hospital Children's Ward in Cleveland, the Third Federal Savings and Loan in Cleveland (1964), the Linda Eastman Branch Library in Cleveland (1980), Luther Redeemer Church, Brook Park, OH (1968), and St. Ann's, Rittman, OH (1969). Solo exhibitions were held in Akron, Ashtabula (OH), Boston, Buffalo, Cleveland, Grand Rapids, New York, Springfield (MA), Youngstown (OH), and Washington (D.C.). Among his honors were a first place award for the S. S. Wiedon Encyclopedia Cover Competition (1930), the Agnes Fund Traveling Scholarship (1935), and the Albert Whitin Traveling Fellowship (1938).—*Stanley L. Cuba*

SOURCES: Irene Piotrowska, "American Painters and Illustrators of Polish Descent," *Polish American Encyclopedia* (Buffalo, NY: Polish American Encyclopedia Committee, 1954, vol. 1); *Who is Who in American Art–2001* (New Providence, NJ: Marquis Who's Who, LLC, 2000).

Dubinsky, David (David Isaac Dobnievski; b. Brest-Litovsk, Poland, February 22, 1892; d. New York, New York, September 17, 1982). Labor leader. An immigrant from the Russian-occupied partition of Poland, Dubinsky became President of the International Ladies' Garment Workers Union and was a major figure in the American labor movement for more than three decades. Though he was born in Brest-Litovsk, he grew up in Łódź where he received his education, first at a Hebrew school, and then at the Poznansky School, endowed by and named for the city's foremost textile manufacturer. However, like his father, he became a baker. At this time he also became a unionist under the influence of the socialist Jewish Labor Bund. Following an arrest for strike activity, he escaped exile in Siberia and fled to the United States, arriving in New York City on New Year's Day, 1911. Soon after his arrival, he entered the needle trades and became a member of the Amalgamated Garment Cutters' Union, Local 10 of the International Ladies' Garment Workers' Union, and the Socialist Party. In each of these organizations he interacted with other Polish socialist labor leaders such as **Leo Krzycki**. He rose to a leadership position in Local 10, becoming general manager in 1921, and then an ILGWU vice president the following year when a civil war broke out within the International. In 1926 communist inspired critics of the ILGWU's socialist leadership gained sufficient power to lead the union into a strike that nearly destroyed it. Emerging from the fray as a foe of the communists, Dubinsky helped save the union from bankruptcy, and in 1929 became general secretary-treasurer and acting president.

On the death of President Benjamin Schlesinger, he became president in 1932 and held this office until his retirement in 1966. Noted as a frugal money manager and staunch anti-communist, Dubinsky led the ILGWU through the Great Depression. A beneficiary of President Franklin D. Roosevelt's pro-union New Deal policies, the ILGWU grew in numbers and influence, coming to be known as "Dubinsky's union." His achievements as president included the elimination of sweatshop working conditions and the introduction of "social unionism" to enhance the lives of the ILGWU membership. The latter featured paid vacations, union-sponsored housing, an impressive vacation resort, and even a hit musical revue with a cast of garment workers.

Accustomed to controversy, Dubinsky as an American Federation of Labor vice-president (1934) was among the founders within the federation of a Committee for Industrial Organization (CIO) to promote industrial unionism. This move led to the ILGWU's suspension from the AFL, but in 1938 Dubinsky declined to join other suspended unions in forming a new Congress of Industrial Organizations. In 1940 he took his union back into the federation. Five years later he again became a vice president, and in 1955 witnessed the merger of the AFL and CIO, which he had strongly supported. In 1957, the AFL-CIO, also to his great satisfaction,

David Dubinsky, president of the International Ladies Garment Workers Union (*OLS*).

adopted a code of ethics to combat labor racketeering.

As a socialist, Dubinsky intensely opposed totalitarianism. In 1934 he helped found the Jewish Labor Committee to fight Nazism, and the following year mobilized the American Federation of Labor to do the same. In 1936, when civil war broke out in Spain, he raised money to fight Fascists in that country. With the German invasion of Poland in 1939, Dubinsky turned to rescuing Jewish labor leaders from the clutches of the Nazis. In addition, the Second World War saw him sounding alarms about the Soviet Union. The Soviet arrest and execution of democratic socialists Henryk Erlich and Victor Alter prompted Dubinsky to lead protests. In 1944 he was a creator and member of the AFL's Free Trade Union Committee designed to check Soviet designs on Western Europe. Five years later he was in London for the founding of the International Confederation of Free Trade Unions.

A force for liberalism, Dubinsky founded two political parties. In 1936 he helped give Franklin D. Roosevelt a second ballot line in New York State through the creation of an American Labor Party. With the ALP veering leftward, Dubinsky abandoned it in 1944 to form a Liberal Party, which had a significant political presence into the 1970s. As a liberal anti-communist, in 1947 Dubinsky was a founder of Americans for Democratic Action. Dubinsky's numerous awards include two honorary degrees, Doctor of Laws (Bard College, 1951) and Doctor of Humane Letters (Temple University, 1964). In addition, he received the Golden Door Award (American Council for Nationalities Services, 1965), Freedom Award (International Rescue Committee, 1966), Presidential Medal of Freedom (United States of America, 1969), and Diamond Jubilee Medal (City of New York, 1973). In 1975 the Fashion Institute of Technology in New York City dedicated the David Dubinsky Student Center. The U.S. Department of Labor inducted him into its National Labor Hall of Fame in 1994.—*Robert D. Parmet*

SOURCES: Max D. Danish, *The World of David Dubinsky* (Cleveland: World Publishing Company, 1957); David Dubinsky and A. H. Raskin, *David Dubinsky: A Life With Labor* (New York: Simon & Schuster, 1977); Robert D. Parmet, *The Master of Seventh Avenue: David Dubinsky and the American Labor Movement* (New York: New York University Press, 2005).

Dudziak, Urszula (b. Straconka, Poland, October 22, 1943; d.—). Musician. Dudziak was born in the Straconka borough of Bielsko-Biała, Poland, where she lived until the age of four. Musically inclined since childhood, she took formal piano lessons at an early age, but became interested in vocal music and jazz in high school through the recordings of Ella Fitzgerald. She began her musical career by singing with several amateur jazz bands in Poland before making her professional solo debut in 1958 as part of the Krzysztof Komeda Band. In 1964 Dudziak embarked on her nearly two decade-long collaboration with jazz violinist **Michał Urbaniak**, and by the late 1960s she was also touring internationally with the Urbaniak Quartet. From 1969–72, she took part in the "Jazz Jamboree" International Jazz Festival in Warsaw—one of the most well-known festivals of its kind in Europe—in the same period that she began experimenting musically with electronic voice modifiers, sound transformers, and amplifiers. Her new technique and style was debuted on her 1972 LP album *New Born Light*—a project on which she collaborated with **Adam Makowicz**. In 1973, Dudziak moved to New York, initially with Urbaniak; however, she soon left the quartet to pursue a solo career, developing her sound and furthering her experimentation with electronic devices. She joined the group, "Vocal Summit," in 1981, in addition to appearing on albums with the Gil Evans Orchestra, and collaborating with the Archie Shepp Band. Throughout this period Dudziak also played in jazz festivals, concerts, and clubs across Europe, the United States, and Canada. The *Los Angeles Times* named her singer of the year in 1979. After years abroad, she returned to Poland to perform with Bobby McFerrin in "Jazz Jamboree" '85. Between 1987 and 1994 Dudziak worked closely with the Krzysztof Zawadzki Band, "Walk Away," with which she produced four albums. Performing on some 50 records throughout her career, she has collaborated and played with such famous recording artists as Dizzy Gillespie, Clark Terry, Wynton and Bradford Marsalis, Sting, Lionel Hampton, and numerous others. She is also known as one of Poland's foremost female jazz musicians. Her work is less familiar to mainstream American audiences, despite years spent performing and recording in the United States. In 2007, her 1976 song "Papaya" became a chart-topping hit in Latin America and Asia.—*Krystyna Cap*

SOURCES: Jan Borkowski, "Urszula Dudziak: Newborn Light," *Jazz Forum*, Vol. 24, no. 4 (1973), 34–35; Ryszard Wolański, "Dudziak, Urszula," *Leksykon Polskiej Muzyki Rozrywkowej* (Warsaw: Agencja Wydawnicza MOREX, 1995), 42–43.

Dudzik, Josephine (Mother Mary Theresa; b. Płocicz, Prussian-occupied Poland, August 30, 1860; d. Chicago, Illinois, September 20, 1918). Catholic nun, social worker. Dudzik was born to a pious peasant family from the village of Płocicz in Flatów County, near Chojnice. Her education was in German for eight years. Subsequently she learned sewing from the Polish Sisters of St. Elizabeth and for some years contributed to the family of six children by employment as a seamstress. A deeply devout young woman, she felt called to serve the needy and poor. In 1881 she accompanied her parents and siblings to Chicago where she was to remain permanently. Like most Polish newcomers, the family settled in an ethnic enclave in the huge parish of St. Stanislaus Kostka. The church, served by the **Congregation of the Resurrection**,

Mother Mary Theresa Dudzik, social worker and founder of the Sisters of the Resurrection (*OLS*).

had the dynamic Rev. **Wincenty Barzysńki**, CR, as pastor. Dudzik soon joined the Third Order of St. Francis, a pious society noted for its profound and demanding spirituality. Becoming a leader, her sense of spiritual duty moved her to invite poor women into the family home, which led to some friction with her mother. In 1894 she proposed to the tertiaries that they collectively serve the poor, an important step in founding a new congregation of religious women. Many of the members agreed and the Rev. Barzyński gave it energetic support since he had long hoped for a local community of Polish nuns. This soon became a formal structure under the patronage of the Blessed Kunegunda, a Polish medieval figure, though years passed before the society received formal recognition from the Catholic Church. Early activity of the new **Sisters of the Resurrection** included staffing the St. Joseph Home for the Elderly. By 1899, the Rev. Barzyński requested the sisters to take in orphans as well, leading to serious overcrowding. The community existed largely on small donations and some support from the parish. With the construction of St. Vincent's Orphanage the nuns were able to better house their charges and their social service work continued.

In 1900, Dudzik, by then known in religious life as Sister M. Theresa, became mistress of novices in addition to her leadership role. As the community grew there was some internal dissension which further complicated the demands of her position. A major initiative she devised was to have the community enter the field of primary education. As with other Polish congregations the early nuns had modest pedagogical preparation and were sometimes only a few years older than their pupils, but Dudzik strongly promoted service in parochial schools. In 1905 a new mother superior, Sister M. Vincent Cyszewski, assumed leadership, though Dudzik functioned as her assistant and became mistress of novices. The reasons for her not being chosen to the head post are unclear but she accepted her new status without complaint. Work with the novices occupied much time since new entrants needed substantial preparation for teaching work as well as formation. Though never again to direct the community, Dudzik demonstrated practical concern for its development. In 1909 she initiated the establishment of a factory to produce vestments as well as fraternal insurance paraphernalia, a successful venture which provided much needed steady income and drew on the impressive sewing skills of many nuns. In her last years she remained in the background, working as a seamstress and helping with gardening and laundry. Her last post was on a commission to compile a Book of Customs and daily prayers for the community. Frail by World War I, she passed away near the conclusion of the conflict.—*William J. Galush*

SOURCES: Sr. Mary Clarenta, "Mother Mary Theresa Dudzik," *Polish American Studies*, Vol. 19, no. 1 (1962), 42–45; Henry M. Malak, *The Apostle of Mercy from Chicago* (London: Veritas, 1962); Sr. Anne Marie Knawa, "Jane Addams and Josephine Dudzik: Social Service Pioneers," *Polish American Studies*, Vol. 35, no. 1–2 (1978), 13–22; Sr. Anne Marie Knawa, *As God Shall Ordain: A History of the Franciscan Sisters of Chicago, 1894–1987* (Stevens Point, WI: Worzalla Publishing Company, 1989).

Duffy, Mickey (William Michael Cusick; b. Philadelphia, Pennsylvania, 1888; d. Atlantic City, New Jersey, August 29, 1931). Gangster. Cusick became involved in criminal activity as a youth and adopted the Irish name Mickey Duffy in an attempt to fit in better with the local Irish-dominated mob. Arrested for assault and battery in 1919, he emerged from prison nearly three years later to find Prohibition enacted and mobsters turning to bootlegging in search of quick profit. Duffy established an illegal brewery in Camden, NJ, quickly increasing his business until he became known as the "Beer Baron of South Jersey." He used his profits to open the stylish Club Cadix at 23rd and Chestnut Streets in Philadelphia and establish an office in the Ritz-Carlton Hotel. Although shot three times in an assassination attempt, he survived only to be gunned down in his sleep at the Ambassador Hotel in Atlantic City. Thousands of people turned out for his funeral, but no one was ever charged with the murder. His date of birth is sometimes given as August 29, sometimes as August 31.—*James S. Pula*

SOURCES: "The Only Good Gangster is a Dead Gangster," *Delmarva Star* (Wilmington, DE), October 25, 1931; Jeff Laushead, "Main Line History: Mobsters on the Main Line," *Main Line Media News*, September 16, 2009.

Dulacki, Leo John (b. Omaha, Nebraska, December 29, 1918; d.—). Marine Corps officer. After receiving his B.S. degree from Creighton University (1941), Dulacki was commissioned as a second lieutenant in the U.S. Marine Corps where he served aboard the aircraft carriers USS *Hornet* and USS *Belleau Wood* during World War II. In 1948 he was assigned as operations officer of the 1st Marine Brigade on Guam, after which he served as assistant naval attaché at the U.S. embassy in Helsinki, Finland (1950–52), a battalion commander in Korea (1952), a member of the United Nations Truce Team in Korea (1953), and an instructor at the Marine Corps facility in Quantico, Virginia (1954–56). He went on to serve as naval attaché at the U.S. embassy in Moscow (1958–61), and with the Defense Intelligence Agency (1961–64), the Naval War College (1964–65), commanding officer of the 5th Marine Division (1968-69), and the 4th Marine Division (1970–73) in Vietnam. In 1965 he earned a M.S. degree from George Washington University. During his career, and following his retirement with the rank of lieutenant general, he was active in a number of organizations including the **Kosciuszko Foundation** where he was a member of the Board of Directors (1974–89), the National Armed Forces Museum, and the Smithsonian Institution. Among his many recognitions were the Distinguished Service Medal (twice), Legion of Merit (four times), Bronze Star (twice), Purple Heart, Order of the Lion of Finland, Korean Presidential Unit Citation, Vietnam Cross of Gallantry, and the U.S. Presidential Unit Citation.—*James S. Pula*

SOURCE: Bolesław Wierzbiński, ed., *Who's Who in Polish America* (New York: Bicentennial Publishing Corporation, 1996), 95.

Dulski, Thaddeus Joseph (b. Buffalo, New York, September 27, 1915; d. Buffalo, New York, October 11, 1988). Congressman. Dulski attended parochial schools, Buffalo Technical High School, Canisius College, and the University of Buffalo. He was also a member of the Chopin Singing Society. From 1940 to 1947, Dulski worked as an accountant for the Bureau of Internal Revenue and a special agent in the Price Stabilization Administration (1951–53). From 1953 to 1958, he served on the Buffalo City Council. Winning election to the Eighty-sixth Congress as a Democrat in 1958, Dulski sat on the Post Office and Civil Service Committee, chairing the committee from 1969 to 1974. This committee generally fought for higher salaries for letter carriers while keeping postal rates low. He led opposition to the Postal Reorganization Act of 1970, but public opinion and President Richard Nixon demanded post office reform. Dulski had more success opposing efforts to abolish the Post Office Committee in 1973. He did not seek reelection in 1974, but following his time in Congress he worked as a congressional lobbyist on behalf of New York Governor Hugh L. Carey until his retirement in 1983.—*Steven L. Leahy*

SOURCES: *New York Times*, October 14, 1988; Richard F. Fenno, *Congressmen in Committees* (Boston: Little, Brown and Co., 1973); "Rep. Dulski, Outstanding Political Figure in New York," *Polish American Journal*, January 23, 1965.

Dutko, John W. (b. Dilltown, Pennsylvania, October 24, 1916; d. Ponte Rotto, Italy, May 23, 1944). Soldier, Medal of Honor recipient. As a private first class in the 3rd Infantry Division, Dutko was involved in the Italian Campaign during World War II. He was awarded the Medal of Honor posthumously for his actions when his unit was pinned down near Ponte Rotto. His citation for the award read: "For conspicuous gallantry and intrepidity at risk of life above and beyond the call of duty, on 23 May 1944, near Ponte Rotto, Italy. Pfc. Dutko left the cover of an abandoned enemy trench at the height of an artillery concentration in a single-handed attack upon 3 machine guns and an 88mm. mobile gun. Despite the intense fire of these 4 weapons which were aimed directly at him, Pfc. Dutko ran 100 yards through the impact area, paused momentarily in a shell crater, and then continued his l-man assault.

Mickey Duffy, gangster (*TU*).

Leo Dulacki, member of the United Nations Truce Team in Korea (*OLS*).

John W. Dutko, Medal of Honor recipient (*NARA*).

Although machine gun bullets kicked up the dirt at his heels, and 88mm. shells exploded within 30 yards of him, Pfc. Dutko nevertheless made his way to a point within 30 yards of the first enemy machinegun and killed both gunners with a hand grenade. Although the second machine gun wounded him, knocking him to the ground, Pfc. Dutko regained his feet and advanced on the 88mm. gun, firing his Browning automatic rifle from the hip. When he came within 10 yards of this weapon he killed its 5-man crew with 1 long burst of fire. Wheeling on the machine gun which had wounded him, Pfc. Dutko killed the gunner and his assistant. The third German machine gun fired on Pfc. Dutko from a position 20 yards distant wounding him a second time as he proceeded toward the enemy weapon in a half run. He killed both members of its crew with a single burst from his Browning automatic rifle, continued toward the gun and died, his body falling across the dead German crew."—*James S. Pula*

SOURCES: R. J. Proft, *United States of America's Congressional Medal of Honor Recipients and Their Official Citations* (Columbia Heights, MN: Highland House II, 2002); *The Medal of Honor of the United States Army* (Washington, D.C.: U.S. Government Printing Office, 1948), 65.

Dutkowski, Mieczysław (b. Słubice, Poland, September 13, 1946; d.—). Polonia activist. Dutkowski was studying at the University of Warsaw when he took part in the massive student demonstrations against the Communist regime in March 1968. Graduating with a master's degree in economics in 1974, he entered the work force and became active in the Solidarność (Solidarity) movement, organizing a Solidarity committee at the KDO ZMD Lift Mounting Company in Warsaw. While he was on vacation abroad, martial law was declared in Poland on December 13, 1981. Dutkowski eventually succeeded in gaining asylum in the United States in 1983. Beginning work in the Los Angeles area as a bookkeeper, by 1992 he had risen to vice president of finance for the same company. In 1988 he became a U.S. citizen. Dutkowski was an active member in numerous **Polonia**, business, and cultural groups and in 1993 was elected president of the Southern California State Division of the **Polish American Congress**. He was sworn in by President Lech Wałęsa. In 1995 he was elected national treasurer of the Polish American Congress. Dutkowski was connected with the creation of the publication *Głos Polonii* (The Voice of Polonia), and was involved in organizing the Polish Credit Union in Los Angeles, the Polish Center in Yorba Linda, CA, and the Polish-American Economic Forum.—*Donald E. Pienkos*

SOURCE: Wojciech Wierzewski, "Sto Trzydzieska Slynnych Polaków w Ameryce" (Unpublished manuscript in the archives of the University of Wisconsin-Milwaukee, 2000).

Dybek, Stuart John (b. Chicago, Illinois, April 10, 1942; d.—). Writer, educator. A second-generation Polish American, Dybek grew up in a family residing in Little Village, a working-class neighborhood on Chicago's Southwest Side. Fascinated with the neighborhood's unassimilated immigrants, especially the World War II refugees called "Displaced Persons," he observed the transition of Little Village from majority Polish and Czech to a majority Mexican population. Despite his constant academic struggles, Dybek graduated from St. Rita of Cascia, a Catholic boys' high school. Music was his first creative outlet. He worked at a jazz record store, played the saxophone in bands and combos, and absorbed the work of Eastern European and other classical composers. Although music inspired him to try writing, Dybek tried several career paths before he found a way to make a professional life in literature. The first member of his family to attend college, he started as a pre-med student at Loyola University, but was placed into remedial English. Again struggling academically, he graduated from Loyola with a bachelor's degree in English in 1964. At the urging of Prof. Tom Gorman, he earned a master's degree in the same discipline from the same institution in 1967. From 1964 to 1966, Dybek served as a Cook County public aid caseworker until he became disillusioned with his inability to help his clients. He first taught on the faculties of St. Martha School in the Chicago suburb of Morton Grove (1966-67) and the Wayne Aspinal School, St. Thomas, Virgin Islands (1968-70). His first published short story was "The Palatski Man," a lyrical, fantastical, and religiously overtoned meditation on the "Old World" ragmen who peddled their wares in Little Village. Like many works to come, Dybek composed "The Palatski Man" while listening to musical recordings—this time one of Janos Starker performing a Zoltán Kodály cello piece. The story appeared in 1970 in the *Magazine of Fantasy and Science Fiction*. Dybek used his payment from the magazine to purchase a typewriter. The story helped him gain admittance to the renowned University of Iowa Writers' Workshop, which awarded him a teaching fellowship (1970–73), and his master of fine arts degree (1973). From 1974 to 2006, Dybek taught in the English department at Western Michigan University in Kalamazoo, earning a reputation for devotion to his students. Over the decades, he steadily published his short stories and poems in well-respected small press literary magazines such as *Poetry, the Paris Review, Antaeus, TriQuarterly*, and *Ploughshare*, and sometimes in wider-circulation magazines such as the *New Yorker, Harper's*, and *Atlantic Monthly*. As of 2008, he had gathered these works into five critically acclaimed books: two poetry collections, *Brass Knuckles* (1979) and *Streets in Their Own Ink* (2004); and three anthologies of interlocking short stories: *Childhood and Other Neighborhoods* (1980), *The Coast of Chicago* (1990), and *I Sailed with Magellan* (2003). Dybek received honors from the Academy of American Poets, the Ernest Hemingway Foundation, the Cliff Dwellers Arts Foundation, the Whiting Foundation, the Society of Midland Authors, and the Catholic Communication Campaign. He received several O. Henry Prizes, two Pushcart Prizes, the Nelson Algren Award, a Lannan Award, and the PEN/Bernard Malamud Prize,

Stuart Dybek, novelist and educator (*OLS*).

as well as a Guggenheim Fellowship (1981) and a National Endowment for the Humanities Fellowship (1982). *The Coast of Chicago* was named the Spring 2004 selection for the Chicago Public Library's One Book/One Chicago reading program. In 2006, Dybek returned to Chicago with his appointment as the first Distinguished Writer-in-Residence at Northwestern University. He continued to teach at Western Michigan University's summer writing program in Prague, Czechoslovakia. In 2007, Dybek was honored with the Rea Award for the Short Story and a MacArthur Foundation Fellowship. Even when Dybek lived away from Chicago, his hometown never ceased to be an essential and wondrous presence in his literary work. As Donna Seaman notes, Dybek's Chicago is "a mythic city of brick and asphalt, desire and dreams, a checkerboard of ethnically defined neighborhoods in which human life in all its striving, absurdity, and beauty dominates, while nature, in all its determined wildness and glory, persists in the city's weedy seams and in the vastness of Lake Michigan."—*Mary Krane Derr*

SOURCES: Maud Casey, "Chicago Stories: A Profile of Stuart Dybek," *Poets & Writers Magazine*, November/December 2003; Deanna Isaacs, "Budding Genius," *Chicago Reader*, September 28, 2007; "Stuart Dybek," *Contemporary Authors Online* (Thomas Gale database, 2007).

Dyczkowski, Eugene M. (b. Philadelphia, Pennsylvania, May 1, 1899; d. North Tonawanda, New York, June 11, 1987). Artist. Dyczkowski's family relocated to Niagara Falls in 1917 where he initially studied with Gleo York and then, through a correspondence course, with noted American cartoonist Eugene Zimmerman (Zim) in Elmira, NY. Following this, he studied at the Albright Art School in Buffalo (1924-25; now the Albright-Knox Gallery), and then privately with John Rummell. He also studied sculpture with Arthur Lee in New York. Dyczkowski worked in a representational style until the early 1950s when he turned to abstract painting. Known for his easel paintings and watercolors of scenes from upstate New York, Gloucester and Rockport (MA), and Kennebunkport (ME), he also pursued teaching and lecturing. He served as Assistant Educational Director of the Albright Art Gallery (1933); developed art lectures for radio broadcasts; taught at the Buffalo Art Institute (1933); and the William Kaegebein School in Grand Island, NY (1955). The first president of the **American Council of Polish Cultural Clubs**, he also served as secretary and later president of the Buffalo Society of Artists and co-founder and president of the Polish Arts Club of Buffalo.

Among his recognitions are the Life Time Achievement Award of the Polish Arts Club of Buffalo (1982); the Hoover Watercolor Award (1939); and the Gold and Silver Medals, with six Honorable Mentions, from the Buffalo Society of Artists.—*Stanley L. Cuba*

SOURCES: Martin F. David, "Eugene M. Dyczkowski: Lusty Realist of Depression-Era Buffalo," *Western New York Heritage*, Vol. 6, no. 4 (Winter 2004); Marlene and Gerald E. Markowitz, "Eugene Dyczkowski Chronology," *New Deal for Art: The Government Art Projects of the 1930s with Examples from New York City and State* (Hamilton, NY: The Gallery Association of New York State, Inc., 1977); *National Exhibition of Paintings by Polish American Artists at Albright Art Gallery*, [Buffalo, NY] *July 22, to August 15, 1949*, exhibition catalog; Irena Piotrowska, *American Painters and Illustrators of Polish Descent* in Revs. Francis Bolek and Ladislaus J. Siekaniec, *Polish American Encyclopedia* (Buffalo: Polish American Encyclopedia Committee, 1954, vol. 1).

Dykla, Edward (b. Chicago, Illinois, April 13, 1933; d —). Polonia activist. After earning a B.A. degree from Benedictine College of Kansas (1957), Dykla taught for nineteen years at Weber High School on Chicago's near north side. During this time he became active in the **Polish Roman Catholic Union** of America. In 1974 he was elected its secretary general (1974–82) and in 1982 became its national treasurer (1982–86). In 1986, he was elected PRCUA president over Frank Rutkowski, who had become acting president in 1985 following Joseph Drobot's retirement due to illness. He held the presidency until 1998 when he left office under the rules of the fraternal's three term limit on tenure. He was succeeded as president by Wallace Ozog of Detroit, Michigan. Dykla served as treasurer of the **Polish American Congress** (1986–92) but was unsuccessful in his bid for a PAC vice presidency at its 1992 election. He was also active as chair of the **Polish Museum of America** and a member of the boards of directors of Chicago's **Felician College**, St. Joseph's Home for Senior Citizens, **St. Mary of Nazareth Hospital**, and the Polish Ministry of the Archdiocese of Chicago. He also served as chair of the Board of the Polish Museum of America. Dykla was known for regularly reminding his audiences that the PRCUA, as the first fraternal society founded in **Polonia** in 1873, was the "Mother of Polish American fraternalism." Among his many honors were the Order of Polonia Restituta from the Polish Government in Exile in London (1986), the Citizen's Award of the Chicago Police Association (1990), the Equestrian Order of the Holy Sepulchre of Jerusalem (1991), the National Citizen of the Year of the *American-Polish Eagle* (1993), and the Fidelitas Medal from the Orchard Lake Schools (1993).—*Angela T. Pienkos*

SOURCES: *American Catholic Who's Who* (Washington, D.C.: National Catholic News Service, 1976); John Radzilowski, *The Eagle and the Cross: A History of the Polish Roman Catholic Union of America* (Boulder, CO: East European Monographs, 2003).

Dymek, Frances (b. Chicago, Illinois, October 16, 1896; d. Chicago, Illinois, August 8, 1979). Polonia activist. Dymek held the office of Ladies' Vice President of the **Polish National Alliance** for twenty-eight years. She was first elected to that office in 1935. After losing her campaign for reelection in 1939 to Mary Czyz, she defeated Czyz in 1943, and went on to continue in that office until her retirement in 1967. Dymek was a member of the PNA "old guard" faction that opposed the "leftists" (or Piłsudskiites) for control of the fraternal in the 1930s. Her first election came against Vice President Maria Milewska, a veteran leader in the left faction. In the later years Dymek became a significant ally of **Charles Rozmarek**, president of the Alliance from 1939 to 1967. An energetic organizer and shrewd politician, Dymek was primarily responsible for enlarging the representation of women in the PNA, both in its Board of Directors and its Supervisory Council. In 1955 she succeeded in bringing about an amendment of the PNA by-laws making its female vice president the first vice president with the right to succeed the president on a provisional basis in case of death or incapacitation. As a result of this, in 1988 Vice President Helen Szymanowicz succeeded to the presidency following the death of President **Aloysius Mazewski**, and in 2005 Vice President Teresa Abick succeeded President **Edward Moskal** on his death. Dymek was also active in leading

Frances Dymek, leader in gaining representation for women in the Polish National Alliance (**PNA**).

the charitable work of the women's divisions and was involved in humanitarian efforts organized by the USO and the Red Cross during the Second World War.—*Donald E. Pienkos*

SOURCE: Donald E. Pienkos, *PNA: A Centennial History of the Polish National Alliance of the United States of North America* (Boulder, CO: East European Monographs, 1984).

Dyngus Day. Beginning as an old Polish folk custom, with still deeper roots in old Slavic traditions, *śmigus-dyngus* is known in the United States as Dyngus Day. On Easter Monday (the first Monday following Easter) people pour water on each other in a custom whose origins are based on the symbolic spring-time cleansing of the body with water from the dirt accumulated during winter. With the advent of Christianity, the tradition gained the additional meaning of cleansing one from sins and marking the end of Lent with a day of feasting and merrymaking. Interestingly, initially *śmigus* and *dyngus* were separate elements of the same celebration. While *śmigus* was related to the symbolic cleansing, *dyngus* represented a customary possibility of "buying" a way out of the second *śmigus* at the same house. Over time, both elements began to merge as "śmigus-dyngus" in Poland. In the United States, the celebration is considered to be an entertaining addition to the Easter celebrations, especially for children.—*Bartosz H. Stanisławski*

SOURCES: Deborah Anders Siverman, *Polish-American Folklore* (Urbana, IL: University of Illinois Press, 2000), 34–38; Sophie Hodorowicz Knab, *Polish Customs, Traditions, & Folklore* (New York: Hippocrene, 1993), 108–10.

Painting depicting the *śmigus-dyngus* tradition (*PMA*).

Dyniewicz, Władysław (Władysław Dywicz; b. Chwałków, Poland, June 13, 1843; d. Chicago, Illinois, February 28, 1928). Publisher, journalist, Polonia activist. Born in the Russian zone of partitioned Poland, Dyniewicz arrived in the U.S. in 1866 after the defeat of the January Insurrection (1863). In 1867 he settled in Chicago, becoming one of the organizers of its influential **Gmina Polska** (Polish Commune) patriotic club. He later founded the first successful Polish newspaper in America, *Gazeta Polska* (The Polish Gazette) of Chicago, and in its pages promoted the idea of a national alliance of patriotic groups working for the independence of Poland. In 1875, Dyniewicz issued a call for such a federation, but it

Władysław Dyniewicz, publisher, journalist, and founder of *Gazeta Polska* (*PMA*).

brought no results. In 1880 he became a major backer of the embryonic **Polish National Alliance**, participating in its founding convention that September. The Dyniewicz publishing company, along with the Smulski printing operation, were the two most active disseminators of materials on Poland's literature, language, and history during the early decades of Polonia in America. One of Dyniewicz's daughters married Roman B. Kwasniewski of Milwaukee, a professional photographer whose massive collection of the Milwaukee Polonia of the era between 1910 and 1940 has been preserved at the University of Wisconsin-Milwaukee library.—*Donald E. Pienkos*

SOURCES: Donald E. Pienkos, *PNA: A Centennial History of the Polish National Alliance of the United States of North America* (Boulder, CO: East European Monographs, 1984); Wacław Kruszka, *A History of the Poles in America to 1908* (Washington, D.C.: The Catholic University of America Press, 1993), Vol. 1; Andrzej Kłossowski, "Władysław Dyniewicz pionier książki polskiej w Ameryce," *Księgarz*, Vol. 13, no. 4 (1969), 54–60.

Dziedzic, Michael M. (b. New York Mills, New York, July 8, 1912; d. New York Mills, New York, July 3, 1991). Polonia activist. Educated in his hometown, Dziedzic was active in many Polish organizations and during the 1920s he helped organize and served as president of the championship Olympics Athletic Club comprised of Polish American youths. In 1934 he was selected to study at the Jagiellonian University in Kraków, Poland, through a **scouting** program sponsored by the **Polish National Alliance** (PNA). Upon his return, he served as scout master and regional coordinator of scouting for the PNA, as well as organizing a PNA drum and bugle corps. He was a charter member and president of the Kopernik Memorial Association and was instrumental in erecting a statue to Mikołaj Kopernik in Utica, NY. In 1946 he began hosting, directing, and producing the Polish Melodies Program over Utica radio station WGAT. Over the years the program moved to WRUN, WBVM, and WUTQ, a run of more than 45 years. In addition to being the longest-running Polish radio program, an independent rating service ranked it the most listened to Sunday radio program in Central New York.—*James S. Pula*

SOURCE: "Michael M. Dziedzic," *Observer-Dispatch* (Utica, NY), July 6, 1991, 6A.

Dziennik Chicagoski (Chicago Daily News). One of many Polish-language newspapers published in Chicago over the years, the paper was founded in 1890 and published continuously until 1971 by the Polish Publishing Company. In 1887, the Rev. **Wincenty Barzyński**, his brother the Rev. Józef Barzyński, and the Rev. Francis Gordon, together with several lay businessmen including **Władysław Smulski** and a third brother **Jan Barzyński**, established the company to publish Catholic literature in Polish including missals and devotional books. Both Smulski and Jan Barzyński had published earlier Polish-language newspapers. The three priests belonged to the **Congregation of Resurrection**, a Catholic order founded by Poles in exile in Paris after the November Uprising (1830-31). The Rev. Wincenty Barzyński, founder of St. Stanislaus Kostka Church, came from Russian Poland where he fought in the war and later joined the Resurrectionist order in Kraków. A Barzyński family story contradicts this location and claims that the two Barzyński brothers joined the order in Rome and were sent to America by the Pope himself. The priests were sent to the United States to organize and direct parish-centered communities for Catholic émigrés. Father Wincenty was an influential leader in the Polish community in Chicago and is credited with the opening of as many as twenty-five additional Catholic churches, several parochial schools, and other institutions in the city.

Soon after its founding, the publishing company, jointly with the **Polish Roman Catholic Union** (PRUCA), published the weekly newspaper *Wiara i Ojczyzna* (Faith and Fatherland) to promote the parish and community efforts of the Resurrectionists. This publication was published concurrently with the *Dziennik Chicagoski* until 1897. In opposition to anti-clerical Polish-language newspapers, but independently of the PRUCA, the Polish Publishing Company began publishing *Dziennik Chicagoski* in 1890. However, the philosophy of the newspaper remained aligned with the views of the Resurrectionists and of the Barzyńskis. The newspaper's founding principles were to promote the interests of the Catholic faith, to encourage the community to learn about and retain the language and culture of their homeland, to support the independence of Poland, and to promote the civic advancement of the Polish immigrants in the United States. The newspaper also published fiction by Polish authors.

Dziennik Chicagoski was the second oldest Polish daily newspaper in the United States. It was the most widely read of the Chicago Polish-language dailies due to the fact that most of the Polish immigrants were Catholics. By 1913 it had a circulation of 15,837. Under the direction of the Rev. Francis Gordon, successor to the Rev. Wincenty Barzyński as the dominant spiritual leader in the community, the newspaper proved to be the most important means of maintaining the Catholic Church's influence in Polonia. The newspaper ceased publication in 1971. The publication by the same name being issued in 2009 was not associated with the original newspaper.— *Daryl Ann Hiller*

SOURCES: Chester Mitoraj, "The *Dziennik Chicagoski*, 1890–1918" (Unpublished M.A. thesis, St. Louis University, 1950); Casimir Wlezien, "A Short History of the Chicago Polish Daily News," *The Vexillum*, Vol. 13 (February 1941); Victoria Granacki, *Images of America: Chicago's Polish Downtown* (Charleston, SC: Arcadia Publishing, 2004); Edward R. Kantowicz, *Polish-American Politics in Chicago 1888–1940* (Chicago: University of Chicago Press, Chicago, 1975); Donald E. Pienkos, *P.N.A.: A Centennial History of the Polish National Alliance of the United States of North America* (Boulder, CO: East European Monographs, New York, 1984); Wacław Kruszka, *A History of the Poles in America to 1908, Part II: The Poles in Illinois* (Washington, D.C.: The Catholic University of America Press, 1994); Karen Majewski, *Traitors & True Poles: Narrating a Polish-American Identity 1880–1939* (Athens, OH: Ohio University Press, 2003); *Poles of Chicago 1837–1937: A History of One Century of Polish Contribution to the City of Chicago, Illinois* (Chicago: Polish Pageant, Inc., Chicago, 1937).

Dziennik dla Wszystkich (Everyone's Daily News). The *Dziennik dla Wszystkich* was a daily newspaper published in Buffalo, New York, from March 11, 1907, to August 12, 1957. Established by Franciszek Ruszkiewicz, this newspaper was written primarily in the Polish language, although an increasingly larger portion of its text was printed in English during the time immediately prior to its closing. With a circulation of approximately 30,000, the *Dziennik dla Wszystkich* was the largest Polish newspaper in the United States during its final 25 years of publication. When founded, the publication promoted a progressive agenda. Later, however, it adopted a moderate orientation. During World War I, the newspaper supported factions aligned with Józef Piłsudski. Editors of the newspaper included **Stanisław Slisz**, Jan J. Kowalczyk, Bronisław Kamienski, **Melania Nestorowicz**, Józef Ruszkiewicz, Adolf Cepura, **Stanley Turkiewicz**, and Alojzy F. Łaszewski. Due to accumulating debt, the publisher was forced to seek relief under the Bankruptcy Act in May of 1957. When reorganization efforts failed, the company was declared bankrupt on August 9, 1957. The newspaper then ceased operations, and the assets of its operating company were liquidated.— *Carl L. Bucki*

SOURCES: Jan Wepsiec, *Polish American Serial Publications: 1842–1966, An Annotated Bibliography* (Chicago: Jan Wepsiec, 1968); "Polish Daily Newspaper Sold Here," *Buffalo Courier Express*, February 27, 1957; "Everybody's Daily Declared Bankrupt, Prints Final Edition," *Buffalo Evening News*, August 9, 1957, 21; "Buffalo Paper Bankrupt," *New York Times*, August 10, 1957, 6.

Dziennik Ludowy (The People's Daily). A Polish-language newspaper published in Chicago for most of its history, it was affiliated with the **Polish Section of the American Socialist Party**. Some sources indicate the paper was first published in New York City but the first issue, dated March 16, 1907, was published in Chicago by the **Polish Socialist Alliance**. The Alliance also published a weekly newspaper, *Robotnik* (The Worker) starting in 1896 at their offices on Milwaukee Avenue near Augusta Street. The Polish Socialist Alliance (Związek Socjalistów Polskich w Ameryce; ZSP) was a loosely affiliated American branch of the Polska Partia Socjalistyczna (Polish Socialist Party; PPS) founded in London (or Paris) by the Alliance of Polish So-

Masthead of the *Dziennik Chicagoski* (*PMA*).

Editors, printers, and staff of the *Dziennik Ludowy* (PMA).

cialists Abroad in 1892. The PPS eventually broke up into two groups, the revolutionary faction associated with General Jósef Piłsudski, and a younger and more left wing group, whose primary concern was workers' rights. In 1907, the younger members began publishing the daily *Dziennik Ludowy* alongside the weekly *Robotnik*. By 1908, due to political friction, this group of members left the ZSP to join the American Socialist Party and took the *Dziennik Ludowy* with them. The Polish Section of the American Socialist Party became of one of the first foreign-language federations to be accepted into the American Socialist Party. The members of the Polish Socialist Alliance who remained loyal to the revolutionary faction were about half the size of the group that left to join the American party. This contracted Polish Socialist Alliance moved *Robotnik* to New York and wrote almost exclusively about the struggle in Poland in their newspaper.

Meanwhile, the newly organized Polish Section of the American Socialist Party took over and continued to publish the *Dziennik Ludowy*. The newspaper's coverage included international and national news but did not dwell on the situation in Poland. Its main focus was the plight of workers in the United States. The *Dziennik Ludowy* was an example of the prolific foreign-language labor press. Of fifteen daily labor newspapers in 1925, nine were foreign-language newspapers. These had the advantage of serving as their readers' primary source of news and were influential in forming their views. The *Dziennik Ludowy* was aided in its efforts by financial support from unions like the International Garment Workers, the Laborers, Meatcutters, Machin-

ists and Amalgamated Clothing Workers. These unions had substantial immigrant Polish memberships. To further its cause, correspondents from the *Dziennik Ludowy* were sent to see and report on the working conditions in mines and manufacturing plants where immigrant Poles worked. They covered factory closings, layoffs, accidents and fires in the workplace. The editors urged its reader to work with the Socialist Party rather than confining themselves to support Polish groups in the homeland. They pointed out that most of the immigrants would be staying in America for a long time even if they planned to return to Poland, and therefore needed to protect themselves from exploitation and bad working conditions. Short-lived attempts were made to establish local editions of the newspaper in New York and Detroit around 1910. Despite the fact that the newspaper was published only in Chicago after the efforts to expand publication to other markets failed, the newspaper enjoyed national readership. In 1913, the newspaper had a circulation of 8,000, about half as many readers as the *Dziennik Chicagoski*, published by the **Resurrectionist** Order, and about a third as many as another local daily in Chicago, the *Dziennik Związkowy* (Alliance Daily News), published by the **Polish National Alliance**. Its circulation had increased to 18,000 by 1918. At the height of its popularity, its readership peaked at 24,188 in 1921.

In February 1913, the Polish National Alliance and the Polish Section

of the American Socialist Party united under the name of the Polish Socialist Federation. In 1919, the newspaper switched its affiliation from the Socialist Party to the Chicago Federation of Labor which launched its own labor party in that year. The *Dziennik Ludowy* ceased publication in 1925. It was succeeded by the **Głos Ludowy** (The Voice of the People). Among the editors of the *Dziennik Ludowy* was Michael Sokolowski.—*Daryl Ann Hiller*

SOURCES: Paul Buhle and Dan Georgakas, *The Immigrant Left in the United States* (Albany: State University of New York Press, 1996); John J. Bukowczyk, *A History of the Polish Americans* (Piscataway, NJ: Transaction Publishers, 2008); Victoria Granacki, *Images of America: Chicago's Polish Downtown* (Chicago: Arcadia Publishing, 2004); *A History of One Century of Polish Contribution to the City of Chicago, Illinois* (Chicago: Polish Pageant, Inc., 1937); Stephen L. Vaughn, ed., *Labor Press* (New York: Routledge, 2007).

Dziennik Polski (Polish Daily News). Established in Detroit in 1904, *Dziennik Polski* became the oldest continuously published ethnic daily in Michigan. Its editors included W. Halicki (1904-?), B. M. Zieliński (1914), Joseph Karasiewicz (1916, 1923–26), Franciszek Barc (1916), W. Barr (1917–19), Stanislaus R. Trojanowski (1920–23, 1930), M. Gmernicki (1931–35), J. Ostrowski (1936–47, 1954–60), and Stanley Krajewski (1960–88). The Great Depression forced the publisher, Ludwik Wójcik, into bankruptcy, but he first transferred ownership of *Dziennik Polski* to the wife of the newspaper's manager, **Franciszek Januszewski**, who assumed the role of publisher. Januszewski, who became extremely anti-union, gained election as treasurer of the Polish Publishers and Editors Guild in the U.S. in 1938. As the new publisher of *Dziennik Polski*, he became active in the Republican Party and, with other Polish editors, formed the **National Committee of Americans of Polish Descent** (Komitet Narodowy Amerykanów Polskiego Pochodzenia, KNAPP) to promote their political views. He was later elected a vice president of the **Polish American Congress** (PAC). Vehemently anti–Soviet, Januszewski, along with **Maximillian F. Węgrzynek**, led in the founding of the **Józef Piłsudski Institute** in New York City, with Januszewski serving as its first president. Under Januszewski's editorship, *Dziennik Pol-*

Masthead of the *Dziennik Polski* (PMA).

ski, along with the New York *Nowy Świat* (New World) edited by Węgrzynek, were the two most vocal newspapers opposing Soviet designs in Poland. During the Detroit newspaper strike of 1955, *Dziennik Polski* increased its circulation from 48,000 to a record 155,000. Over the succeeding years, however, readership declined steadily until 1988 when Stanley Krajewski retired as editor with the daily printing only 12,000 copies. Krajewski continued Januszewski's activism, maintaining membership in the Polish American Congress, the Republican Party, the State Library Commission, and several Polish American organizations. Wojciech Białasiewicz of Chicago succeeded Krajewski as editor, followed by Ewa Ziomecka of Poland, but a declining subscriber list and competition from radio and television, particularly among the assimilated generations, caused *Dziennik Polski* to cease publication in 1989.—*Don Binkowski*

SOURCES: R. Jarzabkowska, "The History of the Polish Press in Detroit," *Poles in Michigan* (Detroit: n.p., 1953), Vol. 1; "Memorializing a Century of the *Dziennik Polski*," *Congressional Record*, September 29, 2004, S9931.

Dziennik Zjednoczenia (The Union Daily).

Dziennik Zjednoczenia was a daily Polish-language newspaper published in Chicago by the **Polish Roman Catholic Union of America** (PRCUA) between 1921 and 1940. The PRCUA had a long track record of publishing newspapers in Chicago but had never attempted the publication of its own daily newspaper (unlike the rival **Polish National Alliance**). Throughout the early years of the organization, it had been closely associated with the activities of the **Congregation of the Resurrection** which operated its own daily newspaper, *Dziennik Chicagoski* (Chicago Daily News). By the time of World War I, the PRCUA was increasingly developing its own institutional character; consequently, interest within the organization in sponsoring a daily paper grew. The original concept of turning the existing PRCUA organ, *Naród Polski* (The Polish Nation), into a daily newspaper was first aired in 1913 by the paper's own editors. The PRCUA convention of 1915 authorized the creation of a daily paper, and the Union began soliciting subscriptions. However, the growing crisis in Europe, the need to create a unified front within **Polonia**, World War I, and the subsequent post-war recession served to delay these efforts. The first edition of *Dziennik Zjednoczenia* appeared in September 1921. It was published in two editions, one for Chicago and the other for the rest of the country with the main difference between the two being the amount of local advertising. The newspaper appeared in the afternoon every day except Sunday and in Chicago was distributed by PRCUA boy scouts. A typical issue featured U.S. and world news on page one, with a significant emphasis on news from Poland. Feature sections included a regular column devoted to the **Polish Falcons**, a "Worker's Section" covering labor and union news, a Health Section, and a Women's Section. The paper continued the practice of printing occasional serialized novels. By the mid–1920s, *Dziennik Zjednoczenia* had added a sports page printed in English as well as a series of Polish cartoon strips drawn by local artists. The high point of its circulation probably occurred in the 1920s. The only extant circulation figures are for the early 1930s. In 1933 the paper had 6,091 subscribers. It was also sent free of charge to many parish priests and religious orders. Readers came from as far afield as Poland, Brazil, and Harbin, China. The mid–1930s proved disastrous for *Dziennik Zjednoczenia*. The effects of the Depression cut deeply into subscriptions. By 1934, paid subscriptions had dropped to 2,198 and fell further the following year. The paper also suffered from distribution problems apparently caused by relying on drivers for *Dziennik Chicagoski* who are said to have often failed to deliver papers to stores or dumped bundles of papers into the street. Libel suits and rising labor costs further added to the paper's difficulties. By 1935, the paper was losing money each quarter. Between 1931 and 1934, the *Dziennik Zjednoczenia* lost $69,000 with other print jobs offsetting some of the losses. By 1940 the membership of the PRCUA voted to discontinue publication.—*John Radzilowski*

SOURCE: John Radzilowski, *The Eagle and the Cross: A History of Polish Roman Catholic Union of America, 1873–2000* (New York: East European Monographs, 2003).

Dziennik Związkowy (The Polish Daily News).

The oldest daily Polish-language newspaper in the United States, *Dziennik Związkowy* began publishing in Chicago on January 15, 1908, as an organ of the **Polish National Alliance** fraternal organization

Dziennik Związkowy **print shop (PMA).**

whose headquarters were in Chicago's Polish Downtown. Published without break from its founding until the present day [as of 2009], it is also the oldest Polish language newspaper in the world published without interruption. The circulation of its weekend edition is about 30,000. The paper is published and sold throughout the Chicago metropolitan area, and, as a subscription, elsewhere in the United States. Copies are also sent for distribution to research libraries in Poland and to the Polish Parliament. The first editor-in-chief was **Franciszek Hieronim Jabłoński** (1908). Following his death, the newspaper was edited in turn by **Tomasz Siemiradzki** (1908–11), Stanisław Orpiszewski (1911–20), Jan Przyprawa (1920–28), Stanisław Zaklikiewicz (1928–31), **Karol Piątkiewicz** (1932–67), **Jan Krawiec** (1968–85), Anna Rychlińska (1985–89), and Wojciech Białasiewicz (beginning 1989). In 2004 the editorial team received the prestigious "Fidelis Poloniae 2004" award.—*Adam A. Zych*

SOURCES: Wojciech Białasiewicz, "85 lat 'Dziennika Związkowego,'" *Dziennik Związkowy*, No. 264 (1993); Wojciech A. Wierzewski, *Polskie Chicago* (Toruń: Wyd. Waldemar Marszałek, 2002).

Dzierozynski, Francis

(Franciszek Dzierożyński; b. Orsza, Russian occupied Poland, January 3, 1779; d. Frederick, Maryland, September 22, 1850). Priest. After the suppression of the Society of Jesus (the Jesuit fathers) in 1773, Tsarina Catherine protected Jesuits in the Russian Empire by refusing to promulgate the papal bull; thus, the 201 mostly Polish and Lithuanian members of the Byelorussian Province were able to continue their traditional work without interruption.

Gradually, a succession of popes expanded the rights and privileges of this Jesuit remnant until the order's universal restoration in 1814. Dzierozynski joined this **Jesuit** province at age fifteen, and worked his way through the long course of studies between 1794 and 1809. Because of the shortage of priests, he was ordained in 1806 after only one year of theological studies. Before ordination, he taught French, physics, music, and grammar for several years at the Kolegium Nobilum in St. Petersburg. After completing his studies, he worked as a professor of philosophy, theology, apologetics, homiletics, and mathematics to Jesuit seminarians and lay students at the *kolegium* in Mogilewo (Mogilev).

When Alexander I expelled the Jesuits from the Russian Empire in 1820, Dzierozynski was sent to Georgetown in the District of Columbia to address the lack of leadership in the Jesuits' Maryland Mission, and to connect American Jesuits with the traditions and spirit of their order, preserved without interruption in Eastern Europe. After his arrival in 1821, he quickly learned English and served as superior of the Maryland Mission from 1823 to 1830. In that capacity, he defined and defended an independent, collaborative profile for the newly restored Society of Jesus *vis-à-vis* the Catholic hierarchy; he normalized internal Jesuit governance; and he re-opened the novitiate, serving as master of novices.

After 1830, he remained a central figure in the Maryland Mission, which became the autonomous Maryland Province in 1833. From 1839 to 1843, he was acting provincial and undertook to expand the educational work of the Jesuits in New England at The College of the Holy Cross. He also served fourteen years as master of novices; taught philosophy and theology at Georgetown College; and served as tertian instructor, supervising the final year of ascetical training for Jesuits. He was a popular retreat director, and translated a number of spiritual works from Latin and Polish into English, including several sermons of Piotr Skarga. In addition, he served as a spiritual director and confessor for women religious, and was the designated theologian for Bishop Benedict Fenwick of Boston at the second Baltimore Council in 1833. At the time of his death, a Jesuit at Frederick characterized him as "a lover of the brethren and a father in Israel, loved by all, without an enemy." Years later, a historian designated him as the "patriarch" of American Jesuits."—*Anthony J. Kuzniewski*

SOURCES: Anthony J. Kuzniewski, S.J., "Francis Dzieroźyński and the Jesuit Restoration in the United States," *The Catholic Historical Review*, Vol. 78 (January 1992), 51–73; Joseph C. Osuch, "Patriarch of the American Jesuits," *Polish American Studies*, Vol. 17, no. 3–4 (1960), 92–100; Mary Neomisia Rutkowska, "A Polish Pioneer Jesuit in America," *Polish American Studies*, Vol. 3, no. 3–4 (1946), 98–103; Franciszek Domański, "Patriarcha amerykańskich Jezuitów O. Franciszkanin Dzieroźyński T.J.," *Sacrum Poloniae Millenium*, Vol. 7 (1960), 459–530.

Dziewanowska, Ada (Władysława Karczewska; b. Poznań, partitioned Poland, January 19, 1917; d.—). Folk dance director, cultural leader, author. After completing her schooling in business education, she worked as a typist before escaping to Sweden after the German invasion of Poland in September 1939. She later reached England and worked for Stanisław Mikołajczyk, the prime minister of the Polish government-in-exile in London, from 1943 to 1945. In 1946 she married **Marian K. Dziewanowski**, a wartime Polish military officer. They soon emigrated to the U.S. where he began his graduate work in history at Harvard University. A celebrated career as a university professor and scholar of Poland and Russia followed, one to which Ada Dziewanowska contributed. Dziewanowska pursued her interest in Polish cultural traditions and dance by studying at the Boston Conservatory of Music. She later served for nine years as the Dance Director and Choreographer of Boston's Krakowiak Polish Dancers. After moving with her husband to Milwaukee in 1979, she became the Artistic Director and Choreographer of the Syrena Polish Folk Dance Ensemble. Dziewanowska led countless workshops on the teaching of authentic Polish dance in the U.S. and nine other countries. In 1997 she authored *Polish Folk Dances and Songs: A Step-by-Step Guide*, which was recognized with the Creative Arts Award from the **Polish American Historical Association** (2000). Dziewanowska is recognized internationally as a leader in the recreation of the Folk Dance movement. On three occasions she has been honored by the government of Poland, and in 1994 received the Cross of Merit of the Polish Republic from President Lech Wałęsa.—*Angela T. Pienkos*

SOURCE: Bolesław Wierzbiański, ed., *Who's Who in Polish America* (New York: Bicentennial Publishing Corporation, 1996).

Dziewanowski, Marian Kamil (b. Żytomierz, Ukraine, June 27, 1913; d. Milwaukee, Wisconsin February 18, 2005). Historian. Dziewanowski came from a Polish gentry family in Ukraine. His family was forced to flee to Poland as a result of the Bolshevik Revolution. While his family had a tradition of military service, he decided to enter into a career in journalism. In 1937, as a correspondent for a Polish news agency, he was stationed in Berlin where he reported on Adolf Hitler's preparation for war. When the war began, Dziewanowski became a member of the 3rd Light Cavalry Regiment in Suwałki where he fought both the Germans and the Russians as they invaded Poland in 1939. He was captured by the Russians, but eventually escaped and made his way, via Sweden and France, to England where he joined the Polish army-in-exile, eventually becoming assistant military attaché for the Polish government-in-exile in Washington. Deciding to stay in the United States when the war ended, he became a U.S. citizen in 1953 and earned a doctorate in history from Harvard University. He began his teaching career at Boston College where he taught until 1965, then moved to Boston University where he taught until he retired in 1978. Less than a year later he went to the University of Wisconsin-Milwaukee where he served as the first professor of Polish history in a new position created by the Wisconsin legislature. Upon his second retirement in 1983, he continued to lecture at Oxford University, the University of Paris, and the University of Bordeaux among others. A prolific researcher and writer specializing in nineteenth and twentieth century Polish and Russian history, he was also affiliated with the Harvard Russian Research Center and MIT's Center for International Studies. Among his lengthy list of publications are *Joseph Piłsudski: A European Federalist, 1918–1922, Poland in the 20th Century, World War II in Europe, War at Any Price, History of Soviet Russia, The Communist Party of Poland*, and *The Polish Campaign of September 1939 in Perspective.—David Stefancic*

SOURCES: *Biography Resource Center* (Farmington Hills, MI: Gale, 2009); Paul J. Best, "M. Kamil Dziewanowski and the Study of Contemporary Poland," *The Polish Review*, Vol. 22, no. 3 (1977), 107–09; Angela and Donald Pienkos, "Marian Kamil Dziewanowski—Recalling a Great Historian Through Two of His Works," *The Polish Review*, Vol. 50, no. 3 (2005), 361–68; obituaries, *Polish American News*, June/July 2005 and *Milwaukee Sentinel*, February 23, 2005; "Dziewanowski," *Contemporary Authors* (Detroit: Gale Research Company), Vol. 29–32, 177.

Dziob, Franciszek "Frank" (b. Poland, December 11, 1887; d. Wisconsin, August 1983). Military officer, Polonia activist. After migrating to the U.S., Dziob was active in the Polish **Falcons Alliance**. During World War I (1914–18), he served as the Falcons' chief national instructor and was engaged in organizing and training eligible Poles living in America to serve in a Polish army formed in this country to fight on behalf of the cause of Polish independence (see **Polish Army in France**). After the U.S. entry into the war in 1917, Dziob was dispatched to France where he served as military adjutant to General Józef Haller, commander of the Polish army there.

Franciszek Dziob in the uniform of the Polish Army in France (*PMA*).

At the same time, he assisted **Ignacy Jan Paderewski** in his political and diplomatic efforts to restore Poland's independence. After the war, Dziob was active in the leadership of the **Polish Army Veterans Association** founded in 1923. From 1939 to 1967 he served as personal secretary to **Charles Rozmarek**, president of the **Polish National Alliance** and **Polish American Congress**. He authored, along with **Karol Piątkiewicz**, many of Rozmarek's speeches.—*Donald E. Pienkos*

SOURCES: Donald E. Pienkos, *One Hundred Years Young: A History of the Polish Falcons of America* (Boulder, CO: East European Monographs, 1987); Wojciech Wierzewski, "Sto Trzydzieska Slynnych Polaków w Ameryce" (Unpublished manuscript in the archives of the University of Wisconsin-Milwaukee, 2000).

Echo z Polski (Echo from Poland). This was the first Polish-language newspaper published in the United States. Devoted to reporting events connected with the January Insurrection of 1863 against Russia, the paper existed from June 1, 1863 until April 22, 1865.

Masthead of *Echo z Polski*, the first Polish-language newspaper published in America (*OLS*).

Based in New York, the first six issues came out three times per month, but the publication appeared weekly starting with the seventh issue. Its editor was Romuald Jaworowski and the publisher was Josef Schriftgieser, a Pole of Jewish heritage who agreed to provide printing and distribution services and other assistance. As an organ of political émigrés, *Echo z Polski* had distinctively political overtones, focusing on news of the uprising taken from publications in Europe. The outbreak of the January Insurrection left many Poles living in America with conflicting loyalties, wondering if they should travel immediately to help fight against Russia in the homeland or use their presence in America to provide assistance through fundraising and publicity. Since the United States was at the time engulfed in its own Civil War, with the fate of the Union still uncertain, Poles serving in the contending armies were left with the further choice of continuing in the service of their adopted homeland or resigning their commissions to rush to Poland's aid in Europe. The large majority of Poles living in the United States favored the Union side in the conflict, with most remaining in America. Only a few left for Poland.—*Anne Gurnack*

SOURCES: James S. Pula, *Polish Americans: An Ethnic Community* (New York: Twayne Publishers, 1995), 10–11; Frank Renkiewicz and A. Bjorkquist, *A Guide To Polish American Newspapers and Periodicals* (St. Paul, MN: Immigration History Research Center, University of Minnesota, 1988).

Education, Polish American. Education in Poland has benefited from sustained interest while suffering from outside interference. The first university was in Kraków, founded in 1364, only the second in Eastern Europe. More broadly influential were parishes of the Roman Catholic Church which for centuries offered religious education, accompanied by basic instruction in literacy. These rudimentary schools utilized the organist as the teacher, establishing a tradition that would persist into modern times and even cross the ocean to America. But state-run elementary education awaited the nineteenth century and developed when the Polish nation had been divided among its aggressive neighbors, Austria, Prussia and Russia. The partitioning powers began to show an interest in government-sponsored schooling after the Napoleonic Wars ended in 1815. Prussia, which emerged from this period of tumult and bloodshed with the northern and western portions of the historic Polish-Lithuanian Commonwealth, was the first. While militaristic and repressive of Polish national aspirations, Prussia was quicker to appreciate the advantages of broad literacy in economic development. By the late nineteenth century a comprehensive elementary education and some higher instruction enriched the German partition. This was a confessional school system with religious instruction as part of the curriculum, initially allowing the teaching of Catholicism in Polish areas. But the *Kulturkampf* in the 1870s under the new German Empire saw the replacement of clergy as school inspectors by government nominees, undermining Polish input into school affairs. By 1886 teachers were removed from control by local elected school boards and subordinated directly to the state, an effort to ensure sympathy for germanization. This meant that most subjects were in German with extensive instruction in that language, including a heavy ideological slant aimed at producing patriotic (i.e., "German") citizens. Poles were increasingly unhappy with the situation and in 1907 a widespread series of school strikes testified to their offended sentiments. During the period of emigration Poles perceived education in the German partition as hostile to their ethnicity even as they benefited from good facilities and well-trained instructors.

The situation in the Kingdom of Poland, the Russian partition, was worse. There, educational development lagged in the characteristic oppressive backwardness of the Russian Empire. The slow development of public education became even less attractive in the wake of the 1863 Uprising when Russian became the sole language of instruction. The census of 1897 revealed an illiteracy rate of seventy percent, indicative of the retarded and inadequate education available. The consequence was the highest proportion of illiterates among these newcomers to America.

The Austrian partition, commonly referred to as **Galicia**, was the most economically underdeveloped but the most open to Polish aspirations in education. With the effective cession of provincial control to Poles by the late 1860s the provincial legislature, which bore the traditional Polish name of Sejm, set up the Provincial School Board in 1869. A law for general elementary education mandated six years of instruction in Polish or the language of the local majority, though this remained only a goal for years. As in German Poland the system was confessional, allowing

Catholics, Orthodox, and Jews to have their own tax-supported schools. While funding increased steadily, the pervasive poverty of Galicia, rather than state hostility, slowed educational improvement.

All of the partitions addressed adult education through voluntary associations. These were most elaborate in Galicia where a sympathetic government permitted the Popular School Society (Towarzystwo Szkoły Ludowej) and the Popular Enlightenment Society (Towarzystwo Oświaty Ludowej) to set up local libraries, provide traveling lecturers and in other ways elevate the cultural level of adults. Some funding came from the provincial government, but wealthy patrons were crucial, even more so in the other partitions. The impetus and instructors came from the intelligentsia, the most nationally-conscious segment of society which by the late nineteenth century recognized that involving the peasant majority was indispensable to fulfilling nationalist goals. This movement made the journey to America but underwent significant change in the new environment.

Immigration of large numbers of Poles to America after the Civil War led to construction of ethnic communities, with the Roman Catholic parish as the largest institution. Entering American Catholicism, they encountered bishops invariably of non–Polish extraction who exhibited an unusually comprehensive commitment to education under church auspices. Although this included secondary and institutions of higher learning, the emphasis was on elementary education. This stemmed from a concern by many American bishops to counter what they perceived as secular or Protestant bias in the proliferating public school system of the later nineteenth century. By the Third Plenary Council of 1884 parochial schools became the goal for every parish. If never achieved *in toto*, the late nineteenth century witnessed an incredible expansion of church-run day schools, distinguishing the American church from its counterparts elsewhere. This occurred without state aid, a subject of complaint by many Catholics but a situation which allowed for freedom from external oversight as well. Aside from rather cursory government inspection prior to World War I Catholics were largely left alone to fashion their vision of education.

Poles found this educational environment strange but stimulating. The Partitions had educational development mainly under hostile state auspices which nonetheless included provision for religious instruction in the public schools. Now there were more choices. Poles settling in cities could send their children free of charge to the local public school, typically housed in a large brick structure much more impressive than anything back in the homeland village or town. While the postbellum years typically saw an exclusion of overt religious instruction, textbooks of the day used a language of generic Protestantism to convey values American educators deemed vital to a proper society. There was also an increasing element of Americanization in the curriculum, about which Poles were ambivalent. On the one hand they generally admired American political institutions and could subscribe to civic tolerance, but they had definite desires to pass on a sense of Polishness to their children. Yet pre–1914 public schools ignored or denigrated ethnicity and as Poles settled permanently they wanted to pass their heritage on to their children in a more systematic manner than simply through the family. This led to a fortuitous coincidence of ethnic with episcopal desires. Unlike contemporary Italian immigrants, who lagged in establishing parish schools, Poles quickly followed the construction of a church with a school. This institution, usually housed in a separate structure, taught not only religion but also ethnicity. The paucity of diocesan school boards meant that there was little external oversight before World War I and bishops eager to promote religious schools were happy to have an immigrant group so interested in setting them up. Left on their own, Poles could experiment in education.

Their first inclination was traditional. Since organists joined the immigration stream and parishes often hired them to provide the church music so beloved by Poles, they were called into service as instructors in many communities. Such teachers usually received $50–$60 a month in the 1890s for both duties and they found themselves fully occupied. Families were prolific so classes ballooned. The ungraded rooms might exceed one hundred children of widely varying ages and preparation. The problem of serving rapidly increasing numbers was a continuing problem. Since lay teachers had no group identity, additions to the teaching staff were difficult to address. Parishes sought more instructors through advertisements in the Polish American and even homeland press but the response was dependent upon individual preference.

The organist-teachers did express some interest in organization. **Antoni Małłek** and others in Chicago set up a society of lay teachers in the late 1890s, but its existence was ephemeral. Subsequent efforts likewise did not result in a durable association, unlike the burgeoning fraternals. While teacher organizations have been ignored by historians, instructors were probably hard to organize due to dispersion in widely separated localities, scarcity of numbers compared to potential mutual aid society members, and transience. Most remained in a parish only for a few years since the pay was modest and demands steadily increased with the influx of new pupils. Unlike in the homeland, there never arose Polish teacher institutes which would have provided a common learning experience and sense of camaraderie. There was no ethnic constituency to demand and support normal schools and government funding was never a prospect. The publicly supported American teacher colleges were indifferent or hostile to ethnicity, and the prevailing assimilationist philosophy made an appeal to multi-culturalism impossible. The supply of lay teachers remained dependent on immigration and many of them moved into other work over time.

The arrival of the Sisters of St. Felix of Cantilice (**Felicians**) in 1874 at the invitation of the Rev. **Józef Dąbrowski** signaled a major turning point in Polonian education. Dabrowski was not only a pastor but an intellectual and activist who strongly felt that nuns were more appropriate types of instructors in parish-linked schools. He chose the Felicians, a new congregation with an orientation toward social work and education, and outlined his educational philosophy in a letter to Mother Superior M. Magdelen: "My reply to your question about the exact kind of schools we are planning, Mother, is that they will be, for the most part, elementary schools in which the subjects to be taught will include catechism, arithmetic, geography, Sacred Scripture, history and perhaps also, fine handiwork for the girls. We must, however, be on a par with the public schools, maintaining a high level since the Protestants strive for a thorough education." The priest was acutely aware of the American environment and wanted Polish schools to be competitive. This sensitivity, coupled with a growing need to conform to state standards, moved Polish institutions into a more and more American-patterned curriculum. He also reflected the general Catholic perspective that the public schools were "Protestant," useful to encourage Poles to stay away from them.

Nuns migrating to the United States were usually young, with some older ones as leaders. They had relatively extensive training and a familiarity with Polish high culture which made them much better educated than most immigrant women. The communities brought with them a tradition of "choirs," internal divisions going back centuries. The first choir was either contemplative — historically seen as spiritually superior — or at least fully professed persons engaged in activity in the "world" such as teaching or hospital work. Contemplatives seemed out of touch with the activist republic and few appeared in America where nuns needed to labor outside the convent. The second choir might not have full vows and were often housekeepers or other subordinates. The democratic American environment and the need to attract additional personnel undermined this traditional system and it largely disappeared by World War I. Polish communities founded in the United States like the **Franciscan Sisters** of Chicago never introduced choirs.

Despite a range of social service experience immigrant sisters found themselves besieged with requests for instructors for parochial schools. Nuns had several attractions for lay people and pastors. First, they were less expensive than lay teachers, usually getting $200–$250 a year before 1914, less than half the wage of a lay person. More subtly but importantly, as one newspaper put it in celebrating their presence, "The Catholic religion, ...that gift of God, ... is inculcated in our Polish school by persons who know it best because more than others they live according to the evangelical teachings in all their impeccable beauty." Their highly regulated lives seemed exemplary compared to the sometimes hard-drinking lay teachers and their often superior cultural level could introduce a higher tone to the school. But while the nuns retained a strong concern for proper behavior their communities had a more proletarian future. The change in cultural background was a product of the incessant need for more sisters. Congregations could only send so many from the homeland and the obvious additional source was recruitment in America. Polonian girls, in fact, were highly responsive to invitations to join communities. The example of devoted nuns before them in school, a strong sense of piety and duty, and perhaps a desire to live with other women of education and have some independence from the patriarchal pattern of Polish families drew more and more young women into service.

These postulants were usually from working class families. Pious immigrant parents made considerable efforts to send their offspring to parochial schools, despite monthly fees of 50 cents to a dollar plus book costs. But such families had little to spare for the traditional dowry, a concrete expression of the metaphor of a nun as a "bride of Christ." Consequently, in America the dowry was another tradition discarded. Indeed, the persistence of the custom in some non–Polish communities was a factor in inclining Polonian girls to look elsewhere. There were a few instances of Polish girls admitted without dowries to such congregations who found themselves relegated to second class status. Such negative experiences led to occasional secessions to form houses based solely on Polish ethnicity. A more positive result of American recruitment was the closure of cultural gaps. Polonian newcomers were unpretentious, familiar with Polish American dialect, and accustomed to the more egalitarian character of American society. Immigrant parents of limited education did not feel out of place in communicating with them and likely they contributed to the popularity of parochial education.

Yet the influx of the American-born created some serious problems. Many were barely out of eighth grade and in their mid-teens when they committed themselves to a sisterhood. Despite the aspiration voiced by the Rev. Dąbrowski for academic excellence, in reality parochial schools were often overcrowded and less well funded than their public counterparts. The pressure to reinforce overworked teaching staffs had the effect of curtailing the already cursory training programs. As one community history delicately put it, the youthful nuns "learned the theoretical and the practical simultaneously under the guidance of an older and experienced sister." The result was inadequately trained teachers.

The weakness in teacher training and other inadequacies of the parochial schools left the door open for criticism from several perspectives. The most radical was from anti-clericals and leftists. These persons, often immigrant intelligentsia uninterested in or hostile to religion, seized the opportunity to condemn parish schools as instillers of clericalism and exemplars of educational incompetence. Some called for the establishment of Polish schools free of religion and urged the Galician provincial government to send well-prepared lay teachers to America to take advantage of freedom from state control to promote enlightened and patriotic instruction. But any appeal to the homeland, even the partition most under Polish control, was a pipedream. School authorities at home had great demands on their limited resources already and their awareness of American **Polonia**'s educational situation was minimal. Sporadic efforts based on domestic resources likewise accomplished little. The example of Czech freethinkers, who had numerous schools, did not resonate with most Poles in America and leftist interest was never consistent or strong. The consequence was a marginalization of the prewar anti-clerical perspective for education.

The secularist mainstream, best represented by the leading fraternal insurance federation, the **Polish National Alliance**, took little action regarding juvenile education before World War I. While not anti-religious in principle and with leaders in smaller settlements often on good terms with local pastors, the PNA nonetheless had a mainly adult focus in its educational activity at this time. The formation of the Education Department (Wydział Oświaty) soon after the turn of the century symbolized its commitment. But it would await the interwar period to see major fraternal efforts to transmit a sense of Polishness to young persons.

Another critique, voicing some of the same complaints, but from a very different orientation, came from the **Polish National Catholic Church**. This denomination, unique in the United States as a dissenting form of Catholicism, emerged in 1897 under the leadership of the Rev. **Francis Hodur**, an immigrant priest from Galicia. The Rev. (later Bishop) Hodur sought to express an ethnic form of the old faith in a more democratic polity. Congregations emerged in most settlements in the next several decades. A common consequence of separation was the withdrawal (or sometimes expulsion) of dissenters' children from the local parochial school. Hodur had to consider how to educate the coming generation. Given his opposition to monasticism, founding teaching sisterhoods was not an option. Yet the PNCC leader and many of his followers liked the concept, if not the Roman content, of parish schools. Unlike the secularists, the PNCC could mobilize resources based on parishes. Hodur encouraged the formation of day schools, but most congregations were too small and poor to support such an ambitious undertaking. Commonly the priest or organist became the instructor in an after-hours school, often in the church basement, where young Polish National Catholics learned the denominational version of religion and ethnicity. Initially dependent on Roman Catholic or homeland texts, in the interwar period the National Catholics developed their own curricular materials. Though affecting only a small minority in most Polish American settlements, Polish National Catholicism offered the only significant alternative to the Roman Catholic schools before World War I.

The most effective critique was internal to Roman Catholicism. Parish committees often assumed an oversight function and pastors had an interest in improving educational offerings. Roman Catholic or independent newspapers published advice and admonition, along with occasional reports on schools. Publicity and parish concern at both official and popular levels made nuns aware of their pedagogical shortcomings. Moreover, internal community observations coincided with outsider opinion. The result was sustained action by congregations, especially after 1900. Often referred to as "educational chapters," conferences of nuns discussed ways to improve the schools. A common response was lengthening the period of community educational instruction. Another was to send nuns to summer school. In the East this usually meant the Catholic University of America or another Catholic institution. The Midwest, where Catholics enjoyed greater confidence based on a presence often coinciding with the beginning of settlement, saw many nuns attend state universities. Here young Polish sisters mingled with non–Catholics, broadening their cultural horizons while addressing pedagogical inadequacies. If still not on a level with public school teachers, the qualifications of nuns improved significantly by World War I.

The Polish Catholic school curriculum steadily moved toward an American model. Parents, pastor, and sisters acknowledged that in the United States instruction the English language and American culture and history had to be included in addition to ethnic and religious instruction. By 1914 commonly half of daily instruction occurred in English, with the tendency to enlarge the presence of the American tongue seemingly inexorable. This pattern emerged with minimal outside pressure since few diocesan school boards existed. The failure of nativist efforts in the early 1890s to compel Americanization through government control in Wisconsin and Illinois made state school superintendents less inclined to intervene, though this varied by state. From an ethnic perspective the situation remained conveniently open.

A basic need was texts. Initially, homeland materials, usually from Galicia, were imported or copies printed here. But they had a more secular character than the parochial instructors were comfortable with. As early as 1879 Polish American works appeared, such as the Rev. Dąbrowski's *Geografia dla szkół polskich* (Geography for Polish Schools). These had not only a stronger religious content but also information or stories about America, providing young Polonians with more relevant instruction. While often critical of Protestantism, texts increasingly spoke favorably of religious toleration, an acceptance of pluralism consonant with Polish tradition but not with the contemporary Catholic theoretical position on Roman Catholicism as the "one true church" deserving privileged status. Fortunately the larger American church never yearned for the European-oriented vision of religious establishment, accepting in practice the presence of diversity. Poles were open to pluralism by virtue of their historic diversity and so, if anything, their schoolbooks anticipated the direction of American Catholic evolution. The books also contained material on being Americans, unlike homeland publications. Seeing no conflict between being good Poles and good Americans, this ethnic group fostered a dual patriotism without qualms.

The parish school had a significant role in the public expression of ethnicity before the war. By 1900 a patriotic liturgical year developed, with commemorations of the January Uprising, Constitution Day in May, Grunwald Day in August, and the November Uprising, to note the more popular. Parochial schoolchildren appeared at rallies, providing choral singing and declamations on patriotic themes. Their presence showed that the next generation was being raised as good nationalists. It also reinforced support for the sisters and church schools since children at public institutions had no comparable training.

Educational activity went beyond the eighth grade and here there was more even competition between religiously oriented Poles and their secularist compatriots. Polish Catholic high schools were few and far between, usually to be found only in large settlements. The earliest example was St. Stanislaus College in Chicago, founded in 1890 and its real status acknowledged later in a name change to Weber High School. The **Congregation of the Resurrection**, active in education as well as pastoral work in the city, began the school in an old frame church. By 1899 it moved to a four-story brick building and in 1914 introduced a two-year commercial curriculum for girls, taught by the School Sisters of Notre Dame. Another Catholic effort at Orchard Lake, Michigan near Detroit became St. Mary's High School in 1915. Such expensive enterprises remained beyond the capacity of most colonies.

The Polish National Alliance provided a secular alternative in 1912 with the founding of a residential high school in Cambridge Springs, Pennsylvania. The support of the largest fraternal federation, and persistent appeals to members to send their children there, allowed it to evolve into **Alliance College** in 1948. The ethnic high schools took in only a small minority of Polonian secondary students. Most went to public schools and the remainder to non-ethnic Catholic institutions. Before World War I there was little educational attention by either religionists or secularists directed at the American-born youth outside of the few high schools.

For adults prewar Polonia had several educational options. In larger colonies private technical education schools taught marketable skills, usually in manual trades. Often English language instruction accompanied this, as well as through independent language schools. Public education in some cities utilized local

The cover of one of the many textbooks published for use in Polish American parochial schools (*OLS*).

elementary or high schools for evening classes, enabling immigrants to inexpensively improve their linguistic skills. Polish newspapers by 1900 frequently carried advertisements for private commercial schools, catering to the significant minority who wanted to enter the economy above the level of manual worker. Though bringing weaker educational backgrounds than German or Scandinavian immigrants, many Poles were interested in acquiring further instruction to advance in American society.

An important if more abstract cultural aspiration made the journey with the immigrants. This was "enlightenment" (*oświata*), a movement associated with socially-conscious intelligentsia in the homeland. With few well-educated immigrants and no wealthy patrons, this developed in a more democratic form in the United States. Many fraternal lodges and parishes set up lending libraries, sometimes supported by dues but often free through subsidies from their parent organizations. Book and periodical lists reveal a wide range of offerings, from scientific to literary to religious/philosophical, varying with the ideological orientation of the sponsor. Newspapers ardently supported these efforts, praising cultural attainment as a mark of a true Pole. There were also drama and singing societies, whose presentations often had strong patriotic or religious overtones, though comedies and melodramas also were popular. By the war there were enlightenment efforts in virtually all Polish colonies.

World War I altered education for Polonia as it did for many other aspects of ethnic existence. When the conflict began in Europe

in the autumn of 1914 the United States proclaimed neutrality, but like other immigrants Poles were deeply concerned about the war. For the host culture the possibility of foreign-born sympathy with one side or another heightened fears of divided loyalty. The Americanization movement, diffuse and uncoordinated before the conflict, became more focused through federal government efforts, especially after U.S. entry on the side of the Allies in the spring of 1917. Public schools, which many Polish children attended, promoted patriotic instruction with an increasingly chauvinistic tenor. Fortunately for Poles, the dominant internal political orientation by 1917 was pro-Allied, with the **National Department** (Wydział Narodowy) stressing loyalty to the United States while pressing the federal government to support the re-establishment of a Polish state. Unlike German Americans, who suffered extensive if usually petty persecution in the last years of the war, conspicuous Polish patriotic enthusiasm, demonstrated by huge bond purchases and army enlistments, gave them some protection from the anti-foreign sentiment of the time. With the U.S. in the war for only eighteen months, parochial schools largely escaped mandated modification of their curriculum. Nonetheless, concerns to appear loyal reinforced the prewar tendency to enlarge the English component of instruction. Heightened sensitivity to public opinion underlay much postwar discussion of education.

There was a fundamental ethnic reorientation in the half-decade following World War I. With the successful establishment of an independent Poland the major unifying goal

came to fulfillment. A series of Emigration Congresses considered what it meant to be a good Pole in the new situation and in 1923 moved from a focus on the homeland to the needs of Polonia. Though the committee formulating new ethnic goals included clerics, and fostering parochial schools became a component of this definition of ethnicity, the postwar formulation never had the singular energy of the movement for independence. Ethnic educational activity became more diverse but lacked an overarching coherent definition of Polishness. Broadly there was increased acculturation, accelerated with the ending of mass immigration due to restrictive laws. The drastic diminution in newcomers meant that education increasingly addressed the American-born.

The postwar era saw several factors fostering acculturation in parochial schools. The rapid development of diocesan boards of education enhanced outside pressure for more instruction in English. In many dioceses the boards created model curricula to be followed by all parish schools, whether territorial or national. This was often accompanied by a list of approved textbooks, seldom from ethnic presses. Indeed, the postwar years saw large American publishing houses become much more active in soliciting parochial school business. They sponsored teacher institutes for educational improvement or made donations designed to draw attention to their wares. Since this was expressed in a value-laden vocabulary of being "modern" and "up to date," it appealed to the more "progressive" (meaning acculturated) nuns. Ethnic presses producing textbooks, usually linked to newspapers which were suffering from a declining Polish language readership, were unequal competitors.

Increasing state pressure for certification of teachers aroused concern. Older nuns were often minimally qualified by American standards and the rush to get native-born women into the classroom before the war had often scanted their education. Attendance at schools offering accredited summer programs increased, along with increased pedagogical preparation in the novitiate, but not until the Second World War were most nuns state certified. Internal changes in communities of sisters reinforced tendencies toward acculturation. The appearance of specially designated inspectors or advisors based in congregational motherhouses brought nuns with the authority to promote change into parochial schools. These visitors were attuned to current pedagogy, which had little concern for ethnicity, though most were not hostile to some curricular component promoting Polishness. The advisors operated in an environment where

St. Hyacinth High School Band in Milwaukee, Wisconsin (*UWM*).

American sisters predominated. Native-born mother superiors appeared for the first time. The younger nuns used English as their tongue of choice, though most had some acquaintance with Polish but often lacked fluency. Such persons were more open to increased use of English. In this milieu Polish tended to move to the periphery of the curriculum.

The parochial schools saw an enrollment decline in the interwar years. The huge immigration of 1900–14 produced numerous marriages and more children, but by 1930 most were beyond elementary age. Simultaneously the Depression constricted incomes and even pious Poles found the free public schools more of an attraction. Conceivably, the decline of Polish instruction also led to parental perception of church schools as less of a bridge between generations and thus less useful than earlier. Though Polish was less central, nuns still sought to instill the ancestral culture through the curriculum, but using texts they deemed more suitable. A series of interwar conferences of Felician sisters, the largest Polonian community, hotly debated the role of English. The predominant opinion was that its extension was inevitable, given almost universal use of English among native-born children. Their inadequacies in the ancestral tongue were accommodated in new publications. Sister M. Cyryla CSSF wrote a large number of schoolbooks for Polish American grade schools. Compared to prewar works, stories were shorter and vocabulary simpler. Polish nationalism was present, but the most important element was religion. These widely used texts addressed the preferences of parochial school instructors and accepted a lower level of Polish proficiency while seeking to instill some knowledge of the homeland language and culture. Use of Polish persisted more in religious instruction than anything else.

The interwar decline of Polish in religious schools went neither unnoticed nor uncriticized. Some secularists called for the establishment of schools to teach the ancestral culture and language without concern for religion, but as before the war there was only weak response. The perennial problem of funding and instructors remained. The weakness of the anti-clerical and leftist perspectives characterized Polonia as much between the wars as before 1914. The Polish government, a potential source of money and materials, showed modest interest in Polonian education between the wars. The Ministry of Education sent texts and two instructors but in comparison with the several hundred thousand children in church schools the enrollment of about 14,000 by 1940 was small. The Polish

Supplementary School Council of America (f. 1926) was an effort to institutionalize this alternative to parochial education. Other alternatives to Roman Catholic schools appeared in less confrontational forms. The fraternal insurance federations, with large treasuries but stagnating memberships in an era of restricted immigration, worked diligently to attract native-born young people to their ranks. The Polish National Alliance and the Polish Roman Catholic Union, the two largest, sought to instill a sense of ethnicity and were often imitated by smaller mutual aid bodies. The Polish Educational Society emerged in 1916 and had 293 "schools" with 22,000 pupils by 1934. The persistent problem of instructors was partially met by the establishment of teacher training courses at the PNA's Alliance College. But children viewed fraternal-sponsored Saturday schools as work and there were persistent problems in encouraging them to attend. More popular were fraternal sports and scouting. Scouting had some ethnic/ideological overlay but less extensive instruction than the supplementary schools.

For high school age and older youth there were fewer possibilities for ethnic instruction. Some fraternals promoted clubs for Polonian high school students, but these relied more on persuasion than parental pressure and seem to have touched few. Some colleges and universities had Polish clubs, here a product usually of student initiative though perhaps benefiting from some local support from mutual aid groups or parishes. At the college level a few Polish organizations appeared, stimulated by the presence of students receiving scholarships from the Polish National Alliance and Polish Roman Catholic Union.

Another approach was to use political clout to insert Polish into the local high schools. In **Hamtramck** the huge ethnic population succeeded in this and by 1935 about thirty public high schools offered Polish as a foreign language. Such novelties depended on a substantial Polish population that could be politically mobilized — more an exception than the norm. Universities occasionally offered Polish, sometimes as a result of the efforts of an interested faculty member but such opportunities remained rare.

Adults continued to show interest in enlightenment but with significant change in participants. The establishment of the Polish Arts Club in 1926 in Chicago seems to have stimulated similar groups elsewhere, as in the Polanie Club of Minneapolis. Unlike the male-dominated enlightenment activities before World War I the new groups welcomed women and indeed they were sometimes preponderant. Coming out of an educated second

generation they used English more than Polish, offering a modified ethnicity that honored the ancestral culture while expressing it in the tongue of the new land. Publications like the *New American* publicized their perspective and concerns. Drama and music continued to be supported, most often in parishes but in large colonies like New York or Chicago with professional companies in the twenties. The Depression undermined the economic viability of these as the spread of radio offered a new and more popular medium, leading to some expression of high culture on the air waves.

The years after 1945 saw a further constriction of education in Polish, modified to some degree by an influx of about 150,000 "displaced persons" of Polish background from refugee camps in Western Europe. About half that number came as emigrants from Communist Poland during 1955–66. The newcomers were superior in education to the largely peasant migration before 1914. In 1952 in Chicago the Polish Teachers Association of America (Zrzeszenie Nauczycieli Polskich w Ameryce) began a long career of promoting Saturday schools largely catering to offspring of the foreign-born. The Saturday schools benefited from a common curriculum and some specialized training for instructors without the ideological overtones that hindered earlier leftist/anti-clerical efforts. A few parishes, usually in large colonies, continued to offer some Polish instruction, but these were rare.

Two major organizations fostering adult enlightenment emerged: the **Polish Institute of Arts and Sciences** (f. 1942) and an offshoot, the **Polish American Historical Association** (f. 1944). The former was a product of wartime émigré concern to preserve Polish culture in an environment safe from the German onslaught and over time it became a leading expression of interest in homeland history and culture. Its periodical, the ***Polish Review***, became a scholarly journal. An America-oriented division evolved into the independent **Polish American Historical Association**, which focused on the American experience and also produced a scholarly periodical, ***Polish American Studies***. Both groups had a core of scholars but appealed to educated laypersons, expanding enlightenment.

Poles in the United States developed extensive educational activities which evolved over time. All age groups could participate and the necessity of voluntary support ensured that offerings remained directly under the control of the ethnic group, keeping it largely free from the politics of public subsidy. Efforts to insert Polish into public education were local and often transitory, but this annoyed mainly some non-religious elites. The long-term concern for cultural preservation is an impressive testimony to the determination of these immigrants to preserve ethnicity in the new land.— *William J. Galush*

SOURCES: For surveys of educational activity in the homeland on the eve of immigration, see Stanisław Michalski, ed., *Dzieje szkolnictwa i oświaty na wsi polskiej do 1918* (Warsaw: Ludowa Spółdzielnia Wydawnicza, 1982); Julian Dybiec, *Mecenat naukowy i oświatowy w Galicji, 1860–1918* (Wrocław: Ossolineum, 1981). For the United States the most comprehensive work is Józef Miąso, *The History of Education of Polish Immigrants in the United States* (Warsaw: Polish Scientific Publishers, 1977); see also the Rev. Francis Bolek, *The Polish American School System* (New York: Columbia Free Press Corporation, 1948); William Galush, *For More than Bread: Community and Identity in American Polonia, 1880–1940* (Boulder: East European Monographs, 2006). Useful articles include Regina Kościelska and Piotr Taras SAC, "Szkoła polonija jako czynnik kulturowej tożsamości w systemie działania spółeczności polonijnej w Stanach Zjednoczonych," *Studia Polonijne,* Vol. 7, 51–125; Dorota Praszałowicz, "The Cultural Change of Polish American Parochial Schools in Milwaukee, 1866–1988," *Journal of American Ethnic History,* Vol. 13 (Summer 1994), 21–45; Ellen Marie Kuznicki, "The Polish American Parochial Schools," in Frank Mocha, ed., *Poles in America: Bicentennial Essays* (Stevens Point, WI: Worzalla Publishing Company, 1978), 435–60; Thaddeus C. Radzilowski, "Polish American Institutions of Higher Learning," in Frank Mocha, ed., *Poles in America: Bicentennial Essays* (Stevens Point, WI: Worzalla Publishing Company, 1978), 461–496; Adam Walaszek, "Images of Neighbors and Poles in Early 20th Century Polish American Schoolbooks," *Polish American Studies,* Vol. 64 (Spring 2007), 5–25; Anthony Kuzniewski, "Boot Straps and Book Learning: Reflections on the Education of Polish Americans," *Polish American Studies,* Vol. 32, no. 2 (1975), 5–26; William J. Galush, "What Should Janek Learn: Staffing and Curriculum in Polish American Parochial Schools, 1870–1940," *History of Education Quarterly,* Vol. 40 (Winter 2000), 395–417.

Egielski, Richard (b. Queens, New York City, New York, July 16, 1952; d.—). Author, illustrator. After attending Pratt Institute and the Parson School of Design, he embarked on a career as an illustrator. Among his publications, containing his own illustrations, are the children's books *Buz* (1995), *The Gingerbread Boy* (1997), *Jazper* (1998), *Three Magic Balls* (2000), *Slim and Jim* (2001), and *Saint Francis and the Wolf* (2005). *Buz* was recognized as one of the top ten illustrated books by *The New York Times.* Egielski won further recognition illustrating the books of other noted authors such as Arthur Yorinks (*Hey, Al*) and Pam Conrad (*The Tub People* series and *The Tub Grandfather*). The American Library Association recognized him with its Caldecott Medal (1987) for illustrating *Hey, Al.* His illustrations in F. N. Monjo's *The Porcelain Pagoda* were included in the American Institute of Graphic Arts Book Show (1976). Among his other awards and recognitions were a Children's Book of the Year citation from the Child Study Association of America for *The Letter, the Witch, and the Ring* (1976); the Society of Illustrators' Certificate of Merit in 1978, 1981, 1984, and 1985; a best book citation from *School Library Journal* for *Louis the Fish* (1980); a plaque from the Biennale of Illustrations Bratislava for *It Happened in Pinsk* (1985); Parents' Choice Picture Book Awards for *Amy's Eyes* (1985) and *The Tub People* (1989); and the Best Illustrated Book designation, *New York Times* for *Jazper* (1998).— *James S. Pula*

SOURCES: Anita Silvey, ed., *Children's Books and Their Creators* (Boston: Houghton Mifflin, 1995), 219–220; Arthur Yorinks, "Richard Egielski," *Horn Book,* July–August, 1987, 436–38.

Ehrenkreutz, Andrzej Stefan "Andrew" (b. Warsaw, Poland, December 19, 1921; d. April 6, 2008, Melbourne, Australia). Historian. Ehrenkreutz grew up in a family with a history of patriotic and civic commitment to the Polish cause. He served in the Polish armed forces in World War II as a member of the 1st Polish Grenadiers in France in 1940, was taken prisoner by the Germans at the front in Lorraine and, except for two escapes, spent the rest of the war in Stalag 4B, a prisoner of war camp near Leipzig. Sent to a displaced persons camp after the war, Ehrenkreutz and his new wife soon were able to join his mother and stepfather in Palestine. There he became interested in the history of the Middle East. In 1947 he began studies leading to a doctorate at the University of London's School of Oriental Studies and post-doctoral research at Yale University. He and his family then moved to Michigan where he began his teaching career. In 1985 he retired as Professor of History and Near Eastern Studies at the University of Michigan in Ann Arbor. Enhrenkreutz's extensive scholarly publications included a biography of Saladin, the great Muslim conqueror during the Crusades, and numerous articles. In 1987 he and his wife moved permanently to Australia to join their son there.

In the 1960s, Ehrenkreutz became active in the **Polish American Congress** and in the mid–1970s was the moving force and co-founder of Studium, the **North American Studies Center for Polish Affairs**. The Center immediately became a leading source of information and analysis about Poland and the democratic opposition to Communist rule. Its quarterly journal, *Studium Papers,* edited by Marian Krzyzowski (known by his pseudonym, Marek Nowak), appeared between 1982 and 1990 and succeeded an earlier Center publication, *Studium News Abstracts,* which began in the late 1970s. *Studium Papers* provided its readers, first among them U.S. government officials focused on Polish affairs, with a steady steam of carefully documented information about the Solidarity movement and its struggle against the Jaruzelski regime. *Studium Papers* also published literary materials and the writings of people inside Poland. Serving on the magazine's editorial board were Marek Zielinski in Poland, Tadeusz Witkowski and David McQuade in Ann Arbor, Sofia Zezmer in New York City, Lillian Vallee in California, and Padraic Kenney, an historian who later went on to direct the Polish Studies Center at Indiana University and head the Polish Studies Association, a national organization of scholars writing on Poland. Frequent contributors included Alina Perth-Grabowska in Munich and Kazimierz Podlaski in Poland.

In point of fact, the Center served as a "think tank" for American **Polonia** and the Polish American Congress during this critical period, thanks to Enhrenkreutz's leadership and his close association with a number of co-founders of the Center, most notably **Jan Nowak-Jezioranski** (then recently retired from Radio Free Europe), **Kazimierz Lukomski** (vice president of the Polish American Congress and chair of its Polish affairs committee), Fabian Polcyn, Stanisław Bask-Mostwin, Hanna Leja, and Peter Swiecicki (later the Center's last president). In fact, more than two hundred academics and professional persons, in the U.S., Canada, and Europe, were engaged in working with and on behalf of the Center, including scholars **Piotr Wandycz, Jerzy Krzyżanowski,** and **Bolesław Wierzbiański,** publisher of the *Nowy Dziennik* (New Daily) of New York. Together they helped in writing a number of "white papers" for U.S. policy makers that outlined the situation in Poland during its crisis years leading to the collapse of communist domination and the birth of pluralistic democracy there from 1989.

Ehrenkreutz visited Washington, D.C., frequently to discuss the Polish situation with U.S. government officials. In addition, he authored many letters to the editor on the Polish situation in newspapers, including pieces published in the *New York Times* and the *Wall Street Journal.* He and his colleagues worked closely with **Aloysius Mazewski,** President of the Polish American Congress, on Poland's behalf. In addition to his political activities, Ehrenkreutz was instrumental in assisting Peter Ostafin in creating the Copernicus Endowment at the University of Michigan, which brought many world renowned Polish intellectuals, scholars, and artists to the University community. In Australia, Ehrenkreutz founded the Australian Institute of Polish Affairs and was active in the Polish-Jewish dialog there.— *Donald E. Pienkos*

SOURCES: Remembrance published by the University of Michigan in 2008 and authored by Marian Krzyzowski; Donald E. Pienkos, *For Your Freedom Through Ours: Polish American Efforts on Poland's Behalf* (Boulder, CO: East European Monographs, 1991).

Eilenberg, Samuel (b. September 13, 1913, Warsaw, Russian Empire; d. January 30, 1998, New York, New York). Mathematician. Born in the Russian Empire and educated in post–World War I Poland, Eilenberg received his M.A. and doctorate in mathematics from the University of Warsaw in 1936 and quickly became one of the foremost researchers in algebraic topology. In 1939, Eilenberg migrated to the United States and traveled to Princeton, New Jersey, where Oswald Veblen and Solomon Lefschetz of Princeton University were assisting European refugee mathematicians to find employment at American universities. From 1940–46, Eilenberg taught at the University of Michigan and at Indiana University from 1946-47. At the University of Michigan he began collaborating with Norman Steenrod on what would become a seminal text in their field: *Foundations of Algebraic Topology* (1952). Eilenberg began teaching at Columbia University in 1947 and held various visiting lecturer and professorships at Princeton (1945-46), the Université de Paris (1950-51 and 1966-67), Tat Institute, Bombay (1953-54 and 1956-57), and the Hebrew University at Jerusalem (1954 and 1970). In the late 1940s, Eilenberg began collaborating with Henri Cartan of the Université de Paris; their work resulted in the book, *Homological Algebra* (1956). Additionally, at the invitation of André Weil in 1949, Eilenberg contributed to a project in concert with a number of French mathematicians who anonymously published under the pseudonym Nicholas Bourbaki. The result was a multi-volume work providing a clear and detailed treatment of the fundamental structures of contemporary mathematics. From 1940–1954, Eilenberg collaborated with Saunders MacLane, one of the most influential American mathematicians of the twentieth century, on fifteen papers on such subjects as cohomology of groups, category theory, and Eilenberg-MacLane space. The papers were published in the 1986 volume, *Eilenberg-MacLane Collected Works*. Privately, Eilenberg was also a collector and dealer of Southeast Asian sculpture art from Indonesia, Cambodia, Nepal, Thailand, and elsewhere. In the late 1980s, his collection was appraised at some $5 million when he donated in excess of 400 pieces to the Metropolitan Museum of Art in New York to assist in raising $1.5 million to endow the Samuel Eilenberg Visiting Professorship in Mathematics at Columbia University. Eilenberg retired from teaching in 1982. Four years later, he was co-winner of the Wolf Foundation Prize in mathematics. Eilenberg was also the recipient of honorary doctorates from Brandeis University (1980), University of Pennsylvania (1985), Columbia University (1987), and the Université de Paris (1989) in addition to holding a prestigious Guggenheim Fellowship and Fulbright Fellowship. He was also a Member of the National Academy of Science and the American Math Society. Eilenberg suffered a stroke in 1995. Bedridden and unable to speak, he lapsed into a coma in June 1997 and passed away seven months later at the age of eighty-four.—*Krystyna Cap*

SOURCES: Alex Heller, *Algebra, Topology and Category Theory: A Collection of Papers in Honor of Samuel Eilenberg* (New York: Academic Press, 1976); Samuel Eilenberg, *Eilenberg-MacLane, Collected Works* (Orlando, FL: Academic Press, 1986); *Asian Works of Art: featuring the Collection of Samuel Eilenberg* (Boston: Bolton, 2001).

Elektorowicz, Emil (Emil Elektorowicz de Ries; b. Tarnopol, Poland, 1880; d. Ossining, New York, October 18, 1933). Polonia activist. The son of wealthy landowners who were also proprietors of a factory in Tarnopol, as a teenager Elektorowicz became active in the Galician Falcons movement. As a student of engineering in Lwów, he won a scholarship of 10,000 francs and in 1906 left Poland for the United States. He eventually became a chief engineer with one of his projects involving construction of the bridges and tunnels for the Inter-borough Rapid Transit Company of New York. In 1912 he became a U.S. citizen and changed his name for professional reasons to Emil de Ryss. Involved in the Falcons from

Emil Elektorowicz, a leader in the "Free Falcons" movement (*OLS*).

the time of his arrival in America, he was a supporter of Józef Piłsudski's direct action approach to regaining Poland's independence. Elektorowicz, who represented Nest 7, was a delegate to the 1909 **Polish Falcons** Alliance convention in Cleveland where he led the walkout of the militants at the gathering from the **Polish National Alliance**-dominated, pro-Dmowski, organization. He was elected president of the "Free Falcons" secessionist group at a counter-convention held the following day, serving as president of the Free Falcons Alliance for two years between 1909 and January 1912, when he resigned because he was convinced that the reunification of the two Falcons groups was a bad idea. He believed the PNA-controlled organization was more of a physical fitness society and was not a good potential partner with the militant Free Falcons organization. Thus he did not attend the reunification meeting of the Falcons in December 1912 in Pittsburgh where **Teofil Starzyński** was elected president. Elektorowicz apparently returned to Poland around the time of the outbreak of World War I and served in Piłsudski's Legion. After the war he attempted to establish a factory in Poland, but the severe inflation that affected the country in 1921 caused his financial ruin and he returned to the United States. He was killed in a shooting accident while duck hunting near Ossining, New York.—*Donald E. Pienkos*

SOURCE: Donald E. Pienkos, *One Hundred Years Young: A History of the Polish Falcons of America* (Boulder, CO: East European Monographs, 1987).

Ellis, Michael B. (b. St. Louis, Missouri, October 28, 1894; d. Chicago, Illinois, December 9, 1937). Soldier, Medal of Honor recipient. The son of Polish immigrants Anthony and Ann Krzyżanowski Eliasz who migrated to American in 1879, his mother died when he was an infant. He quit school when he was twelve to work in a print shop, but in 1912 he enlisted in the army seeing service with Company K, 7th Infantry Regiment, along the Mexican border and at Vera Cruz. Following his discharge, he spent six months as a civilian before re-enlisting. He earned promotion to corporal in April 1917 and to sergeant the following month. During World War I, Ellis served as first sergeant in Company C, 28th Infantry Regiment, 1st Division. He spent some 200 days on the front near Soissons, France, where he was awarded the Silver Star, the citation noting that he "showed unusual courage in carrying supplies and in attacking strong points at Brouil, Pleissy, and Berney-le-Sac." He was awarded the Medal of Honor for combat near Exermont, France, on October 5, 1918. The citation read in part: "During the entire day's

Michael B. Ellis, Medal of Honor recipient (*NARA*).

engagement he operated far in advance of the first wave of his company, voluntarily undertaking most dangerous missions and single-handedly attacking and reducing machine gun nests. Flanking one emplacement, he killed 2 of the enemy with rifle fire and captured 17 others. Later he single-handedly advanced under heavy fire and captured 27 prisoners, including 2 officers and 6 machine guns, which had been holding up the advance of the company. The captured officers indicated the locations of 4 other machine guns, and he in turn captured these, together with their crews, at all times showing marked heroism and fearlessness." Gen. John J. Pershing presented the medal to him in person in St. Louis on December 22, 1919. Because of his heroism, he was invited to be a pall bearer for the interment of the Unknown Soldier in Arlington National Cemetery. Ellis's service was also recognized with the awarding of the French Chevalier Legion of Honor of France and the Croix-de-Guerre with Palm, the Italian Cross of War, the Polish Cross of Valor, and two medals from the government of Morocco. In the postwar years he worked in the U.S. post office in St. Louis. He is buried in Section 6, Grave 9520, at Arlington National Cemetery.—*James S. Pula*

SOURCES: the Rev. Francis Bolek, ed., *Who's Who in Polish America* (New York: Harbinger House, 1943); Arlington National Cemetery Web Site; R. J. Proft, *United States of America's Congressional Medal of Honor Recipients and Their Official Citations* (Columbia Heights, MN: Highland House II, 2002).

Eminowicz, Tadeusz (b. Kraków, Poland, October 10, 1882; d. Detroit, Michigan, April 10, 1917). Actor, director, theatre manager. Eminowicz studied drama in Kraków and probably made his debut in a traveling troupe in 1902. He was also most likely an actor in the Teatr Ludowy in Kraków. In 1907 he left the Austrian partition of Poland and came to America where he was active in Polish ethnic amateur theatrical troupes. In 1908 he founded a Stage Fans' Circle in Chicago and directed one of Schiller's plays as a benefit performed for St. Stanisław Kostka College. He developed a clearly defined program for Polish ethnic theatre in which performances would be held on a continuous basis, with a regular schedule, staged in the Polish ethnic community rather than in downtown districts. Eminowicz's theatre group, named for Juliusz Słowacki, grew to include about forty performers. At the beginning of 1911, Eminowicz and his wife Stefania persuaded the owner of the Kosciuszko Photo Studio, to convert it into a theatre. The new 200-seat Teatr Kościuszko, opened on January 26, 1911, presented a program of one act plays, films, and cabaret songs. In September 1911 Eminowicz became manager and director of the Teatr Popularny in Chicago, but in September 1912 moved to Detroit where he rented the Crescent cinema and in autumn 1912 opened the Teatr Kościuszko. Meanwhile, he and his wife built an entirely new theatre which opened on November 4, 1913, as Teatr Fredro. A splendid edifice with elegant interior and comfortable furnishings, it provided a superb venue for theatrical productions. In addition to their theatrical activities, Tadeusz and Stefania Eminowicz were engaged in national patriotic work, regularly contributing large sums of money to the Polish Legion fund and promoting the Legion in cabaret and other songs. The couple eventually sold their share in the Teatr Fredro and moved to Buffalo, NY, where they opened the Teatr Kościuszko. A year later Eminowicz moved to Cleveland where he set up the Teatr Polonia and ran it for one season. He then returned to Detroit where he opened another Polish ethnic stage, Teatr Ludowy. It appears that Eminowicz was convinced he had a mission to create a permanent network of Polish ethnic theatres in America. To support this, he established in Detroit as early as 1915 the Polish Artistic Club, a professional organization of Polish American artists.—*Emil Orzechowski*

SOURCES: Emil Orzechowski, "Tadeusz Eminowicz," in Marek Eminowicz and Stefan Eminowicz, eds., *The Eminowicz Family. Rodzina Eminowiczów* (Kraków: Drukarnia Związkowa Spoldzielnia Pracy, 1989); Stanisław Dąbrowski and Zbigniew Raszewski, eds., *Słownik Biograficzny Teatru Polskiego 1765–1965* (Warsaw: Panstwowe Wydawn. Naukowe, 1973); Arthur L. Waldo, *Stefania Eminowicz, szkic biograficzny* (Chicago: A. L. Waldo, 1937).

Erdmans, Mary Patrice (b. Grand Rapids, Michigan, June 14, 1959; d.—). Sociologist. Erdmans received her baccalaureate degree in sociology and psychology from St. Mary's College, Notre Dame, IN (1981), and her M.A. (1987) and Ph.D. (1992) in sociology from Northwestern University. From 1982 to 1984 she was a Peace Corps volunteer and worked as a teacher of English as a second language in Thailand. She also taught English to Polish immigrants in Chicago at the **Polish University Abroad** (PUNO) from 1988 to 1991, and business English at the Kraków Industrial Society in Poland in the summer of 1990. Her dissertation explored conflict and cooperative relations between new Polish immigrants and Polish Americans in Chicago working for an independent Poland in the 1980s. This study was the basis of her monograph *Opposite Poles: Immigrants and Ethnics in Polish Chicago, 1976–1990* (1998). Her second book, *The Grasinski Girls: The Choices They Had and the Choices They Made* (2004) explored the meaning of ethnicity, religion, and motherhood among working-class later-generation Polish-American women. Both books were awarded the **Oscar Halecki** Prize from the **Polish American Historical Association**. Her articles and essays have appeared in the *North American Review, Notre Dame Magazine, Journal of American Ethnic History, The Sociological Quarterly, Polish American Studies, Sociological Inquiry*, and *2B Quarterly*. Erdmans was an associate professor of sociology at the University of North Carolina, Greensboro (1992–2001), a visiting associate professor of sociology at The College of the Holy Cross in Worcester, Massachusetts (1999–2002), a research associate at the Center for Social Research, University of Hartford (2002–08), and a professor of sociology at Central Connecticut State University (from 2002). She was president of the Polish American Historical Association (2003–06) and served on its board of directors beginning in 1993. From this organization she received the **Mieczysław Haiman** Award for sustained contribution to the study of Polish Americans (2007) and the Distinguished Service Award (2008). She also received an Outstanding Achievement Award for scholarly contributions to the study of Polish Americans from the **American Council for Polish Culture** (2006). In addition to more than fifty presentations at national and international academic conferences, she has also been an invited speaker at such venues as the Literature to Life Series at the Bushnell Theater, **Polish Genealogical Society of America**, National Public Radio, Connecticut Legislative Briefing, **Sts. Cyril and Methodius Seminary** at Orchard Lake (MI), Fiedorczyk Lecture in Polish American Studies, and the North Carolina Humanities Council.—*Mary Patrice Erdmans*

SOURCES: Bolesław Wierzbiański, *Who's Who in Polish America* (New York: Bicentennial Publishing Corp., 1996), 105; "Erdmans, Mary Patrice," *Contemporary Authors* (Detroit: Gale Research Company), Vol. 177, 160–61.

Ethnic Identity and Assimilation.

There is no one definition of either the concept of ethnicity or assimilation. Ethnicity is often understood as a "sense of peoplehood," or group consciousness based on shared culture and common past, with culture including language, religion, customs, traditions, and values. When a group possesses this "sense of peoplehood," we can say that it has ethnic identity. Ethnicity does not remain constant, but changes over time and generations. It is invented or constructed in response to the historical circumstances every time these circumstances undergo a transformation.

Assimilation is sometimes called Americanization, acculturation, incorporation, or integration of immigrants into the host society, although these terms do not carry identical connotations. According to Milton Gordon's popular stratification, the first stage of the assimilation process is described as "acculturation" or cultural or behavioral assimilation (or Americanization), and it results in the change of cultural patterns to those of the host society. It includes for example a change in some outward appearance, such as rejection of ethnic dress, as well as adoption of English, and general behaviors of the American society. The next stage is "structural assimilation," which conditions "large-scale entrance into cliques, clubs, and institutions of host society, on primary group level," allowing for immigrants to easily interact with persons from outside their ethnic group. The highest level of assimilation is the large scale intermarriage, which, using Gordon's term, leads to "amalgamation."

In the past, scholars considered assimilation as a linear process of losing one's ethnic identity and acquiring general characteristics of the dominant society (Anglo-conformity). Complete disappearance of ethnicity was to be the final outcome of this natural and inevitable process. A competing model of assimilation, the Melting Pot concept, also assumed disappearance of ethnicity, which in this case would not "melt" that much into an Anglo-American form, but rather a new American race.

We now see that assimilation is a much more complicated process. It is neither inevitable nor irreversible. It stems from both individual choices and collective actions, influenced by a number of specific conditions existing within the society at any given time. The process is not one-directional, but rather reciprocal, as ethnic groups are not the only ones that undergo change; they also contribute to the mainstream and change it themselves. Assimilation may proceed differently for different immigrant groups as well as different individuals, depending on their class, gender, human capital, and other variables. Ethnic groups assimilate not only to some generalized Anglo-centric ideal, but also to the specific stratum of the society (the so-called segmented assimilation model), as well as to other ethnic groups, with whom they interact. According to a more recent definition of sociologists Richard Alba and Victor Nee, "Assimilation refers to the results of long-term processes that have gradually whittled away the social foundations for ethnic distinctions; diminishing cultural differences that serve to signal ethnic membership to others and to sustain ethnic solidarity; bringing about a rough parity of life chances to attain socioeconomic goods such as educational credentials and remunerative jobs while loosening the attachment of ethnicity to specific economic niches; shifting residence away from central city ethnic neighborhoods to ethnically mixed suburbs and urban neighborhoods; and, finally, fostering relatively easy social intercourse across ethnic lines, resulting ultimately in high rates of ethnic intermarriage and mixed ancestry."

The historical development of Polish American ethnic identity is intertwined with the story of ethnic resistance and maintenance in the face of conscious Americanization efforts and forces of acculturation, instances of discrimination, and natural advances of assimilation, which affected all ethnic groups in the U.S. It was influenced by economic opportunities and social mobility or lack of thereof, and issues of race, class, and religion. Ethnic identity among American **Polonia** could be further differentiated by gender, region of settlement, occupation, and time of arrival in the United States, and displayed in the form of either private and individual or public and communal ethnicity. Polish American ethnicity was also constructed in response to the events and changes in the homeland, to the arrival of new immigrant waves and new categories of immigrants, such as exiles and émigrés, and to the development of the broader Polish Diaspora. Polish immigrants and their children developed their sense of peoplehood also as a result of their contact and interaction with other ethnic groups in the United States. Sometimes they identified these groups as agents of Americanization, for example the Irish bishops and shop bosses. In other cases, they adopted many of the racial attitudes of the dominant society, for instance towards African Americans and other racial minorities. Often, they brought over prejudices from the Old Country, which complicated the New World relationships, as in case of Jews or Ukrainians. As a result, the emerging Polish American ethnic identity developed both alongside as well as in contrast to other ethnicities.

While some Polish immigrants rejected and resisted assimilation, others embraced it, or at least approved some aspects of it. Generational changes highlighted the issues of advancing assimilation with particular strength. Responses to the progress of assimilation came from individuals and families as well as leaders and organizations, including church. Although many instances of this process were no different in Polonia than in other European groups (especially these from East Central Europe), Polish American experience remains unique. The process of building Polish ethnicity in America was gradual and complicated, as most immigrants first had to learn how to be Polish in America before they could become Polish American.

Early arrivals from Poland who came to America in the seventeenth and eighteenth centuries displayed strong Polish national identity, mostly rooted in their gentry class origins. Since Polonia as a community was yet non-existent, they became individual representatives of the Polish nation, either seeking good fortune of their own, or fighting for "Your Freedom and Ours," as did for example heroes of the Revolutionary War in America and Polish national independence **Tadeusz Kościuszko** and **Kazimierz Pułaski**. Groups of exiles, who arrived in 1831–37 after the fall of the November Insurrection, and following the conspiracy of 1846 and the Spring of Nations of 1848, also showed heightened Polish national consciousness. They were a part of the Polish political Diaspora, scattered in many countries, but interconnected by the Polish national agenda and an exile mission, placing the work for Poland as the central responsibility of immigrants and exiles. While attempting to mobilize the American public opinion for the Polish cause, they forged alliances with American liberals and with other European exiles. Although the political émigrés failed to create a lasting community, and many were gradually absorbed into the American society, their activities did contribute to the early stages of formation of Polish identity in America. As historian **James S. Pula** notes, "The political émigrés left to succeeding generations established organizations, an entrenched spirit of *polskość*, a generally positive image of Poland among the American public, and cooperative ties to other immigrant groups."

The first permanent Polish settlers who in 1854, established their farming community in **Panna Maria**, Texas, and other peasant settlers who arrived before the Civil War, based their identity mainly on their religious and regional affiliation. Since the 1870s, they were joined by a great migration "for bread." These peasant immigrants came with little national consciousness. Their consciousness and identity were often limited to the specific community (*okolica*), village, or parish from which they hailed, and rarely included the supra-local bond to the Polish nation. This state was the result of the feudal and post-feudal conditions in the Polish countryside, its relative isolation, as well as purposefully divisive policies of the partitioning powers. Any type of mobilization of peasant immigrants for the Polish cause attempted by political leaders during and immediately following the January Insurrection failed to arouse much response from immigrant Poles. **Henryk Sienkiewicz**, a Polish writer who traveled in the United States in the mid–1870s, openly expressed his concern about prospects of quick de-nationalization (*wynarodowienie*) of Polish peasants, who, he predicted, would be soon lost in the sea of Americanism.

The Civil War was in many ways a transitional phase in the history of Poles in America, when Polish immigrants demonstrated an increase in their loyalty to America and its government through their voluntary identification with the ideals of either the Union or the Confederacy. Poles participated in the war effort on both sides; for example General **Włodzimierz Krzyżanowski** is best known for his outstanding service in the Union Army, while Major **Gaspard Tochman** was an officer in the Confederate Army. Their activities, as historian Andrzej Brożek emphasizes, revealed "a complex mixture of old Polish traditions and the new elements of consciousness as regards a nascent Polonia," and formed "a kind of bridge between political and economic immigration."

Homeland politics played a central role in defining and redefining of the Polish identity in America. In 1879, **Agaton Giller**, a leading political émigré in Europe after the January Insurrection, called for preserving the loyalty of the masses of Polish immigrants in America threatened by de-nationalization. His letter was published and popularized among Polonia and became a stimulus for the creation of the **Polish National Alliance** (PNA). In time the focus on the fate of Poland and political activism increased, American Polonia adopted a vision of itself as the "fourth partition of Poland," with an obligation to provide a free voice to the subjugated Polish nation.

From the 1870s on, the Polish community in America continued to grow. It established its internal organizational structure, first based on the network of Roman Catholic parishes. Gradually, it began to develop a collective consciousness in both the religious (Catholic) and linguistic and national sense (Polish). A peasant who initially described himself as being from the Mikołajki parish, in response to the pressures of the American society started to see himself as Polish. In time, he developed a sense of belonging to the Polish people in Chicago or Buffalo, and then, under the influence of Polish political and cultural leaders became interested in the cause of Poland. As historian Andrzej Brożek notes, this Polish peasant was thus often "ahead of his contemporaries back in the Polish territories as regards national consciousness." Overcoming of the regional differences became part of the ethnicization process. We have ample evidence that immigrants from **Galicia** (Austrian partition), the Kingdom (Russian partition), and the Prussian partition tended to initially create their own communities and often expressed distrust of and even hostility towards each other. The process of ethnicization after emigration affected not only Poles, but also other Central and Eastern Europeans — such as Germans or Italians.

Historians agree that much of Polonia's ethnic consciousness developed amidst confrontation between two opposing camps, represented by the **Polish Roman Catholic Union** (PRCU) and the Polish National Alliance. As the former defined the role of an immigrant as a Catholic first and Pole second and focused on the work for Polonia, the latter stressed national attachment and activism with no regard for religious affiliation, and centered on the work for Poland. An average Polish immigrant became then an object of struggle for what was termed "a government of the souls" between the leaders of the two organizations: activist priests and their supporters based within the parish structure on one side, and on the other, lay political and cultural leaders, emerging from the ranks of Polish educated elites: gentry and intelligentsia. Assimilation was one of the issues in this conflict. As historian James S. Pula notes, "The PRCU fought to preserve Roman Catholicism by resisting cultural assimilation into American society, while the primary goals of the PNA were to achieve the independence of the homeland and provide assistance to Polish immigrants in America. To achieve its goals, the PNA 'sought to encourage at least some assimilation so as to gain influence in the United States in order to help Poland.'"

The leaders' messages, often contradictory, almost always aggressive, stimulated the immigrant masses in their thinking about their place both in America and in relation to the homeland.

The complicated issues of assimilation and retention of ethnicity permeated in one way or another practically all areas of Polonia's life during the last three decades of the nineteenth century. As mentioned before, the Polish parish became the central unit within Polonia's organizational and social structure. The American Roman Catholic hierarchy dominated by the Irish, German, and French bishops became one of the most insistent agents of Americanization, striving to assimilate ethnically diverse Catholic immigrants and solidify the Vatican's influence over them and through that to strengthen their position among other denominations in the U.S. While refusing to grant growing masses of Polish Roman Catholics representation among the church hierarchy, the bishops insisted on the use of English in church and in parish schools. They also disregarded requests for Polish parish priests. In the minds of average Polish immigrants the "Ajrysze" among the clergy symbolized the American establishment. They responded with protest, defending the right to protect their ethnic traditions within the church in much the same way they did in partitioned Poland, when they confronted Protestant Germans and Orthodox Russians. By insisting on the use of the Polish language and traditionally Polish religious celebrations, immigrants within the parish developed stronger national consciousness, which overcame their regional division. In this sense, the parish resisted assimilation.

Some other aspects of the parish experience, however, contributed to the gradual Americanization of the immigrants. When in their struggle for their place in the church the parishioners implemented concepts of democratic government and equal rights, they were adopting American political models. The consequence became the growth of the independentist movement and subsequent creation of the **Polish National Catholic Church**. Since the process of assimilation is never one-directional, Poles also contributed to the early formulation of multiculturalism within the church through the Rev. **Wacław Kruszka**'s demand for "Polyglot Bishops for Polyglot Dioceses," published in 1901, and their long lasting campaign to break the monopoly in bishop appointments.

The church and ethnically diverse parishes provided ample ground for contacts with other ethnic groups, speeding up the process of formation of different ethnicities, by contrasting one group's identity, language, and history, with the others. For less numerous non–Catholic Poles, religious affiliation more often became a vehicle for Americanization. Although some separate parishes of Polish Protestants, mostly **Baptists** and **Lutherans**, but also Methodists and Presbyterians did exist, most Polish Protestants attended either German Lutheran or other ethnically mixed churches, where they worshiped in English.

The educational system in the United States presented opportunities to both counteract assimilation and advance Americanization, especially among the immigrant second generation. In 1884, the American Roman Catholic church decreed that all Roman Catholics should send their children to parish schools, in order to protect them from "Protestant and secular influences." Polish immigrants did indeed establish an impressive network of parish schools. By the 1920s, fully two thirds of Polish American children attended parochial schools, attesting to Polonia's attachment to their faith. Since initially Polish nuns taught the children religion, Polish religious customs, Polish language, history, and culture, parents regarded parish schools as bastions of Polishness, in contrast to the American public school system which they rightly considered to be an active agent of Americanization. Immigrants regarded parish schools as an important defense line against assimilation reaching the second generation, and often quite consciously sacrificed the level of their education, all too frequently deficient in parochial schools, in order to instead secure the transmission of language and values.

Parents who enrolled their offspring in public schools more often than not appreciated them as vehicles for economic advancement for their children, impossible without some acceptable degree of assimilation: knowledge of "American ways" and the English language. There was, however, a price to pay. Since parish schools reached only elementary level, children and youth who continued their education into high schools and college did so within the public school system. There they were frequently an object of ridicule for their lack of English language proficiency, and singled out for their "foreignness." Teachers berated their nationality and insisted that they adopt supposedly superior American culture. "Fitting in" often required rejection of ethnicity, or at least practice of dual behavior: more American at school and more Polish at home. As in case of parishes, public schools also provided grounds for direct contact with other ethnic groups, bringing opportunities for both conflict and friendships.

The PNA-led criticism of the low educa-tional level in parochial schools at the turn of the twentieth century, reflected not only the organization's disapproval of the church control over them, but also of Polonia's excessive ghettoization and its low economic and political standing in the American society. Education in American public schools was seen as a source of just enough Americanization to improve this standing. At the same time Polish American ethnic identity among the second generation was to be protected by the concerted efforts of parents and the entire community, through, among others, **Saturday schools**, summer camps, sports and leisure activities, and involvement in voluntary youth groups. Such programs proliferated in the 1920s, when parish schools began to abandon Polish language and curriculum, and lose their ethnic character.

The Polish American press, as all ethnic press, was yet another institution, which took upon itself a double role of both an Americanization agent and a protector of ethnicity. In Polonia, press developed early, quickly, and vibrantly. It represented all strides and stripes, reflecting political and social divisions within Polonia. The most heated debates among two opposing ideological camps took place on the pages of Polish American newspapers, shaping the formulation of ethnic identity among the immigrants. The use of the Polish language and the broad and detailed sections bringing news from Poland strengthened Polishness and attachment to the homeland. News on the developments within Polonia built up the Polish American consciousness. Information and commentary on the American society and institutions helped to ease the way immigrants entered the New World and assisted in their Americanization. **Antoni A. Paryski**, publisher of *Ameryka-Echo*, openly encouraged immigrants' citizenship, their participation in American civic and political life, as well as educational achievement and business entrepreneurship. His vision of the modernization of the Polish peasant in America was based on the embracing of American democratic ideals and capitalism. The press, just like an ethnic church and school, underwent its own transformation away from linguistic retention, when it gradually succumbed to the introduction of the English-language pages, and eventually switched from Polish to English almost entirely.

The Polish American publishing, which was closely connected to the press, played a similar role. It provided the immigrants with a variety of reading material in the Polish language, contributing to the language maintenance or sometimes development. As historian **Karen Majewski** shows, the Polish American literature propagated models of behavior, which either stressed attachment to the Polish identity, and rejected full assimilation, or encouraged limited Americanization. It also commented on the relationships with those seen as "others": Americans, Jews, and other immigrant groups. The Polish language sometimes served as a lingua franca; immigrants from other ethnic groups who were familiar with it, such as Ukrainians, Rusyns, Lihuanians, Jews, and some Germans were also consumers of Polish press and publications and listened to Polish radio programs. In *Ameryka-Echo*, their letters to the editor often challenged and confronted the boundaries of immigrant Polishness, as well as broadened them to include the experience of Poland's minorities.

About 85 percent of Polish immigrants settled in urban areas and pursued unskilled occupations in large industries, including mining, meat packing, steel, and automobile industries. Poles established beachheads in some industries using networks of family and friends. In some cases employers favored hiring them as they were stereotyped to be particularly suitable for hard work. They labored together with workers from other ethnic groups, often fellow Slavs and Hungarians. Their foremen and bosses were as frequently Irish, German, and British as native-born American. As members of the American working class, Polish immigrant and other ethnic workers shared the industrial experience, dealt with tough work conditions, exploitative bosses, and frequent economic downturns. As Polish peasants were becoming American industrial workers, their class identity was taking shape alongside their ethnic identity, adding to their overall assimilation.

Employers engaged not only in the discriminatory hiring practices, but also in the "divide and conquer" tactics, designed to halt the cooperation among workers and their unionization efforts. They created ethnically mixed work teams to make communication harder and fanned Old World animosities and prejudice. In the 1880s, the newcomer Poles were sometimes used as scabs, the same way African Americans were also later used as strike breakers. Both the early industrial protests and subsequent organized strike activity brought together many ethnicities, who overcame their divisions and particularisms, and, as historian Adam Walaszek suggests, increased their class consciousness and thus Americanization.

A majority of Polish workers, although not all, had no previous experience with the labor movement. They showed relatively little interest in organized labor, but were not as inactive as some earlier historians suggested. Large American unions, such as the Knights of Labor, and especially the American Federation of Labor, were very reluctant to embrace immigrants and their causes and put little effort in their recruitment. Nevertheless, some individual Poles, such as **Leo Krzycki**, became leaders even on a national level. Since the beginning of the twentieth century, Polish immigrants (both men and women) became union organizers and leaders on a local level in many industries, cooperating with workers from other ethnic groups. Such collaboration based on class rather than ethnic identity was particularly encouraged by socialists, who, although numerically rather weak among Polonia, did impact the formation of the Polish American working class identity. The intersection between ethnicity and class among American Polonia still requires further exploration. As historian **John Bukowczyk** suggests, Polish workers in industrial America created urban villages, in which they combined their ethnic attachments and working class lifestyles. In most cases, this ethnic identity did win over the class considerations, while the immigrant community, church, family, and concerns for homeland remained the object of their primary loyalty.

Until the end of World War I, homeland politics dominated Polonia and affected its nationalization; yet, Polish immigrants also paid attention to American politics. Participation in American politics satisfied the psychological need for belonging in the American society and its democratic institutions, and in some ways, was also considered a measure of one's Americanization. Political influence also meant jobs and patronage, bringing obvious economic advantages, as well as recognition and prestige vis-à-vis other groups. According to **Stanislaus A. Blejwas**, this process was slow for Polish Americans. In 1920, only 28.8 percent of first generation men and women over twenty-one years of age were naturalized. Political clubs and activities appeared as early as the 1870s and 1880s, and some Polish-language newspapers encouraged immigrants to "take out citizenship papers" and vote. Few Poles (especially in proportion to their numbers in many American cities) were elected to local office of importance, and fewer still to either state or federal offices. It is not clear why Polish immigrants and their children failed to capitalize on the advancement in American politics, and interpretations differ depending on localities under study. It is quite apparent, however, that pre–World War II Polonia, unlike other ethnic groups, either rejected or did not succeed in making American politics a vehicle for the group's unity on

the one hand, and for its assimilation on the other.

The process of formation of the ethnic identity was also carried out right in the vibrant immigrant communities and neighborhoods complete with ethnic institutions, churches, businesses, press, etc. Some immigrants rarely left such communities, as they could find there everything they needed for their everyday life. Living around people speaking the same language, worshipping in the same church, and sharing leisure time activities, developed a stronger sense of peoplehood and solidified ethnic identity. This identity shaped often in contrast to others: not only "Americans" but other ethnic groups sharing space in urban America. As historian **Dominic Pacyga** concludes, "neighborhoods were spacially integrated but socially segregated." The extent of this segregation varied. The youth gangs contested ethnic neighborhood boundaries in urban turf wars. The inevitable succession of waves of new immigrants of different nationalities moving into the neighborhoods were also to be resisted. Most of the time, however, despite institutional dominance of one ethnic group in a given area, urban neighborhoods were "crazy quilts" of ethnicities, where immigrants from different countries lived and worked side by side. They frequented local taverns and saloons together, shopped in the same stores, used services of the professional middle class of various backgrounds, attended theater performances and music concerts, rented each other's halls for meetings, and watched (and sometimes participated in) parades celebrating other ethnicities and other national causes. Women and children were particularly important agents in such neighborhood interactions.

Since there is a scarcity of scholarship on the overall experience of Polish immigrant women, we have only a sketchy understanding of how processes of identity formation as well as assimilation differed depending on gender. Immigrant women in general are considered the guardians of ethnicity and religion within families and the main transmitters of ethnic culture to the young generations. Married immigrant women who lived in ethnic neighborhoods and worked within the home usually had fewer opportunities to learn English or to come into direct contact with native-born Americans. Although largely confined to Polonia, these women were very active in the community and the church, fully participating in any developments that pertained to the entire Polonia. Polish working class women also actively engaged in labor protests and support for union-organized strikes. Most single women and these married women were

employed in industrial occupations where they interacted with other nationalities and developed a working class consciousness. They themselves participated in strikes, sometimes becoming their leaders.

The **Polish Women's Alliance**, a national fraternal organization established in 1898, and its newspaper *Głos Polek* became a ground for the activism of middle class Polish women. According to historian Thaddeus Radzilowski, the organization and its publication became "a strong voice for feminism, political reform and progressive goals in American and Polish American society. It favored women's suffrage and the opening of all educational institutions and professional careers to women. It championed the rights of workers and programs of industrial safety. It informed Polish women of the progress of women's causes throughout the world and in the United States. It also tried to help rural immigrant women adjust to life in an urban setting and to become aware of the latest advances in child-rearing, hygiene, education, and nutrition. Finally, the organization worked tirelessly to preserve and propagate the Polish language and culture in America and to win independence." The PWA thus played a double role as a protector of ethnicity and an agent of assimilation aimed at improvement of the position of women within Polonia and the society.

Similarly, Polish and Polish American female religious orders, which created active networks within Polonia communities, represented social mobility options located on the border between the American society and an ethnic community, giving the nuns an opportunity to become links between the two. As Radzilowski explains, through their educational and social activity, the nuns "taught immigrants and their children the meaning of Catholicism in the new American context and sought to create a Polish-American identity that would make the immigrants feel at home in America."

American Polonia did not, of course, build its community in a vacuum. Polish Americans were not immune to nativist, anti-immigrant sentiments and outbursts of xenophobia. They had to respond to serious Americanization pressures coming from the American government, business, reformers, as well as average white Anglo-Saxon Protestant Americans, which were directed towards all immigrant groups. The Poles, just like other nationalities, were perceived as both a potential political threat (due to their alleged lack of democratic skills and adherence to the "despotic" Roman Catholicism), and as a social problem, and blamed for all the ills of growing urban and industrial society. Ethnic discrimination and stereotyping were very real and affected Polish immigrants in numerous ways. The turn of the century pseudoscientific racial theories placed Slavic people in general, and Poles in particular near the bottom of the social ladder. Business owners and employers regarded them as backward, docile, and suitable only for hard manual labor. White middle class reformers saw them as barely civilized, prone to drunkenness and violence, and clinging to their pre-modern ways. The 1910–11 report of the Dillingham Commission further strengthened this negative view of Polish immigrants. In Gary, Indiana, school officials instituted a tracking system, which relegated Polish-American youth to manual trades only. The best example of the intense Americanization campaign within American industry remains the program designed by the Ford Motor Company, which employed many Polish American workers. Under the guise of American patriotism and economic and social advancement, Ford and others sought to strengthen social control and work discipline, and teach the immigrants their proper place in the society as a dependable servant class. Both lay progressive reformers and Protestant reformers targeted Poles and other immigrants for Americanization. Organizations such as the Daughters of the American Revolution or Young Men's Christian Association joined in the campaign of Americanization through foreign language publications, lectures, and classes on American civics and history, and various naturalization programs. Even cooking classes or infant care classes organized in local settlement houses and attended by immigrant women propagated white middle class Protestant standards and values and discredited traditional homemaking skills of Polish women.

In the first decade of the twentieth century Polonia proceeded to affirm and legitimize its place in the American society through the conscious politics of recognition. The struggle between the PNA and the PRCU gradually subsided, especially after 1908 when the Rev. **Paul Rhode** was appointed an auxiliary bishop of Chicago. In 1910, during the lavish Grunwald Year celebrations, monuments to Kościuszko and Pułaski were unveiled in Washington, D.C. Through the commemoration of these Revolutionary War heroes and patriots, Polish immigrants symbolically claimed their place in the American society and history. The creation of the 1912 Komitet Obrony Narodowej (**National Defense Committee**, or KON) became yet another effort to forge Polonia's internal unity. The Russo-Japanese War, subsequent revolution in Russia, and unrest in Poland in 1905, once again firmly focused Polonia's attention on the

homeland. Following the revolution, a new wave of political exiles (often with socialist leanings) arrived from Poland, further politicizing the community, and reinforcing its interest in the events in the Polish lands.

The outbreak of World War I spelled the end of the unified Polonia. Two political organizations, which claimed to represent Polonia and the Polish cause reflected political divisions in Poland. Despite this ideological split within the leadership, Polish immigrants mobilized for Poland's independence with an intensity that would not be duplicated in subsequent decades. Politically, they lobbied the government, most notably through the influence of the statesman-pianist **Ignacy Jan Paderewski**, and supported President Woodrow Wilson and his **Fourteen Points**, which championed Poland's independence. Through social mobilization, Polish immigrants provided material assistance to the destitute people of Poland. And in a show of extraordinary patriotism, 108,000 volunteers created in Canada the Blue Army (see **Polish Army in France**), approximately 20,000 soldiers led by General Józef Haller who fought in France and later on the Polish front.

At the same time, Polish Americans responded to World War I within the American context, proving their growing loyalty to the U.S., while realizing that the resurrection of the independent Polish state would also increase their own status within the American society. During the war years, Polish immigrants, as other ethnic groups, were still subject to the relentless Americanization campaign, which condemned suspect "hyphenated" patriotism and called for "100% Americanism." Often challenged to compete against other nationalities, Polonia massively contributed to Liberty Bond drives and charitable donations. In excess of 215,000 Polish volunteers served in the American Army. By the end of the war, Polish immigrants could be satisfied both with their success as part of the American nation, and as a part of the Polish one. The first phase of the development of their ethnic identity was complete.

The interwar decades of the 1920s and 1930s, again redefined ethnic identity within Polonia, mostly in response to three factors: the resurgence of the independent Polish state in Europe; in America, nativism and Americanization on the one hand, and economic situation on the other; and maturing of the second generation within Polonia. The ethnic identity of American Polonia began its gradual movement from Polish to American of Polish descent, a process that would be largely complete by the outbreak of World War II.

When in 1918, Poland regained independence, American Polonia, the self-proclaimed "fourth partition," lost its unifying cause. The search for a new role *vis-à-vis* the homeland and an independent Polish government proved difficult. Veterans of the Haller Army returned home often disappointed with their reception in Poland as well as with the general conditions there. Poland's economy remained unstable. Fulfilling what they thought was their patriotic obligation, many American Poles invested in the Polish economy only to see their money disappear. Reemigrants who first rushed to a free Poland, now returned back to the U.S., complaining about the volatile political situation, weak democracy, controlling influence of the church, and the lack of economic opportunities. At the same time, Poland's government sought to tie the Diaspora closer to the state and use its international influence for political and economic advantages. It organized cultural and educational programs for Polonia designed to slow down its assimilation. In 1934, it also established the **World Union of Poles from Abroad** (Światpol), an international organization of Polonia communities, which would coordinate their collaboration with Poland's government. The stand that the American Polonia delegation took towards the membership in Światpol, became later recognized as "Polonia's Declaration of Independence." The delegation headed by **Francis X. Świetlik** rejected direct membership in Światpol, while reaffirming support for Poland. The delegates stated: "Regarding ourselves as an inseparable component of the great American nation, we take an active and creative part in every walk of American life, thus contributing to boosting the name of Poland in our country." After returning home, historian **Mieczysław Haiman**, also a member of the delegation, explained: "In the eyes of the Poles in Poland and in other countries we are still only Poles while in fact we are already Americans of Polish extraction." Their declaration found acceptance not only among Polonia, but also among American public opinion.

Polonia's change of focus from Poland-centered to Polonia-centered was also reflected in the slogan "Wychodźstwo dla wychodźstwa" or "Emigrants for Themselves," which called for the support of Polish-American businesses and organizations. Some of these organizations, for example veteran associations and the scout movement enjoyed growing memberships. The expanding domestic focus now included recognition for and preservation of not only Poland's but also Polonia's history and heritage. Several new organizations promoted this idea: in 1925, the **Kosciuszko Founda-**

tion was created in New York; in 1926, the first Polish Arts Club and in 1935, the **Polish Museum of America** were established in Chicago, and since 1937, the Pulaski Parade in New York represented Polonia's achievement in the United States.

Polonia's participation in the ethnic politics of recognitions did not stem only from the rejection of the paternalistic policies of Poland's government. As other American ethnic groups, Polish Americans were also responding to the pressures coming from within the American society as well as opportunities offered by it. The postwar decade continued the heightened Americanization trend. Nativism reemerged through the racial tensions, the Red Scare campaign, and popularity of the Ku Klux Klan, which now expanded its target to include foreigners and Catholics. The passage of the immigration restrictions in the form of the National Origins Quota Act of 1924, drastically reduced the number of immigrants to the U.S. and effectively choked off the influx of new blood to the ethnic communities. At the same time, economic prosperity, which in the 1920s reached all layers of the society, allowed for increased social mobility and expansion of the ethnic middle class.

Polish Americans, as other ethnic groups, became active participants in the materialism and consumerism of the 1920s. They purchased fashionable furnishings, mass-produced cars and radios, and bought on easily available credit. Mass culture and modern American motion pictures provided new role models, for example "*flaperki*" (flappers) for Polish girls or "sheiks" for boys, who wanted to emulate sports heroes like Babe Ruth. Polonia's second generation was maturing and assimilating. In increasing numbers parochial schools were abandoning instruction in Polish and teaching of Polish curriculum, encouraged by the diocesan policies of the American Roman Catholic church. Most Polish youngsters attended public high schools, where they became steeped in American culture. Both at school and in the streets they played and made friends with children and youth from other ethnic backgrounds and English was their main mode of communication. They also played sports on ethnically mixed teams, read American press, watched American movies, and listened and danced to American music. Young business entrepreneurs and those interested in political participation were looking to move beyond the confines of Polonia communities.

Parents and community leaders, anxious about losing their second generation, sprang into action. As historian **William Galush** demonstrates, leading fraternals founded "youth departments" responsible for the creation of their own sport youth groups and baseball and bowling leagues. Others sponsored cultural activities for the younger members, including group singing and dances. Scouting became a popular choice for the children. Some Polish American organizations adopted English as their official language in order to accommodate the native-born and supported establishment of commercial clubs for young second generation professionals. Women's religious groups incorporated American middle-class customs designed to attract young Polish American women (see **Women, Polish American**), like American-style fundraisers, card parties, bridal showers, and weddings. Younger American-born clerics helped to usher in the change from Polish immigrant parishes to Polish American parishes. Since assimilation seemed inevitable, some Americanization became regarded as positive and the proximity between American and Polish history and tradition was emphasized in the search for a common ground.

And yet Polish-language newspapers were full of the older generation's lament over the youth chewing gum, smoking cigarettes, drinking "munszajn" (moonshine), and either corrupting the Polish language or giving it up all together. Parents were blamed for not speaking Polish to their children, and schools for not teaching them about Poland's heroes. As historian Andrzej Brożek notes, torn in two different directions, the second generation dealt with the problem of "how to inhabit two worlds simultaneously. At school they were too foreign, at home, paradoxically, too American. One world was that of their perplexed and nagging parents, Polish priests and teachers who deplored the loosening attachment to things Polish. The other world was that of the public school, American institutions and the friends they spent their time with. Such dilemmas would often arise in the atmosphere of humiliation they were likely to suffer because of their Polish extraction. The picture of Poland as more or less consciously painted for them by their parents was not much to be proud of. Faced with the dilemma of which group to join and which cultural patterns — American or Polish — to adopt, they opted for America." Still, according to William Galush, the Polish American second generation showed a tremendous amount of filial obligation, especially considering what he calls the immigrant hegemony, showcased in the generational exclusivity in office holding, which became a deterrent to the youth's involvement and blocked their way on a traditional route to ethnic status.

The years of the Great Depression, somewhat less studied in the framework of the American Polonia's history, were, nevertheless, very important in the shaping of its ethnic identity. As the stock market crashed and factories began to close, Polonia, like other ethnic groups, started to rely on the community's internal resources, which could not meet the growing needs of people facing lay offs, foreclosures, and evictions. Strangely, the economic catastrophe in some ways helped to halt the assimilation. As historian John J. Bukowczyk puts it, "Cut off from the homogenizing influences of a consumption society, Poles once again clung to their cultural forms. Blocked from occupational mobility, an entire generation of Polonia remained within the immigrant enclave for the lack of anyplace else to go." They were not, however, impervious to assimilation coming from a different source. The ethnic way of life became additionally reinforced by the class considerations. Polonia took vigorous part in the union drives, strikes, and the CIO agitation. Cutting across ethnic lines, Polish Americans embraced the goals of unionization not because they were Polish, but because they were part of the American working class. In the 1930s, the assimilation, which did not reach them through the economic opportunity and mass culture, did affect them as "an ethnic variation of a larger working-class social and cultural pattern born of shared union struggles, political fights, and living and working conditions."

If the 1930s are a less studied decade, we still know less about the World War II years. Although Polonia failed to create another Haller's army, its second generation served with distinction in the American military. On the home front, Polish Americans fully supported the war effort. President Roosevelt courted Polonia as a political group of influence. Seeing itself as an integral part of the American nation, Polonia also mobilized on behalf on Poland, sending charitable donations to Poland as well as Polish refugees scattered around the globe. In 1944, the **Polish American Congress** (PAC) took upon itself the role of a political ethnic lobby, determined to influence the course of American foreign policy in regards to Poland and Polish refugees. Politicization of Polonia was extraordinary, as the unified community again closed ranks on behalf of the homeland, but did it in a clearly American context. The political leadership of Polonia was challenged by a new wave of exiles, who arrived in the U.S. during and immediately after the war, the so-called New Emigration. They not only stimulated Polonia's political involvement and commitment to the Polish cause, but also confronted her Polishness by exposing the degree of her assimilation.

In the 1940s and 1950s, Polonia's ethnic identity evolved in some new directions. The Cold War and McCarthyism effectively eliminated leftist influences within the community. Polonia took steps to solidify its position in the anti-communist camp, which brought her closer to the American mainstream. The PAC continued to speak out on behalf of Polonia and the subdued Polish nation, and did it from the standpoint of Polish Americans as American citizens. At the same time, Polonia's leadership in the struggle for the Polish cause was contested by the activities of the Polish government-in-exile residing in London and other communities of the postwar Polish political Diaspora. In the symbolic case of the so-called **Wyrwa Affair**, Polish Americans declared their loyalty to the American government and its foreign policy goals. Since the 1956 events in Poland, they also acknowledged the Polish nation's agency in the anti-communist struggle, and concentrated more on charitable rather than political actions.

The two postwar decades also brought unprecedented economic boom, which together with the GI Bill, offered opportunities for social mobility to all ethnic groups. More Polish Americans moved to white collar occupations, relocated to the suburbs, bought cars, televisions, and other consumer goods on easily available credit, and immersed themselves in the homogenizing culture of the 1950s. Assimilation pressure was once again on the rise, as the second and third generations distanced themselves from their parents' and grandparents' ethnic past. The Polonia of the past was becoming more fragmented. Although the core urban communities with their ethnic institutions and old fraternal organizations were still active, third generation Polonians more often opted for membership in the new professional and cultural associations. The new arrivals, displaced persons and émigrés, frequently established their own institutional structure, which furthered the cultural fragmentation of Polonia.

These trends continued in the subsequent decades of the twentieth century. It still remains to be determined what the exact impact the civil rights movement, second wave feminism, Vietnam War, and the ethnic revival of the 1960s and 1970s had on Polish Americans. The Polonia community felt effects of rapid social changes most directly on the local level. The New Britain historian Stanislaus Blejwas noted a rapid transformation of the Holy Cross parish from the Polish immigrant parish towards the Polish-American parish. Some older Polish communities were affected by the so-called urban revitalization effort and suffered from the highway building projects

and demolition of the "urban blight" areas. The relationships of Polish Americans and African Americans often remained troubled as both groups frequently competed for the limited resources. Since the passage of the Immigration Act of 1965, the sources of new immigrants to the U.S. changed. Older Polonians now became neighbors with Hispanic, Middle Eastern, Asian, and other immigrants, who streamed into the inner cities. More churches built by Polish immigrants offered Mass in Spanish and traditionally Polish businesses began to lose their client base. In reaction to these changes, together with other European immigrants, Polish Americans moved their identity in the direction of acknowledged whiteness, gradually becoming a part of a group described by sociologists as "white European ethnics."

They did not, however, "melt" either into the American society or into the sea of whiteness. In the 1960s and 1970s, Polonia was hit by a wave of intense anti–Polish sentiment, known as "Polish jokes." Very cruel, vulgar and crude, they portrayed Polish Americans as dumb, uncouth, and primitive. Some Polish Americans internalized this negative image popularized by the media and moved away from their ethnic heritage. Others responded with anti-defamation action, led by the PAC. They wrote protest letters to the press and the TV shows' executives and threatened consumer boycotts of products advertised during the airing of particularly offensive shows. **Edward Piszek**, a Philadelphia based frozen food magnate, poured millions of his own money into a press campaign designed to highlight cultural and scientific achievements of famous Poles and improve the image of Polish Americans as well as Poland. The 1972 National Heritage Act, which, among other things, provided for the more pluralistic curriculum in American public schools, while forging more multicultural values, also contributed to the gradual loss of social approval for ethnic jokes.

Despite these internal efforts, Polonia's image and reputation received the biggest boost from outside circumstances. In 1978, Karol Cardinal Wojtyła was elected the Pope. In 1980, the Solidarity movement in Poland began a political revolution behind the Iron Curtain. A year later Martial Law imposed in Poland sent the Solidarity leaders underground and later created a new wave of exiles. The events in Poland in the early 1980s strengthened the "Polish agenda" in Polonia organizations and again mobilized the community, which responded with charitable actions and political lobby efforts. The visibility of Polish Americans in the society at large increased, as did their political influence in Washington.

As the post–World War II exiles challenged Polonia a few decades before, now post–Solidarity émigrés attempted to do so. According to sociologist **Mary Patrice Erdmans**, the post–Solidarity exiles by and large found a common language with postwar émigrés, but struggled in their attempts to cooperate with older Polonia, as the respective needs of immigrants versus ethnics made this collaboration particularly difficult. The post–Solidarity community, which focused their activities on politics and culture moved in separate circles from both older Polonia and the proceeding 1970s economic immigration from Poland, the so-called "**Wakacjusze.**"

In 1989, Poles in a non-violent revolution voted down the communist government, marking an effective beginning to an end of the communist system in East Central Europe. Polish Americans applauded with pride and immediately proceeded to strengthen the new government with economic investments and political support. Large numbers of more recent immigrants mobilized to vote in the 1992 presidential elections in Poland, laying foundations for tighter transnational ties between them and an independent homeland. Neither did older Polonia disengage from the involvement on behalf of Poland. In mid–1990s, it actively and successfully lobbied for Poland's accession to NATO. It also expanded cultural exchange with Polish universities and other institutions. In response to the public debate about Poland's role in World War II, which followed the publication of Jan Gross's book *Neighbors* in 2000, various groups in Polonia organized scholarly discussions of the historical context and issues of the war years, and became involved in the dialogue with the Jewish-American organizations in the U.S. If any predictions can be made, it seems that Polish Americans will continue to retain a firm focus on the homeland, following events there and reacting to crises through social and political mobilization.

This focus remains particularly strong among post–Solidarity exiles as well as young professionals who arrived in the 1990s. Through their command of English and higher educational achievement, these immigrants joined the American middle class and established themselves in the professions. Their socio-economic status puts them in daily contact with Americans of all ethnic backgrounds and allows for smooth assimilation. Few of them have ties to more traditional and older Polonia organizations and fraternals, which remain a domain of the successors from the turn of the century wave. Yet their identity remains Polish. They predominantly live in the suburbs, but they visit the core communities for ethnic food and shopping, Polish-language church services, Saturday Polish schools for their children, and cultural programs and events. If any of these become threatened, they mobilize in their defense, organizing to demand Polish-speaking priests and Masses in Polish, securing facilities and funds for the schools, scouting or other youth groups, and supporting local universities which offer Polish programs. Despite geographical dispersion, this new Polonia stays connected through family and friendship ties, Polish-language publications, and the Internet, which features an increasing number of discussion forums, virtual groups, web sites, and networks. Many members of this wave lead what some scholars term transnational lives. They repeatedly travel to Poland, follow the recent news on the Internet, establish international businesses, and remain in daily contact with their families in Poland through telephone and skype communication.

On the other side of the ethnic identity spectrum remain those in the third, fourth, and later generations, whose ethnicity Herbert Gans described as symbolic. According to his theory, the symbolic ethnicity satisfies the "ethnic feeling" without the undue burden of organizational membership or excessive economic costs, which could conflict with other ways of life. Some of the symbolic ethnicity practices involve nostalgic and simplified representation of the ethnic past; selective celebration of certain rituals of passage or ethnic holidays; consumption of ethnic foods; support for ethnic politicians who, however, rarely represent ethnic issues; and interest in and support for the Old Country. Sociologist Mary Patrice Erdmans examined ethnic consciousness of the third and fourth generation of Polish American working class women and concluded that "Polishness for later-generation Americans of Polish descent is a consent identity — it is a choice. Like purchasing *kiełbasa* on the West Side, they can buy into their Polish heritage if they want." In the case of Grasinski women their ethnicity as a culture subsides in contrast to their identity as being white. It is not located in the language, membership in ethnic organizations or interest in and knowledge of Poland. But it is still present in the less visible private sphere of food, family stories, familial relationships and religious attachments.

Social scientists have been trying to answer the question about the vitality of Polish and Polish American identity. Will it survive? And in what form? Over the years, scholars of immigration and ethnicity attempted to capture, quantify, and interpret the complicated process of transition from one phase of eth-nicity to another. They identified a number of indicators with which to measure and compare the advances of assimilation among ethnic groups and different generations within them. The most important among those indicators include residential patterns; educational and economic achievement, and social mobility; language maintenance; ethnic self-identification; community structure maintenance; political participation; and intermarriage. By attempting to measure the level of assimilation, scholars also hope to predict the prospects of the group's survival. Although such measurements are often based on imperfect statistical evidence, they do demonstrate major trends in the internal development of Polonia and trace changes affecting its ethnic identity in relation to the passage of time and generations.

Since the 1920s and through the early 1970s, a number of sociologists conducted mostly local community studies of assimilation among American Polonia. In 1975, these studies were reviewed and interpreted by Irwin T. Sanders and Ewa T. Morawska. According to their survey of this research, Polish Americans persisted in the maintenance of separate and well-defined ethnic neighborhoods, located since the 1880s both in the larger cities, such as Chicago and Detroit, and in smaller locales, such as New England or Midwestern towns. Only in some areas, notably Los Angeles, Polish immigrants did not create separate neighborhoods. It is generally accepted that residence in ethnic neighborhoods tends to support persistence of ethnicity and stymies progress of assimilation among their inhabitants. Urban ethnic communities offer job opportunities for businesses and services, including those of ethnic professionals, as well as provide a geographical basis for the development of ethnic organizations and parishes. However, despite the persistence of separate Polish American neighborhoods, already in the mid–1970s some scholars noted a gradual decline of both business and service sectors, which negatively impacted their community's integrative functions. In Buffalo, NY, a large majority of second and third generation Polish Americans were not involved in local ethnic economic enterprises, and most of the younger third generation residents looked for jobs outside the community. By comparison, larger neighborhoods in Chicago and New York were still able to provide support for ethnic businesses. In following decades the decline of the Polish-American ethnic neighborhoods in both small and medium size urban locations accelerated even further.

The residential mobility patterns also showed significant change since the years 1940–1960, as Polish American residents in greater numbers moved either to the suburbs or at least to the transitional or fringe zones outside of the solid core of the community. Such movement was noted in Greater Detroit, Chicago, Salem, Boston, and Bridgeport, and became particularly pronounced among the second and third generations. On the other hand, over fifty percent of Polish displaced persons lived in inner cities and almost forty percent in suburbs. It seems that post–Solidarity immigrants, who brought with them more human capital found their way into the suburbs in even greater numbers and in some cases created their ethnic enclaves there. According to the 2000 census, 73.5 percent of the Polish American metropolitan population already lived in the suburbs.

Educational and economic achievements, which result in social mobility, constitute other indicators of the progress of assimilation among white European ethnic groups. It is generally assumed that the higher the economic and educational status, the weaker connection to ethnicity. At the beginning of the twentieth century, over seventy percent of Polish Americans were unskilled workers. Since then, they have made tremendous strides in occupational improvement, but they still remain behind many other white ethnic groups. In the 1930s, Polish immigrants scored either the lowest or second lowest on the occupational and class ladder among white ethnic groups. In the 1950s, both foreign-born and native-born Polish men were overrepresented among unskilled and semi-skilled workers and operatives, and heavily concentrated in a few specific industrial sectors. By 1970, Polish Americans continued to score decidedly below the national average, with more than half of the males holding manual jobs and 45 percent white collar jobs, with only about sixteen percent as proprietors and managers. However, Polish Americans ranked relatively high as far as both income levels and home and farm ownership; although still below the national average, they placed on par with other central and eastern European groups and often higher than Italians and Greeks. As historian John J. Bukowczyk explains, "These well-paid second- and third- generation blue-collar Polish Americans, like the immigrant shopkeepers before them, had fallen into their own kind of mobility trap. They had done so well in industrial occupations that their children chose to hang onto them instead of grabbing often low-paid bottom rungs of occupational mobility ladder. The chronic disadvantages of class — combined with anti–Polish discrimination — reduced Polish American representation in the upper reaches of the occupational hierarchy and American class structure." Both the 1980 and 1990 census provided evidence of Polonia's advancement in their socioeconomic status. Polish American male workers made strides both on the occupational ladder and in the median income. A 1991 study of the Detroit area by John J. Bukowczyk and Peter D. Slavcheff indicated that most Polish Americans there were no longer members of the working class, but held a variety of jobs, including managerial and professional positions.

Education, which also contributes to the group's standing on the socio-economic scale, generally showed a stronger pattern of improvement between immigrant generations. According to some reports, an estimated 35.5 percent of Poles who came to America in the first decade of the twentieth century were illiterate, and over eighteen percent of children age 10–15 were working for pay. By 1930, the level of illiteracy among Polish Americans dropped to 18.5 percent. Throughout the next two decades, Polish Americans attended school for an average of eight to nine years, with females staying in school for shorter periods. By contrast, the average educational level of Polish displaced persons arriving after World War II was higher. By 1970, Polish Americans still had one of the lowest median years of schooling among other ethnic groups. However, the achievement of the second and third generation was markedly higher than their foreign born parents and grandparents, even outranking other Slavs and Italians. According to some statistics, about 30 percent of Polish men born in 1916–25, attended college, and out of those about half completed four plus years of study, which is below the average for all whites. In the same time period the percentage of Polish women who attended college was one of the lowest among all whites. For the cohort born in 1956–65, however, the same numbers are about 60 percent for both men and women, which is slightly above the average for all whites. According to historian James S. Pula, the 1980 census reported that Polish Americans ranked above the national average in the number of years of schooling and percentage with college degrees, and "by 1990 the U.S. Census showed that 11.4 percent of Polish Americans aged 18–24 had attained a baccalaureate or higher degree, compared with 13.1 percent of the general population."

One of the most direct indicators of assimilation among ethnic groups is usually loss of language. Polish Americans displayed a remarkable attachment to the use of the Polish language, but they could not hold on to it with the passage of the immigrant generation.

Scholars, who studied local communities, remain in agreement over the fact of rapid decline in the use of Polish by Polish Americans. In the 1940 U.S. Census, less than 23 percent of second generation Poles claimed English as their mother tongue, which placed them last among European ethnic groups, and only ahead of Mexicans. The 1969 U.S. Census reported that only 5.5 percent of those identifying themselves as of Polish origin claimed Polish as a language they currently used. In the same time period, other studies indicated that although the second generation still had a chance to use Polish either in parish schools or at home, very few among them had the ability to read newspapers or books in Polish, while the third generation rarely knew or used the language. The displaced persons cohort also noted generational decline in the use of Polish. According to the 1990 census, close to one-quarter of Polish Americans born in 1916–25 spoke Polish at home, compared with less than five percent for those born in 1976–85. Since the 1960s, the Polish language also gradually disappeared from Polish American churches, parish schools, as well as the Polish American press, which suffered a marked decline in this decade.

The progress of assimilation can also be measured by the changes in ethnic self-identification. Scholars noted that in Polonia it progressed from Polish and Polish American in the first generation to largely Polish American in the **second generation**, and Polish American to American in the third. Respondents from all generations agreed that they were perceived as "Polish" by others. Displaced persons in almost eighty percent considered themselves as "Polish," in thirteen percent as "American," and only one percent as "Polish American." It seems that as a rule, women viewed their ethnic background as more important than men. In their majority in all generations, Polish Americans claimed to oppose last name changes, although, especially in the second generation, English first names predominated. According to some statistics, in the early 1960s, 3,000 Detroit Polish residents a year changed their names. With the passing of the Polish joke phase and the general rise in the status of Polish Americans in the American society, the trend to Americanize names seemed to have subsided. Most Polish Americans in all generations continue their preference for Polish food, and persistence of folk customs, both religious and lay, also continues into the second and later generations.

Some scholars claim that another indicator of the progress of assimilation is the weakening of the community structure. This thesis may

indeed relate to American Polonia, which established an impressive number of religious and lay organizations since the period of great migration, but may not apply to other ethnic groups less known for their organizational networks. In case of Polonia, the parish quickly became the main community, serving religious, social and cultural needs of immigrants. This focal position of the parish continued throughout the 1920s, but in the 1930s, according to one study of Chicago's Polonia, the parish began to lose its centrality as the social and cultural leader in the community. This process continued also in the 1950s, and progressed more rapidly in the next decade. Even in places like **Hamtramck**, where the numbers of parish organizations were still high, their membership became gradually limited to lower class females. Some scholars also suggest that the overall position of the priest as a community leader and moral authority declined with the passage of time and immigrant generations, and became restricted more to the purely religious affairs. This view is challenged by multiple examples of activist priests in different locales who, due to their individual leadership skills, were able to organize and mobilize communities around them. For example, in the more recent decades, the service of Polish-speaking priests from the missionary Order of Christ provided a cadre of religious leaders actively involved in community organization among the most recent arrivals from Poland.

On the other hand, American Polonia seems to defy assimilation in the area of ethnic church attendance, which is consistently high throughout generations, particularly among those who live in urban ethnic zones. According to mid-1960s studies, an astonishing eighty percent of respondents in all three generations reported ethnic church attendance. Studies, which differentiated by class noted that there was a slight difference in ethnic church attendance between classes, with working class Polish Americans' attendance scoring higher than that of the intelligentsia. Despite the residential dispersal of the last few decades, which challenged the geographical ethnic parish and ethnic church attendance, Polish Americans, who live in the suburbs, committed themselves to attending a Polish church at least some of the time, and especially on major holidays.

Directly related to church attendance is the issue of support for parochial schools as an indicator of the persistence of ethnic identity and commitment. It is usually assumed that ethnicity of those schools was the main motivating factor for their support, more so than the overall attitude towards educational achievement. Although Polish Americans sent their children to parochial schools in much greater numbers than most other ethnic groups, since the 1930s the overall parochial school enrollment of Polish Americans has been in decline. This trend coincided with the waning of the Polish curriculum and increase in teaching the catechism in English. In the 1968 study of Buffalo, over sixty percent of all three generations' respondents completed elementary education in an ethnic school, while eighty percent of those who went to high schools attended public ones. The more recent immigrant population, which predominantly lives in the suburbs and sends their children to public schools there, remains involved in the maintenance of a well-functioning network of Polish **Saturday schools**, providing supplemental education of Polish language, history, and culture to the Polish American youngsters. These schools, often making use of the facilities belonging to the old Polish American parishes, serve both new immigrants and children of the second and later generations.

Although anecdotal evidence points to the steady decline of Polish American participation in the network of Polonia lay organizations, the numbers gathered for the membership in fraternal organizations in the period of mid–1920s to 1950, show actual growth, perhaps impacted by the arrival of displaced persons. In the early 1960s, one nation-wide study reported seventy percent of respondents claiming active membership in some Polonia voluntary association. These numbers seem to be directly related to the immigrant generations, with the first generation displaying stronger organizational participation than the second and especially third generation. It must be stressed again, that the ethnic organization membership cannot be treated in itself as a major indicator of the persistence of ethnicity. The forms of the participation in the ethnic community change over time. As membership in the fraternals indeed declines, the numbers for national professional organizations either remain steady or grow, and independent local organizations proliferate. With the advent of the Internet, many Polish Americans participate in the virtual forums, discussion groups, and other Internet communities. These new forms of claiming one's ethnicity need to be taken into account and further explored.

A high level of political participation has also been accepted as one of the indicators of assimilation, although some ethnic groups, such as the Irish, successfully pursued political involvement without the loss of ethnic identity. Average Polish Americans generally did not display much interest in American politics. As a rule, they showed more involvement in local politics in smaller communities such as **Hamtramck** or Milwaukee, than in state or national politics. The political ambitions were usually more pronounced among upper class than working class. Some studies suggest that while voting, Polish Americans tended to support ethnicity above issues or party affiliations. Whether due to their own lack of political skill and resources or external obstacles such as well-documented discrimination and competition with other ethnic groups, Polish Americans enjoyed only a very limited success in the political arena. **Angela T. Pienkos** even implied that, once the political leadership in Polonia matured, the forces of "Americanization" deprived it of "the electoral base they needed to attain political recognition." As this author predicts, third and fourth generations of Polish Americans active in local politics may be able to "rekindle the sense of ethnic solidarity on the mass level within the increasingly affluent and better educated Polish American population." It remains to be seen if these slightly contradictory predictions can indeed come true.

According to many scholars, the level of intermarriage is considered the strongest indicator of the progress of assimilation. As in the case of other white European ethnic groups, ethnic intermarriage of Polish Americans rapidly increases with passage of time and generations. Younger Polish Americans and later generations seem to approve of ethnic as well as religious intermarriage in greater proportions than their parents. The preference for Polish (or at least Roman Catholic) spouses, however, remains consistently high. As a study of marriage and baptismal records of the Holy Cross Parish in New Britian, CT, by historian Stanislaus A. Blejwas indicates, the downwards trend in exogamous marriages began already in the period of 1948–62. According to the 1980 census, Polish Americans born in or before 1920 reported that close to 47 percent of their spouses came from the same ethnic group. For the cohort born after 1950, the same number was only 7.2 percent, ranking seventh overall among all European-ancestry groups in U.S. population. The 1990 census showed even more progress in the intermarriage rates of Polish Americans born in 1956–65, with more than three quarters of them entering marriages outside of their ethnic group, which places them above most other white European groups, including Irish, Italian, German, and French. In general, Polish American women are more likely than men to seek a spouse from outside of the group.

Although sociological works shed light on the many complicated aspects of both ethnic assimilation and retention of ethnicity, there are still areas that beg much more scholarly attention and examination. The issue of interethnic relations and interactions has not been explored in depth in relation to American Polonia. The problem of regional ethnicity has not been addressed adequately either, although distinctive cultures of Górale or Kaszubi (see **Góral**; **Kashub**) persisted in Polish American communities for over a century. More recent chain migration from particular regions of contemporary Poland to the same area of settlement, such as New Britain, CT, for immigrants from the Łomża region, may continue to provide conditions for the development of regional identities. The uniqueness of regional cultures and identities should provide fruitful ground for both sociological and historical exploration.

The impact of the location of settlement on the development of ethnic identity remains another subject for further study. As both Galush and Blejwas propose, Polonia formed differently in different regions of the United States, for instance in Chicago and other large urban communities, versus smaller towns in the Midwest or New England. Polish American ethnic identity also developed differently in the rural, more isolated areas as compared to urban and industrial settings. In contemporary times, secondary migration of Polish Americans to the Sun Belt, as John Radzilowski indicates, creates yet another distinctive community.

Despite more recently published studies on the exile or refugee experience versus that of immigrants and ethnics by **Danuta Mostwin**, Mary Patrice Erdmans and **Anna Jaroszyńska-Kirchmann**, the subject of assimilation among refugees and exiles requires further exploration. Similarly, we know little about assimilation and identity formation among Polish American women versus Polish American men. As Thaddeus Radzilowski notes, further study of the experience of the second generation is also critical to our understanding of the process of ethnic identity formation as well as assimilation. Last but not least, this process could and should be studied in relation to both individual and group experience of American Polonia.

In 1901, Polonia's early historian the Rev. **Wacław Kruszka** noted that there existed a separate and distinct type of a Pole in America. He wrote: "This type, not yet fully molded, unclear, and, therefore, imperceptible to the eye of today's historian — it is sure, nonetheless, that such a type is, and has been taking shape ever since the local emigration's history began." Contemporary social scientists also generally agree that there are three basic cultures and ethnic identities within Polonia: Polish, Polish American, and American. These identities, which draw on different cultural sources, can be further complicated by divisions within the group. As sociologist **Helena Znaniecka Łopata** notes, "It is quite probable that each Polish American combines these sources uniquely, drawing different items of Polish, American, and Polonian cultures and identifying with different groups of Poles, Americans, and Polish Americans in his or her ethnic identity package. This is particularly likely to have happened as generational, geographic, educational, occupational, and life-style mobility have de-crystallized the identity packages typical of the many subgroups of the Polish immigrants who have entered America within the past 100 years."

The discussion of ethnic identity and assimilation cannot ever be fully complete, since it is a process, which is in constant flux, affected by changing conditions and choices available to both individuals and groups. There is no doubt that over the decades American Polonia did develop distinctive ethnic identity within the American society, an identity, which, although different for each of the generations, evolves around the common understanding of Polishness in America.— *Anna D. Jaroszyńska-Kirchmann*

SOURCES: Irvin T. Sanders, Ewa T. Morawska, *Polish-American Community Life: A Survey of Research* (Boston: Boston University and the Polish Institute of Arts and Sciences of America, 1975); Richard D. Alba, *Ethnic Identity: The Transformation of White America* (New Haven: Yale University Press, 1990); Richard Alba and Victor Nee, *Remaking the American Mainstream: Assimilation and Contemporary Immigration* (Cambridge, MA: Harvard University Press, 2003); James S. Pula, *Polish Americans: An Ethnic Community* (New York: Twayne Publishers, 1995); Milton M. Gordon, *Assimilation in American Life: The Role of Race, Religion, and National Origins* (New York: Oxford University Press, 1964); John J. Bukowczyk, *And My Children Did Not Know Me: A History of the Polish Americans,* (Bloomington: Indiana University Press, 1987); John J. Bukowczyk, ed., *Polish Americans and Their History: Community, Culture, and Politics* (Pittsburgh: University of Pittsburgh Press, 1996); Angela T. Pienkos, ed., *Ethnic Politics in Urban America: The Polish Experience in Four Cities* (Chicago: Polish American Historical Association, 1978); Stanislaus Blejwas, "A Polish Community in Transition: The Evolution of Holy Cross Parish, New Britain, Connecticut," *Polish American Studies*, Vol. 35, nos. 1–2 (Spring-Autumn 1978), 23–53; Helena Znaniecka Lopata, *Polish Americans*, 2nd revised edition with a new chapter by Mary Patrice Erdmans (New Brunswick: Transaction Publishers, 1994); Andrzej Brożek, *Polish Americans, 1854–1939* (Warsaw: Interpress, 1985); Mary P. Erdmans, *Opposite Poles: Immigrants and Ethnics in Polish Chicago, 1976–1990* (University Park: Pennsylvania State University Press, 1998); Mary P. Erdmans, *The Grasinski Girls: The Choices They Had and the Choices They Made* (Athens: Ohio University Press, 2004); Anna D. Jaroszyńska-Kirchmann, *The Exile Mission: The Polish Political Diaspora and Polish Americans, 1939–1956* (Athens: Ohio University Press, 2004);

William J. Galush, *For More Than Bread: Community and Identity in American Polonia, 1880–1940* (Boulder, CO: East European Monographs, 2006).

Evashevski, Forest (b. Detroit, Michigan, February 19, 1918; d. Petoskey, Michigan, October 30, 2009). Football player, coach. The son of a Polish machine-tool salesman, "Evy" excelled in many sports including track, tennis, baseball, soccer, basketball, and football. Considered too small to play varsity football in high school, he gained weight and joined the team his senior year, playing tackle and linebacker. His career did not last long before he suffered a cerebral hemorrhage after hitting a punt returner. Though doctors said he could no longer play, he worked summers to earn money to attend college. He enrolled at the University of Michigan where he joined the football team coached by Herbert "Fritz" Crisler. Evashevski became a standout quarterback, whom Crisler called the greatest quarterback he ever had. He was named to the All-Big Ten team in 1938–40. A member of the honor society and class president, he majored in sociology. He then coached football at Hamilton College in Clinton, New York. With the onset of World War II, he enrolled in Naval Pre-Flight School in Iowa where he also taught hand-to-hand combat techniques. After the war he took a job as assistant coach at Syracuse University, went on to Michigan State and Washington State, then became head coach at the University of Iowa which had not had a winning season in sixteen years, nor won a Big Ten title in thirty years. Iowa started his tenure with an 0–2 record, then shocked highly touted Ohio State 8–0. The game was voted one of the three greatest upsets of 1952. In 1953, Iowa played to a 14–14 tie with Notre Dame, then ranked number one in the nation. Under Evy's leadership, Iowa continued to improve. In 1956 it defeated Ohio State to win the first Rose Bowl berth in school history, going on to win that game 35–19 over Oregon State. He wrote the book *Scoring Power with the Winged T Offense* in 1959. By the time Evy became athletic director in 1960, he had compiled a 52-27-4 record, but he would become controversial when he was dismissed in 1970 after he and others were accused of "padding" athletic department expense accounts. What cannot be discounted is that he was coach of an Iowa team that scored some of the greatest victories in the school's history.— *Cheryl A. Pula*

SOURCE: Brian Chapman, *Evy and the Hawkeyes: The Glory Years* (New York: Leisure Press, 1983).

Factor, Max, Sr. (b. Factorowitz or Faktorowicz; Łódź, Poland, 1877 (exact date unknown); d. Beverly Hills, California, August 30, 1938). Businessman. Known as the father of modern cosmetics and founder of the Max Factor Cosmetics Company, Faktorowicz grew up in a family of ten children. Since his parents could not afford formal education for their children, at age eight he was placed in an apprenticeship to a dentist-pharmacist. While apprenticing he spent long hours mixing a variety of potions and became fascinated with the human face. As a young adult in Moscow, he opened his first store where he sold hand-made rouges, skin creams, fragrances, and wigs. A theater group wore some of his makeup while performing before Russian aristocracy, which led to his being hired by the Royal Family as its makeup consultant. He also worked in the same capacity for the Imperial Russian Grand Opera. In 1904, Faktorowicz and his family came to America where he began a career selling rouges and creams at the 1905 World's Fair in St. Louis, operating under the name given to him by immigration officials at Ellis Island, Max Factor. From there, believing that actors and actresses in the nascent motion picture business would need make-up and wigs, he moved his family to Los Angeles in 1908. In 1914 he invented greasepaint compressed into a tube, created specifically for movie actors. Unlike theatrical makeup, Factor's greasepaint would not crack or cake. This was the first time he used the term "makeup" to describe the product. Soon movie stars were filing through Max Factor's makeup studio, eager to sample his "flexible greasepaint." Factor is credited with creating a whole new language for screen cosmetics. Inevitably, once actresses had been made to look so stylish on screen, they wanted to maintain the same effect in everyday life, so they wore the new Max Factor "makeup" in personal appearances. Soon, women unconnected with the theatre or the film industry were asking for the makeup, so that they too could look glamorous. During the following two decades, he was responsible for the glamorous looks of celebrities such as Jean Harlow, Judy Garland, Rita Hayworth, Bette Davis, Katharine Hepburn and Joan Crawford, many of whom relied on his services not only for their movie appearances but in their everyday lives. In 1927 Factor started selling his cosmetics to consumers, believing that all women should have the opportunity to look like the stars. In doing so, he was largely responsible for the commencement of the cosmetics industry as we know it today. Many of his Hollywood clients also agreed to appear in magazine ads to market his cosmetics, and the name Max Factor soon became known around the globe. Factor was responsible for a number of cosmetic innovations including the first foundation (known as Pan-cake), which was applied to the face with a silk sponge. Other "firsts" introduced by Max Factor and his company of the same name were false eyelashes, lip gloss, eyebrow pencil, stick makeup, concealer, the mascara wand, water resistant makeup and many others. Following Factor's death in 1938 the company continued to grow under the direction of his son, Max Jr., becoming synonymous with high fashion and glamour. In 1991 the brand name "Max Factor" was sold to its current owner, Procter & Gamble.—*Richard J. Hunter & Héctor R. Lozada*

SOURCES: See Fred E. Basten, *Max Factor: The Man Who Changed the Faces of the World* (Arcade Publishing, 2008), Fred E. Basten, Robert Salvatore and Paul A. Kaufman, *Max Factor's Hollywood: Glamour, Movies, Make-Up* (Stoddart, 1995).

Fajans, Kazimierz (b. Warsaw, Poland, May 27, 1887; d. Ann Arbor, Michigan, May 18, 1975). Chemist. After pursuing his education in Leipzig, Heidelberg and Zürich, Fajans received his doctorate in 1909. In 1910 he began research at Ernest Rutherford's laboratory in Manchester, England, where he was involved in early investigations leading to the identification of the nucleus. Returning to Germany to accept an assistant professorship at the University of Karlsruhe, he undertook extensive research into radioactivity. Accepting leadership of the department of physical chemistry at Munich University in 1917, in 1932 he was named director of the Munich Institute of Physical Chemistry established by the Rockefeller Foundation. Because of escalating discrimination by the Nazis, he moved first to Cambridge and then the United States in 1936 to accept a position as professor at the University of Michigan. He is known in the field of inorganic chemistry for "Fajans' Rules" which explain the diagonal similarities between elements in the periodic table and explain whether a bond will be covalent or ionic. A pioneer in the science of radioactivity and exploration of isotopes, he discovered the radioactive displacement law, identified several elements created through the process of nuclear disintegration including protactinium, used radioactivity to determine the age of minerals, and defined, with Otto Hahn, the formula for understanding the precipitation and absorption of radioactive substances. His research led to important conclusions on chemical bonding, ion hydration, refraction measurements and heat sublimation.—*James S. Pula*

SOURCE: Józef Hurwic, *Kasimir Fajans (1887–1975): sylwetka uczonego* (Wrocław: Zakład Narodowy im. Ossolińskich, 1991).

Falcons *see* **Polish Falcons of America.**

Fangor, Wojciech "Voy" (b. Warsaw, Poland, November 15, 1922; d.—). Artist. Since all Polish art schools and academies were closed by the Germans during World War II, Fangor studied privately with Władysław Witwicki, Tadeusz Pruszkowski, and Felicjan Szczesny Kowarski before enrolling at the reactivated post-war Academy of Fine Arts in Warsaw where he received a diploma in arts (1946). After teaching in the Academy of Fine Arts in Warsaw (1952–61), he accepted a faculty position at the Bath Academy of Art in Corsham, Wiltshire, England (1964–65). He migrated to the United States in 1966, accepting a position at Fairleigh Dickinson University, Madison, NJ (1966–83). After teaching for a year in the American Art School, Lacoste, Vaucluse, France (1995), he returned to Poland in 1999. A noted painter, poster artist, and designer, he had solo exhibitions at various locations in England, France, Germany, Poland, and the U.S. Fangor designed the decorative panneau at the Polish Pavilion in Paris (1954); a frieze at the Fifth World Youth and Student Festival in Warsaw (1955); the Polish Pavilion in Brussels (1956); the mosaic Dworzec Srodmiescia in Warsaw (1960); and decorations for Martha Graham Ballet, Mark Hellinger Theater, New York (1974). Among his many honors are the Złoty Krzyż Zasługi (Gold Service Cross, Warsaw, 1954); a scholarship to the Institute of Contemporary Arts, Washington, D.C. (1962); and the **Alfred Jurzykowski Foundation** Prize, New York (1979).—*Stanley L. Cuba*

SOURCES: Thomas M. Messer and Margit Rowell, *Fangor* (New York: The Solomon R. Guggenheim Museum, 1970); Bożena Kowalska, *Fangor: Malarz przestrzeni* (Warsaw: Wydawnictwa Artystyczne i Filmowe, Wydawnictwo Naukowe PWN, 2001).

Father Justin Rosary Hour *see* **Rosary Hour.**

Faut, Paul (b. Kazan, Russia, May 26, 1898; d. Harris, Texas, March 10, 1984). Radio pioneer. The son of Polish parents who were temporarily residing in Russia, Faut attended the Moscow Theater School and made his stage debut with the Moscow Imperial Theater. In 1921 the family returned to Warsaw where he appeared in five silent films under his mother's maiden name of Mirecki. He left Poland for the U.S. in 1922, settling in Cleveland where he resumed a theatrical career, performing in theaters in Buffalo, Cleveland, Detroit, New York, and Pittsburgh. In 1929, Faut purchased the Polonia Theater which he and his wife Maria turned into a successful venture. In 1931 he founded the Cosmopolitan

Broadcasting Company which, despite the Depression, survived by airing a number of popular ethnic programs in German, Hungarian, Italian, Lithuanian, Polish, and Romanian. One of his innovations was the introduction of the singing commercial. In addition to his radio accomplishments, he also recorded some one hundred Polish records for the Victor Talking Machine Company. His recording of "Polskie Orły" sold over 100,000 copies in only two months.—*James S. Pula*

SOURCE: Joseph Migala, *Polish Radio Broadcasting in the United States* (Boulder, CO: East European Monographs, 1987), 209–11.

Federacja Swieckich Polaków Katolików w Ameryce *see* **Federation Life Insurance of America.**

Federation Life Insurance of America. Originally called the Federation of Polish Catholic Laymen in America (Federacja Swieckich Polaków Katolików w Ameryce), this was a fraternal organization based in Milwaukee that was active from 1911 to 2005. Originally the Federation of Polish Catholic Laymen in America was organized as a movement to support the efforts of **Michael Kruszka**, publisher of the Milwaukee *Kuryer Polski* (Polish Courier) newspaper in his campaign to win Catholic Church approval of the proportional representation of Roman Catholics in the Church hierarchy and to bring about the creation of Polish dioceses administered by bishops of Polish heritage. Kruszka's campaign was itself in support of the strenuous and many faceted efforts of his brother, the historian Rev. **Wacław Kruszka**, pastor of Milwaukee's St. Adalbert parish and long an advocate of this cause. A number of more radical ideas were also approved in the early years of the Federation, including calls for greater lay managerial control of Polish parishes.

The Federation's first convention was held in 1912 when 176 delegates attended and declared they represented 50,000 Polish people in the community. What followed in the wake of that meeting, and others like it, was an intense struggle, one waged in the pages of Milwaukee's Polish language press, within the community, and even the courts, to pressure the Church hierarchy to accept Kruszka's demands. In 1914, some success was achieved with the appointment of **Edward Kozłowski** as an auxiliary bishop in Milwaukee. However, he died the following year and was not succeeded by another Polish American. In 1908 Chicago's **Paul Rhode** had become the first Polish American auxiliary bishop, a result of both the Rev. Kruszka's efforts and the Church's own concerns over the possibility of a substantial Polish Catholic defection into the newly established, schismatic, **Polish National Catholic Church** (PNCC) headed by Bishop **Francis Hodur**. Indeed some Federation activists did leave the church for the PNCC parish in Milwaukee, an action that added to the divisions within the Milwaukee Polonia.

America's entry into World War I in 1917, Michael Kruszka's death in 1918, and growing interest in Poland's independence (proclaimed in November 1918) combined to take the steam out of the Federation's original mission. But, as early as 1913, the Federation had set up its own fraternal insurance program, an idea the ever provocative Michael Kruszka backed as not incompatible with its original political aims. In 1923, in a controversial and hotly debated decision, its leaders formally renamed the organization Federation Life Insurance of America. Insured membership rose from 1,500 in 1926 to 5,500 in 1960. In 1976, membership exceeded 5,600, over 4,000 of whom were in Wisconsin, with local affiliated lodges in Indiana, Michigan, New Jersey, Ohio, and Pennsylvania.

Under its officers, most recently William Kowalkowski, who was president for most of the period from 1968 until 2005, Federation Life Insurance of America was an important contributor to the activities of the Milwaukee Polish American community. But its membership declined to about 2,500 in the early 2000s, and in 2005 its members approved a merger into the **Polish Roman Catholic Union** of America.—*Angela T. Pienkos*

SOURCES: Angela T. Pienkos, *A Brief History of Federation Life Insurance of America, 1913–1976* (Milwaukee: Haertlein Graphics, 1976); Thaddeus Borun and John Gostomski, eds., *We, The Milwaukee Poles* (Milwaukee: Nowiny Pub. Co., 1946); Anthony J. Kuzniewski, *Faith and Fatherland: The Polish Church War in Wisconsin, 1896–1918* (Notre Dame, IN: University of Notre Dame Press, 1980).

Federation of Polish Jews in America.

Founded by Dr. Henry Moskowitz in New York in 1908 as the Federation of Polish Hebrews, the organization was an attempt by East European Jews to promote and create an alternative to the existing Jewish groups in America that were then dominated by Jews from Germany. Initially its purpose was to care for the sick, aged, and orphans, which resulted in the founding of Beth David Hospital in Manhattan in 1912. In 1924 the group was largely reorganized by Benjamin Winter and Zelig Tygel, the latter an active Zionist, into an umbrella organization for over a hundred groups based on regional ties to Poland. With this, its modest membership quickly grew to more than 40,000 and in 1925 its mission was officially changed "to unite all the Polish Jews in America and that it should be the only

body to speak in their name." Although it did not abandon its concern for health issues, the Federation became more actively engaged in providing legal assistance and promoting educational and cultural activities. In 1930 it officially changed its name to "The Federation of Polish Jews in America." By 1939 it claimed 65,000 members, although actual dues-paying membership may have been less than one-third that number. Branch chapters opened in Boston, Chicago, Denver, Philadelphia, Pittsburgh, and St. Louis, as well as various locations in California and Canada. Increasingly between 1925 and the beginning of the Second World War the Federation's leadership focused on promoting the political rights of Jews in Poland. Though frequently critical of Polish policies, the organization generally maintained ongoing relations with Polish officials and invited Ambassador Jan Ciechanowski to its twentieth anniversary celebration. Various attempts by the Federation's leaders to build relationships with Jewish leaders in Poland did not materialize, and efforts by Polish diplomats to win over Polish American Jews to their support in interwar Poland likewise enjoyed little success. In 1930 a joint "Good-Will Committee of Jews and Non-Jews of Polish Extraction" was formed with generally favorable support from Polish leaders, but Jewish leaders were somewhat split between those who favored participation and those who did not. The new Committee organized conferences in several cities, and its leaders appeared at each other's individual events. However, relations deteriorated in 1931 and in 1932 the Federation withdrew from the effort after criticism from other Jewish organizations that it had no authority to speak for them and growing criticism of the status of Jews in Poland. Thereafter, Federation leaders became progressively more strident in their comments on Poland. In 1933, the Federation became increasingly more concerned with the condition of Polish Jews in Germany and, although it remained interested in developments in Poland, especially as restrictions on Jews were implemented following the death of Marshal Józef Piłsudski, it began to concentrate most of its efforts on the situation in Germany. Relations between the Federation and representatives of the Polish government worsened, leading to a complete rupture in relations in late 1936. At the same time, relations between the Federation and the American Jewish Congress also deteriorated with the Congress charging that the Federation was not sufficiently cooperative with other Jewish organizations. Only with the full realization of the attacks on Jews in Germany, and on the eve of World War II, did the Federation adopt

a more conciliatory posture toward the Polish government. In 1939 the Federation took part in a Polish American meeting organized at the Cooper Union in New York by the **Polish National Alliance** and also urged its members to contribute to the Polish National Fund. In the end, the Federation had only limited success because it competed with other larger Jewish organizations and because of the vicissitudes of international Polish-Jewish relations.—*James S. Pula*

SOURCE: Andrzej Kapiszewski, "The Federation of Polish Jews in America in Polish-Jewish Relations During the Interwar years (1924–1939)," *Polish American Studies*, Vol. 56, no. 2 (1999), 45–68.

Felician Sisters.

Founded in Poland in 1855, the Felician Sisters was the first female religious community from Poland that came to the United States to serve the growing number of Polish immigrants between the 1880s and the end of World War I. Officially known as the Sisters of St. Felix of Cantalice, the community's history in America began in 1874 with the arrival of five sisters in rural Wisconsin. Asked by the Rev. **Joseph Dąbrowski**, a missionary priest in America and future founder of **SS. Cyril and Methodius Seminary**, to teach in his parish school in Polonia, Wisconsin, and to open a novitiate, the Felician community begun by Sophia Camille Truszkowska had been in existence for only nineteen years when the original band of Felician pioneers arrived in Wisconsin. The Rev. Dąbrowski's request was actually the second invitation the young community had received to serve Polish immigrants in America. The Felicians were initially asked to minister in the U.S. in 1867 when Mother Angela was serving as the first superior general. On behalf of the **Resurrectionists** who were ministering to the Polish immigrants in Texas, the Rev. Alexander Jełowicki, CR, moderator of the Resurrection Congregation's Polish Missions Center in Paris, asked Mother Angela for sisters to assist their community with pastoral work among the Polish émigrés in Texas. However, in the absence of its pending canonical approval as a legitimate religious institute, and since the young community had not fully completed its reunification following its forcible suppression and disbandment by the Russian government in December 1864, Mother Angela declined this mission to the United States.

At the time of its suppression, the Felician community numbered approximately two hundred members in Poland where they maintained an orphanage, a residence for elderly women, a hospital with forty beds, a school for girls, and conducted classes for religious instruction at their Central House in

Warsaw. In addition, they maintained two other houses in the city, conducted day care programs, and staffed social service centers in twenty-seven villages. In 1860, during its formative years, the Felicians even established a cloistered group within the community. At that time Mother Angela was among the twelve sisters elected by the community to observe a strictly contemplative life. For a year and a half, the foundress was superior of both groups, after which she was recalled to the active choir. By papal decree in 1873, the contemplative group was renamed the Capuchin Sisters of St. Felix. Church approval for the formal establishment of a novitiate came in 1916 and the contemplative group was officially sanctioned as a separate religious community based on the primitive Rule of St. Clare observing the Second Rule.

Following their suppression in the Russian-occupied partition, the Felicians opened a new mother house in Kraków where they had previously staffed a day care center as their only mission outside the Russian area. Once established there, the reunited Felician community experienced an increase in its membership and requests for the services of the sisters multiplied. In August 1874, the Felician community's general chapter voted unanimously to accept an invitation from the Rev. Józef Dąbrowski for the sisters to teach at his parish school in Polonia, Wisconsin. Five sisters ranging in ages from 23 to fifty were selected by the general chapter to begin the American apostolate. Sister **Mary Monica Konwerska Sybilska**, who was the oldest at fifty and had filled several leadership positions during her first eighteen years in religious life, was the designated superior of the group. Sister Mary Cajetan Jankiewicz, who was 35 years old at the time, had completed a normal school program before her profession. During her first seven years in religious life she taught at girls' schools and had also worked with adults at religious conferences. The third member of the group, Sister Mary Wenceslaus Zubrzycka, was 31 years old and had ministered in orphanages and hospitals during her first fourteen years as a Felician Sister. She was a cousin of the Rev. Dąbrowski. At the age of 23, Sister Vincentine Kalwa was the youngest of the five and had entered the community only two years before her departure for America. The newest member of the community was the 32-year-old Sister Raphael Swożeniowska who was invested as a novice with the religious habit on the day before her departure for the U.S.

Beginning on October 24, 1874, at the train station in Wrocław, the Felician pioneers' trip from Poland to Polonia was an arduous journey of 28 days consisting of seven separate travel segments completed by public conveyance as well as extensive walking. Word of the sisters' travel and expected arrival dates had not reached the Rev. Dąbrowski. Their arrival, nonetheless, was anticipated by the priest and people among the American Polonia that had assembled in Chicago for an organizational meeting of the **Polish Roman Catholic Union** (PRCU). The Rev. **Wincenty Barzyński**, C.R., a leading organizer of the Polish Roman Catholic Union, referred to the sisters' arrival in a letter to the Rev. Peter Semeneńko, rector of the Polish Pontifical College in Rome, following the PRCU's first national convention. He said that twelve priests and many representatives from throughout the United States spent three days at the convention where they worked on forming a central Polish Catholic Union. He went on to explain that the aim of the organization was to uphold the Catholic Faith and the Polish national heritage through the promotion of Catholic learning and instruction and that they hoped to invite various Polish sisterhoods, the first of which would be the Felician Sisters who were to arrive shortly, owing to the efforts of the Rev. Dąbrowski.

The initial years in the U.S. were difficult for the city-bred Felicians who were unaccustomed to the hardships of rural living. Enduring dire poverty and two devastating fires in as many months, they found it difficult to cope with the ongoing need for additional personnel while also struggling with the challenges of acculturation. Although the original band of five sisters was never supplemented by European reinforcements, it nevertheless experienced a rapid growth. The congregation eventually extended across the United States from Maine to California and resulted in the formation of seven provinces that included the Livonia, Michigan, province, which was originally established in Polonia, Wisconsin (1874), and the later provinces in Buffalo (1900), Chicago (1910), Lodi (NJ; 1913), Coraopolis (PA; 1920), Enfield (CT; 1932), and Rio Rancho (NM; 1953). Later evangelization efforts by the American provinces extended their ministry boundaries to Mexico (1943–46, 1992), Puerto Rico (1941–46), Germany (1956–77), France (1956–71), Canada (1937–52), and Kenya (1989), and were directly responsible for the establishment of provinces in Curitiba, Brazil (1950), and Mississauga, Ontario (1953).

With the establishment of provinces in the United States, the American Felicians maintained their status as juridical entities under a general administration with its offices at the generalate, originally located in Kraków until 1950 when a provisional generalate was established in Ponca City, Oklahoma. Subsequently, the congregation's generalate was transferred to Rome, Italy, in 1953. Eight of the congregation's twelve superior generals have been American Felicians elected to the community's highest executive office.

Before the end of the nineteenth century, the Felician Sisters, who were originally invited to America to teach the children of Polish immigrants, were responding to other needs that included childcare and healthcare, as well as social services and pastoral ministry. In 1897 the sisters ventured into the field of social services with the acceptance of staffing responsibilities at the St. Joseph Home for Polish Immigrants in New York City, a temporary shelter for Poles arriving in America. From their earliest days at Sacred Heart Parish, the sisters were also engaged in pastoral service to adults of the area and to the native peoples of the region. Childcare became a ministry when the first orphan was brought to the convent doorstep in 1876. By 1900 the sisters were operating four homes for orphans in Wisconsin, Michigan, Illinois, and New York and were also staffing two homes for the elderly. At that time, education remained the Felician Sisters' principal ministry as they continued to accept schools and to print textbooks. By 1900, the American foundation, which included 320 professed members, 40 novices, and 98 postulants, was conducting 41 parish elementary schools in eleven states from Wisconsin to Massachusetts. Nearly a century later, on the threshold of the twenty-first century, the Felician Sisters enrolled 1,600 professed members, five novices, and two postulants serving the American Church in twenty-one states reaching from Maine to California.

Efforts to educate and prepare sisters as qualified teachers resulted in the establishment of a normal school program in Detroit. Upon the advice of the Rev. Dąbrowski, Mother Monica had the school incorporated in 1882 as the Seminary of the Felician Sisters with the right "to provide instruction for the young in the several branches of learning which may qualify them for their position in life." This decision was appropriate not only for its practicality, but also for its anticipation of Canon 205 of the Third Plenary Council of Baltimore in 1884 in which the bishops directed that each religious order was to establish a training school for its novices so there would always be a sufficient number of Catholic teachers trained in the various studies and sciences in methods and pedagogy and other subject areas needed for a sound teacher preparation program. In the decades that ensued, Detroit's normal school program was followed by sponsorship of junior and senior colleges in six of the American provinces, which in most cases began teacher training programs that initially enrolled only the members of the order. In 2009, three of these Felician sponsored institutions continue to operate in Michigan, New York, and New Jersey, educating men and women in the liberal arts and career-oriented programs.

The Felicians of the Livonia, Michigan, province sponsored Presentation Junior College (1937–47), followed by Madonna College in 1947 that was renamed Madonna University in 1991. In 2003 Madonna University acquired as the eighth of its colleges St. Mary's College, Orchard Lake, which had been one of the Orchard Lake Schools founded by the Rev. Dąbrowski in Detroit in 1885. The Felician Sisters of the Buffalo, New York, province conducted Immaculate Heart of Mary Teacher Training College in 1960, which they renamed Villa Maria College of Buffalo in 1961, and which continues as a senior college. The Felicians of the Lodi, New Jersey, province began Immaculate Conception Normal School in 1923, changed it to the Teacher Training Institute in 1935, modified the name to the Immaculate Conception Junior College in 1941, and again changed the name to Felician College in 1942. In 2009 it continued as a senior college.

The three colleges that closed were in Chicago (IL), Ponca City (OK), and Enfield (CT). Beginning in 1926 the Felician Sisters of Chicago conducted Felician College, an extension of Loyola University, opening it as a two-year liberal arts college with a teacher training program for their sisters in 1953. In 1965 it began admitting lay students after which it changed its name in 1988 to Montay College, but in 1995 the college closed. The Felician Sisters of the Ponca City Province (later located in Rio Rancho, New Mexico) conducted Regina Junior College for only three years, 1964 to 1967. From 1935 to 1945, the Felicians of the Enfield, Connecticut, province pursued college courses in extension classes conducted by the Immaculate Conception Junior College of Lodi, New Jersey. In 1945 the Enfield province began sponsorship of Our Lady of the Angels Teacher Training Institute, which they replaced with Our Lady of the Angels Junior College in 1950. In 1970 the institution was renamed Longview Junior College, but it closed in 1972. In 1983, the Felician Central Archives for the American provinces was established in the college building which was renamed the Felician Heritage Center.

Involved in all the usual areas of education at parochial, diocesan, and community sponsored institutions, the Felician Sisters were likewise conducting special education programs for exceptional children and those with learning disabilities and directing academic programs, vocational training, and workshop employment for mentally disabled adults. They continued to sponsor learning centers, a school of music, and remedial programs. With parish school closings and school consolidations of the 1970s, the Felician Sisters broadened the scope of their teaching apostolate to encompass full-time ministry in catechetical centers and religious education programs. In the aftermath of changing child welfare policies at the state level that ended the sisters' residential care of orphans during the 1960s, provinces developed and expanded child day care programs and pioneered adult day care while undertaking new residential programs for the care of children with physical disabilities and the administration of group homes for mentally challenged adults. They also began ministry to African Americans and Native Americans and to later groups of Asian and Latin American immigrants.

During and after World War II, American provinces worked with displaced Polish refugees in the United States, Mexico, Germany, and France. At the heart of Felician ministry to the displaced Polish war refugees were the sisters readiness to serve where needed and their commonality of shared language and understanding of the Poles' religious faith. The fates of the displaced groups were varied, but all bore the indelible scars of homelessness, deprivations, and loss of loved ones.

Entrance into the ministry of healthcare first occurred in 1888 when the Felicians were invited to staff St. Mary Home in Manitowoc, Wisconsin, where the Rev. **Zdzisław Łuczycki**, the pastor of St. Mary Parish, rented two houses for the poor and aged of the district and asked for Felician Sisters to staff the home. The needs of the area were so urgent that he later purchased a twenty-acre site on which he built a larger facility that included a residence for the elderly, housing for orphans, and a ten-bed hospital for the poor. To insure continued operation of the institution, the pastor later transferred ownership to the Felician Sisters before he returned to Poland. In the years that followed, the Felicians took care of the health needs of their sisters, orphans, and of the elderly in their care. It was in the 1930s that healthcare took on a more prominent role in Felician ministry. Requests for Felician Sisters to serve in the healthcare apostolate rose steadily as new provinces were established and the community

was gaining greater visibility in ministry. Prompted by their commitment to the charismatic spirit and vision of their foundress "to remain available for diverse services to the People of God," provinces had already arranged for the education and training of sisters qualified to serve as nurses and other healthcare professionals. Some provinces were asked to sponsor or staff hospitals and nursing care centers and to conduct hospital schools of nursing as well as college baccalaureate nursing programs. In the decades between 1939 and 1962 six provinces administered a total of twenty hospitals in twelve states, Canada, and Puerto Rico that included more than a dozen small community hospitals, of which nearly half closed before 1950.

Reasons for the Felician Sisters' withdrawal from some of the smaller hospitals varied. In some cases it was an ethical decision because sponsors or medical staffs could not be dissuaded from policies and practices that clearly were not in keeping with Church law and moral medical issues. Likewise, because some changes in foreign government regulations imposed serious restrictions on sponsorship, provinces recalled their sisters from these territorial sites. In other cases financial support for construction costs was promised during initial agreements but for various reasons the respective groups did not follow through with earlier commitments as projects were getting underway to replace the temporary facilities where accommodations and inadequate equipment made proper care nearly impossible.

The Felician Sisters, nevertheless, succeeded in sponsoring some of the country's top ranking hospitals in Illinois, Maine, Michigan, Wisconsin, Texas, New Jersey, Pennsylvania, and Florida, only to be confronted in the last decades of the twentieth century by major healthcare issues that put the continued ministry of many Catholic healthcare institutions at risk. In an effort to cope with government regulations, pricing, and ever changing management issues, hospitals sought new ways of ministering to the sick as many institutions struggled with their own survival. In some cases, collaboration, co-sponsorship, or joining other hospital systems were key factors in taking preventive measures that would preclude involuntary closures or financial takeovers.

Additional areas of service in healthcare, pastoral ministry, and related social services which the Felician Sisters assumed included nursing homes, hospice and AIDS ministry, adult day care, senior residence complexes, and a senior clergy village. Still other apostolic services in which they were involved included pastoral ministry and Christian services in parishes; chaplaincies in schools, hospitals and prisons; management of soup kitchens and food pantries; ministry to the homeless and disadvantaged; retreat work; youth ministry; spiritual direction and counseling; house of prayer ministry; and administrative and office positions in diocesan and Vatican offices.

Not long after the Felician Sisters arrived in the United States they were involved in other ministries as they exercised "total availability and compassionate service" in response to the needs of the Polish immigrants and other persons. Nonetheless, because they were the only Polish community in the United States during their first eleven years, they were literally overwhelmed with more requests for teaching sisters than they could possibly accept. In 1885 they welcomed the arrival of the **Sisters of the Holy Family of Nazareth**, a Polish order that the Rev. Barzyński had invited to serve at St. Josaphat Parish in Chicago. In recounting the experiences of earlier immigrants before the arrival of the Felician Sisters and other Polish sisterhoods, there were references to the fact that youngsters had attended parochial schools taught by Polish lay teachers or Polish sisters who were members of German religious communities. With no opportunity to enter Polish communities, some Polish young women who wanted to become nuns joined the German congregations.

Polish immigrants, for the most part, believed very strongly that the parochial school was a bulwark of their faith and the repository of national culture and had come to realize that their faith was best preserved within the stabilizing atmosphere of their national language, traditions, and customs with which Catholic life in Poland had been inextricably woven. Of the 132 Polish parishes in existence during the last decade of the nineteenth century, 122 were conducting parochial schools. Convinced that the sisters' greatest influence was actualized in the parochial school, Father Dąbrowski wrote that "Through the schools, the sisters form good and upright citizens and devout and faithful sons of the Church." It was the shared belief and concern of the Rev. Dąbrowski, the Felician Sisters, and others that parochial schools conducted in Polish parishes would uphold the Catholic faith and preserve the Polish national heritage in the students and their families. On Sunday, November 22, 1874, the day after the Felician Sisters' arrival in Polonia, the Rev. Dąbrowski announced to the parishioners at Mass that the Felician Sisters had arrived from Kraków "to serve the Poles in their new homeland and to work especially for their children by instilling in their young hearts love, faith and obedience to God and the Catholic Church ... as well as love for their national heritage."

The Felician Sisters efforts in preserving the

Polish national heritage in language and culture were multi-faceted in that their endeavors were directed not only to the students in the classrooms, but also to the Felician Sisters American foundation and the new members who would be joining their ranks in the years ahead. In their convents Polish was the language of official correspondence used by the superiors and the language used for internal record keeping. Likewise religious ceremonies and community prayers, with the exception of Latin for public and private Church liturgies and prayer, were in the Polish language. They taught religion and the usual elementary school subjects and also endeavored to preserve the distinctive trait of the Polish parochial schools by teaching Polish language and culture. From the beginning, the sisters used both English and Polish in their schools. The Rev. Dąbrowski, however, insisted that both candidates and sisters should study English under a native American teacher, a tenet to which he adhered for the remainder of his life.

From their earliest years in the American classroom, the Felicians attempted to formulate programs of study that would include the regular curriculum requirements as well as Polish language, literature and history classes suited to the appropriate grade levels. With the later establishment of diocesan school boards and diocesan examinations, as well as with the regulating of county exams in the late 1800s, greater emphasis was placed on English; and the use of Polish was generally confined to Polish reading, religion, and Bible history. In many schools an even distribution between the use of the two languages prevailed. After World War I there were fewer newcomers from Poland due to immigration restriction cutting foreign-born enrollment in the country's Polish parochial schools. An increasing number of the children of immigrants did not understand or speak Polish. Beginning with the early 1920s, however, the American provinces took definite steps to continue the teaching of Polish in schools staffed by the Felicians. Mother Mary Bonaventure Stawska, superior general (1920–34), promoted two recommendations. She proposed that beginning with 1922 each American province would assign one sister to undertake graduate studies in Polish language and literature at the Jagiellonian University in Kraków. Provinces were quick to follow through with this directive so that when American sisters who were enrolled at the Jagiellonian would complete their degree requirements, sisters from their respective provinces would replace them and begin their Polish studies. With Germany's devastation of Poland in 1939 and the onset

Early organizers of the Felician Sisters in June 1900: from left, Sr. M. Anne Wysinski, Sr. M. Angeline Topolinski, Sr. M. Agnes Dzik, Sr. M. Theresa Dudzik (*PMA*).

of World War II, the American Embassy in Poland sent back to the United States by April of 1940 the American Felicians who were studying at the Jagiellonian. This Polish studies program for nuns of the American provinces was never reinstated after the Second World War owing to the communist control of Poland that severely restricted religious communities' involvement in service to the Church and ministry to the laity.

The American Felicians who completed their studies at the Jagiellonian were actively involved in the United States promoting the study of Polish language and culture in grade schools and high schools and at universities and colleges. They were also able to conduct in-service programs in Polish studies for the sisters of their own provinces. In her *Writings of the Felician Sisters in the United States* published in 1955, Sister Mary Charitina Hilburger records thirteen American Felicians who completed theses that were written to fulfill degree requirements at the Jagiellonian University between 1931 and 1939. There were additional sisters who had studied at the Jagiellonian, but whose degree work was interrupted with the onset of the Second World War. Of all these theses, which were written in the Polish language, five had been completed in 1931, two each in 1937 and 1938, and one each in four other years. Among the other 75 sisters who had completed theses to fulfill degree requirements at American colleges and universities, thirteen had done research on topics dealing with Polish issues in science, literature, music or on matters directly related to the Felician Sisters by way of ministry issues, history, or statistical outcomes. Of the 82 theses that Sister Hilburger listed for 1946 to 1954, most Felician Sisters wrote on Polish topics of historic importance or the development of Felician ministries, specific personalities, or provinces.

In her second recommendation, Mother Bonaventure proposed that the American Felicians meet annually to discuss topics of concern in their provinces respective teaching apostolates. This proposal resulted in the formation of the interprovincial Felician Education Association which held its first pedagogical convention in Detroit in 1932 under the leadership of Sister Mary Bronislaus Kajzer, director of education for the Detroit province. The second convention was held in Chicago in 1933; the third, in Buffalo in 1934; subsequent meetings were arranged in Coraopolis, Pennsylvania (1937), Lodi, New Jersey (1939), and Plymouth, Michigan (1941). Conventions were discontinued after 1941 due to wartime travel restrictions. During its brief tenure as a functioning entity, the association identified

mutual pedagogical concerns and proposed to achieve ongoing improvement in all subjects especially in religion and Polish. It issued decisions and directives in an effort to promote the teaching of Polish language and cultural awareness. About ten or more papers were read and discussed during the conventions which usually lasted three days. Printed copies of the papers were available after the conferences, some of which were published in pamphlet form.

Another project designed to encourage national pride and respect for ethnic values while also promoting the study and use of Polish by Felician students was the publication of three monthly periodicals beginning in 1924. Articles and contributions to the Polish-language publications were written mainly by students. A sister from each of the respective Felician provinces was the editor of the periodical. Sister Mary Ursula Górska (1924–39) and Sister Mary Alberica Osinski (1939–49) were editors of *Nasze Pisemko* (Our Pamphlet; 1924–49) published by the Detroit Felicians. *Ave Maria* (Hail Mary), with a lifetime of sixty-one years, was a timely periodical of the Felicians of the Buffalo province (1924–85) and had five editors: Sister Mary Alexander Kucharski (1924–26), Sister Mary Maurice Zalemska (1926–29), Sister Mary Pauline Pawlowski (1929–40), Sister Mary Amandine Faber (1941–51), and Sister Mary Donata Slominski (1951–85). Sister Mary Raymond Wons (1924–47) was editor of *Promyk* (The Ray), a publication of the Chicago (Milwaukee at the time) province. It appears that each of these periodicals, which also had an adult readership, enjoyed wide circulation even in parochial schools staffed by other religious congregations. Articles and contributions to the publications were written mainly by students and the editors. They reported cultural events of the local Polish community and visits of Polish dignitaries, as well as accounts of historical events, religious topics, literary achievements, and items of general interest. Felician Sisters of the Chicago province served as editors of the *Gość Niedzielny* (Sunday Guest) beginning with Sister Mary Paula Wyrozumialska (1916–34). The paper was published by St. Hedwig Printery, a project which the Rev. Francis Rusch established for the vocational training of young men at St. Hedwig Orphanage in Niles, Illinois, a child care institution operated by the Felicians.

What appears to have been a re-awakening of interest in Polish language and culture in Polish American parochial settings and education circles during the 1930s may have been an indirect outcome of the collaborative apostolic efforts of the Felician Sisters in provinces

across America who had studied at the Jagiellonian between 1922 and 1940. This enthusiastic response, as well as improved competence in use of the Polish language, both written and spoken, with an enhanced awareness of Polish history and culture conveyed by the American Felicians was further verification of the success of the European experience. This revival of Polish language and culture in schools generated requests for English-Polish resource materials and textbooks on all grade levels in the elementary and secondary schools. These requests came not just from Felician-sponsored schools and institutions, but from many that were under the sponsorship of other Polish sisterhoods. At the outset of their teaching mission in Polonia, the absence of textbooks in the Polish language was a concern of the Felician pioneers in Polonia. Because the school children and adults, as well, did not understand English at first, and many sisters could hardly understand their spoken Polish, the need for a mutual language denominator was even more critical. Underlying this problem was the fact that the early-arriving Poles from the Prussian partition of Poland spoke a Polish vernacular mixed with Germanisms. Their dialect, therefore, was quite different from that of the Poles of the Russian and Austrian sectors. With the later arrival of Polish-language Bibles, primers, catechisms, and Bible histories, the communication problem was resolved. The need for Polish textbooks, nevertheless, continued and became even more critical as the number of schools increased.

Mother Monica compiled a Polish reader in 1877 using excerpts from European books which she had. The Rev. Dąbrowski purchased additional printing equipment and supplies and taught the sisters and aspirants how to set type, run the press, and bind the books. By the end of 1879 the first Polish reader appeared along with a geography book composed by the Rev. Dąbrowski. Later in 1881, he published an arithmetic manual. Eventually more books on various subjects were published, such as geographies, arithmetic, histories, and readers. The Polish textbooks which the Rev. Dąbrowski and the Felician Sisters compiled were for youngsters who did not know English. The Polish-language textbooks that came out in the 1930s and 1940s were printed for youngsters who did not know Polish and were widely distributed out of a genuine concern about the declining use of the Polish language. While several American Felicians from various provinces prepared Polish textbooks, catechisms, readers, and workbooks that were widely used, no one was as prolific as Sister Mary Cyryla Tabaka of the Chicago province.

Between 1928 and 1940 her sole assignment was the writing of plays, poems, articles, and textbooks promoting the study and appreciation of the Polish language and culture. In all, Sister Cyryla wrote thirteen textbooks that were published between 1933 and 1945: five Polish grammars, five Polish readers, a book on Polish history, a volume on Polish culture, and one book on the history of the Church.

Justice and peace issues, solidarity, multicultural diversity, ecumenism, and responsible stewardship of creation became community watchwords during the 1980s and 1990s. The Felician Community's twenty-first general chapter in 2000 adopted the statement: "Turn to the Lord your God, be Eucharist, be Sister, be Servant to all." Interprovincial meetings and projects, along with Congregational events of 1993 and 1999, enabled many Polish and American sisters to experience one another's camaraderie in their respective homelands. Pope John Paul II proclaimed the foundress Blessed Mary Angela at beatification ceremonies in St. Peter's Basilica in 1993. In 1999 there was a celebration of the Felician Sisters' 125th anniversary in North America.

Analogous to the graduate programs of Polish language and literature studies at the Jagiellonian which American Felicians had begun in 1922, Felician Sisters of the Polish provinces were engaged in the serious study of the English language beginning in the 1990s that continued into the third millennium. One phase of this program called for a yearlong appointment of a qualified American Felician Sister to each of the Polish provinces who was to conduct English language classes for larger groups of sisters. In other aspects of the program, Polish sisters were appointed to an American province with a Felician-sponsored college and access to classes in English as a Second Language through adult education programs in the area. Sisters who were selected for these study programs were later appointed to serve as translators for Congregational assemblies, general chapters and other events as well as translators of community documents, manuscripts and various texts.

Several sisters of the Warsaw province who were sent on a mission to Kenya were also enrolled as English language students in the United States. In addition to the benefits of a working knowledge of English which the Polish sisters acquired, these programs mutually benefited both the Polish and American Felicians in terms of personal contacts and closer relationships with members of the community that resulted in a deeper understanding and appreciation of their respective cultures.

During the first decades of the twentieth century membership in the Felician Congregation continued to increase in the United States as provinces were established according to growth rates and demographic boundaries. The establishment of American provinces started in 1874 ended in 1953 with a total of eight provinces. The life and ministry of the Felician Sisters in the twentieth century reflected the changing scene in American society as well as the Congregation's adaptations in a changing Church. Continuing the ministries which their predecessors had accepted in the last decades of the nineteenth century, the Felician community not only expanded its role of service but also experienced changes in membership that virtually skyrocketed in the 1960s followed by a dramatic decline later that same decade. In the late 1990s, the issue of diminishing membership, along with other concerns, and their impact on the viability of the Felician Sisters' mission in the years ahead came under serious scrutiny.

In an effort to assure the viability of the Felician mission for years to come, the Sisters were engaged in a lengthy process of more than ten years of planning, meetings, discussion, and discernment about the future of the Felician mission in North America. Recognizing the diminishing numbers and aging membership of the North American provinces, the Sisters decided to reconfigure the eight provinces into one juridic entity, a single province. This new, more efficient entity was expected to reduce the number of Sisters needed for administration, maximize the resources of the Sisters for the sake of the province's mission, and allow the Sisters to undertake new ventures for the Church in new places as needed. On November 1, 2008, Sister Mary Barbara Ann Bosch, minister general, announced the establishment of the Our Lady of Hope province effective November 21, 2009, with a membership of nearly 1,000 sisters. Election of the new leadership team for a term of six-years, consisting of a provincial minister, provincial vicar, and six provincial councilors, took place at a Chapter of Elections at the St. John Center in Plymouth, Michigan, on April 20, 2009. Installation of the leadership team was conducted at the opening Mass for the new province in St. Cecilia Church, Rochester, Beaver County, Pennsylvania. Administration offices for the new province were established in the Our Lady of Hope Center. Each of the eight former North American provinces has one sister representing it on the new leadership team. Sister Mary Christopher Moore, provincial minister of the new province, the former provincial minister of Our Lady of the Sacred Heart province, Coraopolis, Pennsylvania said, "For more than a century-and-a-half, the Felician Sisters have pursued the vision of Blessed Mary Angela to be 'sister and servant to all.' This new configuration will allow us to more effectively meet the needs of the times and to fulfill the mission of the Congregation which is to cooperate with Christ in the spiritual renewal of the world."—*M. Janice Ziolkowski*

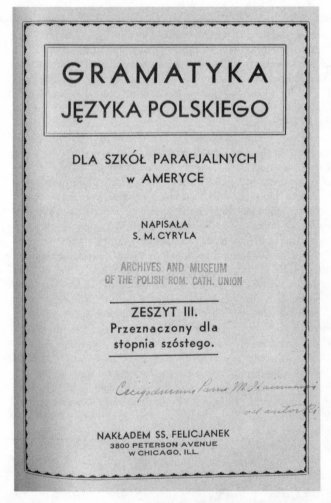

One of the textbooks published by the Felician Sisters to facilitate instruction of Polish grammar (*PMA*).

SOURCES: Dorota Praszałowicz, "Polish American Sisterhood: The Americanization Process," *U.S. Catholic Historian*, Vol. 27, no. 3 (2009), 45–57; Sr. Mary Angela, "The Felician Sisters and Social Service," *Polish American Studies*, Vol. III, no. 1–2 (1946), 21–29; Sr. Mary Charitina, "Writings of the Felician Sisters in the United States," *Polish American Studies*, Vol. III, no. 3–4 (1946), 65–97; Sr. Mary Charitina, "Bibliography of the Writings of the Felician Sisters in the United States 1946–1954," *Polish American Studies*, Vol. 11, no. 3–4 (1954), 78–97; Sr. Mary Amandine, "Seventy-Five Years of Felician Activity in America," *Polish American Studies*, Vol. VI, no. 3–4 (1949), 65–79; Sr. Mary Liguori, "Seventy-five Years of Childcare," *Polish American Studies*, Vol. 10, no. 1–2 (1953), 13–39; Sr. Mary Tullia Doman, "Mother Angela Truszkowska, Foundress of the Felician Sisters," *Polish American Studies*, Vol. 10, no. 3–4 (1953), 65–94; Sr. M. Tullia Doman, ed., "Polish American Sisterhoods and Their Contribution to the Catholic Church in the U.S.," *Sacrum Poloniae Millenium*, Vol. 6, 371–622; Sr. Mary Jeremiah, "Father Dąbrowski and the Felicians," *Polish American Studies*, Vol. 16, no. 1–2 (1959), 12–23; Thaddeus C. Radzialowski, "Reflections on the History of the Felicians in America," *Polish American Studies*, Vol. 32, no. 1 (1975), 19–28; Sr. M. Charitina Hilburger, "Writings of the Felician Sisters in the United States," *Polish American Studies* Vol. 3, no. 3–4 (July–December, 1946), 65–97; Maria Winowska, *Go Repair My House* (Lodi, NJ: Congregation of the Sisters of Saint Felix, 1972); Sr. M. Janice Ziolkowski, *The Felician Sisters of Livonia, Michigan* (Detroit: Harlo Press, 1984); Sr. Ellen Marie Kuznicki, *Journey in Faith: The History of the Immaculate Heart of Mary Province of the Felician Sisters, Buffalo, New York, 1900–1976* (Buffalo: Felician Sisters, Immaculate Heart of Mary Province, 1996); Sister Mary Amadeus Ruda, CSSF, "The New England Province of the Felician Sisters," in Stanlisaus A. Blejwas and M. B. Biskupski, eds., *Pastor of the Poles: Polish American Essays Presented to Right Reverend Monsignor John P. Wodarski in Honor of the Fiftieth Anniversary of His Ordination* (New Britain, CT: Polish Studies Program, Central Connecticut State College, 1982); Josephine Marie Peplinski, *A Fitting Response: The History of the Sisters of St. Joseph of the Third Order of St. Francis* (South Bend, IN: n.p., 1982); Leonard Anthony Drewek, "The Felician Sisters in the United States" (Unpublished M.A. thesis, St. Francis Seminary, 1939); Mary Theophania Kalinowski, "The First Decade of the Sisters of Saint Felix in America, 1874–1884" (Unpublished M.A. thesis, Loyola University–Chicago, 1956).

Ferguson, Christopher John (b. Philadelphia, Pennsylvania, September 1, 1961; d. —). Astronaut. The son of Mary Ann Florkowski Pietras, he received his B.S. degree from Drexel University in 1984 and his M.S. in Aeronautical Engineering from the Naval Postgraduate School in 1991. Earning his wings as a U.S. Navy fighter pilot, he served aboard the aircraft carrier USS *Forrestal* until 1994 when he was chosen as an instructor at the Naval Test Pilot School. In 1995 he was assigned as a pilot aboard the USS *Nimitz* before being selected for the space program in 1998. He served as pilot of the Space Shuttle *Atlantis* on a mission to install solar panels on the International Space Station (2006). His honors include the Navy Strike/Flight Air Medal, three Navy Commendation Medals, and the Navy Achievement Medal.—*James S. Pula*

SOURCE: www.jsc.nasa.gov/Bios/htmlbios/ferguson.html.

Feynman, Richard Phillips (b. New York, New York, May 11, 1918; d. Los Angeles, California, February 15, 1988). Physicist. Born to be a scientist, Feynman taught himself calculus and set up his own laboratory while still a child. A graduate of the Massachusetts Institute of Technology, he received his B.Sc. in 1939 and went on to Princeton. Prior to World War II he worked at the Frankfort Arsenal in Philadelphia helping to develop a mechanical computer for directing artillery. While only in his twenties, he was a group leader at Los Alamos, New Mexico, charged with helping develop the atomic bomb during the Manhattan Project. He did not endear himself to Los Alamos security people by using his spare time to demonstrate how easy it was to crack safes containing classified documents. After World War II, he became a professor at Cornell University, and ultimately the California Institute of Technology. Feynman developed a quantum theory of magnetism and electricity which resolved inaccuracies in earlier theories of quantum electrodynamics pertaining to the actions of atoms in radiation fields. He developed the Feynman diagram to account for atomic particle transformation, which became standard equipment for the study of elementary particles. Feynman has made major contributions to the study of the decay of radioactive particles, the internal structure of the atomic nucleus, and the theory of liquid helium. In 1986, President Ronald Reagan appointed him to the commission investigating the Space Shuttle *Challenger* disaster and he isolated the cause as frozen "O" rings. He is the author of *The Character of Physical Law; QED: The Strange Theory of Light and Matter; What Do You Care What Other People Think; Six Easy Pieces* and *No Ordinary Genius*. His numerous honors

Richard Feynman, the physicist who isolated the "O-rings" as the cause of the space shuttle *Challenger* disaster (OLS).

include the Albert Einstein Award (1954), E. O. Lawrence Award (1962), Nobel Prize in Physics (1965), Oersted Medal (1972), The Niels Bohr International Gold Medal (1973), and the National Medal of Science (1979).—*Cheryl A. Pula*

SOURCES: Richard Feynman, *No Ordinary Genius: The Illustrated Richard Feynman* (New York: Norton, 1994); Richard Feynman, *Surely You're Joking, Mr. Feynman: Adventures of a Curious Character* (New York: Norton, 1985); Richard Feynman, *What Do You Care What Other People Think?: Further Adventures of a Curious Character* (New York: Bantam, 1989); James Gleick, *Genius: the Life and Science of Richard Feynman* (New York: Vintage Books, 1992); John R. Gribbin, *Richard Feynman: A Life in Science* (New York: Dutton, 1997).

Fiction *see* **Literature, Polish American.**

Fidrych, Mark (b. Worcester, Massachusetts, August 14, 1954; d. Northborough, Massachusetts, April 13, 2009). Baseball player. A right-handed pitcher for the Detroit Tigers from 1976 to 1980, Mark Fidrych turned in one of the most spectacular rookie seasons in the history of major league baseball. In 1976, he won 19 games, led the American League in earned run average and complete games, and was selected as the AL starting pitcher in the All-Star game. According to the calculations of the *Total Baseball* encyclopedia, Fidrych was the best pitcher in the American League that year. Nicknamed "The Bird," he became an overnight celebrity and gate attraction owing to his appealing personality and good natured idiosyncrasies on the field, such as talking to the baseball before delivering his pitch. Although he was selected to the All-Star team again in 1977, injuries diminished and shortened his career, and Fidrych won only ten more games over the four seasons that followed his rookie campaign. Following his retirement from baseball, he farmed in his native Massachusetts, and died in an accident involving his truck. In 2009, he was inducted into the National Polish-American Sports Hall of Fame.—*Neal Pease*

SOURCE: Mark Fidrych and Tom Clark, *No Big Deal* (Philadelphia: Lippincott, 1977).

Figas, Rev. Justin (Michael Figas; b. Everson, Pennsylvania, June 24, 1886; d. Buffalo, New York, October 23, 1959). Priest, journalist. The Very Reverend Justin M. Figas served as a provincial of the **Franciscan Friars Minor Conventual** and became a pioneer in the field of religious broadcasting. One of twelve children, at the age of seven he was stricken with infantile paralysis. Praying for a cure, his father promised that if he recovered, his son would lead a life of service to God. To this end, despite having only the limited income of a coal miner, Jacob Figas enrolled his son into St. Francis High School in Trenton, NJ. Michael entered the Franciscan novitiate of the Immaculate Conception in Syracuse at the age of 17, and professed his first vows the following year. As a Franciscan, he then assumed the name of Justin. After attending college in New Jersey, he completed his studies in Rome where he received a doctorate in sacred theology from the Collegio Seraphico. After his ordination, Father Justin returned to the United States in 1911 to begin parish work at St. Josaphat's Basilica in Milwaukee. This assignment lasted only three years as Figas was elected to the position of Secretary of his province in July 1914, moving to the provincial headquarters in Buffalo where he would live for the remainder of his life. In 1921, at meetings in Rome, Figas declined election as secretary general of the Conventual Franciscans, preferring to continue his work in America where he gained election to the position of Provincial of St. Anthony Province in 1923. Although provincials were normally limited to six years of service, he continued in that position until 1939. During his tenure as provincial the Franciscans established St. Hyacinth Seminary in Granby, Massachusetts; St. Joseph Cupertino Novitiate in Ellicott City, MD; St. Francis High School in Athol Springs, NY; and numerous parishes to serve the Polish communities of America. In 1929, he began a radio ministry that became known as *The Rosary Hour*. Conducted in the Polish language, *The Rosary Hour* attracted an estimated audience of five million listeners. Personally delivering more than 750 broadcasts,

The Rev. Justin Figas, originator of the popular *Rosary Hour* radio show (*OLS*).

Fr. Justin continued his radio ministry after completing his term as provincial. As a respected religious leader, he was frequently asked to assume important civic roles, serving as a labor mediator, most notably in the settlement of disputes at the Duffy and Millfoy Silk Mills in Buffalo and at a mill in Milwaukee. In May of 1939, he delivered the homily at services in St. Patrick's Cathedral to celebrate the opening of the Polish Pavilion at the New York World's Fair. During World War II, he twice undertook special missions to Europe. After visiting refugee camps in the Balkans in 1939, Figas wrote a book entitled *Vacuum in Hell* about the plight of Slavic refugees. In 1942, at the request of President Roosevelt, he visited Great Britain to meet with leaders of the Polish underground and to visit Polish and American troops. He described this experience in another of his many books, which he entitled *From Canada to Great Britain by Bomber*. After the Second World War, Father Justin led civic efforts to expand health care service in Western New York through the construction of what became known as St. Joseph's Intercommunity Hospital. His many awards included the title Definitor General, the highest distinction given by the Conventual Franciscan Order; the Fidelitas Medal of **Sts. Cyril and Methodius Seminary**; and the Officer's Cross of Polonia Restituta from the government of Poland.—*Carl L. Bucki*

SOURCES: Stanisław Hajkowski, "Father Justyn and the Rosary Hour," *U.S. Catholic Historian*, Vol. 27, no. 3 (2009), 59–82; "Father Justin, Kindly Friar of 'Rosary Hour' is Dead," *Buffalo Evening News*, October 23, 1959, 27; "Founding of Father Justin Rosary Hour to be Noted," *Buffalo Courier Express*, July 21, 1969, 37; Milton J. Kobielski, ed., *Millennium of Christianity of the Polish People: 966–1966* (Buffalo: Millennium Committee of the Diocese of Buffalo, 1966).

Fine Arts, Polish Americans in. During the past two centuries, the presence of Polish-born and American-born artists of Polish descent in the fine arts in the United States has been impressive. Their participation is documented by exhibition catalogs, books and monographs, and by public sculpture installations in a number of American cities. Prominent Polish artists showed as a group at the World's Columbian Exposition in Chicago (1893), the Mid-Winter Exhibition in San Francisco (1894), and the Louisiana Purchase Exhibition in Saint Louis (1904). At each venue they received prizes and favorable press notices. These international events constituted an important forum of political solidarity and race pride, since Poland did not officially exist at the time, having been partitioned since 1795 among Russia, Prussia and Austria.

Artists of Polish descent have participated in important exhibitions hosted among others by the Metropolitan Museum in New York, Pennsylvania Academy of Fine Arts in Philadelphia, Corcoran Gallery in Washington, D.C., Carnegie Institute in Pittsburgh, Chicago Art Institute, Albright-Knox Gallery in Buffalo, Cleveland Museum of Art and the Milwaukee Art Museum. These artists' paintings, works on paper and sculptures have been acquired by leading American museums and cultural institutions for their permanent collections. Some of the artists have been honored by retrospective exhibitions and are the subject of books and monographs, such as **Richard Anuszkiewicz**, **Julian Stanczak**, **Richard Stankiewicz**, Paul Pletka, **Stanislaus Szukalski**, **Elie Nadelman**, **Arthur Szyk**, **Andrzej Pityński**, and Andrzej Dudziński. Several published books themselves, including **W.T. Benda**, *Masks* (1944), and Stanislaus Szukalski, *Projects in Design* (1931) and *The Work of Szukalski* (1923).

The place of the Polish community in American fine arts has only been sporadically researched and documented. A relatively small number of political exiles came to New York and Philadelphia following the unsuccessful insurrections against Poland's partitioners in 1830-31, 1848, and 1863, but the Polish ethnic group only attained its sizable presence in America in the last quarter of the nineteenth century. The Polish community is generally associated with the ethnic enclaves of large industrial centers in the East and Midwest. Like other immigrant communities of the time, the Poles established many fraternal organizations, parishes (primarily Roman Catholic), newspapers, radio programs, theatrical and literary societies and dance groups. Most of the historical and sociological studies have focused on these aspects of the Polish experience in America because they have been considered traditionally as the essential components of ethnic life.

Although artists of Polish descent often lived in or participated in various Polish communities in the Untied States, they often led very separate lives as artists. This not only resulted from the very nature of the creative process, but also from the fact that as artists they more quickly found acceptance by the American mainstream. Professional contacts with art schools, dealers, galleries, museums and collectors took artists beyond their immediate neighborhood and immigrant community.

The fine arts are missing from or only briefly considered in compendiums about the Polish community in America published on both sides of the Atlantic in the last thirty years. This can be explained by the two conflicting definitions of identity confronting the community for more than a century. Like most immigrant groups in America, the Poles have experienced the strong homogenization and assimilation pressures of American society and culture. At the same time — especially during the era of mass immigration at the turn of the nineteenth century — the Poles in America viewed themselves through the prism of their partitioned homeland. The Polish ethnic community, deprived of a political identity for some 125 years while Poland was under partition, recognized the need to maintain a strong national identity in their new homeland to insure group strength and cohesion.

Against this background, two barometers of accomplishment were at work simultaneously — one for the ethnic community as a whole, and a second of all artists of Polish descent in America. Ethnic groups proudly point to the political and economic recognition accorded individual members by the "establishment" as a measure of achievement for the entire group. Collective striving for economic success to gain acceptance from the large community directly contrasted with the artists' need to preserve individual identity as essential to the creative process.

The artists of Polish descent discussed in this essay were recognized in their day by the professional art critics whose reviews, though not always complimentary, appeared regularly in the American newspapers of New York, Philadelphia, Buffalo, Cleveland, Chicago, and Milwaukee. These cities were also home to some of the largest Polish American communities in the United States. Community support for the fine arts was exemplified by the annual exhibitions held in the late 1920s and 1930s under the auspices of the Polish Arts Club of Chicago, which became the catalyst for the establishment after the Second World War of the American Council of Polish Cultural Clubs (see **American Council for Polish Culture**). These exhibits featured work by artists of Polish descent from the Great Metro Chicago area, such as **Theodore Roszak**, John Szynalik Fabion, Leon Makielski, and Harriet and **Walter Krawiec**. The Polish Arts Club also solicited pieces from Polish artists, such as California-based Max Wieczorek, and from Wojciech Kossak and Gustaw Gwozdecki who had recently visited the United States. Often held at the Home Bank in the heart of Chicago's "Polish Triangle," the club's art exhibitions were reviewed in the *Chicago Tribune*, *Post* and *Journal*. Eleanor Jewett's review of the 1928 exhibition for the *Tribune* ("City's Varied People Do

Their Share in the Art Life of Chicago") not only displayed her dislike of modernism, but also reflected the aloofness of members of the cultural establishment toward "homegrown" American talent of East European origin.

Regardless of controversial reviews and the different historical periods in which they lived, artists of Polish descent have been inspired to create work in America which has become an integral part of the country's cultural heritage. From the standpoint of the European-American relationship, their creative output deserves better exposure in Poland, because they have remained conscious of and cherished their ethnic background. The following sections of this essay survey a select number of them who successfully established themselves in the American cultural milieu. Although not constituting a homogenous group, Polish-born and American artists of Polish descent have been chosen from this two-hundred-year period to illustrate the variety of styles, media and sources of inspiration.

EARLY 19TH CENTURY — POLITICAL ARTIST-EXILES

Known for his military record in Europe and America, **Thaddeus Kościuszko** was also a good amateur artist and the first prominent Pole with a documented portfolio to come to the United States. As one of two Polish-born heroes of the American Revolutionary War, he and his comrade-in-arms, **Casimir Pułaski**, later became subjects for the paintings and sculptures of some of the professional artists of Polish descent working in the United States in the nineteenth and twentieth centuries. A gifted student at the Cadets Corps in Warsaw, a military academy under royal patronage, Kościuszko received a scholarship from King Stanisław Poniatowski to go to France in 1769. There he not only supplemented his knowledge of military engineering which later helped secure Continental victories during the American Revolution, but also studied architecture, painting and drawing at the Royal Academy of Paintings and Sculpture. Several drawings from his Paris sojourn, preserved in the Czartoryski Museum in Kraków, Poland, attest to his artistic talent. He later did a number of portraits and scenes based on his travels in Europe and America.

Following Kościuszko, the first Polish artists active in the United States arrived in New York in 1834. They were part of a group of 235 political exiles whom the Austrian government had forcibly deported from its territory following the collapse of the November 1830 Insurrection against tsarist Russia. Most of them belonged to the Polish gentry class, but their participation in the insurrection re-

sulted in permanent separation from their families and the loss of their fortunes and social position. Although the American public was initially sympathetic to their plight, the funds collected for them by several volunteer committees eventually ran out. Because many of the exiles lacked marketable skills and were not accustomed to hard work, they experienced great hardships while eking out a living as they learned English and adjusted to the new realities of life in Jacksonian America. Most of the exiles remained in the populated states along the Eastern Seaboard, with a smaller number relocating to the Midwest and Far West in search of economic opportunities.

The National Academy of Design in New York, one of the country's leading art institutions at that time, included paintings by F. Faliński and J.A. Nendzyński (Miedzyński) in its annual exhibitions in the early 1840s. Several of the exiles offered private art instruction and gained positions as teachers in local academies or female seminaries, as they were then known. Frederick Hulaniski (Hulanicki), a resident of Auburn, New York in the 1830s, provided initial instruction in wood engraving to John Chester Buttre, who later established a large engraving business in New York.

Felix Gwinczewski, a native of Volhynia and a member of the six-man Polish Committee constituted in New York in 1834, settled in Wilmington, Delaware, where he opened a drawing, painting and French school in 1839. In 1845-46 he was a "teacher of perspective, drawing and painting, etc." at the Wesleyan Female Collegiate Institute in the same city. Gwinczewski's associate on the committee, Martin Rosienkiewicz, studied art as a young man at the Krzemieniec Liceum (Middle School) in Ukraine with Vienna-trained portraitist, Josef Pitschmann, and later taught at the school. Rosienkiewicz spent his first years in the United States in Philadelphia where in 1834 he published a handbook, *Dialogues to Facilitate the Acquisition of the English Language by the Polish Emigrants*. Five years later he moved to Ohio, teaching painting, drawing, dancing and French at the Chillicothe Female Seminary and later "Linear and Perspective Drawing and Painting" at the Wesleyan College for Young Women in Cincinnati where he spent his last years.

Of the Polish artist-exiles in America in the wake of the November Insurrection, Seweryn Cichowski (Severin Cichocki; **Charles Severin**/Severyn) was one of the few who enjoyed a recognized art career. He worked for three decades as a professional lithographer on his own and for leading companies in Philadelphia and New York. A member of the military unit whose attack on the Belvedere Palace on the night of November 29, 1830, triggered the insurrection, he fled with General Gielgud's Corps to Prussia after its collapse and then made his way to France from which he relocated to the United States in 1841.

Initially he was associated with Pierre S. Duval, and then with the firm of Huddy and Duval (both in Philadelphia) for whom he did prints published in the *United States Military Magazine*. By 1845 he was living in New York where he anglicized his name to Charles Severin to facilitate pronunciation and recognition. He produced prints for several important firms, including Currier and Ives. Two of his images occupy an important place in nineteenth-century American lithography: *Peytona and Fashion* (1845), a horse racing print "drawn from nature" of a match held on May 13, 1845, at the Union Course in Queens, New York; and *Husking* (1861), a print of Eastman Johnson's painting of the same title.

Henry Dmochowski-Saunders, Cichowski's contemporary, similarly came via France to the United States where he became a noted sculptor in the decade preceding the American Civil War. A graduate of the University of Wilno (Vilnius) in Lithuania, he engaged in underground political activities in partitioned Poland after the November Insurrection. Apprehended during the Zaliwski Expedition in Galicia (the Austrian sector of partitioned Poland) and imprisoned for four years at Kufstein Castle in Bavaria, he later joined a number of Polish political exiles in France where he belonged to the liberal *Towarzystwo Demokratyczne* (Democratic Society). In Paris he studied sculpture at the Ecole des Beaux-Arts and in the studio of François Rude whom he assisted with the work on Napoleon's sarcophagus.

When Dmochowski arrived in New York in 1852 via England, the city was home to a number of Poles, including Count Marceli Lubomirski of Dubno. Lubomirski befriended Cyprian Norwid during the Polish poet's brief stay in New York (1853-54) where he earned a modest living furnishing elaborate drawings on wood of ornamented initials to Carl Emil Doepler, a German printmaker whom he knew from Alexander Kokular's art school in Warsaw. The initials appeared among 500 illustrations in a sumptuous album, *The World of Science, Art, and Industry, Illustrated from Examples in the New York Exhibition, 1853-54*, jointly published by G.P. Putnam and Company in New York and Sampson Low, Son & Co., in London.

During his American sojourn, Dmochowski resided principally in Philadelphia, but also lived at various times in Washington, D.C., and Savannah, Georgia. Reminiscent of Cichowski's earlier name change, he went by Henry D. Saunders — the pseudonym he previously used during the unsuccessful Zaliwski Expedition in 1833. The decade he spent in America coincided with the maturation of his artistic talent. In the 1850s he showed his marble sculptures and plaster bas-reliefs in the prestigious annual exhibitions of the Pennsylvania Academy of Fine Arts in Philadelphia. His medallions featuring the likenesses of American political figures such as Henry Clay, Andrew Jackson, and Daniel Webster reflected the influence of French sculptor, David d'Angers whom he met in France.

Dmochowski's most frequently-cited works are the monument to his deceased wife, Helen Schaff, and their two infant children at Laurel Hill Cemetery in Philadelphia, as well as his life-size marble busts of Casimir Pułaski and Thaddeus Kościuszko at the U.S. Capitol in Washington, D.C. In 1861 Dmochowski returned to Europe, settling in his native Wilno where he maintained a studio and sculpted statues for the local cathedral. During the January 1863 Insurrection against tsarist Russia he died in a skirmish with a band of Cossack soldiers.

Although not an artist-exile, Max Rosenthal, a native of Turek near Kalisz in the Russian sector of partitioned Poland, merits mention as a lithographer, etcher and painter. He came to the United States in 1849 with his Paris lithographer teacher, Martin Thurwanger, to produce lithographs for the U.S. government. He partnered with his brother, Louis, in Rosenthal's Lithography, printing some of the earliest American chromolithographs. An official illustrator for the United States Military Commission during the Civil War, he did a series of Civil War encampments as well as several hundred portrait prints of famous American political and military figures.

The influx of argonauts to California in the wake of the 1848 Gold Rush included artist-exile lithographer, Alexander (Alex) Zakrzewski (Zakreski). Around 1850 he opened a topographical office in San Francisco where he pursued his profession until 1857, after which he was employed for a time as a draughtsman by the local U.S. Surveyor General's Office. In 1850 he and J.W. Hartman produced a unique documentary lithograph of the procession crossing the Plaza of San Francisco in celebration of California's admission to the Union as a state on October 19 of that year.

The trans-Mississippi west likewise attracted Stanislaus W.Y. Schimonski (Tzschu-

mansky, Schimonsky) who immigrated to the United States around 1850, perhaps a refugee from the Revolution of 1848 in Europe. Settling in the vicinity of Bellevue, Nebraska, about 1852 where he owned and operated a farm, he did pen and ink illustrations tinted with watercolor of Indians and local landmarks which have historical importance as early views of the area.

Two decades later he befriended amateur artist, Bolesław Horodyński, a veteran of the January 1863 Insurrection, who made Nebraska his home in the 1870s. Going by the more pronounceable name of Frank Stadter, Horodyński initially lived in Plattsmouth where he painted portraits of some of the local residents and became an American citizen. From 1877 to 1878 he taught painting and drawing at the University of Nebraska in Lincoln. After returning to his native Poland in 1881, he served as U.S. vice-consul based in Warsaw.

Actively homesteaded after the building of the railroad in the 1860s, Nebraska also figured in the itinerary of Napoleon Ledochowski's sketching trip in the summer of 1870. Resulting in a large number of drawings in pencil, pen and ink and watercolor, the trip was part of an extensive excursion he undertook that year from Chicago through the Great Lakes region to Montréal, Canada, to acquaint himself with his new homeland. Born in France to a Polish father and a French mother, he immigrated to New York in 1869 and soon thereafter established himself as an artist and a teacher of the piano and violin in Chicago where he lived for the rest of his life. He also showed his paintings in the annual exhibitions of The Art Institute of Chicago in the 1880s.

AMERICA'S GILDED AGE

The post–Civil War era through World War I coincided with America's coming of age and development as a world power using the resources from its Western Expansion and Industrial Revolution. The new wealth derived from cheap immigrant labor in mines, mills and factories throughout the country created a new class of plutocrats seeking to display their gentility and sophistication through the construction of huge mansions, creation of art collections, and the endowment of museums and libraries. Their patronage, within the context of creating an American political and economic empire, helped foster an interest in the arts which in turn created opportunities for artists, including those from partitioned Poland.

The largest group showing by Polish artists at an American venue prior to World War I occurred at the World's Columbian Exposition in Chicago in 1893. Organized to commemorate the 400th anniversary of Christopher Columbus's landfall in the New World, the exposition featured an international display of fine art as well as monumental exhibition palaces crammed with the latest achievements in industrial and agricultural production. In Room 62 of the Fine Arts Palace the Society of Polish Artists presented 125 oil paintings by participants, principally from Warsaw and Kraków, plus John Ciagliński from St. Petersburg, Russia.

Among the well-recognized names were Anna Bilińska, Joseph Chelmonski, Wojciech Gerson, A. Kedzierski, Wojciech Kossak, Franciszek Kostrzewski, Jan Matejko, Władysław Podkowiński, Włodzimierz Tetmajer, and Franciszek Zmurko. Although smaller and more modest than the exhibitions mounted by the United States, England, France, Germany and Italy, the Polish contribution was organized without any state support because Poland did not officially exist, but was still in national captivity by Russia, Prussia and Austria. Enthusiastically discussed in the Polish-language press in America, the Polish representation in Chicago in 1893 constituted a departure from the previous practice of Polish artists showing at international exhibitions in the sections allotted to the nation's three partitioners. The Society of Polish Artists' exhibit in 1893 provided an organizational model adopted after 1897 by the Kraków-based Sztuka (Art) group — also known in English as the Society of Polish Artists — for the impressive Polish representation at the Louisiana Purchase Exposition in St. Louis in 1904.

Among the throngs visiting the Chicago Exposition was Milwaukee resident, **Thaddeus Zukotyński**. An alumnus of the Fine Arts Academy in Munich which attracted a number of Polish students in the late nineteenth century, he was part of a group of artists recruited in Germany in the mid–1880s by August Lohr for the American Panorama Company in Milwaukee. At that time the city was in the forefront of panorama painting in the United States. Zukotyński was one of five figure painters working on the *Cyclorama of the Battle of Atlanta* for the city of Atlanta, Georgia, and the *Jerusalem Panorama*, among others. When the panorama business started to wane, he started specializing in the early 1890s in large-scale commissions for Polish and German Catholic parishes in Wisconsin, Illinois, Indiana and Kansas.

The growing number of Polish immigrants establishing parishes in the Northeast and Midwest in the late nineteenth and early twentieth centuries likewise provided employment for other Polish-born artists connected with the Munich School. Felix Bogdański worked for several decades in New Jersey before returning to Poland in 1930; and Stanisław Grocholski, who came to the United States in 1901, eventually settled in Buffalo, New York, where he painted portraits and worked for a time in the local Polish consulate.

Munich Academy alumnus Jan Chelmiński achieved recognition and financial success in Europe and America as a society portraitist and painter of sporting and hunting scenes reminiscent of Maximillian Gierymski. Chelmiński benefited from the promotional resources of Roland Knoedler, his brother-in-law and prominent antique dealer in Paris. Chelmiński, who visited New York in 1884 and later made it his home during World War I, was collected by Poles in Europe and America who related to his canvases of Thaddeus Kościuszko and of the Duchy of Warsaw created by Napoleon. Karl Witkowski, a Galician native and a Munich Academy alumnus, specialized in genre subjects and portraiture in New York and New Jersey in the late nineteenth century. Anecdotal scenes of daily life appealed to the rising American middle class in the post–Civil War era. Analogous to his American counterpart, John George Brown, he depicted newspaper boys, street urchins and youngsters playing baseball and engaging in a variety of pranks which were exhibited at the National Academy of Design in New York and at the Newark Public Library.

Like her better-known colleague Anna Bilińska-Bohdanowiczowa, Kasimira (Casimira) Dziekońska was educated in Paris, the international art capital providing an alternative to the Munich School and similarly attracting a large number of Polish-born artists. Perhaps encouraged by some of the Americans she met there, she relocated to the United States about 1893, living successively in Boston, Chicago and New York where she became known as a portraitist and pastelist. Much like Chelmiński, she maintained contact with Poland, periodically sending her work for exhibition at the Zacheta Gallery in Warsaw to which she retired at age eighty having spent more than three decades in America.

The Society of Polish Artists' display at the World's Columbian Exposition in 1893 and its manifestation of national pride inspired the leadership of Chicago's growing Polish immigrant community to commission a life-size equestrian statue of Thaddeus Kościuszko from Kazimierz Chodziński, a graduate of the Vienna Fine Arts Academy. One of the first large public sculptures on a Polish subject in the United States, it was formally dedicated at Humboldt Park in 1904. The enthusiasm generated by the success of this undertaking turned the Polish American leadership's attention to Washington, D.C. With the influx of Polish immigrants after 1900, they realized the potential of the nation's capital as a forum for underscoring their community's place alongside other more established ethnic groups in the United States. They did so by highlighting the contribution of their forebears — Kościuszko and Pułaski — toward the formation of the American Republic rendered through volunteer service in the American Revolutionary War. The result was two life-size statues whose fundraising was spearheaded by the **Polish National Alliance**, the largest Polish American fraternal society in the United States. Chosen from among seventeen entries exhibited at the Corcoran Gallery of Art in Washington, D.C., in 1906, the Kościuszko monument by Antoni Popiel of Lwów was erected in Lafayette Park across from the White House. It stands in the company of other American Revolutionary War heroes Lafayette, Rochambeau and von Steuben. The Pułaski equestrian statute by Kazimierz Chodziński was placed on 13th and Pennsylvania Avenue, now known as Freedom Park. Both Polish statues were unveiled in Washington, D.C., on May 11, 1910 at ceremonies conducted by the Polish National Alliance and attended by President William Howard Taft and more than 10,000 Polish Americans. The large public gathering also provided the occasion for a congress in Washington devoted to the Polish emigration in different parts of the world.

America's Gilded Age also encompassed the beginning of what has come to be known as the Golden Age of American Illustration spanning the years 1880 to 1930. Prior to the advent of motion pictures and later television and other technical media, periodicals and books provided a major source of public entertainment. This is because "public education and increased prosperity had created a vast literate and leisured population that enjoyed reading for entertainment rather than for information or opinion." The great expansion of the publishing industry in the post–Civil War era with popular magazines like *Century*, *Collier's*, *Cosmopolitan*, *Ladies' Home Journal*, *McClure's* and *Saturday Evening Post* created unparalleled opportunities for a legion of illustrators. They included two Polish-born artists, Sigismund Ivanowski and **Władysław Teodor (W.T.) Benda**.

A member of the Polish nobility, Ivanowski attended the Academy of Fine Art in St. Petersburg, Russia, followed by the Ecole des Beaux-Arts and the Academie Julian in Paris. After marrying Helen Moser Gordon whom he met while studying in France, he moved to Westfield, New Jersey, where he maintained a studio for a number of years. During World War I he briefly returned to Poland as military attaché to **Ignacy Jan Paderewski** where the world-famous pianist and statesman served as the first Prime Minister of the Polish Republic. Apart from his magazine and book illustrations, Ivanowski painted a series of actresses in character for *Century Magazine* prior to World War I.

A student of the fine art academies in Kraków and Vienna, Poznań native Benda came to the United States in 1899 at the invitation of his aunt and famous actress, **Helena Modjeska**, for whom he designed costumes and sets. She helped finance his studies at the Art Students League in New York with Robert Henri after which he embarked on a successful career as a magazine and book illustrator for authors such as Willa Cather and Jacob Riis. He likewise developed a reputation as an authority on masks and was known for his own papier-maché masks used in the Greenwich Village Follies and the original production of Eugene O'Neill's *The Hairy Ape*.

MASS IMMIGRATION — EARLY 20TH CENTURY

Continuing a trend begun in 1890, annual immigration to the United States prior to World War I exceeded one million people in six separate years. These new arrivals, principally from Eastern and Southern Europe, came during the largest immigration period in American history, with Poles and Jews providing some of the more sizable contingents in the first decade of the twentieth century. Seeking economic betterment, freedom from forced military service and religious persecution, they generally gravitated to large cities and industrial sectors in the Northeast and Midwest where many of their compatriots had already congregated and where they could find ready, if often physically demanding employment.

The Polish mass immigration had a largely peasant, blue collar composition, not inherently conducive to fostering artistic talent. For those establishing themselves and their families in America, attaining economic stability and advancement in a frequently alien environment was by nature at odds with an artist's uncertain earning power and unpredictable future professional prospects. Consequently, many first generation immigrant families understandably dissuaded their children from pursuing fine arts careers, later avoiding the burden and social embarrassment of a creative, but financially unsuccessful son or daughter.

Nonetheless, Polish communities in Buffalo, Detroit, Cleveland, Pittsburgh, Chicago and Milwaukee among others — all dating from the mass immigration era — did have painters and sculptors who achieved local and national recognition outside the immigrant milieu. It was due in no small measure to the future artists' strong belief in themselves and their talent despite the prospect of little moral or material support. Many of the young Polish- and American-born artists growing up in the United States during this period benefited from access to local museums and instruction offered by art schools such as the Art Students League and National Academy of Design in New York, Albright Art School in Buffalo, Cleveland Institute of Art, Art Institute of Chicago and the Layton School of Art in Milwaukee. Some of their alumni, such as **Peter Dubaniewicz**, John Szynalik Fabion, and **Edmund Lewandowski**, later found employment as professors/art instructors in Cleveland, Chicago and Milwaukee. Others, including Theodore Roszak, Leon Makielski, John Fabion, Sigmund Kozlow, and Alicia Wiencek won art school scholarships allowing them to further their education in Europe. Artists of Polish heritage participating in the various art programs sponsored by the Federal Government during the Great Depression in the 1930s created murals with local subject matter for post offices, schools and other public buildings.

Art museums and galleries in the aforementioned metropolitan areas, as well as those in more distant New Mexico, Colorado and California, likewise offered Polish and Polish American artists opportunities to show and sell their work in annual juried, group and solo exhibitions. Most often gravitating to the representational style dominating the American art scene prior to World War II, they focused on subjects close at hand. Some found a wealth of material in the form and color of the urban environment, while others preferred the popular genres of portraiture, rural landscapes and still lifes as an alternative to the immigrant experience associated with American cities in the twentieth century.

A major port of entry for visitors and immigrants, New York attracted a steady stream of European and American artists as a leading cultural and educational center. Working in a variety of styles and seeking the exhibition opportunities of the city's various galleries, some artists came as established professionals while others initiated their careers or expanded upon what they had begun elsewhere. Among the new arrivals in the first decade of the twentieth century was sculptor **Adam Dąbrowski**. A student of sculptor Xawery Dunikowski and painters Ferdynand Ruszczyć and

Kazimierz Stabrowski in Warsaw, Dąbrowski operated a wood carving school in Brooklyn furnishing traditional, residential and ecclesiastical decorations for the Frick Mansion and Riverside Church in New York, and later for the Polish Museum of American in Chicago and Protestant and Catholic churches in southern California.

Warsaw native **Elie Nadelman**, who had achieved recognition as a sculptor in Paris where his patrons included Andre Gide and Leo Stein, became a permanent American resident in 1914 shortly after the outbreak of World War I. He came to the United States to execute a commission for the New York salon of Polish-born cosmetic magnate, **Helena Rubinstein**. Four years prior to his arrival, Alfred Stieglitz featured him in the October 1910 issue of *Camera Work* and his sculptures were included in the 1913 Armory Show in New York. Two years later Stieglitz offered him his first solo exhibition at his gallery 291 in Manhattan that introduced to the public both European modernists and young, progressive American artists. Although the financial reversal Nadelman and his wife experienced during the Great Depression forced the dispersal of their large folk art and material cultural collection, American folk objects influenced his choice of subject matter and the use of wood for some of his sculptures after he settled in the United States.

A graduate of the Warsaw School of Fine Arts, illustrator and muralist **Witold Gordon-Jurgielewicz** (later known simply as Witold Gordon) arrived in New York in 1914 and, like W.T. Benda, produced posters for the Polish cause during World War I. After the war he applied his design background to creating murals for New York's Radio City Music Hall and the Rainbow Room at Rockefeller Center, as well as for several pavilions at the 1939 New York World's Fair. For many years he served as design consultant to Helena Rubenstein.

In 1916 painter, sculptor and graphic artist Gustaw Gwozdecki left Paris for New York where he periodically lived and exhibited during and after World War I. His stylized "spiritual portraits" in pencil, Fauvist-inspired canvases, and monotypes were exhibited in solo and group shows at Marius De Zayas's Modern Gallery, Wanamaker Gallery, Decorators Club, Anderson Gallery and the Penguin Club — all in New York. His work earned him positive reviews in *Vanity Fair* (alongside his colleague and friend, Elie Nadelman) and in *Art News*, and was purchased by John Quinn, a well-known American collector and patron of the avant-garde. It also facilitated his contact in 1921 with Katherine S. Dreier of the Societé Anonyme in New York.

The resumption of peace time following the 1919 Armistice and America's perceived economic potential attracted a number of Polish-born artists to New York from war-torn Europe. Born Ivan Gratianovich Dombrowski to Polish parents in 1886 in Kiev (then part of the Russian Empire), John Dombrowski Graham — later shortened to John D. Graham — arrived in New York in 1920 with his wife, Vera, where he lived for the most part until after World War II. He studied at the Art Students League, principally with John Sloan, and became affiliated with the Friends of Modern Art in Baltimore that included collectors Claribel and Etta Cone. One of many immigrant artists contributing to the development of American art in the 1930s and 1940s, he joined the Americans Artists' Congress and The Ten, and organized exhibitions of African and pre–Columbian art in New York.

In the 1920s New York served as the temporary and sometimes permanent home for several Polish artists working in a traditional, representational style. Among them were portraitist **Stanisław Rembski** who was mentored by Edward Hopper and Leon Dabo before relocating to Baltimore, Maryland. Graphic artists Gan Kolski and Max Marek Feldman produced wood engravings and lithographs of the New York skyline symbolizing the whole dynamic of modern civilization that provided a limitless source of inspiration for them and their colleagues, including Howard Cook, Werner Drewes and Louis Lozowick.

Ira Moskowitz, who immigrated to New York with his family in 1927 from Stryj, Poland, where his grandfather was chief rabbi, studied at the Art Students League with Harry Wickey and Jerome Myers. After a few prior trips to New Mexico, Moskowitz and his wife settled in Taos in 1944 where they lived off and on until 1955. During that time he began experimenting with lithography and produced several hundred drawings of the Native American population. A number of them were included in *Patterns and Ceremonials of the Indians of the Southwest* (1949) with text by John Collier, Commissioner of Indian Affairs.

Beginning in 1920, Wojciech Kossak of Kraków made the first of six trips to the United States to develop a new client base for his work. His search took him from coast to coast painting portraits of Colonel Edward House, General John Pershing (West Point Military Academy), Misses Mary and Kathleen Harriman and Polonian leaders Colonel **Francis Fronczak** and Edward Witkowski among others. His first visit resulted in the Kossak Art Society organized by members of the Polish American community to generate

financial assistance for Polish artists in the United States.

Traditional portraitist **Tade Styka** settled permanently in New York in 1929 where he gained notoriety as a society painter and was joined after World War II by his brother Adam, also a painter. In 1904 Tade's first American trip included a visit to the Louisiana Purchase Exhibition in St. Louis, Missouri, where his father Jan Styka displayed his monumental panorama, *The Crucifixion* (*Golgotha*). Like Wojciech Kossak after World War I, the elder Styka hoped that the international venue of the St. Louis exhibition would introduce him to a new and appreciative audience, expanding his European client base.

In the early 1930s Paris-based caricaturist Zdzisław Czermański spent two years traveling the United States at the invitation of the newly-founded *Fortune Magazine*. He depicted political, financial and cultural leaders, Hollywood film stars, as well as scenes from urban and rural American life, some of which were included in his solo exhibition at the Ferargil Galleries in New York in 1932. That same year sculptor Maryla Lednicka-Szczytt, who had studied under Bourdelle in Paris, relocated from Italy to New York where she had several successful solo shows at the Wildenstein Galleries and the Julien Levy Galleries.

After a ten-year stay in the French capital where Sigmund Menkes was a leading member of the Ecole de Paris, the Lwów native first came to New York in 1935 prior to his solo exhibition the following year at the Guild Gallery. Longing for the lifestyle he and his wife enjoyed in Paris, he returned to the French capital on several occasions before permanently settling in New York just prior to the outbreak of World War II. In addition to his extensive output, he taught for many years at the Art Students League in Manhattan and at the Woodstock Summer School north of New York City. During the period between the two world wars New York provided educational and exhibition opportunities for a number of American-born artists of Polish heritage.

Among those studying at the National Academy of Design with Leon Kroll was native New Yorker, Sigmund Kozlow (Zygmunt Kozłowski), a talented painter of landscapes, seascapes and portraits. A Pulitzer Traveling Scholarship enabled him to study in 1936 at the Fontainebleau School of Art and the Ecole des Beaux Arts in France. He later owned the Sigmund Kozlow Gallery near Rockport, Massachusetts, and was president of the Delaware Valley Artists' Association.

After graduation from the Minneapolis

School of Art, sculptor Joseph Kiselewski came to New York in 1921 to study at the National Academy of Design and the Beaux-Arts Institute of Design. Fifteen years later he was elected an Academy Associate and an Academician in 1944. Winning the Parisian Beaux Arts Competition in 1925, he received the Prix de Rome and studied at the American Academy in Rome of which he became an Associate Fellow. Following his return to New York, he executed a number of public sculptures in the Art Deco style in New York and Washington, D.C. His various medal designs, such as the American Defense Service Medal, medals for several branches of U.S. Armed Forces, and those for the Hall of Fame for Great Americans at New York University, earned him in 1970 the J. Sanford Saltus Medal of Excellence in the art of medallic sculpture.

Alicia Wiencek (Mrs. Ernest Fiene) of Chicopee, Massachusetts studied at the Art Students League on a Kenneth Hayes Miller Scholarship in 1937 and at the Warsaw Academy of Fine Arts on a Kosciuszko Foundation Fellowship. During the Great Depression she produced a mural for the United States post office in Mooresville, North Carolina, and assisted Ernest Fiene with his mural at the Needle Trades High School (now the Fashion Institute of Technology) in New York. A member of the National Association of Women Artists and the recipient of a Tiffany Fellowship in 1948, her prints reflect the influence of French artist Georges Rouault.

In December 1937 Theodore Czebotar of Racine, Wisconsin, created a mild sensation with the Bowery, Bronx and Queens subject matter presented in his first solo exhibition at the Walker Galleries on 57th Street in Manhattan. He had been introduced to the gallery's owner, Maynard Walker, by American Regionalist painter, John Steuart Curry, then artist-in-residence at the University of Wisconsin. Czebotar's exhibition earned him a profile in *The New Yorker*'s "Talk of the Town," as well as a show at the Milwaukee Art Institute and a second solo show at the Walker Galleries in 1941. Despite favorable critical reviews and encouraging sales of his work, he later withdrew from the commercial aspects of the art world to a home in Fishkill, New York, where he focused on his work.

With the highest concentration of Polish immigrants in the United States, Chicago proportionately produced the largest number of artists during the mass immigration era. Two of them, primarily known as sculptors, exemplify the different immigration models operating in the Polish community after the turn of the nineteenth century. A native of

Poznań (then in the Prussian sector of Partitioned Poland), **Theodore Roszak** came to the United States as a young child with his parents who permanently settled in Chicago in 1909. An alumnus of the Art Institute, he initially rendered his paintings and graphics in a modernist style. During his European study on the Institute's Anna Louise Raymond Fellowship, he was introduced to the Bauhaus ideology by Czech industrial artists and acquired an appreciation of Cubism, Surrealism and Constructivism. In the mid–1930s he began creating sculptures reminiscent of the Bauhaus style, but abandoned them a decade later in the wake of the destruction left by the Second World War. Thereafter, his welded sculptures incorporated natural forms and established his reputation in the 1950s as one of America's leading Abstract Expressionist sculptors.

Stanislaus Szukalski, the son of a village blacksmith from Warta (then in the Austrian sector of Partitioned Poland), traveled with his mother and sister in 1907 to join his father in Chicago where he became a highly original sculptor. His work brought him critical acclaim when shown at the Art Institute during and after World War I, but his colorful though difficult personality often impeded his professional success. As art critic Roger A. Crane noted, "Szukalski is either worshipped or condemned, never treated with indifference. He is too dynamic to be ignored."

A classic example of the temporary immigrant, he moved back and forth between the United States and Europe exhibiting his work on both continents. In the 1920s two books were published about his work in Chicago, *The Work of Szukalski* (1923) and *Projects in Design* (1929). In Kraków in 1929 he founded the *Szczep Rogatego Serca* (Tribe of the Horned Heart), a group of sixteen young artists who sought inspiration for their work in Old Slavonic culture. Taking on additional members in the early 1930s, the "tribe" lasted until 1936. Fleeing Poland in 1939 after the outbreak of the Second World War during which most of his oeuvre was destroyed, Szukalski and his wife settled in southern California where he spent the rest of his life in relative obscurity.

Similar to Roszak, Vienna-born painter and sculptor, John Fabion (Szynalik) immigrated in 1912 at age eight with his parents to Chicago where he received his elementary and secondary education. He studied on scholarships at the Academia del Belli Arti in Florence, Kunstgewerbeschule (Arts and Crafts) School in Vienna, Akademia Sztuk Pięknych (Fine Arts Academy) in Kraków and the Art Institute of Chicago where he later taught and exhibited for many years. He also served as a combat artist for the United States Marine Corps during World War II and again during the Vietnam War in the late 1960s.

Polish native **Walter Krawiec** similarly grew up in Chicago where for more than thirty years he earned his living as the illustrator-cartoonist for the *Dziennik Polski* (Polish Daily News). A student of established local painters Ralph Clarkson and Walter Clute, he achieved recognition as a painter of circus and horse subjects which he exhibited for more than two decades at the Art Institute of Chicago. Active in local art circles, he was a member of the Chicago Painters and Sculptors, Chicago Gallery Association and the Cliff Dwellers.

In addition to the artists of European origin, Chicago claims a number born to Polish immigrant parents resident in the city. Sister Stanisia (born Monica Kurkowska/Kurk), a member of the School Sisters of Notre Dame, studied with the previously-mentioned Thaddeus Zukotyński, some of whose religious paintings she later restored in Chicago-area churches. Her portraits of religious and secular leaders included Chicago mayor Edward Kelly, Illinois governor Henry Horner, sports figure Knute Rockne, Pope Pius XI, and Cardinals George Mundelein and Samuel Stritch. Harriet Krawiec neé Korzeniowska (Walter Krawiec's wife) took her first art lessons with Sister Stanisia, later becoming an accomplished still life painter in her own right and exhibiting her work at the Art Institute, Corcoran Gallery in Washington, D.C., Carnegie Institute in Pittsburgh and the National Academy in New York. She belonged to many of the same art groups as did her husband, and her work is also in the permanent collection of the Illinois State Museum in Springfield.

Exhibiting at the Art Institute of Chicago and other venues with Walter and Harriet Krawiec were several members of their generation: Norbert Czarnowski, Anthony Mazeski and Adam Szwejkowski, all of whom trained at the Art Institute. Czarnowski came to Chicago from his native Poland when he was eighteen, later volunteering during World War I for the Polish Army commanded by General Haller in Europe. In addition to paintings based on his battlefield sketches, he did scenes of New England fishing ports and provided religious murals and paintings for Catholic churches in Chicago, Milwaukee and Cleveland.

Chicago native Szwejkowski, who specialized in gouaches and oils of the American countryside, later settled in Hollywood where he worked for the motion picture industry.

Mazeski, born in Globe, Arizona, where his immigrant father worked as a copper miner, moved with his family to Chicago. In the summer of 1937 he, Czarnowski and Szwejkowski, studied art in Poland on scholarships from The **Kosciuszko Foundation** in New York which they received for their work on the decorations for the organization's Night in Old Krakow ball at the Waldorf Astoria Hotel. Similarly, Walter and Harriet Krawiec participated in exhibitions in interwar Poland, both winning silver medals at the World's Fair in Poznan in 1929.

Twin daughters Ethel and Jenne Magafan relocated as youngsters for family health reasons from their native Chicago to Denver with their Polish-Greek immigrant parents. Mentored by Colorado artist Frank Mechau after their father died, the Magafans achieved critical recognition for their post office murals painted in the American Regionalist style as participants in the Federal Government art programs during the Great Depression while studying at the Colorado Springs Fine Arts Center. After World War II they were associated with the Woodstock Art Colony.

The exhibition activities of the resident artists of Polish heritage active in Chicago after 1900 created a climate for the establishment of the Polish Arts Club initiated in 1926 by Thaddeus Sleszyński. It encouraged and supported young talent not only in the plastic arts, but also in music, literature and the theater. It organized annual exhibitions of artists from Chicago and elsewhere in the United States at the Home Bank in the heart of the city's Polish community and at the Hamilton Club in downtown Chicago. The juries of selection included Albin Polasek, Pauline Palmer, Charles Wilimovsky, Enrico Glicenstein, and Rudolph Weisenborn.

In addition to mounting exhibitions of local artists, the arts club hosted traveling exhibits of Polish graphic art periodically sent to the United States in the 1920s and 1930s by the Institute for Art Promotion (Instytut Propagandy Sztuki) in Warsaw. The exhibits, less costly to assemble and ship than paintings, aimed to acquaint the American public with reborn Poland after World War I and to provide sales opportunities for the participating artists associated with the well-recognized interwar Polish graphic arts school. They had received favorable notices and won prizes in international exhibitions not only in Europe, but also in Chicago, Los Angeles and elsewhere.

The Polish Arts Club of Chicago served as an organizational model for other similar clubs beginning in 1930 and culminating after World War II in the American Council of Polish Cultural Clubs (ACPCC) (see **American Council for Polish Culture**). Many in the Polish American community regarded the profile and activities of the national organization and its affiliate groups as elitist because they sought to move beyond the confines of the established ethnic community. With varying degrees of success, the arts clubs established important contacts with non–Polish cultural leaders in their communities, helping to publicize their activities in the English-speaking American press.

Although not a Chicago native, Leon Makielski came from South Bend, Indiana (where his family had a picture frame and art supply store) to study with Ralph Clarkson at the Art Institute. Its John Quincy Adams Traveling Scholarship enabled Makielski to spend four years in Paris at the Academie Julien and the Academie de la Grande Chaumiere, exhibiting his work at the Grand Salon. After returning to the United States, he joined the faculty at the University of Michigan at Ann Arbor and also taught at the Meinzinger Art School in Detroit attended by Stanley Twardowicz in 1940. Makielski was a member of the Scarab Club in Detroit whose founder-members included Polish-born artist, Roman Krzyżanowski.

Milwaukee, whose sizable Polish community was somewhat less numerous than Chicago's, had two native sons, Bernard (Ben) Badura and Edmund Lewandowski, who became affiliated with art communities and nationally-recognized art movements. Badura— who initially studied at the State Normal School for Teachers in Milwaukee and later at the Pennsylvania Academy of Fine Art with Arthur B. Carles, Daniel Garber and George Oberteuffer — settled in New Hope, Pennsylvania, in 1930 becoming part of its art community. Exhibiting his paintings locally and nationally, he also gained a reputation for his hand-carved and gilded frames supplied to many Delaware Valley artists.

Lewandowski, an alumnus of Milwaukee's Layton School of Art of which he was later president and where he spent a good portion of his teaching career, became a proponent of Precisionism early on in the Midwest. Like other artists working in this style and depicting American industrial and urban scenes in a precise and ordered manner, he focused on the symbols of the machine age in his paintings of Milwaukee's docks and industries. In 1936 prominent New York art dealer Edith Halpert invited him to join her prestigious Downtown Gallery that also exhibited Ralston Crawford, Louis Guglielmi, Jacob Lawrence, Jack Levine and Mitchell Siporin. After a visit to the mosaic glass in-

dustry in Venice in 1953, Lewandowski executed several mosaic commissions for the Flint Institute of Arts in Michigan and one for the Memorial Art Center in Milwaukee designed by Eero Saarinen.

Similar to Lewandowski, Vincent Nesbert taught for many years beginning in 1928 at the Art Institute of Pittsburgh of which he was later dean. A traditional portraitist like **Stanisław Rembski** and **Tade Styka**, Nesbert immigrated to the United States in 1914 from Poland's eastern borderlands. After studying at the Carnegie Institute of Technology in Pittsburgh and the National Academy of Design in New York, he spent a year in Europe on a Pulitzer Prize. He later showed in the Carnegie Internationals, the oldest North American exhibition of contemporary art from around the globe, whose participants in the 1920s and 1930s included a number of leading Polish artists such as Olga Boznańska, Władysław Jarocki and **Tamara Lempicka**. In the 1930s Nesbert painted five large murals in the imposing lobby of the Allegheny County Courthouse in Pittsburgh for which he is best remembered.

Peter Paul Dubaniewicz, a graduate of the Cleveland Art Institute where he later taught for three decades, applied his representative style to scenes in and around Cleveland, as well as to more distant Central City, Colorado. During World War II he designed camouflage and training aids for the United States Army at Fort Belvoir, Virginia. A long-time member of the American Watercolor Society and president of the Cleveland Society of Artists, he produced a number of murals in Boston, Cleveland and elsewhere in Ohio.

The art activities of Buffalo's Polish community mirrored those in Chicago, although on a somewhat smaller scale. Whether natives or newcomers, a number of its American-born artists of Polish descent exhibited with local art organizations outside their ethnic enclave. **Joseph Mazur** specialized in traditional religious mural paintings for Polish Roman Catholic churches in Upstate New York, New Jersey, Connecticut and Michigan, as well as stained glass memorial windows and sculptures. For many years he was active in the Buffalo Society of Artists and the Buffalo Arts Club.

Also noted for his community art involvement was his colleague, **Eugene Dyczkowski**, whose family relocated from Philadelphia to Niagara Falls when he was a youngster. Unlike most of his fellow Polish American artists in Buffalo who worked in a representational style throughout their careers, Dyczkowski gravitated to abstract painting in the 1950s. He also served as Assistant Educational Director at the

Albright Art Gallery in Buffalo, taught at the Buffalo Art Institute, was a co-founder of the local Polish Arts Club and first president of the American Council of Polish Cultural Clubs.

Like Dyczkowski, Arthur Kowalski moved to Buffalo from Cincinnati as a child. After studying at the Albright Art School, he attended the Arts Students League and Cooper Union in New York and worked in Florence, Italy, in 1933. He was a member of the Saturday Sketch Club in Buffalo, an organization founded by noted printmaker Julius J. Lankes that claimed among its members Charles Burchfield and Alex Fournier. In 1952 Kowalski became president of the Buffalo Society of Artists.

Sculptor-steelworker **Louis Dlugosz** of Lackawanna, New York, received his initial art training at the Buffalo Art Institute. The early recognition received at his solo show at the Nierendorf Gallery in New York in 1940 was interrupted by his wartime military service. Having studied at the Academie de la Grande Chaumiere in Paris on the GI Bill of Rights, he developed his "pretzel-bending" technique of rolling clay into strips and then bending them together in a lattice-work arrangement creating sculptures with an open rather than a solid interior.

The trio of **Joseph Bakos**, Walter Mruk and Augustine Korda, who also attended the Albright Art School, went on to study privately with Buffalo native John Thompson, who spent time in several European art capitals. He introduced them to Post-Impressionism, particularly Cezanne, and encouraged them in plein-air painting. When Thompson relocated to Denver, they joined him there in 1918 taking part the following year in the Denver Art Association's mini–Colorado "Armory Exhibit" shocking the local museum-going public. Korda returned to Buffalo, while Bakos and Mruk moved on to the burgeoning art colony in Santa Fe, New Mexico, where in 1921 they became two of the founder-members of Los Cinco Pintores (The Five Painters), the city's first modernist art group.

In 1920 Tucson became the permanent home of Marylka Modjeska after she married Sidney Pattison, an English professor at the University of Arizona. The daughter of engineer **Ralph Modjeski** and the granddaughter of Shakespearean actress Helena Modjeska (Modzejewska), she studied etching with George Senseney in her native Chicago, in Provincetown, Massachusetts, and later with Georges-Leo Degorce in France. She exhibited her work with the Chicago Society of Etchers, Provincetown Art Association and National Arts Club. After settling in Tucson, her etchings of the Arizona and California landscape were shown at the Tucson Fine Arts Association, Laguna Beach Art Association and the Carmel Art Association.

In the early twentieth century the climate, landscape and art community of Southern California attracted two Polish-born artists: Theodore B. Modra and Stanislaus (Stan) Pociecha Poray. Modra studied in Paris at the Academie Colarossi and in Munich before immigrating to New York City in 1887 where he further trained at the Art Students League with Robert Henri, leader of the New York Eight. In 1915 he settled in Southern California where he did much to promote art appreciation, including organizing exhibitions for the Pacific Southwest Exposition of 1928 and obtaining an appropriation for a permanent art exhibition building at Pomona for the Los Angeles County Fair of which he was art director in the 1920s.

Stan Poray, a native of Kraków where his father Count Michael Poray was an established landscape painter, studied at the city's fine arts academy and later in Paris where he showed in the Autumn Salon. Following his marriage to Mlle. Krzyżanowska in Riga, Latvia, he first lived in Moscow before becoming the art director of the First Art Theater in Tomsk in 1918. Fleeing the Russian Revolution via Vladivostok, he and his wife spent several years in Japan where he painted the Imperial family and other notables. Settling in Los Angeles in 1921, he quickly established his career painting landscapes, coastal scenes, missions and nocturnes. They were augmented later by still lifes based on his study of ancient Chinese culture, philosophy and art.

World War II

The outbreak of World War II which began with the Nazi invasion of Poland on September 1, 1939, stranded some Polish artists then in the United States and provided a refuge for others from their war-torn country. That year, for example, **Bolesław Cybis** and Eliasz Kanarek, two members of the Brotherhood of St. Luke historical painting group in Warsaw, were in the United States preparing murals and decorations for the Polish pavilion at the New York World's Fair. Unable to return home, Kanarek moved to California earning his living as a portraitist, while Cybis and his wife established Cybis Art Productions in 1940 at the Steinway Mansion in Astoria, New York, followed a decade later by Cybis Porcelain in Trenton, New Jersey.

Sculptor Stanisław Ostrowski, creator of the life-size equestrian bronze sculpture of Władysław Jagiełło (King of Poland and Grand Duke of Lithuania) for the entrance to the Polish pavilion at the fair, came to the United States in 1940 where he spent the last seven years of his life. His Jagiełło statue was later placed behind the Metropolitan Museum of Art in New York's Central Park. A graduate of the fine arts academies in Kraków and Florence, he also studied in Rome and Paris where he was a friend of Rodin. He made busts of many important Europeans and Americans, including **Ignacy Jan Paderewski** and Marshal Józef Piłsudski.

In 1940 Polish Jewish miniaturist and caricaturist **Arthur Szyk** arrived in New York, having been sent by Britain and Poland to help publicize the anti–Nazi cause in the United States. He became know for his anti–Axis political illustrations in magazines and newspapers rendered in a distinctive style based on his study of medieval miniaturists and illuminated manuscripts. Awarded the Polish Government Gold Cross of Merit in 1948, he became a citizen of the United States where he died three years later.

After the fall of France in 1940 Irena Lorentowicz, a student at Sorbonne, arrived the following year in the United States where she lived for almost two decades before returning to Poland in 1959. A graduate of the Warsaw School of Fine Arts, she was a set designer for the production of Karol Szymanowski's *Harnasie* at the Paris Opera in 1936, later working in the same capacity at the Metropolitan Opera in New York. She also achieved recognition as a children's book illustrator and installer of the stained glass windows at Holy Trinity Parish in Chicago.

Zdzisław Czermański finally landed in New York in 1941 (where he exhibited a decade earlier), having escaped war-torn Poland with his wife via Wilno, Scandinavia, France, Portugal and Brazil. He quickly re-established his career as a successful illustrator and caricaturist whose works appeared over the next two decades in leading American publications such as *Cosmopolitan, Esquire, Life, Look, Saturday Evening Post, The New Yorker* and *Time*. His series of drawings, *Famous and Infamous*, exhibited at the Gallery of Modern Art in New York and the Butler Art Institute in Youngstown, Ohio, provided a plastic summary of wartime events sharing the suffering of the oppressed, underscoring heroism, and ridiculing conceit and buffoonery.

In contrast to most of the Polish artists coming to the United States preceding and during the war who worked in a more representational style, Teresa Zanower was associated with the Constructivist avant-garde in interwar Poland where she created posters and theoretical designs for residential buildings, sculptures and photomontages. After reaching New York in 1941, she continued working in the same direction until her death eight years later. She provided photomontages for *Obrona Warszawy. Lud Polski w obronie stolicy* (The Defense of Warsaw. The Polish People Defending their Capital, 1942) and exhibited at Peggy Guggenheim's Art of This Century Gallery in 1946.

The title of Zanower's book underscores in a broader context the Polish nation's resistance to the Nazi and Soviet occupations of the respective western and eastern halves of its country. The occupation naturally concerned the American Polonia because of its varying degrees of familial, cultural and political ties with the Old Country. One facet of the wartime occupation was the wanton pillaging and destruction of Poland's cultural treasures. To call attention and provide a counterweight to this unfortunate situation Bolesław Mastai organized two large loan exhibitions of Polish art from American public and private collections. The first one opened at the Metropolitan Museum of Art in New York in February 1944, followed by the second one at the Detroit Institute of Arts in June 1945. Both exhibitions were accompanied by fully-illustrated catalogs. The New York show featured nineteenth-century Polish paintings, while the Detroit version included a number of American-born artists of Polish descent.

In 1937 Polish ambassador, Count Jerzy Potocki, invited **Jan Henryk de Rosen** to Washington, D.C., to paint a large mural, *The Glory of Polish Arms*, for the embassy. Professor of Figure Drawing at the Lwów Polytechnic, the artist had to his credit religious murals at the Armenian Cathedral in Lwów, Sobieski Chapel at Kahlenberg near Vienna, and the private Papal Chapel at Castel Gandolfo near Rome, among others. During World War II he served as an aide at the Polish Embassy in Washington, becoming in 1940 Professor of Liturgical Art at the Catholic University of America. In this capacity he created murals and mosaics for some two dozen churches and monasteries of different faiths, such as the Basilica of the Shrine of the Immaculate Conception, St. Matthew's Cathedral and the National Cathedral all in Washington, D.C.; Cathedral Basilica of Saint Louis in St. Louis, Missouri; and Grace Episcopal Cathedral in San Francisco.

From a financial standpoint, probably the most fortunate Polish artist arriving in the United States during World War II was Tamara de Lempicka (Baroness Kuffner). The Grande Dame of Art Deco in Paris, she visited the United States a decade earlier when her work was included in the Carnegie International Exhibition in Pittsburgh. Under the growing Nazi threat in Europe, her extended American holiday with her husband in 1939 eventually became permanent. She initially enjoyed critical success with solo exhibitions at galleries in New York and San Francisco and at the Milwaukee Institute of Art. But the change in her style and technique undertaken in response to the postwar dominance of Abstract Expressionism in America was not well received so she retired from active life as a professional artist in 1962. However, she lived to see a renewed appreciation of her earlier Art Deco work following her retrospective at the Galerie du Luxembourg in Paris in 1973.

POST-WORLD WAR II ERA

The postwar division of Europe and the onset of the Cold War divided the Polish American community over whether and how to resume connections with Poland following its forcible incorporation into the Soviet sphere of influence in Eastern Europe. For many Americans of Polish descent the new regime tainted and impeded their relations with the land of their forefathers. In the new postwar configuration The Kosciuszko Foundation in New York assumed a new role, moving from the Polish Consulate to a new home in an elegant townhouse off Fifth Avenue in Manhattan. The Foundation's relocation symbolized the onset of a transition occurring at that time as the Polish American community began dispersing beyond its previously-defined ethnic neighborhood boundaries. In addition to the Foundation's scholarship programs, Dr. **Stephen Mizwa**, its founder and first president, initiated through donations a Gallery of Polish Masters focusing on nineteenth- and early twentieth-century Polish painting. He likewise hosted solo exhibitions for Bolesław Czedekowski and W.T. Benda, as well as group exhibitions of American artists of Polish descent that included, among others, Richard Anuszkiewicz, Peter Dubaniewicz, Eugene Dyczkowski and Stanley Twardowicz.

After the Second World War America's — and particularly New York's — cultural and economic ascendancy attracted many artists desirous of experiencing firsthand the city's intense pace and rich cultural milieu. For those from war-torn Europe, New York offered inviting financial and exhibition opportunities. Among the Polish-born artists coming to the United States in the late 1940s and early 1950s were Raymond Kanelba, **Stefan Mrozewski**, and Wiktor Podoski.

Kanelba (Kanelbaum) permanently left his native Warsaw with his young wife for Paris in 1925. There, along with Sigmund Menkes, Moise Kisling, Leopold Gottlieb, Roman Kramsztyk, and Eugene Zak, he became a recognized member of the Ecole de Paris exhibiting in important galleries in the French capital. From London, to which he relocated with his family in 1936, he made several trips to the United States for exhibitions and portrait commissions before making New York his home in 1951 and becoming an American citizen six years later. In the last decade of his life he had important solo shows at the Victor Hammer Gallery and the Associated American Artists Galleries in Manhattan, as well as group exhibitions at the National Academy of Design, Pennsylvania Fine Art Academy and the Detroit Institute of the Arts.

Graphic artists Mrozewski and Podoski both studied in Warsaw with Władysław Skoczylas, founder of the prolific school of modern Polish wood engraving, and belonged to Ryt, an association of Polish graphic artists founded in 1926 and comprising some of Poland's finest modern wood engravers. During the interwar period Mrozewski and Podoski were included in a number of graphic art exhibitions circulated in the United States by the Institute for Art Promotion and by the Polish Art Service based in New York. After World War II, Podoski and Mrozewski immigrated with their spouses to California as guests of the Huntington Hartford Foundation where they spent the remainder of their lives. With the postwar domination of abstract art and the predominance of color in the printmaking medium in the United States, succeeding years were not always kind to both graphic artists who continued producing monochromatic wood engravings in a representational style.

By the early 1950s New York became the center of Abstract Expressionist art whose leading adherents became known collectively as the New York School. They showed in a series of artists' committee invitation exhibitions commencing with the 9th Street Art Exhibition curated by Leo Castelli in 1951 and followed by consecutive exhibitions at the Stable Gallery in New York and the annual exhibitions of painting and sculpture (1953–57). Their participants included several Polish- and American-born artists of Polish descent: **Jack Tworkov** and his sister, Janice Biala, who immigrated to the United States from Biała, Poland, in 1913, and Philadelphia native Richard Stankiewicz. During the 1950s Tworkov used gestural brush strokes in flame-like color, transitioning in the mid–1960s to straight lines and geometric patterns. Stankiewicz, a student of Hans Hofmann in New York and Fernand Leger and Ossip Zadkine in Paris, became known for his "junk sculpture" assemblages found in the permanent col-

lections of a number of leading American and European art museums.

Richard Anuszkiewicz, **Julian Stanczak** and **Edwin Mieczkowski** came to occupy an important place in the Op (Optical) Art Movement in the 1960s and 1970s. The first two are Pennsylvania natives, while Stanczak immigrated as a teenager with his family to the United States from England in 1950 after spending two years in a Soviet labor camp and a Polish refugee camp in British Uganda in Africa. All three participated in major Op Art exhibitions at the Martha Jackson Gallery and the Museum of Modern Art in New York. They continue to explore geometric abstraction in painting, sculpture and the graphic arts.

Although stylistically different, Midwesterners Stanley Twardowicz and **Gerome Kamrowski** both had a New York connection. Despite a difficult childhood, Twardowicz developed into a talented photographer, painter and graphic artist whose style is related to Abstract Expressionism and Color Field Painting, examples of which are in the Museum of Modern Art and the Whitney Museum of American Art in New York. A regular at the Cedar Tavern in New York's Greenwich Village starting in 1953, he became a good friend of New York School painter Franz Kline and of American novelist and poet, Jack Kerouac, a leading representative of the Beat Generation with whom he shared a working-class immigrant childhood.

Kamrowski, whose career spanned two generations, studied and/or associated with some of the twentieth century's leading artists: Hans Hofmann, Jackson Pollock, Robert Motherwell and William Baziotes. He was also introduced to European Surrealists Andre Breton, Max Ernst, Andre Masson and Robert Matta who fled to New York during World War II and greatly influenced him. One of the first American artists to explore Abstract Surrealism and the techniques of automatism, he exhibited at Peggy Guggenheim's Art of This Century Gallery and the Whitney Museum of American Art.

In 1946 he joined the faculty of the University of Michigan at Ann Arbor where he continued to work in Abstract Surrealism through the late 1950s. In the early 1960s he initiated the Hylozoist Group emphasizing the use of technological materials and techniques to explore Surrealist themes. In 1978 he was one of the few Americans to be included in the prestigious *Dada and Surrealism Revisited* exhibition in London.

In the 1960s two well-established artists, **Tadeusz Lapiński** and **Wojciech (Voy) Fangor**, immigrated to the United States quickly attaining a place on the American art scene. Lapiński became known for his largely abstract, split-color lithography, teaching at the Pratt Graphic Center in New York where he met Walter Rogalski and later at the University of Maryland at College Park. Fangor, who taught at Fairleigh Dickinson University in New Jersey and returned to Poland in 1999, shares certain common characteristics of Optical Art and Color Painting with a distinctive manipulation of color-space.

Following them in the 1970s and 1980s for political and/or economic reasons were six other Polish artists: **Jan Sawka**, Andrzej Czeczot, Andrzej Dudziński, **Rafał Olbiński**, Janusz Kapusta, and **Andrzej Pityński**. Five of them with extensive backgrounds in design, illustration and the graphic arts rather quickly established themselves in New York. In addition to notable illustrations for the *New York Times*, *Wall Street Journal*, *Boston Globe*, and *Washington Post*, they produced multi-media presentations and designed stage/concert sets for such diverse venues as the Philadelphia Opera Company, Jean Cocteau Repertory Theater and the Grateful Dead.

Sculptor Andrzej Pityński, affiliated since 1979 with the Johnson Atelier Technical Institute of Sculpture in Mercerville, New Jersey, is known for his sculptures *The Partisans* in Boston and *Katyn 1940* at Exchange Place in Jersey City. Despite a difficult childhood somewhat reminiscent of Stanley Twardowicz's, American-born sculptor **Janusz Korczak Ziolkowski** worked hard to develop his talent that brought him to the attention of Gutzon Borglum whom he assisted at Mt. Rushmore in South Dakota in 1939. He thereafter accepted the invitation of a group of Sioux Indian chiefs to carve Chief Crazy Horse's likeness on Thunderhead Mountain near Custer, South Dakota, where he started working in 1948. He sought to preserve his artistic independence by remaining free of the conditions imposed by government and private grants. Ranked by the *Reader's Digest* in 1976 as one of the seven wonders of the modern world, his work on the monumental Crazy Horse sculpture for more than thirty years is being continued and completed by his family.

Native Americans dominate the work of Neo-Surrealist painter and printmaker, Paul Pletka. A native of San Diego, he grew up in Grand Junction, Colorado, where he became fascinated with the Plains Indians and those of the Southwest. He precedes his depictions of their tribal rituals and moods with painstaking research into their regalia and ceremonial objects to ensure accuracy in rendering his subjects in both group and individual compositions.

Harry Wysocki, born in a Polish American neighborhood in Detroit, later moved to Los Angeles where he initially experimented with the Art Nouveau and Art Deco styles. After World War II he developed a whimsical, signature style depicting small-town Americana including lighthouses, old hotels and railroad stations from the pre-technical age. Lighthouses likewise comprise one of the genres explored by New Jersey artist, **Joseph Konopka**. Working in a modified Photorealist style characterized by large canvases and a muted palette, he has also painted the Tall Ships during the American Bicentennial, the former World Trade Center, New Jersey highways, and everyday intimate scenes often including his wife as the model.

A childhood interest in animation and cartoons led **Ed Paschke** to a career in art. Living briefly in New York in the 1960s where he was exposed to Pop Art, he returned to his native Chicago becoming an internationally-recognized Imagist whose work contains references to Surrealist art. Appropriating his images from popular culture and the electronic media, he infused them with brilliant colors energizing their carefully-worked surfaces.

Paschke was one of a number of American painters, printmakers and sculptors of Polish descent working and exhibiting in Chicago and elsewhere. While Metro Chicago has a sizable group of artists emanating from its large Polish American community, artists of Polish heritage can likewise be found throughout the rest of the country. Whether based in urban areas, small towns and rural environments, their names regularly appear on exhibition rosters, in reference publications and national magazines, as well as on internet websites. Their inclusion is indicative of the various recognition levels accorded their talent by the American community at large.

CONCLUSION

When viewed in its entirety, the past two centuries of activity in the United States by Polish artists and their American-born counterparts of Polish descent are indeed noteworthy. Representing the gamut of social and economic backgrounds and employing a variety of styles, the artists did not form a homogenous group despite their shared ethnic heritage. Not focusing in most cases on Polish themes, they sought out their subject matter in the surrounding American milieu of which they were a part. Their connection to it was reinforced by their membership in various non-ethnic art organizations with which they exhibited.

Their styles reflected their education in Europe and/or America, as well as their individual taste and predilections. The majority of the artists under consideration followed the conservative and naturalistic trends prevalent in nineteenth- and twentieth-century European and American art, with a smaller number pursuing the modernist and abstract ones in vogue after the two world wars.

Working hard to develop their talent, they produced quality work that was accepted in local, regional and national juried exhibitions where it often won prizes. That recognition frequently earned them solo shows at leading art galleries throughout the country. Another barometer of the artists' success was the purchase of their work by American museums and public art commissions awarded them during the Great Depression and in the decades after World War II. Although the careers of a number Polish-born and American artists of Polish descent await complete documentation, their creative output nonetheless remains an integral part of America's shared cultural heritage.—*Stanley L. Cuba*

SOURCES: *Słownik Artystów Polskich* (Wrocław: Zakład Narodowy im. Ossolińskich, 1971–75); Henry C. Pitz, *200 Years of American Illustration* (New York: Random House, 1977); Mieczysław Haiman, *Polish Past in America* (Chicago: Polish Museum of America, 1974); Joseph A. Wytrwal, *Poles in American History and Tradition* (Detroit: Endurance Press, 1969); George C. Groce, *The New-York Historical Society's Dictionary of Artists in America, 1564–1860* (New Haven: Yale University Press, 1957); Mary Sayre Haverstock, *et. al.*, *Artists in Ohio, 1787–1900* (Kent, OH: The Kent State University Press, 2000); Clarissa Bucklin, *Nebraska Art and Artists* (Lincoln, NE: University of Nebraska, 1932); Peter Hastings Falk, ed., *The Annual Exhibition Record of the Art Institute of Chicago, 1888–1950* (Madison, CT: Sound View Press, 1990); *Official Catalogue of Exhibits, Department K Fine Arts, World's Columbian Exposition* (Chicago: W.B. Gonkey Company, 1893); *Who's Who in American Art* (various editions); Anna Lipa, *Gustaw Gwozdecki 1880–1935: wystawa monograficzna* (Poznań: Muzeum Narodowe w Poznaniu, 2002); Eleanor Green, *John Graham: Artist and Avatar* (Washington, D.C.: The Phillips Collection, 1987); Robin West, *Ira Moskowitz: Works on Paper* (Santa Fe, NM: Zaplin Lampert Gallery, 2000); Isaac Bashevis Singer, *et. al.*, *The Drawings and Paintings of Ira Moskowitz* (New York: Landmark Book Co., 1990); Kazimierz Olszanski, *Wojciech Kossak* (Wrocław: Zakład Narodowy im. Ossolińskich, 1976); Jane J. Palczynski, "Chicago Poles Share in City Art History," *Poles of Chicago 1837–1937: A History of One Century of Polish Contributions to the City of Chicago, Illinois* (Chicago: Polish Pageant, Inc., 1937); Stanley L. Cuba and Elizabeth Cunningham, *Pikes Peak Vision: The Broadmoor Art Academy, 1919–1945* (Colorado Springs: Colorado Springs Fine Arts Center, 1989); Katherine Smith-Warren, *Time and Place: One Hundred Years of Women Artists in Colorado 1900–2000* (Denver: The Metropolitan State College of Denver Center for the Visual Arts, 2000); Dennis Barrie *et. al.*, *Artists in Michigan, 1900–1976: A Biographical Dictionary* (Detroit: Wayne State University Press, 1989); "He Labors for Art" (re Louis Dlugosz), *Modern Mechanix*, March 1957, 103–105; Henry C. Pitz, *200 Years of American Illustration* (New York: Random House, 1977); Brian Roughton, "Raymond Kanelba 1897–1960," *Revisiting a Modernist—A Retrospective Exhibition* (Dallas, TX: Roughton Galleries, 2003; Maryla Stikowska, *Wiktor Podoski 1901–1970*

(Warsaw: Muzeum Narodowe w Warszawie, 1979); Irena Piotrowska, "American Painters and Illustrators of Polish Descent," in Francis Bolek and Ladislaus J. Sienkaniec, eds., *Polish American Encyclopedia* (Buffalo: Polish American Encyclopedia Committee, 1954, Vol. l); Stanley L. Cuba, "The Art of Jozef Bakos," *Jozef Bakos: An Early Modernist* (Santa Fe: Museum of Fine Arts, 1988); Stanley L. Cuba, "Walter Mruk: The Elusive Cinco," *El Palacio*, Vol. 105, No. 2, Winter/Spring 2000–01; David F. Martin, "Eugene M. Dyczkowski: Lusty Realist of Depression-Era Buffalo," *Western New York Heritage*, Vol. 6, No. 4 (Winter 2004); Kenneth W. Prescott, James R. Mitchell, *Cybis in Retrospect* (Trenton: New Jersey State Museum, 1970); Eugene Clute, *A Monograph of the Work of Adam Dabrowski, Sculptor in Wood* (Chicago, 1920s, n.d.); Joseph P. Ansell, *Arthur Szyk: Artist, Jew, Pole* (Oxford & Portland, OR: The Littman Library of Jewish Civilization, 2004); *Fangor* (New York: The Solomon R. Guggenheim Museum, 1970); Jean Cassou, *Glicenstein* (New York: Crown Publishers, 1958); Grover A. Whalen, *et. al.*, *American Art Today: New York World's Fair* (New York: National Art Society, 1939); Elizabeth McClelland, "Edwin Mieczkowski: Neo Constructivism" and "Julian Stanczak, "Painted Music," *Harmonic Forms on the Edge: Geometric Abstraction in Cleveland* (Cleveland: Cleveland Artists Foundation, The Beck Center for the Arts, 2001); Karl Lunde, *Anuszkiewicz* (New York: Harry N. Abrams, Inc. 1977); Brady Roberts, *Moving Color: The Art of Stanley Twardowicz* (Phoenix: Phoenix Art Museum, 2001); Eva Ingersoll Gatling, *Stanley Twardowicz* (Huntington, NY: Heckscher Museum, 1974); Glen Bray, ed., *Struggle: The Art of Szukalski*; Foreword by Leonardo and George DiCaprio (San Francisco: Last Gasp, 2000); Evan M. Maurer and Jennifer L. Bayles, *Gerome Kamrowski: A Retrospective Exhibition* (Ann Arbor: University of Michigan Museum of Art, 1983); *Edmund Lewandowski: Fifty Years of Painting* (New York and Greenville, SC: H. V. Allison Galleries, Greenville County Museum of Art, 1990); Douglas Dreishpoon, *Theodore Roszak: Constructivist Works, 1931–1947: Paintings, Constructions, Drawings, Photograms, February 29-April II, 1992* (New York: Hirschl & Adler Galleries, 1992); Barbara Haskell, *Elie Nadelman: Sculptor of Modern Life* (New York: Whitney Museum of American Art, 2003); *Sigmund Menkes, 1896–1986* (Brooklyn: Lipert Gallery, 1993); Baroness Kizette de Lempicka-Foxhall, *Passion by Design: The Art and Times of Tamara de Lempicka* (New York: Abbeville Press, 1987); Gail Stavitsky, *et. al.*, *Precisionism in America 1915–1941: Reordering Reality* (New York: Harry N. Abrams, Inc., in association with The Montclair Art Museum, 1994); Karen Tsujimoto, *Images of America: Precisionist Painting and Modern Photography* (Seattle & London: University of Washington Press, 1982).

First Generation *see* **Generations, Polish American.**

Fletcher, Ann O. (née Kazulewski; b. Latrobe, Pennsylvania, September 22, 1911; d.—). Engineer. Fletcher earned a baccalaureate degree in engineering from Wayne State University (1944) and worked as a patent illustrator with Bendix Aviation in Detroit (1942–47) and Ford Motor Company (1947–68). In 1968 she accepted a position as technical assistant with Shatterproof Glass Corporation in Detroit (1968–80), after which she worked as a free-lance consultant following her retirement. Fletcher was a leader in the American-Polish Engineering Association, serving as its president in 1978-79 and 1988–90. She was a fellow of the Engineering Society of Detroit where she served as a board member (1980–86), served as president of the Detroit chapter of the Society of Women Engineers (1965–68, 1977-78), president of the Society of Engineering Illustrators (1971-72, 1983–85), and vice president of the Michigan Division of the **Polish American Congress** (1973–84). Among her many recognitions were a distinguished service award from the Engineering Society of Detroit (1987), the General K. Pulaski Award from the Polish American Central Citizens Committee of Detroit (1990), and an award for outstanding service from the Polish American Congress (1991).—*James S. Pula*

SOURCE: Bolesław Wierzbiański, ed., *Who's Who in Polish America* (New York: Bicentennial Publishing Corporation, 1996), 111.

Floyar-Rajchman, Henryk (Henryk Reichman; b. Warsaw, Poland, December 7, 1893; d. New York, New York, March 22, 1951). Politician. A politician of the Polish leftist independence movement, Floyar-Rajchman was born into an assimilated Jewish family. During his early education in Warsaw he became an activist in the Polish Socialist Party. Arrested by the tsarist police in 1911, following his release he left for Kraków in the Austrian partition where he continued his education while being an active member of the Shooting Association (Związek Strzelecki), a paramilitary formation connected with the left-wing movement for Polish independence. After the outbreak of World War I, he volunteered for service in Józef Piłsudski's Legions. At this time he began using his pseudonym "Floyar" because, being a Russian subject, he was under the threat of a death sentence in case of capture. After the dismissal of Piłsudski in 1917, he began underground activity in the Polish Military Organization (Polska Organizacja Wojskowa) in Warsaw and changed his name to Floyar-Rajchman. In the years 1918–20 he studied law in Warsaw. At the beginning of 1920 he volunteered for the Polish army. After the Russo-Polish War he actively participated in Piłsudski's May Coup d'État in 1926, after which he moved to Warsaw where he worked in the General Inspectorate of Military Forces. He was promoted to the rank of major in 1928. At the marshal's order, he held the post of the Military and Marine Attaché at the Embassy of the Polish Republic in Tokyo (1928–32). After his return to Poland he served in various political capacities and was elected to the Sejm (parliament) in autumn 1935. He was a supporter of the close circle of Marshal Piłsudski, the so-called "colonel's group." After 1935 he was removed, together with the entire colonel's group, from the highest government positions by another group of Piłsudski's supporters concentrated around Marshal Edward Rydz-Śmigły and the president, Ignacy Mościcki. He spent the last years before the outbreak of war in political retirement.

In September 1939 he volunteered as an officer of the Polish Army where he helped the Minister of Treasure carry abroad the treasure of the Polish Bank. Instead of well-deserved gratitude and reward he had to face the accusations from the ruling political opponents circled around General Władysław Sikorski. After the defeat of France in summer 1940, he escaped to London where he was perceived as one of the main political opponents of the Polish government-in-exile. In 1941 he left for the U.S. where he continued his political activity as a founder of the **Józef Piłsudski Institute** of America. At the same time he was an activist in the **National Committee of Americans of Polish Descent** (Komitet Narodowy Amerykanów Polskiego Pochodzenia), where he often spoke for the honorable treatment of postwar Poland. In exile he was a friend of the outstanding publicist Ignacy Matuszewski and the poet **Jan Lechoń**. After 1945 he supported Piłsudski's camp and the idea of uniting all the factions advocating Polish political independence and excluding the ones that favored compromise with the communists. His funeral in New York became a Polish patriotic manifestation.—*Joanna Wojdon*

SOURCES: Jacek Majchrowski, ed., *Kto był kim w Drugiej Rzeczypospolitej* (Warsaw: Polska Oficyna Wydawnicza "BGW," 1994); Janusz Cisek, *Instytut Józefa Piłsudskiego w Ameryce i jego zbiory* (Warsaw: Biblioteka Narodowa, 1997).

Folejewski, Zbigniew (b. Wilno, Poland, October 18, 1910; d. Victoria, British Columbia, July 28, 1999). Poet, scholar. Folejewski attended Russian schools where his father was in political exile. In 1909 the family returned to Wilno where he attended the Zygmund August Gymnazium and the Stefan Batory University from which he received his M.A. degree in Slavic and Comparative Literature in 1934. Folejewski made his literary debut in 1929 with the publication of short stories and poems, followed in 1933 by a collection of poems *Dom w Gorcach* (A House in Gorce) and then a lengthy poem *Głos w Czeluści* (A Voice in Abyss) which received excellent reviews. In 1935 Folejewski obtained a teaching position in a Polish College in Harbin, Manchuria. In 1937 he went back to Poland, writing for newspapers and lecturing on the radio about his travels in Russia, China, Korea, and Japan. That same year he received an opportunity from the Polish Ministry of Religions and Education to teach Polish at the

University of Stockholm, Sweden. This position was financed jointly by the Polish and Swedish governments. In 1947 he received a teaching position at Uppsala University and in 1949 received his Ph.D. from the same university. His published dissertation on the Polish author Władysław Orkan received excellent reviews in France, Poland, the United States, and England, earning him a place among prominent Slavists at the time. In 1951 he received an offer as instructor at the University of Wisconsin, Madison, where he ultimately became professor and chair of the department. During his fourteen years at Wisconsin he published some forty articles in addition to editorial work, book reviews, and contributions to bibliographies. He also taught at the University of California at Berkeley, the University of Colorado, the University of Toronto, and the University of Illinois. Folejewski was a member of the Royal Swedish Society of Sciences, the Modern Language Association of America, The American Association of Teachers of Slavic and East European Languages (serving as its national president in 1957), the American Comparative Literary Association, and the Canadian Association of Slavists (serving as president from 1974-1975). He was a recipient of a Kumlien Grant for work in England and France, received an honorary degree from the University of Warsaw in 1973, and was honored with an award from the Humanities Research Council of Canada and several other research and publication grants.—*Maria Swiecicka-Ziemianek*

SOURCES: obituary by Jan Solecki, *Canadian Slavonic Papers*, December 2000; "Folejewski, Zbigniew," *Contemporary Authors* (Detroit: Gale Research Company, New Revision Series), Vol. 7, 170–71.

Folkways *see* **Customs, Polish American.**

Food, Polish American. Food has played a major role in binding together Polish American families and communities. This might seem strange in a country where Polish food has never achieved the status of its Italian or Mexican counterparts. Polish food, it seems, has been mostly an affair of the home and the private sphere, something passed down in families and rarely shared with outsiders. In the home during the immigrant generation, food preparation was normally the responsibility of women. The fact that so many Polish women came to America without an extended family network of mothers, grandmothers, and aunts meant that it was necessary to recreate recipes from memory or to rely on the advice and assistance of peers. In addition, women were increasingly able to turn to advice columns in newspapers as well as cook-

books, which were especially helpful in urban areas where ingredients found in American stores were often strange and unfamiliar. Family recipes had to be modified to fit new circumstances and new ingredients and dishes were created using previously exotic ingredients like pasta or tomatoes. The creation of a Polish American cuisine, like the creation of Polish American culture itself, was a supreme act of imagination and courage on the part of the immigrants and their children.

The early Polish immigrants brought an array of hearty rural dishes to America. Soup was a major part of every meal, the varieties being almost endless. The best known was red *barszcz* (borscht), a beet soup that could be served in almost stew-like form with lots of meat and vegetables or as an elegant clear broth on Christmas Eve, accompanied only by small mushroom-filled dumplings. Other common soups ranged from simple potato to the more exotic *żurek* (sour rye soup). Coming from a poorer class where meat was a luxury, Polish immigrants tended to value it and often spent their meager income to include it in their diet. A study of ethnic groups at the beginning of the twentieth century revealed that Poles were most likely to spend extra disposable income on more and better food. Both rural and urban families kept animals for their own table whenever possible. Urban families might also rely on rural relatives for this vital service. Hogs were the least expensive and most commonly kept animal and each fall, after the first hard freeze, Polish families usually slaughtered a pig for the winter, using the entire animal. Pork and beef could appear on the table in many dishes. The best known was *kiełbasa* (sausage). Most families made their own, using recipes passed down from father to son. Flavors varied from region to region and family to family, but garlic, pepper, sage, and (in southeastern Poland) marjoram were the most common spices. Geese, chickens, and ducks were kept by most Polish families in rural areas and often in urban areas prior to enforcement of ordinances meant to restrict country practices in the city. Domesticated fowl provided meat, feathers (for the warm winter comforters called *pierzina*), and eggs.

Gardening was also a necessity. Potatoes, peas, asparagus, cucumbers (for pickles), dill, and cabbage were found in nearly every Polish garden. Farm families also planted fruit trees—apples at a minimum, but also plums and pears when possible. Mushrooms were an absolute necessity; mushroom hunting was a ritual brought from the old country. Favorite mushrooming locations were closely guarded secrets. Another crucial ingredient was poppy

seed, which was usually purchased through local Polish grocery stores.

The high point in the culinary year for Polish immigrants and their American-born descendants was the Christmas Eve dinner or *wigilia*. This intensive ritual begins with the appearance of the first evening star. The table is carefully set with a piece of straw beneath the tablecloth to symbolize Christ' birth in the manger and an extra place is set for any uninvited guest. Dinner begins with *opłatek*, a square wafer of leavened bread. Each family member shares a piece of his or her wafer with every other family member in turn (usually starting from the oldest to the youngest), forgiving all conflicts of the past year, and wishing each other a Merry Christmas and a prosperous new year. When Poles began to disperse to various immigrant communities, the *opłatek* ritual was shared by mail in cards and letters with distant family throughout the world, or with relatives in the military service, symbolically recreating the unity of family separated by distance. Following this, the family would sit down to an odd number of dishes, all meatless. Clear *barszcz* with mushroom dumplings, pickled herring with chopped onions, and some form of *pierogi* were usually on the menu, though these varied widely from family to family. After dinner, the family sang Christmas carols and then, well fortified against the winter's cold and dark, went to midnight Mass. After church, Poles returned home to enjoy a pre-dawn snack (this time with meat) before retiring.

After Polish sausage, *pierogi* became the Polish dish best known to non–Polish Americans, though few are aware of the immense variety of *pierogi* that Poles eat. *Pierogi* came with the earliest Polish immigrants and stayed. Not so with another famous Polish dish, *bigos*, or hunter's stew, a savory mix of meat and cabbage. This dish, originally the province of the nobility, probably did not make much of an appearance in the U.S. until after World War II with the arrival of a new wave of immigration.

No meal was complete without something to wash it down. Polish immigrants were beer-drinkers, both in local saloons and at home where many made their own. There were several Polish-owned commercial breweries in the United States, though none achieved the prominence of their German counterparts and some seem to have gone out of business during Prohibition. Many immigrants fermented wine out of local fruit, and whiskey was also made at home, though more often purchased. Rye whiskey seems to have been preferred, perhaps due to its similarity to the rye vodka many had known in Poland. A common winter concoction was *krupnik* made with honey, spices, and a generous dose of pure alcohol (*spiritus*). This was considered both a form of drink and a medicine for sufferers of the common cold.

A wide range of home remedies and folk medicine using various plants and herbs were practiced by Polish immigrants, though evidence is scant. Some newspapers ran regular columns with titles like "Lekarz Domowy" (Home Physician) that provided advice for housewives on home remedies and more modern public health concerns such as hygiene. Cookbooks became an important way to convey recipes for Polish American families, especially to later generations who did not know Polish. The best-known cookbook is *Treasured Polish Recipes for Americans* published by the Polanie Club of Minneapolis and St. Paul which has sold in excess of 100,000 copies since it first appeared in the late 1950s. Hundreds of other cookbooks were produced in small quantities by various parishes and local cultural groups.—*John Radzilowski*

Sources: John Radzilowski, "Hidden Cosmos: The Life-Worlds of Polish Immigrants in Two Minnesota Communities, 1875–1925," Ph.D. dissertation, Arizona State University, 1999; Irene Jasinski and Marie Sokolowski, eds., *Treasured Polish Recipes for Americans* (Minneapolis, MN: Polanie Publishing Company, 1981); Alina Żerańska, *The Art of Polish Cooking* (Garden City, NY: Doubleday & Company, 1968); Dana Balfour, *Polish Cooking* (London: Marshall Cavendish Book Ltd., 1981); Sherrill Corley, ed., *Polish Cookbook* (Melrose Park, IL: Culinary Arts Institute, 1978).

Foster, Linda Nemec (b. Garfield Heights, Ohio, May 29, 1950; d.—). Poet, educator. Foster's grandparents, whose original name was Niemiec, migrated to the U.S. from villages near Kraków and Nowy Sącz in southern Poland. She grew up in several majority Slavic, working class, immigrant-filled Cleveland area neighborhoods, attended St. Wenceslas Elementary School in Maple Heights (1955–64), and Marymount (now Trinity) High School in Garfield Heights (1964–68). When she was thirteen, her grandmother invited her to correspond with her cousin Maria in Poland, also thirteen. Relatives translated the girls' letters because they did not yet know each other's languages. In 1968, Nemec became the first person in her family to go beyond high school when she moved to Grand Rapids, Michigan, to attend Aquinas College where, she recalled, "I fell in love with poetry. I fell in love with life." She also became best friends and fell in love with Anthony Foster, whom she met in a freshman humanities class. She graduated *magna cum laude* with a B.A. in social science (1972), then worked as a social demographer at the Center for Environmental Study in Grand Rapids. In 1974

she married and moved to Detroit where her husband attended Wayne State University Medical School. There Foster began writing poetry, inspired by the Dylan Thomas work "Fern Hill." The poet Faye Kicknosway, then on the Wayne State faculty, encouraged her work. Foster learned from another prominent poet, Liesl Mueller, "that the most enduring poetry ... has the power of language to communicate, and the power of metaphor to instill mystery." In 1979 she earned her MFA in creative writing with highest commendation from Goddard College. In 1980, she began to teach poetry workshops as well as poetry and writing classes. She taught at the University of Michigan, Oakland University, Ferris State University, Hope College, Aquinas College, and the National Writer's Voice at the Detroit Institute of the Arts. With her husband, she started the Contemporary Writers Series at Aquinas. She conducted workshops through the Creative-Writers-in-Schools Program (later renamed ArtServe) of the Michigan Council for the Arts (1980–2002) and the Michigan Council for the Humanities (1982–87).

By 2009 Foster published over 200 poems, chiefly in small press literary journals. Her work appeared in a wide range of anthologies including *Mother's Nature: Timeless Wisdom for the Journey into Motherhood*, *Riffing on Strings: Creative Writing Inspired by String Theory*, and *Place of Passage: Contemporary Catholic Poetry*. She also worked with Beata Kane to translate the Polish poet Ewa Parma. By the same year she had also published seven books of poetry. Her first, *A History of the Body* (1987), about pregnancy, has been quoted in more than one book encouraging girls' self-esteem. *Contemplating the Heavens* (2001) inspired Steve Talaga to compose a mu-

Linda Nemec Foster, poet and educator (*Linda Nemec Foster*).

sical work that was nominated for the Pulitzer Prize. *Listen to the Landscape* (2006) was a collaborative work with photographer Dianne Carroll Burdick. Foster's best-known book, *Amber Necklace from Gdansk* (2001), arose from her reconnection with her cousin Maria. In 1996, Foster visited Poland and met Maria and other relatives for the first time. In a review of *Amber Necklace*, John Guzlowski calls Foster an "essential" Polish American poet who "asks all of the questions that the best Polish-American writers and thinkers have asked: What did the immigrants lose and gain by coming here, what was Poland like then, what is Poland like now, what is America like, can we understand our immigrant forebears' motives for coming to America, can we understand what they left behind, can we ever find the Poland they left behind, is the Poland of the present even remotely like the Poland they left behind? And finally, she addresses the hardest question: Can any of these questions be answered?"

Foster won numerous honors including four grants from the Michigan Council for the Arts, a nomination for the Laughlin Award from the American Academy of Poets (2002), the Creative Arts Award of the **Polish American Historical Association** (2008), and was named first ever Poet Laureate of Grand Rapids (2003–05).—*Mary Krane Derr*

Sources: Crystal Bowman and Tim Priest, *Amazing Women of West Michigan* (Grand Rapids, MI: William B. Eerdmans, 2006); John Guzlowski, "*Amber Necklace from Gdansk*" [review], *Sarmatian Review* (January 2007).

Fourteen Points. By late 1917 the international status of the Polish Question had been radically changed from the situation at the beginning of World War I. The Central Powers had formally announced the re-creation of the Polish Kingdom in early November 1916 and over the next weeks the Entente Powers had endorsed the idea of some sort of independent Poland emerging from the war. Pres. Woodrow Wilson summarized the state of affairs when, in his famous "Peace Without Victory" speech of January, 1917, he stated that "statesmen everywhere" had agreed that a "united, independent, and autonomous" Poland should be recreated. When the Bolsheviks overthrew the Russian Provisional Government in November, 1917 they quickly announced their support for the recreation of an independent Poland, thus forcing the other belligerents to express themselves on the matter. The Inter-Allied Conference in late November issued a rather lukewarm declaration of support for the Polish cause but did not endorse it as a war aim. This failure let each of the powers issue a separate statement regarding

Poland. Italy declared an "independent and indivisible Poland" an element of a "just and durable peace" in December. The French made a similar declaration as did the British. On January 7, 1918, Wilson met with his closest advisor, Col. Edward House, to formulate American war aims. They had before them the statement on Poland prepared by Roman Dmowski for the Inter-Allied Conference and used that as a basis for preparing the American position. At the same time both pointedly rejected a more cautious statement from the "Inquiry," the body assembled to advise the president on American peace policy. In Wilson's final text American positions were divided into those which "must" be realized and those which only "should" be obtained. Because Poland was regarded as a controversial question it was relegated to the second category unlike, for example, the restoration of Belgium. The next day Poland became the thirteenth of Wilson's celebrated "Fourteen Points" speech in which he said: "An independent Polish state should be erected which should include the territories inhabited by indisputably Polish populations, which should be assured a free and secure access to the sea, and whose political and economic independence and territorial integrity should be guaranteed by international covenant." The Poles greeted the pronouncement with a combination of public jubilation and private misgivings. The term "should" decreased Polish independence from a basic war aim to a moral endorsement and thus did not constitute a binding commitment. The reference to "indisputably Polish population" was dangerously vague and denied Polish claims to restore much of their historic homeland thus introducing the possibility of a narrowly defined ethnographic construction. The reference to sea access was similarly vague and did not promise outright Poland's possession of a port or sea coast. The word "united," important to Polish sensibilities after long years of partition, was noticeably omitted even though it had figured in the "Peace Without Victory" speech of a year earlier. Nonetheless, it associated the recently belligerent and enormously powerful United States with the cause of Polish independence. The Fourteen Points are symbolic of Wilson's, and to a large extent the American, attitude toward the question of Polish independence during World War I. Seemingly ardent proponents of Poland, the Americans were really quite cautious and only expressed themselves after the issue had become well-established in international politics and then with sufficient vagueness to allow considerable room for subsequent maneuver. Nonetheless, support for the idea of Polish independence

by the United States was a vital component in the eventual re-creation of an independent Poland at the close of the First World War.—*M. B. B. Biskupski*

SOURCE: M. B. Biskupski, "Re-Creating Central Europe: The United States 'Inquiry' into the Future of Poland," *International History Review*, Vol. XII (1990), 249–79.

Fox, Paul (Paweł Fuzik; b. Kosjkowice-Cieszyń, Poland, November 16, 1874; d. Chicago, Illinois, May 27, 1961). Musician. After receiving his early education at the gymnasium in Cieszyń, Fox migrated to the U.S. where he earned an A.B. degree from Western Reserve University (1906), a baccalaureate in divinity from Oberlin Theological Seminary (1907), an A.M. from Western Reserve University (1908), and a Ph.D. from Johns Hopkins University (1924). Fox served as a pastor in Ohio and Maryland from 1907 to 1917, after which he taught at the Presbyterian Training School in Baltimore (1917–21). In 1924 he moved to Chicago to head interdenominational Polish social and educational programs, and in 1931 assumed the directorship of the Laird Community House. Beginning two years later he also taught as a part-time instructor in Polish language and literature at Northwestern University. An activist in the Polish American community, he served as president of the Polish People's University in the city, vice president of the University Friends of Poland, an assistant examiner in Polish for the Chicago Board of Education, president of the Kosciuszko Society of the **Polish National Alliance**, a member of the Board of Directors of the Education Department of the Polish National Alliance, a charter member of the Polish Arts Club, and was a member of various other Polish American organizations. He was the author of early volumes on **Polonia** including *The Poles in America* (1922) and *The Polish National Catholic Church* (1957), as well as *The Reformation in Poland, Some Social and Economic Aspects* (1924) and *Essentials in Polish* (1937). His work on the **Polish National Catholic Church** was originally his dissertation submitted to Johns Hopkins University in 1923.—*James S. Pula*

SOURCE: Francis Bolek, ed., *Who's Who in Polish America* (New York: Harbinger House, 1943).

Fox, Rik (Richard Sulima-Suligowski, b. Amityville, New York, December 28, 1955; d.—). Musician, actor. Fox grew up in the Polish neighborhood of Greenpoint in Brooklyn. His father, an amateur historian and Polish heraldry researcher, directly influenced his son's later interest in Polish history. While in high school, being exposed to the early formation of the rock band Kiss, he developed an interest in rock music, especially "glam rock," and pho-

Rik Fox, a heavy metal bassist who also founded a reenactment group based on King John Sobieski's Winged Hussars (*John Radzilowski*).

tography, taking photos of the many early glam rock bands of the New York City music scene, eventually making his onstage debut at the legendary Max's Kansas City club in 1975. While performing in clubs in New York and New Jersey with the Martian Rock Band and Virgin he became acquainted with Peter Criss, drummer for the band Kiss. In 1982 he relocated to Los Angeles and coined the name of the heavy metal rock band WASP. Although his stint with WASP was short-lived, Fox later joined a reformed and successful local Los Angeles band, Steeler. He later formed or played as a heavy metal bassist with such bands as Sin, Hellion, Burn, Surgical Steel, and Thunderball. His active musical career came to a close in the early 1990s after the demise of the Los Angeles metal scene with Thunderball, although he still enjoys the notoriety of his fans in online internet interviews. He then went on to work in the Hollywood film industry as a properties manager and weapons-handler and also acted in various roles including a small role in the soap opera *General Hospital*.

In 1998 Fox formed the first Polish American historical re-enactment organization dedicated to the history of the Polish-Lithuanian Commonwealth, and by 2000 established the first officially recognized portrayal of the legendary Polish Winged Hussar Cavalry in the United States. His winged hussar portrayal in the 2002 New York City **Pulaski Day** Parade marked the first time that a winged hussar was presented in any American parade. Fox's interest in Polish history led him to found The

Polish Nobility Commonwealth Guild, which later changed its name to "Suligowski's Regiment of Sobieski's Command," billed as "America's first living-history re-enactment group of Polish winged hussar knights and military nobility of the mighty Polish-Lithuanian Commonwealth." Fox drew on his recording industry marketing and media experience to present and promote his efforts in an attempt to introduce the winged hussar concept in the United States. The group, based in southern California, appears at Military Timeline Shows, Renaissance Festivals, and other Polish and non–Polish events around the United States with the goal of raising awareness of Polish history and culture, especially that of the era of the sixteenth and seventeenth centuries.—*John Radzilowski*

SOURCE: www.fullinbloommusic.com/rikfox.html.

Frajlich, Anna (Anna Frajlich-Zając; b. Katta Taldyk, Kyrgyzstan, March 10, 1942; d.—). Poet. Born in Kirghizia where her mother escaped after the Nazi attack on Lwów, her family returned to Poland following the war and settled in the city of Szczecin. She earned an M.A. in Polish literature from the University of Warsaw (1965), and in 1969 emigrated to Vienna, Rome, and finally New York City in 1970. She earned a doctorate in Slavic studies from New York University (1991), then became Senior Lecturer of Polish language and literature at Columbia University. The author of twelve volumes of poetry published in Poland, England, France, and the U.S., as well as numerous scholarly publications, the distinguished Polish literary critic Ryszard Matuszewski declared her "one of the most interesting poetic personalities among Polish émigrés." Nobel laureate **Czesław Miłosz** considered her "a very talented poet." Frajlich was the recipient of the 1981 Koscielski Foundation of Switzerland literary prize and the 2003 W. & N. Turzanski Foundation Literary Prize of Toronto, Canada. For her promotion of Polish culture, she was awarded the Krzyż Kawalerski Orderu Zasługi Rzeczpospolitej Polskiej from the Polish government. She was elected to the Board of Directors of the PEN Club Center for Writers in Exile. She was also a member of Polish Writers' Association, the Polish Institute of Arts and Sciences of America, the American Association for the Advancement of Slavic Studies, and the American Association of Teachers of Slavic and East European Languages. Her poetry has been translated into several languages and appeared in many journals including *The Polish Review*, *World Literature Today*, *Terra Poetica*, *Mr. Cogito*, and *Le Journal des Poètes*.—*John Radzilowski*

SOURCES: Bolesław Wierzbiański, *Who's Who in Polish America* (New York: Bicentennial Publishing Corp., 1996), 112; "Frajlich(-Zajac), Anna," *Contemporary Authors* (Detroit: Gale Research Company), Vol. 201, 111–12.

Franciscan Friars, Polish American. The Franciscan Order (*Ordo Minorum* or Friars Minor) arrived in Polish lands sometime during the 1220s, developing into an independent Polish-Bohemian Province in 1238. Promoted both by the royal Piasts and by the burgeoning urban class of Poland, the Franciscans and other mendicant communities integrated themselves into the expanding Polish cities through their pastoral service and social activity in their great Conventual churches. These thirteenth century Franciscan foundations are generally associated with the Conventual Franciscan branch of the Order, popularly known in the Polish lands as "Franciszkanie" (OFM Conv. or Black Franciscans, from the color of their habit). In the fifteenth century the Observant movement fostered a new wave of Franciscan foundations in Poland, spearheaded by the preaching and activity of St. John of Capistrano (1386–1456). The two wings of the Franciscan Order, Conventual and Observant, were juridically divided throughout the Roman Catholic Church by Pope Leo X in 1517, with the Observant foundations popularly called in the Polish lands "Bernardyni" (OFM Obs. or Brown Franciscans) after the name of their principal church in Kraków. The vigor of religious idealism spawned other Franciscan reform movements. The Reformed Franciscans (OFM Ref. or popularly "Reformaci") arrived in Poland from Italy in 1623. All Observant or Reform branches of Franciscanism were amalgamated into the Order of Friars Minor (OFM) by Pope Leo XIII in 1897, with the Conventual branch remaining separate and distinct. All these Franciscan communities continued to grow throughout the early modern period, experiencing the same vicissitudes as the rest of Poland, including the Wars of Religion and the rise to power of both Prussia and Imperial Russia. The expansionist policies of her neighbors was often at the expense of Poland, leading to the elimination of Poland from the European map in the late eighteenth century, dividing the country (and its various Franciscan foundations) into Prussian, Russian, and Hapsburg Austrian possessions.

The unsettled and divided political and ecclesiastical situation in the nineteenth century Polish lands precluded any organized Franciscan foundation from Poland in the United States, although individual Polish friars did immigrate to the New World. In 1852 **Leopold Moczygemba** OFM Conv. formed part of an international group (German, Belgian, Italian, and Polish) of Conventual Franciscan Friars who migrated to the United States to found their community. They arrived in Texas under the auspices of Bishop Jean Marie Odin of Galveston in order to minister to the scattered German settlements in rural Texas in the environs of San Antonio. Moczygemba, a Silesian (see **Silesia**) of probable mixed Polish and German ancestry, sponsored a mass emigration of some fifty Silesian families in 1854, settling in Texas and founding the town of **Panna Maria**, generally acknowledged as the first mass Polish migration into the United States and the first significant Polish settlement in the New World. The early Conventual Franciscan community, however, was much more geared toward ministry among German immigrants, and soon relocated to central New York, where there was a more sizeable and stable German population. The Conventual Franciscan foundation flourished there, gradually spreading to include foundations in New Jersey as well as around Louisville, KY, and southern Indiana. These foundations formed the Province of the Immaculate Conception of the Blessed Virgin Mary in 1872. Moczygemba himself remained sympathetic to his Polish roots, particularly from the 1870s, which led him to transfer first to the Congregation of the Resurrection and finally to the diocese of Detroit, where he is recognized as one of the co-founders of **Sts. Cyril and Methodius Seminary** in Orchard Lake, MI, whose founding mission was to provide diocesan clergy capable of pastoral care in the Polish language.

Augustine Zeytz OFM Ref. escaped Russian persecution of religious life when his friary in Smoleńsk was suppressed in 1872. He received permission to labor in an itinerant ministry in the United States, first in Cincinnati, OH, and predominantly in the coal-mining towns of Pennsylvania. In 1881 he returned to a friary in Kraków, from which he lobbied Polish and Roman authorities to provide Franciscan personnel to minister to Polish immigrants. In 1887 Zeytz received a land grant in Pulaski, WI. He was joined there in 1888 by three friars, to found Assumption of the Blessed Virgin Mary Friary, with Erasmus Sobociński OFM Ref. as mission superior. From this stable foundation the friars both recruited further Franciscan immigration and accepted Polish-American immigrant candidates. These friars served as pastors to Polish communities in Wisconsin (St. Stanislaus, Hofa Park; St. Casimir, Krakow; and St. Mary of the Angels, Green Bay, in addition to Pulaski). In 1890 Jerome Schneider OFM Ref. was named mission superior directly subject to Roman authorities. Schneider's administration was the occasion of a great deal of turmoil within the community, among the parishioners, and with ecclesiastical authorities. In 1894 the Pulaski foundation was joined in an uneasy union with nearby Sacred Heart Province, uneasy both because Sacred Heart Province was predominantly German in population, and because it belonged to a different reformed Franciscan community with different customs, the Recollects. The uneasy union was terminated when the Pulaski friars were recognized as a semi-independent General Commissariate in 1910, which eventually was erected in 1939 as the Province of the Assumption of the Blessed Virgin Mary, with some 200 friars engaged in Polish American ministry.

Increasing immigration from Prussian Poland began to settle in and around the German-language Conventual Franciscan foundations in New York and New Jersey during the 1870s and 1880s. Conventual Franciscan involvement with American **Polonia** reached a turning point with the election of one of these immigrants from Prussian Poland, **Hyacinth Fudziński** OFM Conv., as Minister Provincial of Immaculate Conception Province in 1895. His election to the helm of the German-American province coincided with increasing waves of Polish immigration arriving in the United States, not only from Prussian Poland but increasingly from Austrian and Russian Poland. Imbued with a deep sense of nationalism and uncomfortable with the notion of dependency upon mainly Irish or German clergy, these immigrants quickly desired parochial foundations in their own language and with their own clergy. These early foundations, however, were very often strife-filled, marked by economic tensions, difficulty in assimilating immigrants from tri-partite Poland, philosophical leadership divisions between clericalist and nationalist factions, and differing systems of ecclesiastical property rights and ecclesiastical control in the United States from the home country. Fudziński committed the Conventual Franciscans to pastoral care of struggling parishes in Trenton, NJ (St. Stanislaus); Elmhurst, NY (St. Adalbert); and Corpus Christi in Buffalo, NY, generally regarded as Fudziński's base of operation. Fudziński left office as Minister Provincial of Immaculate Conception Province in 1899, but remained active in connecting Conventual Franciscans to Polish American ministry, expanding commitments in Shamokin, PA (St. Stanislaus Kostka); Chicopee, MA (later to be erected as the Basilica of St. Stanislaus); Holyoke, MA (Mater Dolorosa); and Chelsea, MA (St. Stanislaus). Fudziński brought numbers of Conven-

tual Franciscan friars from Poland to serve these troubled communities, and the absence of common language and common mission fostered the growth of a distinct religious province based upon nationality rather than geographical boundaries. This occurred provisionally in 1904 and definitively in 1906, with the establishment of St. Anthony of Padua Province and Fudziński's election as first Minister Provincial of the new Polish American entity.

As Minister Provincial of St. Anthony of Padua Province Fudziński continued solidification of Conventual Franciscan commitment to Polish America, concentrating heavily upon parish foundations: Baltimore, MD (St. Stanislaus Kostka and St. Casimir); Detroit, MI (St. Hedwig and Our Lady of the Angels); Bridgeport, CT (St. Michael the Archangel); Lawrence, MA (Holy Trinity); and Milwaukee, WI, where in 1909 the Conventual Franciscans rescued the splendid St. Josaphat Church (later Basilica) from near bankruptcy. By the time Fudziński relinquished office in 1920, St. Anthony of Padua Province included approximately one hundred friars involved in Polish American parochial ministry, aided by a Polish American community of religious women in whose foundation Fudziński was instrumental, the **Franciscan Sisters of St. Joseph**, begun in 1896 by Mother Colette Hilbert in Trenton, NJ, and later of Hamburg, NY.

The Catholic Church in the United States, struggling to assimilate the masses of immigrants of diverse nationalities, committed major resources in the second half of the nineteenth century and the first half of the twentieth century to create massive parochial complexes, massive in the sense of edifices and massive in the sense of activities and organizations. These bulwarks of faith served several purposes, including preservation of ethnic identity, gradual assimilation into American culture, and a safe haven to protect and foster Catholic identity in majority Protestant America. Pastors of these parishes presided over elementary schools, religious and fraternal societies, social gatherings, and cultural and athletic organizations, frequently building and rebuilding parish plants to respond to increasing needs, numbers, and complexity. Many of the core foundation parishes of the Conventual Franciscans were presided over by long-serving and legendary pastors, including Lawrence Cyman OFM Conv. in Chicopee, MA; Leonard Pakulski OFM Conv. in Holyoke, MA; Cyprian Adamski OFM Conv. in Chelsea, MA; Eustace Bartoszewicz OFM Conv. in Detroit; Benedict Przemielewski OFM Conv. in Baltimore; and Charles Rata-

jczak OFM Conv. in Bridgeport, CT. The Conventual Franciscans also expanded their parochial apostolate prior to World War II in all of their geographical centers: New England (Fall River, Taunton, Chicopee, Peabody, and New Bedford in Massachusetts, and Danbury and Fairfield in Connecticut); the Middle Atlantic (Clifton and Riverside, New Jersey); western New York (Auburn, Rochester, Ogdensburg, Buffalo, and Athol Springs); and in the Midwest (Chicago, Rockford, and Kewanee in Illinois and St. Joseph, Missouri). The Conventual Franciscan foundations in the Midwest would be divided into a second Conventual Franciscan province with deep roots in American Polonia, St. Bonaventure Province, in 1939.

The full-service immigrant parishes of the pre–World War II period were further served and supported by a host of ministries and institutions of local, regional, or national scope. Very early in their foundation the Franciscans of Pulaski, WI, founded a printing press for the publication of Polish-language materials, which eventually became known as Franciscan Publishers. It produced dozens of varieties of prayer books and religious pamphlets in both Polish and English and published several devotional magazines: *Miesięcznik Franciszkański* (Franciscan Monthly; 1907), *Kalendarz Franciszkański* (Franciscan Almanach; 1912), *Posłaniec Św. Franciszka* (St. Francis Messenger; 1915), *The Paduan* (1932), *Franciscan Message* (1947). Franciscan Publishers also published the only Polish language version of the Bible (*Pismo Święte*) in 1963. The Conventual Franciscans published the devotional magazine *Kronika Seraficka* (Serafin Chronicle), and for a time edited the Wisconsin-based Polish-language daily newspaper *Nowiny Polskie* (Polish News). The Franciscans were heavily committed to itinerant Polish-language preaching: Assumption Province had domestic preaching teams based in Pulaski, WI; Ben Avon, PA; Toledo, OH; Saginaw, MI; Grand Rapids, MI; Canton, MA; and Lake Geneva, WI, while St. Anthony of Padua Province's team was based in Ellicott City, MD. These friars criss-crossed the Atlantic seaboard and upper Midwest, preaching parish missions, devotional sermons, and sacramental ministrations to scattered Polish parochial communities. The education enabling upward economic mobility for second-generation immigrants was the focus of the foundation of St. Bonaventure High School in Sturtevant, WI, by the Franciscans in 1922, and St. Francis High School in Athol Springs, NY, by the Conventual Franciscans in 1927.

From 1923 to 1939 St. Anthony of Padua Province was led by its brilliant Minister

Franciscan Fathers as farmers in Pulaski, Wisconsin, 1923 (*OLS*).

Provincial **Justin Figas** OFM Conv. In addition to his specific Franciscan leadership, Figas was a renowned orator and preacher, both in Buffalo and throughout **Polonia**. In 1926 Figas made a guest appearance on a local Buffalo Polish-language radio comedy program. By popular demand Figas returned on several occasions in a question-and-answer format in response to family, moral, and social problems posed to him. In 1931 Figas formed the independent Great Lakes Radio Network, and began a weekly Sunday evening broadcast of *Godzina Różańcowa Ojca Justyna* (Father Figas's **Rosary Hour**) eventually embracing some seventy-five stations and still broadcasting into the twenty-first century. Figas envisioned the scattered members of Polonia spiritually bonded in a chain by the airwaves in the same way that different beads are joined together in the rosary. Each week a choral selection was followed by a catechetical or moral talk by Figas, followed by responses to questions sent in by listeners, and concluding with a prayer service of Benediction of the Most Blessed Sacrament. Figas' conversational style covered a wide variety of topics not limited to Roman Catholic doctrinal and catechetical issues, topics of great interest to his Depression-era listeners: alcoholism, family strife, adolescent problems, capitalism, labor unions, class warfare, just family wage, American patriotism, and continued loyalty to the newly reconstituted state of Poland. Similarly the Franciscans of Assumption Province operated *Godzina Chrystusa Króla* (Christ the King Hour) from West Chicago, IL, from 1957–1961.

A further requisite for the continuation of this great institutional network of service to Polish Americans was an internal seminary system, useful both for recruiting and training personnel for growth and ministry, and for providing a Polish-language environment in which successive immigrant generations could

be trained in the increasingly forgotten mother tongue. The Franciscans of Assumption Province founded St. Francis Seminary in Burlington, WI, in 1931, and Lourdes Seminary in Cedar Lake, IN, in 1938, with Christ the King Seminary in West Chicago, IL, much later in 1955. The Conventual Franciscans of St. Anthony of Padua Province founded St. Hyacinth Seminary in Granby, MA, in 1927, and St. Joseph Cupertino Novitiate in Ellicott City, MD, in 1931.

The hope engendered by the reformulation of Poland in 1919, coupled with increasingly restrictive American immigration policies in the 1920's, slowed Polish immigration, although Polish American Franciscan provinces continued their steady growth. Already in the 1930's, the great urban parochial powerhouses of the Conventual Franciscans began to show stagnant growth or even gradual decline, as the second and third generations of Polish Americans increasingly began to assimilate into the American mainstream. This assimilation process was accelerated in the post–World War II period, with its suburbanization, greater opportunity thanks to the GI Bill, and homogenization of American Catholics into American life. The Conventual Franciscans added fewer and smaller commitments in this period, in South Boston and Haverhill, MA, and in Sharon, Boswell, and Hollsopple, PA, and the Franciscans of Assumption Province in Saginaw, MI. With the gradual decline in the need for specifically ethnic ministry, both Franciscan communities sought other forms of wider ministry. Assumption Province expanded into secondary education, at St. Anthony of Padua High School in Watkins Glen, NY, in 1946; Bishop Neumann High School in Philadelphia in 1958; and Archbishop Ryan High School in Philadelphia in 1966. St. Anthony of Padua Province expanded its secondary educational apostolate at Bishop Ryan High School in Buffalo, NY, in 1946; Fr.

Baker High School in Lackawanna, NY, in 1958; Cardinal O'Hara High School in Tonawanda, NY, in 1961; Archbishop Curley High School in Baltimore, MD, in 1961; and Kolbe High School in Bridgeport, CT, in 1963. These forays into non-ethnic specific secondary education increasingly attracted non–Poles into Franciscan communities, simultaneously broadening ministerial outreach and diluting specifically Polish ministry. Polish American Franciscans also committed themselves both to domestic and foreign missions: Assumption Province opened a domestic mission in Greenwood, MI, in 1950, and a foreign mission in the Philippine Islands in 1952. St. Anthony of Padua Province labored in Bessemer, AL, beginning in 1940, and in the Amami Oshima Islands off southern Japan since 1952.

The tumultuous period of the 1960's and beyond saw a multiplicity of issues affecting Polish Franciscans, including a drop in vocation recruitment; numbers of departures from religious life; the socio-political unrest of the period; the implementation of the renewal of Franciscan religious life and *aggiornamento* in the Roman Catholic Church; and the final dissolution of the institutional framework created by prior generations of immigrants. In the wake of all the above, Franciscan commitment to multiple ecclesial institutions began to decline. The great Conventual Franciscan urban parochial complexes either began to lose their ethnic character or their populations completely, and by the 1990s diocesan reconfigurations had affected or eliminated a number of these grand old institutions, as the heavy investment in infrastructure made by previous generations could not be sustained by diminished current ones. The specific ethnic religious formation institutions of both provinces collapsed, in favor of smaller programs often in collaboration with other non-Polish entities. Contemporaneously both provinces were re-founding in new non-ethnic specific ministries, in Milwaukee, WI; Rockford and Chicago, IL; and Cleveland, OH, for Assumption Province, and in Kensington and Stafford Springs, CT; Jonesboro and Lithia Springs, GA; and Boynton Beach and Port St. Lucie, FL, for St. Anthony of Padua Province.

In 2010, Assumption Province's commitment to Polish ministry resides in its older historic parochial foundations, which are increasingly Polish only in ancestral memory. In the 1990s Assumption Province also embraced a group of bi-ritual Byzantine Franciscans, adding further diversity to the mix. St. Anthony of Padua Province continues to provide some Polish-language ministry to more recent immigrants by means of fostering immigration of friars from Poland, in Chicopee, Holyoke, and South Boston, MA; Bridgeport, CT; Brooklyn, NY; and Clifton, NJ, as well as the continued, though diminished, broadcast of *Godzina Różańcowa Ojca Justyna* (Father Justin Rosary Hour) from Athol Springs, NY. The transition from ethnic-specific to non-ethnic specific ministry was not a completely tranquil one for St. Anthony of Padua Province, with internal generational contention within the community from the 1950s into the 1980s, and contention with disgruntled parishioners in Bridgeport, CT, in the 1980s, and in Baltimore, MD, in the first years of the new millennium.—*Timothy Kulbicki*

SOURCES: Jerzy Kłoczowski, "Bracia Mniejsi w Polsce średniowiecznej," in Jerzy Kłoczowski and Urszula Borkowska, *Zakony Franciszkańskie w Polsce* (Kraków: Prowincjałat 00. Franciszkanów Konwentualnych,, 1982); Timothy Kulbicki, *Conventual Franciscans in the United States: The First Half Century* (Ellicott City, MD: Companions of St. Anthony, 2002); Jeremiah J. Smith, *History of the Conventual Franciscans in the United States, 1852–1906* (Union City, NJ: Order Minor Conventuals, 1988); Roger Haas, *A History of the American Province of St. Anthony of Padua of the Order of Friars Minor Conventual, 1906–1982* (Ellicott City, MD: St. Anthony of Padua Province, 1984); Dacianus Bluma, *A History of the Province of the Assumption of the Blessed Virgin Mary* (Pulaski, WI: Franciscan Publishers, 1967).

Franciscan Sisters. In the late nineteenth century the burgeoning flow of Poles to the United States came to be accompanied by an increasing number of nuns. Prominent among them were Franciscan sisters who sought to serve the immigrants in the new land. Circumstances in the partitioned homeland favored the movement. While Russian and German authorities showed varying but persistent hostility to Roman Catholicism, hindering but not stopping recruitment of pious young women into the communities, Austrian Poland (**Galicia**) offered more opportunities. The lone Roman Catholic partitioning power, though sometimes using Catholicism to bolster loyalty to the dual monarchy, allowed a much freer expression of religion. In the late nineteenth century this coincided with energetic bishops who sought to improve clerical discipline and education while encouraging more regular practice of religion among the laity. They supported a major expansion of pious societies in parishes, primarily among women. This efflorescence of devotionalism encouraged young women to consider the religious life. Nuns grew almost six times in numbers in Galicia between 1875 and 1914, far more proportionately than male religious. It was this striking evidence of piety that facilitated the rapid expansion of missions among the Polish population in America.

Franciscan sisters came to the United States variously. The most direct involved sending members from a homeland community to America. Such occurred among the Bernardine Sisters of the Third Order of St. Francis in 1901. This cloistered community, located in Zakliczyn in Galicia, responded to an appeal for teaching sisters from the archdiocese of Philadelphia. Characteristically for the young republic the bishop sought nuns active in the world. Responsive to the call, the Bernardines secured a dispensation from enclosure to serve as instructors. Their first leader was Mother M. Veronica Grzedowska, who promptly established a novitiate in Reading, Pennsylvania to prepare recruits for their mission in America. The creation of American motherhouses to train newcomers, drawn more and more from the United States, was typical for the congregations.

New communities could also develop from existing ones. The salience of ethnicity was a powerful stimulus. The mixed congregation of Franciscans in Rochester, Minnesota, had a growing proportion of Polish American women by 1900. In 1907 some Polonian sisters agitated for a separate province but were refused. By 1916 their cause received assistance from Bishop Patrick Heffron of Winona, Minnesota, who urged Mother Leo Tracy to accede to the request from Bishop Joseph Schrembs of Toledo, Ohio, for a new province of Polish nuns. In a frank letter to Mother Leo, Bishop Schrembs asserted that: "The time will certainly come when your Polish sisters, in a spirit of national dissatisfaction will likely appeal to you for a separation from your community. If you anticipate this and form them into a separate province with proper subjection to the motherhouse, you will have successfully thwarted such a movement." The mother superior agreed. Here political exigency fostered a smooth, even cordial, division, with most nuns of Polish background choosing to move to the new house in Sylvania, Ohio.

Separations could be more painful. Polish members of the German-dominated School Sisters of St. Francis of Milwaukee perceived themselves as objects of discrimination. Like most Polonians of the day they came overwhelmingly from working-class origins and so brought no dowry upon entry into the community, a source of annoyance to the German leadership. Polish nuns complained of inadequate preparation for teaching, of being relegated to subordinate positions in sanitaria work, and not being allowed to use Polish in the motherhouse.

In this environment the request for a new Polish community from Father Łukasz Peściński, an immigrant priest serving an ethnic parish in Stevens Point, Wisconsin, received a warm welcome from many discontented nuns. His proposal, seconded by several other Wisconsin Polish clergymen, also benefited from support from Swiss-born Bishop Sebastian Messmer of Green Bay, Wisconsin. Like many other prelates of non–English-speaking origin, he sympathized strongly with the Polish priests' desire for ethnic parochial schools. The new congregation of the Sisters of St. Joseph of the Third Order of St. Francis emerged in 1901 with the motherhouse in Stevens Point.

Some communities started in the United States. The Franciscan Sisters of St. Kunegunda began in 1894 under the leadership of **Josephine Dudzik** in Chicago. A pious immigrant who worked as a seamstress to help support her family, she saw her sisters Katherine and Frances enter religious congregations. A member of St. Stanislaus Kostka Church, a huge parish under the care of the **Congregation of the Resurrection**, she was active in founding the Archconfraternity of the Immaculate Heart of Mary, which saw over forty members become nuns. Her acquaintance with the energetic pastor, the Rev. **Wincenty Barzyński**, CR, led her into the Third Order of St. Francis, a lay pious society of more demanding spirituality. Over time she was moved to help the numerous poor of the locality and in 1894 organized the tertiaries for this purpose. At the suggestion of the Rev. Barzyński she formed a society which quickly evolved into a formal religious community on the pattern of Franciscans.

Josepine Dudzik, in vows known as Sister Theresa, shared with Mother Veronica Grzedowska and the other pioneer leaders of Polonian Franciscans impressive determination and courage in establishing groups of religious in a novel and challenging environment. They began without the wealthy patrons or state assistance which traditionally aided spiritual foundations in the homeland. Instead, they drew support from concerned priests, who often both pressed them to undertake the ventures and mediated with non–Polish bishops. Such men often became community spiritual directors and received considerable deference, though not unquestioning obedience, from the nuns. Undergirding the ventures were the immigrant masses, largely peasant in origin, whose piety and desire to have the services of holy women moved them to dip into their modest resources for donations. They soon became the main source of recruits for the growing communities.

Nuns came with a variety of occupational activities in the homeland, but in the United States the overwhelming cry was for teachers for the parochial schools. Poles here encountered an episcopate in the late nineteenth century committed to day schools attached to parishes as a means to counter the non–Catholic (sometimes anti–Catholic) character of public education. These newcomers eagerly seized on the opportunity to foster not only religion but ethnicity in schools under their control. Polish parishes gratified bishops with their speed in setting up schools, though the episcopate remained much more interested in the inculcation of religion than ethnic consciousness.

Supplying adequate numbers of teachers for the new schools was a major problem. The traditional parochial instructors, organist-teachers drawn from the homeland, proved unsatisfactory due to paucity of numbers, occasional misbehavior and propensity to leave regardless of replacement availability. Unlike the more demographically stable villages, American parishes grew rapidly with immigration and subsequent marriages. Enrollments from the prolific families might lead to over a hundred per class in a few years. Priests and parishioners needed stable and respectable instructors in groups at an affordable cost. Women religious answered the demands.

All the Polish Franciscan foundations proved a reliable source of teachers. The nuns typically received a letter from an interested pastor requesting several members for a new school. Negotiations followed, with nuns usually receiving about $250 per year by 1914 as at St. Hedwig's in Minneapolis, less than half the cost of a lay teacher, and perhaps including agreement to do the clerical laundry and maintain vestments. In addition to pastoral oversight of the school, some parishes had school committees, but all were concerned to have the sisters remain. Communities tried hard to maintain their presence and indeed augment it as necessary, but occasionally conflicts arose over payment of wages or living or working conditions. If a proper convent was not provided or wages scanted, they voiced their discontent in deferential but clear form, and without improvement they might withdraw, the mere threat often prompting a satisfactory outcome.

A persistent difficulty was teacher preparation. Prewar state requirements were low, often nothing more than a brief period of "normal school" which a motherhouse might provide. While many immigrant nuns had extensive education in an environment of less urgency, the persistent calls for more teachers forced Franciscan communities in America to curtail teacher training. This led to public criticism, amplified in the ethnic press, and sharpened awareness of inadequacies in the communities. Their common response was a series of "educational chapters," community gatherings to discuss means of improvement. The period of postulancy lengthened after 1900, with greater provision of formal instruction to supplement the more casual strategy of assigning young nuns to work under older teachers. Varying with community and locale, nuns might also attend public universities in the summer or Catholic institutions, the latter more common in eastern states. While there was progress, they tended to have lower formal qualifications than public school teachers for years to come. However, their schools provided an attractive alternative to the many pious immigrants who wanted their children taught the Catholic faith and Polish culture.

Sisters had important additional functions. They made home visits and provided catechetical instruction for public school children. As music teachers and choir directors, nuns also participated in the public world of Polonia through organizing juvenile presentations for the innumerable rallies sponsored by fraternal insurance societies to encourage Polish patriotism among the immigrants. Their deep national feeling and charitable work involved sisters much more deeply in the ethnic community than public school teachers and perhaps made their pedagogical inadequacies less important to many parents.

Some communities had more varied occupations before the war. The Franciscan Sisters of Chicago under the initial leadership of Sr. Theresa started with the intent to help the many poor among Chicago Poles. To this end her community set up the St. Joseph Home for the Aged and Crippled in 1897 in the Avondale area of the city. Under pressure from the Rev. Barzyński they began an orphanage in an adjacent building in 1899, a ministry that continued for many years. While demands for school teaching led this community into the parochial schools after 1901, they remained more varied than most prewar foundations in their work. In 1904 the Chicago Franciscans opened up the St. Elizabeth Day Nursery, charging ten cents a day and providing two hot meals. Despite a general bias of Catholic intellectuals for a family with the father as the sole provider, the nuns recognized the necessity of some women to work and offered an economical form of assistance. By 1910 they sought to cope with the social disorganization of immigration by adding St. Margaret's Maternity Home to the facility, a residence for unwed pregnant women. Their many ventures received important material support from the Church Vestment Workshop, set up in 1909 at St. Vincent's Orphanage. Not only did the nuns use their sewing skills for elaborate ecclesiastical garments but they also served the demand for fraternal paraphernalia such as badges and society banners. Their deep commitment to service lightened their heavy workload. Some communities also sought charitable donations on a regular basis, but all experienced persistent difficulties about funding their various activities.

World War I cut off immigration and the immediate postwar period saw a series of restrictive laws which blocked much of the traditional influx, especially after 1924. With few nuns coming from the reborn homeland, Franciscan communities came to be dominated by American-born women in the interwar period, including a growing proportion of congregational leaders. This coincided with a general increase in the presence of English in both school curriculums and use in the congregations themselves.

The call to service beckoned Franciscans in another direction in the years between the wars. The influenza pandemic of 1918 brought the Sylvania Franciscans into impromptu nursing and this kindled an interest in a new field of labor. Their ancestral foundation had longstanding ties with the Mayo Clinic in Rochester, Minnesota, and beginning about 1920 Sylvania nuns began training there. Their service often began at the request of a bishop but it might be a lay Protestant, as occurred in 1930 when they received a request to staff a hospital in Branham, Texas. Their devotion and friendliness overcame the suspicions of the largely Baptist community. The expansion of hospital work harkened back in some congregations to homeland practices diminished here initially in response to teaching demands, but nursing became a significant segment of service for many communities and of necessity involved the nuns in more extensive contacts with non–Poles. This likely reinforced the growing use of English and a lessening of the overt expressions of ethnicity.

The years after World War II saw new challenges. State boards of education became more demanding and nuns spent increasingly longer in teacher training to get certification. The Sister Formation Movement of the 1950s also supported improved credentials. Into the sixties parish schools grew in enrollments but the trend toward suburbanization drew more and more out of the old Polish parishes and away from the ethnic enclaves. By the later years of the decade many communities saw their schools close due to insufficient students. Similarly financial and personnel pressures by 1970 forced communities to shrink their hospital work. The entrance of an increasing proportion of persons of non–Polish ancestry also diluted traditional ethnic consciousness and spurred acculturation.

The effects of Vatican II in the sixties, and more subtly the rapid cultural change in the United States, affected the congregations deeply. Most convened chapters to discuss spirituality, dress, community organization, service and other topics in an atmosphere of innovation underlaid with concern. Spiritual life tended to become more individualized, with nuns having more freedom to seek their own paths. In varying forms habits became simpler and less distinctive and perhaps abandoned altogether. Many sisters resumed their baptismal names, interpreted as an entrance into the Mystical Body of Christ which could be validly used while in religious life. Constitutions were often altered to reflect the council call for collegiality and subsidiarity, overall with a greater stress on consensus than hierarchy. The traditional catechetical function changed in the seventies with the appearance of religious instruction coordinators with graduate training and a greater involvement of lay persons.

POLISH AMERICAN FRANCISCAN COMMUNITIES

Professed Nuns	1910	1940	1970	2000
Bernardine Sisters of the Third Order of St. Francis		651	1095	528
Franciscan Sisters of Our Lady of Perpetual Help	29	253	329	148
Franciscan Sisters of St. Joseph		501	496	184
Franciscan Sisters of St. Kunegunda	98	400	368	119
Sisters of St. Francis of Our Lady of Lourdes		306	529	291
Sisters of St. Joseph of the Third Order of St. Francis		894	1159	482

The sixties also saw an increasing imbalance of departures versus entrants. There had always been some women who left the community at different stages but leavers were usually outnumbered by new persons entering. The effect was to increase the average age in the communities and over time to limit their ability to service commitments such as teaching in parochial schools. With a more cosmopolitan membership and the influence of the council the Franciscans became more open to innovation in ministry. They honored their Polish heritage but sought to reach out in new ways to engage themselves in the problems of society. This very American story is still being written.—*William J. Galush*

SOURCES: Dorota Praszałowicz, "Polish American Sisterhood: The Americanization Process," *U.S. Catholic Historian*, Vol. 27, no. 3 (2009), 45–57; Mary Dunstan Klewicki, OSF, *Ventures for the Lord: A History of the Sylvania Franciscans* (Sylvania, OH: Sisters of St. Francis, 1990); Anne Marie Knawa, OSF, *As God Shall Ordain: A History of the Franciscan Sisters of Chicago, 1894–1987* (Stevens Point: Worzalla Publishing Inc., 1989); Josephine Marie Peplinski, SSJ-TOSF, *A Fitting Response: The History of the Sisters of St. Joseph of the Third Order of St. Francis* (South Bend, IN: The Order, 1982); Sr. M. Zygmunta, "A Half-Century on American Soil," *Polish American Studies*, Vol. II, no. 1–2 (1945), 24–28; Sr. M. Edwina, "The Franciscan Sisters of St. Joseph," *Polish American Studies*, Vol. V, no. 1–2 (1948), 8–13; Sr. Mary Alvernia, "The Franciscan Sisters of Blessed Kunegunda," *Polish American Studies*, Vol. 8, no. 3–4 (1951), 92–96.

Franciscan Sisters of Our Lady of Perpetual Help *see* Franciscan Sisters.

Franciscan Sisters of St. Joseph *see* Franciscan Sisters.

Franciscan Sisters of St. Kunegunda *see* Franciscan Sisters.

Freedom for Poland. Freedom for Poland was a political organization founded in Chicago in October 1984 after a Communist officer murdered the Rev. Jerzy Popiełuszko, a Roman Catholic priest in Poland and a vocal advocate of Solidarność and human rights. Its founding president, Andrzej Dudek, had been a member of the National Coordinating Commission of Solidarność. Other key members were Waldemar Kaszubski, Witold Szawłowski, and Józef Kryński. Freedom was incorporated in Illinois in March 1985 as a not-for-profit charitable and educational organization. Its main purpose was to promote anti–Communist sentiment and work with other anti–Communist groups to defeat the Communist political system in Poland. By the late 1980s, Freedom mainly supported a more radical wing of the opposition movement in Poland, Kornel Morowiecki's organization Solidarność Walcząca (Fighting Solidarity). Freedom's main activity was to collect money and send it to the underground opposition in Poland. Money was collected outside of churches, at **Polonia** festivals, political meetings, demonstrations, parades, and other public events in Polonia. Members also paid dues of $5 per month. Freedom members organized demonstrations, circulated petitions, and sponsored opposition leaders' visits to America. In 1988, Freedom had 100 dues-paying members in Illinois, with sympathizers in California, New Jersey, Arizona, and Connecticut, and roughly fifty active members located in the Chicago region. Almost all of its members were Solidarność refugees arriving post–1980; a few others were immigrants who had arrived in the 1960s and 1970s, and two members were World War II émigrés. Several active members were 1970s immigrants who had originally been members of Pomost, and approximately one-quarter of its membership had been **Pomost** members, which led to Freedom being considered a splinter organization of Pomost. The most active members of Freedom had worked as skilled laborers in both Poland and America and had technical vocational educations.—*Mary Patrice Erdmans*

SOURCE: Mary Patrice Erdmans, *Opposite Poles: Immigrants and Ethnics in Polish Chicago, 1976–1990* (University Park, PA: Pennsylvania State University Press, 1998).

Fronczak, Francis (b. Buffalo, New York, October 20, 1874; d. Buffalo, New York, December 27, 1955). Public official, Polonia activist. The son of a participant in the January Insurrection of 1863, Fronczak was one of the earliest Polonia activists to pursue higher education in the United States. After graduating with a B.A. and M.A. from Canisius College, he went on to earn his law degree and his M.D. from the University of Buffalo. In 1896, Fronczak was the first Polish American to be elected to the New York state legislature; in 1910 he was appointed Buffalo's City Health Commissioner, a post he held for thirty-six years. He became one of the country's foremost health authorities, authoring twenty-seven publications in the field of public medicine and frequently representing the United States at international health conferences. In World War I, Fronczak served as a lieutenant colonel in the U.S. Army Medical Corps. Active in the **Polish Roman Catholic Union** fraternal, he came to play a significant role linking the concerns of American **Polonia** with those of the U.S. war effort, first as president of the **Polish Central Relief Committee**. Later he was appointed Polonia's delegate

Francis Fronczak served as president of the Polish Central Relief Committee (*JPI*).

to the Polish National Committee in Paris, the core of a future Polish government headed by Roman Dmowski. In this capacity he represented the Committee to the Allied powers. In France, Fronczak supervised the creation of adequate living and medical conditions for the **Polish Army in France** that assembled on the Allied side. He was also engaged in developing humane conditions there for Polish prisoners of war and refugees. Fronczak was a member of the three-man Council of War of the Polish armed forces in France and a member of the American Red Cross Commission to Poland. After the War, the University of Warsaw and the Jagiellonian University granted him honorary degrees in medicine in recognition of his many services to the Polish cause. After World War II, Fronczak was a medical advisor, observer, and coordinator of the Polish Mission of the United Nations Relief and Rehabilitation Administration (UNRRA).—*Donald E. Pienkos*

SOURCES: Donald E. Pienkos, *For Your Freedom Through Ours: Polish American Efforts on Poland's Behalf, 1863–1991* (Boulder, CO: East European Monographs, 1991); Victor R. Greene, *American Immigrant Leaders 1800–1910* (Baltimore: Johns Hopkins University Press, 1987).

Fronczak, Joseph Eustace (b. Buffalo, New York, February 18, 1894; d. Buffalo, New York, March 3, 1966). Architect. The son of Polish immigrants from the Grand Duchy of Poznań, Fronczak attended Canisius High School and Canisius College, both Jesuit institutions in Buffalo, receiving his A.B. *cum laude* in 1919. During World War I he served in the U.S. Navy, after which he entered the University of Michigan School of Architecture, earning his B.S. degree in 1924. Licensed in New York, Pennsylvania, and Ohio, he completed several major architectural projects in the Buffalo area including church, college, business, and public projects. He also worked on St. Joseph's Byzantine Catholic Church in Cleveland, OH (1933), the **Polish Union of the U.S.A.** of North America in Wilkes-Barre, PA (1936–38), and **Alliance College** in Cambridge Springs, PA. Actively involved in numerous civic, educational, religious and charitable activities, his achievements were honored with the Distinguished Service Medal by the **Polish National Alliance** and by the Professional & Businessmen's Association of Buffalo which named him "Citizen of the Year" in 1965.—*Edward R. Szemraj*

SOURCES: Interview with Joseph Fronczak, *The Buffalo News*, May 5, 1931; "Architect Joseph E. Fronczak Dies after a Long Career," *Buffalo Evening News*, March 5, 1966; "Fronczak, Joseph," *American Architects Directory* (New York: R.R. Bowker Co., 1962, 2nd Edition), 231; "Joseph E. Fronczak Leaves Monuments to the Future," *Am-Pol Eagle*, March 10, 1966, 2; Edward R. Szemraj and Wanda Slawinska, eds., *The Polonian Legacy of Western New York* (Buffalo: Canisius College Press, 2005).

Fudziński, Hyacinth (Ignatius Fudziński; b. Czarnków, Poland, January 9, 1855; d. Poznań, Poland, May 14, 1925). Priest. After completing his secondary education in Poznań, he migrated to the United States in 1872, settling in Syracuse, NY. There he joined the Conventual Franciscan Friars (OFM Conv. or Black Franciscans) of the German American Province of the Immaculate Conception in 1873, taking the religious name Hyacinth. After studying for the priesthood in Louvain, Belgium, he served as apostolic confessor at the Shrine of Our Lady of Loreto in Italy and as apostolic confessor at St. Peter's Basilica in Rome, during which time he earned advanced degrees in theology and canon and civil law. Somewhat surprisingly, he was elected Minister Provincial of his native Province of the Immaculate Conception in 1895. During his sole term as Minister Provincial of Immaculate Conception Province, Fudziński promoted the common life of the friars and heavily committed the predominantly German American Conventual Franciscans to pastoral care of struggling Polish immigrant parishes in the Middle Atlantic states, New England, and in Buffalo, NY, where he founded Corpus Christi Parish in 1898. Fudziński brought numbers of Conventual Franciscan friars from Poland to serve these troubled communities, and the absence of common language and common mission fostered the growth of a distinct religious province based upon nationality rather than geographical boundaries. This occurred provisionally in 1904 and definitively in 1906, with the establishment of St. Anthony of Padua Province and Fudziński's election as first Minister Provincial of the new Polish-American entity.

As Minister Provincial of St. Anthony of Padua Province, Fudziński continued solidification of Conventual Franciscan commitment to Polish America. He accepted further parish commitments in the Middle Atlantic and New England regions, and extended Conventual Franciscan Polish-language ministry into the upper Midwest, most spectacularly in 1909 when he accepted care of the splendid, though nearly bankrupt, St. Josaphat Basilica in Milwaukee. He further began the planning for the province's independent formation program, which would serve to solidify training in Polish for future generations. By the time Fudziński relinquished office in 1920, St. Anthony of Padua Province included approximately one hundred friars involved in Polish-American ministry, aided by a Polish American community of religious women in whose foundation Fudziński was instrumental, the

Franciscan Sisters of St. Joseph, begun in 1896 by Mother Colette Hilbert in Trenton, NJ, and later of Hamburg, NY.

Fudziński lived in semi-retirement at Corpus Christi Parish after 1920. He attended the General Chapter of the Conventual Franciscan Order in Rome in 1924, traveling throughout the continent to renew old contacts in Italy, Belgium, and Poland. During his travels, his health suddenly weakened, and he died in Poland.—*Timothy Kulbicki*

SOURCES: Richard Deptula, *Polish Immigrants, Conventual Franciscans, and Franciscan Sisters of St. Joseph: Corpus Christi Roman Catholic Church, Buffalo, New York, 1898–1939* (Unpublished master's thesis, Catholic University of America, 1989); Timothy Kulbicki, *Conventual Franciscans in the United States: The First Half Century* (Ellicott City, MD: Companions of St. Anthony, 2002); Roger Haas, *A History of the American Province of St. Anthony of Padua of the Order of Friars Minor Conventual, 1906–1982* (Ellicott City, MD: St. Anthony of Padua Province, 1984).

Funk, Casimir (Kazimerz Funk; b. Warsaw, Poland, February 23, 1884; d. New York, New York, January 19, 1967). Biochemist. Born of respected parents in Warsaw, Funk was fluent in Polish, Russian, and German. Following completion of his secondary education, his parents concluded that his future would be brighter outside of Russian controlled Poland and sent him to the University of Geneva, Switzerland, to study biology. He subsequently moved to the Universität Bern to study organic chemistry, defending his doctoral thesis in 1904. After receiving his doctorate, he studied biochemistry under Gabriel Bertrand at the Pasteur Institute in Paris and under Emil Abderhalden at the Emil Fischer laboratory in Berlin. Bertrand's interests included finding trace amounts of metals and other elements in living organisms. Abderhalden was an early researcher into the relationship between protein and health. In 1908, Funk took a position studying infant respiration at Charité, the medical school of the University of Berlin. In 1910, he accepted a position with the Lister Institute in London where, after a year of searching for a substance from which adrenaline could be formed in the body, he published his first English language research paper. His success was rewarded with assignment to research the cause of beriberi, a debilitating disease widespread in Asia that caused pain and paralysis to the victim. Research in the early 1900s had shown that adding the removed rice hulls back into the diet helped chickens recover from similar symptoms. Funk was able to isolate a crystalline substance (thiamin and/or niacin) from the rice hulls which cured pigeons of beriberi. He also isolated apparently identical crystalline substances from yeast, milk, and ox-brain, each curing the pigeons. In publishing his re-

Kazimierz Funk, the discoverer of vitamins (*JPI*).

sults in the *Journal of Physiology* in 1912, he stated: "I have suggested the name vitamine for it as being one of those nitrogenous substances, minute quantities of which are essential in the diet of birds, man and some other animals." Shortly thereafter he published "The Vitamines," a paper suggesting that a variety of diseases could be prevented and cured by making sure that small amounts of certain chemical substances were present in the diet. With that publication, Funk became well known in the scientific community and his work widely discussed throughout the world. His discovery and naming of "vitamins" led to identification of all known vitamins and to the creation of a significant industry. Funk began researching cancer in 1913 and moved to the United States two years later to continue cancer research in private laboratories. In 1917, he became head of research at H. A. Metz and Company, where his attention shifted to production of chemicals to replace those imported from Germany prior to the war. He became a naturalized American citizen in 1920. In 1922 he announced discovery and isolation of Vitamin D, only to have it credited to Edward Mellanby. In 1924 he showed that the pituitary gland's posterior portion produces hormones that regulate water balance and affect muscles. In the 1930s he discovered that the sex hormones, testosterone and estrogen, are effective in treating some diseases. In 1940 he founded the Funk Foundation for Medical Research, focused upon cancer and ulcer research. He published over 140 articles, books, and research reports into vitamins and nutrition, hormones, ulcers, diabetes, and cancer. He was inducted into the Orthomolecular Medicine Hall of Fame in 2010 during the 39th Orthomolecular Medicine Today Conference in Vancouver, British Columbia.—*Brian Bonkosky*

SOURCES: Benjamin Harrow, *Casimir Funk: Pioneer in Vitamins and Hormones* (New York: Dodd, Mead, 1955); Paul Griminger, "Casimir Funk: A Biographical Sketch (1884–1967)," *Journal of Nutrition*, Vol. 102 (1972), 1105–13.

Furgol, Edward Joseph (b. New York Mills, New York, March 22, 1917; d. Miami Shores, Florida, March 6, 1997). Golfer. A childhood accident at the age of twelve left him with a broken left arm that never completely healed, leaving him unable to straighten that arm. Despite this handicap, he developed an unorthodox golf swing that allowed him to rise to the top ranks of the professional golfing world. His championships include the North and South Amateur (1945), the Bing Crosby Pro-Am (1947), the Phoenix Open (1954), the U.S. Open (1954), the Miller High Life Open (1956), the Rubber City Open (1956) and the Agua Caliente Open (1957). He was also a member of the 1957 U.S. Ryder Cup team and was named U.S. Player of the Year in 1954.—*James S. Pula*

SOURCE: James S. Pula and Eugene E. Dziedzic, *New York Mills: The Evolution of a Village* (Utica: Ethnic Heritage Studies Center, Utica College of Syracuse University, 2004).

Gabreski, Francis Stanley "Gabby" (Franciszek Stanisław Gabrzyszewski; b. Oil City, Pennsylvania, January 28, 1919; d. Long Island, New York, January 31, 2002). Military officer. Gabreski was one of the most successful fighter pilots in American military history. He was one of the few pilots to achieve the status of "ace" (five enemy aircraft shot down) in both propeller and jet aircraft. At the time of his death in 2002, he was America's top living fighter ace with a total of 37½ kills to his credit. After attending the Assumption Parish school in Oil City, he attended the University of Notre Dame from 1938 until 1940 when he volunteered for the U.S. Army Air Corps. His early flight training proved difficult and he nearly washed out. After passing his basic flight training, Gabreski went on to graduate from flight school as a lieutenant in March 1941. Assigned to the 45th Fighter Squadron in Hawaii, he was present during the Japanese attack on December 7, 1941. Concerned about what the Nazis were doing in Poland, he asked to be transferred to a Polish squadron of the Royal Air Force. Promoted to captain, in December 1942 he was assigned to 315 City of Dęblin Squadron flying the Spitfire Mark IX. He completed about 30 combat missions with the Polish squadron, gaining valuable skills and experience. In February 1943 he returned to American service with the 61st Squadron, 56th Fighter Group, flying the powerful P-47D Republic Thunderbolt. By June he had been promoted to squadron commander. His unit was assigned to escort American daylight bombing raids and later to conduct ground attack operations against Nazi forces. His first aerial victory came on August 24 over Dreux, France, when he shot down a German Focke Wulf Fw190. From then on, Gabreski racked up kills on a regular basis. On May 22, 1944, he shot down three Fw190s over Germany. Along with his personal combat skills, Gabreski was a highly successful leader, both in the air and on the ground, playing an important role in the growth of the 56th's reputation as one of the best U.S. fighter commands. By July 1944, Gabreski had become the top-scoring U.S. ace in the European theater with 28 kills, surpassing Eddie Rickenbacker's World War I record. In mid–July Gabreski was retired from combat command and ordered home, but he insisted on flying one last mission on July 20. During an attack on a German airfield his plane was damaged and downed. Gabreski was captured and spent the rest of the war as a German prisoner. After the war, following a brief stint in the private sector he rejoined the U.S. Air Force with the rank of lieutenant colonel. He earned a B.S. degree from Columbia University in 1949. In 1951 he returned to combat duty during the Korean War as commander of the 51st Fighter Interceptor Wing, flying the F-86 Sabre jet. He scored his first jet victory on July 5, 1951, shooting down a North Korean MiG-15. On at least one occasion, Gabreski is believed to have shot down a Chinese MiG in Chinese air space. On April 1, 1952, he shot down his fifth MiG to become a jet ace. After

Francis Gabreski, the leading "ace" of the U.S. 8th Air Force in Europe during World War II (*PMA*).

his service in Korea, Gabreski held a variety of command positions in the U.S. Air Force, including Inspector General of U.S. Air Forces in the Pacific. He retired from military service in 1967 with the rank of colonel and took a job with Grumman Aircraft in New York. In July 1978, he was inducted in the Aviation Hall of Fame. Later that year, he was tapped to head up the troubled Long Island Railroad, a position he held for two years. He retired from Grumman in 1987. During his military career Gabreski received numerous awards including the Silver Star with oak leaf cluster, the Distinguished Flying Cross with twelve oak leaf clusters, the Bronze Star, Poland's Cross of Valor, Britain's Distinguished Flying Cross, France's Croix de Guerre and Légion d'honneur, and Belgium's Croix de Guerre. Before his death in 2002, Gabreski summed up his career as follows: "When I think about what has driven me through the years, it comes down to three things: duty, faith, and responsibility."—*John Radzilowski*

SOURCES: Stanley Gabreski, *Gabby: A Fighter Pilot's Life* (New York: Dell, 1992); Edward H. Sims, *American Aces in Great Fighter Battles of World War II* (New York: Harper & Brothers, 1958).

Gadomski, Feliks (b. Warsaw, Poland, July 27, 1898; d. Warsaw, Poland, August 26, 1998). Jurist, journalist, publisher. After studying law in Poznań and Warsaw, Gadomski inherited and ran a publishing house (Biblioteka Dzieł Wyborowych; BDW), served as Warsaw's circuit court judge, and also as vice president of the National Association of Judges and Prosecutors. He left Poland in September 1939, fleeing the German invasion by escaping through Romania and France to London where he worked for the Polish government-in-exile under Gen. Władysław Sikorski as Associate Judge of Appeal of the Polish Maritime Court with jurisdiction over Polish nationals in the United Kingdom. He also edited a literary magazine *Nowa Polska* (New Poland). In 1952 he came to the United States where he was employed by Radio Free Europe from 1952 to 1955. Naturalized as a citizen in 1956, he had also become involved in the **Assembly of Captive European Nations** (ACEN), serving as a member of the Polish delegation (1954–56). On January 12, 1955, while serving as Secretary General of the Polish Democratic Party, Gadomski and Stanisław Olszewski, the party president, decided to join the Polish Council of National Unity and hence recognize **Stefan Korboński** as a chairman of the Polish delegation to ACEN. For ten years (1956–66) Gadomski served as ACEN's secretary for economic, social, and cultural matters, later becoming its secretary general (1966–72). He also served

as editor of the *Survey of Developments in the Captive Nations* and authored many of the organization's appeals and letters addressed to world leaders on behalf of ACEN. A founding member of the Association of Polish Lawyers in Exile in the U.S., he was also an active member of the World Liberal Union in the 1940s, and a founding member of the Liberal Democratic Union of Central Eastern Europe (LDU) on whose behalf he addressed the first ACEN General Assembly on September 20, 1954. In 1972 when ACEN's sponsor, the Free Europe Committee, abruptly terminated all funding, Gdomski joined the organization's chairman, Stefan Korboński, and representatives from eight other captive Eastern European countries to continue their mission as a "voice of the captive people." He assisted in reorienting the organization into a non-profit private organization (ACEN, Inc.) and retained his post of secretary general until 1989. Hence, for over 35 years he worked constantly to advance Eastern Europe's liberation from the Soviet yoke. From ACEN's inception, he had promoted cooperation between East European exiles. Due to his efforts, ACEN's papers (1954–89) were securely deposited in American and Polish archives. In recognition of his services, on April 3, 1996, he was awarded Poland's Officer's Cross of Merit.—*Anna Mazurkiewicz*

SOURCES: *Monitor Polski*, June 17, 1996, no. 36, 356; Feliks Gadomski, *Zgromadzenie Europejskich Narodów Ujarzmionych: krótki zarys* (New York: International Committee on Journalism, 1995); personal data on Feliks Gadomski, Immigration History Research Center, Minneapolis, ACEN 136.

Gałązka, Jacek Michał (b. Wilno, Poland, April 28, 1924; d.—). Businessman, book publisher. Gałązka served as a second lieutenant in the Polish 1st Armored Division with the British Army during World War II. Following the war he earned a baccalaureate degree in business from the University of Edinburgh in Scotland (1948) before moving to the U.S. in 1952. Settling in New York City, he was marketing director for St. Martin's Press (1955–63) before taking a position with Charles Scribner's Sons (1963–85) where he served as manager of the reference department (1963–67), marketing director (1967–74), executive vice president and publisher (1974–83), and president (1983-84). After a merger with Macmillan Publishing Company he served as vice president (1985-86). In 1986 he became publisher of Hippocrene Books and founded **Polish Heritage Publications** where he was responsible for the publication of a wide variety of books and popular calendars on Polish and Polish American themes. He is the translator of *Unkempt Thoughts* by

Jacek Gałączka, founder of Polish Heritage Publication (*Jacek Gałączka*).

Stanisław Jerzy Lec (1962) and Lec's *More Unkempt Thoughts* (1968), author of *American Phrasebook for Poles* (1990), co-author of *Polish Heritage Travel Guide to U.S.A. & Canada* (1992), and editor of the annual *Polish Heritage Calendar* (1987–99).—*James S. Pula*

SOURCE: Bolesław Wierzbiański, ed., *Who's Who in Polish America* (New York: Bicentennial Publishing Corporation, 1996).

Galicia. The principality of Galicia existed from about 1141–1340 encompassing lands adjoining the Dniester River and north of the crest of the Carpathian Mountains in modern Ukraine and extending west into the southern part of modern Poland as far as the area of the Wisłok River. Beginning in the latter year, it became the Województo Ruskie (Palatinate of Rus) within the Polish-Lithuanian Commonwealth for the next four centuries. Following the Partitions, in the era from 1772 to 1918, the term Galicia (Galizien) referred to the province within the Austro-Hungarian Empire that encompassed the area north of the crest of the Carpathian Mountains and stretching from the Cheremosh and Zbruch Rivers in the east to the Czarny Dunajec River west and south of Kraków. When Poles began to leave from this area for the U.S. in large numbers in the late nineteenth century, Galicia was a particularly poor agricultural with minimal living conditions. The average wage for agricultural workers was 40–50 percent lower than that for unskilled industrial workers, while the latter was about 50 percent lower than similar positions in Western Europe. Male agrarian laborers in Poland earned 40–50 percent less for an entire season's work than those in Germany. This economic depression was exacerbated by decreasing landholdings and a rapid increase in the population. Farms were subdivided upon death so that by 1900, when the normal family required an estimated holding of fourteen acres for its support, the average land holding in Galicia was less than six acres. With such small plots of land, families were extremely vulnerable to the vicissitudes of weather and market, with most having barely enough to feed themselves. An estimated 50,000 per year died of starvation. For some, seasonal migrations were an opportunity to earn money in the German-occupied areas. By 1900 these movements were a significant source of income in Poland. A study of a single Galician village, for example, showed that in 1899 seasonal workers brought home an income exceeding the "total income from this village's local farming by 20 per cent." Another option open to Galician peasants was relocation to one of the growing European industrial centers. This allowed for both seasonal and permanent relocation. Regardless of which method was used, the result was an increased prosperity. Similarly, their Galician villages also prospered because migrants, whether temporary or permanent, sent cash home to their families. A third option was to extend these migratory patterns across the Atlantic. In 1891 the average daily wage of $.90 for agricultural laborers in the United States was eight times that available in Galicia. At $1.48 per day, the average wage of an unskilled laborer in the United States was twelve time as high. The conclusion was obvious. As Polish peasant leader Władysław Orkan, a contemporary observer, explained, "For these minds, accustomed to the poor local wages, it was like a fantasy, like a dream pay!" As word of the great opportunities to be had in America spread, it became a very popular option in Galicia with 82,000 migrating to the United States in the 1880s, increasing to 340,000 in the 1890s. It is estimated that between 1899 and 1913, some 47 percent of all Polish immigrants in America came from Galicia. Two-thirds of these were males, and most at least initially planned to earn money and then return home. Once established in America, however, most became sufficiently comfortable to remain so that only one in four actually returned to Poland permanently. Almost 90 percent settled in urban areas in America where they found jobs in the growing industries — especially cities like New York, Utica, Syracuse, Rochester, Buffalo, Pittsburgh, Cleveland, Detroit, Chicago, and Milwaukee. Those who did not follow this typical path generally found employment in the mines of Pennsylvania and West Virginia or, if they remained in agricultural occupations, located in the Connecticut Valley, Up-state New York, and especially the Midwest where farmland was less expensive in Michigan, Wisconsin, Illinois and Indiana.—*James S. Pula*

Sources: James S. Pula, *Polish Americans: An Ethnic Community* (New York: Twayne Publishers, 1995), 16–20; Bolesław Kumor, "The Catholic Church in the Austrian Partition and Emigration," in Stanislaus A. Blejwas and M. B. Biskupski, eds., *Pastor of the Poles: Polish American Essays Presented to Right Reverend Monsignor John P. Wodarski in Honor of the Fiftieth Anniversary of His Ordination* (New Britain, CT: Polish Studies Program Monographs, Central Connecticut State University, 1982); Paul Robert Magocsi, *Galicia. A Historical Survey and Bibliographic Guide* (Toronto: University of Toronto Press, 1983).

Galush, William John (b. Minneapolis, Minnesota, November 4, 1942; d.—). Historian. After receiving his B.A. degree from Carleton College in Northfield, Minnesota (1964), Galush earned his Ph.D. in history from the University of Minnesota (1975). Hired into the History Department at Loyola University Chicago in 1971, he remained there until his retirement in 2006. A specialist in Polish American history, he served as an advisor for the Oral History of Chicago Polonia Project (1976-77). Galush served as managing editor of the scholarly journal *Mid-America* (1980–88) and editor (1988–96). Among his publications are *For More than Bread: Community and Identity in American Polonia, 1880–1940* (2006), and articles in ***Polish American Studies***, *Przegląd Polonijny*, *History of Education Quarterly*, *Catholic Historical Review*, *Records of the American Catholic Historical Society of Philadelphia*, *Polish Americans and Their History: Community, Culture and Politics* (1996), *Ethnicity, Culture, City* (1998), *The Immigrant Religious Experience* (1991), *A Church of Many Cultures: Selected Historical Essays in Ethnic American Catholicism* (1998), and *Immigrants and Religion in Urban America* (1977). He was a member of the Board of Directors of the **Polish American Historical Association** (PAHA; 1991–94, 1999) which he also served as president (1997-98), the Polish Microfilming Project (1971–97), and the editorial board of *Polish American Studies* (2001-). Among his honors are election to the Phi Alpha Theta history society, the Joseph Swastek Prize (1990) for research publication from PAHA, PAHA's **Mieczysław Haiman** Award for sustained contributions to Polish American studies (2000), and the Oscar Halecki Prize for the outstanding monograph, also from PAHA.—*James S. Pula*

Source: Bolesław Wierzbiański, ed., *Who's Who in Polish America* (New York: Bicentennial Publishing Corporation, 1996).

Gąsiorowska, Xenia (Xenia Zytomirska; b. Kiev, Ukraine, October 20, 1910; d. Madison, Wisconsin, July 30, 1989). Poet, novelist, scholar. Gąsiorowska received an M.A. in English literature from Warsaw University, Poland, in 1935 and a Ph.D. in Slavic literatures from the University of California, Berkeley in 1949. From 1949 to 1981, she held a faculty appointment in the Department of Slavic Languages and Literature at the University of Wisconsin in Madison. In 1958-59, she was a visiting professor at Wellesley College. Her first book, *Women in Soviet Fiction, 1917–1964* (1968), published at the height of the second wave of the women's movement, is considered a ground-breaking contribution to the field of women's studies. She is also the author of *The Image of Peter the Great in Russian Fiction* (1979) and numerous articles in scholarly journals. Additionally, she published a novel, *Jan i Malgorzata* (*John and Margaret*; 1945), and three volumes of poetry: *Wiersze* (*Poems*; 1933), *Tlumaczone na wiersze* (*Translated into Poems*; 1938), and *Wiersze wybrane (1933–1945)* (*Selected Poems, 1933–1945*; 1969). Throughout her career, she was strongly committed to making college education affordable to qualified students. To that end, in 1985 she established the Xenia Gasiorowska Fellowship in the Department of Slavic Languages and Literature at the University of Wisconsin in Madison.—*Halina Filipowicz*

Source: Xenia Gasiorowska, *Studies in Honor of Xenia Gasiorowska* (Columbus, OH: Slavica Publishers, 1983).

Gąsiorowski, Wacław (b. Warsaw, Poland, June 27, 1869; d. Konstancin, Poland, October 20, 1939). Editor, Polonia activist. Educated in Poland and France, Gąsiorowski worked in Warsaw as a druggist until 1900, when he gave up that profession and settled in Paris, France, in 1904, where he decided to try his hand at a literary career while making a living as a librarian. Gąsiorowski wrote and published prolifically, with his novels and short stories focused on fascinating themes connected with the Napoleonic era. His most successful work was titled *Pani Walewska* (Madame Walewska; a mistress of Napoleon). Translated into English, the book was made into a Hollywood movie in 1937 starring Greta Garbo and Charles Boyer. In 1914 Gąsiorowski, who was active in the Falcons movement (see **Polish Falcons**), was elected president of the Western European Alliance of Polish Falcons. That year he established *Polonia*, the patriotic weekly of the organization. At the same time he initiated contact at the start of World War I with the Polish Falcons Alliance in the United States with the aim of forming a Polish army to fight alongside France for the Polish independence cause, another reminder of Napoleonic times.

In 1917 Gąsiorowski traveled to the United

Wacław Gąsiorowski, editor and chief administrator of Alliance College (*OLS*).

States to help negotiate an agreement with the U.S. government to recruit Poles for the Polish army. Later, after the army was approved, he appeared in motion pictures to promote the mobilization effort throughout **Polonia**. He went on to hold the rank of captain in the Polish Army. Gąsiorowski was back in the U.S. around 1920 and remained there until 1930, when he returned to Poland. He worked briefly as editor of the Wilkes-Barre, Pennsylvania weekly *Górnik* (The Miner; later renamed the ***Polish American Journal*** and moved to Buffalo, NY). Later he edited ***Gwiazda Polarna*** (Polar Star) in Stevens Point, WI. From 1921 to 1928, he served as chief administrator and director of the **Polish National Alliance**'s School in Cambridge Springs (see **Alliance College**), Pennsylvania, and there was responsible for directing its high school, technical training program, and after 1924 its newly formed junior college. He returned to Poland in 1930 and resumed his writing career, often using the pen name of "Sclavus." His main effort was a two volume history of the **Polish Army in France**. He wrote frequently about American Polonia and was an organizer, and later president, of the Alliance of Journalists and Publicists in the Emigration.—*Donald E. Pienkos*

SOURCES: Donald E. Pienkos, *PNA: A Centennial History of the Polish National Alliance of the United States of North America* (Boulder, CO: East European Monographs, 1984); Donald E. Pienkos, *One Hundred Years Young: A History of the Polish Falcons of America, 1887–1987* (Boulder, CO: East European Monographs, 1987); Andrzej Brożek, *Polish Americans 1854–1939* (Warsaw: Interpress, 1985).

Gatski, Frank (b. Farmington, West Virginia, March 18, 1919; d. Morgantown, West Virginia, November 22, 2005). Football player. The son of a coal miner, Gatski attended Marshall University and Auburn University, playing center and linebacker on their football teams. Following college he played center for the Cleveland Browns (1946–56) and played in the Pro Bowl in 1955. Traded to the Detroit Lions for the 1957 season, he spent a total of twelve seasons in the NFL. Gatski's teams played for the NFL title eleven consecutive times. After his playing career, Gatski was a scout for the AFL Boston Patriots and coached at the West Virginia Industrial School for Boys from 1961 to 1982. He was the first player in Marshall University history to have his jersey number retired. He was elected to the Pro Football Hall of Fame in 1985. Marshall University retired his jersey number 72 in 2006, and on November 18, 2006, the East End Bridge in Huntington, West Virginia, was renamed the Frank Gatski Memorial Bridge.—*Patricia Finnegan*

SOURCE: Richard Goldstein, "Frank Gatski, 84, Hall of Fame Lineman for Powerful Browns," *New York Times*, November 26, 2005, 13.

Gawrychowski, Walenty Piotr (b. Gawrychy, Poland, March 16, 1870; d. Chicopee, Massachusetts, February 1, 1934). Bishop. One of four sons and two daughters, two of his brothers became Roman Catholic priests in Poland. His early education was in Suwalki, after which he studied at the Warsaw seminary and was ordained a Roman Catholic priest in 1893 by Archbishop Popiel. In 1894, he gave a fiery sermon against the oppressive rule of the partitioning powers in Poland and, under threat of arrest and imprisonment to Siberia, he migrated to America. There, he taught at the Polish Seminary in Detroit until 1896 when he renounced his Roman Catholic vows and joined the Independent Polish Catholic movement led by Bishop **Stephen Kamiński** of Buffalo, New York. His first pastorate was at Holy Mother of the Rosary Independent Catholic Church in Chicopee, MA, a parish he helped organize on May 11, 1897. The following year, when the former members of Baltimore's St. Stanislaus and Holy Rosary Catholic Churches organized an Independent Polish Catholic Church on March 17, 1898, he became their first pastor. Baltimore's Independent Polish Catholic congregation bought a former Baptist Church in Fells' Point, the center of the Polish community. Gawrychowski, who arrived in Baltimore on April 13, worked with the new congregation to renovate the church and ready it for worship. On July 24, the church was dedicated by Bishop Kamiński assisted by Gawrychowski and visiting clergy.

In November of 1899, Bishop Kamiński asked Gawrychowski and another priest to visit Philadelphia to meet with the Rev. Wincenty Zaleski, pastor of Our Mother of God Independent Polish Catholic Church. The morning following the meeting, Zaleski was found dead at the foot of the stairs of his house. When police found Gawrychowski's calling card, local newspapers speculated in print about a connection between Gawrychowski and the death of Zaleski, prompting Gawrychowski to threaten legal action against the *Philadelphia Inquirer* "for an unwarranted association of his name with the death of the priest." Eventually the death was ruled accidental, but Gawrychowski's reputation nevertheless suffered, leading to a movement among some members of his church to have him ousted. In fact, the congregation was $18,000 in debt and members accused Gawrychowski of misuse of funds. Kamiński visited the congregation in November and denounced the accusations as "utterly false rumors." Nevertheless, Gawrychowski was sent to Buffalo in 1904 where he joined the Rev. **Franciszek Hodur**'s Polish National Catholic Church. Hodur assigned him a pastorate at Heart of Jesus PNC Church in Bayonne, New Jersey, and in December he was elected vice-president of the First Synod of the PNCC, as well as to the Great Church Council, remaining a member for the rest of his life.

After the death of Kamiński in 1911, Gawrychowski worked with Hodur to bring Kamiński's Independent parishes into the PNCC fold. During his life he organized, or was pastor of twenty-five churches in Baltimore, Maryland; Bayonne, New Jersey; Bridgeport, Connecticut; Buffalo, New York; Central Falls, Rhode Island; Chicago, Illinois; Dickson City, and Philadelphia, Pennsylvania; and Woonsocket, Rhode Island. At the Third Synod of the PNCC in December 1914, Gawrychowski was elected a candidate for bishop. On August 17, 1924, he was consecrated a diocesan bishop of the newly created Eastern Diocese. He returned to Chicopee, Massachusetts, in 1925. In the inter-war period, Hodur brought the PNCC to Poland and Gawrychowski undertook missionary work to establish parishes there. In 1931, he was designated Bishop Ordinary of the PNCC in Poland until a permanent appointment could be established.—*Thomas Hollowak*

SOURCES: Stephen Wlodarski, *The Origin and Growth of the Polish National Catholic Church* (Scranton, PA: Polish National Catholic Church, 1974), 114; *75th Anniversary Holy Mother of the Rosary Polish National Catholic Church* (Chicopee, MA: privately published, 1972), 7.

Gebert, Bolesław Konstanty ("Bill"; b. Tatary, near Tykocin, Poland, July 22, 1895; d. Warsaw, Poland, February 13, 1986). Labor activist, journalist. Arriving in the U.S. in 1912, he worked in the mines in Nanticoke, Pennsylvania, where he soon became a founder of the **Polish Section of the Socialist Party** and, in the 1920s, the Polish Bureau of the Communist Party of the United States (CPUS). Beginning in 1919 he traveled throughout the eastern U.S. as an agitator for the Communist Party, soon becoming a deputy member of its Central Committee. During this time Gebert also worked for the newspaper *Głos Robotniczy* (Workers' Voice) in Detroit. In 1924 he became secretary of the Polish Bureau of the Communist Party and editor of *Trybuna Robotnicza* (Workers' Tribune) in Chicago (1924–28). He was later active in the Polish Section of the International Workers' Order. In 1932 he served as a delegate to XII Plenum of the Communist International (Comintern) in Moscow. After the formation of the Congress of Industrial Organizations (CIO) he became one of the chief organizers among Polish steelworkers and auto workers in the Detroit region. During World War II, as a member of the Polish Bureau in the Central Committee of the CPUS, he supported the Alliance of Polish Patriots and the Polish Army in the Soviet Union, co-founded the **Polish American Labor Council**, the **Kościuszko League**, the "Polonia" Alliance (serving as its president) and the **American Slav Congress**, all of which were organizations manipulated by the Soviet Union to establish pro-Soviet voices within the U.S. Soviet documents suggest that Gebert was a KGB informer. In Detroit he was the editor-in-chief of the newspaper *Głos Ludowy* (The People's Voice), and beginning in 1936 contributed articles to the *Daily Worker*. In September 1947, despite the protests of the CPUS, he returned to Poland to serve in the state-controlled labor unions. In 1949-50 he was a secretary of the World Peace Council, later serving as editor-in-chief of *Głos Pracy* (Labor Voice; 1950–57) and ambassador of the Polish People's Republic to Turkey (1960–67).—*Adam Walaszek*

SOURCES: Bolesław Gebert, *Z Tykocina za Ocean* (Warszawa: Czytelnik, 1982); Louis Budenz, *Men Without Faces: The Communist Conspiracy in America* (New York: Harper, 1950), 55–58, 60–61, 252; Harvey Klehr, *The Heyday of American Communism: The Depression Decade* (New York: Basic Books, 1984), 231; John Earl Haynes and Hervey Klehr, *Venona: Decoding Soviet Espionage in America* (New Haven: Yale University Press, 1999), 234–35, 239.

Geck, Louis William (b. Warsaw, Poland, June 4, 1818; d. Doña Ana, Arizona, June 9, 1890). Merchant. After migrating to the U.S., he enlisted in the 1st United States Dragoons in 1841. At the conclusion of the Mexican War, the unit was assigned to garrison duty in the New Mexico Territory. Geck's company was assigned to the village of Doña Ana where he engaged in several patrols against local Indians. His enlistment expired in February 1851, whereupon Geck chose to remain in Doña Ana. Using his land bounty for his military service, Geck opened a store and over time his holdings grew to four stores including one in Old Mesilla and two in Las Cruces. He became a U.S. citizen in 1854, after which his fortunes increased, ranking him among the most prosperous merchants in the territory. During the Civil War he was named a county justice of the peace by Confederate authorities, while his business sold merchandise to the secessionists. Because of this, his property was later confiscated by Federal authorities. Following the war he rebuilt his business, leading a comfortable life.—*Francis Casimir Kajencki*

SOURCES: Francis Casimir Kajencki, *Poles in the 19th Century Southwest* (El Paso, TX: Southwest Polonia Press, 1990), 15–40; Francis Casimir Kajencki, "Louis William Geck: Soldier, Merchant, and Patriarch of Territorial New Mexico," *Polish American Studies*, Vol. 39, no. 2 (1982), 5–23.

Generations, Polish-American. In immigration history, the term "First Generation" is applied to the initial immigrant generation. The offspring of the immigrants, the first generation born in America, is referred to as the "Second Generation," and so on. In Polish American history, the term "First Generation" not only refers to the initial immigrants, but is also generally used to refer to the period of mass migration between 1870 and 1920. Although not strictly accurate, the term "Second Generation" is sometimes applied to the Interwar period from 1920 to 1940 when a large number of the children of the original immigrants grew to maturity and began to assume leadership positions in the Polish American communities.—*James S. Pula*

Gierat, Stanisław (b. Kozlow, Poland, May 2, 1903; d. Bethlehem, Connecticut, May 30, 1977). Veterans organizer, Polonia activist. Homeschooled until the age of thirteen, in 1916 Gierat enrolled at Sniadecki Gymnasium in Kielce where he entered the

Stanisław Gierat at the second meeting of the Polish American Congress in Philadelphia, 1948, flanked on the left by Bronisław Helczyński, president of Światpol, and on the right by Bolesław Łaszewski, chairman of the Polish veterans central organization in London (*JPI*).

clandestine youth organization "Pet." In 1920 he volunteered for the army to fight against the Bolshevik invasion of Poland. In 1922–31 he studied in the electromechanical department of the Warsaw University of Technology, but without acquiring a degree as he was involved in organizational rather than in academic activities. Until the outbreak of World War II, Gierat was a leader of the youth peasant movement "Wici" (Call to Arms) and co-owner of a prosperous electrical business. His wartime biography began in a telegraphic company in September 1939. He evacuated to Hungary on September 23 and was subsequently interned until January 1940. After his release he joined the Polish Army in France that was evacuated to Great Britain following the French defeat in June 1940. In July 1942 he volunteered for Gen. Władysław Anders' army in Palestine. After the battle of Monte Cassino, Gierat remained in Italy, married Ewa Karpińska in July 1946, and in October moved to London.

In accord with his political beliefs, Gierat decided not to return to communist-ruled Poland. He called for creating an organization of Poles abroad, for resettling Polish displaced persons in countries with large communities of the Polish Diaspora, and for cultivating among them patriotic and anti-communist ideology. He co-founded several organizations including the Federation of Poles in Great Britain, the Polish Veterans in Exile Association (Stowarzyszenie Polskich Kombatantów, SPK) in Great Britain, and the Federation of Polish War Exiles (Zjednoczenie Polskiego Uchodźstwa Wojennego, ZPUW). As a representative of ZPUW he took part in the second convention of the **Polish American Congress** in Atlantic City, NJ, in 1948. Within the framework of ZPUW and the Polish Resettlement Corps, which he joined in 1947, Gierat took an active part in resettling Polish displaced persons. This brought him into co-operation with the **Polish Immigration Committee** in New York.

The Gierats emigrated to the U.S. in May 1951. First they settled in New York City, then in 1955 moved to Bronxville, NY, and in 1969 to Bethlehem, CT. Upon emigration, Gierat was assigned the task of arousing Polish World War II veterans and promoting their membership in the **Polish American Veterans Association** (PAVA). As the conflict between the veterans and PAVA escalated in 1952, Gierat opted for founding an American branch of SPK. In June 1953 the first congress of SPK elected him president. He remained in this office until 1972 with an interlude between 1957 and 1960. Gierat was also an editor of the SPK monthly *Kombatant w Ameryce*.

Active in the London-based World Federation of SPK he took part in its ninth congress in 1971. He maintained regular correspondence with his colleagues in Britain and was informed in detail about the nuances of "Polish London," although he was unable to participate directly in its political actions. He viewed his mission in life as reinforcing **Polonia**'s critical stance toward the communist regime in Warsaw. This was the reason for his engagement in the Polish American Congress and was to be the goal of the World Polonia conference that Gierat had promoted from the 1960s onward. This was also the main objective of founding the North American **STUDIUM** for Polish Affairs in which he actively participated. He was also active as a board member and vice president in the Polish Immigration Committee, the Polish Paratroopers Association, and a board member in the **Piłsudski Institute of America**.—*Joanna Wojdon*

SOURCE: Piotr Kardela, *Stanisław Gierat, 1903–1977* (Szczecin: Działalność społeczno-polityczna, 2000).

Giergielewicz, Mieczysław F. (b. Leczyca, Poland, November 20, 1901; d. New Haven, Connecticut, May 13, 1983). Literary scholar, editor, critic. Upon completion of his studies in Polish philology at the University of Warsaw where he received his B.A., M.A. and Ph.D. degrees, Giergielewicz made his debut as a literary historian in *Ruch Literacki* in 1930. Subsequently, from 1932 to 1938, he worked as an Inspector of Schools in the Warsaw region, chaired the Board of Book Reviews in the Ministry of Religious Professions and Enlightenment, and ultimately, from 1938 to 1939, became editorial director in the publishing house of Gebethner and

Wolff in Warsaw. During World War II, he served in the Polish army in France and later in the Polish Independent Brigade in Scotland as a parachutist. He also lectured to the Polish officers stationed there. In 1944 he was summoned to the Ministry of Education in London to organize advanced courses for teachers in the English language and translation techniques. From 1946 to 1951 he edited *Wiadomości Nauczycielskie* published by the Association of Polish Teachers in Great Britain. Having passed his post-doctoral exams at the Polish University in Exile, he became Professor of Polish Literature there in 1952. In 1957 he left for the United States where he taught Polish language and literature first at **Alliance College** in Cambridge Springs, Pennsylvania, until 1958, and subsequently at the University of California at Berkeley as a lecturer in Polish and Slavic literatures in 1958-59. In 1959 he became a Professor of Polish and Slavic literatures at the University of Pennsylvania where he taught until his retirement in 1970. With a strong interest in comparative literature, he used Polish, Russian, French, German, Ukrainian, Spanish, Italian, and Belorussian in his extensive research. Of his many books, perhaps the most widely read were his works on **Henryk Sienkiewicz**: *Introduction to Polish Versification*, a monumental work which was the first such effort on Polish versification in Western languages at the time, and *Polish Civilization: Essays and Studies*, edited in collaboration with **Ludwik Krzyżanowski**. His other works concerned such prominent Polish writers as Adam Mickiewicz, Cyprian Norwid, Zygmund Krasiński, Juliusz Słowacki, Antoni Małczewski, and Stanisław Wyśpiański, as well as comparative studies on Goncharov and Prus among others. Giegielewicz was a member of the Polish Association of Scholars in London, The **Polish Institute of Arts and Sciences in America**, The American Association for the Advancement of Slavic Studies, The American Association of Slavic and East European Languages, and The Polish Heritage Society in Philadelphia, and served on the editorial board of *The Polish Review* in New York.—*Maria Swiecicka-Ziemianek*

SOURCE: "Giergielewicz, Mieczyslaw," *Contemporary Authors* (Detroit: Gale Research Company, Permanent Series), Vol. 2, 213.

Gieryk, Teodor (b. Kwidzyń, Poland, 1837; d. Radom, Illinois, October 3, 1878). Priest, Polonia activist. Following service as a chaplain in the German army, Gieryk migrated to the U.S. in 1872. He settled in Detroit where he was pastor of St. Adalbert's Parish from 1873–75. There he established the first parish building which opened in 1874

The Rev. Teodor Gieryk (*OLS*).

with 97 students and a Polish Literary Society. During this time he also began publishing the *Gazeta Polska Katolicka* as the first Polish Catholic newspaper in Detroit and called for the first convention of what would later become the national **Polish Roman Catholic Union of America** (PRCUA). Gieryk was elected its first president. In 1875 he moved to Radom, Illinois, as pastor of St. Michael's Parish. In 1934, the PRCUA erected a monument on Gieryk's grave in Radom, Illinois.—*James S. Pula*

SOURCES: Francis Bolek, *Who's Who in Polish America* (New York: Harbinger House, 1943); John Radzilowski, *The Eagle & The Cross: A History of the Polish Roman Catholic Union of America, 1873–2000* (Boulder, CO: East European Monographs, 2003).

Giller, Agaton (b. Opatowek, Poland, January 9, 1831; d. Stanisławów, Poland, August 17, 1887). Polish patriot. A Polish patriot later referred to as the "Godfather" of the **Polish National Alliance**, Giller was a political activist during his early youth in Poland, spending seven years in Siberian exile because of his activities on behalf of Poland. A participant in the January Insurrection against Russian control in 1863, he became a leader in the Polish National Government (or revolutionary council) and was eventually forced into exile in the West following its defeat. In 1879, Giller, who was then living in Switzerland, responded to letters from Polish activists in the United States, most notably **Henryk Kałussowski**, who sought his advice on the most effective way in which to unite the burgeoning immigrant community in America. Giller responded by authoring a lengthy essay published in the Austrian-ruled city of Lwów and titled "On Organizing the Poles in America." In this essay he offered a sound strategy that the Polish immigrants might follow in successfully bringing the emigration together

Agaton Giller inspired Poles in America to organize themselves (*PNA*).

into a mass movement dedicated to both their members' advancement in the U.S. and their effective work on behalf of Poland's eventual independence. In part it read as follows: "How can the Poles best [work for] the Fatherland's cause in America? ... Through organization, since only through organization can our scattered immigrants be unified and their efforts not be wasted.... Having become morally and patriotically uplifted by unifying ourselves, the major task before a Polish organization must be to help our people attain a good standard of living in America. For, when the masses of Poles in America, simply by their very presence in the country, reflect the good name of Poland to all whom they meet, they will be providing an enormously important service to Poland, a service that will be even greater as Poles begin to exert influence on the political life of the United States." Giller's moderate, sensible, and patriotic views inspired the creation of the Polish National Alliance in 1880. When the founders of the Alliance wrote to inform him of their action he responded enthusiastically and congratulated them on their achievement. His letter, read at the second national convention of the Alliance in New York in 1881, has unfortunately been lost. In 1982, Giller's remains were transferred from the Soviet Union to the Powazki Cemetery in Warsaw through the efforts of the Polish National Alliance.—*Donald E. Pienkos*

SOURCE: Donald E. Pienkos, *PNA: A Centennial History of the Polish National Alliance* (Boulder, CO: East European Monographs, 1984).

Gimpel, Bronisław (b. Lwów, Poland, January 29, 1911; d. Los Angeles, California, May 1, 1979). Violinist. Born in the Austrian partition of occupied Poland, Gimpel was the younger brother of the celebrated Polish pianist Jakob Gimpel. After beginning piano and violin lessons as age five, Gimpel studied at the Lwów and Vienna Conservatories before debuting with the Vienna Philharmonic in 1922 at age fourteen. In the following year he went on a successful tour in Italy, and in 1926 joined his brother playing before King Victor Emmanuel III and Pope Pius XI. After successful tours of Europe and South America during the 1930s, he continued his studies at the Berlin Hochschule für Musik. When the Second World War began, an invitation to join the Los Angeles Philharmonic brought Gimpel to the U.S. where he also founded and directed the Hollywood Youth Orchestra. During the Second World War he enlisted in the U.S. Army. Following the war he resumed his musical career as concertmaster with the ABC Radio Symphony, at the same time leading the American Artist String Quartet. In 1947 he went on a solo concert tour of Europe, and in 1950 left ABC to devote his full attention to concertizing. In 1962 he teamed up with his childhood friend Władysław Szpilman, whose wartime ordeal was later the subject of the **Roman Polanski** movie *The Pianist*, to organize the "Warsaw Quintet" which toured Europe and Asia. In 1967, Gimpel accepted a professorship at the University of Connecticut (1967–73), and while there established the well-known New England Quartet. In 1973 he accepted a position at the Royal Northern College of Music (1973–78) in the United Kingdom. At the same time, he performed in concerts in Europe, South America, and the U.S., returning to Los Angeles in 1978.—*James S. Pula*

SOURCE: Arthur Jacobs, *The Penguin Dictionary of Musical Performers* (London: Viking, 1990).

Gladych, Stanisław Z. (b. Warsaw, Poland, January 25, 1921; d. New York, New York, January 1982). Architect. The son of a science teacher and banking clerk, Gladych was educated between Warsaw and Lwów, emigrating from Poland shortly after the outbreak of the Second World War. Traveling through the Middle East, Gladych arrived in England after surviving the torpedoing of the ship he was aboard by enemy forces. The younger brother of Bolesław Gladych, the distinguished Polish fighter pilot, Gladych's hopes to follow into the Polish Air Force were dashed due to recurring ailments, leading him instead to attend the Polish School of Architecture, which was then connected with the University of Liverpool. Completing his studies in London in 1950, Gladych was first assigned to Scotland Yard, designing myriad administrative and penal facilities, including the police headquarters. He was subsequently hired by Alistair McDonald, proprietor of an architectural firm and son of British Prime Minister Ramsay McDonald, where Gladych worked prior to immigrating to the United States. In America, Gladych distinguished himself as a talented innovator, working initially for the prestigious Skidmore, Owings and Merrill as a junior designer and, by 1956, for the firm of C.F. Murray Associates, where he was instrumental in concepting the award-winning Chicago waterworks station. Among Gladych's most well-known architectural endeavors are the Federal Bureau of Investigation Headquarters in Washington, D.C., the First National Bank of Chicago, and O'Hare Airport.—*Krystyna Cap*

SOURCE: Olgierd Budrewicz, *The Melting-Pot Revisited: Twenty Well-Known Americans of Polish Background* (Warsaw: Interpress Publishers, 1977).

Głos Ludowy (The People's Voice). Among the early Polish newspapers in America concerned with worker issues were *Trybuna Robotnicza* (The Worker's Tribune) and *Codzienny Głos Robotniczy* or *Głos Robotniczy* (The Worker's Voice) which began in Pittsburgh before moving to Detroit (1916–18) as a weekly edited by the Socialists Daniel Elbaum and Wincenty Dmowski. *Głos Ludowy* (1924–80) probably evolved from the Polish *Trybuna Robotnicza*, becoming the official organ of the **Polish Section of the Socialist Party**. Historically, the Communist Party of the United States developed out of the ethnic sections of the earlier Socialist Party, thus Jan Wepsiec, in his work on Polonia newspapers, described *Głos Ludowy* as "a labor newspaper giving extensive coverage to news concerning Poland, published by the Communist Party of USA." Incorporated on July 10, 1937, *Głos Ludowy* became a daily, then a weekly, and began to publish in English in 1944. Its editors were Henryk Polski and Tadeusz Radwański (1930–35); Tadeusz Radwański (1936–38); Tomasz Dombrowski (1938–55); Adam Kujtkowski (1955–59); and **Stanisław Nowak** and Kazimierz P. Nowak (who were not related; 1960–80).

The Detroit *Głos Ludowy* became the official organ of the Polonia Society, a Communist Party front organization, in the 1930s. The Stowarzyszenia Polonia (Polonia Society) of the Międzynarodowego Związku Robotniczego (International Workers Order), headed by **Bolesław K. Gebert** and **Wojciech Haracz**, never attracted as many as 10,000 members throughout the United States at the peak when 135 *grupas* (lodges) covering the ten states with the largest Polish American population, although it offered medical benefits as well as life insurance. The IWO, forced to dissolve in 1954, proved to be the most effective Communist Party front group because it allowed the Party inroads into every ethnic group, aiding Gebert in his efforts to organize unions of steel workers and auto workers. Philip Murray, president of the Congress of Industrial Organizations, praised the efforts of *Głos Ludowy* to promote the welfare of workers. In 1975, *Głos Ludowy* published a monthly English supplement, *The Young Outlook*. With a staff of only five, *Głos Ludowy* received a $50,000 annual subsidy from the Polish government in order to survive. An organization, Koło Przyjaciol Prasy Ludowej (Circle of Friends of the People's Press), which supported *Głos Ludowy*, was very active between 1951 and 1979 in the major Polonian cities. Yet, to continue publishing the newspaper was forced to merge with the Toronto *Kronika Tygodniowa* (The Weekly Chronicle) in 1979 when its subscription list numbered only about 1,000. It finally expired in January 1980. A prominent former staffer of the *Głos Ludowy*, journalist Robert Strybel, went on to a distinguished career in Warsaw.—*Don Binkowski*

SOURCES: Jan Wepsiec, *Polish American Serial Publications 1842–1966, An Annotated Bibliography* (Chicago: author, 1968); Margaret C. Nowak, *Two Who Were There* (Detroit: Wayne State University Press, 1989); Robert Keeran, "The International Workers Order and the Origins of the CIO," *Labor History*, Vol. 30, no. 3 (Summer 1989), 385–408; Arthur J. Sabin, *Red Scare in Court* (Philadelphia: University of Pennsylvania Press, 1993).

Głos Polek (The Voice of the Polish Women). The official press organ of the **Polish Women's Alliance of America**, this newspaper was founded in 1902 under the editorship of Frank Wołowski, an associate editor of *Dziennik Narodowy*. It ceased publication after ten months due to financial problems, with the Polish Women's Alliance publishing its own page in *Dziennik Narodowy* until 1910 when the eighth convention of the PWA decided to reactivate *Głos Polek* with **Stefania Laudyn-Chrzanowska** as editor. It was published as a weekly from 1910 to 1956 when it became a semimonthly appearing on the first and third Thursday of each month. In 1995 it became a monthly. Most notable of the editors of *Głos Polek* were Maria Kryszak (1921–39), Jadwiga Karłowicz (1939–51 and 1955–64) and **Maria Loryś** (1964–95). In 1951 an English language section was introduced with Melanie Sokołowska as editor. At its beginning, the English section occupied less than twenty percent of the newspaper, but gradually the proportions of the English and Polish texts have been reversed. Like other fraternal press organs, *Głos Polek* devoted much space to organizational matters, both national and local. It promoted the ideals of the PWA (including feminism, especially at the beginning of the twentieth century) and advertised its insurance plans. It also stressed the need for preserving Polish heritage in Polish American homes, regarding this as an important duty of a Polish American woman.—*Joanna Wojdon*

SOURCE: Angela T. Pienkos and Donald E. Pienkos, "*In the Ideals of Women is the Strength of a Nation*": *A History of the Polish Women's Alliance of America* (Boulder, CO: East European Monographs, 2003).

Głowacki, Janusz Andrzej (b. Poznań, Poland, September 13, 1938; d.—). Playwright. After earning his M.A. degree from the University of Warsaw, he published his first short stories in 1962, achieving popular success with his satirical images of life in contemporary Poland. He left Poland in 1981, settling in the United States where he received fellowships at the University of Iowa in 1981 and 1983. Later, he taught at Bennington College, Yale University, and Columbia University, while achieving popular success writing for the theatre. His contemporary dramas—*Cinders* (1984), *Hunting Cockroaches* (1987), *Fortinbras Gets Drunk* (1990), *Antygone in New York* (1993), and others—have strong satirical overtones but deal with serious social problems, receiving critical acclaim in the United States and in Europe. Among his many honors are the American Theatre Critics Association Award (1986), the Drama League of New York Playwriting Award (1987), and the Hollywood Drama League Critics Award (1987).—*Jerzy Krzyzanowski*

SOURCES: Bolesław Wierzbiański, *Who's Who in Polish America* (New York: Bicentennial Publishing Corp., 1996), 129; "Glowacki, Janusz," *Contemporary Authors* (Detroit: Gale Research Company), Vol. 116, 171–72.

Gmina Polska (Polish Commune). The Gmina Polska or Polish commune (sometimes translated as community or council) was a nationalist organization founded in Chicago in October 1866. Fourteen years later this important organization eventually became one of the founding members of the **Polish National Alliance**. Polish immigrants living on Chicago's Northwest Side came together to organize Gmina Polska as an alternative to the Catholic Saint Stanislaus Society, which had been revived that same year with an ambitious plan to organize a Polish parish and to provide various fraternal benefits. While the St. Stanislaus Society would emphasize the Polish nature of the immigration, the Gmina Polska patterned itself after Polish nationalist organizations that would accept all Poles regardless of religion or political ideology as long as they supported an independent fatherland. The rivalry between the two organizations mirrored ideological issues that soon fractured the immigrant community and would eventually result in the creation of rival national organizations the **Polish Roman Catholic Union** and the Polish National Alliance. Gmina Polska was connected to the national Polish government-in-exile in Switzerland and was part of the worldwide call for Poles living abroad to form such nationalist organizations. **Henryk Kałussowski** began the Gmina movement in the United States in New York City and hoped eventually to create such groups in every Polish community in the United States. In Chicago the task fell to the patriotic twenty-three year old **Władysław Dyniewicz** who first opened a bookstore and then a publishing company in the city. Dyniewicz began to print the *Gazeta Polska* (Polish Gazette) in 1873, Chicago's first Polish language newspaper.

Class differences in the immigrant community seem to have played a part in the early years of both the St. Stanislaus Society and the Gmina Polska. Unlike in Poland, both peasants and gentry lived next to each other in the crowded Polish neighborhoods of industrial Chicago. In many ways the migration had been the great equalizer in the American **Polonia**. At first devout Catholic peasants tended to join the Catholic organization while members of the gentry gravitated towards the more radical Gmina Polska. In the at times confusing disagreements of the immigrant community both organizations worked towards the creation of Polish Catholic parishes. The rivalry between the St, Stanislaus Society and Gmina Polska dragged out for some twenty years and eventually involved the Catholic bishop of Chicago. Charges of freemasonry were often leveled at the Gmina Polska whose membership included atheists as well as Jewish, Protestant, and Orthodox Poles.

Gmina Polska members had long agitated for a strong national organization to represent the Poles in America and to actively agitate for Polish independence. With the founding of the Polish National Alliance (PNA) in 1880 those dreams were achieved. **Maksymilian Kucera**, a representative of the Gmina Polski at the founding convention of the PNA, was elected the first president of the fledgling organization in September 1880. Gmina Polska members played a crucial part in the early years of the PNA and fought successfully to locate its national headquarters in Chicago.—*Dominic A. Pacyga*

SOURCES: Victor Greene, *For God and Country: The Rise of Polish and Lithuanian Ethnic Consciousness in America, 1860–1910* (Madison: The State Historical

Society of Wisconsin, 1975); Joseph John Parot, *Polish Catholics in Chicago, 1850–1920* (DeKalb, IL, Northern Illinois University Press, 1981); Donald E. Pienkos, *PNA: A Centennial History of the Polish National Alliance of the United States of America* (Boulder, CO: East European Monographs, 1984).

Gminski, Mike (b. Monroe, Connecticut, August 3, 1959; d.—). Basketball player. A 6'11" center, Gminski played college basketball at Duke University from 1977 to 1980. In 1979 he was named first team All-American and Atlantic Coast Conference player of the year. He retired as the holder of Duke career records for points scored, rebounds, and blocked shots. Gminski played fourteen seasons as a professional in the National Basketball Association from 1980 to 1994, after being chosen in the first round of the collegiate draft by the New Jersey Nets. After spending his first seven seasons, and part of his eighth, in a New Jersey uniform, he played for three other NBA teams. Following retirement from the court, he appeared on radio and television as a college basketball analyst. In 2003 he was inducted into the National Polish-American Sports Hall of Fame.—*Neal Pease*

SOURCE: "Mike Gminski," National Polish-American Sports Hall of Fame website, www.polishsportshof.com.

Godowsky, Leopold (b. Soshy, Russian Empire, February 13, 1870; d. New York City, New York, November 21, 1938). Musician. Born near present-day Vilnius, Lithuania, Godowsky's father, a physician, died from cholera when the young Godowsky was but eighteen months old and his mother moved the family to Schirwinty where her close circle of friends included amateur musicians. Demonstrating an early aptitude for music, Godowsky was proficient on both the violin and piano, and was largely self-taught, though he benefited from contact with his mother's musical acquaintances. At age seven, he began composing, made his pianistic debut in Vilnius in 1879, and within two years was touring the western provinces of the Russian Empire, as well as Germany. Briefly, Godowsky attended the Berlin Hochschule Für Musik in 1884 before traveling to the United States. He debuted in Boston in December of that year. Two years later, hoping to study under Franz Liszt, Godowsky was forced to alter his plans when Liszt passed away. He therefore traveled instead to Paris where he studied under Camille Saint-Saëns. He returned again to the United States in 1890, in time to perform at Carnegie Hall two weeks after its official opening. In 1891, he married Frieda Saxe and became an U.S. citizen. Between 1894 and 1895 he commuted between New York and Philadelphia where he held positions at the

New York College of Music and the Piano Department of the Broad Street Conservatory of Music in Pennsylvania. In 1895, he moved to Chicago where he served as head of the Chicago Conservatory of Music's piano department until 1900. During these busy years of teaching, Godowsky developed his pedagogical theory of "weight and relaxation" which held that pianistic power should originate from the relaxed use of arm weight, rather than from muscular force. Additionally, it was during this period that some of the earliest of Godowsky's fifty-three pieces collectively titled *Studies on Chopin's Etudes* were published by the well-known U.S. music publisher G. Schirmer. In December 1900, Godowsky returned to Berlin for a successful performance, which solidified his reputation as a piano virtuoso in the European music world. He remained in Berlin until 1909 and continued touring, before he assumed the position of Director of the Piano Master School of the Viennese Academy of Music—a position he held until 1914. Upon his return to the United States, Godowsky performed extensively, moving from New York to Los Angeles and then to Seattle. He continued teaching and composing well into the 1920s. A paralytic stroke suffered while making a phonograph recording in London, England in 1930 effectively ended his musical career. The Leopold Godowsky Collection at the Library of Congress includes holographs of his piano music, printed material, photographs, and other ephemera. Similarly, the John George Hinderer papers at the Minnesota Historical Society and the Vladimir and Wanda Horowitz Collection and Love Family Papers at Yale University, contain various materials relating to his life and musical career.—*Krystyna Cap*

SOURCES: Jeremy Nicholas, *Godowsky, The Pianists' Pianist: A Biography of Leopold Godowsky* (Northumberland: Appian Publications & Recordings, 1989); Leonard S. Saxe, "The Published Music of Leopold Godowsky," *Notes*, Vol. 14, no. 2 (March, 1957), 165–83.

Goeppert-Mayer, Maria (b. Katowice, Poland, June 28, 1906; d. San Diego, California, February 20, 1972). Physicist. Born in Upper Silesia, once German territory, as a child she loved science, later attending the University of Gottingen to study mathematics. She changed her field after attending a lecture on atomic physics, earning a doctorate in theoretical physics in 1930. After meeting and marrying American Dr. Joseph Edward Mayer in 1931, she moved to the United States where she worked at Johns Hopkins University in Baltimore, MD. She eventually became a U.S. citizen (1933) and expanded her field to chemical physics, authoring many papers while

teaching at Columbia University and Sarah Lawrence College, but she did most of her research separating uranium isotopes at S.A.M. Laboratory. She and her husband authored a textbook, *Statistical Mechanics*, the leading text in the field for 44 years. During World War II she worked on the Manhattan Project to develop the world's first atomic bombs. After the war, she moved to Chicago where she continued working in quantum mechanics, studying the movement of electrons within the atom. She taught at the University of Chicago while also working at the Argonne National Laboratory. With Eugene Wigner and Hans Jensen, she developed and published the Elementary Theory of Nuclear Shell Structure, which explained the arrangement of particles in the atomic nucleus. She and Jensen wrote *Elementary Theory of Nuclear Shell Structure* in 1950. In 1959, she became a full professor at the University of California at San Diego, and four years later she and Jensen were awarded the Nobel Prize in Physics in 1963, becoming the first American woman, and only the second woman to win the physics prize (the other was the Pole Maria Sklodowska Curie). Goepper-Mayer became a member of the American Academy of Arts and Sciences, the Academy of Heidelberg, the National Academy of Sciences, and was a fellow with the American Physical Society. She also received honorary degrees from Russell Sage College, Mount Holyoke College, and Smith College.—*Cheryl A. Pula*

SOURCES: Joan Dash, *The Triumph of Discovery: Women Scientists Who Won the Nobel Prize* (Englewood Cliffs, NJ: Julian Messner, 1991); Joseph P. Ferry, *Maria Goeppert Mayer: Physicist* (Philadelphia: Chelsea House, 2003); "Goeppert-Mayer, Maria," *Contemporary Authors* (Detroit: Gale Research Company), Vol. 156, 167–70.

Gola, Thomas Joseph "Tom" (b. Philadelphia, Pennsylvania, January 13, 1933; d.—). Basketball player. The son of a Philadelphia police officer, Tom Gola drew attention from colleges across the country when he led LaSalle High School to the Philadelphia Catholic League Championship. Gola went on to play collegiately for his hometown La Salle University, where he quickly gained a reputation as one of college basketball's all-time greatest players. He played varsity basketball as a college freshman, as LaSalle was one of many smaller universities allowed to use freshmen during the Korean War. In his first year he led the Explorers to a 25–7 record. LaSalle went on to win the 1952 National Invitational Tournament by defeating Dayton in the finals, and Gola won co–Most Valuable Player honors. At the time the winner of the NIT was considered the national champion. In his sophomore year,

LaSalle finished with a 25–3 mark, but lost in the NIT quarterfinals by one point to St. John's. In his junior year the Explorers went 26–4 and won the National Collegiate Athletic Association tournament title by defeating Bradley in the finals as Gola earned MVP honors. By that time, the NCAA tournament had surpassed the NIT. Gola led LaSalle back to the NCAA finals in 1955, his senior year, but the Explorers lost to a powerful University of San Francisco team led by Bill Russell and K. C. Jones. Among his many honors, Gola was named All-American four times, one of just a handful of players so honored. During his four years at La Salle he averaged 20.9 points and 19.0 rebounds during 115 games. He scored a school career record 2,461 points and grabbed an NCAA record 2,201 rebounds. During that time LaSalle had a 102–19 won-lost record and finished in the top 20 nationally each year. Known as "Mr. All-Around," the 6' 6" Gola had the ability to shoot, rebound, and defend as a forward, but he also had the ball handling skills, shooting range, and quickness to play guard.

Following graduation, he was drafted by the NBA with the Philadelphia Warriors as a territorial draft pick. In his rookie season he teamed with all-pros Paul Arizin and Neil Johnston to lead the Warriors to the NBA championship in 1956. Gola concentrated on defense, passing, and rebounding, allowing the other two to be the main scorers. This title made him one of only two players in basketball history to win the NIT, NCAA, and NBA championships. For his ten-year professional career with the Warriors, and later the New York Knicks, he scored over 7,800 points, had over 5,600 rebounds, and averaged 4.2 assists per game. He was named to the All-Pro team five times. In 1968, Gola returned to his alma mater as head basketball coach. During his two-year tenure he led the Explorers to a 37–13 record. He then was elected to the Pennsylvania State Legislature, and later served as Philadelphia City Comptroller. Gola has been named to numerous halls of fame, including the Basketball Hall of Fame in 1976 and the Polish-American Sports Hall of Fame in 1977. In 2008 ESPN ranked him 17th on its list of the 25 greatest college basketball players of all time.—*Thomas Tarapacki*

SOURCES: "In Philadelphia Nearly Everybody Likes Gola," *Sports Illustrated*, December 27, 1954; "Preview: Great Season, Greater Star," *Sports Illustrated*, December 13, 1954.

Gołąbki. A traditional Polish food consisting of boiled cabbage leaves stuffed with various fillings usually including rice or barley, onions, and ground beef or pork. Usually they are baked in a tomato sauce, although recipes vary. The name comes from *gołąb*, the Polish word for "pigeon," because the shape of the stuffed cabbage resembles the body of a pigeon. In the U.S. these are sometimes referred to as "pigs in a blanket" or "cabbage rolls," by other names used for similar dishes in other East European countries.—*James S. Pula*

SOURCE: Irene Jasinski and Marie Sokolowski, eds., *Treasured Polish Recipes for Americans* (Minneapolis, MN: Polanie Publishing Company, 1981.

Goldwyn, Samuel (Szmuel Gelbfisz; b. Warsaw, Poland, August 17, 1879; d. Los Angeles, California, January 31, 1974). Film producer. Gelbfisz migrated to England in 1895 where he adopted the Anglicized name Samuel Goldfish. In 1898 he moved to Canada, and then on to the U.S. in January 1899 where he went to work in a garment factory in Gloversville, New York, and became a naturalized citizen in 1902. The following year he moved to New York City where he became enthralled with the developing motion picture industry. Teaming with entertainer Jesse L. Lasky, theater owner Adolph Zukor, and director Cecil B. DeMille, he founded a company that produced three films and later became Paramount Pictures. After leaving the earlier partnership, in 1916 he teamed with Edgar and Archibald Selwyn to form the Goldwyn Pictures Corporation, with its trademark Lion symbol, the name deriving from a combination of the partner's surnames. Gelbfisz then legally changed his own name to Samuel Goldwyn. The company was eventually purchased by Marcus Loew of Metro Pictures Corporation to form Metro-Goldwyn-Mayer, but Goldwyn took no part in the new enterprise. Goldwyn went on to found the Samuel Goldwyn Studio through which he produced films over three decades that earned a string of Oscar nominations in various categories. Among his hit films were *The Best Years of Our Lives*, *Guys and Dolls*, and *Porgy and Bess*. In 1946 the Academy of Mo-

Producer Samuel Goldwyn with actress Joan Evans (NARA).

tion Picture Arts and Sciences honored Goldwyn with the Irving G. Thalberg Memorial Award, and in 1957 he received the Jean Hersholt Humanitarian Award. In 1971 President Richard Nixon presented him with the Presidential Medal of Freedom. A Beverly Hills theater is named in his honor and he has a star on the Hollywood Walk of Fame.—*James S. Pula*

SOURCE: A. Scott Berg, *Goldwyn: A Biography* (New York: Alfred A. Knopf, 1989).

Golembiewski, Billy (b. Grand Rapids, Michigan, July 31, 1929; d. Coleman, Michigan, January 25, 1998). Bowler. Golembiewski was a prominent professional bowler during the 1950s and 1960s. Based in Detroit, he won the American Bowling Congress Masters championship in 1960 and 1962, and won three other ABC titles. Golembiewski threw five perfect games during his career. In 1961 he issued an instructional recording under the title "Hear How to Be a Better Bowler." He is a member of the ABC Bowling Hall of Fame, and was inducted into the National Polish-American Sports Hall of Fame in 1981.—*Neal Pease*

SOURCES: "Billy Golembiewski," National Polish-American Sports Hall of Fame website, www.polish sportshof.com; *New York Times*, May 12, 1960 and May 19, 1962.

Golombki *see* **Gołąbki.**

Gołota, Andrzej (b. Warsaw, Poland, January 5, 1968; d.—). Boxer. Gołota joined the Warsaw Legia boxing club in 1981 and three years later was nominated as a member of the Polish national junior boxing team. A junior world vice-champion in 1985 and European champion in 1986, he moved to the senior section of the Legia club and in 1987 joined the senior Polish national boxing team. The peak of Gołota's amateur career was a bronze medal in the 1988 Olympic Games in Seoul. In 1991 he migrated to the United States as a result of his marriage to an American citizen of Polish ancestry, and in 1992 he began his professional boxing career. Two years later he had his first opportunity to take part in an HBO Boxing event, fighting Riddick Bowe, but was disqualified for low blows. A riot followed the fight and Gołota was injured by one of Bowe's staff. In a revenge fight he was again disqualified for low blows; nevertheless, his heavyweight career continued. He fought against Lennox Louis in 1997 (Gołota was knocked out), against Tim Witherspoon in 1998 (Gołota won), Mike Grant in 1999 (lost), Mike Tyson in 2000 (lost), and Chris Byrd in 2004 (draw). He had three unsuccessful world title attempts, in 2007 won the IBF North American Heavyweight Title, and in 2008 won the WBA Federation Heavyweight Title. However, in November 2008, fighting for the WBC-USNBC title against Ray Austin, Gołota lost after the first round. He also experienced several legal difficulties beginning with a fight in a disco in Włocławek, Poland, in 1989, after which he was accused of assault and robbery. His migration to the United States let him postpone the trial that eventually took place in 1997. Later he was involved in other fights and in car accidents.—*Joanna Wojdon*

SOURCES: Thomas Myler, *The Sweet Science Goes Sour: How Scandal Brought Boxing to its Knees* (Vancouver, Canada: Greystone Books, 2006); Budd Schulberg, *Ringside: A Treasury of Boxing Reportage* (Chicago: Ivan R. Dee, 2006).

Gonglewski, Zygmunt (b. Suwalki, Russian-occupied Poland, March 27, 1908; d. Meriden, Connecticut, October 15, 1987). Polonia activist. Gonglewski arrived in the United States in 1923. A member of the **Polish Falcons** of America in Meriden, Connecticut, from 1924, he was involved in every aspect of the Falcons in his local group (or "nest") during the next six decades. He was also involved in the activities of the Falcons at the district and national levels. During World War II he served in the U.S. Army and was later an elected local official in Meriden. During and after the war he was also involved in the **Polish American Council** (Rada Polonii Amerykańskiej) and the **Polish American Congress**. In 1939, Gonglewski worked to help organize a Polish American military force in Canada at the behest of Falcons president **Teofil Starzyński**. After the war he was involved in helping in the resettlement of veterans of the Polish armed forces who had entered the U.S. under the Displaced Persons Act of 1948. Gonglewski served as the fifth Grand Master of the Falcons' Commandery of the Legion of Honor from 1972. The Commandery of the Legion of Honor was established in 1925 by the Falcons Alliance under the leadership of Walter Pawlak to honor distinguished service of Falcons' members on behalf of its causes, initially their service in the **Polish Army in France** that had served in France and Poland during and after World War I on behalf of Poland's independence. The first Grand Master of the Commandery of the Legion of Honor was Romuald Ostrowski (1881–1949). In 2009 the Grand Master of the Commandery of the Legion of

Honor and Star of Merit of the Polish Falcons of America was Louis Tremitti of Rochester, New York. Gonglewski was honored for his patriotic and fraternal actions by the Polish government-in-exile in London.—*Donald E. Pienkos*

SOURCE: Donald Pienkos, *One Hundred Years Young: A Centennial History of the Polish Falcons of America, 1887–1987* (Boulder, CO: East European Monographs, 1987).

Góral, Bolesław (b. Koenigsdorf, West Prussia, March 12, 1876; d. Milwaukee, Wisconsin, March 31, 1960). Bishop. Emigrating from Prussia in 1889, Góral attended the **SS. Cyril and Methodius Seminary** in Detroit, Michigan, as well as the St. Francis Seminary near Milwaukee, Wisconsin. A seasoned writer and linguist, fluent in several languages including English, French, German, Greek, Latin, and Polish, Góral began publishing a monthly magazine, *Orędownik Językowy* (The Linguistic Adviser) in 1905. Committed to linguistic purity, the publication was intended to offer Poles a high-brow alternative to other contemporary literary supplements. Due to a lack of funding, Góral and his assistants, **Stanisław Osada** and Karol Barski, were forced to abandon *Orędownik Językowy* four years after its inception. Concurrent with his editorial responsibilities at *Orędownik Językowy*, Góral also edited ***Nowiny Polskie*** (The Polish Daily News), a position which he maintained for nearly two decades, concomitant president and treasurer of the Milwaukee-based publication. Góral had been originally recruited to the position of editor at *Nowiny Polskie* by

The Rev. Bolesław Góral, editor of the influential Milwaukee *Nowiny Polskie* (**OLS**).

Archbishop Sebastian Mesmer who sought an alternative to the vociferously nationalist ***Kuryer Polski*** (Polish Courier) published by **Michał Kruszka**. Although the *Nowiny* was said to have represented the views of the Milwaukee Archdiocese, and had even earned the blessing of the Pope, a polemical battle erupted between the *Kuryer* and the *Nowiny* which lasted for several years. In 1907, Góral launched a new weekly publication, *Nowiny* (The News), with the aid of Albin M. Szybczyński; the success of the paper soon led to its daily publication. From 1908-09, Góral was rector of the Church of St. Vincent de Paul and, soon after, was appointed to replace the Rev. Hyacinth Gulski at St. Hyacinth's parish. Góral managed to repair relations between the parish and its administrators, which had been tense for several years. Góral remained at St. Hyacinth's until his death in 1960. He published several works including a treatise on Polish punctuation, myriad essays and verses, translations of drama and poetry, and an article on the Poles of Milwaukee for the *Catholic Encyclopedia*. He was honored with the Order of Polonia Restituta by the Polish Government in 1924. In 1939, he was elected president of the Alumni Association of the Polish Theological Seminary in Orchard Lake, Michigan, for the Milwaukee District.—*Krystyna Cap*

SOURCE: Anthony J. Kuzniewski, *Faith & Fatherland. The Polish Church War in Wisconsin, 1896–1919* (Notre Dame, IN: University of Notre Dame Press, 1980).

Górale. Native to the **Podhale** region in the southern mountain area of Poland, the Górale Podhalańcy (Podhale mountaineers) developed a culture as unique in Poland as their mountainous homeland was to the great Polish plain that characterized the rest of the nation. Aside from the geographic differences, the *górale* maintained a unique folk culture, dialect, and to a certain extent, a unique economy compared with people in the lowlands. While the main crops in the plains were wheat and rye, in the mountain areas oats and potatoes predominated, along with shepherds tending flocks. As residents of the southern borderlands of Poland, *górale* culture was also heavily influenced by Slovak, Magyar, and to a lesser extent Czech customs. In Polish folklore, the *górale* are imbued with such characteristics as courage, physical strength, pride, impulsiveness, stubbornness, humor, and a strong attachment to freedom. The latter is reinforced in *górale* culture by the belief that their mountain homelands were the only part of Poland not generally subjected to the excesses of serfdom practiced in the balance of the country. Historically, the *górale* often en-

Górale Group No. 3 in Kensington, Illinois, displaying their traditional highland costumes, 1938 (*PMA*).

gaged in seasonal migrations to earn enough money to supplement their rugged and often problematic existence in the mountain climate. Beginning in the last quarter of the nineteenth century, these migrations increasingly led to industrial areas in Europe and then America, eventually leading to more permanent resettlement. One of the most prevalent songs among Poles in America was the sentimental *Góralu, Czy ci nie żal* (Mountaineer, Are You Not Sad) in which a mountaineer laments having to leave his beloved mountains in search of bread. Although *górale* settled throughout the industrial and mining areas of the northeast and Midwest, the largest concentration was in Chicago where a mountaineer or "highlander" community remained quite vibrant in 2010. The Związek Podhalan w Ameryce (**Polish Highlanders Alliance of America**), organized in Chicago in 1928, is the largest and most active *górale* organization in the United States, and the most important serial publication is the newsletter *Tatrzański Orzeł* (Tatra Eagle) published in New Jersey.—*James S. Pula*

SOURCE: Thaddeus V. Gromada, "'Góral' Regionalism and Polish Immigration to America," in Stanislaus A. Blejwas and M. B. Biskupski, eds., *Pastor of the Poles: Polish American Essays Presented to Right Reverend Monsignor John P. Wodarski in Honor of the Fiftieth Anniversary of His Ordination* (New Britain, CT: Polish Studies Program, Central Connecticut State College, 1982), 105–115.

Goralski, Robert Stanley (b. Chicago, Illinois, January 2, 1928; d. McLean, Virginia, March 18, 1988). Journalist. Goralski served in the U.S. Navy in the Pacific during World War II. Following the war he earned a bac-

calaureate degree in journalism and political science at the University of Illinois in 1949. While still an undergraduate, he worked as a full-time news broadcaster with WDWS in Champaign, Illinois, and was hired as news director after he received his degree. Recalled to active duty during the Korean War, he served as a combat journalist. After his discharge he worked for Radio Free Asia in Japan and Pakistan (1952–56) where he wrote, produced, and narrated a series named "The Voice of Asia." In 1956 he moved to the Voice of America in Washington, D.C., as a supervisor of English broadcasts to Asia (1956–61). He joined NBC News in 1961 as a radio and television correspondent covering the White House, State Department, Pentagon, and Energy Department. He was an anchor for the network's coverage of John F. Kennedy's funeral, and for two years went to Asia where he reported on the Vietnam War. He also covered such major stories as the Watergate hearings, the trail of Lt. William Calley for the My Lai massacres, and the 1967 Arab-Israeli War. In 1975 he moved to Gulf Oil Corporation as it director of public relations (1975–83), and later served as senior advisor to the American Petroleum Institute. His book *World War II Almanac, 1931–1945: A Political and Military Record* (1981) was republished several times. His other books include *Press Follies* (1983), *Oil and War* (1987, with Russell Freeburg), an introduction to *The CBS Benjamin Report* (1984), the annual entry on Vietnam in the *Encyclopedia Britannica* (from 1966 to 1975), and contributions to *The Best of Emphasis* (1968). Among his honors are awards

for journalism from the American Television Academy and the Columbia School of Journalism.—*James S. Pula*

SOURCES: "Newsman Robert Goralski Dies; Covered Energy Beat," *Washington Post*, March 20, 1988; "Robert Goralski, News Correspondent, 60," *New York Times*, March 21, 1988.

Gordon, Thomas Sylvy (b. Chicago, Illinois, December 17, 1893; d. Chicago, Illinois, January 22, 1959). Congressman. Gordon attended parochial schools and graduated from St. Stanislaus College, Chicago, Illinois, in 1912. He engaged in the banking business (1916–20), was associated with a Polish-language daily newspaper (1921–42) beginning as a clerk and advancing to head cashier and office manager, served as commissioner of Chicago West Parks (1933–36) and of public vehicle licenses (1936–39), and was a delegate to the Democratic National Convention in Chicago in 1936. Gordon was elected city treasurer of Chicago (1939–42) as a symbol of the continuity of Polish American power in Chicago politics (especially from "Polish Downtown"), being the third Polish candidate in fifty years whom Chicago Democrats successfully placed on the ticket for that office. He was subsequently elected as a Democrat to the Seventy-eighth and the seven succeeding Congresses (January 3, 1943-January 3, 1959). Gordon was chair of the Committee on Foreign Affairs in the Eighty-fifth Congress. In 1945 he was one of four U.S. Representatives who publicly condemned the Soviet Union for unfairly administering United Nations Relief and Rehabilitation aid in Poland. He was not a candidate for re-nomination in

1958, retiring due to ill health.—*Frederick J. Augustyn*

SOURCES: Edward R. Kantowicz, *Polish-American Politics in Chicago, 1888–1940* (Chicago: University of Chicago, 1975), 206, 211; obituary, *Chicago Tribune*, January 24, 1959, part 2, 7.

Gordon, Witold (Witold Jurgielewicz; b. Ciechocinek, Poland, April 16, 1885; d. Southampton, New York, December 1968). Artist. Educated at the Warsaw Academy of Fine Arts, the Ecole des Beaux Arts in Paris, and in Italy, Gordon settled in Manhattan in 1914, living there until the early 1960s when he relocated to Sag Harbor, NY. Gordon was a specialist in murals whose works appeared in the International Casino in New York; the Hotel New Yorker; Radio City Music Hall; the New York World's Fair (1939-40); the Rainbow Room Grill decorative panels in the RCA (now GE) Building in New York; the Rich Family Store in Atlanta, Georgia; and the Richard Mandel House in Bedford Hills, NY. Among his design work were posters for the 1932 Winter Olympic Games in Lake Placid, NY; theater posters, including those for the musical *Oklahoma!*; display cards (Artcraft Lithograph & Printing Co.) for New York theaters; Christmas cards for the American Artists Group (1936–68); Bloomingdale's (New York, 1950s); and costume designs for Enrico Caruso in *Fortza del Destino* at the Metropolitan Opera (1918). He also served as a design consultant for many years to **Helena Rubinstein**. His illustrations were featured on the covers of *The New Yorker*, *Vanity Fair*, *Vogue*, *House and Garden*, Manuel Komroff's *The Travels of Marco Polo*, Sherry Mangan's *Cinderella Married*, and Richard Burton's *The Arabian Nights: An Adult Selection*. Collections of his work are preserved in the Library of Congress, the Cooper Hewitt Museum of the Smithsonian Institution, the Harvard Theater Collection, the Museum of the City of New York Theater Collection, the Whaling Museum of Sag Harbor, and The Grace Museum in Abilene, Texas.—*Stanley L. Cuba*

SOURCES: Irena Piotrowska, *The Art of Poland* (New York: Philosophical Library, 1947); Irena Piotrowska, "American Painters and Illustrators of Polish Descent," in the Rev. Francis Bolek and the Rev. Ladislaus J. Siekaniec, eds., *Polish American Encyclopedia* (Buffalo: The Polish American Encyclopedia Committee, 1947), Vol. 1.

Gore, Joseph E. (Goroszewski; Manhattan, New York, May 2, 1934; d.—). Attorney, Polonia activist. Gore earned his B.S. degree (1955) and J.D. degree (1958) from St. John's University and an L.L.M. degree from New York University School of Law. He was admitted to the practice of law in the State of New York in 1959 and specialized for more than 25 years in the field of corporate law. He was Assistant Corporate Secretary and Assistant General Counsel as well as the head of the Legal Department of the Fortune 500 Forest Products Company spanning a 25-year career through 1984. He was also admitted to practice before the U.S. Supreme Court, the Supreme Court of the State of New York and the U.S. Federal Court and is a member of the American, New York State and New York County Bar Associations. He also taught corporate and business law at Adelphi University and was a consultant in international contracts for the Western Union Corporation. While still a law student, he became a member of the Young Members group of the Kościuszko Foundation (1955–58) and served as its vice chair and treasurer. Following his career as a corporate attorney, he served as the fifth president of the Foundation (March 1987 to November 2008) and its Executive Director. Gore's tenure as President at the Kosciuszko Foundation coincided with a crucial political time in Poland's recent history. Because of this, it became necessary to redefine the Foundation's basic mission concerned with academic and cultural exchange programs between Poland and the United States. Gore's primary and immediate objective was to shift the Foundation's focus of its educational programs to a much broader field of learning and expertise which included consideration of such immediate and vital changes as the privatization of Poland's industries which required trained management as well as legal personnel to operate in an independent world market. He was instrumental in the early 1980's in establishing with UNESCO of Poland and the Ministry of National Education of The Teaching English in Poland a program for Polish high school students. Gore has made frequent trips to Poland to strengthen the relationship between American and Polish academia and institutions as well as governmental agencies in an effort to improve and facilitate the Foundation's educational and many cultural programs. To assist in this task, he opened the Foundation's Warsaw office in the early 1990's where each year Polish and American Advisory Commissions meet to interview prospective Polish academics for the Exchange Program. In the United States, Gore furthered the Foundation's mission of promoting Polish culture through the establishment of geographical chapters: Western New York, Chicago, the Rocky Mountain Chapter in Denver, Houston, Philadelphia, Pittsburgh, the New England Chapter in Springfield, Massachusetts, and the Ohio Chapter in Cleveland. Under his management the Foundation published *Polish Masters from the Kosciuszko Foundation's Collection* and a two volume *Polish English, English Polish Dictionary* (with CD-ROM) as well as a DVD version with American English and Polish pronunciations. Also available is an internet platform whereby subscribers can use the dictionaries online for various periods of time. Gore has long been a student of Polish affairs, with a particular interest in Joseph Conrad. In 2010 he was a member of the Advisory Council of the Polish Institute of Arts and Sciences of America, the Piłsudski Institute of America for Research in the Modern History of Poland, and a member of the National Polish American-Jewish American Council. In 2009 he was elected Chair of the Board of Trustees of the Kosciuszko Foundation. His honors are a Doctor of Humane Letters bestowed by Teikyo Post University, a Silver Medal of the Jagiellonian University in Kraków (1997), a commendation from the Comptroller of the City of New York (1998), and the Knight's Commander Cross awarded by President Kwasniewski of Poland (2000).—*Joseph E. Gore*

Gorski, Chester Charles (b. Buffalo, New York, June 22, 1906; d. Buffalo, New York, April 25, 1975). Congressman. Gorski attended Sts. Peter and Paul Parochial School and Technical High School. He was a member of the Erie County Board of Supervisors (1941–45), serving as minority leader in 1942–45. A member of the Buffalo Common Council (1946–48), he served as both minority leader (1946-47) and majority leader (1948), and was a delegate to Democratic National Conventions in 1948, 1952, 1956, and 1968. He was elected as a Democrat to the Eighty-first Congress (January 3, 1949-January 3, 1951). Gorski's unsuccessful bid for reelection in 1950 and for election in 1952 may have been due in part to Republican gains in New York State engendered when Gov. Thomas E. Dewey was re-elected in 1950 to a third term. Gorski worked for the United States Department of Commerce (1951-52), was again elected to the Buffalo Common Council, and served from January 1, 1954, to February 1, 1956 as its majority leader. He was appointed to the New York State Building Code Commission on February 1, 1956, serving until April 1, 1959. Elected president of the Buffalo Common Council on January 1, 1960, he was re-elected to six succeeding terms. Gorski served in that post until his resignation for health reasons on March 24, 1974. In 1962 the New York State Council of Polish Democratic Clubs very reluctantly endorsed the state ticket after Gorski was not nominated for lieutenant governor.—*Frederick J. Augustyn*

SOURCES: *Biographical Directory of the United States Congress, 1774-Present* (http://bioguide.congress.gov/); *New York Times*, April 26, 1975, 25.

Gorski, Martin (b. Mogielno, Poland, October 30, 1886; d. Chicago, Illinois, December 4, 1949). Congressman. Gorski migrated to the United States with his parents in 1889, settling in Chicago. After attending public high school, he graduated from business college and law school in Chicago in 1917, being admitted to the bar in the same year. Practicing law in the same city, he served as assistant state's attorney (1918–20) and master in chancery of the superior court of Cook County (1929–1942). Gorski was elected as a Democrat to the Seventy-eighth and two succeeding Congresses, serving from January 3, 1943, until his death in 1949 after having been reelected to the Eighty-first Congress. In 1947 he voted with a minority of Democrats and with the Republicans, then in the congressional majority, for a constitutional amendment to limit presidential tenure to two terms in the wake of Franklin D. Roosevelt's unprecedented election to four terms.—*Frederick J. Augustyn*

SOURCES: *Biographical Directory of the United States Congress, 1774–Present* (http://bioguide.congress.gov/); *Chicago Tribune*, December 5, 1949, C6 and December 6, 1949, A7; *New York Times*, December 5, 1949, 23; *Washington Post*, December 5, 1949, B2.

Gorzkie Żale (Bitter Laments). Gorzkie Żale is a weekly Lenten service that originated in the Holy Cross Church in Warsaw during the 1700s and spread throughout Poland before being brought to the United States by immigrants in the latter half of the nineteenth century. The term derives from the hymn *Gorzkie żale przybywajcia* (Come to Us, Bitter Lamentations) and the custom involved a series of devotions on the Sundays during Lent reflecting on the passion and death of Christ.—*James S. Pula*

SOURCE: Sophie Hodorowicz Knab, *Polish Customs, Traditions and Folklore* (New York: Hippocrene Books, 1996).

Goskowicz, Bradley D. (b. Milwaukee, Wisconsin, March 13, 1956; d.—). Speedskater. Goskowicz began his skating career with the West Allis Speedskating Club in Wisconsin at the age of nine. Within ten years he had participated in over 100 competitions. Later, as president of the West Allis club, he introduced innovations, many of which became standard among speed skating clubs. He served as president of both the Wisconsin Skating Association and the Board of the Amateur Skating Union. As chair of the Racing Committee he promoted the standardization of International Skating Union racing rules. As an administrator he organized over fifty long track and short track competitions including the first four U.S. Junior Short Track Championships and the first Short Track

American Cup. He served as a Competitor's Steward during more than 100 competitions and was included on the list for the International Skating Union World Championships. He was elected to the Board of Directors of U.S. Skating in 1991 and its president in 2006, leading a movement to modernize the organization's bylaws and financial structure. He was inducted into the National Speed Skating Hall of Fame in 2009.—*James S. Pula*

SOURCES: Peri Kinder, "U.S. Speedskating Announces the 2009 Hall of Fame Inductees," *U.S. Speedskating*, March 25, 2009; "Goskowicz Wins Title in St. Paul Skating," *Milwaukee Journal*, March 3, 1974.

Grabiarz, William J. (b. Buffalo, New York, January 1, 1925; d. Manila, Philippines, February 23, 1945). Soldier, Medal of Honor recipient. The son of Polish immigrants in Buffalo, New York, he attended local public schools before enlisting in the U.S. Army in 1943 at the age of seventeen. A veteran of combat in the Bismarck Archipelago and New Guinea, he then took part in the invasion of the Philippines where he was killed in action in the streets of Manila on February 23, 1945. His citation awarding the Medal of Honor described the specific act of bravery that served as the basis for that special recognition: "Without warning, enemy machine gun and rifle fire from concealed positions ... swept the street, striking down the troop commander and driving his men to cover. As the officer lay in the open road, unable to move and completely exposed to the point-blank enemy fire, Private Grabiarz voluntarily ran from behind a tank to carry him to safety, but was himself wounded in the shoulder. Ignoring both the pain in his injured, useless arm and his comrades' shouts to seek the cover which

William J. Grabiarz, Medal of Honor recipient (*NARA*).

was only a few yards distant, the valiant rescuer continued his efforts to drag his commander out of range. Finding this impossible, he rejected the opportunity to save himself and deliberately covered the officer with his own body to form a human shield, calling as he did so for a tank to maneuver between him and the hostile emplacement." Grabiarz died before the tank could be repositioned, but his actions did save the life of his commanding officer, Captain John Gregory. In 1948, Grabiarz's body was returned to Western New York where it was buried with full military honors at St. Stanislaus Cemetery. The museum building at the Buffalo and Erie County Naval and Military Park is named in his honor, as is the Pfc. William J. Grabiarz School of Excellence that was opened in November of 2000 near his boyhood home.—*Carl L. Bucki*

SOURCES: "Honor Medal for Life Sacrifice," *New York Times*, December 18, 1945, 11; "Memorial to War Hero to be Urged in Council," *Buffalo Courier Express*, June 7, 1948, 20; Lynn Rzepecki, *The William Grabiarz Story* (Buffalo: privately printed booklet issued on the dedication of the Pfc. William J. Grabiarz School of Excellence, November 9, 2000); R. J. Proft, *United States of America's Congressional Medal of Honor Recipients and Their Official Citations* (Columbia Heights, MN: Highland House II, 2002); *The Medal of Honor of the United States Army* (Washington, D.C.: U.S. Government Printing Office, 1948), 68.

Grabowski, Bernard Francis (b. New Haven, Connecticut, June 11, 1923; d.—). Congressman. Grabowski attended St. Stanislaus Parochial School and graduated from Bristol High School, Bristol, Connecticut, in 1941. He served in the United States Army (1943–45), earned a baccalaureate degree from the University of Connecticut (1949), and a law degree from the University of Connecticut (1952). He was admitted to the bar in 1953, served as a member of the Bristol Town Committee for eight years, and as a Bristol councilman (1953–55). He acted as judge of the Bristol city court (1955–60), coordinator of redevelopment in Bristol (1957–59), and chief prosecutor of the Bristol circuit court (1960–62). Grabowski was elected as a Democrat with significant support from the Connecticut Democratic Party chair John M. Bailey to the Eighty-eighth and Eighty-ninth Congresses (January 3, 1963-January 3, 1967). The relatively unknown Grabowski's name was placed in nomination at the Connecticut state convention in 1962 after Rep. **Frank Kowalski** refused the nod unless it was uncontested. Grabowski handily defeated fellow Democrat Don Irwin at the convention to gain the nomination. He was the last Connecticut Congressman elected to the at large seat, then traditionally reserved by both parties in the state for Polish Americans. Grabowski's ethnicity was highlighted by his fluency in Polish and membership in the Bristol Polish-American Citizens Club and **Polish Legion of American Veterans**. But he was also a member of organizations such as the Knights of Columbus, the Elks, and the Disabled Veterans. Grabowski subsequently won re-election in 1964 when he ran in the newly created Sixth district after the at large position was abolished. But in November 1966, Republican former mayor (later governor) Thomas Meskill, Jr., of Bristol defeated Grabowski by 2,500 votes, perhaps assisted by the third party "peace candidate" Prof. Stephen Minot who received 5,560 votes. Following his defeat, Grabowski resumed the practice of law.—*Frederick J. Augustyn*

SOURCE: *Biographical Directory of the United States Congress, 1774-Present* (http://bioguide.congress.gov/).

Grabowski, Jim (b. Chicago, Illinois, September 9, 1944; d.—). Football player. A heralded football prospect from his native Chicago, Grabowski starred as a fullback at the University of Illinois from 1963 to 1965. He was named most valuable player in the 1964 Rose Bowl, won All-America honors in 1964 and 1965, and received awards as Big Ten and national college football player of the year in 1965. In addition, he was a two time Academic All-American. Chosen in the first round of the professional draft by the Green Bay Packers, Grabowski played in the National Football League for six seasons, 1966–71. His Packers won the first two Super Bowls, in 1967–68. After a retirement from the game hastened by injury, Grabowski broadcast University of Illinois football games for thirty years. He is a member of the College Football Hall of Fame, and in 1993 he was inducted into the National Polish-American Sports Hall of Fame.—*Neal Pease*

SOURCE: "Jim Grabowski," National Polish-American Sports Hall of Fame website, www.polish sportshof.com.

Grabowskii, Arthur Edward Adolphus (b. Russian partition of Poland, 1836; d. Summerville, Georgia, February 25, 1930). Educator. The son of a Polish count employed by the tsarist government, Grabowskii completed studies at the Third Imperial Gymnasium in St. Petersburg, then attended lectures at the University of Bonn before enrolling in the Royal Prussian Institute of Agriculture at Gaisberg to study chemistry (1852–54). In 1856 he migrated to the U.S. where he accepted a position as professor of modern languages at Roanoke College in Virginia. In 1858 he added "instructor of tactics" to his title and organized the Roanoke College Musketeer Guard. In 1860 he left to become com-

mandant of cadets at the Mount Joy Military Academy in Pennsylvania, but left for South Carolina as the secession crisis loomed. There he participated in the bombardment of Fort Sumter initiating the Civil War and enrolled as a volunteer in the 1st South Carolina Infantry. When his three-months service ended, he joined the 4th Virginia Cavalry, but was assigned to the staff of Confederate Adjutant General Samuel Cooper in Richmond. Rising to the rank of colonel, the end of the war found him in command of the warehouses in Greensboro, North Carolina, that were a principal supply base for Confederate armies in the east. In 1866 he was employed as a professor at the Highland Military Academy in Worcester, MA, but soon returned south as a member of the faculty at the Preston and Olin Institute in Blacksburg, VA. In the fall of 1872 he moved to the Montgomery Female College in Christiansburg, VA, where he taught French, German, and mathematics. In 1875 he accepted a position as professor of modern languages and military instruction at the Pennsylvania State University where he enjoyed considerable success, but when financial difficulties forced a reduction in salaries in 1877 he accepted a position as professor of agriculture at the Maryland Agricultural College, the first faculty member to hold a doctorate in the institution's history. Although the college was also in severe financial difficulty, causing the state to withdraw its annual subsidy, Grabowskii presented a plan to reorganize the institution and focus its curriculum on practical education that would appeal to the state's farmers and manufacturers. Once adopted, the institution began to recover and went on to become the University of Maryland. In 1885, Grabowskii was appointed superintendent of the Industrial School for Indians in Lawrence, KS, known

Arthur Grabowskii, educator and college president (*OLS*).

also as the Haskell Institute. Attacked in the popular press for his Confederate service during the war, Grabowskii eventually tendered his resignation as of January 1, 1887. After brief stints in government posts in Louisiana, Colorado, and Utah, he accepted the presidency of Defiance College in Ohio where, during his four-year tenure, he was successful in ending a continuing enrollment decline. In 1895 he returned south to accept the position of principal of the Summerville Academy near Augusta, Georgia, a position he held for the rest of his life.—*James S. Pula*

SOURCES: James S. Pula, "Arthur Grabowskii: Soldier, Educator and Enigma," *Polish American Studies*, Vol. 39, no. 1 (1982), 55–82; Ladislas John Siekaniec, *The Polish Contribution to Early American Education, 1608–1865* (San Francisco: R & E Research Associates, 1976).

Granata, Peter Charles (b. Chicago, Illinois, October 28, 1898; d. Chicago, Illinois, September 29, 1973). Congressman. After attending Chicago public schools, he graduated from Bryant and Stratton Business College in Chicago in 1912. Entering the coal business in 1917, he later became chief clerk to the prosecutor of the city of Chicago (1926–28) and chief deputy coroner (1928–30) under Mayor William Thompson's administration. Elected to the State House of Representatives in 1930 to fill a vacancy, he presented his credentials as a Republican to the Seventy-second Congress and served from March 3, 1931, to April 5, 1932, when he was succeeded by **Stanley H. Kunz**, who had initially been defeated but successfully contested the election on charges of fraud and violence, alleging Granata was an ally of Al Capone. The House voted by 190 to 168 along party lines to unseat Granata. He asserted that the charges of gangster influence were humorous, noting "my character and integrity cannot and shall not be assassinated by the mad charges of a misrepresentative whose greatest obstacle ... was his own notorious character." An unsuccessful candidate for election in 1932, he engaged in the coal and oil business in Chicago until May 1933. Elected to the State House of Representatives, he served from 1933–73, a lengthy term for which he is most remembered. He was also a delegate to the Republican National Conventions from Illinois in 1952, 1956, and 1960; assistant director of finance of the State of Illinois (1941–43); and vice president of a glass company in Chicago.—*Frederick J. Augustyn*

SOURCE: *Biographical Directory of the United States Congress, 1774-Present* (http://bioguide.congress.gov/).

Gray, Gilda (Marianna Michalska; b. Kraków, Poland, October 24, 1901; d. Los Angeles, California, December 22, 1959). Actress,

Gilda Gray (Marianna Michalska), the "shimmy queen" of Hollywood (*OLS*).

dancer. After migrating to the U.S. with her parents in 1909, she settled with them in Milwaukee, WI. A brief marriage to musician John Gorecki ended in divorce after which she moved to Chicago where she performed under the name Mary Gray. There she was discovered by Frank Westphal who took her to New York where his wife, Sophie Tucker, suggested that she change her stage name to from Mary to Gilda because of her golden hair. In 1919 she appeared in *The Gaities of 1919*, adopting an exaggerated dancing style that drew the attention of audiences and critics. Supposedly, when asked about her dancing style she replied "I'm shaking my chemise." Because of her heavy accent, "chemise" sounded like "shimmy" and she was thereafter noted for popularizing the "The Shimmy" as one of the iconic dances of the "Roaring Twenties." Her own popularity soared when she appeared in the Ziegfeld Follies in 1922. Between 1919 and 1936 she made several films, moving to Hollywood after her stint with Ziegfeld. *Aloma of the South Seas* grossed an amazing $3 million in its first three months, leading to a heavy schedule of personal appearances and further offers. In 1927 she made *The Devil Dancer* and *Cabaret*, but she lost most of her money in the 1929 stock market crash. She made ends meet during the Depression dancing at the Palace Theater in New York. Although she later attempted several comebacks, poor health following a heart attack in 1931 interfered with her plans. In 1953 she was featured in an

episode of Ralph Edwards' *This Is Your Life*, with much of the segment dedicated to her efforts to bring six Poles to the U.S. during the Cold War and subsidize their education.—*Patricia Finnegan*

SOURCES: "Shimmy Dancer Gilda Gray Dies," *Los Angeles Times*, December 23, 1959, 2; "Gilda Gray Dead on Coast at 58; Creator of Shimmy Was Singer," *New York Times*, December 23, 1959, 27.

Greenpoint Crew. A major criminal gang operating in the heavily Polish Greenpoint section of New York, 21 of its members were indicted by the United States Attorney's Office in March of 2006 for a wide variety of crimes including armed robbery, drug trafficking, credit card fraud, extortion, gunrunning, theft, and the sale of stolen goods. Working with contacts in Eastern Europe, in addition to Poles the gang included Georgians, Hungarians, and Ukrainians. Accused of leading the group were Krzysztof Spryasak and Ostap Kapelioujnyj. The group was dubbed "Stringfellas" by the New York *Daily News* because of their theft of a valuable Stradivarius violin which they then planned the offer for sale so that they could in turn rob the prospective purchasers.—*James S. Pula*

SOURCES: William Pfeiffer, Jr., "Greenpoint Crew Mobster and International Fugitive Pawel Guzal aka Jaromir Havranek Captured," *Detroit Examiner*, August 28, 2009; "Twenty-one Members of an East European Organized Crime Ring Indicted by a Federal Grand Jury in Brooklyn," press release, United States Attorney's Office, Eastern District of New York, March 8, 2006.

Gregg, Stephen R. (Stefan Grziegorzewski; b. New York, New York, September 1, 1914; d. North Arlington, New Jersey, February 4, 2005). Military officer, Medal of Honor recipient. As a private first class, Gregg served with the 143rd Infantry Regiment, 36th Infantry Division during World War II. After earning a battlefield commission as second lieutenant, he was awarded the Medal of Honor "for conspicuous gallantry and intrepidly at the risk of life above and beyond the call of duty" near Montelimar, France, August 27, 1944. The citation for the Medal read: "As his platoon advanced upon the enemy positions; the leading scout was fired upon and 2d Lt. Gregg (then a Tech. Sgt.) immediately put his machine guns into action to cover the advance of the riflemen. The Germans, who were at close range, threw hand grenades at the riflemen, killing some and wounding 7. Each time a medical aid man attempted to reach the wounded, the Germans fired at him. Realizing the seriousness of the situation, 2d Lt. Gregg took 1 of the light .30-caliber machine guns, and firing from the hip, started boldly up the hill with the medical aid man following him. Although the enemy was

Stephen R. Gregg (Stefan Grziegorzewski), right, receiving his Medal of Honor from General Patch (*NARA*).

throwing hand grenades at him, 2d Lt. Gregg remained and fired into the enemy positions while the medical aid man removed the 7 wounded men to safety. When 2d Lt. Gregg had expended all his ammunition, he was covered by 4 Germans who ordered him to surrender. Since the attention of most of the Germans had been diverted by watching this action, friendly riflemen were able to maneuver into firing positions. One, seeing 2d Lt. Gregg's situation, opened fire on his captors. The 4 Germans hit the ground and thereupon 2d Lt. Gregg recovered a machine pistol from one of the Germans and managed to escape to his other machine gun positions. He manned a gun, firing at his captors, killed 1 of them and wounded the other. This action so discouraged the Germans that the platoon was able to continue its advance up the hill to achieve its objective. The following morning, just prior to daybreak, the Germans launched a strong attack, supported by tanks, in an attempt to drive Company L from the hill. As these tanks moved along the valley and their foot troops advanced up the hill, 2d Lt. Gregg immediately ordered his mortars into action. During the day by careful observation, he was able to direct effective fire on the enemy, inflicting heavy casualties. By late afternoon he had directed 600 rounds when his communication to the mortars was knocked out. Without hesitation he started checking his wires, although the area was under heavy enemy small arms and artillery fire. When he was within 100 yards of his mortar position, 1 of his men informed him that the section had been captured and the Germans were using the mortars to fire on the company. 2d Lt. Gregg with this man and another nearby rifleman started for the gun position where he could see 5 Germans firing his mortars. He ordered the 2 men to cover him, crawled up, threw a hand grenade into the position, and then charged it. The hand grenade killed 1, injured 2, 2d Lt. Gregg took the other 2 prisoners, and put his mortars back into action." Following the war he was an active member of the Polish Legion of American Veterans in Bayonne, NJ.—*James S. Pula*

SOURCES: R. J. Proft, *United States of America's Congressional Medal of Honor Recipients and Their Official Citations* (Columbia Heights, MN: Highland House II, 2002); *The Medal of Honor of the United States Army* (Washington, D.C.: U.S. Government Printing Office, 1948), 68.

Grey Samaritans. At the close of World War I, Polish American women responded to a call to serve their ancestral homeland as "Grey Samaritan" nurses. Their ministry to orphans, malnourished children, and homeless refugees in war-torn Poland formed, according to Sidney Brooks of the American Relief Administration, "a record which has no equal in American relief work in all the countries of Europe." The idea of training young women from American **Polonia** for social service in Poland was raised in late 1918 by Laura de Gozdawa Turczynowicz, the American wife of a Polish aristocrat. She approached the YWCA, whose National War Work Council was among the organizations assisting President Herbert Hoover's American Relief Administration. YWCA officials approved of the venture and dispatched Madame Turczynowicz on a lecture tour of Polish settlements in the northeastern states. Approximately 300 women answered the call for service in Cleveland, Trenton, Chicago, Milwaukee, Detroit, Buffalo, Rochester, Pittsburgh, and other cities. Two hundred of them received initial training, then were sent back to their homes to work among Polish immigrants as nurse's aides. Ninety, judged to be the most hardy and resourceful, moved on to further instruction in New York City, completing courses at the School of Philanthropy and at Teachers College of Columbia University. They also experienced welfare work firsthand in New York City's slums. Outfitted in horizon blue capes and caps reminiscent of the uniforms of General **Haller**'s Polish Army, the first group of twenty Grey Samaritans sailed for Europe on July 17, 1919. Madame Paderewska affectionately welcomed them to Warsaw as her *szare kotki* (grey kittens). Their numbers increased to thirty with the arrival of ten additional women in January 1920. Assigned to Lwów, Pińsk, Wilno, Lublin, Kielce, Łódź, and other areas to distribute food and clothing, organize soup kitchens, and train local volunteers to take over when they moved on to new locations, in a single month the Grey

Grey Samaritans preparing to leave for Poland (*OLS*).

Samaritans were charged with distributing 700,000 sets of children's clothing and feeding more than a million children under auspices of the ARA's Children's Fund. Their orders were to serve the needy "regardless of race, politics, religion, or inability to pay." Grey Samaritan volunteers witnessed and endured difficult conditions in the war-ravaged countryside, often working in refugee camps rife with typhus, smallpox, cholera, dysentery, and tuberculosis. One of them, Anna Kopeć, died of tuberculosis contracted while she was serving in a children's refuge. The suffering they witnessed and helped to alleviate intensified after the outbreak of the Polish-Soviet War. "What is happening in poor Poland at the present is beyond a human being's imagination," Marta Graczyk, one of the Greys from Rochester, wrote to her family. "I thought lately that I would be 'quits' with everything, but when one thinks of the nursery left behind we just cannot refuse to go on." Graczyk endured a trial of another sort late in 1920 while serving near the border of Poland and Lithuania. After crossing into Lithuanian territory, she was arrested by government officials and accused of being a Polish spy. Held for several days while newspapers in her hometown reported her ordeal, she was released with the help of the American minister in Warsaw and returned to her humanitarian work. The Grey Samaritans served in Poland for almost three years, drawing praise from American officials and earning the gratitude of the Polish people. President Hoover observed that "the hardships they have undergone, the courage and resource they have shown in sheer human service is a beautiful monument to American womanhood." The YWCA acknowledged that "their work was an act of devotion to the land of their ancestors." In memoirs written after her return home, Graczyk offered this assessment of the Greys' service: "When one stops to think of the dangers both moral and physical, being in the

thickest of all sorts of diseases ... I cannot help but wonder what it was that kept us young girls out of the many dangers. Was it the daring years of youth or the sacrifice to suffering humanity that pushed us on and on, without a thought for ourselves? ... To one experiencing this adventurous life, it is worth a fortune that no money could buy of moral satisfaction."— *Kathleen Urbanic*

SOURCES: Robert Szymczak, "An Act of Devotion: The Polish Grey Samaritans and the American Relief Effort in Poland, 1919–1921," *Polish American Studies*, Vol. XLIII, no. 1 (Spring 1986), 13–36; Frank W. Thackeray, "'To Serve the Cause of Poland': The Polish Grey Samaritans, 1919–1922," *The Polish Review*, Vol. 35, no. 1 (1990), 37–50; "Memoirs of Marta Graczyk Gedgowd," Hoover Institution Archives (Polish Grey Samaritans collection, box number 3).

Grochowski, Leon (b. Skupie, partitioned Poland, October 11, 1886; d. Warsaw, Poland, July 17, 1969). Bishop. Educated in Siedlce and Warsaw, Poland, he came to the United States in 1905, settling in Baltimore for two years before entering the **Polish National Catholic Church** (PNCC) Seminary in Scranton, PA. He was ordained a priest in the PNCC in 1910. Grochowski proved to be valuable to the fledgling Church as an excellent administrator, and was active in organizing new PNCC parishes and in the Church's mission to Poland. He was consecrated in 1924, two years later becoming bishop of the newly formed Western Diocese of the PNCC, whose see was at All Saints Cathedral in Chicago. In 1949, he was chosen to be the successor to Prime Bishop **Franciszek Hodur** as leader of the denomination. When Hodur died in 1953, Grochowski became the second Prime Bishop of the Church. In 1966, he became the first official of either denomination to suggest a dialogue between the PNCC and the Roman Catholic Church, from which it had split. The following year, for the first time ever, a Roman Catholic clergyman attended a PNCC synod. During Prime Bishop Grochowski's tenure, the

Bishop Leon Grochowski of the Polish National Catholic Church (*OLS*).

PNCC approved publication of Church literature in English as well as Polish, and celebrating the Mass in English. Grochowski was attending a church conference in Poland in 1969 when he died of a heart attack in Warsaw at age 82.—*Martin S. Nowak*

SOURCE: Theodore Andrews, *The Polish National Catholic Church in America and Poland* (London: SPCK, 1953) and Paul Fox, *The Polish National Catholic Church* (Scranton: School of Christian Living, 1961).

Gromada, Thaddeus Vladimir (b. Passaic, New Jersey, July 30, 1929; d.—). Historian. The son of immigrants from the Tatra Mountain region of Poland who came to the United States in the late 1920s and were founders and directors of the Polish Tatra Highlanders Folk Dance Group, Gromada developed an early interest in Polish history and culture as a member of the troupe. Gromada received his Ph.D. under the mentorship of the renowned Polish historian and scholar **Oskar Halecki** who was one of the founders of the **Polish Institute of Arts and Sciences** of America in 1942. An Emeritus Professor of History at Jersey City University since 1992, his articles on Polish history have appeared in the *Slavic Review, The Polish Review, East European Quarterly, Nationalities Papers,* and *East Central Europe*. He and his sister Janina Gromada Kedron are the founders and co-editors of the bilingual quarterly *Tatrzański Orzeł* (The Tatra Eagle). Gromada was appointed by Governor Thomas Kean of New Jersey to chair of the Governor's Commission on Eastern European History which resulted in the publication of a report in 1989 on the status of East European history and social studies in New Jersey's secondary schools. He was a member of the Advisory Council of the De-

partment of Higher Education's Multi-Cultural Studies project of New Jersey, and served as a consultant to the Department of Education, the Smithsonian Institution, the National Education Association, and the **Polish American Congress**, as well as the Learning Corporation of America production of a film about the immigrant experience and a television documentary on Polish Americans. He was a trustee of the **Kosciuszko Foundation**, served as executive director (1971–91), vice president (1991–2008), and president of the Polish Institute of Arts and Sciences of America and president of the **Polish American Historical Association**. He has been honored by the Polish American Historical Association with the Haiman Medal for sustained scholarly contributions to the study of Polonia, received the Cross of Merit and the Commander's Cross of Merit from the President of Poland, and was made an honorary member of the Polish Highlanders Union (Związek Podhalan) for promoting the folklore of the Highlanders.—*Maria Swiecicka-Ziemianek*

SOURCES: Bolesław Wierzbiański, *Who's Who in Polish America* (New York: Bicentennial Publishing Corp., 1996), 141; "Gromada, Thaddeus Wladimir," *Contemporary Authors* (Detroit: Gale Research Company), Vol. 45–48, 204.

Gromek, Stephen Joseph "Steve" (b. Hamtramck, Michigan, January 15, 1920; d. Clinton Township, Michigan, March 12, 2002). Baseball player. Gromek was a pitcher for the Cleveland Indians and Detroit Tigers of the American League from 1941 through 1957. A right-hander, he compiled a career record of 123–108 with an earned run average of 3.41 over the course of seventeen seasons. He was named to the American League all-star team in 1945 when he won nineteen games and was a member of Cleveland's world championship squad in 1948 when he pitched a complete game victory in that year's World Series. In 1981 he was inducted into the National Polish-American Sports Hall of Fame.—*Neal Pease*

SOURCE: "Steve Gromek," National Polish-American Sports Hall of Fame website, www.polishsportshof.com.

Gronouski, John (b. Dunbar, Wisconsin, October 26, 1919; d. Green Bay, Wisconsin, January 7, 1996). Politician. After earning his B.A. degree from the University of Wisconsin in 1942, Gronouski served as a navigator with the Eighth Air Force in Europe, logging 24 combat missions during World War II. Following the war he earned his M.A. and Ph.D. degrees from the University of Wisconsin before joining the Wisconsin Department of Taxation. A fervent Democrat, in 1960 his political activities led to his appointment as

John Gronouski, Postmaster General and Ambassador to Poland (*OLS*).

Commissioner of Taxation. In this position he reorganized the state tax system to make it more efficient. In the presidential campaign his endorsement of John F. Kennedy is believed by many scholars to have been of crucial importance to the senator's campaign. With his election, Kennedy appointed Gronouski Postmaster General, the first Polish American to hold a Cabinet position. There, he quickly became a favorite with the Washington press corps because of his open, frank nature. An outspoken advocate of racial equality in postal employment, he also instituted the five-digit zip code, reorganized the postal service to promote efficiency, and instituted various cost-saving measures. In 1965, Pres. Lyndon B. Johnson appointed him ambassador to Poland, a position he developed into a kind of "roving ambassador" to Eastern Europe, frequently visiting the Soviet Union and other Eastern Bloc nations in an effort to build economic and cultural ties. With the end of the Johnson administration, Gronouski developed a curriculum in public policy and administration for the University of Texas, becoming the founding dean of the Lyndon B. Johnson School of Public Affairs. After stepping down as dean in 1974, he continued as a faculty member until 1989. During the 1970s he served as a court-appointed head of Milwaukee's efforts to desegregate its public schools. In 1974, Pres. Jimmy Carter named Gronouski chairman of the Board for International Broadcasting, charged with operating both Radio Free Europe and Radio Liberty.—*Adam Walaszek*

SOURCES: Joy Anderson, ed., *The American Catholic Who's Who* (Washington, D.C.: National Catholic News Service, 1979); Robert Sobel, ed., *Biographical Directory of the United States Executive Branch, 1774–1989* (Westport, CT: Greenwood Press, 1990); R. McG. Thomas Jr., "John Gronousky," *New York Times*, January 10, 1996, D19.

Gronowicz, Antoni (b. Rudnia, Poland, July 31, 1913; d. Avon, Connecticut, October 16, 1985). Poet, playwright, novelist. Antoni Gronowicz, a Polish émigré, arrived in America in 1938, a year after receiving his Ph.D. from the University of Lwów. A lecturer in creative writing at Columbia University from 1938–40 and at Harvard University from 1941–42, Gronowicz wrote several biographies, social commentaries, plays, and volumes of poetry throughout the course of his life, including biographies on Fryderyk Chopin, **Ignacy Paderewski**, and Sergei Rachmaninoff; a volume on art theory entitled *Harmonizm* (1937); and works on Polish history and culture. Gronowicz won the Polish National Literary Prize in 1938, first prize at the Provincetown Academy of Living Arts One-Act Play Competition in 1970 for his play about Polish stage actress **Helena Modjeska**, and first prize at the 1979 International Playwright Competition in Geneva, Switzerland for *The United Animals*. For many years Gronowicz contributed to *Books Abroad, Saturday Review, Atlantic, New York Times*, and other newspapers and periodicals. Gronowicz achieved public notoriety for his allegedly falsified biography of actress Greta Garbo in 1978, with whom he claimed to have enjoyed a longstanding friendship and even romantic relationship. Garbo had written the foreword to Gronowicz's 1972 novel, *An Orange Full of Dreams*, but denied having known the author in a press release responding to the unauthorized biography's claims. Although the rights to *Garbo: Her Story* were sold to the publishing company Simon & Shuster in 1978, the book remained unpublished until Garbo's death in 1990. Gronowicz also became embroiled in a controversy over his contested biography of Pope John Paul II, for which he claimed over two hundred hours in conversation with the Pontiff. Entitled *God's Broker*, the book was recalled by publisher Richardson & Snyder in 1984 after the Vatican denied Gronowicz's ever having interviewed the Pope. Richardson & Snyder took legal action against Gronowicz, charging him with fraud, but prosecution ended when Gronowicz suffered a heart attack and died in 1985. Gronowicz is buried in Warsaw, Poland.—*Krystyna Cap*

SOURCE: obituary, *Chicago Sun–Times*, April 23, 1990.

Gross, Feliks (b. Kraków, Poland, June 17, 1906; d. New York, New York, November 9, 2006). Sociologist. Gross earned his doctorate in jurisprudence from the Jagiellonian University in Kraków (1931) while teaching in the Sociology Department (1926–31). A labor lawyer and Socialist Party member, he

Feliks Gross, sociologist and president of the Polish Institute of Arts and Sciences of America (*OLS*).

founded and directed Kraków's Labor Social Science School (1934–38). As a member of a prominent Jewish Polish family, Gross, with his wife Priva, fled Poland in 1939, settling in New York City where he taught at Brooklyn College (1946–77) and the City University of New York (CUNY) Graduate Center. Between 1931 and 1977 he held short term positions at the League of Nations, the Eastern European Planning Board, New York University, University of Wyoming, University of Virginia, University of Vermont, and Columbia University, as well as the Universities of Florence, Paris, Rome, and the College of Europe. In 1980 Gross founded the CUNY Academy of Humanities and Sciences, serving as its first president. He was also the Executive Director of the **Polish Institute of Arts and Sciences in America** (1975–88) and its president (1988–99). His scholarship focused on community in diversity, arguing that basic moral norms are universal, if not absolute, and constructing a rational-normative model of ethically acceptable standards for society. He authored more than twenty books beginning with *The Polish Worker* (1945), and a plethora of articles published in many languages. His *Ideologies Goals and Values* (1985) is an important synthesis of his work. His many honors include being named Carnegie International Peace Scholar, Paris (1931); Senior Fulbright Scholar (1956-57); Golden Cross of the Phoenix from the King of Greece (1963); Professor Emeritus of Brooklyn College (1977); Polish Academy of Arts and Sciences (1991); The Order of *Polonia Restituta* (1992); **Alfred Jurzykowski** Award (1992); and the National Archive of the Republic of Poland (1995).— *Jerome Krase*

SOURCES: Jerome Krase, "Feliks Gross: Between Assimilation and Multiculturalism," *The Polish Review*, Vol. 52, no. 2 (2007), 171–87; Grażyna Kubica, "A Real Krakauer: Feliks Gross and His Cracovian Roots," *The Polish Review*, Vol. 52, no. 2 (2007), 147–70; Joseph W. Wieczerzak, "Sociology 75 and Afterwards: Some Reminiscences About Feliks Gross," *The Polish Review*, Vol. 52, no. 2 (2007), 189–91; Jerome Krase, "Feliks Gross: Social Scientist An Elder Brother in Residence," *The Polish Review*, Vol. 46, no. 1 (2001), 100–06.

Gross, Ludwik (b. Kraków, Poland, September 11, 1904; d. Bronx, New York, July 19, 1999). Medical scientist. Gross earned his medical degree from the Jagiellonian University in Kraków in 1929 and served his residency in internal medicine at St. Lazar General Hospital in the same city (1929–32). Following his residency he accepted a position as a researcher at the Pasteur Institute in Paris (1932–39) where he was at the outbreak of World War II. Gross escaped from France and arrived in the U.S. in 1940 where he worked as a cancer researcher at Christ Hospital in Cincinnati (1941–43). After serving as an officer in the U.S. Army Medical Corps (1943–46), he became head of the cancer research unit at the Veterans Administration Medical Center in the Bronx, NY (1946–91), while also teaching at the Mt. Sinai School of Medicine and conducting research at the Sloan Kettering Institute. The author of numerous research studies on cancer and leukemia, his studies on tumor viruses were said to have "revolutionized the modern experimental approach to American cancer research." Gross was a fellow of the American College of Physicians, and a member of the American Medical Association, the National Academy of Science, the International Society of Hematology, the Board of Directors of the American Association for Cancer Research, the American Association for the Advancement of Science, and the **Polish Institute of Arts and Sciences of America**. Among his honors were the Prix Chevillon from the Academie Medicine in Paris (1937), the R. De Villiers Award from the Leukemia Society (NY, 1953), the Walker Prize from the Royal College of Surgeons (United Kingdom, 1962), the Pasteur Silver Medal from the Pasteur Institute (Paris, 1962), a prize from the World Health Organization of the United Nations (1962), the Bertner Foundation Award (1963), the Albert Einstein Centennial Medal (1965), the A. O. Bernstein Award from the Medical Society (NY, 1971), the Albert Lasker Basic Medical Research Award (1974), the Foundations Award from the Cancer Research Institute (1975), the Prix Griffuel (Paris, 1978), the Exceptional Service Award from the Veterans Administration Medical Center (1979), a Doctor honoris causa from Mt. Sinai School of Medicine (1983), the K. Berken Judd

Award from the Memorial Sloan-Kettering Cancer Center (1985), the **Alfred Jurzykowski** Award (1985), and the Chevalier of the Legion d'Honneur (France).—*James S. Pula*

SOURCES: Bolesław Wierzbiański, ed., *Who's Who in Polish America* (New York: Bicentennial Publishing Corporation, 1996); obituary, *New York Times*, July 22, 1999.

Grotnik, Kazimierz J. (b. Jeziorzany, Poland, March 24, 1935; d. Scranton, Pennsylvania, December 9, 2005). Bishop. Grotnik was educated at the Catholic University of Lublin where he received a M.A. degree in 1958 and was ordained in Lublin on April 20, 1958. He migrated to the U.S. in 1969 where he joined the Central Diocese of the **Polish National Catholic Church** as pastor in Middleport, Pennsylvania (1969–83) and St. John the Baptist Parish in Hazleton (1983–99). Grotnik was active in promoting Polish American history and culture and the history of the PNCC and served as archivist of the PNCC (1990–2005). He served on the board of directors of the **Polish National Union of America** and director of its District 8, and was a member of the Bishop Hodur Biography Commission, the **Polish Institute of Arts & Sciences of America**, and the **Polish American Historical Association**. Among his publications were *Index to Nowy Świat* (1984), *Index to Rola Boża* (Vol. I, 1989; Vol. II, 1991), *Polish National Catholic Church: Minutes of the First Eleven General Synods, 1904–1963* (1993), *Polish National Catholic Church of America: Minutes of the Supreme Council, 1904–1969* (1993), *Index to Straż* (Vol. I, 1994; Vol. II, 1997), *A Fifty Year Index to Polish American Studies, 1944–1993* (1998), *The Polish National Catholic Church* (2002), and *The Polish National Catholic Church of America: Minutes of the Supreme Council, 1904–1969* (2004). He obtained a doctorate in Old Catholic theology from the Christina Theological Academy in Warsaw in 1996 and was consecrated bishop in the PNCC in November 1999 and assigned as pastor of St. Stanislaus Polish National Catholic Cathedral in Scranton, Pennsylvania. In 1989 he was recognized as Prelate of Honor with the title Very Reverend."—*James S. Pula*

SOURCE: Bolesław Wierzbiański, ed., *Who's Who in Polish America* (New York: Bicentennial Publishing Corporation, 1996).

Grygier, Casimir Anthony "Cass" (b. Detroit, Michigan, October 16, 1908; d. Beverly Hills, Michigan, June 21, 1993). Bowler. Grygier began his career as a bowler in 1926. Based in Detroit, he won numerous honors and titles in city, state, and Midwestern regional competition. In 1936, Grygier and a teammate won the international doubles championship in Berlin. He is a member of the Detroit Bowling Hall of Fame, and was inducted into the National Polish-American Sports Hall of Fame in 1984.—*Neal Pease*

SOURCE: See "Cass Grygier," National Polish-American Sports Hall of Fame website, www.polishsportshof.com.

Gryglaszewski, Franciszek "Frank" (b. Lwów, Poland, September 24, 1847 (some sources say 1852); d. Santa Fe, New Mexico, November 22, 1918). Polonia activist. Born in the Austrian-ruled partitioned Poland, Gryglaszewski came to America as a youth and settled in Chicago. There he became a member of the **Gmina Polska** (Polish Commune) patriotic society. One of the earliest members of the **Polish National Alliance** and a delegate to its second convention in New York in 1881, Gryglaszewski energetically supported the creation of the Alliance's own newspaper and contributed a considerable sum of money to make it a reality. It was also his suggestion to name the newspaper *Zgoda* (Harmony) to symbolize its commitment to uniting the many different elements of **Polonia**. In 1882, in Chicago, he was elected to the newly created office of vice censor and, the following year, he became censor, a position he held until 1891. For several years he held a federal government office as Inspector of Public Buildings. In this capacity he was able to travel throughout the country, enabling him to promote the PNA to Poles in various locations. Thus, as a kind of "Johnny Appleseed," he enrolled hundreds of new members into the fraternal and helped organize dozens of lodges, mainly in the Midwest.

Franciszek Gryglaszewski, early leader in the Polish National Alliance (*PMA*).

Gryglaszewski served as chairman of the PNA Colonization Commission after 1894, helping several hundred immigrants set up their own farms on lands available through the Federal Homestead Act. In 1895 he was named by the Alliance to be its first chief organizer. A dedicated PNA member and brilliant organizer, the burly, bearded Gryglaszewski was elected PNA commissioner for the state of Minnesota in 1909 and 1911. A "free thinker" who was accused of being a Mason, he also came under fire from some quarters in the early Polonia for his strong support of a Polish National Alliance open to all persons who originated from the lands of the ancient Polish-Lithuanian commonwealth, not just Poles and Catholics. Gryglaszewski also founded the Grygla-Selden cast iron works in Minneapolis.—*Donald E. Pienkos*

SOURCE: Donald E. Pienkos, *PNA: A Centennial History of the Polish National Alliance of the United States of North America* (Boulder, CO: East European Monographs, 1984).

Grynberg, Henryk (b. Warsaw, Poland, July 4, 1936; d.—). Poet, writer. Grynberg and his mother were the only members of their family to survive World War II by remaining in hiding from 1942 to 1944 and using forged "Aryan" papers. Following the war, he resided in Łódź and Warsaw, earning a master's degree in journalism from the University of Warsaw (1959). Entering a career as an actor with the Jewish State Theatre in Warsaw, he became interested in poetry and writing. In 1956 he was recruited by the Polish Agency for Internal Security, but later denied divulging any information and reported his recruitment to the FBI. In late 1967, while on tour in the United States, he refused to return to Poland in protest against the regime's anti–Jewish campaign and the censorship of his writing. In 1971, after two years of graduate study at UCLA, he received an M.A. in Russian literature and moved to the Washington, D.C., metropolitan area. Over the next twenty years he worked for the U.S. Information Agency and Voice of America, as well as a self-employed writer who authored more than twenty books of prose and poetry (including two dramas), mostly on the Holocaust experience and post–Holocaust trauma. A recipient of nearly all major Polish literary prizes, he contributed to the Polish press and English-language journals including essays in *Commentary*, *Midstream*, and *Soviet-Jewish Affairs* (London). Three of his novels have been published in English translation: *Child of the Shadows* (1969), *The Victory* (1993), *Children of Zion* (1998). His writings have been translated into Dutch, French, German, Italian, and Hebrew.—*Włodek Lopaczynski*

SOURCES: Bolesław Wierzbiański, *Who's Who in Polish America* (New York: Bicentennial Publishing Corp., 1996), 145; "Grynberg, Henryk," *Contemporary Authors* (Detroit: Gale Research Company, New Revision Series), Vol. 137, 184–87.

Gryzik, Joseph (b. Katowice, Poland, October 10, 1927; d.—). Soccer player. After migrating to the United States in 1949, Gryzik became active in Chicago-area soccer playing for the Polish American Athletic Club, later known as the Chicago Eagles S.A.C. He was a member of the Chicago All-Stars that played against A.I.K. Stockholm, a visiting Swedish club in 1951. From that time on he was a regular at half back on teams that played visiting clubs from England, Germany, Mexico, and Yugoslavia. He played for the U.S. in the 1963 Pan-American Games, the 1964 Olympics, and the 1966 U.S. World Cup. Gryzik spent his entire career with the Eagles, captaining them to the Peel Cup, emblematic of the Illinois state championship, in 1950, 1954, 1955, 1957, and 1963. He set a record for the Peel Cup with eight goals in a single game, and consistently ranked among the high scorers in both the indoor and outdoor National Soccer League seasons. He retired from competitive play in 1965. In 1972 he was honored with an award for career achievement and sportsmanship by the National Soccer League of Chicago, and the following year he was inducted into the National Soccer Hall of Fame.— *James S. Pula*

SOURCE: national.soccerhall.org.

Grzelachowski, Alexander "Padre Polaco" (b. Kracina, Poland, 1824; d. Puerto de Luna, New Mexico, May 24, 1896). Priest, merchant. Although details of his early life are sketchy, he was probably prepared for the priesthood at a French seminary where he was recruited to serve in the Diocese of Cleveland. After arriving in the U.S. in 1850 he became the first pastor in what would become St. Mary's Church in Avon, Ohio. When a fellow priest, the Rev. Jean Lamy, was named vicar general of the New Mexico Territory, he convinced Grzelachowski to accompany him. They arrived in Santa Fe on August 9, 1851. For the next several years he ministered to mostly Spanish-speaking parishes in San Miguel del Vado and Las Vegas, and then several Indian communities where he became known as "Padre Polaco." He became a U.S. citizen in 1855. During the Civil War he served as chaplain in the 2nd New Mexico Infantry and was later credited with leading Union troops through the mountains to attack Confederate forces from the rear during the Battle of Glorieta Pass (1862) which saved the New Mexico Territory for the Union. Following the war, Grzelachowski left the priesthood

to become a merchant in Las Vegas and also signed contracts to transport government supplies. Around 1874 he moved to Puerto de Luna on the Pecos River where he reestablished his business enterprises, adding ranching and herding cattle, sheep, and horses. His holdings in Las Vegas also continued to operate under the immediate supervision of a partner. Among Grzelachowski's frequent customers were Billy the Kid and Sheriff Pat Garrett. As one of the most influential people in the area, residents referred to him as "Don Alejandro." He served as town postmaster for ten years. He also led a successful fight for irrigation projects and water rights along the Pecos River. When Guadalupe County was established in 1891, he donated land to the county for the construction of the county offices. He was also an early member and supporter of the Historical Society of New Mexico.— *Francis Casimir Kajencki*

SOURCES: Francis Casimir Kajencki, *Poles in the 19th Century Southwest* (El Paso, TX: Southwest Polonia Press, 1990), 79–104; Francis Casimir Kajencki, "Alexander Grzelachowski: Pioneer Merchant of Puerto de Luna, New Mexico," *Arizona & the West*, Vol. 26, no. 3 (Autumn 1984), 243–60.

Gulczynski, Theodore "Ted" (b. Wisconsin, May 8, 1926; d. West Allis, Wisconsin, October 20, 2005). Speedskating official. After serving in the U.S. Marine Corps during World War II, Gulczynski became a speedskating enthusiast, frequenting the Milwaukee rink where he was eventually responsible for the heat box. In this capacity he was well known for his response when skaters complained about who they had drawn in a particular heat, Gulczynski would reply: "You can't beat 'um in the heat, you can't beat 'um in the final!" In 1970 he became a National Official, rising to Chief Clerk in 1972 after which he served in that capacity at every National and North American event held in Wisconsin. A meet director of Wisconsin National and North American events since 1975, he was a delegate to the Amateur Speedskating Union Convention beginning in 1970 and a member of the U.S. Speedskating Advisory Board since 1976. He clerked at all of the Olympic trials, U.S. Speedskating time trials, and International Speed Skating events held in Wisconsin since 1969. A member of the Badger Speed Skating Club and a United States Cycling Federation official, he was elected to the National Speedskating Hall of Fame in 1988.— *James S. Pula*

SOURCE: "Gulczynski, Theodore 'Ted,'" *Milwaukee Journal Sentinel*, October 23, 2005.

Gunther, Bolesław E. "Blair" (b. western Pennsylvania, June 20, 1903; d. Pittsburgh, Pennsylvania, December 29, 1966). Polonia

activist, government official. After graduating from Saint John Kanty College (1922), he earned his law degree from Duquesne University in 1928. Active in local and state politics, he became a county judge in 1942 and later was elected to the Supreme Court of the Commonwealth of Pennsylvania. Gunther was also a leader in the **Polish National Alliance** fraternal in Pittsburgh and was connected for many years with the city's Polish language daily, *Pittsburczanin*. In 1947, he was elected censor of the PNA at its thirtieth national convention in Cleveland, an office he held until 1959. At the second national convention of the **Polish American Congress** in 1948, he was chosen to chair its Committee for the Resettlement of Polish Displaced Persons. This body was created in anticipation of passage of special U.S. federal legislation to permit several hundred thousand World War II refugees from Europe to enter this country apart from the immigration quotas that were then in force. Of the more than 140,000 Poles who entered the United States as a result of the 1948 Displaced Persons Act, as many as 30,000 were assisted in their resettlement through the committee that Gunther headed. In 1957 Gunther was mentioned as a possible candidate to be the first Polish American to become a member of the U.S. Supreme Court; instead, President Eisenhower named William J. Brennan of New Jersey to that office. In 1958, **Censor** Gunther, once an ally of PNA President **Charles Rozmarek**, joined PNA Treasurer Adam Tomaszkiewicz in a strenuous but failed effort to call an extraordinary convention of the Alliance in Chicago, its purpose being to critically review Rozmarek's leadership. The next year, at the thirty-third PNA convention in Hartford,

Blair Gunther, a leader in the Polish National Alliance (*OLS*).

Connecticut, Rozmarek's candidate for censor, Edward Kozmor of New Jersey, defeated Gunther for reelection by a vote of 260–200. Rozmarek defeated Tomaszkiewicz by a 285–172 margin. Thereafter, Gunther limited his activities to his judicial responsibilities.—*Donald E. Pienkos*

SOURCE: Donald E. Pienkos, *PNA: A Centennial History of the Polish National Alliance of the United States of North America* (Boulder, CO: East European Monographs, 1987).

Gurowski, Adam (b. Palatinate of Kalisz, Poland, September 10, 1805; d. Washington, D.C., May 4, 1866). Journalist, political commentator, author. Born into a noble family that lost most of its land holdings for supporting the Kościuszko Insurrection against Russia in 1794, Gurowski was himself expelled from gymnasiums in Warsaw and Kalisz for his participation in revolutionary activities, forcing him to move to Germany where he studied philosophy under Hegel at the University of Berlin, completing studies at the University of Heidelberg in 1823. Returning to Warsaw in 1825, he was imprisoned for continued revolutionary activities, but when released he became active in planning and participating in the November Uprising in 1830-31 for which he was condemned to death *in absentia*. Fleeing to France, he became an active member of the Polish committee in Paris and came under the influence of Charles Fourier. In 1835 he published *La Verite sur la Russie* arguing in favor of a pan-Slavic union. Tsar Nicholas I, who looked with favor upon the idea of pan-Slavism, granted Gurowski a pardon and invited him to return to St. Petersburg, but his properties were not restored. For several years he traveled through Germany, Switzerland and Italy studying, lecturing and adding to his list of publications *La civilisation et la Russie* (1840), *Pensées sur l'avenir des Polonais* (1841), *Aus meinem Gedankenbuche* (1843), *Eine Tour durch Belgien* (1845), *Impressions et souvenirs* (1846), *Die letzten Ereignisse in den drei Theilen des alten Polen* (1846) and *Le Panslavisme* (1848). Migrating to the United States in 1849, he continued his literary activities authoring *Russia as It Is* (1854), *The Turkish Question* (1854), *A Year of the War* (1855), *America and Europe* (1857), *Slavery in History* (1860) and *My Diary*, the latter containing his impressions of the American Civil War. For a time he lectured at Harvard, while also writing articles for the *New York Tribune* advocating the Russian cause during the Crimean War. His work also appeared in the *New American Cyclopedia* and *Atlantic Monthly*. Becoming active in the abolitionist movement, he gained a reputation as a caustic commentator on American politics. Fluent in

Adam Gurowski, journalist, abolitionist, and critic of the Lincoln administration (*PMA*).

eight languages, he gained employment as a translator with the U.S. State Department from 1861–63, but the publication of his diaries in which he was very critical of President Abraham Lincoln, Secretary of State William Seward, and what he considered to be the mismanagement of the Union war effort led to his dismissal. He died of typhoid fever and was buried in the Congressional Cemetery in Washington, D.C.—*James S. Pula*

SOURCES: LeRoy Fischer, *Lincoln's Gadfly, Adam Gurowski* (Norman: University of Oklahoma Press, 1964); Jan Drohojowski, "The United States Versus Adam Gurowski," *Prawo i Życie*, Vol. 5, no. 13 (1960), 8; LeRoy Fischer, "Adam Gurowski and the American Civil War: A Radical's Record," *Bulletin of the Polish Institute of Arts and Sciences in America*, Vol. 1, no. 3 (1942-43), 476–88; Mary Ligouri, "The Pole Who Wrote to Lincoln," *Polish American Studies*, Vol. 10, no. 1–2 (1953), 1–12; Joseph Wieczerzak, "Some Friendly Swipes at Lincoln's Gadfly," *The Polish Review*, Vol. 10, no. 1 (1965), 90–98.

Gutowski, Robert "Bob" (b. San Pedro, CA, April 25, 1935; d. Oceanside, California, August 2, 1960). Pole vaulter. Gutowski attended LaJolla High School where he set a number of California high school records in pole vault events before enrolling in Occidental College. In 1957 he set a world record of 15 feet, 8¹/₄ inches in the pole vault, later jumping 15 feet, 9³/₄ inches in the same year, but the new record was disallowed as a world mark on technicalities. Gutowski failed to make the 1956 U.S. Olympic team in tryouts; however, he was added to the squad when Jim Graham, the winner of the tryouts, was injured. At the games in Melbourne, Australia, Gutowski earned the Silver Medal as he sailed over the 14-foot, ¹/₂ inch bar. Fellow American

Bob Richards won the Gold, giving the United States first and second place honors in the event. In addition to being one of track and field's finest aluminum pole vaulters, Gutowski was also a noted sprinter and a long-jumper with a career best 20'9". Gutowski was killed in an auto accident on August 2, 1960. He was inducted into the **National Polish American Sports Hall of Fame** in 1980.—*Luis J. Gonzalez*

SOURCE: Gerald Lawson Gerald, *World Record Breakers in Track & Field Athletics* (Human Kinetics Publishers, 1997), 191.

Guzik, Jake "Greasy Thumb" (b. near Kraków, Poland, May 20, 1886; d. Chicago, Illinois, February 21, 1956). Gangster. In his youth, Guzik worked as a waiter in his uncle's restaurant which specialized in fried chicken, from which he earned his nickname because of his reputation for carrying the plates to customers with his thumb firmly planted in their meal. As an adult, Guzik displayed an aptitude for accounting leading one author to characterize him as "a financial wizard." Taking an early interest as well in prostitution, he rose through the ranks of organized crime in Chicago's notorious South Side to become the chief accountant for Johnny "The Fox" Torrio's criminal empire. When Torrio passed the leadership of his organization to Al Capone, Guzik continued on as Capone's trusted financial manager and chief bag man for delivering payoffs to local politicians and police, even being sent to meet on Capone's behalf with leaders of the eastern crime families. Following Capone's demise, Guzik remained the chief financial officer for the mob until his death at age 69.—*James S. Pula*

SOURCES: Don Fielding, *Untouchable Chicago: A Ride Through Prohibition* (Chicago: Untouchable Times & Tours, 2008); Robert J. Kelly, *Encyclopedia of Organized Crime in the United States* (Westport, CT: Greenwood Press, 2000); John Binder, *The Chicago Outfit* (Chicago: Arcadia Publishing, 2003).

Guzlowski, John (b. Vienenberg, Germany, June 22, 1948; d.—). Poet, critic, professor. The son of Poles deported to slave labor camps in Nazi Germany, Guzlowski was born in a displaced persons' camp. In 1951 the family, including an older sister, came to the United States as "DPs" (the term which Guzlowski uses to describe the family's status). Eventually he settled with his parents in Chicago where he graduated from St. Patrick High School, took a bachelor's degree at the University of Illinois Chicago Circle Campus, and earned a Ph.D. in English from Purdue University. Guzlowski taught for twenty-five years at Eastern Illinois University, achieving an impressive record as a teacher and scholar. Twice he was presented with Eastern Illinois

University's Faculty Excellence Teaching Award, in addition to two Achievement and Contribution Awards. His scholarship focused on contemporary fiction and Guzlowski emerged as a leading American scholar on the writings of **Isaac Bashevis Singer**. In 2005 he retired from Eastern Illinois University, later moving to Danville, Virginia.

As a sophomore in college, Guzlowski realized that American literature need not be the exclusive domain of white, Anglo-Saxon, Protestant authors and he determined to use literature, especially poetry, to explore, share, and preserve the experiences of his parents in Europe and America. His poems have been published in a wide variety of journals including *Atlantic Review, Spoon River Quarterly, Poetry East, Proteus: A Journal of Thought,* and *Periphery* in the United States and in such venues as *Akcent, Nowa Okolica Poetów,* and *Tygodnik Powszechny* in Poland and *Kalligram* in Hungary. Guzlowski's first collection of poems, *The Language of Mules,* was published in 1999; three years later the collection was translated into Polish and published by the Biblioteka Śląska in Katowice. *Lightning and Ashes,* Guzlowski's second collection, was published in 2007. *Third Winter of War: Buchenwald,* his most recent collection of poems, was also published in 2007. In addition to his own literary work, he created and maintained a network for Polish, Polish American, and Polish Diaspora writers. Named "Writing the Polish Diaspora: News and Information for Polish Writers and Writers of the Polish Diaspora," the network connected writers in the United States, Poland, and around the world who were addressing their Polish roots in order to provide information, advice, encouragement, and writing opportunities for their

efforts; it has also proven a valuable resource to scholars and the literary public as well.

The primary focus of Guzlowski's work has long been his parents' experiences in the slave labor camps of Nazi Germany. In his more recent works he has extended his purview to include his parents' lives in Poland before the war, the family's experiences in the United States, and the legacy of the war not only for his parents but for his sister and himself—and even for his own daughter. In recounting and preserving these experiences, he tells a story which non–Polish Americans in the United States have never heard: the experiences of Polish Christians during and after World War II. In doing so, he has given a voice to perhaps the most silent segment of the Polish American community: the displaced persons of the post–War years. Guzlowski's poetry has been lauded for both its lyric and narrative strengths and has attracted widespread attention and garnered a number of awards. *The Language of Mules* earned an Illinois Arts Council Artist Fellowship Award in 2002 and *Lightning and Ashes* was a finalist for the Eric Hoffer Poetry Award. For *Third Year of War,* Guzlowski was nominated for a Pulitzer Prize. In August of 2009 he received the Cultural Achievement Award of the American Council on Polish Culture. Additionally, he was honored as featured poet by journals such as *Spoon River Review* and *Margie: An American Journal of Poetry.— Thomas J. Napierkowski*

SOURCES: Czesław Miłosz, Review of *The Language of Mules,* http://www.ruf.rice.edu/~sarmatia/904/243 milosz.html; Thomas J. Napierkowski, "*Lightning and Ashes:* The Poetry of John Guzlowski," *Polish American Studies,* Vol. LXV, no. 1 (Spring 2008), 85–93; interview, *Spoon River Poetry Review,* http://everythingsjake.blogspot.com/2007/07/conversation-with-john-guzlowski.html.

Gwiazda Polarna (North Star). A biweekly newspaper begun in 1908 as a continuation of *Rolnik* (The Farmer), it has been published since 1892 by the Worzalla Publishing Company in Stevens Point, Wisconsin. *Gwiazda Polarna* is an independent weekly, not affiliated with any organization or political faction, financed from subscriptions and advertisements. It offers news, practical information, serialized novels, historical and ethnographic information, cultural news, and other features. The newspaper's goal is to disseminate Polish culture and traditions. Originally printed in 6,000 copies, its circulation quickly reached beyond Wisconsin, growing to 49,000 in 1917 and reaching a peak of 90,000 copies in 1929-30 until the Great Depression resulted in contraction. Founded by Paweł Klimowicz who edited it for a long time as a weekly, its other editors included **Wacław Gąsiorowski**, Adam Bartosz, Franciszek Kmietowicz, Alfons

Hering, Leszek Zieliński, and Jacek Hilgier.— *Adam Walaszek*

SOURCE: Jan Wepsiec, *Polish American Serial Publications: 1842–1966, An Annotated Bibliography* (Chicago: Jan Wepsiec, 1968).

Gwiazdowski, Aleksander (b. Suwalki, Poland, September 8, 1883; d. Angola, Indiana, February 26, 1956). Engineer. Sentenced to exile in Siberia by the Czarist government for his socialist activity, Gwiazdowski escaped to America where he instituted in New York the Polski Instytut Ludowy (Polish People's Institute) in 1906. Two years later he participated in the reorganization of the Chicago Polski Uniwersytet Ludowy (Polish People's University). After earning his degree in engineering from Columbia University (1910), he opened a small mechanical workshop in Toledo, Ohio, and began offering courses to prepare young Poles for technical studies. Renewing his association with the celebrated socialist **Aleksander Dębski**, the two cooperated in publishing *Myśl* (The Thought), an illustrated popular magazine on technology. For two years, he taught at **Alliance College** before accepting a position at the University of Toledo in 1914, continuing his work on *Myśl* while also supporting the Detroit Uniwersytet Ludowy (People's University). In 1918, Gwiazdowski established the Stowarzyenie Mechaników Polskich w Ameryce (Polish Mechanics Association of America) and its monthly magazine *Mechanik* (The Mechanic). Following World War I, he returned to Poland where he worked assiduously to found a similar Stowarzyenie Mechaników Polskich while also opening a technical school in Pruszków and publishing a version of *Mechanik.* Later he opened an office and bank in Warsaw. In 1924 he returned to Toledo, later becoming a member of the faculty at the University of Michigan (1928–34). In the 1930s he returned to Poland to expand his technical school into other parts of Poland and to engage in other business ventures. While there, Marshal Józef Piłsudski awarded him the Niepodległości (Independence) medal. Caught in Poland by the Nazi invasion, Gwiazdowski, his wife, and son Richard were sent to German forced labor camps during World War II, despite the fact that they were U.S. citizens. After the war the family returned to America where he taught engineering at Tri-State University in Angola, Indiana until his death. Gwiazdowski's publications include: *Przewodnik dla imigrantów polskich w Ameryce* (1912); *Arytmetyka i trygonometrya ze słownictwem angielskim* (1919); *Machine Shop Practice Laboratory Manual* (1931); *Economics of Tool Engineering; Jig and Fixture Design* (1932); *Course in Machine Shop Practice* (1932); *The Design, Fabrication and*

John Guzlowski, poet, critic and professor (*John Guzlowski*).

Use of Milling Cutters, Twist Drills and Broaches (1932); *Engineering Metallurgy* (1950); *Tool Engineering* (1951); *I Survived Hitler's Hell* (1954); *Ferrous and Nonferrous Tool-and Die Materials* (1955); and *Six Designs of Blanking, Forming, Drawing, Trimming, and Piercing Dies* (1955).—*Don Binkowski*

SOURCES: Francis Bolek, *Who's Who in Polish America* (New York: Arno, 1970 [c1943], 153; Bolesław Wierzbiański, *Who's Who in Polish America* (New York: Bicentennial Publishing, 1996).

Gwizdowski, Józef Julius (b. Gwizdów, Poland, July 7, 1880; d. Detroit, Michigan, May 19, 1940). Architect. Following completion of studies at the Technical Institute in Lwów, Gwizdowski gained employment managing construction of railway stations for the Austro-Hungarian government. Migrating to Chicago in 1904, he continued his studies at Loyola University while obtaining employment with Worthman & Stienbach where he was engaged in planning residential construction projects. After accepting a new position at the W. B. Hartigan architectural firm, he drew up plans for the headquarters of the **Polish Women's Alliance** on North Ashland Avenue. In 1914 he moved to Detroit where he conceived plans for the West Side Dom Polski; the building that became the home of the Polish Art Center; St. Kunegunda Parish School; the Davison Avenue Station of the Detroit Police Department; and the **Hamtramck** Municipal Hospital. Later renamed Saint Francis Hospital, the latter building housed the Hamtramck City Hall in 2008. In 1930 the **Polish National Alliance** selected him to plan the central building at **Alliance College** in Cambridge Springs, Pennsylvania. In 1933 he took a position as Assistant to the Architect of the U.S. Treasury in Washington, D.C., following which he served as Resident Engineer for the Public Works Administration in Detroit. A charter member of the Michigan Society of Architects, he was also a member of the Polish Engineers Society, Polish Falcons Nest No. 31, and the Polish National Alliance.—*James S. Pula*

SOURCE: www.detroitpolonia.org.

Gzowski, Casimir Stanislaus (Kazimierz Stanisław Gzowski; b. St. Petersburg, Russia, March 5, 1813; d. Toronto, Canada, August 24, 1898). Engineer, railway pioneer. The eldest son of an officer in the Russian Imperial Guard, Casimir was sent to the Lyceum of Krzemieniec to study surveying, mathematics, science and languages in 1822 at the age of nine. Graduating at age seventeen in 1830, he was commissioned in the Imperial Corps of Engineers. When an uprising of Poles against the Russian administration broke out in Warsaw on November 29, 1830, he joined the Polish insurgents. Wounded in battle, he retreated with his unit into Galicia, then part of Austria-Hungary, where he and his fellow officers were interned. After negotiations, the United States agreed to accept the internees and in November, 1833, they embarked for New York, arriving on March 8, 1834. On April 1, 1834, he was one of the founders of the Polish Committee in New York, the first Polish organization in America. Within a short time, the exiles dispersed and Gzowski found employment in Pittsfield, Massachusetts, where he learned English while tutoring students in various European languages. Serving as a clerk for attorney Parker L. Hall, he read law and in February, 1837, passed the legal examinations. Gzowski moved to Beaver, Pennsylvania, where he became a U.S. citizen in 1837 and began working for a prominent engineer. As an assistant engineer, Gzowski worked on the Beaver & Lake Erie Canal, then moved to Erie, Pennsylvania, where he supervised construction work on the Erie Railroad. In 1841 Gzowski went to Upper Canada (now Ontario) to investigate whether his firm could obtain construction contracts. The following year in Kingston he met by chance Sir Charles Bagot, the new Governor-in-Chief of the recently united Province of Canada. A former British Ambassador in St. Petersburg, he knew Gzowski's father and was impressed with the younger Gzowski's achievements in the United States. Through Bagot's influence, Gzowski obtained a position in the colonial government as Superintendent of Roads and Waterways in the London District. He was naturalized as a British subject on June 1, 1846. In 1847, Gzowski resigned his position with the colonial government to undertake various private business projects. He was involved in a mining project, then worked as chief engineer in charge of construction of the St. Lawrence & Atlantic Railway. In 1853 he supervised construction of a railroad from Toronto to Guelph. Between 1859 and 1861 he built a railroad from Port Huron, Michigan, to Detroit to connect with lines running south into Ohio and Indiana. Gzowski was involved in surveying the route between Montréal and Québec City, the Port of Montréal in 1850, and the Toronto waterfront in 1853. He became president of the Toronto Rolling Mills Company in 1857, and in 1870, the firm Gzowski, MacPherson and Company constructed the International Bridge spanning the Niagara River. One of the longest bridges in North America, it was considered one of the most important engineering achievements of the time. Gzowski was actively involved in promoting the defense of Canada against the

Sir Casimir Gzowski, engineer and railway pioneer (*OLS*).

Fenian Raids in 1866. In 1872 he was president of the Dominion Rifle Association, a position he held until he retired in 1885. In November, 1872, he was appointed lieutenant-colonel of the Central Division of Toronto Volunteers, and in 1879 gained promotion to colonel in the militia. Among Gzowski's numerous honors were appointment as Honorary Aide-de-Camp to Queen Victoria (1879), chair of the newly-formed Queen Victoria Niagara Falls Park Commission (1886), president of the Canadian Society of Civil Engineers (1889–1892), and Knight Commander of the Distinguished Order of Saint Michael and Saint George at Windsor Castle (1890). The Gzowski Medal became the highest professional award of the Canadian Society of Civil Engineers, while Toronto honored him with Sir Casimir Gzowski Park. Nor did he forget his Polish heritage. In 1879 Gzowski had a statuette made of a Polish lancer to commemorate the November Uprising on which he inscribed the names of all the battles in which he took part. This statuette stood for many years in the Gzowski home known as "The Hall" in Toronto.—*Myron Momryk*

SOURCES: Ludwik Kos-Rabcewicz-Zubkowski and William Edward Greening, *Sir Casimir Stanislaus Gzowski, A Biography* (Toronto: Burns and MacEachern, 1959); Ludwik Kos-Rabcewicz-Zubkowski, "Sir Casimir Gzowski and the Construction of the International Bridge Between Fort Erie, Ont., and Buffalo N.Y.," *The Engineering Journal* (Montréal), Vol. 36, no. 4 (1956), 74–75; H. V. Nelles, "Sir Casimir Gzowski," in Frances G. Halpenny and Jean Hamelin, eds., *Dictionary of Canadian Biography* (Toronto: University of Toronto Press, 1990), Vol. XII, 389–396.

Haendel, Ida (b. Chełm, Poland, December 15, 1924; d.—). Violinist. Haendel took up the violin at age three and four years later was admitted to the Warsaw Conservatory where she studied with Mieczysław

Michałowicz and received a Gold Medal (1933). She later studied with Carl Flesch in London (1935–39) and George Enescu in Paris. Her London debut took place in the Queen's Hall with Sir Henry Wood conducting (1937). During World War II she played in factories and for British and American troops. In 1952 she moved to Montréal where she premiered in Luigi Dallapiccola's *Tartiniana Seconda* (1957*)*. She moved permanently to Miami, FL, in 1979, but continued to perform internationally including a performance in Germany of Allan Petterson's concerto for violin (1989). Among her many honors were the Bronisław Huberman Award at the Young Talents Competition in Warsaw (1934); the Sibelius Prize (1982); the title of a "Commander of the British Empire" (1991); and an honorary doctorate from the Royal College in London (2000).—*Adam A. Zych*

SOURCES: George Grove, Stanley Sadie, and John Tyrell, eds., *New Grove Dictionary of Music and Musicians* (New York: Groves Dictionaries, 2001); Ida Haendel, *Woman with Violin: The Autobiography of Ida Haendel* (London: Victor Gollancz, Ltd., 1970).

Hagel, Charles Timothy "Chuck" (b. North Platte, Nebraska, October 4, 1946; d.—). U.S. Senator, broadcaster. The oldest in a family of four boys, Hagel's father died when he was sixteen. After attending St. Bonaventure High School in Columbus, NE, Hagel graduated from the Brown Institute for Radio and Television in Minneapolis, MN (1966) and the University of Nebraska, Omaha, where he received his baccalaureate degree (1971). He served in the U.S. Army infantry (1967-68) achieving the rank of sergeant and serving a tour of duty in Vietnam in 1968. Hagel's brother Tom also served in combat in Vietnam. Both had volunteered to go in 1967, having grown up in small towns in Nebraska with the expectation to serve in the military. Hagel was wounded twice, "With serious but not lasting wounds." Tom was also wounded (with Chuck, who dragged Tom to safety) and became a Democrat while Hagel became a Republican. Following his military service, Hagel became a newscaster and talk show host in Omaha (1969–71) before accepting a position as administrative assistant to Representative John Y. McCollister (R-Nebraska; 1971–77), a job that helped him frame his political philosophy. As the manager of government affairs (a lobbyist) for Firestone Tire & Rubber Company in Washington, D.C. (1977–80), he was appointed deputy administrator at the United States Veterans Administration (1981-82) and was one of two main speakers at the groundbreaking of the Vietnam Veterans' Memorial in Washington, D.C. From 1982 to 1987 he worked for Vanguard Cellular Systems, a telephone company which he cofounded. Vanguard became the second largest independent cell phone system in the U.S. As an investment banker, he became deputy director and chief executive officer of the Economic Summit of Industrialized Nations (G-7) in 1990. He was elected as a Republican to the United States Senate in 1996, the first elected office that he ever held other than high school student council and later college fraternity president. His Democratic opponent was Governor Ben Nelson, who later became Nebraska's other U.S. Senator. Hagel's basic conservative Republican political philosophy largely informed his voting; that is, he was a supporter of less government, less spending, lower taxes, and less regulation. He was reelected in 2002 by the largest margin ever in a Nebraska Senate contest (83 percent to 15 percent) and served two full terms from January 3, 1997, to January 3, 2009. An internationalist, Hagel sought and received a position on the Senate Foreign Relations Committee. His military experience framed his ideas in arguably a less traditional Republican sense, such as in his opposition to land mines and chemical weapons and skepticism toward the Iraq War. He opposed trade sanctions against Libya and Iran and sought to lift the embargo against Cuba. Known for working across the political aisle in the Senate like his friend and fellow Vietnam War veteran John McCain (with whom he did not entirely agree on campaign finance), there was some speculation that he might run for president in 2008. The Democrat **Zbigniew Brzeziński** said in April 2007 that he would have no hesitation in supporting the Republican Hagel for that office. But Hagel finally decided against that and was not a candidate for reelection to the Senate in 2008. Among his honors is the **Edmund S. Muskie** Public Service Award, which was conferred on him and Ted Kennedy in 2004. His papers are located at the University of Nebraska, Omaha.—*Frederick J. Augustyn*

SOURCES: *Biographical Directory of the United States Congress, 1774–Present* (http://bioguide.congress.gov/); Chuck Hagel, with Peter Kaminsky, *America: Our Next Chapter: Tough Questions, Straight Answers* (New York: Ecco, 2008); Charlyne Berens, *Chuck Hagel: Moving Forward* (Lincoln: University of Nebraska Press, 2006).

Haiman, Mieczysław Albin Franciszek (b. Złoczów, Poland, March 31, 1888; d. Chicago, Illinois, January 15, 1949). Journalist, museum curator, historian. Haiman and his three siblings were orphaned early. In 1906, after completing three classes of high school, Haiman entered the Austrian merchant marine and traveled the world for five years. In 1913 he and his younger brother Adam migrated to the United States. He first worked as a common laborer, then obtained a position as a journalist with Boston's *Kuryer* (Courier) and later with *Polak w Ameryce* (The Pole in America). He also published poetry, which often provided political and social commentary, under the pen-name Nie-Tersytes. In 1927 Haiman published his first historical study *Z przeszłości polskiej w Ameryce* (From the Polish Past in America), which began his life-long exploration of the early Polish history in the United States. The same year Haiman, his wife and their son moved to Chicago where he began work for ***Dziennik Zjednoczenia*** (Alliance Daily) a newspaper published by the **Polish Roman Catholic Union** of America (PRCUA). He continued to prolifically publish on the history of **Polonia** and Poland. The list of his publications includes: *Historia udziału Polaków w amerykańskiej wojnie domowej* (History of the Polish Participation in the Civil War; 1928); *Polacy wsród pionierów Ameryki* (Poles Among American Pioneers; 1930); *Polacy w Ameryce* (Poles in America; 1930); *Polacy w walce o niepodległość Ameryki* (Poles in the Fight for American Independence; 1931); *Poland and the American Revolutionary War* (1932); *Feliks Paweł Wierzbicki i jego Kalifornia* (Felix Paul Wierzbicki and His California; 1933); *J.E. Ks. Biskup Paweł P. Rhode, Jego życie i czyny* (Bishop Paul P. Rhode, His Life and Deeds; 1934); *The Fall of Poland in Contemporary American Opinion* (1935); *Polish Pioneers in California* (1940); *Polish Pioneers of Pennsylvania* (1941); *Kosciuszko in the American Revolution* (1943); *Kosciuszko, Leader and Exile* (1946); *Nauka polska w Stanach Zjednoczonych Ameryki Północnej w latach 1939–1947* (Polish Science in the United States of North America in the Years 1939–

Mieczysław Haiman, journalist, museum curator, initiator of the Polish American Historical Association (*OLS*).

1947; 1948); and *Zjednoczenie Polskie Rzym-sko-Katolickie w Ameryce 1873–1948* (Polish Roman Catholic Union of America; 1948). He also contributed to *Polski Slownik Biograficzny* (Polish Biographical Dictionary), and edited *Annals of the Polish Roman Catholic Union Archives and Museum* and ***Polish American Studies***. In 1934 Haiman visited Poland as a member of the American delegation for the congress of **Światpol**. There he co-authored the document which became known as **Polonia**'s Declaration of Independence. In 1935 Haiman was appointed the first curator of the PRCUA's new archive and museum, which he organized and developed with much success. In December 1942, Haiman became chair of the Committee for Research on Polish Immigration of the **Polish Institute of Arts and Sciences** in America (later the **Polish American Historical Association**). He collaborated with both Polish and American scholars in establishing the organization as a professional historical association, with its own journal and annual conferences. Haiman died probably of stomach cancer at the top of his career in 1949. He was recognized by numerous honors, including Poland's Order of Polonia Restituta, the **Polish National Alliance**'s Gold Honorary Legion, the Polish Academy of Literature's Silver Academic Laurel, the PRCUA's highest honor, and the **Polish Falcons**' Silver Cross Honorary Legion. Haiman is remembered as the "Herodotus of Polonia" due to his pioneering historical scholarship and his role in the organization of the **Polish Museum** in Chicago, and was one of the founding fathers of PAHA.—*Anna Jaroszyńska-Kirchmann*

SOURCES: Robert Szymczak, "The Pioneer Days: Mieczysław Haiman and Polish American Historiography," *Polish American Studies,* Vol. 50, no. 1 (1993), 7–21; Sabina Logisz, "Miecislaus Haiman—Polish American Historian," *Polish American Studies,* Vol. 20, no. 1 (1963), 45–48; Teresa Kaczorowska, *Herodot Polonii Amerykańskiej Mieczysław Haiman, 1888–1949* (Warszawa: Muzeum Wychodźstwa Polskiego im. Ignacego Jana Paderewskiego Łazienki Królewskie, 2008).

Halecki, Oskar (b. Vienna, Austria, May 26, 1891; d. White Plains, New York, September 17, 1973). Historian. Halecki, who was generally recognized as one of the preeminent historians of Poland, earned his doctorate from the Jagiellonian University in Kraków in 1914 where, following postgraduate studies at the University of Vienna (1914-15), he was a lecturer in history from 1915 to 1918. In the latter year he moved to the University of Warsaw as professor of history and served two terms as Dean. He was as an expert advisor of the Polish delegation to the Paris Peace Conference (1918-19), served in the League of Nations secretariat (1921–24), and represented

Oskar Halecki, historian, initiator of the Polish Institute of Arts and Sciences in America (*OLS*).

Poland at the International Historical Congresses in Brussels (1923), Oslo (1928), Warsaw (1933), and Zurich (1938). A foremost authority on Jagiellonian Poland, he lectured widely in Europe and in 1938 came to the U.S. to lecture through the efforts of the **Kosciuszko Foundation**. He was rector of the Polish University in Paris in 1939-40, but due to the outbreak of World War II in the summer of the latter year moved to the U.S. as a visiting professor at Vassar College. Halecki was the prime mover behind the formation of the **Polish Institute of Arts and Sciences** in New York in 1942, serving as its executive director from 1942 to 1945 and president from 1952 to 1964. He was also a member of the Polish Academy of Arts and Sciences in Kraków (1944–61). In 1944 he accepted a position at Fordham University which he held until 1961, offering courses at Columbia University during the same years. The author of seven books and over 150 articles and reviews, his works include *Limits and Divisions of European History, The Millennium of Europe, From Florence to Brest 1439 to 1596, Borderlands of Western Civilization: A History of East Central Europe, History of Poland, Imperialism in Slavic and East European History*, and *Jadwiga of Anjou and The Rise of East Central Europe* (1984). Among his many awards are honorary doctoral degrees from the University of Lyon in France, the University of Montréal, De Paul University, and Fordham University.—*James S. Pula*

SOURCES: Justine Wincek, "Oscar Halecki," *Polish American Studies,* Vol. 24, no. 2 (1967), 106–08; Walter Romig, ed., *The Book of Catholic Authors: Informal Self-portraits of Famous Modern Catholic Writers* (Detroit: Walter Romig and Company, 1945).

Hallerczycy *see* **Polish Army in France.**

Ham, Jack Raphael, Jr. (b. Johnstown, Pennsylvania, December 23, 1948; d.—). Football player. After attending Bishop McCort High School and Massanutten Military Academy in Woodstock, VA, Ham enrolled at the Pennsylvania State University where he was a starting linebacker for three years during which the Nittany Lions went 11–0, 11–0, and 7–3. During his senior year (1970) he was named co-captain, recording 91 tackles and four interceptions while earning All-America recognition. He had 251 career tackles, 143 unassisted, and blocked three punts in 1968, setting a school record that was not tied until 1989. He was inducted into the College Football Hall of Fame in 1990.

In the 1971 National Football League draft Ham was selected in the second round by the Pittsburgh Steelers (34th overall pick). He won the starting left linebacker job as a rookie. Steelers' coach Chuck Noll noted that Ham was blessed with tremendous quickness, while teammate Andy Russell said he was the "fastest Steeler for the first ten yards, including wide receivers and running backs" on a team which included John Stallworth, Lynn Swann, and Frank Lewis. He was one of the few outside linebackers who could play pass defense as well as the NFL's top safeties. Although he was a ferocious hitter, he was known as a player who could not be fooled and was seldom out of position. Maxie Baughan, the great former NFL linebacker, said of Ham, "He was one of the more intelligent players to ever play that position. He was able to diagnose plays. You couldn't ever fool him." In his prime, Ham earned the reputation of being almost a perfect player who defended the run and pass equally well and rarely made a mistake. He was not as colorful as some of his teammates, but was always one of the most popular players among the fans. Steelers fans appreciated his accomplishments on the field and his quiet class off it. His career statistics include 25 sacks, 21 fumble recoveries, and 32 interceptions. Those numbers place him in the Defensive 20/20 Club (20 interceptions and 20 sacks) with only eight other recognized members. As these numbers indicate, Ham had a flair for the big play, guided by some of the best football instincts ever found in a linebacker. Ham won four Super Bowl titles during his twelve year career, all of it spent with the Steelers.

Ham was selected to seven All-Pro teams and named to eight straight Pro Bowls. He was the only unanimous defensive choice on the NFL 1970s Team of the Decade, and was named the greatest outside linebacker of all time by a consortium of professional sports writers, beating out Lawrence Taylor for this honor. In 1987 he was inducted into the **National Polish-American Sports Hall of Fame**, and the following year into the Pro Football Hall of Fame. In 1999 he was ranked number 47 on *The Sporting News'* list of the 100 Greatest Football Players.—*Luis J. Gonzalez*

SOURCE: National Polish-American Sports Hall of Fame website, www.polishsportshof.com.

Hammerling, Ludwik Mikołaj (b. Dorohów, Poland, 1870?; New York City, April 26, 1935). Businessman, politician. Enigmatic and controversial, Hammerling was one of the most influential Poles in America in the World War I era. Born into an impoverished Jewish family, he migrated as a contract laborer to the Hawaiian Islands as a youth before relocating to the anthracite region of Pennsylvania where he quickly became a pioneer in the union movement, playing a major, though unheralded, part in the settlement of the famous 1902 coal strike. Ever enterprising, he became active in innumerable business ventures, particularly the Hearst press network, as well as local politics, serving as a delegate to the Republican conventions of 1904, 1908, and 1912. In 1908, with financial assistance from unclear sources, he created a press network, the American Association of Foreign Language Newspapers, linking the immigrant press in many languages which eventually included over 700 titles with twenty million readers. By placing—or withholding—advertising, he became both influential and wealthy. Hammerling also made considerable money from brewing interests by running anti–Prohibition stories in the press. He undertook a number of international missions for the Taft administration investigating immigration and business matters. Republican officials regarded him as an important access to the immigrant vote. During the First World War, Hammerling received financial payments from the German Embassy to publish material supporting the interests of the Central Powers, actions for which he was later investigated by the American government. In legal and political difficulties he was able to inveigle himself into **Ignacy Jan Paderewski**'s confidence, even entering into business dealings with the maestro's son. Fleeing to Poland after the war, Hammerling quickly used his wealth to become an influential figure in the Polish Peasant Party (PSL-Piast) from whose list he became a Senator of the Republic in 1922. He undertook a number of international financial missions on behalf of the Polish government.

However, his controversial involvement with the Central Powers resurfaced in Poland in 1923, drove him from office, and eventually resulted in his resettling in the United States where he again pursued an amazing series of business ventures. He died, probably by his own hand, in 1935. A convert to Roman Catholicism, Hammerling was widely mistrusted in Polonia for his political and business manipulations. Nonetheless, he enjoyed entrée into the highest reaches of American political and business circles and was regarded as a major figure in the East European immigrant community.—*M. B. B. Biskupski*

SOURCE: Czesław Lechicki, "Hammerling, Ludwik," *Polski Słownik Biograficzny*, 263–264.

Hamtramck. Named after a French Canadian soldier in 1798, Hamtramck Township, located to the northwest of Detroit, remained rural throughout the nineteenth century. Settled first by French explorers and then German immigrants, Hamtramck's population had reached only 3,559 by 1910. But the construction of the Dodge Main auto factory in the 1910s attracted thousands of Polish immigrants, and Hamtramck quickly became an island of Polish American culture within the metropolitan area of Detroit. By 1920, Hamtramck's population had skyrocketed to 48,615. Its current geographic boundaries were set in 1922 when it was incorporated as a politically independent city. Only 2.1 square miles in area, it is surrounded by the city of Detroit on all sides, except for a small section that borders Highland Park. During the 1920s, Hamtramck developed a reputation for political corruption (and as the place for Detroiters to find alcohol during the Prohibition era), but it was also a time of social and institutional organization, as Polish workers formed numerous religious and civic societies, which served as significant sources of strength and support. Particularly important were Hamtramck's three Roman Catholic parishes: St. Florian's (1907), Our Lady Queen of Apostles (1917), and St. Ladislaus (1920). Hamtramck is also home to Holy Cross **Polish National Catholic Church**.

Hamtramck's population peaked during the 1930s, when it topped 56,000. Union activity was particularly strong during this decade, as the United Auto Workers staged the largest sit-down strike in American history at the Dodge Main in 1937. Hamtramck's Polish community also embraced democracy, voting in remarkably high numbers, always consistently Democratic, leading to campaign visits from Franklin Roosevelt, Harry Truman, and John F. Kennedy. Hamtramck thrived in the 1940s and 1950s, thanks in part to a

booming postwar economy, but urban density and increasing prosperity encouraged many Polish families to move to the suburbs, and Hamtramck's population began to decline steadily. In 1940, its population stood at 48,838, of whom 81 percent were ethnically Polish, but fell to 34,137 by 1960, and to 26,245 by 1970. Economic conditions worsened throughout the 1970s, culminating in the Chrysler Corporation's surprising—and economically devastating—decision to close Dodge Main in 1980.

Over the last three decades, Hamtramck has witnessed a remarkable demographic shift. The city has welcomed an influx of newcomers, primarily Muslim immigrants from countries such as Yemen, Bangladesh, and Bosnia, but also new immigrants from Poland. For the first time since 1930, the 2000 U.S. Census registered a population increase in Hamtramck, up to 22,976 from a low of 18,372 in 1990. Forty-one percent of these residents were born outside of the United States, and students in Hamtramck schools speak close to thirty different languages at home, yet Polish Catholics remain the single largest ethnic group at 23 percent. It is unclear how much longer this will be the case, and Hamtramck's longtime Polish residents have faced the challenge of adjusting to a new social situation. Facing an aging Catholic population, the Archdiocese of Detroit has closed all parochial schools in the city, and while Polish Americans have long dominated local politics, a Bangladeshi American became the first non–Pole elected to Hamtramck's City Council in 2003. Hamtramck garnered international attention in 2004 when it became embroiled in a dispute about whether one of the city's several new mosques would be permitted to broadcast the Islamic call to prayer from external loudspeakers, a dispute that brought to the fore Hamtramck's changing political, economic, and social dynamics. This historically Polish-Catholic enclave, which Pope John Paul II visited twice, faces an uncertain future.—*Isaac A. Weiner*

SOURCES: Greg Kowalski, *Hamtramck: The Driven City* (Charleston, SC: Arcadia Publishers, 2002); Frank Serafino, *West of Warsaw* (Hamtramck, MI: Avenue Publishing Company, 1983); Arthur Evans Wood, *Hamtramck, Then and Now: A Sociological Study of a Polish-American Community* (New York: Bookman Associates, 1955); Murray Goodwin, "Hamtramck vs. Ford: A Polish American Retrospective," North American Review, Vol. 223 (May 1932); David A. Sellers, "Hamtramck: A Sociological Study" (Detroit: Unpublished M.A. thesis, Wayne State University, 1957).

Haracz, Wojciech "Albert" (b. Ruda, Poland, April 21, 1885; d. Mokotów, Poland, July 17, 1971). Labor leader. A childhood friend of Stanisław Kot, the renowned scholar and Peasant Party activist, Haracz attended the same agricultural school and maintained a life-long relationship with Kot, although their respective paths diverged. Haracz left Poland in 1907 to escape service in the Austrian army, migrating to Chicago where he worked on an Illinois farm and later in a Wisconsin lumber camp. Joining an aunt in Detroit in 1909, he gained employment at Ford Motor Company while studying English to become an American citizen. Soon he organized the Polish Socialist club Oświata (Knowledge) on Detroit's west side. Taking a leave, he entered Valparaiso University in Indiana to study engineering. Becoming an American citizen in 1915, he worked as a draftsman for American Motors while maintaining his Socialist activity, including working on the newspaper *Trybuna Robotnicza* (Workers' Tribune). Arrested in the infamous Palmer raids, he lost his job in 1920, causing him to return with his family to Poland.

Following the death of his wife while in Poland, and a remarriage, Halacz returned to Detroit without his family in 1928, obtaining work on the Hupp Motors assembly line. Working part-time at the *Trybuna Robotnicza*, renamed **Głos Ludowy** (People's Voice), he became secretary of the American-Soviet Friendship Society until he again lost his job in 1932. Forming a Polish Worker's Club as part of the Unemployed Councils, he was elected president, devoting all his energy to organizing and helping the jobless. At that time, **Bolesław Gebert**, president of the Polonia Society of the International Workers Order (IWO), resided in Detroit. When the International Workers' Order (IWO) offered him a job in New York City, he moved his family there to pursue recruiting members for the Polonia Society under the leadership of Gebert. In 1933 he joined the Communist Party.

During World War II, Haracz associated with the Polish poet **Julian Tuwim**, artist **Artur Szyk**, Czesław Grzelak, and the scholars **Oskar Lange** and Louis Karpiński, as well as the Rev. **Stanisław Orlemański**. Haracz continued to serve as secretary of the Polonia Society until his retirement due to health issues. After the war, Haracz purchased land to build a Polonia Rest Home on the beach north of Traverse City, MI. The home became the center of a small leftist colony, attracting his friends and colleagues from Detroit and Chicago, as well as Communist diplomats from the Polish consulates in Detroit and Chicago and the embassy in Washington, D.C. Haracz's daughter Helen married a Polish diplomat, and when she had children in Poland he returned to his native country in

1951. There, he constructed a building in Dębica which became a community center. In recognition of his work in the Rzeszów area, he was awarded the distinguished Krzyz Oficerski Odrodzenia Polski (Officer's Cross of Reborn Poland), among other medals.— *Don Binkowski*

SOURCES: Don Binkowski, *Leo Krzycki and the Detroit Left* (Philadelphia: Xlibris, 2001); Helen Haracz Lewandowska [Harris], *The Quest of a Perennial Idealist: Remembering Wojciech Haracz* (Berkeley: Author, 2006); Roger Keeran, "The International Workers Order and the Origins of the CIO," *Labor History*, Vol. 30, no. 3 (Summer 1989), 385–408.

Harcerstwo *see* **Scouting, Polish American.**

Hart, Leon (b. Turtle Creek, Pennsylvania, November 2, 1928; d. South Bend, Indiana, September 24, 2002). Football player. Leon Hart played end for the Notre Dame football team from 1946 to 1949, being selected as an All-American three times and playing for three national college championship squads. In 1949, his senior year, he was awarded the Heisman Trophy as the country's top collegiate performer, one of very few linemen ever so honored, and was named Athlete of the Year by the Associated Press. Drafted into the professional ranks, Hart played for the Detroit Lions of the National Football League from 1950 through 1957. His Lions won three NFL championships during that span, and he was named an All-Pro in 1951. Following his retirement from football, Hart worked in business in Michigan for many years. He is a member of the College Football Hall of Fame, and was elected to the **National Polish-American Sports Hall of Fame** in 1988.— *Neal Pease*

SOURCE: "Leon Hart," National Polish-American Sports Hall of Fame website, www.polishsportshof. com.

Heilprin, Michael (b. Piotrków, Russian Empire, February 23, 1823; d. Summit, New Jersey, May 10, 1888). Scholar, journalist. Born to Polish-Jewish parents in the Russian Empire, Heilprin was the eldest of two sons. His early years were spent in Tomaszów where his father — a merchant, but also a scholar well-versed in Jewish literature, the Talmud, Maimonides, and ancient Greek, Arabic, and modern philosophy — undertook his son's education, teaching him languages, history, and philosophy. Michael eventually acquired fluency in some fifteen languages, and by age twelve was composing his own poetry in German, Hebrew, and Polish. Heilprin and his wife, Henrietta Silver, migrated from the Russian Empire to Hungary in 1842 where Heilprin became the proprietor of a bookstore that catered to the liberal-intellectual milieu.

Active in political circles, he spent two years immersing himself in the Magyar language and the history of Hungary. Not long after, he began penning poetry in support of the Jewish cause in the Magyar language, decrying the maltreatment of Jews under Habsburg rule. In contact with the liberal-nationalist movement of which he was an ardent supporter, Heilprin briefly held a post in Lajos Kossuth's government — Secretary of the Literary Bureau, an arm of the Ministry of the Interior — before the 1848 revolt was quashed by Austrian authorities. He and his family were thus forced to flee, arriving in Philadelphia by way of Kraków, Paris, and Ujhely (Hungary) in 1856. Heilprin was briefly an instructor in the Hebrew Education Society's schools before he and his family moved again to Brooklyn, New York. Residing alongside other exiles there, he made a career as a scholar, editor, encyclopedist, journalist, philanthropist, and activist. Upon his introduction to the editors of *Appleton's New American Cyclopedia* (1858), he became an associate editor of many noteworthy articles and worked on the project for over a decade. During 1863-64, Heilprin briefly resided in Washington, D.C., where he returned to the book trade, albeit unsuccessfully, and also founded a short-lived periodical titled *The Balance*. He was also a member of the Polish committee formed to provide assistance to the January Insurrection in Poland. One year later, Heilprin returned to New York where he assumed a position as an ongoing contributor and sometimes editor to *The Nation*. In addition to editing literary reviews, Heilprin also authored political and military pieces, ranging in commentary from European to South American and even African affairs. An outspoken abolitionist, during the Civil War

Michael Heilprin, journalist and abolitionist (***OLS***).

Heilprin protested slavery and offered columns in regards to his position in the *New York Tribune*. Between 1879 and 1880, he published his two-volume *Historical Poetry of the Ancient Hebrews*. News of pogroms in the Russian Empire in 1881 inspired him to action on behalf of Jewish immigrants from the Russian Empire. As a result, he involved himself in projects aimed at the successful resettlement of Jews in connection with the Montefiore Agricultural Aid Society and the Hebrew Emigrant Aid Society. Heilprin personally assisted in the resettlement projects through his fundraising and promotional efforts and aided in the establishment of farming colonies in such states as Kansas, Nebraska, New Jersey, Oregon and the Dakotas. Of his five children, his son Angelo became a well-respected geographer, explorer, and scientist, and his son Louis, an encyclopedist. Heilprin's philanthropic work with Jewish immigrants profoundly influenced the poetry of one of his contemporaries, Emma Lazarus. He also devised a system of transliterating Slavic languages into English that he prepared at the request of the American Library Association. Known as the A.I.A. system, it became the standard system used in the United States.—*Krystyna Cap*

SOURCE: Gustav Pollak, *Michael Heilprin and His Sons: A Biography* (New York: Dodd, Mead & Co., 1912).

Helinski, Theodore M. (b. near Poznań, Poland, April 1857; d. Chicago, Illinois, August 16, 1921). Banker, Polonia activist. Helinski came to America as a boy and was educated mainly in this country. A resident of the town of Poniatowski, Wisconsin, at the time of the founding of the **Polish National Alliance** in 1880, Helinski enrolled as the 245th member of the PNA, organized a lodge of the fraternal in Poniatowski, and was active in the Alliance from that time on. In 1893, he was unanimously elected to the office of **censor** of the PNA, proving to be a strong progressive who championed the admission of women into the Alliance with full membership rights. This objective was achieved at the extraordinary convention of the PNA in 1900. Helinski also argued for a PNA open to all Poles regardless of their politics or religious inclinations. In 1894, he took a leading role in opposing immediate PNA participation in the newly-created **Polish League**, a nationwide federation of Polonia societies dominated by the Rev. **Wincenty Barzyński**, pastor of St. Stanislas Kostka Parish in Chicago and a major force in the rival **Polish Roman Catholic Union**. Helinski and other PNA leaders believed joining the Polish League would lead to the eventual demise of the Al-

Teodor M. Helinski, banker, president of the Polish Central Relief Committee in World War I (*PMA*).

liance as a patriotic movement. Helinski was elected censor of the Polish National Alliance at its 1893, 1895, and 1897 national conventions, and was elected national secretary of the Alliance in 1899, 1901, 1903, and 1905. He later headed the national fund drive to erect a monument in honor of **Tadeusz Kościuszko** in Washington, D.C., a PNA-led effort that was realized in 1910. On November 12, 1899, he spoke at a meeting of the newly formed **Polish Women's Alliance** society in Chicago and urged its members to establish their own national organization. They did so and the Polish Women's Alliance of America held its first national convention in Chicago the following year. During World War I he served first as president of the **Polish Central Relief Committee** (PCKR) and later as first vice president of a committee of the PCKR called the Polish **National Department**. The National Department initially served as the political action arm of the PCKR, although by the end of the First World War it had eclipsed it in significance. He chaired the Military Commission of the National Department which was made responsible for organizing a Polish Army in America. Helinski's career also included a stint as postmaster in Duluth, Minnesota. In 1906 he was named treasurer of the Northwestern Trust and Savings Bank of Chicago, which had been founded by **John Smulski**. He held this position at the time of his death.—*Donald E. Pienkos*

SOURCES: Stanisław Osada, *Historia Związku Narodowego Polskiego i rozwój ruchu narodowego Polskiego w Ameryce Pólnocnej* (Chicago: Nakładem i drukiem Związku Narodowego Polskiego, 1905); Donald E. Pienkos, *PNA: A Centennial History of the Polish National Alliance of the United States of North America*

(Boulder, CO: East European Monographs, 1984); Jadwiga Karłowicz, *Historia Związku Polek w Ameryce: Przyczynki do Poznania Duszy Wychodźtwa Polskiego w Stanach Zjednoczonych Ameryki Północnej* (Chicago: Polish Women's Alliance of America, 1938); Angela T. Pienkos and Donald E. Pienkos, *"In the Ideals of Women Is the Strength of a Nation": A History of the Polish Women's Alliance of America* (Boulder, Colorado: East European Monographs, distributed by Columbia University Press, 2003).

Helminski, Roy C. (b. Wyandotte, Michigan, April 29, 1918; d. Wyandotte, Michigan, July 21, 2002). Speed skater. Helminski was a member of the Wyandotte, Michigan, city fire department for more than 37 years, retiring as assistant chief in 1978. A competitive speed skater from 1930 to 1948, he was active in promoting the sport in Michigan for over forty years and co-founded the Wyandotte Speed Skating Club. An Amateur Skating Union Chief Clerk of Course and Chief Referee, he was also a member of the ASU Board of Control for Michigan (1966–73), First Vice President of the ASU (1977), President (1978–80), and Third Vice President (1980–83). He was the official host for the 1980 Winter Olympics in Lake Placid. Among his many contributions was establishing the National Medallion Program fund in 1981 and actively supporting the Wyandotte Goodfellows movement to provide for needy children at Christmas. In his honor the Roy C. Helminski Fund was created to assist needy families in obtaining children's sporting equipment. He was elected to the National Speedskating Hall of Fame in 1983.—*James S. Pula*

SOURCES: Jim Kasuba, "Man Coached Many in Unique Sport," *The News-Herald* (Wyandotte, MI), January 28, 2004; Jim Kasuba, "Roy Helminski's Dream Lives On," *The News-Herald* (Wyandotte, MI), November 11, 2008.

Henner, Marilu (Mary Lucy Denise Pudlowski; b. Chicago, Illinois, April 6, 1952; d.—). Actress, author. The third of six children of Polish and Greek heritage, the redheaded, green-eyed Henner came from a theatrical background. Her father changed the family name for business reasons, the new name taken from an obscure baseball player. Her mother, Loretta, was president of the National Association of Dance and Affiliated Arts and, for twenty years, director of the Henner Dance School located in the family's garage. Marilu began dancing at two, and by fourteen was teaching classes at the dance school. She attended Madonna High School, then studied ballet at the Illinois Ballet Company. Her first major acting role was with the University of Chicago in the musical *Grease*. The production moved to Broadway in 1971, where she turned down the role of Marty which she had originated, to play the same role in the national touring company with her co-star, John Travolta. By 1977, she had appeared in several other stage productions, making her first appearance in film in *Between the Lines*. Her greatest fame was achieved on the small screen as Elaine Nardo, the single mom and only female cabbie in the comedy hit *Taxi* (1978–83). In 1984 she returned to the big screen opposite Michael Keaton in *Johnny Dangerously* before moving back to television in 1990 for a four-year stint with Burt Reynolds in *Evening Shade*. In addition to being a readily recognizable actress, she has also written several books on health and nutrition including *Marilu Henner's Total Health Makeover*. A vegetarian, she was inspired to write after suffering from bouts of ill health as a child, as well as a battle with being overweight. Her talents for singing and dancing were showcased in her role as Roxy Hart in the musical *Chicago*, which played to standing room only audiences. By 2005, she was on the Discovery Channel, hosting *Shape Up Your Life*, based on her diet books, and the series *America's Ballroom Challenge*. Henner has testified before Congress on behalf of ACES, an organization that aids the government in finding "deadbeat" dads and getting them to assume financial responsibility for their children. She has also taken on the cause of battered women. Among her many awards are five nominations for Golden Globe Awards for her work in *Taxi*.— *Cheryl A. Pula*

SOURCES: Marilu Henner, *By All Means, Keep Moving* (New York: Pocket Books, 1994); "Marilu Henner," *Current Biography* (New York: H.W. Wilson Co., 1999), 259–62.

Hodur, Francis (Franciszek Jan Hodur; b. Żarki, Galicia, Poland, April 1, 1866; d. Scranton, Pennsylvania, February 16, 1953). Bishop. As a youth, Hodur earned a scholarship to the prestigious St. Anne's Gymnasium in Kraków where he graduated with honors in 1889. After briefly considering a career in the theater, he entered the Kraków Diocesan Seminary in October 1891 with religious instructions under the Vincentian Order and academic subjects at the Jagiellonian University. While he was there, the seminary experienced student unrest culminating in a strike over living conditions. Though some activists were expelled, Hodur left voluntarily in December 1892 for the United States. Landing in New York in January 1893, he enrolled in St. Vincent's Seminary in Beatty (now part of Latrobe) in western Pennsylvania. After four months' study, he moved to Scranton where he received major orders, was ordained to the priesthood on August 19, and was assigned immediately as assistant to the Rev. Richard Aust, pastor of Most Sacred Hearts of Jesus and Mary, the city's Polish parish. Aust's tyrannical control over the parish, his fondness for hobnobbing in high society, and his secretiveness in parish finances caused unrest in the parish, as did the demeanor of superiority that he assumed, frequently flaunting his German birth, education, and social superiority over his mostly Galician flock. Hodur stood in stark contrast to Aust. He socialized with parishioners, encouraging the establishment of a parish library, dramatic circle, and lectures, as well as editing the newspaper *Tygodnik Scrantoński* (The Scranton Weekly) in which he praised the secular liberal leaning **Polish National Alliance** fraternal organization over its rival, the clerically controlled **Polish Roman Catholic Union**, and supported the Polish Youth Alliance, a new semi-secret, paramilitary organization with European émigré ties which vehemently opposed "Americanization."

In 1895, following brief service as administrator of Scranton's Slovak parish, Hodur was assigned as the first administrator of a new Polish parish, Holy Trinity, in nearby Nanticoke, where he remained until 1897. During this time he came into conflict with his bishop over issues relating to lay control of parish property and finances, as well as the appointment of priests to parishes. Hodur, a devout Polish nationalist with socialistic inclinations, became an advocate of parishioner control over churches built and maintained by them, the use of the Polish vernacular in the Mass, and, through the use of parish committees, parishioner control over the selection of local pastors. These principles, along with the appointment of Polish bishops, became the cornerstones of Hodur's leadership of dissident parishes in northeastern Pennsylvania and elsewhere. This began when rebellious elements barred the Rev. Aust from St. Stanislaus, Bishop and Martyr, Parish and asked Hodur, without episcopal authority, to assume the duties as their pastor. When he agreed and celebrated Mass in the unfinished church, he was immediately suspended by the bishop.

Hodur established the newspaper *Straż* (The Guard) in which he outlined his vision for a "National Church" (Kościół Narodowy) within the American Roman Catholic ecclesial structure, calling for parishioner ownership of church properties, control of parish finances, and approval of pastors, as well as the appointment of a "Polish" bishop in the American hierarchy. He invited other parishes and clergy to support this new program. In January 1898 he embarked for Rome with a petition from five supporting local parishes and several Polish National Alliance groups, planning to appeal to the Congregation for the Propagation of the Faith, the papal agency then overseeing the American Roman Catholic Church. He left the meeting assuming that the petition would be taken under consideration. However, upon his return to Pennsylvania, Diocesan Ordinary William O'Hara excommunicated Hodur as of September 29, 1898. Hodur's response was to burn the excommunication decree, casting its ashes into a stream near his church. At a parish meeting held on December 16 he rejected the possibility of reconciliation and persuaded most of his parishioners to remain with him as an independent congregation under county charter. At the same time, he continued promulgating his "National Church Program" and was elected administrator by representatives of the dissident parishes pending election of a "Polish" bishop.

Hodur had become a leader in the independent movement in which he rivaled **Antoni Kozłowski** in Chicago and **Stefan Kamiński** in Buffalo for leadership of the dissident movement nationally. When his older rivals died, he became the acknowledged leader of independentism. In July 1904, Hodur, his priests, and lay leaders of "Polish National" parishes issued a call "To all Polish National Churches, patriotic societies and people of good will who have not doubted the future of the Polish nation in exile" (Do wszystkich Kościołów Polsko Narodowych, patriotycznych towarzystw i ludzi dobrej woli, którzy nie zwątpili w przyszłości polskiego narodu na wychodżtwie). Noting the continuing inability of American Polish Roman Catholics to secure their own bishop, it suggested a separate "American Polish National Catholic Church." An assemblage of 146 delegates (fourteen clergy, parish laity and representatives from eighteen Polish National Alliance lodges, and one other lodge) held on September 6–8 was considered the first part of the First Synod of the **Polish National Catholic Church** (PNCC). After voting to break "ties with Rome" and accepting a constitution based on one drafted by Hodur, it elected him bishop.

As Hodur engaged in polemics with Roman Catholic theologians, he also authored plays exposing scandals of neighboring Roman Catholic Polish clergy, giving their characters very slightly disguised names, and he even drew cartoons illustrating his arguments and accusations that were published in *Straż*. Though not yet consecrated, Hodur convened a continuation of the First Synod in 1906, limiting participation to delegates of the church's seventeen parishes. These representatives authorized him to tighten discipline over his priests (several had married, though celibacy was in force, claiming that only a synod could suspend them). After the death of Old Catholic Bishop Kozłowski in 1907, Hodur was consecrated bishop of the schismatic church by the Dutch Old Catholic Archbishop Gerard Van Gul in Utrecht, Holland, and incorporated Kozłowski's parishes into the PNCC, thus increasing the church's membership to over 15,000.

In 1908, Hodur was instrumental in founding the **Polish National Union** (Polska Narodowa Spójnia) as a fraternal insurance organization linked ideologically, but not administratively, with the Polish National Catholic Church. The Second Synod in 1909 affirmed Hodur's recognition of "Word of God preached and heard" as "having sacramental value," and of having the name "Polish National Catholic Church of America" (PNCC) as the full denominational designation. The acceptance of independent parishes, including some of Bishop Kamiński's after his death in 1911, increased church membership significantly. In the meantime, Bishop Hodur wrote a "Confession of Faith," explaining it as a restatement of the essentials of faith for modern times.

At Bishop Hodur's behest, the Fourth General Synod in 1921 voted for the abolition of mandatory clerical celibacy and passed resolutions sustaining his interpretations on the basis of faith, on the complementary aspects of baptism/confirmation, and formalized corporate ("general") adult confession.

During the 1930s, Hodur became depressed that his new church met with little success in an attempt to expand to Poland and devoted

Bishop Franciszek Hodur, founder of the Polish National Catholic Church (OLS).

considerable time to writing his prophetic *Apokalipsa dwudziestego wieku* (Apocalypse of The Twentieth Century). In the meantime, he became increasingly incapacitated by diabetes and cataracts that eventually resulted in over fifteen years of blindness. At its peak, the PNCC attracted about five percent of those of Polish heritage in America.—*Joseph W. Wieczerzak*

SOURCES: Joseph W. Wieczerzak, *Bishop Francis Hodur: Biographical Essays* (Boulder, CO: East European Monographs, 1998); Joseph W. Wieczerzak, "Bishop Francis Hodur and the Socialists: Associations and Disassociations," *Polish American Studies*, Vol. 40, no. 2 (1983), 5–35; Bolesław R. Bak, *A Short History of the Life and Struggles of Bishop Francis Hodur* (Scranton: Polish National Catholic Church, 1954); Francis C. Rowinski, "Francis Hodur—priest Bishop, Founder and Father of the Polish National Catholic Church," *PNCC Studies*, Vol. 5 (1984), 31–41; Hieronim Kubiak, *The Polish National Catholic Church in the United States of America From 1897 to 1980* (Kraków: Państwowe Wydawnictwo Naukowe, 1982).

Hoffman, Eva (Ewa Alfreda Wydra; b. Kraków, Poland, July 1, 1945; d.—). Journalist, literary scholar. Hoffman was born into an assimilated Jewish family where she developed a strong interest in piano music. In 1959 her family migrated to Canada where she continued her education. On graduation from secondary school, she moved to the United States where she earned an M.A. in English at Rice University (1966). She continued to study literature and music at Yale and Harvard, and in 1974 earned her Ph.D. degree. After graduation she worked for *The New York Times* until 1990. Her first book, *Lost in Translation* (1989), launched her international career. The book is an autobiographical account of Hoffman's experience of moving between Poland and North America, but it provides wider insights into the cultural, linguistic, and psychological consequences of emigration and adaptation to the new environment. *Lost in Translation* was translated into many European languages, including Hoffman's native Polish, and was studied by renowned linguists such as Anna Wierzbicka and Mary Besemeres. Subsequently Hoffman wrote three books on historical subjects: *Exit into History* (1993) is an account of her journey to Eastern Europe following the collapse of the Soviet Union, while *Shtetl* (1997) and *After Such Knowledge* (2004) deal with the thorny issue of Jewish-Polish relations before, during, and after the Second World War. In 2001 Hoffman published her first novel, *The Secret*, which hinges on the issue of family relations and genetic engineering. Her second novel, *Illuminations* (2008), Hoffman constructed around ethical issues and music. Her writing also appeared in *The New York Review of Books*, *The Times Literary Supplement*, and *London Review of Books*.—*Piotr Kuhiwczak*

SOURCES: Mary Besemeres, *Translating One's Self* (Oxford, UK: Peter Lang, 2002); Mary Besemeres and Anna Wierzbicka, eds., *Translating Lives: Living with Two Languages and Cultures* (St. Lucia, Qld: University of Queensland Press, St Lucia, 2008); Bolesław Wierzbiański, *Who's Who in Polish America* (New York: Bicentennial Publishing Corp., 1996), 155.

Hoffmann, Roald (b. Złoczow, Poland, July 18, 1937; d.—). Chemist. Hoffmann was a child during the Second World War when his father managed to smuggle him and his mother out of a labor camp to be hidden for the duration of the war by a friendly local family. Following the war he moved to Przemysl and then to Kraków where he attended school. In 1946 he and his mother relocated to displaced persons' camps in Austria and Germany, eventually emigrating to Brooklyn in 1949. In 1955 he entered Columbia University in a premedical program, but it was summer work at the Brookhaven National Laboratory that sparked his interest in research. While completing his graduate work at Harvard, he spent a year at Moscow University on a graduate student exchange program. Receiving his doctorate in 1962, he accepted a Junior Fellowship in the Society of Fellows at Harvard which afforded him the opportunity to refocus his research from the theoretical to applied theory in organic chemistry. In 1965 he accepted a position at Cornell where he became the John A. Newman Professor of Physical Science, being honored with many awards including the American Chemical Society's A. C. Cope Award in Organic Chemistry and a similar award in Inorganic Chemistry in 1982, the only person to have received both of these prestigious honors. Focusing his research on exploration of the electronic structure of stable and unstable molecules, he is credited with developing the extended Huckel Method for the prediction of molecular reactions. In 1981 he received the Nobel Prize in Chemistry for theories "concerning the course of chemical reactions."—*James S. Pula*

SOURCE: Wilhelm Odelberg, ed., *The Nobel Prizes 1981* (Stockholm: Nobel Foundation, 1982).

Hofmann, Josef (Józef Kazimierz Hofmann; pseudonym Michel Dvorsky; b. Kraków, Poland, January 20, 1876; d. Los Angeles, February 16, 1957). Pianist, conductor. The son of a conductor and a singer at the Kraków Theatre in Poland, Hofmann began studying music at the age of three and appeared on European concert tours as a composer-pianist at the age of seven, one of the most precocious musical prodigies in history. After his American debut on November 29, 1887, at the Metropolitan Opera House, and a subsequent series of concerts, Hofmann became a media celebrity and focal point of a controversy about child exploitation. He received a large cash gift that allowed him to retire from concert tours until the age of eighteen and to study music in Germany where he took lessons from Maurice Moszkowski and later became the only private student of Anton Rubinstein, fully assimilating and embodying the older pianist-composer's musical ideals. Hofmann's "adult" debut took place in 1894 in Hamburg, Germany, with Rubinstein conducting his own Piano Concerto No. 4 in D Minor. His international virtuoso career took him frequently to Russia where he famously gave a series of 21 concerts with 255 pieces, not repeating a single work on the program. He was equally popular in central Europe, South America, and the U.S. With a phenomenal music memory (he perfectly remembered and was able to play from memory each piece he heard just once) and a vast repertoire of mostly romantic pieces, Hofmann was the epitome of a pianist-virtuoso. He was also highly successful as director of the Curtis Institute of Music in Philadelphia (1927–38), which he and founder Mary Louise Curtis Bok developed into a model of a music conservatory and an alma mater of the best musicians of the time. His students include Shura Cherkassky and Ruth Slenczynska. Hofmann limited his concert tours during World War II, ending his performing career in 1946. During his heyday (1900–35), Hofmann was recognized as the most original interpreter of the staple classical and romantic repertory (Beethoven, Chopin, Liszt, Schumann), as well as salon music. Hofmann's performing style was recognized for its wide dynamic range, clarity of texture (accomplished with pedaling), technical perfection in bravura passages, heightened emotionalism, and dramatic improvisations. Rachmaninoff dedicated his 3rd Piano Concerto to Hofmann, who never played it, disliking its form and the density and chromaticism of the piano part. Hofmann had very small hands and Steinway built a special piano for him, with narrowed keys. He composed over one hundred compositions (under the pseudonym Michel Dvorsky), mostly for piano and mostly forgotten. His recordings were few and far between even though Hofmann was the first pianist ever recorded by Edison in 1887 (these cylinders were lost). A series of 1913 piano roll recordings for Welte-Mignon survives, and so do recordings of his broadcasts, now reissued commercially. Hofmann never played a piece twice the same way, and he distrusted the mechanical quality of recordings as failing to adequately capture his ever-changeable interpretations. A talented inventor, gifted in mathematics and mechanics, Hofmann continued to work on perfecting recording techniques and held over seventy patents for his inventions that included: a device to record dynamics in reproducing piano rolls, piano mechanisms, pneumatic shock absorbers for cars and planes, a furnace for crude oil, a house revolving with the sun, and a paper clip. He wrote two books on piano performance and was recognized and praised by such contemporaries as Rubinstein, Saint-Saens, Rachmaninoff and Stravinsky as one of the most important romantic pianists. His papers are held at the University of Maryland.—*Maja Trochimczyk*

SOURCES: Harold C. Schonberg, *The Great Pianists from Mozart to the Present* (New York: Simon & Schuster, 1987); Nell S. Graydon and Margaret D. Sizemore, *The Amazing Marriage of Marie Eustis & Josef Hofmann* (Columbia, SC: University of South Carolina Press, 1965).

Hofstadter, Robert (b. New York City, New York, February 5, 1915; d. Palo Alto, California, November 17, 1990). Physicist. Though he demonstrated an early aptitude for mathematics, Hofstadter initially planned to study philosophy in college but was converted to science by Irving Lowen and Mark Zemansky. He graduated *magna cum laude* from the City College of New York (now the City University of New York) with a bachelor's degree in science in 1935. For his exceptional achievements in mathematics and physics, he received the school's Kenyon Prize. Hofstadter pursued a graduate degree at Princeton University, having earned a Charles A. Coffin Foundation Fellowship from the General Electric Company. In 1938, he received his Ph.D., but remained at Princeton to pursue postdoctoral studies. From 1939 to 1940, he became the Harrison Research Fellow at the University of Pennsylvania before assuming the position of instructor of physics at the City College of New York one year later. During the Second World War, Hofstadter served as research assistant and physicist at the National Bureau of Standards (NBS) in Washington, D.C., where he provided support to physicist James Van Allen and worked with colleagues Joseph Henderson and Seth Neddermeyer to create a proximity fuse for bomb detonation in antiaircraft and artillery shells. In 1943, Hofstadter left the NBS for Nordern Laboratories in New York, where he would remain until 1946 working on servo systems, altimeter devices, and aircraft autopilots. In 1950, he joined the Stanford University faculty as an associate professor, where he remained for the rest of his career. At Stanford, Hofstadter undertook his pioneering work on the use of high-energy particle accelerators to study the structure of an atom's nucleus. Soon thereafter, his primary research interest turned to electron-scattering measurements. For his work on nuclear structure, Hofstadter earned the Nobel Prize for physics in 1961— an honor he shared with German physicist Rudolf Moessbauer. Additional honors were bestowed upon him by the City College of New York, which awarded him the Townsend Harris Medal in 1961; the state of California, which named him Scientist of the Year in 1959; and the National Medal of Science in 1986.—*Krystyna Cap*

SOURCES: Peter B. Flint, "Dr. Robert Hofstadter dies at 75; won Nobel Prize in Physics in '61," *New York Times*, November 19, 1990, D11; Jerome I. Friedman and William A. Little, *Robert Hofstadter, 1915–1990: A Biographical Memoir* (Washington, D.C.: The National Academy Press, National Academy of Sciences, 2001; Biographical Memoirs, vol. 79).

Holland, Agnieszka (b. Warsaw, Poland, November 28, 1948; d.—). Film director. Born into a journalist family, Holland studied film direction in Prague (1966–71). After the "Prague Spring" she was arrested for anticommunist activities and spent six weeks in a Czechoslovak jail. As a film director she debuted in Czechoslovakia with *Jesus Christ's Sin* (1970), and in Poland in 1975 with *Evening at Abdon's*. In the 1970s she was an assistant of Krzysztof Zanussi and Andrzej Wajda, cooperated with Krzysztof Kieślowski, and also directed her own films that belong to the "cinema of moral anxiety" (*kino moralnego niepokoju*). Her most successful effort was *Provincial Actors* which won an award at the Cannes Film Festival. Holland was visiting Sweden when Martial Law was introduced in Poland in December 1981, after which she decided not to return to Warsaw. She migrated

Józef Hofmann, child musical prodigy (*PMA*).

to France where she continued her film-making career, directing a documentary on the Paris-based *Kultura* monthly and a film based on Jerzy Popiełuszko's death, *To Kill a Priest*. The movies that brought her international fame were *Angry Harvest* and *Europa, Europa*, both made in Germany and both nominated for Academy Awards. Later she directed films in Europe, including *Olivier, Olivier* (1992) and *Total Eclipse* (1995) and in the United States (including an adaptation of *The Secret Garden* by Frances Burnett for the Warner Brothers (1993), *Washington Square* (1997), and *Copying Beethoven* (2007). Holland is a member of both American and European Film Academies. In addition to directing, she is also a screenplay author and a translator from Czech into Polish. With one of her homes located in Los Angeles (another one is in France), she became involved in the Polish American film community. She entered the Polish Hollywood Connection that was lobbying for the Academy Award for Andrzej Wajda and supported other initiatives promoting Polish and Polish American films in the United States including festivals in Seattle and Chicago. —*Joanna Wojdon*

SOURCE: Agnieszka Holland, *Magia i pieniądze. Rozmowy przeprowadziła Maria Kornatowska* (Kraków: Znak, 2002).

Holy Family of Nazareth, Sisters of the. The Congregation of the Sisters of the Holy Family of Nazareth (CSFN) was founded in 1875 in Rome by the Polish noblewoman, **Frances Siedliska**, known in religious life as Mary of Jesus the Good Shepherd. The life of the foundress and the foundation of the Congregation coincided historically with the immigration of massive numbers of Poles to the United States. They settled in cities such as Chicago, Milwaukee, Detroit, New York, and smaller urban centers and some rural areas in the Midwest. Addressing the religious needs of the growing immigrant population was one of the many concerns of the American bishops who had gathered for the Third Plenary Council of Baltimore on November 9, 1884. As a result of their deliberations, they made it mandatory, among other things, for pastors to establish parish schools in which immigrant children could be educated in the Catholic faith in their own language. Just prior to the gathering of the American bishops, in a letter dated October 13, 1884, the Rev. **Wincenty Barzyński**, a Resurrectionist (see **Resurrection, Congregation of the**) priest and superior of the Polish mission in Chicago, wrote to his confrere, the Rev. Anthony Lechert, CR, spiritual guide to Mother Siedliska's fledgling Congregation. Barzyński wanted sisters to take charge of an

orphanage and parish school for poor Polish children. Upon learning of the request, Mother Siedliska sought counsel from her spiritual director and other clergy, particularly Lucido Cardinal Parocchi, Vicar of Rome, and Giovanni Cardinal Simeoni, the Prefect of the Sacred Congregation for the Propagation of the Faith. Finally, Mother Siedliska experienced a growing conviction to respond affirmatively to the invitation. That same day, on January 11, 1885, she wrote in her diary: "Here, near the Holy Crib, I saw our Nazareth in America, taking roots in the spirit of the Holy Family, a spirit of love and of the liberty of the children of God. It seemed clear to me that Jesus willed to transplant our work even there, so far away."

In February of 1885, Archbishop Patrick Feehan of Chicago, depending on religious orders to implement the decrees of the recent Council of Baltimore, sent a follow-up letter directly to Mother Siedliska, asking her to send the sisters to Chicago by July of that year. At first, only three sisters were to go to America, but Mother Siedliska reconsidered her original decision when, in March 1885, the Rev. Lechert received another request from the Rev. Barzyński asking for ten or twelve sisters, one half of the Congregation's members at the time. Weighing all the factors, Mother Siedliska knew the risks were great. Having been in existence for only ten years, the Congregation was still in its infancy. To send so many would leave only a small number of sisters in Rome and Poland. The fear of inadequate preparation of the sisters for the duties they would have to assume in the U.S., and the challenges of adapting to a new culture, concerned Mother Siedliska as well. However, once convinced she responded with characteristic determination and courage to accept this invitation and take the Congregation to the new land.

On June 18, 1885, accompanied by the Rev. Anthony Lechert, two members of his Resurrectionist community and the nephew and niece of the Rev. Lechert, Mother Siedliska set sail for America with eleven Sisters of the Holy Family of Nazareth. The Rev. Lechert had been delegated by his superior general, the Very Reverend Peter Semenenko, to make the voyage in order to conduct a visitation of the Resurrectionist apostolates in the U.S. and Canada. As spiritual director of the Nazareth Congregation, the Rev. Lechert was also a welcome and trusted advisor to Mother Siedliska in this new venture on foreign territory. The eleven sisters who accompanied Mother Siedliska on the voyage from Naples to the United States on the steamship *Gottardo* were professed. These included Sr. M. Raphael

(Felicia) Lubowidzka who was permanently professed and Sisters M. Frances (Emma) Morgenstern (later Murray), M. Lauretta (Thecla) Lubowidzka, and M. Paula (Maria) Czarnowska who were temporarily professed. Novices included M. Agnes (Caroline) Lukasiewicz, M. Angela (Janine) Czoppe, M. Cecilia (Elizabeth) Sadowska, M. Evangelista (Anna) Kijewska, M. Philomena (Anna) Parzyk, M. Stanislaus (Josepha) Sierpinska, and M. Theresa (Godwin) Dzerminska. The sisters arrived in New York Harbor on July 4, 1885, after nearly two weeks at sea. That evening they boarded a train for their final destination in Chicago. The Rev. Barzyński, both the director of the Polish mission and pastor of St. Stanislaus Parish, and the Rev. John Radziejewski, pastor of St. Adalbert Parish, met the new missionaries. Arriving at St. Josaphat Parish where they would begin their ministry, the sisters found very sparse, unfurnished quarters. There was no church, only a room on the second floor of the rectory which served as a chapel.

Within three days of their arrival, Mother Siedliska, along with Mother Raphael and Sr. Lauretta, paid respects to Archbishop Patrick Feehan and presented letters of introduction to him. They spoke in French as the Archbishop welcomed them and spoke of the "extensive apostolate open to them in Christian education, preserving the faith among the immigrants and for the growth of the Church in the United States." The Archbishop made it clear that the Sisters were needed, and throughout his life continued to be a great support to the sisters. The sisters immediately set about caring for the children in the orphanage, teaching in school, visiting the sick of the parish, holding weekday discussions and prayer with girls of all ages. Given the challenge of adjusting to strange surroundings, meager provisions, and overwhelming drains on their energy, Mother Siedliska was torn between the needs of the people they served and the well-being of the sisters. A particularly trying event occurred when, just one month after their arrival, Sr. Philomena died of typhus. Mother Siedliska seriously considered returning to Rome with her fledgling group. However, with the help of the Rev. Anthony Lechert, and recognizing that the mission was at stake, she decided to have the sisters remain in the United States.

The Congregation and its ministries grew rapidly in the United States. Just two months after the sisters' arrival, St. Josaphat's School opened with 200 students and St. Adalbert's School on the South Side of Chicago had another 500 students. On August 10, 1885, Mother Siedliska admitted the first postulant from the U.S., Albertyna Szopińska (later Sr. Mary Martyna). The number of American-born applicants grew steadily in the years that followed. Within a short time, Mother Siedliska purchased a home in the vicinity of St. Stanislaus parish in Chicago to serve as the central home for the Congregation, as well as a novitiate for new members. She returned to Rome in October 1885, leaving Mother Raphael Lubowidzka as the provincial superior of the American mission. Following her departure from the U.S., Mother Siedliska wrote frequent letters of advice and encouragement to the sisters in the United States. She made two subsequent longer visits (1889-90 and 1896-97) and became a naturalized U.S. citizen on July 26, 1897. She held strong, heartfelt feelings for America, believing throughout her lifetime that this mission would prosper.

Mother Raphael served as provincial superior until August 1888 when she returned to Europe because of health problems. Her niece, Mother Lauretta Lubowidzka, was subsequently appointed to that office and during her tenure as provincial superior (1889 to 1903), the Congregation experienced phenomenal growth. The original ministries of childcare, education and healthcare took root or found new soil for growth as invitations to serve came from other parts of the country. The orphanage at St. Josaphat's Parish in Chicago begun in 1885 was relinquished in August, 1890 to the School Sisters of Notre Dame. The care of Polish orphans, however, began in other parts of the United States. In 1900 in Emsworth, Pennsylvania, Holy Family Orphan Asylum, the forerunner of Holy Family Institute, was established in collaboration with the Holy Ghost Fathers and the Polish parishioners of St. Stanislaus Parish in Pittsburgh. In the early days of its existence, Polish customs and traditions within the institution prevailed because the Polish donors were concerned that these orphans from Polish immigrant families retain their national heritage.

Their Chicago ministry expanded not only to five other parishes in Chicago, including the Lithuanian Parish of St. George (1897), but to parishes in other parts of the country as well. Between 1889 and Mother Siedliska's death in 1902, the Sisters of the Holy Family of Nazareth were teaching in parish schools in Pennsylvania, Indiana, New York and New Jersey. While beginning the work in elementary schools, the sisters also taught evening classes for young women working in factories. These evening classes were the beginning of what became Holy Family Academy, the first high school and boarding school established by the sisters. Informal ministry to the sick began almost immediately upon the arrival of the first eleven sisters. Visiting the sick in their homes or in hospitals was a common practice. In 1894 Mother Lauretta opened a small 24-bed facility, Holy Family Hospital, the forerunner of **St. Mary of Nazareth Hospital** (now Saints Mary and Elizabeth Medical Center). This establishment was opened at the request of Poles who wanted at a time of illness to be able to communicate in the Polish language. Initially recognized informally as the "Polish Hospital," this institution was open to all regardless of nationality.

By the early 1900s, the U.S. province outgrew the building in the Polish neighborhood on Division Street in Chicago. In response to the hospitality offered to him at the CSFN generalate in Rome in 1900, Archbishop James E. Quigley donated eighty acres of land in Des Plaines, a suburb of Chicago, to Mother Lauretta and the sisters. In 1908 a novitiate and a province headquarters was established there. In a world and an era dominated by nationalism, Mother Siedliska envisioned a Congregation whose purpose was to further the Kingdom of God, which included people of every race, language and ethnicity. From its inception, therefore, membership in the Congregation was open to women of every nationality and the ministry of the nuns was extended to all as part of God's family. She consistently encouraged sisters to transcend what she saw as artificial barriers and stumbling blocks to universality. Her desire to have the sisters integrate and become part of the local culture is noted in a letter to her spiritual director in 1896: "The more I observe all that is happening here, the more I implore our Lord and aspire to one thing: that our congregation should eliminate the connotation of being Polish, should draw away from working exclusively among Poles, and associate somewhat with the local American population.... Our sisters will not appear as Poles, but as Americans; they will enter into different relationships and perhaps a small beginning will grow into a large tree bearing fruit."

The vision of a truly international Congregation was tested in 1922 after political events in Europe sparked strong national sentiments among Lithuanian and Polish immigrants in the U.S. In 1918, Lithuania gained its independence from Russia and in 1920, Poland invaded Lithuania. The sympathies of the Lithuanian immigrants for the plight of their country increased, along with the desire to preserve their culture, language and religious traditions. More Lithuanian women entering the Congregation and a growing outreach of the sisters to Lithuanian parishes led a group of Lithuanian pastors and families to try to initiate a Lithuanian province of the Sisters of the Holy Family of Nazareth. Their formal appeal to the Sacred Congregation of Religious in Rome and to Mother Lauretta Lubowidzka, then superior general, was refused because concentration on a single nationality was not in keeping with the original vision established by Mother Siedliska. Subsequently fifteen Lithuanian sisters left the Congregation in 1922. With the help of Bishop Hugh C. Boyle of Pittsburgh, the Franciscan Sisters of Millvale, Pennsylvania and Lithuanian priests and families, these women began the Franciscan Sisters of the Providence of God in Whitehall, PA.

One example of the influence of Polish culture in the Congregation was the establishment of several classes or "choirs" of sisters. This practice reflected the European class system based on economic status with two distinct groups: a wealthy educated class and a larger class of poor uneducated peasants. Mother Siedliska accepted candidates from both classes. The vast differences in language, custom and practical living between women from the wealthier and poorer strata of society called for Mother Siedliska's including this class system. The Original Constitution included three choirs. The sisters in the first choir were destined for leadership in both the ministries and internal services within the Congregation and were titled, "Mother." Those in the second choir taught children in the primary grades, taught women's handcrafts and substituted in certain offices when appropriate or necessary. Sisters of the third choir were dedicated to manual and household occupations. Their religious garb was slightly different from that worn by the other sisters.

Upon advice of the Holy See in 1896, the choir system was limited to two choirs — one engaged in professional ministry and one to household responsibilities. During the General Chapter of 1959, the highest legislative body of a religious congregation, the distinction in apparel was abolished. In the spirit of the 1959 General Chapter and in keeping with the new understanding of the dignity of the person emerging from Second Vatican Council (1963–65), Mother Neomisia Rutkowska and her council sought an indult from the Sacred Congregation to abolish the two-choir system completely. The indult was received on January 20, 1965 and became effective on March 9, 1965. Following Mother Siedliska's death on November 21, 1902, Pope Leo XIII appointed Mother Lauretta Lubowidzka vicar general and later superior general of the Congregation. Her forty-two year leadership as superior general continued, in a remarkable way, to stabilize the Congregation and its mission on American soil. Having met the needs of the initial Polish immigrants whose children were now bi-lingual and integrating into an American way of life, in the ensuing years, the sisters extended their services to a new generation of students. By the time of Mother Lauretta's death in 1942 the sisters' educational ministry had grown to include seventy-two elementary schools and seven high schools. Beyond the early childcare institutions begun during the lifetime of the foundress, the sisters continued to staff homes for children in Conshohocken and later Ambler, Pennsylvania, in Wading River, New York and Mobile, Alabama.

The sisters' service in healthcare expanded also. In addition to Saint Mary of Nazareth Hospital in Chicago, the community subsequently opened hospitals in New Mexico, Pennsylvania, Texas and an additional hospital in Illinois. In total, the Congregation ministered at eleven hospitals in the United States. Records and journals tell stories of collaborative endeavors between sisters, doctors and professionals of many nationalities and of service to a broad population where these facilities were located. From the beginning of the Congregation, despite the length and difficulty of travel, it was a common practice for sisters to serve wherever needed in the world. Travel between the United States and Europe, and to Poland in particular, became difficult with the onset of the World Wars, particularly during World War II and later during the Communist era in Poland. Consequently, for almost fifty years there was little exchange between the sisters in Poland and in the United States. In the intervening years, individual nuns in the United States took upon themselves the goal of preserving Polish culture. One example was Sister Hilary Okon, who received the Gold Cross in 1939 from the Polish government in exile for her efforts. Following World War II, several nuns also received awards for distinguished service to the Polish people or for promoting language and culture. Some examples include Sisters Electa Glowienke and Mary Richard Rutkowska who received the Order of Polonia Restituta for promoting social services for persons displaced by the war. Sisters Liguori Pakowska and Liliosa Melerska were awarded the Gold Cross of Merit for their widespread support of Polish studies among teachers and students. At Sr. Liliosa's initiative, a chair of Polish language and culture was introduced by De Paul University in Chicago on both undergraduate and graduate levels. Sr. Florence Tumasz was named an honorary member of the Polish Heritage Society of Philadelphia. The Society presented Holy Family University (HFU) with a bronze plaque in recognition of Sister Florence's interest and support of the organization's many projects and cultural activities. Meetings of the society are still held at HFU. Sr. Neomisia Rutkowska taught Polish in the Slavic Department in the Catholic University of America, gave talks at the Polish Heritage Society and was an Honorary Member of the Polish Heritage Society in Philadelphia, Pennsylvania.

As the Second Vatican Ecumenical Council encouraged religious congregations to return to their sources and original intent of their foundress, as the world had developed into a global community, and as the new-found freedom following the fall of Communism in Poland in 1989-90 facilitated communication and travel, collaboration had been renewed among the Sisters of the Holy Family of Nazareth in the United States and throughout the world. Through the efforts of the leadership of the provinces in the United States in collaboration with the congregational leadership in Rome and in Poland, a new mutuality of sharing human resources was revived in the 1990s. Approximately twenty sisters came to the United States from Poland, learned the English language and were professionally prepared for service in various ministries throughout the United States. Several sisters from the United States provided English language instruction in Poland. The American provinces provided funds to rebuild deteriorating facilities in Poland which had been confiscated by the government during World War II and afterwards during the communist regime in Poland.

Holy Family University (1954) in Philadelphia, PA, sponsored by the Sisters of the Holy Family of Nazareth, continues to provide educational and ministerial opportunities for Polish nuns. On a broader academic level, under the leadership of Sister Francesca Onley, president, the university provides all its students with opportunities to gain knowledge about the global community and to develop an understanding and appreciation of other cultures by offering scholarships to international students, invitations to guest speakers, special activities and seminars. In particular, Holy Family University has initiated outreach and programming with Poland's universities. Sparked by Professor Stephen Medvec's 2000 presentation on American urban policy to post-diploma students in Suwałki, Poland, higher education links were also initiated with Białystok Technical University, the Catholic University of Lublin and Mazurian University in Olecko. Another example of outreach and collaboration are pilgrimages sponsored by Holy Family Institute and Holy Family University to the original sites of the Sisters of the Holy Family of Nazareth in Poland and Rome. These pilgrimages provide mission education for lay leadership so that they may continue to foster the mission of the Congregation in these organizations.

Individually, some sisters stand out in their service to the Polish community even today. Sister Stella Louise Slomka serves on the Bishop Abramowicz Seminary Board founded in 2000 to bring Polish seminarians to Chicago to serve the area's Polish community. Among many artistic and cultural contributors from among the nuns are Sister Rosarita Liebchen as a member of the Marcella Kochanska Sembrich Chorus of Philadelphia, a group which holds membership in the Polish Singers Alliance of America and Sister Angelica Zajkowski, a member of the Michigan chapter of "The Friends of Polish Art."

After 1918, the Congregation in the United States grew from one central foundation in Des Plaines, Illinois to four other provinces. These included Pittsburgh (1918), Philadelphia (1918), Monroe, Connecticut (1960) and Grand Prairie, Texas (1962). On May 1, 2007, the five provinces merged once again to form a province headquartered in Des Plaines. As of September 2009, 359 sisters serve in the United States in Connecticut, Illinois, Massachusetts, Michigan, New York, Ohio, Pennsylvania, Puerto Rico, Texas. In 2010 the Congregation marked its 125th anniversary in the United States. The current members of the Sisters of the Holy Family of Nazareth stand upon the shoulders of great women whose courage and stout faith was forged in the homes, churches, cities, and villages of Poland. The mutual relationship between this Congregation and Polish Americans in the United States is documented in parish histories, hospital journals and the chronicles in educational institutions. More importantly, although the sisters no longer live or minister in places where they once served, the relationship with the Congregation continues even beyond the United States. Living memories of this relationship is expressed in various ways in a shrine dedicated in 2007 to Mother Siedliska, Blessed Mary of Jesus the Good Shepherd, at St. Stanislaus Parish in Pittsburgh, PA. Pilgrimages to Poland from parishes once staffed by the sisters often include a visit to one of the convents in Poland. A hospital once founded for the needs of Polish immigrants still holds sensitivity to the immigrants of today.

Over the years the internal culture of the community has taken on a distinctly American identity while at the same time honoring the rich Polish heritage of the foundress and the early sisters. Customs and traditions such as celebrating the Christmas Eve **Wigilia**, the sharing of **Opłatek**, the blessing of the Easter food and the celebration of a sister's nameday are still practiced within the Congregation and adapted as women from different ethnic backgrounds enter the Congregation. In 2010, the sisters continued to staff schools, childcare institutions and health care institutions and the other ministries that have evolved in response to the continually changing landscape of family needs in this country.—*Sister Geraldine Wodarczyk and Sister Jude Carroll*

SOURCES: Sister M. DeChantal, CSFN, *Out of Nazareth* (New York: Exposition Press, 1974); Antonio Ricciardi, *His Will Alone: The Life of Mother Mary of Jesus the Good Shepherd* (Oshkosh, WI: Castle-Pierce Press, 1971); Maria Starzyńska and M. Rita Kathryn Sperka, *Hidden Life: A Story Based on the Life and Work of Frances Siedliska* (Chicago: Sisters of the Holy Family of Nazareth, 1977); the Rev. Timothy Stein, *Where God Reigns: A History of the Sisters of the Holy Family of Nazareth in the Diocese of Altoona-Johnstown, 1911–2007* (Altoona, PA: Published by the Diocese of Altoona Johnstown, n.d.); Dorota Praszałowicz, "Polish American Sisterhood: The Americanization Process," *U.S. Catholic Historian*, Vol. 27, no. 3 (2009), 45–57; Sr. M. Liguori, "Seventy-Five Years of Religious Growth," *Polish American Studies*, Vol. 8, no. 1–2 (1951), 1–11.

Home Ownership, Polish American.

In rural Poland where most of the people of the Great Migration between 1880 and 1920 originated, there was a direct relationship between status and land ownership. Although there was little opportunity and no need to purchase large amounts of land in an urban industrial setting in the U.S., the predisposition of Poles to view ownership as a serious status symbol was also carried over into their new environment. This can best be seen in the value they placed upon home ownership. In the U.S. this was often reinforced by the fact that industries developed company towns in which employees rented accommodations from the employer and could be evicted if they went on strike. Thus, home ownership became a source of both social prestige and security, replacing the ideal of land ownership in their native agricultural Poland. Evidence of this can be seen in a 1930 survey in Milwaukee which revealed that 70 percent of Poles owned their own homes as compared to 63 percent of Czechs, 25 percent of Yugoslavs, and about 33 percent of the English and Irish. A similar survey in Nanticoke, Pennsylvania, showed 57 percent of Poles owned their own homes compared to only 23 percent of native-born whites. In Cicero, Illinois, 67 percent of Poles were home owners compared with only 22 percent of native-born whites. Similar results were obtained in other areas.—*James S. Pula*

SOURCES: John Bodnar, "Immigration and Modernization: The Case of Slavic Peasants in Industrial America," *Journal of Social History*, Vol. 10 (1976), 44–71; Janice E. Kleeman, "Polish-American Assimilation: The Interaction of Opportunity and Attitude," *Polish American Studies*, Vol. 42, no. 1 (1985), 11–26.

Horain, Julian Florian (b. Radoszkowice, Lithuania, September 10, 1821; d. Kraków, Poland, March 28, 1883). Journalist, translator. After being unsuccessful in studies in Moscow and failing in an attempt to run the family estate near Lithuanian Minsk, he started to write columns in literary publications in the years 1851–56, soon becoming co-editor of *Dziennik Warszawski* (Warsaw Daily News). Later, after traveling in Germany, Algeria, and Egypt, he returned to Wilno where he taught languages and translated texts from English and French. Seeking financial stability, he left for the United States in 1871, settling in Hoboken, New Jersey, where he lived until 1875. Initially he wrote articles for *Swoboda* (Liberty), soon becoming editor of *Gazeta Nowoyorska* (New York Gazette) in 1874. During the same period, he acted as an American correspondent for the Warsaw press. Seeking new financial opportunities, he moved west to San Francisco but his efforts did not meet with great success. For the American Centennial he published, with N. J. Brett, a *Symbolical Centenary Chart of American History*, which was also published in Polish translation in Kraków in 1883. During his nine years in the United States he mailed at least 150 articles to the Polish press, mainly to the *Gazeta Polska* (Polish Gazette) in Warsaw, which informed a Polish audience about America. His correspondence to people in Poland and America includes unique details about early Polonia life, both on the East and West Coast of the U.S. In 1880 he became a U.S. citizen, but because of a family tragedy he returned to Poland, settling first in Lwów and later in Kraków.—*Halina Florkowska Frančić*

SOURCES: M. Tyrowicz, "Horain Julian," *Polski Słownik Biograficzny*, Vol. IX (1960/61), 613–614; Mirosław Frančić, *Julian Horain i jego korespondencja ze Stanów Zjednoczonych z lat 1871–1880* (Kraków: Zakład Narodowy im. Ossolińskich, 1986).

Hordyński, Józef S. (b. Poland, 1792; d. Poland, 1840). Author, military officer. A major in the 10th Lithuanian Lancer Regiment who had fought under Napoleon Bonaparte, Hordyński participated in the November Uprising (1830-31) and fled to the U.S. with its failure. He arrived in Boston aboard the *Eliza Ann* from Piława on November 9, 1831. He kept in close contact with Polish exiles in Europe, ironically often arguing that they ought to stay in Europe rather than come to the U.S. He wrote to both President Andrew Jackson and the Secretary of State seek-

ing an appointment in the U.S. military, but none was forthcoming. In Boston in 1832 he published *The History of the Late Polish Revolution and the Events of the Campaign*, which was translated into English by a German professor named Gretter and was possibly the first work published in English by a Polish exile in America. It had a significant influence on Robert Carver's later work *Stories of Poland* (1833). As quickly as he arrived in America, he departed and was back in Europe in 1832 where he worked with Joachim Lelewel's patriotic group in Paris and then joined Col. Józef Zaliwski's failed campaign to lead an uprising in Galicia in 1833.—*James S. Pula*

SOURCES: Florian Stasik, *Polish Political Emigrés in the United States of America, 1831–1864* (Boulder, CO: East European Monographs, 2002); Jerzy Jan Lerski, *A Polish Chapter in Jacksonian America: The United States and the Polish Exiles of 1831* (Madison: University of Wisconsin Press, 1958).

Horowitz, Ryszard (b. Kraków, Poland, May 5, 1939; d.—). Photographer. Horowitz moved to the U.S. in 1959. He received a Bachelor of Fine Arts degree from Pratt Institute (1963) before embarking on an acclaimed career with various photographic design firms including establishing his own studio in New York in 1967. His photographic works have been exhibited in New York, Paris, Prague, and Warsaw, and appeared in *Photographie: De la réclame à la publicité* (1990), *Image Hong Kong* (1993), and *Ryszard Horowitz* (1994). He was a member of the board of the Advertising Photographers of America (1987-88), and a member of the American Society of Magazine Photographers. Among his many honors was the Gold Medal of the Art Directors Club of New York (1970), the Gold Award for The One Show (1973), the "Gold Caddie" award as the best in car advertising (1982), All American Photographer of the Year (1983), Best in Special Effects Photography from the Advertising Photographers of America (1991), and various awards from the Art Directors Club of New York.—*James S. Pula*

SOURCES: Michèle Auer, ed., *Encyclopédie Internationale des Photographes de 1839 à nos jours* (Hermance, Switzerland: Éditions Camera obscura, 1985); Bolesław Wierzbiański, ed., *Who's Who in Polish America* (New York: Bicentennial Publishing Corporation, 1996).

Horszowski, Mieczysław (b. Lwów, Poland, June 23, 1892; d. Philadelphia, Pennsylvania, May 22, 1993). Pianist, music educator. Horszowski's father owned a piano shop and his mother, who had been a pupil of Chopin's student Karl Mikuli, was his first teacher when he was only three. As a child prodigy, Horszowski was quickly able to play Bach's two-part *Inventions* from memory, and also began composing. After studying at the

Lwów Conservatory, he went to Vienna with his mother in 1899 to study with Theodor Leschetizky, who had been the teacher of **Ignace Paderewski**, Artur Schnabel, and other prominent pianists of the era. After watching young "Miecio" play, Paderewski was said to have embraced the boy in his arms, hailing him as one who was destined to shine. Horszowski made his concert debut in 1899 before Emperor Franz Josef at the Bosendorfersaal in Vienna. His formal recital debut was in Vienna in 1902, and his orchestral debut was in Warsaw in 1902 as soloist in Beethoven's First Piano Concerto with the Warsaw Philharmonic. Numerous other debuts soon followed, including three notable ones in 1906: London (before Queen Alexandra), at the Vatican (before Pope Pius X), and America (at New York's Carnegie Hall where newspapers compared him with Mozart). After touring extensively for a decade, during which he met many famous composers and musicians and developed friendships with **Artur Rubinstein**, Arturo Toscanini, and Pablo Casals, he then took time off to study philosophy, literature, and the history of art at the Sorbonne (1911–13), before Casals urged him to resume concertizing in 1913. During the interwar period, Horszowski's home was in Milan, but he toured constantly. When Italy entered World War II, he moved to the United States (1941), becoming a naturalized U.S. citizen in 1948. The pianist Rudolf Serkin recruited him to join the faculty of Philadelphia's Curtis Institute of Music in 1942, and he remained a teacher there until his death. Some of Horszowski's students were Murray Perahia, Richard Goode, Andras Schiff, and Peter Serkin.

Known particularly for his interpretations of Beethoven, Chopin, Debussy, and Mozart, Horszowski was also a champion of contemporary composers like Stravinsky and Szymanowski, giving the premiere of the latter's Third Piano Sonata in 1923. In fact, when Horszowski first played Tchaikovsky and Grieg, they were both *new* composers. Although much of the flashy Romantic repertoire was out of his range physically, since, as a diminutive man (barely five feet tall), with small hands and a short reach, he also avoided it by temperament. Unlike the thundering octaves of contemporaries like Vladimir Horowitz, Horszowski was known instead for his gentle and velvety tone, an intellectual who put the music first. Among the numerous noteworthy concerts during his 95-year performing career was a series of twelve recitals in New York covering the complete Beethoven piano works (1954-1955), a cycle of four recitals in New York playing all of the Mozart piano sonatas

in 1960, and many appearances with the NBC Symphony under Toscanini. He performed at the White House for Presidents Kennedy and Carter, appeared with major orchestras all around the world, and was also an eager chamber music player, frequently collaborating with the cellist Pablo Casals (for a half-century) and with the violinist Joseph Szigeti. Horszowski also played as part of the New York Quartet with violinist Alexander Schneider in the 1940s and 1950s, participated annually at the Casals Festivals held in Prades (France) and Puerto Rico, and was affiliated with the Marlboro School and Festival in Vermont, where a scholarship was established in his name in 1967. He received an honorary Doctor of Music degree from the Curtis Institute in 1969.

His eyesight began to fail in the early 1980s, which limited him to solo work and playing from memory, although he continued to give recitals. He made his Japanese debut in 1987 at age 95 to inaugurate Tokyo's Casals Hall, and he gave his last recital in 1991 at the age of 99. Although his family was originally of Jewish origin, they were early converts to Roman Catholicism.—*John Drobnicki*

SOURCES: Bice Horszowski Costa, ed., *Miecio: Remembrances of Mieczysław Horszowski* (Genoa, Italy: Erga edizioni, 2002); John Gillespie and Anna Gillespie, *Notable Twentieth-Century Pianists: A Bio-Critical Sourcebook* (Westport, CT: Greenwood Press, 1995); *Musicians Since 1990* (New York: H.W. Wilson, 1978); obituaries from the *New York Times* and *Philadelphia Inquirer*, May 24, 1993.

Hoskins, Janina (Janina Wanda Ewa Kozłowska; b. Nowa Wilejka, Poland, February 19, 1912, d. Menlo Park, California, October 19, 1996). Librarian. After studying Polish history at the University of Warsaw (1934–38), she moved to Kraków where she enrolled in the Jagiellonian University. During World War II she was a member of the underground opposition to German rule, following which she resumed her studies at the Jagiellonian, earning her doctorate in art history in 1947. In 1949 she escaped from communist-ruled Poland and was granted permanent residency in the U.S. in 1951. When she arrived in the U.S. she was employed as a translator by Representative **John D. Dingell** and Radio Free Europe. She spoke on Radio Free Europe and the Voice of America radio programs and also volunteered time working in the Polish collection in the Library of Congress. In 1952 she was hired at the Library on a part-time basis, and received a full-time appointment in 1955 to the Slavic and East European Division. Under her guidance, the Polish collection grew rapidly, as did the number of active book exchanges with Polish institutions. During her career she assembled in

the Library of Congress one of the best collections of Polish materials outside Poland. She also published a number of selected bibliographies on various Polish-related subjects, and served as a helpful resource for visiting scholars, politicians, Library of Congress staff, and the general public. Among her bibliographic publications were *Casimir Pulaski 1747–1779* (1979), *Tadeusz Kościuszko 1746–1817* (1980), *Victory at Vienna* (1983), *Lafayette in America* (1983), *Ignacy Jan Paderewski, 1860–1941* (1984), *Joachim Lelewel, Scholar, 1786–1861* (1986), and *Visual Arts in Poland: An Annotated Bibliography of Selected Holdings in the Library of Congress* (1993).—*James S. Pula*

SOURCE: Wojciech Zalewski, "In Memoriam: Janina Wójcicka Hoskins (1912–1996)," *The Polish Review*, Vol. 42, no. 1 (1997), 123–26.

Imieniny. The *imieniny* is a Polish tradition in which a person's nameday is celebrated each year. Historically, parents, especially in the Polish countryside, named their newborn infant after one of the saints of the Catholic Church whose feast was celebrated on the day of the child's birth. Thus the nameday of an individual coincided with his or her actual birthday. The calendars published annually by **Polonia** organizations continue to list the names of the various saints whose feast is celebrated each day. There are almost always a number to choose from, if a family wishes to go in this direction in naming the newborn. In modern Poland, a person may be named for a saint whose feast day is not on the actual day of birth. It thus follows that one's nameday (or *imieniny*) is the day that is celebrated by family and friends each year, not the anniversary of one's actual day of birth. This tradition has all but disappeared among Polish Americans, since they, like their fellow Americans, observe birthdays and not namedays and choose the names of their children for many different reasons.—*Angela T. Pienkos*

SOURCE: Eugene E. Obidinski and Helen Stankiewicz Zand, *Polish Folkways in America: Community and Family* (Lanham, MA: University Press of America, 1987).

Immigration Patterns. The beginning of a Polish presence in America lies shrouded in the fog of history. The first definitely recorded migration of Poles to the New World was a small handful of artisans who arrived in the Jamestown colony in 1608, shortly after its founding. The Poles were encouraged to migrate by British mercantile officials eager to use the Poles' expertise at tar, pitch, and glass making to bring economic prosperity to the Virginia colony. The existing records, though scanty, make it clear that the Poles took part in every facet of colonial life, being free men without indentures. With the founding of the Dutch colony of New Amsterdam — later renamed New York by the English — some Protestant Poles who earlier sought the company of their religious compatriots in Holland made the journey across the Atlantic to add their particular cultural heritage to the multi-religious, multi-ethnic colony centered on Manhattan Island. The New Amsterdam Poles represented a cross-section of occupations including soldiers, teachers, farmers, merchants, and government officials. Although small in total number, by the beginning of the American Revolution in 1775, the largest concentration of Poles in America appears to have been in New York City and the neighboring areas of New Jersey. Others mingled among the Dutch colonists in the Hudson and Mohawk Valleys in Upstate New York, among the German settlements in Pennsylvania, and in the Catholic areas of Maryland.

Although these early Poles generally migrated individually, and did not arrive in numbers sufficient to form true Polish communities, they, along with their more famous countrymen **Tadeusz Kościuszko** and **Kazimierz Pułaski** during the American Revolution, provided an early historical presence in North America that could be pointed to with pride by later generations of Polish Americans seeking to place their own historical roots within the formative period of the American mosaic. As historian **Joseph Wieczerzak** explained, Kościuszko and Pułaski were particularly important because they developed "pro-Polish sympathies in the American public through the nineteenth century and afterwards," while also providing later Polish immigrants with "surrogate roots in the American past which psychologically lessened their feelings of being 'strangers' to America."

On three occasions prior to 1860 relatively large groups, at least by the standards of the day, migrated to America. The failure of the November Uprising against Russia in 1830-31 resulted in the arrival in New York of 234 exiled revolutionaries aboard Austrian warships, to be followed by an additional 400 fellow exiles in the following decade. While some settled in the port city of their arrival, most gradually spread out among various cities, with small groups locating in Albany, Troy, Philadelphia, Boston, and Washington, D.C. A few went as far west as Ohio. Although this dispersion prevented them from forming a real Polish colony, they did found the first Polish organization in America as a means of promoting solidarity and lobbying for Polish interests. Since both of these nineteenth century groups consisted of political exiles, the majority did not intend to remain as perma-

nent settlers — although in the end many actually did — but rather to work on Poland's behalf in America until they could return to Europe to participate actively in the liberation of their homeland.

Approximately 500 political exiles also migrated to America in the years following the abortive revolution led by Ludwik Mierosławski in 1846. Like their precursors from the November Uprising, they were mostly educated members of the gentry who found employment in a wide spectrum of occupations from government service to teaching, engineering, and business. While a few settled in Southern cities, especially areas of French influence such as New Orleans, Mobile, and Charleston, most once again chose life in Northern cities. Members of this group formed the Association of Poles in America to foster solidarity, promote Polish interests, and maintain contact with Polish revolutionary organizations in Europe.

The third antebellum group included about 800 Silesians who followed the Rev. **Leopold Moczygemba** to Texas in 1854. Markedly different in education and social class than their predecessors, the Silesians (see **Silesia**) were poor farmers seeking permanent settlement to establish new lives. Unlike earlier groups, they included a much higher proportion of women and children. They settled in and around **Panna Maria** where they pursued farming and established the first true Polish colony in America.

Although the early history of Polish America is primarily that of the migration of individuals and small groups, these early immigrants were generally successful in organizing and exerting some influence on behalf of themselves and Poland. Almost exclusively male, with the exception of the group in Texas, they did not develop the recognizably Polish communities that later immigrants founded. They did, however, exhibit a keen interest in the homeland, founded organizations to pursue their goals, and began, however tenuously, a Polish literary tradition in America. As such, they were the precursors of the ethnic communities founded by the mass migration later in the century.

The great migration following the Civil War began in the Prussian section of partitioned Poland. There, beginning in the late 1850s, German nationalists became increasingly repressive against Polish inhabitants because of the Poles' support for the unsuccessful revolutions in 1846 and 1848. Bad harvests in 1848 and in 1853–56 greatly magnified the Poles' increasing economic difficulties and caused some 1,250,000 acres of land to pass from Polish ownership to German hands in

Poznania and West Prussia between 1846 and 1885. Following German unification in the 1870s, German nationalist sentiments became more strident and less passive. Polish minorities in Germany were traditionally oppressed and exploited, but Chancellor Otto von Bismarck's view of this large minority was even more reactionary. To Bismarck, as Thomas Michalski explains, all non–Germans were *Reichsfeinde* (enemies of the Reich). Because of this attitude, the German Constitution of 1871 contained no provisions safeguarding the rights of ethnic minorities. A systematic persecution of Polish culture soon began (see **Kulturkampf**). The Germans discouraged the use of the Polish language, launched a campaign to force Polish newspapers to print in both languages, and accused the clergy of polonizing Germanic names in an attempt to polonize the German population. The German mail system rejected letters if one wrote the Polish "Gdańsk" instead of the German "Danzig," or if "street" were written in Polish "*ulica*" rather than the German "*strasse.*" Some 7,500 place names were changed from Slavic to German by 1912.

Economic emigrants from the poorer rural areas moved first to the more industrialized areas of western Germany and Western Europe, and then, beginning in the 1870s, to the United States. In a detailed study of immigration from German occupied Poland, Victor Greene concludes that the social, political and economic repression of the German government was a significant contributory cause to emigration, but that the single most important factor in the movement of people out of German occupied Poland was economic dislocation. Some 152,000 Poles migrated from Poznania, East Prussia, West Prussia and Silesia during the 1870s compared to only 2,000 from Austrian **Galicia**. Emigration from the German occupied areas peaked in the 1880s and declined somewhat thereafter. Between 1840 and 1910 some 1,575,000 people migrated from German Poland to the United States, including 877,400 from Poznania, 628,110 from West Prussia, and 70,000 from Russian areas bordering Prussian Poland. This movement had a major influence on America, forming a majority of the early Polish population in New York, Chicago and other northern urban settlements. The Poles from the German occupied partition were at least partly urbanized, had some marketable skills, were on average more highly educated than Poles in the other two partitions, and tended to be young, energetic and optimistic. Many had experience in European factories, mines and foundries, while some were craftsmen, artisans or entrepreneurs. Many opened businesses in the

United States within a relatively short time, forming the basis for the development of a Polish middle class in several northern cities. Further, their experience in Germany made them reluctant to give up their language, culture, and religion, thus causing the formation of distinct communities that resisted acculturation and assimilation for generations.

In Russian Poland, the Tsar abolished serfdom in 1864. By 1875 some 1,000,000 acres of former landed estates were in peasant hands. By 1870, however, a program of Russification sought to eliminate Polish as a language of instruction in schools and limit the influence of the Polish clergy. At the same time, economic conditions deteriorated. In the southern textile center of Łódź, for example, wages for unskilled factory workers between 1880 and 1900 were approximately $.30 per day, one-quarter of the $1.15 paid in the United States during the same decade. The northern portion of Russian Poland remained a poor, economically depressed agricultural area. It was these northern provinces — Suwalki, Łomza and Płock — that accounted for most of the early emigration from Russian Poland to America. As late as 1905, fully one-third of all the Russian Poles who migrated came from Suwalki. In that year, economic problems and civil unrest in both Poland and Russia created serious instability. Thereafter, most of those who left the Russian section were southern industrial workers fleeing a declining economy. Thus, economic motivations also proved the strongest cause for migration from Russian Poland, with some 40,000 journeying to America in the 1880s and 134,000 in the 1890s.

The third partition, Austrian-occupied Galicia, was a particularly poor agricultural area. Located adjacent to the Tatra Mountains, it had a short growing season and the emancipation of serfs came late due to opposition by local Polish nobles. Politically, the Galicians fared considerably better than their German-dominated countrymen. As early as the 1850s the Austrians instituted several liberal reforms including administrative and judicial changes and the institution of self-governing town councils. By 1861 Austria approved the establishment of the Galician Diet as a provincial parliament, with delegates from the Diet attending the Vienna Parliament where they were known as the "Polish Club" because of their actions in favor of their constituents. In 1890 a Polish peasant party was established and in 1907 the Austrian Empire declared universal male suffrage. Thus political and cultural motivations were probably less important in the migration of Poles from Galicia. The key factor again appears to be the general

economic situation which was both chaotic and depressed during the late nineteenth and early twentieth centuries. Victor Greene notes that the Austrian government purposely restrained economic development in order to retain large grain exports from Galicia to the rest of the Empire, particularly the highly industrialized areas in Bohemia and Silesia. It was not until 1910 that a special industrial bank was created to assist economic development in Galicia. Nevertheless, the agricultural population increased from 77 percent in 1890 to 90 percent by 1914. By then Galicia had the smallest urban population of any of the three partitions. Thus it appears that once again economic consideration was the compelling factor in the beginning of mass migration from Galicia.

Conditions in Galicia remained poor. Homes and villages were devoid of any amenities. Peasant dwellings generally contained two large rooms — one for the family and one for livestock, tools, fertilizer, and other supplies. The average pay for agricultural workers was forty to fifty percent lower than that of unskilled industrial workers, while the latter was about fifty percent lower than similar positions in Western Europe. Male agricultural laborers in Poland earned forty to fifty percent less for an entire season's work than those in Germany. The economic depression was exacerbated by decreasing landholdings and a rapid increase in the population. Farms were subdivided upon death so that by 1900, when the normal family required an estimated holding of fourteen acres for its support, the average land holding in Galicia was less than six acres. With such small plots of land, peasants were extremely vulnerable to the vagaries of weather and market, with most having barely enough to feed their families. As a result, male life expectancy was only 27 years, and an estimated 50,000 people per year died of starvation.

In 1891 the average daily wage for agricultural laborers in the United States was eight times that of Galicia. At $1.48 per day, the average wage of an unskilled laborer in the United States was twelve times as high as Galicia. The conclusion was obvious. As Polish peasant leader Władysław Orkan observed, for people "accustomed to the poor local wages, it was like a fantasy, like a dream pay!" As word of the great opportunities in America spread, emigration became popular. In the 1880s, 82,000 Galician Poles migrated to the United States, a number that increased to 340,000 in the 1890s.

An estimated 1,500,000 Poles arrived in the United States between 1899 and 1913. Of these, about 49 percent were from Russian

Poland, 47 percent were Galicians, and only four percent were from German Poland. As World War I approached, the percentage from the Russian areas increased; thus, in 1913, 66 percent came from Russian-occupied Poland, 32 percent from Galicia and only two percent from German-occupied lands. The "typical" Pole who migrated between 1870 and 1900 was male, single, between fourteen and 44 years of age, and an agricultural laborer. Between 1899 and 1913 two-thirds of those who came were males while, even as late as 1913, 55 percent were single. Most listed their occupations as unskilled workers and planned to return home with the money they earned to buy land and make a better life within their native country. Once established in America, however, most became sufficiently comfortable to remain so that only one in four actually returned to the Old Country.

Although 64.5 percent of the immigrants were engaged in agriculture in Poland, almost ninety percent settled in northern urban, industrial areas where they obtained jobs as unskilled laborers in factories. Others who resided outside the major urban centers often found positions in mining or the many small industries that covered New England and the Middle Atlantic states. Of those who chose to remain in agriculture, some located in the Connecticut Valley and Upstate New York, but most settled in the Midwest where farmland was less expensive in Michigan, Wisconsin, Illinois and Indiana. By 1918 the largest group of Polish Americans was concentrated in Chicago with a population of some 400,000. Three of every four who journeyed across the Atlantic came to the United States, and in 1920, of the 1,335,957 Poles living abroad, fully two-thirds (820,595) lived in the United States. This represented 45 percent of the total Slavic immigration between 1899 and 1914.

While much is known about the composition of the Polish mass migration, one question still debated is the actual number of those who came during that period. According to one estimate based on immigration and census records, between 1897 and 1913 U.S. officials counted some 2,000,000 Poles coming into the United States, with the peak year being 1913 when 174,365 immigrants arrived from Poland. These numbers are much in dispute among historians and demographers. The United States census did not record national origin until 1820, and even then immigrants who had not been naturalized were not counted. Also, prior to 1885 the Bureau of Immigration did not list Poland as an option for "country of birth" since during the period of the partitions the nation did not "officially" exist. In practice, Poles entering the country were generally classified as Germans (or Prussians), Austrians, or Russians, and only rarely did a particularly insistent Pole manage to be recorded by the correct ethnicity. This problem was complicated further by the fact that the Bureau of Immigration was not consistent over time, sometimes reporting all entrants together as a lump sum, sometimes reporting immigrants separately from visitors and other non-immigrants, sometimes ignoring departures, and sometimes recording departures and even comparing them with original intent upon entry.

Even when "Poland" was used as a "country of birth," the figures could still be misleading. Poland contained many people with non–Polish heritage who would not consider themselves Poles in the cultural sense. In 1897, for example, Russian Poland contained 64.6 percent Poles, 12.1 percent Jews, six percent Russians, four percent Germans, three percent Lithuanians, as well as varying numbers of Tatars, Bohemians, Rumanians, Estonians, Gypsies, and Hungarians. It was a truly multiethnic area; thus, not everyone listing "Poland" as their place of origin was necessarily "Polish."

The most comprehensive study of this question was published by **Helena Lopata** who made extensive use of the original immigration rolls that differentiated between "country of birth" and "race or people." She found that by using data from the "race or people" category, the highest number of Poles coming in a single year was 174,365 in 1913. Between 1899 and 1932, again based on "Race or People," 1,443,473 Poles arrived and 294,824 returned to Poland for a net gain of 1,148,649. Lopata adds to this those listed by "country of birth" from 1885 to 1898 and 1933 to 1972, when no separate list of "race or people" was maintained, a total of 641,502. By adding these, the maximum number of Poles arriving between 1885 and 1972 would be 1,780,151. In addition to these, there were also 297,590 who arrived and then later left, and 669,392 non-immigrants and temporary residents identified as Poles. Regardless of the specific number, Polish immigration was significant and was based primarily on economic causes.

The outbreak of the First World War slowed migration to a shadow of its prewar magnitude. While hostilities raged in Europe, forces were at work in America to insure that the prewar mass migration would not resume after the end of the conflict. Spurred by a rising tide of prewar nativism, bills to establish a literacy test for immigrants were introduced into Congress between 1913 and 1917, only to be vetoed by Presidents William Howard Taft and Woodrow Wilson. Once the war was over, Congress passed a measure designed to

restrict immigration by allotting quotas to the various ethnic groups based on national origin.

The First Quota Act of 1921 imposed a maximum of 357,803 as the number of immigrants who could enter the United States from outside the Western Hemisphere in a single year. The number was considerably less than the average of 625,629 who entered annually between 1901 and 1920. In addition, each nationality group was given a separate quota based upon three percent of the number of people from that group residing in the United States in 1910. This provision discriminated directly against Southern and Eastern Europeans by purposely reversing the pre-war trend that saw Southern and Eastern Europeans outnumbering Western Europeans by four to one. Under the new law, Poland's first quota of 25,827 was increased to 31,146 in 1922, and then cut to 30,977 in 1923.

The National Origins Act of 1924 reduced the total number of immigrants per year to 164,667, at the same time reducing the quota percentage of each nationality to two percent and moving the base year from 1910 to 1890 (see **Immigration Restriction**). This was a clear attempt to lessen the impact, and therefore the quota, of immigrants from Southern and Eastern Europe who entered in large numbers after 1890. For Poland, this resulted in an annual reduction to 5,982, a loss of almost 81 percent. The final quota established in 1927 recognized Poles as the fifth largest group in the United States behind Germany, Great Britain, Ireland and Italy, assigning them a quota of 6,524.

The result of the quota acts was that fewer Poles came to the United States during the period between 1921 and 1940 than came in any single year between 1900 and 1914. The exact number, of course, depends upon how you defined a "Pole." Helena Lopata compared the arrivals and departures listed by the U.S. Bureau of Immigration by "race or people" and found that between 1920 and 1932, there was a net exodus of 33,618 Poles from the United States. Yet, when she used the figures for "country of birth" there was an increase of 107,476. The discrepancy, which led to some confusion and contradiction among historians and demographers, occurred because of the multinational nature of the Polish republic between the two world wars. Because of this, many who, in conformity with U.S. immigration policies, listed their "country of birth" as Poland were in reality members of other ethnic groups. A review of Polish sources by Edward Kolodziej suggests that of those who left Poland for America during this period, 34.2 percent were ethnic Poles, 6.4 percent

Ukrainians and White Russians, 1.0 percent Germans, 56.9 percent Jews, and 1.4 percent other nationalities or undeclared. Of these, 41.0 percent were farmers, 0.1 percent miners, 18.8 percent industrial workers, 6.9 percent trade workers, 0.3 percent transport workers, 2.7 percent engaged in the learned professions, 3.9 percent provided household service, 8.4 percent were members of unspecified professions, and 17.9 percent were unknown. The vast majority settled in the existing ethnic communities of the northern industrial cities.

With the reestablishment of an independent Poland after World War I, some Poles in the United States elected to return to their homeland. Helena Lopata found that 5,227 Poles arrived in the United States in 1920, while 19,024 left for a net loss of 13,797. In 1921 the outflow continued with a loss of 19,039 and in 1922 the loss increased to 26,075. In 1923, the immediate postwar departure thinned and immigrants thereafter outnumbered those returning to their native land. American sources indicate that 96,832 ethnic Poles returned to Poland between 1918 and 1923. Relying on Polish sources, Kolodziej calculated that between 1918 and 1938 approximately 273,161 Poles migrated to the United States, while 106,793 returned to Poland — a net gain to America of 166,368.

Polish historian Adam Walaszek identified four primary motivations for this re-emigration: some returned to Poland because of failure in the United States, some because they succeeded in earning enough money to return to a better life, some to retire, and some for political reasons. But some of those who returned to Poland were not completely comfortable in Europe. Many reported feeling "different." Some had been away from their homeland for five years, and some for thirty-five. In the intervening years they had changed. They had become accustomed to life in the Polish American urban ethnic enclave. Although few realized it, they had already begun the process of assimilation. At the same time, Poland, too, had changed. Their recollection of Poland was an idealized, even romanticized vision shaped by the forces of time. Upon their return to the Old Country some complained of the low standard of living and poverty in their rural homeland. Some were treated with respect by the Poles, but others were envied by their new neighbors or ridiculed because of the Americanisms in their speech and their unfamiliarity with contemporaneous Poland. Many, having been Americanized more than they realized, no longer fit into Polish society and an estimated 20,000 once again made the voyage across the Atlantic, returning to America after 1924.

The 1930 Census enumerated 1,268,583 people born in Poland and 2,073,615 with one or both parents born in Poland. The effects of the quotas and remigration can be seen as natural attrition began to take its toll on the immigrant generation in the 1930s. By 1940, the Census reported only 993,479 who were actually born in Poland and 1,912,380 with one or both parents born in Poland. Both of these figures represented decreases from 1930. The Second World War brought an influx of political émigrés beginning with the Nazi invasion of Poland in 1939. The dislocations created by the invasion and the subsequent Soviet move into Poland were severe. Data from the Polish Embassy in Moscow show that during the period of the German-Soviet friendship pact, September 1939 to June 1941, some 1,692,000 Poles, Jews, Ukrainians, and Byelorussians were forcibly deported from Poland to the Soviet Union. Between 1936 and 1977, in addition to 101,000 Poles admitted to the United States under the quota system, 19,430 arrived as refugees and 135,302 as displaced persons under special legislation enacted between 1954 and 1977.

The Poles who arrived during the war and its immediate aftermath grew to adulthood in an independent Poland and tended to be very protective of Polish freedom and culture. Among their number, particularly in the months immediately following the Nazi invasion, were a high percentage of intellectuals and professionals. Initially many found they needed additional education or certification before they could practice their professions in the United States, some having to accept menial positions to support themselves until they could obtain positions in their chosen fields. Yet, most came from educated backgrounds and were able to assimilate quite rapidly and to obtain positions at American universities and in their local professional communities.

According to Jan Kowalik, "The many Polish refugee intellectuals driven ashore to America intensified and enriched the activities of younger generations of Americans of Polish descent, creating new organizations, and accelerating a trend toward a renaissance of ethnic self-consciousness." One of the first contributions to the preservation of Polish culture and intellectual life in the Unites States took shape in December 1940 when refugee scholars led by the historian **Oskar Halecki** met in New York to discuss means by which they could organize to carry on their scholarly activities in exile. The group, drawn largely from members of the pre-war Polska Akademia Umiejętności (Polish Academy of Arts and Sciences) in Kraków, determined to form an American branch of the Akademia to "continue Polish scientific activities," to "spread knowledge about Poland and Polish culture in the United States," and to "deepen cultural relations between Poland and America." The scholars elected Halecki their first president, with anthropologist **Bronisław Malinowski** serving as vice president of the new **Polish Institute of Arts & Sciences**.

On July 4, 1943, another group of scholars specializing in the study of modern Polish history met in New York City to found The **Józef Piłsudski Institute for the Study of Modern Poland**. Taken together, the new organizations brought to Polonia an impetus toward cultural and intellectual development. Yet, their effect on mainstream Polonia was limited as the exiles who formed the founding nuclei of these new organizations maintained a European orientation and made little if any effort to reach out to mainstream **Polonia**. Generally, the wartime immigrants and their immediate post-war colleagues, either remained aloof from organized Polonia, or in some instances sought to wrest control of groups from the Polish Americans who then held the elective offices. While they established significant organizations, the wartime exiles proved to be only the initial phase of Polish post-war emigration. At the conclusion of the war, hundreds of thousands of Poles — largely veterans of the Polish armed-forces-in-exile and displaced persons — found themselves in Western Europe, many in the large, poorly supported refugee camps. It has been estimated that by the end of 1946 some 730,000 Poles returned to Poland, while about 240,000, mostly veterans of the Polish army, preferred to stay in the west.

The refugee question quickly became a potent issue among Polish Americans. A variety of groups including Catholic relief organizations, the Red Cross, and a plethora of Polish American organizations conducted fund raising to support European relief efforts aimed at easing the plight of these unfortunates whom political circumstances robbed of both victory and homeland. At the same time, led by the **Polish American Congress**, lobbying efforts sought to influence the American government to modify its strict quota system to permit the entrance of refugees from the Communist areas in Eastern Europe. As a direct result of these efforts, Congress passed the Displaced Persons Act in 1948 and a special law in 1950 allowing Polish veterans into the country. Thus, between 1945 and 1954 some 178,000 Poles entered the country, with another 75,000 gaining entry between 1955 and 1966.

Despite the momentary opening of America's doors, the restrictive quota system remained basically unchanged. The McCarran-Walter Act of 1952, enacted over President Truman's veto, retained the nationality quotas intact. Arguing against this as a "discriminatory policy," Truman cited the sad plight of 138,000 Polish refugees seeking to fill but 6,524 places. It remained for the Immigration and Nationality Act of 1965 to reverse the policy adopted in 1921. The Poles who came to America after World War II added greatly to the heterogeneity of Polonia. Those who arrived during the 1950s, like their counterparts of the 1940s, were primarily political refugees escaping an occupying regime. Although this generation of Polish immigrants contained a cross-section of Polish life, it included a higher proportion of intellectuals, scientists, journalists and exiled leaders of opposition political movements than previous eras. A study by **Danuta Mostwin** revealed that 16.3 percent were executives, 29.5 percent professionals or semiprofessionals, 16.6 percent skilled workers, and only 16.3 percent unskilled workers.

The result was that, unlike the earlier mass migration, the post-war arrivals tended to be better off financially and did not migrate because of economic reasons. Rather, it has been estimated that more that fifty percent migrated because of actual political persecution, another twenty percent fled because of anticipated persecution, and still a further twenty percent were political refugees who stated that their primary reason for leaving was opposition to the political regime. Unlike their earlier compatriots, they also came with the trauma of war, Nazi occupation and Soviet rule sharply etched in their psychological makeup. "Their personalities, attitudes toward the world and man were shaped by this tragic past; many of their kin and friends paid with their lives; they were the survivors," explained **Feliks Gross**.

Research by Maurice R. Davie indicates that, also unlike their predecessors, 96.5 percent of these post-war immigrants came to the United States with the intention of staying in America to take advantage of its freedom and opportunity. Further, although they stayed mainly in the same northeastern urban areas as did the turn-of-the-century immigrants, according to Theresita Polzin they did not settle within the established Polonia settlements. Rather, most of the newcomers chose to reside among the general American population instead of amid the ethnic communities. They came, Polzin concludes, "to escape from a country in which one's life was constantly threatened; where a peaceful life, with even minimal freedom to develop intellectually, culturally, and economically, was blocked." As one immigrant explained, "For the sake of my children who are of school age, I want to stay in the United States. Here we feel like human beings and are not persecuted. Here we can speak our own language if we want, read our Polish newspapers, visit our friends, and go about our business."

The post-war immigrants were different than those who came during the war, or those who formed the great majority of Polish America. While organized Polonia long held as one of its major goals the preservation of Polish history and culture, the degree of "Americanization" among second and third-generation Polish Americans became abundantly clear with the arrival of these new immigrants. To the leaders of Polonia, the newcomers were often regarded as "pushy upstarts," representatives of an educated class that threatened their status as community leaders. Further, the general success of the new immigrants was often resented by the older settlers who felt that the newcomers should work long and hard to succeed as they had. To the immigrants, the established Polonia was only marginally Polish — they spoke a broken, unsophisticated Polish American dialect and knew little of Poland beyond the superficial celebration of holidays and anniversaries that had long since lost their original significance and become mere social events. The new arrivals could not rely solely upon Polonia, as the earlier immigrants had, as a means of cushioning their transition into a new culture.

The post-war immigrants faced the same impediments to success as had the earlier arrivals: the language barrier, unfamiliar customs and values, generally unsympathetic or hostile Americans, significantly different business and professional customs, differences between Polish and American education systems, and the sometimes suspicious and unfriendly disposition of earlier Polish immigrants. But, according to Polzin, the "most disconcerting problem" continued to be the mutual suspicion and misunderstanding between the new and old immigrants that eventually led to "mutual rejection, so that the new immigration formed its own organizations, cultural and otherwise, rather than join those already established." Polzin attributes this to the differences in socioeconomic status between the two groups.

Numerically, Polonia continued to grow in the post-war years. The 1950 census counted 861,184 people residing in the United States who were born in Poland and 1,925,015 with one or both parents born in Poland. By 1960 the number of Polish-born decreased slightly and those with one or both parents born in Poland increased yielding figures of 747,000 and 2,031,000 respectively. In the same year,

in Standard Metropolitan Statistical Areas with a population of 1,000,000 or more and a "foreign" population of 25 percent, Poles ranked as follows: 21 percent of the "foreign" population in Buffalo, 17 percent in Chicago, 16.8 percent in Detroit, 16.4 percent in Milwaukee, 12.9 percent in Cleveland, 11.8 percent in Pittsburgh, 9.8 percent in New York City, 9.1 percent in Philadelphia, and 3.8 percent in Boston. In 1969 the U.S. government estimated there were 4,021,000 Americans who were ethnically Polish, 60.2 percent of whom claimed Polish as their mother tongue and 92.6 percent of whom usually spoke English. Polish Americans argued strenuously that this was an underestimate, maintaining that a more accurate figure would be between six and ten million. Estimates varied due to differences in definition, but Polonia's leaders argued that use of a general ethnological definition regardless of language, sentiments, degree of ethnic stock, and other subjective factors would yield about ten million. When defined culturally, including only those actively conscious of their heritage, an accurate estimate would be between six and seven million.

One of the most important events in determining the future of Polish immigration to America since the nationality quotas were made permanent in 1924 was the Immigration Act of 1965. Eliminating the discriminatory quota system that guided American policy for more than forty years, the new legislation gave priority to immigrants with skills and to the reunification of families. The elimination of the old quota system was consistent with the emphasis on civil rights legislation during the 1960s for it removed the discrimination against immigrants from eastern and southern Europe. As a result, Polish immigration since 1965 was steady, if moderate, and contained a large number of professionals and intellectuals.

The great majority of the post–1965 immigration was comprised of younger people who grew up and were educated in Communist Poland giving them different perspectives and expectations than those who came before them. Feliks Gross identified four distinct categories within the post–1965 group. The first of these included skilled workers who saw in America opportunities for freedom and economic advancement, a group that Gross labeled the "new economic immigrants." Unlike the economic migration "for bread" at the beginning of the century, they were not marginally educated peasants but professionals and skilled artisans who easily found employment in the United States. Given their socialization in a very restrictive society, they were some-

times critical of the excessive freedoms in America that led to violence, self-indulgence and a fixation on money. The second category included idealists disillusioned with the Communist system who sought in America the fulfillment of their utopian dreams. They remained committed to the working-class philosophy, but favored humanism and democratic principles as a means of achieving their goals. Third were the scholars, generally creative and prominent individuals who suffered discrimination in Poland because of their liberal political outlook. Most of these were successful in finding positions in American universities where they pursued their respective specializations. The final group consisted of Polish students; young people seeking a better future. They knew little of pre-war Poland except through their education and cared little about pre-war political legacies.

Despite the differences in age and outlook, the post–1965 immigration nevertheless exhibited a number of general characteristics in common. As Polzin summarized them: they included a large number of intellectuals, professionals, white-collar workers, and scientists; they migrated primarily to find freedom; few expected to return to Poland; they included a high proportion of women and children; they were largely urban dwellers; they often brought money with them; they sought professional positions in competition with other Americans; they joined American rather than Polish ethnic organizations; they valued education; and they sought citizenship early.

The new arrivals were educated and assimilated quickly into American society. Although some rose rapidly to positions of prominence in scholarly and professional organizations, for the most part they did not mix well with the established Polonia which they often regarded as crude and uneducated. The new arrivals generally eschewed older Polonia organizations, creating their own or taking control of organizations established by the post-war exiles. Polonia, in turn, looked to the new arrivals to join their social clubs and take part in Polish American activities. When they did not, Polonians generally viewed the new arrivals as distant and selfish, feeling that, as earlier Polish Americans had about the post-war immigrants, they expected to "get ahead" too quickly without "paying their dues."

The 1970 Census reported 2,437,938 people claiming Polish as their mother tongue including 670,335 Poles of native parentage. The former figure increased slightly from 2,416,000 in 1940. A study by the Census Bureau in 1971 reported that 5,000,000 people claimed both parents to be of Polish origin. Yet, the question that bedevils those who conduct research on Polonia during the Progressive Era still remains today—how do we count Polish Americans? Should we consider anyone descended from one or more Polish immigrants? Or should we only consider those who identify with Polish heritage and culture? Depending upon the answer to that question, Polonia can be estimated to include anywhere from 4,000,000 to 15,000,000 people.

The census of 1980 attempted to answer a number of questions relating to ethnicity, including in its questionnaire an opportunity for estimating the number of people who identified themselves as descended from Polish heritage. Based upon responses to questions on ethnic self-identification, the census projected 8,228,037 people with Polish ethnicity. By 1990 this number jumped to 9,366,106, the sixth largest ethnic group in the United States and 3.8 percent of the total population, with the largest concentrations in the Northeast (6.9 percent of the population) and the Midwest (5.8 percent of the population).

Poles have, then, migrated to America in varying numbers and for various reasons during the last four centuries. In colonial times the movement was small and usually an individual decision based on economic and religious concerns. During the nineteenth century, political exiles formed the bulk of the migration in the first half of the century, followed by large numbers of economic immigrants between 1870 and 1914, the "great migration" that led to the permanent establishment of "Polonia" in America. The twentieth century brought severe legal restrictions on immigration, but the post–World War II era witnessed a gradual lessening of these limitations and an increase in the migration of both political and economic immigrants. The original patterns of settlement in the northeast gradually spread into the northwest, and those areas retain today the highest proportion of Polish Americans. Further, as migration patterns have changed to reflect a broader spectrum of Polish society in the twentieth century, and as educational and employment opportunities have increased during the same period for Polish Americans, the 1990 census indicates that today Polish Americans have made significant socioeconomic progress. By 1990, Polish Americans occupied a broad array of professional and managerial positions, as well as the their more traditional roles in manufacturing and service industries, ranked above the mean in education, above the mean in family incomes, and have become much more geographically dispersed than in previous eras.

The result, then, is that despite the variations in numbers and composition, Polish Americans today form at once a unique ethnic group while participating fully in the broad array of socioeconomic opportunities the United States has to offer. See also **Census**.— *James S. Pula*

SOURCES: Danuta Mostwin, "Post-World War II Polish Immigrants in the United States," *Polish American Studies*, Vol. XXVI, no. 2 (1969), 5–14; Dominic A. Pacyga, "Polish Immigration to the United States Before World War II: An Overview," *Polish American Studies*, Vol. XXXIX, no. 1 (1982), 28–37; Alina Baran, "Distribution of the Polish Origin Population in the USA," *Polish Western Affairs*, Vol. 17 (1976), 139–44; Stanislaus A. Blejwas, "Old and New Polonias: Tensions Within an Ethnic Community," *Polish American Studies*, Vol. XXXVIII, no. 2 (1981), 55–83; Victor R. Greene, "Pre–World War I Emigration to the United States: Motives and Statistics," *The Polish Review*, Vol. VI, no. 3 (1961), 45–68; Jerzy Lerski, "Polish Exiles in Mid–Nineteenth Century America," *Polish American Studies*, Vol. XXXI, no. 2 (1974), 30–42; Helena Znaniecka Lopata, "Polish Immigration to the United States of America: Problems of Estimation and Parameters," *The Polish Review*, Vol. XXI, no. 4 (1976), 85–107; James S. Pula, "American Immigration Policy and the Dillingham Commission," *Polish American Studies*, Vol. XXXVII, no. 1 (1980), 5–31; Joseph Wieczerzak, "Pre- and Proto-Ethnics: Poles in the United States Before the Immigration 'After Bread,'" *The Polish Review*, Vol. XXI, no. 3 (1976), 7–38.

Immigration Restriction, Effect on Polish Americans. The years 1880–1914 marked a period of unprecedented growth in immigration. As arrivals increased, "nativist" sentiments also grew with the rise of voices calling for legislation to limit both the number of new immigrants and the nations from which they were allowed to come. Repeated attempts to pass legislation requiring a literacy test or other restrictive requirements failed until after the end of World War I when increasing racism and anti–Catholicism, combined with the post-war Red Scare, resulted in the passage, on May 19, 1921, of the First Quota Act, the first legislation in American history designed specifically to limit European immigration. Its effect on Polish immigration and Polish Americans was dramatic. Between 1901 and 1920 an average of 625,629 people entered the United States each year. The First Quota Act of 1921 was designed both to limit total immigration to America, and to alter the composition of that immigration in favor of people whose origins lay in the nations of northwestern Europe. To accomplish the first goal, the law imposed a maximum of 357,803 people allowed to legally enter the country from outside the Western Hemisphere in any single year. In addition, each nationality group was given a separate quota based upon three percent of the number of people from that group residing in the United States in 1910. This provision addressed the second goal by discriminating directly against Southern and Eastern Europeans. It did so by using 1910 as a base year rather than 1920, thus eliminat-

ing from the formula by which the quotas were calculated the millions of people, approximately 75 percent of whom traced their origins to Southern and Eastern Europe, who arrived during the decade between census enumerations. Poland's quota was placed at 25,827, slightly more than a quarter of the number of Poles arriving each year before 1914.

In 1924, Congress made the quotas permanent with the National Origins Act, which also reduced the total number of immigrants per year by more than half from 357,803 to 164,667. To further guarantee the predominance of immigrants from northwestern Europe, the quota percentage of each nationality was reduced from three percent to two percent, while the base year was moved from 1910 to 1890. This was a clear attempt to lessen the impact, and therefore the quota, of immigrants from Southern and Eastern Europe who entered en-masse after 1890. For Poland, this resulted in a reduction of its annual quota to only 5,982, some 25 percent of the first quota, and only about six percent of the number of annual arrivals in the decade prior to the beginning of World War I in 1914. The final quota established in 1927 recognized Poles as the fifth largest group in the United States behind those from Germany, Great Britain, Ireland, and Italy, and assigned them a quota of 6,524. The result was that fewer Poles came to the United States during the period between 1921 and 1940 than came in any single year between 1900 and 1914.

The drastic reduction in Polish immigration served not only to cut off the external source of immigrants used to perpetuate the urban ethnic communities, but also cut off direct access to cultural renewal from Poland. In a seminal essay on historical and collective memory, the French sociologist Maurice Halbwachs distinguished three social frameworks that most influenced collective memory — family, religion, and nation. Collective memory is, of course, fundamental to the maintenance of the history and traditions that define group membership. The limitation on Polish immigration deprived Polonia's vibrant ethnic communities of the steady flow of immigrants necessary to maintain vigorous community bonds in each of these social frameworks. Even before the effects of these acts became apparent, the Rev. **Lucyan Bójnowski** warned: "In a few decades, unless immigration from Poland is upheld, Polish American life will disappear, and we shall be like a branch cut off from its trunk."

The family is considered the fundamental unit of socialization for individuals. With the advent of the immigration quotas, temporary family separations became extended, or often permanent. Poles in America were left with the choice of staying in the United States or returning to Poland to visit family and friends, but for those who were not U.S. citizens the trip back to Poland carried with it the uncertainty of whether they would be allowed back into the United States upon their return. Direct contact between families suffered, sometimes resulting in lengthy periods of time between visits or depriving relatives of the ability to come to America to join earlier immigrants. In some cases it led to permanent separations. For Poles, who, research has shown, greatly valued extended family relationships, this situation weakened family bonds while also resulting in a sense of despondency over the loss of some, or all, of the primary support group.

Religion was also a significant factor in the lives of Poles and Polish immigrants in America during the first half of the twentieth century. Upon arrival in America, one of the first collective actions immigrants took was to collect money for a church and lobby the local bishop for the creation of an ethnic parish. But religious life in America was different than it had been in Poland. In the Old Country the local priests and the Roman Catholic hierarchy consisted of fellow Poles. While they may not always have been in concert in their priorities, in the face of foreign occupation during the partitions the church was generally supportive of Polish aspirations to preserve their unique history and traditions. The Church supported Polish culture, often acting as an underground educational, cultural and political institution that sided with the Poles against the efforts of the occupiers to replace Polish culture with their own. By World War I, Polish patriotism and Roman Catholicism had to some extent merged into the collective definition of what it was to be Polish. But in America, Poles found a very different situation with *their* church dominated by the Irish, along with a few Germans. The fundamental institution that formed a building block of what it was to be Polish in the Old Country was in America more often a force promoting assimilation.

For Poles in America, it was vitally important for the preservation of their culture and heritage against what they perceived as the denationalizing forces of American secular schools and society, that sufficient numbers of Polish priests be available to lead Polish ethnic parishes. Immigration restriction had two significant influences on this crucial element of what it was to be Polish. In the first instance, the restrictive quotas severely limited the number of Polish priests available to serve parishes in America, which not only caused a

vacuum in ethnic leadership but also severed the force of vital cultural regeneration that new immigrant priests brought with them from the homeland. Second, the restriction of immigration placed a premium on the training of Polish American priests to serve ethnic parishes, promoting a decided change in leadership from priests born and educated in Poland to those born and educated in America. The decade of the 1920s was particularly pivotal as a new generation of Polish American clergy grew to maturity. The younger clergy were born and raised in America, preparing them to work with greater understanding and sensitivity among **Polonia**'s youth of the second and third generations. While serving their parishes well, American-born priests were by definition less able to dispense contemporary Polish culture to their flocks and more susceptible to the influences of the American environment in which they were raised. Restriction, then, led to acceleration in the transformation of parish leadership from Poles to Polish Americans, and eventually Americans of Polish descent, weakened the bonds of tradition in the face of the forces of Americanization.

There is a significant difference that scholars have recognized which separates the preservation and interpretation of an experience that one has actually lived from one that is passed on by word-of-mouth memory or some other representation. The restriction of immigration essentially disconnected the source of national contemporary consciousness that would otherwise have enriched the continuing conversations that shaped Polonia's consciousness as a group and its unique world view. Gradually, with the elimination of new arrivals, lived memories of Poland gave way to the vague memories of parents, grandparents and others. Increasingly, Polonia's image of Poland became fixed, delimited by the indistinct images of the nineteenth century agricultural villages their ancestors left rather than the developing modern nation that Poland was moving toward during the interwar period. Over time, the quotas that virtually severed the sustaining flow of cultural regeneration also skewed the socialization of Polish American youth toward assimilation. The end result would be an ethnic group no longer bound by the strong ethnic social structures of the immigrant generation, but fourth and fifth generations more concerned with ethnic symbols than with the culture they once represented.

The results of this can be seen in the post–World War II years when cultural differences between new immigrants and the ethnic Polonians arose because of differing needs. As Mary Erdmans has explained, while the new

arrivals needed economic assistance and employment, Polish Americans needed cultural renewal through attachment to Poland and the transmission of ethnic customs. As consequence, ethnic organizations oriented toward meeting ethnic needs were not well positioned to meet the needs of the new post-war immigrants.—*James S. Pula*

Sources: James S. Pula, "United States Immigration Policy and the Dillingham Commission," *Polish American Studies*, XXXVII, No. 1 (1980), 5–31; James S. Pula, "'A Branch Cut Off From Its Trunk'—The Affects of Immigration Restriction on American Polonia," *Polish American Studies*, Vol. LXI, no. 1 (Spring 2004), 39–50; James S. Pula, "The Effects of U.S. Government Policy on Polish Americans, 1900–1925," in James S. Pula and M. B. Biskupski, eds., *The Polish Diaspora. Vol. II: Selected Essays from the Fiftieth Anniversary International Congress of the Polish Institute of Arts and Sciences of America* (Boulder, CO: East European Monographs, 1993), 149–57; Adam Urbanski, "Immigration Restriction and the Polish American Press: the Response of *Wiadomości Codzienne*, 1921–1924," *Polish American Studies*, Vol. 28, no. 2 (1971), 5–21.

Independentism (religious). As Polish and other Catholic immigration to America began its dramatic increase during the 1880s, the Church hierarchy gradually began to recognize that it would need to increase its efforts among these largely non–English speaking groups if it was going to retain their religious loyalty. Organized labor, fraternal groups, and other secular organizations vied for immigrant allegiance along with a variety of other religious denominations. In fact, the Rev. **Wacław Kruszka** estimated that "leakage" to these other groups, or simply to declining interest in religion in general, cost the Church as many as one-third of immigrants who had been Catholic in Europe. At the Third Plenary Council of Roman Catholic prelates in America in November 1884 Church authorities attempted to solidify their control over immigrant communities by decreeing that all American Catholics "should educate their children in parochial schools in order to protect them from Protestant and secular influences." Another policy adopted by the Church to maintain its influence over the ethnic communities was the creation of "national parishes." The Catholic hierarchy in America was organized into parishes and diocese on a geographic basis. Thus, the national parish was an exception; but it was an exception with some precedent. So-called "non-territorial" parishes were first sanctioned in the Fourth Lateran Council in the thirteenth century and later reaffirmed by the Council of Trent in the sixteenth century. Under this principle parishes could be organized according to the "particular character" of the people. In America, the "particular character" was usually language. By 1912 there were almost 1,600 "official" national parishes including 346 German, 336 Polish, and 214 Italian. Through these and other efforts, the hierarchy expected to stem the loss of the faithful to secular organizations or non–Catholic religious groups.

Although the national parish, when staffed by Polish-speaking priests, appealed to most Polish immigrants who retained religious faith, there remained many who were not satisfied with the largely symbolic nature of the national parish. Church authorities exerted strict control over the parishes, demanding title to all property, assigning priests, and otherwise denying meaningful lay participation in decision-making. This conflicted with the Poles' concept of lay involvement and the ideals of democracy and property ownership they equated with America. In partitioned Poland the Roman Catholic Church proved both a unifying factor and a haven for the expression of Polish nationalism. In America, immigrants unfamiliar with the language or culture of their new environment relied upon their religious convictions and institutions as a stabilizing element in their lives, but they often found that in practice the Irish and German bishops that controlled the Church were not at all sympathetic to their traditional cultural expression. In Poland there was a tradition of lay involvement in the founding of parishes. The *ius patronatus* was a long-established "right of patronage" under which the gentry who endowed a parish might nominate a pastor to that parish. Although this right did not directly involve the parishioners, it was well-known among Polish immigrants and established a precedent of lay involvement in parish affairs that they expected would be honored in America as well. Since most of the early Polish parishes in America were begun by lay initiatives rather than by religious authorities, the significant number of Poles believed that the parishioners, as the collective benefactor of the parish, should enjoy the same privileges that accrued to gentry benefactors in Poland.

Most of the Poles' complaints involved their desire for democracy and equality in parish and Church governance, which often took the form of expecting that lay trustees would be responsible for parish finances, holding title to property purchased with the parishioners' money, and exercising decision-making authority on other administrative matters. For their part, Polish priests, often frustrated by lack of career mobility in the national parishes, voiced their own complaints over inequities in assignments and promotions. These grievances generally crystallized around the demand for appointment of Polish bishops.

When the appeals of Polish Catholics authorized by a congress of their representatives that convened in Buffalo in 1901 were ignored by the Vatican, the sentiment for what came to be called "independentism" increased dramatically. While most Poles attempted to work within the Church to secure equality, by the mid–1890s a serious movement toward the establishment of "independent" parishes had already begun. Early dissent appeared in Chicago and Buffalo but soon spread to other communities as lay trusteeship and the appointment of Polish bishops became the focal issues representing equality and Polish nationalism. Church authorities responded quickly and dramatically against the "independents," equating "lay rights" with heresy and labeling them pagans, heathens, atheists, revolutionaries, lawbreakers, and worse. In a concerted effort to crush growing dissent, bishops used discipline and excommunication to enforce obedience from parishioners and priests alike.

Leadership in the independent movement initially rested with Revs. **Stefan Kamiński** of Buffalo and **Antoni Kozłowski** in Chicago. Kamiński, a former Franciscan, began leading the independent Holy Rosary Parish in Buffalo in 1896 and was consecrated bishop two years later by the independent Archbishop Joseph René Vilatte. From 1898 until his death in 1911, Kamiński edited and published the weekly newspaper *Warta* (The Watch). By 1907 he claimed the allegiance of 23 parishes with between 75,000 and 100,000 parishioners, no doubt an inflated number. Kozłowski was also a Catholic priest, but he assumed the leadership of the independent All Saints Parish in Chicago in 1895, the first parish in what Kozłowski labeled the "Independent Polish Catholic Church of America." In 1897, Bishop Edouard Herzog, the Swiss Old Catholic bishop of Berne, Switzerland, consecrated Kozłowski bishop of the "Polish Catholic Diocese of Chicago." He was rewarded with excommunication from the Roman Catholic Church.

With the relatively early deaths of Kamiński and Kozłowski, leadership of the independent movement crystallized around the Rev. **Franciszek Hodur**. As his support increased, Hodur formally established the **Polish National Catholic Church** which retained much of the Roman Catholic tradition and belief, including the hierarchical church organization, but granted authority to local parish councils and made other changes to appeal to the nationalist feelings that spawned its development.

Ironically, while membership in the Polish National Catholic Church never rose above five percent of the Poles in America, and the Roman Catholic hierarchy condemned them as heretics, the same hierarchy eventually began to respond to some of the issues that inspired the original independent movements. In 1952 the Apostolic Constitution *Exsul Familia* guaranteed, for the first time, "the rights of immigrants to proper pastoral care in their own language and traditions," while Vatican II sanctioned the use of the vernacular in the Mass. For further information, see the entries for the individuals and topics highlighted in bold font in this entry.—*James S. Pula*

SOURCES: Hieronim Kubiak, *The Polish National Catholic Church in the United States of America from 1897 to 1980* (Kraków: Państwowe Wydawnictwo Naukowe, 1982); Laurence J. Orzell, "Curious Allies: Bishop Antoni Kozłowski and the Episcopalians," *Polish American Studies*, Vol. 40, no. 2 (1983), 36–58; James B. Earley, "Toward an Understanding of the Historical Context: Roman Catholics and Polish National Catholics in Conflict," *PNCC Studies*, Vol. 18 (1997), 7–23; Joseph W. Wieczerzak, "Setting a Stage: Independent Antecedents of the Polish National Catholic Church," *PNCC Studies*, Vol. 19 (1998), 69–82; Daniel Buczek, "Equality of Right: Polish American Bishops in the American Hierarchy," *Polish American Studies*, Vol. 62, no. 1 (2005), 5–28; Robert F. Trisco, "The Holy See and the First Independent Catholic Church in the United States," in Nelson H. Minnich, Robert B. Eno, and Robert F. Trisco, eds., *Studies in Catholic History in Honor of John Tracy Ellis* (Wilmington, DE: M. Glazier, 1985), 175–238; William S. Shea, "The Polish Independent Church Movement in the United States" (Boston: Unpublished Ph.D. dissertation, Boston College, 1934); James S. Pula, "Polish American Catholics: A Case Study in Cultural Determinism," *U.S. Catholic Historian*, Vol. 27, no. 3 (2009), 1–19.

Ingraham, Laura (b. Glastonbury, Connecticut, June 19, 1964). Attorney, journalist, political commentator. Ingraham graduated from Dartmouth College where she became the first female editor for the prestigious *Dartmouth Review*. After earning a B.A. in Russian and English from Dartmouth College (1985), she worked as a speechwriter in the Reagan White House, as well as with the Department of Transportation and the Department of Education. She later earned a J.D. degree from the University of Virginia Law School (1991) where she was Notes Editor of the *Virginia Law Review*. After graduating, she served as clerk to Supreme Court Justice Clarence Thomas and for Judge Ralph Winter in the U.S. Court of Appeals for the Second Circuit. She became a defense attorney with the firm of Skadden, Arps, Slate, Meagher and Flom in New York before venturing into television with a show on MSNBC called *Watch It!* which was canceled. She then moved to radio with *The Laura Ingraham Show* in 2001, making her one of the few female conservative talk show hosts in a field dominated by men. By 2008 she was rated the number six talk show host in America and was making regular appearances on Fox television's *The O'Reilly Fac-*

tor and other television and radio talk shows. Ingraham is the author of *Shut Up and Sing: How the Elites from Hollywood, Politics and the U.N. Are Subverting America* (2003), *The Hillary Trap: Looking for Power in All the Wrong Places* (2005), and *Power to the People* (2007). As a conservative, Ingraham espouses traditional values such as education and patriotism. Among her awards are the Judy Jarvis Memorial Award for Outstanding Contributions by a Woman on Talk Radio (2008).—*Cheryl A. Pula*

Sources: Jed Babbin, "Laura Ingraham is Fired Up," *Human Events*, Vol. 63, no. 31 (September 17, 2007), 15; Katy Bachman, "Pundit Ingraham Gets Evening Slot," *Media Week*, Vol. 11, no. 17 (April 23, 2001), 14.

Interethnic Relations, Polish American. Interethnic relations can be defined as various types of contact and interaction between two or more ethnic groups, which have impact on the ethnic identity formation, assimilation, directions of community development, and the general ethnic experience. Such contacts may include instances of both conflict and cooperation in their various degrees and manifestations, and can be traced on individual, as well as group, local as well as national levels. Interethnic relations change with the passage of time and generations, and internal and external conditions.

Historians and social scientists interested in issues of immigration and ethnicity have always noted contact and interaction among ethnic groups, frequently stemming from their residence in common areas, especially in urban locations. Most studies on **Polonia**, while acknowledging Polish immigrants' contacts with others within neighborhoods and places of work, paid little attention to any specific aspects of such interactions, unless it focused on conflict, for example between Polonia's parishes and Irish-American Roman Catholic hierarchy. Labor historians emphasized working class cooperation, which cut through ethnic lines, and stressed more issues of class than ethnicity. Over the last three decades, the problem of interethnic relations gained more attention. In some cases, experiences of several ethnic groups sharing space and work were generalized, as evidenced by Ewa Morawska's study of Slavic and Hungarian immigrants in Johnstown, Pennsylvania, or Victor Greene on Slavic and other miners in the anthracite region of Pennsylvania. Other works aimed at contrasting and comparing, for example studies by John Bodnar, Roger Simon, and Michael P. Weber on Blacks, Italians, and Poles in Pittsburgh; Matthew Frye Jacobson on Jews, Irish, and Poles; and Victor Greene on Poles and Lithuanians.

Far fewer studies focused on the direct engagements between two or more groups. Notable exceptions here are a ground-breaking article on Poles and their neighbors in industrial Chicago by **Dominic Pacyga**; Dorota Praszałowicz's study of Polish American and German American relations in Milwaukee, Wisconsin; and studies on Polish American–Jewish American relations in North America. Despite remarkable scholarly potential of this inquiry the state of our knowledge about relationships between Polish immigrants and other ethnic groups continues to generate more questions than answers.

As Dorota Praszałowicz and others argue, migrations from the Polish lands were not a journey from an ethnically homogenous society (nation-state) to a world of cultural plurality. Instead, migration of different ethnic groups from partitioned Poland was a type of "joint venture," in which if one ethnic group initiated migration from a mixed population territory, others usually followed them. At the destination, migrants from the same area often settled close to each other. Chain migration then crossed national boundaries. Following this pattern, Germans, Jews, Ruthenians (Ukrainians), Lithuanians, Czechs, and Slovaks became the closest neighbors to Polish immigrants, sharing an historical past, and often language, traditions, or religion, which facilitated positive interaction. However, common Old Country experience often meant transplantation of hostilities, resentments and conflicts, which brought instant tensions in the New World, causing animosity and deliberate distance.

Polish immigrants did not share historical past or geographical location with others, with whom they lived, worked, and worshipped in the United States, for example their fellow Catholics: the Irish, Italians, and French Canadians; fellow Southern Slavs: Croatians, Serbs, Bulgarians, and Slovenes as well as Hungarians; and fellow industrial workers: African Americans, Mexicans, Puerto Ricans and other Hispanics. By default, their attitudes towards these groups were shaped in the new American context.

The balance of this entry will review major themes of American Polonia's interethnic relations, without attempting to present separate histories of other ethnic groups or indulge in the exhaustive comparing and contrasting of their experiences. Instead, the focus shall firmly remain on the aspects of contact and interaction. The issue of assimilation and retention of ethnic identity vis-à-vis larger American society and the WASPs will be excluded, as it is already discussed under the heading of "ethnic identity and assimilation."

Church

Polish immigrants coming to the U.S. since the mid-nineteenth century were mainly Roman Catholic. The network of parishes that they established became the center of their community life and fulfilled both religious and social functions. Since the Roman Catholic Church in Poland had been instrumental in the struggle against foreign domination and denationalization of the Polish people in each of the three partitions of Poland, Polish immigrants in America expected that the church would continue its role as a protector of their faith as well as their ethnicity. Since early in the nineteenth century, the hierarchy of the American Catholic Church had been controlled by the Irish bishops and priests, giving it a specific Irish character. By the end of the nineteenth century, the Irish bishops became the most fervent Americanizers of their multi-ethnic Catholic flock, often in response to the perceived need to strengthen the church vis-à-vis dominant Protestant denominations. The clash between Polish immigrant parishioners and priests and the Irish American hierarchy became unavoidable.

Polish immigrants detested the church's tight hold on the parish finances and deeds to the land purchased by immigrant money, as well as the church structures built with the sweat and sacrifices of their communities. They demanded greater participation in parish government and affairs. They also wanted to keep the Polish character of their Catholicism through the appointment of Polish pastors and the celebration of Polish feasts. Despite the fact that Poles were one of the largest Catholic groups, they had no representation among the bishops. Polish immigrants felt that the Irish bishops discriminated against them on the grounds of their nationality and protested that the "Ajrysze" were deliberately unresponsive to their needs.

At the turn of the century the campaign for not just representation but equality within the church spurred much public debate as well as efforts at intervention in the Vatican. Although the appointment of Bishop **Paul Rhode** as an auxiliary bishop of Chicago in 1908 largely ended this period of direct conflict, the tensions between Polish immigrants and the Church resulted in the wide-spread movement for independent parishes and eventually establishment of the **Polish National Catholic Church** (PNCC). The Americanization pressure, however, continued. Since 1916, and into the 1920s, the Church proceeded with the centralization and standardization of the curriculum for parish schools, steering them away from their original ethnic character. As historian James R. Barrett notes, second generation youth often found itself in parish schools that "conferred an implicit Irish mentality" and tended to "Hibernicize" them through the influence of the Irish nuns. In 1931, *Przebudzenie* lamented: "Everyone of us Poles understands that in the Irish parochial schools our children are being systematically deprived of their Polish soul, and finally yield to the process of Irishization. But this is not all. The Irish in America were never friendly towards us and they never will be. They consider themselves a higher and more privileged group here and look upon us with contempt."

At the same time these parish schools, which still taught Polish curriculum, frequently reinforced negative ethnic stereotypes, which traveled with the immigrants as part of their cultural baggage of biases and prejudices acquired in the old country. As historian Adam Walaszek documents, textbooks used in parish schools described both Poland's neighbors and other nationalities, including Germans, Russians, Ukrainians, Swedes, Turks, Czechs, Jews, and Hungarians, as enemies, cruel, crude, and untrustworthy. This negative image of the "other" was balanced by the unquestionably positive image of Poles and Poland in general, aimed at rising national feelings in American Polonia. Although the context for those negative images was the history of Poland, one must wonder what impact this depiction had on the second generation Polish American youth and their relationship to the members of other ethnic groups which they encountered in America.

The church provided also a fruitful ground for the development of more positive relationships with other ethnic groups. In turn of the century Cleveland, before they organized their own national parishes, Poles and Russyns initially attended the neighborhood Slovak church. In Willimantic, Connecticut, Poles, who were never as numerous as the Irish, shared the church with them, as well as with the Italians, and, for a time, also French Canadians. Lithuanians, who generally arrived later than Poles, often joined Polish parishes, before they too established their own. Even in decisively Polish parishes, the membership had never been a full one hundred percent Polish.

Milwaukee, Wisconsin, is a good example of evolving interethnic relations between Poles and Germans. When Polish immigrants began to arrive in Milwaukee in the 1860s, they settled on the fringes of the German community and attended the only Roman Catholic parish in this area, the German parish of Holy Trinity, in existence since 1849. The parish welcomed Polish newcomers and the German pastor often invited priests who knew the Polish language to preach there, even though most Poles were familiar with the German language. When in 1866, a first Polish parish was established, the German bishop gave it his blessing, and Holy Trinity's German parishioners participated in the opening festivities and organized a charitable concert. They also shared their cemetery with the Polish congregation. After the Polish parish had built a school, its pastor organized it following the German example and invited teachers from the German order of School Sisters of Notre Dame.

Polish immigrants in Milwaukee also attended other German Catholic churches in the area. Thanks to the pluralistic policy of German bishop Henni, Catholics from different ethnic groups actively supported each other's parishes and participated in celebrations and events such as the blessing of cornerstones, blessing of new church buildings or banners of parish societies. Poles generally modeled both their parish organizational structure and style of celebrations on the German examples. The School Sisters of Notre Dame admitted Polish girls and prepared them to teach in Polish parish schools. Next to Poles, Irish and Czech girls also studied in the order. Polish men attended German St. Francis Seminary, where they had an opportunity to nurture Polish language and culture in a separate student society. Such friendly relationships lasted till the last decade of the nineteenth century.

Praszałowicz ascribes the worsening of Polish-German relations in turn-of-the-century Milwaukee to the increase of national feelings both among the Germans and Poles, in Europe as in America. Much of the tensions played out within the church. The German order of School Sisters of St. Francis, which also admitted Polish girls, began to discriminate against them. The conflict resulted in the creation of the separate Polish order: **Sisters of St. Joseph of the Third Order of St. Francis** in 1902. The rising tensions were most likely further fueled by the Rev. **Wacław Kruszka**'s campaign for Polish rights in the church and for a Polish bishop, which he had pursued since the 1890s. Due to the fact that the Milwaukee hierarchy was controlled not by Irish, but by German bishops, the campaign acquired distinctively anti–German accents.

Instances of both cooperation and hostility also characterized the relationships between German immigrants in Chicago, and Polish immigrants, mostly from the Poznania region of Poland, who initially settled near them, sharing their churches and other public spaces. But with the increased influx of Kashubes, the neighborhood around St. Boniface parish on the Northwest Side of the city began to change its ethnic composition from German to Polish, and the original German inhabitants started to abandon this area and moved farther northwest.

The relationships between Poles and Lithuanians in America also often developed within the framework of the church and parish structure. As historian Victor Greene notices, the two groups possessed a very intimate relationship stemming from centuries of common history in Europe. Lithuanian immigrants, who tended to immigrate to the U.S. somewhat later than their Polish counterparts, often settled either near or within Polish communities, attended mixed Polish-Lithuanian churches, and participated in the life of the community in no small part thanks to their command of the Polish language. Intermarriage was common, and many Lithuanians were either Polonized or Polonophiles. The conflict between Polish pastors and Lithuanian patriot-priest the Rev. Burba in Shenandoah and Plymouth, Pennsylvania, was but one of many serious incidents of tensions. By 1890, the Lithuanian community became the battle ground between nationalists and religionists over the predominant elements of their ethnic identity, reminiscent of the similar conflict, which raged in the Polish community a decade earlier. The Lithuanian nationalists often used anti–Polish rhetoric to create clear borders for their own national identity.

But according to William L. Wolkovich-Valkavičius, despite some perceptions to the opposite, the tensions within Polish-Lithuanian parishes and between Polish and Lithuanian parishes in New England did not carry the marks of serious and long-lasting conflicts fueled by conflicting nationalist aspirations. Instead, most of the tensions were provoked either by the difficult personalities of individual pastors, or by intra-group frictions. On the other hand, there were frequent instances of cooperation within mixed parishes and between Polish and Lithuanian parishes, as parishioners moved from one church to another without a problem, and pastors strove to accommodate the needs of different parts of their congregations. Concluding, Wolkovich-Valkavičius states that there is "no proof of any all-embracing or lasting tensions among Lithuanians and Poles of New England — only embarrassing squabbles."

The Polish National Catholic Church became involved in a number of the interethnic outreach activities, which sought to support independentist movements and churches among other ethnic groups. For example, in

1915, an Italian independent parish in Hackensack, NJ, and its pastor Father Antonio Julio Lenza, switched its allegiance from the Old Catholic bishop to the PNCC, prompting Bishop **Francis Hodur** to make visits to the parish, bless the buildings, administer communion, and preside over church celebrations. Oppression by Irish and German bishops was quoted as a common ground for the collaboration. By the mid–1920s, Bishop Hodur extended his jurisdiction and relationships to several more independent Italian parishes. Similarly, the PNCC developed links to the Hungarian National Catholic parish, as well as some Lithuanian, Slovak, and Czech parishes.

Non-Catholic Poles also attempted to build coalitions with other ethnic groups in order to withstand the pressures of American Protestant denominations. For example, Polish Baptists cooperated with both Ukrainian and Russian Baptist conferences. Since 1917, Poles studied in the Slavic Baptist seminary, the Missionary Training School in Chicago, where they constituted one of the five different nationalities. Polish Lutherans often attended German Lutheran churches, where they worshipped predominantly in German. Chicago-based Rev. Paul Fox is an example of a Progressive Polish Protestant leader, whose activities involved close collaboration with many ethnic groups.

WORK AND LABOR UNIONS

The majority of Polish immigrants who arrived in America before World War I became industrial workers, employed in large urban centers on the East Coast and in the Midwest. They worked side by side with other immigrants, who joined the ranks of the American working class. Poles, Lithuanians, Slovaks, and Hungarians dominated Pennsylvania's anthracite region. Poles, Italians, and African Americans worked hand-in-hand in the steel mills in Pittsburgh. The New England textile industry employed Polish, Irish, and French Canadian workers. In New York Mills, Poles worked together with French Canadian, English, Italian, Syrian, and other workers. The steel mills and packing houses of Chicago employed Poles, Germans, Irish, Czechs, Slovaks, Russians, Ukrainians, and African Americans. In the garment industry as well as construction and many smaller companies, Polish workers shared the workplace with Jews and Italians, Croats, Serbs, and Slovenes.

As Ewa Morawska documents in the case of Cambria mills in Johnstown, Pennsylvania, employers often adopted an informal policy of chain hiring, putting workers of the same ethnic background into homogenous groupings. The author explains that "Natural divisiveness among the immigrants who spoke different tongues and sought each other's familiar company were [sic] deliberately utilized by the Cambria management in its efforts to strengthen control over the workforce." The excuse of efficiency (the boss needed to know just one language) covered up discrimination of unskilled workers, who found it impossible to advance beyond the boundaries of their employment in an ethnic labor gang. The Immigration Commission which investigated employment relations in Johnstown industries concluded that promotion options for some ethnic groups were very limited and "[with some exceptions], the Southern and Eastern European races have gone into the skilled occupations only where there were not enough Americans, English, Welsh, Germans, Irish, and Swedes to supply the demand for that sort of labor."

Purposeful employment of different nationalities in separate departments was aimed also at deepening their differences and making it harder for them to organize in labor unions. Some bosses even spread rumors to fan what they perceived as natural hostility among nationalities. The importation of strike breakers from a different ethnic group, often recruited from among the most recent arrivals, was also a tactic designed to "divide and conquer." In the 1880s, Polish immigrants themselves were sometimes used as scabs, and in 1883, in Bayonne, NJ, oil-refining industry Poles, Slovaks, and Ruthenians were hired to break the strike by American and Irish coopers. In later decades, Polish strikers in many locations battled Italian, French Canadian, or African American strike breakers.

In the case of Johnstown, Morawska also claims that sometimes workers of a particular ethnic group played the system of ethnic employment to their own advantage. First, it allowed them to secure employment for their countrymen, developing well-functioning kinship and friendship networks. Second, it sometimes made it possible for them to move around as a group in search of better opportunities. These benefits were outweighed by class interests which required the unity of workers reaching beyond religious and ethnic divisions. Despite some claims that ethnic differences were the main factor hampering the development of the American labor movement, there is ample evidence showing that workers from different nationalities fought together for their rights.

Victor Greene, who examined labor unrest in the anthracite region of Pennsylvania since the late 1880s and into the first decade of the twentieth century, saw collaboration of Polish, Lithuanian, Slovak, Hungarian, Czech, and Italian workers and miners in a series of strikes and demonstrations, which included the **Lattimer Massacre** of 1897. Entire communities of this ethnically diverse region participated in both decision making and support for the strikes. A famous example of the communal involvement became "Big Mary" Septak, a Polish woman who ran a local boarding house, and organized other Slavic women to attack and run off strike breakers. In the 1912 and 1916 strikes in New York Mills, Poles of Local 357 of the United Textile Workers led successful strikes, which brought together many different ethnicities. During the meetings held in a Polish-owned hall, speeches were given in Polish, French, Italian, Syrian, and English. The company's effort to alienate Poles from others failed, as did an attempt to introduce ethnic rivalry by bringing in Italian workers as strike-breakers. In turn of the century Chicago, large numbers of Poles and Lithuanians, both men and women, joined the Amalgamated Meat Cutter and Butcher Workmen, and struck together in 1904. On the other hand, when the Stockyards Labor Council organized locals along ethnic and racial lines during and after World War I, the labor movement collapsed, proving that multiethnic coalitions brought strength to the struggle.

While Poles bridged some ethnic divisions in order to fight for their rights as part of the American working class, they at the same time distanced themselves from other ethnic groups. In Lawrence, Massachusetts, Italians, Poles, Lithuanians, Russians, Ukrainians, Syrians, Franco-Belgians, Germans, and Jews held together during a grueling 16-week long strike in 1919, while better-paid English-speaking workers, as well as the Irish and French Canadians, and later smaller groups of Greeks, Portuguese, and Turks chose to return to work. The older and more established groups of skilled workers, such as the Welsh, Irish, English, Germans or Dutch were often seen as beneficiaries of favors, including higher pay, skilled positions, and opportunities for promotions. Out of their ranks came the lower management, bosses, and foremen, who occupied the other side of the barricade during labor disputes, as well as police and politicians.

These groups also produced labor leaders, who sometimes clashed with their multiethnic following or competed for influence within ethnic groups. As Pacyga documents, **John Kikulski**, a popular and powerful Polish labor leader in Chicago packinghouses, was murdered following his election as president of the Amalgamated Meat Cutters District No.

9. Polish public opinion blamed Kikulski's death on his Irish rivals within the union, and the Polish-language daily *Dziennik Chicagoski* (Chicago Daily News) commented that "This Pole was like salt in the eye of the Irish. Only after his death are the police looking for killers only because they must." In the end, the Irish-dominated police made no arrest in either Kikulski's murder or in another murder case, that of **Stanley Rokosz**, who succeeded Kikulski in his union position and was murdered less than a year later.

The socialists (see **Socialists, Polish American**), active within the Polish immigrant community called for unity above ethnic and religious divisions. As Adam Walaszek demonstrates for Cleveland, although the socialists in general had only a limited following within **Polonia**, in the 1890s, hundreds of Poles, Croats, and Slovaks took part in the organizational meeting of the Union of Polish Workers (Związek Robotników Polskich). Poles, Czechs, Hungarians, Italians, and others who enthusiastically welcomed Coxey's Army passing through the city, later listened to supportive speeches in many languages, including Polish. Polish socialist leaders cooperated with other socialists within the movement. In 1919, Poles together with Americans, Ukrainians, Jews, Russians, and Hungarians took part in riots organized by the Socialist Party in Cleveland. Similar examples of the grass-root cooperation existed in Milwaukee and Buffalo. The split among the Polish Socialists as well as their eventual demise as a viable center of influence came due to their attitude towards the U.S. participation in World War I and general directions of homeland politics.

During the Great Depression the CIO union drives resulted in Polish American workers joining the labor movement in large numbers. According to Lizbeth Cohen, the CIO consciously and systematically built the culture of unity among various ethnicities. The CIO leaders appointed workers of different backgrounds to their organizational teams and worked closely with representatives of ethnic communities, frequently holding union meetings in rented national halls. They prepared literature in many languages, used radio as their medium, and supported recreational events for families and sports teams. As Cohen emphasizes, "They sought just the right balance between acknowledging ethnic difference and articulating worker unity." However, while developing and strengthening their class consciousness through cooperation with other workers, Polish Americans did not abandon their ethnic attachments and their ethnic communities, which continued to be centers of their culture.

NEIGHBORHOODS, COMMUNITIES, ORGANIZATIONS

Most scholars of American history readily acknowledge that only rarely were urban neighborhoods ethnically homogenous. In reality, many different ethnic groups shared geographical space of ethnic neighborhoods, sometimes making them look like "crazy quilts" of ethnicities. We also know that chain migration as well as time of arrival and economic opportunities often brought the European neighbors together; once in America they settled in each other's proximity. The aforementioned development of mixed parishes illustrates this trend.

Based on his investigation of ethnic Cleveland, Adam Walaszek finds that "The lifestyle in ethnic neighborhoods in the late nineteenth and early twentieth centuries promoted interaction among residents, especially within their own ethnic groups, but also with neighbors of other nationalities. One-story wooden houses often had porches and verandas jutting out into the street, and also little gardens where people met, talked, gossiped, and drank beer on Sundays. Empty lots afforded space for social meetings, particularly in times of tensions and crisis. Public wells and water taps were popular meeting and discussion places for women and the young. The saloon was the magnet for men, serving as a neighborhood rendezvous, a political center, [and] a plebeian "club." Saloon keepers served clientele of many nationalities, as did shop keepers and owners of small businesses. Businesses advertised in ethnic newspapers, and later on ethnic radio programs.

The neighborhood national halls and other buildings were often rented for cultural, union, and social events organized by ethnic associations, and served entire neighborhoods. Ethnic presses of many languages carried announcements about events and encouraged neighborhood participation. Neighbors watched and sometimes joined parades and processions crossing their streets. Representatives of ethnic societies and organizations spoke during cultural events of other ethnic groups, and mixed orchestras, bands, and choirs performed. In Detroit's **Hamtramck**, the Polish language served as a kind of *lingua franca*, with multiethnic audiences listening to Polish radio programs and reading Polish-language press. A popular weekly *Ameryka-Echo* published correspondence from Polish-speaking Ukrainians, Jews, Lithuanians, and Germans in their letters to the editor section.

Some organizations by design had mixed membership, such as the local Slavic Alliance of Cleveland. Fraternals often allowed membership of individuals from other ethnic groups. On the national level the **Polish National Alliance** encouraged membership of Jews, Ruthenians, and Lithuanians, or all immigrants whose ethnic roots were in historical Poland, but the number of non–Polish members remained very limited. Similarly, fraternals on a more local level also sought multiethnic membership. The Association of Poles in the State of Ohio (Związek Polaków w Stanie Ohio, ZPwO), a breakaway group from the PNA established in 1895, saw as its goal to bring together "Poles and Americans of Polish extraction, as well as Lithuanians, Russins, Slovaks, and [other] immigrants and their offspring if they or their ancestors came from the territory of the Polish Kingdom before the partitions." In 1903, group 26 of the ZPwO included 19 Lithuanians. Two other Polish organizations in Cleveland, one insurance-based and the other faith-based, admitted to the membership Slavic and Lithuanian neighbors of Poland. In Minneapolis, the Harmony Society was established in 1884, and shortly affiliated with the PNA. As **William Galush** notes, although its constitution provided for membership of other local Slavs, such as Slovaks and Rusins, the reality of the multiethnic membership was vastly different: "Within a couple of months over fifty men enrolled, a few non–Poles among them. But since the Harmony Society, like most lodges, espoused a fervent Polish patriotism and never elected non–Poles to an officer post, there were significant disincentives for their continued membership. As the numbers of Ruthenians and Slovaks grew, they set up their own ethnically-enclosed societies. Multi-ethnic fraternals seldom persisted despite lip-service in constitutional provisions, more a tribute to Polish insularity than antagonism to others."

Some Polish women who resided in large urban centers had an opportunity to mingle with others through Progressive agencies, such as settlement houses. A good example of an active settlement house, which brought together immigrant women of many different nationalities, was run by Mary Eliza McDowell in the Back of the Yards in Chicago at the turn of the century. McDowell also headed the University Women's Settlement Club, established in 1896, which had eight female vice-presidents, each representing a different ethnic group, including Polish. The women engaged in a variety of improvement programs, holding meetings in English as well as Polish, Czech, and German. In Cleveland Polish and Ukrainian women attended the Broadway Mothers Club, while Harvard Community Club and the University Settlement House brought together Poles, Germans, Italians, Irish, and Slovenes.

If one was to focus solely on friendly neighborhood cooperation, the image of a very idyllic ethnic neighborhood would emerge. It certainly was not always the case. Although it is important to acknowledge positive ethnic interactions within what James Barrett terms a "hybrid ethnic working-class culture," we also need to see conflict and division. Not all neighborhood interactions were friendly; in some cases much hostility was created, as in New York Mills where Polish children were regularly harassed by Welsh kids. In larger urban centers youth gangs carved up their ethnic "turfs" and battled outsiders who attempted to cross the imaginary boundaries. The early Irish gangs became models for later Polish gang activity, and eventually "integrated Poles into broader 'white' gangs," through which "the Irish and other earlier immigrants conveyed a racialized vision of the city with elaborate racial distinctions embodied in racist language and repertories of behavior." According to John Radzilowski, Polish gangs in Chicago were involved in fighting with Jewish, Greek, Irish, Italian, and Mexican gangs, but neither more nor less than other ethnic gangs, for whom "it was proximity, rather than specific ethnic characteristics, that mattered the most." James Barrett also claims that "Poles and other later immigrants, who might have come with all their own prejudices but little awareness of American racial conventions, modeled the Irish hostility toward and conflict with African Americans.... When Mexican immigrants entered the Stockyards and the South Chicago steel mill district in large numbers in the 1920s, they met violent resistance from Polish street gangs who chased them out of playgrounds, a frequent location for ethnic and racial violence, and off neighborhood streets," again copying Irish gangs' actions, considered "standard bearers of Americanization."

Unlike their immigrant parents, Polish American children who grew up in the United States, spoke fluent or almost fluent English, and attended mixed parish schools or public schools, had many more opportunities to interact with peers from different nationalities. They played together in neighborhood streets, parks, and swimming pools. They attended sport events, such as baseball games, and created mixed sport teams. In the 1920s, when Polonia's second generation matured, the siren call of popular mass culture lured them to places of youth entertainment, where they could interact with others of different nationalities, although "dance halls and pavilions brought with them sexual dangers and the

great taboo of intermarriage." Still, despite the growing area of potential mingling, throughout the interwar decades membership in ethnic organizations, including sport teams, was on average 70 to 75 percent homogenous. East Central Europeans in Johnstown, Pennsylvania, continued to stay within social circles of their own ethnic group, consisting of family, friends, and neighbors. The rate of intermarriage was also low, hovering only around ten percent.

Both historians and sociologists who conducted studies on the social preferences among the second and later generations of Polish Americans demonstrated that this trend continued into the twentieth century. Most studies indicate that Poles were found substantially less inclined to venture socially beyond the confines of their families and close networks of Polish American friends. This finding seems to confirm Pacyga's claim that while a "neighborhood" is a geographic term, the term "community" implies social relationship, and on the basis of his study of turn of the century Chicago, ethnic "neighborhoods were spatially integrated but socially segregated."

RACE RELATIONS

Closely connected to the issue of neighborhood is the issue of race relations, as most urban ethnic communities at some point or other undergo a process of race succession. In general, historians still do not know enough about relations between Polish Americans and non-white groups, including African Americans, Latinos, and Asians.

We know very little about contacts between the first Polish immigrants and African slaves, but the scant available sources seem to confirm the image of positive attitudes of Poles towards blacks and their condemnation of slavery. **Thaddeus Kościuszko** provided in his testament conditions for manumission of the slaves granted to him as reward for his contributions to the Revolutionary War. The **Democratic Society of Polish Exiles in America**, created by the post–November émigrés called for work on behalf of oppressed slaves and the abolition of slavery. Some Poles, such as suffragist **Ernestine Potowska-Rose**, were active in the abolition movement. Dr. **Marie Zakrzewska** opened up her nursing school to black women candidates. Some Poles apparently volunteered to serve in the black regiments during the Civil War.

Polish immigrants arriving in America had no previous contacts with blacks in Europe and might have harbored no specific prejudices that in the U.S. were the legacy of slavery. At the end of the nineteenth century they as-

sumed unskilled industrial jobs in the northern cities and began to come into more direct contact with African Americans, as both groups competed for jobs. These first encounters were not always peaceful. In 1893, in Lemont (Chicago), Illinois, Polish workers employed at digging a canal went on strike over pay cuts. They were promptly replaced with African American strike breakers, imported from Georgia. The strikers were unexpectedly attacked by African American scabs that employers armed with rifles. The majority of the dead and wounded were Poles, including one innocent bystander. The incident left an indelible impression on the growing Chicago Polish community. When a year later, in 1894, African American strike breakers were again used against workers in the meat packing industry who went on strike in support of the Pullman strike, the negative image of blacks as scabs had been reinforced. In later years, the Polish American press repeatedly rejected racist theories, realizing correctly that they also affected white ethnic groups.

Despite the fact that the numbers of both Poles and blacks continued to grow and competition for jobs increased, direct confrontations between Polish Americans and African Americans were rather rare. Until World War I, Polish immigrants mostly ignored the developing black community in Chicago. As Dominic Pacyga shows, Poles also restrained themselves from taking part in Chicago race riots in 1919, despite fires burning in their own neighborhood. A local priest, as well as other community leaders and some Polish-language newspapers reminded readers about friendly relations between Polish and black workers and called for calm and self-control, with some even blaming the provocation on the Irish. Several scholarly studies conducted at that time seemed to confirm friendly relations between Polish and black workers.

Following World War I, African American urban communities continued to expand and Polish Americans and other European ethnics began to come into more direct contact with them. At the same time, they themselves experienced increased Americanization pressure, which was coupled with challenges of cultural debate about Prohibition and immigration restrictions. This debate placed Poles, Italians, and other so-called "new immigrants" in a "third racial caste" of not colored, but not entirely white people. According to Hirsch and others, the 1920s became the crucial period when working class, Catholic immigrants from East Central and Southern Europe responded to these challenges by claiming their whiteness and all the privileges that came with it. In the Great Depression, both communities were severely affected by the deteriorating economy. In the 1930s Detroit Polish American workers mobilized in the CIO drives, sometimes collaborating with black union organizers and workers. The car companies again pitted ethnic strikers against African American strike breakers. Shortly afterwards, amid the economic crisis of the early 1940s, Polish Americans and African Americans, both traditionally discriminated against in the economic as well as the social sense, were once more forced to compete for jobs and housing. According to Thaddeus Radzilowski, the housing riots of 1941-42 reflected the frustration and insecurity, rooted in the experience of the Great Depression.

In the postwar period, the main source of conflict between white ethnics and African Americans became racial succession in their urban neighborhoods. Poles, as well as Czechs, Italians, Germans, Greeks, Danes, Swedes, and Irish participated in several race riots spurred by the moving of the racial frontier closer to the traditional white immigrant communities in Chicago in the late 1940s and 1950s. None of those riots was an exclusive confrontation of one nationality group against their African American neighbors; the dividing line ran clearly between "white" and "black." Placed in a position of the peculiar "buffer zone" between expanding black communities in search of better housing and more affluent white suburbs filled with escapees from the inner cities, Polish Americans refused to abandon their property, churches, and cultural centers. The gradual influx of outsiders was seen as the first step towards the destruction of their way of life and the ethnic community they had created. Confrontations between Polish Americans and blacks also occurred in several other cities, such as Dearborn, Buffalo, Bridgeport, Pittsburgh, and Milwaukee.

Polish Americans also tried to preserve the specific ethnic character of their schools. By the end of the 1960s, Polish Americans participated in demonstrations against the policy of busing in Buffalo and Boston. In 1978, the **Polish American Congress** filed an amicus brief in the Bakke case, claiming reverse discrimination and recalling instances of exclusion, discrimination, and disadvantages that Polish Americans suffered in regards to their access to public education over the decades.

In general, all too often Polish Americans have been portrayed as racist and violent white supremacists. At best, they were lumped together with other white ethnics, and depicted as threatened by the political and economic gains of racial groups encroaching on their old urban communities. Their defensiveness al-

legedly led to racist violence and aggression. Some public opinion polls conducted in the 1970s, portrayed them as even more racist than most other white groups. This view needs to be re-examined and perhaps challenged, and more studies are needed to further explore this complex topic and provide us with a more nuanced view of Polish American relations with other racial groups. In the 1960s, Polonia largely rejected George Wallace's racist advances and supported the Civil Rights movement. In 1968 Detroit, the Black-Polish Conference gathered Polish American priests and activists and African American activists and leaders. The Conference remained active until the mid–1970s and worked to create conditions for better cooperation between the two communities. Recent studies by Stephen M. Leahy also demonstrate that Polish American response to the Civil Rights movement in Milwaukee was positive and stereotyping Polonia as either racist or violent had no basis.

PARTY POLITICS AND POLITICS OF RECOGNITION

Another area of interaction between American Polonia and other ethnic groups in the United States was local politics. In general, Polish immigrants entered the world of party politics relatively late and showed limited interest in the competition for office. Scholars present many different reasons for this fact, including lack of prior political experience, slow naturalization rate, increased focus on intra group relations, as well as focus on homeland rather than American politics. These explanations do not fully account for the reality of life in the pluralistic American society, where party politics became an arena of competition among many ethnic groups vying for economic benefits (patronage jobs and neighborhood projects), occupational mobility, and recognition. In this reality, party politics in urban centers were often a domain of the Irish or sometimes German political machines, which played different ethnic groups against each other and controlled the nomination process. Although Irish politicians did court the Polish vote, they rarely supported Polish politicians. Poles were either completely elbowed out of the process or discounted as potential political partners. In response, Poles blamed the Irish for political "trickery" and corruption, while the Irish hold on the offices was perceived as impenetrable. The animosity between Irish and Polish immigrants, which has already been noted in regards to the Catholic Church and labor movement, was also present in party politics.

As Edward Kantowicz demonstrates for

Chicago, Poles found it difficult to form cross-ethnic coalitions necessary for political success, such as that of a Czech, Anton Cermak. The situation might have been different in smaller urban centers, such as Cleveland, where Poles managed to establish a stronger political presence. Czechs, Germans, and Irish were welcome as members of the Polish Republican Club, established in 1889, and Czech candidates often received Polish support. In Milwaukee, where the Germans established their dominance in the city's politics, Poles were nevertheless able to achieve some political recognition and assume offices, including the 1918 election of **John Kleczka** to the U.S. Congress.

More studies are necessary to fully examine Polish American interethnic relations within the world of party politics in the United States. It seems clear that in more recent decades, when the second and later generations entered politics, Polish Americans seemed more willing to seek interethnic support. In 1940s Detroit, **Stanley Nowak** created a Polish American-African American coalition. In Milwaukee, Democrat **Clement Zablocki** was elected to the U.S. House of Representatives sixteen times beginning in 1948 with the votes of a broad working class, ethnic and Catholic constituency.

Politics of recognition did not relate only to successes in party politics, accounted for by the number and level of offices held by the members of an ethnic group. Polish Americans, like other groups, sought to mark their presence in America and emphasize their contribution through a number of more symbolic initiatives. Sometimes such initiatives were undertaken in cooperation with other groups. The Slavic Alliance of Cleveland (Związek Słowian w Ameryce), which existed in the first decade of the twentieth century under Czech and Polish leadership, included Poles, Czechs, Slovaks, Croats, and Slovenes. In addition to organizing social activities for its members, in 1904 the Alliance sponsored the Slavic Handicraft and Industrial Exhibition to advance knowledge about the culture and accomplishments of Slavs in Europe and America.

More frequently, Polish Americans competed with other ethnic groups for recognition within multiethnic communities and vis-à-vis larger American society. When, in 1905, Poles unveiled a monument to Kosciuszko in Cleveland, they followed an example of the Hungarians, who previously erected a statue of Lajos Kossuth. In 1910, monuments to Kościuszko and Pułaski (see **Kazimierz Pułaski**) stood in Washington, D.C., among statues of other Revolutionary War heroes. The "drives for recognition" became especially intense in the 1920s and 1930s, as the second generation began to claim their place in America. In Minneapolis, the Centrala (Central Polish Organization, est. in 1931) lobbied the state senate to designate October 11 as **Pulaski Day** and to support the national action to issue a Kościuszko commemorative postcard. In Cleveland, Polish Americans took part in the Theater of Nations and the Cultural Gardens projects, competing directly with other groups. In Chicago Polonia fought for Polish street names, declaration of Casimir Pulaski Day, and the recognition of May Third as a Polish **Constitution Day**.

Following World War II, the drives for recognition might have changed their character, but they still continued. Much of this activity was led by the Polish American Congress, which during the **Charles Rozmarek** era spearheaded celebrations honoring May Third as the Polish Constitution Day, Pulaski Day celebrations and parades, issuance of the Kosciuszko stamp, **Ignacy Paderewski** commemorations, the 1955 Mickiewicz, and 1957 **Jamestown** celebrations, as well as the 1960 Millennium festivities. During the term of **Aloysius Mazewski**, the Polish American Congress organized the Copernicus commemorations in the early 1970s, and in the mid–1980s, popular **Polish Heritage Month** celebrations. At the same time, Mazewski worked together with representatives of other ethnic groups to liberalize immigration laws, provide for proper representation of ethnic groups in the bi-centennial celebrations, and on a more local level — the revision of the public school curriculum and the implementation of the Ethnic Heritage Act.

Closely related to the issue of recognition was the problem of defamation. The PAC cooperated with other ethnic groups in their anti-defamation activities in the 1970s. In 1972, the Illinois Division of the PAC and the Joint Civic Committee of Italian Americans together created an anti-defamation body called Polish Italian Conference. This collaboration also brought closer relationships between the two groups in other areas. In 1973, Mazewski was honored as a Man of the Year by the Joint Civic Committee of Italian Americans, and in the 1980s, Polish Americans and Italian Americans in Illinois participated in jointly sponsored banquets on St. Joseph's Day.

HOMELAND POLITICS, NATIONALISM, AND THE EXILE MISSION

The patriotic ethos, which permeated much of Polonia's history, focused its attention on homeland politics and called for work for Poland from abroad. Poland's independence often became a rallying cry for closer cooperation with other ethnic groups, especially those which could both identify and sympathize with the problem of the homeland's subjugation. At other times, the role of Polonia as the "fourth partition" and a free voice for the Polish nation brought Polonia into conflict with other ethnic groups, particularly Poland's European neighbors and minorities.

Since the time of the partitions, patriotic Poles proclaimed and actively fought for "your freedom and ours," whenever they joined liberation and revolutionary movements of other nations against not just one of the partitioning powers, but any tyranny. The participation of Kościuszko and Pułaski in the Revolutionary War became a symbol of this attitude. The exile mission, with its specific understanding of immigrant obligation of work on behalf of the homeland included a diasporic concept of the Polish nation, which often called for collaboration and solidarity with any ethnic group ready to lend assistance in the struggle. The experience of the first waves of exiles who arrived in the United States following the November Insurrection, the Spring of Nations, and the January Insurrection are good examples of activities designed to enlist support of other émigrés. As historian Florian Stasik demonstrates, the Polish cause attracted the involvement of such prominent Americans as James Fenimore Cooper, Horace Greeley, Samuel Morse, and Albert Gallatin, who spoke and wrote on Polish behalf and gathered funds in several American cities. The Polish exiles themselves maintained both individual and organizational ties to French, German, Italian, Hungarian, Danish, Norwegian, and other European as well as Cuban émigrés. Representatives of those groups attended the national celebrations commemorating the 1830 Insurrection organized in New York; Poles reciprocated appearing at events sponsored by other groups. The exiles were especially interested in developing closer ties to other Slavs, through, among others, the Polish Slavonian Society, founded in New York in 1846. **Jan Tyssowski**, who became a co-editor of a German liberal émigré newspaper, used this pulpit to promote the Polish cause. Other Poles also published in the German press.

Both Poles and the Irish showed mutual support for their respective aspirations for national independence. Although there were no solid alliances or organizational cooperation between the two groups, they did engage in displays of public solidarity. According to historian James S. Pula, "In 1863, for example, Richard O'Gorman, a distinguished Irish refugee of 1848, spoke at a multinational New York rally in support of the Polish revolution amid a hall decorated with American, French, German, Polish, and Irish flags. Later, on the 125th anniversary of the Polish constitution of 1791 sponsored by the United Polish societies of New York, John Devoy of *The Gaelic-American* was among the principal speakers." Poles, Irish, and Jews also showed support for the Cuban struggle for independence from Spain during the Spanish-American war of 1898, and for the similar independence movement among the Filipinos.

For the most part, Polonia tried to present a unified response to most of the political events in the Polish lands. In cases of the increased tensions between Poland and her neighbors, frictions also rose within the immigrant communities across the ocean. As mentioned before, in Milwaukee the relationships between Poles and Germans within the church suffered due to the intensifying **Kulturkampf** in Europe. The outbreak of World War I brought further aggravation between the two groups, as the Polish-language press evoked old injuries Poles suffered from the German aggressors, and unequivocally supported the Allies and the American entry into the war. Despite this general anti–German sentiment, Poles in Milwaukee made an effort to distinguish between the starving German population and their militaristic government, and supported fund drives organized by Milwaukee's German community. Similarly, although Poles backed banning of the German language from schools, they restrained from any acts of violence or even overly critical attitudes toward their German neighbors in the city. The situation in Chicago was different and antagonism flared up publicly. As Dominic Pacyga notes, "At a meeting held in 1918 at Saint Hedwig's Church it was resolved to attempt to remove all German street names from Twenty-eighth Ward streets. The meeting asked Alderman Adamowski to petition the city council to change street names like Berlin, Frankfort, Coblentz, and Rhine in the now predominantly Polish ward."

World War I also had a potential to activate other conflicts with Poland's neighbors and minorities. In Cleveland, when the Czech press attacked the new Polish state, the Polish press responded in kind, writing about "Czech perfidiousness." The European conflicts did not affect traditionally friendly cooperation between Czechs and Poles in the city. In Chicago Poles and Czechs united in anti–German activity, which included public rallies and demonstrations, as well as a confrontation with German politicians and members of the school board over textbook content.

Poles and Lithuanians, whose relationships

were far more complicated, steered farther apart from each other as a result of the war. The nationalist faction in the Lithuanian community often used their anti–Polish rhetoric to develop the distinct Lithuanian identity. Since the 1880s, Dr. Jonas Sliupas and his newspaper *Ausra* (Dawn) openly condemned Poland's political and cultural dominance and called for total separation from Polonia. The tensions rose, when both Poland and Lithuania established their independent states and began fighting over the border and territorial issues. In 1920, the Polish military captured Vilnus and its region. It immediately caused an uproar within the Lithuanian-American community, which apparently circulated a pamphlet in Chicago showing a bloody hand with a Polish eagle on the sleeve, and engaged in vehement rhetoric in the press condemning Polish aggression.

Ukrainian Americans also reacted strongly to the Polish state's claims to Western Galicia and Volhynia, and Poland's role in the defeat of the Petlura state. Both the Ukrainian and Polish-language press attacked each other, bringing up examples of mutual historic tensions, injuries, and conflicts. In 1922, Ukrainian-American women dressed in ethnic costumes picketed the White House protesting Polish rule of Western Ukraine. One of the signs read: "Down with Polish Tyranny in Eastern Europe." Throughout the 1920s and 1930s, Ukrainian Americans, Lithuanian Americans, and Polish Americans followed the developments in their respective countries and reacted to the news within the American context. Much further study is needed to fully understand the impact that the European politics had on the relationships among these groups in the United States.

The outbreak of World War II in September 1939, mobilized American **Polonia** on behalf of Poland. Throughout the war, as well as during the Cold War, much of Polonia's attention remained dominated by international politics and the situation in the homeland. During this period, various fractions in the community looked for closer cooperation with the ethnic groups who were also interested in the political developments in East Central Europe. In 1942, over two thousand representatives of various organizations established the **American Slav Congress**, founded to promote stronger relationship between the U.S. and the Soviet Union. Socialist labor activist **Leo Krzycki** became its president, and many other Poles with leftist leanings also joined in. Its activities and political profile were rejected by most of Polonia.

Political refugees, who began arriving in the U.S. after the outbreak of the war, quickly be-

came a major force in firmly fixing Polonia's attention on the political issues of the homeland. Among them were émigré intellectuals and exiled politicians, who supported the concept of federalism in East Central Europe, which would provide more protection to the smaller countries in the area. The discussions about federalism involved émigrés from many different countries, including Poland, Czechoslovakia, Hungary, and Romania. The exile elites exchanged views through publications, both formal and informal conferences and meetings, as well as support for common organizations, for example the Central European Federalist (CEF), led mostly by Polish and Czech intellectuals. Individual exiles also maintained private contacts with members of other exiled communities, especially within professional and university circles.

The American government encouraged the collaboration among East Central European groups in exile for political reasons of the Cold War. The CIA-funded National Committee for a Free Europe coordinated establishment of the National Councils in Exile, and eventually led to the creation of Radio Free Europe. Poles as well as other East Central Europeans were also active in the **Assembly of Captive European Nations** (ACEN), established in 1954. Farther away from centers of international politics, émigré scout leaders initiated contacts with scouting organizations established by exiled Ukrainians, Latvians, Lithuanians, Hungarians, and Romanians.

Political events in Europe often provided opportunity for common displays of solidarity. The 1956 Poznań events in which Polish workers demonstrating for "bread and freedom" were attacked by the military, brought together at protest rallies and masses for the victims representatives of the Latvian, Lithuanian, Hungarian, Bulgarian, Estonian, Russian, Ukrainian, Czech, Slovak, Serbian, and Romanian diasporas. Shortly afterwards, the Polish American community had a chance to reciprocate, as Polonia, together with others, showed support for the Hungarian freedom fighters of the 1956-57 revolution. Similar shows of support and solidarity followed the Soviet invasion of Czechoslovakia in 1968, Gdańsk massacre of 1970, introduction of Martial Law in Poland in 1981, as well as the Soviet invasion of Afghanistan in 1979.

The Polish American Congress was often involved with representatives of other ethnic groups from Communist-dominated countries. Historian Joanna Wojdon lists several mostly short-lived initiatives which were to create common organizations for the purpose of political lobbying in the late 1940s and 1950s. But some interactions resulting from

homeland politics had a decidedly confrontational character. In the 1960s, the PAC repeatedly faced the challenge from the German-American delegation to the National Committee on Captive Nations Week, who in the common demonstration in Chicago carried signs demanding the revision of the Oder-Nisse border. The PAC also intervened when the German-American display booth at the International Folk Fair in Chicago exhibited a provocative map of Europe, and finally created a separate commission to monitor the revisionist German propaganda. Post-1956 relationships between the PAC and some Ukrainian organizations in the U.S. were often strained.

Throughout the 1970s and 1980s, the PAC leaders frequently represented Polonia at various events and celebrations sponsored by the East Central European groups in the U.S., and cooperated with them for political purposes, such as protests against the Washington visit of Leonid Brezhnev or an exhibition of Soviet photography; defense of the future of Radio Free Europe; a demand to repudiate annexation of the Baltic republics; or support of the special legislation for the Solidarity refugees. In the post–Cold War period, representatives of various ethnic groups successfully coordinated action supporting the enlargement of NATO.

POLISH-JEWISH RELATIONS

Homeland politics greatly affected relationships between Polish Americans and Jewish Americans in the United States. The story of these relationships is complicated and remains in need of more scholarly inquiry. Although this topic certainly deserves a more detailed treatment, which would include the analysis of conditions in Poland, we will attempt to present here only major themes regarding experiences and contacts of both groups in the United States.

Both Sephardim Jews from Spain and Portugal and Ashkenazi Jews from German-speaking countries settled in America long before the large migrations from the Polish lands had begun. The early relationships between the first Polish immigrants and exiles and Jews in America were friendly, mostly due to their common focus on Poland's independence. Some Polish Jews who were deported alongside their Christian countrymen after the November Insurrection remained active in Polish exile organizations. The Lincoln years have even been called the period of Polish-Jewish amity in America. Polish Jews joined the **Central Polish Committee in New York**, engaged in collection of funds for the Polish cause, and participated in various activities on behalf of Poland, including publication and printing of the first Polish newspapers in the United States.

The mass influx of Jewish immigrants from East Central Europe in the 1880s coincided with the arrival of their Christian neighbors in the industrial centers of America. Both groups, which were familiar with each other in the old country now often settled in the same neighborhoods, where Polish customers and Jewish small business owners continued their economic relationship transplanted from the Polish lands. The re-establishment in the New World of these economic ties strengthened what Ewa Morawska calls "the old country pattern of 'distant proximity' based on continued economic exchange and mutual disdain." Prejudice, anxiety, and suspicion, which previously characterized their relations, were now preserved in a new environment, as both groups perpetuated negative attitudes and stereotypes of each other.

Despite geographical proximity and economic ties, the two communities remained separate. Efforts to unite all "sons of Poland" around the national agenda met with limited success. Although the **Polish National Alliance** allowed membership of non–Catholic Poles and Polish Jews were among the first leaders of the organization, they never had real representation within the PNA ranks. In 1889, an attempt to exclude "notorious unbelievers and Jews" from the PNA membership had been defeated; the strongest arguments against the exclusion came from the national agenda and recollections of the common sacrifice in the fight for Poland's independence. At the same time, the **Polish Roman Catholic Union**, the other leading fraternal organization in Polonia, opted for the total exclusion of non–Catholics.

According to historian **M. B. Biskupski**, in the years before World War I, the political profile of American Polonia began its gradual movement towards the right, following the lead of Endecja, a conservative nationalist party in Poland, hostile to Polish-Jewish cooperation. Negative attitudes towards Jews were sometimes supported by local priests, such as the Rev. **Lucjan Bójnowski** of New Britain, Connecticut, and often found their way into the Polish-American literature. At the same time, a much more positive image of Jews as patriotic countrymen also persisted, and Jewish success in America was generally admired and made into an example to follow for Polonia.

The events in the European homeland had most impact on the connections between the two groups and World War I affected them in the most direct and negative way. While Poles in Poland as well as Polish Americans fought and lobbied for independence, many (although not all) Jews became alarmed about the worsening conditions in the Polish lands during the first period of the war. Some also grew concerned that once an independent Polish state was established, these conditions would further deteriorate and the position of Jews in Poland would become dangerous. In late 1914, Jewish-American newspapers published an open letter by George Morris Brandes, a recognized Jewish-Danish literary critic, who "accused the Poles of common anti–Semitism and of carrying out brutal pogroms against the Jews. He stated that the 'barbaric' Polish nation did not deserve independence." Although much of his information about the situation in Poland was exaggerated and often false, it was widely accepted due to Brandes' reputation. The publication initiated a series of hotly contested exchanges in the press between Polonia defending Poland's name and the Jewish-American critics attacking the Polish record regarding Jews. Internal political changes within both the Jewish-American and Polish-American communities further influenced the alienation, bitterness, and hostility which resulted from their reaction to homeland politics.

As historian Andrzej Kapiszewski chronicles, in 1919, Jewish Americans created a lobby at the Paris Peace Conference to press for the protection of minority rights in East Central Europe. As a result, Poland and other new countries (but not Germany) were forced to sign the Minorities Treaty, whose implementation was to be supervised by the League of Nations. Although the Polish government did not object to granting full rights to the minorities, the notion of a foreign organization supervising Poland's conduct in this area was seen as a humiliating limitation of the state's sovereignty and interference in Poland's internal affairs. The minority rights debates were greatly influenced by the rumors of wide-spread pogroms against the Jews in Poland. Kapiszewski explains that "The largest protests against the alleged pogroms occurred in the United States, home to numerous and politically active Jewish communities. In the spring of 1919, protests, previously mostly limited to critical articles in Jewish newspapers, now took the form of street demonstrations and resolutions sent to President Wilson, to Congress, and to the Department of State. In big cities, Jews organized 'days of mourning.' Jewish workers went on strike to protest against events in Poland. Jewish shop-owners covered windows in black, children were released from schools to participate in demonstrations and war veterans paraded in their American military uniforms to get additional sympathy from the public. Many state governors, city mayors, congressmen and other influential politicians supported the campaign." The largest demonstrations took place in New York and Chicago.

Polish Americans responded to the negative publicity with political efforts in Congress, publications in the press, as well as through their own public protests and rallies. In April 1919, Hugh Gibson was appointed a minister to Poland and charged with the investigation of the situation there. Most of his reports stated that the news about the scale and severity of the pogroms were inaccurate, although he did acknowledge that some violence indeed took place. This assessment was confirmed by the findings of the Morgenthau Commission released in 1920. In March 1921, a new Polish Constitution guaranteed minority rights in Poland. But by then the relationships between Poles and Jews in America seemed irrevocably and permanently damaged. In the interwar period these relationships continued to be affected by the developments in Poland and remained tense at best, especially during the 1930s. The **Federation of Polish Jews in America** was one of the few organizations committed to the improvement of these relationships.

The impact of World War II on both groups had obviously been tremendous. Immediately after the war, both Jewish and Polish Americans were faced with the challenge of rescuing hundreds of thousands of the so-called displaced persons stranded in refugee camps in the territory of Germany and Austria. Both communities were active in efforts to provide special care and protection for their displaced persons and in the lobby to change American immigration laws and allow the displaced persons to resettle in America. As part of this effort, the two groups sometimes collaborated, and competed on behalf of their communities. Refugees, who arrived after the passage of the Truman Directive in 1946 and the Displaced Person Act in 1948, came from the displaced persons camps system that had already segregated them in Europe. They were brought over by either Polish or Jewish organizations, and joined their respective communities after arrival, rarely crossing paths and perpetuating their separateness.

The post-war history of Polish-Jewish relations turned out to be particularly complicated as the experience of the Holocaust became the very center of the Jewish identity in the diaspora. Both Poland's role in World War II and instances of Polish anti–Semitism throughout history became important elements of this identity. Polish Americans challenged and contested this view. Accusations were hurled in both directions: American Jews accused Poles of violent anti–Semitism, and Poles reciprocated with charges of unfounded Jewish anti–Polishness. Much of the conflict played out on the pages of the press, in the media, during the commemoration events, etc., sometimes becoming very vicious. A more detailed treatment of this issue remains beyond the scope of this essay. It needs to be emphasized that both communities produced numerous people of good will who seriously assumed the challenge of opening up the lines of communication. The dialogue was undertaken by the **National Polish American–Jewish American Council**, and Polish American and Jewish American activists collaborated within the United States Holocaust Commission. As new challenges to this process appear (such as the issues of Jedwabne and the March of the Living), the two communities continue to struggle with reconciliation.—*Anna D. Jaroszyńska-Kirchmann*

SOURCES: Dorota Praszałowicz, Krzysztof A. Makowski, Andrzej A. Zięba, *Mechanizmy zamorskich migracji łańcuchowych w XIX wieku: Polacy, Niemcy, Żydzi, Rusini. Zarys problemu* (Kraków: Księgarnia Akademicka, 2004); James R. Barrett, "Aspiration and Coercion: Polish Immigrants Become Polish Americans, 1900–1930," *Przegląd Polonijny*, Vol. 33, no. 4 (2007), 73–89; Dominic A. Pacyga, "To Live Amongst Others: Poles and Their Neighbors in Industrial Chicago, 1865–1930," *Journal of American Ethnic History*, Vol. 16, no. 1 (1996), 55–73; Adam Walaszek, "Images of Neighbors and Poles in Early 20th Century Polish American School Books," *Polish American Studies*, Vol. 64, no. 1 (Spring 2007), 5–25; Adam Walaszek, "Polish Americans," in David C. Hammack, Diane L. Grabowski, and John J. Grabowski, eds., *Identity, Conflict, and Cooperation: Central Europeans in Cleveland, 1850–1930* (Cleveland: The Western Reserve Historical Society, 2002); 185–248; Ewa Morawska, *For Bread with Butter: Life-Worlds of East Central Europeans in Johnstown, Pennsylvania, 1980–1940* (Cambridge: Cambridge University Press, 1985); Dorota Praszałowicz, *Stosunki polsko-niemieckie na obczyźnie: polscy i niemieccy imigranci w Milwaukee, Wisconsin (USA), 1860–1920* (Kraków: Universitas, 1999); Victor Greene, *For God and Country: The Rise of Polish and Lithuanian Consciousness in America* (Madison: The State Historical Society of Wisconsin, 1975); William L. Wolkovich-Valkavičius, "Tensions in Bi-Ethnic Parishes: Poles and Lithuanians in New England," *Polish American Studies*, Vol. 58, no. 2 (Autumn 2001), 75–82; Victor R. Greene, *The Slavic Community on Strike: Immigrant Labor in Pennsylvania Anthracite* (Notre Dame: University of Notre Dame Press, 1968); James S. Pula and Eugene E. Dziedzic, *United We Stand: The Role of Polish Workers in the New York Mills Textile Strikes, 1912 and 1916* (Boulder: East European Monographs, 1990); Dominic A. Pacyga, *Polish Immigrants and Industrial Chicago: Workers on the South Side, 1880–1922* (Chicago: University of Chicago Press, 2003); John Bodnar, Roger Simon, and Michael P. Weber, *Lives of Their Own: Blacks, Italians, and Poles in Pittsburgh, 1900–1960* (Urbana: University of Illinois Press, 1982); William J. Galush, *For More than Bread: Community and Identity in American Polonia, 1880–1940* (Boulder, CO: East European Monographs, 2006); Florian Stasik, *Polish Political Émigrés in the United States of America, 1831–1964*, trans. by Eugene Podraza, ed. and with an introduction by James S. Pula (Boulder. CO: East European Monographs, 2002); Anna D. Jaroszyńska-Kirchmann, *The Exile Mission: Polish Political Diaspora and Polish Americans, 1939–1956* (Athens, OH: Ohio University Press, 2004); Joanna Wojdon, *W imieniu sześciu milionów.... Kongres Polonii Amerykańskiej w latach 1944–1968* (Toruń: Wydawnictwo Adam Marszałek, 2005); Joanna Wojdon, *W jedności siła: Kongress Polonii Amerykańskiej w latach 1968–1988* (Toruń: Wydawnictwo Adam Marszałek, 2005); Matthew Frye Jacobson, *Special Sorrows: Diasporic Imagination of Irish, Polish, and Jewish Immigrants in the United States* (Cambridge: Harvard University Press, 1995); Andrzej Kapiszewski, *Conflicts Across the Atlantic: Essays on Polish-Jewish Relations in the United States During World War I and in the Interwar Years* (Kraków: Księgarnia Akademicka, 2004); *Polin*, Vol. 19, Polish-Jewish Relations in North America, ed. by Mieczysław B. Biskupski and Antony Polonsky; Joseph Parot, "Ethnic versus Black Metropolis: The Origins of Polish-Black Housing Tensions in Chicago," *Polish American Studies*, Vol. 29, no. 1–2 (1972), 5–33; Joseph Parot, "The Racial Dilemma in Chicago's Polish Neighborhoods, 1920–1970," *Polish American Studies*, Vol. 32, no. 2 (1975), 27–37; Rudolph J. Vecoli, "'Ethnic versus Black Metropolis': A Comment," *Polish American Studies*, Vol. 29, no. 1–2 (1972), 34–39; Quintard Taylor, "The Chicago Political Machine and Black-Ethnic Conflict and Accommodation," *Polish American Studies*, Vol. 29, no. 1–2 (1972), 40–66; Thaddeus Radzialowski, "The Competition for Jobs and Racial Stereotypes: Poles and Blacks in Chicago," *Polish American Studies*, Vol. 33, no. 2 (1976), 5–18; James S. Pula, *Black-Polish Tensions: The Reaction of Blacks and Poles to the Civil Rights Movement* (New Britain, CT: Fiedorczyk Lecture, Central Connecticut State University, 1992).

Intermarriage, Polish American. Although extensive quantitative data are often lacking, the patterns of intermarriage between Polish and other Americans tell a fascinating and sometimes unexpected story about both the loss and persistence of ethnic identity down the generations. The focus here will be on Polish Catholics. Information on intermarriage and Polish minorities in the United States is not readily available. There is much on the history of Jewish Americans in general and the question of intermarriage. Yet for many methodological reasons, it remains difficult to reconstruct the history of intermarriage and Polish Jewish Americans *per se*, particularly in a brief article. For example, data on Jewish intermarriage does not always examine the specific national origins of American Jews. It also varies widely in its answers to the highly debated question "Who is a Jew?" However, an early, much-publicized interethnic and interfaith marriage involved none other than a Polish Jewish immigrant. In 1905 writer and radical activist Rose Pastor, a working-class Jewish immigrant from Augustowo, Poland, wed James Graham Phelps Stokes, the son of a wealthy, Anglo-Saxon Protestant New York family. Their marriage provoked immense controversy among both Jews and Christians. Indeed, only two years before the wedding, Pastor herself had written in her advice column for the *Yiddischer Tage-blatt* that intermarriage was "misery and moral death." Although the couple had many happy years together, they experienced growing political differences and divorced in 1926. The end of their storied union verified the wrongness of intermarriage in the eyes of many naysayers.

The first mass migration of Polish Catholics to the United States generally would have agreed with Rose Pastor Stokes' original condemnation of intermarriage. The self-identified *za chlebem* (for bread) wave of roughly 1870 to 1920 included many family groups and already married couples. Facing discrimination in their adopted country, these newcomers formed tightly knit Polonian neighborhoods wherever they settled in substantial numbers, chiefly in the industrial cities of the Great Lakes region. These enclaves offered them safe places to maintain their language, customs, and ethnically specific religious practices. In part because they felt beleaguered by dominant U.S. culture, Polish Americans of the pre–World War I era overwhelmingly married within their own ethnic group, if they were not already married upon arrival in this country.

The portrayal of intermarriage as community betrayal even appeared in early Polish American literature like **Henryk Nagiel**'s 1896 novel *Kara Boża idzie przez oceany* (God's Punishment Crosses the Ocean). Nagiel depicted Polish women's relationships with Russians and Prussians as recipes for long-lasting, wide-spreading disaster. Folklorist **Helen Stankiewicz Zand** noted that in the early days of **Polonia**, "a marriage outside the [ethnic] fold" was considered "a sort of apostasy" even if the non–Polish spouse was Catholic, which was almost always the case, given the Church's prohibition then on interfaith weddings. Zand observed: "It was vaguely assumed that anyone who was a Pole was thereby also a Catholic and anyone not a Pole was not a Catholic." In addition, Zand pointed out that parents had their own practical and emotional reasons for fearing an interethnic marriage, "since they frequently did not speak English, or spoke it but feebly. It meant being cut off from the new household, losing their son or daughter and the grandchildren."

These attitudes toward intermarriage began to subside in the post–World War I era. **Karen Majewski** rediscovered a detective serial novel in a Buffalo, New York, Polish newspaper that communicated a new message about cultural identity. The novel included a marriage between a Polish man and a Native American woman, suggesting both Polish sympathy for another colonized and oppressed group and a new sense of deeper belonging to America among Polish immigrants. Intermarriage was increasing for Polish Americans, both male and female, but only to members of other European groups. The detective novel was making a symbolic point, not recording an actual demographic trend.

During the early 1920s, Julius Drachsler noted the phenomenon of rising intermarriage among second-generation immigrants across diverse European American ethnicities. According to his research on New York City residents, the intermarriage rate grew as much as 100 to 300 percent between the first and second generations of Poles from the Austrian and Russian partitions. Drachsler considered intermarriage "perhaps the severest test of group cohesion," a practice of individuals who "are not under the spell of an intense cultural or racial consciousness." Helen Zand described a more varied picture, noting that some couples "dwelt in an uncertain no-man's land. Unless, of course, one parent gained the ascendancy and gave the home his or her national coloring." She also asserted: "[D]espite the existence of a common ground in American culture and the English language, the non–Polish spouse and the children learn Polish and identify themselves with the Polish American community frequently enough to be a striking fact." But in her view, the opposite situation seldom occurred.

In 1944 and again in 1952, sociologist Ruby Jo Kennedy Reeves conducted historical studies of intermarriage in New Haven, Connecticut, a city with a large European immigrant population. Her findings challenged the then-prevalent belief that American ethnic groups would blend at similar rates with one another into a single "melting pot." She discovered overall declines in intraethnic marriages and an overall increase in intrareligious but cross-ethnic marriages. By the 1940s, Jews, whatever their countries of origin, married other Jews 94 percent of the time. Eighty percent of Protestants — Scandinavians, Germans, and British Americans — married within their own religious group. New Haven's Catholics — predominantly Irish, Italians, and Poles — wed other Catholics at a rate of 85 percent. Kennedy Reeves documented the same patterns during the 1950s. She hypothesized a "triple melting pot" in which ethnicities intermingled, but generally within their own religious group only, whether Jewish, Protestant, or Catholic. Although interfaith marriages rose among all these groups throughout the twentieth century and into the twenty-first, the majority of unions continued to be intrareligious.

As Julius Drachsler predicted, there was indeed an accelerated "amalgamation" of European ethnicities with one another and seldom with other groups such as Blacks, more often than not along the religious lines specified by Kennedy Reeves. By 1969, as many as 59 percent of Polish American men married out of their ethnic group, generally to Catholic women from another European ethnicity. These changing marriage patterns reflected Polish Americans' postwar movement away from the old enclaves of Polonia into the suburbs of Northern cities and even into new territories like California. In these new geographical settings and in their newly multiethnic parishes, Polish Americans mingled more readily with Americans of other, especially other White, backgrounds.

Yet the 1960s marked the resurgence of a Polish American pride and civil rights movement. This movement brought with it deep concerns about whether and how "authentic" identity would survive. These late twentieth century anxieties echoed the late nineteenth century worries of the noted Polish author **Henryk Sienkiewicz**: "But what about the second, third, and fourth generations? What of the children born of German, Irish, or American mothers? Sooner or later, they will forget. They will change everything, even their names." Did this wholescale identity loss and amnesia take place as feared? Folklorist Deborah Silverman made an intergenerational comparison of interethnic couples with one Polish Catholic American member. She observed that Polish American women born around the 1930s most frequently cooked foods from their husband's ethnic group instead of their own. However, couples born in the 1960s and 1970s frequently cooked one another's foods, embraced one another's customs, and even passed the other spouse's folkways down to the children. She even encountered a Swedish-descended woman who made pierogies for Christmas dinner with her Polish-descended husband. While calling for more research on the subject, Silverman came to the "surprising conclusion" that intermarriage need not compromise attachment to one's Polish identity. Arguably, the Polish American and parallel ethnic pride and civil rights movements made it more possible for individuals and families to value and embrace their multiple ethnic origins simultaneously rather than privilege one over the other or try to erase all of them. At the outset of the twentieth first century, multiethnic Americans with Polish Catholic ancestry could be found on all three of these paths. Sinkiewicz's prophecy did not fully come to pass. Interestingly enough, Keren McGinity's 2009 study of Jewish women and intermarriage arrived at a conclusion parallel to Silverman's, that intermarriage need not and frequently enough does not spell assimilation. —*Mary Krane Derr*

SOURCES: John J. Bukowczyk, *And My Children Did Not Know Me: A History of the Polish Americans* (Bloomington: Indiana University Press, 1987); Julius Drachsler, *Democracy and Assimilation: The Blending of Immigrant Heritages in America* (New York: Macmillan, 1920); Julius Drachsler, *Intermarriage in New York City: A Statistical Study of the Amalgamation of European People* (New York: Columbia University Press, 1921); Calvin Goldscheider, "Intermarriage and Jewish Population Changes," in Stephen H. Norwood and Eunice G. Pollack, eds., *Encyclopedia of American Jewish History* (Santa Barbara, CA: ABC-CLIO, 2008), Vol. 1, 61–62; Ruby Jo Reeves Kennedy, "Single or Triple Melting Pot? Intermarriage Trends in New Haven, 1870–1940," *American Journal of Sociology*, Vol. 49 (January 1944), 331–39; Ruby Jo Reeves Kennedy, "Single or Triple Melting Pot? Intermarriage Trends in New Haven, 1870–1950," *American Journal of Sociology*, Vol. 58 (July 1952), 56–59; Karen Majewski, *Traitors and True Poles: Narrating a Polish-American Identity, 1880–1939* (Athens, OH: Ohio University Press, 2003); Karen R. McGinity, *Still Jewish: A History of Women and Intermarriage in America* (New York: New York University Press, 2009); Henryk Nagiel, *Kara Boża idzie przez oceany* (Chicago: Drukiem Spółki Wydaw. Polskiego w Ameryce, 1896); David R. Roediger, *Working Toward Whiteness: How America's Immigrants Became White: the Strange Journey from Ellis Island to the Suburbs* (New York: Basic Books, 2005); Deborah Anders Silverman, *Polish-American Folklore* (Urbana, IL: University of Illinois Press, 2000); Helen Stankiewicz Zand, "Polish-American Weddings and Christenings," *Polish American Studies*, Vol. 16, no. 1–2 (1959), 24–33; Arthur Zipser and Pearl Zipser, *Fire and Grace: The Life of Rose Pastor Stokes* (Athens, GA: University of Georgia Press, 1989).

Irzyk, Albin Felix (b. Salem, Massachusetts, January 2, 1917; d.—). Military officer. Irzyk earned a baccalaureate degree at the University of Massachusetts and a master's degree in international relations at American University in Washington, D.C., and also completed studies at the National War College. During World War II, as a lieutenant colonel he led the 8th Tank Battalion in the 4th Armored Division spearheading Gen. George Patton's Third Army campaigns in France and Germany. Twice wounded, he was awarded the Distinguish Service Cross, the nation's second highest combat award for an action in Germany on March 18, 1945. On that day, Irzyk personally led an assault on German anti-tank positions until his own tank was disabled. Wounded, he nevertheless continued to lead the assault on foot until the objective was secured. For his actions during the war he also received two Silver Stars, four Bronze Stars, two Purple Hearts, the U.S. Legion of Merit, the French Croix de Guerre with star, and the Ceskoslovenský Válecný Kríž. Following the war he commanded the 14th Armored Cavalry Regiment in Europe and served as commander of the U.S. Army

Armor School at Fort Knox for two years. He spent two years in Vietnam (1967–69) where he accumulated 600 hours of combat in helicopters, earning eleven Air Medals and the Distinguished Service Medal, the country's third highest combat award. He retired as a brigadier general in 1971 when he was commanding officer of Fort Devens, Massachusetts. The Albin F. Irzyk Memorial Park in Salem, Massachusetts, was dedicated in 1999.—*James S. Pula*

SOURCES: Albin F. Irzyk, *He Rode Up Front for Patton* (Raleigh, NC : Pentland Press, 1996); Albin F. Irzyk, *Gasoline to Patton: A Different War* (Oakland: Elderberry Press, 2005); Albin F. Irzyk, *Unsung Heroes, Saving Saigon* (Raleigh, NC: Ivy House Publishing Group, 2008); Don M. Fox, *Patton's Vanguard—The United States Army Fourth Armored Division* (Jefferson, NC: McFarland & Company, 2003); Kenneth A. Koyen, *The Fourth Armored Division from the Beach to Bavaria* (Nashville, TN: The Battery Press, 2000).

Ius Patronatus. In the Roman Catholic Church, "ius patronatus," or the "right of patronage," refers to a group of rights and obligations bestowed upon a person, family, or society through ecclesiastical grant. In Poland, there was a tradition of lay involvement in the founding of parishes and it was customary that a patron who donated land or was otherwise the benefactor of establishing a new church would be accorded the right to nominate the pastor of that church. Although this right was conferred upon individuals who were members of the gentry and not upon groups of parishioners, the concept was well-known among Polish immigrants who regarded it as an established precedent of lay involvement in parish affairs. Since the typical founding of a Polish ethnic church in the United States involved a lay committee collecting funds, purchasing land, constructing a building and petitioning the bishop for authorization to form a parish, the lay leadership of these founding groups often attempted to assert rights of patronage in the same manner that benefactors had in Poland. This frequently brought the lay leadership into conflict with the bishops who, during the period between 1870 and 1940, were almost exclusively Irish and German. The element of ethnic distinction was thus added to what became a struggle over property rights, influence in the naming of priests, and Polish ethnic expression. For further information on the schisms that resulted, see "Religious Life, Polish American," "Independentism" and "Polish National Catholic Church."—*James S. Pula*

SOURCE: Patrick Carey, *Priests, People, and Prelates: Ecclesiastical Democracy and the Tensions of Trusteeism* (Notre Dame: University of Notre Dame Press, 1987).

Jablonski, Edward (b. Bay City, Michigan, March 1, 1922; d. New York City, February 10, 2004). Author. Fascinated as a child by airplanes and music, Jablonski turned these early interests into a career authoring respected books in both fields. After serving in the army field artillery where he was awarded a Silver Star during World War II, he obtained his baccalaureate degree from the New School for Social Research in New York City in 1950. In 1949 he was active in the founding of Walden Records. Beginning with an article on Hungarian composer Bela Bartok in a small new literary magazine, Jablonski's articles were soon appearing in the pages of the *Saturday Review*, the *American Record Guide*, *Stereo Review* and the revised edition of Isaac Goldberg's *Tin Pan Alley: A Chronicle of American Popular Music*. Because of a personal friendship with Ira Berlin that began with a fan letter from Jablonski when he was only a child, he was able to gain access to the Gershwin family's personal papers which he used to exceptional benefit in co-authoring the acclaimed book *The Gershwin Years*. His other contributions to the field of music literature include *Gershwin: With a New Critical Discography, The Encyclopedia of American Music, The Gershwin Years in Song, Gershwin Remembered, Somewhere Over the Rainbow: Harold Arlen,* and his final book, *Irving Berlin: American Troubadour*. Nor did he neglect his other childhood fascination — aircraft. Respected for his critical analysis of air combat in World War II, his works include *Ladybirds: Women in Aviation; Flying Fortress: The Illustrated Biographies of the B-17's and the Men Who Flew Them; Double Strike: The Epic Air Raids on Regensburg-Schweinfurt, August 17, 1943; America in the Air War; Doolittle: A Biography; A Pictorial History of the World War II Years; Terror from the Sky; Man with Wings: A Pictorial History of Aviation; Outraged Skies; Atlantic Fever; Seawings;* and the classic four-volume *Air War* series.—*James S. Pula*

SOURCE: "Jablonski, Edward," *Contemporary Authors* (Detroit: Gale Research Company, New Revision Series), Vol. 2, 349.

Jablonski, Frank (Franciszek Hieronim Roman Jabłoński; b. Inowrocław, Poland, August 9, 1863; d. Chicago, Illinois, February 23, 1908). Journalist, Polonia activist. After completing his early education, Jablonski continued his studies in theology in Poznań and at the University of Louvain in Belgium. Migrating to Chicago around 1885, he began work as a teacher at Holy Trinity parish in 1889. At that time, the parish church was closed and Jablonski took a leading part in the struggle to win Church approval for its reopening. During the previous decade mem-

Franciszek Jablonski, editor of *Zgoda* and president of the Polish National Alliance (*OLS*).

bers of Holy Trinity, some of whom were identified with the **Polish National Alliance**, had fought a losing battle against the **Resurrectionists** of St. Stanislas Kostka parish and the Archbishop of Chicago for control over their church. Jablonski was sent to Rome to urge the opening of the parish in the heavily Polish near north side community of Chicago and in 1893 the Vatican concurred. The Rev. Casimir Sztuczko of the Order of the Holy Cross took over as pastor and served in that capacity as a strong ally of the Polish National Alliance until his death in 1949. Because of this success, Jablonski became famous, and at the 1893 PNA convention he was unanimously elected editor of **Zgoda** (Harmony), a post he held until 1897 when he was chosen president of the Alliance. As editor, Jablonski's work centered on defending the PNA from attacks by the Polish clerical faction. Jablonski was the commissioner of the Polish National Treasury for America and an honorary member of the Polish National Museum in Rapperswyl, Switzerland. He was employed by the city treasurer's office in Milwaukee, Wisconsin. In April 1901, he resigned the presidency of the Alliance to accept the editorship of the Milwaukee *Kuryer Polski* (Polish Courier). In 1907 the delegates at the Baltimore convention voted to create a Polish daily *Zgoda* and elected Jablonski to edit the new paper, along with its weekly organ. He died only one month after assuming his new post. Buried in Chicago's St. Adalbert Cemetery, the inscription on Jablonski's tombstone reads, "Here rest the remains of the dearly departed Jablonski, able defender of Holy Trinity Parish and Guardian of the Polish National Alliance."—*Donald E. Pienkos*

SOURCE: Donald E. Pienkos, *PNA: A Centennial History of the Polish National Alliance of the United*

States of North America (Boulder, CO: East European Monographs, 1984).

Jagiello, Walter "L'il Wally" (b. Chicago, Illinois, August 1, 1930; d. Miami, Florida, August 17, 2006). Musician. The son of Polish immigrants from **Galicia**, Jagiello began singing with the Eddie Zima orchestra at the age of eight in the Forest Preserve parks on Chicago's far north side and on Chicago's "Polish Broadway" (Milwaukee Avenue). He taught himself how to play the concertina and the drums. In his late teens he organized his own orchestra, the Lucky Harmony Boys, and continued to perform in Chicago and throughout the United States with his own groups and individually with backup musicians who knew his compositions and style from memory. The diminutive, good looking Jagiello won fame as "Li'l Wally" (Mały Władziu). He possessed an engaging tenor voice and a charismatic persona that underscored the ethnic and peasant character of his style of polka music and his joy in performing for countless thousands of fans, all of which made him the most popular and imitated exponent of the polka in Polish America for more than four decades. His style of music was distinctive in two ways. First it emphasized the peasant character of the two-step polka and differentiated his music from the sophisticated, much larger, orchestras of the eastern states. Second, the Li'l Wally polka was much slower than the eastern brand and was defined by a strong drum, making it easy to dance to by couples of all ages.

Jagiello wrote hundreds of songs and adapted hundreds of Polish folk tunes to the polka, singing in Polish and in English. He amassed seventeen gold records, including such hits as "I Wish I Was Single Again" and "Pukaj Jasiu." Moreover, he unendingly promoted his music in his countless live performances and over the radio. In Chicago his popularity was such that several "Li'l Wally" bands might be playing in the city on the same night with Jagiello traveling from location to location to play for an hour or so at each stop. His Polonia Grove dance hall, now transformed into the Polish Highlanders Hall on the city's southwest side, rocked each weekend for many years.

Jagiello was one of the earliest musicians to set up his own recording company and to distribute his own music on his own label, "Jay Jay Records." He made more than fifty long-playing records and countless singles, and later adapted successfully to the CD market. He delved into a variety of forms, too, including novelty records—*The Polka Twist, Polkas as Performed in France,* and *American "Golden Oldies."* His influence is also felt in Poland.

"Li'l Wally" Jagiello, popular musician (*PMA*).

Jagiello performed several times on the Lawrence Welk national television show and in 1969 was one of the first two individuals to be inducted into the Polka Hall of Fame by the International Polka Association. In 1984 he performed in Rome for Pope John Paul II and received his enthusiastic blessing. Jagiello inspired scores of Polka musicians, among them Marion Lush, **Eddie Blazonczyk**, and Jimmy Sturr, to follow his lead in composing their own pieces, developing their own styles of music within the polka genre, and thus developing a type of polka that is distinctively American and Polish.

Among Jagiello's many compositions were "God Bless Our Polish Pope," "Wish I Was Single Again," "Seven Days and Seven Nights Without You," "Two Bucks Polka," "Johnnie's Knockin'," "Under the Bridge," "Polka Joy," "Flowers for Mother," "Li'l Wally Twirl," "Please Believe Me," "Take Me Baby," "Lucky Stop Waltz," "Broken Hearted," "Utica Polka," "Jolly Fellow," "Leaving for the Service," "A Polka Christmas," "We Love Our USA," and "Old Lady Oberek." His many honors included seventeen gold and four platinum records; being elected Chicago's Polka King by Radio Station WOPA and Polka fans in Chicago, 1956; first elected to Polka Hall of Fame, 1969; Outstanding Service for National Ballroom Operations Association award from the **Polish National Alliance** and All Nations Polka & Folk Dance Committee, 1969; performer for Pope John Paul II, 1984; World Polka King, 1984; Grammy nomination for *Polish Feelings* album, 1985; award of appreciation, **Charles Rozmarek**, president of **Polish American Congress.**—*Donald E. Pienkos*

SOURCES: Joseph Migala, *Polish Radio Broadcasting in the United States* (Boulder, CO: East European Monographs, 1987), 237; Charles Keil, Angeliki V. Keil and Dick Blau, *Polka Happiness* (Philadelphia: Temple University Press, 1992); Victor Greene, *A Passion for Polka: Old-Time Ethnic Music in America* (Berkeley, CA: University of California Press, 1992).

Jamestown Colony, Poles in. Jamestown was founded in 1607 by an expedition organized by the Virginia Company of London. It was destined to become the first permanent English colony in America, though success was far from certain. An earlier attempt in Roanoke, North Carolina, by Sir Walter Raleigh and the 1607 Popham Colony in New England both failed. Meanwhile, hope that gold could be extracted from wealthy Indians soon faded, as did the prospect of a shortcut to China. It appeared the colony would have to work for a living. To accomplish this end the company sent "eight Dutch-men and Poles" and a Swiss man with the "Second Supply" from London aboard the ship *Mary and Margaret* around October 1, 1608. The company recruited as skilled master craftsmen a group of industry specialists in soap-ash, glass, lumber milling (wainscot, clapboard, and "deal"—softwood lumber), naval stores (pitch, turpentine, and tar), and mining. All were hired to teach and organize new industries; not so much to do the work but to train the colonists. Unlike the colonists, who were company shareholders or servants of shareholders, the craftsmen were probably contractors, and their names do not appear on the list of colonists in the ship's manifest. Only the mining and ores specialist is known definitely as a "Zwitzar" (Swiss) man, and even the craft specialty of the others requires a degree of conjecture.

Certainly skilled craftsmen worked in England, so why were Dutchmen and Poles recruited? Few English craftsmen were accustomed to working in virgin forest and primitive conditions, since the great British forests, in this age before coal, had long since gone up chimneys or had been cultivated as tree gardens reserved for use by the Royal Navy. Serious glass industry went to remote forests such as those of Finland or the Tatra Mountains, since a few pounds of glass ship easier than tons of wood. Or, another reason might have been bargain rate labor. As early as 1585, Walter Raleigh was urged to look to Prussia and Poland for "Men skilfull in burning of Sope ashes, and in making of Pitch, and Tarre, and Rozen ... which are thence to be had for small wages." Also, the Polish-Swedish War was current, and wars make for economic refugees and eager, or desperate, recruits.

We know almost nothing about the Poles among the eight Dutchmen and Poles of 1608.

They were likely young, as were almost all the colonists, yet at least in their mid-twenties to have achieved mastery of their craft. Their actions are rarely recorded and their fates are unknown. Captain John Smith gave high marks to the Poles' work ethic, writing that "Only the Dutch-men and Poles, and some dozen others ... knew what a dayes worke was." We know little of them since they apparently worked hard and, unlike the Dutchmen, failed to gain notoriety by fomenting rebellion. Possibly they stayed with the colony and died in the 1610 famine, perhaps they left in 1609-10 by the terms of their contract, or perhaps they even survived to 1611 and beyond.

It is possible, but not probable, that the Poles were Roman Catholic. As special status contractors they may have been exempt from the colonists' requirement to swear they were not "Papists," but anti–Catholic paranoia was high and documents record specific warnings against admitting Catholics to the colony. They could easily have been Protestant Poles since in 1607 the Baltic provinces of the Polish-Lithuanian Commonwealth had large Lutheran and Calvinist populations. Had they been Catholic, the practice of accommodation should have been well understood by the colony's leaders — for example, the English Navy at this time had protocols to follow for Catholic sailors. We know the colony eventually had some religious diversity since, a generation later, up to several dozen Virginia Catholics were exiled. Also, archaeologists have discovered a Catholic-style crucifix from the early Jamestown period, offering an intriguing hint that perhaps the diversity was present from the start. Some accommodation was required in any event since Anglicans were almost non-existent outside Britain, so the craftsmen would not have been members of the official religion of the colony. The safer guess is that the 1608 craftsmen were Protestants, or were at least willing to act the part.

It should be noted as well that the identified "Poles" might have been citizens of the large and diverse Polish-Lithuanian Commonwealth and thus properly so-called; but, ethnically might have been Poles, Lithuanians, Latvians, Rus, Germans, or of any other minority, many of which were readily found in the Commonwealth. When Smith discussed possible labor sources, he mentioned Russia twice, a descriptive term almost as likely to mean the Rus lands of the Polish Lithuanian Commonwealth as the state then usually called Muscovy.

The craft specialty of the Poles is uncertain. We know with some certainty that the lumber mill-men were the three named Dutchmen — Adam, Francis, and Samuel. John Smith states

that these three, and possibly a fourth Dutchman, were sent to do lumber and construction work in December 1608. This leaves the other crafts as candidates. The naval stores and potash men may well have been Poles. Almost no clue can be found in evidence from the early period. Several years later, in 1619, documentation associates Poles with the production of tar, pitch, turpentine, and potash in Jamestown. It is exceedingly unlikely that these were the same 1608 Poles, since there were few survivors from the 1610 "starving time" and the casualty rate in other years was also high. It is plausible that replacements were sought from the same source from whence Captain Smith claimed he had found good service. However, this is a weak brand of speculation, and so they could have been either Dutchmen or Poles.

Most likely, the glassmaker and a possible assistant were probably Poles, but the evidence is weak. Smith mentions both the Dutchmen and Poles in conjunction with the glass-house at Jamestown. The three Dutchmen used it as a hiding place when they smuggled arms out of James Fort. This does not suggest they were glassworkers. Since these were the same people who were probably lumber specialists, they may well have helped build the glass-house, and there were only a handful of named places in tiny Jamestown so this could have been entirely coincidental. Later, Smith tells us, he is near the glass-house when he is attacked by Indians, and there "two of the Poles upon the sands" come to his rescue. This fact is far more suggestive that the Poles were associated with the glass-house, since it carries the implication that they were working there or at least nearby. This is especially significant since lumber, potash, and lye work was performed even further away, as indicated in the following statement: "But 30 of us he conducted downe the river some 5 myles from James towne, to learne to make Clapboard, cut downe trees, and lye in woods."

If three or four Dutchmen were lumber men, and if it is at least possi-

ble that the naval store and potash men were Dutchmen, and since at the very minimum two and probably more Poles existed, there is a "body count" problem if we are to believe that yet another Dutchman or two were the glassmakers. That is, either Dutchmen make up the great majority of the party, which the wording of the primary sources does not seem to imply, or we run out of bodies to which we can assign the work.

Potash making, one of the precursor steps for glass, was familiar to master glass men. Possibly even the glass man or his assistant had responsibility for potash production. If the potash maker was Polish, this may again be a non-coincidental suggestion that the glassmaker was a Pole. This collective evidence seems to favor the Poles as glassmakers.

Beyond that the primary sources are silent. The only new development of the last century of study is the discovery by archaeologists that some of the glassmaking tools, and especially a crucible with glass remnants, were from central Germany, which led some to speculate that this was evidence for a German glassmaker. But some of the crucibles identified were apparently used as metallurgical assay pots. These would be used by the Swiss metallurgist and the English refiners, so the pot's origin and the craftsmen's nationality are dis-

Arthur Szyk's allegorical miniature of the Poles in Jamestown (*OLS*).

connected. Further, crucibles, specialty items made of refractory clay obtainable in only a few places in Europe, were standard international exports that dominated world trade — millions were imported into Britain alone. A commodity export tool does not suggest anything about the nationality of its user. Otherwise, the Dutch, German, and Polish glassmaking industries were all equally robust, so there is nothing inferable from that end.

It should be noted that some publications and internet articles on this subject reference an alleged 1625 primary source — *Pamiętniki Handlowca* or, alternatively, *Memorialium Commercatoris* (A Merchant's Memoir) — which asserts that the glassmakers were Polish and lists with confident authority the names, hometowns, and pedigree of the alleged Polish Jamestown pioneers, as well as detailing their many feats. Various investigations of this source strongly suggest that it is questionable, and likely a fraud.

While Smith always speaks well of the Poles, it is interesting that one of their contributions mentioned in his early reports is dropped in later versions of his history. When "Smith taketh the King of Paspaheigh prisioner," in his first report (Oxford Tract 1613) he wrote: "Long they struggled in the water, from whence the King perceiving two of the Poles, upon the sandes would have fled; but the President held him by his haire and throat till the Poles came in; then seeing howe pitifully the poore Salvage begged his life, they conducted him prisoner to the fort." Later, in his *Generall Historie*, the help was no longer acknowledged and Smith takes somewhat more credit unto himself: "long they struggled in the water, till the President got such a hold on this throat, he neare strangled the King; but having his faucheon to cut off his head seeing howe pitifully he begged his life, he led him prisoner to Jamestowne and put him in chaynes."

The Poles were clearly capable young men who worked hard and did themselves proud, an achievement that created opportunities for other Poles who followed, and we know that Poles were actually present in Jamestown over several decades at least. The evidence and informed reasoning allows speculation that there were at least two and probably three to five Poles, their number likely including a glassmaker and an assistant. Suggestive evidence also supports the theory that the potash and naval stores men were Poles. This is what we know or can reasonably guess. — *Richard J. Orli*

SOURCES: James S. Pula, "Fact vs. Fiction: What Do We Really Know About the Polish Presence in Early Jamestown?" *The Polish Review*, Vol. LII, no. 4 (2008), 477–493; Sigmund H. Uminski, *The Polish Pioneers in Virginia* (New York: The Polish Publication Society of America, 1974); Philip L. Barbour, "The Identity of the First Poles in America," *William and Mary Quarterly*, 3rd Ser., Vol. 21, No. 1 (January, 1964), 77–92; James S. Pula, "Jamestown's 400th Anniversary," *Polish American Studies*, Vol. LXV, no. 2 (2008), 9–17; Richard J. Orli, "The Identity of the 1608 Jamestown Craftsmen," *Polish American Studies*, Vol. LXV, no. 2 (2008), 17–26.

Jan of Kolno. This fifteenth century traveler is alleged to have discovered the Strait of Anian and Labrador in 1476. Joachim Lelewel, a nineteenth century Polish historian, argued that he was Polish. Lelewel cited geographical works dating back to the sixteenth century where Johannes Scolnus, a sailor of King Christian of Denmark, was mentioned and sometimes identified as a Pole. He further interpreted Scolnus as the Latin transcription of the Polish "z Kolna" — that is, "of Kolno." Kolno is a town in Mazovia that prospered in the fifteenth century as a trading center and was home to a number of renowned sailors. A student "Jan z Kolna" was found in the records of the Jagiellonian University from the fifteenth century. Scholars critical of Lelewel's theory argue that "of Kolno" would have been noted as "de Colno" or "Colnensis" in Latin. Some of them transcribe the name as Scoluue, Scolp, Scoluvus, or Scolus and identify him as Norwegian, Danish, or Portuguese. A Polish geographer, Bolesław Olszewicz, who examined the problem carefully in 1933, shared their doubts without questioning the authenticity of the expedition of 1476. Polish artists, including novelist Stefan Żeromski and the artist Jan Matejko, trusted Lelewel and popularized Jan of Kolno as a Pole in their works. The well-known miniaturist Arthur Szyk also executed a painting memorializing Jan z Kolna as a Pole. Today, American scholars generally reject the Polish identification, most arguing a lack of substantial proof that a Pole held a prominent position in the Danish expedition of 1476. — *Joanna Wojdon*

SOURCES: Jacek K. Furdyna, "Scolvus Discovery of Labrador," *Polish American Studies*, Vol. 9, no. 3–4 (1952), 65–77; Bolesław Olszewicz, *O Janie z Kolna, domniemanym polskim poprzedniku Kolumba* (Warsaw: Kasie im Mionowskiego, 1933).

Janda, Victoria (Wiktoria Duda; b. Nowy Targ, Poland, December 17, 1889; d. Hennepin County, Minnesota, April 1, 1961). Poet. After migrating to America with her family at the age of three, Janda was educated in the parochial schools in Minneapolis before earning a baccalaureate degree from the University of Minnesota and embarking on a career in social work. Active in Polish American affairs, she was a president of Group 1530 of the **Polish National Alliance**, president of the local Polanie Club, and a member of several other organizations. Her interest in poetry led to publication of her works in a variety of Polish newspapers and journals including *Zgoda*, *Dziennik Związkowy*, *Nowiny Minnesockie*, *Jaskółka*, *Dziennik Chicagoski*, *Nowy Świat*, and *Antologia Poezji Polsko Amerykańskiej*, and in the English *New American Magazine*, *National Magazine of Poetry*, and *Minnesota Anthology of Verse*. She is also the author of several volumes of poetry for children. — *Sophie Hodorowicz Knab*

SOURCES: the Rev. Francis Bolek, ed., *Who's Who in Polish America* (New York: Harbinger House, 1943); Judith Zając, "Polish American Poetess: Victoria Janda," *Polish American Studies*, Vol. 20, No. 1 (1963), 51–53; Emmanuel S. Nelson, ed., *The Greenwood Encyclopedia of Multiethnic American Literature* (Westport, CT: Greenwood Press. 2005), Vol. 3.

Janis, Byron (Yankilevitch; Yanks; b. McKeesport, Pennsylvania, March 24, 1928; d.—). Pianist, composer. Janis is the youngest of two children of Hattie Horelick and Samuel Yankilevitch, who shortened his surname to Yanks after emigrating to the United States. He moved with his family to Pittsburgh during the Great Depression. Byron began piano lessons in 1933 after demonstrating perfect pitch in kindergarten while performing on a toy xylophone. In early 1936 he moved to New York with his mother and sister, his father remaining in Pittsburgh to operate the family store, to study with Josef and Rosina Lhévinne. After a year they assigned him to their associate Adele Marcus, who became his teacher for six years. He attended composition and harmony classes at the Chatham Square School of Music and academic classes at Columbia Grammar School. Byron Yanks made his recital debut at Pittsburgh's Carnegie Hall in 1937, and a year later, his musical sponsor, Samuel Chotzinoff, decided that Yanks was not a suitable surname for a pianist, so he became Byron Jannes (pronounced *Yannes*).

When Adele Marcus accepted a teaching position in Dallas, Byron followed to continue his studies, soon after changing his surname from Jannes to Janis, since everyone pronounced the J. He made his orchestral debut in 1943 with Toscanini's NBC Symphony Orchestra, conducted by Frank Black. After attending a Janis performance in 1944, Vladimir Horowitz offered to take the fifteen-year-old on as his first student. Following Horowitz's advice, Janis postponed the obligatory New York Carnegie Hall debut, and instead undertook a concert tour to build self-confidence and acquire stage presence. During the Horowitz years (1944–48), Janis made about fifty concert appearances, including a successful tour of South America. At age eighteen he also became the youngest artist signed to a contract by RCA Victor. Janis made his Carnegie Hall debut in 1948, which was hailed by critic Olin Downes in the *New York Times*, and undertook his first European tour in 1952. Janis became front-page news in 1960 when he was invited to give ten concerts behind the Iron Curtain as part of the first U.S.-Soviet Union cultural exchange. Although this was just after the U-2 spy plane incident, the Soviet audiences' responses were overwhelmingly positive, and he was invited back for a similarly successful second tour in 1962. Janis made further musical history in 1967, when he discovered manuscripts of two Chopin waltzes in a chateau outside Paris. He then discovered two completely different versions of the same waltzes at the Yale Music Library in 1973. Janis closely identified with Chopin, and filmed a one-hour documentary for television in 1975, *Frédéric Chopin: A Voyage with Byron Janis.*

In 1973, he was diagnosed with psoriatic arthritis, which eventually caused the distal (tip) joints of nine fingers to fuse, and also caused painful stiffness in his wrists and neck. He kept his condition secret for over a decade, and adjusted his playing technique by changing his fingering and hand positioning. He continued to concertize in Europe and America despite intense pain, eventually limiting himself to solo recitals. He tried many treatments, both medical and alternative, and at times suffered from depression. Janis went public with his illness after a White House concert in 1985, and became a cultural ambassador for the National Arthritis Foundation, giving concerts on its behalf. After an operation on his thumb resulted in its shortening, he returned to songwriting, composing a stage musical, *The Hunchback of Notre Dame.* He subsequently composed music for television and film, as well as a second musical, *The Silver Skates.*

Among Janis's numerous honors are the Harriet Cohen International Music Award/Beethoven Medal (1962); the Grand Prix du Disque (1964); the Chevalier des Arts et des Lettres from the French government (1965); the Distinguished Pennsylvania Artist Award (1985); National Public Radio's "Performance Today Critics Choice Award" (1996) for his recording "Byron Janis Plays Chopin," his first commercial recording after 34 years; and an honorary doctorate from Trinity University in Hartford, Connecticut (1997).—*John Drobnicki*

SOURCES: David Ewen, ed., *Musicians Since 1990: Performers in Concert and Opera* (New York: H.W. Wilson Company, 1978); John Gillespie and Anna Gillespie, *Notable Twentieth-Century Pianists: A Bio-Critical Sourcebook* (Westport, CT: Greenwood Press, 1995); Barbara Goldsmith, "'The First Thing I Had to Conquer Was Fear': The Story of Concert Pianist Byron Janis," *Parade Magazine* (October 13, 1985), 4–7.

Janowicz, Victor Felix "Vic" (b. Elyria, Ohio, February 26, 1930; d. Columbus, Ohio, February 27, 1996). Football Player. Janowicz was a football standout for Ohio State University from 1949 to 1951. In 1950, playing tailback, he was named an All-American and was awarded the Heisman Trophy as the country's top collegiate performer, one of few underclassmen ever so honored. Electing to attempt a career in baseball, he played for the Pittsburgh Pirates for two seasons, 1953-54, but with indifferent success. He then returned to football, joining the Washington Redskins of the National Football League. After two seasons, Janowicz seemed on the brink of stardom in the pros, but in 1956 a serious auto accident ended his days as an athlete. Following his recovery from his injuries, he embarked on a successful career as a businessman and broadcaster in Columbus, Ohio. He is a member of the College Football Hall of Fame, and was elected to the National Polish-American Sports Hall of Fame in 1987.—*Neal Pease*

SOURCE: "Vic Janowicz," National Polish-American Sports Hall of Fame website, www.polishsportshof.com.

Janta, Aleksander (Aleksander Janta-Połczyński; b. Poznań, Poland, December 11, 1908; d. Southampton, New York, August 19, 1974). Writer, poet, journalist. Janta's first short stories were published in 1925 in the hunting journal *Przegląd Myśliwski i Łowiectwo Polskie* (Polish Hunting). Beginning in 1928 he collaborated with several Polish periodicals of different genres and political options including *Życie Literackie* (Literary Life), *Tęcza* (Rainbow), *Dwutygodnik Literacki* (Literary Fortnightly), *Kultura* (Culture), *Dziennik Poznański* (Poznań Daily News), *Wiadomości Literackie* (Literary Information), and *Gazeta Polska* (Polish Gazette). He published essays and poems, but travel stories brought Janta popularity. He started with a trip to France, Great Britain, and the U.S. with his articles appearing in **Nowy Świat** (New World). In 1932 he went to the Soviet Union. Among the countries he visited later were Lithuania, Japan, Afghanistan, Burma, Thailand, China, and India where he met Mahatma Gandhi. During his trip to the U.S. he interviewed President Franklin D. Roosevelt and actor Charlie Chaplin. He traveled as a press correspondent, describing the wars in Manchuria and Ethiopia. In Paris at the outbreak of the World War II, Janta volunteered for the Polish Army in France, becoming a war correspondent. After the German attack on France he fought with the Polish First Grenadier Division commanded by Gen. Bronisław Duch. The division was dissolved when France ca-

pitulated in June, 1940, but the soldiers were ordered to reach England via unoccupied southern France. When Janta and his fellows were surrounded by German forces on their way south, he masqueraded as Rene Lapedagne, a French soldier who actually died in battle. He maintained this French disguise for the next twenty-seven months, first in camp Lorch im Remstal near Stuttgart, then in Lyon beginning in September 1942. He described his war adventures in two books, *I Lied to Live: A Year as a German Family Slave* (1944) and *Bound with Two Chains* (1945). In April 1943 he escaped through Grenoble and Spain, making his way to London in the guise of a German officer. For his actions he was awarded the first of three Crosses of Valor. In London he was assigned to the Ministry of Information and Documentation of the Polish government-in-exile. His application for the Polish Information Center in New York was accepted in March 1944.

Janta arrived in America with the task of enlivening propaganda for the Polish cause. He decided to stay in the United States after the war, but he refused to sever all connections with his homeland, visiting Poland in 1948, an act that led to him being ostracized by émigré leaders and the émigré press. He settled in Buffalo, and in 1949 took a job as a broadcaster on Leon Wysztacki's radio program, then moved to **Dziennik dla Wszystkich** (Everybody's Daily) where he wrote 625 feature stories from October 18, 1949, to January 2, 1952. When the **pierogi** factory he ran went bankrupt in 1954, Janta moved to New York City as the assistant of **Stephen Mizwa** at the **Kosciuszko Foundation**. At the beginning of the 1960s he joined Alexander Hertz in operating an antique bookshop which proved to be a financial success and fulfilled Janta's bibliophilic passion. Living in Elmhurst, NY, he presented the most interesting of his findings in the articles he published beginning in 1966 in a column labeled "Kupa mięci" in the London *Wiadomości* (Information). In America, he translated Russian and Japanese poetry into Polish, and wrote many of his stories and poems, most of which were published privately for a list of subscribers. He served as president of the Polish Art Club in Buffalo in 1949–52 and in this capacity enlivened the city's Polish-American cultural life by organizing exhibits, lectures, and meetings with Polish artists. He continued on the national level as president of the **American Council of Polish Cultural Clubs** between 1952 and 1955. After moving to New York in 1956, Janta became a director of the Paderewski Foundation, and was active in returning the Wawel treasures from Canada to Poland. As a member of the jury for the Alfred Jurzykowski Prize, he promoted Polish writers who could not publish in Poland after the political events of 1968.

Although Janta's bibliography includes more than fifty books and over 800 newspaper and journal articles, the only literary awards he received came at the end of his life. They were the Herminia Naglerowa Prize of the Association of Polish Writers in Exile in 1964 and the Anna Godlewska Foundation award in 1974.—*Joanna Wojdon*

SOURCES: Franciszek Palowski, *Aleksander Janta-Połczyński: ballada o wiecznym szukaniu* (Kraków: Państwowe Wydawnictwo Naukowy, 1990), Jerzy R. Krzyżanowski, ed., *Janta-człowiek i pisarz* (London: Polska Fundacja Kulturalna, 1982).

Januszewski, Frank (b. Łomża, Poland, November 23, 1886; d. Chicago, Illinois, June 12, 1953). Newspaper publisher, Polonia activist. Januszewski took part in the 1905 uprising against the tsar under the leadership of Józef Piłsudski and, following its suppression, had to leave the country for America in 1907. He first settled in Cleveland, where he became active in the Polish **Falcons** Alliance. Soon active in the militant wing of the Falcons which aimed to organize fighting units to help liberate the partitioned homeland, Januszewski became a leader in the "Free Falcons" movement which seceded from the national organization in 1909. Moving to Detroit in 1912, he was employed by the local Polish language newspaper and became a strong supporter of the Polish **National Defense Committee** during World War I. Over the years Januszewski rose to various responsible positions with the *Dziennik Polski* (Polish Daily News) and in 1930 succeeded in purchasing the publication. He became a leading force in the Polish language press of the time and held high office

in the Polish Publishers and Editors Guild of the United States. With the outbreak of World War II in 1939, Januszewski became an outspoken voice for a strong **Polonia** political stance on Poland's behalf. In 1942 he and his friend **Maximilian Węgrzynek**, publisher of the New York *Nowy Świat* (New World), took the lead in founding a new political action organization to promote Poland's objectives in the U.S. This group was the **National Committee of Americans of Polish Descent** (Komitet Narodowy Amerykanów Pochodzenia Polskiego; KNAPP). In 1944 the two men played critical roles in helping organize the **Polish American Congress** together with **Charles Rozmarek**, president of the **Polish National Alliance**. At the PAC's founding meeting, Januszewski and Węgrzynek were elected national vice presidents. Following Węgrzynek's death later that same year Januszewski succeeded him as president of KNAPP, an office he held until his own death. A sharp critic of the policies and methods of Rozmarek from 1946 onward, Januszewski took KNAPP out of the PAC in 1948. He remained a powerful voice for Poland's rights and a strong ally of U.S. Senator Arthur Vandenberg of Michigan, one of the earliest U.S. leaders to call for American diplomatic and military opposition to Soviet postwar expansionism. Always a powerful exponent of the Piłsudski vision of Polish independence, Januszewski was a crucial force shaping the ideological perspective of the PAC and Polonia for years after his own passing.—*Donald E. Pienkos*

SOURCE: Donald E. Pienkos, *For Your Freedom Through Ours: Polish American Efforts on Poland's Behalf, 1863–1991* (Boulder, CO: East European Monographs, 1991).

Jaroszyńska-Kirchmann, Anna Dorota (b. Lublin, Poland, September 6, 1960; d.—). Historian. Jaroszyńska-Kirchmann attended Maria Curie-Skłodowska University in Lublin, receiving an MA with honors in history and a minor in archival studies in 1984. She worked as an assistant professor in the Department of History at UMCS until 1988 when she migrated to the U.S. While in the doctoral program at the University of Minnesota, Jaroszyńska-Kirchmann worked as a research assistant at the Immigration History Research Center at the University of Minnesota and published several archival inventories of the IHRC manuscript collections. In 1997 she earned her PhD from the University of Minnesota after studying American immigration and ethnic history with Professor Rudolph J. Vecoli. The same year, she began working in the Department of History at Eastern Connecticut State University in Willi-

mantic, CT, where she rose to Professor of History. In 2004, she published *The Exile Mission: The Polish Political Diaspora and Polish Americans, 1939–1956*, which was awarded the **Polish American Historical Association**'s **Oskar Halecki** Prize for the best book on a Polish American topic. She also published on different aspects of the Polish postwar political diaspora in the U.S. Two of her articles received PAHA's **Joseph Swastek** Award (2002, 2003). Jaroszyńska-Kirchmann also published on the immigrant press; immigrant letter writing; historical memory and commemoration; ethnic archives, museums, libraries; and ethnic historical associations. Her articles appeared, among others, in *The Polish Review, Polish American Studies, Przegląd Polonijny, Journal of American Ethnic History, The History of Education Quarterly, PNCC Studies*, as well as in several collected works.

Jaroszyńska-Kirchmann served on the editorial board of *Polish American Studies* and *Polish American History and Culture: An Encyclopedia*. She is a member of many professional organizations, including the American Historical Association, Social Science History Association, and the Immigration and Ethnic History Society. She served on the Boards of Directors of the Polish American Historical Association and the **Piłsudski Institute**, the Advisory Board of the **Polish Institute of Arts and Sciences**, and the Board of Directors of the Windham Textile and History Museum in Willimantic, CT. In 2004–07, Jaroszyńska-Kirchmann was First Vice President of the Polish American Historical Association, and in 2007–09 she served as President of PAHA. In 2006, she received an award from the **American Council of Polish Culture** for *The Exile Mission* and other works on the Polish

Franciszek Januszewski, newspaper publisher (*JPI*).

Anna D. Jaroszyńska-Kirchmann (*Anna D. Jaroszyńska-Kirchmann*).

political diaspora. In 2009, she received the **Wacław Jędrzejewicz** History Award from the Piłsudski Institute. At ECSU, she teaches a variety of courses on American history, especially in the more recent periods. Several of her courses focus on different aspects of immigration and ethnic history, immigrant women's experience, immigrants in Connecticut and New England, and the history of East Central Europe.—*Anna D. Jaroszyńska-Kirchmann*

SOURCE: *Nowy Dziennik*, November 17, 2009.

Jasen, Matthew J. (Matthew J. Jasinski; b. Buffalo, New York, December 13, 1915; d. Orchard Park, New York, February 4, 2006). Jurist, civic leader. Jasen grew up in the Polish section of Buffalo, NY, where his father was a tailor who had migrated to the United States from his native city of Kalisz, Poland. After graduating from Canisius College and the University of Buffalo School of Law, Jasen was admitted to the New York State Bar in 1940. He engaged in the private practice of law until shortly after the United States entered World War II when he enlisted in the U.S. Army and received additional training at the Harvard University Civil Affairs School. Serving as a military lawyer and civil affairs officer, Jasen participated in three major European campaigns and was promoted to the rank of captain. After the end of hostilities, he served as president of the United States Security Review Board for the State of Baden-Württemburg, Germany. In 1946, he accepted the position of United States Judge for the Third Military Government Judicial District at Heidelberg. In this role, Jasen exercised civil and criminal jurisdiction over those residents of the American occupied zone who were not subject to military law. After concluding his service in Germany in 1948, Jasen returned to Buffalo where he resumed the private practice of law, while also lecturing extensively about the holocaust and the dangers of genocide. He also became active in **Polonia** affairs, serving as president of the Professional and Businessmen's Association (1953), one of Buffalo's most prominent Polish American organizations. In 1957, Governor Averell Harriman appointed him to fill a vacancy on the State Supreme Court, which in New York functions as the court of general trial jurisdiction. The following year he was elected for a full term as Supreme Court Judge. After ten years of distinguished service on the trial bench, he was elected to the Court of Appeals in November 1967.

As an Associate Justice of the New York Court of Appeals, Jasen earned a reputation for clarity of expression and for commitment

Matthew J. Jasen, jurist and civic leader (*OLS*).

to the law. In 1985 he reached the state's mandatory age of retirement, thereafter returning to private practice. On several occasions the United States Supreme Court appointed Jasen to serve as a special master in complex disputes, including a controversy about the location of the border between Illinois and Kentucky. He also continued his public service through work on a variety of committees and task forces dealing with such matters as judicial conduct, traffic court fairness, and adjudication procedures within state agencies. A highly respected jurist and the first American of Polish descent to serve on New York State's highest court, Jasen published more than 800 written opinions, including approximately 650 opinions on the appellate level.—*Carl L. Bucki*

SOURCES: "A Tribute of Judge Matthew J. Jasen," *Buffalo Law Review*, Vol. 35, no. 1 (Winter 1986); "Retired Court of Appeals Judge Matthew J. Jasen," *The Buffalo News*, February 5, 2006, B6; "Obituary: Matthew J. Jasen," *New York Law Journal*, February 7, 2006, 2.

Jaskulska, Mother Mary Felicia (Magdalen Jaskulska; b. Patnowo, Prussian occupied Poland, 1866; d. Stevens Point, Wisconsin, February 22, 1942). Catholic nun. Known in religious life as Mother Mary Felicia, after completing her elementary education Jaskulska came to the United States with her brother Andrew and stayed with their aunt in Milwaukee. They soon found factory jobs and saved enough money to bring their mother and younger brother and sister to the city. The family settled into life within the Polish community that formed around St. Hyacinth's Parish. In December of 1889 she was accepted into the School Sisters of St. Francis in Milwaukee, but four months later all the candi-

dates had to move to New Cassel, Wisconsin, because the motherhouse of the sisters was destroyed by fire. For the first ten years of her religious life, Mother Felicia taught children of diverse ethnic and cultural background in various parish schools in Missouri, Wisconsin, Illinois, and Michigan. As she experienced the difficulties of being integrated into American life, her commitment to the education of Polish children grew. She wanted to help the children assimilate into American culture without endangering their Polish cultural heritage and Catholic faith. Her determination to accomplish this goal led her and forty-five other School Sisters of St. Francis who were of Polish descent to form a new religious congregation in 1901 with the purpose of serving in Polish parish schools.

At the first general chapter of the **Sisters of St. Joseph of the Third Order of St. Francis** (SSJ-TOSF) in 1902 she was elected superior general at the age of 36. Mother Felicia's strong sense of mission propelled her and the pioneer sisters, among them Mother **Clara Bialkowska** who served as her assistant, to act boldly for the good of the Polish people. Despite the difficulties and hardships that are inherent in any new endeavor, Mother Felicia did her best to respond to the pleas of Polish pastors for teachers in their schools. Fortunately, during the early years of its existence many young women joined the congregation, but they still had to be educated themselves before they could teach. The first three applicants were sent to the Wisconsin Normal School in Stevens Point. Education was indeed a priority for Mother Felicia and she wanted the best for the students of her sisters. By 1902 Mother Felicia made commitments to ten elementary schools; by 1908 five more schools were added to the community's roster of commitments. To the basics of every curriculum that provided a sound academic foundation for the children, the subjects of music and drama were added to enrich the spirits of poor children in the largely rural communities where the sisters served. Big city parish schools in Chicago and Detroit were part of the mission outreach of the sisters from the congregation's beginnings. There the sisters were instructed to stress the English language that was so necessary for Polish people to secure gainful employment in urban centers. The sisters also taught the Polish language and culture and religious instruction so that faith and life were integrated. Mother Felicia did not only make a contribution to the education of Polish immigrants in the United States, she gave birth to a religious congregation dedicated to the education of immigrant peoples.—*Madge Karecki*

SOURCE: Josephine Marie Peplinski, *A Fitting Response: The History of the Sisters of St. Joseph of the Third Order of St. Francis Part II The Growth, 1902–1962* (South Bend: Sisters of St. Joseph of the Third Order of St. Francis, 1992).

Jastremski, Chet (Chester Andrew Jastremski; b. Toledo, Ohio, January 12, 1941; d.—). Swimmer. Jastremski attended Indiana University where he worked with the noted coach James "Doc" Counsilman to invent the "whip kick" which replaced the "frog kick" leading to lowered times in the breaststroke. His prowess at the breaststroke event led to his picture appearing on the cover of the January 29, 1962, issue of *Sports Illustrated*. He won the gold medal at the Pan American Games in 1963 and the bronze medal in the 200-meter breaststroke in the 1964 Tokyo Olympics. During his competitive career he held nine individual and three relay world records, seventeen individual and four relay American records, and sixteen Amateur Athletic Union championships. He was the first person to break the one minute mark for the one hundred yard breaststroke, and was named Breaststroker of the Year in 1965, 1966, 1970, and 1971. A member of the Bloomington Swim Club following his college years, he went on to become a respected physician in Bloomington, Indiana. He was inducted into the International Swimming Hall of Fame in 1977.—*James S. Pula*

SOURCE: Camille Bersamin, "Chet Jastremski, Breaststroker," *Sports Illustrated*, Vol. 94, no. 14 (April, 2, 2001), 16.

Jastremski, Leon (Leon Jastrzębski; b. Soulon, France, July 17, 1843; d. Baton Rouge, Louisiana, November 29, 1907). Soldier, journalist, politician. Arriving in the United States around 1852 or 1853, he received his early education at the Lafayette, LA, public school. In 1854 the family moved to Abbeville, but his parents died two years later and Jastremski went to work as a printer's apprentice on the local *Meridional*. Later he moved to Baton Rouge and New Orleans, finally moving back to Abbeville to work in a drugstore. After the outbreak of the Civil War, the 17-year-old enlisted as a private in the Company E, Louisiana Swamp Rifles, 10th Louisiana Infantry Regiment (July 22nd, 1861). In October his regiment, along with the 14th Louisiana, was attached to Col. **Walerian Sulakowski**'s brigade in Gen. John B. Magruder's army near Yorktown, Virginia. At the beginning of 1862 Jastremski was promoted to sergeant major. The Pole saw only limited action during the Peninsula Campaign until the battle at Malvern Hill on July 1, 1862, when his regiment charged the Federal lines. Jastremski was captured and sent to prison at Fort Delaware, but was exchanged in August and rejoined his command just in time to participate in the battle of Cedar Mountain (August 9, 1862) during which he was taken prisoner again. His second sojourn in captivity was even shorter with Jastremski soon returning to his company. He then fought at Second Bull Run, Chantilly, Harper's Ferry, and Antietam. After Antietam, Jastremski was transferred to Company H, the Orleans Blues, and promoted to first lieutenant. At the Battle of Fredericksburg his regiment saw only limited action, but in 1863 and 1864 he participated in the battles of Chancellorsville, Winchester, Gettysburg, Mine Run, the Wilderness, and Spotsylvania Court House. He was captured a third time at the "Bloody Angle" at Spotsylvania on May 12, 1864. By then a captain, Jastremski and two other officers escaped and, with the help of Southern sympathizers, reached Baltimore, then made their way to Gen. Richard Taylor's army in the Trans-Mississippi just before its surrender. During the war, Jastremski was twice wounded—at Chancellorsville and Gettysburg. After the war he settled in Baton Rouge where he engaged in business. In 1876 he was elected mayor of Baton Rouge. Two years later he assisted in suppressing a panic following the appearance of yellow fever. In 1879 he was one of the delegates to the Constitutional Convention from Baton Rouge, and was instrumental in having the capital restored to his home city. In 1881 he was appointed brigadier general of the Louisiana State National Guard. He was one of the founders of the United Confederate Veterans Association, in which he was a member of Camp No. 1, New Orleans, the Army of Northern Virginia Association, holding the rank of brigadier general on the staff of Gen. John B. Gordon. The governor appointed him vice president of the Louisiana State University and Agricultural and Mechanical College. Jastremski was also an active journalist, being the editor and publisher of the *Louisiana Review*, a weekly newspaper with a large circulation. As a journalist, he was honored with the presidency of the Louisiana Press Association for eleven years, and with the vice presidency of the National Editorial Association. He took an active part in the affairs of the Democratic Party in Louisiana, in 1884 being elected chairman of the Democratic State Central Committee and leading Grover Cleveland's presidential campaign in Louisiana. From November 1893 to July 1897 he was United States consul to Callao, Peru, under the Cleveland administration. Upon his return to Louisiana, he was appointed state commissioner of agriculture and later private secretary to the governor. In 1903 he ran unsuccessfully for governor, and four years later, in a second race for governor he died during the campaign. He was buried in the Old Catholic Cemetery on Main Street in Baton Rouge.—*Piotr Derengowski*

SOURCES: Edward Pinkowski, *Pills, Pen & Politics. The Story of General Leon Jastremski 1843–1907* (Wilmington, 1974); Sigmund H. Uminski, "Two Polish Confederates," *Polish American Studies*, Vol. 23, no. 2 (1966), 67–81.

Leon Jastremski, journalist, politician, soldier (*USMHI*).

Jaworski, Leon (b. Waco, Texas, September 19, 1905; d. Wimberly, Texas, December 9, 1982). Attorney, civic leader. The third of four children, Jaworski's immigrant father became an evangelical minister after settling in the U.S. Graduating from high school at the age of fifteen, Jaworski received a scholarship to attend Baylor University from which he received a law degree in 1925. Shortly thereafter, he became the youngest individual ever admitted to the Texas Bar. After practicing law in Waco for several years, Jaworski accepted an offer to join the Houston firm of Fulbright, Crooker, Freeman & Bates in 1931. Three years later he became a partner in the firm, which eventually changed its name to Fulbright & Jaworski. As head of the firm, Jaworski provided leadership that helped it become one of the largest and most prominent law offices in the U.S. During a career that spanned more than fifty years, Jaworski practiced primarily as a litigator. His clients included Lyndon B. Johnson, on whose behalf Jaworski commenced litigation that enabled Johnson to run for vice-president and the Senate at the same time. Jaworski served as president of the Texas State Bar, the American College of Trial Lawyers, and the American Bar Association. He was also the recipient of

Leon Jaworski, Special Prosecutor in the Watergate investigation (OLS).

the ABA Medal, the highest recognition that the American Bar Association gives for service to American jurisprudence. Recognized for his success as a lawyer in private practice, he is best remembered for his acts of public service. During World War II, he volunteered for the United States Army, where he worked as a military lawyer. After the conflict, he became one of the prosecutors at the Nuremburg trials of Nazi war criminals. However, his most recognized role occurred in his work as special prosecutor of crimes arising from the Watergate Scandal. Appointed to assume the position of special prosecutor after the firing of Archibald Cox from that post in 1973, Jaworski earned respect for the even-handed and expeditious handling of his prosecutorial assignment. His persistence in seeking evidence resulted in the release of taped conversations that linked President Richard Nixon to the Watergate break-in. Ultimately, the special prosecutor's actions led not only to the conviction of several members of the White House staff, but also to Nixon's resignation as president. In 1977, Jaworski accepted yet another assignment, this time to serve as counsel to a House of Representatives committee that investigated allegations of improper relations between members of Congress and a South Korean rice broker. Upon completing his report in 1978, Jaworski returned to his home in Texas. He died suddenly of a heart attack at the age of 77.—*Carl L. Bucki*

SOURCES: "Leon Jaworski, 77, Dies in Texas; Special Prosecutor for Watergate," *New York Times*, December 10, 1982, A1; Leon Jaworski, with Mickey Herskowitz, *Confession and Avoidance: A Memoir* (Garden City, NY: Anchor Press, 1979).

Jaworski, Ronald Vincent (b. Lackawanna, New York, March 23, 1951; d.—). Athlete, sports journalist. Nicknamed "The Polish Rifle" and "Jaws," Jaworski attended Youngstown State University where he played in the Senior Bowl and the Ohio Shrine Bowl. He was drafted by both the Los Angeles Rams of the National Football League and the St. Louis Cardinals of major league baseball. Choosing football, he played 17 seasons as quarterback with the Los Angeles Rams (1973–76), Philadelphia Eagles (1977–86), Miami Dolphins (1987-88), and Kansas City Chiefs (1989). His best year was 1980 when he led Philadelphia to Super Bowl XV, the first in franchise history. In 2008 he still held several records with the Eagles, including passing yardage (27,000) and touchdowns (175). After retiring, Jaworski had his own radio show on station WIP-AM in Philadelphia (1988), and four years later was co-host of Eagles postgame shows on WYSP. He moved to television when he joined ESPN in 1990. Jaworski is part owner of the Arena Football League's Philadelphia Soul, and manages three golf courses. He also is president of the Maxwell Football Club of Philadelphia, the oldest football club in the United States. In 1991 he founded Ron Jaworski Management, Inc., to oversee all his businesses, which include golf courses, a sports clothing store, and the Ron Jaworski Annual Celebrity Golf Challenge. In 2007, he became a commentator on ESPN's broadcasts of *Monday Night Football*. Jaworski is on the Board of PNC Bank and, through charitable work, has raised more than $2 million for youth programs sponsored by United Way. His awards include the NFL Most Valuable Player (1980); Pro Bowl (1980); Bert Bell Award (1980); UPI NFC Player of the Year (1980); Maxwell Football Club Player of the Year Award (1980); Dunlop Rubber Professional Athlete of the Year Award (1980); Youngstown State University Sports Hall of Fame Inductee (1986); National Polish-American Sports Hall of Fame Inductee (1991); Philadelphia Eagles Honor Roll (1992); Professional Football Hall of Fame Nominee (1992); Pinnacle Award from the South Jersey Chamber of Commerce for community service (1997); United Way Volunteer Leadership Award (1998); American Diabetes Association Father of the Year Award (2007).—*Cheryl A. Pula*

SOURCE: Ron Jaworski, *Excellence Now—And For the Future* (Medford, NJ: Beyond Athletics, 1986).

Jax, Anthony (Antoni Jaks; b. Gniezno, Poland, January 1850; d. Chicago, Illinois, May 4, 1926). Playwright. After studying music as a child, Jax migrated from Poland without any formal secondary education, arriving in the U.S. about 1889. He settled in Chicago where he first found employment as a church organist at St. John Kanty and St. Hedwig, and later gave private music lessons. Aside from composing music, Jax became interested in writing for the stage, authoring some forty plays ranging from dramas to comedies, farces, and comedic operettas. His works are noted for their use of action, dialect, and colloquial language, and included historical dramas, social comedies, and parodies with settings in both Poland and America that were quite popular among the general audiences of immigrants that attended productions of his works. His first known published play in America was the tragedy *Genowefa* (Genevieve), while other popular works included the comedies *Niemiec kosynierem* (The German Scythe-bearer), *Peruka profesora* (The Professor's Wig), and *Kuszynka z Ameryki* (The Cousin from America). His use of language, dialect, and linguistic barbarisms was evident in many of his works including

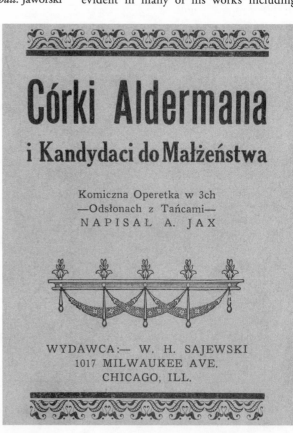

Antoni Jax's operetta *Córki Aldermana i Kandydaci do Małżeństwa* (PMA).

Głupich nie sieją (Fools Are Not Sown), *Panicz w Ameryce* (His Lordship in America), and *Z Pennsylwanii do Kalifornii* (From Pennsylvania to California). Works that focus on themes from the Old Country often dealt with Polish fables and folklore—such as *Zbójca Madej* (Madej the Robber), *Twardowski* (Twardowski), and *Mysia Wieża* (The Mouse Tower)—or historical themes such as in *Oswobodzenie Kościana* (The Liberation of Kościan), *Niemiec i Polka* (The German and the Polish Girl), and *Legionista na Polu Chwały* (A Legionnaire on the field of Glory). Among his more popular satirical works and social comedies were *Wół w Oślej Skórzy* (The Ox in a Donkey's Hide), *Wyrodna Córka* (The Degenerate Daughter), and *Dwaj Hultaje* (Two Rogues). Though sometimes criticized because his plays did not adopt a higher literary standard, his works were nevertheless popular among immigrant audiences in America.—*James S. Pula*

SOURCE: Joseph Krzyszkowski, "Anthony Jax—A Forgotten Playwright," *Polish American Studies*, Vol. 9, no. 1–2 (1952), 17–23.

Jedność (Unity). A Polish term translating as "unity," this term was frequently used by Polish immigrant workers in their struggles to unionize, or by Polish American activists promoting the idea of ethnic unity.—*James S. Pula*

Jędrzejewicz, Wacław (b. Spiczynce, Ukraine, January 29, 1893; d. Cheshire, Connecticut, October 30, 1993). Polonia activist. Jędrzejewicz was a student at the Jagiellonian University in Kraków in 1914. When World War I broke out, he joined the Riflemen's Association (Związek Strzelecki) formed by Józef Piłsudski, one of partitioned Poland's leaders in the struggle for independence and later a founder of the modern Polish nation. Jędrzejewicz was later a founder of Piłsudski's Polish Military Organization (Polska Organizacja Wojskowa) and with Piłsudski was imprisoned by the Germans when he refused to swear allegiance to the German and Habsburg Empires. He later played a military and diplomatic leadership role in newly independent Poland's military entry into the Ukraine and in the subsequent Polish-Soviet War of 1919–21. Jędrzejewicz took part in the signing of the Riga Treaty of March 1921 that ended that war. In the interwar period (1921–39), he held a number of high government posts including Minister of Education. After Germany's invasion of Poland in September 1939 he succeeded in helping evacuate Poland's Treasury for National Defense to Paris, the initial seat of the Polish government-in-exile headed by Gen. Władysław Sikorski. However, Jędrze-

Wacław Jędrzejewicz, Polonia activist (*JPI*).

jewicz was denied the chance to play a leadership role in the Polish exile government due to his close connections with the prewar Piłsudski regime, one that Sikorski had opposed. In March 1941 he traveled to the United States and was soon active in **Polonia** and Polish émigré circles in supporting Poland's postwar restoration and in opposing the policies of Sikorski's government in London. Along with other exiled former Piłsudski-era government officials, among them **Ignacy Matuszewski** and **Henryk Flojar-Raichman**, and Polonia leaders **Francis Januszewski** and **Maximilian Węgrzynek**, Jędrzejewicz was involved in the formation and activities of the New York–based **National Committee of Americans of Polish Descent** (Komitet Narodowy Amerykanów Polskiego Pochodzenia, KNAPP). In May 1944 KNAPP joined with **Charles Rozmarek**, president of the **Polish National Alliance**, and his allies in the Polish American fraternals and Polish American clergy to create the **Polish American Congress** (PAC) in support of Poland's postwar freedom and independence. After KNAPP's withdrawal from the PAC in 1948, Jędrzejewicz wrote the history of the organization. This important book is a source for later publications on the formation of the PAC by **Richard Lukas**, **Donald E. Pienkos**, and others. Jędrzejewicz was a founder of the Józef Piłsudski Institute in New York on July 4, 1943, and served as its first executive director until 1948. Beginning in that year, he taught at Wellesley College and from 1957 to 1963 was director of Slavic studies at Ripon College in Wisconsin. On his retirement from teaching he returned to New York to again serve as director of the Piłsudski Institute. Among Jędrzejewicz's many scholarly articles and books, perhaps his most important contribution is his 1982 biography *Józef Piłsudski: A Life for Poland*. In 1992 he was decorated for his many services to the

cause of free Poland by Pres. Lech Wałęsa.—*Donald E. Pienkos*

SOURCES: Wacław Jędrzejewicz, *Polonia Amerykańska w polityce Polskiej: Historia Komitetu Narodowego Amerykanów Polskiego Pochodzenia* (New York: National Committee of Americans of Polish Descent, 1954); "Jedrzejewicz, Waclaw," *Contemporary Authors* (Detroit: Gale Research Company), Vol. 25–28, 360; Bolesław Wierzbiański, *Who's Who in Polish America* (New York: Bicentennial Publishing Corp., 1996), 173–74.

Jerzmanowski, Erazm Józef Dołęga (b. Tomisławicz, Kalisz, Poland, June 2, 1844; d. Prokocim, near Kraków, Poland, February 7, 1909). Businessman, philanthropist. As a student in the Technical Institute in Puławy, he took part in the January Uprising in 1863 under Gen. Marian Langiewicz. Forced into exile after the failure of the revolt, he completed his education at the University of Paris, graduating from the Polytechnic Institute where he studied chemistry, specializing in the development of safe ways to use natural gas. After taking part in the French-Prussian War in 1870, where he was awarded the Legion of Honor, he arrived in New York in 1873 where he patented the modern gas lamp for street lighting making him the first Polish-American millionaire. In 1882 he co-founded the Equitable Gas Light Company in New York City and for 13 years managed it as vice-president and then president. At the same time, he established similar companies in Chicago and Baltimore, a gas factory in Indianapolis, and businesses in other American cities. He was also among the founders of the Carbit Calcium and Acetylen Company, becoming one of the most prominent figures in the early American gas industry while amassing a personal fortune. In 1896 he returned to Austrian

Erazm Jerzmanowski, businessman and philanthropist (*PMA*).

Poland, settling in Prokocim near Kraków. While in the United States, Jerzmanowski was active in Polonia organizations, especially the **Polish National Alliance**. He organized and presided over the PNA's Central Welfare Committee established in 1886 to assist immigrants on their arrival in New York City, established an immigration bureau, supported the Polish Library (*Czytelnia Polska*) and reading room in New York, and provided financial support for several parochial schools. In 1889, Pope Leo XIII honored him with the Order of St. Sylvester, believed to be the first instance of this award being bestowed on someone in North America. Beginning in 1887 he was active in collecting funds for the Polish National Treasury, and in 1894 he became the North-American Commissioner of the National Treasury in Rapperswyl, Switzerland, which was established to support the struggle for Polish independence. In 1890 he became a member of the Board of Directors of the National Museum in Rapperswyl, to which he contributed significant financial support while convincing others to extend support to this diasporic national institution. However, when the Polish National Democrats began increasing their influence in Rapperswyl, Jerzmanowski slowly withdrew from active participation in the Board and from the Supervisory Commission of the National Treasury. Among the many other causes in Poland to which Jerzmanowski donated funds was the Erazm and Anna Jerzmanowski Foundation, an organization that provided financial support for outstanding scholarly achievements or humanitarian actions. Among those who benefited from the foundation were **Ignacy Jan Paderewski** and **Henryk Sienkiewicz**. Upon his death, his estate went to the Jagiellonian University where it made possible the formation of the Polish Academy of Sciences.—*Halina Florkowska Frančić*

SOURCE: J. Hulewicz, "Jerzmanowski Erazm," *Polski Słownik Biograficzny*, Vol. 11 (1964-65), 178–80.

Jesuits, Polish, in America. The history of Polish Jesuits in the United States begins in 1789 when John Carroll, formerly a Jesuit, became the first Catholic bishop in America. Bishop Carroll established contacts with Polish Jesuits through the Russian Prince Demetrius Augustine Gallitzin who came to Baltimore in 1792 and three years later entered the priesthood there. As an ardent apostle, Gallitzin established the town and parish of Loretto, Pennsylvania, where his memorial is now located. He was well acquainted with the activities of the Jesuits within the Russian Empire and encouraged his bishop to collab-

orate with them to gain devoted priests for the young Catholic Church in the United States. Urged by Gallitzin and others, Bishop Carroll established close contacts with Polish Jesuits working in Belarus (White Russia). When in 1820 the Jesuits were expelled from Russia, members of the Belarus province moved to various European countries, and six of them found their way to the United States including the Rev. **Franciszek Dzierożyński** (1779–1850). Previously a professor of dogmatic theology at Połock Academy (1814–20), as well as its chancellor and secretary, he arrived at Georgetown University toward the end of 1821. Dzierożyński served as superior of the American mission (1823–30), professor of philosophy (1821–25), and professor of theology (1825–38) at Georgetown. Later he supervised the Jesuit novitiate in Frederick (1834–40) and was the Provincial of the first Jesuit province of Maryland (1840–43). He strengthened the organization of the order in America, initiating the establishment of a Catholic university in St. Louis, Missouri, and then the College of the Holy Cross in Worcester, Massachusetts. He also ministered to the few Poles who migrated to the U.S. after the unsuccessful November Uprising against Russia in 1830-31. Considered a great authority on Catholicism, he is regarded as one of the founders of the Jesuit province in America.

Two other Polish Jesuits arrived with Dzierożyński: the Rev. Filip Szczęsny (Beatrix) Sacki (also known as Sacchi, 1791–1850), a professor at Georgetown College and missionary in the states of Maryland and Pennsylvania, and the Rev. Bonifacy Krukowski (also known as Corvin, 1777–1837), who gained fame as a preacher, missionary, and founder of the church in Gospenhoppen. During the European revolutions of the Springtime of Nations (1848-49) and the Jesuit dispersion in the Austrian territories (1848–1852), additional Jesuits left for the United States. Chiefly of Austrian or Czech origin residing in the province of **Galicia**, they knew rudimentary Polish. Among them, the Rev. Kasper Matoga came to New York in 1848, where he graduated in theology from St. John's College at Fordham University and became the first Polish priest to be ordained in America in 1852. Later he moved to Guelph, Ontario, but also worked among the immigrants in Michigan. As he was fluent in Polish, English, French, and German, he was able to achieve much as an itinerant missionary in Guelph, Owen Sound, Kincardine, Southampton, and Mount Forest. Matoga, enjoying a reputation for sanctity, died of exhaustion in 1856, when he was just 33 years old.

ITINERANT MISSIONS OF POLISH JESUITS, 1864–1914

When the first wave of economic immigration began to arrive in the U.S. in the mid–nineteenth century, Polish priests followed. Mainly members of religious orders, the first of their number was the Franciscan Leopold Moczygęba (see **Leopold Moczygemba**) who, in 1854, founded the first Polish settlement at **Panna Maria** in Texas. On the initiative of the American bishops, who realized that pastoral care had to be provided for the rapidly increasing immigrant population, the general of the order recommended to the superiors of the Galician province that Jesuits should be sent as missionaries to work among the people of Polish origin. Thus, from 1864 on, Polish Jesuits have been constantly present in the United States.

In the nineteenth century, Jesuit provinces in the United States enjoyed a period of dynamic growth, focusing their efforts on Catholic secondary and university education, as well as on social welfare and the administration of educational institutions. Initially, Polish Jesuits established contact with large Polish communities, organized Polish parishes and pastoral centers, and founded Polish social and religious organizations which they subsequently managed on their own or handed over either to diocesan clergy or to other orders. In 1896 the general required the Jesuits to relinquish management of their parishes. Since that time, they have worked primarily as itinerant missionaries, supporting diocesan priests who were not always prepared to work in the conditions of the new American environment and needed assistance to establish parishes, Catholic organizations, and programs to enrich the religious lives of their faithful. In this capacity, itinerant Polish Jesuits visited parishes where they led spiritual retreats, ran isolated country missions, worked as confessors, founded Catholic associations, and provided imported prayer books and hymn books for the parishioners' use. The country missions, in particular, were important outreach vehicles providing religious education necessary for an understanding of the basic truths of the faith, preparation for confession and the Eucharist, and visitations to the ill and infirm. These missionaries brought with them from Kraków, where the first Polish Catholic publishing house was opened in 1874, copies of the Bible, prayer and hymn books, religious magazines, and other literature.

In 1900, the Rev. Alojzy Warol described his work on a parish mission: "The way we work on a mission here in America is always the same: either it lasts for two weeks or for a week. A two-week mission in practice has seventeen days without any break, and a one-week mission ten days. In the first case each missionary has fifteen sermons, in the other eight sermons. Confessions occupy the time from 5:00 am to 11:00 P.M. Every second confession is a general one. We have a week to rest between one mission and another, but the time is usually limited ... and again we hear confessions, [and] especially in those towns where there are several Polish parishes the mission works for all of them.... Also, ill people at home and in hospitals would be much disadvantaged — because they cannot come to church — if they were not to enjoy the presence of the missionaries. So we announce at the pulpit that we are ready to visit them, only the address is needed. In this respect, we spare no effort, which really makes an impression on those who are of other denominations, especially in public hospitals and in prisons."

Initially, Jesuits who had come from Galicia lived in the Jesuit houses of residence in St. Louis, Missouri, and worked in that general area. When no parish priest was available, they filled that responsibility. Aleksander Matauschek, a missionary and editor, lived in the international mission centre in Washington, Missouri, and Franciszek Schulak, a missionary and organizer, stayed mainly in Chicago, Illinois. By 1888, the Jesuits' principal area of activity was in Nebraska where they administered newly established Polish parishes. After 1896, when they relinquished parish management, they worked exclusively as itinerant missionaries. From that time on, permanent missions functioned at Jesuit colleges in St. Charles, Missouri (1897-98), St. Louis, Missouri (1898–1908), Milwaukee, Wisconsin (1908–18), Cleveland, Ohio (1903–12) and Toledo, Ohio (1913–34). These groups had their own superiors who, in agreement with diocesan bishops and parish priests, set off on mission trips to parishes and those Polish communities that as yet did not have their churches.

Before the outbreak of the First World War, over twenty Polish Jesuits worked in the United States. They included: Antoni Lenz (1851–59), Ignacy Peuckert (1863–78), Aleksander Matauschek (1864–1907), Franciszek Schulak (1865–1906), Robert Scholtz (1874-75), Marceli Chmielewski (1884–96), Leopold Suchowski (1897–99), Stanisław Wnęk (1897-1900), Jan Beigert (1898–1900 and 1905–09), Alojzy Warol (1900–12 and 1916–28), Jan Rothenburger (1900–06), Karol Janowski (1903–30), Józef Bieda (1903–34), Franciszek Bümann (Bimański; 1907–52), Antoni Boc (1906–13), Józef Pustkowski (1908–11), Fran-

ciszek Mollo (1912–39), and Michał Kurzeja (1912–32). These priests spent most of their time on itinerant missions, preaching, and retreats. During this period, the Polish communities in America were in the process of building their own churches and forming Catholic organizations. To complete these tasks, the assistance of the Jesuits proved especially valuable. Later, when the parishes and Polish centers were established and functioning with their own buildings and sources of funding, the work of Jesuit missionaries gradually became easier. Some, however, could stay in the United States only for short periods since country missions, constant changes of accommodation and the environment, and harsh living conditions were a strain on their health. As a result, they sometimes returned home with their health ruined.

Among the missionaries, special attention should be paid to at least three. The Rev. Aleksander Matauszek (1835–1907) came to the United States in 1864. He worked in Washington, Missouri, and its surroundings establishing Polish settlements and parishes in Krakow (St. Gertrud), Polander (St. Joseph), and in Owensville where he founded a church for Poles and Czechs. He established a Polish mission in St. Louis, and in 1870 published the newspaper *Orzeł Polski* (Polish Eagle), later renamed *Pielgrzym* (Pilgrim), and eventually *Gazeta Katolicka* (Catholic Gazette). In 1880 he became the administrator of Polish parishes in Nebraska, then began the construction of a church in Chojnice and completed arrangements to build a church in Nowy Poznan. In the years 1880–95 he was the parish priest in Washington, Missouri, and superior of the Polish mission house. From 1895 onwards, he worked in St. Louis where, in 1896, he organized a temporary residence house for Polish missionaries. He died in Cleveland on December 18, 1907.

In Chicago, the first priest of Polish origin was the Rev. Franciszek Schulak (1825–1908). Arriving in the United States in 1865, in the following year he established the first Polish organization dedicated to St. Stanisław Kostka. Living mainly at the Jesuit Loyola College in Chicago, he founded a natural history museum with rich collections (sold to the Benedictines after the Second World War) where he gathered specimens from the entire U.S. He participated in the establishment of the first Polish parish centre in Chicago, and when pastoral duties in Chicago were taken over by the **Congregation of the Resurrection**, he devoted much time to itinerant missions, traveling to Massachusetts and Connecticut in the east; to Montana, Colorado, and New Mexico in the west; to Ontario, Canada in the north;

and to Texas in the south. This missionary, who could speak Polish, Czech, Slovak, Hungarian, German, French, and Italian, visited Polish settlements in the majority of the states, organized committees to build Polish churches and chapels, and founded many Polish parishes, pastoral centers, schools, and religious organizations which he subsequently handed over to be administered by diocesan priests. He introduced a number of Polish traditions including the litanies to the Virgin Mary and to the Sacred Heart of Jesus in the months of May and June, respectively, and the Corpus Christi processions. He took part in almost every important event in the life of Polish immigrants at the end of the nineteenth century. He sent specimens of minerals and American fauna and flora to build natural history collections in the Jesuit colleges in Tarnopol and Chyrów, and in 1906 returned to Poland. He left a seven-volume diary in the German language, written at the request of American Jesuits, which describes Schulak's role in the establishment of about seventy Polish parishes, the customs of various nationalities, and the appearance of religious and ethnic antagonisms and conflicts.

Another missionary known and respected by Poles in America was the Rev. Władysław Kamil Sebastyański (1843–1903). He worked in North America beginning in 1884, taking part in sixty missions in ten states. In Nowy Poznan, Nebraska, he built St. Anthony's Church, a residential house, and a school. In Elba he established St. Joseph's Church, and in Boleszyn a church dedicated to St. Stanisław Kostka. He returned to Poland in 1896. His reports from America were published in the magazines *Misje Katolickie* (Catholic Missions) and *Nasze Wiadomości* (Our News).

At the beginning of the twentieth century, many immigrants from Poland felt disadvantaged in America since they were under the religious control of bishops of Irish or German origin. Because of such conflicts, the Rev. **Franciszek Hodur** initiated the **Polish National Catholic Church**, independent from the Holy See, which was joined by other Polish parishes and pastoral centers. Only when the Vatican appointed bishops of Polish origin, and when Roman Catholic priests, mainly Jesuits, launched a counter-campaign, was the growth of that nationally-oriented church stunted. Polish Jesuits provided much assistance to the Detroit seminary — which was later transferred to Orchard Lake, Michigan (see **Sts. Cyril and Methodius Seminary**) — the main U.S. seminary for students of Polish origin, founded in 1884 by the Rev. **Józef Dąbrowski**. It has educated more than 2,000 priests. The Jesuits helped to institute the seminary, and the Rev. Franciszek Schulak, in the first years of its operation, worked there for more than a decade as a spiritual leader and preacher. In the following decades Polish Jesuits offered spiritual exercises as well as various training courses for the alumni.

The history of Polish Jesuits in America also embraces the activities of the Rev. **Wacław Kruszka** (1868–1937), who in 1883–93 completed his religious formation and studies in Poland. He then left the order and went to Milwaukee where he taught Polish in the parish school and worked as a priest. Later he established St. Wenceslas parish in Ripon, where he stayed as the parish priest for thirteen years and at the same time organized the parishes in Oshkosh and Kenosha. Beginning in 1909 he was the parish priest in St. Adalbert parish in Milwaukee where he built a school and a church in 1930. Kruszka was also a social and cultural activist. He set up many religious, social and cultural organizations for people of Polish origin, authored an invaluable publication *Historia polska w Ameryce* (History of Poles in America), where he described the first years of operation of Polish organizations in the United States, and penned his memoirs entitled *Siedm siedmioleci* (Sevenfold Seven Years).

ACTIVITIES OF POLISH JESUITS DURING THE INTERWAR PERIOD

Between the wars (1918–39), the activities of Polish Jesuits developed further, including the publication of the monthly *Posłaniec Serca Jezusa* (The Sacred Heart Messenger) designed to spread the cult of the Sacred Heart of Jesus among Polish Catholics in the United States, and at the same time to help maintain contact between Polish ministerial centers. From 1872 until the outbreak of the First World War in 1914, Jesuit missionaries continued to import large numbers of the *Posłaniec Serca Jezusowego* from Kraków. They were extremely popular and therefore useful, with some 7,600 copies sent to the United States in 1894 alone.

Due to the outbreak of the First World War, importation of books from Poland was interrupted, increasing the need for a publishing facility in the United States. The idea of issuing a monthly publication was first conceived within the **Congregation of the Resurrection** in 1917. The editor-in-chief was a member of the Congregation, the Rev. Paweł Tudyka. The Jesuits, who claimed *Posłaniec* (Messenger) as the monthly of the Society of Jesus, published in various languages all over the world. With this experience behind them, the Jesuits reached an agreement with the Congregation to assume the editorship of the new publication in 1917 after the first two issues had been printed. To that purpose, the Rev. Alojzy Warol returned to America again in 1928 to head the editorial office which was transferred to New York.

The Rev. Warol (1859–1936) was a very popular preacher. During his first sojourn in America (1900–12) he led missions and retreats in the eastern and central states. He was one of the first Polish priests to prepare much needed books, as well as apologetic and homiletic brochures, for the Polish clergy in the U.S. At that time he published *Pamiętnik polskiego misjonarza w Ameryce* (Diary of a Polish Missionary in America), which described the initial phase of his mission work. He also wrote a biography of the Rev. Demetrius Augustine Gallitzin titled *Apostoł Pensylwanji* (The Apostle of Pennsylvania). After his return in 1928 he continued his work as a country missionary and preacher. Warol collaborated with the publishing house Wydawnictwo Apostolstwa Modlitwy in Kraków (1932–36) and edited *Głosy Katolickie* (Catholic Voices; 1935-36). He published *Boskie Serce w przypowieściach* (The Sacred Heart in Parables), *Osnowy kaznodziejskie* (Preacher's Drafts), *Rodzice i dzieci* (Parents and Children) and many other religious prints and articles.

The Rev. Warol and other Polish Jesuits in America also provided financial support to the Jesuits in Poland. During the hardships of the inter-war period, the missionaries in America financed the education of seminary students in Poland, and the Rev. Warol himself contributed to the 1921 purchase of a printer's shop for Wydawnictwo Apostolstwa Modlitwy in Kraków with the funds raised in the U.S. In 1928, the Rev. Warol's editorial duties were taken over by the Rev. Ernest Matzel (1879–1947) who earlier worked as an editor of *Posłaniec Serca Jezusa* in Kraków (1915–21). The Rev. Matzel published a few religious books, along with many dissertations and theological articles both in Kraków and New York. The articles for *Posłaniec Serca Jezusa* were prepared mainly by the editors, but there were also other contributors—Jesuits, nuns, or lay people. The editors strove to adapt the contents of the monthly to the needs of their readers in America by merging Polish and American elements. Therefore, the Apostleship of Prayer developed fairly rapidly, embracing some 543 active Polish communities by 1934. Among people of Polish descent, *Posłaniec Serca Jezusa* promoted the idea of dedicating one's family to the Sacred Heart of Jesus. Between the wars, beside the Apostleship of Prayer, there arose 199 centers of the Eucharistic Crusade under the guidance of the Jesuits. The offices both of the Apostleship of Prayer and the Eucharistic Crusade were usually opened at a solemn celebration during a mission or retreat led by the Jesuits.

Between 1917 and 1934 the editorial office of *Posłaniec Serca Jezusa* was located in the Jesuit college of St. Francis Xavier in New York where there was also a storage house for religious books imported from Wydawnictwo Apostolstwa Modlitwy in Kraków. The monthly was printed first by Lisiecki's company in New York, then by Loyola University Press (1934–46), and later successively by the printing shops of *Dziennik Chicagoski* (Chicago Daily), the Franciscan printing house in Pulaski, Wisconsin, and finally by privately owned firms in Chicago. The editing and distributing responsibilities were fulfilled by Brother Paweł Małecki (1873–1966), who from 1920 onwards assisted the Rev. Warol in managerial functions, initially in New York and later in Chicago. The monthly was promoted in Polish communities thanks to the noteworthy efforts of Brother Andrzej Zemańczyk (1889-1980). Several other brothers were also involved in administrative and distribution tasks including Antoni Bieganski, Tomasz Dziemba, Stanisław Wojtarowicz, Władysław Hadam, Edward Jawor, and Jerzy Piskorek.

Until the 1960s, the circulation of *Posłaniec Serca Jezusa* was between 12,000 and 15,000 copies, but it declined steadily thereafter. By 2000–06, it averaged only about 4,000 copies. Beginning in 1988, beside the monthly *Posłaniec Serca Jezusa*, the Jesuits published a lavishly illustrated calendar of the Apostleship of Prayer. The last issue of *Posłaniec Serca Jezusa* was published in Chicago for July and August 2006, ending ninety years of publication. Since 2006, subscribers have reverted to the pre–World War I practice of receiving the magazine from Kraków. The editors of *Posłaniec Serca Jezusa* included Alojzy Warol (1917–28), Ernest Matzel (1928–47), Zygmunt Jakubowski (1947–61), Franciszek Domański (1961-62, 1969–72), Stanisław Kuźnar (1962–68), Zbigniew Górecki (1972–77), Jan Szuba (1977–81), Stefan Filipowicz (1981–2002), and Paweł Kosiński (2003–06).

In the decade of the 1930s, the five or six Polish Jesuits in America completed 1,456 various pastoral tasks such as retreats or missions, forty-hour services, and meditations. Each of them, on the average 27 times a year, traveled to different parishes or Polish communities. In 1934, Polish Jesuits opened their own residence house in Chicago, having closed their houses in Toledo and New York, at the same time transferring the offices of *Posłaniec Serca Jezusa* to the new house. From that time until the present, Chicago has been the center of activities for Polish Jesuits. This mission house, in the Irving Park area, was acquired in 1933 as an extensive private residence for Leonard and Anna Rutkowski, then, once purchased by the Jesuits, rebuilt to meet their needs. The Society's residence house opened on August 28, 1934. It offered lodgings to country missionaries and preachers who worked among people of Polish origin, as well as serving as the editorial office for *Posłaniec Serca Jezusa*. The missionaries were usually away from the residence, traveling to visit Polish communities, preach during retreats, or say forty-hour services or novenas. Thus, the permanent residents were mainly the editors.

JESUIT ACTIVITIES DURING WORLD WAR II AND ITS AFTERMATH

During the Second World War the Jesuits from Chicago, supported by many Catholics of Polish origin, provided humanitarian aid for Poland and for Poles in German prisoner of war camps. Similarly, after the war, Polish Jesuits, along with their supporters and lay sponsors, organized campaigns to provide assistance to the people in Poland who had suffered so much during the war. This aid largely took the form of food parcels and other items. Of special significance during the war was the achievement of the Rev. Wacław Zajączkowski (1910–92) who arrived in Chicago in 1940. He devoted much time and energy to acquainting the public worldwide with the tragic fate of Poland under Nazi occupation. In 1941 he established the Radio League of the Sacred Heart through which he was able to broadcast a fifteen-minute religious program every Sunday, first in Chicago and then in Hammond, Indiana. The program helped him to organize charitable aid for Poland. His lifetime work was documented in the extensive *Martyrs of Charity* (Washington, 1988–89, 2 vols.), where he documented the names of those Polish men and women living in Poland who lost their lives trying to save Jews from the Holocaust. Among those martyrs were Zajączkowski's mother and other relatives.

During the Second World War, no new Jesuits arrived from Europe provoking a crisis in the Chicago residence. But when the war was over, Chicago welcomed those Jesuits who had been imprisoned in German concentration camps including Czesław Fabisiak, Włodzimierz Konopka, Franciszek Kowalczuk, Józef Krzyszkowski, Józef Mitros, Edward Mruk, Tadeusz Pelczar, and Jan Szopiński. In the ensuing years, as the Cold War began, it was impossible for young Jesuits to travel freely because of the restrictions of the communist regime. Only in the 1960s did

Poland's communist authorities allow a few Jesuits to leave for the United States. Within two decades, thirteen of them visited the U.S. For some, Chicago was only a preparatory stage before their missionary work in Africa. But some settled in Chicago, giving up their plans to go to Africa to remain in the United States.

In the years 1941–1950, when about five Polish Jesuits worked in the United States, there were 1,335 pastoral initiatives. Additional activities were undertaken in the following decade (1950–60) when the number of Jesuits increased to seven, raising the number of retreats, missions, or special church services to 1,804. Yet the records from that period are incomplete, so the scope of their effort was actually higher.

Both before and after the war, Polish Jesuits were increasingly involved in running eight-day retreats for numerous congregations of religious women, both in Chicago and other locations in America. In the years 1925–51 they led 291 such retreats. In the subsequent years, when the missions and retreats for the faithful were less frequent, the number of such works for women's religious orders steadily grew. Until the 1960s, however, the main occupation of the missionaries was to undertake missions, prepare spiritual exercises, and edit *Posłaniec Serca Jezusa*. Although during that decade thirteen Polish Jesuits came to Chicago, the older Jesuits were retiring so that additional new recruits had to be sought.

A few of the Jesuits in America had additional occupations. The Rev. Józef Krzyszkowski lectured on Polish literature at Chicago's Loyola University in 1947–52. The Rev. Józef Mitros graduated from Fordham University after the war, remaining there as a lecturer in philosophy and theology. Among the Chicago Jesuits, history was the specialty field of the Rev. Franciszek Domański (1902–79) who authored a valuable study titled "Patriarcha amerykańskich jezuitów, ks. Franciszek Dzierożyński SJ" that appeared in *Sacrum Poloniae Millennium* in 1960. As vice postulator in the beatification of Archbishop Jan Cieplak, in 1954 he published in Chicago the brochure *Sługa Boży ks. Jan Chrzciciel Cieplak, arcybiskup wileński*.

Between 1951 and 1973, Chicago was home to the Lusaka Mission Service run by the Rev. Stanisław Czapiewski. The Mission Service also included the offices of *Pionierski Trud* (Pioneers' Labour), an occasional magazine. In 1951 the Rev. Czapiewski, as procurator for that mission house, printed the first issue of *Polonia dla Misji Rodezyjskiej* (Polish Migrants for the Rhodesia Mission), which in 1966 became *Wśród Ludu Zambii* (Among the People

of Zambia). Altogether, 44 issues of this richly illustrated magazine were printed. The aim of the publication was to promote the missionary work of Poles in North Rhodesia (now Zambia) and to find sponsors all around the world, mainly among people of Polish descent. The magazine printed 1,500 to 5,000 copies. The Rev. Czapiewski also published albums, brochures, leaflets, and even sold films that reported the activities of the missionaries.

After the war, Polish Jesuits were also engaged in the activities of the Polish Scouting organization in Chicago and its environs. The idea that the Jesuits should be active among Boy Scouts was conceived by the Rev. Jan Wojciechowski (1903–61), a chaplain of the 1944 Warsaw Uprising who came to the U.S. in 1949. Work among the Boy Scouts was continued by other Jesuits including Stanisław Czapiewski, Longin Maj, Leszek Balczewski, Zbigniew Górecki, Jerzy Sermak, Stanisław Czarnecki, and especially Andrzej Pełka. Apart from regular meetings, they organized summer camps for the youth in attractive regions of the U.S. and Canada.

ACTIVITIES OF THE POLISH JESUITS AFTER THE SECOND VATICAN COUNCIL

The changes that affected the Catholic Church all over the world following the Second Vatican Council influenced to a large extent the nature of the work performed by Polish Jesuits. The number of country missions, parish retreats, and forty-hour services declined each year. On the other hand, it became a more common practice to receive the Eucharist, which diminished the popularity of taking the Eucharist on the first Friday of the month and offering the devotion to the Sacred Heart. As the previous activities of Polish Jesuits in America became limited, they offered pastoral help to about ten parishes, mainly in Chicago, which had large Polish populations and often complained about the absence of Polish-speaking priests. These were the parishes of St. Hedwig, St. Josaphat, St. Francis, St. Ladislaus, St. John Brebeuf, St. Constance, St. Priscilla, and St. Fidelis.

Over time, traveling on retreats to other parishes occurred less and less frequently, but the pastoral work going on in the hitherto residence house was ever more varied. The superior of the house, the Rev. Zbigniew Górecki (ca. 1980), invited the faithful to use the chapel at Avers Avenue. On Saturdays and Sundays it was visited by a few hundred people; a couple of years later that number reached more than 2,000. As so many faithful came, another idea arose to extend the chapel, to enable access to the library, and then to seek a new, larger room to hold services and pastoral meetings.

Polish Jesuits had occasionally participated in radio programs since the mid–twentieth century. At first, these were programs connected with important events broadcast by radio stations targeted at Polish audiences. In 1973, in Chicago, the Rev. Stanisław Szewczyk, in co-operation with the Rev. Zbigniew Górecki, initiated a regular weekly radio program *Rev. Stanley's Religious Hour,* broadcast by WOPA every Wednesday. The Rev. Szewczyk was mostly responsible for preparing religious news, while the Rev. Górecki prepared religious conferences. The program was broadcast continually until 1984. When in July 1979 the Rev. Górecki became superior of the house, he introduced a ninety-minute program of the Apostleship of Prayer, broadcast every Sunday by WCEV. This undertaking was possible when a Polish family, the Migałas, acquired half of the shares in the radio station and turned to the Jesuits with a suggestion that Mass could be broadcast live every Sunday morning. The service began at 7:00 am, lasting for forty minutes. Immediately following, listeners were offered religious conferences, news, and local community announcements, interspersed with religious music.

In 1984 the radio shows came under the leadership of the Rev. Leszek Balczewski. He named the twenty-minute Sunday program following Mass "The Hour of Faith." In 1986 the two were separated with "The Hour of Faith" broadcast on Saturday and the Mass on Sunday. The topics of the former program changed depending on the commentator. Initially they were the teachings of Pope John Paul II in Polish, then biblical commentaries and religious news with religious music intermissions.

As the activities of the Jesuits were dependent on various radio stations, the broadcasting times and duration of programs were necessarily different. In 1992, broadcasting responsibilities were assumed by the Rev. Janusz Iwan, assisted by the Rev. Jerzy Sermak who was in charge of the religious conferences section. Andrzej Czuma also became involved in the programs. In January 1995 new equipment was purchased for the studio and attempts were made to broadcast in other states. At the same time, a new thirty-minute "Polonia Varieties Program" previewed on WHLD in Buffalo, NY. Beginning in June 1995, the radio program was edited by the Rev. Jerzy Sermak who, in the following year, introduced interviews and invited guests. Then, in September 1998, Deacon Wojciech Buś began preparing

the programs. He initiated a close co-operation with the Polish section of the Vatican Radio, thus broadening the range of topics and bringing about more variety. Co-operation with the Vatican Radio increased in 1999 due to the Rev. Eugeniusz Senko, formerly an employee of the Vatican station.

When the parish at Avers Avenue continued to attract more and more of the faithful, the former Jesuit chapel became too small since, according to fire regulations, it could not accommodate congregations exceeding eighty people. Moreover, it had neither the necessary parking space nor adequate protection against fire. Therefore, a temporary arrangement was made for use of the Church of the Immaculate Heart of Mary on Spaulding Avenue. Then, in February 2001, as proposed by the superior, the Rev. Paweł Kosiński, a new property was purchased on West Irving Park Road. After the necessary renovations, in 2003 the Jesuit Millennium Center opened dedicated to the Most Sacred Heart of Jesus. The Center has a theatre hall seating 250 people and a library which had been transferred from the previous premises with its collection of about 15,000 volumes. The Center made it possible to carry out more varied pastoral and social activities for the Polish communities of Chicago. In addition to the religious services, there were also meetings of Catholic youth, altar boys, lectors, youth clubs, Catholic families, and special courses for future spouses. Mass was broadcast live from the chapel said first by Revs. Paweł Kosiński and Leszek Balczewski, and then by the Rev. Mariusz Han. None of the programs prepared by Polish Jesuits in Chicago contained advertisements. They were financed solely from listeners' donations.

The superiors of the order's residence house in Chicago were Ernest Matzel (1934–37), Franciszek Mollo (1937–39), Jan Szuba (1942–51), Jan Huchra (1951–57), Franciszek Domański (1957–61), Tadeusz Pelczar (1961–68), Longin Maj (1968-69), Jan Kanty Szuba (1969–76), Leopold Czekaj (1976–78), Edward Mruk (1978-79), Zbigniew Górecki (1979–84), Augustyn Smyda (1984–91), Stefan Filipowicz (1991–94), Leszek Balczewski (1994–99), Paweł Kosiński (1999–2006), and Stanisław Czarnecki (beginning in 2006).

Conclusion

Since 1934, Chicago has been the only permanent place of residence for the Jesuits in America. In exceptional situations, some of them also lived in local parishes. An important Polish center in Detroit hosted, among others, Revs. Franciszek Kowalczuk, Józef Kosman, Bolesław Król, Janusz Iwan, and Stanisław Czapiewski. Between 1966 and 1996, the Rev.

Czesław Fabisiak worked as a priest in an English-language parish of Springfield, Illinois, and in 1975–89, the Rev. Władysław Daleczko worked as a chaplain for the Congregatio Sororum Ancillarum Beatae Mariae Virginis in Woodbridge, NJ, where he prepared publications for the Zambian mission.

In the course of the last twenty years, the ties between Polish and American Jesuits have become stronger. Young Jesuits from Poland study at Jesuit universities in the United States and complete their teaching practice in American colleges, while American Jesuits from various universities teach English to prospective Jesuits in Poland and in general to students in Polish Jesuit universities. Also, American Jesuits of Polish descent visit Poland and start co-operation with Poles.

During the 200 years of collaboration between American and Polish Jesuits, at least 100 Polish Jesuits worked for long periods in the United States. In the early nineteenth century, before Polish economic migrants arrived in the United States, Polish Jesuits played a significant part in the structural development of the Society of Jesus in North America. Since the mid–nineteenth century, Polish Jesuits, while striving to enrich the religious lives of Poles via missions and retreats, were involved in organizing various Polish institutions such as parishes, Catholic associations, and other activities. For Polish Jesuits in America, the 100 years between 1864 and 1964 were spent on mission trips and spiritual retreats. Their spoken word, sermons, and religious teaching were in 1917 supplemented by the printed word: the Polish monthly *Posłaniec Serca Jezusa.* Polish Jesuits did not form a separate Polish province of the order in the United States and left the education and upbringing of young people to their American brethren. After the Second Vatican Council, when their itinerant missions practically came to an end, they undertook new tasks, mainly radio broadcasts and organization of a vibrant pastoral center in Chicago. During the entire period, Polish Jesuits worked mostly for the benefit of those faithful who considered themselves to be Polish.—*Ludwik Grzebień*

Sources: Sr. M. Neomisia Rutkowska, "A Polish Pioneer in America," *Polish American Studies,* Vol. 3 (1946), 98–103; Anthony J. Kuzniewski, "Francis Dzierozynski and the Jesuit Restoration in the United States," *Catholic Historical Review,* Vol. 78 (1992), 51–73.

Johnson, Barbara (Barbara Piasecka; b. Staniewicze, Poland, February 25, 1937; d.—). Philanthropist. Johnson was born in Poland and is regarded as one of world's richest persons with an estimated net worth in 2008 of $2.6 billion which ranked 74 on the list *Forbes*

400 World's Richest People. She was educated at the University of Wrocław where she received both baccalaureate and master's degrees. She migrated from Poland to the United States, via Rome, in 1968, reportedly with a mere $100 in her wallet. In 1973, she became the third wife of Seward Johnson, son of the founders of Johnson & Johnson, having previously served as his housekeeper and home companion. In 1974 the couple established the Barbara Piasecka Johnson Foundation to assist students and professionals from Poland in continuing their studies in the United States. The Foundation also extended significant support to the victims of martial law in Poland as well as to nursing homes, homes for single mothers, and selected health care facilities. Upon his death in 1983, she inherited the bulk of her husband's estate. The inheritance included a golf club, a 226-acre estate, and 36 million Johnson & Johnson shares. As a result of a lawsuit filed by Mr. Johnson's children, she inherited $340 million of the $500 million estate under an out-of-court settlement. After her husband's death, Johnson became involved in numerous charitable and philanthropic activities. In 1990, she offered to invest up to $100 million in the financially troubled Lenin Shipyard in Gdańsk, the birthplace of Solidarity. The deal failed to materialize after a myriad of financial and managerial difficulties emerged, but Johnson remained a personal friend of Solidarity hero Lech Wałęsa. In 2001, Johnson chose Poznań, Poland, as the repository for an important art collection including paintings by Leonardo da Vinci, Rembrandt, Caravaggio, Velázquez, and other works of sculpture, graphic art, and antique furniture.

In furtherance of her extensive work in her native Poland, Johnson also established a "twin sister" foundation in Poland. Her original Barbara Piasecka Johnson Foundation focuses on assistance to children and young adults with autism in Poland. In view of high cost of the therapy, Mrs. Johnson donated to the Foundation her extensive collection of paintings by Polish masters, with the stipulation that all proceeds from its sale would be designated to finance a long-range program designed to increase awareness and understanding of autism and to establish in major Polish metropolitan centers early intervention facilities for small children and group homes for young adults. With her foundation's support, in January 2006 the Institute for Child Development *(Instytut Wspomagania Rozwóju Dziecka)* in Gdańsk — a non-profit organization — began offering science-based therapy to children with autism and assistance to their families. The Institute also conducts scientific studies of autism therapy and offers training for professionals specializing in autism. The Institute is modeled on, and closely cooperates with, the Princeton Child Development Institute in the United States, a world leader in the field.—*Richard J. Hunter, Jr., & Héctor R. Lozada*

SOURCES: Barbara Goldsmith, *Johnson v. Johnson* (New York: Knopf, 1987); David Margolick, *Undue Influence: The Epic Battle for the Johnson & Johnson Fortune* (New York: W. Morrow, 1993).

Jones, Jenny (Janina Stranski; b. Bethlehem, Palestine, June 7, 1946; d. —). Entertainer. The daughter of a Polish army officer who served in World War II, she moved with her family to London, Ontario, Canada, where she broke into show business as a drummer in a touring rock band when she was sixteen. At nineteen, she packed up and moved to Hollywood, eventually getting a job as a backup singer for Wayne Newton before beginning her own band, "Jenny Jones and Company." Deciding that comedy held a better future, she worked as an office manager while appearing briefly on the television shows *Hollywood Squares*, *Match Game*, and *Press Your Luck*. In 1986 she won first prize on *Star Search*, after which she received a number of offers, appearing at Caesar's Palace in Las Vegas, Radio City Music Hall in New York, and the Universal Amphitheater in Los Angeles with headliners such as Sammy Davis, Jr., Tony Bennett, Glen Campbell, Kool and the Gang, The Pointer Sisters, Smokey Robinson, and Dionne Warwick. This experience led her to develop a successful touring comedy show called "Girls Night Out," which set a series of attendance records at various venues. Publicity her show received in *People Magazine*, *Time*, and on the television shows *20/20* and *Larry King Live* led to an offer to host her

Jenny Jones (Janina Stranski), television entertainer (*OLS*).

own talk show, *The Jenny Jones Show*, in 1991. Her show became the first number-one rated daytime talk show, pioneering such innovations as outdoor concerts, makeovers, and pretaped spoofs. Controversy erupted when Scott Amedure, one of her male guests, confessed that he had a romantic interest in another male guest, Jonathan Schmitz, leading a distraught Schmitz to murder Amedure three days later. Amedure's family later sued the show, initially gaining an award of $25 million, but the ruling was later overturned by the Michigan Appellate Court. A decline in viewers led to cancellation of the show in 2003. A philanthropist who does not seek the limelight, Jones provides a scholarship program for disadvantaged students, donates generously to various Chicago-area schools, and donates profits from her biography and cookbooks to breast cancer research. The Jenny Jones Foundation provides millions of dollars in grants to people engaged in community development through its "Jenny's Heroes" program.—*James S. Pula*

SOURCE: Jenny Jones, *Jenny Jones: My Story* (Kansas City, MO: Andrew McMeel Pub., 1997).

Józef Piłsudski Institute. The Józef Piłsudski Institute for Research in the Modern History of Poland was established on July 4, 1943, in New York City as a major research, archival, and science institution for research in the modern history of Poland. Its founders included Polish American community leaders, prominent Polish statesmen, and political exiles. Among them were **Franciszek Januszewski**, publisher of **Dziennik Polski** (Polish Daily News) in Detroit; **Maksymilian Węgrzynek**, publisher of **Nowy Świat** (New World) in New York; and three pre-war Polish government members: Ignacy Matuszewski, **Wacław Jędrzejewicz**, and Henryk Floyar-Rajchman. The purpose of the Institute was to continue the work of the Institute for Research in the Modern History of **Poland** established in Warsaw in 1923. In 1936, the name of Józef Piłsudski was added to the name of the institute. The Institute is governed by a Board of Directors, which in turn chooses a President and an Executive Committee. Every year scholars from around the world use the Piłsudski Institute archives, while other researchers who cannot visit the Institute in person take advantage of preliminary archival research conducted by Institute volunteers.

The mission of the New York-based Institute is to collect, preserve, and make accessible important documents regarding modern Polish history. This was a very important task because during World War II and the Cold War many significant documents were destroyed or hidden from scholars. The Institute houses a rich collection of primary sources covering the period from the Polish January Insurrection in 1863 to the present day. The collection includes documents, photographs, films, posters, periodicals, books, and the personal memoirs of diplomats and political and military leaders. The archival collection contains over one million documents, encompassing 150 linear feet of shelf space. It is one of the largest and most important archives on Polish history outside of Poland. The most important documents relate to the following subjects: the Polish-Bolshevik War of 1919–22; Marshal Józef Piłsudski; the Silesian Uprisings of 1919–21; the diplomatic papers of ambassadors Józef Lipski in Berlin and Juliusz Lukasiewicz in Paris; the papers of General Kazimierz Sosnkowski; and many other documents of prominent diplomats and military officers. The archive also includes records of individual Polish Americans and Polish American organizations. The library contains about twenty thousand books and many rare manuscripts mainly related to the modern history of Poland. It also contains a large magazine, periodical, and newspaper collection of more than 3,000 titles. A separate section contains Polish journals, many published outside of Poland. Among the most important of those are *Na Straży* (On Guard) from Jerusalem, *Tygodnik Polski* (Polish Weekly), **The Polish Review**, and publications from the Polish displaced persons camps following World War II. There are also over 1,350 titles from the Polish Underground press from the mid–1970s to 1990. The independent press collection at the Institute is one of the largest in the United States. About one hundred of these newspapers and periodicals are nearly complete sets. In addition, the Institute possesses other publications such as *Mazowsze Weekly, The Fraternal, Current Information, Solidarity, Opinie* (Opinon), *Spotkania* (Encounter), and *Karta* (Sheet of Paper). The Institute also houses 20,000 photographs covering the period from the beginning of twentieth century and related to Polish and European political, military, and cultural institutions, events, and personalities. These photographs were donated by individuals and organizations such as the **National Committee of Americans of Polish Descent** and The Committee to Help Solidarity. Many photographs in the collection are unique, the most important of which are of Józef Piłsudski and his Polish Legions, and the Polish army and Polish children in the Soviet Union during World War II. Other materials relate to wartime visits to the U.S. by General Władysław Sikorski and to the life of **Ignacy Jan Paderewski**. Photographs from the Institute's collections are frequently used by American and Polish media and in exhibitions and publications.

The Institute houses 2,450 maps from the second half of the nineteenth century through the end of the twentieth century. These are arranged in the following categories: political, administrative, ethnographic, physical, military, and general information. They include a large group of maps published by the Military Geography Institute and a complete set of sketches and maps relating to the Battle of Warsaw in 1920. The Institute contains an art gallery with more than 240 items including oil paintings, watercolors, drawings and illustrations by such artists as Jan Matejko, Józef Chełmoński, Juliusz Kossak, Tadeusz Styka, Alfred Wierusz-Kowalski, Leon Wyczółkowski, Aleksander Gierymski, and Jacek Malczewski. The collection includes portraits of well-known individuals such as Mikołaj Kopernik (Nicholas Copernicus) and **Tadeusz Kościuszko**. Most of the Polish paintings at the Institute are generous gifts from Aleksander Melen-Korczyński, Stanisław and Zofia Jordanowscy, and Janina Czermański. The Institute also houses a collection of military and civilian decorations, regimental badges, stamps, postcards and posters, coins, banknotes, and uniforms.

The Institute's main activities also include acquisition and preservation of historical materials, making them available to the public, and the organization of exhibitions, conferences, seminars, and lectures. The Institute publishes a monthly newsletter and an annual bulletin, as well as books and scholarly publications. Among the studies published by the Institute are: Kazimierz Sosnkowski, *Materialy Historyczne* (Historical Material, 1972), Juliusz Łukasiewicz, *Dyplomata w Paryżu 1936–1939* (Diplomat in Paris, 1988), and **Wacław Jędrzejewicz** and Janusz Cisek, eds., *Kronika życia Józefa Piłsudskiego, t. I–III* (Chronicle of the Life of (Joseph) Józef Piłsudski, 1977–94). During 1948–2004, the Institute published the annual historical journal *Niepodległość* (Independence). The inventory of the Institute's collections, as well as other information, is available on the Institute web site: www.pilsudski.org.

In addition to housing its collections, the Institute has hosted presentations, meetings, lectures, seminars, conferences, encounters with historians, book promotions, documentary film screenings, and other events. Every few years the Institute hosts an Awards Gala to honor achievements of outstanding individuals in the field of history, art, science, literature, and leadership. The Institute also co-operates with major U.S. universities, libraries and other organizations, as well as **Polonia** organizations. After the fall of communism in Poland in 1989, the Institute initiated scientific exchanges with institutions in Poland. Since 2001, the Institute has collaborated with the Head Office of the State Archives, the Foundation for Polish Science, the National Library in Warsaw, the Polish Senate, Semper Polonia Foundation, Stowarzyszenie Wspólnota Polska, and Polish Institute of International Affairs. With funds from the Ministry of Culture and National Heritage and the Polish Senate, the Institute modernized its archival collections and, in 2001, began electronic cataloguing of its library and archival collections.

The Pilsudski Institute and the Head Office of the State Archives in Poland have worked together on conserving, microfilming, and digitizing the Institute's collection of holdings on the Silesian Uprisings of 1919–21, and on a digitalization project beginning in January 2009 that includes the Internet presentation of collections that are housed in Poland and New York. The Pilsudski Institute of America is located at 180 Second Avenue, New York, NY 10003. Its e-mail address is: info@pilsudski.org.—*Iwona Korga*

SOURCES: Michael Budny, "Józef Piłsudski Institute of America for Research in the Modern History of Poland," in Frank Mocha, ed., *Poles in America: Bicentennial Essays* (Stevens Point, WI: Worzalla Publishing Company, 1978), 687–708; Paweł Pietrzyk, "A Brief History of the Mission and Collections of the Piłsudski Institute of America for Research in the Modern History of Poland," *Polish American Studies*, Vol. LX, no. 1 (Spring 2003), 91–98; Tadeusz Święto-chowski, *Guide to the Collections of the Piłsudski Institute of America for Research in the Modern History of Poland* (New York: Piłsudski Institute of America, 1980).

Jurzykowski Foundation *see* Alfred Jurzykowski Foundation, Inc.

Jutrzenka (Dawn). A radical weekly created by the writer, anarchist, socialist and journalist Alfred Chrostowski in Pittsburgh in 1892, *Jutrzenka* was later transferred to Cleveland, OH. During the conflict between the Rev. **Antoni Kolaszewski** and Cleveland's Bishop Ignatius Horstmann the paper took the side of the priest, covering the conflict in detail and in the process becoming the semi-official organ of Kolaszewski's independent party. It also supported workers' organizations, contributing to the formation of the Związek Robotników Polskich (Alliance of Polish Workers). In the summer of 1894, *Jutrzenka* and Chrostowski welcomed Coxey's Army as it passed through Cleveland. The paper ceased publication in 1894. In 1912 a different, conservative weekly with the same title appeared in Cleveland. Beginning in 1915 it became the official paper of the fraternal **Polish Roman Catholic Union** of the Immaculate Heart of Mary, which had been established in Cleveland in 1894. In 1918 it was absorbed by a weekly *Polonia w Ameryce* (Poles in America) which in 1922 changed its title to *Monitor*. The paper ceased publication in 1938.—*Adam Walaszek*

SOURCES: David Van Tassel and John J. Grabowski, *The Encyclopedia of Cleveland History* (Bloomington-Indianapolis: Indiana University Press, 1987); Jan Wepsiec, *Polish American Serial Publications: 1842–1966, An Annotated Bibliography* (Chicago: Jan Wepsiec, 1968); Adam Walaszek, *Światy imigrantów. Tworzenie polonijnego Cleveland, 1880–1930* (Kraków: Nomos, 1994).

Juźwikiewicz, Julian (b. Volhynia, Poland, 1804; d. Versailles, France, February 16, 1837). Author. A notary public in Luck, he was exiled from Poland for his participation in the November Uprising in 1830-31. He was imprisoned by the Austrians, then forced into exile in the U.S. where he arrived in New York on March 28, 1834. He found work as a woodcutter, and then was employed in a textile factory in Fishkill, NY. He left to return to Europe on June 25, 1835, to continue the struggle for the Polish cause. He settled in France where he published *Polacy w Ameryce* (The Poles in America; 1836), in which he described the Polish exile communities in the United States and commented negatively on the institution of slavery, hoping that it might be eliminated through a peaceful process. His publication is an important first-person source on the Polish exiles in America.—*James S. Pula*

SOURCE: Bogdan Grzeloński, *America Through Polish Eyes: An Anthology* (Warsaw: Interpress Publishers, 1988), 73–84.

Kac, Mark (b. Krzemieniec, Poland (now in Ukraine), August 3, 1914; d. Los Angeles, California, October 26, 1984). Mathematician. Kac earned his Ph.D. in mathematics from the Jan Kazimierz University in Lwów (1937) and obtained a scholarship for further study in the U.S. He arrived in the U.S. in November 1938 and obtained a teaching position at Cornell University which he held from 1939 to 1961. In the latter year he accepted an appointment at Rockefeller University in New York City and twenty years later moved to the University of Southern California. He is considered a pioneer in the field of mathematical probability, and especially its application to statistical physics. Among his publications were *Statistical Independence in Probability, Analysis and Number Theory* (1959), *Probability and Related Methods in the Physical Sciences* (1959), *Enigmas of Chance* (1985), and a co-authored book with **Stanisław Ulam**, *Mathematics and Logic: Retrospect and Prospects* (1968). Among his many awards were the Chauvenet Prize

from the Mathematical Association of America (1968) and the George David Birkhoff Prize in Applied Mathematics (1978).—*James S. Pula*

SOURCES: Mark Kac, *Enigmas of Chance: An Autobiography* (New York: Harper and Row, 1985); H. P. McKean, *Mark Kac 1914–1984: A Biographical Memoir* (Washington, D.C.: National Academy of Sciences, 1990); obituary, *Rochester Democrat & Chronicle*, November 11, 1984.

Kaczanowski, Witold Ostoja "Witold-K" (b. Warsaw, Poland, May 15, 1932; d.—). Kaczanowski's father, a psychologist, was an officer in the Polish army and fought with the underground during World War II. Both he and his young son Witold risked their lives by hiding Jewish refugees from capture by the Germans by secreting them in a psychiatric hospital in Pruszków. The son was captured and beaten by the Gestapo who left him for dead. Following the war, Kaczanowski earned a baccalaureate degree and then attended the School of Architecture and Warsaw Polytechnical School of Engineering. After abandoning these studies, he briefly wrote poetry, then enrolled in the Warsaw Academy of Fine Arts where he graduated in 1956. Two years later he was selected the architectural co-designer and muralist of the Cultural Center in the city of Oswięcim (1958–61) which included one of Europe's largest fresco ceiling murals commemorating the victims of the concentration camps. In 1964 he received an award from the Polish Ministry of Culture to study in France and moved to Paris in May of that year. Taking advantage of this opportunity, as a protest over censorship he smuggled some of Boris Pasternak's manuscripts to the west, but was discovered and thus unable to return to Poland. While in Paris he worked with director Anatole Litvak on the film *The Night of the Generals*. In 1968 he traveled to New York to participate in the "Graphics by Masters" exhibit at the La Boetie Gallery in New York City along with Chagall, Picasso, Giacometti, Braque, and Miró. Following the exhibit he moved to California in 1969 where he opened "Witold's Studio" in Beverly Hills. He became an American citizen in 1981, and in the meantime relocated to Denver, Colorado, in 1980. Kaczanowski's works, which number more than 11,000 separate pieces ranging from lithographs and posters to acrylics, appeared in some fifty solo and group exhibitions throughout the U.S. and Europe. Among his many awards were a Medal of Esteem from Pagar, Polish Artists Agency (1990); a Medal of Achievement and Honor from the Republic of Poland (1997); the proclamation of May 15, 1997, as "Witold-K Day in Denver"; and being the first American to be honored with

a solo retrospective at Sotheby's Amsterdam (2007).—*James S. Pula*

SOURCES: Witold Kaczanowski, *Wiltold-K at Sotheby's* (Warsaw: Wydawnictwo MOST, 2007); Witold Kaczanowski, *Witold-K: Paintings and Lithographs, Jan. 8–Feb. 1, 1973: Otis Art Institute of Los Angeles, Los Angeles, California* (Los Angeles: The Institute 1973).

Kaczmarek, Jan A. P. (b. Konin, Poland, April 29, 1953; d.—). Composer, musician. A graduate in law studies from Adam Mickiewicz University in Poznań, Poland, Kaczmarek chose not to pursue a career in the diplomatic corps, opting instead for music and composition to gain artistic freedom. In the 1970s he worked with Jerzy Grotowski's Theater Laboratory in Wrocław, studying the avant-garde with the famous director. Soon after he began composing for the Theater of the Eighth Day in Poznań, before beginning his own orchestra called "The Orchestra of the Eighth Day" in 1977. Kaczmarek and the orchestra toured Europe and North America, performing in such cities as London, Amsterdam, and Karlovy Vary, Czechoslovakia. At the International Music Festival in Karlovy Vary, Kaczmarek received the Golden Spring Prize for Best Composition. The orchestra's American tour ended in 1982, and Kaczmarek recorded his first album called *Music of the End* (Flying Fish Records, Chicago). Seven years later he returned to America, this time permanently, working out of Los Angeles, California. In the early 1990s he composed scores for Chicago's Goodman Theater and Los Angeles' Mark Taper Forum. His score for the New York Shakespeare Festival's 1992 production of John Ford's "'Tis a Pity She's a Whore" won the Obie and Drama Desk Awards. His music has been recorded by Sony Classical, Varese Sarabande, Decca, Milan, and Salvatore Records. Kaczmarek is perhaps better known for his film scores, including *Total Eclipse* (1995), *Washington Square* (1997), *Aimée & Jaguar* (1999), *Lost Souls* (2000), *Quo Vadis?* (2001), *Edges of the Lord* (2001), and *Unfaithful* (2002). His score for the 2004 film *Finding Neverland* earned him a 2005 Oscar for best original score, a nomination for the BAFTA's Anthony Asquith Award for Achievement in Film and Music, and a Golden Globe nomination. Between 2005 and 2006 he was also asked to compose what became known as the "Cantata for Freedom" to celebrate the twenty-fifth anniversary of Solidarity and in 2006, the oratorio "1956" on the fiftieth anniversary of the anti-communist uprising in Poznań. In 2007 Kaczmarek established the Rozbitek Institute to promote European work in film, music, new media, and theater.—*Krystyna Cap*

SOURCE: *Profesor Jan Kaczmarek, Doktor Honoris Causa Politechniki Koszalińskiej, 27, V. 2003* (Kozalin, Poland: Wydawnictwo Uczelniane PK, 2003).

Kaczmarek, Jane Frances (b. Greendale. Wisconsin, December 21, 1955; d.—). Actress. After attending the University of Wisconsin, she continued her studies at the Yale School of Drama. Beginning her career on Broadway, she won praise for parts in "Lost in Yonkers" and "Raised in Captivity," earning recognition with an LA Drama Critics Award. She moved to television in "For Lovers Only" (1982). She has appeared in more than 40 television productions including "Frasier," "Paper Chase," "Law & Order," "Party of Five," and "Pleasantville," but is best known for her role as Lois in "Malcolm in the Middle." She was nominated for Emmy Awards seven times, received three Golden Globe nominations, and two Screen Actors Guild nominations. She was awarded two Television Critics Association Awards (2000, 2001), an American Comedy Award (2001), a Family Television Award (2001), and a Satellite Award (2004). Active in charity work, she founded "Clothes Off Our Back" which auctions celebrity clothing to support children's charities.—*James S. Pula*

SOURCE: Anne Marie Cruz, "Free Association with Malcolm in the Middle's Jane Kaczmarek," *People Magazine*, Vol. 62, no. 5 (August 2, 2004), 116.

Kaczynski, Theodore John (The Unabomber; b. Chicago, Illinois, May 22, 1942; d.—). Mathematician, terrorist. Kaczynski became infamous under the moniker "Unabomber" because of his neo–Luddite campaign of bombing U.S. civilians. A second-generation Polish American, he had a short meteoric academic career. Graduating from Harvard at the age of twenty, he earned his M.A. and Ph.D. degrees at the University of Michigan where he held a National Science Foundation fellowship specializing in geometric function theory. He became an assistant professor of mathematics at the University of California, Berkeley, at the age of 25. Two years later, in 1969, he resigned. During his academic career, Kaczynski published six articles on mathematics and won the University of Michigan's Sumner B. Myers Prize for his dissertation, "Boundary Functions." In 1971 he moved into a remote cabin without electricity or running water that he built himself in Lincoln, Montana. From May 1978 to April 1995, Kaczynski sent 16 bombs to targets around the country including universities and airlines. The name Unabomber was created by the Federal Bureau of Investigation (FBI) from "UNIversity and Airline BOMBER." He was also called the Junkyard Bomber because of the material used to make the bombs—they were all hand-crafted and made with wooden parts. These bombs injured 23 people and killed three. The first serious injury occurred in 1985 when John Hauser, a graduate student and captain in the United States Air Force, lost four fingers and vision in one eye. The first fatality was 38-year-old Hugh Scrutton, a computer store owner in California, in 1985; the last fatality was Gilbert Murray, president of the timber industry lobbying group California Forestry Association in 1995. On April 24, 1995, Kaczynski sent a letter to *The New York Times*, promising "to desist from terrorism" if *The New York Times* or *The Washington Post* published his 35,000-word paper "Industrial Society and Its Future" (later colloquially referred to as the "Unabomber Manifesto"), wherein he explained that he was using terrorist tactics in order to bring attention to the dangers for the human race of technological advancement and the Industrial Revolution. After its publication, the Unabomber's identity was quickly made known to the FBI by his brother, David Kaczynski, who recognized his style of writing and anti-technology beliefs in the manifesto. Agents arrested Kaczynski on April 3, 1996 at his cabin in Montana where they also found a live bomb and originals of the manifesto. A federal court indicted Kaczynski in April 1996, on ten counts of illegally transporting, mailing, and using bombs. He was also charged with killing two people in California and a third person in New Jersey. Kaczynski rejected the advice of his legal team, headed by Montana federal defender Michael Donahoe, to enter an insanity plea to save his life; however, a court-appointed psychiatrist diagnosed Kaczynski as suffering from paranoid schizophrenia. Because Kaczynski often referred to either "we" or "FC" (Freedom Club) in his writing, agents thought he was part of a terrorist group but now believe that he acted alone. On January 7, 1998, Kaczynski attempted to hang himself. To avoid the death penalty, on January 22, 1998, he pled guilty to all charges (a plea he later attempted unsuccessfully to withdraw). He was sentenced to life in prison with no possibility of parole. As prisoner number 04475-046, Kaczynski is serving this sentence in the federal Administrative Maximum Facility prison in Florence, Colorado.—*Mary Patrice Erdmans*

SOURCES: Alston Chase, "Harvard and the Making of the Unabomber," *The Atlantic*, June 2000; Robert D. McFadden, "Prisoner of Rage—A special report; From a Child of Promise to the Unabomb Suspect," *The New York Times*, May 6, 1996; David Johnston, "17-Year Search, an Emotional Discovery and Terror Ends," *The New York Times*, May 5, 1998.

Kajencki, Francis Casimir (b. Erie, Pennsylvania, November 15, 1918; d. El Paso, Texas, July 18, 2008). Military officer, historian. After graduating from Erie's Cathedral Prep in 1937, Kajencki joined the Pennsylvania National Guard when he was unable to secure a congressional appointment to West Point. There he successfully participated in a nationwide competition for the few openings available to Guardsmen, entering the United States Military Academy on July 1, 1939, and graduating on January 19, 1943. During World War II he served in the Pacific Theater of Operations, participating in the campaigns to recapture Guam, the Philippines, and Okinawa. Following the war the army selected Kajencki to enroll in a two-year graduate school in guided missiles at the University of Southern California. He next served at the Guided Missile School at Fort Bliss, Texas, where he taught officer and enlisted students the subject of guided missiles (1949–62), punctuated by a one-year course of studies at the Artillery School at Fort Sill, Oklahoma, and the Command and Staff College at Fort Leavenworth, Kansas. Assigned to command the 548th Guided Missile Support Group in Corlu, Turkey, he returned to the United States in 1962, serving at the Pentagon on the Army Staff in the Force Development Agency. He completed his military service on April 1, 1973, as an Assistant Chief of Information, having earlier attended the University of Wisconsin–Madison where he earned a Master of Science degree in Journalism (1967). Upon retiring he settled in El Paso, Texas, where he served as president of the **Polish American Congress** of Texas from 1984 to 1989. He then took up research and writing, focusing on the activities of Polish immigrants in the New Mexico Territory and Texas during the nineteenth century. Expanding his efforts to the American Revolution and beyond, he authored eight books including *Star on Many a Battlefield: Brevet Brigadier General Joseph Karge in*

Frank Kajencki, historian and military officer (*Peter Obst*).

the American Civil War (1980), *"Uncle Billy's War": General William T. Sherman's Changing Concept of Military-Civilian Relations During the Civil War — From Staunch Civilian Protector to "Cruel Plunderer"* (1989), *Poles in the 19th Century Southwest* (1990), *Thaddeus Kosciuszko: Military Engineer of the American Revolution* (1998), *Casimir Pulaski: Cavalry Commander of the American Revolution* (2001), *Discordant Trumpet: Discrimination of American Historians* (2003), *The Pulaski Legion in the American Revolution* (2004), and *American Betrayal: Franklin Roosevelt Casts Poland into Communist Captivity* (2007).—*James S. Pula*

SOURCE: Bolesław Wierzbiański, ed., *Who's Who in Polish America* (New York: Bicentennial Publishing Corporation, 1996).

Kajsiewicz, Hieronim "Jerome" (b. Slowiki, Poland, December 7, 1812; d. Rome, Italy, February 26, 1873). Priest. Born to the family of an administrator and petty landowner in the Russian Empire, Kajsiewicz was educated at the gymnasium in Sejny before entering the University of Warsaw in 1829 where he studied law and literature. A participant in the November Uprising (1830–31), Kajsiewicz was wounded by Russian troops and taken prisoner; however, he was released by the insurgents shortly before the fall of Warsaw. Kajsiewicz left the uhlans with the rank of second lieutenant and migrated to France where he became a representative of Joachim Lelewel's National Committee. During his time in Paris, he came increasingly under the influence of several romantic nationalist thinkers including Adam Mickiewicz and the zealous Catholic and founder of the **Congregation of the Resurrection**, Bogdan Jański. Kajsiewicz and another disciple of Jański's, Piotr Semeneńko, were encouraged to travel to Rome not only to pursue theological studies, but also to establish a Polish émigré college. Although Jański died in 1840, both Semeneńko and Kajsiewicz were ordained in 1842 and Kajsiewicz served as Superior General of the Congregation in its early years. Kajsiewicz was a strong proponent of the Congregation's internationalization across the Polish émigré community and beyond it. Though originally small, the Resurrectionists established a presence in North and South America. Kajsiewicz spent 1865–66 touring the United States, Canada, and Brazil, inspecting Resurrectionist congregations in Kentucky, Texas and Chicago. In July 1865, he traveled to Ontario, where Wilmont College was renamed St. Jerome's University in honor of his visit. In Rome the Resurrectionists became significant advisors on Polish affairs to the Pontiff, and in particular to Pius IX. A great thinker and writer, Kajsiewicz published several homilies and sermons in the columns of *Przegląd Poznański*

(The Poznanian Review), *Tygodnik Katolicki* (The Catholic Weekly) and *Głos Kapłański* (The Priestly Voice). In 1845, he published his first collected work of sermons in Paris under the title of *Sermons and Incidental Speeches* and in Wrocław, in the same year, *Sermons on Some Sundays and Holidays*. Among Kajsiewicz's more famous writing was an 1863 letter published in Wielkopolska condemning the spirit of the insurrection. In the 1870s, he produced three volumes of writings; however, much of his work remains unpublished. The Church of the Resurrection was approved by the Holy See in 1902. Kajsiewicz suffered a heart attack and died on Ash Wednesday, 1873.—*Krystyna Cap*

SOURCE: John Iwicki, *The First One Hundred Years: A Study of the Apostolate of the Congregation of the Resurrection in the United States, 1866–1966* (Rome: Georgian University Press, 1966).

Kalczynski, Gregory (Grzegosz Józef Wojciech Kalczyński b. Haverstraw, New York, January 14, 1872; d. South Bend, Indiana, March 13, 1958). Polonia activist. The son of a landowner from the Poznań region who had migrated to the United States in 1868, Kalczynski was five when his family moved to South Bend, Indiana, in 1877. Employed as a teenager in the printing trade, he worked on both English and Polish newspapers in town. Later he became editor of the Toledo *Kuryer* (Courier) and served in a similar capacity with the Bay City, Michigan, *Prawda* (Truth) owned by the early **Polish National Alliance** leader Val Przybyszewski. Returning to South Bend in 1896, Kalczynski and several American partners established the weekly Polish-language newspaper *Goniec Polski* (Polish Messenger), a publication with which he was connected for the rest of his life. As editor, he publicized and encouraged the activities of **Falcons** Nest 4, founded in South Bend in 1894. He was elected president of the Falcons at the Alliance's fifth convention in Pittsburgh in 1901, becoming the first American-born leader of that organization. During his tenure (1901–05), the national headquarters of the Falcons moved to South Bend from Chicago. In September 1903, he called a special convention of the Falcons to review its constitution and to more clearly define the aims of the movement and the responsibilities of its officers. This convention also approved changes in the Falcons uniform designed to make it more stylish and affordable than the outfit traditionally mandated since 1894 and borrowed from the movement in Poland. Doing away with the outer mat, the baggy pants, and the cap and feather, the delegates chose to have members wear wide-brimmed hats, dark reddish-purple dress shirts, white ties and slacks. During Kalczynski's presidency, membership grew from less than 400 to about 2,100; how-

ever, Falcons activists who wanted to have closer ties with the supportive Polish National Alliance pushed across a proposal to return its headquarters to Chicago. Kalczynski did not seek reelection at the seventh Falcons national convention in Chicago in 1905. This gathering was momentous and led in 1907 to the Falcons' entry into the PNA as a separate department, with its own elected leadership. Bolesław Lubicz-Zaleski (1876–1953) was elected president to carry forth this agenda. But he failed to maintain a good relationship with the PNA, despite their leaders' substantial financial and promotional support of the Falcons department. In 1912 the controversial merger was terminated with a fully independent **Polish Falcons** Alliance, its membership up to more than 13,000 in all, re-established in Pittsburgh under the leadership of Dr. **Teofil Starzyński**. Although Kalczynski took no further leadership role in the Falcons after 1905, he continued to support its work and was twice honored with the Bronze and Silver Cross of the Falcons Legion of Honor for his many services. His son, Edwin, served eight years as Grand Master of the Commandery of the Falcons of Legion of Honor.—*Donald E. Pienkos*

SOURCES: Donald E. Pienkos, *One Hundred Years Young: A History of the Polish Falcons of America 1887–1987* (Boulder, CO: East European Monographs, 1987); Arthur L. Waldo, *Sokolstwo: przednia straż narodu, dzieje idei i organizacji w Ameryce* (Pittsburgh: Nakł. Sokolstwa Polskiego w Ameryce, Vol. 1, 1953; Vol. 2, 1956).

Kalendarz. A Polish word meaning literally "calendar," among the Polish communities in America the *kalendarz* was a publication

Kalendarz of the Polish National Alliance for 1956 (*OLS*).

much like an annual almanac. It contained historical accounts, details of holiday customs, explanations about American life, and other information of interest to its immigrant readers.—*James S. Pula*

Kalmanovitz, Paul (b. Łódź, Poland, December 27, 1905; d. Tiburon, California, January 17, 1987). Entrepreneur. Kalmanovitz immigrated to the United States by way of Egypt and Palestine after the First World War. Arriving in New York City in 1926, he worked a variety of jobs to support himself, including car washer and building manager. While in New York he married in 1927, the couple traveling first to Chicago, then to Los Angeles, where they purchased a service station. He also took a job working first as a handyman and then as a driver to MGM head Louis B. Mayer. In 1950, Kalmanovitz acquired his first brewery: the Maier Brewing Company of Los Angeles, California, makers of Brew 102. Within twenty years he had so completely reversed the fortunes of the Brewing Company that he began buying lesser local beer and lager companies, like Lucky Lager, and merging them with Maier to form the S & P Corporation. By the 1970s, a rival, Falstaff, was suffering; Kalmanovitz came to its aid with a generous financial support package in exchange for 100,000 shares of preferred stock. The advantage of this position allowed him to gain controlling interest in the company and facilitated his eventual purchase of it. His practice of purchasing once popular brewing companies led to his eventual acquisition of such labels as Ballantine, Narragansett, Jax, Pearl, and, in 1985, Pabst, among others. In addition to acquiring breweries, Kalmanovitz was also an avid real estate investor, purchasing property, including shopping malls, apartment buildings, and ranches in Illinois, Louisiana, New Jersey, and Texas. Throughout his lifetime Kalmanovitz and his wife were also involved in philanthropic work, donating a great deal of their wealth to hospitals, colleges, and universities; a library at the University of California, San Francisco, and a hall at the University of San Francisco bear his name. Around the time of his death, Kalmanovitz's net worth was estimated at some $250 million by the *Forbes 400 List*. Kalmanovitz is buried in Cyprus Hill Memorial Park in Colma, California.—*Krystyna Cap*

SOURCES: Seth Lubove, "Taking No Hostages," *Forbes*, Vol. 155, no. 11 (May 22, 1995), 47; Seth Lubove, "The Legacy of Mr. Paul," *Forbes*, Vol. 155, no. 11 (May 22, 1995), 46–47.

Kałussowski, Henryk (b. Kazimierów, Poland, November 11, 1806; d. Washington, D.C., December 23, 1894). Polonia activist.

Henryk Kałussowski, Polonia activist (*PMA*).

After participating in the unsuccessful November Uprising (1830–31), Kałussowski was forced into exile in Belgium. In 1842, he played a leading role in organizing one of the earliest patriotic groups in the United States, the Society of Poles in America. Involved in 1848 in another unsuccessful Polish revolt, he returned permanently to this country and organized another émigré group, the **Democratic Society of Polish Exiles in America**. During the January Insurrection (1863), he formed the Polish Central Committee headquartered in New York to raise funds for the Polish insurrection in Russian-ruled Poland and to promote popular support for that cause. He was also helpful to Polish immigrants seeking military commissions in the Union forces during the American Civil War. In 1878, he wrote for advice to the Polish exile leader **Agaton Giller**, then in Rapperswil, Switzerland, on how to successfully organize the American Poles in support of patriotic activities on behalf of Poland's independence. Giller's response is credited with leading in 1880 to the formation of the **Polish National Alliance**, the first viable effort to unite the immigrants in support of Poland's restoration. A long time backer of the Alliance in his advanced years, Kałussowski donated his extensive library and collection of personal papers to the PNA in return for its pledge to sponsor a library and reading room open to all in **Polonia**. This collection became the basis for the Alliance's library in Chicago. Following the establishment of **Alliance College** in Cambridge Springs, Pennsylvania, in 1912, Kałussowski's donation was transferred there. Tragically, most of that collection was lost due to a massive fire at the College in 1913. Employed in the U.S. Treasury Department in Washington, D.C., beginning in 1850, Kałussowski lectured frequently on the Polish question. In 1867 he translated the Russian documents for the U.S. purchase of Alaska.—*Donald E. Pienkos*

SOURCES: Donald E. Pienkos, *PNA: A Centennial History of the Polish National Alliance of the United States of North America* (Boulder, CO: East European Monographs, 1984); Leon Orłowski, "Henryk Korwin-Kałussowski (1806–1894), Delegate of the National Polish Government in Washington," *Bulletin of the Polish Institute of Arts and Sciences in America*, Vol. 4 (1945–46), 60–66; Wacław Kruszka, *A History of the Poles in America to 1908* (Washington, D.C.: The Catholic University of America Press, 1993), Vol. 1; *Wielka Encyklopedia Powszechna* (Warsaw: Państwowe Wydawnictwo Naukowe, 1964), Vol. 4; Krystyna Murzynowska, "Henryk Korwin-Kałussowski (1806–1894)," *Problemy Polonii Zagranicznej* (Warsaw), Vol. 4 (1964–65), 117–28.

Kamiński, Janusz (b. Ziębice, Poland, June 27, 1959; d.—). Cinematographer. Kamiński migrated to the United States in 1981 after the imposition of martial law in Poland under the regime of General Jaruzelski. In 1982, he began studies at Columbia College, where he graduated with a degree in film before pursuing his MFA in cinematography at the prestigious American Film Institute in Los Angeles, California. For his debut work, *Lisa* (1988), which was screened at the Illinois Film Festival, Kamiński earned first place. In the early 1990s, he primarily made low-budget and virtually unknown films. His work on the 1991 made-for-television movie *Wildflower*, directed by Diane Keaton, caught the eye of Academy-Award winning director Steven Spielberg, who hired Kamiński initially to shoot the dramatic television production *Class of '61* for which Spielberg was an executive producer. Impressed by his unique camera work and creativity, Spielberg subsequently asked Kamiński to collaborate on his historical film *Schindler's List*. The story of a German businessman who employs Polish Jews from the Kraków ghetto and thereby saves some thousand people from extermination, Kamiński shot the entire film in black and white with handheld cameras to the acclaim of critics who believed the style lent a kind of archival or documentary quality to the film. His breathtaking work on *Schindler's List* earned a National Society of Film Critics Award, a BAFTA Award (UK), and an Academy Award in 1994. Kamiński and Spielberg went on to collaborate on five films including *Amistad* (1997), *The Lost World: Jurassic Park II* (1997), and the Academy-Award winning *Saving Private Ryan* (1998), for which Kamiński earned another Oscar for cinematography. Kamiński's filmography impressively contains several blockbuster and popular mainstream films, including *How to Make an*

American Quilt (1995), *Jerry Maguire* (1997), *Artificial Intelligence: A.I.* (2001), *Minority Report* (2002), and *Munich* (2005). In 2000, he made his directorial debut with the horror film *Lost Souls* starring Winona Ryder and Ben Chaplin, and has since directed the Polish film *Hania* (2007) and *The Night Witch* (2010).—*Krystyna Cap*

SOURCE: Peter Ettedgui, "Janusz Kaminski" in *Cinematography/Screencraft* (Woburn, MA: Focal Press, 1999), 182–91.

Kamiński, Stefan (born Frydryk Raeder; b. Poland, December 1859; d. Buffalo, New York, September 19, 1911). Priest. A one-time parish organist in Detroit, Kamiński joined the Order of the **Franciscan** Fathers (O.M.C) in Pulaski, Wisconsin. In 1896 he was ordained in Cleveland, Ohio, by the independent Archbishop Joseph René Vilatte. From then until May 3, 1907, he served as pastor of Holy Rosary Parish in Buffalo, NY, where he was consecrated bishop on March 20, 1898. An early leader in the Polish independent religious movement in the United States, from 1898 until his death he edited and published *Warta* (The Watch), a weekly newspaper and organ of the independent church. By 1907 he claimed leadership of between 75,000 and 100,000 people in twenty-three parishes, but the number of parishioners is probably inflated. Consecrated bishop of the Polish Independent Church of America by the Old Catholic faction, he was never successful in institutionalizing dissent into a permanent church. Upon his death, the Rev. **Franciszek Hodur** assumed leadership of the independents and succeeded in uniting many of the parishes hitherto loyal to Kamiński and the other leading dissident, Bishop **Antoni Kozłowski** of Chicago, into the schismatic

Bishop Stefan Kamiński (*OLS*).

Polish National Catholic Church.—*James S. Pula*

SOURCE: Joseph W. Wieczerzak, "Religious Independentism Among Polish Catholics in Buffalo, New York," *PNCC Studies*, Vol. 8 (1987), 73–96.

Kamrowski, Gerome (b. Warren, Minnesota, January 29, 1914; d. Ann Arbor, Michigan, March 27, 2004). Painter, graphic artist, sculptor. Educated at the St. Paul School of Art (now the Minnesota Museum of American Art) where he studied with Cameron Booth and Leroy Turner (1932), he went on to study at the Art Students League in New York (1933–34), the New Bauhaus in Chicago (now the Institute of Design, Illinois Institute of Technology) under Laszlo Moholy-Nagy and Alexander Archipenko (1937–38), and the Hans Hofmann summer school in Provincetown, MA (1938). He resided in New York beginning in the late 1930s where he associated with some of the greats of the New York School including Jackson Pollock, Robert Motherwell, and William Baziotes. He also met many of the European surrealists who came to New York during World War II, including Max Ernst, Andre Masson, and Robert Matta. He relocated to Ann Arbor, MI, in 1946 where he accepted a position teaching at the University of Michigan School of Art (1948–82), spending the rest of his life in Ann Arbor. In the 1950s and 1960s he began leaning toward abstraction with brilliant colors and rich textures. Noted primarily as a painter and graphic artist, he also produced sculptures and mosaics.

His solo exhibitions appeared in California, Florida, Illinois, Michigan, and New York, while his works also appeared in group exhibitions in Illinois, New Jersey, New Mexico, and New York, as well as Paris, France. Collections of his works can be found in the Corcoran Gallery of Art, Detroit Institute of Art, Metropolitan Museum of Art, Minneapolis Museum of Art, Museum of Modern Art in New York, Phillips Memorial Gallery in Washington, D.C., University of Michigan Art Museum, Whitney Museum of American Art, and the Worcester Art Museum in Worcester, MA. Commissioned works include two Venetian glass mosaics for the Detroit People Mover in the Joe Louis Arena Station, a series of geodesic dome panels with Buckminster Fuller, and the WPA mural at Northrup Auditorium, University of Minnesota (c. 1935). He has been recognized with awards from the Michigan County Arts (1988); Founders' Society, Annual Michigan Artists Exhibit (1957); Horace H. Rackham Research Grant (1957); and a Guggenheim Fellowship (1938).—*Stanley L. Cuba*

SOURCES: *Artists in Michigan 1900–1976, A Biographical Dictionary* (New York: Greenwood Press, 1988); Evan M. Maurer and Jennifer L. Bayles, *Gerome Kamrowski: A Retrospective Exhibition* (Ann Arbor: University of Michigan Museum of Art, 1983).

Kania, Joseph (b. Tarnowiec, Poland, April 17, 1897; d. Chicago, Illinois, April 12, 1953). Polonia activist. Born in the Austrian-ruled partition of Poland, Kania came to the United States as a child with his parents who settled first in Philadelphia before moving permanently to Detroit. Following his studies in business administration at the Hamilton Institute in Detroit, Kania found employment in a local bank and established a career in that field. He was also active in Detroit civic affairs, gaining appointed to several municipal and county commissions. His involvement in **Polonia** affairs began with his involvement in the **Polish Roman Catholic Union of America** (PRCUA) and later, in the early 1920s, in the Polish **National Department** (Wydział Narodowy). In 1928, Kania was elected vice president of the PRCUA, serving in that office until 1934. That year he was elected PRCUA president, holding the office for two terms until he was required to step down due to the fraternal's two term limit on holding executive office. He was again elected president in 1946 and was in office at the time of his death. As PRCUA president, he established the **Polish Museum of America** in the fraternal's home office building in Chicago. The Museum remains one of the centers of Polish art, culture and ethnic memorabilia in the United States. He was active in the leadership of the Polish American Council, also known as **American Relief for Poland** (Rada Polonii Amerykan-

Józef Kania, founder of the Polish Museum of America (*PMA*).

skiej), which began its most active humanitarian efforts on behalf of Polish refugees after the Nazi and Soviet conquest of Poland in 1939. In 1942 Kania was a founder of the **National Committee of Americans of Polish Descent** (Komitet Narodowy Amerykanów Polskiego Pochodzenia, KNAPP), one of the forerunners of the **Polish American Congress**, founded in 1944. In 1948, Kania and the PRCUA withdrew from the Polish American Congress over opposition to the controversial decision of PAC President **Charles Rozmarek** to set up a formal tie with Stanisław Mikołajczyk, a past prime minister of the Polish exile government in London during World War II.—*Donald E. Pienkos*

SOURCE: Donald Pienkos, *For Your Freedom Through Ours: Polish American Efforts on Poland's Behalf, 1863–1991* (Boulder, CO: East European Monographs, 1991).

Kanjorski, Paul E. (b. Nanticoke, Pennsylvania, April 2, 1937; d.—) Congressman, attorney. After graduating from the United States Capitol Page School in Washington, D.C. (1954), Kanjorski attended Wyoming Seminary in Kingston, PA, Temple University (1957–61), and Dickinson School of Law in Carlisle, PA (1962–65). Although he did not graduate from either college or law school, he passed the Pennsylvania bar exam. He served in the United States Army Reserves (1960–61), after which he established a private law practice. He served as an administrative law judge for workmen's compensation cases (1971–80) before being elected as a Democrat to the Ninety-ninth Congress beginning on January 3, 1985, and to the twelve succeeding Congresses. In his district in northeastern Pennsylvania, Kanjorski is known for his efforts to promote economic development and job creation. He was also concerned about local flood control and may have been helped in his first election by pointing out the incumbent's lack of attention to contaminated water in the district after a flood. He was a centrist within his own party, particularly on cultural issues. Regarded more as an honest policy proponent than a gregarious political person, his tough, yet ultimately successful, re-election fight in 2008 brought in campaign assistance from former President Bill Clinton, former presidential candidate Hillary Clinton, and Scranton native Senator Joseph Biden. As a sixteen-year-old congressional page, Kanjorski was on the House floor in 1954 when Puerto Rican terrorists wounded five Congressmen (he was sprayed by gunfire dust). A strong partisan, he was one of only five House Democrats who voted against all impeachment inquiries aimed at President Bill Clinton in October 1998. He served on the Financial Services Committee where he was the number two Democrat and chair of the Subcommittee on Capital Markets, Insurance, and Government Sponsored Enterprises. He was instrumental in writing the post–Enron scandal bill against corporate fraud, renewing in 2007 the terrorism risk insurance program, and passing the legislation bailing out the financial services industry.—*Frederick J. Augustyn*

SOURCES: *Biographical Directory of the United States Congress, 1774–Present* (http://bioguide.congress.gov/); Borys Krawczeniuk, "Kanjorski Faces Tough Path to Re-Election," *Citizen's Voice* (Wilkes-Barre, PA), October 19, 2008, A1; John J. Mosher, "Kanjorski Fends Off Toughest Challenge," *Morning Call* (Allentown, PA), November 5, 2008, A13; "Washington Talk: Briefing; The House Remembers," *New York Times*, March 2, 1989, B12.

Kaper, Bronisław (b. Warsaw, Poland, February 5, 1902; d. Beverly Hills, California, April 26, 1983). Composer. Also known as Edward Kane, this Polish composer was of great importance in the production of music scores for films and musical theater in Germany, France, and America. A precocious talent, Kaper began playing piano at age six, then went on to study piano and composition at the Warsaw Conservatory and law at Warsaw University. Before ending his studies Kaper was attracted to the musical scene in Berlin, a city of theaters and cabarets where many artists from Eastern Europe were trying to develop a career in show business. After moving to Berlin, he met a composer from Austria, Walter Jurmann, and they decided to work as a team in musical theatre. When the Nazis took power the two moved to Paris in 1933. The advent of sound film opened numerous opportunities for their talents. In France they composed music for films by directors who had fled Hitler. When, in 1935, Louis B. Mayer offered them a seven-year contract with MGM they migrated to the U.S. where they continued working as a team. One of the first American films containing music by Kaper and Jurmann—the song "Cosi-Cosa"—was *A Night at the Opera* with the Marx Brothers (1935). By 1940 Kaper was being assigned complete scores. During his thirty-year career in Hollywood he composed the music for nearly 150 films and won an Oscar for his score for the film *Lili* (1953), whose main tune, "Hi-Lili Hi-Lo," was extremely popular. He composed for films in an incredible variety of subjects, from comic films to suspense dramas, love comedies to horror films. The better known include *Gaslight* (1940), *Chocolate Soldier* (1941), the great Orson Welles film *The Stranger* (1946), *Green Dolphin Street* (1947), *Them!* (a horror film about giant ants), *Mutiny on the Bounty* (1962, nominated for an Oscar), *The Brothers Karamazov* (where he used with great success his knowledge of Russian ethnic music), and *Lord Jim* (1965). He also composed music for the television series *The FBI* (1965–74). Some of Kaper's songs, perhaps due to their melodic and harmonic peculiarities, have become part of the repertoire of many jazz musicians and improvisers. Two of them in particular, "On Green Dolphin Street" (1947) and "Invitation" (1952), have been recorded by such jazz greats as Miles Davis, Bill Evans, Bud Powell, Eric Dolphy, Lee Konitz, Lucky Thompson, and John Coltrane. Kaper served for more than 15 years as a member of the Los Angeles Philharmonic Association Board of Directors. The Bronislaw Kaper Awards for Young Artists are held every year by the Los Angeles Philharmonic to encourage the development of young musicians for the piano and string categories.—*Guillermo Gregorio*

SOURCES: "Kaper, Bronislaw," *American National Biography* (New York: Oxford University Press, 1999), Vol. 12; *The Film Music of Bronislaw Kaper* (Pacific Palisades, CA: Delos Records, Inc., 1975).

Kaptur, Marcy (Marcia Carolyn Kaptur; b. June 17, 1946, Toledo, Ohio; d.—). Congresswoman, urban planner. The granddaughter of Polish immigrants from Burtyn in present-day Ukraine, a lifelong resident of Toledo, and member since her baptism of Little Flower Roman Catholic Parish, Marcy Kaptur grew up in a strongly pro-labor union, working-class family. Her parents worked in auto plants and ran several small grocery stores. Beginning at age thirteen, Kaptur established herself as a prominent volunteer in local Democratic politics. In 1964 she graduated from St. Ursula Academy, a single-sex Catholic school. The first college-educated person in her family, she was awarded a scholarship to the University of Wisconsin at Madison. In 1968 she earned her bachelor's degree in history from the same institution and began working as an urban planner. From 1969 to 1975, Kaptur aided the Toledo and Lucas County Plan Commissions with launching community development corporations for impoverished neighborhoods. In 1974 she achieved her master's degree in urban planning from the University of Michigan. From 1975 to 1977, Kaptur served as planning director at the Washington-based National Center for Urban Ethnic Affairs. President Jimmy Carter then appointed her assistant urban affairs director of his domestic policy staff. After Carter's defeat in the 1980 election, Kaptur enrolled in the Massachusetts Institute of Technology's urban planning and development finance doctoral program. She never finished because Democratic activists from Toledo invited her to run for the U.S. House of Representatives in Northern Ohio's Ninth District.

In 1982 she defeated Republican incumbent Edward Weber with 58 percent of the vote. She was the first woman ever to hold the Ninth District seat. As of mid–2008, Kaptur had been continuously reelected to this seat twelve more times, often by large margins. The most senior of the ninety women in the One Hundred and Tenth Congress, she worked her way up to membership on the Budget and Appropriations Committees. She also joined three different Appropriations subcommittees: Agriculture; Defense; and Transportation, Housing, and Urban Development. During the One Hundred and Tenth Congress, Kaptur launched a last-minute challenge to the ultimately successful bid of Rep. Nancy Pelosi (D-California) to become the first female Speaker of the House. Kaptur made a speech in which she charged the Democratic Party with deserting the working class to fundraise among the wealthy, then withdrew her name from consideration. In 2007, Americans for Democratic Action gave Kaptur a 95 percent rating, which attested to her liberal stances on such issues as civil rights, gun control, war, welfare, and environment. In accord with many of her working-class constituents, Kaptur diverged from the Democratic leadership in her advocacy of international trade barriers and in her pro-life position on abortion. This latter position cost her support from pro-choice feminist groups, even though Kaptur agreed with them on such matters as family planning, parental leave, and maternal child health care programs. She extensively researched and published a book on an often neglected historical topic: the slow rise of women within Congress over the course of the twentieth century. Kaptur contributed to the 2002 book *The Church Women Want*, a project of the Catholic Common Ground Initiative established by Joseph Cardinal Bernardin shortly before his death in 1996. She called for the full equality of women within a "more servantly, less Kingly" Catholic Church. Kaptur also credited the existence of women's rights advocacy within modern times to the struggles and sacrifices of Catholic women religious down the centuries. A member of the Congressional Caucus for Women's Issues, in 2007 she helped re-introduce the Equal Rights Amendment. With her siblings, she founded the Anastasia Fund to memorialize their mother, who died in 1997, and to promote community development and civil liberties in newly democratized Eastern and Central European nations. Kaptur regularly donated her Congressional pay raises to another nonprofit she founded, the Kaptur Community Fund, which focused on Toledo. Among many other nonprofits like the National Association for the Advancement of Colored People, Kaptur was affiliated with the **Polish American Historical Association** and the **Polish Museum of America**.—*Mary Krane Derr*

SOURCES: Adriel Bettelheim, "Rep. Marcy Kaptur, Ohio Democrat: Anti-Abortion Liberal, Stand-Alone Maverick, Veteran Appropriator," *Congressional Quarterly Weekly*, December 28, 2002; Elizabeth A. Johnson, ed., *The Church Women Want: Catholic Women in Dialogue* (New York: Crossroad, 2002); Marcy Kaptur, *Women of Congress: A Twentieth Century Odyssey* (Washington: Congressional Quarterly, 1996).

Kapusta. In the ancient Slavic language, the word kapusta meant a dish made from sweet or sour greens. In Poland, *kapusta* can mean a dish made from fresh cabbage and called *słodka kapusta* (sweet cabbage). This differentiates it from cabbage that has been salted and fermented and called *kwaśna kapusta* (sauerkraut). Among Polish Americans the word is synonymous with the fermented cabbage known as sauerkraut.—*Sophie Hodorowicz Knab*

Karabasz, Antoni (b. Szubin, Poland, August 31, 1867; d. Ambridge, Pennsylvania, March 8, 1934). Polonia activist. Born in the German-dominated section of partitioned Poland, Karabasz was a student in Poznań but came to America as a teenager and became a teacher and church organist in Pittsburgh. There he worked as a teacher and church organist before completing his education as a pharmacist and opening a pharmacy in 1889. Karabasz belonged to the same **Polish National Alliance** lodge as Censor **Leon Sadowski** and in 1911 was himself elected a commissioner for the Pittsburgh region. As commissioner he was influential in the selection of the site for **Alliance College** in Cambridge Springs, Pennsylvania. In 1913 Karabasz was elected PNA censor at the national convention in Detroit, Michigan, beating **Tomasz Siemiradzki**, the candidate of the "left," by a vote of 327 to 259. In March 1914 he and Vice Censor Adolph Rakoczy traveled to Poland to make their own first hand review of the activities of the political parties with which the PNA had become aligned in 1912 when it joined the Polish **National Defense Committee** (KON). Their report concluded that the PNA had erred in supporting the coalition that included the socialist forces headed by Józef Piłsudski. As a result, the PNA formally withdrew from KON and organized its own political action committee, the Independence Department. Within weeks, the KON completely lost is base of mass support in **Polonia**, retaining only the support of Polonia's **socialists** and the **Polish National Catholic Church**. In October 1914, Karabasz became chair of the **Polish Central Relief Commit-**

Antoni Karabasz, Polonia activist (*OLS*).

tee, but in early 1915 he was publicly attacked by the socialist **Dziennik Ludowy** for misdeeds he had allegedly committed before migrating from Poland. Karabasz denied the charges, but also announced his decision to resign as **censor**. The PNA initially refused to accept his resignation, but when he remained adamant it was accepted in April 1915. Karabasz then retired from public life.—*Donald E. Pienkos*

SOURCES: Andrzej Garlicki, "Misja A. Karabasza i A. Rakocznego, *Przegląd Historyczny*, Vol. 52, no. 2 (1961), 232–46; Adam Olszewski, *Historia Związku Narodowego Polskiego* (Chicago: Polish National Alliance, 1957–1963), Vol. II; Donald E. Pienkos, *PNA: A Centennial History of the Polish National Alliance of the United States of North America* (Boulder, CO: East European Monographs, 1984).

Kargé, Joseph (b. near Poznań, Poland, July 4, 1823; d. New York City, New York, December 27, 1892). Educator, military officer. After studying history and linguistics in the University in Wrocław, Kargé took part in the unsuccessful revolutions of the "Springtime of Nations" in 1848. Condemned to death in absentia following the failure of the revolts, he fled to France, then migrated to England and finally to the United States. Arriving in New York in 1851, he earned a living teaching languages and classics until the beginning of the Civil War when he secured a commission as lieutenant colonel of the 1st New Jersey Cavalry. Appointed colonel soon thereafter, his regiment gained a reputation for discipline and esprit de corps. Wounded during the Second Bull Run Campaign in 1862, he returned to duty in time to participate in the Fredericksburg Campaign, but was forced to resign his commission when his wound would not heal properly. After several months of recuperation, he recruited the 2nd New Jersey Cavalry, leading it off to Tennessee as its colonel in November 1863. By April, 1864, he had risen to command a brigade during Gen.

General Joseph Kargé (*LC*).

William T. Sherman's Atlanta Campaign. Kargé also took part in Gen. Benjamin H. Grierson's raids into Tennessee and Alabama. His victory over Confederate Gen. Nathan Bedford Forrest at Bolivar, Tennessee, is believed to be the only time during the war that Forrest was defeated in a pitched battle. Kargé was promoted to brigadier general in April 1865. Following the war he served in the army for several years before accepting a position as chair of the Department of Languages and Literature at the College of New Jersey (later Princeton University), a position he held until his death over twenty years later.—*Francis Casimir Kajencki*

SOURCES: Francis Casimir Kajencki, *Star on Many a Battlefield: Brevet Brigadier General Joseph Kargé in the American Civil War* (Rutherford, NJ: Fairleigh Dickinson University Press, 1980); William Alfred Packard, *Joseph Karge, A Memorial Sketch* (New York: Anson D. F. Randolph and Co., 1893).

Karpowicz, Tymoteusz (b. Zielona, Poland, December 15, 1921; d. Oak Park, Illinois, June 29, 2005). Poet, playwright, translator. An innovative poet, a master of Polish linguistic poetry, a prose writer and a great modernist, Karpowicz studied Polish philology at the University of Wrocław, Poland, received his doctorate and taught there as an assistant to the famous professor Tadeusz Mikulski from 1953 to 1958. During the Nazi occupation he participated in the Polish underground resistance movement, making his literary debut in 1948 with a small volume of poetry *Żywe Wymiary* (Living Dimensions). In 1949 he stopped writing as a result of the socialist realism tendency in literature and did not resume his literary activity until 1956 under the thaw. In 1957 the weekly magazine

Nowe Sygnały (New Signals) that he edited was closed for its nonconforming views, and Karpowicz was also removed as editor of *Poezja* and *Odra* for the same reason. His first postthaw volume of poetry, *Kamienna muzyka* (Stone Music), was published in 1958, the same year he received the Literary Prize of the City of Wrocław. Following this he resigned his academic career and devoted himself entirely to poetry. In the 1970s, supported by scholarships, he was able to go to France, America and Germany. In 1971 he was awarded a fellowship from the Fondation pour une Entraide Intellectuelle Européenne (Paris) and in 1973 he received an invitation to join the International Working Program at the University of Iowa where he defended his postdoctoral dissertation from the University of Wrocław. That same year he received a twoyear position as an Associate Professor of Polish Literature at the University of Illinois at Chicago Circle. During the years 1976–78 he went to Bonn and West Berlin and spent some time teaching at Munich and Regensburg Universities. Upon his return to Chicago in 1978 he was appointed Professor of Polish Literature in the Department of Slavic Languages and Literatures at the University of Illinois at Chicago, where he taught until his retirement in 1992. Karpowicz was considered an expert on Bolesław Leśmian, Cyprian Norwid and Julian Przybos. He wrote some eighty volumes of poetry, twenty plays including radio and theater plays, translations from German, Russian and Serbian and over a hundred articles and numerous reviews. His poetry is difficult, metaphysical, and proverbial. He was a member of the Association of Polish Writers, the Pen-Club, and the World Phenomenological Institute. He was honored with the prestigious **Alfred Jurzykowski Foundation** Award and was twice a recipient of the Illinois Arts Council Annual Award. He was nominated for the Nike Award for *Słóje Zadrzewne* (Rings Behind the Wood), his last volume of poetry published in 1999, for which he received the Odra Literary Prize a year later. This masterpiece was written after his retirement as Emeritus Professor from the University of Illinois in 1992. His literary activity and the innovative aspect of his poetry reflected his mastery of the Polish language and gained him praise for his originality from many, including **Czesław Miłosz**, the Nobel Prize recipient (1980), who insisted that Karpowicz added splendor to Polish poetry. He was a perfectionist and isolationist, an educator, poet, scholar, translator and friend to many. Karpowicz was not interested in widespread acclaim and popularity, but preferred to get the recognition and respect of the elite

few. A dedicated teacher, he is credited with promoting and spreading Polish literature abroad and for having exerted a great influence on many young poets.—*Maria Swiecicka-Ziemianek*

SOURCES: Stanisław Michalski, *Karpowicz* (Warsaw: Wiedza Powszechna, 1979); Joseph Brodsky, et al., *Three Slavic Poets: Joseph Brodsky, Tymoteusz Karpowicz, Djordje Nikolic* (Chicago: Elpenor Books, 1975).

Karski, Jan (b. Jan Kozielewski; Łódź, Poland, April 24, 1914; d. Washington, D.C., July 13, 2000). Soldier, political scientist. With the outbreak of the Second World War, Jan Kozielewski (Karski) served as a soldier in the Polish Army in the initial stages of the German invasion before being captured by the Soviets and held by them as a prisoner of war. Escaping, he reached Warsaw where he worked under several *nommes de guerre* (including "Karski") with the Polish Underground as a courier linking up with various Underground groups and representatives of the Polish Government-in-exile in France and subsequently London. Captured by the Gestapo in 1940, he survived torture and a suicide attempt to escape with the assistance of the Underground. Karski served in a variety of roles until called upon to go as a courier to the Polish government-in-exile in London to convey reports from the various Polish Underground groups in late 1942. This required meeting with all of these groups, including the Polish Jewish Underground (both the Bund and Zionist) groups. After hearing of the horrifying conditions in the Warsaw Ghetto that included starvation, roundups, and deportations, a trip was arranged for Karski to witness these conditions first hand. He later returned to the Warsaw Ghetto to get a more complete sense of the conditions. He also disguised himself as a Ukrainian guard and went to Izbica Lubelska, a "sorting point" for Jews "resettled" to the Nazi extermination facility at Belzec. Sickened by what he had witnessed, Karski resolved to tell the world of the destruction of the Jews. In later years, when Karski found it difficult to speak of these events, he would simply say, "I saw terrible things." Sent to London, he made his reports to the various representatives of the Polish Government-in-exile and sought to convey the news of the Nazi extermination of the Jews to whoever would listen. He also spoke to British representatives and officials who proved to be incredulous or indifferent to Karski's reports. The British government was more concerned about maintaining its alliance with the Soviet Union than supporting the London government-in-exile.

Hopeful that the United States government would be more sympathetic, Karski was dispatched in June 1943 to report to various government officials including President Roosevelt. Committed to warning the United States of growing Soviet threats to Poland, Karski also intended to spread the news of the destruction of Europe's Jews by the Nazis. Roosevelt listened intently and asked many questions. Supreme Court Justice Felix Frankfurter reacted with shock and disbelief. Karski also met with numerous figures within and outside of the Roosevelt administration, with Polish American groups, Jewish American organizations, Roman Catholic church officials, unions, journalists, and anyone who would listen to what he had witnessed, urging them to do what they could to support those resisting the Nazis and Communists.

By spring 1944, as Poland's fate looked bleak after the Teheran Conference, and the fate of the Jews even bleaker, Karski was more determined than ever to promote his cause. Unable to return to the fighting in Europe as his cover had been blown and he was now known to the Nazis, he met a literary agent who obtained for Karski a book contract with Houghton Mifflin. Through the late spring and summer of 1944, he dictated and helped to edit his account of his life in the Underground. With the book, *Story of a Secret State*, slated for publication in the fall, Karski launched a major public speaking tour using the book to promote the cause of an independent Poland and the news of the horrible fate of Europe's Jews. He continued his speaking tour through 1944 to the end of the war in 1945. Exhausted by the tour, the decision at **Yalta** giving Poland to the Soviets and the news of the extermination facilities uncovered by the Allies threw him into deep depression and bitterness. Despite his efforts, he believed he had failed to prevent the Soviet takeover of Poland and the rescue of Europe's Jews. His speaking tours dried up; the new Soviet Communist leaders of Poland replaced the embassy staff he had known. Lost and alienated, Karski was now a man without a country.

Failing in his attempt to secure work in the U.S. State Department and the United Nations, he revived his academic career in 1949, entering the School of Foreign Service at Georgetown University where he received his doctorate in 1953. Hired to teach courses in political science at Georgetown, he remained there until his retirement in 1984. A popular teacher and lecturer, he regularly denounced Communism as a tyrannical form of government, supported the goal of an independent non–Communist Poland, and aided and spoke on behalf of Polish defectors to the West. Yet, in the 1970s he reconnected and kept in close contact with former members of

the Underground who rescued him from the Gestapo.

Karski became a U.S. citizen in 1954 and adopted one of his *nom de guerres,* "Karski," instead of using his given name as that was the name on his U.S. Visa application when he first arrived in 1943. His reputation as an anti–Communist brought him to the attention of the United States Information Service (USIS), where he was hired to go on international lecture tours through Asia, Africa, and the Mediterranean regions (1956–67). Given his experiences as a courier, propagandist, and covert operative for the Polish Underground, Karski was also asked to consult with U.S. intelligence agencies in the 1950s and 1960s.

During his academic life Karski spent most of his time teaching, but also researched and wrote for over a decade his *magnum opus,* a book examining Poland's diplomatic history in the twentieth century, *The Great Powers and Poland: 1919–1945.* The work criticized the small-mindedness of the Polish ruling politicians in the "camp" following Piłsudski's death that prevented them from realistically seeing the threats coming from Germany and the Soviet Union. The work also denounced the abandonment of Polish interests by the Western Allies in favor of Stalin. He also wrote numerous articles for professional and popular audiences and participated in several civic organizations.

His past efforts as a courier of the news of the fate of Europe's Jews came to the attention of Claude Lanzmann who was filming interviews with Holocaust survivors and other witnesses for his film *Shoah.* Despite criticisms of an anti–Polish bias in the film, Karski defended Lanzmann's approach, arguing that the uniqueness of the Holocaust as it impacted the Jews needed to be told.

A renewed interest in those events from the 1970s onward brought attention to Karksi that he initially tried to shun. Elie Wiesel invited him to speak at the 1981 International Liberators' Conference, where Karski spoke openly and emotionally about his mission to the U.S. He and his wife Pola, whose family members perished in the Holocaust, were invited to Israel in 1982, where Karski was listed as a Righteous Gentile by Yad Vashem and planted a tree bearing his name on the Avenue of the Righteous Memorial. He was also made an honorary citizen of Israel. Attention and accolades poured upon Karski as he traveled extensively during the next decade, speaking about his experiences as never before. After the end of communism in Poland, Karski was awarded the Order of the White Eagle by President Lech Wałęsa. Declining health and the death of his wife Pola in July, 1992 curbed

further activities. In her memory, Karski established a $5,000 annual prize to be awarded by the YIVO Institute for Jewish Research to authors documenting or interpreting Jewish contributions to Polish culture and science.— *Romuald K. Byczkiewicz*

SOURCES: David Childs, "Obituary: Jan Karski," *The Independent (London),* July 17, 2000; Jan Karski, *Story of a Secret State* (Boston, MA: Houghton Mifflin, 1944); Michael T. Kaufman, "Jan Karski Dies at 86; Warned West About Holocaust," *The New York Times,* July 15, 2000; E. Thomas Wood and Stanisław M. Jankowski, *Karski: How One Man Tried to Stop the Holocaust* (New York: John Wiley & Sons, Inc., 1994).

Kashubs. Kashubs are inhabitants of Poland's Baltic coast near Gdańsk who have a dialect that was originally part of a series of northwest Slavic dialects that have since become extinct with the exception of Kashubian. During the Middle Ages regional dukes ruled over this area which was sometimes autonomous and at others under the rule of Poland, the Holy Roman Empire, or the Teutonic Order. During the early modern period, Poland ruled over most of the Kashubs but the region fell to Prussia as a result of the partitions of Poland. The Kashubian dialect and culture thus exhibit both Polish and German influence. Most Kashubs were fisherman, small farmers, or foresters. Kashub migration to the New World began in the 1850s, following German migration patterns out of Prussia. The first significant Kashub diaspora community was in Wilno, Ontario, Canada. Founded in 1858, it holds the distinction of being the first Polish community in Canada. Kashubs also began to arrive in the United States, coming directly from Poland and secondarily from Ontario. Most came during the early period of mass Polish immigration, from the 1850s to 1880s. They settled in a number of locations in the Midwest and secondarily on the Great Plains. The Jones Island settlement in Milwaukee began in the 1870s when Kashub immigrants took up land on the shores of Lake Michigan and worked as fishermen. This community was evicted in the 1940s since the original settlers had never obtained title to the land. Identifiable Kashub urban parishes are found in St. Josaphat in Chicago (founded 1884) and St. Hyacinth in Detroit (founded 1907). In most cases, Kashubs were not numerous enough in urban areas to form distinct parishes, though Detroit was home to enough Kashubs to support a company that manufactured traditional Kashub-style snuff tobacco, Goike's Kashub Snuff. The company remained in business into at least the mid–1960s.

The most significant Kashub settlement in the United States was Winona, Minnesota, where the first settlers arrived in the mid 1850s and St. Stanislaus Kostka Parish was founded in 1872. Kashubs formed the majority of Poles in Winona, who by the turn of the century numbered about 5,000. There were a number of nearby satellite communities, including Independence, Wisconsin. Most of the immigrants worked seasonally in the city's sawmills and often maintained small subsistence farms outside of town. Winona's importance as a Kashub center was enhanced by the arrival of **Hieronym Derdowski** a well known Kashub poet and activist who served as editor of the newspaper *Wiarus*. It became the foremost Polish newspaper west of Chicago and Milwaukee until Derdowski's death in 1902. The paper continued under the editorship of his wife until 1919. Although *Wiarus*'s appeal went far beyond Kashubs, Derdowski's reputation and his writing on Kashub topics ensured that is was widely read in most Kashub settlements. Derdowski published occasional poems in the Kashub dialect and, as part of a small book publishing enterprise, edited a Polish-Kashub dictionary, though it is unclear whether any were actually printed. Migrants from Winona, mostly first and second generation Kashubs, settled a number of other farming communities. These included New Brighton and Holloway in Minnesota, Day County, South Dakota, and St. Philips, Montana. Although few Kashubs have come to America in recent decades, Kashub identity remains visible in both Wilno, Ontario, and Winona, Minnesota. In 1997, a small cultural society opened in Minnesota, the Kashub Association of North America.—*John Radzilowski*

SOURCES: John Radzilowski, *Poles in Minnesota* (St. Paul: Minnesota Historical Society Press, 2005); Jan L. Perkowski, "A Kashubian Ideolect in the United States" (Unpublished doctoral dissertation, Harvard University, December 1964); Jan L. Perkowski, "The Kashubs—Origins and Emigration to the U.S.," *Polish American Studies*, Vol. 23, no. 1 (1966), 1–7.

Kaufman, Boris Abelevich (b. Białystok, Poland, August 24, 1897; d. New York City, New York, June 24, 1980). Cinematographer. Following the recreation of an independent Polish state after World War I, Kaufman moved with his parents to Polish-controlled territory. After graduating from the Sorbonne in Paris, he began working in cinematography, working on 32 films in France between 1927 and 1939. With the outbreak of World War II he served in the French army, then escaped to Canada following the fall of France. He moved to the U.S. in 1942 where he worked on 14 documentaries and short films including the wartime *Why We Fight* (1943), *Hymn of the Nations* (1943), and *A Better Tomorrow* (1944). His big break came when he was selected by Elia Kazan to film *On the Waterfront* (1954), which earned Kaufman an

Academy Award for cinematography and a Golden Globe Award (1955). Following his success with Kazan, he directed 24 additional films including such well-know works as *A Family Affair* (1955), *Baby Doll* (1955), *12 Angry Men* (1956), *Splendor in the Grass* (1960), *Long Day's Journey Into Night* (1962), and *The Pawnbroker* (1963). It was Kaufman's *Garden of Eden* (1955) that led to a Supreme Court case, Excelsior Pictures Corp. v. Regents of the University of New York State, which affirmed that nudity in a film was not *ipso facto* obscene.—*James S. Pula*

SOURCES: Boris Kaufman, "Boris Kaufman Papers, 1836–2004" (in the Yale University Archives, New Haven, Connecticut); Boris Kaufman, "Reminiscences of Boris Kaufman: Oral History, 1959" (in the Columbia University Library Archives in New York City).

Kenar, Jerzy Szymon (b. Iwonicz Zdrój, Poland, January 19, 1948; d.—). Sculptor. Educated at the State Higher School of Fine Arts in Gdańsk (1971–73), Kenar left Poland for Sweden in 1973 and in 1979 he migrated to the United States where he opened the Wooden Gallery in Chicago the following year. Working with wood, bronze, and an acrylic-based composite, he created hand-carved sculptures and reliefs involving liturgical art that were installed in more than fifty U.S. churches. His career took off in the mid-1990s with works decorating Chicago's O'Hare Airport, the Harold Washington Library, the interior of St. Constance Church in Jefferson Park, wooden artwork for St. Kevin's Church in South Deering, and the "Millennium Doors" for Holy Trinity. His works were exhibited in several Chicago-area shows. Among his many honors, the Polish Minister of Culture awarded him its prestigious Medal of Honor for an Exceptional Cultural Development within the International Arena (1996), and the Polish Minister of Foreign Affairs, Bronisław Geremek, awarded him an Honorary Diploma recognizing him as one of the outstanding contributing artists to the cultural promotion of Poland in the world (1999). In 1999, Kenar was chosen by the Museum of Architecture and Design as one of the artists featured to be in the "Chicago's Top Ten Artist" exhibition, and both that year and the next the *Chicago Tribune* featured him in its notable *Sunday Magazine* issue. In 2000, he received the prestigious Chopin Award, granted for outstanding contributions to the Cultural and Artistic Development of the World, and the following year was commissioned to create a granite and live-water permanent installation for the Renaissance Public Park by the Chicago Park District. In 2003, the Polish Ministry of Foreign Affairs and *TV Polonia* honored him with the prestigious Freedom Statuette awarded for ex-

ceptional international artistic contributions in helping to raise the awareness of Poland's Culture in the world, and in the same year the Polish American Congress honored him with the Polish Heritage award.—*Adam A. Zych*

SOURCES: Edward B. Kantowicz, *The Archdiocese of Chicago: A Journey of Faith* (Holywood, Ireland: Booklink, 2006); Bolesław Wierzbiański, ed., *Who's Who in Polish America* (New York: Bicentennial Publishing Company, 1996).

Kersten, Charles J. (b. Chicago, Illinois, May 26, 1902; d. Milwaukee, Wisconsin, October 31, 1972). Congressman. Kersten graduated from the Marquette University College of Law in 1925 and established a private law practice in Milwaukee. He served as an assistant district attorney for Milwaukee County from 1937 to 1949, during which time he was a training officer in the Coast Guard Reserve (1943–45) and made his first, successful run for the U.S. Congress in 1946. Defeated in his reelection bid in 1948, he ran again in 1950, winning back the Fifth Congressional District seat he would hold for two more terms (1951–55). During his time in the House, Kersten, a Republican, earned a reputation as one of the most staunchly anti-communist members of Congress. In his first term, he focused much of his efforts on publicly investigating allegations of communist membership in American labor unions. Later, he became well-known for authoring the "Kersten Amendment" to the 1951 Mutual Security Act. This provision allocated $100 million annually to support resistance movements in Soviet bloc nations. It aimed to combine resisters in these countries with recent East European escapees into a fighting "legion of anti-communist exile peoples." These forces would wear their countries' traditional military uniforms, but would be integrated under NATO command. Kersten hoped that the formation of such units, with the active financial support of the United States, would encourage the widespread defection of East European refugees to the West and, in so doing, exacerbate what was quickly becoming a significant problem for Eastern bloc countries. For their part, the Soviets and their Eastern European allies vehemently protested the Kersten Amendment. They argued that U.S. support for the "fascist refugees" constituted an open act of aggression against them, even going so far as to introduce an (ultimately unsuccessful) United Nations resolution against the Kersten Amendment. Kersten's vocal public advocacy forced the Truman administration to step up its efforts to admit and resettle a growing number of East European refugees. His proposal for a refugee fighting force would later be taken up by the Eisenhower administration. Widely supported among Republicans, the plan called for a Volunteer Freedom Corps (VFC) that could potentially enroll as many as 250,000 members. Initially approved by the administration, it was dropped in 1955 as unnecessarily provocative. During his final term in Congress, Kersten also served as chairman of the House Select Committee on Communist Aggression, sometimes called the Kersten Committee. Originally created to investigate the Soviet takeover of Estonia, Latvia, and Lithuania, the committee eventually expanded its remit to investigate "the subversion and destruction of free institutions and human liberties in all other areas controlled, directly or indirectly, by world communism." For these efforts, Kersten would be denounced by the Soviets in the United Nations as an "international criminal." Defeated in his 1954 reelection bid, he served from 1955 to 1956 as a special White House Consultant on Psychological Warfare and then returned to Milwaukee to practice law. He unsuccessfully sought the 1956 Republican nomination for his former Congressional seat and in 1958 became the Secretary General of the World Anti-Communist Congress for Freedom and Liberation. Kersten continued as an attorney in private practice until his death.—*Jonathan Swarts*

SOURCES: *Biographical Dictionary of the United States Congress, 1774–present* (http://bioguide.congress.gov/); "Biographical Note," Charles J. Kersten Papers, Marquette University; Walter L. Hixon, *Parting the Curtain: Propaganda, Culture, and the Cold War, 1945–1961* (New York: St. Martin's Press, 1997), 67–60; Athan Theoharis, "The Republican Party and Yalta: Partisan Exploitation of the Polish American Concern Over the Conference, 1945–1960," *Polish American Studies*, Vol. 28, no. 1 (1971), 5–19; "Guide to the Records of the U.S. House of Representatives at the National Archives, 1789–1989 (Record Group 233): Chapter 22. Records of the Select Committees of the House of Representatives: Select Committee on Communist Aggression (1953–1954)."

Ketchel, Stanley (Stanisław Kiecał; b. Grand Rapids, Michigan, September 14, 1996; d. Conway, Missouri, October 15, 1910). Prize Fighter. The son of Polish immigrants, Ketchel began his career as a professional boxer in 1904. He was a middleweight whose ferocious, attacking style won him the nickname "The Michigan Assassin." Already widely acknowledged as the world's top middleweight fighter by 1907, he won undisputed possession of the title in 1908, becoming the first Polish-American sports champion. That same year he lost the crown to Billy Papke, but promptly regained it in a rematch. In 1909, in his most famous bout, Ketchel challenged titleholder Jack Johnson for the heavyweight championship despite a significant weight disadvantage. He lost the fight by knockout in twelve rounds. While in training on a ranch in Mis-

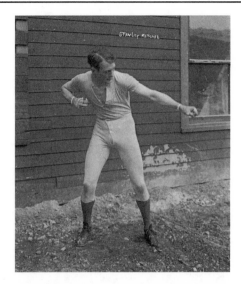

Stanley Ketchel, world champion prize fighter (LC).

souri, he was murdered by gunshot in sordid circumstances. Ketchel is considered one of the greatest middleweights in the history of the sport. He is a member of numerous boxing halls of fame, and was inducted into the **National Polish-American Sports Hall of Fame** in 1984. With a slight change of name, he is the subject of "The Light of the World," a short story by Ernest Hemingway.—*Neal Pease*

SOURCE: "Stanley Ketchel," National Polish-American Sports Hall of Fame website, www.polishsportshof.com.

Kiełbasa. A Polish form of sausage usually made from beef, pork, or a combination of meats, it is available in fresh, smoked, or dried varieties. It can be prepared baked, fried, boiled, broiled, or grilled for use as a meat dish or an ingredient in casseroles, stews, or soups. Traditional Polish *kiełbasa* was based on pork and each region of the country had its own specialty way of preparing it, in addition to individual variety. Popular varieties in the U.S. include thin, dried sausage known as *kabanosy*, thick smoked sausage seasoned with garlic and pepper called *krakowska* because it was associated with the Kraków region, garlic and marjoram spiced pork or veal sausage called *wiejska* usually prepared in a u-shaped ring, and *wesela*, a smoked "wedding" sausage that is also usually prepared in a u-shaped ring. Modern commercially prepared products labeled *kiełbasa* are generally quite different than the originals which can be found in meat markets in Polish American communities. *Kiełbasa* is a standard ingredient in traditional Polish **bigos** or "hunter's stew," as well as soups and casseroles.—*James S. Pula*

SOURCE: *Treasured Polish Recipes for Americans* (Minneapolis, MN: Polanie Club, 1981.

Kielbasa Posse. Organized in the Port Richmond area of Philadelphia, the Kielbasa Posse was a criminal gang comprised of Polish immigrants and Americans of Polish ancestry from the greater Philadelphia metropolitan area and South Jersey. They specialized in drug trafficking (mostly Ecstasy), bookmaking, and loansharking, often rivaling the Irish, Italian, and Russian Mafias for control of territory. Though small in number, the Poles were especially aggressive in moving into areas controlled by the Russian Mafia because many of them were recent immigrants fluent in Russian which allowed them to pass for members of the opposing gang.—*James S. Pula*

SOURCE: Brendan McGarvey, "Pole-Vaulting: Another Group of Eastern-European Gunsels Makes its Mark," *Philadelphia City Paper*, December 12, 2002.

Kiepura, Jan (b. Sosnowiec, Poland, May 16, 1902; d. Harrison, New York, August 15, 1966). Opera singer. Following a brief but spectacular career as a tenor performing in operas at the Teatr Wielki (The Grand Theater) in Warsaw in 1925–26, he performed at the Vienna Staatsoper and then in 1929 debuted at La Scala in Milan. Offered an opportunity to act, he made a number of films in German featuring his powerful and melodious voice. His German experience later resulted in the frequent and completely unfair charge that he was sympathetic to the Nazis. In reality, he was an intensely patriotic Pole—whose mother, incidentally, was Jewish—who had fought against the Germans in 1919 during the Silesian Risings in defense of Polish claims to the area. Though he made a number of European films in the 1930s, his only completely

Jan Kiepura, world renown opera tenor, 1939 (PMA).

American production was the obscure *Give Us This Night*. A wooden actor with limited knowledge of English, Kiepura's films were a string of beautiful arias linked by weak scripts. As a result, he was little known to American audiences though he was enormously popular among Poles in the United States. In 1938 he debuted at the Metropolitan Opera in New York where he starred until 1942. During World War II he tried to join the Polish army-in-exile but was convinced to devote his efforts to fundraising for the Polish cause to which he contributed $100,000 of his own funds. He and his wife, Marta Eggerth, also a singer, made a number of Broadway appearances after the war including *The Merry Widow* and *La Polonaise*. He requested that upon his death he be buried in his beloved Warsaw. In his honor the Polish Parliament proclaimed 2002, the centennial of his birth, "Jan Kiepura Year."—*M. B. B. Biskupski*

SOURCES: Estelle von Wachtel-Torres, "Unforgettable Jan Kiepura," *Bimonthly Newsletter*, Polish American Arts Association of Washington, D.C. (September–October, 2002); Eugene Kusielewicz, "The Polish Caruso," *Polish American World*, May 17, 1963.

Kikulski, John (Jan Teodor Kikulski; b. German-occupied partition of Poland, August 29, 1876; d. Chicago, Illinois, May 21, 1920). Labor leader, Polonia activist. Arriving in the U.S. in 1891, he became an American citizen seven years later. Becoming active in the **Polish National Alliance** (PNA), in 1904 he became one of its directors. He also served as president of the Polish Falcons Alliance (1910–12), an organization affiliated with the PNA. In the summer of 1912 he supported the reunification of the two competing Polish **Falcons** organizations — the PNA–backed Falcons Alliance and the secessionist "Free Falcons" movement — stepping down from his presidency when the unification occurred at the end of the year. While committed to the PNA, he also began working with organized labor at the end of the nineteenth century, gaining the presidency of Local 14 of the Carpenters and Cabinet Makers Union in Chicago in 1908. During World War I, Kikulski emerged as one of Chicago's most active labor leaders, organizing strikes at the International Harvester Company and the Crane Company. An unsuccessful Labor Party candidate for the office of city treasurer, in 1917 he nevertheless gained a reputation as a flamboyant speaker and organizer, using his fluent Polish, Lithuanian, and English while campaigning among ethnically diverse workers in Chicago's packinghouses and slaughterhouses. Elected the president of the Polish Local 554 of the Amalgamated Cutter and Butcher Workmen, which numbered some 16,000

Jan Kikulski, labor leader and Polonia activist, 1911 (*PMA*).

members in January 1918, he also served as secretary of the Stockyards Labor Council (SLC), and later Director of District Council Nine of the packers union. After leading a successful strike in 1919, in the following year he spent three weeks at Wilson and Company encouraging workers to unite, his plea being that "Poles, Irishmen and Lithuanians, all races and all colors, people of all faiths and nationalities should be included [in the union]." His mantra of equality also attracted many African Americans to the union. After racial riots broke out in Chicago in 1919, conflicts arose among the labor organizations leading Kikulski to attempt to create an independent union in January 1920. Accused by J. J. Johnson of financial fraud, Kikulski left the SLC and, with a majority of Polish and Lithuanian members, joined District Council 9 of the Amalgamated, of which he was elected president. On May 17, 1920, unknown assailants shot Kikulski in front of his home; he succumbed to his wounds four days later. Although no one was ever convicted, *Dziennik Związkowy* (The Alliance Daily) echoed the feelings of many of his followers when it openly accused Irish unionists and the SLC of his murder. His funeral became a major union event, uniting once again both Polish and African American workers. In fact, some African American workers proposed to erect a monument on Kikulski's grave at their expense.—*Adam Walaszek*

SOURCES: James R. Barrett, *Work and Community in the Jungle. Chicago Packing House Workers, 1894–1922* (Urbana, IL: University of Illinois Press, 1987); Donald E. Pienkos, *For Your Freedom Through Ours: A History of the Polish Falcons of America 1887–1987* (Boulder, CO: East European Monographs, 1987); Adam Walaszek, *Polscy robotnicy, praca i związki zawodowe w Stanach Zjednoczonych Ameryki, 1880–1922* (Wrocław: Zakład Narodowy im. Ossolińskich, 1988).

King, Betsy (b. Reading, Pennsylvania, August 13, 1955; d.—). Golfer. The daughter of Dr. Weir and Helen Szymkowicz King, Betsy followed her parents in pursuing sports. Her mother, a 1940 graduate of the University of Rhode Island, was elected to the university's Athletic Hall of Fame. She earned five letters and was named best all-around athlete in her senior class. Betsy's father had a football scholarship to Dickinson College in Carlisle, Pennsylvania. King attended Furman University, where she played basketball, field hockey, softball and golf. However, a knee injury led her to concentrate on golf. She was named the University's Athlete of the Year and Woman Scholar Athlete of the Year in 1977 when she led Furman to the National Collegiate Championship. King ranked among the top thirty money winners five times in her first seven years on tour, but did not score her first victory until 1984. She added two more wins that year on her way to capturing the money title and Player of the Year honors. King was the leading money winner on the LPGA Tour in 1984, 1989, and 1993, and finished in the top ten on the money list every year from 1984 to 1995 and again in 1997. She won 34 titles on the tour, including six major championships. She played for the United States in the Solheim Cup five times and was the captain of the 2007 United States team. She lead the team to a 16–12 win over Europe in the 2007 Solheim Cup held in Halmstad, Sweden, September 14–16, 2007. She was named to the LPGA Hall of Fame in 1995, and the National Polish American Sports Hall of Fame in 2001. King served as host of the LPGA's Wachovia Betsy King Classic at Berkleigh C.C. in Kutztown, PA, and has organized the Habitat for Humanity, which has built homes for underprivileged families in Phoenix (AZ) and Charlotte (NC). In the off-season, she has traveled to Romania to work with an orphan relief organization and has been active in the Fellowship of Christian Athletes ministry since 1980.—*Neal Pease*

SOURCE: Mike Sandrolini, ed., *All the Good in Sports: True Stories That Go Beyond the Headlines* (Ventura, CA: Regal Books, 2007).

King, Pee Wee (Julius Frank Anthony Kuczynski; b. Milwaukee, Wisconsin, February 18, 1914; d. Louisville, Kentucky, March 7, 2000). Musician, composer. Young Frankie, as he was called, was taught by his parents to play the violin and accordion. His father led a polka band which the youngster joined at age fifteen. Shortly thereafter he started his own band, the King's Jesters, and took the name Frank King after bandleader Wayne

King. Playing a mixture of polka, cowboy, and pop songs, in 1933 the band became a regular attraction on a local radio show and was hired by a young Gene Autry to be his back-up band. It was Autry who nicknamed King "Pee Wee" for his short stature. After performing with King on a Louisville radio program, Autry left for Hollywood. King stayed in Louisville, in 1936 forming his own country and western band, the Golden West Cowboys. They became so popular that they were invited to join Nashville's Grand Ole Opry, shocking the establishment. Not only was King the first country star from a northern state, his band played country music with polka and waltz rhythms, it was the first to wear flashy rhinestone and sequined suits, and the first to use drums, electric guitar, accordion, and horns at the Opry. King made appearances in Western movies and, for ten years beginning in 1947, had a television show in Louisville that was broadcast nationally for two years. He left vocal chores in the band to others, choosing himself to write songs and play instruments. In 1947 he co-wrote one of the most popular songs of all time, "Tennessee Waltz," which Patti Page took to number one in 1951 and later became the Tennessee state song. Another huge seller was "Slow Poke," also released by King in 1951. Pee Wee King and the Golden West Cowboys were recognized as the best act in country music in the early 1950s, with King becoming one of country's first "crossover" artists whose appeal extended to the world of pop music. He was largely responsible for country music's acceptance into mainstream pop music, which paved the way for the acceptance of rockabilly acts such as Carl Perkins, Johnny Cash, and Elvis Presley. King retired from performing in 1969. He was elected to the Nashville Songwriters Hall of Fame in 1970 and to the Country Music Hall of Fame in 1974, where he was a director until his death.—*Martin S. Nowak*

SOURCE: Wade H. Hall, *Hell Bent for Music: The Life of Pee Wee King* (Lexington, KY: University of Kentucky Press, 1996).

Kiolbassa, Piotr (b. Swibie, Poland, October 13, 1837; d. Chicago, Illinois, June 23, 1905). Polonia activist, political leader, military officer. Kiolbassa migrated to America in 1855, settling in the new Polish settlement of **Panna Maria**, Texas, where he was employed as a teacher and church organist. When the Civil War broke out he served in the Confederate army, was captured, and then enlisted in the U.S. Army where he served in the 16th Illinois Cavalry and as a captain in the Sixth U.S. Colored Cavalry. While awaiting assignment in Chicago in 1864, Kiolbassa was a

Piotr Kiolbassa, political leader and Polonia activist (*PMA*).

leader in the formation of the lay St. Stanislaus Kostka Society. After his discharge on May 1, 1865, he settled in Chicago permanently and emerged as an important political leader. Upon his return, the St. Stanislaus Kostka Society was revived with Kiolbassa as president. It initiated a burial insurance program for its members and raised funds to establish the first Polish Roman Catholic parish in the city in 1867. Kiolbassa took the lead in writing to the **Congregation of the Resurrection** in Poland to plead that a Polish priest be sent to minister to the Poles in Chicago. When the **Polish Roman Catholic Union** was formed at a meeting in Detroit in 1874 as a national umbrella organization to unite local parish organizations, Kiolbassa was elected its initial vice president. He later served as president from 1880 to 1885. Kiolbassa was the first Pole elected to statewide office from Chicago when he won election to the state legislature (1877–79). He later served as Chicago city treasurer (1891–93) where he earned the nickname "Honest Pete" by returning interest earned on city funds to the treasury when the usual practice had been for the treasurer to keep the funds for his personal use. He was elected to the City Council in 1898 and served as Commissioner of Public Works for the city (1902–04).—*James S. Pula*

SOURCES: Helen Busyn, "Peter Kiołbassa — Maker of Polish America," *Polish American Studies*, Vol. 8, no. 3–4 (1951), 65–84; Helen Busyn, "The Political Career of Peter Kiolbassa," *Polish American Studies*, Vol. 7, no. 1–2 (1950), 8–22; Edward C. Różański, "Civil War Poles of Illinois," *Polish American Studies*, Vol. 23, no. 2 (1966), 112–14; Joseph John Parot, *Polish Catholics in Chicago 1850–1920: A Religious History* (DeKalb, IL: Northern Illinois Press, 1981); John

Radzilowski, *The Eagle & The Cross: A History of the Polish Roman Catholic Union of America, 1873–2000* (Boulder, CO: East European Monographs, 2003).

Kister, Marian (b. Mościska, Poland, June 28, 1897; d. New York City, New York, January 6, 1958). Publisher. During World War I, Kister served as a sub-lieutenant in the Austrian Army where he was decorated for courage in action against the Russians. After Poland regained its independence in 1918, he served in the Polish army and fought in the Polish-Bolshevik War. Following the war he enrolled at the Jan Kazimierz University in Lwów, supporting himself by tutoring mathematics. In 1922 he settled in Wilno where he began a publishing business pursuing his life-long love of books. In 1924 he joined a group of writer-businessmen who organized the Rój publishing house in Warsaw, issuing works by **Melchior Wańkowicz**, **Julian Tuwim**, Wanda Wasilewska, Witold Gombrowicz, Bruno Szultz and other leading contemporary Polish authors. Because of his uncanny instinct for recognizing books of literary worth that also had wide appeal, Rój quickly became a leading publishing house of the inter-war period. One of its most successful novels was *Kariera Nikodema Dyzmy*, by Tadeusz Dołęga-Mostowicz, a sensational story of a man's rise to power laced with biting social satire. In addition, Rój published a line of travel books that included the works of outstanding Canadian and American writers. Among these were translations of works by Jack London, O. Henry, William John Locke, Pearl Buck, Erich Remarque, Hermann Hesse, and Upton Sinclair. When World War II began Kister was in London. He never returned to Poland. Together with his wife and two daughters, he migrated to the United States in March 1941. In New York he established Roy Publishers, a very successful enterprise and supporter of the Polish cause in America. Roy published original books in English, Polish and in translation. The first major release in English was Rulka Langer's *The Mermaid and the Messerschmitt* which told a personal story of endurance during the bombardment of Warsaw. Later, *Blessed Are the Meek* by Zofia Kossak gained wide recognition and was included as a "book of the month."—*Peter J. Obst*

SOURCES: Hanna Kister, *Pegazy na Kredytowej* (Warsaw: Państwowy Instytut Wydawniczy, 1980); obituary, *New York Times*, January 7, 1958.

Klawiter, Antoni Leopold (b. Chojnice, Poland, November 12, 1839; d. St. Boniface, Manitoba, September 30, 1913). Priest. After four years of study at the diocesan seminary in Włocławek, Klawiter was ordained to the priesthood in 1859. Following ordination, he ministered at several parishes in the western sector of Russian-occupied Poland, where he participated in the January Insurrection in 1863. In 1873 or 1874, he immigrated to the United States. After serving briefly at a parish in Pittsburgh, he became an assistant pastor at St. Stanislaus Kostka Church in Chicago. Then, starting in the autumn of 1874, he began a series of organizational assignments: as the first pastor of Our Lady of Czestochowa Parish in Blossburg, Pennsylvania; the first pastor of St. Stanislaus Parish in Pittsburgh; founding pastor of St. Anthony Parish in Nowy Poznan, Nebraska; pastor of St. Hyacinth Parish in Dunkirk, New York; founding pastor of St. Adalbert Parish in Buffalo; pastor of St. Casimir Parish in Cleveland; pastor of St. Stanislaus Parish in Newark, New Jersey; first pastor of St. Stanislaus Parish in Meriden, Connecticut; pastor of St. Stanislaus Kostka Parish in Winona, Minnesota; and as a priest ministering to a small Polish settlement in Rapersville, Washington. For part of this time, he served as treasurer of the Association of Polish Roman Catholic Priests in the United States of America.

The year 1895 was a time of transition for the Klawiter. In Buffalo, tensions had arisen between parishioners and a succession of pastors at St. Adalbert, a church that Klawiter had organized in 1886. These tensions reached a climax in May of 1895 when violence erupted over issues of control over the parish treasury. Approximately half of the parishioners then voted to secede from St. Adalbert Parish and to form an **independent** congregation under the name of Holy Mother of the Rosary. On August 30, 1895, Klawiter returned to Buffalo to accept an invitation from leaders of this independence movement to serve as their first pastor. Soon thereafter, Klawiter was excommunicated from the Roman Catholic Church. Klawiter remained at Holy Mother of the Rosary Parish for about six months. After attempting reconciliation with the Roman Catholic Church, Klawiter decided in 1897 to affiliate with the Rev. **Francis Hodur** and his new **Polish National Catholic Church** in Scranton, Pennsylvania. On behalf of the PNCC, he then accepted a new series of organizational assignments at parishes in Dickson City, Pennsylvania; Philadelphia; Fall River, Massachusetts; All Saints Parish in Buffalo; Jersey City, New Jersey; in the Pennsylvania towns of Plymouth, Duryea, and Smithville; in Winnipeg, Manitoba; and in Mikado, Saskatchewan.

In his various assignments, Klawiter developed ambitious plans for social service projects. He organized patriotic observances to commemorate important events in Polish history, and was among the first Poles in America

to plan theatrical performances in the Polish language. One of the earliest proponents of a Polish press, he served as editor and publisher of *Dzwon* (The Bell), a periodical that began publication in Buffalo in 1886. Prior to his death, Klawiter may have reconciled with the Roman Catholic Church as evidenced by the fact that he resided at Holy Spirit Monastery, a facility that the Oblate Fathers maintained in St. Boniface, Manitoba.—*Carl L. Bucki*

SOURCES: Stanley L. Cuba, "Rev. Anthony Klawiter: Polish Roman and National Catholic Builder-Priest," *Polish American Studies*, Vol. 40, no. 2 (Autumn 1983), 59–92; *Pamiętnik Djamentowego Jubileuszu Bazylike Św. Wojciecha, B. M., Buffalo, New York: 1886–1961* (Buffalo: Jubilee Committee, 1961); *Holy Mother of the Rosary Cathedral Polish National Catholic Church 90th Anniversary: 1895–1985* (Buffalo: 90th Anniversary Committee, 1985; Jan Wepsiec, *Polish American Serial Publications: 1842–1966, An Annotated Bibliography* (Chicago: the author, 1968).

Klecko, Joseph Edward "Joe" (b. Chester, Pennsylvania, October 15, 1953; d.—). Football player. Klecko played his high school football at St. James Catholic High School for Boys in Chester before playing for Temple University (1973–76). At the same time he played semi-pro ball with the Aston (PA) Knights under the assumed name of "Jim Jones," claiming to represent the fabricated college "Poland University" in order to keep his NCAA eligibility. He also won two NCAA club boxing titles in the Heavyweight Division. He was drafted in the sixth round in 1977 by the New York Jets as a defensive lineman, becoming part of the "New York Sack Exchange" along with Mark Gastineau, Marty Lyons, and Abdul Salaam. These four combined for 66 sacks during the 1981–82 season, with Klecko credited with 20.5 for which he was named NFL Defensive Lineman of the Year. Klecko played for the Jets from 1977 to 1988, earning selection to the Pro Bowl in 1981, 1983, 1984, and 1985, and All-Pro honors in 1981 and 1985. He was the first player in professional football history to be selected to the Pro Bowl at three different positions: defensive end, defensive tackle and nose tackle. His jersey number 73 was retired by the Jets in December 2004, joining Joe Namath and Don Maynard as the only other Jets players to have their numbers retired. Klecko was traded to the Indianapolis Colts in 1988 and finished his career there. After his retirement, Klecko had a small role in the 1981 Burt Reynolds film *Cannonball Run*, and another Reynolds film *Smokey and the Bandit II*. He also has appeared on the ETWN Network program *Life on the Rock* and is a member of Catholic Athletes for Christ.—*Patricia Finnegan*

SOURCE: Dave Anderson, "Time Has Come for Klecko to Go Into Hall of Fame," *New York Times*, November 8, 2008.

Kleczka, Gerald Daniel (b. Milwaukee, Wis., November 26, 1943). Congressman, accountant. After graduating from Don Bosco High School in Milwaukee, WI (1961), Kleczka attended the University of Wisconsin–Milwaukee (1961–62, 1967, 1970) and was a member of the Wisconsin Air National Guard (1963–69). Elected to the Wisconsin state assembly in 1969, he served there until 1974 and the following year entered the Wisconsin senate (1975–84). He was a delegate to the Wisconsin state Democratic conventions from 1966 to 1984, and a delegate to the Democratic National Conventions in 1980 and 1984. Elected as a Democrat to fill the vacancy caused by the death of Representative **Clement J. Zablocki**, Kleczka was reelected to the ten succeeding Congresses (April 3, 1984–January 3, 2005). An accountant, he appropriately served on the House Budget Committee. During his time in Congress, he favored programs for education, poverty amelioration, and housing needs. In 1999 he unsuccessfully introduced legislation to make seat belts mandatory on all school buses. A dog-owner, he also sought to extend the ban on dog and cat fur in domestic clothing to include imported clothing. Not a candidate for reelection to the One Hundred Ninth Congress in 2004, this Milwaukee South Sider was a member of the **Polish National Alliance**, receiving in 1996 its Outstanding American of Polish Descent award, and a former member of the AFL–CIO. His papers are located in the Wisconsin Historical Society.—*Frederick J. Augustyn*

SOURCES: *Biographical Directory of the United States Congress, 1774–Present* (http://bioguide.congress.gov/); Sherri L. Jackson, "Safety of the Bus," *Milwaukee Journal Times*, January 15, 1999; Dave Umhoefer, "Kleczka Won't Run Again," *Milwaukee Journal Sentinel*, January 24, 2004.

Kleczka, John Casimir (b. Milwaukee, Wisconsin, May 6, 1885; d. Milwaukee, Wisconsin, April 21, 1959). Congressman, judge. The first Polish American elected to the U.S. House of Representatives, Kleczka was educated at St. Stanislaus Catholic School before earning his baccalaureate from Marquette University in 1905. After receiving his degree, he was appointed deputy clerk of the circuit courts of Milwaukee County. He later took law classes at the Catholic University of America in Washington, D.C., and at the University of Wisconsin–Madison, and was admitted to the bar in 1909. Beginning private practice, he won election to the Wisconsin State Senate in 1909 as a member of the progressive wing of the Republican Party. While in the Senate he served on the Executive Committee of the Wisconsin Republican

John Kleczka, judge and congressman (*PMA*).

Party and attended the Republican National Convention in 1912. From 1914 to 1918, Kleczka served as Court Commissioner in the Milwaukee County Circuit Court. In 1918 he won election as a Republican to the Sixty-sixth and Sixty-seventh Congresses (March 4, 1919–March 3, 1923), but then chose to return to the practice of law rather than seek re-nomination in 1922. Following World War I, Kleczka played a decisive role in returning to America on U.S. ships several thousand soldiers who had served in the **Polish Army in France** and later served in Poland in 1921.

Known for his speaking ability, he staunchly advocated Polish independence and the expulsion of anti-war Milwaukee Socialist Representative Victor Berger from the House. As a Representative, Kleczka deviated from the party leadership in voting for higher surtaxes. He also voted for women's suffrage, veterans' bonuses, and against prohibition enforcement legislation. Kleczka received the Cross of the *Order of Polonia Restituta* from the Polish government in 1924 and helped found the Pulaski Council in 1928. He served as a major and judge-advocate for the Army Reserves from 1924 to 1930. While practicing law, Kleczka remained active in politics. His support, as a Catholic, for Herbert Hoover in 1928 against the Catholic Al Smith led the *New York Times* to conclude that religion would not play an issue in the Wisconsin presidential election. After retiring in 1953, Kleczka resumed duties as conciliation judge and court commissioner from 1957 until his death. As a judge, Kleczka was commended for introducing conciliation techniques, substantially lessening case backlogs.—*Steven M. Leahy*

SOURCES: *Milwaukee Journal*, April 22, 1959; Dom Gregory Urbanek, "The First Polish-American Con-

gressman," *Polish American Studies,* Vol. 21 (January–June 1964), 35–38; Donald E. Pienkos, *One Hundred Years Young: A History of the Polish Falcons in America* (Boulder, CO: East European Monographs, 1987).

Klewicki, Ed (b. Pittsburgh, Pennsylvania, May 6, 1912, or May 4, 1911; d. East Lansing, Michigan, July 20, 1997). Football player. Klewicki starred in football as a defensive end at Michigan State College (now Michigan State University) from 1932 to 1934. In his senior year he was named second team All-American. He then played four seasons with the Detroit Lions of the National Football League (1935–38), doubling as end and running back. Klewicki was instrumental in the Lions' victory in the NFL championship game in 1935, his rookie year, and in 1937 he won All-Pro honors. He was inducted into the National Polish-American Sports Hall of Fame in 1982.—*Neal Pease*

SOURCE: "Ed Klewicki," National Polish-American Sports Hall of Fame website, www.polishsportshof.com.

Klub Inteligentsia Katolickiej *see* Brotherhood of Dispersed Solidarity Members.

Kluczynski, John Carl "Johnny Klu" (b. Chicago, Illinois, February 15, 1896; d. Chicago, Illinois, January 26, 1975). Congressman. The son of a butcher and sausage maker from Russian-ruled Poland, Kluczynski attended public and parochial schools in Chicago. During the First World War he served overseas as a corporal with the 8th Field Artillery in 1918 and 1919, subsequently working in the catering business and operating a restaurant after a stint in the stockyards and as a laundry truck driver. He was a member of the Illinois House of Representatives (1933–48), was elected to the state Senate (1948–49) and was elected as a Democrat from the southwest side Fifth District to the Eighty-second Congress. Kluczynski's district included the Bridgeport home base of Richard J. Daley, a fact which became important when Daley became mayor in 1955, although Kluczynski himself was from nearby Brighton Park, then an overwhelmingly Polish American area of the city. Both politicians were raised in this "Back-of-the-Yards" blue collar, ethnic neighborhood with the so-called "Johnny Klu" (to differentiate him in part from his brother, Illinois Supreme Court Justice Thomas C. Kluczynski, who was known as "Tommy Klu") automatically becoming part of the Daley organization. He was affectionately known for his self-deprecating wit, his convivial card playing, and for returning from Washington, D.C. every weekend to his Chicago neighborhood. Reelected to the twelve succeeding Congresses, he served from

January 3, 1951 until his death in 1975. By that time he was chair of the Transportation Subcommittee of the House Public Works Committee, an interest which accounted for his role in helping to build Chicago's expressway, and chair of the select committee that oversaw the House restaurants. The U.S. federal building in Chicago named in his honor a few months after his death attested to Kluczynski's popularity and total loyalty to the Daley organization.—*Frederick J. Augustyn*

SOURCES: *Biographical Directory of the United States Congress, 1774–Present* (http://bioguide.congress.gov/); Michael Barone, Grant Ujifusa, and Douglas Matthews, *Almanac of American Politics* (Washington, D.C.: National Journal, 1974), 270.

Kluszewski, Ted (b. Argo, Illinois, September 10, 1924; d. Cincinnati, Ohio, March 29, 1988). Baseball player. Ted Kluszewski played first base in the major leagues from 1947 to 1961. Over the course of 15 seasons, he hit .298 lifetime with 279 home runs. During his prime years with the Cincinnati Reds, he ranked as one of the top power hitters in the sport. In the span of the four seasons 1953–56, the left handed Kluszewski slammed 171 home runs, played in four straight All-Star games, and three times was named the best first baseman in the major leagues by *The Sporting News*. In various years he led the National League in hits, home runs, and runs batted in. Noted for muscularity, he gained the nickname "Big Klu," and his Reds adopted sleeveless uniform jerseys to allow their slugger to flex his brawny shoulders and arms. He played in the 1959 World Series for the Chicago White Sox. After his retirement as a player, Kluszewski served as a coach for Cincinnati for nine years, and a poll of Reds fans named him the best first baseman in team history. In 1974 he was inducted into the National Polish-American Sports Hall of Fame.—*Neal Pease*

SOURCES: Donald Honig, *The October Heroes: Great World Series Games Remembered by the Men Who Played Them* (Lincoln, NE: Bison, 1996); T. Cohane, "Mighty Kluszewski," *Look*, Vol. 18, August 24, 1954; E. Lawson, "Redlegs One-Man Gang," *Saturday Evening Post*, Vol. 217, March 19, 1955).

Kmiec, Edward Urban (b. Trenton, New Jersey, June 4, 1936; d.—). Bishop. Born in the U.S. to Polish immigrants who had come to America in the early part of the twentieth century, he attended Roman Catholic grammar and high schools in Trenton, then went to St. Charles' College in Catonsville, Maryland, and St. Mary's Seminary in Baltimore, where he received a baccalaureate degree in 1958. Following graduation he studied at the Gregorian University in Rome, Italy, before being ordained on December 20, 1961 at St. Peter's Basilica. He received a degree in theology from the school in 1962. Upon returning to the U.S., he served as associate pastor of St. Rose parish in Belmar, NJ, and was appointed Secretary and Master of Ceremonies to the Bishop of Trenton in 1965. Awarded the title of monsignor in 1977 while serving as pastor of St. Francis in Trenton, he was ordained a bishop in 1982, then served as auxiliary bishop of the Diocese of Trenton until 1992 when he was named the tenth Bishop of Nashville by Pope John Paul II. After twelve years of service in that capacity, Kmiec was appointed the thirteenth Bishop of Buffalo in 2004. Throughout his career, Kmiec served in numerous administrative positions and on diverse church committees, both regional and national. These include chairman of the Bishop's Committee on the Diaconate, and of Region V of the National Conference of Catholic Bishops. He also served on the Bishops' Committees on Human Values, Pastoral Research, the Laity, and Priestly Life and Ministry, as well as the Secretariat for Catholic-Jewish Relations, Catholic-Orthodox Relations, and the Roman Catholic-**Polish National Catholic Church** Committee, Conference of Catholic Bishops' Nominations Committee and Board of Trustees of **SS. Cyril and Methodius Seminary** in Orchard Lake, MI. He is a member of various Polish American organizations and is a Fourth Degree Knight of Columbus.—*Martin S. Nowak*

SOURCE: Matthew E. Bunson, *Our Sunday Visitor's Almanac 2007* (Huntington, IN: Our Sunday Visitor Publishing, 2007).

KNAPP *see* National Committee of Americans of Polish Descent.

Knight, Ted (Tadeusz Władysław Konopka; b. Terryville, Connecticut, December 7, 1923; d. Pacific Palisades, California, August 26, 1986). Actor. One of seven children of Polish immigrants, Knight is best known as the vain, bumbling anchorman Ted Baxter on the *Mary Tyler Moore Show*. He dropped out of Terryville High School to serve in the army in World War II, where he received five Bronze Stars and was one of the first Allied soldiers to enter Berlin. Knight studied acting at the Randall School of Dramatic Arts in Hartford, then the American Theater Wing in New York. He began his career as a radio disc jockey and station manager at stations WCCC and WJAR, then hosted a children's show in Providence, Rhode Island, as an accomplished ventriloquist and puppeteer. He had a fine speaking voice, which led to voice-overs in commercials. In 1948 he married Dorothy Smith and would remain married to her for the rest of his life. He did a stint in Albany, New York, on TV station

Ted Knight, a star of the *Mary Tyler Moore Show* (*OLS*).

WTEN; then moved to Los Angeles in 1957. One of his first movie roles was a non-speaking part in Alfred Hitchcock's *Psycho*. He also appeared in *Combat!, Get Smart, The Twilight Zone, Bonanza*, and other popular television shows. While the role of Ted Baxter brought him well-deserved recognition, it also brought problems as people believed he was the character he portrayed, when he actually was the opposite, a serious actor who was extremely intelligent and articulate. This role identification became so bad that Knight actually asked to be dropped from the show, as it was having an adverse effect on his family. Proud of his Polish heritage, he made many trips home to Connecticut, especially in 1976 to be Grand Marshal of Terryville's bicentennial parade. He appeared on the *Mary Tyler Moore Show* for seven years. After its run was complete in 1977 he appeared in *The Ted Knight Show*, the 1980 movie *Caddyshack* with Rodney Dangerfield, the series *Too Close for Comfort* (1980–1986), and was honored on *This Is Your Life* in 1984. While starring in *Too Close for Comfort*, he was diagnosed with colon cancer. After a year of hospitalization, Knight died at the age of 62. He was buried in the Forest Lawn Memorial Park in Glendale, California, where his headstone bears the name "Theodore C. Konopka." His many awards included six Emmy nominations for best supporting actor for *The Mary Tyler Moore Show*, two Emmy Awards for the "Outstanding Performance by an Actor in a Supporting Role in a Comedy" in 1973 and 1976, and a star on the Hollywood Walk of Fame. In 1987 the town of Plymouth, CT, changed the name of the Canal Street Bridge to the Ted Knight Memorial Bridge in his honor.—*Cheryl A. Pula*

SOURCES: "Ted Baxter and Ted Knight," *TV Guide*, Vol. 19, August 7, 1971. *Press* (Bristol, CT), August 27 and 28, 1986; *Courant* (Hartford, CT), August 27, 1986; *Republican* (Waterbury, CT), May 25, 1975, August 27, 1986, and April 9, 1987.

Kobelinski, Mitchell Peter (b. Chicago, Illinois, August 1, 1928; d. Chicago, Illinois, November 7, 1997). Banker, attorney. After graduating from Loyola University School of Law (Chicago) in 1950, he took a position with the Exchange National Bank of Chicago (1951–59) before becoming a partner in the Parkway Development Company (1960–68). He later served as president and vice-chairman of the Parkway Bank and Trust Company (1968–73) before being named director of the Export-Import Bank of the U.S. (1973–76). Pres. Gerald R. Ford named him administrator of the U.S. Small Business Administration (1976–77), speaking at his swearing in by Supreme Court Justice John Paul Stevens in the White House on February 12, 1976. Following his term with the Small Business Administration, he became president of Kore International Trade (1978–83), later founding and serving as chairman of the Mid-Europe Trade and Investment Co. with offices in Chicago and Warsaw. Deeply attached to his Polish ancestry, Kobelinski served as president of the Copernicus Foundation, chairman of the Chicago-Warsaw Sister City Program, and organized the fiftieth anniversary exhibit of the Warsaw Uprising in Chicago in 1994. The **Polish American Congress** recognized his accomplishments with its Distinguished Service Award (1974).—*Thomas Duszak*

SOURCE: *Chicago Tribune*, September 29, 1994 and November 13, 1997.

Kocialkowski, Leo Paul (b. Chicago, Illinois, August 16, 1882; d. Chicago, Illinois, September 27, 1958). Congressman. Orphaned at an early age, he was educated in private schools which he supplemented by a business course and work in various capacities in several businesses in Chicago. Moving into politics, he engaged in tax appraisal and delinquent tax supervision in Cook County, Illinois, from 1916 to 1932, serving as a delegate to the Democratic National Convention in 1928. He was the first elected ward committeeman from the largely Polish 32nd Ward after its mid-century boundaries were established. He was elected to the U.S. House of Representatives as an independently-minded Democrat by beating political heavyweight **Stanley Kunz**, and to the four succeeding Congresses (March 4, 1933–January 3, 1943). As a member of the newer American-born generation of Polish-Americans, Kocialkowski and his successor as ward committeeman, Joseph Rostenkowski, prevented Kunz in 1936 from returning to politics in the 32nd Ward. In the House he served as chair of the Committee on Insular Affairs in the 74th through 77th Congresses before being unsuccessful in gaining re-nomination in 1942 when he was "purged" for not voting the White House line. He was a member of the Civil Service Commission of Cook County from 1945 to 1949.—*Frederick J. Augustyn*

SOURCE: *Biographical Directory of the United States Congress, 1774–Present* (http://bioguide.congress.gov/).

Kociemski, Stanisław (b. Krotoszyn, Poland, 1827; d. Chicago, Illinois, February 15, 1904). Entrepreneur, Polonia activist. Born in the Prussian-occupied portion of partitioned Poland, Kociemski came to America in 1854 and settled in Chicago where he became the proprietor of a picture frame making factory. Although he became one of the wealthiest Poles in the city, the great Chicago fire of 1871 destroyed his business. Kociemski was a founder of the **Gmina Polska** (Polish Commune) patriotic club in 1866 and one of the earliest supporters of the **Polish National Alliance**, winning election as treasurer (1880–82). In 1882 he was elected president, serving four terms. As president, in 1883 he took the lead in organizing the PNA's celebration of the two hundredth anniversary of King John III Sobieski's victory at the Battle of Vienna, one of the first public displays of patriotism in the early history of the American **Polonia**. He later chaired the Polish National Alliance library and museum at the time of its establishment in 1894.—*Donald E. Pienkos*

SOURCES: Stanisław Osada, *Historia Związku Narodowego Polskiego i rozwój ruchu narodowego Polskiego w Ameryce Pólnocnej* (Chicago: Nakadem i drukiem Związku Narodowego Polskiego, 1905); and Donald E. Pienkos, *PNA: A Centennial History of the Polish National Alliance of the United States of North America* (Boulder, CO: East European Monographs, 1984).

Kolasiński, Dominik (b. Mielec, Galicia, Poland, August 13, 1838; d. Detroit, Michigan, April 11, 1894). Priest. Ordained in Kraków, Poland, on July 25, 1864, his first parish was in the nearby town of Czernichów where his activities caused some complaints. In 1879 he left the parish to study philosophy in Lwów, following which he left for Detroit, arriving on March 30, 1882, to serve as an assistant in St. Adalbert's parish, quickly becoming the pastor (1882–85). He constructed a church, St. Adalbert's, that was impressive in both size and style, but which left the parish and its diocese in serious financial trouble. Kolasiński refused to pay taxes imposed on the parish by Bishop Caspar H. Borgess, also declining to allow the collection within the parish of donations for the Polish seminary near Detroit. Bishop Borgess criticized the high cost of con-

struction, criticism seconded by the Rev. **Józef Dąbrowski**, who at the time was soliciting funds for the new Polish seminary. A scandal arose when Kolasiński was accused of immorality. Although parishioners protested the accusations, Kolasiński was suspended in November 1885. Due to resulting tensions within the parish, the bishop ordered the church closed in December 1885. Half a year later it re-opened under the new pastor, the Rev. Józef Dąbrowski. Supporters of the former pastor immediately clashed with those who supported the new pastor. Kolasiński left Detroit to become the pastor in Warsaw, near Minot, in the Dakota Territory in 1886, but two years later he returned to Detroit, causing new tensions and scandals. Because he was not allowed to serve in St. Adalbert's church he became pastor of the "independent" Sacred Heart of Mary Parish, which he created and led from 1888 to 1894, and where he built a splendid new church consecrated in 1892 by the Jacobite Bishop René Vilatte. Additional clashes took place between Kolasiński and parishioners. On February 18, 1894, Kolasiński reconciled and was pardoned by the Catholic bishop of Detroit, John Foley. He remained pastor in Sacred Heart of Mary to his death.—*Adam Walaszek*

SOURCES: Lawrence Orton, *Polish Detroit and the Kolasinski Affair* (Detroit: Wayne State University Press, 1981); Earl Boyea, "Father Kolasiński and the Church of Detroit," *Catholic Historical Review*, Vol. 74, no. 3 (1988), 420–39.

Kolaszewski, Antoni Franciszek (b. Elżbietów, partitioned Poland, September 5, 1851; d. Cleveland, Ohio, Dec 1, 1910). Priest. Coming to America with his parents in 1859, he studied for the priesthood in Teutopolis, Illinois and Cleveland, Ohio. Bishop Richard Gilmour accepted him in Cleveland to serve Polish immigrants in the city district known as "Warszawa." Ordained on July 1, 1883, Kolaszewski became pastor of St. Stanislaus Church on August 5, 1883. A quickly growing parish, Kolaszewski served not only as pastor but also leader, mediator and advisor to the community. In 1886 he began the construction of a new, neo–Gothic church that was completed in 1891 at a cost of $250,000. It was one of the largest churches in the region, but the financial base in Warszawa did not match the income required to meet the needs of a debt of over $100,000, causing him to impose on parishioners various new taxes and fees that soon brought forth opposition to his leadership and a budding scandal with accusations of financial mismanagement. Bishop Ignatius Horstmann demanded Kolaszewski's resignation in 1892, whereupon he left for Syracuse, NY. In 1894 he returned to Cleveland and,

Antoni Kolaszewski, priest (*OLS*).

with the help of some his supporters, on May 3, 1894 organized the Immaculate Heart of the Blessed Virgin Mary church near St. Stanislaus. The new church was independent of diocesan control and stressed its Polish character. Kolaszewski aggressively challenged Horstmann's authority and policies, yet he was careful to stress that his revolt was not directed against the Catholic Church but against the oppressive local hierarchy. Once constructed, the new church was constructed and blessed by Bishop Joseph René Vilatte of Wisconsin, a member of the Old Catholic Church. With the consecration of the church by the independent Old Catholic bishop, Kolaszewski was formally ex-communicated from the Roman Catholic Church. He tried persistently until 1908 to reconcile with Rome, writing directly to the Apostolic Delegate, Bishop Francesco Satolli in Rome, finally succeeding in September 1908 whereupon the church was accepted into Cleveland's Roman Catholic hierarchy.—*Adam Walaszek*

SOURCE: Charles R. Kaczynski, "'What Mean Ye By These Stones?' Cleveland's Immaculate Heart of Mary Parish and the Construction of a Polish American Rhetoric," *Polish American Studies*, Vol. LV, no. 2 (1998), 25–54.

Kolędy (or Kolendy). Poland boasts a large number of melodic and highly rhythmic Christmas carols that have been preserved for generations in the homes and churches of American **Polonia**. Among these are *Gdy się Chrystus Rodzi* (Christ is Born), *Dzisiaj w Bethlehem* (Today in Bethlehem), *Wśrod Nocnej Ciszej* (In the Still of the Night), *Bóg się Rodzi* (God is Born), *Pojdzmy Wszyscy do Stajenki* (Let Us Hasten to the Stable), *W Żłobie Leży* (In a Manger), and *Lulajze Jezuniu* (Lullaby to the Infant Jesus, the Polish *Silent Night*). These carols are traditionally sung at Midnight Mass on Christmas Eve (Pasterka) following the Christmas Eve (**Wigilia**) supper, and throughout the Christmas season.—*Angela T. Pienkos*

SOURCES: Eugene E. Obidinski and Helen Stankiewicz Zand, *Polish Folkways in America: Community and Family* (Lanham, MD: University Press of America, 1987); Rose Polski Anderson, et al., eds., *Treasured Polish Christmas Customs and Traditions* (Minneapolis: Polanie Publishing Company, 1977).

Komitet Narodowy Amerykanów Polskiego Pochodzenia *see* **National Committee of Americans of Polish Descent.**

Komitet Narodowy Polski *see* **Polish National Committee.**

Komitet Obrony Narodowej *see* **National Defense Committee.**

Komitet Wolnej Europy *see* **National Committee for a Free Europe.**

Konarski, Feliks (pseudonym Ref-Ren; b. Kiev, Ukraine, January 9, 1907; d. Chicago, Illinois, September 12, 1991). Poet, song writer. After receiving his elementary and secondary education in a Polish school in Kiev, in 1921 he moved to Poland where he passed his final exams in Warsaw and began studying law at Warsaw University. During this time he found his calling to the stage after encountering Konrad Tom who helped Konarski begin authoring poems and songs, as well as suggesting the "Ref-Ren" stage pseudonym. In addition to songs, Konarski also wrote satirical plays for theater groups. In 1934 he moved to Lwów where he established a theatre group, wrote poems, and penned the words to what became numerous popular songs. After Lwów was occupied by the Red Army, Konarski performed as part of a traveling orchestra in numerous cities in the Soviet Union. When Nazi Germany attacked, he was in Moscow. In 1941 he enlisted with the Polish Armed Forces in the East. Evacuated to Iran, he headed the Polish Soldier's Theater and served with General Władysław Anders' Polish Second Corps in Italy. There, on the eve of the Poles' victorious storming of Monte Cassino, he wrote the unforgettable and moving anthem, *Czerwone maki na Monte Cassino* (The Red Poppies on Monte Cassino). He was with the Polish Second Corps until it was transported to Britain and demobilized. In the autumn of 1946, he went to London where he organized and conducted the Ref-Ren Theater. Together with his wife and other exiled Polish actors, the theater traveled around the world providing humor and sentimental songs to war scattered Poles. In the 1950s and 1960s he recorded several dozen of these broadcasts for Radio Free Europe, the Polish section of Radio Paris, and

the Polish section of the BBC in London. In 1965, Konarski settled permanently in Chicago where he organized Polish cultural activities and had a radio show called "Czerwone maki" (Red Poppies) for over twenty years, a show that was also broadcast in New York City. He continued to sing and perform on many stages in England, France, and the United States and served as president of the Polish Union for Theatre Artists Abroad (1961–63). For his support of Polish culture in exile, he was twice awarded the Order of Polonia Restituta (Knight's Cross and Commander's Cross). His works include *Serce na dłoni: wiersze i piosenki* (The Heart at the Hand: Poems and Song; 1958), *Historia Czerwonych Maków* (The History of the Red Poppies; 1961), *Miłość w moim życiu* (Love in My Life; 1967), and *Czerwone Maki na Monte Cassino. Wiersze i piosenki 1939–1945* (The Red Poppies on Monte Cassino. Poems and Songs 1939–1945; 2004).—*Adam A. Zych*

SOURCES: Zbigniew Adrjański, *Złota księga pieśni polskich. Pieśni, gawędy, opowieści* (Warszawa: Ofic. Wyd. Volumen, Wyd. Bellona, 1997); Bolesław Klimaszewski, ed., *Mały słownik pisarzy polskich na obczyźnie 1939–1980* (Warszawa: Wyd. Interpress, 1992); Tadeusz Szewera, *Niech wiatr ją poniesie. Antologia pieśni z lat 1939–1945* (Łódź: Wyd. Łódzkie, 1975, 2nd edition).

Kongres Polonii Amerykańskiej *see* **Polish American Congress.**

Konopinski, Emil John (b. Michigan City, Indiana, December 25, 1911; d. Bloomington, Indiana, May 26, 1990). Nuclear scientist. Konopinski earned a Ph.D. from the University of Michigan in 1934. During World War II he worked with Enrico Fermi on the development of the world's first nuclear reactor at the University of Chicago and then in 1943 joined the Manhattan Project which built the first atomic bomb. As a consultant with the Atomic Energy Commission (1946–68) he authored *The Theory of Beta Radioactivity*. Konopinski, who was a professor of physics at Indiana University following the war, proved mathematically that ignition of a hydrogen bomb would not ignite the earth's atmosphere.—*James S. Pula*

SOURCE: obituary, "Emil Konopinski, 78, Atomic Bomb Scientist," *New York Times*, May 28, 1990.

Konopka, Joseph (b. Philadelphia, Pennsylvania, October 6, 1932; d.—). Artist. Educated at the Cooper Union in New York (1950–54), he also studied with Woodman Thompson at Columbia University (1954–55). Following his studies, Konopka served as a U.S. Army illustrator (1956–57) and a military aide at the White House (1957–58). As an artist, he specialized in genre scenes of urban subjects from New York and New

Jersey, including the now non-existent World Trade Center Towers and the Tall Ships–U.S. Bicentennial (1976), as well as Eastern Seaboard lighthouses, all rendered in a modified Photo-Realist style. His work appeared in solo exhibitions in Maryland, New Jersey, New York, and Rhode Island, and in group exhibitions in Connecticut, Delaware, Florida, Illinois, Indiana, Kansas, Maine, Maryland, Mississippi, Missouri, New Jersey, New York, Ohio, Oregon, Pennsylvania, Tennessee, Washington (D.C.), and West Virginia. His professional work includes being a scenic artist at NBC TV for the *Today Show*; the *Tonight Show* (Steve Allen, Jack Paar, Johnny Carson); *Hallmark Hall of Fame*; NBC Operas; *Kraft Music Shows*; Miss America Pageant–Atlantic City; Moon Landing and Apollo Space Shows, Phillco Theater; and *Late Night with David Letterman* and *Conan O'Brien*. He served as vice president of the Associated Artists of New Jersey (1976–85).—*Stanley L. Cuba*

SOURCES: Szymon Bojko, *Z polskim rodowodem. Artyści polscy i amerykanscy polskiego pochodzenia w sztuce Stanow Zjednoczonych w latach 1900–1980* (A Polish Pedigree: Polish Artists and American Artists of Polish Descent in the United States, 1900–1980) (Torun: Oficyna Wydawnicza Kucharski, Archiwum Emigracji, 2007); William D. Gorman, "The Quiet Artist," *New Jersey ArtFormMagazine* (March/April 1981).

Konstanty, Jim (Casimir James Konstanty; b. Strykersville, New York, March 2, 1917; d. Oneonta, New York, June 11, 1976). Baseball player. Konstanty made his debut as a major league pitcher in 1944, but spent most of the next few years serving in the navy, or playing in the minor leagues. In 1948 he reestablished himself in the big leagues as a relief pitcher for the Philadelphia Phillies. A right-hander who relied on a slider, Konstanty enjoyed one spectacular season in 1950. Making an unprecedented 74 appearances on the mound, he won sixteen games and saved a league-high 22, gaining credit for leading his Phillies team to its first pennant in 35 years. He pitched well, though in a losing effort, in that year's World Series. Konstanty gained a shower of honors, and historians of the sport credit his performance that year with having given new glamour and importance to the previously secondary role of relief pitching. He was named the National League's most valuable player, the first reliever so honored, and appeared in the All-Star game. He was also chosen NL pitcher of the year by *The Sporting News*, and athlete of the year by the Associated Press. Over the course of an otherwise solid but unspectacular eleven-year career that ended in 1956, Konstanty won 66 games and saved 74 for five different teams. He was inducted into the **National Polish-**

American Sports Hall of Fame in 2008.— *Neal Pease*

SOURCES: Franklin W. Yeutter, *Jim Konstanty* (New York: A.S. Barnes and Co., 1951); John Thorn, *The Relief Pitcher* (New York: Dutton, 1979).

Koprowski, Hilary (b. Warsaw, Poland, December 5, 1916; d.—). Immunologist. Born to a merchant and one of the first female dentists in Poland, Koprowski earned a degree in piano from the Warsaw Conservatory and, in 1939, his M.D. from the University of Warsaw. With the German invasion of Poland and the occupation of Warsaw in 1939, he escaped to Italy with his family, receiving a degree from Santa Cecilia Conservatory of Music in Rome before fleeing to Brazil as Italy entered the war. In Brazil, he found employment as a piano teacher before meeting a Brazilian physician who had attended the same high school as Koprowski. At the physician's suggestion, he applied for and subsequently accepted a research position funded by the Rockefeller Foundation working on a yellow fever vaccine in Rio de Janeiro. Inspired by his colleagues, Koprowski moved to the United States in 1944 to further his interest in vaccine research with American Cyanamid in New York. In 1946, he was appointed assistant director of American Cyanamid's Lederle Laboratories, where he pioneered vaccines for polio and rabies. In February 1950, after having self-administered an oral dose of an attenuated live-virus polio vaccine without adverse consequence, he conducted the first clinical trial of the oral vaccine on a small group of children and subsequently reported its success in providing immunity. The significance of this breakthrough related to the prevalence of polio outbreaks in summer, his use of an attenuated live polio virus, and perhaps most importantly, its oral form which was much less expensive to administer widely. He continued development of the vaccine, as well as research into rabies, in the following decade. In 1957, he was selected director of the Wistar Institute in Philadelphia. By recruiting top biologists, he led it through 35 years of growth and increased prestige. In 1978, his interest and research in rabies led to a new tissue culture-based vaccine, a vaccine more effective and less painful than the traditional Pasteur technique. It also led to an oral bait vaccine for immunization of wildlife. In the late 1970s, Koprowski pioneered the development and use of monoclonal antibodies to detect cancer antigens. He established the Biotechnology Foundation Laboratories, Inc. (1992) to support medical research and promote medical advances through biotechnology. He and his collogues successfully produced a rabies vaccine in spinach, a cancer antigen in tobacco, and conducted successful clinical trials with Hepatitis B vaccine in lettuce. During his career, Koprowski authored or co-authored more than 875 scientific papers and co-edited several medical journals. He held memberships in the National Academy of Sciences and the American Academy of Arts and Sciences. His honors included the Order of the Lion from the King of Belgium, the French Order of Merit for Research and Invention, a Fulbright Scholarship, a Rockefeller University Fellow, the Nicolaus Copernicus Medal of The Polish Academy of Sciences, and the Casimir Funk Natural Sciences Award from the Polish Institute of Arts and Sciences. Significantly, he was a continuous grantee of the National Institutes of Health for over 50 years. As the new century approached, Koprowski's interest in music also flourished. He began the study of musical composition in 1995 and produced sheet music and recordings of classical/chamber music that he composed.—*Brian Bonkosky*

SOURCES: Roger Vaughan, *Listen to the Music: The Life of Hilary Koprowski* (New York: Springer, 2000); Gerald Garfield, "A Tribute to Hilary Koprowski: Scientist, Musician, and Friend," *Essays of an Information Scientist*, Vol. 5, July 19, 1982, 615–620.

Korboński, Stefan (b. Praszka, Poland, March 2, 1901; d. Washington, D.C., April 23, 1989). Political leader. A pupil of the Russian secondary school in Częstochowa beginning in 1916, Korboński enrolled in the clandestine scouting movement and the illegal Polska Organizacja Wojskowa (Polish Military Organization). He took part in disarming German soldiers in Częstochowa in November 1918, and in defending Lwów against the Ukrainians. Despite his poor health, he volunteered for the Polish army during the Polish-Soviet war of 1920, fighting also in the Third Silesian Uprising in 1921, for which he was awarded the Order of *Virtuti Militari* and the Silesian Cross. Between 1921 and 1925 Korboński studied law at the University of Poznań. At the same time he taught Polish and geography at a secondary school in Pyzdry and worked as a clerk. His cooperation with the peasant political movement began at that time. After an apprenticeship Korboński and his cousin Zygmunt Graliński began their own law practice in Warsaw. Still active in the peasant movement, the young attorney supported the anti–Piłusdskiite political faction. He is regarded as a co-founder of the Polish Secret State during World War II. He represented the People's Party (Stronnictwo Ludowe), and in 1941 was appointed head of the Directorate of Civil Resistance (Kierownictwo Walki Cywilnej, KWC). The KWC supervised the passive resistance of the Polish nation under the Nazi and Soviet occupation. Korboński was instrumental in setting up the radio connection network between occupied Warsaw and London. The peak of his underground career was the post of acting Delegate of the Polish Government-in-Exile from March until June 1945. Arrested by the Soviet NKVD in Kraków on June 29, 1945, he was lucky to be released a month later.

Korboński resumed his law practice in Warsaw and his political activity within the peasant movement. He became one of the national leaders of the Polish People's Party (Polskie Stronnictwo Ludowe, PSL), the only legal anti-communist party in Poland, and its representative in the Polish parliament beginning in January 1947. When the Communist terror spread across the country, and even parliamentary immunity could not guarantee his safety, in November 1947 Korboński and his wife left Poland for Sweden, Great Britain, and finally the United States. He spent the rest of his life in Washington, D.C. He represented the Polish Government-in-Exile and its different organizations, was an active member of the Home Army Circle, of the **Polish Institute of Arts and Sciences of America**, and of the Polish PEN-Club in exile. His main field of activity was the **Assembly of Captive European Nations** where he was elected president for several terms (1958, 1966, 1971–83). He published autobiographical books and studies of the Polish underground state. Both his publications and even his name

Stefan Korboński with President Ronald Reagan (*JPI*).

were banned in Poland before 1989. Only posthumously, in 1995, was he awarded the Order of the White Eagle. His awards in exile included the Home Army Cross (1969), the Alfred Jurzykowski Prize for literature (1973), and the Righteous Among the Nations Medal of the Yad Vashem Institute of Jerusalem (1980).—*Joanna Wojdon*

SOURCES: "Korbonski, Stefan," *Contemporary Authors* (Detroit: Gale Research Company, New Revision Series), Vol. 5, 308–09; Andrzej Krzysztof Kunert, "O Autorze," in Stefan Korboński, *W imieniu Polski Walczącej* (Warsaw: Rytm, 1999), 653–658; Małgorzata Ptasińska-Wójcik, *Stefan Korboński 1901–1989* (Warsaw: Instytut Pamieci Narodowej, 2009); Stefan Korboński, *Warsaw in Exile* (London: George Allen & Unwin, 1966).

Korpanty, Maria (Maria Grosser; Tyczyn, Poland, October 23, 1896; Pittsburgh, Pennsylvania, March 16, 1957). Polonia activist. As a child, Korpanty joined the Galician **Falcons** organization headquartered in the nearby city of Rzeszów in 1910. In 1913 she left Austrian Poland for America and settled in Pittsburgh. Finding work in the home office of the Falcons as a seventeen year old, she became active in the athletic program of the movement at the time it was increasingly focusing on military training exercises. The following year at the national Falcons convention in Buffalo, Korpanty was elected Assistant Chief Instructress of the organization, thereby becoming the first person to hold this newly created position. During the World War I era she worked effectively in cooperation with the Chief Instructors of the Falcons, Witold Rylski and John Bartmanski. In 1917 she married Leon Korpanty, an attorney who served as legal advisor of the Falcons from 1926 until 1933 when he was killed in a train accident. In 1925, Korpanty became vice president of the Falcons and held this office until her death in 1957. An eloquent public speaker who was one of the most popular personalities ever to hold national office in the Falcons movement, Korpanty was especially active in promoting interest in the physical educational work of the organization and in generating enthusiasm for the insurance program it established in 1928. In fact, she practically defined one of the major responsibilities of the office of women's vice president as that of directing the insurance sales efforts of the fraternal. Korpanty represented the Falcons both in America and abroad on numerous occasions and served a term as a national vice president of the **Polish American Congress**. In recognition of her services, the office of vice president was left vacant until 1960 when Genevieve Hartman was elected to succeed her at the twenty-seventh Falcons convention in Newark. For several months beginning in December, 1937

Maria Korpanty, Polonia activist (*OLS*).

until early 1938 Korpanty served as acting president of the Falcons during President **Teofil Starzyński**'s stay in Poland following a serious illness. She again took over as acting president in June 1952, from Starzyński's death until the convening of the twenty-fifth national convention a month later.—*Donald E. Pienkos*

SOURCE: Donald E. Pienkos, *One Hundred Years Young, A History of the Polish Falcons of America, 1887–1987* (Boulder, CO: East European Monographs, 1987).

Korzybski, Alfred Habdank Skarbek (b. Warsaw, Poland, July 3, 1879; d. Sharon, Connecticut, March 1, 1950). Linguist. Educated at the Warsaw Polytechnic Institute, his fluency in Polish, Russian, French, and German led to service as an intelligence officer in the Russian army during World War I. After being wounded, he was sent on a mission to Canada in 1915 where he began studying English. In 1917 he moved to New York to supervise ammunition shipments to Russia. With the collapse of the Tsarist government, he remained in the United States following the war, serving in 1920 on the Polish Commission to the League of Nations. He published *Manhood of Humanity* in 1921 in which he proposed a new theory of "humankind," defining in the process his idea of "time-binding." Korzybski defined the principles of time-binding in *Science and Sanity, an Introduction to Non-Aristotelian Systems and General Semantics* (1933). A survey of prominent scientists in 1950 listed this work as one of the most influential publications of the twentieth century. His insights led to the founding of a new discipline which he labeled "General Semantics," a field of study focusing on "semantic reactions" that seeks to identify the distinction between a word and the object the word describes, the distinction between individual objects all described by the same word, and the effect of time on these relationships. Korzybski argued that human understanding is limited by the structure of the nervous system and the structure of language. Since humans cannot experience everything directly, they do so through "abstractions" originating in the nervous system and the structure of symbolic language. This may lead to misconceptions or reactions that are based on linguistic structure rather than reality; thus people must be trained in the "consciousness of abstracting" which involves the use of scientific and mathematical techniques to better discern the realities from structural abstractions. Korzybski founded the Institute of General Semantics in 1938. His work was influential in the development of Gestalt Therapy, Rational Emotive Behavior Therapy and Neuro-linguistic Programming. During World War II his work was used in the treatment of battle fatigue in the U.S. Army in Europe, while it also influenced the work of notables such as S.I. Hayakawa, Anatol Rapoport, Buckminster Fuller, Alvin Toffler, L. Ron Hubbard, Stuart Chase, and the Belgian surrealist Jan Bucquoy.—*James S. Pula*

SOURCES: Alfred Korzybski, Marjorie Kendig and Charlotte Schuchardt Read, *Alfred Korzybski: Collected Writings 1920–1950* (Englewood Cliffs, NJ: Institute of General Semantics, 1990); Robert P. Pula, *A General-Semantics Glossary: Pula's Guide for the Perplexed* (Concord, CA: International Society for General Semantics, 2000); Robert P. Pula, "Alfred Korzybski,

Alfred Korzybski, founder of General Semantics (*Robert P. Pula*).

1879–1950: A Bio-Methodological Sketch," *Polish American Studies*, Vol. 53, no. 2 (1996), 57–105; Charlotte Read, "Alfred Korzybski: His Contributions and Their Historical Development," *The Polish Review*, Vol. 13, no. 2 (1968), 5–13.

Kościalowski, Napoleon (b. Warsaw, Poland, May 16, 1812; d. Washington, District of Columbia, May 30, 1859). Military officer. After joining the unsuccessful Polish November Uprising (1830–31), he was interned when he fled to Austria, then forcibly exiled to the United States where he arrived in New York on March 28, 1834. As an artist, he found work in Albany, before accepting a teaching position at the Northampton Female Seminary in Massachusetts. Moving to Illinois where he and a group of fellow Poles anticipated a land grant from Congress, he married in 1839 but was unsuccessful as a farmer. Moving then to St. Louis, he opened a surveying and engineering firm with a partner, becoming well-known in the community. As captain, he led the "Kosciuszko Guard," a company of the 3rd Missouri Regiment raised for service in the Mexican War in 1846; however, the regiment was disbanded by the end of the year. In the following year the governor asked for volunteers to help guard the Santa Fe Trail, he recruited and led "Captain Koscialowski's Company, Gilpin's Battalion, Missouri Infantry." Later designated Company E of the Santa Fe Trace Battalion, it left Ft. Leavenworth by October, marching west to engage the Apache and Comanche Indians who were raiding traffic along the Santa Fe Trail. He mustered out with his company on September 30, 1848. Returning to civilian life as an architect, he designed the Illinois Institution for the Blind and was employed by the Illinois State House Board of Commissioners for construction work for the foundation of the state capitol. After completing these jobs, he enlisted in the U.S. Marine Corps in December 1853. He served until 1858, then moved to Washington, D.C., when his health began to fail.—*Francis Casimir Kajencki*

SOURCE: Francis Casimir Kajencki, *Poles in the 19th Century Southwest* (El Paso, TX: Southwest Polonia Press, 1990), 201–17.

Kosciuszko, Thaddeus (b. Andrzej Tadeusz Bonawentura Kościuszko; b. Mereczowszczyzna, Poland, February 12, 1746; d. Soleure, Switzerland, October 15, 1817). Military officer. Although tracing his heritage to the landed gentry, by the time of Kościuszko's birth his family had lost most of its stature and holdings. His father died when the boy was young, leaving his widow to struggle with maintaining the family. Nevertheless, his mother was able to provide him with a classical education in local church schools.

Under the patronage of the powerful Prince Adam Czartoryski, Kościuszko gained entrance to the first class admitted to the new Knight's School in Warsaw where he studied political and military sciences. Upon graduation with the rank of captain, he journeyed to Paris on a scholarship provided by King Stanisław August Poniatowski to continue his studies in art, engineering, and military science. By the time he returned to Poland, his country had suffered through partition, losing much of its land to its neighbors Austria, Prussia, and Russia. Unable to find a suitable position in the reduced Polish military, he returned to Paris where he took an interest in news of the American Revolution.

Journeying across the Atlantic in the late summer of 1776, he arrived in Philadelphia where he was employed to design fortifications for the defense of the Delaware River approaches to Philadelphia. Commissioned colonel of engineers by the Continental Congress on October 18, his engineering talents soon came to the attention of Gen. Horatio Gates who offered him a position as chief engineer when the general was assigned to command of the northern army operating in upper New York State. Kościuszko's first assignment was to assess the defenses of Fort Ticonderoga which he correctly predicted could be rendered untenable if the British placed artillery on Sugar Loaf Hill (now Mt. Defiance). His advice was ignored by the fort's commander, but when the British army under Gen. John Burgoyne arrived at the beginning of July, 1777, its was quick to erect artillery positions on the hill forcing the Americans to abandon the works with the loss of much valuable artillery, equipment, and supplies.

During the American retreat, Gen. Philip Schuyler, who succeeded Gates in command, entrusted Kościuszko with command of the critical rear guard. Using his engineering skills to great advantage to erect barriers, flood lowlands, and otherwise obstruct the British march, he proved so successful that the British were held up for a critical month during which the Americans were able to reorganize and gain reinforcements including professional troops sent from Gen. George Washington's army and militia from the surrounding states. At the crucial Battle of Saratoga that followed, Gen. Gates, who had returned to command of the American army, credited the victory to Kościuszko's skills at selecting and fortifying the American position. In fact, the Pole's engineering skill once again determined not only the battlefield, but forced the British to attack the western flank of the strong American position thereby allowing Gates to anticipate the move and meet it with his best troops. The

victory at Saratoga was a turning point in the Revolution because it led directly to the French alliance which brought that nation, and later Spain, into the war on the side of the Americans. In his comments after the battle, Gates credited Kościuszko with responsibility for the victory.

After Saratoga, Kościuszko received an assignment to design and oversee construction of fortifications at West Point, along the Hudson River north of New York City, to prevent the British from moving toward Albany. Considered by many, including Gen. Washington, to be the key to control of New York State, Kościuszko's work was crucial to the success of the Revolution. His innovative approach to creating a defense in depth, a new concept in fortification, gained lavish praise from American, British, and French engineers alike. When Congress eventually established the United States Military Academy at West Point, an institution Kościuszko actually suggested in a letter to President Thomas Jefferson, *Manoevres of Horse Artillery*, written by the Pole in 1800, was one of the first textbooks used at the new academy. In 1828 the cadets at West Point raised funds to erect a column to his memory, the first monument erected at the Academy.

With the completion of his work at West Point, Kościuszko joined the army in the Carolinas, arriving in the wake of a serious American defeat. Serving under Gen. Nathanael Greene, Kościuszko earned praise for his skill in preparing the escape of the army across the Dan River, where it would be secure from the pursuing British. Throughout the remainder of the campaigns in the South, Greene continued to praise Kościuszko's work as critical to his success. After the war, Greene said of him: "Among the most useful and agreeable of my companions in arms, was Colonel Kosciuszko. Nothing could exceed his zeal for the public service, nor in the prosecution of various objects that presented themselves in our small but active warfare, could anything be more useful than his attention, vigilance and industry."

Praised by Gens. Gates, Green, and Washington, along with nearly everyone with whom he served, Kościuszko was promoted to brigadier general, granted U.S. citizenship, and elected to membership in the prestigious Society of the Cincinnati. He and the Marquis de Lafayette were the only two foreign officers admitted to this prestigious veterans organization for Revolutionary War officers.

Following the war, Kosciuszko returned to Europe in 1784 where he immediately immersed himself in efforts to free his homeland. Commissioned major general in the Polish army in 1789, he fought against a Russian invasion in 1792. Praised for his skillful handling of outnumbered Polish troops, Kościuszko earned promotion to the rank of lieutenant general and was further recognized with one of the first *Virtuti Militari* medals, an award equivalent to the U.S. Medal of Honor. However, when the Polish king capitulated to the Russians, Kościuszko fled to Western Europe where he took part in conspiratorial planning to regain Polish independence. In August of 1792 the French Assembly bestowed upon him honorary citizenship in recognition of his services to the ideals of liberty.

A new partition of Poland in January 1793 caused Kościuszko to accelerate preparations for an uprising which began in Kraków in March 1794. Designated commander-in-chief of all Polish forces, he reached out to peasants, Jews, and other minorities with promises of better treatment and they responded with support; but once again, after initial successes, Polish aspirations for freedom were crushed by numerically superior Russian armies. Gravely wounded, Kościuszko was captured and imprisoned in St. Petersburg. Only after the eventual death of Tsarina Catherine the Great was he finally released by her son, Tsar Paul I, in 1796.

Following his release, Kościuszko returned for a visit to America where he was hailed for his efforts to free his homeland and fêted by his old comrades-in-arms from the American Revolution. Developing a close friendship with Thomas Jefferson, upon his final departure for Europe he penned a will [see **Kosciuszko's Will**], naming Jefferson his executor, in which he left his American property to be used to purchase the freedom of slaves

Tadeusz Kościuszko, engineer of West Point (*OLS*).

and educate them so that they might become self-sufficient citizens. Upon his return to Europe, he wrote to Jefferson following the Virginian's election as president, suggesting that the United States establish an academy, much like the one he attended long ago in Warsaw, to prepare young Americans as military officers.

Settling first in France, and later in Switzerland, Kościuszko continued to support efforts for Polish independence and maintain an active correspondence with Jefferson and other Americans to the end of his life. In his homeland, he is remembered by a *kopiec*, a huge earthen mound outside of Kraków that includes soil from all of his battlefields in Europe and America. His remains were eventually returned to Poland where they now repose in an honored place in the Wawel Cathedral, surrounded by a pantheon of other Polish heroes. In America, among the many public recognitions of him, a prominent statue of him adorns Lafayette Park across the street from the White House in Washington, D.C., and the building in which he lived during his second trip to America was established as a National Park. Thomas Jefferson proclaimed him to be "as pure a son of liberty as I have ever known."—*James S. Pula*

Sources: James S. Pula, *Thaddeus Kościuszko: The Purest Son of Liberty* (New York: Hippocrene Books, 1999); Francis Casimir Kajencki, *Thaddeus Kościuszko: Military Engineer of the American Revolution* (El Paso, TX: Southwest Polonia Press, 1998); Alex Storozynski, *The Peasant Prince: Thaddeus Kosciuszko and the Age of Revolution* (New York: St. Martin's Press, 2009); Gary B. Nash and Graham Russell Gao Hodges, *Friends of Liberty: Thomas Jefferson, Tadeusz Kościuszko, and Agrippa Hull. A Tale of Three Patriots, Two Revolutions, and a Tragic Betrayal of Freedom in the New Nation* (New York: Basic Books, 2008); James S. Pula, "Tadeusz Kościuszko: a Case Study in Constructed Historical Symbolism," *The Polish Review*, Vol. 52, no. 2 (2008), 159–82.

Kosciuszko Foundation. The Kosciuszko Foundation began as the Polish American Scholarship Committee launched in 1923 by Dr. **Stephen Mizwa** to bring Polish students to American universities. Mizwa, in conjunction with Dr. Henry Noble McCracken, president of Vassar College, who had recently returned from a tour of universities and libraries in Eastern Europe, enlarged the Committee's mission to include the promotion of cultural and educational exchange between the United States and Poland. In December 1925, the Committee became the newly-incorporated Kosciuszko Foundation, with Dr. McCracken as president. An internationalist, pacifist, educator, and scholar, McCracken was a modernizing force in American education. A graduate of New York University, he taught in Beirut before returning to the U.S. to teach literature and drama at Yale University and Smith College. Mizwa served as secretary and

executive director of the new Foundation. Under McCracken, the Foundation commemorated the tenth anniversary of Polish independence after World War I in 1928 with a banquet honoring **Ignacy Jan Paderewski** at the Commodore Hotel. In 1933 it established an annual ball to raise funds for its educational and cultural programs. Held at the elegant and prestigious Waldorf-Astoria Hotel, the ball is a major social event for the Polish American community. In 1943, the Foundation helped organize a committee to commemorate the quadricentennial of the death of the great Polish astronomer Copernicus (Mikołaj Kopernik), which resulted in a major celebration held at Carnegie Hall that included Albert Einstein among its guests of honor. In 1949, Howard Hanson of the Eastman School of Music, headed a committee organizing events to mark the centennial of the death of Chopin. These included the inauguration of the Foundation's Chopin Piano Competition by virtuoso Witold Malcuzyński. Held annually ever since, the Competition boasts among its laureates such notables as Van Cliburn, Murray Perahia, and Ian Hobson.

With McCracken's retirement from the Board in 1955, the presidency passed to Mizwa. In the same year, the Foundation established the "Kosciuszko Foundation Medal of Recognition" to honor special friends who significantly contributed to its' mission. The first medal was awarded to McCracken for his efforts in establishing the Foundation. Among the many other notables who have received the Medal are pianists **Artur Rubinstein** and Van Cliburn; conductors **Leopold Stokowski** and **Stanisław Skrowaczewski**; historian **Oscar Halecki**; diplomat **Zbigniew Brzeziński**; and journalist and author Ryszard Kapuściński. In 1959, the Foundation published the *Kosciuszko Foundation English-Polish Polish-English Dictionary* as part of its Polish Millennium Series of publications, which included important biographies and other reference works. This dictionary, which has since been updated and reissued, established itself as the standard reference work of its type in the United States.

Mizwa was followed in the presidency by Dr. **Eugene Kusielewicz** (1970–79), a teacher and scholar who for many years taught history at St. John's University and was one of the founders of *The Polish American World*. At the Foundation, he initiated a Library of Polish Studies which made several important Polish texts available in English, as well as sponsoring biographies, in English and Polish, of Karol Szymanowski, Ignacy Paderewski, and Stanisław Moniuszko. Albert Juszczak, a faculty member at Hunter College in New York City, served as the Foundation's fourth president (1979–86) during the tumultuous years of the Solidarity movement and was responsible for maintaining relations with major institutions in America and Poland during the period of martial law.

Joseph E. Gore, a corporate attorney, succeeded Juszczak as president (1987–2008). Gore's tenure coincided with the most crucial political time in Poland's recent history, during which he succeeded in strengthening the relationship between American and Polish academic institutions and government agencies. To assist in this task, the Foundation opened its Warsaw office, while it also undertook in the 1990s a campaign to establish a Chair of Polish Studies at Columbia University. Under Gore's leadership, in 1996, working with the Film Society of Lincoln Center in New York, the Foundation presented "Revelation and Camouflage," a 60-year retrospective of films from Poland. To celebrate the opening of this program, the Foundation hosted a symposium attended by prominent Polish directors and actors including Andrzej Wajda (an honorary trustee of the Foundation), Krzysztof Zanussi, Agnieszka Holland, Juliusz Machulski (a grantee) and Krystyna Janda. Under Gore's leadership the Foundation issued the *New Kosciuszko Foundation English-Polish Polish-English Dictionary* (2003), the first ever bilingual dictionary of American English that included a CD-ROM, and published "Polish Masters from the Kosciuszko Foundation's Collection." **Alexander Storozynski**, a member of the *New York Daily News* editorial board that received the Pulitzer Prize in 1999, became the Foundations sixth president in November 2008.

The Kosciuszko Foundation fulfills its mission by awarding fellowships and grants to graduate students, scholars, scientists, professionals, and artists, and increases the visibility and prestige of Polish culture in American society through its support of public performance programs, including chamber concerts recorded for broadcast over WQXR-FM, the radio station of *The New York Times*. The Foundation sponsors the annual Chopin Piano Competition, the **Marcella Sembrich** Memorial Voice Scholarship Competition, and the Wieniawski Violin Competition, as well as lectures, films, and exhibitions in New York City and throughout the U.S. in cooperation with its local chapters. It also funds scholarship and exchange programs, a "Teaching English in Poland" program, summer sessions on Polish language and culture held in Poland, and year abroad programs at universities throughout Poland.

In 2010, the Foundation had approximately 2,000 members. Its headquarters were located at 15 East 65th Street on the Upper East Side of Manhattan in a limestone neo–Renaissance four-story mansion built in 1917. The second story ballroom functions as an art gallery, as well as a lecture and concert hall for chamber music and solo recitals. It houses one of the largest public collections of Polish art in America that includes landscapes, portraits, and historical works by such masters as Jan Matejko, Wojciech Kossak, Józef Chełmoński, Józef Brandt, Jacek Malczewski, and **Władysław Benda**. All of the works were sponsored or donated by members, or were gifts of the artists themselves.— *Thomas Pniewski*

SOURCES: Stephen P. Mizwa, *The Story of the Kosciuszko Foundation: How it Came About* (New York: The Kosciuszko Foundation, 1972); Eugene Kusielewicz, "The Kosciuszko Foundation: A Half Century of Progress," in Frank Mocha, ed., *Poles in America: Bicentennial Essays* (Stevens Point, WI: Worzalla Publishing Company, 1978), 671–86.

Kosciuszko Guard. The Kosciuszko Guard of the Wisconsin state militia was the first American military unit organized by Poles in the United States. Formed in June 1874 by immigrants in Milwaukee led by August Rudzinski, the Kosciuszko Guard grew quickly to number one hundred volunteers following an appeal from the pulpit at St. Stanislaus Church on the city's near south side. Soon after, the unit was formally recognized by Gov. William Taylor who authorized providing it with equipment for its members' training activities. The original name of the unit was Company B, since it was the second such formation created in Milwaukee. Initially all commands were given in the Polish language. That the unit was popularly known as the Kosciuszko Guard from the start is an impor-

tant indicator of the respect accorded to **Thaddeus Kosciuszko** in **Polonia** long before monuments in his memory began to be erected in the U.S. The Kosciuszko Guard served as an early launching pad for the election of several Poles to political office. August Rudzinski, its first commander, was elected to the Milwaukee County Board of Supervisors in 1878, thus becoming the first Pole in the U.S. to win office. In 1882, his successor in the Guard, Francis Borchardt, won election to the state legislature. In 1990, yet another Guard leader, August Czerwinski, was elected Milwaukee comptroller, initiating a local tradition (which continued with notable interruptions until 1972) whereby Poles in that office were seen as the city's "Polish mayors." Other successful Polish American politicians and Polonia leaders, most notably Judge Michael Blenski, were also members of the unit. In its military exercises, the Kosciuszko Guard won numerous commendations from visiting army officials from Washington, D.C. The Kosciuszko Guard was also represented by a delegate at the founding convention of the **Polish National Alliance** in September 1880.

On May 4, 1886, Gov. Jeremiah Rusk called on a number of state militia units, including the Kosciuszko Guard, to restore order at the Illinois Steel Company in Milwaukee. There, several thousand employees led by the Knights of Labor, many of them Polish immigrants, were protesting for an eight hour work day. A similar protest had been accompanied by violence in Haymarket Square in Chicago. In the resulting confrontation, shots were fired on the governor's orders and as many as nine demonstrators were killed. The Kosciuszko Guard had been

The "Kosciuszko Guard" in 1931 (*UWM*).

placed in an impossible predicament; its members were severely criticized for having taken part in an action against fellow Poles, although they denied they had used their weapons in the crisis.

In April 1898, members of the Kosciuszko Guard (officially renamed at the time as Company K of the Wisconsin Volunteers) responded enthusiastically to Pres. William McKinley's call for soldiers in the Spanish-American War. However, the war ended before the unit could reach Cuba. In 1915 the Guard was dispatched to the Mexican border as part of Gen. John Pershing's military force following Pres. Wilson's decision to capture the Mexican revolutionary turned outlaw Pancho Villa. In World War I, the volunteers who made up Company K saw extensive military action in France and took many casualties. After the war, Company K was designated Company K of the 127th Infantry, 32nd Division, in Federal recognition of its contributions to victory and those of the 32nd Division. In World War II, the unit served extensively in the Far East, mainly in the campaigns to regain the island of New Guinea and the Philippines from the Japanese. Again, the soldiers of Company K contributed greatly to the U.S. effort, but at an extraordinary price. In the New Guinea campaign alone, from December 1942 to February 1943, 153 of the 165 men in the unit were killed, wounded, or missing in action.

After World War II, the Company was eventually dissolved in the 1950s following a major reorganization and consolidation of National Guard units. From 1895 until it was demobilized in the 1950s, the headquarters of the Kosciuszko Guard was in the Kosciuszko Armory Hall on Milwaukee's near south side. The building was for many years a center of Polish ethnic life and public and patriotic gatherings.—*Donald E. Pienkos*

SOURCE: Frank Krukar, Leo Kosak, and Peter Piasecki, "History of Company K," in Thaddeus Borun and John Gostomski, eds., *We the Milwaukee Poles, 1846–1946* (Milwaukee: Nowiny Publishing Company, 1946), 123–28.

Kosciuszko Home *see* **Thaddeus Kosciuszko National Memorial.**

Kościuszko League. The Kościuszko League was founded in Detroit on November 6, 1943 to represent the views of liberal and left-wing Polish Americans on the contentious Polish-Soviet controversy that threatened Allied unity during World War II. The pro–Soviet positions adopted by the 250 persons in attendance at the inaugural meeting reflected Moscow's attitude on the Polish question. The London-based Polish government-in-exile was condemned as a "prisoner of reaction" and blamed for Stalin's decision to sever diplomatic relations with that government in the wake of the Katyń massacre revelations in April 1943. The Polish claims to the eastern borderlands — annexed by the Soviets in 1939 as a result of the Ribbentrop-Molotov Pact — were dismissed as the preposterous dreams of the displaced pre-war Polish landed aristocracy. These pronouncements immediately placed the new organization at odds with the majority of Polish Americans who supported the Polish government-in-exile as a fighting ally in the war against Nazi Germany.

The impetus for the creation of the Kościuszko League can be attributed to the Rev. **Stanisław Orlemański**, the long-time pastor of Our Lady of the Holy Rosary Parish in Springfield, Massachusetts. The American-born Orlemański had become a severe critic of the Polish government after the break in Polish-Soviet relations. He accused the London Poles of disrupting the Grand Alliance and lambasted Polish American organizations that backed the Polish exile regime and became a frequent contributor of pro–Soviet articles for Detroit's Communist-line *Głos Ludowy* (Peoples Voice) and the leftist *Nasz Swiat* (Our World). When the Soviets announced the formation of a Polish military unit to battle the Germans alongside the Red Army in the spring of 1943, Orlemański saw the development as proof of Stalin's good will toward Poland. Dubbed the "Kościuszko Division," these troops, Soviet-equipped and officered, were commanded by Colonel Zygmunt Berling and placed under the auspices of the Union of Polish Patriots, a group of Communist and left-wing exiles headquartered in Moscow. "I thought it proper for me, as an American citizen of Polish descent to support the move," Orlemański said later. "Kościuszko is our American hero, and bringing Kościuszko to Poland means American democracy." The Soviet-sponsored Kościuszko Division, the priest added, "will help to destroy Hitlerism in Europe, and the Kościuszko League will help to destroy ... pro–Nazi leaders in our [Polish] organizations and also the pro–Nazi leaders among our clergy here in America."

Two forms of activity were proposed at the opening meeting of the Kościuszko League: moral support for the Kościuszko Division in Russia, and a combined campaign to unite Polish Americans in support of the Grand Alliance policy of President Franklin D. Roosevelt, while combating the activities of the "fifth-columnists and appeasers" in both the American and Polish American fields. The Rev. Orlemański, who was present at the proceedings, was elected as the honorary president of the organization. The actual president, however, was Anthony Karczmarzyk, an employee of the **Hamtramck** Broad of Education. Other officers included John Rożycki, vice-president; Adam Kujtkowski, recording secretary; and Vincent Klein, Michigan State Senator **Stanley Nowak**, Marian Jackowicz, Antonina Sajkowska, Leon Chocianowicz, Apolinary Wendolowski, and Adam Nowicki, directors.

On November 24, a lengthy TASS dispatch was published in *Pravda* and *Izvestia* in Moscow quoting the declarations of the Kościuszko League, while the American Communist Party's *Daily Worker* and its Polish-language counterpart, *Głos Ludowy*, warmly praised the group. Orlemański, meanwhile, had embarked on a whirlwind tour through Canada and the Midwest to drum up support for the organization. It is clear that Moscow had anointed Orlemański, **Leo Krzycki**, the veteran labor organizer and president of the **American Slav Congress**, and professor **Oskar Lange**, a socialist economist at the University of Chicago who played a key role behind the scenes in the creation of the Kościuszko League, as the collective "true voice of American Polonia." On December 19, all three of these leftist figures appeared at a Town Hall rally in New York, where they proclaimed a "crusade" against the "reactionary" Polish press and organizations in the United States that supported the Polish London government.

Most Polish Americans disagreed with the aims of the Kościuszko League and a bitter polemical war of words between the two sides ensued. In December, 1943, **Peter Yolles** of *Nowy Swiat* (New World), the main organ of the **National Committee of Americans of Polish Descent**, better known by its Polish initials KNAPP, called the Kościuszko League part and parcel of Moscow's attempt to divide **Polonia** on the Polish issue. KNAPP, the *bête noir* of the "Detroit Poles" for its warnings of Soviet designs on Poland, was labeled a "Fascist organization" by Orlemański, Krzycki, and *Głos Ludowy*.

The Kościuszko League certainly played a role in the Kremlin's concerted propaganda offensive designed to discredit and vilify the London Polish government in the aftermath of the Katyń affair. From the beginning, the pronouncements of the Kościuszko League were indistinguishable in content and even phraseology from those of *Pravda*, the CPUSA's *Daily Worker*, the American Slav Congress, *Głos Ludowy*, and Corliss Lamont's Council on American-Soviet Friendship, with no abatement until a Soviet-controlled regime was locked into power in post-war Poland.

In February 1944, Vyacheslav Molotov, Stalin's foreign minister, proposed to U.S. ambassador Averill Harriman that a new Polish government be formed that might include Orlemański, Krzycki, and Lange—three American citizens—on the basis of friendship with the Soviet Union. In the spring of the same year, the leftist opposition within Polonia scored a major publicity coup when both Orlemański and Lange were invited to confer with Stalin and to visit the Soviet-sponsored Polish troops in Russia. The sensational newspaper headlines produced by the leftist duo's Russian journey served to galvanize American Polonia, which responded with the creation of the **Polish American Congress** in Buffalo at the end of May, a large federation of fraternals and societies representing the vast majority of Polish Americans who supported the Polish government-in-exile.

The Polish-Soviet dilemma carried a potential for domestic political implications that concerned Roosevelt Administration officials in light of the upcoming presidential election. In a confidential report prepared by White House advisor David K. Niles in June, the new Polish American Congress was characterized as "the most representative assembly that was ever called together in the history of the American Poles," while the pro–Soviet Kościuszko League "was not representative of the Polish community." The leaders of the League, Niles noted, were liberals rather than Communists, but "the machinery of the organization is controlled by the Communists." The movement, he concluded "is doomed to failure as far as the broad masses of the Poles in America are concerned." Henceforth, Roosevelt's political advisors would concentrate on keeping the Polish American majority in the Democratic fold with reassurances that Poland would not be abandoned.

The Polish situation, however, unfolded much in the manner predicted by Lange. A Soviet-controlled Committee of National Liberation was installed by the advancing Red Army, a development enthusiastically welcomed by the Kościuszko League, the American Slav Congress, and Professor Lange. The tragedy of the Warsaw Uprising—a last-ditch effort of the Polish Home Army to save Polish independence, is well known. The British and Americans agreed to the "broadening" of the Lublin Committee at Yalta in early 1945, and recognized the Polish Government of National Unity in July. The Polish government-in-exile had been abandoned. In January 1947 the "free and unfettered elections" promised for Poland at **Yalta** proved to be a blatantly fraudulent exercise that made that nation a Communist puppet state for the next four decades.

The efforts of the Kościuszko League, in cooperation with the American Slav Congress and other pro–Soviet groups, had succeeded in creating the impression that Polonia was seriously divided on the Polish-Soviet issue despite the fact that they represented but a small segment of Polish America. Such membership figures that could be unearthed indicate that the Kościuszko League attracted about 1500, with 800 alone from Orlemański's Springfield parish of over 3000. Some League officers were listed as representatives of various CIO unions with large numbers of Polish American workers but carried no union mandate to justify such claims—a standard practice used in other Communist front organizations as well. The imposition of a Stalinist regime in Poland spelled the end of the Kościuszko League within a few short years.— *Robert Szymczak*

SOURCES: Charles Sadler, "Pro-Soviet-Americans: Oskar Lange and Russia's Friends in Polonia," *The Polish Review*, Vol. XXII, no. 4 (Fall 1977), 25–39; Robert Szymczak, "Invitation to the Kremlin: The Adventures of Father Stanislaw Orlemanski, April–May 1944," *East European Quarterly*, Vol. XXV, no. 4 (January 1992), 399–424.

Kościuszko Monument at West Point. The world's second oldest monument to Kościuszko (see **Tadeusz Kościuszko**) after the Kościuszko Mound (Kopiec Kościuszki) in Kraków, the Kościuszko Monument at the United States Military Academy in West Point, New York, was completed in 1828, five years after the Kraków memorial. Following a recommendation to the Corps of Cadets from the Academy's superintendent, Sylvanus Thayer, a small, volunteer committee of Cadets formed to select someone to be memorialized by the monument—preferably a hero of America's War of Independence—and then select a design for the monument and raise the necessary funds. The committee consisted of Charles Petigru, John Mackay, Robert E. Lee, Charles Mason, and E. Basinger. Lee's biographer, Douglas Southall Freeman, in his classic four-volume treatment of the future Confederate leader *R. E. Lee: a Biography*, noted that during Lee's days at the Academy, Kościuszko "was the patron saint of West Point." No doubt because of the Pole's role as chief engineer for original fortifications at West Point, coupled with his positive reputation during the early nineteenth century, the committee chose to honor Kościuszko with the first monument erected at the Academy.

On November 11, 1824, the following notice appeared in *Niles' Register*: "*Kosciusko.* The cadets of the United States Military Academy at West Point have offered a gold medal, of the value of fifty dollars, for the best design for a monument to the memory of Gen. Thaddeus Kosciusko. It is to be erected at West Point, on a romantic spot, situated on a bank of the Hudson, and known by the name of Kosciusko's garden." The winning design was submitted by a former West Point cadet, John H. B. Latrobe, the son of the famous architect Benjamin Latrobe whose work included the United States Capitol building in Washington, D.C.

To finance the monument, each member of the Corps of Cadets assessed himself twenty-five cents from his monthly living allowance, the full cost of the monument being nearly $5,000, a considerable expense at that time. Located on the original site of Fort Clinton, the Kościuszko Monument was dedicated on July 4, 1828. "While your river flows and Country exists," Latrobe commented, "no one will be at a loss to understand the Monument, its purpose, and its location." In his "Oration Prepared for Delivery on the Occasion of Laying the Corner Stone of a Monument Erected to the Memory of Kościuszko by the Corps of Cadets, July 4, 1828," Cadet Charles Petigru closed with these words: "While we join our homage to that which he has already so universally received, and endeavor to associate more closely his name with this place, with which it is already associated by Revolutionary experiences ... amidst the grandeur of the Highland scenery, like his own amiable and simple private virtues, by the side of his more resplendent and exalted qualities of the soldier, the patriot, and the statesman—let us remember that we too are the soldiers of a Republic—that as such we owe the same debt which was by him so nobly acquitted— and proud of the high distinction, let it ever be our ambition to act worthily of it. Let us learn from him that glory in great and honorable undertakings is not dependent upon success—that he who bravely dares for the good of his country, with a willingness to sacrifice himself to her interest, whatever may be the fate of his enterprise or his own, is always sure of the reward in a people's gratitude and in the world's applause."—*Anthony J. Bajdek*

SOURCES: David J. Abodaher, *Warrior on Two Continents: Thaddeus Kościuszko* (New York: Julian Messner, 1968); Monica M. Gardner, *Kościuszko, a Biography* (London: George Allen & Unwin, Ltd., 1942); Miecislaus Haiman, *Kościuszko in the American Revolution* (Boston: Gregg Press, 1972); Francis Casimir Kajencki, *Thaddeus Kościuszko: Military Engineer of the American Revolution* (El Paso, TX: Southwest Polonia Press, 1998); James S. Pula, *Thaddeus Kościuszko: The Purest Son of Liberty* (New York: Hippocrene Books, Inc., 1998); Alex Storozynski, *The Peasant Prince: Thaddeus Kościuszko and the Era of Revolution* (New York: St. Martin's Press, 2009).

Kosciuszko Polish Patriotic League *see* **Kosciuszko League.**

Kościuszko Squadron. At the end of the First World War, Poland became an independent nation for the first time since the 1790s. Its newly-established independence was immediately challenged by Bolshevik Russia which launched a war against the fledgling republic in 1919. At this time of crisis, Merian Caldwell Cooper, a pilot in the American 20th Air Squadron during the war, determined to help the Poles. Cooper's ancestor had served alongside Gen. **Kazimierz Pułaski** in the American Revolution and because of this he took an interest in working with Herbert Hoover in organizing humanitarian relief efforts for Poland, an effort that took him to Galicia and Lwów. With the Bolshevik invasion, Cooper determined to organize an air unit to serve with the Poles. Cooper interested Cedric Fauntleroy, another American pilot, in the venture and the two of them recruited other Americans to join them. The initial group of ten pilots arrived in Poland in September 1919. Together with five Poles under Lt. Ludomił Rayski, the Americans were designated the 7th Air Squadron (7. Eskadra Lotnicza) and assigned to the defense of Lwów. On December 31 the Polish Minister of Military Affairs approved a change in the name to the "7th Polish-American 'Kościuszko' Fighter Squadron." As such, they fought in defense of the Lwów region where they proved invaluable for reconnaissance missions designed to gather intelligence on where enemy forces were located and give warning of impending offensives, for liaison work to deliver messages between units in an era before radio or other modern communication technology, and for attacking ground targets with bombs and machine guns. Without their services, 6th Army headquarters would have been denied valuable information about the enemy while experiencing difficulty communicating with its own widespread units. Major Adam Brzechwa-Ajdukiewicz, head of the 3rd Operational Section headquarters, later concluded: "What were the results of this intelligence? My answer is one word only — fantastic! Quite simply I cannot imagine how the Operational Section could have functioned had it not been for the daily air force reports. All calculations, decisions, and orders were based on them.... During the 2nd Army attack on Berdyczew in April 1920 the 7th Fighter Squadron chased off whole Bolshevik infantry units with ease." Gen. Antoni Listowski commanding the 2nd Polish Army confided in his diary that "The American pilots of the 7th Squadron are performing miracles. They have already reported the cavalry's approach towards Biała Cerkiew. They flew over the city during the unit's entry into the city." In his official report he later wrote: "The American pilots, though exhausted, fight tenaciously. During the last offensive, their commander attacked enemy formations from the rear, raining machine-gun bullets down on their heads. Without the American pilots' help, we would long ago have been done for." Between April 1, 1920, and the ceasefire on October 18, the 7th Air Squadron flew 462 combat sorties. Nine of the American pilots were awarded the *Virtuti Militari* for their efforts on behalf of Polish freedom and independence. Following the war the Americans went home. The squadron was reorganized with Polish pilots as the 111th Pursuit Squadron (111. eskadra myśliwska), but retained the Kościuszko name. In 1939 it fought in defense of Warsaw, and with the fall of the city to the Germans many of its pilots fled to Romania, and then on to France and Britain. There, in 1940, the unit was reconstituted as 303 Kościuszko Squadron flying out of the Royal Air Force fighter base at Northold in defense of London. In the Battle of Britain the Poles shot down more German aircraft than any other Allied squadron, earning universal praise from the British and later the Americans. It served throughout the war, finally being disbanded on December 11, 1946. The name survives today as a fighter squadron in the Polish Air Force, and as a student organization of cadets at the U.S. Military Academy at West Point.—*James S. Pula*

SOURCES: Janusz Cisek, *Kościuszko, We Are Here! American Pilots of the Kościuszko Squadron in Defense of Poland, 1919–1921* (Jefferson, NC: McFarland & Company, Inc., 2002); Robert F. Karolevitz and Ross S. Fenn, *Flight of Eagles: The Story of the American Kościuszko Squadron in the Polish-Russian War 1919–1920* (Sioux Falls, SD: Brevet Press, Inc., 1974); Tomasz J. Kopański and Zygmunt Kozak, *Kościuszko Squadron 1919–1920* (Sandomierz, Poland: Stratus, 2005); Lynne Olson and Stanley Cloud, *A Question of Honor. The Kościuszko Squadron: Forgotten Heroes of World War II* (New York: Alfred A. Knopf, 2003).

Kosciuszko's Garden. While **Tadeusz Kościuszko** was occupied as the chief engineer for the construction of West Point in 1778, he would often climb down one of its cliffs to a secluded spot where he had planted a small garden by carrying bags of soil down the steep escarpment to the isolated location. There he would relax, lost in contemplation for brief moments before going back to work. In 1967 the Polish American Veterans of Massachusetts initiated a "Kosciuszko's Garden Restoration and Perpetual Care Project" to raise funds for the restoration of the garden, the installation of landscaping and modern stairs, and establishment of an endowment fund. The garden was rededicated on June 22, 1969. Today, a modern stairway leads down the cliff to its location below Cullum Hall. Since 2003, the garden has been preserved through the generosity of the "General Edward L. Rowny Family Endowment." Gen. Rowny was a 1941 graduate of the U.S. Military Academy at West Point.—*James S. Pula*

SOURCE: *The Summit Times*, Vol. 10, No. 29 (2003).

Kosciuszko's Garden at West Point (*OLS*).

Kościuszko's Will. Following the American Revolution, **Tadeusz Kościuszko** returned to Europe where he led an unsuccessful revolt against Russian control of Poland. Seriously wounded and imprisoned in Russia, when eventually released by Tsar Paul I he traveled again to the U.S. to settle his financial affairs. As a veteran of the Revolution, the Congress owed him back pay and allowances for his service amounting to $12,280.54, plus interest from January 1, 1793 to December 31, 1797. Before leaving again for Europe, he executed a will that is generally referred to as his "American Will." Signed on May 5, 1798, with John Barnes and John Dawson acting as witnesses and his friend Thomas Jefferson named executor, the text of the final declaration read as follows: "I, Thaddeus Kosciuszko, being just in my departure from America do hereby declare and direct that should I make no other testamentary disposition of my property in the United States, I hereby authorize my friend Thomas Jefferson to employ the whole thereof in purchasing Negroes from among his own or any others and giving them Liberty in my name, in giving them an education in trades or otherwise and in having them instructed for their new condition in the duties of morality which may make them good neighbors, good fathers or mothers, husbands, or wives and in their duties as citizens teaching them to be defenders of their Liberty and Country and of the good order of society and in whatsoever may make them happy and useful, and I make the said Thomas Jefferson my executor of this."

By the time of his death in 1817, Kościuszko's American estate had grown to $17,099, exclusive of the interest which had been paid to him for living expenses in Europe. Jefferson, as executor of the will, soon withdrew from the probate process citing his age. He was seventy-five years old at the time and feared that the probate might be a lengthy process. As it turned out, he was correct. Competing claims to the estate soon came from other claimants. In 1806, while in Paris, Kościuszko authorized a will in which he left a specific sum of money to Kosciuszko Armstrong, the son of his Revolutionary War friend Gen. John Armstrong. A third will, penned in Soleure, Switzerland, in 1816, also appeared in which the Pole bequeathed his French properties. And finally, a fourth will was presented to the court that had been executed in Soleure on October 10, 1817, only five days before Kościuszko's death. In this document he left the largest portion of his estate to the Zeltner family with whom he resided in Switzerland in the last years of his life. The Court delegated the handling of the estate to Benjamin L. Lear of Washington,

D.C. Following his examination of the will, Lear suggested the funds be utilized to endow "The Kosciuszko School" then being planned by the African Education Society of New Jersey. This was the source of a widely held, but incorrect belief repeated in many Polish American publications that Kościuszko's funds were used to endow the school for the benefit of educating African Americans. However, the legal complexities of the four competing claimants to the bequest first had to be adjudicated. The case took years to wind its way through various levels of the court system, but resolution took so long that Lear eventually died in 1832. Col. George Bomford replaced Lear, while Major **Gaspard Tochman** also appeared on the scene representing Kościuszko's Polish heirs who came forward to claim the estate. When Bomford died in 1848 the issue had still not been resolved. In 1852, the complicated international litigations reached the United States Supreme Court under the innocuous legal heading of *John F. Ennis vs. J. H. B. Smith, et. al.* Ennis then represented Kościuszko's Polish relatives who claimed the entire American estate by virtue of a will he signed in 1816, while Smith, acting for Bomford's heirs, argued the case in favor of the primacy of the will of 1798 with regard to the American portion of Kościuszko's legacy. The Polish claimants argued that the 1816 will had previously been proved legitimate under French law, and that it included a standard clause of revocation which read, in English translation, as follows: "I revoke all the wills and codicils which I may have made previous to the present, to which alone I confine myself, as containing my last wishes." This meant that all previous wills were null and void and the new will, that of 1816, was the only legal testament extant at that time. Since no disposition of the American property was made in the 1816 will, and because the 1817 will only bequeathed certain explicit portions of the estate in general, Kościuszko's Polish heirs asserted that the American portion of the legacy was therefore intestate. That is, the American estate not having been bequeathed, it became the property of the next of kin. The Court agreed. Thus, the American estate would go to Kościuszko's relatives. The total amount of the general's estate was placed at $43,504.40. Despite the legalities of the case which led to the final decision, it is clear that what Kościuszko intended was for each of his wills to cover different portions of his estate. Only weeks before his death he wrote to Jefferson that "after my death, you know the fixed destination [of my American estate]." This letter was written well after the will of 1816, and clearly indicates that Kościuszko still

considered his American will of 1798 to be in effect. Regardless, because of legal technicalities his American estate went to his Polish heirs rather than to the purpose he no doubt intended.—*James S. Pula*

Sources: James S. Pula, "The American Will of Thaddeus Kosciuszko," *Polish American Studies*, Vol. 34, no. 1 (1977), 16–25; "Kosciuszko's Will," *Scribner's Monthly*, XVII, No. 5 (March 1879); Louis Ottenberg, "A Testamentary Tragedy: Jefferson and the Wills of General Kosciuszko," *American Bar Association Journal*, Vol. 44 (January 1958).

Kosinski, Jerzy Nikodem (b. Łódź, Poland, June 14, 1933; d. New York, New York, May 3, 1991). Writer. Kosinski was born Jerzy Nikodem Lewinkopf to Polish-Jewish parents. His father, Moses, was a classics professor, and his mother, Elżbieta, a concert pianist. To survive the war and the Holocaust, Moses Lewinkopf and his family assumed Gentile names and identities. With the Soviet advance into Poland, Kosinski's father became a communist supporter and sympathizer; his loyalty was rewarded by a party appointment, which thus allowed Jerzy to lead a comfortable adolescent life after the war. He attended the University of Łódź, first studying sociology, political science, and history under Professor Józef Chałasiński. At the graduate level he pursued social psychology at Warsaw University and Moscow State University, eventually earning a doctorate. Like his parents, Kosinski became increasingly disillusioned with life under communism and soon managed to escape by forging official papers alleging acceptance into an academic exchange program in America. Kosinski fled Poland in 1957 and briefly worked as a truck driver in the U.S. before a Ford Foundation grant permitted him to enroll in a graduate program at Columbia University. While there, he wrote *The Future Is Ours, Comrade* (1960) and *No Third Path* (1962). His works about totalitarianism found a receptive audience in America's anti-communist circles. One particular admirer of Kosinski's early work was the widowed heiress of a West Virginia steel magnate, Mary Hayward Weir. The couple wed in 1962, divorced in 1966, and, in 1968, Weir died of cancer. In that same year Kosinski met and later married the Bavarian aristocrat Katherina "Kiki" von Fraunhofer. While married to Weir, however, Kosinski wrote *The Painted Bird* (1965), his critically acclaimed Holocaust novel about the wanderings of a young boy in Nazi-occupied Eastern Europe. The novel won France's Best Foreign Book Award in 1966; was favorably reviewed by numerous critics, including Elie Weisel; and launched Kosinski's literary career in the United States. A series of prestigious fellowships and teaching positions followed. In 1965 Kosinski became a U.S. citizen and,

Jerzy Kosinski, novelist (*OLS*).

two years later, accepted a Guggenheim Fellowship, which allowed him to teach English at Wesleyan College. While there, he prepared the manuscript for his second book, *Steps* (1968). The novel won the 1969 National Book Award, and Kosinski was soon named a Senior Fellow at Princeton University's Council for the Humanities. In the early 1970s, Kosinski moved again to Yale University to teach drama; produced his third novel, *Being There*, which was adapted into an Academy Award winning film in 1979 starring Peter Sellers; and wrote prolifically, producing *The Devil Tree* (1973), *Cockpit* (1975), *Blind Date* (1977), *Passion Play* (1979), and *Pinball* (1982). His literary fame allowed him access to some of the most famous Hollywood circles. In 1981 he starred as Grigory Zinoviev in Warren Beatty's film, *Reds*. One year later the New York weekly, *Village Voice*, challenged Kosinski's authorship of *The Painted Bird*, *Being There*, and *Steps*, accusing him of plagiarism. The article claimed that Kosinski was not fluent in English at the time of *The Painted Bird*'s publication. Troubled by the accusations, Kosinski was inspired to write *The Hermit of 69th Street* (1988), an "autofiction" about Holocaust survivor Norbert Korsky whose life and work were under similar scrutiny. Kosinski was largely unable to recover from the allegations, thought by some to be orchestrated by Polish communists who had long forbade publication of *The Painted Bird* in Soviet-controlled Poland. Kosinski committed suicide in 1991.—*Krystyna Cap*

SOURCES: James Park Sloan, *Jerzy Kosinski: A Biography* (New York: Dutton, 1996); "Kosinski, Jerzy," *Contemporary Authors* (Detroit: Gale Research Com-

pany, New Revision Series), Vol. 9, 314–18; Vol. 49, no. 1 (2004) of *The Polish Review* is a special issue devoted to Kosinski.

Kosinski, Michelle (b. Cinnaminson, New Jersey, May 6, 1975; d.—). Journalist. Kosinski earned her B.A. and M.A. degrees in journalism from Northwestern University and began her career with WIFR in Rockford, Illinois. After graduate school she moved to WSOC-TV in Charlotte, North Carolina, where she was voted "Best Reporter" in 2001. She left Charlotte for Miami that same year, taking a position with WTVJ where she won a Suncoast Regional Emmy Award in 2003 for her reporting on Haitian immigrants. In 2005 she won a national Emmy Award for election coverage on an NBC news special and was named Woman of the Year by Women in Communications of South Florida. In the same year she became an NBC News correspondent. Among her noteworthy stories were coverage of hurricane Katrina, the New York City transit strike, the killings at Virginia Tech, the murder of Benazir Bhutto, terrorist threats in Europe, and the murder of Caylee Anthony, while contributing regularly to the *NBC Nightly News with Brian Williams*, *Today*, and news broadcasts on MSNBC and CNBC. In 2005 she stirred controversy for an interview she did with Joran van der Sloot, a suspect in the disappearance of Natalee Holloway in Aruba, because the suspect's attorney had not approved the interview.—*James S. Pula*

Kott, Jan (b. Warsaw, Poland, October 27, 1914; d. Santa Monica, California, December 22, 2001). Literary scholar, critic. After earning his Ph.D. at the University of Łódź (1947) and his *habiliticzny* (1952), he became one of the leading Polish authorities on the Marxist interpretation of literature. Active in the Polish Communist resistance movement during World War II, he became deeply involved in promoting Marxist ideology in literary studies early after that conflict. Together with a group of Communist scholars, he was among the founders of the Institute of Literary Studies (IBL) in Warsaw (1952). He had published numerous studies on Polish and World Literature, achieving an international reputation with the publication of his study *Shakespeare, Our Contemporary* (1961, Engl. transl. 1964, 1966), which was translated into fourteen languages. He was made an Honorary Member of the Modern Language Association in 1964. Receiving a Ford Foundation fellowship, he came to the United States in 1966, teaching at Yale University (1966–69), the University of California, Berkeley (1967), the State University of New York, Stony Brook

(1969–83), and the Getty Center, Santa Monica, CA (1985–86). He became a U.S. citizen in 1979. He received numerous honors and awards including The Guggenheim Fellowship (1972–73), the Jurzykowski Foundation Award (1975), the Robert Lewis Medal (1993), the T. Kantor Award (1998), and a number of Polish and French decorations. He was among the most prolific Polish writers and critics, some of his studies being regarded as examples of the highest modern literary scholarship.— *Jerzy Krzyzanowski*

SOURCES: Gerhard M. Vasco and Hélène Volat, *The Publications of Jan Kott* (Stony Brook, NY: State University of New York at Stony Brook, 1979); "Kott, Jan," *Contemporary Authors* (Detroit: Gale Research Company), Vol. 13–16, 465.

Kowal, Charles T. (b. Buffalo, New York, November 8, 1940; d.—). Astronomer. One of the most important astronomers of the last half of the twentieth century, he became interested in astronomy as a young boy. After attending the University of Southern California where he received a baccalaureate degree in astronomy in 1961, he went to work at the California Institute of Technology using the Mt. Wilson and Mt. Palomar observatories to search for supernovae, or exploding stars, eventually finding eighty-one. He also discovered several asteroids and comets that bear his name. In September 1974, Kowal discovered the thirteenth moon of Jupiter, which he named Leda, and the following year found the planet's fourteenth moon, Themisto. By 1977, Kowal began searching for distant objects in the solar system, hoping to find a tenth planet. In November of that year, he discovered a small, strange object between the orbits of Saturn and Uranus that created a sensation. The news media speculated that it might in fact be a tenth planet. Further study showed it to be too eccentric of orbit to be a planet, yet too far from the asteroid belt to be an asteroid, and it did not possess the properties of a comet. Kowal named the object Chiron, after a mythical half-man half-horse known as a Centaur. In the years since Kowal discovered the first, dozens of Centaurian objects have been found. He was awarded the James Craig Watson Medal by the National Academy of Sciences in 1979 for his discoveries. In 1980 he studied Galileo's notebooks and found that the Italian had observed the planet Neptune in 1612, 135 years before its official discovery. In 1986 he moved to the Space Telescope Science Institute in Baltimore to be able to use the Hubble Space Telescope. There he became responsible for monitoring the telescope's instruments and ensuring the quality of its data. Nine years later he took a position at the Applied Physics Laboratory at

Johns Hopkins University in Laurel, Maryland. He transitioned to the job of aerospace engineer and did extensive work on the Near Earth Asteroid Rendezvous (NEAR) mission which orbited the asteroid Eros and landed on it in 2001. Another spacecraft he worked on was TIMED, from 2001 to 2006, which studied the upper atmosphere of Earth. Kowal wrote and ran computer programs that guided these spacecraft. He retired in 2006.—*Martin S. Nowak*

SOURCE: Mark Littman, *Planets Beyond: Discovering the Outer Solar System* (Mineola, NY: Courier Dover Publications, 2004).

Kowalski, Frank (b. Meriden, Connecticut, October 18, 1907; d. Washington, D.C., October 11, 1974). Congressman, soldier. After attending schools in Meriden, Connecticut, he left as a high school junior in 1925 to enlist as a private in the army. Subsequently he took competitive exams to gain admission to the United States Military Academy where he graduated in 1930. In 1937 he received his M.S. degree from the Massachusetts Institute of Technology, and studied international relations at Columbia University in 1945 and 1946. Serving in the army continuously from 1925–58, with service in the European Theater on General of the Army Dwight Eisenhower's staff during World War II, he was director of the program for the disarmament of Germany in 1944 before serving on General Douglas MacArthur's staff as acting chief of the American Advisory Group following the Second World War. In that capacity he helped the Japanese cabinet organize its defenses in 1950 to supplement security forces when many American troops were deployed to the Korean War. In 1954 he organized and was the first commandant of the United States Army Command Management School at Fort Belvoir, Virginia, the first school for senior Army men to learn modern management techniques. Kowalski served in this capacity until his retirement from the service as a colonel on July 31, 1958. He was the recipient of the Legion of Merit with Oak Leaf Cluster and the Bronze Star. A writer on military and management topics, while in England in 1944 he authored interviews with seven Polish-born soldiers who had served in the German army before their capture by the Allies. He also reported on the conditions in Poland following a trip there in October 1945. He favored United Nations intervention in Lebanon, rather than unilateral U.S. involvement, and later recognized the Bay of Pigs invasion in 1961 as a disaster and proposed negotiations rather than another show of force. He invented various military equipment including gas leak preventive valves, improved bullets, and guns

as well as improvements in the design of knitting needles and oil well pumps. Kowalski wrote two book-length works after leaving Congress in 1963. One, *Grace of Heaven (Japan Rearms)*, about the occupation and rearmament of Japan by the U.S., was published in Japanese in 1969, but not in English. The second, *Worms in the Charter Oak*, addressed his work in Connecticut politics and his often unhappy relationship with state Democratic Party boss John M. Bailey. It was never published. Kowalski was chosen by Bailey as the Democratic candidate for the At-Large Congressional seat in Connecticut (which lasted from 1931–64), traditionally reserved by both parties for Polish Americans. In his first election Kowalski defeated the Republican incumbent, a fellow Polish American, **Anthony Sadlak**. He served in the 86th and 87th Congresses (January 3, 1959–January 3, 1963) on the House Committee on the Armed Services and worked as a reformer in combating military manpower waste (he wanted soldiers to serve only in combat, but not in supply or support jobs). He was not a candidate for re-nomination in 1962, but was an unsuccessful candidate for the Democratic nomination for the United States Senate when, as an opponent of nuclear testing and a champion of several labor unions, he opposed the late-entering former governor and Health, Education and Welfare Secretary Abraham Ribicoff, the candidate of Bailey's state party machine. Kowalski was the first member of Congress in 1962 to protest in writing the resumption of nuclear testing while negotiations in Geneva for a total ban continued. He admitted that he was "both the beneficiary and the victim of the Connecticut convention system" as run by Bailey. Appointed by President

Frank Kowalski, congressman (*CCSU-BC*).

John F. Kennedy as a member of the Subversive Activities Control Board, 1963–1966, but not re-nominated by President Lyndon B. Johnson, his continuing propensity for peace was revealed when he marched in October 1967 in an anti–Vietnam War demonstration in Washington D.C.—*Frederick J. Augustyn*

SOURCE: *Biographical Directory of the United States Congress, 1774–Present* (http://bioguide.congress.gov/).

Kowalski, Kazimierz (b. Mława Poland, March 4, 1883; d. Chicago, Illinois, July 23, 1944). Politician, Polonia activist. After migrating to Pennsylvania where he worked in the coalfields, he moved to Milwaukee around 1910. Both he and his wife were active trade unionists, becoming leaders in organizing socialist party units in the Milwaukee Polish community. In 1918 he was elected to a seat on the Milwaukee city council as an alderman-at-large, later serving as a secretary to the city's mayor, Daniel Webster Hoan. Active in the **Polish National Alliance** from the time of the First World War, Kowalski rose to prominence as a leader of the "opposition" or "lewica" faction of the Alliance in the 1920s along with attorney and PNA Censor **Casimir Sypniewski**, and treasurer Max Hencel. A fiery speaker committed to socialism and Piłsudski, he seemed always to be in the eye of the hurricane. He chaired the riotous 25th PNA convention in September 1927, that continued with only the "opposition" delegates remaining, following the walkout of the "old guard" delegates who left because of a bitter dispute over the accreditation of delegates at a convention where the two opposing factions were nearly evenly divided. Kowalski was then elected national secretary by the remaining delegates. When the convention was reassembled by court order in August 1928, Kowalski was confirmed as secretary and went on to serve one three-year term. Defeated for re-election in 1931, he was appointed manager of Alliance Printers and Publishers and held this post for four years. At the time of his death he was working for the Alliance in its real estate department. He was regarded as an authority on fraternal insurance matters and parliamentary rules and procedures.—*Donald E. Pienkos*

SOURCES: Adam Olszewski, *Historia Związku Narodowego Polskiego* (Chicago: Polish National Alliance, 1957–1963); Donald Pienkos, *PNA: A Centennial History of the Polish National Alliance of the United States of North America* (Boulder, CO: East European Monographs, 1984).

Kowalski, Killer (Edward Walter Spulnik, b. Windsor, Canada, August 13, 1926; d. Everett, Massachusetts, August 30, 2008). Wrestler. Although he originally aspired to be an electrical engineer, he moved into wrestling when encouraged to do so by a friend at the local YMCA. Possessing an impressive physique that towered to six feet seven inches, he became a hit shortly after his debut in the late 1940s. With the advent of televised wrestling, he became a star in the 1950s, as famous for leaping onto opponents from the top rope of the ring and applying his "claw hold" on the solar plexus as he was as a prototype villain, he was among the most well-known figures in wrestling entertainment. In a career that lasted over thirty years, he claimed to have appeared in over 6,000 matches. Later in his career he teamed with Big John Studd as the tag team "The Executioners." He retired from active competition in 1977, after which he established Killer Kowalski's School of Professional Wrestling in Malden, MA. His protégés included the popular Triple H and Chyna. Outside the ring, he was noted for his charitable work for special needs children.—*James S. Pula*

SOURCE: *The Glory Days of Wrestling the Way it Was, '50s & '60s* (Longwood, FL: Matrix Video, 1998).

Kozacka, Józef Stanisław (b. Poland, December 24, 1885; d. Tucson, Arizona, April 18, 1966). Engineer. After arriving in America in 1902, he obtained employment at General Electric in Pittsfield, MA (1906–07), Pratt & Whitney Company in Hartford, CT (1907–08), and the Windsor Machine Company in Windsor, VT (1908–09). He enrolled in the Pratt Institute in New York (1910) and was naturalized in 1914, but moved to Flint, Michigan, to work as a toolmaker at the Buick Motor Car Company (1910–11), and the Maxwell Motor Car Company in Dayton, OH (1912–13). He earned a baccalaureate in mechanical engineering from the University of Michigan (1916), and an M.S. from the same institution (1930), the former while working at the Packard Motor Company in Detroit, MI (1911–17). Beginning a teaching career, he taught at Alliance College in Cambridge Springs, PA (1917–29), the Lewis Institute of Technology, Chicago, IL (1930–40), the Illinois Institute of Technology (1940–45), and beginning in 1946 the University of Illinois–Chicago. While teaching in Chicago he worked as a research engineer at the Vascoloy-Ramet Corporation (1945) and in 1944 was elected president of the Polish-American Technical Societies Council, which was organized to aid in Poland's post-war educational and industrial rehabilitation. During World War II he served as supervisor of engineering, science, and management courses at the Illinois Institute of Technology. A member of the American Society of Mechanical Engineers, he served for a time as chair of its Chicago section and director of the Chicago Adult Education Council. His most important publications were J. S. Kozacka, H. A. Erickson, H. W. Highriter, and A. F. Gabriel, "An Investigation of Cemented Tungsten Carbide as Bearing Material: Progress Rept. 2," *Transactions of the ASME*, Vol. 78, no. 7 (October 1956), pp. 1403–1421; W. Baker and J. S. Kozacka, *Carbide Cutting Tools: How to Make and Use Them* (Chicago: American Technical Society, 1949).—*Slawomir Lotysz*

SOURCES: Winfield Scott Downs, ed., *Who's Who in Engineering: A Biographical Dictionary of the Engineering Profession* (New York: Lewis Historical Publications Company, 1948), 1121; obituary, *Chicago Tribune*, April 19, 1966, B8.

Kozakiewicz, Kazimierz (b. Płock, Poland, July 24, 1900; d. Chicago, Illinois, March 27, 1968). Polonia activist. Brought to the United States by his parents at the age of two, he grew up in Lowell, Massachusetts, and earned a doctorate in the field of Oculism from Boston University. Active in the **Polish Roman Catholic Union** of America (PRCUA) from his teens, Kozakiewicz was elected its vice president in 1950 and succeeded to the presidency upon the death of **Joseph Kania** in 1953. He served an additional term in his own right from 1954 to 1958. A leader in the **Polish American Council** relief organization (Rada Polonii Amerykańskiej), Kozakiewicz acted to return the PRCUA to the **Polish American Congress** in 1954. Under President Kania the PRCUA had withdrawn from the Congress out of opposition to **Charles Rozmarek**'s leadership practices. In contrast, Kozakiewicz worked smoothly with Rozmarek and served as Treasurer of the PAC.—*Donald E. Pienkos*

SOURCE: Donald E. Pienkos, *For Your Freedom Through Ours: Polish American Efforts on Poland's Behalf, 1863–1991* (Boulder, CO: East European Monographs, 1991).

Kozłowski, Antoni (b. Zakroczym, Poland, June 1857; d. Chicago, Illinois, January 15, 1907). Priest. Educated in Kraków, Kozłowski was ordained in Taranto, Italy, on August 15, 1885, and came to the United States in 1892. Settling initially in Shamokin, Pennsylvania, in 1894 he moved to Chicago to serve as assistant pastor of St. Hedwig's Parish. In June of the following year he organized the independent All Saints Parish, the first parish in the "Independent Polish Catholic Church of America," which was dedicated June 16, 1895. Because of their independentism, Kozłowski and the members of his parish were excommunicated on September 29, 1895. Regardless, he continued organizing independent parishes and on November 21, 1897, Bishop Edouard Herzog, the Swiss Old Catholic bishop of Berne, Switzerland, consecrated him bishop of the "Polish Catholic Diocese of Chicago." The constitution of Kozłowski's new church generally mirrored the principles of the Old Catholics, but contained a clause stipulating that "the Independent Polish Church considers the Roman Pontiff as Primate of the Occident." On April 26, 1898, Pope Leo XIII personally excommunicated Kozłowski and his flock. Kozłowski was a rival of Stefan Kamiński, and later Francis Hodur, for leadership in the "independent" movement among Polish Catholics in America, but his willingness to reach out to Episcopalians and others for allies and his reluctance to adopt Polish as the language of the Mass led to charges from his rivals that he had betrayed the independent movement's goals of promoting Polish ethnicity and Catholicism. Nevertheless, given the preeminent importance of Chicago within **Polonia**, he remained arguably the most influential independent leader until his death at the relatively young age of fifty.—*James S. Pula*

SOURCES: Laurence J. Orzell, "Curious Allies: Bishop Antoni Kozłowski and the Episcopalians," *Polish American Studies*, Vol. 40, no. 2 (1983), 36–58; Laurence J. Orzell, "A Pragmatic Union: Bishop Kozlowski and the Old Catholics, 1896–1898," *Polish American Studies*, Vol. 44, no. 1 (1987), 5–24; Robert F. Trisco, "The Holy See and the First Independent Catholic Church in the United States," in Nelson H. Minnich, Robert B. Eno, and Robert F. Trisco, eds., *Studies in Catholic History in Honor of John Tracy Ellis* (Wilmington, DE: M. Glazier, 1985), 175–238.

Kozłowski, Edward (b. Tarnów, Poland, November 21, 1860; d. Milwaukee, Wisconsin, August 6, 1915). Bishop. Born in Austrian-ruled Poland and educated at the University of Vienna, Kozłowski migrated to the United States in 1885. He briefly settled in Chicago before moving to Wisconsin where he entered the St. Francis Seminary in Milwaukee. Ordained on June 29, 1887, Kozłowski was first sent to St. Brigid Parish in Midland, Michigan, then to Our Lady of the Rosary Parish in East Saginaw in 1888. During his time in East Saginaw and, one year later, at St. Joseph's Parish in Manistee, Kozłowski raised funds to erect parochial schools, parish houses and even libraries for the parish community. His gift as a skilled mediator even allowed him to pacify restive parishes and repair rifts between congregations. In 1900, Kozłowski was appointed to St. Stanislaus Kostka parish in Bay City, Michigan, where he was instrumental in building a new parochial school; he spearheaded numerous improvements to the parish, including the completion of church furnishings and the installation of a new pipe organ and bell system. At the parishes of St. Hedwig's and St. Anthony's in Fisherville, he led similar improvement projects and initiatives, and in Mt. Forest, Nine Mile and Standish, he created new parishes. Kozłowski played a leading role in several Polish committees and organizations including the Colonization Committee for Polish Farmers, the National Committee in America, and the Association of Polish Priests. On the recommendation of the First Catholic Congress in Baltimore, Maryland, held in 1889, Kozłowski collected statistical information concerning Polish parishes in America, which contributed, among other things, to his periodical writings. In 1913, he was named second auxiliary bishop of the Archdiocese of Milwaukee and consecrated Archbishop, as well as titular bishop of Germia, on January 14, 1914 by Pope Pius X. Within little more than a year following his consecration, Kozłowski contracted blood poisoning and died. His funeral was attended by 30,000 mourners. He is buried in St. Adalbert Cemetery in Milwaukee.—*Krystyna Cap*

SOURCE: Anthony J. Kuzniewski, *Faith and Fatherland: The Polish Church War in Wisconsin, 1896–1918* (Notre Dame, IN: University of Notre Dame Press, 1980).

Kozlowski, Leo Dennis (b. Newark, New Jersey, November 16, 1946; d.—). Businessman. The son of a Newark, New Jersey, reporter for the Associated Press, semi-professional boxer, part-time Republican Party ward heeler, and Public Service Transport investigator, Leo Kozlowski, and Agnes Kozell, a school crossing guard, he grew up in West-Central Newark, with the family attending St. Stanislaus Roman Catholic Church. Kozlowski graduated from West Side High School in 1964 and was educated at Seton Hall University in South Orange, where he received his B.S. in Accounting in 1968. In 1970, Kozlowski became an auditor with SCM Corporation and joined Tyco in 1970. Kozlowski distinguished himself as an "enterprising and effective manager." In 1992, he was promoted to president and chief executive of Tyco Corporation, a multi-national group of manufacturing and services providing companies, active in healthcare, flow control, security, telecommunications and electronics. He led the conglomerate through a series of mega-mergers and unprecedented growth, with Tyco's revenues rising by 48.7 percent from 1997 through 2001. During this same period, his compensation rose from $8.8 million in 1997 to $67 million in 1998 to $170 million in 1990. In 2002, Kozlowski left Tyco in the midst of a controversy regarding his compensation package and published reports of a lavish and extravagant lifestyle, including Tyco's purchase of a $30 million apartment in New York City, featuring a $6,000 shower curtain, and Tyco's paying a $1 million bill (half the cost) for the 40th birthday party of Kozlowski's second wife, Karen, on the island of Sardinia. In that same year, he was indicted for tax fraud for evading $1 million in New York sales tax; a second indictment charged Kozlowski with stealing $170 million from Tyco and $430 million through improper stock sales. A first trial ended in a mistrial. Kozlowski was convicted in a second trial on June 17, 2005 for misappropriating corporate funds and on 22 counts of grand larceny relating to $150 million in unauthorized bonuses. He was also convicted of fraud in the amount of more than $400 million while inflating the value of Tyco's stock. Kozlowski has steadfastly asserted his innocence, noting "Nothing was hidden.... All the information the prosecutors got was directly off the books and records of the company." Kozlowski was sentenced to 8⅓ to 25 years at the Mid-State Correctional Facility in Marcy, New York. A classroom and academic building named for him at his alma mater, Seton Hall University, was renamed Jubilee Hall.—*Richard J. Hunter, Jr., & Héctor R. Lozada*

SOURCES: Anthony Bianco, William Symonds, Nanette Byrnes, and David Polek, "The Rise and Fall of Dennis Kozlowski," *Business Week*, December 23, 2002; Christopher M. Byron, *Testosterone Inc: Tales of CEO's Gone Wild* (Hoboken, NJ: Wiley, 2004); Mark Maremont and Laurie P. Cohen, "Executive Privilege: How Tyco's CEO Enriched Himself," *The Wall Street Journal*, August 7, 2002, A1.

Kozlowski, Linda (b. Fairfield, Connecticut, January 7, 1958; d.—). Actor. Best known for her roles in the *Crocodile Dundee* movies, Kozlowski studied at the Juilliard School in New York as an opera singer. Her acting career began off-Broadway with *How It All Began* at the Public Theater in 1981. She also performed with the New York Shakespeare Festival. Her first important role was "Miss Forsythe," acting with Dustin Hoffman in *Death of a Salesman*, a role that she also performed on television in 1985. A year later she was catapulted to international recognition when she landed the role of photo-journalist Sue Charlton in the movie *Crocodile Dundee* opposite Australian leading man Paul Hogan. She was nominated for a Golden Globe award, and the movie was a world-wide hit, but oddly, she did not receive many more movie offers and eventually starred with Hogan in a sequel *Crocodile Dundee 2* in 1988. In between these two films was a movie with Bill Paxton entitled *Pass the Ammo*. In a case of life imitating art, Kozlowski fell in love with co-star Hogan, just as reporter Charlton did in the movies. Eventually the two married in 1990. She appeared in a television mini-series called *Favorite Son* that created a controversy when she supposedly had a nude bondage scene. She again teamed with Hogan for a third movie, *Almost an Angel*, which was not a success, after which she disappeared from the screen for several years. In 1993 she made *The Neighbor* with Rod Steiger, over the next few years appearing in *Backstreet Justice*, John Carpenter's *Village of the Damned*, and *Zorn*, a Swedish film that was not released in the United States. She tried to break into television with a pilot for a series called *Shaughnessy*, but it never made it to the screen. In 2001 she again teamed with Hogan in the third Crocodile Dundee movie, *Crocodile Dundee in Los Angeles*. She was nominated for a Golden Globe for *Crocodile Dundee* in 1986.—*Cheryl A. Pula*

SOURCE: IMD: The Internet Movie Database.

Kozłowski, Martin (b. Warsaw, Poland, April 24, 1827; d. Kozlowski Ranch, New Mexico, November 15, 1905). Pioneer, rancher. A participant in the abortive "Springtime of Nations" in 1848, Kozlowski fled to England where he stayed for two years before migrating to America. In 1853 he enlisted in the 1st U.S. Dragoons and saw combat against the Apache Indians in the Arizona Territory. When his enlistment expired in 1858, he remained in the area, purchasing a 600-acre ranch along the Santa Fe Trail near Pecos. There, he established a home and tavern serving travelers. During the Civil War he remained loyal to the Union. When Confederate forces invaded the area in 1862, the Kozlowski Ranch became a pivotal piece of real estate since it was strategically located and included a rare water source. Kozlowski offered his home as headquarters for Union Gen. John P. Slough during the campaign that culminated in the Federal victory at Glorieta Pass, provided valuable intelligence information, and turned his tavern into a hospital for the wounded for several weeks following the engagement. By 1866 the ranch became a permanent stop on the stage lines plying the Santa Fe Trail. The business prospered until the railroad opened service in 1880, leading to a precipitous decline in overland traffic. His fortunes declined further when he was found guilty of murder and confined to prison for two years.—*Francis Casimir Kajencki*

SOURCE: Francis Casimir Kajencki, *Poles in the 19th Century Southwest* (El Paso, TX: Southwest Polonia Press, 1990), 47–66.

Krakowiak. A popular Polish dance from the region of Kraków (a former capital of Poland) and the southern part of the country, Małopolska, the dance's common name in English is *cracovienne*, and in German it is known as *Krakauer Tanz*. It is a fast dance in duple meter, using a characteristic syncopated pattern of short-long-short (or eighth-note;

quarter-note; eighth-note) which allows one to recognize the dance form quite easily. Another variant is an eighth-note followed by an accented dotted quarter-note; both are illustrated below:

This pattern alternates with the simpler rhythm of two eighth-notes, plus one quarter-note (or: short-short-long). The phrases are symmetrically arranged in pairs of four measures each, though the texts of songs used in the *krakowiak* are grouped in four lines of six-syllables each. The melodies feature a great variety of patterns, with added extra notes, dotted rhythms, and passages based on triads.

The dance dates back to the sixteenth and seventeenth centuries when it was included in organ and lute tablatures, as well as songbooks, under such titles as *Chorea polnica* or *Polnish Tanz*. However, the first time that the name itself appeared in print was in Franciszek Mirecki's 1816 piano album, *Krakowiaks Offered to the Women of Poland* (1816). In the mid–nineteenth century, the *krakowiak* became a popular ballroom dance in Austria and France and grew to be regarded as a "national dance" of Poland where it competed with the **polonaise**. For Poland, this was the time of partitions and the unsuccessful uprisings (1831, 1848) fought to regain the country's independence. The *krakowiak*, *polonaise*, and even **mazurka**, appeared in the Parisian salons as symbols of solidarity with the oppressed nation and its plight. At the same time, the *krakowiak* became a choice of composers who transformed it into an extensive and even virtuosic form, beginning from Fryderyk Chopin's *Krakowiak (grand rondeau de concert)* for piano and orchestra (op. 14, 1828; including a quotation of the popular "Albośmy to jacy tacy"), and including pieces by Zygmunt Noskowski, **Ignacy Jan Paderewski**, and Roman Statkowski. As the result of this increased artistic stature, even the ballroom form of the dance grew in scope and the dance was transformed into a three-part form, with the music featuring a contrasting central section, and modulations to other keys.

The great popularity of the *krakowiak* among the American **Polonia** has antecedents in its widespread presence in American popular music since mid–nineteenth century. A famous Austrian dancer, Fanny Elssler, presented the *cracovienne* for her debut in New York: dressed in red boots, blue shirt, white jacket and velvet cap, she delighted her audiences and secured the position of this dance in the American popular repertoire. **Aleksander Janta** lists 32 *cra-*

coviennes, four songs *Cracovian Maid*, and five *krakowiaks* in his inventory of Polish dances composed in the U.S. at that time.

In terms of its choreography, the *krakowiak* is set for several couples, among whom the leading male dancer sings and indicates the steps. The *krakowiak* is directed by the leading man from the first pair who approaches the band, sings an improvised verse to a standard melody for the band to follow and starts the dance. There are several figures which appear in the different stages of the dance: the invitation phase, the running, the shuffling, the passing, etc. The three most characteristic steps are: the *galop* (fast running forward), the *hołubiec* (jump with clicking the heels and stamping; pl. *hołubce*), and the *krzesany* (this term is used as a name of a separate dance in the **Podhale** area, but here refers to a sliding motion of the feet with stamping).

The *krakowiak* is the exhibition dance of choice of the Polish American dance ensembles. When performed on the stage, it includes a variety of group figures, in addition to the turns, jumps, running and stamping steps. Dancers wear the *strój krakowski* (Kraków costume) a favorite among the various Polish regional costumes that has come to symbolize the traditional costume of Poland in general, especially abroad. A regional variant from the Nowy Sącz area in south-eastern Poland, called *Krakowiaki Sądeckie* (in the plural form of the noun), is a dance for men only. It consists of a series of *krakowiak* tunes and is a display dance performed in a line, or semi-circle. Its choreorhythmic and musical features place it in-between the dances of the lowlands (Kraków itself) and the mountains (Podhale area).—*Maja Trochimczyk*

SOURCES: Ada Dziewanowska, *Polish Folk Dances & Songs: A Step by Step Guide* (New York: Hippocrene Books, 1999); Aleksander Janta, *A History of Nineteenth Century American-Polish Music* (New York: The Kosciuszko Foundation, 1982); "Krakowiak" entry in Stanley Sadie, ed., *New Grove Dictionary of Music and Musicians* (London: McMillan, 1980), Vol. 10.

Krakowski, Henry P. "Hank" (b. Evanston, Illinois, May 1, 1954; d.—). Engineer, aviation official. After growing up in Chicago, Krakowski graduated from the Parks College of Engineering, Aviation and Technology in 1975, earned a bachelor's degree in aircraft maintenance engineering from St. Louis University, then went on to complete a master's degree in business and management from the National-Louis University in Chicago. For five years he was a member of the Lima Lima Acrobatic Flight Team, performing aerobatics in a navy T-34 trainer that he rebuilt himself. After holding positions with Midway Airlines and Air Illinois Airlines, in 1978 he began a career with United Airlines where he

served as a flight engineer on Boeing 727 and 747 aircraft, and pilot on Boeing 737, DC-8, and DC-10 aircraft. Moving on to become director of flight crew resources, he later served for two years as director of flight operations control, a post he held on September 11, 2001, when he was called upon to direct emergency operations that successfully landed all of United's airborne aircraft in record time. In November 2001 he accepted a position as vice president for safety, security and quality assurance at United Airlines. Following this assignment, he served for two years as co-chair of the Commercial Aviation Safety Team (CAST), a partnership between government and the airline industry that put into service new safety procedures to reduce commercial aviation accidents. He also served as chair of the Star Alliance Safety Advisory Group, as well as being a member of the Air Transport Association Safety Council. After being promoted to vice president for flight operations by United Airlines, in 2007 he was appointed chief operating officer (COO) of the Federal Aviation Administration's Air Traffic Organization where he provided leadership for some 35,000 employees of the U.S. air traffic control system. Among his numerous awards are the Oliver L. Parks Alumni Merit Award from the Parks College of Engineering, Aviation and Technology.—*James S. Pula*

SOURCE: "FAA ATO Gets New Leader," *Air Safety Week*, September 24, 2007.

Krakowski, Jane (Jane Krajkowski; b. Parsippany, New Jersey, October 11, 1968; d.—). Actress. As a child, Krakowski attended the Professional Children's School in New York City and broke into television with a role on the soap opera *Search for Tomorrow* in 1984, gaining nominations for Daytime Emmy Awards in 1986 and 1987. She is probably best known for her role as an office assistant on the hit series *Ally McBeal* (1997–2002) for which she earned a Golden Globe nomination as Best Supporting Actress (1999). In 2006 she began playing a character on *30 Rock*, receiving another Emmy nomination in 2009. While active in television, she also pursued film opportunities, appearing in *National Lampoon's Vacation* (1983), *Fatal Attraction* (1987), *Stepping Out* (1991), *Mrs. Winterbourne* (1996), *Dance with Me* (1998), *Go* (1999), *The Flintstones in Viva Rock Vegas* (2000), *Marci X* (2003), *When Zachary Beaver Came to Town* (2003), *Alfie* (2004), *Pretty Persuasion* (2005), *Mom at Sixteen* (2005), *The Rocker* (2008), *Kit Kittredge: An American Girl Mystery* (2008), *Bygone Days: An Ally McBeal Retrospective* (2009), and *Cirque du Freak: The Vampire's Assistant* (2009). Krakowski also appeared in various theater productions, winning a Tony Award for Best Actress in *Nine* and a Laurence Oliver Award as Best Actress in a Musical for the London production of *Guys and Dolls*. She was also honored twice with Screen Actors Guild Awards for Outstanding Performance by an Ensemble in a Comedy Series for *Ally McBeal* (1999) and *30 Rock* (2008), and a Golden Globe as Best Supporting Actress for the series *Ally McBeal* (1999). As a singer, her vocals have appeared on several records.—*James S. Pula*

SOURCES: "Taking a Bough," *People Magazine*, July 20, 1998; Ernio Hernandez "Nine Nominee Jan Krakowski 'Calls' in a Showstopping Performance," *Playbill*, May 20, 2003; Stephen Holden, "Sorry, Santa, but Naughty Is More Fun Than Nice," *New York Times*, February 3, 2005; Andrew Gans, "Diva Talk: Chatting with Damn Yankees' Jane Krakowski," *Playbill*, July 27, 2008.

Krawczyk, Monica Barbara (née Kowalewska; b. Winona, Minnesota, August 5, 1887; d. Hennepin County, Minnesota, October 31, 1954). Author. The daughter of Polish immigrant parents, Krawczyk had instilled in her from a young age a life-long appreciation of education and learning, as well as Polish arts and culture. After attending Winona State Teachers College, she taught at Washington Elementary School in Winona where she first became involved in social work, assisting the impoverished local Polish community. In the 1930s, Krawczyk founded the Winona Polanie Club, a women's group devoted to exploring Polish heritage and culture. Following additional studies at the University of Minnesota and the School of Social Work in Chicago, she spent much of her later career visiting and counseling at public schools throughout Minneapolis in addition to working with the Polish immigrant community in the northeast of the city. Krawczyk's experience with immigrant culture profoundly shaped her fiction writing, which treats, among other themes, the trials and tribulations of Polish immigrants adjusting to life in America. Her short stories appeared first in local papers in Winona, then in the *Surveyor, Woman's Day, Good Housekeeping*, and the *Journal of National Education*. In 1937, her short story "No Man Alone" won first prize in a short story contest, beating some 5,000 other entries. Krawczyk was recognized by the Polish government in 1939 for her teaching, writing, and social work. In 1950, her short stories were published by the Polanie Club as an anthology called *If the Branch Blossoms and Other Stories*. Her first novel, *Not for Bread Alone*, was never completed and remains unpublished.—*Krystyna Cap*

SOURCES: Edith Blicksilver, "Monica Krawczyk: Chronicler of Polish-American Life," *MELUS*, Vol. 7, no. 3 (1980), 13–20; Melvin Serowiecki, "Monica Krawczyk—Short Story Writer," *Polish-American Studies*, Vol. 20, no. 1 (1963), 49–51.

Krawiec, Jan (b. Bachorzec, Poland, June 15, 1919; d.—). Editor, journalist. An officer in the Polish Army during World War II, he participated in the Polish Underground, writing for an underground newspaper. Arrested in 1943, he spent two years in concentration camps, first in Auschwitz and later Buchenwald, until liberation in 1945. Following the war he worked as a journalist for Polish newspapers in displaced persons camps in Germany before migrating to the United States in 1949. In the 1950s, he worked as a factory laborer (1950–59) before taking a position as city editor with *Dziennik Chicagoski* (Chicago Daily, 1959–63), while attending college at night. After receiving his B.A. in political science from Loyola University in Chicago in 1963, he took a position as a social worker (1963–67). Maintaining an active interest in journalism and politics, he served as editor of *Wiadomości* (The News), a campaign publication of **Aloysius Mazewski** (1963–67), served as an editor at *Ameryka-Echo* (1962–67), and became editor-in-chief of *Dziennik Związkowy* (1968–85). He became one of the closest advisors of Aloysius Mazewski, president of the **Polish American Congress**, on Polish and international affairs, and broadly published on topics of history and politics in the **Polonia** press. His papers are located in the Immigration History Research Center, University of Minnesota.—*Mary Patrice Erdmans*

SOURCE: Donald E. Pienkos, *PNA: A Centennial History of the Polish National Alliance of the United States of North America* (Boulder, CO: East European Monographs, 1984).

Krawiec, Walter (b. Morzewo, Poland, September 24, 1889; d. Chicago, Illinois, June 1982). Painter, cartoonist. Krawiec came to America as a two-year-old with his parents who settled in Chicago. After finding employment as a cartoonist and illustrator with the *Dziennik Chicagoski* (Chicago Daily News) in 1913, Krawiec began his formal studies at the Art Institute of Chicago. There he met his future wife, Harriet Korzeniowska, a fellow student, and a fine artist in her own right. The inspiration for his artistic work, which won him acclaim and many prizes, came from a variety of sources including the lives of ordinary people in Chicago, patriotic events, scenes of horses and other animals, and sports events. He also painted many valued still life subjects, but one of his favored particular interests focused on the world of the circus and its many performers. His realistic-impressionistic style was compared to the work of Toulouse Lautrec and Renoir. Krawiec con-

Walter Krawiec, political and social cartoonist (*PMA*).

tinued at the *Dziennik Chicagoski* until the newspaper closed in 1971. He then moved to the *Dziennik Związkowy* (Alliance Daily), the Chicago organ of the Polish National Alliance, and continued in its employ until he retired a few years later.—*Donald E. Pienkos*

SOURCE: Wojciech Wierzewski, "Sto Trzydzieska Slynnych Polaków w Ameryce" (Unpublished manuscript in the archives of the University of Wisconsin–Milwaukee, 2000).

Kridl, Manfred (b. Lwów, Poland, October 11, 1882; d. New York, New York, February 4, 1957). Literary scholar. Kridl earned his baccalaureate degree in 1906 and his doctorate (1909) from Lwów University. He later continued his studies in literature at Fryburg University in Switzerland where he was active in socialist organizations. From 1907 to 1932 he was a high school teacher except for the World War I years (1914–18) when he served in the Austrian Army. In 1921, Kridl became a professor, and between 1928 and 1932 he lectured on Polish Literature at a university in Brussels. In 1932 he became a full-time professor of history of Polish literature at the University of Wilno. Six years later he became active in the Stronnictwo Demokratyczne (Democratic Party). Following the outbreak of World War II, he fled with his wife and two children in 1940 through Belgium to France, and then to the United States. Between 1940 and 1948 Kridl was a professor of Polish literature at Smith College in Amherst, Massachusetts, and in 1948 became chair of the Katedra Historii Literatury Polskiej (Chair of Polish Literary History) at Columbia University, which was funded by the Soviet-dominated Polish government. An expert on the writings of Adam Mickiewicz and Juliusz Słowacki, he authored *Krytyka i krytycy* (1923) and edited a twenty volume collection of

Mickiewicz's works (1929). In 1934, on the centennial anniversary of Mickiewicz's *Pan Tadeusz*, Kridl edited and wrote the preface to the jubilee edition. He also edited Słowacki's *Letters* and wrote many research articles and reviews published in *Książka, Pamiętnik Literacki, Przegląd Współczesny*, and other journals. In America, Kridl published research articles in *The American Bookman, Comparative Literature*, and *The American Slavic and East European Review*. He edited *Adam Mickiewicz Poet of Poland* (1955) and *An Anthology of Polish Literature* (1957).—*Iwona Korga*

SOURCES: Andrzej Karcz, "Manfred Kridl: The Struggle for the Reform of Polish Literary Scholarship," *The Polish Review*, Vol. 45, no. 2 (2000), 171–82; Zygmunt Wardzinski, "Manfred Kridl," *The Polish Review*, Vol. 45, no. 2 (2000), 251–54.

Krol, John Joseph (b. Cleveland, Ohio, October 26, 1910; d. Philadelphia, Pennsylvania, March 3, 1996). Catholic Cardinal. The fourth of eight children, he was baptized at St. Hyacinth Church, attended the parish elementary school, then continued at Cathedral Latin High School in Cleveland. He was working as the manager of the meat department in a Kroger grocery store when a Lutheran co-worker began challenging Krol regarding teachings of the Catholic faith. Troubled by his inability to explain and defend the Church, Krol began to read and study the Bible, history, and theology. He entered St. Mary's Seminary in Cleveland, being ordained to the priesthood on February 20, 1937. As a young priest he visited Poland just before World War II began, escaping across the mountains to Hungary when German troops arrived. After pursuing postgraduate studies at the Gregorian University in Rome and the Catholic University of America, receiving doctorates in Canon Law from each, he was appointed vice chancellor (1943–51), then chancellor (1951–54). He was appointed auxiliary bishop of Cleveland and Titular Bishop of Cardi by Pope Pius XII on July 11, 1953, and then served as Bishop of Cleveland for eight years before being named by Pope John XXIII as the Archbishop of Philadelphia on February 11, 1961. Krol was a brilliant administrator with the ability to speak eleven languages fluently which served him well during his twenty-seven year term as the archbishop. Archbishop Krol participated in the Second Vatican Council from 1962 to 1965 where he distinguished himself among the American prelates, serving as a permanent undersecretary and a member of the central coordinating committee during the Council. Shortly after the Council, Pope Paul VI elevated him to Cardinal on June 26, 1967. Cardinal Krol expressed concern regarding those individuals

"running away with their so-called renewal" in the Spirit of Vatican II, soon joining the voices of those bishops alarmed by such unauthorized experimentation and calling Catholics to be true to Vatican II. Krol later differentiated the true meaning of the Council found in the Council documents from its various interpretations by progressive Catholic experts. After the military crackdown on the Solidarity movement in Poland in 1981, Cardinal Krol was involved in quiet relief efforts and diplomacy.—*Biff Rocha*

SOURCES: James F. Connelly, "John Cardinal Krol," in James F. Connelly, ed., *The History of the Archdiocese of Philadelphia* (Philadelphia: Archdiocese of Philadelphia, 1976); E. Michael Jones, *John Cardinal Krol and the Cultural Revolution* (South Bend, Indiana: Fidelity Press, 1995); "Krol, John Joseph, Cardinal, 1910–1996," *Our Sunday Visitor*, Vol. 84 (March 31, 1996); Thomas W. Spalding, "Dissimilitude: The Careers of Cardinals Lawrence J. Shehan and John J. Krol," *U.S. Catholic Historian*, Vol. 17 (Fall 1999).

Krotiak, Anthony L. (b. Chicago, Illinois, August 15, 1915; d. Balete Pass, Luzon, Philippine Islands, May 8, 1945). Soldier, Medal of Honor recipient. A private first class in Company I, 148th Infantry Regiment, 37th Infantry Division, Krotiak was an acting squad leader when he led his men into battle against Japanese forces. The citation for his Medal of Honor explained that he was "directing his men in consolidating a newly won position on Hill B when the enemy concentrated small arms fire and grenades upon him and 4 others, driving them to cover in an abandoned Japanese trench. A grenade thrown from above landed in the center of the group. Instantly pushing his comrades aside and jamming the grenade into the earth with his rifle butt, he threw himself over it, making a shield of his body to protect the other men. The

Anthony L. Krotiak, Medal of Honor recipient (*NARA*).

grenade exploded under him, and he died a few minutes later. By his extraordinary heroism in deliberately giving his life to save those of his comrades, Pfc. Krotiak set an inspiring example of utter devotion and self-sacrifice which reflects the highest traditions of the military service."—*James S. Pula*

SOURCES: R. J. Proft, *United States of America's Congressional Medal of Honor Recipients and Their Official Citations* (Columbia Heights, MN: Highland House II, 2002); *The Medal of Honor of the United States Army* (Washington, D.C.: U.S. Government Printing Office, 1948), 76.

Krupa, Gene (Eugene Bertram Krupa; b. Chicago, Illinois, January 15, 1909; d. Yonkers, New York, October 16, 1973). Musician. The youngest of two girls and seven boys, Krupa's father was an alderman and his mother a milliner. Due to his father's death, he went to work at age eleven at Brown Music Company where he learned to play the drums. While still in elementary school, he joined his first band, and then joined another in high school, the Austin High Gang. His parents wanted him to become a priest, and he briefly attended St. Joseph's College in Rensselaer, Indiana, but gave up thoughts of the religious life. He joined the musicians union, becoming friends with some whose names would become household words during the Big Band era — Benny Goodman, Tommy Dorsey, Glenn Miller, Hoagy Carmichael, Bix Beiderbecke, and others. He made his first recordings in 1927. At a time when drummers usually kept the beat for other musicians, Krupa invented the drum solo, one of which made him famous in the song, *Sing, Sing, Sing*. He convinced the Slingerland Drum Company to manufacture drums that could be tuned to different pitches so they could be played for solos. Because of this innovation, Krupa is known as the "father" of the modern drum set. He worked with Avedis Zildjian to develop modern hi-hat cymbals. During his career, he played in Benny Goodman's band, the first to employ black musicians, and the first jazz ensemble to play Carnegie Hall in New York. After tension developed between Krupa and Goodman, he formed his own band which began successfully in Atlantic City, New Jersey. Following this he wrote a book, *The Gene Krupa Method*, began a drum contest, and appeared in several movies. In 1943 he was arrested in San Francisco for possession of marijuana and served ninety days in prison, but the charges were later determined to be bogus. Upon being released he formed another band, and was recruited to play for concerts called Jazz at the Philharmonic, which led to legendary drum battles between Krupa and Buddy Rich. In 1954 he founded

Gene Krupa, popular musician (**PMA**).

a drum school in New York, while a film about him titled *The Gene Krupa Story*, which starred actor Sal Mineo, brought increased fame. In 1960 he suffered a heart attack which slowed his career, leading to his retirement in 1967. He briefly came out of retirement in 1970, but retired permanently in 1973. Oddly, though one of the premier drummers of all time, Krupa never learned to read music. A street in Yonkers was named Gene Krupa Drive in his honor.— *Cheryl A. Pula*

SOURCES: Bruce Crowther, *Gene Krupa, His Life and Times* (New York: Universe Books, 1987); Bruce Klauber, *Gene Krupa: The Pictorial Life of a Jazz Legend* (Los Angeles: Alfred Publishing Company, 2005); Bruce Klauber, *World of Gene Krupa: That Legendary Drummin' Man* (Ventura, CA: Pathfinder Publishers, 1990).

Kruszka, Michael (Michał Kruszka; b. Slabomierz, partitioned Poland, September 28, 1860; d. Milwaukee, Wisconsin, December 2, 1918). Journalist, Polonia activist. After receiving his initial education, economic circumstances forced him to leave school in Wągrowiec. Shortly thereafter he migrated to the United States in 1880, settling in Elizabeth, NJ, where he completed a course at a business school two years later. Unable to find permanent employment, in 1883 he moved to Milwaukee, WI, where he earned a living as an insurance agent. With $28 in capital, he established a small printing press in 1885. Having acquired a deep interest in politics and journalism in Europe, Kruszka began writing letters to Polish periodicals in Europe almost as soon as he arrived in the United States. About six months after establishing his own printing press, he began pursuing his interest in journalism by publishing *Tygodnik Anonsowy* (Advertising Weekly). After about three months he transformed the periodical

into the radical, strongly pro-labor weekly *Krytyka* (The Critique) which he used to rally support for Polish causes and political candidates.

Enjoying some success, in 1888 Kruszka established ***Kuryer Polski*** (Polish Courier), the first Polish-language daily newspaper in the United States. Strongly pro-labor, a vocal advocate of Polish nationalism, and increasingly anti-clerical, *Kuryer Polski* initially tended to back the Democratic Party, but switched to supporting the Republicans in 1900 when Kruszka became angry over what he believed was the reluctance on the part of the Democratic mayor of Milwaukee to appoint Poles to political offices. Always concerned about equality of opportunity for immigrants, Kruszka also used his newspaper to promote Polish causes both in Milwaukee, and later throughout Wisconsin and nationally. Despite his growing anti-clericalism, he was a strong advocate of the appointment of a Polish bishop to minister to Polish Roman Catholics, as well as the pluralism that his brother, the Rev. **Wacław Kruszka**, advocated within the Roman Catholic Church in America. Kruszka used the pages of his newspaper to lobby relentlessly for the inclusion of Polish in the Milwaukee public schools on an equal footing with English and German. Never on very good terms with the local Catholic hierarchy, they viewed his advocacy of the movement to include Polish in the public school curricula as a direct threat to parochial education which, in the Polish parishes, was largely conducted in the Polish language. With public schools also offering instruction in Polish, the clergy reasoned, parochial school enrollment would suffer. This difference greatly widened the gulf between Kruszka and the clergy, sparking an increasingly acrimonious rhetorical exchange in which Kruszka's attacks on the clergy eventually became so strident that in February 1912 Archbishop Sebastian G. Messmer forbade Catholics from reading it. Kruszka reacted by filing suit against five bishops, whom he accused of forming an illegal conspiracy for the purpose of injuring his business. The suit, which sought $100,000 damages, eventually failed when the Wisconsin State Supreme Court ruled that the pastoral letter the bishop had sent to the various parishes was "within the scope of church-discipline."

In 1890 Kruszka was elected to the Wisconsin legislature as a Democrat, serving for two years. He then won election to the State Senate, a position he adroitly used to secure the passage of legislation requiring that government notices, required by law to be published in both English and German, must also

Michael Kruszka, journalist and Polonia activist (***OLS***).

be printed in Polish. The new law led to significant income for Kruszka's publishing business. But Kruszka also used his post to promote causes of interest to working people. He supported legislation that led to the first caucus law in the state of Wisconsin, and worked for the passage of a bill requiring that electric cars have enclosures for the protection of conductors and motormen, the first such law in the United States. He was also a leading advocate for the bill establishing Labor Day as a holiday and supported other laws especially beneficial to workers. Beginning with only 360 readers in 1888, *Kuryer Polski* expanded to 18,000 subscriptions by 1905 with a payroll that included 27 adults and seven children employees, along with 87 delivery staff, a total of 121 employees. As success grew, Kruszka's Kuryer Publishing Company established the literary journal *Niedziela* (Sunday) in 1889, the agricultural weekly *Gazeta Wisconsinska* (The Wisconsin Gazette) in 1892 and the news weekly *Tygodniowy Kuryer Polski* (The Weekly Polish Courier) in 1894. The new publications informed readers that they would be "politically independent" and defend Polish interests. Much like *Kuryer Polski,* they supported higher wages and better working conditions for workers while stressing the importance of maintaining the Polish language and culture in America.

Although his publications were focused on the Polish community, Kruszka also wrote articles in English for the English-language press, invariably promoting Polish interests. Since at the end of the nineteenth century the name of "Poland" had for a century been erased from the European map by partition at the hands of its neighbors, one of his campaigns was to require that census takers list Poles as being born in "Poland" rather than

Austria, Germany or Russia. Kruszka was also active in Polish-American organizations. In 1899 the **Polish National Alliance** elected him a member of its constitutional committee, while he was generous in his financial support of both religious and secular Polish organizations. Throughout his life he was a champion of Polish causes in America, as well as issues affecting workers.—*James S. Pula*

SOURCES: Anthony J. Kusziewski, *Faith and Fatherland: The Polish Church War in Wisconsin, 1896–1918* (Notre Dame, IN: University of Notre Dame Press, 1980); Anthony J. Kuzniewski, "Westward to the Golden Gate: The Kruszka Brothers in Search of America," *Polish American Studies*, Vol. 41, no. 2 (1984), 5–22.

Kruszka, Wacław (b. Słabomierz, Poland, March 2, 1868; d. Milwaukee, Wisconsin, February 28, 1937). As a child, Kruszka experienced the repressive measures of Otto von Bismarck's **Kulturkampf** including the imprisonment of his brother who objected to the suppression of Polish culture. After completing secondary school he entered the Society of Jesus but did not complete his studies before taking a position teaching at the Jesuit high school in Chyrów (1890–91). Moving to Rome, in 1893 he graduated from the Gregorianum and decided to come to the United States. Arriving in New York on November 24, 1893, he traveled to Milwaukee where his brother Michael (see **Kruszka, Michael**) resided, arriving on December 1 and quickly enrolling in St. Francis Seminary where he was ordained in June 1895. Assigned first to St. Josaphat Parish in Milwaukee, he spent less than one year there before being assigned to organize a new Polish parish in the small town of Ripon, Wisconsin. He remained in Ripon for some fourteen years, giving him time to pursue his passion for writing. One of his first projects was to begin collecting information for a history of the Poles in America that he planned to pen. In doing so, he discovered information that thrust him into the vortex of the political and religious squabbles that were then tearing the infant **Polonia** asunder. What Kruszka found was that Poles constituted a large, growing, faithful, and supportive element within the Roman Catholic Church in America, but they wielded virtually no power. Though numbering just under twenty percent of all Catholics in America by the end of the nineteenth century, there was not a single bishop of Polish origin. Father Kruszka, the ardent Polish nationalist, had found his cause.

Although the Catholic hierarchy eventually agreed to establish ethnic parishes, Kruszka was not satisfied with the largely symbolic nature of the national parish. His complaints were largely twofold, involving the desire for equality and democracy in parish and Church governance. The creation of ethnic parishes appeared to him to limit the career mobility of Polish priests who found themselves assigned to these ethnic parishes with no hope for better assignments or promotions. Further, although most Polish parishes began through lay initiatives, Church authorities exerted strict control over them, demanding title to all property, assigning priests, and generally denying lay participation in decision-making. This conflicted with the Poles' concept of lay involvement and the ideals of democracy and property ownership they equated with America. "Equality" thus became a cornerstone of Kruszka's lengthy fight to influence policy change among the Catholic hierarchy.

To Kruszka, the question was one of reconciling the ideals of Polish patriotism and religious belief so the Polish clergy and their flock in America could express their nationalism within the framework of the Roman Catholic faith. In forming his own ideas concept of ethnic pluralism, he was much in advance of its time. To Kruszka, the very existence of the Church throughout the world was proof that it need not be bound by a common language, a common culture, or a common nationality. In early 1901, Kruszka published his ideas in the *New York Freeman's Journal* in an article titled "Polyglot Bishops for Polyglot Dioceses." The Church, he argued, should foster an ethnic pluralism which recognized the dignity and worth of all people, granting them equality of opportunity to attain Church offices and express their own identity. Though a lengthy and often times vitriolic dispute ensued between Kruszka and the American hierarchy, the Pole's views eventually prevailed when, in 1952, the Apostolic Constitution *Exsul Familia* guaranteed, for the first time, "the rights of immigrants to proper pastoral care in their own language and traditions," while Vatican II sanctioned the use of the vernacular in the Mass. Further, the Church became more receptive to the career needs of Polish American priests.

Kruszka's early socialization in the ideals of patriotism and faith also led him to become the first author to pen a comprehensive history of the Polish experience in America. Kruszka's purpose in writing his thirteen-volume *Historya Polska w Ameryce* (1905–08) was to set forth the history of the Polish presence in America in such a way that the Poles' contribution to the development of the United States and the Roman Catholic Church would become widely known. In the process, he hoped to reinforce the validity of his arguments for cultural pluralism. First published in serial fashion in the Milwaukee *Kuryer Polski*, edited by his brother Michał, Kruszka focused his research on the parishes and parochial schools, but he also sought information on agriculture, industry, literature, organizations, demographics, the press, and other secular topics. His work, translated into English and published by The Catholic University of America Press, remains a valuable source for the early Polish experience in the United States and the growth of individual segments of Polonia.

Considered a community leader, Kruszka's chief contributions were his concept of Polish Americanism and his strenuous efforts to popularize it. A Pole in America, Kruszka explained, was certainly not identical to a Pole in Poland—each lived in a different world, faced different daily circumstances, and might even speak different languages. Yet, they remained *rodacy*—compatriots. Kruszka viewed the Polish-American as a new type of Pole, linked to ancestors, native land, and other Poles by the bonds of history, tradition, culture, and blood. A Pole was a Pole by this definition, regardless of where the person might be born or the outward manifestations of religion, language, or material culture. Kruszka's was an open-ended vision of ethnic life, midway between the view of those who desired to force Americanization on newcomers and those within Polonia who advocated separated Polish communities in America or described America's Poles as a "Fourth Partition" of Poland. For Kruszka, the goal of the process was not either assimilation or separatism, but integrated pluralism. His model was progressive because it was open-ended, allowing Polish American identity to continue to evolve under the influence of the American experience. By envisioning cultural identity in these terms, Kruszka broke free from the confining

The Rev. Wacław Kruszka, chronicler of early Polonia (*PMA*).

ties to language that became increasingly unrealistic as ethnic life developed through several generations. Kruszka's vision was a pluralistic view of church and state in which Poles both contributed to and gained from others like so many trees in a forest or parts of a human body.—*James S. Pula*

SOURCES: James S. Pula, "Introduction," in Wacław Kruszka, *A History of the Poles in America to 1908* (Washington, D.C.: The Catholic University of American Press, 1993), Vol. I, xiv–xxiii; Anthony J. Kusziewski, *Faith and Fatherland: The Polish Church War in Wisconsin, 1896–1918* (Notre Dame, IN: University of Notre Dame Press, 1980); Anthony J. Kuzniewski, "Westward to the Golden Gate: The Kruszka Brothers in Search of America," *Polish American Studies*, Vol. 41, no. 2 (1984), 5–22; Mieczysław J. Madaj, "The Polish Immigrant, the American Catholic Hierarchy, and Father Wenceslaus Kruszka," *Polish American Studies*, Vol. 26, no. 1 (1969), 16–29; Alexander Syski, "The Nestor of Polish American Historians in America: Reverend Waclaw Kruszka," *Polish American Studies*, Vol. 1 (1944), 62–70; Anthony J. Kuzniewski, "'Jesteśmy Polakami': Wenceslaus Kruszka and the Value of America's Polish Heritage," *Polish American Studies*, Vol. 44, no. 2 (1987), 25–41; Joseph W. Wieczerzak, "Father Kruszka and Bishop Hodur: A Relational Sketch," *Polish American Studies*, Vol. 44, no. 2 (1987), 42–56; James S. Pula, "Wacław Kruszka: A Polonia Historian in Perspective," *Polish American Studies*, Vol. 44, no. 2 (1987), 57–69.

Kryński, Magnus Jan (b. Warsaw, Poland, May 15, 1922; d. Durham, North Carolina, July 4, 1989). Translator, literary historian, critic. Kryński completed grammar school in Białystok before leaving Poland in 1939. He came to the United States in 1948, enrolled at the University of Cincinnati where he was awarded a baccalaureate in 1952, then went on to earn an M.A. from Brown University (1955), and a Ph.D. in Polish and Russian literature from Columbia University (1962). He taught briefly at Duke University, Brown University (1952–54), Rutgers University (1958–59), the University of Pittsburgh (1961–63), Kenyon College (1964–66), and Ohio State University before becoming chair of the Department of Slavic Languages at Duke in 1966. He retired in 1987. A specialist in twentieth century Polish literature, he authored many articles and translated five volumes of poetry into English in collaboration with R. A. Maguire and T. Różewicz, *The Survivor and Other Poems* (1980); A. Świrszczyńska, *Building the Barricade* (1977); A. Świrszczyńska, *Thirty-four Poems of the Warsaw Uprising* (1977); W. Szymborska, *Salt of Wisdom: Seventy Poems* (1981); W. Szymborska, *Poezje / Poems* (1989).—*Adam A. Zych*

SOURCES: *Dictionary of International Biography* (Cambridge, UK: International Biographical Centre, 1979), 555; Robert A. Maguire, "In Memoriam Magnus Jan Krynski (1922–1989)," *The Polish Review*, Vol. 35, Nos. 3–4 (1990), 158–59.

Krzak, Gregory (Helen Krzak; b. Chicago, Illinois, July 29, 1909; d. Chicago, Illinois, January 22, 1973). Catholic nun. Baptized at St. Casimir Church, Helen Krzak attended St. Casimir Parish School where the Sisters of the Resurrection taught. She entered the Congregation at the age of fifteen in 1924, taking the religious name Sister Gregory, and professed final vows in 1931. Between the years 1926 and 1934 Sister Gregory was involved in the educational ministry of the Congregation. She taught at a parish school in Schenectady, New York, and another in Chicago. The next three years, 1934 to 1937, were spent in nurse training at St. Francis Hospital School of Nursing in Evanston, Illinois. Between the years 1937 to 1945, Sister Gregory was back in education, as a teacher and administrator. Nurse training, hospital experience, and administrative work in the years that followed prepared her for the future. In 1952 she was instrumental in planning for the building of Resurrection Hospital in Chicago. When the hospital was opened in 1953, Sister Gregory was appointed the first administrator, in which capacity she served for twenty-one years. She worked tirelessly to develop the first medical and dental staff for the new hospital, organized and supervised two major additions to the hospital in 1958 and 1961, and coordinated the development of plans for future expansion. She was a strong leader who shouldered the difficult responsibilities of her administrative position with diligence, in spite of suffering from diabetes. Her leadership was recognized when she became the first woman to serve on the Board of the Chicago Metropolitan Health Council. Following her death, the Sister Gregory Chair for Scholarship Activities at West Suburban Hospital in Oak Park, Illinois, was established in recognition of her achievements in hospital ministry.—*Sister Mary Edward Gira*

SOURCE: Eulogy, January 25, 1973, congregation archives.

Krzycki, Leo (b. August 10, 1881, Milwaukee, Wisconsin; d. January 22, 1966, Milwaukee, Wisconsin). Labor leader. The son of immigrants from Prussian Poland, in 1904 he organized a strike of young press tenders in a local Milwaukee lithography plant. Between 1904 and 1908 he served as general vice president of the Lithographic Press Feeders Union, AFL. In 1910 Krzycki organized a strike of clothing workers in Milwaukee, and beginning in 1914 became one of the leaders of Amalgamated Clothing Workers of America (ACWA). His relations with the union continued until 1948 when he retired. Beginning in 1908 Krzycki was also a member of the Socialist Party where he was strongly influenced by the ideas of Eugene V. Debs. In 1912 he was elected an alderman in Milwaukee on the Socialist Party ticket, holding that office for seven years and later serving as deputy sheriff of Milwaukee County. In 1930 he became a member of National Executive Committee of the Socialist Party, becoming its chairman in 1933. He left the party in 1936 because he did not share the Party's opinion of the New Deal and became identified with the Democrats.

During World War I, Krzycki became more involved in the ACWA, working as an organizer and educator of Polish immigrants in the Midwest. In 1919 he became general organizer of the ACWA, working in Chicago, Buffalo, Philadelphia, Milwaukee, Indianapolis, Cleveland, Patterson (NJ), St. Louis, Utica (NY), and several other locales. In 1922 he became a member of its Executive Board, later serving as its vice-president. In 1935 he was among the co-organizers of the Congress of Industrial Organizations and the following year was actively involved in the rubber workers' strike in Akron, Ohio. The ACWA delegated him to work in support of CIO organizational campaigns among steelworkers and miners within the Steelworkers Organizing Committee, a position that brought him into the midst of the Memorial Day Massacre at Chicago's Southside Steelworks in 1937. Krzycki also helped organize the United Auto Workers, and served as a member of the CIO Political Action Committee during the elections of 1944 and 1948.

During World War II, Krzycki attempted to rally Slavic Americans and CIO members to support the alliance with the Soviet Union. Active as president of the **American Slav Congress** (1942–50), he also organized the **American Polish Labor Council**. In 1943 he co-founded the leftist **Kościuszko Polish Patriotic League**. He also supported the **Yalta** agreement that gave substantial portions of Polish territory to the Soviet Union and backed the recognition of the pro–Soviet regime in Poland. In 1945 he visited Europe for the World Federation of Trade Unions conference in Paris, taking the opportunity to visit other countries and to meet with Joseph Stalin for an hour and thirty minute interview. Krzycki destroyed all of his personal papers following his retirement in the wake of rising Congressional interest in investigating communist subversion in the U.S.—*Adam Walaszek*

SOURCES: Don Binkowski, *Poles Together: Leo Krzycki and Polish Americans in the American Labor Movement* (Philadelphia: Xlibris Corp., 2001); Don Binkowski, *Leo Krzycki and the Detroit Left* (Philadelphia: Xlibris Corp., 2001); Eugene Miller, "Leo Krzycki — Polish American Labor Leader," *Polish American Studies*, Vol. 33, no. 2 (1976), 52–64; Edward S. Kerstein, *Red Star Over Poland: Report from Behind the Iron Curtain* (Appleton, WI: C.C. Nelson, 1947).

Krzyżanowski, Ludwik (b. Krosno, Poland, November 10, 1906; d. Wakefield, Rhode Island, March 23, 1986). Literary scholar, editor. Krzyżanowski came to the United States in 1938 as a cultural attaché of Poland and served as a radio broadcaster for WHOM in 1939–40. In 1942, he was one of the founders of the **Polish Institute of Arts and Sciences** in America in Manhattan. He served as editor-in-chief of *The Polish Review*, a scholarly journal published by the Institute, from its establishment in 1956 until his death in 1986. He was also professor of Polish Studies at Columbia University and Political Science at New York University. He was a co-editor *Polish Civilization: Essays and Studies* and *Introduction to Modern Polish Literature*, as well as translator of the early writings of the world renowned anthropologist Dr. **Bronisław Malinowski**. A recognized authority on the novelist Joseph Conrad (Józef Konrad Korzeniowski), a native of Poland and renowned English writer, Krzyżanowski was editor of the *Joseph Conrad Centennial Essays*. A collection of his private and official correspondence, his broadcasting for WHOM, his professional activities and publications are contained in the archives of the Polish Institute of Arts and Sciences in America.—*Maria Swiecicka-Ziemianek*

SOURCES: "In Appreciation of Ludwik Krzyżanowski on the Occasion of the XXVth Anniversary of His Editorship of *The Polish Review*," *The Polish Review*, Vol. 26, no. 1 (1981), 4–15; obituary, *New York Times*, March 26, 1986.

Krzyżanowski, Włodzimierz Bonawentura (b. Rożnowo, Poland, June 9, 1824; d. New York City, New York, January 31, 1887). Military officer, government official. Educated in Poznań, he was involved in the abortive revolution led by Ludwik Mierosławski in 1846, fleeing to the United States to avoid punishment after that movement failed. He settled in New York where he studied English. Employed briefly as a surveyor in Virginia and the Midwest, he married Caroline Burnett in 1854 and settled in Washington, D.C., where he managed Burnett's pottery business. An avid supporter of the infant Republican Party, he gained election as chair of his local District of Columbia Republican Society in 1857. When the Civil War broke out he enlisted as a private soldier in the District of Columbia Militia, but his recruiting activities soon gained him election as captain of the militia's Company B, Turner Rifles, which he led in a skirmish at Great Falls, Maryland, on July 7, 1861.

When his enlistment expired later that month he set about recruiting among the immigrant community in New York City, raising a substantial number of recruits and being named colonel of the 58th New York Volunteer Infantry, known as the "**Polish Legion**." He led his regiment at Cross Keys, Virginia, following which he was placed in command of a brigade in Franz Sigel's corps that he led at Groveton and Second Bull Run. After the latter engagement he was assigned as commanding officer of the 2nd Brigade, 3rd Division, Eleventh Corps under General Oliver O. Howard, and was nominated for the rank of brigadier general in keeping with his duties as a brigade commander. The nomination, however, was rejected by the U.S. Senate.

He led his brigade at Chancellorsville, where he earned praise from his division commander for delaying a Confederate attack long enough for vital artillery and supplies to be evacuated. At Gettysburg his brigade suffered more than fifty percent casualties, but again earned praise for a counterattack that repulsed a Confederate attack on Cemetery Hill. In the fall of 1863 the brigade was sent west where it assisted in relieving the siege of Chattanooga, seeing action at Lookout Mountain, Wauhatchie, and Missionary Ridge, as well as the relief of Knoxville which followed. In April 1864 he was named commander of a brigade assigned to the protection of railroad lines supplying the Union armies operating in Georgia, Alabama and east Tennessee, eventually being confirmed as brigadier general on March 2, 1865.

Following the war he served as founding president of Von Steinwehr Post 192 of the

Włodzimierz B. Krzyżanowski, military officer and government official (*NARA*).

Grand Army of the Republic, a Union veterans organization. During the Reconstruction he was appointed Supervisor of Internal Revenue for the District of Georgia and Florida in 1869. In 1871 he moved to New Orleans as a special agent, and in 1873 was appointed to a similar post in the Washington Territory. Contrary to many assertions, he was never governor of Alaska. Retiring to private life in San Francisco in 1874, he opened a tavern and became active in Union veterans organizations and the local Polish community. His tavern often played host to novelist **Henryk Sienkiewicz** who used the personalities there to create some of the characters in his novels and short stories. While in California, Krzyżanowski was also instrumental in arranging for the American debut of the Shakespearean actress **Helena Modjeska**.

When his business failed during the recession of 1875–77, Krzyżanowski accepted a position as customs agent in Panama, finally transferring to New York in 1882. There he served as special agent for the Port of New York, while remaining active in veterans and Polish affairs and supporting the move for a national Polish American organization. In 1883 he published a series of memoirs in the Polish magazine *Kłosy*. Buried in Greenwood Cemetery in Brooklyn, the general's remains were re-interred in Arlington National Cemetery in 1937 in conjunction with ceremonies marking the fiftieth anniversary of his death.—*James S. Pula*

SOURCES: James S. Pula, *For Liberty and Justice: A Biography of Brigadier General Włodzimier B. Krzyżanowski, 1824–1887* (Utica, NY: Ethnic Heritage Studies Center, Utica College, 2008); M. J. Duszak, "Colonel Kriz of Washington," *Polish American Studies*, Vol. 23, no. 2 (1966), 108–110.

Krzyzewski, Michael William "Coach K" (b. Chicago, Illinois, February 13, 1947; d.—). Basketball coach. While attending the United States Military Academy at West Point, Krzyzewski was an outstanding basketball player, and lettered three years (1967–69). Following graduation he fulfilled his military obligation by serving five years as an army officer (1969–74), during which time he coached service teams. He retired as a captain and immediately began coaching as a graduate assistant at Indiana University under Bobby Knight (1974–75). He returned to West Point in 1975 as head basketball coach, spent five years there, and was then hired as head coach at Duke University (1980). Though the first few years were difficult, "Coach K," as he was nicknamed, turned the struggling Duke program around, building it into one of the most successful collegiate basketball programs in history. Within four years Duke was in the

Mike Krzyzewski, championship basketball coach (OLS).

NCAA tournament, and two years later his team fell just one game short of the national championship. Between 1988 and 1992 he became only the second coach in history to take his team to the Final Four four years in a row, the first being the legendary UCLA coach John Wooden. Krzyzewski won his first national title in 1991 with a second in 1992 and a third in 2010. The same year, he was elected to the Basketball Hall of Fame. Not restricted to college athletics, Coach K also led the United States Olympic Basketball Team to the gold medal in 2008 in Beijing, China. Among his awards are Atlantic Coast Conference Coach of the Year (1984, 1986, 1997, 1999, 2000); Naismith College Coach of the Year (1989, 1992, 1999); Coach of the Year by the National Association of Basketball Coaches (1991); Coach of the Year by *The Sporting News* (1992); Coach of the Year by *Basketball Times* (1986, 1997); CNN Coach of the Year (2001); Time Magazine Coach of the Year (2001); Olympic Gold Medal (2008).—*Cheryl A. Pula*

SOURCES: Greg Doyel, *Coach K: Building the Duke Dynasty: the Story of Mike Krzyzewski and the Winning Tradition at Duke University* (Lenexa, KS: Addax Publishing Group, 1999); Mike Krzyzewski, *Beyond Basketball: Coach K's Keywords for Success* (New York: Warner, 2007); Dick Weiss, *True Blue: a Tribute to Mike Krzyzewski's Career at Duke* (Champagne, IL: Sports Publications, 2005).

Krzyzowski, Edward C. (b. Chicago, Illinois, January 16, 1914; d. Tondul, Korea, September 3, 1951). Soldier, Medal of Honor recipient. A captain in Company B, 9th Infantry Regiment, 2nd Infantry Division, Krzyzowski displayed exceptional courage leading his men in action from August 31 to September 3, 1951. His citation for the Medal of Honor noted that he "distinguished himself by conspicuous gallantry and indomitable courage above and beyond the call of duty in action against the enemy as commanding officer of Company B. Spearheading an assault against strongly defended Hill 700, his company came under vicious crossfire and grenade attack from enemy bunkers. Creeping up the fire-swept hill, he personally eliminated 1 bunker with his grenades and wiped out a second with carbine fire. Forced to retire to more tenable positions for the night, the company, led by Capt. Krzyzowski, resumed the attack the following day, gaining several hundred yards and inflicting numerous casualties. Overwhelmed by the numerically superior hostile force, he ordered his men to evacuate the wounded and move back. Providing protective fire for their safe withdrawal, he was wounded again by grenade fragments, but refused evacuation and continued to direct the defense. On 3 September, he led his valiant unit in another assault which overran several hostile positions, but again the company was pinned down by murderous fire. Courageously advancing alone to an open knoll to plot mortar concentrations against the hill, he was killed instantly by an enemy sniper's fire. Capt. Krzyzowski's consummate fortitude, heroic leadership, and gallant self-sacrifice, so clearly demonstrated throughout 3 days of bitter combat, reflect the highest credit and lasting glory on himself, the infantry, and the U.S. Army."—*James S. Pula*

SOURCE: R. J. Proft, *United States of America's Congressional Medal of Honor Recipients and Their Official Citations* (Columbia Heights, MN: Highland House II, 2002).

Kubek, Tony (b. Milwaukee, Wisconsin, October 12, 1936; d.—). Baseball player, sportscaster. The son of a prominent local sandlot ballplayer in his native Milwaukee, Tony Kubek was an important member of the successful New York Yankees teams of 1957–1965. Primarily playing as a shortstop, he hit .266 over the course of nine seasons. A left handed batter, he won the American League Rookie of the Year award in 1957, and was named to three AL All-Star teams. While he was active, the Yankees won six league pennants and three World Series. Ironically, this sure fielder is best remembered for being the victim of a famous freak play in the seventh and deciding game of the 1960 World Series, a ground ball that took an errant hop and struck him in the throat, opening the door to a comeback victory by the Pittsburgh Pirates. Forced to retire prematurely from the game owing to a chronic back condition, Kubek began a second career as a broadcaster. For three decades before his retirement in 1994, he worked as a well regarded commentator on baseball telecasts for the NBC network, the Toronto Blue Jays, and the Yankees. He was inducted into the **National Polish-American Sports Hall of Fame** in 1982 and in 2008 he received the Ford C. Frick Award from the Baseball Hall of Fame for contributions to broadcasting.—*Neal Pease*

SOURCE: "Tony Kubek," National Polish-American Sports Hall of Fame website, www.polishsportshof. com.

Kubiak, Teresa Wojtaszek (b. Łódź, Poland, December 26, 1937; d.—). Singer. Wojtaszek studied voice at the Łódź Conservatory of Music and won numerous prizes and awards at renowned competitions in Helsinki, Tuluz, and Munich while still a student there. Upon the completion of her studies at the Conservatory, she was hired by the Grand Opera Theater of Łódź in 1965, making her debut in the title role of the acclaimed Polish national opera "Halka" by Stanisław Moniuszko. She also appeared in the same role at the Grand Opera in Warsaw. Five years later Wojtaszek received an invitation to perform at Carnegie Hall, which earned her an excellent review in the *New York Times* and invitations to perform in the United States and abroad, as well as an audition at the Metropolitan Opera. After her performance in Lincoln Center in 1971 she began to use her husband's name Kubiak, rather than her maiden name Wojtaszek, since Kubiak was easier to pronounce outside her native land. In 1973 Kubiak made her debut at the Metropolitan Opera in the role of Liza in Tchaikovsky's "The Queen of Spades," which she continued to perform for over fourteen years. Her final appearance at the Met took place on January 31, 1987 as Elizabeth in Wagner's "Tannhäuser." She performed throughout the United States, as well as in Austria, Bulgaria, Canada, China, Czechoslovakia, Italy, Jordan, Korea, Kuwait, Lisbon, London, New Zealand, the Philippines, Poland, and Spain. Kubiak also gave concert recitals with such prominent symphony orchestras as the London Philharmonic, the Chicago Symphony, the Montreal Symphony, the New York Philharmonic, the Symphony of Munich, and the symphonies of Kraków, Łódź, and Katowice, Poland. She also performed with such internationally famous tenors as Carlo Bergonzi, Placido Domingo, and Luciano Pavarotti. The winner of five national and international vocal competitions, she also judges national and international competitions and teaches master classes throughout the United States, Europe, the Middle East, and New Zealand. Kubiak began her teaching career at Montclair State

College in New Jersey in 1985, then moved to the Jacobs School of Music at Indiana University in 1990.—*Maria Swiecicka-Ziemianek*

SOURCE: "Teresa Kubiak," in Nicolas Slonimsky, ed., *Baker's Biographical Dictionary of Musicians* (New York: Schirmer, 2001).

Kubrick, Stanley (b. New York, New York, July 26, 1928; d. Harpenden, England, March 7, 1999). Film director. After receiving a camera from his father on his thirteenth birthday, Kubrick became an avid photographer. Dropping out of City College of New York, he sold a photo to *Look* magazine and became an apprentice photographer (1946) and avid moviegoer. In 1951 he spent his life savings on a movie he made himself, *Day of the Fight.* He then made several short documentaries for *March of Time,* which produced movie newsreels. These caught the attention of Hollywood producers and he was selected to direct Kirk Douglas in *Paths of Glory* (1956), followed by *Spartacus* (1960). Kubrick moved to England where he directed *Lolita,* followed by *Dr. Strangelove Or: How I Learned to Stop Worrying and Love the Bomb* (1964). This film was so successful that Kubrick virtually had his choice of projects to pursue. His next major film was a science fiction masterpiece, *2001: A Space Odyssey*, based on a novel by Arthur C. Clarke. Noted for demanding technical perfection and dedication from production crews and actors, his next string of films were equally as impressive as his previous efforts: *A Clockwork Orange* (1971); *Barry Lyndon* (1975), *The Shining* (1980), *Full Metal Jacket* (1987), and *Eyes Wide Shut* (1999). Though Kubrick made only thirteen feature length films in his career, most have gone on to become classics. His honors include: Academy Award Best Special Effects 1968 (*2001: A Space Odyssey*); British Academy of Film and Television Awards Best British Film 1964 (*Dr. Strangelove*); Best Film from Any Source 1964 (*Dr. Strangelove*); Best Direction 1975 *(Barry Lyndon)*; Britannia Award for Excellence in Film 1999; Academy Fellowship 2000; Golden Globe Award Best Motion Picture Drama 1961 (*Spartacus*); Boston Society of Film Critics Award for Best Director 1987 (*Full Metal Jacket*); Kansas City Film Critics Circle Award for Best Director 1968 (*2001: A Space Odyssey*); National Board of Review Award Best Director 1975 (*Barry Lyndon*); New York Film Critics Circle Award for Best Director 1964 (*Dr. Strangelove*); New York Film Critics Circle Award for Best Director 1971 (*A Clockwork Orange*); Golden Lion Lifetime Achievement Award 1997.—*Cheryl A. Pula*

SOURCES: John Baxter, *Stanley Kubrick: A Biography* (New York: Carroll and Graf Publishers, 1997); Norman Kagan, *The Cinema of Stanley Kubrick* (New York: Continuum, 1989); Vincent LoBrutto, *Kubrick: A Biography* (New York: D. I. Fine, 1996); Gene D. Phillips, *Stanley Kubrick: A Film Odyssey* (New York: Popular Library, 1975); Alexander Walker, *Stanley Kubrick, Director* (New York: Norton, 1999).

Kucera, Maximilian (b. Poland, January 1840; d. Milwaukee, Wisconsin, March 4, 1904). Polonia activist. Born in partitioned Poland, Kucera took part in the failed January Insurrection in 1863 against tsarist Russian rule. He arrived in the United States sometime later and was employed initially as a laborer. In Chicago, he opened up his own business, a grocery store, and became one of the founders of the **Gmina Polska** patriotic society. He was a delegate from the Gmina Polska group at the founding convention of the **Polish National Alliance** in Chicago in September 1880. At this meeting he was elected the PNA's first president. After serving two one-year terms in office, Kucera was elected treasurer of the PNA in 1885. Relocating to Milwaukee, he was elected vice **censor** of the Alliance in 1899. In 1903 he was made an honorary member of the fraternal. As a leader in the Polish National Alliance in Milwaukee, he took a major role in raising money for the construction of a monument to **Tadeusz Kościuszko** in the city's Kosciuszko Park. The monument was dedicated in 1905.—*Donald E. Pienkos*

SOURCES: Stanisław Osada, *Historia Związku Narodowego Polskiego i rozwój ruchu narodowego Polskiego w Ameryce Pólnocnej* (Chicago: Nakładem i drukiem Związku Narodowego Polskiego, 1905); Donald E. Pienkos, *PNA: A Centennial History of the Polish National Alliance of the United States of North America* (Boulder, CO: East European Monographs, 1984).

Maksymiljan Kucera, Polonia activist (*PNA*).

Kuczynski, Leszek S. "Les" (b. Lubeck, Germany, June 3, 1947; d. Chicago, Illinois, August 19, 2008). Polonia activist. The son of Polish parents who were forcibly removed to Germany following the Warsaw Uprising in 1944, Kuczynski migrated to the U.S. with his parents as displaced persons. He earned a law degree from the University of Minnesota (1972) and an MBA degree from the Keller Graduate School of Management of DeVry University of Chicago (1982). In 1985 he was appointed general legal counsel of the **Polish National Alliance** by President **Aloysius Mazewski**. He continued in this post under PNA Presidents **Edward Moskal** and **Frank Spula**. His fraternal work with the PNA focused on directing its voluntary legal services on behalf of Polish Americans and Polish immigrants in need of such assistance. In 1991, Kuczynski was appointed National Executive Director of the **Polish American Congress** (PAC). In subsequent years he played a crucial role in the PAC on many fronts. He worked closely with **Myra** and **Casimir Lenard** in the Washington, D.C., office of the PAC to coordinate the PAC's efforts to enlist U.S. Senate support for Poland's entrance into the NATO Alliance. Kuczynski was the author of a comprehensive and objective 1999 publication on the PAC's effort to win NATO membership for Poland titled *Expansion of NATO: Role of the Polish American Congress*. Beginning in 1999, Kuczynski led the World War II German Forced Labor Compensation Program on behalf of the PAC and the Polish American community. Initially, he represented **Polonia** in its meetings with the U.S. State Department, later serving as an advisor for the International Organization on Migration, the Geneva-based partner administering the compensation program. After 2002 he was a member of the Appeals Panel that reviewed denied claims of forced labor and personal injury. Through his efforts, more than 4,100 survivors of German forced labor camps residing in the United States and Canada received over $52 million in compensation from German businesses that had exploited them during the war. In all, over $1.6 billion was transmitted to surviving slave and forced laborers around the world, nearly 500,000 of whom were in Poland. Kuczynski also directed the Polish American Congress Charitable Foundation at a time when the Foundation sent more than $150 million in assistance to Poland in the form of donations, medical supplies, pharmaceuticals, and medical texts to Polish hospitals, orphanages, and homes for seniors. In 2002 Kuczynski was elected Chair of the Council of World Polonia (Rada Polonia Świata) for a four-year term. This body is comprised of leaders representing Polonia organizations from around the world. From 2002 to 2005 he was also a member of the Consultative Committee on Polonia Affairs established by the Marshal of the Polish Senate. In 2002 he was appointed (and re-appointed in 2005) to the Advisory Board of the American Red Cross Holocaust and War Victims Tracing Center.—*Donald E. Pienkos*

SOURCE: Donald Pienkos, *Yesterday, Today, Tomorrow: The Story of the Polish National Alliance* (Chicago: Alliance Printers and Publishers, 2008).

Kujawiak. The *kujawiak* is a Polish dance from the region of Kujawy on the Mazovian plains in central Poland after which it is named. The name first appeared in 1827 in a text by T. F. Jaskólski. According to **Ada Dziewanowska**'s description, the *kujawiak* was originally danced with a calm dignity and simplicity, in a smooth flowing manner "reminiscent of the tall grain stalks in the fields swaying gently in the wind," with no vigorous stamps and no drastic changes of tempo. From Kujawy, the dance was taken to Warsaw and other cities, and from there spread all over Poland where it underwent various transformations as, for instance, a tempo alternating from slow to fast and back to slow. According to Roderyk Lange, the *kujawiak* exists in two forms: as a regional folk dance including many varieties, and as the unified "national dance." Both variants include rotations of couples which shift around a large circle of the dance space. The folk versions are notably faster than the national version, and they are also more complicated, with a greater variety and difficulty of steps. The *kujawiak* is set in moderately fast triple meter. The second part of each measure is frequently extended and accented; moreover, the performers often extend (or less frequently, shorten) whole measures of the melody.

According to the entry in *New Grove Dictionary of Music and Musicians*, the "*kujawiak* is characterized by its misplaced accents, usually on the second or sometimes the third beat of the bar, and a tempo of quarter-note = 120–150." In past folk-practice, the main melody was usually performed on the violin, accompanied by the *basy* (low-pitched, bowed string instrument, in two varieties, a larger one and a smaller than the double-bass, modeled on the cello). The *basy* served as a percussion instrument — its two strings were usually played in an open position, with a regular, simple pattern. In performance practice, *kujawiaks* are coupled with faster **obereks**. Traditionally, the *kujawiak* is danced by couples in a circle, either in a flowing walk, with the dancers turning to one another and then leaning away, or in a revolving pattern (with hands

either free or clasped). Polish folk dance groups in the U.S. often use variants of this dance as a display dance for a solo couple, with elaborate and fanciful figures, for example lifting of the female dancer and turns. This practice, in turn, stems from the use of the *kujawiak* by the State Folk Song and Dance Group *Mazowsze*. These "*pas-de-deux*" seem to have more in common with the classical ballet tradition, than with the actual folk practice. In Poland, the State Folk Dance Ensembles replace all these arrangements with a symphony orchestra, and many Polish American dance groups rely on these recordings for their performances before Polonia groups accustomed to the "big-band" style of music.—*Maja Trochimczyk*

SOURCES: Philip V. Bohlman, "Musical Cultures of Europe," in *Excursions in World Music* (Upper Saddle River, NJ: Prentice Hall, 1997), 191–222; Ada Dziewanowska, *Polish Folk Dances & Songs—a Step by Step Guide* (New York: Hippocrene Books, 1999).

Kuklinski, Richard "The Iceman" (b. Jersey City, New Jersey, April 11, 1935; d. Trenton, New Jersey, March 5, 2006). Gangster. Kuklinski, who was of Polish-Irish heritage, was the brother of convicted rapist and murderer Joseph Kuklinski. A former altar boy, Richard dropped out of school following the eighth grade. He began a lifetime of criminal activity after being beaten by members of organized crime for not repaying a financial debt. Once the debt was paid off, Kuklinski began working for the Gambino crime family first by staging a series of robberies and then as a contract killer. Later, he claimed to have killed over 200 people beginning with his first murder at age thirteen, but the veracity of these claims is suspect. His Italian accomplices first referred to him as "The Polak," but he soon became known as "The Iceman" because he would freeze his victims to hide the time of death from investigators. Kuklinski was indicted in 1986 through the testimony of an undercover New Jersey State Police officer. Once incarcerated, he appeared to seek the spotlight by granting frequent interviews including lengthy meetings that formed the basis for two televised documentaries that aired in 1991 and 2001, as well as forming the basis for Philip Carlo's biographical book *The Ice Man* (2006). In 2006 Kuklinski claimed to have been a member of the gang that kidnapped and killed union leader Jimmy Hoffa, but this contradicted earlier statements in which he denied any involvement. Though many of his claims appear to have been without merit, in 1988 he was convicted of five murders which brought consecutive life sentences. In 2003 he also pled guilty to the murder of a New York City police detective.—*James S. Pula*

SOURCES: Philip Carlo, *The Ice Man, Confessions of a Mafia Contract Killer* (New York: St. Martin's Griffin, 2006); Anthony Bruno, *The Ice Man: The True Story of a Cold-Blooded Killer* (New York: Delacorte Press Books for Young Readers, 1993); F. T. Zugibe and J. F. Costello, "The Iceman Murder," *Journal of Forensic Sciences*, Vol. 38 (1993), 1404–08; Douglas Martin, "Richard Kuklinski, 70, a Killer of Many People and Many Ways, Dies," *New York Times*, March 9, 2006.

Kukliński, Ryszard Jerzy (b. Warsaw, Poland, June 13, 1930; d. Tampa, Florida, Feb. 11, 2004). Military officer, intelligence agent. Too young to serve during the Second World War, Kukliński joined the Polish army in the post-war years, rising to the rank of colonel with a posting to the sensitive planning staff of the Polish defense ministry charged with preparations for an eventual war with the nations of the North Atlantic Treaty Organization (NATO). He became convinced that Soviet war planning would cause Poland to be devastated by NATO retaliatory strikes, doubts that were fueled by misgivings over Poland's role in the invasion of Czechoslovakia in 1968 and the killing of Polish workers by communist forces in Gdynia in December 1970. Kukliński believed that Poland's best interests lay with the western alliance and not under Soviet domination. Confident that he could help Poland best by attempting to prevent a war with NATO, in 1972 Kukliński arranged a clandestine meeting with American officials in Europe. Over the ensuing years, he became the most important intelligence agent the United States had in the Soviet bloc, passing along tens of thousands of documents to American intelligence detailing everything from Soviet planning and intentions for a war against NATO, to the location of Soviet troop concentrations and command bunkers, the purpose and result of Warsaw Pact war games, the capabilities of Soviet equipment, and even the personal beliefs of Soviet and Polish officials. During the crisis that led to the imposition of martial law in 1981 he provided American intelligence with Soviet plans to crush Solidarność, as well as the various arguments and proposals made by the differing factions within the Polish and Soviet military establishments. When it appeared that counterintelligence officers were beginning an investigation that might implicate him as a source for the leaked secrets, Kukliński and his entire family escaped to the United States where he was awarded the Distinguished Intelligence Medal, America's highest award for intelligence service. George J. Tenet, director of the Central Intelligence Agency, asserted that "the information that Col. Kuklinski provided assisted the CIA in making critical national security decisions and helped keep the Cold War from escalating." Sentenced to death *in absentia* in 1984, the decree was rescinded following the liberation of Poland from communist rule. He died of stroke at the age of 73 in Tampa, Florida, in 2004 and is buried in the Powązki military cemetery in Warsaw.—*James S. Pula*

SOURCE: Benjamin Weiser, *A Secret Life: The Polish Officer, His Covert Mission, and the Price He Paid to Save His Country* (New York: Public Affairs, 2004).

Kulturkampf. The *Kulturkampf* (Culture Struggle) was a set of far-reaching policies that Prussian Chancellor Otto von Bismarck (1815–98) launched during the 1870s. Their stated purpose was to secularize the imperial government and disentangle it from the political power of the Roman Catholic Church. Bismarck considered these policies essential to the preservation of the recently unified German empire, which he sought to make as culturally homogenous — that is, Germanized — as possible. Bismarck feared that Catholics would ally themselves with the papacy instead of his own regime. He especially feared the prospect of an independent, majority-Catholic Poland as a security threat to the Reich. Poles did represent a large, discontent, and increasingly nationalistic minority group within the Prussian Empire. However, Bismarck's antipathy to an independent Polish state was not simply tactical in nature. According to a number of Polish and sympathetic non–Polish historians, ethnic hostility to Poles was an underrecognized but important component of his *Kulturkampf* agenda. These historians point to the devastation the *Kulturkampf* brought to Prussian-occupied areas of Poland and to Bismarck's own derogatory, unambiguous attitudes towards Polish people, attitudes quite widespread among the Protestant Junker ruling class.

The 1871 Constitution did not recognize the rights of ethnic minorities, whom Bismarck and his supporters detested as *Reichsfeinde* (enemies of the Reich). Bismarck held particular contempt for Poles, whom he considered especially undeveloped and unenlightened in contrast to modern, progressive Germans. Most famously, he wrote to his sister in 1861: "Hit the Poles, so that they break down. If we want to exist, we have to exterminate them; the wolf can also not help it that he was created by God, and nevertheless he is being shot whenever one sees the opportunity." It is worth noting here that German folklore traditionally portrayed wolves as treacherous, deadly shapeshifters, and that a centuries-long campaign to completely exterminate wolves from German lands was then only a few decades from its completion. Norman Davies observes that "although the Kul-

turkampf was not aimed exclusively at the Polish provinces, its impact was soon felt there to maximum effect." As Donald Treadgold, Peter Sugar, and **Piotr Stefan Wandycz** note: "All the elements of the Kulturkampf— state versus church, centralism versus autonomy, authorities versus the citizens — appeared with particular sharpness in Prussian Poland." The chief administrator of Bismarck's *Kulturkampf* was his Minister of Culture Adalbert Falk, a fiercely anti–Catholic and anti–Polish German from Silesia. Between 1872 and 1876, Falk enforced the series of so-called **May Laws** (also known as Falk Laws) that brought extensive and widely resented changes to Prussian-held lands, especially those with large Catholic populations. While continuing to subsidize Protestant institutions, the government discontinued all funds to Catholic organizations. The Reich eliminated its diplomatic ties with the Roman Catholic Church as well as the Catholic Department in the Ministry of Culture. Civil marriages became the only legally recognized kind.

The expansion of state control over Roman Catholic clergy was central to the *Kulturkampf.* The Reich expelled the Jesuit order. Government-appointed boards took over control of congregational properties. The state also assumed control of priest appointments and firings, conducted inspections of seminaries, and mandated examinations in German culture for all seminary graduates. Especially in the Prussian Partition of Poland, the Reich scapegoated Roman Catholic clergy as fomenters of rebellion. The clergy were banned from political engagements of any sort, including protests against *Kulturkampf* policies. In 1874, ninety defiant priests were imprisoned, along with the Archbishop of Poznań, Mieczysław Ledochówski. The Vatican negotiated release into exile for the Archbishop, but was thwarted from installing a replacement for a dozen years.

Because education in the Prussian Partition was so much in the hands of the Roman Catholic Church, the Reich quickly took over the schools in order to secularize and Germanize them. Many members of the clergy were forced out of their teaching posts and replaced with Germans. Teachers were banned from membership in Catholic and Polish ethnic civil society groups. German was made the mandatory language of instruction. Children were punished for speaking Polish at school. Language restrictions were not confined to the schools. The rallying hymn *Boże, coś Polskę* (God Save Poland) often sung at Mass, was banned. Polish-language newspapers were forced to publish in German as well. By 1876, German was the mandatory

language for all government offices and for the legal system. The postal system refused to send letters if they bore the Polish word for street, *ulica,* instead of the German *strasse,* or if they were labeled with Polish city names instead of the Germanized ones (Gdańsk instead of Danzig, Posen instead of Poznań, Breslau instead of Wrocław, and so forth). There was also a push to require certain additional state documents for Polish Catholics and Jews but not for Germans.

By 1879, Bismarck realized that he needed Catholic support in his plans to thwart the rising popularity of socialism, which he perceived as a far greater threat to the Reich than Roman Catholic allegiance to the Pope. He removed Falk from office and declared an official end to the *Kulturkampf.* Yet its repercussions continued and even worsened in Prussian-occupied Poland up through World War I. In 1885, the Prussian police forced 30,000 Polish Jews and Catholics into exile citing their lack of proper government documents. Between 1846 and 1885, as many as 1.25 million acres of land in Poznania and West Prussia went from Polish to German ownership. However, the Reich wanted even more land in German hands. In 1886, Bismarck created the *Ansiedlugskommission,* or Prussian Colonization Commission, which lasted until 1913. Its purpose was to move even more Germans into Prussian-held areas of Poland. Leo von Caprivi, Bismarck's immediate successor (1890–94), a person of partially Slavic (Slovenian) descent, attempted minor relaxations of anti–Polish policies. In 1894, the *Ostmarkenverein,* the Eastern Marches Association, was founded to insist on an even harder line in the Polish territories, especially in regard to land takeovers. Polish landholders were forbidden to build homes for themselves on their own properties. By 1907, the Prussian Colonization Commission had enabled 14,000 Germans to take over 800,000 more acres. By 1912, in another longstanding government strategy to lay claim to the land, fully 7,500 place names had been Germanized.

The *Kulturkampf* and its aftermath awakened an even more intense Roman Catholic and nationalist devotion among Poles. In response to the restrictions on their mother tongue, Poles formed their own thriving literacy societies and libraries. When Poles were dislocated from rural areas, they often moved to cities like Poznań and by their sheer numbers intensified the Polish character of these places. Many rural peasants fought to guard their lands by creating their own farming cooperatives, credit union associations, and land purchase banks. One prominent hero of the resistance was a peasant named Michał Dryzmała (1857–1937). In 1904, he bought land in the Wolsztyn District and resolved to live there despite the laws that forbade him to build a new house. For over a decade, he evaded the authorities & their attempts to evict him by living inside an old circus wagon. His creative persistence won the attention of the German and the international press.

The culture and spirituality of Poles in the Prussian Partition also survived in exile. During the 1870s, fully 152,000 Polish immigrants to the U.S. came from East and West Prussia and Poznań, compared to only 2,000 from Austrian-held **Galicia**. This wave of immigrants subsided in the 1880s. Yet between 1840 and 1910, a total of 1,575,000 immigrants left the Prussian Partition for the U.S., including 877,000 from Poznania, 628,110 from West Prussia, and 70,000 from Russian-occupied areas adjoining Prussian-held lands. These immigrants were often whole families determined to settle in the U.S. Bringing industrial experience, entrepreneurial abilities, and knowledge of skilled crafts with them, they quickly found ways to survive and flourish in their new country, despite its rampant discrimination against them. This first large wave of Polish immigrants established the earliest religious and ethnic institutions of U.S. Polonia, some of which endure into the twenty-first century.

Against the Reich's intentions, the *Kulturkampf* spurred an organized, energetic Polish resistance within the Prussian Partition. This intensified spirit of resistance eventually helped to bring about the independence of the Second Polish Republic. The *Kulturkampf* and its aftermath brought a substantial Polish presence into the United States for the first time and laid the foundations for future waves of immigrants as well. At the same time, the *Kulturkampf* predicated even greater threats to Polish survival and well being, both Catholic and Jewish. In titling his Nazi polemic *Mein Kampf*, Adolf Hitler was quite consciously asserting himself as chief heir to the *Kulturkampf*. In engineering the Holocaust and the Nazi occupation of Poland and other lands, Hitler studied the *Kulturkampf* both as a model to build upon and a cautionary tale about which political tactics to avoid. The enduring legacy of the *Kulturkampf* for Polish people, both in the homeland and in the diaspora, is paradoxical and multifaceted.— *Mary Krane Derr*

SOURCES: Norman Davies, *God's Playground: A History of Poland* (New York: Columbia University Press, 1984); Martin Kitchen, *A History of Modern Germany, 1800–2000* (Malden, MA: Blackwell, 2006); Leo Lucassen, *The Immigrant Threat: The Integration of Old and New Migrants in Western Europe Since 1850* (Urbana, IL: University of Illinois Press, 2005); James S. Pula, *Polish Americans: An Ethnic Community* (New York: Twayne Publishers, 1995); Phillip T. Rutherford, *Prelude to the Final Solution: The Nazi Program for Deporting Ethnic Poles, 1939–1941* (Lawrence, KS: University Press of Kansas, 2007); Donald W. Treadgold, Peter F. Sugar, and Piotr Stefan Wandycz, *A History of East Central Europe* (Seattle: University of Washington Press, 1974); Lech Trzeciakowski, *The Kulturkampf in Prussian Poland* (New York: East European Monographs, 1990).

Kulwicki, Alan (b. Greenfield, Wisconsin, December 14, 1954; d. near Blountville, Tennessee, April 1, 1993). Stock car driver. Kulwicki began stock car racing at local tracks in his native Wisconsin. He joined the NASCAR (National Association for Stock Car Auto Racing) tour in 1986, winning its rookie of the year award. Kulwicki quickly became one of the top NASCAR drivers, winning its Winston Cup championship in 1992, his final season. He died in a plane crash the following year. Kulwicki is a member of the International Motorsports Hall of Fame, and was inducted into the National Polish-American Sports Hall of Fame in 2001.—*Neal Pease*

SOURCE: "Alan Kulwicki," National Polish-American Sports Hall of Fame website, www.polishsportshof.com.

Kuniczak, Wiesław Stanisław (b. Lwów, Poland, February 4, 1930; d. Quakertown, Pennsylvania, September 19, 2000). Novelist. The son of a major general in the Polish army, Kuniczak escaped with his family to Great Britain following the German and Soviet invasions of Poland in 1939. In 1950 he moved to the United States to pursue his education, earning his M.S. in Journalism from Columbia University (1954). Following this, he accepted a position as a writer with *The Citizen-Advertiser* in Auburn, New York (1954–1955), before serving a term in the U.S. Army (1955–57). After his discharge from the army, he went to work for *The Plain Dealer* in Cleveland, Ohio (1957–60). Becoming a U.S. citizen in 1958, he moved to Mexico's Yucatan Peninsula (1961–63) while he prepared his first book for publication. After a brief stint with *The Pittsburgh Post-Gazette* (1968–69), he returned to Europe in 1969 only to be imprisoned in Greece until 1972. His release was secured through the efforts of Edward Piszek of the Copernicus Society of America. From 1972 to 1974 Kuniczak lived in Cyprus where he worked for the *Allied Press Enterprises* in Kyrenia. This provided him with a base for travel in the Middle East, including his participation in the Yom Kippur War. He lost his home in Cyprus during the Turkish invasion of 1974. In the mid–1970s he lived in London and Montréal, finally settling in Denver, Colorado, in 1981. Beginning in 1983 he became a Writer-in-Residence at **Alliance College**, Cambridge Springs, PA (1983–85), then held a similar position at Mercyhurst College in Erie, PA (1985–87), and finally at the Copernicus Society of America where he worked on his monumental task of translating and editing for American readers **Henryk Sienkiewicz**'s Trilogy. He is the author of *The Thousand Hour Day* (1966), *The Sempinski Affair* (1969), *My Name Is Million: An Illustrated History of the Poles in America* (1978), *The March* (1979), *Valedictory* (1983), *The Glass Mountain: An Anthology of Polish Fables, Folk Tales and Legends* (1992). His translations include *With Fire and Sword* (*Ogniem i mieczem*, 1991), *The Deluge* (*Potop*, 1992), *Fire in the Steppe* (*Pan Wołodyjowski*, 1992), and *Quo Vadis* (1993).

It is impossible to overestimate Kuniczak's accomplishments as an American novelist whose first novel, *The Thousand Hour Day*, brought the topic of Poland and her heroic history into the homes of thousands of ordinary American readers through the book's adoption as the main selection by the Book-of-the-Month Club. Kuniczak himself defined *The Thousand Hour Day*, *The March* and *Valedictory* as a Trilogy of the Polish experience in the Second World War. The first volume chronicles the valiant struggle of the Polish nation during the dual German and Soviet invasions of September 1939; the second presents the suffering and martyrdom of thousands of Poles in Siberia and the Katyń Forest at the hands of the Soviets between 1939 and 1944; and the final volume portrays Polish airmen during the Battle of Britain. Critics praise Kuniczak's Trilogy for innovative plot structure, beautiful imagery, and evocative language. The work was nominated for the Nobel Prize in Literature in 1984. Although his novels were translated into seventeen languages, they were never published in Polish. This was attempted, but was abandoned due to political and financial reasons. Kuniczak was also in-

W. S. Kuniczak, novelist (*OLS*).

terested in both the history and the present condition of American **Polonia** as evidenced by his impassioned and controversial speech, "The Silent Emigration," delivered on October 15, 1967, at the Polish Arts Club in Chicago, and from his overview of the history of Polish immigration to the United States in *My Name Is Million*. Kuniczak did not avoid controversy with the publication of his translations from Sienkiewicz. He was criticized for making these nineteenth century classics of Polish literature more compatible with a twentieth century literary aesthetic. Criticism notwithstanding, Kuniczak's translations were widely accepted by American readers. Kuniczak's papers are kept at the Howard Gotlieb Archival Research Center of Boston University in Boston, MA.—*Grażyna J. Kozaczka*

SOURCES: Jerzy R. Krzyżanowski, "Structural Models of W.S. Kuniczak's Major Novels," *The Polish Review*, Vol. 50, no. 3 (2005), 295–305; Jerzy R. Krzyżanowski, "W.S. Kuniczak's *The March*: A Polyphonic Novel," *Polish American Studies*, Vol. 37, no. 1 (Spring 1980), 52–64; Frank Mocha, "History as Literature," *The Polish Review*, Autumn 1967, 78–83.

Kunz, Stanley Henry (b. Nanticoke, Pennsylvania, September 26, 1864; d. Chicago, Illinois, April 23, 1946). Politician, horse breeder. After moving to Chicago with his family at the age of two, he attended public schools, St. Ignatius College, and Metropolitan Business College, all in the city. Entering politics, he gained election to the state Assembly (1888–90) and the state Senate (1902–06) as the first Polish-American in Chicago to do so. A member of the Chicago City Council from the Sixteenth Ward (1898–1921) and the Democratic Party Central Committee of Cook County (1891–1925), he was a delegate to the Democratic National Conventions in 1912, 1916, and 1924. He was elected as a Democrat to the Sixty-seventh and to the four succeeding Congresses (March 4, 1921–March 3, 1931) from the Eighth District of Illinois. He successfully contested the 1930 election of **Peter C. Granata**, an alleged friend of Al Capone, and an earlier opponent, who had unsuccessfully challenged the results of Kunz's 1926 election. The House voted by 190 to 168 along party lines to unseat the recently installed Granata, a Republican, and Kunz again served from April 5, 1932, to March 3, 1933. However, he was an unsuccessful candidate for re-nomination in 1932. Known also as a breeder of thoroughbreds and racing horses, the goateed and pince-nez wearing Kunz, by some accounts powerful but not popular and once the political boss of Chicago's Polish Downtown, was emphatic rather than diplomatic. Nicknamed "Stanley the Slugger" by reformist opponents aligned with Chicago Mayor Carter Harrison, he nevertheless "delivered" for his constituents.—*Frederick J. Augustyn*

SOURCES: *Biographical Directory of the United States Congress, 1774–Present* (http://bioguide.congress.gov/); Edward R. Kantowicz, *Polish-American Politics in Chicago, 1888–1940* (Chicago: University of Chicago Press, 1975), 64–69, 78–79, 175–79.

Kupchak, Mitchell "Mitch" (b. Hicksville, New York, May 24, 1954; d.—). Basketball player. Kupchak played basketball at the University of North Carolina (1972–76) where he was named Atlantic Coast Conference Basketball Player of the Year and won NCAA All-America honors. He also played on the 1976 U.S. Olympic team, winning the gold medal. He was drafted as the thirteenth overall pick by the Washington Bullets in 1976. In his first season he was named to the All-Rookie Team. During his four seasons with the Bullets he helped them win the 1978 NBA Championship before being traded to the Los Angeles Lakers in 1981 at the request of Earvin "Magic" Johnson, but Kupchak injured his knee 26 games into the season and did not play again until the 1983-84 season. He played a key role in the Lakers' 1985 championship series with the Boston Celtics, helping them to win the title, but retired from active playing after the 1985-86 season with over 5,000 career points. While still under contract as a player, he assisted Lakers General Manager Jerry West. Following his playing career he earned an MBA from the Anderson School of Management at UCLA (1987) and became Assistant General Manager to Jerry West, and General Manager in 2000 when West left for the Memphis Grizzlies.—*Patricia Finnegan*

SOURCES: "Nets Have Kupchak on List," *New York Times*, May 5, 2000, 6; George Vecsey, "Kupchak Made it Back," *New York Times*, June 12, 1985.

Kurczaba, Alex (b. Watenstedt, Germany, September 14, 1947; d.—). Literary scholar. After earning his B.A. degree in 1969 from Canisius College in Buffalo, NY, in 1971 he received his M.A. in German Literature from the State University of New York. He continued his interest in arts and literature, earning a doctoral degree in 1978 in Comparative Literature from the University of Illinois, Champaign–Urbana. Kurczaba's research interests involve literature, culture, and film from Poland and Post-Communist Central Europe. In 1980 he published his first book, *Gombrowicz and Firsch: Aspects of the Literary Diary*, a comparative study of the *Tagebucher* of Max Frisch and the *Dziennik* of the exile Polish writer, Witold Gombrowicz, that explored the characteristics of a modern literary diary. In 1983 he received his first fellowship awarded by the National Endowment for the Humanities for research on the *Struggle for Reform in Polish Renaissance Literature*. In 1992 he received a fellowship from the University of Illinois enabling him to pursue research for *Under Native Eyes: Joseph Conrad and Polish Literature*. Later, he co-authored and edited the book *Conrad and Poland* (1996), a collection of essays critiquing Joseph Conrad's publications and his depictions of Polish literature, tradition, and politics. He is also known for his translations of Polish poetry including the works of Adam Asnyk, Cyprian Kamil Norwid, and Krzysztof Kamil Baczyński. He served on the editorial board of **The Polish Review** and the **Sarmatian Review**, as well as a peer-reviewer for *Publications of the Modern Language Association*, the *Slavic and East European Journal*, and the *Canadian Slavonic Papers*. He served as a trustee of the Joseph Conrad Society of America. A member of the faculty of the University of Illinois at Chicago, he is a three time recipient of the Amoco Silver Circle Award for Excellence in Teaching.—*Anamika Dasgupta*

SOURCE: trigger.uic.edu/~kurczaba/.

Kurland, Robert Albert "Bob" (b. St. Louis, Missouri, December 23, 1924; d.—). Basketball player. Basketball's first great seven-foot player, he led Jennings High in St. Louis to two state finals before Henry Iba offered him a scholarship at Oklahoma A&M (now Oklahoma State University). Coach Iba transformed the defensive-minded Kurland into a scoring threat who amassed what was then a season record of 643 points, including 58 in a game against St. Louis University. He led the "Aggies" to back-to-back NCAA championships in 1945 and 1946 while being selected as an All-American three years in a row. Because Kurland often jumped above the bas-

Stanley Kunz, congressman (*LC*).

ket to grab opponents' shots, he was responsible for the NCAA enacting a regulation banning defensive goaltending in 1945. Kurland was the first person to regularly dunk during games. The rivalry between him and De Paul's George Mikan foreshadowed similar matchups between latter-day "Big Men." Kurland never played professional basketball, passing up the newly formed Basketball Association of America and National Basketball League to play for Phillips Petroleum's A.A.U. team, the "66 Oilers." He played for six years with Phillips, winning three championships. Since he never played professionally, he was eligible as an amateur for the 1948 and 1952 Olympics where he became the first player ever to perform on two gold medal–winning Olympic basketball teams. After retiring from competition, he assumed full-time executive responsibilities with Phillips Petroleum where he went on to manage special product sales in the company's marketing division. Kurland, always proud of his Polish heritage, was not sure if his last name was ever shortened. "My father, Albert, told me that his parents came from a Polish province called Courland. Maybe that's where we got the name Kurland." He was elected to the Basketball Hall of Fame (1961) and the **National Polish-American Sports Hall of Fame** (1996).—*Luis J. Gonzalez*

SOURCE: Jerzy Buck, "Basketball's First Great Seven-footer," National Polish-American Sports Hall of Fame and Museum, Inc., http://www.polishsportshof.com/bios/kurland_b_complete.html.

Kurowski, George John "Whitey" (b. Reading, Pennsylvania, April 19, 1918; d. Sinking Spring, Pennsylvania, December 9, 1999). Baseball player. Kurowski overcame childhood osteomyelitis to become one of the premier third basemen in major league baseball in the 1940s. During a nine year career (1941–49), entirely spent as a member of the St. Louis Cardinals, he hit .286 with 106 home runs. In a brief six-season span as a regular, the right hand hitting Kurowski was named to five National League All-Star teams, twice finished among the top ten in balloting as NL Most Valuable Player, and led the league's third basemen in numerous defensive categories. The statistical calculations of the *Total Baseball* encyclopedia rate him as having been among the five most effective non-pitchers in the National League in two seasons. His Cardinals teams won four NL pennants, and three World Series championships. Many observers regarded him as the Cardinals' outstanding performer in the team's victory in the 1942 World Series. After arm and elbow injuries forced a premature end to his playing career, he spent nearly two decades as a manager and coach in the minor leagues. Kurowski was in-

ducted into the National Polish-American Sports Hall of Fame in 1988.—*Neal Pease*

SOURCE: Rich Westcott, *Diamond Greats* (Westport, CT: Meckler, 1988).

Kuryer Polski (Polish Courier). On November 7, 1885, a group of young liberals consisting of **Michał Kruszka**, **Antoni Paryski**, **Stanisław Ślisz**, and **Franciszek Jabłonski** began publishing the *Krytyka* (The Critic) in Milwaukee in support of working class issues. When it failed in 1887, Kruszka, with only $125 in funding, began publishing *Kuryer Polski* on June 23, 1888. Beginning with two assistants and two newsboys, Kruszka built the paper into a major influence in Milwaukee's Polish community and a leading national Polish newspaper. Much like *Krytyka*, the new publication was pro-labor and also waged a lengthy, and at times acrimonious, campaign against the Roman Catholic hierarchy on behalf of Polish representation in the Catholic Church and the recognition of Polish national and religious traditions. His major opponent in this battle was the ***Nowiny Polskie*** (Polish News) edited by the Rev. **Bolesław Góral** with the backing of Bishop Sebastian Messmer. Among the contributors to *Kuryer Polski* were the outspoken leader of the movement for the appointment of Polish bishops in America, the Rev. **Wacław Kruszka**, the publisher's brother. Kruszka was adept at obtaining political support for his newspaper, including a concession for the printing of official state government notices, and continued to edit the paper until his death on December 2, 1918. Although founded with a close allegiance to the Democratic Party, Kruszka switched his support to the Republicans in 1900 in a dispute over the appointment of Poles to positions in the Milwaukee city government. It remained largely Republican in tone since then, although under the later editorship of

Popular actress Gilda Gray looks over an issue of *Kuryer Polski* on a visit to Milwaukee, 1929 (*UWM*).

Czesław Dziadulewicz it supported the Progressive movement headed by Robert LaFollette and then backed Milwaukee's Socialist mayor, Daniel W. Hoan, and the Socialist congressman Victor Berger. In 1939 it began publishing a weekly English-language supplement, and gradually English assumed a greater proportion of the text. Its editors were Michał Kruszka (1888–1918), Stanisław J. Zwierzchowski (1919–28), Czesław Dziadulewicz (1928–36), Józef Kapmarski (1937–40), Adam Kwasieborski (1940–57), Frank Plichta (1958–60), and Jane Sobogne-Bogusławski (1961–63).—*James S. Pula*

SOURCE: Edmund G. Olszyk, *The Polish Press in America* (Milwaukee: Marquette University Press, 1940), 56–57.

Kush, Frank (b. Windber, Pennsylvania, January 20, 1929; d.—). Football coach. Kush played football at Michigan State University (1950–52) earning All-American honors as a defensive lineman, helping the Spartans win a national championship in his senior year. After service in the U.S. Army where he rose to the rank of first lieutenant and coached the Fort Benning, Georgia, football team, he accepted an assistant head coaching position at Arizona State University under former Michigan State coach Dan Devine. When Devine left in 1958 to coach the University of Missouri, Kush became the Sun Devils' head coach. He remained there for 21 years, compiling a record of 176-51-1 with only two losing seasons. In his first eleven seasons, he captured two Western Athletic Conference titles and finished as runner-up five times. After initially deciding to leave Arizona State for the head coach position at the University of Pittsburgh in January 1969, Kush changed his mind and returned to Arizona State. The Sun Devils won the 1970 Peach Bowl and the first three Fiesta Bowls. In 1975, after a 4–7 season, the Sun Devils went 12–0, capping the season off with an exciting 17–14 win over the University of Nebraska in the Fiesta Bowl, where Kush's son Danny kicked five field goals, including the game winner. In 1979, however, former Sun Devil punter Kevin Rutledge filed a $1.1 million lawsuit against both ASU and Kush, alleging both physical and mental harassment by Kush and his staff which caused Rutledge to transfer. Rutledge also accused Kush of punching him in the mouth during a game against the University of Washington. As a result, some overzealous ASU fans set fire to Rutledge's father's insurance company office and issued death threats against the former player. On October 13, 1979, Kush was fired as ASU head coach, just hours before their home game against Washington. ASU Athletic Director Fred Miller charged that Kush was pressuring players and coaches to keep quiet about the Rutledge issue. Kush did coach that game, his team delivered an emotional 12–7 upset against the sixth-ranked Huskies, and the fans carried Kush off the field. After two years in the courts, Kush was found not liable in the case, but it set a precedent for future coaches regarding motivational techniques used on players. In 1981, Kush moved to the Canadian Football League as head coach of the Hamilton Tiger-Cats. In his one season with the team, the Cats were 11-4-1 and earned a berth in the CFL Eastern Conference Championship. In 1982, Kush moved back to the United States when the Baltimore Colts hired him as their head coach. In that strike-shortened season, the Colts went 0-8-1. The team improved the following season to 7–9, but moved to Indianapolis during the off-season. After four wins in fifteen games in 1984, Kush resigned in December. He then accepted the head coaching position with the new United States Football League's Arizona Outlaws, supposedly so he could be closer to his family. The league folded in 1986 and Kush lived off his personal services contract with Outlaws owner Bill Tatham by offering assistance to beginners in a local youth football league. He joked that he was "the highest-paid Pop Warner coach in the country." In 1995, Kush was inducted into the College Football Hall of Fame, and was welcomed back to Arizona State the following year. On September 21, 1996, there was a special ceremony at Sun Devil Stadium, where the field was officially named Frank Kush Field. The Sun Devils went on to upset then top-ranked Nebraska by a score of 19–0, handing the Cornhuskers their first loss in over two years. A bronze statue of Kush was placed outside the stadium, and in July 2000, Kush was officially hired as an assistant to the Athletic Director where he served as a fund-raiser. He was elected to the National Polish-American Sports Hall of Fame.—*Patricia Finnegan*

SOURCE: David Seibert and Sam Freedman, *Frank Kush: The Man, the Philosophy, the Controversy* (Scotsdale, AZ: Valley Sport Focus, 1979).

Kusielewicz, Eugene Francis Vincent

(b. Brooklyn, New York, October 12, 1930; d. New York, New York, December 10, 1996). Historian. Eugene Kusielewicz received his baccalaureate degree from St. Johns University where he eventually returned to teach history in 1955 after earning his doctorate from Fordham University as a student of **Oskar Halecki**. He began his teaching career by teaching in the New York City public schools, then at St. Georges Academy where he became chair of the social studies department. Kusielewicz's specialty was the Paris Peace Conference of

Eugene Kusielewicz, president of the Kosciuszko Foundation (*PAHA*).

1919, the Polish Question, and Woodrow Wilson's role in the rebirth of Poland. Although his primary interest was in the Versailles peace conference and the relations between Pres. Wilson and **Ignacy Paderewski**, he also wrote frequently on the Polish American community and various other topics. He was a frequent contributor on the subject of Poland and Polish-Americans for publications across the country, and was frequently published in *The Polish Review* and *Polish American Studies*. He is best known for his leadership role within the Polish American community where he served as president of the **Kosciuszko Foundation** from 1970 to 1979. During his tenure he instituted the "Library of Polish Studies" series with Twayne Publishers, was instrumental in initiating student exchanges with the Catholic University of Lublin in 1974, served a term as president of the **Polish American Historical Association**, and went on to serve on the Advisory Boards of the **Polish Museum of America** and the **Józef Piłsudski Institute for Research Into the Modern History of Poland**, the Wanda Roehr Foundation, the Catholic Historical Association, and the Polish Institute of Arts & Sciences of America, and was a Trustee of the Brooklyn Public Library. His many honors include the Haiman Award from the Polish American Historical Association, the Annual Award of the Polish Section of the Societé Européenne de Culture, the Distinguished Service Award of the **American Council for Polish Culture**, the Distinguished Service Medal of the Polish Ministry of Higher Education, and induction into the Knights of Malta.—*David Stefancic*

SOURCE: Vol. 56, no. 1 (1999) of *Polish American Studies* contains a symposium of five memorial articles on Kusielewicz.

Kutyna, Donald J.

(b. Chicago, Illinois, December 6, 1933; d.—). Military officer. After attending Lane Technical High School, he attended the University of Iowa for two years, subsequently gaining appointment to the U.S. Military Academy, graduating in 1957. He later earned a master's degree in aeronautics and astronautics at the Massachusetts Institute of Technology (MIT) in 1965. After completing pilot training in September 1958, he was assigned to the 33rd Bombardment Squadron at March Air Force Base, CA, serving as a B-47 combat crew commander until June 1963. Following graduation from MIT, he was assigned to the Aerospace Research Pilot School, Edwards Air Force Base, CA, as a student and later as staff director, training test pilots and astronauts. From December 1969 to January 1971, he served with the 44th Tactical Fighter Squadron at Takhli Royal Thai Air Force Base, Thailand, completing 120 combat missions over the skies of North and South Vietnam. Upon his return from Southeast Asia, he was assigned to Headquarters U.S. Air Force, Washington, D.C., as a development planner in the Office of the Deputy Chief of Staff for Research and Development. In June 1973, he served as executive officer to the Undersecretary of the Air Force. In August 1975, General Kutyna entered the Industrial College of the Armed Forces graduating in July 1976, after which he transferred to the Electronic Systems Division, Hanscom Air Force Base, MA, as assistant deputy for international programs. There he served as program manager for foreign military sales of the E-3A Airborne Warning and Control System (AWAC) aircraft and became assistant program director for the overall E-3A program. In June 1980, he was appointed deputy for surveillance and control systems, responsible for the development and acquisition of the sensors and command centers used by NORAD and the U.S. space program. Kutyna became deputy commander for space launch and control systems at Space Division, Air Force Systems Command, Los Angeles Air Force Station, CA, in June 1982. From this position, he managed the Department of Defense space shuttle program, the design and construction of the West Coast space shuttle launch site at Vandenberg Air Force Base, the acquisition of space shuttle upper stage boosters, and the operational aspects of launching military payloads on the shuttle. Other responsibilities included the development, acquisition and launch support of all Air Force expendable launch vehicles, including the Titan and Atlas space boosters and the new Titan IV heavy lift launch vehicle. His programs for control of space missions encompassed the operations and upgrade of the Air Force satellite control network, and development of Air Force Space Command's Consolidated Space Operations Center, Falcon Air Force Station, CO. In June 1984, he became director of space systems and command, control and communications, Office of the Deputy Chief of Staff, Research, Development and Acquisition. After the loss of the space shuttle *Challenger* in January 1986, he served as a member of the presidential commission investigating the accident and spearheaded the effort to bring expendable launch vehicles back into the nation's space inventory. In June 1986 he was named vice commander of the Space Division overseeing all space system acquisitions, with emphasis on programs associated with the Strategic Defense Initiative (SDI). In November 1987, he became commander of the Air Force Space Command, with headquarters at Peterson Air Force Base, which conducted missile warning, space surveillance and satellite control operations at 46 locations worldwide. In 1990, he assumed command of the North American Aerospace Defense Command and the U.S. Space Command. His military awards and decorations include the Defense Distinguished Service Medal, Distinguished Service Medal, and Legion of Merit with oak leaf cluster, Distinguished Flying Cross with oak leaf cluster, Air Medal with eight oak leaf clusters, and Air Force Commendation Medal with two oak leaf clusters. In June 1987, he received the National Geographic Society's General Thomas D. White U.S. Air Force Space Trophy given to individuals that make outstanding contributions to the nation's progress in space. After retiring from the services in 1992, Kutyna was Vice President, Space Technology, of Loral Space & Communications Ltd., a leading satellite communications company, from 1993 to 1996, and again from 1999 to 2004. He also served as Vice President, Advanced Space Systems, for Lockheed Martin Corporation, a company principally engaged in the research, design, development, manufacture and integration of advanced technology systems, products and services, from 1996 to 1999. From September 2004 through the present, General Kutyna has served as a part-time consultant to Loral Space & Communications Ltd.—*Luis J. Gonzalez*

SOURCE: Aleksandra Ziolkowska, *The Roots Are Polish* (Toronto, Canada: Canadian Polish Research Institute, 1998).

Kuzava, Bob (b. Wyandotte, Michigan, May 28, 1923; d.—). Baseball player. Kuzava was a pitcher in the major leagues from 1946 to 1957. A lefthander, he pitched for eight teams over the course of ten seasons, compiling a record of 49–44 with an earned run average of 4.05. The high point of his journeyman's career came in 1951–53 when he was a member of three straight New York Yankees world championship squads. Pitching in relief, he finished and saved the final and decisive games of two consecutive World Series (1951–52), a feat unmatched in the history of the sport. Kuzava was inducted into the National Polish-American Sports Hall of Fame in 2003.—*Neal Pease*

SOURCE: Leonard Koppett, *The Man in the Dugout: Baseball's Top Managers and How They Got That Way* (Philadelphia: Temple University Press, 2000).

Kwalik, Ted (b. McKees Rocks, Pennsylvania, April 15, 1947; d.—). Football Player. As a tight end on the Pennsylvania State University football team (1966–69), Kwalik set school records for passes caught (86), yardage (1,343), and touchdowns (10). He was the first two-time All American in Penn State history (1968 and 1969). In 1969, he led the Nittany Lions to an 11–0 record and an Orange Bowl victory. Selected as the seventh overall pick by the San Francisco 49ers of the National Football League, he was named to the Pro Bowl three straight seasons (1971–73), and played in three straight NFC West Championship games. In 1972, Kwalik scored nine touchdowns and averaged 18.8 yards per catch average. In 1974, he moved back to Pennsylvania and played for the Philadelphia Bell of the World Football League. When the league folded in 1975, Kwalik signed on with the Oakland Raiders. He played his last three seasons with the Raiders, winning the Super Bowl in 1977 against the Minnesota Vikings. Following his athletic career, he became president and CEO of ProTech Voltage Systems, Inc., a distributor and manufacturer of power conditioning programs. He was elected to the College Football Hall of Fame in 1989 and the National Polish-American Sports Hall of Fame in 2005.—*Patricia Finnegan*

SOURCE: National Polish-American Sports Hall of Fame web site.

Kwasny, Melissa (b. La Porte, Indiana, 1954; d.—). Poet, author, educator. Hearing her high school freshman English teacher read aloud from the *Canterbury Tales* inspired Kwasny to compose her first poems. In 1977 she earned her baccalaureate in English with High Honors at the University of Montana. Although she then moved to San Francisco, she continued to spend time in Montana when possible. In 1986, Kwasny began a decade of teaching through the California Poets in the Schools Program. She was awarded a residency at the Headland Center for the Arts (1987), and in 1990 published her first novel, *Modern Daughters and the Outlaw West*. It realistically, yet lyrically depicts a community of lesbian women around a small mining town in Montana. Kwasny's second novel, *Trees Call for What They Need* (1994), is a fictionalized version of her maternal grandmother's life. It follows the interconnected lives of women friends in an ecologically deteriorating area of Northern Indiana over many decades. By the mid–1990s, Kwasny moved back to Helena, Montana. In 1995 she received a grant from the Money for Women/Barbara Deming Memorial Fund. Returning to the University of Montana for graduate studies, she was awarded the University's Bertha Morton Graduate Fellowship (1996) and an Academy of American Poets Prize (1997). In 1999 she earned her MFA in Poetry and MA in Literature. Kwasny continued to teach and found additional ways of nurturing others' artistic development. She was an instructor and/or visiting writer at the University of Montana (1997, 1998, 2003, 2005); Carroll College (2000–06); Lesley University (2001–); University of Wyoming (2004); and Eastern Washington University (2006). She served as a visiting writer through the Montana Arts Council, the Myrna Loy Arts Plus program, the Missoula Writing Collaborative, and the Helena School District. She coordinated the Montana Writers Read series, Holter Museum of the Arts, Helena (1997–2000); co-founded and ran the Helena Festival of the Book (2001–); and helped select applicants to the Montana Artists Refuge (2004–). After publishing her two novels, she shifted the focus of her writing to poetry and literary criticism, publishing poems in literary magazines such as *Ploughshares, Many Mountains Moving, Feminist Studies,* and *Calyx*. As of early 2009, she had published three books of poetry: *The Archival Birds* (2000) expresses her grief over the growing extinction of species; *Thistle* (2006), winner of the 2005 Lost Horse Press Idaho Prize and *Foreward Magazine's* 2007 Silver Award, meditates on plants in her beloved Montana landscape; *Reading Novalis in Montana* (2008) brings Kwasny's love for such poets as Novalis, HD, and Emily Dickinson into her engagement with that landscape. She also edited a book of criticism, *Towards the Open Field: Poets on the Art of Poetry, 1800–1950* (2004). She was awarded artistic residencies at Norcroft (2003), Hedgebrook (2006), the Virginia Center for the Creative Arts (Wachtmeister Fellowship, 2006), and the Vermont Studio Center (Full Fellowship and National Endowment for the Arts stipend, 2007). She won the Poetry Society of America's Robert H. Winner Memorial Award (2004) and *Cutthroat Magazine's* Joy Harjo Award (2008). Brett Ortler and Maya Zeller identify Kwasny as part of "the great tradition of [women] poets in dialogue with the natural world."—*Mary Krane Derr*

SOURCES: Casey Charles, "Out & About: Interview With Poet Melissa Kwasny," *Out Words*, July 2007; Brett Ortler and Maya Zeller, "A Conversation With Melissa Kwasny, September 29, 2006," *Willow Springs*, No. 54; Caroline Patterson, ed., *Montana Women Writers: A Geography of the Heart* (Helena, MT: Far Country Press, 2006).

Kwiecien, Mariusz (b. Kraków, Poland, November 4, 1972; d.—). Opera singer. Kwiecien studied at the Warsaw Academy of Music and was later a student of the Metropolitan Opera's Lindemann Young Artist Development Program. After debuting at the Kraków Opera in 1993 he rapidly became an internationally recognized baritone known for his handsome voice, incisive musicianship, and captivating stage presence. He performed with the foremost opera companies and symphony orchestras in Europe, North America, and Asia including engagements with the Metropolitan Opera, the Tanglewood Festival, the Boston Symphony Orchestra, and at Carnegie Hall, Hamburg State Opera, Vienna State Opera, Arena di Verona, Bilbao Opera House, Houston Grand Opera, San Francisco Opera, Santa Fe Opera, Seattle Opera, Rotterdam Philharmonic, Warsaw Opera, and the Veroza Japan Company. Among his prestigious awards in several international vocal competitions are First Prize in the 1994 Duszniki-Zdroj International Competition (Poland), the Vienna State Opera and Hamburg State Opera prizes in the 1996 Hans Gabor/Belvedere Competition in Austria, and the Mozart Interpretation Prize and the Audience Choice Award at the 1998 Francisco Vinas Competition in Barcelona. He was selected to represent his native Poland in the 1999 Singer of the World Competition in Cardiff, Wales. He opened the Metropolitan Opera's 2007-08 season with performances of Enrico in a new production of *Lucia di Lammermoor.*—*Włodek Lopaczynski*

SOURCES: Georgia Rowe, "Kwiecien exudes *Don Giovanni," The Contra Costa Times*, May 31, 2007; Craig Smith, "Don Giovanni in Excelsis at Santa Fe," *The New Mexican*, July 5, 2004; Allan Kozinn, "Hints of Youthful Charm and a Dash of the Sublime," *New York Times*, February 5, 2005; Eric Meyers, "Mostly Mariusz," *Opera News*, January 2006, Vol. 70, no. 7; Steven Winn, "Kwiecien's Marcello stirs pulse of Opera's *Bohème," San Francisco Chronicle*, January 8, 2004.

Kwolek, Stephanie Louise (b. New Kensington, Pennsylvania, July 31, 1923; d.—). Chemist. After graduating with a B.S. in sci-

ence from Margaret Morrison College, the women's college of Carnegie Mellon University, in 1946 she accepted a position at DuPont in Buffalo, NY, involving research on condensation polymers designed to develop synthetic fibers for commercial use in tires. In 1950 she transferred her research to Dupont's newly opened Pioneering Research Laboratory in Wilmington, Delaware. In 1965 she discovered a new branch of synthetics, liquid crystalline polymers, which led to the development of exceptionally strong synthetic fibers. Her most famous discovery was poly-paraphenylene terephtalamide, better known as Kevlar, the substance used in bullet-proof protection for police departments and the armed forces. Among its more than 200 other commercial applications are use in airplanes, boats, brake pads, cables, camping gear, fiberoptic cables, ropes, skis, tennis racquets, racing sails, radial tires, safety helmets, spacecraft, and suspension bridge cables. Her discoveries have led to an entirely new field of study, polymer chemistry. When she retired in 1986 she held 28 patents. Among some twenty honors she has received are the National Medal of Technology (1996), the Perkin Medal (1997), the Lemelson-MIT Lifetime Achievement Award (1999), and induction into the National Inventors Hall of Fame (1995).—*James S. Pula*

SOURCES: Robert R. Selle, "Stephanie Kwolek: The Woman Who Created Kevlar," *World and I*, Vol. 19, no. 3 (March 2004), 44; "Stephanie Kwolek," *Biography Resource Center* (Farmington Hills, MI: Gale 2009).

Labor Movement *see* **Organized Labor, Polish Americans in.**

Łabuński, Feliks Roderyk (b. Ksawerynów, Poland, December 27, 1892; d. Cincinnati, Ohio, April 28, 1979). Composer, pianist, music critic. The son of Stanisław, a civil engineer and singer, and Lydia (née Rogowski), a pianist, he spent his childhood in St. Petersburg where he began playing piano four hands with his younger brother, Wiktor. His first piano teacher was Roch Hill, a Polish pianist of English descent, but Łabuński preferred improvisation and composition to practicing. In 1911–14 he studied architecture at St. Petersburg Polytechnic Institute. During World War I he served in the Engineering Corps of the Russian army. Only after returning to Poland in 1922 did he begin the serious study of music with theoretical studies under Lucjan Marczewski in Zakopane and harmony with Witold Maliszewski at the Warsaw Conservatory. In 1924, Łabuński moved to Paris where he studied with Nadia Boulanger and Paul Dukas at L'École Normale de Musique, graduating in 1930. In 1927, along with Piotr Perkowski, Stanisław Wiechowicz, and

Stanisław Czapski, he founded the Association of Young Polish Composers in Paris. A year later, he met the Polish pianist-composer-statesman **Ignacy Jan Paderewski** who became his patron, supporting him financially. After a two-year position as director of music with Polish Radio (1934–36), he emigrated to the U.S., becoming an American citizen in 1941. Between 1938 and 1941 he taught at a number of American and Canadian colleges including New York University, Columbia University, Brooklyn College, Vassar College, Laval University, the University of Kansas, the University of California, Marymount College, and the Curtis Institute of Music. He also gave lectures on the CBS and NBC radio networks and published music criticism in *Musical America, Modern Music,* the *Musical Courier,* and other periodicals. Between 1945 and 1964 he served as professor of composition and orchestration at the Cincinnati College Conservatory of Music. He continued as piano professor and artist-in-residence until 1971. Łabuński's music gained international recognition from the time of the Parisian premiere of his *Triptych Champétre,* a three-movement suite for orchestra, in 1932. From 1941 to 1944 he served as one of the directors of the board of the American section of the International Society of Contemporary Music (ISCM). His *Suite for String Orchestra* including *krakowiak* rhythms was performed frequently during those years. Among his many awards was an honorary doctorate from the Chicago Musical College (1951) and the **Alfred Jurzykowski Foundation** Award (1969).

Fluent in five languages, Łabuński expressed his attachment to Polish culture by the use of folk dance rhythms and melodies (*krakowiak, oberek, mazurka*) and Polish poetry in his cantatas (Kochanowski in *Kantata Polska* in 1932, and Wierzynski in *Ptaki* in 1934). His French training with Nadia Boulanger is evident in the clarity of his neoclassical forms, the logic of his colorful harmonies and the attractive, clear-cut instrumentation. Without interest in experiments, he wanted his music to be expressive and communicate with his listeners. His harmonies were not dissonant, but essentially diatonic. As he said, he believed in "well-defined melody, symmetrical, well-balanced form and economy of means in achieving ultimate results." He wrote a ballet (*God's Man*, 1937), thirteen works for orchestra, mostly suites, about ten vocal instrumental compositions and numerous chamber music and piano pieces.—*Maja Trochimczyk*

SOURCE: James Wierzbicki, "Traditional Values in a Century of Flux: The Music of Feliks Łabuński (1892–1979)," *Polish Music Journal,* Vol. 4, no. 1 (2001).

Lagodzinska, Adele (b. Chicago, Illinois, December 12, 1895; d. Chicago, Illinois, March 20, 1990). Polonia activist. The daughter of respected local Polish community activists, Lagodzinska joined the **Polish Women's Alliance** in 1919 and was elected its national vice president in 1939. She was elected the PWA's fifth president, succeeding **Honorata Wołowska**, in 1947. She went on to serve in that office until her retirement in 1971. Later she was named an honorary president of the PWA. Lagodzinska's 24-year presidency was marked by a notable increase in insured members, growing financial strength, and a focus on reaching out successfully to younger people. Throughout her years as a national officer in the Polish Women's Alliance, Lagodzinska was also a national leader in the **Polish American Council** (Rada Polonii Amerykanskiej), serving for more than twenty years as its secretary general. At the same time, she was also a national vice president of the **Polish American Congress**. Thus she served for more than twenty years as the secretary general of the Polish American Council under the leadership of **Francis X. Swietlik**. At the same time, Lagodzinska was a national vice president of the PAC and worked effectively with both **Charles Rozmarek** and **Aloysius Mazewski**, presidents of the Congress during those years. Beginning in August 1956, she made a number of visits to Poland with the aim of seeing for herself the nature of the country's humanitarian needs and the manner by which Polonia's assistance might be affected following the resumption of contacts between the Polish American Council and the Polish communist regime headed by Władysław Gomulka. Through her efforts, the Polish Women's Alliance and the organizations of **Polonia** extended its aid to a number of hospitals, orphanages and schools in Poland, including the Catholic University in Lublin (Katolicki Uniwersytet Lubelski, KUL) and the School for the Blind in Laski near Warsaw. For many years she was a strong supporter of the **Polish American Historical Association** and served on its Board of Directors. In addition she served as the editor of the English-language section of the official publication of the PWA, *Głos Polek* (The Voice of Polish Women). Following her retirement as PWA president, she was awarded the medal of Polonia Restituta from the Polish government-in-exile headquartered in London. A third generation American of Polish heritage and a person who only mastered the Polish language as an adult, Lagodzinska was a powerful and dedicated Polonia activist on behalf of her ancestral homeland.—*Donald E. Pienkos*

SOURCE: Donald E. Pienkos and Angela Pienkos, *"In the Ideals of Women is the Strength of a Nation": A History of the Polish Women's Alliance of America* (Boulder, CO: East European Monographs, 2003).

Landis, Carole (Francis Lillian Ridste; b. Fairchild, Wisconsin, January 2, 1919; d. Los Angeles, California, July 4, 1948). Actress, model. The daughter of a Polish mother and Norwegian father, the family moved to San Bernardino, CA, in 1922. Landis had a fairly normal childhood but disliked high school so much that she decided to drop out and elope, believing that married women did not need to attend school. Thus, on January 14, 1934, although she was underage, she eloped with Irving Wheeler. In 1935 she ran away from home to San Francisco, hoping to create a career in music for herself. At that time San Francisco was the center of music in California. With her pleasing voice and good looks, Landis was considered one of the most beautiful women in the world in the 1930s and 1940s. She sang in nightclubs until she became so popular that she felt she could go to Hollywood and become what she really wanted to be: a movie star. Upon arriving in Hollywood she caught the eye of director Busby Berkeley, who arranged for her to be an uncredited contract player at Warner Bros. Studios from 1937 until around 1939, when she signed with Republic Pictures and had her first feature roles, generally in B-Westerns. In November 1940 she divorced Wheeler and in July of that year married Willis Hunt, a minor actor in films. The same year she "got noticed" by the public when she was "lent" to Hal Roach Studios and starred in *One Million B.C.* The following year she began working for Twentieth Century–Fox Studios. In 1942, Landis and her friends, Martha Raye, Kay Francis, and Mitzi Mayfair, did a tour of England and Africa under the sponsorship of the War Department. These four left for Europe prior to the first U.S.O. tour and were a success wherever they played. Upon returning to Hollywood, Landis wrote an autobiographical description of this tour which was also filmed by her studio, Twentieth Century–Fox. Both the book and the film were entitled *Four Jills in a Jeep*. During this tour Landis, who had in the meantime divorced Willis Hunt, met and married Tommy Wallace, an American soldier. In 1944 Carole went on another tour with Jack Benny's troupe to the Pacific theater of war. It is said that Landis entertained more soldiers and traveled more miles to do this than any other Hollywood star.

In 1946 she married her final husband, Broadway producer, W. Horace Schmidlapp. At the same time she began working in films in England and became involved in an affair

Carole Landis, actress (*OLS*).

with married actor Rex Harrison. Harrison refused to divorce his wife, and on July 4, 1948, Landis committed suicide, taking an overdose of barbiturates in Hollywood. Her funeral was attended by some of the thousands whose lives she had touched during the war.—*Scott Sheidelower*

SOURCES: E. J. Fleming, *Carole Landis: A Tragic Life in Hollywood* (Jefferson, NC: McFarland, 2005); Eric Gans, *Carole Landis: A Most Beautiful Girl* (Jackson, MS: University Press of Mississippi, 2008); Carole Landis, *Four Jills in a Jeep* (New York: Random House, 1944).

Landowska, Wanda (b. Warsaw, Poland, July 5, 1879; d. Lakeville, Connecticut, August 15, 1959). Musician, historian. Wanda Landowska single-handedly was responsible for the revival of harpsichord music. Born in Russian-occupied Poland, her parents were educated and well-to-do. Her father was a lawyer, and her mother was the first person to translate the works of Mark Twain into Polish. Although ethnic Jews, her parents and grandparents had converted to Christianity. Young Wanda was a musical prodigy who attended the Warsaw Conservatory of Music and at age seventeen went to Berlin for further study where she won several piano competitions. There, she developed an interest in seventeenth and eighteenth century music and met Polish folklorist Henryk Lew. They moved to Paris in 1900 and married. Landowska taught piano in the French capital where she met many of the finest French musicians. Her research into vintage music and instruments led her to the harpsichord. Many compositions had been written for it, but it was supplanted by the piano in the late 1700s. Landowska wanted to perform the old music on the instrument for which it was written, so she began buying old harpsichords, had new ones made, and read old manuscripts that explained the keyboard techniques of masters such as Bach and Couperin. In 1903 she gave her first harpsichord performance, soon becoming very popular while performing in Europe and America. Known for her exquisite dress and stage sets, as well as her superb musical skills, in 1925 she founded the School for Ancient Music in a Paris suburb which became a center for the performance of of old music. She also taught music in Berlin, Basel, and the Sorbonne in Paris. When the Nazis invaded France in 1940 she fled to America where she re-established her career by teaching, recording and performing. Audiences in the U.S. embraced her. She continued her work until shortly before her death in 1959 at age 80. Her legacy is that of a musical historian who introduced the idea of the performance of music as it was originally intended to be played.—*Martin S. Nowak*

SOURCES: Denise Restont, ed., *Landowska on Music* (New York: Stein and Day, 1964); Jan Holcman, "Wanda Landowska (1879–1959)," *The Polish Review*, Vol. 4, no. 3 (1959), 3–6; Bernard Gavoty, *Wanda Landowska* (Geneva: Rene Kister, 1956).

Lange, Oskar Ryszard (b. Tomaszów Mazowiecki, Poland, July 27, 1904; d. London, England, October 2, 1965). Economist, Polonia activist. Despite his poor health as a child, Lange received a thorough education. In secondary school he became secretary of the local branch of the Union of Polish Socialist Youth, following which he studied economics and law in Poznań and in Kraków. He received his LLM (1928), Ph.D. in economics (1928), and habilitation (1930) from the Jagiellonian University. He remained active in the socialist movement, joining the Union of Independent Socialist Youth and, in 1927, the Polish Socialist Party (Polska Partia Socjalystyczna). In 1934 his academic career brought him to the United States where he was a Rockefeller Fellow at Harvard and the University of California–Berkeley. In 1937 he returned to Berkeley, lectured also at Stanford, and in 1938 moved to the University of Chicago. In 1942–43 he was a visiting professor at Columbia University. In his scholarly and popular publications Lange promoted the Marxist economic model of economy, remaining in touch with the Polish socialist movement and making contacts with the Polish American left, including **Leo Krzycki** and **Bolesław Gebert**. According to some researchers, Gebert was instrumental in establishing Lange's position as the Soviet agent

"Friend." Lange's political views, presented in numerous speeches and publications in the American press, supported the Soviet line. He criticized the Polish government-in-exile in London for its hostile attitude toward the Soviet Union and condemned the mainstream Polish American organizations for encouraging such a position. In 1943 he supported the Soviet policy of refusing to recognize the London government-in-exile as the representative of the Polish nation, instead supporting the Stalin-controlled Union of Polish Patriots (Związek Patryjatów Polskich) and the Soviet vision for post-war Poland's boundaries. In 1944 Lange — on Stalin's invitation as a private American citizen (he was naturalized in 1943) though with tacit help of the Roosevelt administration — went to Moscow to discuss Poland's future. In 1945–46, after renouncing his American citizenship, Lange served as ambassador of the Warsaw government in Washington and in 1946–47 also represented Poland in the United Nations Security Council. After returning to Poland, Lange fully supported the Communist regime. He was a founding member of the Central Committee of the Polish United Worker's Party in 1948, a member of the Polish parliament beginning in 1946 and held other political positions as well. His academic carrier included a professorship at the Warsaw School of Economics (in 1949 renamed the Main School of Planning and Statistics) where he was rector in 1952–55, and membership in the Polish Academy of Science beginning in 1952. As one of the very few Poles traveling abroad during those times, Lange lectured in England and Sweden and was a consultant to the governments of India, Ceylon and Egypt. Beginning in 1956

Oskar Lange, economist and Polonia activist (*JPI*).

Lange directed the newly created Economic Council of the Polish government and chaired the political economy programs at the University of Warsaw. He made numerous trips abroad for both academic and political purposes, including a series of lectures at American universities in 1962.—*Joanna Wojdon*

SOURCES: Charles Sadler, "'Pro-Soviet Polish-Americans': Oskar Lange and Russia's Friends in the Polonia, 1941–1945," *The Polish Review*, Vol. 22, no. 4 (1977), 25–39; Robert Szymczak, "Oskar Lange, American Polonia, and the Polish-Soviet Dilemma During World War II: I. The Public Partisan As Private Emissary," *The Polish Review*, Vol. 40, no. 1 (1995), 3–27; Robert Szymczak, "Oskar Lange, American Polonia, and the Polish-Soviet Dilemma During World War II: II. Making a Case For a 'People's Poland,'" *The Polish Review*, Vol. 40, no. 2 (1995), 131–57.

Lansky, Meyer (Maier Suchowljansky; b. Grodno, Poland July 4, 1902; d. Miami Beach, Florida, January 15, 1983). Gangster. Born in Poland to Jewish parents, he migrated to the United States in 1911 and settled in New York City. At the age of 18, Lansky came under the tutelage of the famous gambler Arnold Rothstein. After Rothstein's murder in 1928, Lansky had to go elsewhere for guidance, so he fell in with Charles "Lucky" Luciano, whom he had met in school when Luciano tried unsuccessfully to shake him down for money. They became fast friends, and together they eventually forged a powerful crime empire, assassinating key Mafiosi until they stood at the top of the organization. Known as "The Little Man," Lansky held the purse strings of the Mob, being responsible for millions of dollars. Lansky's stature was such that when there was an important vote, other "dons" waited to see which way Lansky voted, and they would follow suit. With Benjamin "Bugsy" Siegel, he formed one of the most violent gangs in the East. If bootleggers paid his price, he would protect their shipments from government raids. If they did not, he hijacked their goods and sold them. The Mob could be hired for "hits," becoming the antecedent of Murder, Inc., which Lansky eventually ran. He was the brains that held the Luciano empire together, investing millions of Mob money in places like Havana, Saratoga, and other venues including Siegel's Flamingo Hotel in Las Vegas. During World War II, Lansky's mob went to work helping the government break up pro–Nazi rallies and allied with the Office of Naval Intelligence to uncover German infiltrators. He brokered a deal to get Luciano out of jail in return for his providing security at shipyards in New York. After the war, Lansky opened profitable casinos in Havana with a monopoly he personally negotiated with Cuban dictator Fulgencio Batista y Zaldivar for $3 million. Lansky was so powerful he was immune to assassination, often turning enemies over to federal authorities or "fingering" them for assassination by a "hit." The government tried to arrest him in the 1970s for tax evasion, just like Al Capone before him. By then, he had skimmed millions from Las Vegas casinos. He fled to Israel, claiming citizenship under the Law of Return which provided that anyone who had a Jewish mother could be a citizen. But Israel did not want him, and after a protracted legal battle he was deported in 1972. He was put on trial in Miami in 1973, but was acquitted on the tax evasion charges. Lansky was personally worth about $400 million when he died in 1983, but none of his money has ever been found.—*Cheryl A. Pula*

SOURCES: Dennis Eisenberg, *Meyer Lansky: Mogul of the Mob* (New York: Paddington Press, 1979); Robert Lacey, *Little Man: Meyer Lansky and the Gangster Life* (Boston: Little, Brown, 1991); Hank Messick, *Lansky* (New York: Berkley Publishing Company, 1971).

Lapiński, Tadeusz (b. Rawa Mazowiecka, Poland, June 20, 1928; d.—). Artist. During World War II, Lapiński actively participated in the *Szare Szeregi* (Gray Ranks) during the Warsaw Uprising in 1944 against Poland's Nazi oppressor. Following the war he was educated at the Warsaw Academy of Fine Art (1949–55), studying painting with Artur Nacht-Samborski and graphic arts with Józef Tom and Józef Pakulski, receiving a Master of Fine Arts degree in 1955. He initially visited the United States in 1963 at the invitation of Gustav von Groschwitz, director of the Fine Arts Department at the Carnegie Institute in Pittsburgh. After living for nearly twenty years in Porto Alegre, Brazil (1967–86), he migrated to the United States in 1968, becoming a U.S. citizen in 1973. In 1983 he opened the Lapinski Art Center-Museum on the Island of Kirk in Croatia to house his creations. A specialist in split-color lithography, he also engaged in painting and taught at the Pratt Graphic Center, New York (1963–64, 1968–69); the University of Brazil, Porto Alegre (1967–68); and the University of Maryland, College Park (beginning 1972). His works appeared in solo exhibitions in various locations in Austria, Brazil, China, Croatia, England, France, Germany, Italy, Mexico, Poland, Slovenia, the United States, and Yugoslavia, and in group exhibitions in these same nations along with Argentina, Belgium, Canada, Japan, Norway, Puerto Rico, Spain, Switzerland, and Taiwan. His many awards included: Prize, Biennale di Carrara, Italy (1957); Prize, Triennale of Color Graphics, Grenchen, Switzerland (1958, 1961); Biennale of Graphic Arts, Kraków, Poland (1960, 1962, 1970); UNESCO Prize for Graphic Art, Paris (1965); Museum of Art Prize, Porto Alegre, Brazil (1967); Gold Medal, Biennale of Graphic Art, Lausanne, Switzerland (1969); Guggenheim Foundation Fellowship, New York (1970); Medal of Honor, Audubon Artists, New York (1972); Silver Medal, Audubon Artists, New York (1973); Medal of Honor, Painters and Sculptors Association, New Jersey (1975); Grand Prize, Graphic Art Exhibition, Vienna, Austria (1977); Outstanding Achievement Award, University of Maryland at College Park (1982); International Print Competition Prize, Taipei, Taiwan (1983); Statue of Victory Prize, Italy (1985); International Graphic Arts Foundation Award, Greenwich, CT (1990); Students' Teaching Award, University of Maryland at College Park (1993); International Printmaking Award, National Library of France, Paris (2000); Gloria Artis, Polish Government, Warsaw (2008).—*Stanley L. Cuba*

SOURCES: Henry Cliffe, *Lithography: A Complete Handbook of Modern Techniques of Lithography* (New York: Watson-Guptill Publications, Inc., 1965); Fritz Eichenberg, *The Art of the Print: Masterpieces, History, Techniques* (New York: Harry N. Abrams, Inc., 1976); Fritz Eichenberg, *Lithography and Silkscreen: Art and Techniques* (New York: Harry N. Abrams, Inc., 1978); Szymon Bojko, *Z polskim rodowodem. Artysci polscy i amerykanscy polskiego pochodzenia w sztuce Stanow Zjednoczonych w latach 1900–1980* (Torun: Oficyna Wydawnicza Kucharski, Archwium Emigracji, 2007).

Laska, Walter J. (b. Beaver Falls, Pennsylvania, July 20, 1904; d. Pittsburgh, Pennsylvania, May 1984). Polonia activist. Laska took part in the **Polish Falcons** Alliance physical fitness activities as a youngster. A high school student at **Alliance College**, the **Polish National Alliance** school in Cambridge Springs, Pennsylvania, he later studied at Duquesne University where he earned a degree in law in 1931. That year he joined the Polish Falcons of America (PFA; after 1927 a fraternal insurance society) and in 1933 was elected its legal advisor. In 1934 he was elected to the office of treasurer. In 1952 Laska was elected president at the Falcons' twenty-fifth national convention in New Britain, Connecticut, succeeding **Teofil Starzyński**. He served in that office until 1980 when he declined to seek an eighth consecutive term. During President Laska's term in office, the PFA substantially expanded its life insurance program, with its assets rising from $2.3 million to $11 million. The number of insured members rose from 19,600 to 26,500. During his tenure, the PFA made successful efforts to reinvigorate the movement's youth and sports programs, modernized the fraternal's official publication, ***Sokół Polski*** (The Polish Falcon), and established a Falcons Museum at its national headquarters in Pittsburgh. On Laska's recommendation, the PFA ended the practice of admitting non-insured individuals as "social members" in 1956. While the Falcons became an increasingly "American" organization during Laska's years as president, it nevertheless continued to participate in the major **Polonia** organizations, including the Polish American Congress.—*Donald E. Pienkos*

SOURCE: Donald Pienkos, *One Hundred Years Young: A History of the Polish Falcons of America* (Boulder, CO: East European Monographs, 1987).

Lattimer Massacre. Polish, Lithuanian, and Slovak immigrants were increasingly among the unskilled employees hired by the American mining industry beginning in the 1880s. Work in the mines was dangerous, unstable, and low paying, resulting in labor protests. In 1894 organizers of the United Mine Workers of America arrived in Pennsylvania when union president John Mitchell began a campaign to introduce a closed shop. UMW organizer John Fahy went to the region to begin agitation among the Central and Eastern European workers. When the companies in Hazelton introduced new work rules in 1897, a strike followed that demonstrated community support from most of the clergy and the ethnic middle-class for the struggle for justice and better working conditions, as well as inter-ethnic solidarity among Slavic workers. The peaceful strike soon spread to the other counties and companies, eventually involving the entire region. In keeping with the traditions of protest they brought with them from Europe, the immigrant workers marched, paraded, and sang, while at the same time they made it a point in their slogans and through use of the American flag and other symbols that they believed themselves to be a loyal part of American society. On September 5, 1897, unarmed striking miners marched from Harwood to close down the Pardee Company's Lattimer Mine which was still being run by strikebreakers. Sheriff James Martin ordered deputy sheriffs to open fire, killing nineteen people and wounding as many as 39 others — 26 of the victims were Polish. Most of the strikers were shot in the back while trying to escape. Fearing community reaction, state authorities sent the Third Brigade of the Pennsylvania Militia to the region to assist the sheriff. Manifestations of grief and anger took the form of massive attendance at the victims' funerals, while ethnic newspapers labeled the actions "murder" and the perpetrators "beasts." Subsequent rallies condemned the sheriff while demanding that those responsible be placed on trial. Banker Emil Malinowski led local protests, while in Chicago **Piotr Kiołbassa** and **John Smulski** organized rallies in support of the miners, priests called parish meetings and the **Polish National Alliance** issued a strong protest statement. The Lattimer Affair united all of Polonia's political factions in protest and organizing assistance for the victims' families. Austrian Foreign Minister Agenor Gołuchowski and Prime Minister Kazimierz Badeni lodged protests with the American government since most of the victims were citizens of the Austro-Hungarian Empire. Nationwide, the Lattimer Massacre became the symbol of the brutal oppression of workers supported by the alliance between mine owners and state authorities. The tragic events of 1897 paved the way for the success of the United Mine Workers, which became more inclusive for non–English speaking workers and which, during the dramatic and victorious strike of 1902, won significant concessions for workers.— *Adam Walaszek*

SOURCES: Victor R. Greene, *The Slavic Community on Strike: Immigrant Labor in Pennsylvania Anthracite* (Notre Dame-London: University of Notre Dame Press, 1968); Edward Pinkowski, *Lattimer Massacre* (Philadelphia: Sunshine Press, 1950).

Laudyn, Stefania (Stefania Borowska; b. Rochaczów, Poland (now Belarus), January 2, 1872; d. Zakopane, Poland, February 28, 1942). Writer, Polonia activist. By the time Laudyn migrated to the United States in 1909, she had already made a name for herself as an activist for the Polish cause. Born in what is now Belarus, she was influenced as a young girl by veterans of the January Insurrection of 1863 as they returned with stories of their exile in Siberia. Her first husband, Kazimierz Laudyn, was one of those returning insurrectionists. With him she formed part of an active Polish community in Moscow, where she was a "free listener" at Moscow University. Her anonymous series of letters to a St. Petersburg newspaper pleading the Polish cause provoked considerable discussion. When they were gathered and published in booklet form in 1908, Russian censors seized and burned them. Her open letter to Leo Tolstoy on Polish issues prompted Tolstoy to a public response. In addition to contributing regularly to Moscow and Kraków newspapers, Laudyn wrote several plays and political tracts, and in 1907 founded Moscow's Polish Alliance of Women (Związek Kobiet Polskich). It was also in Moscow that Laudyn began an interest in Pan-Slavism that would continue throughout her life.

After her husband's death in 1908, which left her, in the words of a *Głos Polek* article, "free to choose [her] path in life, unfettered and secure," Laudyn struck up a correspondence with Adam Chrzanowski of Chicago, a law student and former foundry worker thirteen years her junior. She emigrated in 1909. This prompted some satirical articles in the

Polonia press. She and Chrzanowski were married in 1910, before which Chrzanowski legally changed his middle name to Laudyn. After her marriage, Laudyn sometimes published under the name Laudyn-Chrzanowska.

In 1910 Laudyn was named editor of *Głos Polek* (The Voice of Polish Women), the official organ of the **Polish Women's Alliance**. Under her editorship the paper expanded to a weekly reaching tens of thousands of readers, while covering a wide range of political, labor, and social issues, paying particular attention to women's rights and the international women's movement. It can be argued that through *Głos Polek* Polish immigrant and ethnic women were more familiar with feminist issues than were American women of their time.

Laudyn was also influential in various Polish and Polonian causes, including the Polish Alma Mater and Chicago-based Polish Society of Writers and Journalists (Towarzystwo Literatów i Dziennikarzy Polskich), of which she was a founding member. It was this activism that caused friction with the Polish Women's Alliance, which accused her of conflicted loyalties and elitism: "We don't know where and when Mrs. Laudyn completed her university studies," *Głos Polek* editorialized, "but we do know that the 12,000 Polish women organized by our Alliance have so much strength of spirit and love for the fatherland that these 'poorly educated' women have built an organization here the likes of which the 'so very enlightened' Mrs. Laudyn never imagined even in the old country." Laudyn left *Głos Polek* in 1912 but evidently was able to repair relations and returned to the paper in 1914, continuing to contribute articles throughout the 1920s. She divided her time between Chicago and Indiana Harbor, Indiana, where Adam Chrzanowski established a law practice. She also continued to write, publishing plays, political tracts, and a collection of short stories, *Galerja obrazów z krainy dolara* (A Gallery of Pictures from the Land of the Dollar, c. 1920), about immigrant life in the United States. But while on issues such as women's rights Laudyn was quite progressive, her reputation as a community leader and political activist was marred by her best-known work, *A World Problem: Jews—Poland—Humanity,* which was blatantly anti-Semitic. Originally published in Polish, it was then issued in a number of English editions by the **Polish National Alliance**.

Laudyn returned permanently to Poland in the mid–1920s, though she occasionally spent time in the United States and continued to contribute to New York's *Kuryer Narodowy* (National Courier). She also renewed her

work on pan–Slavic and women's issues, organizing the Society of Slavic Women (Towarzystwo Kobiet Słowiańskich) in 1929. With Adam Chrzanowski, Laudyn owned the elegant Bristol Hotel in Zakopane where, in 1942, while her husband was interned by the Nazis, Laudyn died. Despite her long work for the Polish Women's Alliance and her visible role in American Polonia, on her death *Głos Polek* could provide only the most perfunctory of information about her life and work. She is buried in Zakopane.—*Karen Majewski*

SOURCES: Karen Majewski, "Laudyn, Stefania (Laudyn-Chrzanowska)," in Rima Lunin Schultz and Adele Hast, eds., *Women Building Chicago, 1790–1990: A Biographical Dictionary* (Bloomington: Indiana University Press, 2001), 492–94; Karen Majewski, "Toward 'A Pedagogical Goal': Family, Nation, and Ethnicity in the Fiction of Polonia's First Women Writers," in Thomas S. Gladsky and Rita Holmes Gladsky, eds., *Something of My Very Own to Say: American Women Writers of Polish Descent* (Boulder: East European Monographs, Distributed by Columbia University Press, 1997), 54–66; Karen Majewski, *Traitors and True Poles: Narrating a Polish-American Identity, 1880–1939* (Athens: Ohio University Press, 2003).

Lechoń, Jan (Leszek Józef Serafinowicz; b. Warsaw, Poland, March 13, 1899; d. New York, New York, June 8, 1956). Poet. Lechoń received his education at Warsaw University (1916–18) where he published his first works and was a co-founder of Skamander, a group of experimental poets, in 1919. During the Russo-Polish War (1919–21) he was employed as a press officer for Józef Piłsudski, and following the conflict he was an active member of the Polish Writers' Union, served as secretary general of the PEN Club, and published two volumes of poetry, *Karmazynowy poemat* (Crimson Poem, 1920) and *Srebrne i czarne* (Silver and Black, 1924) that brought him an award from the Polish Society of Book Publishes (Polskie Towarzystwo Wydawców Książek) in 1925. He also edited the pro-sanacja satirical magazine *Cyrulik Warszawski* (The Warsaw Barber; 1926–29). In 1930 he moved to Paris and the following year was named cultural attaché at the Polish embassy there, a position he continued to hold when the Germans invaded Poland in 1939. With the fall of France in 1940, he escaped through Portugal to Brazil and then moved to New York where he was a member of the group of intellectuals who formed the **Polish Institute of Arts and Sciences** in 1942 and became vice president of its Polish literary history section. Following his arrival in New York he co-edited *Tygodniowy Przegląd Literacki Koła Pisarzy z Polski* (A Weekly Literary Review of the Circle of the Polish Writers) and between 1943 and 1947 edited *Tygodnik Polski* (Polish Weekly) sponsored by the Polish government-

Jan Lechoń, poet (*JPI*).

in-exile in London. During this time Lechoń worked for Radio Free Europe and the Voice of America, published collections of his poems in *Lutnia po Bekwarku* (Bekwark's Lute) and *Aria z kurantem* (An Aria with Chimes, 1945), and published sketches of American culture in *Aut Caesar aut nihil* (Either Caesar or Nothing, 1955) that were later translated into English as *American Transformations* (1959). In 1952 he received a literary award from the London-based Association of the Polish Writers in Exile (Związek Pisarzy Polskich na Obczyźnie). He became a U.S. citizen in 1956, but remained deeply involved in Polish émigré life and a critic of the Communist regime in Warsaw. He committed suicide in 1956, presumably over depression caused by the fate of his homeland under Communist rule.—*Joanna Wojdon*

SOURCES: Beata Dorosz, "New York Secrets of The Life and Death of Jan Lechoń," *The Polish Review*, Vol. 49, no. 2 (2004), 767–90; Charles Kraszewski, ed., *Evening on the Hudson: An Anthology of Jan Lechoń's American Writings* (New York: Polish Institute of Arts & Sciences, 2005); Wanda Łukszo-Nowakowska, *Jan Lechoń: Zarys życia i twórczości* (Warsaw: Tow. Literackie im. Adama Mickiewicza, 1996).

Lednicki, Wacław (b. Moscow, Russia, April 28, 1891; d. Oakland, California, October 29, 1967). Literary historian. The son of a prominent Polish lawyer, Lednicki received his secondary education in the newly founded Medvednikov Gymnasium, attended the University of Moscow, from which he received a diploma of the "first degree," signifying preparation for teaching at a university. He majored in French literature at Moscow University, and also pursued it in his graduate studies in Poland. Lednicki spent some time in the Polish military and diplomatic service. In 1922 he was awarded a doctorate degree from the Jagiellonian University in Kraków, and in 1923 had his first book published, a monograph on Alfred de Vigny, a French author.

His scholarly interests were then redirected in his postdoctoral studies of the history of Russian literature at the Stefan Batory University in Wilno, Poland, in 1926. That same year he was appointed Charge de Cours in Slavic languages and literatures at the University of Brussels. In 1928, Lednicki was appointed associate professor at the Jagiellonian University and later professor until the closing of the University under the German occupation of Poland. Thanks to Belgian intervention, he was able to escape the German occupation and migrate to the United States where he lectured on Slavic literatures at Harvard (1940–44) and at the Ecole Libre des Hautes Etudes in New York (1941–44). In 1944 he accepted an appointment as visiting professor at the University of California–Berkeley where he was later tenured and promoted to full professor in 1945. His career at Berkeley is considered outstanding. He served as department chair for seven years, guiding the department through a period of rapid growth, and trained a new generation of experts and scholars in Slavic studies. A dedicated and inspiring teacher, a fascinating lecturer, an eloquent conversationalist, he supervised students in their graduate pursuits and placed Berkeley on the map as a prominent center in the field of Slavic literature. He was also a very productive scholar, in many respects setting the standard for Slavic studies in the United States and Europe. After his retirement from Berkeley in 1958 as professor emeritus, he continued to write, his primary interest being Romanticism, and especially comparative studies on Pushkin and Mickiewicz. Many of his scholarly works were left in manuscript form; nevertheless, Lednicki's literary legacy is impressive. It consists of some two hundred publications, books, pamphlets, essays, articles, and edited work written in Polish, English,

Wacław Lednicki, literary historian (*JPI*).

Russian, and French. His secondary interests in the history and interpretation of French and Russian literatures, Polish-Russian cultural relations, Eastern Europe and the Near East, and Poland and the West are also well represented in the scholarly works. In 1960, an annual lecture series was established at Berkeley in his honor. Among his recognitions were honorary doctorates from the University of Brussels (1948) and the University of California–Berkeley (1963), the Belgian Order of Leopold I, and Poland's Order of Polonia Restituta. A member of the Polish Academy, an honorary professor at the University of Brussels, and member of numerous European and American scholarly organizations, he was a founding member of the **Polish Institute of Arts and Sciences** in America which offers a prize in literature in his honor.—*Maria Swiecicka-Ziemianek*

SOURCES: Zbigniew Folejewski, "In Memoriam: Wacław Lednicki," *The Polish Review*, Vol. 13 no. 1 (1968), 95–97; obituary, *New York Times*, October 31, 1967.

Legion Młodych Polek *see* **Legion of Young Polish Women.**

Legion of Young Polish Women (Legion Młodych Polek). In response to the needs of the people of Poland at the start of the Second World War, Helen Lenard Pięklo and seven other Polish American women founded the Legion of Young Polish Women on September 2, 1939. These visionary women, and those whom they inspired to follow their lead, were all volunteers. Sending food and clothing to Polish prisoners-of-war and refugees during World War II required not only fundraising skills but also the ability to research what was needed and where food and clothing supplies should be sent. The end of the war and the domination of Poland by a communist regime in the postwar years created a continuing need for aid. The League provided assistance to Polish veterans in Italy, the Polish Mission in Argentina, the Polish Library in Paris, and the Sikorski Institute in London. Within Poland, the Legion continued a tradition of assistance that included the Laski Institute for the Blind, the Catholic University of Lublin, and various senior citizen and children's homes. The Legion supported the Solidarity movement by providing financial aid for the purchase of food, clothing, and medicine. Its "Medical Supplies to Poland Project" provided over $88,000 in assistance to smaller Polish hospitals and clinics that were being bypassed by larger institutional donors from aboard. The Legion contributed over $1.5 million to charitable and cultural causes in the United States, Poland, and elsewhere in the world where there was a need. Over the years, the main recipients of the Legion's assistance have been hospitals, educational, and related institutions in the United States and Poland. In 1961, the Legion established the Chair of Polish Language and Literature at the University of Chicago, which it continues to fund through the Maria Kuncewicz Endowment Fund. In addition, the Legion supported the Polish Studies Program at Loyola University in Chicago, the **Polish Museum of America**, the Pope John Paul II Foundation, the Polish Youth Associations of Illinois, the Ronald McDonald House at Comer Children's Hospital, the Arthritis Foundation, the Home Army/Armia Krajowa Foundation, and the **Polish American Association** (formerly the Polish American Welfare Association). Major donations have been made to scholarship funds such as the Knights of Dąbrowski, to museums such as the Chicago Art Institute and the Milwaukee Art Museum, to the Polish American Immigration and Relief Committee, the **Polish American Congress**'s charitable endeavors, and the Copernicus Foundation. Additionally, the Legion made contributions to the American Cancer Society, Project Hope, the Leukemia Society of America, the Statue of Liberty–Ellis Island Foundation, WTTW Channel 11 (PBS) Broadcasting, Tsunami and Hurricane Relief efforts, Illinois Military Families Relief, the Greek Fire Relief Fund, and various Chicago community funds. The Legion was a major financial supporter for the production of the documentary "In the Name of Our Mothers," honoring Irena Sendler, Israel's 2007 nominee for the Nobel Peace Prize. The Legion of Young Polish Women has only

The Legion of Young Polish Women raised funds to send this ambulance to the Polish Army in England in 1940 (*OLS*).

one major fundraiser, the White and Red Ball. The first Ball was held on February 6, 1940, to benefit Polish relief, and an historic dimension was added to the Ball in 1945 by incorporating the Debutante Cotillion, the first "en masse" presentation ever held in the United States. Providing uninterrupted philanthropy since its inception, this black tie charitable gala, the social event of Chicago Polonia, has always been held at the Hilton Chicago, formerly the Stevens Hotel. Legion members share a common bond through a love of Polish culture and traditions and volunteerism. Every year, members and past debutantes learn to dance the *Polonaise* and the *Biały Mazur* which are showcased at the White and Red Ball. In addition, the Legion members annually organize, according to Polish tradition, a St. John's Festival to celebrate the shortest night of the year.—*Geraldine Coleman*

SOURCES: Geraldine Balut Coleman, ed., *White & Red Ball 2010* (Elgin, IL: Haag Press, Inc., 2010); Shirley L. Dudzinski and Kathy Wojdyla, eds., *Legion of Young Polish Women, 70th Anniversary* (Elgin, IL: Haag Press, Inc., 2009).

Lehmanowsky, Jan J. (b. Warsaw, Poland, 1733; d. Sellersburg, Illinois, January 1858). Educator, clergy. Descended from Jewish ancestors, Lehmanowsky studied at the University of Warsaw and eventually joined the Evangelical Lutheran Church. After serving in the armies of Napoleon, where he claimed to have achieved the rank of colonel, he fled Europe, arriving in Philadelphia in early 1816 where he earned a living teaching languages and music. After a brief foray at farming near Reading, Pennsylvania, he returned to Philadelphia, adding fencing and military science to his teaching repertoire. Around 1825 he moved to Washington, D.C., where he obtained a government position and published his *History of Napoleon, Emperor of the French, King of Italy &c. &c. &c.* (1832). In 1833 he moved west, residing briefly in Ohio before moving on to Indiana where he was licensed by the Evangelical Lutheran Synod of the West at Jeffersonville, KY, in 1834. He was ordained as a Lutheran minister the following year. In 1836 he became an agent for the Immigrants Friend Society charged with organizing schools for the immigrant communities. In the same year he established a school in Cincinnati with lessons being taught in both English and German, and soon after founded a similar school in New Orleans. Various authors have credited him with founding several other schools. In 1839 he was one of two in-dividuals charged with planning a Lutheran theological seminary to be established in the Midwest, with Lehmanowsky being elected treasurer for the venture. Eventually, with the strong recommendation of Lehmanowsky, the group established contact with the English Evangelical Synod of Ohio, but the Lutherans decided to pursue formation of their own seminary in Illinois. Active in the Synod in both educational and theological issues, Lehmanowsky was one of the strongest promoters of the establishment of Hillsboro College (officially the "Literary and Theological Institute of the Far West") in Illinois and a member of its board of trustees. Eventually moved to Springfield, in 1852 it became Illinois State University.—*James S. Pula*

SOURCES: W. A. Sadtler, ed., *Under Two Captains* (Philadelphia: W. A. Sadtler, 1903; Lehmanowsky's autobiography); Ladislas John Siekaniec, *The Polish Contribution to Early American Education, 1608–1865* (San Francisco: R & E Research Associates, 1976).

Łempicka, Tamara de (Maria Górska; b. Warsaw, Poland, May 10, 1898; d. Cuemayaca, Mexico, March 18, 1980). Painter. Educated at the Académie del la Grande Chaumière in Paris, Łempicka's first major show was in Milan in 1925 featuring some 28 new works that she completed in only six months. She quickly became a noted portrait painter for the fashionable *haute bourgeoisie* and aristocracy, painting European duchesses, grand dukes, and socialites. During the 1920s Łempicka immersed herself in the Parisian Bohemian community where she met such luminaries as Pablo Picasso, Jean Cocteau, and André Gide. She won her first major award in 1927, a first prize at the Exposition Internationale de Beaux Arts in Bordeaux for her portrait of her daughter, *Kizette on the Balcony*. In 1929, she painted her iconic work *Auto-Portrait* for the cover of the German fashion magazine *Die Dame*. In the same year she traveled for the first time to the U.S. to paint a commissioned portrait for Rufus Bush and to arrange a show of her work at the Carnegie Institute in Pittsburgh. Despite the Depression, during the early 1930s she painted King Alfonso XIII of Spain and Queen Elizabeth of Greece and in 1933 she traveled to Chicago to work with Georgia O'Keeffe, Santiago Martinez Delgadoi, and Willem de Kooning. In the same year she married her long-time benefactor and lover, Baron Kuffner, abandoning the Bohemian lifestyle for an aristocratic title and a place among the social elite. Sensing the coming war in Europe, Łempicka convinced her husband to sell his estates in Eastern Europe and move his money to Switzerland. In 1939, she moved to the U.S. to arrange a show of her work in New York, after which she and the Baron settled in Beverly Hills, CA. In the succeeding years she did little new work, choosing instead to remake some of her earlier creations in a new style. For example, the crisp and direct *Amethyste* (1946) became the pink and fuzzy *Girl with Guitar* (1963). After the Baron's death in 1962, she moved to Houston, Texas, to be with her daughter and her family. In her latter years she complained that the paints and other artists' materials were inferior to the "old days" and that the people in the 1970s lacked the special qualities and "breeding" that inspired her art. In 1978 she moved to Cuernavaca, Mexico, to live among an aging international set and some of the younger aristocrats.—*Adam A. Zych*

Sources: Alian Blondel and Ingried Brugger, *Tamara de Lempicka: Art Deco Icon* (London: Royal Academy of Arts, 2004); Laura P. Claridge, *Tamara Lempicka: A Life of Deco and Decadence* (New York: C. Potter, 1999); Mori Gioia, *Tamara Lempicka* (Milano: Skira, 2006); Gilles Néret, *Tamara de Lempicka 1898–1980* (London: Taschen, 2000); Stefanie Penck, *Tamara De Lempicka* (London: Prestel, 2004); Kizette De Lempicka-Foxhall and Charles Phillips, *Passion by Design: The Art and Times of Tamara de Lempicka* (New York: Abbeville Press, 1987).

Lenard, Casimir "Cas" (b. Chicago, Illinois, March 10, 1918; d. Washington, D.C., December 7, 2007). Polonia activist. At the age of ten, Lenard was sent to Poland for eight years of study in the Jesuit school in Chyrów. Upon his return to the U.S. he studied at Northwestern University, earning his baccalaureate degree in Economic history. With the outbreak of World War II in Europe in 1939 he entered the Illinois National Guard. In 1941 he was commissioned as a second lieutenant and from 1942 to 1945 he was in combat as a member of the famed 1st Infantry Division ("The Big Red One"), taking part in its campaigns in North Africa, Sicily, and the invasion of Normandy. He then served as a press officer in the Supreme Headquarters of the Allied Expeditionary Forces in Europe. After his discharge in 1945 he married Casimira (**Myra Lenard**) and worked in his family's famed Chicago restaurant, "Lenard's Little Poland." Volunteering for military duty during the Korean War, Lenard served for five years in Germany (1952–57), then on the general staff of the army at the Pentagon after 1962. In 1967 he assumed a command position in Vietnam. From 1968 to 1970, Colonel Lenard worked as a military intelligence analyst at the U.S. Army Institute of Land Combat in Langley, Virginia. In 1970 he retired from military duty after thirty years of distinguished service in three wars. That same year he was appointed the first executive director of the **Polish American Congress**, a post he held until 1974. In subsequent years

he was active in Washington, D.C., in various service and lobbying capacities. One involved his championing a constitutional amendment to protect the American flag from desecration. He was also active in supporting the work of his wife, Myra, who in 1982 was appointed director of the Polish American Congress office in Washington, D.C. He continued to serve in the Washington office of the PAC after his wife's death on May 1, 2000. Lenard was decorated on a host of occasions for his military service and for his devotion to Poland's freedom.—*Donald E. Pienkos*

Source: *Polish American Congress, 1944–1994: Half a Century of Service to Poland and Polonia* (Chicago: Polish American Congress, 1994).

Lenard, Casimira S. "Myra" (b. Poland, May 23, 1924; d. McLean, Virginia, May 1, 2000). Polonia activist. A successful business person, in 1982 Lenard accepted the invitation of Aloysius Mazewski, president of the **Polish American Congress**, to head the PAC's office in Washington, D.C. Her appointment came at a critical time following the suppression of the Solidarity movement in Poland and that country's fall into a deep economic crisis. Over the next eighteen years, Lenard proved to be an extraordinarily dynamic and resourceful lobbyist. Her successes included organizing a series of PAC–sponsored massive shipments of medical supplies, clothing, and foodstuffs to Poland during the 1980s. In this work she cooperated closely with Eugene Rosypal in the Chicago office of the PAC. Working with **Jan Nowak-Jezioranski** and PAC President **Aloysius Mazewski**, Lenard worked tirelessly for passage of the National Endowment for Democracy Act in 1984. This legislation provided U.S. support for the embattled Solidarity movement in Poland. After the collapse of the Polish communist regime in 1989, she worked for the creation of the Polish American Enterprise Fund to support the country's economic recovery. Her efforts and those of her husband, **Casimir Lenard**, PAC President **Edward Moskal**, and PAC Executive Director **Les Kuczynski** were crucial in winning U.S. Senate approval for Poland's admission into the North Atlantic Treaty Organization (NATO) in 1999. For her achievements, Lenard was honored many times by the Polish government and by many organizations in the U.S.—*Donald E. Pienkos*

Source: *Polish American Congress, 1944–1994: Half a Century of Service to Poland and Polonia* (Chicago: Polish American Congress, 1994).

Lenski, Lois Lenore (b. Springfield, Ohio, October 14, 1893; d. Tarpon Springs, Florida, September 11, 1974). Author, illustrator. After graduating from high school in 1911, Lenski moved with her family to Colum-

bus, Ohio, where her father was a faculty member at Capital University. She attended Ohio State University, receiving a Bachelor of Science degree in education in 1915 before pursuing her studies in the visual and fine arts at the Arts Students League in New York. There she met mural painter Arthur Covey, whom she married in 1921. Lenski traveled to London in the 1920s where she attended the Westminster School of Art and worked as an illustrator for publisher John Lane. After illustrating for publishers both in Britain and America for the greater part of a decade, she published her first children's books, *Skipping Village* (1927) and *A Little Girl of 1900* (1928) based on her childhood experiences in Ohio. One year later she gave birth to a son named Stephen whose toddler years inspired her "Mr. Small" series. Lenski has been labeled one of the most prolific writers of children's books of the twentieth century, publishing such popular favorites as *Grandmother Tippytoe* (1931), *The Little Auto* (1934), *Sugarplum House* (1935), *Phebe Fairchild: Her Book* (1936), and *Indian Captive: The Story of Mary Jemison* (1941). In 1946, Lenski won the prestigious Newbery Medal for her book *Strawberry Girl*. One year later she received the Child Study Association Award for *Judy's Journey*, a story of the hardships of migrant work. During her lifetime Lenski authored more than ninety children's books, many of which have been translated into more than twelve languages including Afrikaans, Chinese, and Sinhalese. She donated the majority of her manuscripts, research notes, correspondences, and children's books that she herself collected throughout the course of her life to libraries across the United States, and in particular to the Jackson Library at the University of North Carolina at Greensboro.—*Krystyna Cap*

Sources: Charles M. Adams, ed., *Lois Lenski: An Appreciation* (Chapel Hill, NC: Friends of the Library of the Woman's College, University of North Carolina, 1963); Lois Lenski, *Journey into Childhood* (New York: J. B. Lippincott Company, 1972); Emilie W. Mills, "Lois Lenski's Collection of Early Children's Books," *The Lion and the Unicorn*, Vol. 22, no. 3 (1998), 323–26.

Lerski, Jerzy Jan "George" (b. Lwów, Poland, January 20, 1917; d. San Francisco, California, September 16, 1992). Historian, diplomat. Active in political and educational groups during his youth, he was severely beaten in 1938 by a militant group of right-wing extremists because of his philo–Semitic activities. Lerski studied both law and economics, and was commissioned a second lieutenant in an anti-aircraft artillery unit after completing reserve officers' school. His unit saw action against the German Luftwaffe in 1939. When the Soviet Union invaded Eastern

Poland and occupied Lwów Lerski made his way to France to join the Polish army where he served as an educational officer. After France fell, his unit was evacuated to England and then Scotland. Encouraged by his friend Jan Kozielewski (**Jan Karski**), Lerski agreed to become a courier, undergoing physical conditioning and both paratrooper and covert operations training. He was parachuted into occupied Poland in February 1943 as Prime Minister Władysław Sikorski's personal emissary to the Underground (codename "Jur"), which included the Home Army and the various political groups. He also carried gold, British currency, and $90,000 in U.S. currency, the latter of which was earmarked for Jewish organizations in the Warsaw ghetto. Upon completion of his mission, Lerski worked in the Underground's Department of Information, and he also briefed Zdzisław Jeziorański (**Jan Nowak**) prior to the latter's mission to London. The Underground sent Lerski on a dangerous return mission to the Allies, and the Warsaw Uprising then interrupted plans for Lerski's next mission into Poland, resulting in a posting to Scotland as the Information Representative of the Polish Government. In December 1944, he became private secretary to Tomasz Arciszewski, the Prime Minister of the Polish government-in-exile. He formed the Polish Freedom Movement "Independence and Democracy" (Niepodległość i Demokracja; NiD) and co-authored the government-in-exile's denunciation of the betrayal of Polish independence after the Yalta Conference. Lerski completed his legal studies at Oxford University (LL.M., 1946), and migrated to the United States in 1949, where he attended Georgetown University (Ph.D., History, 1953), becoming a naturalized citizen in 1962. Lerski taught history in Japan (1955–58), Pakistan (1958–60), and Ceylon (1962–64), and was a research fellow at the Asia Foundation (1960–62, 1965–66) and the Hoover Institution (1964–65). He joined the faculty of the University of San Francisco as an associate professor in 1966, and was appointed Professor of Modern European History in 1970. He became Professor Emeritus in 1991. Lerski contributed articles to many historical journals and wrote several books, including *A Polish Chapter in Jacksonian America: The United States and the Polish Exiles of 1831* (1958), which won the "Best Book of the Year" award from the Polish Army Veterans Association; *Herbert Hoover and Poland: A Documentary History of a Friendship* (1977); and a memoir of his war years, *Emisariusz "Jur"* (1984). Lerski was in the process of revising the manuscript of *Historical Dictionary of Poland, 966–1945* at the time of his

death, and it was published posthumously by Greenwood Press in 1996. Among his awards were the Cross of Valor from the Polish Defense Minister (1945), the King's Medal for Courage in the Cause of Freedom from Great Britain (1950), and the honor of "Righteous Among the Nations" by Israel's Yad Vashem (1985). Active in many organizations and known for his staunch anti–Communist views, Lerski was president of the **Polish American Historical Association** (1974) and a National Director of the **Polish American Congress** (1975–77).—*John Drobnicki*

SOURCES: Jerzy J. Lerski, *Poland's Secret Envoy, 1939–1945* (New York: Bicentennial Publishing Corp., 1988); "Lerski, Jerzy (George—'Jur')," in George J. Lerski, Piotr Wróbel, and Richard J. Kozicki, *Historical Dictionary of Poland, 966–1945* (Westport, CT: Greenwood Press, 1996), 298–99; obituary, *San Francisco Chronicle*, Sept. 19, 1992, A16.

Lesinski, John, Jr. (b. Detroit, Michigan, December 28, 1914; d. Dearborn, Michigan, October 21, 2005). Congressman. Lesinski moved to Dearborn at the age of eleven and attended **SS. Cyril and Methodius Seminary** and Fordham High School. He enlisted in the U.S. Navy at the age of eighteen and served from 1933 to 1937. He was recalled to active duty in 1941 and served until 1945, being awarded the Purple Heart and the Navy and Marine Corps Medal. From 1939 to 1943, he also served as vice president of the **Hamtramck** Lumber Company, which had been founded by his father, Congressman **John Lesinski, Sr.** In 1950, Lesinski was elected to the Sixteenth Congressional District seat previously held by his father, who had died earlier that year. He would be re-elected six times, serving in the United States House of Representatives from 1951 to 1965. In 1965, as a result of redistricting, parts of Lesinski's Sixteenth Congressional District in suburban Detroit were combined with parts of the Fifteenth District seat held by fellow Polish American **John Dingell** to create a new Sixteenth District. This created a closely-watched Democratic primary battle between Lesinski and Dingell in September 1965. Chief among the issues in the race were the two candidates' differing stands on civil rights. Whereas Dingell was a supporter of the Johnson Administration's civil rights agenda, Lesinski had moved from an early support for civil rights legislation to open opposition to it. Indeed, Lesinski was the only Northern Democratic congressman to vote against the Civil Rights Act of 1964, saying that the "path is being laid which will lead to the destruction of the rights and liberty of every one of our citizens ... and could put an end to our representative form of government." The contrast with Dingell's support for civil rights focused national at-

John Lesinski, congressman (*LC*).

tention on their 1965 primary contest, with analysts considering it a test of the "white backlash" theory that white voters would punish politicians who were perceived as too supportive of civil rights legislation. In fact, Lesinski was expected by many to win, particularly given the fact that the new Sixteenth District included about ninety percent of his former, overwhelmingly white district. Perhaps for this reason, Dingell sought to downplay the race issue during the campaign. Lesinski, however, made increasingly obvious references to race, with one full-page advertisement in the *Dearborn Press* (though purportedly placed there by a supporter) proclaiming that "John Lesinski is opposed to switch blades and mass demonstrations." In the end, the "white backlash" did not materialize and Lesinski was defeated with only forty-five percent of the vote. While African-Americans seemed to vote almost exclusively for Dingell, race did not seem decisive to most white voters. Lesinski's re-election efforts were particularly hampered by the fact that the state Democratic Party had censured him for his Civil Rights Act vote, and all but one of the new district's Democratic clubs endorsed Dingell, as did the Wayne County AFL-CIO, the United Auto Workers, and the local Teamsters. After his defeat, Lesinski would later serve from 1968 to 1973 as a member of the Wayne County board of commissioners.—*Jonathan Swarts*

SOURCES: *Biographical Dictionary of the United States Congress, 1774–present* (http://bioguide.congress.gov/); Harreld S. Adams, "The Dingell-Lesinski 1964 Primary Race," *The Western Political Quarterly*, Vol. 19, no. 4 (December 1966), 688–696; David R. Jones, "Lesinski, Rights Bill Opponent, Defeated in Michigan Primary," *New York Times*, September 3, 1964, 14; "Calls Bill Unconstitutional," *New York Times*, February 11, 1964, 33; "The Michigan Primary," *New York Times*, September 3, 1964, 28.

Lesinski, John, Sr. (b. Erie, Pennsylvania, January 3, 1885; d. Dearborn, Michigan, May 27, 1950). Congressman. Lesinski's parents moved to Detroit, Michigan, when he was three months old. He attended St. Albertus School, **Sts. Cyril and Methodius Seminary** in Orchard Lake, and the Detroit Business University. At age eighteen he entered the home construction and real estate business. About 4,000 of these homes were in **Hamtramck**, Michigan, a primarily Polish American enclave surrounded by Detroit. He founded the Hamtramck Lumber and Supply Company, the First State Bank of Hamtramck, and the Dearborn Lumber and Coal Company. From 1919 to 1932 he served as president of the Polish Citizens' Committee of Detroit. He helped recruit the **Polish Army in France** during World War I and sold Polish bonds in America, leading the Polish government to award him the Order of Polonia Restituta. Due to a decline in his business interests during the Great Depression, Lesinski ran for a seat in the House of Representatives in 1932 as a Democrat, winning election to the Seventy-third Congress and to eight successive terms, serving from March 4, 1933, until his death. He was a delegate to both the Democratic State Conventions and the Democratic National Conventions in 1936, 1940, and 1944. Recognized as an advocate of organized labor throughout his career, he also chaired the Committee on Invalid Pensions from 1935 to 1945 and the Committee on Immigration and Naturalization from 1945 to 1947. When the Democrats regained a majority in the House in the 1948 elections, Lesinski became chair of its highly partisan Committee on Education and Labor. There he became known for his anti–Communism and his unsuccessful attempts to repeal the Taft-Hartley Act. He also sought federal aid to public schools, and supported proposals to give states the option to finance the transportation of parochial school students. He also refused to sign subpoenas for United Mine Workers official John L. Lewis to testify on labor practices. His son, **John Lesinski, Jr.**, also served in the U.S. House of Representatives.—*Steven M. Leahy*

SOURCE: *Biographical Directory of the United States Congress, 1774–Present* (http://bioguide.congress.gov/).

Leskiewicz, Walter (b. Włodzimierz Woliński, Poland, September 20, 1888; d. Detroit, Michigan, May 21, 1939). Radio pioneer. Leskiewicz enrolled in the University of Lwów, but left his studies to migrate to the U.S. in 1909. He settled in New York where he was employed as a journalist, then moved to Newark (NJ), Cleveland, and finally Detroit in 1929. Once in Detroit he pursued acting, establishing a touring theater company that performed in Polish communities throughout the northeast. When the Depression forced the company to disband, in 1931 Leskiewicz and his wife began a Polish radio program called "Program rozmaitości" (Variety Hour) on WEXL in Detroit. Much of the programming reflected his interest in music, drama, and satire, with the balance including mostly news and commentary. Another popular segment of the show was "Polska Gośposia" (The Polish Homemaker) featuring Leskiewicz's wife Stanisława.—*James S. Pula*

SOURCE: Joseph Migala, *Polish Radio Broadcasting in the United States* (Boulder, CO: East European Monographs, 1987), 232–34.

Lewandowski, John M. (b. Cleveland, Ohio, May 29, 1890; San Diego, California, January 19, 1967). Radio personality. Sometimes called the "Father of Polish Radio in the United States," Lewandowski attended St. Mary's parochial school in Cleveland before obtaining a job at the Peerless Motor Car Company. He joined the city police force in 1915, but enlisted in the U.S. Army in 1917, serving with the 83rd Division in France where he rose to the rank of staff sergeant. Following the war he was involved in organizing American veterans in Ohio and Polish veterans organizations, later serving as national commander of the **Polish Legion of American Veterans**. He established a successful real estate business in 1920 and in 1926 was asked by WJAY, the pioneering Cleveland radio station, to prepare a Polish radio program. The successful program, believed to be the first regularly-broadcast Polish language radio program in America, launched Lewandowski into a lifelong love affair with the new medium. He not only produced and broadcast the program, but lined up guests, musical presentations, and other acts to appear on the show and marketed it to advertisers to pay the program's expenses. He served as an elected member of the Cleveland City Council (1932–39) and became vice chair of the Parks Committee and the Security Council in 1941. As president of the National Broadcasting Association, Inc., he played an important part in the development of similar Hungarian, Italian, and Croatian programs.—*James S. Pula*

SOURCE: Joseph Migala, *Polish Radio Broadcasting in the United States* (Boulder, CO: East European Monographs, 1987).

Lewandowski, Robert "Bob" (Zbigniew Lewandowski; b. Warsaw, Poland, May 13, 1920; d. Chicago, Illinois, September 20, 2006). Actor, radio and television personality. Lewandowski took part in the Warsaw Uprising in 1944, was captured, and spent time in a German prisoner of war camp. After the

Robert Lewandowski, actor, radio and television personality (*PMA*).

war he became involved in theatrical work in Germany, England, and France, and settled permanently in the U.S. in 1951. Initially, he found work at Voice of America and Radio Free Europe. In Chicago by 1953, Lewandowski originated several popular programs on local Polish language radio stations and directed many **Polonia** theatrical programs for the city's substantial postwar Polish immigrant community. In the late 1950s he hosted an hour-long music and variety program, *Polka Go Round* that originated in Chicago and was broadcast nationally over the ABC television network. In 1961 he established a local weekly Polish language television interview and entertainment show that continued into the 1990s. Tall, handsome, and blessed with a fine voice, Lewandowski never quite shook his Polish accent, even while speaking in the best "King's English." He organized a number of documentary programs shown on local television and in Poland, among them films about the 1979 visit of Pope John Paul II to Chicago, the contributions of the Poles to America's history, the "Black Madonna" of Częstochowa, and the celebration at the American Czestochowa shrine in **Doylestown**, Pennsylvania. Lewandowski also wrote regularly for the Polish language press in the U.S. and was a national director of the **Polish American Congress**. In 2003 he was inducted into the Silver Circle of the Midwest Chapter of the National Academy of Television Arts and Sciences.—*Donald E. Pienkos*

SOURCE: Wojciech Wierzewski, "Sto Trzydziesa Slynnych Polaków w Ameryce" (Unpublished manuscript in the archives of the University of Wisconsin–Milwaukee, 2000).

Lewinski, Pauline Agnes (b. Winona, Minnesota, January 20, 1896; d. Chicago, Illinois, October 8, 1988). Catholic nun. A noted instructor and administrator with a long and varied career in the **Sisters of the Resurrection**, Sister Pauline Agnes entered the Congregation when she was seventeen years old. Between the years of 1922 and 1933, she studied at St. Stanislaus College, St. Xavier College, and DePaul University in Chicago. At the latter institution she conducted research for her thesis, "The Secondary School in Poland," which also took her to Poland on a **Kościuszko Foundation** scholarship. Sister Pauline Agnes received a baccalaureate degree from St. Xavier College in 1925 and a M.Ed. degree with honors from DePaul University in 1933. She also took postgraduate classes at Fordham University and the University of Notre Dame. Although her initial role was teaching, her talents led her into administration. She taught for thirteen years in elementary and secondary parish schools in New York State and Chicago, and later served as principal in several of these schools. Her longest assignment in one place was at Resurrection High School in Chicago where she spent twenty-five years, being principal for fourteen. One of Sister Pauline Agnes's first achievements as principal of the high school was to successfully seek accreditation by the University of Illinois, the North Central Association, and the Illinois Department of Education. Out of a deep concern for higher standards in Catholic education, in 1943 she founded and directed Resurrection Teachers' School, a teacher education program affiliated with DePaul University in Chicago. Her goal was to upgrade the training of teachers in parochial schools. She demanded professionalism when she served as supervisor of the Congregation's schools from 1940 to 1943.—*Mary Edward Gira*

SOURCE: Eulogy, October 11, 1988, congregation archives.

Liberace (Władziu Valentino Zuchowski Liberace; Walter Liberace; b. West Allis, Wisconsin, May 16, 1919; d. Palm Springs, California, February 4, 1987). Pianist, entertainer. With a Polish American mother, Frances Zuchowska, and Italian immigrant father, musician and laborer Salvatore, Liberace began studying the piano at the age of four and met his idol, **Ignacy Jan Paderewski**, at the age of eight. Under the tutelage of Florence Bettray Kelly in Milwaukee, with whom he studied for ten years, Liberace gained an astounding piano technique while honing his talent for improvisation. During the Great Depression he earned a living by playing in theaters, on local radio, for dancing classes, clubs, cabarets, and weddings (under the pseudonym

Liberace, musician and entertainment personality (*OLS*).

of "Walter Busterkeys"). A member of an early jazz group, "The Mixers," in 1934, Liberace made his classical début at the age of seventeen at the Society of Musical Arts in Milwaukee. He appeared as soloist with the Chicago Symphony Orchestra on January 15, 1940, playing Liszt's Piano Concerto No. 2. Liberace moved to New York in 1940 to perform mostly in night clubs and popular music venues. In the mid–1940s he refined his new stage persona of a flamboyantly-dressed showman, playing what he called "pop with a bit of classics" or "classical music with the boring parts left out." His programs included variations on classical music themes, especially by Chopin and Liszt, as well as improvisations based on pop tunes, including requests from the audience. Liberace toured the U.S., but after his first appearance in Las Vegas in 1944 settled there for the reminder of his career. A supremely-gifted showman with a talent to connect with his audiences through humor and emotion, Liberace thrived in live performances for which he perfected costumes, lighting, and décor (including elegant white, sparkly tails and a glittering candelabrum on the richly-decorated piano). His show, broadcast in the U.S. and the United Kingdom beginning in 1952, reached audiences of over thirty million, mostly women who also bought his recordings and autobiographies. He recorded over 70 LPs, issued by Columbia and Dot, and received six gold record awards. His most popular single was of variations on Ave Maria, but he was not above playing Chopsticks on the Muppet Show. He was a favorite guest on such TV shows as *The Ed Sullivan Show*, *The Tonight Show*, and *Saturday Night Live*. Since

the 1950s, about 200 fan clubs gathered a quarter of a million member fans. His performances in Las Vegas continued through the 1970s and 1980s when Liberace's outlandish stage persona, covered in furs and diamonds, became a curiosity and an image from the past. Liberace's musical performances resembled his over-decorated outfits and instruments, with outlandish arpeggios, elaborate, dazzling harmonies, and a mixture of simple sentimentality and virtuoso bravado, transforming all music he played into signature Liberace showpieces. A composer of unremarkable pieces (Rhapsody by Candlelight and Boogie-Woogie Variations), Liberace was also a gourmet cook and author of a series of cookbooks. A series of highly publicized lawsuits highlighted his denial of homosexuality, a fact repeatedly alleged in the press and refuted by the pianist. As an actor-pianist, he appeared in films beginning in 1943, with his most interesting role being that of a pair of twins (gangster and pianist) in the TV show *Batman*. Other films included *Sincerely Yours* (1955), *The Loved One* (1965), and *When the Boys Meet the Girls* (1965). His memorabilia may be seen at The Liberace Museum in Las Vegas.—*Maja Trochimczyk*

SOURCES: Liberace, *Liberace: An Autobiography* (New York: Putnam and Co. Ltd., 1973); Liberace and Tony Palmer, *The Things I Love* (New York: Grosset & Dunlap, 1976); Liberace and Michael Segell, *The Wonderful Private World of Liberace* (New York: Harper and Row, 1986); Robert Thomas, *Liberace: The True Story* (New York: St. Martins Press, 1987); Jocelyn Faris, *Liberace: A Bio-Bibliography* (New York: Greenwood Press, 1995); Darden Asbury Pyron, *Liberace: An American Boy* (Chicago: University of Chicago Press, 2000).

Liberkowski, Janusz (b. Nowa Sól, Poland, March 9, 1953; d.—). Engineer. After completing his studies in engineering at the Gdańsk University of Technology in 1981, he moved to the United States in 1984, settling in Silicon Valley in California. In 2006 he won $1 million in ABC television's "American Inventor" contest which attracted some 10,000 entries. His invention was a new design for the Anecia Survival Capsule, a "spherical safety seat" for children that automatically closes during an automobile accident for increased protection through double layers that offer a protective outer shell and a free floating inner shell that cushions the shock from the collision rather than channeling it to the child as is done in conventional children's seat belt systems. By 2008 he held four U.S. patents and jointly holds four others with Intel Corporation, his employer.—*James S. Pula*

SOURCES: "Congratulations Janusz Liberkowski 'Top American Inventor,'" *Polish American News*, June–July, 2006; "One Million Dollars for a Polish Engineer," *Good News* (American Institute of Polish Culture; 2006), 67.

Libeskind, Daniel (b. Łódź, Poland, May 12, 1946; d.—). Architect. The son of Polish-Jewish parents, he attended school in Poland where he learned to play the accordion as a child, quickly becoming a virtuoso player. When his family moved to Israel, he pursued musical studies. In 1960 he won the American-Israel Cultural Foundation Fellowship (together with Itzhak Perlman, with whom he performed). Libeskind moved with his family to New York, but he abandoned musical activities, despite the advice of Isaac Stern, because, according to his own statement in an interview for *Architectural Design*, there was no more technique he could acquire, making it pointless to keep playing. In New York, Libeskind attended the Bronx School of Science, and became a United States citizen in 1965. His architectural education was at the Cooper Union for the Advancement of Science and Art (1970). After graduating, he studied history and philosophy, receiving a postgraduate degree in History and Theory of Architecture at the School of Comparative Studies at Essex University in England in 1972.

Libeskind taught and lectured at many universities in North America, Europe, and Japan and was head of the Department of Architecture at Cranbrook Academy of Art from 1978–85. He was appointed Distinguished Visiting Professor at Harvard University, Ohio State, the Danish Academy of Art in Copenhagen, the University of Naples, the Louis Sullivan Professor at the University of Illinois in Chicago, and, in 1991, the Banister Fletcher Professor at the University of London. From 1986–89, he was invited by the Getty Foundation to become a Senior Scholar. Libeskind was awarded a National Endowment for the Arts Award, the Senior Fulbright-Hayes Fellowship, the Graham Foundation Fellowship, and the First Prize of the Leone di Pietra at the Venice Biennale 1985. In 1987 he won the urban design competition of the International Bauaustellung in Berlin. Among his many honors, Liebeskind was appointed the first Cultural Ambassador for Architecture by the U.S. Department of State (2004), declared Honorary Member of the Royal Academy of Arts in London, England (2004), and received the Gold Medal for Architecture at the National Arts Club (2007).

Libeskind's perspective and works have been linked by several critics and writers to Deconstruction, a critical system which challenges the accepted connections between meaning and form. Derived from the writings of the French philosopher Jacques Derrida, architectural Deconstructionism reached its peak during the 1980s. Libeskind's interests in philosophy, poetry (his book of poetry *Fishing from the Pavement* was published by the Netherlands Architecture Institute, Rotterdam, 1997), and art, as well as his activities as an architectural theorist and professor for many years, did not prevent him from developing a spectacular career related to important enterprises, institutions, and large scale works. Libeskind completed his first building at the age of 52, the Felix Nussbaum Haus in 1998. But his first major international success as an architect was the Jewish Museum in Berlin, completed in 1999. His great notoriety increased when he was selected by the Lower Manhattan Development Corporation to be the master plan architect for the rebuilding of the World Trade Center, which was destroyed in the September 11, 2001 attacks. Libeskind designed museums, concert halls, universities, residences, hotels, shopping centers, and buildings for cultural and commercial institutions. Among the important projects completed by the Studio Daniel Libeskind of New York are the Imperial War Museum North-Greater Manchester, England (1997–2001); the Contemporary Jewish Museum of San Francisco, California (1998–2008); Westside Shopping and Leisure Centre–Bern, Switzerland (2000–08); the extension to the Royal Ontario Museum and renovation of ten of its existing galleries in Toronto, Canada (2002–07); Memoria e Luce, 9/11 Memorial-Padua, Italy (2004–05); The Ascent at Roebling's Bridge, residential condominium building, Covington, Kentucky. Studio Libeskind has many important projects under construction, proposed, and in design. Among them: Creative Media Center, Hong Kong; MGM Mirage City Center, retail and public space on the Las Vegas Strip, Las Vegas, Nevada; New Center for the Arts and Culture, Boston; New Songdo City, Incheon, South Korea; and the Editoriale Bresciana Tower, Brescia, Italy. Daniel Libeskind designed opera sets for Richard Wagner's *Tristan und Isolde* (2001, Saarländisches Staatstheater), for *Intolleranza* by Luigi Nono, and for a production by Deutsche Oper Berlin of *Saint Francis of Assisi* by Olivier Messiaen.—*Guillermo Gregorio*

SOURCES: Daniel Libeskind, *Breaking Grounds* (New York: Riverhead Books, 2004); Daniel Libeskind, *Countersign* (London: Academy Editions, 1991); Christopher Norris and Andrew Benjamin, *What is Deconstruction?* (London, New York: Academy Editions/St. Martin Press, 1988); Andreas Papadakis, ed., *Deconstruction III* (London: Academy Editions, 1990).

Liga Morska (Sea League). Liga Morska is a social and cultural organization that has been active in a number of cities in the United States, mainly on the east coast. Its aim is to promote the causes of a free Poland and its maritime relations with the U.S. The organization dates back to October 1918 when it was founded by a Polish officer in the Russian imperial navy named Kazimierz Porebski. Initially named the Bandera Polska (Polish Banner), it almost immediately received a charter from the newly formed Polish government. By 1921 it claimed 20,000 members around the country. With its new name and official publication, the Liga Morska was active in supporting the development of Poland's new seaport city, Gdynia, in the 1920s. After 1930, it became closely associated with the Polish government of Marshal Józef Piłsudski, and several of his closest followers, among them Gen. Gustav Orlicz-Dreszer and Gen. Kazimierz Sosnkowski, took an interest in its activities. Around this time it also established affiliates in the **Polonia** communities abroad. By 1939, the Liga Morska, which was active as a mass patriotic organization supporting the defense of Poland's interests, claimed a national membership of 993,000. In 1944, Liga Morska ceased its operations in Nazi-occupied Poland but continued operating in the west. In 1949–53 its remaining leadership in Communist-controlled Poland was purged and the organization's name was changed to Liga Przyjaciel Zolnierza (League of the Soldier's Friend). It was then merged into another regime-controlled group, Liga Obrony Kraju (League for the Country's Defense). That organization claimed over 1.1 million members in the 1960s.

In the U.S., the League held its first national congress in 1935 with Władysław Kuflewski elected its president. In the U.S. the league promoted a variety of water and boating activities and organized patriotic manifestations. It also organized youth groups. After World War II it continued these activities. For example, it presented reenactments of the heroic Polish defense at Westerplatte at the start of World War II in 1939. The League was closely connected to the Polish government-in-exile in London. In 2010 its longtime leader was Szczepan Janeczko of New York and the organization was active in supporting the annual **Pulaski Day** parade in New York.—*Donald E. Pienkos*

SOURCE: Szczepan Janeczko, "Liga Morska w Ameryce Polnocnej," (Liga Morska, 2009).

Liga Polska *see* **Polish League** (1894).

Ligowsky, George (b. Madison, Wisconsin, June 27, 1857; d. Cincinnati, Ohio, date unknown). Trapshooter. An avid hunter and target shooter, Ligowsky is said to have conceived the idea for modern clay pigeons in 1880 while watching children skipping shells across the water. He recognized that the concave nature of the shells gave them added stability in the air, and from this developed the saucer-shaped clay pigeons that became standard for the sport of trapshooting, along with the mechanism by which they were launched. His original pigeons were made of baked clay, but he soon developed a better limestone and pitch combination, although the name "clay" continued to be used even though the actual composition of the pigeons changed. They were first used at a competition at Coney Island in New York in 1880. Ligowsky was instrumental in organizing the first national trapshooting competition in New Orleans on February 11, 1885. He also founded the Ligowsky Clay Pigeon Company in Cincinnati to manufacture his invention. He was inducted into the National Trapshooting Hall of Fame in 1969.—*James S. Pula*

SOURCES: W. L. Colville, "Old-Time Sportsmen: Recollections of Men Who Were Prominent in the Early Days of Field and Trap Shooting," *Field and Stream*, May 1909, 55–59; Kenneth P. Czech, "Pottery Pigeons: George Ligowsky and Modern Trapshooting," *Timeline* (Ohio Historical Society), Vol. 11, No. 2 (March–April 1994).

Lipczynska, Waleria (b. Poland, October 4, 1847; d. Grand Rapids, Michigan, February 16, 1930). Polonia activist. After serving as a nurse during the 1863 Polish insurrection against Russian rule, she migrated to the United States in 1869 where she took up residence in Grand Rapids, Michigan. She became a supporter of the **Polish National Alliance** beginning in 1883 and was active in the effort to win equal rights for women in the Alliance. After 1900, when women were admitted as full members of the PNA at an extraordinary national convention called expressly for that purpose, Lipczynska immediately became a leader among the women of the organization and was the first woman to be elected a delegate to a national PNA convention. She participated in every PNA convention from 1901 until her death and led the effort to organize the Women's Division of the Alliance in 1906, which operated as a separate and significant national unit within the PNA into the 1930s. In 1905, Lipczynska was the first woman to be elected to the office of vice censor of the Alliance, and two years later she was elected to the office of commissioner. In 1915, she was elected honorary commissioner for all states and served in this capacity until her death at the age of 83. A well-educated person possessing good organizing skills, Lipczynska earned recognition for her work in recruiting young men for the **Polish Army in France** in 1917. For her efforts on behalf of Polish independence, she was awarded the Golden Cross of Merit in 1927 by the government of Poland.—*Donald E. Pienkos*

SOURCE: Catherine Dienes, Melanie Winiecki, and Donald Pienkos, *Women Make A Difference: The 95th Anniversary of Women's Involvement in the Polish National Alliance* (Chicago: Alliance Printers and Publishers, 1996).

Lipinski, Daniel (b. Chicago, Illinois, July 15, 1966; d.—). Politician. Lipinski received a B.S. in mechanical engineering from Northwestern University (1988), an M.S. in engineering-economic systems from Stanford University (1989), and a Ph.D. in political science from Duke University (1998). He was a professor in James Madison University's Washington Program (2000), served as associate professor at the University of Notre Dame (2000–01), and associate professor at the University of Tennessee (2001–04). His doctoral dissertation, *Shaping Public Perceptions of Congress Through Franked Mass Mailings*, investigated congressional newsletters and targeted mailings. It was subsequently published as *Congressional Communication: Content and Consequences* (Ann Arbor: University of Michigan, 2004). Lipinski served as aide to several U.S. Congressmen from Illinois, including George Sangmeister (1993–94), Jerry Costello (1995–96), and Rod Blagojevich (1999–2000), although he first became involved in politics in 1979 as a campaign volunteer for his father, Congressman William Lipinski. From January until August 1999, he was a communication staff aide to House Minority Leader Richard Gephardt. Although his father had been nominated without opposition in the March 2004 primary, he decided to retire. Still, as Democratic Party committeeman for the 23rd Ward, the elder Lipinski successfully persuaded his party organization to select his son to replace him on the ballot in the general election. Lipinski gained election in November 2004 as a Democrat from the Third District to the 109th Congress and to succeeding Congresses (January 3, 2005–present [as of 2008]). Daniel Lipinski was a member of the House Committee on Small Business, the House Committee on Transportation and Infrastructure (like his father, although the committee's name before 1995 was Public Works and Transportation), and vice chair of the House Committee on Science. He was one of the few members of Congress with an engineering background. He was also concerned with making health care more accessible and affordable.—*Frederick J. Augustyn*

SOURCES: *Biographical Directory of the United States Congress, 1774–Present* (http://bioguide.congress.gov/); Michael Barone and Richard E. Cohen, *The Almanac of American Politics* (Washington, D.C.: National Journal, 2006), 566–68.

Lipinski, Julian (b. Russian-occupied Poland, 1834; d. Buffalo, New York, March 26, 1898). Polonia activist. A founder of the **Polish National Alliance**. Born in the Russian-ruled section of partitioned Poland, Lipinski was a weaver by trade and self-educated. He took part in the Polish January Insurrection in 1863 and afterward spent a number of years in exile in Paris. Active in the Gmina Polska patriotic club in Europe, Lipinski remained involved in exile politics after coming to Philadelphia. There, on February 15, 1880, he took part in the founding meeting of the Polish National Alliance called by **Julius Andrzejkowicz** and was elected treasurer of the new society. Lipinski is identified as the fourth member to join the Alliance and along with Andrzejkowicz, **Julian Szajnert**, John Blachowski, and John Popielinski is remembered as one of the five founders of the PNA. He at-

Waleria Lipczynska, Polonia activist (*OLS*).

Julian Lipinski, a founder of the Polish National Alliance (*OLS*).

tended five national conventions of the PNA. At its 1897 national convention in Philadelphia, he was elected an honorary lifetime member.—*Donald E. Pienkos*

SOURCES: Stanisław Osada, *Historia Związku Narodowego Polskiego i rozwój ruchu narodowego Polskiego w Ameryce Północnej* (Chicago: Nakładem i drukiem Związku Narodowego Polskiego, 1905); Donald E. Pienkos, *PNA: A Centennial History of the Polish National Alliance of the Untied States of North America* (Boulder, CO: East European Monographs, 1984).

Lipinski, Tara Kristen (b. Philadelphia, Pennsylvania, June 10, 1982; d.—). Figure skater. The only child of an oil company executive and a homemaker, Lipinski began her athletic career as a roller skater at age three. She switched to ice skating three years later, then permanently relocated to Sugar Land, Texas. She and her mother moved to Detroit, Michigan, in 1996 to continue training with professional coach Richard Callaghan. When she was twelve, she became the youngest skater ever to win a gold medal at the United States Olympic Festival. Her accomplishments continued when, in 1997, she became the youngest ice skater to win the U.S. Nationals as well as the World Championship. She is the first woman to successfully complete a triple loop/triple loop combination in competition. She won the coveted Olympic gold medal in women's individual figure skating in 1998, not only being the youngest ever to do so, but also the youngest Olympic gold medal winner in the history of the winter games. Following the Olympics, she turned professional, starring in her own skating program called Tara Lipinski's Miracle Match Tour, which raises money for leukemia. She has authored two books about her life. Among her honors are: gold medal at the U.S. Olympic Festival (1994); silver medal at the novice level of the Nationals (1994); silver medal at the U.S. National Junior Championships (1995); fourth place at the World Junior Championships (1995); bronze medal at the U.S. National Championships (1996); fifth at the World Juniors (1996); fifteenth at the World Senior Division Championships (1996); gold medal at the Ladies U.S. National Championships (1997); gold medal at the World Ladies Figure Skating Championships (1997); silver medal at Skate Canada (1997), Bronze Medal Trophee Lalique (1997); Silver Medal Nations Cup (1997); elected Sportswoman of the Year by U.S. Olympic Committee (1997); Silver Medal at the World Championships (1998); Gold Medal in Ladies Figure Skating at the Olympic Games (1998); Silver Medal at Skate America (1998); Silver Medal Trophee Lalique (1998); Elected to U.S. Figure Skating Hall of Fame (2005).—*Cheryl A. Pula*

SOURCES: Tara Lipinski, *Tara Lipinski: Triumph on Ice: An Autobiography* (New York: Bantam Books, 1997); Tara Lipinski, *Totally Tara: An Olympic Journey* (New York: Universe, 1998).

Lipinski, William Oliver (b. Chicago, Illinois, December 22, 1937; d.—). Congressman. The grandson of Polish immigrants, Lipinski graduated from St. Patrick High School in Chicago (1956), attended Loras College in Dubuque, Iowa (1956–57), and served in the United States Army Reserves (1961–67). Lipinski worked for the Chicago Park District as a physical education instructor and area supervisor (1958–75) until elected alderman of Chicago's 23rd Ward on the city's heavily Polish American southwest side. He served on the city council (1975–82), was a delegate to the Democratic National Midterm Convention in 1974, as well as to the Democratic National Conventions in 1976 and 1984 and the Illinois State Democratic Convention in 1977. In 1981, he received the backing of the Cook County Democratic Party organization, then controlled by the sons of the late Mayor Richard J. Daley of Chicago, for a run for Congress in the Fifth district. Supporters of Mayor Jane Byrne preferred Rep. John Fary, who had replaced the deceased Rep. **John Kluczynski** in 1975, to run again as the party nominee in 1982. Lipinski defeated Fary in the primary, subsequently gaining election as a Democrat to the Ninety-eighth and to the ten succeeding Congresses (January 3, 1983– January 3, 2005). Conservative in his social views, he opposed abortion and supported the death penalty and welfare reform. In 1985, Democratic National Committee chair Paul Kirk named him the party's co-chair on the Democratic Council on Ethnic Americans, a task force addressing the concerns of white ethnic voters. In 1984 he had hoped to organize an official ethnic caucus in Congress. Lipinski asserted that Democratic support for firmness in U.S.–Soviet relations would help regain ethnic backing for the party and backed the Reagan Administration's anti-communist policies in Central America. His special focus was on local transportation, since Midway Airport, an important employer, was in his district, and he served on the House Public Works and Transportation Committee. He assisted, through his legislative efforts, in modernizing that airport and building the Orange Line of Chicago's public transit system. After the 1990 census, the Fifth District was merged with the Third, then represented by his congressional colleague Marty Russo. Lipinski defeated Russo in the 1992 Democratic primary and was subsequently re-elected to Congress for the Third District. Lipinski was not a candidate for reelection in 2004. Although he had won the March primary unopposed, by August he decided not to seek reelection and suggested his son, Daniel.—*Frederick J. Augustyn*

SOURCES: *Biographical Directory of the United States Congress, 1774–Present* (http://bioguide.congress.gov/); Michael Barone, Grant Ujifusa, and Douglas Matthews, *Almanac of American Politics* (Washington, D.C.: National Journal, 1998), 479–80.

Lira Ensemble. Founded in 1965 as "The Lira Singers," an amateur group of teenaged singers studying music, the group grew rapidly in number and repertoire. By 2010, the Lira Ensemble included the Lira Symphony, Lira Chamber Ensembles, Lira Chamber Chorus of mixed voices, Lira Dancers, Lira Children's Chorus, and Lira Singers female vocal ensemble. Based in the Chicago area, it was established to promote Polish culture and includes, in addition to performances, English language narratives that tell about the music and dance performed, translate lyrics, explain the Polish or Polish American traditions and customs behind the music, dance, and costumes worn, and give insights into Polish history and the Polish American immigrant experience. During the Communist era in Poland, Lira served as a goodwill ambassador to Poland where the Lira Singers made five concert tours with the cooperation of the United States Department of State and won the acclaim of Polish critics. Lira's sixth tour of Poland in August of 1994, funded mostly by LOT Polish Airlines, demonstrated the role of cultural liaison that the Lira Ensemble continued to play once Poland regained its freedom. The Ensemble presents the full spectrum of Polish music and dance, performing both vocal and instrumental works as well as Polish historic and folk dance. Lira's repertoire includes classical works, ancient music, opera, sacred music, music of various historic periods, folk music, and modern popular music and dance. In addition to Polish Americans, the Ensemble includes people of African American, Latino, Asian American, and other ethnic groups who are interested in the serious study and performance of Polish music. Its performances have won critical acclaim from the *Chicago Tribune, Chicago Sun-Times*, the *Polish American Journal*, and other respected publications. By 2010, it was presenting some sixty performances each year, had produced nine major recordings that were being sold nationwide, and was artist-in-residence company at Loyola University Chicago. Its leaders included **Lucyna Migala**, co-founder of Lira, as artistic director and general manager; Philip Seward and Ruth Lin co-conductors of the Lira Ensemble; Iwona Puc as choreographer and director of the Lira Dancers; and Malgorzata Borysiewicz conductor of the Children's

Chorus. A 501(c)3 educational non-profit organization, the Lira Ensemble is recognized and has received funding from the National Endowment for the Arts, the Illinois Arts Council, the City of Chicago Department of Cultural Affairs, major foundations and corporations in the Chicago area, and prominent Polish American organizations.—*Lucyna Migala*

SOURCE: www.liraensemble.com.

Literature, Polish American. The definitive history of Polish American literature has yet to be written; but the general outline of that history is, by now, clear. And what it reveals is a level of literary activity in need of better appreciation and wider dissemination both because of its value and merit and because of its implications for American literature, for the patterns of American cultural production, and for a better knowledge of the Polish identity in America. This is all the more remarkable because it was long assumed in most circles that the Polish American community—at least the generation of the *stara emigracja* (old immigration), the peasant immigrants of the period from roughly 1880 to 1920—were virtual illiterates who not only failed to produce literature but who, in their struggle to survive in a new land, took little pleasure in reading, much less in literature. Even prominent Polish American scholars have contributed to this impression. One reported, for example, that "remarkable as it may seem, there does not exist a Polish American literature, that is, a literature penned by Polish immigrants and Polish ethnics about their experiences in America." Another explained that "lacking the education and cultural association necessary to the literary life, Polish immigrants concerned themselves with survival, with saving money to purchase land in the United States or in Poland (to which many expected to return), and with work." Such views were perhaps excusable until recently, although a familiarity with the numerous Polish American newspapers and periodicals of the *stara emigracja* has long suggested otherwise; and although we now know that such conclusions are woefully mistaken, impressions of this sort still linger and may be widespread. Consequently, the first task of any review of Polish American literature is to establish that, contrary to popular belief, **Polonia** has, from its early formation, produced a wealth of literature, much of which remains unacknowledged and neglected, especially outside of the Polish American community.

In the last two decades or so, scholarly studies have begun the important task of establishing and reclaiming an impressive record of literary activity in the Polish American immigrant community. None of these studies is more significant than **Karen Majewski**'s *Traitors and True Poles: Narrating a Polish-American Identity, 1880–1939*. In her research, Majewski has singlehandedly documented a remarkable body of Polish-language prose fiction penned by and for the community of the old immigration, the *stara emigracja*. At the heart of this study is a bibliography compiled by the author which alone would have altered our understanding of the literary activity and reading habits of the Polish American community from 1881, the publication date of the first Polonian novel, to 1939, the closing date of Majewski's study when World War II brought a fresh wave of Poles to America and altered the focus of much Polish American literary activity and significantly changed the community's publication industry. Before Majewski's study, no credible bibliography of Polish-language immigrant fiction had ever been compiled. Describing her painstaking search for primary sources, Majewski also hints at the work that remains to be done to complete her bibliography of prose fiction and to establish bibliographies for other genres of literature: "While university repositories facilitated the process, it still meant tracking down clues and half-clues about authors and titles buried in Polish language immigrant histories and memoirs, examining the catalogues and reading the shelves of Polish American organizational libraries and archives, sorting through knee-deep papers strewn on the floors of half-abandoned immigrant bookstores, and scanning hundreds of rolls of microfilmed newspapers. Despite all my efforts to be comprehensive, some works have undoubtedly been missed." The result of this effort is a list of over two hundred novels, novellas, short stories, sketches, and anthologies of short fiction produced between the 1880s and the outbreak of World War II, a list which has profoundly enriched our knowledge of the literary history of Polonia. Remarkably, if Majewski's focus on immigrant identity had not forced her to limit the selection of included works, her list of prose fiction would undoubtedly have been significantly longer; and Majewski estimates that the inclusion of drama and poetry would make any bibliography three times as large. Clearly it is no longer possible to deny Polish Americans a literature of their own. This, however, does not end Majewski's contribution to the history of Polish American letters; her study of this freshly reclaimed body of fiction clarifies patterns of publication in the Polish American community and identifies some of the peculiar circumstances of the history of Poland and of the Polish immigrant community which set Polish American literature apart from that of other immigrant and ethnic groups. Majewski also confirms a level of literary sophistication among writers and readers alike which was extraordinary—and previously unsuspected not only in host-culture commentaries but even in most Polonian circles.

Majewski begins her study with a survey of Polish immigrant publishing which should put to rest forever the notion that Polish Americans of the old immigration lacked "the education and cultural association necessary to the literary life" and were preoccupied "with survival, with saving money to purchase land ... and with work." Along the way, she demonstrates the close link between Polish-language prose fiction and journalism, a connection which "helped shape the physical forms, the literary styles, and thematic content of the literature offered to and created by the immigrant communities." Majewski also provides a summary of the Polish background (e.g., the Partitions, nineteenth century strategies of survival, the literary "conspiracy of understanding," and Polish Positivism) necessary to account for the production and reception of the literature under consideration.

The body of Majewski's study falls into four chapters. The first of these chapters examines Polish American crime and detective novels. Surveying novels such as *Kara Boża idzie przez oceanem* (God's Punishment Crosses the Ocean) by **Henryk Nagiel**, *John Neewen* and *Szumowiny* (The Scum) by Bronisław Wrotnowski, and the anonymous *Przygody polskiego detektywa* (The Adventures of a Polish Detective), Majewski argues that these works were generally read as ethnic and national allegories and that "despite the missing explicit engagement with immigrant social reality, these works reflect the concerns of immigrants at multiple levels, touching simultaneously on personal issues of inheritance and property, on metaphorical concerns about family loyalty and ethnic continuity, and on powerful historical conceptions of a divided Poland betrayed from within, by its allies and its own people." She concludes that "rather than evidence of the lack of literary development [that is, simply popular detective fiction], these multi-leveled works demonstrate the adaptability of popular literary forms to sophisticated collective purposes." Here, then, is not only literature; here is subtle and complex audience response.

Majewski's next chapter, "Emigrant Crossings and Double-Crossings: Family Ties," considers novels and short stories which fall into the general classification of "immigrant sagas"—works which "chronicle the physical, psychological, and cultural process of emigration, from the decision to leave the homeland through the initial period of adjustment in a new country." Like those of other nationalities, Polish narratives in this category "reconstruct the immigrant journey in order to provide their readers with moral and ideological maps by which they can trace the paths which led them from Europe" and in order to orient themselves in America. Unlike other groups, however, Polish immigrants were encouraged "to interpret their own emigration in the context of Poland's political oppression" and "to see themselves as linked with other Poles by a national identity reinforced by ties of shared suffering and exploitation." Furthermore, the journey for Poles was also seen as leading back to Poland—a particularly interesting point since as many as forty percent of all Polish immigrants to America actually did return to Poland.

Reviewed in this section are novels and short stories like Alfons Chrostowski's *Niewolnik polski* (The Polish Slave), Julian Czupka's "Irlandczyk z Smorgonii" (The Irishman from Smorgonia), Bronisław Wrotnowski's *Na szlakiem dolara* (On the Trail of the Dollar), and **Piotr Yolles**' *Trzy matki* (Three Mothers). Once again, Majewski insists that this interesting collection of epistolary narratives, *gawedy* ("a loose chatty form of fiction ... in highly stylized personal language"), and moral tales are evidence not of "Polonia's rudimentary literary development" but, rather, of "a highly nuanced conversation over proper Polishness that could speak to an audience of poorly-educated readers."

The third major section of Majewski's study, "The Use and Abuse of Power: The Family Feud," explores "the literary treatment of institutional responsibility and corruption" and illustrates "the ways opposing factions utilized the same morally-charged rhetoric of treason and betrayal to articulate competing ideologies of group identity and strategies for national survival." Interestingly, only a few of these works concentrate on purely "American" institutions and conditions; most authors "take on specifically immigrant institutions, personages, and power brokers, rather than outsiders." The attacks in these works ranged from the humorous to the vicious; but the criticism always, in one way or another, "centered around failure to serve faithfully the immigrant community and the Polish national ideal," and the usual targets were the clergy, secular institutions, and community leaders.

Noteworthy authors whose works level such charges include **Czesław Łukaszkiewicz**, the notorious and controversial but gifted

anti-cleric; the Rev. **Franciszek Hodur**, founder of the **Polish National Catholic Church**; Kazimierz Neuman, Roman Catholic loyalist; Stanisława Romanowska, political writer; and **Helena Staś**, populist and a favorite of Majewski. These writers, and others, "used novels, short stories, and short tales to challenge (or uphold) delineations of power, to propose (or reject) specific cultural modes, and, not incidentally, to settle old scores with ideological opponents." Here again, Majewski destroys an old myth: she reveals the Polish American community not as powerless, silent, or sullen, as it is often perceived and presented in host-culture literature, but as dynamic, independent, and pro-active, even pressuring American politicians to work for Polish independence.

Majewski introduces the final major section of her study by pointing out that Polish American writing was not exclusively preoccupied with contentiousness and division; it also offered recipes for union or reunion: "If Polish immigrant fiction was often the battleground on which writers enacted their own versions of the national struggle, it was also the field on which an honorable union could be proposed. Such models of reconciliation are most apparent in the 'ethnic romance,' in which questions of collective identity are explored and resolved through the drama (and more rarely the comedy) of sexual attraction and marital alliance. These romance stories articulate most explicitly the varied criteria by which Polishness could be measured and circumscribed." Such a pattern, Majewski recalls, had precedents in post-insurrection Poland where writers resituated "Polishness in the mind and heart, rather than the battlefield or halls of state." Thus, Polish American romance narratives of love, sex, and marriage associated family with nation in order to model "an ethnic identity rooted in familial intimacy," to embody "Polish peoplehood, if not in an independent political state, then in the state of marriage," and to draw "compelling blueprints of an enduring Polishness." Here again, Polish American authors give a different twist to their treatment of marriage than do host-culture writers: for Polonian authors, marriage is not a device for assimilation and the resolution of nativist-immigrant differences; it involves the creation and preservation of ethnic identity.

Here also a wealth of Polish American authors and works are used to illustrate Majewski's analysis—among them, Helena Staś (*Marzenie czy rzeczywistość*; Dream or Reality), **Stanisław Osada** (*Z pennsylwańskiego piekła*; From a Pennsylvania Hell), Iza Pobog ("Ich syn"; Their Son), and Melania Nestorowicz (*Sprzedawaczka z Broadwayu*; The Salesgirl

from Broadway). As in the other sections of her study, Majewski concludes with a reminder of the metaphoric use of marital alliance and misalliance, suggesting yet again not just unexpected literary production but a complex handling of material.

Majewski closes her study with an examination of the demise of this body of Polish-language fiction. She also points to "common patterns of production, form, and theme, as well as very particular issues and concerns" between the literature of the *stara emigracja* and of current immigrant cohorts from Poland. Modern immigrants, she reminds us, "may not need an American experience to awaken an awareness of themselves as Poles, but they do continue to write about the transformations of identity which living in emigration imposes"—for example, disagreements about just who is Polish, about the obligations of Polishness, and about the proper political and social actions on behalf of Poland. All of this, of course, documents from the inside both the continuities and the evolving nature of the Polish American community.

Karen Majewski has re-shaped the study of Polish American literature. She has, for one thing, reopened the pages of a long-forgotten body of Polish prose which will never be overlooked again and which demands to be included in the canon of non–English-language American literature. She has forced a re-consideration, and likely a reformulation, of commonly accepted paradigms of ethnic American literature by showing a body of work which simply doesn't fit existing models. And she has demonstrated a counterpoint to the prevailing image of Polish Americans in host-culture literature: "Even the most sympathetic of these often portray the Polish immigrant as inarticulate, passive, almost primeval, as faceless symbols of a primitive life force and as voiceless victims of social injustice and economic exploitation. Naturally, they may have appeared so to outsiders with whom they could not easily communicate. But the view from within Polonia was of an active, vibrant, and complex community, and most relevantly the sound from within was not silence but conversation, argument, laughter. The only way to hear these voices is by eavesdropping on the literature these communities produced by and for themselves, with no intention of cultural mediation with America-at-large, but with very particular agendas relevant to the immigrants themselves, their institutions, and even to the shape of the world map. All this is lost unless we hear them in their own language."

Another important legacy of Majewski's study is the necessity she has created to recover the remainder of Polish-language fiction — and poetry and drama — and to restore the entire landscape of Polish American literature. As Majewski suggests, one of the reasons why Polish American literature has been overlooked and lost is that the bulk of Polonia's early literary efforts was written in Polish. Writing in one's language of origin is, of course, common enough in immigrant communities; but the peculiar circumstances of Polish-language literary production in the United States once again have no clear analogies among other immigrant or ethnic groups — with the possible exception of Cuban Americans — and are one of the distinguishing features of Polish American literature. This aspect will be addressed in more detail later in this essay; but for now a brief review of early poetic and dramatic activity, also overwhelmingly conducted in Polish, is necessary to document the range of early Polish-language literature in the United States.

The fields of poetry and drama have received nothing at all like the study which Majewski has focused on fiction; but there are several sources, both primary and secondary, which point to a wealth of literary production and which await examination. In the area of poetry, the task of recovering a substantial body of the works composed until World War II will be even more daunting than it was for fiction; but the *Antologia Poezji Polsko-Amerykańskiej* (Anthology of Polish-American Poetry) edited in 1937 by Dr. Tadeusz Mitana under the auspices of the Polish Arts Club of Chicago provides a good beginning and suggests that the recovery will be worthwhile. A brief history of the *Anthology* and its contents establishes an important perspective on Polish American poetry. Once the project of the anthology was approved by the Polish Arts Club, "poems were solicited through a series of announcements in every Polish newspaper in the United States and Canada, and a great mass of poetry was received." The result was a collection of one hundred and seventy-eight poems by fifty-five poets; one hundred and thirty-six of the poems are written in Polish, and forty-two in English. Approximately one-third of the Polish poems had been previously published, some in separate collections but most in a wide range of Polish-language newspapers; a similar percentage of the English poems had also been previously published. The credits in the anthology are somewhat unclear, but it appears that while the bulk of the poems were written close to the date of the anthology's publication, several were composed much earlier — the oldest dating from 1913.

Among the poets with multiple entries in

Polish are Walery Fronczak, M. A. Niedzwiecki, Janusz Ostrowski, and Irena Poplawska-Leineweber. Bridging the gap between the Polish and English languages is **Victoria Janda**, who was later nominated for a Pulitzer Prize, with four poems in Polish and six in English, while writing exclusively in English was Alan Edward Symanski with eight entries. Interestingly, even **Mieczysław Haiman**, perhaps the leading Polish American scholar of his day, has an entry.

Beyond the poetry itself, Mitana's notes to the reader, one version in Polish and another in English, shed important light on the project of an anthology of poetry and on the then current Polish American literary scene. For one thing, Mitana, speaking rather prophetically, suggests that the anthology will be especially valuable because in the future the majority of these materials will likely be forgotten and covered with dust. Nonetheless, he assures us that "the future historian of Polish poetry in America will find a wealth of material for intriguing study, both in the number of Polish American poets and the great wealth of poetry generated in various Polish publications throughout the United States." Regarding the evaluation of the collected poems, Mitana insists that their achievement lies not so much in formal or aesthetic criteria but in their "degree of candor and truthfulness of emotion." Moreover, like literary scholars of the present decade, Mitana stresses the importance of the insiders' view which these poets supply: "They are not only revealing to the understanding hearts of their readers a singular pathos of the process of adjustment, but are also lifting the curtain that for so long has hidden the very nature of the spiritual aspirations of the Polish people in America. It is no exaggeration to say that between its covers, the *Anthology* gives for the first time, both an insight into the qualities of the Polish mind in America and a cross section of its emotional content. This volume is truly an index of the ever-changing world of human aspirations on the one hand, and of the distinctively Polish orientation to its dream land on the other." Finally, Mitana acknowledges the inevitable replacement of Polish by English for literary efforts in Polonia.

The Anthology of Polish American Poetry edited by Tadeusz Mitana is comparable to *The Book of American Negro Poetry* edited by James Weldon Johnson in 1922, a time when the Black American community was still struggling to promote an appreciation for its contributions to American literature; both books are as important for what they suggest as for what they contain. Like the pioneering effort of the Black American editor, Mitana's volume

demands further study for its own sake and for that of its subject area. In any case, the Mitana *Anthology* points to a large body of poetry from the period of the *stara emigracja* which remains to be recovered and studied. It has also prompted the theory that poetry, not fiction, may have been the preferred literary genre of the early Polish American community. Although poetry is today the minority field of literature, this has not always been so. Further, the personal nature and relative brevity of most lyric poetry might have made it more appealing, manageable, and publishable than fiction or drama.

Polish-language drama in America has already been remarkably well documented but inadequately studied — especially given the scope of dramatic activity. A brief sketch of some of the milestones in its documentation will have to suffice as an indication of the recovery and critical analysis which remains to be done. By 1890 Polish American amateur theatre was so well established and pervasive that visiting Polish literary historian Karol Estreicher wrote an essay entitled "*Teatr polski za oceanem*" (Polish Theatre Beyond the Ocean), published both in Europe and America, in which he supplies a valuable description of performances and stresses the importance of the theatre in immigrant life. The essay lists scores of plays performed in a range of Polish American communities in cities ranging in size from Chicago and New York to Winona, Minnesota, and Grand Rapids, Michigan. Indeed, Estreicher reports that drama is more vibrant in the "young" Polish American community than it is in Poland where "the foreign atmosphere" produced by the partitions has "poisoned" the experience for many.

Almost fifty years later, in the essay "The Amateur Theatre Among the Poles" written for inclusion in the book *The Poles of Chicago*, Natalie Kunka provides a brief history of the amateur theatre in Polonia and documents an astounding number of dramatic clubs and circles in the Chicago area alone. According to Kunka, dramatic activities originated in virtually every Polish Roman Catholic parish of the area — some parishes supporting more than one dramatic circle. She also identifies many dramatic societies in the city operating independently of church affiliation. Kunka estimates that dramatic activity in the parishes peaked in 1917 and attributes its decline at least partially to the popularity of motion pictures. This notwithstanding, she notes that her essay is written on the tenth anniversary of the Alliance of the Polish Literary Dramatic Circles of America, a nation-wide federation of parish and independent dramatic clubs established to promote friendly relations, support, and cooperation. The very existence and longevity of the Alliance attest to a tradition of drama still vital on the eve of World War II.

Also noteworthy is the essay "Polish American Theatre" by **Artur Waldo** which was published in 1983 in the collection *Ethnic Theatre in the United States*. In this important piece Waldo begins with a sketch of the early amateur drama circles which he, like Kunka, overwhelmingly associates with immigrant parishes; indeed, Waldo points out that the popularity of amateur performances was so great that they rapidly became natural fundraisers for the churches. Along the way, he presents summaries of the careers of leading figures in amateur theatrical circles such as **Teofilia Samolińska** and **Szczęsny Zahajkiewicz**. The main focus of Waldo's essay, however, is Polish American professional theatre in Chicago, New York, Milwaukee, Detroit, Buffalo, and Cleveland; here Waldo devotes a great deal of attention to the life and career of Thaddeus Dołęga-Eminowicz (see **Tadeusz Eminowicz**), the leading organizer and performer in professional circles. Finally, Waldo analyzes the decline of Polish-language theatre, identifying four causes for its ultimate demise: "(1) restriction of immigration from Poland after 1920; (2) the introduction of radio and later of television into all homes; (3) the Anglicization of all ethnic groups; and (4) the economic crisis of 1929–1933." Even this did not put an end to Polish drama, for Polish theatre directors and managers themselves moved into radio to continue their work — a topic which itself deserves much more study than it has received.

More recently, in 1989, Emil Orzechowski published a book-length study of Polish American drama, *Teatr polonijny w Stanach Zjednoczonych* (The Polonian Theatre in the United States), through the prestigious Ossolineum Press in Poland. This is by far the most ambitious study yet done, but it has had a greater impact in Poland than in the United States. American scholars, especially Polish American but also host-culture scholars, need to follow Orzechowski's lead, learn from his research, and finish the task of recovering, studying, and evaluating Polish-language immigrant drama in America. If they do not, this impressive and important body of dramatic literature will remain unnoticed or, worse, will literally be discarded; and an important aspect of Polish American life will be lost. There did, then, exist an impressive body of Polish-language literature produced in America by and for the Polish American community up to the beginning of World War II.

In the last decade or two, students of Amer-ican literature have been directing more and more attention toward works, both past and contemporary, written in languages other than English by residents of the United States, many of them immigrants but a significant number of them the children of immigrants, and even by visitors to this country. Scholars like Werner Sollors are insisting that American literature is historically and properly multilingual, are calling for support for the recovery of important foreign-language texts, and are promoting an openness to current authors writing in languages other than English. This most recent expansion of the canon requires the study and appreciation of the literary works in the languages in which they are written; but it also demands quality translations of the works if the general public is to recognize and profit from the experiences and insights of these authors and their ethnic/racial groups.

This is an exciting and long overdue development in the study of American literature — but one which has, with few exceptions, brought little attention and benefit to Polish Americans. The most important step in correcting this situation will be completion of the work begun by Karen Majewski: recovery of the impressive body of literature — fiction, poetry, and drama — penned by Polish immigrants to the United States from the very beginning of their community in this country. Retrieval of these works, until so recently ignored or denied, will call attention to the literary achievements of Polonia and demand the attention which they deserve.

This extensive body of literature produced before 1939 was not followed by an equally extensive body of Polish American literature in English. The reasons for this require careful investigation; but some factors, a few of them already mentioned, certainly contributed to the situation. With the arrival of post–World War II immigrants from Poland, the Polish American community again found itself caught between two worlds, both culturally and linguistically. Culturally, the new immigrants reinvigorated the Polish roots of Polonia; but their focus on Poland seems to have detracted from an emerging American agenda for the community. Similarly, the revitalized use of Polish may have psychologically discouraged the use of English as a literary language for the community. This, combined with a general indifference to non–English literature on the American literary scene, no doubt took its toll.

In an opposite vein, until the advent of the Civil Rights Movement and the ethnic awareness movement of the 1960s, overwhelming pressure for assimilation devalued Polish American topics as a subject area for literature and encouraged aspiring writers to look elsewhere for their vision and their voice. Most Polish Americans at mid-century grew up and were educated without a single image of themselves or their community in the literature of the United States which they studied and which was heralded by the literary establishment. Furthermore, despite the incentive of the ethnic movement documented and promoted by works like Michael Novak's *The Rise of the Unmeltable Ethnics*, Polish Americans, as the archetypical blue-collar immigrant Americans, often found themselves branded as racists and super patriots, a primary source of America's domestic problems and supporters of unpopular wars abroad. It did not really matter that hard evidence disproved the first charge or that ethnics had little to say about American foreign policy and were drafted to fight in high percentages. There was little reason for Polish Americans even to aspire to write about their ethnic identity or community (unless to repudiate or demean them) — let alone to try to find a national audience for such literature.

Whatever the causes, English-language literature had not yet been composed in great volume by the Polish American community; on the other hand, despite the lack of inducements, by mid-century Polonia produced a growing number of authors writing in English. In the area of fiction, **Antoni Gronowicz** (*Bolek*, 1942; *Four from the Old Town*, 1944), **Monica Krawczyk** (*If the Branch Blossoms*, 1950), Wanda Kubiak (*Polonaise Nevermore*, 1962), Richard Bankowsky (*A Glass Rose*, 1958; *After Pentecost*, 1961; *On a Dark Night*, 1964; *The Pale Criminals*, 1967), and Darryl Ponicsan (*The Last Detail*, 1970; *Goldengrove*, 1971; *Andoschen*, 1973; *The Accomplice*, 1975) illustrate the inevitable but occasionally difficult move to English. Writing with varying degrees of sophistication about the Polish American experience and in widely different styles, these authors and others achieved some considerable success — even a share of national notoriety and critical attention — and document a continuing literary fascination, through even the third and fourth generation, of the Polish American identity. Furthermore, regardless of what has already been said about these mid-century authors, especially by some host-culture critics, they are figures whose very identity and status as ethnic writers call for further clarification, whose handling of ethnicity (their own and that of the Polish American community at large) deserves continuing debate, and whose literary strengths and accomplishments demand closer examination, especially if scholars are serious about diversity in the canon of American literature.

This movement to English as the preferred literary language of the Polish American community is also seen in an increasing number of poets from the period. By the 1930s poets such as Edmond Kowalewski (*Deaf Wall*, 1934), John Drechney (*Nature Smiles*, 1947), Edward Symanski (*Against Death in Spring*, 1934; *From the Fourth Province*, 1952; *Fallen Stars*, 1961), and **Victoria Janda** (*Star Hunger*, 1942; *Walls of Space*; 1945; *Singing Furrows*, 1953) writing primarily in English, drew not only ethnic audiences but also significant national attention. As mentioned earlier, Janda was nominated for the Pulitzer Prize for Poetry for her volume *Singing Furrows*; and Edmond Kowalewski's book *Deaf Walls* was reviewed in such newspapers as *The New York Times*, *The New York Herald Tribune*, and *The Saturday Review of Literature*; the book also received endorsements from such prominent literary figures as Hervey Allen, Alfred Kreymborg, John Farrar, William Alexander Percy, and Vachel Lindsay. Interestingly, Kowalewski's book was recently re-issued by Kessinger Publishing and hailed as a "contemporary lyric sensation" and "a new symphonic revelation in poetry." Bridging the gap between fiction and poetry in this period of transition to English and testifying to the vitality of both the ethnic experience and of literary experimentation was *Let the Blackbird Sing* (1952), a verse novel by Helen Bristol whose struggle for identity in America reflects a common theme among Polish American poets.

Despite this movement to English, especially but not exclusively among the children and grandchildren of the *stara emigracja*, temporary and permanent Polish residents in the United States have continued to write in Polish. Focusing for the moment on the mid-century, one can discern at least three major waves of authors: the war years; the post-war period, including the resettlement of displaced persons and the relocation of political émigrés; and the era of the Cold War.

Leading scholars of Polish literature produced in the West tend to focus attention on writers such as **Jan Lechoń**, **Kazimierz Wierzyński**, **Józef Wittlin**, and Aleksander Polczyński as particularly prominent during the war years. In the decade and more which followed World War II, figures such as **Danuta Mostwin**, Alicja Iwanska, Aleksander Hetrz, and **Wiesław Kuniczak** emerged as significant writers living and writing in the United States — although Kuniczak, unlike the others, came to write in English and will be discussed later. Finally, during the Cold War, Polish writers such as Maria Kuncewicz, **Melchior Wańkowicz**, **Leopold Tyrmand**, and, most prominently, **Czesław Miłosz** settled and wrote in this country.

The writings of most of these Polish displaced persons and political refugees who arrived in the United States in the aftermath of World War II and during the Cold War are, in all likelihood, the least publicized works of Polish American literature. The reasons for this are multiple. Because these authors wrote in Polish, most had little or no access to general American audiences and even limited audiences in the Polish American community itself since the children and grandchildren of the earlier immigrants of the late nineteenth and early twentieth centuries were themselves less and less fluent in the language of their parents and grandparents. Additionally, the Polish-language authors of this generation frequently told a story which the United States had no desire to hear since it treated the surrender of the longest fighting member of the Allied Nations to Soviet hegemony. To complicate matters even more, these authors had no qualms about disabusing people in the West about the failings of Communism at a time when a good many Western intellectuals, politicians, media pundits, and literary figures were sympathetic to both the Communist experiment and the Soviet Union. Only two of these writers have received serious study in English: Czesław Miłosz and Danuta Mostwin — and even these two only belatedly. Until he received the Nobel Prize in 1980, Miłosz had only a very small American audience and, for the most part, published abroad; and Mostwin has only in the last few years begun to receive critical attention in the United States.

In the past thirty years or so, yet other waves of immigrants have arrived from Poland (for example, Solidarity refugees from martial law and more recently immigrants from free Poland). These latest groups of immigrants have also produced writers of note. Perhaps even more than earlier Polish immigrant authors, these writers represent divergent experiences and interests. Most write initially in Polish, although several employ both Polish and English, and others increasingly turn to English as the language of choice for their writings. Many of these authors reside in the United States only temporarily and do not really examine the American scene, while others have taken up permanent residence in this country and more and more write about their American experiences and, like earlier generations of writers, the difficulties of dual identities and of their new lives. Included among these recent waves of writers are **Anna Frajlich**, **Stanisław Barańczak**, **Henryk Grynberg**, Joanna Rostropowicz-Clark, Tadeusz Chabrowski, Maciej Patkowski, Adam Lizakowski, and others.

Thus, the long tradition of Polish language literature written in the United States, dating back to the earliest arrival of Poles in America, continues today. In the last several decades, however, a new generation of Polish American authors writing in English, for the most part the grandchildren of immigrants, are emerging and are being recognized and honored, creating a virtual renaissance of Polish American literature. It is to representatives of this new generation that we now turn.

Several writers of fiction on the contemporary scene have found in their ethnic background powerful material for their short stories and novels; and although none of these authors writes exclusively about his or her Polish American identity, it is clear that identity plays a major role in both the formation of their literary voices and their incentive to write.

Anthony Bukoski is a case in point. A native of the Polish American east side of Superior, Wisconsin, and a professor at the University of Wisconsin–Superior, Bukoski has already published five heralded volumes of short stories (as of 2009). His work has also appeared in a wide range of national journals including *New Letters*, *The Literary Review*, *Western Quarterly*, *New Orleans Review*, *Writer's Forum*, *Beloit Fiction Journal*, and *The Louisville Review*. All of Bukoski's collections of short stories, but especially the last four (*Children of Strangers*, 1993: *Polonaise*, 1999; *Time Between Trains*, 2003; *North of the Port*, 2008), examine aspects of Polish American family, community, and religious life largely ignored by host culture writers and generally neglected by even some other descent writers since the shift away from Polish-language literature; what's more, he does so unabashedly with a sensitivity and skill rare for any ethnic writer. Bukoski has revealed himself as intimately familiar with both the light and dark sides of the Polish American community and its experiences; and he presents them with an uncommon command of language, dialogue, characterization, and setting which has won for him growing national and international interest and acclaim.

Bukoski has received numerous literary awards and honors. He has twice won Outstanding Achievement Awards form the Wisconsin Library Association and twice the Anne Powers Book-length Fiction Award for Wisconsin Writers. In 2002 he was named the R.V. Cassill Fellow in fiction by the Christopher Isherwood Foundation. In a different vein, in 1997 Bukoski was featured along with Diane Glancy and Paul Gruchov in the PBS video *A Sense of Place*. In 2003 a week of stories from *Time Between Trains* was broadcast on Wisconsin Public Radio; and in 2004 actor Liev Schreiber read the title story from the same collection at Symphony Space in Manhattan as part of the *Selected Shorts: A Celebration of the Short Story*— a reading which was later broadcast on National Public Radio. Additionally, *North of the Port* has been praised for its "heart-piercing, poetic fiction of place and ethnicity" and recommended by the *Boston Globe* as one of five short gems worthy of summer reading. Though focusing primarily on the Polish American community of Superior, Bukoski has struck a universal cord with readers and critics of divergent backgrounds and has been compared by them to Flannery O'Connor, Sherwood Anderson, and William Faulkner.

Another writer whose popular and critical recognition attests to the growing success of English-language fiction by Polish American authors is **Suzanne Strempek Shea**. This former reporter from western Massachusetts has in quick order published five very well received novels and three memoirs. The first four of the novels deal with "the view from the author's window" and are set in Polish American communities suspiciously like Three Rivers, Massachusetts. Shea did not set out to write Polish American or ethnic novels: her intent was simply to write about something familiar; but the accuracy and power of her insights and the quality of her writing have made her works instant successes. Shea treats universal themes such as coming of age within the particular context of the Polish American experience; and she does so with a control of point of view, characterization, setting, and action which is remarkable for any writer.

Strempek Shea is earning a national reputation as the Amy Tan of the Polish American community. She has done book tours from coast to coast, appeared on the *Today Show* and the *Tom Snyder Show*, and sold the film rights to her first novel, *Selling the Lite of Heaven*. So closely have Shea's works identified her with Polonia that recently, along with such national figures as former United States National Security Advisor **Zbigniew Brzeziński**, singer **Bobbie Vinton**, actress **Stefanie Powers**, and United States Senator **Barbara Mikulski**, she was featured in *The Polish Americans*, a part of the heritage film series produced for public television. Her works have been translated and published abroad in Germany, Korea, and Poland. Suzanne Strempek Shea is providing readers with a view of the Polish American community which most writers simply do not know.

Yet another important literary figure in the contemporary Polish American community, and likely the best known internationally, is **Anne Pellowski**. Founder and former director of the Information Center on Children's Culture, a section of UNICEF, Pellowski is a storyteller, teacher, and author of children's literature who has consulted and performed in well over one hundred countries. Among her many honors are the Grolier Award of the American Library Association and the Constance Lindsay Skinner Award of the Women's National Book Association; the citation for the latter award honors Pellowski for her "extraordinary contributions to the world of books and, through books, to society."

Beyond her technical and scholarly works, Pellowski has published a tetralogy of children's books (*Stairstep Farm: Anna Rose's Story* 1981; *Willow Wind Farm: Betsy's Story* 1981; *First Farm in the Valley: Anna's Story* 1982; and *Winding Valley Farm: Annie's Story* 1982) which have both helped to establish a new standard for children's literature and which serve as models for the treatment of ethnicity in American literature. These stories which chronicle four generations of a Polish immigrant family settling the Latsch Valley of Trempealeau County, Wisconsin, address children honestly, treating sadness as well as joy, fear as well as courage, and death and pain as well as life and birth — but always in a context of security and love. In short, Pellowski's tetralogy not only entertains young people; it also arouses their curiosity, and helps them to develop their intellects and to clarify their emotions. As ethnic literature, these stories ground their material in the reality of immigrant life in a way which acknowledges but does not distort that reality; as one critic has stated, "Without apology or chauvinism Pellowski presents an identity different from that of White, Anglo-Saxon, Protestant Americans, establishes an appreciation for that identity, and manages to touch those universals which are the common bond of all humanity."

In the tetralogy Pellowski's handling of characterization, action, language, and setting vividly portray the realities of farm life, living conditions, and social adjustments through a period of more than one hundred years. Particularly impressive is Pellowski's ability to tell the stories from the point of view of a series of six-year-old daughters and nieces while supplying all the information necessary to a clear grip of the narratives; it is a feat which enhances the pleasure of the works for children and adults alike. Here is Polish American literature which displays literary mastery, fresh direction in its field, and new insights into Polonia.

Also noteworthy in the current generation of Polish American authors is novelist **Leslie Pietrzyk** whose first novel, *Pears on a Willow Tree*, was applauded as a major achievement in highly regarded literary circles at home and abroad. *The Times* of London, for example, praised the work as "a remarkable first novel"; and the *Washington Post* dubbed Pietrzyk "a genuine and fully developed talent." A tale of four generations of Polish American women in the Marchewka family, *Pears on a Willow Tree* treats universal questions such as the complexity of mother-daughter relations, the complicated identities women must forge, and the obvious and subtle effects of immigration in the context of a Polish American milieu, demonstrating the uniqueness of each individual while giving a human face to the Polish American experience. Indeed, the overarching motifs of the novel are storytelling and each of the women's response to the stories of her family and heritage. Pietrzyk and her novel also contribute powerfully to the feminist dimension of the Polish American literary scene. There can be little doubt that *Pears on a Willow Tree* has established Leslie Pietrzyk as a talent of the first order capable of providing new insights to the Polish American story and its literature.

In addition to those whose primary focus is the world of letters, other authors whose training and careers are far afield have been motivated to tell the story of their Polish American background. A case in point is **Ken Parejko**, who holds a doctorate in aquatic ecology and for years taught biology at the University of Wisconsin–Stout. Parejko has published two novels, the first of which, *Remember Me Dancing*, tells the story of a Polish immigrant family settling in Wisconsin in the early years of the twentieth century. The novel has been praised for its historical veracity, its sensitive but candid portrayal of the internal world of immigrant life, and its literary power; it is, in at least some respects, reminiscent of Polish Nobel Laureate Władysław Reymont's tetralogy *Chłopi* (The Peasants).

Mention should also be made of Polish and Polish American writers such as **Jerzy Kosiński**, **Wiesław Kuniczak**, and **Stuart Dybek** who would regard their work as outside any Polish American literary tradition. These authors, nonetheless, have, from time to time, been associated with the Polish American community — occasionally, one senses, to their chagrin.

More open to his Polish and Polish American roots and experiences is Gary Gildner, author of seventeen books, including a novel, several books of poetry, a collection of short stories, and *The Warsaw Sparks*, a memoir on his experiences coaching a baseball team while on a Fulbright appointment in Poland. This winner of numerous awards—among them the Theodore Roethke Prize and the William Carlos Williams Prize for Poetry—not infrequently draws on his Polish American background. Especially prominent in Gildner's work is his Polish immigrant grandfather who is the title figure in *My Grandfather's Book: Generations of an American Family* (2002). The recognition of Polish ethnicity, even among a writer generally regarded as a consent author, reinforces the legitimacy of the Polish American community as a source of literary inspiration.

Perhaps nowhere is this more evident than among a new generation of Polish American poets who are confidently drawing on their ethnic identity and experiences as a source for their poetic explorations and, along the way, achieving recognition in the literary world. Certainly one of the most accomplished of these poets is **John Guzlowski**, author of three volumes of poetry and poetic entries in journals such as *Atlantic Review*, *Poetry East*, *Proteus*, and *Periphery*. Born in a displaced persons' camp to a Polish couple freed from slave labor in Nazi Germany, Guzlowski has focused the majority of his poetry on preserving the memory of his parents' experiences as slave laborers during the war, the family's life as displaced persons, their adjustment to life in America, and the legacy of the war for his parents, his sister, himself—and even for his daughter. This is particularly urgent because the Polish experience in World War II is still little known in the West and because the story of Polish displaced persons in America has received minimal attention even in the Polish American community. The passion of Guzlowski's poetry does not reside only in the nature of his subject matter. The lyric-narrative poetry which he writes displays impressive mastery of the skills peculiar to both narrative and lyric literature. His deft handling of characterization and action lends power to his stories; and his control of verse and meter, clarity of diction, and skilled conversational tone communicate but also control the emotion which his lyrics convey. In addition to his other recognitions, Guzlowski has been awarded an Illinois Arts Council Artist Fellowship, was nominated for a Pushcart Prize for Poetry, and honored as featured poet by journals such as *Spoon River Review* and *Margie: An American Journal of Poetry*. In 2008 he was nominated for the Pulitzer Prize.

Another poet of note who draws on his Polish American background is John Surowiecki. This poet and verse dramatist has authored two collections of poetry (*The Hat City after Men Stopped Wearing Hats*, 2007, and *Watch-*

ing Cartoons before Attending a Funeral, 2003), and five chapbooks. A third collection—fifty poems about his parents, family, and neighbors entitled *Barney and Gienka*—is in preparation. Many of his poems treat the people of the large and active Polish American community in which he was raised—"the people history tends to pass by." Surowiecki writes with the expectation that poetry can trump history; he insists that the people in his background provide worthy example "from their dignity in the face of suffering, from their sentimentality and warmth and loyalty, and just the way they embrace life, without condition or compromise." His many honors suggest that he is achieving his goals. He has won the 2006 Pablo Neruda Prize, the 2006 Washington Prize, and First Prizes from *Common Ground Review* and *Georgia State University Review*; he was also a finalist for the Robert Penn Warren Award.

Approaching her work in a similar vein and with similar motivation is **Linda Nemec Foster** who does not write solely from a Polish American perspective but whose focus on the universal is grounded in the reality of a particular ethnic background and a particular place in history: "a woman and a wife, a daughter and a sister, a mother and grandmother of Polish immigrants." Thus, her efforts to communicate with her readers by transforming her life into the imagery and metaphor of poetry frequently reflect that perspective. Foster has authored eight collections of poetry including *Amber Necklace from Gdańsk* which was nominated for over ten book awards, among them the Paterson Poetry Prize and the Laughlin Award, and *Living in the Fire Nest*, a finalist for the Poet's Prize. Her poems have appeared in over two hundred and fifty magazines and journals.

Two other poets who draw inspiration from their Polish American heritage are Cecilia Woloch and Leonard Kress. Woloch's poems frequently trace her "journey of identity" and have appeared in a score of anthologies and dozens of journals and magazines. She is the author of four books of poetry and the winner of numerous prizes and awards. Woloch freely acknowledges the Polish American dimensions of her youth and family but does "not believe that 'Polish American' is an apt description of either my identity or my writing." That notwithstanding, her sense of "otherness" from "more Americanized" neighbors has helped to shape her "as a person and a writer."

Listed here primarily for his work as a poet, Leonard Kress is also a playwright, fiction writer, and translator of growing note. In this respect and by virtue of his life experience, he nicely rounds out this brief survey of contem-

porary Polish American authors. Although born into a family of Polish and Lithuanian immigrants of the *stara emigracja*, Kress was raised in the suburbs of Philadelphia in a household that "lacked any sense of Polish identity or culture" and "in a fairly non-religious Jewish environment"; but when he began to write fiction and poetry, he "gravitated inexorably toward *Polishness*." He pursued Slavic studies at Indiana University and at the Jagiellonian University in Kraków. He is the author of four books of literature; and his poetry, prose, and translations have appeared in numerous journals and anthologies. He is also the recipient of several grants and awards. In all these respects Kress typifies the experiences and achievement of contemporary Polish American writers.

We are just beginning to appreciate the existence and scope of the literature created by Polish Americans. In the case of Polish-language literature, an enormous task of discovery and recovery lies ahead; translations of at least some of the works are in order; and critical studies remain. The road will be long, costly, and difficult; but the work of Karen Majewski has demonstrated that it will also be exciting and rewarding. English-language literature also requires further study; too often scholars have been content simply to note its existence and to report on its reception but have failed to inquire into its antecedents and to analyze its literary qualities. Finally, Polish American writers on the contemporary scene suggest that the last chapter of this story has yet to be written, that Polish American literature is beginning to capture a national audience, and that it is serving its own needs as well as contributing to those of the larger American community.

The definitive history of Polish Americans and literature has yet to written; but there is now every reason to be confident that when it is, it will document that Polonia has contributed not just economically, politically, and physically to the fabric of American life but artistically, culturally, and spiritually as well. It will also preserve the memories of the community and protect them from distortion and falsehood.—*Thomas J. Napierkowski*

SOURCES: Stanislaus Blejwas, "Voiceless Immigrants," *Polish American Studies*, Vol. 45, no. 1 (1988), 5–11; Thomas S. Gladsky, *Princes, Peasants, and Other Polish Selves: Ethnicity in American Literature* (Amherst: The University of Massachusetts Press, 1992); Karen Marie Majewski, *Traitors and True Poles: Narrating a Polish American Identity: 1880–1939* (Athens, OH: Ohio University Press, 2003); Thomas S. Gladsky and Rita Holmes Gladsky, *Something of My Very Own to Say: American Women Writers of Polish Descent* (Boulder, CO: East European Monographs, 1997); Artur L. Waldo, "Polish-American Theatre," in Maxine Seller, ed., *Ethnic Theatre in the United States* (Westport, CT: Greenwood, 1983), 387–417; Natalie Kunka, "The

Amateur Theatre Among the Poles," in *Poles of Chicago, 1837–1939* (Chicago: Polish Pageant, 1937), 67–90; Thomas J. Napierkowski, "Anne Pellowski: A Voice for Polonia," *Polish American Studies*, Vol. 42, no. 2 (1985), 89–97.

Litscho, Daniel (possibly Liczko; b. Koszalin, Poland, date unknown; d. New Amsterdam, New Netherlands, 1662). Military officer, government official. One of the earliest settlers in the Dutch colony of New Amsterdam, Litscho rose to the rank of lieutenant in the Dutch colonial military force. He took part in Governor Peter Stuyvesant's campaign against Swedish settlers along the Delaware River in 1651 and commanded the force that supported the governor in the following year when he reasserted his control over Rensselaerswyck (the area around modern Albany). Because of his support for the governor, he was appointed city fire inspector and took part in the deliberations of the Council of Burgomasters and Schepens. Around 1648 he opened a tavern that became a gathering place for supporters of the governor.—*James S. Pula*

SOURCES: Haiman, *The Polish Past in America 1608–1865* (Chicago: Polish Museum of America, 1974), 16–17; E. B. O'Callaghan, *History of New Netherland, or, New York Under the Dutch* (Salem, MA: Higginson Book Company, 2006; reprint of 1846 edition).

Logisz, Sabina Phyllis (b. Chicago, Illinois; November 10, 1916; d. Chicago, Illinois, November 9, 2010), Librarian. Sabina Logisz received her Associate Bachelor of Arts degree from Wright College before beginning a life-long association with the **Polish Roman Catholic Union of America** (PRCUA). Her enthusiasm for the newly founded **Polish Museum of America** (PMA) led her to begin work there in 1936, an affiliation she maintained until her retirement in 2002. From 1936 until 1948 she used her organizational skills to assist **Mieczysław Haiman**, the first curator of the PMA, in organizing archival materials; then, in 1958 PRCUA president Stanislaus Turkiewicz requested that she become his secretary, a post she held for 23 years for several PRCUA presidents. During her tenure as secretary, Sabina engineered the financial success of the Museum's most significant fundraiser, "The Summer Ball." Additionally, from 1968 to 1989 she authored an English language column, "Sabina's See Saw," for the PRCUA's bi-monthly publication *Naród Polski* (Polish Nation). Although she was offered the position of Executive Editor of *Naród Polski* in 1981, she chose instead to become part of the Museum's library staff. This opportunity allowed her to use her editorial skills in preparing the publication of *Autographed Letters of Thaddeus Kosciusko in the American Revolution* (1977) and the re-issuing of Haiman's *Polish Past in America* (1991).

Sabina Logisz, secretary, assistant and librarian (*PMA*).

During her tenure with the Museum library, and her 66 year affiliation with the PRCUA, Logisz served as the PMA's secretary, cataloguer of book donations, instructor in the intricacies of the English language to numerous library employees, and the liaison between the library and Chicago's Polonia community. For decades she assisted scholars in their research, being recognized as the "heart" of the Museum library and its "encyclopedia" of archival information. Logisz has been an active member of many educational, social, and philanthropic organizations including the **Polish American Historical Association**, the Polish Arts Club of Chicago, the **Legion of Young Polish Women**, and the Auxiliary of **St. Mary of Nazareth Hospital**. She received numerous awards for her contributions to **Polonia** including the "Woman of the Year" award from the Polish American Scholarship Fund (1976); the Officer's Cross of Polonia Restituta (1990) for publishing material on Polish culture, the award for Meritorious Service to Polish Culture from the Minister of Culture and Arts of the Republic of Poland (1998); and the highest cultural award given by the Republic of Poland outside of Poland, the Golden *Gloria Artis*, for her cultural contributions (2007).—*Geraldine Coleman*

SOURCE: Ryszard Brykowski, ed., *Polish Museum of America History and Collection Guide* (Warsaw: Polish Community Association Center for Polish Cultural Heritage, 2003).

Lopat, Eddie (Edmund Walter Lopatynski; b. New York, New York, June 21, 1918; d. Darien, Connecticut, June 15, 1992). Baseball player. After an unusually long apprenticeship at lower professional levels, Lopat began a successful career as a major league pitcher in 1944. Over the course of twelve seasons

hurling for three different teams in the American League, he won 166 games. Lopat enjoyed his greatest success as a member of the starting pitching rotation for the New York Yankees when the team won an unmatched five consecutive world championships from 1949 to 1953. During that span, Lopat won eighty regular season decisions, and four World Series games. He was named to the American League All-Star team in 1951, and the statistical calculations of the *Total Baseball* encyclopedia rank him as having been the third best pitcher in the AL that year. In 1953, he led the league's pitchers in earned run average and won-lost percentage. A lefthander, Lopat threw a variety of slow pitches, a repertoire that gained him the nickname "The Junkman." After his playing days ended in 1955, he remained in baseball for more than a decade as a manager in the minor leagues, and as a coach, manager, and executive at the major league level. Lopat was inducted into the National Polish-American Sports Hall of Fame in 1978.—*Neal Pease*

SOURCE: Donald Honig, *The October Heroes* (Lincoln, NE: Bison, 1996).

Lopata, Helena Znaniecka (Helena Znaniecka; b. Poznań, Poland, October 1, 1925; d. Milwaukee, Wisconsin, February 12, 2003). Sociologist. A pioneer in the field of gender studies, Lopata was the daughter of internationally known sociologist **Florian Znaniecki**. She married Richard Lopata in 1945. She received her M.A. in Sociology and Philosophy from the University of Illinois (1947) and her Ph.D. in Sociology (1954) from the University of Chicago where she wrote her dissertation, "The Functions of Voluntary Association in an Ethnic Community: Polonia." She taught at DePaul University (1956–60) and Roosevelt University (1964–69) before joining the Sociology Department at Loyola University in Chicago (1969) where she remained until her retirement in 1997. Her early academic articles represent her theoretical development of the concept of social roles, while over the course of her career she also studied the social roles of women. Her first book, *Occupation: Housewife* (1971), examined a hitherto overlooked role for women. Her study of widows was also groundbreaking in its topic and scope. Publications from this research include *Widowhood in an American City* (1973), *Women as Widows: Support System* (1979), *Current Widowhood: Myths and Realities* (1996), an edited two-volume work *Widows: The Middle East, Asia, and the Pacific* (1987), and *Widows: North America* (1987). In 1972, she established the Center for Comparative Study of Social Roles at Loyola University from which she launched her study of women working in urban areas and developed her expertise as a symbolic interactionist focused on the study of sex roles and gender. From her research on women's changing occupational roles, she co-authored with Cheryl Miller and Debra Barnewolt a two-volume work, *City Women: Work, Jobs, Occupations, Careers* (1984, 1986). She was also series editor for *Current Research on Occupations and Professions* (previously titled *Research on the Interweave of Social Roles*) which published seven volumes between 1980 and 1997. In the mid-1970s, she returned to the study of **Polonia**, focusing on social status, organizational roles, and national identities. First published in 1976, *Polish Americans: Status Competition in an Ethnic Community* was revised, updated, and reissued in 1996 as *Polish Americans*. She received many awards and honors in her career including faculty member of the year at Loyola University, Chicago (1975), the Mieczysław Haiman Award from the **Polish American Historical Association** (1987), the Distinguished Scholar Award from the Family Division, Society for the Study of Social Problems (1989), the Burgess Award from the National Council on Family Relations (1990), the Distinguished Career Award from the Section on Aging, American Sociological Association (1992), the Mead Life Achievement Award from the Society for the Study of Symbolic Interaction (1993), and the Bronisław Malinowski Award from the **Polish Institute of Arts and Sciences in America** (1995). She was president of the Illinois Sociological Association (1968–70), Midwest Sociological Society (1975–76), Society for the Study of Social Problems (1982–83), and Sociologists for Women in Society (1993–94).—*Mary Patrice Erdmans*

SOURCES: Helena Znaniecka Lopata, "Life Course of a Sociologist" in Sarah Fenstermaker and Ann Goetting, eds., *Individual Voices, Collective Visions: Fifty Years of Women in Sociology* (Philadelphia: Temple University Press, 1995), 185–99; David R. Maines, "Coming to Grips: Aspects of the Life History of Helena Z. Lopata," *Midwest Feminist Papers*, Vol. 4 (1983), 112–24; Barbara Ryan, "Helena Znaniecka Lopata," in Mary Jo Deegan, ed., *Women in Sociology: A Bio-Bibliographical Sourcebook* (New York: Greenwood Press, 1991), 263–72; obituary, *Chicago Tribune*, March 8, 2003.

Lopata, Stan (b. Delray, Michigan, September 12, 1925; d. —). Baseball player. Lopata played for thirteen seasons in the major leagues from 1948 to 1960, mostly for the Philadelphia Phillies of the National League. A right-handed hitting catcher, he compiled a career batting average of .254 with 116 home runs. Lopata played in the 1950 World Series as a member of Philadelphia's National League pennant winning squad. He had his best seasons in 1955 and 1956 when he hit 22 and 32 home runs respectively, and was named to the National League all-star team. He is a member of the Pennsylvania Sports Hall of Fame, and was inducted into the National Polish-American Sports Hall of Fame in 1997.—*Neal Pease*

SOURCE: "Stan Lopata," National Polish-American Sports Hall of Fame website, www.polishsportshof.com.

Lorentz, Leopold (b. Camden, New Jersey, September 15, 1918; d. Mexico City, April 4, 1967). Journalist, military officer. The son of Polish immigrants, Lorentz grew up in Rochester, NY, where he became involved in the activities of St. Casimir's **Polish National Catholic Church** and local **Polonia**. The onset of World War II affected him greatly, and he began to write a column about Poland's cause for *Zgoda* (Harmony). In 1941 he enlisted in the Polish Army at Windsor, Ontario, and authored a new column titled "Diary of a Polish Soldier," carried in *Zgoda*, *Dziennik Polski* (Polish Daily News), and *Sokół Polski* (Polish Falcon). Lorentz chronicled life at camp while stationed with the Polish First Armored Division in Scotland, and life at the front as the division advanced through France, Belgium, and Holland. His articles presented the war from the view of Polish soldiers, describing their daily routines, sacrifice, and heroism. Wounded in 1944 at the battle for the Mark Canal, Lorentz was awarded a battlefield commission as lieutenant and honored with the Cross of Valor (Krzyżem Walecznych). He remained in service with the Polish Army until 1948, assisting with repatriation of 500 American and Canadian recruits, including invalids in British hospitals. Returning to the U.S., Lorentz and his wife Olga Puławska, a veteran of the Home Army, helped resettle hundreds of Polish refugees in Rochester. He turned his energies to community activities and chaired the 1966 convention of the American Council of Polish Cultural Clubs (see **American Council for Polish Culture**) hosted by the local Polish Arts Group. Lorentz's memoir *Caen to Wilhelmshaven* (1947) is a tribute to the men of the First Armored Division offered by "an American soldier of Polish descent who came from the other side of the ocean to fight for the liberty of his forefathers' country."—*Kathleen Urbanic*

SOURCE: Kathleen Urbanic, "Alliance of Hearts: Leopold Lorentz and the Ideals of Polish Heritage," *Polish American Studies*, Vol. LVII, no. 1 (Spring 2000), 25–54.

Loryś, Maria (Maria Mirecka; b. Ulanów, Poland, February 7, 1916; d. —). Polonia activist, author, journalist. Mirecka was studying law at the Jan Kazimierz University in Lwów when World War II began. During the war she was active in the resistance and rose to the position of commandant (and later captain) of the Armed Women's service of the Armia Krajowa (Home Army; AK) for the Rzeszów region. Arrested and imprisoned by the Polish security police after the Communist regime came to power under Soviet auspices in 1945, she was freed in a general amnesty declared on September 1. Subsequently, a new arrest warrant was issued against her but she was able to leave Poland via an underground escape route. In Italy in 1946, she married Lt. Henry Lorys, a reserve officer in the II Corps of the Polish Army. She and her family migrated to the United States in 1951, where she was active in several **Polonia** organizations, most notably the **Polish Women's Alliance** headquartered in Chicago. Maria Lorys served as the editor in chief of the PWA official publication, *Głos Polek* (The Voice of Polish Women) from 1964 to 1995. She was also a national director of the **Polish American Congress**. Acting on behalf of PNA/PAC President **Aloysius Mazewski**, Lorys organized the transfer of the remains of **Agaton Giller**, a leader in the Polish insurrection against Russia of 1863 and the "godfather" of the Polish National Alliance, from Stanisławów, then in the Soviet Union, to a prestigious final resting place in Warsaw's Powazki Cemetery. Lorys authored the second volume, in Polish, of the history of the Polish Women's Alliance. Following her retirement from the PWA and the death of her husband, she retired to live in Poland. Both of the children of Maria and Henryk Lorys, Jan and Ewa, became active in the Polish American community in Chicago.—*Donald E. Pienkos*

SOURCES: Angela T. Pienkos and Donald E. Pienkos, "*In the Ideals of Women is the Strength of the Nation*": A History of the Polish Women's Alliance of America (Boulder, CO: East European Monographs, 2003); Wojciech Wierzewski, "Sto Trzydziesta Slynnych Polaków w Ameryce" (Unpublished manuscript in the archives of the University of Wisconsin–Milwaukee, 2000).

Lotarski, Casimir (Kazimierz Lotarski, b. Youngstown, Ohio, February 4, 1918; d. Chevy Chase, Maryland, November 15, 1998). Banker, Polonia activist. In 1922, Lotarski's parents returned to their native Poland with their family. He completed his secondary education in 1937 and was enrolled in a polytechnic institute (1937–39). In 1935, he began a series of aviation courses through the Aero Club of Poland and was licensed as a glider operator and pilot for all civilian airplanes. In 1939, he volunteered and served as a bomber pilot in defense of Poland against the German invasion. As an American citizen, he was arrested and imprisoned by the Germans in December 1941 after Germany declared war on the U.S. He returned to Youngstown in 1942 under an exchange of German and American citizens. There he pursued a general course of studies at Youngstown University (1942–44) and a special program in insurance and real estate at the Millard Fillmore College of the University of Buffalo (1952–53). Lotarski moved to Buffalo in 1948, where he was active in city and western New York civic affairs. He was secretary of the Division of Water of the City of Buffalo under Mayor Chester Kowal (1962–65), served as Deputy Commissioner of Finance for Erie County in charge of the Treasury Division (March 1974–October 1981), and was a New York State delegate to the 1976 Republican National Convention committed to Governor Nelson Rockefeller. He also was a member of the Committee for Rapid Transit, regional chair of the Catholic Charities Drive, and Commissioner on Condemnation Proceedings by appointment of the New York State Supreme Court. Lotarski was a banker and businessman, his positions including terms as director (1952–80) and president (1970–80) of the Fillmore Savings and Loan Association in Buffalo, originally founded by Polish immigrants as "Kasa" Savings and Loan. He arranged Fillmore's merger in March 1980 into the Buffalo Savings Bank, later re-named Goldome, and served on the board of both (1980–90). He was also owner and president of the Lotarski Insurance and Real Estate Agency managed by his wife Anna.

Lotarski was a charter member of the **Polish American Congress** and was the youngest participant at the Congress's May 1944 convention in Buffalo. He was a delegate to all subsequent PAC conventions and was elected a National Director at the ninth convention in 1972 in Detroit, a position he held until resigning in November 1997. He served as president of the PAC Western New York Division and was a director of the PAC's Washington Metropolitan Area Division from 1986 until his death in 1998. He was a delegate to the **American Relief for Poland** in December 1948 and a member of National Treasury. Appointed chair of the Displaced Persons Committee by New York Governor Averell Harriman, Lotarski helped arrange sponsors, jobs, and homes in Western New York for hundreds of Polish war refugees. Lotarski was a leader in the **Polish National Alliance**, being elected **censor** (chair of the Supervisory Council) for the 1971–75 term, after serving as vice censor for 1968–71. He founded PNA Lodge 3085, "Społem," in Buffalo in 1949, served as president of PNA Council 19 for twelve years, was a delegate to nine national conventions, and was secretary of the 1951 PNA convention in Buffalo. Lotarski served as chair of the board of trustees of **Alliance College** in Cambridge Springs, Pennsylvania,

1971–75, and vice chair in 1968–71. Passionate about educational opportunities for Polish Americans, he was president (1980–98) of the Copernicus Educational Aid Association, Inc., founded in Buffalo in 1914 to provide scholarships for Polish American youth of both sexes, and earlier served as its treasurer. In 1998, the Association transferred a $45,000 fund to Villa Maria College of Cheektowaga, New York, operated by the **Felician Sisters**, for management and award of "Copernicus Scholarships" to Polish American youth.

Lotarski was awarded a Doctor of Humane Letters by Alliance College in 1977; the Polish National Alliance awarded him the Gold Cross of the Legion of Honor in February, 1978; Western New York's Polish American weekly, the *Am-Pol Eagle*, honored him with the Citizen of the Year Award for Fraternalism in 1969; and his services to Poland and the Polonia were recognized by the Polish Government in London.—*Donald E. Pienkos*

SOURCES: Donald E. Pienkos, *PNA: A Centennial History of the Polish National Alliance of the United States of North America* (Boulder, CO: East European Monographs, 1984); *Perspective—A Publication of Buffalo Savings Bank*, Vol. III, no. 1 (Spring/Summer 1980; "Casimir Lotarski, Former PNA Censor, Dies at 80," *Dziennik Związkowy*, November 25–26, 1998; Wojciech Wierzewski, "Sto Trzydziesska Slynnych Polaków w Ameryce" (Unpublished manuscript in the archives of the University of Wisconsin–Milwaukee, 2000).

Lubanski, Eddie (b. Detroit, Michigan, September 3, 1929; d.—). Bowler. An accomplished bowler from youth, Lubanski returned to the sport as a professional at age 21 after spending several seasons as a minor league baseball pitcher. He was one of the last top notch bowlers to use a two finger delivery. Lubanski reached the peak of his career in 1959 when he was named Bowler of the Year and rolled two perfect games in a row. His lifetime average of 204 in American Bowling Congress tournament play is the highest on record, and he compiled eleven sanctioned 300-games. Lubanski is a member of the United States Bowling Congress Hall of Fame, the Michigan Sports Hall of Fame, and was elected to the National Polish-American Sports Hall of Fame in 1978.—*Neal Pease*

SOURCE: "Eddie Lubanski," National Polish-American Sports Hall of Fame website, www.polishsportshof.com.

Łuczycki, Zdzisław (b. Berejów, Poland, October 9, 1858; d. Bochotnicy, Poland, June 13, 1929). Priest, journalist. Łuczycki grew up in the Russian-occupied partition of Poland from which he was forced into exile because of his participation in patriotic conspiratorial activity. After spending some time in Rome, he arrived in the U.S. in 1886 and took up pastoral duties in the Immaculate Conception

of the Blessed Virgin Mary Parish in Manitowoc, Wisconsin, as well as smaller congregations in Two Rivers and Northeim. In the same year he arrived in his new parish, Łuczycki founded the first Polish-language newspaper in Manitowoc, the religious *Wszystko Przez Serce Jezusa i Maryi* (All Through the Heart of Jesus and Mary). The first issue of the publication appeared on December 27, 1886, and the last on December 29, 1890. There followed the short-lived publications *Dzwon* (The Bell), *Gość* (The Visitor), and the newspaper supplement *Tryumf Ewangelii* (Triumph of the Gospel), as well as a bookstore that the priest owned and operated. The proceeds from these enterprises Łuczycki used to partially fund, in 1887, the construction of the St. Mary's Home for the Aged People and the Orphanage of the Sweetest Heart of Jesus and Mary in Manitowoc. To this orphanage he later added a hospital, eventually turning ownership of the facilities over to the **Felician Sisters**. By 1894, however, the economy soured and Łuczycki experienced increasing difficulties keeping his publications, bookstore, and printing enterprise financially viable. In the same year, discouraged by the downturn in his business efforts, he returned to Poland. He returned to America in 1902 as pastor of the small Sacred Heart Parish in Two Rivers, and in the following year began publishing *Biblioteczka Rodzinna* (The Family Library), a series of publications of about 64 pages each that ceased publication in the same year when Łuczycki moved to new Britain, Connecticut as assistant to the Rev. **Lucian Bójnowski**. The following year he moved to Stamford, Connecticut where he founded Holy Name Parish and constructed a church and school. In 1906 he returned to Poland where he settled in Nałęcz and later constructed a convent and a home for aged and infirmed priests.—*James S. Pula*

SOURCE: Casimir Stec, "Pioneer Polish-American Publisher," *Polish American Studies*, Vol. 18, no. 2 (1961), 65–83.

Lujack, Johnny (John Luczak; b. Connellsville, Pennsylvania, January 4, 1925; d.—). Football Player. As a college sophomore, Johnny Lujack played on Notre Dame's national champion football squad in 1943 before entering military service. Upon returning to Notre Dame, he quarterbacked the Fighting Irish to consecutive national titles in 1946–47, earning All-America honors both seasons. In 1947, as a senior, he won the Heisman Trophy as the top collegiate player in the country, and was named Athlete of the Year by the Associated Press. Drafted into the professional ranks, Lujack starred for four seasons in a brief career with the Chicago Bears. He won first team All-Pro honors as quarterback in 1950, and played in the Pro Bowl in 1950 and 1951. Injuries led to his premature retirement from the sport. Lujack is a member of the College Football Hall of Fame, and was elected to the National Polish-American Sports Hall of Fame in 1978.—*Neal Pease*

SOURCE: "Johnny Lujack," National Polish-American Sports Hall of Fame website, www.polishsportshof.com.

Lukas, Richard (Richard Conrad Lukaszewski; b. Chicago, Illinois, August 29, 1937; d.—). Historian. Lukas earned his doctorate in history from Florida State University in 1963 and went on to teach at a number of universities, most notably Tennessee Technological University. His many publications include several important works that deal with Poland and its relationship to the United States during and after World War II, including *The Strange Allies: Poland and the United States, 1941–1945* (1978). In 1986, Lukas authored what one scholarly reviewer characterized as a "carefully researched" book, *The Forgotten Holocaust, The Poles under German Occupation, 1939–1944*. This book was sharply criticized in a controversial exchange published in the American academic journal, *The Slavic Review*. The main criticism involved Lukas's daring decision to use the word "Holocaust" in writing about the catastrophe visited on the Polish people in World War II. Lukas continued to publish on these subjects, his later work including *Out of the Inferno: Poles Remember the Holocaust* (1989). He received numerous awards and honors for his scholarly publications, including the Janusz Korczak award from the Anti-Defamation League of the B'nai B'rith (1994).—*Donald E. Pienkos*

SOURCES: Wojciech Wierzewski, "Sto Trzydziesta Slynnych Polaków w Ameryce" (Unpublished manuscript in the archives of the University of Wisconsin-Milwaukee, 2000); Bolesław Wierzbiański, *Who's Who in Polish America* (New York: Bicentennial Publishing Corp., 1996), 270; "Lukas, Richard C.," *Contemporary Authors* (Detroit: Gale Research Company), Vol. 33–36, 526.

Łukaszkiewicz, Czesław (b. Kraków, Poland, April 19, 1882; d. Chicago, Illinois, January 7, 1946). Writer, Polonia activist. The son of an 1863 insurrectionist, Łukaszkiewicz joined secret patriotic societies as a schoolboy and spent his adult life promoting Polish political causes as a writer and journalist. After studying law, philosophy, and psychology, he did educational work among Polish workers in Kraków, Vienna, and Budapest, working as a correspondent, founding schools, and writing books. After a stint in Warsaw and Berlin, he edited a miner's newspaper in Silesia until expelled by the Prussian government. Moving to Paris, he underwent training

as a rifleman. With the outbreak of World War I in 1914, he was sent to the United States to organize a Polish American fighting force under the Komitet Obrony Narodowy (KON; see **National Defense Committee**). Lecturing and publishing on Polish history and politics, he also organized schools for military officers in New York. Reports differ, but it appears that in 1917, denounced by local Polish American priests as a German sympathizer, Łukaszkiewicz was detained for six months by the United States government at Fort Oglethorpe, Georgia, before being freed through the efforts of Dr. **Paul Fox**. If clergymen were indeed the cause of Łukaszkiewicz's imprisonment, he had his revenge with a series of very popular anticlerical novels set in **Polonia** beginning with *Księży chleb* (Priestly Bread), first published in 1919. Other titles include *Zakonny welon* (The Nun's Veil, 1920), *Ucieczka grzesznych* (Refuge of Sinners, 1928), and *Listy Księ dza Świeczki* (Father Swieczka's Letters, 1930). His 1923 novel *Dziwna dziewczyna* (The Strange Girl) exposed political and economic opportunism within Detroit Polonia in the early days of Poland's newly-regained independence. And *Anioł stróż i djabeł stróż* (Guardian Angel and Guardian Devil), published in 1931, may well be the best Polish immigrant novel written in Polish during his generation. Łukaszkiewicz had a wicked sense of humor, a sharp political mind, and a prolific pen. His many other works include poetry, plays, translations, histories, and political analyses. He spent protracted periods of time in Toledo, Chicago, Detroit, and New York, but did much of his writing at his farm in Mattoax, Virginia. Throughout his peripatetic career, he served as editor and/or correspondent to the Toledo *Ameryka-Echo*, Chicago's *Chicagoski Kuryer Niedzielny* (Chicago Sunday Courier), *Dziennik Ludowy* (People's Daily News), *Dziennik Związkowy* (Alliance Daily News), and *Kuryer Narodowy* (National Courier), the Detroit *Dziennik Polski* (Polish Daily News), New York's *Nowy Świat* (New World), *Kuryer Nowoyorski* (New York Courier) and *Wici* (The Weaver), the Buffalo *Dziennik dla Wszystkich* (Everyone's Daily News), Scranton's *Straż* (The Guard), and Baltimore's *Postęp* (Progress). An active lecturer and organizer, he was a supporter of the **Polish National Catholic Church**, Polish singing groups, the Klub Małopolski (Little Poland Club), and the Uniwersytet Ludowy (People's University), establishing branches of the latter in Buffalo (1922) and Scranton (1926). In 1930 Łukaszkiewicz returned to Poland where he lectured, continued to contribute to newspapers in Poland and the United States, and was active in the **Liga**

Morska (Polish Sea League), Związek Pionierów Kolonialnych (Union of Colonial Pioneers), and Towarzystwo Polsko-Estońskie (Polish-Estonian Friendship Society), and served as president of the Związek Przyjaciełł Litwy (Alliance of Friends of Lithuania). He returned permanently to the U.S. in 1934, spending several years in Virginia before taking on the editorship of *Ameryka-Echo* in 1941, then joining the effort in Chicago to organize the **Polish American Congress**. He received many honors for his work on behalf of Poland, including the Polish Legionnaire's Cross, Independence Cross, Order of Polonia Restituta, the Order of the Colonial Commandery from France, and Estonia's White Eagle Cross. His biography in the *Polish Biographical Dictionary* claims that Łukaszkiewicz died on June 12, 1954. But numerous Polish American newspapers reported on his death and funeral in January 1946. He is buried in Chicago's Irving Park Cemetery.—*Karen Majewski*

SOURCE: Karen Majewski, *Traitors and True Poles: Narrating a Polish-American Identity, 1880–1939* (Athens: Ohio University Press, 2003).

Lukomski, Kazimierz (b. Bitajcie, Lithuania, March 16, 1920; d. Chicago, Illinois, December 18, 1991). Polonia activist. In 1929, Lukomski's family moved to Poland where he graduated from high school in 1938 and enlisted in the Polish Army. During the Second World War he served with the First Polish Paratroop Brigade of the Polish Armed Forces under British and U.S. command. After the war he resettled in London, arriving in the United States in 1955 as a refugee under the Displaced Persons Resettlement Act of 1954. Settling in Chicago, he worked as an accountant for Papermate and Barton Brands, Ltd. In 1968 he was elected vice president of the **Polish American Congress**, in the same year becoming chairman of the PAC's Polish Affairs Commission where he was the driving force in formulating and implementing PAC's policy toward Poland. He served as the interim chief of the PAC after the death of **Aloysius Mazewski** in August 1988 and before the election of **Edward Moskal** in November, but resigned in 1991 as a protest against the policies of then President Moskal. Lukomski was an active member of the **Polish Army Veterans Association**, president of the Mutual Aid Association of the New Polish Immigration, and co-chairman of the **National Polish-American Jewish American Council**. Lukomski advocated cooperation with other immigrant communities within the United States, including Lithuanians, and was a pioneer in establishing dialogue between Polish and Jewish Americans. He helped to coordinate Black Ribbon Day, an annual protest of the Molotov-Ribbentrop Pact that established German and Soviet spheres of influence in East Central Europe. A collection of his papers is housed at the University of Illinois at Chicago library of special collections.—*Mary Patrice Erdmans*

Sources: Mary Patrice Erdmans, *Opposite Poles: Immigrants and Ethnics in Polish Chicago, 1976–1990* (University Park, PA: Pennsylvania State University Press, 1998); Donald E. Pienkos, *For Your Freedom Through Ours: Polish American Efforts on Poland's Behalf, 1863–1991* (Boulder, CO: East European Monographs, 1991).

Lutherans, Polish American. The Rev. **Paul Fox**, in his history of the Reformation in Poland, writes, "Owing to this remarkable degree of religious toleration, Poland became a land of refuge for persecuted religious dissenters and reformers of other European countries ... and because of the close proximity of Great Poland to Saxony and Wittenberg, Luther's reforms reached it quickly." Luther's teachings took hold among the Polish speaking **Mazurians** living in the southern districts of former East Prussia and the western half of Suwalki, Poland. Karl Krueger found on the eve of migration to the United States, "The Mazurians were a distinct community with a unique culture — a Polish-speaking Protestant culture, a deviation in the popular paradigm that labeled Germans as Protestants and Poles as Catholic." Economic factors of land scarcity and employment opportunities in the largely agrarian region whose population was experiencing a surge forced many to migrate to the United States in the decades following the American Civil War. Though some migrated to industrial areas like Detroit or Scranton, the majority chose agricultural communities, settling in Milwaukee and Pound County, Wisconsin; Decatur, Illinois; Benton County, Minnesota; and Baltimore County, Maryland.

Arriving in America without clergy or means to establish their own congregations, the Mazurians from East Prussia were able to fulfill their spiritual needs by attending German Lutheran churches. The Rev. Ferdinand Sattelmeier, who spoke Polish and would be instrumental in reaching out to these Polish Lutherans in Michigan, Pennsylvania, and Maryland, noted in his autobiography that among Detroit's German Lutheran congregations almost fifty percent were comprised of Poles. Polish Lutherans from Suwalki only spoke Polish, therefore worshiping with a German congregation was not possible. They required a Polish-speaking pastor and their scarcity in America resulted in this group creating a *Gromadki* unit, or semi-self-sufficient worshipping community whose needs for a pastor were occasional. In a *Gromadki* the

members worshipped in the home of a member of the community who led the service in the absence of the pastor. This was true of Polish Lutherans in Baltimore County, Maryland, in the early 1900s where the Rev. Sattelmeier, who at the time was pastor of a Polish Lutheran congregation in Scranton, visited the community four times a year to teach the children their catechism, visit the sick, and administer the sacraments. This arrangement functioned well for two years, but it took a toll on the Rev. Sattelmeier who eventually became exhausted from the train ride and the problems of caring for two growing congregations. At Sattelmeier's urging, the worshipping community wrote a constitution of seven paragraphs and organized as the First Polish Lutheran Evangelical Church on March 20, 1904.

Once the congregation was established, the Eastern District of the Lutheran Synod assumed responsibility for the congregation and secured Kazimierz Mikulski, a Polish Lutheran cleric born in Łomza, to act as minister. Because the community was not in a financial position to support the Rev. Mikulski, the Eastern District provided a salary of $700. After beginning his pastoral duties, a delighted Mikulski wrote the editors of *Przyjaciel Ludu* (Friend of the People), "I am very happy that I will be able to be a pastor to my compatriots. This was the desire of my heart for eight years when I left the fatherland."

By 1906 the Missouri Synod's missionary board estimated there were 2,500 Polish Lutherans being served by six Polish-speaking clerics: three German and three Polish. The group began publishing a newspaper, *Kościół Reformacyjny w Ameryce* (The Church of the Reformation in America) with Sattelmeier serving as editor. Its four pages contained articles on religion and parish news, attracting the attention of Polish Lutherans throughout the United States and Canada. At the height of its popularity there were 250 subscribers in North America, as well as twenty-five in Russian Poland. In 1908 the national meeting of the Missouri Synod incorporated the Polish Mission of the Eastern District into its Foreign Language Missions. This provided financial assistance for congregations such as Baltimore whose members were farm workers unable to raise more than a few hundred dollars to purchase land and build a church and school. As a result the Polish-speaking clergy were able to stabilize the ministry, transforming the *Gromadki* form of worship into eventual self-sustaining congregations with constitutions, clerics, and churches. Although it was willing to subsidize church construction, the national synod refused to assume liability for

the Polish newspaper whose cost exceed its income and eventually the newspaper ceased publication.

At the time of America's entry into the First World War the Polish mission estimated there were twelve Polish Lutheran congregations lead by Polish-speaking clergy numbering 4,900 members. The coming war led to opportunities that eventually transformed the agrarian workers into industrial employees. Bethlehem Steel purchased property in eastern Baltimore County at Sparrows Point. The three-hundred acre property produced ships for the war and became a major employer attracting fellow Polish Lutherans from Pennsylvania. As the next generation left farm work for industry they also spoke English instead of Polish outside of the home and in the early 1920s the Polish Lutheran ministry introduced English into its services. With each succeeding generation the use of Polish in the service became less and eventually the congregations became Polish in name only. Gradually, this nomenclature disappeared as well, though many of the congregations still exist strong in the Lutheran faith of their Polish ancestors.— *Thomas L. Hollowak*

Sources: Karl Krueger, *Psalms and Potatoes: The Congregations of the Polish-speaking Protestant Mazurians in East Prussia, Suwalki, Poland, and the United States* (Ph.D. Dissertation, University of Michigan, 1992, 2 vols.); Frederick A. Sattelmeier, *Man in Action: The Happy Life of a Clergyman and His Family, with a Short Sketch on the Origin of Religion, God's Unfolding Purpose* (Palm Springs, CA: F. A. Sattelmeier, 1966).

Luzinski, Gregory Michael (b. Chicago, Illinois, November 22, 1950; d.—). Baseball player. Known as "The Bull" for his massive build, Luzinski was widely recruited to play college football, but chose instead to play professional baseball, and made his major league debut with the Philadelphia Phillies in 1970. In the course of a fifteen season career, Luzinski hit .276 with 307 home runs, playing for two teams. A right handed power hitting left fielder, he had his greatest success with the Phillies over a four year stretch from 1975 through 1978. During that span, Luzinski hit 128 homers, and in 1975 led the National League in runs batted in. In all four seasons, he was named to the National League All-Star team, and placed among the top ten in balloting for the league's Most Valuable Player award, finishing second twice. His teams reached postseason play five times, and in 1980 his Phillies won the first World Series championship in the history of the franchise. Retiring as a player after the 1984 season, he coached in the major leagues. Luzinski was inducted into the **National Polish-American Sports Hall of Fame** in 1989.—*Neal Pease*

SOURCE: "Greg Luzinski," National Polish-American Sports Hall of Fame website, www.polishsportshof.com.

Lynn, Janet (Janet Lynn Nowicki; b. Chicago, Illinois, April 6, 1953; d.—). Figure skater. As a figure skating prodigy, Janet Lynn—she used her given middle name for competitive purposes—won the U.S. Junior championship in 1966, at age 12. She won the U.S. Ladies' Singles championship five straight years, 1969–1973, as well as the North American Ladies' title in 1969. She competed in the 1968 and 1972 Olympics, claiming a bronze medal on the latter occasion. Very popular with the public, Lynn then became a professional performer. Although her career was interrupted by health problems, she continued to skate into the 1980s. Lynn was inducted into the **National Polish-American Sports Hall of Fame** in 1990.—*Neal Pease*

SOURCE: Christine Brennan, *Inside Edge: A Revealing Journey into the Secret World of Figure Skating* (New York: Anchor, 1997).

Lytell, Delphine (Delphine Mackowski; b. South Bend, Indiana, October 10, 1944; d.—). Polonia activist. After earning a baccalaureate degree in English literature at **St. Mary's College** in Indiana, Lytell worked as a high school teacher and librarian. Involved in the **Polish Women's Alliance** from childhood (her mother was a PWA District 3 president), Lytell was appointed editor of the English language section of the PWA's official publication, ***Głos Polek*** (The Voice of Polish Woman) in 1984. In 1987 she was elected the fraternal's vice president, and in summer 1992 she joined President **Helen Wojcik** and *Głos Polek*'s editor, **Maria Loryś**, to represent the Alliance at the world congress of Polonia held in Warsaw and Kraków. There, the PWA donated three medical transport vans the fraternal's members had purchased to help meet the needs of handicapped children. In 1995 she was elected to succeed Wojcik as PWA president, defeating Lucyna Migala of Chicago in a second ballot run-off. As a national officer, and a leader in the **Polish American Congress**, Lytell was involved in a number of humanitarian efforts on Poland's behalf. In June 1996 Lytell and Treasurer Olga Kaszewicz represented the PWA in a Vatican meeting with Pope John Paul II. The meeting brought together the leaders of a number of American societies that were raising funds to support the creation of the **Pope John Paul II Cultural Center** being planned in Washington, D.C. At the PWA's thirty-third national convention in 1999 Lytell narrowly lost her reelection bid to national director Virginia Sikora of Detroit. Following her presidency, Lytell continued to be active in the Polish

Women's Alliance and from 2003 to 2007 she served as president of its District One (Illinois) unit. She was also Librarian of the Moraine Valley Community College in Palo Hills, Illinois.—*Angela T. Pienkos*

SOURCE: Donald E. Pienkos and Angela Pienkos, *"In the Ideals of Women is the Strength of a Nation": A History of the Polish Women's Alliance of America* (Boulder, CO: East European Monographs, 2003), 223.

Machrowicz, Thaddeus Michael (b. Gostyn, Poland, August 21, 1899; d. Bloomfield Township, Michigan, February 17, 1970). Congressman, attorney, judge. Migrating to the United States with his parents in 1902, he settled in Chicago, later moving to Milwaukee where he was naturalized in 1910. Attending parochial school in Milwaukee, he did undergraduate work at **Alliance College** (1912–16), Cambridge Springs, PA, before enrolling in the University of Chicago in 1917. During the First World War he served as a lieutenant in the Polish Army organized and trained in Canada for service in France and Poland between 1917 and 1920. He served with the American Advisory Commission to the newly created Polish government (1920–21), the American Relief Mission headed by Herbert Hoover, and became a war correspondent with Floyd Gibbons in Poland (1919–21). Returning to the U.S., he attended De Paul University in 1921, graduated from the Detroit College of Law in 1924, was admitted to the Michigan bar in 1924, and began practice in Detroit. He served as the city attorney of **Hamtramck**, Michigan, in 1934–36; legal director of the Michigan Public Utilities Commission in 1938–39; and municipal judge in Hamtramck, 1942–50. He was a delegate to the Democratic Party National Conventions from Michigan in 1952, 1956, and 1960, and a member of the War Labor Board during World War II. Elected as a Democrat in 1950 from Detroit's East Side to the 82nd Congress and the five succeeding Congresses, Machrowicz served on the House Judiciary, Public Works, and Ways and Means Committees, and was a leader in creating the St. Lawrence Seaway. Machrowicz was a member of the House Select Committee to Conduct an Investigation and Study the Facts, Evidence, and Circumstances of the **Katyń** Forest Massacre (1951–52). He resigned to become a judge appointed by President John F. Kennedy to the United States District Court for the Eastern District of Michigan where he served until his death. He helped to establish the Michigan chapter of the **Polish American Congress**, serving as its first president, and recorded Polish language broadcasts for Voice of America.—*Frederick J. Augustyn*

SOURCES: Marek Święcicki and Róża Nowotarska,

The Gentleman from Michigan (London: Polish Cultural Foundation, 1974); *Biographical Directory of the United States Congress, 1774–Present* (http://bioguide.congress.gov/).

Maciejewski, Anton Frank "Whitey" (b. Anderson, Texas, January 3, 1893; d. Chicago, Illinois, September 25, 1949). Congressman, coal merchant. After attending public schools in Cicero, Illinois, and the Lewis Institute, which later became the Illinois Institute of Technology, he became engaged in the wholesale and retail coal business in Cicero in 1916. From 1925 to 1928 he served as assistant agent in charge of relief in Cook County, which includes Chicago and a number of adjacent towns and suburbs. He was a member of the Democratic State and National Committees, a delegate to the Democratic National Conventions in 1928 and 1940, and supervisor and treasurer of Cicero (1932–39). Elected as a Democrat to the 76th and 77th Congresses, he served from January 3, 1939, until his resignation on December 8, 1942, when he took over as an elected member of the Board of Trustees of the sanitary district of Chicago, which he also served as president. He later resumed the wholesale and retail coal business, and engaged in the construction of defense housing during World War II.—*Frederick J. Augustyn*

SOURCE: *Biographical Directory of the United States Congress, 1774–Present* (http://bioguide.congress.gov/).

Maciora, Lucien J. (b. New Britain, Connecticut, August 17, 1902; d. New Britain, Connecticut, October 19, 1993). Public official, Congressman. Maciora attended local schools in New Britain and worked as a young man at his father's grocery business. He was a partner in a furniture and undertaking business in the 1930s, worked as an agent for the Metropolitan Life Insurance Company in the 1940s, and helped found the People's Bank of New Britain. Maciora was active in a number of Polish American associations and was a former president of the **Polish American Congress**, having attended its founding meeting in Buffalo in 1944. He began his political career on the New Britain common council, serving from 1926 to 1934. Subsequently, he was part of a successful effort by Democrats to break the longstanding Republican hold on seats in the Connecticut House of Representatives. He was elected to the Connecticut House in 1931 and served to 1937. In addition, he was the chairman of the New Britain police board from 1934 to 1940. With the support of the Pulaski Federation of Democratic Clubs of Connecticut, Maciora was nominated at the 1940 state Democratic Party convention to challenge incumbent Republican Congressman **Boleslaus J. Monkiewicz**, the first Pole ever elected to Connecticut's at-large House seat. He defeated Monkiewicz and served one term in the House of Representatives (1941–43). However, he lost his reelection bid in 1942, with Monkiewicz regaining his seat. He returned to New Britain politics, serving with the support of both parties as the city tax collector from 1950 to 1969.—*Jonathan Swarts*

SOURCES: *Biographical Dictionary of the United States Congress, 1774–present* (http://bioguide.congress.gov/); Stanislaus A. Blejwas, "The '44 Club: Second Generation Polonia," *Polish American Studies,* Vol. 51, no. 1 (1994), 49–64; "L. J. Maciora; Served Term in Congress," *Hartford Courant,* October 20, 1993, D11.

Maciuszko, Jerzy J. (b. Warsaw, Poland, July 15, 1913; d.—). Literary scholar. A distinguished scholar, writer, and educator, Maciuszko dedicated his life to the study, preservation, and advancement of Polish cultural heritage in the United States. After earning a degree in English language and literature at the University of Warsaw (1936), he served in the Polish Army during World War II, being captured by the Germans and held in a prison camp until the end of the war. During his captivity, he won the first of many literary honors when his short story *Koncert F-Moll* was awarded first prize in a competition among prisoners of war sponsored by the International Young Men's Christian Association. Following his liberation at the end of the war, he moved to London where he became a contributor to several professional journals. Maciuszko began his academic career after emigrating to the United States in 1951 when he accepted a position as a lecturer in Polish language and literature at **Alliance College** in Cambridge Springs, Pennsylvania. Shortly thereafter, he moved to Cleveland where he earned a master's degree in library science from Western Reserve University (1953) and held the position of assistant head of foreign literature at the Cleveland Public Library (1953–62). After earning his doctorate in library science in 1962, Maciuszko was promoted to director of the prestigious John G. White Collection at the Cleveland Public Library, a position he held until 1969. Throughout these years he was also a lecturer in Polish language and literature at Western Reserve University. In 1969 he was appointed chair of the Slavic Studies Department at Alliance College. During his tenure there he established the first international student exchange program between the Jagiellonian University in Kraków and an American college. He also expanded the activities of Alliance's Center for Polish Studies, which attracted to the College the noted writer **W. S. Kuniczak** and other international scholars. In 1974 he left Alliance College to become director of the Ritter Li-

brary, as well as professor at Baldwin-Wallace College in Berea, Ohio. He continued as library director until 1978, remaining as professor thereafter.

A prolific writer, Maciuszko contributed biographical entries to such publications as the *Encyclopedia of World Literature in the 20th Century* (1975) and *The Encyclopedia of Cleveland History* (1987). Among his other publications were *The Polish Short Story in English: A Guide and Critical Bibliography* (1968) and *Half-a-Century of the Polish Institute of America, 1942–1992* (1997). In addition to his academic work, Maciuszko was active in various Polish American civic and cultural organizations including the **Polish American Congress**, the **Alliance of Poles in America**, the Cleveland Society of Poles, the **Polish Institute of Arts and Sciences of America**, and the Association of Polish Writers Abroad. He was also a founding member of the John Paul II Cultural Center in Cleveland. Among his numerous awards were the Gold Medal from the World Federation of Polish Veterans Association in London (1988), the Polonia Foundation Heritage Award for Distinguished Community Service (1990), the American Biographical Institute's Man of the Year (1990), the Officers' Cross and the Order of Merit from the Republic of Poland (1993), and the Polish Heritage Award from the Cleveland Society of Poles (2000).—*Ben S. Stefanski II*

SOURCES: Maria Szonert-Binienda, "Director Jerzy J. Maciuszko—Ambassador of Polish Culture," *Forum,* February 2006, 4–5; "Maciuszko, Jerzy J.," *Contemporary Authors* (Detroit: Gale Research Company), Vol. 25–28, 447.

Madaj, Mieczysław J. (b. Illinois, June 15, 1912; d. Cook County, Illinois, July 31, 1986). Priest, Polonia activist. Madaj attended St. Mary of the Lake Seminary in Mundelein, Illinois. After his ordination in 1937 he served in various parishes until he enrolled in the Vatican School of Archival and Library Science in 1952. He continued his educational pursuits with a M.A. degree in music and history and a doctorate in history from Loyola University in Chicago (1956). In the following year he pursued post-doctoral studies at Oxford University in England. After serving for several years on the faculties of St. Norbert College in Wisconsin and St. Joseph's College in Indiana, in 1968 Madaj was assigned to St. Mary of the Lake Seminary as a member of the faculty and archivist for the Archdiocese of Chicago, a position he held for sixteen years. A long-time **Polonia** activist, Madaj served four terms as president of the **Polish American Historical Association**, editor and then corresponding editor of the *PAHA Newsletter,* and executive secretary from 1970

to 1984. In the latter capacity he was responsible for establishing a permanent headquarters for PAHA at the **Polish Museum of America** in Chicago and PAHA's acceptance as an affiliate member of the prestigious American Historical Association. Among his recognitions was PAHA's Haiman Award for sustained contributions to research and dissemination of Polish American history and culture.—*James S. Pula*

SOURCE: *Polish American Studies,* Vol. XLIII, no. 2 (Autumn 1986), inside cover.

Maida, Adam Joseph (b. East Vandergrift, Pennsylvania, March 18, 1930; d.—). Catholic Cardinal. After earning his baccalaureate degree in philosophy from St. Vincent's College in Latrobe, Pennsylvania, he enrolled in St. Mary's University in Baltimore, Maryland, where he earned a licentiate in Sacred Theology in 1956. Maida was ordained on May 26, 1956, following which he went on to study in Rome where he earned another licentiate in Canon Law from the Pontifical Lateran University in 1960. His Doctorate in Civil Law, awarded in 1964, was from Duquesne Law School in Pittsburgh, Pennsylvania. He served as an Assistant Professor of Theology at La Roche College and Adjunct Professor of Law at Duquesne. On November 8, 1983, after serving in the diocese of Pittsburgh, he was installed as the ninth Bishop of the Diocese of Green Bay on January 25, 1984. In May of 1990 Pope John Paul II named him Archbishop of Detroit and four years later proclaimed him a cardinal. Maida became one of the founding forces behind the **Pope John Paul II Cultural Center** in Washington, D.C. In April 2005, following the Pope's death, Cardinal Maida traveled to the Vatican to participate in the papal conclave that elected Cardinal Joseph Ratzinger as Pope Benedict XVI. In June 2006 he celebrated the fiftieth anniversary of his ordination to the priesthood. In 2008, Cardinal Maida was the eldest active member of the American hierarchy.—*Biff Rocha*

SOURCE: "Detroit Gets a New Archbishop," *Our Sunday Visitor,* Vol. 79 (May 27, 1990), 17.

Majer, Dominik A. (b. Russian Poland, December 28, 1838; d. St. Paul, Minnesota, March 11, 1911). Priest. An important early figure in American **Polonia**, Majer was a founding member of three major Polonia fraternal organizations, played a critical role in the early conflicts between the **Polish National Alliance** and the **Polish Roman Catholic Union of America**, and was crucial in the development of Polonia parish communities in Minnesota. In 1906 he became the first Polish priest in the United States to be granted the title of monsignor. Majer studied classics and philosophy in Warsaw before completing a degree in theology at the University of Vienna in 1861. He was ordained a priest that same year. During the January Insurrection of 1863 the young priest served as a chaplain in an insurgent unit. Following the defeat of the Polish uprising, Majer fled to Austrian Poland, but like many ex-insurgents was forced to leave due to the hostility of the Austrian authorities. After a brief sojourn in Italy, he spent some time in Prussian Poland. In 1873, he was sent to the United States to conduct missionary work among Polish immigrants. Assigned to the Polish parish in Berlin, Wisconsin, he later served for five years as pastor of St. Adalbert Parish in Chicago, then as pastor in Pine Creek, Wisconsin. In September 1883, he was assigned to the new Polish parish of St. Adalbert in St. Paul, Minnesota where he served as pastor for the next twenty-eight years, until his death in 1911. During this time, he helped to found several other Polish parishes including Holy Cross, Minneapolis (1886); St. Casimir, St. Paul (1892); and St. John the Baptist, New Brighton (1902). Majer's long tenure at St. Adalbert was unusual in that, unlike many early Polonia parishes, it never experienced a major internal conflict nor did it come into serious conflict with the powerful Americanizing archbishop of St. Paul, John Ireland.

Majer was originally recommended for the pastorate in Chicago by the powerful Chicago **Resurrectionist**, the Rev. **Wincenty Barzyński**. Initially, Majer seems to have worked closely with Barzyński as a founding member

The Rev. Dominick Majer, leader of a faction of priests allied with the Polish National Alliance (*OLS*).

of the Polish Roman Catholic Union of America. However, he soon had a falling out with Barzyński over the direction of the new organization and Barzyński's role in picking assignments for Polish priests in Chicago. By 1887, Majer had gravitated to the Polish National Alliance, leading a group of fellow priests to defect from the PRCUA and join the PNA. Known as the "Alliance Priests," they favored an organization that was both strongly nationalist and confirmed the centrality of Catholicism among Polish immigrants. By 1889, the Alliance Priests fell afoul of radical anti-clerical elements in the PNA and were forced out. In 1890, Majer founded his own fraternal, the **Polish Union of America** (Unia Polska) which he intended to be a "third way" between the PNA and PRCUA that would, he believed, unify American Polonia. In 1900, Majer seems to have lost control of the organization which moved its headquarters to Buffalo. The Polish Union later split into three groups: the **Polish National Alliance of Brooklyn**, the Polish Union of America (Buffalo), and the **Polish Union of the United States** (Wilkes Barre, PA). After 1900, Majer's influence nationally seems to have declined and he focused primarily on local issues, though he continued to write occasional articles for the Polonia press. His last major project was the building of a new church for own parish of St. Adalbert which was completed just after his death in 1911.— *John Radzilowski*

SOURCES: John Radzilowski, "Hidden Cosmos: The Life Worlds of Polish Immigrants in Two Minnesota Communities, 1875–1925" (Ph.D. dissertation, Arizona State University, 1999); "The Right Reverend Monsignor Dominic A. Majer," *Acta et Dicta* (St. Paul), Vol. 3, no. 1 (July 1911), 206–13.

Majewski, Karen (b. Chicago, Illinois, April 21, 1955; d.—). Historian. After receiving her baccalaureate (1977) and M.A. (1981) degrees in English from Southern Illinois University–Carbondale, Majewski went on to earn a Ph.D. in American Culture from the University of Michigan (1998), with postgraduate work at the Center for International Studies Intensive Summer Language Program (Hungarian) at Beloit College (2003) and the Archival Practice Summer Training Program held at the Polish National Archives in Warsaw (2001). Her teaching career included an appointment as instructor in English composition at Inver Hills Community College in Minnesota (1981–83), as lecturer in composition and literature at North Carolina State University (1983–88), and appointment to the faculty of English, Polish and East Central European Studies at **St. Mary's College** in Michigan (1994–2003) where she rose from

adjunct instructor to associate professor before the institution closed. She also served as director of the Polish and Rare Book Collection at St. Mary's and the Orchard Lake (MI) Schools beginning in 1996, and director of the Archives of **Polonia** at Orchard Lake beginning in 2008. In the latter two positions she was responsible for organizing, cataloguing, and preserving the extensive holdings of book and archival materials. Majewski was elected mayor of **Hamtramck**, Michigan, in 2006 after having served on the City Council (2003–05) and as President/Mayor Pro Tem (2004–2005). She was a member of the Board of Directors of the Michigan Municipal League (beginning 2008), Executive Director of the **Polish American Historical Association** (1998–2007), newsletter editor of the Polish American Historical Association (1998–2004), an appointee to the Hamtramck Historical Commission (2002–03), Exhibit Researcher for the "Polish Presence in Detroit" exhibit at the Detroit Historical Museum (2001–02), a member of the Michigan Women's Hall of Fame Selection Committee (2001), a Board Member of the Dekaban Foundation (1999–), a Board Member of the Polish American Historical Association (1997–98), and a member of the Exhibit Organizing Committee for the "Polish Literary Milestones" exhibit at the Detroit Public Library (1995). An expert on Polish American literature and women's studies, Majewski's book *Traitors and True Poles: Narrating a Polish American Identity, 1880–1939* (2003) explored and preserved a largely unknown literary tradition among Polish immigrants of the mass migration, earning her recognition and "best book" awards from the Polish American Historical Association (2004) and the **Polish Institute of Arts & Sciences of America** (2005). Among her many other honors are the Distinguished Service Award from the Polish American Historical Association (2003), an American Council of Learned Societies Foreign Language Study Grant (2002), and the Halecki Prize for a Distinguished Dissertation in Polish American studies from the Polish American Historical Association (2000).— *James S. Pula*

Majka, Debbie (Deborah Mary Filipek; b. Philadelphia, Pennsylvania, April 14, 1946; d.—). Polonia activist. Educated at St. Hubert's High School and Villanova University, Majka earned an M.S. in Counseling and Human Relations. She was employed professionally in the Monomers Marketing division of Rohm and Haas Company, taking an early retirement in 2006. She served as president of the **American Council for Polish Culture**

(ACPC) in 1993–99 and 2003–07, and was a member of the ACPC Pulaski and Skalny Scholarship Committees, the General Pulaski Memorial Committee and a co-chair of the ACPC National Convention. In 2006 she became Vice-President for Cultural Activities of the **Polish American Congress**, a new position especially created for her, in addition to serving on the Financial Development Committee and representing ACPC.

On the local level, she was active in the Polish Heritage Society of Philadelphia, an affiliate of ACPC, serving several terms as president. In 2005 she was the chair for the ACPC convention in Philadelphia. She was a charter member and president of the **Marcella Sembrich-Kochanska** Female Chorus, No. 321, **Polish Singers Alliance of America**, and, together with the members of the Chorus, sponsored the Adam Mickiewicz Polish Language School Junior Chorus No. 22. She taught Polish language to children and adults at the Adam Mickiewicz Polish Language School based at the Associated Polish Home in Northeast Philadelphia. She served as the Polish Home's president, was its financial secretary for over ten years, and also functioned as membership chair. A member of the Philadelphia-Torun Sister City Committee, she is also the producer and host of a half-hour radio program in English on Polish topics entitled *Polonia Today*, heard in the Greater Delaware Valley on 1540 WNWR AM and host of the *Polonia View* segment of the local Polish TV program *Kalejdoskop* on Channel 35 WYBE.

Among her many honors are the Medal Zaslugi (Polish Army Veterans); Distinguished Woman of the Year (Polish Heritage Society of Philadelphia); Polish American World Newspaper Citizen of the Year; the ACPC Founders Award; Poland's Krzyz Kawalerski, Orderu Zaslugi (Cavalier Cross of the Order of Merit); the Pulaski-O'Neil Medal (City of Savannah); the Polish American Historical Association's Civic Achievement Award; recognition by the Pauline Fathers of the **National Shrine of Our Lady of Czestochowa**, Doylestown, PA, for her volunteer efforts for more than 20 years; and *Am-Pol Eagle* National Citizen of the Year for 2006 (Buffalo).—*Peter J. Obst*

SOURCE: Bolesław Wierzbiański, *Who's Who in Polish America* (New York: Bicentennial Publishing Corp., 1996), 278.

Makowicz, Adam (Adam Matyszkowicz; b. Hnojnik, Czechoslovakia, August 18, 1940; d.—). Pianist. Makowicz's family, ethnic Poles who came from the disputed Zaolzie border region of Poland and Czechoslovakia, moved to Poland in 1946. His mother was a piano teacher and singer, and he pursued studies in classical piano at music schools in Rybnik, Katowice, and the Chopin High School of Music in Kraków. As a teenager, he was inspired by the American jazz he heard via Voice of America's broadcasts of the Jazz Hour on Willis Conover's program, *Music USA*. Shortly thereafter, Makowicz appeared in Helicon, a jazz club in Kraków, for several months. He then moved to Warsaw in 1956 where he quickly established working relationships with such important Polish jazz musicians as the Novi Singers, **Urszula Dudziak**, and the **Michał Urbaniak** Group. In 1962, together with trumpet player Tomasz Stańko, Makowicz formed The Jazz Darlings, a quartet that won the First Prize at a jazz competition in Poland in 1964. Around that time Makowicz also formed his own trio and toured Poland, India, Australia, New Zealand, and Cuba. By the mid–1960s, Makowicz's performances began to appear on the Polish Muza record label, as well as the Swiss Exlibris, West German Saba, and Czech Supraphon labels. By 2009, Makowicz had recorded over forty solo and ensemble albums all around the world. He performed at the Tallin International Jazz Festival in Estonia in 1967, and the Warsaw Jazz Jamboree in 1976, the latter of which was attended by Benny Goodman who recommended Makowicz for an engagement in New York. These performances led to his being discovered by John Hammond, the legendary record producer and talent scout. Hammond invited Makowicz to appear for a ten-week engagement at The Cookery, one of the most famous jazz clubs in New York City. Makowicz's successful American debut in May 1977 led to a solo performance at Carnegie Hall, where he shared the stage with such jazz legends as Earl "Fatha" Hines, George Shearing, and Teddy Wilson. Both the Carnegie Hall concert and Makowicz's highly acclaimed 1978 solo album on Columbia Records were produced by John Hammond. Makowicz settled in New York in 1978, becoming a U.S. citizen in 1986. An active supporter of the Solidarity movement, he returned to Poland after the fall of communism in 1989, presenting a concert of his own compositions with the Warsaw Philharmonic String Quartet. Since that time Makowicz has made numerous tours of Poland and appeared in concert throughout the world. A long-time resident of New York, in 2006 Makowicz resettled to Toronto, Canada. Voted the Number One European jazz pianist in the *Jazz Forum* reader's poll in 1977, Makowicz was lauded in June of 1977 by *Down Beat Magazine*, quoting Willis Conover's opinion that he is "one of the top ten jazz pianists in the world today." Makowicz developed his unique and highly virtuoso style from his earliest days of jazz playing in Poland. Art Tatum's brilliant technique with rapid right-hand runs and powerful left hand stride are at the foundation of Makowicz's pianistic style, together with influences of Duke Ellington, Erroll Garner, Bud Powell, Bill Evans, and Oscar Peterson, whose legacy of jazz standards find a creative outlet in this extraordinary Polish jazz virtuoso.—*Krysta Close* and *Marek Zebrowski*

SOURCES: *Jazz Forum Magazine*, 1977; *Down Beat Magazine*, June 1977.

Malinowski, Bronisław K. (b. Kraków, Poland, April 7, 1884; d. New Haven, Connecticut, May 14, 1942). Anthropologist. A student at Kraków's Jagiellonian University where his father had been a professor, Malinowski earned his doctorate in 1908. He then pursued further study at the University of Leipzig with Wilhelm Wundt and Karl Wilhelm Buecher before enrolling at the London School of Economics in 1910 where he developed his powerful ideas about anthropology. During World War I, he conducted research on New Guinea's Trobriand Islanders on which his groundbreaking book *Argonauts of the Western Pacific* (1922) was based. He returned to London in 1927 where he played a major role in the International Institute of African Languages and Cultures. He also popularized anthropology, recruiting talented young scholars such as E. E. Evans-Pritchard and Hortense Powdermaker for his seminars. In 1938 he came to Yale University, remaining there after the outbreak of World War II. Malinowski co-founded the **Polish Institute of Arts and Sciences in America**, serving as its first president in 1942.

Malinowski helped replace older methods of ethnography with the modern method of participant observation. In his own work he attempted to connect "civilized" and "primitive" societies by showing how both share rationality and scientific attitudes. He also demonstrated the orderliness of "primitive culture," and how "primitive" people, like their modern "civilized" counterparts, manipulated and deviated from rules of their community. Along with Emil Durkheim and Alfred R. Radcliffe-Brown, Malinowski is credited with developing the Structural-Functional paradigm that became one of the most influential social scientific theories of the twentieth century. This theory argued that culture was essentially an instrument for the satisfaction of basic human needs such as reproduction and security. For Malinowski, anthropology's primary goal was the discovery of universal laws governing human conduct, while he also sought to prove the underlying unity in cultural diversity.—*Jerome Krase*

SOURCES: Roy Ellen, et al., ed., *Malinowski Between Two Worlds: The Polish Roots of an Anthropological Tradition* (Cambridge, England: Cambridge University Press, 1990); Raymond Firth, *Man and Culture: An Evaluation of the Work of Bronisław Malinowski* (London: Routledge and Kegan Paul, 1957); Konstantin Symmons-Symonolewicz, "Bronisław Malinowski: An Intellectual Profile," *The Polish Review*, Vol. 3, no. 4 (1958), 55–76; Konstantin Symmons-Symonolewicz, "Bronisław Malinowski. Individuality as a Theorist," *The Polish Review*, Vol. 5, no. 1 (1960), 53–65; Konstantin Symmons-Symonolewicz, "The Origin of Malinowski's Theory of Magic," *The Polish Review*, Vol. 5, no. 4 (1960), 36–44; Feliks Gross, "Young Malinowski and His Later Years," *American Ethnologist*, Vol. 13, no. 3 (August 1986), 556–70.

Małłek, Antoni (b. Ogorzeliny, Poland, May 5, 1851; d. February 4, 1917, Chicago, Illinois). Musician, conductor. In 1871, escaping military service, Małłek crossed the Atlantic arriving in Chicago on March 31, 1871. In 1872 he took the post of organist in St. Stanislaus Kosta Church where he organized the parish's first choir. In 1873–74 he worked in St. Stanislaus Church in Milwaukee before moving to St. Casimir Church in Northeim, WI (1875–80). There he organized various choirs in Polish, German, and Irish churches. In 1879 he was elected a Justice of the Peace in Manitowoc County. Beginning in 1880 he served as organist in Holy Trinity Church in Chicago where he organized and conducted various choirs including "Harmony" (1883), "Wanda" (1888), "Chopin" (1888), and later others. While at Holy Trinity, Małłek, who was a member of the **Polish National Alliance** (PNA) and its secretary general from 1889 to 1895, was engaged in the conflict between the PNA and the **Resurrectionists**.

Małłek's mission in life was to propagate the culture of music among **Polonia** and through music to raise feelings of ethnic nationalism among the first and second generations of Poles in America. In 1884 he bought a special printing machine that enabled him to publish music literature, song books, scores, and manuals for singers. The first issue of his publication *Ziarno* (Seed) appeared in July 1886. Aside from his organizational and publishing contributions, he also composed songs, hymns, and marches, and organized music contests. On November 29, 1888, with the participation of representatives of choirs from Chicago, Milwaukee, La Salle (IL), and St. Paul (MN), Małłek and his brother Konstanty formed The **Polish Singers Alliance** in America. With its headquarters in Milwaukee, Konstanty served as first president and Antoni as director general, both until 1897. Stressing Polish patriotism, both advocated close ties to the Polish National Alliance in the conflicts with the **Polish Roman Catholic**

Antoni Małłek, musician, conductor and Polonia activist (*PMA*).

Union for influence within Polonia. The first general convention met in 1889, but by 1897 the internal strife that plagued Polonia led to a split at the convention held in Grand Rapids, MI. As a result, the Małłeks and their supporters left the convention while the remaining representatives formed the rival United Polish Singers Alliance in America headquartered in Chicago, with the Małłek faction retaining control of *Ziarno*. A reconciliation in 1903 led the two organizations to re-unite, but the Małłeks took a progressively diminishing role. From 1911 to 1913 Małłek worked as organist and teacher at the Church of Our Lady of the Angels in Chicago where he remained very active on the musical scene, composing songs and conducting choirs. He co-founded the Association of Polish Organists in Chicago in 1892, and in 1904 founded the St. Cecilia Association of Polish and Lithuanian Organists in America. Well known and respected as a teacher and educator, he numbered among his students Jadwiga Smulska and Agnieszka Nering, both of whom were well-known Polish American singers.—*Adam Walaszek*

SOURCES: Stanislaus A. Blejwas, *The Polish Singers Alliance of America: Choral Patriotism* (Rochester-Woodbridge: University of Rochester Press, 2005); Franciszek German, "Antoni Małłek," in *Polski Słownik Biograficzny*, Vol. 19, 450–51.

Mankiewicz, Joseph Leo (b. Wilkes-Barre, Pennsylvania, February 11, 1909; d. Mt. Kisco, New York, February 5, 1993). Screenwriter, director, producer. The youngest of three children born to Jewish immigrants of Polish ancestry, Mankiewicz attended Man-

hattan's prestigious Stuyvesant High School and earned a baccalaureate in English from Columbia University (1928). While at Columbia he sold his first piece of writing to *Life* magazine for six dollars under the pseudonym Joe Mason, in order not to besmirch the family name. To supplement his allowance, he taught English to the foreign-born at a night school earning $150 per semester for teaching three evenings a week. During the summer he was a dramatics counselor at a summer camp owned by the Marx Brothers where, foreshadowing his future career, he taught the campers to perform small dramatic sketches in preparation for parents' visiting day. Following graduation from Columbia, he moved to Germany to pursue graduate studies at the University of Berlin, but instead he landed a job as a junior reporter in the Berlin office of the *Chicago Tribune* and a second job translating intertitles from German to English for foreign motion picture release. In 1929 he accepted a position for $60 a week as a junior writer at Paramount Hollywood studios writing titles for silent movies such as *The Mysterious Dr. Fu Manchu* and *The Virginian*. In 1931 he was promoted to scenarist and dialogue writer, receiving his first Oscar nomination for *Skippy* starring Jackie Cooper. Between 1929 and 1934, he received dialogue credit for eight films, and screenplay credit for eight more including *Million Dollar Legs*, *If I Had a Million*, and *Alice in Wonderland*. In 1935 Mankiewicz moved to Metro-Goldwyn-Mayer where he worked as a producer until 1942. Among the eighteen films he produced were *Three Godfathers*, *Fury*, *Three Comrades*, *A Christmas Carol*, *Adventures of Huckleberry Finn*, *Strange Cargo*, *Philadelphia Story*, and *Woman of the Year*. In 1943 he moved to Twentieth-Century–Fox under Darryl F. Zanuck, remaining until 1952. It was there that he did his best work as screenwriter and was finally permitted to direct. He won a record four Academy Awards for Best Director and Best Screenplay for *Letter to Three Wives* and *All About Eve*. In 1950 he was elected President of the Screen Directors Guild, and battled communist-phobic Cecil B. DeMille over the requirement for the union membership to pledge loyalty oaths in the midst of the blacklist era. He directed *La Boheme* at New York's Metropolitan Opera in 1952 and the film version of *Julius Caesar* in 1953. In his final period Mankiewicz remained very productive. In 1954 he directed, produced, and wrote the screenplay for *Barefoot Contessa*, and the following year he directed and wrote the screenplay for *Guys and Dolls*. He directed, produced, and wrote the screenplay for *The Quiet American* (1955), directed *Suddenly Last*

Summer (1959), and directed and was co-screen writer for the Richard Burton–Elizabeth Taylor fiasco, *Cleopatra* (1963). His last film, *Sleuth* (1972), garnered Mankiewicz his final directorial Academy Award nomination.—*David Koenigstein*

SOURCES: Kenneth L. Geist, *Pictures Will Talk: The Life and Times of Joseph L. Mankiewicz* (New York: Scribner's, 1978); Bernard F. Dick, *Joseph L. Mankiewicz* (Boston: Twayne, 1983).

Manzarek, Ray (Raymond Daniel Manczarek; b. Chicago, Illinois, January 12, 1939; d.—). Singer, musician. Born in Chicago, he spent his childhood on the south side of the city, attending St. Rita's High School. His parents were second generation Polish Americans, Raymond and Helen (nee Kolenda) Manczarek, who encouraged young Ray to study piano. At the same time he was influenced by the African American blues he heard in Chicago. Manzarek received a baccalaureate degree from DePaul University. After being discharged from the Army in 1963, he went to Los Angeles where he received a master's degree in film at UCLA. He met Jim Morrison there in 1965 and shortly thereafter the two teamed up with John Densmore and Robbie Krieger to form the Doors, a group that became the hottest band on the Sunset Strip. It was not long before their first record was released, and worldwide fame followed. Manzarek's haunting and melodic organ and piano playing can be heard throughout the Doors' songs, many of which he co-wrote. Their most famous song is the instantly recognizable "Light My Fire," one of the most popular rock and roll songs ever recorded. Their record albums were quite unlike any done before, peppered with Morrison's mysterious poetry and Manzarek's keyboard artistry. Other hits included "Touch Me," "Love Her Madly," and "Riders on the Storm." The band broke up not long after Morrison's death in 1971, and Manzarek went on to record on his own, write novels, produce films and videos, and team up with poet Michael McClure for performances. In 2000, Manzarek and Krieger reunited to tour with a new band, Doors of the 21st Century, later taking the name Riders on the Storm after a legal dispute. Manzarek continued to tour with the band, which features the music of the original Doors.—*Martin S. Nowak*

SOURCE: Ray Manzarek, *Light My Fire: My Life with the Doors* (New York: G. P. Putnam's Sons, 1998).

Marcella Sembrich Opera Museum. The Marcella Sembrich Opera Museum is an institution dedicated to preserving the memory of **Marcella Sembrich**, one of the first singers to receive broad acclaim on the American opera scene. The museum is located in the village of Bolton Landing, NY, on the shores of Lake George on an estate that Sembrich had used as a summer residence. After retiring as an opera performer in 1909, Sembrich became a pioneer in music education who founded the vocal departments at both the Juilliard School in New York City and the Curtis Institute in Philadelphia. Each summer, from 1922 until her death in January of 1935, Sembrich brought select students to Bolton Landing for special voice instruction. Sembrich's daughter-in-law, Julliette de Coppet Stengel, converted the residence into a museum, which opened for the first time in 1937. The museum has preserved the pristine environment that Sembrich enjoyed during her lifetime. Visitors can still stroll along 1,000 feet of shoreline paths, where they can view Lake George and the surrounding Adirondack Mountains. Meanwhile, the house and studio now serve as a repository for artifacts related to Sembrich's exemplary career. These include paintings, sculptures, musical scores, and autographed photos of such Sembrich contemporaries as Brahms, Caruso, Liszt, Mahler, Puccini and Rachmaninoff. The collection also contains twenty complete costumes that Sembrich wore during her operatic career. The museum is open daily from mid–June to mid–September. During this season, it also conducts a variety of programs, including concerts and symposia on opera history.—*Carl L. Bucki*

SOURCES: *Notes*, the newsletter of The Marcella Sembrich Opera Museum; "Marcella Sembrich Opera Museum," at www.thesembrich.org.

Marchibroda, Ted (b. Franklin, Pennsylvania, March 15, 1931; d.—). Football player, coach. A standout collegiate quarterback at St. Bonventure and the University of Detroit, Marchibroda ranked first nationally in total offense in 1952. Chosen in the first round of the 1953 professional draft by the Pittsburgh Steelers, he played four seasons in the National Football League, three years with Pittsburgh and one with the Chicago Cardinals, in a career cut short by military service and injury. Marchibroda was a head coach in the NFL for twelve seasons, with the Baltimore Colts (1975–79), Indianapolis Colts (1992–95), and Baltimore Ravens (1996–98). His teams made the playoffs in four seasons, winning three division championships. He was also an assistant coach for two other NFL teams. Following the end of his coaching days, Marchibroda became a radio commentator for Indianapolis Colts game broadcasts. He was inducted into the National Polish-American Sports Hall of Fame in 1976.—*Neal Pease*

SOURCE: "Ted Marchibroda," National Polish-American Sports Hall of Fame website, www.polishsportshof.com.

Marciniak, Edward A. (b. Cook County, Illinois, December 21, 1917; d. Chicago, Illinois, May 23, 2004). Community activist. A lifelong Catholic activist promoting social justice, particularly among the urban poor, Marciniak was a leader in the movement for a lay-centered church pre-dating the Second Vatican Council. He was prominent among the group that established the Christian Family Movement, the Cana Conference, the Catholic Social Action Conference, and the Chicago Inter-Student Catholic Action, as well as supporting national organizations such as the Catholic Worker Movement, the Young Christian Workers, the Young Christian Students, the Catholic Committee on Urban Ministry, and the National Conference on Interracial Justice. He was the principal author of "A Chicago Declaration of Christian Concern" (1978) which cautioned against overemphasis on the ceremony and trappings of the Church while overlooking the practical need for social justice in daily life. "In the last analysis," he wrote, "the church speaks to us and acts upon the world through her laity. Without a dynamic laity conscious of its personal ministry to the world, the church, in effect does not speak or act." The author of over 500 articles on social issues in the *New Republic*, *America*, *Commonweal* and other leading magazines, he also published *Tomorrow's Christian* in which he wrote about the role of the secular Christian in actualizing the Church's theology within the modern world. During the late 1960s and early 1970s he served as Chicago's deputy commissioner of development and planning, a position he used to promote improved public housing and race relations. During the administration of Mayor Richard J. Daley, Marciniak served as director of the city's Commission on Human Rights, and later directed the Institute of Urban Life at Loyola University.—*James S. Pula*

SOURCE: *National Catholic Reporter*, September 3, 2004.

Marszalek, John Francis, Jr. (b. Buffalo, New York, July 5, 1939; d.—). Historian. After graduating from Canisius College in 1961, he enrolled in graduate studies at the University of Notre Dame where he earned an M.A. degree in 1963 and a Ph.D. in 1968. After appointments to the faculty of Canisius College (1967–68) and Gannon University (1968–73), he accepted a position at Mississippi State University in 1973. In 1994 he was named William L. Giles Distinguished Professor. When he retired from teaching in 2002 he was named Giles Distinguished Professor Emeritus. Following retirement he directed the Mississippi State University Distinguished

Scholars Program. A specialist in the period of the American Civil War, Marszalek published twelve books and over 150 articles, the former including *Court Martial: A Black Man in America* (1972; later made into a movie); *A Black Businessman in White Mississippi, 1886– 1974* (1977); *The Diary of Miss Emma Holmes, 1861– 1866* (1979); *Sherman's Other War: The General and the Civil War Press* (1981); *A Black Physician's Story: Bringing Hope in Mississippi* (1985); *Grover Cleveland, A Bibliography* (1988); *Encyclopedia of African-American Civil Rights: From Emancipation to the Present* (1992); *Sherman: A Soldier's Passion for Order* (1993; nominated for a Pulitzer Prize and featured as an Alternate Book-of-the-Month Club selection); *Assault at West Point: The Court-Martial of Johnson Whittaker* (1994); *American Political History: Essays on the State of the Discipline* (1997); *The Petticoat Affair: Manners, Mutiny, and Sex in Andrew Jackson's White House* (2000); and *Commander of All Lincoln's Armies: A Life of General Henry W. Halleck* (2004; a History Book Club selection). Among his awards and honors are the Richard Wright Literary Award for Lifetime Achievement (2002) and the B.L.C. Wailes Award for National Distinction in the Field of History from the Mississippi Historical Society (2004). In 2002, Mississippi State University established the John F. and Jeanne A. Marszalek Lecture Series in his honor.—*James S. Pula*

SOURCE: "Marszalek, John F.," *Contemporary Authors* (Detroit: Gale Research Company, New Revision Series), Vol. 14, 309.

Martin, Ross (Marcin Rosenblatt; b. Grodek, Poland, March 22, 1920; d. Ramona, California, July 3, 1981). Actor, director. Ross earned an M.A. degree in psychometrics, a law degree, and could speak English, French, Italian, Polish, Russian, Spanish, and Yiddish. He began a career in entertainment as one half of the comedy team of Ross & West. His first notable film credit came in *The Colossus of New York* (1958), followed by a convincingly terrifying portrayal in *Experiment in Terror* (1962). Throughout the 1950s and early 1960s he was a regular on such television game shows as *The Ad-Libbers* (1951), *Pantomime Quiz* (1950–63), and *Stump the Stars* (1962–63). After a supporting role in *The Sheriff of Cochise* (1956–60), he costarred as Andamo in *Mr. Lucky* (1959–60) before emerging as one of the great character actors in early television history. His role as Secret Service agent Artemus Gordon in *The Wild, Wild West* (1965–69), where he costarred with Robert Conrad who played James West, provided him with an opportunity to exhibit his acting versatility. After a serious heart attack, he finished his career directing *Here's Lucy* (1968–74) and doing voiceovers.—*James S. Pula*

SOURCE: "Ross Martin," *Almanac of Famous People* (Detroit: Thomson Gale, 2007).

Matejka, James J., Jr. (b. Chicago, Illinois, October 27, 1916; d. Oak Park, Illinois, November 30, 1979). Philatelist. An internationally recognized philatelist specializing in stamps featuring Newfoundland airmails, Czechoslovakia, and the postal history of the Alaska–Yukon Territory, Matejka was a member of various philatelic societies in the Chicago area and was an organizer of the first Combined Philatelic Exhibition of Chicagoland in 1958 and the four succeeding exhibitions. For his efforts he received the Newbury Award from the Chicago Philatelic Society (1959). He was an officer in the Society for Czechoslovak Philately, the American Air Mail Society, and the Society of Philatelic Americans. He also served three terms on the U.S. Postmaster General's Citizens' Stamp Advisory Committee (1961–63, 1965–69, 1975–78) and was a frequent judge at international exhibitions. His many publications include several editions of *Newfoundland Aerophilately*. His recognitions include the Philatelic Specialists Society of Canada Medal (1958), the Walter J. Conrath Memorial Award from the American Airmail Society (1963), inclusion on the Roll of Distinguished Philatelists (1979), induction into the American Philatelic Society Hall of Fame (1981), and induction into the Aerophilatelic Hall of Fame (1991).—*James S. Pula*

SOURCE: www.stamps.org.

Matuszewski, Ignacy (b. Warsaw, Poland, November 1, 1891; d. New York, New York, August 3, 1946). Diplomat, journalist. A son of a renowned literary critic, Matuszewski studied philosophy at the Jagiellonian University in Kraków, architecture in Milan, law in Dorpat, and agriculture in Warsaw. In December 1914 he began serving in the Russian army where he organized a meeting of Polish soldiers in St. Petersburg in 1917, just before enlisting in the First Polish Corps under the command of Gen. Józef Dowbór-Muśnicki. In 1918 he was sentenced to death *in absentia* by both the Germans and the Bolsheviks. Escaping to Kiev, he enrolled in the Polska Organizacja Wojskowa (Polish Military Organization) where he organized an unsuccessful revolt against Gen. Muśnicki. When Poland regained its independence in November of that year, Matuszewski was employed in the Polish army intelligence service. He took part in the Polish-Soviet peace talks in Riga in 1921, and was later appointed military attaché in Rome (1924–26), ambassador in Budapest (1928–29), minister of the Treasury (1929–31), and editor of *Gazeta Polska* (1932–36)

and *Polityka Narodów* (National Politics). Matuszewski admired Józef Piłsudski despite their disagreement on budget issues in the early 1930s, but he was critical of the Sanacja governments formed after Piłsudski's death in 1935. In his publications he blamed Piłsudski's successors for their political naïveté and insufficient military preparations for the war that was about to come. When his pessimistic prognoses came true in September 1939, he managed to organize, together with his friend **Henryk Floyar-Rajchmann**, the transportation of 75 tons of gold deposited in the Bank of Poland from Warsaw to Paris via Romania, Turkey, and Syria. While in France, he published articles critical of both the pre-war governments and most of the Polish army commanders of the "September campaign." After the capitulation of France, he left for Spain, but was arrested while crossing the border. Released after a five-month imprisonment, he arrived to Portugal in March 1941.

In August 1941, Matuszewski sailed to the United States where he settled in New York. He soon contacted his friends Floyar-Rajchmann and **Wacław Jędrzejewicz**, and together with the Polish American activists **Maximilian Węgrzynek** and **Frank Januszewski** established the **Józef Piłsudski Institute of America** and the **National Committee of Americans of Polish Descent** (Komitet Narodowy Amerykanów Polskiego Pochodzenia, KNAPP) in order to promote their political views. While still in Europe, Matuszewski had become extremely critical of Prime Minister Władysław Sikorski's policies toward the Soviet Union. Węgrzynek and Januszewski were happy to publish his political articles in the New York *Nowy Świat* (New World) and Detroit *Dziennik Polski* (Polish Daily News). Before his death in 1946 Matuszewski wrote more than 500 articles for the Polish American press and authored several political brochures. A talented and extraordinarily energetic journalist, he became a spokesman of the anti-Sikorski, and later anti–Mikołajczyk opposition. Sikorski and his supporters reacted with accusations that Matuszewski left Europe without the government's permission, even suggesting that he deserted from the army, and that his anti–Soviet attitude made him profascist or fascist-like. This last argument also was raised by the Polish American left. It was probably these accusations that resulted in a letter from the Department of Justice dated March 11, 1943, asking Matuszewski to register as an agent for a foreign power under provisions of the Foreign Agent Registration Act of 1938 (amended in 1941). His foreign agent status was to be clearly indicated in all his publications and the Department of Justice was to be given a copy of each publication. This did not prevent his continuing activities. He was among the co-founders of the **Polish American Congress** and represented KNAPP at the United Nations conference in San Francisco in 1945. Critical of the provisions of the Yalta conference that completely disregarded the principles of the Atlantic Charter, he urged the Poles in exile to prepare for a third world war as the only hope for a free and independent Poland.—*Joanna Wojdon*

SOURCE: Sławomir Cenckiewicz, "Ignacy Matuszewski (1891–1946)—emigracyjne losy," *Arcana*, Vol. 1, no. 5 (2000), 100–20.

Maurer, Jadwiga (Jadwiga Graubard; b. Kielce, Poland, September 24, 1932; d.—). Literary scholar. Maurer received her Ph.D. in Slavic studies from the University of Munich, Germany, in 1959. She held faculty appointments at the University of California, Berkeley (1959–65), Indiana University (1965–69), and the University of Kansas (1970–2001). A specialist in Polish literature, Polish Jewish studies, and Slavic linguistics, her research reflects a special interest in Adam Mickiewicz and his ties to Judaism. She is the author of "*Z matki obcej...*": *Szkice o powiązaniach Mickiewicza ze światem Żydów* (Of a Foreign Mother Born: Adam Mickiewicz's Ties to the World of the Jews; 1996), a book that addresses long-standing misconceptions about Mickiewicz's biography and work. She also published articles on taboo topics in Mickiewicz studies. In addition to several important articles, she published three collections of short fiction: *Liga ocalałych* (The League of Holocaust Survivors; 1970), *Podróż na Wybrzeże Dalmacji* (A Trip to the Coast of Dalmatia; 1982), and *Sobowtóry* (Doubles; 2002). For *Liga ocalałych,* she received the 1970 Literary Prize awarded by the journal *Wiadomości* (Information) in London for the best book published in Polish by a Polish émigré writer. In 2001, the University of Kansas recognized her outstanding teaching and mentoring with the Distinguished Teaching Award.—*Halina Filipowicz*

SOURCE: Bolesław Wierzbiański, *Who's Who in Polish America* (New York: Bicentennial Publishing Corp., 1996), 290.

Maxwell, William S. (Dzwoniecki; b. Warsaw, Poland, May 13, 1899; d. Brooklyn, New York, July 10, 1989). Naval officer, environmental manager. Maxwell migrated to the U.S. as a teenager and enlisted in the U.S. Navy where he rose from apprentice seaman to rear admiral. He retired from the Navy in 1950 and accepted a position as Deputy Director of the New York City Bureau of Smoke Control (1950–52) where he earned a reputation as a forceful advocate for clean air and

pursuer of polluters including government agencies. Among his achievements was a legal action against the Consolidated Edison Company resulting in a court order requiring Edison to pay $3.74 million to reduce pollution from its generators. In 1955 he was named chair of the Board of Standards and Appeals in the New York State Labor Department and in the same year was honored as Power Engineer of the Year by the National Association of Power Engineers.—*James S. Pula*

SOURCES: Edward Pinkowski, "Soviet Trainees in U.S.A. in World War II," *Russian Review*, Vol. 6, no. 1 (Autumn 1946), 11–16; Glenn Fowler, "William S. Maxwell, 89, Is Dead; Ex-Admiral and Pollution Official," *New York Times*, July 12, 1989.

May Laws *see* **Kulturkampf.**

Mazeroski, William "Bill" "Maz" (b. Wheeling, West Virginia, September 5, 1936; d.—). Baseball player. Mazeroski played second base for the Pittsburgh Pirates for seventeen seasons, from 1956 through 1972. Never more than an ordinary hitter, he is generally regarded as the greatest defensive second baseman in the history of the sport. Especially noted for his proficiency at turning the double play, Mazeroski won Gold Glove awards in eight different seasons as the outstanding fielder at his position. He played in ten All-Star games, and during his career the Pirates reached postseason play four times, and won two world championships. "Maz" received election to the National Baseball Hall of Fame in 2001, one of very few so honored primarily for defensive credentials. In 1979 he was inducted into the **National Polish-American Sports Hall of Fame**. Although offensive prowess was never his long suit, Mazeroski is best remembered for one of the most dramatic

Bill Mazeroski scoring the winning run on a home run in the 1960 World Series (*OLS*).

blows ever struck by a batter. On October 13, 1960 he hit a home run to win the seventh and decisive game of the World Series, giving his Pirates an unlikely championship over the favored New York Yankees. This was the first time a home run had ended a World Series. The feat inspired *The Sporting News* to recognize Mazeroski as the major league player of the year for that season. A historical marker on the University of Pittsburgh campus, where Forbes Field once stood, identifies the spot where his legendary home run cleared the left field wall of the ballpark.—*Neal Pease*

SOURCE: John T. Bird, *Twin Killing: The Bill Mazeroski Story* (Birmingham, AL: Esmeralda, 1995).

Mazewski, Aloysius A. (b. North Chicago, Illinois, January 5, 1916; d. Portage, Wisconsin, August 3, 1988). Polonia activist. Becoming active in the **Polish National Alliance** as a teenager, he rose to leadership in Council 41 during the 1930s. He energetically organized youth activities as a high school and college student and was president of the Polish Students' Club at Lane Technical High School, the Chicago Polish Students' Association, and the Polish American Junior League which included seventeen Chicago high school units. After earning a law degree from DePaul University in 1940, he volunteered for military service following the outbreak of World War II, serving as an intelligence officer, and later became a military hospital chief administrator. Mazewski completed his military duties in 1946 with the rank of major. Mazewski was active in the Polish National Alliance from the time of his teenage years. He was elected to its national Board of Directors in 1947 and reelected to a second four year term in 1951. Ambitious to lead the Alliance, he was instead "dumped" from the Board at the 1955 PNA convention by President **Charles Rozmarek**. In 1959, Mazewski backed the unsuccessful candidacy of Adam Tomaszkiewicz for the presidency and in 1963 he waged his own unsuccessful campaign for the office against Rozmarek. In 1967, however, Mazewski bested Rozmarek at the 35th quadrennial convention in a closely fought and bitter contest, winning the presidency by a vote of 221 delegates to 189. Thereafter, he was reelected to five additional terms with little or no opposition. In August 1968, Mazewski also succeeded Rozmarek as president of the **Polish American Congress** and went on to lead that organization without opposition for the next twenty years. As head of the Polish National Alliance, the largest Polish American fraternal insurance benefit society and the largest such organization having an ethnic membership basis in the United States,

Mazewski modernized the business operations of the company and introduced a number of new types of insurance plans of benefit to its purchasers. While overall insured PNA membership declined during his presidency, the assets of the organization rose from $133 million in 1967 to $204 million in 1987 and insurance coverage provided by the PNA in this period also rose, from $302 million to $516 million. Under Mazewski's leadership, the national office of the PNA moved from its location in the old **Polonia** section of Chicago's near north side to a new and modern building on the city's northwest side in 1977. The PNA purchased its first radio station, renamed WPNA, in 1987 to serve the Chicago area Polish American community. The Alliance's two newspapers underwent a modernization as well to make them more attractive to younger readers and newcomers from Poland. PNA sponsorship of the massive **Polish Constitution Day** parade, an annual Chicago event since 1904, continued, but the parade was rerouted to the downtown "Loop" section of Chicago and out of its traditional locale in a historic Polonia neighborhood where very few persons of Polish heritage still lived. For years after, the parade was also televised to further increase its audience.

In 1987, Mazewski received approval from the PNA leadership to close the failing **Alliance College** established in 1912 and located in Cambridge Springs, Pennsylvania. The reasons for this difficult decision involved declining student enrollment, rising costs, and the school's loss of academic accreditation. In

Aloysius Mazewski, president of the Polish American Congress and Polish National Alliance (*JPI*).

place of the college, Mazewski considered, but did not act on, a plan to establish an "Alliance Institute" to promote knowledge of the Polish experience through publications and conferences. He did back the creation of a PNA college scholarship program for eligible PNA members. Established in 1987 as a fund distributing $75,000 annually, the program in 2008 was committing $250,000 to support the studies of meritorious college students belonging to the PNA.

As president of the **Polish American Congress**, Mazewski worked to improve the Congress's visibility in the nation's capital and built a productive relationship between Polonia and each successive U.S. President from Richard Nixon through Ronald Reagan. He was on excellent terms with Vice President George H. W. Bush and was a frequent visitor to the White House and Congress to promote the PAC position in support of a free Poland. A skilled politician and excellent public speaker, Mazewski's strong Republican identification also helped him greatly, since the era of his presidency coincided with Republican control of the White House (only one Democrat, Jimmy Carter, held the presidency during his tenure and it was President Carter who delivered the main address at the centennial anniversary celebration of the PNA in 1980).

Mazewski's closest political tie with a U.S. president was, perhaps, with Gerald Ford. It was Mazewski who led the effort to support Ford's election in 1976 among U.S. ethnic organizations, especially after Ford's gaffe in his foreign policy debate with Carter. Mazewski also enjoyed excellent relations with a series of governors in the state of Illinois, with a succession of Chicago mayors, and with such U.S. powers in Washington as Congressmen **Daniel Rostenkowski** and **Edward Derwinski** of Illinois and **Clement Zablocki** of Wisconsin.

Mazewski made substantial efforts to broaden the mission of the Polish American Congress. In 1971 he established a PAC charitable foundation to promote humanitarian activities of concern to the PAC. During the crisis in Poland following the Communist regime's suppression of the Solidarity movement in 1981, the Foundation shipped more than $130 million in medical and food supplies to Poland. At home, Mazewski spoke out against the defamation of Poland and Polish Americans in the mass media, a highly sensitive issue in Polonia from the 1970s. He also initiated a continuing dialog between the Jewish-American and Polish-American communities to discuss matters of mutual concern. Mazewski later served as one of two Polish-

Americans on the 62 member National Holocaust Memorial Commission, where he regularly voiced his views as head of the Polish American Congress.

As head of the chief political organization speaking for the largest Polish ethnic community in the emigration, Mazewski represented the PAC at countless American government meetings and ceremonies and on those occasions when the representatives of the worldwide Polonia gathered. He hosted many visits to America of dignitaries of the Polish Church, including that of Karol Cardinal Wojtyła of Kraków in 1976. Mazewski attended Wojtyła's investiture as Pope John Paul II in 1978 as a member of the official United States delegation which traveled to Rome. In 1981 he became the first PAC president to visit Poland when he flew to Warsaw as part of the American delegation for the funeral of Stefan Cardinal Wyszyński. There he met with Solidarity's leader, Lech Wałęsa, and remained a powerful voice in support of Solidarity's aims throughout the 1980s.

Mazewski strongly supported Radio Free Europe and Radio Liberty and actively backed the creation of the National Endowment for Democracy, an agency that played a signal role in providing support to the underground Solidarity cause after 1981. He was an outspoken advocate of just treatment of the thousands of individuals who sought U.S. residency status following the invoking of martial law by the Polish communist regime in December 1981.—*Donald E. Pienkos*

SOURCES: Donald E. Pienkos, *PNA: A Centennial History of the Polish National Alliance of the United States of North America* (Boulder, CO: East European Monographs, 1984); Donald E. Pienkos, *For Your Freedom Through Ours: Polish American Efforts on Poland's Behalf* (Boulder, CO: East European Monographs, 1991).

Mazoń, Janusz (b. Bytom, Poland, November 3, 1960; d.—). Ballet dancer, teacher, choreographer. A graduate of the Bytom Ballet School (1979), Mazoń became a solo dancer with the Bytom State Opera. In 1980 he joined Teatr Wielki (the Polish National Ballet) in Warsaw where he was named Principal Dancer in 1982 and First Soloist in 1983. He received the Gold Medal at the Polish Professional Ballet Competition (1982) and the Leon Wójcikowski Medal (1983), awarded annually to the most promising Polish ballet dancer. In 1985 Mazoń was offered a contract with the Hamburg Ballet in Germany by its director and the world-renowned ballet choreographer John Neumeier. As a Principal Dancer with the Hamburg Ballet, he danced leading roles both in classical ballets and in Neumeier's original productions, and toured extensively throughout Europe (Paris Opera,

Mariinsky Theatre in St. Petersburg, and Bolshoi Theatre in Moscow), Asia, South America, and the U.S. During his collaboration with the Hamburg Ballet, he solidified his position as an exceptional dancer of superb talent, immaculate technique, and remarkable sensitivity. In 1997 he moved to the United States to join the Georgia Ballet in Marietta, Georgia, where he assumed the position of Principal Dancer and Ballet Master. His artistry immediately captured and delighted the Georgia Ballet audiences, bringing him recognition in the art community. Mazoń danced the leading roles in classical ballets such as *Sleeping Beauty* (Prince Desiré), *Nutcracker* (Cavalier), *Swan Lake* (Sigfrid), and *Serenade*, as well as in original productions choreographed by the founder of the Georgia Ballet, Iris Hensley (for example, the role of Burt in *The Adventures of Mary Poppins*).

The collaboration with the Georgia Ballet resulted in Mazoń's growing interest in choreography. As a choreographer, he created several original ballets for the company including *American Dreamer* with Stephen Foster's music (2001), *Interruptions* with Leroy Anderson's music (2005), *A Sleepy Hollow Story* based on a classical American tale by Washington Irving with music by various twentieth century composers (2006), *The Firebird* (2007), and in 2009 *A Young Dancer's Guide to the Orchestra* with music by Benjamin Britten (arranged by Michael Alexander)—an innovative partnership with a symphonic orchestra. In his productions, Mazoń realized his creative vision in its entirety—starting from the choice of music and the arrangement of ballet dances, through costumes and stage setting to minute production details. He enriched the Georgia Ballet repertoire incorporating contemporary movements into classical ballet. Both as a dancer and as a choreographer he has always aimed at the utmost level of professionalism and artistry.

When his wife, Gina Hyatt-Mazoń, became Artistic Director of the Georgia Ballet in 2003, they together created a new syllabus for the Georgia Ballet School building the artistic course for the School. Mazoń also contributed to the advancement of the Georgia Ballet community outreach program, which resulted in a significant growth in the number of young audiences attending the Georgia Ballet productions.

Mazoń is a distinguished and widely recognized Ballet Master. His students have been inspired by his professionalism, creativity and artistry, as well as his personal charms, modesty, and pure humanity. He is considered a very demanding, yet generous teacher. Under his coaching, the students feel compelled to always raise the bar and strive for perfection. Due to Mazon's influence, the professional dancers of the Georgia Ballet have made a tremendous improvement in their technique and artistry that can be compared to international standards. On the whole, the company has advanced to a higher status among ballet companies in the U.S. Mazón is also a graduate of the Life University College of Chiropractic in Marietta, Georgia. Since 2002 he has operated his own chiropractic practice, Mazon Chiropractic Clinic. In 2009 he received an Ovation Award for Outstanding Dance Performance.—*Bozena U. Zaremba*

SOURCES: Marcus E. Howard, "Georgia Ballet Marks 50 Years," *Marietta Daily Journal*, June 22, 2009; Sally Litchfield, "Ballet in Their Blood," *Marietta Daily Journal*, July 10, 2009; Marcus E. Howard, "Georgia Ballet to Begin 50th Season," *Marietta Daily Journal*, October 3, 2009; Sally Litchfield, "Ovation Awards Laud Residents," *Marietta Daily Journal*, October 30, 2009.

Mazovia *see* **Mazurian.**

Mazur *see* **Mazurka.**

Mazur, Józef C. (b. Buffalo, New York, March 17, 1897; d. Buffalo, New York, April 23, 1970). Artist. Educated at the Albright Art School in Buffalo and the Art Students League in New York, where he studied with Frank Vincent Dumond, Leopold Seyfert, Mahonri Young, George Bellows, and Luis Mora, Mazur emerged as a leading mural painter, sculptor, and stained glass artist. His murals decorated Blessed Trinity, St. Stanislaus Bishop and Martyr, St. Ann, St. Adalbert (Wojciech), and Our Lady of Peace, **Polish National Catholic** Cathedral, all in Buffalo; St. John Gualbert and Villa Maria Academy in Cheektowaga, NY; Holy Trinity in Niagara Falls, NY; St. Stanislaus in Rochester, NY; St. Stephen in Perth Amboy, NJ; Holy Cross in Trenton, NJ; St. John Cantius in Detroit, MI (Del Ray Section); St. Stanislaus in New Haven, CT; the Polish Village Restaurant in Buffalo; and the Chopin Club Room in Cheektowaga. His sculptures are located in St. Aloysius, Springville, NY; the Chopin Monument, Buffalo; the **Casimir Pulaski** equestrian statute (proposed) for the Pulaski Skyway, New Jersey. Stained glass memorial windows were located at Fordham University, Bronx, NY (dedicated to the memory of Cardinal Farley); Grace Episcopal Church, SS. Rita & Patrick in Buffalo; St. Barbara, Lackawanna, NY; Our Lady of Czestochowa, North Tonawanda, NY; the 16th Regiment Chapel, Chicago, IL; the Polish Room, SUNY at Buffalo (Marie Curie, Nicholas Copernicus; as well as a stained-glass chandelier depicting Frederic Chopin, Adam Mickiewicz, Juliusz Slowacki and **Ignacy Paderewski**); and the Artists and Architect's Club, Philadelphia.—*Stanley L. Cuba*

SOURCES: *Złota księga parafji św. Szczepana w Perth Amboy, N.J., 1892–1942* (Perth Amboy: Golden Jubilee Book, St. Stephen's Parish, 1942); the Rev. Stanisław J. Wysociński, ed., *Album pamiątkowe złotego jubileuszu parafji św. Wojciecha, B.M., Buffalo, New York, 1886–1936* (Buffalo: St. Adalbert's Jubilee Committee, 1936); *Buffalo Arts Journal*, January 1927; *Księga pamiątkowa złotego jubileuszu osady polskiej i parafiji św. Stanisława B. i M. w Buffalo, New York, 1873–1923* (Buffalo: Program Committee, 1923).

Mazurki, Mike (Michał Mazurewski; b. Tarnopol, Poland, December 25, 1907; d. Glendale, California, December 9, 1990). Actor. After arriving in the U.S., Mazurki graduated at the top of his class with a baccalaureate degree from Manhattan College (1930). An accomplished sportsman as well, he played basketball and American minor league football with the Wessington Passaic Red Devils (NJ) in 1936, then embarked on a career in professional wrestling. A recipient of the Professional Wrestling Hall of Fame's New York State Award, presented to an individual for significant contributions to the sport of Professional Wrestling in the Professional Wrestling Hall of Fame's home state of New York, he also refereed championship matches in the U.S., Europe, and Asia, and founded the "Cauliflower Alley Club," a nonprofit organization that awarded scholarships and financial assistance to retired or injured wrestlers and their families.

Mazurki also pursued a career in film. Because of his height and his intimidating facial features, he was typecast into parts as strongmen, gangsters, and bullies, the direct opposite of his intelligent, sensitive nature. His first film appearances were without attribution in *Gentleman Jim* (1942) and *About Face* (1942). He went on to appear in nearly fifty movies by the end of the decade, including an acclaimed performance as the ex-con "Moose Malloy" in the film noir thriller *Murder, My Sweet* (1944), and the gruesome "Splitface" in *Dick Tracy* (1945). He continued in similar roles throughout the 1950s and 1960s, often showing an adeptness for deadpan comedy in films including *Abbott and Costello in Hollywood* (1945*)*, *Some Like It Hot* (1959), *It's a Mad Mad Mad Mad World* (1963), *The Disorderly Orderly* (1964), the Western *Cheyenne Autumn* (1964), *Donovan's Reef* (1963), *The Adventures of Bullwhip Griffin* (1967), and the children's film *Challenge to Be Free* (1976). Even as demands for film roles diminished in the mid–1960s and 1970s, Mazurki began appearing in TV guest roles in series such as *Adam-12, Gilligan's Island, The Beverly Hillbillies*, and a short-lived 1971-72 series, *The Chicago Teddy Bears*. One of Mazurki's last roles was in the 1990 Warren Beatty remake of *Dick Tracy*. In all, he appeared in over one hundred movies during his long career.—*Patricia Finnegan*

SOURCES: Obituary, *New York Times*, December 12, 1990; "Mike Mazurki," *Almanac of Famous People* (Detroit: Thomson Gale, 2007); "Mike Mazurki," *Contemporary Theatre, Film, and Television* (Detroit: Gale Research, 1991), Vol. 9.

Mazurian. On April 10, 1525, Albrecht of Hohenzollern (1490–1568), a Grand master of the Order of Teutonic Knights, walked into Kraków's Market Square, knelt before his uncle, Poland's King Sigismund I (1467–1548), and pledged his allegiance to the Polish crown. In the presence of Catholic bishops and Polish nobles, the Lutheran Albrecht promised to dissolve the Teutonic Order and convert its lands into a Duchy protected by the Polish kingdom. Having secured assurances from Poland's leadership, Albrecht returned to the small realm on the Baltic Sea and in July 1525, announced the establishment of a Lutheran state. The arrangement of a Catholic monarch sanctioning and protecting a Lutheran territory was exceptional at this time, but the agreement ended two centuries of fighting and secured Poland's northern border. Three separate cultures lived within the realm: a Lithuanian in the eastern districts, a Polish in the southern, and a German that was concentrated in the districts around and to the west of Königsberg. The districts settled by Polish-speaking colonists from neighboring Mazovia included Soldau (Działdowo), Osterode (Ostróda), Neidenburg (Nidzica), Ortelsburg (Szczytno), Sensburg (Mrągowo), Johannisburg (Pisz), Lötzen (Giżycko), Lyck (Ełk), and Oletzko (Olecko). Having farmed the sandy soil of Mazovia for centuries, the Polish-speaking colonists who migrated to Teutonic Prussia in the fifteenth century were the ideal settlers for this region of a thousand lakes, extensive forests, and a soil that was by nature stingy. With the passage of time a unique culture that combined Polish and German elements developed among the inhabitants in the southern districts. At the beginning of the nineteenth century the term "Pole" was reserved for the descendants of the Mazovian gentry or Polish-speaking landowners, while "Mazur" was applied to the landless Polish-speaking peasants. With the partitioning of Poland, it appears that Polish Protestant landowners in an attempt to distinguish themselves from the recently incorporated Polish Catholic population adopted the word "Mazurian" when referring to themselves and their districts in Prussia.

On the eve of the Second German Empire (1871), life in the impoverished Mazurian districts was difficult. As a result of agrarian reform most Mazurian peasants had lost their small farms and were barely able to hold on to their little one- or two-room cottages. At that time two new forces entered the districts: Rhenish pietists that introduced prayer societies (Gromadki) and German Baptist missionaries. The pietistic prayer meetings found a receptive audience among the Mazurians, and by 1884 church officials knew of 343 prayer societies in Neidenburg and 160 in Ortelsburg. It is estimated that 80 percent of the Mazurian population in East Prussia belonged to a prayer conventicle. Membership provided these Protestants with important pre-migration experiences. Participants developed leadership skills by organizing and leading home meetings. German Baptist missionaries were equally successful among the Mazurian population. Like the Pietists, they encouraged lay leadership. German and Polish nationalist movements emerged in the Mazurian districts in the final decades of the nineteenth century but were in their infancy when the Mazurians started to emigrate, which means that the majority who left East Prussia saw themselves politically as Prussian Poles.

As affordable land became scarce in the Mazurian districts and Suwałki, young couples looked for alternatives. In the 1860s Mazurian Baptists in Ortelsburg emigrated to Volhynia in Ukraine, but by the 1880s were dissatisfied and, like their Lutheran kin in the Mazurian districts, decided to relocate to the Ruhr Valley or immigrate to the United States. Since most of the new arrivals from East Prussia were listed as Germans or German Poles and those from Suwałki as Polish, it is difficult to track the Mazurian migration to America. From church records we know that Lutheran Mazurians from Osterode settled in Decatur, Illinois, while farmers from Soldau/Neidenburg relocated to Reading, Pennsylvania, and then to Benton County, Minnesota. Baptists migrated to Buffalo, New York, and Marinette County, Wisconsin. Mazurians coming from Suwałki, Poland, in the first decade of the twentieth century found employment in the mines and factories of America's cities. Each group, regardless of where they settled, assembled in homes or in the basement of neighboring churches to worship. They recreated the prayer societies (Gromadki) that sustained them in their homeland and eventually established bilingual congregations (German/Polish) in Benton County, Minnesota; Westfield, Massachusetts; Scranton, Pennsylvania; Dundalk, Maryland; Detroit, Michigan; Chicago, Illinois; and Pound, Wisconsin. Ten Polish Lutheran congregations were formed and ultimately affiliated with the Lutheran Church–Missouri Synod because that denomination had several bilingual candidates (German/Polish) from the Russian partition of Poland in their seminaries. Within the walls of these churches the Mazurians transplanted their pre-migration spirituality using their Polish Bibles and the beloved *Kancyonal*, that they carried with them or had shipped from Königsberg. Mazurians in Benton County organized parish celebrations around the traditional customs of hunters' stew (bouja/**bigos**) and the procession of the angels (Jutrznia) on Christmas Eve. On that night young boys wearing their fathers' white shirts with a piece of rope tied around the waist, processed to the altar then to one of the corners of the wooden church singing "Narodził się nam Zbawiciel" (Unto Us a Savior Is Born). Clergy corresponded with the editors of newspapers in East Prussia and Poland (*Mazur, Gazeta Ludowa, Przyjaciel Ludu*) and copies of the Prussian Protestant Almanac, *Kalendarz Królewsko Pruski*, were shipped to the United States and survive in the archives of the parish in Sauk Rapids, Minnesota. Clergy in the United States that ministered to the Polish Lutheran congregations also published a newspaper in America, *Kościoł Reformacyjny w Ameryce* (The Reformed Church in America). Started in 1906, the newspaper eventually had 250 subscribers in the U.S. and Poland but ceased publication in 1908. Copies have survived in Poland. Most parishes, Lutheran and Baptist, discontinued Polish worship services after World War II, but a few Lutheran congregations were able to sustain a ministry in Polish into the 1970s with the help of Polish Lutheran pastors who emigrated after the war. A truly unique aspect of the Mazurian experience, Baptist and Lutheran, was the loss of their identity. With no advocates to explain or promote their unique heritage, a short-lived newspaper, and denominations that disapproved of membership in non-congregational fraternal societies, the churches became isolated ethnocentric centers in which subsequent generations matured with little or no understanding of their history and their culture. As English replaced Polish and German as the language of home and church, the American born descendants could no longer read any records or resources left by the first-generation. Genealogical research has prompted individuals to inquire about their ancestors and their stories and may lead to some new examinations of this under studied group.—*Karl Krueger*

SOURCE: Karl Krueger, *Psalms and Potatoes: The Congregations of the Polish-speaking Mazurians in East Prussia, Suwalki, Poland, and the United States* (Ph.d. dissertation, University of Michigan, 1992).

Mazurka (or Mazur). The *mazur* and *mazurek* (i.e., small mazur), or in English *mazurka*, are general terms for a series of Polish folk dances in triple meter, which originated in the plains of Mazovia around Warsaw. The people of the province were called *Mazurs*; thus, the dance *mazur* bears the same name as the male inhabitant of the region. The dances, known abroad as *mazurkas*, comprise more than one type: *mazur* or *mazurek*, the *obertas* or **oberek**, and the **kujawiak** from the neighboring district of Kujawy. There are many other folk dances that fall into this category: *ksebka, obertas, okrągły* (round), *okrąglak* (round), and *owczarek* (shepherd). These dances are linked by common rhythmic and choreographic traits, especially the *mazurka* rhythm consisting of a pattern of two sixteenths followed by two eighth-notes (in a three-eighths meter), i.e., two short and two long notes. According to current research, it is not possible to describe traits which would unequivocally distinguish an *oberek* from a *mazur* or a *kujawiak*. Oskar Kolberg stated in the first volume of his monumental folklore collection, *Pieśni ludu polskiego (Songs of the Polish people* 1857), that *kujawiak*, i.e. *obertas*, was the most popular dance in the whole country. In his later writings, Kolberg distinguished between these dances differing in tempo, with the *mazur* occupying the middle ground between the slow, lyrical *kujawiak* and the furiously fast-paced *oberek*. Moreover, he described a common performance practice of dancing a set of three dances, a *chodzony* (walking dance, folk version of the *polonaise*), followed by a *kujawiak*, and a *mazur* or an *obertas* (*oberek*).

The name is much younger than the dance itself, and appears for the first time in J. Riepel's music dictionary published in Germany in 1752. The dance was known as early as the sixteenth century; early lute and organ tablatures feature many instances of the *mazurka* rhythm in pieces entitled *Polish dance*, or in Latin, *Chorea polonica*. During the seventeenth century the dance spread over Poland and began to appear also in neighboring countries; distinct versions of these dances could be found in the repertoire of the countryside (the folk *mazur*-type dances and the *mazur* of the nobility), and the towns (urban *mazurka*). Augustus II, the Elector of Saxony and King of Poland (1697–1733) was very fond of this dance and introduced it into the courts of Germany. Following Poland's loss of independence, the dance became fashionable in higher social circles in Paris, then London, and other centers of Western Europe. In the 1830s and 1840s, the *mazurka* enjoyed its greatest popularity in the Western salons; along with the *krakowiak* and the *polonaise*, it served as a sign of solidarity with the oppressed Polish nation. Paradoxically, after the partitions of Poland, the *mazurka* also became popular among the Russian aristocracy and peasantry.

The basic dance pattern is derived from 8-, 7- or 6- syllable verses of the *mazur* folk song; the strophes are structured regularly and consist of four verses set in eight measures of the music. Strong accents are irregularly placed on the second or third beat of the measure. The tempi vary greatly between the various types of the dance, and also geographically getting faster in the south of the country. The *oberek* or *obertas* is usually the fastest, with MM = 160 – 180; while the regular *mazur* is performed in the tempo range of MM = 120 – 40 (the *kujawiak* is still slower). The music consists of two or four parts, each part having six or eight bars, and each part is repeated. The most common ensemble performing in the Mazowsze region consists of a violin, a large drum, and later, a Polish folk accordion and clarinet. Folk fiddlers often play many variants of the same melody, with different, elaborate ornamentation in each of the variants. The folk dance is improvisatory in character; it is danced by couples who rotate around the hall and alternate the rotating motion with a variety of steps and gestures. The position of the body resembles that of the *polonaise*— head held high, torso erect, graceful motion of the hands. The difference of the character stems primarily from the faster tempo and the presence of irregularly spaced accents, stomps and clicks of the boots. There are a number of basic steps: *bieg mazurowy* (running step), sideways step, sliding step, and the *hołubiec* (clicking heels together, similar to the step in the *krakowiak*). There are also many hand positions, figures, and turns that could be used by couples performing this dance. A different set of group figures is available for ensembles. Thus, the dance leaves much room for the creativity of its choreographer and the spontaneity of individual dancers. There are four versions of the *mazur* that could be presented by a Polonian folk dance group: the dance of the nobility (in seventeenth-century costumes), the salon dance of the Napoleonic era (in the appropriate military [men] and salon [women] mixture of clothing), the dance of urban folk or a peasants' dance from central Poland. Each type of dance would emphasize different class characteristics of portrayed strata of Polish society.

The introduction of the *mazurka* to art music is usually credited to Fryderyk Chopin, though his predecessors included Maria Szymanowska, and others. While Chopin's borrowings from folk, urban, or salon types of the *mazurka* have been extensively discussed by scholars, certain melodic, harmonic, rhythmic and formal traits point to their close relationship with the features of the folk *mazur*-type dances. Several stylized *mazurs* of the nobility appear in the operas *Halka* and *Straszny Dwór* (The Haunted Manor) by Stanisław Moniuszko. Other Polish composers interested in the mazurka include Aleksander Tansman, Karol Szymanowski, and Roman Maciejewski.

An important fact in the history of the *mazurka* is its appearance in the Polish national anthem. *Mazurek Dąbrowskiego* (Dąbrowski Mazurka) was created in 1797 as a *Song of the Polish Legion* for the troops of General Jan Dąbrowski, serving Napoleon during his conquest of Europe with the hope of regaining Poland's independence. The melody of the anthem is of anonymous, folk origin; the text was penned by Józef Wybicki. Thus, the fast-paced, energetic dance became a national symbol in several distinct ways. In America, the *mazurka* (the title was usually in this spelling) appeared in 1840s; salon composers wrote the *mazurkas* as dances associated with Poland and its celebrated loss of independence, or as fashionable dances dedicated to society ladies. In some variants the *mazurka* is crossed with the *polka*— a salon dance, not its folk counterpart. **Aleksander Janta** lists about 30 mazurkas in his study of nineteenth-century American-Polish music.—*Maja Trochimczyk*

SOURCES: Ada Dziewanowska, *Polish Folk Dances & Songs: A Step by Step Guide* (New York: Hippocrene Books, 1999); Aleksander Janta, *A History of Nineteenth Century American-Polish Music* (New York: The Kościuszko Foundation, 1982); "Mazurka," entry in Stanley Sadie, ed., *New Grove Dictionary of Music and Musicians* (London: McMillan, 1980), Vol. II.

McCosky, Barney (b. Coal Run, Pennsylvania, April 11, 1917; d. Venice, Florida, September 6, 1996). Baseball player. Barney McCosky played for four major league baseball teams from 1939 to 1953. A left-handed hitting outfielder, he compiled a .312 batting average over a career of eleven seasons interrupted by a three year stint in the navy during World War II. McCosky had his best season in 1940 when he led the American League in hits and triples and his Detroit Tigers won the AL pennant and played in the World Series. He was inducted into the **National Polish-American Sports Hall of Fame** in 1995.— *Neal Pease*

SOURCE: William M. Anderson, *The Detroit Tigers: A Pictorial Celebration of the Greatest Players and Moments in Tigers' History* (Detroit: Wayne State University Press, 1999).

Medal of Honor. For Polish American recipients see **Sylvester Antolak, Charles Cawetzka, John W. Dutko, Michael B. Ellis, William J. Grabiarz, Anthony L. Krotiak, Edward C. Krzyzowski, John Mihalowski, Edward J. Moskala, Robert J. Modrzejewski, Nicholas Oresko, Joseph J. Sadowski, Joseph R. Sarnoski, Matt Urban, David Urbansky, Frank Witek, Fred W. Zabitosky.**

Menkes, Sigmund (Zygmunt Menkes; b. Lwów, Poland, May 6, 1896; d. Riverdale, New York, August 20, 1986). Artist. Educated at the Industrial Art School in Lwów (beginning in 1912), he at the same time worked as a church painter. Continuing his education at the Academy of Fine Arts in Kraków, where he studied with Józef Pańkiewicz and Wojciech Weiss (1919–22), he moved to Berlin in 1922 to work in Alexander Archipenko's studio. The following year he moved to Paris where he became a leading member of the Ecole de Paris based in the Montparnasse district. A close friend of Eugeniusz Zak and Marc Chagall, he traveled to the United States in 1930, presenting his work in Cleveland and New York. After spending time in Berlin in 1928, and touring Spain in 1935 with Artur Nacht-Samborski, he relocated to New York in 1935 where he spent the rest of his life. He taught at the Art Students League in New York for many years, and at the Woodstock Summer School beginning in 1948. His illustrations appeared in Jakob Apenszlak and Józef Wittlin, *Poezje ghetta z podziemia żydówskiego w Polsce* (Ghetto Poetry from the Jewish Underground in Poland; 1945). His career included solo exhibitions in New York and Philadelphia, as well as France, Germany, Israel, and Poland, while his work also appeared in group exhibitions in California,

Sigmund Menkes, artist and illustrator (*Stanley L. Cuba*).

Chicago, Cleveland, Detroit, Minneapolis, Philadelphia, Washington (D.C.), Colby College in Maine, Mary Washington College in Virginia, the University of Illinois, the University of Iowa, the University of Nebraska, and several locations in New York, as well as France and Poland. Menkes' work was recognized with the Paul Purinas Memorial Prize, National Academy of Design (1979); **Alfred Jurzykowski Foundation** Award, New York (1967); National Academy Award for Foreign Painters (1963); Andrew Carnegie Award, National Academy of Design (1955); Carol H. Beck Prize, Pennsylvania Academy of Fine Arts (1944); and W. A. Clark Prize, Corcoran Gallery, Washington, D.C. (1941).—*Stanley L. Cuba*

SOURCES: Irena Kossowska, "Zygmunt (Sigmund) Menkes" at www.culture.pl; *Sigmund Menkes* (Brooklyn: Lipert Gallery, 1993).

Meskowski, Walter "Wally" (b. Indiana, October 14, 1915; d. Greenwood, Indiana, January 1980). Race car owner. A very demanding owner, Meskowski was one of the top car owners on the United States Auto Club's Midwest and Eastern circuits during the 1960s. Among the drivers who ran his cars were Mario Andretti, Johnny Rutherford, Jim Hurtubise, Johnny Parsons, Jack Howerton and Billy Vukovich. Nine drivers who piloted Meskowski's cars later won Indianapolis 500 championships. He was elected to the National Sprint Car Hall of Fame.—*James S. Pula*

SOURCE: Joe Scalzo, "Wally Meskowski," National Sprint Car Hall of Fame & Museum web site.

Michaels, Lou (b. Swoyersville, Pennsylvania, September 28, 1935; d.—). Football player. Michaels was a standout defensive lineman at the University of Kentucky from 1955–57, twice winning All-America honors. Selected in the first round of the professional draft by the Los Angeles Rams, he played thirteen seasons in the National Football League from 1958 through 1971, performing for four different teams. A star defensive end and placekicker, he appeared in two Pro Bowls and was a member of the Baltimore Colts squad that played in the 1969 Super Bowl. Michaels is a member of the College Football Hall of Fame, and in 1994 he was inducted into the **National Polish-American Sports Hall of Fame**. His brother Walt Michaels also was a noted football player and coach, and a member of the Polish-American Sports Hall of Fame.—*Neal Pease*

SOURCE: "Lou Michaels," National Polish-American Sports Hall of Fame website, www.polishsportshof.com.

Michaels, Walt (b. Swoyersville, Pennsylvania, October 16, 1929; d.—). Football

player, coach. After starring as a collegiate football player at Washington and Lee University, Michaels was chosen in the seventh round of the 1951 professional draft by the Green Bay Packers of the National Football League. He went on to play eleven seasons in the NFL, and one in the American Football League. Michaels spent the bulk of his pro career as a standout linebacker with the Cleveland Browns. As a member of that team, he appeared in five Pro Bowls, was named first or second team All-Pro in five different seasons, and played for two NFL champion squads. After his retirement as a player, he entered the coaching ranks, notably as head coach of the New York Jets for six seasons (1977–82). During that span, his Jets made the playoffs twice, and he was honored as American Football Conference coach of the year in 1978. Michaels also served as an assistant coach for three other NFL teams, and spent two seasons as head coach of the New Jersey Generals of the United States Football League. In 1997, he was inducted into the **National Polish-American Sports Hall of Fame**. His brother Lou Michaels also was a noted football player, and a member of the Polish-American Sports Hall of Fame.—*Neal Pease*

SOURCE: "Walt Michaels," National Polish-American Sports Hall of Fame website, www.polishsportshof.com.

Michelson, Albert Abraham (b. Strzelno, Poland, December 19, 1852; d. Pasadena, California, May 9, 1931.) Physicist. Born in the German partition of Poland, Michelson migrated to the U.S. in 1854 when he was only two years old. He was nominated by President U.S. Grant to the Naval Academy in Annapolis and graduated in 1873 after which he was appointed an instructor in physics and chemistry at the Academy where he taught for two years. He applied for leave to study physics at several universities in Europe, remaining there for two years before returning in 1879 and being assigned to the Nautical Almanac Office in Washington, D.C. While lecturing at Annapolis, Michelson conducted his first experiments on the speed of light, which would become his lifetime field of study. He returned to Europe for two more years of study, and while in Berlin began to construct the basic parameters for his "interferometer." The interferometer measured the "aether," the substance that scientists then proposed was a medium in the atmosphere used to carry light vibrations. During his time at the Nautical Almanac Office, Michelson had come into contact with James Clerk Maxwell. Maxwell had inquired about measuring the velocity of the solar system by observing the eclipses of

Jupiter's moons. Michelson extrapolated on this idea to begin his study of measuring the velocity of light.

Michelson resigned from the Navy and in 1883 became a professor of physics in Cleveland, Ohio. While there, he collaborated with a colleague, Edward Morley, in a joint project that would become known as the Michelson-Morley experiment for measuring the aether in the atmosphere. Michelson had already begun his study of the speed of light, and in conjunction with Morley finalized construction of the Michelson interferometer. This instrument produced the most accurate figures for the speed of light known at that time. Michelson continued improving this device for the next forty years. He and Morley conducted their experiments under different conditions and the results were at first baffling. Michelson initially perceived his experiment a failure, with the conclusion that the speed of light did not change. This would become the experimental foundation for Einstein's theory of relativity, and would earn Michelson the Nobel Prize in 1907, the first American scientist to be awarded this honor.

In 1890 Michelson taught at Clark University in Massachusetts, and in 1892 became the head of the physics program at the University of Chicago. He rejoined the Navy during World War I, serving until the end of the war. Michelson returned to teach at Chicago and in 1925 was appointed to a Distinguished Service Professorship. He resigned in 1929 to work at Mount Wilson Observatory in Pasadena, California. Michelson was the first scientist to measure the angular diameter of stars, beginning by measuring the size of Betelgeuse. He continued to contribute to the field of astronomy with several volumes, *Velocity of Light* (1902), *Light Waves and Their Uses* (1899–1903) and *Studies in Optics* (1927). He served as president of the American Physical Society (1900) and president of the National Academy of Sciences (1910–11, 1923–27). Among his many honors were the Copley Medal (Royal Society, 1904), Nobel Prize (1907), Draper Medal (National Academy of Sciences, 1912), Franklin Medal (Franklin Institute, 1923), and the Duddell Medal (Physical Society, 1929).—*Susan Sanchez-Barnett*

SOURCE: B. Jaffe, *Michelson and the Speed of Light* (Westport, CT: Greenwood, 1979).

Mieczkowski, Edwin (b. Pittsburgh, Pennsylvania, November 26, 1929; d.—). Artist. Educated at the Yale–Norfolk Summer Art School where he received a fellowship (1953), he went on to study at the Cleveland Institute of Art (BFA, 1957), and Carnegie Mellon University in Pittsburgh (MFA, 1959).

In 1959, he became a co-founder with Frank Hewitt and Ernst Benkert of the Anonima group which worked together in New York and Cleveland, declaring itself free from the pressures of the art market and the pursuit of personal fame. Specializing in Op Art and geometric abstraction as a sculptor and painter, he taught at the Cleveland Institute of Art (1959–98) and the Western Reserve University (1963–66). Solo exhibitions of his work appeared in Akron (OH), Burlington (VT), Cleveland, Columbus (OH), Dayton (OH), New York, North Olmstead (OH), and Santa Fe (NM), while his works also appeared in group exhibits in various cities in the U.S, as well as London, Paris, Warsaw, and Zagreb. His murals can be found in Denmark, Israel, and Poland. His honors include a National Endowment for the Arts Award (1965), the Cleveland Arts Award (1966), and an Ohio Arts Award (1977).—*Stanley L. Cuba*

SOURCES: Elizabeth McClelland, "Edwin Mieczkowski: Neo Constructivism," *Harmonic Forms on the Edge: Geometric Abstraction in Cleveland* (Cleveland: Cleveland Artists Foundation, 2001); Edward B. Henning, *Mieczkowski: Paintings and Constructions* (Akron, OH: Akron Institute of Art and New Gallery of Contemporary Art, 1977); Richard H. Janson and William C. Lipke, *Anonima Group Retrospective 1969–71* (Burlington, VT: Robert Hull Fleming Museum, University of Vermont, 1971).

Migała, Joseph (b. Chicago, Illinois, February 17, 1913; d. Antioch, Illinois, January 22, 1999). Polonia activist, radio personality. Migala was active in the Polish rural cooperative movement. Leaving Poland in 1947 with his family, he settled in Chicago where he directed Polish language programs on several radio stations. The founder of his own station in Chicago, WCEV, he included his children Lucyna, George, and Diana in various programs broadcast to the Chicago **Polonia** community. Lucyna Migala is active in the **Polish Women's Alliance** and is the founder of the Lira Singers ensemble, an outstanding group that has toured the country since the 1990s with its faithful presentations of Polish folk

Slawa and Joseph Migala, Polonia radio pioneers (OLS).

and classical music. George Migała has been active in Chicago politics and in the **Polish American Congress**. Joseph Migała earned his doctorate from the University of Warsaw in 1981 and published his dissertation in the U.S. in 1987 as *Polish Radio Broadcasting in the United States*. The work was a history of Polish language radio broadcasting in America.—*Donald E. Pienkos*

SOURCES: Wojciech Wierzewski, "Sto Trzydzieska Slynnych Polaków w Ameryce" (Unpublished manuscript in the archives of the University of Wisconsin-Milwaukee, 2000); Joseph Migala, *Polish Radio Broadcasting in the United States* (Boulder, CO: East European Monographs, 1987), v–vii; Bolesław Wierzbiański, ed., *Who's Who in Polish America* (New York: Bicentennial Publishing Corp., 1996), 300.

Migala, Lucyna (b. Kraków, Poland, May 22, 1944; d.—) Polonia activist, journalist, performing arts director. Migała migrated to the U.S. from Poland as a young child. She received her journalism degree from Northwestern University and studied under a postgraduate fellowship program at the Washington Journalism Center. Additionally, she studied voice and dance during her undergraduate years at Northwestern University, as well as studying voice at the Chicago Conservatory College and dancing at Northwestern and the Stone-Camyrn School in Chicago. Her first introduction to journalism and cultural activism was through her parents Estelle and **Joseph Migała** who were popular Polish-language radio personalities in the Chicago area. During her thirteen-year tenure as a producer, writer and reporter, Migała worked for NBC News as a reporter for *Nightly News* and the *Today Show*. In 1974, she won an Emmy Award from the National Academy of Television Arts & Sciences, Cleveland Chapter, for her excellence in news reporting. Additionally, she reported on Pope John Paul II's first visit to Poland in June 1979. Migała left the national scene to create an ethnic-concept radio station with members of her family and became vice president and program director of WCEV 1450 AM, one of metropolitan Chicago's major multi-ethnic radio stations. Since 1965, Migała has directed, along with Alice Stephens, *The Lira Ensemble*, a professional performing arts ensemble which specializes in Polish music, song, and dance. Migała was recognized with many awards and distinctions including the Cavalier's Cross of Merit from the President of Poland for her contribution in popularizing Polish culture. She served as a national board member of the **Polish Women's Alliance of America**, and a member of the board of directors of the Illinois Arts Alliance and the Illinois Humanities Council. She is a founding member of the Ethnic and Folk Arts Panel of the Illinois

Arts Council and the founder and former president of the Chopin Piano Competition, Chicago chapter.—*Geraldine Coleman*

SOURCES: Margaret Gawlak, ed., *White and Red Ball 2005* (Chicago: Mid-City Printing, 2005); Jack Winans, ed., *Malibu East Dialogue* (Chicago, March 2001).

Mihalik, Zigmund John "Red" (b. Ford City, Pennsylvania, September 22, 1916; d. Ford City, Pennsylvania, September 25, 1996). Basketball player, referee. Born to Polish immigrant parents who settled in Pennsylvania in the early 1900s, Mihalik enjoyed a long and respected career as a basketball player and referee well remembered as an official for his extraordinary fairness, commitment, knowledge, and integrity. But it may never have happened if not for a snow storm. When the officials could not make it through the snow to work a high school game, the home town coach tapped Mihalik and a fellow teammate to referee the game. After serving in the U.S. Army Air Corps during World War II, he began refereeing on the collegiate level, soon developing a reputation as an official who kept control of the game, but did not upstage the players or interfere with the game's excitement; instead, he let the players play to their maximum skills with as little interference as possible from his officiating. In 1951 he gained nationwide attention when Dell Publications proclaimed him the best official in the nation. The article stated, "Mihalik makes strong calls and has the respect of both players and coaches. He's not whistle-happy and he has the guts to make the big call without hesitation." Mihalik had the reputation of always being mentally and physically prepared for every game. Pete Newell, who coached at Michigan State University, the University of San Francisco, and the University of California, said of Mihalik: "I never saw anyone more physically or emotionally ready for an important game. He brought an intensity to his work that matched the greatest athletes." It was his ability and toughness, based on his sense of fairness and sportsmanship, which helped him make tough calls in the face of angry coaches and hostile crowds, and made him such a respected figure on the court. During his career he worked six NCAA championship finals, officiated three National Invitational Tournaments, and two Olympics (Tokyo 1964 and Mexico City 1968). Although he also officiated in the National Basketball Association, he preferred officiating amateur and collegiate contests. In the early 1970s, knee problems forced him to give up officiating on the international and major college level even though he continued to referee high school and women's college basketball games. In 1986, largely through ef-

forts initiated by North Carolina Coach Dean Smith, Mihalik was inducted into the Basketball Hall of Fame. In 1996, he became the first person selected to the **National Polish-American Sports Hall of Fame** as an official. He was a beloved figure in his native Ford City, Pennsylvania, where fellow citizens named both a gymnasium and a softball field in his honor.—*Luis J. Gonzalez*

SOURCE: Thomas Tarapacki, "Red Mihalik — You Have to Have the Guts," National Polish-American Sports Hall of Fame.

Mihalowski, John (b. Worcester, Massachusetts, August 12, 1910; d. Largo, Florida, October 29, 1993). Naval officer, Medal of Honor recipient. Mihalowski enlisted in the U.S. Navy in 1927. After rising to the rank of Chief Torpedoman, he trained as a diver and served in that capacity in the Experimental Diving Unit (1933–37) and aboard the *USS Falcon* (1937–41). On May 23, 1939, he played a key role in rescuing survivors from the sunken U.S. submarine *Squalus* for which he was awarded the Medal of Honor. The citation for the award read: "For extraordinary heroism in the line of his profession during the rescue and salvage operations following the sinking of the U.S.S. *Squalus* on 23 May 1939. Mihalowski, as a member of the rescue chamber crew, made the last extremely hazardous trip of the rescue chamber to attempt to rescue any possible survivors in the flooded after portion of the *Squalus*. He was fully aware of the great danger involved, in that, if he and the other member of the crew became incapacitated, there was no way in which either could

John Mihalowski, Medal of Honor recipient (*NARA*).

be rescued. During the salvage operations Mihalowski made important and difficult dives under the most hazardous conditions. His outstanding performance of duty contributed much to the success of the operations and characterizes conduct far above and beyond the ordinary call of duty." During World War II, Mihalowski was promoted to warrant officer and later received a commission for his work salvaging ships that sank in Pearl Harbor in an accident in 1944 and for his work on damaged ships during the invasion of Okinawa in 1945. After retiring to the Fleet Reserve in 1948, he was recalled to duty in September 1950 during the Korean War. He was promoted to lieutenant commander in 1952 and commander in 1954, retiring with that rank in 1958.—*James S. Pula*

SOURCE: R. J. Proft, *United States of America's Congressional Medal of Honor Recipients and Their Official Citations* (Columbia Heights, MN: Highland House II, 2002).

Miklaszewski, James Allen "Jim" or "Mik" (b. Milwaukee, Wisconsin, July 8, 1949; d.—). Journalist. Miklaszewski began his broadcast career as the news director for radio station KRXV in Forth Worth, Texas, in the 1970s, using the on-air name "James Allen." By 1979 he had become account executive for the station before moving to television where he became one of the CNN "originals" as a national correspondent covering the Reagan administration before moving from CNN to join NBC in 1985. He served as a floor reporter at the Democratic and Republican conventions in 1984, 1996, and 2000. During the administration of President George H. W. Bush, he served as NBC's chief White House correspondent, reporting on the first Gulf War, summits with Soviet leaders Mikhail Gorbachev and Boris Yeltsin, and covering the Bush reelection campaign in 1992. He was also White House correspondent during the administration of President Bill Clinton. Nicknamed "Mik," he has had considerable foreign reporting experience, covering wars in Lebanon, El Salvador, and the Falkland Islands, as well as the U.S. air raid in Libya and the so-called "tanker wars" in the Persian Gulf. He has been the moderator for two CNN public affairs programs, *Election Watch* and *Newsmaker Sunday*. On September 11, 2001, he was the first correspondent on the scene during the terrorist attacks on the Pentagon, where he had his office. He was NBC's leading reporter on the war in Afghanistan. His awards include the Edward R. Murrow Award for Journalism for the series *After Nam* and the Cable ACE Award.—*Cheryl A. Pula*

SOURCE: Allison Gilbert, *Covering Catastrophe* (Santa Monica, CA: Bonus Books, 2002).

Mikos, Michael (Michael Jacek Mikoś; b. Warsaw, Poland, October 3, 1939; d.—). Literary scholar. Educated at the Catholic University of Lublin where he received a baccalaureate in English in 1963 and Brown University where he earned his doctorate in linguistics in 1977, he has been a member of the faculty of the University of Wisconsin–Milwaukee since the latter year. During his career he received several National Endowment for the Humanities and **Kosciuszko Foundation** research awards, as well as the American Association of Teachers of Slavic and East European Languages (AATSEEL) Award for Outstanding Achievement in Scholarship (1995), the Polish Pen Club Translation Prize (1995), and the Turzanski Foundation Award for popularizing Polish literature in the United States (1996). His most important achievement was the publication of a series of annotated anthologies of Polish literature ranging from the Middle Ages to the end of the twentieth century—*Medieval Literature of Poland: An Anthology* (1992); *Polish Renaissance Literature: An Anthology* (1995); *Polish Baroque and Enlightenment Literature: An Anthology* (1996); *Polish Romantic Literature: An Anthology* (2002); *Polish Literature from 1864 to 1918—Realism and Young Poland: An Anthology* (2006); and *Polish Literature from 1918 to 2000: An Anthology* (2008). Among his other books are volumes on Adam Mickiewicz and **Henryk Sienkiewicz**, as well as translations of the poetry of Juliusz Słowacki and Jan Kochanowski. Mikos has been a member of the editorial boards of *Slavic and East European Journal, Sarmatian Review, The Polish Review, Milwaukee History,* and *Etnolingwistyka.* He also has been active in Polish American affairs, conducting academic summer tours to Poland (1981–2007) where he presided over a course of study in Polish language and history at the Catholic University of Lublin. Mikos's achievement is rich and varied; he is one of the few American Polish scholars who have been able to obtain and retain a full time professorial position in Polish subjects at an American university.—*Ewa Thompson*

SOURCE: Bolesław Wierzbiański, *Who's Who in Polish America* (New York: Bicentennial Publishing Corp., 1996), 302.

Mikulski, Barbara Ann (b. Baltimore, Maryland, July 20, 1936; d.—). U.S. Senator. The granddaughter of Polish immigrants, Mikulski was born and raised in East Baltimore where she was the eldest of three daughters. As a child, she helped her father in the family-run grocery store, Willy's Market, often assisting in the delivery of groceries to the elderly. Long interested in community and public service, upon graduating from Mount Saint Agnes College (now part of Loyola College in Maryland) with a degree in sociology in 1958 she earned a master's degree in social work from the University of Maryland School of Social Work in 1965. Mikulski worked for various welfare and social service agencies including the Associated Catholic Charities (1958–61), the Baltimore Welfare Department (1961–63), and with such groups as Responding to the Elderly's Ability and Sickness Otherwise Neglected (REASON), Narcotics Anonymous, and the Southeast Community Organization (SECO). In 1966 she became assistant chief of community organizing for the Baltimore Department of Social Services. Her community activism began at the grassroots level. She encouraged African-Americans to register to vote, organized tenant strikes, and struggled to preserve many of Baltimore's ethnic neighborhoods. Mikulski was particularly instrumental in organizing a coalition of Baltimore residents to assist in blocking a plan to construct a 16-lane highway which would have run through parts of East Baltimore, including Fells Point, the Inner Harbor, and the first African American home-ownership neighborhood. In 1971 she was elected to the Baltimore City Council, serving until 1976 when she successfully ran for and was elected to Congress as a representative of Maryland's Third District. Ten years later she was elected to the Senate, making history as the first Democratic woman to have ever been elected to both houses of Congress in her own right. In 1987 she was only one of two women in the Senate. Mikulski distinguished herself politically as a strong supporter of women's issues, including health and reproductive rights, domestic violence, and workplace policies relating to sexual harassment and discrimination. Additionally, she has been a strong advocate of funding NASA's space station, a staunch opponent of predatory lending, and a supporter of issues relating to education, health insurance, and the elderly. Between 1993 and 1995, Mikulski held the position of assistant Senate Democratic floor leader of the 103rd Congress and has served on several major committees and subcommittees including labor, public works, and the environment. In 2009 Mikulski was the senior female senator and the dean of women in the United States Senate. For her public service she has received numerous awards and honors and holds several honorary doctorates. Mikulski is also a member of the National Association of Social Workers and the **Polish Women's Alliance.**—*Krystyna Cap*

SOURCE: Eric Pianin, "The Abrasive Lady From Baltimore Polishes Her Act," *The Washington Post,* June 14, 1987, W17.

Milewski, Stanley E. (b. Detroit, Michigan, November 30, 1929; d.—). Priest, college administrator, Polonia activist. Milewski completed his studies for the priesthood in 1955 at St. John's Provincial Seminary in Plymouth, MI. His first parish ministry was in Detroit. Beginning in 1957 he taught Polish, religion, and history at **Saint Mary's College** in Orchard Lake, MI, where he went on to hold a number of administrative duties at the College and responsibilities in the administration of the schools located there, which included a seminary for the training of candidates for the priesthood from **Polonia** and Poland, a four year liberal arts College, and a high school located on the grounds. Milewski was appointed Chancellor of the Orchard Lake Schools and served in this capacity from 1977 to 2000. Monsignor Milewski was been deeply involved in the revival of the **Polish American Priests Association** nationally, was active in several Polish American fraternals, and was a national director of the **Polish American Congress**. His many involvements in these organizations and in his priestly work in the Archdiocese of Detroit have been recognized on many occasions by **Polonia** and Church groups, the government of Poland, Pope John Paul II (in 1990), and Pope Benedict XVI (in 2007). He is an Honorary Canon in both the Dioceses of Płock and Łomza, Poland.—*Donald E. Pienkos*

SOURCES: Wojciech Wierzewski, "Sto Trzydzieska Slynnych Polaków w Ameryce" (Unpublished manuscript in the archives of the University of Wisconsin–Milwaukee, 2000); Bolesław Wierzbiański, *Who's Who in Polish America* (New York: Bicentennial Publishing Corp., 1996), 304.

Miłosz, Czesław (b. Seteniai, Lithuania, June 30, 1911; d. Kraków, Poland, April 14, 2004). Poet. A son of a road engineer, Miłosz spent his early childhood traveling in Russia. After returning to Lithuania in 1918, he was educated at the home of his grandparents who were members of the Lithuanian gentry. He then attended the Polish secondary school in Wilno (Vilnius) between 1921 and 1929. Later he regarded his secondary education as the most helpful for his future American academic career. A law student at the Stephen Batory University between 1929 and 1934, Miłosz closely cooperated with the Polish philology students and the literary journal *Żagary.* He published his first poem in *Alma Mater Vilnensis* in 1930, took his first trip to Paris in 1931, had his first book published in 1933, and received his first literary award from the weekly *Pion* in 1938. After a one-year scholarship in Paris (1934–35) Miłosz worked for the Polish Radio in Wilno (Vilnius) and in

Warsaw. The outbreak of World War II forced Miłosz to flee to Romania, but in January 1940 he came back to Wilno, then under Lithuanian administration. When Lithuania was incorporated into the Soviet Union in the summer that year, Miłosz fled to Warsaw where he took a job at the university library. At the same time he became active in organizing conspiratorial Polish literary life, publishing his poems illegally under the pseudonym Jan Syruć. After the end of the Warsaw Uprising in October 1944, Miłosz managed to escape from the transit camp in Okęcie, finding shelter in villages near Kraków.

Following World War II, Miłosz published not only poems, but also feature articles in **Dziennik Polski** (Polish Daily) and other periodicals. Later he characterized this phase of his journalism as "consciously descending into disgust." In December 1945 he began his diplomatic career at the New York consulate of the People's Republic of Poland, moving in 1947 to the embassy in Washington, D.C. Miłosz was instrumental in establishing the Adam Mickiewicz Chair of Polish Culture at Columbia University in 1948 under the sponsorship of the Communist government in Warsaw. In 1950 he moved to a position at the Polish embassy in Paris, but in February 1951 asked for political asylum in France. Officially condemned in Poland and welcomed with reserve by the London émigrés, Miłosz presented his views on the Sovietization of Poland in *The Captive Mind* and *The Seizure of Power*, books published in the "Kultura Library" series in Paris.

In 1960, Miłosz came to the United States as a visiting lecturer at the University of California–Berkeley where he was granted a tenured position the following year. Apart from lecturing on Polish and Russian literature, he published poetry and prose in both Polish and English, translated Polish poetry into English, and translated the books of the Bible from Greek and Hebrew into Polish. His works brought Miłosz recognition within Polish communities abroad, as well as in American professional circles. Among his many Polish honors were the "Kultura" literary prize in 1957, the Polish Writers in Exile Association award in 1958, the Alfred Jurzykowski Prize in 1968, and the Polish PEN Club award in 1974. Additional honors included a Guggenheim Fellowship (1976), an honorary Doctor of Letters from the University of Michigan (1977), and the Neustadt International Prize for Literature and Berkeley Citation (1978). The Nobel Prize in Literature for 1980 gave him worldwide recognition, as well as clearing the way for his first visit to Poland since 1950

and for the publication of his works in Poland. During that visit he received an honorary doctorate from the Catholic University of Lublin. Other honorary degrees soon followed including New York University (1981), Brandeis University (1983), Jagiellonian University (1989), Harvard University (1989), Vytautas Magnus University of Kaunas (1991), Bologna University (1991), and Universita di Roma (1992). In 1981–82 Miłosz gave the Charles Eliot Norton Lectures at Harvard University, and in 1989 he was recognized as one of the Righteous Among Nations by the Yad Vashem Institute.

After the collapse of the Communist regime in Poland, Miłosz made regular visits to Poland, dividing his time between Berkeley and Kraków. His new works continued to bring acclaim. *Piesek przydrożny* brought him the "NIKE" literary award in 1997. He also received several high government decorations including the Order of the White Eagle (Poland, 1994) and Order of the Lithuanian Grand Duke Gediminas, Second Class (Lithuania, 1995). He is buried at historic Skałka church in Kraków.—*Joanna Wojdon*

SOURCES: Andrzej Zawada, *Miłosz* (Wrocław, 1996); Czesław Miłosz, et al., *Conversations with Czesław Miłosz* (San Diego: Harcourt Brace Jovanovich, 1987); Leonard Nathan and Arthur Quinn, *The Poet's Work: An Introduction to Czeslaw Milosz* (Cambridge, MA: Harvard University Press, 1991); Edward Możejko, *Between Anxiety and Hope: The Poetry and Writing of Czesław Miłosz* (Edmonton, Canada: University of Alberta Press, 1998).

Minczeski, John (b. South Bend, Indiana, July 8, 1947; d.—). Poet. Minczeski earned his B.A. from the University of Minnesota in 1973 and an M.F.A. in poetry from Warren Wilson College in 1990. He has been a staple of Minnesota arts and cultural life for decades, publishing four collections of poetry, including *The Reconstruction of Light* (1981), and the well-received *Circle Routes* (2001), the latter a winner of the Akron Poetry Prize. Minczeski has also edited two volumes of poetry, including *Concert at Chopin's House: A Collection of Polish-American Writing* (1988). The recipient of several awards and honors, Minczeski has received fellowships from the Minnesota State Arts Board (1976), the Bush Foundation (1981), the National Endowment for the Arts (1984), and was also named the Edelstein-Keller Distinguished Fellow at the University of Minnesota for the 2004–2005 academic year. His poetry has appeared in such journals as *Agni, Meridian, Mid-American Review, Free Lunch, Cream City Review, Quarterly West*, and others. Minczeski has taught creative writing and poetry to students in elementary schools, high schools, and colleges throughout Minnesota, including Ham-

line University, St. Paul; Macalester College, St. Paul; and St. Cloud State University in St. Cloud. He is also an instructor at the Loft Literary Center, one of the largest literary centers in America, which offers classes, workshops, seminars, and mentorship programs to aspiring and published writers. Minczeski served as president of the Loft's board of directors between 1976 and 1978. He is also an affiliate of COMPAS (Community Programs in the Arts) which is a St. Paul–based not-for-profit organization promoting activities in the arts and offering grants to people of all ages.—*Krystyna Cap*

SOURCE: "Poetry—Gravity by John Minczeski," *The Virginia Quarterly Review*, Vol. 68, no. 1 (Winter 1992), 28.

Mish, John Leon (b. Śląsk region of Poland, 1909; d. Hawthorne, New York, August 22, 1983). Linguist, librarian. Mish earned his Ph.D. in Chinese and Japanese literature at the University of Berlin in 1934. He taught Oriental Studies in Warsaw, then taught German in Baghdad, and later worked in British Intelligence in Bombay resulting in the British government awarding him the King's Medal for Service to the Cause of Freedom in 1946. One of the world's great linguists, he knew numerous languages including all of the Slavic and Romance languages, as well as Arabic, Chinese, Japanese, Korean, Turkish, Sanskrit, Malay, Hindi, Manchu, and others. While in Bombay he was invited to join the Oriental Branch of the New York Public Library which he accepted 1948, becoming chief of the division and greatly expanding its collections of Asian materials. In 1955 he also became chief of the Slavonic Division, the only person to hold both positions simultaneously, positions which he held until his retirement in 1978. In addition to aggressively building the collections of both divisions, he was also a prolific author. His most important publications dealt with early Chinese history, especially those relating to Manchu texts, an area in which he was internationally renowned. He published an introduction to a standard history of Japan, and authored or co-authored several bilingual dictionaries, among them one for Turkish-English and another for Arabic-English. He was awarded a Guggenheim fellowship in 1957 and on a Fulbright Fellowship in 1959–60 he discovered in the Vatican Library a very early seventeenth century work by the Italian Jesuit missionary Guido Aleni, The *His-Fang-Ta-Wen*, written to explain Europe to the Chinese. Mish published the Chinese text in 1964 in *Monumenta Serica*, with his introduction, translation, and notes. During his tenure at the New York Public Library he taught at various institutions including the Asia Institute (1946–51), Dropsie College (1961–63), Seton Hall University (1963–76), Fordham University (1967–69), and Barnard College (1970–73). He also established book exchange programs with libraries in East and West Europe.—*James S. Pula*

SOURCE: Thomas W. Ennis, "John L. Mish, Library Official and Language Expert, Dead," *New York Times*, August 24, 1983, A20.

Mizerak, Steve (b. Perth Amboy, New Jersey, October 12, 1944; d. Boca Raton, Florida, May 29, 2006). Pocket billiards player. Mizerak began playing pocket billiards, or pool, professionally at age thirteen, though for much of his life this was a side venture to his career as a schoolteacher. He won the U.S. Open Pocket Billiards championship four consecutive years (1970–73), won the World Open twice (1976, 1978), and captured three straight Professional Pool Players Association world championships (1982–84). Known by the nicknames "The Miz" and "The Machine," he gained celebrity in 1978 by performing trick shots in a television commercial for Miller Lite beer. Mizerak appeared as a pool-playing opponent of Paul Newman in the 1986 film *The Color of Money*. He is a member of the Billiards Congress of America Hall of Fame, and was the author or co-author of numerous instructional books on pool.—*Neal Pease*

SOURCE: "Steve Mizerak, National Pool Champion, Is Dead at 61," *The New York Times*, June 2, 2006.

Mizwa, Stephen Paul (Stefan P. Mierzwa, b. Rakszawa, Poland, November 12, 1892; d. Houston, Texas, January 16, 1971). Polonia activist. A poor peasant boy of seventeen from Eastern Poland (then part of the Austro-Hungarian Empire) Mizwa arrived in America in 1910 with $15 in his pocket. He learned English quickly and enrolled in the American International College in Springfield, Massachusetts, where he finished grammar school and college preparatory courses while working in a basket factory. With a scholarship, he graduated *cum laude* in 1920 from Amherst College earning a Phi Beta Kappa key. He received a full tuition scholarship from Harvard, earning an A.M. degree in 1921. Before pursuing his Ph.D. he taught courses in economics at Drake University in Des Moines, Iowa. While there, a magazine article by Dr. Henry Noble MacCracken, President of Vassar College, concerning his lectures at various European universities including the Jagiellonian University in Kraków, intrigued Mizwa. MacCracken had been greatly impressed with the intellectual atmosphere at the Jagiellonian, the

enthusiasm of its students for learning and their desire to become acquainted with the United States and American literature. This revived an idea originally inspired by his student advisor at Amherst, President Alexander Meiklejohn, about creating an organization which would promote the exchange of students, professors, and culture between Poland and the United States similar to organizations already in existence between the United States and several European countries. Following a meeting with MacCracken, who was encouraging, the Polish American Scholarship Committee was organized with Dr. Władysław Wróblewski, Polish Minister to the United States, serving as its president. The Committee raised over $9,000 in public contributions from 1924 to 1925 and was able to grant scholarships to the first group of nine Polish students. In 1925 the Committee was transformed into the **Kościuszko Foundation** to continue the Committee's mission. Rather than erect another monument to **Tadeusz Kościuszko** on the occasion of the 150th anniversary of his arrival to fight in the American Revolutionary War, which was to take place in 1926, Mizwa proposed a living memorial in the form of a foundation. An all American team constituted the first Board of Trustees. In addition to MacCracken, the trustees included Samuel Vauclain, president of Baldwin Locomotive Works of Philadelphia, Pennsylvania; Willis H. Booth, vice president of the Guaranty Trust Company of New York, New York; Colonel Cedric Fauntleroy of Chicago, commander of the Kościuszko Air Squadron during the Polish-Bolshevik War of 1920; Dr. Robert H. Lord, professor of history at Harvard; Professor Paul Monroe of Columbia Teachers College; and Mizwa. The first headquarters was a room with donated furniture in the Polish Consulate building located on Third Avenue and 57th Street, New York City. At the end of World War II the change in the Polish government required a new headquarters. In 1945 the Kościuszko Foundation acquired a town house at 15 East 65th Street in New York City. With the onset of the 1929 depression, the Foundation was not able to support a full-time director. Accordingly, in 1929 Mizwa became president of **Alliance College** in Cambridge Springs, Pennsylvania, and remained president until 1932. Thereafter, he devoted the rest of his life in making the Kościuszko Foundation a leading American institution. During the Second World War, Mizwa worked to aid Polish refugee scholars such as **Oskar Halecki**. He helped to establish a school in Switzerland for Polish soldiers interned there after the fall of France and worked tirelessly, seven days a

week, never taking a vacation and for very little money with neither medical insurance nor a pension. Whatever spare time he had he spent promoting Polish culture. Mizwa was the author of biographies of Frederick Chopin and Copernicus and editor of Great *Men and Women of Poland*, as well as the monumental *Kosciuszko Foundation Polish-English, English-Polish Dictionary*. Mizwa retired on the 45th anniversary of the founding of the Foundation, December 23, 1970, to a nursing home in Houston, Texas.—*Joseph E. Gore*

SOURCES: Stephen P. Mizwa, *The Story of the Kosciuszko Foundation—How It Came About* (New York: The Kosciuszko Foundation, 1972); Elizabeth A. Daniels, *Bridges to the World—Henry Noble MacCracken and Vassar College* (Clinton Corner, NY: College Avenue Press, 1994); Eugene Kusielewicz, ed., *A Tribute to Stephen P. Mizwa* (New York: Czas Publishing Company, 1972); *The Kosciuszko Foundation Monthly News Letter*, Vol. XXV, no. 1 (September 1970), Vol. XXV, no. 5 (January 1971), and Vol. XXV, no. 6 (February 1971); Eugene Kusielewicz, "In Memoriam. Stephen Mierzwa (1892–1971)," *The Polish Review*, Vol. 16, no. 2 (1971), 116.

Mlotkowski, Stanisław (b. Volhynia Province, Poland, April 19, 1829; d. Egg Harbor, New Jersey, August 19, 1900). Military officer. After taking part in the abortive Mierosławski Insurrection in 1846, Mlotkowski escaped to Hungary, made his way to Paris, and then to the U.S. where he settled in Philadelphia and earned a living as a painter. When the Civil War broke out, he enrolled as a first lieutenant in Battery A, Pennsylvania Light Artillery, on September 11, 1861, and was assigned to Fort Delaware outside Philadelphia. He was promoted to captain and given command of the battery on March 1, 1862. In the following month some 258 Confederate prisoners-of-war were consigned to the fort, turning it into a prison camp. Although Mlotkowski was described as a "Black Republican," a term that meant he was abolitionist in sentiment, he gained a reputation as a fair and considerate officer among rebel prisoners. One observed, the captain "treats the Rebels with kindness; cordially shakes hands with the Confederate officers, and admits that a prisoner not only has a right to try to make his escape, if not on parole, but that his duty to his government requires him to do so, if possible. His fairness, his respect for the rights of others and his determination to recognize the goodness of human beings were exemplary." Another observed that Mlotkowski was "very popular" with the rebel prisoners. After the war ended, Mlotkowski was mustered out at Camp Cadwallader on July 1, 1865. Following the war he was a member of a group that developed the Atlantic coast resort at Egg Harbor City, New Jersey, where he was a member of Gen. Stahel Post No. 62

and the Grand Army of the Republic veterans organization.—*James S. Pula*

SOURCES: John A. Kowalewski, "Capt. Mlotkowski of Ft. Delaware," *Polish American Studies*, Vol. XXIII, no. 2 (1966), 89–92; *Mlotkowski Memorial Room: Fort Delaware—Pea Patch Island* (Fort Delaware, DE: Captain Stanislaus Mlotkowski Memorial Brigade Society, ca. 1976); W. Emerson Wilson, *Fort Delaware* (Newark, DE: University of Delaware Press, 1957); Isaac W. K. Handy *United States Bonds; or Duress by Federal Authority: Journal During Imprisonment of Fifteen Months at Fort Delaware* (Baltimore: Turnbull Brothers, 1874), 403.

Mocha, Frank (Franciszek Mocha; b. Babice, Silesia, Poland, February 18, 1923; d. New York, New York, May 1, 2001). Philologist, educator. Mocha was in the Polish army when Germany invaded in 1939, then made his way to France to join the Polish army-in-exile. Captured in France in 1942, he spent three years in prisoner of war camps in Alsace (Neu Breisach), Bavaria (Stalag VIIA), and Austria (Stalag XVIIB). Eventually escaping, he made his way over the Pyrenees to Gibraltar where he rejoined the Polish army in England. Following the war he studied economics and history at the University of London (1946–48) on a British government scholarship. He migrated to the United States in 1951, becoming a naturalized American citizen in 1956. While working as a proofreader for Retnak Press in New York City, he studied Slavic literature at Columbia University, from which he received a B.S. degree in 1961, *magna cum laude* and Phi Beta Kappa. He then pursued graduate studies at Columbia, receiving his M.A. as a National Defense Foreign Language Fellow in 1963, and a Ph.D. in 1970. Both his master's thesis and his doctoral dissertation were later published in *Antemurale*, the journal of the Polish Historical Institute in Rome.

Mocha's first academic appointment was teaching Polish and Russian at the University of Pittsburgh where he was instructor (1966–68) and then assistant professor (1968–71). During 1971–72, he was an exchange scholar in Russia through the International Research and Exchanges Board, and subsequently a research scholar at the **Kosciuszko Foundation** (1972–73). After teaching at New York University's School of Continuing Education (1974–76), where he developed courses on the U.S. Bicentennial, Mocha moved to the University of Illinois, Chicago Circle, where he was associate professor of Slavic languages and literature (1976–79). He then joined the faculty of Loyola University Chicago, where he was a lecturer in modern languages (1979–1982), and then adjunct professor of modern languages (1982–1984). He simultaneously held an appointment at the Chicago branch of the **Polish University Abroad**, where he was Dean of Humanities and Professor of Slavic Philology (1979–84). Mocha retired from both institutions in 1984 to devote himself to writing full-time.

Mocha contributed articles and reviews to numerous scholarly journals, including the *Slavic Review*, the *Polish Review*, the *Slavic and East European Journal*, and a two-part memoir of his early years in Silesia in *Modern Age*. He presented papers at many scholarly conferences in both the United States and Europe, and was editor of two books: *Poles in America: Bicentennial Essays* (1978); and *American "Polonia" and Poland* (1998). Mocha was also co-editor of *Poland's Solidarity Movement* (1984), which contained papers presented at the International Symposium on Poland's Solidarity Movement held at Loyola University Chicago in 1982. He was active in numerous scholarly organizations, including the Modern Language Association, the **Polish American Historical Association**, the American Association of Teachers of Slavic and East European Languages, the American Association for the Advancement of Slavic Studies, and the **Polish Institute of Arts and Sciences in America**, for whom he served on the Board of Directors (1974–77), was chair of the Literary Section (1974–77), and associate editor of the *Polish Review* (1973–75). Mocha was also president of the Polish Arts Club of Chicago (1977–79), a member of the Board of Directors of the Illinois Division of the **Polish American Congress** (1977–78), and president of the Polish American Educators Association (1981–84). He was quick to write letters to newspaper editors correcting errors and clarifying points, especially in articles on Polish topics.—*John Drobnicki*

SOURCE: *Who's Who in the Midwest, 1982–1983* (Chicago: Marquis Who's Who, 1982), 480.

Moczygemba, Leopold Bonaventura Maria (Moczygęba; b. Płużnica, Poland, October 18, 1824; d. Dearborn, Michigan, February 23, 1891). Priest. Born in Upper Silesia, Moczygemba is best remembered today as the founder of the first permanent Polish settlement in the United States at **Panna Maria**, Texas, in 1854. In later life he helped build the core of Franciscan Minor Conventual parishes and friaries in the eastern United States, was instrumental in establishing the **Polish Roman Catholic Union**, served the **Congregation of the Resurrection**, and with the Rev. **Joseph Dąbrowski** was one of the founders of the Polish Seminary in Detroit, Michigan.

Moczygemba grew up in the villages of Płużnica and Ligota Toszecka in the Opole Regency, part of Prussian Upper Silesia. He attended German-operated schools in the market towns of Gliwice and Opole. Then in his early twenties, he made the momentous decision to become a priest, traveling to northern Italy in the fall of 1843 to begin his novitiate in the Friars Minor Conventual. Ordained on July 25, 1847, the order transferred him to Bavaria where he met the Rev. Jean-Marie Odin, Bishop of Galveston, who had come from America in 1852 to solicit aid and to recruit missionaries to serve in his diocese, which comprised the entire state of Texas. He made arrangements in Bavaria for the Friars Minor Conventual to care for several of his German immigrant parishes, and among the priests he brought back was twenty-nine-year-old Leopold Moczygemba, an ethnic Pole who was fluent in German. The young priest saw the material prosperity of his German parishioners and began writing letters home to family friends in Upper **Silesia** about the life he observed in the New World. In time he organized the movement of several parties of Poles from his home region to Texas. Starting to arrive in December 1854, they established at a place Moczygemba called Panna Maria the first permanent Polish settlement, Catholic parish, and Polish school in the United States. Moczygemba remained in Texas only through late 1857, when he departed for several months in Europe.

Moczygemba returned to the United States in November 1858, this time to the eastern states, where the Friars Minor Conventual had been given several German ethnic parishes. As the commissary general for a newly elevated canonical province of Friars, he worked with others to build parishes in places including Philadelphia, Pennsylvania; Utica and Syracuse, New York; Louisville, Kentucky; and Jeffersonville, Indiana. Traveling to Europe in 1861, he came back with more money for the American efforts. He again went to Europe in 1868, this time spending two years, during which time he published a pocket ritual for use by missionary priests in America, *Enchiridion Sacerdotum Curam Animarum Agentium* (1870). Moczygemba received temporary exclaustration from the Franciscans in 1870 in order to work outside the order in a diocesan parish to earn money to assist his aged mother. He then traveled back to America, where in early 1871 he became pastor in Litchfield, Illinois; in 1873 at Terre Haute, Indiana; in 1875 in Jeffersonville, Indiana; and in 1877 in Louisville, Kentucky. During this time Moczygemba became more involved with Polish immigrant life. He helped establish the Polish Roman Catholic Union and was elected its third president in 1875. His interest in working among Poles in part prompted the

The Rev. Leopold Moczygemba, founder of the first Polish American settlement at Panna Maria, Texas (*PMA*).

priest's last trip to Europe in 1878. It resulted in Pope Leo XIII approving his transfer from the Friars Minor Conventual to a nationalistic Polish order, the Congregation of the Resurrection.

In 1880 Moczygemba returned to America, spending the next two years working with the Rev. **Wincenty Barzyński** at St. Stanislaus Kostka parish in Chicago. During this time he also assisted with parish duties at Eaton, now Poland, Wisconsin. For five years, from 1882 to 1887, he undertook the last major works in his life. While working actively in creating a new Polish parish at Lemont, Illinois, he concurrently collaborated with the Reverend Joseph Dąbrowski in creating a first-ever Polish seminary in America. Moczygemba contributed several thousand dollars of his personal funds as seed money for creation of **Sts. Cyril and Methodius Seminary** just outside Detroit, Michigan, participating in the laying of its cornerstone in 1885. The aging priest spent his last years in declining health working in parishes at Parisville, Hilliards, and Detroit, Michigan. In 1974 his mortal remains were transferred from Michigan to Panna Maria in Texas. There they were reinterred beneath the very same historic oak under which he offered the first mass of thanksgiving for the Silesian immigrants in December 1854.— *T. Lindsay Baker*

SOURCES: T. Lindsay Baker, "The Reverend Leopold Moczygemba: Patriarch of Polonia," *Polish American Studies*, Vol. LXI, No. 1 (Spring 1984), 66–109; Joseph Swastek, *Priest and Pioneer: Rev. Leopold Moczygemba* (Detroit: Conventual Press, 1951).

Modjeska, Helena (Jadwiga Benda; b. Kraków, Poland, October 12, 1840; d. New-port Beach, California, April 8, 1909). Shake-spearean actress. Although her paternity has been contested by claims that Modjeska was illegitimately fathered by Prince Władysław Sanguszko, Jadwiga Benda (later christened Helena Opid), was born into a family that traveled in artistic circles. Despite their relative poverty, from a young age Modjeska was influenced by her adopted musician father, Michał, and his literary and artistic friends. In 1861 Modjeska married Gustave Sinnmayer Modrzejewski, who had supervised her early education and promoted her fledgling acting career. In the same year she made her first on-stage appearance in a one-act comedy named *The White Camellia*. Although her husband died in 1866, she continued her career in Poland, remarrying in 1868. Her second husband, Count Karol Bozenta Chłapowski, was a well-known Polish patriot and journalist. Throughout the late 1860s and early 1870s, she continued to receive critical acclaim for her various roles on the Warsaw stage. In the years prior to emigration, she and her husband briefly traveled to Kraków, where Chłapowski published a partisan journal and where Helena became active in Polish politics. Upon return to Warsaw, the radical nationalist position held by both Modrzejewska and Chłapowski resulted in increasing harassment by Russian authorities, and led the pair to leave Warsaw for America in 1876. Thus she migrated to California with her son from her first marriage, Ralph (later a well-respected civil engineer; see **Ralph Modjeski**), Chłapowski, and a handful of Polish friends and colleagues, including Julian Sypniewski and **Henryk Sienkiewicz**.

Modrzejewska and her husband purchased a twenty-acre farm in Anaheim, established a ranch there, and with their Polish friends, intended to found a utopian Polish farming colony. When plans failed owing to a lack of agricultural knowledge (and lacking the funds to return home), Modjeska traveled to San Francisco, where she began English language lessons with the intention of returning to the stage. Not long after, with the assistance of several Poles resident in San Francisco, she approached Barton Hill and John McCullough of the California Theater for a role. It was Mc-Cullough who suggested that she shorten her name to Modjeska to make it easier for American audiences to pronounce. On August 20, 1877, Modjeska made her American debut in San Francisco in an Ernest Legouvé and A. E. Scribe play, *Adrienne Lecouvreur*. Achieving critical acclaim for her successive roles, including Ophelia and Juliet, she soon began touring American stages in a variety of roles, appearing in Boston, Buffalo, Kansas City,

Helena Modjeska, noted Shakespearean actress (*PMA*).

New Orleans, New York, and elsewhere. In 1878 Modjeska briefly toured theaters in Russian Poland and traveled to England in 1880. Upon her return to America in 1882, she produced and starred in a version of Henrik Ibsen's *A Doll's House*. In America, Modjeska became famous chiefly for her portrayal of several Shakespearean roles, including Juliet, Desdemona, Rosalind, Queen Anne, and Ophelia. In May 1893, she was invited to speak at an international conference at the Chicago World's Fair, where she delivered a stirring speech on the status of Polish women, uttering several highly patriotic remarks regarding the injustice of Poland's eighteenth-century partitions. In Russia her speech met with the ire of tsarist authorities, who issued an *ukase* prohibiting her from ever returning to Russian Poland. Modjeska died in 1909 at her home on Bay Island in Newport Beach, California; however, Chłapowski buried her remains in Kraków. One year later, her memoirs were published in America and thereafter translated into Polish. Throughout her career, Modjeska played in over 225 towns and cities throughout the United States and Canada. In popular culture, Modjeska inspired Susan Sontag's novel, *In America* (1999), which was awarded the National Book Award. Sontag's novel was based on Modjeska's life after emigration and came under public scrutiny for allegedly having plagiarized passages from Modjeska's own memoir and other biographical sources. A small collection of primary and secondary materials on Modjeska's career in Poland and the United States is housed in the Special Collections and Archives of the University of California, Irvine.— *Krystyna Cap*

SOURCES: Ellen K. Lee, "The Catholic Modjeska," *Polish American Studies*, Vol. 31, no. 1 (1974), 20–27; "Helena Modjeska," in Charles H. Shattuck, ed., *Shakespeare on the American Stage: From Booth and Barrett to Sothern and Marlowe* (London: Associated University Presses, 1987), Vol. 2, 125–36; Arthur P. Coleman and Marion Moore Coleman, *Wanderers Twain: Modjeska and Sienkiewicz. A View of California* (Cheshire: Cherry Hill Books, 1964); Marion Moore Coleman, *Fair Rosalind: The American Career of Helena Modjeska* (Sheshire: Cherry Hill Books, 1969); Antoni Gronowicz, *Modjeska: Her Life and Loves* (New York: Thomas Yoseloff, 1956); Helena Modjeska, *Memories and Impressions of Helena Modjeska: An Autobiography* (New York: Benjamin Blom, 1969); Beth Holmgren, "Virility and Gentility: How Sienkiewicz and Modjeska Redeemed America," *The Polish Review*, Vol. 46, no. 3 (2001), 283–96.

Modjeski, Ralph (Rudolf Modrzejewski; b. Bohnia, Poland, January 27, 1861; d. Los Angeles, California, June 26, 1940). Engineer. The son of noted Shakespearean actress **Helena Modjeska** (Modrzejewska), he came to the United States with his mother in 1876 and settled in Anaheim, CA. He changed his name from Modrzejewski to Modjeski on becoming an American citizen in 1883. After studying civil engineering at the Ecole des Ponts et Chaussees in Paris, France, where he graduated with honors (1885), he apprenticed with American bridge engineer George Morison. He later established his own engineering company, Modjeski and Masters (1895), based in Harrisburg, PA. The Government Bridge at Rock Island, Illinois built in 1895, was his first independent project. He served for a while as a consulting engineer for the city of Chicago, but gained his reputation primarily from the construction of bridges including the Bismarck Bridge for the Northern Pacific Railroad; the Columbia and Willamette River Bridges for the Portland & Seattle Railway; the McKinley Bridge at St. Louis; the Broadway Bridge in Portland, Oregon; the Columbia River Bridge in Cecilo, Oregon; the Cherry Street Bridge in Toledo, Ohio; the Memphis Bridge in Tennessee; the Delaware River Bridge (later renamed the Benjamin Franklin Bridge) between Philadelphia and Camden, New Jersey; the Tacony-Palmyra Bridge over the Delaware River in Northeast Philadelphia; the Mid-Hudson Bridge in New York State; the New Orleans Bridge and the Huey P. Long Bridge in New Orleans; the Thebes Bridge over the Mississippi River at Thebes, Illinois; the Iowa-Illinois Memorial Bridge at Davenport; the Calvert Street Bridge in Washington, D.C.; the Trans-Bay Bridge between San Francisco and Oakland in California; and the Blue Water Bridge connecting Port Huron, Michigan, and Sarnia, Ontario, Canada. Among his more important works was re-designing a poorly conceived Quebec Bridge in 1907, a project that is still the longest cantilever bridge

Ralph Modjeski, engineer and bridge builder (*Peter J. Obst*).

in the world. His work on the Thebes Bridge led to his being named "A Man of Illinois" by the State Assembly. Altogether he was associated with building over forty major bridges in the United States. Labeled by the *New York Times* as "the world's leading bridge builder," he was honored with the Howard N. Potts Medal of the Franklin Institute, Philadelphia (1914); the John Scott Medal in Philadelphia (1924); the John Fritz Gold Medal (1930), the most prestigious engineering award in America; the Washington Award of the Western Society of Engineers (1931); the Grand Prix Medal of the Exposition of Industry and Science in Poznań, Poland (1929); and Knight of the Legion of Honor from France. He also received honorary doctoral degrees from the Pennsylvania Military College (1927; now Widener University) and the Polytechnic University in Lwów (1931).—*Peter J. Obst*

SOURCES: *Biography of Ralph Modjeski, Medalist for 1930* (New York: John Fritz Medal, 1930); Józef Glomb, *A Man Who Spanned Two Eras* (Philadelphia: The Kosciuszko Foundation, 2002, a translation of a Polish text); William Frederick Durand, "Biographical Memoir of Ralph Modjeski 1861–1940," in *Biographical Memoirs* (Washington, D.C.: National Academy of Sciences, Vol. 23); Jacek Przygoda, ed., *Polish Americans in California 1827–1977 and Who's Who* (Los Angeles: Polish American Historical Association, California Chapter, 1978).

Modrzejewski, Robert Joseph (b. Milwaukee, Wisconsin, July 3, 1934; d.—). Military officer, Medal of Honor recipient. Modrzejewski graduated from Pulaski High School in Milwaukee in 1953 and earned a B.S. from the University of Wisconsin–Milwaukee four years later. He was commissioned a second lieutenant in the U.S. Marine Corps reserve in June 1957, completed training at Quantico,

Virginia, and was assigned as a platoon leader with the 3rd Battalion, 3rd Marines, 3rd Marine Division. Promoted to first lieutenant in 1958, he was transferred to Camp Lejeune, North Carolina and promoted to captain in May 1962. After various assignments he was ordered to Vietnam in early 1966 to command Company K, 3rd Battalion, 4th Marines, 3rd Marine Division. His actions from July 15–18 during Operation Hastings resulted in the awarding of the Medal of Honor which he received from President Lyndon B. Johnson on March 12, 1968. The citation read as follows: "For conspicuous gallantry and intrepidity at the risk of his life above and beyond the call of duty. On 15 July, during Operation HASTINGS, Company K was landed in an enemy-infested jungle area to establish a blocking position at a major enemy trail network. Shortly after landing, the company encountered a reinforced enemy platoon in a well-organized, defensive position. Maj. Modrzejewski led his men in the successful seizure of the enemy redoubt, which contained large quantities of ammunition and supplies. That evening, a numerically superior enemy force counterattacked in an effort to retake the vital supply area, thus setting the pattern of activity for the next $2^1/_2$ days. In the first series of attacks, the enemy assaulted repeatedly in overwhelming numbers but each time was repulsed by the gallant marines. The second night, the enemy struck in battalion strength, and Maj. Modrzejewski was wounded in this intensive action which was fought at close quarters. Although exposed to enemy fire, and despite his painful wounds, he crawled 200 meters to provide critically needed ammunition to an exposed element of his command and was constantly present wherever the fighting was heaviest, despite numerous casualties, a dwindling supply of ammunition and the knowledge that they were surrounded, he skillfully directed artillery fire to within a few meters of his position and courageously inspired the efforts of his company in repelling the aggressive enemy attack. On 18 July, Company K was attacked by a regimental-size enemy force. Although his unit was vastly outnumbered and weakened by the previous fighting, Maj. Modrzejewski reorganized his men and calmly moved among them to encourage and direct their efforts to heroic limits as they fought to overcome the vicious enemy onslaught. Again he called in air and artillery strikes at close range with devastating effect on the enemy, which together with the bold and determined fighting of the men of Company K, repulsed the fanatical attack of the larger North Vietnamese force. His unparalleled personal heroism and indomitable leadership inspired his men to a significant victory over the enemy force and reflected great credit upon himself, the Marine Corps, and the U.S. Naval Service."

Modrzejewski was promoted to major in January 1967 while still in Vietnam. Upon his return to the U.S. in June of that year he was assigned to duty at the U.S. Naval Academy, and later to the Marine base at Kaneohe, Hawaii. In 1976, while still on active duty, he earned a master's degree in education from Pepperdine University. He retired in 1986 with the rank of colonel. In addition to the Medal of Honor, he was also recognized with the Purple Heart, Presidential Unit Citation, National Defense Service Medal, Legion of Merit, Vietnam Service Medal with two bronze stars, Vietnamese Cross of Gallantry with Gold Star, and the Republic of Vietnam Campaign Medal.—*James S. Pula*

SOURCE: R. J. Proft, *United States of America's Congressional Medal of Honor Recipients and Their Official Citations* (Columbia Heights, MN: Highland House II, 2002).

Modzelewski, Dick (b. West Natrona, Pennsylvania, February 16, 1931; d.—). Football player, coach. Modzelewski first gained notice for his football prowess as a tackle at the University of Maryland (1950–52). He was twice named All-American, and in 1952 was awarded the Outland Trophy as the best collegiate interior lineman. Chosen in the second round of the 1953 professional draft, Modzelewski played defensive tackle for four National Football League teams over fourteen seasons (1953–66). "Little Mo"—so called as the younger brother of Ed Modzelewski, also a noted college and pro footballer—appeared in one Pro Bowl, and won two NFL championships with the New York Giants (1956) and Cleveland Browns (1964). After his playing days, he became interim head coach for Cleveland in 1977, and served stints as an assistant coach for five other NFL teams. He is a member of the College Football Hall of Fame, and was inducted into the **National Polish-American Sports Hall of Fame** in 1986.—*Neal Pease*

SOURCE: "Dick Modzelewski," National Polish-American Sports Hall of Fame website, www.polishsportshof.com.

Mokrzycki, Gustaw Andrzej (pseud. Gustav M. Andrew; b. Lwów, Poland, October 1, 1894; d. Fullerton, California, January 22, 1992). Engineer. Mokrzycki studied at Lwów Polytechnic Institute until the outbreak of World War I when he was drafted into the Austrian army where he became interested in aviation and joined a secret patriotic organization of Polish aviators. Following the war he studied at the Ecole Superieure d'Aeronautique in Paris and in 1927 accepted a position on the faculty of the Warsaw Institute of Technology. With the outbreak of World War II he fled to France, and then to Great Britain, Canada and the U.S. in 1944. During his career, he worked for Convair, the Ryan Aeronautical Company, Boeing Corporation, and the U.S. Air Force Flight Test Center at Edwards Air Force Base. A specialist in flight stability and automated flight controls, Mokrzycki was instrumental in solving the problem of aerodynamic stability through use of an autopilot, a discovery that was later used in the controls of jet aircraft such as the B-52 and B-70, and unmanned missiles. The author of more than 100 scientific articles in four languages, Mokrzycki was awarded the Cross of Polonia Restituta by the Polish government-in-exile in London in 1978 and the Sylvanus Albert Reed Award from the American Institute of Aeronautics & Astronautics for "distinguished contributions to the aeronautical sciences."—*James S. Pula*

SOURCE: *Polish Americans in California* (Washington, D.C.: National Center for Urban Ethnic Affairs, 1995), Vol. II.

Monkiewicz, Boleslaus Joseph (b. Syracuse, New York, August 8, 1898; d. New Britain, Connecticut, July 2, 1971). Congressman. Moving with his parents to New Britain, CT, in 1899, he attended public school and graduated from New Britain High School in 1917 before joining the U.S. Navy as an apprentice seaman on October 3, 1918. Monkiewicz later graduated from the law program at Fordham University and was admitted to the bar in 1933. He commenced law practice in New York and Connecticut while also engaged in banking and serving as clerk of the New

Boleslaus J. Monkiewicz, congressman (*CCSU-BC***).**

Britain city and police court from July 1932 to August 1933. He was prosecuting attorney in the police court from 1937 to 1939 until he was elected as a Republican to the 76th Congress (January 3, 1939–January 3, 1941) as the congressman-at-Large, the seat in Connecticut that during its existence between 1931 and 1964 was ordinarily reserved by both parties for Polish Americans. An unsuccessful candidate for reelection in 1940, he was elected to the 78th Congress (January 3, 1943–January 3, 1945), but failed to gain reelection in 1944. He resumed the practice of law, was appointed to the federal parole board on the recommendation of House Speaker Joseph Martin, and also held the position of unemployment compensation commissioner of Connecticut. He was a member of the United States Board of Parole in Washington, D.C., 1947–1953. After resuming the practice of law in New Britain he served as judge of the circuit court of Connecticut from 1961 to 1968.—*Frederick J. Augustyn*

SOURCE: *Biographical Directory of the United States Congress, 1774–Present* (http://bioguide.congress.gov/).

Monuments, Polish American. Beginning in the last decade of the nineteenth century, groups of Polish Americans have been active in organizing efforts to fund and erect monuments in their communities which have as their aim the broadening of pride and awareness of the Polish heritage and creating enduring symbols of the Polish presence in this country. Such activities began in earnest in the late 1890s with monument building campaigns in honor of Brig. General **Tadeusz Kościuszko** and Brig. General **Kazimierz Pułaski**, who both contributed their talents to America's victorious war for independence and who were at the same time fighters for the freedom of Poland. These efforts peaked in the early 1930s in connection with commemorations marking the 150th anniversary, on October 11, 1929, of Pułaski's death at the Battle of Savannah. Many monuments to these heroes have been erected, all of them underscoring the fact that the values of both men are symbolic of the unity of values shared between the American and Polish peoples.

The first Pułaski monument was erected in 1825 in Savannah, Georgia. The first Kościuszko monument, in the form of a pedestal, was erected in 1828 at the U.S. Military Academy at West Point. Apparently, Poles played no role in these actions. The first **Polonia**-sponsored monument, an equestrian statue of Kościuszko, was dedicated in September 1904 in Chicago's Humboldt Park. It became the locus of countless **Polonia** patriotic manifestations over the next seventy-five years, until the statue was moved to a new site on the

Polish American scouts posing in front of the Kościuszko Monument in Milwaukee, 1930s (*UWM*).

city's lakefront. The Polish community of Cleveland, Ohio followed suit in May 1905 in dedicating a second Kościuszko monument; only a month later, the Polonia in Milwaukee, Wisconsin, dedicated their own monument to the Polish and American hero of independence. In 1903, the U.S. Congress appropriated $50,000 to honor its historic commitment to erect a monument in Washington, D.C., in memory of Pułaski. In 1904, the **Polish National Alliance** won the support of President Theodore Roosevelt for a comparable monument to honor Kościuszko in the nation's capital. The site for the statue — which was paid for by the PNA and other Polonia groups and presented to the American nation as a gift of the Polish people in America — was in LaFayette Square, just in front of the White House. The Pulaski monument was placed on Pennsylvania Avenue. The two monuments were dedicated on May 11, 1910 in the presence of President William Howard Taft and a large audience that included several thousand Polish Americans. There is a dramatic, but too little appreciated, story involving Polonia's effort to win the government's support for the erection and placement of the monuments. In involves the influential connection the leaders of the PNA developed with President Theodore Roosevelt in the face of the hostility of the Russian and German empires to any talk of the idea of an independent Poland, the idea symbolized in the lives of Pułaski and Kościuszko. This story is told by three historians of the Polish National Alliance,

Stanisław Osada, Romuald Piątkowski, and Adam Olszewski, in books they authored in the Polish language.

In 1913, Polish Americans funded a Kościuszko monument at **West Point**. It was placed atop the site's historic pedestal. In the years since at least six other significant Kościuszko monuments have been erected, in Boston, Philadelphia, Stamford (CT), Fall River (MA), Saratoga (NY), and Detroit. Monuments in memory of Pułaski are found in Hartford and Meriden (CT), Baltimore (MD), Northampton (MA), Utica (NY), and Milwaukee, Cudahy and Stevens Point (WI).

Numerous other famous people connected with Polish heritage have also been commemorated with monuments in the U.S. Statues honoring the great astronomer Nicolaus Copernicus (Mikołaj Kopernik) are found on Chicago's lakefront near the Kościuszko monument, in Utica (NY), and in Philadelphia. There are likenesses of composer

Frydryk Chopin in Buffalo (NY) and in Milwaukee. Statues or busts of the pianist-patriot **Ignacy Jan Paderewski** are in New York City, UCLA in California, and at Arlington Cemetery outside of Washington, D.C. Paderewski's heart is in the Church of Mary, the Mother of Jesus Christ, at the shrine of the American Częstochowa in **Doylestown**, Pennsylvania. Statues to Pope John Paul II are in Cheektowaga (NY) and at the Cultural Center bearing his name in Washington, D.C. A great equestrian statue of King Władysław Jagiełło is in New York's Central Park, a gift of Poland brought to New York for the World's Fair held there in 1939. Famed actress **Helena Modjeska**'s statue is found in Anaheim, California.

Other notable monuments testifying to the Polish presence in America are those of Gen. **Włodzimierz Krzyżanowski**'s **Polish Legion** (58th New York Infantry) on the grounds of the Gettysburg battlefield in Pennsylvania, a marker recalling the arrival of the very first Poles in America at **Jamestown**, Virginia, and another marker commemorating Polish settlers in **Panna Maria**, Texas (1854). Baseball Hall of Famer **Stan Musial** has a statue in St. Louis, Missouri. Members of the post–World War II Polish immigrations have made their mark by drives to erect monuments in memory of

„Uncle Sam" odsłania pomniki polskich bohaterów.
(Z „Evening Star".)

A newspaper cartoon depicting the unveiling of the Kościuszko and Pułaski monuments in Washington, D.C. (*OLS*).

the Polish officers murdered in the **Katyń** Forest in 1940; these are in Jersey City (NJ), New Britain (CT), and Doylestown (PA). Monuments recalling the murdered Solidarity supporter the Rev. Jerzy Popieluszko are found in New Britain (CT) and Greenpoint, Brooklyn (NY). A statue honoring the World War II Polish patriot and postwar American scholar, **Jan Karski**, is in Manhattan (NY).

There are innumerable shrines honoring the Mother of Jesus as depicted in the famed icon of the Częstochowa Madonna, most notably in Doylestown (PA). An outdoor icon of the "Black Madonna" adorns the wall of St. Stanislaus Bishop and Martyr Church in Milwaukee. The chapel on the grounds of the Orchard Lake Polish seminary is yet another special monument to the Częstochowa Madonna.

There are of course many more modest physical memorials to Polish heritage. These are found inside the churches established by Polish immigrants and their offspring, and in schools and colleges having a connection with the Polish heritage; for example, Milwaukee's Pulaski High School has a bust of Pulaski in its main hall. Not insignificantly, monuments honoring many of Polonia's leading personages, especially those in politics, fraternal life, commerce, and the Church, can be found in the many cemeteries across the U.S. where large numbers of Polish Americans were laid to rest. The practice of expending large sums of money to establish these memorials had largely ended by the time of World War II. But those already in existence remind us of the many Polonia leaders who contributed much to their community's development. Whatever the cost of these many and diverse statues, reliefs, or plaques, to the famous and less famous, all testify to the desire of Polish Americans to preserve knowledge of their ethnic legacy for future generations.—*Donald E. Pienkos*

SOURCES: Jacek Galazka and Albert Juszczak, *The Polish Heritage Travel Guide to the U.S.A. and Canada* (Cornwall Bridge, CT: Polish Heritage Publications, 1992); Donald E. Pienkos, *For Your Freedom Through Ours: Polish American Efforts on Poland's Behalf* (Boulder, CO: East European Monographs, 1991).

Moskal, Edward J. (b. Chicago, Illinois, May 21, 1924; d. Chicago, Illinois, March 22, 2005). Polonia activist. Moskal joined the **Polish National Alliance** fraternal after army service in World War II. In 1963 he was elected to its national Board of Directors and in 1967 he was elected treasurer of the PNA. Moskal served in that office for the next twenty-one years. On October 12, 1988, he was elected president by the PNA Supervisory Council in a special vote following the death of **Aloysius Mazewski** two months earlier. A

month later Moskal also succeeded Mazewski as the third president of the **Polish American Congress**. Subsequently, he was reelected president of the Polish National Alliance at its 1991, 1995, 1999, and 2005 national conventions, and president of the Polish American Congress in each of its successive biennial elections.

High school educated and by profession a real estate salesman and caterer, Moskal enjoyed a most successful career as an elected PNA national officer. Following his election as PNA treasurer, he never faced an opponent in winning reelection to that office; as president his only opposition came in 1999 when he easily defeated Director Aloysius A. Mazewski, Jr., of Chicago, the son of the past PNA president, and in 2003, when he won overwhelmingly over Vice President Stanley Jendzejec of Coventry, Rhode Island. He enjoyed similar success in his elections as PAC president. As PNA president, Moskal modernized the computerized insurance operations of the fraternal, improved the look of the PNA official publication, *Zgoda* (Harmony), put the PNA's Chicago-based daily newspaper "in the black" financially, and enhanced the profits of its Chicago-based radio station, WPNA. He introduced several new PNA insurance plans and promoted strengthening the PNA sales force. In 1999, the PNA opened its first bank in the suburb of Niles, north of Chicago. Nevertheless, insured PNA membership declined from 283,000 to 193,000 between 1987 and 2003, even as the financial position of the Alliance improved substantially. In 1987, the fraternal's total assets amounted to $205 million; in 2003 they were reported at the 44th PNA national convention to be $374 million. Total PNA insurance in force also rose greatly in the period from $516 million to $812 million. The PNA's fraternal commitment to its annual scholarship program also rose significantly, from $75,000 in 1987 to $200,000 in 2003.

In 1991, Moskal ended PNA sponsorship of the annual Polish **Constitution Day** parade, which it had underwritten since 1904; the parade continues under other auspices. At the same time he supported a number of significant programs highlighting Poland's cultural heritage under PNA aegis, most notably the "Land of the Winged Horseman" exhibition in Baltimore and Chicago (1999) and "Leonardo da Vinci and the Splendor of Poland" in Milwaukee, Houston, and San Francisco (2001–02), along with a number of public concerts of Polish music. The PNA was a major supporter of the **Pope John Paul II Cultural Center** in Washington, D.C. and several other initiatives during his presidency.

As president of the Polish American Congress, Moskal, who had not been active in the Congress while Mazewski headed the organization, was quick to take an active role in supporting the Solidarity trade union movement in its efforts to come to power in 1989 and to bring an end to failed communist rule in Poland. In October 1989, he traveled to Poland as head of a PAC delegation to meet with the leaders of the newly elected Solidarity-headed democratic government. From that time onward, Moskal both visited Poland a number of times and welcomed Polish democratic leaders to Chicago, including Lech Wałęsa, Solidarity's leader, and later Poland's first popularly elected president, and Tadeusz Mazowiecki, Poland's first democratically chosen prime minister.

Moskal was a strong supporter of U.S. economic assistance to Poland and, working with the PAC's representatives in Washington, D.C., **Myra Lenard** and her husband, Casimir (see **Casimir Lenard**), backed the creation of the Polish American Enterprise Fund to assist Poland in its economic transformation from socialism to a market economy. In concert with Senate leaders like **Barbara Mikulski** of Maryland and Paul Simon of Illinois, he successfully lobbied President George H. W. Bush in 1990 to back an international agreement that fully guaranteed Poland's border with the newly united German Federal Republic. Moskal also played a critically important, though generally ignored, role in successfully leading the lengthy **Polonia** effort to persuade the U.S. government to support Poland's admission into the North Atlantic Treaty Organization, the NATO Alliance. In spring 1999 Poland was admitted to NATO and for his work Moskal was honored at a ceremony at the Polish embassy in Washington, D.C. Working with Moskal to win Poland's entry into NATO were many PAC activists, including its national executive director Atty. Leszek Kuczynski and Myra and Casimir Lenard.

Moskal's political style and leadership, which made him virtually unchallenged within the PNA and the PAC, played him false, however, when he expressed his views in larger surroundings. Thus in November 1989, his undiplomatic words and impulsive actions alienated the long time PAC vice president for Polish affairs, **Kazimierz Lukomski**, who resigned after publicly criticizing him for failing to consult with the executive officers of the Congress before making public declarations. After the 1995 Polish presidential election won by a former communist leader, Aleksander Kwasniewski, over Wałęsa, Moskal came in for sharp criticism in Poland and in the U.S. over an intemperate letter he wrote to the new president that was made public in Warsaw. At a national PAC meeting in 1998, he became embroiled in an unseemly personal dispute with PAC director **Stanislaus Blejwas** of Connecticut, a historian of Poland who also co-chaired the **National Polish-American Jewish-American Council**. Soon after, the Council, a dialog group co-sponsored by the Polish American Congress and the American Jewish Committee, voted to end its formal relationship with the PAC. In 2001, Moskal initiated an incendiary campaign against journalist **Jan Jeziorański Nowak**, an icon in Washington, D.C., due to his long career of opposition to communism at Radio Free Europe, and a former PAC vice president for Polish affairs. At Chicago's annual **Pulaski Day** ceremony in March 2002, Moskal made a gratuitously hostile attack on one of the candidates for U.S. Congress from the heavily Polish district previously represented by **Daniel Rostenkowski**. This led some in the local media to brand his words as "anti–Jewish." In 2003 Moskal opposed Poland's entry into the European Union as president of the PAC without having received the approbation of the Congress. The result of these actions tarnished the record of his genuine achievements as Polonia leader in a time of great change in Polonia and turbulence in Poland and the world.

After Moskal's death, he was succeeded in June 2005 by PNA National Secretary Frank Spula as president of the PNA, and later as president of the PAC. On his election, Spula promised an "open door" administration and a forward-looking approach in dealing with the challenges facing both organizations.— *Donald E. Pienkos*

SOURCES: Donald E. Pienkos, *Yesterday, Today, Tomorrow: The Story of the Polish National Alliance* (Chicago: Alliance Printers and Publishers, 2008); Donald E. Pienkos, "Witness to History: Polish Americans and the Genesis of NATO Enlargement," *Polish Review*, Vol. 44, No. 3 (1999), 329–337; Leszek Kuczyński, *Expansion of NATO: Role of the Polish American Congress* (Chicago: Polish American Congress, 1999).

Moskala, Edward J. (b. Chicago, Illinois, November 6, 1921; d. Okinawa, Ryukyu Islands, Japan, April 9, 1945). Soldier, Medal of Honor recipient. A private first class in Company C, 383rd Infantry Regiment, 96th Infantry Division, Moskala took part in the invasion of Okinawa. His citation for the Medal of Honor read: "He was the leading element when grenade explosions and concentrated machine gun and mortar fire halted the unit's attack on Kakazu Ridge, Okinawa, Ryukyu Islands. With utter disregard for his personal safety, he charged 40 yards through withering, grazing fire and wiped out 2 ma-

Edward J. Moskala, Medal of Honor recipient (*NARA*).

chine gun nests with well-aimed grenades and deadly accurate fire from his automatic rifle. When strong counterattacks and fierce enemy resistance from other positions forced his company to withdraw, he voluntarily remained behind with 8 others to cover the maneuver. Fighting from a critically dangerous position for 3 hours, he killed more than 25 Japanese before following his surviving companions through screening smoke down the face of the ridge to a gorge where it was discovered that one of the group had been left behind, wounded. Unhesitatingly, Pvt. Moskala climbed the bullet-swept slope to assist in the rescue, and, returning to lower ground, volunteered to protect other wounded while the bulk of the troops quickly took up more favorable positions. He had saved another casualty and killed 4 enemy infiltrators when he was struck and mortally wounded himself while aiding still another disabled soldier. With gallant initiative, unfaltering courage, and heroic determination to destroy the enemy, Pvt. Moskala gave his life in his complete devotion to his company's mission and his comrades' well-being. His intrepid conduct provided a lasting inspiration for those with whom he served."—*James S. Pula*

SOURCES: R. J. Proft, *United States of America's Congressional Medal of Honor Recipients and Their Official Citations* (Columbia Heights, MN: Highland House II, 2002); *The Medal of Honor of the United States Army* (Washington, D.C.: U.S. Government Printing Office, 1948), 84.

Mostwin, Danuta (Danuta Pietruszewska; b. Lublin, Poland, August 31, 1921; d. Ruxton, Maryland, January 11, 2010). Sociologist. Mostwin is renowned for her scholarly and literary work on the process of immigrant adjustment in which she combines sociological and psychological research with personal in-

sight. She began her higher education at the Warsaw Underground Medical School (1940–44) before migrating with her family to England where she continued her studies at the Paderewski Teaching Hospital School of Medicine in Edinburgh. In 1951, with her family, she came to the United States, settling in Baltimore. She earned a degree at the National Catholic School of Social Service of The Catholic University of America in Washington in 1959, and in 1970 earned a doctorate in Social Work from Columbia University. Her professional life in America was equally varied. Beginning in the Maryland Department of Social Service (1956–60), she then served as director of the Maryland Children's Aid (1960–69), director of The Family Study Center and Professor of Social Work and Mental Health at the Catholic University of America DC (1969–80), and finally Professor of Psychology at Loyola College in Baltimore (1980–87). She is the author of many nonfiction and fiction books including her landmark sociological work *The Transplanted Family* (1980); the highly acclaimed *Ameryko! Ameryko!* (1961), *Trzecia wartość* (The Third Value; 1985), *Emigranci polscy w USA* (Polish Immigrants in the USA; 1991), *Cień księdza Piotra* (In the Shadow of Father Peter; 1985), *Tajemnica zwyciężonych* (The Clandestine Conqueror; 1992), and *Testaments: Two Novellas of Exile and Emigration* (2005). The recipient of numerous civic, scholarly, and literary awards, Mostwin was also nominated for the Nobel Prize in Literature in 2006. Other honors include the Polish Literature Award (1965), Doctoral Dissertation Award of the **Kosciuszko Foundation** (1971), Anny Godlewska Literature Award (1975), *Wiadomości* Award (1979), Bolesław Prus Award (1985), W. Pietrzak Literature Award (1987), Distinguished Service Award from the American Council for Polish Culture (1991), Polish Heritage Association of Maryland Award (1992), and the World Federation of Polish Combatants Association Award (1993).—*Jerome Krase*

SOURCES: Bolesław Wierzbiański, *Who's Who in Polish America* (New York: Bicentennial Publishing Corp., 1996), 313; "Danuta Mostwin, Doctor and Acclaimed Writer," *Polish American Journal*, Vol. 99, no. 2 (February 2010), 16.

Mrozewski, Stefan (b. Częstochowa, Poland, April 12, 1894; d. Walnut Creek, California, September 7, 1975). Artist, printmaker. At the age of eleven Mrozewski took part with his mother in a street demonstration in Sosnowiec, Silesia, demanding the teaching of Polish in local schools. Educated at Jerzy Lehman's private evening school in Łódź (1920), he then studied at the School of Decorative Arts in Poznań (1921), the Ludwika and Wilhelm Mehoffer School of Painting and Drawing in Kraków (1922), and the School of Fine Arts in Warsaw (1923–25). During the Polish-Soviet War he served in the cartographic unit of General Władysław Sikorski's Fifth Army (1920). He later lived in Paris (1925–32; 1945–47), Amsterdam and Helvoirt in North Brabant (1933–35, 1948–51), and London (1935–37). During World War II he was a member of the Polish underground Armia Krajowa (Home Army). He left Poland illegally in the summer of 1945, migrating to Paris and then to the United States in 1951, settling in California. Specializing in wood engravings, he also created frescoes, stained glass, mosaics, pastels, and terracotta sculptures. His book illustrations appeared in the works of nearly thirty authors in English, Polish, German, and French. Solo exhibitions of Mrozewski's work were held in Belgium, Canada, England, France, Germany, Ireland, the Netherlands, Poland, and the United States. Among his honors were the Silver Medal at the Poznań International Fair, Poland (1929); First Prize at the First International Woodcut Exhibition, Warsaw, Poland (1933); City of Warsaw President's Prize (1934); Second Prize, Polish National Olympic Arts Competition for the XI Olympiad in Berlin (1936); Grand Prix, Exposition Internationale Arts et Techniques, Paris (1937); First Prize, Nederlandse Bijbelgenootschap, Amsterdam, Holland (1948); Huntington Hartford Foundation Fellowship (1952, 1962); Graphic Art Prize, 56th Annual Exhibition, Washington Water Color Club, Washington, D.C. (1953); and he was posthumously awarded the Home Army Cross and Partisan Cross from Poland.—*Stanley L. Cuba*

SOURCES: Elżbieta Wróbel and Teresa Kulisiewicz, *Stefan Mrozewski—piękno drzeworytu* (Częstochowa, Poland: Wydawnictwo Graffiti, 2005); Agata Pietrzak, et. al., *Czarodziej rylca: wystawa w sto dziesiąta rocznice urodzin Stefana Mrozewskiego 1894–1975* (Warsaw: Biblioteka Narodowa, 2004); Bartlomiej Szyndler, *Stefan Mrozewski (1894–1975), Polski Słownik Biograficzny*, Vol. 22, no. 2, 1977; Stanley L. Cuba, *Stefan Mrozewski 1894–1975: Wood Engravings, a Posthumous Exhibition, November 5–21, 1976* (New York: The Kosciuszko Foundation, 1976).

Mruk, Joseph (b. Buffalo, New York, November 6, 1903; d. Lancaster, New York, January 21, 1995). Congressman. A bachelor his entire life, Mruk entered the retail jewelry business, opening his own successful store in Buffalo, NY, in 1926. He became interested in politics, gaining election to the city council in 1937 as a Republican, representing his heavily Polish American district for five years. Despite having one of the largest concentrations of Polish American residents for decades, in 1940 the city of Buffalo still had not had a Congressman or mayor of Polish descent.

Mruk changed that. He was popular enough to be nominated by the Republicans for Congress from New York's 41st district in 1942, winning the general election to become the first Polish American to serve Buffalo in the U.S. House of Representatives. Because he opposed certain Republican policies, the party bosses did not nominate him for re-election in 1944 so he ran as an independent and lost. Nevertheless, Mruk stayed active in party politics, soon being nominated for mayor on the Republican ticket in 1949. He easily won the general election, once more becoming a trailblazer for Buffalo's **Polonia** as the first Polish American mayor in the city's history. Despite a small scandal involving one of his appointees, his term represented a generally uneventful, prosperous time for the city. Nevertheless, he did not run for re-election, serving only one four year term. Mruk later made another bid for his party's nomination for Congress, and also for mayor, but was unsuccessful. He held appointments to positions in city government, then returned to running his jewelry store. He closed that business in the 1970s, retired, and died at age 91.—*Martin S. Nowak*

SOURCE: Michael F. Rizzo, *Through the Mayor's Eyes* (Morrisville, NC: Lulu Enterprises, 2005); Melvin G. Holli and P. d'A. Jones, eds., *Biographical Dictionary of American Mayors, 1820–1980: Big City Mayors* (Westport: Greenwood Press, 1981); *New York Times*, Jan. 20, 1995, A20.

Mummers *see* **Polish American String Band.**

Munchak, Michael Anthony "Mike" (b. Scranton, Pennsylvania, March 6, 1960; d.—). Football player. After a standout career as a fullback and linebacker at Scranton Central High School, he played college football for Joe Paterno's Penn State Nittany Lions. In 1982 the Houston Oilers selected him in the first round of the National Football League draft, the first lineman selected and the eighth overall pick. Munchak won the starting left guard position as a rookie, going on to play twelve seasons (1982–93) and 159 games (156 starts), all with the Oilers. During his career he demonstrated that hard work, determination and well developed skills can carry a player to a new level of competition in sports. Running behind the Munchak-led offensive line, Hall of Fame back Earl Campbell and the Houston Oilers led the NFL in total offense in 1990 and passing offense in 1990 and 1991. In 1991 the Oilers offensive line finished second in the AFC and fourth in the NFL in the fewest quarterback sacks allowed. His Oilers teams had seven consecutive playoff appearances (1987–93). Munchak was known as a fierce competitor on the field. During his career he made nine Pro Bowl appearances,

was named an All-Pro in 1987, 1988 and 1989, and accorded All-Pro Second Team honors in 1983, 1984, 1985, 1988, 1990, 1991, 1992 and 1993. Munchak was a seven-time All-AFC choice and four-time All-AFC Second Team selection. He was named to the NFL's All Decade Team of the 1980s, and to Pro Football Hall of Fame (2001). Following his playing career he was an assistant coach with the NFL Tennessee Titans.—*Luis J. Gonzalez*

SOURCE: Ron Smith, *Pro Football's Heroes of the Hall* (St. Louis: Sporting News Books, 2003).

Murkowski, Frank Hughes (b. Seattle, Washington, March 28, 1933; d.—). U.S. Senator, governor, banker. Of Polish descent on his father's side, like him, Murkowski initially became a banker. He attended the public schools of Ketchikan, AK, then enrolled in the University of Santa Clara, CA (1951–53), graduating from Seattle University in Seattle, WA (1955). He served in the U.S. Coast Guard (1955–56) before becoming Alaska Commissioner of Economic Development (1966–70) and president of the Alaska Chamber of Commerce in 1977. Murkowski was elected as a Republican to the United States Senate in 1980 and reelected in 1986, 1992, and 1998 for the term ending January 3, 2005. He served from January 3, 1981, to December 2, 2002, when he resigned, having been elected Governor of Alaska. In the Senate, he was chair of the Committee on Veterans' Affairs (Ninety-ninth Congress) and the Committee on Energy and Natural Resources (One Hundred Fourth through One Hundred Sixth Congresses; One Hundred Seventh Congress [January 20, 2001–June 6, 2001]). As Senator, he fought unsuccessfully for oil drilling in the Arctic National Wildlife Refuge

Frank Murkowski, U.S. senator and governor of Alaska (*NARA*).

(ANWR). Favoring sustainable development of natural resources, he reflected many Alaskans' viewpoint in opposing "no-growthers." He said: "Pushing production out of America to nations without our environmental standards increases global environmental risks." Also like many Alaskans, Murkowski was skeptical about governmental interference in personal life as well as in economics. Somewhat frustrated in the Senate by being unable to open up ANWR, he was elected governor to an open seat (incumbent Tony Knowles retired at that time since he was term-limited). Murkowski thereby ended a twenty-year lock by the Democrats on the Alaskan governor's office. He served as governor from 2003 to 2007, but came in third in the 2006 Republican gubernatorial primary which Sarah Palin easily won with a majority of the votes. Murkowski's purchase of a gubernatorial jet with state money, despite legislative opposition, became an unwanted symbol of spending which led to his defeat for re-nomination. He had also eliminated funding for the longevity bonus program, which had provided Alaska seniors a monthly stipend regardless of their income. His papers are located at the University of Alaska.—*Frederick J. Augustyn*

SOURCES: *Biographical Directory of the United States Congress, 1774–Present* (http://bioguide.congress.gov/); *Who's Who in Polish America* (New York: Bicentennial Publishing, 1996).

Murkowski, Lisa (b. Ketchikan, Alaska, May 22, 1957; d.—). U.S. Senator, lawyer. The first U.S. Senator born in Alaska, and the only woman ever elected to Congress from her state, Murkowski attended public schools in Fairbanks, AK. Due to her father's first job as a banker, her family moved all over Alaska, including Wrangell, Juneau, Fairbanks, and Anchorage. She attended Willamette University in Salem, OR (1975–77), earned a B.A. in Economics from Georgetown University (1980) and a J.D. from Willamette College of Law (1985). As an attorney, she was a member of the Alaska Bar Association, an Anchorage District Court attorney (1987–89), and maintained a private practice from 1989 to 1996. She served on the Mayor's Task Force on the Homeless (1990–91), the Anchorage Equal Rights Commission (1997–98), and was elected to the Alaska State House of Representatives (1999–2002). For the 2003 session of the State House, she was named Majority Leader, but before she assumed that post she was appointed on December 20, 2002, to the U.S. Senate by her father, Governor **Frank Murkowski**, to fill out the two remaining years of his term. Her father had said that he sought someone as his replacement who basically shared his philosophy and values. Nev-

ertheless, many conservatives in 2002 opposed her re-election to the State House because of her support of a tax hike (specifically she successfully pushed for the nation's highest levy on alcoholic beverages) and her largely (but not consistent) pro-choice views. Despite the political talk that this appointment caused (the legislation passed a law preventing a governor from making such an appointment in the future and this was the first time that any U.S. governor had appointed his child to the Senate), she was elected senator in 2004 in her own right for the term ending January 3, 2011. She maintained that politically she was her own person and did not get advice from her father. In that contest, Murkowski defeated former Governor Tony Knowles, whom her father had succeeded in 2003. Murkowski served on the following committees: Appropriations; Energy and Natural Resources; Health, Education, Labor, and Pensions; and Indian Affairs. Long-time family friend Sen. Ted Stevens, for whom she once interned, said that she was "a hell of a lot better senator than her dad ever was." More of a centrist than her father, she nevertheless, like her father, pushed for Alaska-centric issues such as opening up the Arctic National Wildlife Refuge (ANWR) to oil drilling.—*Frederick J. Augustyn*

SOURCES: *Biographical Directory of the United States Congress, 1774–Present* (http://bioguide.congress.gov/); "Lisa Murkowski," in *Women in Congress, 1917–2006* (Washington, D.C.: Government Printing Office, 2006); Adam Clymer, "Challenges Expected for Alaska Senator," *New York Times*, June 4, 2003, A28.

Musial, Stan (Stanisław Franciszek Musiał; b. Donora, PA, November 21, 1920; d.—). Baseball player. By common consent, Stan Musial ranks among the brightest stars in the history of baseball, and is regarded as the greatest American athlete of Polish ancestry. He was born of mixed Slavic parentage, but always identified with the ethnic background of his Polish-born father. A gifted athlete, the young Musial caught the eye of baseball scouts as a potential pitcher, but a shoulder injury prompted his conversion to the outfield and rapid emergence as one of the finest hitters ever to play the game. He made his debut with the St. Louis Cardinals in 1941, and spent his entire career with that team, interrupted only by service in the Navy during the Second World War. Over the course of 22 seasons, Musial recorded a lifetime batting average of .331, with 475 home runs, playing primarily as an outfielder and first baseman. His Cardinals teams won four National League pennants, and three World Series championships. Few players in the annals of baseball can match Musial's lengthy list of accomplishments. He won the National League Most

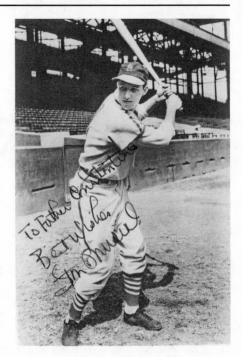

"Stan the Man" Musial (*PMA*).

Valuable Player award three times, in 1943, 1946, and 1948. In particular, his performance in 1948, when he narrowly missed winning the "Triple Crown" (topping the league in batting, home runs, and runs batted in), is regarded as one of the most impressive of individual seasons. A seven time batting champion, he led the National League in nearly every important hitting category in multiple years. Musial played in 24 All-Star games, and was named "Player of the Decade" 1946–55 by *The Sporting News*. A left hander who hit out of an odd, distinctive stance, peeking around his front shoulder at the pitcher, he acquired the nickname "Stan the Man"—a moniker bestowed on him in fearful tribute, as the story goes, by rival fans who winced every time "that man" came to the plate. He ended his playing days in 1963 as the holder of 55 major league or National League career records, including most lifetime hits. Upon retirement, Musial continued to work for the Cardinals organization in various capacities, and pursued business interests in the St. Louis vicinity. That city still recognizes him as the greatest player ever to wear the uniform of the local team, and his statue stands in Stan Musial Plaza outside the Cardinals' Busch Stadium. He has lent his name and efforts to numerous charitable and civic activities. In 1972, the government of Poland named him the first foreign recipient of its highest national award for sport. While many of his records have been surpassed, he remains consistently ranked by baseball experts as one of the two or three best leftfielders the game has ever seen. He received election to the National Baseball Hall of Fame in 1969, his first year of eligibility, and in 1973 the National Polish-American Sports Hall of Fame named him its first inductee.—*Neal Pease*

SOURCES: James N. Giglio, *Musial: From Stash to Stan the Man* (Columbia: University of Missouri, 2001); Stan Musial and Bob Broeg, *The Man Stan: Musial, Then and Now* (St. Louis: Bethany Press, 1977); Neal Pease, "Diamonds Out of the Coal Mines: Slavic Americans in Baseball," in Lawrence Baldassaro and Richard A. Johnson, eds., *The American Game: Baseball and Ethnicity* (Carbondale: Southern Illinois University, 2002).

Muskie, Edmund Sixtus (b. Rumford, Maine, March 28, 1914; d. Washington, District of Columbia, March 26, 1996). U.S. Senator, diplomat. Muskie attended public schools where he was often the target of taunts because of his Polish ancestry, his Roman Catholic religion, and his father's Democratic Party politics. His father, a tailor, had somewhat Americanized his name from Marciszewski, but he would not further assimilate by becoming a Republican. Muskie graduated from Bates College in Lewiston, Maine, in 1936, and Cornell University Law School in Ithaca, NY, in 1939. He was admitted to the Massachusetts bar in 1939 and the Maine bar in 1940, beginning the practice of law in Waterville, Maine, in 1940. During the Second World War he enlisted in the U.S. Navy and served in the Atlantic and Pacific Theaters (1942–45). He was a member and secretary of the Waterville Board of Zoning Adjustment (1948–55), district director for the Maine Office of Price Stabilization (1951–52), and city solicitor of Waterville (1954). Elected to the state House of Representatives in 1946, 1948, and 1950, he was Democratic floor leader in 1949–1951. Elected governor of Maine (1955–59), the first Democratic governor of Maine in twenty years, he was elected as a Democrat to the United States Senate in 1958, then reelected in 1964, 1970, and 1976, serving from January 3, 1959, until his resignation on May 7, 1980, to enter the Cabinet. In the Senate he was chair of the Committee on the Budget (Ninety-third through Ninety-sixth Congresses). He was often called "Mr. Clean" in recognition of his responsibility for the passage of such bills as the 1963 and 1965 Clean Air Acts and the 1965 Water Quality Act. Muskie was the leading anti-pollution authority in Congress in his time. He also favored restraint over executive privilege and the systematic declassification of secret government documents. Muskie was known for his height (6′4″), his temper, his modesty, his humor, his New England cadences, his independence, and his frequent invitation to hecklers on the campaign trail to join him on stage

in order to debate the issues. Muskie was the unsuccessful Democratic candidate for Vice President of the United States in 1968. That surprising, yet popular selection arguably made him the most nationally prominent Polish American politician, a position he retained for several years. It positioned him as the frontrunner before the primaries began for the 1972 Democratic presidential nomination, which he did not win, in part because of his angry, arguably tearful, defense of his wife against the editorial attacks of the Manchester, New Hampshire, *Union Leader* newspaper. Whether he had or not, Muskie appeared to weep at a time when male politicians usually did not. Muskie became the surprise Secretary of State in the Cabinet of President Jimmy Carter (1980–81) when he replaced Cyrus Vance, who had resigned in protest over the attempted (as it turned out, unsuccessful) military rescue of the American hostages in Iran. Ironically, Muskie took the post on the condition that the influence of Carter's hawkish National Security Advisor, Muskie's fellow Pole **Zbigniew Brzeziński**, would be constrained. The Senate assured him of its promise of support in the event of a disagreement between the two. Muskie mused after he left office that, had it not been for the hostage situation, he might not have become Secretary of State. But had it not been for the hostages remaining in captivity for so long, he might have served much longer in that post and President Carter might have been re-elected. He made the cover of *Time* magazine three times, once with his running mate Hubert Humphrey in 1968, once in 1971, and again in 1980. He was awarded the Presidential Medal of Freedom on January 16, 1981. He was a member of the President's Special Review Board (the "Tower Commission") in 1987, and practiced law until his death from a heart attack in Washington, D.C. His legacy

echoes with awards bearing his name such as the Edmund S. Muskie Distinguished Public Service Award from the Center for National Policy (which Muskie chaired from 1985–94) and the Edmund S. Muskie Graduate Fellowship Program, established by Congress in 1992 within the U.S. State Department to encourage democracies in Eurasia. His papers are located at Bates College in Lewiston, ME.—*Frederick J. Augustyn*

SOURCES: *Biographical Directory of the United States Congress, 1774–Present* (http://bioguide.congress.gov/); William Lee Barnett, "An Analysis of the Rhetorical Effectiveness of the 1972 Presidential Primary Election Campaign of Senator Edmund S. Muskie" (Ph.D. dissertation, University of Pittsburgh, 1976); Robert F. Blomquist, "Senator Edmund S. Muskie and the Dawn of Modern American Environmental Law: First Term, 1959–1964," *William & Mary Environmental Law & Policy Review*, Vol. 26 (Spring 2002), 509–612; Theo Lippman, Jr., and Donald J. Hansen, *Muskie* (New York: W.W. Norton & Co., 1971); David Nevin, *Muskie of Maine* (New York: Random House, 1972); *Edmund S. Muskie (1914–1996), Late a Senator from Maine: Memorial Tributes in the Congress of the United States* (Washington: Government Printing Office, 1996, 104th Cong., 2d sess.).

Nadelman, Elie (b. February 20, 1882, Warsaw, Poland; d. December 28, 1946, Bronx, New York). Artist. After enrolling in the Warsaw Art Academy at age nineteen, Nadelman spent six months studying art exhibitions in Munich before moving to Paris in 1904 where he was influenced by the work of Auguste Rodin. His first individual show in Paris in 1909 met with considerable success, with some of his works subsequently being exhibited in the Armory Show in 1913 and led to the publication of a series of his drawings under the title *Toward a Sculptural Unity*

Elie Nadelman, sculptor (*LC*).

Edmund Muskie holding a campaign bumper sticker with his original Polish surname (*OLS*).

(1914). When World War I began, Nadelman moved to London and then on to New York City, where his individual exhibition at Alfred Stieglitz's Gallery 291 in 1915 attracted several important patrons including Leo Stein and Helena Rubinstein. In 1919 he married Viola Spiess Flannery, a wealthy socialite, with whom he founded the Museum of Folk and Peasant Art (later the Museum of Folk Arts) in Riverdale, New York. The Great Depression brought with it financial difficulties that caused the closing of the museum, while the accidental destruction of much of his work in 1935 effectively ended his public career. Nadelman's interest in exploring the sculptural relationship between volume and geometry and his abstract style led to the development of his trademark curvilinear human figures that are said to have greatly influenced early twentieth century American sculpture.—*James S. Pula*

SOURCES: Lincoln Kirstein, *The Sculpture of Elie Nadelman* (New York: Museum of Modern Art, 1948); Lincoln Kirstein, *Elie Nadelman* (New York: Eakins Press, 1973); John I. H. Baur, *The Sculpture and Drawings of Elie Nadelman* (New York: Whitney Museum of American Art, 1975).

Nagiel, Henryk (b. Warsaw, Poland, January 19, 1859; d. Lwów, Poland, December 2, 1899). Writer, journalist, editor. Although he spent less than ten years in the United States, Nagiel was influential in the early development and chronicling of Polish American intellectual and cultural life. He received his law degree from Warsaw University, and in 1888 migrated to Paris. Despite his profession as a lawyer, Nagiel was interested in literature from an early age, and began publishing humorous poems at 15. As a university student he edited the magazine *Wędrowiec* (The Wanderer), and in Paris worked as a typesetter. He arrived in the United States around 1889, immediately beginning work as a journalist affiliated with the loosely socialist Manhattan-based Ognisko Group of writers and artists, who formed an intellectual hub for early **Polonia**. Although Chicago eventually replaced New York as Polonia's most influential center in America, the Ognisko Group formed a progressive and colorful, if short-lived, subculture. Its members produced a number of newspapers, magazines, and other publications, often satirical, and in addition to Nagiel included important early Polonian writers Alfons Chrostowski and Julian Czupka.

During his short time in the U.S., Nagiel worked on many of Polonia's newspapers, including *Kukuryku* and *Krytyka* in Buffalo, *Kuryer nowoyorskie i brooklyński* in New York, and *Nowe Życie, Reforma,* and *Telegraf* in Chicago. He was an editor of the influential *Dziennik Chicagoski* from 1892 until his return to Poland in 1896. His involvement in immigrant journalism led Nagiel to write *Dziennikarstwo polskie w Ameryce i jego 30-letnie dzieje* (Polish Journalism in America and Its 30-Year History), published in 1894. It was the first in-depth look at the subject, and is made all the more interesting by Nagiel's firsthand experience. But Nagiel also used his experiences to write fiction. Even before he arrived in the U.S., he had published two potboiler novels, *Tajemnice Nalewek* (Mysterious Nalewek; 1888), which was made into a film in 1921, and *Sęp* (The Vulture; 1889). His enormously popular *Kara Boże idzie przez oceany: powieść na tle stosunków polskich w Ameryce* (God's Punishment Crosses the Ocean: A Novel Based on Polish Conditions in America) appeared in 1896. A Polish immigrant who-done-it of political espionage, murder, and romance with a multiethnic cast of characters, the sensational novel was reprinted in serial form in 1912. Reportedly unable to bear conditions in America any longer, Nagiel returned to Europe in 1896, settling in Lwów, where he contributed to *Słowo polskie* (The Polish Word). Long ill with tuberculosis, he died in Lwów in 1899, barely forty years old.—*Karen Majewski*

SOURCE: Karen Majewski, *Traitors and True Poles: Narrating a Polish-American Identity, 1880–1939* (Athens: Ohio University Press, 2003).

Nagorski, Andrew (b. Edinburgh, Scotland, May 3, 1947; d.—). Journalist. Nagorski migrated to the U.S. with his parents soon after he was born. He earned his baccalaureate degree with honors at Amherst College (1969) where he was a member of the Phi Beta Kappa honorary and studied at the Jagiellonian University in Kraków. After teaching high school social studies (1969–73), he joined the staff of *Newsweek International* magazine in 1973 as associate editor and became assistant managing editor in 1977. He served as a regional editor and Hong Kong Bureau Chief (1978–80), and in 1982 gained international recognition when his reporting resulted in his expulsion from the Soviet Union. Following two years as bureau chief in Rome, Italy, he was assigned to the same position in Bonn, Germany. In 1990 was named bureau chief in Warsaw, and in 1995–96 returned again to the Soviet Union as bureau chief in Moscow. From 1996 to 1999 he served as bureau chief in Berlin, while also covering stories throughout Central Europe. In 2000 he was assigned as *Newsweek's* senior editor in New York, a position he held until 2008 while he played a major role in developing the magazine's foreign language editions including *Newsweek Arabic* (2000), *Newsweek Polska* (2001), *News-*

Andrew Nagorski, journalist (*OLS*).

week Russia (2004), and *Newsweek Argentina* (2006). In 2008 he joined the East-West institute as vice president and director of public policy. His reporting has been honored three times with awards from the Overseas Press Club, and in November 2009 Polish Foreign Minister Radosław Sikorski awarded him the *Bene Merito* award for his international promotion of Poland during the Solidarity era. Nagorski is the author of *Reluctant Farewell: An American Reporter's Candid Look Inside the Soviet Union* (1985), *The Birth of Freedom: Shaping Lives and Societies in the New Eastern Europe* (1993), and *The Greatest Battle: Stalin, Hitler and the Desperate Struggle for Moscow That Changed the Course of World War II* (2007), the latter of which was named one of the best books of 2007 by the *Washington Post*. He is a member of the Council of Foreign Relations and the board of directors of the Polish-American Freedom Foundation.—*James S. Pula*

SOURCES: David L. Wilson, "Washington's Movers and Shakers; Security," *National Journal*, September 9, 1989; "Nagorski, Andrew," *Contemporary Authors* (Detroit: Gale Research Company), Vol. 93–96, 387.

Nanoski, John "Jukey" (b. Philadelphia, Pennsylvania, June 14, 1918; d.—). Soccer player. Nanoski began playing soccer when he was twelve years old, continuing the game at Stetson High School and then for the Westmoreland Soccer Club, Lehigh Soccer Club, and the Kensington Quoit Club, all in the Philadelphia area. In 1937–38 he began playing for the Kensington Blue Bells, an excellent team that won the Pennsylvania League title in 1938. He was paid three dollars per game for a win, two dollars for a tie and one dollar for a loss. During his first season he led the league in scoring with 54 goals while leading his team to the championship. Following the season he moved to Brooklyn to play center forward for the St. Mary's Celtic of the American Soccer League where he scored three of the five goals leading his team to the championship in the National Open Cup in 1939, the second year in a row the team emerged with the championship. He later played for the Brooklyn Wanderers and Trenton Highlanders, as well as the Philadelphia Americans who won the American Soccer League championship in 1944, 1947, and 1948. Nanoski was the league's leading goal scorer in 1942 and 1947. In 1942 he played with the Metropolitan All-Stars against the Atlante club from Mexico, and in 1948 he was on the Philadelphia Stars when they played the English club from Liverpool. He was inducted into the National Soccer Hall of Fame in 1993.—*James S. Pula*

SOURCE: national.soccerhall.org.

Napieralska, Emilia (b. Chicago, Illinois, April 21, 1882; d. Hinsdale, Illinois, February 18, 1943). Polonia activist. Napieralska joined the **Polish Women's Alliance of America** in 1901 and in 1910 was elected its secretary general. In 1918 she was elected president of the PWA, thereby becoming the first person born in the U.S. to hold that office. She continued as president until 1935. As a PWA activist and feminist, Napieralska was an effective and dynamic speaker in both Polish and English. She first won acclaim in **Polonia** by her attendance at the International Women's Peace Conference held in The Hague, Netherlands, in 1915.

Emilia Napieralska, president of the Polish Women's Alliance (*JPI*).

At this gathering she made a speech draped in the colors of the U.S. and Poland. In it she objected to the Conference's call for "peace at any price" without first recognizing the need for justice and freedom for the oppressed and partitioned Polish nation. The Congress accepted her position, although its efforts to bring an end to the conflict met with failure. As president of the PWA from 1918 to 1935, she oversaw a great expansion in the fraternal from 21,000 to 65,000 insured members. She began sponsorship of regular PWA tours to visit the new Poland in 1928 in what the PWA originally called "pilgrimages" to the old homeland. Active in Chicago and Cook County politics, Napieralska was vice president of the Cook County Civil Service Commission. She was also successful in winning city approval to rename Crawford Avenue as Pulaski Road, in honor of the great Polish and American patriot. Her dynamism and leadership skills made her the pride of **Polonia** in her day. In the words of **Karol Wachtl** in a book published in 1944, she was "undoubtedly one of the most remarkable women that Polonia in America ever produced." In 1939, she was named honorary president of the PWA.—*Donald E. Pienkos*

SOURCE: Angela Pienkos and Donald Pienkos, "*In the Ideals of Women is the Strength of a Nation": A History of the Polish Women's Alliance of America* (Boulder, CO: East European Monographs, 2003).

Napierkowski, Thomas J. (b. Chicago, Illinois, 1943; d.—). Literary scholar, critic. Napierkowski was born and raised in South Chicago, a heavily Polish American and industrial community within the southern limits of the City of Chicago. His family belonged to St. Mary Magdalene Parish, and he attended the parish grade school. In 1961 he graduated from Archbishop Quigley Preparatory Seminary; and after taking a year off to work, he enrolled in the University of Wisconsin–Oshkosh, majoring in English literature. After graduation, he received a scholarship to do graduate work in English literature at the University of Colorado at Boulder where he specialized in the study of medieval literature. After completing his Ph.D. in 1971, Napierkowski and his family moved back to Wisconsin where he taught for two years in the University of Wisconsin System. In 1973 he received an appointment to the English Department of the University of Colorado at Colorado Springs where he spent the balance of his career. Napierkowski has written that his decision to study medieval literature was significantly influenced by his inability to find a reflection of himself— his economic, ethnic, and religious identity — in the canon of American literature. In 1968, however, an oppor-

tunity arose which changed the course of his career. Following the assassination of Dr. Marin Luther King, Jr., Napierkowski was asked by his graduate department to help develop and to teach a course on African American literature, both on the campus of the University and, as an extension course, at a Denver inner-city high school. These experiences not only provided Napierkowski with new areas of scholarly and teaching interest, they quickened within him a passionate desire to study Polish American literature. Finding literature of high quality among then relatively obscure Black American authors convinced him that an equally significant body of immigrant, especially Polish American, literature remained to be discovered and appreciated. His study of African American literature also shaped his critical approach to Polish American literature and determined the theories of minority American literature which he has championed.

A member of the Medieval Academy of America and the Early English Text Society of Oxford, England, Napierkowski continues to teach and research Middle English literature; but he has also promoted the recognition and value of Polish American literature in the world of American letters. In 2004 he was honored with a Distinguished Service Award by the **Polish American Historical Association**, an organization he also served as president. The citation read at the presentation of that award nicely summarizes Napierkowski's efforts: "perhaps Dr. Napierkowski's most notable contribution to PAHA has been the promotion and study of Polish American literature through numerous articles, reviews, conference papers, and personal correspondence. Himself a winner of a national prize for his essay 'Stepchild of America: Growing Up Polish American,' Napierkowski has championed Polish American literature, bringing to it the attention of a wide audience and arguing for its legitimate place in the American canon."

Harriet and Thomas Napierkowski, literary scholars (*Thomas J. Napierkowski*).

Napierkowski has actively worked with numerous Polish American authors to encourage appreciation and critical analysis of their works. Recently he has also worked to support the recognition of American literature as historically and properly multilingual and to guarantee an acknowledgement of the wealth of American literature written in the Polish language. Within the **Polonia**, Napierkowski has repeatedly promoted a greater awareness of the importance of literature to a preservation of the history of the Polish American community and to a correct recognition of Polonia within the wider world of American culture. Finally, he has actively campaigned for the preservation of the literature of the *Stara Imigracja* (Old Immigration) which, he argues, is endangered of being lost because of inadequate archiving funds and efforts.—*Harriet Napierkowski*

Naród Polski (The Polish Nation). *Naród Polski* is the newspaper of the **Polish Roman Catholic Union of America** (PRCUA). It was founded in 1897 as the official organ of the PRCUA and has remained in continuous publication ever since. Prior to the creation of *Naród Polski* the PRCUA had published two other organs, *Gazeta Polska Katolicka* (Polish Catholic Gazette), an unofficial organ, and *Wiara i Ojczyzna* (Faith and Fatherland), the first official organ. It is likely that the PRCUA did not own the latter periodical outright. As such, the creation of a new organ wholly owned by the PRCUA would have been a logical step since during the late 1890s the PRCUA was reforming its structure and developing a greater degree of centralization. There are approximately five distinct stages in the history of *Naród Polski* up to the present. The first occurred during the period from its founding through 1921. During this era, the paper was published weekly, usually in eight-page editions though supplemental pages were sometimes added. During this era, *Naród Polski* remained relatively closely tied to the larger universe of **Resurrectionist**-directed enterprises, sometimes sharing staff and resources. For example, early **Polonia** historian **Karol Wachtl** was editor of *Naród Polski* from 1903 to 1907, then became editor of *Dziennik Chicagoski* (Chicago Daily News) until 1911 when he returned to *Naród Polski*. A typical issue contained a mixture of organizational information and a wide range of news from Poland, the United States, American Polonia, and the wider world of the Catholic Church. Devotional items and serialized novels were also mainstays. The paper's editorial line was strongly loyal to Roman Catholicism, opposing the positions of the secularist **Polish Na-tional Alliance**, anti–Catholic radical factions, and the schismatic **Polish National Catholic Church**. At the same time, after 1900 the paper provided a platform for clerics such as the Rev. **Wacław Kruszka** who remained firmly within the Catholic fold but sought a larger role for Polish Americans. During World War I, the paper enthusiastically supported the Allied war effort and **Polonia**'s mobilization on behalf of Polish independence. An important and remarkable feature of this period of the newspaper's development was its strong focus on social reform within the Polish American community. *Naród Polski*'s editors assailed a wide range of social problems in unflinching terms: alcoholism, family breakdown, violence, crime, and juvenile delinquency. An important component of this approach was a strongly written women's page, which was probably edited by one of the PRCUA's female officers in the Chicago home office. The page contained articles on the important role of women in social reform, notable achievements of Polish women, and practical columns such as "Lekarz Domowy" (home doctor).

The second phase of *Naród Polski*'s development occurred after the creation of the PRCUA daily newspaper, *Dziennik Zjednoczenia* (Union Daily News) in 1921. Freed from the necessity of printing world and national news, *Naród Polski* began to focus almost exclusively on PRCUA issues. During the mid to late 1920s, the paper was reduced to a bi-monthly periodical.

The third stage began when pressure from Union members and the financial problems experienced by *Dziennik Zjednoczenia* resulted in a return to the weekly format by the early 1930s in a form similar to the pre–1921 editions. One important change, however, was the addition of an English-language page which focused on sports and youth concerns.

The next major change in the newspaper's format occurred in the 1950s when *Naród Polski* began to focus far more on internal PRCUA matters and reduced its coverage of news. This marked an important watershed when the newspaper lost its function as a source of outside news and information to a community which was increasingly bi-lingual and able to read English-language papers and was exposed to radio and television. The paper remained a bastion of the Polish language and if anything, English declined in the post-war period as long-time editor **Zygmunt Stefanowicz** attempted to hold the line against the decline of Polish in the younger generations of the Polish community.

In the 1970s, the newspaper switched over to a mostly English-language format after the retirement of Stefanowicz. In the 1980s, it began a gradual process of technical modernization, further under the auspices of the first female editor, Kathryn Rosypal. *Naród Polski* also revamped its Polish-language section and added sections of cultural news. Although circulation has declined due to the fall in PRCUA membership, *Naród Polski* remains one of the most important and widely read periodicals in Polonia.—*John Radzilowski*

SOURCE: John Radzilowski, *The Eagle and the Cross: A History of Polish Roman Catholic Union of America, 1873–2000* (New York: Columbia University Press/East European Monographs, 2003).

National Committee of Americans of Polish Descent (Komitet Narodowy Amerykanów Pochodzenia Polskiego; KNAPP). KNAPP was a political action organization formed in June 1942 in New York under the leadership of **Maximilian Węgrzynek**, editor and publisher of the Polish language daily newspaper *Nowy Świat* (New World). It aimed to mobilize the major organizations of the Polish ethnic community in giving strong and vocal support to the cause of a restored and fully independent post–World War II Polish state. KNAPP's founders included **Frank Januszewski**, editor and publisher of the Detroit-based *Dziennik Polski* (Polish Daily News) and three Polish émigrés who had held cabinet-level positions in interwar Poland during the rule of Marshal Józef Piłsudski, the key figure in the Polish government from 1926 to 1935: **Ignacy Matuszewski**, **Wacław Jędrzejewicz**, and **Henryk Floyar-Rajchmann**. KNAPP's leaders were profoundly skeptical of the efforts of General Władysław Sikorski, head of the exile Polish government-in-exile in London, whose efforts, they believed, were insufficient in defending Poland's national interests against Soviet Russia. In September 1939, the USSR and Nazi Germany had invaded and destroyed the Polish state; however, in June 1941, Soviet Russia was attacked by Germany and immediately became an ally of Britain and, ominously, Poland. The United States joined the anti–Nazi alliance after Pearl Harbor in December 1941, thus making political action by **Polonia** on Poland's behalf imperative.

Until 1942, Polonia had not been politically engaged. The **Polish American Council** (Rada Polonii Amerykańskiej), led by **Polish National Alliance** leader **Francis X. Swietlik**, had been limited to humanitarian efforts on behalf of Polish refugees and prisoners of war. But in early 1942, advocates of a close U.S. alliance with Soviet Russia created the **American Slav Congress** (ASL) which made the exaggerated claim that it represented fifteen million Americans of Slavic origin. Led by

National Committee of Americans of Polish Descent meeting in San Francisco in 1945: from left, Lucjusz Kaupferwasser, Wacław Jędrzejewicz, Franciszek Januszewski, Walenty Porański, Ignacy Matuszewski, Józef Plich, Wacław Gawroński (*JPI*).

labor unionist and longtime socialist **Leo Krzycki**, the ASL, along with another Krzycki-led group, the **American Polish Labor Council** (which claimed to represent no fewer than 600,000 Polish working people), won Washington's attention thanks to its loud support of President Franklin D. Roosevelt and the U.S.–Soviet alliance and the backing it received from influential friends in the Administration. Roosevelt, ever concerned about maintaining unity with the United States' allies — Britain and the Soviet Union — regarded KNAPP as a problem; indeed, Sikorski himself denounced KNAPP. As a result, the U.S. government went so far as to require KNAPP's Polish émigré activists, most notably Matuszewski, to register as agents of a foreign power and kept them under close surveillance.

In early 1944, Węgrzynek and his associates came to an agreement with the leaders of the main Polish American fraternal organizations and Polish American representatives of the Roman Catholic and **Polish National Catholic** Churches to form a new national political action federation on Poland's behalf. This organization, the **Polish American Congress** (PAC), came into being in June 1944 at a massive convention held in Buffalo, New York. Not only was the PAC program much influenced by KNAPP, Węgrzynek and Januszewski were both elected national vice presidents at the gathering. Following the "Big Three" **Yalta** summit in February 1945, KNAPP's worst concerns were proven correct. Poland fell into the Soviet orbit and the new Polish state, stripped of its eastern territories, was forced into satellite status. The PAC condemned the Yalta agreement on Poland in the sharpest terms and soon became part of a broad-based anti-Soviet U.S. coalition that quickly became dominant in defining the "Cold War" foreign policy views of the Re-

publican Party and, later, the Democratic Party as well.

In 1948, PAC president **Charles Rozmarek** established a formal tie with Stanisław Mikołajczyk, who had been prime minister of the London exile government (1943–44) after Sikorski's death. The Rozmarek-Mikołajczyk arrangement was controversial: in 1945, Mikołajczyk had returned to Poland with the goal of defeating the Soviet-run Polish provisional government in a fair national election. KNAPP and others had condemned that move as both hopelessly naive and one that gave the communist regime an undeserved aura of respectability. After his effort was crushed in January 1947 in rigged parliamentary elections, Mikołajczyk was forced to flee to the U.S. While his resulting alliance with Rozmarek was short-lived and without impact, it led to KNAPP's decision to withdraw from the PAC in protest. The **Polish Roman Catholic Union** followed suit, but returned in 1954. KNAPP disbanded in the mid–1950s; by then it had become marginalized by the far larger, more influential, and militantly anti-communist activism of Rozmarek and the PAC.—*Donald E. Pienkos*

SOURCES: Wacław Jędrzejewicz, *Polonia Amerykańska w Polityce Polskiej: Historia Komitetu Narodowego Polskiego Pochodzenia* (New York: National Committee of Americans of Polish Descent, 1954); Richard Lukas, *The Strange Allies: The United States and Poland, 1941–1945* (Knoxville, TN: University of Tennessee Press, 1978); Piotr Wandycz, *The United States and Poland* (Cambridge, MA: Harvard University Press, 1980); Donald E. Pienkos, "The Polish American Congress, Polish Americans, and the Politics of Anti-Communism," in Ieva Zake, ed., *Anti-Communist Minorities in the U.S.* (New York: Palgrave Macmillan, 2009).

National Defense Committee (Komitet Obrony Narodowej; KON). Formed in Pittsburgh in late 1912 in support of Józef Piłsudski and socialists in **Galicia** who supported Polish independence, the KON sought to unify all Polish American groups under a single umbrella organization except for the schismatic **Polish National Catholic Church** (PNCC). It was anti–Russian in sentiment, favored direct military action to free the homeland from domination by the partitioning powers, and viewed the role of American **Polonia** in the struggle for Polish independence as largely one of fund raising to support the cause. The organization was strongly supported by Polish American socialist leaders **Aleksander Dębski** and Bronisław Kulakowski; the militantly nationalist editor of *Zgoda*, Tomasz Siemiradzki; "conservative nationalists" including Catholic priests and the **Polish Roman Catholic Union**; and the "center nationalists" of the **Polish National Alliance** (PNA). Soon after the Pittsburgh meeting the headquarters was transferred to Chicago where the more moderate and conservative forces led by **Kazimierz Zychlinski**, president of the Polish National Alliance and a supporter of Piłsudski's rival Roman Dmowski, gained the ascendancy in

National Defense Committee: left to right, back row, J. K. Płonka, director; J. B. Ogłoziński, director; Aleksander Hinkelman, secretary; Michał Sokołowski, director; front row, Fr. Przybyłowicz, director; Fr. Woszczyński, vice president; Jan M. Sienkiewicz, president; Stanisław Obszula, secretary (*JPI*).

the KON. In 1913 the issue of membership by the PNCC prompted a walkout by Roman Catholic clergy and the more conservative fraternal organizations, leaving the socialists, the PNA, the **Polish Falcons Alliance**, the **Polish Women's Alliance** (PWA), and the PNCC to carry on the KON's work. The groups that had withdrawn formed their own organization, the Rada Narodowa (**Polish National Council**). In September 1913 a number of KON activists were elected to the PNA executive board, leading the fraternal to turn its treasury over to the Piłsudskiites in **Galicia**, a move that severed longstanding PNA ties to the National Democratic movement in Poland. In 1914, however, as a result of criticism of the Galician group by **Ignacy Jan Paderewski** and reports of its own fact-finding mission to Poland, the PNA withdrew from the KON, followed shortly thereafter by the Falcons and the PWA. The KON was left with only the socialists and PNCC as active supporters. KON's influence declined significantly; by the outbreak of World War I it was actively engaged only in New York, New Jersey, and Connecticut. It continued to operate during the war, but was greatly encumbered by its reputation as socialist and anti–Catholic and by its support for the Central Powers. By 1918 it claimed only 6,934 members nationwide, compared to 126,000 PNA adherents. It had raised approximately $250,000 to support its wartime causes, compared to about $10 million raised by nationalist and conservative organizations. During the 1920s and 1930s, KON activists gained ground in **Polonia** after Piłsudski's May 1926 *coup d'etat*. Piłsudski's enthusiasts even won control of the PNA and tried to forge close ties with Poland in backing the creation of the **Światpol** international organization headquartered in Warsaw. But their efforts failed in the PNA national conventions of 1931, 1935, and 1939 due to the efforts of **Francis Swietlik**, **Charles Rozmarek**, and their followers. Still, KON partisans were visible in their support of the World War II era, New York based, **National Committee of Americans of Polish Descent** (KNAPP). Significantly, KNAPP activists played an active part in the creation of the **Polish American Congress** in 1943–44.—*Donald E. Pienkos*

SOURCE: Donald E. Pienkos, *For Your Freedom Through Ours: Polish American Efforts on Poland's Behalf, 1863–1991* (Boulder, CO: East European Monographs, 1991).

National Department (Wydział Narodowy). The National Department, or Polish National Department, was created as a political action subcommittee under the auspices of the **Polish Central Relief Committee** (es-

National Department: front row from left, Capt. K. Kleczkowski, the Rev. Władysław Zapała, Jan Smulski, Bishop Paul Rhode, Dr. Seyda, Henryk Setmajer, Lt. Marszewski; back row, N. L. Piotrowski, J. Magdziarz, Kazimierz Sypniewski, Anna Neumann, Peter Rostenkowski, the Rev. B. Celichowski, Zygmunt Stefanowicz, Jan Rybicki, Dr. B. Klarkowski, Maria Sakowska, T. Blachowski, Kazimierz Żychliński (*OLS*).

tablished in October 1914 three months after the outbreak of World War I). From 1916, the National Department, headed by Chicago banker, former Illinois state treasurer, and **Polonia** activist **John F. Smulski**, overshadowed the Relief Committee as Polonia's main lobby for Polish independence. The National Department enjoyed three advantages in leading Polonia over its rival, the Polish **National Defense Committee** (KON), formed in 1912, namely: (1) it included nearly all of the major Polonia organizations; (2) its presentation of Poland's cause benefited from its close association with the internationally renowned virtuoso pianist and patriot, **Ignacy J. Paderewski**; and (3) it had close ties with the Polish National Committee in France led by Roman Dmowski, head of the National Democratic Party in occupied Poland. Dmowski's Committee, an erstwhile postwar Polish provisional government, maintained close ties with France and Britain (and after April 1917 the United States) in the conflict against imperial Germany. The National Department's signal achievement came in August 1918 when it convened a Congress of the Polish Emigration (Sejm Wychodźtwa) in Detroit, a gathering of nearly 1,000 delegates from across Polonia. These delegates were chosen in a fashion that was later imitated by the **Polish American Congress** when it was organized in 1944. Both Paderewski and Dmowski addressed the Congress, which resolved to collect $10 million in support of the expected postwar independent Polish state. At the Congress, Smulski was elected president of the National Department. **Kazimierz Zychliński**, president of the **Polish National Alliance**, was elected vice president and President Nikodem Pi-

otrowski of the **Polish Roman Catholic Union** was chosen to be its treasurer. Leaders of Polonia's fraternals dominated its Board of Directors. World War I came to an end only ten weeks later, on November 11. The fund drive subsequently faltered and did not reach its goal. Moreover, Marshal Józef Piłsudski, the hero of KON in America, eclipsed Dmowski in leading the newly independent Poland. For his part, Smulski did try to convert the National Department into a permanent lobby for Poland. But many in Polonia disagreed, arguing that, with independence attained, it was no longer needed. Following its fourth national convention in Cleveland in 1923, the National Department disbanded.—*Donald E. Pienkos*

SOURCES: Louis J. Zake, "The National Department and the Polish American Community 1916–1923," *Polish American Studies*, Vol. 38, no. 2 (1981), 16–25; William Galush, "American Poles and the New Poland: An Example of Change," *Ethnicity Magazine*, Vol. 1, no. 3 (1974); Donald E. Pienkos, *For Your Freedom Through Ours: Polish American Efforts on Poland's Behalf, 1863–1991* (Boulder, CO: East European Monographs, 1991).

National Medical and Dental Association, Inc. Founded as the Polish Medical and Dental Association of America at a meeting in Detroit, Michigan, in 1910, the organization was incorporated in the state of Ohio in 1924, changing its name after World War II. Following the First World War, responding to a request from the U.S. government, members assisted in developing a public health program in the newly independent Polish Republic. A leader in this movement, Dr. **Francis E. Fronczak** of Buffalo, New York, was honored by both the Polish and American governments for his efforts. With the outbreak of the Second World War, the organization raised funds and gathered medicine and equipment it used to assist wounded Polish soldiers serving in the Polish Armed Forces in exile on the Allied side, with additional aid assisting in the building of hospitals and clinics in war-ravaged Poland following the conflict. Association member Conrad M. Mietus received a commendation for his work in establishing a facility for blind children in Poland. Similar efforts have been made over the years through financial donations, volunteer services, fundraising activities and acquisition of equipment to support hospitals and health facilities in areas of Polish immigrant settlement in the United States. In 2008, local chapters existed in Boston, Buffalo, Chicago, Cleveland, Detroit, New York City, Newark, Philadelphia, and Pittsburgh. The organization hosts an annual convention including medical-related and social events, as well as the election of officers and presentation of an annual Man of the Year Award. The Association also supports a scholarship fund for Polish Americans studying in the fields of medicine and dentistry and publishes *The Bulletin of the National Medical and Dental Association*. In 2008, its headquarters were located at 1133 West Wilson Avenue, Chicago, Illinois, 60640.—*James S. Pula*

SOURCE: *The Bulletin of the National Medical and Dental Association.*

National Polish American/Jewish American Council. The Polish-American/Jewish-American Council owed its origins to local efforts in the Detroit area where the then president of **St. Mary's College** in **Orchard Lake**, Michigan, the Rev. Leonard Chrobot, the Rev. Ronald Modras, and leaders of the Detroit chapter of the American Jewish Committee (AJC) including its chairman Harold Gales and the Michigan division of the **Polish American Congress** (PAC) had engaged in discussions of Polish-Jewish issues. On September 13, 1979, this group convened a meeting at St. Mary's College between local and national representatives of the AJC and representatives of Polish American cultural, civic, religious, and academic organizations. This meeting resulted in the publication of an Orchard Lake statement on Polish-Jewish relations.

Shortly thereafter a meeting was held in New York that included Rabbi Marc Tanenbaum and George Szabad of the American Jewish Committee, Professor Lucjan Dobroszycki of YIVO and the Rev. **John Pawlikowski**, OSM, of the Catholic Theological Union in Chicago. This meeting focused on the possibility of transforming the Detroit ini-

tiative into a truly national effort. The conclusion of the discussion was positive, resulting in immediate steps to implement the decision.

The American Jewish Committee leadership decided that the proposed national council would best be located in AJC's program on ethnic pluralism in America funded by the Ford Foundation directed by David Roth out of AJC's Chicago office. It was David Roth who was largely responsible for laying solid foundations for the work of the Council. He had already been in contact with national leaders of the Polish American Congress based in Chicago, particularly **Aloysius A. Mazewski** and **Kazimierz Lukomski**. Lukomski in particular gave strong support to the idea of such a Council.

The National Council soon became reality as David Roth negotiated an agreement with AJC and the Polish American Congress to serve as the institutional co-sponsors of the Council. The co-chairs of the original local initiative in Detroit, the Rev. Leonard Chrobot and Harold Gales, were designated as the first co-chairs of the National Council with David Roth assuming the position of the Executive Director. A board was assembled that included representatives from AJC and the Polish American Congress as well as people with ties to various Polish American and Jewish American organizations and academics. Important relations were also forged with staff persons at the Polish embassy in Washington (which gave the Council strong support) and to a lesser extend with Israeli diplomats based in the United States. The new United States Holocaust Memorial Museum in Washington likewise became an important partner of the Council, especially during the chairmanship of Miles Lerman who had served in the Jewish resistance movement in Poland during the Nazi era.

As the new National Council formulated its goals, emphasis was placed on the contemporary situation facing the two communities, not on the past historical relationships. Issues included those shared in common, as well as providing support for the other community on matters of particular importance to Polish Americans and Jewish Americans respectively. It became quickly apparent, however, that staying away from past history or confining its work solely to the American domestic scene was impossible. Both communities saw international dimensions as important for their identities (Israel for Jews; Poland for Polish Americans) and historical controversies, particularly involving World War II, continued to impact the consciousness of Polish Americans and Jewish Americans alike.

Over the years the Council gave its attention

to a range of issues reflecting its diverse goals. Among the most important were working on immigration matters connected with the exodus of Soviet Jews and Poles leaving Poland for the United States in connection with the crackdown on the Solidarity movement, joint support for Poland's entry into NATO, joint delegation to important World War II commemorations in Poland, joint analysis of Claude Lanzmann's controversial documentary film *Shoah*, discussions of anti–Semitism and the term "Holocaust," a joint declaration during the contentious debate over the convent at Auschwitz, and collaboration with the United States Holocaust Memorial Museum on a week-long program on Polish victimization and rescue efforts and a comprehensive evaluation of signage at the Museum which referenced either Poles or Poland. With regard to the last of these activities the three Council members who simultaneously served on the board of the Holocaust Museum—**Stanislaus Blejwas**, John Kordek and the Rev. John Pawlikowski—played a central role in organizing these efforts in collaboration with the Museum's chair, Miles Lerman. The Council also played an important role in facilitating use of the Warsaw airport as a transfer point for departing Soviet Jews when the previous facility in Vienna was suddenly closed by the Austrian government. On Council matters involving Poland, **Jan Nowak-Jeziorański** exercised a significant role.

The Council survived two important crises. The untimely death of the Council's director David Roth in July 1995 left a void as he had become the Council's driving force, a person highly respected on both sides of the aisle. Subsequent directors Jeffrey Weintraub and Guy Billauer did a commendable job but neither had the stature or influence of Roth.

In April 1996, Polish American Congress President **Edward Moskal** began an open attack on the Council and accused Polish President Aleksander Kwaśniewski of excessive submission to Jewish demands. AJC Director David Harris responded by declaring that the Council could no longer sustain ties with PAC. Some PAC divisions rejected Moskal's statements and continued to cooperate with the Council. Nowak-Jeziorański resigned from the PAC board over the situation.

After these developments the Council went into low gear, never quite recovering its initial energy. In June 2009 a decision was made by Council members to end the work of the Council believing that much of its original agenda had been completed, that the political situation had changed significantly, and that the global economic crisis had made Council funding highly problematic. The Council formally closed with a celebratory event at the Polish Consulate in New York. —*John Paw-likowski*

SOURCE: Anthony Polonsky and Mieczysław B. Biskupski, eds., *Polin: Studies in Polish Jewry* (Oxford: The Littman Library of Jewish Civilization, Vol. 19, 2007).

National Polish-American Sports Hall of Fame.

Housed within the American Polish Cultural Center in Troy, Michigan, this organization espouses the mission of honoring accomplished American athletes of Polish descent. It was originally founded in 1973, when its first inductee was the baseball standout Stan Musial. There are now more than 100 inductees drawn from numerous sports. The Hall of Fame also maintains a museum of artifacts and exhibits relating to Polish-American sports. —*Neal Pease*

SOURCE: website of the National Polish-American Sports Hall of Fame, www.polishsportshof.com.

National Polish Center.

In the late 1970s and early 1980s, Poles and Polish Americans were making monumental contributions to society. Karol Wojtyła began his leadership of the entire Roman Catholic world as Pope John Paul II. Lech Wałęsa spearheaded the revolt in Poland that led to Poland's emancipation from communism and ultimately to the dissolution of the Soviet empire. For a time, **Zbigniew Brzeziński** crafted American foreign policy as President Carter's national security adviser. In 1985, the **American Council for Polish Culture** conceived the idea of establishing a national center in Washington D.C., through its President **Blanka Rosenstiel**, which could become a showcase for the art and culture of Poland in the nation's capital. This would ensure that the contributions of Polish Americans to the United States would neither go unnoticed by contemporaries nor be forgotten by future generations. A goal was set to raise a million dollars for the acquisition of a suitable property to house the organization. Alexander and Patricia Koproski, of Connecticut, led the fund-raising effort, themselves contributing an initial $110,000. Then, in October 1989, the American Center of Polish Culture was officially incorporated in Washington, D.C., as a tax-exempt non-profit organization under section 501(c)(3) of the United States Internal Revenue Code. Two years later, the organization purchased a building at 2025 "O" Street, N.W., in the heart of Washington, to house the Center, which recently adopted as its official designation The National Polish Center (The American Center of Polish Culture, Inc., d.b.a.). The first Executive Director of the Center was Dr. Kaya Ploss. The National Polish Center presents concerts, lectures, discussions, exhi-

bitions, seminars and other events for adults and children in its Salon, which is decorated with pictures and sculptures of Polish and Polish American artists. Among its exhibits is a significant art collection bequeathed by Irene Nurkiewicz of New Jersey, while it also maintains the Amber Art Gallery, where temporary art exhibitions take place. It makes available its collection of folk art and costumes for display at community events, and maintains a large collection of Polish posters from the 1960s and 1970s, which depict the free voice of the Polish people under Communism. The Center issues a publication, *Center Line*, which is sent to all members, as well as to educational organizations. The Center reaches out to introduce public school students in Washington, D.C., to the culture of Poland, and maintains contacts with Poland and the Polish Embassy. The Center also sponsors an annual tribute to General **Kazimierz Pułaski**, on his birthday, in Washington D.C. —*Al Koproski*

SOURCE: www.nationalpolishcenter.org.

National Shrine of Our Lady of Czestochowa *see* Czestochowa.

Nedzi, Lucien Norbert (b. Hamtramck, Michigan, May 28, 1925; d. —). Congressman, attorney. Born in what was a Polish enclave surrounded by Detroit, Nedzi graduated from Hamtramck High School, **Hamtramck**, MI (1943). He served as a combat infantryman in the Philippines with the U.S. Army during World War II and the Corps of Engineers during the postwar occupation of Japan (1944–46) before obtaining a baccalaureate degree from the University of Michigan (1948). After attending the University of Detroit Law School in 1949, he earned his J.D. from the University of Michigan Law School (1951). As a member of the U.S. Army Reserve (1946–53) he served in the Korean War, after which he was admitted to the Michigan bar in January 1952 and to the District of Columbia bar in 1977. A delegate to the Democratic National Conventions in 1960 and 1968, he was elected as a Democrat to the Eighty-seventh Congress, by special election, to fill the vacancy caused by the resignation of **Thaddeus M. Machrowicz** who had been appointed a judge. Nedzi was reelected to the nine succeeding Congresses (November 7, 1961–January 3, 1981), serving as chair of the Select Committee on Intelligence (Ninety-fourth Congress), the Joint Committee on the Library (Ninety-third through Ninety-fifth Congresses), and the Committee on House Administration (Ninety-sixth Congress). Nedzi's chairmanship of the House Intelligence Committee fell during the investigation of the Watergate scandal. He ap-

parently did not use his position as chair to garner publicity for himself. He was not a candidate for reelection to the Ninety-seventh Congress in 1980. His papers are located at the University of Michigan. —*Frederick J. Augustyn*

SOURCE: *Biographical Directory of the United States Congress, 1774–Present* (http://bioguide.congress.gov/).

Negri, Pola (Barbara Apolonia Chałupiec; b. Lipno, Poland, December 31, 1894 [her actual birth date varies depending on the source]; d. San Antonio, Texas, August 1, 1987). Actress. When her father was arrested by Russian authorities and sent to Siberia, she was raised by her mother in poverty in Warsaw where she studied ballet. By the end of World War I she had become a popular actress, appearing both on the stage and in films. Her film debut came in *Niewolnica zmysłów* (Slave of the Senses) in 1914. Adopting the stage name "Pola Negri" in recognition of the Italian poet Ada Negri, she played roles in a number of Polish films including *Żona* (The Wife), *Bestia* (The Beast), *Studenci* (The Students), and *Kochanka apasza* (A Street Ruffian's Lover). With fame came an opportunity to move to Berlin in 1917 to appear in films under the acclaimed directors Max Reinhardt and Ernst Lubitsch. Her roles in *Carmen* (1918) and *Madam DuBarry* (1919) brought great popularity, with each being released in the U.S. under the titles *Gypsy Blood* and *Passion*. Her popularity in these roles brought her to Hollywood where she signed a contract with Paramount Pictures in 1923, a year after Reinhardt and Lubitsch, who pre-

Pola Negri, popular actress and early screen *femme fatale* (*LC*).

ceded her to the U.S. In America she quickly earned a reputation as the *femme fatale* of silent films, as well as gaining notoriety for affairs with several of Hollywood's glamorous leading men including Charlie Chaplin and Rudolph Valentino. Among her more than three dozen films were the especially popular *The Spanish Dancer* (1923), *Forbidden Paradise* (1924), *A Woman of the World* (1925), and *Hotel Imperial* (1927). At one time she was said to be the most popular and richest actress of her day, but the advent of sound film and the Hays Code for motion pictures in 1930 caused her career to decline. "Talkies" revealed her heavy accent which audiences did not embrace, while the Hays Code ban on "scenes of passion" and "lustful" kissing greatly curtailed her *femme fatale* screen image. Negri starred in her first talking movie, *Loves of an Actress*, in 1928, but made her last American film, the "talkie" *The Woman from Moscow*, in the same year. Losing her fortune in the Wall Street Crash of 1929, she returned to Europe to make *The Way of Lost Souls* in England in the same year. Thereafter she made only a few films in England and Germany. Although her role in the Willi Forst movie *Mazurka* led to a brief resurgence in popularity, she fled Germany for France in 1938, then moved to Portugal and from there, in 1941, returned to the United States. After a small role in the 1943 film *Hi Diddle Diddle*, she became a U.S. citizen in 1951 and appeared in her final film, *The Moon-Spinners*, in 1964. She received a German award for her contributions to film and is enshrined with a star on the Hollywood Walk of Fame. In retirement she moved to San Antonio, Texas, where she died from pneumonia. Her life was the subject of the film *Life Is a Dream in Cinema: Pola Negri* directed by Mariusz Kotowski.—*James S. Pula*

SOURCES: Pola Negri, *Memoirs of a Star* (New York: Doubleday Press, 1970); Wiesława Czapińska, *Pola Negri—polska królowa Hollywood* (Warsaw: Philip Wilson, 1996).

Nemkovich, Robert Michael (b. Grove City, Pennsylvania, November 27, 1942; d.—). Bishop. Nemkovich attended Youngstown University and Westfield State College, after which he prepared for the priesthood in the **Polish National Catholic Church** at **Savonarola Theological Seminary** in Scranton, PA. He was elected Bishop Ordinary of the Western Diocese based in Chicago at the Eighteenth General Synod in 1990. He was elected Prime Bishop at the Twenty-First General Synod in 2002.— *Theodore L. Zawistowski*

SOURCE: "Appointed Senior Priest," *Straż*, August 28, 1980, 4.

Nestorowicz, Melania (Melania Habdank Białobrzeska; b. Warsaw, Poland, May 30, 1876; d. Wilkes-Barre, Pennsylvania, February 21, 1951). Writer, Polonia activist. Nesterowicz originally intended to study medicine in Switzerland, but her future was irrevocably changed when, in 1894, at the age of seventeen, she married pharmacist Stefan Nesterowicz who was 25 years her senior. As a result of her husband's business failures, the Nesterowicz family emigrated to the growing Polish settlement of Curitiba, Brazil. Discouraged by the backbreaking work there, around 1902 Stefan, Melania, and their two children came to the United States. The example of Antoni and Michał Paryski (see **Antoni Paryski**), successful booksellers and publishers in America, set Nesterowicz and her husband on a new path. Though Stefan periodically sought work as a chemist and pharmacist, both he and his wife would spend most of their working lives in journalism. Stefan became a traveling book agent as well as writer and editor for ***Ameryka-Echo***, Antoni Paryski's hugely successful newspaper and book publishing company in Toledo, Ohio. Melania Nesterowicz began as an editor for Paryski, but was soon publishing her own political tracts and short works of fiction. Her early stories, like *Z życia analfabety* (From the Life of an Illiterate, 1907), reflected the issues facing the immigrant community of which she was a part. Her first job in America had been sewing hats for thirty cents a day, and she was always sympathetic to the struggles of immigrant families, and especially those of working women. These concerns were also reflected in the editorials and articles she published, either anonymously or under the pseudonym "Jan Kłos."

In 1917 Nesterowicz began working for Buffalo's ***Dziennik dla Wszystkich*** (Everyone's Daily News), where she served as editor-in-chief from 1921 to 1933, and to which she continued contributing long after. It was in Buffalo that she produced her most important works of fiction, inspired by the real-life dramas she encountered as a journalist. Novels like *Stella z Buffalo* (Stella from Buffalo, 1926–27), *Hot-cha-cha* (1934), and *Tajemnica nieślubnego dziecka* (The Secret of the Illegitimate Child, year unknown) told the stories of second-generation Polish American "flappers" as they sought careers, romance, and autonomy, often in conflict with their ethnic communities. Her most popular novel, *Sprzedawaczka z Broadwayu* (The Salesgirl from Broadway, 1932) was published in multiple editions and was turned into a play. It even found a contemporary audience when it was reprinted in Detroit's *Świat Polski* (Polish World) in the 1990s. About these novels, Nesterowicz said, "I didn't care at all about any kind of renown as a novel writer.... I cared above all about a pedagogical goal." She received numerous honors from the Polish government, including the Polish Legionnaire's Cross (1925), the Polonia Restituta (1936), the Independence Cross (1930), and the Silver Laurel of Merit from the Academy of Literature (1938). Even with these recognitions, "J.K.," writing for Detroit's ***Dziennik Polski*** (Polish Daily News) in 1947, chastised American Polonia for neglecting a woman who had served her community for decades while earning less than her male counterparts.—*Karen Majewski*

SOURCE: Karen Majewski, *Traitors and True Poles: Narrating a Polish-American Identity, 1880–1939* (Athens: Ohio University Press, 2003).

Neumann, Anna (b. Osiecin, Poland, July 23, 1860; d. Chicago, Illinois, April 4, 1947). Polonia activist. Neumann came to America as a child and settled with her parents in Chicago. Employed as a seamstress, she joined the **Polish Women's Alliance**, the first independent Polish women's "fraternal" organization in the United States, in 1900, two years after its creation. In 1902 she was elected president of the fraternal, succeeding **Stefania Chmielińska**, the founding leader of the Alliance. Neumann served as president between 1902 and 1906 and again from 1909 to 1918. She was a particularly prominent leader in the Polish American community as the PWA's representative in a number of significant groups working on behalf of the cause of Polish independence and on humanitarian matters during the First World War (1914–18). She is perhaps best remembered for her decision to volunteer the then sizable sum of $3,000 on behalf of the PWA to a request for funds for the cause of Polish independence made by **Ignacy Jan Paderewski** at a meeting held with **Polonia** fraternal leaders in New York in September 1914, shortly after the outbreak of the war. The other leaders, all of them men, demurred, stating they needed to receive the approval of their fellow officers before acting on the request. But Neumann immediately declared her organization's support of Paderewski's request. The maestro in reply declared: "Women aren't content to advise; they act" ("Kobiety nie radza, a czynia"). Under Neumann's leadership, the Polish Women's Alliance raised thousands of dollars for Polish independence through its Fundusz Bojowy (War Fund). Neumann was the Polish Women's Alliance representative in the **Polish Central Relief Committee**, the largely immigrant Polonia's main humanitarian aid organization, and the Polish **National Department** (Wydział Narodowy), the community's chief political action federation throughout World War I. Following her retirement as

PWA president, Neumann continued on as its honorary president for nearly all the remaining years of her long life. She was later appointed the PWA's librarian and helped found its museum, located in the fraternal's national headquarters. She was honored by the government of independent Poland with the Gold Cross of Achievement.—*Donald E. Pienkos*

SOURCE: Angela Pienkos and Donald Pienkos, "*In The Ideals of Women is the Strength of a Nation*": *A History of the Polish Women's Alliance of America* (Boulder, CO: East European Monographs, 2003).

New Immigration (Nowa Emigracja). This is a reference to the Polish wartime refugees and displaced persons (DPs), who arrived in the United States during and immediately after World War II (1939–53). According to the Immigration and Naturalization Service statistics, about 15,000 Polish quota immigrants were allowed into the U.S. in 1939–45. About 17,000 more came in 1945–48. As a result of the Displaced Persons Act of 1948, and its 1950 Amendments, in 1948–51, close to 140,000 DPs born in Poland were resettled in the U.S. An estimated 40,000 of them were Polish Jews, who settled mostly in Jewish communities. The refugee wave was part of the larger Polish postwar Diaspora of more than 400,000 Poles dispersed on all continents. Their decision to stay in exile was mostly politically motivated, as Poland became dominated by Communism. The unwritten mission of the Diaspora focused on the refugees' responsibility to work from abroad on behalf of a free Poland; to represent the Polish cause to the other nations through the active support of the political lobby efforts by the London-based Polish government-in-exile and its political parties; to keep the culture, heritage, and language alive, and transmit them to the next generation; and to care for the prewar and war history of the generation.

Most members of this distinctive immigrant wave were people who spent their lives in the independent Poland of the interwar period. The majority of DPs were of either peasant or working class background, while the wartime exiles and a minority among DPs represented intellectual and political elites. Veterans were present both among the DPs and in a group of over 11,000, who came together with their families from Great Britain due to the special provisions of the 1950 Displaced Persons Act Amendments. The majority of the refugees were relatively young; there were among them a large number of children, who survived the war or were born in the DP camps.

THE WARTIME EXILES

The wartime wave, which settled predominantly in the New York and Chicago areas, although numerically weak, spearheaded the formulation of the exile mission and created the first postwar refugee communities in the U.S. In New York the refugees established the Polish War Refugee Association in the United States (Zrzeszenie Uchodźców Wojennych z Polski w Stanach Zjednoczonych), headed first by Stefan Zagórski, and then Władysław Korczak. In Chicago a smaller Circle of Polish Refugees (Koło Uchodźców Polskich) was formed. During the war and until July 1945, when the West withdrew its recognition, Polish refugees in the Diaspora could count on modest subsidies of the Polish London government. In the U.S. a charitable Polish American organization, the **Polish American Council** (Rada Polonii Amerykańskiej), supported both refugee organizations with money distributed to the sick, destitute, old, and unable to work in 1940–45. Despite financial problems and frequent health care issues, the memoirs of the refugees (see for example Irena Lorentowicz, **Alexander Janta**, **Jan Lechoń**, Klaudiusz Hrabyk) depict a community which kept together and maintained an active social life. The Polish Consulate General in New York became a center for information exchange, as did a neighboring restaurant, Ognisko, while hotels operated by refugees in the Adironacks and Sea Cliff in Long Island became popular vacation spots.

The wartime exile group included a disproportionate number of prewar Polish intelligentsia, intellectuals, artists, journalists, scholars and scientists, as well as politicians. Some became founders of the **National Committee of Americans of Polish Descent** (Komitet Narodowy Amerykanów Polskiego Pochodzenia, or KNAPP), a political organization established in New York in 1942. Among its creators were **Ignacy Matuszewski**, **Wacław Jędrzejewicz**, and **Henryk Floyar-Raychman**, all former ministers in the prewar government. The same group also became involved in the establishment of the **Józef Piłsudski Institute** in New York in 1943. In 1942, Polish scholars in exile established in New York the **Polish Institute of Arts and Sciences in America** (PIASA; in Polish, Polski Instytut Naukowy w Ameryce, PIN). Among the founding members were historians **Oskar Halecki** and Jan Kucharzewski, legal historian Rafał Taubenschlag, anthropologist **Bronisław Malinowski**, historian of Slavic literatures **Wacław Lednicki**, and chemist Wojciech Świętosławski. One of the most active PIASA committees focused on research on Polish immigration and was in time transformed into the **Polish American Historical Association** (PAHA).

The wartime exiles also established the Polski Teatr Narodowy (the Polish National Theater) in New York, and later the Polski Teatr Artystów (Polish Artists' Theater), which featured works of some of the most popular prewar actors, actresses, and directors, as well as stage designers, including Jadwiga Smosarska, Janina Wilczówna, Zofia Nakoneczna, Lunia Nestorówna, Karin Tiche, Stanisława Nowicka, Maria Modzelewska, **Antoni Cwojdziński**, and Irena Lorentowicz. *Tygodnik Polski* (The Polish Weekly) dominated the New York and Diaspora literary scenes from its inception in January 1943, until it closed for financial reasons in 1947. Remaining under the editorship of renowned poet Jan Lechoń, *Tygodnik* featured contributions from exiled poets **Kazimierz Wierzyński** and **Józef Wittlin**, writer Zenon Kosidowski, and a plethora of other essayists, journalists, intellectuals and politicians. Throughout the entire period of the weekly's existence, Lechoń used it to formulate and propagate a concept of the postwar Diaspora seen as a conscious continuation of the ideals of the Great Emigration, which followed the November Uprising of 1830, and called for the exiles to take on the responsibility of working for Poland from abroad. The majority of the refugees, who initially had planned to return to Poland after the war's end, remained in exile after 1945.

THE WARTIME DISPLACEMENT AND DISPLACED PERSONS CAMPS

As a result of the outbreak of the war in September 1939, several million Polish citizens found themselves outside Polish borders. They included soldiers and officers of the Polish Armed Forces in the West, for example a Polish army in France, the First Polish Corp and the First Polish Armored Division, Carpathian Brigade and other units under the British command, as well as prisoners of war from the September Campaign in 1939, placed by the Germans in *Oflags* and *Stalags*, or forced to work in the German war economy. Some Polish citizens from the areas directly annexed to the Reich were forcefully conscripted into German military units. Groups of Polish children were removed from Poland for Germanization purposes, and families from ethnically mixed areas resettled in the German territories. The largest category of migrants from Nazi-occupied Poland were forced laborers, captured in Poland and transported to the Reich to perform slave labor in German agriculture and industry. According to some estimates, close to three million Poles were at some point employed in German war economy. Political prisoners and prisoners of the concentration camps constituted another large group deported to Germany, perhaps as large as

200,000, in addition to about 68,000 Poles deported from Warsaw after the collapse of the Warsaw Uprising in 1944. In the last month of the war, more Polish prisoners were transported from Nazi prisons and concentration camps in Poland to Germany.

Many civilians also fled Poland through different channels. A large number of refugees followed the retreating Polish government to Romania and Hungary, others crossed illegally through the so-called "green border," and some managed to leave with false passports at the very outset of occupation. They joined those Poles who were temporarily outside of Poland when the war broke out. After getting out of Poland, civilian refugees joined the Polish army, established successful intelligence networks, joined local resistance movements, and continued to work for the government-in-exile. They established communities complete with elementary and high schools for children, higher learning institutions and courses for adults, press and publishing, political parties, scientific associations, and other social, cultural and educational organizations. Such communities existed in the various stages of their displacement in Hungary, Romania, France, Switzerland, and Great Britain.

Poles from the Polish territories under Soviet occupation also faced forced deportations. About 15,000 Polish officers were murdered by the Soviet NKVD in the **Katyń** massacre in 1940. Approximately 350,000 civilian Poles were placed in Soviet prisons and penal colonies. In 1939–41, Soviet authorities deported some 1,500,000 Polish citizens to labor camps in Siberia, where they were faced with brutal labor, harsh climate, poor living conditions, and starvation. Following the Sikorski-Maiski pact of 1941, the deportees were allowed to leave the camps. Large groups joined General Władysław Anders' Polish Army, others were eventually evacuated from the Soviet Union. The evacuees were then placed in refugee camps in Iran; India; eastern parts of Africa, including Uganda, Kenya, and Tanganyika; the Middle East, including Lebanon; as well as New Zealand and Mexico. Those serving with the Second Polish Corps were incorporated into the British forces in the Middle East and participated in the African and Italian campaigns.

At the end of the war, about ten million displaced people of various nationalities waited to return home to their countries. Poles were a part of this group. In May 1945, almost 1.9 million Poles were stranded in Germany: about 1.2 million in the American, British, and French occupation zones, and approximately 700,000 in the Soviet occupation zone. Smaller groups of Poles were also in Austria and Italy (excluding the Second Corp). The great majority of the DPs spent the war as forced laborers, but there were also others: prisoners of concentrations camps, POWs, September and Warsaw Uprising veterans, Polish Armed Forces in the West, and others. DPs of different nationalities were placed in the so-called Displaced Persons camps, remaining under the supervision of the Allied occupation forces, and until 1947, the United Nations Relief and Rehabilitation Administration (UNRRA). In 1945–47, UNRRA repatriated to Poland about 550,000 Polish DPs from the American, British, and French zones in Germany and more than 15,000 from the camps in Austria and Italy. The Soviets repatriated 700,000 Poles from their zone. As a result close to 1.4 million Poles returned to Poland (74 percent of all the Poles who were in the DP camps in May 1945). In 1947, UNRRA was replaced by the International Refugee Organization (IRO). In 1947–1951, the IRO resettled more than 350,000 Polish citizens in 47 countries. The largest groups settled in the U.S., Australia, Canada, Israel (Polish Jews), Great Britain (where the Second Polish Corp as well as refugees from the Middle East, Africa, India, and other places, were resettled), France, Belgium, the Netherlands, Brazil, Argentina, Paraguay, and Venezuela. They became the backbone of the postwar Polish political Diaspora.

The DP camp experience became a direct preparation for the life in exile for Polish refugees. In most of the camps, Polish DPs had to deal with poor living conditions, inadequate food and clothing supplies, and often unfriendly attitudes of the UNRRA officials as well as German civilians. They were plagued by health problems, uncertainty and anxiety about their future, post traumatic stress disorders, and apathy resulting from the lack of meaningful occupation and dependence on the benevolence of international organizations. Despite these adverse conditions, Polish DPs made the camps into strong and vibrant exile communities, complete with a vast network of schools of different levels, youth scouting organizations, trade organizations, press and publishing, political parties, self-government, religious life, as well as flourishing cultural and sport activities. The DP camp sojourn then became an important stage in the development and adoption of the exile mission.

THE AMERICAN RESETTLEMENT EXPERIENCE

In December 1945, President Harry S Truman issued an executive order (the so-called Truman Directive) that allowed 40,000 DPs of different nationalities to come to the U.S. in 1947–48. In June 1948, the U.S. Congress passed the Displaced Persons Act (amended in 1950), which allowed 400,000 DPs to enter the country over the four-year period till the end of 1951. Polish Americans, led by the **Polish American Congress** (PAC) actively participated in lobbying efforts organized by different American ethnic groups to pass these laws. According to the INS statistics, under the Displaced Persons Act between June 1948 and June 1953, some 140,000 Polish citizens entered the U.S.

The resettlement program was possible due to the work of three major Polonia resettlement agencies working with the federal Displaced Persons Commission and other accredited organizations: Rada Polonii (**American Relief for Poland**), the Polish Immigration Committee, and the **American Committee for the Resettlement of Polish Displaced Persons** (ACRPDP). The majority of refugees settled in large urban centers with Polonia populations such as Chicago, Detroit, New York, Milwaukee, and Buffalo. Those initially resettled in rural areas (favored by the special agricultural provisions in the Displaced Persons Act), gradually migrated to the cities, attracted by better employment opportunities and contact with other Poles. This tremendous resettlement effort became a success story despite time pressure, complicated legal and bureaucratic requirements, limited finances, and overstretched human resources. In general, serious conflicts between individual sponsors and DPs were infrequent, and usually stemmed from misinterpretation of rules and regulations guiding the resettlement program.

ORGANIZATIONAL LIFE OF NOWA EMIGRACJA

Some DPs joined older Polonia religious and lay organizations and parishes upon their arrival in the U.S., but many preferred to establish their own organizations, which often revitalized and reinvigorated Polish American communities, although it also resulted in a certain organizational duality within Polonia. An example of the self-help organization was Chicago's Samopomoc Nowej Emigracji, formed in 1949. It assisted with job and housing searches, and translation of documents, established its own library and a popular news program, and sponsored dance parties and performances by Polish exiled artists. Stowarzyszenie Nowych Amerykanów (Association of New Americans), a similar organization in Milwaukee, Wisconsin, provided the new arrivals with pertinent information, English-language classes, and financial loans, and organized picnics, theater performances, and even sponsored a choir and a soccer team. Both organizations relied on cooperation with old Polonia, using existing facilities, and collaborating with some of the leaders.

The Ogiński Choir is another example of the cultural organization, transplanted to the New York area from the DP camp in Wildflecken, Germany, where it was first established in 1945. The choir, still in existence, gained much popularity and performed on various occasions for both Old and New Polonia. Several theaters featuring Polish prewar artists and directors also performed in Polonia centers. Nasza Reduta entertained Polonia audiences in Chicago in 1950–73. Other theater groups and variety shows included: Teatr Dramatyczny (Dramatic Theater); Teatr Aktora (Actor's Theater); Radiowy Teatr Wyobraźni (Radio Theater of Imagination), Teatr Ref-Rena (Ref-Ren's Theater); Wesoła Czwórka (Jolly Foursome), and Wesoła Lwowska Fala (Jolly Lwów Wave). Theater groups were also active in New York, Detroit, Los Angeles, and Boston. Some traveled with their performances to smaller Polonia communities.

Other Nowa Emigracja organizations had an educational or professional character. Their membership level and longevity differed greatly. Some examples include Polski Związek Akademików (Polish Academic Association); Koło Byłych Wychowawców i Wychowanków Polskich Szkół Średnich z Niemiec (Circle of Former Teachers and Pupils of the Polish High Schools from Germany); Stowarzyszenie Prawników Polskich w Stanach Zjednoczonych (Association of Polish Jurists in the United States), and Związek Lekarzy Polskich na Wychodźstwie (Association of Polish Physicians in Exile). The veteran associations constituted another large organizational group. Stowarzyszenie Polskich Kombatantów (SPK, the **Association of Polish ex–Combatants**) undertook mutual welfare, social, and political goals, and for a time, competed with the **Polish Army Veterans Association in America** (Stowarzyszenie Weteranów Armii Polskiej, SWAP), an older **Polonia** organization, which also attracted a sizeable number of postwar veterans. Among other veteran organizations were: Stowarzyszenie Lotników Polskich (Association of Polish Pilots); Związek Polskich Spadochroniarzy w Ameryce (Polish Airborne Forces Veterans Association in America); Samopomoc Marynarki Wojennej (Polish Navy Veterans Association of America); Okręg Armii Krajowej na Stany Zjednoczone (Home Army Veterans Association); Stowarzyszenie Saperów Polskich w USA (Polish Sappers Veterans Association in the USA), and Stowarzyszenie Byłych Żołnierzy

1.szej Dywizji Pancernej (First Armored Division Veterans Association).

Scouting leaders and educators, who developed the vigorous scouting movement in many exiled communities during the war, including the DP camps, re-established it later in the United States. Separate scouting troops for the New Emigration youth appeared in Polonia communities immediately after the resettlement. According to some estimates, approximately 20,000 young people moved through the ranks of Harcerstwo (Scouts; see **Scouting**) in 1949–77. Many of the leaders were women, who were also represented among teachers and supporters of the **Saturday schools** for Polish children and youth. Both scouting and the schools aimed at transmitting Polish language and heritage as well as patriotic messages to the young generation, expected to continue the exile mission.

The majority of DPs claimed attachment to Roman Catholicism as their religion. However, although many DPs joined the traditional Polish parishes in the Polonia communities, the centrality of the parish in the lives of the new arrivals as compared with the old Polonia, had diminished. Although only a fraction of exiled intelligentsia was openly anti-clerical, and most attended church, they often favored lay political and professional organizations over the parish structure. Those DPs who moved farther away from the Polonia enclaves, found it difficult to travel longer distances to participate in parish activities. Some sociological studies suggested that only about 39 percent of new immigrants in the early 1970s belonged to a Polish American parish and that about 22 percent did not belong to any parish.

POLITICAL TIES TO POLONIA AND THE DIASPORA

Most postwar refugees claimed political motivation as justification for their decision to remain in exile. It is difficult to clearly distinguish between such motivation and other motives for emigration, such as economic or individual reasons. Since the exile mission placed the responsibility of political activism on the refugees, several centers of political influence competed for the Diaspora leadership in this area. The most important was the Polish government-in-exile in London, since 1949 split into two opposing factions. The Polish political parties, which existed in Europe, all had their counterparts in the United States also, although significantly less numerous and less active.

Although Polish refugees who resettled in the U.S. mostly professed their loyalty to the London government, they were fully aware of

their unique position as potential lobby leaders vis-à-vis the American government, perceived as a world leader in the fight with Communism. They positioned themselves as uncompromising anti-communists, supportive of the American Cold War aims, and determined to keep the Polish cause in the international spotlight. They made use of the National Committee for a Free Europe (NCFE; Komitet Wolnej Europy, KWE), established in 1949, secretly sponsored by the CIA and the State Department. They also actively participated in the international lobby organization **Assembly of Captive European Nations** (ACEN), as well as explored possibilities of forming Polish military forces during the Korean War. As illustrated in the so-called **Wyrwa Affair**, the questions of loyalty towards the American government versus the Polish government in London were complicated ones and had a potential of dividing the exile community.

The largest political umbrella organization in Polonia, the **Polish American Congress** (PAC) was established in 1944 with the support of the wartime exiles gathered within KNAPP. The postwar arrivals quickly became very active within its ranks, undertaking political cooperation with the Old Polonia leaders and utilizing the Old Polonia structures to pursue their political goals of work for Poland. By 1978, eleven of the 29 presidents of the PAC state divisions were from the postwar wave. Throughout the 1980s, the PAC's committees on Polish affairs were dominated by the exiles who designed the main directions of the PAC policies towards Poland, wrote memoranda and statements, lobbied the American government, and generally contributed to the shape of U.S.–Poland relations in the postwar decades. One of the main architects of those policies was **Kazimierz Łukomski**, the PAC's vice president since 1968, and the Chair of the PAC Polish Affairs Committee. In the 1970s, the exiles involved the PAC in international initiatives to unite and coordinate efforts of "Polonias in the Free World." In 1975, an international meeting "Polonia 75" took place in Washington, D.C., sponsored by the PAC and Polish Canadian Congress. The next such meeting, "Polonia 1978–Polonia Jutra," in Toronto brought together 175 delegates from 18 countries in addition to representatives of the largest Diaspora organizations, such as press, scouting, and veteran organizations. The conference established a Coordinating Council of Polonia of the Free World, which held meetings attended by the PAC representatives in Toronto, Rome, and London in the 1970s and 80s.

The Diasporic ties of Polish exiles in the

U.S. also had private and personal dimensions, as they maintained relationships with others resettled in different places in the world. The exchange of information, ideas, and cultural expressions happened during frequent letter writing, travels, and visits. These bonds were strengthened by the widely circulating press and publications, which often focused on the common generational experience as well as elements of the exile mission. Polish exiled intellectuals and artists who settled in the U.S. participated in several international meetings of the postwar Diaspora: in London in 1957; New York in 1966; the Congress of Polish Science and Culture in Exile in 1970; and the Congress of Polish Culture in Exile in 1985.

TENSIONS BETWEEN NEW AND OLD POLONIA

The work for Poland usually united Old and New Polonia. There were also numerous examples of good will and cooperation on both sides, with many individuals demonstrating their understanding, friendship, and ethnic solidarity. Organizations too made special efforts to extend their welcome to members of other waves and generations, willingly shared resources, and collaborated on common projects. However, the relationships between the two waves were often marked by a certain degree of tension, which stemmed from several different sources. First, when Polonia activists lobbied in support of the community for new legislation and later rallied around the resettlement program, they developed a polarized image of the refugees: as helpless victims of the international organizations' mistreatment on the one hand, and as sturdy, energetic and anticommunist immigrant material ready to contribute to America on the other. In the propaganda efforts, this image became confusing to an average Polish American and sometimes even lost its human dimensions. Additionally, the two groups had very little knowledge about each other's wartime experiences. Polish Americans found it especially difficult to fully comprehend the impact of traumatic events on the DPs, including death, destruction, military duty, concentration camps, family separation, loss of one's country, years of suffering and displacement, as well as survivor's guilt. The refugees bristled when told to forget about their past and look only into the future. The two cohorts also had only limited knowledge about the history of Polonia on the one hand, and the history of the independent Polish state in the interwar period on the other. The refugees did not realize how much work and effort it took Polonia to build their communities and get established within the American

society. Polish Americans imagined that the refugees came from the same Poland of remote villages their ancestors had left and found it hard to believe in the progress and change of the interwar period.

Although both groups looked forward to their reunion on American soil, their mutual expectations were unrealistic. The Old Polonia anticipated welcoming their social replicas, grateful for the help and ready to start at the bottom and slowly work their way up without any complaints. The DPs imagined Polonia communities as more affluent, powerful, and politically involved than they really were. Some expected that Polonia would show signs of gratitude for the refugee war contributions and that the country that endorsed betrayal at Yalta had an obligation to now extend a helping hand to its victims. These refugees who had acquired education, work, and language skills during different stages of their displacement and especially in the DP camps, hoped to reestablish their lives at higher levels than the unskilled ground work.

As mentioned before, the demands of the resettlement program also created a conflict prone environment. In the rush to meet the DP Act expiration deadlines, it was easy to misinterpret the rules as well as intentions of both the resettlement agencies and Polish-American sponsors, and the newly arrived DPs. Both groups assumed that the other had more obligations than they really did, and accused each other of ungratefulness, failing to fulfill their promises, exploitation and manipulation.

Differences between the needs of refugees as a special immigrant category and second and later generation ethnics also played a role in the development of tensions. For the refugees, the experience of migration was usually much more acute, as they were forced rather than chose to leave their homelands. They arrived with fewer resources and information, and more psychological baggage, including often severe post-traumatic stress disorder. Practical concerns of finding jobs and housing and establishing themselves in the new environment became their primary goals. They preferred to associate themselves with others who shared their experiences. Political motivations of their migration decision demanded that they get involved in the implementation of the exile mission. On the other hand, second and later generation immigrants, such as Polish Americans, who function well within their societies, focused more on the preservation of cultural heritage frequently defined as ethnic traditions developed already post-migration. They might be much less interested in political activities, as they relegated

such concerns to their leaders and their government.

The level of assimilation and language maintenance created additional frictions. While the refugees saw themselves as "really Polish," they questioned the Polishness of older immigrants, charging them with being too Americanized. They ridiculed their language skills, abhorred their low intellectual level and negligible position within the American society. Some tensions stemmed from the class differences. The painful loss of social and professional status by the intelligentsia and the inability of mostly working class Polish Americans to relate to their experience further contributed to the rift between them. While some of the intelligentsia contemptuously rejected peasant/working class culture and habits of Polish Americans, members of Old Polonia derisively suggested that the "gentlemen and ladies" from Poland would finally have a good chance to learn how to work hard.

The tensions between Old and New Polonia were played out on the pages of the Polish-American press in a lively debate about the meaning of Polishness and immigrant obligations, during meetings of Polonia organizations, when both groups competed for leadership, as well as on a neighborhood and family level. The difficulties in the adjustment between more established immigrant waves and the refugee newcomers were not unique for American Polonia. Polish communities in other countries experienced them too, as did other ethnic groups in the U.S., for example Ukrainians, Jews, Latvians, Hungarians, and others.

Similar tensions marked relationships between the Polish postwar exiles and later waves of Polish immigrants, whom the exiles often saw as tainted by their upbringing in Communist Poland and accused of lack of patriotism, insularism, and materialism. They resented the newcomers' attempts to speak for Poland and to reach for leadership without proper understanding of the functioning of both Polonia and the American political system. These tensions decreased when both groups worked on behalf of Poland during the Solidarity and Martial Law period, organizing a vigorous political lobby and humanitarian help for the Polish nation in the 1980s.

TOWARDS INDEPENDENT POLAND

The year 1956 was a turning point in the history of postwar Diaspora. By then it became obvious that a speedy return to a free Poland was not realistic and the Cold War was there to stay. The outbreak of the politically motivated working class protests in Poznań and the October events in Warsaw proved the political maturity and determination of the Polish nation, moving the Diaspora's efforts to the margins. In the United States Old and New Polonia came together to protest the conditions in Poland and to lobby on behalf of the Polish nation. The Diaspora's efforts were now to focus on diplomatic activities, aimed at keeping the Polish cause alive and in the international spotlight. When the passport requirements were liberalized in the late 1950s, some former refugees began visiting Poland and reestablished relations with their families, while making a careful distinction between help for the Polish nation and the rejection of contacts with Poland's Communist authorities. Only a small number returned permanently. Both Old and New Polonia were challenged by the arrival of the new immigrant waves: mostly economic immigrants in the 1970s and Solidarity era refugees in the 1980s. The influence of the London government in the Diaspora steadily decreased and postwar exiles accepted American citizenship.

In 1989, Poles in Poland overthrew the communist government. In December, 1990, Ryszard Kaczorowski, the last president-in-exile, handed over the insignia of the state to the democratically elected President of the Republic of Poland, Lech Wałęsa. Polish postwar exiles supported political and economic changes in Poland, lobbying for foreign investments, organizing cultural exchanges, and strengthening a positive image of Poland abroad. They also became involved in activities designed to preserve and propagate their historical experience and make it a part of the larger Polish history, which was previously denied to them. In the United States, the exiles saw their second generation come to maturity, as they now treated America as their second home. Very few returned to live in Poland permanently, although they frequently visited. Never entirely integrated into the Old Polonia community, they continued to identify themselves mostly with the postwar diaspora.—
Anna D. Jaroszyńska-Kirchmann

SOURCES: Anna D. Jaroszynska-Kirchmann, *The Exile Mission: The Polish Political Diaspora and Polish Americans, 1939–1956* (Athens: Ohio University Press, 2004); Czesław Łuczak, *Polacy w okupowanych Niemczech, 1945–1949* (Poznań: Pracownia Serwisu Oprogramowania, 1993); Mary Patrice Erdmans, *Opposite Poles: Immigrants and Ethnics in Polish Chicago, 1976–1990* (University Park: Pennsylvania State University Press, 1998); Danuta Mostwin, *The Transplanted Family: A Study of Social Adjustment of the Polish Immigrant Family to the United States after the Second World War* (New York: Arno Press, 1980); Elżbieta Wróbel and Janusz Wróbel, *Rozproszeni po świecie: obozy i osiedla uchodźców polskich ze Związku Sowieckiego, 1942–1950* (Chicago: Panorama, 1992); Stanislaus A. Blejwas, "Old and New Polonias: Tensions Within an Ethnic Community," *Polish American Studies*, Vol. 38, no. 2 (Autumn 1981), 57–60.

Neyman, Jerzy (b. Bendery, Russia, April 16, 1894; d. Oakland, California, August 5, 1981). Mathematician. Descended from Polish nobility, Neyman was born in the Russian Empire. As a lawyer, his father traveled frequently, moving the family from Bendery to Kherson, Melitopol, and Simferopol in the Crimea. When Neyman's father died of a heart attack in 1906, the family moved to Kharkov where Neyman's mother had family. In 1912, he undertook studies at the University of Kharkov (later Maksim Gorky University). Briefly, Neyman demonstrated an interest in physics, but soon shifted his attention to mathematics under the tutelage of the eminent S. N. Bernstein. In 1916, he became a lecturer at the Kharkov Institute of Technology, a position he held until 1921; with the outbreak of war and revolution Neyman, identified as an enemy of the state due to his Polish noble heritage, was temporarily imprisoned. In 1920 he moved to Poland upon the outbreak of the Russo-Polish War. There, he was employed as a statistical analyst for the National Agricultural Institute in Bydgoszcz and in 1923 became director of the Biometric Laboratory of the Nencki Institute for Experimental Biology in Warsaw. He also offered lectures at the Central College there. Upon completing his doctorate in 1924, Neyman began teaching statistics and mathematics at the University of Warsaw. A postdoctoral fellowship earned one year later allowed him to travel to England to conduct research at the Biometric Laboratory at University College. Under the mentorship of Karl Pearson, he met his son, Egon, with whom he undertook a five-year-long correspondence after Neyman's return to Poland. Together they published two joint papers and collaborated on what became known as the Neyman-Pearson theory, which posits that margins of error can be reduced if the optimal test is chosen to examine a statistical hypothesis. In 1933 Pearson invited Neyman to London in the capacity of visiting professor at University College. Three years later, he had achieved a full professorship. In 1934 Neyman developed a theoretical framework for cluster sampling—a valuable contribution to modern public polling as used by Gallup. Three years later, he received and accepted a lectureship offer from the University of California, Berkeley. Neyman once again taught courses in statistics and mathematics, and was on course to establish a center to train American statisticians, but the outbreak of the Second World War led him instead to assist in military research, applying his knowledge and work with statistics to bombsight and target accuracy. After the war, he served as an election observer in Greece before returning to

America where he finally succeeded in establishing statistics as a department separate from mathematics at Berkeley in 1955. He is remembered as having laid the groundwork for the development of sequential inference, statistical decision theory, and asymptotic theory. Throughout his career, Neyman authored more than 200 research papers, monographs, articles, and reports. For his numerous scholarly contributions, among other honors he was awarded the prestigious Cleaveland Prize of the American Association of the Advancement of Science (1958), the Guy Medal from the Royal Statistical Society (1966), and the Medal of Science from President Lyndon B. Johnson (1969). In addition, he received several honorary degrees including doctorates from the University of Chicago, the University of California, Berkeley, and the University of Warsaw.—*Krystyna Cap*

SOURCES: D. G. Kendall, et al., "Jerzy Neyman. 16 April 1894–5 August 1981," *Biographical Memoirs of Fellows of the Royal Society*, Vol. 28 (November 1982), 379–412; Constance Reid, *Neyman—From Life* (New York: Springer-Verlag, 1982).

Niekro, Joe *see* **Phil Niekro.**

Niekro, Phil (b. Blaine, Ohio, April 1, 1939; d.—). Baseball player. Of Polish descent on both sides of his family, Phil Niekro carved out a long and successful career as a major league pitcher. Playing for 24 seasons from 1964 to 1987, primarily for the Milwaukee and Atlanta Braves, Niekro won 318 games, and was named to five National League All-Star squads. He pitched a no-hitter in 1973, won five Gold Glove awards for fielding excellence at his position, and in various seasons led his league in wins, earned run average, and won-lost percentage. His Braves teams reached the postseason playoffs on two occasions. Niekro was a right hander who specialized in throwing the knuckleball, an unusual and deceptive pitch that can be tossed with relatively little stress on the arm. This allowed him to play in the major leagues until the advanced age of 48, and he ranks near the top of many lifetime statistical categories. Upon retiring from baseball, Niekro worked as a consultant to a toy manufacturer, and took part in charitable and community service.

His younger brother Joe Niekro (b. Martins Ferry, Ohio, November 7, 1944) also recorded a substantial career as a major league right-handed knuckleball hurler, playing 22 seasons for seven teams from 1967 to 1988. *The Sporting News* selected Joe as the National League pitcher of the year in 1979, when he won 21 games for Houston, and he contributed a victory to the Minnesota Twins' World Series championship in 1988. Between them, the brothers Niekro won 539 games, more than any other fraternal pair. Both Niekros have been inducted into the National Polish-American Sports Hall of Fame, and Phil won election to the National Baseball Hall of Fame in 1997.—*Neal Pease*

SOURCE: Gary Caruso, *The Braves Encyclopedia* (Philadelphia: Temple University Press, 1995).

Niemcewicz, Julian Ursyn (b. Skoki, Poland, now Lithuania, February 6, 1757; d. Paris, France, May 21, 1841). Writer, statesman. Born into the minor nobility in Skoki, Poland, as the eldest of 16 children, Niemcewicz joined the Cadet Corps in Warsaw and entered the army upon graduation. He took the first of several trips through Europe in 1784. Four years later he was elected to the Polish parliament where he was an exemplary speaker, and began a prolific writing career. He played an important role in drawing up the May 3, 1791, constitution (see **Constitution of the Third of May**). In the 1794 insurrection to rid Poland of foreign armies, he served beside **Tadeusz Kościuszko** as his aide-de-camp. After the Poles were defeated, both men were imprisoned by the Russians in St. Petersburg. Released in an amnesty two years later, they sailed for America and arrived in Philadelphia in 1797. Cultured, witty, and intelligent, with knowledge of English, Niemcewicz quickly became popular in New York City society where he familiarized Americans with Polish culture. He became friends with John Jay and Alexander Hamilton, was introduced to President John Adams and Vice President Thomas Jefferson, and traveled to Georgetown, D.C., where he met retired President George Washington who invited Niemcewicz to visit his Mount Vernon home. On June 2, 1798, Niemcewicz arrived for a twelve day stay. A habitual diarist, the details of his visit provide historians with a look at the home life of the former president and are a source of the only detailed account of the lives of the estate's African American slaves. In 1800 Niemcewicz married an American woman, Susan Livingston Keane, and they made their home in Elizabeth, New Jersey. Two years later he returned to Warsaw to settle his father's estate and did not return to New Jersey until 1804 when he resumed his life as a gentleman farmer, philosopher and traveler. In 1807, when he received word that Napoleon had chased the Russians out of Poland and created the Duchy of Warsaw, he returned to Poland. Ever hopeful that his homeland could again become free, he served as the Duchy's Secretary of the Senate, as well as holding academic positions. After Warsaw was retaken by Russia, Niemcewicz remained, became president of a committee for a new Constitution, and held political posts in the opposition. He continued writing plays, poems, and history. Many of his works were inspirational to the Polish cause for independence. He was a supporter of the November Uprising of 1830-31 and went to London to try to procure military aid from Britain. That mission having failed, and the insurrection defeated, he joined other Polish exiles in Paris where he died in 1841.—*Martin S. Nowak*

SOURCES: Metchie J. E. Budka, ed., *Under Their Vine and Fig Tree* (Elizabeth, NJ: Grassmann Pub. Co., 1965); Ludwik Krzyżanowski, *Julian Ursyn Niemcewicz and America* (New York: Polish Institute of Arts and Sciences in America, 1961); Eugene Kusielewicz, "Niemcewicz in America," *The Polish Review*, Vol. 5, no. 1 (1960), 66–79; Barbara W. Low Budka, "Julian Ursyn Niemcewicz, "Man of Enlightenment: His Portrait of America 1797–1799, 1806," *The Polish Review*, Vol. 46, no. 3 (2001), 261–70; Sigmund H. Uminski, "Julian Ursyn Niemcewicz in America," *Polish American Studies*, Vol. 2, no. 3–4 (1945), 89–94.

Nikodym, Otton Marcin (b. Zabłotów, Poland, August 13, 1887; d. Utica, New York, May 4, 1974). Mathematician. One of the founders of the famous "Polish School" of mathematics, Prof. Otton Nikodym had, between the two World Wars, obtained his education at the Universities of Lwów and Warsaw, taught at the Jagiellonian University in Kraków and the University of Warsaw, and lived through the Warsaw Uprising of 1944 together with his wife Stanisława, herself a mathematician and painter. In 1947 he accepted an invitation to teach in the United States at Kenyon College, Ohio, where he remained until 1964 when he retired to the Polish American community in Utica, New York. Nikodym published over 100 research papers in the most prestigious mathematical journals of Europe. Among his most important works are "Sur une généralisation des intégrales de M. J. Radon" in *Fundamenta Mathematicae* (1930), "Sur le principe de minimum dans le problème de Dirichlet" in *Annales de la Societé Polonaise de Mathematique* (1931), and his crowning achievement, *The Mathematical Apparatus for Quantum Theories* (1966), created mainly in America and completed in Utica. Throughout his life he was an invited guest lecturer in mathematical centers of Europe and America, especially at the Sorbonne in France, and in Belgium, Germany and Italy. In America he held many grants from the National Science Foundation and the Atomic Energy Commission. He is buried in the "Illustrious Poles" Cemetery of the "American Częstochowa" Shrine in Doylestown, Pennsylvania. His papers are at the Archives of American Mathematics at the University of Texas at Austin.—*Eugene P. Nassar*

SOURCES: Alicja Derkowska, "Otton Marcin Nikodym," *Roczniki Polskiego Towarzystwa Matematy-* *cznego*, Vol. 25 (1983), 74–88; Wacław Symański, "Who Was Otton Nikodym?" *The Mathematical Intelligencer*, Vol. 12, no. 2 (1990), 27–31 (1990).

Nobel Prize. For Polish American recipients see **Roald Hoffmann**, **Robert Hofstadter**, **Albert A. Michelson**, **Czesław Miłosz**, **Isidor Isaac Rabi**, **Andrew V. Schally**, **Isaac Bashevis Singer**, **Frank Wilczek**.

North American Center for the Study of Polish Affairs *see* **Studium.**

Novak, Milan V. (b. Illinois, December 24, 1907; d. Springfield, Illinois, January 5, 1992). Speed skating official. A speed skating enthusiast, Novak served as a National Timer for the Amateur Skating Union's (ASU) Board of Control, ASU Parliamentarian, and Chair of its Hall of Fame Committee. He co-edited the ASU *Handbook*, co-authored *Speedskating, What You May Want to Know* (1959), and with his wife founded and co-edited *Racing Blade* magazine. He and his wife founded the Novak Trust Fund for the support of novice skaters. A five-time recipient of the Amateur Skating Union's Certificate of Appreciation, he received an ASU award for outstanding service and dedication, and was elected to the National Speedskating Hall of Fame in 1979.— *James S. Pula*

SOURCE: www.nationalspeedskatingmuseum.org.

Nowa Emigracja *see* **New Immigration.**

Nowak, Henry James (b. Buffalo, New York, February 21, 1935; d.—). Congressman. Nowak attended public elementary schools in Buffalo, graduated from the city's Riverside High School in 1953, then earned a baccalaureate degree from Canisius College (1957) and a J.D. from the University of Buffalo Law School (1961). Admitted to the New York bar in 1963, he began practice in Buffalo, served in the U.S. Army (1957–58, 1961–62), and then obtained a position as assistant district attorney of Erie County, NY, in 1964. He served as Erie County comptroller (1964–74), a delegate to the New York State Democratic convention (1970), and a delegate to the Democratic National Convention (1972). Before his political career, Nowak gained renown as a basketball player for the Canisius College Golden Griffs, graduating as that college's scoring leader. While he was a player, Canisius made three of its four appearances at the NCAA tournament and Nowak was dubbed "Hammerin' Hank" for his aggressive play. He turned down an offer to play for the St. Louis Hawks in order to go to law school. He was elected as a Democrat to the Ninety-fourth and to the eight succeeding Congresses (January 3, 1975–January 3, 1993), but was not a candidate for renomination in 1992. As a congressman, Nowak focused more on constituent services rather than on formulating national policy. His political tactics were similar to those he used on the basketball court; that is, he spoke softly to get results. Detail oriented, he was a successful, but relatively obscure legislator.—*Frederick J. Augustyn*

SOURCES: *Biographical Directory of the United States Congress, 1774–Present* (http://bioguide.congress.gov/); Rose Ciotta, "Hank's Place: Henry Nowak Has Been in Washington for 17 Years, but His Heart Belongs to Buffalo," *Buffalo News*, March 8, 1992, M6.

Nowak, Stanley (Stanisław Nowak; b. Przemyśl, Poland, March 14, 1903; d. Detroit, Michigan, April 26, 1994). Labor leader. Arriving in Chicago in 1913, Nowak worked in the Chicago garment industry where, in 1922, he first met **Leo Krzycki**, an organizer for the Amalgamated Clothing Workers of America. This marked the beginning of his active participation in the American labor movement. During the Great Depression, he joined the Proletarian Party which J. Edgar Hoover characterized as "the more radical branch of the Communist Party." According to FBI records, Nowak joined the Communist Party in 1934, becoming a paid staff member two years later. Hired by Local 174 of the United Auto Workers, he soon became a member of the leadership of the Communist Party's Committee of Polish Unionists. At the request of United Auto Workers president Homer Martin, CIO president John L. Lewis dispatched Leo Krzycki to aid the UAW in their organizing efforts. Meeting at a Polish rally, Krzycki urged Martin to make use of Nowak as an organizer among Polish workers. With Krzycki's support, Nowak formed the Polish Trade Union Committee (PTUC), sponsored by the newly organized Polish section in UAW, on June 26, 1936 at the Dom Polski (Polish Home) in Detroit. Early members included the Polish unionists Jan Zaremba, Wincenty Klein, Antoni Plezia, W. Sylwestrowicz, Adam Poplawski, Jan Rusak, Edward Danielewski, and Jan Przepiorka. Supported by the newspaper *Głos Ludowy* (The People's Voice), the PTUC organized programs on Polish radio and attacked the fiercely anti-union *Dziennik Polski* (Polish Daily News), which it labeled *Dziennik Niepolski* (Daily Non-Polish News).

In 1938, Nowak was elected a Michigan state senator, notwithstanding attacks by his opponents on his communist affiliation which they printed on red paper. During his ten years in office, he advocated many reforms including unemployment benefits, fair housing, civil rights, and supported other worker rights. A member of the Civil Rights Congress, he was long devoted to the cause of civil liberties,

including African American civil rights. In 1940 he became a member of the International Workers Order, serving as vice chairman of the American Committee for the Protection of Foreign Born. It was not until 1939 that the FBI opened their file on Nowak, who was indicted three years later for neglecting to state that he was a Communist when he applied for citizenship in Detroit in 1937. Since the application did not contain the question, the case was dismissed.

He was denounced regularly by the *Dziennik Polski* and other papers like the South Boston *Polish Daily Courier*, which charged him with being the "leader of a fifth column to sow discord and confusion among the Poles in the United States." He took a leading role in denouncing the creation of the **Polish American Congress** prior to its founding meeting. In return, he was the subject of numerous protests by the Polish American Congress which rejected his radical views and Communist affiliation. Among the latter, he served as executive secretary (1944) and a member of the Development Commission (1943–45) of the communist-oriented **Kościuszko Patriotic League**; national vice president of the International Workers Order (1944); Chairman (1944) and secretary of the national **American Slav Congress**; a member of the American Committee for the Protection of Foreign Born; American Committee to Aid Poland; and Poles for Peace. In 1948, he was one of the original organizers of the Progressive Party in Michigan. Relinquishing his senate seat, Nowak ran for Congress in 1950 following the death of veteran Congressman **John Lesinski**. He was called to testify before the House Un-American Activities Committee in

Stanley Nowak, labor leader (*OLS*).

1952, 1956, and 1959, with deportation proceedings being initiated in 1952. Although he lost the first two rounds of his deportation case, the U.S. Supreme Court reversed the lower court decision after six years, citing a lack of credible evidence.

Nowak directed the newspaper *Głos Ludowy* as its editor (1960–80). A Stalinist throughout his career, Nowak visited Poland five times. The Detroit Urban League honored him with its Warrior's Award in 1982. As a loyal Stalinist, Nowak actively campaigned against Solidarność despite the fact that the Polish union received financial support from the UAW and other CIO unions. Nowak's name is commemorated by a plaque on the Wall of Labor at the Michigan Labor Legacy Project.—*Don Binkowski*

SOURCES: Donald E. Pienkos, *For Your Freedom Through Ours* (Boulder, CO: East European Monographs, 1991); Conrad Komorowski, *The Strange Trial of Stanley Nowak* (Detroit: Stanley Nowak Defense Fund, 1954); Margaret Collingwood Nowak, *Two Who Were There* (Detroit: Wayne University Press, 1989); Don Binkowski, *Poles Together: Leo Krzycki and Polish Americans in the American Labor Movement* (Philadelphia: Xlbiris, 2001); Don Binkowski, *Leo Krzycki and the Detroit Left* (Philadelphia: Xlbiris, 2001).

Nowak-Jeziorański, Jan (Zdzisław Antoni Jeziorański; b. Berlin, Germany, October 3, 1914; d. Warsaw, January 20, 2005). Journalist, diplomatic courier, Polonia activist, soldier. After studying economics at the university in Poznań, he lectured there from 1936 to 1939. When Germany invaded Poland, he enlisted as a non-commissioned officer of artillery. Eventually captured by the Germans, he quickly escaped to join the underground Polish Home Army (Armia Krajowa) where he took the *nom-de-guerre* "Jan Nowak." In the Home Army, he organized Akcja N that printed fake German newspapers and other items to spread misinformation and despondency within the German forces. He also became a courier between the command of the Polish Home Army in Poland and the Polish government-in-exile in London. He made five trips between Warsaw and London, including bringing the first news of the Warsaw Ghetto Uprising in 1943. He returned to Poland just in time to take part in the Warsaw Uprising of 1944, where he conducted daily radio broadcasts to tell the world what was happening. He was ordered to leave just before the surrender of Warsaw and returned to London with documents and photos of the German atrocities. He spent the rest of the war in London. Nowak-Jeziorański stayed in the West after the war to fight against the Soviet domination of Poland. He became a regular commentator on the BBC starting in 1948. In 1952, he moved to Munich to head the Polish

Jan Nowak-Jeziorański speaking at a celebration of the 70th anniversary of regaining Polish independence (*JPI*).

division of Radio Free Europe. He retired in 1976, and became active in the **Polish American Congress** as a director from 1979 to 1996. He was an advisor to the National Security Council under Jimmy Carter and Ronald Reagan, and a major proponent of Poland joining NATO in 1999 and later the European Union. He returned to Poland in 2002 where he continued to be active as a political commentator in radio and television work until his death. He is the author of many publications including his memoirs, *Courier from Warsaw*. He was a recipient of many awards including the Order of Virtuti Militari, the Order of the White Eagle, the Commander's Cross of Polonia Restituta, and the American Medal of Freedom.—*David Stefancic*

SOURCES: Jan Nowak-Jezioranski, *Courier from Warsaw* (Detroit: Wayne State University Press, 1981); obituary, *International Herald Tribune*, January 22, 2005.

Nowiny Polskie (The Polish News). This Milwaukee Polish language newspaper was established as a weekly in 1906 and a year later became a daily. It was created on the orders of the Archbishop of Milwaukee, Sebastian Messmer, for the purpose of combating the Milwaukee *Kuryer Polski* (Polish Courier), a daily owned and operated by **Michał Kruszka**. Kruszka had been increasingly critical of the archbishop over a variety of issues and his publication was seen as a threat to the loyalty of the large Polish Catholic population in Milwaukee to the Church. The rise of religious **independentism** in other parts of the country and the forming of the **Polish National Catholic Church** may have played a role in Messmer's thinking. The *Nowiny Polskie* (Polish News) was not the first anti–Kruszka publication in the city; earlier failed efforts to battle the *Kuryer Polski* had included the newspapers *Słowo* (The Word) and *Dziennik*

Milwaucki (Milwaukee's Daily). The Rev. **Bolesław Góral** was chosen to be the editor of the *Nowiny Polskie* and took his duties very seriously. The rivalry between the two papers and Góral's own antipathy toward Kruszka's half-brother, the Rev. **Wacław Kruszka**, himself an equally strong-willed person, intellectual, and frequent contributor to the *Kuryer Polski*, only deepened the conflict. The *Nowiny Polskie* never surpassed its rival in circulation, even after Messmer and his fellow Wisconsin bishops ordered Polish Catholics to cease reading Kruszka's paper under pain of excommunication. In fact, the Church leadership's attacks may have helped increase *Kuryer Polski* readership and build its circulation nationally as well. In 1929 the paper was sold; its new owners maintained its previous editorial policy until 1948 when it closed.—*Donald E. Pienkos*

SOURCES: Thaddeus Borun and John Gostomski, eds., *We, The Milwaukee Poles* (Milwaukee: Nowiny Polskie Publishers, 1946); Anthony Kuzniewski, *Faith and Fatherland: The Polish Church War in Wisconsin* (Notre Dame, IN: University of Notre Dame Press, 1980); Donald E. Pienkos, "Politics, Religion and Change in Polish Milwaukee, 1900–1930," *Wisconsin Magazine of History*, Vol. 61, no. 3 (Spring 1978).

Nowy Dziennik (New Daily News). In 2009, with a circulation of 22,000–25,000 for its weekday edition and 27,000–30,000 on Friday through Sunday, this newspaper had the widest circulation of any Polish-language newspaper outside Poland. Founded in 1971 by **Bolesław Wierzbiański** and a group of Polish American activists, it is edited and published in New York by Bicentennial Publishing Co., Inc. *Nowy Dziennik* presents information relevant to the Polish American community; it covers local news from New York and surrounding states, current national affairs, and social and political news from Poland. Its classified section constitutes an important source of information about legal and medical services (especially those provided by Polish speaking professionals), English as a Second Language courses, and employment opportunities. Besides the daily newspaper, *Nowy Dziennik* also publishes two weekly magazines, *Przegląd Polski* (Polish Review; which appears on Fridays) and *Weekend*. The main objective of *Przegląd Polski* is to help the Polish American community stay in touch with Polish culture, art and history, and to record the presence and contribution of Poles and Polish Americans in the world's art and culture. Issues covered by *Przegląd Polski* include news about upcoming cultural events in the U.S. featuring Polish artists; reviews of recent literary publications, movies, concerts, fine arts shows and theatrical productions; interviews with notable Polish artists; information and

commentaries about cultural life in Poland; reports about forgotten chapters in Polish history or new viewpoints on historical events. The *Weekend* magazine targets young adult readership, featuring essays each week on various topics that pertain to the life of the young generation of immigrants, and providing a multifaceted outlook on the problems and choices they face. The staff of *Nowy Dziennik* consists of seasoned editors and journalists with experience reporting on both Polish and American life. The newspaper maintains regular correspondents in the U.S., Poland, London, Rome, and Kiev. *Nowy Dziennik* is available on newsstands and via home-delivery subscription. An electronic subscription of *Przegląd Polski* is available, reaching Polish-speaking communities all over the world. *Nowy Dziennik* maintains a comprehensive website, which presents many of its feature articles in electronic format and provides links to various services, such as advertising, subscription, and archives. Additionally, the newspaper operates a bookstore, which offers publications in Polish and English. *Nowy Dziennik* organizes poetry readings, walking tours, and meetings with artists and officials. It also manages an art gallery (launched in 1989) where notable Polish artists can exhibit and sell their artwork. *Nowy Dziennik* collaborates with WNYC radio as a part of the Feet in Two Worlds program. In 2009, newsstands accounted for 75 percent of its total sales, with the remaining 25 percent being subscriptions. At that time, Czesław Karkowski served as editor-in-chief of *Nowy Dziennik*, Julita Karkowska was senior editor of *Przegląd Polski*, and Jan Latus edited *Weekend*. Editors of *Nowy Dziennik* included Bolesław Wierzbiański (1971–2003), Barbara Wierzbiańska (2003–2008), Malina Stadnik (2008–2009), and Tadeusz Kondratowicz (since 2009).—*Bozena U. Zaremba*

SOURCES: Wiesława Piątkowska-Stepaniak, *Nowy Dziennik w Nowym Świecie. Pismo i jego rola ideowo-polityczna* (Opole, Poland: Uniwersytet Opolski, 2000); Wiesława Piątkowska-Stepaniak, ed., *Autoportret zbiorowy. Wspomnienia dziennikarzy polskich na emigracji z lat 1945–2002* (Opole, Poland: Uniwersytet Opolski, 2003); Bolesław Wierzbiański, *Wybor pism* (New York: Bicentennial Publishing Corporation, 2007).

Nowy Świat (New World). The Polish language daily newspaper *Nowy Świat* was published in New York City between 1922 and 1971. After its demise, another New York–based daily, **Nowy Dziennik** (New Daily News) was established in its place by Polish émigré and one-time **Światpol** activist **Bolesław Wierzbiański**. It continues in operation under his widow's direction. *Nowy Świat*'s Polish-born editor and publisher **Max-**

imilian Węgrzynek was its most prominent and influential force. A long-time activist in support of Józef Piłsudski and his regime in Poland after 1926, Węgrzynek ardently supported the cause of Polish independence after the outbreak of World War II in 1939. He became a key figure backing the activities of the **National Committee of Americans of Polish Descent** (KNAPP) after 1941. This New York–based organization sharply criticized the policies of the Polish exile government in London headed by General Władysław Sikorski toward the Soviet Union. The USSR had invaded and occupied eastern Poland in September 1939 following the signing of the Nazi-Soviet non-aggression pact just a week before the outbreak of the war. In May–June 1944, Węgrzynek was one of the founders of the **Polish American Congress** and was elected one of its vice presidents at its first national convention. All these matters received continuing and prominent coverage in the newspaper. Węgrzynek and *Nowy Świat* vigorously endorsed the presidential candidacy of Republican Governor Thomas E. Dewey of New York in the 1944 election and alleged that President Franklin D. Roosevelt had accepted Poland's postwar dominance by the Soviet Union and the loss of its eastern territories at his November 1943 Teheran Summit meeting with Soviet leader Josef Stalin. Events subsequently proved the newspaper correct. However, Roosevelt was reelected to an unprecedented fourth term, winning an estimated ninety percent of the Polish American vote.—*Donald E. Pienkos*

SOURCES: Richard Lukas, *The Strange Allies: The United States and Poland, 1941–1945* (Knoxville, TN: University of Tennessee Press, 1978); Donald E. Pienkos, *For Your Freedom Through Ours: Polish American Efforts on Poland's Behalf, 1863–1991* (Boulder, CO: East European Monographs, 1991).

O, Karen (Karen Lee Orzolek; b. South Korea, November 22, 1978; d.—). Singer. Orzolek grew up in New Jersey before she attended Oberlin College and the Tisch School of the Arts at New York University. As the lead singer for the alternative rock band The Yeah Yeah Yeahs, formed in 2000, she is best known for her over-the-top fashions and outrageous stage behavior during concerts. As of 2009, the band's works included two albums, four extended play discs, eight singles, six music videos, and one video album. Their first release reached the number one position on the British Indie Chart in 2003. She received the Sex Goddess Award from *Spin Magazine* in 2004 and 2005, and was named one of the hottest women in rock by *Blender* (2006). She collaborated on the soundtrack for the movie *Jackass 2*, and contributed to other movie soundtracks.—*James S. Pula*

SOURCE: Brian Hiatt, "Karen O," *Rolling Stone*, April 16, 2009, 32.

Oberek. Also known as *obertas* (common in the nineteenth century), or *ober* (the name used less frequently), the *oberek* is, in its stage versions performed by Polish folk dance ensembles, the most vivacious and acrobatic of the so-called five national dances (with **polonaise**, **mazur**, **kujawiak**, **krakowiak**). The oberek originated in the villages of Mazowsze in central Poland; it is danced by couples to instrumental music in triple meter. The name *oberek* is derived from the verb *obracac się*—to spin. The dance's main movement is rotational: the dancers spin and twirl around the room. The term *obertas* appeared for the first time in 1679, in the book *Lanczafty* by Korczyński. *Oberek* belongs to the group of dances which feature the so-called *mazurka* rhythms. The dances include *kujawiak* (the slowest), *mazur* or *mazurka* (in a moderate tempo), and *oberek* (the fastest dance of this group). According to Oskar Kolberg, in central Poland dances from the family of the *mazur* (*kujawiak*, *mazur*, *oberek*) were often performed in a set preceded by a *chodzony* (walking dance, a folk *polonaise*) and organized in an increasing tempo. The set ended with a frenzied *oberek* (MM = 160 – 180). This 19th-century practice was abandoned early in the 20th century when the *obereks* became even faster. In central Poland, the music for the *oberek* was typically performed by a *kapela*, a small village band dominated by the violin. The size and exact make-up of the *kapela* depended on the part of the region from which it originated; it always included the violin, accompanied by a percussion instrument, plus a folk accordion or a clarinet. The accompaniment for the dance was inseparably connected with singing. The musicians responded to the initial couplet sung by a soloist who "called on them" to play, at times mocking their skills and ridiculing their poverty, at other times teasing other dancers and participants in the social occasion. The *obereks* were often danced in wedding celebrations and a variety of texts contain sexual overtones. A notable feature of the sung *oberek* is the presence of meaningless syllables and phrases, *oj dana, dana*, or *uch, ucha-cha*, or *oj dziś, dziś*.

The music includes the same type of *mazurka* rhythms as the *kujawiak* and *mazur*. In instrumental *obereks* the longer notes of the melody are filled in with fast-paced sixteenth-note figuration, often following the outline of a triad *arpeggio*. The lead violinist shows off his skill by playing ever new variants of the same melody; the tempo is either steady, or gradually increases towards the end of the dance, making the performance (both of the musicians and the dancers) more and more virtuosic. Each phrase of the music usually consists of four or eight measures and they are grouped in pairs. The main accent usually falls on the third beat in each measure. As mentioned above, the *oberek* is the quickest of the five national dances and in folk performances reaches dizzying speeds.

In classical music, the name *oberek* was used by composers of stylized dances starting with Oskar Kolberg who collected *obereks* from Mazovia in four volumes of his study dedicated to the Mazowsze region and in two volumes from the Kujawy region. Other Polish composers of *obereks* include Henryk Wieniawski (obertas for violin and piano), Roman Statkowski, Karol Szymanowski, Aleksander Tansman, and Grażyna Bacewicz (who composed *obereks* as self-standing works for violin and piano, as well as movements in more extended compositions, e.g. the finale of her Piano Sonata no. 2). Needless to say, the fastest Mazurkas by Fryderyk Chopin are also examples of *obereks*; for instance, his Mazurka op. 56 no. 2. In contrast to the *mazurka*, *polonaise* and *krakowiak* (*cracovienne*) the title *oberek* is very rare in the music of Western composers, and it does not occur among the titles of Polish dances composed in 19th century America.

The *oberek* is danced by couples who are placed in a circle and rotate both around the whole circle and around their own axis (to the right). The dancers follow the direction "against the sun" (*pod słońce*, counterclockwise). The strongest dancer may ask for a change of direction of the whole group which then would dance "*ze słońcem*" (with the sun, clockwise). The most difficult change of direction involves a simultaneous change of the rotation around the personal axis, performed to the left only by the best dancers. At times the women turn around the men; sometimes the men vary the motion of their legs, performing a wider "twisting" gesture on the third beat. The dancers in a couple do not separate (with the exception of quick turns performed by the woman) and tend to hold their hands throughout. There are few steps to provide variety in the course of the dance; its enjoyment stems from the very fast tempo, regularity of turns and the simultaneity of changes of direction.

The costume of choice for the *oberek* is the colorful striped costume of the Łowicz area. Women wear wool skirts made of striped cloth woven from vivid hues over layers of white petticoats finished with lace and ruffle. The men wear pants made from the same striped cloth, high black boots, long dark vests and white shirts. The costumes are extremely rich in color and ornaments — hence their popularity among Polish American folk dance groups. The *oberek* has also become a recreational dance growing in popularity and providing competition to the Polish American *polka.*—*Maja Trochimczyk*

SOURCES: Ada Dziewanowska, *Polish Folk Dances & Songs: A Step by Step Guide* (New York: Hippocrene Books, 1999); "Oberek," entry in Stanley Sadie, ed., *New Grove Dictionary of Music and Musicians* (London: McMillan, 1980), Vol. 15; Maja Trochimczyk, "Oberek" entry, Polish Dance in Southern California website, University of Southern California, Polish Music Center, 2000.

Odrowąż, Edward (b. Galicia, Austrian-occupied Poland, 1840; d. New York, New York, January 20, 1889). Polonia activist, journalist. Born in partitioned Poland to a respected aristocratic family, Odrowaz took part in the 1863 insurrection against Russian rule and paid dearly for his efforts, losing his entire estate. After a period of time in exile in Paris, he came to New York in 1875. In 1880 he participated in the founding meeting of the **Polish National Alliance** in Chicago where he was elected by acclamation to be its first national secretary. The following year, at the second PNA convention in New York, he was elected editor of the newly created official newspaper of the Alliance, *Zgoda* (Harmony). However, Odrowaz refused to be a candidate for the editorship when the delegates to the 1882 convention voted to move the paper's office to Chicago. An early journalist in **Polonia**, Henryk Nagiel, described Odrowaz's work with *Zgoda* as "well edited in a patriotic spirit. From its first issue *Zgoda* played an important role among New York Poles.... *Zgoda*'s language was clear, concise and its style well-turned, its editorials objective and its general tone truly didactic."—*Donald E. Pienkos*

SOURCES: Donald E. Pienkos, *PNA: A Centennial History of the Polish National Alliance of the United States of North America* (Boulder, CO: East European Monographs, 1984); Stanisław Osada, *Historia Związku Narodowego Polskiego i rozwój ruchu narodowego Polskiego w Ameryce Pólnocnej* (Chicago: Nakładem i drukiem Związku Narodowego Polskiego, 1905).

Okolica. This is a Polish word meaning "neighborhood." In the urban environment in which most Polish immigrants of the mass migration (1870–1920) found themselves, the neighborhood became the basic unit of social identification after the family. These early urban Polish-Americans generally identified closely with their parish, proudly claiming to be from "Stanisławowo" (St. Stanislaus), "Wojciechowo" (St. Adalbert), or wherever they worshipped. To say this implied more than just a church, but an entire neighborhood, a community, an ethnic enclave within the larger urban environment, a place where the immigrant could feel secure interacting with people who understood the same language, culture, and world view. More often then not, one's job, social activities, school, and virtually all other facets of life took place within the confines of this urban neighborhood. As a report from investigators in Buffalo, NY, in 1910 concluded, the Poles "are in the Buffalo community, but they are not of it. They have their own churches, their own stores and business places, their own newspapers. They are content to live alone, and the rest of the population generally knows little about them and cares less." The okolica was a self-contained urban community in which Poles fashioned lives for themselves in which they could feel comfortable amid the uncertainty of the large urban environment that was otherwise fraught with uncertainty and often hostility.—*James S. Pula*

SOURCE: James S. Pula, *Polish Americans: An Ethnic Community* (New York: Twayne Publishers, 1995), 22–24.

O'Konski, Alvin Edward (b. Kewaunee, Wisconsin, May 26, 1904; d. Kewaunee, Wisconsin, July 8, 1987). Congressman, educator, journalist. Born to Polish parents, O'Konski attended local public schools and the University of Iowa before graduating from the State Teachers College at Oshkosh in 1927. He then did graduate work at the University of Wisconsin and the University of Iowa before accepting a teaching position in high schools at Omro, Oconto, and Pulaski, WI (1926–29). He was a member of the faculty of Oregon State College at Corvallis (1929–31), served as superintendent of schools in Pulaski, WI (1932–35), and then accepted a position on the faculty of the University of Detroit (1936–38). He was editor and publisher of *The Iron County Miner* (1940–42) in Hurley, WI. He was elected as a Republican to the Seventy-eighth and the fourteen succeeding Congresses from Wisconsin's old 10th District (January 3, 1943–January 3, 1973). While in Congress, he founded the NBC TV affiliate in Rhinelander and owned and operated radio stations in Wausau and Merrill. A member of the House Veterans Affairs, Public Works, Education and Labor, and Armed Services committees, he was co-author of the GI Bill of Rights, signed in 1944, which gave servicemen a chance at higher education and more easily obtainable home mortgage loans. O'Konski also served on the House District Committee where, during the 1960s, he opposed the creation of a rapid rail metro system as too costly. He was an unsuccessful candidate for the Republican nomination in 1957 to the U.S. Senate to fill the vacancy caused by the death of Joseph McCarthy. O'Konski was an unsuccessful candidate for reelection in 1972 to the Ninety-third Congress after the 1970 census results caused Wisconsin to lose a Congressional district. This forced O'Konski's and Democratic incumbent Congressman David Obey's districts to be merged. O'Konski once described himself as a "New Deal Democrat domestically and a rabid conservative internationally." An ardent anti–Communist, in 1945 he denounced the **Yalta** agreement stating that the postwar partition of Poland was "the most ghastly crime of all ages known to man or beast." In 1956 he threatened to resign from Congress when Eisenhower invited Yugoslavian President Marshall Tito to Washington. After his defeat due to reapportionment, O'Konski became head of the World League to Stop Communism. In 1945, he was voted the most distinguished American by the foreign language press, and was awarded "Polonia Restituta" the highest medal of Free Poland. Shortly before he died of a heart ailment, he underwrote a monument on the county courthouse lawn in Kewaunee honoring the war dead. His papers are in the Nicolet College and Technical Institute in Rhinelander, WI.—*Frederick J. Augustyn*

SOURCES: *Biographical Directory of the United States Congress, 1774–Present* (http://bioguide.congress.gov/); obituaries, *Chicago Tribune*, July 9, 1987, Sec. 2, 11; *Los Angeles Times*, July 11, 1987, 34; *Minneapolis Star and Tribune*, July 10, 1987, 6B; *Newsday*, July 9, 1987, 45; *New York Times*, July 9, 1987, A25; *Washington Post*, July 9, 1987, B4.

Okręg Armii Krajowej na Stany Zjednoczone *see* **Home Army Veterans Association.**

Oladowski, Hypolite (b. Russian partition of Poland, ca. 1798; d. Columbus, Georgia, August 16, 1878). Soldier, government official. A captain in the Russian Army, he joined the Polish Insurrection of 1830, was captured and sentenced to life imprisonment in Siberia, but escaped through the aid of a Polish lady who changed clothes with him in prison. He traveled to the United States where his military experience secured for him a non-commissioned appointment in the U.S. Army. For the next thirty years he was associated with the Federal Ordnance Department, during which time he also took part in the Mexican War. At the outbreak of the Civil War, Oladowski was assigned to the arsenal in Baton Rouge, Louisiana, with the rank of Ordnance Sergeant. Gen. Braxton Bragg, who was organizing troops in Florida, secured for him an appointment as a captain of artillery in the Confederate regular service and made him Chief of the Ordnance Department of the Army of Pensacola. From that time, he accompanied Bragg through most of the war. In late March 1862, when Bragg joined Albert

Sidney Johnston's command in Corinth, Mississippi, Oladowski was appointed Chief of Ordnance of the Army of Mississippi. In May he was promoted to the rank of lieutenant colonel, a nomination confirmed by the Congress of the Confederacy in October. Oladowski remained in this position during Bragg's invasion of Kentucky. After the collapse of the invasion the army was renamed the Army of Tennessee. Oladowski held his position until mid–1864 despite the fact that Bragg was relieved of command by Joseph E. Johnston in December 1863. There is no information about Oladowski's service during the next six months, but on January 11, 1865, he was appointed Chief of Ordnance in the Department of North Carolina under the command of Braxton Bragg. In this position Oladowski served until the end of the war. After the war Bragg secured Oladowski's services making improvements in the harbor of Mobile Bay, and later the U.S. government employed him working on the river and harbor in this district. Oladowski died after a long illness and was buried two days later in the Magnolia Cemetery in Mobile, Alabama.—*Piotr Derengowski*

SOURCES: "Death of a Polish Refugee," *The New York Times,* August 25, 1878; Ella Lonn, *Foreigners in the Confederacy* (Chapel Hill: University of North Carolina Press, 2002).

Olbiński, Rafał R. (b. Kiecle, Poland, February 21, 1945; d.—). Artist. After earning a degree from the Warsaw Polytechnic Institute, Olbiński migrated to the U.S. in 1982, and three years later he accepted a position with the School of Visual Arts in New York. His popular illustrations have appeared in prominent publications such as *Atlantic Monthly, Business Week, Der Spiegel, Newsweek, New York Times, New Yorker, Omni, Playboy,* and *Time,* as well as specialized professional journals such as *Art Magazine in America* (New York), *Graphis* (Zurich), *High Quality* (Munich), *Idea* (Tokyo), and *Universe des Artes* (Paris). In 2002 he was acclaimed for his design of the stage settings for the Philadelphia Opera Company's production of *Don Giovanni.* His paintings have been included in collections of the Carnegie Foundation, the Library of Congress, and the National Arts Club in New York. Among his many honors are the International Oscar for the World's Most Memorable Poster, *Prix Savignac 1994,* in Paris.—*James S. Pula*

SOURCES: Rafał Olbiński and Magdalena Fudala, *The Best of Rafał Olbiński* (Kielce: Świętokrzyski Urzad Wojewódzki, 2005); Rafał Olbiński, *Rafał Olbiński* (Kielce: Muzeum Narodowe w Kielcach, 2000); Rafał Olbiński, *Rafał Olbiński, Posters* (New York: Nahan Editions, 1996).

Olczyk, Edward Walter "Eddie" (b. Chicago, Illinois, August 16, 1966; d.—).

Hockey player. Growing up in Illinois, he began his enthusiasm for the game of hockey in the early 1970s at the age of six. Success came early as a member of the Illinois midget team that won the 1982 national title against a Detroit Compuware squad that featured future National Hockey League (NHL) stars Pat LaFontaine and Al Iafrate. He played for the 1984 United States Olympic hockey team at the age of 16. Olczyk was drafted by the Chicago Blackhawks in the first round of the 1984 NHL Entry Draft as the third overall pick. During his NHL professional career he was traded frequently, playing for a number of teams. In 1987 he was traded to Toronto by the Blackhawks and traded again in 1990 to Winnipeg. In 1992 he was traded for the third time in his career, this time to the New York Rangers, but would miss most of the 1993-94 season recovering from a thumb injury. However, he recovered in time to win the Stanley Cup with the team that season. In 1995 he was again traded, this time back to Winnipeg. In 1996 he signed as a free agent with Los Angeles, but he did not finish the season because he was traded to the Pittsburgh Penguins. He finished his career with his original professional team the Chicago Blackhawks. A gifted playmaker with speed and a quick release, he was also solid on his skates and not easy to bump off the puck. His big league career was one of the most productive ever by an American player. Olczyk played 1,031 NHL games and produced 342 goals and 452 assists for a total of 794 points between 1984 and 2000. After retiring as a player he signed as the Pittsburgh Penguins' head coach from 2003 to 2005. During the 2004-2005 season, despite adding marquee free-agents, the Penguins started the season with a disappointing 8-17-6 record, leading to Olczyk's dismissal on December 15. Beginning with the 2006-07 NHL season, Olczyk was the game analyst for the Chicago Blackhawks television broadcasts, as well as being the lead game analyst for *The NHL on NBC.* He was inducted into the National Polish-American Sports Hall of Fame in 2004.—*Luis J. Gonzalez*

SOURCES: Brian McFarlane, *Brian McFarlane's History of Hockey* (Champaign, IL: Sagamore Publishing, 1997), 201; Harvey Wittenberg, *Tales from the Chicago Blackhawks* (Champaign, IL: Sports Publishing LLC, 2003), 99.

Olejniczak, John (b. Chicago, Illinois, March 21, 1886; d. Chicago, Illinois, November 8, 1963). Polonia activist. As a child, Olejniczak moved to South Bend with his parents. There he became active in business and local politics. In the latter capacity he served as an alderman and chairman of South Bend's

John Olejniczak, Polonia activist and fraternal leader (*OLS*).

City Council. He was an unsuccessful candidate for the U.S. House of Representatives in 1936. An active fraternalist, he rose to local leadership in the **Polish Falcons** Alliance and went on to win election to national office in the **Polish Roman Catholic Union of America,** serving as PRCUA president from 1928 to 1934 and again from 1941 to 1946. Olejniczak was also national treasurer of the **Polish American Council** (Rada Polonii Amerykanskiej) Polish relief organization in World War II and one of the founders, and the first national treasurer, of the **Polish American Congress** in 1944.—*Donald E. Pienkos*

SOURCE: Donald E. Pienkos, *For Your Freedom Through Ours: Polish American Efforts on Poland's Behalf, 1863–1991* (Boulder, CO: East European Monographs, 1991).

Opłatek. A Polish and Polish American Christmas tradition, *opłatek* remains very popular in Polish American homes. This tradition is celebrated just before the **Wigilia** or Christmas Eve supper, which is itself an elaborate meatless meal in Poland and in many **Polonia** homes. The *opłatek* is a large Communion-like wafer embellished with a Christmas design. Tradition has each member at the supper breaking off a piece of the *opłatek* and sharing it with each person present. In doing so, each person offers the other his or her best wishes for the coming year. *Opłatki* (the plural of *opłatek*) are also mailed to family and friends during the Christmas season along with the usual Christmas greeting cards. This tradition continues to be widely practiced among Polish Americans and members of

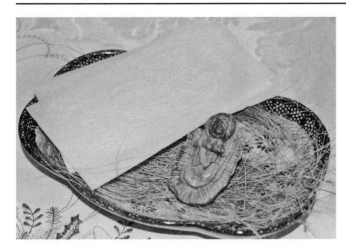

Opłatek wafers on a bed of straw (*Ann Gunkel*).

other ethnic communities of East Central European origin.—*Angela T. Pienkos*

SOURCES: Eugene E. Obidinski and Helen Stankiewicz Zand, *Polish Folkways in America: Community and Family* (Lanham, MD: University Press of America, 1987); Rose Polski Anderson, et al., eds., *Treasured Polish Christmas Customs and Traditions* (Minneapolis: Polanie Publishers, 1977).

Oral History Archives of Chicago Polonia. Created in 1976 from the federal Ethnic Heritage Studies Program, 32 interviewers working under the direction of Mary Cygan recorded first-hand autobiographies of immigrants who arrived in the U.S. between 1880 and 1930, as well as second generation Polish Americans born during that period. The material collected is unique because at that time it was still possible to contact living witnesses from the turn-of-century immigration. The project provides information about the immigrants' origin, journey, occupation, training, work, contacts with the other ethnic groups, living conditions, neighborhood life, family life, celebrations and customs, religious life, organizational life, and other aspects of the history and culture of Polish Americans during that period. By December 1976, 140 people were interviewed, yielding 350 hours of tape. The originals are stored in the Chicago Historical Society, with copies in the **Polish Museum of America** in Chicago and Loyola University in Chicago. The material, which is mostly in English, is indexed and also available in typed transcription.—*Adam Walaszek*

SOURCES: *Oral History Archives of Chicago Polonia: Passages* (Chicago: Chicago Historical Society, 1977); *Master Index for the Oral History Archives of Chicago Polonia* (Chicago: Chicago Historical Society, 1977).

Orbach, Jerome Bernard "Jerry" (b. Bronx, New York, October 20, 1935; New York City, New York, December 28, 2004.) Actor. The son of a Jewish German father and a Catholic Polish American mother, Orbach

was raised Catholic. After studying acting at the University of Illinois and Northwestern University, he moved to New York to study at the Actors Studio. He worked on several off Broadway productions, but his first major role came in the long-running hit *The Fantasticks*. From there he went on to play in *The Threepenny Opera, Carnival,* a revival of *Guys and Dolls* for which he received a Tony Award as Best Featured Actor in a Musical, the original production of *42nd Street* for which he was nominated for a second Tony, and a revival of *The Cradle Will Rock*. He made occasional television and film appearances in the 1970s, but shifted to those genres in earnest in the following decade. He played a corrupt detective in *Prince of the City*, Jennifer Gray's father in *Dirty Dancing*, and a gangster in *Crimes and Misdemeanors*. On television he starred in the short-lived 1987 crime drama *The Law and Harry McGraw*, was a regular on *Murder, She Wrote*, and a celebrity guest panelist on *What's My Line?* and *Super Password*. In 1991 he did a voice appearance in the Academy Award–winning animated musical *Beauty and the Beast*, and in the same year made an appearance as a defense attorney on the series *Law & Order*. He joined the cast of *Law & Order* a year later as a regular, playing a recovering alcoholic police detective. During his twelve years on the show he became one of its most popular characters with *TV Guide* naming him among the top fifty television detectives of all time. Signed to continue his role in the sequel *Law & Order: Trial by Jury*, he appeared in only two episodes before his untimely death. The day following his death, the marquees on Broadway were dimmed in mourning, one of the highest honors of the American theatre world.—*Patricia Finnegan*

SOURCE: Jerry Orbach, *Remember How I Love You: Love Letters From an Extraordinary Marriage* (New York, NY: Simon & Schuster, 2009).

Orbansky, David *see* **Urbansky, David.**

Orchard Lake Archives *see* **Central Archives of American Polonia.**

Orchard Lake Seminary *see* **Saints Cyril and Methodius Seminary.**

Oresko, Nicholas "Nick" (b. Bayonne, New Jersey, January 18, 1917; d.—). Soldier,

Medal of Honor recipient. During World War II, Oresko served as a master sergeant and platoon leader in Company C, 302nd Infantry Regiment, 94th Infantry Division. He landed in Europe in August 1944 and his unit was part of a reinforcement sent to help halt the German breakthrough in the Ardennes Forest during the Battle of the Bulge that December. In late January his unit was ordered to attack enemy positions near Tettingen, Germany, but successive assaults over a two day period were thrown back. On January 23, Oresko ran forward alone, braving German machine gun fire to knock out the two bunkers holding up the American advance even though he was himself wounded. The citation for his Medal of Honor read: "M/Sgt. Oresko was a platoon leader with Company C, in an attack against strong enemy positions. Deadly automatic fire from the flanks pinned down his unit. Realizing that a machinegun in a nearby bunker must be eliminated, he swiftly worked ahead alone, braving bullets which struck about him, until close enough to throw a grenade into the German position. He rushed the bunker and, with pointblank rifle fire, killed all the hostile occupants who survived the grenade blast. Another machinegun opened up on him, knocking him down and seriously wounding him in the hip. Refusing to withdraw from the battle, he placed himself at the head of his platoon to continue the assault. As withering machinegun and rifle fire swept the area, he struck out alone in advance of his men to a second bunker. With a grenade, he crippled the dug-in machinegun defending this position and then wiped out the troops manning it with his rifle, completing his second self-imposed, 1-man attack. Although weak from loss of blood, he refused to be evacuated until assured the mission was successfully accomplished. Through quick thinking, indomitable courage, and unswerving devotion to the attack in the face of bitter resistance

Nicholas Oresko, Medal of Honor recipient, at his welcome home ceremony (*NARA*).

and while wounded, M /Sgt. Oresko killed 12 Germans, prevented a delay in the assault, and made it possible for Company C to obtain its objective with minimum casualties."—*James S. Pula*

SOURCES: R. J. Proft, *United States of America's Congressional Medal of Honor Recipients and Their Official Citations* (Columbia Heights, MN: Highland House II, 2002); *The Medal of Honor of the United States Army* (Washington, D.C.: U.S. Government Printing Office, 1948), 87.

Organic Work *see* **Positivism, Polish American.**

Organizational Life, Polish American

(see also **Religious Life**). The arrival of large numbers of Polish immigrants to the United States in the decades after the American Civil War (1861–65) made possible their creation of a large and complex set of organizations formed in response to their many social needs. The most important of these, in their number and the size of their adherents, were the approximately nine hundred churches that were built and supported by the immigrants and their offspring. These mainly Roman Catholic churches, together with their many companionate structures (which included parochial schools, convents, orphanages, social service and charitable agencies, seminaries, convents, and cemeteries) were the dominant institutions of **Polonia** from the start. They have remained important, though on an increasingly reduced level, especially over the past forty years. But the Polish Roman Catholic parish, and to a small extent, the **Polish National Catholic**, Independent Catholic, and Protestant churches, were by no means the only institutions of the Polish people in America. This essay examines the so-called "secular" organizations of the Polish people in the U.S., their original and evolving missions, their scope of operations and bases of popular support, accomplishments, limitations, and current conditions.

The secular and religious organizations of the Polish community in America can well be compared and contrasted in gaining an appreciation as to what each set of structures has been about. What makes them similar has been their character as voluntary social groups, which have grown, declined, evolved, and sometimes disappeared in response to their members' changing needs and interests. A second similarity involves the explicit original self-definition of their mission as serving the needs of a distinctive "Polish" or "Polish American" following. A third similarity recognizes the interconnected character of operations that have linked most Polonia religious and secular organizations to one another. There have been only a few exceptions to this generalization, most notably the **Polish Socialist Alliance** that operated in a number of Polish immigrant communities in the U.S., mainly before the First World War. Practically all of the rest of the secular and religious organizations operated more or less closely and harmoniously with one another, and have continued to do so.

Differences also exist between the goals and character of the two sets of Polonia organizations. For the most part, the religious institutions of Polish Americans, with the exception of the Polish National Catholic Church, have been neighborhood structures. Nationally, the Polish Roman Catholic parishes in the U.S. are part of the Roman Catholic Church and have no formal and separate existence. Efforts to build such a distinctive Roman Catholic identity separate from the Catholic church in the U.S. have been unsuccessful, for example in the failures of a series of Polish Priests associations to achieve a degree of enduring status, and in the reluctance of the American bishops to support the appointment of Polish bishops for Polish immigrants. In contrast one may compare the Polish experience with the more recent one of Latinos in the Catholic Church.

For their part, many if not most of Polonia's secular organizations have strived, sometimes very successfully, to establish themselves beyond the local neighborhood Polonia and to forge national organizations promoting their distinctive missions. This has been especially true of a number of fraternal insurance benefit societies to be discussed below, most notably the **Polish National Alliance**, the **Polish Roman Catholic Union**, and the **Polish Women's Alliance**. In these and other cases, churchmen of Polish origin have found themselves in the role of supporters, rather than as leaders in Polonia.

Another difference between the religious and secular organizations lies in the limitations that follow from a parish's physical "rootedness" in a neighborhood. Secular Polonia organizations like fraternals, veterans groups, cultural associations, business and labor groups, political action organizations, newspapers and the electronic media, can, and have readily moved physically with their members; churches cannot readily do so. Over time, neighborhoods once populated by large concentrations of Polish Americans have lost their ethnic definition. Non-Polish people have replaced them and the result has involved the loss of the historic Polish ethnic character of many once Polish parishes, and in many cases their entire disappearance. In some cases, parishes with time honored Polish names have been changed to meet the supposed expectations of new parishioners of non–Polish heritage. There are examples where even the statuary and artifacts of a once Polish parish has been discarded.

In contrast, few examples of the loss of ethnic identity are to be found among the secular organizations of Polonia, although most have had to change their modes of operation to respond to new conditions. Few continue to conduct their operations in the Polish language, for example. Some have merged with other organizations. Others have disappeared. Let it be noted here that many historically Polish parishes do remain and retain a semblance of their original ethnic identity. These structures represent significant embodiments of the Polish heritage to their members and to secular Polonia leaders.

KEY SECULAR POLONIA ORGANIZATIONS

From a look at their functions, one may readily identify the following types of secular organizations in American Polonia: (1) fraternal insurance benefit societies; (2) newspapers and periodicals, and electronic media; (3) veterans' associations, cultural associations and entertainment groups, educational societies, business and labor organizations; and (4) political action organizations.

THE FRATERNALS

Clearly the second largest set of mass membership organizations in American Polonia after the churches have been the fraternals. These organizations are not for profit mass membership organizations whose aim is one of providing a range of benefits to their members, most notably life insurance protection, educational aid, cultural and social enrichment, all in an environment that celebrates the Polish heritage in some significant fashion.

The first successful fraternal society was the Organization of Poles in America (Organizacja Polska w Ameryce) founded in Detroit in 1873. The OPA was committed to uniting the emigration around the goals of establishing Polish Catholic parishes and schools in America and organizing humanitarian and charitable work on behalf of the least fortunate in the immigration. In 1874 the OPA moved its headquarters to Chicago and became the Polish Roman Catholic Union of America (Zjednoczenie Polskie Rzymsko-Katolickie w Ameryce, ZPRKwA in Polish). It also came under the leadership of the Rev. **Wincenty Barzyński**, the zealous and vigorous leader of the **Resurrectionist Order** of priests in Chicago and the pastor of Polonia's first great parish church, St. Stanislaus Kostka on Chicago's near northside.

Barzyński's autocratic and controversial

leadership had important consequences for Polonia. Locally, his parish eventually became home for some 50,000 people and the members of his Resurrectionist order came to organize more than a dozen parishes in Chicago. In the PRCUA, Barzyński's leadership went unchallenged as long as he lived (until 1899). In 1894, he even put together a federation of Polonia organizations, the **Polish League** (Liga Polska) in an effort to direct the national mission of the organizations of the immigration along the lines he believed in.

The Polish National Alliance (PNA; Związek Narodowy Polski or ZNP) was the second major Polonia fraternal organization to come into being. Under the leadership of **Julius Andrzejkowicz**, an immigrant businessman and Polish patriot, it was established in Andrjekowicz's home city of Philadelphia in February 1880 and that September held its first convention in Chicago. Its leaders, who included several priests who had left the PRCUA due to disagreements with Barzynski, organized the PNA around the principle of uniting the immigrants behind the cause of Polish independence, something they believed to be lacking in the PRCUA. In 1881, the PNA established its own newspaper, called *Zgoda* (Harmony) and in 1886 created the very first fraternal life insurance program for the Poles in America, an action that the PRCUA quickly imitated. That same year the PNA recast its national leadership into the "central government" (*rzad centralny*) of the immigrant community, an action that provoked the enmity of its opponents. As a result, the PNA and the PRCUA found themselves in a struggle for leadership in the still small but rapidly growing Polonia. This conflict came to a gradual end only after Barzyński's death.

Three issues were at the core of the conflict. One had to do with the priorities of Polonia — service to the immigration versus a concern for Poland. PNA activists believed their organization could do both; Barzysńki emphasized the former to the near exclusion of the latter. A second issue was one of leadership; should priests be dominant or could lay persons do the job? Thirdly, there was the question of membership: could a "Polonia" organization invite non–Poles and non–Catholics into its ranks? The PNA argued yes, because they believed all those in America with roots in the old pre-partition Polish-Lithuanian state that had been destroyed in the eighteenth century could be part of the Alliance. They included Lithuanians, Ukrainians, Jews, believers and non-believers. This idea, they argued, did not make them anti–Catholic, but simply more inclusive.

All three issues were eventually resolved. By the First World War (1914–1918) the PRCUA was generally endorsing the PNA position in favor of Poland's independence in complementing its traditional Catholic and immigration concerns. Lay leaders began coming to the fore throughout the immigrant community. And the PNA for its part had dropped its emphasis on recruiting non–Poles and had come to be identified with the Catholicism of the great majority of the Poles in America; after all, they made up both its membership and intended audience.

But while a certain coexistence between the two large fraternals was achieved by 1914, this did not lead to the unification of the fraternal movement. Instead, something quite different occurred and involved the proliferation of fraternals in Polonia. This trend had several dimensions. The first involved actions by local fraternalists in the two big organizations in breaking off to form their own organizations, usually based on some disagreement with the national leaderships in Chicago. Examples of this behavior exist and include the creation of the **Polish Association of America**, centered in Milwaukee, and the **Polish National Alliance of Brooklyn**, both of which left the PRCUA. Another example, among several, was the creation of the Alliance of Poles based in Cleveland that seceded from the PNA.

A more serious development involved the forming of alternative fraternal organizations distinctive from the PNA and PRCUA in some significant fashion. The most obvious example here involves the forming of the Polish Women's Alliance of America (Związek Polek w Ameryce) in Chicago in 1898–1900. The founders of the PWA were increasingly angered over the two main fraternals' resistance to admitting women into their ranks and on the basis of full equality with men. (Soon after their formation, the PNA and PRCUA did grant women what they had demanded, something other fraternals did too in the years after.) The PWA gradually rose to be the third largest Polonia fraternal (or perhaps more properly, the largest Polonia sisterhood).

A major and lasting contribution of the Polish Women's Alliance, the smaller Polish American women's "fraternals" that formed in its wake, and the women who joined the existing formerly all-male fraternals as equals with men was the enhancement of Polonia's cultural mission. This mainly involved their establishment and management of libraries and reading rooms, study programs in English, Polish literature and history for the general population, and the teaching of skills of value to women as wives and mothers, e.g., sewing. In sum, the creation of the PWA brought about an expansion of the fraternal mission in the Polonia.

In 1890, several priests who believed in the idea of a fraternal combining the principles of the rival PRCUA and PNA formed a fraternal they named the **Polish Union of America** (Unia Polska). Ironically, this organization itself later split in two, one with its headquarters in Wilkes-Barre, Pennsylvania, the other in Buffalo. A third separate fraternal movement was the **Polish National Union** (or Spojnia) created under the auspices of the breakaway Polish National Catholic Church in Scranton, Pennsylvania in 1908.

Yet a fourth similar and notable development came with the **Polish Falcons** Alliance in the years between 1887 and 1894. Originally formed as a physical fitness society for young people with a patriotic mission as well, the Falcons imitated the structure and practices of a number of organizations created earlier

Polish Cultural Club of Greater Hartford, Connecticut, joins in a local parade (*CCSU-BC*).

Polish Falcons Hall No. 1, Milwaukee, Wisconsin, 1930s (*UWM*).

in Europe. After the Spanish-American War of 1898, the Falcons developed a kind of military training program for their members. The idea was for its members to somehow prepare themselves to fight for Poland's freedom should that opportunity arise. At the same time, the Falcons Alliance grew ideologically close to the much larger, well financed, Polish National Alliance; between 1905 and 1912 it actually merged with the PNA. (It was in these years that the PNA also attempted to forge mergers with a number of other like-minded but previously independent organizations, for example, the **Polish Singers Alliance**, formed in 1889, and the Alliance of Polish Young People, formed in 1890.)

After reasserting its independence, the Falcons took the lead in sending its members to serve in the **Polish Army in France** formed in 1917 to fight for Poland's independence. In the late 1920s it went a step further and set up its own fraternal insurance program to complement its athletic and physical fitness activities, a move that in fact gave it "a new lease on life."

By the 1930s at least eighteen different Polish American fraternals were in operation with a combined membership of nearly 700,000 men, women and children, or approximately fifteen percent of the entire Polish population in the U.S. They ranged in size from the large and nationally organized PNA (with nearly 300,000 members at the time), the PRCUA (nearly 180,000), and the PWA (over 60,000) to the smaller but not insignificant fraternals like the Falcons, the Polish National Union, the Polish Beneficial Association, the two Polish Unions, the Sons of Poland (with about

20,000 each) and a number of even smaller organizations, which usually operated in only one or a few states.

Initially several of the fraternals that came into existence after 1880 adopted programs that imitated the patriotic orientation of the PNA. However, a number aligned themselves ideologically more closely with the PRCUA. In time, these original distinctions faded, with nearly all the fraternals establishing programs (in addition to their sales of life insurance) that combined the aims of the two early major organizations. Thus all included a patriotic concern for Poland's freedom, service to Polonia, ethnic work among the youth (through their organizing dance and singing societies, libraries and reading rooms, sports and scouting programs, and Polish language and culture courses), support for the Polish parishes, commemorations of Polish anniversaries, and assistance to immigrants and needy Polish Americans. Nearly all maintained publications for the benefit of their members. All elected their officers from the local lodge to the national level as well.

Since the 1980s, a number of the smaller fraternals have merged into the larger organizations. This has been a result of their inability to maintain their memberships and their financial stability in the face of changes occurring in the ever more Americanizing Polish community, and the stiff competition they were experiencing from commercial insurance companies. In 2008, nine Polish American fraternals remained in operation: the PNA, PRCUA, PWA, Polish Falcons, Polish National Union, Polish Beneficial Association, Sons of Poland, Polish Union in Wilkes-Barre and Polish Union in Buffalo.

The combined membership in the Polish American fraternal movement has also declined; in the early 2000s it totaled less than 500,000, compared to a highpoint of more than 800,000 in the early 1960s. This trend has been due to: (1) the Polish fraternals' inability or unwillingness to turn to professional means of selling their insurance products as a way to supplement the recruitment and insurance sales work traditionally performed by cadres of volunteers who in the past served as local lodge organizers and secretaries; (2) the growing competition they faced from commercial insurance companies; (3) the success of many working people in the U.S. in gaining group life insurance benefits through their employers, which reduced their need for insurance from the fraternals; (4) the gradual assimilation of many people of Polish ancestry and their resulting loss of contact with, and awareness of, the fraternal organizations, the activities of their local neighborhood lodges,

their media, and the fraternal benefits they offered (which in 2010 included generous college scholarship programs and a variety of youth, sports, and social activities).

TOTAL POLISH AMERICAN FRATERNAL MEMBERSHIP: 1900s TO 2006

1905–1908	92,000	13 frat'ls
c.1925	531,000	18 frat'ls
c.1935	698,000	18 frat'ls
c.1955	820,000	17 frat'ls
1978	675,000	17 frat's
2006	460,000	9 frat'ls

THE MEDIA OF AMERICAN POLONIA

The earliest publications in the Polish language date back to the 1860s with **Echo z Polski** (New York), which appeared briefly beginning in 1863. In 1870, the first Polonia oriented Polish paper appeared, *Orzeł Polski* (Polish Eagle). Later titled *Pielgrzym* (The Pilgrim), it was published in Union, Missouri, and continued until 1874.

The editors of this paper, **Ignacy Wendziński** and **Jan Barzyński**, can be called the fathers of Polonia journalism. In 1873 **Władysław Dyniewicz** established the *Gazeta Polska* (Polish Gazette) in Chicago and the following year Jan Barzynski set up the *Gazeta Katolicka* (Catholic Gazette) in Detroit. In 1881, the fledgling Polish National Alliance approved the establishment of its own paper, **Zgoda** (Harmony), which was first published in New York and sold to the public. It continues to this day as the fraternal's official organ and is issued to its adult members at no charge.

It was not until the mid–1880s, when Polish immigration was substantial enough, that publications in the Polish language began to appear more frequently and to be more viable. According to Andrzej Brożek, ten Polish language publications were operating in 1888, 24 in 1895, 68 in 1915, and over 100 in 1923. Indeed the rise of publishing in Polonia assumed a remarkable degree of significance and diversity; by 1940, nearly 1,200 different publications had come into existence.

The first successful daily Polish language newspaper was **Michael Kruszka**'s **Kuryer Polski** (Polish Courier), established in Milwaukee in 1888. In the years after, a number of dailies were founded, among them the **Dziennik Chicagoski** (Chicago Daily News) of Chicago in 1890 and sponsored by the **Resurrectionist** religious order, and Chicago's *Dziennik Narodowy* (National Daily News), set up with the backing of the Polish National

Society of St. Kazimierz, New York Mills, New York, 1920s (*James S. Pula*).

Alliance in 1897. Other early dailies were Buffalo's ***Polak w Ameryce*** (The Pole in America), established in 1897, and the Toledo-based ***Ameryka-Echo*** under the ownership of **Anthony Paryski**, from 1902. This paper, like the *Kuryer Polski*, aspired to reach a nationwide readership and at the height of its success claimed as many as 100,000 subscribers. Other dailies established in the years that followed were the *Pittsburczanin* in Pittsburgh, the *Kuryer Polski* (Boston), the *Kuryer Narodowy* and the ***Nowy Swiat*** (New World) in New York, the *Dziennik Polski* (Polish Daily News; Detroit), the *Monitor* and later the *Wiadomość Codzienny* (Daily Information; Cleveland), along with a second Milwaukee paper, the Catholic *Nowiny Polskie* (Polish News), whose policy was always opposed to Kruszka's *Kuryer Polski*. Nevertheless, Chicago remained the capital of the Polish dailies. In 1908 no fewer than four operated simultaneously in the "Windy City": the ***Dziennik Chicagoski***, *Dziennik Narodowy*, the socialist ***Dziennik Ludowy*** (People's Daily News), and the ***Dziennik Związkowy*** (Alliance Daily News), initiated by the PNA. In the 1920s, the *Dziennik Narodowy* merged with its PNA rival; soon after, a new publication came into operation, the ***Dziennik Zjednoczenia*** (Union Daily News), funded by the PRCUA. In addition many weekly and bi-weekly publications came into existence, such as the ***Gwiazda Polarna*** (Polar Star) of Stevens Point, Wisconsin.

The larger Polish American fraternal insurance and benefit societies made it a priority to establish publications for their own members; most notable of these were the already mentioned *Zgoda* of the PNA, the PRCUA's

Narod Polski (The Polish Nation), which superceded the ***Wiara i Ojczyzna*** (Faith and Fatherland), the first PRCUA organ, the Falcons' ***Sokół Polski*** (The Polish Falcon), the Polish Women's Alliance's ***Głos Polek*** (The Voice of Polish Women), the Polish National Union's ***Straż*** (The Guard), and the PNA of Brooklyn's *Czas* (Time). The smaller fraternals issued their own publications as well, though on a less frequent basis. These newspapers' importance lies in their wide distribution; they went out to their members at no charge and thus served both to reinforce the thinking of those Polish Americans who read the commercial press and to touch many others who for some reason could not, or would not, subscribe to a Polish language and ethnic paper. Indeed, the fraternal publications also regularly reprinted a great amount of news and information about Poland and its political situation from the commercial Polonia press. For decades published solely in Polish, from the 1930s, these papers gradually began giving increased space to the English language. By the 1980s all were primarily English language publications.

To be noted too is the important role enterprising publishers in Polonia played in setting up printing houses that issued large numbers of books catering to their readers' interests, both in popular fiction and Polish history. Their inexpensively priced publications included works that had already appeared in Poland; but they also included original writings by Polish American authors and translated editions of non–Polish authors. Major publishers included Chicago's Dyniewicz and **John Smulski**, the Worzalla Brothers of Stevens Point, Wisconsin, and Michael Kruszka

in Milwaukee. Indeed it was Kruszka who published, in 1908, the very first extensive history of the Polish people and their communities in the U.S. This seminal work was authored by his brother, the Rev. **Wacław Kruszka**. But by far the most successful of all of Polonia's publishers was Anthony Paryski, whose Ameryka-Echo company produced over 2,000 titles in five to eight million copies.

Readership for these works was most popular in the years before World War I; a steady decline began in the 1920s, as growing numbers of Polish Americans turned for entertainment and enlightenment to English language reading materials, along with movies and radio. As late as 1945, ten Polish language dailies operated in the U.S., two of them in Chicago, two in Milwaukee, one in Buffalo, Boston, Cleveland, Detroit, Pittsburgh, and New York. In all, they enjoyed a daily readership amounting to perhaps 250,000 adults. And the dailies were but the tip of the iceberg. Below the surface were countless secular and church based publications that reached out to still more readers, locally or regionally.

Most significantly, perhaps, by this time the editorial policies followed by the press had come to have a remarkably unified outlook. Prior to the First World War, divisions along the lines of the PNA-PRCUA rivalry had been most prominent, along with conflicts between the conservative versus the socialist and PNCC camp. In the interwar years (1918–39) sometimes sharp differences over the government in Poland preoccupied editorialists in the press, with some backing General Józef Piłsudski's regime established by a military coup in 1926 and some opposed. But the outbreak of the Second World War in 1939 forged a consensus in the press in support of Poland's independence, the need for humanitarian aid to its people in the face of Nazi and Soviet occupation and oppression, a commitment to the Polish exile government's wartime alliance with the United States after 1941, and a powerfully expressed solidarity on behalf of Poland's liberation from Soviet domination after 1945.

This press consensus gave no quarter to the rather few leftist activists of Polish ethnic background who sympathized with the Soviet Union and its aims. The United States' failure to adequately defend Poland's sovereignty at the **Yalta** conference of 1945 was a point of special press condemnation, as was its deep opposition to Soviet communism. This consensus was further bolstered by the Polonia press' solidarity with the Polish American Congress, the political action federation formed in 1944 to voice support for Poland's post war freedom and independence in the U.S. The unity within the Polish American Newspaper Guild, the organization of Polish journalists further underscored this consensus.

Developments in recent times: In the decades after World War II, the significance of the print media in Polonia declined precipitously. By the first decade of the 21st century, only three Polish language dailies were in operation, two in Chicago (*Dziennik Związkowy* funded by the PNA, and a new paper, *Dziennik Chicagoski*, operated by post 1970s emigrants) and one in New York (*Nowy Dziennik*, established in the 1970s after the closing of the New York *Nowy Swiat*). The others had failed, due to a lack of Polish language readers, the preference of Polish Americans for sources of news and entertainment, especially television and radio, one they shared with their fellow Americans of other ethnic and racial origins, and the lack of sufficient advertising revenue.

Polonia's major publications had already suffered readership declines dating back to the interwar years, due to the "Americanization" of the second and third generations of Polish Americans, the end of substantial Polish immigration after 1924, and the resultant decline in Polish language usage, especially among people born in the U.S. Including a larger number of stories and features in English, especially in covering U.S. sports, did not reverse this decline. Radio for a time played a significant role in the community, but its decline in the face of television after 1950 was not accompanied by a surge in local TV programming of an ethnic type, aside from the occasional Polka show. The rise of cable TV has also been little taken advantage of in Polo-

nia, although a Polish cable station, TV Polonia, has subscribers in the U.S.

In a few cases, English language publications have tried to reach out to Polish Americans, most notably the *Polish American Journal*, published in Buffalo, and the *Polonia Today*, in Chicago. But overall, the reality is that for the overwhelming majority of Polish Americans in recent times, their sole source of information about Poland and Polish culture has been served up, and very sparingly, by the American mass print and electronic media. In its best form, this information has been valuable in bringing great personages, like Pope John Paul II, to the attention of Americans, and linking him and his work with his Polish heritage. Similarity, Polish Americans could not help but feel pride in the creation, vision, and heroic accomplishments of the men and women of the Solidarity trade union movement from 1980 on, and Poland's achievement of freedom and independence from Soviet communist domination after 1989.

The U.S. mass media has also served up more than its fair share of negative commentary about Poland, Polish Americans, and things Polish. These have included the "Polack" jokes that descended on the country in the 1970s (mainly via television) and the more recent, and more ominous, characterizations of Poland as an anti-semitic nation. It is impossible to accurately appraise the effects, and affects, of such media-borne characterizations of "Polishness" on the consciousness and sense of ethnic identification and pride among Polish Americans,

particularly those who are far removed by generations from any direct contact with Poland and its people. But they have hardly helped to generate a positive sense of heritage among persons of Polish ancestry in the U.S.

One might note here that in 1990, the number of persons who asserted their Polish origins in the decennial U.S. census survey of national ancestry rose significantly from the first such enumeration in 1980; this count was held in the wake of ten years of very impressive commentary about "the Pope from Poland" and Solidarity. In the 2000 census survey, in contrast, the number of Polish identifiers dropped considerably from the previous decade. Over the decade of the 1990s, stories about the free and democratic Poland were covered very little in the media, Solidarity itself fell from power, and the aging and physically debilitated Pope was less often associated with Poland.

The absence of a mass Polonia media, save for the publications of the fraternals (whose monthly reach was most certainly in the early 2000s no more than 500–600,000 readers each month in a population of 9–10 Polish Americans), was thus a serious obstacle in enabling the organizations to tell large numbers of Polish Americans "their story" on a continuing and consistent basis.

VETERANS, CULTURAL, SOCIAL, AND EDUCATIONAL GROUPS IN POLONIA

A fascination with forming military-like societies was noticeable in Polonia already in the last decade of the nineteenth century. The

Polish Army Veterans Post in Milwaukee, Wisconsin, 1931 (*UWM*).

Polish Falcons Alliance added to this interest by creating paramilitary training groups in the years immediately following the smashing U.S. victory in the Spanish-American War of 1898. In a few cities, most notably Milwaukee, Polish Americans even had their own regiments in the National Guard. But the main impetus in the forming of organizations of a military character came after World War I, when returnees from service in the Polish Army raised in the United States established the **Polish Army Veterans Association** (PAVA, or Stowarzyszenie Weteranow Armii Polskiej, SWAP) in 1921. That same year, Polish Americans who had served in the U.S. military forces in World War I formed their own organization, which came to be known as the **Polish Legion of American Veterans** (PLAV).

Both organizations continue in operation, with PAVA transformed after World War II into an organization admitting Poles who had served in the Polish military during that conflict. Yet a third significant veterans organization is the Polish Combatants Association, which came into being in 1952, organized by participants in the various Polish military groups that took part in World War II on the western front, in Italy, in occupied Poland itself, and in the East.

Memberships in these organizations peaked at about 15,000 in each case in the 1960s, but have since dwindled, due to the effects of the aging of their members and a general reluctance of Polish American veterans of the U.S. armed forces since that time to join. This reluctance is not unique and poses a problem for all of the many American veterans organizations.

Nonetheless, the Polish veterans groups have played, and continue to play, a highly visible and important role in the Polonia, especially in connection with their uniformed presence at the various patriotic Polish observances that take place each year around the country in the community. The Veterans groups have also been significant factors in adding muscle to the anti–Soviet and anti-communist policy positions taken by the Polish American Congress political action federation on Poland's behalf. For instance, in the Détente era in the 1970s, they were a key element in helping the PAC steer clear of any association with communist-run Poland, at a time when the Gierek regime briefly, but aggressively, tried to cultivate Polonia by asserting its ties with the emigration.

Cultural societies have always been part of Polonia life, many of them connected at the neighborhood level with the Church and the fraternals and taking the form of choral societies. At the national level, one early cultural federation was the Polish Singers Alliance, formed in 1889 by activists in the Polish National Alliance led by **Anthony Małłek**. Another national federation, already noted, was the Polish Falcons Alliance, which stressed physical fitness activities aimed at younger men and women combined with programs stressing pride and patriotism toward Poland. Initially their physical fitness program focused on gymnastics activities; in time they extended to track and field competitions.

A highpoint in the Falcons program was, and is, the Falcons' national meet, or *zlot*, held every four years in conjunction with the organization's national convention. From the 1920s, the Falcons sports program broadened still further to include American team sports like baseball and activities like bowling, swimming, wrestling, and soccer. Yet another late 19th century cultural activity involved the formation of the **Polish Youth Alliance** (Związek Młodzieży Polskiej) in 1894. This movement became part of the PNA in 1905. A Catholic counterpart to this group was the Polish Alma Mater (Macierz Polska). It too entered into the PNA, but much later, in 1986.

Already by the beginning of the 20th century, a large and diverse number of local theater, opera, orchestral, dance, and singing societies became significant contributors to the cultural life and vitality of the Polonia community at the local level, with some attaining broad recognition for the quality of their programs. One of these was the Polanie women's cultural club formed in Minneapolis, Minnesota. It came to play a crucial role in disseminating the music and cultural heritage of Poland by its sponsorship of a series of well received books of Polish songs and traditions.

Following the spirit and example of Polanie, a number of other local cultural organizations were formed; after World War II many of them joined together into a loose confederation they named the American Council of Polish Cultural Clubs. This highly diverse grouping of organizations was later renamed the **American Council for Polish Culture**. The groups belonging to the ACPC promote many different Polish cultural activities in their communities, including piano and violin competitions, scholarship competitions, art festivals, lectures on Polish and Polonia themes, and dance and singing programs. They participate in the various Polish and ethnic festivals held around the United States each year. They have been important supporters of performances by musical ensembles from Poland. And they sponsor tours to Poland as well. One notable achievement by members of the ACPC is a building named the **National Polish Center** located in Washington, D.C.

Nationally, the leading cultural organization promoting knowledge of the Polish cultural heritage is the **Kościuszko Foundation**, established in 1925 by Dr. **Stefan Mizwa** (Mierzwa) and headquartered in New York City. Since its creation the Foundation has raised funds to invite scholars from Poland to do research and lecture in this country and provided fellowships for young American scholars to do their doctoral research in Poland. The Foundation also supports study in Poland for college age Americans and offers awards to Polish Americans doing graduate work in this country as well.

At the academic and professional level, there is the **Polish Institute of Arts and Sciences in America** (now of America). The Institute was established in 1942 in New York City by scholars led by Historian **Oskar Halecki**. All found themselves in the west after Poland's occupation at the start of World War II. Dedicated to keeping Poland's culture alive in the face of the Nazi and Soviet destruction of the country, the PIASA is today an active American scholarly association that publishes its own quarterly journal, *The Polish Review*, and organizes an annual national academic conference.

A second scholarly organization is the **Polish American Historical Association** (PAHA) also founded in 1942. Organized under the leadership of Professor Halecki, the PAHA has grown into a widely regarded academic body under the leadership of a number of scholars dedicated to the subject, beginning with Polonia historian **Mieczysław Haiman**, director of the Polish Museum of America located in Chicago. The PAHA also sponsors a semi-annual scholarly journal, *Polish American Studies*, and an annual national conference that meets in conjunction with the American Historical Association. There it confers a variety of honors to scholars and Polonia activists in recognition of their dedication to researching and sharing knowledge of the Polish experience in America. The organization is currently headquartered in Connecticut. A third, smaller, scholarly grouping is the Polish Studies Association.

Other notable centers of Polish culture in America have included two institutions of higher education. One was **Alliance College**, located in Cambridge Springs, Pennsylvania and established in 1912 by the PNA. The school closed in 1987; in the previous 75 years it graduated over 6,000 students and organized many educational programs dealing with the Polish cultural heritage, including a summer studies program in this field of learning. The Polish Seminary (see **Sts. Cyril and Methodius Seminary**), established in 1886, in Detroit,

Michigan, moved to nearby Orchard Lake in 1908. The institution later sprouted both a high school and a liberal arts college on its grounds. The Seminary continues; the college closed in 2001. In addition, a number of Polish studies programs of varying significance are to be found around the country.

POLITICAL AND CIVIC
ACTION ORGANIZATIONS

Polish American involvement in American political and civic affairs is a subject covered in another essay in this work (see **Politics, Polish Americans in**). Here suffice it to be noted that this activity has been multifaceted and substantial, with large numbers of persons of Polish origin and ancestry taking full advantage of the opportunities they have had in the U.S. to organize and operate freely in this country in the political arena on behalf of the causes that concerned them.

The most significant areas of civic and political activity centering in Polonia have, of course, involved the creation of organizations dedicated to the cause of Poland, the old "fatherland" (*ojczyzna*) of the Polish immigration, its members' children and descendants born in the United States.

Before the advent of massive immigration following the American Civil War, a series of relatively short-lived Polish groups working for Poland's independence were formed, usually in connection with the efforts of the early immigrant activist **Henryk Kałussowski** (1806–1894). These included the Association of Poles in America (1842), the **Democratic Society of Polish Exiles in America** (1852) and the **Polish Central Committee** of New York (1864, formed to support the cause of the "January" Polish insurrection against the Russian tsar.)

By 1880, the size of the Polish immigrant population had grown enough to make possible the forging of more viable political action organizations on the national level. The first of these was the Polish National Alliance, one of whose supporters was the 74-year-old Kałussowski, and whose mission supported the cause of Poland's restoration to national independence. While this effort did not succeed in uniting the immigration behind the PNA leadership, it did lead to a rise in interest in this idea. Thus in 1891, several organizations in Chicago organized public manifestations in honor of the centennial anniversary of the promulgation of the Polish **Constitution of May the Third**, 1791. In 1894, the Reverend **Wincenty Barzyński** organized his Polish League (Liga Polska), whose purpose was to unite Polonia behind his community-focused programs in America. The Polish National Al-

liance opposed his action and it failed. The PNA was already committed to supporting an earlier Polish League formed in Switzerland with supporters in the partitioned homeland; its leaders feared that its patriotic message would be marginalized in Barzyński's League.

In the years that followed, both the PRCUA and PNA devoted considerable time and effort to forming nationwide organizational efforts aimed at uniting **Polonia** under their banners. PRCUA efforts included Catholic-centered efforts initiated in 1896, 1901, 1902, 1904, and 1908. PNA initiatives took place in 1905 (in conjunction with its national convention) and 1910. All of these actions, though failing to create a united Polonia, were nonetheless important in drawing immigrant opinion in the direction of giving general support to the PNA mission supporting Poland's independence.

A significant example of this trend came in the growing enthusiasm for a number of projects to erect monuments in honor of **Tadeusz Kościuszko**, the widely admired participant in the American War of Independence and the populist leader of the failed Polish uprising for independence of 1794. **Monuments** to Kościuszko were funded by the early 1900s in several major Polonia centers, most notably, Chicago, Milwaukee, and Cleveland. A Kosciuszko monument was also funded by the PNA and its allies in Washington, D.C. and dedicated with great pomp and pageantry in the nation's capital in 1910, along with a monument funded by the U.S. Congress to honor General **Kazimierz Pułaski**, the Polish patriot and American Revolutionary War hero who gave his life to the American independence cause at the battle of Savannah on October 11, 1779. Yet another Kościuszko monument was later erected at the U.S. Military Academy at **West Point**, New York.

In 1903, the Polish **Constitution Day** parade became an annual event in Chicago. Similar manifestations were also held in other Polonia centers. In New York, beginning in 1937, an annual parade in honor of Pułaski became a staple of pride in the East. In 1910, in conjunction with the celebration of the dedication of the Pułaski and Kościuszko monuments, the PNA organized a Congress of Polonia to discuss the central issues facing the community. There, the President of the PNA put forth a motion calling for Poland's restoration to independence.

In 1912, the organizations of Polonia reached an agreement in Pittsburgh to form the first true national confederation of the Polish emigration in America. The decision followed their presence at the reunification of the Polish Falcons Alliance. They named the federation

the **National Defense Committee** (Komitet Obrony Narodowej, KON).

But this decision did not hold. Leaders from the PRCUA and the Catholic clergy soon withdrew over KON's inclusion of the small schismatic **Polish National Catholic Church** and the radical **Polish Socialist Alliance**; their action was followed soon after by the PNA, Polish Women's Alliance and Polish Falcons. By the time of the outbreak of World War I in August 1914, KON had become a marginal factor; it continued on into the 1920s only because of its identification with General Józef Piłsudski, Poland's most prominent political figure after the country regained its independence in 1918.

In September 1914, the PRCUA, PNA, PWA and Falcons, together with the clergy created a new organization, the **Polish Central Relief Committee** (Polski Centralny Komitet Ratunkowy, PCKR), whose mission was to gather supplies for shipment to partitioned Poland, already a killing ground in the conflict between its warring rulers, imperial Germany and Russia. From the start, the relief organization, headed by the Chicago banker, politician and Polonia leader **John Smulski**, established a close working relationship with the Polish independence committee operating in France led by Roman Dmowski and represented in America by the Pianist **Ignacy Jan Paderewski**. The PCKR included a political action subcommittee, the Polish **National Department** (Wydział Narodowy). By 1916 this body had swung into action to present Poland's case for independence in the U.S., one in line with the policies of Britain and France, soon to become America's closest allies when it entered the War. Soon, the Department completely overshadowed its parent body. In addition to its propaganda work, the National Department also played a key role in organizing a Polish Army in America of more than 20,000 young men. This force was dispatched to France where it saw a bit of action before the War's end in November 1918 as part of a much larger Polish army that was then sent to Poland. There its members took part in the Polish-Bolshevik war of 1919–21. After their return home, many formed the Polish Army Veterans Association noted above.

In September 1918, the National Department organized a Congress of the Emigration in Detroit attended by over 1,000 Polonia leaders. There the delegates heard addresses by Dmowski and Paderewski. When the War ended only a few weeks later, and with Poland's independence apparently recognized by 1921, the rationale disappeared for a permanent Polish National Department. In 1925 it dissolved, and no comparable all–Polonia federation replaced it in the years up to the outbreak of World War II and the Nazi-Soviet conquest of Poland in September 1939.

In the late 1920s, Poland attempted to form an organization, the **World Union of Poles from Abroad** (Światowy Związek Polaków ze Zagranicy, "Światpol") that aimed to bring together the organizations of the emigration around the world that would operate in co-operation with its government. The second congress of "Światpol" was convened in Warsaw in August 1934, with 40 delegates from American Polonia present at the gathering. But they refused to swear allegiance to "Światpol," on the grounds that Polish Americans constituted an inseparable part of the great American nation, and were not to be seen as members of some kind of separate Polish colony in the U.S. Nevertheless, those present affirmed their pride in Poland's achievements and culture, their past work on behalf of Polish independence, and their desire to work with Poland to promote the Polish heritage in America. Interestingly, at the first world congress of the Polonia organized in 1992 in Poland following the end of communist rule, American representatives acted in much the same fashion as in 1934. On the one hand they declined to be part of a Poland-sponsored world coordinating council of Polonia but expressed their support for close cooperation with the organizing body of the congress, Wspólnota Polska, or The Polish Community.

With the outbreak of World War II in 1939, Polonia's organizations returned to the mission

Banner of the Society of St. Stanislaus, Bishop and Martyr, in New York Mills, New York (*Eugene E. Dziedzic and James S. Pula*).

that had animated them in the First World War. Within weeks of Poland's conquest by Nazi Germany and Soviet Russia, the organizations, together with the clergy, formed a new humanitarian federation they named the **Polish American Council** (Rada Polonii Amerykańskiej, RPA, more commonly known in the U.S. as American Relief for Poland). The RPA, headed by **Francis X. Swietlik, censor** of the PNA, went on to play a noteworthy role in delivering millions of dollars in supplies to Poles afflicted by the war, primarily those who had become refugees, the inmates of the prisoner of war camps, and Polish soldiers fighting on the Allied side in Britain. But for several reasons it was constrained from playing any role as a political action organization.

By 1942, two groups of Polish Americans were politically active. One was linked with leftist and pro–Soviet groups in this country and included the **American Slav Congress** and the **American Polish Labor Council**. Its leaders stressed their support for the Roosevelt administration and the establishment of a close U.S.–Soviet alliance. The second was a group formed in New York City, the **National Committee of Americans of Polish Descent** (Komitet Narodowy Amerykanów Polskiego Pochodzenia, KNAPP). Headed by several former exiled officials of the pre–1939 Polish government, most notably the publicist **Ignacy Matuszewski**, it also included Polish Americans who shared a deep apprehension over the Soviet Union's intentions toward Poland and sharply criticized General Władysław Sikorski, the head of the Polish exile government for his perceived weakness in representing Poland's interests to the U.S., Britain, and Soviet Russia in their allied war effort against Nazi Germany. Neither group had widespread backing, with most Polish Americans remaining politically passive on the issue of Poland, aside from the general support many gave to the work of the RPA.

In 1943, three big events changed things dramatically. In April the graves of thousands of murdered Polish military officers were discovered in the Soviet forest with blame for the crime fixed by many on the Soviet Union. In July General Sikorski was killed mysteriously in a plane crash. And following the November summit meeting between Soviet leader Josef Stalin and President Roosevelt at Teheran, Iran, rumors grew that the President had made a secret deal with the Soviet boss at Poland's expense.

In May 1944 a new political action organization, the Polish American Congress (PAC or Kongres Polonii Amerykańskiej) was created at a massive gathering of over 2,600

elected representatives of Polonia in Buffalo, New York. The work of the leaders of the major Polish American fraternals, the clergy, and the KNAPP organization, the PAC elected **Charles Rozmarek** of the PNA as its president and approved an action program dedicated to achieving a free and independent postwar Poland and reaffirming Polonia's total support for the American war and its aims. The war resulted, not in a free and independent Poland, but in a communist puppet state under Soviet control with radically altered borders. Thus the PAC was obliged to continue in action, unlike its World War I era predecessor, the National Department. In the next decade it became a powerful element in the growing anti-communist coalition that became a dominant force in influencing U.S. politics and this country's policies toward the Soviet Union long after Stalin's death in 1953. The PAC, moreover, unswervingly maintained its position in support of Poland's freedom from communist domination under Rozmarek's successors as president, **Aloysius Mazewski** (1968–88) and **Edward Moskal** (1988–2005). At every juncture in the efforts of the Polish people to assert their freedom from Soviet domination — in 1947, 1956, 1970, and 1980 — the PAC strongly expressed its concern for Poland to the leaders of the U.S. government.

In August 1980, the PAC came out in support of the Solidarity trade union only days after its creation in Gdańsk. It backed a hard line against the communist regime after it tried to destroy the Solidarity movement in December 1981. And it strongly backed the policies of the new Polish democratic government that came into existence in September 1989. In the early years of democratic Poland, the PAC succeeded in gaining U.S. government approval of a series of economic aid policies on Poland's behalf. In 1999, Poland, with considerable PAC lobbying, became an ally of the United States when its membership in the multi-state NATO alliance was approved. Since then, and while PAC support for a close strategic relationship between the U.S. and Poland remain very important, the PAC in other respects can readily be described as an organization in search of a redefined mission.

THE FUTURE

Poland's achievement of sovereignty and democracy after 1989 and its entry into NATO in 1999, along with the death of Pope John Paul II in 2005, may be seen as climactic watershed dates for Polonia, Poland, and their relationship. In Polonia, fewer individuals belong to the fraternals than at any time since the 1920s. The percentage of foreign born Poles, about five percent, is lower than at any time over the past century. The media reaches a very small audience. Relatively few persons of Polish descent know the Polish language. Intermarriage between persons of Polish heritage with persons of other ethnicities, religious traditions, and even racial backgrounds is increasing in line with the general pattern found among other American ethnic populations. The great events of the heroism of the Polish people, as manifested most recently during the Solidarity era that began with the election of John Paul II in 1978, have apparently come to a close. Since 1989, Poland has, instead, increasingly become a "normal" country, and thus a land "off the front page" of the American consciousness.

Looking at the state of American Polonia from this vantage point presents a rather dismal picture. But there is another perspective that is worth considering. It lies in the existence of a number of cultural organizations around the country whose members are both knowledgeable about Poland, its history, culture, literature, language, and the Polish experience in America, and dedicated to sharing this knowledge with others. This body of organizations includes the **Kosciuszko Foundation** and the small but solid cadre of university professors who regularly share their expertise about "things Polish" with their students, academic colleagues, and interested members of the communities where they work. It includes the still substantial number of Polish American fraternals, whose members are committed to their heritage and traditions. It includes the activists who direct the Polish cultural centers and museums that are scattered about the country and are a source of continuing enlightenment for those people who enter their premises. It includes the festivals of Polish and **Polonia** culture that take place across the country each year and which direct their attention to popular culture, as it is presented in polka music and the old, reliable, tasty, Polish peasant soul foods, as well as the "high" Polish culture identified with Chopin and scores of other renowned contributors to the world's great music, literature, and art.

There is lastly, the state of Poland, since 1989 a sovereign democracy no longer separated from the U.S., western Europe, and even its own diasporas by the politics of discredited and prejudiced rulers submissive to an alien system of thought. This Poland can be a major source of energy for Polonia in the future, yes, a smaller Polonia in terms of organizational membership, but rich in its heritage and its aspirations. Poland is a land that can be readily visited too, and is thus a source of endless learning and renewed enthusiasm for those who travel there, even for short periods of time.

Perhaps the Polish American Congress might be the Polonia organization, working with the ethnic community's main cultural organizations and the Polish government, that will convene a summit meeting bringing all together. At such a summit an agenda might be seriously and systematically discussed about their common interests and concerns, with a practical action program for the future agreed upon. Through such a summit, a process to build and broaden awareness of the Polish and Polish American heritage in the U.S. might begin which would be of benefit to all concerned.—*Donald E. Pienkos*

SOURCES: Walter Zachariasewicz, "Organizational Structure of Polonia," in Frank Mocha, ed., *Poles in America: Bicentennial Essays* (Stevens Point, WI: Worzalla Publishing Company, 1978), 627–70; Andrzej Brozek, *Polish Americans 1854–1939* (Warsaw: Interpress Publishers, 1985); Anna D. Jaroszyńska-Kirchmann, *The Exile Mission: The Polish Political Diaspora and Polish Americans* (Athens, Ohio: Ohio University Press, 2004); Wacław Kruszka, *A History of the Poles in America to 1908, Part I* (Washington, D.C.: The Catholic University of America Press, 1993; James S. Pula, ed.); Helena Znaniecka Lopata, *Polish Americans: Status Competition in an Ethnic Community* (Englewood Cliffs, New Jersey: Prentice Hall, 1976, 1994); Michael J. Mikos, "Towards a History of Polonistyka in the United States," *The Polish Review*, Vol. 53, no. 2 (2008); Frank Mocha, ed., *Poles in America: Bicentennial Essays* (Stevens Point, WI: Worzalla Publishing Company, 1978); Donald E. Pienkos, *For Your Freedom Through Ours: Polish American Efforts on Poland's Behalf, 1863–1991* (Boulder, CO: East European Monographs, 1991); James S. Pula, *Polish Americans: An Ethnic Community* (New York: Twayne Publishers, 1995); Frank Renkiewicz, "An Economy of Self-Help: Fraternal Capitalism and the Evolution of Polish America," in Charles A. Ward, Philip Shashko, and Donald E. Pienkos, eds., *Studies in Ethnicity: The East European Experience in America* (Boulder, CO: East European Monographs, 1978); Piotr S. Wandycz, *The United States and Poland* (Cambridge, MA, and London: Harvard University Press, 1980); Joseph A. Wytrwal, *Behold! The Polish Americans* (Detroit: Endurance Press, 1977).

Organized Labor, Polish Americans in. Initially the labor movement in the United States was focused on skilled laborers and organized locally; a local union of the same trade mainly dealing with the protection of trade standards and economic power. During the 1830s, these local unions combined their forces for purposes of mutual defense and local action. After 1850 national unions came into existence to define larger purposes. The American Federation of Labors (AFL) was one of the first and largest federations of unions. Although its' main focus was trade unions, it had always included a number of industrial unions such as the United Mine Workers of America (UMW) as miners were considered skilled workers. In the late nineteenth and early twentieth centuries the support for unions grew as increasing numbers of workers faced difficult working conditions, long work-weeks, and low wages. This formation of the labor activity was inspired by economic forces within the American society; their participants were mostly of European origin.

Older immigrant groups, originating from the northern and western part of Europe, dominated the American labor movement. They responded with hostility toward the more recent migrants from Eastern and Southern Europe, and tried to exclude them from the labor movement. They argued that these newcomers were not needed as the labor market was filled to capacity. Recent migrants were also blamed for being willing to work for lower wages. In this fashion, labor leaders argued, these new immigrants would undermine the effectiveness of trade unionism. The American labor movement therefore believed in a restricted labor market. It applauded the outcome of the **Dillingham Commission** and supported the quota system limiting immigration of Eastern and Southern Europeans. The unions also felt that the newcomers had no understanding of labor organizations. Cultural and language barriers played a role in this. Since most Eastern and Southern European immigrants initially did not speak English and had a different background than immigrants of Anglo-Saxon origin, they often were misunderstood. These cultural differences, next to competition for jobs, housing, and status, cut deeply into the labor movement and failed to unite the workers. Company owners reinforced the ethnic diversification frustrating class cooperation even more.

Over the years the hostility toward immigrants declined. The introduction of new work processes strengthened interethnic ties as different ethnic groups were now working side by side in the same departments. The labor movement also realized that it needed the new immigrants. Initially the trade unions did not bother with the struggle of the industrial — unskilled — workers. As most immigrants were industrial workers, they were excluded from the trade unions. However, due to increasing mechanization of industrial processes fewer skilled workers were needed undermining the power of the unions. The trade unions realized that they could not exclude the unskilled industrial workers any more and opened their ranks. AFL unions also changed their policy toward the newcomers and made some adjustments. Ethnic leaders were recruited and immigrants were addressed in their own language. Consequently, immigrants from Eastern and Southern Europe, who had often formed their own independent union locals, became involved with the national American labor movement.

Initially, the Poles were not considered very active in the American labor movement. Negative and racial stereotypes colored this typecast. Poles were portrayed as docile and seemingly content with the poor working conditions. The unions also complained that the Polish immigrants were shunning their organizations and were not participating in labor conflicts. This stereotype was rooted in the conviction that migrants from peasant origin — as were most Polish migrants — were passive victims of American capitalism, frustrating unionization. Later scholarship proved that this stereotype was false and that the Poles actually were quite active in the labor movement. That most early Polish immigrants were mainly of peasant origin did not mean that they were docile. The Poles proved to be active unionists and became involved in its organizations more and more.

INVOLVEMENT OF POLES IN THE EARLY LABOR MOVEMENT

Most Poles who came to the U.S. before 1900 were used to hard working conditions, long workdays, and low wages. Working conditions for the early Polish immigrants in the United States were very hard as the majority were employed as unskilled laborers. At least eighty percent of the Polish immigrants ended up in industrial towns engaged in the lower and menial jobs. They were employed inside the plants of the meat packing industries in Chicago, the textile mills in New England, as well as the steel factories and the coal mines in Pennsylvania. Most of these early Polish immigrants came with the intention to work hard and save as much money as possible. They either wished to send their savings to their families in Poland, or use it to buy land in the homeland. As **"birds of passage"** — people who intended to return someday to Poland — they tolerated the poor working conditions in order to save the money they would need to establish for themselves and their families a better life in Poland. As it turned out, it proved to be difficult to put aside enough money and it gradually became clear that their goal of returning to their homeland was unrealistic. Most Polish migrants realized they would not be able to return as a rich man so their outlook on life in the United States changed. This resulted in a more critical attitude toward their working conditions which they no longer accepted. The culture the Poles brought with them from Europe stressed group decisions and communal approval, making them militant strikers, community oriented, and supportive of local unions. Their strikes were often spontaneous and, as community events, involved the whole

family. Men, women, and children would join these activities, marching on picket lines, throwing stones, and engaging in other support activities.

Although few Poles joined the early trade unions, as largely unskilled industrial workers they responded positively to the call of unions seeking to enroll and organize industrial workers. An exception among trade unions was United Mine Workers which opened its ranks to Polish miners. The miners' union introduced some adjustments to address its members of Polish origin; for example, it made important documents available to them in Polish. John Fahy, the popular union leader in the anthracite region of Pennsylvania, recruited ethnic leaders to assist him in addressing and organizing the immigrants. The UMW's policy also proclaimed a new constitution incorporating the principle of brotherhood by prohibiting discrimination based on race, nationality, or creed. Thus, the UMW proved to be ethnically friendly and pluralistic. Its president, John Mitchell, became very popular among the Poles.

LATTIMER MASSACRE

The **Lattimer Massacre** in 1897 was a traumatic event for the Polish labor movement. A strike started as a protest against the harsh working conditions in the mines and the "alien tax" in the company stores. During this strike, launched by Slavic coal miners in Luzerne County, Pennsylvania, a peaceful march of 400 people in Lattimer was met with brutality by James Martin, the county sheriff. The marchers were halted and commanded to leave. Without any warning, sheriff's deputies began firing into the crowd killing 19 people and wounding 38. The Lattimer Massacre therefore has been characterized as one of the most serious acts of violence against American laborers in general, and the Polish community in specific, with twenty-six Poles injured or killed. It became a symbol of mass martyrdom that inspired Polish workers to become engaged in the union cause.

POLES IN THE TWENTIETH CENTURY LABOR MOVEMENT

The first two decades of the twentieth century were a period of increasing mechanization and rationalization of industrial processes leading to deteriorating working conditions and loss of control for the workers. Not only had the industrial worker become an extension of the machine and therefore a small part of the production process (for instance, a shoemaker would not make the whole shoe anymore, but might only cut out button holes instead). Like the parts of a machine, the

workers had become replaceable, increasing job insecurity. Becoming unemployed had become an element of the rationalized industry. Consequently, more labor conflicts and clashes occurred. The workers employed by the industries protested against the hardships and wrongs, against the new discipline. They demanded higher wages, better workings conditions, fewer hours, and relaxation of the discipline. They wished to reform industry. This time the Poles' involvement was more structured as those who had arrived after 1900 were more experienced with rural populist and urban political movements, and an increasing percentage realized that their future lay permanently in America.

As the American unions realized that they needed the immigrants, some adjustments to include them were introduced. The Amalgamated Meat Cutters and Butcher Workmen (AMCBW) in Chicago, for instance, employed translators, as well as organizers who were familiar with East European languages. This policy was successful, and immigrants joined the union in great numbers, especially Polish meat packers. Consequently, the Poles' influence on the policy of the union also grew.

Other industries also profited from increasing Polish involvement. Due to the large percentage of Polish workers in the textile mills of New York and New England, the United Textile Workers of America (UTWA) decided to recruit Polish organizers and print union materials in Polish. As the Poles formed the majority of the workforce in the mills, they took the initiative to organize local lodges of the UTWA. For instance, the Poles took a leading role in the founding of UTWA Local 753 of New York Mills, New York, and subsequently led successful strikes in 1912 and 1916. When the Poles went on strike the company officials responded by hiring strikebreakers and provoking violent actions. The strikers remained disciplined throughout and asked other unionists to join them. The first strike resulted in a compromise; more pay and a promise for better work conditions. Immediately after the strike ended the company broke its promise and the union organizers were fired. Another strike began in 1916 lasting for four months. This strike was more successful and most demands were honored including recognition of the union by the company. The Poles also became a major force in the UMW which, in 1912, began publishing the weekly *Górnik Polski* (Polish Miner) addressed to Polish workers.

There was widespread support for unionism and collective action among Polish workers before World War I. As the involvement of the Poles with the labor movement grew, they

An encampment of striking Polish America workers and families of Local 753, United Textile Workers of America, in New York Mills, New York, 1916 (*Eugene E. Dziedzic and James S. Pula*).

took leading roles during strikes and became well represented on strike committees. Being represented in strike committee was considered very important since the committee was in full control during the strikes. These were organized according to grassroots structures with each plant having its own strike committee. In one example, during a textile strike of Passaic, New Jersey, in 1919 the Poles formed their own union, the Independent Union of General Workers of the Textile Industry of Passaic and Vicinity headed by Mateusz Płukarz. Although Polish involvement in the organization of strikes continued to increase during this period, their importance was mainly limited to local communities. Nevertheless, Poles rose to important local union positions such as **Jan Kikulski** in the Stockyard Labor Council (SLC) in Chicago and Anton Piławski in the National Committee for Organizing the Iron and Steel Workers in Cleveland.

THE STEEL STRIKE OF 1919

Despite efforts to include immigrants, the labor movement remained divided and therefore its influence was limited. Consequently, the early unions were not very successful improving the workers' conditions. During World War I this situation improved somewhat as employers tried to prevent the outbreak of strikes. Moreover, the government protected the unions because of the need to maintain wartime production. Some changes were introduced such as higher wages, but overall working conditions continued to be very hard and workweeks long. The unions' request to change the twelve hour workday

for seven days a week into fewer and shorter workdays had not been honored. Once the war was over the improvements that had been gained did not last. Although the increase in wages was not reversed, inflation after the war made it even more difficult for workers make ends meet.

After the war the unions resumed their fight for improvement of the workers' conditions. One of the most important strikes was the Steel Strike of 1919, a bitter attempt by the American labor movement to organize the steel industry and reclaim its power. It started in Pennsylvania when thousands of steelworkers went on strike on April 1, 1919. They felt betrayed by the broken promises of employers and the government to keep prices low, raise wages, and improve working conditions. The strike evolved into a general national steelworkers' strike starting on September 22, 1919. Later, workers from other companies joined the strike that shut down about fifty percent of the steel industry including mills in Pennsylvania, Illinois, Ohio, West Virginia, Colorado, and New York. But the steel companies had seriously misjudged the strength of worker discontent. The unrest eventually involved more than 350,000 workers demanding higher wages, an eight-hour workday, and recognition of unions. Among them were tens of thousands of Polish Americans.

THE POLISH SOCIALIST LABOR MOVEMENT

Despite Polish workers' labor activism, the general stereotype persisted that they were quite conservative. Another challenge to this

viewpoint was Polish involvement in the socialist labor movement. Unlike the trade unions, socialist unions called for industrial unionism and actively sought to recruit immigrants by employing organizers fluent in various languages and publishing its materials in those languages. Poles not only join these unions, but became actively involved in the organization's leadership. The Polish association with the socialist labor movement started before World War I. In 1912, a Polish section of the Socialist Party (PS-SP) was established that consisted of 134 locals and 2,500 members, more than any other ethnic group (see **Socialists, Polish American; Polish Section, Socialist Party of the United States;** and **Polish Socialist Alliance of America**). Through the PS-SP's newspaper, the ***Dziennik Ludowy*** (People's Daily) that circulated among 18,000 Poles, and popular theatrical productions, a thriving socialist subculture was created.

The Polish socialists in the United States were heavily influenced by the homeland politics. Consequently, Polish socialist workers were divided into three groups. The pro-independence socialists influenced **Polonia** considerably as they took leadership roles in the **Polish National Alliance** and the **National Defense Committee**. The anti-independence socialists, those who supported the concept of a Polish socialist country that would belong to a larger international communist state, were also quite influential in the PS-SP despite their numerical weakness. The third Polish socialist group was formed by the nationalists. Their position was more difficult to sustain among American **Polonia** because they supported Józef Piłsudski's strategy of allying with Germany against Russia during World War I. Later, when Piłsudski changed sides to fight against the Germans, his strategy was heavily criticized by Polonia. These divisions within the Polish socialists fractured the movement, weakening its potential influence.

The socialist movement in Polonia lost momentum throughout the 1920s, but regained some influence during the Great Depression when a new generation of Polish socialists proved to be less radical than their predecessors. This new leadership attempted to reach Polish American workers through existing institutional, community, and parish networks. By the end of the 1930s, about 600,000 Polish Americans were enrolled in the left-leaning Congress of Industrial Organizations (CIO). The CIO, created by John L. Lewis in 1932, was a federation of unions that organized workers in industrial unions in the United States and Canada. It was born out of protest against the American labor movement that was reluctant to organize unskilled industrial workers who formed the majority of workers in America. Lewis started the CIO within the AFL but, facing increasing hostility from AFL's leadership, he led eight industrial unions out of the AFL to form the independent CIO in 1935. The CIO proved to be highly successful and within a few years it had organized steel, automobile, rubber, and other major industries. In 1955, the CIO merged with the AFL to form the AFL-CIO. Under the banners of the CIO and the New Deal of Franklin D. Roosevelt, workers in Chicago revitalized the labor movement that had suffered from the failed strikes in 1919. Research has suggested that as much as forty percent of the membership of the CIO in the 1930s consisted of Slavic workers.

POLISH LEADERS IN
THE LABOR MOVEMENT

Throughout the development of the labor movement in the United States, Polish Americans have held leadership positions on both the local and national levels. Prominent early national leaders included **David Dubinsky**, president of the International Ladies' Garment Union; **John Kikulski**, a prominent leader in the Chicago stockyards; and **Leo Krzycki**, a leader in the Amalgated Clothing Workers of America. **Stanley Nowak**, an influential organizer of the United Auto Workers in Detroit, became editor of *Głos Robotniczy* (The Workers' Voice) in 1924. He was later elected to the state senate in Michigan in 1938. **Frank Wachter** was a national official in the early Knights of Labor; **Bolesław Gebert, a** co-

founder of the **Polish American Labor Council**, served as editor-in-chief of the ***Głos Ludowy*** (The People's Voice); **Stanisław Rokosz** was a successful organizer among steelworkers in Pittsburgh and Chicago slaughterhouses; while **Richard Trumka**, an AFL-CIO executive, was named by President Barack Obama to the President's Economic Recovery Advisory Board in 2009.

One of the more famous Polish American labor leaders was **Joseph Yablonski**. In 1934, Yablonski was elected as a union officer and became a representative to the international executive board of the United Mine Workers by 1940. In 1958, he was appointed president of UMW District 5. A noted reformer, by 1963 he clashed with union president W. A. "Tony" Boyle over how the union should be run. In May 1969 he challenged Boyle by announcing his candidacy for president of the union. Although Boyle won the elections by fraud, he decided to eliminate his rival. Yablonski, his wife, and his daughter were killed in their home during the evening of December 31, 1969. Three days later their killers were arrested and later convicted. Eventually, Boyle's involvement with the murder became known and he was sentenced to prison. The murder of Yablonski had a major impact and began a democratic reform movement within the mine workers' union.—*Pien Versteegh*

SOURCES: John Bodnar, *Immigration and Industrialization: Ethnicity in an American Mill Town, 1870–1940* (Pittsburgh: University of Pittsburgh Press, 1977); John Bodnar, Roger Simon, and Michael P. Weber, *Lives of Their Own: Blacks, Italians, and Poles in Pittsburgh, 1900–1960* (Urbana, IL: University of Illinois Press, 1982); Mary E. Cygan, "The Polish-American Left" in Paul Buhle and Dan Georgakas, eds., *The Immigrant Left in the United States* (Albany: State University of New York Press, 1996), 148–84; William G. Falkowski, "Labor, Radicalism and the Polish-American Worker," in John J. Bukowczyk, ed., *Polish Americans and their History: Community, Culture, Politics* (Pittsburgh: University of Pittsburgh Press, 1996), 39–57; Victor R. Greene, *The Slavic Community on Strike: Immigrant Labor in Pennsylvania Anthracite* (London: University of Notre Dame Press, 1968); Ewa Morawksa, *For Bread with Butter: The Life-Worlds of East Central Europeans in Johnstown, Pennsylvania, 1890–1940* (Cambridge: Cambridge University Press, 1985); Margaret Collingwood Nowak, *Two Who Were There: A Biography of Stanley Nowak* (Detroit: Wayne State University Press, 1989); Paul John Nyden, "Miners for Democracy; A Struggle in the Coal Fields" (Ph.D. diss., Columbia University, 1979); Dominic A. Pacyga, "Villages of Steel Mills and Packinghouses: the Polish Worker on Chicago's South Side. 1880–1921" in Frank Renkiewicz (ed.), *The Polish Presence in Canada and America* (Toronto: The Multicultural History Society of Ontario, 1982), 19–27; Frank Renkiewicz, "Polish American Workers, 1880–1980," in Stanislaus A. Blejwas and Mieczysław B. Biskupski, eds., *Pastor of the Poles: Polish American Essays Presented to Right Reverend Monsignor John P. Wodarski in Honor of the Fiftieth Anniversary of His Ordination. Polish Studies Program Monographs* (New Britain, CT: Central Connecticut State University, 1982), 116–136; Adam Walaszek, "Was the Polish Worker Asleep? Immigrants, Unions and Workers' Control in America, 1900–1922," *Polish American Studies*, Vol. 64, no. 1 (1989), 74–96; James S. Pula and Eugene E. Dziedzic, *United We Stand: The Role of Polish Workers in the New York Mills Textile Strikes, 1912 and 1916* (Boulder, CO: East European Monographs, 1990); Victor R. Greene, "The Poles and Anthracite Unions in Pennsylvania," *Polish American Studies*, Vol. 22, no. 1 (1965), 10–16; George Dorsey, "The Bayonne Refinery Strikes 1915–1916," *Polish American Studies*, Vol. 33, no. 2 (1976), 19–30; Neil Betten, "Polish American Steelworkers: Americanization through Industry and Labor," *Polish American Studies*, Vol. 33, no. 2 (1976), 31–42; Edward F. Keuchel, "The Polish American Migrant Worker: The New York Canning Industry 1900–1935," *Polish American Studies*, Vol. 33, no. 2 (1976), 43–51; Eugene Miller, "Leo Krzycki—Polish American Labor Leader," *Polish American Studies*, Vol. 33, no. 2 (1976), 52–64; Lucille O'Connell, "The Lawrence Textile Strike of 1912: The Testimony of Two Polish Women," *Polish American Studies*, Vol. 36, no. 2 (1979), 44–62; Tadeusz Z. Grabinski, "Polish Contract Labor in Hawaii, 1896–1899," *Polish American Studies*, Vol. 39, no. 1 (1982), 14–27; John J. Bukowczyk, "Polish Rural Culture and Immigrant Working Class Formation, 1880–1914," *Polish American Studies*, Vol. 41, no. 2 (1984), 23–44; Victor Greene, "The Polish American Worker to 1930: the 'Hunky' Image in Transition," *The Polish Review*, Vol. 21, no. 3 (1976), 63–78; James S. Pula and Philip Bean, "The Anatomy of Immigrant Strikes: A Comparison of Polish and Italian Textile Workers in Central New York," *The Polish Review*, Vol. 41, no. 3 (1996), 273–92; Georg Schrode, "Mary Zuk and the Detroit Meat Strike of 1935," *Polish American Studies*, Vol. 43, no. 2 (1986), 5–39; Vol. 46, no. 1 (1989) of *Polish American Studies* contains a symposium of eight articles on Polish workers in Europe and America.

Orlemański, Stanisław (b. Erie, Pennsylvania, December 12, 1889; d. Springfield, Massachusetts, March 16, 1960). Priest, Polonia activist. After attending seminaries in Orchard Lake, Michigan, and Montréal, Canada, Orlemański began work as a Catholic priest in Springfield, Massachusetts, in 1918. In 1932, he authored a pamphlet titled *Wychodźstwo Polskie w Ameryce* (Polish Emigrants in America). Although a Roman Catholic, he was sympathetic toward socialism and in 1943 helped to found the **Kościuszko League**, which sympathized with the pro–Soviet Związek Patriotów Polskich (Society of Polish Patriots). Orlemański was named the Kościuszko League's Honorary State Chairman at its meeting in Detroit in 1943. On April 27, 1944, he arrived in the Soviet Union for a visit, where he met with Wanda Wasilewska and other members of Związek Patriotów Polskich. On April 28, 1944, Orlemański met with Stalin and visited Poles living in Soviet Russia. After he returned to the United States, he met with President Roosevelt to report on his trip. Throughout the war, Orlemański was a close collaborator to pro–Soviet elements including **Bolesław Gebert**, **Oskar Lange**, and **Leo Krzycki**. His activities were not welcomed by the Roman Catholic hierarchy, which ordered him not to get involved in political activities outside his parish. Orlemański spent the rest of his life as a parish priest in Springfield.—*Iwona Korga*

Source: Eric Estorick, "Polish American Politics," *Nation*, no. 158 (1944), 591–93.

Orlick, Warren (b. Detroit, Michigan, July 9, 1912; d. Birmingham, Michigan, May 17, 2003). Golfer. First associated with golf at age eight as a caddie at the Grosse Isle Golf and Country Club, Orlick went on to a career of over 71 years, including 29 years at the Tam O'Shanter Country Club in Orchard Lake, Michigan. He was a noted teacher, and it has been estimated that more than thirty of his assistant professionals went on to become head professionals themselves. The 1956 and 1960 he was named Michigan PGA Golf Professional of the Year, and in 1960 he was named Professional Golfer of the Year for his all-around ability and contributions to the game. Orlick gained international recognition as golf's "Mr. Rules" by conducting National PGA Rules Workshops for professionals and amateurs, as well as making important rulings while serving on committees of every major golf tourney for over three decades — the Masters, PGA Championship, U.S. Open, Tournament Players Championship, Ryder Cup, and PGA Seniors. His term as PGA President (1971–72) saw the development of the PGA Apprentice and PGA Master Professional programs. A long-time supporter of the disabled community, Orlick established a weekly Adaptive Golf Clinic that assisted people with impairments to regain some dexterity. He started Adaptive Golf leagues and tournaments as well as designing many devices to make it easier for golfers with disabilities to play and continue to enjoy the game. In recognition of his contributions, he was presented with the 2002 Rick Knas Lifetime Achievement Award for his significant contributions to Michigan's athletes with disabilities. Orlick was elected to the Michigan Sports Hall of Fame in 1979 and the National Polish-American Sports Hall of Fame in 1983. The Michigan PGA named Orlick the first recipient of its Lifetime Achievement Award, which later was renamed the Warren Orlick Award in his honor. In 1996, he was the second honoree of the Legends of The PGA Program. The annual Warren Orlick Memorial Golf Outing is named for him.—*Luis J. Gonzalez*

Source: "Par Excellence in All Phases of Golf," National Polish-American Sports Hall of Fame, http://www.polishsportshof.com/bios/orlick_w_complete.html, May 2008.

Osada, Stanisław (b. Pruchnik, Poland, April 14, 1869; d. Poland, July 28, 1934). Polonia activist, journalist. Early in life Osada moved to Lwów where he obtained work as a clerk in a government office, but he soon joined a group of patriotic conspirators in **Galicia** working for the freedom and independence of Poland. Conscripted into the Austrian army, he quickly began organizing soldiers and students and eventually deserted, fleeing to Switzerland to join the patriotic group headed by Zygmunt Miłkowski where he served as secretary of the Towarzystwo Polskie (Polish Society). In August of 1893 he was dispatched to the U.S. to organize Poles there in support of the national cause. After a brief residence in Buffalo, he moved to Chicago where he became a dynamic force for promoting Polish culture and political ideals through both the Polish and English-language press. He became active in the **Polish National Alliance** and the **Polish Falcons**, serving the latter as its third secretary general. He was a member of the organizing committee for the **Polish National Congress** in 1910, the organizing committee for the **National Defense Committee**, and secretary of the **Polish National Council**. The energetic Osada was secretary of the **Polish Central Relief Committee** and led efforts to conduct a detailed census of American **Polonia** (1915–18). As a journalist, Osada edited *Tygodnik Milwaucki* (Milwaukee Weekly, 1901–05), and assumed editorship of *Sztandar* (The Standard, 1893–1902) and *Zgoda* (Harmony, 1905–10). Later, with the PNA increasingly a battleground between the nationalists and the "left" supporters of Józef Piłsudski, Roman Dmowski's chief rival in the movement for Polish independence in the homeland, Osada had to find employment with other newspapers, most notably publications of a conservative and nationalist persuasion. He was a regular contributor to other newspapers such as *Reforma* (Reform), *Kuryer Polski* (Polish Courier), *Dziennik Milwaucki* (Milwaukee Daily News), *Tygodnik Milwaucki* (Milwaukee Weekly), *Dziennik Polski* (Polish Daily News), and *Wiadomości Codzienne* (Daily Information). During World War I, he was editor of *Free Poland*, the publication of the Catholic and conservative Polish National Council. In 1920 he worked with the Polish consulate in Chicago on a $10 million fundraising drive in support of his newly-independent homeland then defending itself from Bolshevik invasion. In 1922 he returned to Poland, but returned to America in 1924 in an attempt to encourage Poles to re-emigrate to Poland. Between 1928 and his death in 1934 he edited *Sokół Polski* (Polish Falcon), the organ of the Polish Falcon Alliance. As a promoter of Polish culture, he was active in the theater movement among Polish immigrant communities, and as a writer he contributed much to documenting the early history of Polonia, in-

Stanisław Osada, journalist and Polonia leader (*PMA*).

cluding two major works that remain of particular interest to historians: *Historya Związku Narodowego Polskiego* (History of the Polish National Alliance, 1905) and *Jak się kształtowała polska dusza Wychodźtwa w Ameryce* (How the Polish Spirit of the Emigration in America Formed Itself, 1928). Both works stand out as extraordinary compositions that go far beyond the writing of history as this subject is generally understood. Thus, his outstanding PNA history was at the same time a fervent argument for PNA leadership of a consolidated and significant Polonia dedicated to the independence cause — nothing less than Poland's "fourth partition." His 1928 work was a spirited recalling of the past achievements of the ethnic community and the obligation of its members to remain conscious of their heritage. Osada's intense opposition to Piłsudski's rule in Poland after 1926 led him to take a leading role in writing against the new regime's efforts to build up its ties with the major American Polonia organizations. As a delegate to the second congress of the World Union of Poles from Abroad (**Światpol**), which was held in Warsaw in August, 1934, he was set to oppose the formal entry of American Polonia into this government-sponsored organization. His position prevailed and the forty-member American delegation did not take any formal part in the congress. But Osada had died in Poland just days before the Congress's opening session.—*Donald E. Pienkos*

Sources: Stanislaus A. Blejwas, "Stanisław Osada: Immigrant Nationalist," *Polish American Studies*, Vol. 50, no. 1 (1993), 23–50; Donald E. Pienkos, *PNA: A Centennial History of the Polish National Alliance of the United States of North America* (Boulder, CO: East European Monographs, 1984).

Joseph Osajda, Polonia leader (*PMA*).

Osajda, Joseph L. (b. Evanston, Illinois, May 26, 1909; d. Chicago, Illinois, July 7, 1979). Polonia activist. After graduating from Holy Trinity High School in Chicago, Osajda was initially employed in the business office of the Sherman Hotel where he rose to the rank of general manager and vice president of the hotel. Along the way, he earned a law degree and Master of Business Administration. Active in the **Polish Roman Catholic Union** of America from 1929, he became one of the fraternal's most successful insurance salesmen. After having served as the PRCUA's counsel, he was elected its president in 1970, serving until 1978. During his term, the fraternal celebrated its centennial in 1973–74 and the activities of the **Polish Museum of America** were revitalized. Osajda was also active in attempting to make innovations in the insurance offerings of the PRCUA. He served as treasurer of the **Polish American Congress** under the leadership of President **Aloysius Mazewski**. In 1977 Osajda was incapacitated by a stroke, retiring a year later to be succeeded as PRCUA president by Joseph Drobot of Detroit.—*Donald E. Pienkos*

SOURCES: Donald E. Pienkos, *For Your Freedom Through Ours: Polish American Efforts on Poland's Behalf, 1863–1991* (Boulder, CO: East European Monographs, 1991); Sandra Pesmen, "Immigrant's Success Story," *Chicago Daily News*, November 2, 1970.

Oskie, James "Jimmy" (b. Maywood, California, February 8, 1946; d.—). Sprint car driver. Oskie began driving sprint cars at age sixteen when he told race officials he was eighteen in order to qualify as a driver. He began competing in the California Racing Association events in 1963. Following a two-year stint in the U.S. Navy, he was named Most Improved Driver in 1968 when he finished second in point totals. In 1969 he won the point championship, and the following two years competed in the United States Auto Club event in the Midwest. Returning to California, he finished second in point total in 1972 and 1973, winning the title in 1974, 1976, 1977, and 1979. He retired in 1990 with 58 main event victories to his credit. At the time, he was the all-time leader with 56 dash trophy victories. He is a member of the National Sprint Car Hall of Fame.—*James S. Pula*

SOURCE: www.sprintcarhof.com.

Oskierko, Edward Daniel (b. Chicago, Illinois, April 9, 1893; d. Tempe, Arizona, February 1985). Radio pioneer. After completing his elementary education, Oskierko went to work in the steel plants of South Chicago. Active in various Polish organizations and cultural groups, it was not until 1929, when he was thirty-six years old, that he began producing "The Polish Variety Program" on WJKS (later WIND) in Gary, Indiana. With the Depression, Oskierko was able to find only enough advertisers to pay for the radio time, so he kept the program alive by working without remuneration, continuing his labors in the steel mill for a livelihood and conducting his radio activities in his spare time. Transferring the program to WWAE (later WJOB), he experimented with installing a teletype to provide the latest news, broadcasting religious events, providing information on local Polish organizations and their events, and broadcasting live masses including the traditional Polish Christmas Eve Mass. The recipient of numerous awards for his radio and civic achievements, he was also named director of ethnic programming at WJOB in 1954.—*James S. Pula*

SOURCES: Joseph Migala, *Polish Radio Broadcasting in the United States* (Boulder, CO: East European Monographs, 1987), 214–16; Karen Fiasco, "Calumet City Resident, Polish Broadcaster Feted for 50 Years on the Air," *Sun Journal* (Calumet City, IN), November 6, 1980.

Osmanski, Bill (b. Providence, Rhode Island, December 29, 1915; d. Chicago, Illinois, December 25, 1996). Football player, coach. Osmanski was a standout fullback for the College of the Holy Cross (1936–38), winning All-America honors in 1938. Chosen in the first round of the professional draft in 1939, he played seven seasons as running back for the Chicago Bears of the National Football League from 1939–47, missing two years while serving in the Marines during the Second World War. Despite the brevity of his career, Osmanski played for four NFL champion Bears squads, and appeared in three Pro Bowls. As a rookie in 1939, he led the NFL in rushing and was named All-Pro. He was honored as a member of the NFL All-Decade team for the 1940s. After his playing days, Osmanski turned in two seasons as head football coach for Holy Cross (1948–49), and subsequently practiced dentistry in Chicago. He is a member of the College Football Hall of Fame, and was inducted into the National Polish-American Sports Hall of Fame in 1977.—*Neal Pease*

SOURCE: "Bill Osmanski," National Polish-American Sports Hall of Fame website, www.polishsports hof.com.

Ozark, Danny (Daniel Leonard Orzechowski; b. Buffalo, New York, November 24, 1923; d. Vero Beach, Florida, May 7, 2009). Baseball manager. During World War II, Ozark served in the U.S. Army and fought in the Battle of the Bulge. Following his discharge in 1946 he played in the minor league organization of the Brooklyn Dodgers where he also coached after his playing career. In 1964 he joined the Los Angeles Dodgers as a coach, but in 1972 accepted the manager position with the Philadelphia Phillies. He led the Phillies to three successive National League East titles (1976–78), the first time the team had reached the playoffs since 1950. He finished with a .538 winning percentage as Phillies manager and was named Manager of the Year in 1976 by the *Associated Press* and *Sporting News*.—*James S. Pula*

SOURCE: Tom Tarapacki, "Ozark Passes," *Polish American Journal*, Vol. 98, no. 7 (July 2009), 17.

Paciorek, Tom (b. Detroit, Michigan, November 2, 1946; d.—). Baseball player. Paciorek played in the major leagues from 1970 through 1987, performing for six different teams. A right-handed hitting outfielder and first baseman, he compiled a batting average of .282 over the course of eighteen seasons. He appeared twice in postseason play, in the 1974 World Series with the Los Angeles Dodgers and in the 1983 American League championship series with the Chicago White Sox. In 1981, while playing for the Seattle Mariners, he was named to the American League all-star team and finished near the top of many AL hitting categories. He was inducted into the National Polish-American Sports Hall of Fame in 1992.—*Neal Pease*

SOURCE: "Tom Paciorek," National Polish-American Sports Hall of Fame website, www.polishspor tshof.com.

Packer, Billy (William Paczkowski; b. Wellsville, New York, February 25, 1940; d.—). Sportscaster, author. The son of a Leigh University basketball coach, Packer attended Liberty High School in Bethlehem, Pennsylvania, then Wake Forest University in Winston-Salem, North Carolina (1958–62), where he played basketball as a guard (1960–62), winning All-Atlantic Coast Conference honors. Graduating with a degree in economics, he remained at Wake as assistant basketball coach (1965–69) before beginning a broadcasting career in 1972, serving as a fill-in for a nationally televised game. Through this, he was asked to do broadcasts on a regular basis the following year, teaming with well-known sportscaster Curt Gowdy. For over three decades Packer was color commentator on various sporting events, most notably college basketball. From 1974 to date [2008] he broadcast every NCAA Division I (Men's) Basketball Championship as well was the Final Four. In 1992 he covered the Winter Olympics. Those who work with him say he is always exceptionally prepared and has a knack for knowing what will happen before it does. Packer voices his opinions without hesitation, often getting into trouble by taking unpopular views. In 1996 he referred to Allan Iverson, an outstanding guard for Georgetown University and an African-American, as a "tough monkey." Though Iverson was not offended by the remark, Packer made a national apology, saying he meant it only as a compliment to Iverson's tenacious play. Four years later, he apologized again when he made sexist remarks to female ticket takers at a Duke University men's basketball game. Again, in 2004, he was involved in a controversy when he questioned the choice of St. Joseph's University for a top-seeded berth in the NCAA men's basketball championships, and in 2006 when he blasted the NCAA for including so-called "mid-major" teams in the tournament. Packer has worked for two major networks, NBC (1974–81) and CBS (1982 to present [2008]). He also does broadcasts of ACC basketball games, and has done so since 1972. His awards include a Sports Emmy Award for Most Outstanding Sports Personality/Analyst (1993) and the Marvin Francis Award for notable achievement in covering the Atlantic Coast Conference (2005). He was elected to the National Polish-American Sports Hall of Fame in 1988.—*Cheryl A. Pula*

SOURCE: Billy Packer, *Hoops! Confessions of a College Basketball Analyst* (Chicago: Contemporary Books, 1985).

Pacula, Joanna (b. Tomaszów Lubelski, Poland, January 2, 1957; d.—). Actress. After graduating from the Theater Academy in Warsaw (1979), she became a member of the Warsaw Dramatic Theater where she played parts in *Romeo and Juliet*, *Othello*, and *As You like It*. Her film debut came in Krzysztof Zanussi's *Barwy ochronne* (1997). She gained national recognition in Poland when she starred in *Nie Zaznasz Spokoju* (1997) and *Zycie Kamila Kuranta* (1981). In Paris when

the Communist government declared martial law in Poland in 1981, she migrated to the United States the following year. In 1983 she starred with William Hurt and Lee Marvin in *Gorky Park*, receiving a Golden Globe Award nomination. Following this, she appeared in *Not Quite Jerusalem* (1984), *Escape from Sobibor* (1987), *Sweet Lies* (1988), *The Kiss* (1988), *E.A.R.T.H.Force* (1990), *Marked for Death* (1990), the television series *The Colony* (1990), *Husbands and Lovers* (1992), *Tombstone* (1993), *The Haunted Sea* (1997), *Virus* (1999), and *When Nietzsche Wept* (2007). She was chosen by *People Magazine* as one of the fifty "Most Beautiful People" (1990) and ninth on the *FHM Magazine* list of the one hundred "Sexiest Women of All Time." *Premiere Magazine* ranked her role in Gorky Park as the 57th best performance of all time.—*Bartosz H. Stanisławski*

SOURCE: Joan Dupont, "In From the Cold: Stranger in Hollywood," *International Herald Times*, April 9, 1993, 18.

Pacyga, Dominic A. (b. Chicago, Illinois, May 1, 1949; d.—) Historian. Pacyga's grandparents arrived in the United States before World War I from the Podhale region of Poland. His early employment experience included working as a livestock handler and security guard in Chicago's Union Stock Yards. That experience, along with growing up in Sacred Heart Parish in Chicago's Back of the Yards neighborhood, has shaped much of his work as an historian. He received his doctorate in history from the University of Illinois at Chicago in 1981, after which he served as associate director of the Southeast Chicago Historical Project in the city's Steel District. He has been a member of the faculty of Columbia College–Chicago since 1984, and has served the college in various other capacities. Pacyga has worked in the fields of Polish American history and American urban history, publishing *Polish Immigrants and Industrial Chicago* (1991, reprinted 2003) for which he was recognized with the **Oscar Halecki** Award. He has co-authored several other works on Chicago including *Chicago: A Biography* (2009). His work has appeared in various academic journals, encyclopedias, and as chapters in books, and he has presented papers across the United States as well as in Poland and Canada. Pacyga has served on various editorial boards, held various offices in professional organizations, had a great deal of experience as a peer reviewer for academic presses and journals, and served for more than five years on the Peer Review Board of the Fulbright Senior Scholars Program. He was a member of the Chicago–Warsaw Sister Cities Committee for several years. He has been widely quoted in the

Chicago and national press concerning immigration, ethnicity, labor, and race relations. He was honored by Columbia College with its Excellence in Teaching Award (1999), and in 2005 was a Visiting Scholar at Campion Hall, Oxford University.—*Kathleen Alaimo*

SOURCE: "Pacyga, Dominic A.," *Contemporary Authors* (Detroit: Gale Research Company), Vol. 128, 309.

Pączki. Deep fried, these yeast-leavened desserts, comparable to berliners or jelly donuts, are a staple of Polish cuisine in both North America and Poland. Pączki (singular: pączek) are thought to have been part of Polish cuisine since the Middle Ages. Injected with custard or raspberry, prune, rosehip, apple, strawberry, or other preserves, these pastries are coated generously with either powdered sugar or a sugar-based glaze. Although available year round, these donuts are especially popular before Lent, enjoyed prior to the **Gorzkie Żale**, or bitter lament services. In previous centuries their consumption was linked to last-minute efforts at utilizing remaining eggs and fat before the Lent fast began. In Poland this day is known as Tłusty Czwartek (Fat Thursday); however, in America, these donuts tend to be eaten instead on Mardi Gras (Fat Tuesday), Ostatki Wtorek (Shrove Tuesday), or Pączki Day, owing to the influence of the New Orleans Carnival. Pączki Day is celebrated in Chicago, Cincinnati, Detroit, Indiana, Ohio, and in other states and communities populated by Polish Americans. In 2001, the sale of pączki totalled some $300 million nation-wide.—*Krystyna Cap*

SOURCES: John J. Bukowczyk, *And My Childen Did Not Know Me: A History of the Polish Americans* (Bloomington: Indiana University Press, 2008); Robert Strybel, "Paczki time — Polonia's Mardi Gras," *Polish American Journal*, February 1, 2001.

An example of the tasty *pączki* dessert (*Anne Gunkel*).

Paczyński, Bohdan (b. Wilno, Poland, February 8, 1940; d. Princeton, New Jersey, April 19, 2007). Astronomer. Paczyński's father was a lawyer and his mother a teacher of Polish literature. Born in Wilno when it was still part of Poland, his family moved to Kraków in 1945 after the shifting of borders, and in 1949 to Warsaw. Paczyński received his education in his native Poland. He studied astronomy at the University of Warsaw, receiving his M.A. degree in 1962 and his Ph.D. (dr. hab.) in 1964. He spent twenty years at the Copernicus Astronomical Center in Warsaw. In 1974 he became a "Docent" and in 1979 was promoted to the rank of professor. He served as a member of the Centre of Astronomy of the Polish Academy of Sciences and at the age of thirty-six became the youngest member of the Polish Academy of Sciences. In 1981 Paczyński visited the United States and lectured at numerous universities. As a result of the declaration of martial law in Poland, he decided to stay in the U.S., joining the faculty of Princeton University in 1982. He was appointed the Lyman Spitzer Jr. Professor of Theoretical Astrophysics in 1989.

Paczyński was the initiator of the Optical Gravitational Lensing experiment in Warsaw, which earned him an international reputation. He is also acknowledged to have coined the term "microlensing." He received numerous medals and awards including being the first astronomer to receive all three major awards of the Royal Astronomical Society, the Gold Medal, the Eddington Medal and the George Darwin Lectureship (1999). He was also given the title of doctor honoris causa from Wrocław University in Poland in 2005 and from the Nicolaus Copernicus University in Toruń, Poland, in 2006. He received the Henry Morris Russell Lectureship of the American Astronomical Society that same year, and was named a member of both the Polish Academy of Sciences and the American Academy of Sciences. He is recognized as a prominent scientist in the theory of the evolution of stars, accretion disc and gamma ray bursts. He maintained strong relations with the astronomical community in Poland, but martial law prevented him from returning. He constantly hosted scientists from his native land and kept in touch with them. He apparently regretted not being able to make one last trip to Poland before he died. A well respected scholar and a well-liked colleague and teacher, he published over two hundred and eighty books and articles.—*Maria Swiecicka-Ziemianek*

SOURCE: David Spergel, *Bohdan Paczynski, 1940–2007* (New York: American Institute of Physics, 2007).

Paderewski, Clarence Joseph "Pat" (b. Cleveland, Ohio, July 23, 1908; d. San Diego, California, July 9, 2007). Architect. After completing high school in Los Angeles, Paderewski earned a baccalaureate degree in architecture from the University of Califor-

nia–Berkeley in 1932. In 1939 he began teaching in the San Diego school system and soon began offering extension courses through the University of California Extension. Gradually building a local reputation as an architect specializing in school design, he soon opened the firm of Paderewski, Mitchell and Dean with partners Delmar S. Mitchell and Louis A. Dean. He is often recognized as the first architect to use colorful schemes in elementary schools, and designed the first school to make use of radiant heat (1947). Paderewski, Mitchell and Dean was the first to use pre-fabricated plywood wall and roof panels to meet the demand for expanding school construction after the Second World War. In 1956 he designed the first all-glass exterior elevator for the El Cortez Hotel, and later planned a futuristic geodesic dome on the campus of Pamona College. An active promoter of Polish-American causes, he was one of the founders of the House of Poland in Balboa Park and the San Diego Polish American Association in 1936. As a relative of **Ignacy Jan Paderewski**, he signed the release to have the maestro's body returned to Poland in 1992, accompanying it aboard Air Force II on the flight to Warsaw.—*James S. Pula*

SOURCES: "Clarence J. Paderewski San Diego's Noted Architect," *Polish American Journal*, December 1974; obituary, *News of Polonia*, Pasadena, California, July 2007, 1, 16.

Paderewski, Ignacy Jan (b. Kuryłówka, Russian-occupied Poland, November 6, 1860; d. New York, New York, June 29, 1941). Pianist, diplomat. Paderewski began studying piano at age three, later studying in the Warsaw Conservatory and in Berlin. He began teaching at the Warsaw Conservatory at age eighteen and, after additional study, gained international acclaim with tours throughout Europe and the United States, South America, South Africa, Australia, and New Zealand. With the outbreak of World War I, Paderewski worked tirelessly in the Polish cause, speaking on behalf of Polish independence and holding benefit concerts for the relief of Polish war victims. He supported the creation of a **Polish Army in France** from among volunteers in the United States and Canada and was recognized as the representative of the Polish people in negotiating with the American government in 1917 and 1918. He was a leader in the formation of the first independent postwar Polish government, attended the Paris Peace Conference on behalf of Poland, and served as premier of Poland in 1919. Among American **Polonia** he is primarily remembered as the leader of efforts to provide relief for Poland and to reestablish the independence of Poland. Among his many awards were honorary doc-

Ignacy Jan Paderewski, internationally renowned pianist and diplomat (*PMA*).

toral degrees from the University of Lwów (1911), Yale University (1917), the Jagiellonian University (1919), Oxford Univesity (1920), Columbia University (1922), the University of Southern California (1923), the Adam Mickiewicz University in Poznań (1924), the University of Glasgow (1925), and Cambridge University (1926), as well as an Honorary Knight of the Grand Cross of the Order of the British Empire, the Order of Leopold of Belgium, Grand Cross of St. Maurice et Lazare of Italy, Grand Cross of the White Eagle of Poland, the Polonia Restituta, the Virtuti Militari, and the Légion d'honneur.—*James S. Pula*

SOURCES: M. B. Biskupski, "Paderewski as Leader of American Polonia, 1914–1918," *Polish American Studies*, Vol. 43, no. 1 (1986), 37–56; Zofia Sywak, "Paderewski in America," in Frank Mocha, ed., *Poles in America: Bicentennial Essays* (Stevens Point, WI: Worzalla Publishing Company, 1978), 371–386; Mary Lawton, ed., *The Paderewski Memoirs* (London: Collins, 1939); Bronisław A. Jezierski, *Paderewski: Patriot and Statesman* (Meriden, CT: Sentinel Publishing Company, 1942); Antoni Gronowicz, *Paderewski, Pianist and Patriot* (New York: Thomas Nelson & Sons, 1949); Rom Landau, *Ignace Paderewski, Musician and Statesman* (New York: Crown, 1934); Marian Marek Drozdowski, *Ignacy Jan Paderewski: A Political Biography* (Warsaw: Interpress, 1981).

Padre Polaco *see* **Alexander Grzelachowski.**

Painting *see* **Fine Arts.**

Paluszek-Gawronski, Halina (Halina Wolff; b. Kutno province, Poland, November 7, 1896; d. unknown). Polonia activist, journalist, radio pioneer. Growing up in Warsaw, Wolff attended a school for girls, but when her father died and her mother remarried, her new stepfather brought the family to the United States where she arrived in 1913. After settling in Chicago, she enrolled in evening classes to learn English while she worked in a tailor shop during the day. She joined the **Polish Women's Alliance** in 1915, soon becoming chair of its Helena Paderewski Young Ladies Circle and secretary of its recruiting efforts on behalf of the **Polish Army in France**. In 1919 she married Ludwig Paluszek, the co-owner of an advertising agency, and moved with him to New York where she obtained a position on the editorial staff of the newspaper *Nowy Swiat* (New World). She returned to Chicago with her family in 1929 when her husband accepted a position as director of advertising for *Dziennik Zjednoczenia* (Alliance Daily News). She began doing radio commercials for WBBM and WGES, which led to developing and hosting some of the first purely Polish radio programs in the city. She left radio in 1943, and the following year was selected by the Polish Women's Alliance to develop and organize their library. In 1951 she was chosen editor of the PWA's bilingual newspaper *Głos Polek* (The Voice of Polish Women) to which she added regular features on Polish history, literature, and culture. Ludwig died in 1952 and she later married Wacław Gawronski. Her memoirs appeared in a series of articles in the newspapers *Dziennik Chicagoski* (Chicago Daily News), *Gwiazda Polarna* (The North Star), and *Polonia.—James S. Pula*

SOURCE: Joseph Migala, *Polish Radio Broadcasting in the United States* (Boulder, CO: East European Monographs, 1987), 216–24.

Panna Maria, Texas. Established by immigrants from Upper Silesia in December 1854, Panna Maria, Texas, holds the distinction of being the first permanent Polish settlement in the United States. It also is known as the site for the oldest Polish church and school in America. To this day it remains a quiet rural community sixty miles southeast of San Antonio. Panna Maria came into existence through the efforts of the Reverend **Leopold Bonaventura Maria Moczygemba**. In his twenties in 1852, the young priest came to Texas to work among the German immigrants already living there. Seeing the material success of his parishioners, the pastor wrote letters home to his friends and family in the Opole Regency of Prussian Upper Silesia, encouraging them to come to the New World as a means of bettering their lives. In fall 1854 the first of several immigrant parties departed Upper Silesia first by train to Bremen and thence by ship to Galveston on the Texas coast. They made their way inland to San Antonio, where Moczygemba met them and led them to the site he had prepared for their settlement at the confluence of the San Antonio River and Cibolo Creek in Karnes County.

On arrival he offered a Christmastime mass beneath an oak on a rise overlooking the stream valleys. This place became the center of the village. Eventually more Upper Silesians came in 1855 and 1856. The Poles named their community Panna Maria in honor of the Virgin Mary. They began farming and erecting houses. Things went well until drought struck in 1856–57, searing their crops and forcing the newcomers to spend what money they still had from Europe just to buy food.

Hoping to become wealthy in the New World, the immigrants instead grew poor. Difficult living conditions caused a breach between the Poles and their pastor; he departed the colony in fall 1856, never to return except for occasional visits in later years. The drought had hardly ended before the Poles at Panna Maria found themselves involved in a war among the Americans. Texas seceded from the Union in February 1861, and eventually many men from the Polish settlement became soldiers in the Confederate army. One reason the Silesians had left Europe was to avoid conscription into the Prussian army, so they resented being forced into the military in their new land. Following the war, some Southerners living around Panna Maria took out their resentment over defeat by harassing the Unionist Poles at Panna Maria. Eventually, in April 1869 the U.S. Army established the nearby short-lived Post of Helena in part to protect the loyal Poles. In time the farmers at Panna Maria became increasingly integrated into life among the surrounding Americans and other immigrants.

The Catholic parish at Panna Maria,

named after St. Mary, had its beginning with the arrival of the first immigrants at the behest of Father Moczygemba. The initial church, erected between spring 1855 and fall 1856, was a modest structure with twenty-foot-tall stone walls. It was reconstructed in the 1870s and remains at the site to this day. Two pastors served the Poles in Texas following Father Moczygemba's departure in 1856. Then in 1866 several priests from the **Congregation of the Resurrection** arrived to care for the spiritual needs of the Poles. Under the pastorate of Father **Adolf Bakanowski**, in 1867 the settlers at Panna Maria began construction of a two-story stone school, which opened for classes as St. Joseph's School in spring 1868, even though instruction had been offered since 1866. This was the first exclusively Polish school in the United States.

Panna Maria became the mother colony for multiple Polish communities in Texas. Just the year after Panna Maria was founded, Silesian Poles began moving to the pre-existing American town of Bandera, west of San Antonio, where they established a Catholic parish. Concurrently other Silesians located in urban San Antonio, where they organized yet another Polish Catholic parish. About the same time Silesians also located on Martinez Creek between San Antonio and Panna Maria in Bexar County at a place they called St. Hedwig, again founding a parish. At both Myersville and Yorktown in DeWitt County, Silesians formed communities, establishing their own church in the latter town in 1867. Poles also moved northward up Cibolo Creek from Panna Maria into the area of Czestochowa in

An allegorical miniature of the Polish settlement in Panna Maria, Texas, by Arthur Szyk (OLS).

the 1870s, starting a parish there in 1877. Polish settlement continued in that northerly direction, with Silesians starting a parish at Kosciuszko, thirteen miles from Panna Maria, in 1892. Even before this the San Antonio and Aransas Pass Railroad laid tracks west of Panna Maria and Czestochowa in the mid–1880s, creating a new town called Falls City in 1884. Many younger Poles from the older communities moved there, where they started another ethnic church in 1902. Much farther away, in the Texas Panhandle, Silesians joined Poles and others in 1910 to found the community of White Deer, which also had its own Catholic parish. Finally, in the 1920s and 1930s Poles from the Panna Maria area moved into extreme South Texas, establishing an ethnic enclave at McCook in Hidalgo County that has its own Polish Catholic church.

Panna Maria served as the mother colony for about half of the Polish settlements in Texas. Many of the Poles in the state today trace their lineage to this original colony. Its significance stems from its having attracted the first organized migration of Polish peasants to the United States. They were the forerunners of thousands of Poles who started coming to America only a decade later.—*T. Lindsay Baker*

SOURCES: T. Lindsay Baker, *The Early History of Panna Maria, Texas* (Lubbock, TX: Texas Tech University Press, 1975); T. Lindsay Baker, *The First Polish Americans: Silesian Settlements in Texas* (College Station: Texas A&M University Press, 1979); Joseph Jaworski, *Panna Maria: An Image of Polish Texans* (Wimberley, TX: Dorsoduro Press, 1991); *Silesian Profiles: Polish Immigration to Texas in the 1850s* (Panna Maria, TX: Panna Maria Historical Society, 1999–2004, 2 vols.); Andrzej Brożek, "The Roots of Polish Migration to Texas," *Polish American Studies*, Vol. 30, no. 1 (1973), 20–35.

Parazynski, Scott Edward (b. Little Rock, Arkansas, July 28, 1961; d.—). Astronaut. After graduating with a B.S. in biology from Stanford University in 1983, he completed his medical studies at Stanford Medical School in 1989. He is the author of several articles on space physiology, and his research has largely addressed the problem of human adaptation to stressful environments. Entering the astronaut program in 1992, he qualified as a mission specialist and served successively as a crew representative in the Astronaut Office Mission Development Branch, the Astronaut Office Operations Planning Branch and Chief of the Astronaut Office Extra Vehicular Activity Branch. Following the *Columbia* disaster, he was assigned as Astronaut Office Lead for Space Shuttle Thermal Protection System Inspection and Repair. His space missions include the Atmospheric Laboratory for Applications and Science-3 (ATLAS-3) aboard the *Atlantis* (1994), a second mission aboard the *Atlantis* to dock with the Russian Space Station *Mir* (1997), a mission aboard the *Discovery* to deploy the Spartan solar-observing spacecraft and test the Hubble Space Telescope Orbital Systems Test Platform (1998), and a mission aboard the *Endeavor* to install a robotic arm on the International Space Station *Alpha* (2001), a total of over 1,019 hours in space. His honors include the Wilderness Medical Society Research Award, the Space Station Team Excellence Award, two NASA Exceptional Service Medals, four NASA Space Flight Medals, and the NASA Distinguished Service Medal.—*James S. Pula*

SOURCE: *Forty Careers in Medicine* (Palo Alto, CA: Stanford University School of Medicine Office of Alumni Relations, 2000).

Parishes, Polish American. Of the many institutions established by Polish immigrants and their descendants in America, none has played a more significant role than the parish. Scholars beginning with William I. Thomas and **Florian Znaniecki**, authors of *The Polish Peasant in Europe and America* (1927), have recognized that the Polish American parish effectively filled not only religious but also educational, fraternal, social, and cultural needs. During the *za chlebem* (for bread) wave of immigration (1870–1920), hundreds of Roman Catholic parishes were formed in America by Poles, principally in the northeastern and mid-western states. Typically, the first Polish immigrants to arrive in an area joined together for the purpose of establishing a church where their language could be spoken and their religious traditions maintained. In some cases, an adventurous Polish priest arrived to provide leadership. In others, the immigrants appealed to the local bishop for help in bringing a priest from their homeland. After land was purchased and a modest church constructed, the parish complex generally expanded to include a rectory, meeting hall, school, and a convent for female members of a religious congregation who provided the immigrants' children with bilingual instruction. As more immigrants arrived and congregations grew, most Polish parishes replaced their original church buildings with newer, often magnificent structures that reflected Polish tradition and culture in architecture and artwork.

Entire neighborhoods drew their identity from parishes, particularly in large cities where there was more than one Polish church. There might be a community known as "Stanisławowo" with St. Stanislaus Church as its center, and another known as "Wojciechowo" radiating from the location of St. Adalbert's Church. These affectionate names reflected the parish's role as a center of Polish community life, encompassing not only religion but also education, culture, tradition, economic welfare, and social opportunities. Parishes often included a lending library, credit union, immigrant aid society, theater group, choir, insurance fraternals, athletic teams, and an assortment of religious and cultural groups for men, women, and children. Pastors who oversaw these impressive networks played a powerful role in Polish American communities, and the Sisters who provided education and other services earned parishioners' deep and abiding affection.

The intense sense of ownership Polish immigrants felt for their parishes contributed to a conflict that erupted in many communities at the close of the nineteenth century and the early years of the twentieth century. Those who feared that the Roman Catholic Church in America would suppress their ethnic and national identity, or who resented the bishop's control over parish property and finances, broke away in an unprecedented independent church movement, the greatest expression of which was the **Polish National Catholic Church**. Like their Polish Roman Catholic counterparts, parishes formed under the auspices of the Polish National Catholic Church served as centers of community life and offered an array of services emphasizing Polish American identity.

Over succeeding decades, the parish continued to occupy a central role in the Polish American experience, welcoming new waves of immigrants, offering a point of reference for new members of **Polonia**, and providing a reliable focus for heritage and tradition. In recent years, some Polish parishes have diminished or closed, affected by change in neighborhoods, lack of identification with heritage on the part of later generations, lower numbers of practicing Catholics overall, and a shortage of priests. The closure of Polish parishes has been met with sometimes fierce opposition expressed in rallies, vigils, and legal attempts to prevent suppression of the heart of a once thriving "Stanisławowo." At the same time, many parishes remain vital institutions of **Polonia**, continuing to fulfill their longstanding role as religious, cultural, and social centers. Increasingly, the beautiful churches built by the first immigrant generation are recognized as architectural and historical landmarks worthy of preservation, as well as repositories of Polish tradition and culture.—*Kathy Urbanic*

SOURCES: Joseph J. Parot, *Polish Catholics in Chicago, 1850–1920* (DeKalb, IL: Northern Illinois University Press, 1981); Stanislaus A. Blejwas, *St. Stanislaus B. & M. Parish, Meriden, Connecticut: A Century of Connecticut Polonia* (New Britain, CT: Central Connecticut State University, 1991); Anthony J. Kuzniewski, *Faith and Fatherland: The Polish Church War in Wisconsin, 1896–1918* (South Bend, IN: University of Notre Dame Press, 1980).

Parker, Frank "Frankie" (Franciszek Andrzej Pajkowski; b. Milwaukee, Wisconsin, January 31, 1916; d. San Diego, California, July 24, 1997). Tennis player. Parker's talent for tennis was discovered while he worked as a ball boy at a local club in Milwaukee. He ranked among the ten best men's players in the United States for seventeen straight years (1933–48), a record that stood until 1968. He won consecutive championships in both the U.S. Open (1944–45) and the French Open (1948–49). He also won the U.S. doubles crown (1943, with Jack Kramer) and the Wimbledon doubles title (1949, with Pancho Gonzales), and was a five time Davis Cup player. Parker is a member of the International Tennis Hall of Fame, and was inducted into the National Polish-American Sports Hall of Fame in 1988.—*Neal Pease*

SOURCE: "Frankie Parker," National Polish-American Sports Hall of Fame website, www.polishsportshof.com.

Parker, Jean (Louise Stephanie Zelinska; b. Butte, Montana, August 11, 1915; d. Los Angeles, California, November 30, 2005). Actress. Parker moved with her family to California when she was six years old. She made her film debut in 1932 in *Rasputin and the Empress* and appeared in more than eighty films during the next three decades. In 1932 the attractive, petite Parker starred with Joan Bennett and Katharine Hepburn in *Little Women*, with Marion Davies in *Operator 13*, and in 1934 with Russell Hardie in *Sequoia*, which many critics consider her best film. She evolved from ingénue roles to more sophisticated and hardened types. She made her Broadway debut in *Loco* in 1946 and continued to act there while her film career gradually wound down in the 1950s. She starred there in *Burlesque* with Burt Lahr and *Born Yesterday*, replacing Judy Holliday. She also played regional theater and did a traveling nightclub act. She coached young actors for some time in the 1970s, but gradually became a recluse. In 1998 she moved to the Motion Picture and Television Country House and Hospital. Her birth name is frequently given as Lois Mae Green. Parker explained this in a 1972 interview with Marcia Barie when she said that at age sixteen she changed her name to Green, after an actress then very popular, and her birth place to Deer Lodge, Montana, which she believed was more romantic.—*James S. Pula*

SOURCE: Tom Vallance, "Jean Parker," *The Independent*, February 6, 2006.

Paryski, Antoni Alfred (Antoni Panek; b. Bocheń, Poland, July 11, 1865; d. Toledo, Ohio, April 24, 1935). Publisher, journalist, entrepreneur. In 1883, most likely escaping from conscription into the Russian army, Panek left Poland, migrated to the United States, and changed his name to Paryski. After laboring on a farm, he found work as typesetter for *Gazeta Narodowa* (National Gazette; Detroit), *Gazeta Polska w Chicago* (Chicago Polish Gazette), and *Gazeta Katolicka* (Catholic Gazette) in Chicago, learning journalism in the process. Closely associated with Polish socialists in Europe and America until 1886, he became an organizer of the Knights of Labor where he claimed to have organized over forty locals. When he lost his job in Chicago, he moved to Winona, Minnesota, but soon returned to Chicago and later to Milwaukee where he continued to act on behalf of the Knights. In 1886, he was nominated General Organizer of the union, but a conflict with Knights of Labor leader Terrance V. Powderly, whom Paryski accused of financial irregularities in January 1887, caused Paryski to abandon his position and leave Milwaukee. The same year he began editing the newspaper **Wiarus** (The Veteran) in Winona, and in 1887 took over editorship of *Krytyka* (Critic) in Milwaukee. In the latter year he also bought the weekly *Gwiazda* (The Star). He founded the weekly *Ameryka* in Toledo, Ohio, in 1889, and merged it with the *Echo* in 1904 to form **Amerika-Echo**. A publication of decidedly liberal, pro-union, and anti-clerical orientations, *Ameryka-Echo* became one of the most popular **Polonia** newspapers with Paryski retaining ownership until his death. It was the largest Polish American newspaper not affiliated with a major organization, with

circulation reaching a peak of 120,000 in the late 1920s prior to the Great Depression.

In 1894, Paryski established the Paryski Publishing Company in Toledo which published thousands of titles including both reprints of Polish literature and original titles. Organized along modern lines with paid distribution agents, the publishing company enjoyed great success printing the novels of Dumas, **Sienkiewicz**, Mickiewicz, and other contemporary European and Polish authors; popular histories of Poland, Polish America, and America; children's books; textbooks; handbooks, guides and calendars; translations of labor literature; and original anticlerical novels, as well as the catechism and the lives of the saints. Paryski authored numerous press articles, brochures on various topics, and a Polish translation of the U.S. Constitution. Although he was critical of mainstream Polish American life, Paryski's publishing activities had a significant influence on creating and sustaining Polish and Polish-American identity.—*Adam Walaszek*

SOURCES: Victor Rosiński, *Życie, praca, czyny 1865–1935* (Toledo: Ameryka-Echo 1945); Czesław Łukaszkiewicz, *Nauczyciel wychodźtwa: Antoni A. Paryski (1865–1935)* (Toledo: Ameryka-Echo, 1938).

Paschke, Ed (b. Chicago, Illinois, June 22, 1939; d. Chicago, Illinois, November 25, 2004). Artist. Paschke's childhood interest in animation and cartoons led him toward a career in art. Educated at the School of the Art Institute of Chicago (BFA, 1961; MFA, 1970) where he studied with John Fabion and Steele McKinnon, he traveled to Mexico in 1961 before being drafted into the U.S. Army in 1962. He was stationed in Fort Polk, Louisiana, as a Specialist Fourth Class assigned to illustrate training ads to explain weapons and procedures to incoming troops. After his discharge in 1964 he lived briefly in New York where he was exposed to Pop Art philosophy. Moving to Chicago, he became a leading Imagist painter with his work exhibiting clear influences from non–Western and Surrealist art, and images appropriated from popular culture and the electronic media infused with brilliant color noted for their energized, carefully-worked surfaces. His style incorporates elaborate masks and depersonalized, partial figures. He was a member of the faculty of Northwestern University, Evanston, IL (1978–2004), and also taught briefly at the School of the Art Institute of Chicago, St. Louis Community College–Meramec in Kirkwood, MO, and Barat College in Lake Forest, IL. Paschke had more than fifty solo exhibitions at locations throughout the United States and in France, Italy, Korea, Poland, Scotland, Spain, and Switzerland. His work was also featured in group exhibitions in the United States, Brazil,

Antoni Paryski, journalist and publisher (*PMA*).

Canada, England, France, Germany, Japan, Mexico, Poland, Scotland, and Switzerland. His commissioned work included 28 creations appearing in *Playboy* magazine (1962–69). His work can be found in public collections in Austria, England, France, Mexico, the Netherlands, and numerous institutions in the U.S.—*Stanley L. Cuba*

SOURCES: Ed Paschke, *Ed Paschke, Electronicon* (Jacksonville, IL: Lewis and Clark Community College Foundation Press, 2007); Ed Paschke and Donald Kuspit, *Ed Paschke* (New York: Ballery B.A.I., 1999); Neal Benezra, Dennis Adrian, John Yau, Carol Schreiber, *Ed Paschke* (New York: Hudson Hill Press, 1990); *Ed Paschke: Selected Works 1967–1981* (Chicago: Renaissance Society of the University of Chicago, 1981).

Patelski, Kazimir J., Jr., "Casey" (b. Chicago, Illinois, January 1, 1928; d.—). Engineer. Growing up on the northwest side of Chicago, Patelski became interested in aeronautics early in life when his father took him on visits to the Chicago Municipal Airport (today Midway Airport). After graduating from Lane Technical High School, he took flying lessons, but was stricken with polio that left him able to walk only with difficulty using leg braces and a cane. Despite the difficulty caused by this handicap, he enrolled in the Aeronautical Engineering program in the University of Illinois extension program in Chicago, then transferred to the university's main campus where he completed his B.S. degree in 1952. Moving to Southern California, where he accepted a position with the Douglas Aircraft Company, he worked on propulsion systems for the DC-8, DC-9, B-66, C-124, and C-133 aircraft. In 1957, Douglas promoted him to Group Design Leader for the Thor rocket program, an assignment that led to a two-year stint in England working in conjunction with the Royal Air Force before he returned to California as Project Engineer for the Delta rocket program. In 1965 he joined the McDonnell-Douglas Saturn Apollo Program as Deputy Manager of Systems Engineering where he was responsible for developing systems design requirements. In 1968 Patelski was chosen as Lead Engineer for the Saturn V moon rocket which required him, in addition to his engineering skills, to plan, organize and establish the staff and procedures for Mission Control in his capacity as Managing Director of Rocket Flight Control Operations. Among other accomplishments, it was Patelski's team that developed the emergency procedure for attaching the square carbon dioxide filter of the Command Module to the round filter of the Lunar Module that helped to save the lives of the Apollo 13 crew on its aborted mission to the moon. Patelski and his engineering team were recognized

Kazimir "Casey" Patelski, aeronautical engineer (*OLS*).

with the Presidential Medal of Freedom (1970) for their work during the Apollo 13 crisis. Following the Apollo program, Patelski was assigned to lead the team developing the Skylab. Many of the innovations developed for the successful design of Skylab were later incorporated into the International Space Station. After the conclusion of the moon landing program, Patelski accepted a position as a Project Engineer designing petroleum plants (1974–82), after which he was named Vice President for Engineering with Flour Arabia, a company specializing in the construction of petroleum refineries, petrochemical facilities, and power plants (1982–86). He held these two positions for about twelve years until he accepted a position back with McDonnell-Douglas (1986) as head of the program to develop the Geo-Positioning Satellite (GPS) System. He retired in 1990.—*James S. Pula*

SOURCE: Ann O. Fetcher, Bonnie Patelski, and Ronald M. Wolosewicz, eds., *A Tribute to Kazimir J. Patelski, Jr., An Outstanding Aeronautical Engineer and Manager* (American Polish Engineering Association, 2002).

Pawelczyk, James Anthony "Jim" (b. Buffalo, New York, September 20, 1960; d.—). Astronaut. After obtaining two baccalaureate degrees in biology and psychology at the University of Rochester (NY) in 1982, he completed an M.S. degree in physiology at the Pennsylvania State University in 1985 and a Ph.D. in physiology at the University of North Texas in 1989. The co-author of *Blood Loss and Shock* (1994), he has authored more than twenty refereed journal articles and three invited book chapters on cardiovascular regulation and cardiovascular physiology. He served as Assistant Professor of Medicine at the University of Texas Southwestern Medical Center (1992–95), Director of the Autonomic and Exercise Physiology Laboratories, Institute for Exercise and Environmental Medicine, Presbyterian Hospital of Dallas (1992–95), and Assistant and Associate Professor of Physiology and Kinesiology at the Pennsylvania State University (1995–). In 1998 he took a leave of absence to fly aboard *Columbia* as a payload specialist for the Neurolab conducting experiments on the effects of microgravity on the brain and nervous system. Logging 381 hours in space, he was awarded the NASA Space Flight Medal. In 1999 he was one of three astronauts to visit the Republic of Poland to present a Polish flag carried aboard the Space Shuttle *Columbia*.—*James S. Pula*

SOURCE: National Aeronautics and Space Administration, Lyndon B. Johnson Space Center, http://www.jsc.nasa.gov/Bios/PS/pawelczy.html.

Pawlak, Walter (b. near Płock, Poland, June 30, 1888; d. Pennsylvania, November 1962). Polonia activist. Pawlak arrived in America at the age of fourteen in 1902. He became active in the **Falcons** movement in Pittsburgh practically from that time onward and served the organization in many capacities, initially as a local lodge (or "nest") officer, as a physical exercise and athletics instructor in District Four of the Falcons (a region encompassing the Falcons nests located in western Pennsylvania), and as chief instructor on a national basis in 1916 and again from 1920 through the end of 1925. In World War I, Pawlak volunteered for service in the **Polish Army in France** created in **Polonia** and rose to the rank of captain. He later saw action in the Polish-Soviet War in 1920. As chief physical instructor after the war, Pawlak revitalized the gymnastic and athletic program of the organization. He was also responsible for the establishment of an order of merit to formally recognize the achievements of dedicated members of the causes embraced by the Falcons movement. Initially his proposal was rejected by the then president of the Falcons, Roman Abczyński, but Abczyński's successor, **Teofil Starzyński**, wholeheartedly supported another version of Pawlak's idea. The revised plan to establish the Falcons' Commandery of the Legion of Honor was approved at an extraordinary Falcons convention in Detroit, Michigan, in November 1925. The order continues to the present time. A fine all-around athlete and gymnast, Pawlak was particularly recognized for his staging of musical and dance pageants focusing upon Polish patriotic themes. He helped organize a Falcons tour to Poland in 1925 in which a number of Polish Americans were able to take part in the "*zlot*" (athletic meet) held in Warsaw and sponsored by the Falcons movement in Poland. Pawlak resigned as national instructor effective December 31, 1925. Appointed to succeed him was **Gustav Pieprzny** of Chicago, who remained in the post, with one interruption, until his death in 1970.—*Donald E. Pienkos*

SOURCES: Arthur L. Waldo, *Sokolstwo: przednia straż narodu, dzieje idei i organizacji w Ameryce* (Pittsburgh: Nakł. Sokolstwa Polskiego w Ameryce, 1956); Donald E. Pienkos, *One Hundred Years Young: A History of the Polish Falcons of America* (Boulder, CO: East European Monographs, 1987).

Pawlikowski, John T. (b. Chicago, Illinois, November 2, 1940; d.—). Priest, educator. Pawlikowski received his Ph.D. from the University of Chicago in 1970. A Servite priest, he has served as professor at the Catholic Theological Union, part of the ecumenical cluster of theological schools at the University of Chicago, where he is also director of the Catholic-Jewish Studies Program. A noted scholar of Catholic ethics and Christian-Jewish Studies, he is also a leader in the Christian-Jewish dialogue nationally and internationally. He has served as President of the International Council of Christians and Jews (ICCJ), and serves on its Board. His lengthy list of contributions to scholarly study includes ten books, notable among them especially *Catechetics and Prejudice, Sinai and the Calvary, The Challenge of the Holocaust for Christian Theology, Christ in the Light of the Christian-Jewish Dialogue,* and *Jesus and the Theology of Israel.* He served as the editor of *New Theology Review,* and a member of the editorial boards of the *Journal of Ecumenical Studies, Journal of Holocaust and Genocide Studies,* and *Shofar: An Interdisciplinary Journal of Jewish Studies.* His efforts on behalf of Christian-Jewish understanding led President Jimmy Carter to appoint him as a founding member of the United States Holocaust Memorial Council in 1980, and to his re-appointment by President George H. W. Bush and two reappointments by President Bill Clinton. Pawlikowski served on the Council's Committee on Conscience and its Academic Committee, and chaired its Committee on Church Relations. He served on the Advisory Committee on Catholic-Jewish Relations of the United States Conference of Catholic Bishops for over twenty years, and is a member of the National Advisory Council of the **Polish Institute of Arts and Sciences** and vice president of the American Association for Polish-Jewish Studies. He twice chaired the **National Polish-American/Jewish-American Council** of which he was a founder, and was a member of the Board of Trustees of the Parliament of the World's Religions, a member of the Board of the United States Committee of the World Conference of Religions for Peace, and a member of the Board of Directors of the Annual Conference on Holocaust, Genocide and the Church Struggle. He was also a member of the Vatican Delegation for the International Jewish-Catholic Dialogues in Baltimore (1992), Jerusalem (1994), and New York (2001). Among his recognitions are the Raoul Wallenberg Humanitarian Award for Distinguished Contributions to Religion, the Distinguished Service Award from the American Jewish Committee in Chicago, a Person of the Year Award from the Polish Council of Christians and Jews in Warsaw, the Nostra Aetate Award from the Archdiocese of Chicago, and the Army Cross of Merit for Distinguished Service to the Polish Nation from the Republic of Poland.—*James S. Pula*

SOURCE: "Pawlikowski, John T.," *Contemporary Authors* (Detroit: Gale Research Company, New Revision Series), Vol. 24, 355–56.

Payak, John (b. Rossford, Ohio, November 20, 1926; d. Bowling Green, Ohio, February 27, 2009). Basketball player, official. John Payak, Jr., played collegiate basketball at Bowling Green State University from 1944 to 1949, interrupted by a stint in the U.S. Navy. A guard-forward, he played two seasons as a professional in the National Basketball Association with Philadelphia and Waterloo in 1949–50, and Milwaukee in 1952–53. In addition, Payak played for the Toledo Mercurys, a traveling opponent of the Harlem Globetrotters. After retiring as a player, he spent seventeen seasons as a college basketball referee, eventually becoming supervisor of officials for the Mid-American Conference. Payak is a member of the Bowling Green State University Athletics Hall of Fame, and in 1982 he was inducted into the National Polish-American Sports Hall of Fame.—*Neal Pease*

SOURCE: "John Payak," National Polish-American Sports Hall of Fame website, www.polishsportshof.com.

Peckwas, Edward Alan (originally Przekwas; b. Chicago, Illinois, May 1, 1942; d. Chicago, Illinois, June 25, 1993). Businessman, genealogist. The son of a businessman, contractor, and developer who designed and built Chicago's Midway Motel and operated Drake Motor Sales and Crane Motor Sales, Peckwas attended Hannibal-LaGrange College in Missouri where he earned an A.A. in Commerce (1962) and Northern Illinois University where he earned a B.S. in Liberal Arts (1968). Gaining employment as treasurer of Program Control and Information Systems, Inc., a computer data processing company (1970–71), he and his wife then established the Kiddie Corner Nursery School in Chicago in 1974. They later opened Captain Kidd Preschool (which closed in 1993), and then Children's Crossing Learning Center. A founding member and president of the Illinois Child Care Association, he was an advocate for the concerns of private child care providers, and was instrumental in bringing those concerns to the attention of state legislators. Peckwas also owned and operated Ed Peckwas Construction Company beginning in 1979, a company involved in the construction of strip malls and the remodeling of child care centers.

Long interested in genealogy and heraldry, Peckwas was president of Heraldry Unlimited, Inc., from 1970–74, which specialized in detailed researching of individual family trees and heraldry, including the preparation of hand colored family crests for clients. Building on this, in 1978 he founded the Polish Genealogical Society with the goal of assisting its members with genealogical research and providing a forum to exchange information. Peckwas served as its first president (1978–91), as well as editor of the Society's *Newsletter* (1979–92), the title of which was later changed to *Rodziny* (The Family). In 1992, the organization changed its name to the **Polish Genealogical Society of America**. Several articles that Peckwas wrote for the *Post Eagle* newspaper were published as *Collection of Articles on Polish Heraldry* (1978). He also wrote the introductions to two small books that the Polish Genealogical Society translated into English: *Register of Vital Records of Roman Catholic Parishes Beyond the Bug River* (1984), and *A Historical Bibliography of Polish Towns, Villages, and Regions (Except Warsaw and Krakow)* (1990). Peckwas was a highly sought speaker on Polish heraldry and genealogy. During his tenure as president, the PGSA grew in membership from nine original members to nearly 900, and the *Newsletter* received first prize in the National Genealogical Society's Newsletter Competition. After his death, the family opened the Edward A. Peckwas Preparatory Academy (a private elementary school) in 1996, and Peckwas' extensive book collection was donated to the Library of the Polish Museum of America. Peckwas served on the Board of Directors of the **Polish Museum of America**, vice president of the National Child Care Association, and president of Society Number 1516 of the **Polish Roman Catholic Union of America**. He was awarded the Commander's Cross of the *Order of Polonia Restituta* in 1985 from the Polish Government-in-Exile.—*John Drobnicki*

SOURCES: obituary, *Chicago Tribune,* June 26, 1993; Mary Keysor Meyer and William P. Filby, eds., *Who's Who in Genealogy & Heraldry* (Detroit: Gale Research Company, 1990); *Who's Who in Polish America* (New York: Bicentennial Publishing, 1996).

Pellowski, Anne (b. Trempealeau County, Wisconsin, June 28, 1933; d.—). Author, children's advocate. A fourth-generation Polish

American, Pellowski was raised in the Latsch Valley of Wisconsin where she graduated from Cathedral High School in Winona, MN, before earning a baccalaureate degree from the College of St. Teresa in Winona. After a Fulbright Scholarship to Ludwig Maximilian University in Munich, Germany, she was awarded a master's degree in library science from Columbia University in New York. From 1957 to 1966 she was employed by the New York Public Library as a children's librarian, storyteller, and group work specialist. In 1966 she established the Information Center on Children's Culture, a division of UNICEF, serving as director of the Center until 1983. Beginning in 1984 she worked as an independent consultant, lecturer, writer, and storyteller. Pellowski authored scores of books, monographs, chapters, and articles and produced a wide range of recordings, discs, tapes, and videos. Among her scholarly books, four are particularly noteworthy for their acclaim and lasting impact on the fields of storytelling and children's literature: *Made to Measure: Children's Books in Developing Countries* (1980), *The Story Vine* (1984), *The Family Storytelling Handbook* (1987), and *The World of Storytelling* (1990). Several of Pellowski's books have been adapted and translated into foreign languages; *Made to Measure*, for example, has been adapted for editions in French, Spanish, Japanese, and Farsi. Pellowski is also a highly acclaimed author of children's literature who earned a reputation as a groundbreaker in the establishment of a more honest, yet nurturing adolescent literature and a pioneer in the handling of ethnicity in the genre. She emerged as a leading voice in Polish American children's literature with her Wisconsin farm tetralogy (*Stairstep Farm: Anna Rose's Story*, 1981; *Willow Wind Farm: Betsy's Story*, 1981; *First Farm in the Valley: Anna's Story*, 1982; *Winding Valley Farm: Annie's Story*, 1982), books which tell the story of four generations of a single Polish American family, her family, from its settlement in the Latsch Valley in the second half of the nineteenth century until the last quarter of the twentieth century. The books are models of literary narrative directed at adolescents but appealing as well to adults.

Pellowski is more than simply a scholar, she is an advocate. In addition to her administrative duties, she worked as a volunteer through the International Board on Books for Young People (IBBY), giving workshops in developing countries. Her workshops concentrate on the creation of books for children in minority languages in which such books are virtually nonexistent. Among the languages she has championed are Yekuana, Carib, Guajiro, Arawak, and Yagua in Venezuela; Quechua and Ashaninka in Peru; Caqchiquel and Quiche in Guatemala; Bahasa and Sumatran in Indonesia; Guarani in Paraguay; Venda in South Africa; and Kriolu in Cape Verdi. She has received numerous awards and honors, prominent among them the Grolier Award of the American Library Association (1979), the Cutts Lifetime Service Award of the United States Board on Books for Young Children (2009), and the Constance Lindsay Skinner Award of the Women's National Book Association (1980) for "extraordinary contributions to the world of books and, through books, to society." — *Thomas J. Napierkowski*

SOURCES: Bernard Koloski, "Children's Books: Lois Lenski, Maia Wojciechowska, Anne Pellowski," in Thomas S. Gladsky and Rita Gladsky, eds., *Something of My Very Own to Say: American Polish Writers of Polish Descent* (Boulder, CO: East European Monographs, 1997), 144–69; Thomas J. Napierkowski, "Anne Pellowski: A Voice for Polonia," *Polish American Studies*, Vol. VLII, No. 2 (1985), 89–97; "Pellowski, Anne," *Contemporary Authors* (Detroit: Gale Research Company, New Revision Series), Vol. 9, 392.

Perranoski, Ron (Ronald Perzanowski; b. Paterson, New Jersey, April 1, 1936; d.—). Baseball player. Ron Perranoski ranked as one of the top relief pitchers in major league baseball in the decade of the 1960s. Over the course of a thirteen-season career lasting from 1961 through 1973, pitching for four teams, he won 79 games, saved 179, and posted a lifetime earned run average of 2.79. A lefthander, he commanded a repertoire of three different pitches. With him as their relief ace, the Los Angeles Dodgers won three National League pennants and two World Series championships. With the Dodgers, Perranoski led his league in various seasons in games pitched and won-lost percentage. In 1963, he saved a game in the World Series, finished third in voting as NL Most Valuable Player, and according to the statistical calculations of *Total Baseball*, was the league's third most effective hurler. After joining the Minnesota Twins, he put together back to back brilliant seasons in 1969–70 to help the team reach postseason play. In both years, Perranoski led the American League in saves, and won *The Sporting News* award as the AL's top reliever. By the reckoning of *Total Baseball*, in 1969 he was the best pitcher in the American League. After retiring as a player, he coached for many years in the major leagues, mainly with his old team, the Dodgers, and worked in the front office of the San Francisco Giants. He was inducted into the National Polish-American Sports Hall of Fame in 1983. — *Neal Pease*

SOURCE: Bob Cairns, *Pen Men* (New York: St. Martin's, 1992).

Peszke, Michael Alfred (b. Dęblin, Poland, December 19, 1932; d.—). Historian, psychiatrist. The son of a Polish Air Force officer, he left Poland as a child during the German and Russian invasion of 1939 and travelled widely throughout Europe before settling in Great Britain in 1941. He graduated from Trinity College, Dublin, Ireland, with a medical degree (1956). After advanced training in psychiatry in the U.S., Peszke had a long and distinguished career in the medical profession including teaching positions at Yale University, the University of Chicago, the University of Maryland and the University of Connecticut Medical School. He was also on the faculty of the University of Connecticut School of Law. During this time he produced a series of major papers dealing with a broad array of mental problems, especially schizophrenia and the interface between law and psychiatry. He was president of the Hartford Psychiatric Society, and advisor to the Connecticut General Assembly and court system regarding mental health issues. He was a member of an investigative team which made breakthrough findings regarding the treatment of schizophrenia. He retired from the profession in 1999 as Distinguished Life Fellow of the American Psychiatric Association. Peszke's next career was that of an historian specializing in Polish military history and the history of the Second World War. In this new field he has published three major books — *Battle for Warsaw, 1939–1944* (1995), *Poland's Navy, 1918–1945* (1999), *The Polish Underground Army, the Western Allies, and the Failure of Strategic Unity in World War II* (2005) — as well as many essays and reviews and has presented a large number of papers at learned conferences in both Europe and America, authoring a lengthy bibliography of scholarly works in his second career. Peszke has been a tireless supporter of Polish studies in the United States serving, among others, as vice president of the Friends of **Kosciuszko** at **West Point** and chair of the Advisory Board of the Polish Studies Program at Central Connecticut State University. He is a member of the **Polish Institute of Arts and Sciences of America** and the Royal United Services Institute in London. — *M. B. B. Biskupski*

SOURCE: Bolesław Wierzbiański, *Who's Who in Polish America* (New York: Bicentennial Publishing Corp., 1996), 352.

Pett, Edward (b. Detroit, Michigan, February 8, 1918; d. unknown). Polonia activist. Pett became active in the sports and youth programs of the **Polish Falcons** of America fraternal from the early 1930s and competed as a swimmer in the national Polish Olympics held in Pittsburgh, PA, in 1938. As an assistant physical fitness instructor in his Falcons Nest from 1936 until he entered military service in

World War II, Pett supported his own children's involvement in the Falcons' athletic programs in the 1950s and 1960s while he was employed in a series of responsible positions with the Ford Motor Company. He became active again in the Falcons after 1968, focusing on sports programs run by the Falcons in Michigan and northern Ohio. Following the death of **Gustav Pieprzny** in 1971, Pett became Chief Instructor and continued in this post for many years, working well with several chief women's instructors of the Falcons. One of their successes was in organizing a succession of national PFA sports tournaments to coincide with the quadrennial national conventions of the PFA. In addition to his many PFA activities, Pett was involved in the **Polish American Congress** and also served as a director of the **Polish American Sports Hall of Fame** located in Orchard Lake, Michigan.— *Donald E. Pienkos*

SOURCE: Donald E. Pienkos, *One Hundred Years Young: A History of the Polish Falcons of America, 1887–1987* (Boulder, CO: East European Monographs, 1987).

Piasecki, Frank Nicholas (b. Landsdowne, Pennsylvania, October 24, 1919; d. Haverford, Pennsylvania, February 11, 2008). Engineer. Piasecki received a B.S. degree in Aeronautical Engineering in 1940 from the Guggenheim School of Aeronautics at New York University. With partners, he founded a company, the P-V Forum, to build and fly the second successful helicopter in America (1943) becoming the first helicopter pilot licensed by the FAA. He then developed the tandem rotor helicopter on contract for the U.S. Navy. His design raised the status of the helicopter from a small aerial observation platform to that of an aircraft with broad military, commercial and humanitarian applications. To manufacture these helicopters, popularly known as the "Flying Banana" because of their upturned fuselage, in 1947 he organized the Piasecki Helicopter Corporation which grew to employ over 6,000 workers. In 1955 he sold his interest in the company, which was renamed the Vertol Helicopter Corporation and was later acquired by Boeing Aircraft. Eventually, Piasecki's concepts in vertical flight evolved into the Chinook and Sea Knight helicopters used by the American armed forces and in many countries around the world. Among his innovations were the flying jeep, a fan-driven two-man vertical take-off vehicle built for the U.S. Army, and the Heli-Stat, an airship-helicopter hybrid for making heavy aerial lifts. He experimented with ring-tailed compound helicopters and attempted to blend the best features of fixed wing and rotor aircraft. During his long aviation career, Piasecki was the

Frank Piasecki, aeronautical engineer and helicopter designer (*Peter Obst*).

recipient of many patents and numerous honors. In 1986 President Ronald Reagan honored him with the National Medal of Technology and in 2005 he was awarded the Smithsonian National Air and Space Museum's Lifetime Achievement Award. He served on the boards of several organizations including The **Kosciuszko Foundation** and The American Institute of Aeronautics and Astronautics (AIAA).— *Peter J. Obst*

SOURCES: Obituary, *Philadelphia Inquirer*, February 12, 2008; Jay P. Spencer, *Whirlybirds: A History of the U.S. Helicopter Pioneers* (Seattle: University of Washington Press, Seattle, 1998).

Piast Institute. Established in 2002 by Thaddeus Radzilowski and Virginia Skrzyniarz, the mission of the Piast Institute is to serve as a think tank on Polish and Polish American affairs. In 2006 it was designated an official United States Census Bureau Information Center, through which it makes available demographic information on the Polish American community. It is also approved as an official site to offer assistance to immigrants with visa and related documentation issues. The Institute also takes an interest in anti-defamation activities and cooperates with the Dekaban Liddle Foundation to promote faculty exchanges between universities in Canada, Poland, the United Kingdom, and the United States in the fields of agriculture, economics, and engineering. The Institute is located in **Hamtramck**, Michigan.— *James S. Pula*

Piątkowski, Romuald (b. Sokal, Poland, February 12, 1857; d. Orchard Lake, Michigan, November 30, 1939). Educator, Polonia activist. An immigrant in 1892 from Russian-

ruled Poland, Piątkowski taught first at the Polish Seminary (see **Sts. Cyril and Methodius Seminary**) then located in Detroit, Michigan, between 1892 and 1909. Active in the **Polish National Alliance** and an unsuccessful candidate for the office of national secretary in 1907, in 1908 he was appointed to head the Polish Press Information Bureau of the Alliance, a post he held until 1911. Piątkowski played an important role in organizing the PNA–sponsored **Polish National Congress** (in fact a world congress of Polish activists) in Washington, D.C., and was appointed recording secretary for that meeting. The gathering was held in May 1910, coinciding with the unveiling and dedication of monuments honoring **Kościuszko** and **Pułaski** in the nation's capital. Piątkowski's massive book published in 1911 and titled *Pamiętnik wzniesienia odsloniecia pomników Tadeusza Kościuszki i Kazimierza Pułaskiego tudziez polaczonego z ta uroczystoscia pierwszego Kongresu Narodowego Polskiego w Washingtonie, D.C.* (On the Dedication of the Monuments to Kościuszko and Pułaski and the Proceedings of the First Polish National Congress held together in Washington, D.C.) provides a masterful and comprehensive report on these two great moments in the history of American **Polonia**. Piątkowski was appointed the first rector of the newly-created **Alliance College** in Cambridge Springs, Pennsylvania in 1912, but resigned from the post in 1916 over a dispute concerning the use of English instead of Polish in classroom instruction. He then returned to teach at the Polish Seminary, by then relocated to Orchard Lake, Michigan.— *Donald E. Pienkos*

SOURCES: Adam Olszewski, *Historia Związku Narodowego Polskiego* (Chicago: Polish National Alliance, 1957–1963), Vol. 2; Donald E. Pienkos, *PNA: A Cen-*

Romuald Piątkowski, educator and Polonia activist (*PMA*).

tennial History of the Polish National Alliance (Boulder, CO: East European Monographs, 1984).

Piekarski, Frank (b. Nanticoke, Pennsylvania, August 17, 1879; d. Pittsburgh, Pennsylvania, August 14, 1951). Football player. Piekarski was a four-year letter-winner as a guard for the University of Pennsylvania football team from 1901 to 1904. In 1903 he was named to Walter Camp's third All-American team, and was a consensus All-American in 1904. Playing at 6-foot 3-inches and 200 pounds, Piekarski led the University of Pennsylvania Quakers to a 12-0-0 record and the national championship of college football in 1904. The Quakers were so dominant that they shut out 11 of 12 opponents, and outscored their opposition by a combined score of 222–4. The only score allowed during the entire season was one field goal, which at that time counted for four points. During Piekarski's four years, the Quakers had a record of 40-12-0. Following graduation with a degree in law, he became an attorney, later serving as Pittsburgh City Solicitor, attorney for the Auditor General of Western Pennsylvania, and judge of the Allegheny County Court. He was inducted into the **National Polish-American Sports Hall of Fame** in 2005.—*Luis J. Gonzalez*

SOURCES: Thomas Tarapacki, "Frank Piekarski; The First Polish All-American," *Polish American Journal*, September 2005; *Philadelphia Evening Journal*, August 15, 1951.

Pienkos, Angela T. (Angela Therese Mischke; b. Chicago, Illinois, May 15, 1941; d.—). Historian. In 1949 Mischke moved with her family to Milwaukee when her father, a printer, took a position with the *Milwaukee Journal*. After graduating from Marquette University (B.A. and M.A.), she completed her doctoral studies at the University of Wisconsin in Modern European history in 1971. She also studied at Laval University in Quebec, the Sorbonne (Paris), and the University of Warsaw. Her focus was on nineteenth century Polish-Russian relations. She married political scientist **Donald E. Pienkos** in 1967, after which she taught at Ripon College (1968–69) and Alverno College of Milwaukee (1969–76). In 1976 she was appointed Chief Administrator of Divine Savior Holy Angels High School (DSHA) in Milwaukee and served there until 1997. During her administration, DSHA earned a Federal commendation from President Ronald Reagan as one of America's Exemplary schools. She greatly enhanced the school's curriculum, its foreign study programs, its extracurricular opportunities, and put the school on a firm financial footing. She was principal at Kettle Moraine High School in Wales, Wisconsin

Donald and Angela Pienkos, historians (*Donald and Angela Pienkos*).

(1997–2000) and was the second Executive Director of the Polish Center of Wisconsin, founded in 2000, from 2001 to 2003.

Pienkos joined the **Polish American Historical Association** in 1971 and was its president (1980) and executive director (1985–86). She and her husband received the **Mieczysław Haiman** Medal from PAHA in 2005 for their contributions to the study of the Polish experience in America. She is also active in the **Polish Institute of Arts and Sciences of America**. A frequent visitor to Poland since 1960, she has lectured publicly on Polish and Polish American subjects in the U.S. Her publications include *A Brief History of Polanki, Polish Women's Cultural Club of Milwaukee, 1953–1973* (1973), *A Brief History of Federation Life Insurance of America, 1913–1976* (1976), *Ethnic Politics in Urban America: The Polish Experience in Four Cities* (1978), *The Imperfect Aristocrat: Grand Duke Constantine Pavlovich and the Polish Congress Kingdom* (1987), and *"In the Ideals of Women is the Strength of a Nation": A History of the Polish Women's Alliance of America* (with Donald E. Pienkos, 2003). In 2003 she received the Civic Achievement Award of the Wisconsin Polish American Congress.—*James S. Pula*

SOURCE: Bolesław Wierzbiański, *Who's Who in Polish America* (New York: Bicentennial Publishing Corp., 1996), 354.

Pienkos, Donald E. (b. Chicago, Illinois, January 23, 1944; d.—). Political scientist, Polonia activist. Pienkos received his B.A. from DePaul University and his M.A. and Ph.D. degrees from the University of Wisconsin. An expert on Polish and East European Studies, Russia, and the Polish ethnic community in the U.S., he served as professor of political science at the University of Wisconsin–Milwaukee, coordinator of its International Studies major, and was a founder of its Russian and East European Studies and Polish Studies committees. Pienkos was a member of the Council of National Directors of the **Polish American Congress** from the

1980s and was twice elected to the Board of Directors of the **Polish National Alliance**, serving from 1987 to 1995. He was president of the Wisconsin Division of the Polish American Congress for twelve years, attended the first Congress of "Wspólnota Polska" (the "Polish Community" organization established in democratic Poland to bring together the Polonias throughout the world) in 1992, and has lectured widely in Poland. He was active in the effort to include Poland as a member of the NATO Alliance. He served on the Board of Directors of the **Polish Institute of Arts and Sciences of America** beginning in 1999, and has been a member of the editorial board of *The Polish Review* since 2008. Pienkos was president of the **Polish American Historical Association** (2001–03). His many publications include *PNA: A Centennial History of the Polish National Alliance of the United States of North America* (1984), *For Your Freedom Through Ours: Polish American Efforts on Poland's Behalf, 1863–1991* (1991); *One Hundred Years Young: A History of the Polish Falcons of America* (1987), "*In the Ideals of Women Is the Strength of a Nation": A History of the Polish Women's Alliance of America* (2003, with his wife **Angela Pienkos**, herself a historian of Poland and Polonia).—*Maria Swiecicka-Ziemianek*

SOURCE: Bolesław Wierzbiański, *Who's Who in Polish America* (New York: Bicentennial Publishing Corp., 1996), 354–55.

Pieprzny, Gustaw Tomasz (b. Kielce, Poland, July 12, 1894; d. Dortmont, Pennsylvania, November 1970). Polonia activist. Born into a family whose members had been active for years in the country's independence struggle, in 1904 the entire family left Poland, eventually settling in Chicago's near north side. As a child, Pieprzny took part in the calisthenics and exercise classes held by **Falcons** Nest 2 under the direction of Wojciech Rajski, himself a past national chief instructor of the movement. In 1912 Pieprzny formally became a member of the **Falcons** at the age of eighteen and tried to enter the paramilitary training courses the organization was sponsoring. Refused entry because of his youth, he joined the Illinois National Guard and in 1915 served in General John Pershing's expedition into Mexico against Pancho Villa. In 1917 he was active in helping organize the Polish officers training program in Canada established by the Falcons, and in December of that year he was one of the first soldiers sent to France. There he took part in a number of actions against the Germans as a captain of the 1st Battalion, 1st Division of the Polish Army, winning a number of medals for heroism. Following the Armistice on the Western Front,

Gustaw Pieprzny in his uniform of the Polish Army in France (*OLS*).

A plate of *pierogi* (*Anne Gunkel*).

Pieprzny remained in the **Polish Army in France** under General Józef Haller and by spring, 1919, he was in Poland. There he took part in the Polish expedition to Kiev and later in the great Battle of Warsaw in August 1920, as well as in several other major military actions. Returning to America in 1921, he later served as the chief instructor of Nest 2 in Chicago. In February 1926 he was appointed chief instructor of the Falcons following the resignation of **Walter Pawlak**. He held this post until his death in November, 1970, with the exception of a thirty-month period (1960–63) when the office was filled by Edward Biestek. Pieprzny, a loyal friend of President **Teofil Starzyński**, was an energetic promoter of the physical education and athletics endeavors of the Falcons.—*Donald E. Pienkos*

SOURCE: Donald E. Pienkos, *One Hundred Years Young: A History of the Polish Falcons of America, 1887–1987* (Boulder, CO: East European Monographs, 1987).

Pierogi. Widely regarded as a plebian food of Eastern European Slavs, *pierogi* (singular: *pieróg*) are dough-based dumplings, stuffed with a variety of fillings, both sweet and savory. Etymologically, it has been suggested that *pierogi* draw their name from the proto–Slavic word, "*pir*," meaning "festivities" or "celebration." Although they are a staple of Polish cuisine, variants exist across Central and Eastern Europe, including "*vareniki*" in the Latvian, Russian, and Ukrainian kitchens, translating roughly as "boiled things," and "*derelye*" in the Hungarian kitchen. As names for the dumpling vary regionally, so does the stuffing. Western Slavs, including Poles, Czechs and Slovaks, favor more vegetarian fillings of cabbage, sauerkraut, potatoes, onions, mushrooms, and cheese. Russian, Latvian, and Ukrainian variants are frequently meat-based in stuffing and the dough possesses a denser, more bread-like quality. Though the origins of *pierogi* are speculative at best with comparable entities existing in Italian (*ravioli*), Chinese (*jiaozi*), Korean (*mandu*), Caucasian (*khinkali*), Lithuanian (*kolduny*), Ashkenazi Jewish (*kreplach*), and Turkish (*manti*) cuisines, Poles often attribute their arrival to the Italian Queen Bona who profoundly influenced Polish cuisine and culture during her reign in the sixteenth century. Alternatively, the origins of *pierogi* have been linked to China, to the Caucasus, and to the Mongol influence in Eastern Europe. Although *pierogi* are stuffed with myriad fillings including meat, cheese, sauerkraut, potato, mushroom, and fruit, "*ruskie pierogi*" are among the most popular, filled with potatoes and cheese and named after their assumed place of origin in the region surrounding Lwów. At the Polish *Wigilia*, or Christmas table, a sauerkraut and mushroom variant is often served. Dessert *pierogi* are more common in the summer and can be stuffed or topped with blueberries, strawberries, prunes, apples, and powdered sugar and jam. In North America, *pierogi* are sometimes topped with maple syrup. *Pierogi* are remarkably common in delis and grocery stores across North America.—*Krystyna Cap*

SOURCE: Robert Strybel, "Where Do Pierogi Come From?" *Polish American Journal*, August 31, 2003.

Pietrowicz, Felix (b. Poznań, Poland, September 1864; d. Cook County, Illinois, May 29, 1940). Polonia activist. The son of a jeweler, he migrated with his family to Chicago in 1880. Aware of the activities of the **Polish Falcons** movement in partitioned Poland, Pietrowicz worked to organize a Falcons group on Chicago's near north side that was modeled after the Polish Falcons nest operating in Lwów. In doing so he obtained assistance from several existing Turnverein having similar aims that were already operating in Chicago's Czech and German immigrant communities. The new nest was formally established on June 12, 1887, with the blessings of the **Polish Roman Catholic Union** and **Polish National Alliance**. Pietrowicz, a land agent and real estate salesman, was elected its secretary and led its gymnastics exercises. In 1889, he moved to Milwaukee and thereafter was no longer active in the Falcons; however, he helped organize exercise programs within the community's **Kosciuszko Guard**, a unit within the Wisconsin National Guard. In 1891, the Chicago group Pietrowicz had been involved in organizing became inactive, but it was reorganized the following year, taking the designation of Nest 2 of the newly-formed Falcons Alliance. There is no record of Pietrowicz's involvement in the Falcons after the mid–1890s.—*Donald E. Pienkos*

SOURCES: Arthur L. Waldo, *Sokolstwo: przednia straż narodu, dzieje idei i organizacji w Ameryce* (Pittsburgh: Nakł. Sokolstwa Polskiego w Ameryce, 1956), Vol. 1; Donald E. Pienkos, *One Hundred Years Young: A History of the Polish Falcons of America, 1887–1987* (Boulder, CO: East European Monographs, 1987).

Pietrzyk, Leslie (b. Iowa City, Iowa, June 24, 1961; d.—). Novelist, short story writer. Although she was raised in Iowa City, where her father was a chemistry professor at the University of Iowa, Pietrzyk has often recalled with fondness a special bond with her Polish grandmother and relatives in the Polish American enclaves of Detroit. After completing her elementary and secondary education in Iowa City, Pietrzyk obtained a bachelor's degree in English and creative writing from Northwestern University in 1983. Two years later she earned a Master of Arts degree in creative writing from American University in Washington, D.C. For more than seven years Pietrzyk worked as the Director of Communications for the Arlington, Virginia, Chamber of Commerce while honing her skills as a fiction writer. Eventually, she committed her energies full-time to her writing career and to occasional university appointments and writer-in-residence positions. Pietrzyk has published two exceptionally well received novels, *Pears on a Willow Tree* (1998) and *A Year and a Day* (2004), and authored scores of short stories which have appeared in a wide range of anthologies and in an impressive number of highly regarded journals such as *Columbia*, *Epoch*, *Gettysburg Review*, *Iowa Review*, *New England Review*, and *Shenandoah*. Her fiction has been very favorably reviewed, and Pietrzyk has been recognized with several prestigious awards, grants, and honors, including fellowships from the Virginia Center for the Creative Arts, the Bread Loaf Writers' Conference, and the Sewanee Writers' Conference; an Editors' Choice Award for Fiction (*Columbia*, 1999); the Jeanne Charpiot Goodheart Prize for Fic-

Leslie Pietrzyk, novelist and short story writer (*Leslie Pietrzyk*).

tion (*Shenandoah*, 1996); and several Pushcart Prize nominations. Pietrzyk has also published nonfiction essays and reviews in *The Washington Post Magazine*, *The Sun*, and *The Washington Post Book World*.

Pietrzyk's first novel, *Pears on a Willow Tree*, deserves special note. Billed as "a multigenerational roadmap of love and hate, distance and closeness, and the lure of roots that both bind and sustain us all," *Pears on a Willow Tree* is the story of four generations of Marchewka women: Rose, the great grandmother, who immigrated from Poland to the United States; Helen, Rose's daughter, who has a foot in two worlds, adjusting as best she can to the family's new life in America while still honoring her mother and the Old Country; Ginger, Helen's alcoholic daughter, who flees from Detroit and a close-knit family which she regards as oppressive; and Amy, Ginger's daughter, who eventually discovers in her heart a place, even a need, for the Old World and the New. *Pears on a Willow Tree* was greeted with extraordinary acclaim. *The Times* of London, for instance, hailed it as "a remarkable first novel" while praising Pietrzyk's deft presentation of theme as "powerful and subtle." *The New York Times Review of Books* singled out Pietrzyk's "skill at characterization" and her "gifts of eye and ear" for particular praise. And *The Washington Post* insisted that the publication of *Pears on a Willow Tree* marked "the debut of a fully developed talent with a most promising future." The themes which Pietrzyk addresses in *Pears on a Willow Tree* are traditional — mother-daughter relations, the accommodations of immigration, and the quest of women for identity in a

changing world; but they are placed in a setting with which few American readers are familiar, thus providing a human identity for Polonia and an enriched world for other Americans.— *Thomas J. Napierkowski*

SOURCES: Ann Harleman, "The Matriarchs," *New York Times Book Review*, October 4, 1998, 21; Amina Hafiz, "On Being A Writer, Food, And Stubbornness: An Interview with Leslie Pietrzyk," *Folio: A Literary Journal at American University* (Winter 2005); Roland Merullo, "*Pears on a Willow Tree*: An Immigrants' Tale That Bears Plentiful Fruit," *Washington Post*, October 19, 1998, D09.

Piłsudski Institute *see* **Józef Piłsudski Institute.**

Pinkowski, Edward G. (b. Holyoke, Massachusetts, August 12, 1916; d.—). Journalist. At the age of fourteen he moved with his family to the hard coal fields of Pennsylvania where his father and grandfather previously worked in coal mines in the Mount Carmel area. There he started a writing career while still in high school. During World War II he was a writer in the U.S. Navy, rising to the rank of Chief Specialist (X). An avid researcher of Polonica, he is credited with locating **Tadeusz Kościuszko**'s last residence in America, saving it for the purpose of creating a national monument, and placing an historical marker at the corner of 3rd Street and Pine Street in Philadelphia. In 1976 the house-turned-museum opened as the **Thaddeus Kościuszko National Memorial** under the auspices of the National Park Service. He was a member of the Philadelphia Historical Commission from 1969 to 1985, and earlier was president, for four years, of the Spring Garden Civic Association in Philadelphia and the first lay chairman of the nominating committee and vice president of the **Polish American Historical Association** (PAHA). He was chairman of the Ethnic Council and vice president of the Philadelphia 1976 Bicentennial Corporation. A founder of the Polish Heritage Society of Philadelphia, an affiliate of the **American Council for Polish Culture** (ACPC), he also was responsible for erecting a monument on **Anthony Sadowski**'s grave 300 years after his birth. In 1989 he earned the **Mieczysław Haiman** Award from PAHA for outstanding contributions in the field of Polish American studies. In 1997 the ACPC recognized his lifetime of contributions to research in Polish American history by awarding him its Distinguished Service Award. In 1996 he presented evidence that **Kazimierz Pułaski**'s remains were buried in a brick vault under a monument in Savannah and was recognized by the mayor of Savannah with a key to the city for rescuing Pułaski's body from oblivion. In 2001, Pinkowski was a recipient of the Cava-

lier's Cross of the Order of Merit awarded by the President of Poland, Aleksander Kwaśniewski. Among his other awards are the Ellis Island Medal of Honor (2004) and the **Kosciuszko Foundation** medal (2006).—*Peter J. Obst*

SOURCE: *Marquis Who's Who in the East 1972–1973* (Chicago: Marquis, 1972–73).

Piotrowski, John L. (b. Detroit, Michigan, February 17, 1934; d.—). Military officer. After graduating from high school in Dearborn, Michigan, in 1951, Piotrowski enlisted in the U.S. Air Force the following year. In July 1953, he was assigned to the Fighter Weapons School at Nellis Air Force Base in Nevada where he was an F-4 instructor pilot, academic instructor, and project officer for the operational test and evaluation of the Walleye missile program. He then pioneered the use of the Walleye in combat with the 8th Tactical Fighter Wing in Southeast Asia. While on duty he attended Arizona State University, Florida State University, and earned a B.S. degree from the University of Nebraska at Omaha (1965). He did postgraduate work at the University of Southern California and Auburn University, and graduated from the Air Command and Staff College at Maxwell Air Force Base in Alabama (1965), the Armed Forces Staff College in Norfolk, Virginia (1968), and the Royal Air Force College of Air Warfare in Manby, England (1971). In 1968 he was assigned to duty at U.S. Air Force headquarters in Washington, D.C. In 1971 he was assigned to Bitburg Air Base in Germany as deputy commander of the 36th Tactical Fighter Wing, and the following year assumed command of the 40th Tactical Air Group based in Aviano, Italy. In 1974 he was assigned to the chief of staff of Maxwell Air Force Base, becoming vice commander of the Keesler Technical Training Center at Keesler Air Force Base in 1975. In the following year he assumed command of the 552nd Airborne Warning and Control Wing at Tinker Air Force Base in Oklahoma where he played a key role in activating the E-3A Sentry Airborne Warning and Control System. Piotrowski was named deputy commander for air defense in September 1979, and in April 1981 he was assigned as deputy chief of staff for operations at Langley Air Force Base in Virginia. He assumed his present command in October 1982. Promoted to lieutenant general in 1982, he was then assigned to command of the 9th Air Force with headquarters at Shaw Air Force Base in South Carolina. A command pilot with more than 100 combat missions and 210 combat flying hours to his credit, his honors include the Distinguished Service Medal, Legion of

Merit, Meritorious Service Medal with two oak leaf clusters, Air Medal with two oak leaf clusters, Air Force Commendation Medal with one oak leaf cluster, Presidential Unit Citation, and Air Force Outstanding Unit Award ribbon with three oak leaf clusters.—*James S. Pula*

SOURCE: *Zgoda*, April 15, 1985.

Pipes, Richard Edgar (b. Cieszyn, Poland, July 11, 1923; d.—). Historian. Born into an assimilated Jewish family in Austrian Silesia, Pipes displayed an early interest in music (piano), art history (Giotto), and philosophy (Nietzsche), before the family was forced to flee after the German invasion in 1939. Traveling on forged papers, the family eventually made its way to Rome where the Polish ambassador issued them Polish passports enabling them to migrate to the United States in 1940. Pipes became a naturalized United States citizen in 1943, the same year he joined the U.S. Army Air Corps. He applied for the Army's Specialized Training Program and was assigned to study Russian at Cornell, where he received a baccalaureate degree in 1945. After being discharged from the Army in 1946, he studied history at Harvard, receiving his M.A. in 1947 and Ph.D. in 1950. Appointed an instructor at Harvard in 1950, he was granted tenure in 1958 and served on the faculty until his retirement and appointment as Professor Emeritus in 1996. Pipes' major contribution to historical literature was his rejection of the accepted view that the Bolsheviks had the popular support of the proletariat and that the rulers of the Soviet Union behaved rationally. Pipes traced the origins of Soviet totalitarianism and autocratic traditions to Tsarist times. Unlike those who thought that Stalin was an aberration, Pipes firmly believed that Stalinism derived directly from Leninism. He compared Bolsheviks to Nazis, warning that since the USSR thought it could win an offensive nuclear war the idea of détente was a dangerous fallacy. His hard-line speeches and writings brought him to the attention of politicians, resulting in an appointment by CIA Director George H. W. Bush in 1976 to head "Team B," a group of non-government experts who critically evaluated the CIA's estimate of Soviet strategy for nuclear weapons. After serving on Pres. Ronald Reagan's transition team in 1980, Pipes became head of the National Security Council's East European and Soviet Desk from 1981 to 1983, where he argued for strong sanctions against the Soviet Union after the declaration of martial law in Poland. Pipes' stance against the Soviets infuriated liberals, one of whom dubbed him "Reagan's Dr. Strangelove." His many books include *The Russian Revolution, Russia Under the Bolshevik Regime*, and a two volume biography of the Russian economist and intellectual Peter Struve. Pipes' first book, *The Formation of the Soviet Union*, was awarded the American Historical Association's George Louis Beer Prize in 1955. Among his many honors are an honorary doctorate from the University of Silesia, which was conferred by its Cieszyn branch (1994); honorary citizenship of Cieszyn (1994); the Commander's Cross of Merit of the Republic of Poland (1996); honorary consul and honorary citizenship, Republic of Georgia (1997); and the National Humanities Medal (2007) awarded by Pres. George W. Bush for "peerless scholarship on Russia and Eastern Europe and for a life in service to freedom's cause."—*John Drobnicki*

SOURCE: Richard Pipes, *Vixi: Memoirs of a Non-Belonger* (New Haven, CT: Yale University Press, 2003).

Piszek, Edward (Edward John Piszczek; b. Chicago, Illinois, October 24, 1916; d. Fort Washington, Pennsylvania, March 27, 2004). Businessman, philanthropist. Piszek moved with his family to Pennsylvania as a child and earned a degree in business from the prestigious Wharton School at the University of Pennsylvania. In 1946, when he was working at General Electric, workers went out on strike so he and a friend sold crab cakes at a local tavern. When they did not all sell, he placed the remaining cakes in a freezer and found that customers enjoyed them when they were later thawed. With this idea, he and his friend John Paul put together $350 and went into business manufacturing frozen fish. In the 1950s, Piszek bought out his partner and his business Mrs. Paul's Kitchens became widely popular for its fish sticks and other frozen seafood. In 1982 he is reported to have sold his company to Campbell Soup for some $70 million. A noted philanthropist, he gave millions of dollars to fight tuberculosis and fund Little League Baseball in Poland. He spent a half-million dollars on a national advertising campaign and established the Copernicus Society, both to promote knowledge of Poland and its people and culture. Piszek also purchased the residence in Philadelphia where **Tadeusz Kościuszko** resided during his second visit to America. He donated the building to the National Park Service and it became the **Thaddeus Kościuszko National Memorial**.—*James S. Pula*

SOURCES: Edward J. Piszek and Jake Morgan, *Some Good in the World: A Life of Purpose* (Boulder: University Press of Colorado, 2001); Douglas Martin, "Edward J. Piszek, Who Founded Mrs. Paul's Brand, Dies at 87," *New York Times*, March 30, 2004, C15.

Pitass, Jan (b. Piękary, partitioned Poland, July 3, 1844; d. Buffalo, New York, December 11, 1913). Priest. Growing up in German-occupied Silesia, he went to Rome to study as a seminarian at the Gregorian University in Rome. There, in 1872, he was recruited by Buffalo's Bishop Stephen Ryan to minister to a small but growing community of Polish immigrants. After arriving in the Diocese in May of 1873, Pitass completed his studies at Niagara University and was ordained on June 7, 1873. On the following day, he called a meeting to organize St. Stanislaus Bishop and Martyr Church, the first Polish parish in the Diocese of Buffalo. As pastor for more than forty years, Pitass saw his parish grow from 82 families to approximately 5,000. Beyond these numbers, however, Pitass played a significant role in defining the character of **Polonia** in Western New York by creating a multidimensional service organization that would become a prototype for 24 other Polish parishes in the diocese. As pastor, Pitass established a school that would achieve a peak enrollment of more than 2,000 students, introduced the **Felician Sisters** to Western New York, and helped to organize numerous fraternal organizations and societies. After other Catholic cemeteries notified Pitass that they would no longer accommodate the deceased members of his parish, he promptly developed a twenty acre farm into the Saint Stanislaus Roman Catholic Cemetery. Due to his many successful efforts, in 1894 the bishop designated Pitass as dean of all Polish parishes in the diocese. Pitass also extended his leadership into many aspects of community life. He owned a daily newspaper, *Polak w Ameryce*, in which he often expressed political positions, and became an acquaintance of Theodore Roosevelt who visited Pitass at his parish. As president, Roosevelt directed his personal emissary to suggest that the Vatican consider Pitass for a hierarchical appointment. On a national level, he worked to organize American Polonia into a more united community. With Msgr. **Dominik Majer** of St. Paul, Minnesota, Pitass established the **Polish Union of America**. He helped to organize the first Polish Catholic Congress, which met in Buffalo in September of 1896, and in 1901, at the second Polish Catholic Congress which again met in Buffalo, Pitass successfully promoted the concept of sending a mission to Rome for the purpose of presenting a petition advocating a greater Polish presence within the Catholic hierarchy of America. At his passing, his wake attracted more than 20,000 mourners, with 188 priests participating in his funeral services. Traveling from Chicago, Bishop **Paul Rhode**, the first Pole to be consecrated a bishop in America, delivered the funeral oration at St. Stanislaus Cemetery.—*Carl L. Bucki*

SOURCES: Sister M. Donata Slominska, "Rev. John Pitass, Pioneer Priest of Buffalo," *Polish American Studies*, Vol. XVII (1960), 28–41; Claudia Buczkowski, "Seventy Years of the Pitass Dynasty," *Niagara Frontier*, Vol. 24, no. 3 (1977), 66–75; "20,000 See Body of Father Pitass Borne to Church," *Buffalo Courier*, December 15, 1913; *One Hundred Years of Grace—1873–1973—Commemorating St. Stanislaus B. & M. Parish* (Buffalo: Centennial Committee, 1973).

Pityński, Andrzej (b. Ulanów, Poland, March 15, 1947; d.—). Artist. Educated at the Academy of Fine Arts, Kraków, Poland, where he studied with Professors Jan Sliwiński and Jerzy Badura (1968–74), he continued his studies at the Art Students League in New York (1975). In 1974 he migrated from Poland to the U.S., becoming an American citizen in 1987. A specialist in enlarging and casting monuments in bronze, he was affiliated with the GZUT Foundry, Gliwice, Poland (1974) before serving as an assistant to Alexander Ettel modeling and enlarging monuments at Sculpture House in New York (1974–79). He held teaching posts in sculpture at Rider University (1992–97), Rutgers University (1997–2002), and Johnson Atelier Technical Institute of Sculpture (beginning 1979). His public monuments include *Ignacy Jan Paderewski*, Kraków, Poland (1973); *The Partisans I,* Boston, MA (1979); *Marie Skłodowska-Curie*, Public Library, Bayonne, NJ (1987); *Rev. Jerzy Popieluszko*, St. Jadwiga's Church, Trenton, NJ (1987); *The Avenger* (1988) and *General Władysław Anders* (1995), American Częstochowa Shrine, Doylestown, PA; *Pope John Paul II*, Ulanów, Poland (1988–89); *Katyń—1940*, Exchange Place, Jersey City, NJ (1988–91); *Pope John Paul II*, St. Stanislaus Bishop and Martyr Church, New York (1991); *The Blue Army*, Grunwald Square, Warsaw, Poland (1998); *The Partisans II* (1999) and *The Sarmatian* (2001), Grounds for Sculpture, Hamilton, NJ; *The Flame of Freedom—Katyn*, Inner Harbor East, Baltimore, MD (2000); *Tadeusz Kościuszko* (2001), Williams Park, St. Petersburg, FL; and *Juliusz Tarnowski*, A. Surowiecki Square, Tarnobrzeg, Poland (2003).

Pityński's bas reliefs include *Queen Jadwiga* (1974); *Michał Krupa* (1982) and *Maria Konopnicka* (2004), Ulanów, Poland; *Our Lady—The Home Army* (1984), *Maksymilian Kolbe* (1985), *Urn—Heart of Ignacy Jan Paderewski* (1986), *Miracle on the Vistula* (2000), *Jan Lechoń* (2006) all in Doylestown, PA; *Polish Heraldic Eagle* (1990), Consulate of the Republic of Poland, New York, and Embassy of the Republic of Poland, Washington, D.C.; *Wolyniak* (1997), Tarnawiec, Poland. He also executed medals including *Leap* (1974); *Pulaski Police Association*, New York (1979); *Polish-Slavic Center*, Greenpoint, NY (1980); *Światowid* (1980); *Nowy Dziennik*

(1981); *Our Lady of Częstochowa* (1982); *Warsaw Uprising* (1984); *Baczyński* (1984); *Popiełuszko/Piłsudski* (1985); *Cardinal Krol* (1986); *Baptism of Rus* (1988); *Ulanów/John Paul II* (1988); *National Treasure—London* (1989); *Captain Mirecki* (1989); *General Sikorski* (1993); *Ulanów High School* (1994); *Pope John Paul II/Gdańsk Millennium* (1997); *Blue Army/America* (1998); *Wolyniak* (1998); *Professor Sulimirski* (1998); *Wounded Polish Eagle* (2000); *General Kościuszko* (2002); *Rev. Lucjiusz Tyrasiński* (2006); *Paderewski/Association of Polish Army Veterans in America* (2008).

Among his many honors are the Audubon Artists' Silver Medal of Honor (1997–98) and Gold Medal of Honor (1996); Allied Artists of America Silver Medal of Honor (1985); Elliott Liskin Memorial Award (1989); Members & Associates Award (1994); Polonia Restituta Cross from the Polish Government-in-Exile, London (1989); Gold Order of Merit of the Republic of Poland (Warsaw, 1990); Commander of the Order of Merit of the Republic of Poland (1996); Perennial Wisdom Medal, Monuments Conservancy, Rockefeller Center, New York (1999).—*Stanley L. Cuba*

SOURCES: Donald Martin Reynolds, *Masters of American Sculpture: The Figurative Tradition from the American Renaissance to the Millennium* (New York: Abbeville Press, 1993); Irena Grzesiuk-Olszewska and Andrzej K. Olszewski, *Andrzej Pitynski Sculpture* (Lesko, Poland: Wydawnictwo Bosz, 2008).

Podhale. The name Podhale denotes an extensive geographical-ethnic region in Poland delineated by the Tatra Mountains to the south, the Nowy Targ Lowlands lying along the Dunajec River and the Gorce Mountains to the north, the Beskidy in the west, and the Pieniny Mountains in the east. In reality, Podhale is composed of three major regions—Spisz, Podhale and Orawa—along with smaller sub-regions, but most often these are all lumped together under the name Podhale. See **Górale; Polish Highlanders Alliance of North America**.—*Sophie Hodorowicz Knab*

Podres, Johnny (b. Witherbee, New York, September 30, 1932; d. Glens Falls, New York, January 13, 2008). Baseball player. Johnny Podres was one of the more prominent pitchers in major league baseball from 1953 to 1969. Over a career lasting sixteen seasons, he won 148 games and compiled an earned run average of 3.68, hurling for three teams. A lefthander who relied on control, Podres is best remembered for having won two games in the 1955 World Series, including a shutout in the seventh and decisive match, giving the Brooklyn Dodgers their first and only world championship. In recognition of his feat, he was named the Most Valuable Player of the

Series, and *Sports Illustrated* named him its Sportsman of the Year. In 1957, he led the National League in earned run average, and the statistical calculations of *Total Baseball* rank him as the second best NL pitcher that season. After the Dodgers moved to Los Angeles, Podres formed part of an imposing pitching staff that led the team to three more World Series titles between 1959 and 1965. While overshadowed by more celebrated teammates such as Sandy Koufax and Don Drysdale, Podres led the league in won-lost percentage in 1961, and he was named to three NL All-Star squads. In all, his Dodgers teams claimed five National League pennants and four world championships, and Podres logged an impressive 4–1 lifetime record in World Series competition. After retiring as a player, he coached for several major league teams. Podres was inducted into the National Polish-American Sports Hall of Fame in 2002.—*Neal Pease*

SOURCE: Donald Honig, *The October Heroes* (New York: Simon and Schuster, 1979).

Poetry *see* **Literature, Polish American.**

Pogonowski, Iwo Cyprian (b. Lwów, Poland, September 3, 1921; d.—). Engineer, author. Pogonowski spent five and one-half years in a series of German concentration camps, most notably Auschwitz and Sachsenhausen, from December 1939 until April 1945 when he escaped and crossed into the U.S. military zone of Germany. He migrated to the U.S. in 1950, earned a B.S. and an M.S. degree in civil and industrial engineering at the University of Tennessee, and became a civil engineer specializing in oil research. Working in Venezuela and the U.S., he developed more than fifty patents in his field of work. After deciding on an early retirement, Pogonowski devoted himself to his two passions, the creation of a series of Polish-English dictionaries, and the compilation of a number of historical works devoted to Poland. One of the latter, *Poland—A Historical Atlas*, appeared in 1987. A second, *Jews in Poland—A Documentary History*, appeared in 1993. He was also active as a polemicist on controversial topics involving Poland and its history.—*Donald E. Pienkos*

SOURCE: Wojciech Wierzewski, "Sto Trzydziesta Slynnych Polaków w Ameryce" (Unpublished manuscript in the archives of the University of Wisconsin–Milwaukee, 2000).

Polak w Ameryce (The Pole in America). *Polak w Ameryce* was a Polish language newspaper founded by the Rev. **John Pitass,** the pastor of St. Stanislaus Church in Buffalo, New York. The publication began as a weekly on April 1, 1887, became a semi-weekly in

1890, and was then published daily beginning in 1895. During its early years of publication, *Polak w Ameryce* claimed to be "the only Polish daily in the Eastern Central States." Eventually changing its name to *Telegram*, the newspaper converted into a weekly journal in 1928 and would eventually cease publication around 1934. Although noted for advancing a conservative perspective, *Polak w Ameryce* shifted its allegiance between the Democratic and Republican parties. In 1894, it became the center of a controversy that resulted in a landmark legal decision called *Krug v. Pitass*, a case which helped to define the law of libel in New York State. During the course of its operations, the newspaper employed fourteen different editors, among them the noted **Polonia** historian **Mieczysław Haiman**.—*Carl L. Bucki*

SOURCES: Henry M. Senft, "The Pole in America: A Study of Pioneer Polish Newspaper of Buffalo, N.Y. 1887–1920" (Buffalo: Unpublished master's thesis, Canisius College, 1950); Jan Wepsiec, *Polish American Serial Publications: 1842–1966, An Annotated Bibliography* (Chicago: Jan Wepsiec, 1968); Frank H. Severance, "The Periodical Press of Buffalo: 1811–1915," *Buffalo Historical Society Publications*, Vol. 19 (Buffalo: Buffalo Historical Society, 1915); *Krug v. Pitass*, 162 N.Y. 154 (1900).

Poland, History of. By the middle of the tenth century the rudiments of a state had emerged among the Western Slavs on the eastern margins of Europe. It is generally believed that the Western Slavs migrated into the area between the Oder and Vistula Rivers from regions bordering the upper and middle Dnepr River. Most were farmers who supported themselves by growing crops. In contact with the Roman Empire, the Western Slavs gradually began to develop similarly to western European nations, while the Eastern and Southern Slavs began to look to Byzantium and eventually adopted Orthodox Christianity. Early Western Slav groups included the Samo (623–58), the Principality of Mazovia (ca. 8th century–833), the Principality of Nitra (ca. 8th century–833), and Great Mazovia (833–907). Primitive, east of an older Europe which had based its civilization on the Roman inheritance, and still pagan by 900, the Poles were late additions to the European community. The Bohemians to the south and the Eastern Slavs to the east created discernible centers at about the same time. To the west the largely German Holy Roman Empire, a Christian state and the inheritor of the Roman tradition of imperial claim to all of Europe, was several generations older and at a more advanced stage of organization and culture. The immediate prospects of Poland were not auspicious.

Poland's political evolution over the next two centuries was dramatic with both major triumphs and serious setbacks. The Christianization of the country in 966 under Mieczko I (ca. 945–992) and its ability to place its church directly under Rome and avoid subordination to the Holy Roman Empire was a major success as it foreclosed the Empire's claim to a missionary right at Polish expense. The gradual emergence of a native dynasty founded by Mieczko and consolidated by his son Bolesław Chrobry, named after the legendary first ruler, Piast, meant a considerable degree of stability and discernible frontiers. The dynasty would last for some four centuries. The tribal system was gradually replaced by a more complex social organization with crude institutions of local administration. Several vigorous monarchs—including Kazimierz I (1037–58) and Bolesław III Wrymouth (1102–38)—expanded the borders markedly, and elevated Poland to a major regional power. However, an unwise decision to divide the national territory under the various branches of the ruling family, and thus dissolve political unity, led to grave difficulties which were only repaired more than a century later under the vigorous leadership of Władysław I Łokietek (1260–1333) and his more famous son, Kazimierz III Wielki (1310–1370).

Under the Piasts, Poland emerged as a unified state, with its capital at Kraków, that included various ethnic and religious minorities. Jews in particular, persecuted in Western Europe, arrived in large numbers to take advantage of Poland's relative religious freedom. A uniform legal code was enacted, educational opportunities expanded with the founding of major universities, and cultural activities expanded. Kazimierz's success paved the way for the transformative events of 1385 when the heiress to the Piast legacy, Jadwiga of Anjou, was betrothed to the leader of Lithuania, Jagiełło. This political arrangement reflected the congruence of Polish and Lithuanian strategic interests. The Lithuanians had emerged suddenly on the map of Europe as a rapidly expanding pagan people based on the shores of the Baltic. After 1240, and the destruction of the Kievan state by the Mongols, the Lithuanians expanded rapidly into the territory of the old Kievan patrimony. The result was a large heterogeneous state ruled by a Lithuanian warrior minority but containing a large Eastern Slavic Orthodox population. By the mid–fourteenth century this large but ramshackle edifice faced many threats: the Mongols to the east, the crusading order of the Teutonic Knights in the Baltic, and Poland in the west, an obvious rival.

On the Polish side the prospects were almost equally challenging. Even though the Mongol invasion of 1241 was blunted at Legnica, Poland was under constant threat. The Teutonic Knights to the north threatened to remove Poland as a Baltic power and dominate all of northern Poland. The Piast dynasty had just expired leaving only the child Jadwiga, a distant relative of Kazimierz.

This situation led to political marriage between Jadwiga and Jagiełło, and the associated Treaty of Krewo (1385) which was the first of a series of links between Poles and Lithuanians. The intimacy and essential nature of this relationship remains an object of controversy between Polish and Lithuanian historians. The latter tend to diminish its significance, the former see it as the initial step in the eventual union of Poland and Lithuania. Regardless of the real nature of the agreement, Lithuania accepted Christianity through a Polish intermediacy, a major development in the history of that people.

The allies scored a major victory with the defeat of the Teutonic Knights at the Battle of Grunwald in 1410. Whereas Grunwald did not eliminate the Order—that would take several more generations and more than one war—it did remove the immediate threat and proved to both Poland and Lithuania the value of the new relationship. Here we should mention the striking efforts of Paulus Vladimiri (Paweł Wlodkowic, 1370–1435) to defend Poland by the assertion of an early version of human rights in the diplomatic struggle with the Knights. The victory at Grunwald led directly to the 1410 Union of Horodło whereby the weak links of Krewo were considerably strengthened by an agreement in which Polish noble clans "adopted" their Lithuanian counterparts, which symbolically began the process of creating a joint upper class for the conjoined states. A social bond now reinforced a tenuous political alliance.

For Poland the relationship with Lithuania was a turning point in national history. Under the Piasts, Poland was a Central European state, a latecomer to the heritage of old Rome of rather modest territorial expanse. After Krewo, Poland turned eastward and became a huge joint state with vast territory and a large population not of Polish ethnic stock or language, a community of Eastern Slavs who were Orthodox Christians. Poland now bordered the rapidly emerging power of Muscovite Russia. Thus, in one process were born several traditions which were to pervade Poland forever after: Poland as a multi-national conglomeration over vast territory rather than a compact ethnic state, and Poland and Russia as rivals for the dominance of the east of Europe. Poland began its career as an Eastern European power without abandoning its Central European status, thus bequeathing to Polish culture the question of whether Poland was a western state in the east or an eastern state on the borders of the true westerners, the Germans.

Poland's pluralism was further underscored by the emergence of a large Jewish community which had migrated east from the German lands. By the time of the Treaty of Krewo, the Jewish population of Poland was already substantial and growing. Originally a western Polish phenomenon, the Jews gradually spread throughout the Polish-Lithuanian territories especially to the southeastern border regions. Unlike the Christian population, overwhelmingly peasant and hence rural, the Jews were largely an urban population, with strict barriers to regular intercourse with the majority population and administered by laws and customs peculiar to themselves and guaranteed by the national authorities. The Jews in Poland were not an integrated portion of the national mosaic. This would be a much later development long after the tradition of separation had generations to develop.

The large German population of western and southwestern Poland meant that Poland had western minorities as well as the huge Eastern Slavic and Lithuanian populations to the east and such exotica as Armenian and Tatar communities. Poland was, after 1385, the most nationally diverse nation in Europe, a phenomenon later praised as a characteristic feature of Poland's absorptive capacities and condemned as dooming the large state to inevitable disunion.

The crowning achievement of Poland's eastern orientation was the 1569 Union of Lublin which essentially dissolved the barriers between Polish lands and Lithuanian and Eastern Slavic territories to the east. This agreement made of Poland-Lithuania essentially one political community — the Polish "Commonwealth" (Rzeczpospolita Polska) — an interpretation, however, later rejected by Lithuanians who wished to emphasize their individuality from Poland.

Lublin was the first of a series of late sixteenth century acts which transformed Poland. In 1572, the last Jagiellonian died, leaving Poland in profound crisis. The response was to create a unique structure — an elective monarchy in which the numerous *szlachta* (nobility) were allowed to vote for the next king who, in turn, would be required to sign a contract (the *pacta conventa*) which restricted his prerogatives and invested the nobility with broad authority. This Royal Republic resulted in a state which had singular merits and defects. The notion that a large state would exhibit the nucleus of republican institutions with a large class of the population enjoying political rights and with the king limited in authority prefigured the later democratic evolution in Europe and made Poland, in the words of a contemporary, the freest state in Europe. On the other hand, the weak monarchy made Poland unable to respond vigorously to national threats and opportunities; the king could only function with the consent and cooperation of a large and unwieldy nobility which was more jealous of its political liberties than inclined to cooperate with the monarch. This threat of paralysis in crisis was merely that, a threat, when Poland was at the height of its power from the mid–sixteenth century for the next several generations. However, as the state fell into a series of crises after 1648, these very institutions which had been in the van of European political evolution became a crippling burden to a government attempting to react to huge and mounting difficulties.

Slightly after the Lublin accord, the 1573 Warsaw Confederation codified religious toleration for all creeds, a striking contrast to the religious strife engulfing much of Europe. The Poles had for centuries been a Catholic people and their faith had proved vital in the formation of the nation. Nonetheless, some in Poland had converted to Protestantism: Lutheranism among the German burghers and Calvinism among some of the nobility for the most part, although this phenomenon proved short lived. Many Poles were convinced that Polish toleration, coupled with the political liberties of the Royal Republic, made Poland an unusually progressive member of the European community. Poland became a "haven for heretics" as many fleeing religious persecution elsewhere came to Poland.

The creation of the elective monarch, the Warsaw confederation, along with the Union of Lublin, was complemented by the controversial Union of Brześć (Brest). This 1596 agreement was essentially a religious pact between the large Orthodox population of the southeast — that is, Ukraine and the majority Roman Catholics. Former Orthodox thereafter became Uniates (Greek Catholics) in communion with Rome; those who remained Orthodox resented the actions of their former co-religionists. The fact that the Union was something that affected the Orthodox population from the top down — the upper classed accepting it, the lower rejecting it — made the Union a bone of contention in the southeastern portions of the state where the Orthodox population was the overwhelming majority. We can see Brześć as the religious counterpart to Lublin, both aiming to enhance unity within the state by lessening if not eliminating barriers to national consolidation. The late sixteenth and early seventeenth century marked the zenith of Polish power. A series of victories over Russia in the Livonian Wars and even a temporary Polish occupation of the Kremlin made Poland's powerful position in the east obvious.

These years are often referred to as the "golden age" of Poland and certainly the era produced more than just political innovation, but major cultural advance as well. In addition to the Jagiellonian University in Kraków (1364), a new university opened in Wilno (1586), and later in Lwów (1660). The era is resplendent with great names in various fields. In literature we have the founder of Polish letters Mikołaj Rey (1505–69) — like many other Poles of the Renaissance era, a Protestant — whose famous remark that "Poles are not geese, but have their own language" (Polacy nie gęsi, iż swój język mają) may be considered the birth of literary consciousness among the Poles. An even larger figure, one of the greatest of all Slavic writers, was Jan Kochanowski (1530–84) who virtually invented Polish poetry. His *Treny* (Laments), heart-breaking reflections of his bellowed daughter's death, remain enormously moving half a millennium later.

Andrzej Frycz Modrzewski's (1503–72) work *De republica emendanda* (Improving the Commonwealth) is a classic treatise in the evolution of Western — and not just Polish — political thought and one of the key documents in the creation of democratic thought in Poland. Another great scholar was Maciej Miechowita (1457–1523) whose work presented the geography of Eastern Europe for the first time. Mikołaj Kopernik (Copernicus, 1473–1543) became famous throughout the world for his *De revolutionibus orbium coelestium* in which he presented his heliocentric theory that the sun, rather than the earth, was the center of the solar system, thereby launching modern astronomical research.

However, in the mid–seventeenth century Poland was plunged into a crisis which led directly to its ruin at the end of the next century. In 1648, the Cossack rebellion broke out among the Ukrainian Orthodox community of the southeast. Prompted by the extension of regular Polish administration to the previously frontier region, and fueled by religious and ethnic grievances, the rebellion was essentially a protest against the consolidation of a Polish state. The rebellion rapidly spread with Catholics, Uniates, and Jews, all representatives of the post–1596 Poland, especially targeted and suffered devastating losses. This civil war was soon expanded when Russia invaded Poland ostensibly in support of the Orthodox population. Peace only came in 1667 with enormous territorial losses to Russia under the Treaty of Andruszów. The settlement with the Ukrainians was more a testimony to mutual exhaustion than reconciliation. No sooner did these wars end, when a Turkish invasion began another conflict which witnessed King Jan Sobieski's dramatic victory at Vienna in 1683, but caused further damage to the Commonwealth by the time hostilities ended in 1699. The new dynasty in Poland, the worthless Saxon monarchs, then recklessly plunged Poland into the Great Northern War (1699–1721) as Russia's ally against Sweden, a strategic blunder of major proportions. By the time these wars ended, the Commonwealth was a ruined country — enormous population losses, economic devastation, shattered administration, corruption, and demoralization. The elective monarch had revealed its worst features as foreign powers, principally Russia, intervened in Polish elections playing a major role in politics. The country was able to assert its sovereignty only with difficulty. Witness to this confusion was the ill-fated Confederation of Bar (1768). Among those who gained prominence in the Confederation was **Kazimierz Pułaski**, who later died leading American troops at Savannah in the American Revolutionary War.

The last years of the eighteenth century were a contest between a growing reform movement which attempted to resurrect the country from the morass, and increasing foreign intervention which played upon national enfeeblement and a corrupt political system. In 1772, the First Partition was the verdict on Poland's long decline. By this act substantial territories were seized by the Russians, Prussians, and Austrians and the country found itself in dire straits. The shock stimulated a frenzy of reform symbolized by the famous **Constitution of the Third of May** (1791) which suggested that Poland was at least on the road to rejuvenation. The signs of renewed vigor in Poland provoked the concern among its neighbors who had grown used to regarding Poland as too feeble to protect its national interests. The result was the Second Partition in 1792. This was truly the death knell of old Poland as it left the country so reduced in size that its continued existence was brought into question. A last great effort at national resistance through insurrection, the Kościuszko Insurrection of 1794, led by the famous figure of the American Revolution, the heroic **Tadeusz Kościuszko** (1746–1817), failed to stem the tide, and Poland was erased from the map of Europe by the Third Partition of 1795.

The demise of Poland also fundamentally transformed the minority communities so characteristic of the Commonwealth. Ukrainians and Belarusians in the east began the slow process by which they would either assimilate to Russian culture or, later, develop a sense of separatist nationalism sundering their connections to the Commonwealth's traditions. The Jews, who had been virtually immune from assimilation before 1795, began their slow movement toward Russification in the east and Germanization in the west with the later phenomenon of Zionism all competing with Polish loyalties to claim their adherence.

Poland was the capital of the Jewish world after the fourteenth century. By the late sixteenth century this had coalesced into the famous Council of Four Lands (Wielkopolska, Małopolska, Wołyń and Ruś to use their Polish names). But the next century brought widespread devastation to the Jews of southeastern Poland as a result of the Cossack Wars (after 1648). As the old Commonwealth came to an end a distinctive form of emotive Judaism spread among the lower classes of the Jewish community, Hasidism, which was in stark contrast to the more ascetic tradition closely associated with the rabbinate, especially the rabbinic center at Wilno. Simultaneously a small but passionate messianic movement (Frankism) further complicated and enriched the Jewish community of Poland. By the time of the Partitions the Jewish community of Poland had a turbulent and fractious history, with traditions both mystical (kabbalah) and messianic among many others which had extended over half a millennium.

Learning and culture flourished in the Commonwealth, which became an important center for the development of modern social and political philosophies and known throughout Europe for its religious tolerance at a time when religious wars rent the peace of Western Europe. The Commonwealth was home to important political philosophers such as Andrzej Frycz Modrzewski (1503–72), Wawrzyniec Grzymała Goślicki (1530–1607), and Piotr Skarga (1536–1612), the historian and cartographer Martin Kromer (1512–1589), mathematician and astronomer Jan Brożek (1585–1652), and Baal Shem Tov who founded Hasidic Judaism (1698–1760). Religious art flourished, especially the use of black marble for altars, fonts, monuments, and tombstones, while nobles supported composers and musicians, founded choirs and orchestras, and in other ways sponsored the development of the arts. Much of this was informed by the multiplicity of ethnic and religious traditions that collectively interacted in Commonwealth Poland. By the mid–1500s, about eighty percent of the Jews in the world lived in Poland. By 1618, it has been estimated that the population of Poland included 4.5

million Poles, 3.5 million Ukrainians, 1.5 million Belarusians, 750,000 Lithuanians, 750,000 Prussians, 500,000 Jews, and 500,000 Livonians. About ten percent of the population were nobles, fifteen percent burghers, and the balance overwhelmingly peasants.

Following the Third Partition, a Polish state did not exist for 123 years. The Partitions visited upon the Poles profound questions as well as national subjugation. Had Poland deserved its own destruction? Was this history's verdict on Poland's career? Or were the Partitions the rapacious act of foreign powers preying upon temporary weakness, the type of weakness that all nations suffer but from which none had been forced to lose all? In other words, the question for Poles to contemplate until 1918 was: was it our fault or theirs? A second question was posed by the Partitions: could a nation survive without a state? Could Poles exist without a Poland to define them? Would the parceling out of Polish territory to three neighbors dissolve the bonds of a territory so long united? Would the heterogeneous Polish Commonwealth be replaced by a series of ethnic communities contesting for the territory of a once common patrimony? And, finally, the "Polish Question" was posed: Could Poland regain its independence and, if it proved possible, how could it be done and what would be the result? The nineteenth century was a long trial of survival in difficult circumstances.

The death of old Poland coincided with the tumultuous events of the French Revolution and the attendant Napoleonic wars (1789–1815). Poles were divided in their reaction. Some saw in France, and particularly in Napoleon, a deliverer. After all, France was the opponent of Austria and Prussia, both Partitioners, and Russia, the third enemy was also intermittently a French opponent. Hence could France's military victories destroy the system which shackled Poland? On the other hand, Napoleon was regarded by many Poles — notably Kościuszko — as a cynical and unscrupulous actor who would praise or abandon the Poles as circumstances suggested. In the end Polish support for Napoleon was ill-rewarded. The Poles gained considerable success and much stuff of subsequent legend by their military exploits in Napoleon's service, but Poland did not re-emerge as a result. The Congress of Vienna (1815), which ended the wars, did not resurrect Poland and the new arrangements merely confirmed the partitions, albeit with some territorial modifications. After 1815, we must follow developments in three Polands; the Austrian, Prussian, and Russian Partitions. These three separate lines of development embedded Poland in the history of three often antagonistic countries and did much to dissolve the historic unity of old Poland.

Russian Poland, by far the largest portion, was itself divided into two segments. A central nucleus was designated the "Congress Kingdom" and enjoyed a constitution, separate administration, and considerable freedoms within the confines of the Russian Empire, the result of the liberality of Tsar Alexander I and the efforts of his intimate advisor, the Pole Adam Prince Czartoryski (1770–1861). However, the former eastern territories of the Commonwealth enjoyed no such benefits and were increasingly amalgamated into the Russian empire. Polish efforts to regain independence in 1830 (the November Uprising) only meant the end of the quasi-independence of the Congress Kingdom and a worsening status for the eastern territories. A renewed effort in 1863 (the January Insurrection), was also crushed and ushered in an era of harsh and increasingly pervasive Russification designed to extirpate the Polish elements of the eastern lands.

Romanticism — which stressed sacrifice for the sacred cause of the Fatherland and had a profound effect on the Poles — was largely discredited by the failed uprisings. Nonetheless, its representatives, like Fryderyk Chopin (1810–49), Adam Mickiewicz (1798–1855), Juliusz Słowacki (1809–49), Artur Grottger (1837–67), as well as the somewhat later "Father" of Polish opera Stanisław Moniuszko (1819–72), remained inspiration to future generations. These notions acted as a spiritual bond for the numerous exile community caused by the insurrections, the Great Emigration. However, after the collapse of the January Insurrection, in place of Romanticism a new, apolitical doctrine, "**organic work**," supported by Polish **Positivism**, stressing social and economic progress, coupled with acceptance of the political status quo characterized Polish political thought for a generation and more.

The last decades of the nineteenth century brought transformation to Russian Poland. Peasant emancipation in the 1860s, explosive industrialization in the following decades, and a rapid population growth, worked a social revolution in the country. Whereas urbanization could absorb some of the increase, many Poles now found themselves forced to emigrate, at first to Western Europe, and by the last years of the century across the Atlantic. The "emigration for bread" (*za chlebem*) had begun.

Simultaneously there was a revolution in the nationality structure of old Poland. Ethnic nationalism spread rapidly among both the Poles and the former minority peoples of the old Commonwealth. Polish nationalism increasingly identified "Poles" not as the children of a common fatherland but those of Polish blood and language and Roman Catholic by faith. Similar doctrines among Ukrainians, Lithuanians and, to a lesser extent, Belarusians, meant that many hostile communities now populated Poland's historic lands. Among the Jews a peculiar transformation was being worked. By the late nineteenth century many Jews were leaving the traditional separation of their communal lives and joined the Poles through assimilation, but the more virulent strands of Polish nationalism were characterized by anti–Semitism and did not welcome these newcomers. Not surprisingly Zionism, which stressed the "peoplehood" of the Jews, became a Jewish form of nationalism making the Jews yet another contestant in the heterodox lands of former eastern Poland. The old Commonwealth was collapsing internally, unable to meet the challenges of modern times. The lack of a Polish state to sustain them meant that Poland could not survive as a multinational structure.

In German Poland, national antagonism between Poles and Germans intensified markedly during the post-partition era. Originally, after 1815, the Prussians were quite generous in their administration of former Polish territories and social relations between Poles and Germans were civil, if not cordial. However, with the creation of the German Empire in 1871 national chauvinism became the characteristic feature of Berlin's treatment of the Poles. Discriminatory legislation, and colonization of Polish territories was complimented by public efforts to de-polonize the German east by crowding out all public aspects of its once Polish character. Polish Jews, increasingly Germanized, saw the German state as a more attractive model than the remnants of old Poland which was increasingly a faded memory. Thus, as Jews modernized, they also Germanized. This led to increasing animosities with the ethnic Polish community which saw the Jews as abandoning them.

Aggressive nationalism among the Germans was met with an equally uncompromising Polish response. Germany, unlike Russia, was a modern state with an advanced economy, and a quality educational system. Hence, Polish efforts to organize to respond to the German threat made the German Poles the best organized, wealthiest, and best educated Poles in the partitioned lands. When population pressures forced these Poles to emigrate — a generation before the Russian Poles — they became the leaders of the Poles in emigration due to their social, organizational, and edu-

cational superiority. Contesting with the Germans had made the Poles into a more modern people. The early Polish urban communities in America were largely peopled and developed by these early arrivals who often lived in German neighborhoods and worshipped in German churches in the U.S. until sufficient numbers of Poles existed to form their own parishes.

Austrian Poland was an exception to this pattern. Originally, Austrian rule over Polish territory was a mixture of neglect and exploitation. However, the ramshackle Austrian state faced destruction after its defeat by Prussia in 1866 which threatened to dissolve the Hapsburg Empire along ethnic lines. In an effort to compromise with its most implacable minorities, Vienna gave autonomy to the powerful Hungarians and wide latitude to the Poles of **Galicia**. The result was that Poles from the upper classes, the major landowners and the urban intelligentsia, were substantially won over to cooperation with — if not support of — the monarchy. In exchange for being *Kaisertreu* (loyal to the Kaiser), the Poles received the right to govern Galicia according to their own preferences and were granted a powerful position in the political affairs of the Empire. The poorer Poles of rural Galicia gained little from this arrangement, and thus was created a two tiered system: a pro–Habsburg upper class and an apathetic majority mistrustful of its social betters. With the end of the century, Galicia began sending waves of immigrants to the New World and the Austrian Poles rivaled, if not surpassed, the Russian Poles in numbers of immigrants, both exceeding the older German Polish wave considerably.

The minority populations of Galicia, the Ukrainians, and the Jews were a complicating factor. The Habsburgs liked to play off the Poles against the Ukrainians thus gaining greater leverage by exacerbating ethnic rivalries. In eastern Galicia, where the population was heavily Ukrainian, this led to considerable bitterness as nationalism gained rapid ground among both Poles and Ukrainians. The Jews were caught in a difficult position. Traditionally they tried to propitiate the governing power to protect their minority interests, something they had done in old Poland. But in Galicia that meant choosing Vienna over Poles or Ukrainians. Many Jews assimilated to Polish culture, fewer to Ukrainian; most tried to avoid conflict in an increasingly charged atmosphere.

Across partition boundaries, Polish thought and culture were enlivened at the turn of the century — a period of remarkable cultural efflorescence — by a return to the themes and attitudes of the Romantic era. The best exemplars of this neo-romanticism were the novels of **Henryk Sienkiewicz** (1846–1916) set in the turbulent decades of the late seventeenth century and filled with battle and passion. The return to the heroic was further exemplified in painting in the canvases of Jan Matejko (1838–93), Juliusz Kossak (1824–99) and especially Wojciech Gerson (1831–1901) and Wojciech Kossak (1857–1942) among others who often depicted military glories. The younger generation included the Dali-like Jacek Malczewski (1854–1929), a symbolist obsessed with Polish martyrdom.

The overlapping "Young Poland" (Młoda Polska) movement continued the neo-romantic theme but shifted attention to the sacred mission of the artist and celebration of decadence in opposition to bourgeoisie stultification. In this phenomenon we should mention the novelist Stefan Żeromski (1864–1925) and the multi-talented Stanisław Wyspiański (1869–1907) whose play *Wesele* (The Wedding) captured a Poland torn by conflicting feelings of torpor and passionate desire to regain independence through the resurrection of the heroic values of old Poland. Władysław Stanisław Reymont's (1868–1925) novel *Chłopi* (The Peasants) was written in this era and would win him the Nobel Prize in 1924.

By the twentieth century Poland was incomparably different than the old Commonwealth. The multi-national state was replaced by a conglomeration of ethnic rivalries. Village torpor was increasingly replaced by urban industrialization; millions were leaving for temporary, and increasingly permanent, emigration. By 1900, modern politics made its appearance. Populism spoke for the village and focused on uniting the peasant majority into a body capable of protecting the economic and social interests of the farmer. Populism avoided enunciating answers to the perennial Polish Question and concentrated on the quotidian concerns of rural life. It was, relative to its huge numbers, a movement of little influence in crafting a national policy for the divided Polish nation. The heartland of Populism was in Austrian Poland where peasants even served in parliament and gained experience in modern politics. Among the leaders of the movement we should note the controversial Jan Stapiński (1867–1946) and the later more famous Wincenty Witos (1874–1945).

The working class of urban Poland was attracted to socialism which posited the worker as the engine of progress, and thus differentiated between peasant backwardness and proletarian modernity. The landowner was as a result looked upon as a social anachronism, and the rising middle class as an exploiter of labor. Socialism's appeal was complicated by a profound division. The Social Democratic movement preached internationalism and argued that Polish workers were fundamentally that, workers, who had common cause with others workers regardless of nationality and which should view the capitalist class, even when Polish, as enemies. However, there also existed a patriotic socialism: the Polish Socialist Party which attempted to combine socialism with calls for independence and argued that worker freedom could only be fully realized when Poland was restored. Particularly strong in the cities of Russian Poland, socialism's most prominent figure was Józef Piłsudski (1867–1935).

The third powerful movement was Polish nationalism. Nationalism is to be understood as essentially a modernizing force, not a traditionalist creed; it is hence not conservative. The nationalists posited a revolutionary redefinition of Poland as a nation composed exclusively of Roman Catholic ethnic Poles and rejected the multi-national heritage of the pre-partition state. With their modern nationalism — then in vogue in Europe — rejection of conservative traditionalism and stress on a practical rational approach to life-reminiscent of the "organic work" movement of a generation earlier, the nationalists were, as their main proponent Roman Dmowski argued, illuminating a "modern Pole."

While Europe moved toward war in the early years of the century, two different "orientations" appeared among the Poles. A future war would match the western democracies, England and France, and their authoritarian ally Russia, against Germany and Austria, the so-called Central Powers. The nationalists favored support for the first coalition, reasoning that a victory for the Central Powers would be a disaster for the Poles as it would mean German control of all Polish territory. Given the increasingly bad relations between Germans and Poles — perhaps best captured in Maria Konopnicka's (1842–1910) bitter and stirring *Rota* (Oath, 1908) — this was a dire prediction. The problem for the nationalists was that whereas France and England were attractive, Russia was repulsive and made it very difficult to argue in favor of support for England and France if Russia was part of the combination. Followers of Piłsudski rejected support of any combination involving Russia. As a result they favored working with Austria, where Polish influence was not inconsiderable, and reluctantly accepted the perforce association with Germany. Any enemy of Russia, according to this logic, was a friend of Poland.

The two orientations had different approaches to the means by which independence could be achieved, the pro–Western nationalists emphasized diplomacy and a public relations campaign to win support for the Polish cause; they envisioned a gradual approach whereby all Polish lands would be united — unfortunately under Russian control — and independence would only come later. Piłsudski, by contrast, placed his hope on armed struggle: the creation of small symbolic military units (the Legions) and efforts to prepare a general insurrection at a propitious time. Charismatic and decisive, Piłsudski captured the imagination of Poles everywhere and rapidly became the symbol of a resurrected Poland.

At the start of the war none of the belligerents favored the creation of an independent Poland. However, the course of the war brought the so-called "Polish Question" to the fore. Not long after hostilities commenced, the Russians announced concessions to Polish desiderata, but soon much of Russian Poland passed to Austro-German occupation. The war's devastation brought great suffering to the Polish population and made the plight of the Poles an international cause, especially in the United States. Pianist-turned-statesman **Ignacy Jan Paderewski** (1860–1941) arrived there in 1915 and quickly emerged as the leader of American **Polonia**, as well as the main spokesman for Polish interests. He was able to win considerable public and political support, even gaining the ear of President Woodrow Wilson by 1916. **Polonia**, however, was split between the supporters of Piłsudski, politically to the left, organized into the **National Defense Committee** (KON), and the far larger **National Department** (WN) — based originally on the relief organization the **Polish Central Relief Committee** (PCKR) — which was dominated by Paderewski and the Polonia right. The latter was able to recruit a sizeable army to fight alongside the Western Allies after 1917 (see **Polish Army in France**), Polonia's greatest success.

In Poland, Piłsudski's Legions distinguished themselves fighting alongside the Austrians. Piłsudski, however, was unable to use these minuscule Legions to leverage major concessions for Poland from the Central Powers. He had hoped to turn this shadow Poland into the nucleus of a reborn state. However, the Germans were insincere in their support for Poland. Piłsudski broke with them and was eventually incarcerated by the Germans. His position regarding the war seemed to be in shambles.

By 1916, the Germans gambled that the recreation of an independent Poland, albeit in name only, would rally the Poles behind the German war effort, then desperate for manpower. This resulted in the November 5, 1916 "Two Emperors" declaration establishing an amorphous Kingdom of Poland. The "Polish Question" had returned to the agenda of Europe. The western powers feared that the Germans would win the Poles to their side and rapidly issued a series of statements supporting the idea of restoring Poland. Dmowski succeeded in creating a virtual government-in-exile for Poland in Paris, the **Polish National Committee** (or KNP from its Polish version, the Komitet Narodowy Polski). Paderewski—in the U.S.—and Dmowski worked in tandem to gain western support for the Polish cause.

The year 1917-18 revolutionized the Polish Question. Russia collapsed and Germany seemed the only power with a voice in Polish affairs. Poland was substantially reunited, albeit under German aegis. This position proved ephemeral; however, the Germans were defeated in 1918, shortly after foundering Austria disintegrated. With the ruin of the Central Powers, all three partitioners were temporarily in chaos. The Germans released Piłsudski in the hopes of having someone to work with in Warsaw; a necessity given the vast German forces stranded in the east which would be forced to cross Poland to return home.

Piłsudski arrived in Poland a national hero and announced the recreation of an independent Poland (Independence Day, November 11, 1918). Paderewski rapidly returned as well, but had to agree to a power-sharing arrangement with Piłsudski which left the latter in the dominant position. Dmowski remained in Western Europe and hoped to use his influence with the Western powers to become the focus for Polish affairs. Although the situation was chaotic, Poland was free.

The first stage of Polish independence was kaleidoscopic in its developments. Poland fought minor border skirmishes with all its neighbors and a major war with the new Bolshevik Russia. This war, which began in 1919, witnessed a series of dramatic turns. In August 1920, Piłsudski engineered a great victory before Warsaw and routed the Russian forces which were pursued eastward. However, exhausted by long combat, the Poles failed to achieve a decisive victory over the Russians and had to settle for a compromise peace, the Treaty of Riga in 1921, which left much of eastern Poland under Russian control. Thus, the full territorial damage of the Partitions remained unredeemed. Piłsudski's hope to resurrect a Poland reminiscent of the pre-partition Commonwealth with close relations with the Ukrainians, Lithuanians, and Belarusians was not realized. This would have required not only evicting the Russians from the eastern borderlands of Poland, but convincing the various nationalities of the area to work in harmony with the Poles. Neither of these requirements was fully satisfied. The Russians were driven back, but not vanquished. The several minorities, mistrustful of what they espied as Polish imperialism, refused to support a close relationship among the peoples who had inhabited pre-partition Poland.

Meanwhile the Poles suffered a series of disappointments at the Paris Peace Conference convened in 1919 to reconstruct Europe from the chaos of the war. Dmowski and Paderewski, Poland's spokesmen, failed to convince the powers to support a large Poland and had to settle for modest borders which placed Poland at a strategic disadvantage to Germany in the west. The vital port of Danzig (Gdańsk) was not made a part of Poland but rendered a Free City, proving an irritant in Polish-German relations. Mineral-rich Upper Silesia was divided and questionable plebiscites removed much of the Baltic coast from Poland and produced the odd geography of the "Polish Corridor." Wilson, who had been reckoned as a friend of the Poles, supported the idea of an independent Poland, but was opposed to a large state. The result was a paradox—Poland was free, but exposed in the west and only partially victorious in the east, a state strategically vulnerable and a far-cry from the pre-1795 nation.

Free Poland, deemed the Second Republic (1918–39), struggled with daunting structural problems—a vulnerable strategic position, entrenched poverty, and a restive minority population (perhaps one-third the total) which no longer regarded Poland as their historic home. The large and discontented Ukrainian population, perhaps 12–15 percent of the national total, remained substantially un-reconciled to being Polish citizens. In the west, the smaller but locally powerful German minority looked across the border to the new Germany, especially after Adolf Hitler came to power in 1933, as its true homeland. The small Belarusian minority exhibited restiveness due to dire poverty, but was more an economic than a national problem. The Jews, as ever, were a case apart. Few Jews had assimilated into Polish culture by 1918. Many wanted to establish a kind of autonomy within Poland—a very unpopular notion to the Polish majority. A wave of anti–Jewish excesses marred the birth of the Second Republic as the two nationalities continued suspicious and mistrustful of each other.

Politically, the Second Republic had a troubled history. Piłsudski, the dominating figure, was unpopular with the political right. The first president, Gabriel Narutowicz (1865–1922), was assassinated almost immediately after his election by a demented rightist, an attack symbolically aimed at Piłsudski. Civil war seemed possible. Although this was averted, the constant wrangling between Piłsudski and the *sejm* (parliament), and frequent changes of government, led Piłsudski to retire bitterly. He returned to power via *coup d'état* in 1926, creating an authoritarian, though not dictatorial, regime. After his death in 1935, his lesser followers attempted to profit from his legendary status to maintain a government whose chief claim to legitimacy was that it was led by devotees of Piłsudski. At the same time, an increasingly powerful rightist movement seemed to gain support among the general public. This created increasing friction with the minority population, especially the Jews, which the right regarded with hostility. By the late 1930s, the Second Republic had serious political problems but had avoided either civil war or dictatorship. Its future looked troubled, though perhaps not bleak.

Relations with Poles abroad proved challenging for the new Poland. American Polonia was enamored of Paderewski who was the dominant Polish figure in World War I America. But Paderewski had a brief and unhappy career in post–1918 Poland and spent the interwar period in virtual exile in Switzerland. Piłsudski, who was the outstanding political figure of interwar Poland, was not well known in the United States and supporters in Polonia were a distinct minority. Efforts by the Warsaw regime to work more closely with Polonia were little more than a fiasco, and the refusal of many of the leading Polonia figures to join Światpol (Światowa Organizacja Polaków) in 1934, was a major event. By declaring themselves Americans of Polish descent rather than Poles in America, Polonia's leaders either declared their independence—as partisans would have it—or severed Polonia's ties with its Polish roots.

Post-war Poland was an imperfect solution. For all its structural flaws and intractable problems, it represented the restitution of Polish independence and thus had inestimable symbolic value. Moreover, the Republic created a functioning parliamentary state with all the machinery of government with an educational system, a judiciary, and all the other trappings of modernity. It re-knit the fissure in Polish history.

Artistically, the twenty years of Polish independence continued in only slightly diminished magnitude the earlier cultural triumphs of the pre-war era. The *Skamander* movement influenced by the brilliant Leopold Staff (1878–1957), featured a galaxy of major poets including Julian Tuwim (1894–1953), Kazimierz Wierzyński (1894–1969), Antoni Słonimski (1895–1976), and **Jan Lechoń** (1899–1956). The major composer Karol Szymanowski (1882–1937), one of the musical giants of the century, deserves particular mention. Painting saw the work of the polymath Stanisław Witkiewicz (1895–1939), whose suicide after the Russian invasion of Poland in 1939 is a romantic commentary on the passions of restored Poland and its tragic demise. A similar symbol of the drama of modern Poland is Bruno Schultz (1892–1942), writer and artist, at once a Jew and a Polish patriot killed by the Nazis during the Holocaust.

By 1939, Poland was essentially isolated in a dangerous Europe. Hitler's Germany was on a course to war and signed a non-aggression treaty with Moscow (August 23). Stalin's Russia was a great threat to Poland's east. Neither of these two traditional enemies had reconciled to the existence of a free Poland. In the face of this, Poland had diplomatic links to France and rather weaker ties to Great Britain. These were tested — and found meaningless — when Germany invaded on September 1, and the Soviets poured across the border on the September 17. Poland was defeated and occupied, suffering 200,000 casualties. For the next six years the Germans subjected the population to brutal occupation including the systematic slaughter of virtually the entire Jewish population of the country among millions of casualties. In the east, the Soviets attached eastern Poland to their state and deported hundreds of thousands to brutal exile. The war was a nightmare for Poland.

At the beginning of World War II the population of Poland numbered some 35 million people. During the war, the Germans murdered three million of the 3.3 million Jews in Poland, ninety percent of the entire Jewish population, mostly in concentration camps that they established in the country to eliminate not only Polish Jews but Jewry from all over Europe. The Germans murdered over two million Polish Catholics, concentrating especially on intellectuals, political and military leaders, and clergy. Twenty-five percent of the Catholic clergy were eliminated, 25 percent of scientists, and twenty percent of school teachers. An estimated 200,000 children were deported to Germany, about 75 percent of whom never returned. But the Germans were not the only perpetrators. Invading Soviets murdered some 21,000 Polish officers and officials in the Katyń Forest and elsewhere. Over 1.5 million Poles were deported to Siberia and Kazakhstan, with an estimated eighty percent losing their lives either directly or indirectly because of outright murder or maltreatment and deprivation. Tens of thousands of others were murdered by the NKVD for political reasons. When it was over, 6.5 million civilians, and an estimated 664,000 combat deaths — the latter was more than the combined battlefield deaths of the United Stated and Great Britain. Poland lost over twenty percent of its entire prewar population during the conflict. No other European nation lost as a high a proportion of its population.

During the war, Poland contributed more armed forces to the Allied cause than any nation other than the United States, Great Britain, and the Soviet Union. While they fought, Germans systematically attempted to eradicate Polish culture. Public cultural events were banned, schools closed, printing Polish-language books was prohibited, and other cultural expressions were suppressed. They robbed Poland of its artistic treasures, murdered its political and intellectual leadership, and looted or destroyed its cultural artifacts. German authorities estimated that they removed about ninety percent of all valuable artworks from Poland and shipped them to German museums and private collections. Poles were considered to be subhuman (*untermenschen*) and could be killed with impunity by the German occupiers. Death was the immediate penalty for even minor crimes, and assisting a Jew in any manner at all was punishable by death. By war's end, Poland lost about 45 percent of its prewar physicians, 57 percent of its lawyers, 30 percent of its teachers, 40 percent of its scientists and university professors, and 28 percent of its clergy.

Despite the repression, a Polish underground state emerged, complete with a government and an underground military force, the Armia Krajowa (Home Army). The underground staged plays, conducted educational programs, published newspapers, and in other ways continued Polish cultural life in defiance of the brutal occupation. The Poles also formed Żegota, an organization whose mission it was to aid Jews in escaping the Germans by providing false documents, shelter, food, and other support. The Polish underground military force was the largest in occupied Europe, numbering in excess of 400,000 combatants. Its intelligence contributions to the Allied cause were exceptional, including cracking the German enigma code and the remarkable feat of stealing, disassembling, and smuggling to Great Britain an entire German rocket-propelled missile.

While the Polish underground fought its guerilla war against the Germans, the Polish government, which had refused to surrender, was reconstituted in the West under General Władysław Sikorski. This government was eventually able to collect scatted units into a considerable force and fought on all major fronts against the Germans. Initially heralded by the British, especially after the remarkable role of the Poles in the Battle of Britain, by 1941 there was a dramatic change in British attitudes. Germany invaded the Soviet Union and the erstwhile allies became enemies. The British at once realized the necessity of keeping Russia in the war against the Germans by all means. When the Americans became belligerents in December 1941, they adopted this British disposition. Hence the Poles were forced into a pathetic situation. Russia was Poland's enemy, but the most vital ally of Britain and the United States. Poland's position collapsed in the West as it became a nuisance to close cooperation among the three major allies.

Polish Americans were again split in their opinions. The leftist KNAPP (**National Committee of Americans of Polish Descent**) had virtually no resonance outside of Polish ranks, and the Rada Polonii Amerykańskiej (**American Relief for Poland**) and the later **Polish American Congress** (PAC) had little more. Efforts to raise an army in support of Poland were a dismal failure.

In 1943, the Germans discovered the mass graves at Katyń where the Russians had murdered several thousand Poles in 1941. This caused a rupture in Soviet relations with the Sikorski government as the Russians denied the atrocity, a position that was accepted by London and Washington. A few months later Sikorski died in a plane crash at Gibraltar. The position of the Polish government-in-exile was in ruins. In August, 1944, as Russian troops advanced on Warsaw, the Poles staged a mammoth uprising. They hoped to evict the retreating Germans before the Russians liberated the capital. However, the Germans decided to stay and crush the uprising and the Soviets not only provided little aid, but largely prevented Western assistance. After 63 days of fighting, the Polish underground army was devastated and Warsaw was destroyed. Heinrich Himmler, leader of the Nazi SS, ordered that "The city must completely disappear from the surface of the earth and serve only as a transport station for the Wehrmacht. No stone can remain standing. Every building must be razed to its foundation." German forces did their best to carry out the order, completely destroying 85 percent of the city. In 2005, total losses of property were estimated at $54.6 billion in Warsaw alone. Estimated casualties for the uprising included about 16,000 Polish fighters killed, up to 25,000 wounded, and 15,000 captured. Estimates of civilian deaths during the uprising range from 150,000 to 200,000.

After the Germans crushed the last resistance and leveled Warsaw, the Soviets finally advanced into the desolated shell of the city. By 1945, Poland was a ruined country with massive material damage, the loss of six million people, including nearly its entire Jewish population of about three million in the Holocaust, and abject demoralization. Poland was now occupied by the Soviets and became part of the Eastern Bloc.

The post-war borders of Poland were redrawn by the Soviet Union, radically altering modern Poland. The historic eastern lands, including such ancient Polish cities as Wilno and Lwów, were taken, and new territories in the west were seized from a defeated Germany including the large cities of Wrocław (Breslau) and Szczecin (Stettin). These lands had historic links to Poland, but that relationship was centuries old. The considerable minority populations of Poland vanished. Germans were expelled brutally, the Jews had been annihilated by the Nazis during the war, and the eastern minorities, Belarusians and Ukrainians, had been lost to the Soviets. This was a smaller Poland, homogenous perhaps for the first time in its millennial history. The historic territorial ties of Poland with the pre-partitioned Commonwealth were severed.

While Soviet troops occupied Poland, the London-based government-in-exile continued to exist. Although soon discredited by the British and Americans, it maintained its exile mission until the eventual fall of Communism in Poland finally reunited, if only symbolically by that time, the two divergent factions. Between 1945 and 1989, Poland was a Soviet satellite in which the Soviets constructed a socialist system modeled on that of the USSR. The career of the communist regime is most uninspiring. At first seemingly moderate to pacify a stunned country, the regime became increasingly repressive by the late 1940s as the opposition was crushed. Oppressive Stalinism made Poland seem permanently locked behind the Iron Curtain. In 1956, however, widespread demonstrations threatened a Soviet invasion. Władysław Gomułka, who had a reputation as a patriot, albeit a communist one, was returned from prison and launched a reform era in the PRL (Polska Rzeczpospolita Ludowa, the Polish People's Republic). The Soviets decided against invasion once the situation cooled, and Poland avoided the fate of Hungary whose more belligerent defiance of Soviet rule resulted in a bloody invasion (1956–57). An amelioration of the worst features of Communism and Russification was worked, and the population had exacted concessions from the regime; the first episode in a process which would eventually return freedom to the country.

Poland in the 1960s was characterized by a dreary society and economic incompetence fostered by the Soviet system. In 1968, internal discord in the regime provoked an attempt to stir up nationalist passions and spread anti–Semitic propaganda. The chief actor here was General Mieczysław Moczar. The major result of this sorry spectacle was to make Poland appear both repulsive and ridiculous in foreign eyes. Demonstrations by students against intellectual repression, however, did not provoke similar action among the general population. There was as yet no "solidarity," but the episode left some people in jail and provoked substantial emigration.

Economic hardship and frustration brought demonstrations and riots along the Baltic coast in 1970, leading to brutal suppression by the authorities. The repressive reaction of the regime only worsened the situation and resulted in spontaneously formed organizations like the Komitet Obrony Robotników (Workers' Defense Committee, KOR), which arose to protect the workers from further government reprisals. These organizations were in many ways the ancestors of the later Solidarność (Solidarity) movement.

The election of Karol Wojtyła as Pope in 1978 had an electrifying effect on the country, not only for its religious significance for overwhelmingly Roman Catholic Poland. This was the first national triumph since the defeat of the Russians before Warsaw in 1920. John Paul II proved a stimulant to opposition to the regime and an immense boost to the country's self-confidence. The linkage between the Papal election, his first trip to Poland in 1979, and the 1980 Solidarity movement is easy to argue. The enthusiasm of 1978 emboldened the country to organize spontaneous opposition to the governments' efforts to quash worker unrest in the port cities. Lech Wałęsa emerged as a flawed but charismatic national figure who led a movement which began as a group of united workers and developed into a trade union, then a social movement of some ten million people with even more supporters. The famous Gdańsk shipyard strikes and the eventual unification of the workers' movement with intellectuals and other elements of society, which had not occurred in 1968 or 1970, led to the development of Solidarity as a virtual counter-government.

The regime's clumsy efforts to control Solidarity failed by 1981, and in its desperation the authorities declared martial law on December 13, 1981, and ordered mass arrests and internment of Solidarity leaders. The regime, now headed by General Wojciech Jaruzelski,

attempted to rally patriotic support around the idea that only a communist regime could forestall domestic chaos and Soviet intervention. The Jaruzelski effort failed, and Poland went into an economic tailspin as the regime was unable to consolidate its position. The opposition went underground, attracted significant international support, and became a *cause celèbre* among Polish Americans. The murder of the charismatic priest Jerzy Popieluszko by the Security service in 1984 further discredited the regime. Martial law was eventually lifted in 1983, but thousands of Poles moved abroad, a large number of them permanently, because of the period of repression.

Mikhail Gorbachev's policies of *glasnost* and *perestroika* meant that the Soviet Union began to crumble in the mid–1980s. In Poland, by 1989 Jaruzelski became convinced that some *modus vivendi* had to be found with the opposition and commenced the "Round-Table" negotiation with the Church acting as intermediary between representatives of Solidarity and the government. These negotiations have remained controversial because many have criticized the Solidarity leaders for allowing too large a role for adherents of the regime in the post-communist order. The result, critics argue, was that former communists survived what should have been a thorough house-cleaning, leaving Poland with a heavy burden of corrupt communists in key positions in society.

With the Communist Bloc dissolving and the Cold War ending, the regime essentially negotiated its own demise by allowing elections in 1989 which resulted in a smashing victory for the opposition in the first free elections in Poland since World War II. Now exposed without national support, communism collapsed. After a brief and grotesque interlude when Jaruzelski remained as president while Solidarity formed a government, Wałęsa became the first president of the new Poland in 1990 with long-time dissident Tadeusz Mazowiecki as prime minister. Former opposition leaders played prominent roles in the new government.

The transition from Communism proved rocky. There was no model for the undertaking and Poland had to save a faltering economy while rebuilding a democratic polity. A rapid adjustment to a market system (so-called "shock therapy" associated with economist Leszek Balcerowicz) plunged the economy into a crisis before the rapid recovery of the 1990s. One result was yet another wave of immigration abroad in response to the economic situation. Whereas the rudiments of democracy spread rapidly throughout society, the new government was in a state of perpetual turmoil due to internecine squabbling, which was not helped by the mercurial Wałęsa. This unhappy situation led to the emergence of a post-communist left party the Sojusz Lewicy Demokratycznej (Social Democratic Union, SLD) led by former Communist Party stalwarts. The bizarre spectacle of Poland choosing to return to power the very people it had replaced just a few years before is explained by the choice offered between Wałęsa, seeking a second term, and the SLD leader, the youthful Aleksander Kwaśniewski. It was essentially a referendum on whether Poland wished to engage in a long-period of retrospective "score settling" or try to ignore the past and concentrate on a post-communist future — ironically championed by former communists. After two terms (1995–2005), Kwaśniewski was ejected only after his regime had demonstrated obvious corruption and incompetence. This uninspiring era was relieved by Poland's admission into NATO in 1999 and the subsequent entrance of Poland to the European Union in 2004.

In 2005 the SLD was replaced by a coalition of populist parties which emphasized nationalism, a paternalistic state, and rooting out vestiges and adherents of the former communist regime (*lustracja*). The new regime was ill-served by political antics including such unsavory populist figures as Andrzej Lepper representing a rural Poland, which had benefited little from market reforms and found the new capitalist system very difficult to accept.

Polish politics in the first years of the twenty-first century witnessed a tripartite division. On the Left was some version of the SLD which had evolved into a liberal-left coalition. The populist right was represented chiefly by the Prawo i Sprawiedliwość (Law and Justice, PiS) party led by the twins Jarosław and Lech Kaczyński, with adherents from a few smaller political formations. This faction preached a paternalistic populism, with European integration, rooting out corruption and protection of traditional Polish values including Roman Catholicism. It became closely associated with a concerted effort to expose those tainted by collaboration with the former communist authorities, a campaign variously labeled a cleansing of the national conscience. Even Wałęsa, a national hero, was accused of youthful collaboration with the Communists, a charge not yet elucidated but characteristic of the passion loosed by the issue.

The third faction, the Platforma Obywatelska (Civic Platform, PO) led by Donald Tusk, was a proponent of market capitalism and European integration. Regarded as modernizing and indifferent to traditional Polish values by the PiS, the existence of two anti-leftist factions made Polish politics confusing to Western observes who mistakenly regarded the PiS and the PO as sharing common values. Indeed, the PiS's welfare state notions, coupled with nationalism and overt religiosity, in contrast to the self-conscious cosmopolitanism of the PO, makes Polish politics challenging to analyze. Most of the Poles in the U.S. who voted in Polish elections cast their ballots overwhelmingly for the PiS, while **Polonia** in Western Europe voted largely for Tusk and the PO.

The balance sheet on post-communist Poland is complicated but must be regarded as essentially positive. Poland has had a rapidly expanding economy despite temporary slumps, democracy is firmly rooted, and politics are democratic if fractious. No truly radical party enjoys a sizeable following and the basic values of the new Poland enjoy consensus. The attribution of anti–Semitism, long damaging to Poland, no longer adheres as Poland has exhibited a determination to come to terms with even the more unsavory aspects of its past, as evidenced by its resolve in addressing issues such as the controversy over the World War II Jedwabne massacre. The minuscule Jewish community is showing signs of revitalization. Poland is a stable and increasingly prosperous member of the European community.

There are serious problems, especially regarding security issues, the perennial Polish nightmare. An increasingly aggressive disposition by Russia threatens the east of Europe: Moscow's subtle, and not so subtle, efforts to destabilize Ukraine and the invasion of Georgia (2008) are merely two examples. The reaction of the European Union to Russian aggression has been most disappointing and is not likely to improve. Germany, the chief EU power, is heavily dependent of Russian energy imports and hence unlikely to adopt a resolute position regarding Moscow. The EU in turn will not contradict Berlin's disposition despite occasional voices to the contrary. This leaves Poland in a vulnerable position in the east in which Warsaw can count only on a series of weak states that were formerly parts of the Soviet Bloc.

Poland's membership in NATO and the EU are intriguing aspects of its security. The German-Polish honeymoon, so prominent after the fall of Communism, has faded and

Map of Poland. The outline shows its borders in the 18th century, while the dashed lines depict the areas absorbed by Austria, Prussia, and Russia after the partitions (*OLS*).

the two countries have bickered over a number of issues, including public differences over World War II. Here, the plan to build an Expellees' Center in Berlin is particularly galling to Poland because it seems to equate German suffering with the Poles' fate at German hands in the war years.

Moreover, American support for Warsaw in the face of a Russian threat is problematical. Washington has always been quick to endorse Polish independence but reticent to support it. Distracted by Middle Eastern issues, the U.S. finds Europe a decreasing focus of its attention. Within Europe, Poland has never occupied a major position in American eyes. The likelihood that NATO ties would prompt Washington's action on Poland's behalf is not high.

The Third Republic has openly courted the United States and a pro–American alignment is a cornerstone of national policy as well as being endorsed by the population. Poland's support for American efforts in Afghanistan and Iraq — undertaken in the face of strong criticism from other European states — has gained it little from Washington. There is growing fear that Polish efforts to build a special relationship with the Americans — and thereby increase its leverage in Europe — are in vain.

The questions about the Third Republic are fascinating but only present distractions. The larger sweep of Polish history raises profound issues that must be confronted to understand the country's evolution. Merely restricting ourselves to the modern era, we may ask whether the newly independent Poland which emerged in 1918 was really a restored state or something quite new using old references. Much smaller, with discontented minorities and a form of government radically different from the pre–1795 state, did it really link a Poland separated by 123 years of division and separate paths of historical development? In other words, was the Second Republic a renewal or an invention? We may also ask ourselves the larger question of what relationship the pre–1795 Poland has with its modern counterparts. The second obvious question is whether the Third Republic is the legitimate heir of the Second, or was the half-century of Communism a real interruption in Polish history? What is the legacy of the Communist era? Is the Second Republic a model for the Third, or just as much an antique as the pre-partition state?

This raises the fundamental question of who, or perhaps better stated, what has won the contest for Poland first launched at the end of the nineteenth century, a question which implicates the whole of Polish history.

Was Piłsudski right, or was Dmowski? In other words is the Piast model for Poland, a Central European state with an ethnically defined nation living within relatively limited borders favored by Dmowski, the real Poland? Or, is Poland a state of the east with a multinational heritage, large and heterogeneous? Certainly Poland's constricted borders in the post–1918 world, with a virtual absence of national minorities since 1945, would suggest that Dmowski has prevailed. Ironically, recent evidence demonstrates that it is Piłsudski, and not Dmowski, who retains a hold on Polish national sentiment. Insofar as history is a guide for the emotions of the Poles, it is a history associated with Piłsudski. This is a paradox at the center of modern Polish political culture.

Has the peasant question finally disappeared in the twenty-first century? Is rural Poland still, in some ways, a place foreign to the urban population? The failure to establish a vigorous, revived Peasant Party since 1989 suggests that the peasants are now fully citizens and no longer guided by class issues. Voting trends in post–1990 elections certainly exhibit a much stronger appeal of populism, in whatever form, in rural areas. Economic progress lags behind in the countryside.

Is Polonia no longer of any consequence for Poland? Certainly the contribution of the exile and immigrant community to the history of Poland is problematical and has usually been exaggerated by Poles living beyond the national borders, especially in North America. Polonia's support for Poland's admission to NATO is a lonely exception. Recent trends have indicated that the new international Polonia is located in places like the British Isles and not Chicago. American Polonia is too completely absorbed into American society to be anything more than a curiosity with many frozen class and cultural characteristics. This is perhaps best symbolized by the career of **Czesław Miłosz** (1911–2004) who was long resident in the United States but never a member of Polonia. His status as a Polish poet made the Polish American community in the United States seem uncongenial to him. When the Polish governments of the twenty-first century consider what role Polonia has for Poland they will be concerned about Poles living in Wrocław but working in London, or a large Polonia in Dublin, and not the activities of the **Polish National Alliance** or the weak lobbying efforts of the **Polish American Congress**. American Polonia has only a sentimental significance.

Is Poland, like much of Europe, on the way to irreparable demographic crisis? The years of a youthful Poland, with a large population

increase yearly, are over. Poland produces few children. In fact, Poland now has one of the poorest rates of national increase in a continent which is known for low numbers. Can Poland survive with a declining population? In other words, is an aging Poland, with obvious economic consequences, the sorry spectacle which awaits the current generation?

Finally, is Poland ceasing to be Poland? Is the movement toward European integration dissolving the traditions and peculiarities which have for generations made Poland a unique member of the continent's population? Certainly a pressing problem for many Poles is whether Catholicism, the national faith for so long, can withstand the forces of secularization which have eroded it in much of Europe. Will Poland become a Slavic Holland? Similarly, the powerful urgings of Polish patriotism have for many generations been associated with the notion of the "Fatherland being in jeopardy." Can a secure Poland prompt a similar devotion? Is history, which for more than a century sustained the Poles by arguing that the national tradition can survive even the most profound challenge, still a meaningful repository for the nation? Is a Polish population indifferent to the passions of Polish history still Polish? If Poland is secure, is profound national loyalty unnecessary and hence dispensable? How much longer will the *Warszawianka* be played? In this context, Poland is in 2010 the recipient of immigration from the east, while return-migrants from the west bring with them cosmopolitan elements.

Despite the grave concerns, we must remember that Poland at the start of the twenty-first century is more secure than at any time since Sobieski. Poland is free, a member of powerful alliances possessed of a stable political structure, with no clamorous minorities and a rapidly developing economy. Such a Poland exceeds the hopes of many Polish generations. This is a good Poland indeed.— *M. B. B. Biskupski*

SOURCES: M. B. Biskupski, *The History of Poland* (Westport, CT: Greenwood Press, 2000); M. B. Biskupski, James S. Pula, and Piotr Wróbel, eds., *The Origin of Modern Polish Democracy* (Athens, OH: Ohio University Press, 2010); Norman Davies, *God's Playground* (New York: Columbia University Press, 1982, 2 vols.); Adam Zamoyski, *The Polish Way: A Thousand-Year History of the Poles and Their Culture* (New York: Hippocrene Books, 1987); M. K. Dziewanowski, *Poland in the 20th Century* (New York: Columbia University Press, 1977); Paul Knoll, *The Rise of the Polish Monarchy: Piast Poland in East Central Europe, 1320–1370* (Chicago: University of Chicago Press, 1972); Samuel Fiszman, *The Polish Renaissance in Its European Context* (Bloomington, IN: Indiana University Press, 1988); Harold B. Segel, *Renaissance Culture in Poland: The Rise of Humanism, 1470–1543* (Ithaca, NY: Cornell University Press, 1989); Janusz Tazbir, *A State Without Stakes: Polish Religious Toleration in the*

Sixteenth and Seventeenth Centuries (New York: The Kosciuszko Foundation, 1973); Piotr S. Wandycz, *The Lands of Partitioned Poland, 1795–1918* (Seattle, WA: University of Washington Press, 1975); Stanislaus A. Blejwas, *Realism in Polish Politics: Warsaw Positivism and National Survival in Nineteenth Century Poland* (New Haven: Yale Concilium on International and Area Studies, 1984); Wiktor Sukiennicki, *East Central Europe During World War I: From Foreign Domination to National Independence* (Boulder, CO: East European Monographs, 1984, 2 vols.); Antony Polonsky, *Politics of Independent Poland, 1921–1939: The Crisis of Constitutional Government* (Oxford: Clarendon Press, 1972); Piotr S. Wandycz, *Polish Diplomacy, 1914–1945: Aims and Achievements* (London: Orbis Books, 1988); Józef Garliński, *Poland in the Second World War* (New York: Hippocrene Books, 1985); Richard C. Lukas, *The Forgotten Holocaust: The Poles Under German Occupation* (Lexington, KY: University of Kentucky Press, 1986); Stefan Korboński, *Fighting Warsaw: The Story of the Polish Underground State* (New York: Funk & Wagnalls, 1956); Norman Davies, *Rising '44: The Battle for Warsaw* (New York: Viking, 2003).

Poland, Polish American Aid to.

Poland, partitioned by its neighbors at the end of the eighteenth century, regained independence on November 11, 1918. Polish Americans' aid to their homeland began even before that date. Not only did individual Polish immigrants help their relatives in their home towns and villages, but also institutional aid was organized in support of different organizations and groups struggling for free and independent Poland. Of the two main central Polish American organizations founded during World War I, the **National Defense Committee** (Komitet Obrony Narodowej) acted in favor of Józef Piłsudski and his activities, while **National Department** (Wydział Narodowy), on **Ignacy Jan Paderewski**'s suggestions, supported Polish national democracy and the Paris-based **Polish National Committee** (Komitet Narodowy Polski). During World War I, Paderewski and his wife organized the Polish Victims Relief Fund and the **Polish White Cross** as purely charitable, non-political organizations. Polonia also urged the American Red Cross to aid the Poles in Europe.

In August, 1918, Paderewski proclaimed a $10 million fund drive in support of Poland, but only half of the sum was eventually collected. Most of that money was used to buy food for Poland and to support Polish charitable institutions. In 1920 Poland, fighting against the Bolsheviks for its independence, was in desperate need of money. Polish American clergy supported the Catholic Church in Poland and Polish American fraternals and other organizations sent funds for different Polish projects. They included the struggle to protect the Polish borders (Śląsk and Gdańsk won the most widespread support while few supported movements to secure the Eastern border regions), but also financing Polish political parties. The latter objective was criti-

cized by many Polish Americans and became one of the factors discouraging them from further aid to Poland. Gradually, **Polonia** tired of constant appeals for funds, many of which were spent ineffectively or simply embezzled. Polish Americans became generally disillusioned with their home country, its poor economy and management and with its attitude toward Polonia. The slogan "We have done our part now let them do theirs" began to gain popularity.

After 1923 Polish Americans concentrated on their own problems. The Great Depression reduced even individual aid sent to families in Poland, although according to Tadeusz Radzik about $8 million was sent to Poland each year during the 1930s compared to $35 million before World War I. However, when Hitler's demands for the "Polish corridor" were revealed, with the threat of a new war becoming more and more apparent, and when the National Defense Fund (Fundusz Obrony Narodowej, FON) was promoted in Poland, new fundraising efforts were organized in the U.S. in support of Poland. Before the outbreak of World War II, a million dollars were collected for FON.

The German invasion of Poland on September 1, 1939, sparked a new wave of generosity for the Polish cause. Polish Americans concentrated on the relief activities, coordinated by the Rada Polonii Amerykańskiej (**Polish American Council**) that registered as a foreign aid agency with the Department of State in September 1939, and in 1942 joined the National War Fund under the name of the Polish War Relief. As neither the German nor the Soviet occupiers of Poland were willing to allow foreign relief agencies to operate in Polish territories, most of the beneficiaries of this aid were Polish prisoners of war in German camps and Polish refugees worldwide. By 1945 the Rada collected in excess of $6.5 million.

After the end of World War II, the Rada Polonii Amerykańskiej, its name changed to the American Relief for Poland, helped the United Nations Relief and Rehabilitation Administration resettle Polish displaced persons in Europe to Poland and other countries including the United States. American Relief for Poland also maintained contacts with the authorities in Warsaw to distribute aid in Poland. Its offices were closed by the Warsaw regime in 1951, but it resumed activities in 1956. In 1955–57 new agreements were signed between Poland and the Soviet Union regarding the repatriation of Poles from the USSR. The fund and clothes drive in support of the repatriates was the last large charitable campaign in American Polonia prior to the 1980s. The flow of individual packages and money

transfers did not stop, however. Polish American organizations lobbied for lower custom dues and postal charges both in Poland and in the U.S. Polish American aid sent through to the Catholic Church in Poland also continued. Following World War II it was coordinated by the **Catholic League for Religious Assistance to Poland** and used American and Polish Church channels to collect, transfer and distribute goods.

Church channels and institutions of the Polish political emigration in Europe were involved in transferring Polish American funds in support of anti-communist opposition in the 1970s. At first, these were individual actions organized after the massacre of Polish workers in December 1970, using as a conduit primarily London-based émigré institutions. After the formation of the Komitet Obrony Robotników (Workers' Defense Committee) in 1976, the **Polish American Congress** established the **Polish Workers' Relief Committee** in Chicago. It coordinated assistance to the democratic opposition in Poland until 1990. Special events in support of the opposition in Poland also were held in other cities with large Polish American populations. Some Polish American donations supported campaigns organized by the Warsaw government; for example, "1000 New Schools for the Polish Millennium" in the 1960s, reconstruction of the Royal Castle in Warsaw in the 1970s and of "Panorama Racławicka" in the 1980s. Polonia also participated in smaller fundraising drives for the Polish Olympic Committee and for the childrens hospital in Warsaw.

Another large Polish American charitable campaign began in 1981 in response to the catastrophic economic situation of Poland and appeals from both the Polish Episcopate and the Solidarity trade union. Solidarity concentrated on healthcare, while the Episcopate focused its efforts on relieving food shortages. Those two campaigns occurred simultaneously under the name "Relief for Poland" coordinated by the Polish American Congress Charitable Foundation. The campaigns involved assistance from the largest American pharmaceutical companies, clinics and philanthropic organizations including Project HOPE, CARE and Catholic Relief Services. The Polish American Congress Charitable Foundation solicited surplus food and medicines, shoes and clothes, medical equipment and transportation facilities, money and other donations. Polish American Congress activities in 1981–83 were dominated by these charitable actions. Both the Washington and Chicago offices of the organization served as the logistic centers, while nearly all other Charitable Foundation programs were suspended. Between 1981 and 1990 the PAC Charitable Foundation received almost $5.6 million in donations and transferred goods valued at almost $169 million in over 800 shipments to Poland.

In 1989, Polish Americans supported the Solidarity parliamentary campaign. One of the largest actions in the 1990s was organized to provide relief for the flood victims of 1997. By the end of the 1990s, economic conditions in Poland improved considerably, with Polish American assistance once again centering on individual aid through family connections.—*Joanna Wojdon*

SOURCE: Donald E. Pienkos, *For Your Freedom Through Ours: Polish American Efforts on Poland's Behalf, 1863–1991* (Boulder, CO: East European Monographs, 1991).

Polański, Roman (Rajmund Roman Liebling; b. Paris, France, August 18, 1933; d.—). Film director, producer. In 1937 his family moved from France back to Poland, settling in Kraków. When Poland was occupied by Nazi Germany, Polański, being of Jewish origin, was forced into the Kraków ghetto but escaped and went into hiding. Polański's mother perished in the Auschwitz-Birkenau concentration camp while his father survived the Mauthausen-Gusen concentration camp in Austria. During the era of Soviet-imposed communism, Polański became a student of film directing at the Polish film school in Łódź where he made some short films including the acclaimed *Dwaj ludzie z szafą* (*Two Men and a Wardrobe*; 1958) and *Gdy spadają anioły* (*When Angels Fall*; 1959). His feature debut was *Nóż w wodzie* (*Knife in the Water*; 1962). Made from a script written jointly by Jerzy Skolimowski and Polański, *Knife in the Water* is an exploration of power struggles lying at the center of all human interaction. With only three characters isolated in a boat in laboratory-like conditions, the most minimal dialogue, oppressive close-ups, and free jazz scores, Polański exhibits deep pessimism about human relationships, a subject-matter of all of Polański's films. *Knife in the Water* earned Polański his first Academy Award nomination (Best Foreign Language Film, 1963). After this film, he chose to leave Poland.

In *Knife in the Water* images of confinement serve Polański's purpose of reflecting on human struggles for power. In the cycle of films he did outside Poland, most notably *Repulsion* (1965) and *Le Locataire* (*The Tenant*; 1976), confinement is used to convey madness or the distorted perceptions of reality of disturbed characters. In *Cul-de-Sac* (1966), too, Polański's favorite image of confinement reappears, this time in the form of a secluded cas-

tle. Since the characters' struggle for domination is here reduced to absurdity, critics have pointed out the film's affinity with Ionesco and Beckett. *Cul-de-Sac* earned Polański The Golden Bear award at the Berlin Festival. *The Fearless Vampire Killers* (1967) was Polański's first feature to be photographed in color and using a widescreen 2.35:1 aspect ratio. The presence of vampires in this film also relates to his pervasive theme of the master, the slave, and the struggle for power. A vampire, as Ewa Mazierska observes, is a victim and perpetrator in one entity: someone who becomes a bloodsucker after being attacked by another bloodsucker. The theme of the master's oppression of the slave resurfaces in some of Polański's later films such as *The Pirates* (1986) and *Death and the Maiden* (1994).

In 1968, Polański migrated to the United States, where he established his reputation with the success of a horror-thriller *Rosemary's Baby* (1968), based on the novel of the same name by Ira Levin. Polański's screenplay adaptation earned him a second Academy Award nomination. On August 9, 1969, Charles Manson's sect murdered Sharon Tate, his second wife, who was eight months pregnant with the couple's first child. Polański left the United States for Europe. In 1971, Polański made a film version of Shakespeare's *Macbeth*, his first feature following Sharon Tate's murder. In 1974 he returned to the United States and reinterpreted the film noir in *Chinatown* (1974). However, charged with illegal sexual intercourse with a minor, Polański fled to Europe.

Tess (1979), a film rendition of Thomas Hardy's novel *Tess of the D'Urbervilles*, was Polański's first film after leaving the United States. Although *Tess* is set in a framework of melodrama, as Ewa Nawoj points out, this film was made more profound by a reflection on the issue of guilt and punishment unknown to the melodramatic genre. Polański's *Tess* earned him his fourth Academy Award nomination, his second nomination for Best Director, and his second nomination for best picture and best original score. In addition, *Tess* earned him three Oscars (best cinematography, best art direction and best costume design).

Polański's *The Pianist* (2002) seems to be the culmination of his career. Made when he was in his seventies, *The Pianist* represents Polański's first attempt to address the traumatic experiences of the war he lived through as a child.—*Silvia G. Dapía*

SOURCES: Barbara Leaming, *Polanski, the Filmmaker as Voyeur: a Biography* (New York: Simon and Schuster, 1981); Ewa Mazierska, *Roman Polanski: the Cinema of a Cultural Traveler* (London: I. B. Tauris, 2007); John Orr and Elżbieta Ostrowska, eds., *The*

Cinema of Roman Polanski: Dark Spaces of the World (London: Wallflower Press, 2006).

Polish American Association (PAA). The original antecedent of the PAA, the Polish Welfare Association (PWA), was incorporated in Chicago on August 16, 1922, under the auspices of the Chicago Society of the **Polish National Alliance**, to combat the increase in juvenile delinquency among Poles in Chicago. Its first organizational move was to recruit a group of Polish American and Polish businessmen, professionals, and clergy to support their mission of educating Polish parents and their children. Their goals were to lessen the cultural and educational gap between the Polish people and the greater Chicago community, and to assist Polish immigrants in understanding and accepting their community responsibilities. The PWA's charter stated its objective thusly: "To secure the greatest amount of cooperation from the citizens of Polish extraction, to promote the moral and physical welfare of the Polish people, to cooperate with the legal agencies and various welfare organizations in the handling of juvenile and adult delinquency, and to carry on a campaign of education and information into the home to reduce delinquency."

In its first three years (1922–25) the Polish Welfare Association attracted only one volunteer, **Maria Sakowska**. In October 1925, Mary Midura became the PWA's first professional employee with experience in casework services. From 1926 to 1931, it operated with a staff consisting of Midura, two full-time caseworkers, and one part-time caseworker. During the Great Depression, when funding decreased drastically, Midura had no professional staff and often no salary. In 1934, Monsignor Thomas P. Bona of the Archdiocese of Chicago, in order to increase funding for the PWA, instituted an array of social benefit events such as card parties, fashion shows, and banquets. Two years later, the PWA was renamed the Polish Welfare Association of the Archdiocese of Chicago (PWAAC) with an amalgam of male-only members' chapters, women auxiliaries, and volunteers who were associated with Roman Catholic parishes throughout Chicago. That same year, it appointed its first executive director, John T. Nering, a position Nering held until his death in 1962 at the age of 99.

With the onset of World War II, and with most young men leaving to join the armed forces, the PWAAC disbanded its Youth Problems Committee and began to concentrate on mental health issues and the concerns of homeless men and women. In the postwar years, the PWAAC focused on veterans' issues and the resettlement of Polish displaced persons. On July 7, 1954, the PWAAC reverted to its original name of Polish Welfare Association, while continuing to focus on the problems of Polish displaced persons. During the decades of the 1960s and 1970s, the PWA continued to provide clients with Polish language assistance and intervention services. As the 1980s approached, under its executive director Theresa Chamberlain the organization established a clothing and food pantry, appointed a public relations person to promote the PWA's significance within the community, and through the Refugee Program of 1980, which was funded through federal and state support, assisted Poles displaced as a result of the Solidarity Movement. With increased immigration from Poland, the PWA hired additional immigration counselors to serve the several thousand Polish political refugees who arrived through the National Amnesty Program. On July 1, 1986, Chicago's Mayor Harold Washington formally opened the PWA's long-awaited day shelter for homeless men. In February 1988, with over 50,000 Polish elderly comprising Chicago's largest ethnic group with limited English-speaking skills, the PWA established a Senior Center on Chicago's Southwest Side.

Under its new executive director, Karen Popowski, the PWA established its Learning Center in 1989. In that year, the Center served 8,300 adults in 500 classes with over 300,000 hours of instruction in English and U.S. civics. Over the next five years, with more than 50,000 immigrants from Poland comprising Chicago's largest group of legal immigrants, the PWA's office was constantly filled with those seeking help. In 1996, under Popowski's leadership, the PWA's name was officially changed to the Polish American Association (PAA) to reflect the strength of the organization and the PAA established a website. As a human services agency, the PAA serves the diverse needs of the Polish immigrant community with over 30 programs and services. It provides to its clients the resources needed for changing their lives and enhancing their ability to become contributing members of the community. Educational services include teen counseling, computer classes, English-as-a-Second Language classes, U.S. citizenship exam preparation courses, career counseling, and a vocational training program for certifying nursing assistants and physical rehabilitation aides.

The PAA has provided employment services since 1981, adult education since 1989, and vocational training, which was approved by the State of Illinois in 1992. In the area of social services, the PAA offers programs for families, senior citizens, battered women, youth development, the homeless, and those suffering from substance abuse. Additional programs include a day center for homeless men, intensive outpatient alcohol treatment, a food pantry and kitchen, parenting education, and youth outreach. In 2006, the PAA's educational, sociological, informational, and emigrational services and programs rendered assistance to more than 13,400 clients, with over 1,000 clients requesting assistance in each of the following services: senior citizens, English-as-a-Second Language instruction, KidCare (an Illinois State health insurance program), and immigration and outreach programs. In 2008 the staff consisted of approximately 90 full-time and 75 part-time bilingual staff members. The majority of the PAA's funding, approximately 75 percent, is from state, city, and federal agencies. Approximately 20 percent of its funding is provided by foundations, corporations, special fundraising events, individual contributions, program fees from clients, and the United Way of Greater Chicago.

The Polish American Association is governed by a 27-member volunteer board of directors composed of professionals and community representatives, whose aim is to establish a programmatic direction that best responds to the needs of its clients. With a grant received from the Illinois Department of Commerce and Community Affairs in 2000, the PAA was able to establish a much-needed facility on Chicago's Southwest Side. In 2010, the PAA had three locations: its Main Office and Learning Center on Chicago's Northwest Side and its Southwest Side offices. The PAA is accessible through its website: www.polish.org.—*Geraldine Coleman*

SOURCES: Merril F. Krughoff, *The Polish Welfare Association of Chicago* (Chicago: n.p., 1934); Walter Duda, "A Study of the Polish Welfare Association of Chicago" (Unpublished M.Doc.Ad. Thesis, Loyola University–Chicago, 1951).

Polish American Bowling Association. Incorporated in Milwaukee in January 1928, the purpose of the Polish American Bowling Association was to establish a national umbrella organization for Polish American bowlers. Its founders were John A. Schultz, John J. Kotlarek, Roman D. Pankowski, and John J. Ludka. The organization sponsored an annual tournament sanctioned by the American Bowling Congress beginning in 1928. A women's division was added in 1942. Although striving for a national participation, most of those who attended the tournaments were from Milwaukee and Chicago, with the tournament alternating annually between these two cities. Interest began to decline during the 1950s with the last tournament held in 1962. The records of the PABA are housed in the archives of the University of Wisconsin–Milwaukee.—*James S. Pula*

Polish American Congress (*Kongres Polonii Amerykańskiej*). The Polish American Congress (PAC) is a broadly based national civic and political action federation that since 1944 has sought to represent the interests and concerns of Americans of Polish origin. Membership in the PAC is open to organizations and individuals. The former include fraternal benefit societies like the **Polish National Alliance**, the **Polish Roman Catholic Union**, the **Polish Women's Alliance**, and the **Polish Falcons of America**; veterans organizations such as the **Polish Army Veterans Association** and the **Polish Combatants Association**. The members of these organizations are indirectly members of the PAC. Individuals may also join on a direct basis.

The PAC is organized territorially into thirty divisions and chapters; these units are located in eighteen states and the District of Columbia. The governing body of the PAC is its Council of National Directors, which meets twice annually and includes approximately 140 members. They are elected by state divisions or by the national organizations affiliated with the Congress. Ten "at-large" directors are also elected. The day to day operations of the PAC are directed by an executive committee composed of the president, six vice presidents, a secretary general, and a treasurer. These officers are elected by the Council of National Directors and serve two year terms. The national headquarters of the PAC has traditionally been in Chicago; however, the organization has always maintained an office in Washington, D.C., to coordinate lobbying activities. Several key committees deal with Polish Affairs, the "American Agenda," anti-bigotry matters, and the annual observance, in October, of **Polish American Heritage Month**.

Between 1944 and 1976, the PAC followed the practice of holding national conventions, generally at four year intervals and a few months before the American presidential elections. Ten conventions were held during this period. The first two drew large numbers of delegates. More than 2,600 **Polonia** activists took part in the founding gathering in Buffalo, New York, in 1944. In 1948, more than 1,200 delegates attended the second PAC convention in Atlantic City, New Jersey, a time when emotions were high over Poland's fall under Soviet control. Thereafter, attendance gradually diminished. In 1976 fewer than 600 delegates were present, despite the appearance of both major presidential candidates seeking the Polish vote in the coming election. Thereafter the PAC by-laws were amended and the national convention discontinued.

From its founding in 1944, the president of the PAC has also been president of the Polish National Alliance. **Charles Rozmarek** (PNA president 1939–67) led the PAC from 1944 until 1968. He was succeeded in 1968 by **Aloysius Mazewski** (PNA president 1967–88), in 1988 by **Edward Moskal** (PNA president 1988–2005), and in 2005 by **Frank J. Spula** (PNA president from 2005). The close connection between the PAC and the PNA, though understandable, has been controversial as some in the Polish American community have believed that the Congress is too closely associated with the Alliance. Benefits of the relationship include the financial support and publicity it regularly receives from the PNA's newspaper *Zgoda* (Harmony) and the PNA's Chicago-based Polish language paper *Dziennik Związkowy* (The Alliance Daily). Further, the civic action objectives of the PAC and the PNA are practically identical in emphasizing the importance of uniting the Polish American community behind the causes of Poland's independence and the advancement of Polonia.

FORMATION OF THE PAC

With the outbreak of World War II in 1939 and Poland's conquest by Nazi Germany and Soviet Russia, Polonia's charitable and relief agency, the **Polish American Council** (Rada Polonii Amerykańskiej; RPA), headed by PNA leader **Francis Swietlik**, gathered money and materials on behalf of Polish war victims. But because the RPA received financial subsidies from a U.S. government agency, it was prohibited from engaging in political lobbying on behalf of Poland. This remained the case even after America entered the conflict in December 1941 and became an ally of Great Britain (itself allied to Poland's exile government in London) and the Soviet Union (which had been invaded by its former Nazi ally in June 1941 after having participated in Poland's destruction twenty months earlier). No such restriction limited the activities of pro–Soviet Polish Americans who took part in organizing the **American Slav Congress** and the **American Polish Labor Council**. These organizations claimed to represent millions of Polish and Slavic Americans in their support of the Soviet-American military alliance, although they were silent about Poland's post war fate. The absence of a Polish American political lobby caused the creation of an anti–Soviet and émigré-led New York based group formed in 1942, the **National**

Committee of Americans of Polish Descent (Komitet Narodowy Amerykanów Polskiego Pochodzenia; KNAPP). Suspicious of both Soviet intentions toward Poland and of the benefits of the policies followed by the Polish exile government toward Moscow, KNAPP nevertheless remained ineffective in **Polonia** until 1943. That April, the corpses of several thousand Polish army officers missing since 1940 were discovered in Soviet territory. News of the "Katyn Massacre" followed in July 1943 by the shocking and mysterious death of the exile Polish leader General Władysław Sikorski, awakened Polonia to the threat to Poland posed by Soviet Russia. By 1944, Poland's postwar fate was a matter of growing concern to Polonia. In that year, leaders of KNAPP met in Chicago with the heads of the Polish American fraternals and representatives of religious groups. Their meetings resulted in the calling of a national congress of Polish Americans to unite the representatives of Polonia's main secular and religious organizations and to provide a forum for them to express support for Poland's postwar restoration as a free and independent state. The 1944 Buffalo meeting was described as an event that would "go down in history."

President Roosevelt took an interest in the PAC proceedings due to his concern that it might influence Congress in weakening Polonia's support for America's alliance with Soviet Russia and somehow even jeopardize his re-election plans. Despite these fears, the PAC adopted an agenda that emphasized Polonia's dedication to America's military victory and a just peace for Poland based on the principles of the Atlantic Charter. However, Roosevelt's view on postwar Poland differed markedly from what the PAC understood it to be. In November 1943, at the first great power summit meeting in Teheran, Roosevelt had secretly agreed with Stalin on significant postwar concessions of Polish territory to the USSR. In November 1944, Roosevelt was elected to an unprecedented fourth presidential term with the overwhelming support of Polish American voters, who were kept ignorant of his actual policy toward Poland. At the Yalta Summit in Soviet Russia in January 1945, Roosevelt accepted a process by which a Soviet-controlled provisional government was established to run the post-war Polish state. His action led to an immediate denunciation by the PAC as a repudiation of the principles embodied in the Atlantic Charter. Poland's submergence as a Soviet-controlled satellite after 1945 meant that the Polish American Congress needed to remain in operation to defend Poland's right to freedom.

THE PAC'S HISTORICAL RECORD

The history of the Polish American Congress falls into four periods. The first spans the years 1944–1960, when Poland came to be dominated by an imposed communist regime governed from the Soviet Union. The second and longest period extends from 1960 into 1980, when communist rule in Poland came to be an accepted fact in international relations. A third period of PAC operation began in 1980 with the appearance of the Solidarity Independent Free Trade Union movement led by Lech Wałęsa, and extended to 1999 when Poland, with the support of the PAC, became a member of NATO. With Poland free and independent, a member of NATO, and since 2003 a member of the European Union, the PAC entered a fourth period in its existence, where the question has been one of defining its mission anew.

1944–1960

This first period in the life of the PAC was one of extraordinary activism. Rozmarek and his colleagues traveled about the country and abroad to express their concerns over the fate of a postwar Poland under Soviet domination. They criticized the U.S. government for its failure to oppose Stalin's takeover of Eastern Europe. They attended the founding meeting of the United Nations in San Francisco to present their views on Poland. They even traveled to Western Europe to argue Poland's case and visited refugee camps in Germany to demand better treatment for Poles in the camps. The PAC raised new funds to enable it to continue its operations. It lobbied successfully for U.S. legislation (approved in 1948) to permit more than 140,000 Polish war refugees and military personnel to enter the country. It supported the creation of Radio Free Europe (in 1949), successfully called for a U.S. Congressional investigation of the **Katyń Massacre**, and in 1952 endorsed the Republican party's action to include language in its political platform to support the liberation of Eastern Europe from Soviet domination.

In 1956, following the death of Josef Stalin in 1953, a more moderate communist regime in Poland led by Władysław Gomulka caused the PAC to modify its position away from "liberation" to accept a U.S. policy promoting the gradual independence of Poland from Moscow's control. Nevertheless, the militant opposition of the PAC to communism continued to make it an influential factor in U.S. politics. In 1960, both candidates for the presidency, Vice President Richard Nixon and U.S. Senator John Kennedy (along with outgoing President Dwight Eisenhower) addressed the PAC leadership in their efforts to win over the Polish American electorate. Polonia's support for Kennedy proved to be a major factor in his narrow victory.

1960–1980

After 1960 the PAC had to face the reality of the gradual normalization of U.S. relations with Moscow, a development that affected American policy towards Poland. Moreover, U.S. involvement in the protracted Vietnam War pushed the issue of Soviet domination in Eastern Europe to the back burner. In the early 1970s, Nixon's détente policy with Moscow provided Polish communist party leader Edward Gierek's regime (in power from 1970 to 1980) with the opportunity to present itself as a normal and legitimate government seeking only businesslike relations with the U.S. and American Polonia. This the PAC, under its second president, Aloysius Mazewski, stubbornly opposed. Through these years the PAC continued to push its 1940s position in favor of U.S. recognition of Poland's western boundary with Germany, a view Washington rejected until President Ford's acquiescence to an international agreement on security and cooperation in Europe at Helsinki, Finland, in 1975. Ford's action placed the U.S. on record in opposing any change in the boundaries of the signatory states without their consent. In this way, the United States at last ratified, albeit indirectly, the postwar western Polish border.

In summer 1980, Poland's deepening economic crisis led to the birth of the Solidarity union. The PAC, working closely with the émigré-led **North American Center for Polish Affairs**, closely followed the dramatic events in Poland and worked to play a role in transmitting its views on the crisis to the U.S. government. President Mazewski's success in building a positive relationship with a series of American presidents, and his contacts with President Jimmy Carter's national security adviser, the Polish-born Soviet scholar **Zbigniew Brzeziński**, added to the Congress' visibility. Following the repression of Solidarity in December 1981, the PAC vocally supported President Reagan's actions in condemning the declaration of martial law by General Wojciech Jaruzelski. It acted, through its Polish American Congress Charitable Foundation, to ship food and medical supplies to Poland in cooperation with Roman Catholic Church leaders. By 1990, the PACCF had sent over goods valued at more than $160 million.

The PAC strongly backed Solidarity throughout the 1980s. Already in October 1989, the new PAC president, Edward Moskal, acted decisively to lead a delegation of Polonia leaders to Poland where they met with the heads of the new democratic Solidarity-led coalition and to express the community's support for the new government. The PAC lobbied for legislation to provide $800 million in assistance to Poland through the Support East European Democracy (SEED) Act. It supported the creation of a Polish American Enterprise Fund through a U.S. grant of $240 million to further help Poland in its early efforts to restructure its economy along free market lines. It also supported Poland on the foreign policy front. Thus in 1991, the PAC persuaded President George H.W. Bush to support full international recognition of the borders between Poland and the newly reunited Germany. And, beginning in 1993, it worked for Poland's admission into NATO. Significantly, at the Congress' fiftieth anniversary gathering in Buffalo in November 1994, both President Wałęsa and Prime Minister Waldemar Pawlak were present to offer Poland's thanks for the PAC's unceasing commitment to Poland.

In 1999, the PAC helped persuade President Bill Clinton in favor of a NATO expansion treaty, which was approved by the Senate by a vote of 80–19. Poland's entry into NATO stands out as one of the PAC's greatest achievements and largely completed its historic mission. Since 1999, the PAC has found itself wrestling to redefine its mission. President Moskal was unable to accomplish this objective and too often interposed himself into arguments occurring inside Poland. Notably he opposed Poland's entry into the European Union, a position overwhelmingly supported by the Polish voters in a 2003 referendum. The task of defining its mission anew is a complicated one and rests with Moskal's successor, Frank Spula, and his colleagues in the PAC Council.

Domestic Matters

The PAC has also sought to address the interests and concerns of Polonia. A priority of the late 1940s and early 1950s was supporting the admission and resettlement of World War II era Polish refugees into the United States. Beginning in the late 1960s, the aim was to develop a comprehensive "American agenda" to win the appointment of Polish Americans to government offices, fighting ethnic defamation, and building coalitions with other ethnic communities. One result of this third objective was a U.S. government decision to add a national ancestry survey component to its 1980 census, although it was discontinued after 2000. In the late 1970s, the PAC opposed the Federal government policy of "affirmative action," which it saw as a form of reverse discrimination hurtful to Polish Americans.

In 1984 the PAC began to promote an annual observance of Polish American Heritage Month to broaden public awareness of the contributions of Poles to culture, science, and civic life. In the mid 1980s, the PAC succeeded in winning permission for thousands of Polish refugees, in America after the repression of Solidarity, to remain permanently in this country. In 1991, it collected nearly $600,000 to help build the Ellis Island Immigration Museum; earlier in the mid 1980s it had raised more than $150,000 in a project to help restore the Statue of Liberty. These efforts notwithstanding, it must be noted that the organization's record with respect to its "American Agenda" has been much overshadowed by its exertions for Poland. There are at least three reasons for this. First, the Polish issue has riveted the attentions of the leaders and members of the organization, many of whom have been Polish-born. Poland's restoration was the reason for the creation of the PAC. Second, it has been difficult to adequately define and fund Polonia's domestic agenda. Among these concerns one might note the maintenance of Polish language, knowledge of the Polish heritage, promotion of ethnic self-identification, the never ending struggle against defamation, and efforts to preserve the historic churches and patriotic monuments of Polonia in the face of urban renewal — all in an environment in which the Polish American population has grown less cohesive and more dispersed. Third, while the "Polish issue" has for the most part served to unite Polish Americans across the country, the "American Agenda" has almost by definition had a centrifugal, localized, and even divisive character. It is always fashionable to talk of Polish Americans in monolithic terms, but they differ markedly from one another in educational attainment, social economic class background, the strength of their religious inclinations, their areas of residence, and their political orientations.

A special issue for the PAC is the development of better relations between Americans of Polish and of Jewish heritage. Such a dialog was initiated in the late 1960s between the PAC and the Anti-Defamation League of the B'nai B'rith, one that was revived in the late 1970s under the leadership of the Rev. Leonard Chrobot, a Polish American, and Harold Gales of the American Jewish Committee. Their work eventually won PAC and AJC sponsorship on the national level; and this dialog continued into 2007, but only under AJC sponsorship, as the **National Polish American/Jewish American Council**. But far more needs to be done to better educate Jewish and Polish Americans alike about their historic relationships in Poland and their perceptions of one another in America today. Unlike the diplomatic Mazewski, Moskal's antagonistic words and actions brought an end to PAC co-sponsorship of the national dialog. An effective dialog must lead to cooperation between the two communities in America where Jewish Americans and Polish Americans are in substantial accord.

THE FUTURE

With the achievement of Poland's independence, will the PAC continue to have a reason to exist? Can it begin to focus on developing a more America-centered agenda aimed at strengthening appreciation of Polish and Polish American heritage, generating greater recognition of the contributions of Polish Americans to American society, and engaging Polish Americans to work for its realization? If the PAC fails to do so it will eventually disappear.—*Donald E. Pienkos*

SOURCES: Zbigniew Kruszewski, "The Polish American Congress, East-West Issues, and the Formulation of American Foreign Policy," in Mohammed E. Ahrari, ed., *Ethnic Groups and U.S. Foreign Policy* (New York: Greenwood Press, 1987); Donald E. Pienkos, *For Your Freedom Through Ours: Polish American Efforts on Poland's Behalf, 1863–1991* (Boulder, CO: East European Monographs, 1991); Donald E. Pienkos, "Witness to History: The Polish American Congress and NATO Expansion," *The Polish Review,* Vol. 44, no. 3 (1999), 329–37; Leszek Kuczynski and Wojciech Bialasiewicz, *Expansion of NATO: Role of the Polish American Congress* (Chicago: Alliance Printers and Publishers, Inc., 1999); Stanislaus A. Blejwas, "The Republic of Poland and the Origins of the Polish American Congress," *Polish American Studies,* Vol. 55, no. 1 (1998), 23–33; Richard C. Lukas, "The Polish American Congress and the Polish Question, 1944–1947," *Polish American Studies,* Vol. 38, no. 2 (1981), 39–53.

Polish American Congress Anti-Defamation Commission. During the 1940s and 1950s the **Polish American Congress** (PAC) protested films and books that insulted Poles and **Polonia**, but the subsequent popularity of so-called "Polish jokes" led to a 1969 meeting called by PNA president **Aloysius Mazewski** to deal with the problem. Thaddeus Maliszewski, the first president of the **Polish American Congress** Civic Alertness Commission, believed that only a strong stance against the source of the defamation could stop the problem. Thus, he planned a series of legal actions against media outlets disseminating objectionable material. This stance was shared with Thaddeus Kowalski who succeeded Maliszewski in 1970. It was Kowalski who organized the Polish American Congress Anti-Defamation Commission and its network of local branches in every state division of the PAC. President Mazewski and both offices of the PAC (Chicago and Washington) also pursued anti-defamation activities. Protests led by the PAC Anti-Defamation

Commission, along with other Polish American organizations and general Polish American public support, brought some positive results with the publication in the Detroit *Free Press* of a series of positive articles about Polish heritage and adjustments to the screenplay for *The End,* a film featuring negative portrayals of Polish Americans. The Commission pursued other anti-defamation legal cases throughout this period, while letters of protest and telephone calls were its most important popular instruments. In 1971 the Commission published an *Anti-Defamation Guide* to inform Polish Americans how to send letters of protest to publishers, to radio and television stations, and to Congress. In 1973 Kowalski sued ABC-TV over its promotion of anti–Polish programs. The Polish American Congress demanded that the Federal Communications Commission revoke the station's license, but the case was dismissed by the FCC as incompatible with the constitutional freedom of speech. The PAC appealed to the Supreme Court, but it sustained the FCC's decision. Thus, legal means were exhausted without results. However, Polish American protests were widely noted by publishers and broadcasters, with the result that by the end of the decade observers noted a significant drop in the amount of the anti–Polish media portrayals. Although the PAC's Commission was partly responsible for this, the positive image of National Security Advisor **Zbigniew Brzeziński**, the election of the Polish Cardinal Karol Wojtyła as Pope John Paul II, the later rise of Solidarność under Lech Wałęsa, and other factors all contributed to a better image for Polish Americans. Kowalski resigned in 1977. Under the leadership of Jeannette Szulec of Detroit the Commission changed its name to the American Sentinel Committee, only to be renamed the Defamation and Discrimination Committee in 1979 under the management of Leonard Walentynowicz in Washington, D.C. Since 1980, Frank Milewski of New York, head of the Anti-Bigotry Committee, has concentrated on improving the image of the Poles during the Second World War, and especially their role in the Holocaust.—*Joanna Wojdon*

SOURCE: Joanna Wojdon, *W jedności siła. Kongres Polonii Amerykańskiej w latach 1968–1988* (Toruń: Wydawnictwo Adam Marszałek, 2008), 134–146.

Polish American Congress Anti-Defamation Committee of California *see* **Polish Anti-Defamation Committee.**

Polish American Council (Rada Polonii Amerykańskiej; RPA). American Relief for Poland was a central Polish American chari-

table organization formed in 1936 by leaders of the primary Polish-American fraternals in response to encouragement from the Polish consulate in Chicago to create an umbrella organization to coordinate Polish American social and cultural activities and to cooperate with the Warsaw-based **Światpol**. Initially founded under the name of Polska Rada Międzyorganizacyjna (Polish Interorganizational Council), the organization changed its name to Rada Polonii Amerykańskiej during its third convention in 1938. Its chair was **Francis Swietlik**. It also changed its interests from contacts with Poland to representing the Polish-American community in the United States. The influence of the RPA grew with the outbreak of World War II when it became the main organization coordinating humanitarian aid for Polish war refugees. On November 19, 1939, it registered as an aid agency with the Department of State. It was also recognized by the Polish government-in-exile in London as the central organization for Polish war relief in the United States. Its 36 regional districts organized fund drives and collected food and clothes to be sent to Europe and to Africa, Palestine, Persia, India, Mexico, and New Zealand where Poles expelled from their homes could be found. The Polish and American Red Cross, as well as the Committee for Polish Relief (Hoover Committee), were used to transport goods to Polish refugees, prisoners of war, and military personnel. By 1942 the total value of contributions exceeded $1.6 million.

After the United States entered the war and the National War Fund was established, the RPA joined the Fund as the only representative of the Polish ethnic group under the name of "Polish War Relief" (PWR). Its new task was to present the needs of Polish war refugees to local war chests. By 1945 the National War Fund had provided more than $5.3 million

Emblem of the Polish American Council (*JPI*).

Supplies collected for the relief of Poland (*PMA*).

II," *Journal of American Ethnic History*, No. 3 (2003), 3–30.

Polish American Health Association. Established in October of 1990 by a group of approximately forty physicians, biomedical scientists, and other individuals from the Washington metropolitan area, the organization's purpose was to provide a forum for health care and biomedical professionals of Polish descent. The name was selected to indicate that not only physicians but also other health care professionals and biomedical scientists were among those who founded the organization. The group was spearheaded by Dr. Lucas Kulczycki, Professor of Pediatrics at Georgetown University, who was its founder and first president. The group is organized and operates exclusively for educational, scientific, and charitable purposes through conducting and promoting meetings, workshops, and symposia on biomedical, scientific, medical, and health-related issues; providing support and expertise to medical schools, universities, and biomedical research institutions in Poland; and soliciting donations from the public to support non-profit service and relief agencies for the sick, elderly, handicapped, and underprivileged. The group's activities also include public discussion groups and fundraising for the benefit of various humanitarian, nonprofit organizations in Poland. Its causes include Doctors of Hope, the Equestrian Therapy Project, and the Children's Home in Poznań, Poland, as well as providing computers to a center for disadvantaged children in Poland and initiated a fundraising program to support the purchase of the first Cyberknife for Poland.—*Włodek Lopaczynski*

SOURCE: Władysław Zachariasiewicz, *Etos Polonii Amerykańskiej* (Warsaw: Oficyna Wydawnicza RYTM, 2005).

Polish American Heritage Month. Polish American Heritage Month is an annual event that observes the successes Polish Americans have made in America and celebrates the strong pride held by the ethnic group. By the early 1980s, the state of Pennsylvania held numerous celebrations to honor its various ethnic residents. Despite their significant numbers in the state, no such celebration existed to honor Polish Americans. Consequently, Michael Blichasz, president of the Polish American Cultural Center in Philadelphia, decided to organize a month-long event that would unite the many Polish Americans in the state. First celebrated in August 1981, Polish American Heritage Month enjoyed great success in its initial year. Event coordinators chose August due in part to the frequency of vacations, amusement park visits, gatherings, and other travel events which occur during that partic-

to Polish relief programs. Critics of the Polish War Relief admitted that Poles were in this regard behind many other nationalities, but the amount was much more than the PWR was able to solicit among the Polish American communities. According to National War Fund regulations, Polish War Relief had to remain an apolitical body, but its reluctance to raise questions regarding the future of Poland evoked criticism from the Polish government-in-exile in London and the New York–based **National Committee of Americans of Polish Descent** (KNAPP). As a result, in the spring of 1944 the Polish American Congress was established to pursue political issues while the Polish War Relief retained its purely charitable character.

After the end of the war, the RPA signed an agreement with the United Nations Relief and Recovery Administration to continue its relief activities on behalf of Polish refugees in Europe. At this time its name was changed once again to the "American Relief for Poland" (ARP). Its European headquarters were located in Geneva, Switzerland, with offices in Salzburg, Paris, Rome, Munich, Hamburg, Frankfurt, and Zirndorf-Valka. Liaison officers worked in Brussels, Copenhagen, Amsterdam, Oslo, Stockholm, and Barcelona. According to estimates, more than 1.5 million Poles in German territory, over 112,000 in France, and in excess of 16,000 in Austria benefited from the ARP's assistance. In 1948, Swietlik reported that between 1939 and 1948, American Relief for Poland had collected $11,435,000 in donations and shipped approximately 18,000 tons of clothing, medical

supplies, and foodstuffs to Europe. Between 1949 and 1954, donations of American **Polonia** to ARP contributed nearly another $480,000. Until 1951, ARP cooperated with the Warsaw government, assisting Polish refugees in their repatriation to Poland, providing them with food and clothes, and delivering aid to people in need in Poland. In April 1951 the ARP Warsaw office was closed by the communist authorities who took over its property and archives, arguing that the cost of ARP operations (office rent and transportation) were too high for the Polish government, especially since the government already ran a public welfare network. The European offices were closed in 1957-58 upon the completion of the resettlement of Polish displaced persons under provisions of the Displaced Persons Act of 1948 and the Refugee Relief Act of 1953.

American Relief for Poland operated in the United States until the early 1970s with its main scope of activities unchanged: collecting and distributing aid to Poles in need in Poland and worldwide. In 1956 it organized a special drive for repatriates from the Soviet Union arriving in Poland. After 1956 it resumed its activity in Poland, concentrating its efforts on assisting Polish hospitals, orphanages, and the Catholic University of Lublin. It became involved in the U.S. program for shipping surplus food to Poland, but that program ended in 1969. The last ARP financial report is dated November 23, 1974.—*Joanna Wojdon*

SOURCES: Donald E. Pienkos, *For Your Freedom Through Ours* (Boulder, CO: East European Monographs, 1991), 73–104; Bradley Fels, "'Whatever Your Heart Dictates and Your Pocket Permits': Polish-American Aid to Polish Refugees During World War

ular month. The goal was to unite cultural, civic, religious, and social organizations for a month long celebration which highlights Polish traditions, culture, and history. Celebrated in a variety of ways including youth activities, parades, and social festivities, the event became an immediate success in Pennsylvania and the city of Philadelphia. While the event continued to be celebrated as a local and state-wide affair, Blichasz, along with the Polish American Cultural Center and the **Polish American Congress**, lobbied politicians in both Pennsylvania and Washington, D.C., to place Polish American Heritage Month on the national register. In 1984, the United States Congress, by House Joint Resolution 577, designated August as Polish American Heritage Month. To commemorate the event, President Ronald Reagan issued a proclamation urging all Americans to celebrate Polish American Heritage Month. As a national celebration, Polish American Heritage Month received enthusiastic support by major Polish American organizations as well as Polish American parishes throughout the country. Over 3,000 groups and 750 churches became registered participants. Communities and organizations across the country used the event as a means to renew interest in Polish history, language, and culture among local populations.

In 1986, committee members decided to move the celebration of Polish American Heritage Month from August to October. The decision to make the switch resulted from two motivations: first, a number of schools and educators wished to become involved in the celebration and sponsor their own events which could take place during the school year, and second, to celebrate the event on the same month that the first Polish settlers came to America, landing in **Jamestown**, Virginia, in 1608. With the inclusion of schools in the festivities, the National Heritage Month Committee started coloring and essay contests as well as introducing themes for each annual celebration, such as honoring **Kazimierz Pułaski** or the anniversary of Columbus's voyage to the New World. By 2010, Polish American Heritage Month enjoyed much involvement by Polish American communities across the United States. With the help of the Polish American Cultural Center, preparations for Polish American Heritage Month are made months in advance. Numerous activities are sponsored including parades, fairs, fundraisers, and cultural displays in libraries, community centers and the Polish Consulate in New York City. Although fewer groups now participate in the annual celebration than in past years, the event is attracting involvement from a number of non–Polish American organizations. For example, several major bookstores located in areas with significant numbers of Polish American residents hold special events that celebrate and highlight Polish authors, while other ethnic groups increasingly show their support by sponsoring events.—*Michael T. Urbanski*

SOURCE: Official Polish American Heritage Month website at PolishAmericanHeritageMonth.com.

Polish American Historical Association. With the assistance of the Polish government-in-exile in London and the support of several Americans and American Poles, on May 15, 1942, a group of Polish émigré scholars who had fled the Nazi onslaught founded the **Polish Institute of Arts and Sciences in America** (PIASA) in New York City. According to historian and PIASA president Jan Kucharzewski, the new Polish Institute vowed "to assemble, preserve, and harness for posterity the values of a nation" and "to represent Polish thought in the world." PIASA was organized into four "Scholarly Sections," including a section devoted to the "Historical and Political Sciences," headed up by the renowned Polish émigré historian **Oskar Halecki**. At the first meeting of the latter, on September 11, 1942, Halecki proposed creating "a special Committee for the study of the history of Poles in the United States" and, once approved, enticed **Mieczysław Haiman** of the **Polish Museum** in Chicago to head it. Open to "all students of the Polish immigrant," without regard to their ethnic background, and headquartered at the Polish Museum in Chicago, the new Commission on Research on Polish Immigration held its first conference and meeting December 29–30, 1943, in New York City. At its second meeting, held at Orchard Lake Seminary (see **Saints Cyril and Methodius Seminary**) in Michigan in October 1944, the organization changed its name to the Polish-American Historical Commission and that year began to publish its own scholarly journal, *Polish-American Studies*. In June of 1947, both the organization and journal dropped the hyphen from their names, and the Commission formally joined both the American Historical Association (AHA) and the Catholic Historical Association.

After the death of Haiman in January 1949, leadership of the organization increasingly shifted to American-born Poles, prominent among whom were nuns and priests. The most active was the Rev. **Joseph Swastek** who served as president of the organization and its long-time journal editor. In that year, the Commission also changed its name to the Polish American Historical Association (PAHA). Reflective of the growing role of Polish American religious in PAHA affairs, in 1950 the organization moved its headquarters to **St. Mary's College** in **Orchard Lake**, Michigan. The role of Polish American religious in the life of PAHA remained prominent through the long tenure of service of the Rev. **M. J. Madaj**, a past president and long-time executive secretary. The Rev. Madaj—together with a few other lay officers like **Eugene Kusielewicz**—spearheaded the modernization and professionalization of PAHA, including the creation of local chapters (now defunct), a 1965 resolution to hold PAHA annual meetings in concert with the annual meeting of the American Historical Association, and the creation in 1965 of an annual scholarly award, the Haiman Award, the first of many prizes and awards that the organization would establish in future years. In 1969, Madaj oversaw the movement of PAHA headquarters from Orchard Lake to St. Mary of the Lake Seminary in Mundelein, Illinois, and shortly thereafter back to the Polish Museum in Chicago.

Leaders of the Polish American Historical Association at its first convention in New York in 1943. Left to right: The Rev. Franciszek Bolek, Heliodor Sztark, Arthur L. Waldo, Prof. Oskar Halecki, Zygmunt Umiński, Mieczysław Haiman, Prof. Jan Kucharszewski, the Rev. Józef Swastek, Prof. Konstanty Simons-Symonolewicz, the Rev. Antoni Bochenski (*PAHA*).

On October 16, 1972, PAHA was incorporated in Illinois as a 501(c)(3) not-for-profit organization, finally ending its formal connections to PIASA, and in 1975 the group was accepted as an affiliate society of the American Historical Association. In 1980, PAHA became a contributor to the AHA's National Coordinating Committee for the Promotion of History (NCC).

During these years, increasing professionalization of PAHA was accompanied by increasing secularization, as a generation of university-educated doctorally-trained Polish Americans took up service as PAHA officers and council members and in editorial roles for the journal. By the mid–1980s, both the organization and journal had become, for all intents and purposes, lay professional projects. In 1981, the organization conferred its first annual Halecki Prize for the best book on Polish American history or culture and first annual Swastek Award for the best article published in *Polish American Studies*; subsequently, the organization created the Stanley A. Kulczycki Prize for graduate and post-doctoral research in Polish American studies, a Distinguished Service Award, a Civic Achievement Award, a Creative Arts Award, the Amicus Poloniae Award, and a Graduate Research paper award. In 1998, PAHA's headquarters returned to St. Mary's College at the Orchard Lake Schools campus in Orchard Lake, Michigan, and in 2004 found a permanent home at Central Connecticut State University in New Britain, Connecticut, under the sponsorship of the CCSU Polish Studies Program and the Polish Chair named after the late CCSU professor and past PAHA president Stanislaus A. Blejwas.

Since its founding in 1942, PAHA has become a modern, secular, interdisciplinary academic and professional organization with a diverse, international membership of individuals and institutions. PAHA sponsors an annual conference, held in conjunction with the yearly meeting of the American Historical Association; awards about a dozen annual scholarly, publication, and civic prizes and awards; publishes a semi-annual journal, *Polish American Studies*, and a semi-annual newsletter; and is a funder of the Ohio University Press Polish and Polish American Studies Series and, on an ad hoc basis, a sponsor of various other publication and scholarly projects, conferences, and public programs. In 2008, *Polish American Studies* joined the History Cooperative developed by the University of Illinois and also accepted an invitation to participate in the JSTOR (Journal Storage) archival project, the premier academic repository for full-text electronic history journals.—*John J. Bukowczyk*

SOURCES: John J. Bukowczyk, "'Harness for Posterity the Values of a Nation'—Fifty Years of the Polish American Historical Association and *Polish American Studies*," *Polish American Studies*, Vol. 50, no. 2 (1993), 5–99; John J. Bukowczyk, "The Polish American Historical Association," in James S. Pula and M. B. Biskupski, eds., *The Polish Diaspora. Vol. II: Selected Essays from the Fiftieth Anniversary International Congress of the Polish Institute of Arts and Sciences of America* (Boulder, CO: East European Monographs, 1993), 99–102; Anna D. Jaroszyńska-Kirchmann, "The Polish American Historical Association: Looking Back, Looking Forward," *Polish American Studies*, Vol. 61, no. 1 (2008), 57–76; Angela T. Pienkos, "The Polish American Historical Association and Its Role in Research on Polish America: An Assessment," *Polish American Studies*, Vol. 38, no. 1 (1981), 63–73; James S. Pula, "The Role of the Polish American Historical Association in the 1980s," *Polish American Studies*, Vol. 39, no. 1 (1982), 6–13; Frank Mocha, "The Polish Institute of Arts and Sciences in America: Its Contributions to the Study of Polonia: The Origins of the Polish American Historical Association (PAHA)," in Frank Mocha, ed., *Poles in America: Bicentennial Essays* (Stevens Point, WI: Worzalla Publishing Company, 1978), 709–24; *Polish American Historical Association 1942–1951* (Orchard Lake, MI: Polish American Historical Association, 1951).

Polish American Immigration and Relief Committee. Incorporated in New York on April 26, 1947, under the name of the American Commission for Relief of Polish Immigrants, the goal of this organization was to help Polish displaced persons resettle in the United States and other countries. Under the leadership of its first president, the Rev. Felix Burant of the New York City parish of Saint Stanislaus Bishop and Martyr, co-founders of the Commission included Polish American businessmen from New York and journalists from the New York newspaper *Nowy Świat*. They regarded existing Polish-American organizations as incapable of dealing with the problems of the Polish displaced persons who were about to enter the United States in great numbers under the provisions of the Displaced Persons Act of 1948. The provisions of this act, along with the Refugee Relief Act of 1953, largely determined the Committee's activities until 1957. Committee members provided assurances and affidavits of support for refugee Poles in Western Europe, welcomed displaced persons at American ports in Baltimore, Boston, New Orleans, New York, and Philadelphia, and assisted them in their first steps on American soil with support such as legal advice, translation services, arranging transportation to a sponsor or renting an apartment. It also offered loans that were to be repaid after individuals found jobs.

The Commission was instrumental in bringing large groups of some 2,500 Poles from Germany to farming communities in New York and Connecticut, it found sponsors for almost one hundred Polish widows and women with children who otherwise would have been denied immigration visas, and it

assisted Poles who wished to migrate to the U.S. not only from Europe, but also from South America and Canada. The Committee's contacts were used to distribute CARE parcels among "hard core cases" in Europe; that is, those who could not qualify for immigration. The Committee also cared for Poles detained on Ellis Island, offering them clothing, books and newspapers, and also legal advice and moral support. The Committee worked to postpone the deportation of those denied entry, while it sought other destinations to which they might migrate. Good working relationships with the New York Congressional delegation led to support and some individual bills designed to assist Poles attempting to avoid deportation. Despite some initial tensions and conflicts, the Committee received substantial economic assistance from the **Polish American Congress** and the **Polish American Council** (Rada Polonii Amerykańskiej) in the 1940s and at the beginning of the 1950s.

At the end of the 1950s, the Committee had to accommodate itself to the atmosphere of "détente" and to the financial exigencies of its sponsors. The Rev. Burant claimed that despite some reforms in Poland, Polish political refugees still appeared in Europe and therefore the mission of the Committee would not be over "as long as political circumstances force the people to escape to freedom." On this basis the Committee lobbied the Immigration and Naturalization Service to treat Polish immigrants as political refugees and for reforms in U.S. immigration law that would allow more Poles to enter the United States.

The American Commission for Relief of Polish Immigrants changed its name to the Polish American Immigration and Relief Committee in 1958. In order to get direct access to American **Polonia** and its generosity, it opened local branches in cities with larger Polish American populations including Buffalo, Chicago, Cleveland, Detroit, Hartford, Houston, Los Angeles, Milwaukee, Philadelphia, Springfield (MA), Yonkers (NY), and one branch for the state of New Jersey. At the same time, European offices were established in Brussels, Frankfurt, Hamburg, Munich, Nuremberg, Paris, Rome, Salzburg, and Vienna. These replaced the recently closed offices of the Polish American Council in registering Polish refugees and assisting them before their further migration to the United States or other countries. The Committee co-operated with the National Catholic Welfare Conference and worked within the framework of the United States Escapee Program sponsored by the Department of State. Beginning in the mid–1960s federal funds played a significant role in the Committee's finances.

Due to the collapse of Communism in Poland at the end of the 1980s the problem of Polish political refugees ceased to exist, causing the Department of State to terminate the Committee's registration and withdraw financing from it. In 1990, the Committee's European offices were closed, as were its local branches in the U.S. From that time on, the Committee concentrated its efforts on assisting homeless and jobless Poles of the New York City area who could not adapt to the American reality. The Committee dissolved in 2000. According to the findings of Janusz Cisek, between 1947 and 2000, the Committee aided 70,000 Poles to migrate to different countries, not including those who benefited from its material help or legal advice. Committee presidents included the Rev. Feliks Burant (1947–64), the Rev. Franciszek Kowalczyk (1965–68), the Rev. John Karpinski (1968–88), and the Rev. Joseph Marjanczyk (1988–2000). Executive directors were **Walter Zachariasiewicz** (1950–62), Ignacy Morawski (1964–69), Heronim Wyszynski (1969–74), Frank Proch (1975–81), and Janusz Krzyżanowski (1981–2000).—*Joanna Wojdon and Donald E. Pienkos*

SOURCES: Janusz Cisek, *Polish Refugees and the Polish American Immigration and Relief Committee* (Jefferson, NC: McFarland Publishers, 2006); Walter Zachariasiewicz, "The Polish American Immigration and Relief Committee," in Frank Mocha, ed., *Poles in America: Bicentennial Essays* (Stevens Point, WI: Worzalla Publishers, 1978).

Polish American Journal. Founded in October 1911, as a small Polish-language newspaper named *Zorza* (The Dawn), in Pittston, Pennsylvania, under the editorship of Ignatius Haduch, the predecessor of the *Polish American Journal* moved to Wilkes-Barre two years later under the name *Republika* (Republic). In 1918 its editor moved to Scranton, the location of a Polish-language weekly *Górnik Pennsylwanski* (The Pennsylvania Miner). Both newspapers were experiencing financial difficulties but were saved from suspension by John Dende. Although a comparatively recent arrival in the United States, Dende had already made his mark on the Polonias of Scranton and Wilkes-Barre. After first purchasing *Republika*, in 1920 he also obtained *Górnik Pennsylwanski*, whereupon he combined the two under the title of *Republika-Górnik Pennsylwanski*. In 1926 Dende purchased and remodeled The Farr Building in Scranton where he established the Dende Press. The combined newspaper soon became influential throughout the hard coal fields, its editorial views often being quoted in Polish publications in other parts of the country. Dende became a national figure in Polish American circles, traveling extensively to attend important affairs conducted in the inter-

est of Americans of Polish origin. Following Dende's death on December 18, 1944, the newspaper continued to be published by his sons Henry, as editor, and Richard, as publisher. Realizing that more Americans of Polish descent were conducting their lives in the English language, the Dende brothers decided to cease publication of the Polish-language newspaper. On January 25, 1948, the new *Polish American Journal* became the first Polish American weekly to be printed entirely in the English language. At that time, the decision was met with disapproval from other editors who continued to print Polish-only papers. The change from Polish to English was motivated by the then six million Americans of Polish descent, five million of whom were American-born and better versed in English. The move proved correct as evidenced by an increase in circulation of a thousand percent. Moreover, the *Polish American Journal* acquired national stature as it became the only national English language voice of Americans of Polish ancestry. The *Polish American Journal* became the only Polish American publication that had established direct contacts with members of Congress, government officials, national civic and political leaders, the leaders of Free Poles here and abroad, and with numerous anti–Communist crusaders

throughout the world. In this capacity, it became the most referenced Polish American publication in the *Congressional Record*. In 1962, **Henry Dende** became the first Polish American newspaper editor to travel behind the Iron Curtain. He documented his trip on over 3,000 feet of film and discussed his findings at 125 public events over the next several years. In addition to the plight of Poles in Poland, Dende was concerned of the vitality of **Polonia**'s fraternal benefit societies, which were shrinking in membership with the passing of the immigrant generation. Starting in 1962, Dende convinced leaders of Polonia's fraternal benefit societies to use the *Journal* as their official publication, a move that would save the groups money and streamline operations. Over the next few years, the *Journal* became the official publication of the **Polish Union of North America** (Wilkes-Barre, PA); the Polish Beneficial Association (Philadelphia); The **Polish National Alliance of Brooklyn**, USA; and the Association of the Sons of Poland (Jersey City, N.J.). With the support of these fraternals, Dende was able to bring Polish Americans continuous coverage of the events in then Communist-controlled Poland, as well as news from Polish communities across the United States and Canada. As the *Journal* approached the 1980s, the

Offices of the *Republika Górnik*, the predecessor of the *Polish American Journal* (OLS).

Dende brothers began to entertain thoughts of retirement. Henry was especially concerned that before Dende Press closed its doors, a new home for the *Journal* had to be found. Across the nation, Polish American publications were closing upon the retirement of their publishers. In 1979, a group of young, Polish American college graduates in Buffalo, New York, invested their limited income in what was considered to be an up and coming part of an increasingly specialized industry — computerized typesetting. They formed the Panagraphics Corporation and began publishing a Polish American newspaper, the *Polonia Reporter* under the auspices of the **Polish Union of America**, which rented office space to Panagraphics at its home office in Buffalo. News of the new Polish pope and the fledgling Solidarity movement filled the pages of the paper. When the Polish Union of America decided to limit its news to strictly fraternal activities, Panagraphics decided to start its own publication. The new paper was called the *Polish American Voice*. Henry Dende was watching these developments from Scranton and, after several meetings, decided that the *Journal* should begin publishing in Buffalo with the premier issue being August 1983. In December of that year, Panagraphics purchased and remodeled a new office building and began publishing both the *Voice* and the *Journal* as separate newspapers. However, to avoid both dual subscriptions and duplication of news in each, they decided to merge the publications. The result was the expanded *Polonia's Voice: The Polish American Journal*. Edited since 1998 by Mark A. Kohan, in 2002 the *Polish American Journal* joined the growing practice of e-commerce. Soon the entire newspaper was being written, composed and edited by writers and staff in locations throughout the United States and Poland. Today, the *Polish American Journal* is a monthly, English language newspaper dedicated to the promotion, preservation and continuance of Polish American culture. It is published by Panagraphics, Inc., in Boston, New York, with a web site located at www.polamjournal.com.—*Mark A. Kohan*

SOURCE: Charles Allan Baretski, "A Content Analysis of the Polish American Journal Newspaper in Reflecting the Political Attitudes, Issues and Perspectives of the Polish-American Group During the Period, 1950–1966" (Unpublished Ph.D. dissertation, New York University, 1969).

Polish American Labor Council *see* **American Polish Labor Council.**

Polish American Priests Association (PAPA). Founded in 1990 at San Antonio, Texas, by a unanimous decision of priests of Polish descent attending the twentieth anniversary celebration of the Texas Polish American Priests Association, PAPA is a national fraternal organization of priests of Polish heritage and those involved in ministry to **Polonia** in the United States. At the San Antonio meeting a steering committee was selected to guide the informal, yet to be named group, and sub-committees were established to formulate by-laws, a convention program, and nominations for officers. During the historic PAPA Constitutional Convention held in Chicago, April 8–11, 1991, participants adopted a mission statement and by-laws for the association, which were subsequently amended at the 2001 Convention in Albany, NY. The first elected officers were: the Rev. **John Yanta**, San Antonio, TX, president; Canon Anthony Iwuc, Central Falls, RI, vice-president; the Rev. Richard Klajbor, Chicago, IL, secretary; and Msgr. Walter Gorski, Linden, NJ, treasurer. The Board of Directors included: the Rev. David Bialowski, Buffalo, NY; the Rev. Henry Fiedorczyk, Hartford, CT; the Rev. Bruno Janik, Chicago, IL; the Rev. John Lazar, Brooklyn, NY; the Rev. Philip Majka, Warrenton, VA; Msgr. Thaddeus Malanowski, Belleaire Bluffs, FL; the Rev. Leon Prozny, Utica, NY; the Rev. Joseph Sredzinski, Everson, PA; and Msgr. Bernard Witkowski, Philadelphia, PA. In addition, Msgr. Joseph Marjanczyk of Bayonne, NJ, then serving as Polish Apostolate Representative to the United States Catholic Conference Bishops' Committee on Migration, was made an ex-officio member of the board. The Rev. John Yanta, the originator of PAPA, who became auxiliary bishop of San Antonio (1994) and later bishop of the Diocese of Amarillo, TX (1997), appointed Mrs. Louise Janysek Jurgajtis as Executive Secretary to the National Office located at 5035 Bernadine, San Antonio, TX.

According to its mission statement, members of PAPA, under the patronage of Our Lady of Częstochowa as Catholic clergy of Polish heritage in the United States in union with the Holy See, desire to be faithful to a millennial tradition of faith handed down by their ancestors, evangelize by proclaiming Christ in Word and Sacrament, promote fraternity, and serve the unique needs of the spiritual and cultural dimensions of the Catholic Church in the United States. PAPA's mission is to be a religious, educational, and non-profit association of clergy who share a common ethnic heritage and/or support its goals, purpose, and objectives. Through various means of communication, networking, national conventions, and mutual encouragement, the Association promotes the pastoral, spiritual, and cultural identity of its members, fulfilling the hope of Pope John Paul II for "a constant fidelity and a new responsiveness to the needs of today's church and of Polonia as it exists in the world today." The objectives of PAPA are to foster fraternity, solidarity, unity and mutual support among Polish American priests; to promote and encourage renewal and preservation of liturgical customs, traditions, and heritage of American Polonia; and to develop Polish American priestly identity by advocating the rights of persons and pastoral agents and supporting them.

PAPA collaborates with the **Orchard Lake Schools** in implementing an effective pastoral program for the spiritual needs of **Polonia**. The Association promotes the acceptance and integration of Polish-born priests and seminarians into American society and dioceses in the United States; it fosters vocations to the priesthood, religious life, and diaconate within the Polish American community, and supports lay ecclesiastical ministry. Through solidarity and a network of communication between diocesan or regional Polish American priests' groups, the Association offers a national forum for a common vision to assist in resolving questions arising in local Polish American communities. It also provides individual priests a forum for expressing their personal experiences and concerns. PAPA cooperates, where feasible, with all organizations and agencies which promote the religious, educational, social, economic, and political welfare of the Polish American community. Thus, it contributes to the mosaic of American Catholicism by sharing the treasures of a millennial tradition of Polish Catholicism. The Association represents Polish American clergy and cooperates with laity in various departments of ecclesiastical and civil government. Finally, PAPA also serves as a significant voice of the Polish American clergy in the United States Conference of Catholic Bishops.

Membership is open to diocesan and regional Polish American priests' organizations and all priests in the United States of Polish ancestry. PAPA has become an umbrella organization for many already existing Polish clergy groups, for example, the Association of Polish Priests of Connecticut, which boasts a century of service. Similar Polish priest groups may be found in New Jersey, New York, Pennsylvania, Massachusetts, Michigan, Ohio, Indiana, and Texas. Groups range in size from five in Cleveland, OH, to as many as 123 in Newark/Paterson, NJ. A list compiled by Louise Janysek Jurgajtis in 1993 revealed 14 affiliated Polish clergy groups comprising 558 members, and 202 individual memberships. Members may be found in all fifty states, the District of Columbia and ten foreign countries. The Association also maintains communication with its members through a newsletter. In 2008 the mailing list to Polish American clergy included 3,690, plus all hierarchy and bishops in the United States and Poland.

Since the first national gathering of Polish American priests in 1990 at San Antonio, TX, each year over a hundred priests involved in Polish ministry and the Polish apostolate have gathered to pray, to share issues important to their ministry, and to update themselves on how to more effectively bring Christ to the people of God. The Association annually grants the Father **Leopold Moczygemba** Award.—*Frank B. Koper*

SOURCES: *Polish American Priests Association Constitution (P.A.P.A.)* (Orchard Lake, MI: The National Association of the Polish Apostolate, n.d.); the Rev. Msgr. Stanley E. Milewski, ed., *Polish American Priests Association PAPA Bulletin* (Orchard Lake, MI: The Orchard Lake Schools, December 2004–November 2007).

Polish American String Band.
Organized in the Polish ethnic community in Philadelphia in 1933, by 2000 the band numbered more than 90 volunteer performers who combined Polish heritage with the traditions of the famous Philadelphia Mummers. Dressed in the elaborate, colorful costumes of the Mummers, the band consists of banjos, accordions, bells, and various bass, percussion, and saxophone instrumentation. It has played at social, political and sporting events throughout the United States, as well as appearing in Poland, Cuba, and elsewhere. Its record in the annual New Year's Day Philadelphia Mummers Parade is unprecedented, being honored with (by 2000) eleven first place finishes and fourteen second place recognitions, and finishing in the top ten 64 times. Its first place finishes are the most by any string band in the parade, and only twice in its long history of participation in the event has it finished out of the top ten.—*James S. Pula*

SOURCE: *Polish-American Association String Band* (Philadelphia: Polish-American Association String Band of Philadelphia, an annual periodical published since the early 1990s).

Polish American Studies.
Published by the **Polish American Historical Association** continuously since 1944, *Polish American Studies* is a refereed scholarly journal that publishes articles, edited documents, reviews, and related materials dealing with all aspects of the history and culture of Poles in the Western Hemisphere. The preeminent publication dealing with Polish American history and culture, it is an interdisciplinary publication that accepts contributions from any discipline in the humanities and social sciences, and especially those that place the Polish experience in historical and comparative perspective by examining its relationship to other ethnic groups. The journal is a member of the prestigious JSTOR and History Cooperative electronic databases and is regularly abstracted in *Historical Abstracts, America: History and Life,* and *The Catholic Periodical and Literature Index.* Sample acceptance rates include 36.4 percent in 2005, 47.2 percent in 2006, 28.6 percent in 2007, and 36.4 percent in 2008. The journal's editors have been Constantin Symonolewicz (1944–45), **Joseph Swastek** (1946–69), Ladislas J. Siekaniec (co-editor, 1968–69), **Frank Renkiewicz** (1969–81), and **James S. Pula** (1982–).—*James S. Pula*

SOURCES: Frank Mocha, "The Polish Institute of Arts and Sciences in America: Its Contributions to the Study of Polonia: The Origins of the Polish American Historical Association (PAHA)," in Frank Mocha, ed., *Poles in America: Bicentennial Essays* (Stevens Point, WI: Worzalla Publishing Company, 1978), 709–24; polishamericanstudies.com.

Polish Anti-Defamation Committee.
Several committees of the **Polish American Congress** had used *anti-defamation* in their title, but one of the most vocal groups was the Polish American Congress Anti-Defamation Committee of California. The group was founded in 1986, with Teodor Polak as chair, after the California State Education Department proposed a mandatory model curriculum on Human Rights and Genocide which neglected the treatment of Poles during World War II. The group's lobbying proved successful when a Polish section was added to the final version of the curriculum that was adopted for use in the state's public schools. The Anti-Defamation Committee also publicized and protested any slights directed toward Poles, especially those in the media. Any time a magazine, newspaper, or television program referred to "Polish death camps" or made a Polish joke, a letter or press release from the Committee would follow, and an article about the slight or slur would appear in the group's newsletter, *Alert,* edited for many years by Artur Zygmont. In 1993, the Anti-Defamation League of B'nai B'rith went to court claiming that it had exclusive use of the service mark "anti-defamation," and the central office of the Polish American Congress in Chicago eventually agreed to abandon further use of the name, leading the California group to change its name in 1995 to the Polish American Defense Committee (PADC). Strongly believing that Poles were co-victims of the Holocaust along with Jews, the group defended the presence of the Carmelite convent at Auschwitz and criticized authors (**Jerzy Kosiński** and Yaffa Eliach), books (*Maus* and *Neighbors*), films (*Shoah* and *Schindler's List*) and subjects (Kielce and Jedwabne) which they felt presented a biased view of Polish-Jewish relations. In 1999, the PADC joined with the Polish American Congress and six Polish victims in filing a motion to include Poles among the victims of Nazi persecution who would receive $1.25 billion in a Swiss bank settlement. However, the motion was denied, as was the appeal.—*John Drobnicki*

SOURCES: Eugene Kusielewicz, "B'nai B'rith Versus the Poles," *Polish American Journal* (December 1992), 4; Teodor Polak, "Polish Victims of the Holocaust Excluded from the Swiss Banks Settlement by New York Judge," *Alert,* no. 22 (June 2000), 1; "We're Still Here February 1995," *Alert,* no. 16 (Feb. 1995), 1–2; Artur Zygmont, "Polish American Congress Anti-Defamation Committee of California: Prevent Defamation of Poles and Polish Americans and the Distortion of Polish History," in *Polish Americans in California,* Volume II (National Center for Urban Ethnic Affairs & Polish American Historical Association, 1995).

Polish Army in France
("Haller's Army"). When the United States declared war on Germany on April 6, 1917, the dream of an independent Poland advanced toward realization. Polish immigrants in America, especially the **Polish Falcons**, had, from the start of World War I, struggled for this goal. What had seemed a faint possibility now appeared closer to being accomplished. **Ignacy Jan Paderewski**, whom many recognized as the voice of Poland in America, addressed the Falcons in Pittsburgh later that month. He proposed the creation of "Kościuszko's Army," consisting of 100,000 men who would fight as part of the American Expeditionary Force. Canada, at Britain's bidding, was already secretly training 23 Falcons to serve as officers in a future Polish military unit. Three of these men, in uniform, also spoke at the same meeting.

The idea of an ethnic unit in the American army had no prospect of success from the start for various reasons. But France took advantage of Polish aspirations, and in early June formally established the Polish Army in France by presidential decree. In August the French sent a delegation to America to negotiate recruitment of Polish immigrants for the army. It included **Wacław Gąsiorowski**, head of the Falcons in France, whose assignment was to work out the details with the Polish **National Department** (Wydział Narodowy). France's unilateral proclamation of the army pleased neither Britain nor the United States, but by October both reluctantly agreed to cooperate with their ally in the matter. Recruitment formally began that month in Chicago, even though volunteers left for the Polish Army camp at Niagara-on-the-Lake, Ontario, before the public inauguration of the effort. The Falcons were ready to do their duty for Poland as they saw it and predominated among the first volunteers.

The camp, a summer bivouac for the Canadian Army, was hastily prepared to accommodate the recruits. Colonel Arthur D'Orr

A St. Louis recruiting office for the Polish Army in France. Note the red and white arm bands and the flags of the western Allies — Britain, the United States, and France (*PMA*).

LePan supervised the work of the men sent to Canada for officer training, including a total of 137 who came north during the summer. They erected tents for the recruits and Colonel LePan made plans to construct more substantial housing for the volunteers, who were expected to embark quickly for France. Transportation problems delayed their departure, while an early frigid winter set in. Two subsidiary camps were opened at St. Johns, Quebec, and Fort Niagara, New York to house the growing ranks of the army. The first transport of over 600 volunteers sailed for France in December. Their departure relieved the crowding in the camps. Regular sailings continued through 1918, and the American recruits soon formed the majority of the army. The transports also allowed the Canadians to close St. Johns and Fort Niagara.

In Europe the American volunteers continued preparation for battle. The first unit actually entered the trenches in Champagne in July as part of the French Fourth Army. That same month General Józef Haller left Russia for France, where he immediately became a member of the **Polish National Committee** headed by Roman Dmowski. Haller was an Austrian officer whose unit mutinied in February on learning of the Treaty of Brest-Litovsk. By this pact Germany and Austria-Hungary consigned areas that Poles regarded as Polish territory to the Ukrainian Republic. The Central Powers signed this agreement to force the Bolsheviks to seriously negotiate Russia's withdrawal from the war. Crossing into Russian territory, Haller was accepted as commander of a unit formed from former Polish soldiers in the Russian Army. German pressure on the Bolsheviks forced his retreat to Moscow, whence he withdrew to Murmansk for evacuation to Britain.

The French also recruited among prisoners of war of Polish origin from the German Army. Their number augmented the Polish Army, which continued its steady growth as a result of transports from America. Another source was Polish soldiers in the Russian Expeditionary Force in France. In October the Polish National Committee, to which the French government in March had granted a say in the army's management, named Haller commander of the Polish Army after consultation with the French military authorities. This is why the Polish Army in France was subsequently known as Haller's Army. The powder blue uniforms the men wore in France gave the army its colloquial name the "Blue Army."

By this time the American **Polonia** had sent over 13,000 men to the army, with a few of the recruits also being residents of Canada. The flu epidemic then raging probably halted the transports in September. When they resumed in October, another 7,400 men sailed for Europe. A surprising increase in volunteers after the Armistice caused the Polish Military Mission to require of them a promise to serve six months in the army in Europe. Some of these men no doubt saw the army as a convenient way to check on their families in Poland. The final group departed in March, 1919.

The Germans vociferously protested the plan to send the Polish Army to Poland through Danzig. They feared the army would seize the city for Poland. Meanwhile, Polish prisoners of war in Italy were incorporated into the Polish Army in France, outnumbering the volunteers from the New World. Prolonged negotiations eventually allowed the army to transit Germany by train on the way to Poland. The transfer began on April 16 and took two months.

Józef Piłsudski, Poland's head of state, persistently demanded the repatriation of the army, which was one of several Polish military formations during World War I. Those based in Poland acknowledged his leadership. In Western Europe, his quondam association with Germany, despite subsequent internment at Magdeburg, made him suspect to the Entente, which felt more comfortable with the Polish National Committee. Dmowski and Piłsudski differed over their vision of Poland's future. The army, when it entered Poland, numbered some 68,000 men and arrived with French equipment and advisors, including Captain Charles de Gaulle. It was then the best organized and supplied military unit in

Blessing of the flags of the Polish Army in France in June 1918. General Haller is seen to the right of the flags (*OLS*).

Poland. Potential conflict over its relationship to other military formations in the restored republic never developed, because Haller subordinated his force to Piłsudski.

Marshal Piłsudski, in turn, recognizing the need to merge all these units into the Polish Army (Wojsko Polskie), did so in September, as disputes with Germany, Ukraine, and Bolshevik Russia threatened to destabilize Poland. The Hallerczycy, as soldiers in the Polish Army were known, encountered some resentment from their comrades who had spent the war in Poland. This, plus disillusionment with the situation in Poland, led some 12,500 volunteers to opt for return to America, where they established the **Polish Army Veterans Association**. Congressmen Adolph Sabath of Chicago and **John Kleczka** of Milwaukee cosponsored a bill authorizing the return of veterans of the Czecho-Slovak and Polish Armies in France to the United States.—*Joseph T. Hapak*

SOURCES: Paul S. Valasek, *Haller's Polish Army in France* (Naples, FL: Whitehall Printing, 2006); Joseph T. Hapak, "The Polish Military Commission, 1917–1919," *Polish American Studies*, Vol. 38, no. 2 (1981), 26–37; Joseph T. Hapak, "Recruiting a Polish Army in the United States, 1917–1919" (Ph.D. dissertation, University of Kansas, 1985); Stanley R. Pliska, "The 'Polish-American Army' 1917–1921," *The Polish Review*, Vol. 10, no. 3 (1965), 46–59; Wincenty Skarzyński, *Armja polska we Francji w świetle faktów* (Warsaw: Tłoczono w Zakładach graficznych Straszewiczów, 1929); Józef Sierociński, *Armja polska we Francji: Dzieje Wojsk Generała Hallera na obczyznie* (Warsaw: Nakł. własnym, 1929); Wacław Gąsiorowski, *Historja armji polskiej we Francji, 1910–1915* (Warsaw: Dom Książki Polskiej Spółka Akcyjna, 1931); Wacław Gąsiorowski, *Historja armji polskiej we Francji, 1915–1916* (Łódź: Dom Książki Polskiej, 1939).

Polish Army Veterans Association (Stowarzyszenie Weteranów Armii Polskiej). An organization of Polish American veterans, it was established in 1921 by the former soldiers who served in Gen. Józef Haller's **Polish Army in France** during World War I. The idea of creating the organization emerged before the soldiers returned to the United States, with the first posts organized in 1920 in Buffalo, Chicago, Detroit, Milwaukee, New Britain (CT), Passaic (NJ), and Youngstown (OH). The first convention of PAVA took place in Cleveland on May 28–30, 1921, with **Teofil Starzyński** elected its first president (1921–28). By 1939, twelve regional districts had been organized with 141 posts and 4,450 members. One post also opened in Bydgoszcz, Poland. Membership was open only to former soldiers of the Polish Armed Forces — including, but not limited to, Haller's army. In 1925 a separate organization, the Polish American Veterans Association Auxiliary Corps, was created for non-combatants willing to support PAVA. In 1940 it had 113 posts. The primary goal of PAVA was to help Polish American veterans, especially the disabled, ill, poor, jobless or homeless, and their widows and orphans. PAVA paid special subsidies to existing shelters or organized new shelters for Polish American veterans in several cities with large Polish American populations. Membership dues did not suffice to meet the veterans' needs, so PAVA solicited funds from Polish-American organizations and the general public. Fundraising campaigns were supported by **Ignacy Jan Paderewski** and Gen. Józef Haller, but PAVA's efforts to secure for Polish Army veterans the medical and social privileges accorded to American army veterans was not successful until 1976. In 1938 an agreement was signed with the government of the Republic of Poland guaranteeing a yearly subsidy of $3,000 for disabled Polish American veterans, but due to the outbreak of World War II the subsidy was paid only once, in March 1939.

In its relations with interwar Poland, PAVA refrained from involvement in political issues, attempting to cooperate with each Polish government for the benefit of Polish American veterans. Because of its efforts, Polish funds were provided to cover the expense of transporting Polish American veterans who had remained in Poland to America in 1922. The Association also attempted to assist those who decided to stay in Poland. It gave special loans to those who chose to settle on land offered to the veterans by the Polish government and it organized an agricultural cooperative in Kuligi near Brodnica that was supposed to serve as a shelter for disabled veterans. Both ventures proved to be financial failures. Very few Polish Americans decided to pursue farming in Poland and those who did were usually too poor to repay the loans. Similarly, in Kuligi the veterans proved incapable of collective work, leading to the closure of the cooperative which cost PAVA some $30,000.

PAVA's American ventures were more successful. Although it was incorporated as a non-profit organization, economic activities such as canteens, room rental, and the organization of events, helped many posts earn considerable funds, some of which were used to purchase homes or recreational facilities. PAVA's press organ, *Weteran* (The Veteran), began returning a profit in the mid–1930s. The association also produced films; organized exhibits, lectures, theatrical performances, Polish and Polish-American anniversary celebrations; operated libraries and reading

General Joseph Haller Post of the Polish Army Veterans organization in Chicago, 1935 (*PMA*).

rooms; and sponsored a two-volume history of the Polish Army in France authored by **Wacław Gąsiorowski** and published in Warsaw in 1931 and 1939.—*Joanna Wojdon*

SOURCE: Teofil Lachowicz, *Weterani polscy w Ameryce do 1939 roku* (Warsaw: Oficyna Wydawnicza Rytm, 2002).

Polish Association of America (Stowarzyszenie Polaków w Ameryce, SPA). A Polish American fraternal insurance and benefit society established in 1895 in Milwaukee, Wisconsin, it was formed by several local lodges of the **Polish Roman Catholic Union of America**. At its height it had members in 150 lodges in Wisconsin, where it was strongest, and in Illinois, Michigan, Ohio, Indiana, Nebraska, New York, and New Jersey. The organization was staunchly Catholic in character and its leadership included a number of Milwaukee-based pastors. Membership in the SPA exceeded 10,000 members until the middle 1930s. In the 1970s it officially changed its name to Northern Fraternal Life Insurance to attract a wider membership base. In the 1990s it was merged into the Catholic Family Life Fraternal based in Massachusetts; by then its membership was about 2,500.—*Donald E. Pienkos*

SOURCES: Thaddeus Borun and John Gostomski, eds., *We, The Milwaukee Poles* (Milwaukee: Nowiny Pub. Co., 1946); Wacław Kruszka, *A History of the Poles in America to 1908* (Washington, D.C.: The Catholic University of America Press, 1993), Vol. 1; Andrzej Brożek, *Polish Americans 1864–1939* (Warsaw: Interpress, 1985).

Polish Brigade. At the outbreak of the American Civil War in 1861, Polish exile **Gaspard Tochman** presented to the Confederate government, then located in Montgomery, AL, a plan to raise troops for the South from among the nation's immigrant population. He opened an office in New Orleans in May, 1861, issued an appeal to "Fellow-Countrymen of the Old World," and within six weeks had recruited 1,415 men of foreign birth and 28 born in the U.S. The troops were organized into the 14th and 15th Louisiana Infantry regiments which went on to serve with great distinction in the Army of Northern Virginia. Although known as the "Polish Brigade," few of the recruits were actually Polish, the majority being Irish, French, and German. Tochman resigned in a dispute over rank and never served with the command in the field.—*James S. Pula*

SOURCES: Maria J. E. Copson-Niećko, "The Poles in America From the 1830's to 1870's: Some Reflections on the Possibilities of Research," in Frank Mocha, ed., *Poles in America: Bicentennial Essays* (Stevens Point, WI: Worzalla Publishing Company, 1978), 45–302; Edward Pinkowski, *Pills, Pen & Politics: The Story of General Leon Jastremski* (Wilmington, DE: Captain Stanislaus Mlotkowski Memorial Brigade Society, 1974); Francis C. Kajencki, "The Louisiana Tiger," *Louisiana History*, Vol. XV, no. 1 (Winter 1974), 49–58; Mary W. Schaller and Martin N. Schaller, *Soldiering for Glory: The Civil War Letters of Colonel Frank Schaller, Twenty-second Mississippi Infantry* (Columbia, SC: University of South Carolina Press, 2007), especially chapter 3, 37–48.

Polish Catholic Laymen in America *see* **Federation Life Insurance of America.**

Polish Central Relief Committee (1914–18). Following the virtual disintegration of the **National Defense Committee** (KON), **Polonia** was without overall political leadership in the early days of World War I. Under the urging of the prominent activist **Jan F. Smulski** the **Polish National Alliance** convened an emergency meeting of Chicago **Polonia** leadership on September 25, 1914. Responding to the passionate call for action and coordination animating Polonia, the meeting created a new body, less grand in its ambitions than the KON and reflecting the rightist politics of the recently established Chicago based National Council (Rada Narodowa). Twenty-four leaders, overwhelmingly representing the clerical-right faction in Polonia, established the Polish Central Committee (Polski Centralny Komitet). The specific charge of the new body was to coordinate and urge the solicitation of funds for the relief of Poland. It was openly critical of the KON and urged Poles not to support its efforts.

Despite its seemingly restricted goals, the Committee harbored larger political ambitions. In late October it deemed its mission "consolidating the entire emigration for active aid to the Fatherland," claimed to be the "single legal authority" for Polish Americans and announced a stunningly broad agenda to "decide all questions of Polish policy," represent Polonia before American authorities, and establish relations with Poland. This vast agenda was soon reduced to emphasize relief efforts and the name of the organization was altered to the **Polish Central Relief Committee** (Polski Centralny Komitet Ratunkowy); "Relief" being added to lessen the obvious political ambitions, a change probably suggested by Bishop **Paul Rhode**. The leadership of the PCKR included representatives of all the major organizations of a clerical-right orientation. It worked very closely with the Rada Narodowy and the latter's' journal *Free Poland* was effectively the voice of the PCKR. The organization was, from its inception, dominated by Chicago Poles and boasted the three leading clerics on its Executive Committee. President **Antoni Karabasz**, the controversial **censor** of the Polish National Alliance, was seconded by **Piotr Rostenkowski** of the **Polish Roman Catholic Union** and **Anna Neumann** of the **Polish Women's Alliance** as vice-presidents.

Quickly the PCKR adopted a definitive attitude toward the war, denouncing Germany and endorsing the Entente Powers. Among the first initiatives of the PCKR was to involve itself in the complex and ultimately fruitless effort to create military formations to join the war in conjunction with the Entente; an effort suspended in November, 1914. This would later return as a major Polonia ambition which ultimately assumed the form of the **Haller Army**. A transformation was worked within the PCKR by its affiliation with the Vevey Committee in Switzerland, an international agency led by **Ignacy Jan Paderewski** and **Henryk Sienkiewicz**, designed to channel

Leaders of the Polish Central Relief Committee in Chicago, 1914–1918 (*PMA*).

material aid to war-ravaged Poland. More than half of Vevey's funds were provided by Polonia, and 117 of its 174 local branches were in America. Rhode, Smulski, and Karabasz of the PCKR became Polonia's delegates to Vevey. However, efforts to solicit support from the larger American community were a dismal failure. The 1915 arrival in America of Paderewski was crucial for the history of the PCKR. Paderewski quickly assumed leadership of Polonia basing his actions on the organizational framework of the Committee. By 1915 the Committee was working closely with the so-called Lausanne Committee (Centralna Agencja Polska) which was increasingly an instrument of rightist and pro–Entente European Poles.

By late 1915 the CAP was under the effective control of Roman Dmowski who decided to establish close relations with Paderewski and Polonia by dispatching Jan Jordan Rozwadowski to the United States in 1916. Rozwadowski's mission was to establish close coordination with the PCKR and stimulate the collection of funds for political purposes. These measures would require a much more efficient organization of Polonia. Rozwadowski met with Paderewski who endorsed his mission and then traveled to Chicago to meet the PCKR leadership. Rozwadowski set himself the goal of "concentrating all national work ... in one common organization." The basis for this was the PCKR's decision in April 1916 to create a "Committee for Political Affairs" under the direction of Smulski to engage in specifically political work. Close financial and political links were quickly established between the CAP and the PCKR with Rozwadowski acting as intermediary.

The political committee subsumed the Rada Narodowy organ *Free Poland*, planned to create a permanent lobbying office in Washington and in June 1916 re-named itself the "**National Department**" or Wydzial Narodowy. Although the PCKR continued to function, it was completely eclipsed by its own creation, the WN, and restricted its activities to fund raising. Despite its virtual demise after mid–1916, the PCKR proved to be the body upon which political activity during the war was constructed, the base of operations for Paderewski, and the institutional link between Polonia and the Poles of Europe, principally the Dmowski faction. The PCKR, a project of the clerical-right, succeeded in the goals originally set by the KON in 1912, becoming a quasi-directing body for American Polonia during the war.—*M. B. B. Biskupski*

SOURCE: M. B. Biskupski, "The United States and the Rebirth of Poland, 1914–1918" (Ph.D. dissertation, Yale University, 1981).

Polish Constitution Day. An annual Polish American tradition, this holiday commemorates May 3, 1791, when the Polish parliament (or Sejm) approved a new Constitution at a critical time for the country. The "May Third Constitution" provided for a thoroughgoing governmental reform aimed at strengthening the state's sovereignty. It formally guaranteed religious toleration to all of the nation's people; a radical act in 1791 in Europe, but one practiced in Poland for centuries. In many ways it had much in common with the U.S. Constitution ratified in 1789. Both were products of the human rights-conscious European Enlightenment. In response, the rulers of Prussia and imperial Russia reacted to passage of the May Third Constitution by invading the country and revoking the Constitution. Poland was then subjected to a second seizure of part of its territory in the Second Partition. Though Poland was wiped off the map of Europe in a Third Partition in 1795, generations of freedom-loving Poles saw the 1791 Constitution as a symbol of the nation's aspirations for independence and liberty and its capacity to govern itself effectively. In the United States, the May Third Constitution was recalled by Poles on various occasions in the nineteenth century. In 1891, on the centennial anniversary of its promulgation, the Constitution was commemorated in Chicago for the first time on a massive scale and in an extraordinary manner. That year, the **Polish National Alliance** fraternal and its opponent, the Rev. **Wincenty Barzyński**, head of the **Resurrectionist** Order and Pastor of St. Stanislaus Kostka Church, were unable to work together to hold a single commemoration of the anniversary. As a result, two celebrations were held. The first, on Saturday May 2, had the PNA sponsoring a spirited parade through Chicago's near north side culminating at the City's Central Music Hall. There a series of speeches were delivered by **Polonia** leaders and city officials, choral presentations, and a sound and light show depicting patriotic events in Polish and American history. On Sunday May 3, the Rev. Barzyński organized a High Mass honoring the Constitution at his church to kick off a three day anniversary commemoration.

Thereafter, the idea of a Polish Constitution Day parade in Chicago languished. But in 1904 it was resumed under PNA auspices. The parade, which grew in size over the years, kept to a route through Chicago's heavily Polish north side ending in its Humboldt Park. There at the site of the newly erected statue of **Thaddeus Kościuszko**, speeches praising the Constitution and the Poles' hopes for Poland were given. This event became an an-

nual affair, only departing from the Humboldt Park destination in 1974, when the parade moved to Chicago's downtown loop area. In 1978, the Kościuszko monument was also moved to the Chicago lakefront. Over the years, the May Third event drew thousands of marchers and as many as 150,000 spectators. It was also a day of Polonia unity and an occasion for speeches by national leaders of the United States, officials of Poland, and during the Cold War, émigré activists. The event was and continues to be celebrated in other American cities where large numbers of Polish Americans reside. In 1992 the PNA discontinued its sponsorship of the Chicago parade. Since then the event has been coordinated by Polonia activists connected with various organizations, most notably the Alliance of Polish Clubs.

Other holidays uniting Polish Americans in celebrating Poland's, and America's, shared values are **Casimir Pulaski** Day, first celebrated on October 11, 1929, the 150th anniversary of the patriot's death in the battle of Savannah in the American War for Independence, and Polish Independence Day (commemorated on November 11 in free Poland and the U.S. since 1991 and coinciding with Veterans Day and the end of World War I in 1918).—*Donald E. Pienkos*

SOURCE: Donald E. Pienkos, *PNA: A Centennial History of the Polish National Alliance of the United States of North America* (Boulder, CO: East European Monographs, 1984).

Polish Falcons of America (Związek Sokolstwo Polskie w Ameryce). The Polish Falcons of America (PFA) is a not-for-profit fraternal insurance benefit society licensed to sell insurance and annuity products in nine states. It is the fourth largest fraternal insurance benefit society, in members and assets, of the more than twenty that have been established in the United States by persons of Polish birth and origin. In 2005, the Falcons had a membership of 25,808 plus 2,909 owners of annuities, with fraternal assets of $47,446,382 and insurance in force amounting to $64,290,000. The PFA is organized along the principles of representative self-government with all officers, from the local nest through the national convention, elected by the membership. All adult members are eligible for election to its national convention (*Zjazd*). At the conventions, held every four years since 1936, the national leadership is elected and its future program and budget approved. The national officers include a president, two vice presidents, a secretary-treasurer and a board of twelve directors, one elected from each of the regional districts into which the PFA is divided. The Falcons publish a

Leaders of the Polish Falcons, 1905–07: seated, from left, Antoni Dobrzański, secretary general; Bolesław Zaleski, president; Stanisław Osada, editor of *Sokół Polski*; standing, from left, Jan Wutkowski, director; Leon Romanowski, department head; Józafat Latuszewski, vice president; Władysław Skwarczyński, department head; Leon Czesławski, secretary; Antoni Mazur, department head (*OLS*).

twice-monthly journal, **Sokół Polski** (The Polish Falcon).

The story of the Falcons is distinctive, though little known. The PFA dates its origins to June 12, 1887, when the first Polish Falcons society in America was established in Chicago, Illinois. Its founder was **Feliks Pietrowicz**, a twenty-four year-old immigrant from Poznań. Pietrowicz's aim was to create an organization modeled after the Falcons movement, in existence since 1867, in Poland. The earliest Falcons or "Sokół" societies established among the Slavic peoples were formed in the Czech lands of the Austrian empire in 1862. Thereafter, the Czech, and later the Slovak "Sokóls" grew into thriving mass movements both in Europe and America. These may have been influenced by the earlier German "Turnverein" or "Turner societies," which date back to the 1830s, which stressed the flexing of arms, legs, and torso, or "turning." The Poles who organized Falcons societies in America used the pan–Slavic word "*sokół*" to describe their groups, and in fact benefited from their early contacts with already established Czech societies in Chicago. At the same time, the English language name they officially used for many years was the "Polish Turners Alliance in America."

The Falcons movement brought together men and women to take part in organized gymnastic programs. But the Falcons society was more than a physical fitness club. Its premise was that a person's physical health was closely related to intellectual and moral development, including pride in the national heritage. The Falcons' adopted an ancient motto, borrowed from the Romans, "W zdrowym ciele, zdrowy Duch!"—"A healthy spirit in a healthy body." The emblem of the Falcons dates to 1914, the time of its military involvement in the Polish independence cause. It depicts a falcon perched on an exercise weight; its beak is breaking the chains of Poland's oppression. Behind it is a sword and a bayoneted rifle. To the left are the laurels of athletic victory, to the right are the initials ZSP w A Związek Sokolstwa Polskiego w Ameryce). In the background is the great burial mound of the Falcons' patron, **Tadeusz Kościuszko**, near Kraków, itself brightened by the sunshine of freedom. Surrounding the emblem are the words "Czołem Ojczyźnie Szponem Wrogowi!"—"Hail to the Fatherland, Talons to the Enemy!" The Falcons possess a set of unique terms that further distinguish their organization. Male members are addressed as *Druh* (comrade or friend), women members as *Druhna*. Members salute one another with the words *Czolem* (hail!) or *Czuwaj* (be prepared!). A male member is a *Sokół*, a female a *Sokolica*. The local lodge or group is a nest (*gniazdo*), and the local gymnastics center is a *Sokolnia*. An officer having a traditionally important role at every level of the organization is the physical instructor (*naczelnik*, female *naczelniczka*).

The ties between encouraging physical fitness and a commitment to building in them a strong sense of patriotic feeling led the early leaders of Chicago's Polish immigrant **Polonia** to support enthusiastically the development

of the Falcons society. The Falcons movement in America was also distinctive because it is the only secular Polonia organization whose origins were in Poland. The first Polish Falcons society came into existence in 1867 in Lwów in Austrian-ruled Poland. Pietrowicz was in contact with its leaders and with their blessings organized the first Falcons nest in Chicago. Following the formation of the first Polish Falcons society, at least twelve groups, or nests, were organized, several of them in Chicago. On January 7, 1894, representatives from four of these established the Związek Sokolstwa Polskiego w Ameryce (ZSPA). In 1896, the Falcons began holding an organized athletic competition (*zlot*) modeled after the newly reborn international Olympic meet in Athens to coincide with the Falcons' regular national convention. These meets remain a part of the life of the organization and continue to be held at the national and district levels of Falcons life.

In the Falcons' first constitution the aims of the movement were defined as promoting physical education programs, training instructors, developing patriotic feeling among the members, and working for Poland's freedom "by all legal means." The early leadership of the Alliance even authorized a special uniform for its members. In the later years, especially in the wake of the Spanish-American War of 1898, many nests also became involved in organizing paramilitary exercises in nearby forests and woods in the expectation that they might somehow be enlisted to go to Poland itself to participate in its struggle for independence. In 1914 the Polish Falcons Alliance adopted a new charter that emphasized its role as a paramilitary force. During its first decade, membership in the Polish Falcons Alliance remained modest: a decade after its creation in 1905 the Alliance counted only 1,800 members in fewer than fifty nests. But in that year the PFA president, Bolesław Zaleski, led the Falcons into a union with the **Polish National Alliance**. The resulting "Alliance of Polish Falcons Department of the Polish National Alliance" immediately began receiving a substantial amount of publicity and financial support from the much larger 45,000 member PNA. Not surprisingly, membership in the Falcons Department grew to 3,200 members in 89 nests in 1907 and to 6,000 members in 176 nests by 1910. But dissidents among the Falcons bitterly resisted the merger, which they argued would lead to the loss of their movement's distinctive identity.

In 1906 a secessionist "Union of Polish Falcons in America" centered in Connecticut formed in opposition to the Chicago-based PFA Falcons Department. Partisans of Józef

Newspaper cartoon by Wincenty Gawron showing the Falcons clasping hands across the Atlantic (*OLS*).

Piłsudski in partitioned Poland objected to the PNA's close ties with rightist Roman Dmowski, Piłsudski's main rival in the homeland. There was friction, too, between President Zaleski and the PNA leadership that climaxed at the 1909 Falcons *zjazd*. There he and his followers walked out of the hall and immediately created a rival organization they called the "Free Falcons Alliance." The Connecticut secessionists joined them. Between 1909 and 1912, the two Falcons Alliances were in competition. The Chicago-based PNA Falcons climbed to 9,300 members and the New York–centered "Free Falcons" claimed 3,200 followers. By 1912 both factions were facing pressures to unite, a move that was facilitated by the decision of the PNA, ironically led by past Falcons president **Kazimierz Zychliński**, to end the merger with its Falcons Department. In December 1912, delegates from the two organizations met in Pittsburgh, agreed to unite, and elected a new national leadership headed by Dr. **Teofil Starzyński**, a Free Falcons activist. The unified Polish Falcons Alliance set up its new national headquarters in Pittsburgh, where Starzyński resided.

Upon the outbreak of the First World War, militants in the Falcons Alliance tried to make their way to Poland to take part in the Legions led by Piłsudski. But Starzyński declared that no military mobilization could be initiated until the United States entered the war. He did back the creation of an officers training program, however. The first of these was set up at **Alliance College** in Cambridge Springs, Pennsylvania. In 1917, a clandestine officers training program for Falcons members was established in Canada. In April 1917, President Woodrow Wilson obtained a declaration of war against Germany from the U.S. Congress. America's entry into the conflict on the side of Britain, France, and the Russian empire came at the very time of an extraordinary Falcons *zjazd* in Pittsburgh. There the pianist-patriot **Ignacy Paderewski**, acting as the representative of the Dmowski-led Polish National Committee in France, called for the creation of a 100,000-man army of Poles in America to serve on the side of the Allies. Starzyński was named to a three member military recruiting commission. The commission enlisted more than 38,000 volunteers, of whom about 9,000 were members of the Falcons. Eventually, 22,000 men (of whom perhaps 5,000 were Falcons) were shipped to France after a basic training program and there became part of a 90,000-man Polish army under the command of General Józef Haller (see **Polish Army in France**). Haller was himself a one-time military instructor in the prewar Falcons movement in Austrian Poland. It is notable that the very first member of the Polish Army from America to be killed in action in France was Second Lieutenant Lucjan Chwałkowski, a member of the Falcons' nest in Brooklyn, New York.

With the war's end on November 11, 1918, most of the "Haller army" was dispatched to the newly independent Poland. Many Falcons were in this force, among them Starzyński who resigned as president to serve. Over the next three years they saw action in various theaters of the wars Poland was obliged to fight in defending its new borders. It should also be noted that several thousand Falcons who were ineligible for service in the Polish American army because they were already U.S. cit-

Group No. 2 of the Polish Falcons in Chicago, 1926 (*PMA*).

izens also served in the armed forces of the United States. Upon their return to the United States, many Falcons resumed their involvement in the Alliance, creating, in 1921, the **Polish Army Veterans Association** (Stowarzyszenie Armii Weteranów Polskiej; SWAP), which continues to the present time and whose members include veterans who served in the Polish armed forces in World War II. After World War I, Polish Americans who had served in the U.S. armed forces set up their own organization, the **Polish Legion of American Veterans**, PLAV, which also remains active.

With Poland independent, the Falcons' activity as a paramilitary training force was no longer needed. The Falcons' mission as a youth and sports organization was also challenged when the Polish American fraternals received permission by American insurance regulatory bodies to enroll children and young adolescents in their ranks. Accordingly they quickly began organizing their own youth and sports departments. At an extraordinary convention in Detroit in 1925, the delegates redefined the Falcons' mission and established a system of life insurance for all members. The move was critical in reversing the slide in membership, from 25,688 in 1914 to 13,545 in 1926. By 1928 the number of enrolled individuals had risen to 23,310 and by 1940 it was 25,410. Financially, the decision to create an insurance program also strengthened the organization considerably. The Falcons' assets in 1928 were $28,000, but by 1940 they were more than $528,000. The mission of the organization, renamed the Polish Falcons of America, was restated to promote its new fraternal insurance program and step up its sports and physical fitness activities and to include a number of American team sports into its program.

During World War II, the PFA supported Polonia's activities on behalf of Polish refugees, prisoners-of-war, and members of the Polish armed forces through its involvement in the **Polish American Council** (Rada Polonii Amerykańskiej, RPA). In 1944, Starzyński helped found the **Polish American Congress**. Three of his successors, **Bernard Rogalski** (president 1980–88), Lawrence Wujcikowski (president 1988–96), and Wallace Zieliński (president from 1996), have served as national secretaries of the PAC.

Two members of the Falcons have attained national recognition for their athletic achievements. **Stella Walasiewicz Walsh** won a gold medal as a representative of the Polish team at the 1932 Olympics in Los Angeles, and in 1936 she won the silver medal at the Berlin Olympics. Another outstanding athlete and Falcon is Baseball Hall of Fame great **Stan "The Man" Musial** who played for the St. Louis Cardinals between 1941 and 1963.

In 1960, Falcon membership was 27,807 and assets were reported at $4,676,943. Within twenty years these rose by 1980 to a membership of 29,135 (91.3 percent insured) and assets of $11,352,017. In 1986, the PFA surpassed the thirty thousand membership figure.—*Donald E. Pienkos*

SOURCES: Stanisław Osada, *Sokolstwo Polskie, Jego Dzieje, Ideologia i Posłannictwo* (Pittsburgh: Nakładem i drukiem "Sokola Polskiego," 1929); Arthur L. Waldo, *Sokolstwo Przednia Straż Narodu* (Pittsburgh: Polish Falcons of America, 5 vols., 1953–84); Donald E. Pienkos, *One Hundred Years Young: A History of the Polish Falcons of America, 1887–1987* (Boulder, CO: East European Monographs, 1987); Joseph Hapak, "The Polish Military Commission, 1917–1919," *Polish American Studies*, Vol. 38, no. 2 (1981), 26–38.

Polish Genealogical Society of America. Though it was not officially founded until 1978, the Polish Genealogical Society of America (PGSA) grew directly out of social and political transformations that gained momentum during the 1960s. The movement for African American civil rights and the ensuing "Black Pride" cultural movement, inspired many other historically marginalized groups, including Polish Americans, to organize their own anti-discrimination efforts and to more explicitly express pride in their own ethnic heritage. At the same time, growing numbers of Americans no longer lived in the same geographic localities as their extended kinship networks. Third- and fourth-generation Polish Americans, for example, were relocating and marrying beyond established Polonian neighborhoods and communities at unprecedented rates. Many Americans, including Polish Americans, longed to revive lost family and ethnic connections, or even create new ones altogether. In 1976, author Alex Haley published *Roots*, a best-selling book that traced seven generations of his family back to West Africa. A television depiction of his work attracted a record number of viewers in 1977. The book and the television series helped spur Americans of all races and ethnicities to seek out and uncover their unknown or incompletely known family histories. Polish Americans were no exceptions to the genealogy "craze" that followed *Roots*. At the same time, other factors such as the publication of Michael Novak's book promoting the "New Ethnicity," **Edward Piszek**'s sponsorship of "Project Pole," increasing anger over the spread of defamatory "Polish jokes," and the increasing prominence of Polish leaders on the world scene—Pope John Paul II, **Zbigniew Brzeziński**, Lech Wałęsa, and the rise of Solidarność—all led to increasing ethnic consciousness among Polish Americans.

When *Roots* became so wildly popular, the library staff at the **Polish Museum of America** was inundated with phone calls from people eager to discover their family histories. The Museum is housed within the historic **Polish Roman Catholic Union of America** building on Milwaukee Avenue in Chicago's earliest Polish neighborhood. One of the Museum's librarians encouraged these callers to join forces, with the Museum sponsoring a genealogy workshop on August 23, 1978. Within two weeks, the participants began to lay the groundwork for a national nonprofit organization devoted to Polish American family history. The PGSA bylaws list **Ed Peckwas**, Lawrence Janowiak, Carol Carlin, Genevieve Wojcik, Joseph Dressel, Betty Guzak, and Edward Piegzik as the founders, with Peckwas elected its first president at the workshop. The Polish Genealogical Society was officially established as an Illinois nonprofit corporation, the words "of America" being added to the name in 1992. Within days of its launch, the organization claimed dues-paying members from almost all fifty states. Its mission was "to collect, disseminate and preserve information on Polish and Polish-American family history and to help its members use that information in their own research." In January 1979, PGSA published the first issue of its official periodical *Rodziny* (Families). The articles from this inaugural bulletin speak of ongoing genealogical concerns, from "Basic Understanding of Polish Names" and "Aids to Research" to "In Search of Grandpa Guzak" and "Konwinskis of Aiken, SC Meet Konwinskis of Gniezno."

From its beginning, PGSA has facilitated research on Polish families both before and after their arrival in the United States. Both areas of research pose large technical challenges and often call on knowledge and skills that the average family history researcher may not possess. For example, Polish immigrants to the U.S. have often been working class persons who left behind less, or less obvious, written documentation of their lives than more privileged people. Surviving records are sometimes in Polish, a language their descendants may not be fluent in or even know at all. Records from the lives of ethnic and religious minority members within Poland, such as Jews or Belarusians, may be in still other languages unknown or little known to their descendants. Languages of occupying powers, such as German and Russian, also appear frequently in historical records. Indeed, immigration records may note a Polish person's original nationality not as Polish but as that of the occupying power in his or her home region. For example, some late nineteenth century immigrants from Poznań are identified as "Prussian."

While immigrants often passed on rich oral histories, sometimes they preferred to speak little or not at all of the economic and political traumas behind their moves to the U.S. Genealogical research and access to necessary records have also been greatly complicated by the complex historical permutations and erasures of the Polish nation itself. Even if one has identified a definite name for an ancestral place, locating it on a map may not be a simple task. The location may have undergone any number of name changes and belonged at different times to different political jurisdictions. Access to the appropriate records within Poland may not have been possible until after the Soviet era. PGSA members have not only identified such frequent barriers to Polish American family history research, they have developed and shared the knowledge and skills necessary to navigate these obstacles.

As of 2008, PGSA received substantial monetary support from its dues-paying members. It was classified by the Internal Revenue Service as a 501(c) (3) tax-exempt nonprofit. Its logo featured the Polish Eagle and the Crown of Poland. The organization had some 2,000 members from throughout the U.S. and ten other countries, including Poland, Great Britain, and Australia. Among PGSA's leaders were Paul Valasek and Jan Lorys, and its part-time volunteer staff continued to operate from and archive their records at the Polish Museum of America Library. The PGSA remained an organization distinct from the Museum, despite their close relationship. For several regularly scheduled hours per week at the Library, PGSA genealogists gave in-person guidance on genealogy research methods to interested members of the public. The emphasis was on teaching family history researchers how to do their own work, rather than having PGSA staff do it for them. PGSA also held quarterly meetings and an annual conference in the Chicago area. It contributed to the burgeoning field of Jewish genealogy, as well as the United Polish Genealogical Society meeting held at the Family History Library, Salt Lake City, Utah, every two years. Along with *Rodziny*, PGSA offered an ever-expanding array of print and electronic publications through its official website at www.pgsa.org. Titles for purchase include *Going Home: A Guide to Polish American Family History*, *Translation Packet*, and *Polish Parish Records of the Roman Catholic Church*. PGSA also made a number of online reference guides and databases available on the website

itself at no charge. These included historical map data from various regions of present-day Poland, as well as indexes of church jubilee books, **Haller's Army** records, and Polish American newspaper death notices. PGSA continued to "encourage its members to communicate with each other and share leads, research sources, and any other information that may prove mutually beneficial." In other words, despite its 1970s founding date and its primary appeal to American-born Polonians, PGSA continued the same spirit of mutual aid that moved so many groups started by and for first-generation immigrants.—*Mary Krane Derr*

SOURCE: Rosalie Lindberg, "Polish Genealogical Society of America (PGSA)," in *The Polish Museum of America Information Guide* (Chicago: Polish Museum of America, 2006), 3.

Polish Heritage Foundation. Established in July 2006 in the Greater Washington Metropolitan Area, its purpose is to promote knowledge of the history of Polish American contributions to American society. Its first president was Andrzej Drozd of Potomac, Maryland, with the Board of Directors comprised of Edwarda Buda, Zbigniew Okreglak, Włodek Lopaczynski and Andrzej Rabczenko. In addition, Mariusz Brymora of the Polish Embassy was instrumental in establishing the goals and initial activities of the Foundation. The goals of the organization are to increase awareness about Poland; to promote and preserve Poland's history, language and culture including dissemination of relevant information about the country; and to promote and preserve Polish heritage and the activities of Polish Americans. The objectives of the Foundation are pursued by means of organizing and supporting research and publication, establishing fellowships at major academic institutions and diverse activities of cultural or scholarly merit in a variety of related fields. These activities are supplemented by a series of the multi-disciplinary events that present all aspects of Polish culture to the public at large. One of its initial activities was sponsorship of a series of concerts and performances of Polish artists in Washington, D.C., and a special event at which Mariusz Brymora unveiled a book commemorating the 400th anniversary of the arrival of the first Polish settlers in **Jamestown**, Virginia.—*Włodek Lopaczynski*

Polish Heritage Publications. A private imprint created by Jacek Galązka when he joined Hippocrene Books as publisher in 1986, its first edition appeared in 1987 in the form of a Polish art calendar featuring thirteen paintings from the **Kosciuszko Foundation**

in New York. In all, thirteen "Polish Heritage Art Calendars" were published (1987–99) and the Polish **Falcons** ordered a special edition of the 1987 calendar to commemorate its 100th anniversary. The calendars for 1988, 1989, and 1990 featured forty Polish paintings in public and private collections in North America, including The **Polish Museum** in Chicago, The Gallery in Orchard Lake, Michigan, and the **Piłsudski Institute** in New York. The 1991 calendar of paintings in the Warsaw National Museum was the first to feature a Polish museum. The next three calendars were illustrated with paintings from museums of Poznań, Kraków, and Lwów. The 1995 edition was the only calendar that was entirely based on a private collection in Warsaw, that of the famous Polish tenor and art collector Wiesław Ochman. The 1996 calendar included paintings from the Polish Museum in Rapperswil, Switzerland, two paintings by **Jan de Rosen** in the Papal Chapel in Castel Gandolfo, and additional works from the Warsaw Museum. The 1997 calendar was based on the Wrocław National Museum. The last two calendars took a different approach; 1998 featuring paintings which celebrated Wilno and 1999, the last in the series, dedicated to Kraków. The series included 165 Polish paintings by some eighty artists, most from the early nineteenth century. Over 150,000 calendars found their way into American homes and just about every Polish American organization, most of them members of the **American Council for Polish Culture**, took part in the promotion and sale of the series. In addition to the calendars, Polish Heritage Publications also issued *Polish Heritage Travel Guide to U.S.A. and Canada* (1992), *American Phrasebook for Poles* (1990, 1993, 1995, 1997), *A Treasury of Polish Aphorisms* (1997), *Song, Dance and Customs of Peasant Poland* (1996), and *The Polish Heritage Songbook* (1990).—*Jacek Galazka*

Polish Highlanders Alliance of North America (Związek Podhalan w Północnej Ameryce; ZPPA). This fraternal organization represents immigrants from the **Podhale** region of Poland. The Związek Podhalan w Północnej Ameryce or ZPPA was founded in 1929 in Chicago as a result of a series of lectures given by the Polish geographer Dr. Stefan Jarosz who encouraged Polish Highlanders (**Górale**) to celebrate and maintain their regional customs. Jarosz, originally from Podhale and educated at the Jagiellonian University in Kraków, was a proponent of the Ruch Podhalański (Highlander) movement. Jarosz electrified audiences in Chicago, the largest settlement of immigrants from Podhale, who responded by creating two important organizations, the Polsko-Amerykańskie Towarzystwo Tartrzańskie (Polish American Tatra Society) in 1928, which was open to all Polish Americans, and the Związek Podahlan w Północnej Ameryce (Polish Highlanders Alliance of North America) the following year. These joined the Związek Podhalan formed in Poland in 1919 as part of the movement to preserve Highlander culture and community. In 1934 the two American organizations merged resulting in the current association, which unites all Górale in North America.

Most Polish Highlanders settled in Chicago. After the original organizational meeting of the ZPPA, six circles or *koło* were quickly organized, four in Chicago, one in Detroit and one in Passaic, New Jersey. Chicago's Jan Sabała Circle is the oldest local koło. Henryk Lokański served as the first president of the national organization with Józef Lopatowski as the first Secretary General. The first national congress or *Sejm* opened on June 8, 1930, with a novena at Sacred Heart of Jesus Church in Chicago's Back of the Yards neighborhood and a meeting at nearby Słowacki Hall (Columbia Hall). These congresses continued to be held at regular intervals in Chicago, where since the 1950s a Dom Podhalan (Podhalan or Highlanders' Hall) has been maintained as the national headquarters. Highlanders' Hall is located on Archer Avenue on the Southwest Side of the city in a building that was turned into a Polish mountain chateau. The organization grew quickly, spreading to Polish Highlander communities across the United States and Canada. By 1979, twenty-one circles had been organized. In 2009, over sixty circles existed, a result of continued migration from Podhale to North America.

The Polish Highlanders Alliance is more than a fraternal insurance company providing help to sick members and the families of the deceased, it actively promotes Highlander culture, music, and dance both in the United States and Poland. Highlander theatrical plays have been performed since the beginning of the ZPPA. The Passaic Circle alone produced more than fifty such events in the first fifty years of its existence. The American organization helped to preserve authentic Polish Highlander folk songs, recording them in the United States for the Victor Label. It has also helped celebrate Podhalan Culture in Poland.

The connection of the Polish Highlanders Alliance in North America with Polish-based Podhale organizations took place almost immediately. In 1928 a representative of the ZPPA attended a convention in Kościelisko, Podhale. In 1934, despite the Great Depres-

sion, members of the ZPPA raised funds to help erect a statue in memory of Władysław Orkan in Nowy Targ, Podhale. Orkan, a great writer and promoter of Podhalan culture in Poland, died in 1930. This link with Podhale has been maintained over the years with the exception of the Stalinist era during which official connections with the Polish Tatra organizations ceased. After Joseph Stalin's death and the establishment of a somewhat more open Polish Communist regime in 1956, the lines of communications were reestablished and have since remained strong. The Górale make up a large and active part of the American **Polonia** maintaining their traditions and dialect across the continents.—*Dominic A. Pacyga*

SOURCES: *Pamiętnik 2-go Sejmu Związku Podhalan w Północnej Ameryce* (Chicago: Polish Highlanders Association, 1933); *Pamiętnik III Sejmu Związku Podhalan w Północnej Ameryce* (Chicago: Polish Highlanders Association, 1935); Thaddeus V. Gromada, "50 Years of the 'Ruch Podhalański' in U.S.A.," *Tartzanski Orzeł*, Vol.32, No. 2 (Summer 1979).

Polish Institute of Arts & Sciences of America (Polski Instytut Naukowy w Ameryce). The outbreak of World War II found several Polish scholars, members of the Polska Akademia Umiejętności (Polish Academy of Arts & Sciences) of Kraków, in the United States. In December 1942, six of these prominent scholars—anthropologist **Bronisław Malinowski**, historians **Oskar Halecki** and Jan Kucharzewski, literary historian **Wacław Lednicki**, chemist Wojciech Swiętoslawski, and historian of Ancient Roman law Rafał Taubenschlag—met in New York City to found The Polish Institute of Arts & Sciences in America (PIASA) to assure the continuity of Poland's intellectual and cultural development. Supported initially by the Polish government-in-exile in London, and led by its initial executive director, Oskar Halecki (1942–52), the organization operated as an academy-in-exile, an outpost of the prestigious Kraków institution that was forcibly closed by the German occupiers. The Institute's first president was the prominent anthropologist Bronisław Malinowski. Upon his early death in 1942 he was succeeded by Jan Kucharzewski (1942–52); Oskar Halecki (1952–64); Zygmunt Nagorski, Sr. (1964–65); Stanisław Mrozowski (1965–74); **John A. Gronouski** (1974–87); **Feliks Gross** (1988–99); **Piotr S. Wandycz** (1999–2008); and **Thaddeus V. Gromada** (2008–).

Instead of independence and a return to democracy, the end of World War II brought to Poland a communist dominated regime under firm Soviet control. When the Polska Akademia Umiejętności was reestablished in Kraków under communist control in January

1945, members of the Institute elected not to return to their shackled homeland but to remain in America to oppose communist rule in Poland. At the same time, they refused to place PIASA under the jurisdiction of its former parent organization in Kraków, with Halecki declaring that he preferred to face serious financial difficulties rather than give up the Institute's full freedom and independence. Thus, on June 22, 1945, PIASA amended its charter in the State of New York and became an independent American corporation. From that point through 1989, PIASA scrupulously avoided any official contacts with the "Polish People's Republic" so as not to give it any semblance of legitimacy or recognition. It did not hesitate to speak out forcefully and protest in defense of academic freedom and human rights in Poland whenever warranted during the Cold War era. Since 1956, however, individual members of the Institute visited Poland to do research or to attend scholarly or scientific conferences. Between 1942 and 1946, the Institute published its proceedings in a quarterly *Bulletin of the Polish Institute of Arts and Sciences*, and in 1956 it began publishing **The Polish Review**, a multi-disciplinary scholarly journal devoted to Polish studies. First edited by Stanisław Skrzypek (1956), its succeeding editors were **Ludwik Krzyżanowski** (1956–86), **Stanisław Baranczak** (1986–90), Joseph E. Wieczerzak (1991–2008), and Charles S. Kraszewski (2008–).

During the 1970s, the Institute began to shed its image as a Polish émigré organization. Some of the younger émigrés, veterans of the Polish armed-forces-in-exile who refused to return to communist dominated Poland, completed their higher education at American universities in the 1950s and eventually gravitated to PIASA. Although there were very few American-born members in the Institute's ranks during the first two decades of its existence, that began to change in the 1960s when the children of early Polish immigrants entered academia and were elected to PIASA membership. Eventually, these Polish Americans rose to positions of leadership. In 1972, PIASA affiliated with the American Association for the Advancement of Slavic Studies (AAASS) which broadened its contacts with other scholars working in fields of Slavic studies, and in 1978 the Institute's annual meetings were transformed into scholarly conferences following the model used by other American academic societies.

The trend toward Americanization of the Institute was reinforced by the election of John A. Gronouski as the first American-born president of PIASA on April 14, 1974. Before assuming the presidency Gronouski, Dean of the Lyndon B. Johnson School of Public Affairs at the University of Texas at Austin, had served as Postmaster General in John F. Kennedy's administration and U.S. Ambassador to Poland under Lyndon B. Johnson. Although supporting the Institute's traditional mission to preserve and disseminate Poland's historical, cultural, and intellectual heritage, Gronouski also advocated that more attention be paid to **Polonia** as the Institute's natural constituency and that it become more concerned with issues in American mainstream society. These views were supported by Feliks Gross, Professor Emeritus of Sociology at Brooklyn College CUNY, who was elected Executive Director in 1975, and by his successor, Thaddeus V. Gromada, Professor of History at Jersey City State College. During this period PIASA began to attract the attention and support of the Rockefeller Foundation, the National Endowment for the Humanities, and other private and public foundations. The former provided a substantial grant for a "Sociological-Historical Research Project on the Polish American Ethnic Group," and later provided funding for the organization and preservation of the Institute's archives and launch its Oral History project.

The dramatic events occasioned by the rise of Solidarność (Solidarity) in Poland, and particularly the imposition of martial law in December 1981, led to creation of a "Committee to Aid Polish Scholars" (1981–88) and to close cooperation with the National Endowment for Democracy to aid people in the Solidarity movement. The eventual collapse of communism in Poland in 1989 finally led to a normalization of relations between the Institute, the Polish government, and academic and cultural organizations in Poland. Particularly important was the reestablishment of relations with the Polska Akademia Umiejętności, including the exchange of formal visits and the opening of a symbolic station of the Akademia in PIASA's Manhattan headquarters. In 2000, PIASA held its 58th Annual Meeting in Kraków in cooperation with the Akademia and the Jagiellonian University, an event that was hailed in the Polish media as a triumphant return to the PIASA's Kraków roots.

In 2010, PIASA was a non-profit, 501(c) tax exempt, academic and cultural organization with a mission to advance knowledge about Poland and Polish Americans and to serve as a liaison between American and Polish academic circles. From its headquarters in the Murray Hill section of New York City, the Institute maintains a specialized reference library of over 25,000 volumes and valuable archival collections, publishes books under the "PIASA Books" imprint, conducts an annual awards

program, manages a yearly scholarly conference, and organizes lectures, authors evenings, and art exhibits.— *Thaddeus V. Gromada*

SOURCES: Stanisław Strzetelski, *Polish Institute of Arts & Sciences in America: Origins and Development* (New York: Polish Institute of Arts & Sciences, 1960); Frank Mocha, "The Polish Institute of Arts and Sciences in America, Its Contributions to the Study of Polonia: The Origins of the Polish American Historical Association," in Frank Mocha, ed., *Poles in America: Bicentennial Essays* (Stevens Point, WI: Worzalla Publishing Company, 1978), 709–24; Stanisław Flis, "The Archives of the Polish Institute of Arts & Sciences of America," *Polish American Studies*, Vol. 60, no. 1 (2003), 81–90; Thaddeus V. Gromada, "The Polish Institute in Historical Perspective: 1942–2005," *The Polish Review*, Vol. 50, no. 4 (2005), 425–33; Thaddeus V. Gromada, "Polish Institute The First 50 Years: An Historical Survey," *PIASA's 50th Anniversary Album* (New York: Polish Institute of Arts & Sciences, 1993).

Polish Institute of Science and Culture, Inc. *see* **Polish University Abroad.**

Polish Joke. Generations of Polish Americans have encountered the Polish joke, a large genre of ethnic insults also known as the "Polack joke." The term "Polack" originated in mockery of the word *Polak*, meaning in Polish a male Pole. Polish Americans consider "Polack" a derogatory term, especially from non–Polish mouths, just as African Americans consider the "n-word" a derogatory term, especially from non–Black mouths. **Mary Patrice Erdmans** names the Polish joke "a vestige of the racist eugenic theories of the early twentieth century" and a symbol of the "stupidity, vulgarity, racism, anti–Semitism, illiteracy, and filth" attributed to Polish Americans. Garland Allen identifies the Polish joke as a legacy of eugenics, which "help[ed] reinforce or create class divisions during the most intense period of the labor conflict in United States history." This was also a period of heightened immigration, including Polish immigration. Among other punitive actions against "inferior" groups, eugenicists sought to restrict immigrants instead of altering or replacing social institutions that excluded the newcomers. Folklorist Roger Welsch argues that the Polish joke is one form of the "American numskull tale," which "probably represents a reaction to the imagined threats posed by a sudden influx of an immigrant group at a particular point in history." A previous American numskull tale was the "Pat and Mike" joke that became rampantly popular in the mid–nineteenth century with the influx of refugees from An Gorta Mór, Ireland's Great Hunger.

The African American civil rights movement of the 1960s inspired many other marginalized groups, including Polish Americans, to take pride in their own unique cultural identities and assert their own human rights. As part of this social transformation, ethnic

jokes of all varieties came under increasingly greater scrutiny and challenge. However, as it became more socially unacceptable to tell Black jokes, many Americans simply retold these as Polish jokes. They even justified their actions on the grounds that it was non-racist and sophisticated to target Polish Americans instead of other ethnic groups for ridicule. Polish Americans who objected were often told that they lacked a sense of humor and the ability to laugh at themselves. Eugene Obidinski understood this intensification of ethnic "humor" against Polish Americans to be "symbolic aggression," a more socially acceptable but still harmful substitute for the "sticks and stones of the past," which included spitting and other, more violent and humiliating physical assaults.

Polish Americans reacted in a variety of ways to the redoubled popularity of the Polish joke. Polish Americans with multigenerational roots in the community often regarded the Polish joke as a significant irritant or threat. Yet more recent arrivals often felt that **Polonia** faced more pressing concerns. Some Polish Americans responded to the Polish joke like Angel, a participant in Mary Patrice Erdman's study *The Grasinki Girls*. Angel said she did not get offended because "wherever I've worked, I've always managed to convince them that I was much smarter than they were." Unlike Stanley Kowalski, the stereotypical anti-hero of Tennessee Williams' play *A Streetcar Named Desire*, Angel did not feel compelled to the "defensive moan, 'I am not a Polack ... I am a hundred percent American!'" While such a strategy for coping with the Polish joke may speak of ethnic and personal self-confidence and dignity, it also may speak of social pressure to prove that one does not measure down to the stereotypes. Responses like Angel's may only underscore the insistence of **James S. Pula** that the Polish joke was "far from harmless. The constant derision, often publicly disseminated through the mass media, caused serious identity crises, feelings of inadequacy, and low self-esteem for many Polish Americans."

The mass media did indeed tell Polish jokes on a very wide scale, particularly during the 1960s and early 1970s. In 1965, the book *It's Fun to be a Polak* was published, although it was withdrawn when Polonians objected. Many of the era's best-known entertainers engaged in anti–Polish routines, including Steve Allen, Morey Amsterdam, Carol Burnett, Johnny Carson, Phyllis Diller, Dean Martin, Don Rickles, Joan Rivers, Rowan and Martin, and Frank Sinatra. For example, in 1968 Carol Burnett performed a skit on CBS-TV about a "Slavic" airplane with dirty flight attendants and an oafish pilot. Highly popular television sitcoms of the period regularly featured characters who perpetuated Polish-joke stereotypes. *All in the Family*'s Archie Bunker famously castigated his Polish American son-in-law as a "meathead." *Laverne and Shirley* included a none-too-bright character named Lenny Kosnowski, who fancied himself to be "89th in line to the Polish throne."

Anti-defamation groups such as the **Polish American Congress** monitored and protested these "comic" ethnic insults, but non–Poles did not always fathom how to make amends. For example, when challenged to offer positive rather than negative images of Polish Americans, NBC-TV responded ineptly with the short-lived series *Banacek* starring George Peppard. On the one hand, the title character, a Polish American detective, was highly intelligent and indeed sought after for his ability to puzzle out difficult-to-solve disappearances and thefts. On the other hand, Banacek's name was spelled in the Czech rather than the Polish fashion. His trademark was the utterance of fake "old Polish proverbs" such as "if you're not sure it's potato Borscht, there could be orphans working in the mine."

During the late 1970s and early 1980s, globally broadcast events ushered in a new and much-welcomed phase in the history of the Polish joke. In 1978, the learned and charismatic Cardinal of Kraków, Karol Józef Wojtyła, became Pope John Paul II, the first Pole ever to head the Roman Catholic Church. The Gdańsk shipyard strikes of 1980 marked the birth of the Solidarność movement under the leadership of another compelling figure, Lech Wałęsa. The mass media could not help but showcase the very qualities of Polish culture, such as intellectual prowess and passionate concern for social justice, that were absent from the stereotypes expressed in the Polish joke. To the delight of many Polish Americans, there ensued a sudden and lasting dropoff in the Polish joke's popularity. At the same time, Polonians were moved to their own triumphant remasterings of the Polish joke, as folklorist Lydia Fish documented in examples like the following. "Did you hear about the Pope's first decree? Wafers of kielbasa will now be used for Communion. Instead of using wine in the Mass now they're using a shot and a beer."

In a special report to the *New York Times*, Michael T. Kaufman suddenly discovered that the "real Polish jokes" told in Poland were witty and intelligent commentaries on the shortcomings of the Soviet-dominated regime. These jokes expressed the very same creative spirit of resistance that led to that regime's downfall by the end of the 1980s. A member of the "Solidarność" wave of immigrants, Jaga Urban-Klaehn, recalls that "thanks to these jokes Poles were able to release their tension, stress and a feeling of frustration with the Communistic system." After her arrival in the U.S., Urban-Klaehn was "stunned" to read an old ethnic joke book from the 1970s and discover that "the so-called 'Polish jokes' were exactly like the policemen jokes we had laughed at in Poland! The word 'a policeman' was just replaced by 'a Pole.' Did we laugh at ourselves through all these years? Hard to give a simple and straightforward answer."

Although it undeniably waned, the Polish joke did persist into the opening years of the twenty-first century. David Ives' 2003 drama *Polish Joke* occasioned bitter controversy. The playwright — born David Roszkowski into a working-class Polish family on Chicago's South Side — characterized his work as a comic depiction of ethnic stereotypes and the quest for self-acceptance. Yet the iconographer Marek Czarnecki characterized *Polish Joke* as "a vehicle" for the playwright's "own self-hatred as a Polish-American and lack of connection to his own deep patrimony, which is used only as an occasion for ridicule." In 2007, a character on Fox-TV's *Back to You* uttered the line, "Bowling is in your Polish blood, like kielbasa and collaborating with the Nazis." Protesters informed Fox of massive Polish resistance to the Nazi occupation. While Fox apologized and promised not to re-air the clip, it also insisted that the offensive line came from an "ignorant" and "clueless" character.

On February 19, 2007, the *New Yorker* magazine published a cartoon that depicted one child telling another: "My parents named me Zbigniew because they were drunk." When Polonians expressed their outrage over the cartoon, the *New Yorker* denied that it had committed any ethnic slur. On July 21, 2008, the *New Yorker*'s cover depicted soon-to-be President Barack Hussein Obama, as a "Muslim terrorist" and his wife Michelle Obama as a gun-toting "Black militant." When African Americans and the Obama campaign itself objected, the *New Yorker* again denied — tellingly — that it was guilty of any ethnic slur. African Americans, Polish Americans, and other minority ethnic groups had made undeniable strides. Yet, as these incidents showed, racism and jokes originating in and perpetuating it were hardly dead. — *Mary Krane Derr*

SOURCES: Garland E. Allen, "Radical Politics and Marxism in the History of Science," in Garland E. Allen, ed., *Science, History, and Social Activism: A Tribute to Everett Mendelsohn* (Boston: Kluwer Academic Publishers, 2002); Joe Babcock, "'Polish Joke' Leads to Anger vs. Magazine," *New York Daily News*, February 22, 2007; John Bukowczyk, *And My Children Did Not Know Me: A History of the Polish Americans* (Bloomington: Indiana University Press, 1987); Mary Patrice Erdmans, *The Grasinki Girls: The Choices They Had and the Choices They Made* (Athens, OH: Ohio University Press, 2004); Mary Patrice Erdmans, *Opposite Poles: Immigrants and Ethnics in Polish Chicago, 1976–1990* (University Park: Pennsylvania State University Press, 1998); Lydia Fish, "Is the Pope Polish? Some Notes on the Polack Joke in Transition," *Journal of American Folklore*, Vol. 93, No. 370 (October/December 1980), 450–54; Lara Foley, "Eugenics," in Judith A. Baer, ed., *Historical and Multicultural Encyclopedia of Women's Reproductive Rights in the United States* (Westport, CT: Greenwood Press, 2002), 77–78; Richard Huff, "Shamed Fox Apologizes for Polish Slur on *Back to You*," *New York Daily News*, November 21, 2007; Michael T. Kaufman, "Real Polish Jokes Thrive in Real Polish Socialism," *New York Times*, May 11, 1986, 10; Eugene Obidinski, "American Polonia: Sacred and Profane Aspects," *Polish American Studies*, Vol. 32, no. 1 (Spring 1975), 5–18; James S. Pula, *Polish Americans: An Ethnic Community* (New York: Twayne, 1995); Jaga Urban-Klaehn, "Political Jokes in Poland versus Polish Jokes in America," *Polish American Journal*, October 2007; Roger L. Welsch, "American Numskull Tales: The Polack Joke," *Western Folklore*, Vol. 26, no. 3 (July 1967), 183–86.

Polish League (1894; Liga Polska). This early attempt to form a unified federation of Polish immigrant societies was the brainchild of two men, the Rev. **Wincenty Barzyński** and **Erazm Jerzmanowski**. Barzyński was pastor of the enormous St. Stanislaus Kostka Parish in Chicago, head of the **Order of the Resurrection**, and the dominant figure in the **Polish Roman Catholic Union** of America fraternal society. Jerzmanowski lived in New York. He was a Polish exile and an early **Polonia** industrialist, inventor, and philanthropist who in the 1880s had become a tireless supporter of the **Polish National Alliance**, the main rival of Barzyński and the PRCUA. The two agreed to create a single national organization whose mission was to unite the many Polish parishes and secular societies in the small but rapidly growing immigrant community. At first their efforts won much favor, and numerous PNA leaders expressed enthusiasm for the idea. But PNA Censor **Theodore Helinski** objected strongly to the Polish League and his view prevailed. At the first convention of the Polish League in May 1894, a meeting attended by some 233 delegates, the PNA members in attendance expressed their objections to the organization, which was largely responsible for its disappearance by 1896. PNA opposition to the Polish League focused on the belief that formal representation in the League too greatly favored the parishes, to the disadvantage of the fraternals, and the belief that the League's mission placed too much of a focus on the internal needs of the immigrant community and too little attention on the cause of Polish independence. Most significant, however, was the distrust many PNA leaders had regarding Barzyński's true motives which they suspected were to use the League to dominate **Polonia** and the PNA, a consequence of years of bitter rivalry between the "Catholic" and "nationalist" wings in the community. Despite a series of substantial efforts to create an all-inclusive civic action federation in Polonia in the years after the failure of the Polish League, it was not until the Second World War (1939–45) that this goal was actually realized, first through the creation of the Rada Polonii (or **Polish American Council**, a charitable federation) in 1939, and the **Polish American Congress**, a political action organization, in 1944.—*Donald E. Pienkos*

SOURCES: Donald Pienkos, *PNA: A Centennial History of the Polish National Alliance of the United States of North America* (Boulder, CO: East European Monographs, 1984); Wacław Kruszka, *A History of the Poles in America to 1908* (Washington, D.C.: The Catholic University of America Press, 1993), Vol. 1; Stefan Barszczewski, *Związek Narodowy Polski w Stanach Zjednoczonych Ameryki Północnej* (Chicago: Druk. Zgody, 1894); Stanisław Osada, *Historja Związku Narodowego Polskiego i rozwój ruchu narodowego Polskiego w Ameryce Północnej: w dwudziestga piąta rocznice zalozenia Związku* (Chicago: Nakladem i drukiem Związku Narodowego Polskiego, 1905); Mieczysław Haiman, *Zjednoczenie Rzymsko-Katolickie w Ameryce, 1873–1948* (Chicago: Zjednoczenie Polskie Rzymsko-Katolickie w Ameryce, 1948); Andrzej Brożek, *Polish Americans 1854–1939* (Warsaw: Interpress, 1985).

Polish Legion (31st New York Volunteer Infantry).

Organized largely from the New York City metropolitan area under the leadership of Col. Calvin Pratt, the regiment, nicknamed the "Montezuma Regiment," left the state to join the Union troops guarding Washington, D.C., on June 24, 1861. Serving first in Franklin's Division, then the First Corps, and beginning May 1862 in the Sixth Corps, the regiment fought at the First Battle of Bull Run, the Seven Days Battles, Antietam, Fredericksburg, Chancellorsville, and several other smaller skirmishes before being mustered out at the completion of its two years of service at New York City on June 4, 1863. During its service the regiment lost 71 officers and men killed, 168 wounded and 140 missing, an aggregate loss of 379. Company C of the regiment, raised by Capt. **Alexander Raszewski**, was composed largely of Polish volunteers and was sometimes referred to as the "Polish Legion" because Raszewski had been recruiting a unit under that name for service in the Union Army when his men were consolidated with other unfinished units to form the 31st New York. Raszewski was eventually promoted to major. The other officers who served in Company C were Capt. Louis Domanski, 1st Lt. Vincent Kochanowski, 1st Lt. Theodore F. Rich, 1st Lt. Louis Solyon, 2nd Lt. Valentine Wawelski, and 2nd Lt. Julius Ehrhard. Following the First Battle of Bull Run in August 1861, the regiment's col-

This drawing of the Polish Legion (31st New York) appeared in a German newspaper during the Civil War. Note the square-cornered Polish military hat (*PMA*).

onel wrote that then Captain Raszewski and First Lieutenant Domanski were among those "to whose coolness and judgment I am indebted." Company C wore distinctive four-cornered hats modeled on the Polish *rogatywka*. A drawing of the uniform and cap that appeared in the German press is often attributed to Col. **Włodzimierz B. Krzyżanowski**'s 58th New York, but was actually an illustration of Company C, 31st New York.—*James S. Pula*

Polish Legion (58th New York Volunteer Infantry).

On August 20, 1861, in an effort to raise troops quickly during the American Civil War, the War Department authorized **Włodzimierz B. Krzyżanowski** to raise a regiment of infantry that he planned to call the "United States Rifles." When his unit did not complete its organization, it was combined with three other incomplete units to form the 58th New York Volunteer Infantry. One of the units with which it was combined was a force being raised by Julian Allen which he called the "Polish Legion." Although Krzyżanowski became colonel on the basis of having enrolled more men than the other recruiters, the regiment eventually adopted the "Polish Legion" moniker. The regiment consisted mainly of immigrants and their sons, the majority being German but with a wide mixture of other nationalities including men from Poland, France, Italy, and other European nations. It left the state on November 7, 1861, and was assigned to Gen. Ludwig Blenker's "German" division composed of regiments that were mainly German in character. Under Blenker

the regiment fought at Cross Keys on June 8, 1862, where it received favorable comments from its brigade and division commanders. Assigned to the First Corps, Army of Virginia, with Krzyżanowski elevated to brigade command, the regiment fought under Gen. Franz Sigel along the Rappahannock River and at Second Bull Run in August 1862, again acquitting itself well. In September it became part of the Eleventh Corps of the Army of the Potomac, serving with it in the Union disaster at Chancellorsville where the 58th New York and 26th Wisconsin, under Krzyżanowski's direct command, held the crucial right flank of the Union line for vital minutes that allowed the successful withdrawal of artillery and wagons when the Union position was overrun by "Stonewall" Jackson's flanking attack on May 2, 1863. Two months later it fought at Gettysburg where it helped to hold the key Union position on Cemetery Hill. Following Gettysburg the regiment was sent west to help relieve the Confederate sieges of Chattanooga and Knoxville. When the Eleventh and Twelfth Corps were merged in the spring of 1864, the 58th New York, by this time greatly reduced in strength because of its difficult service, was assigned to guard federal railroads and supply lines in Northern Alabama and Southeastern Tennessee. During its service the regiment lost four officers and 28 enlisted men killed or mortally wounded; three officers and 60 enlisted men died from disease or accident; five officers and 63 enlisted men wounded; three officers and 38 enlisted men missing.—*James S. Pula*

SOURCE: James S. Pula, *For Liberty and Justice: The Life and Times of Brigadier General Włodzimierz B. Krzyżanowski, 1824–1887* (Utica, NY: Ethnic Heritage Studies Center, Utica College, 2008).

Polish Legion of American Veterans, U. S. A. (PLAV).

Following World War I, veterans throughout the United States began to organize to keep their mutual bond of patriotic national service alive and promote friendships with other comrades-in-arms. Most prominent among the founding organizations was the Alliance of American Veterans of Polish Extraction of the State of Michigan headquartered in **Hamtramck**, MI; the Alliance of American Veterans of Polish Extraction headquartered in Chicago, IL, and operating in Illinois, Ohio, and Wisconsin; and the Polish Legion of the American Army headquartered in Brooklyn, NY, and operating in New York and New Jersey. Representatives of these three organizations met in Cleveland, OH, September 5–7, 1931, out of which emerged the Polish Legion of American Veterans with Stanley Halick serving as its first national commander. The new organization

The Polish Legion of American Veterans on parade in Milwaukee, 1920s (*UWM*).

adopted the non-profit charter of the Michigan group and, with some alterations, its constitution and by-laws, and adopted an organizational emblem. The latter was altered in September 1946 to include the World War II Victory medal in deference to the new veterans joining its ranks. At its Ninth National Convention in September 1948 the letters "U.S.A." were added to the organization's name. In 1957 the PLAV began publication of *The National PLAV News*, and ten years later the national commander and five other PLAV members were invited to act as technical advisors to the U.S. Veterans Advisory Commission. In November 1974 the PLAV became an associate member of the National Veterans Day Committee, and on December 2, 1978, the Service Officers of the PLAV were recognized officially as "Claims Agents" for the processing of veterans claims before the Veterans Administration Appeals Board. On July 23, 1984, President Ronald Reagan signed an act of Congress granting a federal charter to the Polish Legion of American Veterans, U.S.A. In 1992 the PLAV dropped its ethnic requirement for membership.

Dating its origin from the initial meeting in **Falcons** Hall in Chicago in 1920 that formed the original Alliance of American Veterans of Polish Extraction, the PLAV celebrated its 75th anniversary in 1995 by acting as host for the National Veterans Day Observance at Arlington National Cemetery on November 11. During the 1990s it joined other veterans organizations in a concerted effort to assure continuing veterans benefits for those who had served their country, especially speaking out against the closure of veterans hospitals and other facilities. In 2009, the mailing address of the PLAV national headquarters was P.O. Box 42024, Washington, D.C., 20015.—*Joseph L. Pudlo, Jr.*

SOURCE: *The History of the Polish Legion of American Veterans, U.S.A.: Chartered by Act of Congress: 1920–2003* (n.p.: Polish Legion of American Veterans, 2003).

Polish Mechanics Association of America (Stowarzyszenie Mechaników Polskich w Ameryce). One of the most important industrial achievements of the American **Polonia** at the beginning of the 1920s, the Polish Mechanics Association of America was one of many organizations created after World War I with the intention of transferring its activities to Poland. With the reestablishment of Polish independence following World War I, there was a tendency among many Poles living in America to return to Poland. Among their slogans was "Our profits and dividends will be a rich and happy Poland." Among the approximately 200 Polish American industrial and entrepreneurial corporations and cooperatives that were established during this period, the PMA was the largest and the economically strongest. Created in Toledo, Ohio, in 1919, by **Aleksander Gwiazdowski**, the association had strong ties with socialist circles and the Polish **National Defense Committee**. Its budget amounted to $3 million in capital. In 1921 the number of members reached 18,343, with about 1,000 of them returning to Poland. Having transferred its activity to Poland, PMA bought tool, lathe, and machine plants in Pruszków, Warsaw, and Zawiercie (Poręba), as well as the steelworks and enameled dish plant in Wyszków. It also owned a PMA Bank in Warsaw (which went bankrupt in 1924), two brickworks in Bydgoszcz, and a technical school in Pruszków. The company published a professional journal called *Mechanik* until 1927. It also had shares in the New York daily newspaper *Nowy Świat* (New World). In 1923 the entire company moved to Poland, changing its name to the Polish Mechanics Association from America. In the second half of the 1920s, due to conflicts among the shareholders and board of directors, as well as difficulties in the stock market, PMA went through a crisis. It survived thanks to the intervention of the Polish Commercial Bank and the help of the government. Beginning with the 1920s, a number of the most renowned engineers specializing in the machine tool in-

The John Robak Post PLAV band, 1930s (*Eugene E. Dziedzic*).

dustry cooperated with the PMA. The outbreak of World War II in 1939 brought a halt to the organization's activities.—*Adam Walaszek*

SOURCE: Adam Walaszek, "Stowarzyszenie Mechaników Polskich w Ameryce, 1919–1945," *Przegląd Polonijny*, Vol. 12, no. 2 (1986).

Polish Medical Society. Established in 1946, the purpose of the Society was to facilitate social and professional relations along with improving the status of Polish émigré physicians in American institutions. It is a charitable, non-profit, tax-exempt organization. In the 1960s and 1970s its activities included various publications, erection and maintenance of the Nicholas Copernicus monument in Chicago, and celebration of the millennium of Poland. These led to better recognition of Polish science and culture in the United States. A member organization of the Chicago Medical Society, the Polish American Congress, and the Federation of Polish Physician Organizations Abroad, the Society plays a key role in supporting Polish medical emigration to the U.S. Its members represent various medical specialties and many are professors at Chicago area universities. Over the years the Society has organized fundraisers for charitable causes including two Educational Funds of the Polish American Medical Society, medical assistance for needy Poles during martial law in Poland, and donations to the **Polish Museum of America**, the **Lira Ensemble**, the **Polish American Association**, A Gift of the Heart Foundation, victims of floods in Poland in 1997 and 2001, the Charitable Foundation of the **Polish American Congress**, and the **Kosciuszko Foundation**. The Society also organizes the prestigious annual Physicians' Ball, picnics, alpine skiing and tennis competitions, and participates in local actions for **Polonia**; but, most importantly, it unites and represents medical, dental, and veterinarians of Polish descent. In 2009 the Society had over 400 members. Founded by its first president, Bolesław Zietak, its succeeding presidents were Aleksander Rytel, Władysław Cebulski, Barbara Roniker, Józef Mazurek, Marek Gawrysz, Anna Szpindor, and Bronisław Orawiec.—*Anna Szpindor*

SOURCE: *History of the Polish Medical Society of Chicago 1915–1966* (Chicago: Polish Medical Society, 1966).

Polish Microfilm Project. In August 1971 the **Alfred Jurzykowski Foundation** provided a grant of $10,000 in response to a proposal to preserve Polish-language newspapers published in the U.S. The project, proposed jointly by the **Kosciuszko Founda-**tion, the **Polish Institute of Arts and Science of America**, and the Immigration History Research Center at the University of Minnesota, received equal matching funds from the National Endowment for the Humanities. In succeeding years Polish Americans contributed an additional $45,000 which was also matched by the NEH, providing funding that made possible the microfilming of a wide variety of newspapers that would otherwise have been largely inaccessible and eventually deteriorated to the point where they would no longer be available for researchers. The project was administered by the Immigration History Research Center.—*James S. Pula*

SOURCE: Edward V. Kolyszko, "Preserving the Polish Heritage in America: The Polish Microfilm Project," *Polish American Studies*, Vol. 32, no. 1 (1975), 59–63.

Polish Museum of America. Established in 1935 by the **Polish Roman Catholic Union of America**, the Polish Museum of America (PMA) is one of the oldest ethnic museums in America and is believed to be the largest museum devoted to a single ethnic group. The PMA opened on January 12, 1937, with a mission to promote Polish culture and document the history and culture of Poles and Polish Americans. The prominent early **Polonia** historian and collector **Mieczysław Haiman** was appointed its first curator, archivist, and chief librarian, and under his direction the Museum quickly became the most important repository of Polonia-related archival materials in the United States. Among the PMA's collections are paintings, sculptures, and other art works from renowned Polish and Polonia artists; folk costumes and handicrafts including a large collection of *pisanki* (decorated Easter eggs); an extensive coin collection; a wide variety of historical documents and rare books dating to the fourteenth century; nearly a thousand jubilee books from Roman Catholic parishes; the recruiting records of the **Polish Army in France**; a major collection of costumes, documents, and artifacts belonging to the Shakespearean actress **Helena Modjeska**; the largest collection of materials on **Ignacy Jan Paderewski**; and major collections of documents relating to **Tadeusz Kościuszko** and **Kazimierz Pułaski**. The museum also sponsors a wide variety of cultural activities including museum exhibitions, lectures, art exhibits, films, musical recitals, and the annual **Pułaski Day** celebrations for the city of Chicago. The library contains over 60,000 books and 250 periodicals in Polish and English. The PMA is located at 984 North Milwaukee Avenue, and its web site can be accessed at www.polishmuseumofamerica.org. In 2010, the Museum's president was Maria Cieśla and the chair of its Executive committee was Wallace M. Ozog.—*James S. Pula*

SOURCES: *The Polish Museum of America—History and Collections—Guide* (Warsaw: Argraf, 2003); Richard Kujawa and Joann Ozog, *The Polish Museum of America: Information Guide* (Chicago: Polish Museum of America, 2006); *The Polish Museum of America Library (1915–2005), 90 Years of Service* (Chicago: Polish Museum of America, 2005); Sabina P. Logisz, *Fiftieth Anniversary, 1935–1985: Polish Museum of America* (Chicago: Polish Museum of America, 1985); Jan Loryś, "The Polish Museum of America," *Polish American Studies*, Vol. 60, no. 1 (2003), 23–25; Stephan S. Grabowski, "P.R.C.U. Archives and Museum in Chicago," *Polish American Studies*, Vol. 18, no. 1 (1961), 37–40.

Polish Museum of America and Polish Roman Catholic Union of America offices, 1930s (*PMA*).

Polish Music Center. The Polish Music Center (PMC) was established in 1985 as the Polish Music Reference Center at the University of Southern California (USC) in Los Angeles through an endowment given by Dr. **Stefan** and **Wanda Wilk**. Renamed the Polish Music Center in 2000, it houses the largest public collection of Polish music materials in the U.S., and is the only such collection at an American university devoted exclusively to Polish music. It contains approximately 10,000 items, including books, scores, manuscripts, recordings, periodicals, documents, and other items related to Polish music, with a primary focus on contemporary music. In cooperation with the USC community, the PMC organizes concerts and music festivals, and publishes the Polish Music History book series, a monthly online newsletter, and the *Polish Music Journal* (1998–2003). Launched in 1994, the Polish Music Center website contains biographies and catalogues of works, recordings and repertoire by Polish composers, as well as articles on the history of Polish music and dance. Initially a part of the USC Music Library, the PMC Collection was moved into its own space in October 1987 and became associated with the Thornton School of Music. Appointed by the Music School Dean, Wanda Wilk served as the first Director of the PMC. In this capacity she lectured at the Los Angeles Music Center, local universities, music organizations and Polish American associations, including the **American Council of Polish Cultural Clubs**. Under the auspices of the Friends of Polish Music, a fundraising and outreach group established by Wanda Wilk in 1981, Wilk wrote the first monograph, *Karol Szymanowski* (1982), in the Polish Music History Series (PMHS). Published by the Polish Music Center in conjunction with Figueroa Press, the series includes (as of 2008) ten volumes on subjects such as Grażyna Bacewicz, Polish music since Chopin, the vocal music of Karol Szymanowski, Maria Szymanowska, and **Zygmunt Stojowski**, among others. Wanda Wilk also initiated the unique PMC manuscript collection by soliciting gifts of original scores from Witold Lutosławski and **Stanisław Skrowaczewski** in 1984. Today, the PMC has one of the world's most important collections of manuscripts by modern Polish composers, including works by Bacewicz, Baird, Laks, Meyer, Penderecki, **Ptaszyńska**, Schaeffer, and Tansman, among many others. Donated in 2005, the manuscript collection also includes the archives of Sigismond and Luisa Stojowski and the newly discovered manuscripts of symphonic music by **Henry Wars**. In 1982 the Wilks established a competition for the best English-language essays on Polish music. The Wilk Essay Prize for Research in Polish Music and the Wilk Book Prize for Research in Polish Music were given until 2002; winners included Stephen Downes, Jeffrey Kallberg, Martina Homma, James Parakilas, Sandra Rosenblum, and others. Wilk retired as the Director of the PMC in 1996, but continued as the Honorary Director and President of the Friends of Polish Music. Wilk was succeeded as director by Dr. Maria Anna Harley (Maja Trochimczyk) who initiated several new programs and events, including establishing the Henryk Górecki residency (1997), enlarging the manuscript collection, creating and serving as editor-in-chief of the online *Polish Music Journal*, and improving the PMC website. In 2002, Trochimczyk established the Annual Paderewski Lecture–Recital series designed to introduce prominent Polish composers and musicians to audiences in Southern California. Marek Żebrowski, a pianist and composer with a distinguished worldwide concert and academic career, became the director in 2004. His experience as a performer and concert organizer led to performances at USC by some of the most prominent composers and interpreters of Polish music, and their collaborations with USC students and Southern California musicians. Żebrowski re-established the Paderewski Festival in Paso Robles, CA, in 2006 and facilitated relationships with music festivals, competitions, and government institutions in Poland. In 2007, he spearheaded the effort to bring a monument to Paderewski to the USC campus, paving the way for the donation of the Paso Robles Paderewski Collection to the University in 2008. Żebrowski served as editor-in-chief of the PMHS. He also published *Paderewski in California* (2009). The full-time position of PMC Manager and Librarian was created in 2004, as the PMC was reorganized and moved into a new space in Stonier Hall on the USC campus. Krysta Close, a graduate of the USC Vocal Arts Program who has concertized throughout the United States, currently serves at PMC Manager and Librarian, overseeing website and collection maintenance, the monthly newsletter production, preparation of concert programs, and other administrative tasks. The PMC also relies on part-time work-study students to assist in its operations.—*Krysta Close* and *Marek Zebrowski*

SOURCES: *About the Polish Music Center* (Los Angeles: USC Thornton School of Music, 2004); Greg Wagner, "Music Reviews All-Polish Program at USC," *Los Angeles Times*, October 30, 1987, 20.

Polish National Alliance (Związek Narodowy Polski w Stanach Zjednoczonych Polnocnej Ameryki; ZNP). In 2010, the Polish National Alliance of the United States of North America was the largest fraternal insurance benefit association of the more than twenty such organizations established by people of Polish origin in the U.S., both in terms of total membership, assets, and the amount of insurance it provides to members. Founded in 1880, the Polish National Alliance is also the largest ethnic or nationality-based American fraternal. As of December 31, 2005, the PNA reported total membership of 184,600 current life insurance policy holders and 8,200 annuity holders. It declared $412,246,660 in assets and provided life insurance protection of $825,473,000 to its members. The PNA has members in every state and is licensed to conduct business in thirty-six states and the District of Columbia. Since its founding, an estimated 2.2 million people have belonged to the Alliance.

FRATERNAL CHARACTER

The PNA is a fraternal insurance benefit association. Nearly one hundred such organizations operate in the United States. They are quite diverse from one another in size, memberships, particular histories, traditions, and activities. But all share several key features in common. According to the National Fraternal Congress of America, a fraternal is "any incorporated society, order or supreme lodge, without capital stock whose activities are conducted solely for the benefit of its members and their beneficiaries and not for profit and which possesses a local lodge system having a ritualistic form of work a representative form of government, and which makes provision for the payment of benefits." Membership in the Polish National Alliance is based on the purchase of a PNA life insurance policy or, since 1995, its annuity product. All members in good standing who have reached the age of sixteen have the right to participate in electing their leaders. All adult members are eligible to seek any elective office in the fraternal, from the local lodge to the national level. The financial yields the PNA earns from its investments are used for the benefit of its members through dividends paid to its insurance holders and as fraternal benefits. The latter include a wide variety of sports, youth, and cultural programs, along with a college scholarship program. In 2005 alone, the PNA distributed over $227,000 in community service benefits, more than $500,000 in fraternal activities support, and $265,000 in scholarship funds. Adult members also receive, at no cost, the PNA fraternal publication, *Zgoda* (Harmony). In addition, funds are dispensed to members and non-members when the need arises. For example, the PNA provided aid to victims of the 1992 Florida hurricane, the 1993 flooding of the Missouri River, the 1994 Los Angeles earthquake, and Hurricane Katrina (2005). The needy in Poland have also received substantial PNA aid. For example, in 1997 the Alliance sent more than $4 million in supplies to Poland in the aftermath of floods that engulfed the southern part of the country.

ORIGINS AND IDEOLOGICAL FOUNDATIONS

The Polish National Alliance was established on February 15, 1880, in Philadelphia, Pennsylvania, by a group of Polish émigrés who were invited by **Julius Andrzejkowicz**, the proprietor of a chemical company, to form a nationwide organization in support of the independence of partitioned Poland (which had been under foreign domination since 1795) and to give humanitarian aid to its people. The idea was not new; there had been several earlier, unsuccessful, efforts dating back to 1842, to unite patriotically minded Poles in America around these causes. But by 1880 the rapid growth of Polish immigration to the United States resulted in an estimated 400,000 Poles in the U.S., creating a critical number that made a national organization more feasible than the dispersed individuals and families of earlier times. Heeding advice from **Agaton Giller**, a participant in the failed Polish uprising of 1863 against czarist Russian rule living in exile in Switzerland, the founders of the Alliance promoted the advancement of immigrants in all aspects of American life in order that they might be in a better position

to aid the cause of Poland. As Giller wrote: "Because the Polish emigration in America constitutes an undeniably great force, it should be the task of those who are motivated by true patriotic feelings to direct this force so that our fatherland's cause will be presented to its best advantage (in America).... In what way can we best direct the realization of Poland's cause? Through organization, we reply, since it is only through organization that our scattered immigrants can be unified. Only organized work will enable us to channel their concerns so that individual efforts (on Poland's behalf) will not be wasted, but rather consolidated for the good of the Fatherland.... Having become morally and patriotically uplifted by the fact that we have unified ourselves, the major task before a Polish organization must be to help our people attain a good standard of living in America. For when the masses of Poles in America, simply by their very presence in the country, reflect the good name of Poland to all whom they meet, they will be providing an enormously important service to Poland. In time, this service will be even greater as Poles begin to exert influence upon the political life of the United States...."

Seven months later, in September 1880, Andrzejkowicz and his colleagues held a founding convention (*sejm*) of the new PNA in Chicago. There they approved a constitution and set of by-laws for their society and elected their first slate of national officers. Andrzejkowicz accepted the important post of **censor**, or chief judge of the organization. **Maximilian Kucera** of Chicago, a participant in the 1863 rising, was elected the first PNA president. At the second PNA convention in New York in 1881, the delegates voted to establish an official weekly PNA publication, which they named *Zgoda*. It continues as the twice-monthly official organ of the PNA. The first PNA constitution called for the organization to work to bring about Poland's independence "by whatever peaceful means possible." The document also included a program supporting the economic betterment of the mushrooming Polish immigration. Interestingly, PNA membership was made open to all persons who originated from the lands of the old Polish pre-partition

state and was not restricted to Poles or persons who were Roman Catholics. This led to an early conflict between the PNA and the **Polish Roman Catholic Union** of America, established in 1873 with a requirement that its members adhere to the Catholic faith. The often contentious debate between the two organizations, both headquartered in Chicago, went on for decades.

In 1886 the PNA set up its own life insurance benefit plan, the first such program to go into effect on behalf of the Polish immigration. In the years after, the insurance program of the PNA proved to be very important in transforming the Alliance into a mass membership organization. The PNA's mission, restated over the years, is to "form a more perfect union of the Polish people in America with the rest of the citizenry of the United States and to transmit this relationship to future generations; to insure to them a proper moral, intellectual, economic and social development; to foster and cherish the best traditions of the cultures of the United States and of Poland; to preserve the mother tongue, and to promote all legitimate means leading to the restoration and preservation of the independence of Poland." In 1996, an article in *Zgoda* defined the aims of the Alliance as "promoting the material and civic betterment of its members, who may be of Polish birth or ancestry or of other cultural backgrounds, by offering high quality life insurance and annuity products to help them realize their financial objectives and to enhance the security of their loved ones, by providing them with a variety of valued fraternal benefits, by assisting people in need whether or not they belong to the PNA, by cherishing patriotism and civic involvement in American life, and by instilling a wider and deeper appreciation of the Polish heritage in the United States."

PROGRAMMATIC ACTIVITIES

From the start, PNA activists endeavored to unite the immigrant community in working for Polish independence. While these efforts were generally unsuccessful, the Alliance continued to commit itself to this objective in a variety of ways. In 1887, for example, the PNA initiated a nationwide fund raising effort, Skarb Narodowy (Polish National Treasury), on behalf of Poland's independence. In 1891, it organized the first **Polish Constitution Day** parade in Chicago to commemorate Poland's Constitution of May 3, 1791 (see **Constitution of the Third of May**). From 1904 on, this parade became an annual popular manifestation in Chicago and elsewhere, linking the Polish cause to the principles of the American constitution. Early in the twentieth century, the

A 25th anniversary drawing of leaders of the Polish National Alliance: from left, Marian Stęczyński, president; Antoni Schreiber, censor; and Prof. Romuald Piątkowski (*JPI*).

Emblem of the Polish National Alliance (*OLS*).

PNA worked to forge close ties with a number of smaller patriotic movements. In 1905, it briefly merged with the **Polish Falcons Alliance**, a youth-oriented patriotic and physical fitness society formed between 1887 and 1894. But this effort failed and in 1912 the Falcons resumed operations as an independent organization. In 1910 the PNA hosted a national congress in Washington, D.C., bringing together the leaders of most of the organizations of the Polish community and even representatives from partitioned Poland. This gathering took up the issues of Polish independence, U.S. immigration law, and the improvement of the social and economic conditions of the Polish population in America. It coincided with the dedication of monuments to the American Revolutionary war heroes and Polish patriots, **Kazimierz Pułaski** and **Tadeusz Kościuszko**. The cost of the Pułaski monument was borne by the U.S. government. The Kościuszko monument, in Lafayette Square adjacent the White House, was funded by the PNA, one of several its members erected in cities where large numbers of Poles lived, namely Chicago, Cleveland, Buffalo, and Milwaukee. Among the many leading PNA activists of this era was **Marian Stęczyński** who was president of the PNA between 1903 and 1912.

The outbreak of World War I in 1914 caused the PNA to work more cooperatively with other organizations in the Polish community. Working alongside other fraternals, the PNA helped create the **Polish Central Relief Committee** for the purpose of gathering funds, clothing, and medical supplies for shipment to the war torn homeland. In 1916 the PNA helped form the political action committee of the relief operation, the Polish **National Department** (Wydział Narodowy). This body worked closely with the Polish American businessman, politician and one-time PNA activist **John Smulski**, the famed pianist-patriot **Ignacy Paderewski**, and Polish independence activist and politician Roman Dmowski. Dmowski headed an incipient Polish government-in-exile, the Polish National Committee in France. The U.S. entry into the war in 1917 enhanced the ability of the **National Department** to promote the cause of Poland's independence. That same year it was also given permission to begin recruiting Poles in the United States into a military formation that would eventually include over 22,000 members. These soldiers sailed to Europe to become part of an army of more than 100,000 men serving on the side of Britain, France and the U.S. against the German empire (see **Polish Army in France**). A highpoint in the work of the National Department came with its convening of a Congress of the Polish Emigration in Detroit in August 1918. Both Paderewski and Dmowski addressed this gathering of more than one thousand Polish community leaders, who then committed the Polish community to the task of raising $10 million on behalf of the country's postwar reconstruction. All these efforts had the backing of the PNA and its president, **Casimir Zychliński** (president, 1912–28).

In the inter-war years (1918–39), the PNA maintained its policy of cooperation with other **Polonia** organizations as the best way to realize the goal of uniting the organized Polish American community. But relations between the PNA and independent Poland became strained after General Józef Piłsudski seized power there in 1926. A so-called "leftist" faction of PNA activists who admired Piłsudski pushed for closer ties with his new regime. This group was ultimately defeated in a series of PNA national conventions by backers of what became popularly known as the "old guard" faction. Curiously, the "old guard" achieved its success under the leadership of two younger, American-born attorneys of Polish origin, **Francis X. Swietlik** of Milwaukee (**censor** of the PNA, 1931–47) and **Charles Rozmarek** (PNA president, 1939–67).

The Nazi German and Soviet invasions and the ruthless partition of Poland in September 1939 signaled the start of World War II. This tragedy brought about an immediate renewal of the PNA's support of the Polish people. Not only did the Alliance and its members commit massive amounts of money on behalf of the humanitarian needs of the Polish people, Swietlik, as chairman of the **Polish American Council** (Rada Polonii Amerykańskiej) charitable federation, played a key leadership role in organizing a Polonia-wide wartime and postwar humanitarian effort. This effort also operated in cooperation with the U.S. government and a host of other charitable agencies. For his part, Rozmarek became a leader in establishing a new all–Polonia political action federation, the **Polish American Congress**, PAC (Kongres Polonii Amerykańskiej). Founded in Buffalo, New York in May 1944 at a gathering of more than 2,500 delegates elected from Polish community organizations across the country, the PAC pledged Polonia's total support for both America's military victory against the Axis powers and the restoration of Poland's full post-war independence. But the war's end in 1945 did not bring about Poland's restoration as a free and sovereign state. Instead the devastated country came under Soviet military occupation and a Polish communist regime was installed illegitimately under the auspices of Moscow. In these circumstances, the PAC had no option but to continue in operation as the voice of free Poland in the West.

Rozmarek went on to serve as president of the Polish National Alliance until 1967. Then, at the 35th PNA national convention in Detroit, he was defeated in his quest for an eighth term in office by a Chicago attorney and long time PNA activist, **Aloysius Mazewski** (PNA president 1967–88). The year after, Mazewski also replaced Rozmarek as president of the PAC. Upon Mazewski's death, he was succeeded as head of both the PNA and PAC by **Edward Moskal** of Chicago (president, 1988–2005). On Moskal's passing, **Frank J. Spula** of Chicago succeeded him as the head of both organizations. PNA leadership of the Polish American Congress can be explained in terms of the size, financial strength, and significance of the Alliance. But just as important is the fact that the civic action aims of the PNA and PAC were quite identical and PNA leadership of the PAC represented its historic objectives to lead the Polish American community.

Organization and Structural Development

In 1881, at its second *Sejm*, the PNA set up its own official publication, *Zgoda*. Initially a weekly in the Polish language, *Zgoda* became a bi-monthly in 1947. Since 1968, the sixteen-page publication has appeared mainly in English. In 1908 the PNA established its own daily newspaper, *Dziennik Związkowy* (The Alliance Daily), aimed at the general Polish language readership in Chicago and beyond. In 1987, the Alliance added to its communications activities by inaugurating its own radio station, WPNA, to serve metropolitan Chicago. In 1999 the PNA announced the creation of its own Bank in Chicago; since then a second Chicago area bank location has been established, beginning operation in Brooklyn, New York, in 2008.

The Alliance's insurance plan, established in 1886, was officially chartered by the State of Illinois in 1896. That same year the PNA established its first home office on Chicago's near north side in a district having a high concentration of Polish residents. A second and larger building was dedicated in the same neighborhood in 1938. In 1977 a third national headquarters was established on the city's northwest side.

In March 1900 the PNA formally approved the admission of women as full members of the Alliance at a special convention called for that purpose. This move, adopted twenty years before the ratification of the Women's Suffrage Amendment to the U.S. Constitution, was crucial to the growth and dynamism of the PNA in the years to come. In 1900, the Alliance counted 15,288 members. By 1910, this number had risen to 71,335 members. This growth continued, with membership at the time of its twentieth convention exceeding 100,000. By 1920 membership rose to 126,521; in 1930 it stood 286,526; thereafter, membership stabilized at approximately 300,000 insured members, a development adversely affected by the Great Depression. Membership once again began growing after World War II with its peak years coming in the early 1960s. At the Alliance's 1963 convention, it reported an all-time high to that point of 351,166 members. Women members not only accounted for approximately half of this total; women activists in the Alliance were responsible for managing a wide variety of fraternal activities in all levels of the organization. At the national level, a number of women activists made notable contributions to the PNA, including **Maria Sakowska**, the first woman to serve on its Board of Directors, and **Frances Dymek**, who was vice president of the PNA from 1935–1939 and from 1943 to 1967.

PNA membership growth in the twentieth century is also due to at least two other developments. One came with the approval it received in 1917 to provide insurance for children under the age of sixteen. The PNA immediately began enrolling youngsters into its ranks and formed a youth and sports department on their behalf. In the early 1930s the PNA also formed its own scouting organiza-

Delegates to the 7th Sejm of the Polish National Alliance held in St. Paul, Minnesota, September 1887 (*PMA*).

tion, one modeled after Poland's scouting movement, or Harcerstwo (see **Scouting, Polish American**). Before this effort disbanded in the early 1940s due to objections from the Boy Scouts of America, it enrolled more than 50,000 youngsters into its ranks and played a positive role in stimulating ethnic pride in this new generation of the American-born of Polish heritage.

After World War II, PNA membership again rose due to its success in recruiting thousands of Polish refugees who had been allowed to enter this country under special legislation approved by the U.S. government. From the start, many of these newcomers involved themselves in the Alliance with a fresh appreciation of its members' cultural heritage and devotion to the cause of Poland's liberation from Soviet domination. Entry into the PNA has traditionally come via a person's enrollment into one of its local groups or "lodges" (*grupy* or *towarzystwa*). Since 1880, more than 3,200 have existed; of these about 800 were still in operation in 2009. The lodge is an autonomous, grass roots unit in the PNA structure. Its members elect their officers and manage their own particular fraternal activities. Groups of lodges join together to set up councils (*gminy*) whose representatives are responsible for promoting the recruitment and fraternal activities of their member lodges and holding elections at which delegates to the PNA national conventions are chosen. Conventions, originally held every year, have, since 1927, been held every four years. The national convention is the highest decision-making body of the Alliance. There, the delegates elect their national officers, determine the fraternal's budget, and approve its policies for the next four years. In 2009, national officers include a president, three vice presidents, a secretary, a treasurer, and a board of fifteen national directors. The PNA's chief ju-

dicial officers are the censor and a deputy or vice censor. They, together with the PNA's thirty-four district commissioners, are elected at the convention and oversee the insurance sales and fraternal activities of the Alliance at the local and regional level. There are no limits to the terms of the six executive officers of the Alliance, the censor and vice censor; a change in the by-laws approved in 1975 restricts directors and commissioners to serving two consecutive four-year terms in the same office.

An enduring aspect of PNA fraternalism has been its many-faceted interest in its members' educational advancement. As early as 1891, the Alliance began to set up libraries and reading rooms in Chicago and other centers of Polish immigration. Student loans, scholarships, citizenship, and night school courses began to be offered from the late 1890s. In 1912, the PNA established its own educational institution, the **Alliance College** (Kolegjum Związkowe) in Cambridge Springs, Pennsylvania, twenty miles south of Erie. Eventually transformed into a four-year, co-educational institution with a peak enrollment of more than 600 students in the 1960s, Alliance College graduated more than five thousand young people in its seventy-five years of existence. However, in 1987 its failure to increase enrollments, the rising cost of maintaining the institution, and concerns over its future accreditation obliged the elected national leadership of the PNA to close the College. Over the years the Alliance had expended $20 million on its behalf.

In place of the College, the PNA initiated a significant scholarship program on behalf of its members at the 40th convention in Chicago in 1987. There, $300,000 was set aside over the next four years for scholarships. In the years since, each quadrennial convention allotment of scholarship funds has continued

Group 2066 of the Polish National Alliance, New York Mills, New York, ca. 1925 (*James S. Pula*).

to increase. At the 2007 convention, $1 million in scholarships was approved, or $250,000 per year. Overall, more than $3.6 million in scholarships had been funded by 2009. In addition the PNA has given substantial financial support to the many Polish "**Saturday Schools**" operating in the U.S. Awards are also made to qualifying students in graduate and professional studies.

Conscious of assimilation's impact on the millions of persons of Polish origin who have entered the American mainstream, PNA leaders have worked to maintain their awareness of the Alliance's mission and their involvement in its activities. Thus, by the 1960s English had replaced Polish as the dominant language of the fraternal. Beginning with the presidency of Aloysius Mazewski in 1967, the PNA began developing a variety of new insurance plans to better meet the needs of the ever more diverse population of Americans of Polish origin and heritage. Under his successor, Edward Moskal, this initiative was complemented by new efforts to train, expand, and professionalize its sales force in its efforts to more effectively enroll new members and stem the decline that has affected the PNA, and all Polish fraternals, since the 1960s. Under Presidents Mazewski, Moskal, and Spula, the PNA has also succeeded in admitting a number of smaller Polish American fraternals into the Alliance. These have included the Polish Alma Mater and the Union of Polish Women, both of Chicago, and the Alliance of Poles of Cleveland. The most recent example is the inclusion of the **Polish National Alliance of Brooklyn** into the PNA in 2007.

The decline in membership is a subject of concern, as is the case for nearly all American fraternals. In the PNA case, membership in its centennial anniversary year of 1980 was 297,000, a substantial drop from its reported high of 351,000 in 1963. In 1999 at its 43rd convention, the figure was 216,000. The obstacles facing the PNA include the need to further professionalize the sale of its insurance and annuity products, to be more competitive in reaching out with the PNA message to the millions of Americans of Polish ancestry who are two, three and even four generations removed from immigration, and to find ways to interest the elusive newcomer generation of Poles who have settled in the U.S. since the 1980s about the benefits of fraternal insurance and the value of PNA membership. Financially the PNA has experienced continued growth. In 1900 its assets were $98,339; in 1920, $5,656,563; in 1950, $56,298,000; and in its centennial year of 1980, $167,355,216. In the year 2005, it was $412,246,660, not including the substantial assets of the banks operated by the PNA.

The slogan of the Polish National Alliance is "W Jedności Siła, w Zgodzie Potęga" (In unity there is strength, in concord authority). The historic PNA emblem is a shield showing an eagle, a knight on horseback, and the Archangel Michael. These symbolize, respectively, Poland, Lithuania, and Ukraine — the three main regions of the old Polish commonwealth that ex-isted from the end of the fourteenth century until its destruction in 1795. This emblem was used in the uprising of 1863 and underscored the Poles' aim to rally all three peoples in the fight for freedom from foreign domination. Above the shield, two hands clasp, symbolizing fraternal solidarity. The shining sun represents the cause of freedom — for America and Poland. — *Donald E. Pienkos*

SOURCES: Stanisław Osada, *Historia Związku Narodowego Polskiego i Rózwoj Ruchu Narodowego w Ameryce, 1880–1905* (Chicago: Alliance Publishers, 1905, 1957); Adam Olszewski, *Polish National Alliance* (Chicago: United Press Publishers, 1964), 4 Vols.; Donald E. Pienkos, *PNA: A Centennial History of the Polish National Alliance of the United States of North America* (Boulder, CO: East European Monographs, 1984); Donald E. Pienkos, *Yesterday, Today, Tomorrow: The Story of the Polish National Alliance* (Chicago: Alliance Printers and Publishers, 2008); Frank Renkiewicz, "An Economy of Self-Help: Fraternal Capitalism and the Evolution of Polish America," in Philip Shashko, Charles Ward and Donald Pienkos, eds., *Studies in Ethnicity: The East European Experience in America* (Boulder, CO: East European Monographs, 1980).

Polish National Alliance of Brooklyn (Zjednoczenie Polsko-Narodowe w Brooklyn). The Polish National Alliance of Brooklyn was a fraternal established by members of the **Polish Union of America** (founded 1890) fraternal in New York who broke away from the PRCUA in 1903. Its membership rose from 5,400 in the era of World War I to about 16,000 in the 1930s, and peaked in 1960 at about 23,800. Thereafter it experienced a decline to 13,000 in 1983, and to less than 10,000 by the 1990s. Its Polish language fraternal publication *Czas* (The Times) was published until 1976. Over the years the Polish National Alliance of Brooklyn developed a close and supportive relationship with the **Kosciuszko Foundation** of New York, with Dr. **Eugene Kusielewicz**, the Foundation's president in the 1970s and early 1980s, being

Flag of the Polish National Alliance of Brooklyn (*OLS*).

a member of its Board of Directors. In 2007, the PNA of Brooklyn, under Christine J. McMullan, its president from 1978, merged with the **Polish National Alliance** of the United States of North America (PNA) headquartered in Chicago. Its imposing main office in Brooklyn was also scheduled to become the home of the PNA Bank in the Borough.—*Donald E. Pienkos*

SOURCES: Donald E. Pienkos, *PNA: A Centennial History of the Polish National Alliance* (Boulder, CO: East European Monographs, 1984); Donald E. Pienkos, *Yesterday, Today, Tomorrow: The Story of the Polish National Alliance* (Chicago: Alliance Printers and Publishers, 2008).

Polish National Catholic Church.

The Polish National Catholic Church (PNCC) traces its origins to 1897 when the Rev. **Franciszek Hodur** became pastor of the independent St. Stanislaus Bishop and Martyr Parish in Scranton, Pennsylvania (see **Independentism**). The PNCC was a reaction to longstanding grievances that many Polish Catholics had with the hierarchy of the Roman Catholic Church in the United States. These were encapsulated in Hodur's program for what he called the "Kościół Narodowy" (National Church) that he initially hoped would exist within the Catholic ecclesiastical structure in America. His program called for ownership of parish properties by the parishioners, the governance of parish affairs by lay parish committees, parishioner approval of the appointment of priests, and the appointment of Polish bishops to minister to the Polish communities in the U.S. Hodur began to openly criticize the Roman Catholic hierarchy and to contest various Catholic doctrines, including papal infallibility, in the pages of his newspaper, *Straż* (The Guard). As a result, he was excommunicated on September 29, 1898. On Christmas Eve, 1900, Hodur celebrated the first mass in Polish, which soon became the norm throughout the dissident parishes. By the following year, the National Church had attracted ten affiliated parishes in Pennsylvania, New Jersey, and Massachusetts.

In July 1904, Hodur, his priests, and lay leaders of the "National" parishes issued a call for a general meeting to form a separate church. Some 146 delegates attended what became the First General Synod of the Polish National Catholic Church on September 6–8. The synod voted to officially disassociate itself from the Roman Catholic Church, to elect Hodur as the first bishop of the new PNCC, to adopt *Straż* as its official newspaper, to elect a Great Church Council comprised of clergy and laity, and adopted a Constitution. The PNCC retained much of Roman Catholic tradition and belief, including the hierarchical church organization, but the liturgical language changed from Latin to Polish and the church calendar expanded to include many additional feast days commemorating events in Polish history. In the following year it established **Savonarola Theological Seminary** to prepare clergy for the growing number of parishes that the independent movement was attracting. By 1907, membership in the PNCC had increased to more than 15,000 and in 1908 it established the **Polish National Union of America** (Spójnia) as a fraternal insurance organization that was linked ideologically, but not administratively, with the PNCC.

The Second General Synod in 1909 affirmed Hodur's recognition of the "Word of God preached and heard" as "having sacramental value," and of having the name "Polish National Catholic Church of America" (PNCC) as the full denominational designation. Representation at the General Synods was accorded on the basis of one delegate for every fifty active members in a parish. The acceptance of independent parishes, including some hitherto supporting the independent Bishops **Antoni Kozłowski** and **Stefan Kamiński** after their deaths in 1907 and 1911 respectively, increased church membership significantly. Bishop Hodur wrote a "Confession of Faith," explaining it as a restatement of the essentials of faith for modern times. Three Provincial Synods (Wilkes-Barre, Pennsylvania; Chicopee, Massachusetts; Passaic, New Jersey) voted its acceptance in 1912. The Third General Synod, held in Chicago in 1914, added its vote. With the church's membership increase to nearly 40,000 and its geographical extension to the far Midwest and Canada, the delegates approved Hodur's request for three non-bishop suffragans. It also mandated the future establishment of the church in a free Poland and sought endorsement of a *Polish* Polish National Catholic Church by Józef Piłsudski, the nominal future leader of independent Poland. The request was rejected, but Hodur continued to plan for extension of the PNCC into Poland.

The Polish mission encountered many obstacles. Petitions for government recognition as a Polish Christian denomination (as were Roman Catholics, Orthodox, Lutherans, and Calvinists) were disapproved, and it was categorized as a proselytizing American church (as were Methodists, Mormons, and Seventh Day Adventists). At local levels, its clergy were harassed and arrested for impersonating Roman Catholic priests, using Catholic vestments, and employing the title *ksiądz* (literally priest). Vital statistics registration bureaus located in Roman Catholic Church rectories would not register births, marriages, and deaths of people associated with the PNCC. Things turned violent with the severe beatings of Bishops Hodur and **Francis Bończak** by students incited by a priest. Hodur also faced internal problems engendered by quarreling among the clergy, leading to secessions and calls for removal of the "Hodurite" church when he designated Bończak as bishop of the Polish diocese. At home, his Polish missionary activities were criticized as being costly and diverting needed attention from the PNCC in America.

At Bishop Hodur's behest, the Fourth General Synod in 1921 voted for the abolition of mandatory clerical celibacy and passed resolutions sustaining his interpretations on the basis of faith, on the complementary aspects of baptism and confirmation, and formalizing corporate ("general") adult confession. Foregoing co-consecrators, he consecrated four bishops elected at the Fifth General Synod in 1924: **Valentine Gawrychowski**, Francis Bończak, and **Leon Grochowski** to head its three diocese and John Gritenas as Lithuanian diocese bishop. At various times, Hodur also had Italian, Czech, Slovak, and Hungarian parishes under his jurisdiction. In reaction to post–World War I "Americanizing" campaigns by Roman Catholic bishops, the PNCC made significant gains in members and new parishes through the 1920s. In 1923 it established *Rola Boża* (God's Field) as the official Church organ, and continued its expansion with creation of a Western Diocese in 1926, a Buffalo-Pittsburgh Diocese in 1928 under Bishop John F. Jasiński, and the Polish Diocese in Warsaw in the same year under Bishop Władysław Faroń.

Hodur's life took a negative turn by the 1930s. The Sixth General Synod in 1931 saw a thoroughly depressed Prime Bishop Hodur decrying the lack of spirituality in the American church and expressing shock by betrayal in the Polish church. Although he requested release from his duties as bishop to resume service as a simple preacher, he rescinded the request after pleading by the delegates, thereafter devoting time to writing his prophetic *Apokalipsa dwudziestego wieku* (Apocalypse of The Twentieth Century; 1930). In the meantime, he became increasingly incapacitated by diabetes and cataracts which eventually caused over fifteen years of blindness.

The decade of the 1930s witnessed the election of Bishop John Misiaszek to head the Central Diocese (1935), creation of the rank of Senior Priest (1935), election of Bishop Joseph Padewski (1935), and consecration of Bishop Joseph Lesniak to lead the Eastern Diocese. The Seventh General Synod established intercommunion with the Episcopal

Church in 1946, a relationship that lasted until 1978 when it dissolved over the issue of Episcopal ordination of women. Bishop Grochowski was elected the PNCC's second Prime Bishop in 1947. Another important event of the decade occurred in 1943 when Josephine Walentynowicz bequeathed the 600-acre "Warsaw Village" located in the Pocono Mountains in Thornhurst, Pennsylvania, to the PNCC. Its summer cottages were used as a vacation spot and became a valuable adjunct to the church's activities.

The decade of the 1950s brought the tragedies of Bishop Padewski's death in a Communist prison, the defection of the Polish Diocese which became the "Polish Catholic Church," and the death of the PNCC's founder, Bishop Hodur, in 1953. With fewer and fewer young people fluent in Polish, the Tenth General Synod approved the use of English in the Mass in 1958. Yet, expansion continued. In 1963 Bishop Eugene Magyar was elected by Czech and Slovak parishes, the first National Youth Conference convened in Buffalo, and a Canadian Diocese was created in 1967. The Thirteenth General Synod elected Bishop **Thaddeus Zieliński** as the third Prime Bishop in 1971, and he was succeeded by Bishop **Francis Rowiński** who was elected by the Fifteenth General Synod in 1978, Bishop **John Swantek** who was elected by the Seventeenth General Synod in 1985, and Bishop **Robert M. Nemkovich** who was elected by the Twenty-First General Synod in 2002.

The PNCC entered into dialogue with the Roman Catholic Church toward repairing the strained relations between the two groups in 1984. This led to a lengthy series of discussions culminating in an agreement on limited intercommunion. Another result was the publication of *Journeying Together in Christ: A Report of the Polish National Catholic Church-Roman Catholic Dialogue* (1990) and *Journeying Together in Christ: the Journey Continues—The Report of the Polish National Catholic-Roman Catholic Dialogue 1989-2002* (2003). At the same time, relationships with other groups deteriorated. In 2003 the International Bishop Conference of the Union of Utrecht voted to expel the PNCC because of increasing doctrinal differences.

PNCC membership rose steadily to between 60,000 and 85,000 in more than fifty parishes by 1926. By the time of Hodur's death in 1953 it numbered more than 130,000. At its peak, the PNCC attracted about five percent of Polish Americans. In 2009, a census of its parishes indicated its active membership had shrunk to less than 10,000.—*Joseph W. Wieczerzak*

SOURCES: Theodore L. Zawistowski, "The Polish National Catholic Church: An Acceptable Alternative," in Frank Mocha, ed., *Poles in America: Bicentennial Essays* (Stevens Point, WI: Worzalla Publishing Company, 1978), 423-34; Paul Fox, *The Polish National Catholic Church* (Scranton, PA: School of Christian Living, n.d.); Hieronim Kubiak, *The Polish National Catholic Church in the United States of America from 1897 to 1980* (Kraków: Państwowe Wydawnictwo Naukowe, 1982); Joseph Wieczerzak, *Bishop Francis Hodur: Biographical Essays* (Boulder, CO: East European Monographs, 1998); Stanislaus A. Blejwas, "'Equals With Equals': The Polish National Catholic Church and the Founding of the Polish American Congress," *Polish American Studies*, Vol. 44, no. 2 (1987), 5-23; Lawrence Orzell, "A Minority within a Minority: The Polish National Catholic Church, 1896-1907," *Polish American Studies*, Vol. 36, no. 1 (1979), 5-32; Frank S. Mead, "Polish National Catholic Church of America," *Handbook of Denominations in the United States (10th Edition)* (Nashville, TN: Abingdon Press, 1995).

Polish National Committee (1831). Claiming to represent the Polish nation abroad after the November 1830 insurrection, the Polish National Committee was formed under the auspices of the Marquis de Lafayette in Paris, France. Lafayette, who was sympathetic to the Polish national cause and to the radical democratic wing of the Polish emigration, presided over a sister organization called the *Comité polonaise*. The Polish National Committee was composed primarily of members of the democratic wing of the Polish emigration and stood in opposition to a similar body formed under the leadership of Bonawentura Niemojowski. The Committee was established on December 8, 1831, and resembled, in composition and political orientation, the Warsaw Patriotic Club, which had, at the start of the November Uprising in Russian Poland, spoken out against the conservative Administrative Council for attempting negotiations with the czarist authorities for a peaceful resolution to the cadet's revolt. The Committee's first organizational meetings were held in late December 1831, naming Polish historian and republican nationalist Joachim Lelewel president and Maurycy Mochnacki, an émigré publicist, secretary. Among the Committee's first actions was the release of a proclamation condemning the conservative political leadership—represented by such figures as Prince Adam Jerzy Czartoryski—for the failure of the insurrection and calling upon Poles to follow the new democratic liberal leadership toward the goal of a reconstituted Poland. The overall function of the Polish National Committee was to provide material support for the émigré community (both civilian and military), to make continuous appeals to the French and British governments to condemn the partitions of Poland, and to promote the Polish cause in both cultural and political spheres. Culturally, Lelewel and Mochnacki established a scientific association, which actively published Polish literature in English, French, and German translation. Politically, the Committee advanced a program for a reconstituted Poland, which advocated a return to Poland's pre-partition borders and rejected the gentry democracy of the Polish-Lithuanian Commonwealth in favor of a federated republic based on socioeconomic and ethnic equality. The Committee also condemned despotism in general, and czarism in particular, proclaiming the continuing struggle by Poles against the partitioning powers until independence was achieved. Successive proclamations denounced czarist policy in the aftermath of the Uprising, including Nicholas I's Organic Statute, which abolished the constitutional provisions granted to the Kingdom of Poland by Alexander I such as the Sejm, Congress Poland's own army, and its regional autonomy. A June 1832 appeal written by Lelewel and Polish poet Adam Mickiewicz, entitled "To Our Russian Brothers," appealed to the Slavic heritage of Russians and Poles, and recalled their political cooperation in such revolts as the 1825 Russian Decembrist Uprising. The intended aim of the appeal was to gain sympathy from the more democratic and liberal Russian circles for the Polish plight. Because of the anti-czarist tone of the appeal, the Russian Ambassador in France, Pozzo di Borgo, pressed the French government to expel Lelewel and all co-signers of the document. Despite widespread public sympathy for the Polish cause, the French government remained suspicious of the émigré community and of Polish political aims, particularly as it influenced their diplomatic relations with states such as Russia. In December 1832 the government of Louis Philippe dissolved the Committee and by 1833 its officers had been expelled from France. Many of the Polish exiles from the November Uprising who went to the U.S. maintained their ties with this group of revolutionaries. For further information on their activities in American, see **Democratic Society of Polish Exiles in America**.—*Krystyna Cap*

SOURCES: Joan S. Skurnowicz, *Romantic Nationalism and Liberalism: Joachim Lelewel and the Polish National Idea* (Boulder, CO: East European Monographs/Columbia University Press, 1981); Jerzy Jan Lerski, *A Polish Chapter in Jacksonian America: The United States and the Polish Exiles of 1831* (Madison, WI: University of Wisconsin Press, 1958).

Polish National Committee (Komitet Narodowy Polski; 1917). The Polish National Committee, better known as the KNP from its Polish name, Komitet Narodowy Polski, was formed in Lausanne, Switzerland, in the summer of 1917. It is not to be confused with an organization of the same name which emerged in Russia shortly after the beginning of the war and combined conservative and nationalist factions to work with the tsarist authorities in promoting Polish issues. By the late summer of 1917, Polish leaders in Western Europe realized that some new and larger efforts were necessary to coordinate Polish efforts internationally. The Austro-German creation of a Polish Kingdom the previous November had done much to internationalize the Polish Question. The declaration by the new Russian (Provisional) government endorsing the creation of an independent Poland and the address by Woodrow Wilson in January, 1917 (the Peace Without Victory speech), offering Polish independence as an example of a just outcome of the war, had greatly advanced Poland as an international issue. American support became more important with the U.S. declaration of war in April, 1917. Moreover, protean efforts to create a Polish army, including **Ignacy Jan Paderewski**'s call for recruiting in the United States (April) and the French government's announcement of its support for an army (June) had brought the issues of a Polish force fighting in conjunction with the Western Powers to the fore. Some political directing body to coordinate the emerging army was imperative. In August, 1917, a meeting in Lausanne of a group of prominent Poles led by Roman Dmowski laid the outlines of a Polish National Committee to "represent Polish political interests before the Western allies." Dmowski had left Russia and was traveling about Western Europe promoting the Polish cause and was universally regarded as the leader of the nationalist right in Polish politics. Also in attendance were Jan Jordan Rozwadowski who had earlier been instrumental in fostering the establishment of the Polish **National Department** in the United States (Wydział Narodowy; WN) and Jan Maria Horodyski from the United States where he acted as Paderewski's trusted lieutenant. In August the KNP took on its definitive form in its new headquarters, Paris, where it was to reside thereafter. Representatives were designated in a number of capitals and Horodyski was tasked with winning Paderewski to the role of serving as KNP representative in Washington. From its inception the KNP was dominated by Dmowski and his allies on the Polish right.

Representatives of the Polish left or any minority populations were excluded. From the beginning the KNP regarded steering the myriad plans to raise a Polish army in the West as its principle task. Closely associated with this were efforts to win support in the United States for recruiting and gaining the close cooperation of Paderewski in dealing with the American authorities. The KNP made it very clear that it wished to have a representative of the National Department (WN) join its ranks, though it seems that full membership was not to be accorded the **Polonia** representative. In addition the KNP sought to act as an overall political representation for international Polonia and provide quasi-consular protection for Poles living abroad. The KNP was devoted to the Western Powers regarding the war. Polish efforts to work with the Central Powers, which were in occupation of the bulk of Polish territory, were specifically excluded. Paderewski was initially averse to joining the KNP: not only did he have qualms about an organization which was almost exclusively the product of the right, but he was in the midst of complex negotiations to create his own international political directing body for Poland with himself as head. It was only with considerable reluctance and after his own efforts proved unavailing that the maestro agreed to join the KNP and then only with assurances that he would be given a free hand in America and not be under KNP supervision. In the last half of 1917, Paderewski's principal activities were to win American support for the Polish army projects and convince Washington to recognize the KNP as an official Polish organization. Washington was reluctant to move on either matter which it rightfully regarded as intertwined. The State Department was in a muddle regarding the army issue — it was "frightfully mixed up" according to a senior official — and Secretary of State Robert Lansing was attempting to leave open various options for American Polish policy. Lansing briefly explored working with the political adventurer **Jerzy Jan Sosnowski**. Sosnowski, in turn, had ties to the Austrian representative in the United States, Adam Count Tarnowski, as well as representatives of the **National Defense Committee** (KON). Lansing even toyed with the idea of sponsoring a Polish Provisional government under American auspices. Both these initiatives proved ephemeral but indicate the fluidity of Washington's policy at this time.

By September, the British were convinced that recognition of the KNP would bring some clarity to Polish issues especially the Army "muddle" and pressed Washington for a response. Lansing's notions of a Provisional Government were rejected by London which regarded them as too large an imitative. The British were inclined to follow the American lead regarding Poland. Lansing turned to President Woodrow Wilson to ask him his pleasure regarding the KNP. The president responded that he was unwilling to take steps before consulting with Paderewski who had, by this time, become Wilson's major if not sole source of guidance regarding Polish matters. Paderewski had, of course, already made up his mind as he was tied to the KNP and would obviously support its *desiderata*. The maestro informed Wilson that the National Department had just joined the KNP and that he would function as their joint representative. Thus Paderewski pressed the State Department for conjoint approval of recruiting and recognition of the KNP. Despite these urgings the Americans were excruciatingly slow in making a determination regarding the KNP. They first canvassed the opinions of all the Allied governments. The British had hesitated because of Lansing's scheme for a Provisional Government and hence waited for an American initiative which was long delayed. In the meanwhile the French recognized the KNP and the Italians were pressing for a similar step if the British would act. Only in October did Wilson seek a formal request from the KNP in Paris — this despite Paderewski's earlier request. Finally in November, after agonizing negotiations with the Russians who did not wish the Americans to work with the KNP, did the United States extend recognition to the Committee but then bizarrely kept the issue secret for another month. The KNP had established close relations with the "Polish Council of United Parties" (Rada Polska Zjednoczenia Międzypartyjnego or RPZM), the chief Polish political organization in Russia, and sought to appoint an American representative, from the WN, to its ranks to consolidate its relations with Polonia. Accomplishing these goals would effectively put the KNP at the head of organized international Polonia. Paderewski was given *carte blanche* to select the Polonia candidate. The maestro chose Dr. **Franciszek Fronczak**, Health Commissioner of Buffalo and a socially prominent Polonia activist. The Americans designated Fronczak a major in the American Expeditionary Force Medical Corps and assigned him as liaison to the KNP thus facilitating his travels. Though prominent, Fronczak was not a politically significant figure in Polonia and, not being a Chicagoan, was not from the center of Polonia power. He was accepted into KNP ranks in December 1917, but played no serious role in the organization: his status as Polonia representative was essentially ceremonial. Neither Paderewski nor the WN provided Fronczak with direction. The KNP continued to function until August 15, 1919, when it held its last meeting. By then a Polish government had been established in Warsaw. Although never recognized as a Polish government-in-exile, it had essentially that function until the end of the war and was the chief agency of the right as regards Polish matters internationally.—*M. B. B. Biskupski*

SOURCE: M. B. Biskupski, "The United States and the Rebirth of Poland, 1914–1918" (Ph.D. dissertation, Yale University, 1981).

Polish National Congress (1910). On May 10, 1910, ceremonies were held in Washington, D.C., to celebrate the unveiling of two great monuments; one honored **Kazimierz Pułaski**, its cost underwritten by the U.S. government. The second depicted **Tadeusz Kościuszko** and was paid for mainly by the **Polish National Alliance**. Thousands of Polish Americans attended the ceremonies, joined by William Howard Taft, President of the United States, and many government representatives. Following the ceremonies, a National Congress of **Polonia** leaders, joined by representatives from partitioned Poland, took part in a four-day series of meetings (May 11–14) to discuss a variety of issues concerning Poland and Polonia. The gathering was called by the PNA and brought together more than 200 delegates from the Alliance and those Polonia organizations that belonged to its "patriotic" camp; most notably, the **Polish Women's Alliance**, **Polish Falcons**, **Polish Singers Alliance**, Young Peoples Alliance, Alliance of Polish Armies, and **Polish Socialist Alliance**. Representatives from the Catholic fraternals and the clergy who had attended the monument dedication ceremonies did not take part in the Congress. The delegates took up three sets of issues. Participants in the Economic-Emigration Section reviewed U.S. policy toward the Polish immigration and came up with a series of resolutions connected with both the treatment of Polish immigrants in America and problems facing Polish emigrants in partitioned Poland. The Educational Section dealt with a number of matters having to do with the improvement of educational opportunities for the immigrants, the wider dissemination of Polish reading materials in schools, better health safety in the work place, and greater efforts to provide immigrants with accurate information about medical remedies being sold in Polonia, hygiene, and the problem of alcoholism. The Political section dealt with uniting Polonia under the leadership of the PNA on behalf of Poland's freedom, issued a resolution calling for Poland's restoration to independence (a controversial declaration at the time), and a proposal to set up a permanent national organization uniting the Polish people in America around the cause. **John Smulski**, **Thomas Siemiradzki**, **Alexander Dębski** (head of the Polish Socialist Alliance), and **Marian Stęczyński** (president of the PNA), were the key figures in organizing the Congress. **Romuald Piątkowski** served as its secretary; the extraordinary publication he put out in 1911 is a gold mine of information about

the meeting and the dedication ceremonies that preceded it. The Polish National Congress failed to bring together the entire Polish community of the time and did not become a permanent institution. Significantly, the federations working for Polish independence that came after, most notably the Polish **National Defense Committee** (KON; 1912) and the Polish **National Department** (Wydział Narodowy; 1916) succeeded as more inclusive federations, at least at first in the case of KON, and were not PNA–dominated.—*Donald E. Pienkos*

SOURCES: Donald E. Pienkos, *For Your Freedom Through Ours: Polish American Efforts in Poland's Behalf, 1863–1991* (Boulder, CO: East European Monographs, 1991); Romuald Piątkowski, *A Memorial Commemorating the Unveiling of the Kościuszko and Pułaski Monuments along with the Holding of the First Polish National Congress in Washington, D.C.* (Chicago: Polish National Alliance, 1911).

Polish National Council (Rada Narodowa). A **Polonia** federation formed in 1914 in support of Poland's independence and its inhabitants' well being, the organization was active during the First World War (1914–18). From the emergence of a substantial Polish immigration to the United States after the American Civil War (1861–65), repeated attempts were made to create an organization that could unite the Poles under one banner. Notable early efforts in this direction were the establishment of the Organization of Poles in America (Organizacja Polaków w Ameryce, later the **Polish Roman Catholic Union** in America) in 1873, the **Polish National Alliance** (Związek Narodowy Polski) in 1880, and the **Polish League of 1894**. All failed to achieve their goal. In the early 1900s, the **Polish National Alliance** renewed its efforts in this direction, meeting with partial success, by developing close ties with a number of "nationalist" organizations in the community, most notably the **Polish Falcons Alliance** and **Polish Women's Alliance**. However, the May 1910 **Polish National Congress** that the PNA promoted failed to attract representatives from the Catholic wing in Polonia. In September 1912, on the occasion of a general meeting of organizational leaders in Pittsburgh that was called to witness the reunification of the Polish Falcons Alliance as an independent organization, a new national federation was created, the **National Defense Committee** (Komitet Obrony Narodowej, KON). But the supporters of this federation were seen as too closely associated with anti–Russian Polish independence activists in partitioned Poland led by Józef Piłsudski. Consequently, Polonia activists identified with **Ignacy Jan Paderewski** and Roman Dmowski, head of the anti–German National Democratic movement in Poland,

withdrew from KON in June 1913 and formed the Polish National Council (Rada Narodowa). The president of the PRCUA, Stanisław Adamkiewicz became the head of the Council and Bishop **Paul Rhode** of Chicago was named its honorary chair.

Following the outbreak of World War I, the Council initiated a weekly propaganda and information publication titled *Free Poland*. This publication continued until 1919. In October 1914 the Rada Narodowa leadership, together with the Polish National Alliance, the Polish Falcons Alliance, and the Polish Women's Alliance, each of which had also seceded from the KON, united in Chicago to create the **Polish Central Relief Committee** (Polski Centralny Komitet Ratunkowy, PCKR). In 1916, it greatly strengthened the scope of responsibilities of its political affairs subcommittee, the **National Department** (Wydział Narodowy). This body represented the main Polonia fraternal and church leadership except for the small Polish Socialist Party and the **Polish National Catholic Church**, both of which remained aligned with KON. The most prominent figure in the National Department was the respected Chicago banker, politician, and leader **John F. Smulski**, who maintained close ties with both Paderewski and Dmowski and supported America's alliance with France and Britain as the best way in which to secure Polish independence after the war. Ironically, it was Piłsudski who became the most prominent Polish leader following the regaining of Poland's independence in 1918. But this did not much help KON, which remained a marginal factor in Polonia. Moreover, the idea of a united Polonia remained only a hope until World War II with the creation of the **Polish American Council** (or Rada Polonii) in 1939 and the **Polish American Congress** in 1944.—*Donald E. Pienkos*

SOURCES: Andrzej Brożek, *Polish Americans 1854–1939* (Warsaw: Interpress, 1985); A. M. Jasienski, "The Polish National Council of America," *Free Poland*, Vol. I (July 1, 1915).

Polish National Union of America. Also known as Spójnia, the Polish National Union of America is a not-for-profit fraternal benefit society founded in 1908 by Prime Bishop **Franciszek Hodur**, the organizer of the **Polish National Catholic Church** (PNCC). Headquartered in Scranton, Pennsylvania, the Polish National Union provides its members with life insurance, mortgages, retirement plans and annuities, and operates a credit union. It is affiliated with the PNCC. Bishop Hodur saw the need for a fraternal organization for PNCC members since many of them were being barred or facing discrimination from existing Polish American fraternals because of their church affiliation. The Union provides financial assistance to PNCC parishes and publishes the monthly newspaper *Straż* (The Guard) which debuted in 1897. The Union is organized into more than 100 branches. It supports a home for the aged and disabled in Waymart, Pennsylvania, provides stipends and scholarships to deserving youths, sponsors sports activities for young and old, and organizes youth retreats, tours of Poland, and Polish cultural events. Through the years, the Union has been active in charitable programs and provided assistance to national disaster relief efforts, without regard to religious affiliation. In the 1980s the organization initiated the "Medical Bridge to Poland" program, which has provided well over a million dollars worth of medical aid to that country.—*Martin S. Nowak*

SOURCE: Stephan Wlodarski, *The Origin and Growth of the Polish National Catholic Church* (Scranton: Polish National Catholic Church, 1974).

Polish Printers Association (Stowarzyszenie Drukarzy Polskich). The Polish immigrants who arrived in the United States before 1900 came in two waves. The first were those who emigrated after the defeat of the insurrection in 1863. These immigrants were mostly from noble families and came to establish a new homeland; they were fiercely attached to the cause of Polish independence. The second wave, which began around 1890, was comprised of immigrants seeking a better life, the so-called *emigracja za chlebem* (emigration for bread). For both of these groups, the Polish-language press was very important. But the publication of newspapers comprised only a part of the output of the early Polish press. There was also great demand for fiction and non-fiction books, theatrical plays, music, religious publications, and text books. Although some publishers printed books, newspapers were the main provider of published materials and often serialized fiction. As early as 1872, **Władysław Dyniewicz** edited and published a newspaper, the *Gazeta Polska* (Polish Gazette), in which he espoused his views; he also was one of the organizers of the **Gmina Polska** patriotic club, which took part in the founding of The **Polish National Alliance** (PNA) in the early 1880s, and which, in turn, established the Alliance of Printers and Publishers. Those who were aligned with the Roman Catholic St. Stanislaus Kostka Society, the Rev. **Wincenty Barzyński**, and Francis Gordon, published the rival *Gazeta Polska Katolicka* (Polish Catholic Gazette). Eventually they founded, with **Władysław Smulski**, the Polish Publishing Company, a disseminator of Catholic literature. In conjunction with the **Polish Roman Catholic**

Union of America, they first published *Wiara i Ojczyzna* (Faith and Fatherland), a weekly, and subsequently a daily newspaper, the ***Dziennik Chicagoski*** (Chicago Daily News).

Jan I. Migdalski, who emigrated from Warsaw in 1899, is credited with founding the Polish Printers Association in 1894. First employed as the director and an editor by the newspaper *Wiara i Ojczyzna*, he soon established his own print shop, interestingly located at the same street address as the PNA. Unfortunately, soon after attending a union convention in South Carolina in 1895, he succumbed to tuberculosis, which was often called the "printers disease." It is possible that it was he who started the newspaper *Telegraf* (Telegraph) in its earliest incarnation in the

early 1890s. After Migdalski's death, the fledgling union struggled to survive due to friction between political factions. One faction consisted of the "Alliancists," members of, or those sympathetic to, the PNA's patriotic agenda. On the other side were the "Unionists," strongly influenced by the Catholic-oriented Polish Roman Catholic Union of America. However, the two fraternal organizations had common goals — both were committed to preserving the Polish language, culture, and community in the United States.

Although Migdalski was an editor and later an independent publisher, most union members were typesetters at various Polish language print shops. The more activist members worked at the Polish-language newspapers. During this early period these included the

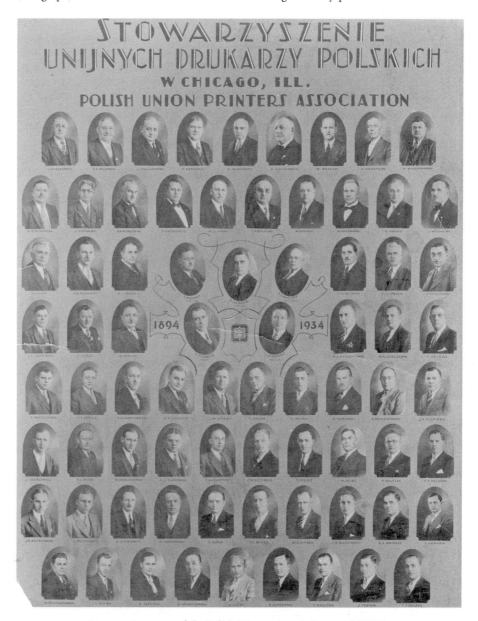

A composite group of the Polish Printers Association, 1934 (*PMA*).

daily *Dziennik Chicagoski* owned by the **Resurrectionist** Order, the semi-monthly ***Narod Polski*** (The Polish Nation), the official publication of the PRCUA, and two PNA–sponsored newspapers, the weekly ***Zgoda*** (Harmony), the national publication of the PNA, and the ***Dziennik Związkowy*** (Alliance Daily News), its Chicago-based daily. Other newspapers included the ***Dziennik Zjednoczenia*** (Union Daily News), the interwar Chicago daily sponsored by the PRCUA, and the ***Dziennik Ludowy*** (People's Daily News), operated under the auspices of the Polish Socialist Alliance.

The Polish Printers Association affiliated with the International Typographical Union in 1895 and was renamed The Chicago Polish Typographical Union No. 358. Later regaining its independence, it then rejoined the ITU again in 1902, at which time it became part of ITU Local No. 16 until the ITU merged into the Communications Workers of America. In 1902, the Association was renamed The Chicago Polish Typographical Union No. 546. Eventually all Polish-language print shops in Chicago were organized, including the PRCUA newspapers, those of the **Polish National Alliance**, and several socialist newspapers. Illness and death benefits were provided to members in addition to the union's main mission of improving pay and working conditions for printers. It also provided safety and technical education to members. At the turn of the century, the linotype machine was invented and the union trained typesetters in the new technology. A periodical trade paper, *Drukarz* (The Printer), began publication in 1902 under the direction of Jan Chonarzewski, an ardent union supporter who pushed for the Polish Printers' second affiliation with the national union. Historical notes disclose that the Polish Printers Association raised money for schools in Poland, the statue of General **Kościuszko** in Chicago's Humboldt Park (now relocated to the lakefront) and the Printers Home (an old age facility and tuberculosis sanatorium) in Colorado Springs, Colorado.

Among those responsible for establishing and maintaining the union were Jan Olbiński, Stanisław Zawiliński, brothers Antony and Jan Chonarzewski, Antony Kołodziejski, Jan Grzeca, Piotr Liske, Jan Habrylewicz, Edward Reichel, Roman Neumann, Stanisław Zloczewski, Józef Koleta, Władysław Panek, A. Eichstaedt, E. Blachowski, F. Cienciara, Peter Kotowski, Edward L. Kolakowski, and A. Janecki.—*Daryl Ann Hiller*

SOURCES: *Poles of Chicago 1837–1937; A History of One Century of Polish Contribution to the City of Chicago, Illinois* (Chicago: Polish Pageant, Inc., 1937); Donald E. Pienkos, *P.N.A.: A Centennial History of the Polish National Alliance of the United States of North America* (Boulder, CO: East European Monographs, 1984).

The Polish Review. *The Polish Review* (ISSN 0032-2970) is a peer-reviewed, scholarly quarterly with editorial offices in New York City. It has been published continuously since 1956 by the **Polish Institute of Arts and Sciences of America**, with headquarters in the Murray Hill section of Manhattan. The history of *The Polish Review* began in 1942 when **Bronisław Malinowski**, **Oskar Halecki**, and other members of the Polish Academy of Arts and Sciences (Polska Akademia Umiejętności), forced into exile by the Nazi-Soviet occupation of Poland during World War II, called PIASA into being in order to carry on the academic traditions of PAU, repressed by the German occupiers of Kraków. The new Institute soon began holding scholarly meetings after the manner of PAU, with the meeting reports, along with scholarly articles by members and other texts of interest, published in *The Polish Review*'s direct predecessor, the PIASA *Bulletin* (*Biuletyn*). As PIASA modeled itself on PAU, so the *Bulletin* followed in the footsteps of previous PAU publications, reporting on the section meetings held by all Institute members encompassing both the physical sciences and the humanities. Although PIASA members continue to represent all fields of academic endeavor, the mission of *The Polish Review* has been to be the premier English-language outlet for Polish-centered scholarship. Thus, although articles in the physical sciences are no longer to be found in its pages, the quarterly continues to be a multi-disciplinary journal regularly publishing scholarship in the fields of Polish literature, history, art history, culture, music, and film, as well as sociology, political science, economics, and related fields dealing with Poland and Poles. Although primarily concerned with Poland, *The Polish Review* also accepts articles on American and global **Polonia**. Less frequently, it features noteworthy translations of Polish literature and interviews with important figures. Book reviews appear in every issue. Since 1956, its editors-in-chief have included Stanisław Skrzypek (1956), **Ludwik Krzyżanowski** (1956–1986), **Stanisław Barańczak** (1986–1990), Joseph W. Wieczerzak (1991–2007), and Charles S. Kraszewski (2008–). *The Polish Review* celebrated its fiftieth anniversary in November 2006 with publication of an anthology of notable works that first appeared between its covers —*Fifty Years of Polish Scholarship: The Polish Review, 1956–2006. The Polish Review* maintains an Internet home at www.thepolishreview.org.—*Charles S. Kraszewski*

SOURCE: Frank Mocha, "The Polish Institute of Arts and Sciences in America: Its Contributions to the Study of Polonia: The Origins of the Polish American Historical Association (PAHA)," in Frank Mocha, ed., *Poles in America: Bicentennial Essays* (Stevens Point, WI: Worzalla Publishing Company, 1978), 709–24.

Polish Roman Catholic Union of America (Zjednoczenia Polsko-Rzymsko Katolickie w Ameryce). The Polish Roman Catholic Union of America (PRCUA) is the oldest extant Polish-American national organization. It is the oldest fraternal society and as of 2007 was the second-largest Polish American organization. The PRCUA was founded in 1873 in Detroit at a meeting attended by representatives of several early **Polonia** enclaves. Three individuals were essential to the organization's founding: the Rev. **Teodor Gieryk**, a Detroit priest, **Jan Barzyński**, a newspaper editor, and the Rev. **Wincenty Barzyński**, the pastor of St. Stanislaus Kostka parish in Chicago, the city's first Polish parish. The following year, the organization relocated to Chicago and the parish of St. Stanislaus where it came under the leadership of the redoubtable the Rev. Barzyński. The exact nature of the early PRCUA is unclear due to conflicting accounts, rivalries, conflicts, and the animosity of many non–PRCUA leaders toward the Rev. Barzyński and his fellow **Resurrectionists**. The Rev. Gieryk and several other early Polonia leaders sought to create an organization for anyone who identified as Polish-American, while the Rev. Barzyński wanted an organization that would be both Polish and Catholic, thus leaving out non–Catholics. In 1880, the **Polish National Alliance** (PNA) would emerge as the secular alternative to the PRCUA, open to members whatever their religious inclinations. At the heart of this difference were two distinct visions of **Polskość** (Polishness) in America. One was that of secular nationalism, heavily influenced by a concern for the liberation of the Polish homeland from foreign domination. The vision ultimately enshrined by the PRCUA was that of the "parish-community," an American version of the okolica (a Polish village community). A Catholic version of Polish **positivism**, and especially the idea of "organic work," were important influences on the PRCUA's founders and leaders. For the Rev. Barzyński, Polishness in a local community centered on a parish church. These ideas shaped the early structure of the PRCUA which resembled a loose confederation of independent parish death-benefit societies more than a centralized organization. Until 1887, the PRCUA had no central benefit structure — death benefits were provided entirely by the local affiliated societies. Even after benefits were centralized, it took several years for all PRCUA societies to actually join the fund.

Among the early activities of the PRCUA were the creation of rural colonies in Nebraska, the promotion of Polish parochial schools and seminary, and the publishing of Catholic-oriented newspapers. The Union did not have an official organ until 1887 when it created *Wiara i Ojczyzna* (Faith and Fatherland). Prior to this, *Pielgrzym* (The Pilgrim) and *Gazeta Polska Katolicka* (Polish Catholic Gazette) served as unofficial PRCUA organs under the editorship of Jan Barzyński. In 1897, the PRCUA established a new organ, *Naród Polski* (The Polish Nation). The 1880s and 1890s were characterized by both rapid growth and intense rivalry with the newer Polish National Alliance. Until about 1896, the PRCUA had more members, but after this date, the PNA outpaced the PRCUA in memberships. This may have been due to the fact that the PNA allowed for the creation of more local societies than did the PRCUA. At the start of the twentieth century, the PRCUA was heavily concentrated in Chicago, Pennsylvania, and Michigan which together accounted for sixty percent of all the local societies in the organization. The Union made few inroads into New England until after 1900. Almost a quarter of all Union societies were in Chicago and its environs. This reflected the close tie between the PRCUA and the **Congregation of the Resurrection**. The PRCUA societies were all based in parishes and thus closely tied to the development of Polish American **religious life**. This was reflected not only in the importance of pastors within local societies, but also in the symbols and requirements of membership. All members were required to be Catholics in good standing. The PRCUA developed as part of a larger universe of Resurrectionist-led enterprises which included newspapers, schools, hospitals, and even a temperance society. It was quite common for PRCUA publications to share editors with Resurrectionist counterparts such as *Dziennik Chicagoski* (Chicago Daily News). The PRCUA also served as the main Catholic loyalist organization. It never wavered from its full support for the American bishops and its opposition to dissidents, atheists, radicals, and schismatics such as Bishop **Francis Hodur** of the **Polish National Catholic Church** (PNCC). Nevertheless, after the death of the Rev. Barzyński in 1899 the organization began to moderate its position in several respects. Thus it began to provide a forum to the Rev. **Wacław Kruszka** in his efforts to gain a Polish-American bishop and it began to gradually separate itself from other Resurrectionist enterprises. Although the PRCUA continued to work closely with the Chicago Resurrectionists, it operated with far greater autonomy after 1899. This was reflected in the growing significance of lay leaders whose importance and power within the PRCUA grew in the first three decades of the twentieth century.

Unlike its rival, the PNA, the PRCUA never saw itself as the "fourth partition" of Poland, nor did it seek to gather other Polonia organizations under its control. Instead, it focused on grassroots social development and sought alliances with allied groups. Significantly, the PRCUA newspapers reflected the rhetoric and concerns of the Progressive Era: social problems such as family breakdown, alcoholism, crime, and juvenile delinquency took up far more space than the plight of the Polish homeland. During World War I, however, the PRCUA, led by Bishop **Paul Rhode**, mobilized its resources on behalf of Polish independence. It became a critical part of Bishop Rhode's Polska Rada Narodowa (**Polish National Council**; RPN) and supported the exclusion of the PNCC as well as socialists and other radicals from membership. It also took part in the Polski Centralny Komitet Ratunkowy w Ameryce (**Polish Central Relief Committee**; PCKR) and the **National Department** of the PCKR. Union headquarters in Chicago was a recruiting station for both the U.S. Army and the **Polish Army in France** under Gen. Haller. Its publishing arm produced the PNC's English-language materials including the magazine *Free Poland*, while its business office managed the finances of the PCKR and oversaw collection of the National Fund.

Following the war, the PRCUA—like many ethnic fraternals—developed a new set of programs for the community's expanding cohort of youth and young adults, including sports programs, scout troops, a summer camp, youth insurance policies, and educational programs. In the 1930s, the Union provided the major support for the creation of the **Polish Museum of America**. The PRCUA also established its own daily newspaper, *Dziennik Zjednoczenia* (The Union Daily News), but the effort fell victim to the economic woes of the Depression and was discontinued in 1940.

During World War II, the PRCUA again played a significant role in mobilizing Polonia to support the Polish cause and to support the American war effort. Union presidents such as **Joseph Kania** and **Jan Olejniczak** were the first leaders to press for the creation of what would later become the **Polish American Congress** (PAC). Despite its early role in the development of the PAC, the Union eventually played a secondary role to the rival PNA after the congress' formation in 1944. PRCUA presidents served as PAC treasurers and often complained that they were treated as second class citizens by their rivals. Between 1948 and 1953, the PRCUA withdrew from the PAC when President Joseph Kania had a falling out with PNA President **Charles Rozmarek**.

After the war, the PRCUA focused more heavily on the insurance business. From a financial standpoint the organization did well and was able to acquire significant property in the city of Chicago. Nevertheless, the aging of the Polish-American community and residential and economic changes in the country as a whole resulted in a gradual decline of membership, as did the decline in the number of heavily Polish "ethnic" parishes, the historic base of support for the PRCUA. During the late 1960s, the Union's dynamic young president Joseph Pranica sought to break this cycle of decline by acquiring a mainstream insurance company, Nathan Hale insurance. The idea seems to have been that it would allow the PRCUA to sell insurance to non–Poles and non–Catholics and use the proceeds to

A board of directors meeting of the Polish Roman Catholic Union in the 1930s (*PMA*).

enhance the Union's overall finances. It would also help to circumvent the practice of using amateur salespeople from the Union's local branches (who received a commission on each new policy and were understandably loath to give this up). Nathan Hale's professional salespeople could sell PRCUA policies and reach out to Polish Americans beyond the traditional Polonia enclaves where the majority of the Union's activity had been focused. The Union also acquired a bank as part of the deal. This bold move, however, backfired due to political infighting and mismanagement.

Although PRCUA membership has continued its steady decline, the organization has continued to develop financially, culturally and spiritually. It remains the second-largest Polonia organization after the PNA. The election of Pope John Paul II in 1978 was a major event for the organization, resulting in the creation of several new societies. The Union supports a wide variety of cultural activities and events, including **Saturday Schools**, folk dance ensembles, and, perhaps most important, the **Polish Museum of America**.—*John Radzilowski*

SOURCES: John Radzilowski, *The Eagle and the Cross: A History of Polish Roman Catholic Union of America, 1873–2000* (Boulder, CO: East European Monographs, 2003); Miecislaus Haiman, *Polish Roman Catholic Union of America, 1873–1948* (Chicago: Polish Roman Catholic Union of America, 1948).

Polish Section, Socialist Party of the United States. The largest of three organizations supported by the Polish American left prior to World War I, the Polish Section of the Socialist Party had its genesis with a group of young Polish immigrant radicals who began publishing *Dziennik Ludowy* (People's Daily News) in Chicago in 1907 under the editorship of Michał Sokołowski. In the following year, sixteen socialist locals formed the Polish Section of the Socialist Party, the first foreign language federation accepted within the Socialist Party, under the leadership of M. Sokołowski, Z. Piotrowski, and F. Cienciara. Unlike the weekly *Robotnik* (The Worker), the official organ of the **Alliance of Polish Socialists**, which focused mostly on original local reporting, *Dziennik Ludowy* initially offered its readers more international and American national news and commentary, including extensive coverage of industrial struggles in the U.S. and developments within the American labor movement. The Polish Section advocated ignoring considerations of race, ethnicity, and language in order to achieve social ownership of the means of production. Leaders of the Polish Section strongly supported industrial unionism and the Industrial Workers of the World. By the end of 1912, there were 134 Polish locals numbering approximately 2,500 members, half of whom were also union members. Readership of the *Dziennik Ludowy* increased to 8,000 by 1913. After 1912, the Polish Section questioned the policy of Alliance of Polish Socialists which it charged with ignoring worker issues and focusing primarily on the issue of Polish independence. In 1913, there was a short-lived attempt to reconcile the Polish Section and the Alliance of Polish Socialists under the name Polish Federation of the Socialist Party, but this existed only until 1916. After 1916, the Polish Section and the Alliance of Polish Socialists split over their support for rival European factions. In 1919, when some of its activists were deported, the Polish Section regrouped as the Polish Federation of the Communist Party, and in the 1920s it created the Polish Bureau of the Communist Party U.S. led by **Bolesław Gebert**, T. Radwański, J. Kowalski, and **Stanley Nowak**, with the *Głos Robotniczy* (Worker's Voice) and *Trybuna Robotnicza* (Worker's Tribune) as its press organs.—*Adam Walaszek*

SOURCES: Mary E. Cygan, "The Polish American Left," in P. Buhle and D. Georgakas, eds., *The Immigrant Left in the United States* (Albany: State University of New York Press, 1996); K. Groniowski, "Socjalistyczna emigracja polska w Stanach Zjednoczonych (1883–1914)," *Z Pola Walki*, 1977, no 1; D. Piątkowska-Koźlik, *Związek Socjalistów Polskich w Ameryce (1900–1914)* (Opole: WSP, 1992).

Polish Singers Alliance of America (Związek Spiewaków Polskich w Ameryce). Founded in Chicago in 1889 on the initiative of **Antoni Małłek**, a leader in the **Polish National Alliance**, the goal of the Polish Singers Alliance of America was to "propagate and cultivate Polish national song among the Poles of America." It was, from its inception, what **Stanislaus Blejwas** called an "ideological organization" whose goals were to inculcate and preserve Polish patriotism, not merely serve as a forum for the enjoyment of song. The Alliance's founding reflected the tradition of choral singing in Poland as a means of promoting patriotism. It emerged at a time when **Polonia** was groping towards organizational structure amidst competing visions of the national community. The Alliance grew rapidly in its early years and boasted sixteen choirs by 1896, all in the Midwest with six in Chicago alone. However, a bitter factional dispute soon erupted which lasted until 1903, with the Singers Alliance barely resisting an effort by the Polish National Alliance to assume control. Factionalism plagued the Singers Alliance which endured another serious split in 1913 that radically diminished membership. Despite this and wartime disorders, there were more than 100 choirs involved by 1918. But the numbers were deceiving as the organization, faction ridden and impoverished, was near dissolution by war's end. The situation stabilized during the long presidency of Władysław Panka (1928–47), with the split of 1913 finally ending in 1929. The efforts of the government of independent Poland to act as patron of the singers' movement led to its revitalization. The Singers Alliance began again to expand in numbers as well as geographic dispersal, but with characteristic volatility: of 260 registered choirs in 1937 only 100 were active. In an effort to appeal to Polish Americans, what had been exclusively Polish selections began to include a variety of other compositions in the interwar years.

World War II was a difficult era for the Singers Alliance as income fell and many choirs became inactive; membership declined almost sixty percent with only 44 choirs remaining active by 1944. The national treasury had scarcely $100. After the war, the Alliance moved its national headquarters from Chicago to New York (in 2008 it was located in Buffalo), but the organization continued to flounder. Under the leadership of Józef Czechlewski (1950–80) a brief revival occurred in the early 1950s with new choirs joining, including the first Canadian affiliates, and choirs representing the post-war emigration appeared. Nevertheless, the Alliance gradually became split between the newer immigrants and "old Polonia." The severance of ties with Poland, then under Communist rule, also affected the organization. Membership peaked in 1956 reaching its pre-war height, but dropped precipitately thereafter. When Czechlewski left the presidency the Alliance was but half the size it was when his tenure began, a decline characteristic of many Polonia organizations during that era. The decline in continuing emigration and an aging Polonia made the Alliance an ethnic rather than an immigrant organization. The characteristic use of English rather than Polish became increasingly apparent by the 1980s. By its centennial, the Alliance had only about forty active choirs with membership hovering at approximately 1,500. A number of changes of leadership and headquarters have proven disruptive, while the financial health of the Alliance remained precarious.

For most of its existence the Alliance, a reservoir of patriotism, has endeavored to preserve Polish traditions and loyalties during times of hardship. Whether the re-emergence of a prosperous and free Poland will allow the Alliance to survive in Blejwas's words as a "purely cultural organization," or whether it needs to bear witness to the Polish cause to endure, functioning as an "ideological" organization, remains unclear.—*M. B. B. Biskupski*

SOURCES: Stanislaus A. Blejwas, *The Polish Singers Alliance of America, 1888–1998: Choral Patriotism* (Rochester, NY: University of Rochester Press, 2005); Leon T. Blaszczek, "The Polish Singers' Movement in America," *Polish American Studies*, Vol. 38, no. 1 (1981), 50–62.

Polish Slavonian Literary Association

(Polsko-Słowiańskiego Stowarzyszenia Literackiego). Aside from their continuing political interest in Poland and the cause of Polish independence, the exiles from the November Uprising (1830–31) and the later equally unsuccessful Mierosławski revolt (1846) were very much interested in promoting awareness of Polish history and culture in America. To this end, **Gaspard Tochman** founded the Polish Slavonian Literary Association in New York on March 26, 1846. He was assisted in this effort by **Paweł (Paul) Sobolewski, Feliks Paweł Wierzbicki**, Jósef Podbielski, and **Henryk Kałussowski**. Formed with the purpose of promoting knowledge and the history, literature, and scientific achievement of the Slavic people among the American public, the organization grew rapidly to more than 200 members including such leading Americans as the historian Jared Sparks, editor and publisher of the New York *Daily Tribune* Horace Greeley, U.S. Attorney General Reverdy Johnson, Secretary of the Treasury Levi Woodbury, poet and editor of the New York *Evening Post* William Cullen Bryan, poet F. G. Halleck, New York political leader William H. Seward, future presidential candidate Samuel Tilden, Albert Gallatin, and Samuel Gridley Howe. Hoping to form a society that would continue to attract American illuminati, the Poles enticed Georgia Senator John M. Pherson to be president, with J. J. Astor as treasurer and other equally influential people holding the other officer positions. Unfortunately, a continuing lack of funds greatly curtained operations, causing attendance at meetings to plummet. A noble effort, in the end its accomplishments were few.—*James S. Pula*

SOURCES: Florian Stasik, *Polish Political Emigrés in the United States of America, 1831–1864* (Boulder, CO: East European Monographs, 2002; transl. Eugene Podraza, ed. James S. Pula), 106–08; Zygmunt Wardziński, "The Oldest Slavic Magazine in the United States: 'Poland: Historical, Literary, Monumental, Picturesque' and its Article on Copernicus (1842)," *The Polish Review*, Vol. 19, no. 3–4 (1974), 83–98.

Polish Socialist Alliance in America

(Związek Socjalistów Polskich w Ameryce; ZSP). Founded in 1900 in Buffalo, NY, by the congress of the **Polish Section of the Socialist Party of America** (founded in 1894), the group numbered about 1,000 members, most of whom were active in Chicago, Cleveland, Detroit, Milwaukee, and the industrial centers

Polish Socialist Alliance headquarters and print shop for its newspaper *Robotnik*, 1902 (*PMA*).

of Pennsylvania and the East Coast. The Alliance sought to combine the struggle for the independence of Poland with the struggle for workers' rights. After 1909, the ZSP gave its full moral and material support to the newly established Polish Socialist Labor Party of America (SPA), including transferring a portion of individual membership dues to the Socialist Party. The Alliance participated in Socialist Party federal and municipal election campaigns, also encouraging both individual members and local branches to join the SPA. Continual discussions were held within the Alliance on the possibility of merging with the SPA, but the Alliance remained a separate organization to emphasize the importance of the independence of Poland which it believed was an indispensable condition for fulfilling the rightful demands of Polish workers. Interestingly, in 1907, the Socialist Party of America set up its own Polish Section, which weakened the ZSP. Within the sphere of Polish politics, the ZSP followed the Polish Socialist Party (PPS) and Józef Piłsudski's political thought. Many ZSP activists were emissaries of the Polish Socialist Party to America, with **Aleksander Dębski** the most prominent and active among them. The ZSP provided funds to the PPS, especially during the revolutionary period of 1905–07 that occurred in connection with the Russo-Japanese War. In 1912, activists of the Polish Socialist Alliance were among the founders of the Polish **National Defense Committee** (KON), remaining its backbone until 1919. The Alliance organized libraries, reading rooms, and theater performances for Polish American workers, as well as publishing

Robotnik Polski (The Polish Worker), a weekly newspaper appearing from 1897 to 1967. In 1910 the Alliance established the Workmen's Aid Fund, and in 1912 founded the Polish People's University in New York. During the First World War it devoted most of its energies to the Polish question. After 1918 many ZSP leaders re-emigrated to Poland, weakening the organization in America. Some of its local chapters thereupon joined SPA, but individual locals operated into the 1970s.—*Joanna Wojdon*

SOURCES: Mary E. Cygan, "Polish American Socialism," in Paul Buhle and Dan Georgakas, eds., *Immigrant Radicalism* (Albany: State University of New York Press, 1996), 148–84; Mary E. Cygan, "Political and Cultural Leadership in an Immigrant Community: Polish American Socialism, 1880–1950" (Ph.D. dissertation, Northwestern University); Danuta Piątkowska-Koźlik, *Związek Socjalistów Polskich w Ameryce (1900–1914)* (Opole: Wyzsza Szkoła Pedagogiczna w Opolu, 1992).

Polish Studies Programs in the United States.

In discussing programs on Polish studies, reference is usually made to programs involving two or more academic persons at a particular college or university who teach courses in, and write about, the history, language, literature, political experience, and culture of the Polish people in Poland and the experience of Polish emigrants and their descendents living outside of Poland. Such programs may exist as formally established Polish studies programs, or operate more informally as recognized groupings of scholars interested in the Polish experience. They almost always involve instruction in the Polish language, along with courses taught on Polish literature and Polish history; they may also include courses in political science, film, theater, art, and society, along with the study of **Polonia**. Polish studies also may be understood in broader terms, as **Stanislaus A. Blejwas** has argued in a 1994 article published in *The Sarmatian Review*, that is, by including national scholarly organizations whose mission is to promote knowledge of the Polish experience, along with the Polish studies programs at American universities and colleges. Most notable among these organizations are the **Polish Institute of Arts and Sciences of America**, the **Polish American Historical Association**, and the Polish Studies Association. They also include institutions like the **Kosciuszko Foundation** and cultural associations operating in various localities, many of which belong to the **American Council for Polish Culture**. These latter organizations are covered elsewhere in this work.

One compilation of Polish studies programs at American universities lists as many as sixty-six such groupings, most of which involve informal activities of faculty members in disciplines like Polish language and literature, Polish and East Central European history, and collateral areas like the social sciences, theater, and film studies. A closer analysis of this list indicates that several programs in Polish studies are particularly strong in terms of the size of their Polish studies faculties, their academic focus on Polish studies, and records of achievement over the years. Notable programs in Polish studies, in alphabetical order, include those at the following institutions: Central Connecticut State University in New Britain, Connecticut; Columbia University; Indiana University; University of Illinois at Chicago; University of Michigan; University of Rochester; and the University of Wisconsin–Milwaukee. Here special mention might be made about the establishment of a chair in Polish and Polish American studies at Central Connecticut State University through the energetic efforts of Stanislaus A. Blejwas. Among Blejwas's other initiatives was an annual lecture series devoted to the Polish ethnic experience in America.

Columbia University's involvement in Polish studies dates back to the 1950s and as of the early 2000s eight academic faculty were engaged in the program, which is part of the university's East Central European Institute and master's degree in International Affairs. Indiana University's Polish Studies Center goes back to the early 1970s and has received federal funding for its programs, which include an association with the University of Warsaw. The University of Illinois at Chicago has had faculty in Polish language and literature and Polish history for many years. In

2009 the University received a bequest of more than nine million dollars from a local Polish American to establish endowed chairs in Polish history and Polish literature. The University of Michigan, in addition to faculty in language, literature, and history, boasts the Copernicus Endowment, initiated in 1973, the 500th anniversary of his birth, which supports academic study in Polish affairs and an annual lectureship that has brought a long list of prestigious scholars, scientists, and artists of Polish origin to speak on the campus.

The Skalny Center for Polish and Central European Studies at the University of Rochester dates to 1994. In 2007, it adopted its present name, thanks to substantial endowments from the Louis **Skalny family**, which is prominent in the area. The Center maintains a close connection with the Jagiellonian University in Poland. A number of prominent faculty members from that institution have been visiting scholars at the university. The University of Wisconsin–Milwaukee's Polish Studies committee dates back to 1979 and at its height in the early 1990s included six faculty members having a strong scholarly interest in the fields of Polish language and literature, history, the geography of Poland and East Central Europe, Poland's political experience, and the Polish immigration and ethnic experience in the U.S. Polish studies at UW–M resulted from pressure from the Polish community, support from state legislators of Polish heritage, and cooperation from one of the university's officials and several of its faculty members.

Solid faculty-based programs in Polish studies are also to be found at Boston College; Rutgers University; University of North Carolina; University of California at Berkeley; University of Washington; Yale University; and University of Wisconsin–Madison (the site of the very first Polish Studies program in the U.S. in 1935, one headed by Dr. Edmund Zawacki, 1908–93). It might also be noted that Polish studies programs have existed in several universities in the past, but are no longer active on the same level. This is due to faculty retirements and the decisions of their institutions not to replace them with new personnel having similar academic interests. The continuing viability of Polish studies programs in the U.S. depends on three factors: (a) the existence (and availability) of academic professionals trained in one of the fields of Polish studies (b) faculty and administration support for the appointment of such programs, and (c) the involvement of Polish American community activists (and possibly in the future the Polish government) in pressing for the appointment of faculty specializing in some area of Polish studies and the creation and main-

tenance of such programs. Professor Blejwas argued in the above-noted 1994 *Sarmatian Review* article that a summit meeting of Polish American organization leaders was needed to begin charting a national strategy to develop Polish studies in the U.S. While a conference of academic specialists was held on this subject in 1995 under Polish embassy sponsorship, it did not lead to the all–**Polonia** summit that Blejwas had envisioned.—*Donald E. Pienkos*

SOURCES: "Questionnaire" in *The Sarmatian Review*, Vol. 14 (1995); Angela Pienkos and Donald E. Pienkos, "Marian Kamil Dziewanowski" in *The Polish Review*, Volume 50, no. 3 (2005), Appendix 1; Frank Mocha, "The Polish Institute of Arts and Sciences of America and the Polish American Historical Association," in Frank Mocha, ed., *Poles in America: Bicentennial Essays* (Stevens Point, WI: Worzalla Publishers, 1978).

Polish Union of America (Unia Polska w Ameryce). In 2008, the Polish Union of America was a fraternal benefit society chartered under the laws of the State of New York to provide insurance and fraternal services to its membership. Formed in 1890 by Msgr. **Dominik Majer** of St. Paul, MN, and the Rev. **John Pitass** of Buffalo, NY, because of their belief that the secular foundation of the **Polish National Alliance** and the religious priority of the **Polish Roman Catholic Union** should be brought together in a new, united **Polonia** fraternal. Majer left the PNA after its 1889 convention where the delegates rejected his proposal that the Alliance follow a Catholic religious orientation, and not a secular one open to all religious and non-religious persons. He had already broken with the PRCUA because it was not "patriotic" enough. The new Polish Union of America was originally organized from three parish societies at Saint Adalbert's Church in St. Paul, and the Sons of the Queen of Poland Society at St. Stanislaus Church in Buffalo. From its inception, delegates from the various lodges have gathered periodically for meetings of the grand convention. Initially, each such convention reserved the right to designate the headquarters, which was relocated from St. Paul, to Buffalo, to St. Paul, to Wilkes-Barre, and then back to Buffalo. At the 1910 convention in Chicago, a dispute regarding this designation led the organization to break into two parts. The first retained the name of the Polish Union of America with headquarters in Buffalo. The second established operations in Wilkes-Barre and became known as the **Polish Union of the United States of North America**. Since this split, the Polish Union of America has continuously maintained headquarters in Buffalo or in one of its nearby suburbs.

For the first 25 years of its existence, the Union was an unincorporated association serving as an umbrella for a number of parish societies. Generally, these societies charged dues on a per capita basis and provided a death or disability benefit to their members without regard to any actuarial calculation. In 1914, the State of New York intervened to enforce the mandates of the state insurance law. After a period of transition to achieve compliance, the Polish Union of America was formally incorporated on July 16, 1917. In addition to the delivery of insurance protection to its membership, the PUA undertook a broad program of fraternal activities. These included scholarships, the development of a senior citizen housing project, and support for religious and ethnic events throughout Western New York. At one time or another, more than 400 lodges were affiliated with the PUA.—*Carl L. Bucki*

SOURCES: *A History of the Polish Union of America* (Buffalo: Program for 32nd Grand Convention of the Polish Union of America, August 1990); Henryk Lokanski and I. Smolczynski, *Album oraz Historya Osady Polskiej w Buffalo, N.Y.* (Buffalo: Wydane staraniem i nakładem Polskiej Spółki Wydawniczej, 1906); Stanisław Bubacz, *Historya Unia Polskiej w Ameryce* (Buffalo: Rekord-Unista, 1930).

Polish Union of the United States of North America.

The Polish Union of the United States of North America originated in 1890 when the Rev. **Dominik Majer** of St. Paul, Minnesota, took the lead in founding the **Polish Union of America**. The "Patriarch of the Poles" in Minnesota, Majer had previously been one of the organizers of the **Polish Roman Catholic Union of America** (PRCUA) and was later very active in the **Polish National Alliance** (PNA). He left the PRCUA

after a dispute with the Rev. **Wincenty Barzyński** of Chicago, the leading force in the PRCUA during its first quarter century in operation. In 1889, he and his priest-colleagues withdrew from the PNA when the delegates at the eighth PNA national convention in Buffalo rejected his resolution to bar non–Catholics from membership. Majer and several of his allies in the clergy and laity then organized the Polish Union of America, whose mission was to unite the immigrant community by underscoring its commitment to the Catholic focus of the PRCUA and the patriotic objectives of the PNA. Its original national headquarters were in St. Paul; however, in 1896 the headquarters were moved to Buffalo, New York, in view of that city's more central location in the growing Polish community nationally.

In 1908, at its eighth national convention in Chicago, the Polish Union of America split into two competing and nearly evenly divided groups. One retained the name of Polish Union of America and maintained its headquarters in Buffalo. The second group was reconstituted as the Polish Union of the United States of North America, with its headquarters in Wilkes-Barre, Pennsylvania. In 1935–36 it included about 30,000 adult members, had organized its own youth division, and published its own fraternal newspaper. During World War II, it took part in the **Polish American Congress** and was engaged in humanitarian actions in support of the work of the **Polish American Council** (Rada Polonii Amerykańskiej). After World War II, the

dominant figure in the Union was **Henry J. Dende**. In 1948 Dende took over the family-owned local Polish language newspaper *Republika Gornik* (Miner Republic) and reorganized it as an English language publication which he renamed the ***Polish American Journal***. He sold the publication in 1983 to a firm based in Buffalo. In 1965, Dende was elected president of the Polish Union of the U.S. of North America; he served in this capacity until his death in 2001. During his presidency he modernized and expanded the organization's insurance and fraternal programs and worked to broaden knowledge of the Polish heritage, especially among its younger members. In 2005 the Union was headed by Rose Wartko with a membership of 9,020 and assets of $8.9 million. The Polish Union of the United States of North America is licensed to operate in Pennsylvania, Illinois, Michigan, and New Jersey. Its publication, *The Fraternal Journal*, began appearing online in 2006.—*Donald E. Pienkos*

SOURCES: Stanisław Osada, *Historja Związku Narodowego Polskiego Rozwój Ruchu Narodowego Polskiego w Ameryce Północnej* (Chicago: Polish National Alliance, 1905, 1957); Andrzej Brożek, *Polish Americans 1854–1939* (Warsaw: Interpress, 1985); John Radzilowski, *The Eagle and the Crown: A History of the Polish Roman Catholic Union of America* (Boulder, CO: East European Monographs, 2003).

Polish University Abroad

(Polski Uniwersytet na Obczyźnie; PUNO). The Polish University Abroad was founded in London in 1939, and the Chicago branch was organized in the late 1970s. Between 1978 and 1987, PUNO was composed of several university professors in Chicago who gave occasional lectures to the Polish community. In 1988 the Chicago branch was more fully developed by members of the Solidarity emigration, in particular, Hubert Romanowski. The purpose of PUNO in Chicago was to promote Polish culture, history, and tradition among Polonia, and help new immigrants to assimilate into American occupational, professional, and educational institutions. Through lectures, seminars, courses, and conferences, PUNO served the new immigrant community. PUNO offered courses in English as a Second Language, computers, business, and finance. It held seminars to explain the system of higher education in the United States and the processes by which professionals could recertify their credentials. Under the directorship of Romanowski, PUNO was incorporated as the Polish Institute of Science and Culture, Inc. (PINIK) in 1989 as a non-profit educational organization. In cooperation with the Kraków Industrial Society, PUNO/PINIK organized a summer business school in Kraków in 1990, and, with a grant from the German Marshall

Polish Union of the United States of America meeting in Wilkes-Barre, Pennsylvania, 1915. In the center of the front row are Ignacy Jan Paderewski and Madame Paderewska. On the left of the first row is the Rev. J. Gryczka, and to Paderewski's right is Jakób Dembiec. The other identified individuals are (6) Dr. J. J. Koncyan, (7) W. Płoński, (8) J. Sosnowski, (9) Dr. Teofil A. Starzyński, (10) I. Haduch, (11) F. Boguszewski, and (12) S. Mitarnowski (*OLS*).

Fund, they sent business teachers to Poland to support its emerging capitalist economy. Between 1989 and 1990, PUNO was awarded SLIAG funds (State Legalization Impact Assistance Grants) from the U.S. government to teach English to immigrants newly legalized through the Immigration and Reform Act of 1986. In cooperation with the Roman Dmowski Institute and the **Polish Museum of America**, PUNO organized a conference to celebrate the seventieth anniversary of independent Poland in November 1988. In 1990, Romanowski stepped down as the director of the Chicago branch of PUNO when he assumed his new position as Counsel General of the Polish embassy in Chicago. Beverly Sweeney and then Dennis Kolinski each served as Executive Director of PUNO/PINIK, but within a few years the Chicago branch became inactive.—*Mary Patrice Erdmans*

SOURCE: Helena Znaniecka Lopata, *Polish Americans* (New Brunswick, NJ: Transaction Publishers, 1994).

Polish Veterans Association (Stowarzyszenie Polskich Kombatantów; SPK). Comprised of former soldiers who served in the Polish Armed Forces in the West during World War II, the SPK was established by veterans residing in the U.S. Most of the soldiers arrived in America under provisions of the Displaced Persons Act of 1948 and the Refugee Relief Act of 1953. In 1949 an agreement was signed between the SPK in Great Britain and the **Polish Army Veterans Association** (PAVA) in the United States providing that the newly-arrived combatants would join PAVA. In practice, conflicts between the newcomers and the veterans of the First World War soon arose. The newcomers particularly criticized the three-year waiting period before they could run for the organization's offices, as well as undemocratic organizational decision-making procedures. They experienced further discrimination when, in 1952, an amendment to PAVA's by-laws stipulated that officers must have American citizenship. Their reaction was to create their own organization. The first meeting, under the name of the "Second World War Veterans of the Polish Armed Forces in Exile," was held in New York on November 16, 1952. The first national convention took place on June 6–7, 1953, with **Stanisław Gierat** elected the first president, a position he held until his resignation in 1957, and then again from 1960 to 1972 when vice president Janusz Krzyżanowski assumed the office. Initially, the SPK was supervised by the headquarters in London, receiving both instructions and financial assistance from Britain. At Gierat's initiative, in 1963 the

World SPK was decentralized and transformed into the World Federation of SPK, while its American branch became one of the member organizations. At that time the SPK in America reached a membership of 3,000. It closely cooperated with the SPK in Canada.

The SPK's activities were twofold: to assist its members and to struggle for the Polish cause. In the first respect, the greatest success of Polish American veterans' organizations was passage of federal legislation on October 14, 1976, providing "hospital and medical care to certain members of the armed forces of nations allied or associated with the United States in World War I or World War II." Social events sponsored by the SPK reflected the strong anti-communism and Polish patriotism of the organization's leadership. They were usually organized in conjunction with Polish historical anniversaries or with the visits of the Polish generals in exile. Keeping the Polish cause on the agenda of American **Polonia**, and especially of the **Polish American Congress** (PAC), was regarded as the most important mission of the SPK, which denied the legal authority of the pro-communist Warsaw regime and took care to make sure that all official PAC documents reflected that attitude. The association initiated conferences of the world Polonia in 1975 and 1978, and played an important role in establishing the Free World Polonia Organizational Council.—*Joanna Wojdon*

SOURCE: Piotr Kardela, *Stanisław Gierat, 1903–1997: Działalność społeczno-polityczna* (Szczecin: Wydawn. Promocyjne "Albatros," 2000).

Polish Welfare Association *see* **Polish American Association** (PAA).

Polish White Cross (Polski Biały Krzyż). The Polish White Cross existed for approximately two decades as a civil organization with a paramilitary character. Its main objective, both in the United States and Poland, was the welfare of Polish soldiers during periods of war and in times of peace. Established without any preparatory work, real planning, or organization, the White Cross began operations almost spontaneously with money raised by Polish Americans during World War I. During the war, it prepared the Polish army in America for battle while providing the **Polish Army in France** with much needed medical attention. After moving to Poland following the war, the organization continued its efforts by providing relief for civilians and returning soldiers. During the inter-war period, the White Cross successfully eliminated illiteracy among Polish military ranks while creating new avenues of cultural appreciation for soldiers. The eruption of World War I in Au-

gust 1914 gave Poles everywhere the renewed hope of an independent Poland. Many viewed the United States, with its democratic principles and large Polish immigrant population, as the ideal setting to secure the support needed for Polish independence. The leader behind the organization of relief for the citizens of Poland was the Polish pianist **Ignacy Paderewski** who, along with the newly formed **National Department** (Wydział Narodowy), assumed the daunting task of unifying Polish American organizations behind the Polish cause and initiating relief efforts. One issue, which had yet to be addressed, was the lack of materiél and medical care being given to Polish soldiers fighting in France. Although the French military paid wages to Polish soldiers, they made no provision for their care either on or off the battlefield. In the United States, Paderewski and the National Department were preparing to organize their own army of Polish American men to assist General Józef Haller and his Polish forces on the Western Front. Therefore, the need for a military relief organization became an increasing necessity. In late 1917, Paderewski's wife, Helene, already deeply involved in the Polish Victims Relief Committee and the **Polish Women's Alliance**, had planned to open a Polish section of the Red Cross. Although Poles and Americans eagerly made charitable donations to the Polish cause, no one took an active role in creating the facilities and gathering the supplies Polish soldiers needed. Helene Paderewski's efforts to create a Polish branch of the Red Cross proved impossible as the Red Cross could exist only in an independent nation. Undeterred, she decided to create a substitute organization, the Polish White Cross, to carry out her objectives.

Officially established on February 2, 1918, the Polish White Cross (PWC) started operations with Helene Paderewski as its president. The organization had three main objectives: to ensure that all Polish and Polish American soldiers were outfitted with the proper clothing needed in battle; to provide care for the families of soldiers, especially in the event of death or permanent disability; and, most importantly, to make quick and adequate medical attention readily available to the Polish Army in France. These objectives were somewhat overwhelming considering that by the end of 1918 the Polish Army in France numbered somewhere in the region of 100,000 soldiers. To fulfill their objectives, Ignacy and Helene Paderewski travelled the country to explain the importance of the PWC to both Polish and American audiences. Numerous organizations and individuals responded to the appeal. In Chicago, 140 members of the Polish Women's Alliance became volunteers for the PWC, and numerous groups across the country started fund drives. The Polish clergy, in particular, eagerly came to the aid of the PWC, organizing parish fundraisers, charitable gatherings, and donating supplies. Polish American women formed numerous sewing groups in their homes and local church basements in order to make underclothing, socks, hats, scarves, and other items needed by Polish soldiers. The massive public support of the White Cross greatly aided the organization in accomplishing its goals. Not only were Polish soldiers properly outfitted and receiving medical attention for the first time, but the PWC was able to send supplies, newspapers, cigarettes, medicine, bandages, provide fourteen medical vehicles and open a medical hospital. In June 1917, prominent Polish physicians in New York formed training courses for those who volunteered to serve as nurses on the Western Front. In all, forty-two nurses served alongside the Polish Army in military hospitals and medical barracks. These nurses were of great benefit since they spoke Polish, were able to translate, and gave wounded soldiers a general sense of comfort.

After the signing of the Armistice on November 11, 1918, the Paderewskis immediately returned to Poland where Ignacy accepted the position as Prime Minister of the Second Republic. However, as one war ended for Poland, another began with the invasion of Russian Bolsheviks into the newly independent country. Despite their exhaustion, Polish soldiers on the Western Front, including those from America, willingly travelled to Poland to save their homeland. With the end of World War I, government officials in the United States formally requested the liquidation of the Polish White Cross claiming it violated the authority and jurisdiction of the American

A group of the Polish White Cross in Philadelphia between 1914 and 1918 (*PMA*).

Red Cross. Consequently, in January 1919, the PWC ceased operations in the United States. With the support of Józef Piłsudski, Helene Paderewski quickly re-established the Polish White Cross in Poland and extended its relief programs to civilians. Surprisingly, the opening of the PWC created no issues with the newly formed Polish Red Cross which, due to the Bolshevik war, already operated in Poland. This mutual cooperation was possible since the Polish Red Cross concerned itself with war victims, soldiers injured in battle and their families. The Polish White Cross, on the other hand, concentrated their efforts on the general welfare and health of soldiers both on and off the battle field. To achieve this end, Helene Paderewski and the PWC formed canteens, stores, hotels, and libraries throughout Poland for the use of soldiers. In February 1919, with the financial support of Polish Americans, Helene opened the White Cross hospital in Warsaw which served members of the military needing surgical attention at no cost. The hospital contained one hundred beds, each subsidized by an individual or organization. On July 23 1919, the PWC received recognition by the Polish government as the nation's key social and philanthropic organization. The White Cross maintained partnerships with 228 other charitable organizations, managed over 19,000 volunteers, and administered 145 hotels, forty sewing facilities, thirteen cleaning facilities, and 64 libraries. Much of the Polish White Cross'

work in Poland during the Bolshevik War was accomplished thanks to the National Department. The organization assumed control of PWC activities once it left the United States and continued to collect funds, make clothing and gather medical supplies for battle stricken Poland. Between 1919 and 1920, the National Department, in conjunction with the American Red Cross, sent seven supply ships to Poland; the majority slated for use by the PWC. One such cargo transport contained 7,768 crates weighing approximately five tons and held a value of about two million dollars. The organization also established the volunteer "Rescue Section of Polish Women" that travelled to Poland to aid the PWC and administer the supplies sent from the United States.

American support of the White Cross in Poland was short lived. Following the November Armistice ending World War I, Polish American support of relief organizations declined steadily. Despite the transport of goods to Poland, the decrease in financial assistance put strain on the PWC. With the dissolution of the National Department and its humanitarian pursuits in 1921, aid from the United States ended altogether. Although greatly championed by Polish officials, assistance from the financially beleaguered government was never enough to support the various PWC programs. In 1920, the White Cross hospital, in particular, lost the support of several donors and no longer functioned solely on the generosity of others. In order to preserve the hospital, Helene Paderewski used her own personal resources to make up the difference in operating costs. A year later, the hospital closed due to a significant drop in external support and the inability of Helene Paderewski to continue funding the facility on her own. After two years, Poland managed to protect its borders from the Russian-Bolshevik onslaught. The country, devastated by nearly a decade of warfare, finally began to recover. Towards the

Flag of the Polish White Cross serving with the Polish Army in France during World War I (*OLS*).

end of the war, the Polish White Cross focused more of its energy on being a humanitarian organization helping war victims in addition to soldiers returning from battlefields. Although the PWC could no longer rely on money from the United States, it still controlled a large number of resources and assets throughout Poland. This allowed the PWC to open shelters and homes of convalescence for adults, children, and soldiers. Yet, at its core, the main focus of the White Cross remained on serving the Polish army. Throughout the inter-war period, the Polish White Cross served as an educational and cultural organization for the military. The organization worked with military officials to improve the educational and social position of soldiers throughout the ranks. Between 1923 and 1939, the PWC opened and maintained projection theaters, training centers, reading rooms, libraries and numerous cultural institutions specifically designed for the Polish military. The PWC proved successful and vital in eliminating illiteracy among soldiers while improving their cultural outlook. By 1937, however, Polish military officials lost interest in the need to educate soldiers and in the PWC. By 1939, the relationship between the two deteriorated and the Polish White Cross ceased operations prior to the onset World War II.—*Michael T. Urbanski*

SOURCES: Józef Orłowski, *Helena Paderewska; na piętnastolecie Jej pracy narodowej i społecznej, 1914–1929* (Chicago: 1929); Aneta Niewęgłowska, *Polski Biały Krzyż a wojsko w latach 1919–1939* (Torun: Mado, 2005); Tadeusz Radzik, "Działalność Polskiego Białego Krzyża i Sekcji Ratunkowej Polek w Stanach Zjednoczonych Ameryki w Latach 1918–1920," Przegląd Polonijny, Vol. 61, no. 1 (1990), 99–110.

Polish White Eagle Association.

The Polish White Eagle Association (PWEA) was a small, Minnesota-based fraternal association founded in the early twentieth century that merged with a non–Polish fraternal group in 2001. The precise origins of PWEA are unclear, but its original membership seems to have been drawn from Minnesota **Polish National Alliance** (PNA) members who became disenchanted with the explicitly secular nature of the Alliance. Although similar in its nationalist orientation to the PNA, unlike the larger fraternal the PWEA members had to be practicing Roman Catholics in good standing with the church to join. Initially membership was open to Poles, Ruthenians, and Slovaks, or their spouses, though in its final years this stipulation was dropped. PWEA was headquartered in the largely Polish section of northeast Minneapolis where it owned a small office building and a social hall. At its height the association had about twenty societies around the state of Minnesota, with the ma-

jority in Minneapolis and St. Paul and few in other **Polonia** communities in southeast and central Minnesota. It is unlikely that individual societies had their own halls or other property.

The association was at its height in the first half of the twentieth century and played a significant role in Minnesota Polonia up through the 1940s. It drew almost all of its members from immigrants who had come to the U.S. before World War I. It seems to have attracted only a few members from the post–World War II wave of immigrants. After World War II, PWEA was increasingly a social organization. From the late 1960s onward, there seems to have been an ongoing dispute over the Polish character of the organization. A significant group within the organization sought to explicitly de–Polonize PWEA. As membership fell and Polish immigrants began to move out of traditional ethnic neighborhoods like Northeast Minneapolis, this group grew in strength and became increasingly militant in its demands to strip the Polish character from the organization. In the 1990s, the organization changed its name to Eagle Fraternal in an effort to attract members of other ethnic groups. This effort failed and in 2001, with declining membership and under pressure from state regulators, the organization merged its business activities with the St. Paul–based Degree of Honor fraternal. Several local PWEA chapters continue to exist informally as social groups. No history of the organization has ever been written although many of its records were deposited at the Immigration History Research Center at the University of Minnesota.—*John Radzilowski*

SOURCE: John Radzilowski, *Poles in Minnesota* (St. Paul: Minnesota Historical Society Press, 2005).

Polish Women's Alliance of America

(Związek Polek w Ameryce). The Polish Women's Alliance of America is the third largest fraternal insurance benefit association created by Americans of Polish origin and is the largest fraternal organized by women of Polish ancestry. The PWA (or "Women's Alliance") is also the second largest fraternal formed by women based on membership, and the third largest in assets. As of December 31, 2005, the PWA reported a total of 47,711 insured members and 2,749 annuity holders. Its assets amounted to $52,806,487 and it provided insurance amounting to $110,632,000. Since its founding in 1898, more than six hundred thousand individuals have belonged to the organization.

FRATERNAL CHARACTER

The Polish Women's Alliance of America is a not-for-profit fraternal insurance benefit so-

ciety. It is incorporated in the state of Illinois and is licensed to sell life insurance and annuity products in sixteen states and the District of Columbia. It operates solely for the benefit of its members and their beneficiaries and is organized on the basis of a representative form of government. All insured adult members in good standing are eligible to participate in the governance of the Alliance. They do so by their involvement in the more than four hundred PWA local groups, by voting for their local lodge officers and by holding such responsibilities themselves, by serving as elected delegates to the national conventions the fraternal has held every four years since 1931, and by seeking election to its national leadership. Leadership in the Women's Alliance is invested in a General Administration headed by a president and including a vice president, a secretary-treasurer and five directors. Other elective offices include those of district presidents — the PWA is organized into fourteen territorial districts. In the Women's Alliance, past presidents have been accorded the title of honorary president and are invited to meetings of the General Administration. Until 1947, membership in the PWA was composed solely of women. In that year, males under the age of sixteen were made eligible to be insured members. In 1987, adult males were also extended this privilege. As of 2007, however, no male member has held, or sought, elective office in the organization.

The PWA invests its funds into U.S. government securities, corporate bonds, and home mortgages granted to its members. The earnings derived from these investments are returned in large part to the membership in two forms — as dividends on the insurance they have purchased and as fraternal benefits. The latter include college scholarships (which all PWA members attending college on a full time basis may receive), along with a variety of social, ethnic, and sports programs. All active insured members receive, at no cost, the fraternal publication of the PWA, *Głos Polek* (The Voice of Polish Women).

Throughout its history, the Polish Women's Alliance of America has dedicated considerable resources to gathering funds for the civic causes its members have regarded as significant. Aside from its substantial relief activities on behalf of Poland over the years, the PWA raised over one million dollars through member donations in the mid–1980s to assist in the repair of the Statue of Liberty in New York Harbor, to help develop the Immigration Museum at Ellis Island, to back the creation of the **Pope John Paul II Cultural Center** adjacent to the Catholic University of America in Washington, D.C., and to support a variety of other worthy objectives. From the 1960s, the Alliance strongly supported the construction of the national shrine to the Virgin of Częstochowa in **Doylestown**, Pennsylvania. Beginning in the 1950s, the organization also contributed to a number of Polish causes, including the Catholic University in Lublin. The PWA was a strong supporter of the **Polish American Historical Association** (PAHA) from its inception in 1942. For decades, the Women's Alliance also provided financial support to **St. Mary's College** and **Saints Cyril and Methodius Seminary** located in the community of Orchard Lake, Michigan, west of Detroit.

ORIGINS, IDEOLOGY, AND PROGRAMMATIC DEVELOPMENT

The Polish Women's Alliance of America was established in Chicago, Illinois, over a period of eighteen months beginning in May 1898. For some years before, women activists in the Polish immigrant community in Chicago had attempted, without success, to gain entry into the existing immigrant fraternal societies. On May 22, 1898, several of them gathered at the invitation of **Stefania Chmielińska** (1866–1939; president 1899, 1900–02, 1906–10), an immigrant seamstress who was dedicated to the causes of women's equality (Równouprawnienie) and the restoration of partitioned Poland's independence. Together, they created the Polish Women's Alliance in America Society. Five months later, in October 1898, they published and distributed an appeal calling on other women to join them in setting up their own national women's federation. The spirit of their undertaking is evident from this document, which reads in part as follows: "Not long ago there arose from the bosom of the Polish women of Chicago the idea of establishing a greater women's organization, its task the uniting of the Polish women in America, the payment of death benefits, the maintenance of the patriotic spirit in the ranks of its members, and the preservation and inculcation of this feeling within the Polish youth.... We are hopeful that our words will not die away without even an echo, and that they will resound among our Polish countrywomen, who will support our aims and join with us in ties of harmony, friendship and work for the general good."

When the **Polish National Alliance**, the premier progressive immigrant fraternal in Chicago, failed to take up the cause of women's inclusion at its national convention in September 1899, Chmielińska and her friends, together with representatives of two other women's groups, met that November and proclaimed the creation of the Polish

Women's Alliance in America. As early as June 1900, the leaders of the fledgling organization called their first national convention in Chicago. Twenty four delegates representing 264 members in eight societies, seven from Chicago and one from Pennsylvania attended. This gathering elected national officers, adopted a constitution, and began work to establish a fraternal insurance program. In the PWA's first decade of activity, Chmielińska and several other activists, most notably another weaver named **Anna Neumann** (president 1902–06, 1910–18) succeeded in making it a substantial and respected organization, one dedicated to the causes of women's equality in the Polish community, the educational and economic advancement of Polish women, Poland's independence, and the providing of a sound insurance benefit program for its members. Early on, contact was made with the Polish poet, patriot, and women's rights activist, Maria Konopnicka, who strongly supported its mission. Soon after, the PWA established an educational committee (Wydział Oświaty) to set up reading rooms and night school educational programs for members of the immigrant community. Already in 1906, the PWA had purchased a small building to be its headquarters; in 1912, it built a much larger home office on Chicago's heavily Polish near north side. That building was substantially expanded in the 1930s. In 1979, the Women's Alliance moved its headquarters to the suburb of Park Ridge, northwest of Chicago. It remained there until 2004, when it transferred its operations back to Chicago's northwest side.

In 1910, after earlier unsuccessful attempts, the PWA established its official publication, *Głos Polek*, as a weekly newspaper. The PWA soon won the respect of the immigrant community in Chicago and beyond by its success in rapidly growing its membership, despite the opposition it faced from the existing male-run fraternals. All of them had acted quickly to admit women into their ranks in response to the forming of the Women's Alliance. The organization grew from 4,302 members in 1906, to 10,930 (1912), 31,787 (1924), and 65,321 (1931). Membership growth only stalled during the Depression years of the 1930s and the World War II period (1939–45), the latter period a time when the organization had focused its attentions on Polish relief work and efforts to lobby the U.S. government for Poland's postwar reconstitution as an independent state. In 1947, membership was reported at 67,899 at its twentieth convention, an event held on the eve of the PWA's fiftieth anniversary. Membership then again began expanding substantially; at the 24th convention in 1963, it stood at 91,101, its all-time high.

Over the past forty-five years, the Polish Women's Alliance of America, not unlike nearly all other Polish American fraternals, has experienced the impact of the assimilation process in the ethnic community upon its overall membership. In 1975, total membership was 82,000, in 1995, it was 58,000, and in 2005 it had declined further, to just over 50,000. At the same time, the organization's assets have continually grown, from $15,085 in 1906 to $99,314 (1912), $1,107,762 (1924), $3,090,207 (1931), $9,914,582 (1947), $23,664,666 (1963), $30,707,809 (1975), $44,264,618 (1995), and $52,806,487 (2005). One decision that spurred the membership growth came in 1917 with the state insurance regulatory commission's decision to permit fraternals to sell life insurance to children and juveniles under the age of sixteen. The PWA acted quickly to encourage their members to "sign up" their children and grandchildren into the organization. Its leaders also began developing youth, sports, and ethnic programs designed for youngsters through their local groups. The most successful of these were the PWA youth circles, called Wianki (Garlands). In 1963, the fraternal's youth department included 17,489 juveniles, the high point of its success in this area. By the 1940s, the PWA also began organizing regular national and regional youth conferences; these have featured a wide variety of entertaining sports, cultural, and folk dance activities.

The Polish Women's Alliance of America's commitment to raising public awareness and appreciation of the contributions of women to the larger community is symbolized by its nomination of a select number of outstanding women role models of Polish origin to be its honorary members. Maria Konopnicka was the first to be so recognized at the 1903 PWA convention. Honorary membership status has since been conferred upon novelists Eliza Orzeszkowa and Maria Rodziewiczówna, the two-time Nobel laureate Maria Składowska Curie, actress Helena Modrzejewska (**Modjeska**), Helena Paderewska, the wife of pianist-patriot **Ignacy Paderewski** and a leader in the humanitarian efforts for World War I Polish victims, Helena Sikorska, widow of Poland's World War II Prime Minister, General Władysław Sikorski, and United States Senator **Barbara Mikulski** of Maryland. In 2007, Irena Sendler, who was personally responsible for saving the lives of some 2,000 Jewish children trapped in the Warsaw Ghetto in World War II and who was herself captured and tortured by the Nazis for her heroic acts, was named the ninth Honorary Member of the PWA.

The Polish Women's Alliance of America's interest in supporting the cause of Poland's freedom and well-being within the organized Polish ethnic community (**Polonia**) was made dramatically evident during the First World War. The PWA contributed its own resources and collected tons of goods and substantial sums of money from its members and the general community for Polish relief purposes during the conflict. It helped recruit soldiers into the 24,000 member Polish army raised in America which served on the side of the United States in France at the end of World War I. The Women's Alliance took a leadership role in the humanitarian work of the **Polish Central Relief Committee** and in the political lobbying efforts of the Polish **National Department** (Wydział Narodowy), a political action federation led by **John Smulski** (1867–1928), a nationally known Chicago civic leader. In 1915, an American-born PWA activist, **Emilia Napieralska** (secretary general 1910–18, president 1918–35), made her way to the international women's peace congress held in the Netherlands. There she eloquently and successfully argued the justice of Poland's independence cause and declared that the rights of Europe's oppressed nations took precedence over the congress' stated aim of "peace at any price."

The Nazi-Soviet invasion and destruction of the interwar Polish state in September 1939 touched off World War II and ignited a new period of PWA activism on behalf of its members' ancestral homeland. Under **Honorata Wołowska** (president 1935–47), the PWA again took a leading role in raising funds and collecting goods for the relief of Polish war victims, especially mothers and children, and was a major force in the Polish American Council charitable federation chaired by Marquette University law school dean and Polonia leader **Francis Swietlik**. Its members' patriotism in support of the U.S. war effort even included purchases of U.S. war bonds that were sufficiently great to lead the American government to name two of its bomber planes in honor of the organization. On the political front, Wołowska, in 1944 took a leading role, with **Charles Rozmarek**, president of the Polish National Alliance, John Olejniczak, president of the **Polish Roman Catholic Union of America**, and **Teofil Starzyński**, president of the **Polish Falcons of America**, in founding the **Polish American Congress** (PAC, in Polish Kongres Polonii Amerykańskiej, KPA). The PAC reiterated Polonia's commitment to America's victory in the War and exhorted the U.S. government to back Poland's postwar reconstitution as an independent and democratic state with its pre-war borders intact. When

Poland was occupied by the Soviet Union and a communist regime placed in command of the devastated country, the Polish American Congress continued, with strong PWA support, to vociferously object to Soviet domination of the old homeland. Upon her election as PWA president in 1947, **Adele Łagodzińska** (president until 1971) also became a vice president of the Polish American Congress. The Chicago-born Łagodzińska was a strong critic of the communist regime, although she was one of the first Polonia leaders to take the controversial action of visiting Poland in spring 1956 to learn for herself about the critical situation there. While in Poland, she committed Polonia to renewing its humanitarian commitment to the old homeland. Following the collapse of Stalinist rule in Poland in October 1956, Łagodzińska returned to Poland, this time as head of a "pilgrimage" of PWA members that re-established a tradition of organized cultural visits that had been interrupted by the war and the subsequent Soviet occupation. Her successors have continued this tradition.

In the 1980s, **Helen Zielinski**, who followed Łagodzińska as president (1971–87), took a leadership role in supporting the Polish American Congress Charitable Foundation's shipments of medical goods and foodstuffs to Poland. There the economy had come apart, due to the failed policies of the communist regime and the radical increase in oil prices imposed by the Middle Eastern states and their allies. Zielinski promoted PAC support for the Solidarity independent trade union movement from its birth in 1980, and joined her fellow PAC officers in condemning the communist regime's imposition of martial law in December 1981, an ultimately unsuccessful effort to destroy the democratic opposition. Her successors, **Helen Wójcik** (president, 1987–95), **Delphine Lytell** (1995–99), and Virginia Sikora (1999–), continued with these policies. In October 1989, Wójcik traveled to Poland as a member of a PAC delegation to reaffirm Polonia's support of the new Solidarity-led democratic government that had come to power a month before.

Symbols of Organizational Objectives

Over the years, the Women's Alliance has adopted a number of mottos to define its mission. The first of these was Czyn (service). In 2010, its motto was Bóg i Ojczyzna (God and Country). Yet another popular slogan is Ideał Kobiety to Siła Narodu (In the Ideals of Women is the Strength of a Nation), an eloquent pronouncement of the organization's patriotism and specific brand of feminism.

Emblem of the Polish Women's Alliance (*OLS*).

The first emblem of the Polish Women's Alliance was very much the same as that of the Polish National Alliance, a shield showing the Polish eagle, the Lithuanian knight on horseback, and the Archangel Michael that symbolized its commitment to the restoration of Polish independence. In the 1920s, this emblem was dropped in favor of one that shows two women — one from Poland, the other from America — extending their hands in solidarity with one another across the Atlantic Ocean. Between them is a shield emblazoned with the stars and stripes of the United States and the Polish Eagle. In the background a shining sun symbolizes the ideals of freedom and opportunity that women cherish for themselves, their families, and their homelands and the pride that PWA members have for their fraternal. In 1931, the PWA approved a resolution to place the portrait of the Madonna of Częstochowa on the obverse side of its banner, a symbol of its members' respect for Poland's patroness. — *Angela T. Pienkos and Donald E. Pienkos*

SOURCES: Jadwiga Karłowicz, *Historia Związku Polek w Ameryce: Przyczynki do Poznania Duszy Wychodźtwa Polskiego w Stanach Zjednoczonych Ameryki Północnej* (Chicago: Polish Women's Alliance of America, 1938); Maria Lorys, *Historia Związku Polek w Ameryce* (Chicago: Polish Women's Alliance of America, 1980); Helen Zielinski, *Historia Związku Polek w Ameryce: Sprawy Organizacyjne, 1898–1979* (Chicago: Polish Women's Alliance of America, 1981); Angela T. Pienkos and Donald E. Pienkos, *"In The Ideals Of Women Is The Strength Of A Nation": A History of the Polish Women's Alliance of America* (Boulder, CO: East European Monographs, distributed by Columbia University Press, 2003).

Polish Workers' Relief Committee

(Komitet Pomocy Rodzinom Prześladowanym w P.R.L.; since 1978, Komitet Obrońcom Praw Człowieka w Polsce; since 1986, Krajowy Komitet Pomocy dla Opozycji Demokratycznej w Polsce). Founded in Chicago on October 3, 1976 by local leaders of the Polish Veterans' in Exile Association (SPK) and the Illinois Division of the **Polish American Congress**, the organization's goal was to assist the democratic opposition in Poland, first through the newly-created Workers' Defense Committee

(Komitet Obrony Robotników, KOR), and later, after some discussion, through other formations such as the Movement for Defense of Human and Civic Rights (Ruch Obrony Praw Człowieka i Obywatela, ROPCiO) and Polskie Porozumienie Niepodległościowe (PPN). Jan Jurewicz was elected its first president, but was replaced by Bonawentura Migała in 1978, who in turn resigned in 1988 in favor of Grażyna Cioromska. In 1986 the Committee became a member of the national Polish American Congress (PAC). Although most of its work was still done in Chicago, and the majority of its funds were collected there, other state divisions of the PAC often helped the democratic opposition in Poland on their own.

During the legal existence of Solidarność (Solidarity) in Poland in 1980–81, the Committee concentrated on charitable activities coordinated by the Polish American Congress and addressed to the Polish nation in general, not only to the opposition activists. It was argued that Solidarność had many other sources of financial assistance from abroad, including American trade unions. The Committee's action in relief of the Polish opposition resumed with the introduction of martial law in Poland in December 1981. Special parcels were sent to the families of Solidarność members who were imprisoned, interned, or jobless. The Committee also generously supported the independent publishing movement, with assistance continuing until the collapse of the communist regime in Poland.

From its inception, most of the Committee's funds were transferred to Poland with the help of Jerzy Giedroyc and his Paris-based *Kultura* monthly. **Polonia** trusted Giedroyc, who claimed expertise on the Polish opposition movement. Acknowledgements of donors were printed in *Kultura* and Giedroyc charged no fee for transferring monies to Poland. Occasionally the Committee used other means of sending money including official postal services, the assistance of the London office of the Komitet Obrony Robotników (Workers' Defense Committee) run by Eugeniusz Smolar in the 1970s and the Solidarity office in Brussels in the 1980s. The Rev. Plater-Zyberek in Paris also transferred donations to the Primate Committee on Prisoners and Internees Relief (Prymasowski Komitet Pomocy Uwięzionym i Internowanym). To obtain the necessary funds, the Committee solicited donations from Polish-American organizations and sponsored fund drives in Polish-American communities. In the 1980s, the largest donations were collected by **Freedom for Poland**, an organization of newly arrived Polish immigrants, during special fund raising events,

masses, and parties. All the donations were sent to Poland with the Committee members working as volunteers and local banks covering the administrative costs. According to a report by **Jan Krawiec**, donations worth $487,028 were transferred to Poland as of November 8, 1987. Andrzej Czuma estimates that the total value of the Committee's assistance between 1976 and 1990 was $190,000 in cash and $750,000 in material goods. —*Joanna Wojdon*

SOURCES: Andrzej Czuma, "Dla niepodległości Polski. Zarys historii Komitetu Pomocy dla Opozycji Demokratycznej w Polsce działającego w Chicago w latach 1976–1990," (Chicago: Unpublished typescript, 1993); Joanna Wojdon, *W jedności siła. Kongres Polonii Amerykańskiej w latach 1968–1988* (Toruń: Wydawnictwo Adam Marszalek, 2008), 386–87, 402–05.

Politics of Polish Americans in U.S.

Polish Americans have been interesting and on occasions significant factors in the political life of the United States from the time when a substantial Polish immigration began settling in this country. As early as 1880, perhaps 400,000 Poles were living in the U.S., about one percent of the U.S. population. By 1900, the Polish population, by then composed mostly of immigrants plus their offspring, had risen to more than two million, 2.5 percent of the total population. In 1914, the number was about four million persons of Polish birth or ancestry, comprising about four percent of the U.S. population, which by then surpassed 100 million.

The rapid increase in the Polish ethnic population in the U.S. was part, and typical, of the larger story of the post–Civil War industrialization of the U.S. and America's "open immigration" policy toward Europe. After World War I (1914–18) and the restoration of an independent Polish state for the first time in over 120 years, Polish immigration declined sharply, mainly after federal legislation in 1921 and 1924 that severely reduced the number of immigrants from all countries to 150,000 annually. Between 1900 and 1914, as many as one million people had entered in some years, with over 170,000 coming from Poland alone in one year. The law was particularly prejudicial to Poles and other eastern, central, and southern Europeans and only a relatively small number of Poles entered the country over the next twenty-five years. After World War II, Congress in 1948 approved special legislation that permitted some 200,000 Poles to enter this country under special dispensation. Some had served in the Polish armed forces on the U.S. side in the war; most were refugees from Nazism who had had to work as slave or forced laborers in often brutal conditions. None of these people were willing to return to Poland, which fell under Soviet communist domination at war's end. The trickle of Polish

immigrants to the U.S. increased a bit following passage of the Immigration Reform Act of 1965, which ended the discriminatory aspects of the 1924 law. In the late 1970s, a third wave of Polish immigration appeared as a result of the communist's authoritarian mismanagement of the country's economy.

Together, the members, offspring, and descendants of these three rather disparate immigrations have comprised the "Polish American community" or **Polonia**. In the 2000 U.S. Census Survey of the national origins of Americans, approximately 9.1 million persons were officially estimated to be of Polish ancestry out of a total population of 278 million. In 1980, the first such census survey had identified 8.2 million Polish Americans out of 210 million; the 1990 census estimated the number as 9.5 million out of 240 million. In 2000, about 95 percent of the Polish American population was U.S. born. This represented a major change from the situation as late as 1940, when perhaps one fourth of all persons of Polish heritage were foreign born, with the rest composed of their "second generation" U.S.–born sons and daughters and their grandchildren.

Census data indicate that the Polish American population has traditionally been concentrated in the northeastern and Midwestern states of the country, mainly in New York, Pennsylvania, Illinois, Michigan, New Jersey, Massachusetts, Ohio, Wisconsin, Connecticut, Maryland, Indiana, and Minnesota. In the 2000 census survey, many Polish Americans were residing in Florida, the American Southwest, and California, due mainly to their retirement there. While most Polish immigrants to the U.S., especially in the first two waves, originated from rural areas of Poland, most Polish Americans have resided in urban areas, often in particular neighborhoods where they often made up a large part of the population. These factors have helped to make the Polish vote salient in local, state and national elections, especially after the 1920s. By that time, many, if not most, Polish immigrants, and all their American-born children and descendants were citizens with the right to vote.

Polish Americans' political orientations have been widely recognized as leading them to favor candidates of the Democratic, as opposed to the Republican, Party. Moreover, most Polish Americans who have won elective office at the state and national levels, and nearly all who have won office over the past thirty years, have been Democrats. This is so for three distinctive, interrelated reasons. On their arrival in America, most Polish immigrants, especially those who settled in cities, came to identify with the Democrats, then regarded as the "party of the workingman." The Democrats' opposition to the prohibition of alcoholic beverages may have also enhanced Polish voter support. But the strongest reason for Polish support for the Democratic Party, especially at the national level, came with their response to the election in 1932 of Franklin D. Roosevelt. It was Roosevelt who implemented a set of "New Deal" pro-employment, pro-union, and social welfare programs aimed at confronting the worst aspects of the great economic depression that gripped the nation after 1929. Many Polish Americans, along with Americans of other largely immigrant and ethnic working class groups, would retain a strong loyalty to the Democratic Party for decades after Roosevelt's own death in 1945.

A second influence on their politics and outlook is a result of the deep attachment most Polish Americans have felt for the Roman Catholic Church in America. On their arrival into this country, the mostly poor Polish immigrants quickly recognized that the Church was the one significant social institution that closely resembled what they had left behind. In time, countless immigrants, their children and grandchildren became involved in the construction and maintenance of as many as 900 Roman Catholic parish churches in the U.S., nearly as many parochial schools, and a host of ancillary religious agencies. The Church in **Polonia** proved to be its most significant institution. In addition to its central role in providing spiritual guidance and a sense of community to its members, the Church was also a political force in Polonia, especially at the neighborhood level and in the decades before a substantial stratum of well educated lay persons of Polish origin had arrived on the scene. Obviously, the priestly pastors of the Polish parish were powerful forces in the neighborhood community. As respected, educated men, they could, and frequently did, exert a considerable influence on their parishioners at election time. Generally, the members of the clergy were also Democratic in their politics. This was perhaps partly due to the fear that to do otherwise might expose the poorly paid workingmen of the early Polonia to more radical political forces the clergy usually referred to as the "godless socialists." Since the 1970s, the Roman Catholic Church has exerted a different kind of influence on Polish Americans, one based on its strong opposition to legalized abortion. This position has since been adopted by the Republican Party and has become a key "wedge issue" at election time. The identification with the "pro-life" cause by John Paul II, the revered "Pope from Poland," further shaped the thinking of many Polish American

Catholics, who were already "trending Republican" because they agreed with the Party on other policy issues of the day.

A third influence on Polish American political thinking has been Poland. Of course, most Poles, like many other immigrants from Europe over the past 150 years, came to the United States to work and attain a better life—"for bread" in **Henryk Sienkiewicz**'s words. At the same time, a small but steady stream of Polish immigrants entered this country with a highly defined commitment to working for Poland's freedom and independence. Here, they were able to organize, promote their views, and join with like-minded people from the vast "for bread" immigration to create mass-member civic action organizations dedicated to the independence cause. The story of the once great state of Poland's loss of independence in the partitions era (1772–95) and the saga of a series of heroic, but failed insurrections to regain Polish independence, beginning with **Tadeusz Kościuszko**'s national uprising in 1794 and running through the revolts of 1830, 1848, and 1863, each left its mark on patriotic Poles whose involvement in an uprising forced them into foreign exile. They came to hold a set of common aims: to work from abroad for Poland's independence, to cooperate where possible with Poles in the partitioned homeland to advance this cause, and to mobilize the "for bread" immigration, especially in the U.S., to identify with Poland's eventual restoration.

Political exiles in the U.S. made organizational efforts in the years between 1830 and 1880, but these proved ephemeral because the number of Poles in America was too few to sustain concerted activity. But by 1880 the situation had changed significantly. That year saw the creation of the **Polish National Alliance**, whose action program linked the work for Poland with a mass appeal having a fraternal, social uplift character. From 1880 to 1918, numerous patriotic Polonia organizations followed in the wake of the PNA, most significantly, the **Polish Falcons** of America (1887) and the **Polish Women's Alliance** (1898). These groups represented the Polish cause to leaders of the U.S. government and undertook activities to promote knowledge of Polish history and culture. Together, they led movements to fund monuments around the country to memorialize the two Polish patriots who served in the American Revoltion, Kościuszko and **Kazimierz Pułaski**, and whose lives symbolized the tie between America's values and Poland's hopes. They also organized an international congress to promote the cause of Polish independence in Washington, D.C., in 1910, and political action feder-

ations for Poland's freedom in Pittsburgh (1912) and Chicago (1914, 1916). In so doing, these groups made the Polish cause a central and continuing topic for discussion in the extensive Polish language press of the time. Eventually they also won over the many Polonia organizations that had initially focused on Catholic concerns rather than Polish independence. As a consequence of Poland's restoration to independence at the end of World War I in 1918, and for decades after, the patriotic elements in Polonia, led by the fraternal leaders and people like the Chicago banker and politician **John Smulski** made Poland's independence important to the Polish American community. They added a new set of heroes of Polish freedom to the pantheon of patriotic figures of the past, among them the virtuoso pianist **Ignacy Paderewski** and General Józef Piłsudski, the founder of modern Poland.

In World War II, a new Polish American political action federation came into existence in 1944, the **Polish American Congress** (PAC). When Poland fell under Soviet Communist domination at war's end, the PAC, led by its first president, **Charles Rozmarek** (president from 1944 to 1968) was obliged to continue in operation as a deeply anti-communist pressure group that worked with other organizations to affect U.S. policy toward Poland and the Soviet Union. Under its second president, **Aloysius Mazewski** (1968–88), the PAC continued to champion these causes. Mazewski's successor, **Edward Moskal** (like his predecessors president of the Polish National Alliance), remained an uncompromising advocate of Poland. When the Solidarity trade union movement and its allies won power after their historic June 1989 election victory over the communists, the PAC gave its full support to the new Polish democratic government and was a key actor in pushing for Poland's admission, in 1999, into the NATO military alliance.

In short, the existence and activities of a succession of Polonia political action organizations going back more than a century have served to unite large numbers of Polish Americans around the cause of Poland's independence and freedom. These activities have strengthened among many Polish Americans their sense of ethnic identity and purpose. At the same time, they have helped make the issue of Poland, and the votes of Polish Americans at election time, a salient feature in the strategies of the two major political parties and their candidates.

U.S. PRESIDENTIAL ELECTIONS AND POLISH AMERICANS

As early as 1899, Polish Americans entered U.S. national affairs in serious fashion when a coalition of immigrant leaders in Chicago's Polonia organizations addressed an appeal to President William McKinley on behalf of the cause of Polish independence. This effort may have had the effect of bringing the Polish community's concerns to the attention of McKinley's successor, Theodore Roosevelt, who became president after McKinley's assassination in 1901. Roosevelt met the representatives of the Polish National Alliance at the White House in 1907 following its national convention in nearby Baltimore. He selected the model for the Kościuszko monument that stands in Lafayette Square across from the White House, a monument paid for by the PNA. In 1910 his successor, William Howard Taft attended the dedication of the monuments to Kościuszko and Pułaski; in 1912 Taft took part in the ceremony dedicating the newly created **Alliance College** in Cambridge Springs, Pennsylvania.

During World War I, Polonia's leaders, working closely with Paderewski, the emissary of the Polish national committee in France, urged President Woodrow Wilson to support Poland's independence. In January 1918 Wilson included Polish statehood in his "**Fourteen Points**" address to Congress listing the United States' aims in the war. It was, however, the coming of the great economic depression after 1929 and Polonia's support for the Democratic Party's presidential nominee in 1932, Franklin D. Roosevelt, that shaped Polish American loyalty to the Democrats for the next forty years. Indeed, in the 1930s the "Polish vote" for Roosevelt reached as high as ninety percent in many parts of the country. With the exception of the 1952 and 1956 elections, won by the popular Republican Party nominee Dwight Eisenhower, at least 78–80 percent of Polish Americans remained loyal to Democratic presidential nominees in every election until 1968.

In two elections, in 1944 during World War II and in 1948, the Polish vote was an important factor affecting the outcome. In 1944, FDR won reelection to a fourth term and carried eight states having sizeable Polish populations—New York, Pennsylvania, Massachusetts, Connecticut, Illinois, Michigan, New Jersey, and Maryland. But in nearly all these states his margin of victory was very narrow. Significantly, FDR's actual wartime policies toward Poland and his secret dealings with Poland's enemy, Josef Stalin, were unknown in Polonia during the campaign; had they been widely publicized even a few weeks before the vote the result of the election might have been different.

In 1948, the Polish vote was again a key to President Truman's hopes for election. Truman, who had succeeded FDR upon his death in April 1945, won by a narrow margin in an intense campaign over his Republican Party opponent, New York Governor Thomas Dewey. Interestingly, eighty percent of the Polish vote went his way; however, he won the electoral votes of only two states having significant Polish ethnic populations—Wisconsin and Ohio.

In both these campaigns Poland and its takeover by the Soviet Union following World War II was a salient issue. In 1948 in particular, the PAC and other groups called on traditionally Democratic Polish Americans to turn against Truman because of FDR's "sell out" of Poland at the infamous **Yalta Conference** of 1945. But already by early 1947 Truman had become an increasingly militant critic of the behavior of the Soviet Union. His "hard line" campaign efforts paid off in his narrow "whistle stop" campaign victory.

In 1952 and 1956, the Polish Democratic vote fell to approximately fifty percent due to some extent perhaps to the Republican Party's powerful anti-communist opposition to Soviet domination of post–World War II Poland. In 1952 many PAC activists became identified with the Republican Party presidential nominee, General Dwight Eisenhower. But the Polish American shift to Eisenhower can also be explained in part by Eisenhower's stature as a World War II military hero who stood above parties. Significantly, it did not yet signal a permanent change of party allegiance for the masses of still mainly working class Polish American voters.

In the 1960 Presidential election, Polish Americans voted 4–1 for the Democratic presidential nominee, John F. Kennedy, a Roman Catholic of Irish heritage; in 1964 they backed his successor, Lyndon B. Johnson, by about the same margin in his landslide win. In the 1960 contest, their support was indeed critical to making possible Kennedy's exceedingly slim election victory. Kennedy carried eight states having substantial Polish ethnic populations—New York, Illinois, Pennsylvania, Massachusetts, Connecticut, Maryland, and Michigan. His opponent, Vice President Richard Nixon, won only in Wisconsin and Ohio. Overall, Kennedy won the popular vote by only 120,000 votes out of more than 68 million cast. He carried Illinois by fewer than 8,000 votes.

The 1960 presidential election is also memorable because it represents a key moment in American, and Polish American, politics. In that campaign both candidates vied throughout to show Polonia, and of course the entire electorate, that he was indeed the greatest opponent of Soviet Communism and the best champion of a free Poland. As a result, the issue of anti-communism was embraced by both parties and ceased playing any real role as a dividing factor between presidential candidates in the years after. As a result, other issues, like social security, federally funded medical insurance, civil rights, law and order, and opinion about the war in Vietnam, came to play increasingly important roles in election year public debates.

One occurrence of interest came in the 1968 presidential election. In it, the Democrats, demoralized and deeply divided over the country's involvement in the Vietnam War, chose a Polish American, U.S. Senator **Edmund S. Muskie** of Maine, to be the party's vice presidential nominee. Running with presidential nominee Hubert H. Humphrey in the wake of the party's disastrous convention in Chicago, Muskie was an excellent campaigner and a genuine asset to the ticket. But the Republican Richard Nixon narrowly won in an election notable for its lack of focus. Polish American support for the Democrats fell to a "low" of 56 percent in a three way race that included Alabama segregationist George Wallace, who received fourteen percent of the overall popular vote. In 1972, Muskie was an early favorite to win his party's presidential nomination. A moderate Democrat, like most Polish Americans, he campaigned in a period of ideological polarization and was knocked out of the race early, a victim of his own centrism, the "dirty tricks" employed against him by his opponents, and perhaps his own hot temper.

In 1976, the issue of Poland came up unexpectedly during a Presidential debate between the incumbent Gerald Ford, who had replaced Nixon following his forced resignation in 1974 due to the Watergate scandal, and his Democratic Party opponent, "Jimmy" Carter. There Ford made an incredible gaffe in asserting that Poland and other communist-ruled countries in Eastern Europe were not under Soviet domination. Ford narrowly lost the election, despite the Heruclean efforts of PAC President Aloysius Mazewski and other pro–Republican ethnic organization leaders to persuade the stubborn Ford to acknowledge his blunder. Carter won sixty percent of the Polish American vote and six of the ten most heavily Polish states, coming in on top in the electoral vote by 297–241.

In 1980 and 1984, Polish Americans continued to vote for the Democratic Party nominees but by steadily narrowing margins against the conservative, strongly anti-communist Republican presidential candidate, Ronald Reagan of California. In both contests, Reagan won every state with a large Polish population in gaining and then holding the presidency. His successor, George H.W. Bush, did nearly as well in winning office in 1988. In all these contests, the Republican anti-communist message, their projection of military strength against Soviet expansion, and the economic conditions at the time of each vote were buttressed by Reagan and Bush's good fortune in running against three weak Democratic Party nominees.

In summer 1989 Poland, led by Solidarity and inspired by the words of John Paul II, regained its full freedom from Soviet domination. The sudden and unexpected demise of communist rule everywhere in Eastern Europe followed soon after; astonishingly, between August and December 1991 the Soviet Union itself disintegrated. With its demise came an end to the Cold War between the USSR and the U.S. and the end of anti-communism as an issue in American, and Polish American, politics.

In the years since, Polish American voting preferences have come to be defined in ways not dissimilar to those of other Americans of eastern, central, and southern European ethnic ancestry, with the added note that many Polish Americans remain attuned to issues raised by the Roman Catholic Church, especially abortion. Large numbers of Polish Americans, many of them college educated, better paid, and professionally trained residents residing in the suburbs of the very cities where their parents and grandparents had lived, had already begun to move politically to the Republican Party. But this move was not as significant as it might appear at first glance. Even most working class Polish Americans had been among the more socially concerned members of the old New Deal Democratic coalition, and their support had always been strongest in connection with its pro-welfare, pro-social security, and pro-union programs.

An interesting footnote about Polish American political thinking involved the appearance of the "new ethnicity" idea in the late 1960s. The "new ethnicity" was a response to the "Black Pride" concept that emerged as part of the Civil Rights movement in the 1960s. It rejected the "melting pot" thesis that proposed the gradual disappearance of ethnic identity among the immigrants' descendants. Author Michael Novak was the chief exponent of the "new ethnicity"; his book *The Rise of the Unmeltable Ethnics* became a basic text for the movement he tried to build. But the U.S. political establishment was cool to the idea, particularly since both major parties had since the 1940s run their own ethnic divisions to mobilize voter support for their candidates. Moreover, many Polish Americans, like most other ethnic Americans, did not fully buy into

Novak's argument. A mini surge in discussions about ethnic pride and assertiveness did occur in the 1970s in Polonia and elsewhere, most of it centered around discussions among some of the young generation of mainly American born academics and professionals of ethnic heritage. This resulted in much published research on immigration and ethnic life in the U.S. On the larger stage, the "new ethnicity" led to rising complaints about "defamation" in the mass media, most notably in a growing resentment about the "Polack joke" plague that infected the country in the 1970s. For its part the PAC supported the inclusion of questions about national ancestry into the decennial U.S. census. Congress approved and a survey of American national ancestry has been conducted in 1980, 1990, and 2000. Its main result has been to provide interested persons with a better sense of the cultural richness and diversity of America, one going far beyond traditional distinctions based on race and foreign birth. The PAC also backed two "friend of the court" initiatives in the late 1970s in cases heard by the U.S. Supreme Court in questioning the constitutionality of "affirmative action"; its briefs criticized affirmative action for racial minorities and women as not going far enough in responding to past and continuing prejudice directed against the ethnic and immigrant origins of individuals. Several cultural programs were also funded by Washington in the 1970s to promote greater understanding of Polish heritage in the U.S. Another less successful initiative sought to create a "dialog" between Polish and Jewish Americans aimed at building understanding and cooperation between the two communities on various issues of mutual concern.

At the national level, a handful of Americans of Polish origin have gained political prominence over the past fifty years. Muskie was the most notable among them; he served several terms as governor of Maine before winning election to the U.S. Senate in 1958. After unsuccessful runs for the vice presidency in 1968 and the presidency in 1972, President Carter appointed him U.S. Secretary of State in 1980, making him the highest public official of Polish heritage in U.S. history. Two other Polish Americans have served in a president's cabinet: **John Gronouski**, who was Postmaster General of the U.S. under President Johnson and later America's Ambassador to Poland in 1965, and **Edward Derwinski**, an articulate, deeply anti-communist former U.S. Congressman from Illinois who became Secretary of Veterans Affairs under President George H.W. Bush in 1990.

Pehaps the most influential Polish American in national affairs, after Muskie and along

with Derwinski, is **Zbigniew K. Brzeziński**. The son of a career Polish foreign service officer based in Canada in World War II, Brzeziński came to the U.S. as a graduate student, became a U.S. citizen, and rose to a professorship in Soviet affairs at Harvard and Columbia Universities. One of a select number of policy-oriented scholars to engage in government service at a high level (others include Henry Kissinger and Daniel Patrick Moynihan) Brzeziński was President Carter's National Security Advisor from 1977 to 1981. Afterward he continued to play an active and highly visible role as a commentator, and presidential advisor in foreign affairs. A gifted writer and public speaker, he was, and is, unique among Polish Americans in U.S. politics.

In addition, several Polish Americans elected to the U.S. Senate and House of Representatives have gained positions of signal national influence. They include U.S. Senator **Barbara Mikulski** of Maryland, and Congressmen **Daniel Rostenkowski** of Illinois, **John Dingell** of Michigan, and **Clement Zablocki** of Wisconsin. Senator Mikulski has been a highly visible national figure since her election to the House of Representatives in 1976. On several occasions she has taken important and highly praised positions on matters pertaining to Poland. Rostenkowski gained prominence as chair of the Ways and Means Committee of the House of Representatives, its most powerful legislative body. Dingell, the longest serving Polish American Congressman in history (he was first elected in 1954) has been a dominant force in the House. Zablocki served as Chair of the House International Relations Committee for fifteen years and gained prominence as a sponsor of the controversial, possibly unconstitutional, "War Powers Act" that sought to limit the prerogatives of the President as commander in chief of the armed forces after the Vietnam War. Zablocki also won praise for sponsoring a U.S. funded children's hospital in Kraków, Poland during the Cold War. Other Polish Americans elected to the Senate have been Alaska Republican **Frank Murkowski**, who was succeeded by his daughter, **Lisa Murkowski**, and Nebraska Republican **"Chuck" Hagel**. A few Polish Americans have been state governors, most notably Democrats Muskie of Maine, Ted Kulongoski of Oregon, and Republican Tim Pawlenty of Minnesota.

CONGRESSIONAL AND LOCAL POLITICS

Over the ninety years beginning with the 1918 Congressional elections and ending with the 110th Congress in January 2009, fifty-four Polish Americans have won election to the

House of Representatives. The first, in 1918, was **John C. Kleczka**, a Republican from Milwaukee. Since then at least one person of Polish origin has been in the body in every session, with the largest number, twelve, elected in 1962, 1982, and 1984. The trend since has been downward, with six Polish Americans in the House in 2008.

A look at Polish Americans in the House through three successive overlapping thirty year periods provides the following facts. In all, twenty Polish Americans were elected to the body between 1918 and 1948, 28 were elected between 1948 and 1978, with 21 between 1978 and 2008. Over time, the average number of years Polish Americans have held office increased steadily: in the first thirty year period the average for the twenty congressmen was slightly less than eight years; between 1948 and 1978 the 26 congressmen elected in that period held office for an average of 11 years. Between 1978 and 2008, the 21 individuals in office in that period were in office for twelve years. In the first thirty year period, twelve Democrats and eight Republicans won office; between 1948 and 1978, 22 Democrats and six Republicans won; in the most recent thirty year interval only one of 21 has been a Republican.

John Dingel, Jr., of Michigan has served the longest; he was first elected in 1954 and is still serving in 2008 (Dingel's father preceded him in office from 1932. His original name was Dziegielewicz). Daniel Rostenkowski was in office from 1959 until 1995; Clement Zablocki from 1949 to his death in 1984. In all, most Polish Americans in Congress have served heavily Polish constituencies. For example, thirteen Congressmen have come from metropolitan Detroit alone, ten from Chicagoland, six from Buffalo, and four from Milwaukee. Between 1938 and 1962 seven individuals were elected to Congress from Connecticut, but none since (as of 2010). Interestingly, Chicagoland possessed four Congressmen of Polish origin from 1959 to 1973, but in 2009 had only one. Detroit had one, where it once had as many as three. Milwaukee and Buffalo have none. While there has never been a "Polish Caucus" in the House, Polish Americans in Congress have invariably supported the Polish cause, some in very notable fashion.

At the local level, several hundred persons of Polish ancestry have held office in state legislatures, the judiciary, and a wide variety of county, city, and town council positions. In only a few cases has a Polish American been elected to a big city mayorship, most notably in Detroit and Buffalo. Perhaps the most significant, talented, if unsuccessful, Polish

American candidate for mayor was **Benjamin Adamowski**, a Democrat turned Republican who ran a strong and controversial race against Richard J. Daley and his Chicago "machine" in 1963. The lack of success by ambitious Polish Americans in winning high local office, and the decline in the number of Polish Americans in the House of Representatives may be due to three factors. One involves the declining importance of a large and politically homogeneous "Polish vote" as a foundation for one's being taken seriously for public office. Second, in the modern age, candidates need substantial financial resources to be serious candidates for mayoral, Federal, and statewide offices. In the past, a heavy concentration of Polish votes in a particular area was an undeniable asset to the claims of Polish American candidates for consideration for office. Also, in the era of political machine politics, money was less essential than was party organization in "getting out the vote." Third, there is the fact that over the past fifty years the number of congressional seats allotted to states with significant Polish American populations has declined. As recently as 1960, the ten most populous Polish American states had a total of 190 congressional seats. In 2008 this number declined to 144.—*Donald E. Pienkos*

SOURCES: Andrzej Brożek, *Polish Americans 1854–1939* (Warsaw: Interpress, 1985); Edward R. Kantowicz, *Polish American Politics in Chicago, 1888–1940* (Chicago: University of Chicago Press, 1975); Angela T. Pienkos, ed., *Ethnic Politics in Urban America: The Polish Experience in Four Cities* (Chicago: Polish American Historical Association, 1978); Stephen M. Leahy, *The Life of Milwaukee's Most Popular Politician, Clement J. Zablocki: Milwaukee Politics and Congressional Foreign Policy* (Lewiston, Maine: Edward Mellen Press, 2002); Jack L. Hammersmith, "Franklin Roosevelt, the Polish Question, and the Election of 1944," *Mid-America*, Vol. 59, no. 1 (1977), 5–17; George H. Janczewski, "The Significance of the Polish Vote in the American National Election Campaign of 1948," *The Polish Review*, Vol. 13, no. 4 (1969), 101–09; Stanley P. Wagner, "The Polish Vote in 1960," *Polish American Studies*, Vol. 21, no. 1 (1964), 1–9; Edward R. Kantowicz, "The Emergence of the Polish-Democratic Vote in Chicago," *Polish American Studies*, Vol. 29, no. 1 (1972), 67–80; Athan Theoharis, "The Republican Party and Yalta: Partisan Exploitation of the Polish American Concern over the Conference, 1945–1960," *Polish American Studies*, Vol. 28, no. 1 (1971), 5–19; Arthur W. Thurner, "Polish Americans in Chicago Politics, 1890–1930," *Polish American Studies*, Vol. 28, no. 1 (1971), 20–42; Charles Allan Baretski, "How Polonia Reacts to Inadequate Recognition in the Political Arena," *Polish American Studies*, Vol. 28, no. 1 (1971), 43–53; Fred B. Misse, "Franklin Roosevelt and the Polish Vote in 1944," *Midwest Quarterly*, Vol. 21 (1980), 317–32; Athan G. Theoharis, "Ethnic Politics and National Policy: Polish-Americans and Yalta," *Intellect*, March 1976, 470–73; Peter H. Irons, "'The Test is Poland': Polish Americans and the Origins of the Cold War," *Polish American Studies*, Vol. 30, no. 2 (1973), 5–63; Craig R. Bucki, "Ethnic Appeals: The 1960 and 1968 Presidential Elections in Buffalo's Polish American Community," *Polish American Studies*, Vol. 60, no. 2 (2003), 25–57.

Polka. The favorite of American **Polonia**, the *polka* is a lively couple-dance in a moderately fast duple meter. Because of its acceptance as an ethnic symbol by Polish immigrants to North America, the *polka* is gradually increasing its position among Polish dances and is often present in the repertoire of Polish folk dance ensembles in the U.S. The dance, however, is not Polish and it is not included among the five "national" dances of Poland: **polonaise**, **kujawiak**, **mazur**, **oberek**, and **krakowiak**. *Polka* is not a meaningful symbol of Polish culture for Poles from Poland. According to the *New Grove Dictionary of Music and Musicians*, the *polka* originated in Bohemia around 1830 as a round-dance, and became popular throughout Europe and in America in the course of the nineteenth century. The name "*polka*" is derived from Czech words for "field" or "half;" in other interpretations the name relates to the Czech term for a Polish girl, "*polska*," in reference to the *krakowiak* dance-songs which the Bohemians adopted for their *polkas*. It is interesting to note that the word "*Polka*" means "Polish woman" in Polish.

The nineteenth-century *polka* was characterized by a frequent occurrence of a rhythmic motive consisting of two sixteenths followed by an eighth note (two short and a long), in a duple meter:

The tempo of the *polka* was that of a military march played rather slowly, at 52 bars (MM = 104) per minute. The music was usually in ternary form with eight-bar sections, sometimes with a brief introduction and a coda. Such *polkas* were cultivated by all the leading ballroom dance composers of the latter part of the nineteenth century. Later, *polkas* increased in tempo and became very fast, vivacious, and energetic. Music with the *polka*'s characteristics appears in various collections written about 1800 for practical use by village musicians. Since the 19th century, *polkas* were written by the leading composers of ballroom music (including both Johann Strausses) and classical music, such as Smetana, Dvorak, Stravinsky, and others. The *polka* was soon performed in many countries, including Austria, Germany, France, England, the U.S., Canada, Mexico, Argentina, and even India. It attained extraordinary popularity, so that clothes, hats, streets and even dishes were named after the *polka* (e.g. "polka dots"). Local choreographers introduced their own variants, for instance, the *polka-mazurka*, which combined *polka* steps with the 3/4 time of the *mazurka*, popular in the 1840s and brought to the U.S. in the mid–1860s.

Polkas appear in the repertoire of folk ensembles of the whole of Poland, including even the **Podhale** area of the Tatra Mountains from which other national dances of Poland were absent. The most common association of the *polka* is with urban folklore. As an exhibition dance, the *polka* includes a variety of gestures, with special steps, jumps, and kicks, lifting the women, dancing in a circle, etc. The particular array of steps depends on the choreographer and the image of a tradition that he/she wants to evoke (e.g. early 20th century working-class Warsaw, nineteenth-century middle-class, various regions with local *polka* variants, Rzeszowskie, Małopolska, Wielkopolska, and so on).

The modern American *polka* is distant from its European roots. Charles Keil lists six different *polka* styles, some of which have intermingled in the U.S. since the 1920s, resulting in the present-day *polka* of the Polish American ethnic community: Slavic *polkas* (Polish, Slovenian), Germanic *polkas* (German, Czech-Bohemian), and southwestern *polkas* (Mexican and Papago-Pima). All the ethnic terms in this list should be hyphenated with "American" (e.g. Polish American); moreover, all of the *polkas* "have come to define a certain persistent quality of ethnic working-class identity." The distinct Polish American version of the *polka* has roots in working class communities of the East Coast and the Midwest with mixed Polish, German and Czech populations. Musicians of the Eastern *polka* tradition included Walt Solek and Walter Dana Daniłowski. In the 1950s Chicago emerged as a major center and the source of the dominant style of the *polka* which crystallized in the music of Li'l Wally [see **Jagiello, Walter**] (slower tempo, expressive lyrics and the ensemble including the clarinet, trumpet, and concertina). Polish American *polka* bands are so widespread now, and the genre so well-established that there is a separate category at the Grammy Awards dedicated to the *polka* as well as numerous websites on the Internet (e.g. PolkaNet.com).

Among contemporary popular and ethnic dance genres, the *polka* has kept its image of the working-class dance providing enjoyment and relaxation after long days of hard, physical labor. With the "*polka* happiness" providing the keyword to its meaning (term borrowed from the title of a 1992 study by Charles and Angeliki Keil), the dance is slowly gaining popularity as a recreational activity for amateur dancers who relish the *polka*'s lively tempo and enjoy the strenuous exercise that it provides. The musical styles continue to evolve and the Polish American *polka* remains one of the few dances historically linked to Poland which are alive in social practice. The *krakowiaks*, *mazurs* or *zbójnickis* are exhibition dances performed by semi-professional Polish folk dance ensembles for Polish and American audiences. The *polonaise* kept its function as a high-status musical symbol of Polishness and its name is used in publications and events of Polish American cultural organizations. Only the *polka* is danced by everyone.—*Maja Trochimczyk*

SOURCES: Ada Dziewanowska, *Polish Folk Dances & Songs: A Step by Step Guide* (New York: Hippocrene Books, 1999); Charles Keil and Angeliki V. Keil, *Polka Happiness* (Philadelphia: Temple University Press, 1992); Victor Greene, *A Passion for Polka* (Berkeley, CA: University of California Press, 1992); Ann Hetzel Gunkel, "The Polka Alternative: Polka a Counter-Hegemonic Ethnic Practice," *Popular Music and Society*, Vol. 27, no. 3 (Winter 2004); "Polka," entry in Stanley Sadie, ed., *New Grove Dictionary of Music and Musicians* (London: McMillan, 1980), Vol. 15; Janice Ellen Kleeman, "The Origins and Stylistic Development of Polish-American Polka Music" (Berkeley, CA: Unpublished Ph.D. dissertation, University of California–Berkeley, 1982); Maja Trochimczyk, "Polka," entry, Polish Dance in Southern California website, University of Southern California, Polish Music Center, 2000; Vol. 61, no. 2 (2004) of *Polish American Studies* is a theme issue on the polka.

Polonaise (Polonez). The *polonaise* is a stately Polish processional dance, performed by couples who walk around the dance hall. The music is in triple meter and moderate tempo. The dance developed from the *Polish dance* (*taniec polski*) of the eighteenth century; this form, in turn, was derived from the *chodzony* (walking dance) which was popular in the seventeenth century and known as a *pieszy* (pedestrian), or *chmielowy* (hops) dance. The latter form had its roots in the folk wedding dances, from which it separated and then entered the dance repertoire of the nobility. The Polish name of the dance, *polonez*, stems from the polonized form of the French term *polonaise* which was introduced in the seventeenth century. The earliest Polish source is a 1772 manuscript collection by Joseph Sychra that included 62 *polonaises*. The court *polonaise*, according to the *New Grove Dictionary of Music and Musicians*, "was played by musicians in the galleries of the great reception halls while the assembly, dressed in great splendour, danced it below in processional figures [...] In this form it was transformed into the most highbred expression of the Polish national spirit and became in the process the most representative of Polish dances throughout Europe." The dance has been used in formal contexts and during public ceremonies and festivities, particularly at weddings, or, recently, as the first dance of a formal ball. Dancing the *polonaise* requires a straight, upright posture with no movement of hips, smooth and elegant hand gestures, and the head held high, with pride, as it were. According to **Ada Dziewanowska**, "the man should display dignity and polite attentiveness not only to his partner, but to others around. The woman should carry herself with grace and a certain timidity." There are two characteristic rhythmic patterns that allow one to recognize the *polonaise*: (1) the succession of one eighth-note, two sixteenths and four eighth-notes at the opening of the dance (depicted below), and (2) the cadential formula of four sixteenths followed by two quarternotes (depicted below).

After 1800, the instrumental *polonaise* began to be cultivated in Poland by composers, the greatest of whom was Fryderyk Chopin whose works for piano made this dance the musical symbol of Poland and Polishness. According to the inventory of Polish dances in American popular music edited by **Aleksander Janta**, the *polonaise* appeared in the U.S. in 1815. Janta lists 29 editions of *polonaises*, as well as two *polonaises* attributed to **Tadeusz Kościuszko**.—*Maja Trochimczyk*

SOURCES: Ada Dziewanowska, *Polish Folk Dances & Songs: A Step by Step Guide* (New York: Hippocrene Books, 1999); Aleksander Janta, *A History of Nineteenth Century American-Polish Music* (New York: The Kosciuszko Foundation, 1982); Józef M. Reiss, and Maurice J.E. Brown, "Polonaise," in Stanley Sadie, ed., *New Grove Dictionary of Music and Musicians* (London: McMillan, 1980), Vol. 15.

Polonia. Polonia is the Latin word for Poland that refers to the Polish diaspora; that is, Polish communities outside of Poland's geographic borders. Immigrants in the United States began using this term in the nineteenth century to refer to their own communities. In the twentieth century the term was used to refer to numerous Polish ethnic communities around the world. Polonian communities are located in all regions of the United States, but they are heavily concentrated in Illinois, New York, Pennsylvania, Michigan, Ohio, Wisconsin, New Jersey, Connecticut and Massachusetts. The first Polonia community established in the United States was in **Panna Maria**, Texas, in 1854. In addition to the United States, Polonian communities can be found in Britain, Canada, France, Germany, Sweden,

Ireland, South Africa, Australia, Brazil, Spain and the Netherlands.—*Mary Patrice Erdmans*

Polonia Technica (Society of Polish Engineers). The association "Polonia Technica" was officially registered on May 16, 1941 in New York City, New York, as a non-profit organization. The main goal of the society was to help Polish engineers and technicians migrate to the United States from a Europe overrun by Germany and Russia during the Second World War. Originally intended to last for the duration of the war, after demobilization of the Polish Army in England in the 1950s, a large group of Polish engineers and technicians arrived in the U.S. with the intention of staying, thus reviving the society. Their main goal became the integration of newcomers and mutual assistance in assimilating into American society, including help with finding housing, employment, the exchange of experiences and education. Every year the society awarded a number of scholarships for Poles majoring in engineering, including many in Argentina where a large Polish population was established. The organization also sent a considerable number of technical books and periodicals to Poland. Beginning in the early 1990s, the organization offered computer courses on new technologies to its members, organized hundreds of lectures, training classes and seminars in many disciplines, and in 1994 in New York organized an event called "ComPract," a technical show of computer applications. Through these meetings, within a few hours over 1,000 members and supporters had a chance to familiarize themselves with practical uses for computers. In the mid–1990s the Internet took the world by storm. Polonia Technica was among first societies to educate Polish professionals and students about this new technology. For many years, Polonia Technica sponsored the Investors Club which hosted monthly meetings with Wall Street specialists. Polonia Technica cooperated with the Polish Student Union in New York to organize meetings called "Studia 4U" with the motto "The future of **Polonia** lies in the education of its Youth." The society took an important role in the calendar of Polish events with over 800 listeners.

The association celebrated its sixtieth anniversary in 2001. On this occasion it published a monograph titled *Historical Details in Years 1941–2001* that reviewed the history and achievements of Polish engineers in the United States including such luminaries as **Tadeusz Sendzimir**, Jan Grzybowski Holm, Bolesław Przedpelski, Wacław Szukiewicz, Zdzisław J. Starostecki (designer of the "Patriot" rocket), Wojciech Rostafiński, **Frank**

Piasecki, **Alina Szczesniak**, **Andrzej Targowski**, and **Janusz Romanski**. In 2010, Polonia Technica had over 300 members, while its database held the names of over 750 people associated with the society as its supporters. Its goal was then to bring together professionals who work in technical fields to develop their social network and national bonds. The society worked to develop professional cooperation, technical education, exchange of information about new technologies, and the integration of Polish emigrants in the U.S. Polonia Technica has transferred all its archives to digital media. Most of the materials are available through the Internet, via the Idaho University server, and in the archives of the **Polish Institute of Arts & Sciences** in New York.—*Janusz W. Romanski*

Sources: Zbigniew Piasek, ed., *Encyclopedia of World Research and Engineering Heritage of Polish Engineers in the USA, Canada, Europe, Argentina and Singapore* (Kraków: FOGRA Oficyna Wydawnicza, 2006); Marek Szczerbiński, *Polonia Technica: Stowarzyszenie Inżynierów i Techników Polskich w Stanach Zjednoczonych Ameryki Północnej: zarys historii w latach 1941–2001* (Częstochowa and New York: Światowa Rada Badań nad Polonią, Akademia Polonijna, 2001).

Polski Instytut Naukowy w Ameryce *see* **Polish Institute of Arts & Sciences of America.**

Polski Uniwersytet na Obczyźnie (PUNO) *see* **Polish University Abroad.**

Polskość (Polishness). A Polish term that literally means something of Polish origin, or someone of Polish language and customs, the term is used by scholars of the Polish experience in America to refer to "Polishness," the quality of being Polish. It is often used in the context of preserving Polish culture and traditions in America.—*James S. Pula*

Pomost (Platform). One of the largest and most active organizations during the Solidarność era, Pomost, headquartered in Chicago, was organized for the purpose of providing publicity and financial support for the democratic opposition movement in Poland, in particular the activities of the Solidarity labor union. Prominent leaders of this group included Christopher Rać, Waldemar Wlodarczyk, Roman Koperski, and Marian Sromek. Pomost was an outgrowth of two smaller organizations founded in the mid–1970s, the Polish Student's Union at the University of Illinois, Circle Campus, and the **Polish National Alliance** lodge Pokolenie. Although the fraternal lodge and student organization helped to bring together a group of Polish immigrants and Polish Americans interested in Polish affairs, these organizations were not useful for organizing political activity. First,

both organizations were embedded in larger structures that limited their activities. Second, neither organization could raise large amounts of money. Pokolenie was useful because it became an organizational member of the **Polish American Congress**, thus allowing new immigrants to become delegates and committee members in the PAC Illinois Division. The student organization helped to attract an educated membership. In 1979 this group decided to publish a "social-political" quarterly called Pomost for a Polish reading audience. Between 1979–84, Pomost circulated 1,500–2,000 copies of each issue, except during martial law times (1982) when it printed nearly 7,000 copies. The articles focused almost exclusively on Poland, relations between the United States and Poland, and the relationship between Polonia and Pomost. Some 92 percent of the articles were written in Polish. Pomost was incorporated in 1982 in Illinois as a charitable educational organization. The founders and most of the members were recent immigrants who had arrived in the 1960s and 1970s; however, Pomost also attracted some young Polish Americans and older World War II émigrés. During its peak years in 1982–83, Pomost boasted 6,000 sympathizers nationwide and 900 dues paying members. Its main activities were publishing the quarterly, organizing demonstrations in Chicago, raising funds for the opposition in Poland, and eventually engaging in lobbying activities to influence U.S. foreign policy toward Poland. **Magnus Jan Krynski**, an émigré who arrived in the United States as a child in 1939, was the main lobbyist for Pomost in Washington, D.C. The lobbying activities brought Pomost in direct competition with the Polish American Congress, especially as the two disagreed over such issues as lifting the sanctions against the Jaruzelski regime in Poland. Pomost and the PAC eventually became bitter enemies, with both organizations working to discredit the other. By the mid–1980s the organization was dissolved.—*Mary Patrice Erdmans*

Sources: Mary Patrice Erdmans, *Opposite Poles: Immigrants and Ethnics in Polish Chicago, 1976–1990* (University Park, PA: Pennsylvania State University Press, 1998); Mary Patrice Erdmans, "Conflict and Cooperation Between Pomost and the Polish American Congress," *Polish American Studies*, Vol. 52, no. 1 (1995), 52–69; Polish American Archives, Central Connecticut State University, Files of Dr. Magnus Jan Krynski, Box 4, Folder 22.

Pope John Paul II Cultural Center. Located at 3900 Harewood Road, N.E., in Washington, D.C., this Cultural Center was an outgrowth of a proposal for a "Catholic Center" made by Bishop **Joseph Maida** to Pope John Paul II in 1988. Work on the project began in 1997 and was completed in

2001. The site chosen was a twelve-acre tract adjacent to the Catholic University of America in the vicinity of The Basilica of the National Shrine of the Immaculate Conception. An online museum, a place of pilgrimage, and a spectacular work of architecture, the Cultural Center was designed with a wing-shaped roof and contains themes on papal history, Polish history, works of art, audio-visual presentations, music, books, religious items, and souvenirs. It has galleries with technology for visitors to explore their own faith and to interact with others. It offers a display of personal memorabilia, works of art, and photos of encounters with Pope John Paul II. The Center also became a place of scholarly research on the teachings of John Paul II and inter-religious dialogue. It has a chapel, three auditoriums, a café, and two gift shops. The Pope John Paul II Cultural Center was initially dedicated in November, 2000, by the American Cardinals Maida, Anthony Joseph Bevilacqua and William Henry Keeler and the Apostolic Nuncio to the United States, Gabriel Montalvo Higuera. On March 22, 2001, it was officially opened to the public after a dedication by President George W. Bush and presided over by American Cardinals, Maida, James Aloysius Hickey, William Henry Keeler and Theodore Edgar McCarrick, the Polish Cardinal Franciszek Macharski and the Governor of Vatican City, Cardinal **Edmund Casimir Szoka**. The dedication was also attended by many other prominent clergy and officials. Located outside the Cultural Center is a ten-foot statue of Pope John Paul II donated by the Polish Conference of Catholic Bishops, a sign of their support of the mission of the Cultural Center. It was unveiled during the Polonia Day Celebrations on June 9, 2001, by the Polish Cardinals Franciszek Macharski and Henryk Roman Gulbinowicz and the American Cardinal Maida. The Polish Heritage Room, which was reopened by the Pope John Paul II Cultural Center on Sunday, October 28, 2007 to the public, is exclusively devoted to Pope John Paul II.—*Maria Swiecicka-Ziemianek*

Popieliński, John N. (b. Poland, ca. 1850; d. unknown). Polonia activist. Popieliński had already served as president of the Kosciuszko Patriotic Club in Philadelphia when he was invited by **Julius Andrzejkowicz** to attend the first meeting of what became the **Polish National Alliance** on February 15, 1880. In a letter he wrote late in his life to **Stanisław Osada**, author of the 1905 history of the PNA, Popieliński gave a glimpse of the founding meeting: "We called Poles together at 347 Third Street in Philadelphia on February 15,

1880.... Besides [Julian] **Szajnert**, Andrzejkowicz, I, and [Julian] **Lipiński**, around fifteen others came to the meeting.... Andrzejkowicz called the meeting to order, stated its aims, and a majority backed the idea and elected Andrzejkowicz president, Szajnert secretary, Lipiński treasurer. At the first meeting eleven people signed the declaration and decided to send Polish exile leader **Agaton Giller** a letter and to send out an announcement to other groups as well. Some groups praised us, others criticized, but they didn't stop us." Popieliński was honored for his involvement in the Alliance at its 1897 national convention in Philadelphia and is remembered as one of the five founding members of the PNA.—*Donald E. Pienkos*

SOURCES: Stanisław Osada, *Historia Związku Narodowego Polskiego i rozwój ruchu narodowego Polskiego w Ameryce Pólnocnej* (Chicago: Nakładem i drukiem Związku Narodowego Polskiego, 1905); Donald E. Pienkos, *PNA: A Centennial History of the Polish National Alliance of the United States of North America* (Boulder, CO: East European Monographs, 1984).

Poplawski, Stephen John (b. Poland, August 14, 1885; d. Racine, Wisconsin, December 9, 1956). Inventor. The inventor of the electric blender migrated to the U.S. with his parents at age nine, settling in Racine,

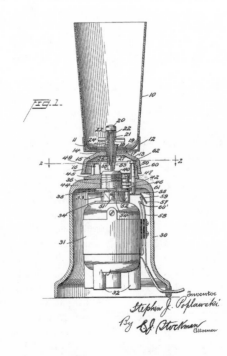

A drawing of the original electric blender invented by Stephen Poplawski (*U.S. Patent Office*).

Wisconsin. In 1918 he established Stephens Tool Company and a year later Arnold Electric Company engaged him to devise an automated mixer for Horlick's malted milkshakes. In 1922 Poplawski added blades to an electric motor placed at the bottom of a cup-shaped vessel and received a patent for the first electric mixer. The following year he developed the first liquefier blender, and in 1926 sold his company to Hamilton Beach Manufacturing Company with Poplawski joining Hamilton Beach as a member of its research and development staff. In 1932 Poplawski was granted a patent on a device that would convert fruits and vegetables to liquids. In 1940, Poplawski founded the Stephens Electric Company and patented a home mixer for use in the kitchen. This device was used in the popular Waring Blender, and when Poplawski retired and sold his company to John Oster in 1946 it became the template for the lucrative Osterizer.—*James S. Pula*

SOURCES: Gerald P. Poplawski, *The Life Story of S. J. Poplawski* (self-published, 2006); obituary, *Racine Journal-Times*, December 10, 1956.

Positivism, Polish American. Positivism emerged in Poland in the mid- to late 1860s as a response to the failure of the January 1863 insurrection. Centered in Warsaw, the Positivists appealed to Poles to strengthen the nation from within through the practice of "organic work"— a term referring to actions aimed at improving and strengthening Polish culture, society, and economy through activities including the building and establishment of schools, universities, cultural associations and groups, and credit and loan banks. In America, Polish Positivism was a blend of social issues and activism with romantic national ideals. It was profoundly influenced not only by the writing of the Polish positivists, but also by the émigrés of 1864 who contributed to the debate between the "romantics" and the "realists." The ideas of strengthening Polish society through associations and organizations designed *by* Poles for the benefit of *all* Poles led to the creation of such important groups as the **Polish Roman Catholic Union of America** (PRCUA) and the **Polish Women's Alliance in America**, and shaped the work of such influential immigrant writers as **Helena Staś**. The idea of organic work, in particular, also influenced the activities of Polish expatriates and refugees like the Rev. **Wincenty Barzyński** (a founder of the PRCUA) and the Rev. **Józef Dąbrowski** (founder of the Polish Seminary in Detroit, MI), who adopted positivist programs to promote Polish-Catholic morals and Polish national values through associations, networks, farming colonies, and religious and educational institutions. The PRCUA and its program of organic work differed markedly from the orientation of the **Polish National Alliance** (PNA), which was heavily influenced by Poland's early nineteenth-century tradition of Romantic nationalism, and which prioritized activities aimed at furthering the cause of Poland and the Polish nation abroad over aiding the Polish community in America.—*Krystyna Cap*

SOURCES: Karen Majewski, *Traitors and True Poles: Narrating a Polish-American Identity, 1880–1939* (Athens, OH: Ohio University Press, 2003); John Radziłowski, *The Eagle and the Cross: A History of the Polish Roman Catholic Union of America, 1873–2000* (Boulder, CO: East European Monographs, 2003).

Post, Christian Frederick (b. Chojnice, Poland, 1710; d. Germantown, Pennsylvania, April 29, 1785). Minister, pioneer, explorer. Post arrived in the U.S. with a group of Moravian missionaries in 1742. Shortly after arriving he settled in a village of Delaware Indians, married one of their number, and proceeded to learn their language and customs. After the death of his wife he returned briefly to Europe to organize another group of missionaries, but his attempt to found a missionary outpost in Labrador in 1752 failed due to the hostility of the natives. Moving back to Pennsylvania, he was credited with paving the way for the treaty that brought peace between the Indians and English settlers in the Wyoming Valley. In 1758 he undertook a dangerous mission into western Pennsylvania in an attempt to convince the Delaware and other area tribes to abandon their allegiance to the French and ally instead with the English. His efforts were largely responsible for driving a wedge between the French and their Indian allies, the loss of which eventually caused the French to abandon Fort Duquesne and western Pennsylvania.—*James S. Pula*

SOURCES: Joseph A. Borkowski, "Polish-born Pennsylvania Pioneer," *Polish American Studies*, Vol. 20, no. 2 (1963), 81–86; Francis Bolek, ed., *Who's Who in Polish America* (New York: Harbinger House, 1943).

Powers, Stefanie (Stefania Zofia Federkiewicz; b. November 2, 1942, Hollywood, California; d.—). Actor. The second child of Polish American parents, Powers was raised Roman Catholic by her mother and grandparents. A graduate of Hollywood High School (1960), she originally pursued singing and dancing, appearing on stage at the age of 15 in *West Side Story*. She took acting classes at Twentieth Century–Fox, beginning her career as "Taffy Paul." Changing her stage name permanently in the 1960s, she appeared in various movies including *Experiment in Terror* and *If a Man Answers,* both in 1962. One of her first major roles was with John Wayne in *McClintock*. Her beauty landed her the featured role in the television series *The Girl from U.N.C.L.E.* She is best known as the character Jennifer Hart in the series *Hart to Hart* (1979–1984), co-starring with Robert Wagner as a pair of rich amateur sleuths. Powers became an advocate for wildlife conservation, establishing in 1981 the William Holden Wildlife Foundation, named for her partner and becoming director of the Mount Kenya Game Ranch in Africa. In 1984 she was in the miniseries *Mistral's Daughter*, followed by the television movie *Beryl Markham: A Shadow on the Sun* (1988). In 2001 she toured England as Anna Leonowens in the musical *The King and I,* which also toured the United States in 2004-05. In 2003 she released a musical CD entitled *On the Same Page*. She is also the author of two books, *Stefanie Powers: Superlife!* (1985) and *Power Pilates: Stefanie Powers' Guide to Longevity and Well-Being Through Pilates* (2004). An outstanding polo player, she was one of the first foreign members of England's Royal County of Berkshire Polo Club. Powers speaks seven languages: English, French, Italian, Polish, Spanish, Swahili, and some Mandarin Chinese. Her awards include: a Laurel Award nomination as "Top New Female Personality" (1962), the People's Choice Award for "Favorite Female Performer in a New TV Program" (1980), two Emmy nominations (1981, 1982), five Golden Globe nominations for "Best Television Actress" (1980–1984), a star on Hollywood Walk of Fame (1992), the Sarah Siddons Award in 1993 for *Love Letters*, and an Honorary Fellow of the Chester Zoo in England for her work in wildlife conservation.—*Cheryl A. Pula*

SOURCE: Ephraim Katz, ed., *The Film Encyclopedia* (New York: Thomas Y. Crowell Co., 1979).

Press, Polish-American. One of the most important influences on the Polish-American community was the development of a Polish-language press. In Poland, the press was viewed as an authority on virtually any subject and played a prominent role within the Polish community, especially in areas where high illiteracy gave the written word an aura of added mystery. In America, the Polish-language press provided local news and information from Poland for people unable to speak English, carried organizational news, imparted information about American customs, laws, and naturalization procedures, and generally assisted in the adjustment of immigrants to their new environment. In this sense, the Polish press was both an educational force for maintaining ethnic identity and a change agent that eventually assisted immigrants to understand and take part in the larger American society.

The first known Polish-language newspaper in the U.S. was ***Echo z Polski*** edited by Romuald Jaworowski in New York City in 1863 as an organ of the émigré community. It purpose was to provide to Poles in the U.S. news of the Polish January Insurrection of 1863 and other conspiratorial activities of Poles who were seeking to free their homeland from occupation by the partitioning powers — Austria, Prussia, and Russia. With the beginning of the mass migration following the American Civil War, Polish-language newspapers began to flourish in the 1870s. In 1893 **Henryk Nagiel** surveyed the Polish press and found that 105 periodicals appeared since the *Echo z Polski*. Half were still being published in 1893. "Unlike the first publications of the political refugees who concentrated on Poland's survival and European politics," Jan Kowalik explained in his *The Polish Press in America*, "the immigrant press of the later period dealt with adaptation problems, served the community interests, and [was] determined to operate on a sound financial basis. In order to reach the farmer and factory worker, it had to lower the literary niveau and tailor the content to its readers' needs and likings. Although most of the papers were typographically poorly outfitted and some lacked even the diacritical markings of the Polish alphabet, they did more than their share to educate the often illiterate immigrant masses and promote their ethnic and religious self-consciousness." The first such publication devoted to Polish American concerns appears to have been *Orzeł Polski* (The Polish Eagle) which began publishing on February 22, 1870, in Washington, Missouri.

Just as **Polonia** contained a plethora of political, regional, economic, religious, and secular perspectives, so too did the Polish-American press mirror these various viewpoints. Among the most influential nineteenth century newspapers was Chicago's *Gazeta Polska* (Polish Gazette) whose editor, **Władysław Dyniewicz**, did much to popularize newspapers among early immigrants. The weeklies ***Zgoda*** (Harmony) and ***Naród Polski*** (The Polish Nation) served as the house organs of **Polish National Alliance** and the **Polish Roman Catholic Union** respectively, with a combined circulation in excess of 100,000 copies. The **Polish Women's Alliance** published ***Głos Polek*** (Polish Women's Voice) beginning in 1910.

Many of the early influential newspapers enjoyed religious backing including ***Polak w Ameryce*** (The Pole in America) founded by the Rev. **Jan Pitass** in Buffalo in 1887 and edited by **Stanisław Ślisz**, *Gazeta Katolicka* (Catholic Gazette) published by **Władysław Smulski** in Chicago, and *Orzeł Polski* (Polish

Eagle) edited by the Rev. Aleksander Matauszek and **Ignacy Wendziński** in Missouri beginning in 1870. The latter only lasted two years, but was replaced by *Pielgrzym* (Pilgrim), published and edited by **Jan Barzyński**, which subsequently became the respected *Gazeta Polska Katolicka* (Polish Catholic Gazette) in Detroit.

One of the leading liberal, anti-clerical publications was *Ameryka-Echo* founded in Toledo by **Antoni Paryski** in 1889. Often referred to as the "Polish Hearst," Paryski was a very talented individual who popularized folk literature while at the same time engaging in "Yellow Journalism" rivaling that of William Randolph Hearst. Paryski produced hundreds of thousands of copies of books, pamphlets, and other publications that his traveling agents sold throughout Polonia. Other anti-clerical publications included such journals as the weekly *Gwiazda Polarna* (The Northern Star), the New York organ of the **Polish Socialist Alliance in America** *Robotnik Polski* (The Polish Worker), and the leftist *Dziennik Ludowy* (The People's Daily) which later became *Głos Ludowy* (The People's Voice) published by the Polish Bureau of the Communist Party of the United States.

The first Polish daily in the United States was *Kuryer Polski* (Polish Courier) founded in Milwaukee in 1888 by **Michał Kruszka**. To counter influence of *Ameryka-Echo* and *Kuryer Polski*, the **Resurrectionist Order** in Chicago founded *Dziennik Chicagoski* (Chicago Daily News) in 1890, one of the best and most popular of Polish newspapers. Another popular publication was Detroit's *Dziennik Polski* (The Polish Daily News), as was the conservative Catholic *Polak w Ameryce* (The Pole in America) founded in Buffalo by the Rev. Jan Pitass.

The *Polish American Journal* was the first English language Polish-American newspaper with nation-wide appeal. Gradually, as the second generation gave way to the third, many publications followed the lead of Kruszka's *Kuryer Polski* which added an English-language supplement in 1939 to appeal to Polish Americans of the younger generations.

The Polish press provided valuable information to immigrants in America, keeping them in touch with the Old Country and assisting them in their transition to American society. In addition, it also served to solidify Polonia, increase ethnic self-awareness and informed public opinion. In 2010, leading Polish American newspapers included *Nowy Dziennik*, *Zgoda*, *Naród Polski*, *Dziennik Związkowy*, *Polish American Journal*, and *Gwiazda Polarna*.—*James S. Pula*

SOURCES: Anthony J. Kuzniewski, "The Polish-American Press," in Sally M. Miller, ed., *The Ethnic Press in the United States* (Westport, CT: Greenwood Press, 1987); Jan Kowalik, *The Polish Press in America* (San Francisco: R & E Research, 1978), 39–40; Bernard Pacyniak, "An Historical Outline of the Polish Press in America," in Frank Mocha, ed., *Poles in America: Bicentennial Essays* (Stevens Point, WI: Worzalla Publishing Company, 1978), 509–30; Samuel Bonikowski, "The Polish Press in Wisconsin," *Polish American Studies*, Vol. II, no. 1–2 (1945), 12–23; Eugene Obidinski, "The Polish American Press: Survival through Adaptation," *Polish American Studies*, Vol. 34, no. 2 (1977), 38–55; Alphone S. Wolanin, *The Polish Press* (Chicago: University of Chicago Press, 1952); Lubomyr Wynar, *Encyclopedia Directory of Ethnic Newspapers and Periodicals in the United States* (Littleton, CO: Libraries Unlimited, Inc., 1972).

Prokop, Stanley A. (b. Throop, Pennsylvania, July 29, 1909; d. Lake Ariel, Pennsylvania, November 11, 1977). Congressman. Educated in the public schools in Throop and Dickson City, PA, Prokop earned B.A. and B.S. degrees from Villanova University. During World War II he served in the army's 30th Infantry Division, rising from private to captain. Following the war he served as supervisor of Lackawanna, PA, before being elected as a Democrat to the Eighty-sixth Congress (January 3, 1959–January 3, 1961). After an unsuccessful bid for reelection, he served as a member of the Board of Assessment Appeals of Lackawanna County and for fourteen years as director of veterans' affairs for the county.—*James S. Pula*

SOURCE: *Biographical Directory of the United States Congress, 1774–Present* (http://bioguide.congress.gov/).

Prosky, Robert (Robert Joseph Porzuczek; b. Philadelphia, Pennsylvania, December 13, 1930; d. Washington, D.C., December 8, 2008). Actor. Born into a Polish immigrant family, Prosky's introduction to the theater came as stage manager for a production of *Our Town* while he attended Roxborough High School. After graduating from Temple University in 1952, where he continued his involvement in student productions, he enlisted in the Air Force during the Korean War. Following his discharge he dabbled in local community theatre, including the Old Academy Players, then entered and won a televised talent contest run by Michael Ellis. This led to a professional summer stock production at Ellis' Bucks County Playhouse (1955) alongside Walter Matthau and William Windom. Prosky then earned a New York Drama League scholarship to study for two years at the American Theatre Wing's School in New York, where he worked as a bookkeeper during the day at the Federal Reserve Bank and acted in off Broadway shows at night. In 1958 he won a part in the Arena Stage (Washington, D.C.) production of *The Front Page*. In twenty-three seasons at Arena Stage (1958–82), Prosky appeared in over 130 roles including Willy Loman (*Death of a Salesman*) and Galileo Galilei (*Galileo*). Arena Stage, the first American theatre company to tour the Soviet Union (1973), provided Prosky with both a steady income and job security to raise a family in Washington, D.C. A role as a mobster in the 1981 film *Thief* led to additional Hollywood supporting roles (*Monsignor*; *The Natural*), and then to a Tony-nominated role as Shelly Levene in David Mamet's *Glengarry Glen Ross* (1984), which won a Special Drama Desk Award for Outstanding Ensemble Performance. When actor Michael Conrad, who played Sgt. Phil Esterhaus on *Hill Street Blues*, died in 1983, Prosky joined the cast as Sgt. Stan Jablonski from 1984 to 1987. Ironically, Prosky had earlier turned down the role of Coach in *Cheers* in 1982, not wanting to sign a long-term contract that would interfere with his family life. Prosky earned a second Tony nomination in 1988 for his role as Botvinik in Lee Blessing's *A Walk in the Woods*, for which he also received an Outer Critics Circle Award. Among his other awards are the Helen Hayes Award for Outstanding Lead Actor in a Resident Play (1995), the American Express Tribute to an American Actor (1998), and the Jewish Council for Aging's Productive Aging Award (2006). Although he played both priests and Jewish roles during his long acting career, Prosky was baptized an Episcopalian, though descended from Roman Catholics.—*John Drobnicki*

SOURCES: Laurence Hooper, "The Grocer's Kid: Tony Award Nominee Robert Prosky is a Working Stiff of Stage and Screen," *Philadelphia*, Vol. 79 (October 1988); Simi Horwitz, "Face to Face: Robert Prosky. Defying God in 'The Golem,'" *Back Stage*, Vol. 43 (April 19, 2002); and Diana McLellan, "Do You Know Me? Robert Prosky Perfected His Craft at Arena Stage. Now He's Learning to be a Star," *Washingtonian*, Vol. 28 (August 1993).

Przybyszewski, Walenty "Val" (b. Poland, February 1862; d. Michigan, February 24, 1924). Polonia activist. Migrating to America in 1873, he settled in the heavily Polish town of Bay City, Michigan. A fiery leader who was active in both local politics and Polish patriotic affairs, Przybyszewski organized the St. Casimir Society, Group 12 of the **Polish National Alliance** in 1880, becoming the 312th member of the Alliance. Elected PNA vice **censor** (or deputy chief judge) in 1885, he won election as president at the 1886 PNA convention held in Bay City. Through his efforts, the entire PNA board of directors elected at this convention came from Bay City and Przybyszewski succeeded in having the national headquarters of the Alliance moved there from Chicago for the one and only time in its history that it was located outside Chicago. At the next PNA annual convention

Walenty V. Przybyszewski, Polonia activist (*OLS*).

in 1887, however, the Chicago faction, headed by members of the **Gmina Polska** group, won control and brought the administration back to Chicago. In 1891, Przybyszewski defeated **Franciszek Gryglaszewski** for the office of **censor**, although his disagreements with the leadership in Chicago and the editor of the PNA official publication, *Zgoda* (Harmony), deadlocked the organization during his two year term in office. In 1893, he declined to seek reelection and **Theodore Heliński** of Chicago was elected unanimously to succeed him. Przybyszewski remained active in the Alliance for many years thereafter. In 1912, Lodge 192 in Philadelphia named itself after him. Przybyszewski remains the only person in the PNA to be elected to the Alliance's two highest offices.—*Donald E. Pienkos*

SOURCES: Stanisław Osada, *Historia Związku Narodowego Polskiego i rozwój ruchu narodowego Polskiego w Ameryce Pólnocnej* (Chicago: Nakładem i drukiem Związku Narodowego Polskiego, 1905); Donald E. Pienkos, *A Centennial History of the Polish National Alliance of the United States of North America* (Boulder, CO: East European Monographs, 1984).

Ptaszyńska, Marta (b. Warsaw, Poland, July 29, 1943; d.—). Composer, musician. After graduating from the State Higher School of Music in Warsaw (now F. Chopin University of Music) with degrees in composition, percussion, and music theory (1962–68), in 1969–70 she studied with Nadia Boulanger in Paris on a scholarship from the French government. In 1972–74 she continued her studies at the Cleveland Institute of Music where she received an Artist Diploma Degree in per-

cussion. In 1974–77 she taught at Bennington College in Vermont, and in 1977-78 served as a guest professor at the University of California, Berkeley. In 1979-80 she was a composer in residence at the University of California, Santa Barbara, and in the 1980s and 1990s she taught composition and percussion at Northwestern University, the University of Chicago, and Indiana University, Bloomington. Since 1998, she has been a tenured professor of composition at the University of Chicago. Ptaszyńska's academic credentials are coupled with an impressive track record of awards that include prizes from the Percussive Arts Society (1974 for Siderals, 1976 for Classical Variations, and in 1987), second prize at the UNESCO International Rostrum of Composers (1986 for *La Novella di'inverno*), 2006 Benjamin H. Danks Award of the American Academy of Arts and Letters, The Fromm Music Foundation Award, the Officer Cross of Merit from Poland (1995), a medal from the Polish Composers' Union (1988), and a lifetime Achievement Award from the **Jurzykowski Foundation** (1996).

Ptaszyńska's music can be described as an individual brand of sonorism, with the best examples provided by her percussion works. Her affinity for percussion timbres is apparent in her choice of percussion instruments as soloists in her concerti and as important elements in her chamber works. Although percussion is often seen as a source of rhytmic drive, in Ptaszyńska's music the timbral variety of percussive instruments takes a priority. Ptaszyńska has the synaesthetic ability to "hear" in color not only pitches and chords, but also percussive timbres; her music is often inspired by surrealist painting and colorful poetic images from her texts. She set to music poems by Paul Verlaine (*Un grand sommeil noir*, 1978), Rainer Maria Rilke (*Sonnets to Orpheus*, 1981), William Shakespeare, Leopold Staff, and Frederico Garcia Lorca (the latter three in *Songs of Despair and Loneliness*, 1989), and contemporary American poets (M. Duffy in *Liquid Light* and *Cantiones Jubilationis*). Her chamber music sparkles with a kaleidoscopic array of colors and subtle sound effects often supported by traditional formal models of the sonata allegro form, concerto, rondo or variations. She frequently selects titles relating to space, dreams, light, imagination, and nature (*Dream Lands, Magic Spaces*, 1978; *Moon Flowers*, 1986; *Linear Constructions in Space*, 1998). Ptaszyńska's chamber music reveals a preference for subtle sonorities of the harp, flute, and voice, often joined by a marimba or vibraphone and a variety of exotic sounding rattles, shells, bells, drums, and other instruments. Since 1965 she composed 10 collections

of children's pieces and co-authored a percussion textbook in five volumes as well as a children's opera, *Mr. Marimba* (1995). This light hearted opera to a witty text by Agnieszka Osiecka highlights her fascination with Asian musicians has few precedents in her dramatic works, including the television opera *Oscar of Alva*, 1988. Another opera for youth, *Magiczny Doremik,* was premiered in 2008. The list of Ptaszyńska's politically oriented works includes a series of compositions on Polish themes, such as cantata *Listy Polskie* (*Polish Letters*, 1988), and a monumental *Holocaust Memorial Cantata* to Leslie Woolf Hedley's *Chant for all the People on Earth* and texts by Yehudi Menuhin (1992). Recent works include *Drum of Orfeo, Percussion Concerto (*2008) for Evelyn Glennie. Ptaszyńska's music is published by PWM in Poland and by Theodore Presser in the U.S. Recordings have been issued by CD Accord-Universal, Muza Polish Records, Chandos, Olympia, Dux, Bayer Records, and Pro Viva Sonoton labels.—*Maja Trochimczyk*

SOURCES: Philip Hong Chan, "A Study of Marta Ptaszynska's Holocaust Memorial Cantata" (DMA Dissertation, University of Cincinnati, 1996); Maria Anna Harley (now Maja Trochimczyk), "Percussion, Poetry and Color: The Music of Marta Ptaszynska," *Musicworks*, Vol. 74 (Summer 1999), 34–47; Maja Trochimczyk, "Marta Ptaszynska" in Kristine H. Burns, ed., *Women and Music in America Since 1900: An Encyclopedia* (Westport CT: Greenwood Press, 2002), Vol. 2; R. Zierolf, "Composers of Modern Europe, Australia and New Zealand," in K. Pendle, ed., *Women and Music* (Bloomington: Indiana University Press, 1991), 187–207, esp.199–202; Barbara Smolenska-Zielinska, "Concerto for Marimba by Marta Ptaszyńska," *Percussive Notes*, Vol. XXIX, no. 4 (1991), 78–82.

Pucińska, Lidia (Stanisława-Lidia Jędrzejowska; b. Kraków, Poland, April 29, 1896; d. Chicago, Illinois, October 25, 1984). Actor, director, radio broadcaster. Born to a gentry family that owned a well-known restaurant in Kraków, when her mother and sister emigrated to the United States following her father's death in 1907, she remained in Kraków to study drama with Marian Hoffman Marski and perform with the *Gwiazda* (Star) drama circle. Around 1912, she married Michał Puciński, after which the couple moved to Chicago's Northwest Side to join her family. There, Pucińska became a distinguished actor in the Polish American theater, debuting in 1913. The early twentieth century marked a "golden age" for ethnic-language drama in the U.S. This was as true for Polish Americans as any other immigrant group. At one time, Chicago alone boasted over a dozen Polish-language theatres. These and their counterparts in other Polish American communities enabled Pucińska's career to flourish. She capitalized on her celebrity status to promote the World War I work of Madame Helena

Paderewska, head of the **Polish White Cross** and spouse of pianist and statesman **Ignacy Jan Paderewski**. Pucińska also recruited Polish Americans for the **Polish Army in France**. After the war she organized theatrical benefits to aid Polish flood victims. By 1929, when the stock market crashed and the Great Depression set in, she faced immense difficulties as a divorced, single mother whose cherished profession was rapidly becoming economically untenable. The Depression brought about a rapid decline in Polish-language and other ethnic theatres. Pucińska quickly and creatively reinvented herself so that she could employ her dramatic talents and still support her family. Particularly during the 1930s and 1940s, she directed and performed in Polish-language dramas staged not at permanent theatres, but church and school auditoriums. In 1933 she wed Stefan Rutkowski, but used her established professional surname, Pucińska, for the rest of her life.

During the early 1930s, Pucińska launched her Polish-language program "Godzina Słoneczna" (The Sunshine Hour) on WEDC 1240 AM, a station on Chicago's Northwest Side. The "Sunshine Lady," as she was known, featured news from **Polonia** and Poland, interviews with prominent persons, household and family advice, and cultural affairs. She often included her own skillful dramatic readings, performing all the voices herself, and exhorted her listeners to feed the sparrows. As she did with her theatrical work, Pucińska often advocated for community causes through her radio show. During World War II, she sold millions of dollars in war bonds, funding the purchase of a whole P-51 squadron as well as a heavy bomber dubbed "Polonia of Chicago." After the war, she focused on fundraising for Polish war refugees, especially disabled military veterans who no longer had an independent nation willing to take responsibility for their care. She supported the March of Dimes, originally an anti-polio initiative, and sent Braille typewriters and books to blind children in Poland. Pucińska was an early leader and supporter of many significant Polonian institutions including the Polonez Choir, the Polish Actors Guild, the **Polish American Congress**, and the **Polish National Alliance**. In 1963 several Polonian organizations sponsored a "Golden Jubilee" celebration of Pucińska's civic and artistic achievements. In 1971, she was honored by the Immigrant Service League and named "Woman of the Year" by the Polish-American Scholarship Fund. Three years later, the National (U.S.) Shrine of Our Lady of Częstochowa in Pennsylvania [see **Doylestown**] named Pucińska "Polonia Mother of the Year." In 1978, the Restore Ellis

Lidia Pucinska, actress, director and radio broadcaster (*PMA*).

Island Committee recognized her as an "outstanding immigrant." On September 26, 1979, the CBS TV Evening News interviewed Pucińska about her radio program and her listeners' joyous anticipation of Pope John Paul II's Chicago visit that October.

Without interruption, Pucińska broadcasted her "Sunshine Hour" for over fifty years, until just a few weeks before her death at age eighty-eight. Through her pioneering, enduring work in ethnic-language theatre and radio broadcasting, she sustained Polish American culture and advocated for causes of great importance to Polish and other Americans. The Lidia Pucińska Papers are located in the **Polish Museum of America**, Chicago, Illinois.—*Mary Krane Derr*

SOURCES: Emma A. Kowalenko, "Stanisława-Lidia Jędrzejowska Pucińska," in Rima Lunin Schultz and Adele Hast, eds., *Women Building Chicago 1790–1990: A Biographical Dictionary* (Bloomington, IN: Indiana University Press, 2001), 722–24; Sabina Logisz, *Woman of the Year 1971: Presentation Honoring Lydia Pucinska Friday, March 19, 1971* (Chicago: Polish American Scholarship Fund, 1971); Marilynn Preston, "Mother Pucinska Puts Her Polish on Her Polish News," *Chicago Tribune*, April 19, 1977; Joseph Migala, *Polish Radio Broadcasting in the United States* (Boulder, CO: East European Monographs, 1987), 224–226.

Pucinski, Roman C. (b. Buffalo, New York, May 13, 1919; d. Chicago, Illinois, September 25, 2002). Congressman, Polonia activist. A graduate of Chicago's John Marshall Law School, Pucinski served in the U.S. Army Air Corps in the Pacific theater during World War II. His active service during the war earned him the Distinguished Flying Cross and promotion to the rank of captain. For some twenty years into the late 1950s Pucinski worked as a staff reporter and investigative writer for the *Chicago Sun Times*. His most

significant service during those years was his work as the chief investigator for the Select Committee of the U.S. House of Representatives in 1951-52 which reviewed the facts of the 1940 **Katyń** Forest Massacre of more than 10,000 Polish officers at the hands of the Soviet security police operating under orders of Joseph Stalin. In 1958 Pucinski won a seat in the House of Representatives on his second try for that office. He went on to serve fourteen years in Congress where he was an influential member of the Education, Labor, and Veterans Affairs committees. As a Congressman, Pucinski was a leader in the development of community colleges in the United States. He also worked with U.S. Senator Richard Schweiker (R, Pennsylvania) in pushing through legislation supporting ethnic cultural studies in the U.S. In 1972 Pucinski was defeated in his bid to unseat Republican Charles Percy for the office of U.S. Senator from Illinois, but in April 1973 he won election as alderman from Chicago's heavily Polish 41st Ward, an office he held until April 1991. In 1977 he campaigned unsuccessfully as a maverick opponent of his party's slated nominee, Michael Bilandic, in seeking the Democratic Party nomination for the office of Mayor of Chicago, which had become vacant following the death of Mayor Richard J. Daley. Until his run for the mayorship in this special election, Pucinski had been a faithful member of the Daley organization. He served for many years as a leader in the **Polish American Congress** in the Chicago area and president of its Illinois State Division. In this post he worked

Roman Pucinski, congressman (*PMA*).

closely with both **Charles Rozmarek** and **Aloysius Mazewski** during their tenures as national PAC president. He was especially involved in work on behalf of Polish immigrant newcomers to Chicago. In November 1988, Pucinski was a candidate for the presidency of the PAC following Mazewski's death, but lost to **Edward J. Moskal** with whom he had worked in the past. In November 1990, he was elected a national PAC vice president along with **Helen Wojcik** and **Kazimierz Lukomski**, serving in that office until 1994. Pucinski was the owner of a Chicago-based radio station, WEDC, where his mother Lydia was a well-known personality throughout **Polonia** for some fifty years. Pucinski's daughter, Aurelia, was active in local politics and in 1988 was elected clerk of the Circuit Court of Cook County.—*Donald E. Pienkos*

SOURCE: Donald E. Pienkos, *For Your Freedom Through Ours: Polish American Efforts on Poland's Behalf* (Boulder, CO: East European Monographs, 1991); *Biographical Directory of the United States Congress, 1774–Present* (http://bioguide.congress.gov/).

Pula, James Stanley (b. Utica, New York, February 18, 1946; d.—). Historian. After graduating from New York Mills High School, Pula earned his B.A. degree at the State University of New York at Albany (1968), an M.Ed. at the University of Maryland (1979), and M.A. (1970) and Ph.D. (1972) degrees in history from Purdue University. He joined the faculty of Voorhees College in Denmark, SC, in 1973, then taught history and sociology with the University of Maryland University College (1975–79) in Japan, Korea, Germany, Italy, and the College Park, MD, campus. His administrative career began in 1979 with appointment as Director of Administration at Southeastern University in Washington, D.C. He accepted a position as Associate Dean and Director of Continuing Education at St. John Fisher College in Rochester, NY (1980–86), followed by appointments as Director of the Division of Career and Interdisciplinary Studies at SUNY-Binghamton (1986–89), Associate Dean at SUNY-Empire State College (1990–93), Dean of Metropolitan College at The Catholic University of America (1993–99), Dean of Graduate and Continuing Education at Utica College of Syracuse University (1999–2004), and Vice Chancellor for Academic Affairs at Purdue University North Central beginning in 2004. A specialist in ethnic and immigration studies and nineteenth century American history, his publications include *For Liberty and Justice: A Biography of Brigadier General Włodzimierz B. Krzyżanowski, 1824–1887* (2008), *New York Mills: The Evolution of a Village* (2004), *Thaddeus Kościuszko The Purest Son of Liberty* (1998), *The Sigel Regiment: A History of the 26th Wisconsin Volunteer Infantry, 1862–1865* (1998), *Polish Americans: An Ethnic Community* (1995), *United We Stand: The Role of Polish Workers in the New York Mills Textile Strikes, 1912 and 1916* (1990), *For Liberty and Justice: The Life and Times of Wladimir Krzyżanowski* (1978), *The History of a German-Polish Civil War Brigade* (1976), and *The French in America* (1975). His edited and co-edited works include *The Polish American Encyclopedia* (2011), *The Origins of Modern Polish Democracy* (co-edited, 2009), and numerous other works.

An active member of various Polonia organizations, he served as president of the **Polish American Historical Association** (1981), Treasurer (beginning 1998), and a member of the Board of Directors (since 1978). He was a member of the Board of Directors of the **Polish Institute of Arts and Sciences of America** (beginning 1989) and Secretary (1994–2009), Vice Chair of the Rochester–Krakow Sister Cities Committee (1981–86), a member of the Advisory Board of the Friends of Kościuszko at West Point (beginning 2004), a member of the Advisory Board of The American University in Poland (2003–08), and a Trustee of the International Sister Cities Committee (1981–86). As a professional educator he served as Chair of Region II, National University Continuing Education Association (1985–86), Chair of the Division of Budget and Finance, National University Continuing Education Association (1987–89), Chair of the Continuing Education Committee, Rochester Area Colleges Consortium (1982–84), Chair of the Board of Directors of the Orphan Foundation of America (1997–98), and a member of the Boards of Directors of the Luke C. Moore

James S. Pula, historian (*James Pula*).

Academy (Washington, D.C., 1998–2000), the Washington Association for Foster Care Children (1998–2000), The Orphan Foundation of America (1994–98), and the Oneida County Historical Society (2001–04).

He edited PAHA's scholarly journal ***Polish American Studies*** and served as Chair of the Publications Committee (1982–), was the founding editor of *Mohawk Valley History* published by the Oneida County Historical Society, and a founding member and president of the Daniel Butterfield Civil War Roundtable. He also established the Winifred and Stanley Pula Scholarship Fund at Utica College which supports local students studying history. His honors include being named National Continuing Education Professional of the Year in 1985, two Oskar Halecki Prizes for the best book on Polish American history and culture (1991, 1996), the Gambrinus Prize in History (1999), the Distinguished Service Award of the Polish American Historical Association (2000), Honorary Membership in the Iron Brigade Society (2000), the Michael Dziedzic Award for contributions to **Polonia** from the Kopernik Memorial Association (1999), the Distinguished Service Award from the **American Council for Polish Culture** (1998), an award from the Educational Opportunity Center/College Board for contributions and support of outreach education in Washington, D.C. (1997), an award from the Community Preservation and Development Corporation for promoting education among low income residents of Washington, D.C. (1997), an award for "outstanding contributions" from Adelante, Inc., a Latino community service agency in Washington, D.C. (1995), the **Mieczysław Haiman** Award from the Polish American Historical Association (1988), a Doctoral Dissertation Award from the **Kosciuszko Foundation** (1974), a Dr. Stanislaw Chylinski Fellowship from The Kosciuszko Foundation (1973), an *Amicus Poloniae* award (1971), and five awards for excellence in academic program development from the National University Continuing Education Association (1981, 1983, 1986, 2000, 2003).—*James S. Pula*

SOURCE: Bolesław Wierzbiański, ed., *Who's Who in Polish America* (New York: Bicentennial Publishing Corporation, 1996), 375.

Pula, Robert Paul "Bob" (b. Baltimore, Maryland, December 3, 1928; d. Baltimore, Maryland, January 11, 2004). Educator, writer, civic leader. A teacher, human communication consultant, scholar of Polish history, and leader in Baltimore's **Polonia**, Pula was also an author, editor, and lecturer in the field of General Semantics, and an amateur pianist, composer, and artist. He wrote over

200 published papers in general semantics, history, biography, musicology, and the epistemology of science. A third-generation Polish American, he was born in Baltimore's "Little Poland" where he grew up. During the Korean War he was stationed in Texas (1950) and South Central England (1951–53) as an Air Force medic. Following the war he attended Loyola College where he received his B.S. in Social Sciences and received the medal for excellence in English (1958). He pursued graduate study in English and education at the University of Maryland and Johns Hopkins University. At public schools and local colleges, and at Forts Meade and Holabird, Pula taught English composition and literature, speed reading, general semantics, and Polish culture. He consulted in human communications and staff relations for organizations across the U.S.

Beginning in 1967, Pula lectured for the Institute of General Semantics (IGS) at universities and meetings in the U.S., Canada, and Poland. In 1980, Educational Cassettes, Inc., recorded his seminars on audiotape. He received the Irving J. Lee Award for Excellence in Teaching General Semantics in 1996, and in 2000 he presented the 49th annual invitational Alfred Korzybski Memorial Lecture. A frequent contributor to IGS publications, Pula was editor of the annual *General Semantics Bulletin* (1977–85), Director of the IGS (1983–86), and later Director Emeritus. At the time of his death, he was researching and writing the first full-length biography of General Semantics founder **Alfred Korzybski**, residing in Warsaw during the academic year 1999–2000 to conduct part of this research. He is the author of *A General-Semantics Glossary: Pula's Guide for the Perplexed* (2000).

A cultural leader in Baltimore's Polonia, Pula wrote articles on Polish topics for many publications. In 1979, he partnered on several articles with Stanisław Bask-Mostwin, then Chairman of the American Jewish-Polish Committee, and a former World War II soldier and Polish resistance paratrooper. Later, he worked to see Mostwin honored as a Righteous Gentile. Pula cooperated on committees to have a memorial erected for victims of the 1940 **Katyń** massacre. In 1998, he received a Senatorial citation through **Barbara Mikulski**, recognizing his research supporting Poland's admission to NATO. At various times, he was a member of the Polish Students' Association (PSA), Polish Heritage Association of Maryland, **Polish National Alliance** Council 21, **Polish Legion of American Veterans, Polish American Historical Association**, and **Kosciusko Foundation**. He was a past president of the Polish Students' Association.

Robert P. Pula, educator (*Dorothy Strohecker*).

Pula also expressed his Polish identity through the arts. He sang in the PSA choir, and founded, directed, and conducted the Polonia Renaissance Chorus. He composed dozens of original piano works, sometimes performed them at cultural functions, and published many of them on a sound recording by Bank Street Records (1980). Especially notable works include his choral setting of Mickiewicz's sonnet "Ackermann Steppe" and his Janusz Korczak Sonata in D Minor. Pula sometimes exhibited his oil paintings at Baltimore's Polish Festival. Subjects included portraits of notable Poles, including Mikołaj Kopernik, Adam Mickiewicz, and other Polish historical themes, such as a nighttime landscape of Warsaw burning while the Polish spirit endures in the person of Fryderyk Chopin playing the piano in the foreground. Following his death, his family established the annual Robert P. Pula Memorial Scholarship.—*Dorothy Pula Strohecker*

SOURCES: "Robert Pula, Leader in Baltimore's Polonia," *Polish American Journal*, April 30, 2004; "Bob Pula: Memories and Tributes," *Time-Bindings*, Spring 2004.

Pulaski, Edward C. (b. near Green Springs, Ohio, February 9, 1868; d. Coeur d'Alene, Idaho, February 2, 1931). Inventor, forest ranger. "Big Ed" Pulaski worked as a ranch foreman, railroad worker and miner in the northwestern U.S. before becoming a ranger with the Forest Service in 1908. One of his jobs as a ranger was to monitor and fight forest fires. In the summer of 1910 a large area of western Montana and northern Idaho was engulfed in a fire that became known as "the Big Blow-up." Pulaski headed out from Wallace, Idaho, with a group of 45 men to battle

the blaze and save the town. His crew, like many others, became trapped by the firestorm. He led his men to an abandoned mine shaft and ordered them to lie down, threatening to shoot any who tried to leave. Pulaski and 40 of the men survived the fire, for which he is considered a hero and legend in firefighting lore for this lifesaving feat. In 1911, Pulaski, tired of carrying two separate implements to fight fires, one to chop and one to hoe, combined an axe and a grub hoe. Now he could chop with one side and hoe the ground with the other. It went into production and became known as the Pulaski Tool, and to this day is still in use as basic forest firefighting equipment. Pulaski never patented the tool, so he never realized any money from his invention. He worked as a ranger until 1930 and died the following year from injuries suffered in a car accident. The mine tunnel where Pulaski and his crew took refuge, and the trail leading to it, were restored in 2006 and is now the Pulaski National Historic Site. His original Pulaski Tool is exhibited at the Wallace, Idaho, Mining Museum and Visitors Center.—*Martin S. Nowak*

SOURCE: Stephen J. Pyne, *Year of the Fires: The Story of the Great Fires of 1910* (New York: Viking, 2001).

Pułaski, Kazimierz (b. Warsaw, Poland, March 6, 1745; d. near Savannah, Georgia, October 9–10, 1779). Military officer. Born into a landed gentry family, Pułaski's parents sent him to Warsaw to pursue the best education their relatively prosperous economic circumstances could afford. After completing legal and military studies, he assumed a position in the court of the Duke of Courland, but returned to Warsaw when Russian troops arrived to bring Poland under the influence of the Tsar. Soon he became actively engaged in the Confederation of Bar, a revolutionary movement formed in 1768 by his father Józef whose purpose it was to free Poland from Russian control. Quickly gaining a reputation for shrewd and tenacious military ability, Kazimierz led forces in several campaigns against the Russians, defeating troops under the leadership of the famous Marshal Suvarov. His heroic and successful defense of Częstochowa in 1771 against a greatly superior Russian force has been immortalized in Józef Chełmoński's famous 1875 painting "Pułaski at Częstochowa." When Russian numerical superiority finally overwhelmed the Confederation, Pułaski fled his homeland for Turkey.

Eventually making his way to France, Pułaski arrived in Paris where he met Benjamin Franklin, the emissary of the American revolutionary government to France. In the letter of introduction that he wrote on behalf of the Pole, Franklin described him as "an officer famous throughout Europe for his bravery and conduct in defense of the liberties of his country." Upon his arrival in America, Pułaski initially served as a volunteer on the staff of General George Washington until the Continental Congress approved his commission. In this capacity, at the Battle of Brandywine he was credited with leading a cavalry force against an attempt by the British to outflank Washington's army, thereby giving the commanding general time to prevent being outflanked and to withdraw his forces in safety. Following Brandywine, Congress confirmed Pułaski as a brigadier general and "Commander of the Horse," making him the ranking officer in charge of all mounted troops. Often known as the "Father of the American Cavalry," he instituted a regular training routine that brought discipline and purpose to the American cavalry. After leading his force in several campaigns, Pułaski encountered difficulties with some American officers who resented reporting to a foreigner, as well as having to answer financial questions arising from lax bookkeeping practices. These experiences prompted him to resign his position. Nevertheless, he remained in America to raise the independent Pułaski Legion which he organized along European lines as a joint force of cavalry and infantry. In fact, Pułaski's horsemen became so proficient that a British officer later proclaimed them to be the best cavalry the Americans had throughout the en-

tire war. The Legion's flag was crafted by the Moravian Nuns in Bethlehem, Pennsylvania, as immortalized in Henry Wadsworth Longfellow's poem "Hymn of the Moravian Nuns."

Sent south to oppose British operations in the Carolinas, Pułaski and his troops successfully defended Charleston, South Carolina, following which they participated in the joint Franco-American attack on Savannah. In an assault on the British fortifications, Pułaski was mortally wounded while rallying the troops to charge the British entrenchments. Although his body was long believed to have been buried at sea, more recent research suggests that it may be buried in a vault at the base of his monument in Savannah. As a hero of the American Revolution, his name has been taken by numerous cities and counties throughout the country. Fort Pulaski was named in his honor in Savannah, and his statue can be found in various cities including Freedom Plaza in Washington, D.C. By presidential proclamation, October 11 is reserved each year for the commemoration of "Pulaski Day." On November 6, 2009, President Barack Obama signed joint legislation by the House and Senate bestowing American citizenship on Pułaski.—*Francis Casimir Kajencki*

SOURCES: Francis Casimir Kajencki, *Casimir Pulaski, Cavalry Commander of the American Revolution* (El Paso, TX: Southwest Polonia Press, 2001); Francis Casimir Kajencki, *The Pulaski Legion in the American Revolution* (El Paso, TX: Southwest Polonia Press, 2004).

Pulaski Day. Kazimierz Pułaski was one of the founders of the Confederation of Bar which sought to defend the politically ailing Polish-Lithuanian Commonwealth against Russian aggression. As a military commander and later paid mercenary, he distinguished

himself against the Russians at Berdichev (1768), Żwaniec (1769), and The Holy Trinity Trenches (Okopy Święty Trójcy, 1769). After an abortive attempt to kidnap King Stanisław August Poniatowski and allegations of intended murder, Pułaski fled Poland, briefly residing in Paris before participating in Turkish assaults against Russian forces in 1774. Returning to Paris after the conclusion of a peace treaty between Russia and Turkey, he met Benjamin Franklin who recommended him to George Washington as a potential military commander to aid the colonists against the British during the Revolution. In 1777, Pułaski came to America and once again distinguished himself in fighting, commanding the American cavalry at Brandywine and Germantown. With the permission of Congress, Pułaski established his own unit, the "Pulaski Legion," composed of some 120 men, a mixture of cavalry and infantry. In 1779 this legion was dispatched to recapture Savannah, Georgia from the British. Pułaski was wounded in a cavalry charge in the Battle of Savannah on October 9, dying of his wounds two days later. He has since been commemorated in monuments and place names throughout America. In 1867 a bust of Pułaski was placed on Capital Hill and in 1919 a monument of him on horseback was added to the main square of Washington, D.C. Pułaski monuments also exist in Baltimore, Detroit, Utica (NY), and elsewhere, and several U.S. states bear the town, county, highway, bridge, park, street, or school named for him. In 1929, Ignace Werwinski, a businessman in South Bend, Indiana, petitioned President Herbert Hoover to mark October 11 as Pulaski Day. Six years later Congress adopted a resolution along these lines, allowing the president to

Kazimierz Pułaski, Revolutionary War general (*OLS*).

The First Pulaski Day Parade, New York City, 1937 (*KF*).

proclaim October 11 as a day of observance and commemoration of the death of Kazimierz Pułaski. A commemorative stamp was also released by the U.S. Post Office. In the 1970s, the state of Illinois passed a bill, introduced by Senator Leroy W. Lemke, which designated the first Monday in March Pulaski Commemorative Day. In Wisconsin, March 4 also marked the official date of observation, although it is still generally observed in October. Pulaski Day festivities are marked by parades and other patriotic activities in such states as Georgia, Indiana, Nebraska, and Wisconsin. The largest Pulaski Day parade takes place annually in New York City on the first Sunday in October when the parade route proceeds up Fifth Avenue from 29th Street to 53rd Street.—*Krystyna Cap*

SOURCE: Leszek Szymański, *Casimir Pulaski: A Hero of the American Revolution* (New York: Hippocrene Books, 1994).

Pulaski Legion. Upon his arrival in America to fight for the rebels in the Revolution, **Kazimierz Pułaski** played an important role during the Battle of Brandywine and was soon thereafter named "Commander of the Horse," which placed him in command of all cavalry units in Gen. George Washington's army. Disagreements with American officers and recurring financial questions caused the Pole to resign from his command on February 28, 1778. Following his resignation, Congress authorized Pułaski to recruit a unit that would consist of 68 cavalrymen and 200 infantry. Most of the officers were French, with a few Poles and Americans and a smattering of others. The rank and file were predominantly Americans with the majority being from

Maryland. The Pulaski Legion was largely funded by its commander. Its flag, a gift of the Moravian Nuns in Bethlehem, PA, was immortalized in Henry Wadsworth Longfellow's poem "Hymn of the Moravian Nuns." The banner is preserved in the Maryland Historical Society. In its introduction to combat, the Legion suffered a serious defeat when a former Hessian who had been assigned by Congress to the Legion deserted and led a force of British troops that surprised the Legion's pickets at Little Egg Harbor, NJ, killing and wounding nearly thirty including the Legion's infantry commander, Lt. Col. Carl von Bose, who was killed. After a brief stint on the frontier area along the Delaware River, the Legion was ordered south to meet British threats in the Carolinas and Georgia where it rendered distinguished service. At Charleston, SC, the Legion attacked the leading elements of the British advance on May 11, 1779, and, although suffering losses, was credited with disrupting the British movement and saving the city. At the siege of Savannah in October 1779 the French were also favorably impressed by the Legion, and historian Alexander A. Lawrence concluded that "Among the American regulars only Pulaski's outfit was to impress the French." British Brigade Major F. Skelly called the Pulaski Legion "the best cavalry the rebels ever had." Following Pułaski's death from wounds received at Savannah in October 1779, the Legion's survivors were consolidated into a partisan unit led by Col. Charles Armand.—*Francis Casimir Kajencki*

SOURCE: Francis Casimir Kajencki, *Casimir Pulaski, Cavalry Commander of the American Revolution* (El Paso, TX: Southwest Polonia Press, 2001).

The presentation of the Pułaski Legion banner by the Moravian Sisters in Bethlehem, Pennsylvania. It is preserved in the Maryland Historical Society (*OLS*).

PUNO *see* **Polish University Abroad.**

Putski, Ivan (Józef Bednarski; b. Kraków, Poland, January 21, 1941; d.—). Wrestler. The Polish-born Bednarski migrated to the United States with his parents at age nine, and began professional wrestling in the early 1970s under the assumed name "Ivan Putski." Noted for his strength, he became a popular performer on the pro wrestling circuit, known by the nickname "Polish Power." In 1979, Putski won the World Wrestling Federation World Tag Team championship in combination with Tito Santana. He is a member of the World Wrestling Entertainment Hall of Fame.—*Neal Pease*

SOURCE: "Ivan Putski," World Wrestling Entertainment website, www.wwe.com/superstars/halloffame/ivanputski/.

Quinn, Jack (Janos Pajkos (?); b. Štefurov, Austria-Hungary (?), July 1, 1883 (?); d. Pottsville, Pennsylvania, April 17, 1946). Baseball player. The athlete known to baseball fans as Jack Quinn compiled a long and distinguished career as a major league pitcher. Much uncertainty surrounds the date and place of his birth, as well as his original name, but it is now generally accepted that he was born in what now is Slovakia, not in Pennsylvania, as long believed. Recent research also suggests that he was of Rusyn parentage, although his Polish identity was taken for granted during his life. Over 23 seasons, hurling for eight teams from 1909 to 1933 (New York Highlanders, Boston Braves, Baltimore Terrapins, Chicago White Sox, Boston Red Sox, Philadelphia Athletics, Brooklyn Robins/Dodgers, Cincinnati Reds) Quinn won 247 games, with an earned run average of 3.29. A righthander, he relied on the spitball, and he was one of a few pitchers permitted to continue to throw this delivery after it was banned from the sport. The statistical methods of the *Total Baseball* encyclopedia rank him as having been one of the best pitchers in the short lived Federal League in 1914. His career was most notable for exceptional longevity, attributed to a fitness and training regimen unusual for his time. Quinn played in four different decades, and pitched in his last game at age fifty. He set several major league records based on seniority, among them being the oldest pitcher to have won a game, and the oldest player to have hit a home run (since broken) and to have appeared in a World Series game. In the later stages of his career, Quinn became one of the first pitchers to specialize in relieving, and he led the National League in saves in 1931 and 1932. His teams won three pennants, and two world championships. He was inducted into the **National Polish-American Sports Hall of Fame** in 2006.—*Neal Pease*

SOURCES: E. Michael D. Scott, "John 'Jack Quinn' Picus: Not Polish, Not Welsh, and Not Born in America at All," *Nine*, Vol. 16, no. 2 (2008), 93–106; "Jack Quinn," National Polish-American Sports Hall of Fame website, www.polishsportshof.com.

Rabi, Isidor Isaac (b. Rymanów, Poland, July 29, 1898; d. New York City, New York, January 11, 1988). Scientist. Brought to New York by his family in 1899, he received his B.S. in chemistry from Cornell University in 1919 and Ph.D. from Columbia University in 1927 with a specialization in the magnetic properties of crystals. Following two years of post-doctoral work in Europe, in 1929 he assumed the position of lecturer in theoretical physics at Columbia, rising to the rank of professor in 1937. In 1940 he received leave to assume the post of associate director of the Radiation Laboratory at the Massachusetts Institute of Technology where he worked on projects related to the development of radar and the atomic bomb. Returning to Columbia in 1945, he also pursued his work at the Brookhaven National Laboratory for Atomic Research on Long Island, a facility exploring peaceful uses of atomic energy. The author of numerous articles in *The Physical Review* and other scholarly journals, he served as president of the American Physical Society in 1950 and was appointed to the Board of Governors of the Weizmann Institute of Science in Israel. In 1955 he served as the U.S. delegate and vice-president of the International Conference on Peaceful Uses of Atomic Energy in Geneva, Switzerland. He was a member of the Science Advisory Committee of the International Atomic Energy Commission, and his contributions have been recognized by numerous awards and citations. In 1939 the American Association for the Advancement of Science honored him with its prize, in 1942 he received the Elliott Cresson Medal from the Franklin Institute, and in 1944 he was honored with the Nobel Prize in Physics "for his resonance method for recording the magnetic properties of atomic nuclei." He was awarded the Medal for Merit, the highest civilian award of the Second World War, in 1948, the same year he received the King's Medal for Service in the Cause of Freedom. He was also an Officer of the Legion of Honor.—*James S. Pula*

SOURCES: John S. Rigden, *Rabi, Scientist and Citizen* (New York: Basic Books, 1987); Isidor I. Rabi, "Reminiscences of Isidor Isaac Rabi: Oral History," (Thesis, Columbia University, 1985).

Rada Narodowa *see* **Polish National Council.**

Rada Polonii Amerykańskiej *see* **Polish American Council.**

Radicalism, Polish American. Anarchist tendencies were most prevalent among some Polish immigrants toward the end of the nineteenth century, mostly in the intellectual circles on the East Coast, but also among some immigrant workers participating in the May 1886 strikes in Chicago and Milwaukee who were influenced by the International Workingmen's Association in the Midwest. In New York, some members of the Ognisko (Bonfire) and Równość (Equality) groups were associated with the Alliance of Polish Workers (Związek Robotników Polskich) in Russian Poland, which included elements of anarchist ideology. Anarchist ideas were present in several popular plays of the era, including *Nihilists* written by the journalist, author, and publisher Alfons Chrostowski. The play, centered on the assassination of Tsar Alexander II, was written by I. Hryniewiecki in 1881 and performed broadly in ethnic theatres in America. Interest in anarchist ideology among Polish Americans appears to have peaked in 1894–95. Among the leaders of the movement were Józef Rybakowski, Stanisław Bombiński, and Adolf Nelson who created the Alliance of Polish Workers in America (Związek Robotników Polskich w Ameryce) in Chicago, along with its newspaper *Gazeta Robotnicza* (Worker's Gazette). Rybakowski organized and led a group of Polish participants who marched to Washington, D.C., with Coxey's Army in 1894. The popularity of anarchist ideology declined sharply after the Polish American anarchist **Leon Czołgosz** assassinated President William McKinley in 1901. It was widely believed at the time that Czołgosz was influenced by the speeches of Emma Goldman, which were later depicted in a strongly anti-socialist novel written by the conservative nationalist **Stanisław Osada**. Polish American organizations, and the Polish press in America, including those with socialist leanings, strongly condemned Czołgosz's act.

Some Polish American workers responded positively to appeals from the Industrial Workers of the World, including distributing IWW literature in Polish and forming the first Polish locals in 1907. By 1914 there were approximately 700 Polish "Wobblies," as IWW members were labelled, the most stable locals operating in Chicago, Baltimore (MD), and Fall River, Holyoke, and New Bedford (MA). Twelve locals were unquestionably Polish, but Poles were also members of many other locals that were not exclusively Polish in character. In 1910, the IWW began publishing the Polish language organ *Solidarność* (Solidarity) in Buffalo under the editorship of W. A. Zieliński and B. Szrager. The publication moved to Chicago where it continued from 1913 to 1917. It supported industrial unionism and a strategy of direct action, publishing mostly original materials rather than reprints from the English language *Industrial Worker*. The publication and the Polish locals generally declined following government restrictions imposed in 1917.—*Adam Walaszek*

SOURCES: K. Groniowski, "Socjalistyczna emigracja polska w Stanach Zjednoczonych (1883–1914," *Z Pola Walki*, 1977, no. 1; Adam Walaszek, "Polish Emigrants Among the Industrial Workers of the World, 1905–1917" in Orm Oveland, ed., *In the European Grain. American Studies from Central and Eastern Europe* (Amsterdam: VU University Press, 1990, European Contributions to American Studies, Vol. XIX), 116–31.

Radwan, Edmund Patrick (b. Buffalo, New York, September 22, 1911; d. Buffalo, New York, September 7, 1959). Congressman, attorney. After attending local public schools, Radwan graduated from the University of Buffalo Law School in 1934. He began his career as an athletic coach of East High School, Buffalo (1929–34), was admitted to the New York bar in 1935 and began the practice of law in Buffalo. He served as village attorney of Sloan, NY (1938–40) and was a member of the faculty at the Catholic Labor College in Buffalo in 1941. With the outbreak of World War II, he served as a corporal in the U.S. Army (1943–45). Following the war he was elected to the State Senate from 1945 to December 31, 1950, and was elected as a Republican to the Eighty-second and to the three succeeding Congresses (January 3, 1951–January 3, 1959), being first elected when he was still in the army. A representative of New York's 41st and 43rd Districts, he was not a candidate for renomination in 1958 because of ill health. He was well-known for his legislative efforts on behalf of veterans. Both Radwan and **Henry Nowak** represented the district in western New York that was the birthplace of the **Polish American Congress**.—*Frederick J. Augustyn*

SOURCES: *Biographical Directory of the United States Congress, 1774–Present* (http://bioguide.congress.gov/); obituaries, *New York Times*, September 8, 1959, 35; *Washington Post*, September 9, 1959, B2; *Washington Evening Star*, September 9, 1959, B4.

Radzimiński, Charles (b. Warsaw, Poland, 1805; d. Memphis, Tennessee, August 18, 1858). Military officer, surveyor. Little is known of Radzimiński's early years, and there is some question as to whether he was born in 1805 or 1817, but it is known that he participated in the unsuccessful November Uprising of 1830-31, was interned by the Austrians, and then exiled to the United States, arriving in New York on March 28, 1834. After moving to Washington, D.C., he was employed as a civil engineer by the James River and Kanawha Canal Company of Richmond, VA, in 1840. With the outbreak of the Mexican War in 1846 he enlisted as a second lieutenant in the

3rd U.S. Dragoons, acting later as quartermaster and then adjutant. Discharged in 1848, he joined the Northeast Boundary Commission reconstructing survey maps of the Maine-Canada boundary. The following year he was assigned to complete a re-survey of the Mason-Dixon Line for the curved portion separating Pennsylvania and Delaware. He completed this in 1850, whereupon he was assigned to the U.S.–Mexican border survey required under the terms of the Treaty of Guadalupe-Hidalgo ending the Mexican War. Appointed Principal Assistant Surveyor, he arrived in El Paso in June 1851. Between April and May 1852 he surveyed the boundary between roughly Doña Ana and Frontera along the Western Rio Grande for a distance of 90 miles; between June and October 1853 he completed work on the 241 miles between Ringgold Barracks and the Gulf of Mexico; and between 1854 and 1855 served as secretary of the Boundary Commission for the survey from the Rio Grande to the Colorado River, some 530 miles. In the process, he concluded the "United States–Mexico Agreement of November 14, 1853" delineating the international boundary from Brownsville to the gulf coast. He was one of the commissioners who laid the foundation for International Boundary Marker No. 1 on January 31, 1855. Following his service on the Boundary Commission, Radzimiński accepted a commission as first lieutenant in the 2nd U.S. Cavalry (1856–58), and was then assigned to Texas under the leadership of Lt. Col. Robert E. Lee. The command engaged in several skirmishes with Indians, but Radzimiński's deteriorating health led to absences on sick leave. He left for the east on July 24, 1858, but died of tuberculosis within the month. In his honor, the 2nd Cavalry named a post on Otter Creek near the Wichita Mountains "Camp Radziminski," and a nearby prominence "Mount Radziminski."—*Francis Casimir Kajencki*

SOURCES: Francis Casimir Kajencki, *Poles in the 19th Century Southwest* (El Paso, TX: Southwest Polonia Press, 1990), 121–97; Francis C. Kajencki, "Charles Radzimiski and the United States Mexican Boundary Survey," *New Mexico Historical Review*, Vol. 63, no. 3 (1988), 211–40.

Radziwill, Anthony Stanislas (Antoni Stanisław Albrecht Radziwiłł; b. Lausanne, Switzerland, August 4, 1959; d. New York, New York, August 10, 1999). Producer, television executive. The son of Prince Stanisław Albrecht Radziwiłł, a native of Poland, and Lee Bouvier, sister of Jacqueline Kennedy Onassis, he was a friend and cousin of John F. Kennedy, Jr., and nephew of President John F. Kennedy. President Kennedy was godfather to him and his younger sister, Krystyna Radzi-

will. After growing up in England, he graduated from Boston University in 1982 with a baccalaureate degree in broadcast journalism. He began his career in 1988 as an associate producer for NBC sports, covering the Summer Olympics in Seoul, South Korea, for which he received an Emmy Award for sports journalism, an award considered the television equivalent to the Oscars. In 1989 he joined ABC News on *Prime Time Live* as an executive and producer, where he worked with Diane Sawyer among others. In 1990 he received a Peabody Award, an international award for excellence in radio and television broadcasting and that same year received second Emmy Award. Radziwill joined HBO in 1997 as vice president for documentation where he was nominated for still another Emmy Award. He was considered an extremely talented, tireless, decent, and well liked journalist. He battled cancer for some ten years prior to his death.—*Maria Swiecicka-Ziemianek*

SOURCE: Carole Radziwill, *What Remains—A Memoir of Fate, Friendship and Love* (New York: Scribner, 2005).

Raszewski, Aleksander (b. Żytomierz, Poland, 1805; d. Fremont, New York, October 10, 1884). Polonia activist, military officer. After completing his education as a cadet for the Polish army, he joined the November Uprising (1830–31) and when it failed he fled first to France and then to the U.S. He became a U.S. citizen on May 21, 1860. With the outbreak of the Civil War in 1861 he was commissioned captain of Company C, 31st New York Infantry, comprised of Poles that he

Aleksander Raszewski, officer in the American Civil War and Polonia activist (*USMHI*).

raised and outfitted with red four-cornered Polish military caps. He was promoted to major in the spring of 1862, but resigned his commission in October of that year in a dispute over further promotion. An active member of the **Democratic Society of Polish Exiles**, when the January Insurrection broke out in Poland in 1863 he was a leader in calling for a meeting of Poles and supporters in Steuben Hall in New York City. The meeting, held in March 1863, resulted in the formation of a Central Committee to coordinate efforts to disseminate information and solicit funds to aid the Polish revolutionaries. Raszewski was elected a member of the Committee and was very active in meeting with potential American supporters.—*James S. Pula*

SOURCES: Florian Stasik, *Polish Political Emigrés in the United States of America, 1831–1864* (Boulder, CO: East European Monographs, 2002); Frederick Phisterer, *New York in the War of Rebellion, 1861–1865* (Albany: J. B. Lyon & Co., 1912).

Ratzenberger, John Deszo (b. Bridgeport, Connecticut, April 6, 1947; d.—). Actor, philanthropist. The son of Deszo and Bertha Grohowski Ratzenberger, his first foray into acting was at St. Ann's elementary school where he sang "With a Shelalee Under My Arm and a Twinkle in My Eye." After attending Sacred Heart University in Fairfield, Connecticut, where he majored in English literature, he performed in one-man shows and served as a director at the Stowe Playhouse in Vermont, then relocated to London, England, where he had parts in films such as *A Bridge Too Far* and *Superman*. He founded a theatrical duo, "Sal's Meat Market," which did improvisation and played to standing room only audiences. He was also a screenwriter and producer for the BBC, Paravision, the Royal Court Theater, Hampstead Theatrical Club, Royal Academy of Dramatic Arts, and Granada TV. Returning to the United States in 1981, he landed his best known role as mailman and bar denizen Cliff Clavin in the Emmy Award winning television comedy series, *Cheers*. Originally, he auditioned for the part of Norm Peterson, which was given to actor George Wendt. Ratzenberger suggested that the show needed another character as Norm's friend, a wise-cracking know-it-all. He did a five minute, off-the-cuff demonstration, and the producers liked the idea, created the role on the spot, and "Cliff" went on to become an American TV icon. Ratzenberger has also done voices for various animated movie and television series, as well as hosting the series *John Ratzenberger's Made in America* on the Travel Channel in which he features American working people. He is co-founder of Nuts, Bolts and Thingamajigs Foundation, which raises awareness among youngsters of the engineering and skilled trades. Not confined to acting, he has developed a biodegradable alternative to plastic packing "peanuts" made from recycled paper, called Quadra-Pack, which is used by Hallmark and other businesses. To raise money for the Special Olympics, he rowed a boat non-stop around Vashon Island in Washington, the only person ever to complete the 36 mile trip. He is chairman of Children With Diabetes, the world's largest internet web site dealing with diabetes information and research. Ratzenberger is also National Walk Chairman for the Juvenile Diabetes Foundation, serves on the Board of Trustees of Sacred Heart University, and is Honorary Chairperson for the Board of Trustees of the Willie Ross School for the Deaf. Among his honors are the TV Land Awards Legend Award (2006), two Emmy Award nominations (1985, 1986), Father's Day Council of America Father of the Year Award (1996), American Diabetes Association Outstanding Role Model Award (1996), and Honorary Doctorate in Humane Letters, Sacred Heart University (2002).—*Cheryl A. Pula*

SOURCE: "An Interview with John Ratzenberger: John Ratzenberger, Star of 'Cheers' Talks With ACTE About Career and Technical Education (CTE) and His Nuts, Bolts & Thingamahigs Program," *Techniques*, Vol. 85, no. 1 (January 1, 2010), 14+.

Reed, Ron (b. LaPorte, Indiana, November 2, 1942; d.—). Baseball player. Reed was a major league baseball pitcher from 1966 through 1984, hurling for four different teams over nineteen seasons. A right-hander, he compiled a lifetime record of 146–140 with an earned run average of 3.46 and 103 saves in relief. Reed appeared in postseason play in seven seasons, notably in two World Series with the Philadelphia Phillies. In 1980, he contributed one save as the Phillies won the first World Series championship in franchise history. As a member of the Atlanta Braves, Reed was named to the National League all-star squad in 1968. He was also accomplished at basketball, playing college ball at Notre Dame and two seasons for the Detroit Pistons of the National Basketball Association (1965–67). He was inducted into the **National Polish-American Sports Hall of Fame** in 2005.—*Neal Pease*

SOURCE: "Ron Reed," National Polish-American Sports Hall of Fame website, www.polishsportshof.com.

Re-Emigration to Poland. At the time of the mass migration (1870–1924), Poles were drawn to America by the promise of socioeconomic advancement. Yet for many, the expectation was not a permanent move but rather a temporary emigration to earn sufficient funds to better their family's life in Poland. These people defined "hope" within the context of the immigrants' own culture. For better or worse, work in the fields for the largely peasant immigration afforded a living. Using the funds they received from those who had emigrated abroad, those who remained in Poland could build a house (often called "American houses"), achieve greater status, and, foremost, buy more land. The rapidly expanding economic situation in the United States at the end of the nineteenth century offered peasants an opportunity to fulfill these aspirations for socioeconomic advancement. During two weeks in America one could earn as much as during a whole season in German or Hungarian agriculture. They worked hard, saved, and became members of the proletariat—all in order to buy land in the old country. Yet, despite their original intentions, emigrants often abandoned their plans to return because of a variety of circumstances they encountered in America.

Poles migrating from the German occupied partition were generally more influenced to migrate by the exceptional religious and national oppression endured under the *Kulturkampf* that sought to eradicate Polishness from German-occupied lands. Because of this, fewer emigrants planned to return to Poland than from the Austrian or Russian occupied partitions. Consequently, the rate of return from the German-occupied areas was less than from the other two regions. Since fewer intended to return to Poland, this group began adapting to America earlier, experienced some socioeconomic advancement, and became organizers and leaders of future Polish American communities.

Return migration from America to the Polish territories prior to World War I is estimated at approximately thirty percent of the original emigration. In some villages the percentage was higher—examples in Galicia included 35 percent in Broniszów in 1914, 42 percent in Żmiąca, and 53 percent in Babica. Between 1908 and 1918, 221,176 Poles (according to the "race and nationality" classification) left the U.S., while between 1908 and 1914 returns averaged about 30,000 annually. Among those who left, U.S. statistics show that 54 percent went to Austria, 0.5 percent to Hungary, 0.7 percent to Germany, and 42.4 percent to Russia. During the nineteenth and early twentieth centuries, circular migration was also a common phenomenon. In Babica, at least thirty percent of migrants crossed the Atlantic several times. Returnees brought savings with them. In 1902, Polish immigrants sent from America $3.5 million in money orders to Austrian Poland alone. Ewa Morawska calculated that during one year $12 million entered the Polish economy from immigrants to America. This resulted in improvements in lifestyle, and the purchase of land, houses, and tools.

Following World War I, return migration differed significantly. Between 1919 and 1923, the press often described re-emigration as a "fever." The long break in communication during the war and the patriotic slogans of the wartime era strengthened the desire to return. Altogether, slightly more than 100,000 Poles returned during those four years. Three-fourths were males, 73.6 percent in the age category between 16 and 44, and 23.6 percent were over 45 years of age. Most returned after a stay of five to ten years (72.2 percent), while some eight percent returned after ten to fifteen years abroad. According to American statistics, 53.7 percent of the returnees were unskilled workers, 6.2 percent skilled, 10.6 percent were self-defined as farmers, and 25 percent fell into category "other jobs." Polish statistics offered a different picture with 52.9 percent as workers, 33 percent farmers, and 10.4 percent representing "other jobs." This portrait is similar to that of other European ethnic groups. Post–World War I re-emigration had often been presented as a patriotic hysteria, but the movement really was motivated either by homesickness or speculative hopes of fulfilling original plans for economic advancement. There were even cases where returnees attempted to found businesses in Poland, but nearly all eventually failed. Those who thought that in a new Poland they would easily make fortunes or enlarge their property were most often wrong. Post-war economic crises and inflation frequently consumed their savings, and returnees were also targets of swindles and exploitation. News of these bad experiences, together with the introduction of new American immigration quotas, greatly reduced returns, except for those who were naturalized U.S. citizens and who chose to visit relatives in Poland. The onset of the Depression further eliminated incentives for re-emigration.

In the post–World War II era, immigrants to America generally had no intention of returning to a Poland dominated by the Soviet Union since their migration had largely been caused by political and ideological reasons. Beginning in the 1970s, there were some "returns of retirement," that is, people who received U.S. pensions and benefits returned to Poland in retirement because the currency exchange rate provided them with a favorable economic status. Another chapter in return migration opened with the collapse of Communism in Poland in 1989, although the number of returnees is unknown. At the same time, the declining exchange rate of the dollar reduced the number of retirees who viewed a return to Poland as a viable option for their retirement years.—*Adam Walaszek*

SOURCES: Ewa Morawska, "Labor Migrations of Poles in the Atlantic World Economy, 1880–1914," *Comparative Studies in Society and History*, Vol. 31, no. 2 (1989); Adam Walaszek, "Return Migration from the USA to Poland," in Daniel Kubat, ed., *The Politics of Return. International Return Migration in Europe* (New York: Center for Migration Studies, 1984).

Religious Life. Polish tradition has Christianity entering Poland through the missionary work of Ss. Cyril and Methodius, with the seminal date the baptism of Duke Mieszko I in 966 AD marking the conversion of the Polish lands. Germans influenced the development of Polish Christianity heavily, bringing the emerging state within the orbit of western or Roman Catholicism rather than eastern Orthodoxy. Loyalty to Roman Catholicism has characterized the Poles ever since.

While Catholicism was to remain the predominant expression of religion in what became Poland, the late medieval and early modern periods witnessed the incorporation of diverse faiths as the country expanded, giving the state a pluralism in religion and ethnicity which lasted until the terrible events of World War II. In the eastern lands White Russian and Ukrainian populations retained their early preference for Orthodox forms of Christianity. The Polish crown, unlike the more ethnically uniform kingdoms such as France or Spain, followed a policy of accommodation of religious diversity throughout most of its history. Orthodox affiliation among the inhabitants of the eastern lands co-existed with Catholic adherence among most nobles and Polish settlers who slowly moved eastwards. By 1500 pluralism was an accepted reality, though kings of Poland had to be of the Catholic faith.

Further enriching this mixture was another element, important throughout much of Polish history. By the eleventh century Jews entered the state, becoming a mercantile and artisan element in the developing cities. As early as 1264 Polish magnates and later kings granted them the right to practice their religion and considerable communal self-government as well. Jews tended to be urban dwellers, with legal prohibitions against rural landownership reinforcing a historic preference for trade. Despite varying tensions with Christians their presence became generally accepted and Polish rulers continued to afford them legal protections.

The Reformation of the sixteenth century introduced even more religious variety. Germans in the north and west for the most part adopted Lutheranism while some Poles, especially nobles and artisans, were drawn to the Calvinist persuasion. A wide range of Protestants appeared in the sixteenth and seventeenth centuries but, with the exception of German adherents, failed to root permanently. The appearance of the Society of Jesus in the late sixteenth century led to an effective, and occasionally repressive, counter-evangelism and the conservative Polish peasantry never saw much attraction in the new churches. In the same period a portion of Ukrainians switched allegiance to the papacy, with an agreement guaranteeing retention of religious customs and language in 1596. This became the Greek Catholic (Ukrainian) rite and further enlarged the range of religious expression in the state.

The vicissitudes of the eighteenth century led to the dissolution of the Polish-Lithuanian commonwealth in a series of partitions among neighboring countries, culminating in 1795 with the complete disappearance of this historic state from the map of Europe for over a century. The new rulers, Russia, Prussia (later Germany) and Austria-Hungary, were less tolerant about religion, especially in the instances of Orthodox Russia and Protestant Prussia.

The official hostility to Catholicism in the Russian and German partitions had the paradoxical effect of increasing Polish allegiance to their ancestral faith in the nineteenth century. Catholicism became an aspect of national consciousness, though the rise of secular and even anti-clerical philosophies such as socialism and positivism provided competing alternative orientations of considerable attraction, especially to urbanites and intellectuals. But the large majority of Poles were peasants and they displayed a stubborn attachment to their traditional faith.

In the latter nineteenth century the Roman Catholic Church showed increasing institutional vigor. Bishops promoted a more vigorous lay piety and enhanced discipline over priests. The growth of pilgrimages to shrines such as Częstochowa brought increasing numbers of persons from different partitions into a powerful shared religious experience, diminishing through religion the distinctiveness of partitional boundaries. Particularly in Austrian Poland, the sole partition dominated by a Catholic monarchy, vocations to religious life increased significantly by 1900, providing more priests and nuns to serve the laity. Even in the other partitions religious activity revived, stimulated by intermittent state oppression in the Russian "Kingdom of Poland" and the ***Kulturkampf*** in the new German Empire. While some bishops and clergy sought accommodation with the foreign rulers most priests and nuns were quiet but effective voices for the preservation of a sense of Polishness (***Polskość***). This enhanced identification with a distinct ethnicity, which by the end of the nineteenth century came to include aspirations for an independent Poland, made clerics the bearers of a form of nationalism.

Material developments in the 1800s combined to powerfully change Polish society. The nineteenth century saw the general population more than double, with consequent pressure on the land by an ever more numerous peasantry with declining economic prospects. The spread of railroads in the latter part of the century and the emergence of seasonal migration for farm labor from the Russian and Austrian partitions to Germany and other parts of Europe accustomed Poles to geographical movement. From its historic role as an immigrant destination, especially for Jews and Germans, the Polish lands became sources of outward movement. This was driven mainly by economic necessity, with an overlay of cultural and religious oppression in the German and Russian-held lands.

The preferred overseas destination for Poles was the United States. Far more than Canada or Latin America the American giant attracted newcomers. The incredible economic dynamism which made the United States the leading manufacturing country by 1880 required vast numbers of laborers and mechanization of production processes and steadily decreased skill requirements. Polish peasants, strong and willing to work hard, were ideal for industrial labor from the perspective of employers. The result was a startlingly large movement from the Polish lands, beginning with the German partition in the 1850s and accelerating powerfully after the end of the American Civil War in 1865. These newcomers often arrived as family units, leaving behind a hostile economic environment where the anti–Catholic attitudes of the German state powerfully reinforced an inclination to depart permanently. By the 1880s the Russian and Austrian partitions began sending emigrants. These were more often single young men, whose venture to America had a design to earn money to buy land at home upon return not many years hence. But women increasingly entered these emigration streams and contributed to an inclination to permanent settlement which came to mark them as well. By 1914 there were about one and a half million Poles in the United States.

Poles tended to settle in lower-class areas of American cities, with a declining minority seeking farms. Agriculturalists here were early arrivals, predominantly from the German partition and settled in the Midwest (see **Agriculture**), and often clustered in preferred rural districts. An important result of this pattern of residential concentration was institutional formation. These immigrants proved adept at forming voluntary associations bounded by ethnicity and often religion. The first society was almost always a fraternal benefit association, a very practical collective protection against the vicissitudes of life. Such groups were overwhelmingly male before 1900, with women participating in significant numbers only in the twentieth century. A portent for the long term character of American **Polonia** was the early but ephemeral presence of Jews and non–Polish Christians from the historic Polish-Lithuanian commonwealth. The emergence of a Polish-centered nationalism and some anti–Semitism, coupled with desires for independent expression of ethnicity and religion among Ukrainians, Lithuanians and Jews, made the fraternal movement increasingly mono-ethnic. But mutual aid, even with its social and patriotic dimensions, was inadequate to give a full sense of place and meaning to life. Polish immigrants sought fulfillment of fundamental spiritual needs in religion.

The story of their parish formation contrasts with the episcopally-directed pattern of the twenty-first century. Poles entered America in a period of unprecedented immigration of Catholics from all parts of Europe. The early nineteenth century mass immigration of Irish Catholics, distantly seconded by Germans, ballooned Roman Catholics from about one percent of the population around the Revolution to ten percent by the Civil War. Irish numbers and political astuteness guaranteed that this ethnic group — conveniently English-speaking and overwhelmingly inclined to permanent settlement — came to dominate the American hierarchy. The only significant minority among bishops were Germans, mostly found in the sees of the Midwest, with a scattering of other nationalities, none of them Poles before 1908. In the post-bellum era "liberal" bishops, meaning those who admired the United States and wanted Catholics to be accepted as Americans, favored acculturation of newcomers. A "conservative" orientation in the hierarchy was often more sympathetic to ethnicity as a support to faith and viewed America more critically. The liberal element was more dynamic and much of the tensions within the episcopate revolved around how to be Catholic in a largely non-Catholic and officially non-religious country. Arriving when they did, Poles encountered a well-structured Catholic Church run by non-Poles and who often displayed little understanding of the traditions and desires of the newcomers.

The pioneers of a local settlement found partial satisfaction for their religious needs in whatever Roman Catholic Church was nearby. While this might be an English-speaking territorial parish, they were often drawn to a German Catholic Church if one were available. Poles from the German and Austrian partitions frequently had some knowledge of German and churches run by order priests such as Franciscans might even have persons of Polish background among them. Attendance at a German church also brought their attention to an important fact: American Catholicism in the antebellum period had come to allow ethnically-enclosed parishes due to German pressure. The example of "national" (ethnic) congregations was powerfully attractive.

These East Central Europeans drew upon their experience of voluntarism in fraternals and other small societies to form parishes. They did not wait upon the bishops to recognize their presence but took initiative on their own. When Poles achieved a certain size of settlement, usually in the hundreds, pious persons convened a meeting of activists and community members and elected a parish committee (*komitet parafialny*). Sometimes they were officers in Roman Catholic fraternals but almost invariably they were wealthier and more established than the average immigrant. The committeemen promoted collection of funds either for the purchase of empty lots for future construction or occasionally bought an existing church. Often this was a small Protestant edifice whose members sought to relocate as the neighborhood became more Polish.

Somewhere in the process the immigrants had to contact the local bishop. The prelate invariably was non–Polish, but in some large dioceses the ordinary had suffragans or consultors who spoke a Slavic language, providing him with advice and information. Regardless, the committeemen presented themselves to the bishop to get official recognition. This entailed the bishop dedicating the edifice and assigning a priest. At this point the bishop faced a choice: should he bless the effort or withhold his approval? Up to World War I ordinaries were inclined to support such lay initiatives since they had enormous demands on their time and preferred to accommodate newcomers who were pious enough to organize their religious community. While liberal bishops like John Ireland of St. Paul disliked national parishes in principle even they realized that not allowing ethnically distinct congregations would lead to massive protests. The outcome was usually favorable and soon the bishop appeared to consecrate the new church, a major event in community life and always recalled with pride in parish anniversary books.

Another dimension of the process was less attractive to Poles. Lacking a patron or state subsidy the community itself raised all funds for the enterprise. Yet the bishop required that title to all parish property be signed over to the diocese. Whether established as a sole corporation sole Chicago or the more common group corporation of bishop and other officials, the diocese demanded ownership and got it. This aggravated the property-conscious newcomers but they realized that legitimate status in American Catholicism necessitated surrender of title.

With the formation of the church the parish committee usually persisted in some form. Typically, in accordance with canon law potential members were selected by the pastor and elected by the parishioners at an annual meeting. Occasionally it had a more independent status, chosen without pastoral input. The ubiquity of the committee form, annoying to many bishops, institutionalized a lay voice in these congregations and satisfied immigrant sensibilities that those who paid should have a say in parish affairs. Prudent pastors worked with the committees, which were useful for mobilizing support for the numerous building programs to accommodate rapidly growing parishes in a period of heavy immigration.

Pastors before World War I were normally born in the Polish lands and often educated there, though American bishops made increasingly strenuous efforts to recruit young clerics and give them some time in American seminaries. Unlike the similar-sized influx of Italians whose spiritual guides were less prone to emigrate, Poles insisted on a priest of their own ethnicity. Clerics in congregations were an early source, notably the **Resurrectionists** who served the first parish (f. 1854) of **Panna Maria** in Texas but whose ministry shifted to burgeoning Chicago where they sought — unsuccessfully — to monopolize national parishes. **Franciscans**, who might be in mixed communities of Poles and non–Poles, appeared in many cities. Jesuits were more often missioners, itinerant priests who gave missions at various parishes on the pattern of the German-dominated Redemptorists.

Diocesan priests soon came to prevail in the immigration stream, though their departures were mainly the product of individual preference. The United States offered numerous openings and rapid promotion since most congregations had only a single priest, creating pastors among clerics who might be assistants at home. Salaries were also considerably higher in America. While a few were fleeing personal problems in the homeland, the vast majority were sincerely interested in serving their countrymen in a new environment. Some moved around, investigating openings and sometimes negotiating with parish committees directly, but the preferred route was to seek incardination in a diocese and an assignment to a Polish parish. The paucity before 1900 of educated laymen gave the early intelligentsia strata a more clerical overtone than at home.

The status of the clergy was higher than in the homeland and this reverence persisted in the face of increasing competition from lay intelligentsia seeking power and recognition. The novel and often threatening urban environment challenged the mostly peasant immigrants and created a strong desire for security, most obviously represented by traditional religion. Priests had an enhanced pastoral role, defining proper behavior and exhorting their overwhelmingly young congregants to lead morally upright lives in a situation of temptations not found in the homeland villages. Drunkenness, a traditional curse exacerbated by the prevalence of saloons in Polish areas, was a particular threat, though Polish priests were seldom drawn to the contemporary movement for outright prohibition of alcohol. Sermons denounced urban temptations and stressed the development of moral character. The sad prevalence of infant deaths due to overcrowding and disease brought them close to grieving young parents as valued consolers. In addition, their superior education and knowledge of English often cast priests as cultural brokers, helping newcomers adapt to the strange new society.

With considerable social distance from the laity and only non–Poles as bishops, priests felt a need for social contacts and defense of their position. One solution was a society of priests. The first was founded in 1875 by the Resurrectionist **Wincenty Barzyński** as a lodge in the **Polish Roman Catholic Union**. His dominating personality and perhaps links to a congregation prompted a separate organization a few years later by diocesan priests in the rival **Polish National Alliance**. Various bodies came and went, with the largest and most durable forming the Union of Polish Priests in 1911. With state units and periodic meetings it provided social interaction and allowed clergy to meet to discuss issues of common import. While there were no equivalents in the homeland, the society was a useful tool for defending clerical interests in the new land.

If priests were enlarging their roles in the new land the laity were changing as well. Most immigrants were young men with basic education, growing in extent through the steady spread of elementary schools in rural areas. The vitality of youth and the ambition characteristic of immigrants made the new parishioners more assertive.

The parish committees were the most obvious manifestation of a tendency toward democratization of society. Without any nobles and few lay intelligentsia but in an environment of greater economic opportunity, a new class of upwardly mobile persons emerged in the settlements. Small entrepreneurship rather than extensive education marked the new elite, an occupational orientation which stressed the practical and made income a more common marker of status. Such men were disproportionately recognized by their fellows through election to fraternal and other organizational posts, giving societies a leadership decidedly less proletarian than the general membership. The selection of leaders through election seemed suited to church as well as lay organizations and parish committeemen were often successful businessmen. In turn they saw popular support as the basis for their official legitimacy, giving them more confidence in dealing with clerics than was the situation for peasants at home.

Parish life was not only more democratic but more organized. Women were especially quick to form pious groups such as a Rosary Society or the Society of St. Agnes. Under whatever name they offered a basis for fellowship outside the home and provided some experience in office holding since women held all posts save chaplain. Spiritual uplift and common prayer developed ties across class lines and varied homeland origins. There was a social dimension and probably an exchange of advice and help, compensating for the pre–1900 exclusion from the fraternal movement. As measured by the size and number of societies in parishes, rates of participation were higher in the United States. Men lagged here, with most finding their organizational outlets in fraternalism or more specialized groups outside the parish. The emphasis on patience, long suffering and other virtues associated with women may have limited the appeal of devotional groups. The contemporary rise of the Holy Name Society bypassed Poles and it remained for the next generation of men to move into devotionalism. But voluntarism in America made Polish parish life varied and vigorous.

Though only immigrants from the German partition came predominantly in family groups, the growing proportion of single women made it increasingly common to marry here and begin families. Most Austrian and Russian men forsook their plans to return home with earnings in favor of permanent settlement in America. By preference they sought brides from their own locality (*okolica*) but the greater variety of origins in Polonian settlements encouraged unions from more distant parts of the homeland, even from other partitions. Seldom did Poles marry outside their ethnic group; endogamy remained the pattern for immigrants. Marriages here were for love; the absence of parents and matchmakers and the example of American culture promoted romance and individual choice, though roles and expectations for husband and wife remained traditional in the first generation. Weddings were occasions of great celebration, welcome breaks from the routine of strenuous labor. The lengthy and often raucous parties following the nuptial Mass were nonetheless shorter than at home, where the absence of industrial discipline allowed them to last several days. Yet they went on far into the night, leading priests and newspaper editors to denounce them for encouraging drunkenness and degrading the public reputation of Poles. The pressure for respectability had limited effect among the immigrants but would greatly change wedding patterns among their children.

The unions were soon blessed with offspring. Poles tended to have large families, frequently five or more. Baptisms provided another important occasion for laity and priest to come together, bonding them in celebrating the entrance of a new person into the faith. The event was also the occasion of a party, smaller than a wedding reception but still a welcome occasion for enjoyment.

An important effect of life in America was a significant decline in illegitimate births. At home about fifteen percent of children were born out of wedlock around 1900. The clerical stress on sexual morality and earlier marriage facilitated by higher income made pre-nuptial births much less common. Parish records suggest illegitimacy here declined to about one percent. This addressed a fear of priests and lay leaders at home about the moral dangers of emigration. Far from falling into ethical chaos in the new environment, Polish immigrants were generally successful in rapidly creating a stable and morally authoritative ethnic order which provided norms and community.

Immigrant parishes were dynamic and inclusive, the product of collaboration between a committed clergy and a youthful laity. Pastors and lay leaders usually addressed the question of what it meant to be a good Pole in America by not being overtly ideological. Thus they avoided much of the controversy which divided the fraternal movement. There the religiously-oriented societies demanded an overt commitment to Catholicism while the more secular and tolerant ones held religion to be a personal option. Pastors were aware that they served a diverse audience and they sought to bring people in rather than fence them out. The same attitude characterized parish committees, which were acutely conscious of the need to finance burgeoning churches and the negative financial effects of an exclusionary policy.

Pre–1914 Polish Roman Catholic parishes expanded their physical and spiritual structure through periodic enlargement of facilities. After the church the most important addition was a school (see **Education**). From the perspective of the hierarchy, committed after 1884 in principle to each parish having a school, Poles were very cooperative. In reality these immigrants saw a school as not only promoting religion but culture, an important aid to the transmission of Polishness to the American-born. By 1910 most of the 510 national parishes had schools, an impressive accomplishment by an overwhelmingly working class ethnic group. These were housed in successively larger and more elaborate buildings, without precedent in the homeland and a tribute to the piety and concern for the preservation of Polishness of these newcomers. After an initial staffing by lay teachers from the homeland nuns took over instruction virtually everywhere. Individually they worked for much less and were available in groups while their presence had an aura of superior spirituality. The parish assumed responsibility for their housing, unlike for lay instructors, but early convents were more modest and crowded than rectories.

The Polish parish school system could not have arisen without strong lay support. Immigration was an act of hope and the newcomers had a saying: "That our children may have it better." The novel environment fostered aspirations for advancement and this included their offspring. If parents sent their children to public schools they at least usually enrolled them in catechism classes, mainly taught by nuns. Again instruction in Polish reinforced ethnic consciousness as well as religion and transmitted culture to the coming generation.

The creation of ethnic parishes did not always proceed peacefully. As noted previously, lay desires for input contradicted the more authoritarian vision of the church held by bishops and priests. Sometimes this led to actual ruptures and no division in **Polonia** proved more durable than the religious.

The rise of "independentism" (see **Polish National Catholic Church**) epitomized the intense Catholicity of these immigrants.

Protestant efforts at evangelism, pursued by Baptists, Methodists, Presbyterians, and others, produced only a few thousand converts by 1914. Much more significant were efforts to break with the Roman Catholic Church while retaining Catholic spirituality and traditions. Although there were occasional independent parishes before 1890, often ephemeral, the last decade of the century saw more elaborate challenges to traditional allegiances. Several dissenting priests, the reverends **Stefan Kamiński** of Buffalo, **Anthony Kozłowski** of Chicago and **Francis Hodur** of Scranton, challenged Roman Catholicism by forming independent but Catholic denominations. The most important was Father Hodur, a Galician immigrant of great determination, organizational skill and vigor, who began his **Polish National Catholic Church** in 1897 in the coalfield district of Pennsylvania. Reflecting current anthropology, Hodur argued that each "race" or people had a particular religious genius which required institutional expression. More concretely, he denounced the American Catholic Church for undermining Polishness and oppressive governance. Hodur asserted that his new denomination properly honored ethnicity and had a more democratic structure. A Polish National Catholic parish held title to its property and the laity had a voice in selecting the pastor and administering the congregation through an elected council. Hodur secured consecration in 1907 as bishop from the Old Catholic Church in Europe, giving him the legitimacy of the apostolic succession and gradually absorbed his competitors. The denomination spread to most Polish communities over the next several decades, acting as a refuge for local dissenters and providing priests, counsel and comfort. Democracy and ethnicity appealed to persons dissatisfied with their pastor and parish, but in all settlements only a minority joined the PNCC.

Roman Catholic reaction was intensely hostile. Priests and bishops denounced the National Catholics as heretics, schismatics and worse while the independents attacked the old church, alleging tyranny, indifference to Polishness and often immorality by the pastor. The Roman response stressed loyalty to the true church and emphasized the Polish character of the parish while defending Roman Catholic polity. The general religious conservatism of this group worked in favor of the traditional affiliation and after their initial growth the independents seldom subsequently increased their numbers. The departure of the most vocal dissatisfied laity eased the situation for the Roman Catholic clerics and they pursued a policy of isolation of the independents. The overall effect was to establish a permanent

though small religious alternative among these Catholic immigrants.

One consequence of the rise of independentism was a growing demand for Polish representation in the Roman Catholic hierarchy. While a multiple hierarchy based on dividing American Catholicism into ethnically-based segments never was a realistic possibility, even if desired by some German and Polish Catholics, Poles did get some modest recognition. In 1908 the Rev. **Paul Rhode** became a suffragan bishop of Chicago and *de facto* national bishop for Poles in America. With the exception of **Edward Kozlowski** as bishop of Green Bay, Wisconsin for 1914–1915 Rhode was the sole Roman Catholic prelate into the interwar period. During that time a handful of Polonians became suffragans or ordinaries of minor dioceses like Grand Island, Nebraska. Desires for recognition through elevation to important sees would await the period after World War II.

The unexpected outbreak of World War I was to prove a watershed in Polonian religion and society. By the end of 1914 immigration from the Polish lands had almost completely ceased as belligerents forbade the departure of men of military age and naval warfare disrupted sea travel. For Polonia this meant the cessation of newcomers bringing the homeland culture to the new land, something not immediately appreciated as attention focused on the plight—and opportunity—for the divided homeland.

Polish parishes had customarily been sites for patriotism as well as religion, and priests shared the vision of national independence. Though intensity of pastoral interest varied, the war invigorated the role of the parish for nationalistic activities. Roman and National Catholic congregations vied to demonstrate their superior patriotism—and hence Polishness. Overall the advantage lay with the more numerous and better organized Roman Catholics, aided by developments abroad.

The story of the independence movement is complex, but broadly a more religiously-oriented perspective grouped in America as the **National Department** (Wydział Narodowy) competed with a secular one under the **National Defense Committee** (Komitet Obrony Narodowej), with the latter perforce attracting Polish National Catholic support since it was open to religious variety. Local committees formed in settlements, with the National Department often situated in Roman Catholic parishes.

The conservative or religionist camp, led by Roman Dmowski and **Ignacy Jan Paderewski**, favored the Allies and the circumstances of war and diplomacy ultimately favored them. For tactical reasons the secular orientation, under the leadership of Józef Piłsudski, linked with the Central Powers as the most likely to allow the re-emergence of a Polish state, but by 1917 this approach had not borne fruit. By contrast, the United States entered the war in April, 1917 on the side of Great Britain, France and Russia, and the National Department stigmatized the Committee as pro–German. Able to use Roman Catholic parish facilities and often supported from pulpits, the conservatives marginalized the secularists in 1917–18. This also diminished the influence of the Polish National Catholics in the independence movement.

Allied victory led to the restoration of Polish independence, an event joyously celebrated in parishes across America. Yet the revived state inevitably did not fulfill the glorious dreams of its Polish American supporters and within a few years incessant pleas for aid, partisan politicking and a sense that **Polonia** had done its part led to a portentous change in perspective. Following the war a series of National Department–sponsored Emigration Congresses initially emphasized aid to the homeland. But by 1922 religionist leaders, including the sole bishop, Paul Rhode, discussed the need to refocus Polonian concerns. The 1923 Congress ratified their new position, which stressed the maintenance of ethnicity here, support for parochial schools and other points which had an internal, not Polish, concern.

Underlying the emphasis on America was a growing recognition of the importance of the second generation. The interwar years were the era of massive maturation of the American-born, whose sense of identity was inevitably different from their immigrant parents. For clergy the transmission of the faith took precedence over nationalism, although they did not so much reject ethnicity as try to reformulate it. Priests sought to retain some traditional Polish expression of religion, strikingly seen in the tendency for the subject of religion to be taught in Polish longer than any other. Yet they recognized that this required adaptation and innovation, bringing young persons into parish life in new ways.

One was particular emphases or organizations linked to age. There was a proliferation of juvenile pious societies. Various sodalities devoted to Mary or a saint emerged for children and youth, sometimes distinguished by gender as well. Masses for schoolchildren gave them a sense of distinctiveness in Sunday worship.

The presence of gymnasiums provided another basis for reaching young people. The native-born showed strong interest in team sports even before the war and following it the expansion of educational facilities included a growing appreciation of athletics, partly as a means to link them to parishes in an enjoyable way. Immigrants may have regarded sports as a waste of time but some of them found it attractive too, fostering additional links across generational lines.

As the second generation reached adulthood, other associational forms appeared or were modified. The Rosary Society under a variety of names had been the most common immigrant devotional group among women. In the interwar years a significant variant appeared, often referred to as an "English unit." The second generation was less fluent in the old language, understanding more than it spoke. In turn this modified ethnic identity as Polish lost its monopoly as the lay medium of religious expression. The same pattern appeared in fraternals, leading the immigrant-dominated lodges to increasingly become the habitats of the elderly.

Male Polonians, though traditionally less attracted to organized piety, began to enter it in larger numbers among the American-born. This was itself an aspect of acculturation. In the later nineteenth century the Holy Name Society became the most popular vehicle for masculine piety, attracting large numbers of English-speaking Catholics but with little impact among Poles. The youth, speaking English well and increasingly wanting to mingle with successful young Catholics outside their ethnic group, found Holy Name congenial. Since it was linked to the diocese, it provided

occasions where Polonians worked and prayed with non–Poles. The consequence was a broadening of contacts and horizons, religiously enclosed but ethnically inclusive. The link of faith made such ties acceptable.

Increased contact with non–Polish Catholics, as well as inculcation in parochial school or catechism class of the legitimacy of the authoritarian model of church government had the effect of increasing deference toward the priestly office. This included an acceptance of clerical dominance in parish affairs, the arrangement in territorial parishes. The effect was to lessen the role of parish committees, which declined or even disappeared, sometimes under episcopal pressure. In seeming paradox, as social relations between American-born laity and clergy became more casual and egalitarian the prewar inclination to demand a lay role in polity declined.

This expansion of parish activities reflected important changes among the religious. Poles born here demonstrated an attachment to religion as strong as their parents, if sometimes expressed differently. But one definite continuity was a willingness to enter religious life. Seminaries and motherhouses benefited immensely from this as young men and women offered themselves to Christ through taking vows. Yet the American-born were different in significant ways. The new priests and nuns used English as their first language, especially for those in the diocesan seminaries where Polish was often absent. The establishment in Michigan of the **Ss. Cyril and Methodius Seminary** (f. 1885) to provide an ethnic en-

The interior of Saints Cyril and Methodius Church in Milwaukee, Wisconsin. Polish Americans took great pride in their churches as symbols of their community (*UWM*).

vironment never educated more than a small fraction of clergy. Although male and female congregations continued to respect the ancestral culture, even their graduates were usually more comfortable in English. Since the younger laity shared this preference they literally communicated more easily than many immigrant clergy. Moreover, young religious were products of American egalitarianism. Polish nuns in the United States dropped the distinction between first (contemplative, seen as more purely spiritual) and second (active) choirs. Likewise they eliminated the dowry, facilitating the entrance of poor but pious women. Young priests likewise mixed more casually with their increasingly educated and affluent lay peers. Social distance between laity and clergy decreased in the second generation.

Internal distinctions among priests were linked largely to generation. Senior clergy might acquire the title of monsignor or become diocesan consultors and they were the mainstays of the Union of Polish Priests. While able to communicate in English they often preferred Polish. Their American-born subordinates were native speakers of English but less fluent in the ancestral tongue. The young men did not have much interest in the UPP, much to the dismay of its leaders. This was not so much because the curates were indifferent to ethnicity, but that they felt one could be a good Pole in America and still speak English. UPP concern for the ancestral culture and tongue seemed excessive to them and they preferred to socialize with their peers or the more educated and affluent laity. Thus Polonian priests developed more outside contacts but at the cost of unity with their immigrant seniors.

Clergy began to mingle with outsiders more as well. World War I had frequently led to contacts with "Americans" for relief or money-raising activity, accustoming even immigrant pastors to more external contact. After the war many dioceses elaborated their bureaucracies with boards for education or other supra-parochial activity and Polish priests were assigned to many of them. The curates found such work more comfortable since their facility in English and American education gave them more commonalities with non–Poles. Yet bishops customarily staffed their national parishes exclusively with clergy of Polish extraction, seen as prudent in view of ethnic preferences.

The 1920s particularly were a period of building as increased size and affluence required new edifices. Poles favored the Romanesque over the Gothic, associated with Irish and Germans, and had a fondness for baroque interiors of often striking magnifi-

The Rev. Aleksander Fijałkowski with a First Communion class at St. Mary, Our Lady of Częstochowa, Parish in New York Mills, New York, during the 1930s. (*James S. Pula*).

cence. Churches might have some statuary or stained glass with Polish elements but décor emphasized common Catholic themes. Faith expressed in stone or brick often made the church the largest building in the locality, a potent symbol of ethnic presence.

The American episcopate turned against national parishes by 1920, though a few still formed in the interwar years. Ethnicity had always been a difficulty for most bishops and the heightened American nationalism of the war and an upsurge in nativism enhanced many bishops' desires to make the Church seem less "foreign." With immigration restriction laws in 1921 and 1924 drastically slowing the influx of Europeans there was also less pressure to form national parishes. Prelates such as George Mundelein, cardinal archbishop of Chicago from 1915 to 1939, addressed ethnicity by forming new churches in outlying parts of the city as territorial parishes but staffed by Polish priests where they comprised large majorities of parishioners. Americanization within Catholicism accelerated through official encouragement.

The Polish American middle class grew dramatically after the war and increasingly the more affluent American-born sought better housing and its attendant status outside the ethnic ghettoes. These young persons maintained family ties and returned on holidays to their childhood districts but interacted more and more with non–Poles. This went along with steadily increasing exogamy. Young Polonians far more than their parents met and married outside the ethnic group, especially in areas where Poles were less numerous to

begin with. Most unions were with other Catholics, but a growing minority chose a person outside the ancestral faith. The Roman Catholic Church viewed marriage with non–Catholics with some alarm, insisting on agreements to have any children raised as Catholics but was unable to halt the process. Polish priests may have preferred endogamy but they were unlikely to counsel against marriage to another Catholic, though they shared concerns of bishops for marriage with non–Catholics. The general effect of intermarriage and removal from the ethnic districts was to attenuate ties with historic ethnicity and less often Catholicism.

The Polish National Catholic Church also reflected the evolution of the interwar environment. By World War II the rate of parish formation had slowed. Immigrant attitudes about church governance likely touched the American-born less and ethnicity among youth encompassed English as the normal tongue, lessening the appeal of ethnicity and democracy. Internally, however, the PNCC retained its strong emphasis on Polishness and democracy but as with Roman Catholics increasing second generation dispersal made church-going more arduous as congregations remained in Polish districts. Possibly some residents in outlying areas began attending more conveniently located Roman Catholic Churches.

For the working-class majority of Poles in America the advent of the Great Depression in 1929 was a major blow. Massive layoffs in manufacturing, a disproportionate source of employment for this ethnic group, inevitably had a negative effect on income for both Roman and Polish National Catholic congregations. Churches saw debt increase as mortgage payments were deferred or only partially paid. Roman Catholic parochial schools saw a sharp decline in enrollment as children were transferred to free public schools to save the modest but still significant tuition. The Polonian birthrate also dropped, reflecting a general American trend but possibly linked to a growing acceptance of birth control practices. The latter was cause for clerical condemnation but also indicated acculturation among women, the culturally most conservative element.

The outbreak of World War II, begun with the invasion of Poland in September, 1939, created a crisis for Polonia unmatched in a generation. Yet the response was quite different from twenty-five years previous. The now elderly immigrants were too old to consider the militant response of the last war, which saw over 20,000 men enlist in the **Polish Army in France**. The second generation considered themselves Americans first and the overwhelming tendency was to seek to aid Poland through relief efforts. Parishes often became centers for relief collection, coordinated through the **Polish American Council** (Rada Polonii Amerykańskiej) and the American Red Cross. Hostile Nazi and Soviet authorities made distribution very difficult, with collection efforts exceeding ability to ensure materials actually reached needy Poles. The entrance of the United States into World War II in December 1941 made this even harder. But the parishes were very supportive of the American war effort, proudly listing in their newsletters the young men and women in service and taking part in a great national — and nationalizing — effort which hopefully would also lead to the re-establishment of an independent Poland.

By war's end there were 946 Polish Roman Catholic parishes, about the peak of their number, compared to 143 much smaller Polish National Catholic congregations which grew slowly in number to 166 by 1966 and declined to 108 in 2007, with a total membership in the latter year of about 25,000. For both groups, the environment in the United States after 1945 presented powerful challenges. The postwar economic boom and unprecedented access to higher education through the G.I. Bill elevated more Polish Americans into the middle class than ever before. Affluence and suburbanization drew more and more away from the older urban areas into new communities where ethnic identity was less of an identifier than race. New suburbs were havens of "whiteness," with virtually no African Americans but also with no national parishes for

Roman Catholics. Membership in territorial congregations and intermarriage became common, though most Polonians married Roman Catholics in religious, but not ethnic, endogamy. Their departure impoverished old ethnic parishes since the middle class enjoyed superior income and confirmed the traditional Polish districts as enclaves of the elderly.

After several decades of sparse immigration, America opened its doors to a limited extent after 1945 by allowing in "displaced persons" outside of quota restrictions. A significant number were Poles, often veterans of the Polish army formed by the western Allies and now reluctant to return to a Communist-dominated homeland. Others were liberated slave laborers forced to work in Nazi Germany or simply refugees who fled Poland. About 200,000 came in the late 1940s and into the 1950s, arriving impoverished but with impressive human capital in the form of education and often command experience as military officers.

The meeting with the established Polish American community was not always easy. Pre–1914 immigrants and their children, who controlled the institutions of Polonia, extended much assistance but implicitly saw themselves as guides and models. The newcomers advanced more rapidly in the economy than was the case for the previous immigrants and they appeared reluctant to participate in Polonian organizational life, though many attended Polish parishes until they moved to more affluent areas. Hopes for a reinvigoration of traditional Polish districts proved unfounded, and while parishes enjoyed some access of younger Polish-speakers these arrivals dispersed more rapidly than their predecessors and provided less long-term support.

Into many of the old districts came other newcomers, often dark of skin and Protestant by heritage, a reversal of the Catholicization of much of urban America in the nineteenth century. Even if they were Catholic Hispanics they were different and parishes formed on ethnic exclusiveness had to consider how to adapt. Some closed but more allowed in the new arrivals, often with Spanish Masses and new customs which could both enrich and disturb the old Polish members. Celebration of the liturgy might become tri-lingual, with Masses in Polish, English and now Spanish. From the 1960s Poles began appearing as leaders of major dioceses, such as **John Krol**, cardinal archbishop of Philadelphia. Such bishops were aware of their ethnic heritage but had to consider the needs of the entire diocese, occasionally leading to unpopular closings or consolidation of national parishes. Recognition came late to this ethnic group

and may not have satisfied the hopes of many Polonians.

The so-called People's Poland (Polska Ludowa) of the Communists somewhat surprisingly became a modest source of immigrants. Unlike other Soviet-bloc states Poland by the late 1950s allowed some persons to leave, varying with the political climate but most notable in the 1980s with outflow of Solidarity-era persons and continuing after 1989 from an independent homeland. The stream of newcomers by the late twentieth century included priests, especially from the Society of Christ (Towarzystwo Chrystosowe). Welcomed by American bishops who confronted sharp declines in seminary enrollments by 1970, these clergymen and also immigrant nuns served in national parishes. They brought a Catholicism little modified by Vatican II and their conservatism gratified some but irritated other Polish Americans. As with the displaced persons, there was some conflict over who was a Pole and how religion should be practiced. The result could be a kind of separation, with some parishes becoming centers for recent immigrants and others being more mixed and predominantly American-born.

By the twenty-first century Catholicism among the majority of persons of Polish extraction or birth was less ethnic and more broadly religious. The rise of ecumenicism produced a useful dialog between Polish National and Roman Catholics which may in the future reunite these branches of Catholicism. But intermarriage, increasingly across ethnic lines, has made Poles much more integrated into the Roman Catholic Church in the United States.—*William J. Galush*

SOURCES: Religion appears as a major topic in general histories of Polonia such as John J. Bukowczyk, *And My Children Did Not Know Me: A History of the Polish Americans* (Bloomington: Indiana University Press, 1987); James S. Pula, *Polish Americans: An Ethnic Community* (New York: Twayne Publishers, 1995). Community studies stressing the role of religion include William J. Galush, *For More Than Bread: Community and Identity in American Polonia, 1880–1940* (Boulder, CO: East European Monographs, 2006); Anthony J. Kuzniewski, *Faith and Fatherland: The Polish Church War in Wisconsin, 1896–1918* (Notre Dame: University of Notre Dame Press, 1980); Joseph John Parot, *Polish Catholics in Chicago, 1850–1920* (DeKalb: Northern Illinois University Press, 1981). On ethnic education of clergy see Frank Renkiewicz, *For God, Country and Polonia: One Hundred Years of the Orchard Lake Schools* (Detroit: Harlo Press, 1985). For the Polish National Catholic Church see Hieronim Kubiak, *The Polish National Catholic Church in the United States of America from 1897 to 1980* (Warsaw: Państwowe Wydawnictwo Naukowe, 1982).

Rembski, Stanisław (b. Sochaczew, Poland, October 8, 1896; d. Baltimore, Maryland, September 14, 1998). Artist. Educated at the Fine Arts School, where he studied with Stanisław Lentz and at the Technological Institute in Warsaw, he continued his studies at the Ecole des Beaux-Arts in Paris, the Royal Academy of Fine Arts in Berlin, and the Art Students League in New York. In 1922 he relocated to the United States where he spent the rest of his life, living initially in New York (1922–40) where he had a studio in the Ovington Building in Brooklyn Heights. He later moved to Baltimore, MD (1940–1998), and also maintained a summer studio at Deer Isle, ME. His mentors included Leon Dabo and Edward Hopper. A noted portrait painter, he also taught at the Maryland Institute College of Art in Baltimore (1952–55). His works were seen in solo exhibitions at the Dudensing Galleries, New York (1927); Carnegie Hall Gallery, New York (1934); Arthur Newton Galleries, New York (1935); H. Chambers Co., Baltimore (1940); Baltimore Museum of Art (1947); Baltimore Institute of Art (1950); Calvert Gallery, Washington, D.C. (1990); and Salmagundi Club, New York (1996). Group exhibitions where his works appeared included the Neighborhood Club, Brooklyn (1924–29); Brooklyn Society of Artists (1924–29); Brooklyn Museum of Art (1927); Society of Independent Artists (1931, 1936); Roerich Museum, New York (1932); Carnegie Hall Gallery, New York (1932); Anderson Galleries, New York (1936); and Detroit Institute of Arts (1945).

Collections of his work may be found in Baltimore at the Babe Ruth Museum, Board of Education, Goucher College, Johns Hopkins University, and Loyola College; Carnegie Hall Archives, New York; Carnegie Institute, Pittsburgh, PA; Museum of Art, Fort Lauderdale, FL; Franklin D. Roosevelt Library and Museum, Hyde Park, NY; Museum of Arts and Sciences, Daytona Beach, FL; Museum of the City of New York; National Academy of Design Museum, New York; Newark Museum, NJ; Polenmuseum, Rapperswil, Switzerland; State Historical Society of Wisconsin, Madison; State House, Annapolis, MD; University of Maryland, College Park, MD; White's Hall, Gambrills, MD; and Woodrow Wilson Museum, Washington, D.C. Murals included the triptych on the Life of St. Bernard of Clairvaux, St. Bernard's School, Gladstone, NJ (1931) and "I am the Life," Memorial Episcopal Church, Baltimore (1962).—*Stanley L. Cuba*

SOURCES: Robyn Nissim, "The Old Master," *Baltimore Sun*, May 1995; Fred Rasmussen, "Stanislav Rembski, 101, Renowned Artist," *Baltimore Sun*, 1998.

Renkiewicz, Frank Anthony (b. New York, New York, May 16, 1935; d. Bronx, New York, October 11, 1993). Historian. After receiving his baccalaureate degree from St. Peter's College in Jersey City, NJ, in 1956,

Renkiewicz attended graduate school at the University of Notre Dame, earning an M.A. (1958) and a Ph.D. (1967) in history. His master's thesis was on "The Polish Immigrant in New York City, 1865–1914," while his doctoral dissertation was a study of "The Polish Settlement of St. Joseph County, Indiana, 1855–1935." Renkiewicz began teaching history as an instructor at the College of St. Teresa in Winona, MN, in 1962, gaining promotion to assistant professor (1967) and then associate professor (1971). He served as chair of the History Department from 1971 to 1975, before taking a two-year leave (1975–77) to serve as a research associate at the University of Minnesota's Immigration History Research Center. Renkiewicz returned to the College of St. Teresa as Professor of History (1977–81), and subsequently was on the faculty of St. John Fisher College, where he served as Director of Polish Studies (1981–83). He then moved to **St. Mary's College** (Orchard Lake, MI), where he was both Professor of History and Director of the Orchard Lake Center for Polish Studies (1983–87), as well as its Dean of Students (1983–85). Renkiewicz joined the National Park Service in 1990, working as an historical interpreter at the Ellis Island Museum until his death from heart failure in 1993. A specialist in immigration and American ethnic history, he presented papers at many scholarly conferences and contributed journal articles and book chapters that gained him a respected reputation in the field. He was the author of *For God, Country and Polonia: One Hundred Years of the Orchard Lake Schools* (1985), and compiler/editor of *The Poles in America: A Chronology and Fact Book* (1973), *The Polish Presence in Canada and America* (1982), and *A Guide to Polish Amer-*

Frank Renkiewicz, historian (*PAHA*).

ican Newspapers and Periodicals (1988). He also served as an assistant editor for the project to translate the Rev. **Wacław Kruszka**'s *Historia Polska w Ameryce* into English, working primarily on the reference notes in Volume 1 (1993). Renkiewicz served as president of the **Polish American Historical Association** in 1976, and editor of its scholarly journal, *Polish American Studies*, from 1969–1981. He received the **Kosciuszko Foundation** Doctoral Dissertation Award (1969), PAHA's **Mieczysław Haiman** Award (1978) for sustained scholarly effort in the field of Polish American studies, and the PAHA's **Oskar Halecki** Prize (1986) for the best book on a Polish American topic (*For God, Country and Polonia*).—*John Drobnicki*

SOURCES: *Directory of American Scholars* (New York: Bowker, 1982); obituary, *New York Times*, October 15, 1993, B10.

Resurrection, Congregation of the. The Congregation of the Resurrection, commonly known as the Resurrectionists, began in Paris in 1836. While composed overwhelmingly of Poles for much of its existence, its French origins reflect the exile status of the founders. The three original members—Bogdan Jański, Peter Semeneńko, and **Hieronim Kajsiewicz**—were fervent Polish patriots and their sense of Polishness long pervaded the Congregation. Of peasant extraction but unusual talent, Jański received a university education but fell into a dissolute life and a failed marriage. By the early 1830s he was drawn to Catholicism through contacts with liberal priests after fleeing his homeland following the unsuccessful November Uprising (1830-31) against the Russian occupiers. His previous interest in social justice took on a more specifically Catholic dimension and he joined Adam Mickiewicz's United Brethren in 1834 to engage in prayer and works of mercy. The Brethren did not prosper but Jański attempted to preserve it in a Brotherhood of National Service. His first companion was Kajsiewicz. The founder saw it as promoting both practical Christianity and Polish nationalism. Other émigrés, including Semeneńko, joined what became the basis for a new Roman Catholic community of men, eventually called the Congregation of the Resurrection. The intensely nationalistic character of the early members profoundly influenced the community's development and carried over to the United States.

In the wake of the American Civil War, the Resurrectionists received calls from American bishops for priests to serve the rapidly growing Polish immigration. More than most newcomers, Poles demanded priests of their own ethnicity and homeland clergy responded generously. The Congregation first appeared in the unlikely locale of Texas in 1866. Yet, there was the first Polish American parish, a small settlement of Silesian Poles centered around the town of **Panna Maria**. Resurrectionist priests cared for souls there and established the first Polish parochial school in America, even founding an ephemeral community of teaching nuns, the Sisters of the Immaculate Conception (1875–81). But the lack of growth prospects in Texas and limited resources inclined the community to change its geographic focus. In 1868 the bishop of Detroit requested their presence in what became a major Polish community. In 1869 the Rev. Jan Wolkowski preached the first mission in Chicago and a year later Bishop Thomas Foley begged the Resurrectionists to come to serve Poles in the burgeoning western metropolis. In negotiations with Kajsiewicz the bishop agreed in 1871 to give the Congregation the right to administer all non-diocesan Polish parishes for a ninety-nine year period. Impressed with the rapid growth of Chicago **Polonia**, the community made Chicago the center of Resurrectionist activity in the United States.

The leader in America in the period of the Resurrectionists' development was the Rev. **Wincenty Barzyński**, who entered Chicago in the early 1870s. A man of iron will, his vision of nationalism required a commitment to Catholicism. He soon promoted an organization of Polish priests, formed as a lodge in the **Polish Roman Catholic Union** (f. 1873), a pioneering effort to give structure — and greater influence — to Polish clergy in the United States. In the contentious atmosphere of late nineteenth century **Polonia**, many diocesan priests perceived this as an attempt to increase Resurrectionist power and rival clerical societies soon arose. More significant for Barzyński and the Congregation was pastoral work, which operated in a novel environment. In post-bellum America, Poles reopened an old debate about the extent of democracy in Catholicism. Accustomed to lay involvement in homeland parishes, both as state intervention and patronage from wealthy parishioners, the largely peasant immigrants felt their financial support entitled them to a voice. Most parishes grew out of lay committees, often sponsored by a fraternal insurance society, as was the case for St. Stanisław Kostka in Chicago. Here the parish had a constitution which incorporated a lay role in governance. The secularist fraternal lodge **Gmina Polska** (Polish Commune) vied with the more clericalist elements in the Tow. Św. Stanisława (St. Stanislaus Society) over influence on the first Chicago parish, which emerged in 1867.

Barzyński followed a series of Resurrectionist pastors who served only a few years each; he was to be pastor for close to a quarter century. As shepherd of a rapidly growing flock, which by his death in 1899 would number close to 50,000 — the largest parish in America — the Resurrectionist was painfully aware of numerous difficulties affecting the Polish newcomers. His solution was what Joseph Parot has aptly termed the "community parish," in which the church formed a wide range of institutions designed both to address problems and to encompass life apart from work. These included a parochial school, orphanage, old age home, parish bank and innumerable societies devoted to piety, charity, intellectual improvement and mutual aid. This institutional proliferation had been advocated by the Rev. Semeneńko in his guidebook entitled "Instrument for Conducting a Parish." This embodied the strong social justice as well as pious dimensions of Resurrectionist spirituality, important in a country with an undeveloped welfare system. The results were impressive. In the first decade of the twentieth century the parish included sixty-one pious societies, seven confraternities, eleven fraternals, several choirs and two drama groups. The school had over 4,000 children taught by sixty-seven nuns and six lay teachers. If there were occasional failures, such as the collapse of the bank, the multi-faceted effort provided immigrants and their offspring with an ethnically enclosed support system for material and cultural purposes.

A series of progressively larger orphanages signified community social concern. Beginning with St. Josaphat's Orphanage in 1885, the Chicago effort culminated in the establishment of St. Hedwig's Industrial School in 1911. Situated on the northwest side in several large buildings, the name included "industrial school" in order to qualify for state assistance. Served by Polish nuns the children received a basic education in an in-house school as well as manual training for future employment. In reality some residents were not orphans but rather youngsters from broken or impoverished homes. Parents sometimes used the institution to tide the family over a major crisis. The Congregation and local Polonia accepted this and in effect provided a private welfare system as well as care for parentless children.

For those families struggling but still intact the Congregation tried to provide day care. From 1904 to 1916 Polish nuns ran St. Elizabeth Day Nursery. For pennies a day a child received oversight and meals in a safe environment. This provided an ethnic alternative to secular or Protestant settlement houses, whose non–Catholic and non–Polish character

were viewed with suspicion by clergy. St. Adalbert Cemetery was the symbolic end to this institutional elaboration. The Resurrectionts were aware of Poles' desire to be buried among their own and provided a large cemetery near St. Hedwig's Industrial School. The cemetery was also an income source while providing Catholic internment in an ethnic context.

The early period of community development coincided with religious dissent. Poles were uniquely drawn to expressing their dissatisfaction with the Roman Catholic Church in Catholic form. Beginning about 1893 a long and complex struggle began at the Resurrectionist parish of St. Hedwig where an assistant, the Rev. **Antoni Kozłowski**, eventually led some parishioners away from the Roman allegiance. A priest influenced by the dissenting Old Catholic movement in Europe and an ardent nationalist, Kozłowski wanted the liturgy in the ancestral tongue and other changes in spirituality and governance. This brought him into sharp conflict with the pastor, the Rev. Józef Barzyński, brother of Wincenty. In 1895 Kozłowski set up the independent church of All Saints and soon founded a competing denomination, the Polish Old Catholic Church. Following his death this joined with the more successful **Polish National Catholic Church** (f. 1897) under the leadership of Bishop **Francis Hodur**. While never more than a small minority of Chicago Poles, the movement agitated the local Polonia.

The Congregation of the Resurrection, though distracted by dissent and controversy from time to time, continued to enhance its range of service. Resurrectionist concern for education extended beyond the elementary level. In 1890 the community founded St. Stanislaus College, which was in reality a high school. It offered post-elementary training mainly in commerce and business, a practical emphasis for the offspring of workers rather than the college preparatory orientation of local Jesuit institutions such as St. Ignatius. Instruction was largely in English, a recognition of the need for fluency in America that grew over time. Polish parents supported basic education but were much less interested in high schooling so the Congregation initially had to work hard to get students. Tuition was purposely low at twenty-five cents a month at a time when day laborers earned one to two dollars a day, but only gradually did parental attitudes change. In 1926 the name changed to Weber High School, after a Resurrectionist archbishop, and the school has persisted to the present.

The Congregation also sought to influence

the general Polonia through the most popular medium of the nineteenth century — a newspaper. In 1890 the *Dziennik Chicagoski* (Chicago Daily News) appeared. This quickly became one of the most prominent Polonian newspapers espousing a Catholic perspective. It carried a mixture of local, national and international news in Polish with occasional works of fiction, a pattern common in the ethnic press. By 1939 the paper introduced an English section, again a typical interwar recognition of the linguistic abilities of its readers. Its political orientation moved from Democratic to independent after World War I. In the 1930s support for Edmund Jarecki, a prominent local judge not part of the Chicago Democratic political machine, led to conflict with Cardinal Mundelein, closely aligned with the Democrats locally and nationally. This eventually forced the resignation of the editor, the Rev. Michael Starzyński, an example of the limits of Resurrectionist independence from powerful local prelates.

The Polish patriotism of the Congregation shone most brightly during the grim years of World War I. Nationalist sentiment had always marked Polonia but with the outbreak of conflict in 1914 hopes soared at the prospect of a revived homeland. Yet factionalism divided American Poles. Dissatisfied with the nationlist umbrella organization, the **National Defense Committee** (Komitet Obrony Narodowy; f. 1912), Roman Catholic–oriented groups set up what came to be known as the Polish **National Department** (Wydział Narodowy Polski). The Congregation naturally gravitated to the National Department, which in the course of the war became the dominant expression of Polish nationalism in America.

The Rev. **Władysław Zapala** was the most active community patriot and worked well with **Ignacy Paderewski**, the leading lay figure. With the accomplishment of Polish independence in 1918, the Resurrectionists turned to rebuilding their disrupted European houses and services and Zapala became the head of the American community in 1920.

While the Congregation was most active in Chicago Resurrectionists spread through Illinois and elsewhere in the United States in the twentieth century and even before. An early effort was the colony of New Posen in Nebraska, with the church of St. Anthony erected in 1877. The rural settlement drew heavily from Chicago and the Rev. Józef Barzyński served there before his pastorate at St. Hedwig's in the city. The community turned over care to other missionaries in 1884, similar to diocesans assuming the pastorate at St. Wenceslaus (f. 1875) in Pine Creek, Wisconsin, after several years of Resurrectionist presence. In the twentieth century the community appeared in Massachusetts, New York, California, and even Kentucky, Alabama, and Utah. In western and southern states this often meant service to predominantly non–Polish congregations.

The increase of work among non–Poles stimulated discussion over the dimensions of ethnicity in the Congregation. Bishops often solicited Resurrectionist services but with an assimilationist perspective before the 1960s they pressured the community to become more "American." In Chicago George Cardinal Mundelein, an ardent Americanizer, epitomized this attitude and in 1935 sermons in English were introduced in local Polish parishes. This was not solely a response to episcopal pressure; the American-born of Polish descent were seldom fluent in the homeland tongue and English was the language of the larger society that they aspired to enter.

Internal community developments also supported greater use of English. While the Depression was a period of heightened vocations novices often did not know Polish well and sometimes had little interest in learning. The entrance of more and more non–Poles into the American Congregation created further pressure for the use of English. The general trend was a decline, though by no means disappearance, of Polish.

After World War II the Congregation sought to adapt to a changing Polonia. An indicator was Gordon Technical High School, founded in 1953 and named after the noted Rev. Francis Gordon. It had a curriculum not only for manual and commercial practice but also a strong college preparatory component. This reflected the increasing aspirations for upward mobility among children and grandchildren of immigrants and the school grew steadily in the fifties and sixties. Students became increasingly non–Polish and the curriculum was essentially in English.

The Congregation's most important center, Chicago Polonia, came under siege in the postwar period from urban development and suburbanization. St. Stanislaus Kostka, the original parish, suffered along with others in the vicinity from expressway construction which cut up the neighborhood and promoted an exodus of parishioners. Younger people often moved willingly to suburbs for more space and better housing. At the same time the innovations of Vatican II were only slowly accepted by the increasingly elderly congregation. At St. Hedwig's the arrival of Hispanic immigrants in the area exemplified another challenge: integrating Catholic newcomers into a historically Polish parish.

Clerical education also changed. St. John Cantius Seminary in St. Louis was affected by the Second Vatican Council. Seminarians became more questioning and the curriculum reflected new interest in ecumenism, pastoral counseling and social studies. With the establishment of a **Jesuit** school of theology at St. Louis University the Congregation took advantage of the possibility of a larger faculty and better facilities to send students there. This had the effect of further integrating a historically Polish community into a more general "American" setting. The Congregation of the Resurrection in the United States has persisted with a conviction of its Polish heritage that adapts to the society it serves. From an ethnic body of religious men laboring in Polonian settlements the Congregation has expanded to work in varied areas of America.— *William J. Galush*

SOURCES: John Iwicki, C.R., *The First One Hundred Years: A Study of the Apostolate of the Congregation of the Resurrection in the United States, 1866–1966* (Rome: Gregorian University Press, 1966); John Iwicki, C.R., *Resurrectionist Charism: A History of the Congregation of the Resurrection* (Rome: Gregorian University Press, 1992), 3 vols.; Joseph John Parot, *Polish Catholics in Chicago: A Religious History, 1850–1920* (DeKalb: Northern Illinois University Press, 1981).

Founders of the Congregation of the Resurrection: from left, Bogdan Jański, Piotr Semeneńko, Hieronym Kajsiewicz (*OLS*).

Resurrection of Our Lord Jesus Christ, Sisters of the. The Congregation of the Sisters of the Resurrection was founded in Rome by a young widow, Celine Borzęcka and her daughter, Hedwig. In 1875 they met the Rev. Peter Semeneńko, Superior General of the Congregation of the Resurrection (see **Resurrection, Congregation of the**), at the Church of St. Claude. He became their spiritual director. The Rev. Semeneńko wished to form a women's Resurrectionist community and encouraged the Borzęckas toward this goal. In October of 1884 the Sisters of the Resurrection began under the leadership of Mother Celine and Mother Hedwig. They, and five candidates, moved into an apartment on Via Arcone 88 in Rome and lived in community. They lived a simple existence, dividing time between prayer, study, lessons, and the training of the sisters. The Rev. Semeneńko supervised their spiritual life and visited once a week for informal conferences. Mother Celine and Mother Hedwig introduced the Resurrectionist Rule into daily observance and the sisters devoted themselves to a charitable and pedagogical apostolate in which they taught catechism, cared for the poor, and visited the sick. Mother Celine, in compliance with the wishes of the Rev. Semeneńko, desired that the community promote Christian education. Born into a noble family, she was well educated in classic literature, the arts, modern languages, and religion, and desired to offer the same education to the girls in the new Resurrectionist school on Via Arcone. Unexpected help in religious training came through a young priest, Monsignor James della Chiesa, son of a Marquis who lived in an apartment in the same building. He became their chaplain, taught religion, and later became Pope Benedict XV.

January 6, 1891 marked the official acceptance of the Congregation of the Sisters of the Resurrection of Our Lord Jesus Christ by the Church. Mother Celine and Mother Hedwig professed final vows, three sisters made their profession of first vows, and all received religious habits. In the summer of 1891 Mother Celine went to Poland where she established the first foundation at Kęty. As the community spread, it began to develop a sense of missionary work. Unlike many female religious orders of the time, the Resurrectionist nuns were not cloistered, but were in contact with the world, living and working among lay people. Work and duties varied with the talents, preparation, and preference of each sister. All sisters were considered equal, with only a single choir (internal status division), a novel idea for the period. By 1899 the Congregation had already established foundations in three countries:

Italy, Poland, and Bulgaria. In the New World, the Resurrectionist Fathers, finding themselves welcomed enthusiastically by the Polish immigrants, felt that the Sisters of the Resurrection would be excellent collaborators in the work of educating the women in the parish and the children in the parish schools. In December of 1899, the new Superior General, the Rev. Paul Smolikowski, with the Rev. John Kasprzycki, C.R., came to Mother Celine in Rome with an insistent plea to send sisters to staff the school in the new parish of St. Mary of the Angels in Chicago. The Archbishop of Chicago, Monsignor Patrick Feehan, had given permission for them to teach in the archdiocese.

On February 2, 1900, four Sisters of the Resurrection arrived at St. Mary's. The four pioneers sent by Mother Celine were Sister **Anne Strzelecka**, Sister Matylda Surrey, Sister Casimira Szydzik, and Sister Sophie Podworska. The huge building of St. Mary's included the temporary church, school classrooms, and the nuns' living quarters. The sisters immediately began preparations for their apostolic ministry in the parish school. Under the direction of the pastor, the Rev. Francis Gordon, C.R., preparations proceeded briskly and efficiently with a definite American tempo.

On February 19, 1900, the sisters opened the parish school. The first day, 425 children were enrolled in grades one through eight. Several grade levels of students were assigned to each of the four classrooms. The sisters not only faced the challenge of the large numbers of students in each class, but also that of learning a new language, a new curriculum, and adapting to a new culture. Within a month of the arrival of the first nuns in Chicago, Sister Anne Strzelecka wrote to Mother Celine in Rome requesting more sisters to meet the needs of the school and parish. Sister Laura Jezewska, experienced in pedagogical methods, arrived with Sister Caroline Klenart in August 1900, bringing new energy, interest, and enthusiasm to the pioneers. Additional help for the school came from the young women living in America who joined the sisters in living community life and were accepted into the Congregation. Though young and inexperienced in religious life as well as in teaching, they had one advantage. They knew American children, their virtues and their faults. In September 1901, the Resurrectionist nuns opened their second mission in the city to serve Polish immigrants on the southwest side of Chicago at the Church of St. Casimir. The Rev. Albert Furman, the pastor, directed the work of the sisters. Four more nuns arrived from Poland to meet the rapid enrollment in grades one

through eight. The sisters gave special care and concern to the poorest families in the parish and everything was done to give financial help to those in need. Inspired by the ideal of raising the status of women, Sister Anne Strzelecka brought the mothers of the school children together into a Women's Auxiliary to support the ministry of the nuns.

The rapid expansion of the Congregation and its wide-reaching activities soon caused Mother Celine to fear that the rapid increase in numbers in the community might have a detrimental influence on their religious life, especially in America. In an effort to strengthen the community's spiritual bonds, in 1902 Mother Celine and Mother Hedwig visited the United States. During a second visitation in 1909 Mother Celine worked with the nuns, teaching them music and even directing their instruction in foreign languages. Candidates to the religious life began to apply in increasing numbers and the American nuns pointed out the need for a novitiate in Chicago. Mother Celine and Mother Hedwig preferred to train and form the American postulants in Rome or Kęty. After much discussion, permission was finally given to establish a canonical novitiate in Chicago. On December 17, 1906, the first convent of the Sisters of the Resurrection was blessed and dedicated, located directly across from St. Mary of the Angels Church. It became the novitiate and central home of the community.

For the next five years, the apostolate focused on the development of schools in Polish parishes. Invitations, requests, and pleas came from clergy and Polish immigrants themselves, asking for nuns to teach in their parish schools. In 1906 the sisters opened a new mission in Chicago Heights, a suburb south of Chicago, which enrolled 250 children in its school. The following year the sisters were called to their first mission in the eastern part of the United States, in Schenectady, NY. The eastern mission expanded to include schools in Yonkers (NY) and Stamford (CT) in 1910 and New York City in (1913). At St. Mary Clemens in New York City, children of every race and nationality studied and learned in harmony.

The community also accepted work in rural areas. In 1908 three nuns were sent to Cracow, NE, at the request of immigrants who, with the pastor, were all from the same part of Poland. The convent and the parish school were located on a large farm, with the number of students varying with the seasons and the work needed on the family farm. There was also a boarding school for children who lived at a distance. The sisters catechized after school and on Saturdays in neighboring parishes, and soon expanded their teaching to the neighboring parishes of Silver Creek, Genoa, and Fullerton. A few years later, Resurrectionists appeared in Chojnice (NE) and Warsaw (ND). In the latter state rural public schools sometimes employed nuns. However, in this period the state of North Dakota had an "Anti-Garb Law" which prohibited the wearing of habits. Thus, nuns teaching in the public schools wore secular dress.

In consideration of the increase in activities in the United States, Mother Celine decided to appoint Sister Helen Kowalewska, mistress of the novitiate in Kęty, as delegate over all the homes in the United States. For an assistant, she nominated Sister Mary Zubylewicz, the superior in Kęty. Sister Helen remained in America from 1904 until her death in 1924. A highly cultured person, deeply spiritual and educated, she endeavored to raise the intellectual and moral standards in the schools. She organized educational courses for the sisters, visited the schools, wrote magazine articles, and composed short school dramas that were popular with the children. Sister Mary strengthened the religious spirit of the nuns.

Sister Anne's vision of expanding the community's apostolate in education included opening a private high school for girls. In 1912, the community purchased land in Norwood Park, a neighborhood of farmlands outside the city of Chicago. In 1915, Resurrection Academy was built on the grounds and opened its doors as an elementary school with a limited number of boarders. The Academy developed in enrollment and grade levels and, in 1922, Resurrection High School in Norwood Park welcomed its first students. Fourteen young women enrolled and four seniors graduated in 1926. Enrollment steadily increased, and by the middle of the 1970s reached 1,500. In 2009 it remains one of the finest high schools on the northwest side of Chicago.

In 1927, the Sisters began teaching at the two year Commercial High School founded by St. Casimir Parish. Located on the southwest side of Chicago, the neighborhood consisted of a dense population of Polish families. The new school was a great success. It offered professional training for young girls, which in turn meant jobs and work and much needed financial help for the immigrant families. The community also staffed the elementary school with forty-five nuns, teaching 2,500 pupils by 1929. In the years between 1900 and 1930, the Congregation founded, staffed, and managed parish schools across the United States. To facilitate the organization and direction of the apostolic ministry of the sisters, the homes and ministries of the Congregation in the United States were divided into the Immaculate Conception Province in Chicago and the St. Joseph Province in Castleton, New York.

In 1930, the Chicago Province opened a mission in Kewanee, Wisconsin, at the request of the pastor. Two years later it also staffed schools in North Creek and Arcadia, as well as parishes in Indiana. The province expanded to the South when it accepted the invitation of the bishop of Mobile, Alabama, to take over St. Magdalene School, a three room building in an abandoned factory in Tuscaloosa. Eighty-seven children, mostly Baptists, were enrolled, but all studied religion and attended religious functions. In 1958 the province established a high school in Panama City, Florida.

Following World War II more specialized institutions emerged. In 1947, both Provinces cooperated to establish the Mother Celine House of Studies in Harrison, New York. A first in the Sister Formation Movement, it was affiliated with Fordham University to provide professional training for the young Sisters needed to prepare them for their future ministry in education. The eastern province opened a catechetical center in Greenwich, Connecticut, in 1956. The following year, another such center was established in Herkimer, New York, which later became a parish school. In 1957 the St. Joseph Province assumed the administration and staff of Maria Regina, the new diocesan high school for girls in Westchester County.

During the postwar era, the sisters of the Chicago Province spread to suburban Chicago. They staffed the new school of St. Bede in Fox Lake and Queen of the Rosary in Elk Grove Village. They also expanded their work in rural areas such as St. Peter and Clarke, Nebraska. Reaching out increasingly to non–Catholics, in 1962 four sisters went to the second parish of the Resurrection Fathers in Panama City, Florida, Our Lady of Grace. This was a small, poor school for black children, not many of them Catholic. The children were taught during the school day and the adults in evening classes. Adult education offered information on finance, nutrition, insurance, and other practical subjects. The nuns also offered tutoring to parents to acquire skills in reading, English, and mathematics.

In 1963, the Sisters from the eastern province went to Vancouver, Canada, to collaborate with the Oblate Fathers in their apostolic ministry among the Polish immigrants living there. The nuns taught in the parish school of St. Casimir and actively engaged in the full life of the parish. They directed the choir, organized the sodality and clubs for women, and helped with the celebrations of all the liturgical functions and traditional Polish events.

In 1976, the Chicago Province sent three Sisters to work with the Franciscan Fathers (see **Franciscan Friars Minor Conventual, Order of**) and Brothers in St. Anthony Parish in Parma, Ohio. In addition to teaching in the parish school and in the Confraternity of Christian Doctrine (CCD) program, they also worked with the Franciscan brothers visiting the sick and the elderly in the nursing homes and retirement centers within the parish. A number of the residents in these homes were old Polish immigrants who enjoyed the opportunity to converse with someone in their native language.

In the beginning, the apostolate of the sisters in the parish schools was directed basically to the children and through them and because of them, to their parents and family members. After the 1960s, lay teachers were added to the staff of the parish schools. Enrollment grew in the schools and additional sisters were not available to meet the need. The nuns became the means of forming and maintaining an integrated faculty. Parents were better educated and contributed constructively to the school community. Parish school boards were formed with the sisters, clergy, and laity working together to form school policies and to participate in decisions concerning the school, but the sisters continued to play a central role in the parish school. In the last quarter of the century, the population grew in the cities and suburbs, but decreased in the rural areas, especially among the younger generation. Modern consolidated schools established by the public school districts led to decreased enrollments in the parish schools. To meet this challenge, the dioceses organized programs for the religious instruction of children in public schools which replaced the catechetical centers. Founded in parishes that served predominantly Polish ancestry, the schools also experienced racial and ethnic population change from the original Polish character of many of the neighborhoods the nuns originally served. Although nuns still staffed parish schools, though in limited numbers, the Sisters began to focus more of their efforts on maintaining high schools for girls, regardless of ethnic background.—*M. Edward Gyra*

Sources: Dorota Praszałowicz, "Polish American Sisterhood: The Americanization Process," *U.S. Catholic Historian*, Vol. 27, no. 3 (2009), 45–57; Teresa Florczak, C.R., *The Double Knot: Sisters of the Resurrection* (Sisters of the Resurrection, 2002); Gilla Vincenzo Gremini, M.S.C., *Celine Borzecka, Foundress of the Sisters of the Resurrection of Our Lord Jesus Christ* (Sisters of the Resurrection, 1953); John Iwicki, C.R., *Resurrectionist Charism: A History of the Congregation of the Resurrection* (Rome: Tipografia Poliglotta della

Pontificia Università Gregoriana, 1986), 3 Vols; Teresa Kalkstein, *Witness to the Resurrection: The Servant of God Mother Celina Borzecka Foundress of the Congregation of the Resurrection of Our Lord Jesus Christ* (Castleton-on-Hudson, NY: Sisters of the Resurrection, 1967); Sr. Mary Catherine, "Mother Celine Borzęcka CR, Foundress of the Resurrection Sisters," *Polish American Studies*, Vol. 10, no. 3–4 (1953), 95–103; Sister Ligoria, "Mother Hedwig Borzęcka CR, Co-Foundress of the Resurrection Sisters," *Polish American Studies*, Vol. 10, no. 3–4 (1953), 103–111.

Reszke *see* **de Reszke.**

Rey, Nicholas A. (Mikołaj Andrzej Rey; b. Warsaw, Poland, January 23, 1938; d. Georgetown, District of Columbia, January 13, 2009). Diplomat. Rey was not yet two years old when his parents fled Poland in the wake of the German invasion in 1939, hiding, with the full knowledge and assistance of U.S. Ambassador Anthony J. Drexel, among a convoy of U.S. diplomats who left via Austria. Escaping to the United States, the family became citizens in 1946. After earning degrees from Princeton and Johns Hopkins Universities, he rose to become managing director with the firms Merrill Lynch and Bear Stearns. In 1990 he was named vice chair and director of the Polish-American Enterprise Fund, a $240 million U.S. government program designed to stimulate private enterprise in Poland. President Bill Clinton appointed him U.S. ambassador to Poland in 1993, a position he held until 1997, being involved in supporting the entry of Poland into NATO. Following his service as ambassador, he was active in Democratic Party politics, and was a cofounder in 2003 of the American Polish Advisory Council (APAC), an organization of Polish-Americans whose mission it was to lobby on behalf of Poland.—*Edward L. Rowny*

SOURCE: Robert Strybel, "Ambassador Nicholas Rey Fondly Remembered," *Polish American Journal*, Vol. 98, no. 2 (February 2009), 19.

Rhode, Paul Peter (b. Wejherowo, Poland, September 18, 1871; d. Green Bay, Wisconsin, March 3, 1945). Bishop, Polonia leader. Rhode came to America at the age of nine with his mother, the family settling in Chicago. He later studied philosophy and theology at St. Francis Seminary near Milwaukee and was ordained a priest in 1894. In 1908, he was consecrated an auxiliary bishop for the Archdiocese of Chicago after having served some twelve years as pastor at St. Michael's Parish on the city's far south side. His elevation made Rhode the first Polish bishop in the United States. His selection followed a strenuous campaign led by the Rev. **Wacław Kruszka** of Milwaukee to persuade the Church hierarchy to appoint bishops of Polish origin to serve the needs of the large, rapidly growing, and sometimes troubled Polish community. Rhode remained auxiliary bishop in Chicago until 1915 when he was appointed bishop of the diocese of Green Bay, Wisconsin, an office he held until his death. Rhode was active in the life of the Polish community throughout the country and took very seriously his duty to serve as a responsible and concerned church leader far beyond the Archdiocese of Chicago. He was a founder of the Polish Priests' Association in the United States and served as honorary national chaplain of the **Polish Roman Catholic Union** of America fraternal. Rhode was prominent in **Polonia** patriotic organizations in World War I, most notably as Honorary Chairman of the **Polish National Council** and was especially visible in humanitarian efforts in Polonia on behalf of the

Polish people, during the War and after. Historian Andrzej Brożek summed up Rhode's core beliefs about the Polish people in America as follows: preservation of the Polish Catholic tradition in the U.S. and commitment to the Poles' active participation in American life; and opposition (in the 1930s) to both **Polonia**'s involvement in Poland's internal political affairs and the idea that Poland had a duty to enlighten and teach Polish Americans about their responsibilities as U.S. citizens. He was succeeded as Bishop of Green Bay, with but one exception, by clergymen of Polish origin in the decades after his passing: by Stanislaus Bona (1945–1967), Aloysius Wycislo (1968–1983), **Joseph Maida**, later Archbishop of Detroit (1984–1990), and David Zubik (since 2003). The one exception in this line was Bishop Joseph Banks (1990–2003).—*Donald E. Pienkos*

SOURCES: Donald E. Pienkos, *For Your Freedom Through Ours: Polish American Efforts on Poland's Behalf, 1863–1991* (Boulder, CO: East European Monographs, 1991); Andrzej Brożek, *Polish Americans 1854–1939* (Warsaw: Interpress, 1985).

Rodziński, Artur (b. Split, Dalmatia, January 1, 1892; d. Boston, Massachusetts, November 27, 1958). Musician, conductor. Rodziński studied music in Lwów before moving to Vienna where he enrolled in both law and music programs. He was wounded in action during World War I and after his discharge returned to Lwów where he accepted a position as chorus master at the city Opera House. In 1920 he debuted as conductor of Verdi's *Ernani*, and in the following year moved to Warsaw where he was employed as conductor of the Warsaw Philharmonic Orchestra. There, Leopold Stokowski heard Rodziński conduct Wagner's *Die Meistersinger von Nürnberg* and invited him to conduct the Philadelphia Orchestra. Rodziński accepted and, as Stokowski's assistant, conducted in the Philadelphia Grand Opera from 1925 to 1929. In the latter year he assumed the position of conductor of the Los Angeles Philharmonic Orchestra, and in 1933 moved to the same post with the Cleveland Orchestra (1933–43) where he led the Orchestra in a series of popular recordings on Columbia Records and was credited with turning the Cleveland Orchestra into one of the finest in the nation. During this time he also performed occasionally with the New York Philharmonic Orchestra, the NBC Symphony Orchestra, and the Vienna Philharmonic Orchestra. In 1943 Rodziński became conductor of the New York Philharmonic Orchestra where he also continued recording for Columbia Records and hosted a popular weekly broadcast on CBS radio, but in 1947 left to become conductor of the

Nicholas A. Rey, U.S. Ambassador to Poland (*OLS*).

Bishop Paul Rhode, the first Polish American elevated to the rank of bishop (*PMA*).

Artur Rodziński with an admirer (*JPI*).

Chicago Symphony Orchestra. He left Chicago after one year and returned to Europe in failing health, but continued to perform in appearances with various European orchestras and to record for Westminister Records. In 1958 he returned to Chicago to conduct for the Lyric Opera Company, but died later that fall.—*James S. Pula*

SOURCES: Halina Rodziński, *Our Two Lives* (New York: Charles Scribner's Sons, 1976); Kazimierz Wierzyński, "Artur Rodziński (1892–1958): Tribute of a Friend," *The Polish Review*, Vol. V, no. 2 (1960), 3–7; obituary, *Los Angeles Times*, November 28, 1958.

Rogalski, Bernard B. (b. Jackson, Michigan, May 20, 1918; Jackson, Michigan, October 27, 1994). Polonia activist. The son of an organizer of local Nest 336 of the **Polish Falcons** Alliance in 1912, Rogalski served in the U.S. Navy in World War II after which he found employment as a tool and die designer with Hancock Industries. In 1959 and 1960, Rogalski set records in recruiting new insured fraternal members into the Falcons. He was recognized as the Falcons' "champion sales person" and elected its vice president at PFA's 1960 convention in Newark, New Jersey. In 1968 he was appointed the Falcons' national field manager with the mission of promoting its insurance sales, in 1972 he was elected PFA national secretary and in 1980 he was elected the fraternal's national president, succeeding Walter Laska. During his first term, Rogalski also served as acting editor of the Falcons' fraternal publication, *Sokół Polski* (The Polish Falcon). During his eight year tenure as president, which coincided with the centennial of the PFA in 1987, and the publication of its first English language history, the membership and assets of the fraternal continued to rise. Rogalski was reelected president in 1984 and

two years later was also elected national secretary of the **Polish American Congress**. The outgoing, friendly and active Rogalski was universally respected as the "very embodiment of fraternalism" in the PFA and in **Polonia**.—*Donald E. Pienkos*

SOURCE: Donald E. Pienkos, *One Hundred Years Young: A History of the Polish Falcons of America, 1887–1987* (Boulder, CO: East European Monographs, 1987).

Rokosz, Stanisław (b. 1859; d. April 20, 1921). Polonia activist, labor leader. Arriving in the United States in 1885, Rokosz quickly became active in the union movement, organizing and serving as president of a meat cutters' local. Eventually gaining ownership of a saloon, he became active in the **Polish National Alliance** in 1889, co-founded *Dziennik Narodowy* (National Daily), participated in the PNA *sejms* (conventions) from 1891 to 1901, and served as vice president from 1899 to 1901. When **Franciszek H. Jabłoński** resigned in 1901, Rokosz replaced him as president, but in 1903 he was defeated for re-election by **Marian B. Stęczyński**. During World War I, Rokosz became active as a union organizer, agitating successfully among steel workers in Pittsburgh in 1919 and in the Chicago slaughterhouses in 1920. After the tragic death of **Jan Kikulski**, Rokosz replaced him as leader of the Polish and Slavic unionists. In August 1920 he was elected president of District Council Nine. On April 8, 1921 he was attacked and beaten with baseball bats on South Ashland Avenue in Chicago. He died April 20, 1921. His wife Maria was among the founders of the **Polish Women's Alliance of America**, and served as treasurer of that organization.—*Adam Walaszek*

Stanisław Rokosz, labor leader and Polonia activist (*PNA*).

SOURCES: Stanisław Osada, *Historia Związku Narodowego Polskiego* (Chicago: Polish National Alliance, 1957), Vol. 1; A. Olszewski, *Historia Związku Narodowego Polskiego* (Chicago: Polish National Alliance, [n.d.]), Vol. 3; Adam Walaszek, *Polscy robotnicy, praca i związki zawodowe w Stanach Zjednoczonych Ameryki, 1880–1922* (Wrocław: Zakład Narodowy im. Ossolińskich, 1988).

Rola Boża (God's Field). The official organ of the **Polish National Catholic Church**, *Rola Boża* was established in 1923 by Bishop **Franciszek Hodur** who served as its first editor. Although an official publication, the contents of the newspaper do not always articulate the official doctrine of the church, but contain articles and letters expressing other views as well.—*James S. Pula*

SOURCES: Casimir J. Grotnik, *An Index to Rola Boża—God's Field Volume I 1923–1953* (Scranton, PA: Polish National Catholic Church Commission on History and Archives and Bishop Hodur Biography Commission, 1989); Casimir J. Grotnik, *An Index to Rola Boża—God's Field Volume II 1954–1970* (Scranton, PA: Polish National Catholic Church Commission on History and Archives and Bishop Hodur Biography Commission, 1991).

Romanski, Janusz Wojciech (b. Warsaw, Poland, March 14, 1943; d.—). Mechanical engineer. Romański's father, a professional officer in the Polish army, died in the Warsaw Uprising of 1944. After receiving his doctorate in mechanical engineering from Gdańsk University of Technology (1978) he began a teaching career at the same institution. Migrating to the U.S., he joined the faculty of the Department of Materials Engineering at Drexel University in Philadelphia (1981–88). In 1991 the accepted a position at the Piasecki Aircraft Corporation as senior structural and materials engineer. Following this, he returned to teaching in the Department of Mechanical Engineering at Widener University in Chester, Pennsylvania (beginning in 2003). The author of over fifty scientific publications on the subject of stress and materials in application to military helicopters, he is co-author of several research projects for the U.S. Air Force and Navy. As an expert in the area of Stress and Materials, he conducted several industry and research projects on modifying and upgrading flight performance of military helicopters such as AH-1W-Cobra, AH 60-Apache, and SH-6O F Black Hawk. He has also published many articles in the Polish American press. He served as chair of the Philadelphia Chapter of the Society of Manufacturing Engineers; secretary and director of the American Helicopter Society Chapter; vice chair of the Association of Polish Engineers in the U.S. (**Polonia Technica**); a board member of the Eastern District of the **Polish American Congress**; and vice-chair of the **Polish People's University**. In recognition of his scientific and professional contributions he received the Cavalier Cross of the Order of Merit (Poland), Silver Cross of Merit (Poland), 1,000th Anniversary Medal of the City of Gdańsk, 100th Anniversary Medal of Gdańsk University of Technology, the Medal of the Polonia Technica in the U.S., the 90th Anniversary Medal from the Association of Polish Engineers in France and other awards.—*Peter J. Obst*

SOURCE: Zbigniew Piasek, ed., *Encyclopedia of World Research and Engineering Heritage of Polish Engineers in the USA, Canada, Europe, Argentina and Singapore* (Kraków: FOGRA, 2006).

Romaszkiewicz, Jan (b. Merecz, Poland, October 3, 1873; d. 1949). Polonia activist. After coming to America as a high school age youth, Romaszkiewicz completed his education in business in Boston, later working in banking. A member of the **Polish National Alliance** beginning in 1893, he was elected a vice **censor** of the Alliance at its 1907 national convention and two years later won election as a district commissioner. His activities included fund raising work on behalf of the Polish National Fund (Skarb Narodowy) and involvement in the east coast work of the Polish **National Department** (Wydzial Narodowy) during World War I. Committed to promoting the cause of Poland's independence among young people, he strongly supported close ties between the PNA and the **Polish Falcons Alliance**. He was an enthusiast of Józef Piłsudski in Poland and became active in the "opposition" faction of the PNA in the 1920s. He was elected president of the Alliance at its controversial twenty-fifth convention in Chicago's Sherman Hotel in 1927 at which the members of the "old guard" faction walked out of the conclave. A year later his election was confirmed when the delegates to a reunified PNA convened a second time on court order. Ro-

maszkiewicz was comfortably reelected president at the 1931 convention, but won by only eight votes over **Charles Rozmarek** in 1935, 260–252. Four years later and ailing, he lost to Rozmarek in Detroit, 269–262. In 1943, he faced Rozmarek again, this time as a challenger in his home town of Boston, but was routed by a 444–87 vote at the convention. Romaszkiewicz's main accomplishment in office was his creation of the PNA scouting movement, or **Harcerstwo**. Modeled after the Harcerstwo movement in Poland, the PNA effort at its peak numbered 52,000 youngsters during the 1930s and helped enliven interest in the Alliance among many in the younger, American-born generation. Romaszkiewicz's position, both in the PNA and with Harcerstwo, was increasingly weakened after 1931 by the Great Depression's deepening impact on the PNA coupled with the decline of the "opposition" faction as a political force in the fraternal. After he left office, his successor also terminated the Harcerstwo organization.—*Donald E. Pienkos*

SOURCES: Adam Olszewski, *Historia Związku Narodowego Polskiego* (Chicago: Polish National Alliance, 1957–1963); Donald E. Pienkos, *PNA: A Centennial History of the Polish National Alliance of the United States of North America* (Boulder, CO: East European Monographs, 1984).

Romatowski, Jenny (b. Wyandotte, Michigan, September 13, 1927; d.—). Softball player, field hockey player. After starring in Detroit-area fast-pitch softball competitions in her high school years, Romatowski played for nine seasons in the All American Girls Professional Baseball League, from 1946 through 1954. Over the course of her career, playing catcher, third base, and outfield for seven teams, she hit .204. In the off season, Romatowski earned a degree in physical education from Michigan State Normal School (now Eastern Michigan University), and was later elected to the EMU Athletic Hall of Fame in 2000. Her final season of 1954 was also her best, as her Kalamazoo team won the last AAGPBL championship while she was named the All-Star catcher for the year. After the Girls League shut down, Romatowski took up field hockey, and became a member of the U.S. national team and touring all-star teams in the 1950s and 1960s. She also taught school for more than thirty years in suburban Detroit before retiring to Florida. Romatowski was inducted into the **National Polish-American Sports Hall of Fame** in 1999, the only female baseball player so honored. She appeared briefly in the popular 1992 film *A League of Their Own* that was based on the theme of the AAGPBL.—*Neal Pease*

SOURCE: W. C. Madden, *The Women of the All-American Girls Professional Baseball League: A Biographical Dictionary* (Jefferson, NC: McFarland, 1997).

Rompala, Mary Jerome (b. Chicago, Illinois, March 10, 1919; d. Chicago, Illinois, April 2, 1999). Catholic nun. One of the outstanding educators in the Immaculate Conception Province of the Congregation of the **Sisters of the Resurrection**, Rompala was baptized Martha Mary Rompala. When Martha was in the seventh grade she already knew that she wanted to be a nun. After finishing eighth grade at St. Mary of the Angels School, she went to Resurrection High School, entered the novitiate in 1937, and professed final vows in 1943. She then became known as Sister Mary Jerome. She was destined to have a long and fruitful career in education. Beginning in 1938 she taught in several elementary schools in Chicago and in 1950, the same year she earned a baccalaureate degree in education from DePaul University, she was assigned to teach English and journalism at Resurrection High School. She spent the next 34 years sharing her expertise with hundreds of students. She was advisor or moderator for many student organizations, including the school newspaper, *The Res Banner*, and was also advisor for the school yearbook for ten years. Both of these publications won numerous awards and acclamations over the years. In 1961 she earned an M.A. degree from the University of Notre Dame. Her activity in journalism led to election as vice president of the Illinois State Press Association (1972–73). Because Sister Mary Jerome spoke Polish fluently, her talent in this field was utilized many times. She was the official translator at a congregational assembly held in Lake Placid, New York, in 1983. She translated the proceedings of the general chapter of the Congregation held in Rome in 1986, and when the fall of Communism made contact with Poland easier in 1991 she traveled there with a group of nuns and served as translator. In 1984 she left Resurrection High School to spend more time translating Congregational materials. She was actively involved in many community endeavors, served as an office assistant at St. Casimir High School for four years, and later served at the Information desk at Our Lady of the Resurrection Medical Center for about ten years.—*Mary Edward Gira*

SOURCE: Sister Mary Barbara Sniegowski, Eulogy, April 5, 1999, congregation archives.

Rosary Hour. The Rosary Hour was a weekly religious program that has been broadcast in the Polish language over a radio network that extended into much of the United States and Canada. The program had its origin in 1926 when the Kolipinski Brothers Furniture Company sponsored a half-hour Polish Variety Program on radio station

Jan Romaszkiewicz, creator of the Polish National Alliance scouting movement (*PNA*).

WEBR in Buffalo, New York. At that time, the St. Anthony Province of the Conventional Franciscans maintained its headquarters in that city. The Franciscan provincial, the Rev. **Justin Figas**, O.F.M., Conv., agreed to make a guest appearance on the radio program. Due to an overwhelmingly positive response, the program sponsors persuaded the Rev. Figas to become a regular contributor. Shortly thereafter, "Father Justin," as he was universally called, initiated his own program which he called "The Rosary Hour." Based on its success in the Buffalo market, Fr. Justin established the Rosary Hour Network in 1931. In its first year, the Rosary Hour Network carried Fr. Justin's program to markets in Buffalo, Chicago, Detroit, Pittsburgh, Scranton and Cleveland. By 1959, the network had expanded to include 79 radio stations in fourteen states and Canada, and reached an estimated weekly audience of five million listeners. In 1964, the Network received more than 80,000 letters from its listeners. Although the number of affiliated states has since declined, the Rosary Hour has expanded to offer access over the internet and on cassette and compact disk.

The Rev. Figas directed the Rosary Hour Network for 28 years during which he produced more than 750 programs. After Father Justin's death in 1959, the Rev. Cornelian Dende assumed the position of director, continuing in that capacity until 1996. Subsequent directors have included the Rev. Marion Tolczyk and the Rev. Wladek Mezyk. The Rosary Hour is produced at its headquarters in Athol Springs, New York, although the program has occasionally incorporated taped segments such as remarks by Pope John Paul II. In its original format, the program included a twenty-five minute talk by the director, a question and answer segment, and religious songs by visiting choirs. The Rosary Hour would then conclude with benediction and a singing of the traditional Polish hymn, *Boże Coś Polskę* (God, Protector of Poland). During the 1990s the Rosary Hour format changed from an hour long program that was produced for eight months, into a half-hour program that was produced throughout the year.—*Carl L. Bucki*

SOURCES: Stanisław Hajkowski, "Father Justyn and the Rosary Hour," *U.S. Catholic Historian*, Vol. 27, no. 3 (2009), 59–82; "Founding of Father Justin Rosary Hour to be Noted," *Buffalo Courier Express*, July 21, 1968, 37; Milton J. Kobielski, ed., *Millennium of Christianity of the Polish People: 966–1966* (Buffalo: Millennium Committee of the Diocese of Buffalo, 1966).

Rose, Ernestine Potocka (b. Piotrków, Russian-occupied Poland, January 13, 1810; d. Brighton, England, August 4, 1892). Women's rights activist. Growing up as the daughter of a strict Orthodox rabbi, Potocka came to resent the limitations placed on women both within her father's religion and in the context of early nineteenth century East European society. As a result, she became rebellious in her youth and as an adult was disaffected from religion while actively attempting to further the cause of women's rights. In 1827, at the age of seventeen, she left for Berlin, but finding little opportunity there she moved on to Holland, Belgium, and then Paris where she met and became a supporter of Adam Mickiewicz and the Polish revolutionary movement headquartered among the Polish exiles in the French capital. Frustrated in an attempt to return to Poland with the revolutionaries, she next moved to London where she came under the influence of Robert Owen's utopian socialism. She became active in Owen's movement, learned enough English to become a speaker at meetings, and married fellow Owenite William E. Rose. The couple moved to New York in 1836 where Ernestine Rose became active in several of the social reform movements of the day including education, temperance, abolitionism, and women's rights. For her own special cause she selected the issue of women's legal rights. At the time, when a woman married the husband legally became the owner of any and all of her property, she had no legal say in the raising of the children, she could not sign contracts, could not sue in court without her husband's permission, and was otherwise treated as if she did not exist in the eyes of the law. Eleanor Flexner, historian of the women's rights movement in America, concluded that Rose was "one of the first women to try to improve the position of her

Ernestine Potocka Rose, responsible for the first married woman's property law in the U.S. (*PMA*).

sex through legislative action." Her major achievement was leading the movement that resulted in the New York State legislature adopting, in 1848, the first law in the nation guaranteeing women the right to own their own property within marriage. Rose attended the first and succeeding national women's rights conventions, took on in public debate the venerable liberal Horace Mann who had argued against women's right to vote, went on several national lecture tours, and continued to be in the forefront of those advocating full civil and political rights for women. In 1869 she returned with her husband to England, but visited the U.S. and remained an active voice for women's rights until her death.—*James S. Pula*

SOURCES: James S. Pula, "'Not as a Gift of Charity'—Enrestine Potocka Rose and the Married Woman's Property Laws," *Polish American Studies*, Vol. 58, no. 2 (2001), 33–73; Yuri Suhl, *Ernestine L. Rose and the Battle for Human Rights* (New York: Reynal & Company, 1959); Carol A. Kolmerten, *The American Life of Ernestine L. Rose* (Syracuse, NY: Syracuse University Press, 1999).

Rosen, John de *see* **de Rosen, John.**

Rosenstiel, Blanka A. (Blanka Aldona Wdowiak; b. Warsaw, Poland, 1929; d.—). Polonia activist. Following World War II, she studied art in Brussels, Belgium. In 1956 she moved to the United States where she married Lewis S. Rosenstiel, Chairman of Schenley Industries, a great humanitarian and philanthropist, in 1967. Widowed in 1976, she divided her time between Miami Beach during the winter season and her home at Blandemar Farm in Charlottesville, Virginia, in the summer. Noted for her avid interest in the arts, dedication to helping young artists, and desire to promote Poland's heritage while fostering culture in her American homeland, in 1972 she established the **American Institute of Polish Culture**, Inc. (AIPC) in Miami. The Institute shares with the American society the rich heritage of Poland and also serves as a center of educational facilities and resources for the encouragement and promotion of scientific and aesthetic endeavors of Americans of Polish descent. She participated in, organized and/or sponsored hundreds of concerts, lectures, seminars, poetry readings, radio and television programs, book signing parties and a Polish Film of the Month series. She conceptualized and sponsored two traveling exhibitions—a 60-panel exhibition titled "The Polish Perspective," which was inaugurated at Duke University and traveled to more than one hundred American universities, and "Polish Music Today" featuring musical scores of eleven contemporary Polish composers on 26 panels. She has also helped to bring contemporary Polish filmmakers and their work to the Miami International Film Festival. In 2004 she also produced a documentary about the Warsaw Uprising titled *Honor of the City*, which was distributed free of charge to American schools, libraries, organizations, and individuals. She helped establish the Kościuszko Chair of Polish Studies at the University of Virginia in 1998, which has since been transferred to the Institute of World Politics in Washington, D.C. She established the Harriet Irsay Scholarship which awards ten to fifteen grants each year to talented students, preferably of Polish descent. The scholarships are awarded to students majoring in fields such as journalism, communication, education, film, history, international relations, liberal arts, Polish studies, or public relations. She also sponsors several students each year to take part in summer courses at universities in Poland.

Rosenstiel initiated translation and publication of more than twenty books, including the five volume history of Poland *Saga of a Nation* by Pawel Jasienica and the rare *Accomplished Senator* by Wawrzyniec Grzymała Goślicki (1530–1607). The annual magazine *Good News* is sent to all members and distributed to interested parties during the year. She has presided over the annual International Polonaise Ball, Christmas and Easter celebrations, and poetry evenings which serve as fund-raising events. In 1977, she established the Chopin Foundation of the United States, a national organization dedicated to helping young American musicians and promoting Chopin's music in the United States through concerts, television projects, publication of *Polonaise* magazine, and international exchange programs for musicians and musicologists. Regionally, the Foundation operates through its Councils, which are now active in Miami, New York, and San Francisco. Every five years, the Chopin Foundation organizes the National American Chopin Piano Competition in Miami for American pianists. Apart from substantial cash prizes, the four top winners are sent to Warsaw, Poland, to officially represent the United States in the prestigious International Chopin Piano Competition. In 1984, at a National Convention held in Washington, D.C., Rosenstiel was elected president of the American Council for Polish Culture, a national body with more than forty member organizations. She held this post for two years and initiated, among others things, the establishment of an American Center for Polish Culture in Washington, D.C. In 1998 she was appointed an Honorary Consul of the Republic of Poland.

Among her many honors are a Doctor of Humane Letters, *Honoris Causa*, from **Alliance College** (1976); an American Council of Polish Cultural Clubs National Award (1978), a National Humanitarian Award from the National Advocates Society and **National Medical and Dental Association** (1981); and Ambassadors Award from **St. Mary's College** in Orchard Lake, MI (1981); a Miami Ballet Society Humanitarian Award (1983); a National Parkinson Foundation Humanitarian Award (1983); an American Council of Polish Cultural Clubs Award (1984); Lady of the Sovereign Order of St. John of Jerusalem, Knights of Malta (1984); an Am-Pol Eagle National Citizen of the Year Award (1985); a Florida International University Society of Founders Award (1989); a Greater Miami Youth Symphony Award (1994); an Ellis Island Medal of Honor (1995); the Cavalier's Cross of Polonia Restituta Order (1996); the Jose Marti Medal (1998); the Polish Commander's Cross of the Order of Merit (2004); and the Gloria Artis Medal (2007).—*Włodek Lopaczynski*

SOURCE: Bolesław Wierzbiański, *Who's Who in Polish America* (New York: Bicentennial Publishing Corp., 1996), 386–87.

Rosienkiewicz, Martin (Marcin Rosienkiewicz; b. Wołyń region, Poland, date unknown; d. Cincinnati, Ohio, 1847). Educator, Polonia activist. A professor at the Polish

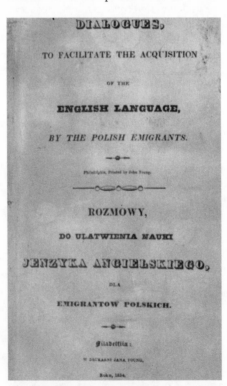

Cover of the first English language instruction book for Polish immigrants published in America by Marcin Rosienkiewicz, Philadelphia, 1834 (*PMA*).

lyceum in Krzemieniec, he supported the November Uprising (1830-31) resulting in his exile to America where he arrived in 1834. One of six people elected to a committee by the exiles to speak on their behalf, he was one of three chosen to go to Washington, D.C., to represent the exiles before Congress and was generally recognized as the group leader. When it became apparent that the exiles could not all remain in New York, Rosienkiewicz led a group of about thirty to Philadelphia where, with the financial assistance of a local group of American supporters, in 1934 he established the first English school for Polish immigrants in Philadelphia. Rosienkiewicz also published in 1834 an English-Polish conversational handbook which is generally considered the first Polish language book published in America. Following the closing of the school, he continued to teach English and French.—*James S. Pula*

SOURCES: Ladislas John Siekaniec, *The Polish Contribution to Early American Education, 1608–1865* (San Francisco: R & E Research Associates, 1976); M. Theodosetta (Lewandowska), "The Poles in Philadelphia to 1914," *Polish American Studies*, Vol. VIII, no. 1 (1951), 12–20; M. Ligouri Pakowska, "The First Polish Book Printed in the United States," *Polish American Studies*, Vol. V, no. 1 (1948), 1–7.

Rostenkowski, Daniel David "Dan," "Rosti" (b. Chicago, Illinois, January 2, 1928; d. Genoa City, Wisconsin, August 11, 2010). Congressman. From a Polish family, he apparently used the last name "Rosten" while in high school in an attempt to be assimilated. But when he entered politics at the age of 24 he went back to his ethnic last name. He graduated from St. John's Military Academy in 1946 and attended Loyola University. He served with the U.S. Army infantry in Korea (1946–48) before being elected to the state House of Representatives in 1952. He was a delegate to the Illinois State Democratic Convention every four years beginning in 1952, and a delegate to the Democratic National Conventions in 1960, 1964, 1968, 1972, and 1976. He served in the state Senate (1954–56), and was then elected as a Democrat to the Eighty-sixth and the seventeen succeeding Congresses (January 3, 1959–January 3, 1995). Unsuccessful in a bid for reelection to the One Hundred Fourth Congress, he was dogged by charges of political corruption for allowing the relatively unknown Republican Michael Flanagan to serve for one term. He was chair of the Committee on Ways and Means (Ninety-seventh through One Hundred Third Congresses) and the Joint Committee on Taxation (Ninety-seventh through One Hundred First Congresses). Rostenkowski, one of the most powerful figures on Capitol Hill in his position as Chairman

Congressman Daniel Rostenkowski with President John F. Kennedy (*PMA*).

of the Ways and Means Committee (1981–95), presided over a district on Chicago's North Side designed for him. Resident in a city that values local politics, he retained his alderman position when he was in Congress. Rostenkowski had at times been mentioned as a possible mayor or, nationally, as Speaker of the House. His home district encompassed diverse ethnicities, including Polish American neighborhoods ranged around St. Stanislaus Kostka Church near Pulaski Park. Not an ideologue, but a believer in the institutional process, he concentrated on getting things done. Gruff, old-fashioned, he purveyed typical Illinois partisan Congressional politics. But after serving 36 years in Congress, Rostenkowski pled guilty to two of seventeen charges of corruption and was convicted of payroll padding and use of government allowances for private purchases. He served approximately a year in a minimum security prison, not permitting any friends or relatives to visit him there. His papers are at the Loyola University in Chicago.—*Frederick J. Augustyn*

SOURCES: *Biographical Directory of the United States Congress, 1774–Present* (http://bioguide.congress.gov/); Richard E. Cohen, *Rostenkowski: The Pursuit of Power and the End of Old Politics* (Chicago: Ivan R. Dee, 1999); James L. Merriner, *Mr. Chairman: Power in Dan Rostenkowski's America* (Carbondale, IL: Southern Illinois University Press, 1999); Randall Straham, *Dan Rostenkowski: A Study in Congressional Power* (Washington, D.C.: Congressional Quarterly Press, 1993); Randall Straham, *Reed and Rostenkowski: Congressional Leadership in Institutional Times* (Armonk, NY: M.E. Sharpe, 1992).

Rostenkowski, Piotr (b. Tucholski district, Poland, October 1868; d. Chicago, Illinois, June 17, 1936). Polonia activist, politician. Rostenkowski came to America as a child with his parents, settling first in Stevens Point, Wisconsin. At age eighteen, he relocated to Chicago where he became involved in real estate and mortgage lending activities

on the city's near north side **Polonia** district dominated by St. Stanislaus Kostka parish. With his younger brother Albert, later a successful politician himself, Rostenkowski organized the St. Joseph Credit Union and became active in the **Polish Roman Catholic Union** of America (PRCUA). From 1913 to 1917 he was elected national president of the PRCUA; he later served as the fraternal's treasurer. During World War I, Rostenkowski was a leader in the **Polish Central Relief Committee** and a founder of the Polish **National Department**; in 1926 he received the *Polonia Restituta* medal from **Ignacy Jan Paderewski** for his many services to Poland. Rostenkowski was active in the Democratic Party in his district and in 1912 was a delegate to the Democratic Party national convention where Woodrow Wilson was nominated to run for president. Rostenkowski and his wife Katarzyna, née Giersch, became heads of a family of politicians. Their son Joseph, known as "Joe Rosty," was active in local politics from an early age and in 1930 was elected to the Illinois State legislature. In 1931 he won office as Alderman of Chicago's 32nd ward and later

Piotr Rostenkowski, politician and Polonia activist (*OLS*).

became the ward's Committeeman, in the process defeating the political boss in the district, **Stanley Kunz**, Chicago's first Polish American in the U.S. House of Representatives. For his loyalty to the Democratic Party political machine of Mayor Richard J. Daley, he was rewarded with a lifetime city job; in 1958, Mayor Daley slated his son, **Daniel Rostenkowski**, to be the party's candidate for a seat in the House of Representatives from Chicago's near north side.—*Donald E. Pienkos*

SOURCES: John Radzilowski, *The Eagle and the Cross: A History of the Polish Roman Catholic Union of America* (Boulder, CO: East European Monographs, 2003); Edward Kantowicz, Polish American Politics in Chicago (Chicago: University of Chicago Press, 1978); Richard E. Cohen, *Rostenkowski: The Pursuit of Power and the End of the Old Politics* (Chicago: Ivan Dee, 1999).

Roszak, Theodore (b. Poznań, Poland, May 1, 1907; d. New York, New York, September, 2, 1981). Sculptor, graphic artist. After emigrating with his family to Chicago at the age of two, he was educated at the School of the Art Institute of Chicago, the National Academy of Design, and in private study with George Luks. He also pursued courses in logic and philosophy at Columbia University (1926). During World War II he worked at the Brewster Aeronautical Corporation, Newark, NJ. Beginning a teaching career part-time at the Art Institute of Chicago, he soon became a full-time instructor of drawing and lithography (1927–28) before moving to the Laboratory School of Industrial Design in New York (1938–40). During World War II he taught at the Stevens Institute of Technology, Hoboken, NJ, then served on the faculty of Sarah Lawrence College (1941–55). Roszak had solo exhibitions at galleries in Albany (NY), Chicago, Fort Lauderdale, Los Angeles, Madsion (WI), Minneapolis, New York, Paris (France), San Francisco, Waterville (ME), Wichita (KS), and Youngstown (OH). His works also appeared in numerous group exhibitions throughout the U.S. In addition to his artistic works, he authored "Some Problems of Modern Sculpture" in *Magazine of Art* (1949) and *In Pursuit of an Image* (1955). He was a member of the Advisory Board of the National Committee of Arts and Government (1956–58); U.S. Delegate to International Art Council Congress, Vienna Austria (1960–61); Advisory Committee on Cultural Presentation Program, U.S. State Department, Washington, D.C. (1961–67); Board of Trustees, Tiffany Foundation (1962); Board of Governors, Skowhegan School of Painting and Sculpture, Maine (1962); Fine Arts Commission, Washington, D.C. (1962–66); Delegate and Participant on Higher Education in American Republics, Lima, Peru (1964); National Institute of Arts and Letters, New York (1964–65); Charter Member, Drawing Society (1965); Fine Arts Commission, New York (1969–75); Board of Trustees, American Academy in Rome, Italy (1970–72). His honors include the National Art Contest for Public Schools by the *Chicago Herald-Examiner* (1920); American Traveling Fellowship from the Art Institute of Chicago to visit East Coast museums and practice lithography in Woodstock, NY (1927–28); Anna Louise Raymond Fellowship for European Study to spend eighteen months in Europe: Prague (attended Exhibition of Contemporary Culture in Brno, Czechoslovakia), Paris, Italy, Austria, Germany (1929–30); Silver Medal from the Tenth National Exhibition, Poznań (1929); Tiffany Foundation Fellowship (1931); Eisendrath Award for Painting from the Art Institute of Chicago (1934); Frank Logan Medal from the Art Institute of Chicago (1948, 1951); Faculty Fellow at Sarah Lawrence College (1951); International Award and Purchase, Institute of Contemporary Arts, London (1951–52); American Award, International Competition, Museum of Modern Art, New York (1952); George E. Widener Gold Medal Award for Sculpture, Pennsylvania Academy of Fine Arts (1956); Ford Foundation Grant (1959); Griner Award, Indiana (1962); Century Association Medal, New York (1967).—*Stanley L. Cuba*

SOURCES: Douglas Dreishpoon, *Theodore Roszak: Constructivist Works, 1931–1947: Paintings, Constructions, Drawings, Photograms: [Exhibition] February 29 to April 11, 1992* (New York: Hirschl & Adler Galleries, 1992); Howard E. Wooden, *Theodore Roszak: The Early Works, 1929–1943: An Exhibition of Sculptures, Paintings, and Drawings* (Wichita, KS: Wichita Art Museum, 1986); Paul Cummings, *The Theodore Roszak Bequest [Exhibition] January 21–March 18, 1984* (New York: Whitney Museum of American Art, 1984).

Rowinski, Francis C. (b. Dickson City, Pennsylvania, September 10, 1918; d. Chicago, Illinois, August 4, 1990). Bishop. After attending **Savonarola Theological Seminary** in Scranton, PA, Rowinski was ordained a priest in the **Polish National Catholic Church** (PNCC) in 1939. He served as pastor of Chicago parishes for twenty years before being consecrated a bishop in 1959 and installed as Bishop of the Western Diocese of the PNCC at All Saints Cathedral in Chicago. In 1978 he was elected the fourth Prime Bishop of the PNCC, a position he held until 1985. During his tenure as head of the Church, the PNCC began a dialogue with the Roman Catholic Church in 1984. Called "Journeying Together in Christ," the talks have reduced animosity between the two denominations and resulted in a limited intercommunion. After leaving the Prime Bishop's seat, Rowinski became Bishop of the Buffalo-Pittsburgh Diocese of

the PNCC at Holy Mother of the Rosary Cathedral in Buffalo, NY, and held that position at the time of his death.—*Martin S. Nowak*

SOURCE: Hieronim Kubiak, *Polish National Catholic Church in the United States of America from 1897 to 1980* (Kraków: Państwowe Wydawnictwo Naukowe, 1982).

Równouprawnienie (Equality of Rights). As the mass migration of Poles beginning in the 1870s dramatically increased the number and percentage of Poles among the Roman Catholic population in the United States, Polish clergy found themselves assigned to ethnic parishes with little or no opportunity for advancement. At the same time, the Polish American laity, accustomed to a Church hierarchy in Poland dominated by their countrymen, felt increasingly alienated from the Irish and German-dominated Roman Catholic hierarchy in America. One of the leaders in the resulting movement to gain appointment of Polish bishops in America was the Rev. **Wacław Kruszka** whose article "Polyglot Bishops for Polyglot Dioceses" argued that bishops who could not understand the language of large portions of their flock committed a mortal sin by accepting appointment as their shepherd. Kruszka argued for "equal treatment" in the appointment of Polish clergy to the ecclesiastical hierarchy, coining the phrase "Równouprawnienie" which came to be a byword for the Polish struggle for "equality of rights" within the Roman Catholic hierarchy in America.—*James S. Pula*

SOURCES: Wacław Kruszka, "Polyglot Bishops for Polyglot Dioceses," *The New-York Freeman's Journal and Catholic Register*, August 3, 1901; Michael A. Guzik, "Trent Recalled and Vatican II Prefigured: The Underlying Ecclesiology of "Polyglot Bishops for Polyglot Diocese," *Polish American Studies*, Vol. LIX, no. 2 (Autumn 2002), 17–28.

Rowny, Edward L. (b. Baltimore, Maryland, April 3, 1917; d.—). Military officer, diplomat. After distinguished field service during World War II commanding a battalion in the 92nd Infantry Division on the Italian front from 1944 to 1945, Rowny served with the Operations Division of the War Department General Staff in Washington, D.C. (1945–47), where he worked on strategic plans for the completion of the war against Japan as well as for the design of the post-war army. After earning master's degrees in international relations and civil engineering from Yale University in 1949, he was assigned to the Far East where he served under General Douglas MacArthur and was one of the officers involved in the planning of the Inchon landings during the Korean War. In September 1952, he reported to the Infantry School, Fort Benning, GA, as an instructor, and attended

the Airborne Course at the time the Army began to integrate helicopters into service for reconnaissance, attack, logistics, and evacuation of casualties. One of his ideas was to assist infantry ground assaults by troops attacking behind enemy lines via helicopter. From Fort Benning, Rowny went to the Armed Forces Staff College at Norfolk, Virginia, in February 1955, and from there was assigned as deputy secretary and later secretary of the general staff at SHAPE (Supreme Headquarters, Allied Powers, Europe). In 1958 Rowny was assigned to the National War College and after graduation was appointed the Army member of the Chairman's Staff Group, U.S. Army Element, Office of the Joint Chiefs of Staff, Washington, D.C., where he was promptly promoted to brigadier general.

In September 1961, Rowny was assigned to the 82nd Airborne Division at Fort Bragg, NC. Here he became involved in the testing of helicopters in nuclear situations, "sky cavalry" roles for land warfare, and counterinsurgency techniques as director of testing operations. He was later assigned to Vietnam as chief of the Army Concept Team in Vietnam. In 1965, he went to Europe as the commanding general of the 24th Division, and deputy chief of staff to the United States Command for Europe in Stuttgart for a year before returning to the United States to become deputy chief of research and development, U.S. Army. This position lasted a short time after which he was sent to Korea in July 1970 to become commander of I Corps where he was promoted to lieutenant general in September 1970. In July 1971, he became deputy chairman for the NATO military committee. He was then appointed chairman of MBFR (Mutual and Balanced Force Reductions), a new group established by Rowny, and later was the military representative to the Strategic Arms Limitation Talks (SALT), holding that post under Presidents Richard Nixon, Gerald Ford and Jimmy Carter. In 1979, he retired from the SALT team and the U.S. Army after policy disagreements with the Carter administration.

In 1981, Rowny was appointed to the rank of ambassador as President Ronald Reagan's chief strategic negotiator to the Strategic Arms Reduction Treaty (START) where he served for four years, later serving as Special Advisor for Arms Control to Presidents Reagan and George H. W. Bush until 1990 when he retired from the government to become an international consultant. Subsequently he authored *It Takes One to Tango* (1992), a memoir of his service to five presidents and his dealings with the Soviets. In 1992, he fulfilled a fifty-one year ambition by becoming the honorary chairman of the committee to return the re-

Edward Rowny, military officer and diplomat (*JPI*).

mains of **Ignacy Jan Paderewski** to Poland. In 1994, Rowny became president of the Paderewski Living Memorial to perpetuate the legacy of the Polish patriot and internationally acclaimed composer and pianist. He was a founding member of the American Polish Advisory Council. In 2004, he established the Paderewski Scholarship Fund to bring Polish university students to the United States for study. Rowny earned a B.S. in engineering from Johns Hopkins University, a B.S. degree from West Pont, two master's degrees from Yale University, and a Ph.D. from American University (International Studies). His military decorations include two Distinguished Service Medals, four Legions of Merit, three Silver Stars and the Bronze Star Medal (combat). He was awarded the Presidential Citizen's Medal in 1989.—*Luis J. Gonzalez*

SOURCES: Edward L. Rowny, *It Takes One to Tango* (Washington, D.C.: Brassey's, 1992); *Good News* (Miami, FL: American Institute of Polish Culture, 2005–06); Bolesław Wierzbiański, *Who's Who in Polish America* (New York: Bicentennial Publishing Corp., 1996), 389.

Royko, Michael, Jr., "Mike" (b. Chicago, Illinois, September 19, 1932; d. Chicago, Illinois, April 29, 1997). Journalist. Royko grew up in the Polish neighborhoods along Milwaukee Avenue on Chicago's Northwest Side. He was the third of four children born to a Ukrainian immigrant father and Polish-American mother who operated a cleaning and tailoring business. The family later owned a tavern, living upstairs. Royko skipped two grades at Salmon Chase Grammar School, graduated at twelve, then worked as a bowling pin setter, stocker, and movie usher. His parents sent him to Morgan Park Military Academy and then Montefiore, a public school for troubled youth. He dropped out at sixteen

but earned his high school diploma from the Central YMCA in 1951 and took some college courses. Royko became an Air Force radio operator stationed near Seoul, Korea, and in Blaine, Washington. In November 1954, he married Carol Duckman, a childhood friend. When Royko transferred to the military base at Chicago's O'Hare Field, he avoided military police duty by claiming he had reported for the *Chicago Daily News* which gained him an appointment as base newspaper editor.

After his discharge in 1956, Royko reported for the *Lincoln-Belmont Booster* and the legendary City News Bureau. He covered county government for the liberal afternoon *Daily News* with such wit that he received his own column in 1963. Soon Royko's very popular column appeared five times each week. It was during this time that he established his favorite career-long themes, including sports, especially baseball and sixteen-inch softball, and his passionate defense of "ordinary people." He opposed the Vietnam War, lambasted racists, mocked corrupt, hypocritical politicians, and chastised heartless bureaucrats. In 1967 he held a dog show for mongrels at Soldier Field. Royko developed an "everyman" alter ego, Slats Grobnik, boyhood chum turned drinking buddy. Royko frequented taverns, particularly the famous Billy Goat. Pop psychology and New Age spirituality inspired another Royko character: Dr. I. M. Kookie, a self-styled expert "on a lot of things." Royko regularly shared with readers the angry letters he received, especially from people who misunderstood his satire.

Royko was awarded the Heywood Broun Award (1968), the National Headliner Award (1971), and the Pulitzer Prize for commentary (1972). In 1971 he published his only book besides anthologies of his columns, *Boss*, a scathing look at Chicago mayor Richard J. Daley and his political machine. It was nominated for a National Book Award, even as the mayor's wife tried to ban it. In 1978, the *Daily News* ceased publication. Royko's column reappeared on page two of the *Chicago Sun-Times* and was syndicated to an ever-growing number of papers. In September 1979, Carol Royko died unexpectedly from a brain hemorrhage. Royko memorialized his wife in "A November Farewell," one of his most loved columns. He was elected to the Chicago Journalism Hall of Fame (1980), given the H. L. Mencken Award (1981), and the Ernie Pyle Award (1982). In 1982 he launched the popular Royko Ribfest.

In 1984, tabloid tycoon Rupert Murdoch bought the *Sun-Times*. Royko resigned, protesting that "no self-respecting fish" would allow itself to be wrapped in a Murdoch newspaper.

He found a new home on page three of the *Chicago Tribune*, which eventually syndicated him to over 600 other newspapers. In 1985, he cut back to four columns a week. During the 1990s, he provoked more controversy than ever. Arrested for drunk driving (1995), he made homophobic insults against the police officers. Mexican Americans protested outside the Tribune Towers in response to his mockery of the immigration debate (1996). After decades of heavy drinking, smoking, and driven work habits, he died of heart failure at age 64. Chicagoans stopped asking each other what they thought of "today's Royko," instead speculating over how he would have reacted to current absurdities and outrages. Royko's family and friends gleaned and published two career retrospectives from the 8,000-plus columns he had written since the 1960s. Royko's papers and artifacts, including cigarette butts, were donated to the Newberry Library. As Jacob Weisberg remembered, Mike Royko could "make you laugh and make you think, stir outrage ... or bring a tear to the eye when he flashed a glimpse of the heart hidden beneath his hard shell ... with a regularity and prominence that no ... columnist ... can match today."—*Mary Krane Derr*

SOURCES: F. Richard Ciccone, *Royko: A Life in Print* (New York: Public Affairs, 2001); Doug Moe, *The World of Mike Royko* (Madison: University of Wisconsin Press, 1999); Mike Royko, *Boss: Richard J. Daley of Chicago* (New York: Dutton, 1971); Mike Royko, *Dr. Kookie, You're Right!* (New York: Dutton, 1989); Mike Royko, *For the Love of Mike: More of the Best of Mike Royko* (Chicago: University of Chicago Press, 2001); Mike Royko, *I May Be Wrong, But I Doubt It* (Chicago: H. Regnery, 1968); Mike Royko, *One More Time: The Best of Mike Royko* (Chicago: University of Chicago Press, 1999); Mike Royko, *Sez Who? Sez Me* (New York: Dutton, 1982); Mike Royko, *Slats Grobnik and Some Other Friends* (New York: Dutton, 1973); Mike Royko, *Up Against It* (Chicago: H. Regnery, 1967); Don Terry, "Mike Royko, the Voice of the Working Class, Dies at 64," *New York Times*, April 30, 1997.

Rozanski, Edward (b. Chicago, Illinois, March 7, 1915; d. Chicago, Illinois, 1993). Polonia activist. Born to an immigrant couple who opened a photography studio in Chicago before World War I, the family returned to Poland when Rozanski was five. In 1931, he returned to Chicago where he graduated from Crane Technical High School and, in 1948, from the Illinois College of Optometry with a Doctor of Optometry degree. In 1939–42, he worked as a photographer-journalist for the Polish-language daily *Zgoda* (Harmony) in Chicago. In 1942 he moved to Washington, D.C., where he served with the U.S. Coast and Geodetic Survey until 1945. After completing his service, he returned for a time to *Zgoda*, but in 1950–75 he worked as a color specialist for the gravure Cuneo Press in Chicago. Beginning in 1975 he served as general manager of the Alliance Printer and Publishers, retiring in 1985. An active member of **Polish National Alliance** District 13, Rozanski served as a PNA director in 1967–71. In 1966–70 and 1978–79 he was president of the Illinois State Division of the **Polish American Congress**, developing a vigorous program of preservation and propagation of Poland's and **Polonia**'s history. In 1971 the United Polish American Councils named him "Man of the Year." He contributed to the organization of two international conferences, Polonia '75 and Polonia Jutra '78, as well as being a member of the **Polish Roman Catholic Union of America** and the **Polish Falcons** Nest 2 in Chicago. Rozanski was actively involved in the erection of several historical monuments, as well as the organization of observances of the Civil War Centennial, the U.S. Bicentennial, the Mikołaj Kopernik Quincentennial, and the Pułaski Bicentennial. He cooperated closely with the **Polish Museum of America** in Chicago, and served on its board, donating thousands of volumes of published materials and manuscripts, artifacts and other memorabilia to many libraries and scholarly institutions in the U.S., Poland, France, and Great Britain. The Orchard Lake Schools opened the "Dr. Edward C. and Loda Rozanski Room" housing parts of their private collections. Another major recipient of the manuscript records which Rozanski often salvaged from destruction became the Immigration History Research Center at the University of Minnesota, which holds Rozanski's personal papers. Throughout the years, he was also involved in many veterans organizations, chairing the Commission on the Care of Polish Military Cemeteries, the 1964 General Sikorski Memorial Committee, and was one of the organizers of the **Katyń** Forest Massacre observances in 1970. Rozanski consciously bridged a gap between older **Polonia** and postwar refugees and displaced persons; he served as a president of the Chicago chapter of the **Polish American Immigration and Relief Committee**, and supported the Mutual Aid Association of the New Polish Immigration in Chicago. Rozanski's church involvement included service as a permanent deacon at the St. Hyacinth Church in Chicago. Rozanski received numerous awards and distinctions from Poland's government, Polish London government-in-exile, and Polish and Polonia organizations.— *Anna D. Jaroszyńska-Kirchmann*

SOURCE: Anna D. Jaroszyńska-Kirchmann, *Inventory to the Papers of Edward C. and Loda Rozanski* (St. Paul, MN: Immigration History Research Center, 1996).

Rozmarek, Charles (Ignacy Karol Rozmarek; b. Wilkes-Barre, Pennsylvania, July 25, 1897; d. Chicago, Illinois, August 5, 1973). Polonia activist. Coming from a poor family, Rozmarek nonetheless succeeded in earning his degree in law from Harvard University in 1925. After returning to Wilkes-Barre, he held several public offices in the field of justice. Already active in the **Polish National Alliance**, in 1931 he was appointed to the school board that managed the PNA's **Alliance College** in Cambridge Springs, Pennsylvania. In 1935 he was a candidate for the presidency of the Alliance, losing narrowly to the incumbent, **John Romaszkiewicz**, 260–252. In September 1939, at its 28th national convention in Detroit, Rozmarek was elected president of the PNA in a rematch with Romaszkiewicz, 269–262. He went on to hold that office for a record twenty-eight consecutive years. During his presidency, membership in the PNA surpassed 300,000 for the first time, peaking at 351,000 in 1963. Its net assets also rose, from $30 million to $133 million. On June 5, 1944, Rozmarek was a key party to the U.S. Supreme Court decision in the case of National Labor Relations Board vs. the Polish National Alliance. The Court ruled against him and upheld the right of PNA employees to organize a labor union. Rozmarek argued that the PNA, as a not-for-profit fraternal, was not obliged to do so under the terms of the Wagner Act. During World War II, Rozmarek played a leading role in organizing the **Polish American Congress** (PAC) in support of the cause of Poland's freedom. He was elected its president at the PAC's massive founding convention in Buffalo, New York, in June 1944. He held this office until 1968.

As president of the PAC, Rozmarek was one of the first Americans to publicly denounce Franklin D. Roosevelt's actions at the **Yalta** Conference of February 1945, which accepted the Soviet Union's postwar domination of Poland. In the years after, he met frequently with a succession of U.S. presidents about Poland and spoke on hundreds of occasions throughout the country in support of a free Poland. In October 1945 he led a PAC delegation to the founding meeting of the United Nations in San Francisco where he worked tirelessly on behalf of the Polish cause. In 1946 he traveled to Europe to observe the living conditions of thousands of Polish displaced persons in refugee camps in postwar Germany. On his return to the U.S. he criticized their treatment by U.S. government authorities in Europe. He championed passage of the Displaced Persons Act of 1948, which enabled 140,000 Polish refugees to settle under special dispensation in this country.

Rozmarek led the successful effort to get a special committee of the House of Representatives to investigate the murder of thousands of Polish officers in World War II. In 1952 the committee found the Soviet Union responsible for the **Katyń** Massacre, a conclusion eventually acknowledged by Russia's own leaders, Mikhail Gorbachev (1990) and Boris Yeltsin (1992). He was a prominent supporter of the creation of Radio Free Europe in 1949. He regularly represented the PAC at the hearings of the platform committees of the two major political parties at their national conventions and identified in the early 1950s with the idea of the "national liberation" of Eastern Europe from Soviet control. But after 1956 he backed a series of new U.S. policies that provided material aid to Poland as a way to advance its independence from Moscow. He was a constant proponent of U.S. recognition of Poland's northern and western post war borders, something finally achieved at the Helsinki conference of 1975.

In October 1944 Rozmarek was invited to

Edward Rozanski, Polonia activist (*PMA*).

Charles Rozmarek, Polonia activist (*PMA*).

meet with Franklin D. Roosevelt following FDR's final campaign visit to Chicago just prior to the November election. There, Roosevelt pressured Rozmarek to support his reelection to a fourth term in office. Rozmarek, at that time unaware of FDR's private acceptance at his November 1943 summit meeting in Teheran of Stalin's demands for Soviet postwar control of Poland, provided his personal endorsement, but his words were broadcast as the Polish American Congress' endorsement of the president's reelection.

The zenith of Rozmarek's stature in **Polonia** may have come in 1960, when both U.S. presidential candidates, Richard M. Nixon and John F. Kennedy, along with retiring President Dwight D. Eisenhower, all made visits to Chicago to speak to audiences brought together by Rozmarek to win the Polish vote in the coming election.—*Donald E. Pienkos*

SOURCE: Donald E. Pienkos, *PNA: A Centennial History of the Polish National Alliance of the United States of North America* (Boulder, CO: East European Monographs, 1987).

Rozmarek, Wanda (Wanda Blinstrub; b. Russian-occupied Lithuania, February 2, 1904; d. Chicago, Illinois, January 24, 1994). Educator, Polonia activist. After her family's arrival in Boston her father established a successful and prominent restaurant. Blinstrub graduated from Boston University in 1925 and earned her Master's Degree in education the following year. With **Charles Rozmarek**, whom she married while both were students, she organized a "Polish Circle" or club for college students of Polish heritage in the city. Along with teaching French and Spanish in Wilkes-Barre, Pennsylvania, her husband's home town, she was active in organizing a club for women in the professions and business and was active in the **Polish National Alliance**, holding leadership positions at the lodge, council, and women's division level of the fraternal. From the 1930s on, she taught at the college level at several schools, including **Alliance College** where she taught the Polish language. She also organized college student clubs in Pennsylvania and Chicago. She was the author of a Polish language textbook that was widely used for many years. Rozmarek was a major ally of her husband, who became president of the Polish National Alliance in 1939 and president of the **Polish American Congress** in 1944. In the late 1940s she opened the Rozmarek family home in Chicago as a place for newly arrived Polish immigrants to stay temporarily until they found suitable lodgings and work.—*Donald E. Pienkos*

SOURCE: Donald E. Pienkos, *PNA: A Centennial History of the Polish National Alliance of the United States of North America* (Boulder, CO: East European Monographs, 1987).

Rubinstein, Artur (b. Łódź, Poland, January 28, 1887; d. Geneva, Switzerland, December 20, 1982). Pianist, conductor. Rubinstein began playing music at the age of two before he learned to speak, and within a year his precocious talent was recognized by German violinist Joseph Joachim. Rubinstein took lessons in Łódź and Warsaw in preparation for giving his first concerts at the age of seven, but in 1897 he returned to study music in Berlin with Joachim, Heinrich Barth (piano), and Max Bruch and Robert Kahn (music theory). In December 1900, at the age of 13, he appeared in Mozart's Concerto K 488 and Saint-Saëns's G minor Concerto with Joachim conducting. Further concerts throughout Europe and the U.S. included appearances in Paris (1904) and at the Carnegie Hall (1906) with the Philadelphia Orchestra. After commencing an international career as a touring virtuoso, Rubinstein did not continue regular music studies but often traveled to study privately with Paderewski in Switzerland. His talent for sight-reading, enthusiasm, and brilliant technique, along with romantic emotionalism, were the hallmarks of his earlier style. After his London debut in 1912, Rubinstein settled there and spent the war years as a military interpreter (he spoke eight languages) and chamber musician, paying with Eugene Ysaÿe. During travels to Spain and South America (1916–17; he performed in Argentina, Uruguay, and Chile), Rubinstein discovered the music of Isaak Albéniz, Manuel de Falla, Enrique Granados and Heitor Villa-Lobos. He frequently included their pieces on his concert programs, which always featured

Artur Rubinstein, pianist and conductor (PMA).

Chopin. Beginning in 1914, Rubinstein refused to perform in Germany, though continued to include German composers in his repertoire (Bach, Mozart, Beethoven and Brahms were his favorites). A devotee of modern music, he championed Debussy, Dukas, Poulenc, Ravel, Stravinsky, Szymanowski, and the Spanish composers mentioned above. In 1921 Rubinstein toured the U.S. with violinist Paweł Kochański, a lifelong friend, and Karol Szymanowski. At that time, he made numerous piano roll recordings of live concerts for AMPICO and Aeolian Duo-Art, while continuing to record profusely using different technologies throughout his career. After marrying Aniela (Nela) Młynarska, daughter of conductor Emil Młynarski, in 1932, Rubinstein withdrew from the concert stage to study his repertoire and work on his technique, to better balance the brilliance, emotionalism, and dynamism of his personality with more profound reflection and formal discipline. His return to the concert stage in an American tour in 1937 was greeted with universal critical acclaim in which he was recognized as one of the greatest romantic pianists of his time. His repertoire was vast and his energy unbounded—he could play several concerti in one evening well into his 80s. In addition to countless solo appearances around the world and hundreds of recordings, Rubinstein enjoyed performing chamber music with such eminent partners as Jasha Heifetz, Gregor Piatigorsky, Paul Kochanski, and Henryk Szeryng. His more than 200 recordings include the complete piano works of Chopin and three different interpretations of the Beethoven piano concertos. Rubinstein's life-long passion for the music of Fryderyk Chopin (his favorite encore was the Nocturne Op. 15 No. 2) was one expression of his Polish roots, which also included fluency in Polish, attachment to Polish culture, and support for Polish musicians from Szymanowski to Krystian Zimerman and Jadwiga Falkowska. In the 1960s and 1970s he won five Grammy awards for chamber and solo music, as well as a posthumous lifetime achievement award of 1994. In 1976, he became an honorary Knight Commander of the Order of the British Empire. He also received the U.S. Medal of Freedom. A secular Jew, he was greatly attached to Israel and was buried in Jerusalem in 1983, a year after his death. The Arthur Rubinstein International Music Society now organizes a triennial piano master competition in his honor.—*Maja Trochimczyk*

SOURCES: Harold C. Schonberg: *The Great Pianists: From Mozart to the Present* (New York: Simon & Schuster, 1987); Harvey Sachs and Donald Manildi, *Rubinstein: A Life* (New York: Grove Press, 1995); Artur Rubinstein, *My Young Years* (New York:

Knopf, 1973); ArturRubinstein, *My Many Years* (New York: Knopf, 1980).

Rubinstein, Helena (Chaja Rubinstein; b. Kraków, Poland, December 25, 1870 or 1871; d. April 1, 1965, New York City). Businesswoman. The eldest of eight children of a shopkeeper in Kraków, she became the founder and eponym of Helena Rubinstein, Incorporated, a cosmetics firm that made her one of the world's richest women. At the age of eighteen she obtained work as a governess in Australia before working as a waitress in a Melbourne café, and later at the Winter Garden tea room, an artists' haunt. In 1902, she discussed her plans to sell medical formulas and ointments she claimed were imported from the Carpathian Mountains with J. T. Thompson, manager of the Robur Tea Co., who provided £100 for the venture. Chaja changed her name to Helena and opened a salon selling Crème Valaze, a face cream allegedly concocted from sheep oil whose odor was disguised with scents of lavender, pine bark and water lilies. Although there was little to distinguish Crème Valaze from the dubious patent medicines advertised at the time, in a stroke of marketing genius Rubenstein began claiming that its recipe included "rare herbs from the Carpathian mountains" and had restorative powers. In 1905 Rubinstein went to Europe to study skin treatment with European specialists, after which she began the Valaze Institute offering various skin conditioners, followed by the Valaze Massage Institute in Sydney and an agency in New Zealand.

In 1908 Rubinstein left for London with £100,000 to invest. Within a year she opened Helena Rubinstein's Salon de Beauté Valaze; within another year, she claimed, a thousand society ladies were paying her a special subscription of £200 a year for weekly beauty treatments. She later acquired a salon in Paris, but with the outbreak of World War I she opened a salon in New York in 1916 and brought her sister Manka from London to help establish salons in San Francisco, Boston, Philadelphia, Chicago and Toronto. She also permitted selected department stores to stock her products, while retaining the right of training and inspection. In 1928 she sold her American business, but bought it back cheaply when the Wall Street crash slashed the share price from $60 to $3. After the war Rubinstein returned to Paris where she established, on the Île St. Louis, a salon for artists and writers, and indulged a voracious appetite for collecting, among other things, jewelry, antique miniature furniture, modern art, and African sculpture. In 1938 she established a gentlemen's product line through the House

Helena Rubinstein with Artur Rubinstein (*JPI*).

of Gourielli in New York City, and in 1953 founded the Helena Rubinstein Foundation. Through the foundation she funded the Helena Rubinstein Pavilion for Contemporary Art at Tel Aviv, and in 1957 established the Helena Rubinstein traveling art scholarship in Australia. In 1964 she published her memoirs, *My Life for Beauty.* The bulk of her personal estate of $1 million was left to be administered by the foundation; the total value of the business was estimated at more than $60 million. During her life she enjoyed the cut and thrust of business, especially on Fifth Avenue where her feud with Florence Nightingale Graham (Elizabeth Arden) and Charles Revson, founder of Revlon, reached extraordinary levels of bitterness and ingenuity, and lasted a lifetime. Nonetheless, and according to the *New York Times*, "Madame Rubinstein was probably the greatest female American entrepreneur of all."—*Richard J. Hunter, Jr., and Héctor R. Lozada*

SOURCES: J. R. Poynter, "Rubinstein, Helena (1870–1965)," *Australian Dictionary of Biography* (Volume 11, Melbourne University Press, 1988), 475–77; Seymour Brody (author), Art Seiden (illustrator), *Jewish Heroes & Heroines of America:150 True Stories of American Jewish Heroism* (Hollywood, FL: Lifetime Books, 1996); Marie J. Clifford, "Helena Rubinstein's Beauty Salons, Fashion, and Modernist Display," *Winterthur Portfolio,*

Vol. 38 (2003), 83–108; Lindy Woodhead, *War Paint* (London: Virago Press, 2004).

Rubinstein, John Arthur (b. Los Angeles, California, December 8, 1946; d.—). Actor, director. The son of the famous pianist **Artur Rubinstein** and dancer Aniela Młynarska Rubinstein, he attended UCLA before making his acting debut in *Pippin* (1972), for which he earned a Theater World Award. His role in *Children of a Lesser God* (1980) brought him a Tony Award, as well as awards from Drama Desk, the Los Angeles Drama Critics Circle, and a Drama-Logue Award. He went on to appear in *Fools, The Caine Mutiny Court-Martial, M. Butterfly, Getting Away with Murder, Rosencrantz & Guildenstern Are Dead, Urban Blight, Cabaret Verboten, Counselor-at-Law, The Rover, Love Letters,* and *Wicked.* In addition to his work on the stage, he appeared in more than 150 television episodes in such productions as *Family, Crazy Like a Fox, Perfect Murder, Perfect Town, Angel, The Guardian, The Practice, Star Trek: Enterprise, Barber Shop, The Two Mrs. Grenvilles,* and *Friends.* His work in feature films included roles in *21 Grams, Red Dragon, Mercy, Another Stakeout, Someone to Watch Over Me, Daniel, The Boys from Brazil, Rome and Jewel, Jekyll, Kid Cop, Getting Straight, Zachariah, The Trouble with Girls, The Delivery,* and *The Car.* In addition to his work as an actor, Rubinstein also composed and conducted musical scores for five feature films. He spent six years as host for the radio production *Carnegie Hall Tonight.*—*James S. Pula*

SOURCES: "John Rubinstein," *Contemporary Theatre, Film, and Television* (Detroit; Gale, 2009), Vol. 93; "John Rubinstein," *Almanac of Famous People* (Detroit: Thomson Gale, 2007).

Ryter, Joseph Francis (b. Hartford, Connecticut, February 4, 1914; d. West Hartford, Connecticut, February 5, 1978). Congressman, attorney. Ryter attended parochial schools and St. Thomas Seminary in Bloomfield, CT. He graduated from Trinity College in Hartford, CT, in 1935, from Hartford College of Law in 1938, and was admitted to the bar in 1938. After beginning the practice of law in Hartford, he served as assistant clerk of the Hartford Police Court (1939–41) and of the Hartford City Court (1941–43). He was a delegate to the Democratic National Convention in 1940, and served as president of the Pulaski Federation of Democratic Clubs of Connecticut 1939–42. Elected as a Democrat to the Seventy-ninth Congress as a Congressman at Large (January 3, 1945–January 3, 1947), he served as a member of the House Foreign Affairs Committee during which time he visited Eastern Europe (1946) and reported on United Nations relief and rehabilitation programs. Ryter was an unsuccessful candidate for reelection in 1946 to the Eightieth Congress, after which he resumed the practice of law.—*Frederick J. Augustyn*

SOURCES: *Biographical Directory of the United States Congress, 1774–Present* (http://bioguide.congress.gov/); obituary, *Boston Globe*, February 8, 1978, 33.

Ryterband, Roman (b. Łódź, Poland, August 2, 1914; d. Riverside, California, November 17, 1979). Musical conductor, composer. Ryterband was educated at the State Academy of Music in Łódź and then earned a degree in law from the University of Warsaw. He was visiting France at the time of the German invasion of Poland in 1939 and managed to escape to Switzerland before the fall of France in 1940. In Switzerland, he earned an M.A. in musicology at the University of Bern while composing and working as a conductor. In 1955 he moved to Montréal where he worked as music director for the CKVL radio station and lectured at McGill University. In 1960 he accepted a position on the faculty of the Chicago Conservatory College, and four years later he was honored as the Outstanding New Citizen by the Chicago Citizen Council. Ryterband was involved in conducting Polish musical organizations in Chicago, but moved to Palm Springs, California, in 1967. There he composed *Tunes of America* for the U.S. Bicentennial celebrations, founded the Palm Springs Festival of Music and Art, and taught at California State University in Los Angeles. As a composer, he wrote a wide variety of works from chamber music and symphonies to choral works and pieces for harp, organ, and piano. The Roman Ryterband Academy and Institute in Chicago was named in his honor.—*Maja Trochimczyk*

SOURCE: "Roman Ryterband," in Nicolas Slonimsky, ed., *Baker's Biographical Dictionary of Musicians* (New York: Schirmer, 2001).

Rzewski, Frederic Anthony (b. Westfield, Massachusetts, April 13, 1938; d.—). Musician. After taking up the piano at age five, Rzewski attended Harvard and Princeton Universities before journeying to Italy to continue his studies and begin a concert career. He was a co-founder of Musica Elettronica Viva, a pioneer in electronic instrumentation and improvisation bringing together classical and jazz avant-garde musicians. He returned to New York in 1971, but six years later accepted a position as professor at the Conservatoire Royal de Musique in Liège, Belgium, and continued to teach occasionally at various universities in Europe and the U.S. Among his more popular works are *The People United Will Never Be Defeated, Coming Together, North American Ballads, Night Crossing with Fisherman, Fougues, Fantasia, Sonata, The Price of Oil, Le Silence des Espaces Infinis, Les Moutons de Panurge, Antigone-Legend, Nanosonatas*, and *Cadenza con o senza Beethoven.*—*James S. Pula*

SOURCES: "Frederic Rzewski" in Stanley Sadie, ed., *The New Grove Dictionary of Music and Musicians* (London, Macmillan Publishers Ltd., 1980); *The Concise Edition of Baker's Biographical Dictionary of Musicians* (New York: Schirmer Books, 1993, 8th edition, revised by Nicolas Slonimsky).

Rzeznik, Johnny (John Joseph Theodore Rzeznik; b. Buffalo, New York, December 5, 1965; d.—). Singer, songwriter, musician. The lead singer of the Goo Goo Dolls rock group, Rzeznik was born to Joseph and Edith Rzeznik in a working class Polish American neighborhood. Both his parents died by the time he was sixteen. He was a self-described "good little Polish boy," serving as an altar boy for a time. He learned to play accordion and guitar at an early age, briefly attended Buffalo State College, then formed a band with fellow musicians Robby Takac and George Tutuska, who was later replaced by Mike Malinin. First called the Sex Maggots, the group changed its name to the more inoffensive Goo Goo Dolls. For nine years they released records and performed nationwide in small venues or as an opening act before hitting it big with the song "Name" in 1995. Over the years other hits followed, such as "Iris," "Slide," and "Broadway." Rzeznik is co-writer, lead singer and guitarist on most of the band's recordings, which have sold tens of millions of copies. Although he moved to the Los Angeles area, he continued to draw inspiration from visits to his hometown, and the Goo Goo Dolls continue to be one of the most successful musical acts in the business.—*Martin S. Nowak*

SOURCE: "Talking with Johnny Rzeznik," *Time*, Vol. 170, no. 21, 26.

Rzeznik, Marion Michael (b. Kowenic, Poland, December 15, 1899; d. Buffalo, New York, August 8, 1979). Artist. An accomplished artist whose work graces many churches in Western New York, Rzeznik studied bronze sculpture at a technical school in Sanbor, Poland, and developed his skill as a painter in Kraków, Vienna, and New York City. He established a studio in Buffalo where he initially specialized in metal arts. In the late 1920s, Rzeznik turned to the creation of religious murals, embarking on a career that would earn him a reputation as one of Buffalo's most accomplished ecclesiastical artists. Among his early church paintings was a mural for Our Lady of Victory Basilica in Lackawanna, NY, where he worked with the renowned Professor Gonippo Raggi. By the mid–1930s, Rzeznik's religious art was in demand, and he completed murals and paintings for churches in New York and other northeastern states. One of his most ambitious projects was a rendering of Raphael's "Disputa" for St. Casimir's Church in Cleveland, Ohio. He devoted months of arduous, painstaking work to this expansive mural (68 feet long by 34 feet high), which features 36 figures of heroic proportions. The Polish Arts Club of Buffalo presented an exhibit of Rzeznik's work in 1982. Benedict Rozek, chair of the exhibit, praised Rzeznik's "masterful interpretation of artistic form. Using the style of the eighteenth century baroque, his technique brought out the color, the roundness, the flesh and blood of the period.... He is survived by the legacy of outstanding artistic creations which inspire mankind to praise the Almighty God."—*Kathleen Urbanic*

SOURCE: "Marion Rzeznik: Master of Religious Art" in Benedict A. Rozek, *Polish Heritage*, Vol. XXXIII, no. 4 (Winter 1982), 5.

Sabin, Albert (Albert Bruce Saperstein; b. Białystok, Poland, August 26, 1906; d. Washington, District of Columbia, March 3, 1993). Immunologist. With his parents, Sabin moved to the United States while still in his teens, settling in Paterson, NJ, in 1921. Speaking no English when he arrived in the U.S., he was tutored and subsequently graduated from Paterson High School. Encouraged by an uncle's offer to finance his college education in dentistry, he enrolled at New York University. His interest in microbiology led him to switch to the study of medicine and a nearby outbreak of polio likely influenced his decision to research the causes of this disease. He earned his B.S. degree in 1928 and his M.D. in 1931. While completing his studies, he became an American citizen in 1930 and changed his name to Sabin. His first contribution was proving that a skin test given to determine susceptibility was not valid. During an internship at Bellevue Hospital, he became the first to document a case of human B-virus infection in a patient bitten by a monkey. Sabin named the virus, related to herpes, for the patient's surname initial. Following his internship, Sabin continued his research at the Lister Institute and the Rockefeller Institute before accepting a position at the University of Cincinnati. During World War II, he joined the army, rising to the rank of lieutenant colonel in the Surgeon General's Office, investigating infectious diseases such as sand fly fever in combat areas and helping develop a vaccine against dengue fever. Returning to the University of Cincinnati following the war, Sabin continued his research into polio. Building upon the polio vaccine work of Jonas Salk, Thomas Francis, Herald Cox, **Hilary Koprowski** and his own research, Sabin developed an attenuated live-virus vaccine in mid–1950s which, like Koprowski's, was administered orally. Sabin's vaccine addressed all three types of polio, provided intestinal as well as bodily immunity, and afforded longer lasting immunity. It underwent successful trials before being recommended by the World Health Organization for wider application abroad in the late 1950s. In 1961, the vaccine was endorsed by the United States Public Health Service and became the vaccine generally credited with eradicating polio. In the following decades, Sabin remained involved with his polio vaccine as well as vaccines for other infectious diseases such as swine flu. He became president of the Weizmann Institute of Science in the early 1970s and a research professor at the Medical University of South Carolina from 1974 until 1982 when, at age 76, he became a consultant to the John E. Fogarty International Center of the U.S. National Institutes of Health in Bethesda, MD. During his career he was the recipient of more than forty honorary degrees and numerous awards including the U.S. National Medal of Science in 1970 for "numerous fundamental contributions to the understanding of viruses and viral diseases, in development of the vaccine which has eliminated poliomyelitis as a major threat to human health." In 1986, he was awarded the Presidential Medal of Freedom. He is buried at Arlington National Cemetery.—*Brian Bonkosky*

SOURCE: Joseph L. Melnick, *Homage to Albert Sabin* (London: Academic Press, 1993).

Sadecki, Ray (b. Kansas City, Kansas, December 26, 1940; d.—). Baseball player. Sadecki was a major league baseball pitcher from 1960 to 1977, hurling for six different teams over eighteen seasons. A lefthander, he compiled a career record of 135–131 with an earned run average of 3.78. In 1964, he won twenty games for the St. Louis Cardinals during the regular season and contributed a victory to the team's World Series championship. Sadecki appeared as well in the 1973 World Series with the New York Mets, saving one game in relief. He was inducted into the **National Polish-American Sports Hall of Fame** in 2007.—*Neal Pease*

SOURCE: "Ray Sadecki," National Polish-American Sports Hall of Fame website, www.polishsportshof.com.

Sadlak, Antoni Nicholas (b. Rockville, Connecticut, June 13, 1908; d. Rockville, Connecticut, October 18, 1969). Congressman, attorney, judge. Born to a Polish immigrant family, Sadlak attended parochial school, graduated from George Sykes Manual Training and High School in 1926, and from

Antoni Sadlak, a congressman, at a Pulaski Day Parade in Hartford, Connecticut (*CCSU-LC*).

the Georgetown University School of Law, Washington, D.C., in 1931. The latter institution also awarded him a Doctor of Laws degree in 1958. He began his career as a special inspector for the Department of Justice from July 1941 to December 1942, where he rounded up enemy aliens in California. He then served as assistant secretary-treasurer of the Farmers' Production Credit Association in Hartford, CT (1944–46). Sadlak learned politics as secretary to former Representative at Large **Boleslaus Joseph Monkiewicz** in 1939, 1940, 1943, and 1944. He served in the U.S. Naval Reserve in New Guinea, the Philippines, and China from March 1944 to April 1946, assigned as communications watch officer with top secret clearance on the staff of Admiral Thomas Kincaid, Commander of the Seventh Fleet. Sadlak was the educational supervisor in the Connecticut Department of Education from July 1 to September 15, 1946. He was elected as a Republican to the Eightieth and the five succeeding Congresses (January 3, 1947–January 3, 1959) as Connecticut's Congressman at Large. He served on the House Ways and Means Committee where he worked on behalf of tax reform, especially tax reduction. Sadlak was an unsuccessful candidate for reelection during the big Democratic year of 1958. Thereafter he served as regional assistant manager of the Veterans' Administration in Hartford, CT, from March 30, 1959, to May 2, 1960, and engaged in lecturing and legislative consultation. In 1966 he was elected judge of probate for the Ellington-Vernon District, serving until his death. He was a member of the Knights of Columbus. His papers are in the Connecticut Historical Society.—*Frederick J. Augustyn*

SOURCES: *Biographical Directory of the United States Congress, 1774–Present* (http://bioguide.congress.gov/); obituary, *New York Times*, October 19, 1969, 92.

Sadowski, Antoni (b. Poland, ca. 1669; d. Amity Township, Pennsylvania, April 22, 1736). Pioneer. Little is known of Sadowski's early life, although family tradition suggested that he received a classical education as a youth. He apparently left Poland at the time of the Swedish invasion, arriving in New York some time during the first decade of the eighteenth century, probably between 1702 and 1706. The first known mention of him in America is a record dated May 21, 1709, listing him as a witness to a will drawn up in Freehold, New Jersey. After marrying and residing in New Jersey, Sadowski moved to Pennsylvania where he purchased 400 acres of land along the Schuylkill River outside Philadelphia on January 21, 1712. There he settled down to the life of a farmer while also trading with the local Indians and acting as an interpreter. In one instance he is said to have acted as a peacemaker between the colonists and the indigenous population when some dispute broke out that threatened the peace. Sadowski's trading activities led him west where he explored into western Pennsylvania and along the shores of Lake Erie in Ohio. Legend has it that the city of Sandusky, Ohio, was named for him, although no direct evidence of this has surfaced.—*James S. Pula*

SOURCES: Edward Pinkowski, *Anthony Sadowski—Polish Pioneer* (Philadelphia: Sadowski Memorial Commission, 1996); Edward Pinkowski, "The Sadowskis—First Polish Family in Pennsylvania," *Gwiazda*, September 15, 1966; Mieczysław Haiman, *Polish Pioneers of Virginia and Kentucky* (Chicago: Archives and Museum of the Polish Roman Catholic Union of America, 1937); Joseph A. Borkowski, "Sandusky—Indian or Polish Origin?" *Polish American Studies*, Vol. 25, no. 1 (1968), 6–9.

Antoni Sadowski in frontier attire in a miniature by Arthur Szuk (*OLS*).

Sadowski, George Gregory (b. Detroit, Michigan, March 12, 1903; d. Utica, Michigan, October 9, 1961). Congressman. After graduating from Northeastern High School in Detroit in 1920 and the University of Detroit law program in 1924, he was admitted to the bar in 1926 and began practice in Detroit, while at the same time becoming involved in real estate and building businesses. Elected to the State Senate (1931–32), he was a member of the State Democratic Central Committee from 1930 to 1936 and a delegate to the Democratic National Conventions from Michigan in 1932, 1936, 1940, 1944, and 1948. In 1932 he was elected to Congress, serving in the House of Representatives from March 4, 1933 to January 3, 1939. Unsuccessful in his effort to gain re-nomination in 1938, he was later re-elected to the House from January 3, 1943 to January 3, 1951. Both within and outside of Congress after World War II he opposed the rebuilding of Germany lest it lead to the outbreak of another war. He also argued for more rapid release of the military's building materials for civilian postwar domestic construction. Generally left of center in his votes, Sadowski opposed funding the House Committee on Un-American Activities. He was unsuccessful in gaining re-nomination in 1950.—*Frederick J. Augustyn*

SOURCES: *Biographical Directory of the United States Congress, 1774–Present* (http://bioguide.congress.gov/); Angela T. Pienkos, ed., *Ethnic Politics in Urban America: The Polish Experience in Four Cities* (Chicago: Polish American Historical Association, 1978), 53; *Washington Post*, October 11, 1961, B14.

Sadowski, Joseph J. (b. Perth Amboy, New Jersey, December 8, 1916; d. Valhey, France, September 14, 1944). Soldier, Medal of Honor recipient. As a sergeant with the 37th Tank Battalion, 4th Armored Division, Sadowski was awarded the Medal of Honor for conspicuous bravery during the Second World War. The citation for his award read: "For conspicuous gallantry and intrepidity at the risk of his life above and beyond the call of duty at Valhey, France. On the afternoon of 14 September 1944, Sgt. Sadowski as a tank commander was advancing with the leading elements of Combat Command A, 4th Armored Division, through an intensely severe barrage of enemy fire from the streets and buildings of the town of Valhey. As Sgt. Sadowski's tank advanced through the hail of fire, it was struck by a shell from an 88-mm. gun fired at a range of 20 yards. The tank was disabled and burst into flames. The suddenness of the enemy attack caused confusion and hesitation among the crews of the remaining tanks of our forces. Sgt. Sadowski immediately ordered his crew to dismount and take cover

Joseph J. Sadowski, Medal of Honor recipient (*NARA*).

in the adjoining buildings. After his crew had dismounted, Sgt. Sadowski discovered that 1 member of the crew, the bow gunner, had been unable to leave the tank. Although the tank was being subjected to a withering hail of enemy small-arms, bazooka, grenade, and mortar fire from the streets and from the windows of adjacent buildings, Sgt. Sadowski unhesitatingly returned to his tank and endeavored to pry up the bow gunner's hatch. While engaged in this attempt to rescue his comrade from the burning tank, he was cut down by a stream of machine gun fire which resulted in his death. The gallant and noble sacrifice of his life in the aid of his comrade, undertaken in the face of almost certain death, so inspired the remainder of the tank crews that they pressed forward with great ferocity and completely destroyed the enemy forces in this town without further loss to themselves. The heroism and selfless devotion to duty displayed by Sgt. Sadowski, which resulted in his death, inspired the remainder of his force to press forward to victory, and reflect the highest tradition of the armed forces."—*James S. Pula*

SOURCES: R. J. Proft, *United States of America's Congressional Medal of Honor Recipients and Their Official Citations* (Columbia Heights, MN: Highland House II, 2002); *The Medal of Honor of the United States Army* (Washington, D.C.: U.S. Government Printing Office, 1948), 91.

Sadowski, Leon (b. Mława, German-occupied Poland, April 12, 1869; d. Pittsburgh, Pennsylvania, April 12, 1927). Polonia activist. Sadowski came to the U.S. with his parents as a child. His family settled in Detroit where Sadowski studied at the Polish Seminary. Later he completed his medical training at the University of Pittsburgh and became a practicing physician. He joined the **Polish National Alliance** in 1890 and was elected its

censor in 1899, serving in that office for three terms, or six years. This was a period of enormous growth as membership tripled from 15,000 to 45,000 and the assets of the Alliance rose from $88,000 to $300,000. A strong supporter of women's equality, Sadowski was responsible for calling a special convention of the PNA in March 1900 to admit women as equal members with men in the Alliance. As U.S. Commissioner for the Polish National Fund in Switzerland, Sadowski was sent to Europe by the delegates of the 1903 convention to determine how money from America was being used by the exile movement. On his return in 1904 he defended the Alliance's continued support of the Fund in a report he published in ***Zgoda*** (Harmony), the official newspaper of the Alliance. Sadowski further urged that the Alliance maintain its traditionally close ties with the National Democratic movement in Europe. His stance brought him some opposition from those in the Alliance who supported the Socialist cause in Poland led by Józef Piłsudski (with a war going on between tsarist Russia and Japan this was a time of intense rivalry between the National Democrats and the Socialists). While the PNA leadership was solidly aligned with the National Democrats in Europe, Sadowski was defeated for reelection at the 1905 Buffalo convention by **Anthony Schreiber**, a prominent businessman and brewer in the host city. In 1909 at the PNA convention in Milwaukee he again ran, unsuccessfully, for the office of censor against Schreiber.—*Donald E. Pienkos*

SOURCES: Stanisław Osada, *Historia Związku Narodowego Polskiego i rozwój ruchu narodowego Polskiego w Ameryce Północnej* (Chicago: Nakładem i drukiem Związku Narodowego Polskiego, 1905); Adam Olszewski, *Historia Związku Narodowego Polskiego* (Chicago: Polish National Alliance, 1957–1963).

Saint Joseph, Sisters of the Third Order of St. Francis *see* **Felician Sisters.**

Saint Mary of Nazareth Hospital. In 1875, **Frances Siedliska** founded the **Sisters of the Holy Family of Nazareth** in Poland. She came to Chicago in 1885 in response to pleas from pastors in Polish parishes to help in establishing schools. On her second trip to Chicago, Mother Frances became aware of the critical need for a hospital to serve the Polish speaking community. The sisters obtained a deed for property at 1714–22 West Division Street and, in 1894, opened Holy Family Hospital with 24 beds. The sign on the door read "Szpital Polski" (Polish Hospital). However, as is the practice until the present day, all religions, races, and nationalities were admitted. After 1899, when twenty beds were added, admissions continued to rise rapidly. In 1900,

Saint Mary of Nazareth Hospital in Chicago (*PMA*).

the foundation for a new 297-bed St. Mary of Nazareth Hospital was laid in a square block bounded by Oakley Boulevard and Haddon, Leavitt, and Thomas Streets. That hospital, announced by *Dziennik Chicagoski* (Chicago Daily News) as the "Pride of Polonia Chicagoska," opened in 1902. Dr. Albert Ochsner, a highly respected surgeon, was chief of staff at the hospital for 36 years. He initiated many surgical innovations and was instrumental in launching the St. Mary of Nazareth School of Nursing in 1900. By 1986, when the school closed, it had 3,000 graduates. The hospital also administered schools for nurse anesthetists, radiologic technology and medical technology which were operational from the 1930s to the 1980s.

As continued demands for the hospital's services increased, a decision was made to build a new hospital. On January 5, 1975, John Cardinal Cody dedicated a 496-bed facility with the cornerstone of the hospital reading "Saint Mary of Nazareth Hospital Center." A feature that attracted national attention was that each patient would enjoy a private room. Sister Stella Louise Slomka, CSFN, appointed chief executive officer in 1959, guided the hospital in this transition and implemented many positive clinical and management changes during her forty-year tenure. Saint Mary of Nazareth Medical Center was recognized for its identity with the Polish American community. In 1976, it was selected by the City of Chicago as the official welcoming site for a delegation of the Epis-

copate of Poland headed by Karol Cardinal Wojtyła, later to become Pope John Paul II. In 1997, the hospital co-sponsored a Chicagoland tour of "Adoramus," a singing group of Sisters of the Holy Family of Nazareth from Warsaw, Poland. Over the years, the hospital featured numerous cultural and art exhibits and observances reflecting its appreciation of the ethnic heritages of the many communities the hospital continues to serve. Among these are annual tributes to **Polish Constitution Day**, celebration of a Mass in honor of Our Lady of Częstochowa, and the hospital's women's auxiliary observance of "**Pączki** Day."

In 2001, the Sisters of the Holy Family of Nazareth and the **Sisters of the Resurrection**, a religious congregation tracing its origin to Poland, signed an agreement to co-sponsor Resurrection Health Care. As Saint Mary of

Nazareth Hospital Center and other hospitals and medical centers joined, Resurrection Health Care grew rapidly to be the largest Catholic health care organization in the Chicago area. In 2003, Saint Mary of Nazareth Hospital Center and Saint Elizabeth Medical Center combined and began operations as a single entity.—*Joseph W. Zurawski*

Sources: *The Healing Touch, 1894–1944: Jubilee Memoir: St. Mary of Nazareth Hospital, Chicago* (Chicago: St. Mary of Nazareth Hospital, 1944); Charles W. Sanford, Jr., *A History of Healing, a Future of Care; Saint Mary of Nazareth Hospital Center: Celebrating a Century of Catholic Hospitality* (Flagstaff, AZ: Heritage Publishers, Inc., 1994); Joseph W. Zurawski, *Historical Archives Catalog; Saint Mary of Nazareth Hospital Center* (Chicago: Saint Mary of Nazareth Hospital Center, 1997); M. Florian Jendrycki, "Fifty Years at St. Mary of Nazareth Hospital, 1894–1944" (Washington, D.C.: Unpublished M.S. thesis, The Catholic University of America, 1960); M. Carmelita Zencka, "History of St. Mary of Nazareth School of Nursing Chicago, Illinois, 1900–1955" Washington, D.C.: Unpublished M.S. thesis, The Catholic University of America, 1957).

Saint Mary's College (Michigan). In 1885, the Rev. **Józef Dąbrowski** founded a Polish seminary in Detroit which added a minor preparatory school named for St. Mary in 1888. The school developed into a high school and junior college by 1892. Seeking room for expansion away from the city, in 1909 he purchased land and facilities along Orchard Lake to the west and north of Detroit from the defunct Michigan Military Academy. The facilities included "The Castle," a home built in 1858 by a retired judge that had been enlarged as a hotel in 1872, and a large academic building constructed for the Military Academy in 1877. In 1927 the schools were reorganized into three separate entities, **Saints Cyril and Methodius Seminary**, St. Mary's Preparatory School, and the private St. Mary's College offering a liberal arts curriculum. The college gained accreditation by the North Central Association in the early 1970s. In 2003, with an enrollment that had dwindled to only some 130 students, St. Mary's College

The Orchard Lake Schools in Michigan, home to St. Mary's College, 1940s (*OLS*).

merged with Madonna University to become St. Mary's College of Madonna University. In this form it constituted one of the academic colleges of the university with curricula leading to baccalaureate degrees in sacred theology, philosophy, and Polish studies. *See also*— **Central Archives of American Polonia**.—*James S. Pula*

SOURCE: Thaddeus C. Radzilowski, "Polish American Institutions of Higher Learning," in Frank Mocha, ed., *Poles in America: Bicentennial Essays* (Stevens Point, WI: Worzalla Publishing Company, 1978), 461–96.

Saints Cyril and Methodius Seminary. A four-year, free standing inter-diocesan graduate school of theology popularly known as the "Polish Seminary," SS. Cyril and Methodius was founded in 1885 in Detroit, Michigan, for the education and formation of bi-lingual Polish-American priests. Approval for founding the seminary was granted on January 14, 1879, by Pope Leo XIII upon the petition of Father **Leopold Moczygemba**, O.F.M. Conv. Realization of the seminary fell to a younger priest, Father **Joseph Dąbrowski**, who originally conceived of the idea of a Polish seminary in America. By 1884 both agreed on Detroit as the site for the seminary because it was centrally located among the main Polish colonies. Initially a venture of faith based largely on Dąbrowski's conviction of its necessity, the rest — funds, faculty, students, site, buildings — was to materialize over time. As the first rector, Dąbrowski was authorized on March 14, 1884 by Bishop Caspar Borgess of Detroit "to solicit aid for this important undertaking in our diocese, and beg to recommend you to the kind consideration of the Right Reverend Bishops of other Dioceses who may share in the benefit of the institution." Thus, under the jurisdiction of the Bishop of Detroit, the seminary was to serve the needs of dioceses throughout America. In April 1884 Dąbrowski purchased two and a half acres of land for constructing a building on St. Aubin Avenue, with ground breaking on May 19, 1885. The seminary was dedicated to SS. Cyril and Methodius during the laying of the cornerstone on July 22, 1885 at an impressive ceremony with Bishop Ryan of Buffalo presiding and Bishop Borgess assisting. The feast of the Apostles to the Slavs, Cyril and Methodius, had been incorporated into the liturgical calendar of the Church in 1880, and millennial jubilee celebrations of their achievement were held widely in 1885. The choice of the patronal name thus reflected the hope that the new seminary would appeal to other Slavic immigrants in America. As an expression of popular piety the seminary was also dedicated to the Immaculate Conception of Mary, with the new school being named St. Mary's or SS.

Cyril and Methodius Seminary, but more often known in its early years simply as the "Polish Seminary." Following the ceremony for laying the cornerstone, Dąbrowski said in an interview: "I have in view the education of the Polish candidates for the priesthood and the education of others, so that they may be on a par with other young men in this country. Heretofore we have been obliged to procure Polish priests from Europe, but they cannot speak English and cannot do what a native [born] American might. We Poles have the right to enjoy complete liberty in this country, but liberty cannot be enjoyed by uneducated people. The better a people is educated, the better they enjoy liberty and the better citizens they become of America.... I deem the erection of this seminary more necessary than the building of expensive churches. Intelligence only makes men free."

On December 16, 1886, the seminary officially opened. The curriculum included classical or preparatory studies as well as theological disciplines. In 1890 the seminary produced its first sacerdotal fruits with ordinations taking place at St. Albertus Church under Bishop John Foley, successor to Bishop Borgess. The first ordinands were the Rev. John Gulcz for the diocese of Harrisburg and the Rev. Casimir Wlajtys for the diocese of Detroit. Increasing enrollment and the need for additional space led the Rev. Witold Buchaczkowski, the seminary's second rector, to transfer the institution in 1909 from Detroit to the site of the former Michigan Military Academy in the rural village of Orchard Lake, northwest of Detroit. As early as 1888, the Polish Seminary embraced two schools, the theology department which attracted greater public interest and motivated founding the seminary, and the classics course, later known as the high school. The original academic program consisted of ten years of studies: five in the preparatory classical department and five in the upper division including two in philosophy and three in theology. In 1927 three administratively independent schools were established: SS. Cyril and Methodius Seminary, **St. Mary's College**, and St. Mary's Preparatory, known collectively in the later half of the last century as the **Orchard Lake Schools**. The reorganization effectively put the Seminary on the graduate level.

The Seminary had been incorporated in 1917, but its corporate status lapsed in 1934 because it had failed to file the required annual reports with the State of Michigan. After the administrative reorganization in 1927, the other two departments were incorporated as "St. Mary's Polish High School and College" in 1929 in the State of Michigan and were granted a charter to offer secondary and undergraduate courses without restriction. In 1941 Archbishop Edward Mooney initiated the restructuring of the Seminary and its allied schools. As a result the corporation decided to amend the charter and the collective name was changed to "SS. Cyril and Methodius Seminary, St. Mary's College, St. Mary's High School" and the purpose of the Seminary, to provide "facilities for the training of priests as are prescribed by the Canon Law of the Church," was added formally to that of the High School and College. Ownership of the school property, originally vested in the Bishop of Detroit, was transferred to the newly re-named corporation of which the Archbishop of Detroit was a member *ex officio*. On February 24, 1941, a new charter created a fifteen member board of trustees. In 1971 the Board of Trustees replaced itself and the old Corporation with a Board of Regents. Ex officio membership on the new Board included the Archbishop of Detroit, major ad-

Saints Cyril and Methodius Seminary, 1940s (*OLS*).

ministrators, alumni, and **Polonia** leaders. Each of the schools had its own sub-board drawn from the Regents: a Board of Directors for the Preparatory, a Board of Trustees for the College, and a Board of Consultants chaired by the archbishop of Detroit for the Seminary. Later, the boards of the Preparatory and Seminary were designated as Trustees also.

The Seminary's existence as a national institution was brought into question from its very beginning. Administrators at Orchard Lake were constantly challenged by the predominantly Irish and German Church hierarchy in America to justify its existence. During the patriotic era of the First World War and the 1920s many Church leaders hoped that ethnic identities would disappear into a common American nationality. The so-called "melting pot theory" of assimilation added support to this view. The 1917 Code of Canon Law affirming the territorial nature of the Catholic parish, diocesan insistence upon English as the language of instruction in Catholic schools, and different notions of the social basis of the Catholic Church in America all contributed to promoting further Americanization of immigrants. The leadership at Orchard Lake revealed the process of Polish-Americanization that dominated the development of the Seminary between the World Wars. Polish Americans found Orchard Lake an acceptable form of transition from immigrant family and neighborhood life into professional and business careers which required dealing with a larger world than that into which they had been born. With a few modifications, the Orchard Lake way of daily life that emerged in the 1920s and 1930s persisted until the 1960s and in some important ways until the 1970s. Perhaps the single most significant deviation from Roman-American seminary discipline at Orchard Lake was the practice of admitting students before they had been sponsored by a diocese.

In the post-conciliar era, the Seminary responded within the framework of experimentation encouraged by the Second Vatican Council. As priestly vocations declined, outreach, lay ministry, and graduate programs made it a pioneer in religious education. A Center for Pastoral Studies, established in 1968, offered education and formation of permanent deacons, pastoral formation for seminarians, and continuing education for adults. In the ensuing years, the seminary introduced the Master of Divinity degree (1973) for priesthood candidates, religious, and lay men and women; the Master of Religious Education (1989); and Master of Arts in Pastoral Ministry (1989), an upgrading of the Certifi-

cate in Pastoral Ministry which had been in existence since 1975. SS. Cyril and Methodius Seminary in 1971 became an associate member of the Association of Theological Schools of the United States and Canada (ATS). In 1992 the seminary was granted candidacy for accredited status in the association and undertook a two-year self study as part of the process leading toward accreditation. It obtained initial accreditation by ATS in January 1995, subsequently gaining reaffirmation in 2000 and 2005.

In the early 1980s, as the Seminary redefined its primary mission — the formation of priests — and embarked upon a Polish American Vocation Awareness Program and a formal recruitment program, the programmatic innovations of the 1960s and 1970s remained in place. The need for Polish-speaking priests in America encouraged the Seminary to accept mature Polish seminarians to complete their theology, learn English, and seek sponsorship by American dioceses. As a result the proportion of native Poles increased well beyond what it had been in the heyday of the "Polish" Seminary, but the greater sensitivity of American bishops to cultural pluralism and the needs of ethnic communities argued strongly for their admission. The return to "basics" in the 1980s was apparent in the appointment of directors of spiritual formation and admissions, and in a surge of applications from Polish-born and Polish-trained seminarians. The new direction raised the possibility of a "Polish" seminary that even the Rev. Dąbrowski had not envisioned. Yet, history has its own rhythms. SS. Cyril and Methodius Seminary and St. Mary's Preparatory have stood the test of time. By its 120-year anniversary in 2005, the Seminary continued to recruit seminarians from Poland for priestly service in American dioceses as well as students for lay ecclesial ministry in the Church. St. Mary's Preparatory was thriving with a multicultural, religiously pluralistic enrollment of over 550 students. Only the College proved fragile, closing its doors in 2003. With the demise of the College, the Orchard Lake Center of Madonna University began offering a satellite program of undergraduate studies at the Orchard Lake Schools campus. — *Frank B. Koper*

SOURCES: Joseph V. Swastek, "The Formative Years of the Polish Seminary in the United States," in *Sacrum Poloniae Millenium*, Vol. VI (Rome: Typis Universitatis Gregortanae, 1959), 29–150; Thaddeus C. Radzilowski, "Polish American Institutions of Higher Learning," in Frank Mocha, ed., *Poles in America: Bicentennial Essays* (Stevens Point, WI: Worzalla Publishing Co., 1978), 461–96; Thaddeus C. Radzilowski, "Father Jozef Dąbrowski, the Orchard Lake Schools and the Shaping of Polish American Catholicism," *U.S. Catholic Historian*, Vol. 27, no. 3 (2009), 83–107; Frank Renkiewicz,

For God, Country and Polonia: One Hundred Years of the Orchard Lake Schools (Orchard Lake, MI: Center for Polish Studies and Culture, 1985); John A. Michnowicz, "America's First Polish College," *Polish American Studies*, Vol. 22, no. 2 (1965), 65–77; Mary Edwin Bozek, "Early History of SS. Cyril and Methodius Seminary" (Notre Dame, IN: Unpublished M.A. thesis, University of Notre Dame, 1943).

Sajak, Pat (Patrick Leonard Sajdak; b. Chicago, Illinois, October 26, 1946; d.—). Television host. After graduating from high school in 1964, Sajak attended Columbia College in Chicago. He joined the army in 1968 and went to Vietnam where he worked on Armed Forces Radio in Saigon. After his discharge, he worked playing music on WSM in Nashville before being hired to do a weather broadcast on KNBC television in Los Angeles. He was then hired to host the daytime version of *Wheel of Fortune* in 1981, and hosted both the daytime and evening versions of the show from 1983 to 1989). He dropped the daytime show when he began hosting a late night talk show on CBS in January 1989. *Wheel of Fortune* was the top-rated game show of the 1990s. Sajak made a number of guest appearances on various television shows, including guest host on *Larry King Live* and *Live with Regis and Kelly*. He served as a member of the Board of Trustees at Hillsdale College and the Board of Directors of the Claremont Institute. He is also the benefactor of the Lesly and Pat Sajak Pavilion at the Anne Arundel Medical Center in Annapolis, Maryland. He was also an important donor to the Ronald Reagan Presidential Library. — *James S. Pula*

SOURCE: Jack Hittinger, "Buying Vowels With Pat Sajak," *The Collegian* (Hillsdale College), September 20, 2007.

Pat Sajak, the popular host of the game show *Wheel of Fortune*, with Vanna White (*NARA*).

Maria Sakowska, first woman elected to the board of directors of the Polish National Alliance (*OLS*).

Sakowska, Maria (Mary; b. Nanticoke, Pennsylvania, 1879; d. Chicago, Illinois, May 13, 1963). Polonia activist. One of the earliest women leaders in the **Polish National Alliance** and the first woman to be elected to its Board of Directors (1909), Sakowska served in that capacity until 1918. In 1924 she was elected vice president of the PNA. She was deeply involved in the formation of the Alliance's system of **Saturday schools** and in the work of organizing libraries and reading rooms sponsored by the PNA around the country. Sakowska was a delegate at the first **Polish National Congress** held in Washington, D.C., in 1910. During the First World War she was active in the work of the **Polish Central Relief Committee** and in recruitment in the U.S. for the **Polish Army in France**. During the 1920s and early 1930s, Sakowska was a leader of the "old guard faction" during its struggles with the "left," or pro–Piłsudski, faction that vied with one another for control of the PNA during the interwar years.—*Donald E. Pienkos*

SOURCE: Catherine Dienes, Melanie Winiecki, and Donald Pienkos, *Women Make A Difference: The 95th Anniversary of Women's Involvement in the Polish National Alliance* (Chicago: Alliance Printers and Publishers, 1996).

Salomon, Haym (b. Lissa (now Leszno), Poland, 1740; d. Philadelphia, Pennsylvania, January 6, 1785). Broker, financier. The son of a rabbi, Salomon traveled widely in Western Europe where he is believed to have become conversant in eight languages and gained considerable experience as a broker in international trade. He returned to Poland in 1770, but left after the beginning of the partitions in 1772 and arrived in New York City in 1775 as the American Revolution was beginning. He opened an office as a broker for international trade. He was sympathetic to the patriot cause, which led to his arrest by the British who charged him with spying. After several months in prison he was released, but was arrested again in 1778. He escaped from the city and traveled to Philadelphia where he became acquainted with Robert Morris, the Superintendant of Finance for the Continental Congress. Salomon brokered the sale of some $658,000 in Continental securities which helped to finance the American Revolution and loaned $20,000 to Congress to finance the move of Gen. George Washington's army south for what would be the decisive Yorktown Campaign. He also loaned money to several members of the Continental Congress, including James Madison, Thomas Jefferson, James Monroe, and James Wilson, that allowed them to remain in Philadelphia. He never sought repayment of the loans. During World War II a Liberty Ship was named for him, and in 1975 a U.S. commemorative postage stamp was issued in his honor.—*James S. Pula*

SOURCES: Lionel Koppmen, *Guess Who's Jewish in American History* (New York: Shapolsky Books, 1986); Howard Fast, *Haym Salomon: Son of Liberty* (New York: Julian Messner, Inc., 1941); Charles Edward Russell, *Haym Salomon and the Revolution* (New York: Cosmopolitan Book Corp., 1930).

Sambora, Richie (Richard Stephen Sambora; b. Woodbridge, New Jersey, July 11, 1959; d.—). Musician, singer. Sambora began playing the guitar at age twelve and played in several bands before joining Jon Bon Jovi as lead guitarist. He composed music for Bon Jovi and also released his own solos including *Stranger in This Town* (1991) and *Undiscovered Soul* (1998). He composed the theme songs for the television shows *Entertainment Tonight* and *The Insider*, was featured singing in Steven Seagal's movie *Fire Down Below*, recorded "One Last Goodbye" for *The Three Bang Sisters*, and provided music or vocals for several other television shows and movies. In addition to his music, Sambora was known for his marriage to actress Heather Locklear (1994–2007) and for his charity benefits for Dream Street, the Steve Young Forever Young Foundation, the Michael J. Fox charity for Parkinson's disease, and cancer research. Among his many recognitions are an honorary doctorate from Kean University (2004) and induction, along with Jon Bon Jovi, into the Songwriters Hall of Fame (2009).—*James S. Pula*

SOURCE: "Richie Sambora," *Contemporary Musicians* (Detroit: Gale Group, 1999), Vol. 24.

Samolińska, Teofila (Teofila Cwiklińska; b. Poland, April 22, 1848; d. Chicago, Illinois, December 1, 1913). Poet, Polonia activist. Samolińska arrived in Chicago in the 1860s and soon became active in the cultural life of the tiny but growing Polish community there. Her involvement with Chicago's **Gmina Polska** society eventually led her to be one of several individuals who wrote to **Agaton Giller** in 1878 for advice on building a viable national Polish patriotic organization in America. Giller was a respected figure who lived in exile in Switzerland following the failure of the Polish insurrection against Russian rule that had begun in January 1863. Giller's reply to these requests (in the form of an article he published in Poland) is seen as providing the impetus for the formation of the **Polish National Alliance** in 1880.

Samolińska's activities centered on writing.

Richie Sambora, musician and composer (*OLS*).

Teofila Samolińska, poet and Polonia activist (*PNA*).

She authored plays, poems, essays, and fictional stories, and was a passionate public speaker focused on building patriotic sentiments among the growing immigrant population in Chicago. She published in a variety of Polish newspapers including *Orzel Polski* (The Polish Eagle) and *Przyjaciel Ludu* (People's Friend) while remaining active in the Gmina Polska. She was a strong proponent of the PNA, but was unable to persuade its founders that women should be admitted with equal rights into the Alliance. In 1887 she founded the Central Association of Polish Women in Chicago, a society of female activists that continued to exist after her own death. Although Samolińska was in touch with a number of individuals who founded the **Polish Women's Alliance** of America in Chicago between 1898 and 1900, she did not join that organization. She is also identified as a supporter of the **Polish Falcons Alliance**, which from its inception in 1887 admitted women into the organization as non-voting members.—*Donald E. Pienkos*

SOURCES: William Galush, "Purity and Power: Chicago Polonia Feminists, 1880–1814," *Polish American Studies*, Vol. 47, no. 1 (Spring 1990), 5–24; *Teofila Samolinska 1848–1913* (Chicago: Samolinska Memorial Service, 1988); Arthur L. Waldo, *Teofila Samolińska: Matka Zwiazku Narodowego Polskiego w Ameryce* (Chicago: A.L. Waldo, 1980); Arthur L. Waldo, *Pierwsza Sokolica: Teofila Samolińska* (Pittsburgh: Sokolstwo Polskie w Ameryce, 1975).

Sand, Mary (Mary Novak; b. Hennepin County, Minnesota, February 17, 1939; d.—). Speed skater. Active in skating from a young age, Sand was the first skater to win the National Outdoor Championship at every class from Midget through Senior. She won eighteen National and North American Outdoor and Indoor Championships, setting seven records in the process. Following her competitive career she founded several skating clubs and was active in coaching. She was elected to the National Speedskating Hall of Fame in 1972.—*James S. Pula*

SOURCE: www.nationalspeedskatingmuseum.org.

Sarmatian Review. *The Sarmatian Review,* an academic newsletter published three times a year on Polish and Central European affairs, was founded by Professor Ewa Thompson of Rice University in December 1981 under the title of *The Houston Sarmatian.* In 1988 the journal was renamed *The Sarmatian Review,* and in 1998 a separate nonprofit entity, the Polish Institute of Houston, was created to serve as publisher. The financial base for *The Houston Sarmatian* and *The Sarmatian Review* has been provided by subscribers and donors, with no financial support from any government or political organization. Its web version is distributed by Rice University; its archives, in PDF format, are available at the Central and East European Library (ceeol.com); and reformatted versions of the journal are also available through various databases. *The Sarmatian Review* publishes scholarly articles related to Poland and non–Germanic Central and Eastern Europe. It also publishes translations of social, political, and cultural documents, as well as translations of literary works. The publication of primary sources in translation is central to the journal's mission. Each issue contains at least a dozen book reviews. Among the *Sarmatian Review* texts that have proven most popular are the *Memoirs* of Dmitrii Shalikashvili, father of the former Chairman of the Joint Chiefs of Staff, Gen. **John Shalikashvili**; texts by Krzysztof Rak and Mariusz Muszynski on Polish-Russian and Polish-German relations; papers given at the joint Jewish-Polish meeting at the Holocaust Museum Houston in 1998; the poetry of Krzysztof Baczynski; **Alex Kurczaba**'s paper on Polish Studies in America; an interview with Andrzej Wajda; and an interview with Zbigniew Herbert. *The Sarmatian Review* has published numerous archival texts pertaining to Polish history and society that have never before been translated into English. Some of these texts are crucial to the understanding of Polish society in the post–World War II years. The editorial offices are located in the Department of History at Rice University.—*Ewa Thompson*

Sarnoski, Joseph Raymond (b. Simpson, Pennsylvania, January 30, 1915; d. Buka, Solomon Islands, June 16, 1943). Soldier, Medal of Honor recipient. After spending his early years working on the family farm, Sarnoski enlisted in the Army Air Corps in 1936. After receiving specialized training he gained promotion to sergeant in 1940, was assigned as a bombardier on the new B-17, and then assigned as a bombing instructor. Following the outbreak of World War II, Sarnoski was assigned to Australia in 1942 and promoted to technical sergeant and then master sergeant in the 43rd Bomb Group. Moving to the advanced base at Port Moresby, New Guinea, he was awarded a Silver Star for actions in combat, along with a battlefield promotion to second lieutenant. On June 16, 1943, while on a photo reconnaissance mission over Buka off the northern tip of Bougainville Island in the Solomons, his plane was attacked by Japanese fighters. Sarnoski was wounded but continued to man the nose gun, shooting down two enemy fighters. Although blown completely out of the nose compartment by an exploding shell, and severely wounded, Sarnoski climbed back into his position and continued firing on

Joseph R. Sarnoski, Medal of Honor recipient (*NARA*).

the attackers until he died at his post. For his actions he was awarded the Medal of Honor. The citation read: "For conspicuous gallantry and intrepidity in action above and beyond the call of duty. On 16 June 1943, 2d Lt. Sarnoski volunteered as bombardier of a crew on an important photographic mapping mission covering the heavily defended Buka area, Solomon Islands. When the mission was nearly completed, about 20 enemy fighters intercepted. At the nose guns, 2d Lt. Sarnoski fought off the first attackers, making it possible for the pilot to finish the plotted course. When a coordinated frontal attack by the enemy extensively damaged his bomber, and seriously injured 5 of the crew, 2d Lt. Sarnoski, though wounded, continued firing and shot down 2 enemy planes. A 20-millimeter shell which burst in the nose of the bomber knocked him into the catwalk under the cockpit. With indomitable fighting spirit, he crawled back to his post and kept on firing until he collapsed on his guns. 2d Lt. Sarnoski by resolute defense of his aircraft at the price of his life, made possible the completion of a vitally important mission."—*James S. Pula*

SOURCES: R. J. Proft, *United States of America's Congressional Medal of Honor Recipients and Their Official Citations* (Columbia Heights, MN: Highland House II, 2002); *The Medal of Honor of the United States Army* (Washington, D.C.: U.S. Government Printing Office, 1948), 91.

Satalecki, S. F. Adalia (b. Lwów, Poland, 1848; d. Lwów, Poland, 1919). Polonia activist. Born in the Austrian-controlled partitioned Poland, Satalecki settled in Chicago in 1887 where he practiced law. A fine public speaker, fluent in several languages, he was also a prolific essayist and ran unsuccessfully for local public office on a number of occasions. Elected vice president of the **Polish National**

Alliance in 1889, Satalecki served as president for two eventful two-year terms (1891–1895) in the life of early **Polonia**. During his tenure, the competing elements in Polonia came together to raise money to put up an exhibition hall in Lwów to commemorate the centennial of the **Kościuszko** uprising of 1794. They also cooperated in sponsoring a "Polish Day" celebration during the Columbian Exposition of 1893 in Chicago and in opposing a proposed American-Russian treaty that was believed to be adverse to the cause of an independent Poland. It was also during Satalecki's presidency that the **Polish League**, inspired by the Reverend **Wincenty Barzyński**, the dominant figure in the **Polish Roman Catholic Union** at the time, was formed, only to collapse due to PNA opposition led by **Censor Theodore Heliński**. PNA opponents of the League believed the PNA and its Polish independence rationale for existence would be submerged in a federation led by Barzyński. Several PNA leaders initially supported the mission of the Polish League, including Vice President Wiktor Bardonski and **Erazm Jerzmanowski**. Satalecki's position is unclear. In any event, the PNA's withdrawal brought an end to the Polish League. Satalecki's association with **Henry Kałussowski** is believed to have led Kałussowski to donate his personal library to the PNA. This collection of more than six thousand volumes served as the basis of the Alliance's later efforts to provide immigrants with reading materials on Poland's history and literature and led to the creation of a PNA library and reading room in Chicago. Satalecki's connections with Polish émigrés in Europe also strengthened their ties with the PNA. In 1894, a North American branch of the Polish National Treasury was set up under PNA direction to facilitate the collection and forwarding of money to assist the work of the Polish national democratic movement centered in Switzerland. Satalecki did not seek reelection in 1895 and disappeared from the scene, except for the years between 1899 and 1901 when he was back in Chicago and again active in PNA matters. "A mysterious and romantic figure," in the words of the PNA historian Adam Olszewski, he apparently spent time in the American West and even in Alaska engaged in various business interests. He is believed to have died in Poland in 1919 while employed by the Austrian government in the resettlement of Poles returning from America.—*Donald E. Pienkos*

SOURCES: Stanisław Osada, *Historia Związku Narodowego Polskiego i rozwój ruchu narodowego Polskiego w Ameryce Pólnocnej* (Chicago: Nakładem i drukiem Związku Narodowego Polskiego, 1905); Adam Olszewski, *Historia Związku Narodowego Polskiego* (Chicago: Polish National Alliance, 1957–1963).

Saturday Schools, Polish American. The concept of a supplementary Polish Saturday school was first formulated by the **Polish National Alliance** (PNA) to promote and preserve interest in the Polish language and culture for future generations of Polish Americans. As far back as the beginning of the twentieth century, the PNA established a committee, the *Wydział Oświaty* (Education Department), to oversee educational matters pertaining to the PNA. In 1916, dissatisfied with the quality or lack of Polish language studies in schools, and to accommodate both public and parochial school students, a group of progressive **Polonia** leaders, in cooperation with the *Wydzial Oświaty* and its educational counterpart in Poland, first conceived the idea of the Polish Saturday school. In 1926, with the help of the Polish government, the Polish Supplementary School Council of America (PSSCA) was established. This council helped to develop supplementary schools which taught Polish language, history, geography, and culture to children of Polish heritage. These schools, provided with textbooks published in Poland, were staffed by Polish immigrant teachers who had been educated in Poland. The PSSCA thrived on the East Coast of the United States until World War II inhibited its further development. In the early 1940s, there were some 195 schools with approximately 14,000 students throughout the United States, but by 1967 the number had fallen to 43 schools. A decrease in the number of traditional Polish parochial schools and the decline of Saturday schools funded by the PNA continued into the 1960s. As young Polish American families moved out of the old **Polonia** neighborhoods into the suburbs, Polish American communities contracted and Polish language proficiency declined. However, the influx of Polish émigrés after World War II brought a renewed interest in Polish language and cultural instruction. These immigrants were different than their predecessors in their sociological characteristics. Their advocacy for the education of their children through a consortium of Polish Saturday schools reinvigorated the growth of that movement.

The Polish Teachers Association in America (PTAA; Zrzeszenie Nauczycieli Polskich w Ameryce) was formed in Chicago in 1952. Its first Polish Saturday school, named for **Tadeusz Kościuszko**, was located near the Polish Triangle neighborhood on Chicago's northwest side. That same year, the **Kazimierz Pułaski** Saturday School was also established in Chicago. The objectives of the new PTAA were to propagate Polish culture, history, and language by establishing and increasing the number of Polish Saturday schools; to offer

assistance in organizing new Saturday schools in the Chicago area and throughout the United States; to publish textbooks; to acquire and distribute teaching materials; to organize interschool activities; to cooperate with other organizations in the interest of Polish educational, cultural, and charitable issues; and to contribute to other charitable causes. These schools offered programs in Polish education at both the elementary and secondary levels, with the intent of providing children access to subjects that the parochial schools were not able to accommodate.

Saturday school teachers faced many obstacles and challenges including the teachers' own limited English language skills, inadequate textbooks, and difficulty in finding adequate classrooms. Through the resourcefulness of their advocates, these ethnocentric community-based schools were generally able to obtain inexpensive facilities, although sometimes the buildings were not particularly suitable for teaching. They also tended to use textbooks that were published or imported from England, Germany, or, in some cases, the Middle East, and were thus not well adapted to the American experience. Danuta Schneider, an authority on Polish Saturday school education, explained the textbook history this way: "You know that during the end of World War II there were many Poles who were exiled in England, and toward the end of the war over 150,000 Poles from the Siberian labor camps were being transported to England by way of Iraq, Persia (Iran), and/or Palestine. Also, after the war, many Poles were placed in displaced persons camps in Germany, as well as Austria. Wherever Polish refugees arrived or were taken, Polish schools were started, and there were always refugee teachers in these camps who were eager to teach. Even if there were only six children, a school was started. Since there were no textbooks available, these teachers developed their own. Through the help of various agencies, these teachers were able to have them published. This is where the Polish Saturday schools got their first textbooks." Needless to say, many of these were not professionally prepared.

Since the 1980s, Polish Saturday schools have filled a void that most public schools and parochial schools were unable to fill. As new immigrants arrived from Poland during the Solidarity movement of the 1980s and the decade that followed, the number of Saturday school students and teachers increased dramatically. For example, in 1983, there were 18 Polish Saturday schools in the Chicago metropolitan area, with 130 teachers and 3,000 students, ranging from four to 19 years of age.

However, by 2000, there were 27 Polish Saturday schools with 608 teachers serving approximately 12,658 students in the same area. In addition, there were approximately 7,300 students and 466 teachers in 16 other states.

Today, most Polish Saturday schools share a programmatic identity with their American counterparts. Helena Ziolkowska attributes one of the successes of the Polish Saturday schools to "a mandatory standardized program," by which a uniform curriculum is followed by each school in each grade. The textbooks and supplementary materials, which are now published by the PTAA, are the same for all PTAA schools and consistent by grade level. This standardized approach provides all students the opportunity to change schools, if the need arises, without any basic interruption of their Polish language education. Also, teachers are able to benefit by this standardized approach. By fully understanding their responsibilities, teachers confidently create an educational atmosphere of enrichment and an arena in which to share their ideas. Students are motivated by intraschool and interschool competitions in creative writing, art, and other academic areas. Ziolkowska and Schneider, editors of *Głos Nauczyciela* (The Teacher's Voice), the Polish Saturday schools' professional periodical, point out that Polish Saturday schools in the Chicago area have never been owners of their facilities. The schools' administrators did not want to be hampered with mortgages and all that is involved in building maintenance. Instead, they chose to negotiate rental contracts for facilities. The schools rent space from Polish American organizations, Catholic or public schools, as well as in publicly owned city facilities. This enables Polish Saturday schools to focus on educational issues and concerns.

The goals of the PTAA were updated in the 1980s to include organizing teachers' conferences, supplementary courses and methodical workshops during which papers on didactic matters are discussed; evaluating and observing open lessons; updating educational programs; searching for sponsors and other sources for financial and material support; and supervising educational standards. In addition, parents have been at the center of the Saturday School movement. Ziolkowska credits the Parents' Association (Komitet Rodzicielski), an organized parental council established in 1955, with much of the Saturday schools' success. It requires that parents be responsible for finding suitable teaching facilities if the need arises, and for raising money for rent, educational equipment, and, of course, teachers' salaries. Thus, parents are responsible for all the financial aspects of the school, and for ad-

ministering to all of the Saturday schools' needs, such as keeping the school in order during class periods and supervising the entire facility while school is in session. The teachers do the teaching and the principal supervises the teachers. Also, the teachers and principal are solely responsible for the educational aspects of the schools, from the preparation of class work, to the realization of the programs, and selection of textbooks. Additionally, since the Polish Saturday School system publishes its own textbooks, funds it receives from the sale of these textbooks help pay expenses. A growing concern within the Polish Saturday School system is its lack of accreditation by a respected American accreditation system, such state boards of education or the regional accrediting associations. The efforts of the Polish Saturday school principals to gain formal accreditation have, thus far, been unsuccessful. In Illinois the Polish Saturday schools are permitted to certify each graduating high school student as having graduated from a foreign language school and having passed a school-supervised exam. This certification enables a student to take a college or university proficiency exam, which, if passed, may give the student one or two years of college credit in foreign language.—*Geraldine Coleman*

SOURCES: Helena Ziolkowska, ed., *1952–2002: Fiftieth Anniversary of the Polish Teachers Association of America, 50 lat działalności Zrzeszenia Nauczycieli Polskich w Ameryce w służbie Polonii* (Chicago: Polish Teachers Association of America, Inc., 2002); Helena Ziolkowska and Richard Lysakowski, *Polish Saturday Schools in Chicago Area: Their Growth and Development* (Chicago: Polish Teachers Association of America, Inc., 1982).

Savonarola Theological Seminary. The First Synod of the **Polish National Catholic Church**, held in 1904 in Scranton, PA, recognized the need to establish a theological seminary for the training of priests to serve the new denomination and a dues mechanism was created to help raise the necessary funds. Candidates for the priesthood soon began to be accepted. These included interested laymen, former Roman Catholic priests, and priests from the Polish religious **independent movement** in America. The Rev. **Franciszek Hodur**, elected the first bishop of the PNCC by the Synod, undertook organizing the seminary and conducting the training of the first candidates. Over the next quarter of a century, the students were housed at various times in the rectory of St. Stanislaus Bishop and Martyr Cathedral Parish and the Straż Building, both in Scranton, and the facilities of Good Shepherd Parish in Plymouth, PA. In 1926, a building was purchased in Scranton exclusively for the seminary. In 1927, the PNCC established a sister seminary in

Kraków, Poland. In 1950–51, the Scranton building was remodeled and extended. It contains a chapel, offices, dormitory rooms, library, classroom, exercise area, dining hall, and kitchen. As many as 28 students and staff have resided in the building at one time. Over the century, several hundred priests from America and Poland have graduated from or been re-trained at Savonarola Seminary. The largest influx of new students came after World War II, many of them veterans. During 1942–45, while World War II was raging, U.S. seminaries were not permitted to accept new students, thus there were many who enrolled in the immediate postwar years that would normally have done so earlier. More then seventy new priests were ordained between 1935 and 1946. The several Prime Bishops of the PNCC exercised overall supervision over the Seminary. Outstanding rectors or vice-rectors have included: the Rev. Dr. Theophilus Czarkowski, a scholar of Biblical languages and literatures, and the Rev. Bronisław Krupski.—*Theodore L. Zawistowski*

SOURCES: Casimir J. Grotnik, ed., *Polish National Catholic Church: Minutes of the First Eleven General Synods, 1904–1963* (Scranton, PA: Polish National Catholic Church of America Central Diocese and East European Monographs, Boulder, 2002); Casimir J. Grotnik, ed., *Polish National Catholic Church of America: Minutes of the Supreme Council, 1904–1969* (Scranton, PA: Polish National Catholic Church of America Eastern Diocese and East European Monographs, Boulder, 2004).

Sawka, Jan (b. Zabrze, Poland, December 10, 1946; d.—). Artist. Educated at the Institute of Technology in Wrocław, Poland, where he received a Master of Arts degree in Architectural Engineering (1972), he went on to further study at the Fine Arts Academy in Wrocław (MFA in Painting and Printmaking, 1972). He served as artistic director of the Stodola Gallery in Warsaw and the Summer Arts Festival on the Baltic coast (1973–74). A freelance artist and graphic designer in the mid–1970s, in 1976 he migrated via Paris to the United States where he pursued a career as a painter, printmaker, poster artist, illustrator, and sculptor. He is also known for his work on the large-scale concert set for the Grateful Dead (1989) and for his designs for the Wrocław Jazz Festival, Bam Art Theater, *New York Times*, Harold Clurman Theater, Samuel Beckett Theater, and the Jean Cocteau Repertory Theater in New York. He likewise has to his credit multimedia sculptures and other presentations in Abu Dhabi, United Arab Emirates (1996); Lisbon, Portugal (1998); Essen, Germany, Houston, Texas (1999); and Fujisawa, Japan (2004). He is the author of *A Book of Fiction* (1986) and *70 Views En Route to Venice* (1991). Sawka's work appeared in solo exhibitions in the Czech Republic, Finland, France, Germany, Hungary, Italy, Japan, the Netherlands, Poland, Switzerland, and the United States. Among his honors are the Most Outstanding Young Poster Designer, Katowice, Poland (1973); Second Place, Sixth National Graphic Art Exhibition, Warsaw (1973); Warsaw's Best Poster award (1973–81); LOT Polish Airlines Award, 5th International Poster Biennial, Warsaw (1974); Golden Pin Award, *Szpilki* (Pins), Warsaw (1974); Oscar de la Peinture and Special Prize of the President of France, Cagnes-sur-Mer (1975); Gold Medal and First Place, Seventh International Poster Biennial, Warsaw (1978); Pride of Honor, 3rd Biennial of Poster Design, Lahti, Finland (1979); Eyes and Ears Foundation Award, Los Angeles (1979); Book of the Year Award, New York Times (1986); Silver Medal, 14th Biennial of Graphic Design, Brno (1990); Artist Laureate, Seventh Colorado International Invitational Poster Exhibition, Fort Collins (1991); Japanese Cultural Agency Award (1994); Award of Merit, Ninth Colorado International Invitational Poster Exhibition, Fort Collins (1995); Premio di Lorenzo Il Magnifico Gold Medal in Multimedia, Florence, Italy (2003).—*Stanley L. Cuba*

SOURCES: Joseph S. Czestochowski, ed., *Contemporary Polish Posters in Full Color* (New York: Dover Publications, Inc., 1979); Zdzisław Schubert, *The Polish Poster 1970–1980* (Warsaw: Krajowa Agencja Wydawnicza, 1982); Stanley Cuba, *Jan Sawka: A Selected Retrospective* (Arvada, CO: Arvada Center for the Arts and Humanities, 1990); Marek Rostworowski, *The Returns* (Kraków: Muzeum Narodowe w Krakowie, 1991).

Sawko, Chester S. (b. Poland, January 15, 1930; d.—). Businessman, inventor. Sawko and his family were deported to Siberia by the Soviet authorities in 1939 and only survived the experience by finding a way out of the Archangel region to Iran where he was sent to the Santa Rosa colony established by the Polish Relief organization, Rada Polonii Amerykańskiej (**Polish American Council**). He remained there until the war's end. Sawko served in the U.S. Army during the Korean War. Returning to Chicago, he established his own business in 1959, the R.C. Coil Spring Company, in Glendale Heights, Illinois. His very successful firm was a leader in the production of compression springs, wire forms, stampings, and rings used in the automotive industry, in construction, and in other fields. Sawko studied at **Alliance College** after the war and later served on its Advisory Council. He received an honorary degree from the College in 1975. Sawko was a generous benefactor of numerous Polish and **Polonia** charitable causes and funded the monument of Pope John Paul II and Cardinal Stefan Wyszyński

located in the Jasna Gora Monastery in Częstochowa, Poland.—*Donald E. Pienkos*

SOURCE: Wojciech Wierzewski, "Sto Trzydziesta Slynnych Polaków w Ameryce" (Unpublished manuscript in the archives of the University of Wisconsin–Milwaukee, 2000).

Schakowsky, Janice D. "Jan" (b. Chicago, Illinois; May 26, 1944; d.—). Congressman, teacher, consumer rights advocate. Schakowsky attended Sullivan High School in Chicago before earning a B.S. in elementary education from the University of Illinois (1965). In 1969 she led a fight, with the National Consumers Unite group that she founded, to put freshness dates on grocery products. She was also a member of the consumer group Illinois Public Action. She served as director of the Illinois State Council of Senior Citizens (1985–90), and in 1989 organized a protest by elderly people against Representative **Dan Rostenkowski**'s Medicare Catastrophic Health Care law, leading Congress to repeal it as inadequate. She was a leading advocate for social issues such as preventing violence against women immigrants, establishing transitional housing for victims of abuse, and fostering a single payer government health insurance. Elected to the Illinois General Assembly (1990–98), she was then elected as a Democrat to an open seat in the One Hundred Sixth and to the five succeeding Congresses (beginning January 3, 1999). Schakowsky was a member of the Congressional Progressive Caucus and served as the Democratic Chair of the bipartisan Congressional Caucus on Women's Issues. In 2003 she opposed the Republican-sponsored prescription drug bill. She briefly considered running for the U.S. Senate in 2004, but decided instead to remain in the House. In 2008, Schakowsky easily beat the first challenger she faced in a Democratic Party primary since she was elected in 1998. She was a member of the Committee on Energy and Commerce, the Permanent Subcommittee on Intelligence, and was a chief deputy party whip in the House.—*Frederick J. Augustyn*

SOURCES: *Biographical Directory of the United States Congress, 1774–Present* (http://bioguide.congress.gov/); "Janice Schakowsky" in *Women in Congress, 1917–2006* (Washington: Government Printing Office, 2006); "Schakowsky Cruises to Primary Victory," *Daily Herald* (Arlington Heights, IL), February 6, 2008, 18.

Schally, Andrew Victor (Andrzej Wiktor Schally; b. Wilno, Poland, November 30, 1926; d.—). Physiologist, endocrinologist. During the Second World War, Schally survived the Holocaust, moving to Great Britain in 1946. He completed his high school education in Scotland, after which he studied chemistry at the University of London, soon joining the prestigious National Institute of

Medical Research. In 1952 he moved to McGill University in Montréal where he participated in research on brain functions and endocrinology at the Allan Memorial Institute of Psychiatry. In 1955 he and a colleague demonstrated for the first time the existence of hypothalamic hormones regulating pituitary functions. After receiving his doctorate from McGill in 1957, he accepted a position at the Baylor University College of Medicine in Texas where he served as both assistant professor of Physiology and a Senior Research Fellow of the U.S. Public Health Service. Becoming a U.S. citizen in 1962, he was in the same year named Chief of the Endocrine and Polypeptide Laboratories being established by the Veterans Administration in New Orleans. Upon taking the new position Schally also served as associate professor of Medicine at Tulane University, being promoted to professor in 1966. In 1973 he was named a Senior Medical Investigator, a prestigious honor of the Veterans Administration. Schally gained an international reputation for his research on endocrinology and growth hormones, including the neurohormone GnRH and the isolation and synthesis of somatostatin, TRH (thyrotropin-releasing hormone), and LHRH (luteinizing hormone-releasing hormone). He is the author of more than 2,000 publications. His research has been honored with the Van Meter Prize of the American Thyroid Association, the Ayerst-Squibb Award of the U.S. Endocrine Society, the Veterans Administration's William S. Middleton Award, the Charles Mickle Award of the University of Toronto, the Gairdner Foundation International Award from Canada, the Edward T. Tyler Award, the Borden Award of the Association of American Medical Colleges, the Albert Lasker Basic Medical Research Award, the Laude Award from Spain, and honorary doctorates from nearly twenty universities including the Jagiellonian University in Kraków, the Sorbonne in Paris, McGill and the University of Madrid. In 1977 Schally was awarded the Nobel Prize in Physiology of Medicine for "discoveries concerning the peptide hormone production of the brain" and "development of radioimmunoassays of peptide hormones."—*James S. Pula*

SOURCE: Wilhelm Odelberg, ed., *The Nobel Prizes 1977* (Stockholm, Sweden: Nobel Foundation, 1978).

Schemansky, Norbert (b. Detroit, Michigan, May 30, 1924; d.—). Weightlifter. Schemansky took up weightlifting as a youth, and competed in his first world championship meet at age 17. As a member of the United States Olympic team, he won a gold medal in 1952 (middle heavyweight division), silver in

1948 (heavyweight), and bronze in 1960 and 1964 (heavyweight). He was the first weight-lifter to earn four Olympic medals. Scheman-sky was recognized as middle heavyweight world champion in 1951, 1953, and 1954, and won numerous American championships. He is a member of the International Weightlifting Federation Hall of Fame, and was inducted into the National Polish-American Sports Hall of Fame in 1979.—*Neal Pease*

SOURCE: "Norbert Schemansky," National Polish-American Sports Hall of Fame website, www.polish sportshof.com.

Schermann, Antoni (or sometimes Sher-man; Antoni Smagorzewski or Smarzewski; b. Wagrowice, Poland, May 24, 1818; d. Chicago, Illinois, September 1900). Businessman, Polo-nia activist. Sherman arrived in Chicago with his wife and three children on June 1, 1851, where he found work with the Chicago & Alton Railway Company. Arriving with vir-tually nothing, in 1867 he opened a tavern and grocery store at the corner of Noble and Bradley Streets, and later a bookstore. In 1868, he was named an immigration agent for Chicago and opened the "Polish Agency" at his business location. An early **Polonia** activist, he was a founder of the St. Stanislaus Kostka Society in 1864 and St. Stanislaus Kostka Parish three years later. In 1870 the so-ciety purchased lands adjacent to Sherman's property for the construction of a church. He became one of the richest Poles, and possibly the richest, in the United States during his lifetime.—*James S. Pula*

SOURCES: Edward R. Kantowicz, *Polish-American Politics in Chicago* (Chicago: University of Chicago Press, 1975), 14, 230; Wacław Kruszka, *A History of*

The Chicago business owned by Anton Schermann (Antoni Smarzewski) sold steamship tickets and acted as a foreign exchange bank (*PMA*).

the Poles in America to 1908 (Washington, D.C.: The Catholic University of America Press, Vols. I, II); *Album Pamiątkowe z Okazji Złotego Jubileuszu Parafii św Stanisława K Chicago, Illinois, 1867–1917* (Chicago: St. Stanislaus Kostka Parish, 1917).

Schoepf, Albin Francis (b. Podgórze, Poland, March 1, 1822; d. Washington, D.C., May 10, 1886). Military Officer. After gradu-ating from the Vienna Military Academy in 1841 as a lieutenant of artillery, he served in Hungary as a captain in the Austrian army. Upon the outbreak of the Magyar Revolution, Schoepf resigned his commission and enlisted in the Hungarian revolutionary forces in the newly formed Polish Legion under Lajos Kos-suth, a lawyer who became president of Hun-gary during the war between Austria and Hungary (1848–49). Enlisting as a private in the legion, he rose in the ranks to major. When Kossuth abdicated in 1849, Schoepf was exiled with Kossuth to Turkey where he served with and trained the Ottoman Empire's army before migrating to the United States in 1851. Arriving in Washington, D.C., he found employment as a hotel porter. Here he was befriended by Joseph Holt, U.S. patent com-missioner, who recommended Schoepf for a drafting position in the patent office. With Holt's star rapidly rising in national political circles, the fortunes of Schoepf also rose. Appointed Secretary of War by President James Buchanan, Holt made arrangements for Schoepf's transfer to the War Department, and then dispatched him to Virginia where he was authorized to prepare a military sur-vey.

With the outbreak of the Civil War, Schoef was appointed a brigadier general in the Union army in September 1861. He commanded his brigade in a victory at Wildcat Mountain, repuls-ing Confederates under Felix Zollicoffer, and led troops at Logan's Cross Roads where Zollicoffer was killed. Proving himself an aggressive and able field commander, Schoepf was promoted to division com-mand in August 1862, but often found himself at odds with Gen. Don Car-los Buell, commander of the Army of the Ohio, es-pecially after being denied orders to attack until late in the Battle of Perryville. Appointed to a board of inquiry investigating Buell during the campaign,

Schoepf made no secret of his disapproval of Buell's actions, so much so that Buell raised Schoepf's hostility as an issue. Not wanting his involvement to affect the Buell investiga-tion's outcome, Schoepf asked army com-mander Henry W. Halleck to transfer him to another assignment. On April 13, 1863, Schoepf was ordered to report to Fort Delaware, serving there as commanding officer of a prisoner-of-war complex for the balance of the war. In this assignment his fairness earned him the respect not only of his subordinates, but also of the imprisoned Confederate soldiers. Dur-ing his posting at Fort Delaware he acquired a reputation of a man of sobriety and com-passion and, his supervision and administra-tion of the fort was one of forbearance and efficiency.

On January 15, 1866, Schoepf was dis-charged from the Army. Upon his return to civilian life, he obtained the title of principal examiner in the Patent Office and served there in honorable employment until his death (likely due to stomach cancer). He was buried in the Congressional Cemetery in Washington, D.C.—*Luis J. Gonzalez*

SOURCES: Charles A. Baretski, "General Albin Francis Schoepf—A Preliminary View," *Polish Amer-ican Studies*, Vol. XXIII, no. 2 (1966), 93–96; Mieci-slaus Haiman, "General Albin F. Schoepf," *Polish Amer-ican Studies*, Vol. II, no. 3–4 (1945), 70–78.

Schreiber, Antoni (Antoni Pisarski; b. Raciaz, Poland, January 12, 1864; d. Buffalo, New York, November 8, 1939). Entrepreneur, Polonia activist. Born in the Prussian-ruled partition of Poland, Schreiber earned a degree in chemistry at the University of Berlin, later emigrating to the U.S. where he settled in Buffalo and opened the Schreiber Brewing Company. In 1886 he joined the **Polish Na-tional Alliance** as its 1,797th member. In 1905 he was elected **censor** of the PNA, hold-ing that post for the next eight years. During his tenure, the PNA established a new system of elected officers at the regional level to help direct the activities of the rapidly expanding membership in the Alliance. Together, these individuals met under the chairmanship of the censor. One of the Council's duties was to elect national officers of the Alliance, the election occurring between its national conventions. In 1908 the PNA established its own daily newspaper in Chicago, *Dziennik Związkowy* (The Alliance Daily). In 1910 the fraternal sponsored a Polish national congress in Washington, D.C., to express **Polonia**'s po-sitions on the issues of Poland's independence and Polish immigration to the U.S. The congress took place immediately following the dedication of monuments to **Kazimierz Pułaski** and **Tadeusz Kościuszko** by President

Antoni Schreiber, entrepreneur and Polonia activist (*OLS*).

William Howard Taft. The Kościuszko monument was underwritten by the PNA with Schreiber's strong support. Schreiber was also involved with fund raising work on behalf of the Polish National Treasury (Skarb Narodowy), a PNA cause going back to the late 1880s. In 1911 the PNA approved the establishment of its own school in Erie, Pennsylvania. Named **Alliance College**, it was another major area of activity for Schreiber, who was the proprietor of his own brewery in Buffalo, New York, producing, among other beverages, a beer named "Manru" after **Ignacy Jan Paderewski**'s opera. One of the most energetic and effective of PNA censors, Schreiber was honored in 1931 at the 26th PNA national convention in Scranton, Pennsylvania, with admission into its Legion of Honor in recognition of his services to the Alliance and **Polonia**.—*Donald E. Pienkos*

SOURCES: Adam Olszewski, *Historia Związku Narodowego Polskiego* (Chicago: Polish National Alliance, 1957–1963), Vol. 2; Donald E. Pienkos, *PNA: A Centennial History of the Polish National Alliance of the United States of North America* (Boulder, CO: East European Monographs, 1984).

Schwatka, Frederick (b. Galena, Illinois, September 29, 1849; d. Portland, Oregon, November 2, 1892). Explorer. After graduating from the U.S. Military Academy at West Point (1867–71), Schwatka was appointed 2nd lieutenant in the 3rd Cavalry and was assigned to duty in the Dakota Territory until 1877. During his service he studied law and was admitted to the Nebraska bar in 1875, the same year

he also received a medical degree from Bellevue Medical College in New York. He led an expedition into King William's Land (1878–80) in the Arctic where he discovered the remains of Sir John Franklin and his missing party, completing in the process the longest sledge journeys on record. In 1883 the army assigned him to explore the Yukon River, which he completed to the Bering Sea in the longest journey by raft in history. He rejoined his regiment in 1884, but resigned his commission in 1885. In the following year he led an expedition to Alaska funded by the *New York Times*. The explorers climbed Mt. St. Elias to a height of 7,200 feet. In 1889 he led an expedition to Mexico, then, in 1891 he headed another expedition into hitherto unexplored regions of Alaska. He later undertook two private expeditions to Alaska and three to Mexico. As a foremost Arctic explorer, he authored a dictionary of the Eskimo language and published several books on his exploits including *The Search for Franklin* (1882), *Along Alaska's Great River* (1885), *Nimrod in the North* (1885), *The Children of the Cold* (1886), *In the Land of Cave and Cliff Dwellers* (1893), and *A Summer in Alaska* (1894). He was honored for his achievements with several prestigious American and international awards including the Roquette Arctic Medal from the Geographical Society of Paris, a medal from the Imperial Geographical Society of Russia, and honorary membership in geographical societies in Bremen, Geneva, and Rome. Mount Schwatka in Alaska and Schwatka Lake in the Yukon are both named for him.—*James S. Pula*

SOURCES: William H. Gilder, *Schwatka's Search: Sledging in the Arctic in Quest of the Freanklin Records* (New York: C. Scribner's Sons, 1881); *The Search for Franklin: A Narrative of the American Expedition Under Lieutenant Schwatka, 1878 to 1880* (Edinburgh and London: T. Nelson, 1881); *Dictionary of American Biography* (New York: Scribner, 1928), Vol. XVI, 481–82; *The National Cyclopaedia of American Biography* (New York, J.T. White Co., 1893), Vol. III, 285.

Scouting, Polish American (*harcerstwo*). World scouting developed at the end of the nineteenth and beginning of the twentieth centuries under the spiritual leadership of Robert Baden-Powell and his wife Olave. In Poland, Andrzej and Olga Małkowski founded a Polish scouting movement known as *harcerstwo*. From its inception, Polish *harcerstwo* emphasized patriotic upbringing of the youth and work towards Poland's independence. The Małkowskis visited the United States and **Polonia** communities before World War I and soon afterwards the first publications about scouting and manuals for scouting instructors appeared in Polonia. The greatest development of Polish American scouting, which was spon-

sored by Polonia fraternals, took place in the 1930s, inspired by the wide-spread concern about the progress of Americanization among the younger generation born and raised in America. Scouting became one of the vast array of youth programs designed to provide attractive social alternatives to Polonia youth and keep them within the community. The movement, however, declined by the end of the decade and eventually disintegrated with the outbreak of World War II. In the postwar years, a new *harcerstwo* organization was established by the exiles and refugees from the Polish political diaspora (see **New Immigration**). Strengthened by the subsequent waves of Polish immigration to the U.S., the Polish Scouting Organization (Związek Harcerstwa Polskiego, ZHP), which is affiliated with the Polish Scouting Association, a world organization headquartered in London, continues to attract newest arrivals within Polonia communities.

The **Polish Roman Catholic Union** (PRCUA) formed the first scout troops in Chicago in the early 1920s, but scouting did not become officially a part of the fraternal until 1933. The PRCUA's scouting organization affiliated with the Boy Scouts of America, following an example of other similar ethnically based movements. By 1934, the PRCUA sponsored 74 male scout troops with 6,600 members and 15 female scout troops with more than 460 members. According to John Radziłowski, the PRCUA's "scouting activities expanded with the formation of Cub Scouts, Junior Daughters, Senior Daughters, and Sea Scouts.... By 1941, 215 Union scout troops existed." The bi-lingual newspaper *Ognisko* (Campfire) served as the PRCUA's scouting publication.

In 1935, the PRCUA boy and girl scouts journeyed to Poland for an international jamboree in Spała celebrating the 25th anniversary of the organization in Poland. Together with president **Józef Kania** and other PRCUA leaders, the youth travelled around Poland visiting historic places. Among others things, they laid flower wreaths at the tomb of Józef Piłsudski and at the Eaglets' Cemetery in Lwów. The trip helped to emphasize the Polish character of the organization, which, according to some of its critics, ushered in Americanization of Polonia youth through its affiliation with American scouting. In 1939, the PRCUA's Youth Department bought extensive camp grounds located to the south of Chicago, and named them Camp Gieryk, after one of the fraternal's founders. Camp Gieryk proved a perfect location for scout jamborees, meets, summer camps, and various educational and art programs and sports events for the younger generation.

Beginning in 1931, the **Polish National Alliance** (PNA) started to form *harcerstwo* troops, independent of the Boy Scouts of America. The idea originated with **John Romaszkiewicz**, a new PNA president. He wanted to create a counterbalance to some of the American activities for youth — such as baseball, bowling, and basketball — and instead linked the *harcerstwo* program and methods to the traditions of the **Polish Falcons** and to the ZHP in Poland. As a PNA president, Romaszkiewicz automatically became the head of the *harcerstwo*, pouring much of his own ideas and energy into the development of the organization. According to **Donald Pienkos**, Romaszkiewicz "established his youth groups in conscious imitation of the Polish model and encouraged the wearing of uniforms of the Polish *harcerstwo*, and the teaching of Polish songs, language and sport activities that were popular in the ancestral homeland. Through all these programs Romaszkiewicz and his followers believed it possible to reinvigorate ethnic feeling among Polonia's youth by identifying with post war Poland."

In 1932, Stanisław Kołodziejczyk was appointed the head scoutmaster of the PNA organization and immediately launched the first scout training workshop in Chicago. On May 3, 1932, the Consul of Poland presented the *harcerstwo* with a banner. Two years later, *harcerstwo* included 23,000 active members grouped in 486 troops. According to some estimates, by 1938, this number quadrupled and reached close to 80,000 members. In addition, several thousand instructors, leaders, and other adult supporters were also actively engaged in the many scouting activities.

The PNA *harcerstwo* developed an active relationship with scouting in Poland. Between 1933 and 1938, Polish American scouts visited Poland five times, participating in camps,

jamborees, and summer courses. With the support of **Światpol**, Polish scoutmasters organized training workshops for their counterparts in both Canada and the U.S.; for example, in **Alliance College** in Cambridge Springs, Pennsylvania.

The close collaboration with Poland's government, and particularly with the Piłsudski regime, the paramilitary character of the organization, and its refusal to affiliate with American scouting, drew criticism from the conservative faction in the PNA led by **Francis Swietlik**. At the same time, the Boy Scouts of America continued to pressure the PNA to join the American organization and to begin paying membership dues. In 1938, **Karol Rozmarek**, Swietlik's supporter, was elected the new PNA president. On his initiative, the PNA convention in Detroit discontinued the name, the uniforms, and other symbols of the *harcerstwo*, reorganizing the movement under the name of *Drużyny Młodzieżowe* (youth troops), subordinate to the PNA's Department of Youth and Sports. The move proved detrimental to further development of the organization, as the new youth troops enjoyed far less support and popularity. With the outbreak of World War II, many devoted instructors joined the military and the organization further declined.

During World War II, *harcerstwo* in Poland continued its activities underground, particularly in the form of *Szare Szeregi* (Grey Ranks) and *Hufce Polskie* (Polish Brigades). The organization was also revived among Polish refugees and exiles scattered around the globe. Wherever Polish exile communities formed, there the new scouting troops were created. In the autumn of 1939, the Head Committee (*Komitet Naczelny*) of ZHP resumed its activity first in France, and then in London. In the Middle East, scouting troops,

sponsored by the Carpathian Brigade, were established in 1940. After the evacuation of Polish civilian deportees from the Soviet Union, the numbers of children, as well as experienced scout instructors in the Middle East, grew dramatically. ZHP was quickly reconstructed there with the help of the Second Corps under the command of General Władysław Anders.

Polish refugees in Africa, Great Britain, New Zealand, India, Santa Rosa in Mexico, as well as in the occupation zones of Germany, Austria and Italy, also re-established local scouting organizations. In the Displaced Persons camps in Germany and Austria, where the environment was particularly inadequate for the proper physical and mental development of children, exiled instructors immediately began organizing boy and girl scout troops. In the conditions of forced exile, the young generation of Poles was given a chance to learn, bond, and retain traditional patriotic values. In December 1945, *harcerstwo* in Germany included about 25,000 members, with 120 instructors leading 800 troops. As a result of repatriation to Poland and resettlement in other countries, the organization continued to diminish, but in 1950 Polish scouting in Displaced Person camps in Germany still included about four thousand active members.

Many scouting instructors and leaders migrated to the United States, where they immediately began building the structures of a new Polish *harcerstwo*, which was a part of the larger political Diaspora's ZHP organization with headquarters located in London. In 1949, the first boy and girl scout troops were formed in Chicago, Detroit, New York, New Jersey, and Connecticut. An important element of the movement became the patriotic upbringing of the youth in the pre-war Polish spirit. An example of such spirit was the inscription

Group No. 2 of the Harcerstwo (Scouts) in Milwaukee, Wisconsin (*UWM*).

in the Chicago troop's chronicle in the 1950s, written by a young Polish *harcerka* (female scout) who adopted it as her life motto: "Through *harcerstwo* to a free Poland!" Polish *harcerze* and *harcerki* dressed in their uniforms represented patriotic Polish youth during national celebrations, religious commemorations, and ethnic parades.

The ZHP District for the U.S., established in 1951, eventually set up four regional districts: Chicago; Detroit; "Atlantyk" (New York, Connecticut, Massachusetts, New Jersey, Pennsylvania, and Washington, D.C.); and "Pacyfik" on the West Coast. By 1990, about two thousand Polish girl and boy scouts were members of *harcerstwo*. ZHP in the U.S. continued traditional activities developed in pre-war Poland, which included camps, jamborees, and meets organized on a local and national scale, as well as various educational, sports, and arts programs. Working relationships were also established between ZHP and other ethnic scouting organizations. The activities of troops were aided by Koła Przyjaciół Harcerstwa (The Friends of *Harcerstwo* Circles), grouping parents and other adults supporting the movement. Scouting publications and press also developed, including *Czuj Duch* (Stay Alert), *Spójnik Terenowy* (Local Connector) *Wici 75-Lecia* (75th Anniversary News), and *Znicz* (The Torch). In the 1980s, the archives of the ZHP found their home in a special room within the **Central Archives of Polonia** in Orchard Lake, Michigan.—*Anna D. Jaroszyńska-Kirchmann*

SOURCES: John Radziłowski, *The Eagle and the Cross: A History of the Polish Roman Catholic Union of America* (Boulder, Co: East European Monographs, 2003); Donald E. Pienkos, *PNA: Centennial History of the Polish National Alliance of the United States of North America* (Boulder, Co.: East European Monographs, 1984); Anna D. Jaroszyńska-Kirchmann, *The Exile Mission: The Polish Political Diaspora and Polish Americans, 1939–1956* (Athens: Ohio University Press, 2004); Ewa Gierat, *Powojenna Historia Harcerstwa w Stanach Zjednoczonych* (Detroit: Zarząd Okręgu ZHP, 1990).

Sculpture *see* Fine Arts.

Second Generation *see* Generations, Polish American.

Sejda, Jan (b. Poland, December 27, 1927; d. San Francisco, California, October 10, 1982). Dancer, choreographer, poet. After studying ballet, theatre arts, and choreography in Poland, Sejda traveled throughout the countryside seeking and preserving Polish regional folk songs and dances. One of the original members of the Polish national dance ensemble Mazowsze, and a noted expert on Polish culture and customs, he was an outstanding choreographer and directed performances involving over 3,800 singers and

dancers in Silesia, Poland. After he moved to the United States, he founded the Kujawiaki Dancers and Singers, a student ensemble group of **Alliance College**, serving as its director from 1965 to 1972. In the latter year he moved to the San Francisco Bay area to become artistic director of the Khadra International Folk Ballet and choreographer for the Łowiczanie Polish Folk Dance Ensemble. At folk dance camps and seminars he gave sessions involving a variety of folk arts, costuming, folk songs, stories, and even Polish paper cutting. His publications include: *To... Ty. Poezje* (It's... You. Poetry; 1964), *Dwadzieścia pieśni polskich* (Twenty Polish Songs; 1969), and *Polish Folk Dances* (1969).—*Adam A. Zych*

SOURCE: Adam A. Zych, *Na mojej ziemi był Oświęcim: Oświęcim w poezji współczesnej* (Oświęcim: Wydawn. Państwowego Muzeum w Oświęcimiu, 1987).

Sejm Wychództwa *see* Congress of the Emigration.

Sembrich, Marcella (Prakseda Marcelina Kochańska; b. in Wiśniewczyk, Eastern Galicia, Poland, February 15, 1858; d. New York, New York, January 11, 1935). Opera singer. After studies in the Lemberg Conservatory and the Vienna Conservatory, Sembrich debuted in Athens, Greece, in 1877 as Elvira in Bellini's *I Puritani*. Later she performed in Vienna, Dresden, Warsaw, and London. In 1880 she married Wilhelm Stengel (1880), her former teacher and later a manager. In 1881 she performed in St. Petersburg, London, Moscow, and several other venues. Her debut in the U.S. took place on October 24, 1883, in the Metropolitan Opera, New York, where she played Lucia in Donizetti's *Lucia di Lammermoor*. Between her opening engagement and her last appearance at the Metropolitan Opera in 1909, Sembrich made over 450 performances. After European tours she returned to the U.S. in 1898 and for twenty seasons (with the exception of 1900–01) performed there. Sembrich sang for the last time in Warsaw on May 10, 1909, after which she performed in Vienna, Berlin, and St. Petersburg. She was considered one of the best coloratura sopranos in the world, and her repertoire included works in Italian, German, French, Russian, Spanish, Polish, and English. Retiring to Les Vergers, Switzerland, in 1912, Sembrich returned to America in 1914, becoming honorary president of the Polish National Relief Fund. Her active involvement in charitable causes included efforts to inform American audiences about the living conditions Poland during World War I. In January 1915 Sembrich became president of the American Polish Relief Committee in New York where she initiated a series of charity concerts, during

Marcella Sembrich, opera singer (*PMA*).

which she also sang, to collect funds for humanitarian aid to the Polish people. Cooperating with other organizations, she maintained close contact with **Henryk Sienkiewicz**'s Polish relief committee in Vevey, Switzerland, through which she transferred money intended for Polish relief. She left the presidency of the APRC at the end of 1915. After 1917, Sembrich taught in music schools in Philadelphia and New York, founding in New York in 1940 the Marcella Sembrich Memorial Association which cultivates her memory and organizes contests for operatic artists. The **Marcella Sembrich Opera Museum** is located in Bolton Landing, New York, and the **Kosciuszko Foundation** in New York City sponsors an annual "Marcella Sembrich Voice Competition." Her personal papers and musical scores are preserved in the Music Division of the New York Public Library.—*Adam Walaszek*

SOURCES: E. Vincentelli, "Sembrich, Marcella," in ed. Judy Barrett Litoff and Judith McDonnell, eds., *European Immigrant Women in the United States. A Biographical Dictionary* (New York–London: Garland Publishers, 1994), 277–78; H. Goddard Owen, *A Recollection of Marcella Sembrich* (New York: DaCapo Press, 1982).

Sendak, Maurice (Bernard Sendak; b. Brooklyn, New York, June 10, 1928; d.—). Illustrator, designer, author. Born to parents who married in America after migrating from small *shtetls* near Warsaw before World War I, Sendak developed an interest in drawing as a child. While attending high school in Brooklyn, he worked for All-American Comics filling in backgrounds for a comic strip they published. His first book illustration that was professionally published was for a textbook, *Atomics for the Millions* (1947). After completing high school, he did window displays at the toy store FAO Schwarz while attending classes at New York's Art Students League. In 1950, while at Schwarz, Ursula Nordstrom, Harper's legendary children's book editor, saw his work and was impressed. She arranged for him to illustrate *The Wonderful Farm*. That same year he also illustrated *Good Shabbos, Everybody* for the United Synagogue Commission on Jewish Education. In 1952 Sendak illustrated his first "concept" book, *A Hole Is to Dig*, earning enthusiastic comments from critics and a *New York Times* Best Illustrated Book Award. He won the same award four more times during the 1950s and was also nominated for two Caldecott Awards during the same decade. Initially, all of his art work complemented other people's text, but in 1956 he wrote and illustrated *Kenny's Window*.

In 1960 he authored and illustrated *The Sign on Rosie's Door* and in 1962 created the four diminutive books of *The Nutshell Library*. In 1963 he wrote and illustrated *Where the Wild Things Are* which won a *New York Times* Best Illustrated Book Award, the following year being awarded a Caldecott Medal. His work earned five more *New York Times* Best Illustrated Book Awards during the 1960s. In 1970 Sendak became the first American to receive the Hans Christian Andersen International Medal for his work in children's illustration. That year he published *In the Night Kitchen* which won several awards including being named a Caldecott Honor Book in 1971. During the 1970s he became involved in other media, serving as director and lyricist for *Really Rosie, Starring the Nutshell Kids*, an animated special broadcast on CBS in 1975. In 1978 he worked as set designer and lyricist for the musical *Really Rosie*, which reached New York in 1980. At the same time, he continued to work on book illustrations, twice earning *New York Times* Best Illustrated Book Awards during the 1970s.

In 1981, his *Outside Over There* was named a Caldecott Honor Book, a [Boston] Globe/Horn Book winner, and in 1892, an American Book Award. In 1983 he won the Laura Ingalls Wilder Award for his corpus of work, and in 1996 a National Medal of Arts for his contribution to the arts in the United States. The Swedish government bestowed on him the first Astrid Lindgren Memorial Award (2003), an international prize for children's literature. During the decades following 1980, he turned his attention to opera and theater design. In 1980 he designed Mozart's *The Magic Flute* for the Houston Grand Opera, later serving

as lyricist, set and costume designer for the opera *Where the Wild Things Are*, produced in New York in 1984. He designed a total of six operas for major companies during the 1980s. During the 1990s he co-founded and served as artistic director of a national children's theater, The Night Kitchen. In 2000 he designed the opera *Brundibar*, a children's opera written by Jews during the Holocaust and performed at Terezin, a Nazi concentration camp. In 2003 he gave the Arbuthnot lecture and in 2005 designed the opera *The Comedy on the Bridge*. Sendak enjoyed a long and distinguished career, receiving almost every possible prize for children's literature. He has also transformed the genre, allowing it to express darker emotions than it had prior to the publication of *Where the Wild Things Are*.—*Scott Scheidlower*

SOURCES: John Cech, *Angels and Wild Things: The Archetypal Poetics of Maurice Sendak* (University Park: Pennsylvania State University Press, 1995); Selma G. Lanes, *The Art of Maurice Sendak* (New York: Abrams, 1980).

Sendzimir, Michael (b. Shanghai, China, November 21, 1924; d. Waterbury, Connecticut, August 31, 2008). Engineer, businessman. Educated as a youth in Poland, Switzerland, and New York, Sendzimir served as a second lieutenant in the U.S. Army during the Second World War. He earned a baccalaureate degree in industrial engineering from the Columbia School of Engineering (1951), and received honorary doctorates in science (1986) and law (1993). He began working with his father's firm, T. Sendzimir, Inc. (see **Sendzimir, Thaddeus**) in 1948 and served as president for more than four decades. When his father died in 1989, Sendzimir replaced him as chairman of the board as well. Considered a world authority on multi-roll rolling mills for flat products, he was largely responsible for development of the Sendzimir cold strip mill used almost exclusively for stainless steel and special applications in rolling silicon steel. Sendzimir served as chair of the board of directors of the **Kosciuszko Foundation**, and for many years was on the board of directors of the **Polish Institute of Arts & Sciences**, and a member of several other boards including the Salvation Army, the Waterbury (CT) Symphony Orchestra, the Waterbury Hospital, and the Biotechnology Foundation. President Lech Wałęsa of Poland honored him with the Gold Order of Merit of the Polish Republic in 1992.—*James S. Pula*

SOURCE: "Michael G. Sendzimir (1924–2008)," *The Polish Review*, Vol. 53, no. 3 (2008), 411–412.

Sendzimir, Thaddeus (Tadeusz Sędzimir; b. Lwów, Poland, July 15, 1894; d. Jupiter, Florida, September 1, 1989). Engineer,

inventor. Sendzimir gave his name to a revolutionary method of processing steel and metals employed throughout the industrialized world. Educated in the Gimnazjum Klasyczne in Lwów, he entered but never graduated from the prestigious Politechnika Lwówska because once Russian troops captured Lwów the Polytechnic Institute was closed. Sendzimir worked for a time in auto services in Kiev and in the Russian-American Chamber of Commerce where he learned both Russian and English, but was forced to flee Russia during the Russian Revolution. Moving first to Vladivostok and then to Shanghai, he built the first factory in China producing screws, nails, and wire. By 1929 he began experimenting with new ways to galvanize steel, but was unable to enlist the support of any American industrialists or investors in his project. He arrived in San Francisco in 1930 but returned to Poland in 1931 where he obtained support for the construction of the first industrial-scale galvanizing unit and placed into operation several cold strip mills. Sendzimir later founded a steel mill in Butler, Pennsylvania, in 1936 and two years later he formed a partnership, the Armzen Company, with Armco Steel to oversee the burgeoning galvanizing and mill technologies. Sendzimir left Paris in 1939 to establish residence in Middletown, Ohio. Soon thereafter he founded T. Sendzimir, Inc. in Waterbury, Connecticut, an operation that eventually had plants in thirty-four countries worldwide. While honored in interwar Poland with the award of the Golden Cross of Merit in 1938, his achievements were never properly recognized in "socialist Poland" until he was awarded the Officer Cross of the Order *Polonia Restituta* by then first-secretary Edward Gierek. Later, in 1975, he was awarded the title doctor *honoris causa* by the AGH University of Science and Technology in Kraków. In the West, he was awarded the Bessemer Gold Medal of the Iron and Steel Institute in 1965 and in 1974 received the Brinell Gold Medal from

Thaddeus Sendzimir, engineer and inventor (*OLS*).

King Gustav of Sweden — the equivalent of the Nobel Prize for engineering. His processes were introduced into mills in Great Britain, Japan, and Canada in the 1950s and 1960s. By the 1980s, nearly 90 percent of the world's production of stainless steel passed through the Sendzimir processes with plants in Poland, France, the United Kingdom, Japan, and Canada having purchased his steel mills and processes over the prior decades. By the time of his death he held 120 patents in mining and metallurgy. Sendzimir was also a major supporter of the **Kosciuszko Foundation**, establishing a fund for research, and cultural and scholarly exchanges between the United States and Poland; the **Polish Institute of Arts and Sciences**; and the now-closed **Alliance College** in Pennsylvania. In 1990, Poland's largest steel plant was renamed the Tadeusz Sendzimir Steelworks (*Huta Sendzimira*) in recognition of his unique contribution to science and engineering throughout the world. Perhaps most fittingly, however, on the centennial of the Statute of Liberty, Sendzimir was honored as one of America's most prominent immigrant sons by New York Mayor Edward I. Koch.— *Richard J. Hunter, Jr., and Héctor R. Lozada*

SOURCE: Vanda Sendzimir, *Steel Will: The Life of Tad Sendzimir* (New York: Hippocrene Books, 1994).

Severin, Charles (Seweryn Cichocki; b. Galicia, Poland, 1806; d. New York, New York, February 24, 1890). Artist. In 1820 he entered the military school in Kalisz, Poland, and five years later was assigned to the Grenadier Guards. In 1827 he transferred to the Officer Cadet School for Infantry in Warsaw and the following December became a founding member of its secret organization led by Piotr Wysocki. Although resigning from the army in 1830, he remained active in the organization and was part of the detachment attacking the Belvedere Palace in Warsaw on the night of November 29, 1830, seeking to assassinate Grand Duke Constantine. Re-entering military service, Cichocki was assigned to General Sołtyk's regimental staff and soon joined the Mounted Lublin Regiment with whom he fought at the Battles of Białołęka and Grochów. In 1831 he was wounded while serving as a lieutenant in Captain Zaliwski's partisan squad operating near Ostroleka. Following the Battle of Wilno, Cichowski transferred to the newly-formed Sixth Mounted Riflemen. After the defeat of the November Uprising (1830–31), he crossed into Prussia with General Gielgud's Corps, later making his way to France.

In exile, Cichowski received financial help from his brother Adolf Cichowski, publisher of *Kurier Warszawski* (Warsaw Courier) during the Uprising, who in exile was an art collector, a member of the Polish émigré community in Paris, and a supporter of the Bibliotheque Polonaise. With this support he continued his studies in Paris, also living for brief periods in Bourges and Rouen. In 1841 he migrated to Philadelphia where he worked in the lithography firm of Pierre S. Duval, who himself had relocated there from France a decade earlier. For Duval he produced *La Tres Ste. Vierge* (after Murillo). He also drew several lithographed images of volunteer militia groups published by Huddy and Duval for the *United States Military Magazine*. About 1842 he relocated to New York where he worked on his own and through the 1860s was periodically associated with several well-known lithography firms including Currier & Ives, H. R. Robinson, Eliphalet M. Brown, and George W. Hatch. His most notable prints include: *Kossuth in New York, Barnum's American Museum, The American Expedition, Under Commodore Perry, Landing in Japan*, plus two valuable images for Currier and Ives — *Peytona and Fashion* (1845) and *Husking* (1861) — the "only work of the painter Eastman Johnson that Currier & Ives reproduced and [is] among the finest of their prints." Collections of his work may be found in the Bibliotheque Polonaise — Paris; Kornik Library of the Polish Academy of Sciences — Poland; New York Public Library; New York Historical Society; National Museum of American Art — Washington, D.C.; and Library of Congress.—*Stanley L. Cuba*

SOURCES: Janet A. Flint, *The Print in the United States from the Eighteenth Century to the Present* (Washington, D.C.: Smithsonian Institution Press, 1981); Janusz M. Michałowski, "Seweryn Cichowski," *Słownik Artystów Polskich* (Wrocław: Zakład Narodowy imienia Ossolińskich, Instytut Sztuki Polskiej Akademii Nauk, 1971), Vol. 1; George C. Groce and David H. Wallace, *The New-York Historical Society's Dictionary of Artists in America, 1564–1860* (New Haven: Yale University Press, 1957); Harry T. Peters, *Currier & Ives, Printmakers to the American People* (Garden City, NY: Doubleday, Doran & Company, Inc.,1942); Bronisław Pawłowski, "Seweryn Cichowski," *Polski Słownik Biograficzny* (Kraków: Polska Akademia Umiejętności, 1938), Vol. 4.

Seymour, David "Chim" (David Szymin; b. Warsaw, Poland, November 20, 1911; d. near Suez Canal, Egypt, November 10, 1956). Photojournalist. After studying printing and graphic arts at the Akademie für Graphische Kunst in Leipzig (1929–31), Seymour attended the Sorbonne in Paris (1931–33) where he became interested in photography. In 1933 he opened a small darkroom that he shared with Robert Capa and Henri Cartier-Bresson while adopting the pseudonym "Chim." During the 1930s his photojournalism career began in earnest covering notable political events including the Spanish Civil War where his empathetic images of the toll of war on civilians in Barcelona were published initially in *Regards* and *Life* to widespread acclaim. He migrated to the U.S. in 1939 where he again changed his name to Seymour. During World War II he served in the U.S. Army as a photo interpreter. In 1947 he established Magnum Photos along with other photographers including Capa and Cartier-Bresson. In 1948, while working for the United Nation Educational and Scientific Organization (UNESCO), Seymour's photographs of children broken physically and spiritually by war once again brought him worldwide attention. The photos were later published in *Children of Europe* (1949). Other collections of his photography include *The Vatican* (1950) and *David Seymour ("Chim")*(1966). He was killed while covering the Arab-Israeli war in 1956.—*James S. Pula*

SOURCES: David Seymour, *David Seymour—"Chim," 1911–1956* (New York: Grossman Publishers, 1974); Werner Adalbert Bischof, *The Concerned Photographer: The Photographs of Werner Bischof, Robert Capa, David Seymour ("Chim"), André Kertész, Leonard Freed, Dan Weiner* (New York: Grossman Publishers, 1968).

Shalikashvili, John Malchase David (b. Warsaw, Poland, June 27, 1936; d.—). Military Officer. Born to Georgian parents that fled Georgia after it was occupied by Soviet troops in 1921, his parents met in Poland where his father, a veteran of the Imperial Russian Army of Czar Nicholas II and the Army of the Democratic Republic of Georgia from 1918 to 1921, served in the Polish Army as a contract officer. Moving to the United States, Shalikashvili was conscripted into the army in 1959, graduated from Officer Candidate School, and was commissioned a second lieutenant in an artillery unit. For the next 23 years he served in several command and staff positions in Alaska, the continental United States, Germany, Italy, Vietnam (1968 to 1969 as an advisor for the South Vietnamese Army), and Korea. In 1982, he gained promotion to brigadier general and was posted as deputy director for strategy, plans and policy on the U.S. Army General Staff. In 1984, he returned to Germany as an assistant division commander for the 1st Armored Division. Two years later he was promoted to major general and re-assigned to the Army General Staff as assistant deputy chief of staff for operations and plans and director of strategy, plans, and policy. From June 1987 to August 1989, he served as commander of the 9th Infantry Division in Fort Lewis, Washington. Promoted to lieutenant general in August 1989, he returned to Germany to assume duties as deputy commander-in-chief of the United

Gen. John Shalikashvili, Chairman of the Joint Chiefs of Staff (*OLS*).

States Army, Europe, and Seventh Army. In April 1991, he assumed command of Operation Provide Comfort, the relief operation that returned hundreds of thousands of Kurdish refugees to Northern Iraq, and in August 1991, he was called back to Washington, D.C., to become assistant to the chairman of the Joint Chiefs of Staff. He next served as Supreme Allied Commander for Europe (SACEUR) and commander-in-chief of the United States European Command from June 1992 to October 1993, when he returned to Washington to assume the position of thirteenth chairman of the Joint Chiefs of Staff. He was the first foreign-born person to hold this position. In this capacity he served as the principal military adviser to the President, the Secretary of Defense and the National Security Council. In September 1997 he stepped down and retired from the army. Following retirement he served as a visiting professor at the Center for International Security and Cooperation and a senior adviser to the Preventive Defense Project, a research collaboration of Stanford and Harvard Universities. Shalikashvili received a baccalaureate in mechanical engineering from Bradley University and an M.S. in international affairs from George Washington University. His military education included completion of the Naval Command and Staff College and the United States Army War College.—*Luis J. Gonzalez*

SOURCES: "Shalikashvili, John" in *Current Biography Yearbook* (New York: H.W. Wilson, 1995), Vol. 56; John M. Shalikashvili, et al., *An Oral History of General John M. Shalikashvili* (Carlisle Barracks, PA: U.S. Army Military History Institute, 2008).

Shea, Suzanne Strempek (Suzanne Strempek; b. Palmer, Massachusetts, December 7, 1958; d.—). Author. Educated at the

Portland School of Art in Portland, Maine (currently the Maine College of Art) where she earned a B.A. in photography, she embarked on a journalistic career spending the next fifteen years working as a reporter for Springfield newspapers and the *Providence Journal* (Rhode Island). Encouraged by her husband, the journalist Thomas J. Shea, she started writing fiction, and the success of her first novel, *Selling the Lite of Heaven,* allowed her to resign from her newspaper job and devote herself to writing full time. Devoting most of her writing to an artistic exploration of her Polish American heritage, especially a fictional portrait of her own strongly ethnic community in the area of Springfield, MA, her subsequent publications include *Hoopi Shoopi Donna* (1996), *Lily of the Valley* (1999), *Around Again* (2001), *Songs from a Lead-Lined Room: Notes — High and Low — from My Journey Through Breast Cancer and Radiation* (2002), *Becoming Finola* (2004), *Shelf Life: Romance, Drama, and Other Page-Turning Adventures from a Year in a Bookstore* (2004), and *Sundays in America: A Yearlong Road Trip in Search of Christian Faith* (2008). Undoubtedly there are strong autobiographical elements in most of her fiction and non-fiction although three of her most recent publications, *Songs from a Lead-Lined Room, Shelf Life,* and *Sundays in America,* can be classified as memoirs. The first two, powerfully emotional, chronicle Strempek Shea's struggle with breast cancer and with the difficult return to "normal life." The writer candidly discloses her feelings about herself and those around her and is not afraid to present her own failings. *Sundays in America,* records her year-long journey through the American religious landscape. There, Strempek Shea describes Sunday services at fifty Christian places of worship where she hopes to find a genuine sense of connection both with her God and neighbor. Her religious journey is set against her Polish American Roman Catholic background. Human relationships as well as issues of identity are very important in her fiction. The heroines of her novels are thirty-something women who confront a need to make sense of their lives and define their identity as they face conflicts between the dominant culture and the ethnic traditions of their Polish American families and communities. Especially in *Selling the Lite of Heaven, Hoopi Shoopi Donna,* and *Lily of the Valley,* Strempek Shea creates a masterful group portrait of Polish Americans from the working class enclaves of New England. With great affection and pride, she records a vanishing ethnic culture of the late twentieth century. In *Around Again,* the heroine's journey to understanding, forgiveness and love is set

against the plight of the small Polish American farmers in Massachusetts. *Becoming Finola* is the only novel that Strempek Shea set outside a Polish American community; and although it takes place in Ireland, the main character also has Polish roots. Strempek Shea is the author of numerous short stories and essays which have been published in such magazines as *Yankee, The Bark, Obit, The Boston Globe, The Philadelphia Inquirer,* and others. She taught writing at Emerson College in Boston, University of South Florida at Tampa, and the University of Southern Maine's Stonecoast MFA Program, as well as conducting numerous writing workshops both in the United States and Ireland. Her work has been recognized with the New England Book Award for Fiction (2000) and honorary degrees from Elms College, Chicopee, MA; the University of Scranton, Scranton, PA; and Western New England College, Springfield, MA.—*Grażyna J. Kozaczka*

SOURCES: Thomas S. Gladsky and Rita H. Gladsky, eds., *Something of My Very Own to Say: American Women Writers of Polish Descent* (New York: Columbia University Press, 1997); Grażyna J. Kozaczka, "The Invention of Ethnicity and Gender in Suzanne Strempek Shea's Fiction," *The Polish Review,* Vol. XLVIII, no. 3, 327–45; John Merchant, "Recent Polish-American Fiction," *The Sarmatian Review,* January 1998.

Sherman, Anthony *see* **Schermann, Antoni.**

Shipley, Ruth (Ruth Bielaski; b. Montgomery County, Maryland, April 20, 1885; d. Washington, D.C., November 3, 1966). Government administrator. After finishing high school in Washington, D.C., Bielaski accepted a position as a clerk in the U.S. Patent Office in 1903. She married Frederick Shipley in 1909 and after a residence of several years in Panama where her husband was employed, they returned to Washington, D.C., where she obtained a position in the State Department through the assistance of her brother, **A. Bruce Bielaski,** head of the Justice Department's Bureau of Investigation. She worked in the Department for forty-one years, rising to become a special assistant to the Assistant Secretary Alvey Adee and in 1928 an appointment as the first head of the Passport Division. In 1930 she served as a delegate to the Conference on the Codification of International Law at The Hague in the Netherlands. She became the center of controversy when, acting under authority granted by Congress, she used her position to deny passports to prominent American leftists including Paul Robeson, Arthur Miller, Leo Szilard, Linus Pauling, W. E. B. Du Bois, Herbert Aptheker, and others based solely on political grounds. The result was a legal action, Aptheker v. Secretary of

State (1964), in which the Supreme Court found that the State Department had not provided the plaintiff with due process. The State Department recognized her services with its Distinguished Service Award upon her retirement in 1955. — *Thomas Duszak*

SOURCES: H. W. Erskine, "You Don't Go if She Says No," *Collier's*, Vol. 132 (1953), 62–65; Andre Visson, "Watchdog of the State Department," *Independent Woman*, Vol. 30 (1951), 225–26; obituary, *New York Times*, November 5, 1966; obituary, *Washington Post*, November 5, 1966.

Siedliska, Frances Anna Josephina (b. Roszkowa Wola, Poland, November 12, 1842; d. Rome, Italy, November 21, 1902). Catholic nun. The foundress of the Congregation of the **Sisters of the Holy Family of Nazareth**, Siedliska (in religion known as Mary of Jesus the Good Shepherd), was the first child of Adolphe Siedliski, a Polish nobleman and ardent patriot, and Cecilia de Morawska, daughter of Poland's Minister of Finance. In youth, she appeared destined for a life of wealth and social prominence. Educated at her parents' ancestral estates by several governesses, her formal education also included instruction in music and the social arts, all designed to fashion a highly cultured young woman. As was often typical of nineteenth century Polish nobility, religious indifference characterized the Siedliska home. However, at the age of twelve, under the direction of the Rev. Leander Lendzian, a noted Capuchin priest, Frances began religious instruction in the Roman Catholic faith. A person of poor health from birth, she was confined to bed with a protracted illness when her spiritual director informed her that

Mother Frances Siedliska, founder of the Congregation of the Sisters of the Holy Family of Nazareth (*PMA*).

she was to begin a new religious community. On July 2, 1873, at age 31, Siedliska pronounced private vows and resolutely set about the task. The Congregation, modeled on the life of the Holy Family of Nazareth, was established in Rome in 1875. Intentionally not limited to a specific charitable work, but motivated by an intense love for the church and dedication to the renewal of Christian families, Mother Siedliska directed the formation of the Congregation and its work with determined energy.

The first mission of the Congregation was opened in Kraków in 1881. In 1885 the foundress journeyed with eleven sisters, half of the Congregation's total membership, to the United States to minister to the immigrant Poles then flooding American cities. Between 1885 and 1897, she made two more trips across the ocean to ensure a firm base for the American foundation. Mother Siedliska became a naturalized American citizen on July 26, 1897. Beginning with schools, a hospital, and an orphanage in Chicago, IL, the work of her Congregation in the United States continued to exist in 2010 in Connecticut, Illinois, Massachusetts, Michigan, New York, Ohio, Pennsylvania, Puerto Rico, and Texas. Following her death in 1902, the cause for Beatification was introduced in 1920 and on April 23, 1989, Pope John Paul II declared her "Blessed." The feast of Blessed Mary of Jesus the Good Shepherd is celebrated on November 21. — *Geraldine Wodarczyk* and *Jude Carroll*

SOURCES: Antonio Ricciardi, *His Will Alone: The Life of Mother Mary of Jesus the Good Shepherd* (Oshkosh: Wisconsin Castle-Pierce Press, 1971); Katherine Kurzo Burton, *Where There is Love: The Life of Mother Mary Frances Siedliska of Jesus the Good Shepherd* (New York: J.P. Kennedy & Sons, 1951); Mary Theophame, "Frances Anne Josephine Siedliska: An Educator (Unpublished master's theses, University of Ottawa, Canada, 1958); Maria Starzynska and M. Rita Kathryn Sperka, *Hidden Life: A Story Based on the Life and Work of Frances Siedliska, Foundress of the Sisters of the Holy Family of Nazareth* (Chicago: Saint Mary of Nazareth Hospital Center, 1997); Sister M. Liguori, "Mother Mary Frances Siedliska in America," *Polish American Studies*, Vol. III, no. 1–2 (1946), 30–34; Sr. M. Liguori, "Seventy-Five Years of Religious Growth," *Polish American Studies*, Vol. 8, no. 1–2 (1951), 1–11.

Siemaszko, Kazimierz A. "Casey" (b. Chicago, Illinois, March 17, 1961; d. —). Actor. The brother of actress **Nina Siemaszko**, he was the son of a Polish Underground fighter and survivor of the Sachsenhausen concentration camp. After graduating from DePaul University in Chicago, he played major roles in a number of popular movies including *Stand By Me* (1986), *Young Guns* (1986), *Back to the Future Part II* (1989), *Of Mice and Men* (1992), *The Phantom* (1996), *The Bronx Is Burning* (2007), and several other films. Siemaszko had a recurring role on the hit ABC

television series *NYPD Blue* as Internal Affairs Captain Pat Fraker. He also made guest appearances on television shows such as *St. Elsewhere*, *The Facts of Life*, *Law & Order*, and *Law & Order: Criminal Intent*, and lent his voice-over talents to several video games. He narrated the 1999 feature *The Polish-Americans*. — *James S. Pula*

SOURCE: "Casey Siemaszko," in *Contemporary Theatre, Film, and Television* (Detroit: Gale, 2009), Vol. 87.

Siemaszko, Nina (Antonina Jadwiga Siemaszko; b. Chicago, Illinois, July 14, 1970; d. —). Actress. The daughter of a World War II Polish underground and Sachsenhausen concentration camp survivor and sister of actor **Casey Siemaszko**, Siemaszko graduated from DePaul Univeristy in Chicago. Her first feature film was the role of Karen Lundahl in the 1986 comedy *One More Saturday Night*. She played Natalie Anderson in the 1988 comedy *License to Drive* and actress Mia Farrow in the CBS miniseries *Sinatra* (1992). She played Mona Ramsey in the PBS miniseries *More Tales of the City* (1998) and had roles in *Airheads* (1994), *The American President* (1995), *Suicide Kings* (1997), *Goodbye Lover* (1998), *Jakob the Liar* (1999), *The Big Tease* (1999), and *The Haunting of Molly Hartley* (2008). She also made guest appearances on several television shows including *Red Shoe Diaries*, *Judging Amy*, *The West Wing*, *CSI: Crime Scene Investigation*, *A Christmas Carol*, *Private Practice*, and ten episodes of the *Mystery Woman* series. — *Patricia Finnegan*

SOURCE: "Nina Siemaszko," *Contemporary Theatre, Film, and Television* (Detroit: Thomson Gale, 2006), Vol. 70.

Sieminski, Alfred Dennis (b. Jersey City, New Jersey, August 23, 1911; d. Vienna, Virginia, December 13, 1990). Congressman, businessman. After attending public schools in Jersey City, Sieminski attended the New York Military Academy in Cornwall-on-the-Hudson and graduated from Princeton University with a degree in political science in 1934. While there, he was a member of a crew team that raced at the Henley Regatta in England. Sieminski was a student at Harvard Law School in 1935 and 1936 and also studied at Hamburg University in Germany and the University of Warsaw in Poland. He was employed as comptroller and vice president of Brunswick Laundry in Jersey City beginning in 1937, a company owned by his father. He enlisted in the United States Army as a private in 1942, served in the Italian campaign with the 92nd Division in 1944 and 1945, and rose to the rank of captain. He took part in the Military Government Division in Austria in 1945 and 1946, served with Tenth Corps in

Korea in 1950, and was discharged to the Infantry Reserve as a major in 1950 where he was promoted to lieutenant colonel in 1956. He was elected as a Democrat while he was fighting in the Korean War (his wife campaigned for him) to the Eighty-second (by a recount victory of 57 votes) and to the three succeeding Congresses (January 3, 1951–January 3, 1959), serving on the House Appropriations Committee. He was an unsuccessful candidate for re-nomination in 1958 when the Democratic machine selected another candidate. Following his terms in Congress, he served as administrative vice president of the Hun Preparatory School in Princeton, engaged in administrative education and project development, and worked at the Medical and General Reference Library of the Veterans' Administration in Washington, D.C. (1962–73). Among his military decorations were the Legion of Merit and the Bronze Star.—*Frederick J. Augustyn*

SOURCES: *Biographical Directory of the United States Congress, 1774–Present* (http://bioguide.congress.gov/); obituaries, *Boston Globe*, December 15, 1990, 35; *New York Times*, December 16, 1990, A50; *Washington Times*, December 17, 1990, B4.

Siemiradzki, Tomasz (b. Nowogródek, Minsk, March 13, 1859; d. Cleveland, Ohio, March 26, 1940) Journalist, politician. Siemiradzki studied classical languages and Roman law, becoming a professor in gymnasiums in Kielce, Łomża and Odessa. Early in his career he was a member of the Zet and National League organizations, being arrested twice because of his activism as a Warsaw journalist. In 1895 the Education Department of the **Polish National Alliance** invited him to the United States for a series of popular lectures, after which he chose to remain in the U.S. teaching classical languages in the Orchard Lake Schools. In the Polish National Alliance he energetically worked to expand Polish national democratic influences among Polish Americans and supported the patriotic involvement of **Polonia** in Polish affairs and politics. A Polish intellectual and ideologist, he committed his whole life to the development of Polonia as an active political diaspora that supported close ties with Poland. During the first two decades of the twentieth century he was one of the leading voices in the formulation of Polish national goals in America.

Siemiradzki earned a living mostly from writing, collaborating with **Antoni A. Paryski** and the Paryski Publishing Company in the development of outlines of Polish history, as well as writing for Paryski's newspaper, the ***Ameryka-Echo***. When elected editor of the weekly ***Zgoda*** (Harmony; 1901–07, 1908–12) he moved from Orchard Lake to Chicago. He

also edited *Pobudka* (Awake), the organ of the Young Men's Alliance in America, and in 1900 published his *Dzieje polityczne Polski w zarysie* (Outline of Polish Politics) which was reprinted many times. Active in the **Polish Falcons Alliance** in Detroit and Chicago, Siemiradzki understood the movement as preparation for the formation of a Polish military force to free the homeland. His publications show some ideological transformations, but throughout life he fought for the political unification of American **Polonia**. Until 1912 he believed that unification should occur under the banner of the Polish National Alliance. Around 1900 he recognized the National League as the "authority of the Polish state," but in 1903 he came into conflict with **Stanisław Osada** and two years later with **Jan Smulski** causing him to abandon the National Democratic movement after 1905. Clearly sympathetic toward the nationalistic wing of the socialist movement led by **Alexander Dębski** and Stanisław Rayzacher, he supported their approach to addressing labor problems in Poland and America. In *Dzieje polityczne* he warmly referred to Polish socialists and the Galician Peasant Party, and in the 1906 edition he underlined the workers' role in the society. In 1907 he defended the progressive and leftist viewpoints in *Zgoda*; indeed, under his editorship the weekly devoted much space to the labor movement including support for the 1910 Chicago textile strike and similar labor actions in the steel industry in 1919 and 1920.

In 1908 Siemiradzki was nominated chief editor of ***Dziennik Związkowy*** (Alliance Daily News), at the same time holding the editorship of *Zgoda*. During the **Polish National Congress** in Washington, D.C., in May 1910

Tomasz Siemiradski, journalist and politician (*PMA*).

he presided over the important political section that strongly supported the vision of an active struggle for Polish independence and appealed for the unification of all Polish organizations. During the 1912 movement to unify the Falcons he was one of the architects of, and enthusiastically supported the formation of a pro–Piłsudskite **National Defense Committee**. From then until the end of his life, he remained loyal to this organization, serving as treasurer and publishing his political polemics in its organs *Wici, Narodowiec*, and *Free Poland*. In 1918 he moved to Cleveland, Ohio, where he was associated with the liberal, leftist and pro–Piłsudski groups. Between 1918 and 1937 he edited *Wiadomości Codzienne*, a liberal, pro–Piłsudski paper, while also writing regularly to ***Dziennik dla Wszystkich*** (Everyone's Daily News; Buffalo) and ***Dziennik Polski*** (Polish Daily News; Detroit). During the period between the two world wars, he was among those who retained contacts with Poland, supported it and defended Piłsudski's May *coup d'etat*, for which he was strongly criticized by Polish right wing politicians, and especially the national democrats. In 1925 he became president of the United Committees of Józef Piłsudski which worked for the unification of independent leftists and coordinated works in support of Poland. Between 1927 and 1931 he regained some influence within the Polish National Alliance, while continuing to advocate the idea of political unification of Polonia.—*Donald E. Pienkos & Adam Walaszek*

SOURCE: Adam Walaszek, "Tomasz Siemiradzki: An Intellectual in Ethnic Politics," *Polish American Studies*, Vol. LXII, no. 2 (2005), 47–73.

Sienkiewicz, Henryk (Henryk Adam Aleksander Pius Sienkiewicz; b. Wola Okrzejska, Poland, May 5, 1846; d. Vevey, Switzerland, November 15, 1916). Author. Known as "The Patriot Novelist of Poland," Sienkiewicz was one of the most prolific Polish writers of the later half of the nineteenth century. Sienkiewicz attended the University of Warsaw where he studied law, medicine, literature, and history, soon discovering his writing talent when he wrote for a student newspaper. He became an admirer of the works of Sir Walter Scott and Alexandre Dumas, which led him to pen his own historical work *Ofiara* (The Sacrifice), but no copy is known to exist. After authoring some strong satirical pieces, he traveled to America in 1876, and upon returning to Poland, published his impressions in Polish newspapers. His journey gave him a great deal of material he could use in other works, including the short story *The Lighthouse Keeper* (1882) and character traits that he later used in developing the characters of his more fa-

Henryk Sienkiewicz, Nobel Prize–winning author (*PMA*).

mous novels. He became co-editor of the newspaper *Słowo* (The Word), and a co-founder of the Mianowski Foundation and the Literary Foundation (1889). Sometimes using the pseudonym "Litwos," much of his writing reflected historical themes, and this held true for some of his most well-known works, a trilogy of titles about seventeenth century Poland: *Ogniem i Mieczem* (With Fire and Sword; 1884), *Potop* (The Deluge; 1886), and *Pan Wołodyjowski* (Pan Michael or Fire in the Steppe; 1888). A trip to Italy led to his most famous work, *Quo Vadis*, about the persecution of Christians in early Rome. He continued to write about Poland for the remainder of his career, and became wildly popular not just in Poland, but all over the world, resulting in his works being translated into some fifty languages. Some of his supporters even raised money to purchase a castle for him, which had been the home of his ancestors. When World War II began, he fled to neutral Switzerland. Between 1948 and 1955 a complete edition of his works was published encompassing sixty volumes. Eight years after his death, his body was returned to Poland. He was awarded the Nobel Prize in Literature (1905) for "outstanding merits as an epic writer."—*Cheryl A. Pula*

SOURCES: Monica Mary Gardner, *The Patriot Novelist of Poland, Henryk Sienkiewicz* (New York: E. P. Dutton, 1926); Mieczysław Giergielewicz, *Henryk Sienkiewicz* (New York: Twayne, 1968); Wacław Lednicki, *Henryk Sienkiewicz, 1846–1946* (New York: Polish Institute of Arts and Sciences in America, 1948); Sr. M. Nobilis, "Sienkiewicz and the Poles in America," *Polish American Studies*, Vol. II, no. 1–2 (1945), 34–37; Beth Holmgren, "Virility and Gentility: How Sienkiewicz and Modjeska Redeemed America," *The Polish Review*, Vol. 46, no. 3 (2001), 283–96.

Sikorski, Gerald Edward (b. Breckenridge, Minnesota, April 26, 1948; d.—). Congressman, attorney. After graduating from Breckenridge High School in 1966, Sikorski earned a baccalaureate degree from the University of Minnesota (1970) and a J.D. from the University of Minnesota Law School (1973). He was admitted to the Minnesota bar in 1973 and began the practice of law in Stillwater in 1974. Elected to the Minnesota Senate (1976–82), he was subsequently elected as a Democrat to the Ninety-eighth and the four succeeding Congresses (January 3, 1983–January 3, 1993). He was an unsuccessful candidate for reelection in 1992, having been implicated in overdrafts on the House Bank as well as characterized by a windy speaking style not suitable to the short sound-bites favored by the media. His papers are in the Minnesota Historical Society.—*Frederick J. Augustyn*

SOURCE: *Biographical Directory of the United States Congress, 1774–Present* (http://bioguide.congress.gov/).

Silesia (Śląsk). Silesia lies in Central Europe in the areas of what is today southwestern Poland, southeastern Germany, and the northern Czech Republic. It is largely a relatively flat plain split by the Oder River and its tributaries and bordered on the south by the mountains separating modern Poland from the Czech Republic. The region changed hands many times throughout history, largely because of its strategic position and abundant resources. From the earliest times, it was populated by a mixture of people speaking German, Czech, Polish, and a Silesian tongue that some consider a dialect of Polish while others argue is a separate language in its own right. In the tenth century it became part of the early Polish realm under Mieczko I, but later passed to Bohemian control, then to the Holy Roman Empire in the fourteenth century. Its major cities included Wrocław and Katowice, although its borders have frequently changed with the shifting political fortunes of the area. In 1742 it came under the control of Frederick the Great as a province of Prussia, and later the German Empire. When mass migration began to America in the last three decades of the nineteenth century, the Silesian plain was a rich agricultural area while the mountainous area to the south contained valuable coal mining and industrial complexes. Many of the Silesian Poles settled among German communities in the United States and attended German churches until sufficient numbers of Poles arrived to construct their own houses of worship and build their own urban communities. Other Silesian Poles, experienced as miners in their homeland, settled in Pennsylvania and West Virginia where they found similar work in the expanding coal fields.—*James S. Pula*

SOURCE: William John Rose, *The Drama of Upper Silesia: A Regional Study* (Brattleboro, VT: Stephen Daye Press, 1935).

Simmons, Al (Aloysius Harry Szymanski; b. Milwaukee, Wisconsin, May 22, 1902; d. Milwaukee, Wisconsin, May 26, 1956). Baseball player. A native of the Polish-American south side of Milwaukee, the young Aloys Szymanski attracted notice as a baseball prodigy on the local diamonds of his home town. By the time he entered the major leagues in 1924, he had changed his name for professional purposes, and as Al Simmons he won renown as one of the outstanding hitters of his era. He was called "Bucketfoot Al" for an unorthodox, self taught batting stance that flouted textbook form, but over the course of a twenty year career as an outfielder for seven teams, he compiled a lifetime average of .334 with 307 home runs. Simmons enjoyed his finest seasons with his original team, the Philadelphia Athletics, and he contributed mightily to the exploits of the A's in 1929–1931, when they won three American League pennants and two World Series; named his league's Most Valuable Player in 1929, Simmons followed that performance with consecutive batting championships in 1930 and 1931. In various years, he also led his league in runs, hits, total bases, and runs batted in, and played in three All-Star games. His skills diminished in the later years of his career through the combined effects of age and drink, but he still ended his playing days in 1944 as holder of the record for most hits by an American League right handed batter. After serving several seasons as a coach for the Athletics and Cleveland Indians, Simmons spent his final years in retirement in Milwaukee. He entered the National Baseball Hall of Fame in 1953, the first player of Slavic descent to earn that honor, and he was inducted into the **National Polish-American Sports Hall of Fame** in 1975.—*Neal Pease*

SOURCES: Ed "Dutch" Doyle, *Al Simmons, The Best: A Fan Looks at Al, the Milwaukee Pole* (Chicago: Adams Press, 1979); Neal Pease, "Diamonds Out of the Coal Mines: Slavic Americans in Baseball," in Lawrence Baldassaro and Richard A. Johnson, eds., *The American Game: Baseball and Ethnicity* (Carbondale: Southern Illinois University, 2002); George Reimann, *Sandlot Baseball in Milwaukee's South Side* (Milwaukee: Robert W. Wiesian, 1968).

Simonek, Richard H. "Dick" (b. Wayne, New Jersey, June 15, 1907; d. Ormond Beach, Florida, November 13, 1997). Sprint car machinist. Beginning his career working with Fred Peters's machine shop in New Jersey's "Gasoline Alley" during the 1930s, Simonek teamed with Ted Horn to open a machine shop in Paterson, NJ, following World War II. The partners fielded three cars, one of which was driven by Horn to the American Automobile Association National Championships for three straight years (1946–48). Simonek was credited with developing a new piston that reduced the weight by half while also resulting in higher revolutions. He also fabricated his own carburetors before the development of fuel injection systems. Following his career as a race car machinist, he operated what was then the only engine-balancing shop on the east coast. From the late 1950s until 1967 he worked with the National Association for Stock Car Auto Racing (NASCAR) as a technical inspector for engines. He was elected to membership in the National Sprint Car Hall of Fame. —*James S. Pula*

SOURCE: Larry L. Ball, Jr., "Dick Simonek," National Sprint Car Hall of Fame & Museum web site.

Singer, Isaac Bashevis (Icek Hersz Zynger, Yitzchak Bashevis; b. Leoncin, Poland, November 21, 1904; d. Surfside, Florida, July 24, 1991). Author. The son of a rabbi and descendant of generations of rabbis, Singer grew up in relative poverty because his father earned only a meager living as a judge of a *beth-din* (a religious court). Many of his early childhood memories would later be recreated in amazing detail in his writings. Singer attended the traditional religious primary schools in his own home and those of other rabbis, studying both the mysticism of his Hassidic father and the rationalism and skepticism of his mother and older brother Israel Joshua, his mentor and also a future author. At age ten, Singer read his first secular book, *Crime and Punishment* by Dostoyevsky, in Yiddish translation. This book, a gift from his brother, was to have a profound effect on the youngster, who decided that he wanted to be such a writer. Due to their poverty, Singer and his mother left German-occupied Warsaw in 1917 to live in his maternal grandfather's town of Bilgoray where he studied Hebrew and immersed himself in rural Hasidic folk culture. In his late teens, Singer pursued secular studies including German, Polish, and the philosophy of Spinoza. He wrote short stories and poems in Hebrew, taught Hebrew for an income, and returned to Warsaw in 1923 where he obtained a proofreading job for the Yiddish periodical, *Literarishe Bletter*. Between 1925 and 1929, Singer had his short stories published in various Yiddish newspapers. In 1932, he sold several of his short stories to *Globus*, a literary magazine, which also serialized his first novel, *Satan in Goray*. In 1935, fearing a German invasion, Singer migrated to New York to work as a freelance journalist at *Forverts*, the world's largest Yiddish newspaper. Almost all of Singer's future short stories and novels would

Isaac Bashevis Singer, internationally recognized author (*OLS*).

first appear in serialized versions in the *Forverts*. "Gimpel the Fool," translated by Saul Bellow and first published in *Commentary* in 1953, brought Singer instant fame. This would be followed by eighteen novels (two National Book Awards), ten volumes of short stories, and fourteen books for children (two Newbery Honor Book Awards). His works have been translated into dozens of languages, and have been adapted into motion pictures (*Yentl, Enemies*), plays, and even an opera (*Gimpel*). He wrote about Yiddish-speaking, pre–Holocaust Polish Jewry, and those who migrated to the United States. His themes include morality and passion, good and evil, tradition and modernism, the mundane and the metaphysical, saints, superstitions, illicit sex, and old world demons. Without having completed a day of college-level education, Singer received eighteen honorary doctorates, professorships at Queens College of CUNY, Bard College, and the University of Miami, membership to the National Institute of Arts and Letters, two Louis Lamed Prizes, and three streets named in his honor in New York, Florida, and Poland. —*David Koenigstein*

SOURCES: Irving H. Buchen, *Isaac Bashevis Singer and the Eternal Past* (New York: New York University Press, 1968); Janet Hadda, *Isaac Bashevis Singer: A Life* (New York: Oxford University Press, 1997); Paul Kresh, *Isaac Bashevis Singer, the Magician of West 86th Street: a Biography* (New York: Dial, 1979).

Sisters of St. Felix of Cantalice *see* **Felician Sisters.**

Sisters of St. Francis of Our Lady of Lourdes *see* **Franciscan Sisters.**

Sisters of St. Joseph of the Third Order of St. Francis *see* **Franciscan Sisters.**

Sisters of the Holy Family of Nazareth *see* **Holy Family of Nazareth, Sisters of the.**

Sisters of the Resurrection of Our Lord Jesus Christ *see* **Resurrection of Our Lord Jesus Christ, Sisters of the.**

Skalny Family and Foundation. The Louis Skalny Foundation Trust was established by Ludwik and Aniela Skalny, natives of southern Poland. Ludwik Skalny was born in 1889 in Bieliny and Aniela Mierzwa was born in 1892 in Rudnik-nad-Sanem. Although they grew up just five miles from each other, they did not meet until after each migrated to America. Ludwik learned the art of weaving at an early age living in a region where willow grew naturally and the villagers depended on making furniture and baskets as their livelihood. However, work options were limited in Poland at that time so in anticipation of economic gains Ludwik sailed to Boston in 1907 at the age of eighteen. There he worked as a weaver for the next several years. Aniela sailed to Boston in 1909 at the age of seventeen. She came to stay with family who were already living in the Boston area. One Sunday she and her girlfriends attended a social event in a Boston park where immigrants from Bieliny and Rudnik-nad-Sanem would gather. There she met Ludwik and the two were married on February 26, 1911, at St. Hedwig's Roman Catholic Church in Cambridge. To secure employment as a weaver, Ludwik and Aniela left Boston in 1912 to work in Rochester, New York. After a short time, they decided to move to **Hamtramck**, Michigan, but soon returned to Rochester where he was offered a job with the Bidlack Basket Company in 1920. There they spent more than sixty years, joining St. Casimir's **Polish National Catholic Church** and raising a family of five children — John T., Joseph, Anna, Edward, and Bernard. In 1928 Ludwik established his own basket business using their home as a base. Soon he was selling his carefully crafted baskets to florists, produce markets, food stores, and other retail shops around the city. Through hard work, entrepreneurial skill, and a quality product, he gradually expanded the business by renting a downtown Rochester warehouse and, years later, purchasing a huge building that once housed a bakery business, converting it into the L. Skalny Basket Company.

During World War II, John T. Skalny worked at the Bausch and Lomb Optical Corporation in Rochester on war projects; Joseph enlisted in the army and rose from private to captain in the Signal Corps; Edward became a staff sergeant in the Marines; Bernard was an aviation radar technician in the Navy; and their daughter Anna joined the WACs and served four years in England. After the war, at the height of the business boom, the L. Skalny Basket Company employed 45 weavers and provided many of the new wave of Polish immigrants to Rochester with their first opportunities to work and adjust to their new surroundings. By the mid–1950s the firm had become one of the largest importers of basket goods in the USA. Through the efforts of Louis and his children, the company imported 95 percent of their products from over thirty countries. Their products included over 700 varieties of wicker-ware. During this period the structure of the business changed as the company made the transition to a family corporation with Louis as chairman of the board; John T. as president; Joseph as executive vice president; Edward serving as vice president; Bernard as secretary; and Anna as treasurer.

When Louis Skalny died in 1969 at the age of eighty, his sons and daughter continued the business. Out of respect for their father, they decided in 1971 to establish the Louis Skalny Foundation. The initial directors of the Foundation were John, Joseph, Bernard, Anna, and their mother Nellie. The Louis Skalny Foundation, classified as a 501(c)(3) not-for-profit organization, provided grants, scholarships, and financial assistance in the areas of health, education, religion, and community services. In 1975, a significant connection was created between Rochester and Poland. This was the appointment of John T. Skalny as the first chairman of the Kraków-Rochester Sister Cities Committee by Mayor Thomas Ryan. John T. had the distinction of chairing the first sister cities connection that was with a country still dominated by the Soviet Union and located behind the "Iron Curtain." Funds from the Louis Skalny Foundation assisted the Committee in establishing a successful Summer Study Scholarship for Rochester students to attend the Jagiellonian University in Kraków that continued for over fifteen years.

In 1981 the Foundation made a substantial commitment to St. John Fisher College with an initial gift of $100,000 to develop the Institute for Polish Studies. The Institute officially closed in 1992 after eleven years of service to the college and the community. During its existence, the Institute offered students a course of study in Polish history, literature, and language, and brought to the community an impressive list of guest speakers and scholars from Poland and throughout the United States through the Skalny Lecture and Artist Series. Two distinguished members of the **Polish American Historical Association** have served as directors of the Institute: Dr. **James S. Pula** and Dr. **M. B. Biskupski**.

Through the assistance of both Drs. Pula and Biskupski, the Louis Skalny Foundation has, since 1982, been a major underwriter of the PAHA publication *Polish American Studies*. During this timeframe, two additional endowments were created at St. John Fisher College: John T. and his wife Leona Skalny created the Louis and Nellie Skalny Scholarship fund for study in European History, and Joseph and his wife Irene Skalny established the Joseph and Irene Skalny Endowed Scholarship fund which was to financially help Rochester area high school students attend Fisher.

In the early 1990s, with the deaths of John T. and Bernard, the composition of the Foundation directors changed. Stasia Skalny replaced her husband Bernard, and Frederic Skalny replaced his father, John T. Another significant change occurred in 1993 when the directors of the Louis Skalny Foundation decided to once again underwrite a Polish Studies Program. A proposal submitted by Dr. Ewa Hauser and Dr. William Scott Green from the University of Rochester led to creation of the Center for Polish and Central European Studies in 1994 at the University with a multiyear grant from the Foundation. In that same year, a group from the University including President Thomas Jackson accompanied Stasia and Frederic from the Foundation and other Skalny family members to Kraków for an official ceremony recognizing "the Agreement for Scholarly Collaboration and Exchange between the Jagiellonian University and the University of Rochester." The Center at the University offered an undergraduate course of study in Polish history, literature, arts, language, government, and religion. In addition, the Center offered a new Skalny Lecture and Artist Series for the college and Rochester community, scholarships for summer study at the Jagiellonian, and the Skalny Visiting Professor Exchange Program between the Center and the Jagiellonian. President Jackson, at the signing ceremony at the Jagiellonian, mentioned that "the Center has been supported, tangibly and emotionally, by the Skalny family and the Louis Skalny Foundation,

whose commitment to this relationship has played an integral role.... To the Skalny family, today is your day as much as ours."

Underwriting the Center for Polish and Central European Studies added to the Skalny legacy of pride in its Polish heritage. In 1998 this legacy was recognized by the Polish American Historical Association when it presented the directors of the Foundation with its Distinguished Service Award in recognition of the Skalny's generous support over many years of Polish and Polish American projects. In November 2000 a special reception was held by the University of Rochester during which the Center was officially renamed the Skalny Center for Polish and Central European Studies. At this event, the Polish Consul General Agnieszka Miszewska decorated the directors Joseph, Anna, Stasia, and Frederic with the distinguished Cavalier Cross of Merit from the Republic of Poland in appreciation of their support of Polish culture in America. In 2009 the Polish American Historical Association recognized the Louis Skalny Foundation and the Skalny family by renaming its Civic Achievement Award as the "Skalny" Civic Achievement Award. This award is given annually to honor individuals or groups who have advanced PAHA's goals of promoting research and an awareness of the Polish experience in America.

The Foundation honors the passing of its original directors — Nellie Skalny died in 1993 at the age of l00; Louis died in 1969; John T. in 1991; Bernard in 1992; Stasia in

Standing, from left, Ben (Bernard) Skalny, William Pickett (president of St. John Fisher College), Joseph Skalny; seated, from left, M. B. Biskupski, Anna Skalny, John T. Skalny (*PAHA*).

2004; Joseph in 2008; and Anna in 2009. In 2010, the mission of the Foundation was in the care of directors Frederic Skalny and Gloria Skalny Sciolino, children of John T. and Leona; Gregory Skalny and Diane Skalny Campbell children of Bernard and Stasia; and Scott Skalny, grandson of Edward and Alice. The directors of the Foundation support national organizations like the **American Council for Polish Culture** with a multi-year scholarship in honor of Louis and Nellie Skalny, the Polish American Historical Association, and the **Kosciuszko Foundation**. At the local level they continue to underwrite the Skalny Center for Polish and Central European Studies at the University of Rochester, special programs of the Kraków-Rochester Sister Cities Committee, the prestigious Polish Heritage Society of Rochester, and other community based human service agencies in Rochester.—*Frederic Skalny*

SOURCES: "American Odyssey of the Skalnys," *Straż*, March 12, 1987, 1, 6, and June 18, 1987, 1, 6; "One Hundred Thousand Dollars for Polish Studies," *Straż*, October 22, 1981, 1; "Polish Studies Program Expands at St. John Fisher," *Straż*, October 24, 1985, 1.

Skoniecki, Alfons A. (b. Zielenia, Poland, July 16, 1894; d. Montagne, Massachusetts, July 26, 1975). Priest. Ordained in the U.S. in 1917, during World War I he actively supported recruitment efforts for the **Polish Army in France**. Skoniecki served as assistant pastor of Saints Peter and Paul Parish in Three Rivers, Massachusetts, before being named pastor of St. Mary's Parish in Turners Falls in 1925, a parish he would lead for 23 years. In 1928 he built a new and expanded church building, and throughout his pastorate he encouraged the formation of parish and community organizations and the promotion of Polish culture and traditions. He edited or contributed to various local Polish newspapers and periodicals and served as a delegate to the **Polish National Congress**, and in 1934 was a delegate to the World Congress of Poles Abroad held in Warsaw. He was elected president of Chapter 1 of the **Polish American Council** in Massachusetts, and served for seven years as president of the Massachusetts district of the Union of Polish Priests in America. During World War II, he gained prominence as an early promoter of Polish war relief, and later served as executive secretary of the Coordinating Committee of American Polish Associations in the East, a strongly anti–Soviet group that supported U.S. involvement to guarantee Poland's territorial and political integrity. In 1948 he was assigned to serve Saints Peter and Paul parish, a Polish American church in Three Rivers, Massachusetts. There he founded the Mothers' Club, and led the

parish out of serious financial difficulty. In recognition of his services to the Polish cause, in 1954 the Polish government-in-exile in London conferred upon him the honorary title of colonel in the Polish army. Among his other awards, Skoniecki was decorated by the Polish government-in-exile with the Haller's Swords medal and the Gold Cross of Merit of the Polish army, and also received the Gold Cross of Merit from the **Polish Roman Catholic Union** of America.—*James S. Pula*

SOURCE: Daniel S. Buczek, *Last of the Titans: Monsignor-Colonel Alphonse A. Skoniecki of Massachusetts* (Sterling Heights, MI: Society of Christ in America, 1986).

Skoronski, Bob (b. Ansonia, Connecticut, March 5, 1934; d.—). Football player. Skoronski played college football at Indiana University where he starred as an offensive lineman from 1953 to 1955. Chosen in the fifth round of the 1955 professional draft, he played eleven seasons for the Green Bay Packers between 1956 and 1968, in a career interrupted by military service. Playing tackle and center, Skoronski was a key member of the Packers dynasty of the 1960s that won five NFL championships, as well as the first two Super Bowls. He was named to the Pro Bowl in 1966. Skoronski is a member of the Green Bay Packers Hall of Fame and the Indiana University Athletic Hall of Fame, and was inducted into the National Polish-American Sports Hall of Fame in 2000.—*Neal Pease*

SOURCE: "Bob Skoronski," National Polish-American Sports Hall of Fame website, www.polishsportshof.com.

Skowron, William "Bill" (b. Chicago, Illinois, December 18, 1930; d.—). Baseball player. Skowron attended Purdue University on a football scholarship, but elected to pursue a career in major league baseball. Over the course of fourteen seasons, from 1954 through 1967, he hit .282 with 211 home runs, playing for five teams. A muscular, right handed power hitting first baseman, he was known as "Moose," a childhood nickname conferred not for size or strength, but for a supposed resemblance to Benito Mussolini. Skowron is best remembered as a stalwart for his original team, the New York Yankees, in an era when they dominated the sport. In nine seasons as a Yankee, he was named to five American League All-Star squads, and played for seven pennant winners and four World Series champions. After being traded from the Yankees, Skowron won one more World Series title with the Los Angeles Dodgers in 1963, and represented the Chicago White Sox in the 1965 All-Star game. Following retirement, he resided in the Chicago area, and worked for the White Sox organization. Skowron was in-

ducted into the National Polish-American Sports Hall of Fame in 1980.—*Neal Pease*

SOURCE: Dom Forker, *Sweet Seasons: Recollections of the '55–'64 New York Yankees* (Dallas: Taylor, 1989).

Skrowaczewski, Stanisław (b. Lwów, Poland, October 3, 1923; d.—). Conductor, composer. At the age of four, Skrowaczewski's mother, an amateur pianist, began giving him lessons. By age eight he composed his first symphony, and in the same year the Lwów Philharmonic performed one of his overtures. Dividing his studies at the Lwów Music Society between piano and violin, Skrowaczewski gave his first piano recital at age eleven, two years later conducting and soloing in Beethoven's Third Piano Concerto. He volunteered for the army at the outbreak of World War II, and during the two-year period that Lwów was occupied by the Soviet Union, he continued to play and conduct music. A German bombing raid in June 1941 broke both of his hands and also did nerve damage, ending any thought of pursuing a career as a virtuoso, after which he concentrated on composing and conducting. He worked as a bricklayer under the Nazi occupation, eventually graduating from the University of Lwów in 1945, where he studied physics, chemistry, and philosophy, also receiving diplomas in composition and conducting from the Lwów Conservatory. After further study at the Kraków State Higher School of Music, Skrowaczewski obtained his first conducting position as music director of the Wrocław Philharmonic Orchestra (1946–47). His "Overture 1947" received second prize at the Szymanowski Competition in Warsaw (1947). A fellowship from the French Ministry of Culture and Art enabled him to go to Paris to study composition with Nadia Boulanger and conducting with Paul Kletzki from 1947 to 1949. He also cofounded the avant-garde group "Zodiaque," along with Maurice Ohana. Returning to Poland, he led three prominent orchestras in succession: the Silesian Philharmonic Orchestra in Katowice (1949–54), the Kraków Philharmonic Orchestra (1955–56), and the National Philharmonic Orchestra in Warsaw (1957–59). During this time he attained recognition as both a composer and a conductor, receiving first prize in Rome's Santa Cecilia International Competition for Conductors in 1956. His String Quartet, which had previously received second prize at an International Composers Competition in Belgium (1953), was awarded a gold medal at a competition of composers in Moscow (1957). During a Warsaw concert on its 1957 European tour, the Cleveland Orchestra's music director George Szell invited Skrowaczewski to make his American debut with Cleveland the following year. He guest-conducted in Cleveland again in 1959 (giving the U.S. premiere of his "Symphony for Strings"), as well as in 1960 with Pittsburgh, Cincinnati, and the New York Philharmonic, where he substituted for Dmitri Mitropolous, who had just died. After a world-wide search, Skrowaczewski was hired in 1960 to succeed Antal Dorati as music director of the Minneapolis Symphony (later renamed the Minnesota Orchestra). He became a naturalized American citizen in 1966. Many of Skrowaczewski's earliest works, mostly string quartets and other chamber works, were lost when he fled Lwów in 1945. He began to actively compose again in 1969 after the Philadelphia Orchestra premiered his Oboe Concerto. Among his many compositions are four symphonies; four string quartets; two overtures; concerti for English horn (1969), clarinet (1980), and violin (1985); six piano sonatas, as well as music for opera, ballet, films, and theatre. In Minnesota, Skrowaczewski introduced many important Polish works to American audiences, including compositions by Szymanowski (Symphony No. 2), and Lutosławski (Funeral Music), as well as the American premiere of Penderecki's "The Passion and Death of Our Lord Jesus According to St. Luke." He also lobbied tirelessly for the construction of Orchestra Hall. He made his debut as an opera conductor in 1964 at the State Opera in Vienna and his Metropolitan Opera debut in 1970. After nineteen years leading the Minnesota Orchestra, he decided not to renew his contract and became conductor laureate in 1979, wanting to concentrate on composing, teaching, and guest conducting. However, after several years, he agreed to become Principal Conduc-

tor of the Hallé Orchestra in Manchester, England, from 1984–91. He also served as Musical Adviser to the St. Paul Chamber Orchestra (1986–88), and the Milwaukee Symphony (1992–94). In 2007, he became principal conductor of two Tokyo orchestras: the Nippon Symphony and the Yomiuri Nippon Symphony. Among his honors are the Commander's Cross of the Order of Polonia Restituta; Second Prize in the International Competition for String Quartet (1953); the Kennedy Center Friedheim Award (1976); and the Gold Medal, Bruckner-Mahler Society (1999). He received honorary doctorates from Hamline University (1961), Macalester College (1977), the University of Minnesota (1979), and the Royal College of Music, Manchester (1986).—*John Drobnicki*

SOURCES: *Current Biography Yearbook* (New York: H. W. Wilson, 1964); *Musicians Since 1990* (New York: H. W. Wilson, 1978); *Who's Who in Polish America* (New York: Bicentennial Publishing, 1996); Herbert Elwell, "Talk With Polish Conductor Whets Musical Thought," *Cleveland Plain Dealer*, December 27, 1959.

Ślisz, Stanislaus Thomas (b. Kołaczyce, Poland, March 4, 1856; d. Buffalo, New York, October 10, 1908). Editor, journalist. Ślisz received his education in Jasło and Chyrów before enrolling in the Jagiellonian University in Kraków where he earned a degree in law. He migrated to the U.S. in 1885, settling in Buffalo, NY, where he edited the weekly newspaper *Ojczyzna* (Fatherland, 1885–87) which reflected an orientation toward the Democratic Party. When this newspaper failed, he moved to Milwaukee in 1887 to edit the weekly *Krytyka* (The Critic), and from 1887 to 1889 served as editor of **Wiara i Ojczyzna** (Faith and Fatherland), the organ of the **Polish Roman Catholic Union**, and

Kropidło (The Aspergillum) in Chicago. Moving back to Buffalo in 1889, he assumed editorship of **Polak w Ameryce** (The Pole in America, 1889–1908), a successor to the earlier *Ojczyzna*, and *Polak Amerykański* (Polish American, 1908–09). Ślisz also authored a number of short stories and contributed to other newspapers, adhering throughout to support of Roman Catholic issues.—*James S. Pula*

SOURCE: Francis Bolek, ed., *Who's Who in Polish America* (New York: Harbinger House, 1943).

Sliwa, Curtis (b. Brooklyn, New York, March 26, 1954; d.—). Community activist, radio personality. The son of a Polish father and an Italian mother, Sliwa graduated from Canarsie High School. In May 1977, during a time when New York City as experiencing a wave of violent crimes on its subways, he created a crime-fighting organization he named "The Magnificent 13." As the group grew in numbers it was eventually renamed "The Guardian Angels." Their distinctive uniform of a military-style red beret and white insignia t-shirt became instantly recognizable. Their work drew both positive and negative reactions from police, public officials, local residents, and the media, as they began to court media attention. As president of the group, Sliwa saw the organization grow to include operations in nine countries and 82 cities around the world, with a membership of some 5,000. The Angels' New York City activities eventually became confined mostly to patrolling the Restaurant Row neighborhood in Manhattan. In July 1992, a stolen taxi picked Sliwa up near his East Village home and a gunman hiding in the front passenger seat jumped up and fired several shots, wounding Sliwa in his groin and legs. He escaped the kidnapping attempt by jumping out the window as the cab was moving. Federal prosecutors charged John A. Gotti, the son of organized crime boss John Gotti, with attempted murder. It was said that the younger Gotti was angered by comments supposedly made by Sliwa about the elder Gotti. After three failed attempts to try Gotti on the charges, they were eventually dropped. Sliwa went on to become a radio talk show host on WABC in New York, and later on WNYC. In 1994, after four months at WNYC, Sliwa went back to WABC and in 1999 became the co-host, with attorney Ron Kuby, of the long-running show *Curtis and Kuby in the Morning*. The show lasted eight years until Citadel Broadcasting replaced them with Don Imus, but the station kept Sliwa in a late-night time slot. As a broadcaster, he was also known for his "Sliwaisms," malapropisms such as "They

Stanisław Skrowaczewski, composer and conductor (**PMA**).

Stanisław Ślisz, editor and journalist (**OLS**).

kidnapped the Limburger baby" and "a skimpily-clad bikini." —*Patricia Finnegan*

SOURCES: "Curtis Sliwa, live!" *New Yorker*, Vol. 70, no. 3 (March 7, 1994), 34; Mark A. Uhlig, "Sliwa, Angels' Founder, A Herald, Not A Cherub," *New York Times*, June 17, 1988, 1; "Sliwa's Angels Empowered New Yorkers in the Fight on Crime," *New York Times*, December 9, 1992, 22.

Slovik, Edward Donald "Eddie" (b. Detroit, Michigan, February 18, 1920; d. Sainte Marie aux Mines, France, January 31, 1945). Soldier. During his youth, Slovik amassed a history of arrests beginning with breaking and entering at age twelve and including several instances of disturbing the peace and theft for which he was imprisoned in 1937, but paroled in the following year. After crashing a stolen car while driving drunk, he was sent back to prison in 1939, but was paroled in 1942. Originally classified by the draft board as 4-F because of his criminal background, he was reclassified 1-A in November 1943 and conscripted into the army in January 1944. In August 1944 he was ordered to France where he was assigned as a replacement to the 109th Infantry Regiment. En route to his assignment he and another soldier took cover during an artillery bombardment and were separated from the other replacements. Eventually taken into custody by a Canadian military police unit after some six weeks, the other soldier finally wrote to the commander of the 109th Regiment to explain their absence. When they finally reported for duty, no charges were filed but they were informed that any further unauthorized absence would result in a charge of desertion. The day after reporting, Slovik informed his company commander that he was "too scared" and asked to be reassigned to a rear echelon unit. He threatened to run away if he was not reassigned. Slovik persisted in his threats to run away, eventually deserting a second time. Taken into custody in Belgium, he was charged with desertion and imprisoned. A court martial found him guilty of desertion, following which Gen. Dwight D. Eisenhower refused Slovik's appeal for clemency, probably in an attempt to curb a rising desertion rate. Slovik was executed by a firing squad on January 31, 1945, becoming the only American soldier executed for desertion since the Civil War. —*James S. Pula*

SOURCE: William Bradford Huie, *The Execution of Private Slovik* (New York: Dell Publishing, 1972).

Smagorzewski, Antoni *see* **Schermann, Anthony.**

Smolinski, Joseph, Jr. (b. Quebec, Canada, October 19, 1845; d. Washington, District of Columbia, 1912). Military officer, government official. The son of Joseph Smolinski, Sr., he was educated at the University Institute in Nogent-sur-Marne, France, the Polish National School in Paris, and in London. When the American Civil War broke out he enlisted in the proposed "United States Lancers" that his father was attempting to raise, but efforts were unsuccessful and Smolinski was consolidated into the 9th New York Cavalry in which he served throughout the war. When the regiment was mustered out at the end of the war, Smolinski enlisted in the U.S. Marine Corps, then took a position as a clerk in the War Department in Washington, D.C. (1875–1909), where he rose to become chief of the Military Information Department. In 1909 he became an attorney and general agent with the Patent Office (1909–12), following which he served as Commissioner of Deeds in Amsterdam, NY (1912). He represented Poles in America before the Senate Committee on Immigration during the 57th Congress; served as secretary of the committee for raising funds for the **Kościuszko** statue at West Point; was a founder of the Polish Businessmen's Association; a corresponding member of the Polish National Museum at Rapperswyl, Switzerland; a member of the Loyal Legion of the United States; a founder of the United States Marine Legion with the rank of colonel; an organizer of the Fenian Brotherhood; a member of the Grand Army of the Republic and organizer of its Lafayette Post; and a member of the National Association of Naval Veterans in Philadelphia. —*James S. Pula*

SOURCES: William Simmons, *History of the National Association of Naval Veterans from the First to the Tenth Annual Convention Inclusive* (Philadelphia: Dunlap Printing Co., 1895), 125; Francis Bolek, ed., *Who's Who in Polish America* (New York: Harbinger House, 1943); Stanisław Łempicki, *Historja Związku Młodzieży Polskiej w Ameryce* (Chicago: Nakł. Wydziału Oświąty Z.M.P., 1905).

Smolinski, Joseph, Sr. (Józef Smoliński; b. Płock, Poland, March 16, 1809; d. Washington, District of Columbia, December 21, 1886). Military officer, political activist. During the Polish November Uprising (1830–31) against Russian influence, Smolinski served as a sergeant major in the 4th Regiment and won praise for his bravery at the Battle of Grochów on February 19–20, 1831, for which he was promoted to second lieutenant and awarded the Virtuti Militari. Later promoted to first lieutenant, he fled to France after the revolt collapsed. In 1832–33 he served in Algiers with the French Foreign Legion, then migrated to the U.S. in 1834. After journeying to New York, where he became an American citizen, he left for France, then spent a year in Brazil before settling in Quebec, Canada, in 1842. When the Crimean War broke out he enlisted with the British forces where he was assigned to recruiting duties and was quickly promoted to major and then colonel. He took part in the Siege of Sebastopol where his conduct brought the award of a gold medal from Queen Victoria and the Order of Medjidieh from Turkey. During the American Civil War, on June 15, 1861, Smolinski applied for permission to raise a regiment of cavalry to defend the Union, however his efforts met with only limited success and he lost his opportunity for command when his incomplete unit was merged into the 9th New York Cavalry. He returned to Washington, D.C., where he worked as a clerk in the Census Office until March 1863 when he left to fight in the Polish January Insurrection. With the failure of the revolt, Smolinski attempted to reach an agreement with Confederate officials in Richmond for grants of land for Poles who volunteered to serve in the Southern armies. After the end of the Civil War, he became involved in some dubious land schemes, all of which failed, and then returned to the U.S. where he signed an oath of allegiance on November 9, 1867, and obtained a position as a clerk in the U.S. Treasury Department in Washington, D.C. Quite soon, however, he became involved in General John O'Neill's Fenian Rebellion that sought to separate Canada from British control. In June of 1869 he was appointed a general and organizer of the Irish Republican Army in Virginia, Maryland, Delaware, and the District of Columbia. He succeeded so well that he was appointed chief of staff to the president of the Fenian Brotherhood. Smolinski also became involved in attempts to found a Polish colony in Virginia, but once again the effort failed. Destitute, he was able to regain his clerkship in the Treasury Department in 1882 at the advanced age of 73. —*James S. Pula*

SOURCES: Francis Bolek, ed., *Who's Who in Polish America* (New York: Harbinger House, 1943); Maria J. E. Copson-Niećko, "The Poles in America from the 1830's to 1870's: Some Reflections on the Possibilities of Research," in Frank Mocha, ed., *Poles in America: Bicentennial Essays* (Stevens Point, WI: Worzalla Publishing Company, 1978), 45–302.

Smulski, Jan Franciszek (real name Jachiński or Jakiński; b. Trzemeszno, Poland, February 4, 1867; d. Chicago, Illinois, March 18, 1928). Attorney, banker, politician, Polonia activist. In 1881, Smulski migrated to the U.S. where he studied law at Northwestern University, later becoming an attorney in Chicago. Joining the **Polish National Alliance**, he was elected to the Board of Directors in 1893. He also became active in the Polish **Falcons** in America, serving as vice president in 1899. Turning to politics, he won election to the Chicago City Council on the Republican ticket in 1898, gaining reelection in 1899 and 1901. In April 1903 he was elected the city's attorney where he gained a reputation for struggling against city corruption. Elected city treasurer in 1906, he resigned at the end of 1907 to devote his entire energy to business and Polish ethnic affairs. Following the death of his father in 1897, he became responsible for operations of the Smulski Publishing Company which, in 1920, merged with **Władysław Dyniewicz**'s printing company. With two other investors, Smulski established a mining company in California called the "Polish Gold Mine," yet his primary business venture was a partnership with other Polish businessmen that resulted in 1905 in the founding of the first Polish-owned bank in Chicago, the Northwestern Trust and Savings Bank. Popularly known as the "Smulski Bank," it became the largest Polish-owned commercial lending operation in the United States. The institution was also involved in real estate, resulting in Smulski becoming the first Polish millionaire in Chicago.

Known within **Polonia** for his political association with the National Democratic wing of the **Polish National Alliance**, and the National Democratic program espoused by Roman Dmowski in partitioned Poland, he wielded considerable influence during the **Polish National Congress** in Washington, D.C. (1910), where he opposed the leftist nationalistic group within the PNA identified with the views of Dmowski's rival in Poland, Józef Piłsudski. Particularly important was Smulski's role during World War I and its aftermath when he co-founded the **Polish Central Relief Committee**. As treasurer of the PCRC, Smulski collaborated closely with **Ignacy Jan Paderewski** during the virtuoso's visits in the

Jan Smulski, attorney, banker, politician, and Polonia activist (*PMA*).

U.S., introducing him to many important American politicians. Due largely to his initiatives, organizations associated with the PCRC founded their own political body, the **Polish National Department**, in 1916 with Smulski as president of the executive committee. The National Department raised millions of dollars for Polish war victims and organized in America a Polish Army of some 25,000 men that fought alongside the Allies during World War I (see **Polish Army in France**). His contributions to the success of the Allied war effort and the recovery of Polish independence were recognized with the French Legion of Honor and the Polish government's highest honor, the Order of Polonia Restituta.

Smulski was among the organizers of the Congress of the Polish Emigration in Detroit in August 1918, presiding over it and analyzing the organizational and political situation of **Polonia**. His speeches were published in a brochure *Ratujmy przede wszystkim Polskę!* (Let us save Poland first of all!). A supporter of Paderewski's idea of creating a Polish National Fund of $10 million, Smulski advocated immediate American aid to Poland (1918–20), helped to create Polish diplomatic missions in the U.S., and supported Paderewski and the National Democratic groups in the Polish diaspora and Poland. Smulski supported the National Democrats in Poland both in speeches and with financial contributions leading up to the plebiscites and the Silesia Uprisings, including financial support for the Polish newspaper *Rzeczpospolita* whose subventions were severely criticized by the Polish left. Although his bank stood to profit by a two percent commission on each sale, Smulski was largely unsuccessful in arranging for the sale of Polish Bonds in American Polonia. Elected president of the Executive Council of the National Polish Committee of America, which was expected to function as a nation-wide Polonia umbrella group, his ties to Paderewski and the Polish National Democrats declined during 1919–20. By the time of the Polish congress in Cleveland in April 1923, Smulski sensed a major change in ideology within Polonia, which was becoming more concerned with itself and less with the internal politics of Poland. This prompted him to step down from the presidency of the National Department. Two years later he also dramatically addressed the question of Polish American identity and policies.

In the mid–1920s Smulski concentrated his efforts on business activities of the Northwestern Trust and Savings Bank, which by that time had grown to some $20.5 million in deposits. Toward the end of his life he became seriously ill, necessitating a series of operations

that left him in such depression that he committed suicide on March 18, 1928. Following his death the Northwestern Trust and Savings Bank collapsed during the Depression.—*Adam Walaszek*

SOURCES: Donald E. Pienkos, *P.N.A. Centennial History of the Polish National Alliance of the United States of North America* (Boulder, CO: East European Monographs, 1984); Donald E. Pienkos, *For Your Freedom Through Ours: Polish American Efforts on Poland's Behalf, 1863–1991* (Boulder, CO: East European Monographs, 1991); Edward R. Kantowicz, *Polish American Politics in Chicago 1880–1940* (Chicago: University of Chicago Press, 1975); Joseph J. Parot, *Polish Catholics in Chicago, 1850–1920* (DeKalb: Northern Illinois University Press, 1981).

Smulski, Władysław Teodor (Władysław Teodor Jakiński; b. Gniewkowo, Prussian Poland, June 1, 1836; d. Chicago, Illinois, October 1897). Journalist, publisher. After completing high school in Trzemeszno, Jakiński worked as a clerk. Migrating to the U.S. in 1868, he changed his name to Smulski. In 1874 he began working in **Władysław Dyniewicz**'s printing house editing *Gazeta Polska w Chicago* (Chicago Polish Gazette), which supported the **Gmina Polska** (Polish Commune), and later the **Polish National Alliance**, in opposing the policy and ideology of the **Resurrectionists**. Teaming with **Jan Barzyński**, Smulski published and edited the weekly *Gazeta Polska Katolicka*, which became the *Gazeta Katolicka* (Catholic Gazette) in 1880. Barzyński and Smulski founded the Polskie Towarzystwo Literackie (Polish Literary Society) on January 1, 1875, but ideological differences soon ended the partnership with Smulski becoming sole owner in January 1884. He was also very active in the organizational life of **Polonia**, being among the founders of Chicago's Nest No. 2 of the **Polish Falcons** and taking part in the creation of the Polish National Alliance. His first attempt to publish the daily *Kuryer Chicagoski* (Chicago Courier) failed after three months, but in 1886 he opened a printing house, the Smulski Publishing Company, in Chicago. The new venture became one of the most important printing houses of Polonia, publishing textbooks for Polish American schools, reprints from Poland, novels, popular books, and original works such as those by Modest Maryański. After Smulski's death his son John took over management of the company.—*Adam Walaszek*

SOURCE: J. Myszor, "Smulski, Władysław Teodor," *Polski Słownik Biograficzny* (Wrocław: Zakład Narod. Im. Ossolinskich, 1999), Vol. 39, no. 3, 394.

Sobieski, John (b. Warsaw, Poland, September 10, 1842; d. Los Angeles, California, November 12, 1927). Soldier, attorney, politician. A direct descendant of King John III Sobieski of Poland who defeated the Turks at

Vienna in 1683, Sobieski's father was executed by the Russians in 1846 for his patriotic activities and the remaining family members were sent into exile. Migrating to the U.S. in 1855, he enlisted in the army and served on the frontier until the outbreak of the Civil War when he served with the Army of the Potomac. Following the war he joined the Mexican revolutionaries fighting against Emperor Maximilian. Rising to become chief of staff to Gen. Escobedo, Sobieski was a witness to Maximilian's execution in 1867. Returning to the U.S., he settled in Minnesota where he was elected to the state legislature in 1868 and introduced a bill to allow women to vote. A founder of the state's Prohibition Party, Sobieski frequently put himself forward for other elective office on its ticket, including eyes on the governorship. Admitted to the bar in 1870, he was later admitted to practice before the Supreme Court of Nebraska. He also authored his memoirs and a *Life of King John Sobieski, John the Third of Poland* (1915).—*James S. Pula*

SOURCES: John Sobieski, *The Life-Story and Personal Reminiscences of Col. John Sobieski* (Shelbyville, IL: J. L. Douthit & Son, 1900); Francis Bolek, ed., *Who's Who in Polish America* (New York: Harbinger House, 1943).

Sobieski, Lee Lee (Liliane Rudabet Gloria Elsveta Sobieski; b. New York, New York, June 10, 1982; d.—). Actress. Lee Lee Sobieski grew up in New York City, although she also spent considerable time in France. Although she has claimed descent from King John III Sobieski, genealogists question the claim. She was educated at the Trevor Day School and Brown University where she studied literature and art. She had leading parts in *A Horse for Danny* (1995) and *Jungle 2 Jungle* (1997), but gained acclaim for her appearances in *Deep Impact* (1998) and as a nymphet in *Eyes Wide Shut* (1999). Her role in *A Soldier's Daughter Never Cries* (1998) won her a Chicago Film Critics Award as Most Promising Newcomer. Her role in the television movie *Joan of Arc* (1999) brought nominations for an Emmy for Best Lead Actress in a Miniseries or Movie, a Golden Globe for Best Actress in a Miniseries or Television Movie, and a Satellite Award for Best Actress in a Miniseries or Television Film. Since then she has appeared in some two dozen other films, earning another Golden Globe Best Actress nomination for the television movie *Uprising* (2001).—*James S. Pula*

SOURCES: "Don't Walk All Over Leelee," *News of the World Sunday Magazine*, February 3, 2008, 28; "Leelee Sobieski Biography," *Theatre, Film, and Television Biographies* (Detroit: Gale Research Co., 2004).

Sobolewski, Edward (b. Königsberg, East Prussia, October 1, 1804; d. St. Louis, Missouri, May 17, 1872). Musician. Largely forgotten by contemporary historians of music, Johann Friedrich Eduard Sobolewski (later Edward) demonstrated from a young age unique musical abilities with particular aptitude on the violin and piano, performing, at age sixteen, as first violin in the Zander Quartet chamber group. Educated in Berlin and Dresden, Sobolewski studied composition with Carl Friedrich Zelter, Carl Maria von Weber, and later counted amongst his musical acquaintances Felix Mendelssohn and Franz Liszt. He returned to Königsberg, where he became Kapellmeister of the Königsberg Theater in 1830. His ascendancy to success and esteem in the music world was rapid: in 1835 he became cantor of the Altstädtische Kirche; in 1838, conductor of the newly-established Philharmonische Gesellschaft; and in 1843 conductor of the chorus of the Music Academy. His lifelong interest in vocal music inspired his 1841 publication *The First Elements of Vocal Instruction*. During this period he also became a correspondent of the Königsberg music scene for Robert Schumann's *Neue Zeitschrift für Musik* (New Journal for Music), writing under the pseudonym J. Feski ("J," for Johann, "F" for Friedrich, and "-ski" for the suffix of his Polish name). Additionally, he was the music critic for the *Ostpreussische Zeitung* (The East Prussian Gazette). The turbulent political upheavals of 1848–50, coupled with the emergence of younger musical talent in Königsberg, led Sobolewski to move to Bremen where he assumed directorship of the theatre there. Despite attempts to secure more prestigious and higher paying positions through his various contacts, he was unsuccessful, and continued to compose in Bremen with limited success. He enjoyed wider recognition for his operatic works, with his opera

Edward Sobolewski, musician, critic, and author (*OLS*).

Vinvela debuting in 1853 in Weimar, and later in London, where his daughter, Malvina, sang in the Exeter Hall performance. In 1859, Sobolewski migrated to the United States, settling in Milwaukee—a center for German musicians and political exiles of the 1848 Revolutions. He eked out a living through advertising his academic credentials and his prestigious associations, which permitted him to continue his operatic composition. What soon followed was a unique work on the subject of the American Revolution—*Mohega, die Blume des Waldes* (Mohega, the Flower of the Forest). The opera, the first of its kind in subject-matter, debuted with the assistance of the Milwaukee Musical Society on October 11, and told the story of a love triangle between the daughter of an Indian chief, Mohega, the granddaughter of a man who eradicated an Indian tribe, and both women's infatuation with the Revolutionary War hero, **Kazimierz Pułaski**. Sobolewski was particularly active on the American music scene. In 1860 he founded and conducted the Milwaukee Philharmonic Society Orchestra before moving to St. Louis, Missouri, where he assumed the position of conductor of the Philharmonic Society. Six years later, Sobolewski left the Philharmonic Society to devote himself more fully to composition and teaching. As regards the latter, he assumed a professorship, teaching music at Bonham's Female Seminary until 1872. Sobolewski died of an apoplectic stroke.—*Krystyna Cap*

SOURCE: Robert T. Laudon, "Eduard Sobolewski, Frontier Kapellmeister: From Königsberg to St. Louis," *The Music Quarterly*, Vol. 73, no. 1 (1989), 94–118.

Sobolewski, Paul (b. Warsaw, Poland, June 16, 1818; d. Chicago, Illinois, May 30, 1884). Author, editor. Educated in Humań by the Basilian Fathers, Sobolewski left school to participate in the November Uprising (1830–31) and with its failure went into exile in Austria where he continued to be active in patriotic conspiratorial groups. In May 1833 the Austrian authorities arrested him and deported him to the U.S. because of his political activity. He arrived in New York along with 235 other Polish exiles on April 2, 1834, at the young age of seventeen. Sobolewski settled in Philadelphia (1834–40) where he worked for James Longacre, the editor of *National Portrait Gallery of Distinguished Americans*. In 1836, after acquiring some facility in English, Sobolewski published English translations of *Jeszcze Polska nie zginieła*, which became the Polish national anthem, and *Warszawianka*. After publishing a series of brief articles in various magazines, in 1841 Sobolewski moved to New York where he joined the **Polish Slavonian Literary Society** and became a fre-

Paul Sobolewski, author and editor (*PMA*).

quent participant in city social events. In New York in January or February 1842 he began editing and publishing *Poland: Historical, Literary, Monumental, Picturesque*, an illustrated literary magazine "Dedicated to the People of the U.S. of America." The journal, though short-lived, enjoyed several distinctions as the only English-language periodical published by the antebellum political exiles in the U.S., the first publication of the Polish American press, and the first Slavic literary magazine in the U.S.—*James S. Pula*

SOURCE: Zygmunt Wardziński, "The Oldest Slavic Magazine in the United States: Poland: Historical, Literary, Monumental, Picturesque" and its Article on Copernicus (1842)," *The Polish Review*, Vol. 19, no. 3–4 (1974), 83–98.

Socialists, Polish American.

Polish Americans have little remembered the substantive history of socialists within their ranks, in large part because the Soviet Union so dominated Poland after World War II. Periodic cycles of "red-baiting" in U.S. culture as a whole have reinforced this ethnic amnesia. In addition, as Mary Cygan points out, non–Polish historians depict Poles and other immigrant ethnic minorities within the U.S. socialist movement as "alien and unsympathetic to American concerns, not as victims of American nativism themselves." Delving into Polish-language sources, Cygan finds "a very different picture ... [of] a complex socialist movement" whose diverse "perspectives and forms of organization ... stemmed not so much from abstract debate over ideological principles as from differing preimmigration experiences."

Beginning in the 1870s, Bismarck's *Kulturkampf* escalated land seizures and religious and cultural persecution to Poznania and other Prussian-occupied areas of Poland. Entire families fled and settled together permanently in the U.S. Despite their agricultural backgrounds, they gravitated to the industrial Great Lakes cities to meet the demand there for laborers and artisans. Like other industrial workers, these early Polish immigrants typically were paid two dollars or less per day to perform grueling, dangerous tasks ten to twelve hours per day, six days a week. Soon they joined with other Americans to challenge and improve these appalling conditions. Polish Chicagoan tinsmiths and carpenters joined their Czech and German coworkers in the International Working People's Association (IPWA), an anarchist group that advocated radical direct action. During 1886, a campaign for an eight-hour work day swept the nation. The devastating Haymarket Affair of 1886 was a reaction against IWPA activities in this campaign.

Many Polish Americans in Milwaukee, Wisconsin, joined the Knights of Labor through factory-based assemblies or all–Polish units. During the city's general strike of May 1886, they figured prominently, as well as tragically, in the eight-hour work day campaign. The state militia fired on demonstrators outside the Bay View steel rolling mill, which primarily employed ill-paid, ill-treated Polish immigrants. Seven were killed and an unknown number injured. A five year old boy named **Leo Krzycki** never forgot the dead and wounded brought to his father's tavern for identification. He grew up to be a prominent leader in the Amalgamated Clothing Workers of America, the American Socialist Party, the Congress of Industrial Organizations, and the **American Slav Congress**. In New York City during the 1880s, intellectual and political émigrés founded the utopian mutual benefit society and newspaper *Ognisko* (The Forge). Some members broke off into a Marxist group called Równość (Equality) that organized Polish locals of the Socialist Labor Party in several states. These locals formed the umbrella organization Związek Oddziallow Polskisch (ZOP). The ZOP persuaded the **Polish National Alliance** to change its membership ban against socialists. However, the ZOP soon fractured internally over the question of aiding Polish independence. Against this backdrop, Galician immigrant **Franciszek Hodur** launched the **Polish National Catholic Church** (PNCC) at the opening of the twentieth century. Although never wholly a partisan of any one socialist organization, Hodur strongly gravitated to religious socialism because of his poor background, exposure to European socialism at the Jagiellonian University

in Kraków, and influence from the Roman Pope Leo XIII's 1891 encyclical *Rerum Novarum*. Hodur's affinity for socialism deeply shaped the PNCC's politics of worker solidarity.

Meanwhile the rift within ZOP over Polish independence intensified with changing immigration patterns. By 1900, most Polish immigrants were single young men from the Russian partition of Poland who aspired to work in the U.S. several years and return home. In 1900, pro-independence ZOP chapters broke away and started the **Polish Socialist Alliance**, Związek Socjalistów Polskich (ZSP). In 1901, **Leon Czolgosz**, who had loose ties to ZOP, assassinated President William McKinley, in the aftermath of which the ZOP deteriorated further. The ZSP and its official newspaper *Robotnik* (The Worker) increasingly used mass education and mobilization methods to raise money and recruit volunteers for the Polish independence struggle, its highest priority, while also addressing labor concerns in the U.S. After the 1905 Russian Revolution, younger members left the ZSP and began publishing the widely read *Dziennik Ludowy* (People's Daily) in Chicago in 1907. The following year they launched the Polish Section within the recently established democratic Socialist Party of America. The Polish Section prided itself on its popular education and culture projects. By World War I, there were Polish-language socialist papers in five cities. On the eve of World War I, the ZSP organized politically wide-ranging Polonian groups to form the Komitet Obrony Narodowy (KON; **National Defense Committee**). The KON briefly united Polonians in support of Józef Piłsudski's military campaigns against the Russian czar. Although **Polish Section** called for the ZSP to be more critical of alliances with centrist and right-wing groups, in 1913 the two factions merged into the Polish Federation of the Socialist Party.

Under Piłsudski's leadership, the Second Polish Republic became independent in 1918. During the 1920s and 1930s, a new generation of Polish-American socialist leaders pursued strategies of interethnic cooperation. Even when Polish-born, these leaders grew up and received their political educations largely or entirely within the U.S. Leo Krzycki drew thousands of Polish Americans into the CIO. Already a well-established feminist and labor activist, Rose Wieslander Pastor Stokes cofounded the American Communist Party and agitated for the equal inclusion of African American members. **Bolesław Gebert** became secretary of the Party's Polish Federation and co-editor of its Polish-language newspaper.

Stanley Nowak creatively and successfully used Polonian ethnic media, meetings in ethnic social halls, and other community channels to recruit for the United Auto Workers. He also brought in other Eastern Europeans and African Americans.

During the 1940s, the **Katyń** Massacre and the Soviet "liberation" and domination of Poland severely discredited socialism within the Polish American community. Especially with the influx of World War II refugees, a staunch anti–Communism ruled Polish American politics for the entire Cold War. Widely seen as monolithic, socialism was equated with Stalinist dictatorship and anti–Polish racism, and more than ever with the rejection of religion. These developments occurred alongside McCarthyism and the widescale dismantling of organized U.S. socialism during the 1950s. At the same time, fiercely anti–Communist Polonians continued to advocate labor and other causes that many Americans would deem leftist. **Polonia** also overwhelmingly supported the Democratic Party until the 1980s when the Reagan Revolution caused some to begin to vote Republican. The "Solidarność" immigrants of the 1970s and 1980s arguably represented a new socialist presence within Polish America. They were named for the Solidarity trade union movement which was then leading the ultimately successful mass nonviolent resistance to Communist and Soviet domination of Poland. The Solidarność immigrants were economic refugees from severe food shortages, and/or political refugees whom the Communist authorities forced into exile. The Solidarity movement baffled many leftists around the world and occasioned debate about its relationship, if any, to socialist values and aspirations. Here, finally, was workers' revolution, but one against an avowedly socialist regime, deeply shaped by Roman Catholicism, and backed by such staunchly anti–Communist, conservative world leaders as Margaret Thatcher and Ronald Reagan. Yet, Solidarność supporters located themselves within a politics of democratic socialism and criticized the Polish regime as falsely socialist. They made demands that socialists would not support, but Reagan and Thatcher would. For example, Lech Wałęsa and the Gdańsk shipyard strikers of 1980 called for universal health care, paid maternity leave, state-funded child care, and equity-driven food distribution.

The Solidarność immigrants to the U.S. clashed frequently with the Polonian establishment, dominated as it was by World War II refugees and "ethnics." Socialist-versus capitalist-influenced understandings of community and personal responsibility may help explain these conflicts, in concert with the growth of Polish American Republicans. For example, established Polonians often attributed the new arrivals' difficulties with employment to poor work habits and a culture of welfare dependency. Yet, the Solidarność immigrants themselves believed that established Polonians should help them with jobs and the U.S. government should provide for basic needs like health care. According to Mary Patrice Erdmans, such disagreements hindered the Polish-American community on vital issues from immigrants' social welfare to support for the anti–Communist resistance within Poland.

Polish immigrants to the U.S. after the fall of Communism called themselves the "post-Solidarity" wave. They came principally for economic opportunities then unavailable in Poland. Yet, after Poland joined the European Union (2004), many returned to their homeland. The wish for guaranteed social welfare benefits was one factor. As one young couple explained, "We don't have health insurance.... We pay all the taxes, but we get nothing in return." Meanwhile, demands for such government benefits increased across Americans of all ethnicities, including Polonians with longer roots in the U.S. However, as of 2009, the Democratic Socialists of America (DSA), the country's largest organized socialist group and a descendant of the old Socialist Party, had only 10,000 members and focused upon influencing progressive Democratic Party politics. Although cofounder Motl Zelmanowicz and a few individual members were Polish Americans, the DSA lacked a presence in the community. Social welfare concerns with substantial historical ties to organized socialism did survive among Polonians, but not under the name they had worn less than a century before.—*Mary Krane Derr*

SOURCES: Mary E. Cygan, "The Polish American Left," in Paul Buhle and Dan Georgakas, eds., *The Immigrant Left in the United States* (Albany: State University of New York Press, 1996); Mary Patrice Erdmans, *Opposite Poles: Immigrants and Ethnics in Polish Chicago, 1976–1990* (State College, PA: Pennsylvania State University Press, 1998); Leon Fink, *Workingmen's Democracy: The Knights of Labor and American Politics* (Champaign-Urbana, IL: University of Illinois Press, 1985); Rob Jones, "The Rise and Fall of Solidarność," *Socialism Today* (March 2002); Eugene Miller, "Leo Krzycki—Polish American Labor Leader," *Polish American Studies*, Vol. 33, no. 2 (Autumn 1976), 52–64; Margaret Collingwood Nowak, *Two Who Were There: A Biography of Stanley Nowak* (Detroit: Wayne State University Press, 1985/1989); Joseph Wieczerzak, "Bishop Francis Hodur and the Socialists: Associations and Disassociations," in Theodore L. Zawistowski, ed., *Bishop Francis Hodur: Biographical Essays* (Scranton, PA: Central Diocese, Polish National Church (Boulder, CO: East European Monographs, 1998); Arthur Zipser and Pearl Zipser, *Fire and Grace: The Life of Rose Pastor Stokes* (Athens and London: University of Georgia Press, 1989).

Society of Jesus *see* **Jesuits.**

Society of Polish Engineers *see* **Polonica Technica.**

Sojourners *see* **Birds of Passage.**

Sokół Polski (The Polish Falcon). The *Sokół Polski* is the official organ of the **Polish Falcons** of America and one from the oldest bilingual Polish-English periodicals in the U.S. Originally established under the title *Sokół* (The Falcon) on September 1, 1896, in Chicago, it was published from 1896 to 1912, but was merged in 1913 with *Sokół Polski w Ameryce* (The Polish Falcon in America) published in New York from 1909 to 1913, to become *Sokół Polski*. The new publication was edited in Pittsburgh, Pennsylvania, largely in the English language with some articles in Polish. It was published weekly between 1913 and 1953, biweekly from 1953 to 1956, then as a monthly. The founder and first editor-in-chief of *Sokół* was **Stefan Barszczewski** (editor 1896–1901), and after his return to Poland it was edited in turn by **Stanisław Osada** (1928–34), Mieczysław J. Wasilewski (1934–79), Thomas A. Suski (1979–2004), and Timothy L. Kuzma (2004–). The main sections of the monthly include Falcon News, Junior Falcon, News from Poland, Falcon Focus on Poland, The Polish-American Scene, Reason to Celebrate, Chaplain's Corner, In Memoriam, Calendar of Events, PFA Book and Video Service, and reviews of new books. In 2010 the address was 615 Iron City Drive, Pittsburgh, PA 15205-4397 and the Internet address: http://www.polishfalcons.org.—*Adam A. Zych*

SOURCE: Jan Wepsiec, *Polish American Serial Publications: 1842–1966, An Annotated Bibliography* (Chicago: Jan Wepsiec, 1968), 148.

Solidarity Immigration. The term "Solidarity Immigration" refers to almost 500,000 Poles who migrated to the United States at the end of the twentieth century. This immigrant cohort is characterized mostly by Poles arriving in the late 1970s and 1980s as a result of worsening economic and political conditions in Poland that eventually led to the collapse of the Polish People's Republic in 1989. In the first half of the 1960s, roughly 7,000 Poles were admitted annually into the United States. When the Immigration and Nationality Act of 1965 revised immigration laws, the number of Polish newcomers rose steadily throughout the 1970s and 1980s with the arrival of political refugees and an increase in temporary visitors. The 1968 upheaval in Poland created a new wave of political refugees. Unrest in the universities, initiated by intellectuals but manipulated by factions within the Polish Communist Party, led to an anti–Semitic and anti-reformist backlash. Most of the Jewish émigrés went to Israel while ethnic Poles came to the United States. A larger wave of refugees began arriving in the late 1970s. National strikes in Poland in 1976 and again in 1980 led to the formation of the trade union *Niezależny Samorządny Związek Zawodowy* (Independent Self-Governing Trades Union), known in Poland as *Solidarność* (Solidarity). In December 1981, the Polish state declared martial law, disbanded Solidarity, and jailed opposition activists. Between 1961 and 1992, the U.S. admitted 48,685 political refugees, and over eighty percent of them were admitted between 1979 and 1989 as a result of their involvement with the Solidarity movement.

Along with the political dissidents were a much larger number of economic immigrants. Dissatisfaction with both political and economic conditions in Poland was reflected in the escalating number of temporary visitors to the United States, particularly "visitors for pleasure," known within the community as *wakacjusze* (vacationers) or *turyści* (tourists). The number of visitors for pleasure rose from an average of 24,000 admitted annually in the 1970s, to 36,000 in the 1980s, to almost 50,000 in the 1990s. Many of these "vacationers" worked without authorization and a significant number overstayed their visas (in some cases, for decades). Estimates in the mid–1980s were that 95,000 Poles were living (and working) in the U.S. illegally, the second largest population of illegal immigrants. In 1992 in Chicago, 27 percent of all illegal immigrants came from Poland. Efforts to reduce this illegal population through the 1986 Immigration Reform and Control Act gave amnesty to more than 16,000 Poles and another 2,000 of their dependents. In 1996, the estimate of this illegal population was down to 70,000.

In addition to these temporary visitors and undocumented workers, 381,641 permanent Polish immigrants were admitted between 1960 and 2000, nearly half of them after 1989, the year marking the formal collapse of the communist system in Poland. The transitional capitalist market in Poland created unequal rates of development, high rates of inflation that outpaced increases in income, high rates of unemployment (fifteen percent for most of the 1990s), and, resultantly, a reserve immigrant labor force. While the great majority of Poles migrated to Germany (71 percent in the 1990s), the United States continued to attract Poles, especially with the more expansive immigration policies enacted in the 1990s. The Immigration Act of 1990 raised immigration ceilings which benefitted all countries, but Poles were helped particularly by the new "Diversity Visas" available to people from countries adversely affected by the Immigration and Nationality Act of 1965. Between 1992 and 1997, 53,000 Poles were admitted under this program (known within the community as the "lottery") before the admission procedures changed. Adding together the amnesty recipients, lottery winners, and general immigration, 180,035 Polish immigrants were formally admitted in the 1990s, more than twice the number admitted in the 1980s (81,578), and four times the number admitted in the 1970s (42,378).

The majority of the new immigrants arrived with craft, technical, and professional skills, especially those emigrating from urban areas (83 percent of all emigrants from Poland in the 1990s came from urban areas). In 1980, a third of all Polish immigrants had at most an eighth grade education, while only fifteen percent had post secondary degrees; by 2000, only five percent had an eighth grade education or less, and a third had post secondary degrees (rates similar to the native-born American population).

New immigrants were over represented in service and manual labor occupations. According to the 1990 census, only a quarter of the Polish foreign born worked in professional managerial occupations: thirty percent of those who arrived before 1980 worked in these occupations compared to seventeen percent of those arriving in the 1980s. Even after the influx of a fairly well educated cohort in the 1990s, Polish immigrants were still under represented in professional and managerial occupations and over represented in manual labor and service positions. According to the 2000 census, 45 percent of Polish immigrants worked in professional, managerial, technical, and sale administration occupations (compared to 63 percent of the U.S. native–born population, and Polish immigrant women were twice as likely to have these positions as men (56 percent compared to 26 percent). Polish men were more likely to be working in skilled and unskilled labor positions in the construction and manufacturing sectors: fifty percent of all Polish men worked in these industries. Polish women were more likely to work in the professional and personal service industries (child care, elder care, and home cleaning).

The new immigrants often resettled near established Polish American communities. According to the 2000 census, over half of all foreign-born Poles lived in Illinois and New York, and another fifth lived in New Jersey, Connecticut, and Michigan. In addition, immigrants built new communities in Florida and California. Recent immigrants, temporary migrants, and undocumented workers were the most likely to live in the older urban Polish neighborhoods in places like Chicago and New York. Because of limited English-language skills (in 2000, roughly a third of the Polish foreign born were living in linguistically isolated households), new immigrants were the clientele for Polonia's commercial and professional community, which had grown significantly (the Chicago Polish-language phone book had more than 1,500 pages in 2001). In *Jackowo*, a prominent Polish immigrant community in Chicago in the 1980s, almost all of the businesses were owned by Poles and served primarily Polish customers. By 2000, an increasing number of new immigrants were resettling in suburban areas. In Chicago (the destination for one-third of all new Polish immigrants), the number of new arrivals listing a suburban zip code as their intended residence more than doubled, from 16 to 36 percent, between 1983 and 1998. The presence of immigrants in the suburbs was also evident by the growth of Polish Saturday Schools (schools organized and funded by members of **Polonia** to teach Polish language, history and culture to the children of immigrants). In 1983, there were eighteen Polish Saturday schools in the Chicago metropolitan area, and all but one were located in the city; by 2002, there were 27 schools and fourteen of them were located in the suburbs.—*Mary Patrice Erdmans*

SOURCES: Mary Patrice Erdmans, "New Polonia: Urban and Suburban," in John Koval, Larry Bennet, Michael Bennet, Roberta Garner, Fassil Demissie, and Kiljoong Kim, eds., *The New Chicago* (Philadelphia: Temple University Press, 2006), 115–27; Mary Patrice Erdmans, "Polonia in the New Century: We Will Not Fade Away," *Polish American Studies*, Vol. 57, no. 1 (2000), 5–24; Mary Patrice Erdmans, *Opposite Poles: Immigrants and Ethnics in Polish Chicago, 1976–1990* (University Park, PA: Penn State Press, 1998); Marcin Kula, "Emigration from a Communist Country—Both Economic and Political: A Post-Communist Perspective," *Journal of American Ethnic History*, Vol. 16, no. 1 (1996), 47–54.

Solidarity, Polish American Support for. In the United States there were twelve groups known as Support of Solidarity (SOS) committees. These were located in Arlington (MA), Berkeley (CA), Boston, Cleveland, Detroit, Los Angeles, New Haven (CT), New York, and Philadelphia, as well as Ohio, Southern California, and Western Massachusetts. There were also seven chapters of Solidarity California (in Orange County, Concord, Los Angeles, San Diego, Sacramento, Santa Barbara, and Central California), and at least twelve other groups created to support Poland's democratic opposition movement—Freedom California, Maryland Action for

Poland, Central New Jersey Solidarity, Solidarity International (in New Britain (CT) and New York), North Carolina Committee for Solidarity with "Solidarity," Friends of Solidarity (Washington, D.C.), Solidarity Support Committee of Rhode Island, Committee of Solidarity — Former Political Prisoners (Maywood, NJ), Friends of Solidarity Families Project (Buffalo, NY), Friends of Solidarity, Inc. (Vienna, VA), **Polonia** Solidarity Association (Reading, PA), Solidarity and Human Rights Association (Buffalo, NY), and *Solidarność* Association (Seattle, WA). The most prominent international organization was the Conference of Solidarity Support Organizations (CSSO). In the late 1980s, there were seven CSSO coordinators in four countries. In addition, there were at least 26 Solidarity support organizations in Canada, twenty in Europe, and organizations in Japan, Australia, New Zealand, Venezuela, and Mexico.—*Mary Patrice Erdmans*

SOURCE: Polish American Archives, Central Connecticut State University.

Somalski, Richard J. (b. Bay City, Michigan, September 19, 1926; d.—). Speedskating coach. The founder of Bay Landscaping, Inc. (1948), Somalski also established the Bay County Speedskating Club in 1946. He was the first coach of seven-year-old Terry McDermott, filling that role until 1960 when McDermott made his first Olympic team. He went on to become an Olympic Gold Medal winner in 1964. Somalski was elected president of the Michigan Skating Association in 1964 and served as a member of the U.S. International Speedskating Association Board (1968–92) and later treasurer (1984–92). He was elected to the National Speedskating Hall of Fame in 1991.—*James S. Pula*

SOURCE: www.nationalspeedskatingmuseum.org.

Soroka, Wacław (b. Zborca, Poland, January 18, 1917; d. Stevens Point, Wisconsin, April 22, 1999). Historian. After receiving his university education at the Catholic University of Lublin where he was a student with Karol Wojtyła, he was involved with the Polish Peasant Party before World War II. During the war he served as a lieutenant in the Polish Home Army (Armia Krajowa, AK) and a teacher in the underground government. Following the war, he was forced to flee, settling in France for a short while where he worked with Stanisław Kot, a leader in the International Peasant Union. In addition to his political work, he earned a law degree from the European University in Belgium. Shortly afterward he came to the United States where he earned a degree in library science and helped to expand the Slavic holdings of both

Indiana University and the University of Illinois. He came to the University of Wisconsin–Stevens Point in 1963 where he taught Russian and East European history for twenty-five years and helped create the Russian and East Central European Studies Program, serving as its first director. Out of this program evolved two very important projects, an oral history project and a speakers series. The oral history project helped to preserve the memories of early Polish immigrant life in Portage County, Wisconsin, while the other project created the Annual Lectures on Poland Program which brought outstanding speakers to central Wisconsin. Both of these projects helped to educate people about Polish history and culture and maintained a Polish identity in an area where it could have faded away. Among his publications are *Under the Horror of the Swastika and the Red Star* and *Polish Immigration to the United States*. Soroka was the first American to receive the Merit Award from the Jagiellonian University in Kraków, Poland.—*David Stefancic*

Sosnowski, John Bartholomew (b. Detroit, Michigan, December 8, 1883; d. Detroit, Michigan, July 16, 1968). Congressman, real estate broker, military officer. After attending parochial schools he enlisted as a private in the 7th United States Cavalry during the Spanish-American War, serving in Cuba and the Philippine Islands. After the war he continued in the service on detached duty at the United States Military Academy, West Point, N.Y. He was honorably discharged on December 26, 1906, returning to Detroit to engage in the real estate and brokerage business. He served as a captain and adjutant in the 31st Infantry Regiment, Michigan National Guard, from 1909 to 1916, including service on the Mexican border against Pancho Villa in 1916. Turning to politics, he became a member and chairman of the board of water commissioners of the city of Detroit (1918–1924) before being elected as an anti–Prohibition Republican to the Sixty-ninth Congress (March 4, 1925–March 3, 1927.) Sosnowski, immediately regarded as the chief rival of Speaker Nicholas Longworth as the best dressed man in the House, opposed Federal legislation in 1926 designed to close all stores, theaters, and ballparks on Sunday. He proclaimed: "What this country needs is not less but more amusements." An unsuccessful candidate for re-nomination in 1926, he resumed his real estate and brokerage business, but later served as a delegate to the Republican National Conventions in 1932, 1936, 1940, and 1944. Chosen as a Wendell Willkie presidential elector for Michigan in 1940, he was an unsuccessful candidate for election to Congress

in 1942, 1944, and 1946. He later served as a hearing examiner for the Michigan Liquor Control Commission in 1947–1951.—*Frederick J. Augustyn*

SOURCE: *Biographical Directory of the United States Congress, 1774–Present* (http://bioguide.congress.gov/).

Spójnia *see* **Polish National Union of America.**

Sports, Polish Americans in. Participatory and spectator sport stands as one of the defining elements of contemporary American civilization. Few, if any, leisure activities exert such a powerful influence on everyday life and popular culture in the United States. In their most basic form, such pursuits provide exercise and friendly competition for ordinary folk of all ages, while at the most exalted ranges of these sweaty entertainments, accomplished athletes match skills in contests that command the attention and patronage of millions, and support an enormous sporting industry of pervasive reach. This was not always so. The emergence of modern American sport began in earnest in the era of industrialization, growth, and urbanization that followed the Civil War, and continued steadily through the twentieth century — in other words, the same period that saw the arrival on American shores of the masses of immigrants from Southern and Eastern Europe, and their subsequent development as permanent settlements within the United States. The newcomers could not help but be drawn into the realm of American athletics, which intersected with ethnicity on many levels. For the Poles and other immigrant peoples, sport offered a vivid and attractive entry into the distinctive way of life of the United States. Gaining proficiency in the American games could serve the various functions of fostering integration into the broader culture, winning acceptance from the skeptical native majority, and promoting solidarity and group pride within the gritty neighborhoods of **Polonia.** Because professional sport operated as a meritocracy of muscle, not dependent on advantages of status and breeding, over the years it tended to recruit from the ranks of urban, working class males looking for a way out of the slums or the coal mines, frequently the sons or grandsons of immigrants. For many Polish Americans, sport supplied enjoyment and relief from toil and care; for some, it opened a path to social advancement; while for a lucky few, it afforded a livelihood, and might even lead to fame. As was often the case with immigrants, athletics was the first calling of high profile and prestige in which Polish Americans attained distinction and recognition, and the ethnic community held their sports heroes in special esteem as examples of success, glamorous proofs that they could make the grade in America. In sum, sport has played a considerable and colorful part in the history of Polonia, while conversely, the story of American sport has been much enhanced by the contributions and achievements of notable athletes of Polish heritage.

THE FIRST GENERATION

Of the many things that mystified immigrant Poles about their new surroundings in the United States, none baffled them more than the fact that in America many grownups played strenuous games, or cared about games played by others. The republic that had originated as a colonial outpost of the British Empire had inherited a rich English culture of sport, and had begun to adapt it according to Yankee tastes. The essential American sporting repertoire took shape in a burst of recreational and entrepreneurial creativity in the later nineteenth century. To the established pastimes of horseracing and prizefighting were added team games of native invention, sometimes as twists on foreign precursors. The first was baseball, which gained a wide following and recognition as the national game of the United States. The popularity of baseball led to its organization as a commercial enterprise, establishing the model of professionalization that other sports would copy at a later date. Before long, American football and basketball made their debut, though they remained predominantly amateur activities for several decades. Beyond these developments, this era of athletic innovation also saw the first running of the Boston Marathon, and the adoption of the British imports of golf and tennis as genteel diversions of the well to do.

The Polish transplants found the American appetite for physical play entirely alien and bewildering. Like most other immigrants from the east and south of Europe who passed through the gates of Ellis Island, they regarded games as childish amusements, not worthy of adult attention. Moreover, Poles worked at the hardest and most taxing jobs, while indulging in sport required leisure time, space, and spare energy, all luxuries in short supply in the working class districts of the Atlantic coast or Great Lakes cities, or the mining towns of Pennsylvania. The typical Polish immigrant male took no interest in the American variety of sport, either as participant or spectator, and preferred to seek relaxation in taverns or ethnic clubs.

Nor did the offspring of this Polish first generation enter into the sporting life of their new homeland quickly or without resistance. Parents discouraged their children from taking up the American games, objecting to them as

The championship St. John Kanty baseball team, Milwaukee, 1922 (*UWM*).

frivolities that exerted a bad influence on their youth and enticed them to abandon the ways of the Old World. Nor did Polish youngsters receive the benefit of athletic exposure and training they might have gained as an accompaniment to formal education, since most did not advance far in school, but went to work at an early age to supplement family income.

Although **Oscar Bielaski** played for five seasons in the inaugural years of major league baseball in the 1870s, gaining distinction as the first Polish American professional athlete, his otherwise forgettable career was anomalous and notable mainly for its singularity. Still more familiar with the customs of Poland than of their new surroundings, and not yet initiated into American sport, the early Polonia found its main athletic outlet in New World variants of the Central European fraternal patriotic and exercise societies, such as the German Turners and the Czech Sokols. An outgrowth of an organization founded in the Polish lands twenty years before, the **Polish Falcons** formed in Chicago in 1887, and quickly spread to other cities. Its combined emphasis on physical fitness and advocacy for Poland and its diaspora would make the Falcons an important influence on Polish American history.

TURN OF THE CENTURY

By the time the First World War broke out, Polish Americans had begun to integrate into the sporting culture of the United States, at roughly the same pace, and in roughly the same way as other European immigrants of their era. The driving force of this development was the recreational preference of the

American born sons of the Polish newcomers, keen to blend in by acquiring the language and customs of their native land, including its growing zeal for vigorous physical play. In effect, the younger, second generation voted with its limbs and its lungs by eagerly taking up the American sports as their own, both as participants and as fans. Partially responding to the athletic enthusiasm of these youths and partially out of concern for their upbringing, institutions and advocates of social uplift now encouraged them in this direction. The idea had taken root that sport provided a wholesome outlet for juvenile energy and a training ground for adult virtues. Progressive reformers recommended the health benefits of exercise for urban tenement dwellers and argued that when immigrant children learned American sports, especially the national game of baseball, they learned American and democratic values along with them. So the Falcons and other Polonia organizations broadened and Americanized their athletic programs. Parishes, schools, workplaces, and Polish owned businesses founded and sponsored teams and leagues. The result was an explosion of local amateur and semiprofessional Polish American sports activity that would continue to thrive until after World War II. This grassroots network of ethnically based recreation had the dual, seemingly paradoxical effect of fostering pride and a sense of identity within the community while also speeding its acculturation into the larger society. Over the years, many of the finest Polish American athletes got their start on these rough neighborhood sandlots and playgrounds before graduating to the big time and national stardom.

Baseball quickly became the leading sport among Polish American youth in these initial years of the twentieth century, but they would require time to gain the proficiency needed to shine at the highest levels of the well entrenched national pastime, long dominated by players of earlier immigrant stock, above all the Irish. On the other hand, the sons of Polonia were present at the creation of professional football, and established a precocious prominence in the sport that eventually would surpass even baseball in popularity. Football had started as a college boys' hobby, strongly associated with blueblood Ivy League elites; the pro version sprang from plebeian beginnings in the scruffy mining and steel towns of Pennsylvania and the upper Midwest. This roughneck competition attracted many players of Polish and other East European heritage, suited to its rigors by occupations demanding brawn and heavy exertion. It did not take long for the football public to notice the frequency of Polish surnames in their game, and this reputation for excellence on the gridiron would become a lasting tradition of Polish American sport.

The leisure and sporting preferences of Polonia during the Ragtime decades reflected its profile as an urban, blue collar populace that liked its amusements elemental and unsophisticated. Corner poolrooms and taverns continued to be favorite gathering places. In particular, bowling parlors began to proliferate in the Polish city districts. They drew a bustling clientele, and their proprietors often became figures of personal and political influence within the community. The link between Polish Americans and bowling became an enduring stereotype, one of those with some basis in fact. Prizefighting and wrestling also commanded a wide following. Boxing offered scrappy dead end kids a puncher's

chance to escape the mean streets, so Poles and other ethnics made up more than their share of the pugs in local clubs, especially in the lighter weight divisions. One of them, **Stanley Ketchel** (Kiecał), became the first acknowledged Polish American sporting champion when he captured the world middleweight crown in 1908; his reign, like his life, was short and tempestuous, and ended two years later in his death by gunshot. The Polish born wrestler **Stanley Zbyszko** (Cyganiewicz) began touring in America in the opening years of the century, and became such a draw that he adopted the United States as his home and base of professional operations. Zbyszko attained near legendary status within Polonia and remained a sometime titleholder and premier gate attraction until his retirement in 1928 at the advanced age of 47.

The Jazz Age and the Depression

After the First World War the American fascination with sport shifted into higher gear as part of the revolution in popular culture initiated during the decade of the "Roaring Twenties." Prosperity allowed people to spend more freely on entertainment, and the emergence of mass media such as the radio, newsreel, and motion picture stimulated and fed an unprecedented public interest in celebrity. So attendance at sporting events rose to record levels, and fans eagerly cheered the exploits of superstars like Red Grange, Jack Dempsey, and above all the baseball colossus Babe Ruth, the most famous man in America. Like most other industries, the sports business took a nosedive during the Great Depression of the thirties, as economic straits caused gate receipts to plummet, but Americans continued to follow their teams and athletic heroes just as avidly in the newspapers or over the air. In

good times and bad, sport had become a consuming national passion.

The conditions of the period had the curious effect of both speeding the channeling of Polonia into the American sporting mainstream while, for the time being, reinforcing its separate, enclosed system of ethnic athletics. Restrictions on immigration naturally weakened the ties of Polish America with the ancestral homeland, and the sheer passage of the years worked in favor of its gradual absorption into the American way of life and sport. It became common practice for the Polish language press to use English as the language of its sports pages, a telling indicator of both the leisure and linguistic preferences of its readership. Still, Polish Americans remained tightly bound to their big city enclaves, and the institutions and organizations that gave it structure. Local Polish amateur and semipro leagues flourished as never before, and neighborhood contests regularly drew crowds in the thousands. During the Depression, when the price of a ticket to a premier sporting event seemed out of reach, the nearby sandlots provided an inexpensive, homegrown alternative. Bowling, too, continued to offer affordable and convivial recreation for the working class Polonia rank and file who had to have their entertainment cheap or not at all.

The interplay between Americanization and the maintenance of the established immigrant group support system showed in the continued expansion and diversification of the various intramural Polish American athletic programs. A notable addition to the staple repertory of baseball, football, and bowling was basketball, an urban game with a pronounced ethnic accent in those days. By the later 1930s the Polish Falcons had introduced its own national bowling tournament and staged the first Polish American "Olympics." As if to prove that they had not forgotten their origins in the Turner tradition, Falcon entrants frequently took top honors in gymnastic competitions sponsored by the Amateur Athletic Union.

By this time, an increasing number of Polish Americans succeeded in pushing their way into the ranks of stardom. Baseball fans noticed that Polish and Italian names had begun to outnumber Irish ones on major league rosters. The pitcher **Stan Coveleski** (Kowalewski) won twenty games or more in five different seasons during the span of his prime, 1918 to 1925, and a few years later the outfielder **Al Simmons** (Szymanski) established himself as one of the top hitters in the game; eventually, these two became the Polish American players of earliest vintage to gain induction into the National Baseball Hall of

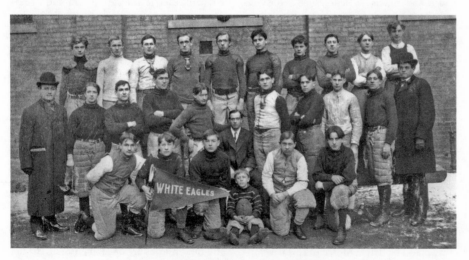

Chicago's **White Eagles** football team (*PMA*).

Fame. Collegiate football likewise made more room for the descendants of Poles and other immigrants with the spread of the sport to middlebrow land grant colleges and the availability of athletic scholarships to open the doors of higher education to those sons of the unwashed adept at blocking and tackling. **Alex Wojciechowicz** won All-American honors as a lineman at Fordham in the mid-thirties, and went on to carve out a stellar professional career. The boxer **Teddy Yarosz** captured the world middleweight crown in 1934 before injuries contributed to his loss of the title the following year.

THE GLORY DAYS OF POLISH-AMERICAN SPORTS, 1941–1970

Roughly sixty years after their ancestors starting crossing the Atlantic in the millions, Polish American athletes attained their historic height of visibility and accomplishment within the arena of sport in the United States during the Second World War and the subsequent quarter century of the postwar baby boom. Several reasons combined to bring about this golden age of Polonia's sporting prowess and recognition. For one thing, Polish Americans collectively had learned to play the American games, and play them well. The extensive system of Polish American athletics taught and practiced in neighborhood clubs, churches, gyms, and sandlots had thrived for forty years, and was primed to yield a rich harvest of trained talent. World War II created opportunities of diverse sorts for this up-and-coming generation of sportsmen. Some got an immediate crack at the big time when the military draft opened vacancies in professional sporting ranks by putting experienced players in the different uniforms issued them by Uncle Sam. Others went to college on the G.I. Bill after serving their wartime stint in the armed forces, or as part of the increasing democratization of higher education, and took advantage of the chance to offer their skills to the varsity teams. At the same time, Polonia still remained largely a blue collar crowd standing on the lower rungs of status, schooling, and opportunity, the social stratum that classically grabs at the slim chance of becoming sports stars since it has no chance of becoming lawyers or doctors. In a larger sense, the Polish-Americans were taking their chronologically defined turn in one of the recurrent themes in the history of sport in the United States, that of successive waves of athletic ascendancy by various immigrant peoples and racial and ethnic minorities. The Irish and Germans had come before them; the blacks and Hispanics would follow them; this was Polonia's moment in the winner's circle.

The Polish impact on major league baseball reached an all time high. Indeed, the image of a burly Slavic slugger became widely accepted as an archetype of the power-hitting brand of ball played in the 1950s. Beyond personifying the game, Polonia produced several of the most glittering stars of the period. The honor roll begins with **Stan Musial**, who debuted as leftfielder for the St. Louis Cardinals in 1941; he retired in 1963 as the holder of the lion's share of National League hitting records. Musial appears on everyone's short list of the very greatest ballplayers, and is regarded, by consensus, as the most storied of Polish American athletes. Similar to Musial in many ways, Boston Red Sox leftfielder **Carl Yastrzemski** gained recognition as the outstanding player in the American League during the later 1960s. While not nearly their equal with the bat, Pittsburgh second baseman **Bill Mazeroski** joined "Stan the Man" and "Yaz" in the Hall of Fame thanks to his reputation for matchless defensive work at his position.

The particular aptitude of muscular Polish Americans for football, evident from its infancy, became yet more striking now that more of them were entering the college ranks and the game itself rose to challenge the position of baseball as the premier sporting attraction in the country. During the four consecutive years 1947–1950, three gridiron stars of Polish background —**Johnny Lujack**, **Leon Hart**, and **Vic Janowicz**— received the Heisman trophy awarded annually to the nation's top collegiate performer. **Forest Evashevski** and **Hank Stram** won accolades as coaches at the college and professional levels, respectively. In his biography and hardnosed persona, **Mike Ditka** almost seemed to sum up the story of football, from his origins and college exploits in western Pennsylvania, to his later identification with the Chicago Bears first as standout player, then as coach, lifting him to iconic stature as the embodiment of the big shouldered capital city of Polish America.

In the meantime, Polonia continued to excel in the rough and ready indoor pastimes that reflected its established urban character. **Johnny Crimmins** was named national bowler of the year in 1942, and **Eddie Lubanski** claimed the same prize in 1959. **Tony Zale** became the third world middleweight boxing king of Polish heritage in 1940. Unlike his two predecessors, he enjoyed a lengthy tenure as champ, and held on to his crown, with one brief interruption, until 1948.

Even so, as a sign of changing times, Polish Americans were starting to make inroads and headlines in sports just entering into broad popularity, or formerly associated with WASP swells. As the first seven-footer to shine in basketball, **Bob Kurland** led Oklahoma A & M to two straight NCAA titles in 1945–46, and made the All-America team three times. **Tom Gola** topped that, at least numerically, by being named All-American in four seasons, and college player of the year to boot in 1954, when his LaSalle squad captured the national championship; he went on to become a frequent all-pro in the National Basketball Association. Tennis courts were scarce in the crowded Polish neighborhoods of the country, but that did not stop **Frankie Parker** (Pajkowski) from winning four Grand Slam events in his career, the U.S. Open in 1944 and 1945, and the French Open in 1948 and 1949.

WOMEN AND SPORT

Until recent times, sport has been regarded as a male preserve *par excellence*, not suited for

Milwaukee's Kosciuszko Reds, championship semi-professional baseball team (*UWM*).

women on the grounds that it was unladylike and too demanding for the female frame. This was all the more emphatically so among Polish Americans, whose religious and cultural values reinforced traditional ideas of family and sex roles. Womenfolk were expected to tend to home, nursery, shop, and church, and to reflect prevailing norms of femininity. The result was that relatively few women of Polonia cared for athletic pursuits, or had leisure time to devote to them, and those who did ran the risk of social disapproval and resistance. For instance, Polish American women in Chicago had to overcome the objections of their husbands to organize their own Falcon and bicycling sororities in the 1890s. The daunting, dominant belief that women and sport should not mix slowly eased with the passage of time, as it did in mainstream America, frequently tied to notions of the salutary benefits of exercise. By the 1920s Polish American newspapers began to endorse athletics as an aid to the enhancement of women's health and appearance.

Because of their scarcity and limited opportunities, not to mention minimal public interest in their doings, Polish American sportswomen only occasionally gained popular attention before the rise of feminism in the 1960s and 1970s. The first celebrated female athlete to emerge from within Polonia was the track and field standout **Stella Walsh** (Walasiewicz), born in Poland but brought up in the United States by immigrant parents. Competing for her native country, Walsh won the gold medal for the 100 meter run in the 1932 Olympics. Over the course of a lengthy career, she set many world or American records. Walsh received a measure of posthumous notoriety when, upon her death, she was discovered to have been sexually androgynous. This revelation has stirred controversy about the legitimacy of her exploits, but also has been

cited as a precedent in the subsequent relaxation of gender determination tests by international sporting authorities. A conspicuous number of players in the All American Girls Professional Baseball League (1943–1954) were of Polish stock, largely due to the fact that most of its teams were based in medium sized industrial towns ringing Lake Michigan.

Women's sport is a late blooming phenomenon, having come into its own only since the final decades of the twentieth century, so it is no surprise that many of the most prominent and successful Polish American women athletes made their mark during this stretch of years. **Carol Blazejowski** was named a college basketball All-American three seasons running at Montclair State College, and national player of the year in 1978. Golfer **Betsy King** won the U.S. Women's Open in 1989 and 1990, and the LPGA championship in 1992.

SPORT IN THE CONTEMPORARY ERA

The Polish American community and its way of life changed dramatically after the Second World War, and these changes — most of them indicative of socio-economic advancement — could be measured in athletic terms, as well as the more solemn gauges of social scientists. As in the past, looking at Polonia through the lively lens of sport could tell much about its sense of identity, its circumstances, and its status and degree of integration within American society. Like other immigrants, Poles had arrived in the United States as strangers to its sporting culture; had adopted the American games as their own as they exchanged their ancestral customs for those of the New World; and, in time, produced more than their share of athletic champions, as the urban working classes always did.

But increasingly, Polish Americans of the third and fourth generations were graduating from college, and entering professions and white collar offices. Polonia was moving up and out into the world: up into the middle class, and out into the suburbs.

The migration of Polish Americans away from the old neighborhood reduced the importance of sport as a communal activity and rallying point, while the greater opportunities now open to their youth meant that relatively fewer of them sought and won stardom on the playing field. The exodus from the city led to the slow decline of the downtown Polish parishes and clubs, and with them the complex of instructional programs and sandlot leagues that had trained, vetted, and encouraged the budding athletes of Polonia. Beyond that, now that they stood a reasonable chance of getting into law or medical school, physically talented Polish American youngsters who, in earlier times, might have taken the gamble of choosing sport as their livelihood now elected to hit the books rather than baseballs. Those who still did follow the siren call of athletics ran into the obstacle of stiffer competition, as blacks and Hispanics came into their own as the newly dominant elements in sport, displacing the white ethnics who had held sway for the previous century.

To be sure, Polish America continued to contribute notables to the world of athletics. Knuckleballer **Phil Niekro** won 318 major league games, more than all but a handful of hurlers in baseball annals, and his mastery of this fluttery delivery punched his ticket into the Hall of Fame. By any measure, **Mike Krzyzewski** ranks among the premier coaches in the history of college basketball. To date, "Coach K." has won three NCAA championships at Duke University, multiple national coach of the year awards, and guided the U.S. men's basketball team to a gold medal in the 2008 Olympics. A stock car racer on the NASCAR circuit, **Alan Kulwicki** won the Winston Cup crown in 1992, just before his promising career was cut short by a fatal air crash. Kulwicki was known as the "Polish Prince," an exotic presence within the southern-fried milieu of NASCAR, but for the most part the sporting public, and Polonia itself, tended to take less notice of the Polishness of these latter day luminaries than earlier observers would have done. They were no longer pigeonholed as "ethnic" stars, or held up as role models for a people struggling to better itself. Now they were thought of simply as standouts in the rich pageant of American sport, much as the descendants of immigrants from the Polish lands had become an inextricable part of the story of America.—*Neal Pease*

A Polish American soccer club parading in Hartford, Connecticut (*CCSU-LC*).

SOURCES: Neal Pease, "Diamonds Out of the Coal Mines: Slavic Americans in Baseball," in Lawrence Baldassaro and Richard A. Johnson, eds., *The American Game: Baseball and Ethnicity* (Carbondale: Southern Illinois University Press, 2002), 142–61; Neal Pease, "The Kosciuszko Reds, 1909–1919: Kings of the Milwaukee Sandlots," *Polish American Studies,* Vol. 61, no. 1, 11–26; Thomas M. Tarapacki, *Chasing the American Dream: Polish Americans in Sport* (New York: Hippocrene, 1995); Thomas M. Tarapacki, "Poles," in George B. Kirsch, Othello Harris, and Claire E. Nolte, eds., *Encyclopedia of Ethnicity and Sports in the United States* (Westport, CT: Greenwood Press, 2000), 363–68; Casimir J. B. Wronski, "Early Days of Sport Among Polish Americans of Chicagoland," in *Poles of Chicago, 1837–1937* (Chicago: Polish Pageant, 1937), 145–48.

Stadnitski, Pieter (Piotr Jakub Stadnicki; b. Amsterdam, The Netherlands, April 2, 1735; d. Amsterdam, The Netherlands, September 29, 1795). Banker, financier. A descendant of a prominent Calvinist family from Podgorze, Poland, who migrated to Amsterdam during the Reformation, Stadnitski never set foot in North America yet he played a significant role in the success of the American Revolution. At the beginning of the Revolution, the infant government was in great need of funds to pay and equip an army to oppose the British. The first American government under the Articles of Confederation lacked the power to tax the people directly, and the lack of a federal bank or the power to make long-term loans made it difficult for the revolutionary government to raise funds or borrow money. As the war continued for several years, a crisis loomed and John Adams was sent to Amsterdam in the United Dutch Provinces, then the banking capital of Europe, to obtain a loan to prevent the American government from defaulting on its obligations and destroy its credit rating. A syndicate organized by Stadnitski was the first to arrange significant financial support for the American treasury, eventually purchasing some $1,340,000 in American securities. By 1788, Thomas Jefferson considered Stadnitski to be America's principal banker. In the same year Stadnitski sent an agent to the United States to investigate opportunities for financial speculation. Based on his favorable report, in 1789 Stadnitski formed another syndicate to purchase American securities and began speculating in American lands in 1792. By 1795 his efforts led to formation of the Holland Land Company that eventually purchased over 5,000,000 acres of land in central and western New York and western Pennsylvania. After investing in internal improvements such as roads to make the land more attractive for settlement, the partners sold off individual lots to settlers. Although the venture did not return the quick profits Stadnitski hoped for, it did remain solvent and helped provide the framework for the growth and development of New York State. Stadnitski continued serving as the company's leader until his death. The company remained in business until 1849 when it disposed of its remaining lands.—*James S. Pula*

SOURCES: Paul D. Evans, *The Holland Land Company* (Buffalo: Buffalo Historical Society, 1924); James Jan Kaminski, "Pieter Stadnitski: America's Principal Broker and Land Developer," *Polish American Studies,* Vol. XLIV, no. 1 (Spring 1987), 56–66.

Stanczak, Julian (b. Borownica, Poland, November 5, 1928; d.—). Artist. In February 1940 the Russians forcibly sent him and his family to a labor camp in Perm (Molotov) where pneumonia, encephalitis, starvation, and a severe beating cost him the use of his right arm. Released from Siberia with thousands of other Poles in 1942, he briefly joined the Polish Army-in-Exile in Persia at age thirteen. After spending his teenage years in a Polish refugee camp in British Uganda, Africa, where he learned to paint left-handed, he later moved to England where he was educated at the Borough Polytechnic Institute in London (1948–50). He emigrated with his family to the U.S. in 1950 where he continued his education at the Cleveland Institute of Art (BFA, 1954) and, studying with color theorists Josef Albers and Conrad Marca-Relli, at Yale University (MFA, 1956). Following graduation, he accepted teaching positions at the Art Academy of Cincinnati (1957–64), Cleveland Institute of Art (1964–95), and Artist-in-Residence at Dartmouth College (1964). He soon became recognized, along with Richard Anuszkiewicz, as one of the foremost exponents of the Op (Optical) Art Movement in the 1960s and early 1970s.

Stanczak's works were featured in solo exhibitions in England, Kenya, Poland, and various locations in the U.S. His work was recognized with the Cleveland Fine Arts Prize for Visual Arts (1970); Outstanding American Educator, Educators of America (1970); Award for Excellence in Painting, Ohio Arts Council (1972); Model of Excellence Award, Cleveland Institute of Art (2001); Victor Schrekengost Award, Cleveland Institute of Art (2004).—*Stanley L. Cuba*

SOURCES: *Who is Who in American Art 2008* (New Providence, NJ: Marquis Who's Who, LLC, 2007); Joe Houston and Dave Hickey, *Optic Nerve: Perceptual Art of the 1960s* (London: Merrell Publishers, Ltd., 2007); Robert C. Morgan, *Julian Stanczak, Construction and Color: Four Decades of Painting* (New York: Stefan Stux Gallery, 2005); Elizabeth McClelland, *Julian Stanczak, Retrospective: 1948–1998* (Youngstown: Butler Institute of American Art, 1998); Floyd Ratliff and Sanford Wurmfeld, *Color Function Painting: The Art of Josef Albers, Julian Stanczak and Richard Anuszkiewicz: Selections from the Collection of Neil K. Rector* (Winston-Salem: Wake Forest University Fine Arts Gallery, 1996); Jacqueline Shinners and Rudolf Arnheim, *Julian Stanczak: Color = Form* (Traverse City: Northwestern Michigan College, 1993); Rudolf Arnheim, Harry Rand and Robert Bertholf, *Julian Stanczak: Decades of Light* (Buffalo: The Poetry/Rare Books Collection, State University of New York at Buffalo, 1990); Gene Baro, *Serigraphs and Drawings of Julian Stanczak 1970–1972* (Washington, D.C.: Corcoran Gallery of Art, 1972).

Stanczyk, Stanley Anthony (b. Armstrong, Wisconsin, May 10, 1925; d.—). Weight lifter. As a young child Stanczyk moved with his family to Detroit where he joined the Boy's Club and became interested in a variety of sports. Soon he began to excel at weight lifting and started training under the guidance of the noted Johnny Krill. With the outbreak of World War II he was drafted into the army in 1943 right after winning the Junior Nationals the same year. He served in the Pacific, earning a Purple Heart. Following the war Stanczyk placed third in the 1946 Senior Nationals, breaking the record in the 165-pound class for the clean and jerk. He won the 1946 North American Championships as a middleweight, and the World Lightweight Championship in Paris, France, the same year, setting a new world record in the process. In 1947, lifting as a middleweight, he broke another world record, won the Senior Nationals, and at the World Championships in Philadelphia broke four American and three world records. At the 1948 Olympics he won the gold medal in the light-heavyweight class. He won three more world championship in 1949, 1950, and 1951, a gold medal in the 1951 Pan American Games, and a silver medal in the 1952 Olympics in Helsinki, Finland. He then opened and operated a bodybuilding and weightlifting gymnasium in Miami, Florida. In 1955 he opened a bowling alley, restaurant, bar, and lounge.—*James S. Pula*

SOURCES: Arthur Gay, "TERRIFIC is the word for Stanczyk," *Your Physique*, December 1947; Chester O. Teegarden, "Stanczyk's Workout," *California Weight Lifter's Association Bulletin*, November 1949, 2).

Stankiewicz, Richard (b. Philadelphia, Pennsylvania, October 18, 1922; d. Worthington, Massachusetts, March 27, 1983). Sculptor, printmaker. Following the death of his father in a railroad accident, the family relocated to Detroit in 1928. Educated at Cass Technical High School, he went on to further education at the Hans Hofmann School of Fine Arts (1948–49) and the Atelier Fernand Leger and Ossip Zadkine Studio in Paris (1950–51). During World War II he served as a radio operator in the U.S. Navy (1941–46). After a stint as a freelance mechanical draftsman (1952–64), he began a teaching career at the State University of New York, Albany (1967–82), Skowhegan School of Art (1972, 1977), and Artist-in-residence at the University of Southern Florida and Tampa Art Institute (1965), Amherst Collage (1971), and

Dartmouth College (1979). He is best known for his assemblage "junk sculptures." Stankiewicz held solo exhibitions in Australia, England, France, Switzerland, Yugoslavia, and various locations in the U.S. His work was recognized with the Creative Arts Award from Brandeis University (1966).—*Stanley L. Cuba*

SOURCES: Adam D. Weinberg, Emmie Donadio, Jon Wood and Martin Friedman, *Miracle in the Scrap Heap: The Sculpture of Richard Stankiewicz* (Andover, MA: Addison Gallery of American Art, Phillips Academy, 2003); Emmie Donadio, *Richard Stankiewicz: Sculpture in Steel* (Middlebury, VT: Middlebury College Museum of Art, 1994).

Stara emigracja. A Polish phrase meaning "old emigration," it was frequently used among scholars to refer to the generation of immigrants arriving in the U.S. between 1870 and 1920.

Stary kraj. A Polish phrase meaning "Old Country," it was frequently used among the immigrant communities of 1870–1920 when speaking of their homeland in Poland.

Starzenski, Victor (b. Clayton, Kansas, July 20, 1886; d. Schenectady, New York, May 1974). Lacrosse player, coach. After graduating from Hoboken Academy in New Jersey, Starzenski attended the Stevens Institute of Technology where he earned a degree in mechanical engineering (1907) and played lacrosse. Following graduation he embarked on a successful career in engineering for Westinghouse, eventually accepting positions as a general supervisor for the Adirondacks Power Corporation, general manager for the Schenectady Power Company, and vice president of the Hudson Valley Fuel Corporation (1936–45). He founded and coached the lacrosse program at three colleges: Union College in Schenectady, NY (1922–28), Rensselaer Polytechnic Institute in Troy, NY (1944), and the University of New Mexico (1946), then returned to Union College (1948–50). In 1947 he was recognized by the United States Intercollegiate Lacrosse Association as the person who had contributed most to lacrosse. He was inducted into the National Lacrosse Hall of Fame in 1995.—*James S. Pula*

SOURCE: apps.uslacrosse.org.

Starzyński, Teofil A. (b. Trzemeszno, Poland, April 14, 1878; d. Pittsburgh, Pennsylvania, June 9, 1952). Politician, Polonia activist. In 1887 Starzyński arrived in the United States with his mother, settling with the family in Pittsburgh. He studied pharmacy and later medicine at the University of Pittsburgh, earning an M.D. degree in 1904 and opening a practice in Pittsburgh. In 1897 he organized Nest No. 8 of the **Falcon** (Sokół) movement in Pittsburgh, and the same year

was elected president of District IV, an office he held several times. He opposed the movement of some Falcons to affiliate with the **Polish National Alliance**, becoming in 1909 a leader of the "Free Falcons" who left the national movement over its merger with the PNA. When the two groups were eventually reunified in 1912, he was elected president and transferred the organization's headquarters from Chicago to Pittsburgh. Except for the years 1918–24, he served as president of the Falcons until his death in 1952. Under his leadership the Falcons had a strong commitment to the formation of the **National Defense Committee**, with Starzyński also being numbered among the founders of the **Polish Central Relief Committee** and serving as a member of its Executive Committee. Beginning in 1913 he was one of the early advocates of Falcon military training to support the Polish independence movement. He constantly appealed to American authorities, trying to convince them to support the idea of Polish independence and charitable relief activities on Poland's behalf. In the beginning of 1917 he was among those who formed military camps in Niagara-on-the-Lake, Ontario, and Cambridge Springs, Pennsylvania, to train Poles to fight in Europe. In the same year he initiated the recruitment of volunteers for the **Polish Army in France**. In 1918 he resigned to join the Polish Army with the rank of major to fight for Polish independence in France and later in **Galicia** in 1919 where he was promoted to the rank of colonel. Upon his return to the U.S. in 1924 he was re-elected president of the

Teofil Starzyński, politician and Polonia activist (*JPI*).

Falcons and served without serious opposition thereafter. He also helped organize and became president of the **Polish Army Veterans Association**; in 1939 he was decorated with the association's Cross of Merit. During World War II, Starzyński assisted in organizing the **Polish American Congress**, but later differed from most of those involved in the Congress because he believed that Polish Americans should be in contact with postwar communist Poland. He supported the new Polish western border imposed at **Yalta**, another break with mainstream **Polonia**, and accepted the fact that Poland had lost its eastern territories. He further marginalized himself by condemning the Warsaw Uprising and applauding Soviet agrarian policies in Poland. As a result, he resigned from his position in the Polish American Congress, but continued to lead the national Falcons organization. Starzyński was honored with a Falcons college scholarship program named in his memory.—*Adam Walaszek*

SOURCES: Szymon Szytniewski, "Teofil Starzyński's Activities to Recruit Polish Soldiers in Canada During the Second World War," *Polish American Studies*, Vol. 63, no. 2 (2006), 59–77; Adam Walaszek, "*Teofil A. Starzyński*," *Polski Słownik Biograficzny*, Vol. 42, no. 2 (Warszawa 2004), 174; Donald Pienkos, *One Hundred Years Young: A History of the Polish Falcons in America 1887–1987* (New York: Columbia University Press, 1987).

Staś, Helena (Helena Męczyńska Staś; b. Pietrkowo, Poland, May 9, 1868; d. Kalisz, Poland, April 23, 1930). Author, Polonia activist. Staś was one of early **Polonia**'s most prolific and outspoken writers, producing a long string of novels, novellas, and stories based on the immigrant experience, as well as poems, social and political commentaries, and spiritual tracts. Along the way, she founded what was probably the first Polish women's monthly magazine in the United States, worked off and on as a journalist for numerous newspapers and journals, was a frequent lecturer on national, women's, and spiritual subjects, and was active in the **Polish Women's Alliance** and the **Polish Falcons**. Despite her many activities, the pieces of Helena Staś's life form a difficult puzzle to reconstruct. She migrated to the United States with her tailor husband, Theodore Męczyński, sailing on the *Moravia* and landing in New York on Christmas day, 1888. According to Staś's writings, her first years in the United States were spent apart from **Polonia**. Only after the death of her husband and daughter did she begin to write. In 1907 a flurry of short stories, novellas, letters to the editor, and polemical pieces began to appear in Polish American newspapers like the Detroit *Dziennik Polski* (Polish Daily News). While other writers of her era sometimes published anonymously or under a pseudonym, Staś admitted, despite the lack of a formal education, she wanted to make a name for herself while serving Polonia and the Polish cause.

Early novellas like *Anioł miłosierdzie* (Angel of Mercy, 1907), *Marzenie czy rzeczywistość* (Dream or Reality, 1907), *Na falach życia* (On the Waves of Life, 1907), and *Polski pień* (The Polish Trunk, 1907) dealt particularly with the experiences of Polish immigrant women. In 1909 Staś founded *Ogniwo* (The Link), a monthly magazine for women, which lasted until 1911. Her only full-length novel, *Na ludzkim targu* (In the Human Market, 1910), whose protagonist was a struggling woman writer, was outspokenly critical of Polish American institutional power in Chicago. By this time Staś was also deeply involved in the theosophical movement, and the combination of her spiritual unorthodoxy and this confrontational novel were probably what motivated her to leave Chicago for Milwaukee around 1911.

For the next ten years Staś moved in and out of public life, running a candy store for a time but also lecturing, teaching, writing, and organizing spiritual study groups. In 1915 she worked as a traveling subscription agent for the English-language monthly *Free Poland,* and traveled as far as California lecturing on behalf of Polish independence. She published a popular cookbook in 1920, and a collection of children's stories, *Moje koraliki* (My Corals) in 1921. Around this time Staś became editor of the women's and children's section of Milwaukee's *Kuryer Polski* (Polish Courier), while also establishing a theosophical monthly, *Nowa era* (New Era). In 1927 *Kuryer Polski* organized a tour of Poland with Staś traveling along as a correspondent. On this trip she reestablished ties with her family overseas, from whom she seems to have been estranged, and in failing health and going blind, she returned to Poland, dying in Kalisz in 1930.—*Karen Majewski*

SOURCES: Karen Majewski, "Toward 'A Pedagogical Goal': Family, Nation, and Ethnicity in the Fiction of Polonia's First Women Writers," in Thomas S. Gladsky and Rita Holmes Gladsky, eds., *Something of My Very Own to Say: American Women Writers of Polish Descent* (Boulder, CO: East European Monographs, 1997), 54–66; Karen Majewski, *Traitors and True Poles: Narrating a Polish-American Identity, 1880–1939* (Athens: Ohio University Press, 2003); Danuta Pytlak, "The Ongoing Story: The Image of the Polish American Family in the U.S.A. (1880–1939) in Polish American Fiction," in Marta Wiszniowska, ed., *Local Colors of the Stars and Stripes* (Torun: Wyd. Uniwersytetu Kopernika, 2001).

Stęczyński, Marian Bogdan (b. near Kraków, Poland, March 24, 1866; d. Pennsylvania, December 8, 1939). Polonia activist.

After migrating to the U.S., Stęczyński settled in Chicago and became a member of the **Polish National Alliance** in 1896. Already associated with émigré political activists in Switzerland at the time, he rose quickly to a prominent place in the Alliance. Elected president of the PNA in 1903, he worked for the merger between the PNA and a number of smaller patriotic organizations focused on the younger generation, such as the **Polish Falcons Alliance**. The Falcons, in fact, joined the PNA in 1905. However, this merger, while leading to a rapid expansion in the membership of the Falcons with PNA support, led to the secession of activists who opposed the tie. In 1912, the Polish Falcons Alliance was reunited as an independent organization under a new president, Dr. **Teofil Starzyński**.

Under Stęczyński's leadership, the PNA established its own Polish language daily newspaper, *Dziennik Związkowy* (The Alliance Daily) in 1908, and organized a system of district leaders (commissioners) to help direct the insurance and fraternal operations of the rapidly growing Alliance. PNA membership rose from 36,000 to 100,000 between 1903 and 1913. In 1907 he succeeded in arranging the first meeting of PNA representatives with a president of the United States, Theodore Roosevelt, at the White House. In 1910, working with PNA **Censor Anthony Schreiber**, he succeeded in inviting President William Howard Taft to dedicate the monuments to **Kazimierz Pułaski** (paid for from Federal funds) and **Thaddeus Kościuszko** (underwritten by the PNA) in Washington, D.C. Coinciding with these ceremonies, Stęczyński took the lead in organizing a **Polish National Congress** where the issues of Polish independence and immigration could be discussed in the nation's capital by delegates from **Polonia** and Europe. At the Congress, Stęczyński proposed an eloquent resolution declaring that "We Poles have the right to existence as an independent nation and we believe it is our sacred duty to strive for the political independence of our fatherland, Poland."

In 1912, the Polish National Alliance approved the creation of its own school, **Alliance College**, in Cambridge Springs, Pennsylvania. At this point Stęczyński resigned the presidency of the PNA. He was succeeded by **Casimir Zychlinski**, his long time friend and a former leader of the Falcons Alliance. Stęczyński was appointed business manager of the new school. He remained the business manager at Alliance College until his death in 1939. A horticulturalist by training, Stęczyński journeyed to Poland after World War I and brought back seedlings from the Tatra Mountains that sprouted later into a luxuriant forest of evergreens.—*Donald E. Pienkos*

SOURCES: Stanisław Osada, *Historia Związku Narodowego Polskiego i rozwój ruchu narodowego Polskiego w Ameryce Północnej* (Chicago: Nakładem i drukiem Związku Narodowego Polskiego, 1905); Adam Olszewski, *Historia Związku Narodowego Polskiego* (Chicago: Polish National Alliance, 1957–1963), Vol. 2; Romuald Piątkowski, *Pamiętnik wzniesienia i odsłonięcia pomników Tadeusza Kościuszki i Kazimierza Pułaskiego tudzież połączonego z tą uroczystoiścią Pierwszego Kongresu Narodowego Polskiego w Washingtonie, D.C.* (Chicago: Nakładem Zwiazku Narodowego Polskiego w Połnocnej Ameryce, 1911); Donald E. Pienkos, *PNA: A Centennial History of the Polish National Alliance of the United States of North America* (Boulder, CO: East European Monographs, 1984).

Stefanowicz, Zygmunt (b. Lida, Poland, November 8, 1884; d. Łódź, Poalnd, April 26, 1978). Editor, Polonia activist. After coming to the United States as a young man, he completed studies begun in Wilno at Valparaiso University in Indiana. Finding work as a journalist, he was employed as an associate editor and editor in a number of Polish Catholic newspapers, becoming editor-in-chief, in 1938, of the *Dziennik Zjednoczenia* (Polish Union Daily), the daily newspaper of the Chicago-based **Polish Roman Catholic Union** of America. At the same time he held identical responsibilities with the PRCUA's fraternal publication, *Narod Polski* (The Polish Nation). Stefanowicz remained in charge of *Narod Polski* practically through the remainder of his life. Active in patriotic **Polonia** affairs from the time of World War I onward, he was involved in the **Wydział Narodowy**, the Polish Welfare Council in America, and the **Polish American Council** (Rada Polonii). In 1944 he was a founder of the **Polish American Congress** (PAC). For many years he was

Marian Stęczyński, president of the Polish National Alliance (PMA).

the national secretary of the PAC, also serving as the national secretary of the **Polish Museum of America**. Together with such activists as **Stefan Barszczewski**, **Stanisław Osada**, **Karol Piątkiewicz**, and **Arthur Waldo**, Stefanowicz was one of the leading publicists in Polonia of the era between the First World War and the 1960s. In his final years, he retired to Poland.—*Donald E. Pienkos*

SOURCE: Donald E. Pienkos, *For Your Freedom Through Ours: Polish American Efforts on Poland's Behalf, 1863–1991* (Boulder, CO: East European Monographs, 1991).

Stemkowski, Peter "Pete" (b. Winnipeg, Canada, August 25, 1943; d.—). Hockey player. A product of the Toronto Maple Leafs farm system, Stemkowski played in his native Winnipeg before moving to Toronto at the age of 17 to play with the Ontario Hockey Association's Toronto Marlboros, the Leafs' junior team. After splitting his first three professional seasons between the Leafs and their American Hockey League farm team in Rochester, NY, he spent the 1966-67 season with the Leafs in the National Hockey League, a year in which Toronto won the Stanley Cup with Stemkowski contributing twelve points in twelve games. Known to his teammates also as "Stemmer" and "The Polish Prince," he was traded to the New York Rangers where he played for seven seasons including three straight twenty-goal seasons from 1972-73 to 1974-75. During the 1971 Stanley Cup semifinals against the Chicago Blackhawks, Stemkowski scored the game-winning goal in Game 1 after 1:37 of overtime. The Rangers lost Game 5 in overtime, only to be in the same position in Game 6. Facing elimination, the Rangers forced a deciding seventh game when Stemkowski scored at 1:29 of the third overtime—a total of 41:29 of extra time. This game is still the longest in Rangers history. The MSG Network special "The 50 Greatest Moments in Madison Square Garden History" placed the Game 6 triple overtime winner at number 18. His best season may have been the 1973-74 year when he tied his career-high of 25 goals and also notched a career-high 70 points. In 1977-78, Stemkowski finished his career by playing for the Detroit Red Wings and Los Angeles Kings. He served a stint as the television (1992–96) and radio color commentator (2000–05) for the San Jose Sharks and then the New York Rangers on a part-time basis. He was inducted into the National Polish-American Sports Hall of Fame in 2002.—*Luis J. Gonzalez*

SOURCE: "The Polish Prince," National Polish-American Sports Hall of Fame and Museum, Inc.

Stepniewski, Wiesław Zenon (b. Kamieniec Podolski, Poland, January 4, 1909; d. Springfield, Delaware, December 9, 1998). Aeronautical engineer. A graduate of the Warsaw University of Technology in 1933, Stepniewski taught aerodynamics courses at Lwów University of Technology until 1939. His career combined both academic and industrial engineering work ranging from directing the design of sailplanes, motor gliders, and light planes to participation in design teams for large military rotorcraft. Stepniewski left Poland during World War II, spending time in Romania, France, and England. He settled in Canada in 1941, where he headed the Aerodynamic and Stress Analysis Department of De Havilland Canada in Toronto. Beginning in 1946 he devoted his talent and energy to the field of rotor-wing science and technology, and became dedicated to the development of helicopters and VTOL rotorcraft. In 1947 he joined the Piasecki Helicopter Company in Morton, PA, where he worked as chief aerodynamicist on several military helicopters including the XHJP-1, HUP-2, H-16, H-21, Vertol 107CH "Sea King," and CH-47—Chinook, all of which have been used successfully by the U.S. armed forces and other countries around the world. In 1955, as Director of Advance Research at the Boeing-Vertol Company, he conducted research on tilt-wing rotorcraft. His design concept and construction was well known as Vertol-V76 (VZ2), which was the first tiltrotor in the world to achieve full transition from vertical to forward flight, and became a model for future rotorcraft design such as the XV-15 and the V-22 Osprey. In 1969 he was appointed adjunct faculty full professor at Princeton University, NJ, where he taught advanced courses on helicopter aerodynamics. He also served on the Ph.D. Scientific Board at Princeton and Drexel University, Philadelphia, PA. He retired from Boeing-Vertol in 1975, but continued to serve there as a consultant until 1992. He also established his own company named International Technical Associates in Springfield, PA.

Stepniewski published over fifty scientific and research papers, and participated in numerous scientific conferences and professional society meetings as a keynote speaker, lecturer, advisor, and consultant. He is the author of *Introduction to Helicopter Aerodynamics* (1950), which at that time was the first book in the U.S. in its field. In cooperation with C. N. Keys of Boeing, he wrote the well known *Rotary-Wing Aerodynamics* which has become a classic textbook used by universities and helicopter professionals around the world. With his friend Tadeusz Kaczyński, he translated numerous technical publications from French and Russian. He was an Honorary Fellow of the American Helicopter Society and Polish Rotor-Wing Society; Fellow of New York Academy of Sciences; and an Associate Fellow of the Royal Aeronautical Society in Great Britain. He was a recipient of the Enoch Thulin Medal of the Swedish Aeronautical Society, the I. B. Laskowitz Gold Medal Award of the New York Academy of Sciences, and an honorary member of the **Association of Polish American Engineers** "Polonia Technica." In recognition of his scientific and technical achievements in helicopter aerodynamics, the main auditorium at the Aerodynamics and Aviation Department at Warsaw University of Technology carries his name. His name is also displayed at the American Helicopter Museum at West Chester in Pennsylvania.—*Janusz W. Romanski*

SOURCES: Polonia Technica *Bulletin*, Vol. 2 (2001); Marek Szczerbiński, *Polonia Technica: Stowarzyszenie Inzynierów i Techników Polskich w Stanach Zjednoczonych Ameryki Pólnocnej: zarys historii w latach 1941-2001* (New York: Swiatowa Rada Badan nad Polonia, Akademia Polonijna, 2001).

Stereotype, Polish American. The period between 1880 and the beginning of World War I in 1914 marked a period of unprecedented growth in immigration. As the influx increased, fears of crime and labor unrest caused many of the earlier residents to become more hostile toward newcomers. This was reflected in an emphasis among nativist writers on the natural superiority of the so-called Anglo-Saxon race and calls for the use of a literacy test as a requirement for entry into the country. In the U.S. Senate, F. M. Simmons from North Carolina bemoaned what he called the growing threat from "the degenerate progeny of the Asiatic hoards [*sic*] which, long centuries ago, overran the shores of the Mediterranean." Ellwood Cubberly, "the father of school administration in the United States," wrote in 1909 that "These Southern and Eastern Europeans are of a very different type from the Northern Europeans who preceded them. Illiterate, docile, lacking in self-reliance and initiative and not possessing the Anglo-Teutonic conceptions of law, order, and government, their coming has served to dilute tremendously our national stock, and to corrupt our civic life." A study of popular literature between 1900 and 1930 by T. J. Woofter revealed a marked change in public sentiment toward immigration that reflected the increasing writings of nativists who emphasized "the undesirability of certain racial elements." Typical of this new genre was Madison Grant's *The Passing of the Great Race*, published in 1916, which argued that the pure, superior American racial stock was being diluted by the influx of "new" immigrants from the Mediterranean, the Balkans and the Polish ghettos.

The stereotype of the Polish American that found its way into literature, film, and the popular conscious of the twentieth century took root during this period. As Janice Kleeman explained, "Mainstream America's reluctance to embrace the Poles was rooted in three discriminatory stances: *religious prejudice* (Protestant America eschewing Catholicism), *racism* (Anglo-Saxon/Teutonic America depreciating the Slavic Poles) and *general resentment of immigrants* as alien and as competitors in the job market." This was "legitimized" in the findings of the Dillingham Commission (see **Immigration Restriction**) which characterized Polish immigrants between 1870 and 1910 as submissive, undisciplined, prone to violence, of limited mental capacity, and noted for their excessive use of alcohol and criminality. According to Karel D. Bicha who studied the derivation of the derisive term "Hunky" applied to East Europeans, "implied a combination of physical strength and mental insufficiency." Gradually, as Poles came to predominate, the term "Polack" replaced "Hunky," even for non–Poles from Eastern Europe. Regardless of the derivation, by 1920 the image of the "Hunky" was firmly fixed in American stereotypy and quickly developed into the stereotypical "hard-hatted, beer-bellied Joe Sixpacks" of the 1960s. These images were later ingrained in American thinking through repetition in popular films and television productions such as Michael Stivic in *All in the Family*, Andy Renko in *Hill Street Blues*, Lenny Kosnowski in *Laverne & Shirley*, or Victor Isbecki in *Cagney & Lacy*. One study suggests that no fewer than 78 percent of the television characterizations of Polish Americans from 1948 through 1992 featured them as stereotypical muscular dimwits or in some manner socially dysfunctional. In less than a half-dozen cases during that entire period were major Polish American television characters portrayed in a positive light.—*James S. Pula*

SOURCES: James S. Pula, "American Immigration Policy and the Dillingham Commission," *Polish American Studies*, Vol. 37, no. 1 (1980), 5–31; James S. Pula, "Image, Status, Mobility and Integration in American Society: The Polish Experience," *Journal of American Ethnic History*, Vol. 16, no. 1 (1966), 74–95; Karel D. Bicha, "Hunkies: Stereotyping the Slavic Immigrants, 1890–1920," *Journal of American Ethnic History*, Vol. 2 (Fall 1982), 16–38; Eugene Obidinski, "Polish American Social Standing: Status and Stereotypes," *The Polish Review*, Vol. 21, no. 3 (1976), 79–101.

Stewart, Martha (Martha Helen Kostyra; b. Jersey City, New Jersey, August 3, 1941; d.—). Businesswoman. Stewart earned a baccalaureate degree in history and architectural history at Barnard College while she worked as a model. After gaining success as a stockbroker (1967–73), she opened a catering company with a friend whom she later bought out. Her cookbook *Entertaining* became a bestseller, vaulting her to national prominence and the publication of *Martha Stewart's Quick Cook* (1983), *Martha Stewart's Hors D'oeuvres* (1984), *Martha Stewart's Pies & Tarts* (1985), *Weddings* (1987), *The Wedding Planner* (1988), *Martha Stewart's Quick Cook Menus* (1988), *Martha Stewart's Christmas* (1989). These successful ventures, along with regular newspaper columns and magazine articles, solidified her reputation as America's foremost expert on household matters. In 1990 she founded the magazine *Martha Stewart Living* which reached a circulation of two million copies per issue by 2002. Building on the magazine, in 1993 she began a half-hour weekly television program which expanded to an hour with a daily format. In 1997 she reorganized her various activities into Martha Stewart Living Omnimedia. In 2004 Stewart was convicted of lying to investigators about the circumstances surrounding her sale of stock and was sentenced to five months in prison. Once released, she resumed leadership of her faltering business enterprises and soon had them returning increasing profits, including *The Martha Stewart Show*, a syndicated talk show titled *Martha*, and guest appearances on a number of prominent television shows.—*James S. Pula*

SOURCES: Christopher Byron, *Martha Inc.: The Incredible Story of Martha Stewart Living Omnimedia* (New York: Wiley, 2002); Lloyd Allen, *Being Martha: The Inside Story of Martha Stewart and Her Amazing Life* (Hoboken, NJ: John Wiley, 2006); Patricia Sellers, "Remodeling Martha," *Fortune*, November 14, 2005, 49–62; *Good News* (Miami: American Institute of Polish Culture of Miami, 2005–06).

Martha Stewart, entrepreneur (*OLS*).

Sto Lat. "Sto Lat," meaning "A Hundred Years," is a spoken exclamation for wishing someone a long life. It may or may not precede a toast. However, the phrase figures largest as the title of a short celebratory song familiar to and beloved by Poles and Polish Americans alike. In many Polish American families, even those who have become quite "Americanized," the knowledge of "Sto Lat" has persisted down through generations. Like many traditional folk songs, "Sto Lat" has an unknown composer and date of origin. Although additional and varied verses exist, generally only the first verse is sung. The Polish American Cultural Center of Philadelphia provides the following sheet music and English translation for the first verse. As shown here, "Sto Lat" is most frequently sung in unison. Here it appears in 4/4 meter, although some attribute a 2/4 meter to it.

"Sto Lat" is sometimes called the Polish "Happy Birthday." Polish Americans often pair these two songs together during birthday parties. However, in both Poland and the United States, "Sto Lat" is a fixture at a much wider array of occasions, including but not limited to dinners, weddings, anniversaries, and name days. It can be either directed at all present or, like the British "Jolly Good Fellow," used to honor a specific person. Polish Americans frequently request "Sto Lat" from ***polka*** bands, and indeed the noted *polka* band leader Gene Wisniewski (1921–2002) recorded it.

"Sto Lat" has been a part of momentous public as well as private occasions in both the United States and Poland. Numerous Polish American Catholic parishes have titled their centennial celebration booklets *Sto Lat,* not simply because of the phrase's literal meaning, but its evocation of the song. In 1979, when Pope John Paul II returned to his native Poland for the first time since becoming pontiff, he joked with an enthusiastically serenading youth group in Kraków: "How can the Pope live to be a hundred years when you shout him down?" When he visited the U.S. the same year, tens of thousands of Polish

Chicagoans sang "Sto Lat" so exuberantly for him that he quipped: "If we keep this up, they're going to think it's the Polish national anthem." As Solidarność was born during the 1980 Gdańsk shipyard strike, the ship builders carried Lech Wałęsa on their shoulders and struck up "Sto Lat." At the First Solidarność Congress in 1981, the delegates sang the song to Marek Edelman, a Jewish physician and leader as an adolescent of the Warsaw ghetto uprising. Although its own beginnings are unknown, "Sto Lat" nevertheless serves as a marker and bearer of Polish and Polish American history, personal and political alike.—*Mary Krane Derr*

SOURCES: Timothy Garton Ash, *The Polish Revolution: Solidarity* (New Haven, CT: Yale University Press, 2002); Desiree De Charms and Paul F. Breed, *Songs in Collections: An Index* (Detroit: Information Service Incorporated, 1966); Laurie Gomulka Palazzalo, *Horn Man: The Polish American Musician in Twentieth Century Detroit* (Detroit: Wayne State University, 2003); Deborah Anders Silverman, *Polish-American Folklore* (Urbana: University of Illinois Press, 2000); George Weigel, *Witness to Hope: The Biography of Pope John Paul II* (New York: Harper Perennial, 2005).

Stojowski, Zygmunt

(Zygmunt Denis Antoni Jordan de Stojowski; b. Strzelce, Poland, May 4, 1870; d. New York, New York, November 5, 1946). Composer, pianist, teacher. As a young child, Stojowski began piano lessons with his mother Maria (née Bogdenska), later enrolling at the Kraków Conservatory where he studied with composer Włodzimierz Żeleński. In 1887, as a seventeen-year-old student, he appeared as a soloist in Beethoven's Concerto No. 3 in a public concert (two years earlier he played the same work in the salon of Countess Czartoryska, a pupil of Chopin). The next year saw his move to Paris to study piano with Louis Diemer and composition with Leo Delibes. He received three top prizes when graduating from the Conservatoire National in Paris — for piano, counterpoint, and fugue. He was also a private student of **Ignacy Jan Paderewski** (he began studies with him in 1891 and became his life-long friend), Saint Saëns, and Massenet. Before moving to the U.S. in 1905, Stojowski was well established as a promising composer and virtuoso pianist. In 1898, his Symphony in D minor, Op. 21, received first prize in the Paderewski Music Competition in Leipzig. The work was premiered during the inaugural concert of the Warsaw Philharmonic under the baton of Emil Mlynarski to great acclaim.

Frank Damrosch's invitation to head the piano department at the Institute of Musical Arts in New York (1905–11) resulted in emigration to Stojowski's new homeland. From 1912–17 he was a professor at the Von Ende Music School in New York, later teaching pri-

Zygmunt Stojowski, composer, pianist, and educator (*PMA*).

marily in his private Stojowski Studios and giving master classes at the Juilliard School of Music in 1932, 1940–46. He traveled throughout the Americas giving recitals and master classes in Buffalo, Chicago, Denver, Detroit, Los Angeles, Pittsburgh, Portland, San Francisco, Seattle, Washington, D.C., Havana, Lima, Rio de Janeiro, and elsewhere. As a composer and musician, Stojowski had conservative tastes (he did not understand the music of Debussy or Ravel, let alone Schoenberg) and wrote in a romantic style, reminiscent of Paderewski, Tchaikovsky, or Rachmaninoff. His catalogue includes 43 opus numbers and numerous smaller pieces, including two piano concertos (No. 1 in F-sharp minor Op. 3, and No. 2 in A-flat Major Op. 32), Rhapsodie symphonique for piano and orchestra Op. 23; Violin Concerto Op. 22; Cantata A, Prayer for Poland, to a text by Zygmunt Krasinski, Op. 40; and numerous sonatas for piano, violin and cello, as well as romances, dances, etudes and other pieces for ensembles with piano or for piano solo. During World War I Stojowski assisted Paderewski with fundraising for the Polish cause, and throughout his career was a champion of Poland and Polish culture in the U.S. He was active in numerous organizations, co-founded the Polish Institute of Arts and Culture of America in 1943, and published pedagogical texts on teaching piano performance and interpreting Chopin and other romantic works. Stojowski's nearly forgotten contribution to music currently sees a modest revival championed by pianist Jonathan Plowright, conductor Joseph Herter, his biographer, and the Polish Music Center at USC where his manuscripts and papers have been housed since 2006.—*Maja Trochimczyk*

SOURCES: Joseph Herter, "The Life of Zygmunt Stojowski," *Polish Music Journal*, Vol. 5, no. 2 (2002); Joseph A. Herter, *Zygmunt Stojowski: Life and Music* (Los Angeles: Polish Music Center, 2007; Polish Music History Series Vol. 10).

Stokowski, Leopold Anthony

(Leopold Antoni Stanisław Bolesławowicz Stokowski; b. London, England, April 18, 1882; d. Nether Wallop, England, September 13, 1977). Conductor. In spite of Stokowski's claim to have been born in Kraków, Poland, in 1887, it is well known that the *maestro* was born in London in 1882 of Polish descent on his father's side and of Irish extraction on his mother's side. He began a precocious and brilliant formative career in England. Between 1896, the year Stokowski entered the Royal College of Music, and 1903, the year he earned a Bachelor of Music degree at Queen's College, Oxford, Stokowski sang in the choir of St. Marylebone Church, was assistant organist at Temple Church, was elected to membership in the Royal College of Organists at age 16, formed the choir of St. Mary's Church — where he played organ and trained choirboys — and in 1902 was appointed organist and choir director of St. James Church, Piccadilly. In 1905 Stokowski met with great success in New York as organist and choir director at St. Bartholomew's Church. However, he resigned in order to pursue his career as an orchestral conductor and moved to Paris for additional instruction. In 1909 he made his official conducting debut in Paris and, shortly after, in London. That same year he was appointed conductor of the Cincinnati Symphony Orchestra. Stokowski enjoyed great success in Cincinnati. Brimming with innovative ideas, he conducted the American premieres of new works by European composers, but due to frustrations with the politics of the orchestra he resigned in April 1912. That same year, in October, Stokowski was appointed director of the Philadelphia Symphony Orchestra where he remained until 1940. During those years he shaped the "Philadelphia Sound" — what was actually the "Stokowski sound" — while he conducted the American and world premieres of many works by renowned old and new composers. After leaving the Philadelphia Orchestra he founded the All-American Youth Orchestra, its players' ages ranging from 18 to 25. With that orchestra he toured South America (1940) and North America (1941). In 1944 Stokowski helped to form the New York City Symphony Orchestra, and in 1945 he founded the Hollywood Bowl Symphony Orchestra. The following year he became Guest Conductor of the New York Philharmonic.

In 1951 Stokowski began a new international career, conducting the Royal Philharmonic Orchestra, the Berlin Philharmonic, the Suisse

Romande Orchestra, the French National Radio Orchestra, the Czech Philharmonic, and others, touring in Germany, Switzerland, Holland, Portugal, and Austria. Between 1954 and 1963 he conducted the NBC Symphony Orchestra, later known as the Symphony of the Air. From 1955 to 1961 he was the music director of the Houston Symphony Orchestra, which premiered many important works. In 1962 he founded the American Symphony Orchestra and, in 1972, at the age of 90, he returned to England. His last public performance took place in July 1975 during the Vence Music Festival in France where he conducted the Rouen Chamber Orchestra in several of his Bach transcriptions. Stokowski was very fond of experimentation. He experimented with the orchestra by altering the conventional seating of the instrumentalists and encouraging "free bowing" from the string section and "free breathing" from the brass section. The tonal quality that he could command from an orchestra—which some critics felt may have been sometimes injudiciously applied—has never been equaled. He was well-known for his arrangements and the liberties he took in works by famous composers such as Beethoven, Bach, Brahms, Tchaikovsky, and others. Stokowski experimented with space, light and new sources of sound, and promoted the use of electronic instruments (once he asked the famous Russian inventor of electronic instruments, Leon Theremin, to construct one that would lend support to the low bass notes of the orchestra, almost under the limit of audibility). Inventor Maurice Martenot demonstrated his famous electronic instrument, the *ondes martenot*, for the first time in America, playing it in New York with the Philadelphia Orchestra in a concert conducted by Stokowski in 1930. He also premiered the Concerto for Theremin and Orchestra by Anis Fuleihan with the New York Symphony Orchestra in 1945. In October 1952, during an introductory speech to four pieces of new tape music by Luening and Ussachevsky at the New York Museum of Modern Art, Stokowski predicted a time in the future when the composer would be able to shape the music directly—without previous notations—by using electronic devices. Stokowski was a tireless advocate for the latest developments in music. As early as 1922, conducting the Philadelphia Orchestra, he gave the official American premiere of *Le Sacre du printemps* by Igor Stravinsky, and the first New York performance of Arnold Schoenberg's Five Orchestral Pieces. In his role of supporter and performer of the music by the ultra-moderns, in November 1924 Stokowski conducted *Hyperprism* by avant-garde composer Edgar

Varèse in Philadelphia and New York. Stokowski was engaged by Varèse for occasional concerts at the International Composers Guild, an organization that intended to cover the full spectrum of contemporary music. He conducted *Renard* by Stravinsky for the ICG in 1923, and Schoenberg's *Serenade* in 1925. The premiere of Varèse's *Integrales* by Stokowski at the ICG concert in March 1925 in Aeolian Hall gave another boost to that composer's visibility. As a part of his New York concerts with the Philadelphia Orchestra, Stokowski presented Leo Ornstein's *Piano Concerto No. 2* (in 1925), Edgar Varese's *Ameriques* (in 1926) and *Arcana* (dedicated by the composer to Stokowski) in 1927, and Wallingford Riegger's *Study in Sonority* (1929). In addition to Varèse, Stokowski promoted other new American composers such as Alan Hovhaness (the director commissioned the composer to produce his single most famous work, *Mysterious Mountain*, for his inaugural concert with the Houston Symphony in 1955) and Lou Harrison. Leopold Stokowski conducted many premieres of difficult contemporary works including the premiere of the Fourth Symphony by Charles Ives in a legendary performance in 1965.

Stokowski had a definite tendency to flamboyant exhibitionism which, along with his considerable abilities, brought him fame early in his career. Always conducting without a baton (free-hand performing style), he would place himself in spotlights at his platform or even hide the orchestra behind a curtain so that the sound seemed to proceed from him alone. Additional glamour came from his affair with Greta Garbo, and his appearance in Walt Disney's film *Fantasia*, collaborating with the director, conducting the music—including his own orchestrations of Bach—and

Leopold Stokowski, conductor, 1937 (*PMA*).

shaking hands with Mickey Mouse.—*Guillermo Gregorio*

SOURCES: Abram Chasins, *Leopold Stokowski* (New York: Da Capo Press, 1979); Daniel Oliver, *Leopold Stokowski: A Counterpoint of View* (New York: Dodd, Mead & Company, 1982).

Storozynski, Alex (b. Greenpoint, New York, August 26, 1961; d.—). Journalist, Pulitzer Prize recipient. After graduating with a degree in political science from the State University of New York at New Paltz (1983), Storozynski earned his Master's degree from the Columbia University Graduate School of Journalism (1985) and did postgraduate work at the University of Warsaw. He held positions as a reporter for *The Legislative Gazette* in Albany and McGraw Hill Information Systems in New York, after which he served as managing editor of *The Queens Chronicle* (1988–89) and editor of *Empire State Report,* a political magazine (1989–93). Later he became deputy director of public information for the New York State Thruway Authority (1993–95) and press secretary for the Attorney General of New York (1995–96). In 1996 he joined the editorial board of the New York *Daily News* and wrote editorials on public policy issues, leading to recognition with a Pulitzer Prize for editorial writing (1999), the George Polk Award (1999), the Sigma Delta Chi Award (1999), two Deadline Club Awards (1999, 2001), four Associated Press Awards for editorial writing (1996, 1997, 1998, 2000), and two Silurian Awards (1997, 2001). He left the *Daily News* in 2003 to become editor in chief of *amNew York* where he broke an important story about financial mismanagement by the Statue of Liberty/Ellis Island Foundation. In 2005 he was named city editor of the *New York Sun,* and in 2008, president of the **Kosciuszko Foundation.** He is a former chairman of the board of the Polish and Slavic Federal Credit Union and author of the acclaimed *The Peasant Prince: Thaddeus Kosciuszko and the Age of Revolution*, a biography of **Tadeusz Kościuszko.** His articles have appeared in *The Wall Street Journal, Chicago Tribune, New York Post, New York Newsday* and other publications.—*James S. Pula*

SOURCE: "The 2007 Annual Awards Dinner Program" (Washington, D.C.: National Polish Center, May 5, 2007).

Stowarzyszenie Mechaników Polskich w Ameryce *see* **Polish Mechanics Association of America.**

Stowarzyszenie Polaków w Ameryce *see* **Polish Association of America.**

Stowarzyszenie Polskich Kombatantów *see* **Polish Veterans Association.**

Stowarzyszenie Weteranów Armii Polskiej *see* **Polish Army Veterans Association.**

Stram, Hank (Henry Louis Wilczek; b. Chicago, Illinois, January 3, 1923; d. Covington, Louisiana, July 4, 2005). Football coach, broadcaster. Stram was the son of Henry and Nellie (Boots) Wilczek. The elder Wilczek was a tailor who had wrestled professionally under the name Stramm — German for "sturdy" — and the family's surname was eventually changed to Stram. To make ends meet for him and his sister after his father's death (1938), his mother opened a restaurant with support from the local **Polish National Alliance** lodge. Stram remained grateful, and later organized the Hank Stram/Tony Zale Silver Bell Sports Award Banquet, held every year to raise scholarship money for local graduating high school seniors of Polish and Slavic descent. Stram would recruit high profile friends from around the country to appear at the annual banquet in Indiana, guaranteeing its success.

After lettering in four sports (football, baseball, basketball, and track) at Lew Wallace High School in Gary, Indiana, Stram accepted a scholarship to Purdue University, but was drafted after his sophomore year into the U.S. Army Air Forces (1943–46). After returning to Purdue, he received the Big Ten Medal, awarded to the conference's best all-around scholar-athlete. Upon graduation (1948), Stram was hired to be Purdue's backfield coach (1948–55), and also coached the baseball team. Among the players he recruited to Purdue was quarterback Len Dawson. When head coach Stu Holcomb left, Purdue bypassed Stram for the job, so he became offensive coach at Southern Methodist for one year (1956–57). When SMU also passed him over for the head coaching job — Stram believed it was because he was a Roman Catholic — he moved to Notre Dame as backfield coach for two seasons, and then became an assistant coach at the University of Miami.

In 1960, Lamar Hunt hired Stram to be head coach of the Dallas Texans of the fledgling American Football League, which Hunt had formed after the National Football League resisted expansion efforts. The Texans won the AFL championship after their third season, before moving to Kansas City to become the Chiefs. After winning the franchise's second AFL championship, the Chiefs lost to the Green Bay Packers in the first NFL–AFL World Championship game in January 1967, later known as Super Bowl I. The Chiefs won a third AFL championship in 1969, and then beat the heavily favored Minnesota Vikings

in Super Bowl IV, which was the last game prior to the NFL–AFL merger. Stram was the only head coach who had lasted the entire history of the AFL (1960–69), and was also its winningest coach. Known as "The Mentor" and considered a master innovator, Stram popularized the I-formation, the moving pocket, the two tight end offense, the zone defense, the triple-stack defense, and also instituted weight-training and off-season mini-camps. He took players who were cast-offs from other teams, including Len Dawson, and coached them to success. Five of Stram's players were voted into the Hall of Fame, and he encouraged diversity on his teams, recruiting heavily from historically black colleges.

After being fired by Hunt in 1974, Stram became a football broadcaster for CBS, before spending two dismal seasons as head coach of the New Orleans Saints (1976–77). He then returned to CBS, where he worked on both television and radio, including a very successful 16-year pairing with Jack Buck broadcasting Monday Night Football games on CBS Radio. His professional coaching record over sixteen seasons (including playoffs) was 136-100-10.

An impeccable dresser (which he credited to his father), Stram became a fan favorite after wearing a hidden microphone for NFL Films on the sideline during Super Bowl IV, during which he made many humorous comments, which some critics saw as gloating. Stram was voted AFL or AFC coach of the year four times, and was inducted into both the Kansas City Chiefs Hall of Fame (1987) and the Pro Football Hall of Fame (2003). He was elected to the National Polish-American Sports Hall of Fame in 1985. — *John Drobnicki*

SOURCES: Hank Stram, with Lou Sahadi, *They're Playing My Game* (New York: William Morrow and Company, 1986); *Scribner Encyclopedia of American Lives* (New York: Charles Scribner's Sons, 2007), Vol. 7.

Straż (The Guard). The *Straż* newspaper first appeared April 17, 1897, a month after the Rev. **Franciszek Hodur** arrived in Scranton, PA, to accept a call to lead St. Stanislaus Bishop and Martyr Parish, which was in the process of beginning to break its relationship with the Roman Catholic Church. The paper, which carried general **Polonia** news and articles pertaining to the **independent** movement in Scranton and other Polish communities in the United States, was distributed locally and to other Polish immigrant settlements. Although remaining independent, *Straż* became, *de facto*, the official organ of the **Polish National Catholic Church** when the Church formally constituted itself at the First Synod in 1904. When the Church-related but inde-

pendent fraternal benefit society, the **Polish National Union of America** (*Spójnia*), was organized in 1908, it became the official organ of that organization as well. In 1923, *Rola Boża* (God's Field) became the official organ of the PNCC, but *Straż* continued to carry Church news into the next century. In the early years, *Straż* was published almost exclusively in the Polish language but, as the decades passed, English began to appear and eventually predominated. *Straż* was published weekly into the twenty-first century and, for a time, was the oldest continuously-published Polish American weekly in America. In late 2009 it changed to an electronic-only format. *Straż* has been edited at various times by hired editors, PNCC clergy, and PNU officers. The first official editor was Stanisław Dangel-Langowski with Zdzisław Łopatyner acting briefly as co-editor. Other official editors included Stanisław Klukowski, Czesław Łukaszkiewicz, Stanisław Staruszkiewicz, Józef Mastalski, Theodore L. Zawistowski, Regina Gorzkowska, Wanda Cytowska, and Mitchell Grochowski. Among regular columnists and contributors have been **Henry Archacki**, Leopold Dende, Lawrence Orzell, **Edward Pinkowski**, Robert Strybel, and the Rev. Senior **Joseph L. Zawistowski** under his own name and *nom de plume* Stanisław Okopiszczak. Straż Printery was one of the earliest union print shops in Pennsylvania. In addition to printing most of the periodicals, books, and other imprints of the PNC Church and PNU, it was a general job printer and printed several unrelated weekly, monthly, and other publications. The Straż Building originally housed the home offices of the PNU, which eventually bought the paper, the printery, and the building. Under its various auspices, the Polish National Catholic Church was the second largest publisher of Polish language imprints in America in the twentieth century. — *Theodore L. Zawistowski*

SOURCES: Casimir J. Grotnik, ed., *An Index to Straż-The Guard, Volume I, 1897–1915, Volume II, 1916–1925, Part I and Part II* (Scranton, PA: Polish National Union of America, 1994 and 1997, respectively); Casimir J. Grotnik, ed., *Polish National Catholic Church: Minutes of the First Eleven General Synods, 1904–1963* (Scranton, PA: Polish National Catholic Church of America Central Diocese and East European Monographs, 2002); Eugene Obidinski, "Straż and the Polish National Catholic Church as a Source of Polonian Ethnic Expression," *PNCC Studies*, Vol. 16 (1995), 47–58.

String Band *see* **Polish American String Band.**

Strzelecka, Anne (b. Lubielski, Poland, February 11, 1863; d. Castleton, New York, March 5, 1934). Catholic nun. One of the first **Sisters of the Resurrection**, Strzelecka's par-

Mother Anne Strzelecka, one of the first Sisters of the Resurrection in America (*OLS*).

ents gave her an excellent education with studies in Paris at the Sorbonne. In spite of potential honors, fame, and wealth, in 1893 she entered the newly formed Congregation of the Sisters of the Resurrection to dedicate her life and work to God. Nine years after the foundation of the Congregation, the Sisters of the Resurrection responded to the request of the **Resurrectionist** priests in Chicago to send sisters to minister to the city's Polish immigrant families. On January 19, 1900, Sister Anne was one of the four nuns who left Naples, Italy, headed for their new mission at St. Mary of the Angels Church. The challenge of living in a new land, learning a new language, a new culture, and a new ministry was imposing. Sister Anne directed the organization of the school, overcoming the many difficulties she encountered, after which she served as superior of the first convent in Chicago. In this capacity she helped organize a novitiate for the training of new members, established a day nursery for children of working parents, maintained a boarding home for working women, and undertook the supervision of a huge building project that developed into a prestigious high school for girls. In all these endeavors, Sister Anne was supported by the Women's Auxiliary which she organized at the beginning of the mission. Possessing great determination, dedication, and commitment, she was likewise astute in business and legal matters.—*Mary Edward Gira*

SOURCE: Mary Edward Gira, C.R., ed., *Letters and Journal of the First Resurrectionist Sisters in America, 1900–1913* (Rome, Italy: Sisters of the Resurrection, 1987).

STUDIUM. The STUDIUM North American Center for the Study of Polish Affairs, headquartered in Ann Arbor, Michigan, was created in 1976 by Profs. Andrzej Ehrenkreutz and Czesław Maliszewski to educate and inform the American and Canadian populations about Polish affairs and to assist **Polonia** organizations in their efforts to support the democratic opposition in Poland and later, the newly established Solidarność trade union. The goal of STUDIUM was to work on behalf of Polish sovereignty and serve as an intellectual arm for the **Polish American Congress**. It was composed mainly of educated professionals who were mostly World War II émigrés including Andrew Targowski, Andre Błaszczynski, Tomasz T. Arciszewski, and Barbara Hanna Kwasnik. STUDIUM worked with the national Polish Affairs Committee of the **Polish American Congress** in its efforts to direct and influence U.S. foreign policy toward Poland. One of its main activities was the dissemination of information to the English-speaking American public through opinion essays placed in major newspapers and writing briefs for lobbyists. Between 1982 and 1990, they published a quarterly periodical, *STUDIUM Papers* that targeted a Polish and Polish American audience in the United States. The majority of the articles were in English, focusing on Poland's political and economic conditions. STUDIUM worked cooperatively with the PAC in lobbying efforts in Washington, D.C., to help secure Poland's independence.—*Mary Patrice Erdmans*

SOURCES: Paul J. Best, "Polish-American Scholarly Organizations," in Stanislaus A. Blejwas and M. B. Biskupski, eds., *Pastor of the Poles* (New Britain, CT: Polish Studies Program Monograph, 1982), 153–165; Mary Patrice Erdmans, *Opposite Poles: Immigrants and Ethnics in Polish Chicago, 1976–1990* (University Park, PA: Pennsylvania State University Press, 1998); Helena Znaniecka Lopata, *Polish Americans* (New Brunswick, NJ: Transaction, 1994).

Stupak, Bartholomew Thomas "Bart" (b. Milwaukee, Wisconsin, February 29, 1952; d.—). Congressman. After receiving his baccalaureate degree in criminal justice from Saginaw Valley State College (1977) he went on to earn his *juris doctorate* from the Thomas M. Cooley Law School (1981). He served as a trooper with the Michigan Department of State Police (1973–84) before being elected as a Democrat to represent the 1st Michigan Congressional District in the Upper Peninsula beginning with the 103rd Congress in 1993. Reelected seven times by 2006, he was a member of the House Energy and Commerce Committee. He was present when President Bill Clinton signed public laws 386 and 390 during the 105th Congress providing educational assistance for families of slain officers and for penalties for criminals with guns. During the 108th Congress, Stupak recognized Pope John Paul II on the 25th anniversary of his papacy and urged President George W. Bush to confer upon him the Presidential Medal of Freedom.—*Thomas Duszak*

SOURCE: *Biographical Directory of the United States Congress, 1774–Present* (http://bioguide.congress.gov/).

Styka, Adam (b. Kielce, Poland, April 7, 1890; d. New York City, New York, September 23, 1959). Artist. The son of acclaimed Polish artist Jan Styka and brother of **Tadé Styka**, Adam Styka studied at the Academie de Beaux Arts in France and exhibited his early works in Parisian galleries where he received favorable reviews. He graduated from the Fountainbleau, the French military academy, and served as an artillery officer in the French Army during World War I, earning the Cross of Merit and a grant of French citizenship. Following the war he traveled in North Africa where he became fascinated with the lives and landscapes of the desert that were reflected in many of his subsequent works. His use of color, lighting, and shadow to illuminate his African scenes won for him the appellation "the Artist of Sunlight." After moving to the U.S., Styka created highly regarded paintings of the American west, and later in life turned to religious art.—*James S. Pula*

SOURCE: Adam Styka, Czesław Czapliński, Jan Styka, Tadeusz Styka, *The Styka Family Saga* (New York: Bicentennial Publishing Corporation, 1988).

Styka, Tadeusz "Tadé" (b. Kielce, Poland, April 12, 1889; d. Los Angeles, California, September 11, 1954). Artist. Born in the Russian-occupied partition of Poland, Styka was the elder of two sons of the famed Polish painter Jan Styka (1858–1925), creator of the massive 360 foot long "Battle of Racławice Panoroma" that was first displayed in Lwów in 1894 and since 1985 has been on permanent display in Wrocław, Poland, and the 210 foot long "Golgotha" Panorama, which is on permanent display at Forest Lawn Cemetery in Los Angeles, California. Tadé Styka studied painting as a youngster under his father's direction and continued his studies as a portrait artist in Paris. Pronounced a young "prodigy" by one of the country's leading art critics, he was granted membership in the Associé Nationale and awarded the Legion of Honor at the age of 24. Among his most famous subjects as a portrait painter were Leo Tolstoy (1903), opera greats Enrico Caruso, Tito Ruffo, and Boris Chaliapin (1912), Marshal Ferdinand Foch (1919), movie actress **Pola Negri** (1920), President Herbert Hoover (1930), President Harry Truman (1948), and General Władysław Anders (1950). Styka's 1930 portrait of **Ignacy Jan Paderewski** is in the great hall where the "Golgotha" painting is displayed. This work was later chosen by the U.S. Postal Service as the likeness of Paderewski it used for the stamp issued to memorialize the great pianist and Polish patriot. As reported by David Mc-

Tadé Styka, artist, standing by his portrait of French Marshal Ferdinand Foch, 1930 (*PMA*).

Cullough in his 1992 biography of Harry Truman, Styka's portrait of the president was completed in October, just weeks before the 1948 presidential election. It appeared on page one of all 72 Polish-language newspapers on the eve of the election. Truman won eighty percent of the Polish American vote on his way to a totally unexpected election victory. Styka also painted scenes of nature and wildlife. Styka's younger brother, **Adam Styka** (1890–1959) won fame mainly for his paintings of the Sahara and depictions of Moroccan and Mexican life. He also painted many scenes from the Bible (as did his father and his brother).—*Donald E. Pienkos*

SOURCES: Adam Styka, Czesław Czapliński, Jan Styka, Tadeusz Styka, *The Styka Family Saga* (New York: Bicentennial Publishing Company, 1988); *Wielka Encyklopedia Powszechna* (Warsaw: Państwowe Wydawnictwo Naukowe, 1968), Vol. 11.

Sulakowski, Walerian (b. Russian partition of Poland in 1827; d. New Orleans, Louisiana, June 19, 1873). Engineer, military officer. After taking part in the Hungarian uprising in 1848, during which he served on the Hungarian general staff, Sulakowski was exiled to the U.S. where he first settled in Houma, Terrebonne Parish, Louisiana. There he devoted his attention to surveying and civil engineering. Soon afterwards he moved to New Orleans. When the Civil War broke out, Sulakowski, along with **Gaspard Tochman**, organized the **Polish Brigade** in New Orleans. He took command of the 1st Regiment (later the 14th Louisiana Infantry) with the rank of colonel. After training in Camp Pulaski, fifty miles from New Orleans, he was sent to Virginia. Sulakowski was ordered to report to Gen. John Bankhead Magruder who was defending the York Peninsula. Recognizing the

Walerian Sulakowski, engineer and military officer (*PMA*).

military abilities of the Polish officer, Magruder placed Sulakowski on his staff as his chief engineer and gave him command of the 7th Brigade consisting of the 10th and 14th Louisiana Infantry Regiments. But Sulakowski's pride was offended in some way and on February 15, 1862, he tendered his resignation which was accepted. He returned to his home in New Orleans where he was soon arrested by Federal Gen. Benjamin Butler, but after a vigorous protest he was released. In October 1862 Sulakowski enlisted in the Confederate service once again and was assigned to fortify numerous Confederate defensive positions in Louisiana and Texas, including those along the Teche River and at Velasco, Quintana, Galveston, and Sabine Pass. At some time not later than July 1863 Sulakowski offered to go to France to induce Polish exiles there to enlist in the Confederate service. Finally, after some negotiations in the spring of 1864, Sulakowski started his journey to Europe on board the schooner *Dodge* but it was captured by U.S. ships blockading the Confederacy and the plan collapsed. Again talking his way out of possible arrest, Sulakowski made his way to Matamoras, Mexico, and eventually to Europe, but he returned to America just in time to see the end of the war. After the war he returned to his home in New Orleans, quickly resuming his profession as civil engineer. In 1871 he was appointed to the United States Land Office as a surveyor. He died of apoplexy in his residence in New Orleans.—*Piotr Derengowski*

SOURCES: Francis C. Kajencki, "The Louisiana Tiger: Sulakowski," *Polish American Studies*, Vol. 23, no. 2 (1966), 82–88; Ella Lonn, *Foreigners in the Confederacy* (Chapell Hill, NC: University of North Carolina Press, 2002); *The Daily Picayune* (New Orleans), June 20, 1873; *The New Orleans Times*, June 20, 1873; *New Orleans Daily Picayune*, June 20, 1873.

Swanson, Gloria (Gloria May Josephine Svensson; b., Chicago, Illinois, March 27, 1899; d. New York, New York, April 4, 1983). Actress. The daughter of Joseph Svensson and Adelaide Klanoski (also spelled Klanowski), she worked as a sales clerk until 1914 when she gained a part as an extra in the silent movie *The Song of Soul*. Although she had not planned on an acting career, Essanay Studio hired her for several features including *His New Job* with Charlie Chaplin, after which she was featured in the famous Keystone Cop movies before signing with Paramount Studios in 1919. There, under the direction of Cecil B. DeMille, she became a leading lady in romantic films including an appearance with the legendary Rudolph Valentino in the 1922 movie *Beyond the Rocks*. During the mid–1920s, she was Hollywood's highest paid actress making $250,000 a week. In 1928 she was nominated for an Academy Award for *Sadie Thompson*, which she produced on her own as an independent film after turning down a contract renewal with Paramount. A year later, she starred in *Queen Kelly*, directed by Erich von Stroheim and bankrolled by Joseph P. Kennedy, Sr. Unlike many silent movie stars, Swanson successfully made the transition to "talkies" with *The Trespasser*. Even so, her career began to decline until the 1950s when she staged a remarkable comeback in the classic *Sunset Boulevard* which gained her another Academy Award nomination. Her last major movie was *Three for Bedroom "C"* in 1952. She portrayed herself in *Airport 1975* and an episode of the television show *The Beverly Hillbillies*. Outside of acting, the United Nations asked her to design a stamp for the Decade of Women, and it became a collector's item. She also wrote her autobiography, *Swan-*

Gloria Swanson was the most popular actress of her day (*NARA*).

son on Swanson. Her honors include the Academy Award for Best Actress in 1950; a Golden Globe Award for *Sunset Boulevard* in 1951; Italian Syndicate of Film Journalists' Silver Ribbon Award in 1951; a Jussi Award as the Best Foreign Actress in 1951; an Academy of Science Fiction, Fantasy and Horror Special Award in 1975; and a Special Achievement Award in 1980.—*Cheryl A. Pula*

SOURCES: Richard M. Hudson, *Gloria Swanson* (South Brunswick, NJ: A.S. Barnes, 1970); Axel Madsen, *Gloria and Joe* (New York, NY: Arbor House/ William Morrow, 1988); Lawrence J. Quirk, *The Films of Gloria Swanson* (Secaucus, NJ: Citadel Press, 1984); Gloria Swanson, *Swanson on Swanson* (New York, NY: Random House, 1980).

Swantek, John F. (b. Wallingford, Connecticut, May 15, 1933; d.—). Bishop. Swantek was educated at Clark Union, the University of Connecticut, and **Savonarola Theological Seminary** in Scranton, PA, after which he became a priest in the **Polish National Catholic Church.** He was elected bishop at the Fifteenth General Synod in 1978 and appointed Bishop Ordinary of the Buffalo-Pittsburgh Diocese (1979–86). In 1986 the Seventeenth General Synod elected him Prime Bishop, a position he held until 2002. He was one of the promoters of a 1992 Healing Service held in Scranton and attended by Roman Catholic Cardinal Edward I. Cassidy, president of the Pontifical Council for Promoting Christian Unity, as an effort to advance relations between the two groups. It was the first service of its kind in the United States and led to the Roman Catholic Church recognizing the validity of PNCC Holy Orders and affirming that the PNCC has the same sacramental status as the Orthodox Church.—*Theodore L. Zawistowski*

SOURCE: *Bishop Swantek's 25th Anniversary of Ordination* (Scranton, PA: Straż Publishing, 1983).

Swastek, Joseph Vincent (b. Detroit, Michigan, March 10, 1913; d. Pontiac, Michigan, September 5, 1977). Priest, Polonia activist. Swastek served as professor of history at **St. Mary's College** in Michigan (1940–77), editor of *Polish American Studies* (1946–70), and was four times president of the **Polish American Historical Association** (PAHA; 1949, 1950, 1951, 1953). He was also the archivist of the Archdiocese of Detroit and of the Orchard Lake Schools where he was largely responsible for developing one the largest and most important collections of archival materials on **Polonia** in the country. Among his lengthy list of publications were *Korczak Ziolkowski, Mountain Carver* (1950, 1982), *The Polish American Story* (1953), *The Formative Years of the Polish Seminary in the United States* (1959), *Poland's 1000th Anniver-*

The Rev. Joseph Swastek, editor of *Polish American Studies* and four-time president of the Polish American Historical Association (*PMA*).

sary, 966–1966 (1963), *Kapłan polonijny: ks. Józef Dąbrowski* (Polish Priest: the Rev. Joseph Dabrowski; 1969), and *Detroit's Oldest Polish Parish, St. Albertus, 1872–1973, Centennial* (1973). In recognition of his services to the PAHA and his lengthy editorship of its journal, PAHA created the Joseph Swastek Prize for the best article appearing in each volume of *Polish American Studies.*—*James S. Pula*

SOURCE: obituary, *The Catholic Historical Review*, Vol. 64 (1978), 138.

Światowy Związek Polaków z Zagranicy *see* **World Union of Poles from Abroad.**

Światpol *see* **World Union of Poles from Abroad.**

Święconka. A Polish and Polish American Easter tradition, this blessing of Easter baskets is a popular Polish Catholic tradition that is observed by many Polish American Catholics. This highly symbolic practice takes place on Holy Saturday, following Good Friday services, where the Crucifixion and death of Jesus is observed, and prior to Easter Sunday, the

Święconka basket (*Ann Gunkel*).

joyous day of His Resurrection. On Holy Saturday, family members bring a basket of symbolic Easter foods (decorated hard boiled eggs or *pisanki*, bread, sausage, ham, horseradish, butter, often molded in the shape of a lamb, and other foods) to the church to be blessed by the priest. These foods will be eaten at an Easter Sunday breakfast to celebrate the Resurrection. This meal comes after the forty-day long period of Lenten fast and abstinence.—*Angela T. Pienkos*

SOURCE: Eugene E. Obidinski and Helen Stankiewicz Zand, *Polish Folkways in America: Community and Family* (Lanham, MD: University Press of America, 1987).

Świeczkowska, Clara (Klara Schroeder; b. Detroit, Michigan, September 1, 1890; d. Detroit, Michigan, August 26, 1986). Polonia activist, government official. Affectionately known to her friends as "Panna Klara" (Miss Clara), Świeczkowska was probably the most active woman in the history of Michigan **Polonia.** Born to Kaszubian parents as Clara Schroeder, she was adopted in 1914, changing her name to Świeczkowska. In adulthood, she applied her talents and exceptional energy in many endeavors and organizations. Baptized at St. Albertus, Detroit's first Polish Catholic Church, she received her primary education at the Felician Academy and Orphanage across the street from the church. She supported the **Felician Sisters** and the Roman Catholic Church throughout her life. The Rev. **Joseph Swastek,** president of the **Polish American Historical Association** and editor of *Polish American Studies,* praised her as "the most active worker on behalf of the Polish cause at St. Albertus Parish during and immediately after the war." Historian **John Bukowczyk** concluded, "One woman whose activities have earned her a place in Polish American history is Clara Swieczkowska." As early as 1912, she served as secretary of the Polish American Relief Society, continuing to at least 1923. She became the secretary of the Detroit Polish Women's Relief Commission in 1915, which collected $120,000 in goods that it sent to war victims in Poland, and was also active in numerous other organizations attempting to free Poland. In recognition of her outstanding work, she was twice decorated by Poland after World War I.

As a journalist, she worked for the *Rekord Codzienne* (Daily Record) in Detroit from 1919 until its bankruptcy in 1935, when she moved to the *Dziennik Polski* (Polish Daily News) as the editor for religious and educational news. In 1923 she was elected president of the **Polish Welfare Association.** Świeczkowska's greatest achievement came with the founding of the local Polish Activities League in 1923, St. Elizabeth Community House in Detroit, and St. Anne's Community House in **Hamtramck**. She served as the League's first president (1931–36), as well as its executive secretary (1935–48). With the assistance of former Michigan governor Alex Groesbeck, and a donation of land from State Senator Cass Jankowski, Świeczkowska helped to establish St. Mary's Summer Camp for children. Later, it became a home for Polish Army Veterans known as Wanda Park. Detroit Mayor Frank Murphy recognized her talents by appointing her to the Detroit Mayor's Unemployment Commission (1932) and naming her his appointee to a board which helped establish the social security law. In 1937 she became the first Polish American woman appointed by the governor to the Detroit Recorders Court Jury Commission. She participated in the citizens' committee investigating the cigar makers' strike, and later helped organize the Federated East Side Improvement Association (1958), an organization of property owners. In 1960, Democratic Governor G. Mennen Williams appointed her to the Michigan Welfare Commission. Upon her death in 1986, a friend commented: "She was the outstanding Polish woman of her generation in metropolitan Detroit.... For sixty years, she had been in the forefront in serving the Polish community. Indeed, her loyalty to Polish culture and language was only surpassed by her devotion to Catholicism." She was also active in the **Polish Women's Alliance** for many years and in 1935 was an unsuccessful candidate for president, losing to **Honorata Wołowska**. Among her many awards were the *Order Pro Ecclesia et Pontifice* from Pope Pius XI (1934), the only Polish American woman ever so honored, and being named Woman of the Year by the Orchard Lake Women's Auxiliary (1976).—*Don Binkowski*

SOURCES: Francis Bolek, *Who's Who in Polish America* (New York: Arno, 1970 [c1943], 441; *Polish Women for Progress* (Detroit: Polish Activities League, 1973); Frank Renkiewicz, *The Poles in America* (Dobbs Ferry: Oceana Publications, Inc., 1973); Rachel Brett Harley and Betty Macdowell, *Michigan Women Firsts and Founders* (Lansing: Michigan Women's Studies Association, Inc., 1992), 73–74; John J. Bukowczyk, "In Search of Clara Swieczkowska, 1892–1986 — Detroit Social Worker and Community Activist," *Sarmatian Review*, Vol. 16, no. 2 (April 1996), 385–92.

Swietlik, Francis X. (b. Milwaukee, Wisconsin, November 24, 1889; d. Milwaukee, Wisconsin, December 12, 1983). Polonia activist. After earning a law degree from Marquette University in 1914, Swietlik soon became involved in the activities of the **Polish National Alliance** fraternal. During World War I, he was delegated by the Alliance to evaluate the conditions of Polish refugees living in Canada, later serving in the U.S. Army

in Europe where he rose to the rank of captain. Following the war, and after a decade in private legal practice, Swietlik joined the Marquette University Law School faculty in 1930 and in 1934 was appointed its dean. He held this position until 1953 when he resigned after his appointment to be a judge of the Wisconsin Circuit Court in Milwaukee.

In the 1920s Swietlik became recognized as a leader of the "old guard" or anti–Piłsudski faction of the PNA. This group opposed the leadership of **Censor Casimir Sypniewski**, elected in 1924, and head of the "left" or pro–Piłsudski faction in the Alliance. At the 1931 PNA national convention in Scranton, PA, Swietlik defeated Sypniewski for censor with 282 delegate votes to 235 for his opponent. He went on to serve as **censor** for four four-year terms, until 1947, when he declined to run again. Swietlik's tenure is notable for several reasons. In August 1934, he led a 40-member delegation of Polish Americans to the second congress of the **World Union of Poles from Abroad** (Światowy Związek Polaków z Zagranicy; "Światpol"), an organization created by the Polish government to strengthen its relations with the vast Polish emigration that existed throughout Europe and the Americas. But, led by Swietlik and counseled by the U.S. Ambassador to Poland, the American delegation refused to swear allegiance to Poland at the outset of the congress and stayed on only as observers of the gathering. Famously, Swietlik declared American **Polonia**'s "independence" from Poland in emphasizing that the ethnic community's first loyalty was to the United States, though its members' cultural ties to Poland remained important and valued. This sensible and far-sighted orientation has remained the key to understanding American Polonia's relations with Poland ever since.

Second, Swietlik led the effort within the Polish National Alliance to redirect its investment policies away from a traditionally heavy reliance on home mortgages, a risky business during the Great Depression of the 1930s, and into more secure investments in bonds. This move led to an enormous enhancement of the financial stability of the Alliance.

Third, Swietlik worked to bring about greater cooperation between the PNA and the other major Polish fraternals by stressing their common concerns in the charitable and humanitarian areas of fraternal life. A key result of this effort was the creation, in 1936, of what became the **Polish American Council** (Rada Polonii Amerykańskiej), later also known as American Relief for Poland. During and after World War II, this national Polonia federation raised more than $20 million ($200 million

in 2008 dollars) on behalf of needy Polish refugees, war victims, prisoners of war, and Polish military personnel.

Swietlik's leadership of a charitable federation that depended on U.S. government support obliged him to remain outside of the **Polish American Congress**, founded in 1944 as a political lobby on behalf of the Polish exile government in London. The PAC was led from the start by PNA president **Charles Rozmarek**, who increasingly regarded Swietlik as a political rival in and outside the Alliance. Relations between the two leading national **Polonia** figures deteriorated after the war to such a degree that Swietlik publicly criticized the president's autocratic actions in his report to the delegates at the 1947 PNA convention. He did not run again for office at the gathering and was succeeded by Rozmarek's candidate for censor, Judge **Blair F. Gunther** of Pennsylvania. In 1951 Swietlik did seek the office of censor, but lost decisively, 381–138, to Gunther. Ironically, Gunther himself became an opponent of Rozmarek a few years later and even attempted, unsuccessfully, to call an extraordinary national convention of the Alliance to review Rozmarek's leadership of the Alliance.

Swietlik continued to chair the Polish American Council into the early 1970s and his organization played a noteworthy role between 1963 and 1969, distributing tons of surplus foodstuffs to Poland during the presidency of Lyndon B. Johnson. In 1974, the organization ceased its activities and transferred its existing funds into the Polish American Congress Charitable Foundation, established in 1971 by Rozmarek's successor, PNA president **Aloysius Mazewski**.—*Donald E. Pienkos*

As Polish National Alliance censor, Franciszek X. Swietlik declared American Polonia's "independence" from Poland (*PMA*).

SOURCES: Adam Olszewski, *Historia Związku Narodowego Polskiego* (Chicago: Polish National Alliance, 1957–1963), Vols. 4–6; Donald E. Pienkos, *PNA: A Centennial History of the Polish National Alliance of the United States of North America* (Boulder, CO: East European Monographs, 1984); Donald E. Pienkos, *For Your Freedom Through Ours: Polish American Efforts on Poland's Behalf, 1863–1991* (Boulder, CO: East European Monographs, 1991).

Swit, Loretta (b. Passaic, New Jersey, November 4, 1937; d.—). Actress. A singer, stage and television actress, Loretta Swit is probably best known for her role as the Army nurse, Margaret "Hot Lips" Houlihan in the hit 1970s–1980s television series, *M*A*S*H*. She began her acting career at age seven in a school production of *The Snow Queen,* and seriously as an adult over the objections of her mother and acting agents, who suggested she change her name and get a nose job, which she was not willing to do. She studied at the American Academy of Dramatic Arts, then spent a few years with the Gene Frankel Repertory Company. One of her first big roles was in a road company stage play in Las Vegas, where she was housekeeper to Susan Hayward's Auntie Mame in *Mame.* She broke into television around 1970, with small roles in programs such as *Hawaii Five-O, Gunsmoke,* and *Mission: Impossible.* Settling in Hollywood, California in 1971, she landed the role of Major Houlihan a year later and rocketed to stardom playing the nurse opposite Alan Alda. She was with the show for its entire eleven year run and appeared in all but ten episodes, receiving two Emmy Awards. She also made a pilot episode for a police show called *Cagney and Lacey* in 1981 but could not get out of her *M*A*S*H* contract to be in the series. Swit became the first *M*A*S*H* cast member to visit Korea, and later narrated a documentary series entitled *Korea, the Forgotten War.* She was given a star on the famous Hollywood Walk of Fame in 1989, and has an extensive number of credits on Broadway, starring in

such productions as *Same Time Next Year* and *The Mystery of Edwin Drood.* She had roles in over 25 movies, among which were *Games Mother Never Taught You* and *A Killer Among Friends.* Her television appearances included singing and dancing on *The Muppet Show* with Miss Piggy. For five years, she was the host of a program on the Discovery Channel called *Those Incredible Animals,* which is seen in 30 different countries around the world. Due to her tireless efforts on behalf of animals, she has been named Woman of the Year by two organizations, the International Fund for Animal Welfare and the Animal Protection Institute. Her honors include Emmy Awards in 1980 and 1982; a People's Choice Award in 1983; The Genie Award; The Silver Satellite Award (honoring women who have made significant contributions to electronic media and related fields); The Jean Golden Halo Award; The Sarah Siddons Award (Chicago's highest theatrical honor) for *Shirley Valentine* in 1990; and a Star on the Hollywood Walk of Fame.— *Cheryl A. Pula*

SOURCES: Stuart Jeffries, "Arts: Inside Story: War is Awful, Acting Isn't Brain Surgery, and Women Should Be Proud of Their Bodies ... Loretta 'Hot Lips' Swit Shares Her Insights With Stuart Jeffries," *The Guardian* (London), December 7, 2001, 13; Eric Stimac, "Loretta Swit: Connecting is the Key," *Back Stage,* Vol. 40, no. 36 (September 3–9, 1993), A2; Angela Fox Dunn, "Loretta Swit's Only Goal Was to Act," *Boston Globe,* February 13, 1983, 1.

Switlik, Stanisław "Stanley" (b. Lwów, Poland, December 4, 1891; d. Trenton, New Jersey, March 4, 1981). Businessman. Switlik migrated to the U.S. at age sixteen. In 1920 he purchased a canvas and leather goods manufacturing company which, in the 1930s, became the Switlik Parachute & Equipment Company, the largest manufacturer of parachutes in the country. The company outfitted the expeditions and record attempts of Amelia Earhart, Wiley Post, and Admiral Richard Byrd. In 1934, Switlik and George Palmer Putnam, Amelia Earhart's husband, formed a joint venture to build a 115-foot tower on Switlik's farm in Ocean County. Designed to train airmen in parachute jumping, the first public jump from the tower was made by Earhart on June 2, 1935. The company manufactured parachutes for airmen during World War II, the Korean War and the Vietnam conflict. At the same time it developed and manufac-

tured rescue equipment such as inflatable lifeboats, life vests, survival tents and ancillary equipment, which came to form its main product line. As a pioneer in parachute development, Switlik was named to the Aviation Hall of Fame and received the Fred. L. Wehran Industrial Achievement Award. He was involved in real estate development in Florida and donated land for parkland preservation to the state of New Jersey.— *Peter J. Obst*

SOURCES: obituary, *New York Times,* March 7, 1981; *Pol-Am Journal,* July 1981.

Sybilska, Mother Mary Monica (Monika Kowerski; b. Warsaw, Poland, December 6, 1824; d. Detroit, Michigan, September 15, 1911). Catholic nun. Educated in Warsaw, Sybilska was one of a group of **Felician** nuns sent to the U.S. in 1874 at the request of the Rev. **Józef Dąbrowski** to serve as teachers in the parish school at Polonia, Wisconsin. Sybilska was named the first provincial-superior of the American Foundation of the Felician Sisters, serving from 1874 to 1896. In 1880 she built a new convent in Detroit, Michigan, and in 1882 transferred the motherhouse, novitiate, and orphanage there from Polonia. Under her leadership a girls academy was established in Detroit, thirty-six schools were established in various parishes, land was purchased for establishing the Immaculate Heart of Mary Province in Buffalo, New York, and the St. Mary's Home for the Aged opened in Manitowoc, Wisconsin.— *James S. Pula*

SOURCE: Francis Bolek, ed., *Who's Who in Polish America* (New York: Harbinger House, 1943).

Sypniewski, Kazimierz W. (b. Poznań, Poland, January 17, 1877; d. 1958). Polonia activist. Sypniewski came to America with his family and settled in Pittsburgh where he eventually became an attorney. Active in the national conventions of the **Polish National Alliance** as early as 1909, during World War I he chaired the Polish **National Department** (Wydział Narodowy) under the leadership of **John Smulski** and represented this **Polonia** political action federation in Paris. He was also involved in the **Polish Falcons Alliance** prior to and during the war. In 1918 Dr. **Teofil Starzyński**, president of the Falcons, resigned to enter the **Polish Army in France** being formed in the U.S. in service to the Allied cause and in support of reestablishing a postwar independent Poland. In the special election of the Falcons' Board of Directors to replace Starzyński on an interim basis, Sypniewski lost to Falcons Secretary General Adam Plutnicki by a vote of 6–5. An admirer of Józef Piłsudski's leadership in Poland, Sypniewski

Loretta Swit, seen here with the cast of the hit television show *M*A*S*H,* played the part of Major Margaret "Hot Lips" Houlihan (*NARA*).

Kazimierz W. Sypniewski, Polonia activist and chair of the National Department (*OLS*).

Julian Szajnert, a founder of the Polish National Alliance (*OLS*).

was active in the "opposition" or "left" faction of the Polish National Alliance, which was particularly influential in the eastern part of the U.S. in the 1920s and 1930s. In 1924 he was elected **censor**, or chief judge, of the PNA at its 24th national convention and was re-elected to this post in 1928. But Sypniewski's tenure as censor of the Alliance was controversial and the PNA was torn by chronic internal conflict between two nearly equal factions, the "old guard" and "the opposition" or "left." This struggle was punctuated by legal suits and political battles at nearly every level of Alliance life and led to a near civil war in the PNA at its 1927 convention in Chicago. Only by a judge's order was the conflict resolved, with Sypniewski's faction narrowly winning control of the Alliance at the reconvened gathering in 1928. But Sypniewski's highly partisan decisions during this period damaged whatever claims his reputation had for fairness. A key objective for Sypniewski involved strengthening PNA ties with the Polish government in Warsaw. But he lost his bid for reelection at the 1931 PNA convention to attorney **Francis X. Swietlik** of Milwaukee, the 41 year old, U.S.–born candidate of the "old guard" faction. By the end of the decade, the "old guard" had won complete control over all the top national offices in the PNA. Sypniewski's defeat ended his involvement in the Polish National Alliance.—*Donald E. Pienkos*

SOURCES: Adam Olszewski, *Historia Związku Narodowego Polskiego* (Chicago: Polish National Alliance, 1957–1963); Donald E. Pienkos, *PNA: A Centennial History of the Polish National Alliance of the United States of North America* (Boulder, CO: East European Monographs, 1984).

Szajnert, Julian (b. Poland, ca. 1848; d. Minneapolis, Minnesota, October 20, 1928).

Polonia activist. Szajnert's early years in America were spent in Philadelphia where he was one of the organizers, in 1871, of the **Tadeusz Kościuszko** patriotic society. He took part in the founding meeting of the **Polish National Alliance** called by **Julius Andrzejkowicz** in Philadelphia on February 15, 1880. There he was elected the group's secretary and together with Andrzejkowicz authored the first announcement calling on Poles throughout America to join the Alliance. Over the years Szajnert assumed the role of an "elder statesman" who in critical times offered his counsel to the movement. In the years 1911–18 and 1924–28 he held the office of honorary commissioner for all states and during the latter period took an active leadership role within the "old guard" faction in its struggle against the "opposition" headed by **Censor Casimir Sypniewski**. He is remembered in the **Polish National Alliance** as one of its five founders, along with Andrzejkowicz, John Blachowski, **John Popieliński**, and **Julian Lipiński**.—*Donald E. Pienkos*

SOURCES: Stanisław Osada, *Historia Związku Narodowego Polskiego i rozwój ruchu narodowego Polskiego w Ameryce Pólnocnej* (Chicago: Nakładem i drukiem Związku Narodowego Polskiego, 1905); Adam Olszewski, *Historia Związku Narodowego Polskiego* (Chicago: Polish National Alliance, 1957–1963), Vols. 3–4.

Szarkowski, Thaddeus John (b. Ashland, Wisconsin, December 18, 1925; d. Pittsfield, Massachusetts, July 7, 2007). Photographer. Szarkowski graduated from high school in 1942 and served in the army during World War II. Following the war he earned a degree in art history from the University of Wisconsin (1948) and began a career as a photographer, an interest he maintained since childhood. As a staff photographer for the Walker Art Center, he spent his leisure time pursuing photography

as well, with his first exhibition held in Minneapolis in 1949, followed by publication of his works in his *The Face of Minneapolis* (1958). In 1950 he moved to Buffalo where he taught in the Albright Art School, and in the process held another exhibition where he showed work he did in the western New York area. A grant from the Guggenheim Foundation in 1954 allowed him to take a series of images of the architectural work of Louis Sullivan which he published in *The Idea of Louis Sullivan*. In 1961 Szarkowski received a second Guggenheim Foundation grant, and in the following year the famed photographer Edward Steichen selected him as his replacement as director of photography for the Museum of Modern Art in New York City. During his tenure, Szarkowski purchased thousands of photographs for the museum's collections and directed 160 exhibitions.—*James S. Pula*

SOURCES: "Ordinary Pictures and Accidental Masterpieces: Snapshot Photography in the Modern Art Museum," *Art Journal*, June 22, 2008; "Master of the Medium: Maria Morris Hambourg on John Szarkowski (1925–2007)," Artform international, October 1, 2007; "John Szarkowski 1925–2007," *Art in America*, September 1, 2007.

Szczesniak, Alina Surmacka (b. Warsaw, Poland, July 8, 1925; d.—). Scientist. Szczesniak moved to the U.S. following World War II, studied at Bryn Mawr College, and earned a graduate degree in food science from the Massachusetts Institute of Technology. She was employed by General Foods Central Laboratories (1952–86) where she specialized in studies of food texture and developed the Sensory Texture Profile Analysis which became the industry standard in the field. She was the founding editor of the *Journal of Texture Science* (1969). In 1981 she was elected a fellow of the Institute of Food Technologists (IFT), and in 1985 was honored with the Nicholas Appert Award from the IFT for her "pioneering work on food texture that led to its recognition as an important quality attribute affecting consumer acceptance and to its organization as a subdiscipline of food science." Active in **Polonia** affairs, she was for many years a member of the Board of Directors of the **Polish Institute of Arts and Sciences in America**.—*James S. Pula*

SOURCE: "People News: Alina S. Szczesniak," *Food Technology*, September 2002, 16.

Szlachta. The origins of the Polish nobility, or *szlachta*, are the subject of debate among scholars. Although academics generally agree that the *szlachta* was consolidated as one of the Polish-Lithuanian Commonwealth's five estates beginning with the reign of Kazimierz Wielki (Casimir the Great, 1333–70), the formative years are still a matter of speculation. One prominent though somewhat discredited theory maintains that the *szlachta*'s origins lay in the ancient Slavic clan structure of tenth and eleventh century Poland. Some consider this theory supportable owing to the unique character of Polish heraldry, which, unlike its Western European counterparts, assigned mottos and insignias to groups of frequently unrelated noble clans, rather than to individual families. This practice was known as *wspólność herbów*, or the "holding of arms in common." Throughout the fifteenth and sixteenth centuries, economic and commercial developments led increasing numbers of Polish knights and nobles to involve themselves in agriculture and in estate management. This eventually led to the landed status of many gentry families and to the relationship between material wealth and political power. Although all Polish nobles were theoretically equal, property — and more specifically the number of estates in a family's possession — determined positioning in the noble hierarchy. Magnate families, such as the Lubomirskis, Potockis, Radziwiłłs, and Zamoyskis were considered among the wealthiest in the Commonwealth, with upwards of fifteen village estates per family. Many nobles, however, owned fewer than five estates, if any at all; the existence of landless nobles was not uncommon.

The percentage of Polish nobles in comparison to the rest of the Commonwealth's population was disproportionately high, numbering an estimated 10–12 percent by the end of the eighteenth century in comparison to 1–2 percent in France and England and five percent in Hungary and Spain. Also unique to the Polish *szlachta* was its relative ethnic homogeneity, with the majority of nobles either of Polish descent or of Ruthenian, Lithuanian, Baltic German, or Tatar ancestry, but culturally and linguistically Polonized. Perhaps most unique to the Polish nobility was the system of privileges attained through royal concessions over successive generations. Where Western European nobles enjoyed privileges that were largely fiscal in nature, the privileges of the *szlachta* — in addition to their tax exemption — afforded them numerous legal and political rights. As a result, the *szlachta* wielded considerable influence over the election of representatives to the local dietines, or *sejmiki*, and over the appointment of officials, bureaucrats, county judges, and other important stations. More directly, their involvement in the political life of the Polish-Lithuanian Commonwealth — and the relative impotence of the Polish monarch — led to the development of a bicameral parliamentary system in which they were directly represented, though the in-

stitution was often ineffective as a result of the pursuit of personal, regional, and political interests by individual nobles and their families. The Commonwealth earned the appellation of a "gentry democracy" and a "Republic of Nobles," but the political well being of the state suffered from prolonged political infighting and the meddling of foreign powers into the affairs of the Commonwealth. The first partition of Poland in 1773 led to an attempt to reduce the power of the *szlachta* and to increase monarchical authority through the Constitution of May 3, 1791; however, these efforts were unsuccessful. After the final partition in 1795, the property rights and privileges of the *szlachta* were determined by the various policies of the partitioning empires. In Congress Poland, the Russian authorities permitted local autonomy until the 1830–31 Uprising. Self-government was also granted to the province of **Galicia** by the Habsburg Empire after 1867. The partitioning empires, however, began stripping the rights and privileges of petty nobles, leading the *déclassé* gentry to find employment in the state bureaucracy or the army. Other members of the *szlachta* migrated, most often due to political persecution. Though of relative numerical insignificance in comparison to the flood of Polish peasants and workers arriving after 1870, many members of the *szlachta* who participated in the Polish Uprisings of 1830–31 and 1863–64 migrated to the United States as an alternative to Western Europe. The March 1921 Constitution of the Second Polish Republic abolished the hereditary nobility as a legal class, though it remained a socially and economically recognizable group until its complete elimination by the post–World War II government of the People's Republic of Poland. — *Krystyna Cap*

SOURCE: Norman Davies, "Szlachta: The Nobleman's Paradise," in *God's Playground: A History of Poland*, vol. 1: The Origins to 1795 (New York: Columbia University Press, 1982), 201–55.

Szmanda, Eric Kyle (b. Milwaukee, Wisconsin, July 24, 1975; d.—). Actor. Known mostly for his role of Greg Sanders on the television drama *CSI: Crime Scene Investigation*, he graduated from Mukwonago High School (1993) and Carroll College in Wisconsin. One of three children and the great-nephew of Ray Szmanda, who is known as the spokesman for the Menard's chain of home improvement stores in the Midwest, he began his career in films and television in 1998 when he appeared in the TV series *The Net*. After landing a part in his first movie, the producer requested that he change his name, but he refused. He has since had parts in the films *The Rules of Attraction*, *True Vinyl*, and *Little*

Athens. Not limited to television and movies, he also had a one-man show on stage called *Hyenas*, and appeared in a production of Shakespeare's *A Midsummer Night's Dream*. He served as a music consultant for the feature film *Life as a House*. In his role on *CSI*, Szmanda proved it was possible to be an intellectual "lab rat," and still have popular appeal with his spiky hair, penchant for Marilyn Manson music, and wearing "in" clothing. Among his honors are: Screen Actor's Guild Award for Outstanding Performance by an Ensemble in a Drama Series for *CSI* (2004, 2005); Nominated for Screen Actor's Guild Award for Outstanding Performance by an Ensemble in a Drama Series for *CSI* (2002 and 2003). — *Cheryl A. Pula*

SOURCE: "Eric Szmanda," *Contemporary Theatre, Film, and Television* (Detroit: Gale, 2009), Vol. 91.

Szoka, Edmund Casimir (b. Grand Rapids, Michigan, September 14, 1927; d.—), Catholic Cardinal. Szoka was educated for the priesthood at St. Joseph's Seminary in Grand Rapids, Sacred Heart Major Seminary in Detroit, and St. John's Provincial Seminary in Plymouth, Michigan. Ordained on June 5, 1954, he was assigned to a parish in Manistique, Michigan, but was soon appointed secretary to Bishop Thomas Noa in Marquette. He studied canon law in Rome (1957–59), returned to Michigan, and in 1971 was consecrated Bishop of Gaylord. He served as president of the National Conference of Catholic Bishops (NCCB) from 1971 to 1977, while also holding the office of treasurer and secretary of the Episcopal Conference of Michigan. On March 21, 1981, he was named Metropolitan Archbishop of Detroit by Pope John Paul II, serving also as president of the administrative council of St. John Seminary in Plymouth and **Saints Cyril and Methodius Seminary** in Orchard Lake, and a member of the executive committee of The Catholic University of America, administrator for the National Shrine of the Immaculate Conception, and treasurer of the NCCB. In 1990 he was named president of the Prefecture for the Economic Affairs of the Holy See, a position he held until 1997. He was elevated to cardinal on June 28, 1988, and on October 15, 1997, named president of the Pontifical Commission for Vatican City State. He was a member of the papal conclave in 2005, with special responsibility for arranging housing for the delegates. Upon reaching the mandatory retirement age of 75, he submitted his resignation to Pope John Paul II in 2002, and it was accepted by Pope Benedict XVI in 2006. — *James S. Pula*

SOURCES: "Szoka looks back upon his retirement," *Grand Rapid Press*, June 24, 2006; "Time to Retire,"

Michigan Catholic, September 14, 2007; "Cardinal Szoka, Gaylord's First Bishop, Announces He'll Retire from Vatican," *Gaylord Herald Times*, June 28, 2006; "Former Detroit Cardinal to Retire from Vatican Post," *Detroit Free Press*, June 22, 2006; "Szoka Plans to be Active in Retirement," *Detroit Free Press*, June 26, 2006; "Former Archbishop of Detroit Brought Capitalism to City's Budgetary Chaos," *Wall Street Journal*, April 8, 2005; "Szoka Shines as Pope's Go-to Guy at the Vatican," *Detroit News*, July 27, 2000.

Szulc, Gustave (Nils Gustaf Ulric Schoultz; b. Kuopio, Finland, October 7, 1807; d. Kingston, Ontario, Canada, December 8, 1838). Engineer, revolutionary. Born into an upper-class family, Szulc's grandfather had been a distinguished army officer and his father a chief circuit court judge in Rautalampi, Sweden, where the family had been forced to flee when the Russians invaded Poland in 1808. Szulc followed in his grandfather's footsteps, entering the military academy at Karlberg, then the Swedish army before receiving a discharge in 1830. As a student during the November Uprising (1830–31) in Warsaw, he fought alongside Polish army cadets against the Russian army. With the fall of the uprising, Szulc fled to Italy and France before leaving Europe for the United States in 1836. Initially settling in Salina near Syracuse, New York, he worked as a chemical engineer, refining a salt extraction process for use on the salt spring water areas of Salina, eventually receiving the first Polish patent in America (number 298) for his extraction process. While working as a recruiting officer in New York, Szulc altered his surname to "Nils Szolteocky Von Schoultz," an alleged tribute to his possible Polish roots, and later in Canada became known as Szulc. Additionally, he began claiming that he was Polish and had been a major in the November Uprising. Drawn into one of the secret societies formed in the northern United States to free the Canadas from British rule, Szulc was recruited in 1838 by John Ward Birge for participation in the Prescott Campaign. Leading a schooner of approximately 200 men, the *Charlotte of Toronto*, and successfully becoming the only vessel to reach Prescott, he launched a valiant defense against British forces and staved them off for five days before he and his men were captured and taken to Fort Henry where they awaited court martial. His defense attorney, a young lawyer named John A. Macdonald—later first Prime Minister of Canada—was employed as Szulc's counsel. Szulc was condemned to death by hanging. At his request, the words "Native of Poland," were added to his tombstone. He is buried at St. Mary's Cemetery in Kingston, Ontario.—*Krystyna Cap*

SOURCE: Ella Pipping, *Soldier of Fortune: The Story of a Nineteenth-Century Adventurer*, trans. Naomi Walford (Boston: Gambit, 1971).

Szyk, Arthur (b. Łódź, Poland, June 3, 1894; d. New Canaan, Connecticut, September 13, 1951). Artist. Educated at the Academie Julian in Paris (1909) and the Academy of Fine Arts in Kraków (1913), Szyk served as Artistic Director in the Department of Propaganda for the Polish Army in Łódź during the Polish-Soviet War (1919–20). During World War II he was sent by the Polish government from Britain to the U.S., via Canada, in 1940 to help publicize the anti–Nazi cause. In this capacity he became widely known for his anti-Axis political illustrations, caricatures and cartoons, as well as his illustrations for books, magazines and newspaper articles done in a distinctive style based on his study of medieval miniaturists and illuminated manuscripts. Following the war he became an American citizen on May 22, 1948. A prolific artist, he had solo exhibitions in Kalisz, Łódź, and Warsaw in Poland; Geneva, Switzerland; London, England; Toronto and Montréal, Canada; and throughout the United States. His illustrations also adorned many books including publications in English, French, German, and Polish. His popular cartoons appeared in *American Hebrew*, *American Magazine*, *American Mercury*, *The Answer*, *Cavalry Journal*, *Chicago Sun*, *Collier's*, *Time*, *Compass*, *Esquire*, *Fortune*, *France-Amerique*, *Free World*, *Jewish Forum*, *Jewish Veteran*, *Liberty*, *Look*, *Menorah Journal*, *New York Post*, *PM*, *Polish Review*, *Reader's Scope*, *Saturday Review of Literature*, *Time and Tide* (London), and *Vestnik* (Toronto). He also developed advertisements for Casco, Coca Cola, General Motors, North American Aviation, Philco, and U.S. Steel, as well as patriotic advertisements for U.S. Treasury War Bonds and fundraising stamp series for the British American Ambulance Corps, Polish Relief, and Bundles for Britain. Among his

Arthur Szyk, artist (*OLS*).

many works is a series on the highlights of Polish American history.

Among his awards were the Gold Cross of Merit from the Polish Government (1931) and the George Washington Medal (1934). His works may be found in the Art Gallery of Ontario, Toronto; The British Museum, London; The Coca-Cola Company; FDR Library, Hyde Park, NY; Fine Arts Society PLC, London; The Jewish Museum, New York; The **Kosciuszko Foundation**, New York; Library of Congress, Washington, D.C.; National Library, Warsaw, Poland; Queens' Royal Collection, Windsor Castle; United States Memorial Holocaust Museum; U.S. Naval Academy Museum, Annapolis, MD; Yeshiva University Museum, New York; and YIVO Institute of Jewish Research–New York.—*Stanley L. Cuba*

SOURCES: Irvin Ungar, *Justice Illuminated: The Art of Arthur Szyk* (Berkeley and Burlingame: Frog Ltd. and Historicana, 1999); Steven Luckert, *The Art and Politics of Arthur Szyk* (Washington, D.C.: United States Holocaust Memorial Museum, 2002); Joseph P. Ansell, *Arthur Szyk: Artist, Jew, Pole* (Oxford, England and Portland, Oregon: The Littman Library of Jewish Civilization, 2004).

Szymanowicz, Helen (b. Erie, Pennsylvania, February 12, 1909; d. Erie, Pennsylvania, March 20, 2005). Polonia activist. Active in the **Polish National Alliance** for many years, Szymanowicz was elected vice president of the PNA at its 36th national convention in 1971. She went on to serve in this office for twenty years until her retirement in 1991. She succeeded **Aloysius Mazewski** as president of the PNA on his death in August 1988, thereby becoming the first woman to hold this office in the Alliance. Szymanowicz was not a candidate for reelection to the presidency and in October 1988 the PNA Supervisory Council elected Treasurer **Edward J. Moskal** to succeed her as head of **Polonia**'s largest fraternal insurance association. Szymanowicz was active from the late 1920s as an organizer for the PNA in the Erie area. As vice president, she headed the women's units within the PNA and enhanced their many charitable undertakings. She took a notable role in efforts by the PNA and the **Polish American Congress** to collect money, clothing, and medical items for shipment to Poland during its economic and political crisis in the 1980s. She energetically promoted the establishment of **Saturday schools** whose mission was to educate youngsters in their Polish heritage, a program that eventually included nearly ten thousand children in the Chicago area alone and which received substantial financial support from the PNA and other **Polonia** organizations. Szymanowicz also chaired the massive Polish Constitution Day parade in Chicago for many years. She was honored on many occasions for her fraternal, educational, and humanitarian work.—*Donald E. Pienkos*

SOURCES: Donald E. Pienkos, *PNA: A Centennial History of the Polish National Alliance of the United States of North America* (Boulder, CO: East European Monographs, 1984); Wojciech Wierzewski, "Sto Trzydzieska Slynnych Polaków w Ameryce" (Unpublished manuscript in the archives of the University of Wisconsin–Milwaukee, 2000).

Szymanski, Frank (b. Detroit, Michigan, July 6, 1923; d. Detroit, Michigan, April 26, 1987). Football player, jurist. Szymanski played college football, as a center and linebacker, at Notre Dame in 1943–44, and was a key member of the Fighting Irish national championship squad in his first season. After being drafted in the first round of the professional draft in 1945, he played five seasons (1945–49) for three different teams in the National Football League. He was the starting center for the NFL champion Philadelphia Eagles in 1948. After retirement from football, Szymanski served as judge for the Wayne County Probate Court from 1959 until his death in 1987. He was inducted into the National Polish-American Sports Hall of Fame in 1995.—*Neal Pease*

SOURCE: "Frank Szymanski," National Polish-American Sports Hall of Fame website, www.polishsportshof.com.

Szymanski, Henry Ignatius "Red" (b. Chicago, Illinois, July 4, 1898; d. Colorado Springs, Colorado, November 6, 1959). Military officer. Appointed to the U.S. Military Academy from Illinois at age nineteen, he finished a war emergency course in eighteen months and was commissioned first lieutenant on November 1, 1918. Following the end of World War I he returned to West Point for six additional months of instruction before graduating in the Class of 1919. A strong athlete, he was a member of the U.S. Olympic wrestling team that participated in Belgium before being assigned to ROTC duty at Northwestern University. While there he earned a B.S. degree in 1929. He resigned from the army to enter private business, but voluntarily re-entered the army when the Japanese bombed Pearl Harbor. Assigned to the 33rd Infantry Division, while serving as morale officer he devised a new system of exercises designed to increase stamina. It was so successful that the army later published it in a pamphlet, "Take Your Tip from the Army," for distribution to the general public. Because of his fluency in Polish, he was assigned as liaison officer to the Polish Second Army Corps under Gen. Władysław Anders. There he authored two reports of historical significance. The first dealt with the Soviet obstruction that prevented him from joining the Polish troops in Russia, placing the Soviets in a bad light for

being uncooperative with the Western Allies. The second report provided detailed information on the **Katyń** murders. Due to wartime politics, both of these reports were suppressed by the War Department Military Intelligence Division G-2. Promoted to colonel, Szymanski accompanied the Poles to North Africa and Italy, serving with them during the costly fighting at Monte Cassino. In 1944 he was awarded the Polish Order of Polonia Restituta. In December 1944 he was assigned to the Supreme Headquarters, Allied Expeditionary Force (SHAEF) where he served on Gen. Dwight Eisenhower's staff as an expert on Polish affairs. With the approval of SHAEF, he organized guard battalions from former Polish prisoners to protect supply lines on the Western Front, thereby releasing many U.S. and British troops for combat operations. Szymanski returned to the U.S. in December 1945 and retired from the army in 1953. Moving to Colorado Springs, he was employed as director of public relations for the Exchange National Bank. In 1957 he founded the Academy Life Insurance Company, serving as its president until his death.—*Francis C. Kajencki*

SOURCE: U.S. Military Academy archives.

Szymanski, Richard "Dick" (b. Toledo, Ohio, October 7, 1932; d.—). Football player. After starring as an All-City athlete in baseball and basketball at Libbey High School in Toledo, Ohio, Szymanski enrolled at the University of Notre Dame where he became a four-year starter (1951–54), playing on the Irish's 1953 national championship team and earning All-America honors. Drafted by the Baltimore Colts in the second round with the sixteenth overall pick of the 1955 NFL draft, he started at center as a rookie, earning All-Pro honors in 1955. After serving a tour in the U.S. Army, he returned to the Colts in time for the 1957 season which saw him move from center to linebacker. For the next five seasons Szymanski played both positions until returning full-time to the center position in 1962. He was named All-Pro three times (1956, 1963, 1965), played on three championship teams (1958, 1959, 1968), and concluded his career in Super Bowl III in January 1969. He was named to the Colts' Silver Anniversary Team in 1977. After fourteen seasons with the Colts, Szymanski retired as a player, but remained with the Colts with a variety of front office responsibilities including scout, assistant personnel director, offensive line coach, director of player personnel, executive vice president, and general manager. In 1982 he left the Colts after 27 years to accept a job as scout with the Atlanta Falcons, and in 1985 he joined the NFL Alumni as vice president for

chapter relations, overseeing the operations of the charitable organization's national network of thirty chapters. He was named the executive director in 1991–92. Szynamski was inducted into the **National Polish-American Sports Hall of Fame** in 1994.—*Luis J. Gonzalez*

SOURCE: Don Horkey, "Few Played the Game with His Intensity," National Polish-American Sports Hall of Fame and Museum, Inc.

Szymczak, Miecislaus Stephen (b. Chicago, Illinois, August 15, 1894; d. Evanston, Illinois, April 1978). Economist. Szymczak earned his baccalaureate degree at St. Mary's College (1914), attended Mount St. Mary's Seminary in Cincinnati (1914–17), and received A.B. (1917) and A.M. (1918) degrees from DePaul University in Chicago. He taught mathematics at St. Mary's College (1913–14) and both mathematics and history in the DePaul University Preparatory School (1914–19). Szymczak was on the faculty of DePaul University beginning in 1919, before beginning a career in business as vice president of the Hatterman & Glanz State Bank (1927–28). He organized and directed the Ridgemoor Building & Loan Association in 1928, then went into politics with his election as clerk of the Cook County Superior Court in 1929. Two years later he was appointed City Comptroller, which was a stepping stone to being appointed to the Board of Governors of the Federal Reserve System. Active in many community organizations, he was also among those who established the **American Council for Polish Culture** at a meeting in New York in 1939.—*James S. Pula*

SOURCE: Francis Bolek, ed., *Who's Who in Polish America* (New York: Harbinger House, 1943).

Szypula, George (b. Philadelphia, Pennsylvania, June 24, 1921; d.—). Gymnast. While attending Temple University, where he competed as a gymnast at the national level, he won the AAU National Tumbling Championships (1940–43). Following service in the armed forces during World War II, he returned to gymnastics, establishing himself as the first coach of the new gymnastics program at Michigan State University in 1947. He stayed as the university's coach until his retirement in 1989. During his tenure, the Spartan gymnastics team captured 45 Big Ten and 18 NCAA individual titles. The 1958 Michigan State gymnastics team achieved the highest team honors of Szypula's coaching career, gaining a share of the NCAA national team championship with Big Ten rival Illinois. The Spartans also finished in the top five in the team championships eight different times under Szypula. In 1968, his team captured the Big Ten gymnastics' team championship. His teams also finished second five times and took third place honors eleven times. Szypula served as president of the National Association of Gymnastics Coaches and chairman of the selection committee for the Gymnastics Hall of Fame. After 1989 he served as gymnastics coach at East Lansing High School, while also running a recreational gymnastics program for young people of all ages. He authored several books on competitive gymnastics including *Contemporary Gymnastics* (1977), *Beginning Trampolining* (1968), and *Tumbling & Balancing for All* (1968). In 1977, The National Association of Collegiate Gymnastics Coaches presented him with its prestigious "Honor Coach Award" for his outstanding thirty-year career and service to the sport of gymnastics. In 1978, the U.S. Gymnastics Federation conferred on him its "Master of Sports" award, and in 1984 the U.S. Gymnastics Federation's Junior Olympic Boys Program again honored Szypula with the Frank Cumisky award in recognition of his contributions made to the youth gymnastics programs in the United States. He received a meritorious services citation from the Michigan State Senate after his retirement from MSU in 1989. He was inducted into the Gymnastics Hall of Fame, the Temple University Hall of Fame, and the National Polish-American Sports Hall of Fame. In January 2002, the eighty-year-old Szypula was chosen as torchbearer for the Olympic flame for the 2002 Salt Lake City Winter Olympic Games.—*Luis J. Gonzalez*

SOURCES: "A Lifetime Dedicated to Gymnastics," National Polish-American Sports Hall of Fame and Museum, Inc.; Jack Seibold, *The Spartan Sports Encyclopedia: A History of the Michigan State Men's Athletic Program* (Champaign, IL: Sports Publishing LLC, 2003), 260.

Taberski, Francis Andrew "Frank" (b. Stuyvesant Falls, New York, March 15, 1889; d. Schenectady, New York, October 23, 1941). Pocket billiards player. Taberski decided to play competitive billiards after attending a championship and coming away convinced he could play as well as the winners. After placing third in his first pocket billiards championship, he went on to win ten consecutive championships, an unheard-of feat. At the time, a ruby and diamond studded gold traveling medal was awarded to the champion with the proviso that anyone who won ten successful championship challenges could keep the award. No one had previously won more than five in a row. Taberski won his first championship in 1916, and by 1918 had achieved the seemingly impossible mark of ten straight, three in 1916, six in 1917, and one in 1918. He won again in 1925, twice in 1927, and twice in 1928. During his career he won twenty con-

secutive world championship challenge matches without a loss, 307 consecutive 100 point games, and set the world's record for a high run in an exhibition game at 271. In 1975 he was inducted into the Billiards Congress of America Hall of Fame.—*James S. Pula*

SOURCE: Francis Bolek, ed., *Who's Who in Polish America* (New York: Harbinger House, 1943).

Tanana, Frank (b. Detroit, Michigan, July 3, 1953; d.—). Baseball player. A standout high school athlete, Tanana turned down numerous college basketball scholarship offers to become a professional baseball pitcher. In 21 major league seasons, from 1973 through 1993, pitching for six teams, he won 240 games with an earned run average of 3.66. A lefthander, Tanana enjoyed his greatest success in the first phase of his career with the California Angels, when he possessed one of the most potent fastballs in the game. As an Angel, he led the American League in strikeouts and earned run average in different years, and was named to three AL All-Star squads. The statistical calculations of the *Total Baseball* encyclopedia rank Tanana as having been one of the five best pitchers in the American League in three consecutive seasons. An arm injury in his sixth season deprived him of the speed that was his best asset. Forced to remake himself as a hurler relying on guile and breaking balls, he never recovered the brilliance of his youth, but remained an effective major league pitcher for fifteen more years. In both seasons that his teams reached postseason play, 1979 and 1987, Tanana won the game that clinched the division championship. He was inducted into the National Polish-American Sports Hall of Fame in 1996.—*Neal Pease*

SOURCE: "Frank Tanana," National Polish Sports Hall of Fame website, www.polishsportshof.com.

Targowski, Andrew (b. Warsaw, Poland, July 15, 1937; d.—). Engineer. Targowski received his Ph.D. from the Warsaw University of Technology in 1967. A pioneer of business computing and inventor of INFOSTRADA (Poland 1972), which triggered the Information Superhighway wave in the U.S., he was a head of the Polish National Computer Development Program (1971–74) and Poland's Delegate to the United Nation's Group on Automation. In 1980 he moved to the U.S. where he was granted political asylum. After accepting a teaching position in Computer Information Systems at Western Michigan University, his professional career in the U.S. combined his interests in computer engineering and business into modeling enterprise systems and exploring the role of information and knowledge in human development. He

served as president of the International Society for the Comparative Study of Civilizations, chair of the Advisory Council of the Information Resource Management Association (1996–2004), chair of the board and later project director of the *TeleCITY* of Kalamazoo (1992–99), and president of Colleagues International (2001–03), a non-profit supported by the U.S. Department of State which brought foreign professionals from the former Soviet Union to Kalamazoo for business practice. He was also chair of the World Research Council of Poles Living Abroad (2001–07), and in 2004 he organized the Council of Polish Engineers in North America. He is a member of the **Polish Institute of Arts and Science** in New York, a Foreign Member of the Academy of Engineering in Poland, and has been active in numerous Polish American professional societies including **Polonia Technica**. His scholarly work included over seventy papers and 22 books including *Cognitive Informatics and Wisdom Development* (2010), *Information Technology and Societal Development* (2009), *Enterprise Systems Education in the 21st Century* (2006), *Electronic Enterprise, Strategy and Architecture* (2003), and *Global Information Infrastructure* (1996). In recognition of his scientific and professional contributions, Targowski received the Cavalier Cross of the Order of Merit from Poland, the Medal of the "Polonia Technica" in the U.S., and various other awards and diplomas.—*Janusz W. Romanski*

SOURCES: Zbigniew Piasek, ed., *Encyclopedia of World Research and Engineering Heritage of Polish Engineers in the USA, Canada, Europe, Argentina and Singapore* (Kraków: Oficyna Wydawnicza FOGRA, 2006); Marek Szczerbiński, *Polonia Technica: Stowarzyszenie Inzynierów i Techników Polskich w Stanach Zjednoczonych Ameryki Północnej: zarys historii w latach 1941–2001* (New York: Światowa Rada Badań nad Polonią, Akademia Polonijna, 2001).

Tarski, Alfred (real name Tajtelbaum or Teitelbaum; b. Warsaw, Poland, January 14, 1901; d. Berkeley, California, October 26, 1983). Mathematician. Tarski attended secondary school in Warsaw before entering the University of Warsaw intending to study biology. After Poland regained its independence in 1918, the university became a leading research institution in logic, foundational mathematics, and the philosophy of mathematics. Convinced by his professors to switch from biology to mathematics, he became the youngest person ever to complete a doctorate at the University of Warsaw (1924). Tarski taught logic at the Polish Pedagogical Institute, mathematics and logic at the University of Warsaw, but these positions paid poorly so he also taught mathematics at a Warsaw secondary school, a not uncommon experience for

European intellectuals prior to World War II. In 1930, Tarski visited the University of Vienna and, thanks to a fellowship, was able to return to Vienna during the first half of 1935 to work with Carl Menger's research group. From Vienna he traveled to Paris to present his ideas on truth at the first meeting of the Unity of Science movement, an outgrowth of the Vienna Circle. Tarski's ties to this movement saved his life, because they resulted in his being invited to address the Unity of Science Congress held in September 1939 at Harvard University. Thus, he left Poland in August 1939, on the last ship to sail from Poland for the United States before the German invasion and the outbreak of World War II.

Once in the U.S., Tarski held a number of temporary teaching and research positions. In 1942, he joined the Mathematics Department at the University of California at Berkeley, where he spent the rest of his career. He became an American citizen in 1945. In addition to teaching, he lectured widely including visiting professorships at University College in London (1950, 1966), the Institut Henri Poincaré in Paris (1955), the Miller Institute for Basic Research in Science in Berkeley (1958–1960), the University of California at Los Angeles (1967), and the Pontifical Catholic University of Chile (1974–1975). Tarski's mathematical interests were exceptionally broad for a mathematical logician. His collected papers run to about 2,500 pages, most of them on mathematics, not logic. In 1924, he and Stefan Banach proved that, if one accepts the Axiom of Choice, a ball can be cut into a finite number of pieces, and then reassembled into a ball of larger size, or alternatively it can be reassembled into two balls whose sizes each equal that of the original one. This result is now called the "Banach-Tarski paradox." In a decision method for elementary algebra and geometry, Tarski showed, by the method of quantifier elimination, that the first-order theory of the real numbers under addition and multiplication is decidable. In his 1953 *Undecidable Theories*, Tarski et al. showed that many mathematical systems, including lattice theory, abstract projective geometry and closure algebras, are all undecidable. One of the foremost logicians, he produced axioms for logical consequence, and worked on deductive systems, the algebra of logic, and the theory of definability. His semantic methods, which culminated in the model theory he and a number of his Berkeley students developed in the 1950s and 1960s, radically transformed Hilbert's proof-theoretic metamathematics.

Among many distinctions garnered over the course of his career, Tarski was elected to the United States National Academy of Sciences, the British Academy, and the Royal Netherlands Academy of Arts and Sciences. He received honorary degrees from the Pontifical Catholic University of Chile in 1975, Marseilles' Paul Cézanne University in 1977, and from the University of Calgary in 1981, the same year he received the Berkeley Citation. Tarski presided over the Association for Symbolic Logic (1944–1946) and the International Union for the History and Philosophy of Science (1956–1957). He was also an honorary editor of *Algebra Universalis*. His works include *Pojęcie prawdy w językach nauk dedukcyjnych* (Notion of Truth in Languages of Deductive Sciences; 1933); *O logice matematycznej i metodzie dedukcyjnej* (About Mathematical Logic and Deductive Method; 1936); *A Decision Method for Elementary Algebra and Geometry* (1948); *Cardinal Algebras* (1949); *Undecidable Theories* (with Andrzej Mostowski and Raphael M. Robinson; 1953); *Ordinal Algebras* (1956); *Cylindric Algebras* (with Leon Henkin and Donald Monk; 1971, 1985); *Logic, Semantics, Mathematics* (1983); *Introduction to Logic and the Methodology of Deductive Sciences* (1984); *A Formalization of Set Theory Without Variables* (with Steven Givant; 1987); and *The Collected Papers of Alfred Tarski* (1986), 4 vols. —*Adam A. Zych*

SOURCES: Robert L. Vaught, "Alfred Tarski's Work in Model Theory," *Journal of Symbolic Logic*, Vol. 51 (1986), 869–82; Steven Givant, "A Portrait of Alfred Tarski," *Mathematical Intelligence*, Vol. 13 (1991), 16–32; Anita Burdman Feferman, "Alfred Tarski," in John A. Garrity and Mark C. Carnes, eds., *American National Biography* (New York: Oxford, 1999), Vol. 21, 330–32; Anita Burdman Feferman and Solomon Feferman, *Alfred Tarski: Life and Logic* (Cambridge: Cambridge University Press, 2004).

Tatrzański Orzeł (The Tatra Eagle). The folklore quarterly of the **Polish Highlanders Alliance** was established in Passaic, NJ, in August 1947 and was later edited in Hasbrouck Heights. Published in Polish, with some articles in English, the publication was originally titled *Tatrzanin*, but was renamed *Tarzański Orzeł*. The focus of the journal is cultural life of the Tatra Highlanders in the United States, but it also includes information from the **Podhale** and Tatra regions in Poland. Founded by Jan Władysław Gromada, who served as editor-in-chief from 1947 to 1951, it has been edited since then by the brother and sister team of **Thaddeus Vladimir Gromada** and Janina Gromada Kedron. Its contents usually include sections on literature (poetry and prose), Podhale history, interviews, and a review of publications on subjects related to the Tatra Highlanders. The masthead of the journal is decorated with a woodcut portraying the flight of an eagle over the Tatra Mountains and dancing highlanders designed by Wincenty Gawron. —*Adam A. Zych*

SOURCES: Zygmunt Alt, "Góralskie skrzydła czyli o jubileuszu 45-lecia 'Tatrzańskiego Orła,'" *Dziennik Związkowy*, No. 217 (1992); Anna Brzozowska-Krajka, "Narodowość i etniczność w publicystyce polonijnej na przykładzie 'Tatrzańskiego Orła,'" in T. Żabski, ed., *Literatura i kultura popularna* (Wrocław: Uniwersytet Wrocławski, 1997), Vol. 6; Zuzanna Bednarek, "Życie społeczne i kulturalne górali z Passaic w latach 1947–1989 w świetle 'The Tatra Eagle,'" in A. Judycka, Z. Judycki, H.W. Żaliński, eds., *Podhalanie w świecie. Historia i współczesność* (Kraków: Wydawnictwo Naukowy AP, 2005).

Taubenschlag, Rafał (b. Przemyśl, Poland, May 8, 1881; d. Warsaw, Poland, June 25, 1958). Professor of law. Taubenschlag earned his doctorate in law from the Jagiellonian University in Kraków in 1904 and served in the Polish court system from 1904 to 1919, while also lecturing in Roman law beginning in 1913. In 1919 he accepted a professorship in Roman law at the Jagiellonian University, rising to dean of the Philosophy Department by 1939. With the outbreak of World War II he fled via Romania to France where he lectured at the Aix-Marseille University in Aix-en-Provence before migrating to the U.S. in October 1940. As a visiting professor of law at the New School for Social Research in New York, he was actively involved in founding the **Polish Institute of Arts and Sciences** and served as its initial associate director (1942–45). In 1942 he moved to Columbia University (1942–45). An authority on Roman and Canon Law, he published some eighty monographs on Roman, Grecian, and Medieval Polish law, with some of his works being published in Polish, English, French, German, and Italian editions. His most recognized contribution to the study of ancient law is *The Law of Greco-Roman Egypt in the Light of the Papyri 332 B.C.–640 A.D.* (1944). While at Columbia he also founded the *Journal of Juristic Papyrology* in 1946. In 1947 he returned to Poland to become chair of the Department of Ancient Law at the University of Warsaw. In 1954 the Polish government awarded him its Commander's Cross with Star. —*James S. Pula*

SOURCES: Francis Bolek, ed., *Who's Who in Polish America* (New York: Harbinger House, 1943); *The Journal of Juristic Papyrology, Founded by Rafael Taubenschlag* (Warsaw: Polish Scientific Publishers, 1971); Rafał Taubenschlag, Iza Biezunska-Malowist, Henryk Kapiszewski, Józef Modrzejewski, *Symbolae Raphaeli Taubenschlag Dedicatae* (Warsaw: Ossolineum, 1956); Adolf Berger, *Rafal Taubenschlag, 1881–1958* (New York: Polish Institute of Arts and Sciences, 1958 [see also *The Polish Review*, Vol. 3, no. 3 (1958)]).

Tenerowicz, Rudolph Gabriel (b. Budapest, Hungary, June 14, 1890; d. Hamtramck, Michigan, August 31, 1963). Physician, Congressman. Migrating to the United States with his parents in 1892, Tenerowicz attended the Polish **SS. Cyril and Methodius Seminary** in Orchard Lake (MI), St. Bonaventure College in Allegany (NY), and St. Ignatius College in Chicago (IL) before obtaining his medical degree from Loyola University in Chicago (1912). He practiced medicine in Chicago (1912–23) where he was a member of the Chicago Medical Society, the Cook County Medical Association, and the American Medical Association. Active in Polish organizational matters, he was elected **censor** of the **Polish Union of America**. During World War I he served as a first lieutenant in the U.S. Army Medical Corps (September 10, 1917–December 26, 1918), after which, as a captain, he was a member of the Medical Reserve Corps (1919–34). After completing a postgraduate course in surgery at Illinois Post Graduate School, Tenerowicz moved to **Hamtramck**, MI, in 1923. There, he was elected mayor (1928–32; 1936–38) but was convicted of conspiracy to operate houses of ill-fame in Hamtramck in 1931. The Michigan Supreme Court upheld the conviction on appeal in *People v. Tenerowicz* (March 6, 1934). After serving a nine-month prison sentence, he was pardoned by Governor William Comstock on grounds that the prosecution was politically motivated. Following this he served as a member of the Wayne County Board of Supervisors for seven years and was an upset winner over Congressman **George G. Sadowski** in the primary election on September 13, 1938. He was subsequently elected as a Democrat to represent Michigan's First Congressional District encompassing Detroit and Hamtramck to the 76th and 77th Congresses (January 3, 1939–January 3, 1943). He introduced House Joint Resolution 430 on January 16, 1940, to provide $15 million to relieve starvation and prevent epidemics in Poland. A pro-labor advocate, he argued on January 23, 1940, that attacks on the Wagner Act and the National Labor Relations Board were an attempt to weaken New Deal reforms. He also gave an impassioned speech in favor of aid to the Polish people in German-occupied Poland on February 6, 1940. He was an unsuccessful candidate for renomination to his former congressional seat in 1942, and for election as a Republican in 1948, 1950, 1952, 1954.— *Thomas Duszak*

SOURCES: Bruce A. Ragsdale and Kathryn Allamong Jacob, eds., *Biographical Directory of the United States Congress 1774–1989* (Washington, D.C.: U.S. Government Printing Office, 1989), 1921; *Michigan Reports: Cases Decided in the Supreme Court of Michigan*, Vol. 266 (1935); *New York Times*, January 3, 1939, 10.

Thaddeus Kościuszko National Memorial. The smallest national park in the Untied States is a building located at 301 Pine Street on the corner of 3rd Street in Philadelphia, PA. In this house, located in the Society Hill section of the city, **Thaddeus Kościuszko** rented an apartment from Ann Relf during his visit to the United States between August 1797 and May 1798. It was in this building that Kościuszko met frequently with Thomas Jefferson, discussing politics and cementing a bond that would last for the rest of their lives. Still suffering from the effects of wounds he received during the Kościuszko Insurrection in Poland in 1794, the Pole spent most of his time recuperating while receiving a variety of prominent visitors with whom he discussed everything from memories of the American Revolution to science and politics. The building is now the Thaddeus Kościuszko National Memorial, administered by the National Park Service as part of the Independence Hall National Park. First listed on the National Register of Historic Places on December 18, 1970, it was authorized as a national memorial on October 21, 1972. Opened in 1976 and renovated in 2008, it contains period furniture and interpretive materials on Kosciuszko's life.— *James S. Pula*

SOURCE: Thaddeus Kosciuszko National Memorial web site (http://www.nps.gov/thko/).

Theater, Polish American. The subject of Polish theater outside of Poland has, until recent years, received little treatment from historians except for the period of the Second World War. This can be partially explained because Polish ethnic theater in the U.S. was largely the creation of a single generation. Its creators seldom left written records, while their descendants, most of whom did not preserve their ancestral language, displayed little interest in cultivating their own ethnic theatrical tradition. Another reason for the limited interest in Polish ethnic theater among scholars has been the widespread belief that it comprised only relatively uninteresting, occasional amateur productions of local character. This characterization was supported by English language publications that promoted the stereotypical view that Polish ethnic theater consisted of productions based on Polish folk traditions. Thus, researchers tended to accept this view without criticism and, with the exception of ethnographers studying folk traditions, to avoid the subject.

In fact, Polish ethnic culture in America was an extremely complex phenomenon. The analysis of source materials proves that it manifested itself in rich variety. This variety derives from the origin of Polish migration itself: early migration was primarily political in nature with a large percentage of intelligentsia; between 1880 and 1920 it was largely comprised of farmers and agricultural workers migrating for economic reasons; and following World War II it was once again dominated by political migration and the intelligentsia. What was overlooked in this general scheme was that the economic immigration between 1880 and 1920 also included members of the intelligentsia. Although they were not especially numerous, they were important figures in the organization of cultural life in the Polish ethnic communities that developed.

The beginnings of Polish American theater were indeed associated with occasional amateur productions. These were not, however, purely popular theater as the stereotype would have it; rather, most of these, regardless of whether they were the creations of independent drama or literary societies or were sponsored by patriotic or workers organizations, were based on a repertoire of drama of acknowledged literary value. About 1890, the Polish ethnic theater movement became partly subordinated to ethnic religious parishes. In Chicago, for example, over twenty different societies staged their performances in a hall on Bradley Street that was owned by St. Stanisław Kostka Parish and adapted for theatrical purposes. The most influential person in **Polonia** theater at that time was **Szczęsny Zahajkiewicz**, a dramatist, director, and actor who had been brought from Poland by the **Resurrectionist** Order for that purpose. Other Polish ethnic parishes followed this example with priests giving their support to the amateur theater movement. Since the parish at that time formed the center of ethnic community activity, theater became a central activity of ethnic cultural life with important ideological significance for both religious and patriotic reasons. Additionally, the ethnic theater became an important means of publicizing Polish culture to American society through semi-theatrical events such as street parades organized by members of amateur troupes.

While much of the theatrical movement during this time was associated with religious parishes, another element existed independent of clerical influence. Local lodges of the **Polish National Alliance** and other labor and patriotic ethnic organizations sponsored theater groups, including troupes of socialists who were generally excluded from religiously affiliated theaters. These productions were often financial successes, the proceeds from which were used for the benefit of the sponsoring organizations. The value of the property owned by amateur troupes — often including halls, libraries, costumes, scenery, and related items — and income from performances and accompanying events — dances, balls, rallies, commemorations, and so on — often amounted to many thousands of dollars per year.

The repertoire of the various theater groups was diverse. Parish troupes performed mainly religious, folk, patriotic plays, and melodramas. Independent theatrical and literary circles tended to choose plays of recognized literary value. The most controversial repertoire was that of the socialists, who usually chose plays dealing with workers' problems or national patriotic dramas, with the latter frequently being interpreted differently than similar topics presented in parish theaters. Regardless of their ideological differences, nearly all theatrical troupes arranged their repertoire according to the same unwritten rule: they preferred to perform plays by Polish authors. A great number of such plays were published in America, and some were also written by Poles in the U.S. Foreign plays were rarely produced, and then only by literary circles and the socialists. Folk and patriotic dramas were the most popular themes, as is easily understood if one takes into consideration the social background of the audience.

Some differences also existed between the various Polish American communities that can be seen reflected in the performances. Chicago was home to the richest theatrical life, but numerous theaters were also active in New York City and its surrounding area, Detroit, Buffalo, Cleveland, Pittsburgh, Milwaukee, and Newark (NJ). Performances were less frequent in smaller communities because of the much smaller size and consequently the ability to support multiple theaters, but the existing documents prove that productions were staged in these smaller communities in dozens places all over America.

Polish American theater can generally be divided into five segments. The first and least known period can be labeled the "Period of Amateur Troupes Before 1906." This period was dominated by amateur ethnic theater, a unique tradition at the time. The second period can be described as a time "Between Amateur and Professional Theater." This was generally characteristic for the period between the 1906 and 1910 which was especially rich in new initiatives. In 1906 the first semi-professional theater group came into being in Chicago. It had its roots in the amateur movement, but was organized as an independent theater society governed by its own statutes. The actors of this theater, labeled proudly "National" and "Polish," were divided into categories and paid by the theater. Performances took place in hired theater halls, and a dramatic school was organized in conjunction with the theater. The National Theater existed for only about two years (1906–08). Although

some historians ascribed its demise to financial troubles, it is more likely that it suffered from competition with the amateur parish theaters and a lack of support by priests or important Polish ethnic organizations.

After the demise of the National Theater a new, semi-professional troupe came into being in Chicago. Initially called the "Society of Lovers of Polish Theater," it later changed its name to the "Juliusz Słowacki Society of Lovers of Polish Theater." The organizer was an immigrant from Kraków, **Tadeusz Eminowicz**. The group used the St. Stanisław Kostka parish theater hall, but its repertoire was independent of the parish's influence. The basic difference between this theater and the amateur groups was twofold. Its members were experienced players, and, more importantly, its productions appeared with regularity, offering a new premiere every two weeks. The group was active until 1910.

The National Theater and the Society of Lovers of Polish Theater were examples of the tendency of the Polish ethnic theater movement to become professional and independent of parish influence and control during this second phase. Beginning in the closing years of the nineteenth century, attempts were made to systematically train the actors, organize drama competitions, and even to build a presentable Polish American theater in Chicago. In 1901 the idea was strongly supported by the famed Shakespearean actress **Helena Modjeska** (Modrzejewska), her son **Ralph Modjeski**, and the noted pianist **Józef Hofmann**. The fact that this goal was never realized may

have been due to the hostility of the clergy, especially the **Resurrectionists**, who feared the loss of their ideological influence on the audience, as well as potential financial losses.

The third period in the development of the Polish ethnic theater movement can be labeled "Troupes and Performances in the Years 1907–1939." It encompasses a time when the movement had already split into professional and amateur productions. Amateur theaters were still sporadic and mainly organized by parish groups. The most ambitious repertoire, however, was that of independent groups which called themselves literary-dramatic societies or circles. They were managed by people like Jan Kochanowicz and **Karol Wachtl** who had knowledge of both dramatic literature and stagecraft. At the same time, the professional groups developed a new organizational form which was a logical consequence of previous experiences which proved that Polish American audiences were capable of giving sufficient financial support to groups that performed regularly. For the actors who played in such groups, theater automatically became the sole or primary source of their income. The theater became their place of professional work.

The first Polish American professional theaters were founded in Chicago in 1910 with performances taking place in a hall belonging to a German, but his Lola Theater was adapted mainly for movies and was not a comfortable place for actors. A year later, in 1911, Marcin Moneta, a photographer, opened the first theater owned by a Pole. His Kościuszko Theater was home to a group founded by Tadeusz

The Modjeska Theater, Milwaukee, ca. 1910 (*UWM*).

Eminowicz. A year later, the Theater of Premiers, the first building constructed solely as a Polish American theater, opened. In the succeeding years, new ethnic theaters opened in Detroit, Buffalo, Cleveland, Newark (NJ), and Milwaukee, including the sumptuous Fredro Theater built by the Eminowicz family in Detroit. These theaters were not subsidized by parishes or other organizations, their existence depending solely on the audience's attendance, which was in turn determined by the attractiveness of the program. Thus the program had to be of a popular nature addressed to the general public which was not well educated and did not demand an ambitious repertoire. Usually plays were combined with movies and songs. One performance each week was generally devoted to regular drama and there were no movies shown on that evening.

The period between the wars, at least until the Great Depression, was a time of extensive

development of professional theaters. The most ambitious were the initiatives undertaken by Tadeusz and Stefania Eminowicz, Stanisław Zenon, and Gertruda Wachtel. Their theaters were the most characteristic of the Polish-American professional theater. The activities of Władysław and Teodozja Ochrymowicz and Ludwik Kowalski, who were active in New York, ought to be regarded as a specific variety of this type of theater. The basic difference was that they had an ambition to stage not only dramas, but operettas and even operas, while another significant difference was that their Polish Theater was an itinerant group. Some of these actors were invited to perform in Poland, and Kowalski, an impresario of actors and sportsmen, was even successful in staging Polish national operas by Stanisław Moniuszko. Among his productions were *Halka*, *Straszny dwór* (The Haunted Manor) and others which included performances by outstanding singers from Poland.

Kowalski's initiatives were also connected with the activity of two prominent orchestra conductors, Władysław Grigajtis and Jerzy Bójanowski. The latter was one of the most talented Polish conductors of his generation. It was thanks to him that Moniuszko's operas were included in the program of the Civic Opera House in Chicago, some of them with Jan and Ladis Kiepura [see **Jan Kiepura**] and other internationally famous opera stars.

The fourth developmental period may be defined as the "War Years 1939–1945." This was a time when numerous artists from Poland were trapped in the U.S. by the outbreak of the war or arrived after having fled the violence in Europe. These new arrivals tended to organize their own theater groups including the Polish Artists Theater in New York. This group, harboring professional ambitions, presented a new repertoire based in part on spectacles inspired by wartime themes. The fates of its members illus-

trate the demarcation between emigrant and ethnic theater. Following the war, some of those involved in the wartime emigrant theater returned to Poland, while others decided to stay in America but usually did not identify themselves with the established Polish-American community.

The fifth period in the development of the Polish American theater is the "Postwar Years 1945–1980." During these years numerous new initiatives were undertaken, with most of them originating with a new wave of postwar emigration. These included the Ref-Ren Theater established by **Feliks Konarski** in Chicago, Nasza Reduta established by L. Krzemienski and his wife, also in Chicago, and theaters established by Lydia Pucinska, W. Zbierzowska Frydrych, and others. As the activities of the older theaters owned by representatives of the previous emigration gradually declined, new groups founded by the wartime and post-war emigration rose to prominence. Their social backgrounds differed considerably from members of the older Polish ethnic community originating in the emigration at the turn of the century. Yet, in the postwar years Polish ethnic theater was not able to maintain its old status of a professional, repertory theater. Its historic role began to yield to other forms of Polish ethnic culture. Of the two major forms of Polish ethnic theatrical productions, only the amateur form exhibited continued vitality in the postwar years. One of the most successful of these amateur groups operated in Buffalo (NY) where some eighty performers representing varied generations staged over a dozen different plays in church halls for audiences ranging up to more than a thousand people. Much of its success was due to its director, Kazimierz Braun, a well known theater artist in Poland before his migration to America.

Finally, one might label the years following the imposition of martial law in Poland as "The Years After 1980" since this period saw the beginning of a new wave of well-educated immigrants fleeing the communist crackdown. Included in this group were some professional actors who attempted to found theater groups in the New York metropolitan area, Chicago, and some of the other larger Polish communities. Most had no lasting success.—*Emil Orzechowski*

SOURCES: Emil Orzechowski, *Teatr polonijny w Stanach Zjednoczonych* (Polish Theater in the United States; Wrocław, Ossolineum, 1989); Karol Wachtl, *Polonja w Ameryce* (Philadelphia: Karol Wachtl, 1944); Arthur L. Waldo, *Stefania Eminowicz* (Chicago: A. L. Waldo, 1937); Stanley L. Cuba, "Polish Amateur Theatricals in America: Colorado as a Case Study," *Polish American Studies*, Vol. 38, no. 1 (1981), 23–49; Matthew J. Strumski, "The Beginnings of the Polish American Theatre," *Polish American Studies*, Vol. 4,

A poster announcing a performance of Maxim Gorky's "Lower Depths" at the Teatr Polski (*UWM*).

no. 1–2 (1947), 31–36; Artur L. Waldo, "Polish-American Theatre," in Maxine Seller, ed., *Ethnic Theatre in the United States* (Westport, CT: Greenwood, 1983), 387–417; Natalie Kunka, "The Amateur Theatre Among the Poles," in *Poles of Chicago, 1837–1939* (Chicago: Polish Pageant, 1937), 67–90.

Tochman, Gaspard (Kacper Tochman; b. Łętownia, Poland, 1797; d. Mattaponi, Virginia, December 20, 1880). Attorney, Polonia activist. During the November Uprising (1830–31) Tochman served as a second lieutenant in the Polish forces, although he later claimed to have been a major and to have been awarded the prestigious *Virtuti Militari* decoration. With the failure of the revolt he fled to France, and then in 1837 to the U.S. where he became a naturalized citizen in 1841. Between 1840 and 1844, he traveled throughout the U.S. delivering over one hundred speeches in support of the Polish cause to audiences including several state legislatures. Despite these efforts on Poland's behalf, he seems not to have been very involved in the Polish exile organizations in America. He was the leading force behind the establishment of the **Polish Slavonian Literary Association** in New York in 1846, an attempt to promote knowledge and the history, literature, and scientific achievement of the Slavic people among the American public. The organization grew rapidly to more than 200 members, including such leading Americans as the historian Jared Sparks, editor and publisher of the New York *Daily Tribune* Horace Greeley, U.S. Attorney General Reverdy Johnson, Secretary of the Treasury Levi Woodbury, poet and editor of the New York *Evening Post* William Cullen Bryan, New York political leader William H. Seward, and future presidential candidate Samuel Tilden. In 1845 he passed law examinations in New York and Maryland, after which he practiced law in Albany (NY) and Washington, D.C.

He was admitted to practice before the U.S. Supreme Court in the same year he began practice and represented the heirs of **Tadeusz Kościuszko** in the adjudication of the Revolutionary hero's American will before the highest court until protests from the Russian Minister to the U.S. forced him to relinquish involvement to two other American attorneys. When he was unsuccessful in obtaining a consular or other government appointment from the presidential administrations of James Buchanan and Abraham Lincoln, in May 1861 he offered his services to the infant Confederate government in Montgomery, AL. Under the impression that he had the approval of the Confederate government, Tochman opened an office in New Orleans where he issued a call to arms addressed to "Fellow-Countrymen of the Old World." In only six weeks he

Gaspard Tochman, 1860s (*PMA*).

had enlisted 1,415 men of foreign birth and 28 born in the U.S. into two regiments that would be known as the "**Polish Brigade**"— the 14th and 15th Louisiana Infantry Regiments. The units went on to serve with great distinction in the Army of Northern Virginia under the command of Gen. Robert E. Lee. Few of the men were actually Polish, the majority being Irish, French, and German.

Convinced that he was entitled to the rank of brigadier general for his efforts, he spurned the offered rank of colonel and settled into private life where he carried on a lengthy campaign in a vain attempt to obtain compensation for his efforts from the Confederate government. These difficulties notwithstanding, in 1863 he offered to raise for Confederate service thousands of Polish volunteers from among Poles exiled in France and other European countries. Poles in the North and Europe were dismayed by his allegiance to the South. The Polish Democratic Society branches in France and England each adopted resolutions of censure and called upon him to explain his support for the South. Following the war he attempted to found a Polish colony in Spotsylvania County, Virginia, but the effort failed.—*James S. Pula*

SOURCES: Maria J. E. Copson-Niećko, "The Poles in America From the 1830's to 1870's: Some Reflections on the Possibilities of Research," in Frank Mocha, ed., *Poles in America: Bicentennial Essays* (Stevens Point, WI: Worzalla Publishing Company, 1978), 45–302; Maria J. E. Copson-Niećko, "The Polish Political Emigration in the United States 1831–1864," *The Polish Review*, Vol. XIX, No. 3–4 (1974), 45–82; Florian Stasik, *Polish Political Emigrés in the United States of America, 1831–1864* (Boulder, CO: East European Monographs, 2002); Béla Vasvady, Jr., "The 'Tochman Affair': An Incident in Mid-Nineteenth Century Hungarian Emigration to America," *The Polish Review*, Vol. 25, no. 3–4 (1980), 12–27; Sigmund H. Uminski, "Two Polish Confederates," *Polish American Studies*, Vol. XXIII, no. 2 (1966), 65–81.

Tomasik, Edward J. (b. Chicago, Illinois, November 11, 1921; d. Cuhahy, Wisconsin,

August 2, 2004). Optometrist, Polonia activist. After service in World War II, Tomasik relocated to the Milwaukee area where he became involved in the **Polish American Congress** in the mid 1960s and became a tireless advocate of a strategy he called the "Wisconsin Plan." In short, this plan involved an effort to reach, organize, and mobilize Polish-Americans in large numbers around the country and to engage them in communicating directly with their elected representatives in Washington, D.C., on matters pertaining to Poland and **Polonia**. Repeatedly rebuffed in his efforts to win approval for his proposal by **Charles Rozmarek**, the president of the Polish American Congress until 1968, Tomasik backed **Aloysius Mazewski** for leadership of the Congress in the expectation that he would be favorable to his Wisconsin Plan idea. He proved to be mistaken, and as a result became one of Mazewski's sharpest critics. From 1976 to 1982 Tomasik served as a PAC national vice president and president of its Wisconsin State Division for one term. Among his other activities was chairmanship of the statewide Polonia committee formed to commemorate the life and work of the astronomer Nicolaus Copernicus (Mikołaj Kopernik) in 1973, the 500th anniversary year of his birth. Here his efforts went beyond directing a giant banquet honoring Copernicus and extended to organizing groups of teachers and engineers for the purpose of expanding knowledge of Copernicus in the wider community. For more than twenty years, Tomasik was a voice of the "loyal opposition" in his constant, and often emotion-filled, appeals for greater Polish American Congress grassroots activism on issues concerning Poland and Polonia.—*Donald E. Pienkos*

SOURCE: Donald E. Pienkos, *For Your Freedom Through Ours: Polish American Efforts on Poland's Behalf, 1863–1991* (Boulder, CO: East European Monographs, 1991).

Toski, Bob (Robert John Algustoski; b. Haydenville, Massachusetts, September 18, 1926; d.–). Golfer, golf instructor. The son of Polish immigrants, Toski won five events on the Professional Golfers' Association tour and was the top PGA money winner in 1954, the same year in which he won the World Championship of Golf. After retiring as a player, he became a noted golf teacher credited with developing such professionals as Tom Kite, Bruce Crampton, Jane Blalock, Pat Bradley, Bruce Devlin, and Judy Rankin. He has written or produced numerous instructional books and videos on the sport. Toski is a member of the World Golf Teachers Hall of Fame, and in 1987 he was inducted into the **National Polish-American Sports Hall of Fame**.—*Neal Pease*

SOURCE: Bob Toski and Dick Aultman, *Bob Toski's Complete Guide to Better Golf* (New York: Atheneum, 1977).

Totenberg, Roman (b. Łodz, Poland, January 1, 1911; d.—). Musician, teacher. Beginning his musical education in Russia, Totenberg continued his studies at the Warsaw Conservatory (1921–25). In 1923, at the age of 11, he debuted as a soloist with the Warsaw Philharmonic Orchestra. Between 1925 and 1929 he was a student at the Fryderyk Chopin Higher School of Music in Warsaw, with Mieczysław Michałowicz (violinist) and Witold Maliszewski (composer, teacher of Witold Lutosławski), graduating with a Gold Medal. His post-graduate education included a year of studies with Karl Flesch in Berlin (1929) and five years (1933–38) with Romanian composer George Enescu and French conductor Pierre Monteux in Paris. Beginning in 1925 he performed as a soloist with orchestras around the world, his first performances in London and New York dating to 1932. In the same year he won the International Mendelssohn Prize in Berlin, later moving to Paris where he joined the international circle of musicians and artists and befriended Pierre Monteaux, Karol Szymanowski, Darius Milhaud, and others. In 1938 he moved to the U.S., receiving American citizenship in 1943. In 1947 he became a music professor and chairman of the strings department at the Music Academy of the West in Santa Barbara, California. He taught at Mannes College (1951–57), the Peabody Conservatory of Music, the Aspen School of Music (1950–60), and Boston University (1961–78) where he directed the strings department. He gave regular master classes at Aspen, Salzburg, and the Tanglewood Festivals. In 1978 he became director of the Longy School of Music in Newton, Massachusetts, a post he held until 1985.

In 1934–36 Totenberg went on concert tours with Karol Szymanowski, and in 1937 he performed with **Artur Rubinstein** in South America. As a soloist, he appeared with the major orchestras of the world, conducted, among others, by **Leopold Stokowski**, **Artur Rodzinski**, Grzegorz Fitelberg, Witold Rowicki, Jan Krenz, and Antoni Wit. Totenberg premiered works by Hindemith, William Schuman, and Darius Milhaud. His rich repertoire included over thirty concertos and numerous solo and chamber pieces, ranging from Bach to the contemporary. His recordings appeared on Deutsche Grammophon, Telefunken, Philips, and other labels. In the first decade of the 2000s, Shar Company has reissued his Bach recordings and other collections on CD. In 1988, the Polish government recognized his contributions to Polish culture with the Medal of Merit, and in 1996 he received the Metcalf Cup and Prize, the highest teaching honor at Boston University.—*Maja Trochimczyk*

SOURCE: Martin Bernheimer, "Roman Totenberg," *New Grove Dictionary of Music and Musicians*, online (2000).

Towarzystwo Demokratyczne Wygnańców Polskich w Ameryce *see* **Democratic Society of Polish Exiles in America.**

Traditions *see* **Customs, Polish American.**

Tramiel, Jack (Idek Trzmiel; b. Łódź, Poland, December 13, 1928; d.—). Entrepreneur, computer pioneer. Following the German invasion of Poland in 1939, he was sent with his family to the Auschwitz concentration camp where he was selected for forced labor in Ahlem, near Hanover, Germany. Tramiel migrated to the U.S. in 1947 and joined the U.S. Army where he learned how to repair office equipment. After leaving the army he opened an office repair shop in New York City which he named Commodore Portable Typewriter. His business went public in 1962 and began marketing the Commodore 64, the first mass-produced desktop computer designed for home use. Tramiel left his company in 1984 to found Tramiel Technology Ltd., which he hoped would take a leading role in designing the next generation of personal home computers. Later that same year his new company purchased the Consumer Division of Atari, Inc., and renamed his merged enterprises Atari Corporation. He sold his interest in the new company in 1996.—*James S. Pula*

SOURCE: Brian Bagnall, *On the Edge: The Spectacular Rise and Fall of Commodore* (Winnipeg: Variant Press, 2005).

Trammell, Alan (b. Garden Grove, California, February 21, 1958; d.—). Baseball player. Alan Trammell was a standout major league shortstop for twenty seasons from 1977 to 1996, batting .285 lifetime with 185 home runs. Trammell played his entire career with the Detroit Tigers of the American League, and he and longtime second base partner Lou Whitaker played more games as teammates than any other pair in major league annals. A right handed hitter, he was named to six American League All-Star squads, and won four Gold Gloves for defensive excellence as a shortstop. Trammell enjoyed his best season in 1987, when he finished second in voting as AL Most Valuable Player, and was, by the statistical methods of the *Total Baseball* encyclopedia, the second best player in the league. His Tigers reached postseason play twice, and won the world championship in 1984, when Trammell was chosen as Most Valuable Player of the World Series. Since retiring as a player, he has managed and coached in the major leagues. He was inducted into the National Polish-American Sports Hall of Fame in 1998.—*Neal Pease*

SOURCE: Donald Honig, *The Greatest Shortstops of All Time* (Dubuque, IA: William C. Brown, 1992).

Trcziyulny, Charles (b. Poland, date unknown; d. Bellefonte, Pennsylvania, July 9, 1851). Surveyor. Trcziyulny was apparently educated as a military engineer before migrating to Philadelphia in 1794 where he obtained employment as a surveyor of land claims. In this capacity he laid out the plans for the town of Phillipsburgh where he later managed a grist and saw mill and was proprietor of a general store. Trcziyulny surveyed Osceola Mills, and in 1809 was named deputy surveyor for Clearfield and McKean Counties. In 1814 he was named one of three commissioners to determine the boundaries of Rush Township, and in 1817 journeyed north to New York where he joined Robert Brooke as surveyors for a canal that would connect the Tioga River with Seneca Lake. Appointed to the Pennsylvania Board of Canal Commissioners, he was instrumental in selecting the route for the Pennsylvania Canal from Pittsburgh to Philadelphia. Entering politics, Trcziyulny was appointed postmaster of Bellefonte where he owned 329 acres of land, and was then elected Justice of the Peace for Center County in 1833.—*James S. Pula*

SOURCE: Joseph A. Borkowski, "Pennsylvania's Polish Surveyor," *Polish American Studies*, Vol. 21, no. 2 (1964), 118–22.

Tripucka, Frank (b. Bloomfield, New Jersey, December 8, 1927; d.—). Football player. The son of a Polish immigrant father, Tripucka played quarterback as a collegian at Notre Dame from 1946–48, and was named All-American as a senior. After being chosen in the first round of the professional draft in 1949, he played quarterback for fifteen seasons for six teams in the National Football League, the Canadian Football League, and the American Football League. As a member of the Denver Broncos, Tripucka played in the AFL Pro Bowl in 1962. His son, Kelly Tripucka, became a noted college and professional basketball player. Tripucka was inducted into the National Polish-American Sports Hall of Fame in 1997.—*Neal Pease*

SOURCE: "Frank Tripucka," National Polish-American Sports Hall of Fame website, www.polish-sportshof.com.

Tripucka, Kelly (b. Glen Ridge, New Jersey, February 16, 1959; d.—). Basketball player. Tripuka was a three-year starter on his high school basketball team, earning First

Team All-State and All-American honors twice. He went on to star at the University of Notre Dame where he led the Irish to the NCAA Tournament in each of his four years. After his graduation in 1984, Tripucka was chosen by the NBA's Detroit Pistons. With the Pistons he proved to be a prolific scorer, but was criticized for poor defensive skills. After the 1984-85 season he was traded to the Utah Jazz for Adrian Dantley, but Tripucka and Jazz head coach Frank Layden did not get along well. At the time, Layden was building the Jazz offense around budding stars Karl Malone and John Stockton, with the result that Tripucka saw less and less playing time. In the NBA Expansion Draft in 1988, the Jazz left Tripucka unprotected and the new Charlotte Hornets selected him. During his time with the Hornets he was among the team's leading scorers. Tripucka is one of five Detroit Pistons players to have scored forty or more points in a playoff game. After his retirement as a player, he became a color commentator for the Detroit Pistons televised games on FSN Detroit and WKBD for eight seasons (1993–2001). In 2001 he took a full-time radio job with the New Jersey Nets. From 2003 to 2005 he was the color commentator for Nets games on the YES Network. In 2008 he joined the New York Knicks' MSG Broadcast team. He is also a scout for the New York Knicks. In 2000, Tripucka was named to the National Polish-American Sports Hall of Fame.—*Patricia Finnegan*

SOURCES: National Polish-American Sports Hall of Fame website, www.polishsportshof.com; "Nets Pick Tripucka as Radio Analyst," *New York Times*, September 11, 2001.

Trumka, Richard (b. Nemacolin, Pennsylvania, July 24, 1949; d.—). Labor leader. Trumka was born in a small Pennsylvania mining town. While attending Pennsylvania State University, where he eventually graduated with a Bachelor of Science degree in 1971, he worked in the Jones and Laughlin coal mines near his hometown, sometimes alongside his father Frank, a second-generation miner. In 1974, Trumka earned his law degree from Villanova University and soon joined the legal staff of the United Mine Workers of America (UMWA) in Washington, D.C. He left this position briefly in 1978 to return to the mines; however, within three years, he was elected to the organization's Board of Directors and by 1982, to the office of president of the UMWA—a position he held until 1995. A defining event during Trumka's years in office was the strike against the Pittston Coal Company which has been widely characterized as one of the largest demonstrations of civil labor disobedience in modern history, encompassing

nearly 1,700 workers. In addition to failing to guarantee miner job security, a modest wage increase, and the creation of an Education and Training Trust Fund to subsidize unemployed mine worker retraining or reeducation, the Pittston Coal Company refused to pay into the health and retirement fund created in the 1950s and even terminated vital healthcare and pension benefits to miners. Emerging victorious in the Pittston strike, Trumka's new leadership style and emphasis on community solidarity heralded a period of reform. In 1995, Trumka became Secretary-Treasurer of the American Federation of Labor-Congress of Industrial Organizations (AFL-CIO) and the youngest elected member. Trumka was re-elected four times by 2009 and served on several key committees including the Executive Council, Strategic Approaches Committee, Finance Committee and Capital Stewardship Committee. In 2008, he delivered a ground-breaking speech against racism in the presidential election, becoming the first labor leader to earn more than 500,000 cyberspace viewers on the popular online video website YouTube. In 2009, President Barack Obama appointed Trumka to the President's Economic Recovery Advisory Board (PERAB), tasked with advising Obama on responses to the economic crisis and potential directions for economic policy. Trumka was honored for his continuing work through such distinctions as the Gompers-Murray-Meany Award from the Massachusetts AFL-CIO, the Labor Responsibility Award from the Martin Luther King, Jr., Center for Nonviolent Social Change and The Jewish National Fund Tree of Life Award from the State of Israel.—*Krystyna Cap*

SOURCE: John H. M. Laslett, *The United Mine Workers of America: A Model of Industrial Solidarity?* (University Park, PA: Pennsylvania State University Press, 1996).

Turkiewicz, Stanley (b. Buffalo, New York, March 22, 1898; d. Buffalo, New York, November 8, 1983). Journalist, Polonia activist. Turkiewicz served as city editor of Buffalo's Polish newspaper, ***Dziennik dla Wszystkich*** (Everybody's Daily) until it closed in 1957. He was later managing editor of Buffalo's weekly ***Am-Pol Eagle*** during the 1970s. Long active in the **Polish Roman Catholic Union of America** (PRCUA), Turkiewicz served one term as its president from 1958 to 1962. Earlier, he had worked extensively on behalf of the **Polish American Council** (Rada Polonii Amerykańskiej) and, in the years immediately after World War II, had been responsible, with his wife, for aiding hundreds of displaced Poles in their resettlement in America. Turkiewicz also served as treasurer of the **Polish American Congress** during his term as

PRCUA President. Turkiewicz and his wife spent three years in Warsaw between 1962 and 1965 directing the Rada Polonii's activities in Poland to insure that the materials collected in **Polonia** were properly distributed. A civic activist in Buffalo, he served on the city's Public Library Board of Trustees. He was also an amateur actor.—*Donald E. Pienkos*

SOURCE: John Radzilowski, *The Eagle & the Cross: A History of the Polish Roman Catholic Union of America* (Boulder, CO: East European Monographs, 2003).

Turyści *see* **Wakacjusze.**

Tuwim, Julian (b. Łódź, Poland, September 13, 1894; d. Zakopane, Poland, December 27, 1953). Poet. Born into the assimilated Jewish family of a bank clerk, Tuwim published his first poem, "Prośba" (Request), in *Kurier Warszawski* (Warsaw Courier) in 1912 when he was still in secondary school. In 1917 he withdrew from his law studies after just one year to devote himself entirely to literature and during the 1920s his political sympathies supported Józef Piłsudski. In the next decade these gradually faded as Tuwim was particularly disappointed by the decisions that subjected his poems to censorship and by the anti–Semitic attacks he suffered from the press. Since he could not present his political views, he switched to children's poetry, a genre for which he has been best-known ever since. After the outbreak of World War II, Tuwim fled first to Romania, then through France and Portugal to Brazil, and finally, on May 19, 1941, he arrived in New York City. During the war he came to the conviction that cooperation with the Soviet Union was the only positive solution for the Polish cause. These beliefs resulted in his break with former friends including **Jan Lechoń** and **Kazimierz Wierzyński**, and his collaboration with leaders of the Polish American left including **Oskar Lange**, **Bolesław Gebert**, **Leo Krzycki**, and Stefan Arski. In his speeches delivered at Polish American workers meetings in Detroit, Tuwim mocked the Polish government-in-exile in London, accused all those who criticized the Soviet Union of being fascists, and enthusiastically presented the vision of a People's Poland tightly bound with the USSR. He supported the Union of Polish Patriots organized in Moscow and the Polish Workers' Party that started operating in the Polish territory.

Upon receiving information about the Holocaust, Tuwim appealed to Polish Jews in the U.S. to establish a fund to support Jewish children in Poland. In 1944 he took part in the New York rally commemorating the first anniversary of the Warsaw ghetto uprising. In exile, he wrote one of his most important poems, *Kwiaty Polskie* (Polish Flowers). In June 1946 the poet returned to Poland where he was welcomed by officials, provided with comfortable living conditions, and isolated from the problems of everyday life. As the artistic director of the Teatr Nowy (New Theater) in Warsaw (1947–51), Tuwim presented old, unambitious plays, and took part in mass propaganda events. His publications of this period are rather scarce, but they reveal his admiration for Polish and Soviet communist leaders. Conversely, Tuwim used his influence in the communist hierarchy to lobby for a pardon for Jerzy Kozarzewski, a Polish nationalist underground soldier sentenced to death, organize research on Gypsy culture in Poland, and secure government care for his mentor, the poet Leopold Staff. Tuwim was awarded the city of Łódź literary award in 1928 and in 1949, the Polish PEN-Club award in 1935, an honorary doctorate from the University of Łódź in 1949, and the state award in 1952.—*Joanna Wojdon*

SOURCE: Mariusz Urbanek, *Tuwim* (Wrocław: Wydawn. Dolnośląskie, 2004).

Tworkov, Jack (b. Biała, Poland, August 15, 1900; d. Provincetown, Massachusetts, September 4, 1982). Artist. Tworkov migrated to the United States in 1913 where he studied at Columbia University (1920–23), the National Academy of Design in New York (1923–25), privately with Ross Moffett (1924–25), and at the Art Students League in New York (1925–26). He became a United States citizen in 1928. During the Depression he worked on the U.S. Treasury Department Public Works of Art Project (1934) and the Federal Art Project of the Works Progress Administration (Easel Division, 1935–41). During World War II he served as a tool designer (1942–45). Becoming a member of the New York School in 1949, he shared adjoining studios with Willem de Kooning (1948–53), becoming a noted American abstract expressionist painter and graphic artist. His teaching career included the Fieldston School of Ethical Culture, New York (1931); School of General Studies, Queens College, New York (1948–55); American University, Washington, D.C. (1948–51); Indiana University, Bloomington (1954–55); University of Mississippi, Oxford (1955); Pratt Institute, Brooklyn (1955–58); University of Minnesota, Minneapolis (1957); Yale University (Chairman of the Art Department, 1963–69; Leffingwell Professor of Painting, 1963–69); American Academy, Rome (1972); Dartmouth College, Columbia University (1973); Royal College of Art, London (1974). Tworkov was an artist-in-residence at the American Academy, Rome (1972) and Dart-

mouth College (1973). He was a visiting artist at Black Mountain College, NC (1952); School of Art and Architecture, Yale University (1961); University of Illinois, Urbana (1961); Columbia University, New York (1973); Cooper Union School of Art, New York, and New York Studio School (1975); University of California, Santa Barbara (1976); California State University, Long Beach (1979). Tworkov's work appeared in solo exhibitions in Scotland and various locations around the U.S. Among his honors are an Honorary Degree from the Rhode Island School of Design, Providence (1979); Distinguished Teaching Art Award, College Art Association of America, New York (1976); Painter of the Year Award, Skowhegan School of Painting and Sculpture, ME (1974); Doctor of Humane Letters, Columbia University, New York (1972); Doctor of Fine Arts, Maryland Institute of Art, Baltimore (1971); Fellowship, John Simon Guggenheim Foundation (1970); William A. Clark Prize and Corcoran Gold Medal (1963).—*Stanley L. Cuba*

SOURCES: *Jack Tworkov: Red, White & Blue* (New York: Mitchell-Innes & Nash, Ameringer/Howard/Yohe, 2002); Richard Armstrong and Kenneth Baker, *Jack Tworkov: Paintings 1928–1982* (Philadelphia: Pennsylvania Academy of the Fine Arts; Seattle and London: University of Washington Press, 1987); Andrew Forge, *Jack Tworkov, Fifteen Years of Painting: The Solomon R. Guggenheim Museum, New York* (New York: Solomon R. Guggenheim Museum of Art, 1982); Edward Bryant, *Jack Tworkov* (New York: Whitney Museum of American Art, Frederick A. Praeger, 1964).

Tykociner, Joseph (Józef Tykociński; b. Włocław, Poland, October 5, 1877; d. Urbana, Illinois, June 11, 1969). Engineer. Tykociner grew up in a Polish Jewish family, but left for the U.S. at age eighteen to pursue further studies. In 1897 he went to Germany to study at the Höheres Technisches Institut, after which he moved to England where he obtained a job with Guglielmo Marconi's infant Marconi Company. In 1901 he was present when the first radio signal was transmitted across the Atlantic Ocean. In 1903 he took a position with Telefunken in Berlin, and with the outbreak of the Russo-Japanese War in 1904 he worked with the Russian government to establish radio communication links for their navy. He continued to work for the Russians until the outbreak of the October Revolution when he returned to Poland and served the Polish government during the Russo-Polish War (1919–21). In 1920 he left again for the U.S. where he obtained a position with the Westinghouse Research Laboratory, and the following year accepted a research position at the University of Illinois. His research led directly to his greatest contribution, the addition of sound to motion pictures which he demonstrated publicly for the first time in

1922. In the mid–1920s he began experimenting with radio antennas, work that laid the foundation for the development of radar. He later created a new field of research he labeled "zetetics," the study of the relationship between science and art. In 1964 the National Electronics Conference honored him with its Award of Merit, and in the same year he was further honored by being named a Fellow of the Institute of Electrical and Electronic Engineers.—*James S. Pula*

SOURCES: Joseph T. Tykociner, "Photographic Recording and Photoelectric Reproduction of Sound," *Transactions of the SMPE* (Society of Motion Picture Engineers), No. 16 (1923), 90–119; Edward W. Kellogg, History of Sound Motion Pictures, First Installment," *Journal of the Society of Motion Picture and Television Engineers*, June 1955, 291–302; Sławomir Lotysz, "Joseph Tykociński-Tykociner (1877–1969), Pioneer of Sound on Film," *Gazeta: Newsletter of the American Association for Polish-Jewish Studies*, Vol. 13, no. 3 (2006).

Tyler, Tom (Vincent Markowski; b. Port Henry, NY, August 9, 1903; d. Hamtramck, Michigan, May 3, 1954). Actor. Already a champion boxer and weightlifter, Markowski entered the motion picture industry as a stuntman in silent films in 1924. His career grew quickly, successfully bridging the gap between silent and sound films, when he began to star in the popular western genre. With the advent of sound, his deep voice led to casting in roles as a villain such as the homicidal Luke Plummer in *Stagecoach* (1939) and a hot-tempered strikebreaker in *Talk of the Town* (1942). In 1940 he landed the role of the Mummy in *The Mummy's Hand*, followed by title roles in *The Adventures of Captain Marvel* in 1941 and *The Phantom* in 1943. Increasingly severe rheumatoid arthritis limited his career thereafter to supporting roles as the boxing referee in Abbott and Costello's *Buck Privates*, a soldier in John Ford's *She Wore a Yellow Ribbon*, and several other minor appearances.—*James S. Pula*

SOURCES: Mario DeMarco, *Tom Tyler and George O'Brien: The Herculeses of the Cinema Range* (West Boylston, MA: M. DeMarco, 1986); Mike Chapman, *The Tom Tyler Story: From Cowboy Star to Super Hero* (Newton, IA: Culture House Books, 2005); Buck Rainey, *Heroes of the Range: Yesteryear's Saturday Matinee Movie Cowboys* (Metuchen, NJ: Scarecrow, 1987).

Tyrmand, Leopold (b. Warsaw, Poland, May 16, 1920; d. Fort Myers, Florida, March 19, 1985). Writer, journalist. Born into an assimilated Jewish family, Tyrmand graduated from secondary school in Warsaw in 1938 before journeying to Paris to study architecture. Back in Poland in the summer of 1939, he fled to Wilno when Warsaw surrendered to the Germans. On July 28, 1940, the first of over 140 feature articles that he authored appeared in *Prawda Komsomolska* (Comsomol Truth), an organ of the Communist Alliance of Lithuanian Youth. There is disagreement about whether this job was only a cover for his underground activities, actions for which he was arrested in April 1941 and sentenced to eight years in prison. When Germany attacked the USSR in June 1941, Tyrmand escaped from a train that was about to transport him to Russia. In Wilno, then under German occupation, he volunteered to work in Germany using fake French documents. His jobs included translator, railway worker, attendant, waiter, stoker, and shoeblack in Wiesbaden, Frankfurt, and Vienna. In 1944 he was hired as a steward on a German merchant ship sailing to Norway. He hoped to find a way into neutral Sweden, but upon disembarkation was arrested and sent to a camp in Grini near Oslo. After the war he worked for the International Red Cross in Norway, the Polish press agency Polpress, and the Polish legation in Copenhagen.

In 1946 Tyrmand returned to Warsaw, took a job at Agencja Prasowo-Informacyjna (Press-Information Agency) and launched the first jazz club in post-war Poland. From 1947 to 1950 he worked for the weekly *Przekrój* (The Section), but was fired for his report on the Polish-Soviet boxing contest in Warsaw when he praised Polish fans while the Communist authorities found their behavior anti-Soviet. His collaboration with *Tygodnik Powszechny* (Popular Weekly) ended in 1953 when the regime disbanded the editorial staff of this Catholic weekly. Deprived of any opportunity to publish, Tyrmand earned a living as a private teacher. On January 1, 1954, he started his famous "Diary 1954" which he dropped on April 2, 1954, after signing a contract for the publication of the detective story *Zły* (Evil). Published in December 1955, *Zły* proved a great success not only in Poland, but also abroad, earning the author both fame and money. Tyrmand could now publish again: short stories, press articles, the novel *Filip*, and the first history of jazz in Polish. In 1958, however, the political climate in Poland changed again and Tyrmand's publishing contracts were annulled. Moreover, his application for a passport was rejected until 1964.

When he finally left Poland, he journeyed across Europe and Israel to the U.S., arriving in New York on January 20, 1966. There, he undertook a three-month tour sponsored by the Department of State; his notes of that journey were published by *The New Yorker* in 1967 as "The American Diary." By 1970, Tyrmand, who settled in New York City, wrote more essays for *The New Yorker* comparing the American and Communist ways of life. These essays were published in 1970 as *Notebooks of a Dilettante*. His articles also appeared in the

American and Polish émigré periodicals *Reporter, Interplay, New York Times Magazine, Kultura,* and *Wiadomości.* Tyrmand prepared an English anthology of his articles published in *Kultura* (*Kultura Essays,* 1970), gave lectures on the principles of the Communist system, and was a visiting professor of Slavic literature at Columbia University (1968–69). After 1971 his conservative anti–Communist views did not receive recognition from the mainstream American media. Tyrmand moved to New Canaan, Connecticut, where he published "The Media Shangri-La" (1976) in *American Scholar.* This brought him to the attention of John A. Howard, the rector of Rockford College and director of the Rockford College Conservative Institute, who offered Tyrmand a position as college vice-president. In 1976 Tyrmand moved to Rockford, Illinois, and a year later launched the conservative bimonthly *The Chronicles of Culture,* serving as editor-in-chief until his death. A member of the conservative "Philadelphia Society" since the 1980s, the originator of the Ingersoll Prizes in Literature and the Humanities in 1983, and the secretary of its jury, Tyrmand promoted conservatism in the United States. He was awarded the George Washington Medal by the Freedom Foundation in 1981.—*Joanna Wojdon*

SOURCES: Mariusz Urbanek, *Zły Tyrmand* (Warsaw: ISKRY, 2007); Katarzyna Kwiatkowska and Maciej Gawęcki, *Tyrmand i Ameryka* (Tczew: Wydawn. Bursztyn, 1998).

Tyssowski, John (Jan Józef Tyssowski; b. Tarnów, Poland, March 8, 1811; d. Washington, D.C., April 5, 1857). Polonia activist, government official. After completing studies in philosophy at the University of Lwów, Tyssowski studied law for three years but became actively engaged in the November Uprising (1830–31) against Russia. Although the revolt failed, Tyssowski's revolutionary spirit did not. Barred from further study in Lwów because of his revolutionary activities, he enrolled at the University of Vienna where he completed his law studies, receiving a doctorate in law in 1835. In 1842 he accepted a position as secretary to Prince Władysław Sanguszko, but by 1844 was deeply involved once again in conspiratorial activities in the Tarnów district. Two years later, Tyssowski was named a member of a six-man committee, representing **Galicia,** called together by the revolutionary leader Ludwik Mierosławski. Although the leader was betrayed and arrested in Poznań, Tyssowski proclaimed the Republic of Kraków, with himself as dictator, in February 1846 and proceeded with the doomed rebellion. Driven from the city by Austrian troops, he crossed the border into Saxony where he was discov-

Jan Tyssowski, government official (*PMA*).

ered, arrested, and eventually forced into exile. He arrived in the U.S. in July 1847, becoming a naturalized citizen in 1852. Shortly after his arrival he became associated with the *Deutsche Schnellpost* published in New York City, becoming an assistant editor and in 1848 becoming co-owner of the publication with the noted German liberal Karl Heinzen. In the same year he and fellow exile **Henryk Kałussowski** founded a Polish Committee in New York affiliated with the Paris group. In both of these positions, as a newspaper editor and committee activist, Tyssowski promoted the Polish cause, especially in his attempts to gain the support of the large German American community. Failure of the "Springtime of Nations" led to a decrease in subscriptions since news from Europe was no longer as popular, eventually forcing Tyssowski and Heinzen to sell the newspaper. Moving to Washington, D.C., in 1849, he accepted a position as a draughtsman with the U.S. Congressional Committee on Public Lands. In 1853 he joined the U.S. Patent Office as a Second Class Clerk, rising to Assistant Examiner in 1855. In exile, in addition to his continuing activities on behalf of Poland, he also assisted newly arrived Polish immigrants and fellow exiles.—*James S. Pula*

SOURCE: M. Neomisia Rutkowska, *John Tyssowski* (Chicago: Polish Roman Catholic Union of America, 1943).

Ulam, Adam B. (b. Lwów, Poland, April 8, 1922; d. Boston, Massachusetts, March 8, 2000). Political scientist. Ulam was sent to college in America on August 20, 1939, just days before the outbreak of World War II and two weeks before he was originally scheduled to leave Poland. His father's decision to send him early saved his life — everyone else in his

Adam Ulam (*OLS*).

family perished in the war, except for his older brother Stanisław (see **Stanisław Ulam**), who was also in the U.S. Rejected for military service in World War II due to poor eyesight, Ulam went on to complete his academic studies during the conflict. He began teaching at Harvard University in 1947 and continued there until his retirement in 1992. During his distinguished career he authored twenty books and scores of articles dealing with the Bolshevik Revolution, Soviet politics, and Soviet foreign policy, and became well known as one of America's leading "Kremlinologists." Among Ulam's most significant books are his biography of Joseph Stalin, his foreign policy works on the Soviet Union (most notably *Expansion and Coexistence* and *The Rivals: The United States and Russia Since World War II*), and his many studies of the Russian Revolution and the men who made it, first among them *The Bolsheviks*. Ulam was one of a select number of highly influential American scholars of Polish origin who contributed enormously to defining the threat the Soviet Union posed to U.S. national security. The two other most prominent scholars in this circle are **Zbigniew Brzeziński** and **Richard Pipes**.—*Donald E. Pienkos*

Sources: Wojciech Wierzewski, "Sto Trzydzieska Slynnych Polaków w Ameryce" (Unpublished manuscript in the archives of the University of Wisconsin–Milwaukee, 2000); Mark Kramer, "Memorial Notice: Adam Bruno Ulam (1922–2000)," *Journal of Cold War Studies*, Vol. 2, no. 2 (Spring 2000), 130–32.

Ulam, Stanisław Marcin (b. Lwów, Poland, April 3, 1909; d. Santa Fe, New Mexico, May 13, 1984). Mathematician. An early interest in astronomy and physics led Ulam to teach himself calculus while in secondary school. In 1927 he enrolled at the Lwów Poly-

technic Institute where, before receiving his doctorate in 1933, he collaborated on an algebraic topology problem which led to the Borsuk-Ulam Theorem. This theorem brought him to the attention of Solomon Lefschetz and John von Neumann at Princeton University, leading to an invitation to study at Princeton's Institute for Advanced Study in 1936. Ulam spent the next four years at Princeton and Harvard, returning home each summer. In 1940 he was offered an assistant professorship at the University of Wisconsin. Three years later he obtained American citizenship, receiving in the same year an invitation from John von Neumann to join him and some colleagues working on the Manhattan Project to develop the atomic bomb at Los Alamos, New Mexico. Following the end of the war he accepted a university faculty position and shortly thereafter was struck by encephalitis, requiring major surgery. While recovering, he played the card game solitaire and pondered whether the chances of winning could be determined. In doing this, it occurred to him that simply playing 100 games and counting the victories might produce an adequate approximation of the possible combinations and results. With this insight and his knowledge of an emerging technology, Ulam immediately understood how it could be applied to physics. He used the opportunity of an invitation to return to Los Alamos to discuss a new project to outline the concept to Dr. von Neumann. The emerging technology was the electronic computer which made such calculations possible, and Ulam's insight came to be known as the "Monte Carlo" simulation, now widely used in science and business. The new project was the hydrogen bomb, and Ulam was asked to remain at Los Alamos to work on it. The concept of a hydrogen bomb belonged to Dr. Edward Teller whose design emerged as the favored one in the late 1940s, leading Ulam and Dr. Cornelius Everett to explore the feasibility of the approach mathematically. Their conclusion in early 1950 was that the approach would not work. That conclusion was soon confirmed by computer. The following year, Ulam proposed a variation of Teller's design that was successfully tested in November 1952 as the Teller-Ulam design. He remained at Los Alamos until the mid-1960s, serving as a visiting professor at several leading universities and a consultant in government and industry. He continued work on the Monte Carlo approach he pioneered as it migrated into other fields. He and Everett did pioneering work on nuclear powered spacecraft, work he considered his greatest legacy. Ulam joined the University of Colorado as chair of its mathematics department and served

in that role for ten years before retiring. His accomplishments include several books, over 150 articles published in technical publications, and service on President Kennedy's Scientific Advisory Committee.—*Brian Bonkosky*

Source: Stanisław M. Ulam, *Adventures of a Mathematician* (New York: Charles Scribner's Sons, 1976).

Uminski, Sigmund (Zygmunt Henryk Umiński; b. Jersey City, New Jersey, January 6, 1910; d. Teaneck, New Jersey, March 31, 1975). Journalist, editor, accountant. Uminski studied at St. John's University, Columbia University, New York University, and the Pace Institute's School of Accountancy and Business Administration. In 1935 he became associate editor of New York's *Nowy Swiat* (The New World). An ethnic activist, Uminski served as president of the **Polish American Historical Association** (PAHA), a founder and president of The American Polish Writers Association, founder and president of The Polish Book Guild, Inc., and a life trustee and president of The Polish Publication Society of America. As a journalist, he combined his profession with his interests in **Polonia** as author of *Poland's Contribution to the World's Civilization*, *Tales of Early Poland*, *Poland Discovers America*, and *The Polish Pioneers in Virginia*. As an active member of the PAHA, he was the moving force behind creation of "The Poles in the Americas," a projected series of books detailing the history and culture of Poles in the Western Hemisphere, of which he authored the first two volumes. Additionally, he authored articles in *Nowy Swiat* that provided useful information to Polonia's youth on such topics as "Planning Your Life," "How to Study," and "Making Good in High School." He authored several texts on youth leadership that were published and used by the **Polish National Alliance** (PNA). Active in youth groups, he served as director of the PNA's youth camps in Connecticut, New Jersey, and New York (1933–42). He was elected to the Gallery of Living Catholic Authors (1942), and was a member of the Research Commission on Polish Immigrants organized by the **Polish Institute of Arts and Sciences** in 1943, the origin of the Polish American Historical Association.—*James S. Pula*

Source: Francis Bolek, ed., *Who's Who in Polish America* (New York: Harbinger House, 1943).

Unia Polska w Ameryce *see* **Polish Union of America.**

United States Immigration Commission *see* **Immigration Restriction, Affect on Polish Americans.**

Urban, Matt (Matthew Louis Urbanowicz; b. Buffalo, N.Y., August 25, 1919; d. Holland, Michigan, March 4, 1995). Military officer, Medal of Honor recipient. Urban is the most decorated combat veteran in United States history. He received 29 U.S., French, and Belgian medals, including the Medal of Honor, America's highest decoration for valor. His legendary exploits in the summer of 1944 led the Germans to dub him "the Ghost" for his ability to keep coming back after suffering near-fatal wounds. Urban was wounded seven times. He ended the war at the rank of lieutenant colonel. Although he was recommended for the Medal of Honor during the war, the application was misplaced and Urban did not receive the medal until 1980.

In 1937, Urban was accepted into Cornell University, graduating in 1941. While at Cornell, he joined the Reserve Officer Training Corps. After graduation he received his military training at Fort Bragg, NC, before being assigned to the 2nd Battalion, 60th Infantry Regiment, 9th Infantry Division. Urban participated in combat operations in North Africa and Sicily in 1942 and 1943, gaining promotion to captain and serving as company commander. Following the D-Day invasion in June 1944 he distinguished himself as a combat leader during fighting in Normandy's bocage country. On June 14, near Renouf, France, his unit was pinned down by heavy enemy fire. Urban armed himself with a bazooka, advanced toward the enemy tanks, exposing himself to German fire, and destroyed both tanks. This action rallied his men who counterattacked and routed the enemy. Later that day, he was severely wounded but refused evacuation before he was wounded a second time. While recovering at a hospital in England in mid–July, Urban heard his men had suffered heavy casualties and were badly demoralized. He checked himself out of the hospital and hitchhiked back to his unit. Limping, using a cane, he arrived at the front on July 25. Urban found his men stalled by an enemy strong point. A supporting force of tanks came forward to assist, but the lieutenant in charge of the tanks was killed. Urban dashed though withering enemy fire and despite his leg wound climbed on top of the tank. Manning the tank's external machine gun, he ordered it forward. Completely exposed to enemy fire, he led the attack, placing heavy suppressing fire on enemy positions. Urban's men rallied and overwhelmed the enemy. Wounded again in early August, Urban refused evacuation. He was promoted to commander of the 2nd Battalion on August 6 and wounded again on August 15. On September 3 his battalion led an attack across the Meuse River in Belgium. When the attack faltered, Urban rallied his troops and led the attack on

Lt. Col. Matthew Urban, America's most decorated soldier, at the ceremony awarding him the Medal of Honor (*NARA*).

the river crossing point. Urban was hit in the neck and though bleeding and almost unable to speak he again led his battalion to rout German defenders and secure the position.

Following the war, Urban lived in Holland and Monroe, Michigan. He worked as executive director of the Monroe community center and community recreation director. He was a member of the **Polish Legion of American Veterans**, Veterans of Foreign Wars, American Legion, American Red Cross, Golden Gloves Committee, and Boy Scouts of America. He was buried with full military honors at Arlington National Cemetery. His Medal of Honor citation summed up his remarkable military career: "Captain Urban's personal leadership, limitless bravery, and repeated extraordinary exposure to enemy fire served as an inspiration to his entire battalion. His valorous and intrepid actions reflect the utmost credit on him and uphold the noble traditions of the United States Army."—*John Radzilowski*

SOURCES: Arlington National Cemetery official biography; Anthony Bajdek, "Matt L. Urban: Buffalo's Own Was Most Decorated Soldier in World War II," *Amherst Times* (NY), November 19, 2007; Matt Urban, *The Matt Urban Story: Life and World War II Experiences* (Holland, MI: n.p., 1989); Marzena Ziejka, "The Most Decorated U.S. Soldier of World War II," *Zgoda*, October 15, 2001, 16.

Urbaniak, Michał (b. Warsaw, Poland, June 22, 1943; d.—). Musician, composer. Known for his violin, lyricon, and saxophone skills, Urbaniak began studying music at age six. Widely regarded as a child prodigy, he gave numerous recitals and concerts throughout his native Poland and competed among adults at various music competitions. He was

awarded a prestigious scholarship to study under famed musician David Ojstrach in Moscow, which he declined in order to continue his studies at the Music Secondary School in Łódź. Here he began experimenting with jazz, playing in a Dixieland band called Tiger Rag. Although Urbaniak had been classically trained on the violin and pursued it under the tutelage of Tadeusz Wroński at the Academy of Music in Warsaw, he quickly achieved proficiency on the sax before joining Zbigniew Namysłowski and the "Jazz Rockers," with whom he performed during the Jazz Jamboree Festival of 1961. Soon after, Urbaniak received an invitation to play with Andrzej Trzaskowski and "The Wreckers," and by 1962 he was touring jazz clubs and festivals throughout the United States, appearing in Newport, San Francisco, Chicago, and New York. Upon his return to Poland, Urbaniak began collaborating with Krzysztof Komeda's Quintet and appeared in the 1965 film "Jazz aus Polen," made for West-German television by Joachim Berendt. The group went on to tour Scandinavia. In 1965 Urbaniak left the Quintet to establish his own self-titled group with singer Urszula Dudziak, pianist Adam Makowicz, and others. The Michał Urbaniak Group recorded their first international album, *Parathyphus B*, and went on to play at several jazz festivals. One year later, Urbaniak was named Best Soloist at the Montreux Jazz Festival and was subsequently offered a scholarship to the Berklee Music School in Boston, which he declined. He migrated to the United States in 1973 with his wife, **Urszula Dudziak**. In America, he was signed by Columbia Records, which subsequently released a series of his albums under the band name Michal Urbaniak Fusion. Throughout the late remainder of the 1970s and 1980s, he played with such influential American jazz musicians as Ronnie Burrage, Joe Caro, Kenny Davis, Tom Guerin, and Steve Jordan. Urbaniak appeared at jazz clubs, concert halls, and music festivals across the eastern seaboard and frequently returned to Europe on tour. His music has been described as a fusion of jazz and Polish folk elements, R & B, hip hop, and classical, and he has been credited as influential in the jazz fusion movement of the 1970s and 1980s and the acid jazz movement of the 1990s.—*Krystyna Cap*

SOURCES: Michael Bourne, "Rhythm and BLU," *Down Beat*, Vol. 54 (February 1987), 15; Becca Pullium, "The Tone Doctor Is In," *Down Beat*, Vol. 58 (November 1991), 26–27.

Urbanowicz, Clarent Marie (b. Johnstown, Pennsylvania, January 2, 1910; d. Lemont, Illinois, February 27, 2002). Catholic nun. Urbanowicz joined the Franciscan Sisters

Sister Clarent Marie Urbanowicz (*PAHA*).

of Chicago in 1925 and took her vows in 1931. She received her baccalaureate degree at De-Paul University (1941) in Chicago, her M.A. degree at St. John College (1946) in Cleveland, completed a certificate in theology at Xavier College in Chicago (1952), and did additional graduate work at Rosary College (IL), Youngstown University, the University of Notre Dame, St. Mary's College (IN), and Marquette University. She was an elementary and secondary school teacher in various schools, and served as principal of the Saturday Polish Language School in Youngstown, Ohio, and the St. Sanislaus School in Chicago. The author of various pamphlets and brochures for the Franciscan Sisters of Chicago, she was the organizer and president of the Youngstown, Ohio, chapter of the **Polish American Historical Association** and was a long-time member and active on the national board of directors of PAHA. Among her many honors were the Gold Medal of Honor from the Polish government-in-exile in London, Woman of the Year honors from the Polish American Scholarship Fund, the Gold Medal of Honor from the Polish Ministry of Education in London, and a medal from the Polish veterans organization in Youngstown (OH).—*James S. Pula*

SOURCE: Bolesław Wierzbiański, ed., *Who's Who in Polish America* (New York: Bicentennial Publishing Corporation, 1996), 476.

Urbanowicz, Witold (b. Olszanka, Poland, March 30, 1908; d. Glendale, New York, August 17, 1996). Military officer. After joining the Polish Air Force in 1930, he rose to become an instructor at the Dęblin Air Academy at the time of the German invasion in 1939. Following the fall of Poland, he led the remaining cadets by foot to then neutral Romania. They boarded a ship for France where they fought in the 1940 campaign. Following the fall of France, he flew with the 145th Squadron of the British Royal Air Force. Transferred to the new Polish 303 **Kościuszko Squadron**, he fought in the Battle of Britain as the Polish squadron commander of the highest scoring squadron during the battle. In late 1940 he assumed command of the Polish 11th Fighter Group, and in 1941 he organized and commanded the First Polish Fighter Wing. Having endured his share of dogfights, he was posted to Canada and Washington where he served the Polish Government-in-Exile as assistant air attaché. However, desk jobs soon bored him and, intrigued by what was going on in China, he went through some refresher training with the American 14th Army Air Force and was posted in China in October 1943. He became the first foreign volunteer pilot to report to Gen. Claire Chennault's Flying Tigers. At age 36, he was also the second oldest pilot in the unit after General Chennault. Flying a P-40 Warhawk, he escorted bombers and transport planes, dropped food and ammunition to Chinese troops and sank fifteen Japanese riverboats. Once he found himself alone battling six Japanese Zero fighters deep in enemy territory and made it to a friendly airfield with not a drop of fuel to spare. He returned to Washington in 1944 as air attaché with the rank of colonel. After the war, he settled in the United States and worked for American Airlines, Eastern Airlines and Republic Aviation as an executive in production control. He retired from Republic in 1973 but continued as a security consultant to the aviation industry until 1994.

Witold Urbanowicz (*PMA*).

Poland's foremost fighter ace of World War II, he scored seventeen confirmed aerial victories (some sources claim as many as 28 confirmed aerial victories to his credit). For those exploits he was awarded Poland's highest decoration for valor, the Order of Virtuti Militari. Among his many other decorations were the British Order of Merit and the Distinguished Flying Cross. Before his death in 1996, then Polish President Lech Wałęsa honored General Urbanowicz with a formal promotion to general in the Polish Air Force.—*Luis J. Gonzalez*

SOURCE: Wolfgang Saxon, "Gen. Witold Urbanowicz, 88, Polish Fighter Ace in World War II," *New York Times*, August 20, 1996.

Urbański, Edmund Stefan (b. Ostrów Wielkopolski, Poland, July 6, 1909; d. Washington, D.C., October 6, 1996). Latin Americanist, educator. After receiving his early education in Poland and Sweden, Urbański earned his M.A. (1943) and doctorate (1946) degrees from the National University of Mexico and did post-doctoral study at the University of Barcelona, the University of San Marcos in Peru, and the University of California. After beginning research in Polish and Scandinavian studies, he was greatly intrigued by the diversity of cultures found in Latin America and spent the rest of his career exploring these civilizations, and the Polish presence in the region. His teaching career spanned four decades and a variety of institutions from lecturer at the National University of Mexico (1942–46) to the Federal University of Parana in Brazil (1979), with stops at Marquette University, the University of San Francisco, University of Idaho, University of Notre Dame, John Carroll University, the State University of New York at Buffalo, Western Illinois University, Western Michigan University, Howard University, and the University of Warsaw. Among his many publications were *Los eslavos ayer, hoy y mañana* (The Slaves Yesterday, Today and Tomorrow, 1944), *Historia de la literatura polaca* (History of Polish Literature, 1946), *Studies in Spanish Literature and Civilization* (1964), *Angloamérica e Hispanoamérica: Análisis de los civilizaciones* (Anglo-America and Hispanic America: Analysis of the Civilizations, 1965), *American Hispanic America and its Civilizations* (1978), *Hispanic America and its Civilizations: Spanish Americans and Anglo-Americans* (1978), *Wśród indian, metysów i murzynów w Hispanoameryce* (Among Indian, Mestizo and Blacks in Hispanic America, 1994), and *Polish Contributions to Latin American Culture* (1996). Among his honors was election to the Academy of History of Santander, the Peruvian Instituto de Estudios Humanos (1966), the Academia de Historia of Columbia (1968), the International Social Science Honor Society, the Cross of Merit from the Republic of Poland (1938), the Medal of Honor from the Mexican government (1965), and the Order of Polonia Restituta from the Polish government-in-exile in London (1987).—*James S. Pula*

SOURCES: "Urbanski, Edmund Stephen," *Contemporary Authors* (Detroit: Gale Research Company, New Revision Series), Vol. 23, 434; Bolesław Wierzbiański, *Who's Who in Polish America* (New York: Bicentennial Publishing Corporation, 1996), 477–78.

Urbansky, David Aarin (b. Lautenburg, Prussian Poland, 1843; d. Piqua, Ohio, January 22, 1897). Soldier, Medal of Honor recipient. Urbansky came to the U.S. at age fifteen. After a three-year residence in New York City, he moved to Columbus, Ohio, where he opened a business as a cabinetmaker. When the Civil War erupted, he enlisted as a private in Company B, 58th Ohio Volunteer Infantry, on October 28, 1861. He fought at Shiloh, Tennessee, in 1862 and at Vicksburg, Mississippi, in 1863. In the first Union assault on the Confederate fortress at Vicksburg, Urbansky's company commander fell badly wounded and the enlisted man "went back amidst shot and shell and carried him back to his regiment." He was awarded the Medal of Honor on August 2, 1879, for "gallantry in action" at Shiloh and Vicksburg. After he was mustered out on January 14, 1865, he settled in Piqua, Ohio. His name is sometimes rendered as "Orbansky."—*James S. Pula*

SOURCES: Isadore S. Meyer, *The American Jew in the Civil War* (New York: American Jewish Historical Society, 1962); Harry Simonhoff, *Jewish Participants in the Civil War* (New York: Arco Publishing, 1963).

David Urbanski, Medal of Honor recipient (*NARA*).

Valentine, Greg "The Hammer" (John Anthony Wisniski, Jr.; b. Seattle, Washington, September 20, 1950; d.—). Wrestler. The son of wrestler Johnny Valentine, Wisniski dropped out of college to become a wrestler, debuting in the ring in July 1970. Gaining a reputation as a tough, rugged competitor, he became a top-ranked superstar during the 1970s, 1980s and 1990s. Beginning his career under the ring name "Baby Face Nelson," he later changed to "Johnny Fargo," one half of The Fargo Brothers with Don Fargo between 1971 and 1974. The Fargo Brothers initially competed in the Buffalo and Cleveland-based National Wrestling Federation before moving on to Texas. When the Fargo Brothers split in 1974, Wisniski went to Florida where he began performing as "Johnny Valentine, Jr." He later changed his ring name to Greg "The Hammer" Valentine, and was billed as Johnny Valentine's brother, not his son, because of fears that the elder Valentine would be thought of as too old to be a legitimate threat. He remained in Florida for a year while also working in Los Angeles and Japan under Antonio Inoki in 1975 and early 1976. He remained in the wrestling profession for many years and in 2004, after a colorful and very profitable career in the ring, he was inducted into the WWE Hall of Fame by his former manager Jimmy Hart. The following night, at Wrestle-Mania XX at Madison Square Garden, he received loud applause when the class of 2004 was introduced. Shortly after being inducted into the WWE Hall of Fame, he dedicated the plaque he received to his late father.—*Luis J. Gonzalez*

SOURCE: Oliver G. Johnson, *The Pro Wrestling Hall of Fame: The Heels* (ECW Press, 2007), 81.

Van Dam, Rob (Robert Szatkowski; b. Battle Creek, Michigan, December 18, 1970; d.—). Wrestler. Szatkowski began a professional wrestling career in 1990, adopting the ring name "Rob Van Dam," often shortened to RVD. A popular performer for many years, he is credited with numerous championships. Van Dam has made many appearances on television and films. Outside the ring, he is known as an advocate of the legalization of marijuana.—*Neal Pease*

SOURCE: "Rob Van Dam," World Wrestling Entertainment website, www.wwe.com/superstars/wwealumni/rvd.

Vars, Henryk *see* Wars, Henryk.

Verbinski, Gregor "Gore" (b. Oak Ridge, Tennessee, March 16, 1964; d.—). Movie director. The son of a Polish physicist who worked on the nuclear program at the Oak Ridge Laboratory, he moved to southern California with his family in 1967. After earning

Gore Verbinski, film director (*OLS*).

his baccalaureate in film at the UCLA Film School (1987), he began his career working on music videos before directing commercials for Canon, Coca-Cola, Nike, Skittles, and United Airlines. He was awarded the prestigious Silver Lion at Cannes (1993) and four Clio Awards for designing the popular Budweiser advertising campaign featuring the croaking frogs. His first films as a director were *The Ritual* (1996), *Mousehunt* (1997), *The Mexican* (2001), and *The Time Machine* (2002). His first real "hit" came with *The Ring* (2002) which grossed over $230 million, but his rise to prominence was solidified with *Pirates of the Caribbean: The Curse of the Black Pearl* (2003), which grossed more than $650 million, garnered five Oscar nominations, and earned a Saturn Award for best director. Following *The Weather Man* (2005), he completed *Pirates of the Caribbean: Dead Man's Chest* (2006) which set a record for an opening weekend earning $135,600,000, grossed in excess of $1 billion, and earned four Oscar nominations and one award. His third hit in the series was *Pirates of the Caribbean: At World's End* (2007) which received two Oscar nominations.—*James S. Pula*

SOURCE: "Gore Verbinski," *Contemporary Theatre, Film, and Television* (Detroit: Gale, 2003), Vol. 46.

Verdeur, Joe (b. Philadelphia, Pennsylvania, March 7, 1926; d. Bala Cynwyd, Pennsylvania, August 6, 1991). Swimmer. As a collegiate swimmer at LaSalle University (1946–1950), Verdeur was named an All-American four times. Competing for the United States, he won a gold medal in the 200 meter breaststroke event in the 1948 Olympics. He broke the world record for the butterfly-breaststroke twelve times. He is a member of the International Swimming Hall of Fame, and in 2009 was inducted into the National Polish-American Sports Hall of Fame.—*Neal Pease*

SOURCE: "Joe Verdeur," International Swimming Hall of Fame website, www.ishof.org/honorees/66/66 jverdeur.html.

Vinton, Bobby "The Polish Prince" (Stanley Robert Vintula, Jr.; b. Canonsburg, Pennsylvania, April 16, 1935; d.—). Singer. Forming his first band at the age of sixteen, he earned money playing clubs in the Pittsburgh area to finance his education at Duquesne University. Following service in the U.S. Army, he appeared on Guy Lombardo's *TV Talent Scouts* which led to a contract with Epic Records in 1960 but was not successful until he recorded as a single a previously rejected song entitled *Roses Are Red (My Love)* which became the number one song in the country for four straight weeks. His *Blue Velvet* reached number one in 1963, followed by two No. 1 hits the following year, *There! I've Said It Again* and *Mr. Lonely*. During the decade between 1962 and 1973, he had more recordings reach number one on the charts than any other male soloist, causing *Billboard Magazine* to label him "the most successful love singer of the 'Rock-Era.'" In 1972 Epic Records terminated its contract with Vinton, but the singer staged a remarkable come back with *My Melody of Love*, a song sung partially in Polish that rose to number one and sold several million copies. Vinton turned the hit into a gold album, *Melodies of Love*, followed by the successful *Bobby Vinton Variety Show*, a syndicated production that reached over 140 cities in the U.S. and Canada between 1975 and 1978. Awarded over a dozen gold records, Vinton sold more than 75 million records and had more Billboard No. 1 hits than any other male vocalist, including such greats as Elvis Presley and Frank Sinatra. He was honored

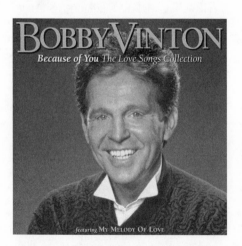

The cover of one of Bobby Vinton's hit albums (*OLS*).

with a bronze star on the Hollywood Walk of Fame.—*James S. Pula*

SOURCE: Bobby Vinton, *Bobby Vinton: The Polish Prince* (New York: M. Evans and Company, Inc., 1978).

Virginette, Sister Mary, C.S.S.F (Anna Chlebowska; b. Wilmington, Delaware, February 13, 1903; d. Lodi, New Jersey, September 17, 1995). Felician Sister. The fifth of seven children, Anna Chlebowska entered the **Congregation of Sisters of St. Felix of Cantalice** in 1921. She pursued her baccalaureate studies at Fordham and Villanova Universities receiving her Master of Philosophy from the Jagiellonian University in Kraków, Poland, where she studied from 1933 to 1938. Her thesis was a biography of Teodor Potocki entitled "Wielki Prymas Teodor Potocki." She taught at Immaculate Conception High School in Lodi, directed its aspirant program, and served as principal. She also translated three plays: *Còrka Milionerska* (The Millionaire's Daughter) and *Niespodziewani Aniołowie* (Unexpected Angels) and Dorothy Clark Wilson's drama, *The Lost Star* (Zaginiona Gwiazda). She read her "Wycieczki Jako Czynnik Szkolny" (Excursions: An Important Factor in Education) at the Felician Pedagogical Convention in Plymouth, Michigan in 1941. Other essays include "The Importance and Dignity of Catholic Education" (1944) and "Educating for Tomorrow" (1946). She translated children's prayer books for First Holy Communion: *Pray Always* by the Rev. Alphonse Sausen, O.S.B. translated as *Módl Się Zawsze* (1939) and *Jesus, I Love You* by the Rev. Joseph Mary Lelen translated as *Jezu Kocham Cię* (1940). In addition, she compiled a 220-page prayer book entitled *Raj Duszy* (A Soul's Paradise; 1942). One of the founding members of the **Polish American Historical Association**, she served as its first female president. In 1946 she became a member of the provincial administration in the Lodi province where she helped to establish the **Catholic League for Religious Assistance to Poland** in 1948. As the seventh provincial superior of the Lodi province from 1959 to 1970, she initiated construction of the five-story extension called the Mother Angela Wing that was blessed on May 31, 1961. She served on the boards of trustees of St. Mary's Hospital in Orange, New Jersey and St. Joseph Hospital in Philadelphia. Elected superior general of the worldwide congregation of 4,000 Felicians on February 2, 1970, she served until 1976, leading the expansion of Felician College in Lodi into a four-year college for women. During her tenure as superior general, she implemented the changes of the Second Vatican Council, including the transition to a more secular

garb, and was active in the Conference of Major Superiors of Women and Consortium Perfectae Caritatis. In 1992, she received the papal "Pro Ecclesia et Pontifice Cross." Archbishop Theodore McCarrick presided at her funeral Mass at the Immaculate Conception Convent Chapel on September 20, 1995. She is buried in the Felician Sisters cemetery in Lodi.—*Thomas Duszak*

SOURCES: "In memoriam: Sister Virginette (Anna) Chlebowski," *PAHA Newsletter*, Vol. 51, no. 4 (December 1995), 6; Sister Mary Bonaventure Grabowski, *Felician Sisters: History of the Congregation of the Sisters of St. Felix of Cantalice* (Newark, NJ: Johnston Letter Co., 1993).

Wachowski Brothers. Laurence "Larry" (b. June 21, 1965) and Andrew Paul "Andy" (b. December 29, 1967) Wachowski were both born in Chicago where they graduated from Whitney Young High School. Larry attended Bard College in New York, while Andy went to Emerson College in Boston, but both left without graduating. Returning to Chicago, they operated a carpentry business and produced comic books for Marvel Comics and EPIC Comics. In 1995 they had their big break as writers of the script for the popular movie *Assassins*, the success of which led to them writing and directing *Bound* (1996). Their major achievement in film came when they wrote, directed, and produced the hit Matrix series—*The Matrix* (1999), *The Matrix Reloaded* (2003), and *The Matrix Revolutions* (2003). They also wrote and produced *The Animatrix* (2003). They wrote and produced *V for Vendetta* (2006); wrote, directed, and produced *Speed Racer* (2008); and produced *Ninja Assassin* (2009). In 2003 they established Burlyman Entertainment to publish comic books based on the Matrix series, and they also wrote and directed the popular games *Enter the Matrix* (2003) and *The Matrix: Path of Neo* (2005).—*James S. Pula*

SOURCE: Mark Miller, "Matrix Revelations," *Wired*, Vol. 11, no. 11 (November 2003).

Wachtel, Stanley (Stanisław Zenon Wachtel; b. Jarosław, Poland, May 11, 1887; d. Detroit, Michigan, June 18, 1959). Actor, playwright, radio pioneer. Born in the province of **Galicia** when it was controlled by the Austro-Hungarian Empire, Wachtel received an education in agronomy. He then fulfilled his compulsory military duties in the Austrian cavalry before obtaining leave for a visit to his brother **Karol Wachtl** in Chicago in October of 1912. There, the activities of Polish amateur drama circles captivated his imagination. He fell in love with and married one of its stars, Gertrude Irene Wieckowska, on August 10, 1914. They seemed destined to devote their talents to the Polish stage where knowledge of

Poland's literary classics and works of outstanding dramas could be performed for audiences thirsting to hear their native Polish tongue. Thus inspired, a troupe of like minded actors prepared an ambitious repertoire which was presented over the years in Chicago's Chopin, Polonia, Wolna Polska, Big Ashland, Davis, Union, Premier, Juno, Fredro, and Ochlylski theaters. The group also performed in Detroit's Fredro, Martha Washington, Rozmaitości, Wolna Polska, Ludowy, and Farnum theaters; in Cleveland's Polonia; in Newark's The Polonia; and in Buffalo's Fillmore Theater. Each of these accommodated full season repertory enterprises, with play lists ranging from dark tragedies to light-hearted folk comedies or French frocked farces. Elaborate musicals were great audience favorites. The introduction of "talkies" by the movie industry and the grimness of the Great Depression brought this gay theatrical era to a halt, but not before the Polish government awarded Wachtel its Order of Polonia Restituta (1928) in recognition of his part in the preservation of Polish culture in the United States.

Wachtel turned to radio in 1933 when he debuted on Detroit's station WEXL where he scripted a mystery series for Ted Zając's night time program. Walenty Jarosz also had Wachtel contribute to a morning program on WMBC; then Władysław Leskiewicz employed him to direct a full morning hour program at station WJBK. In 1938 WMBC changed its call letters to WJLB and moved its studies to the Broderick Towers in downtown Detroit. The station owner, John Lord Booth, contracted Wachtel to direct a "Polish Morning Variety Show" with a live orchestra, vocalists, news commentators, and actors in dramatic serials. Live audiences were a unique and exciting feature. This successful project ended in 1944 when foreign language programming was suspended for security reasons during the Second World War. Manuscripts, plays and photographs relating to Wachtel's works are archived in "The Stanley Wachtel Collection" at the Burton Historical Library of the Main Library of Detroit.—*Estelle Phyllis Wachtel-Torres*

SOURCES: Józef Migała, *Polish Radio Broadcasting in the United States* (Boulder, CO: East European Monographs, 1987); Emil Orzechowski, *Teatr Polonijny w Stanach Zjednoczonych* (Wrocław: Zakład Narodowy im. Ossolińskich, 1989).

Wachter, Frank Charles (b. Baltimore, Maryland, September 16, 1861; d. Baltimore, Maryland, July 1, 1910). Congressman, labor official. Wachter attended private schools and St. Paul's Evangelical School at Baltimore, Maryland. He learned the trade of clothing cutter and in 1892 became engaged in the cloth-shrinking business. He was a member of the local Knights of Labor and as a union official presided in 1889 over the national convention of cutters and trimmers meeting in Rochester, New York. He opened a cloth-sponging business in 1892, was active in various clubs, and a member of the Second Lutheran Church. He was a member of the jail board of Baltimore (1896–98) and an unsuccessful candidate for police commissioner of Baltimore in 1898. He was elected as a Republican to the Fifty-sixth Congress in part because he favored the welcoming of new immigrants, then mostly from Poland and Italy, whom many of the Irish in the Democratic Party sought to exclude. He was re-elected to the three succeeding Congresses (March 4, 1899–March 3, 1907), but was not a candidate for re-nomination in 1906. Wachter was nominated for mayor of Baltimore but did not win the general election, resuming his former business pursuits in Baltimore. He was a member of the board of managers of the Maryland Penitentiary from 1909 until his death. Wachter's grandfather's Polish ancestry, who presumably came from the German-occupied part of partitioned Poland, may have influenced the Congressman's support for the erection of the equestrian statue of **Pułaski** and its placement in Washington's Lafayette Square.—*Frederick J. Augustyn*

SOURCES: *Biographical Directory of the United States Congress, 1774–Present* (http://bioguide.congress.gov/); Edward Pinkowski, "Fascinating Pol-Am History: The World of the Wachters," *Zgoda* (January 1, 2008), 16.

Wachtl, Charles (Karol Henryk Alphonse Wachtel; b. Jarosław, Poland, November 11, 1879; Philadelphia, Pennsylvania, January 26, 1946). Editor, journalist. After completing his secondary education in Lwów, Wachtl enrolled in the University of Lwów where he took a great interest in journalistic and cultural pursuits, becoming a member of the editorial board of *Wiadomości Artystyczne* (Artistic News) and an editor for the Catholic daily newspaper *Przedświt* (Predawn). In 1903, Wachtl accepted a position with *Promień* (Ray of Light), a Polish-language newspaper in La Salle, Illinois, eloped with his sweetheart and headed for America. He soon left *Promień* to assume editorship of the official organ of the **Polish Roman Catholic Union** in Chicago, *Naród Polski* (The Polish Nation), a position he held for four years. In 1905 he also began editing *Polonia* (**Polonia**), a weekly children's newspaper also published in Chicago. In 1907 he became co-editor of the widely-read ***Dziennik Chicagoski*** (Chicago Daily News), becoming editor from 1917 to 1923. Aside from his journalistic efforts, Wachtl was artistic director for the first permanent Polish theater in Chicago and an active member of the committees that erected the **Kościuszko** monument in Chicago (1904) and the Kościuszko and **Pułaski** monuments in Washington, D.C., in 1910. During World War I he served as secretary and a member of the executive committee of the **Polish National Council** and editor of its newspaper *Free Poland*. He was a member of the **National Department** where he led the press section, was active in recruiting volunteers to serve with the **Polish Army in France**, and received personal thanks from Pres. Woodrow Wilson for translating the *Star Spangled Banner* into Polish. His efforts on behalf of Poland were recognized with the Haller Swords, the Silesian Star, and the Cross of Merit of the Polish Army.

In 1920 Wachtl earned a Ph.D. in philology, literature, and history from DePaul University in Chicago. Following World War I, he returned to Poland with his family, settling in Warsaw where he edited *Gazeta Niedzielna* (Sunday Gazette) and *Rozwój* (Development). These publications were not successful and as a supporter of Roman Dmowski and **Ignacy Jan Paderewski**, after their rival Józef Piłsudski rose to power in May 1926, Wachtl determined to return to America. In his later writings he expressed some bitterness about his treatment in Poland, as well as the attitude of Poles toward other returning Polish Americans. He arrived in New York in October 1926 where he edited the *Kuryer Narodowy* (National Courier), then moved to Philadelphia in 1935 to edit *Gwiazda* (The Star) until 1946. During the Second World War he was active selling war bonds and spoke on behalf of Poland and the war effort on a regular Sunday radio program. Wachtl was a founding member of the **Polish American Historical Asso-**

Karol Wachtl, journalist and editor (*PMA*).

ciation and contributed many historical writings on early **Polonia** including his *Z.P.R.K. Dzieje Zjednoczenia Polskiego Rzym.-Kat. w Ameryce* (History of the Polish Roman Catholic Union of America, 1913) and *Polonja w Ameryce* (Polonia in America, 1944). The former is more properly described as a history of early Polonia as well as the Polish Roman Catholic Union, while the latter work, though much criticized for its organization and methodology, provides considerable information for future researchers.—*Donald E. Pienkos*

SOURCES: Anna M. Cienciala, "Foundations of Polish-American Scholarship: Karol Wachtl," *Polish American Studies*, Vol. 50, no. 1 (1993), 51–73; Andrzej Brożek, *Polish Americans 1854–1939* (Warsaw: Interpress, 1985).

Wagner, Wieńczysław Józef (b. Moscow, Russia, December 12, 1917; d.—). Law professor. Wagner earned an L.L.M. from the University of Warsaw (1939) and a diploma from the Brun Institute of Commercial Sciences, also in Warsaw (1940). During World War II he joined the Armia Krajowa (the Home Army underground, 1942–44) where he served as a second lieutenant, as a junior judge, legal counsel, and editor-in-chief of an underground publication. Captured, he spent time in a German prisoner of war camp. When freed at the end of the war, he moved in Paris where he became president of the Home Army Association, chair of the Polish War Refugees in France, vice president of the Polish Catholic Students' Association, and earned an L.L.D. from the University of Paris (1947) and a certificate from the Academy of International Law in The Hague (1947). Migrating to the U.S. in 1948, he obtained a position as visiting professor of Polish language and literature at Fordham University in New York, but soon moved to Chicago where he earned an L.L.M. (1950) and J.D. and S.J.D. (1957) degrees from Northwestern University. His teaching career encompassed positions as a fellow of comparative law at Northwestern University (1950–53) and the University of Notre Dame (1953–62), a professorship at Indiana University (1962–71) and the University of Detroit (1971–89), a visiting Distinguished Professor of Law at Seton Hall University (1979–80), and visiting positions at the Jagiellonian University in Kraków (1990–92), the Catholic University of Lublin (1991–93), and the Mikołaj Kopernik University (1993–94). During this time Wagner was also a visiting professor at the Universities of Paris and Rennes (1959–60), Cornell University (1961–62), Nice, France (1968–69), Warsaw (1979–80), and London (1986–87).

In Chicago, Wagner organized chapters of the Home Army Association and the Pad-

erewski Foundation. He was admitted to the bar in Indiana in 1960, and undertook a rigorous schedule of summer lectures that took him to England, France, Luxembourg, Germany, Switzerland, Greece, Italy, the Caribbean, Guatemala, Bolivia, Chile, Argentina, Uruguay, Brazil, Algeria, Morocco, Senegal, Rhodesia, Zaire, Zimbabwe, Togo, Burkina Faso, Cameroon, Egypt, Jordan, India, Pakistan, Cambodia, and South Korea. Wagner edited or authored over 250 books, articles, reviews, and prefaces which were published in English, Polish, French, German, or Portuguese. Notable among these was his collaborative compendium on *Polish Law Throughout the Ages*, intended as a contribution to Poland's millennium celebrations, and articles explaining Polish law in history, such as the comparison of the *liberum veto* to the American "filibuster," which, he explained, may not be held in a bad light when used judiciously. Another important work was his collaborative research on Wawrzyniec Grzymała Goślicki (Laurentius Grimaldius Goslicius), whose book *The Accomplished Senator* may even have influenced the U.S. Constitution. A sixteenth century political philosopher, Goślicki argued that law is above the ruler and the ruler must respect the people's will. Wagner's piece, the "Conspiracy in Civil Law Countries," was cited by the Criminal Tribunal for Rwanda and other scholars writing on the subject.

Wagner was chairman of the International Meetings Commission of the American Comparative Law Association (1962–90), the vice president of the Catholic Lawyers International Movement *Pax Romana*, president of the **Polish Institute of Arts and Sciences in America**, a member of the Executive Council of World Federalists, president of the American Council of Polish Culture, and committee president of the Polish American Bicentennial Committee. In 1973 he was named "Outstanding Educator of America." He is also Knight Commander, Sovereign Order of Malta, and has been a member of some thirty American, Polish, French, and international organizations. Among his decorations are the *Polonia Restituta* Commander's Cross, the Golden Cross of Merit, and various military decorations. He received a French government grant in 1945, four Fulbright Foundation grants, and a Ford Foundation Fellowship, as well as a *doctor honoris causa* from the Mikołaj Kopernik University in Poland.—*Wanda Slawinska*

SOURCES: Bolesław Wierzbiański, *Who's Who in Polish America* (New York: Bicentennial Publishing Corp., 1996), 481; *Dictionary of International Biography: A Biographical Record of Contemporary Achievement* (Cambridge, UK: International Biographical Centre, 1999); "Wagner, Wenceslas Joseph," *Contemporary Au-*

thors (Detroit: Gale Research Company), Vol. 37–40, 580–81.

Wakacjusze. This term, meaning "vacationers," has been used by sociologists and historians, along with the term *turyści* (tourists), to refer to the large number of Poles who came to the U.S. on tourist visas during the period of martial law in Poland and into the early 1990s. Many, if not most, worked illegally in the U.S., motivated by the poor economic conditions and lack of employment opportunities in the years of martial law and the subsequent transition to a market economy.—*James S. Pula*

SOURCE: Anna D. Jaroszyńska-Kirchmann, *The Exile Mission: The Polish Political Diaspora and Polish Americans, 1939–1956* (Athens, OH: Ohio University Press, 2004).

Waldo, Arthur Leonard (b. Radom, Poland, November 6, 1896; d. Phoenix, Arizona, September 29, 1985). Journalist. After completing his secondary school education, Waldo migrated to the United States in 1913. Employed as a traveling reporter with the Polish weekly *Zorza* (Dawn) published in Pittston, Pennsylvania, he immediately joined the **Polish Falcons Alliance** and was appointed a captain in the Falcons military forces in 1914. In 1917 he volunteered for the Polish army being formed in the United States and saw action in France in 1918 and in Poland during the Polish-Soviet war of 1920 before returning to the United States in 1921. Employed as an editor with several newspapers, most notably Chicago's ***Dziennik Zjednoczenia*** (Polish Union Daily; owned by the **Polish Roman Catholic Union** of America), Waldo authored more than fifty plays and numerous historical studies, among them *An Outline of the History of Polish Literature in America* and *The Polish Theater in America*. Following on the earlier historical research of the Rev. **Wacław Kruszka** of Milwaukee and **Mieczysław Haiman** of Chicago on the first Poles in the **Jamestown** colony of Virginia in 1608, Waldo actively promoted public recognition of their place in American colonial history beginning in the 1930s. He was greatly responsible for two commemorations of the first Poles in the Jamestown colony, one in 1953 and a second, more substantial event, in 1958, which marked the 350th anniversary of their arrival. Through his efforts, a plaque memorializing the first Poles' arrival was approved by the Polish Falcons of America for placement at the Jamestown site. Waldo's publications on this subject include his *First Poles in America* and his *True Heroes of Jamestown*. However, the scholarship of Waldo's research on the first Jamestown Poles has since come in for serious criticism from historians who question the authenticity of his primary historical source, a purported memoir of one of Jamestown's original Polish settlers.

In 1939, Waldo was appointed an advisor on American **Polonia** matters by the **World Union of Poles from Abroad** (Światowy Związek Polaków ze Zagranicy), headquartered in Warsaw. Just as he arrived there, war broke out. Waldo volunteered for military duty in the Polish Army and saw some action before returning to the U.S. in March, 1940. Thereafter, he was employed for a time by the U.S. Coordinator of Information for Polish Affairs. In 1952, Waldo contracted to write a history of the Polish Falcons of America. His research led to what became a massive, five-volume, 2,000-page, lavishly illustrated and documented history of the movement in the Polish language. Due to the highly detailed character of this work, the exorbitant length of time it took him to complete his work, and its cost, Falcons President Walter Laska removed Waldo from the project before its completion. The incomplete history — only the first forty-seven years of the Falcons' organization were covered in the five published volumes, titled *Sokolstwo: Przednia Straz Narodu* (The Falcons Movement: Vanguard of the Polish Nation) — remains an extraordinary publication of great value to future historians. A sixth, unpublished volume took the story up to 1965.

Waldo received many awards for his services to Poland and Polonia, including military honors from the governments of France and Poland, and the Haiman Award for his scholarly contributions to Polonia studies from the **Polish American Historical Association**. On September 28, 1985 Waldo received the highest honor to be bestowed by the Polish Falcons of America by its president, **Bernard Rogalski**, at a testimonial banquet in Phoenix, Arizona. On receiving the Gold Legion Cross of the Polish Falcons Legion of Honor, Waldo told his well wishers, "This is my last hurrah."

During the night he died in his sleep. — *Donald E. Pienkos*

SOURCES: Donald E. Pienkos, *One Hundred Years Young: A History of the Polish Falcons of America* (Boulder, CO: East European Monographs, 1987); *Sokół Polski* (The Polish Falcon), October 15, 1985, page 1; Joseph Wiewiora, *Jamestown Pioneers from Poland* (Chicago: Polish American Congress, 1958, 1976, 2007).

Wallace, Jean (Janina Walasek; b. Chicago, Illinois, October 12, 1923; d. Beverly Hills, California, February 14, 1990). Actress. A precocious fashion model, Wallace moved to Hollywood when very young and had a number of minor roles, debuting as a chorine in *Ziegfield Girl* (1941). She married the much older actor Franchot Tone the same year while still a teenager. Reportedly Tone was able to help get her larger roles, but she never became a star. The two were divorced in 1948. She married actor Cornel Wilde three years later. With Wilde she formed Theodora Productions which made a number of films in the 1950s with Wallace starring opposite Wilde. None of these was either an expensive production or a critical success. They were the only films in which Wallace had a starring role. Perhaps the best known of these features was the last, 1963's *Lancelot and Guinevere* with the couple in the title roles. In the last film the two did together, the well-regarded 1967 war film *Beach Red*, she had a lesser part. The two were divorced in 1981. Her career was effectively over by the end of the 1950s, other than a scarce film or television appearance. Wallace was a striking blonde beauty, but evaluation of her acting talents is mixed. Some reviews were critical while others credited her with unrealized talent. Thrice married, Wallace had a difficult personal life, attempting suicide twice, in 1946 and 1949. — *M. B. B. Biskupski*

SOURCE: obituary by Glenn Fowler, "Jean Wallace, 66, Screen Actress Known for 1940's and 50's," *New York Times*, February 18, 1990.

Walsh, Stella (Stanisława Walasiewicz; b. Wierzchownia, Poland, April 3, 1911; d. Cleveland, Ohio, December 4, 1980). Athlete. The future Olympian track star came to the United States as a two year old when her entire family emigrated from Poland, eventually settling in Cleveland. A member of the **Polish Falcons** as a youngster, Walsh further developed her athletic skills in Poland after the First World War as a student at the Physical Education Institute in Warsaw. In 1929 she won the 100-meter dash at the International Slav Złot (Meet) in Poznan. With the approach of the 1932 Olympic Games, which were scheduled to be held in Los Angeles, Walsh sought to join the American team, but was ruled ineligible because of her Polish citizenship. Walsh competed anyway, representing Poland, and won a gold medal in the 100 meter dash. In 1936 she competed in the Berlin Olympic Games and there won a silver medal in the same competition. During an illustrious career spanning more than five decades (she was still competing successfully in meets in her 60s), Walsh won over 500 prizes and set more than 300 records including 61 world and national track records in the 60, 70, 100 and 200 meter dashes, many of them wearing the insignia of the Polish Falcons of America. In 1962, Walsh was honored by the Falcons as a life-time honorary member in recognition of her great achievements in amateur sports. In 1974, she became the second inductee into the **National Polish-American Sports Hall of Fame**, and the following year was inducted into the U.S. Track and Field Hall of Fame. Following her death, a controversy arose over her gender. Although her original birth records indicated that she was a female, postmortem examination revealed apparent male genitalia and that she possessed both XX and XY chromosomes

Arthur Waldo, journalist (*JPI*).

Jean Wallace, movie star (*OLS*).

Stella Walsh, Olympic athlete (*OLS*).

making gender ambiguous. The issue remains unresolved, although her records are still recognized.—*Donald E. Pienkos*

SOURCES: Donald E. Pienkos, *One Hundred Years Young: A History of the Polish Falcons of America* (Boulder, CO: East European Monographs, 1987); Timothy L. Kuzma, ed., *Polish Falcons of America: District History Series* (Pittsburgh: Polish Falcons of America, 1987); "Walsh, Stella," in *American National Biography* (New York: Oxford University Press, 1999), Vol. 22.

Wandycz, Piotr Stefan (b. Kraków, Poland, September 20, 1923; d.—). Historian. Growing up in Lwów where his father was a petroleum engineer and a member of the Piłsudski Legions, he crossed into Romania with his family when the Soviets and Germans invaded Poland in 1939. In 1940 the family moved to France where he studied at the Université de Grenoble before moving to Great Britain in 1942 to join the Polish armed forces in exile as a second lieutenant. Following the war Wandycz studied at Cambridge University, earning B.A. and M.A. degrees, and at the London School of Economics where he received his doctorate in 1951. Migrating to the United States, he accepted a position at Indiana University, moving to Yale in 1966. There, as director of graduate studies in Russian and East European studies, and chair of the Council on Russian and East European Studies, he established himself as arguably the pre-eminent scholar of Poland abroad, eventually being named Bradford Durfee Professor of History in 1989. The author of twenty books and more than 400 shorter works, Wandycz has written extensively on Poland in international affairs and also published on a broad range of topics including the evolution of East Central Europe and the development of Polish-American relations. His *France and Her Eastern Allies, 1919–1925* was recognized with the American Historical Association's prestigious George Louis Beer Prize, while *The Twilight of French Eastern Alliances, 1926–1936* received the Wayne S. Vucinich Prize from the American Association for the Advancement of Slavic Studies. A member of the Polish Academy of Science, the Polish Academy of Arts and Sciences, and the **Polish Institute of Arts and Science of America**, he holds honorary doctorate degrees from the Catholic University of Lublin, the Jagiellonian University in Kraków, the Sorbonne, and the University of Wrocław. Among his other honors are the Commander's Cross of the *Order of Polonia Restituta*. He retired from teaching in 1997, after which he was elected president of the Polish Institute of Arts & Sciences of America.—*M. B. B. Biskupski*

SOURCE: Bolesław Wierzbiański, *Who's Who in Polish America* (New York: Bicentennial Publishing Company, 1996).

Wanniski, Jude Thaddeus (b. Pottsville, Pennsylvania, June 17, 1936; d. Morristown, New Jersey, August 29, 2005). Journalist. Drawn to the field of politics and journalism as a child, Wanniski obtained a baccalaureate in political science (1958) and a master's degree in journalism (1959) from the University of California, Los Angeles. After brief assignments on local newspapers in Culver City (CA), Anchorage (AK), and Las Vegas (NV), he took a position in 1965 with *The National Observer* covering news on Capitol Hill. In 1972 he was named associate editor of *The Wall Street Journal*. Wanniski is credited with coining the phrase "supply-side economics" in a 1976 editorial to distinguish this new approach from the accepted Keynesian economic theories. His book *The Way the World Works* (1978), which argued for a revival of the classical approach to economics, was recognized by the *National Review* as one of the one hundred most influential books of the twentieth century. An unswerving advocate of reduced trade barriers, elimination of capital gains taxes, and a return to the gold standard, he became an advisor to Pres. Ronald Reagan (1978–81) where he was responsible for devising the tax cuts that revived the economy following the "stagflation" of the Carter presidency. Republican leader Jack Kemp called him "the Thomas Paine of the Reagan Revolution." Winniski also founded Polyconomics in 1978, a firm providing advice to business and government on the consequences that political and economic events might have on national and world-wide economic markets. He is also credited with developing the "Two Santa Claus Theory" (1974) in which he argued that when one political party campaigns on promises of spending, the other cannot effectively campaign on not spending but must instead find other ways to appeal to voters.—*James S. Pula*

SOURCE: Adam Bernstein, "Jude Wanniski Dies; Influential Supply-Sider," *Washington Post*, August 31, 2005, B6.

Wardzinski, Felix (Andrzej Feliks Wardziński; b. Poland, 1801; d. Harris County, Texas, 1848). Soldier. After taking part in the Polish November Uprising of 1830–31, Wardzinski was forced into exile in America. Making his way to New Orleans, he enlisted in Captain Turner's Infantry Company B of the Texas revolutionary army under Gen. Sam Houston and arrived in Texas with that unit in 1836. At the decisive Battle of San Jacinto, he was with a party that destroyed a key bridge on the Vance River which helped to defeat the Mexican army under General Antonio Lopez de Santa Anna, who held the office of president of Mexico. Wardzinski was among the group

*Feliks Wardzinśki, soldier (**PMA**).*

that discovered and captured President Santa Anna when he attempted to escape notice by disguising himself in the uniform of a common soldier. Following the successful conclusion of the Texans' fight for independence, Wardzinski returned to civilian life on August 5, 1837, becoming a farmer in Harris County where he received 320 acres of land for his service during the Texas revolt. In 1845 he enlisted in the U.S. Army during the Mexican War, fought with the Texas volunteers at the Battle of Monterrey, and served until February 2, 1848.—*James S. Pula*

SOURCE: Stephen L. Moore, *Eighteen Minutes: the Battle of San Jacinto and the Texas Independence Campaign* (Dallas: Republic of Texas Press, 2004).

Warner Bros. The famous Hollywood moguls were children of Polish-Jewish immigrants from the north-central town of Krasnosielc. The name Warner is probably altered from its unknown original form, which the Warner Bros. studio web site claims was "Wonskolaser." The two oldest brothers, Hirsch (1881–1958, known as Harry) and Aaron (1883–1967, Albert) were born in Poland, while Szmul (1887–1927, Samuel) and Itzaak (1892–1978, Jack) were born after the family arrived in North America; Samuel in Baltimore, and Jack in London, Ontario. Pioneers in the motion picture business, the Warners' studio is one of the oldest continuously functioning companies in Hollywood. After a series of minor ventures into films early in the century, the brothers re-located to Hollywood where they catapulted to fame due to a series of films with the dog Rin-Tin-Tin (26 films commencing in 1924) and the first "talkie" film *The Jazz Singer* (1927). The studio subsequently produced a great many popular and critically-acclaimed films. The Warners' relationship with Poland and the Poles was not positive. Two films produced in the early 1930s (*The Life of Jimmy Dolan* and *How Many More Knights*) featured foul characters with the highly symbolic names of "**Pulaski**" and "**Kosciuszko**." This led to a bitter exchange with the Polish government which deemed the films "anti–Polish propaganda" and banned all Warner productions from Poland. In turn, studio head Sam Warner denounced the Polish government as "anti–Semitic." Later in the decade Warner Bros. released *As the Earth Turns* which portrayed Polish immigrants to the United States as primitives and *Black Fury* (1935) which depicted a Pole as a simple-minded lout. Given the scarcity of Polish characters in American films, these portrayals were significant. During World War II, Warner was responsible for the film *In Our Time* (1944) which was a scurrilous attack on inter-war Poland that elicited wide-spread protests from the Polish community in America. In *Edge of Darkness*, a 1942 release set in occupied Norway, the Polish character is a Nazi collaborator. **Polonia** was again outraged. The Poles also figure marginally in the infamous pro–Soviet propaganda film *Mission to Moscow* (1943) where they are cast in a most negative light. Warner Bros. was the most relentlessly hostile studio in Hollywood regarding Polish themes. The motives for this disposition regarding Poland cannot be reconstructed, and Jack's memoirs (*My First Hundred Years in Hollywood*) mentions Polish matters in several places without particular animus. In general Warner Bros. should be regarded as an extreme example of the traditional Hollywood disdain for Poland and the Polish American community.—*M. B. B. Biskupski*

SOURCE: Cass Warner Sperling and Cork Milner, *Hollywood Be Thy Name: The Warner Brothers Story* (Lexington, KY: University of Kentucky Press, 1998).

Wars, Henryk (original surname was Warszawski or Warszowski; b. Warsaw, Poland, December 29, 1902; d. Beverly Hills, California, September 1, 1977). Composer. A graduate of the Warsaw Conservatory of Music, Wars also completed military training at the officers' school in Włodzimierz. Strongly influenced by American jazz, he began composing but had his career interrupted by the German invasion in 1939. Joining the Polish army again, he was taken prisoner by the Germans but escaped into the Soviet Union where he organized a theatrical troupe that toured major cities. In 1941 he joined the Polish army in Russia being created by Gen. Władysław Anders. He moved with the army into the Middle East and then to Italy where Anders' Second Corps was attached to the British army. His main function during this period was providing, through his theatrical group, entertainment and relaxation for Polish and Allied military personnel and civilians. While in Italy his troupe was recognized with a first prize in a contest between various Allied performing groups. Upon his discharge from the army in 1947 he migrated to the U.S. After some time he was able to obtain an appointment with Columbia Pictures to work on the score for *The Big Heat* which won for him recognition that led to offers from other studios. During his ensuing career he worked on 39 films and had his songs recorded by popular artists such as Jimmy Rogers, Doris Day, and Bing Crosby. He also wrote scores for several television shows including *Daktari*, *Flipper*, and *Gunsmoke*.—*James S. Pula*

SOURCE: Jacek Przygoda, *Polish Americans in California 1827–1977 and Who's Who* (Los Angeles: Polish American Historical Association, California Chapter, Loyola Marymount University, 1978).

Wasie, Stanley (Stanisław Wasielewski; b. Austrian Poland [?], May 8, 1899; d. Minneapolis, Minnesota, July 13, 1974). Businessman, philanthropist. Wasie was instrumental in the development of the overnight shipping industry, long-haul trucking, and numerous innovations that streamlined that business. After arriving in the United States with his parents in 1906 (probably from **Galicia**), the family settled in Northeast Minneapolis, a heavily Polish district of the city. During World War I, he worked for the Minneapolis Machine Company. After the war, he found employment as a shipping clerk and dispatcher for Pratt's Express, a local trucking company. Shortening his name to Wasie during the 1920s, he entered the trucking business when it was in its infancy, a time when shipping was dominated by railroads and trucking was primarily a short-haul enterprise. In 1927, Wasie started his own company, Merchants Motor Freight, Inc., with a single truck and an office in Northeast Minneapolis. The firm handled local transport, hauling freight between Minneapolis and St. Paul. However, the company soon added other operating outlets: Des Moines, Chicago, Kansas City, Detroit, Cleveland, Denver, and St. Louis. The growing Mayo Clinic in Rochester, Minnesota, was an early customer. By the 1950s, Merchants had over 800 trucks and a chain of terminals and warehouses throughout the Midwest. Merchants was one of the first trucking companies to offer direct city-to-city overnight shipping. Wasie was also among the first to automate his terminals with conveyor belts and pneumatic tubes, among the first to use computers to process billing, and the first to equip his trucks with two-way radios. One of Wasie's greatest innovations was the creation of an industry-wide transport paperwork clearing house that streamlined the billing process, especially for small carriers. Wasie pioneered the creation of a cooperative equipment pool for the trucking industry. He served as a founding member of several industry associations and was the first president of the Middle West Motor Freight Traffic Bureau, vice president of the American Trucking Association, and president of the National Trailer Pool, Inc. Following his retirement, Wasie and his wife set up the Wasie Foundation which donates money for hospitals and clinics in Minnesota, as well as providing college scholarships for Polish and Polish American youth. Wasie

Although movie producer Jack Warner was Polish by birth, his studio portrayed Polish characters in his movies in a negative light (*NARA*).

Henryk Wars, composer (*OLS*).

stated, "I'm proud I grew up on the East Side [Northeast Minneapolis]. Those kids over there don't have the same chance [as wealthier groups]. If I can help their situation a little bit, I'd be happy."—*John Radzilowski*

SOURCE: John Radzilowski, *Poles in Minnesota* (St. Paul: Minnesota Historical Society Press, 2005).

Wasie Foundation *see* **Wasie, Stanley.**

Wasielewski, Thaddeus Francis Boleslaw "Thad" (b. Milwaukee, Wisconsin, December 2, 1904; d. Milwaukee, Wisconsin, April 25, 1976). Congressman, attorney. After attending the parochial schools and South Division High School of his native city, Wasielewski earned a baccalaureate degree from the University of Michigan (1927) and a J.D. from Marquette University (1931). He was admitted to the bar in 1931 and began practice in Milwaukee. He served as census supervisor in 1940 and was elected as a Democrat to the Seventy-seventh and to the two succeeding Congresses (January 3, 1941–January 3, 1947), but was an unsuccessful candidate for re-nomination as a Democrat in 1946 and an unsuccessful Independent candidate for election in 1946. He was a delegate to the Democratic National Convention in 1948, and a member of the Wisconsin State Central Committee (1942–48). Following his political career he resumed the practice of law and was an active member of the **Polish National Alliance**. His papers are located at the University of Wisconsin–Milwaukee.—*Frederick J. Augustyn*

SOURCE: *Biographical Directory of the United States Congress, 1774–Present* (http://bioguide.congress.gov/).

Wasilewski, Mieczysław (b. Stanisławow, Poland, December 9, 1897; d. Pittsburgh, Pennsylvania, May 1979). Journalist, editor. A student in Lwów when he first became active in the Polish scouting movement, or **Harcerstwo**, Wasilewski was too young to be accepted for military service in Józef Piłsudski's Polish Legion during World War I. Nevertheless, he served as a messenger on the Russian-Austrian front where he was captured by the Russians, held prisoner for eighteen months, and tortured by Bolsheviks. Finally freed and permitted to return to Poland, he volunteered for service in the newly established Polish Army. Wasilewski later studied physical education at the University of Poznań. Until 1926 he worked as both a physical instructor with the **Polish Falcons** organization and as a director in the Polish scouting movement. Invited to the United States in early 1926 to organize training programs for young Falcons by *Sokół Polski* (Polish Scout) editor Karol Burke, Wasilewski was actively engaged in this

Mieczysław Wasilewski, journalist and editor (*JPI*).

work for several years throughout the Eastern section of the country. Working also as a journalist, he was appointed editor of *Sokol Polski* in 1934 upon the death of **Stanisław Osada**, a post he retained until his death. Wasilewski also directed the operations of the Falcons' print shop and in the 1960s established the Falcons Museum in the fraternal's national headquarters in Pittsburgh. He cooperated with **Arthur Waldo** in the publication of his history of the Falcons movement and was largely responsible for the appearance of the third and fourth volumes of that massive work. Although his first love had been the field of physical education, the post of chief instructor in the Falcons had already been filled by **Gustaw Pieprzny** prior to Wasilewski's coming to America. He and Pieprzny became close friends and their joint commitment to the Falcons and its president, **Teofil Starzyński**, created a harmonious atmosphere which greatly strengthened the organization. Moreover, with Pieprzny, Wasilewski carried on Starzyński's philosophy in the pages of *Sokół Polski* for many years after Starzyński's own death in 1952.—*Donald E. Pienkos*

SOURCE: Donald E. Pienkos, *One Hundred Years Young: A History of the Polish Falcons of America, 1887–1987* (Boulder, CO: East European Monographs, 1987).

Watrous, Albert Andrew (b. Yonkers, New York, February 1, 1899; d. Royal Oak, Michigan, December 3, 1983). Golfer. Moving to Michigan at an early age, in 1922, the same year in which he obtained his first position as golf professional at the Redford Golf

Club, Watrous won the Canadian Open in Montréal and the Michigan PGA title. At age 23, he became the youngest to win the Michigan title. Over the years he went on to win a total of nine Michigan PGA titles, more than any other golfer, and in the process became not only the youngest, but also the oldest (1954) person to win the title. In 1926 he finished as the runner-up to the legendary Bobby Jones at the British Open Championship. In the same year he became a member of the unofficial United States team that played the British in the forerunner of the Ryder Cup Competition. In 1927 and 1929, he took part in the Ryder teams that represented the United States. In 1957 he defeated Britain's John Burton in Scotland for the World Seniors professional title after qualifying by winning the National PGA Seniors' Championship for the third time (1950, 1951, 1957). Watrous has the rare distinction of scoring twelve holes-in-one at professionally sanctioned tournaments during his professional career. He also has the distinction of competing in the first Masters tournament at Augusta National. He went on to play in eight other Masters. He won six Michigan Opens (1926, 1927, 1929, 1930, 1943, 1949), nine Michigan PGA Championships (1922, 1924, 1932, 1936, 1938, 1939, 1941, 1952, 1954), five Michigan PGA Senior championships (1953, 1954, 1956, 1957, 1961) and two Michigan Pro-Ams (1952, 1954). Watrous served as pro at both Grand Rapids Highlands and Meadowbrook before taking over at renowned Oakland Hills for an unprecedented 37 years. Following his career in golf, he became an executive with General Motors. He was inducted into the National Polish-American Sports Hall of Fame in 1979 and the Michigan Golf Hall of Fame in 1982.—*Luis J. Gonzalez*

SOURCE: "Michigan's Most-Titled Professional Golfer," National Polish-American Sports Hall of Fame and Museum, Inc., http://www.polishsportshof.com/bios/watrous_a_complete.html, May 2008.

Węgrzynek, Maximilian Franciszek (b. Rudnik, Poland, February 27, 1893; d. November 8, 1944). Publisher, Polonia activist. Węgrzynek came to America in 1914, settling in New York City where he graduated from the City College of New York in 1917. Beginning in 1922 he was the publisher of New York's Polish language daily, *Nowy Swiat* (New World), the most progressive **Polonia** newspaper at the time, and between 1928 and 1938 he also published a Hungarian language daily in the city, *Amerikai Magyar Nepszava* (The Hungarian American News.) With the outbreak of World War II in 1939, Węgrzynek became a director of the **Polish American Council** (Rada Polonii Amerykańskiej; also called American Relief for Poland). In 1942 he, along with **Frank Januszewski**, publisher of the ***Dziennik Polski*** (Polish Daily News) of Detroit, helped organize the **National Committee of Americans of Polish Descent** (Komitet Narodowy Amerykanów Polskiego Pochodzenia, KNAPP), whose aim was to speak in the U.S. for occupied Poland's postwar independence and national interests. Working with Węgrzynek, who was elected KNAPP's first president, were **Joseph Kania**, the former president of the **Polish Roman Catholic Union** fraternal, Walter Cytacki, a former vice **censor** of the **Polish National Alliance** (both from Detroit), New Yorkers Ignacy Nurkiewicz and Ignacy Morawski, Alex Hinkelman of Chicago, and several émigrés from Poland who held high office in the Polish government before 1939, most notably **Ignacy Matuszewski** and **Wacław Jędrzejewicz**. All identified themselves closely with Poland's chief pre-war leader, Józef Piłsudski (1867–1935). Led by Węgrzynek, KNAPP aggressively argued Poland's position to the American public and in **Polonia** in the face of withering left wing and communist criticisms that branded his group "fascist" and "anti–American." KNAPP was also highly critical of General Władysław Sikorski, leader of the Polish exile government in London and a pre-war Piłsudski foe, who was seen as too accommodationist in his relations with the Soviet Union, a participant with Nazi Germany in the conquest and partition of Poland in September 1939. Already seriously ill, Węgrzynek was a founder of the **Polish American Congress**, and elected a national PAC vice president, even though he was unable to attend its massive gathering in Buffalo, New York, in June 1944. In the 1944 presidential election campaign, Węgrzynek's newspaper published numerous articles and editorials that argued the U.S. government under President Franklin D. Roosevelt had undermined Poland's future freedom and independence in his talks with Soviet leader Joseph Stalin at the Teheran Conference of November 1943. As a result, Węgrzynek and Januszewski gave their editorial support to Roosevelt's opponent in the 1944 presidential election, New York Governor Thomas E. Dewey. Węgrzynek died on November 8, 1944, on the heels of Roosevelt's surprisingly narrow election to a fourth presidential term. Roosevelt's victory was aided greatly by the votes he received from hundreds of thousands of Polish Americans who were unaware, like PAC President **Charles Rozmarek** (who gave his own personal endorsement to Roosevelt's campaign just days before the election), of FDR's words and deeds at Teheran. A fiery and militant nation-

Maximilian Węgrzynek as a student, 1918 (*PMA*).

alist and an uncompromising Piłsudski loyalist, Węgrzynek was honored twice by the Polish government for his actions. He also served as a vice president of the **Kosciuszko Foundation** of New York. He was honored by the Polish government with both the Officer's Cross of Polonia Restituta and the Commander's Cross of Polonia Restituta. He was a director of District No. 4 of the Polish American Council, a member of the Board of Directors of the Polish Welfare Bureau in New York, the founder and president of the importing firm AMPOL, Inc. (1932–39), and grand marshal of the Pulaski Memorial Parade held in New York City in 1938.—*Donald E. Pienkos*

SOURCES: Donald E. Pienkos, *For Your Freedom Through Ours: Polish American Efforts in Poland's Behalf, 1863–1991* (Boulder, CO: East European Monographs, 1991).

Weiss, Hymie (Earl J. Wojciechowski; b. Chicago, Illinois, January 25, 1898; d. Chicago, Illinois, October 11, 1926). Gangster. Weiss became involved in petty crime as a youth growing up on the north side of Chicago where he became a friend of another teenager named Dion O'Banion. With the support of Weiss and George "Bugs" Moran, O'Banion later organized the North Side Gang that eventually controlled bootlegging and other illegal activities in northern Chicago. The North Side Gang was the chief rival of Johnny Torrio and Al Capone for control on the Chicago criminal underworld. When O'Banion was murdered by Torrio's gang in November 1924, Weiss took control of the North Side Gang. He and Moran ambushed Torrio, but the intended victim, though severely wounded, survived the attempted "hit." The two were also responsible for a failed at-

tempt on Capone at the Hawthorne Hotel on September 20, 1926. When negotiations to conclude a ceasefire between the rival gangs failed, Weiss was gunned down on State Street on October 11, 1926. Although his killers have never been identified, it is generally believed that one was Jack "Machine Gun" McGurn.—*James S. Pula*

SOURCES: Herbert Asbury, *Gem of the Prairie: An Informal History of the Chicago Underworld* (DeKalb, IL: Northern Illinois University Press, 1986), 353–58; Michael Lesy, *Murder City: The Bloody History of Chicago in the Twenties* (New York: W. W. Norton & Co., 2007).

Wells, Cory (Emil Lowendowski; b. Buffalo, NY, February 5, 1942; d.—). Singer. The son of a Canadian father and American mother whose grandfather had been an opera singer in Poland, Wells was raised by his mother. At a young age he became fascinated by early rock and roll music and was a member of some local bands in his teens. He then joined the Air Force where he formed an interracial musical group. After being discharged, Wells moved to Los Angeles, where he became a member of a rock group called the Enemys, who, in the mid–1960s, became the house band at the legendary Whisky-A-Go-Go nightclub and had a couple of minor hit records. In 1968 he formed a new rock group with Danny Hutton and Chuck Negron which featured the three as lead singers backed by a four piece band. Named Three Dog Night, it quickly became one of the most popular musical groups in the world. From 1969 to 1974, Three Dog Night had more top ten hit records than any other act. Some of its hit songs, many featuring Wells as lead singer, include "One," "Joy to the World," "Never Been to Spain," and "Shambala." The band broke up in 1975 but re-formed six years later. Cory Wells continued to tour with the revamped Three Dog Night. He has been an avid fisherman all his life and has written several articles for outdoor magazines and been an editor with *Outdoor Life* magazine.—*Martin S. Nowak*

SOURCE: Joel Cohen, *Three Dog Night and Me* (Los Angeles: Open Horizons, 1971); www.allmusic.com.

Wendziński, Ignacy Błażej Andrzej (b. Bydgoszcz, Poland, January 23, 1828; d. Milwaukee, Wisconsin, December 30, 1898). Journalist, Polonia activist. Born in Prussian-ruled Poland and educated in Trzemeszno to be a teacher, Wendziński took part in patriotic efforts during the "Spring of the Nations" of 1848 and was imprisoned for two years for his activities. In 1863 he participated in the Polish insurrection against Russia, following which, after a few years in exile in Western Europe,

Ignacy Wendziński, journalist (*OLS*).

he came to America in 1870. Employed as a teacher at St. Stanislaus Kostka School in Chicago in 1872, and later St. Adalbert's School in the same city, he also worked as an editor for such newspapers as *Orzeł Biały* (The White Eagle), *Gazeta Polska* (The Polish Gazette), and *Przyjaciel Ludu* (The Friend of the People) before becoming editor of the official publication of the **Polish National Alliance**, *Zgoda* (Harmony) at the 1882 PNA convention in Chicago. His election came following the refusal of the paper's first editor, Edward Odrowąż, to move to Chicago from New York when the convention delegates voted to transfer the newspaper's headquarters to Chicago. Wendziński served as editor until 1886, a period when *Zgoda* was actually printed in Milwaukee. Under Wendziński, a sharp opponent of those in the Polish clerical camp who accused the PNA of being an anti-religious organization, *Zgoda* grew rapidly in circulation. But, by the mid–1880s opinion within the Alliance had shifted to favor a less combative policy and **Zbigniew Brodowski** replaced Wendziński. Later, he worked as an editor for several Milwaukee Polish newspapers and a teacher, also remaining active in the PNA. He is sometimes known as the "Father of Polish-American Journalists."—*Donald E. Pienkos*

SOURCES: Wacław Kruszka, *A History of the Poles in America to 1908* (Washington, D.C.: The Catholic University of America Press, 1993), Vol. 1; Stefan Barszczewski, *Pierwsza historia Z.N.P.: wydana w roku 1894 na pamiątkę setnej rocznicy Powstania Kościuszkowskiego* (Chicago?: n.p., 1894); Stanisław Osada, *Historia Związku Narodowego Polskiego i rozwój ruchu narodowego Polskiego w Ameryce Pólnocnej* (Chicago:

Nakładem i drukiem Związku Narodowego Polskiego, 1905).

Wiadomości Codzienne (*Polish Daily News*). Established in 1914 by the socialists S. A. Dangel and Paweł Kurdziel in Cleveland, Ohio, this newspaper grew out of the earlier leftist weekly *Narodowiec* (Nationalist) that had published between 1909 and 1914. Published in "Kantowo," a working-class Polish district in the city, it was a moderately leftist paper that supported the political program of Józef Piłsudski in Poland and the **National Defense Committee** in the U.S. Under the editorship of **Tomasz Siemiradzki** between 1918 and 1937, it was pro-labor, covering tensions in American industry and the workers' struggles after World War I. At the same time, in the post–World War I years *Wiadomości* still presented moderate freethinking views, but engaged in a harsh polemical battle with the nationalistic camp and the Catholic position as it appeared in the pages of *Monitor Clevelandski* (est. 1925). In brief, it reflected the policies of the Polish interwar government while arguing that the Polish diaspora should play a significant role in Polish history. *Wiadomości Codzienne* strongly criticized Polish and **Polonia** right wing politics. On June 13, 1938, *Wiadomości* purchased *Monitor* and the paper became much more centrist. When Paweł Kurdziel, the owner of *Wiadomości* since 1921, died in 1940, the daily passed into the hands of his son August J. Kurdziel, with Zygmunt Dybowski becoming editor. On October 15, 1966, *Wiadomości* suspended publication due to increasing costs and difficulty in recruiting bilingual personnel.—*Adam Walaszek*

SOURCES: Adam Walaszek, *Światy imigrantów. Tworzenie polonijnego Cleveland* (Kraków: Nomos, 1994); David D. Van Tassel and John J. Grabowski, eds., *The Encyclopedia of Cleveland History* (Bloomington-Indianapolis: Indiana University Press, 1987).

Wiara i Ojczyzna (Faith and Fatherland). *Wiara i Ojczyna* was the first official newspaper of the **Polish Roman Catholic Union of America** (PRCUA), published in Chicago between 1887 and 1898. Prior to its creation, the PRCUA did not have an official publication but relied on **Jan Barzyński's** *Gazeta Polska Katolicka* (Polish Catholic Gazette) as a kind of unofficial organ. *Wiara i Ojczyzna* was created to replace this publi-

Front page from *Wiara i Ojczyzna* (*PMA*).

cation, to provide information for PRCUA members and societies, and to complement other Catholic newspapers in Chicago such as ***Dziennik Chicagoski*** (Chicago Daily News) and *Kropidło* (Aspergillum). As such, it played an active role in the political and rhetorical disputes that convulsed Chicago **Polonia** in the 1890s. A typical issue of *Wiara i Ojczyzna* was between eight and twelve pages. The front page usually featured news about the PRCUA and reports from local societies. The next few pages usually carried a round-up of American and foreign news culled from other Polish-language newspapers and letters from subscribers. Another regular section covered news from Polonia communities around the United States. Serialized novels, including those of **Henryk Sienkiewicz**, and somewhat sensationalized nonfiction pieces were also popular. A typical issue from January 1896, for example, contained an exposé on the dangers of Freemasonry translated from English and a memoir on the plight of Polish exiles in Siberia. *Wiara i Ojczyzna* also played a role in publishing the annual *Polish Catholic Almanac in America* which seems to have contained articles from many of the same sources and on the same subjects as the newspaper. In 1897, the PRCUA created a new official organ, **Naród Polski** (The Polish Nation). *Wiara i Ojczyzna* seems to have continued publication as a private newspaper into 1898 but folded after a short time due to lack of support.—*John Radzilowski*

SOURCE: John Radzilowski, *The Eagle and the Cross: A History of the Polish Roman Catholic Union of America, 1873–2000* (New York: Columbia University Press/East European Monographs, 2003).

Wiarus (The Veteran). Also known as *Katolik* (The Catholic), *Wiarus* was an important early **Polonia** newspaper and one of the few truly national publications not produced in a major urban enclave. It was published between 1885 and 1919 in Winona, Minnesota. The newspaper was founded in 1885 by the Rev. Romuald Byżewski, pastor of St. Stanislaus Kostka parish in Winona. At that time, Winona and its immediate environs had a Polish population of nearly 5,000 people making it the largest Polish community in the Upper Mississippi Valley and the largest west of Chicago and Milwaukee. The Rev. Byżewski invited **Hieronim Derdowski** from Detroit to be editor of the new periodical. No extant copies of the first months of publication exist, so it is unclear when the first issue was printed or whether the Rev. Byżewski himself edited the first editions prior to Derdowski's arrival in early 1886. The paper soon gained a significant following throughout the upper Midwest, especially in the many smaller farming communities being established in Wisconsin, Minnesota, and the eastern Dakotas. Judging from correspondence published in the paper there also seems to have been significant readership in Nebraska, Texas, Illinois, and Michigan. Derdowski's reputation as a Kashubian poet and polemicist also helped to draw in readers with roots in the **Kashub** region who would prove to be some of *Wiarus*' most loyal subscribers even during the paper's declining years. One secret to the paper's success was the editor's willingness to publish news and polemics from numerous small farming communities of the Midwest and Great Plains. Although some of the contributions were ungrammatical even to the point of being unreadable, they provided a window on the world and forum for many small and otherwise isolated settlements. These articles provide a glimpse of life in small **Polonia** communities and include news of community celebrations, tragedies, as well as poems and songs composed by these early immigrants. Derdowski also attracted significant controversy. A skilled polemicist, he acted as Polonia's gadfly, equally irritating supporters of all of Polonia's major organizations. Although a staunch Catholic, he seems to have felt little in common with other strong loyalist periodicals such as *Wiara i Ojczyzna* or *Naród Polski* and on occasion printed protests against

Irish bishops whom he felt were acting against the interests of Polish parishioners. He had a particularly bitter conflict with **Michał Kruszka**, editor of *Kuryer Polski* (The Polish Courier). Even many in his home state turned against him. In a letter to a rival paper, two Minneapolis businessmen denounced *Wiarus* and its "gypsy editor" and stated that their stores would no longer sell the paper.

Wiarus appeared in weekly editions throughout its existence. Between June 1, 1893 and August 15, 1895, the paper was renamed *Katolik*. The reason for the change was unclear and the content of the paper remained unchanged. Throughout its first decade, the paper was sold by subscriptions gathered by local agents — often storekeepers, rural postmasters or saloonkeepers — who apparently got a small fee for this service. After the turn of the century, these agents seem to have become less significant. In 1902, Derdowski died at the age of fifty after several years of poor health. His wife Joanna assumed the editorship of the paper and would continue for the remaining seventeen years of the paper's existence. By this time, however, *Wiarus* had been eclipsed by the rapid growth of the Polonia press elsewhere in the U.S. The farming communities of the Midwest were no longer growing as they once had and new waves of Polish immigrants went increasingly to industrial centers and mining towns. *Wiarus*' focus became increasingly centered on Winona, although loyal subscribers could still be found in abundance from throughout Minnesota, the Dakotas, Wisconsin and Texas. In 1918, a group of Polish businessmen in St. Paul founded *Nowiny Minnesockie* and the following year purchased *Wiarus*' subscriber mailing list from Joanna Derdowska. The last known edition of the newspaper was published on August 5, 1919. Microfilmed copies of the extant copies of *Wiarus* are available at the Archives of the Minnesota Historical Society in St. Paul.—*John Radzilowski*

SOURCE: John Radzilowski, *Poles in Minnesota* (St. Paul: Minnesota Historical Society Press, 2006).

Wicik, Stefan (b. Kórnik, Poland, May 3, 1924; d. Chicago, Illinois, February 10, 2001). Opera singer. Wicik was sent to Germany as a forced laborer following the outbreak of World War II. After the war he studied voice in Cologne, Germany. Arriving in the United States in 1951, he continued his vocal studies as a tenor at the American Conservatory of Music in Chicago. He made his operatic debut in 1954 in Chicago and successfully took part in many operatic programs and competitions in subsequent years. Between 1964 and 1969 he was a soloist with

Chicago's Lyric Opera. He also performed in the opera houses in Vienna and Salzburg, Austria, in Germany, and England. He made his first Polish appearance in Poznań in 1978. For years after he continued to perform in musicals, operettas, and cabarets. Wicik was awarded the Order of Polonia Restituta and the Cavalry Cross by the Republic of Poland.—*Donald E. Pienkos*

SOURCE: Wojciech Wierzewski, "Sto Trzydziesta Slynnych Polaków w Ameryce" (Unpublished manuscript in the archives of the University of Wisconsin–Milwaukee, 2000).

Wieczerzak, Joseph W. (b. Newark, New Jersey, January 1, 1931; d.—). Historian, editor. Wieczerzak received his baccalaureate degree in English from Brooklyn College in 1952. After serving in the U.S. Army in Europe from 1952 to 1955, he earned his M.A. (1958) and Ph.D. (1962) in East European history, with a focus on Poland, from New York University. A fellowship from the **Kosciuszko Foundation** in 1962 enabled him to do research in Poland. In 1967 he received the Foundation's doctoral dissertation award for his work *A Polish Chapter in Civil War America* which was published that same year. Wieczerzak served as president of the **Polish American Historical Association** (PAHA) in 1970 and 1978, was an associate editor of its publication, *Polish American Studies*, and a long time member of its Advisory Council. He chaired the History Commission of the **Polish National Catholic Church** and beginning in 1981 edited its annual publication, *PNCC Studies*. While continuing to publish on Polish American history, beginning in 1966 Wieczerzak was also an associate editor of *The Polish Review*, the quarterly journal of the **Polish Institute of Arts and Sciences of America**. In 1991, Wieczerzak was appointed editor-in-chief of *The Polish Review*, succeeding **Stanisław Barańczak** of Harvard University. In 2007 he was named editor emeritus and was succeeded as editor by Charles Kraszewski of King's College. His seventeen-year tenure as editor was second only to that of **Jerzy Krzyżanowski**, who served from 1956 to 1986. Wieczerzak received the Haiman Award from PAHA in 1980 for his scholarship on **Polonia** and services to the association. In January 2000, he received PAHA's **Oskar Halecki** Award for his book *Bishop Francis Hodur: Biographical Essays* (1999). He was a member of the faculty of Bronx Community College of the City University of New York where he is professor emeritus of history.—*Donald E. Pienkos*

Wierzbiański, Bolesław (b. Bachórz, Poland, November 16, 1913; d. New York, New York, March 26, 2003). Journalist. After his father died when he was a child, Wierzbiański spent his pre-school years with his mother near Tarnopol. He came to Kraków to attend secondary school where he was active as a scout. In 1933 he began the study of law and economics at the Jagiellonian University, becoming involved in the Alliance of Polish Democratic Youth (Związek Polskiej Młodzieży Demokratycznej, ZPMD). In 1934 he enrolled in Warsaw University. Still active in the ZPMD in 1936, he was elected president of its Warsaw chapter, and in 1937 president of the national ZPMD. He founded the Patriotic Left in 1935 as a federation of youth organizations opposed both to nationalism and communism. Before World War II, Wierzbiański was also an active member of the clandestine youth organization "Zet" and of the Polish Western Alliance (Polski Związek Zachodni). He organized groups of Polish youth abroad in Czechoslovakia, East Prussia, Pomerania, Silesia, Bukovina, and Latvia, becoming one of the leaders of the **World Alliance of Poles from Abroad** (Światpol). His poor health prevented his military participation in World War II. Instead, he worked to restore Światpol in exile, first in France and later in Britain. He transformed Światpol into a press agency that provided information about Poles living abroad, while the Światpol publishing house printed books about the Polish diaspora.

Wierzbiański decided not to return to postwar Poland under Communist rule. He was among the co-founders of several organizations of Polish exiles including the Polish Freedom Movement "Independence and Democracy" (Polski Ruch Wolnościowy "Niepodległość i Demokracja," NiD), the Federation of Poles in Great Britain, and the International Federation of Free Journalists from East-Central Europe (IFFJ). In 1956 he migrated to the United States, settling in New York where he studied at Columbia University (1957–60). In 1958 he organized the Foreign News Service, an information agency dealing with the problems of countries behind the Iron Curtain. He also worked for Radio Free Europe and the Voice of America, lobbying for more jobs for Polish journalists in those institutions. Later, in the 1980s, he organized material help for independent journalists in Poland. His magnum opus became ***Nowy Dziennik*** (New Daily News), a Polish daily founded in 1971, after the bankruptcy of ***Nowy Świat*** (New World). *Nowy Dziennik* became the only Polish American daily in New York, with Wierzbiański serving as editor until 2000. He also owned Bicentennial Publishing, the firm that published not only *Nowy Dziennik*, but also a series of books on Polish topics. A

Bolesław Wierzbiański, journalist (*JPI*).

member of the International Press Institute in Zurich and in London, he promoted freedom of the press. Wierzbiański was active in Polish American organizations including the **Polish American Congress** where he was a member of its board of directors and a representative of the PAC for the last stage of the Polish Round Table talks in Warsaw in 1989. He was also active in the **Polish Institute of Arts and Sciences of America** and the **Kosciuszko Foundation**, as well as being a member of the **Assembly of Captive European Nations** and the Council of National Unity in the U.S. In 1981–89, Wierzbiański was appointed Commissioner of the Human Rights Commission of the City Council of New York. Among his numerous awards were honorary membership on the Board of Trustees of the **Kosciuszko Foundation** (1998), honorary presidency of the Union of Polish Journalists (Stowarzyszenie Dziennikarzy Polskich, SDP; 1990), the Bolesław Prus Prize from the Union of Polish Journalists (1990), the Commander's Cross of the Order of Polonia Restituta (1987), the Commander's Cross with Star of the Order of Polonia Restituta (1994), and the Order of the White Eagle (1999).—*Joanna Wojdon*

SOURCES: Wiesława Piątkowska-Stepaniak, *"Nowy Dziennik" w Nowym Świecie* (Opole 2000); Marek Rudzki, "Bolesław Wierzbiański 1913–2003," *Zeszyty Historyczne*, Vol. 144 (2003), 181–87.

Wierzbicki, Feliks Paweł (b. Czerniawka, Poland, January 1, 1815; d. San Francisco, California, December 26, 1860). Physician. At the age of fifteen he took part in the November Uprising (1830–31), suffering deportation to America where he arrived in New York in 1834. In 1836 he published *French Grammar for Beginners* which some believe to be the first book on French grammar actually published in the U.S. After teaching French at the Northampton Female Academy in Massachusetts (1837–38), he moved to Providence,

RI, to practice medicine. In 1846 he assisted in forming the **Polish-Slavonian Literary Association**, as well as writing a series of articles in the New York *American Whig Review* in defense of Polish independence. In the same year, with the Mexican War raging, he enlisted in Col. Jonathan D. Stevenson's Regiment as a physician, taking a ship to California where he arrived in early 1847. When his commission was not honored, he applied for and received an honorable discharge. After traveling about the state for some four months dispensing medical services, he settled in San Francisco, authored the first article on the history of medicine published in California, and was a member of the group that established the first medical society in the state. Due to his knowledge of metals, when the U.S. mint established a branch in San Francisco he secured a position with the facility. As an author, his *Idealny Czlowiek* (The Ideal Man; 1841) proved popular among émigré circles, but he is best known for *California as it is and as it may be, or a Guide to the Gold Region* (1849), generally considered the first book in English published west of the Rocky Mountains. Two editions were published in 1849; it is considered one of the best contemporary descriptions of California during the period of the Gold Rush.—*James S. Pula*

SOURCES: Ladislas John Siekaniec, *The Polish Contribution to Early American Education, 1608–1865* (San Francisco: R & E Research Associates, 1976); Gillian Olechno-Huszcza, "Felix Pawel Wierzbicki in California," *Polish American Studies*, Vol. 42, no. 1 (1985), 59–69; Felix Paul Wierzbicki, *California as it is and as it may be, or a Guide to the Gold Region* (San Francisco: Grabhorn Press, 1933; this reprint contains a biography of Wierzbicki by George D. Lyman).

Wierzyński, Kazimierz (Kazimierz Wirstlein, b. Drohobycz, Austrian Poland, August 27, 1894; d. London, England, February 13, 1969). Poet. Of Austrian heritage, Wierzyński became one of the most noteworthy modern poets of Poland. Among all of the "Skamander" poets of the Interwar period, he continues to be, along with **Julian Tuwim**, arguably the most relevant. He studied at both the Jagiellonian University in Kraków and the University of Vienna — exploring Polish, Romance, Germanic, and Slavic languages and literatures, and philosophy — before volunteering for the Polish Eastern Legion upon the outbreak of World War I in 1914. One year previously, the family name had been officially changed to Wierzyński. Captured on July 7, 1915, at the battle of Kraśnik, he was a Russian prisoner of war until his escape in January 1918. Returning to Warsaw via Kiev, where he enlisted in the Polska Organizacja Wojskowa (Polish Military Organization), he also took part in the Polish-Soviet War of 1919–21. As a poet, his early volumes such as *Wiosna i wino* (Spring and Wine, 1919), *Wróble na dachu* (Sparrows on the Roof, 1921), and *Pamiętnik miłości* (A Love Diary, 1925) set him firmly in the nineteenth century epigone tradition of the Skamander group, with whom he associated. Others, like *Wielka niedźwiedzica* (The Great She-Bear, 1923), with its war poems, display a more developed individual style based upon personal experience. *Laur olimpijski* (The Olympic Wreath, 1927) won the gold medal in a literary contest at the ninth modern Olympics held in Amsterdam in 1928. Other volumes of poetry from the pre-war era include *Rozmowa z puszczą* (Conversation with the Wilderness, 1929), *Pieśni fanatyczne* (Fanatic Songs, 1929), and *Gorzki urodzaj* (Bitter Harvest, 1933), many of which strike a pessimistic tone of foreboding, as well as *Wolność tragiczna* (Tragic Freedom, 1936) dedicated to Marshal Piłsudski.

The outbreak of World War II saw Wierzyński evacuated from Warsaw to Lwów, from where he went to France. After the fall of that country he migrated to the United States by way of Portugal and Brazil. Settling in Sag Harbor, Long Island, for almost twenty-five years; he returned to Europe (Rome and then London), in 1964. As for many Poles of his generation, World War II was doubly tragic for Wierzyński. First, most of his family members, who remained behind in Poland, died during the conflict, including his parents and two brothers. These tragic events find their echo in his wartime poems, which include the volumes *Ziemia-Wilczyca* (Shewolf-Land, 1941), *Róża wiatrów* (Wind Rose, 1942), and the postwar *Krzyże i miecze* (Crosses and Swords, 1946). Secondly, the postwar imposition of Soviet rule on Poland induced him to remain in exile. Although he was never officially blacklisted by the publishing houses of the Communist era, his work was censored. Poems such as "Ballada o Churchillu" (Ballad of Churchill, 1944), "Barbakan Warszawski" (The Warsaw Barbacan, 1940), "Podzwonne na kaprala Szczapę" (The Bell Tolls for Cpl. Szczapa, 1945), and the prewar "Kurhany" (1938) were never published in Poland during the Communist years, even in his collected works.

Wierzyński was an early member of the **Polish Institute of Arts and Sciences of America**. He published in *The Polish Review*, the London *Wiadomości* (News), and the New York *Tygodnik Polski* (Polish Weekly). His postwar volumes are very interesting. Unlike his friend and fellow émigré **Jan Lechoń**, Wierzyński outgrew the traditional nineteenth-century versification that marked the early Skamandrites and experimented with more contemporary verse forms. His volumes of poetry published after the war include *Korzec maku* (A Bushel of Poppyseed, 1951), *Siedem podków* (Seven Horseshoes, 1954), *Tkanka ziemi* (Tissue of Earth, 1960), *Kufer na plecach* (Coffer on One's Back, 1964), *Sen mara* (Dream Nightmare, 1969), and *Czarny polonez* (Black Polonaise, 1968). These last two volumes are important for two reasons: they contain a good number of historically interesting polemical verses aimed at the Communist régime in Poland, and, especially in the case of *Czarny polonez*, they show Wierzyński's contemporary prosody to its best effect. His experiments with puns, propaganda-parodies, and Communist "newspeak" foreshadow the linguistic poetry of later dissidents such as **Stanisław Barańczak**. As a prose writer, Wierzyński composed short stories, literary and theatrical criticism, and essays. His most famous prose work, originally published in English with an introduction by **Artur Rubinstein**, is the biography *The Life of Chopin* (1953).—*Charles S. Kraszewski*

SOURCES: Clark Mills, Louise Bogan, Mary Phelps, Oscar Halecki, Ludwik Krzyżanowski, "Kazimierz Wierzyński: A Symposium," *The Polish Review*, Vol. V, no. 1 (1960), 91–100; Jolanta Dudek, *The Poetics of W. B. Yeats and K. Wierzyński. A Parallel* (Kraków: Zeszyty naukowe Jagiellonian University, 1993); Charles S. Kraszewski, "The Harmonic Bell-Jar: Wierzyński, Barańczak and the Poetics of Anti-Heroic Dissent," *The Polish Review*, Vol. LII, no. 2 (2007), 193–214.

Wiewiora, Joseph (b. Poland, March 10, 1909; d. Hammond, Indiana, November 14, 1987). Editor, journalist. Wiewiora came to America in 1926 with his parents from the region around Zywiec in Southwest Poland. Residing in East Chicago, Indiana, Wiewiora first worked at the daily newspaper *Dziennik Zjednoczenia* (Union Daily News) published by the **Polish Roman Catholic Union** and in 1930 worked in Stevens Point, Wisconsin, for the *Gwiazda Polarna* (North Star) Polish weekly. Returning to Chicago, he was again employed by the *Dziennik Zjednoczenia* until World War II when he worked in the military supply division of the Pullman Standard Company before joining the army. After the war, Wiewiora was active in Hammond, Indiana, politics before working as a writer for the **Polish American Congress** and as an assistant editor of *Dziennik Związkowy* (Alliance Daily News). Beginning in January 1968, he served as editor of *Zgoda*. In this capacity, he made the newspaper into a bilingual publication with the first section in English followed by information in Polish. Equally important, he transformed the function of *Zgoda* from one largely limited to organizational information from the **Polish National Alliance** into something of a broader news publication providing news about Poland, American **Polonia**, and the Polish American Congress along with PNA stories.—*Donald E. Pienkos*

SOURCE: Donald E. Pienkos, *PNA: A Centennial History of the Polish National Alliance of the United States of North America* (Boulder, CO: East European Monographs, 1984).

Wigilia. The Wigilia, a Christmas Eve supper, is one of the most significant and enduring of Polish customs transplanted to America. The festivities begin when the *Gwiazdka*, the first star to appear in the eastern sky, is sighted. Before sitting down to dinner guests break the traditional wafer of unleavened bread, the *opłatek*, and exchange wishes for good health and happiness in the new year. The traditional *Wigilia* differs from other evening meals in that the number of courses is fixed at seven, nine or eleven. Similarly, tradition dictates that there must be an even number of guests or someone present will not live to see the next Christmas. A lighted candle is placed in the window as a welcome and an extra place is set at the table for Christ or any uninvited guest. This tradition is a reflection of the Polish adage "A guest in the home is God in the home." The table is covered with a white cloth, under which some hay is placed as a reminder of the manger where Christ was born. The *Wigilia* meal is meatless, a custom no doubt originating in the longstanding abstinence mandated by the Roman Catholic Church on the day before Christmas. Although Church laws have changed, and many families no longer adhere to the strict meatless tradition, the occasion continues to be observed in individual homes and in ceremonial fashion in Polish American communities throughout the country. Typical foods on this occasion might include mushroom or red beet (*barszcz*) soup, boiled potatoes, pickled herring, fried fish, *pierogi*, beans, sauerkraut, dried fruit compote, sweet bread, assorted pastries, nuts and candies. Following the meal, the guests sing Polish Christmas carols, or *kolendy*, and exchange small gifts. The evening generally ends with a visit to the local church for midnight Mass, the *Pasterka*, at which people join the choir in the singing of traditional *kolendy*.—*James S. Pula*

SOURCES: Sophie Hodorowicz Knab, *Polish Customs, Traditions & Folklore* (New York: Hippocrene Books, 1993); Rose Polski-Anderson, ed., *Treasured Polish Christmas Customs and Traditions* (Minneapolis, MN: Polanie Publishing Company, 1980); Anna Chrypinski, *Polish Customs* (Detroit: Friends of Polish Art, 1972).

Wilczek, Frank (b. Queens, New York, May 15, 1951; d.—). Physicist, mathematician. After receiving his B.S. in mathematics from

Frank Wilczek, Nobel laureate (*OLS*).

the University of Chicago in 1970 and his M.A. in mathematics and Ph.D. in physics from Princeton University in 1972 and 1974 respectively, he accepted a position on the faculty at Princeton. In 1980 he moved to the University of California at Santa Barbara, but in 1989 returned to Princeton as a professor at the Institute for Advanced Study. In 2000 he accepted a position as the Herman Feshbach Professor of Physics in the Center for Theoretical Physics at the Massachusetts Institute of Technology. An expert in pure particle physics, the application of particle physics to cosmology, the application of field theory techniques to condensed matter physics and the quantum theory of black holes, he is a member of the American National Academy of Sciences and has been honored with the Dirac Medal in 1994, the Lorentz Medal from the Royal Netherlands Academy of Arts and Sciences in 2002, and the Michelson-Morley Prize also in 2002. In 2004 he was honored with the Nobel Prize in Physics "for the discovery of asymptotic freedom in the theory of the strong interaction." This discovery led to the development of the entirely new physical theory of quantum chromodynamics (QCD).—*James S. Pula*

SOURCE: Tore Frängsmyr, ed., *Les Prix Nobel. The Nobel Prizes 2004* (Stockholm, Sweden: Nobel Foundation, 2005).

Wilk, Stefan Piotr (b. Kamienobród, Poland, September 2, 1917; d. Los Angeles, California, March 25, 2008). Physician. Orphaned early in life, Wilk was raised in several foster homes. From 1931 until 1935 he studied at the Niepokalanów Seminary near Warsaw, an institution founded by Father Maximilian Kolbe in 1927. Wilk returned to the city of Lwów in 1935 where he worked as a private tutor to finance his studies. He obtained a

high school diploma and enrolled in the Lwów Polytechnical Institute, concentrating in mathematics and engineering, but his education was interrupted by the outbreak of World War II. In the early months of the war, he escaped from occupied Poland to Yugoslavia, and then to France where he joined a Polish Army battalion attached to the French Army. Fluent in French, German, and Russian, he also served as a military interpreter. After the French defeat in June of 1940, his unit retreated to neutral Switzerland where he was interned for the duration of the war. Thanks to a special grant secured by the joint efforts of **Ignacy Jan Paderewski** and the **Kosciuszko Foundation** in New York, Wilk studied medicine in Winterthur and at the School of Medicine at the University of Zurich. He graduated with a medical degree on January 29, 1949, continuing in an advanced degree program in biochemistry and radiology at the University of Bern. Wilk arrived in the United States in 1952, settling in Los Angeles where he obtained a medical license and a Radiology Board Certification. He joined the UCLA School of Medicine in 1954 as an assistant professor. In 1959 he became Director of the Radiology Department at the Queen of Angels Hospital where he also started a school of x-ray technology, the first of its kind in Los Angeles. Wilk initiated many programs in hospitals and educational institutions and authored pioneering works in tomography and image diagnostics. He also translated books on radiology from German into English, including *The Human Spine in Health and Disease* (1959) and *Borderlands of the Normal and Early Pathologic in Skeletal Roentgenology* (1968). The author of a wealth of scientific papers and articles, Wilk was recognized as a leading specialist in the field of radiology throughout the United States and some of his early research on tomography helped lay the groundwork for the development of CAT scan technology. During the 1970s he conducted some of the first transmittals of x-rays via television. He was the recipient of many awards, including the 1962 Special Award from the Radiological Society of North America, the 1978 Doctor of the Year Award from the Queen of Angels Hospital, the 1983 Distinguished Service Award from Santa Marta Hospital, and the 1986 Regina Angelorum Award. Wilk's other important contribution in the field of medicine

Stefan and Wanda Wilk (*OLS*).

is the Children's Medical Care Foundation, which he endowed in 1981 and chaired for many years. The Foundation provides young Polish pediatric physicians with practical training at the world's leading medical schools, including the University of Southern California, Harvard Medical School, and Columbia School of Medicine, as well as universities and medical schools in Paris, Frankfurt, and Zurich. The Children's Medical Care Foundation also helps sustain pediatric hospitals in Poland and the Ukraine. Wilk's charitable efforts were recognized by the Polish government in 1990 with a Cross of Polonia Restituta. In 1952, Wilk married Wanda Harasimowicz (**Wanda Wilk**). Together they established and endowed the Polish Music Reference Center (now the **Polish Music Center**) at the University of Southern California in 1985. Ars Musica Poloniae, another charitable foundation established in 1993 by the Wilks, facilitates a variety of projects in Polish music from publishing and recording to scholarships for Polish students in Los Angeles. Wilk was a recipient of the Directors' Award from the USC School of Music in 1983. Together with his wife, he also received the Gold Medal from the Polish Composers' Union in 1988 and the Polonia Award from the **Polish American Congress** in 1989. Wilk received an honorary doctorate from the University of Warsaw in 1990 for his outstanding scientific, educational, and humanitarian achievements.—*Krysta Close* and *Marek Zebrowski*

SOURCE: Gillian Olechno-Huszcza, "Stefan Wilk: Humanitarian Par Excellence," in Henrietta Simons, ed., *Polish Americans in California — Vol. II* (Washington, D.C.: National Center for Urban Ethnic Affairs & Polish American Historical Association, 1995), 98–99.

Wilk, Wanda (Wanda Harasimowicz; b. Hamtramck, Michigan, January 13, 1921; d. Los Angeles, California, February 18, 2009). Educator, musician. Having earned her Bachelor of Music degree from Wayne University in Detroit in 1943, specializing in Music Education, Harasimowicz taught for several years in public schools in Detroit before moving with her parents to Los Angeles in 1949. She enrolled in a graduate program at the University of Southern California, but interrupted her studies to teach in conjunction with the UCLA Teacher's Education Program, while continuing to perform as a pianist at various charity benefits and Polish functions. In 1952 she married Dr. **Stefan P. Wilk**. In 1974, she returned to the USC School of Music to finish her Master's degree, alongside her daughter Diane who was enrolled at USC in the School of Architecture. Her thesis on Polish music led to a summer session at the Jagiellonian University in Kraków. In 1976 Wilk completed her thesis and graduated from USC with a Master of Music degree, but the lack of reference materials on Polish music at USC and throughout the U.S. had planted in her the seed of an idea that would eventually come to fruition in the Polish Music Reference Center. In 1980 Wilk received the Mayor's Certificate of Appreciation for her participation in the Polish Cultural Exhibit at the California Museum of Science and Industry in Los Angeles, for which she organized the music section and presented seventeen musical programs. In 1981 she secured the sponsorship of the USC School of Music for a Szymanowski Centennial. There she established the Friends of Polish Music and organized a week-long series of symphonic concerts, recitals, lectures, discussions, a banquet, and an outdoor festival with the participation of artists, musicologists, and students from England, Poland, and various parts of the United States. Between 1983 and 1984 she prepared a traveling exhibit on Szymanowski which was shown in 24 university libraries throughout the U.S. and Canada. In 1983, she received the Perspectives' Award from *Perspectives Magazine* in Washington, D.C.

In 1985, the Polish Music Reference Center (now the **Polish Music Center**) at USC was established with a joint endowment gift from Dr. Stefan and Wanda Wilk. She was appointed the Director of the PMRC by the Music School Dean and in this capacity was invited to give lectures at the Los Angeles Music Center, local universities, music organizations, and Polish-American associations, including the American Council of Polish Cultural Clubs. She authored *Karol Szymanowski* (1982), the first monograph in the Polish Music History Series, of which she subsequently served as Editor. She also authored articles about Polish women composers, and many other subjects pertaining to the history

of Polish music, for various Polish-American media. In 1993, the Wilks established Ars Musica Poloniae, which funds efforts to promote Polish music throughout the U.S., and in 1994 she initiated the creation of the Polish Music Center website, now recognized as an important tool for scholars world-wide.

In 1988, Dr. Stefan and Wanda Wilk were awarded the Polonia Award from the Southern California chapter of the **Polish American Congress**, and a Gold Medal from the Polish Composers' Union (ZKP), an organization of which Ms. Wilk is an honorary member. The **American Council of Polish Clubs** honored her in 2004, and her efforts at USC have been lauded by the University many times, including the Director's Award from the USC School of Music (1982), the Torchbearers' Award (1992), and the President's Commendation (2005). In 2008, she was made an honorary citizen of her hometown, **Hamtramck**, MI. In 1996 Wilk retired as Director of the PMRC, but continued as the Center's Honorary Director and President of the Friends of Polish Music. In the same year as her retirement, her devotion to Polish music earned her the highest state award of Poland, the *Polonia Restituta* medal. Wanda Wilk's enthusiasm and achievements have encouraged the awareness and appreciation of Polish music both nationally and internationally, and will continue to be an inspiration for generations.—*Krysta Close* and *Marek Zebrowski*

SOURCES: Gillian Olechno-Huszcza, "Wanda Harasimowicz Wilk: Tireless Promoter of Polish Music," in Henrietta Simons, ed., *Polish Americans in California—Vol. II*. 1995: (Washington, D.C.: National Center for Urban Ethnic Affairs & Polish American Historical Association, 1995), 101–02; "Wanda Wilk, Biography" (1997), Polish Music Center; "Wanda Wilk, Polish Music Patron, Passes," *Polish American Journal*, Vol. 98, no. 4 (April 2009), 1, 10.

Wilkowski, Jean Mary (b. Rhinelander, Wisconsin, August 28, 1919; d.—). Diplomat. After earning her master's degree in journalism, Wilkowski pursued a career in the U.S. Foreign Service where she developed an expertise in commercial affairs. She helped negotiate the expansion of the General Agreement on Tariffs and Trade, which led to the creation of the World Trade Organization. In 1972 she was appointed ambassador to Zambia (1972–79) where she was instrumental in establishing American policy in southern Africa. Following her service as ambassador, she took part in forming the American policy statement regarding a proposed world conference on science and technology sponsored by the United Nations.—*James S. Pula*

SOURCE: Jean M. Wilkowski, *Abroad for Her Country: Tales of a Pioneer Woman Ambassador in the U.S. Foreign Service* (Notre Dame, IN: University of Notre Dame Press, 2008).

Winiarski, Warren Paul (b. Chicago, Illinois, October 22, 1928; d.—). Vintner. After enrolling in the University of Chicago, he left school to engage in agriculture and mining in Colorado. He earned a baccalaureate degree from St. John's College in Maryland (1952), then re-enrolled in political theory at the University of Chicago. While spending a year studying in Naples, Italy, he became interested in winemaking. After gaining experience with other winemakers, in 1970 he purchased fifty acres of land in California's Napa Valley that he converted into a winery, producing American-French hybrids under the label Stag's Leap Wine Cellars. In 1976 his first vintage was awarded first place in the prestigious Paris Wine Tasting. In 2007 he sold his interest in his winery to UST Inc. and Marchese Piero Antinori for $185 million.—*James S. Pula*

SOURCES: Warren Winiarski, "Zut alors! The French like California wine," *Wines & Vines*, Vol. 72, no. 4 (April 1991), 28; George M. Taber, *Judgment of Paris: California vs. France and the Historic 1976 Paris Tasting that Revolutionized Wine* (New York: Scribner, 2005); Bolesław Wierzbiański, ed., *Who's Who in Polish America* (New York: Bicentennial Publishing Corporation, 1996), 500.

Wirkus, Faustin E. (b. Dupont, Pennsylvania, November 16, 1897; d. Brooklyn, New York, October 8, 1945). Soldier, "King of La Gonave." The son of a Polish American coal miner, Wirkus enlisted in the U.S. Marine Corps when he was seventeen. By 1925 he had worked his way through the ranks to gunnery sergeant, serving with his unit in Haiti, when he was assigned to administer the small island of La Gonave whose 12,000 residents were beset by domestic disputes. There he was surprised to encounter black residents with Polish surnames, the descendants of survivors from the legionnaires sent to Haiti by Napoleon Bonaparte. Another surprise was the natives' belief that Wirkus was the reincarnation of a previous ruler, leading to his investment as the island's King Faustin II. Wirkus ruled La Gonave from 1925 to 1929, learning the local Creole language, taking part in voodoo ceremonies, and acquiring considerable knowledge of the local culture and religious beliefs. According to the e-magazine at Haitiwebs.com, Wirkus proved to be "a thoroughly decent, charitable & good-humored man with a genuine regard for the black islanders, & he endeavored to wield his considerable authority & influence as judiciously as possible. So it was that, while Sgt. Wirkus spent the first part of his Haitian duty hunting down caco insurgents along mountainous trails, he spent the latter half settling domestic disputes, importing improved livestock & seed, delivering & doctoring babies, building houses, repairing chimneys & attending (as the sole caucasian) esoteric native ceremonies." Haitian officials eventually forced his abdication in 1929, the same year that he left the Marine Corps, returned to the United States, and took a job selling financial securities in New York City. He rejoined the Marines in 1939 as a recruiter, later being assigned as a gunnery instructor.—*James S. Pula*

SOURCES: Faustus Wirkus and Taney Dudley, *The White King of La Gonave* (Garden City, NY: Doubleday Doran, 1931); Henry Archacki, "Faustus Wirkus the White King of La Gonave," *Straż*, February 25, 1971; "Fantastic Career of Faustin Wirkus, Coal Miner who Became a King, Ended by Death," *United Mine Workers Journal*, November 15, 1945; J. P. Folinsbee, "Yankee King of the Tropics," *Coronet*, May 1951, 87–90.

Wisniewski, Stephen "Wiz" (b. Rutland, Vermont, April 7, 1967; d.—). Football player. Wisniewski played as a very successful guard for Pennsylvania State University, being twice named an All-American (1987, 1988). He was a key contributor on the Nittany Lions' 1986 national championship team. During his senior season he played in the Hula Bowl and the Japan Bowl, graduating with a baccalaureate degree in marketing in 1989. The 6'4", 305 pound Wisniewski was a second round draft pick (#29 overall) of the Dallas Cowboys in the 1989 NFL Draft, but was traded to the Oakland Raiders before the start of his first professional season, spending twelve seasons with the Oakland/Los Angeles Raiders as an offensive guard. Known among his teammates and fans as "Wiz," he was an eight-time Pro Bowl selection and named to the NFL's All-Decade Team for the 1990s. Following his professional career he took a position marketing computer software for Cima Systems. He was inducted into the **National Polish-American Sports Hall of Fame** in 2004.—*Luis J. Gonzalez*

SOURCE: National Polish-American Sports Hall of Fame and Museum, Inc.

Witek, Frank Peter (b. Derby, Connecticut, December 10, 1921; d. Mount Santa Rosa, Guam, August 3, 1944). Soldier, Medal of Honor recipient. At the age of nine his family moved to Chicago, Illinois, where he finished his education at Crane Technical High School, following which he went to work at the Standard Transformer Company. In January 1942, he enlisted in the U.S. Marine Corps and was initially stationed in Hawaii. His family received a letter in January 1943 stating that he was in New Zealand in transit to the front lines. His first combat assignment was on Bougainville in the Solomon Islands where he saw action in three major battles. After a rest and relaxation period, he was shipped out again on July 21, 1944, with the 1st Battalion, 9th Marines, 3rd Marine Division for the invasion of Guam. There, he served as a Brown-

ing automatic rifleman and a scout behind the Japanese lines. He was killed in action during the struggle for Mount Santa Rosa at Finegayen on August 3, 1944. His citation for the Medal of Honor read: "For conspicuous gallantry and intrepidity at the risk of his life above and beyond the call of duty.... When his rifle platoon was halted by heavy surprise fire from well-camouflaged enemy positions, Pfc. Witek daringly remained standing to fire a full magazine from his automatic at point-blank range into a depression housing Japanese troops, killing 8 of the enemy and enabling the greater part of his platoon to take cover. During his platoon's withdrawal for consolidation of lines, he remained to safeguard a severely wounded comrade, courageously returning the enemy's fire until the arrival of stretcher bearers, and then covering the evacuation by sustained fire as he moved backward toward his own lines. With his platoon again pinned down by a hostile machine gun, Pfc. Witek, on his own initiative, moved forward boldly to the reinforcing tanks and infantry, alternately throwing hand-grenades and firing as he advanced to within 5 to 10 yards of the enemy position, and destroying the hostile machine gun emplacement and an additional 8 Japanese before he himself was struck down by an enemy rifleman. His valiant and inspiring action effectively reduced the enemy's firepower, thereby enabling his platoon to attain its objective, and reflects the highest credit upon Pfc. Witek and the U.S. Naval Service. He gallantly gave his life for his country." Initially buried in the Army, Navy, and Marine Corps Cemetery on Guam, his remains were reinterred in the Rock Island National Cemetery, Rock Island, Illinois, in 1949. On Sunday, 20 May 1945, 50,000 persons, including his mother and Gen. Alexander A. Vandergrift, Commandant of the Marine Corps, honored his life and memory in Soldier's Field, Chicago. In February 1946, the Navy christened one of its fastest 2,400 ton Gearing Class destroyers as the *USS Witek* in his honor. In 1999, Witek's hometown of Derby, Connecticut, named the PFC Frank P. Witek Memorial Park in his honor; the Marine Corps Scholarship Foundation awards a memorial scholarship in his name, and the area near the village of Yona on Guam, where Witek perished, was named Marine Camp Witek. Although the camp closed decades ago, Guam natives still refer to the area as "Camp Witek."—*Luis J. Gonzalez*

SOURCES: R. J. Proft, *United States of America's Congressional Medal of Honor Recipients and Their Official Citations* (Columbia Heights, MN: Highland House II, 2002); *Who's Who in Marine Corps History* (United States Marine Corps History Division, February 2007).

Wittlin, Tadeusz (b. Warsaw, Poland, June 19, 1909; d. Washington, D.C., October 4, 1998). Poet, journalist. Wittlin received a master's degree in law in 1932 and a Master of Arts in 1933, both from the University of Warsaw. Initially he worked as an assistant prosecutor for the Warsaw District Court but moved into journalism, becoming an editor of *Cyrulik Warszawski* (The Warsaw Barber; 1931–34). He served with the Polish Army during the September 1939 Campaign, was taken prisoner, and spent time in Soviet Gulag camps. After the German invasion of Russia he was able to join Gen. Władysław Anders' army and as a platoon leader and public relations officer in the Second Corps attached to the Polish Armed Forces in the West (1942–46). During this time he edited *Parada* (Parade) in Cairo, Egypt. After the war he worked for Radiodiffusion Française in Paris (1950–51). He migrated to the United States in 1952 where he worked as a free-lance writer and for the broadcasting services of Voice of America and Radio Free Europe. He also worked as a translator in the Motion Picture Service Branch of the United States Information Agency in New York City (1952–58). From 1958 to 1971 he was the editor of the Polish language magazine *Ameryka*, published by the State Department to promote the United States in Poland. He later supported himself by writing and lecturing at George Washington University (D.C.), North Carolina College, Southwestern University (TX), and McGill University (Canada). Wittlin is the author of: *Trasa na Parnas* (poems; 1929), *Marzyciel i goscie* (1933, recognized as the best book of fiction by a young writer), *Zlamane skrzydla* (1934), *Przekreslony czlowiek* (1935), *Radosne dni* (1945), *Pieta Achillesa* (1949), *Wyspa Zakochanych* (1951), *A Reluctant Traveler in Russia* (1952), *Modigliani: Prince of Montparnasse* (1964), *Time Stopped at 6:30* (1965); a critically acclaimed book about the Katyn massacre), *Commissar: The Life and Death of Lavrenty Pavlovich Beria* (1972), *Ostatnia cyganeria* (1974), *Piesniarka Warszawy, Hanka Odon—wna i Jej Swiat* (1985), *Nad szarej Wisly brzegiem* (1990), *An Evening with Anton Chekhov and Maxim Gorky* (play; 1987), and *Szabla i Kon* (about Wieniawa Dlugoszowski; 1989). His books were published in English and Polish, many appearing also in French, German, Italian, and Japanese versions. He also translated books into Polish including *The Last of the Mohicans* by James Fenimore Cooper.—*Peter J. Obst*

SOURCES: Bolesław Wierzbiański ed., *Who's Who in Polish America* (New York: Bicentennial Publishing Corporation, 1996); "Wittlin, Jozef," *Contemporary Authors* (Detroit: Gale Research Company, New Revision Series), Vol. 3, 610–11.

Wojciechowicz, Alexander Francis "Alex" (b. South River, New Jersey, August 12, 1915; d. South River, New Jersey, July 13, 1992). Football player. Following an outstanding career at South River High School, he attended Fordham University on a football scholarship, earning All-America honors in 1936 and 1937 as a linebacker and center of the famed "Seven Blocks of Granite" offensive line. A fun-loving, light-hearted person who was very popular with his teammates, once on the field he was a fierce competitor who played with great tenacity. Fordham was a national power during his time there, losing just two games in three seasons. In 1937 the Rams had a 7-0-1 record, and were ranked third in the nation. The number one draft pick of the Detroit Lions in 1938, he immediately became a starter, gaining a reputation as one of pro football's last great "iron men" who played both offense and defense. Better known as a center, he may have been an even better linebacker with excellent pass coverage skills. In 1944 he intercepted 7 passes for the team, something no defensive back had done, a team record that stood for a number of years. Wojciechowicz earned All-Pro honors for the Lions in 1939 and 1944, but he yearned to play for a championship contender. He also wanted to be close to his business interests in the East. In 1946 the Lions honored his wishes by trading him to the Philadelphia Eagles, who wanted to use him primarily as a defender. The 6-foot, 200-pound athlete immediately became a team leader and the linchpin of the defensive platoon. He and Joe Muha were the linebackers in Coach Greasy Neale's innovative 5-2-4 alignment that helped the Eagles to three straight division titles (1947–49) and two NFL titles (1948, 1949). He retired after the 1950 season to work in real estate, but also helped found the NFL Alumni Association to assist former pro football players in need. He was elected to the College Football Hall of Fame (1955), the Pro Football Hall of Fame (1968) and the **National Polish-American Sports Hall of Fame** (1975).—*Thomas Tarapacki*

SOURCES: Ben Chestochowski, *Gridiron Greats: A Century of Polish Americans in College Football* (New York: Hippocrene, 1977); George Sullivan, *Pro Football's All-Time Greats: The Immortals in the Pro Football Hall of Fame* (New York: G. P. Putnam's, 1968).

Wojciechowska, Maia Teresa (aka, Maia Rodman, Maia Larkin; b. Warsaw, Poland August 7, 1927; d. June 13, 2002, Long Beach, New Jersey). Poet, author, translator. The daughter of a staff officer in the Polish Air Force, Wojciechowska was educated in Poland, France, and England. She moved to the U.S. in 1942 and became a naturalized cit-

izen in 1950. A woman of varied interests, she is best known as the author of children's books, although she has published other works as well. Her numerous books for teens involve the search for identity. She was recognized with the prestigious Newbery Medal (1965) for her children's book *Shadow of a Bull* which the medal committee believed "epitomizes all humanity's struggle for conquest of fear and knowledge of self." The same book was also accorded the Children's Spring Book Festival Award from the *New York Herald Tribune*. She was also the founder and president of Maia Productions Inc.—*James S. Pula*

SOURCES: Bernard Koloski, "Children's Books: Lois Lenski, Maia Wojciechowska, Anne Pellowski," in Thomas S. Gladsky and Rita Gladsky, eds., *Something of My Very Own to Say: American Polish Writers of Polish Descent* (Boulder, CO: East European Monographs, 1997), 144–69; Alan Hedblad, ed., *Something About the Author: Facts and Pictures about Authors and Illustrators of Books for Young People* (Detroit: Gale Group, 1999), Volume 104; "Wojciechowska, Maia," *Contemporary Authors* (Detroit: Gale Research Company, New Revision Series), Vol. 4, 602–03.

Wojcik, Helen (Helena Siwek; b. Chicago, Illinois, August 3, 1923; d. Cook County, Illinois, March 14, 1996). Polonia activist. Active in the **Polish Women's Alliance** from her youth, Wojcik's mother, Veronica Siwek, served as a national director of the PWA for 28 years. In 1971 Wojcik was elected vice president of the PWA and worked for sixteen years with President **Helen Zielinski** before her own election to the presidency in 1987. As president, she continued Zielinski's work in both the PWA and as a vice president of the PAC. In October 1989 she traveled to Poland as part of a **Polish American Congress** leadership delegation to meet with the heads of the new Solidarity government that had just come into office. In 1993 she took part in discussions with Vice President Albert Gore in Milwaukee and President William Clinton in Washington, D.C. over Poland's admission into the North Atlantic Treaty Organization (NATO). In 1994, she chaired the fiftieth anniversary celebration of the founding of the Polish American Congress in Buffalo, New York, an event attended by President Lech Wałęsa, Prime Minister Waldemar Pawlak, U.S. Ambassador to the United Nations Madeleine Albright, and many other dignitaries. Wojcik chaired the **Polonia** committee responsible for collecting funds in support of the Immigration Museum being created at Ellis Island in New York Harbor. This effort raised more than $560,000, over twice its original goal. In 1994 she commissioned the first English language history of the PWA. The book appeared in 2003. Wojcik retired in 1995.—*Donald E. Pienkos*

SOURCE: Angela T. Pienkos and Donald E. Pienkos,

"In the Ideals of Women is the Strength of a Nation": A History of the Polish Women's Alliance of America (Boulder, CO: East European Monographs, 2003).

Wolman, Abel (b. Baltimore, Maryland, June 10, 1892; d. Baltimore, Maryland, February 22, 1989). Engineer. The son of Jewish immigrants from Poland, Wolman earned a B.A. degree from Johns Hopkins University (1913) and a B.S in engineering (1915). In 1914 he accepted a position with the Maryland State Department of Health, rising to chief engineer, a position he held from 1922 to 1939. During this time he established the standards by which municipal water supplies were chlorinated, resulting in significant reductions in the death rate from water-borne contaminants and a corresponding increase in life expectancy. Wolman became recognized as an expert in the field of environmental engineering (at that time called sanitation engineering), and his career included consulting appointments with various local, state and federal government agencies including the Atomic Energy Commission, the Department of Defense, the National Research Council, the National Resources Planning Board, the National Science Foundation, the Tennessee Valley Authority, the U.S. Geological Survey, the U.S. Public Health Service, the Pan American Health Organization and the World Health Organization. He served as president of the American Public Health Association (1939) and the American Water Works Association (1942).

In 1937 Wolman established the Department of Sanitary Engineering at Johns Hopkins, chairing it until his retirement in 1962. The author of four books and over 300 articles, he served as associate editor of the *American Journal of Public Health* (1923–27), editor of the *Journal of the American Water Works Association* (1921–37), and editor of *Municipal Sanitation* (1929–35). Among more than sixty awards and honors, Wolman was recognized with the Albert Lasker Public Service Award from the American Public Health Association (1960), the National Medal of Science (1975), the Tyler Prize for Environmental Achievement (1976), the Environmental Regeneration Award from the Rene Dubos Center for Human Environments (1985), the Health for All by 2000 Award from the World Health Organization (1988), an honorary doctorate from Johns Hopkins University (1937), and the renaming of the Baltimore city public works building in his honor (1986).—*James S. Pula*

SOURCES: *Memorial Tributes* (Washington, D.C.: National Academy of Engineering of the United States of America Press, 1992), Vol. 5; C. ReVelle, "Abel Wolman, 1892–1989," *EOS*, Vol. 70 (August 29, 1989); *APWA Reporter*, Vol. 56 (October 1989), 24–25.

Wołowska, Honorata (b. Torun, Poland, 1875; d. Pittsburgh, Pennsylvania, June 5, 1967). Polonia activist. Wolowska came to the U.S. in 1890, settling first in Chicago and later in Pennsylvania in 1896. Trained as a teacher and social worker, she taught in night school classes for coal miners for many years. An activist in the **Polish Women's Alliance** of America from the time of its first national convention in 1900, Wołowska worked to build its membership in Pennsylvania while at the same time toiling to win equal membership rights for women in that youth-oriented patriotic organization. Wołowska's **Polonia** involvements extended to serving a term as vice president of the **Polish Falcons Alliance** during World War I and directing her energies to recruiting men into the **Polish Army in France** established after April 1917 in the U.S. She also was active in forming the Polish **Grey Samaritans** nursing corps which traveled to Poland following the war to work with the poor and orphaned victims of the conflict. She went to Europe herself where her many services to Poland were recognized by the Polish government with the Krzyż Walecznych (Cross of Valor) from Marshal Józef Piłsudski. Elected president of the Polish Women's Alliance in the dramatic 1935 PWA convention in Chicago, Wołowska served three terms before retiring from office in 1947. She continued on for the next twenty years giving her active support to the PWA as an honorary president of the Alliance. Wołowska's activities during World War II were extensive and the focus of much of her energies. As PWA President, Wołowska issued a dramatic appeal in 1939 to "all women and mothers of the world" and to the press of the United States, Britain and France to bring an immediate end to the brutal devastation of the Polish nation by the

Honorata Wołowska, Polonia activist (*PMA*).

Nazis. Under her leadership, the Women's Alliance organized drives to "Save the Infants" and to provide "Shoes for Polish Children." The PWA also established a fund to raise $100,000 for the benefit of Polish children wherever they lived. Wołowska also worked to win PWA support of the American war effort, especially in the purchase of U.S. War Bonds, both by individual members and by the Alliance itself. From the proceeds of these purchases, the U.S. government procured two B-25 bombers which carried the name of the Polish Women's Alliance. She was a key officer in the work of the **Polish American Council** (Rada Polonii Amerykańskiej) relief organization, from 1944 playing a key leadership role in the creation and early activities of the **Polish American Congress**. At the founding convention of the PAC, Wolowska was elected one of its national vice presidents. —*Donald E. Pienkos*

SOURCE: Angela Pienkos and Donald Pienkos, "*In the Ideals of Women is the Strength of a Nation*": *A History of the Polish Women's Alliance of America* (Boulder, CO: East European Monographs, 2003).

Wolski, Dariusz Adam (b. Warsaw, Poland, May 7, 1956; d.—). Cinematographer. After studying at the national film institute in Łódź, he moved to the U.S. in 1979, settling in New York. He supported himself working as a production assistant on student films at Columbia University, and then as an assistant on several BBC documentaries. He moved to Los Angeles (1986) where he began working on music videos for Virgin Records and MTV. His films include *Chains of Gold* (1991), *Fifteenth Phase of the Moon* (1992), *Romeo Is Bleeding* (1993), *The Crow* (1994), *Crimson Tide* (1995), *The Fan* (1996), *Dark City* (1998), *A Perfect Murder* (2001), *The Mexican* (2001), *Bad Company* (2002), *Pirates of the Caribbean: The Curse of the Black Pearl* (2003), *Hide and Seek* (2005), *Pirates of the Caribbean: Dead Man's Chest* (2006), *Pirates of the Caribbean: At World's End* (2007), *Sweeney Todd: The Demon Barber of Fleet Street* (2007), *Eagle Eye* (2008), *Little Minx Exquisite Corpse: Come Wander with Me* (2008), and *Alice in Wonderland* (2010). He was nominated for an MTV Video Award for cinematography for *Janie's Got a Gun* (1990), an ASC Award for *Crimson Tide* (1996), and an MTV Video Award for *Stan* (2001). —*James S. Pula*

SOURCE: "Dariusz Wolski," *Contemporary Theatre, Film, and Television* (Detroit: Gale, 2008), Vol. 83.

Wolszczan, Aleksander (b. Szczecinek, Poland, April 29, 1946; d.—). Astronomer. After receiving his doctorate in physics from the Nicholas Copernicus University in Toruń in 1975, he worked in the Department of Radio Astronomy at the University's Institute

of Astronomy. In 1973, he visited the newly constructed Max Planck-Institute radio telescope in Effelsberg, Germany, kindling his interest in radio-astronomy. Between 1979 and 1982 he worked at the Polish Academy of Sciences' astronomical center in Toruń. Accepting a position at Cornell University in New York in 1982, he migrated to the United States to pursue his interest in astronomy and especially pulsars. He later accepted a position at Princeton University before joining the faculty of Pennsylvania State University as a professor of astronomy in 1992. He and a colleague were credited as the first to discover a planet outside our solar system. In subsequent years, he led teams using radio and optical telescopes to discover other planets and to develop a better understanding of the universe. Continuing his research into pulsars, he was using the Arecibo Observatory in Puerto Rico in 1990 when he discovered the pulsar PSR B1257+12. Pulsars are neutron stars formed following super novas (explosions) at the end of their lives as stars. These remnant, collapsed stars are very small (tens of kilometers in diameter), incredibly dense, and rotate rapidly. Pulsars were first discovered in 1968 and distinguish themselves by possessing an electromagnetic field which momentarily points to earth with each revolution, much as a lighthouse does. PSR B1257+12 was noted to be of a class of pulsars which rotate faster than 100 times per second. Theory holds that such pulsars are the remnants of binary stars, two stars that formerly orbited each other and the leftover material of the second sun could have formed into planets. Wolszczan continued to observe, record, and analyze signals emanating from PSR B1257+12, noting some irregularities. This analysis, published in 1992, concluded that there were at least two and possibly three planets orbiting PSR B1257+12. That finding, subsequently verified by others, is recognized as the first confirmed discovery of planets outside our solar system. Following the discovery, Wolszczan remained active in astronomy, continuing to publish his new discoveries. In 2005, along with Dr. Maciej Konacki, he announced discovery of the smallest planet discovered, a fourth orbiting PSR B1257+12, 1,500 light years away. A year later, he announced discovery of a disk of debris around another pulsar 13,000 light years away. Such debris may be planet-building material in the early stages of formation. The discovery was made using an orbiting infrared telescope which detected the "warm" glow of the disk. In 2007 Wolszczan, leading a Pennsylvania State University team which catalogued hundreds of giant stars as candidates for planets, announced discovery of a planet orbiting a giant red star 300 light years from Earth. The discovery was made using the Hobby-Eberly optical telescope in Texas. Wolszczan was the 1996 recipient of the American Astronomical Society's Tinsley Prize. In 1999 he was recognized along with Albert Einstein by the science magazine, *Nature*, as providing one of the fifteen most fundamental works in physics ever published by the magazine.—*Brian Bonkosky*

Sources: Robert Naeye, "The Pull of the Planets," *Discover*, Vol. 16, no. 1 (January 1, 1995), 34–35; "There Goes the Galactic Neighborhood," *Popular Science*, Vol. 245, no. 3 (September 1994), 31; Tim Friend, "Three Planets Found Outside Solar System," *USA Today*, April 22, 1994, 1D.

Women, Polish American. The initial phase of Polish migration to America was predominantly a male experience. There were a few male artisans in **Jamestown**, occasional migration of Polish Protestants to the Dutch New Amsterdam colony, and some other individuals scattered throughout New York, New Jersey, Pennsylvania, and the Catholic colony of Maryland, but few women. Although the first federal census in 1790 enumerated 462 Poles in United States, including 221 women, it is doubtful that the latter number represents actual Poles and is more likely a reflection of non–Poles married to Polish men whose nativity was ascribed to the whole household. The first arrival of multiple families of Poles in America came with the movement of Silesian Poles, led by the Rev. **Leopold Moczygemba**, to Texas in 1854. Only with their arrival were there sufficient numbers of Poles in a single location to form a truly Polish settlement with a developed family, social, and religious life. Despite their very limited numbers in antebellum America, some Polish women nevertheless made noteworthy contributions. Chief among these were **Marie Elizabeth Zakrzewska** and **Ernestine Potocka Rose**. One of the first women to receive a medical degree in the United States when she graduated from the Western Reserve College of Medicine in 1856, Zakrzewska was a leader in establishing the New York Infirmary for Women and Children in 1857. Two years later she was appointed professor of obstetrics on the faculty of the New England Female Medical College before convincing its Board of Directors to establish the New England Hospital for Women and Children in 1862. The new hospital was unique in having an all-woman staff. She later opened the first professional nursing school in America, and the first to admit black students. In addition to her medical work, Zakrzewska was an active abolitionist, a speaker for women's rights, and

earned the sobriquet "Mother of Playgrounds" for inaugurating the movement to establish urban playgrounds for children.

Ernestine Potocka Rose migrated to the United States in 1836 after a brief residence in England where she became an active member of the "Owenites," a group of utopian socialists led by Robert Owen. Deeply concerned with social issues, she was immediately drawn to the major social movements of the day—education, temperance, abolitionism, and women's rights. Particularly concerned about the legal rights of women who, when married, saw their assets immediately become the legal property of their husbands with them having no say in financial or other property decisions, Rose quickly became a leader in the burgeoning women's rights movement. Historian Eleanor Flexner credits Rose with being one of the first women to seek legislation to improve the status of women. And in fact, Rose was primarily responsible for the passage of the first married woman's property law act in New York State, giving married women the right to own property in their own name.

In the years following the American Civil War, one of the most significant contributions made by a Polish woman to America was that of **Helena Modjeska** (Modrzejewska), the noted Polish Shakespearean actress. Arriving in San Francisco in 1876 following triumphal appearances in Kraków and Warsaw, she studied English and soon became a favorite on the American stage where her various roles included Ophelia, Juliet, Desdemona, Cleopatra, and Lady Macbeth. An honorary member of the **Polish Women's Alliance** of America, she participated in the Columbian Exposition in Chicago in 1893 on the invitation of local women's organizations.

WOMEN AND FAMILY

Large-scale migration from Poland to the United States began during the 1870s with the movement of individuals and families primarily from the German-occupied section of the country. These were followed in increasing numbers by Poles from the Austrian partition beginning in the 1880s and the Russian partition in the 1890s. While large numbers of women were included in this movement, they still represented a small proportion in the early years of this vast migration. Nevertheless, the beginning of the mass movement of Poles to America affected the lives of hundreds of thousands of Polish women. Those who stayed behind while their husbands sought opportunity in America were forced to assume new roles. With the husband away, Polish women had to raise their children alone, and

to assume other roles outside the home customarily performed by the male. These included dealing with business people and local officials, performing social obligations within the parish and village, and engaging in economic life through real estate transactions, the purchase of supplies, and other traditional male activities. Often the husband would send instructions or advice from America, but as the separation grew longer there was a tendency for the woman to ignore attempts to control the household from afar and to become increasingly independent. When eventual reunions occurred, women were very reluctant to give up this new self-sufficiency.

Those who migrated with their husbands to America found themselves in family and social situations often quite different from those they were used to in Poland. In the economy of rural agrarian Poland, where most immigrants originated, large extended families were the basic economic unit and every member had specific functions to perform for the overall survival of the group. In America, this same tradition allowed Polish families to adapt to the demands of the factory system. Despite the surface changes, the family remained the central economic unit. Men, women and children all contributed in one form or another, pursuing what sociologist Ewa Morawska called "penny capitalism," the accumulation of funds to meet family goals.

In America, Polish women were expected to fulfill the traditional Old World roles of keeping house, sewing, cooking, and caring for children. Within the household, in fact, women generally wielded considerable influence, often controlling internal family decisions. According to historian John Bodnar, women were "pre-eminent at home and assumed a wide range of responsibilities including management of family finances." Usually women were responsible for the family budget, serving as fiscal managers to whom the husband and children relinquished their pay. Women also increasingly served as disciplinarian for the children when husbands were forced to work long hours in mines or factories. The female was usually responsible for the family garden, using the produce to supplement the family diet or to sell or barter outside the home. Women baked bread, churned butter and cheese, produced noodles, canned food for the winter, and sewed much of the family's clothing, all of which contributed to the family's financial and physical well-being.

Most adult male family members obtained jobs as unskilled workers, but with wage scales for unskilled labor at very low levels, families could not exist on the income of a single wage earner. Thus, women took on yet another new role. In Poland, women were discouraged from working outside the home lest they acquire a negative "reputation." In America, the necessity of earning additional income forced an accommodation to this traditional prohibition. As soon as women began migrating in large numbers they were forced to seek employment outside the home as unskilled workers, domestics, factory operatives, and service workers to supplement the family income. In many cases Polish households in America began taking in boarders—first single relatives and then expanding to include non-relatives. Though frowned on in Poland and generally not an option of choice in America, renting spare rooms to boarders could be very lucrative. In fact, Poles had a higher percentage of households with boarders or lodgers than any other European ethnic group, some 48.4 percent as compared to an average of 32.9 percent. When boarders were present, the female members of the household were responsible for cooking and often washing clothes and housekeeping for them, usually for an additional payment beyond simple room rent.

In families where the wages of two working parents were often barely enough to support a subsistence level existence, children were also called upon to contribute to the family finances. In rural Poland children were an economic asset; additional workers who could do household chores and later contribute in the fields and through outside employment once they matured. In industrial America this tradition continued with children expected to assist by caring for boarders, taking jobs in factories, or helping in the family business when a family was fortunate enough to own one. All too often economic necessity required that children be encouraged to leave school at an early age to earn money to support the family. Older children who worked were expected to turn their money over to the family, and were generally given an allowance of a few cents a week for candy or entertainment. Some studies suggest that economic necessity caused as many as eighty percent of Slavic children to drop out of school after the sixth grade. By age fifteen, nearly all male children were employed. Young females worked as maids, servants, or unskilled mill workers. As a result, the sons and daughters of the immigrant generation generally obtained only a rudimentary education and followed their parents into the mills and mines that first lured their ancestors across the Atlantic. Education levels and social mobility were thus seriously inhibited in the second generation for both men and women.

Women, the Work Force, and Organized Labor

Before World War I, the vast majority of single Polish women worked outside the home, and approximately twenty percent continued to do so after marriage. To a certain extent, the need to work after marriage was partially a function of the industry that predominated where the person resided. Where mining and heavy industries such as steel manufacturing were the major employers, the higher wages paid to men and the relative lack of opportunity for women resulted in fewer women working outside the home. Where textile mills, meatpacking, or light industry prevailed, the lower wages paid to men often required women to work outside the home. Further, the nature of the textile mills and meatpacking houses meant there were more jobs available for women as weavers, packers, and unskilled machine operatives. "Young Polish girls were seldom given the opportunity to finish even a grammar-school education," historian Joseph Parot concluded. Out of economic necessity, they were "hustled into any one of several dozen sweatshops." Parot found that by 1900, 38.7 percent of Polish women employed in Chicago worked in the garment trades, 7.3 percent were laundry workers, and only 1.9 percent were classified in "professional" occupations.

Beginning with World War II, women found employment in a much wider spectrum of jobs and careers than ever before, many moving into positions outside the local Polish community. Because of the entry of larger numbers of women into the workforce, and the importance of employment issues to the welfare of the family, Polish women were among the earliest supporters of organized labor. Although women were usually excluded from leadership positions in the early union movements, they formed a significant proportion of union membership and were among the leaders in the well-known Pennsylvania anthracite strike in 1897, the Brooklyn sugar refinery strike in 1910, and the Chicago packinghouse strike in 1921–22. **Mary Zuk** led a popular Meat Strike in Detroit in 1935, and Polish female weavers were active in initiating and sustaining the famous Lawrence textile strike of 1912 and similar strikes in Little Falls (NY) in 1912 and New York Mills (NY) in 1912 and 1916, as well as dozens of other labor actions in the textile, garment, packinghouse, and cigar making industries. Even when not in leadership positions, it was often the women who provided logistical support, walked picket lines, and provided the emotional support for resistance. "Time and again," noted historian **Frank Renkiewicz**, "women, wives usually, bolstered the flagging spirits of their men and took the lead in demonstrations and in sustaining resistance." Women once again played prominent roles in the CIO organizing drives of the 1930s, and during World War II, like other women, entered the workforce in increasing numbers as jobs that had been largely closed to them in the prewar years were now available. In the postwar years Polish women were among the most loyal unionists in America.

The period between the world wars witnesses a broadening of occupational opportunity for women who increasingly appeared in the **second generation** as store clerks, teachers, and a variety of service occupations that provided some economic and social mobility. Following World War II, many of the new female immigrants were better educated than their predecessors, allowing them to move into white collar positions more readily. Beginning in 1960, the economic migration of the **wakacjusze** (vacationers) resulted in a large number of newly-arrived females taking employment, often illegally, as maids, cleaning ladies, child care, elder care, and other service occupations. Their experience was vividly described in Zofia Mierzyńska's popular novel *Wakacjuszka*. Beginning in the 1980s, female members of the Solidarity and post–Solidarity immigrations were, like their male counterparts, generally well-educated and found professional positions.

The Polish Women's Alliance of America

During the second half of the nineteenth century an indigenous self-help movement swept Poland, leading people in local areas to band together in mutual aid societies to better their lives. As emigration to the United States increased between 1880 and 1900, Poles brought this concept with them and applied it to their new environment in urban America. Local organizations proliferated as immigrants in ethnic enclaves attempted to provide for their mutual needs and protect themselves against what they perceived to be a hostile outside world. In 1880, they attempted to form an umbrella organization to unite **Polonia** throughout the United States into the *Związek Narodowy Polski* (**Polish National Alliance**; PNA). A patriotic fraternal benefit organization to which any Pole could belong regardless of religious affiliation, the PNA was dominated by men and would not admit women to full membership. Consequently, in 1898 **Stefania Chmielińska** took the lead in organizing the *Towarzystwo Związek Polek w Ameryce* (Polish Women's Alliance Society of

America) to serve the organizational needs of women. In the following year two other societies joined the group, drafted a new constitution, and became the *Związek Polek w Ameryce* (**Polish Women's Alliance** of America; PWA), one of the earliest fraternal benefit societies formed by women in the United States.

The PWA was organized along lines similar to the PNA with local member groups and an annual congress where major organizational decisions were taken by representative democratic vote. Taking the lead in founding the new organization, Chmielińska, a seamstress imbued with the spirit of self-help who believed that women could become self-sufficient and provide for their own economic security while at the same time strengthening neighborhood bonds and preserving their ethnic heritage. While serving as the PWA's first president, Chmielińska established contact with leaders in the international women's movement, initiated an organizational newspaper for communication and mutual support, and formed an education committee. Her efforts were later recognized by the Polish government with its Gold Service Cross.

Among the other founders and early leaders of the PWA were **Anna Neumann**, **Emilia Napieralska**, and **Honorata Wołowska**. Neumann, also a seamstress, served two terms as president (1902–06 and 1910–18) during which membership in the PWA tripled and its assets increased sevenfold. Napieralska, the first president born in the United States, was a major leader in the International Women's Peace Conference in 1916 and an effective voice in support of immigrants' and women's rights. Wołowska was instrumental in the **Polish American Council**'s efforts to bring relief to Polish war victims, and in the formation of the **Polish American Congress** as a political lobbying organization in 1944. Among its other early efforts, the PWA provided relief and political support to Poland during World War I, funded the purchase of radium for the Nobel Prize–winning scientific inquiries of Marie Skłodowska Curie, and gathered funds for the purchase of a bomber for the U.S. Army Air Corps in World War II. In the latter years of the twentieth century, the PWA organized relief efforts for Poland during the period of martial law, provided support for Polish immigrants, and lobbied for the inclusion of Poland in NATO.

Founded to meet the economic and social needs of women and **Polonia**'s youth, the PWA, from its very foundation, was an early and outspoken advocate of the right of women to higher education, to equality of employment and pay, to enter the professions,

and to purchase insurance, hold property, and transact business in their own names. Based on a strong tradition of Polish patriotism, historian Frank Renkiewicz explained that the PWA believed above all else that "the emancipation, education, and protection of women would strengthen the nation and preserve **Polskość** (Polishness) through the influence of women upon the family and the rearing of children." With this philosophical mission, the PWA interested itself in education, service work, political lobbying, and publications designed to promote Polish heritage and women's issues.

In 1904 the PWA numbered 41 groups with 2,040 members and a treasury of $9,310. By the end of the first decade its success forced the PNA and the **Polish Roman Catholic Union**, its religious counterpart, to change their rules so that women could be admitted to full membership, and women began to be elected to their national boards and as department heads. The PWA, however, rejected all overtures designed to bring its members back into the PNA and continues to maintain its independence as a national organization.

Within two decades of its founding the PWA numbered more than 25,000 members and began sponsoring summer camps in the countryside for city children. Its community libraries included reading rooms containing books, newspapers, and journals from both Poland and America, while its educational programs sponsored classes in Polish language, history, and culture, as well as typing, sewing, and other practical skills that could generate income. Chief among its patriotic and educational services, the Alliance began publishing in 1910 the newspaper ***Głos Polek*** (The Voice of Polish Women) that defined the organization's purpose thusly: "Let us join hands — women who do hard labor and women of words and thoughts — let us believe in each other, let us respect each other's work ... all classes, ranks and conditions — forward! Let us clear the road to enlightenment and the future! Let us not divide but unite; let us not destroy but shape and create what Polish women want and need."

Owned and managed by women, the readers of *Głos Polek* were, according to historian Thaddeus C. Radzilowski, "probably as knowledgeable about the problems and activities of contemporary women as any group of people in America." Its columns offered women everything from practical tips on running a household, cooking, consumer advice, shopping, health, and child raising, to serialized novels, essays on famous women, and analyses of foreign and domestic affairs. The regular column "Kronika Kobieca" (Women's Chron-

icle) extolled women's accomplishments, while "Z Ruchu Kobiecego" (From the Women's Movement) offered commentary on the women's suffrage movement, the struggle for equal education for women, and other issues of the day. The newspaper was also vocal in its support for workers causes, especially when they affected the rights of women. *Głos Polek* emerged, Radzilowski explained, "as a strong voice for feminism, political reform, and progressive goals.... It favored women's suffrage and the opening of all educational institutions and professional careers to women. It championed the rights of workers and programs of industrial safety. It informed Polish women of the progress of women's causes throughout the world and in the United States. It also tried to help rural immigrant women adjust to life in an urban setting and to become aware of the latest advances in child-rearing, hygiene, education, and nutrition. Finally, the organization worked tirelessly to preserve and propagate Polish language and culture in America and to win Polish independence."

As the second generation of Polish American women grew to maturity the Polish Women's Alliance continued to grow in strength and activity. In the twelve years beginning in 1924 it increased its membership from 50 percent to 300 percent every four years and its assets rose to $4,500,000 by 1935. By 1975 its insurance and investments totaled approximately $40 million in assets, with 80,000 members organized in 14 Districts, 38 Commissions, and 548 Groups. The PWA also operates 481 youth groups with more than 15,000 members. By the beginning of the twenty-first century, it remained, according to Radzilowski, "one of the most important organizations founded by immigrant women of any ethnic group in the United States."

The Polish Women's Alliance, with its network of local groups, offered women in the long decades before the success of the feminist movement an opportunity to become leaders, business managers, financial experts, and entrepreneurs not generally available in American society. In 1975, Radzilowski mused, the *New York Times*, with great fanfare, announced the founding of a Women's Bank with $3,000,000 in capital. At the same time, the Polish Women's Alliance managed over $40,000,000 in assets, more than thirteen times that of the Women's Bank. Within a few years the latter institution failed, but the PWA exists to this day, its position stronger than ever.

In 2001, the Polish Women's Alliance was licensed in seventeen states and offered a variety of insurance, annuity, and other financial products to its members. While still promoting its ethnic heritage and traditions, it continued to speak out on women's issues, education, and other timely social topics. Its recent activities have been as diverse as contributing to the restoration of the State of Liberty and Ellis Island, supporting the **Pope John Paul II Cultural Center** in Washington, D.C., and providing funds for the Pope John Paul II Pilgrim Home in Rome.

WOMEN AND
COMMUNITY SERVICE

Service has always been a high priority for Polish women. Aside from the organized efforts of the Polish Women's Alliance, tens of thousands of other women served their local communities or were affiliated with national and regional service efforts. Locally, though the names of the organizations varied from community to community, Polish women served in groups whose purpose it was to raise money for local parish projects, provide social support for members and the general parish community, and create educational and children's programs. One of the most effective local female activists was Clara Świeczkowska who founded the Polish Activities League of Detroit in 1923 to increase political awareness and influence among Poles and to promote social welfare for Catholic women. Świeczkowska was also instrumental in establishing the St. Elizabeth Community House in Detroit, and later the St. Anne's Community House in **Hamtramck**.

Nationally, Polish women served in the various relief efforts during World War I, including the Red Cross, the War Council, and the National Catholic Welfare Conference. In one of the more unique relief efforts the Young Women's Christian Association recruited bilingual Polish-American girls whom it trained as nurses for work in Poland. Ninety young women were selected and sent to New York City for a six-month training program during which they underwent "welfare training in the slums of the city, attended lectures at the New York School of Philanthropy, and were given Red Cross courses in cooking, health, and hygiene." They underwent further training in business principles and arts and crafts at Columbia University, as well as attending YWCA lectures on social manners. Seventy-five graduated, receiving badges and grey uniforms from which they took their name—**Grey Samaritans**—and reciting the following pledge: "I,—, in accepting the Polish Grey Samaritan uniform, pledge myself to uphold the highest ideals of womanhood in every action of my life; To be faithful in the fulfillment of the duties of a Polish Grey Samaritan; To be obedient to the orders of my Superiors; To serve the cause of Poland; To allay suffering and bind up the wounds of those by the wayside; Believing that in so doing I serve the cause of humanity."

The first group of twenty of the "Grey Samaritans" sailed for Europe in July, 1919, aboard the *SS Rochambeau*. They were assigned to hospitals as nurses' aides and also sent out as social workers to make home visits and distribute food and clothing. Amy Pryor Tapping of Utica, New York, assigned to oversee the Grey Samaritans in Poland, recalled that Madame Paderewski "calls them *szare kotki*, little grey kittens. For so do they look in their blue-grey uniforms. And ... they are my job, these Polish American girls; I wish that you might know them in their youth and enthusiasm. They are Poles and to be a Pole is to be a patriot. They have been in America and America has given them something to bring back to their newly reconstructed country. And here they are, ready to serve, my basket of *szare kotki*."

The Grey Samaritans treated wounded soldiers from the Russo-Polish War in a hospital which Josephine Tarkowska of Cleveland described as "a death trap" where the wounded had no sheets or blankets, subsisted on black bread and bitter coffee, and lay about for weeks without proper medical treatment. Despite the disease and privation, the Grey Samaritans served in Poland almost three years. A YWCA report concluded that "Their work was an act of devotion to the land of their ancestors," while APA director and future President Herbert Hoover asserted that "the hardships they have undergone, the courage and resource they have shown in sheer human service is a beautiful monument to American womanhood."

During World War II, Polish American women, distinguished themselves in their work with the Red Cross and other charitable organizations, especially in those involving relief and humanitarian work. They were particularly active in the **American Relief for Poland** (Rada Polonii Amerykańskiej), the Polish immigration Committee, the **American Committee for the Resettlement of Polish Displaced Persons**, the **Catholic League for Religious Assistance to Poland**, and the **Polish American Council**. They were particularly active in the efforts to support Polish displaced persons and resettled them in America where many of the efforts were led by **Wanda Rozmarek** who personally signed hundreds of assurances that allowed people entry into the United States and even brought them into her own home. She, and many others, sought jobs and housing for new arrivals, and otherwise made every attempt to ease their successful transition to life in America.

Led by Helen Lenard Pięklo, the **Legion of Young Polish Women** (Legion Młodych Polek) was established on the day following the German invasion of Poland. Its purpose was to provide relief to Polish refugees, prisoners of war, and soldiers. In the postwar years it continued to provide assistance to Polish veterans and medical and other humanitarian assistance to Poland, as well as supporting several educational and cultural causes in the United States and American Polonia. Within

A women's organization at St. Mary, Our Lady of Częstochowa, Parish, New York Mills, New York, ca. 1930s (*Eugene E. Dziedzic and James S. Pula*).

other organizations of mixed gender, women were also quite active, but remained foremost in positions such as secretary and those responsible for auxiliary functions such as food preparation, youth activities, artistic presentations, decoration and cleaning, and in providing staff for festivals, dinners, and church events. Although all of these services were essential, they often went underappreciated while male leaders in the organizations held most of the leadership positions, gave speeches, and represented the public face of the organizations in the community.

WOMEN'S RELIGIOUS ORGANIZATIONS

By the end of the nineteenth century, Poland had been an occupied nation for a century. During that period of national prostration, the local parish became a center of not only religious and social life, but cultural renewal and patriotic expression. By the mid-nineteenth century there developed a growing trend toward religious vocations among Polish women seeking inspiration for social and religious service under the auspices of the Virgin Mary. Polish Marianism formed a very strong impetus to the formation of sisterhoods between 1850 and 1890. Without doubt, the most significant contributions of any group of Polish American women, and the most significant source of opportunity prior to World War II, were the religious congregations. Over time, women's religious work was a mainstay in the development of Polish parochial schools in America and the most significant element in shaping the religious, cultural, and social values of the second and third generations of Polish Americans.

The initial congregations were transplanted from Poland by sisters who crossed the Atlantic to minister to the needs of Polish immigrants in America. These sisters tended to be members of the middle and upper socioeconomic classes who were interested primarily in careers as teachers and in fields otherwise unavailable to them in Poland. Once in America they attracted as novices some of the urban poor because, in the words of Corinne Azen Krause, "the church brought solace, comfort, and social contact to women who were coping with the difficulties of poverty and adjustment to a strange society."

As the founding nuns from Poland gradually passed away or became a small minority in their own congregations, leadership passed to women born in America. Immigrant women or their daughters also founded seven orders, a majority of Polish women's religious orders in America. The congregations generally grew rapidly once established because, in addition

to their religious aspects, they provided Catholic women with opportunities for occupational mobility often not readily available to them in secular society. "The religious life appealed to women who were interested in positions of power, responsibility, travel, social status, and education," explained Radzilowski, "It also represented a chance to leave home and offered an attractive alternative to marriage, domestic service, or factory work."

The religious orders appealed to women for both personal and professional reasons. Religion was always important in the life of the Polish woman, both in Poland and in America where, as Krause noted, "Religion became 'the very bone and sinew of ethnicity,' for it gave meaning, a system of moral values, and community to the immigrants." Many women chose to enter the religious orders to preserve this sense of community and to pass it along to others, and in fact the various Polish sisterhoods, whether formally through their teaching or informally through their social and cultural activities, were a major factor in the preservation of not only religion, but Polish heritage and culture.

Professionally, women were interested in social work, teaching, caring for the poor, aged and infirm, and other service occupations that were more or less open to them in secular society, but the religious orders also offered other opportunities, both in the order itself and in the various organizations the orders administered, to fill other roles not generally open outside the religious congregations. Women religious enjoyed the opportunity to fill administrative and management positions, to function as financial officers, and to be decision-makers

on any level. As William J. Galush observed, "nuns were unusual among nineteenth- and early twentieth-century women in having direct control of large institutions and numerous personnel. Furthermore, sisters mobilized impressive amounts of capital for major projects whose scope and purpose they largely defined." A study of Detroit by Peter A. Ostafin in 1905 revealed that over two-thirds of all of the Poles with a professional or semi-professional position were women religious employed in schools, orphanages, hospitals, clinics, day care centers, and other largely service institutions. At their peak, Polish sisterhoods managed 34 hospitals, 15 orphanages, five homes for the aged, and 126 other social institutions.

To Radzilowski, "The growth of the religious orders represented the mobilization of the talents of thousands of Polish American women for service to their struggling new communities. The orders also acted as a major agency for social, educational and occupational mobility for women at a time when the world outside was seen as threatening and dangerous to community and faith.... Their choice of a vocation to the religious life also conferred honor and status on their families. It gave the women who joined the order the kind of respect from their male relatives they would not otherwise have gotten, as well as a certain moral authority over them."

See also **Felician Sisters; Franciscan Sisters; Holy Family of Nazareth, Sisters of the; Religious Life.**

WOMEN AND EDUCATION

Chief among the activities of the Polish sisterhoods was staffing the elementary and sec-

The Polish women's organization "Koło Polskich Dziewczat" in Connecticut (*CCSU-LP*).

ondary schools that served the Polish American communities. The experience of Poles during the later nineteenth century when the mass migration to America began was dominated by a century of occupation by foreign powers which, to a greater or lesser degree, all made attempts to restrict Polish political expression and cultural heritage. To cope with this, Poles relied very heavily upon the local parish churches to provide them with sanctuary to preserve their social and cultural heritage, educate the young in Polish language and traditions, and foster a sense of Polishness (Polskość).

With their recent experience etched in their minds, Polish immigrants to America faced the dilemma of wishing to educate their children while also harboring fears that the public education system was anti–Catholic and would lead to their denationalization as Poles. To solve the dilemma the Poles invested heavily in the establishment of parish schools that would provide education, while at the same time valuing their religion and heritage. "The Polish school stands right next to the church in importance in America," wrote the Rev. **Wacław Kruszka** in his pioneering *Historya Polska w Ameryce* (Polish History in America). "In the fullest sense of the word, it is the foundation of the Polish church abroad. Without a Polish school, the Polish church, if it is to remain Catholic, will certainly become Irish, English, and 'American.' The Polish churches, where the Poles so often hear the word of God in their native language, are citadels of patriotism; arks and vessels that protect the Polish people in exile from the flood of the deluge of denationalization and foreignness. But the foundations of these citadels, the hulls of these arks and vessels, are the Polish schools! Without them, the Polish church would sink like a bottomless vessel is a sea of Anglo-Americanism. Polish schools are the best sources and propagators of Polish nationality and patriotism on the foreign American soil. Here, in these Polish parochial schools not only do our children learn that which is offered in 'public' or government-supported schools — that is, to read, write, and count — but they also learn faith in God and love for our homeland — Poland. In the other schools our Polish children would hear about Poland only as much as, or even less than, they might hear about the wild tribes of Australia or distant islands."

The Polish parochial schools faced a daunting task. During the 1870s, when large-scale immigration to the United States began, only 39 percent of the children of school age in the Austrian-controlled Polish area of **Galicia** were actually enrolled. As late as 1895, illiteracy in the Russian section of partitioned Poland was about 70 percent. Among Polish immigrants arriving between 1901 and 1904, 27.5 percent were illiterate, a number that rose to 32.2 percent for those arriving between 1905 and 1908. The Rev. Anthony Kuzniewski estimates that by 1900 approximately 35 percent of all Polish Americans were illiterate. With this disadvantage, the educational opportunities available to Polish Americans were crucial to their successful transition into the American socio-economic milieu.

The parochial school movement gathered considerable impetus after 1884 when the Third Plenary Council of Roman Catholic bishops mandated the establishment of parish schools as a means of preserving Catholicism. In 1887 a total of about 75 Polish parochial elementary schools enrolled 14,510 children. By 1914 this increased to 395 schools serving 128,500 students, and by 1918, 511 parochial schools with 3,658 teachers educated 219,711 children. Kuzniewski found that in 1921 some 67 percent of Polish American children attended parochial schools, and as late as 1957 there were still 769 schools serving 214,000 students. In fact, a national study by Andrew Greeley and Peter H. Rossi in 1966 concluded that 73 percent of all children of Polish extraction had at least some parochial school background.

The backbone of these efforts was the orders of teaching nuns who dedicated their lives to the task of educating Polish youth. By 1901, Kruszka calculated that Polish parochial schools were already serving almost 70,000 students. At their peak, the various orders staffed some 1,000 schools, developed their own curricula, wrote and published their own textbooks, and administered every other aspect of the educational enterprise. It is due largely to their efforts to promote Catholicism and Polish heritage that scholars have found the Poles in America to retain the strongest religious and ethnic ties of any of the primary European immigrant groups. Largely because of the efforts of the parochial school system, the illiteracy rate among Polish Americans, which stood at about 35 percent in 1900, declined rapidly to only 3 percent in 1924. Further, the parochial school system succeeded amply in preserving religious faith and Polish heritage among Polish Americans. A number of studies have shown that the values of Polish culture and Roman Catholicism remained strong among Polish Americans even in the last decade of the twentieth century. The nuns had a particular effect in opening education to women who might otherwise not have persisted in the public schools. The results can be seen in the 1980 census which reported that over 90 percent of Polish American women

under the age of 25 had completed high school, a higher percentage than any other group reported. "Possibly no one in Polonia did more to shape the consciousness of Polish Americans than did the Felician sisters," asserted Radzilowski, "defining Polish American identity through their schools and textbooks, shaping its institutions, channeling its human resources and surplus capital into educational and charitable endeavors, tying together its neighborhoods and educating its youth.... From the beginning they helped to socialize the immigrants from the villages of the Polish plain into the confusing world of urban, industrializing America.... [T]hey preserved the Polish language, literature and traditions and at the same time taught us, above all, to be loyal Americans. For better or worse, they did their best with love under sometimes difficult conditions, and Polonia owes them an incalculable debt."

Aside from the considerable contributions of the religious orders to the education of Polonia's youth, women were deeply involved in more informal educational activities in the home where they were the primary transmitters of culture, customs, oral histories, and language. Outside the home, women were the backbone of organizing and staffing **Saturday schools**, organizing cultural events. Research by Ewa Gierat and Anna Jaroszyńska-Kirchmann suggests that as many as seventy percent of the post–World War II leaders in the **scouting** movement were women, while others were engaged in educational activities in libraries, museums, and other organizations largely staffed by women. Traditionally, it has been women who are most involved in passing along folk art such as creating wycinanki, pisanki, folk costumes, decorations, and performing arts such as music, dance, and theater. In recent years, women authors such as **Susanne Strempek Shea** and **Leslie Pietrzyk** have found a wide audience for their short stories based on Polish American life.

See also **Religious Life, Polish American; Politics, Polish Americans in; Fine Arts, Polish Americans in; Literature, Polish American; Organizational Life, Polish American.**—*James S. Pula*

Sources: Laura Anker, "Women, Work and Family: Polish, Italian and Eastern European Immigrants in Industrial Connecticut, 1890–1940," *Polish American Studies*, Vol. 45, no. 2, pp. 23–49; John J. Bukowczyk, "Holy Mary, Other of God: Sacred and Profane Constructions of Polish-American Womanhood," *The Polish Review*, Vol. 48, no. 2, pp. 195–203; Sr. M. Tullia Doman, "Polish American Sisterhoods and Their Contributions to the Catholic Church in the U.S.," *Sacrum Poloniae Millennium* (Rome, Italy), Vol. 6, pp. 371–622; Mary Patrice Erdmans, *The Grasinski Girls: The Choices They Had and the Choices They Made* (Athens: Ohio University Press, 2004); William J. Galush, "Purity and Power: Chicago Polonia Feminists, 1880–

1914," *Polish American Studies*, Vol. 47, no. 1, pp. 5–24; Thomas S. Gladsky and Rita Holmes Gladsky, eds., *Something of My Very Own to Say: American Women Writers of Polish Descent* (Boulder, CO: East European Monographs, 1997); Corrine Azen Krause, "Ethnic Culture, Religion, and the Mental Health of Slavic-American Women," *Journal of Religion and Health*, Vol. 18, No. 4 (1979); Joseph John Parot, "The 'Serdeczna Matko' of the Sweatshops: Marital and Family Crises of Immigrant Working-Class Women in Late Nineteenth-Century Chicago," in Frank Renkiewicz, ed., *The Polish Presence in Canada and America* (Toronto: The Multicultural History Society of Ontario, 1982); Thaddeus C. Radzilowski, "Family, Women, and Gender: The Polish Experience," in John J. Bukowczyk, ed., *Polish Americans and Their History: Community, Culture, and Politics* (Pittsburgh: University of Pittsburgh Press, 1996); Thaddeus C. Radzilowski, "Immigrant Women and Their Daughters" (New Britain, CT: Fiedorczyk Lecture, Central Connecticut State University, 1990).

World Union of Poles from Abroad (Światowy Związek Polaków z Zagranicy; Światpol). An organization established by the Polish government, its purpose was to promote closer ties between Poland and the many and varied Polish emigrant communities throughout the world (it may be noted here Poland was by no means unique in making such an effort). The largest and most significant of these was in the United States. Planning for the organization took several years, with a first Congress of Poles from Abroad held in July 1929. Światpol was itself established in July and August 1934 at a large gathering in Warsaw of Polish government officials and **Polonia** representatives from more than twenty countries. The largest foreign contingent, numbering forty members, was from the United States. However, the Polish American delegation, which was led by **Censor Francis Swietlik** of the **Polish National Alliance**, followed the advice of the U.S. ambassador to Poland and declined to formally join Światpol on the grounds that it was sponsored by the Polish government. This decision was accepted by Światpol and the Polish Americans attended the congress as its guests. The decision not to join Światpol has been called American Polonia's "declaration of independence" from Poland. Indeed, the Polish Americans' statement to the congress, after praising the achievements of newly restored independent Poland and noting **Polonia**'s part in supporting the Polish cause, asserted that: "The emigrants constitute a strong and lasting link between Poland and her sincere and disinterested friend, the United States of America. We regard ourselves as an inseparable component of the great American nation. We take an active and creative part in every walk of American life, and thus contribute to boosting the name of Poland in our country. The emigration does not intend to cease its work in the future but, on the contrary, to continue it.

That is why we delegates from Polish organizations in the United States composed of American citizens, in the name of those organizations declare our readiness to collaborate with the World Union of Poles from Abroad in the field of culture on the understanding that our decision is subject to approval by the supreme authorities of our organizations." In fact, several Polonia organizations did take issue with the decision not to join Światpol, most notably the **Polish Falcons** of America.

Three observations regarding Polonia's relation with Poland as expressed in the 1934 declaration are in order. First, the statement is very much the same in spirit to the advice given by émigré leader **Agaton Giller** to Polonia prior to the founding of the Polish National Alliance in 1880. Second, it reflected a view held by many Polonia activists in the 1930s, that Polish Americans and their communities were distinct from Poland and that the "Polish issue" should be subordinated to the domestic concerns of "Americans of Polish extraction"—a term used by historian **Mieczysław Haiman**. This "Polonia for Polonia" view (or in the language of the time, "Wychodźtwo dla wychodźtwa," "Emigrants for the Emigrants") had first been expressed in 1921 and led to the disbanding of **John Smulski**'s **National Department** federation in favor of a Polonia-focused Polish Welfare Council in America (Polska Rada Opieki Społecznej w Ameryce). In fact the division was also generational in nature and perhaps a reflection of the enduring split between Piłsudski and Dmowski supporters in America. Third, in fact, Polonia continued to be powerfully concerned about Poland, as manifested in the community's responses to Poland's destruction at the hands of Nazi Germany and Soviet Russia in September 1939 and the subsequent creation of the Rada Polonii Amerykańskiej (**Polish American Council**) relief organization and the **Polish American Congress** political action federation.

During the Second World War, Światpol, then re-located in the West, continued propagandizing in support of the cause of Polish independence. In 1993, a new Poland-based organization, Wspólnota Polska (The Polish Community) called its first worldwide congress of representatives from the Polish communities abroad. Its efforts to bring the Polish American organizations into formal membership also failed, and for reasons that were similar to those of 1934.—*Donald E. Pienkos*

SOURCE: Donald E. Pienkos, *For Your Freedom Through Ours: Polish American Efforts on Poland's Behalf, 1863–1991* (Boulder, CO: East European Monographs, 1991).

Wos, Aldona Zofia (b. Warsaw, Poland, March 26, 1955; d.—). Diplomat, physician.

The daughter of a former member of the Polish Home Army (Armia Krajowa), a survivor of the Flossenburg Concentration Camp, and a recipient of the "Righteous Among the Nations" medal from Yad Vashem, Aldona Wos obtained her medical degree at the Warsaw Medical Academy before moving to New York City to complete her residency. A specialist in HIV and AIDS prevention, she is a member of the American College of Physicians, the American Women's Medical Association, and the American College of Chest Physicians. In 2004, Pres. George W. Bush appointed her Ambassador to Estonia. For her services in that position, she was awarded the Estonian Order of the Cross of Terra Mariana, 1st Class, the Distinguished Service Cross of the Estonian Defense Forces and the Cross of Merit of the Estonian National Police Board. She was also appointed by Pres. Bush to serve on the United States Holocaust Memorial Council. In 2006 the Institute of World Politics in Washington, D.C., recognized her with an honorary degree.—*James S. Pula*

SOURCE: Richard P. Poremski, "Aldona Wos, Mark Brzezinski and Ian Brzezinski Awarded in Polish Consulate in Washington, D.C." *Polish-American Journal*, April 5, 2007.

Wozniak, Stephen Gary "Woz" (b. San Jose, California, August 11, 1950; d.—) Computer engineer, inventor, businessman. Wozniak was the son of an engineer from Lockheed Corporation. Basically self-educated, he built his first computer at age 13 and was president of the electronics club at Homestead High School in California. He flunked out of the University of Colorado and later withdrew from the University of California, Berkeley in 1975 and started working for Hewlett-Packard. He had previously become friends with Steve Jobs, also a Homestead graduate, working in a summer job in the same business where Wozniak was working on a mainframe computer. Both Wozniak and Jobs were involved with a group of young scientists and inventors who called themselves the Homebrew Computer Club. Selling Wozniak's HP scientific calculator and Jobs' VW van, the pair raised $1,300 and later assembled the first prototypes in Jobs' bedroom and garage. Wozniak's computer, which he named Apple I, was a fully assembled and functioning unit that contained a $20 microprocessor on a single-circuit board with ROM or "Read-Only Memory." It was the world's first personal computer. In April of 1976, Jobs and Wozniak formed Apple Computer, with Wozniak assuming the position of Vice President in charge of research and development. The first Apple I was priced at $666.66. In addition to designing the hardware, Wozniak also wrote most of the software. In 1980, Apple went public, with a stock value of $117 million, creating two instant multi-millionaires. Apple I became Apple II, the profits from which enabled Apple to develop the Macintosh. Due to a serious design flaw, the Apple III had to be recalled in 1981. Wozniak suffered a serious plane crash in February 1981 and did not return to Apple. Instead, he returned to Berkeley where he completed his undergraduate degree in 1986 under the name "Rocky Raccoon Clark" (a combination of his dog's name and his wife's maiden name), majoring in computer science/electrical engineering. Wozniak ended his full time employment with Apple in 1987. Since that time he has engaged in numerous activities and projects including developing the first universal TV remote control, teaching fifth grade students, supporting a technology program for his local school district, and a variety of educational and philanthropic projects. He has received honorary degrees from the University of Colorado, North Carolina State University, Kettering University, and Nova Southeastern University, as well as the National Medal of Technology in 1985 from President Ronald Reagan, and was inducted into the Inventors Hall of Fame in 2000. In 2000 he also received the prestigious Heinz Award for Technology. In 2001 Wozniak founded Wheels of Zeus, or WoZ, focusing on wireless hardware for using GPS to track the physical location of enabled objects. The company shut down operations in March 2006 and Wozniak, now known as the "Wizard of Woz," and other former Apple colleagues co-founded Acquicor Technology, a shell-company created for acquiring and developing high-tech companies.—*Richard J. Hunter, Jr., & Héctor R. Lozada*

SOURCES: Stephen Wozniak, with Gina Smith, *IWoz: From Computer Geek to Cult Icon: How I Invented the Personal Computer, Co-Founded Apple, and Had Fun Doing It* (Old Saybrook, CT: W.W. Norton, September 2006); Andy Hertzfeld, Steve Capps, and Alan Noren, *Revolution in the Valley: The Insanely Great Story of How the Mac Was Made* (Beijing: O'Reilly Media, Inc., 2005).

Woznicki, Stephen Stanislaus (b. Miners Mills, Pennsylvania, August 17,1894; d. Saginaw, Michigan, December 10, 1968). Catholic bishop. Woznicki attended St. Mary High School in Detroit before entering Saints **Cyril and Methodius Seminary** in Orchard Lake, Michigan. He later attended St. Paul Seminary in Minnesota and was ordained in Detroit on December 22, 1917, at the age of 23. Assigned to a parish in Danville, Pennsylvania, in 1919 he was appointed secretary to Bishop Michael Gallagher in Detroit. He was appointed auxiliary bishop of Detroit on December 13, 1937, and bishop of the Diocese

of Saginaw in 1950. He served for a total of 51 years as a priest and just short of thirty years as a bishop.—*James S. Pula*

Wspólnota Rozproszonych Członków NSZZ Solidarność *see* **Brotherhood of Dispersed Solidarity Members.**

Wyrwa, Tadeusz (b. Warsaw, Poland, March 15, 1926; d.—). Soldier. A soldier of the Home Army in Poland during the Second World War, a displaced person in the United States following the war, then a retired professor in France, Wyrwa became the center of the so-called Wyrwa Affair (Sprawa Wyrwy). In 1941, at the age of sixteen, he joined his father Józef Wyrwa in active military duty with the Home Army's guerilla unit in the forests of the Kielce region. After being arrested and imprisoned by the communist authorities in 1945, both Wyrwas escaped from Poland and made their way to the displaced persons camps in Germany. In 1949, they migrated to Chicago, and in August 1950 the 25-year-old Tadeusz was drafted into the American army. In a published statement he refused to join because, as a Polish citizen and a Polish officer, he was obliged to only follow the orders of the Polish government in London. Both the Polish American and American press picked up the issue, initiating a heated debate on the responsibilities of refugees toward the country which admitted them, as well as their native homeland. Polonia's opinion was divided with some praising Wyrwa and others condemning him. Detroit's *Dziennik Polski* (Polish Daily News), Chicago's *Dziennik Związkowy* (Alliance Daily News), and New York's *Nowy Świat* (New World), among others, carried editorials and letters to the editor discussing the issue. The debate focused on U.S. leadership in the Cold War, loyalty toward the American versus the Polish London government, the need to keep Poland's plight in the international focus, as well as the duties of exiles and refugees toward their adoptive countries. In response to the Wyrwa Affair, the London government issued a statement that Polish citizens should not serve in foreign armies, which reflected a belief that the Korean War might turn into an international conflict in which the Polish army-in-exile could then fight for Poland's independence from communist domination. In June 1951 the U.S. Congress closed a loophole by passing a new law stating that foreigners residing in the U.S. were now eligible for compulsory military service. In January 1952, Tadeusz Wyrwa received another draft notice. Since he had no intention of complying, he applied for an emigration visa to leave the U.S. His application was denied because he was a male of draft age.

Although the London government now recommended that Wyrwa obey American law, he again refused to serve, was briefly arrested, and then released on bail. The continued debate in Polonia featured voices concerned about the image of Polonia as unpatriotic, as well as those that called for making the Wyrwa Affair into an international case highlighting the Polish cause. In September 1952, Wyrwa's case was finally dismissed on the grounds of his long military service in the Home Army. Disappointed by the lack of support for his uncompromising stance, Wyrwa and his father left the U.S. They first settled in Spain, where Tadeusz received a doctorate in political science with a specialization in international law. Since 1960, Wyrwa has lived in Paris, France, where he earned three more doctoral degrees. He is the author of numerous books and other publications on the history of Poland.—*Anna D. Jaroszyńska-Kirchmann*

SOURCES: Józef Wyrwa, *Pamietniki Partyzanta* (London: Oficyna Poetow i Malarzy, 1991); Anna D. Jaroszyńska-Kirchmann, *The Exile Mission: The Polish Political Diaspora and Polish Americans, 1939–1956* (Athens: Ohio University Press, 2004).

Yablonski, Joseph Albert "Jock" (b. Pittsburgh, Pennsylvania, March 3, 1910; d. Clarksville, Pennsylvania, December 31, 1969). Labor leader. Going to work in the mines as a boy, Yablonski was propelled into union activism by the death of his father in a mining accident. Quickly establishing himself as a leader, he gained election to the international executive board of the United Mine Workers in 1940 and became president of District 5 of the UMW in 1958. When William A. "Tony" Boyle became UMW president in 1963 the two quickly clashed over Boyle's attempts to concentrate power in his office and Yablonski's belief that Boyle was not representing the real interests of the union members. Since district presidents were then appointed, in 1965 Boyle removed Yablonski as president of District 5. In May 1969 Yablonski announced his intention to run against Boyle for UMW president, campaigning on promises of greater democracy within the union and more responsiveness to rank-and-file concerns. When Boyle defeated Yablonski in an election many viewed as fraudulent, Yablonski conceded, but then filed five legal actions in federal court and requested that the U.S. Department of Labor launch a probe of election fraud. When Yablonski, his wife and daughter were murdered on December 31, 1969, subsequent investigations determined that Boyle had arranged the "hit," paying for it with money he embezzled from the union. Yablonski's murder resulted in formation of the "Miners for Democracy" movement, a federal investigation that overturned the results of Boyle's 1969 election, and the election of Arnold Miller, the "Miners for Democracy" candidate, at a special election overseen by the Department of Labor in December 1972. Boyle was convicted of murder and sentenced to three consecutive life terms. **Charles Bronson** played the part of "Jock" Yablonski in the 1986 HBO movie *Act of Vengeance*, while the murder was also featured in *Harlan County USA*, a 1976 documentary by Barbara Kopple.—*James S. Pula*

SOURCE: Trevor Armbrister, *Act of Vengeance: The Yablonski Murders and Their Solution* (New York: E. P. Dutton & Co., Inc., 1975).

Yalta. To Polish Americans, the word "Yalta" is synonymous with "betrayal." Poland was the first nation to take up arms against German Fascism. It fought for six long years, contributing more armed forces to the defeat of Germany than any nation other than Great Britain, the United States, and the Soviet Union, and suffering inestimable human and physical damage. It lost over six million citizens killed, and only Yugoslavia suffered a higher percentage of deaths during the war than Poland. Yet, at the end of the war the "Big Three"—Franklin D. Roosevelt, Winston Churchill, and Joseph Stalin—met in the Yalta Conference in the Crimea to reaffirm secret protocols agreed to at the earlier Teheran Conference. Poland, a loyal ally that had contributed and suffered so much during the war, was treated as if it were a defeated enemy. Poland was forced to relinquish some 70,000 square miles of territory to the Soviet Union including the historic and beloved city of Lwów. Although Poland was later "compensated" with 40,000 square miles of German territory east of the Oder and Neisse Rivers at the Potsdam Conference in the summer of 1945, it remained the only allied nation to *lose* territory and population by being on the winning side in the conflict. Further, at the same time the Soviet-organized Lublin puppet government was officially recognized as the legitimate government of Poland, while the Polish government-in-exile in London, which had loyally supported the Allied cause throughout the war, was cast aside. Poland was also the only Allied nation *not* invited to San Francisco to participate in the formation of the United Nations. Outrage over the Yalta agreements dominated much of Polish American politics in the decade following the end of the war in 1945, and continued to be a sore point for decades thereafter.—*James S. Pula*

SOURCES: William Larsh, "Yalta and the American Approach to Free Elections in Poland," *The Polish Review*, Vol. 40, no. 3 (1995), 267–89; Athan G. Theoharis, "Ethnic Politics and National Policy: Polish-Americans and Yalta," *Intellect*, March, 1976, 470–71; James S. Pula, *Polish Americans: An Ethnic Community* (New York: Twayne Publishers, 1995), 102–15.

Yanta, John Walter (b. Runge, Texas, October 2, 1931; d.—). Priest. The fifth of eight children, his paternal and maternal ancestors migrated to **Panna Maria**, Texas from the Opole region of Silesia in 1854 and 1855. Yanta attended the Runge Public Schools before moving to San Antonio, Texas, where he graduated from Central Catholic High School while beginning his seminary studies as a high school sophomore. After studying briefly in Kirkwood, Missouri as a postulant of the Society of Mary, he entered St. John's Seminary in San Antonio, but transferred to Assumption Seminary for theologate studies. Yanta was ordained to the priesthood on March 17, 1956 at San Fernando Cathedral in San Antonio. His first assignment was as second assistant pastor at St. Ann's Parish in San Antonio. In 1962 he was named director of the archdiocesan Catholic Youth Organization (CYO), subsequently being named youth director for the Archdiocese of San Antonio in 1963. In 1965 he founded the San Antonio Neighborhood Youth Organization (SANYO), serving as its executive director until 1971 while growing it into a federally funded anti-poverty program providing work training for needy youth in San Antonio. In 1971 he founded and became first president of the **Polish American Congress** of Texas. He later served as president of the Texas Catholic Conference of Priest Senates (1978–82) and was editor of the archdiocesan newspaper *Today's Catholic* (1981–83). Yanta received the Bishop Odin Award from the Texas Conference on Ethnic Community Affairs in 1980. In November 1981 he founded the Catholic Television of San Antonio (CTSA), the first Catholic television station in the United States, and served as its first executive director. A lifelong advocate for the unborn, Yanta was arrested on January 22, 1983 for blocking the entrance of an abortion clinic in San Antonio. On November 29, 1989 he was elevated to the title of monsignor in the Roman Catholic Church, and the following year organized the **Polish American Priests Association** (PAPA). On December 30, 1994, in an outdoor Mass in Panna Maria, Texas, Yanta was ordained auxiliary bishop of San Antonio and titular bishop of Naratcata. On January 21, 1997, Pope John Paul II appointed Yanta to the Diocese of Amarillo, Texas, where he was installed on March 17, 1997. Yanta is as a member of the Catholic Relief Service Board of Directors, the Kennedy Memorial Foundation, and treasurer of the Texas Conference of Churches. On December 12, 2005, Bishop Yanta approved the Constitutions of the Missionaries of the Gospel of Life, a society of apostolic life for priests, deacons and lay missionaries to support the pro-

file cause in the United States and internationally.—*Eric Opiela*

SOURCE: Bolesław Wierzbiański, *Who's Who in Polish America* (New York: Bicentennial Publishing Corp., 1996), 518–19.

Yarosz, Teddy (b. Pittsburgh, Pennsylvania, June 24, 1910; d. Monaca, Pennsylvania, March 29, 1974). Prize Fighter. The son of Polish immigrants, Yarosz began his professional boxing career in 1929. He won the world middleweight championship in 1934, defeating Vince Dundee. The following year, Yarosz lost the crown to Babe Risko. He continued fighting until 1942, never regaining a world title, but defeating such highly regarded opponents as Billy Conn and Archie Moore. Four of his brothers boxed at various levels; one of them, Tommy, became a ranked light heavyweight. Yarosz is a member of the International Boxing Hall of Fame and the World Boxing Hall of Fame, and was inducted into the **National Polish-American Sports Hall of Fame** in 2005.—*Neal Pease*

SOURCE: "Teddy Yarosz," National Polish-American Sports Hall of Fame website, www.polishsportshof.com.

Yastrzemski, Carl (b. Southampton, New York, August 22, 1939; d.—). Baseball player. The son of Polish American potato farmers on Long Island, Yastrzemski succeeded the legendary Ted Williams as left fielder for the Boston Red Sox in 1961, and became one of the greatest stars of the game in his own right. Over the course of a career spanning 23 seasons, he compiled a .285 lifetime batting average with 452 home runs. A left handed hitter, he won three American League batting championships. As a left fielder, Yastrzemski won eight Gold Glove awards for defensive excellence at that position before moving to first base in his later years as a player. He was named to eighteen American League All-Star squads, and his Red Sox teams played in two World Series. "Yaz" is best remembered for his exploits in 1967, when he turned in one of the finest individual seasons in the annals of the game. Already an established standout, he won the "Triple Crown" that year by leading his league in batting average, home runs, and runs batted in, a feat that, as of 2009, had not been duplicated by any major leaguer. In addition, Yastrzemski drove the undermanned Red Sox to an unexpected and dramatic American League pennant, their first in more than two decades. His performance won him the annual Most Valuable Player award, and *Sports Illustrated* named him its "Sportsman of the Year." After the heroics of 1967, Yastrzemski turned in several more seasons of comparable brilliance, and remained a fixture in the Boston lineup until 1983. He retired from the game at or near the top of many lifetime statistical categories, a testimony to his rare combination of quality and longevity. In 2009, Yaz remained the only player in the history of the American League to have reached the career levels of both 3,000 hits and 400 home runs. In his career he played in 3,308 games, had 3,419 hits, 452 home runs, and 1,844 RBIs. He was elected to the National Baseball Hall of Fame in 1989, and inducted into the **National Polish-American Sports Hall of Fame** in 1986.—*Neal Pease*

SOURCES: Carl Yastrzemski and Gerald Eskenazi, *Yaz: Baseball, the Wall, and Me* (New York: Doubleday, 1990); Carl Yastrzemski and Al Hirshberg, *Yaz* (New York: Viking, 1968); Robert B. Jackson, *"Let's Go Yaz": The Story of Carl Yastrzemski* (New York: Henry Z. Walck, 1968).

Yellen, Jack (Jacek Selig Jeleÿ; b. Raczki, Poland, July 6, 1892; d. Springville, NY, April 17, 1991). Songwriter, screenwriter. Yellen migrated to the United States from Poland with his parents at the age of five. Living in Buffalo, N.Y., he began writing songs in his teens. After graduating from the University of Michigan, he served a brief stint as a reporter, then came to New York City where he soon began writing material for singers, one of whom was Sophie Tucker for whom he wrote the 1925 piece "My Yiddishe Momma." During his career, Yellen wrote the lyrics to more than 200 popular songs and scored dozens of Broadway plays and movies. His most famous songs were "Ain't She Sweet" (1927), "Hard Hearted Hannah" (1929), and "Happy Days Are Here Again" (1930). The latter became the theme song of Democrat Franklin D. Roosevelt's 1932 presidential campaign, although Yellen was a Republican. He was a board member of the American Society of Composers, Authors and Publishers (ASCAP) from 1951 to 1969, and was among the first inductees into the Songwriters Hall of Fame in 1969. He always maintained a home in the Buffalo area and commuted to New York for business.—*Martin S. Nowak*

SOURCE: Richard Hanser, *Buffalo Melody Makers: Jack Yellen, One Little Nap Too Many Sent Him to Tin Pan Alley to Fame and Fortune* (Buffalo: Buffalo Times, 1931).

Yolles, Piotr Paweł (pseudonym Włóczęga (The Wanderer); b. Zabłotów, Poland, February 25, 1892; d. New York, New York, August 26, 1958). Editor, journalist. Yolles received his early education in Stanisławów and graduated from the University of Czerniowce (now in Ukraine) with a degree in law (1914). He was drafted into the Austrian army at the beginning of World War I, was wounded and contracted malaria. He migrated to the U.S. in 1920 where he attended Columbia Univer-

sity, earned an M.A. degree in social science in 1925, and enrolled in journalism classes at New York University. For the rest of his life, Yolles combined journalism and social work. After serving as associate editor of *Dziennik Nowoyorski* (New York Daily News, 1920) and editor of *Telegram Codzienny* (Everyday Telegram, 1921–24), he began a long-term stint with New York's *Nowy Świat* (New World), where he held editorial positions for the rest of his life and established the paper's Social Services Department. *Nowy Świat* was aligned with the **National Defense Committee**. In addition, he founded and directed the South Brooklyn Polish Day Nursery. Yolles was an active writer on many fronts. His short articles frequently appeared both under his own name and under the pseudonym Włóczęga (The Wanderer), perhaps an allusion to his Jewish background. It was under this pseudonym that his 1930 novel, *Trzy matki* (Three Mothers), was serialized in *Nowy Świat*. Never published as a stand-alone novel and never translated into English, *Trzy matki* was a sophisticated exploration of restrictive social, religious, and gender issues in pre–World War II Poland, which Yolles presents in contrast to the dream of individual opportunity in America. A 1953 novel, *Ciernie* (Thorns), is set in World War II Poland. Besides contributing daily pieces in the Polish American press, he also served as correspondent for numerous papers in Europe and North and South America, and his articles were translated into many languages, including Chinese and Greek. His English-language monograph, *Social Aspects of the Housing Problem in New York City,* was published in 1925. He contributed a chapter to the English-language book *I Am an American* and analyzed the Polish ethnic community in William Seabrook's *Americans All* (1938).

Yolles also had his own weekly radio program on New York's *Two Edwards* show, which did much to support Polish war relief. He served as president of the Stowarzyszenia Wydawców i Dziennikarzy Polskich (Association of Polish Editors and Journalists) and the Związek Dziennikarzy Polskich w Ameryce (Alliance of Polish Journalists in America). In 1946, he was one of the organizers of the **Polish American Immigration and Relief Committee,** for the aid of refugees from Poland. On the 25th anniversary of his journalistic career, *Nowy Świat*'s readers offered Yolles the gift of a car. He accepted an ambulance instead, which was sent to the Polish army in England. He was an active member of the **Polish National Alliance** and the **Polish Falcons.** Among his many awards were the Cross of the Legion of Honor from the Polish Fal-

cons and the Swords of General Haller from the **Polish Veterans Association** in America. Outlining his long career after his death, New York's *Robotnik Polski* issue of September 7, 1958, noted that Yolles "was above all a good man." Yolles' papers are held by the **Polish Institute of Arts and Sciences in America** (PIASA), in New York.—*Karen Majewski*

SOURCES: Karen Majewski, *Traitors and True Poles: Narrating a Polish-American Identity, 1880–1939* (Athens, OH: Ohio University Press, 2003); William Seabrook, *Americans All: A Human Study of America's Citizens from Europe* (London: G.G. Harrap, 1938); Peter Yolles in *I Am an American,* Robert Spiers Benjamin, ed. (New York: Alliance Book Corp., 1941), 48–49; Francis Bolek, ed., *Who's Who in Polish America* (New York: Harbinger House, 1943).

York, Edward Joseph "Ski" (Edward Joseph Cichowski; b. Batavia, New York, August 16, 1912; d. San Antonio, Texas, August 31, 1984). Military officer, Doolittle raider. Upon graduation from high school, he enlisted in the army in 1930, serving with the 7th Infantry Regiment based in Alaska. Deciding on a military career, he applied to and was accepted at the West Point Preparatory School in San Francisco. In 1934 he received a senatorial appointment to the U.S. Military Academy at West Point, graduating in 1938. While at West Point, he changed his surname to York, but friends continued to call him by his nickname "Ski." Choosing the Army Air Corps as his branch of service, he trained at Randolph Field in Texas, receiving his pilot's wings in 1939. At the outbreak of World War II, York commanded the 95th Bombardment Squadron, but volunteered for secret special duty in early 1942. Reporting to Lt. Col. James Doolittle, York was named operations officer and was involved in training pilots at Eglin Field in Florida. On April 18, 1942, York piloted one of sixteen B-25 bombers that took off from the deck of the aircraft carrier *USS Hornet* under Col. James Doolittle to bomb Tokyo. With his fuel exhausted, he successfully landed his plane near Vladivostok, Siberia, where he and his crew were interned by the Soviets before escaping in April 1943. Returning to the United States, he volunteered for combat duty and was assigned as deputy commanding officer of the 483rd Bombardment Group in Italy. After flying twenty-four combat missions, he was recalled home, then assigned as Air Attaché at the U.S. embassy in Warsaw (1945–47). During this period he flew Ambassador Arthur Bliss Lane on diplomatic missions in Europe. Following this assignment he commanded the Air Force Officers Candidate School at Lackland Air Force Base in Texas. In 1950 he was assigned to the Military Advisory Assistance Group (MAAG) in Copenhagen, Denmark, returning to the U.S. to attend the Air War College in 1953 before being assigned to Headquarters, U.S. Air Force, as head of the Air Attaché Branch. Following five years with the Military Air Transport Service (MATS), he spent a year with the Air Materiel Command. His final two assignments were as commander of the Site Activation Task Force at Larson Air Force Base in Washington and Chief of Staff of the U.S. Air Force Security System in San Antonio, Texas. He retired from active duty on August 13, 1966. Following retirement from the Air Force he served as city manager of Olmos Park, Texas. His honors include the Distinguished Flying Cross awarded for his participation in the Doolittle Raid, the Legion of Merit with oak leaf cluster, the Air Force Commendation Medal, the Chinese Order of Lun Hui, and various theater and campaign medals.—*Francis C. Kajencki*

SOURCES: Nelson Craig, *The First Heroes: The Extraordinary Story of the Doolittle Raid—America's First World War II Victory* (New York: Viking, 2002); Duane P. Schultz, *The Doolittle Raid* (New York: St. Martin's Press, 1988); Carroll V. Glines, *The Doolittle Raid: America's Daring First Strike Against Japan* (New York, NY: Orion Books, 1988).

Za Chlebem. The Polish term *"za chlebem"* means "for bread." Between the mid–1880s and the beginning of World War I in 1914, approximately 1.5 million Poles migrated to the United States. Most of these new arrivals were rural farm workers who left the homeland to escape harsh economic conditions. They were generally undereducated and are often referred to by historians as *"za chlebem"* immigrants, particularly those who came after 1890, because they sought better economic conditions. However, the group also included a small number of intellectuals, revolutionaries, and clergy, especially among the Poles who arrived prior to 1890. The *"za chlebem"* immigration was the largest wave of Polish immigration to reach America.—*Anne Gurnack*

SOURCE: Victor Greene, "Poles" in S. Thernstrom, ed., *Harvard Encyclopedia of American Ethnic Groups* (Cambridge, MA: Harvard University Press, 1980).

Zabitosky, Fred William (b. Trenton, New Jersey, October 27, 1942; d. Lumberton, North Carolina, January 18, 1996). Soldier, Medal of Honor recipient. While serving in Vietnam with the 5th Special Forces Group, on February 19, 1968, Zabitosky voluntarily risked his life to save fellow soldiers. His citation for the Medal of Honor read: "Sergeant First Class Fred W. Zabitosky, United States Army, Studies and Observations Group, then a Staff Sergeant, distinguished himself while serving as an assistant team leader of a nine-man Special Forces long-range reconnaissance patrol operating deep within enemy held ter-

Fred W. Zabitosky receiving the Medal of Honor from President Richard Nixon (**NARA**).

ritory in Laos. On 19 February 1968, they were attacked by a numerically superior North Vietnamese Army unit. Rallying his team members, he deployed them into defensive positions and exposed himself to concentrated enemy fire in order to better direct their return fire. He covered their withdrawal to a landing zone for extraction. Rejoining the patrol, now under increased enemy pressure, he positioned each man in a tight perimeter defense, encouraging them one by one and controlling their fire. Inspired by his example, the patrol maintained its position until the arrival of the rescue helicopter. The North Vietnamese pressed their attack when the helicopters arrived, and Sergeant Zabitosky again exposed himself to their fire, allowing the helicopter gunship to adjust suppressive fire. He positioned himself beside the helicopter door-gunner and fired on the enemy as the ship took off. The helicopter crashed after being engulfed in a hail of bullets and Sergeant Zabitosky was thrown from the craft. Recovering consciousness, he ignored his painful injuries and moved to the flaming wreckage where he pulled the severely wounded pilot and copilot from the blaze. He made repeated attempts to rescue his fellow patrol members but was driven back by the intense heat. Despite his own serious burns and crushed ribs, he dragged the unconscious pilots through a curtain of enemy fire to within ten feet of a hovering rescue helicopter before collapsing."—*James S. Pula*

SOURCE: R. J. Proft, *United States of America's Congressional Medal of Honor Recipients and Their Official Citations* (Columbia Heights, MN: Highland House II, 2002).

Zablocki, Clement John (b. Milwaukee, Wisconsin, November 18, 1912; d. Washington, District of Columbia, December 3, 1983).

Congressman. The son of a laborer and a neighborhood grocery store owner, Clement Zablocki was born in the South Side of Milwaukee. He attended school at St. Vincent's Catholic School and then Marquette University High School before enrolling in Marquette University where he received a degree in communications in 1936. Active as a church organist, choir leader, and civics instructor for immigrants, the personable, popular Zablocki was a natural candidate for public office. Elected State Senator as a Democrat in 1942, he lost the 1948 election for Milwaukee City Comptroller, a position often held by a prominent Polish American in previous years. Desiring to purge leftist and pro–Soviet radicals from the Wisconsin Democratic Party, Zablocki succeeded in winning the traditionally Democratic-leaning and heavily Polish American Fourth District seat in the U.S. House of Representatives in 1948, serving in Congress from 1949 until his death. A noted defender of labor and Catholic interests, he was instrumental in helping William Proxmire and Gaylord Nelson win state offices and in John F. Kennedy's campaign for the presidency. Zablocki helped change the Foreign Affairs Committee from an insignificant panel to an important power base. A Wilsonian internationalist, Zablocki advocated using foreign aid to foster economic development. He also served as a congressional expert on Poland. A strong supporter of the Vietnam War—even to the point of chairing Lyndon B. Johnson's doomed 1968 Wisconsin primary campaign—once he realized that the unpopularity of the war threatened his position, Zablocki

Clement Zablocki, congressman (**PMA**).

transformed his image from a militant hawk to an arms control advocate. He later secured the passage of legislation designed to restrain the "Imperial Presidency." Most importantly, he was the primary author of the War Powers Resolution of 1973, whose constitutionality remains a bone of contention between advocates and critics of presidential leadership in foreign policy matters. In subsequent years, Zablocki sought to maintain presidential flexibility with strict accountability after controversial decisions. In 1977, he became chair of the International Relations Committee (later renamed again the Foreign Affairs Committee) despite strong opposition from the supporters of Israel. As chair, Zablocki attempted to implement a bipartisan foreign policy in an age of increasing political polarization. Zablocki was also responsible for the establishment of a children's hospital in Kraków paid for by the U.S. government. A life-size statue of the diminutive Zablocki stands at the entrance to the hospital. Zablocki was also a key Congressional ally of presidents **Charles Rozmarek** and **Aloysius Mazewski** of the **Polish American Congress** on matters pertaining to Poland, and on behalf of funding Radio Free Europe. His popularity in his Congressional district was such that he rarely needed to do any fundraising, and his only serious challenge came in his last years, but this too proved unsuccessful.—*Steven M. Leahy*

SOURCE: Stephen M. Leahy, *The Life of Milwaukee's Most Popular Politician, Clement J. Zablocki: Milwaukee Politics and Congressional Foreign Policy* (Lewiston, NY: E. Mellen Press, 2002).

Zaborowski, Olbrecht (b. Pokrzywna, Poland, about 1638; d. Hackensack, New Jer-

Olbrecht Zaborowski portrayed in a miniature by Arthur Szyk (*OLS*).

sey, September 11, 1711). Entrepreneur, government official. Zaborowski arrived in the Dutch colony of New Amsterdam in 1662. There, he engaged in trading and learned the local Indian language well enough to become an interpreter. Apparently successful at business, he eventually owned title to much of what is today northern New Jersey. In 1682 he was named the first Justice of the Peace in Upper Bergen County. He was a founder of the Lutheran Church in Hackensack, NJ. The family, whose name was later changed to Zabriskie, enjoyed a long and influential role in New Jersey history.—*James S. Pula*

SOURCES: Mieczysław Haiman, *The Polish Past in America 1608–1865* (Chicago: Polish Museum of America, 1974), 17–19; Richard Wynkoop, "Zabriskie Notes," *The New York Genealogical and Biographical Record*, Vol. XXIII, 26.

Zabriskie *see* **Olbrecht Zaborowski.**

Zabriskie, Christian Brevoort (b. Fort Bridger, Wyoming Territory, October 16, 1864; d. February 8, 1936). Businessman. Descended from Olbrecht Zaborowski, who migrated to the Dutch colony of New Amsterdam (later New York) in 1662, Zabriskie served as a telegrapher with the Virginia & Truckee Railroad in Carson City, Nevada, before gaining employment in the Esmeralda County Bank in Candelaria. In 1885 his life took a dramatic turn when Francis M. "Borax" Smith offered him a managerial position with his Harmony Borax Works in 20 Mule Team Canyon. Five years later Smith purchased the holdings of a rival company which he consolidated with his own business under the name Pacific Coast Borax Company. Adept at management, Zabriskie earned promotion to vice president and general manager, positions he held for thirty-six years. Under his leadership, the Pacific Coast Borax Company prospered. Its "20-Mule Team Borax" slogan became a household phrase, especially through its sponsorship of the popular television program *Death Valley Days* first hosted by the "Old Ranger" played by Polish-American actor Stanley Andrews. Because of his lengthy association with the borax industry and the area surrounding 20 Mule Team Canyon, a popular tourist spot located in the Amargosa Mountains within the Death Valley National Park was named Zabriskie Point in his honor. Zabriskie retired in 1933, the same year the National Park was established.—*James S. Pula*

SOURCE: Hugh Tolford, *Zabriskie Point and Christian Brevoort Zabriskie, the Man* (Pasadena, CA: Castle Press, 1976).

Zachara, Franciszek (b. Tarnów, Poland, December 10, 1898; d. Tallahassee, Florida, February 2, 1966). Composer, musician. After receiving his early education in a state gym-

nasium in Warsaw, he pursued the study of music at the Imperial Conservatory in Saratov, Russia, where he graduated in 1919. He undertook further studies at the Imperial Conservatory in St. Petersburg, graduating in 1921, after which he taught piano at the State Conservatory in Katowice, Poland (1922–28). He made his American debut in New York on November 18, 1928, receiving positive reviews from critics. Following an American tour, he accepted a position teaching piano at Brenau College in Georgia, later being named Dean of Music. Zachara became a U.S. citizen in 1946, the same year in which he moved to New York. Two years later he accepted a position at Florida State University. Known for composing in the Polish romantic tradition, Zachara composed more than 150 works for piano, a symphony, several works for band, and numerous chamber pieces.—*James S. Pula*

SOURCES: Mark J. Froelich, *The Franciszek Zachara Collection at the Warren D. Allen Music Library: Catalog and Biographical Notes* (Tallahassee, FL: Florida State University College of Music, 2005); obituary, "Music Prof. F. Zachara dead at 67," *Tallahassee Democrat*, February 3, 1966).

Zachariasiewicz, Władysław "Walter" (b. Kraków, Poland, November 7, 1911; d.—). Polonia activist. A graduate of the Jagiellonian University in the fields of law and administration, Zachariasiewicz was president of the Polish Democratic Youth Association at the university. An officer who took part in the defense of Poland in 1939, he spent time in Soviet prison and labor camps before being released through the efforts of the Polish government-in-exile in London. In 1946 he was evacuated with the Polish army of Gen. Władysław Anders to Britain and in 1948 was able to migrate to the United States. By that time Zachariasiewicz had already become active in Polish relief and immigration work in Europe and continued in this capacity in the U.S. after Pres. Truman signed the Displaced Persons Act into law. Finding employment in the U.S. Post Office, he enjoyed a long and productive career, rising to the rank of special assistant to the Postmaster General of the United States. Zachariasiewicz was involved in a number of **Polonia** organizations devoted to promoting knowledge of Poland's cultural heritage. These included his service as president of the Polish American Arts Association in Washington, D.C., and the **American Council of Polish Cultural Clubs**, and his membership on the Advisory Council of the **Polish Institute of Arts and Sciences of America**. He was also active in the **Polish American Congress** and served as a member of its Polish Affairs Committee. In the 1990s he was personally named by Pope John Paul

II to serve as a member of the board of directors of the Pope John Paul II Foundation. Zachariasiewicz was politically engaged and headed the effort with American ethnic communities to promote the presidential election campaigns of Sen. John F. Kennedy in 1960 and Pres. Lyndon B. Johnson in 1964. He also served on the board of directors of Radio Free Europe/Radio Liberty. In 2006, Zachariasiewicz published his study of American **Polonia** titled *Etos Niepodległościowy Polonii Amerykańskiej* (The Independence Ethos of American Polonia).—*Donald E. Pienkos*

SOURCE: Bolesław Wierzbiański, *Who's Who in Polish America* (New York: Bicentennial Publishing Corp., 1996), 520–21.

Zadora, Pia (Pia Alfreda Schipani; b. Hoboken, New Jersey, May 4, 1954; d.—). Singer, actress. The daughter of an Italian father and a Polish mother (Saturnina Zadorowski, whose maiden name Zadora shortened as her stage name), Zadora attended the American Academy of Dramatic Art while still a child in order to get rid of her shyness. After playing Bialke on Broadway in *Fiddler on the Roof* (1964–66), she starred in the film *Butterfly* (1981) for which she was recognized with a Golden Globe Award as New Star of the Year; however, her effort was also "rewarded" with two Razzie Awards in 1982 as "Worst New Star" and "Worst Actress." In 1983 she received yet another Razzie as "Worst Actress" for her portrayal of a victim of sexual assault in *The Lonely Lady*. The Razzie Awards later named her "Worst New Star of the Decade" for the 1980s. In 1983 she appeared in a *Penthouse* magazine pictorial, and later became the focus of criticism when she and her husband purchased Pickfair, the former home of screen icons Mary Pickford and Douglas Fairbanks Sr., and proceeded to demolish the mansion and subdivide the property. Her chief fame came in her singing career which began in the 1960s under the stage name "Little Pia." She later rose to fame as a pop singer during the 1980s. She was nominated for a Grammy Award in 1984 for "Rock It Out."—*Patricia Finnegan*

SOURCES: "Pia Zadora," *Contemporary Theatre, Film, and Television* (Detroit: Gale Research, 1991), Vol. 9; "Pia Zadora," *Almanac of Famous People* (Detroit: Thomson Gale, 2007).

Zahajkiewicz, Szczęsny (b. Stanisławów, Poland, April—, 1861; d. Chicago, Illinois, October 1, 1917). Poet, editor, Polonia activist. Educated in Horodenka, Kołomyja, and Stanisławów, Zahajkiewicz graduated from the Teachers College (Seminarjum Nauczycielskie) in Stanisławów before taking a position as a teacher in Dolina and later Stanisławów. After serving as a private teacher for Count Adalbert Dzieduszycki for three years, he took a teaching position at Piramowicz School in Lwów, where he edited the weekly newspaper *Światełko* (Light), and contributed poetry to the newspapers *Szczutek* (Fillip) and *Śmigus* (Propeller). On request of the **Fathers of the Resurrection** from Chicago, and on the recommendation of Cardinal Pużyna, he came to U.S. in 1889 as a teacher at St. Stanislaus Kostka parochial school in Chicago. In 1891 he organized and served as president of the St. Stanislaus Parish Dramatic Circle, and two years later was co-founder of the **Polish Falcons** of America, of which he was elected vice president. In 1894 he backed the creation of the **Polish League**, a national federation of **Polonia** parishes and community organizations led by the Rev. **Wincenty Barzyński**, pastor of St. Stanislaus Kostka parish and head of the **Resurrectionist Order**. The League was centered on the goal of working for the development of **Polonia**, but it failed because of opposition from the **Polish National Alliance**, which included a commitment to actively supporting independence for partitioned Poland on its own agenda.

In 1899 Zahajkiewicz was one of the signers of the first all–Polonia memorandum supporting the cause of Poland's freedom that was addressed to the president of the United States in connection with the international peace conference called by the tsar of Russia for the Hague, Netherlands. The Polonia appeal called on the U.S., and the other participants at the meeting to take up Polish independence as a key element in bringing about peace and stability in Europe. Between 1900 and 1901 he taught Polish literature and history at Holy Family Academy and St. Stanislaus Kostka High School. In 1900 he began publishing and editing the humorous weekly newspaper *Komar* (Mosquito), after which he published over 150 short stories, poetry, plays, and the books *Zbiór Poezji* (Poetry Collection; 1894), *Złota Księga* (Golden Book; 1897), *Życie i Czyny Polaków w Ameryce* (Life and Achievements of the Poles in America; 1890), and *Powinszowania i Deklamacje* (Congratulations and Declamations; 1890).

Zahajkiewicz was himself a major supporter of the **Polish Roman Catholic Union of America** fraternal organization dominated by the Rev. Barzyński. He was also editor in chief of the ***Dziennik Chicagoski*** (Chicago Daily News) newspaper, which was closely identified with the Resurrectionist Order. In 1897 he completed the first published compilation of Polonia parishes and clergy in America. Historian Andrzej Brożek identifies Zahajkiewicz as one of the greatest teachers in early Polonia.—*Donald E. Pienkos*

SOURCES: Donald E. Pienkos, *One Hundred Years Young: A History of the Polish Falcons of America* (Boulder, CO: East European Monographs, 1987); Andrzej Brożek, *Polish Americans 1854–1939* (Warsaw: Interpress, 1985); Donald E. Pienkos, *For Your Freedom Through Ours: Polish American Efforts on Poland's Behalf, 1863–1991* (Boulder, CO: East European Monographs, 1991); Mary Angela Musial, "American Literary Productions of Szczesny Zahajkiewicz" (Chicago: Unpublished M.A. thesis, DePaul University, 1944).

Zakrzewska, Marie Elizabeth (b. Berlin, Germany, September 6, 1829; d. Jamaica Plain, Massachusetts, May 12, 1902). Physician. Born into a family of Polish nobility that had lost its land because of its opposition to Russian control, Zakrzewska became interested in medicine early in life when she accompanied her mother in her work as a midwife at a local hospital. At the age of twenty she en-

Szczęsny Zahajkiewicz, editor and poet (*PMA*).

Marie E. Zakrzewska, physician (*PMA*).

rolled in the midwifery curriculum at the Royal Charité Hospital in Berlin. Although she proved proficient in her studies, eventually being named head of midwifery at the hospital, she grew increasingly frustrated over the lack of opportunity for women as physicians. This led her to migrate to the United States in 1853 to pursue further medical studies, only to find few American doors open to women interested in the medical profession. Her break came when she met Dr. Elizabeth Blackwell, one of only two or three female physicians in America, who managed to arrange for her admission to the Cleveland Medical College (later Western Reserve University).

Following graduation in 1856, Zakrzewska joined Elizabeth and Emily Blackwell in New York where they planned to open a hospital for women and children. Thanks in part to Zakrzewska's fundraising, the New York Infirmary for Women and Children, today known as Beth Israel Medical Center, opened in 1857. Two years later Zakrzewska moved to Boston where she accepted a position as professor of obstetrics on the faculty of the New England Female Medical College. After becoming disenchanted with the management and standards of the institution, she left to open the New England Hospital for Women and Children, now the Dimock Community Health Center, in 1862. In addition to being only the second hospital in America to have an entirely female staff of physicians and surgeons, the hospital also hosted intern Dr. Caroline Still, believed to be the first African-American female physician in America. In 1872 Zakrzewska opened the first professional nursing program in the United States, which, among other "firsts," graduated the first African-American professional nurse in the country, Mary Elizabeth Mahoney. In addition to her managerial and fundraising activities, she also pursued a private practice in gynecology. Zakrzewska's pioneering work was largely responsible for the gradual opening of professional doors to women seeking to pursue careers in medicine.

A personal friend of leading reformers such as William Lloyd Garrison, Karl Heinzen, and Wendell Phillips, she was a champion of women's rights and the abolitionist movement in addition to her work in the medical field.—*James S. Pula*

SOURCES: Arleen Marcia Tuchman, *Science Has No Sex: The Life of Marie Zakrzewska, M.D.* (Chapel Hill, NC: University of North Carolina Press, 2006); Ishbel Ross, *Child of Destiny: The Life Story of the First Woman Doctor* (New York: Harper & Brothers, 1949); *Marie Elizabeth Zakrzewska, A Memoir, 1829–1902* (Boston: New England Hospital for Women and Children, 1903); Marie Zakrzewska, *A Woman's Quest* (New York: Appleton and Company, 1924); Sr. Mary Liguori, "Marie Elizabeth Zakrzewska: Physician," *Polish American Studies*, Vol. 9, no. 1–2 (1952), 1–10.

Zale, Tony (Anthony Zaleski; b. Gary, Indiana, May 29, 1913; d. Portage, Indiana, March 20, 1997). Prize fighter. Zale rose from the slums and steel mills of his hometown to become twice holder of the world middleweight boxing championship, first from 1940 to 1947, then again in 1948. After becoming a professional prizefighter in 1934, he was recognized as middleweight titleholder in 1940, and continued to hold that distinction during three years of absence from the ring while serving in the U.S. Navy during the Second World War. He was nicknamed "The Man of Steel" for his strength, durability, and solid build. Between 1946 and 1948, Zale retained, lost, and regained his championship in a series of three bouts with Rocky Graziano that are regarded by boxing aficionados as one of the classic rivalries in the history of the sport. His first victory against Graziano led *Ring Magazine* to name Zale its Boxer of the Year. Within months of recapturing the middleweight crown, he lost it to Marcel Cerdan. After retiring from the ring, he taught and coached boxing in the Chicago area for many years. Zale is a member of numerous boxing halls of fame, and was inducted into the **National Polish-American Sports Hall of Fame** in 1975.—*Neal Pease*

SOURCES: "Tony Zale," National Polish-American Sports Hall of Fame website, www.polishsportshof.com; James E. Rasmusen, "Tony Zale, Gentleman from Indiana," *Sport*, Vol. 5, September 1948.

Zalinski, Edmund Louis Gray (b. Kórnik, Poland, December 13, 1849; d. New York City, March 10, 1909). Engineer, military officer. Migrating to the United States with his parents in 1853, he settled in Utica, NY, before attending school in Seneca Falls and Syracuse. He then volunteered for service as a private in the 2nd New York Cavalry at the age of fifteen in 1863. During the Civil War he served as aide-de-camp to Gen. Nelson A. Miles, winning praise for gallant and meritorious conduct at the Battle of Hatcher's Run, Virginia, before being commissioned second lieutenant in the 2nd New York Heavy Artillery in February 1865. Following his discharge from the volunteer service on September 29, 1865, he was commissioned second lieutenant in the 5th U.S. Artillery on February 23, 1866, gaining promotion to first lieutenant on January 1, 1867, and captain on December 9, 1887. While serving in the army, he was assigned to duty as professor of military science at the Massachusetts Institute of Technology from 1872 to 1876. Among his many inventions were a pneumatic gun that could fire dynamite charges over a great distance, a pneumatic torpedo-gun that also used dynamite as its charge, the electrical fuse, an

Edmund L. G. Zalinski, military officer and inventor (*OLS*).

entrenching tool, a ramrod-bayonet, a telescopic sight for artillery pieces, and a device that made allowances for wind deviation in the sighting of artillery and rifles. In 1876 he was one of thirteen founders of the Military Historical Society, established to investigate military history, and especially the American Civil War. Zalinski served as military attaché to Russia in 1889–90 before retiring due to ill health in 1894.—*James S. Pula*

SOURCES: David M. Hansen, "Zalinski's Dynamite Gun," *Technology & Culture*, Vol. 25, no. 2 (April 1984), 264–79; *New York Journal*, February 17, 1898.

Zamka, George David "Zambo" (b. Jersey City, New Jersey, June 29, 1962; d.—). Astronaut. Zamka earned a B.S. degree in mathematics from the U.S. Naval Academy (1984) and an M.S. in engineering management from the Florida Institute of Technology (1997). As an officer in the U.S. Marine Corps, he flew 66 combat missions over Kuwait and Iraq in F/A-18D Hornets during Operation Desert Storm. In 1994 he graduated from the U.S. Air Force Test Pilot School and four years later entered the astronaut training program. He made his first space flight as pilot of STS-120 (*Discovery*) in 2007 and his second as commander of STS-130 (*Endeavor*) in 2010. Among his honors are six Navy Strike Air Medals, the Navy Commendation Medal with Combat V, four NASA Superior Accomplishment Awards, and various other academic and campaign awards. In 2010, he was a colonel in the U.S. Marine Corps with more than 5,000 flight hours in over thirty different aircraft and more than 692 hours in space.—*James S. Pula*

SOURCE: http://www.jsc.nasa.gov/Bios/htmlbios/zamka.html.

Zand, Helen (Helena Stankiewicz; b. Łódź, Poland, March 2, 1901; d. Erie, Pennsylvania, February 2, 1996). Educator, social worker. Migrating with her parents to the United States in 1907, she settled in Buffalo, NY. In 1921 she graduated from Cornell University (Phi Beta Kappa, junior year) where she helped organize and serve as first president of the Women's Cosmopolitan Club of Cornell. She continued her education in the Law School of the University of Buffalo, and in Paris and New York, in 1923 received her *Juris Doctorate* from Buffalo. Following graduation she worked as a social worker, sociologist and teacher, affiliated with many social service organizations in Buffalo, Detroit, Rochester (NY), and New York City. Married to a Polish aviation pioneer, aeronautical engineer, and inventor Dr. **Stefan J. Zand**, the couple became friends of *Nowy Świat* editor **Maksymilian Węgrzynek**, a **Polish American Congress** activist.

In 1928 she published a translation of Polish writer Stefan Żeromski's novel *Popioły* (Ashes) in Alfred Knopf's series "Genii Linguarum." In 1947 she moved to Erie, PA, where she taught sociology and Polish at Gannon University (1948–61 and 1960–73), while maintaining close ties with the school and participating in many college events in later years as professor emeritus. She also taught sociology at the Berkshire Community College in Pittsfield, MA (1961–64). Her professional interests were child protection, ethnic family life, and intercultural relations. She was a pioneer in research on Polish folklore, the everyday life of the Polish ethnic group and family, and Polish customs that survived in America. She began work on these subjects in 1937 with a series of short articles published in daily newspaper *Nowy Świat*. In the meantime, she began interviewing people to amass sociological data for a more scholarly investigation of the subject of Polish American culture. She published her results in a series of eleven articles in **Polish American Studies** between 1949 and 1961. These articles were reprinted in book form in 1987 with an introduction and epilogue by Eugene Obidinski. In 1961 she published *Polish Proverbs* which was reprinted four times. Zand was an active member of the **Polish Institute of Arts and Sciences of America**, the **Polish American Historical Association** (vice president in 1950) and throughout her life pursued her interest in Polish-American culture.—*Adam Walaszek*

SOURCE: Bolesław Wierzbiański, *Who's Who in Polish America* (New York: Bicentennial Publishing Corporation, 1996), 526.

Zand, Stefan J. (b. Łódź, Poland, September 18, 1898; d. Massachusetts, January 24, 1963). Engineer. A pioneer aeronautical engineer and inventor, Zand began serious research on acoustical problems dealing with internal noise on aircraft while working for Sperry Corporation. With the development of the innovative Douglas DC-1, one of the problems that emerged with its use as a passenger aircraft was the excessive internal noise created by the dual Wright radial engines. Zand developed a new sound-absorbing material that successfully reduced internal noise in the passenger compartment of the DC-2 to a level less than that in a contemporary railroad car. He remained as senior project engineer at Sperry from 1932 to 1945, rising to the position of director of the Vese Memorial Aero Laboratory at the Sperry Gyroscope Company. During the Second World War he served in Europe as a colonel in the technical intelligence service, making use not only of his engineering expertise but also his fluency in five languages. He was a member of the group that prepared the postwar report on the effects of strategic bombing on the German aircraft industry. Following the war he went to work for the Lord Corporation where he encouraged long-range research. Among his awards and honors were the Presidential Medal of Merit, the Wright Brothers Medal, as well as being named a Fellow of the Royal Aeronautical Society and a Fellow of the Institute of Aeronautical Sciences.—*James S. Pula*

Zapała, Władysław J. (b. Łapanów, Poland, September 26, 1874; d. New York, New York, June 16, 1948). Priest, editor. After receiving his early education in Nowy Sącz and Kraków, in 1890 Zapała entered the Order of the Fathers of the Resurrection where he was ordained in 1897. Three years later he migrated to the U.S. where he taught Polish at St. Stanislaus Kostka College (1901–09) in

The Rev. Władysław Zapała (*OLS*).

Chicago, later serving as rector of that institution (1909–20). Active in **Polonia** affairs, he was a member of the Polish American delegation to the 500th anniversary celebration of the Battle of Grunwald held in Kraków in 1910, and served as editor of *Przegląd Kościelny* (Catholic Review) and **Dziennik Chicagoski** (Chicago Daily News). During World War I he was general secretary of the Polish National Council of America and secretary of the Union of Polish Priests in America. Rising to Superior General of the **Resurrectionists**, he resided in Rome, Italy, until his return to the U.S. in 1940. Among his honors, he was awarded the *Polonia Restituta* by the Republic of Poland.—*James S. Pula*

SOURCE: Francis Bolek, ed., *Who's Who in Polish America* (New York: Harbinger House, 1943).

Zarnecki, Euzebiusz "Zeb" (b. Kalisz, Poland, May 13, 1894; d. Chicago, Illinois, August 1984). Radio pioneer. Raised under Russian rule, Zarnecki joined an underground student organization in Kalisz. Following his mother's death in 1910, he migrated to the U.S. where he found employment in a steel mill in South Chicago. He enrolled in Crane College to study English, became active in local Polish organizations, and eventually married and opened a vegetable stand which he operated until it was forced to close during the Depression. Interested in radio, in 1935 he developed a show called "Tance w stodole" (Barn Dances) reasoning that since most of the Polish immigrants in the Chicago area came from rural backgrounds they would find the folk music appealing. He added John Piwowarczyk's folk orchestra and the popular singer **Marysia Data**, and the innovation of broadcasting directly from locations where live dances were taking place. During World War II, hundreds of thousands of dollars worth of U.S. bonds were sold through these dances and broadcasts, and following the war they were also used to benefit a variety of charities. In 1945 he obtained an FM license and opened the first Polish radio station in metropolitan Chicago, WLEY-FM. He retired in 1955.—*James S. Pula*

SOURCE: Joseph Migala, *Polish Radio Broadcasting in the United States* (Boulder, CO: East European Monographs, 1987), 228–32.

Zawadzki, Bohdan (b. Turbov, Ukraine, March 10, 1902; d. New York, New York, September 22, 1966). Psychologist. After attending a Polish elementary school in Kiev, he was repatriated to Poland in 1920 where he completed secondary school in Warsaw. In 1928 he earned a Ph.D. from the University of Warsaw and accepted a position as director of the Psychological Laboratory at the Central

Institute of Physical Education in Warsaw. He completed special studies at the University of Berlin (1929–30), University of Vienna (1932–33), and Harvard and Columbia Universities (1933–34). After serving as associate professor and director of the Psychological Institute at the Stefan Batory University in Wilno from 1935 to 1939, he migrated to the United States in March 1940 where he was a lecturer in psychology at Wellesley College (1940–41). In September 1941 he accepted a similar position at Sarah Lawrence College in Bronxville (NY). A specialist in the field of personality and clinical psychopathology, Zawadzki authored many monographs that were published in Polish and English including *Wykłady z psychopatologii* (1959) and *Wstęp do teorii osobowości* (1970).—*Adam A. Zych*

SOURCES: Elwira Kosnarewicz, Teresa Rzepa, and Ryszard Stachowski, eds., *Słownik psychologów polskich* (Poznań: Zakład Historii Myśli Psychologicznej, Instytut Psychologii UAM, 1992); Jerzy Siuta and Andrzej Beauvale, eds., *Słownik psychologii* (Kraków: Zielona Sowa, 2005).

Zawistowski, Józef Lebiedzik (b. Rzeszów, Poland, August 31, 1877; d. Davie, Florida, January 29, 1967). Priest, journalist. Arriving in U.S. prior to World War I, Zawistowski entered the seminary of the **Polish National Catholic Church** of America (PNCC) and was ordained a priest in 1915. He served a number of parishes as pastor during his fifty-year career. As the first chancellor of the PNCC Western Diocese (Chicago), he obtained formal recognition of the PNCC as a denomination in Canada and was elevated to the rank of Senior Priest in 1935. He was sent to Poland in 1931 to review the PNCC mission there, at which time he received the military medal Krzyż Waleczności. He returned to Poland again in 1946 with relief aid, following which he headed the largest fund-raising drive in PNCC history to that point for aid to the PNCC mission and people in Poland. He taught at **Savonarola Theological Seminary** and was honored as an active supporter of the **Polish National Union of America**. Zawistowski began publishing articles in PNCC and other Polish American publications soon after his ordination. His column "Przez moje okno" (Through My Window) appeared for many years and he frequently used the pen names Stanisław Okopiszczak, Stanisław Piersna, and Stanisław Cibski. The author of several books as well, these publications include *Prace i Pisma Księdza Biskupa Franciszka Hodura* (later translated into English as *Works and Writings of First Bishop Franciszek Hodur*), *Kazania na Puszczy* (Sermons in the Wilderness), *Prezent Ślubny* (Wedding Present), and

Wieniec Laurowy (Laurel Wreath). He also published a series of booklets that were later compiled into a book. One of the first priests in the PNCC to marry, he helped bring about an end to mandatory celibacy in the Church.—*Theodore L. Zawistowski*

SOURCES: Kazimiera Zawistowski, "From My Memories," *Straż*, October 1, 1981 through October 8, 1981; Theodore L. Zawistowski, "From the Memoirs of Kazimiera Zawistowski, the Binghamton Segment," *PNCC Studies*, Vol. 8 (1987), 49–54; Theodore L. Zawistowski, *Zawistowski Collection: Library & Papers of Józef Lebiedzik Zawistowski* (Storrs, CT: University of Connecticut, 1972).

Zawistowski, Theodore L. (b. Philadelphia, Pennsylvania, November 27, 1936; d.—). Editor, journalist. Zawistowski earned his B.A. degree from the Southeastern Massachusetts University (1969), M.A. in sociology from the University of Connecticut (1972), and M.A. in psychology from Marywood University (1985). A founding member of the **Polish National Catholic Church** (PNCC) Commission on History and Archives and the first editor of its *PNCC Studies*, Zawistowski served as editor of *Straż* (The Guard, 1973–82), when it was the official organ of the **Polish National Union of America** (Spójnia). A prominent writer and compiler of information on the PNCC, he was the editor and translator of *Bishop Francis Hodur: Biographical Essays* by Joseph W. Wieczerzak, *Polish National Catholic Church: Minutes of the First Eleven General Synods, 1904–1963, Polish National Catholic Church: Minutes of the Supreme Council, 1904–1969, Sermon Outlines and Occasional Speeches: 1899–1922* by Bishop **Franciszek Hodur**, *Hodur: A Compilation of Selected Translations*, and *The Polish Year* by Zofia Kossak. He taught at the **Savonarola Theological Seminary** (1980–85), the Pennsylvania State University–Dunmore, and Marywood University. Zawistowski served as treasurer of the **Polish American Historical Association**, editor of the *PAHA Newsletter*, president of the **Polish American Congress** of Northern Pennsylvania, president of the Emergency Medical Services of Northeastern Pennsylvania, and president of the United Nations Association of Greater Scranton. He was co-founder of The Zawistowski Collection at the Immigration History Research Center, University of Minnesota, and co-recipient of the Kościuszko Medal of Recognition presented by the **Kościuszko Foundation**. Following a move to Florida, he worked as a counselor/therapist with male juveniles and adult sex offenders at Charlotte Behavioral Health Care (1999–2008).—*James S. Pula*

SOURCE: Bolesław Wierzbiański, *Who's Who in Polish America* (New York: Bicentennial Publishing Corp., 1996), 531.

Stanley Zbyszko, wrestler (*UWM*).

Zbyszko, Stanley (Stanisław Jan Cyganiewicz; b. Stanisławów, Poland, April 1, 1881; d. St. Joseph, Missouri, September 23, 1967). Wrestler. Sources disagree on the year and exact place of his birth in the vicinity of Kraków. Following his graduation from the University of Vienna, he began a career as a wrestler and strongman in Europe at the turn of the twentieth century. He was noted for exceptional strength, and took the professional name "Zbyszko," after a fictional hero in the novels of **Henryk Sienkiewicz**. As his career flourished, he moved to the U.S. in 1909, making it his principal residence and base of operations. Depending on the source, he is described as having been acknowledged as the world heavyweight wrestling champion on various occasions between 1914 and 1925. Zbyszko enjoyed enormous popularity among Polish-Americans, and he continued his wrestling career to an advanced age. In retirement, he worked as a sports promoter. Widely regarded as one of the greatest wrestlers from the early days of the sport, he is a member of the Professional Wrestling Hall of Fame, and was inducted into the **National Polish-American Sports Hall of Fame** in 1983. Zbyszko was a man of multiple talents: he spoke numerous languages, wrote memoirs, and portrayed wrestlers in two feature films.—*Neal Pease*

SOURCE: "Stanley Zbyszko," National Polish-American Sports Hall of Fame website, www.polishsportshof.com.

Zelazny, Roger Joseph (pseudonym, Harrison Denmark; b. Cleveland, Ohio, May

13, 1937; d. Santa Fe, New Mexico, June 14, 1995). Author. As a child Zelazny enjoyed writing and sold his first short story, "Mr. Fuller's Revolt," in 1954 at the age of seventeen. In 1959 he graduated from Western Reserve University with a B.A. in English. He continued his studies at Columbia University where, in 1962, he was awarded an M.A. in Elizabethan and Jacobean Drama. During this period, from 1960 until 1966, Zelazny was in both the National Guard and the Army Reserve. He drew upon this experience in several of his works, such as *Damnation Alley* (1969). From 1962 to 1969 he worked for the Social Security Administration full-time and wrote part-time. Most of his writing during this period consisted of short stories and novellas. When he quit the Social Security Administration in 1969 in order to write full-time, he started to write novels as well. In 1975 he moved from Baltimore, Maryland, where he had been living since 1969, to Santa Fe, New Mexico, where he remained for the rest of his life.

Zelazny received a Hugo Award nomination for his short story "A Rose for Ecclesiastes" in 1963. Two years later he was nominated for a Hugo for his short story "Devil Car." He finally won the Hugo in 1966 for the story "...And Call Me Conrad." That same year he also won a Nebula Award for his novella "He Who Shapes" and one for his novelette "The Doors of His Face, the Lamps of His Mouth." In 1966 he published his first two novels, *This Immortal* and *The Dream Master*, followed in 1970 by *Nine Princes in Amber*, the first of his ten "Amber" novels. In 1972 the French edition of *Isle of the Dead* won the *Prix Apollo*. Several of Zelazny's works won major awards in 1976, including the novella "Home is the Hangman" which claimed both the Hugo and the Nebula, and *Doorways in the Sand* which the American Library Association named one of the Best Books for Young Adults. In 1980 he published his first book of poetry, *When Pussywillows in the Catyard Bloomed*, while also receiving the Balrog Award for his story "The Last Defender of Camelot." His collection *Unicorn Variations* won a Balrog Award (1984) and a Daison award for its Japanese translation. *Trumps of Doom* received a Locus Award for Best Fantasy novel, while *A Dark Travelling* was chosen as an American Library Association "Science Fiction Highlight of the Eighties." He received additional Hugo Awards for the novel *Lord of Light*. (1968), *Unicorn Variations* (1982), "24 Views of Mount Fuji by Hokusai" (1986), and "Permafrost" (1987).

Zelazny continued writing until his death from cancer. He is credited as one of the authors of Science Fiction's "New Wave," a group of writers including Harlan Ellison who moved science fiction from concentrating on space westerns to creating more interesting plots based in characters and their psychology.—*Scott Scheidlower*

Sources: Jane M. Linkskold, *Roger Zelazny* (New York: Twayne's United States Authors Series, 1993); "Roger (Joseph) Zelazny," in Everett Franklin Bleiler, ed., *Science Fiction Writers: Critical Studies of the Major Authors from the Early Nineteenth Century to the Present Day* (New York: Charles Scribner's Sons, 1982.

Zgoda (Harmony). The official publication of the **Polish National Alliance**, *Zgoda* has been in continuous existence since 1881. During its early years, it was frequently at odds with *Naród Polski* (The Polish Nation), the organ of the **Polish Roman Catholic Union**, in the lengthy disputes that went on between the two organizations for hegemony over American **Polonia** before the outbreak of the First World War in 1914. The first editor was **Edward Odrowąż** in New York who established its patriotic and nationalist tone in keeping with the spirit of the PNA, but when the 1882 PNA convention voted to move the publication to Chicago he resigned and was replaced by **Ignacy Wendziński** (1882–86). In the early years, the editor was elected annually with Wendziński's successors including **Zbigniew Brodowski** (1886–89), Stanisław Nicki (1889–93), **Franciszek Jabłoński** (1893–97, 1908), **Stefan Barszczewski** (1897–1901), **Tomasz Siemiradzki** (1901–13), and Stanisław Orpiszewski (1913–21). In 1915 the editorship became appointive with Orpiszewski continuing in office. His successors included Jan Przyprawa (1921–28), Stanisław Zaklikiewicz (1928–31), **Karol Piątkiewicz** (1931–67), and **Joseph Wiewiora** (1967–). Wiewiora turned the newspaper into a bilingual publication with a beginning section in English followed by a Polish-language section. He also revamped its content from largely PNA news to include not only Alliance information, but news from **Polonia** and Poland, as well as matters of special interest to Polish Americans. *Zgoda* appears twice each month. In 2008 its editor was Wojciech Wierzewitski.—*Anne Gurnack*

Delivery trucks of the *Zgoda* and *Dziennik Związkowy* (PMA).

Sources: Jan Wepsiec, *Polish American Serial Publications: 1842–1966, An Annotated Bibliography* (Chicago: Jan Wepsiec, 1968); Jan Kowalik, *The Polish Press in America* (San Francisco: R&E Research Associates, 1978).

Zielinski, Bronisław (b. Jasło, Poland, July 1, 1907; d. Chicago, Illinois, November 11, 1951). Radio and television pioneer. Arriving in the U.S. as a baby in 1908, Zielinski attended St. Barbara's parochial school and graduated from Harrison High School in 1926. In 1930 he originated the radio program "Godzina Grunwaldzka" (The Grunwald Hour) on WEDC which featured popular comedy sketches written by Bronisław Mroz about "The Troubles of the Siekierski Family" in adjusting to life in America. Zielinski is credited with beginning the first Polish television program in America in 1957, "It's Polka Time," which was broadcast by the American Broadcasting Company (ABC) to 29 stations. In 1979 his achievements were recognized with the Heritage Award from the state division of the **Polish American Congress**.—*James S. Pula*

Source: Joseph Migala, *Polish Radio Broadcasting in the United States* (Boulder, CO: East European Monographs, 1987), 227–28.

Zielinski, Helen (Helena Kloc; b. Ralphtown, Pennsylvania, August 7, 1911; d. Crown Point, Indiana, August 10, 2007). Polonia activist. Zielinski became active in the **Polish Women's Alliance** of America in Merrillville, Indiana, where she and her husband raised their three children. She was elected its vice president in 1959. In 1971, she was elected president of the PWA and went on to serve sixteen years in office. Following her retirement, she was named its Honorary President. As a PWA officer and president, Zielinski devoted her energies to building membership in the fraternal. In 1979, she oversaw the organization's move out of its home office on Chicago's near north side to a newer, modern building in the northwest Chicago suburb of Park Ridge, Illinois. Zielinski loved music and dance and worked to enhance the Women's Alliance's fraternal programs in these areas. In 1979 she was the author of the third volume, in Polish, of the story of the Polish Women's Alliance. As vice president of the **Polish American Congress**, Zielinski was involved in nationwide fund raising campaigns to build a Polish pilgrims' hostel in Rome to honor Pope John Paul II, to sup-

Helen Zielinski, president of the Polish Women's Alliance (*Polish Women's Alliance of America*).

port the restoration of the Statue of Liberty in New York harbor, and to preserve the shrine of Our Lady of Czestochowa in **Doylestown**, Pennsylvania. In December 1981, Zielinski was invited to the White House with PAC President **Aloysius Mazewski**, PAC Treasurer Joseph Drobot, and **John Cardinal Krol** of Philadelphia to discuss America's response to the Polish regime's suppression of the Solidarity movement and its imposition of martial law with President Reagan.—*Donald E. Pienkos*

SOURCES: Angela T. Pienkos and Donald E. Pienkos, "*In the Ideals of Women is the Strength of a Nation*": *A History of the Polish Women's Alliance of America* (Boulder, CO: East European Monographs, 2003); "In Memoriam Honorary President Helen Zielinski," *Głos Polek*, May 2007, 1–2.

Zielinski, Thaddeus F. (b. Wilkes-Barre, Pennsylvania, December 26, 1904; d. Scranton, Pennsylvania, August 11, 1990). Bishop. Ordained a priest in the **Polish National Catholic Church** (PNCC) in 1927 after attending **Savonarola Theological Seminary** in Scranton, PA, Zielinski was first assigned to St. John the Baptist parish in Frackville, then to St. Adalbert's in Dickson City, PA. He was consecrated a bishop in 1954 and headed the Buffalo-Pittsburgh Diocese of the PNCC at Holy Mother of the Rosary Cathedral in Buffalo, N.Y. Bishop Zielinski was a strong advocate of the use of the English language in the Church, since he observed that third generation Polish Americans in the PNCC were not familiar with Polish, then its official language. He personally translated PNCC prayer books, catechisms and other literature into English. Upon Prime Bishop **Leon Grochowski**'s death in 1969, Zielinski

was elected the PNCC's third Prime Bishop. During his tenure, the PNCC suspended and eventually terminated its thirty year intercommunion with the Episcopal Church over the latter's decision to ordain women. Bishop Zielinski retired in 1978.—*Martin S. Nowak*

SOURCE: The Rev. Stephan Wlodarski, *The Origin and Growth of the Polish National Catholic Church* (Scranton: PNCC, 1974).

Ziółkowska-Boehm, Aleksandra (b. Łódź, Poland, April 15, 1949; d.—). Journalist. After earning doctorates at the University of Warsaw (1979) and University of Toronto (1982), she married Norman Boehm. Working as a research assistant to the well-known Polish journalist **Melchior Wańkowicz**, she published a number of recollections and critical studies devoted to him. In the 1970s she moved first to Canada and, in 1990, to the United States where she became interested in the history of American Indians through the influence of her relative, the sculptor **Korczak Ziolkowski**, who began carving a monument to Chief Crazy Horse in South Dakota. Having published a number of books on Poland, she turned her interest to Canada and wrote journalistic reports on that country, eventually publishing studies on Polish personalities in the United States including *The Roots Are Polish* (1998) and a history of American Indians, *Otwarta rana Ameryki* (America's Open Wound; 2008). She received a number of awards and followships.—*Jerzy Krzyzanowski*

SOURCES: Bolesław Wierzbiański, ed., *Who is Who in Polish America* (New York: Bicentennial Publishing Company, 1996); *International Authors and Writers Who's Who* (Cambridge, UK: International Biographical Centre, 1999–2000).

Ziolkowski, Korczak (b. Boston, Massachusetts, September 6, 1908; d. Crazy Horse, South Dakota, October 14, 1982). Sculptor. Orphaned at an early age, Ziolkowski earned enough money to enroll in a local technical school, after which he became an apprentice at a Boston shipbuilding firm. Around 1918 he began to experiment with wood carving, gaining a reputation as a maker of fine furniture. He completed his first marble sculpture, a bust of Judge Frederick P. Cabot who had encouraged his boyhood interests in the fine arts, in 1932, and soon gained a reputation for his work throughout New England that allowed him to open a successful studio in West Hartford, Connecticut. In 1939 his reputation received a major boost when his marble work "Paderewski, Study of an Immortal" received a first prize at

the New York World's Fair. In the same year he also began assisting Gutzon Borglum who was beginning his famous presidential carvings on Mount Rushmore. Because of the publicity generated from his World's Fair success and his work on Mount Rushmore, Chief Henry Standing Bear of the Lakota tribe, whose heritage held the Black Hills of the Dakotas to be sacred land, contacted Ziolkowski with the suggestion that he create a memorial similar the Mount Rushmore as a tribute to America's Indian heritage. Intrigued by the idea, Ziolkowski met with representatives of the Lakotas, examined several potential sites and began preliminary research for a massive sculpture that would be carved into the side of Thunderhead Mountain.

The outbreak of World War II interrupted planning for the monument when Ziolkowski volunteered for service in the U.S. Army. After landing on Omaha Beach during the Normandy invasion, he was wounded in action. Following his recovery and the end of the war, Ziolkowski moved to the Black Hills in 1947 to begin work on the "Crazy Horse Memorial," projected to be the largest sculpture in the world at 563 feet high and 641 feet wide. He had exactly $147 at the time and lived in a tent at the worksite. Sculpting commenced in 1948 with the dynamiting of the hillside to expose the rock and prepare the preliminary base for the final sculpture. For the next thirty-four years Ziolkowski worked on the immense project, refusing to take any salary for his efforts. But work progressed slowly since Ziolkowski would not apply for grants or other funding, instead relying on admission fees paid by people interested in observing his work. Upon his death in 1982, his remains were buried at the base of the mountain. His wife and several of his children have carried on his work.—*James S. Pula*

SOURCES: Joseph Swastek, *Korczak Ziolkowski: Mountain Carver* (Detroit: The Conventual Press, 1950); Vinson Brown, *Great Upon the Mountain: The*

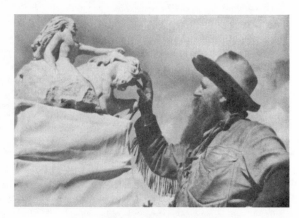

Korczak Ziolkowski, sculptor (*OLS*).

Story of Crazy Horse, Legendary Mystic and Warrior (New York: Macmillan, 1975).

Zioncheck, Marion Anthony (Antoni Zajączek; b. Kęty, Poland, December 5, 1901; d. Seattle, Washington, August 7, 1936). Congressman, attorney. Migrating to the United States in 1905 with his parents who settled in Seattle, Washington, he grew up poor in the Beacon Hill area overlooking the original Skid Row before attending the University of Washington. There, as an iconoclast and an egalitarian (and as elected student body president in 1928), he opposed the "lofty status" of fraternities and athletics on campus. In response, he was kidnapped and dunked into Lake Washington. He graduated from the law program in 1929 after time off to earn money working in logging camps and fisheries, was admitted to the bar the same year, and began practice in Seattle earning renown as president of the Municipal Utilities Protection League. In this capacity he helped engineer the recall of Mayor Frank Edwards in 1931. He was a delegate to the Democratic State conventions in 1932 and 1934, being elected as a self-described radical Democrat, supported until 1936 by the socialist Washington Commonwealth Federation. Elected to the 73rd and 74th Congresses from the First District, he served from March 4, 1933, until his death by suicide (after exhibiting erratic behavior, he jumped from a building and was killed instantly). Zioncheck was outspoken, energetic, and ambitious. He denounced J. Edgar Hoover and clashed with Rep. Thomas Blanton of Texas over the teaching of communism in District schools. Zioncheck may have deliberately sought to garner publicity by making good copy, or possibly he became mentally ill since he was hospitalized in a Maryland mental institution for several weeks before escaping by jumping a fence and taking a train back to Seattle. Always restless, increasingly impatient with congressional decorum, he saw more than a dozen candidates enter the race for his office as he lost support. He initially declared for re-election, then withdrew when he might have faced a recall, but declared himself in the race again days before his death. His suicide note revealed his commitment to distributing economic wealth and opportunities, and presumed disheartenment, when he wrote: "My only hope in life was to improve the condition of an unjust economic system...." Dubbed by various publications a sot, a playboy, and "the Pagliacci of Pennsylvania Avenue," Zioncheck nevertheless had a massive funeral at a Seattle auditorium and still looms as a local popular culture figure.—*Frederick J. Augustyn*

SOURCES: *Biographical Directory of the United States Congress, 1774–Present* (http://bioguide.congress.gov/);

Phil Campbell, *Zioncheck For President: A True Story of Idealism and Madness in American Politics* (New York: Nation Books, 2005).

Zisk, Richie (b. Brooklyn, New York, February 6, 1949; d.—). Baseball player. Zisk played in the major leagues for four different teams from 1971 through 1983. A righthanded hitting outfielder and designated hitter, he compiled a career batting average of .287 with 207 home runs over thirteen seasons. In 1974 and 1975, Zisk appeared in postseason play with the Pittsburgh Pirates, his original team. He was named to the American League all-star squad twice, in 1977 with the Chicago White Sox and in 1978 with the Texas Rangers. In 2004, he was inducted into the **National Polish-American Sports Hall of Fame**.—*Neal Pease*

SOURCE: "Richie Zisk," National Polish-American Sports Hall of Fame website, www.polishsportshof.com.

Zjednoczenia Polsko-Rzymsko Katolickie w Ameryce *see* **Polish Roman Catholic Union of America.**

Znaniecki, Florian Witold (b. Świątniki, partitioned Poland, January 15, 1882; d. Champaign, Illinois, March 23, 1958). Sociologist. Educated as a philosopher at the Jagiellonian University in Kraków, Znaniecki spent several years abroad studying sociology, philosophy, and the theory of science at universities in Geneva, Zurich, and Paris. As his interest in sociology grew, it was in this academic discipline that he was the most influential. In 1913, while holding an administrative position in Warsaw, he met William I. Thomas who was beginning a significant empirical study concerning European immigrants in the United States. Thomas arranged for an appointment for Znaniecki at the University of Chicago where the two worked together on a project focusing on Polish immigrants which eventually had a great impact on the new field of social history with the publication of the five volume work titled *The Polish Peasant in Europe and America* in 1927. This pioneering study of newly arrived Polish men from the Russian and Austrian partitions of Poland sought, in part, to investigate whether there might be differences in the immigrants based on the section of the partitioned nation from which they originated. Additionally, Thomas and Znaniecki sought to explain Polish immigration through what they viewed as "common sense sociology" through which they sought to explain social problems by examining the relationship of the individual and his surrounding society. The key to understanding immigration, they posited, rested not in looking at government, but in focusing on the

family, neighborhood, and surrounding communities to understand how Poles were bound together by social ties. Together, they invented what became known as the "life study method," the essence of which involved encouraging immigrants to tell their life stories or in locating letters or documents that charted their life experiences. The generation of sociological researchers influenced by the *Polish Peasant* was labeled the "Chicago School." In addition to immigrant communities, the scholars used labor movements and city stockyards as their laboratories. They explained the importance of ethnic communities in protecting the identity of Polish immigrants; however, Thomas and Znaniecki eventually concluded that Polish immigrant communities suffered from what they termed "social disorganization," were in a state of decline, and would eventually self-destruct. Modern scholars have reevaluated this thesis and have found the conclusion was not accurate because many elements of Polish culture in fact persisted over time. By the end of World War II, the importance and influence of *The Polish Peasant* declined as social science researchers turned their attention to theoretical works and quantitative studies.

Eventually Thomas experienced legal and political difficulties at the University of Chicago, losing his position there. Znaniecki returned to teach in Poland until the 1930s when he accepted a position as Professor at the University of Illinois Urbana–Champaign at the beginning of World War II. He remained there until the time of his death in 1958. During those years he achieved considerable recognition in academe. In 1953, he was elected president of the American Socio-

Florian Znaniecki, sociologist (*OLS*).

logical Association. Until recently, however, his work was not appreciated in Poland, where he is now recognized as an important figure in both sociology and philosophy. His great work, *Social Relations and Social Roles: The Unfinished Sociology* was published posthumously by his daughter **Helen Znaniecka-Lopata.**—*Anne Gurnack*

SOURCES: John Bodnar, "Immigration and Modernization: The Case of Slavic Peasants in Industrial America," *Journal of Social History*, Vol. 10 (1976); Eli Zaretsky, ed., *The Polish Peasant in Europe and America* (Urbana and Chicago: University of Illinois Press, 1984); Joseph C. Gidyński, "Florian Znaniecki: Original Thinker, Philosopher and Sociologist," *The Polish Review*, Vol. 3, no. 4 (1958), 77–87; Tamara K. Obrębska, "Florian Znaniecki," *The Polish Review*, Vol. 3, no. 1–2 (1958), 3–5; Hyman Henry Frankel, "The Sociological Theory of Florian Znaniecki" (Urbana, IL: Unpublished dissertation, University of Illinois, 1958).

Zuk, Mary (Mary Stanceusz; b. Neffs, Ohio, November 19, 1904; d. Troy, Michigan, July 17, 1987). Labor leader. After her father died in a mining accident, Mary was forced to live with a sister in Detroit who worked in the auto factories. She married Stanley Zuk on August 26, 1922, before becoming involved in community activism with the **Hamtramck** Unemployment Council during the Great Depression. Out of these years of frustration over rising prices with little or no income, she led a few desperate housewives in **Hamtramck** to voice their concerns by engaging in a boycott of meat that received national publicity. As the head of the Kobiecy Komitet Akcji Przeciwko Drozyzenie (Women's Action Committee Against High Prices), she wired President Franklin Roosevelt and Secretary of Agriculture Henry A. Wallace asking for appointments to discuss economic concerns. Subsequently, Zuk led a delegation of five women to advocate the abolition of the Agricultural Adjustment Act, processing taxes to reduce costs by twenty percent. Expanding their protest to include the high cost of milk, the women also formed the Kobieca Liga Walki z Drozyzna (Women's League for Struggle Against High Prices) with Zuk as president. Ultimately, the protest ended after most of the AAA legislation was declared unconstitutional by the U.S. Supreme Court. As consumer issues captured the attention of working-class Americans during the 1930s, Zuk spoke at the United Labor Conference for Political Action in 1935.

Gaining a national reputation for her leadership of the meat strike, Zuk ran for election to the Hamtramck City Council on a platform focused on working-class issues. She was one of the first white politicians to reach out actively to black voters, her platform containing a call for "Full social and political rights to the Negro citizens." Though she was endorsed by the People's League, her opponents labeled her a communist and circulated literature asking people to vote against her to "Defeat Communism." She was subjected to personal attacks, continual harassment, and attempts to disrupt her speeches by her opponents throughout her campaign. When she won election as the first woman to sit on the Hamtramck City Council in 1936, the *Detroit News* called her "a flaming evangel of the workingman and his womenfolk and children." Following her election, Zuk worked closely with the Farmer-Labor Party and also actively urged Mayor **Rudolph Tenerowicz** to hire an African American medical doctor as the city's physician.

In addition to her work on the Hamtramck City Council, Zuk served on the Wayne County Board of Supervisors. She was later active in the Polish Trade Union Committee (PTUC) led by **Stanley Nowak**. When women cigar makers requested Nowak's guidance, he brought in Zuk, a former Dodge worker, to assist. In this capacity she participated in many picket lines, strikes, and labor rallies. Her support of workers brought CIO President John L. Lewis to Detroit. There, she, along with Councilman John Kuberacki, met Lewis at the Union Depot. She was involved in the founding of the short-lived Polish Local 187 of the United Auto Workers Union in October 1936. Mayor Tenerowicz, however, remained loyal to Zuk, appointing her to Hamtramck's new Water Department. Later, after passing an FBI examination, she worked briefly for the U.S. Department of Labor. Zuk's memory is preserved by a plaque on the Wall of Labor in the Michigan Labor Legacy Project.—*Don Binkowski*

SOURCES: Don Binkowski, *Poles Together: Leo Krzycki and Polish Americans in the American Labor Movement* (Philadelphia: Xlibris, 2001), 286–301; Don Binkowski, *Leo Krzycki and the Detroit Left* (Philadelphia: Xlibris, 2001); Georg Schrode, "Mary Zuk and the Detroit Meat Strike of 1935," *Polish American Studies*, Vol. XLIII, no. 2 (Autumn, 1986), 5–39; Annelise Orleck, "'We Are That Mythical Thing Called the Public': Militant Housewives During the Great Depression," *Feminist Studies*, Vol. 19, no. 1 (Spring, 1993), 147–72.

Zukotynski, Thaddeus (Tadeusz Żukotyński; sometimes Zuckotinsky; b. Przewrocie, Ukraine, April 1, 1855; d. Chicago, Illinois, December 7, 1912). Artist. Educated at the Polytechnic in Riga, Latvia, he studied business (1875–79) and was a member of the Arkonia Fraternity. He later studied figure, landscape, and still-life painting in atelier classes at the Academy of Fine Arts in Munich, Germany (1879–85). In 1880 he was among sixteen Polish artists in Munich who sent a congratulatory telegram to the commemorative celebration for painter Juliusz Kossak in Kraków. During the mid–1880s he was part of a group of artists recruited in Germany by August Lohr for William Wehner's American Panorama Company in Milwaukee. The artists painted the *Cyclorama of the Battle of Atlanta* for the City of Atlanta, Georgia, and the *Jerusalem Panorama*, along with several other works. Arriving in the United States in 1886, he was one of the *Cyclorama's* five figure painters. Settling in Milwaukee, where he was later associated with Adolph Liebig in the fresco painting firm of A. Liebig & Company, he was also hired by the Milwaukee Glass Works. He permanently relocated to Chicago in 1893 where he spent the rest of his life. While there he taught drawing at St. Stanislaus Kostka College. His best-known student was Sister Mary Stanisia Kurkowski (Kurk), a portrait painter and teacher who was primarily a painter of religious subjects for Catholic churches in Wisconsin, Illinois, Indiana, and Kansas.

In addition to the *Cyclorama of the Battle of Atlanta* and the *Jerusalem Panorama*, his secular works included still life and figure paintings and drawings at the **Polish Museum of America** in Chicago and illustrations for *St. Nicholas Magazine* (1890s). He executed over one hundred religious paintings that adorn St. John Cantius, St. Stanislaus Kostka, St. Hedwig's, St. Hyacinth's Basilica, and Holy Cross in Chicago; St. Josaphat's Basilica, St. John the Evangelist Cathedral (fire destroyed paintings in 1892), St. Michael's, and the School Sisters of Notre Dame Adoration Chapel (destroyed) in Milwaukee; the Chapels of the Angels and St. Rose of Viterbo Convent in LaCrosse, Wisconsin; St. Hedwig's Church in South Bend, Indiana; St. Joseph's in Mishawaka, Indiana; St. Benedict's in Terre Haute (fire destroyed some of his paintings in 1930), Indiana; the Church of the Immaculate Conception at Saint Mary-of-the-Woods, Indiana; St. Mary's Catholic Church in Benedict, Kansas. His work was also displayed in group exhibitions by the Towarzystwo Pryzjaciół Sztuk Pięknych (Society of the Friends of the Fine Arts) in Kraków, Poland (1881–86). Among his awards was the Silver Medal of the Academy of Fine Arts, Munich, Germany (1883).—*Stanley L. Cuba*

SOURCES: Dr. Peter C. Merrill, *German Academic Painters in Wisconsin* (West Bend: West Bend Gallery of Fine Arts (West Bend Art Museum; 1989); Gary A. Lane, *Chicago Churches and Synagogues: An Architectural Pilgrimage* (Chicago: Loyola Press, 1982); Irena Piotrowska, *American Painters and Illustrators of Polish Descent* in the Rev. Francis Bolek and the Rev. Ladislaus J. Siekaniec, eds., *Polish American Encyclopedia* (Buffalo, NY: Polish American Encyclopedia Committee, 1954), Vol. 1; the Rev. Francis Bolek, ed., *Who's Who in Polish America* (New York: Harbinger

House, 1943); obituary, *Dziennik Chicagoski*, December 10, 1912.

Związek Narodowy Polski w Stanach Zjednoczonych Północnej Ameryki *see* **Polish National Alliance.**

Związek Polek w Ameryce *see* **Polish Women's Alliance of America.**

Związek Socjalistów Polskich w Ameryce *see* **Polish Socialist Alliance in America.**

Związek Sokolstwo Polskie w Ameryce *see* **Polish Falcons of America.**

Związek Śpiewaków Polskich w Ameryce *see* **Polish Singers Alliance of America.**

Zwierzchowski, Stanisław J. (alias Zowski; b. Srem, Poland, April 27, 1880; d Michigan ?, January 10, 1940). Engineer. After completing his studies in mechanical engineering at the Polytechnic in Charlottenburg, Germany, in 1905, he migrated to the United States where he found work as an engineer constructing water turbines in Dayton, Ohio. After joining the Allis-Chalmers Company in Milwaukee, he was transferred to Montréal, Canada. In 1907 he accepted a position on the mechanical engineering faculty of the University of Michigan, and four years later was named Professor of Hydromechanical Engineering, the only position of its kind in America. His success led to his promotion to department head. In 1913 he developed a new form of turbine that was used widely in the U.S. and Poland for the next generation. He was named editor of the daily newspaper *Kuryer Polski* (Polish Courier) in 1918, and elected director of the Polish National Committee in Chicago in the same year. During this time, President Woodrow Wilson named him to a committee charged with gathering historical and statistical information for use at the Paris Peace Conference following World War I. His work played a large part in settling the issue of Poland's borders when the nation regained its independence. Returning to Poland in 1922 after his homeland regained its independence, he accepted a position as director of the hydromechanical engineering program at Warsaw Polytechnic, he visited the U.S. each summer in conjunction with the Kuryer Polski Publishing Company of which he remained president. Following the German invasion of Poland in 1939, he fled back to the United States.—*James S. Pula*

SOURCES: www.linkinghub.elsevier.com; *World Pumps*, Vol. 2005, no. 465 (June 2005), 22–29.

Żychliński, Kazimierz (b. February 24, 1854, Poznań, Poland; d. August 27, 1927, Chicago, Illinois). Polonia activist. In 1876 Żychliński emigrated with his family to the U.S., settling in New York where he joined the **Polish National Alliance** in 1881. Two years later he moved to Chicago where he became a community leader, being among the organizers of the second **Polish Falcons** nest on the city's South Side in 1888. In 1894 he was elected president of the Polish Falcons Alliance. Under his leadership the organization grew steadily, establishing the newspaper *Sokół* (Falcon) in 1899. Żychliński moved to South Bend, Indiana, in 1899, but returned to Chicago in 1903 and was elected president of Falcons District Two. He was also a member of the Polish National Alliance where, in 1901, he joined with **Tomasz Siemiradzki**, **Marian Stęczyński**, and **Jan Smulski** to promote closer Falcons involvement in the PNA. These efforts resulted in the merging of the Falcons organization with the PNA in 1905. In 1901 Żychliński was a member of the Central Board of the PNA, working in its Education Department. In 1911 he became a national director of the PNA, and in 1912 was elected president of the PNA following the resignation of his friend Stęczyński. He thus became one of the crucial figures on the Polish American scene in the World War I years to come. He remained in this post until his death in 1927.

Prior to and during World War I, Żychliński took a leading part in **Polonia's political life**. When, in 1912, the **Polish National Defence Committee** (KON) was established as an umbrella organization uniting all Polonia factions to support the independence of Poland, Żychliński was a key supporter resulting in his election as president of the new KON in 1913. Soon after his election, however, he began to distrust the pro–Piłsudski faction supported by the KON and allied himself with the Polish National Alliance and the national democrats who supported **Ignacy Jan Paderewski**. Because of this Żychliński's opponents labeled him a "Russophile." Working with the **Polish Women's Alliance**, the Polish National Alliance, and the **Polish Roman Catholic Union**, Żychliński was active with Jan Smulski in forming the **Polish Central Relief Committee** to organize support in America for humanitarian assistance to Poland. In 1916 the PCRC created the **National Department** as its political action subcommittee, with Żychliński becoming vice president. He assisted in the recruitment of the **Polish Army in France** and, following the war, attempted to organize relief efforts for Poland. Żychliński also supported the post-war self-help movement among Polish Americans epitomized in the slogan "Emigrants for Themselves." Despite internal tensions within the PNA, Ży-

Kazimierz Żychliński, Polonia activist (*OLS*).

chliński remained president until his death. His passing, just a week before the 1927 PNA convention, weakened the "old guard" faction of the Alliance and led, in 1928, to the victory of the "leftist" or Piłsudski faction in winning control over the fraternal. It was not until 1939 that this faction was fully defeated at the national level of PNA leadership.—*Adam Walaszek*

SOURCES: Donald E. Pienkos, *PNA: A Centennial History of the Polish National Alliance of the United States of North America* (Boulder, CO: East European Monographs, 1984); Donald E. Pienkos, *One Hundred Years Young: A History of the Polish Falcons of America, 1887–1987* (Boulder, CO: East European Monographs, 1987).

Żychliński, Ludwik (b. Wielkie Księstwo, Duchy of Poznań, Poland, 1837; d. Brúsno, Poland, 1901). Soldier. Growing up in partitioned Poland, Żychliński participated in the unsuccessful Polish insurrection against Prussia in 1848, then moved to Italy where he served in the Papal army before joining Garibaldi's campaign in Sicily. With Garibaldi's failure, Żychliński fled to the United States where he landed in New York in April 1862. With the American Civil War raging, he enlisted in the Independent Battalion of New York Volunteer Light Infantry, known as "Les Enfans Perdu," and fought with them during Gen. George McClellan's peninsula campaign. Injured during maneuvers, he went to Boston to recuperate and claimed in his memoirs to have then rejoined the Union army but this later service has not been verified by existing records. During his recuperation in Boston he penned a memoir titled *Pamiętniki z wojny amerykańskiej* (Memoir of the American War; 1862). With the outbreak of the January Insurrection in Poland, Żychliński returned to his homeland to participate in the rebellion. Exiled to Siberia upon the revolution's collapse, he later published additional memoirs titled *Przygody Wielkopolanina w Azji i Ameryce* (The Adventures of a Pole in Asia and America; 1882), *Wrażenia i przygody zesłanego w Sybir Wielkopolania* (Impressions and Adventures of An Exiled Pole in Siberia; 1883), *Przygody więźnia politycznego* (The Adventures of a Political Prisoner; 1884), and *Pamiętniki byłego dowódcy dzieci warszawskich* (Memoir of the Former Leader of the Children of Warsaw; 1885). Although his 1862 memoir appears to be an accurate description of his service, his subsequent memoirs have been criticized by historians as suffering from inflation and assertions that cannot be corroborated. In one, for example, he describes a meeting of Poles in America with President Abraham Lincoln, but his description of the time frame is so vague that it cannot be verified. Nevertheless, his memoir from 1862 is an extremely rare source from a Union regiment that is otherwise largely undocumented.—*James S. Pula*

SOURCES: James S. Pula, ed., Eugene Podraza, transl., *The Memoirs of Ludwik Żychliński: Reminiscences of the American Civil War, Siberia, and Poland* (Boulder, CO: East European Monographs, 1993).

Zygmund, Antoni Szczepan (b. Warsaw, Poland, December 25, 1900; d. Chicago, Illinois, May 30, 1992). Mathematician. Zygmund attended elementary school in Warsaw but his education was interrupted by the advent of World War I. His family was relocated in the Ukraine, but after the war they returned to Warsaw. Zygmund had always been interested in astronomy, but that field of study was not offered at the collegiate level. Instead, he decided to study the field of mathematics at the University of Warsaw where he researched functional mathematical analysis. His professor, Aleksander Rajchman, assisted in the direction of his studies, and Zygmund gained a life-long interest in trigonometric series. In 1920 he entered the Polish army during the Russo-Polish War, returning to his studies in 1922. He was appointed an instructor in the Department of Mathematics at Warsaw Polytechnic School while completing his Ph.D. which he received in 1923. Zygmund's dissertation analyzed the Riemannian theory of trigonometric series.

Zygmund continued to teach at both the University of Warsaw and the Polytechnic School. During the years 1929–30 he studied and taught at Oxford on a Rockefeller scholarship. In 1930 he was appointed mathematics chair at the Stefan Batory University in Wilno, Poland. In 1939 he was drafted into the Polish Army Reserve, serving until its defeat in October of that year. In the following year Zygmund, with his wife and son, escaped to the U.S., where he taught at the Massachusetts Institute of Technology. In 1947 he accepted a position at the University of Chicago, where he remained for forty-five years until his retirement. In 1948 Zygmund visited South America where he met Calderón, whom he mentored to continue his studies of mathematics. Calderón returned to Chicago with Zygmund, where their summative work in mathematical analysis led to the Chicago School of Mathematics. Another mathematical area Zygmund contributed to was Fourier analysis and its application to differential equations. His book *Trigonometric Series* (1935) remains the classic standard in its subject. Other major works include *Analytic Functions* (1938) and *Measure and Integral* (1977).

Zygmund's work in harmonic analysis was applicable in the scientific field of wave theory and vibrations. The mathematical descriptions he solidified became integral for the design of spacecraft, crystallography, and laser holography. In 1986 he was awarded the National Medal of Science for contributions in Fourier analysis and for creating the strongest mathematical analysis institution in the world. His academic works in total include six books and more than 180 papers. His honors include the American Mathematical Society Colloquium Lecturer (1953), London Mathematical Society Honorary Member (1967), American Mathematical Society Steele Prize (1979), and National Medal of Science (1986).—*Susan Sanchez-Barnett*

SOURCES: *Modern Scientists and Engineers* (New York: McGraw-Hill, 1980), Vol. 3, 370–371; *Colloquium Mathematicum*, Vol. 60–61 (1990; volume dedicated to Zygmund).

Index

Numbers in **bold italics** indicate pages with illustrations.